THE CONTINUUM COMPANION TO TWENTIETH CENTURY THEATRE

THE CONTINUUM COMPANION TO TWENTIETH CENTURY THEATRE

EDITED BY COLIN CHAMBERS

continuum
LONDON · NEW YORK

First published 2002 by
Continuum
The Tower Building, 11 York Road, London SE1 7NX
370 Lexington Avenue, New York, NY 10017–6503

British Library Cataloguing-in-Publication Data
A catalogue record for this book is available from the
British Library
ISBN 0–8264–4959-X

Typeset by Wyvern 21 Ltd, Bristol
Printed and bound in Great Britain by Bath Press Ltd, Bath

CONTENTS

PREFACE AND ACKNOWLEDGEMENTS

Planning for the *Companion* began more than a decade ago, towards the end of the century that forms its backdrop. In the intervening years between conception and birth, the world of theatre has altered significantly—and rapidly—but the main aim of the book has stayed the same: to take the reader a first few steps down many of the criss-crossing paths that open up behind the deceptively plain door marked 'theatre'. Hence a companion rather than a dictionary or an encyclopaedia. There was no single reader in mind, just anyone interested in theatre, whether the new student, the established specialist or those who simply enjoy going to or making theatre. The book, however, would find its chief audiences in English-speaking cultures, and the prism through which we looked was the theatre of those cultures in their international context.

From the outset, the idea was to define theatre broadly and as a live and continuing activity. As someone working in the theatre at that time, I was determined to follow through this approach not only in the range of subjects to be covered but also more importantly in the choice of contributors. Alongside the academic and journalistic commentators writing on their topics of particular expertise, I wanted people who earned their living in the theatre to bring their own crafts, skills and disciplines to life: the wig maker, the fight arranger, the sound designer, the actor, the voice teacher, the composer, the playwright, the director, the choreographer, the lighting designer, the prop maker, the scenographer, the costume designer, the production manager, the stage manager, the literary manager, the casting director; and beyond them, the administrator, the publicist, the photographer, the publisher, the architect. As an example, the entry that offers a brief historical survey of the development of directing in the century is off-set by an account of what it means to be a director, written by a director; or, to take another case, the biographical and analytical entry on one of the landmark playwrights, say, Brecht, Ibsen, or O'Neill, is accompanied by a brief description of performing that writer's work written by an actor distinguished in his or her interpretation of it.

The focus of the *Companion* is the century of unprecedented change in theatre yet the historical starting point was kept loose deliberately in order to allow coverage of the impact of the preceding century. The twentieth century for our purposes was deemed to run up to the end of the year 2000, although a few later events and books published subsequently have been included. Naturally, other centuries are present as well; we live in a constant interaction with our understanding of the past. There are entries on the influence and interpretation of previous eras, from the ancient Greeks and Romans through the medieval, Elizabethan and Jacobean ages to the Restoration, in addition to the nineteenth century.

Influences are also worldwide and cross not only the barrier of time, but of language and geography too. Theatre institutions, key towns and cities, countries, genres, trends, a basket-full of '-isms', the various branches of theatre-making, and the individuals who practice and have practised related skills, are all to be found here from across five continents. This breadth is matched by the span of some 280 contributors, who are based in 20 countries.

Radical conceptual and linguistic changes occurred during the century, and are occurring still, as boundaries are transgressed and 'high' and 'low' artistic divisions are challenged. Consequently, dramatic theory has an entry as do, for instance, audience, body art, cabaret, carnival, circus, escapology, the Internet, magic, waxworks, pop music, fireworks, food and fashion. Entries on television, radio, cinema, opera and dance are included for similar reasons, with more space allocated to dance-related subjects because of its close interaction with theatre.

Definitions throw up other problems too, notably differences in usage at different times in the century, and between as well as within countries. This is especially tricky in contested areas of life that concern identity, for example in dealing with 'ethnicity' or 'disability' or even what to call a female performer. More strikingly, political reality—the disappearance or formation of a new state, a change in a place name—can overtake works such as this. Sometimes it is possible to rewrite adequately, sometimes not. Similarly, it is not always possible to keep up with mortality.

The choice of the more than 2,500 entries was mine, but, apart from editing entries in order to maintain a consistency in form and presentation to aid the reader, the contents of each entry is the responsibility of the contributor and inclusion does not mean that I neces-sarily agree with everything that appears. Contributors were asked to provide certain basic facts but facts can be slippery things, as a quick glance at any two reference books on the same subject reveals. While I endeavoured to double check as much of the information as was humanly possible (and bearable), I am aware of areas of doubt and incompleteness, and that new research will demand revisions. I would welcome information from readers that might help in that task.

Contributors were also asked to provide a bibliography for their entries. However, in an attempt to be both up-to-date and wide-ranging, and keeping the final extent of the work within manageable proportions, titles were often added later or deleted without the contributor's involvement. Bibliographies, therefore, are not the contributors' responsibility. Books written by the subject of an entry are contained within the entry. To save space published play texts were excluded. Websites have not been listed because the *Companion* does not seek to be a directory or handbook, and electronic publishing was in its infancy when the book was locked into its final stages of production. A selective general reference bibliography is included, and this does contain some relevant Internet entries.

The huge stylistic and organizational challenges posed by a book of this scope and scale were made more onerous by the complexity and duration of the whole production process, which, in turn, was made more testing by a change of publisher along the way. Some things had to be abandoned, such as illustrations (too costly). The solutions to various problems used in those parts of the *Companion* that did survive are described in the Reader's Guide. The general rule was to make sense of the book for the reader rather than to follow slavishly a 'house' style.

Acknowledgements

At the beginning of the project, I was given invaluable support and guidance by a group of advisors: Professor Vera Gottlieb, John

Gunter, Genista McIntosh, Ian McKellen, and Rob Marx, who continued to help on matters American. Each one has also contributed to the *Companion*, and without them, the book would never have taken off at all.

At the other end of the project, the *Companion* would never have survived to publication without the patient, tireless efforts of Veronica Higgs, my Project Manager at Continuum Publishing.

Thanks also to: Gillian Bromley, Janet Godden, Francesca Greatrorex, Colin Hutchens, Ben Jancovich, Michael Patterson, Alyn Shipton; to those subjects of entries who volunteered biographical information; to those contributors who helped me with queries that were not related to their own entries; and to innumerable individuals in colleges, libraries, theatre organizations and theatre companies who helped me in small but always important ways, in particular: Dr Janet Birkett at the Theatre Museum, London; the Institut Français, London; Wendy Seyb and Kevin Winkler at the New York Public Library for the Performing Arts; Richard Bapty, Glasgow University Library; and Dilys Grant, Playmarket, New Zealand.

Colin Chambers
London, 2002

READER'S GUIDE

The *Companion* consists of more than 2,500 entries written by some 280 contributors from 20 countries. In editing the entries, certain stylistic and organizational rules were followed wherever possible in order to help the reader make sense of the content provided.

These are the main principles:

1. Entries are arranged in alphabetical order, word by word. Names beginning with Mc and Mac are filed in one sequence at the beginning of the letter M, arranged alphabetically according to the letter following the prefix. The positioning of prefixes/suffixes in names varies from language to language; normal usage and subject's preference have generally been followed. Additional, alternative, or names not normally used, are presented within square brackets (e.g. Eliot, T[homas] S[tearns]; Marx, Groucho [Julius]), but are ignored in the alphabetical arrangement. Institutions known by a number, e.g. 7:84 or 25th Street Theater, are filed as if the number had been spelled out.

2. Where possible place and full date of birth and death are provided. If unknown or doubtful, a question mark is added, or information is given as recorded in birth and death registers. The country may not be given if the place is sufficiently well known or, in the case of deaths, is the same as that of birth. For those affected by the new calendar introduced in Russia in 1918, the new dates are given.

3. Boxed entries are written by theatre practitioners about their own area of work.

4. Names or topics which appear in small capital letters within an entry indicate that there is a separate entry for that subject.

5. The date accompanying a play is the date of first production, unless otherwise stated or made clear from the context, e.g. the date of a production in an entry on a director or actor.

6. Transliteration has been standardized wherever possible, e.g. on the spelling of proper names such as Stanislavsky. When used in titles of plays or theatre companies, we have followed the convention of the contributor and have tried to be consistent across entries.

7. Non-English titles of plays, books and theatre companies, etc. have where possible

been given in the original language, transliterated when necessary. The English version of such titles is also given, though for popular plays with many titles in English not every version is listed. If, to the best of the contributor's knowledge, there is no English version, a translation is offered where possible and is signified by being placed within single quotation marks. If no translation is given, it usually means either that the title is the same in English or that it has not been translated into English and there is no English equivalent.

8. Further reading bibliographies at the end of entries are a combination of titles provided by contributors and those added by the editor. Published playtexts are not listed for space reasons, and titles by the subjects are included in the entries themselves. There is also a selective general reference bibliography.

CONTRIBUTORS

David Adams
Arts journalist

Christopher Akerlind
Lighting designer

Karim Alrawi
Playwright/literary editor

Elaine Aston
Lancaster University

Laurie Atkinson
Critic

Joe Aveline
Theatre consultant

Robert Ayers
Nottingham Trent University

David Ayliff
Theatre consultant

Ronald Ayling
University of Alberta

Martin Banham
University of Leeds

David Barbour
Entertainment Design, New York

Clive Barker
New Theatre Quarterly

Peter Barnes
Playwright

Nick Barter
Royal Academy of Dramatic Art

Neil Bartlett
Lyric Theatre, Hammersmith, London

Richard Beacham
University of Warwick

Susan Bennett
University of Calgary

Eugene Benson
University of Guelph

Günter Berghaus
University of Bristol

Leonard Berkman
Smith College, Northampton, MA

Cicely Berry
Voice director

Ian Bevan
Theatre historian

Evita Bier
Warehouse Theatre, Croydon, Surrey

Brian Birch
University of Hull

Lauren Bishop
Northern Stage, Newcastle upon Tyne

William Bland
Balkan expert

John M. Blundall†
Puppeteer

Sari Bodi
Theatre researcher

Travis Bogard
Independent scholar

Gerald Bordman
Theatre historian

David Bradby
Royal Holloway, University of London

George Brandt
University of Bristol

Christopher Brereton†
Architect

Yvonne Brewster
Director

Jon M. Brokering
Chuo University, Tokyo

Peter Brook
Director

John Broome
Festival Theatre, Stratford, Ontario

Rexton S. Bunnett
Theatre historian

Ramsay Burt
Dr Montfort University, Leicester

Ophelia Byrne
Linen Hall Library, Belfast

John Calder
Publisher

Simon Callow
Actor

Luisa Cariaga
Deaf West Theater Company, Los Angeles

Marvin Carlson
City University of New York

Christie Carson
Royal Holloway, University of London

Peter Cheeseman
Director

Robert Cheesmond
University of Hull

Lynne Clark
Queen Margaret University College,
  Edinburgh

Ian Clarke
Loughborough University

Claire Cochrane
University College Worcester

Martha Coigney
International Theatre Institute

Thomas F. Connolly
Suffolk University, Boston

Leonard W. Conolly
Trent University, Peterborough, Ontario

Contributors

Mossamiliano Cossati
Actor/director

Cathy Courtney
Freelance writer

Richard Crane
University of Sussex

Cyril Cusack†
Actor

Phil Dale
English National Opera

Kim Dambaek
International Theatre Institute, Denmark

Lyn Darnley
Voice teacher

Gillian M. Day
Independent scholar

Thomas DeFrantz
Massachusetts Institute of Technology

Maria Delgado
Queen Mary, University of London

Gillian Diamond
Casting director

Joseph M. Diaz
Freelance writer

Leonard E. Doucette
Theatre historian

Oliver Double
University of Kent at Canterbury

Neil Dowden
Freelance arts journalist

Jeremy Eccles
Arts journalist

Gwynne Edwards
University College of Wales, Aberystwyth

Sveinn Einarsson
Ministry of Culture, Reykjavik, Iceland

Alfred Emmet†
Director

Joan L. Erdman
Columbia College, Chicago

Michael Evans
Rogaland Teater, Stavanger, Norway

Richard Eyre
Director

Felicity Firth
University of Bristol

Christopher Fitz-Simon
Writer/director/scholar

Anne Fletcher
Independent scholar

Lorna Flint
The Shakespeare Institute,
    Stratford-upon-Avon

Kathy Foley
University of California, Santa Cruz

Helena Forsås-Scott
University College London

Sandra Freeman
University of Sussex

Ted Freeman
University of Bristol

Karen Fricker
Irish Theatre Magazine, Dublin

Donald H. Frischmann
Texas Christian University, Fort Worth, TX

Maggie Gale
University of Birmingham

Michael Gambon
Actor

Kurt Gänzl
Encyclopedia of the Musical Theatre

Simon Garrett
Learning Media, Wellington, New Zealand

Anna Wheeler Gentry
University of Missouri-Kansas City

Jools Gilson-Ellis
University College Cork, Ireland

Steve Gooch
Playwright

Martin Gottfried
Theatre historian

Vera Gottlieb
Goldsmiths College, University of London

Tony Graham
Unicorn Theatre, London

Frances Gray
University of Sheffield

Francesca Greatorex
Theatre researcher

Alexis Greene
New York University

Gillian Greer
Independent scholar

Richard Griffiths
Kings College, University of London

Firenza Guidi
European Live Arts Network Wales

John Gunter
Designer

Maik Hamburger
Dramaturg/translator

Kaiser Haq
University of Dhaka

Martin Hargreaves
De Montfort University, Leicester

Peter Harlock
Publicist

Alamgir A. Hashmi
Explorations, Islamabad

Mark Hawkins-Dady
Editor and writer

John Haynes
Photographer

Peter Hepple
The Stage, London

Katharine Herbert
English Touring Opera, London

Nick Hern
Publisher

Roger Hill
National Association of Youth Theatres

Philip Hobsbaum
University of Glasgow

Alison Hodge
Royal Holloway, University of London

Terry Hodgson
University of Sussex

Peter Holland
The Shakespeare Institute,
  Stratford-upon-Avon

Stuart Hopps
Choreographer

Jane House
Independent scholar

Pamela Howard
Scenographer

Tony Howard
University of Warwick

Anthony Hozier
Rose Bruford College, London

Alan Hughes
University of Victoria, British Columbia

Adriana Hunter
Theatre researcher

Michael Huxley
De Montfort University, Leicester

John Istel
Stagebill, New York

Anthony Jackson
The University of Manchester

Ann Jellicoe
Playwright

Jeffrey Eric Jenkins
Theatre critic

Sue Jennings
Drama therapist

Sharon Jensen
Non-Traditional Casting Project,
New York

Claudia Durst Johnson
Independent scholar

Cathy Joyce
Arts manager

Anna Karabinska
Independent scholar

Michael Karp
Clown/actor/movement specialist

Ben Kingsley
Actor

Pirkko Koski
University of Helsinki

Joanna Krakowska-Narożniak
Theatre historian

Ananda Lal
Jadavpur University, Calcutta

Ellen Lampert-Gréaux
Entertainment Design, New York

Harry Lane
University of Guelph, Ontario

Jessica Lange
Actress

Steve Lawson
Williamstown Theatre Festival,
 Massachusetts

Robert Leach
University of Birmingham

Brenda Leedham
Royal Shakespeare Company,
 Stratford-upon-Avon

John A. Leonard
Sound designer

Dick Linklater†
Arts administrator

Charles London
Theatre historian

John London
Independent scholar

Felicia Hardison Londré
University of Missouri-Kansas City

Frank Long
Freelance writer

Joseph Long
University College Dublin

Tomas MacAnna
Abbey Theatre, Dublin

Dick McCaw
Royal Holloway, University of London

Jan McDonald
University of Glasgow

Robert David MacDonald
Translator/actor/writer

Frank McGuiness
Playwright

Genista McIntosh
Royal National Theatre

Ian McKellen
Actor

Linda MacKenney
Independent scholar

Anna McMullan
Trinity College, Dublin

G.H. McWilliam
University of Leicester

Petar Marjanović
Theatre historian

Karen Marshalsay
Royal Scottish Academy of Music
   and Drama

Robert Marx
Essayist/producer/foundation director

Daniel Massey†
Actor

Judy Meewezen
Freelance writer

Mei Sun
Victoria University of Wellington,
   New Zealand

Daniel Meyer-Dinkgräfe
University of Wales, Aberystwyth

Gábor Mihályi
Theatre historian

Julia Miles
Women's Project and Productions,
   New York

Patrick Miles
Translator

Bob Millington
Freelance writer

Mitch Mitchelson
Circus specialist

Michael Morley
Flinders University, Adelaide, Australia

Linda Moss
Freelance writer

Roland Muldoon
Hackney Empire Theatre, London

Christopher Murray
University College Dublin

Paul Nadler
New York University

Paul Newham
Voice expert

Olu Obafemi
University of Ilorin, Nigeria

Dunbar H. Ogden
University of California, Berkeley

Osita Okagbue
University of Plymouth

Kole Omotoso
University of the Western Cape,
    South Africa

Vicky Ooi
University of Hong Kong

M. Elizabeth Osborn†
Theatre researcher

Fintan O'Toole
Journalist/critic

Avraham Oz
University of Haifa

Derek Paget
University College Worcester

Stewart Parker†
Playwright

Susan Pastika
University of California, Davis

Susan Pauly
Mount Mercy College, Cedar Rapids,
    Iowa

D. Keith Peacock
University of Hull

Arthur Penn
Film director

Maria Petchell
Freelance writer

Edward Petherbridge
Actor

Litz Pisk†
Choreographer

Alan Plater
Playwright

Joanne Pottlitzer
Writer/director/producer

Sharon Pressburg
University of California, Davis

Hal Prince
Director/producer

Marian J. Pringle
The Shakespeare Centre,
    Stratford-upon-Avon

Orla Pulton
Freelance writer

Gerald Rabkin
Rutgers University

Helen Rappaport
Freelance translator/researcher

Kenneth Rea
Guildhall School of Music and Drama,
    London

Dan Rebellato
Royal Holloway, University of London

Beatriz J. Rizk
Independent scholar

Jason Robards†
Actor

Brian Roberts
Goldsmiths College, University of London

Rosemary Roberts
Freelance editor

Geoffrey Robertson, QC
Barrister

Christopher Robinson
Christ Church, Oxford

Pieter Rogers
Producer

George Rowell
University of Bristol

Donald Roy
University of Hull

Domhnall Ruadh
Freelance writer

Allen Saddler
Journalist

Helen Salmon
International Theatre Institute

Ian Saville
Magician

Lesley-Anne Sayers
Independent scholar

George Schaefer
University of California, Los Angeles

Ekkehard Schall
Actor

Michael R. Schiavi
New York Institute of Technology

David Schneider
Actor

Claude Schumacher
Theatre historian

Wendy Scott
Freelance writer

Adrienne Scullion
University of Glasgow

Richard Seaford
University of Exeter

Linda Sears
University of California Davis

Richard Seaver
Publisher

David Self
Freelance writer

Nabil Shaban
Actor

Dominic Shellard
University of Sheffield

Maria Shevtsova
Goldsmiths College, University of London

Rachel Shteir
Depaul University, Chicago

Jeanette Siddall
Battersea Arts Centre, London

Lizzie Slater
Freelance writer/performer

Irene Slatter
University of Durham

Robin Slaughter
University of Bristol

Barry Smith
Nottingham Trent University

Sarah A. Smith
Theatre researcher

Andrew Solway
Freelance writer

Michael Sommers
Freelance writer

Eva Šormová
Theatre Institute Prague

David Staines
University of Ottawa

Stuart Stallard
Mask maker

Sarah Stevenson
Theatre researcher

John Stokes
King's College London

Judy S. J. Stone
Freelance writer

Ronald W. Strang
University of Kent at Canterbury

Janet Suzman
Actress

Jeannie Swales
Stephen Joseph Theatre, Scarborough

Dorothy L. Swerdlove
formerly, Curator, The Billy Rose Theatre
    Collection, New York Public Library

Lowell and Nancy Swortzell
New York University

Carolyn Talarr
Theatre researcher

Peter Thomson
University of Exeter

John Tiffany
Traverse Theatre, Edinburgh

Denise Tilles
Freelance editor

Carlos Tindermans
Theatre historian

Jennifer Tipton
Lighting Designer

Ruth Tompsett
Middlesex University

Rudolf Valkhoff
Translator

Rob van der Zalm
Theater Instituut Nederland, Amsterdam

Chris Vine
New York University

Jeffrey Wainwright
Manchester Metropolitan University

Mick Wallis
Loughborough University

Harriet Walter
Actress

J. Michael Walton
University of Hull

Micheline Wandor
Writer/critic

Donald Watson
Translator/theatre historian

Marie Wells
University College London

Arnold Wesker
Playwright

Debora Weston
Actress

Billie Whitelaw
Actress

Peregrine Whittlesey
Agent

David Williams
Dartington College of Arts, Totnes, Devon

David A. Williams
University of California, Davis

Faynia Williams
University of Sussex

R. Clive Willis
University of Manchester

Steve Wilsher
Fight director

Sue Wilmington
Costume designer

Noel Witts
University College Scarborough

Laurie Wolf
Goldsmith College, University of London

Sarah Woodcock
Theatre Museum, London

Guy Woolfenden
Composer

Gus Worby
The Flinders University of South Australia

Nick Worrall
Middlesex University

Barbara Wright
Translator

Barry Yzereef
University of Calgary

SELECTIVE REFERENCE BIBLIOGRAPHY

Arata, Esther S. *More Black American Playwrights: A Bibliography*. Metuchen, NJ: Scarecrow Press, 1978.

Arata, Esther S. and Nicholas John Rotoli. *Black American Playwrights, 1800 to the Present: A Bibliography*. Metuchen, NJ: Scarecrow Press, 1976.

Archer, Stephen M. *American Actors and Actresses: A Guide to Information Sources.* Detroit: Gale, 1983.

Aston, Elaine and Janelle Reinelt, eds. *The Cambridge Companion to Modern British Women Playwrights.* Cambridge: Cambridge University Press, 2000.

Atkinson, Patrick W., comp. *Theatrical Design in the Twentieth Century: An Index to Photographic Reproductions of Scenic Designs.* Westport, CT: Greenwood Press, 1996.

Banham, Martin, ed. *The Cambridge Guide to African and Caribbean Theatre*. Cambridge: Cambridge University Press, 1994.

Banham, Martin, ed. *The Cambridge Guide to Theatre,* 2nd ed. Cambridge: Cambridge University Press, 1995.

Bean, Annemarie. *A Sourcebook of African-American Performance: Plays, People, Movements*. London: Routledge, 1999.

Berthold, Margot. *The History of World Theater. Volume 1: From the Beginnings to the Baroque.* New York: Continuum, 1999. New paperback edition.

Bordman, Gerald. *American Theatre: A Chronicle of Comedy and Drama, 1869–1914.* Oxford: Oxford University Press, 1994.

Bordman, Gerald. *American Theatre: A Chronicle of Comedy and Drama, 1914–1930.* Oxford: Oxford University Press, 1995.

Bordman, Gerald. *American Theatre: A Chronicle of Comedy and Drama, 1930–1969.* Oxford: Oxford University Press, 1996.

Bordman, Gerald. *The Oxford Companion to American Theatre,* 2nd edition. New York: Oxford University Press, 1992.

Brandon, James R., ed. *The Cambridge Guide to Asian Theatre.* Cambridge: Cambridge University Press, 1997.

British Theatre Directory, 2001. London: Richmond House Publishing, 2001.

Brown, John Russell, ed. *The Oxford Illustrated History of Theatre.* Oxford: Oxford University Press, 1997.

Bryan, George B. *Stage Deaths: A Biographical Guide to International Theatrical Obituaries, 1850–1990.* 2 vols. Westport, CT: Greenwood Press, 1991.

Bryan, George B. *Stage Lives: A Biography and Index to Theatrical Biographies in English.* Westport, CT: Greenwood Press, 1985.

Cassell Companion to Theatre. London: Cassell, 1997.

Cavanagh, John. British Theatre: A Bibliography, 1905–85. Mottisfont, Hants: Motley Press, 1989.

Contemporary American Dramatists. New York: St James Press, 1994.

Contemporary British Dramatists. New York: St James Press, 1994.

Contemporary Dramatists, 6th ed. New York: St James Press, 1998.

Contemporary Women Dramatists. New York: St James Press, 1994.

Cortes, Eladio et al, eds. Dictionary of Latin American Theatre. Westport, CT: Greenwood Press, 2000.

Coven, Brenda. American Women Dramatists of the Twentieth Century: A Bibliography. Metuchen, NJ: Scarecrow Press, 1982.

Demastes, William W., ed. American Playwrights, 1880–1945: A Research and Production Sourcebook. Westport, CT: Greenwood Press, 1995.

Demastes, William W. and Katherine E. Kelly, eds. British Playwrights, 1880–1956: A Research and Production Sourcebook. Westport, CT: Greenwood Press, 1996.

———. British Playwrights, 1956–1995: A Research and Production Sourcebook. Westport, CT: Greenwood Press, 1996.

Dramatists Sourcebook: Complete Opportunities for Playwrights, Translators, Composers, Lyricists and Librettists, 20th edition. New York: Theatre Communications Group, 2000.

Dunton, Chris. Nigerian Theatre in English: A Critical Bibliography. Oxford: Hans Zell, 1998.

Durham, Weldon B., ed. American Theatre Companies, 1888–1930. Westport, CT: Greenwood Press, 1987.

———. American Theatre Companies, 1931–1986. Westport, CT: Greenwood Press, 1989.

Epstein, Lawrence S., ed. A Guide to Theatre in America. New York: Macmillan, 1985

France, Rachel, ed. A Century of Plays by American Women. New York: Richard Rosen Press, 1979.

Franklin, Joe. Joe Franklin's Encyclopedia of Comedians. New York: Bell Pub. Co., 1979.

Frick, John W. and Stephen M. Vallilo, eds. Theatrical Directors: A Biographical Dictionary. Westport, CT: Greenwood Press, 1994.

Gänzl, Kurt. The Encyclopedia of the Musical Theatre, 2nd ed. 3 vols. New York: Gale, 2001.

Gänzl, Kurt. Ganzl's Book of the Broadway Musical. New York: Schirmer/Prentice Hall International, 1994.

Gänzl, Kurt. The Musical: A Concise History. Boston, MA: Northeastern University Press, 1997.

Gänzl, Kurt. Musicals: The Complete Illustrated Story of the World's Most Popular Live Entertainment. London: Carlton, 1995.

The Grey House Performing Arts Directory, 2002, 2nd ed. Millerton, NY: Grey House Publishing, 2001.

The Guide to Selecting Plays for Performance, 90th ed. London: Samuel French, 2000.

Hischak, Thomas S. The American Musical Theatre Song Encyclopedia. Westport, CT: Greenwood Press, 1995.

Hischak, Thomas S. American Theatre: A Chronicle of Comedy and Drama, 1969–2000. Oxford: Oxford University Press, 2001.

Hochman, Stanley, ed. McGraw-Hill Encyclopedia of World Drama, 2nd ed. 5 vols. London: McGraw-Hill, 1984.

Innes, C.D., et al. Twentieth-Century British and American Theatre: A Guide to Archives. London: Ashgate, 1999.

International Bibliography of Theatre, 1994–95. New York: Theatre Research Data Center, 1997.

International Dictionary of Theatre. 3 vols. Detroit: Gale Research, 1992–95.

Jowers, Sidney and John Cavanagh, eds. Theatrical Costume, Masks, Make-up and Wigs: A

Bibliography and Iconography. London: Routledge, 2000.

Kaye, Phyllis Johnson, ed. *National Playwrights Directory*, 2nd ed. Waterford, CT: Eugene O'Neill Theater Center, 1981.

Kullman, Colby H. and William C. Young, eds. *Theatre Companies of the World.* 2 vols. Westport, CT: Greenwood Press, 1986.

Londré, Felicia Hardison. *The History of World Theater, Vol. 2: From the English Restoration to the Present*. New York: Continuum, 1999. New paperback edition.

Londré, Felicia Hardison and Daniel J. Watermeier. *The History of North American Theater: From Pre-Columbian Times to the Present.* New York: Continuum, 1998.

Loney, Glenn. *20th Century Theatre.* 2 vols. New York: Facts on File, 1983.

McNeil, Barbara and Miranda C. Herbert, eds. *Performing Arts Biography Master Index,* 2nd ed. Detroit, Mich: Gale Research, 1981.

MacNicholas, John, ed. *Twentieth-Century American Dramatists,* 2 vols. Detroit, Mich: Gale Research, 1981.

Mapp, Edward. *Directory of Blacks in the Performing Arts*, 2nd ed. Metuchen, NJ: Scarecrow Press, 1990.

Matlaw, Myron. *Modern World Drama: An Encyclopedia.* London: Secker and Warburg, 1972.

Meyer-Dinkgräfe, Daniel, ed. *Who's Who in Contemporary World Theatre*. London: Routledge, 2000.

Mikotowicz, Thomas J., ed. *Theatrical Designers: An International Biographical Dictionary.* Westport, CT: Greenwood Press, 1992.

Murphy, Brenda, ed. *The Cambridge Companion to American Women Playwrights.* Cambridge: Cambridge University Press, 1999.

New York Public Library, Research Libraries. *Catalog of the Theater and Drama Collections. Parts I-III*. Boston, Mass: G.K. Hall, 1967–76.

Norton, Richard C. *A Chronology of the American Musical Theater.* 3 vols. Oxford: Oxford University Press, 1998.

Parsons, Philip and Victoria Chance, eds. *Companion to Theatre in Australia.* Sydney: Currency Press, 1995.

Pavis, Patrice. *Dictionary of the Theatre: Terms, Concepts and Analysis.* Toronto: University of Toronto Press, 1998.

Peterson, Bernard L. *Profiles of African American Stage Performers and Theatre People, 1816–1960*. Westport, CT: Greenwood Press, 2000.

Rees, L. *A History of Australian Drama.* 2 vols. Melbourne: Angus & Robertson, 1978.

Rigdon, Walter, ed. *The Biographical Encyclopedia and Who's Who of the American Theatre.* New York: Heinemann, 1966.

Rubin, Don, ed. *World Encyclopedia of Contemporary Theatre.* 6 vols. London: Routledge, 1994–1999.

Segel, Harold B. *Twentieth Century Russian Drama from Gorky to the Present.* New York: Columbia University Press, 1979.

Shafer, Yvonne. *American Women Playwrights, 1900–1950.* New York: Peter Lang, 1955.

Shiach, Don. *American Drama 1900–1990.* Cambridge: Cambridge University Press, 2000.

Silvester, Robert. *United States Theatre: A Bibliography from the Beginning to 1990.* New York: G.K. Hall, 1993.

Stanton, Sarah and Martin Banham. *Cambridge Paperback Guide to Theatre.* Cambridge: Cambridge University Press, 1996.

Stratman, Carl Joseph. *American Theatrical Periodicals, 1798–1967: A Bibliographical Guide.* Durham, NC: Duke University Press, 1970.

Styan, J.L. *Modern Drama in Theory and Practice.* 3 vols. Cambridge: Cambridge University Press, 1981.

Swortzell, Lowell, ed. *International Guide to Children's Theatre and Educational Theatre: A Historical and Geographical Sourcebook*. Westport, CT: Greenwood Press, 1990.

Trapido, Joel, gen. ed. *An International Dictionary of Theatre Language*. Westport, CT: Greenwood Press, 1985.

Trussler, Simon, ed. *Cambridge Illustrated History of British Theatre*, new edition. Cambridge: Cambridge University Press, 2000.

Wearing, J.P. *American and British Theatrical Biography: A Directory*. Metuchen, NJ: Scarecrow Press, 1979.

White, Kerry R. *An Annotated Dictionary of Technical, Historical and Stylistic Terms Relating to the Theatre and Drama: A Handbook of Dramaturgy*. Lampeter: E. Mellen, 1995.

Who Was Who in the Theatre, 1912–1976. Detroit, Mich: Gale Research, 1978.

Wilmeth, Don B. and Christopher Bigsby, eds. *The Cambridge History of American Theatre*. 3 vols. Cambridge: Cambridge University Press, 1998–2000.

Wilmeth, Don B. and Tice L. Miller, eds. *The Cambridge Guide to American Theatre*. Cambridge: Cambridge University Press, 1996.

Websites

Dramatists Play Service, Inc.
http://www.dramatists.com

Inter-Play: An On-Line Index to Plays in Collections, Anthologies and Periodicals
http://www.portals.org/interplay

International Bibliography of Theatre 1996 [Theatre Research Data Center, Brooklyn College]
http://www.rxwbc@cunyvm.cuny.edu

The International Theatre Design Archive: Project 2000.
URL: http://www.siue.edu/PROJECT2000

McCoy's Guide to Theatre and Performance Studies.
URL: http://www.stetson.edu/departments/csata/thrguid.html

SIBMAS International Directory of Performing Arts Collections
http://www.emmettpub.co.uk

Theatre Central
http://www1.playbill.com/cgi-bin/plb/central?cmd=start

A

Abbey Theatre The Irish Literary Theatre, founded by AUGUSTA GREGORY (Lady Gregory), EDWARD MARTYN and W. B. YEATS in 1898 with its first production a year later, became the Irish National Theatre Society in 1903 (absorbing the National Dramatic Society of William and Frank FAY) as well as the lessees of the old Mechanics' Theatre in Abbey Street, Dublin, subsequently known as the Abbey Theatre. The first production (on 27 December 1904) was a double bill of Lady Gregory's folk comedy *Spreading the News* and Yeats's VERSE DRAMA *On Baile's Strand*. The society's earliest financial benefactor was ANNIE HORNIMAN, later founder of the GAIETY THEATRE, Manchester.

The aim of the founders at this time of rising national sentiment was to present new plays by Irish writers, preferably on Irish subjects and with Irish actors and technicians. This objective has been maintained. There are two stages, the Abbey and the smaller Peacock, which opened in 1925, both operating 52 weeks of the year with a repertoire of new Irish plays, plays by Irish writers of the past (especially Farquhar, Goldsmith, Sheridan, Boucicault, WILDE, SHAW, Yeats, SYNGE and O'CASEY), and selected international classics.

At the beginning of the twentieth century Lady Gregory favoured rural or folk themes. Yeats was interested in something more 'remote, spirtual, ideal', and drew his inspiration from Celtic mythology, contemporary European writers and artists such as MAETERLINCK and Doré, and the Japanese *noh* theatre. The more domestic mode prevailed, notably in the work of COLUM, MURRAY, MACNAMARA, MAYNE and ROBINSON. Under William Fay, who directed most of the early productions, a remarkably 'natural' performace style was developed, which became the hallmark of the Abbey Theatre ensemble for almost half a century and which suited the majority of new plays written in what came to be termed the 'Irish Ibsenite' tradition. In 1918 Robinson and Yeats founded the Dublin Drama League from within the Abbey, along with others outside, to present plays from abroad (by O'NEILL, COCTEAU, PIRANDELLO). It ran for ten years.

The earliest playwright associated with the Abbey Theatre to gain international recognition was J. M. Synge. His comedy of the fantastic hero Christy Mahon, *The Playboy of the Western World* (1907), is a masterpiece of Western drama. After his death in 1909, with the Fays removed by Horniman and her financial support removed a year later (partly because Yeats refused to close the theatre during Edward VII's funeral), Yeats and Gregory steered the theatre to its next important phase. O'Casey dominated the Abbey Theatre during the 1920s; his 'Dublin trilogy', *The Shadow of a Gunman, Juno and the Paycock* and *The Plough and the Stars*, are more frequently revived than any other plays in the repertoire, though the last of the three was greeted by riots at its première. O'Casey left the Abbey and Ireland when the theatre rejected *The Silver Tassie* in 1928. During the period 1930–50 the most popular playwrights were GEORGE SHIELS, ST JOHN ERVINE, P. V. CARROLL, Louis Dalton, M. J. MOLLOY and Walter Macken.

Among the many Abbey players destined to find fame via the emerging (mainly US) film industry were MÁIRE O'NEILL, Maureen Delany, Eileen Crowe, May Craig, SIOBHÁN MCKENNA, BARRY FITZGERALD, F. J. MCCORMICK, Arthur Sinclair, ARTHUR SHIELDS, CYRIL CUSACK and Denis O'Dea. Lennox Robinson directed the majority of stage productions from 1910 to 1935; HUGH HUNT was resident director 1935–8, followed by Frank Demody (1938–48) and then RIA MOONEY.

From 1941 to 1972 the managing director was Ernest Blythe.

In 1951 the theatre was accidentally burned down and the company was accommodated in the Queen's Theatre until the new building designed by Michael Scott was opened on the original site in 1966. A new Peacock was opened in 1967. Since then, TOMÁS MACANNA, Hugh Hunt, Alan Simpson, Lelia Doolan, JOE DOWLING, Christopher Fitz-Simon, Vincent Dowling, GARRY HYNES, PATRICK MASON, and Ben Barnes have held the post known as artistic director.

The Abbey Theatre has produced new plays by EUGENE MCCABE, BRIAN FRIEL, TOM MURPHY, THOMAS KILROY, HUGH LEONARD, JOHN B. KEANE and many others. TOM MACINTYRE, Graham Reid, Neil Donnelly, Seán McCarthy and BERNARD FARRELL are among the highly successful playwrights of the following generations, while subsequent younger writers whose work has been initially produced or taken up by the Abbey Theatre include FRANK MCGUINNESS, SEBASTIAN BARRY, MICHAEL HARDING, Dermot Bolger and MARINA CARR.

The Abbey Theatre was the first company in the English-speaking world to recieve annual state subsidy (1925). It is administered by a board of seven, two of whom are appointed by the Taoiseach (prime minister). CHRISTOPHER FITZ-SIMON

Mícheál hAodha, *Pictures at the Abbey* (1983)
Hugh Hunt, *The Abbey* (1979)
Robert Welch, *The Abbey Theatre, 1899–1999: Form and Pressure* (1999)

Abbott, George [Francis] (b. Forestville, NY, 25 June 1887; d. Miami, Fla., 31 Jan. 1995) Director, producer, play-doctor and playwright. At the age of 102, Abbott was still directing on Broadway. In 1987 he directed a revival of his first playwriting hit *Broadway* (with Philip Dunning, 1926). He had begun his professional theatre career as an actor in 1913, but won his greatest renown as a director of musical comedies, many of which he co-authored, including the Pulitzer Prize winning *Fiorello!* (1959). Abbott worked on over 120 productions, winning six Tony awards and numerous other honours. His colourful autobiography, *Mister Abbott* (1963), chronicles decades of American showbiz. FELICIA HARDISON LONDRÉ

Abdoh, Reza *see* EXPERIMENTAL THEATRE

Abel, Lionel *see* DRAMATIC THEORY; METATHEATRE

Abell, Kjeld (b. Ribe, Denmark, 25 Aug. 1901; d. Copenhagen, 5 March 1961) Playwright and stage designer. Kjeld's plays, which included *Melodien, der blev voek* (*The Melody that got Lost*, 1935; London 1936),

were greatly influenced by the work of Hans Christian Andersen; they had a strong note of social criticism couched in poetic language. Though highly regarded as one of Denmark's greatest playwrights, little has been seen in English. ADRIANA HUNTER

Robert Corrigan, *Masterpieces of Scandinavian Theatre* (1967)

Abramovic, Marina *see* BODY ART

absurd, theatre of *see* THEATRE OF THE ABSURD

Achard, Marcel [Marcel Auguste Ferréoll] (b. Sainte-Foy-les-Lyon, France, 5 July 1899; d. Paris, 4 Sept. 1974) Playwright. His plays are rooted in Marivaux and the COMMEDIA DELL'ARTE. Such early comedy as *Jean de la Lune* (1929) rates quite as highly as the famous *Patate* (1957, also translated as *Rollo*). Several of his plays appeared in New York. He also wrote for the screen (*Orage*, 1934). TERRY HODGSON

Achurch [Sharp], Janet (b. Lancs, 17 Jan. 1864; d. Ventnor, Isle of Wight, 11 Sept. 1916) Actress who worked with FRANK BENSON and was committed to the promotion of advanced drama, IBSEN in particular. She made her major contribution to the cause when she appeared as Nora in the British première of *A Doll's House* (1889), a production she organized with her husband, Charles Charrington. She and Charrington, in association with the INDEPENDENT THEATRE SOCIETY, undertook a tour of *A Doll's House* and SHAW's *Candida*, in which she played the lead. Before retiring in 1913 she organized and acted in other plays by Ibsen and Shaw. A play based on her correspondence with Shaw was seen in London in 1978. IAN CLARKE

Ackland, Rodney [Norman Acland Bernstein] (b. Rochford, Essex, 18 May 1908; d. Richmond, Surrey, 6 Dec. 1991) Actor and playwright. His acting career began with GORKY's *The Lower Depths* (1924). He worked for many of the repertory and CLUB theatres, including J. B. FAGAN's Oxford Players. He appeared in KOMISSARZHEVSKY's production of *Three Sisters* (1925), which inspired him to write, and he earned the label of the English CHEKHOV. His playwriting career began with *Improper People* (1929); other plays include *The Dark River* (1942), about England on the edge of war, and *The Pink Room* (written 1946, first staged 1952), set at the end of the Second World War. Revised as *Absolute Hell*, it was broadcast on BBC television (1991) and given a successful production at the NATIONAL THEATRE (1995). He co-authored works with the actor Robert Newton, including *Cupid and Mars* (1945), and was known for his adaptations of Russian plays by BUL-GAKOV, Dostoevsky and Ostrovsky. MAGGIE GALE

Charles Duff, *The Lost Summer* (1995)

Acquart, André (b. Vincennes, Paris, 12 Nov. 1922) Designer. He began designing in Algiers, where he was educated, and in 1951 moved back to Paris, where he became a key figure in the new theatre movement, applying his architectural and minimalist approach to plays by AUDIBERTI, BRECHT, DURAS, FRISCH, IONESCO, VALLE-INCLÁN and VINAVER. He worked with leading directors such as ROGER PLANCHON, JEAN-MARIE SERREAU and JEAN VILAR, and is particularly remembered for his association with ROGER BLIN on GENET's *The Blacks* (1959) and *The Screens* (1966). CHARLES LONDON

acrobatics *see* CIRCUS; CLOWN

acting In the twentieth century the process of acting underwent more thorough analysis and experimentation than at any other time in the history of Western theatre. Previously, written reflections on the craft were mostly anecdotal, and an actor's development relied largely upon practical experience both through the immediacy of performance and through informal apprenticeships. Western practitioners tended to prioritize the rehearsal and performance of a play over sustained, self-conscious systems of actor training. At the beginning of the century widespread interest in the acting process took hold. The increasing influence of objective scientific research encouraged the search for absolute, objective languages of acting. Further inspired by a growing awareness of Eastern traditions of training and performance as well as innovations in other art forms, practitioners began to experiment. These investigations were led by the first of a new breed in the theatre – the director – whose rational examination of the whole construction of the actor's role and preparatory training became the foundation for many of the landmark productions of the period. KONSTANTIN STANISLAVSKY was the first fully to analyse the actor's process. Working initially at the MOSCOW ART THEATRE, he established a 'grammar of acting' in 1906 when struggling with his performance of Dr Stockmann in IBSEN's *An Enemy of the People*. He found it was necessary to develop techniques that would encourage the creative interpretation and expression of a character, but would not rely on inspiration alone. In three seminal texts – *An Actor Prepares*, *Building a Character* and *Creating a Role* – Stanislavsky outlined his psycho-physical system through a student actor's experience of it. He wished to establish strategies which could be useful to any actor in any form of

theatre, and although his name became synonymous with psychological realism (for which the Moscow Art Theatre was famous), he went on to explore much more widely, working with SYMBOLISM, OPERA and VERSE. The impact of realism, which had been growing since the mid-nineteenth century, retained a powerful influence and encouraged a psychologically based style of performance which is associated with Stanislavsky, and came to be adapted by LEE STRASBERG and the key exponents of the METHOD in the United States. The Method's emphasis on individual expression and psychological revelation led to an acting style in which the actor 'personalizes' the role to an intense, almost inseparable degree of engagement. Many leading theatre and film actors (BRANDO, PACINO, Newman, de Niro, PAGE) were trained in this approach, which dominated American acting from the 1950s. At the same time, realism and naturalism were rejected by many practitioners early in the century, and different acting systems, such as those of JACQUES COPEAU and MICHAEL CHEKHOV, soon began to emerge. VSEVELOD MEYERHOLD favoured a more presentational style of performance, preferring the possibilities of the actor as *cabotin* – as a singer, dancer, juggler and tumbler. In his BIOMECHANICAL system of training, Meyerhold laid a strong emphasis on reflexive and rhythmical impulses of the body as the resource for the actor's creativity, emphasizing ensemble playing in a highly physical form of theatricalized performance. However, Meyerhold never forgot the importance of the intellect: 'I have no use for actors who know how to move but cannot think.' Following another trajectory, BERTOLT BRECHT, acutely sensitized by the political extremism of prewar Germany, dismissed the emotional acting he associated with Aristotelian drama, accusing the actors of going 'into a trance and taking the audience with them'. He wished for a theatre that allowed the audience to engage critically with the performance, including its social and political implications. Although Brecht's EPIC THEATRE techniques demanded an understanding of the psychological life of a character, he believed the actor should also critically examine the character during performance. In *A Short Organum for the Theatre*, the notion of 'gestus' was proposed – in part a theory of gestural expression which helped distance the audience from the action, inviting a greater awareness of the social and economic forces at play. Brecht's legacy was immense, and many practitioners continued working with the possibilities of the more politicized role of the actor, including JOAN LITTLEWOOD's THEATRE WORKSHOP and JOSEPH CHAIKIN's OPEN THEATER. Towards the end of the century the Brazilian-born cultural activist AUGUSTO BOAL developed Forum Theatre, in which the empowered spectator becomes the 'spect-actor', actively contributing to the performance in order to engage physically with themes of exploitation and oppression. The second half of the century saw a major shift in the actor's function in the experimental, collaborative and devised theatres of Europe and the United States. By the 1960s many practitioners were seeing actors as more than interpreters of the text; they were repositioned at the centre of the theatre-making process. ANTONIN ARTAUD provided a significant reference point in this context. Artaud's *The Theatre and its Double* called for performance which celebrated the non-verbal elements of consciousness that could arouse therapeutic emotions within his spectators. While Artaud left no concrete technique for actors to work with, his belief in the actor's physical potential – 'an affective athleticism' in which an actor could 'make use of his emotions as a wrestler makes use of his muscles' – influenced much of the physical theatre of the late twentieth century, notably in the work of PETER BROOK, the LIVING THEATER, Joseph Chaikin and JERZY GROTOWSKI. The growing concentration on the physicality of the actor was encouraged by a practical engagement with non-Western forms. Artaud's vision of a THEATRE OF CRUELTY was inspired by his encounter with Balinese dance-drama; others, such as Peter Brook and EUGENIO BARBA, have undertaken wide-ranging practical research within Eastern performance traditions (*see* EASTERN THEATRE, ITS INFLUENCE ON THE WEST).

The increasing centrality of the actor as the creative hub of theatre led to highly disciplined PHYSICAL PREPARATION. Jerzy Grotowski's POOR THEATRE abandoned all external 'trappings' of theatre, and insisted on an intense vocal and physical training which would free the actor's body to become an 'obedient instrument capable of performing a spiritual act'. Grotowski described his methodology of training as a process of elimination – a 'via negativa' through which the actor, rather than building skills, eradicated blocks. Through a process of self-penetration the actor performs a sacrificial act of revelation, against which the spectator could measure themselves. Grotowski described this form of acting as *re*-acting, and worked on it with a small group of collaborators in intense privacy. Although his intimate productions were witnessed by small numbers of people, his own writings were published in *Towards a Poor Theatre* and have been widely disseminated.

Unlike any other art form, the actor uniquely utilizes her or his 'self' as the instrument through which an action, image, persona or narrative is communicated to an audience. In the late twentieth century the question of how the actor might utilize this notion of 'self' again became destabilized by rapidly changing cultural, political and social circumstances and beliefs. New questions concerning identity, ethnicity, interculturalism, gender and ecology have entered the continuing debate on the nature of acting. ALISON HODGE

See also DIRECTING; PERFORMANCE, PREPARING A PART.

Antonin Artaud, in *Actors on Acting*, ed. Toby Cole and Helen Krich Chinoy (1970)
Bertolt Brecht, *Brecht on Theatre*, ed. John Willet (1978)
Jerzy Grotowski, *Towards a Poor Theatre*, ed. Eugenio Barba (1981)
Vsevelod Meyerhold, in *Twentieth Century Actor Training*, ed. Alison Hodge (2000)
Shomit Mitter, *Systems of Rehearsal* (1992).

· An actor reflects ·

'They act a lot ... I wish there was not so much acting,' said ANTON CHEKHOV during the fourth rehearsal of *The Seagull* at the Alexandrinksy Theatre, St Petersburg, in October 1896. The production was a failure, but Chekhov was persuaded to allow a new company, the MOSCOW ART THEATRE, to produce the play, and now the seagull emblem on the stucco façade of the Moscow Art Theatre has outlived the emblem of the Communist Party's hammer and sickle, which was for a long time its companion. Chekhov's relationship with the Moscow Art Theatre in general and its director STANISLAVSKY in particular was a complex one – but it might be safely said that, by and large, the company did *not* act too much. In fact we are told (by THEODORE KOMISSARZHEVSKY) that they were known in their early days among the rest of the Moscow acting fraternity as 'The Whisperers'.

After the revolution, in 1923, Stanislavsky led part of the company on a foreign tour to Berlin and Paris, but it was in the United States that they made their major impact. They gave special Friday matinées attended by hundreds of actors. John BARRYMORE, who was enjoying a triumph as Hamlet on BROADWAY, attended one of these matinées at the Jolson's Theater on 59th Street, and wrote that it was 'the most amazing experience I have ever had by a million miles in the theatre' – high praise from someone whose reputation for dissolution is stronger than it is for discernment. Indeed, Charlie Chaplin wrote that Barrymore had 'a nonchalance that treated everything rather contemptuously; whether it was a performance of *Hamlet* or sleeping with a duchess, it was all a joke to him.' Since both JOHN GIELGUD and LAURENCE OLIVIER were enthralled by Barrymore's Hamlet in London in 1925, we may, perhaps, value Barrymore's opinion of the Moscow Art Theatre.

Two of its company – RICHARD BOLESLAVSKY and Maria Ouspenskaya – stayed behind in New York and the American Laboratory Theater was founded under their tutelage. There followed the THEATER GUILD and the GROUP THEATER. Significantly, CLIFFORD ODETS, looking back on his youthful days as an actor and then playwright with the Group Theater in the early 1930s, said, 'Without the Group Theater, I doubt that I would ever have become a playwright. I might have become some other kind of writer, but the Group Theater and the so-called "method" forced you to function out of the kind of person you are, not as you thought the person had to function, or as another kind of person, but simply using your own materials.' The METHOD, as interpreted by the New York ACTORS' STUDIO, founded by distinguished Group members in 1947, became quite simply the most famous acting style the world has ever known. From the early 1950s, if you'd stopped anyone in the street in any town or village in the world where American films were shown, they'd have been able to give you their own definition of 'Method Acting'.

The London theatre had been bypassed by the foreign tour of the Moscow Art Theatre in the 1920s, and felt then – and for some time to come – no very strong urge to emulate the great repertoire ensembles of Europe. It was dedicated to commercial runs of single plays, eight performances a week for at least a year at a time, rehearsed invariably for no more than three weeks, with occasional excursions into the classics, particularly Shakespeare, both at the OLD VIC and out at STRATFORD-UPON-AVON. This 'island' theatre made do with Stanislavsky's books *My Life in Art* and *An Actor Prepares*. So, it was not 'The Whisperers' (who'd never whispered, of course) but the 'mutterers and scratchers' of the silver screen of the early 1950s who exerted the big influence on young English actors in films such as *On the Waterfront* and *A Streetcar Named Desire*. But, just as an apparently anti-theatrical style was becoming fashionable (could it have originated from those words of Chekhov's: 'They act a lot – I wish there was not so much acting'?), a new theatricality asserted itself.

In 1956 the BERLINER ENSEMBLE visited London just after BRECHT's death. Still a young company, its influence was more revolutionary than the Moscow Art's visit two years later, though the bulk of that company had worked with Stanislavsky himself. Brecht's influence won the day, though he himself was capable of enjoying, even admiring, the legacy of the famous Russian actor, director and teacher. For good measure, in the 1960s London had the world's theatre on its doorstep with an annual WORLD THEATRE SEASON. The Italians brought, among other things, something very like traditional *COMMEDIA DELL'ARTE*, the Japanese brought their traditions of *noh* theatre, *kabuki* and *bunraku* puppets, the Greeks sang and danced in Aristophanes, Czechoslovakians mimed and, no doubt, if MEYERHOLD had not been shot for formalism in 1940, we would have had his company presenting classics in the biomechanical style. The same period saw in London the Peking Opera and the *kathakali* dancers of India. In fact all these companies, including the COMÉDIE-FRANÇAISE, *acted a lot*.

It's a dangerous oversimplifiction, but there is evidence to support the notion that it was a tame, complacent, conventional, nearly moribund British theatre which was so challenged and stimulated by foreign influences in the 1950s and 1960s. In the same year as the Brechtian invasion there came from the United States ARTHUR MILLER's play *A View from the Bridge*, which, because of one aggressive kiss by the male hero on the mouth of his daughter's would-be suitor, was denied the LORD CHAMBERLAIN's licence for public performance and had to be performed in hastily organized CLUB conditions. 'It seemed an exotic play to the English at the time,' wrote Miller in his autobiography *Timebends*, 'especially when their own theatre was so middle-class, so bloodlessly polite.'

The arrival of the seven-year-old Berliner Ensemble in London in 1956, followed in 1958 by the 60-year-old Moscow Art Theatre's visit, were remarkable enough simply as cultural manifestations of a political 'thaw' in the Cold War, with all the curiosity value of a privileged peep behind the impenetrable Iron Curtain. But if we thought Miller's achievement in creating a tragedy portraying the working-class life of New York's longshoremen and their women, which opened out effortlessly from vivid workaday realism into ancient Greek dimensions, 'exotic', then do not forget that in anticipating what we might describe as the 'shock of the old' in the Moscow Art Theatre, we were also recovering from seeing a company the bulk of whose regular audience was bussed in from the factories of Berlin. The ALIENATION EFFECT was the most talked-about acting phenomenon, along with EPIC THEATRE: POLITICAL THEATRE with a capital 'P'. The words 'ENSEMBLE' and 'repertoire' had a thrilling, urgent, almost mystic ring in a London which had no national theatre yet, no permanent troupes – it still has none, but then the idea of belonging to such an institution was a consummation devoutly to be wished. The actress playing Madame Ranevskaya in the Moscow Art's visiting production of *The Cherry Orchard* had joined the company in 1916. Her c.v., like so many of the others in the company, listed such awards as the Red Banner of Labour, the Order of Lenin and several Stalin prizes. How, we wondered, had this great bourgeois, pre-revolution theatre survived to become *the* cultural communist flagship; where had Stanislavsky's pursuit of truth in acting led these actors within the straitjacket of official socialist realism? 'We act withour voices,' wrote KENNETH TYNAN, 'they act with their lives.' Once more the awe we felt at the foreign product carried with it an implicit rebuke to our homegrown article.

By the time of the first World Theatre Season in 1964, our NATIONAL THEATRE was one year old and the ROYAL SHAKESPEARE COMPANY had a home in London as well as Stratford, and a repertoire that included classics other than Shakespeare as well as contemporary English and foreign plays, drawing classical and contemporary acting technique and style healthily closer to one another. The security of tenure which European actors enjoyed never materialized, but gradually new patterns of work did. The 'security' of eighteen-month runs in the WEST END in light commercial pieces was broken down by the growing importance and attractiveness of television. Television destroyed the provincial audience for actors in the treadmill of 'weekly rep' – hasty copies of West End successes. In 1960 there were still 70 such provincial companies. State subsidy for non-commercial provincial rep gave actors more rehearsal time and more adventurous repertoire.

What had sustained the notion of a 'great' British theatre throughout this traumatic transformation decade from the mid-1950s to the mid-1960s, dazzled as we were by American and European achievements? We had lost an empire, but still the English language – the language of Shakespeare and the King James I translation of the Bible – was also the great international language (as it has increasingly since become in the fields of politics, commerce and science). As a glorious language of poetry and rhetoric, of scintillating comedy and towering tragedy, its finest acknowledged exponents were actors. Surely they had developed deftness with gold cigarette cases, doorknobs, silver teapots, throwaway lines and all manner of British middle-class understatement. The famous American quip about our restraint – 'One can see the reins but where's the damn horse?' – still applied. But in this twenty-first century when we read or see the best plays of the first half of the twentieth century we realize in some surprise what protean challenges they still present to actors. Even a reading of SOMERSET MAUGHAM's commercial hit *The Circle* of 1921 astonishes when we appreciate what a roller-coaster of serious social, sexual and, yes, moral ambiguity and surprise English drawing-room comedy could and still can be, somehow carrying on the tradition which stretched through Goldsmith and Sheridan right back to Congreve and Wycherley. Laurence Olivier's National Theatre company, founded in 1963, had a great tradition to draw upon as well as a vital new path to forge. SHAW, GALSWORTHY, GRANVILLE BARKER, PINERO, WILDE, COWARD and Maugham were all crying out to be revived, and the 'kitchen sink' drama of the 1950s had certainly not annihilated the acting technique required to revive them. Indeed the contemporary playwrights ARDEN, PINTER, STOPPARD, to name but three, positively required at least something of what Bernard Shaw said his plays required: a technique wholly rhetorical and hyperbolical.

Olivier's ashes rest in Poet's Corner in Westminster Abbey together with those of Sir HENRY IRVING, and the corners of their two small paving stones, marking the place, touch. Nearby the name of Oscar Wilde glows in stained glass. It was placed there in a window in 1995, exactly a century after the ruination of his theatrical and literary careers when, on the day of the announcement that Irving had become Britain's first knight of the realm, Wilde was committed to two years' hard labour. At Olivier's memorial service in the Abbey in 1989, the British actors who made up the core of the congregation formed an assemblage perhaps unprecedented in the whole history of acting since Thespis, in that among them they had been part of the ransacking of the world's repertoire of drama. They had looked for the truth in the widest ever selection of the theatrical game of 'Let's Pretend' to date. Their technique had been challenged by the widest selection of styles and conventions, and their imaginations had been privileged to identify with the widest selection of vision; maybe they had misfired more wildly, and connected more miraculously than any other actors before them. PEGGY ASHCROFT, born 82 years before, walked to the lectern and spoke some lines from Milton's poem 'Lycidas': 'Weep no more, woeful shepherd, weep no more, For Lycidas your sorrow is not dead.' Nor, it seemed, was theatrical tradition! The still vigorous athletic music of Ashcroft's voice seemed to render negligible the span of theatrical time between that moment in the Abbey and some notion we might have had of how ELLEN TERRY, Henry Irving's leading lady, might have spoken the same lines a century earlier at Irving's funeral in 1905.

Terry had worked for 30 years with Irving, the undisputed head of the profession, at the LYCEUM THEATRE, doing lavish Shakespeare, romantic melodrama, Alfred Tennyson's *Becket*, a version of Goethe's *Faust*. Under Irving, the Lyceum had gained the status of a national theatre, but Irving's resistance to the progressive IBSEN and Bernard Shaw was absolute. In 1903, at the age of 55 and under her own management, with her own money, Terry risked Ibsen's *Vikings* with revolutionary designs by her son, ex-Lyceum actor GORDON CRAIG. And in 1906 she appeared at the Royal Court in Shaw's *Captain Brassbound's Conversion*, becoming the first actor of the century to descend from the high pedestal of establishment stardom to play in Sloane Square in the work of a controversial modern playwright whose work the West End managers wouldn't touch, although they caught up with him later. They often do.

When Sir Henry was laid to rest in Poet's Corner in 1905 Shaw refused to attend, 'Authorship,' he wrote, 'having no place at Irving's graveside.' A huge part of the future, however, *was* represented at Irving's funeral, by a diminutive 16-year-old actor and music-hall performer who was there by virtue of the fact that he happened to be playing a small part in a West End theatre at the time. Charlie Chaplin was appearing at, of all theatres, the Lyceum, and by virtue of being in West End employ, had a pass for the ceremony. It was Shaw who noted the link between Irving and Chaplin. Irving, he wrote, 'was utterly unlike anyone else. He could give importance and a noble melancholy to any sort of drivel that was put into his mouth and it was this melancholy, bound up with an impish humour, which forced the spectator to single him out as a leading figure with an inevitability that I never saw again in any other actor until it rose from Irving's grave in the person of a nameless cinema actor who afterwards became famous as Charlie Chaplin.' If Irving had spurned the new playwrights, Chaplin was to have no need of playwrights at all. The silent film era reintroduced comic improvisation, a Hollywood *commedia dell'arte* on an unprecedented scale in terms of time, money and audience, and Chaplin and Buster Keaton became the actor–poets of the cinema, each creating a unique mask of his own. Now we can see that Chaplin, Keaton and the tramps of BECKETT's *Waiting for Godot* are all relatives.

What was it, though, in the early 1900s, that the Shaws, Craigs and Terrys were leaving behind of the old century? The great classics of opera and ballet, when still staged traditionally, are the best clue: *Swan Lake*, *Giselle*, *La Traviata*, *Tosca*. We have John Gielgud's word for it that the influence of all this lingered on. He remembers as a boy of 12 seeing Ophelia brought in, dripping, on a bier after the willow speech to produce an effective curtain. And it is the applause at the successful theatrical scene endings to which he constantly refers in his notes on his own Hamlet, published in 1937. 'I know only too well that my own performance had been cluttered with these things. I have never been sufficiently experienced or sufficiently original to dare to direct a play or play Hamlet without including a great deal of this kind of theatricalism.' The fine romantic actor LEWIS WALLER, who failed in the modern drama and died in 1915, leaves us a sound recording of Henry V's 'Once more unto the breach . . . ' delivered in a long, generalized, rhetorical forte with his diaphragm working overtime to provide a vibrato on every open vowel. (It has to be said that Gielgud's early Parlophone recording of the same speech is in precisely the same vein with not one tremulo less.)

The small change of workaday naturalism is often seen as our modern cure as actors for the old-fashioned grandeur which we suspect was not underpinned with a fully explored truth. If the old stage characters were created too much within the frame of theatrical convention and not exposed to the less predictable, more disturbing currents of life itself, maybe the acting, especially on the grander scale, suffered similarly. If there is any truth in these subjective speculations, we mustn't fall into the trap of believing that there is something about the everyday behaviourist approach of our modern naturalistic style which more easily attains the stamp of truth. No; it is another convention and, like all conventions, continually falls prey to cliché. Conventions we can never escape, though we can have fun with them, juggle with them, swap them and pretend that they are not there. Cliché we can, and must, avoid, and perhaps the avoidance of cliché is the most important item in the actor's stock-in-trade.

However naturalistic, however stylized, whether disturbingly avant-garde or reassuringly conventional, whether the auditorium is awash with empathy or bristling with Brechtian alienation, the actor seeks one thing, that the audience shall believe, and so the actor's quest is towards truth. This is the common ground that unites the thespian behind the mask, in the sunshine of ancient Greece, and the actor in his key light in the film studio. Our work might be edited, recorded digitally and bounced off a satellite to be seen a thousand miles away and after we are dead, but what we do, what we produce in the studio and on the stage, remains stubbornly as part of that dwindling proportion of human-kind's handmade products, a personal, primitive yet infinitely complex and lively ritual of enacting ourselves to ourselves in which we still believe there may be some truth to be glimpsed within the pretending, some new way of seeing our lives – some vital way of confronting our real life roles as human beings.

EDWARD PETHERBRIDGE

activism A term associated with the utopian but socially active wing of anti-war EXPRESSIONISM around the time of the First World War; playwrights CARL ZUCK-MAYER and Johannes Becher were briefly part of the trend. COLIN CHAMBERS

Actor's Company (UK) *see* EDDISON, ROBERT; McKELLEN, IAN

Actor's Company (US) *see* LA JOLLA PLAYHOUSE

Actors' Equity Association *see* UNIONS

Actors' Studio A professional workshop established in New York in 1947 by GROUP THEATER members ELIA KAZAN, CHERYL CRAWFORD and ROBERT LEWIS. Membership is by invitation, and is granted only to those who pass exhaustive auditions; but it is granted for life. A fundamental premise is that an actor can always improve on his or her work, that there is never a definitive performance or acting style. The Studio does not charge its members tuition fees; it is not a school of acting, but rather offers the opportunity to explore acting techniques, using improvisation and team criticism.

In 1949 LEE STRASBERG joined the Studio, and he became its artistic director in 1951. Strasberg owed much of his ability as a trainer of actors to the ideas of STANISLAVSKY, and he developed his own 'Method' for helping actors to work. It was under his directorship that the Studio's members became great exponents of METHOD acting. The powerful, idiosyncratic and often intensely erotic naturalistic performances of the Studio's actors are best displayed in Kazan's films, *A Streetcar Named Desire* (1951), *On the Waterfront* (1954), both with MARLON BRANDO, and *East of Eden* (1955) with James Dean.

Towards the end of the 1950s the Studio set up corresponding workshops for playwrights, directors and producers, and in 1963 established a short-lived theatre of its own. It is chiefly remembered, however, for its influence on acting. It has nurtured many acclaimed performers including Paul Newman, Marilyn Monroe, GERALDINE PAGE, DUSTIN HOFFMAN, Robert de Niro and Meryl Streep. Many Hollywood stars travel to New York in order to benefit from the workshops. Supporters admire the psychological depth and natural truth of Studio actors' performances. Critics condemn the psychological explorations as self-indulgent and the nat-

uralness – typically manifested as sniffing, scratching and mumbling – as mannerism. Most agree, however, that the Studio has irrevocably influenced American acting – indeed, has come to represent the contemporary American style – and that Method acting achieves outstandingly credible film performances.

Following Strasberg's death in 1982, ELLEN BURSTYN and AL PACINO became directors of the Actors' Studio, and, after a period when Arthur Penn was in charge (*see* ACTORS' STUDIO FREE THEATER AT RAW SPACE), they were joined in the leadership by actor Harvey Keitel.

ADRIANA HUNTER

See also ACTING; AN ACTOR REFLECTS.

D. Garfield, *A Player's Place: The Story of the Actors' Studio* (1980)

F. Hirsch, *A Method to their Madness: The History of the Actors' Studio* (1984)

L. Strasberg, *A Dream of Passion: The Development of the Method* (1988)

Actors' Studio Free Theater at Raw Space In 1994 the ACTORS' STUDIO launched a new initiative with the New York New School for Social Research, a marvellous university that had been established by John Dewey and others at the time of the First World War and had survived since then through considerable adversity. The Studio introduced a three-year postgraduate programme for actors, directors and playwrights, inspired by a programme that had been offered at the New School in the 1940s under the leadership of ERWIN PISCATOR. Initial expectations were well exceeded, and the success of the programme led to the establishment of a unique theatre on 42nd Street, which matches its political and artistic audacity by being free. Dramatic theatre had been squeezed out of BROADWAY by the influx of British musicals, and the smaller theatres, which in the 1960s and 1970s had been able to be take risks, had become beholden to their subscribers; this had taken away their capacity for adventure, caught, as they now were, between commerce and art. For instance, the idea of staging a new play with 20 actors had become an impossibility.

An ex-National Guard armoury called Raw Space was found which had been used for independent film shooting spaces; one space proved too small for the cinema's needs and it was donated to the Actors' Studio. The premier American theatre architect Hugh Hardy revamped the space and turned it into a flexible auditorium, wide but not deep, seating 94. The first production, *Major Crimes* by Jay Presson Allen, was directed by Arthur Penn and opened in 1997.

With no box-office income, the money to support the Free Theatre has come from the Studio's association with the New School and the sale to cable television of in-depth craft sessions given by Actors' Studio veterans, such as ELLEN BURSTYN, Paul Newman and AL PACINO. ARTHUR PENN

Actors' Theater A theatre company established as the Equity Players in 1922 by the United States Actors' Equity Association to present serious drama, both new and classical. They enjoyed considerable success with a production from their first season, Jesse Lynch Williams's *Why Not?*; but most of their work – though highly valued by the critics – was little appreciated by audiences. In 1924 the company underwent considerable restructuring and changed its name to the Actors' Theater. As such it enjoyed several successful seasons. In 1927 it became a part of KENNETH MACGOWAN's company. ADRIANA HUNTER

Actors Theatre of Louisville Nonprofit professional theatre, founded in Louisville, Kentucky, in 1964 by Richard Block and Ewel Cornett and led by Jon Jory from 1969 to 2000, when Marc Masterson took over. It is best known for its festival of new American plays, produced every spring since 1977 and attracting national and international attention. The festival in its early years was especially important to the development of Southern and women playwrights such as BETH HENLEY (*Crimes of the Night*, 1979) and MARSHA NORMAN (*Getting Out*, 1977). In the 1990s the festival grew more diverse, presenting new work by the likes of Anne Bogart, Suzan-Lori Parks, DAVID HWANG, Regina Taylor, TONY KUSHNER and David Margulies, whose 1999 Pulitzer Prize play *Dinner with Friends* was given its première at the festival in 1998. The theatre received a special Tony award in 1980. M. ELIZABETH OSBORN

Actor's Workshop A regional theatre company founded in 1952 by HERBERT BLAU and Jules Irving, both professors at San Francisco State College. It focused on the furthering of the individual performer's abilities – hence the position of the apostrophe in the title – and became famous for its performances of contemporary political and experimental pieces such as *Mother Courage* and *Waiting for Godot*. The company instigated a special workshop for the prisoners at San Quentin, and it performed at the Brussels and Seattle World's Fairs.

The Actor's Workshop disintegrated after Blau and Irving left in 1965. ADRIANA HUNTER

Actresses' Franchise League A British all-woman suffrage society founded in 1908 that presented plays to further the cause of all women. The AFL provided entertainment for political meetings and had a play department to meet the considerable demand. Its first big success was a farce by CICELY HAMILTON, *How the Vote Was Won* (1909), directed by ELLEN TERRY's daughter EDITH CRAIG (and reprinted in 1985 as the title play in a collection of suffragette plays). The pair teamed up again later that year for *A Pageant of Great Women*. By 1913, a men's group for actors and writers had been formed and an independent Women's Theatre Company set up but war intervened and the AFL joined the fight, organizing entertainment for the troops under LENA ASHWELL's direction. The granting in 1917 of the vote for women over 30 saw the end of the AFL, but its spirit survived for a few years more in the PIONEER PLAYERS, which had been founded by Craig in 1911. COLIN CHAMBERS
See also WOMEN IN THEATRE.

Julie Holledge, *Innocent Flowers: Women in the Edwardian Theatre* (1981)

Adamov, Arthur (b. Kislovodsk, Caucasus, 23 Aug. 1908; d. Paris, 15 March 1970) French playwright of Russian origin, son of a family which owned oil wells, appropriated by the state after 1917. Having been sent to Switzerland in 1914, Adamov moved with his family to Germany in 1922 and then to France in 1924; here, with his knowledge of Russian and German, he obtained commissions to translate many classics. He also developed a small reputation as a SURREALIST poet and met ARTAUD and others which began his interest in the theatre. In three autobiographical volumes, *L'Aveu* (*The Confesssion*, 1946), *L'Homme et l'enfant* (*Man and Child*, 1968) and *Je . . . Ils* (1969), he talks of the events that anguished his life.

Adamov's theatrical career really began only after the Second World War. He became the third of the trio of ABSURD playwrights whose names are bracketed together by critics, along with BECKETT and IONESCO; he was the most political of the three and the only one to join the Communist Party (in 1960). His first original postwar play, *La Parodie* (*The Parody*, written 1945, first performed 1948) was followed during the next few years by *L'Invasion* (*The Invasion*, 1948); *La Grande et la Petite Manoeuvre* (*The Big and the Little Manoeuvre*, 1950); *Le Professeur Taranne* (*Professor Taranne*, 1953), the first in a fruitful collaboration with the director ROGER PLANCHON; *Tous contre tous* (*All Against All*, 1950); and his principal successes, *Le Ping-Pong* (*Ping Pong*, 1955) and the most overtly political *Paolo Paoli* (1957). They portray the confusion of waking reality with dream, sexual humiliation and the depiction of scenes of fascist brutality that also suggest the atmosphere of Kafka.

Thereafter Adamov fell increasingly under the influence of BRECHT and O'CASEY, and his plays became closer to everyday reality, dealing mainly with historical events. His biggest success was *Le Printemps '71* (*Spring '71*, 1961), set during the Paris Commune, and *Les Âmes mortes* (*Dead Souls*, 1960) after Gogol. Plagued by unhappiness and alcoholism, afraid of failure and death, politically committed to the left, penurious and living in small hotels, he eventually died by his own hand. His other major plays, still virtually unknown in English, are *La Politique des restes* (*Scavengers*, 1962, performed, as was *Spring '71*, by the amateur UNITY THEATRE, London), *Sainte Europe* (1966), *Monsieur le modère* (*Monsieur the Moderate*, 1967), *Off Limits* (1968) and *Si l'été revenait* (*If Summer Came Again*, 1969).   JOHN CALDER

John J. McCann, *The Theater of Adamov* (1975)
John H. Reilley, *Arthur Adamov* (1974)

Adams, John   *see* OPERA; SELLARS, PETER

Adams, Maude [Kiskadden]   (b. Salt Lake City, Utah, 11 Nov. 1872; d. Tannersville, NY, 17 July 1953)   Actress. Assuming her actress mother's unmarried name, she began performing while still a child in San Francisco and nearby mining camps. She moved east in 1888 and played increasingly important supporting roles with major stars of the time. But it was only after producer CHARLES FROHMAN took the pale-haired, grey-green-eyed, graceful young lady under his aegis that she won the stardom which made her America's most popular actress until her retirement on Frohman's death. Her singular charm was evident in such plays as *Rosemary* (1896) and five by J. M. BARRIE: *The Little Minister* (1897), *Quality Street* (1901), *Peter Pan* (1905), *What Every Woman Knows* (1908), and *A Kiss for Cinderella* (1916). She returned to the stage only twice after this, working instead as a lighting adviser and drama teacher.
GERALD BORDMAN

P. Robbins, *Maude Adams: An Intimate Portrait* (1956)

adaptation/translation   Since these two terms can cover similar territories, whose frontiers are the subject of frequent border disputes, 'translation' should be understood as meaning straightforward 'changing into another language retaining the sense' (Samuel Johnson), and 'adaptation' as 'the process of modifying to suit new conditions' (*OED*), either by altering an original dramatic work to fit a new context or presentational concept, or by converting to theatrical use a work (usually narrative) not originally intended for that medium – a process sometimes known as dramatization.

The progress of translation and adaptation in the twentieth century, or more accurately its second half, was one of gradual but continual expansion. In England in the early 1900s little was noticeable except a few lacklustre imports of French plays, French having been since the mid-seventeenth century by and large the only generally accessible foreign tongue. Since the forming of the *entente cordiale*, German culture was no longer a paramount influence; French was once again fashionable, and, it was always slightly to be hoped, a trifle indecent. The First World War, fought as it was on a fairly restricted front, made little difference to this rather smug state of things, and the interwar years, while they produced certain versions of elegance and distinction, produced none that seriously dented the cultural complacency of a public that, having to support the arts unaided, naturally favoured products which could be relied on to contain nothing to disturb the values for which that public stood. This, and a pendulum swing to propriety, stifled what scant appetite for change there was. 'French, eh?' says the Customs man in Evelyn Waugh's novel *Vile Bodies* (1930), '. . . and pretty dirty, too, I shouldn't wonder . . . If we can't stamp out literature in the country, we can at least stop it being brought in from abroad.'

The first great expansive impulse came from the Second World War, which, fought on multiple and extended fronts, repatriated, at its end, a multitude of soldiery with a new appetite and respect for 'bloody abroad': as soon as rations permitted, the English cuisine began to veer ponderously towards the beckoning hearths of Italy and France, and as soon as money permitted, the Labour government initiated direct subsidy of, *inter alia*, the theatre. The subsequent fortunes of translated work have been directly connected to the amounts given to, and the standards set by, the subsidized theatre. As the grant system, though firmly entrenched, found no welcome in the self-help ethos of the right, it was no surprise, during the 1980s, to witness the rise of the accountant as a policy-defining figure, whose baleful influence was cast on publishing, concert programmes and the theatre repertoire. This, in turn, favoured the (in theory) cost-effective practice of engaging, in the event of being forced to present foreign-language work, star authors to lend their name and fame to work regardless of their degree of familiarity with the original language of the work.

However this practice may have affected the quality of the work done, it did, perhaps paradoxically, enhance the status of the translator, who, from being the harmless literary drudge whose name by no means always appeared on the title page, became a valued collaborator whose name often appears, even in reviews.

Because the theatre likes to preserve its mystery by insisting that only a true 'theatrician' can ever hope to know how to write for it, it tends to think that a literal translation prepared by a bilingual hack can be transmuted in the alembic of monoglot genius into the pure gold of a semi-original masterpiece, a view as tendentious as saying that work of quality is possible only at the hand of a linguist/stylist. The truth, as so often, lies disappointingly in between. Translation is 'the art of the least intolerable sacrifice ... the instinctive choice between competing imperfections' (David Luke), and the significant prerequisite is an instinctive affinity of one writer for another, to allow the conducting of a sort of conversation with the original author, permit the liberties taken with intimates, even the suggestion of things that may not have occurred to him or her. That these affinities need not depend on a knowledge of the original language becomes clear when a foreign writer becomes popular with readers or audiences who experience similar affinities, instinctual or elective.

Stravinsky said that 'All sins against the spirit begin with a sin against the letter,' and the theatre – not, after all, the home of academic exegesis – can often be accused of allowing a vague dedication to the 'spirit' to excuse breathtaking inaccuracies. There are two extreme situations for a translator: the technical document and the opera libretto. In the one, inaccuracy can have possibly disastrous repercussions; in the other, preordained stress, pitch and volume limit the translator's choices to a point where absolute accuracy can be tortuous, ludicrous and sometimes downright undesirable. In between these extremes lies imaginative literature, combining both headaches. The better the writer, the less replaceable the choice of words – the best the translator can hope for is to convey the overtones in the wider context of a whole passage rather than word by word. Secondly, every prose sentence has a rhythm as taut as a line of verse, any extension of which will cause an alarming sag: translations, in an effort to convey precision of meaning, nearly always end up slightly longer than the original. Nowhere is this more dangerous than in dramatic dialogue.

Adaptations of original plays to fit new circumstances can be said charitably to give renewed currency to work temporarily or unjustly out of public favour, much as the work of Nahum Tate and David Garrick on the plays of Shakespeare, though now considered barbaric, did much to maintain Shakespeare's reputation at a time when he himself was considered barbaric. (The reverse situation, when a play already popular is exploited in another theatrical medium – e.g. the extraction of *My Fair Lady* from *Pygmalion* – usually does little more than purchase charm at the expense of bite.) Other than this, the function of such adaptations seems otiose: there is less inclination now than there was in 1950 to think that a neatly equivalent ambience for any foreign situation can be found somewhere or other in one's own country, nor is it still thought essential for the understanding of a work to transport it bodily and more or less violently into a region where it does not belong: such variants will blur as much and more of the play as they will reveal.

In adapting novels, the effect of transferring them into an alien medium is similar to that of an engraving or a piano transcription; certain things are revealed more clearly and more immediately than on the wider canvas of the original, due to the less discursive nature of the theatrical experience, and to the need to pick out essentials, not to burden the spectator with details impossible to absorb in the limited time available. Beginning in the nineteenth century, when demand for the theatre started to outstrip the supply of work worth performing in it, most successful novelists – Dickens, Scott, Balzac, Dumas *père* – attracted by the superior short-term financial rewards awaiting the equally successful dramatist, adapted or permitted adaptations of their works. With the new century, particularly in continental Europe, the new breed of directors began to use the adapted novel as a vehicle for their ideas on the new theatre, which were often less easy to express within the conventional framework: STANISLAVSKY, MEYERHOLD, PISCATOR and REINHARDT all at one time or another turned to novels in an attempt to expand the theatrical territory. Clearly, in such ventures the adaptor becomes a key figure whose contribution could be more considerable sometimes even than that of the original author, who may have given little beyond the first galvanic impulse and a famous title. Again an affinity is necessary; but whereas a translation will be a love affair, sometimes unrequited, between an author and an admirer, an adaptation will be like a descendant spending, sometimes imprudently, the wealth inherited from a rich relative, on things that interest him regardless of the source of his money.

Finally, the whole question of both translation and adaptation remains bound up with the fact that the theatre is a modish, transient medium. Works are created for a particular set of circumstances and a particular set of collaborators at a particular time; once these conditions cease to obtain, the work's effectiveness will be diminished. It might be no bad thing were all such works to be equipped with an auto-destruct mechanism to volatilize them after a statutory period. What an author, and indeed a public, finds compelling in a novel in 1990 is not what it would have found compelling in 1950, nor what it will find compelling in 2020; though the primary works remain unchanged, the adaptations will date and the translations become frowsty, a mystery like a fake painting which, after a period of successful deception, can suddenly reveal its falsity to all but the most casual observer. An artifical trade, against whose excesses Vladimir Nabokov warns: 'What is translation? On a platter / a poet's pale and glaring head: / a parrot's screech, a monkey's chatter, / and profanation of the dead.' ROBERT DAVID MACDONALD

Theo Hermans, ed., *The Manipulation of Literature* (1985)
Hanna Scolnicova and Peter Holland, eds, *The Play Out of Context: Transferring Plays from Culture to Culture* (1989)
Outrun Zuber, ed., *The Languages of the Theatre: Problems in the Translation and Transposition of Drama* (1980)

Ade, George (b. Kentland, Ind., 9 Feb. 1866; d. Brook, Ind., 16 May 1944) Humorist and playwright. Ade triumphed in the theatre with his comic operetta librettos, *The Sultan of Sulu* (1902) and *The Sho-Gun* (1904), and with small-town comedies, *The County Chairman* (1903) and *The College Widow* (1904). He had three hits on Broadway in 1904, all celebrated for their evocative American idiom. FELICIA HARDISON LONDRÉ

Lee Coyle, *George Ade* (1964)

Adelaide Founded in 1836, the state capital of South Australia has always seen itself as the most 'English' and 'cultured' of Australia's cities, distinguished by a continuing commitment to theatre in every form. The entrepreneur George Coppin, an English comic actor, ran theatres and hotels in Adelaide in the mid-nineteenth century, moved to Victoria with the gold rush, returned to Adelaide in 1868 and subsequently continued his career in both Adelaide and Melbourne. One of the theatres he controlled in Adelaide, The Queen's, remains the oldest dedicated theatre on the mainland, and is now a national heritage site. Even more than Melbourne and Sydney, Adelaide theatre has been characterized by a thriving amateur tradition, dating back to the early twentieth century, and the influence of figures such as the Welsh composer and dramaturg Bryceson Treharne, who sought to establish a repertoire of 'intelligent' theatre from the rest of the world, combined with the fostering of local playwrights. Between 1940 and the mid-1960s, the role of amateur theatre was crucial in South Australia, with professional productions offered only by touring companies such as the OLD VIC, J. C. Williamson and the AUSTRALIAN ELIZABETHAN THEATRE TRUST. But with the founding of the Adelaide Festival in 1960, which has become the major international arts festival of the southern hemisphere

and which (unlike EDINBURGH, on which it was modelled) takes place every two years, the move towards the establishment of a major subsidized professional theatre company gained momentum. This led to the setting up of the South Australian Theatre Company in 1972, which has remained the focus for theatre activity in the state which styles itself 'the Festival State'. Adelaide's wish to define itself as the major 'cultural' location, *vis-à-vis* its larger, wealthier rivals, is perhaps best characterized by the fact that when the Australian Grand Prix, which had been staged in the city for several years, was 'stolen' by Melbourne, the State Government, the Department of the Arts and State Opera all joined forces to mount (in 1998) a production of Wagner's *Ring* tetralogy, the first time an Australian company had attempted the work. MICHAEL MORLEY
See also FESTIVALS.

Adler, Jacob [P.] (b. Odessa, Russia, 12 Feb. 1855; d. New York, 1 April 1926) He had begun to establish himself as an actor in Russia and London before first coming to America in 1887. He failed, returned to Europe, then made a second, more successful attempt to win over Jewish American audiences two years later. A commanding actor – his name in German means, appropriately, 'eagle' – he quickly became the YIDDISH THEATRE's most admired player and a matinée idol as well. He won applause in new Yiddish plays such as *The Wild Man*, in freewheeling adaptations such as *The Yiddish King Lear*, and in more faithful translations such as that of *The Merchant of Venice*. He eventually brought his Shylock to Broadway (1903, 1905), where he performed in Yiddish while the other actors spoke English. His book, *Life on Stage*, was translated by Lulla Rosenfeld in 1999. Sara, his wife, six of his seven children (Celia, Luther, Stella, Charles, Jay and Julia) and his niece Francine Larrimore were also actors, three of whom rose to prominence: Celia (1890–1979) on the Yiddish stage; Luther (1903–84), who went from Yiddish theatre to the PROVINCETOWN PLAYERS and then the GROUP THEATER, with which he created the lead in CLIFFORD ODETS' *Golden Boy* (1937); and Stella (1902–92), who went from Yiddish theatre to study at the American Laboratory Theater, joined the Group Theater and married its co-founder HAROLD CLURMAN. As well as directing, she founded the Stella Adler Conservatory of Acting (1949), having retired as a performer. She had studied under STANISLAVSKY and based her method on imagination in contrast to STRASBERG's memory approach. Her ideas can be found in *Stella Adler on Acting* (1988). GERALD BORDMAN
See also THEATRE FAMILIES.

L. Rosenfeld, *Bright Star of Exile: Jacob Adler and the Yiddish Theatre* (1977)
Joanna Rotte, *Acting with Adler* (2000)

Adler, Luther   *see* ADLER, JACOB

Adler, Stella   *see* ADLER, JACOB

administration   *see* MANAGEMENT

Adrian [Bor], Max   (b. Ireland, 1 Nov. 1903; d. Surrey, 19 Jan. 1973)   Actor who found his most successful persona as a sardonic comedian in a series of West End intimate REVUES when he inherited the throne vacated by HERMIONE GINGOLD: *Tuppence Coloured* (1947), *Oranges and Lemons* (1948), *Penny Plain* (1951), *Airs on a Shoestring* (1953), *From Here and There* (1955) and *Fresh Airs* (1956). As the vogue for intimate revue faded, he resumed his long career as a general actor, begun in 1926 and highlighted by the creation of Dr Pangloss in the HELLMAN/BERNSTEIN musical version of *Candide* (1956) and a worldwide tour of his one-man show as GEORGE BERNARD SHAW in *An Evening With G.B.S.* (1966). He was a founder member of the ROYAL SHAKESPEARE COMPANY.   IAN BEVAN

advertising   *see* MARKETING

Afinogenov, Alexander [Nikolaevich]   (b. Skopin, Ryazan Province, Russia, 4 April 1904; d. Moscow, 29 Oct. 1941)   Playwright. He joined the Communist Party in 1922 and from 1926 to 1929 worked as a dramatist, literary manager and director of the Moscow Workers' Proletkult Theatre which staged his dramatization of Jack London's stories, *Po tu storonu shcheli* ('On the other side of the crack', 1926), *Na perelome* ('At the crossroads', 1926) and *Malinovoe varenye* ('Raspberry jam', 1928). In 1929 *Chudak* ('The eccentric') was produced by the MOSCOW ART THEATRE Second Studio, which also staged his *Strakh* (*Fear*, 1930–31), a play influenced by GORKY in its treatment of the intelligentsia. Secretary to the theatre section of the Russian Association of Proletarian Writers and, in 1934, editor of *Theatre and Drama*, Afinogenov wrote more than 26 plays, often an unusually complex blend of socialist realism and psychological depth. They include: *Dalekoye* (*Distant point*, 1935, subsequently produced by London's UNITY THEATRE, 1940); *Salyut, Ispaniya!* ('Greetings, Spain!', 1936); *Moskva, Kremil* ('Moscow, Kremlin', 1938); the popular *Mashenka* (1940, translated as *Listen, Professor*); and *Nakanune* (*On the Eve*, 1942). VERA GOTTLIEB

African American theatre   *see* BLACK THEATRE

Agate, James [Evershed]   (b. Seedley, Manchester, 9 Sept. 1877; d. London, 6 June 1947)   Theatre critic. After working for the *Daily Despatch*, *Manchester Guard-ian* and *Saturday Review*, in 1922 Agate joined the *Sunday Times* as theatre critic. His learned and forceful writing soon earned him unrivalled respect and authority although, obsessed as he was with BERNHARDT and IRVING, his views could be eccentric. Some saw his nine volumes of autobiography, tellingly entitled *Ego* (1932–47), as evidence of a growing self-importance; but his outspokenness was often valuable: his recommendation of SHERRIFF's *Journey's End* (1928) led to a successful West End production. His prodigious output included film and book reviews, many of which were collected and published.   DAN REBELLATO

J. Harding, *Agate* (1986)

agents   People who represent actors, writers, directors, designers, composers, illustrators, even whole productions in order to sell the artists' talents to casting directors, publishers, theatre managers, directors and the public. The role first emerged in the nineteenth century for writers but mushroomed in the twentieth century to become big business across the profession. Agents' skills are paramount in negotiating complex contracts, fees, royalty advances, copyright deals, television, film, video and theatrical rights, while ensuring the artist's interests are kept at heart. For this they take a percentage as fee – famously 10 per cent, though this can vary. In addition to this financial and legal role, they often act as advisers, career shapers and 'morale boosters' to their clients. Notable play agents include Elizabeth Marbury, Audrey Wood (US) and PEGGY RAMSAY (UK).   MARIE PETCHELL

agitprop   The term originates with the formation of the Department of Agitation and Propaganda in the USSR (1920), though the *agitbrigady* ('propaganda units') of the Revolution and Civil War period (1917–21) provided models in the arts. Active in all media, the Department formed consciousness-raising BLUE BLOUSE theatrical troupes to take informational entertainment into the countryside. Techniques included the MASS DECLAMATION and the LIVING NEWSPAPER. Their style was influenced by MEYERHOLD and EISENSTEIN, and by traditional entertainments. Their programmes were flexibly staged and collectively devised. Performers were multi-talented, and used the direct methods of VARIETY and MUSIC HALL. The nearest equivalent in previous Western theatre history is the MEDIEVAL moral interlude. Agitprop spread in Europe (especially in Germany, 1924–33), and as far as the United States through the network of international communism. Agitprop-type entertainments were produced by BRECHT and PISCATOR, by Britain's UNITY THEATRE and by the groups of America's Workers' Theater League. After the Second World War, political activity in the West led to a resurgence of agitprop (1968–75), and the methods are still useful in Third World countries, where they provide a voice for oppositional ideas. Agitprop can be dismissed as crude and unsophisticated, but that is to ignore the historical and political contexts which are its *raison d'être*. DEREK PAGET

Colin Chambers, *The Story of Unity Theatre* (1989)
Eugène van Erven, *Radical People's Theatre* (1988)
Richard Stourac and Kathleen McCreery, *Theatre as a Weapon: Workers' Theatre in the Soviet Union, Germany and Britain 1917–34* (1986)

Aidoo, [Christina] Ama Ata (b. Abeadji Kyiakor, Ghana, 1942) Playwright, former education minister in Ghana and one of the major female voices in theatre in West Africa (she now lives in Zimbabwe). She has published short stories, novels and two plays: *The Dilemma of a Ghost* (1964) and *Anowa* (1970); the latter is a memorable and moving indictment of the male responsibility for slavery and slave trading in West Africa in the nineteenth century. KOLE OMOTOSO

Jane W. Grant, *Ama Ata Aidoo: The Dilemma of a Ghost* (1980)

Ailey, Alvin (b. Rogers, Tex., 5 Jan. 1931; d. New York, 1 Dec. 1989) The most famous African American dancer and choreographer of the latter twentieth century, he founded the Alvin Ailey American Dance Theater in 1958. Successful from the start, the company of mostly African American dancers excelled in works that explored African American experience, including Ailey's *Blues Suite* (1958) and his unequivocal masterpiece *Revelations* (1960). His CHOREOGRAPHY resisted 'ethnic' classification, and his broad output included pointe ballets, modern dance ballets and staging for theatre, including the Leonard Bernstein *Mass* (1971). His dances employed a blatant theatricality, and often rely on glamorous settings and costumes. He suffered a nervous breakdown in 1980, and later died of AIDS. His company and its associated school, incorporated in 1967, continued under the direction of former star dancer Judith Jamison, and remains the most celebrated and active company of American modern dance artists. THOMAS DEFRANTZ

See also DANCE; MOVEMENT, DANCE AND DRAMA.

Jennifer Dunning, *Alvin Ailey: A Life in Dance* (1996)

Ainley, Henry [Hinchliffe] (b. Leeds, 21 Aug. 1879; d. London, 31 Oct. 1945) Actor and manager who specialized in romantic and Shakespearean roles. He first made his mark as the eponymous lead in PHILLIPS's *Paolo and Francesca* (1902). Later notable performances include Leontes in GRANVILLE BARKER's *The Winter's Tale* (1912), Ilam Carve in ARNOLD BENNETT's *The Great Adventure* (1913), and the lead in FLECKER's *Hassan* (1923) at His Majesty's, in the management of which he was involved. After illness, he returned to the stage in ST JOHN ERVINE's *The First Mrs Fraser* (1929) with MARIE TEMPEST, and played Hamlet a year later. IAN CLARKE

Aitmatov, Chingiz (b. Sheker, Soviet Khirgizia, 12 Dec. 1928) Author of novels, short stories, film scripts and plays. His most famous play, written with Kaltai Mukhamedzhanov, is *Voskhozhdenie na Fudziyamu* (*The Ascent of Mt Fuji*, 1973, subsequently put on in Washington DC and London). Son of a victim of Stalin's purges, Aitmatov's work explores themes of collective guilt, morality, exile and youthful idealism versus official brutality. His use of parable, metaphor and legend, and his criticisms of Soviet life, distinguish him as a writer of 'The Thaw'; his subjects include Stalin's camps in *The Ascent of Mt Fuji*; the destruction of ethnic culture in *Belyi parokhod* (*The White Steamship*, 1970), or the abuse of power in *Proshchai, Gulsary!* (*Farewell, Gulsary!*, 1967). VERA GOTTLIEB

Akalaitis, JoAnne (b. Chicago, 29 June 1937) Director. A founding member of the experimental MABOU MINES, Akalaitis has worked with the company since 1970 as performer, designer, director and creator (e.g. *Dressed Like An Egg*, 1977). Her other directorial credits range across the United States and Europe, from BECKETT and KROETZ to *The Photographer* (1982) with score by PHILIP GLASS, her former husband, and *'Tis Pity She's a Whore* (1992). Akalaitis directed *Henry IV, Parts 1 and 2* (1991) for the PUBLIC THEATER, New York, where she was named artistic director that year. She was sacked in 1993 by the board because of declines in finances, critical approval and audience support. ELLEN LAMPERT-GRÉAUX

Akimov, Nikolai [Pavlovich] (b. Kharkov, Russia, 3 April 1901; d. Moscow, 6 Sept. 1968) Director and stage designer. His first independent production was a controversial *Hamlet* (1932), with music specially composed by SHOSTAKOVICH. A master of the comic grotesque, and especially associated with the plays of YEVGENII SHVARTS, he headed the Leningrad Comedy Theatre from 1935 until his death. NICK WORRALL

Akins, Zoë (b. Humansville, Mo., 30 Oct. 1886; d. Los Angeles, 29 Oct. 1958) Playwright, screenwriter, novelist and poet. *The Magical City* (1916), a free-verse one-act tragedy, won some acclaim in its WASHINGTON SQUARE PLAYERS production, with set design by LEE SIMONSON. Her ability to address women's concerns through lively dialogue can be seen in her Broadway successes. They include *Déclassé* (1919), which starred ETHEL BARRYMORE, *Daddy's Gone A-Hunting* (1921), *The Varying Shore* (1921), *The Texas Nightingale* also known as *Greatness* (1922). *The Old Maid* (1935), adapted from an Edith Wharton story, won the Pulitzer Prize. Screenplays include EDNA FERBER's *Showboat* (1931), *The Right to Love* (1930), from SUSAN GLASPELL's *Brook Evans*, and *Camille* (1936), starring Garbo.   JANE HOUSE

Aksyonov, Vasiliy [Pavlovich]   (b. Kazan, Russia, 20 Aug. 1932) Novelist and playwright. He acquired a reputation during the 1960s which was enhanced with emigration to the United States in 1980. Son of Evgenia Ginzburg, who wrote a key account of Stalinist terror *Journey into the Whirlwind*, his own early novel, *Ticket to the Stars*, was accused of misrepresenting Soviet youth; his Western-influenced satire-cum-musical *Vsegda v prodazhe* (*Always on Sale*) was a hit with young people when staged by EFREMOV in 1965. Other plays, written during the 1970s, are the fantastico-satirical *Vash ubiytsa* (*Your Murderer*) – 'An Anti-Alcoholic Comedy' – and *Tsaplya* (*The Heron*) – 'A Comedy in Rhyme with Intervals' – both containing satirical jibes at Soviet popular culture.
NICK WORRALL

Harold B. Segel, *Twentieth-Century Russian Drama* (1979)

Aktie Tomaat (Action Tomato)   *see* NETHERLANDS

Al-Hakim, [Husay] Tawfiq [Ismail Ahmad]   (b. Alexandria, 9 Oct. 1898; d. Cairo, 26 July 1987) Novelist, and the Arab world's most accomplished playwright. Some of his early plays deal with the pressing issues of the day, from the British occupation to the emancipation of women, while others take a more absurdist and philosophical turn: *Pygmalion* (1942), *The Tree Climber* (1962), *The Fate of a Cockroach* (1966). But it is his unpretentious social dramas, collected in 1950 in a volume entitled *The Theatre of Society*, that will probably remain his most enduring achievement.   KARIM ALRAWI

Richard Long, *Tawfiq al-Hakim – Playwright of Egypt* (1979)
Paul Starkey, *From the Ivory Tower – A Critical Study of Tawfiq al-Hakim* (1987)
Gilbert Tutunji, *Tawfiq al-Hakim and the West* (1966)

Albanesi, Meggie [Margharita]   (b. London, 8 Oct. 1899; d. Broadstairs, Kent, 9 Dec. 1923) Actress. Early roles included Sonia in EDITH CRAIG's production of HEIJERMANS' *The Rising Sun* (1919), for which the press hailed her as one of the great actresses of the future. After playing Jill in GALSWORTHY's *The Skin Game* (1920), she played Sydney Fairfield in CLEMENCE DANE's *A Bill of Divorcement* (1921) to great acclaim. Playwrights such as

BARRIE, COWARD and Dane applauded the freshness and poignancy of her technique. An intestinal perforation caused her early death, which was seen as a great loss. A plaque designed by Eric Gill was placed in the St Martin's Theatre, London, in her memory, and a scholarship named after her was established at her old drama school, the Royal Academy of Dramatic Art.   MAGGIE GALE

E. M. Albanesi, *Meggie Albanesi* (1928)

Albania   Although archaeological evidence establishes that drama played a significant role in the life of the ancient Illyrians (the ancestors of the Albanian people) as far back as the fourth century BC, the modern Albanian theatre dates only from the nineteenth century, when a number of amateur dramatic societies were set up in the main towns. The first original play in the Albanian language was *The Wedding in Lunxhëria* by Koto Hoxhi (1824–95), the première of which took place in the Albanian town of Gjirokastra in 1874. The proclamation of independence in 1912 brought little development to the Albanian theatre, and was soon followed by the foreign occupations of the First and Second World Wars. However, one actor of Albanian origin – Aleksandër Moisiu (1879–1935) – did achieve international fame. Following the establishment of the People's Republic (later the People's Socialist Republic) of Albania in 1946, the Albanian theatre made notable progress in sociological terms. A country of only three million people, it boasted eight professional drama theatres (as well as 15 variety theatres and 26 puppet theatres). The first drama school was opened in 1946. Although each theatre company has its own premises, it spends half the year playing to audiences in the countryside. The repertory of the drama theatres includes translations of foreign plays, but priority has been given to the development of a national theatre, which has already produced a number of talented playwrights, actors and directors.

After the Communist Party lost power in the early 1990s the theatre system remained more or less intact while being opened up to a wider range of external developments and was affected by the strife in the area.   WILLIAM BLAND

K. Bihiku, *A History of Albanian Literature* (1980)

Albee, Edward [Franklin, III]   (b. Washington DC, 12 March 1928) Playwright. He was adopted as an infant in 1929 by the rich and powerful Albee family, who owned a circuit of 70 VAUDEVILLE theatres around America. After graduating from Trinity College, Hartford, Albee chose to make his way in New York, thanks to a family legacy, and worked at various casual jobs while pursuing a writing career. His debut with the

AVANT-GARDE and the THEATRE OF THE ABSURD was followed by more intense drama examining American postwar complacency and its emotional cost. His first play, *The Zoo Story*, at the time considered too unconventional for New York audiences, was premièred in Berlin in 1958, and he followed this with other short, absurdist plays like *The Death of Bessie Smith* (1959), which tackled racism, and *The Sandbox* (1960) and *The American Dream* (1961), both of which caricatured American middle-class values. Albee's reputation was slow to establish itself in the United States, and he had already gained considerable success with his work in Europe before the explosive *Who's Afraid of Virginia Woolf?* (1962), with its clever and savagely funny orchestration of intellectual angst, brought him accolades as a major American playwright who was compared to O'NEILL and WILLIAMS. The expectations raised by the success of this work were, however, not fulfilled in Albee's next plays, several of which were adaptations, like *The Ballad of the Sad Café* (1963, from CARSON MCCULLERS), *Breakfast at Tiffany's* (1966, from Truman Capote) and *Lolita* (1980, from Vladimir Nabokov). In *Tiny Alice* (1964) he produced a bold, mythic play but one of his least accessible, and his career hit a low point. Albee continued to experiment in various theatrical styles, as in the more intimate musical plays like *Box-Mao-Box* (1968) and the radio play *Listening* (1975) or the solo harangue of the audience in *The Man Who Had Three Arms* (1982), which mirrors his own career. Popular success evaded him, with the exception of *A Delicate Balance* (1966), which was staged in New York and London and returned to the themes that had worked so well for him in *Virginia Woolf*. Both plays were filmed. The awarding of the Pulitzer Prize for *A Delicate Balance* was repeated in 1975 for his play *Seascape*, which he directed himself. While he has not recaptured the critical acclaim of his early years, signs of rehabilitation were evident with *Three Tall Women* (1992) which was followed by successful revivals of earlier plays.

HELEN RAPPAPORT

C. W. E. Bigsby, *Albee* (1969)
Ruby Cohn, *Edward Albee* (1969)
Mel Gussow, *Edward Albee: A Singular Journey* (2000)
Anita M. Stenz, *Edward Albee: The Poet of Loss* (1978)

Albery, Bronson   *see* ALBERY FAMILY

Albery, Donald   *see* ALBERY FAMILY

Albery family   Theatrical dynasty founded by James Albery (1838–89), a successful playwright and adapter of plays from the French. (His record-breaking *Pink Dominos*, 1877, was being revived well into the twentieth century.) Albery was also a heavy drinker and died penniless, leaving his widow **Mary** (née Moore, b. London, 3 July 1861; d. London, 6 April 1931) to support three sons. This she did by becoming an actress with the actor, manager and author **Charles Wyndham** [Culverwell] (b. 23 March 1837; d. London, 12 Jan. 1919), whom she married in 1916. Knighted in 1902, he ran the Criterion, where *Pink Dominoes* had played, and the theatre bearing his own name, which had housed *Mrs Dane's Defence* (1900) and the English première of *Cyrano de Bergerac* (1903). Mary proved to be not only a delightful light comedienne but also a brilliant businesswoman, and it was largely her efforts that established the group of fashionable WEST END theatres (Criterion, Wyndhams and, the third of Charles's theatres, the New) of which her second son, **Bronson Albery** (b. Greenhithe, Kent, 6 March 1881; d. London, 21 July 1971), inherited control along with his step-brother Howard Wyndham (Charles' son by his first wife Emma). An active producer for more than 30 years (notably of *A Pair of Silk Stockings*, 1914; SHAW's *Saint Joan*, 1924; *French Without Tears*, 1936; *Our Town*, 1946), he was also an office-holder in many theatrical organizations, and was knighted in 1949 for his work in the theatre. In 1962 control of Wyndham Theatres Ltd passed to his son **Donald** [Arthur Rolleston] (b. London, 19 June 1914; d. Monte Carlo, 14 Sept. 1988), who expanded the group by buying the Piccadilly Theatre, the company's only freehold property. He proved the most innovative producer of the family (GRAHAM GREENE's *The Living Room*, 1953, and *The Potting Shed*, 1958; BECKETT's *Waiting for Godot*, 1955; West End transfers of JOAN LITTLEWOOD's productions from the THEATRE ROYAL, STRATFORD EAST; and the firm's biggest ever commercial success, the musical *Oliver!*, 1960). He was knighted in 1978, like his father for services to the theatre, and retired soon after to live in the south of France, having sold the firm to Associated Newspapers Ltd but leaving his son **Ian** (b. London, 21 Sept. 1936) with a contract to run it. The newspaper giant lost patience with show business in 1984 and sold the group to new owners who parted company with Ian and in 1988 parted company with the theatres, not quite 100 years after James Albery's death. The family name was given a West End memorial in 1973 when the New Theatre was renamed the Albery. Ian went on to run SADLER'S WELLS and his son, **Tim** (b. 20 May 1952), became a successful director.   IAN BEVAN

See also THEATRE FAMILIES.

Wendy Trewin, *All on Stage: Charles Wyndham and the Albery's* (1980)

Albery, Ian   *see* ALBERY FAMILY

Albery, Tim   *see* ALBERY FAMILY

Aldredge, Theoni V. [Theoni Athanasiou Vachlioti] (b. Salonika, Greece, 22 Aug. 1932) Costume designer. She studied at the Goodman School of Theater in Chicago, where she did her first professional work. Afterwards, besides regularly working with the NEW YORK SHAKESPEARE FESTIVAL, she created the clothes for such diverse Broadway successes as *Sweet Bird of Youth* (1959), *Who's Afraid of Virginia Woolf?* (1962), *A Chorus Line* (1975), and *La Cage aux Folles* (1983).
GERALD BORDMAN

Aldwych farces Long-running series of 13 farces staged at London's ALDWYCH THEATRE (1922–33). BEN TRAVERS provided nine consecutive successes between 1925 and 1933, including *A Cuckoo in the Nest*, *Rookery Nook*, *Thark* and *Plunder*, for a skilful ensemble led by TOM WALLS, Ralph Lynn, Robertson Hare, Mary Brough and Winifred Shotter. Loosely plotted around the suspicion of sexual improprieties, but enlivened by Travers' playful language, eccentric characters and deft routines, the plays enjoyed accumulated popular goodwill and an almost legendary theatrical status. RONALD W. STRANG
See also FARCE.

Aldwych Theatre CHEKHOV might have enjoyed the irony: the London theatre that saw the first production in England of *The Cherry Orchard* (in 1911, six years after the 1,100-seater opened) became best known for giving its name to the ALDWYCH FARCES, a series of hits mostly by BEN TRAVERS that ran from 1922 to 1933. It remained a conventional WEST END theatre except for the years 1960–82 when the ROYAL SHAKESPEARE COMPANY made the Aldwych its London home and staged many outstanding productions there. Alongside transfers from STRATFORD-UPON-AVON, these ranged from PETER BROOK's production of *Marat/Sade* (1964) and several PINTER premières to DAVID JONES's GORKY productions and *Nicholas Nickleby* (1980). From 1964 to 1975 (excepting 1974), the RSC hosted at the Aldwych the annual WORLD THEATRE SEASON. COLIN CHAMBERS

Aleichem, Sholom [Solomon Rabinowitz] (b. Pereyaslav, Russia, 2 March 1859; d. New York, 13 May 1916) Yiddish writer of stories, novels, essays and plays who, with down-to-earth philosophy and humour, chronicled the world of the Jewish *shtetl* and used a pseudonym inspired by the Hebrew greeting. An important figure in YIDDISH THEATRE, he is best known for the Broadway musical adaptation of his stories about 'Tevye the Milkman', *Fiddler on the Roof* (1964).
ANNE FLETCHER

Alexander, Bill *see* BIRMINGHAM REPERTORY THEATRE

Alexander, F[rederick] Matthias (b. Wynard, Tas-mania, 20 Jan. 1869; d. London, 10 Oct. 1955) Actor. By experimentation, he discovered a way of creating and maintaining an improved harmony in the body through conscious control and correct alignment. The 'Alexander Technique' is used successfully in education, drama and music schools, and professional theatre, and by doctors and physical therapists. Believing that the involuntary muscular contractions caused by misalignment drastically reduce the ability to stand, move and speak with relaxed ease, Alexander perfected a system for replacing familiar, and therefore comfortable, poor habits (misuse) with a mentally guided correction of the whole physical structure. From 1904 he was based in London, and he published four books on his principles: *Man's Supreme Inheritance* (1910), *Constructive Conscious Control of the Individual* (1923), *The Use of Self* (1932) and *The Universal Constant in Living* (1941). Among his pupils were HENRY IRVING, LILLIE LANGTRY and GEORGE BERNARD SHAW. JOHN BROOME

Frank Pierce Jones, *Freedom to Change: The Development and Science of the Alexander Technique* (3rd ed. 1997)

Alexander, George [Gibb Samson] (b. Reading, 19 June 1858; d. Chorley Wood, Herts, 16 March 1918) Actor and manager. Having acted with IRVING at the Lyceum, he became manager of the Royal Avenue and then took over the St James until he retired in 1917. Here, following a policy of presenting indigenous new writing, he produced some of the most important plays of the period, notably WILDE's first staged play, *Lady Windermere's Fan* (1892) and *The Importance of Being Earnest* (1895), in which he created the part of Jack Worthing; PINERO's *The Second Mrs Tanqueray* (1893), which launched MRS PATRICK CAMPBELL as a star, and *His House in Order* (1906); and STEPHEN PHILLIPS' *Paolo and Francesca* (1902). He was knighted in 1911.
CHARLES LONDON

A. E. W. Mason, *Sir George Alexander and the St James's Theatre* (1935)

Alexander [Quigley], Jane (b. Boston, 28 Oct. 1939) Actress. Her understated performances, both on stage and in film, attracted notice in the 1970s. Her most notable early stage performance was in HOWARD SACKLER's Pulitzer Prize winning *The Great White Hope* (1967), playing the white girlfriend of a black prize-fighter, Jack Jefferson. She followed this with further critical acclaim, playing Lavinia in *Mourning Becomes Electra* (1972) and making appearances in *First Monday in October* (1978), *Monday after the Miracle* (1982), *Shadowlands* (1990) and *The Sisters Rosensweig* (1992). She became the first performing artist to hold the prestigious position of chair of the NATIONAL ENDOWMENT FOR THE ARTS (1993–97).

She wrote about this in *Command Performance: An Actress in the Theatre of Politics* (2000). HELEN RAPPAPORT

Alexander Technique *see* ALEXANDER, F. MATTHIAS

Alfreds, Mike [Michael Guy Alexander] (b. London, 5 June 1934) Director. After training in the United States (1957–60) and living in Israel (1970–5), Alfreds founded the influential SHARED EXPERIENCE company and directed its first production, *The Arabian Nights* (1975), which pioneered a form of vivid theatricalization of old texts. He also adapted for them Dickens' *Bleak House* (1977) and Evelyn Waugh's *A Handful of Dust* (1982), and directed much innovative work with them up to 1986. He has worked at the NATIONAL THEATRE (e.g. a highly energized *The Cherry Orchard*, 1985) and worldwide. He was director of the Cambridge Theatre Company (later Method and Madness) from 1991 to 1999. CATHY JOYCE

alienation effect (A-effect) Unfortunate English translation of *Verfremdungseffekt*, BRECHT'S concept of distancing or estrangement whereby the spectator is able to maintain a critical detachment and see the familiar anew. In English it has mistakenly led to the notion of alienating, i.e. putting off, the spectator.
COLIN CHAMBERS
See also MODERNISM.

Allan, Maud (b. Toronto, 27 Aug. 1873; d. Los Angeles, 7 Oct. 1956) Dancer, choreographer and teacher. She performed in the 'Greek' revivalist style, an approach which took its inspiration mainly from figures on ancient Greek vase painting and stressed the expressive interpretation of the performer, rather than a particular dance technique. Its most famous exponent was ISADORA DUNCAN. Like Duncan, Allan performed barefoot in loose clothing in a manner that challenged both the dominance of classical ballet as expressive dance and Victorian ideals of propriety for middle-class women. In this respect, Allan was among the first pioneers of modern dance. She frequently set her dances to Mendelssohn, but her most famous, and indeed infamous, dance was *The Vision of Salome* (1903), to the music of Marcel Rémy. She toured internationally but settled in England, where she opened a school in 1928. Her memoir, *My Life and Dancing*, appeared in 1908.
LESLEY-ANNE SAYERS
See also DANCE; MOVEMENT, DANCE AND DRAMA.

F. B. Cherniavsky, *The Salome Dancer: The Life and Times of Maud Allan* (1991)

Allen, [William] Chesney (b. London, 5 April 1894; d. Midhurst, Sussex, 13 Nov. 1982) Comedian and theatrical agent. A solo VARIETY artist and manager to the MUSIC HALL artist FLORRIE FORDE prior to his stage

and film partnership with BUD FLANAGAN from 1924 to 1944. For the second half of this period, the pair were part of the CRAZY GANG, with whom Allen introduced the songs 'Underneath the Arches' and 'Run, Rabbit, Run'. He retired from the stage in 1946 due to ill health, but returned in 1981 for a musical celebration of the Crazy Gang entitled *Underneath the Arches* (Chichester). REXTON S. BUNNETT

Allen, David (b. Birmingham, 4 Jan. 1936) Playwright. He taught drama in Britain before moving to Uganda (1966–70) and Adelaide (1972). He co-founded Troupe, South Australia's major alternative professional theatre company, for which he wrote and directed his first plays (e.g. *Gone with Hardy*, 1978). His works have been staged in Australia, Britain and America, and though sometimes criticized for a 'rootlessness' which matches that of some of the characters, the plays are well crafted and show to advantage his ear for sharp dialogue and gift of deft and exuberant characterization. Plays include *Buckley!* (1981), *Cheapside* (1984), *Pommies* (1986) and *Modest Expectations* (1990). He has also written widely for film, radio and television.
MICHAEL MORLEY

Allen, Gracie *see* BURNS, GEORGE

Allen, Jim *see* ENGLISH STAGE COMPANY

Allen, Viola (b. Huntsville, Ala., 27 Oct. 1867; d. New York, 9 May 1948) Actress, the sheltered daughter of touring actors, who rose to become the leading lady of an imposing nineteenth-century actor, John McCullough. In 1886 she played Desdemona to TOMMASO SALVINI's Othello. Following five seasons (1893–8) with CHARLES FROHMAN, she toured as a star until 1918, with notable successes in Hall Caine's *The Christian* (1898) and several Shakespeare plays.
FELICIA HARDISON LONDRÉ

Alley Theater (Nina Vance Alley Theater) One of the oldest, most prestigious regional theatres in the United States. Founded by Mr and Mrs Robert Atfield and Nina Vance in 1947, it began as an amateur group in a rented dance studio at the end of an alley in Houston, Texas. In 1949 it moved to a fan factory and used some professional actors; in 1954 it became one of America's first three professional companies, the others being the ARENA STAGE and the CLEVELAND PLAY HOUSE. A modern theatre complex was opened in 1968 and named after Vance when she died in 1980. The Alley provides a balanced repertoire of new and classical works, as well as supporting both a playwright in residence and the Merry-Go-Round, America's largest theatre school for young people. It conducted a unique exchange in 1983 with the STEPHEN JOSEPH THEATRE in England. ROBERT WILSON has used the theatre since 1993 as his base in the United States. SUSAN PAULY

Joseph Wesley Zeigler, *Regional Theatre: The Revolutionary Stage* (1973)

Allgood, Sara (b. Dublin, 15 Oct. 1883; d. Hollywood, 22 June 1950) Actress. She created many parts from the opening of the ABBEY THEATRE (1904), in plays by GREGORY, SYNGE, YEATS and others. From 1913 much of her work was in Britain, Australia and the United States in the commercial theatre. She had an unprecedented succcess at the Abbey in 1924 as Juno in the first production of O'CASEY's *Juno and the Paycock*, and as Bessie Burgess in the first London production of *The Plough and the Stars* (1926). Her later career was mainly in films, where she tended to be cast in stereotyped Irish roles. Her sister was the actress MÁIRE O'NEILL.
CHRISTOPHER FITZ-SIMON

Allio, Rene (b. Marseille, France, 8 March 1924; d. Paris, 27 March 1995) Stage designer, director and screenwriter. In the late 1950s he worked with the influential director ROGER PLANCHON at the newly established Théâtre de la Cité in Lyon and was involved in the design of the cultural centre there. Allio's advocacy of an adaptable theatre space, not restricted to any one particular shape, led to the imaginative redesign of several theatres (including plans for Centre 42 to convert London's ROUND HOUSE) before he started writing and directing his own films. Important in France because of his Brechtian approach, he also designed for WILLIAM GASKILL at STRATFORD-UPON-AVON and at the NATIONAL THEATRE (e.g. his seminal production of *The Recruiting Officer*, 1963; *Armstrong's Last Goodnight*, 1965; and *The Beaux' Stratagem*, 1970). HELEN RAPPAPORT

Almeida Theatre In 1981 Pierre Audi re-opened an erstwhile music hall in Islington, north London, which had originally been a nineteenth-century literary and scientific institution, as a 300-seat centre for European performing arts. In 1988 IAN McDIARMID and Jonathan Kent took over, changing its direction towards the literary, and since 1990 it has been a full-time producing theatre. Despite continual financial difficulties, it has presented many acclaimed revivals and successful premières, including works by HOWARD BARKER, HAROLD PINTER and DAVID HARE, several of which transferred to the WEST END. It has won many awards, including the 1993 Laurence Olivier award for outstanding achievement. Acclaimed performances include DIANA RIGG in *Medea* (1992) and RALPH FIENNES in *Hamlet* (1995, at the HACKNEY EMPIRE), both of which were seen on BROADWAY. The Almeida has specialized in this kind of careful balancing of well-chosen stars and classic texts. In 1998 Hollywood luminary Kevin Spacey triumphed in O'NEILL's *The Iceman Cometh*; the company also achieved the remarkable feat of running two Racine tragedies in repertoire, starring Diana Rigg, in the West End. Fiennes returned in 2000 as Richard II and Coriolanus (at the revamped Gainsborough Film Studios). The Almeida moved into a temporary home in 2001 while its theatre was being refurbished and the artistic directors announced their resignation from 2002. DAN REBELLATO

Aloni, Nissim (b. Tel Aviv, Israel, 24 Aug. 1926; d. Tel Aviv, 13 June 1998) Playwright. His first play, *Most Cruel of All The Kings* (1953), based on the biblical account of the split of the Hebrew kingdoms, departed from the prevalent realism and attempted to constitute a new dramatic style of historical themes rendered through poetic idiom, a style rarely followed later by Israeli playwrights including himself. Aloni spent a year in Paris, where he became closely acquainted with the new European drama which henceforth had a crucial influence on his plays. Upon his return to Israel he developed a journalistic career, and in 1961 wrote and directed his next play, *The King's Clothes*, a modern symbolic sequel to Hans Christian Andersen's fairytale, which introduced into Israeli drama MODERNIST influences of existentialist plays and particularly the dramatic idiom of GHELDERODE and DÜRRENMATT. In 1963 he was among the founders of the Seasons Theatre, a theatrical venture that lasted for about four years, where he produced one of his major plays, *The American Princess* (1963). Acclaimed as one of Israel's foremost dramatists during the 1960s and early 1970s, he wrote and produced plays for most of the country's major companies. His language developed a personal lyrical rhythm, at once mysterious and highly accessible. His plays include *The Revolution and the Chicken* (1964), *The Bride and the Butterfly Hunter* (1967), *Napoleon, Dead or Alive* (1967), *Aunt Lisa* (1968), *The Gypsies of Jaffa* (1971), *That Scapegoat* (1973), and *Eddy King* (1975). He published one collection of short stories, *The Owl* (1975), and a volume of journalistic sketches, *Notes of an Alley Cat* (1996). Critically acclaimed for his plays and translations of drama into a lively, exuberant Hebrew, Aloni's most popular works were his satirical sketches and songs written for the highly successful trio Hagashash, which had an enormous impact on idiomatic Hebrew slang. His work has been translated into French and English. Two years before his death, Aloni was awarded the Israel Prize for theatre. AVRAHAM OZ

alternative theatre/alternate theatre A term that gained currency in Britain in the late 1960s and 1970s as a loose movement of individuals, groups and venues grew around a set of theatrical ideas opposed to the mainstream, which by then included the subsidized theatre that had once been the alternative to the commercial theatre. FRINGE was seen as marginal and defined in relation to the mainstream rather than countering it. Generally, the term is applied to any theatrical practice that offers values in opposition to those of the predominant drama. Usually politically as well as aesthetically inspired, it often embraced an ENSEMBLE ideal. COLIN CHAMBERS

See also EXPERIMENTAL THEATRE; INDEPENDENT THEATRE; POLITICAL THEATRE; THIRD THEATRE.

Alton [Hart], Robert (b. Bennington, Vt., 28 Jan. 1897; d. Hollywood, 12 June 1957) Choreographer. After starting his career as a chorus boy in *Take It from Me* (1919), he worked his way up until he was allowed to create dances for *Hold Your Horses* (1933). Among his subsequent hits were *Ziegfeld Follies of 1934*, *Anything Goes* (1934), *Leave It to Me!* (1938), *Pal Joey* (1940) and *By Jupiter* (1942). He was one of the first choreographers to dispense with regimented chorus lines, breaking lines into small groups and even solo turns.

GERALD BORDMAN

See also CHOREOGRAPHY; DANCE; FOLLIES.

Álvarez Quintero, Serafín (b. Utrera, Spain, 26 March 1871; d. Madrid, 12 April 1938) and **Joaquín** (b. Utrera, 21 Jan. 1873; d. Madrid, 14 June 1944) Brothers who wrote prolifically in collaboration. Helen and HARLEY GRANVILLE BARKER adapted several of their plays, including *Puebla de las mujeres* (*The Women Have Their Way*, 1912) and *El amor que pasa* (*Love Passes By*, 1904), as an antidote to the ponderous nature of much English drama of the period. The brothers' work was also known in North America. JOHN LONDON

Amalrik, Andrei [Alekseevich] (b. Moscow, 12 May 1938; d. Guadalajara, Spain, 11 Nov. 1980) Russian dissident, author of the celebrated 1969 essay *Will the Soviet Union Survive till 1984?* His plays revived the Russian absurdist tradition of Kharms and Gogol, with overtones of political satire. They include *Vostokozapad* (*East–West*, 1963), *Konformist li dyadya Dzhek?* (*Is Uncle Jack a Conformist?*, 1964) and *Moya tyotya zhivyot v Volokolamske* (*My Aunt Lives in Volokolamsk*, 1966). After serving in a labour camp, he emigrated in 1976.

PATRICK MILES

amateur theatre Although all theatre has its origins in amateur theatre, it is only in the twentieth century that the amateur theatre can be regarded as attaining some degree of maturity. When the story-teller, surely the first actor, summoned the aid of one or two others to help make the story more entertaining, amateur theatre

was born. When such a little group decided to tour the countryside for a living, performing its stories or interludes wherever it could, professional theatre had grown out of the amateur. By the time Shakespeare wrote *A Midsummer Night's Dream*, the kind of rustic amateur theatre he depicted must have been widespread. Peter Quince's company was the local village dramatic society, and the village drama club of the present century is directly in the same tradition. Its social importance now, as then, lies in the fact of its being an expression of the life of the small community. Such was the increase in amateur theatrical activity subsequently in Britain that by the mid-1840s T. H. Lacy was able to establish a profitable business (later taken over by Samuel French) as publisher of acting editions of plays for amateurs, together with practical handbooks. (*See* THEATRE PUBLISHING.)

At the beginning of the twentieth century, what WILLIAM ARCHER had called 'the new movement' in the theatre, together with the development of the national theatre movement, was creating an ambience of a more serious attitude to the theatre generally. No doubt this also affected the more thinking leaders in the amateur theatre, who began to see a place for amateur theatre in the scheme of things. The Stockport Garrick Society, which founded its own LITTLE THEATRE in 1901, claimed to be the first amateur group to produce the plays of IBSEN and SHAW. The People's Theatre, NEWCASTLE UPON TYNE, was founded in 1911 as the Clarion Dramatic Society for the purpose of raising funds for the British Socialist Party, but gradually moved away from a purely socialist aim until it claimed its object as 'the furtherance of Art'; its earliest reputation had been built on the production of plays by Shaw, with a sprinkling of GALSWORTHY, Ibsen and SYNGE; also in 1911, NUGENT MONCK left the professional theatre to found the Guild of Norwich Players, later setting up the well-known MADDERMARKET THEATRE, often seen as an outstanding example of what an amateur theatre could aspire to.

An amateur theatrical tradition in the labour and co-operative movement had been developing in the early years of the century, encouraged, for instance, by the National Organization of Clarion Dramatic Clubs and the Workers' Educational Association. This led to a politically committed theatre movement of which UNITY was the best-known group.

A new concept in the field of amateur theatre had been the formation in 1899 of the National Operatic and Dramatic Association. While NODA was primarily an association for mutual help among its member operatic societies and did not aim at providing leadership, later national organizations were strongly influential, particularly in encouraging higher standards. The Village

Drama Society, founded by Mary Kelly in 1918, did much to promote and inspire village community groups, in addition to providing practical assistance. The VDS was later absorbed into the British Drama League (*see* BRITISH THEATRE ASSOCIATION), which was founded by GEOFFREY WHITWORTH in 1919 'to assist the development of the art of the Theatre and to promote a right relation between Drama and the life of the community'. There was a considerable upsurge of amateur dramatic activity at the end of the First World War, and the founding of the BDL came at the very moment when elements in the amateur theatre were ready to respond to its leadership. Many amateur groups, including new ones being formed, were greatly influenced by the ideals it propounded, both in respect of drama as a community activity and in respect of the amateur theatre as an art. Whitworth continually preached that the old 'amateur theatricals' had been replaced by a new concept of the 'amateur drama', and by so saying he helped to make it happen.

The BDL was soon pressing on the Board of Education the case for the educational value of drama. The acceptance of this idea by the Board did much to change the climate in which the amateur theatre functioned, giving it a new respectability. This paved the way for the recognition of suitably constituted groups and little theatres as educational charities, with exemption from entertainments duty and income tax. This was itself an encouragement to the more permanent type of dramatic society to re-examine and re-define its policy and constitution.

University theatre has had a long tradition, going back even to Elizabethan times, when it was firmly associated with education. The two best-known university dramatic societies, the OXFORD OUDS and the CAMBRIDGE ADC, have been the nursery of much professional talent. The newer universities and polytechnics often produced more AVANT-GARDE and EXPERIMENTAL work, seen at the EDINBURGH FESTIVAL FRINGE or in the annual Student Drama Festival.

Between the two world wars there was a great variety of amateur theatre groups. A number of new amateur Little Theatres were founded, as were many independent amateur societies, some of which held together to establish their own theatres after the Second World War (e.g. the QUESTORS). Many church dramatic societies were formed, following an earlier pattern; business firms, banks and factories inaugurated their own drama clubs, often subsidised; branches of the Women's Institute, Townswomen's Guild, YWCA and YMCA had dramatic sections, helped and encouraged by professional drama advisers attached to central headquarters; schools and colleges almost invariably had a dramatic society. In short, wherever there was a community within the wider community, the practice of amateur theatre became a natural activity. Many short-lived groups, however, mushroomed and folded, usually due to lack of determined leadership.

Much emphasis was being placed on the importance of artistic standards as a justification for amateur theatre work. Among its other activities, the BDL gave a lead in organizing training courses for amateur actors and producers, which soon proliferated round the country. In 1927 the Carnegie UK Trust inaugurated a policy of grant aid for amateur drama through the establishment of County Drama Committees and the employment of County Drama Advisers, partly paid for by the Trust. The function of the drama advisers was to give advice and assistance to the adult groups in their area, and to organize training courses and workshops, etc., aimed at promoting higher standards. The establishment of drama classes as part of adult education was spreading widely.

Despite all this emphasis on improving standards, it was only in exceptional cases that the artistic quality of work could challenge that of even lesser professional companies. Sometimes, though, it did, and that was often with plays that the professional theatre would regard as non-commercial.

On the outbreak of war in 1939 most amateur theatre activity came to an abrupt halt. Some, however, continued or soon revived, coping with the difficulties caused by air raids, loss of personnel, shortage of clothing coupons to make costumes, timber licences to make scenery and petrol coupons to travel to rehearsals, in order to provide much-needed entertainment. Help was given by the COUNCIL FOR THE ENCOURAGEMENT OF MUSIC AND THE ARTS (CEMA, later reorganized as the ARTS COUNCIL OF GREAT BRITAIN). In the first year of the war the membership of the BDL dropped by one-third. Three years later it showed a remarkable resurgence, substantially contributed to by hundreds of service units, wanting to borrow plays for play readings and productions. After the war there was a great revival of amateur theatre activity. Groups that had closed down were started up again as members returned from the forces; other new groups were launched, sometimes by those who had had their first taste of amateur acting or directing while in the services. There was a remarkable increase in the number of little theatres. The scope of amateur theatre was also extending. It was no longer seen as primarily an adult activity. There was a gap to be bridged between drama in schools and the adult dramatic society. This led to the establishment of youth drama clubs under the Youth Service of the Education Authorities. The 1950s saw the establishment by the BDL of the Junior Drama League (1955), which held its first residential school in 1958; Michael Croft founded the NATIONAL YOUTH THEATRE in 1956; the British Children's Theatre Association was formed in 1959. Youth drama festivals often produced imaginative and lively work. Many little theatres and established societies started their own youth groups or junior sections, which provided an easy transition, particularly when accompanied by training courses for actors.

One of the most important ways in which amateur groups can, and do, contribute to the theatre is by the presentation of new plays and the encouragement of new playwrights. Another is in keeping theatre alive in areas deprived of good professional theatre. In both these cases the question of standards is of great importance; a poor production of her or his play may do a young author more harm than good; an indifferent performance of an indifferent play may fail to give the audience the unique experience of live theatre and drive them back to their television screens. Standards will always be a problem in the amateur theatre (as, indeed, in the professional theatre). In even the best of little theatres the standard is liable to vary. It is arguable that in the amateur theatre the most important thing is the process as a community undertaking rather than the result, that it is not so much the standards actually achieved as the commitment to striving for them that is of benefit to the community. By any such measure the advance of the amateur movement in the twentieth century was considerable.

Financial support for the amateur theatre is haphazard. The Arts Council persistently refused to recognize the place of the amateur theatre and its grants were entirely confined to the professional theatre. There was no general policy of aid by regional arts associations, though some gave a certain amount of grant aid for projects. Much the same applies to local authorities, which have the power but seldom use it generously. Adult education classes are usually subsidized, but do not often lead to sustained activity. From the late 1980s there was a considerable increase in commercial sponsorship.

There is no way of accurately quantifying the number of dramatic societies in Britain. The Central Council for Amateur Theatre, formed in 1977 to give a united voice to all the national bodies concerned with amateur theatre, conducted a statistical survey in 1978 which estimated some 8,000 regular theatre groups in England. This figure is almost certainly a substantial underestimate. *Amateur Arts in the UK* (1991) by Robert Hutchison and Andrew Feist said that amateur opera and drama productions involved nearly 1.8 million people.

The amateur theatre is strong in most European countries, though the development has followed a different pattern, especially in the east.

Its distinguishing feature as compared with Britain or the United States is the high level of state subsidy, both in the west (with one or two exceptions, such as France) and in the east (although here political changes in the 1990s threw doubt on continuing state support). In most cases, any organization of the amateur theatre movement has developed since the Second World War; in the west by the formation of national organizations, subsidized as educational activities – in the Scandinavian countries, for instance, and in Belgium and the Netherlands; in the former socialist countries by the state taking over responsibility for the administration, usually through the ministry of culture. Under the old, stricter east European regimes an amateur group could not exist without some semi-official sponsor such as a trade union or agricultural cooperative; in this way control was exercised, even over the choice of play, which had to be approved. As the professional theatre was controlled by the same authority, there was substantial cooperation between professional and amateur, and leading actors from the professional theatre even directed for or acted with amateur groups. Such a degree of cooperation is seldom seen in the western countries, and in France and Italy in particular the gulf between professional and amateur, though narrowing, is still deep. In all countries there is great emphasis on training courses at all levels, and these are almost invariably subsidized, often totally.

In the nineteenth century there had been a tradition in those countries suffering from oppression or occupation by a foreign power of a vigorous amateur theatre, often student-based, linked with a national movement or struggle for national freedom. This tradition of POLITICAL THEATRE of protest seems to have had an echo, for instance, in POLAND, where student theatre since the mid-1950s has been seen as a major force in the theatrical AVANT-GARDE of Europe. Most European countries keenly support international theatre activities, often through the INTERNATIONAL AMATEUR THEATRE ASSOCIATION; drama FESTIVALS, including international festivals, are an important part of amateur theatre activity.

The Little Theatre movement has never really caught on in continental Europe. On the other hand, leading groups in both west and east often retain a production in their repertoire for long periods, touring it to other areas and giving a large number of performances; this can result in very high standards, e.g. in work from Sweden (Teater Schahrazad), Hungary (Studio K) and Poland (Teatr STU and Teatr KUL). Most of these groups, while starting as amateurs, were verging on the professional and have since become fully professional – a more normal ambition than in Britain.   ALFRED EMMET

See also CIVIC THEATRE; COMMUNITY THEATRE; LITTLE

THEATRE; STUDENT THEATRE; THEATRE FOR YOUNG PEOPLE; YOUTH THEATRE.

John Allen, *Theatre in Europe* (1982)
G. W. Bishop, ed., *The Amateur Theatre Dramatic Year Book and Community Theatre Handbook, 1928–29* (1929)
Peter Cotes, *A Handbook for the Amateur Theatre* (1957)
Bonamy Dobree, *The Amateur and the Theatre* (1947)
Mary Kelly, *Village Theatre* (1939)
Norman Marshall, *The Other Theatre* (1947)
Robert G. Newton, *Together in Theatre* (1954)
Adrian Rendle, *Everyman and his Theatre* (1968)
George Taylor, *History of the Amateur Theatre* (1976)

American Academy of Dramatic Arts *see* DRAMA SCHOOLS

American Conservatory Theater (ACT) Founded in 1965 in Pittsburgh by director WILLIAM BALL, it moved the following year to Stanford University before finding a permanent home at San Francisco's Geary Theater in 1967 and adding a second, smaller house, the Marine's Memorial Theater, in 1968. Known popularly as ACT, its company is the only major American theatrical troupe to operate in traditional repertory fashion, rotating its programme every night or two. The repertory ranges from classics to modern European successes, but only since Ball's retirement in 1986 has a serious effort been made under Edward Hastings (1987–91) and Carey Perloff to introduce new works. It also runs a training programme. The troupe performed in other venues until the earthquake-damaged Geary was restored in 1996. GERALD BORDMAN

J. R. Wilk, *The Creation of an Ensemble: The First Years of the American Conservatory Theater* (1986)

American Laboratory Theatre *see* ACTING (AN ACTOR REFLECTS); BOLESLAVSKY, RICHARD

American National Theater and Academy Founded in 1935 under a congressional charter as a national, 'people's' theatre, it foundered because the government expected it to be self-supporting. It was reappraised in 1945 with a new board of directors composed mainly of people working in the theatre and became the American branch of the INTERNATIONAL THEATRE INSTITUTE. In 1950 it took over the Guild Theater in New York as its headquarters; renamed the Anta Playhouse, this briefly became a venue for experimental productions and was later leased for commercial ventures, although ANTA retained its offices there.

During construction of the LINCOLN CENTER FOR THE PERFORMING ARTS, ANTA organized the building of a temporary home on Washington Square for the Center's repertory company. With the loss of its theatre, which was sold in 1981, ANTA's activities went into decline. HELEN RAPPAPORT

American Negro Theater Established in Harlem, New York, in 1940 by Abram Hill and FREDERICK O'NEAL, this company was one of several black ensembles which came into being as a result of the FEDERAL THEATER PROJECT's encouragement of African American theatre in the 1930s. The huge success of the group's production of *Anna Lucasta* (1944, with O'Neal in the lead), led to a three-year run on Broadway followed by a season in London in 1947. This success, however, exhausted the company artistically. It lost funding and had to move to more expensive premises. It struggled to survive, returned to London in 1953 and subsequently toured Europe before disbanding. HELEN RAPPAPORT
See also BLACK THEATRE.

American Repertory Theatre The original company was founded in 1946 by EVA LE GALLIENNE, CHERYL CRAWFORD and MARGARET WEBSTER in an old theatre on New York's Columbus Circle. The aim was to create the equivalent of London's OLD VIC, and the first season offered an eclectic range from Shakespeare, IBSEN and SHAW to BARRIE and O'CASEY. It was, however, also the last season: the venture closed through lack of support. The second company to use the name is a nonprofit professional theatre in Cambridge, Massachusetts. Operating since 1979, in association with Harvard University, under the leadership of ROBERT BRUSTEIN ART grew out of the theatre launched at Yale in 1966 by Brustein, who announced his retirement at the end of the 2000–1 season. One of the few theatres in the United States to maintain a resident acting company, ART produces new American plays and neglected works from the past, but is best known for unconventional explorations of classic texts, staged by European-born directors (e.g. ANDREI SERBAN), or by such American innovators as JOANNE AKALAITIS, Anne Bogart, RICHARD FOREMAN and ROBERT WILSON. In 1986 ART received a special Tony award. In 1987 the theatre established a two-year programme of advanced training. Former ROYAL SHAKESPEARE COMPANY director Ron Daniels ran the company for a five-year period in the 1990s. M. ELIZABETH OSBORN

American Shakespeare Festival *see* AMERICAN SHAKESPEARE THEATER; LANGNER, LAWRENCE

American Shakespeare Theater Founded in 1951 in Stratford, Connecticut by LAWRENCE LANGNER as the American Shakespeare Festival Theater and Academy, it built its own theatre, loosely based externally on drawings of London's Elizabethan Globe but up-to-date inside and covered. It opened in 1955 with *Julius Caesar*. From 1963 non-Shakespearean plays were also staged, beginning with SHAW's *Caesar and Cleopatra*. In 1959 special spring performances for students were introduced, and in 1972 the name was shortened. Five years later the Connecticut Center for the Performing Arts was set up there to expand activity, but in 1982 the theatre went bankrupt. The state bought the theatre and various attempts were made to revive it, including one in 1989 by a company from the AMERICAN CONSERVATORY THEATER. In 1998 a new body, the Stratford Festival Theater, was given permission to acquire the theatre and restore it but progress was slow and the theatre's future remained uncertain. Among actors to appear there in its heyday are MORRIS CARNOVSKY, KATHARINE HEPBURN, JAMES EARL JONES, CHRISTOPHER PLUMMER and JESSICA TANDY.   CHARLES LONDON

See also SHAKESPEARE FESTIVALS.

R. Cooper, *The American Shakespeare Theatre, Stratford, 1955–1985* (1986)

Ames, Winthrop (b. New Easton, Mass., 23 Nov. 1871; d. Boston, 3 Nov. 1937)   Producer. A student of GEORGE PIERCE BAKER, Ames studied abroad and was influenced by the INDEPENDENT THEATRES of Europe. Fed up with commercial theatre, in 1909 he joined other wealthy investors to found the short-lived New Theater (1909–11), hoping to create a modern repertory theatre along the lines of the MOSCOW ART THEATRE. He became the leading proponent of the 'new stagecraft' in America but the New Theater failed after only two years, due to a number of diversions from the European ensemble style it sought to imitate: the theatre was too large, seating 3,000 with an enormous acting area; his employment of star players inhibited the chemistry of the young company; and there was no core of enduring native American plays to give coherence to the repertoire. Ames continued to practise his ideals in two other theatres which he built in New York, the Little Theatre (1912) and the Booth Theatre (1913). He invited MAX REINHARDT to New York and encouraged the lighting innovations of NORMAN BEL GEDDES. Among Ames' noteworthy productions were SCHNITZLER's *The Affairs of Anatol* (1912), KAUFMAN and CONNELLY's *Beggar on Horseback* (1924) and a series of GILBERT and SULLIVAN revivals in the 1920s. He remained an influential leader until his death.   DAVID A. WILLIAMS

ancient Greek drama in the twentieth century

In Britain and the United States at the beginning of the twentieth century, classical theatre meant almost exclusively the plays of Shakespeare and his contemporaries. In his projected renewal of the theatre the leading interpreter of Shakespeare, HARLEY GRANVILLE BARKER, saw no real future for Greek plays, the acknowledged

fountainhead of Western drama. But this was also a period in which traditional classical education, of which Greek drama formed a central part, was more widespread and prestigious than it later became. Since then, whereas production of Greek drama has moved from a peripheral to a much more central (albeit somewhat uncertain) place in the classical repertoire, the study of the plays themselves as texts has, in the educational and cultural sphere, moved in the opposite direction. Inherent in this dual process is the progressive detachment of production from classical education. Such productions and play readings as did occur at the beginning of the century were still to a large extent associated with the schools and universities. It is no accident that the dominant figure was a professor of Greek, Gilbert Murray (1866–1957). His personal enthusiasm for production, and the immense popularity of his translations of TRAGEDY, represent a partially successful attempt to take Greek drama outside the confines of the academic world. On the other hand, the translations seem from a later perspective hopelessly unsuitable for production, with their high-flown late Victorian poetic diction and their scant sense of the visual dimension of the Greek theatre.

It was as a result of developments within MODERNISM around the time of the First World War that the situation began to change. The poets Pound, YEATS and ELIOT were all, for different reasons, interested in Greek tragedy. In Ireland, Yeats's interest and his translation of Sophocles' *Oedipus Rex* led to a notable production by the ABBEY THEATRE in Dublin in 1927; and in Britain, Eliot's attack on Murray's translations played an important role in opening up the originals to contemporary writers no longer encumbered by the rhetoric of a dead poetic tradition and with a better understanding of theatrical practicalities. Eliot's own plays were heavily influenced by Greek tragedy, and so assisted its integration into the tradition. In this respect Eliot was not a solitary figure. In the United States the monumental efforts of EUGENE O'NEILL to develop modern tragedy in plays like *Mourning Becomes Electra* and *The Iceman Cometh* were saturated with the values and assumptions of the ancient models, and had the same effect of encouraging audiences and practitioners to see the plays as part of a living theatrical language accessible to writers and producers alike. In both countries, however, the lack of publicly subsidized major theatre companies was a handicap to the development of productions of the original plays themselves. The infrequent opportunities to see them depended, in Britain, on the efforts of enlightened managers such as ANNIE HORNIMAN with her Manchester Company, who gave the young SYBIL THORNDIKE a notable opportunity to play Hecuba and Medea in the early 1920s. But even these companies, of which LILIAN BAYLIS's OLD VIC was the most prominent before the Second World War, found it very difficult to integrate Greek drama within the normal repertoire. Baylis's dedication to the work of bringing Shakespeare within the orbit of a new theatregoing public led to the complete neglect of ancient drama in the prewar Old Vic; and it was not until 1945 that LAURENCE OLIVIER played his outstanding Oedipus there, in Yeats's translation of Sophocles.

The developments within contemporary poetry and drama had not been the only influence on the production of ancient drama. The Greek plays no longer seemed to belong to the classical scholars, but the manner of their production continued to be influenced (albeit indirectly) by academic work, which was itself rapidly changing. Two of the various factors deserve emphasis. The first is the new interest created by archaeological rediscovery of evidence for ancient production (costume, masks, gesture, etc.), and in particular of the ancient open-air theatres themselves. This has contributed to the recent widespread recognition, in literary and scholarly interpretation of the plays, that the visual dimension must not be ignored. Interest in the original conditions of production accompanied the establishment in 1932 of the Greek National Theatre, which began to produce the plays, with a success that continues to this day, in the ancient theatres themselves, especially renovated for the purpose. The company's 1939 tour to London was influential, in particular the production of Sophocles' ELECTRA with KATINA PAXINOU in the title role. Equally successful were their tours nearly 30 years later in the WORLD THEATRE SEASONS at the ALDWYCH THEATRE, with tragedies and comedies directed by KAROLOS KOUN. The gradual rediscovery of the theatricality of what had for centuries been disembodied texts extended even to an influence on the design of modern theatres. The abolition of the proscenium arch and the development of the modern thrust stage has led theatre architects to re-examine the design precepts of the Greek theatres to find what is relevant to modern design problems. Perhaps the most notable example of this influence is the Olivier auditorium of the NATIONAL THEATRE in London, which is directly based on the proportions of the theatre at EPIDAUROS. The second important respect in which production has been indirectly influenced by academic progress is one element in a gradual, basic shift in our perception of Greek culture as a whole. The Victorian concept of Greek society as a pure and rational source of moral, political and aesthetic values was from the beginning of the century being gradually subverted by a more historical perspective. The work of the Cambridge school, which explored the

close relationship of Greek drama to ritual, acquired a social and political dimension in the work of Professor George Thomson, which has had an influence well beyond the academic world. Thomson combined various disciplines, notably archaeology and anthropology, to relate the development of Attic tragedy out of RITUAL to the transition of Attica from a tribal society to a democratic state. The idea of drama as an expression of fundamental social change may have been particularly attractive in periods of political turmoil (and stories from Greek drama have been revisited by playwrights as diverse as HAUPTMANN, COCTEAU, BRECHT, SARTRE and ANOUILH as well as practitioners of ALTERNATIVE THEATRE such as the LIVING THEATER). But the conversion of Greek drama from a merely aesthetic to a social product has had an enduring appeal. For example, the recognition that the alien quality of Greek drama derives from a society fundamentally different from our own has perhaps facilitated the success in Britain of such recent non-European adaptations as the Nigerian WOLE SOYINKA's *Bacchae* (1973), LEE BREUER's black gospel music version of Sophocles' *Oedipus at Colonus* (1983), and the Japanese NINAGAWA company's *Medea* (1985). This range of idiom is one symptom of a general increase in the number and variety of productions of Greek drama in the last decades of the century, which saw some notable work (e.g. by PETER STEIN, ANDREI SERBAN and ARIANE MNOUCHKINE). This has extended even to occasional productions of Aristophanes, an author whose grotesque rumbustiousness may have had an influence on some drama of the 1960s (JOE ORTON, for example, was a devotee of Aristophanes), but whose comedies are notoriously difficult to produce – at least in the English-speaking world; the visit to London of Koun's production of the *Acharnians* provided a splendid glimpse of the Greeks' gift for beautifully controlled anarchy. One obstacle was removed by the abolition in 1968 of the LORD CHAMBERLAIN's CENSORSHIP in 1968, which allowed full exploitation of the obscenity which is one of the more accessible features of Aristophanes for a modern audience. However, tragedy has continued to predominate. Notable productions have included two ambitious attempts to combine more than one tragedy in a single performance: the ROYAL SHAKESPEARE COMPANY's cycle *The Greeks* (1979) and the National Theatre's *Oresteia* (1981). These productions represent the culmination of a 60-year progress of ancient Greek drama from the margins of professional theatre to its central institutions. They also represent diametrically opposed approaches. *The Greeks* was deliberately modernistic, using new versions of the plots written largely by JOHN BARTON, and no attempt was made to simulate ancient conditions or technique; whereas the *Oresteia* used masks, music, formal chorus procedures, an all-male cast and a concentration on formality and ritual, in conscious imitation of the original techniques of production. Both approaches, inevitably, had their admirers and detractors, but of more importance to the future of Greek drama in production was the fact that both productions were enormous box-office successes. Such a public response seems to justify optimism for the future of Greek drama in the theatre. Recent years have also seen the establishment at Oxford University of an archive for modern productions of ancient drama. Granville Barker's gloomy prognostications have finally been dispelled. RICHARD SEAFORD

See also ARCHITECTURE; GREECE.

Richard Beacham and J. Michael Walton, *Living Greek Theatre: A Handbook of Classical Performance and Modern Production* (1987)
Marianne Mcdonald, *Ancient Sun, Modern Light: Greek Drama on the Modern Stage* (1992)
Oliver Taplin, *Greek Tragedy in Action* (1978)
George Thomson, *Aeschylus and Athens* (1941)
J. Michael Walton, *The Greek Sense of Theatre* (1984)
David Wiles, *Greek Theatre in Performance: An Introduction* (2000)

Anderson, Judith [Frances Margaret Anderson] (b. Adelaide, 10 Feb. 1898; d. Santa Barbara, Calif., 3 Jan. 1992) Actress. After her stage debut in Sydney (1915), she moved to the United States in her late teens. Major roles followed in New York and London, including in *Mourning Becomes Electra* (1932), *Come of Age* (1934), *The Old Maid* (1935), *Hamlet* (as Gertrude opposite GIELGUD, 1937), *Macbeth* (opposite OLIVIER, 1937), *The Tower Beyond Tragedy* (1941), *The Three Sisters* (as Olga, 1942), *John Brown's Body* (1953) and *The Seagull* (as Arkadina, 1960). Her signature role was *Medea* (1947). She toured as Hamlet (in the early 1970s) and also worked extensively in film and television. In 1984 she had a theatre in New York named after her. She was the first Australian actress to be created a dame (1960). DAVID BARBOUR

Anderson, Laurie *see* LIVE ART; MODERNISM; MULTI-MEDIA THEATRE; MUSIC THEATRE

Anderson, Lindsay [Gordon] (b. Bangalore, India, 17 April 1923; d. Péngueux, France, 30 Aug. 1994) Stage and film director. An Oxford graduate, he became a film critic and documentary film maker before joining the ENGLISH STAGE COMPANY at the ROYAL COURT in 1957, where his productions included WILLIS HALL's *The Long and The Short and The Tall* (1959), JOHN ARDEN's *Sergeant Musgrave's Dance* (1959) and MAX FRISCH's *The Fire Raisers* (1961). In 1969 he joined WILLIAM GASKILL and

ANTHONY PAGE in running the Court and began his distinguished collaboration with DAVID STOREY, directing with a sinewy poetic realism *The Contractor*, *In Celebration* (both 1969), *Home* (1970), *The Changing Room* (1973), *The Farm*, *Life Class* (both 1974) and later, at the NATIONAL THEATRE, *Early Days* (1980), *The March on Russia* (1989) and *Stages* (1992). His first feature film was *This Sporting Life* (1967), followed by *If* (1968), two of the best British films of their day. FRANK LONG

G. Lambert, *Mainly About Lindsay Anderson: A Memoir* (2000)

Anderson, [James] Maxwell (b. Atlantic, Pa., 15 Dec. 1888; d. Stamford, Conn., 28 Feb. 1959) Playwright. After initial commercial success with the ribald war play *What Price Glory?* (in collaboration with Laurence Stallings, 1926), Anderson attempted to revive poetic drama in the prosaic era of the 1930s. Whether historical (*Elizabeth the Queen*, 1930; *Mary of Scotland*, 1931; *The Masque of Kings*, 1937; *Anne of the Thousand Days*, 1948) or contemporary (*Winterset*, 1935; *High Tor*, 1937; *Key Largo*, 1939) in subject matter, Anderson's plays do not deny social injustice; they deny dogmatic political solution. In defence of personal freedom, they consistently argue the necessity, if also the futility, of resistance to *all* oppressive authority, a theme made explicit in the title of one of his non-verse dramas, *Both Your Houses* (1933). He collaborated with KURT WEILL on *Knickerbocker Holiday* (1938) and *Lost in the Stars* (1949), and was a founder of the PLAYWRIGHTS' COMPANY. GERALD RABKIN

Alfred S. Shivers, *The Life of Maxwell Anderson* (1983)

Anderson, Robert [Woodruff] (b. New York, 28 April 1917) Playwright. Anderson led his time in developing new insights into gender development and extending theatrical treatment of sexual and social bonds. Depicting adultery as rational, potentially moral behaviour, his controversial hit *Tea and Sympathy* (1953, directed by ELIA KAZAN) challenged prevalent ideas of masculinity, conventional compassion, homophobia and (implicitly) McCarthyism. He was elected to the PLAYWRIGHTS' COMPANY in 1953. Other plays include *All Summer Long* (1954); *Silent Night, Lonely Night* (1959); two combinations of short plays – *You Know I Can't Hear You when the Water's Running* (1967) and *Solitaire/Double Solitaire* (1971); *I Never Sang for my Father* (1968, filmed 1969); *The Last Act is a Solo* (1992); and *The Kissing Was Always the Best: Scenes from a Divorce* ((1993).
LEONARD BERKMAN

T. Adler, *Robert Anderson* (1978)

Andrews, Harry [Fleetwood] (b. Tonbridge, Kent, 10 Nov. 1911; d. Salehurst, E. Sussex, 7 March 1989)

Actor. Andrews was a fine classical actor who owed much to the presence lent him by his great stature and resonant voice. At 24 he made his London debut as Tybalt in GIELGUD's *Romeo and Juliet*. He took a series of key classical parts, enjoying great acclaim as Laertes in *Hamlet* (1939). From 1945 he played a succession of Shakespearean roles at the OLD VIC and in STRATFORD-UPON-AVON; later he performed with equal success in contemporary works (e.g. as BOND's *Lear*, 1971) and was a noted film actor. ADRIANA HUNTER

Andrews [Wells], Julie [Elizabeth] (b. Walton-on-Thames, 1 Oct. 1935) Actress and singer who made her stage debut at the age of 12. Born into a showbusiness family, Andrews appeared regularly in VARIETY shows, REVUES and concerts before making her first appearance on BROADWAY in *The Boy Friend* (1954). The highlight of her stage career was her creation of the role of Eliza Doolittle in *My Fair Lady* (1959–60), which she followed with a long run in *Camelot* (1960–2), again on Broadway. She moved into musical films, won an Academy award for her first role in *Mary Poppins* (1964), and topped this with the huge box-office success of *The Sound of Music* (1965). She was created a dame in 1999. HELEN RAPPAPORT

J. Cottrell, *Julie Andrews: The Story of a Star* (1968)
R. Windeler, *Julie Andrews* (1970)

Andreyev, Leonid [Nikolaevich] (b. Orel, Russia, 21 August 1871; d. Kuokkala, Finland, 12 Sept. 1919) Playwright. Author of 21 full-length and 7 short plays, Andreyev wrote his first, *Kzvezdam* (*To the Stars*) in 1905, having previously written stories and a novel. With the outbreak of the First World War, Andreyev became passionately pro-war, and was equally passionate in his opposition to the Bolshevik Revolution, emigrating to Finland, where he died. Controversial and pessimistic, even nihilistic, Andreyev's plays may be divided into two kinds: the more 'realistic' plays, like *Dni nashie zhizni* (*Days of Our Life*, 1908), *Anfisa* (1909), *Gaudeamus* (1909) or *Professor Storitsyn* (1912); and the SYMBOLIST and mystical plays, such as *Zhizn cheloveka* (*The Life of a Man*, 1907), directed by STANISLAVSKY in Moscow and by MEYERHOLD in St Petersburg in the same year; *Anathema* (1909), a parable play on the life of Christ which caused a scandal and accusations of blasphemy; *Tsar Golod* (*Tsar Hunger*, 1907); and *Chernye maski* (*Black Masks*, 1908). The most famous of his symbolist plays is *Tot, kto poluchaet poshchechiny* (*He Who Gets Slapped*, 1915), in which 'He', a clown, is slapped for the entertainment of others in in the circus – a metaphor for life. It was seen in New York (1922) and London (1927), and made into a silent film (1924). VERA GOTTLIEB

A. Kaun, *Leonid Andreyev: A Critical Study* (1924)
James B. Woodward, *Leonid Andreyev: A Study* (1969)

Anglin, [Mary] Margaret (b. Ottawa, 3 April 1876; d. Toronto, 7 Jan. 1958) Actress and producer. After years of apprenticeship she won fame as Roxane to RICHARD MANSFIELD's Cyrano in 1898, then consolidated her reputation in *Mrs Dane's Defence* (1900). Another high point was her proper New Englander in *The Great Divide* (1906). But the rich-voiced, statuesque player also carved a niche in revivals of Shakespeare, WILDE, and, most importantly, ancient Greek tragedies. These last appealed only to a limited coterie, and by modern standards were outlandishly overproduced. Her refusal to bend to changing tastes and her difficult personality eventually removed her from the spotlight, though she continued to perform in modern plays until the 1940s. GERALD BORDMAN

Angola *see* PORTUGUESE-SPEAKING AFRICAN THEATRE

angry young man The term can be traced back to the title of an autobiography by author Leslie Paul (1951), but became current in the mid-1950s in England largely through the play *Look Back in Anger* (1956) by JOHN OSBORNE and his central character, the disillusioned Jimmy Porter. Osborne says that the ROYAL COURT's part-time press officer George Fearon first used the phrase, which was soon popularly applied to anyone, although particularly in the arts, who was vociferously critical of postwar Britain or just thought to be a rebel. The tag did not acquire an equivalent female form. COLIN CHAMBERS

Annenkov, Yuri [Pavlovich] (b. Kamchatka, Russia, 11 July 1889; d. Paris, 18 July 1974) Designer and director. A pioneer of modernist theatre, he staged a number of experimental productions at the Fledermaus Theatre, Moscow, and the Crooked Mirror Theatre, St Petersburg, before collaborating with EVREINOV on a mass spectacle, *The Storming of the Winter Palace* (1921). NICK WORRALL

Anouilh, Jean [Marie Lucien Pierre] (b. Bordeaux, 23 June 1910; d. Lausanne, 3 Oct. 1987) Playwright. Anouilh was inspired by GIRAUDOUX, influenced by PIRANDELLO and an admirer of the surrealist VITRAC. In spite of his self-styled grouping of the plays into 'black', 'rose', 'grating', 'baroque', etc., he worked firmly in the tragicomic mode, haunted by Molière, whom he liked to define as *inconsolable et gai*. Renowned as a master craftsman, a reputation he relished, he proclaimed himself a mere entertainer, keeping abreast of every new fashion: for Greek subjects he used flashbacks, 'play within the play', the 'monologue-style', the revival of farce; for

27

political subjects, he used pseudo-philosophical and ABSURDIST drama – trends he could both follow and satirize in the same play. He rejoiced in attacking the beliefs and attitudes of a bourgeois audience, assuaged by his more traditional play construction, ready wit and dislike of intellectual pretension. He rarely sired a flop, yet for all his stylistic variations, he always rang the changes on the same characters, themes and devices, and he had the knack of infuriating critics, in France and in Britain, for his 'escapist whimsy' and for inviting what the critic Ivor Brown labelled 'a tranquil snooze'.

From the Second World War, however, into the early 1960s he held a dominant international position, with plays such as *Antigone* (1941), *Point of Departure* (originally *Eurydice*, 1941), *L'Invitation au château* (1946, translated by CHRISTOPHER FRY as *Ring Round the Moon*), *La Répétition* (*The Rehearsal*, 1946), *La Valse des toréadors* (*The Waltz of the Toreadors*, 1952), *L'Alouette* (*The Lark*, 1953) and *Becket* (1959). Beneath the froth lurks 'a man of the theatre' vainly striving to come to terms with reality. What is truly real and how true is it? Anouilh's world is indeed a stage, his realism plainly artificial, his game-playing 'real' and, if consistency is any guide, sincere. Play-making and living coalesce as his 'pure' young idealists grow up with him, appearing more intransigent when contrasted with flawed and crapulous middle-age – a shift of sympathy first adumbrated in his Creon and Antigone. Time plays tricks with identity and Anouilh with time as his search for himself leads, from *Le Voyageur sans bagage* (*Traveller without Luggage*, 1936) and his Pirandellian 'play the author couldn't write', *La Grotte* (*The Cavern*, 1960), to his final encapsulation as the lame *Oedipe* (1986). DONALD WATSON

John Harvey, *Anouilh: A Study in Theatrics* (1964)

H. G. McIntyre, *The Theatre of Jean Anouilh* (1981)

Edward O. Marsh, *Jean Anouilh: Poet of Pierrot and Pantaloon* (1953)

Leonard C. Pronko, *The World of Jean Anouilh* (1961)

Philip Thody, *Anouilh* (1968)

Ansky [An-Ski], Simeon Akimovich [Solomon Samuel (Seinwill) Rappoport] (b. Vitebsk, Belorussia, 8 Nov. 1863; d. Warsaw, 8 Nov. 1920) Yiddish writer, ethnologist and author of the most famous of Yiddish plays, *The Dybbuk, or Between Two Worlds*, a mystical drama from an Hasidic legend about demonic possession. It was written in Odessa in 1916, first performed in Yiddish by the Vilna Troupe in 1920, and then in Hebrew by the Moscow HABIMAH company, directed by VAKHTANGOV. It spread across Europe and to America, and has remained in the international repertoire since. As a member of the Jewish Socialist Bund, Ansky also wrote their song, 'The Oath'. VERA GOTTLIEB

See also YIDDISH THEATRE.

anthropology *see* THEATRE ANTHROPOLOGY

anti-play A theatre work in which the creator sets out to subvert and counter the theatrical conventions of the day, e.g. by the use of long silences, inactivity, non-sequential plotting or nonsense dialogue. The term 'anti-theatre' was also used, mainly after the Second World War, to describe plays that flouted the accepted conventions. Examples range from JARRY's *Ubu Roi* (1896) to HANDKE's *Offending the Audience* (1966). As categories dissolved towards the end of the twentieth century, the terms became rarely used.
COLIN CHAMBERS

See also DADA; HAPPENINGS; THEATRE OF THE ABSURD.

anti-theatre *see* ANTI-PLAY

Antigua *see* CARIBBEAN

Antoine, André (b. Limoges, France, 31 Jan. 1858; d. Le Pouliguen, 19 Oct. 1943) Actor and director. In spring 1887 he gathered together a group of amateur actors and founded the Théâtre Libre (Free Theatre). Hiring a small hall in Montparnasse with savings earned as a clerk in the Paris Gas Company, he became the first great practitioner of naturalism, the prevailing form of twentieth-century theatre, repudiating the dominant MELODRAMA, FARCE and romantic costume plays and the newer SYMBOLIST theatre of MAETERLINCK. He later moved to a theatre in the Paris Latin Quarter and then to the Théâtre des Menus-Plaisirs. For seven years he provided a showcase of predominantly one-act plays by over 50 authors, most of them aged under 40. He directed 111 plays, including non-naturalist VERSE DRAMA and semi-poetic plays such as HAUPTMANN's *Hannele*. He brought a new and scrupulous realism to both acting and stage design. He banished wings and footlights, employed natural light sources, built solid doors in box-sets and rented everyday furniture. Famous productions include IBSEN's *The Wild Duck* (1891), STRINDBERG's *Miss Julie* (1893) and Hauptmann's *The Weavers* (1893). His theatre, however, lost money and he found himself seriously in debt. He left in 1894 but founded the Théâtre Antoine in 1897 and became director of the ODÉON (1906–14), where he established a serious approach to Shakespeare. Before the First World War he dominated the French AVANT-GARDE theatre until the arrival of JACQUES COPEAU, who owed much to him. Antoine stimulated new playwrights such as EUGENE BRIEUX and François de Curel (1854–1928), and developed a new, restrained acting style appropriate for the social realism of his preferred authors. 'It is the environment,' said Antoine, 'which determines the characters, not the movement of the characters which determines the environment.' His example inspired OTTO BRAHM in Berlin and J. T. GREIN in London to found INDEPENDENT THEATRES.

After the First World War he encouraged young writers such as Georges Duhamel (1884–1966) and JULES ROMAINS, and became an influential drama and film critic. His memoirs are contained in *Le Théâtre* (2 vols, 1932–3). TERRY HODGSON

J. Chotia, *André Antoine* (1991)
John A. Henderson, *The First Avant-Garde* (1971)

Antrobus, John (b. London, 2 July 1933) Playwright. A comic SURREALIST, sympathetic to the abnormal and distrustful of modern science. Plays include *You'll Come to Love Your Sperm Test* (1965), and *Hitler in Liverpool* (1980). Antrobus wrote *Goon Show* radio scripts and – with the comic SPIKE MILLIGAN – the post-apocalyptic farce *The Bed-Sitting Room* (1963).
TONY HOWARD

Apollinaire, Guillaume [Wilhelm Apollinaris de Kostrowitzky] (b. Rome, 26 Aug. 1880; d. Paris, 9 Nov. 1918) The foremost French poet of the first half of the twentieth century, who coined the word SURREALISM. As an art critic he was the first to recognize the importance of painters like Picasso, Matisse, Braque and Duchamp. The author of only five plays, his importance to theatre rests upon just one of them, *Les Mamelles de Tirésias* (*The Breasts of Tiresias*, 1917), a 'surrealist drama in two acts and a prologue', which is a crucial link in the history of theatre between JARRY's *Ubu Roi* and IONESCO's *Bald Prima Donna*. (The only professional production of *The Breasts of Tiresias* in Britain was staged at Nottingham in a double bill with *The Bald Prima Donna* in November 1987.) In this play, a wife rebels against her reproductive duties, gets rid of her breasts (a red and a blue balloon) and turns into a man. Within a day she becomes soldier, MP, general, minister, senator, while her husband, forced to wear her skirt, produces 40,049 children, all crying together. A prologue rejects outmoded realism and stresses the importance of chance, of joyfulness, of voluptuousness. CLAUDE SCHUMACHER

Scott Bates, *Guillaume Apollinaire* (1967)
David Berry, *The Creative Vision of Apollinaire* (1982)
Claude Schumacher, *Alfred Jarry and Guillaume Apollinaire* (1985).

Apollo Theater, New York One of the most important showcases for black talent in its heyday, from 1935 to the mid-1970s. Originally a BURLESQUE house for an all-white audience, opened in 1913 in Harlem, New York, it was renamed the Apollo in 1928 by impresario Bill Minsky. On his death in 1932, the Apollo was turned into an all-black VAUDEVILLE house. For the next 40 years, the theatre instituted a variety show format – later copied by the HACKNEY EMPIRE, London – that featured every form of popular entertainment: comedy, drama, gospel, blues, jazz, rhythm and blues, rock and roll, and soul music. The theatre was vacant for several years in the mid-1970s, but in 1986 renovations were made to bring it up to date as a performance venue.
DENISE L. TILLES

J. Schiffman, *Uptown: The Story of Harlem's Apollo Theater* (1971)

Appen, Karl von (b. Düsseldorf, 12 May 1900; d. Berlin, 22 Aug. 1981) Painter and designer. Von Appen is best known for his work with the BERLINER ENSEMBLE, which he joined as chief designer in 1954. His designs for the last of BRECHT's own productions and his continuing influence until 1977 did much to establish the style of Brecht productions worldwide.
CLIVE BARKER

See also DESIGN.

Appia, Adolphe (b. Geneva, 1 Sept. 1862; d. Nyon, Switzerland, 29 Feb. 1928) Designer and theoretician; a major innovative force in SOUND and LIGHTING design. At the end of the nineteenth century Appia laid out both the theoretical and practical foundations for a permanent change in theatrical art. Through his extensive commentary, detailed scenarios and unprecedented designs – all inspired by his analysis of Wagnerian opera – Appia first provided a complete and devastating critique of the disastrous state of contemporary practice, and then, with astonishing foresight, suggested the solutions which would re-establish it upon an entirely different basis.

In his revolutionary work *Music and the Art of the Theatre* (1899), Appia suggested that the musical score itself should dictate not only the duration of the performance, but also all the movement and gestures of the actors, and by extension, the physical area itself – the scenic space in which the performance took place. He called for three-dimensional scenery; for the use of creative, form-revealing light (developing the concept of the 'lighting plot'); and for settings which would be expressive of the inner reality *as art* of works of musical drama. He demanded that the actor be set free from the mockery of flat, painted settings, in order to perform within a supportive and responsive setting. Light, symbolic colouring and a dynamic, sculptured space should evoke mood, atmosphere and psychological nuance, with all these expressive elements coordinated by the new theatrical artist, whom Appia termed the 'designer-director'. The audience should no longer be thought of as mere passive spectators; Appia believed that experiments along the lines he suggested could more fully involve them in the theatrical act in order both to experience and to determine it more directly.

The second phase of Appia's creative career arose from his involvement from 1906 with the system of eurhythmics devised by his fellow countryman, EMILE JAQUES-DALCROZE. This was designed to enhance performers' sensitvity to musical rhythm and tempo through the responsive movement of their own bodies. Appia saw in it the key to realizing his earlier theoretical principle that the performer must be motivated by music and through his movement determine the nature of the scenic environment. He prepared a series of designs, termed 'rhythmic spaces', which further revolutionized scenic practice. These were abstract arrangements of solid stairs, platforms, podia and the like, whose rigidity, sharp lines and angles, and immobility, when confronted by the softness, subtlety and movement of the body, would, by opposition, take on a kind of borrowed life.

Together with Dalcroze, Appia presented at Dalcroze's Institute in Hellerau, Germany, a series of demonstrations highlighting the potential of eurhythmics for both performance and design. In 1912 and 1913 they held festivals there, the centrepiece of which was an influential production of Gluck's *Orpheus and Eurydice* without a proscenium arch. The lighting, operated from a central 'organ', was carefully coordinated with the music and movement as well as the emotional 'flow' of the performance. Appia met GORDON CRAIG in Zurich in 1914, and in 1922 they exhibited together in Amsterdam. Appia also became a friend of COPEAU. Although Appia's *Tristan and Isolde* (1923) at La Scala, Milan, did not win popular approval, in 1924 he was asked to stage the entire *Ring* cycle at Basel. Unfortunately, the production of *The Rhinegold* and *The Walkyrie* provoked such outrage among a minority of reactionaries that the rest of the project was cancelled. At his death his ideas were still thought too advanced by many, and full recognition came only in 1951 with the advent of the 'New BAYREUTH Style' under the director WIELAND WAGNER, who, in his productions of his grandfather's operas, wholeheartedly embraced Appia's vision. His influence, though less widely acknowledged than that of Craig, most of whose ideas he anticipated, is immense, and was absorbed into the practice of many of the most notable designer and directors of the century.

RICHARD BEACHAM

See also ARCHITECTURE.

R. Beacham, *Adolphe Appia, Theatre Artist* (1987)

——*Adolphe Appia: Artist and Visionary of the Modern Theatre* (1994)

W. Volbach, *Adolphe Appia: Prophet of the Modern Theatre* (1968)

——*Adolphe Appia: Essays, Scenarios and Designs*, ed. and trans. R. Beacham (1989)

Arab theatre   *see* MIDDLE EAST AND NORTH AFRICA

Arbuzov, Alexei [Nikolaevich]   (b. Moscow, 13 May 1908; d. Moscow, 20 April 1986)   Playwright, actor and director. Orphaned after the Revolution and homeless until taken in by an aunt, Arbuzov started work with Proletkult in Leningrad in 1923, studied acting in drama school (his only formal education), and in 1928 organized touring theatre groups and ran the literary section of the first Kholkhoz Theatre. In 1939 he had his first real success with the popular 'lyrical drama' *Tanya* (a play often given radio production), and founded the Moscow Studio Theatre with Plyuchek, scripting plays from improvisations and workshops – the first of which, *Gorod na zare* (*The Town at Dawn*), played to front-line troops in 1941. He wrote over 30 plays and his work engaged the talents of leading figures in the Soviet theatre (e.g. SIMONOV, OKHLOPKOV, TOVSTOGONOV, EFROS). Arbuzov's popular *Irkutskaya istoriya* (*Irkutsk Story*, sometimes translated as *It Happened in Irkutsk*, 1959) has also been turned into a ballet, *Angara*. Equally successful was *Moi bednyi Marat* ('My poor Marat', 1965, translated as *The Promise*, produced simultaneously throughout the Soviet Union and seen in London's West End with JUDI DENCH and IAN MCKELLEN). Along with these two plays, several others have been successfully produced abroad, e.g. *Dvenadtsaty chas* (*The Twelfth Hour*, 1959), *Skazki Starogo Arbata* (*Once Upon a Time*, 1970) and *Staromodnaya Komediya* (*Old World*, 1975), produced by the ROYAL SHAKESPEARE COMPANY (1976) with PEGGY ASHCROFT and ANTHONY QUAYLE.

VERA GOTTLIEB

Archer, William   (b. Perth, Scotland, 23 Sept. 1856; d. London, 27 Dec. 1924)   Drama critic, playwright and translator. Archer was a major force from the 1890s onwards in the promotion of advanced drama, especially IBSEN. In addition to his theatre criticism, his greatest practical achievement lay in his translations of Ibsen's plays, produced in a collected edition of 11 volumes (1906–8). Most notable, not least for the furore they provoked, were *A Doll's House*, staged in 1889, and *Ghosts* (1891). In contrast to his commitment to progressive drama, the one successful play of his own, *The Green Goddess* (1923), seems curiously conventional. His critical works include *English Dramatists of Today* (1882), *Masks or Faces* (1888) and *The Old Drama and the New*

(1923), in which he continued to champion contemporary plays in the face of what he saw as a widespread conservative emphasis on the classics.   IAN CLARKE

architecture   Designing theatres belongs to a specialized and subtle branch of architecture. At the beginning of the twentieth century it was a form which, with just a few but significant exceptions, and also with national variations, was rooted in a tradition which had developed consistently during the previous 250–300 years. Nevertheless, there already existed three types of theatre building which, under a combination of artistic and economic influences, were to become increasingly distinct as the century wore on, although at different times and in varying degrees as developments in one category exerted their influence on the others. These three categories may be termed *commercial, civic* and *artistic,* and they appealed to three basic groups of audience: the *masses,* the *middle* and the *minorities.* In audience as in the forms of the buildings themselves, some crossing-over between categories occurred, but rarely from one extreme to the other.

Arts

These are most characteristic of countries where, prior to the mid-twentieth century, there was no tradition for state or civic involvement in the theatre, e.g. Britain and America. In 1900 a major boom in commercial theatre building was at its height, having started in the 1890s; it was to continue until the outbreak of the First World War in Europe and until around 1930 in America. Whether intended primarily for the presentation of plays, for which a capacity of about 1,000 was typical, or for musical shows and star comedy turns, with capacities of between 1,500 and 2,500, commercial theatres were almost invariably built on tight city-centre sites. Their purpose was, after all, to produce a profit, and in order to maximize revenue the bulk of the building containing the auditorium and stage was usually hidden behind relatively narrow entrance façades which were flanked by shops and offices, often part of the same development. Architectural practices had developed which specialized in theatre construction and they became expert in achieving the maximum possible seating capacity on a given site within tolerable limits for sightlines and comfort, although in the latter case this was often of minimal standard for the cheaper seats in the upper levels. In Britain, among the most prolific specialists during the period up to the First World War were FRANK MATCHAM, Bertie Crewe (d. 1937) and W. G. R. Sprague (d. 1933). Sprague was usually employed to design theatres of moderate seating capacity (about 1,000) by today's standards, primarily intended for the presentation of plays and smaller musical entertain-

ments. They were in a direct line of development from Victorian theatres built for similar purposes, and were usually in the form of a slightly raked main floor with two, or at most three, balconies above, facing a formal proscenium frame to the stage and with boxes projecting from the side walls. Behind the proscenium, which was usually an almost standard width of about 30 feet, the stage was enclosed within a tall structure called a fly tower with a gridiron from which scenery could be suspended, usually 50–55 feet high. Auditorium design differed most notably from earlier theatres built in the latter half of the previous century in that steel cantilever construction allowed for much deeper balconies, extending far over the main floor and over each other. The rows of seating in these balconies were usually only slightly curved so that they could be brought closer to the stage without creating poor sightlines at the sides. This form of design could result, however, in some loss of theatrical atmosphere when compared with earlier theatres which had shallow balconies laid out on a horseshoe or lyre-shaped plan (e.g. the OLD VIC, London, 1871). The side seats in these, although not perfect in respect of sightlines, nevertheless contributed strongly to a linking of the audience with the action on the stage and to a lively sense of enclosure and audience self-awareness. Characteristic of Sprague's theatres and others of similar scale of this period are the ALDWYCH (London, 1906) and the Globe (London, 1906), renamed the GIELGUD in 1994.

The basic form of design of the smaller and medium-sized theatres was also applied on an increased scale to the big VARIETY theatres built in Britain during this period. Typical are the LONDON PALLADIUM (1910, Matcham, 2,300 seats) and the Palace Theatre, Manchester (1913, Crewe, 2,180 seats). Although large in scale, these auditoriums achieve a remarkable degree of intimacy by setting a reasonable limit on the distance from the stage front to the rear rows (about 75– 80 feet), and instead achieved the large seating capacities by an increase in width (about 90 feet). Proscenium openings are compatible with the widths of the auditoriums and suitable for spectacular shows (Palladium, 47 feet 6 inches; Palace, Manchester, 42 feet 6 inches) although stage depths rarely exceed about 40 feet. The high but relatively narrow spaces between the balcony fronts and the proscenium were ornately treated with elaborate compositions of boxes framed by columns on the side walls and by domed or coved ceilings. Architects cleverly made use of limited site areas by fitting foyers and bars within voids under the steep rakes of the huge balconies.

American theatre architecture for the first three decades of the century, until further building was curtailed by the effects of the Depression, tended to be somewhat

31

formulaic in basic design, if not in decorative treatment. Auditoriums tended to be of considerable width, and wide prosceniums (40 feet and more) were the norm. Single balconies were more common than two, and boxes were frequently arranged to step down towards the stage but were generally so widely angled away from the stage as often to be merely decorative rather than useful. Ornate ceilings usually covered the whole space of the auditorium up to the rear wall and although architecturally impressive they tended further to emphasize the lack of intimacy. As in Britain, some architects became specialists in theatre design; among these were Herts and Tallent, Thomas Lamb, William Lehman, Eugene de Rosa, Walter Ahlschlager, Frank Grad, John Eberson, and Rapp and Rapp. Styles adopted for the fibrous plaster decorations range from a fairly restrained Adamesque manner often employed by Lamb (e.g. the Newark Theater, 1917) to extremely lavish interpretations of French or Spanish Renaissance (e.g. the George Theater, Staten Island, 1929 by de Rosa). From the 1920s architects were increasingly responsible for cinemas as well as theatres, and the relatively small number of 'legitimate' theatres which continued to be built compared to the great boom in cinema construction were inevitably influenced by the requirements of the cinema where, in particular, intimacy was not a consideration. Theatres were often fitted with projection booths so that they could readily switch over to showing films. Although historically derived decorative schemes continued to be used up to *c*.1930, art deco developed alongside and reached a peak of inventiveness in the early 1930s; but interiors of theatres proper were restrained compared with the almost wild opulence used in some cinema and cine-theatre auditoriums. From *c*.1933 the Depression began to bite, and when recovery came in the 1940s, the cinema supplied the needs of mass entertainment.

The small number of post-First World War commercial theatres to be built in Britain also reflected the influence of cinema design and, through that, of American cinema and theatre design, albeit in a very much watered-down form. Typical of the 1920s in Britain are four big variety theatres designed by the Milburn brothers – the Empire, Liverpool (1925); Empire, Southampton (1928), Edinburgh Empire (1928) and the Dominion Theatre, London (1929), which soon went over to films but later returned to theatre. In their basic structural form they follow on from the prewar theatres, with two deep and wide balconies above the stalls (although the very American Empire in Liverpool has only one balcony). They are sparsely decorated with classical plasterwork and have token boxes filling the space between the ends of the balconies and the proscenium. As large theatres they function well, but they lack the vibrancy still evident in theatres built at the tail-end of the old tradition which died before the war. A few medium-sized theatres were built in London in the late 1920s and early 1930s, again following the familiar basic form of slightly curved, deeply overhanging balconies. One or two, like the Savoy (1929, gutted by fire in 1990 and later refurbished) and the Adelphi (1930), successfully integrated restrained art deco decorative schemes, but more typical are the Cambridge (1930) and the Saville (1931, now gutted), where large areas of blank side-wall showed the influence of contemporary cinema design and had the effect of distancing the audience seated in the balconies from the stage. Theatres built outside London in the 1930s are very rare and again strongly exhibit the influence of the cinema, with sparsely applied art deco motifs, e.g. the New Theatre, Oxford (1933); Royal Court, Liverpool (1933); Alexandra, Birmingham (1935); Opera House, Blackpool (1939). By this time, the cinema had overtaken the theatre as the supplier of popular entertainment and the building of new commercial theatres virtually ceased in Britain.

In most European countries theatres were built by civic authorities or the state, and it was only in the largest cities that commercial theatre also flourished. In Paris or Berlin, theatres built for plays tended to follow the traditional form which had developed in the design of court and other official theatres of a number of relatively shallow tiers of horseshoe layout surrounding a spacious open well. Earlier examples adopted historically derived decorative schemes, rococo being the most common; later ones, in the 1920s and 1930s, were simpler, with surfaces covered with polished wood veneer and incorporating art deco motifs, e.g. Théâtre Pigale, Paris. Oskar Kauffmann produced some delightfully idiosyncratic designs in Berlin in the 1920s, e.g. the Kurfürstendamm Theater. Very large commercial theatres like those in Britain and America were rare in Europe, although the Alhambra in Paris is an example; but this was designed by an English firm of architects, Gray & Evans of Liverpool, in partnership with a French architect, Georges Gumpel. In Italy, the few commercial theatres which were built tended to be designed as a stripped-down version of the traditional Italian multi-tiered horseshoe design. The Teatro Eliseo, Rome, is a late example, built in 1936 (architect Luigi Piccinato).

Civic theatres
In many European countries, particularly Germany, Austria, Italy and France, there has been a tradition, going back in some cases to the mid-seventeenth century, for theatres to be built by municipal authorities or

state governments. In smaller or medium-sized cities, theatres were often multi-purpose, presenting both drama and opera; but in large cities there was usually separate provision, with theatres being built specifically for drama. They often took their place among the major public buildings of a city centre, forming the dominant feature of a square, or placed in order to terminate the vista along a boulevard – in striking contrast to countries such as Britain where there was no such tradition. By the outbreak of the First World War the majority of European cities had been provided with a publicly funded theatre building. These almost invariably continued the development of the forms which had matured at the end of the previous century with the designs of specialist architects such as Fellner & Helmer, or Heinrich Seeling in Austria and Germany. Auditoriums typically had two or three shallow balconies continuing into slips and boxes at the sides, curving round an open well to meet a formal proscenium arch. Stages were deep, with high fly towers, and often had a lower rear-stage for use in special scenes or for the storage and handling of scenery during a production. These theatres were also provided with public areas of a degree of spaciousness entirely unknown in the commercial theatres of Britain and America. Relatively few civic theatres were built, or needed to be built, in Europe between the First and Second World Wars, and those that were, particularly in northern Europe, tended to be influenced by contemporary cinema design, with shallowly raked stalls, one or two deeper balconies and areas of blank side wall. The small number of theatres which were built in Italy were usually of traditional Italian type, e.g. the Teatro Communale, Sulmona, of 1933, with a horseshoe of four shallow tiers supported on rings of columns, and mostly containing boxes.

In Britain before the Second World War there were no purpose-built theatres paid for with public money. One theatre, the SHAKESPEARE MEMORIAL THEATRE at STRATFORD-UPON-AVON, might perhaps be included in this section, however, not because it was built or subsidized from public funds (the company did not receive its first public subsidy until the 1960s), but because it was not a commercial venture, and also because in terms of architectural scale it was comparable with the civic theatres of Europe. Designed by Elizabeth Scott and opened in 1932, it was strongly influenced by contemporary cinema architecture, having a fan-shaped auditorium and one balcony with a raised-up but not overhanging gallery behind. The slightly curved rows met large areas of plain plastered side walls. The action on the stage was made to appear even more remote by being recessed within a succession of heavily emphasized wood-panelled frames. Although a narrow fore-stage

stepped down into the stalls, this was unsuited for general use, and most of the action took place 30 feet from the front row of seats and 95 feet from the back row of the balcony, which was extremely remote for a theatre with a total seating capacity of 1,000. (It is worth noting that 65–70 feet is the approximate distance beyond which it is normally no longer possible to discern facial expressions and when hearing becomes difficult without amplification.) After four attempts to alter this unsatisfactory actor–audience relationship, including the removal of the panelled recessed frames of the proscenium, the company successfully achieved a major improvement in 1976 by introducing a three-sided forestage thrusting into the auditorium and linking the audience in the balcony and gallery to the action on it by forming two levels of slips stepping down the side walls. Further improvements have been made since.

The Second World War resulted in the destruction of many civic and state theatres in Europe, particularly in Germany, and here, as soon as improvements in economic conditions allowed in the early 1950s, a major rebuilding programme got under way, often considerably aided by state lotteries. In scale these postwar theatres are similar to their predecessors, ranging in seating capacity from about 800 to about 1,200 (the upper limit being determined by the need to maintain an acceptable level of intimacy). In their backstage facilities they are, however, usually even more lavish than before, with side as well as rear stages common, together with extensive scenery workshops and storage, rehearsal rooms, etc. Some of the theatres of the early 1950s displayed considerable evidence of the influence of cinema design, e.g. the Schiller Theater, West Berlin, of 1951 by Volker and Grosse (1,090 seats). In the late 1950s and early 1960s some architects adopted the BAYREUTH Opera House mode of a single rake of seats, e.g. the National Theatre in Mannheim (1957 by Gerhard Weber, 1,200), the Schauspielhaus, Stuttgart (1962 by Volkart), Wuppertal (1966 by G. Graubner) and Düsseldorf (1969 by B. Pfau). Unlike Wagner's Opera House, however, the side walls of which are broken up by a series of buttress-like projecting walls and columns parallel to the proscenium, these theatres have plain, flat walls which are deadening in effect. The declared intention for such designs was that they were 'democratic', abolishing the so-called hierarchical disposition of the traditional multi-tiered auditorium, but in fact there is little that is democratic in viewing a stage from the distant rear third of such a great expanse of seating.

Architects who understood the special requirements of theatre design, as against those of the cinema or the concert hall, had the courage to learn from the accumulated evidence of the past and to reinterpret traditional forms, but without resorting to pastiche. The lively, truly theatrical atmosphere generated within the auditorium of the Stattheater, Münster (1956, by Rave, von Hausen and Runhau, 956 seats) may be compared with the frigid prairie at Düsseldorf (1,008 seats). The most important single practical difference is that at Münster half the total number of seats are stacked vertically in three shallow balconies which overhang the rear and sides. More innovatory than Münster is the Stattheater at Gelsenkirchen (1959 by Rave, von Hausen and Runhau, 1050 seats) which achieves an even greater sense of liveliness and intimacy of relationship between audience and actor. This is done by putting more seats into the overhanging balconies; not by means of over-deepening them, but instead by stepping down the side walls a series of balconies/boxes with cleverly contrived sightlines, thus enclosing the space three-dimensionally with people. The effect of such a carefully considered design may also be measured in purely practical terms by comparing the maximum distance from the stage at Gelsenkirchen of 65 feet and at Düsseldorf of 97 feet 6 inches. Common to many of these theatres are unemphasized openings to the stage, adjustable in width, and adaptable fore-stages/orchestra pits.

In other European countries, particularly northern ones, civic theatres were built or rebuilt in the postwar period where needed and were often influenced in their design by those in Germany. In Britain during the 1950s and 1960s a great many commercial touring theatres went out of business because of the popularity of the cinema and television. Some of the smaller ones were taken over by repertory companies which got subsidies from the ARTS COUNCIL and local authorities. Where existing theatres were not available or were unsuitable, some of the more enlightened local authorities began to build new civic theatres. This was a novel concept in Britain. Few were comparable in the scale of their facilities with those abroad, particularly in Germany, and by no means all were true civic theatres, several being built by trusts responsible for running repertory companies and with only part public funding. The first proper CIVIC THEATRE in Britain was the Belgrade Theatre, Coventry (1958, capacity 910, designed by the City Architects' Department). It is in a Festival of Britain mode of design, and although serviceable is somewhat rigid and dull. The single, almost straight-rowed balcony is set rather too high up and feels cut off from the stalls, although the stepped boxes which project from the side walls go some way to offset the cinema feel. The proscenium is fairly formally treated within deep, wood-panelled splays, but some concession is made to flexibility with a narrow fore-stage/orchestra pit. That architects were unused to designing theatres at this time is amply illustrated by

two horrors: the Ashcroft Theatre, Croydon (1962) and the OXFORD PLAYHOUSE, both with long, narrow auditoriums with a straight-rowed balcony far away at the rear and acres of bare wall. One of the first really successful designs was the NOTTINGHAM Playhouse (1963, capacity 750, architect Peter Moro). The front-of-house spaces, the auditorium with its semicircular drum and the fly tower are well articulated externally. Internally, the embracing curves of the balcony front and the auditorium walls, which imperceptibly open into the stage, achieve a sense of intimate contact between audience and actor. If there is a fault, it is that the balcony is set rather too high and this is also the main defect of the Yvonne Arnaud Theatre, Guildford (1965, capacity 574, architects Scott, Brownrigg and Turner), which is otherwise a successful small theatre for a repertory company. Other designs opt for a 'democratic' single rake. With a relatively low capacity this may come off, e.g. the Thorndike Theatre, Leatherhead (1969, capacity 526, architect Roderick Ham), although one is rather too aware of the blank side walls covered with tiles, but the sea of seats at the BIRMINGHAM REPERTORY THEATRE (1971, capacity 900, architects S. T. Walker & Partners) is reminiscent of Düsseldorf or Wuppertal. The lessons learned by some architects in Germany in re-interpreting a baroque handling of space in modern terms (e.g. Gelsenkirchen) had their influence in Britain. The Forum Theatre, Billingham (1968, capacity 650, architects Elder, Lester & Partners) has only 12 rows of seats in the stalls, the rest of the audience being stacked vertically around the rear and side walls in three shallow tiers linked to stepped balconies/boxes. The larger Eden Court Theatre at Inverness (1976, capacity 830, architects Law and Dunbar-Nasmith) carries the traditional approach further, and the sense of the audience embracing the action on the stage is enhanced by the ends of the boxes overlapping the 'invisible' proscenium. The opening is adjustable in width, and its flexibility of use is increased by canting the front of the fly tower over the fore-stage. The Barbican Theatre, London (opened 1982 but conceived in the late 1960s, capacity 1,200, architects Chamberlain, Powell and Bonn) was designed specifically to fit the requirements of the ROYAL SHAKESPEARE COMPANY. The auditorium is shallow in depth and of reasonable width, and its intimacy is further ensured by the curious but successful device of making each of its three shallow balconies jut out over the one below, and the ends of the balconies dip down along the side walls towards the stage. In this way a remarkable degree of intimacy is achieved for the 1,200 seats, with no member of the audience further than 65 feet from the 'point of command', which was defined as about 8 feet behind the front of the stage. The transition between auditorium and stage was also designed to achieve maximum flexibility, with the opening capable of being as wide as the front part of the auditorium, with ramps up to the acting area from each side; panels may be moved in from the wings to form a proscenium 35 feet wide. The Lyttelton Theatre of the NATIONAL THEATRE, London (opened 1976 but conceived and designed in the 1960s, capacity 890, architect Sir Denys Lasdun) is retrogressive in its flat-on rigidity. It is claimed for the Olivier (capacity 1,165) that it is an 'open-stage' theatre. In reality it is an extremely wide fan-shaped auditorium (150 feet wide at the rear) facing an unemphasized structural opening to the scenic stage 58 feet wide, in front of which a fore-stage with a three-sided front edge projects 25 feet into the auditorium. Only 44 of the total number of seats are forward of the front edge of this fore-stage. No attempt is made to improve intimacy by providing overhanging areas of seating – the very large rear 'balcony' projects by only one row over the stalls seating in front of it. As a result, the distance from the 'point of command' to the rear row in the middle of the 'balcony' is as much as 78 feet; but even more damning than this for a theatre which was designed specifically for drama is the fact that because of the great width of the auditorium, the actor is perceived by any member of the audience who is not sitting in the centre block of the stalls as being dwarfed by its vast overall volume. Similar in basic concept but theatrically far more successful is the Haymarket Theatre, LEICESTER (1973, capacity 703). The seating rows are faceted rather than curved in plan, but most importantly the balcony overhangs the stalls, thus bringing those seated in it correspondingly closer to the stage. The width of the auditorium is reasonable and is further reduced visually by dropping the end sections of the balcony down to a lower level, which at the same time improves contact with the stage. The Theatre Royal, Plymouth (1981, architect Peter Moro) adopts a similar plan form, although it is proportionately less wide and has a fore-stage of smaller projection. It differs most, however, in having a variable seating capacity, from 1,280 for opera, musicals, etc, to 724 for more intimate productions. This is achieved by lowering the ceiling to cut off the large second balcony.

Flexibility of capacity is a feature possessed by a number of American theatres built after the Second World War, but particularly from the 1960s, often to satisfy a need created by the loss of commercial theatres. These buildings are typically funded by higher education establishments, civic authorities and private non-profit making bodies, sometimes in partnership. One of the principal advocates of this multi-purpose type of theatre has been GEORGE IZENOUR, theatre consultant, who believes that theatres can only be successful if their design is subject to the application of scientific criteria intended to produce perfect sightlines and acoustics. This almost invariably results in hall- or cinema-like auditoriums, often of great size in their maximum capacity format, which may be of 2,000 or more seats in order to provide an economic return from unsubsidized productions. Capacities may be lowered for smaller-scale productions by the use of suspended panels to screen rear areas of seating and to bring down the ceiling height. Representative examples are the Jesse H. Jones Hall, Houston (1966) and the Edwin Thomas Hall, Akron, Ohio (1973). But even in their minimum capacity format, a sense of theatre is almost entirely lacking – the inevitable result of two-dimensional rather than three-dimensional planning. Theatre design cannot be reduced to a formula.

Arts theatres

This rather nebulous category belongs, at least in its early years of development, to the AVANT-GARDE and EXPERIMENTAL; a world of directors, writers, stage designers and some architects who reacted against what they saw as the tyranny of traditional theatre forms. Ideas which emerged from the end of the nineteenth century and during the first three decades of the twentieth developed into a constant search for ideal solutions. This produced a bewilderingly diverse progeny, some of it continuing to be of an experimental and often small-scale nature, and some developing into accepted forms which were adopted for the building of major theatres, often with part or whole civic funding. Some of the first moves towards a break with tradition were, however, based on a desire to recreate a historically authentic past rather than to produce new ideas for the future. In the 1880s and 1890s, particularly after the discovery in 1888 of the copy by von Buchel of De Witt's drawing of the Elizabethan Swan Theatre, London, there were a number of fixed-set and simple platform productions of Shakespeare, e.g. by WILLIAM POEL in England and Max Kruger in Germany. There were also revivals of ancient Greek plays in simplified productions without conventional painted illusionistic scenery, and some which were done in the OPEN AIR in small-scale reconstructed versions of Greek theatres. A further development was also related to the influence of the Greek theatre plan as modified by Gottfried Semper and taken up by Wagner at his Bayreuth Opera House in 1876 with his rejection of the multi-tiered, multi-directional baroque horseshoe type in favour of a unidirectional single rake of seats. In 1908 the architect Max Littmann built the Künstlertheater in Munich, which took the Bayreuth plan and reduced it to a smaller scale for drama. He kept the single steep rake of seating but cut off the sides of the fan.

Although this form did not attempt to remove the proscenium which separated the 'real world' from the *Glanzwelt*, its insistence on a single-minded concentration on the stage picture had a tremendous influence on future theatre design. But this did not necessarily mean that intimacy of contact was considered to be of particular importance. Although the Künstlertheater had only 640 seats, the last row was as much as 75 feet from the front of the stage. Early versions of the Künstlertheater type appeared with the Birmingham Repertory Theatre in 1913 (architect S. N. Cooke) and the theatre at the Cologne Werkbund exhibition of 1914 by Van de Velde. Both had long, narrow auditoriums, somewhat cold and lecture theatre-like in atmosphere.

At this time the influence of innovatory directors and stage designs began to exert particular influence, especially the scenic ideals of ADOLPHE APPIA in Germany and his British follower GORDON CRAIG, who rejected conventional illusionistic scenery with painted flats and borders and instead used imaginative lighting and simple platforms, ramps, steps, etc. to create three-dimensional effects. It was, however, the work of the producer and impresario MAX REINHARDT which led to the first truly architectural expression of a rejection of the separation of auditorium and stage. In 1919 architect Hans Poelzig reconstructed a Berlin Circus building as a 3,500-seat space for Reinhardt's spectacular production of plays, including classical Greek plays. Its most revolutionary feature was its thrust or peninsular stage, which projected from a scenic stage to be surrounded on three sides by a semicircular amphitheatre of stepped seating without balconies. The central space was covered by a vast dome decorated with plaster stalactites. The Grosses Schauspielhaus was not a success, largely because of its great size and the poor view of the scenic stage from the side seats, and because of bad acoustics. Apart from some unrealized projects it was some time before the peninsular stage/scenic stage form re-emerged. The Municipal Theatre in Malmö, Sweden, opened in 1944 and has 1,595 seats on a main floor and single balcony laid out concentrically from the peninsular stage which does not, however, project as far into the auditorium as that of the Grosses Schauspielhaus. It is from this type of theatre that the Olivier Theatre in London is also derived; but, as mentioned above, the front of stage there has retreated to the extent that it is barely enclosed by audience at all. This progressively smaller degree of stage projection/audience enclosure reflects the basic difficulty of combining the peninsular and scenic stage types in that those two-thirds of the audience seated at the sides of a full peninsular stage have a very restricted view of action on the scenic stage.

The omission of the scenic stage would allow for the full exploitation of the peninsular form. This was done with great success in 1948 by TYRONE GUTHRIE for his production of *The Thrie Estaitis* in the mid-nineteenth century Assembly Hall of the Church of Scotland for the EDINBURGH FESTIVAL. In 1957 Guthrie was involved in the design of a purpose-built peninsular stage theatre at STRATFORD, Ontario. The Festival Theater (architects Rounthwaite and Fairfield) is large, with a total of 2,250 seats on two levels with the rows concentrically arranged around the stage. The GUTHRIE THEATER, MINNEAPOLIS (1963, architect Ralph Rapson) is similar in concept, although not so large, with 1,400 seats. The CHICHESTER FESTIVAL THEATRE, England (1962, architects Powell and Moya) is within a hexagonal envelope. It has nearly the same seating capacity as Minneapolis, but the central block of seats extends back by a further six rows because there is no balcony. All of these theatres suffer from the same basic fault of being too big. Although the maximum distance as measured directly from the stage to the rear rows is not great, the actor is actually seen in relation to the very considerable volume of the total space in which s/he is standing. The Crucible Theatre, SHEFFIELD, England (1971, 1,000 seats, architects Renton Howard Wood Associates) sets a reasonable limit on size and achieves a successful actor–audience relationship in the peninsular stage form. It is an example of this avant-garde form being adopted for a municipally funded theatre.

An OPEN STAGE concept which began to develop at about the same time as the peninsular type was the open-end stage. This is a form which places the acting area within the same space as the seating, which is unidirectional. It was again largely the result of experimental work by directors or producers, and one of the first examples was initiated by the Swiss director EMILE JAQUES-DALCROZE at Hellerau near Dresden. The Festival Theatre there was designed by Heinrich Tessenow in 1910–11 for the performance of EXPRESSIONIST mystery plays and had a single bank of raked seating facing an open stage arranged as a series of platforms linked by steps. These were designed, together with the lighting, by Appia. In 1919 LOUIS JOUVET converted the existing Théâtre du Vieux Colombier, Paris, into the open-end stage form for JACQUES COPEAU. The proscenium was removed to open up the stage into the rectangular auditorium and, as at Hellerau, a permanent set of platforms and steps was constructed. In another conversion of an existing building, in 1926 TERENCE GRAY removed the entire proscenium wall of the 1816 Theatre Royal at Barnwell, Cambridge. He stepped the front of the stage down into the stalls and built a permanent cyclorama across the full width of the rear wall. The sensation thus created was in this case the more remarkable in that the old auditorium was retained in its multi-tiered horse-shoe form. Such experiments as these tended, however, to be relatively short-lived as they depended to a large extent on the talents of their initiators, and in any case audiences soon tired of the sameness of productions with permanent settings. A later example of the open-end stage was the conversion of a former warehouse to form the MERMAID THEATRE, London, in 1959. This did not have a permanent set and so a variety of settings was possible; but even so, the limitations of not having space for movement at the sides of the stage or provision for suspension above it were apparent. In the case of the Mermaid, although the form was deliberately chosen, it was also unavoidable because of the enclosing structural walls. The length of the auditorium also meant that the rear third of seats were remote from the stage relative to the capacity of 500. That the form could be successful, if on a small enough scale, is demonstrated by the Phoenix Theatre, LEICESTER (275 seats) or the HAMPSTEAD THEATRE, London (157 seats).

From the late 1950s in Germany and the 1960s in Britain, it came to be realized that the same basic actor–audience relationship could be achieved by allowing the side walls of an auditorium to merge imperceptibly into the stage without the intervention of any sort of frame, and yet at the same time the stage itself could be endowed with wing space and flying facilities. Considerable flexibility could be achieved within the zone of transition between auditorium and stage, allowing for different widths of opening and different degrees of projection of the stage into the volume of the auditorium. It was this approach which was adopted from the 1960s for many of the theatres in the civic category. It was also successfully used, often with variations, for more modest theatres more properly belonging to the present category, some of which will be referred to later.

A more uncompromising form of open stage theatre is that where the audience entirely surrounds the acting space, usually known as THEATRE IN THE ROUND. In 1922 NORMAN BEL GEDDES, who worked with Reinhardt, designed a project for a theatre with eight concentric rows of seats surrounding a circular acting area which rose up from a well on a stepped podium. However, as with other projects by Geddes, it was not built. In Moscow in the late 1920s and early 1930s there were experimental stagings in existing buildings by the director NIKOLAI OKHLOPKOV. Further experiments in this form were made at American colleges in the 1930s, and in 1940 a small purpose-built theatre in the round was constructed at the University of Washington, Seattle, designed by Carl Gould. It had a circular acting area surrounded by three rows of seats with a capacity of 180, enclosed within a circular drum with ancillary accommodation attached. Other permanent or semi-permanent theatres in the round followed in America, mostly at universities, and were successful because of their relative smallness. Due to the fact that it is inevitable in this form that the actor has her/his back to part of the audience all the time, the distance to the rear row should preferably not exceed about 32 feet 6 inches, which in practice means about six or seven rows of seats and a capacity of about 400. Another consideration is that, as with the peninsular or thrust stage, the actor is perceived in relation to the *total* volume of the space and can, therefore, be dwarfed by it if it is too large.

The ARENA STAGE, Washington DC (1961, architect Harry Weese and Associates) was built to house a professional repertory company. It is square in plan with a square acting area surrounded by 750 seats in seven rows. It is rather too large and lacks the intimacy needed if this form is to be successful. The ROYAL EXCHANGE THEATRE, MANCHESTER (1976, 700 seats, architects Levitt Bernstein), although similar in capacity to the Arena Stage, aims to achieve as intimate a relationship between actor and audience as possible by limiting the seating at stage level to 450 in five rows and placing the other 250 seats above in two galleries of two rows each. The result is very successful, although the sightlines in the upper gallery are stretched to the limit, with the audience looking down at the tops of the heads of the nearest actors! It is certainly a very exciting space, being contained within a seven-sided tubular steel and glass structure, free-standing within the vast Exchange hall.

Theatre in the round is, however, a form which by its nature is perhaps best suited to ad hoc fit-ups within existing spaces to meet the needs of a particular production, rather than to being formalized as a permanent structure.

Adaptability as an end in itself is another concept in theatre design within this category which developed during the twentieth century and produced a few unrealized 'ideal' projects, a number of small studio theatres which achieved flexibility by manual means with some success, and some rather more ambitious theatres which attempted to be adaptable by mechanical means, usually with less success. In the 1920s various projects for adaptable theatres emerged from the BAUHAUS School of Design in Germany, and in 1927 its director, WALTER GROPIUS, designed for the theatre director ERWIN PISCATOR a scheme for a *Totaltheater*. This was an elaborate mechanized concept, the whole of which – including the auditorium – would serve as a place of action. It was intended that a circular acting area should move from within one end of an oval configuration of seating to its centre, or that the circular acting area be covered with seats and the stage be in a more conventional position outside one end of the oval. The project was never realized, but its influence on the ideas of others was considerable.

In the 1930s, the ideas of ANTONIN ARTAUD became known in Europe. He advocated that 'We abolish the stage and auditorium and replace them by a single site, without partition or barriers of any kind ... a direct communication will thus be established between the spectator and the spectacle ... abandoning the architecture of today, we will rent some kind of barn or hangar.' His influence has inevitably been most evident in the work of directors, notably PETER BROOK, who had the Bouffes du Nord music hall, Paris, gutted and filled with benches for his new theatre. Others continued to attempt to translate the concept of adaptability into purpose-built form. It was again in the American universities that experimentation was particularly active. The Ring Theater at Miami University (1950) allowed for in-the-round or peninsular stage performances by means of the manual movement of sections of raked seating, which is feasible where there is ample free labour available.

The Germans, having been in at the beginning of ideas for adaptability, had by the post-Second World War period generally come to be of the opinion that built-in adaptability rarely produces a satisfactory solution to any one of the forms it is attempting to combine, and that it is better to choose one form and design a solution for it as carefully as possible. In the theatre rebuilding boom of the 1950s and 1960s, only about two theatres were designed for adaptable seating/staging – the small theatres attached to the main ones at Mannheim and Gelsenkirchen (it had already been decided that adaptability of size was an impractical concept). In both cases the mechanical adaptability available is rarely made use of, and they usually remain fixed into the form in which they are most effective – an open-end stage.

One of the most ambitious of the mechanically adaptable theatres in this category is the Loeb Drama Center at Harvard University (1960, designed by Hugh Stubbins and Associates with Izenour). In front of 12 fixed rows with 400 seats there is a block of 200 seats with a wide gangway separating the two. Together, these may face a wide proscenium stage. Alternatively, the smaller block may be split in the middle and each half mechanically swung round to face the other across a peninsular stage brought forward to project from the proscenium. As a third form, the smaller block may be moved into the position of the proscenium stage to face across a traverse stage towards the block of permanent seating. All of this may be made to operate quickly and smoothly, but whether it works theatrically is another matter. There is a sense of compromise with all three forms, with too much imbalance of size between the areas of seating, and too much 'space left over' around them. Another version of this design is the Rodney Theater, University of New Mexico (1974). A better balance is achieved and more flexibility (though non-mechanical) is possible at the amateur QUESTORS THEATRE, Ealing, London (1964, capacity 330–478, architect Norman Branson). It is, however, most successful when its permanent horseshoe of stepped seating encloses the peninsular stage, with the scenic stage and cyclorama behind. Other examples in Britain of small, non-mechanical adaptable theatres are the Octagon, Bolton (1967), 322–356–422 seats in thrust, open-end or in-round; the Gulbenkian, Hull University (1969), with up to 200 seats in the same variations plus proscenium; and the New Vic Studio, BRISTOL (1973), again with thrust, end and in-round forms. A further development of the arts theatre type in Britain which has paralleled, in simpler form, developments in the design of larger theatres, has arisen from the reinterpretation of some elements of traditional theatre buildings. This has been with the objective of enhancing the three-way relationship of actors with audience and of members of the audience with each other – the latter being an essential element of true theatre. The sources which have been returned to have been the Shakespearean theatre, in respect of both the performances which took place in the galleried courtyards of inns and those in purpose-built theatres, and the simple theatres of Georgian country towns, like that at Richmond, Yorkshire (1788). A characteristic of both of these is the 'peopling of space' by means of the use of shallow galleries, returned along the side walls to form a strong visual link with the action on the stage, thus strengthening the performance and the audience's enjoyment of it. One of the first designs to adopt this idiom was the theatre at Christ's Hospital, Horsham, Sussex (1974), the nearest historical precedent for which is the square-plan, galleried Fortune Theatre, London (1600). The galleries are supported on timber posts and have open timber balustrades. In 1977 the Cottesloe Theatre (conceived by Iain Mackintosh) opened as the third, and arguably the most successful, auditorium of the National Theatre, London. A rectangular space of 65 by 55 feet is capable of being adapted to a scenic end stage with a raked main floor of seating enclosed by three levels of galleries of one row each, or to an open-end stage, or to a theatre-in-the-round, both again making use of the galleries. It is also possible to remove the lower gallery and make a level floor over the whole space. The capacity is variable from 200 to 400 seats. In 1986 the Swan Theatre, Stratford-upon-Avon (architects, Michael Reardon & Associates), was formed within an existing semi-circular brick shell dating from 1879, which had survived from the fire which destroyed the predecessor of the present Shakespeare Memorial Theatre. There are two levels of shallow galleries carried on timber posts and with open timber balustrades. The middle sections of the galleries conform to the semicircular shape of the enclosing structure and the side arms embrace an open-end stage. Building on and refining the concept of the Cottesloe, the Wilde Theatre, Bracknell (1984, capacity 330–400, architects Levitt Bernstein) is one of the most successful of this group, consistently and elegantly designed and endowed with a delightfully festive atmosphere by the brightly coloured steelwork of its three galleries.

Theatres such as these, modest though they are, represent a return to a proper understanding of the special requirements of theatre architecture – a successful climb-back after years of trial and error from the mid-century trough. At the end of the century in Britain, the National Lottery allowed a new wave of theatre building to occur, the results of which will be tested in the new millennium. CHRISTOPHER BRERETON

T. Hardin, *Theatre and Opera Houses: Masterpieces of Architecture* (1999)
Iain Mackintosh, *Architecture, Actor and Audience* (1993)

Arden, John (b. Barnsley, Yorkshire, 26 Oct. 1930) Playwright. He came to prominence during the 1950s new wave at the ROYAL COURT, when his use of verse, song and emblematic staging were unfamiliar to British theatregoers more accustomed to naturalism and his early work was considered bewilderingly enigmatic. *Serjeant Musgrave's Dance* (1959), for instance, was accused of lacking a clear moral perspective but has since come to be regarded as a modern classic. *The Workhouse Donkey* (1963) was the first new play to be performed at the CHICHESTER FESTIVAL THEATRE, and two years later the NATIONAL THEATRE staged *Armstrong's Last Goodnight* there before taking it to the OLD VIC. (It was first seen in 1964 at the Glasgow CITIZENS' THEATRE.) Increasingly, and in collaboration with his wife Margaretta [Ruth] D'Arcy (b. 1922), he tried to broaden the base of theatre and work in the community. He devised plays for specific occasions and groups, such as the members of his parish church, trades union groups and Girl Guides, and held a month-long festival of theatre based at his own house. In 1969 a visit to India, where Arden encountered both censorship and appalling poverty, clarified the socialist perspective always apparent in his work; together with D'Arcy, he began to work with politically committed groups such as 7:84 and CAST. He also became one of the few writers on the British left to concentrate upon the question of the British presence in Northern Ireland. *The Ballygombeen Bequest* (1972) explored the relationships between Northern Ireland, Britain and the Irish Republic, centring upon the issue of land prices. Arden and D'Arcy also co-authored a more allusive study of British colonialism for the ROYAL SHAKESPEARE COMPANY, *The Island of the Mighty* (1972), a poetic play which depicted a King Arthur struggling to preserve the Roman imperialistic values he has been taught in the face of an energetic Celtic underclass. Feeling that the company was distorting the anti-imperialist stance of the play, the authors picketed the theatre and Arden vowed never to write for the British theatre again. Subsequently they have been active in community theatre in Ireland, most notably in a work reflecting the influence of Indian epic theatre, *The Non-Stop Conolly Show* (1975). This 26-hour celebration of the Republican hero brought together British and Irish actors, students, trades union groups and children of the Fianna. Author or co-author of some two dozen stage plays, Arden has also written extensively for radio, including *Pearl* (1978) and a nine-part study of the politics of early Christianity, *Whose is the Kingdom?* (1988). He has written novels and, with D'Arcy, two sets of articles collected as *To Present the Pretence* (1977) and *Awkward Corners* (1988), both of which explore the relationship between theatre and politics. FRANCES GRAY

Michael Anderson, *Anger and Detachment* (1976)
Colin Chambers and Mike Prior, *Playwrights' Progress* (1987)
Frances Gray, *John Arden* (1982)
Albert Hunt, *Arden: A Study of his Plays* (1974)

Ardrey, Robert (b. Chicago, 16 Oct. 1908; d. Cape Town, 14 Jan. 1980) Playwright. Author of *Casey Jones* (1938) but best known for *Thunder Rock* (1938), which charts a man's move from nostalgic withdrawal into political action in the face of fascism, and *Shadow of Heroes* (1958), which deals with the Hungarian uprising of 1956. CLIVE BARKER

Arena Stage A pioneer in the American regional theatre movement, co-founded in 1950 in Washington DC by Zelda Fichandler, Thomas C. Fichandler and Edward Mangum, all of whom were associated with the George Washington University. It moved from the Hippodrome, an old cinema, to the converted old Heurich Brewery in 1956 and in 1961 to its own new complex in which four performance spaces were gradually opened: the 800-seat Arena Stage, renamed the Fichandler Stage in 1992 in honour of the founding directors; the 514-seat Kreeger; the Old Vat, a basement cabaret; and The Scene Shop, added in 1983. This non-profit company has always developed new plays, and supported the

work of American and international directors. Among its successes have been HOWARD SACKLER's *The Great White Hope* (1967), ARTHUR KOPIT's *Indians* (1969) and MICHAEL WELLER's *Moonchildren* (1971, seen in London the previous year as *Cancer*). In 1976 Arena Stage was the first theatre outside New York to be honoured with a Tony award for artistic excellence. Zelda Fichandler served as artistic director until 1991, when Douglas C. Wagner took over. Molly Smith followed in 1998.
ELLEN LAMPERT-GRÉAUX

L. Maslon, *The Arena: The First Forty Years* (1991)

arena stage   *see* THEATRE IN THE ROUND

Arent, Arthur   (b. Jersey City, 29 Sept. 1904; d. New York, 18 May 1972) Playwright. *Injunction Granted* (1936), *Triple-A Ploughed Under* (1936), *Power* (1937) and *One-Third of a Nation* (1938) stand as peak achievements of the US FEDERAL THEATER PROJECT. In these works Arent developed the LIVING NEWSPAPER to new levels of artistic and political effectiveness. He also contributed to the popular trades union revue *Pins and Needles* (1937).   CLIVE BARKER

Argentina   *see* SOUTH AMERICA

Aristotle   (384–322 *BC*) Greek philosopher whose *Poetics* is perhaps the single most influential document on Western drama and gave dramatic criticism many of its standard terms (e.g. 'catharsis'). In a famous essay of about 1930, BRECHT itemized those elements of the *Poetics* which he considered conservative of social injustice. The implication of the spectator in the TRAGEDY of the isolated heroic individual, which is a necessary prelude to catharsis, carried with it, for Brecht, an acceptance of humankind as unalterable and a consequent wearing down of the spectator's capacity for action. Half a century later AUGUSTO BOAL, in *Theatre of the Oppressed*, repeated and elaborated Brecht's opposition to Aristotle's 'coercive system of tragedy', whose objective is 'to eliminate all that is not commonly accepted, including the revolution, before it takes place'. The continuing urge to oppose the first great dramatic theorist is, of course, a kind of homage, a livelier consciousness of the Aristotelian vision than that implicit in the title of George Steiner's influential *The Death of Tragedy* (1961). It is worth remembering, in the context of Marxist attacks on the *Poetics*, that Aristotle's *Politics* and *Ethics* have regularly fuelled Marxist raids on the feudal concept of a social contract as the necessary binding of naturally independent individuals. But Brecht and Boal should not be disregarded. The perception of Aristotle's magnitude has been and, extraordinarily, can still be used to downgrade other kinds of magnitude

which are possible. Thus, while playwrights have escaped the tyranny of the 'three unities', the theatre has not. It is the almost unvarying intention of the theatrical director to discover and to demonstrate the unity of a play, too often at the cost of its diversity, and what began with Aristotle's brilliant perception of a 'unity of action' in the work of Sophocles has become the theatre's own postmodernist cliché.   PETER THOMSON

Arlen, Harold [Hyman Arluck]   (b. Buffalo, NY, 15 Feb. 1905; d. New York, 23 April 1986) Composer. Although most of Arlen's best and most successful work was done for films (e.g. *The Wizard of Oz*), he had his share of Broadway productions. Beginning in 1930 he wrote some music for REVUES. His biggest Broadway hit was *Bloomer Girl* (1944). An even better score was lost in the failure of *House of Flowers* (1954). His last show for New York was *Saratoga* (1959). Most of his most popular material (e.g. 'Stormy Weather') was based on classic jazz traditions, notably the blues, and on other black musical idioms.   GERALD BORDMAN

Edward Jablonski, *Harold Arlen: Happy with the Blues* (1961)

Arliss[-Andrews], [Augustus] George   (b. London, 10 April 1868; d. London, 5 Feb. 1946) Actor. Distinctive and autocratic, he developed a talent for playing famous historical figures. He had numerous successes in London productions such as *The Second Mrs Tanqueray* (1901), *Hedda Gabler* (1904) and *Rosmersholm* (1907). His appearance in New York in the title role of *Disraeli* (1911) attracted the attention both of the public – he toured the part for four years – and of Hollywood, and established a successful career for him in films: he won an Oscar (1929) for his film portrayal of Disraeli in an early talkie (having played the part in a 1921 silent version). It was 22 years before he was able to return to the London stage, in 1923, in one of his most famous roles as the Rajah in WILLIAM ARCHER's *The Green Goddess*. His last great stage performance was as Shylock in *The Merchant of Venice* (1928). He also wrote or collaborated on several plays and published his memoirs, *Up the Years from Bloomsbury* (1927) and *My Ten Years in the Studios* (1940).   HELEN RAPPAPORT

Armenia   *see* SOVIET UNION

Armstrong, William   (b. Edinburgh, 30 Nov. 1882; d. Birmingham, 5 Oct. 1952) Actor and director. He had a long and varied career, but found his true vocation from 1923 to 1944 as director of the LIVERPOOL PLAYHOUSE, where he set high standards and created a fine training ground for acting talent. Among his many 'graduates' were REX HARRISON and MICHAEL REDGRAVE. He was less influential when he transferred to the BIRMINGHAM REPERTORY THEATRE in 1945, but enjoyed some success as a WEST END director, including *The Rivals* in modern dress, with conversations in vivid red telephone boxes (1945).   IAN BEVAN

Armstrong-Jones, Anthony   *see* THEATRE PHOTOGRAPHY

Arnaud, Yvonne [Germaine]   (b. Bordeaux, France, 20 Dec. 1892; d. London, 20 Sept. 1958)   Actress who contributed much the same professional 'Frenchness' to the London stage as MAURICE CHEVALIER did to the Hollywood screen. Despite marriage to an Englishman and a lifetime's residence in England, she never permitted herself to lose her accent or her continental mannerisms, which she exploited brilliantly in a series of comedies and farces (e.g. *Tons of Money*, 1922, and *A Cuckoo in the Nest*, 1925). She had her first great solo success in FREDERICK LONSDALE's *Canaries Sometimes Sing* (1929), followed after the Second World War by more major successes with Arthur Macrae's *Traveller's Joy* (1948), which ran for two years, and Alan Melville's *Dear Charles* (1952), which ran for one. The Yvonne Arnaud Theatre (1965) in Guildford, Surrey, near where she lived, is named after her.   IAN BEVAN

Aronson, Boris   (b. Kiev, 15 Oct. 1900; d. Nyack, NY, 16 Nov. 1980)   Artist and stage designer. Having studied with EKSTER in Russia, Aronson left for Berlin and then the United States. He began his New York career in the YIDDISH THEATRE, his scope broadening to include BROADWAY (e.g. *Three Men on a Horse*, 1935), the GROUP THEATER (e.g. *Awake and Sing*, 1935), and, ultimately, the big-budget musical (e.g. *South Pacific*, 1949). Cubism and constructivism characterize his work, and he was particularly influenced by Marc Chagall, as can be seen in his designs for MACLEISH's *JB* (1958). Capable of designing in a more realistic vein, Aronson's work was at its best when he was afforded the opportunity to experiment freely with line and form – for example, in his innovative 'projected scenery' (colour projected on to a neutral background, first used in 1940). While he designed new plays by the likes of MILLER, SAROYAN and WILLIAMS, he achieved lasting fame with *Fiddler on the Roof* (1964) and his long-standing association with producer HAL PRINCE that also included *Cabaret* (1966), *Company* (1970) and *A Little Night Music* (1973).
ANNE FLETCHER

Lisa Aronson and Frank Rich, *The Theatre Art of Boris Aronson* (1987)

Arrabal [Terán], Fernando   (b. Melilla, Spanish Morocco, 11 Aug. 1932)   Playwright and novelist. Son of a Republican loyalist killed in the Spanish Civil War and a Royalist Catholic mother who betrayed him, Arrabal exiled himself to France in 1954 and thereafter wrote in French. A prolific reinventor of poetic ceremonial drama, Arrabal's plays reveal situations and relationships that blend innocence and evil, erotic fantasy and much self-mockery in language that is intended to surprise and shock. But they also contain much humour. Derived largely from SURREALISM and especially ARTAUD's THEATRE OF CRUELTY, Arrabal's drama is usually classified as ABSURDIST, closer to BECKETT than IONESCO, especially in his construction of dialogue that is colourful, brittle, fast-moving and euphoric. The influence of Baudelaire, de Sade, APOLLINAIRE and JARRY is also evident, as can be seen in the early plays, e.g. *Oraison* (*Orison*, 1958, his first). In the mid-1960s he moved towards a more delirious style that he labelled the THEATRE OF PANIC. In *Pique-Nique en campagne* (*Picnic on the Battlefield*, 1959) the parents of a conscripted soldier picnic with him in the middle of the carnage; they decide, after meeting an enemy conscript, that wars are really unneccessary but are killed all the same. Other plays, some not performed, include *Le Cimetière des voitures* (*The Car Cemetery*, 1966); *Guernica*, in which the heroics of that battle are debunked; *Le Labyrinthe* (*The Labyrinth*, 1967); *La Bicyclette du Condamné* (*The Condemned Man's Bicycle*, 1966); *L'Architecte et l'empereur d'Assyrie* (*The Architect and the Emperor of Assyria*, 1967), in which two men trapped on a desert island destroy each other; *Le Grand Cérémonial* (*The Grand Ceremonial*, 1966); *La Communion solenelle* (*The Solemn Communion*, 1964); *Le Couronnement* (*The Coronation*, 1965); *Cérémonie pour un noir assassiné* (*Ceremony for a Murdered Black*, 1966); and *Le Jardin des délices* (*The Garden of Delights*, 1969), a study in sado-masochism.
JOHN CALDER

Luis Oscar Arata, *The Festive Plays of Arrabal* (1982)
Thomas John Donahue, *The Theater of Arrabal: A Garden of Earthly Delights* (1980)
Peter L. Podol, *Fernando Arrabal* (1978)

Artaud, Antonin [Antoine Marie-Joseph]   (b. Marseille, 4 Sept. 1896; d. Ivry, nr Paris, 4 March 1948)   Theatrical theorist, playwright, actor and poet. One of the most prolific and discussed personalities of the twentieth-century performing arts, Artaud was the son of a sea captain and a Levantine mother from Smyrna; his two grandmothers were sisters. He suffered from meningitis as a child after a fall and this, combined with childhood misadventures and the bankruptcy of his father when he was 13, may have contributed to the nervous depression and poor health which dogged his life. It also prevented his conscription in 1914; he spent much of the First World War in hospitals and sanatoria, already writing poetry and contributing to periodicals. In 1919 he started to paint and to experiment with opium. In 1921 he contributed to *Littérature*, the new journal of the SURREALISTS, met ANDRÉ BRETON, Philippe Soupault, Louis Aragon, Max Jacob and others, and became a leading member of the group. That same year he began his career as an actor after joining a new company founded by CHARLES DULLIN; the following year he played many roles and involved himself in scene and costume design as well as stage direction. In 1923 he began his famous correspondence with Jacques Rivière, editor of the *Nouvelle revue française*, who rejected his poems but with such creative criticism that it turned Artaud in a new direction. Publication of poems and critical writing in both surrealist and other publications followed. He played Marat in Abel Gance's film of *Napoléon* (1925) and, in spite of increasing addiction to opium, pursued a successful career as writer and actor, occasionally editing some issues of the leading surrealist magazines; his earnings, however, were meagre. His best-known publications appeared in the late 1920s and 1930s: *Art and Death* (1929), *Heliogobale or the Anarchist Crowned* (1934), *The New Revelations of Being* (1937) and, especially, *The Theatre and its Double* (1938), which contained manifestos for a TOTAL THEATRE and from which the ideas of PETER BROOK in particular, but also of CLAUDEL, JEAN-LOUIS BARRAULT and the LIVING THEATER, are largely derived. He advocated a new theatre that depended not on the dramatic use of language alone, but on the use of many elements, including music, special effects, painting brought alive and primitive elements such as are found in the Balinese theatre, to disturb the audience (*see* EASTERN THEATRE, ITS INFLUENCE ON THE WEST). The role of the theatre is not to mirror everyday life but to bring out in the spectator all that is most primitive that culture and civilization have submerged. Art should not be a shadow of reality, but should strive as far as possible to be that reality itself, to bring real passions and sufferings out of the shadows. Panic and the maniacal are a necessary part of such theatre and 'the scream' one of its most potent manifestations. The THEATRE OF CRUELTY devised by Artaud (he gave the title to his experimental season in 1934) and revived by Peter Brook in the 1960s thus forces audiences to find in the theatre not escape, but the realization of their worst nightmares and deepest fears. Every facet of total theatre that can be brought into play to increase the sense of violence and increase the disorientation of the audience is justified.

Artaud's theories are realized in his playlet *Le Jet de Sang* (*The Spurt of Blood*, 1925) and particularly in *Les Cenci* (*The Cenci*, 1935), adapted from Shelley, but in his long career as a director and actor he was involved in a variety of plays from the Greek and Roman classics to those of STRINDBERG and Artaud's surrealist friends, especially ROGER VITRAC, with whom he and Robert Aron founded the Théâtre Alfred Jarry in 1927. He wrote scenarios for several films, some of which were realized on the screen, including the surrealist *La Coquille et le Clergyman* (1928), and made many more appearances as an actor in films: his protrayal of the monk in Carl Dreyer's *Passion of Joan of Arc* (1927) is particularly powerful. He fell out with Breton after Vitrac was expelled from the surrealist group, but they were later reconciled. In 1936 he went to Mexico, where he lectured on the theatre at the university and made contact with Mexican artists, in the following months involving himself in both theatrical and political activity. Returning to France, he went to a clinic to curb his addiction to drugs, now much advanced. During the rest of that year he scandalized France and Belgium with a series of hallucinatory lectures, and it was clear that his mental state was perilous. In Ireland, which he visited in search of druidic remains and St Patrick's staff, he was arrested; after being held for some weeks he was returned to France and committed to an asylum. He remained at various asylums until transferred to Rodez, where he wrote his famous series of *Letters*, which contains writing of extraordinary lucidity mingled with hallucinatory visions. Released in 1946, he died less than two years later.

Artaud's life was composed of pain and melancholy, but never, even when most drug-addicted, did he cease to write: there is much verse poetry, but the essays, prose poems and euphoristic prose are also poetry of a kind. His ideas, based partly on the decadent romanticism of nineteenth-century literature (Baudelaire, Gautier and Rimbaud, among others), and partly on the new freedoms in sensual perception of reality brought about by DADA and surrealism, have been derided by many, but his influence on the theatre in particular has been evident since the 1960s, when he became a cult figure, particularly in France (e.g. ARRABAL, GENET, BLIN, PLANCHON), and Poland, where GROTOWSKI was one of his most ardent admirers. In addition to his theatrical work, there is much writing on the cinema. Artaud also kept up a voluminous correspondence with many of the leading figures of his day in art, literature and the theatre. JOHN CALDER

See also DRAMATIC THEORY.

Martin Esslin, *Artaud* (1976)

Naomi Greene, *Antonin Artaud: Poet without Words* (1970)

Bettina Knapp, *Antonin Artaud: Man of Vision* (1969)

Claude Schumacher, ed., *Artaud on Theatre* (1997)

Arts Council of Great Britain   The body which, until 1994, dispensed central government money to the arts. It was established in 1945 and incorporated by Royal Charter the following year, succeeding the wartime COUNCIL FOR THE ENCOURAGEMENT OF MUSIC AND THE ARTS (CEMA), which had admirably demonstrated the importance of the arts in the life of the nation. The Arts Council's objects, slightly adjusted over the years but in all essentials the same as they were at first, are (a) to develop and improve the knowledge, understanding and practice of the arts; (b) to increase the accessibility of the arts to the public; and (c) to advise and cooperate with departments of government, local authorities and other bodies.

Originally its grant-in-aid was received direct from the Treasury, but in 1964 the government appointed for the first time a Minister for the Arts, the relevant department became responsible and there was a significant increase in the total available. (A new ministry was created in 1992 and the new government in 1997 changed its name to the Department of Culture, Media and Sport.) The Scottish Arts Council and the Welsh Arts Council were virtually autonomous within the parent Council: the chairman and another member of each served on the ACGB, and they appointed their own advisory panels and staff.

In 1994 the ACGB was divided into the Arts Council of England, the Scottish Arts Council and the Arts Council of Wales. The Arts Council of Northern Ireland was already separate. The Arts Council is not a government department, and its staff, led by the secretary general, are not civil servants. It is independent and autonomous, making its decisions free from government influence: since the appointment of a Minister for the Arts the 'arm's length' principle has been maintained, although this has been to some extent eroded since the 1980s. The independence of the Arts Council and of its clients has been fundamental and fiercely guarded since the Council's inception.

The Councils appoint advisory Drama Panels (or Theatre Committees) of men and women actively engaged in the theatre, who serve voluntarily for a period of years. An application for subsidy is processed by the Drama Department, then considered by the Drama Panel, whose recommendation is normally approved (very rarely not) by the Council itself.

In 1945 the Arts Council was, for the first time in Britain, an across-the-board dispenser of state patronage of the arts, and therefore it supported only non-profit-distributing companies which were registered as charities, though not AMATEUR THEATRE. The commercial theatre in the West End or touring, and the hundred-odd commercial repertory companies, could not be given subsidy and did not then need it. Nor did variety theatre or the music hall.

A legacy from the war was touring to theatreless areas, mostly the mining districts of Wales, the midlands and the north-east of England, playing one- and two-night stands in schools or welfare halls. These tours were produced and managed by the Council's Drama Department, and were of a remarkably high standard under difficult conditions, employing distinguished directors, designers and actors. The need for these tours steadily lessened with the growth of the REPERTORY MOVEMENT, and as petrol rationing ended, so that people could get to entertainment away from home: the tours were stopped altogether in 1960.

In Bristol, Coventry and Salisbury, where there was a clear demand for theatre and no organization to keep one going, the Arts Council directly managed repertory companies for several years until independent bodies were established to take them over. Other initiatives include the additional, and for the first time earmarked, grant made available in 1965 for housing the arts, which was used as pump-priming; the inquiry, also in 1965, into THEATRE FOR YOUNG PEOPLE which led to the creation of a Young People's Theatre Panel that five years later was merged with the main drama panel; the New Drama scheme begun in 1952, which followed the special grants given the year before as part of the Festival of Britain to companies producing new plays; the extension of the scheme to cover second productions (later dropped); the help to writers via bursaries, royalty supplements, commissions and attachments to companies; a variety of professional training schemes or apprenticeships, which began in 1961 with a scheme to help young designers, expanded towards formal qualification for administrators and led in 1968 to the formation of a training committee; after some controversy, the funding of what became known as the FRINGE; the setting up of the Theatre Investment Fund to aid touring; and the recognition of the need to challenge the problems of disability.

Drama policy has been influenced by the grants given to the national companies, which would not have existed without the support of the Council, and by the imbalance between the amount spent in London and elsewhere. (In 1967 the Scottish and Welsh committees were given increased independence.) Having been complementary to the commercial sector, the Council helped shape the publicly subsidized sector which became dominant. The Council funded the 12 Regional Arts Associations (later Boards) and, from 1984 and the publication of its paper *The Glory of the Garden*, encouraged devolution to the regions. The break-up of the ACGB in 1994 (into the Arts Council of England, the

Scottish AAs Council and the Arts Council of Wales – the Arts Council of Northern Ireland was already a separate body) furthered this process, but without a consequent shift in power 'outwards'. At the same time it reversed traditional thinking and embraced the market; government funding would be pegged in real terms, while new money was to come from private sponsorship. Management and buildings seemed to become more important than artists, and consultants sprang up everywhere as applying for grants became more complicated – a trend exacerbated by the arrival of the National Lottery in 1995, which at first gave money via the Council only to capital projects and threatened the commitment of government to adequate revenue funding. The Lottery doubled the amount of money available to the Council and allowed it to support a much wider range of activities than before. There was, however, a strong sense by the late 1990s, when it slimmed down the governing body, that the Council had become both supine and impotent, and had let the theatre world down. Following various reviews, however, the Council in 2000 announced the largest ever rise in FUNDING for theatre as well as the abolition of the Regional Arts Boards, which would 'unite' with the Arts Council of England to create a single body. There was still much to play for.

DICK LINKLATER & COLIN CHAMBERS

R. Hutchinson, *The Politics of the Arts Council* (1982)
Janet Minihan, *The Nationalization of Culture: The Development of State Subsidies to the Arts in Great Britain* (1977)
Andrew Sinclair, *Arts and Cultures: The History of the 50 Years of the Arts Council of Great Britain* (1995)
R. Witts, *Artists Unknown: The Alternative History of the Arts Council* (1998)

Arts Lab[oratory]   The short-lived (January 1968– October 1969) but influential ALTERNATIVE multimedia venue founded by Jim Haynes in London's Drury Lane two years after he left the TRAVERSE in Edinburgh. The PIP SIMMONS THEATRE, the PEOPLE SHOW, Portable Theatre and Freehold all sprang from this informal, chaotic set-up inspired by the American underground. The Arts Lab inspired the establishment of a new FRINGE network after its demise.   COLIN CHAMBERS

J. Haynes, *Thanks for Coming* (1984)

Arts Theatre   Opened under the presidency of BRONSON ALBERY   in London's WEST END in 1927 with eating and drinking facilities as a CLUB THEATRE, thereby escaping the Lord Chamberlain's CENSORSHIP powers, the Arts was immediately successful. In 1928 the Chamberlain lifted the ban on *Young Woodley* by JOHN VAN DRUTEN, having seen it performed at the Arts, and

allowed it to play at the SAVOY, beginning not only a long sequence of many such commercial transfers but also the gradual loosening of stage censorship, which eventually came to an end in 1968. The intimate 340-seat theatre, with the smallest capacity in central London, hosted famous foreign visitors – e.g. YVETTE GUILBERT, COMPAGNIE DES QUINZE – and from 1942 to 1952, under ALEC CLUNES, transformed London theatre with an ambitious repertoire that might have graced a national theatre. As well as staging 13 full-length SHAW plays, Clunes' management presented the premières of *The Lady's Not for Burning* (1948) by CHRISTOPHER FRY and *Saint's Day* (1951) by JOHN WHITING. This innovation continued under subsequent directors, with English premières of BECKETT (*Waiting for Godot,* 1955), IONESCO, BETTI, ANOUILH and ALBEE. The première of *The Caretaker* (1960) by HAROLD PINTER was followed by a ROYAL SHAKESPEARE COMPANY experimental season, including the startling *Afore Night Come* (1962) by DAVID RUDKIN, and, under MICHAEL CODRON, *Entertaining Mr Sloane* (1964) by JOE ORTON. As the FRINGE grew, the Arts declined and became noted for housing fringe transfers – Robert Patrick's *Kennedy's Children* (1975), TOM STOPPARD's *Dirty Linen* and *New Found Land* (1976) – and for the work there of the UNICORN children's theatre, which was resident there from 1967–99.

COLIN CHAMBERS

Wendy Trewin and J. C. Trewin, *The Arts Theatre, London, 1927–81* (1986)

Asche, Oscar [John Stanger Heiss]   (b. Geelong, Australia, 26 Jan. 1871; d. Marlow, Bucks, 23 March 1936) Actor, director and manager. Made his London stage debut in 1893 and achieved success as an actor, often aided in classical roles by his fine physique. In 1911 he staged the first production of EDWARD KNOBLOCK's *Kismet*, with himself as Hajj, and acquired the taste for oriental splendour which led to his greatest success when he devised, wrote, directed and starred in the musical *Chu Chin Chow*. This spectacular and melodic retelling of an Arabian Nights tale opened at His Majesty's Theatre, London, on 31 April 1916 and ran until 22 July 1921, a total of 2,235 performances, which remained a record in the English musical theatre until *Salad Days* in 1954. There have been several revivals of *Chu Chin Chow*, including one on ice, but the piece had had its day. Asche's autobiography, *His Life*, was published in 1929.   IAN BEVAN

Ashcroft, Peggy [Edith Margaret Emily]   (b. Croydon, 22 Dec. 1907; d. London, 14 June 1991)   Actress. After studying under FOGERTY, Ashcroft made her debut at the BIRMINGHAM REPERTORY in 1926. A sense of powerful innocence brought her great success in FEUCHTWANGER's *Jew Süss* (1929) and this quality, fused with courage and optimism, became one of her hallmarks, both on stage and off, where she was an indefatigable campaigner for civil liberties, justice and peace. Her reputation as a fine classical actress began when she played Desdemona to PAUL ROBESON's *Othello* (1930) – a production which opened her eyes to racism because of the outrage it caused in some circles – and continued at the OLD VIC (1932–3) under BAYLIS with Shakespeare's Imogen, Perdita and Rosalind and SHAW's Cleopatra. After playing Juliet (1935) in GIELGUD's production of *Romeo and Juliet*, she became the outstanding actress of her time, with peaks of achievement in both classical and modern roles stretching across the next half century. She partnered Gielgud on many occasions, in CHEKHOV, Sheridan, Webster, WILDE and in Shakespeare as Beatrice, Cordelia, Ophelia, Portia and Titania; a poetic lucidity in her verse speaking allowed her to play such parts over a relatively long timespan.

She created the parts of Evelyn Holt in *Edward, My Son* (1947) by ROBERT MORLEY and Noel Langley, and Hester Collyer in RATTIGAN's *The Deep Blue Sea* (1952). While her portrayals were noted for their determination, none came stronger than her Hedda Gabler (1954), which won international acclaim. She became a member of the artistic committee of the ENGLISH STAGE COMPANY, for which she played Shen Te in BRECHT's *The Good Woman of Setzuan* (1956) in its inaugural season at the ROYAL COURT. She was a founder member, and later a director, of the ROYAL SHAKESPEARE COMPANY, with whom she had many successes, from Margaret in the seminal *Wars of the Roses* (1963) and Mrs Alving in *Ghosts* (1967) to the Countess of Rousillon in *All's Well That Ends Well* (1981), as well as lead roles in new plays by ARBUZOV, ALBEE, DURAS, GRASS and PINTER. She played Winnie in BECKETT's *Happy Days* (1976) in the opening performance of the NATIONAL THEATRE at its new home on the South Bank. Much honoured, she was a member of the ARTS COUNCIL (1962–5) and had a theatre named after her in her birthplace (1962). Late in life she enjoyed success in film and television, and won an Oscar for her role in David Lean's film *A Passage to India* (1985). Her second husband of three was the director KOMISSARZHEVSKY. She was much honoured and was created a dame in 1956.

COLIN CHAMBERS

Michael Billington, *Peggy Ashcroft* (1988)
Gary O'Connor, *The Secret Woman: A Life of Peggy Ashcroft* (1997)

Ashton, Frederick *see* CHOREOGRAPHY; DANCE

Ashwell [Pocock], Lena (b. on board ship, River Tyne, 28 Sept. 1872; d. London, 13 March 1957) Actress, manager and producer. She made her name on stage in *Mrs Dane's Defence* (1900). While manager of the Kingsway Theatre, at first an independent cooperative, she was involved with the ACTRESSES' FRANCHISE LEAGUE and was responsible through the AFL for organizing entertainment for troops during the First World War. After 1918 she continued to organize work for unemployed artists at the Century Theatre (formerly the Bijoux Theatre), where she staged new plays. Likened to ANNIE HORNIMAN and LILIAN BAYLIS, she also adapted classics (e.g. Dostoevsky's *Crime and Punishment*, 1927) and helped set up the BRITISH DRAMA LEAGUE. She wrote several books, including an autobiography, *Myself a Player* (1936). MAGGIE GALE

Asian American theatre Asian American theatre was initiated in the 1960s as American performers of Asian descent began creating companies in which they were the primary performers and directors. By the 1970s playwriting workshops associated with these and other American theatres were instituted to develop new scripts dealing with the life experiences of this group.

Asian American theatre should be distinguished from the immigrant theatre of each Asian community which replicated artistic traditions and narratives of the homeland. Ethnically based theatre which served as a locus of community social and cultural life was created and in some instances continues in various Asian immigrant communities in the United States. Chinese opera and puppetry came to California and Hawaii with immigrants working in plantation and railroad industries in the mid-1800s. Various regional Chinese opera forms have again received impetus with the influx of Chinese immigrant artists in the post-1980 liberalization of relations with China. *Kabuki* dance was widespread in the Japanese communities of Hawaii and the West Coast in the early part of the twentieth century and vestiges remain in dance schools which are often loosely associated with cultural programmes at Japanese Buddhist temples in the United States. Indian dance theatre, especially Bharata Natyam, has been common in Indian communities of the late 1970s to the present, and Indian dance performances, from traditional stories like the *Ramayana* to the more acculturated offerings, like a Bharata Natyam *Nutcracker*, abound. But rather than focusing on new work for the new life, these theatres are largely attempts to continue Asian sources and 'enculturate' the next generation in the ideas of the home country. While this mode of performance generally appeals to the first generation of immigrants and may maintain support into the second generation, it rarely has appeal to the third generation.

By contrast, Asian American theatre is about the experience of living as Americans. While some first-generation artists (e.g. Tisa Chang of the Pan Asian Repertory in New York, or Yuriko Doi of Theater of Yugen in San Francisco) have become involved in this movement, it is more routinely the preserve of artists who have been born and educated in America. The theatrical genres presented correlate to American styles, from realism to GUERRILLA THEATRE to postmodernism, rather than to Asian artistic genres. Early scripts like Gladys Li's *The Submission of Rosie Moy* (1928) exist, but were little produced. The widespread emergence of Asian American voices came only with the socio-political transformations of the later era. African American and Chicano theatres, which developed along with the civil rights movement in the late 1950s and early 1960s, created a model of identity-based theatre which would create work by, for and about a specific group. Artists two or more generations removed from Asian life experience sought to create solidarity with peers across the cultural divides that would split the group in an Asian cultural context. Filipino, Chinese, Japanese, Okinawan and Cambodian might have little in common in an Asian framework, where religion, history, politics and ethnic difference often put one group in opposition to the next; Americans of these different groups, however, saw their past conflicts as history and felt that their treatment in America had created common ground among them. Their physical features marked them out from the Caucasian majority and, as affirmative action created an ethnic category which employers and schools began to identify from the 1970s on as 'Asian American', solidarity was created. Artists working together found a common theme – the reality of being a minority member of Asian descent in a society that takes the Euro-American as the norm.

Companies of Asian American performers were established in major cities between the 1960s and the 1980s. East West Players in Los Angeles was established in 1965 with Mako, a noted film actor, as artistic director. In addition to producing classics of the Euro-American canon with all-Asian casts, the company sponsored play competitions that promoted the generation of new scripts. From the late 1960s the group fostered the development of voices like Wakako Yamauchi, whose *And the Soul Shall Dance* was widely produced in the mid-1970s. This play portrayed the lonely lives of Japanese American women in the Imperial Valley agricultural community in California in the early part of the century. By the early 1970s more companies had been founded and were consciously seeking scripts that represented the Asian American experience. In New York, China-born Tisa Chang established the Pan Asian Repertory Theater, which has supported the work of many of the East Coast Asian American actors, directors and writers. In Honolulu the Kumu Kahua players at the University of Hawaii fostered new work by Asian and Pacific islanders. In Seattle the Asian Exclusion Act (now the Northwest Asian American Theater Company) developed with Judy Nihei as founding artistic director. The Asian American Theater Company in San Francisco, with actors like Lane Nishikawa, created spaces for the work of authors such as Genny Lim and Philip Kan Gotanda. Genny Lim's *Paper Angels* (1980) deals with the experience of Chinese immigrants in the Angel Island immigration detention centre, a prime entry point for Chinese coming into the United States. Yuriko Doi's San Francisco-based Theater of Yugen works from Japanese *noh/kyogen* as a movement base but develops new work which has ranged from a *noh*-inspired *Christmas Carol* to a flamenco- and *kabuki*-influenced adaptation of LORCA's *Blood Wedding* set in Hispanic California. The Angel Island Theater Company and Minna-Sama-No in Chicago are other groups that have fostered Asian American talent.

Since the 1970s a number of significant writers have been produced by these companies or, increasingly in the 1980s, by major American repertory companies like the AMERICAN CONSERVATORY THEATER and the Berkeley Repertory in San Francisco; the MARK TAPER FORUM in Los Angeles; LA MAMA, the PUBLIC THEATER, the MANHATTAN THEATER CLUB and even on BROADWAY in New York. Frank Chin's *Chickencoop Chinaman* was widely produced in the early 1970s, presenting a strong male voice in contestation of the emasculated stereotype of the Asian American male portrayed in Euro-American work. Chin laid the groundwork for the political and social protest which was to be a basic theme of the Asian American writers. He was soon to take issue with major author Maxine Hong Kingston as she, along with other female authors, represented the sexism of Chinese American life in novels like Kingston's *Woman Warrior* (translated to the stage in the 1990s). While Asian American women have often sought to deconstruct the patriarchy that underlies the Asian American or Asian female experience, Chin has accused this group of contributing to the negative stereotype that the Asian American male must confront. This male–female debate has continued as a subtheme of writing in the Asian American community to the present day. DAVID HWANG's *FOB* (i.e. 'fresh off the boat') was produced at the Public Theater in New York in 1980 and dealt with the self-hate with which the assimilationist Asian American is taught to look at Asian culture. Three characters meet in a restaurant: Grace, who immigrated from Taiwan as a child;

Steve, a fresh-off-the-boat Hong Kong man; and Dale, a second-generation Chinese American male. Grace is alerted to her woman warrior potential through her Asian American studies at the university. Steve, although starving, still considers himself strong like the Chinese god of war. Only Dale seems hopelessly alienated from his Chinese identity. Hwang's *M. Butterfly* (1988) uses the historical incident of a French diplomat's long-term relationship with a Peking opera star to take the emasculation of the Asian male by the Western stereotype to its fullest extent. The story of how a female impersonator could keep his European lover oblivious to the fact of the impersonator's masculinity throughout a lifelong affair highlights the blindness of the Westerner to the reality of the Asian or Asian American 'other'. More recently, Hwang's *Golden Child* (1996) confronts the conundrum of modernity for Chinese through the story of a Chinese girl whose father orders her feet unbound so she can live a modern life. The script questions which parts of the past can be imported into this new, Westernized way of being. Philip Kan Gotanda's *Yankee Dawg You Die* (1988) takes the stereotypes of Asians portrayed in American media as its starting point. A Chinese American actor who has made a career representing Japanese stereotypes in Second World War films is confronted by a supposedly politically aware young Asian American performer of the new generation. Velina Hasu Houston's *Tea*, which explores the experience of Japanese war brides in America, was produced by the Asian American Theater Company in 1985 and at the Manhattan Theater Club in 1986. Ping Chong's PERFORMANCE ART-influenced theatre, with its strong visual emphasis, has won praise from postmodern audiences. The number of scripts by Asian American authors has grown exponentially since the 1970s, but only Hwang has received extensive production by mainstream American theatre.

Also of importance in the 1990s is the emergence of Asian American SOLO performers. Lane Nishikawa's *I'm on a Mission from Buddha* takes a comic look at growing up Asian American. Brenda Wong Aoki is a solo storyteller whose *Uncle Gunjaro's Girlfriend* (1998) looks at the story of her great-uncle, the first Japanese to marry a Caucasian in California, evoking the wrath of racist, anti-miscegenation society and causing his wife to lose her American citizenship.

With cutbacks in government support for the arts in the 1990s some companies, like the Asian American Theater in San Francisco, have experienced economic difficulty; others, like the North West Asian American Theater Company and Theater of Yugen, have turned consciously to collaborative efforts with Japanese companies to fund new work. The large influxes of Asians into the United States in the last quarter of the twentieth century brought with them some increase in immigrant theatre, but for most Asian American artists the quest for representation by, for and about Asian Americans remains the core. Meanwhile David Hwang looks beyond ethnicity to question that the Euro-American norm is indeed the norm. He argues that authors, actors and audiences should not be pigeonholed by ethnic identity and that the work of such artists should not be labelled Asian American theatre, but be recognized for what it is – American theatre. KATHY FOLEY

Misha Bernon, ed., *Between Worlds* (1990)

Yuko Kurahashi, *Asian American Culture on Stage: The History of the East West Players* (1999)

Joann Faung Jean Lee, *Asian American Actors: Oral Histories from Stage, Screen and Television* (2000)

Josephine Lee, *Performing Asian America: Race and Ethnicity on the Contemporary Stage* (1997)

Asian theatre in Britain   *see* BLACK THEATRE; ETHNIC THEATRE; TARA ARTS

Askey, Arthur [Bowden]   (b. Liverpool, 6 June 1900; d. London, 16 Nov. 1982)   Comedian. What he lacked in height he made up for in his billing as 'Big Hearted Arthur'. Fame came with the radio programme *Band Wagon* (1938), which led to a successful broadcasting, television, film and stage career, including VARIETY, PANTOMIME (as DAME), and musical comedies. He created such catch phrases as 'Hello Playmates', 'Aythangyow' and 'Before Your Very Eyes' – which was also the title of his autobiography (1975). REXTON S. BUNNETT

Astaire, Adele   *see* ASTAIRE, FRED

Astaire, Fred [Frederick Austerlitz]   (b. Omaha, Nebr., 10 May 1899; d. Los Angeles, 22 June 1987)   Dancer, singer and actor. With his sister **Adele** (b. Omaha, Nebr., 10 Sept. 1898; d. Phoenix, Ariz., 25 Jan. 1981) he began in VAUDEVILLE; they made their Broadway debut in 1917. Their modern stepping, to jazz-based rhythms and with a humorous undercurrent, pushed them to stardom in *For Goodness Sake* (1922; as *Stop Flirting*, London, 1923), *Lady, Be Good!* (1924), *Funny Face* (1927), *Smiles* (1930), and *The Band Wagon* (1931). After Adele's retirement that year, Fred performed as a solo star in *Gay Divorce* (1932, which included Cole Porter's song 'Night and Day') before his spectacular and influential career in films. Adele was considered to have a greater gift for comedy. Fred's autobiography, *Steps in Time*, appeared in 1959. GERALD BORDMAN

S. Green and B. Goldblatt, *Starring Fred Astaire* (1973)

H. Prompson, *Fred Astaire* (1970)

T. Satchell, *Astaire: The Biography* (1987)

At the Foot of the Mountain Theatre company. Formed in 1974 in MINNEAPOLIS, it became a women's COLLECTIVE in 1976 featuring the plays of one of its founders, Martha Boesing (b. 1936), such as *Raped* (1976), a reworking of BRECHT's *The Exception and the Rule*, and the collaboratively created *The Story of a Mother* (1978). While retaining its feminist orientation, it also embraced multicultural issues and in 1985 worked with SPIDERWOMAN THEATRE. The group, which folded in 1991, also presented plays by MEGAN TERRY, MARIA IRENE FORNES and ADRIENNE KENNEDY.

CHARLES LONDON

See also WOMEN IN THE THEATRE.

Athey, Ron *see* BODY ART

Atkins, Eileen (b. London, 16 June 1934) Actress. Her early career was transformed by her award-winning performance as Childie in FRANK MARCUS's *The Killing of Sister George* (1965), in which her wayward, eerie intensity first made a serious impact. Although she has worked with distinction in film and television, her most interesting performances have been on the stage, both in the UK and in the United States, where she has played often, notably in two different accounts of the life of Virginia Woolf, *A Room of One's Own* and *Vita and Virginia*. She has played many of the major classical parts (including Viola, Rosalind and Medea), but her greatest success has been in twentieth-century work, especially in the plays of TENNESSEE WILLIAMS, SHAW and EDWARD ALBEE. She co-created two successful television series (*Upstairs Downstairs* and *The House of Elliot*) and wrote the screenplay for a film adaptation of Virginia Woolf's novel *Mrs Dalloway*. She was created a dame in 2001.

GENISTA MCINTOSH

Atkins, Robert [Alexander] (b. London, 10 Aug. 1886; d. London, 10 Feb. 1972) Actor and director who specialized in Shakespeare. He was a member of BEERBOHM TREE's company (1906–9), and then successively played with other distinguished actor–managers: MARTIN HARVEY, FORBES-ROBERTSON and GREET. He brought a fine sense of tradition to his staging of classic plays after the First World War, which carried through to his work as director of productions at the SHAKESPEARE MEMORIAL THEATRE, STRATFORD-UPON-AVON (1944–5) and as director at the OPEN-AIR THEATRE in London's Regent's Park (1933–60). In 1932 he directed and played the title role in *Napoleon*, written by the Italian dictator Benito Mussolini and adapted into English by John Drinkwater, an esoteric achievement which earned Atkins the Knighthood of the Order of the Crown of Italy. IAN BEVAN

Atkinson, [Justin] Brooks (b. Melrose, Mass., 28 Nov. 1894; d. Huntsville, Ala., 13 Jan. 1984) Drama critic. Educated at Harvard University during the tenure of GEORGE PIERCE BAKER, Atkinson served as assistant drama critic for the *Boston Daily Evening Transcript* (1918–22) before joining the *New York Times* as literary editor (1922) and succeeding STARK YOUNG as drama critic in 1926. Except for the war years, Atkinson held this position until 1960, then served as critic-at-large until 1971. His deep knowledge of theatre and his incisive, literate criticism for America's most powerful newspaper gave him greater influence than any other US critic. Atkinson used his power honestly and thereby commanded enormous respect. At the end of his unequalled tenure, the Mansfield Theater in New York was renamed in his honour. His literary output includes *Broadway Scrapbook* (1948), *Brief Chronicles* (1966), *Broadway* (1970) and *The Lively Years: 1920–1973* (1974). JOSEPH M. DIAZ

Atlanta Best known as the corporate headquarters of Coca-Cola and the host of the 1996 Summer Olympic Games, Atlanta, Georgia is a thriving, progressive city with a substantial metropolitan area. It is thus a city with great potential for professional theatre. Yet theatre has had a difficult time gaining a stronghold in Atlanta. The first attempt to establish a professional theatre presence came in 1968, when the Atlanta Municipal Center was built to house the new Atlanta Repertory Theater, as well as the Atlanta Ballet, Opera, and Symphony. A splashy grand opening, designed to showcase the work of all the resident companies, was a massive financial disaster, leading to the demise of the Atlanta Repertory less than a year later. Out of its ashes, however, arose the Alliance Theater, which gamely stepped in with an attempt at a more manageable season. After a precarious beginning, the Alliance has grown to be one of the largest and most respected regional theatres in America.

Several other theatre companies, with smaller, more focused goals, have also found a niche in Atlanta. These include an African American theatre, Jomandi Productions, Inc. (1978), and an inter-Celtic theatre, the Theater Gael (1984). The intimate Horizon Theater Company (1983) is devoted to feminist issues and urban Southern themes. The foremost educational theatre is the Academy Theater (1956). Shakespeare has his due through the Shakespeare Tavern (1990) and musical theatre is represented through the Theatrical Outfit (1976). SARAH STEVENSON

Joseph Wesley Ziegler, *Regional Theater: The Revolutionary Stage* (1977)

Auckland Theatre Company Founded in 1993 after the closure of the only full-time, professional, repertory company in the New Zealand city of Auckland, the MER-CURY THEATRE, in 1992. The ATC has neither a permanent company nor a theatre, but under the leadership of Simon Prast since its inception has mounted seven productions a year in one of the three major theatres in the city.   GILLIAN GREER & LAURIE ATKINSON

Auden, W[ystan] H[ugh]   (b. York, 21 Feb. 1907; d. Vienna, 29 Sept. 1973)   English-born, later naturalized American poet, playwright, librettist and essayist; one of the major literary figures of the twentieth century. The focal figure in an OXFORD University artistic group that included STEPHEN SPENDER, Auden quickly established himself as a leading poet, influenced by Marx and Freud. In 1932 he was invited to write for the newly formed GROUP THEATRE and became for a few years a guiding light, writing ambitious experimental pieces, such as the EXPRESSIONIST *The Dance of Death* (1934) on the collapse of the bourgeois class, and espousing TOTAL THEATRE. With his friend from childhood CHRISTOPHER ISHER-WOOD, he wrote for the Group three bold poetic plays owing something to BRECHT and further examining political and personal impulses, including their own homosexuality: *The Dog Beneath the Skin* (1936), *The Ascent of F6* (1937) and *On the Frontier* (1938). Auden's travels, which had taken him to Weimar Berlin and Republican territory in the Spanish Civil War, in 1939 led him with Isherwood to America, where they both settled and renounced their political pasts.

Auden's stage writing subsequently concentrated on libretti and lyrics; 17 such projects included Benjamin Britten's *Paul Bunyan* (1941) and, with his lover Chester Kallman, *The Rake's Progress* (1951) and three Brecht pieces, *The Caucasian Chalk Circle* (1948), *The Seven Deadly Sins* (1958) and *Mahagonny* (1963), as well as works with Hans Werner Henze. Auden wrote four radio plays and five film documentaries, and adapted work by COCTEAU, Goldoni, Shakespeare, TOLLER and Webster. His dramatic poem *The Age of Anxiety* (1947) won the Pultizer Prize and found its title widely used to describe the period of postwar pessimism in which it is set.
COLIN CHAMBERS

E. Callan, *Auden: A Carnival of Intellect* (1983)
Humphrey Carpenter, *W. H. Auden: A Biography* (1981)
Edward Mendelson, *Early Auden* (1988)

Audiberti, Jacques   (b. Antibes, France, 25 March 1899; d. Paris, 10 July 1965)   Playwright, novelist and poet. Many of Audiberti's plays depict the monstrous eruption of hidden, evil forces. His drama combines verbal virtuosity, farce, fantasy and melodrama. Plays include *Quoat-Quoat* (1946), *Le Mal court* ('Evil spreads',

1947) and *La Fourmi dans le corps* ('Ants in the flesh', 1951).   ANNA MCMULLAN

Gérard-Denis Farcy, *Les Théâtres d'Audiberti* (1988)
George E. Wellwarth, *The Theater of Protest and Paradox* (1964).

audience   The role of the theatre audience has been both preserved and challenged in the twentieth century. The set of conventions for mainstream theatre, requiring a particular response to the on-stage dramatic presentation, has remained remarkably constant: audiences continue to take their seats in an orderly way, agree to virtual silence and physical passivity at the dimming of the lights and/or the raising of the curtain, and offer applause at the requisite moment(s). This scenario demands a homogeneity of response which, not surprisingly, is achieved as an effect of the homogeneity of the audience itself. In order to ensure ticket sales – particularly in the case of reliance on advance sales of subscription packages – repertoires are devised to fit within the dominant ideology of the cultures they serve, and a perceived lack of innovative theatre has in many cities brought problems of diminishing audiences for the mainstream theatres. This, and generally rising costs, have led to ever-escalating ticket prices, thereby further limiting accessibility of mainstream productions to prospective audiences. Many theatres have responded by conducting market research into their support. Yet if homogeneity characterizes the audiences to be found in the theatres of BROADWAY or the WEST END, or any of the major theatres in the urban centres of the Western world, this is neither a given nor a target for the producers of ALTERNATIVE THEATRE/drama. Many alternative theatre practices have been elaborated to challenge spectators to take up an active and creative role in performance.

Early in the century, the concerted challenges of theorist/practitioners such as APPIA, CRAIG, REINHARDT, PISCATOR, ARTAUD, MEYERHOLD, MARINETTI and (perhaps most importantly) BRECHT established important models for reconstructing the performance–spectator contract. For Meyerhold and for Brecht, the political arena provided the ideas and the shapes for the drama. The audience for such work was to be a co-creator of the dramatic text, inspired to carry on thinking about the play's topic(s) outside the specificity of performance: in short, to become a politically active subject. For Marinetti, the nightclub or CABARET, with its multiple activities (entertainment, eating, drinking, smoking, socializing and so on), became the model for a single space where performers and spectators could act and interact. (*See* FOOD AND DRINK.) The different and disparate experiments of such key figures have brought

49

about a devolution of theatre as well as a continuing attempt to establish new products in new venues for new audiences. As a result, at the end of the twentieth century there was a multiplicity of theatre practices which sought out the theatre audience as co-creator of performance.

Theatre introduced (or re-introduced) to regional cities and towns as well as to rural communities has often pragmatically involved its local constituency in the development of repertory. The proliferation of theatre 'FRINGE' events has made available a range and diversity of performance which has demanded new and different skills from its audiences. Many theatre companies work directly with their target audiences. Some have worked on specific community issues, writing a script with the help of local 'expertise' or around a significant local history – the shared context becoming the determining factor of the performance–audience relationship. Other groups have worked with interest groups, particularly in the fields of feminist, anti-racist, anti-homophobic or class concerns. In such circumstances, the theatre audience is not only the receiver of the performance, but often the creator of the performance script and devisor of its production methodology. A well-documented example of such work is the 'theatre of the oppressed' created by AUGUSTO BOAL. Here spectators are trained and transformed into actors in the drama with the goal of empowering their lives in a non-theatrical context.

The theorizing of the role of the audience has, until recently, been almost entirely neglected. While in 1941 Jan Mukařovský examined the roles of actor and spectator, finding them 'much less distinguished than it might seem at first glance', it is only in the last part of the century that the blurring of apparently demarcated roles became the site of detailed investigation. These more recent studies have considered the 'history' of specific theatre audiences – their class, race, gender, sexual preference – and their relationship to the type(s) of theatre they choose to attend. Semiology has attempted the codifying of signifying systems in on- and off-stage situations as well as the processes by which theatre audiences arrange and place in a hierarchy the multiple components of performance into a structure that generates meaning. Psychoanalytic, and especially Freudian, criticism has paid attention to the pleasures of spectatorship, while feminist criticism has examined the gendered 'gaze' of both film and theatre audiences. The processes of perception in receiving a dramatic text are particularly complex and the practices (and problems) of spectatorship have only just begun to be sketched.

SUSAN BENNETT

See also ARCHITECTURE; COMMUNITY THEATRE.

Daphna Ben Chaim, *Distance in the Theatre: The Aesthetics of Audience Response* (1984)

Susan Bennett, *Theatre Audiences: A Theory of Production and Reception*, 2nd edn (1997)

Herbert Blau, *The Audience* (1990)

Jill Dolan, *The Feminist Spectator as Critic* (1988)

Jan Mukařovský, *Structure, Sign, and Function*, ed. and trans. John Burbank and Peter Steiner (1977)

C. D. Throsby and G. A. Withers, *The Economics of the Performing Arts* (1979)

audition A dirty word in the lexicon of many performing artists, the audition – a term borrowed from music – only came to have its theatrical meaning in the twentieth century. It involves presenting oneself, generally in direct competition with other performers, for inspection, interrogation, judgement and even measurement by potential employers, who may be directors, producers, authors, choreographers, musical directors, casting directors, designers, sponsors or occasionally their spouses. They might even be other performers. There are three main types of theatre audition: singing, dancing and acting. The first two, involving specific vocal or dance requirements, are more straightforward than the third. A singer who cannot comfortably reach a required note, or a dancer who cannot safely accomplish a specific step, is clearly unsuited technically to the part. Acting ability is not so easily determined. Young artists will often audition with set speeches in which they have been carefully tutored at drama school. Older artists will sometimes refuse to audition, but will mostly agree 'to meet the director for a chat'. In the hands of a skilful director, this turns out to be an audition in all but name. With the young artist, the experienced director will disregard the set speech and endeavour to judge ability to respond to direction. The dancers who contributed to the writing of *A Chorus Line* (1975) provided an accurate (if sentimental) picture of a mass dancing audition – known with reason as 'a cattle call'. The only reason auditions continue is that no one has thought of a better way to winnow their particular wheat from the chaff.

There is another type of audition known as a 'backers' audition'. This mostly applies in the MUSICAL THEATRE and involves the writers reading and playing through their show to people who may invest in the fund needed to put it on. As RODGERS and HAMMERSTEIN admitted to going through the ordeal more than 40 times to raise the money for *Oklahoma!*, it is not considered *infra dig* for writers to do this. IAN BEVAN

See also CASTING.

Australia The country's first conventional theatre was opened in 1796 by an ex-convict, Robert Sideaway – and closed two years later after a spate of robberies on the unattended homes of theatre patrons. None the less, from the 1820s onwards the several colonies of nineteenth-century Australia supported an increasing number of theatres and theatrical performances. Few of the 600 or so plays written and performed in their public houses, converted halls and purpose-built theatres between 1834 and 1914 have survived, but those that have witness a shift from theatre as a place of free and easy entertainment to the Georgian mode of comfort, respectability and increasing technical sophistication. American actors arrived with the rush for gold, the first of them in 1853. None was more influential than J. C. Williamson and Maggie Moore, who established what became known as 'the Firm' – an organization that dominated commercial theatre in Australia for 80 years. Williamson declared: 'Australians will not have Australians on the stage.' Others disagreed. During the 1870s and 1890s, the 'golden age of melodrama', writers such as George Darrell, Alfred Dampier, Garnet Walsh and BLAND HOLT confirmed and refined the stock of Australian characters: the bushman, the new chum, the girl of the bush and the loyal 'mate' – and the status of the local actor–manager.

At the start of the twentieth century LOUIS ESSON, sometimes called the father of Australian theatre, perceived two countries, one in danger, the other dangerous. The end of that century saw the 'illusion of theatre' and the conventions of privileged spectatorship identified as 'the primary logic' in the construction of an historical process of 'continually becoming' Australian. It has even been suggested that the very sense of Australian community was fashioned in the first theatrical performance in Sydney in 1788, just months after the first settlement – or invasion – of the island continent. These are but two versions of history which struggle to account for the last 200 years of presence in a place which has for scores of thousands of years known and practised what Westerners call 'culture'.

After just 100 years of British occupation, Esson's dangerous Australia was a 'settled' place, peopled by opportunists for whom landscape meant real estate, silence signified consent and motion the mindless pursuit of the spoils of progress. The endangered country was a land of opportunity and mystery – radical in persuasion and sentiment, independent in speech, thought and action. These ideas continue to contribute to contested representations of 'nation'. In a learning piece, prophetically entitled *The Time is Not Yet Ripe* (1912), Esson urged a species of anarchy upon hoped-for and future audiences, knowing full well that for the 'settlers', vastness, silence and stillness were perceived more as enemy than inspiration. They were happy to identify with the land through the homely and conventional characters of bucolic comedy and fable – with Dad and Mother Rudd and their sentimental, battling family in the popular play and film versions of Steele Rudd's *On Our Selection* (1912). They did not want to celebrate a place of contradictions, moods and caprices – less still a land which was at some fundamental level not theirs at all. For Esson, battling and struggle were not merely pioneer virtues, they were part of a much more complex state of being, both political and metaphysical.

New theorists and historians have framed the discussion somewhat differently in their evaluation of theatre's role in remapping, restaging and questioning the colonial project in Australia. They talk of 'counter-events' and 'quiet but significant little revolutions' which have identified the making and changing of a culturally diverse and pluralist nation. The story of Australian theatre (not *the* Australian theatre) which follows recognizes and is influenced by both radical tendencies.

It was in response to such theatrical precedents that Esson co-founded the Pioneer Players (1922), a small ensemble dedicated solely to the production and promotion of plays written by Australians for Australians, performed in a way which avoided both the clichés of popular MELODRAMA and the imported if well-meaning solemnities which dominated the repertory movement established in Melbourne in 1911 by GREGAN MCMAHON – once called the GRANVILLE BARKER of the Australian theatre.

For Esson, Australia was always 'the new thing, the unknown', *terra Australia incognita*. He defined the sense of excitement, quest, fear and struggle inherent in all great art as quintessentially Australian – thus Sophocles was an Australian, and Shakespeare. It was at once an ironic reflection on a new nation's response to what was seen as an intimidating cultural void and a passionate exhortation to those brave enough to challenge the very notion of emptiness. The purpose was to unsettle and indeed subvert the self-comforting and habituated view of a supposedly innocent, honest, active and perpetually 'youthful' people. In their efforts at reform the Pioneers set the agenda for later generations: establish a company; declare an artistic philosophy; match theatre practice to politics; investigate the legends and assumptions of the past; develop an acting style; find a local voice and accent; experiment with form; admit influences but avoid models. In Esson's case, the influences came principally from turn-of-the-century bohemian Romantics as well as advocates of working-class culture and literature such as short-story writer and poet Henry Lawson who wrote for the 'bushman's Bible', the *Bulletin* newspaper, from the late 1880s. He also admired YEATS,

SYNGE and the ABBEY THEATRE experiment in Dublin, and espoused an idiosyncratic socialism.

There were home-grown, contemporary theatrical encouragements for the Pioneers. In Adelaide, where he founded the Literary Theatre in 1908, Bryceson Treharne was advocating the establishment of theatre ensembles as an aid to the development of a national theatre. Melbourne's William Moore promoted Australian Drama nights between 1909 and 1912. Arthur Adams, an early advocate and practitioner of 'Australian' playwriting, saw his works *The Wasters* (1910) and *Mrs Pretty and the Premier* (1913) performed and received with interest. Journalist Leon Brodzky encouraged the development of a reflexive drama through his Australian Theatre Society (1904) and in numerous articles. Most important of all, McMahon of the Melbourne Repertory Theatre presented the earliest of Esson's plays (1910).

At the same time, the commercial theatre and the newly introduced medium of cinema (1896) were trading successfully on stereotypes taken from popular theatrical melodrama, and the repertory movement was competing for the loyalties and attention of the bourgeoisie. For a fledgling theatre of ideas, 'mood' and social conscience, to ignore the importance of lively traditions of popular and intellectual culture was to deny a variety of truths about Australia and Australians. Esson's folk theatre, deliberately distanced from such traditions and practices, was hard put to make its presence felt. By 1926 dream turned to disillusionment and Esson quit the theatre along with his collaborators, Hilda Esson, Nette Palmer, VANCE PALMER and Stewart Macky, leaving behind a handful of scripts to be revived half a century later. Many of these works, but by no means all, derived from the 'bush' genre of the 1890s, but most questioned bush mythology in some way even as they acknowledged it. For example, Esson's plays *The Woman Tamer* (1910), *Dead Timber* (1911) and *Mother and Son* (1923) used role reversals to undermine masculinist assumptions and the supposedly subordinate and marginal place of women in such a culture, and revealed in the process a range of hitherto unexplored and exotic subcultures, types and environments.

Though Esson has been labelled 'father' of Australian theatre by patriarchal convention, neither theatrical nor sociological practice has offered an equivalent ascription to any of the many women who have contributed to and sustained that theatre. Yet one of the most impressive of all plays of the time, and one in sympathy with the aims of the Pioneers, was written by an influential and politicized woman, KATHARINE SUSANNAH PRICHARD. The play was *Brumby Innes*. Written as a companion piece to *Coonardoo*, her novel of cattle-station life in the far north-west, it addressed issues of class, race, sexuality and environment with a frankness which prevented production until 1972 yet drew accolades as early as 1927. Prichard dared to reveal a brutality in her outback hero which profoundly questioned the preferred asexual, rough-diamond image of a man of the land. Moreover, she wrote honestly of domestic and racial entrapment, exploitation and rape, in a manner which exposed contradictory codes of behaviour at the heart of an apparently down-to-earth and straightforward society. Using the symbol of the wild horse – the brumby – she pursued with powerful dramatic logic the process of transformation of personality and psyche in an alien place and relationship. These conflicts, and the convolutions of time and the timeless, would also become a preoccupation of later playwrights, especially the generation of the 1970s which rediscovered *Brumby Innes*. Unlike the mood pieces favoured by Esson and Palmer, this work admitted a vast landscape and opened with the remarkable song, dance and ritual celebration of a corroboree – ascribed to the Ngaala-Warrngga speaking South Pandjima people – which serves as an encapsulation of the tensions which shape the whole.

After Prichard came a string of successful and important left-wing women writers, theatre directors and administrators, whose claim to influence through their practice is as great as Esson's. This is certainly the case in the New Theatre movement of the 1930s which, in a sense, assumed the mantle forsaken by the Pioneers. While advocating an internationalist politics through its Melbourne and Sydney theatres in particular, the New Theatre advanced a national cause in its encouragement of local writers, actors, designers, technicians and directors. Its history is marked by classic left-wing productions like *Waiting for Lefty* (1936), but is equally notable for its topical, community-issue plays like *The Thirteen Dead* (1936), *War on the Waterfront* (1939) or *Reedy River* (1951), which celebrates the great Queensland shearers' strike of 1891 in folk-ballad opera form. This play has been regularly produced throughout Australia and overseas, including a London showing by UNITY THEATRE. Prichard contributed, along with many left-wing artists, to New Theatre writing, ethics and aesthetics. From the 1930s to the radical 1960s and 1970s playwright–novelists of international standing such as BETTY ROLAND, Dymphna Cusack and Frank Hardy have had their work produced alongside the revues, AGITPROPS and issue plays penned by celebrated company members. These include Oriel Gray's *Lawson* (1943) and *The Torrents* (1955), and Mona Brand's *Here Under Heaven* (1948) and *Barbara* (1966). The New Theatres in Sydney and to a lesser extent Melbourne continue to survive, though the movement from which they take their names is long since past.

Roland wrote her classic *The Touch of Silk* (1928) seven years before the formation of the New and was, by 1935, already a significant and politically committed writer. Like Prichard and others, such as Henrietta Drake-Brockman in *Men Without Wives* (1944), she took as her principal theme the isolation of women in an alien environment. Whereas Prichard chose the remote north-west, Roland invoked the closed society of the country town. The play gathered together familiar figures from the bush tradition. Her stroke of genius was to add to this array a French war bride. Jeanne's sense of dislocation and her ultimate capitulation to the stigma of 'difference' turned potential melodrama into a social tragedy in which personal and community catastrophe is linked to elemental forces of drought and flood. These in turn are connected to constricted ideas of love and fears of impotence. The 'touch of silk' defines cultural prejudice and misrepresentation in an Australian drama increasingly preoccupied with lost innocence and the trauma of personal disintegration. These writers were aware of the paradoxical characterization of the land as feminine, hard and fickle and of the 'woman of the bush' as the personification of unswerving constancy and maternal comfort. Tropes of barrenness, denial and betrayal in successive generations of plays have served to reinforce the contradictions. Contemporary women playwrights have consequently given much time to rewriting those views without denying the achievements of their predecessors. Elaine Ackworth's *Composing Venus* (1995), for example, sheds new light on playing the past as present reality in the lives of three generations of country women in one family.

By the end of the 1930s images other than those of bush and sheep station had claimed the attention of a nation reshaped by war and Depression. The popular stage gave rise to an urban figure which defined an economically divided society. It was down at heel, shiny-arsed, overdressed in dark suit and spats and wore a painted, woebegone expression like a tragicomic mask beneath its fedora. This was an expression like no other – part larrikin, part 'lair' and mischief-maker, part foolhardy skite. It belonged on the face of Mo, perhaps the most famous and enduring Australian clown figure apart from BARRY HUMPHRIES' archetypal and monstrous Edna Everage.

Mo, the alter ego of VAUDEVILLE Dutch-Jewish comedian Roy Rene, was the epitome of lost soul and lost innocence combined. He made an art form of innuendo and gave a rallying cry, half prayer and half oath, to the people of his generation and to those which were to follow: 'Strike me lucky.' Throughout the 1930s and 1940s, however, the belief in luck was repeatedly called into question by writers such as Palmer, George Landen Dann and Sydney Tomholt. Indeed, the 'lucky country' epithet was used later with some degree of irony, and contemporary playwrights have acknowledged this in their examination of the increasingly complex and uncertain dream worlds of their characters.

By the beginning of the Second World War the evolving Australian theatre had acquired some significant features: a call for a national theatre; a fascination with symbol and subversion; the courage to deal with sexuality, racism and xenophobia, and admit the fusion of landscape and personality; a social conscience; a taste for agitation and propaganda; a variety of responses to endemic isolation and loneliness; and a talent for masking, 'turns' and knockabout. There were, however, no permanent professional companies to explore any of the implications of such features. Musicals from America or companies such as the OLD VIC from England, with their classical productions and 'stars', continued to be imported. This pattern was interrupted by the war, when home-grown musical comedy favourites like GLADYS MONCRIEFF in *Maid of the Mountains* (1942) found a ready and enthusiastic public. Peace brought its own form of cultural reoccupation and Australians, with rare exception, returned to playing second fiddle to imported leads or went overseas to gain both experience and status in the eyes of home managements and public alike. Amateur or semi-professional LITTLE THEATRES provided the only alternative engagement and entertainment. After the beginning of public broadcasting in Australia in 1923, daytime radio actors helped to keep such theatres alive by night. Companies like Sydney's Independent (1930), Melbourne's Little Theatre (1930) and Perth's Patch (1930) produced English standards, contemporary European plays and classics by turn and in the repertory fashion. When tight budgets permitted they presented local product, but there was no subsidy for such theatres nor any extensive, full-time and formal training for their artists until 1958, when the National Institute of Dramatic Art took its first students. In a sense, then, Australian theatre was still a scattering of writers, actors, directors and designers in search of each other and a receptive public.

The 1940s yielded a number of plays of increasing complexity. Three in particular brought new ideas and the techniques of poetic drama, DOCUMENTARY and EXPRESSIONIST-influenced design and characterization to the Australian stage. Two of the playwrights, DOUGLAS STEWART and SUMNER LOCKE ELLIOTT, presented reworked images of folk heroes which challenged and at the same time confirmed their status and place in popular consciousness. In *Ned Kelly* (1942), Stewart attempted to unmask the celebrated bushranger and to differentiate between outlaw and outcast – between the living and the dead heart of a people. Locke Elliott, in *Rusty Bugles* (1947), sought to account for the effects of enforced isolation and inactivity on enlisted men imbued with a spirit of action and obligated to mateship. In both plays, characters struggled to find words and voice to match, or replace, deeds. Both investigated the implications of ritual and routine on the inner life of character and society. This fascination with RITUAL must be added to the list of features and influences which continue to shape contemporary Australian theatre, as must the preoccupation with the fragmented and fractured self.

PATRICK WHITE's expressionist *The Ham Funeral* (1947) joined *Ned Kelly* and *Rusty Bugles* to look beyond accepted roles, uniforms and masks and to probe and articulate the subconscious. Like them, it unmanned the Australian theatre and prepared the way for new perceptions of the absurd and the sublime. It found logic in ambiguity and salvation in fragmentation, and dwelt on the process of coming to terms with substance, not image, in its personification of youth, will, lust and inspiration.

Each of these plays encountered difficulty in transition from script to stage, principally because there was no theatre movement dedicated to their presentation. Such works were dependent on the programming policies of the little, independent and repertory theatres. *Ned Kelly* was thus first taken up by the émigré director Dolia Ribush and a company assembled for the purpose; *Rusty Bugles* received its initial production at Doris Fitton's Independent Theatre in Sydney; and *The Ham Funeral* was adopted by the Adelaide Theatre Guild as a *cause célèbre*.

It is a sign of their times that the plays were respectively considered unproduceable, unpatriotic and undesirable. Yet the challenges, censorship and discrimination which first greeted them gave much-needed focus and direction to a proto-theatre in search of a place and a future. In time, the poetic turn of phrase, barrack-room language and grotesque but comic imagery were to become hallmarks of a 'new wave' tendency and style. Police and government interference in the presentation of *Rusty Bugles* was to be remembered 20 years later when actors in JOHN ROMERIL's agitprop piece *Whatever Happened to Realism?* (1969) and ALEX BUZO's *Norm and Ahmed* (1968) were brought to court. The decision of the board of the first Adelaide Festival of Arts (1960) to reject *The Ham Funeral* was recalled when White's *Signal Driver* was presented as a feature of the 1984 Festival and with each of three subsequent premières and numerous revivals of White's plays in that festival city.

Some historians, however, cite 1953 as the most significant year in the development of drama in Australia. That year saw the first professional legitimate repertory theatre, the Union Theatre Repertory Company (UTRC), established on the campus of Melbourne University and the AUSTRALIAN ELIZABETHAN THEATRE TRUST, under British expatriate HUGH HUNT, set up to give financial assistance to the performing arts. Opinions are divided as to whether these events advanced or hindered the 'Australian theatre' cause. To understand this division, it must be remembered that Esson had dissociated himself from the repertory movement under McMahon's leadership in Melbourne because it looked away from its society for artistic and stylistic inspiration. The UTRC (later called the MELBOURNE THEATRE COMPANY), under John Sumner's 35-year artistic leadership, was to face the same criticism in the debate over Australia's right to cultural autonomy. Both McMahon and Sumner supported Australian work but did not commit to it as Esson had done. Sumner is credited with encouraging RAY LAWLER's *The Summer of the Seventeenth Doll* (1955) and other artists and work thereafter but, like McMahon, he was also seen by regionalists and pro-nationalists as an appropriator rather than an innovator. It was argued that repertory directors' interest lay elsewhere by definition: in the known and tried classics and their traditions, in certain contemporary British and American works, and above all in the box office.

The case against the reps in its simplest and least partisan form was that Australian artists would never develop a sense of their own significance or any creative momentum while they had to wait their turn. These artists were reputed to be great imitators, perhaps the best in the world. As such, they inevitably succeeded on terms other than their own. The prime example of this referred excellence had come in 1949 with TYRONE GUTHRIE's fanciful and thoroughly colonial suggestion – in response to a federal government request for advice – that an Australian National Theatre Company should be established and trained in England, where many expatriate performers, such as Cyril Richard, Madge Elliott, John McCallum, Peter Finch, Coral Browne, Merle Oberon and Leo McKern, had found employment. It was reasoned that a national theatre should be proficient in the classics and trained accordingly. But an Australian theatre could not thrive, ultimately, by playing other people's actions, speaking other people's words in other people's accents, moving to increasingly alien rhythms, responding subliminally to political, social and psychological influences which had second-hand meaning.

Paradoxically, the success of 'The Doll', both in Australia and overseas, presented a number of problems to any potential theatre movement, not the least of which was the expectation of like successes. In many ways 'The Doll' was an old fashioned well-made play, the type of play to which conservative audiences were accustomed. To those who argued for an Australian theatre of experiment in form as well as content the play was therefore only half satisfying, even though Lawler had pushed traditional and sentimental views of domestic relationships to breaking point, confined the outdoorsman, questioned mateship and broken the mould of the competent and long-suffering girl–woman. Lawler gave, to the generation of the 1950s, a clear image of collective crisis and personal nightmare which influenced much of what was to follow, but in a familiar and comfortable form.

Despite subsequent bids to break with a circumscribed past and attempts throughout the decade by writers like Gray, Cusack, Barbara Vernon, Richard Beynon, John Hepworth, PETER KENNA, ALAN SEYMOUR and HAL PORTER to push home the sense of shock and bewilderment at the heart of Lawler's revelations, many Australians continued to read in 'The Doll' a sentimental affirmation of old values and traditions – of 'going forward looking back', as one contemporary playwright has observed. They saw only a personal tragedy. They imagined reconciliation between characters and ignored the broader signs. This made the need for change more pressing and the chance of achieving it less assured. The play evokes complex reactions to the effect of 1950s consciousness on the Australian psyche, as Robyn Nevin's outstanding 1996 touring production indicates.

Seymour, hard on the heels of Lawler, also stressed the end of a dream in his *One Day of the Year* (1960). In the belligerent assertion of middle-aged Alf Cook's opening line, 'I'm a bloody Australian and I'll always stand up for bloody Australia,' lay the seeds of betrayal of a radical tradition. A one-time principle of survival had become a statement of loss, bigotry and delusion. Seymour urged his audiences to re-think Australianness, not simply to react to jingoistic catch cries about Australians and Australia, and created a new-generation Australian to bear the brunt of the anger and insecurity which came with losing grip on past glories. The principal target for Alf's rage is Hughie, his son, a working-class boy with prospects. He is the first of the upwardly mobile, university-educated characters to appear on the modern Australian stage. Since that appearance, the culture has been dominated by the Hughie Cook generation.

Was reconciliation between generations and ideologies possible in 'fair go' Australia? What choices were to be made? These were questions writers of the late 1960s and early 1970s pursued in their plays through the torments of madness and self-deception and, by magic, beyond death itself. The Australian theatre movement itself was to become increasingly mad, bad and dangerous to know.

Theatre workers in all disciplines, shaped by the 1960s, formed the basis of what was called the New Wave of Australian drama: the alternative drama. The names of the writers became well known, particularly DAVID WILLIAMSON, JACK HIBBERD, Romeril, Buzo, RON BLAIR, BARRY OAKLEY, Michael Boddy, DOROTHY HEWETT, ALMA DE GROEN, Bob Ellis and Rodney Milgate. Some of them worked beyond the theatre as public intellectuals. They attempted to free themselves of the residual influences of a tenacious 'old' Australia in plays such as *Beware of Imitations* (Oakley, 1973) and *Last Day in Wooloomooloo* (Blair, 1976). The theatres in which they worked have acquired their own folklore – Jane Street (1966), La MaMa (1967), The Pram Factory (1970), NIMROD (1970). The styles and working methods they espoused have provided a unique terminology and critical vocabulary: cartoon vaudeville; quasi-naturalism with absurdist overtones; imagism with a personal style of surrealism; bivouac theatre; pramocracy; monodrama; and so on. This was Australian theatre's 'shock of the new'. It was 'rough, relevant and ribald', as Hibberd put it. It was also eclectic, world-wise but aggressively local and regional in its reference and application.

It has been suggested that this surge of theatrical energy was part of a neo-nationalism which purportedly brought to power the first Labor government (1972) in 23 years. The party slogan was 'It's Time'. Those who reject chauvinist, nationalist imputations point to global factors such as the emergence of an influential left-wing youth movement and growth of a counterculture in the West, and the concurrent interest in non-Western cultural practices and forms. They acknowledge a resistance to postwar colonialism, brought into focus by Australia's involvement in the war in Vietnam, as a crucial factor in the renaissance of critical interest in expressions of Australian identity and identity politics. It was argued that new Australian theatre and film were far from parochial in application and relevance. They were in fact taking their legitimate place in a critique of a changing world – a world to be challenged, satirized and fantasized, not merely to be accepted and described.

There was debate, too, about the validity of the term 'new wave'. Like 'theatre of the absurd', it was declared a critical convenience to permit the linking together of disparate forces. Certainly there were differences between Sydney-style new theatre and Melbourne's equivalent. Yet the participants in this nationwide (not just eastern states) phenomenon seemed happy enough to share the title for political reasons in what was an 'us and them' struggle against establishment force and influence. Their particular targets were the large theatres like the Melbourne Theatre Company, Sydney's OLD TOTE THEATRE Company and the flagship Australian Opera and Ballet Companies, which, after 1968 and the creation of the Australia Council for the Arts, received a major proportion of government subsidy. Privileged organizations and their supporters argued, in return, that an Australian theatre should satisfy the various needs of the existing public, not merely the predicates and prophecies of a left-wing, popularist minority campaigning for future generations. Between 1968 and the constitutional 'coup' – or dismissal – which brought down the Whitlam Labor government in 1975, the battle for minds and public money was engaged.

These years were crucial for the advocates of change as they worked past Lawler's prophetic breakdown in relationships through crises of identity, location and mythology. They mocked the lucky streak and admitted fantasies of violence, humiliation and dislocation in absurd land, sea and street-scapes. In so doing they celebrated their right to a freedom of idiom, rhythm, tone, performance space and subject-matter. This marked a release from linguistic and behavioural constraints imposed by disapproving fathers and a laundered history. It also marked the first faltering steps toward the postmodern and a serious consideration of theory by Wal Cherry at the Emerald Hill Company (founded in Melbourne in 1962, growing out of Theatre 60). STANIS-LAVSKY, BRECHT, LITTLEWOOD, PINTER, BECKETT, IONE-SCO, GROTOWSKI, BROOK, BECK and MALINA, SCHUMANN and SCHECHNER, as well as Shakespeare and Sophocles, were now grist to the mill of local invention. They too were now what Esson would have called 'Australians'.

Plays such as *Norm and Ahmed* and *Rooted* (1969) by Buzo; *The Legend of King O'Malley* (1970) by Boddy and Ellis; Hewett's *The Chapel Perilous* (1971); *The Removalists* (1971) and *Don's Party* (1971) by Williamson; *Dimboola* (1969) and the outstanding *A Stretch of the Imagination* (1972) by Hibberd; and *The Floating World* (1974) by Romeril epitomized these times. So did the political agitation of Queensland's Popular Theatre Troupe and the improvisatory experiments of the Performance Syndicate and Rex Cramphorn. Throughout the 1970s 'experiment' in Australian theatre became a sign of wider change, a means of political expression and a focus for community action. There was talk and growing evidence of women's theatre, black theatre, community theatre, multicultural theatre, Theatre in Education, youth theatre, theatre of the deaf, bilingual theatre. Theatre spaces themselves became sites of protest. Sauce factories, shirt factories, pram factories, brothels and stables were converted and made over by designers like Peter Corrigan of the Australian Per-

forming Group and Larry Eastwood at Nimrod. Their legacy exists in the work of later exponents such as Shaun Gurton, Jenny Tait and Stephen Curtis. Their inspiration derived from an earlier generation of painter–designers such as Desmonde Downing, Sydney Nolan and Wendy Dickson. Production, publication and debate increased – much of it to the rhythm of original music composed by Martin Friedl or Lorraine Milne, Sara de Jong, Carl Vine or Alan John.

In the Back Theatre at the Pram Factory the women of the influential Australian Performing Group devised and presented a defiant and entertaining *And Betty Can Jump* (1972) in response to the growing number of plays about blokes, mates and beer. Thus began a renewed process of feminization in Australian theatre which has aided and contextualized the work of writers like Jennifer Compton, Alma De Groen, Gillian Jones, Jill Shearer and HANNIE RAYSON, Joanna Murray-Smith, Tobsha Learner, Hilary Bell, Debra Oswald, Cherie Imlah, Samantha Bews and Tee O'Neill; companies such as Home Cooking, Just Wisteria, Legs on the Wall, Woman Action Theatre and the germinal Vitalstatistix; performer–directors Kerry Dwyer, Anna Volska, Robin Laurie, Gale Edwards, Margaret Davies, Ros Horin, Doreen Warburton, Christine Johnston, Mishline Yasmine Jammal and Rosealba Clemente; solo performer–writer–directors Robyn Archer, Evelyn Krape, Jenny Kemp, Virginia Baxter, CATHY DOWNES, Jean Kitson, Sue Ingleton and Leah Purcell; and executive producer Christine Westwood – to name but some of an ever-increasing number of women who continue to enhance and diversify the 1970s alternative tradition. The range of address and form is remarkable, from reclaiming and redefining inner as well as public space, through auto-performance and biography, cabaret and circus, community education and stand-up, to projects like Women in Theatre (1981–2) which tackled fundamental issues of representation and put complex and contested ideas about gender and power into action. Moreover, these readings have been extensively theorized by Peta Tait, Susan Pfisterer and Helen Gilbert.

In Redfern the National Black Theatre devised its first revue, *Basically Black* (1973), featuring Jack Charles and Bob Maza, and performed Robert Merritt's landmark play *The Cake Man* (1974). Thereafter JACK DAVIS, Australia's senior indigenous playwright, produced an outstanding trilogy of plays in his work with the Marli Biyol/Black Swan Company in Western Australia; Merritt has established the Eora cultural centre in inner-city Redfern; and Broome's Jimmy Chi has written his inspirational musicals *Bran Nue Dae* (1990) and *Corrugation Road* (1996). Bryan Syron and Justine Saunders, in their direction, performance and promotion of indigenous arts, have inspired and supported two generations of playwrights, actor–entertainers, film-makers and media personalities like Kevin Gilbert, Tracy Moffatt, Ernie Dingo, Eva Johnson, Roger Bennett, Rachel Maza, Lydia Miller, Richard Walley, Rhoda Roberts, Wesley Enoch, Deborah Mailman and Martin Buzzacott. Indigenous artists are now making the most effective use of the theatre, dance and allied arts in Australia – witness the success of Bangara, Kooemba-Tolarra or Ilbijerri. For them there is a wealth of contemporary and traditional culture on which to draw, and urgent political and social agendas which encompass land, health, rights and race. Non-indigenous theatre workers and commercial film-makers are lending their support, as Andrew Ross has shown in his work with Jimmy Chi, and Nicholas Parsons and Bryan Brown in their respective productions of *Dead Heart* (1993; 1996).

A publishing house for Australian plays was established by Philip Parsons and Katharine Brisbane in 1971. Its title, Currency, harked back to the name given the first generation of white Australians who identified with the new country. They were not the Sterling breed of the Old Dart. Playlab (1978) and Yackandandah Publishing (1982) also took up and sustained the cause. These newly released texts found their way on to school and university syllabuses; performing arts courses proliferated as part of a boom in tertiary education. This coincided with the advent of new theatres, or the resurgence of old theatres transformed: La MaMa, Hoopla, Troupe, HOLE-IN-THE-WALL, La Boite, the Q Theatre and the Stage Company. Each produced or supported its share of new plays and writers – BARRY DICKINS, Roger Pulvers, DAVID ALLEN, DOREEN CLARKE, Jill Shearer, STEVE J. SPEARS, Rob George and Clem Gorman. The subsidized companies and the small independents such as Sydney's Ensemble also increased their exposure to Australian works and in some cases provided playwriting residencies.

From the mid-1970s and through the 1980s, in the suburbs of all capital cities, there emerged experimental, community, youth and regional theatres and their networks – Arena, WEST, Theatreworks, Toe Truck, Magpie, Sidetrack, Anthill, Handspan Puppet Theatre, Salamanca, Shopfront Theatre for Young People, Zootango, Deckchair, Street Arts, Junction, Melbourne Workers' Theatre, Six Years Old and Barking Gecko Theatre – determined to make theatre from the everyday lives and experiences of a diverse, increasingly multicultural population. County towns and provincial cities boasted their own companies, like the now-famous Flying Fruitfly Circus from the twin rural centres of Albury–Wodonga, New Moon from northern Queensland or Mainstreet from south-eastern South Australia. These companies encountered and tackled the 'mechanisms of forgetfulness' which have isolated not only black Australians but other minorities. In this process of change, especially since the early 1980s, works by theatre artists of non-English-speaking background such as RON ELISHA, Janis Balodis, and, more recently, Tess Lyssiotis, Tom Petsinis, Teresa Crea and the Doppio Teatro/ doppio parallelo companies, and director–animateur Don Mamouney, have dramatized (even popularized, in the 'wog boy' case of Nick Giannopoulos) an Australia preoccupied with different concerns and customs from those of the dominant group of 1970s playwrights of Anglo-Irish or Celtic tradition or extraction.

Yet between the excitement of the early 1970s and the contemporary legacy of such excitement came an 'eerie calm', a dose of 'the proscenium arch blues'. It seemed that the best efforts of those who had pursued change had been all too easily absorbed by the institutions and ideologies of mainstream culture. Cultural democracy and the democratization of culture were debated fiercely, and the slippery concept of excellence again raised its head. Whereas one-time rebel writers, performers and directors found acceptance, contracts and commissions in all branches of the performing arts and media, others found life on the dole or in the doldrums intolerable, and quit. Was this, they asked, a repetition of the dream–disillusionment cycle experienced periodically over half a century?

To the outside observer there was a clear answer. Some things had changed. The importance of the 1970s lay as much in the diaspora of ideas and personalities as in the confrontations with the establishment, funding struggles or the attempted exorcism of that ubiquitous stereotype, the 'ocker' Australian. Comedy, cabaret, community theatres and theatre in education, for example, drew on the resources and performance innovations of that decade – cherishing and developing its gift of athletic and highly energized routines, the preference for skits and shows rather than plays, the love of live music and music theatre and the enthusiasm for lively exchanges of banter across crowded playing spaces. The spectacular and renowned Circus Oz (1978) had its origins in such an amalgam, rather than in the conventional circus tradition which began in Van Diemen's Land in 1847. The emergence and popularity of theatre restaurants and comedy rooms like the Flying Trapeze, the Last Laugh, the Comedy Café and Kinselas have also vindicated and sustained the struggles of alternative against establishment to the point where all capital cities now have comedy venues and Melbourne regularly hosts one of the world's largest comedy festivals. Theatre comedy has had great effect on Australian popular television.

For those who saw the theatre's health and development in its playwriting, or at best in the collaboration of writer, director and company with a known audience, an apparent lack of a further wave in the late 1980s was alarming – the more so since writers above all other theatre practitioners had fought hard to gain both recognition and constant employment. In fact, a growing rift between developments in performance style and experiments in writing caused some experienced campaigners – Buzo and Hibberd for example – to attempt to establish writers' theatres to provide support, context and critical feedback for those who were not fortunate enough to be taken up by established and fund-favoured theatre companies. The fear was that a few well-known and marketable writers would have their commissioned work produced once in each heavily subsidized state playhouse and the remainder would languish for the want of connection. The prospect offered an altogether unsatisfactory reading of new and unknown.

In the 1980s and recession-affected early 1990s these favoured institutions did indeed call the tune as smaller, once influential, theatres like the Pram Factory and Nimrod closed or shifted both location and artistic stance. Few new writers found equivalent ensemble focus for their work – though the Griffin Company (1981) and the Company B cooperative (1984) maintained something of a nexus in Sydney, as did the Church and the important Playbox (1976) in Melbourne; and there were new companies hoping to take their chance. In part compensation, there is an annual National Playwrights' Conference (1972) and a Playwrights' Centre (1986) and advisory service. Whereas small companies once claimed and were accorded the right to fail with their experiments, political and financial pressure nowadays all but forbid the suggestion. While there is evidence of wide-ranging theatrical activity, it is more precarious than was the case in the late 1980s and early 1990s. This has much to do with a changing economic climate and the recession and crash of 1987. It also reflects the change in political philosophy of new conservatism in all states but one, and in the attitude of the federal Liberal-National government (1996) towards the arts in context. There was a net increase in 'culture' spending in the 1990s, but the targets were new technology or spectacular bicentennial, millennial or Olympic style events. Even in the cultural mainstream, artistic directors and managers staked and lost their reputations on the principle of theatrical research and development. A notable example concerns the failure, after two seasons, of the admired Australian Playhouse concept at the STATE THEATRE COMPANY OF SOUTH AUSTRALIA. The executive producer proposed five seasons of classic and new Australian works with attendant critical analysis in 'retro-prospect' of the new millennium. The

objective was to use the theatre as a feature of public debate and discourse in a manner which seemed consistent with the objectives of the pioneering 1920s and alternative 1970s.

All-Australian seasons aside, certain writers, who once were stalwarts of alternative theatre and innovation beyond the mainstream, have become established if not establishment figures within it. They at least serve to connect generations. White, Nowra, Romeril, STEPHEN SEWELL, Hewett, Hannie Rayson and MICHAEL GOW carry the authority of literary and theatrical tradition, both Australian and European. The occasional but quite deliberate coincidence of such writers with former alternative theatre directors such as Jim Sharman and a core of sympathetic actors, to form ensembles in major playhouses, was as much a phenomenon of the theatre of the 1980s as was the shoestring and stayput ensemble a feature of the 1970s. It might be argued, therefore, that the Melbourne performer-focused alternative style has shaped the development of community and cabaret, while Sydney-style director-influenced alternatives have more successfully infiltrated the mainstream. The argument can be pursued further to include schools of formal practical and intellectual training. On the one hand, the University of New South Wales and the National Institute of Dramatic Art have their influence: on the other, Melbourne and Monash Universities and the Victorian College of the Arts (especially in the first decade of its operation, 1976–86) have theirs.

These are not exclusive divisions. Other institutions and collaborations in other cities – especially in Adelaide and Perth – make their contribution and more than enough has been made of eastern-seaboard rivalries, with comparisons between Sydney's spangled Shakespeare and Melbourne's brutal Brecht. But the preoccupation with antipodean approaches to Shakespeare by Cramphorn and JOHN BELL and a commitment to the work of new Australian authors at Nimrod and the symbolist–expressionist and occasionally romantic propensities of Sydney's short-lived Paris Theatre Company (1978) seemed to result in an influential alliance which claimed national attention and pre-eminence in the 1980s. Theatre practitioners from around the country travelled to the Emerald City to reinforce the impression. White, Nowra, Sewell and then Gow joined with directors Sharman, Aubrey Mellor and Neil Armfield to explore both psyche and contemporary circumstance through plays of dream and vision, whose central characters are in extremis, voyaging inwards to apocalypse or apotheosis. Postmodern experiments in the early 1990s by the Sydney Front confirmed a further 'reinvention' of Australia and its drama, as did the multiple perspectives of feminist works like *The Serpent's Fall* (1987) by Sarah Cathcart and Andrea Lemon, or Pam Leversha's *Early Days under the Old Hat* (1991).

It must be recognized that these writers and animateurs are not the only ones whose sense of displacement and relocation has impelled them to cast their characters adrift or urge them through and beyond the mirror which purports to represent nature. Plays which take this journey, such as *A Stretch of the Imagination* (1972), *The Floating World* (1974), *Crossfire (1975)*, *The Man from Mukinupin* (1979), *The Dreamers* (1982), *Signal Driver* (1982), *Too Young for Ghosts* (1985), *The Golden Age* (1985), *Dreams in an Empty City* (1986), *Two* (1986), *Rivers of China* (1987), *Shimada* (1987), *Furious* (1991), *Funerals and Circuses* (1992), *The Gap* (1993), *Tear from a Glass Eye* (1998), *The Dogs Play* (1999), *Meat Party* (2000) and *Look at Everything Twice for Me* (2000), offer insight into the preparedness of the Australian theatre to continue to deal with more than surface reality, Europhilia or -phobia, so-called 'asianization' and problems of national identity.

The works, through their stylistic spirals, juxtapositions and self-conscious appropriations, set out to tackle the material and metaphysical self as *terra Australis incognita*. They continue to summon the dark side of the 'Sunny South' and release repressed and un-settled life without, as yet, entirely sacrificing the celebratory quality which has consistently informed the drama. They play with emblematically inscribed Australias and fashion theatre into trilogies, sequences and self-conscious layers of work and knowledge. Recently, such approaches have been associated with what conservatives call a 'black armband' view of Australian history. Many artists reject the typification and the construction.

There is one writer, however, whose success lies in his determination to reflect and refract contemporary reality with its brittle surfaces, hollow rituals, imperfect social mechanisms and its moral dilemmas. David Williamson, perhaps the most successful and prolific of contemporary Australian playwrights, assumes the role of 'storyteller to his tribe' – not shaman or prophet. He is a fascinating and adept wordsmith, but stands outside the tradition of poet–dramatists and is tied by fashion to another lineage which is said to include Lawler, Seymour and to some extent Kenna, the increasingly popular, versatile and accomplished Nick Enright of *Mongrels* (1991) fame, Hannie Rayson in plays of compromise and emotional complexity like *Hotel Sorrento* (1993), and Rayson and Andrew Bovell in their collaboration *Scenes from a Separation* (1995). Williamson's so-called naturalism disguises his origins in the alternative 1960s and a satirist–absurdist's view of the behaviour of his middle-class, middle-aged tribe. Williamson is playwright to

middle (and now middle-aged) Australia and is thereby the most performed of contemporary writers. Whether he is also the most accomplished of such writers remains a moot point. Certainly, from *The Coming of Stork* (1970) to *The Great Man* (2000) he has committed to theatre, film and television his fascination with power games, the hidden face of violence, institutionalized corruption of values, the frailties of family and friendship, and the gap between ideals and the capacity to meet them. He has also unleashed his wit and vented his spleen on academia and the theatre and film industries which sustain him. Adherence to a somewhat mechanistic and occasionally moralistic view of society has repeatedly drawn laughter of self-recognition as well as demands for a firmer stand on the issues raised in the plays. He refuses to be drawn in his work, but is still an outspoken public figure.

Whereas Williamson's characters act out the found-form routines of urban Australia-as-we-know-it, other playwrights choose to gain insight through imagined relocation and distanciation. In their displacements they examine the experiences of existential, cultural and political dependence and speculate on the need for change. Since the late 1980s, Australian theatre has ceased to be the influential and culturally dynamic or transforming medium it was in the 1970s. Yet the performative, physicalized and spectacular aspects of expression which the theatre championed and which have for so long been admired by Australian audiences remained evident across a range of media, forms, representations and arts organizations – despite increasingly hard times, during which the language of the arts has become the language of business, and management discusses its achievements in terms once reserved for artists: quality of performance, innovation, creativity and excellence. Commercial managements are steadily encroaching on 'art' space. And yet it is argued by some that theatre is exciting and well placed to carry its practitioners and its audiences into the new millennium with daring and in style in response to the pressure to diversify. A glance at the performing arts directories of the mid-1990s will reveal, for example, a register of more than 200 performance directors and creators of special events; over 130 practising playwrights and scriptwriters; 300 or more theatre groups and a further 40 music theatre companies and groups; and 320 theatre and concert venues, with continued investment by corporations and governments in large-scale multipurpose houses in the hope of generating revenue from 'cultural tourism'. This professional superstructure sits atop the many hundreds more up-and-coming, flash-in-the-pan (or quality) amateur groups, organizations and contributors which draw consistently and deliberately on the labours of the previous 30 years of vigorous Australianiz-ation. Some indication of this grassroots culture can be gleaned from the hundreds of acts which register to per-form at fringe and comedy festivals in capital cities. Cur-rency Press lists 440 titles for such groups to access (if they are not creating their own material), and the rate of self-devised and unpublished performance will match that number many times over.

There is also clear evidence of diversification such that successful practitioners in one medium also work in others. This is a function of necessity but also marks a shift in flexibility and the conception of the performing artist and writer in the last twenty years of the century. Many work in clubs and some in television or film to support the theatre, just as theatre artists once sup-ported fledgling movie, radio and television industries in the 1910s and 1920s, the 1930s and 1950s. They also contribute to the increasing number of festivals which identify places, industries, communities, seasons and issues – from Adelaide's Fringe, to the Sydney Gay and Lesbian Festival and the Mardi Gras; from Melbourne's Next Wave to the Woodford Festival in Queensland; from the Rotnest Festival in the West, the Darwin Glendi and the Cultural Olympiad to NAIDOC week and Sur-vival Day or Wired celebrations and performances across the country. Such events owe their existence and popularity in some part to the community theatre and arts movements of the 1970s and 1980s as well as to increasing 1990s corporate and state tourism marketing involvement in public celebration.

Beneath and around structural and sectoral changes, the issues which have affected and shaped the theatre since the 1920s are resurfacing, perhaps as a function of 'millennialism', perhaps because there is much about the mainstream politics of the arts and the country which remains steadfastly backward- rather than for-ward-looking. There is an ideological and teleological struggle in progress for possession of cultural definition. 'Progressive' concepts, policies and practices such as multiculturalism, indigenous rights and representation, freedom of speech and cultural pluralism are under pres-sure if not attack from an electorally re-invigorated, cen-sorial and censorious right. Publicly funded institutions in general (and in the arts as a matter of course) fear cuts and programme accordingly. But stringencies also pro-voke dissent within and beyond institutions, and it is surfacing once again.

At a forum at the end of the 1996 National Perform-ance Conference, the struggles of at least half a century of painstaking liberalization were recounted and the rapid erosion of achievements resentfully and incredu-lously acknowledged. Unlike crisis debates on the arts in the 1920s, 1950s, 1970s and early 1980s, however, this forum dealt with more than the immediate threat of contraction or of disillusionment in the sector. Under-pinning all discussion was an awareness of history – apparently repeating itself, but *not* new. Participants could talk of a 'few but roses' approach to funding or of encouraging 'a thousand flowers to bloom' and recog-nize in the dichotomy their own historiography, narrat-ive and process. There could be discussion of the merits of establishing a national theatre to consolidate pre-cious funds, this time without reference to any Knight of the Empire; or discussion of the merits of establishing state performance ensembles without reference to an East London, East German or West Coast American model. Changes in the 'landscape of the theatre' could be contemplated without reference to a map drawn half a world away. There were space, time and knowledge to permit three generations of experience to be recounted and for connections between experiences to be made – intuitively and routinely. It was possible to say that such-and-such a strategy was a quarter of a century old and to have that quarter-century reckoned in long-term Australian theatre memory by people still working in the sector after that length of time. An equivalent meet-ing in the early 1970s also held in Melbourne had no such sense of context or continuity. It was possible to consider the merits of regionalism and responsibility of artist to community and know the 'to what and to whom' of the reference. There was a critical sensibility – at work and unexceptionable – which absorbed postco-lonial and present-pragmatist critiques without disin-genuous or rabid contestation.

The issues are indeed familiar, just as the circum-stances which frame them are tough and bound to get tougher, despite the official rhetoric of sustained eco-nomic growth. But the theatrescape has changed to the extent that artists know much more about the struggle, what is to be lost and what must be preserved. Articles published in the mid- to late 1990s asked equally famil-iar questions: 'Is the text-based drama dead?' 'Australian theatre in crisis – (again)?' There were pronouncements on 'the narrowing of the theatre in the 1990s', with critics such as Len Radic, Geoffrey Milne and Alex Buzo adding their voices to others which have debated similar issues over a quarter of a century: Katherine Brisbane, Garrie Hutchinson, James Waites, Angela Bennie, John McCallum, Veronica Kelly, Helen Thomson, Harry Kippax, Virginia Duigan, Peter Ward, the Open City group and many more.

Is the Australian theatre narrower than it was, and tex-tually moribund? Any up-to-the-minute answer will have to speak of tendencies rather than certainties, since the construct of an Australian theatre is changing along with changing ideas of reliable historical narrative. It has been argued, for example, that theatricality and performative aspects of *many* forms of public cultural expression have gained more rather than less prominence. This may have produced a corresponding diminution of theatre as a discrete, text-dependent and interpretative discipline and affected playwriting as well. But that which is still identified as theatre by its use of text, space, personnel, technique and technology has its own niche values and influences. Scripts published by Playlab and the Australian Script Centre at the end of the 1990s would suggest that the appeal of new 'plays' remains. The writing is diverse and lively. New names appear: Tim Connigrave, Christine Evans, Niamh, Nicholas Hammond, Owen Love, Raemondo Cortese. There is not the obvious power of a 'Movement' or 'Wave' to give their work collective impetus, but there is an infrastructure and an awareness of their contribution to a living theatre which supports them.

The 2000 National Playwrights' Conference produced competent work-in-progress, but nothing to compare in efficacy and relevance to that trialled at the National Aboriginal and Torres Strait Islander Playwrights' Conference held in the same week. Here the power of the written-to-be-performed text in context was palpable. Both conferences served the theatre, but one struck at the foundations of nationalism and the assumptions of nation. One added its voice to defining issues for Australians: reconciliation, indigenous deaths in custody, the human rights infringements of certain mandatory sentencing laws; the other preoccupied itself with craft and form.

If theatre is alive and well, its presence should be felt in the major arts festivals which mark cultural seasons and cycles. Evidence in Perth, Adelaide and Sydney can be said to suggest directions and mark achievements in the articulation of cultural values in hybrid partnership with music, dance and the material arts. They indicate a renewed political engagement as well – through intercultural collaborations such as the Landmines Project, which brings playwrights together from Australia, Vietnam, Thailand, Malaysia, Singapore and Cambodia, or in Big hART's community projects with the young and disadvantaged.

Is the theatre in crisis (again)? One answer is: hopefully, yes. In this region, 'crisis' sometimes translates as 'creative danger'. Australian needs such a theatre, whether it produces splendid adaptations such as Tim Winton's *Cloud Street* (1999), hitherto undiscovered and untranslated works such as Theo Patrikareas' *The Promised Woman* (2000), or imperative stories of dislocation and trauma, as in Jane Harrison's *Stolen* (1998). Another answer is that theatre, as a discreet and singular way of encapsulating and acting out Australia, is struggling to

find a place for itself in the 'hybridization' and mediation of public communication. This form of crisis is not so good for those who serve a particular cause in art. It raises questions of sectoral relevance; but also draws attention to those who are exploring ways 'out'. Once we asked: 'What Australian theatre?' At least the question now is: 'Which Australian theatre?'

Theatre in Australia may not be the medium of the moment or of the generation; it may not be sufficiently funded; the local produce may be overshadowed by blockbuster imports; but at conferences, in classrooms and in every home-made performance it continues its compelling and complex voyage from imitation, through contrivance to representation and thence to translation – of experience from one state to another, from one language to another, from one time to another. The Australian theatre is defined, as Esson suggested, by the determination in each and every new performance to mark, name, speak, utter, embody and sing into knowledge the existence of peoples inhabiting the oldest continent on earth, strung between Old Worlds east and west, first and third, facing indigenous cultures and a complex history older than Old.

The new and unknown Australian theatre plays for us all. GUS WORBY

G. Blundell, *Australian Theatre* (1997)
K. Brisbane, *Entertaining Australia* (1992)
C. Chesterman, *Playing with Time: Women Writing for Performance* (1995)
P. Fitzpatrick, *After the Doll* (1979)
R. Fotheringham, *Community Theatre*, rev. edn (1992)
H. Gilbert, *Sightlines: Race, Gender and Nation in Contemporary Australian Theatre* (1998)
P. Holloway, *Contemporary Australian Drama*, rev. edn (1987)
V. Kelly, ed., *Our Australian Theatre in the 1990s* (1998)
H. Love, ed., *The Australian Stage* (1984)
D. Malouf, *A Spirit of Play* (1998)
P. Parsons, ed., *Companion to Theatre in Australia* (1995)
L. Radic, *The State of Play* (1991)
L. Rees, *A History of Australia Drama*, 2 vols (1978)
P. Tait, *Converging Realities* (1994)
D. Walker, *Dream and Disillusion* (1976)

Australian Elizabethan Theatre Trust Established in 1954 in Sydney to commemorate the Queen's first visit to Australia. The Trust's purpose as laid down in its charter was to develop the performing arts at a time when there was little activity in that area. In the early 1960s, its aim shifted towards a policy of regional development, and this coincided with moves by the various states to establish their own companies, rather than one company trying to fill national requirements. Since

then, it has filled a variety of roles with differing degrees of success: as entrepreneur, bringing, in its words, 'the best entertainment from around the world'; as a pioneer in promoting developments in the performing arts in Australia; and as a promoter of serious works with an Australian content, and of more popular Australian productions of hit shows from New York and London. However, with changes in theatre funding and the advent of new production organizations, the Trust was left with no role to fill, and it ceased functioning in the 1990s.
MICHAEL MORLEY

Austria At the beginning of the twentieth century Austrian theatre's outstanding figures were members of the Young Vienna group of artists, the playwrights Hermann Bahr, ARTHUR SCHNITZLER and HUGO VON HOF-MANNSTAHL. With the Austrian director MAX REIN-HARDT, one of the towering figures of the modern European theatre, Hofmannstahl founded the Salzburg Festival, which became a leading international theatrical gathering after the First World War. The fall of the Austro-Hungarian Empire, however, and later the rise of Nazism, saw the development of Austrian drama increasingly intertwined with that of Germany (*see* GERMAN-LANGUAGE DRAMA). Austria nevertheless continued to make its own distinctive contribution. Playwrights OSCAR KOKOSCHKA, ARNOLT BRONNEN and FRANZ WERFEL were early exponents of EXPRESSIONISM. Actors such as FRITZ KORTNER, Werner Krauss and Max Pallenberg earned reputations in both Germany and Austria, particularly at the Vienna Burgtheater, a major European theatre revitalized briefly under playwright and director Anton Wildgans (1881–1932). Alongside the peasant and folk plays of Richard Billinger (1890–1965) and Max Mell (1882–1971), and the historical works of writers like Alexander Lernet-Holenia (1897–1976) and Richard Beer-Hoffman (1866–1945, another member of the Young Vienna group), there were plays with a more modern sensibility by Franz Csokor (1885–1969), KARL KRAUS, FERDINAND BRUCKNER and the Hungarian ODÖN VON HORVÁTH, who lived and worked in Austria. Nazism dispersed many of these artists, like the writers STEFAN ZWEIG and FRITZ HOCHWÄLDER, and it took several years for Austrian theatre to recover after the Second World War. Director Walter Felsenstein stayed in Germany, while BERTOLD VIERTEL returned to Austria after making his mark in Germany to direct the rebuilt Burgtheater in 1951, but soon a new generation focused on another Vienna Group were challenging the postwar orthodoxy. Konrad Bayer (1932–64) led the way by reviving the traditional folk figure Kasperl in grim farces that set the tone for the harsh worlds of plays by PETER HANDKE and WOLFGANG BAUER. A different kind of alienation is at work in the other major Austrian playwright of the postwar years, THOMAS BERNHARD, whose ironic, symphonic pieces have often caused offence at home. Other writers of note include George Tabori, Werner Schwab (b. 1958) and the Nobel Prize winner Elias Canetti (1905–94), whose plays from an earlier period, such as *The Marriage* (written 1932), excited interest in a new generation. CHARLES LONDON

avant-garde Term applied since the end of the nineteenth century to theatre as well as other arts and practitioners involved in introducing original and experimental ideas, forms and techniques. Examples range from JARRY and APOLLINAIRE to CAGE and ROBERT WILSON. MARVIN CARLSON
See also EXPERIMENTAL THEATRE; MODERNISM; PERFORMANCE ART.

B. Cardullo and R. Knopf, eds, *Theater of the Avant-Garde 1890–1950: A Critical Anthology* (2001).
C. Innes, *Avant Garde Theatre, 1892–1992* (1993)

Avignon Festival Founded by JEAN VILAR in 1947, as part of the decentralizing of French theatre. Vilar, director of the THÉÂTRE NATIONAL POPULAIRE (1951–63), continued to develop the Festival until his death in 1971. It runs when French theatres are closed for the month of July – originally it was a week – and is a major showcase and inspiration for French and international theatre, encouraging experimental use of unorthodox spaces. Major directors or companies to appear include the LIVING THEATER, with *Paradise Now* (1968), ROBERT WILSON, with *Einstein on the Beach* (1976), TADEUSZ KANTOR, with *Qu'ils crèvent les artistes* (*Let the Artists Die*, 1985) and PETER BROOK, with *Mahabharata* (1985).
ANNA MCMULLAN
See also FESTIVALS.

awards and prizes Theatre is swamped with prizes, some designed to boost sales of current productions, some awarded in genuine tribute – or a mix of both. At one end of the financial and status scale is the international Nobel Prize, inaugurated in 1901 by gunpowder manufacturer Alfred Nobel and awarded annually for a body of work in six categories, including literature which embraces drama. Several playwrights have received this prestigious honour, including BJØRNST JERNE BJØRNSON (1903), JOSÉ ECHEGARAY (1904), MAURICE MAETERLINCK (1911), GERHART HAUPTMANN (1912), RABINDRANATH TAGORE (1913), ROMAIN ROLLAND (1915), Knut Hamsun (1920), W. B. YEATS (1923), GEORGE BERNARD SHAW (1925), JOHN GALSWORTHY (1932), LUIGI PIRANDELLO (1934), EUGENE O'NEILL (1936), T. S. ELIOT (1948), PÄR LAGERKVIST (1951), ALBERT CAMUS (1957), SAMUEL BECKETT (1969),

Elias Canetti (1981), WOLE SOYINKA (1986), DEREK WAL-COTT (1992) and DARIO FO (1997). SARTRE was awarded it in 1964 but turned it down.

In America, among the 50 or so significant awards, several have come to prominence: the Pulitzer Prize was founded by Joseph Pulitzer to honour an original American play and first awarded in 1918; dissatisfaction with the Pulitzer led to the creation of the New York Drama Critics' Awards in 1935; the Tony awards, named after ANTOINETTE PERRY, were established in 1947 to mark distinguished achievement. In Britain, the Evening Standard awards were inaugurated in 1955 and the LAURENCE OLIVIER awards in 1976 (as the Society of West End Theatre awards; the name changed in 1984).

CHARLES LONDON

Axelrod, George (b. New York, 9 June 1922) Playwright, director and producer. In the 1950s he wrote three superior comedies: *The Seven Year Itch* (1952), *Will Success Spoil Rock Hunter?* (1955) and *Goodbye, Charlie* (1959), also directing the last two. He sometimes directed and co-produced the plays of others, but by the mid-1960s had largely retired from theatre.

GERALD BORDMAN

Ayckbourn, Alan (b. London, 12 April 1939) Playwright and director. Ayckbourn is a prolific writer of over 50 farces and comedies, an acute commentator on suburban mores and one of the most successful dramatists now writing. Possibly because of this popularity, and because his writing is always 'accessible', he is sometimes under-rated as a playwright and dismissed as 'merely' an entertainer. Yet he merits his many commissions as writer and director from the ROYAL NATIONAL THEATRE, and the comparisons that have been made between his work and that of COWARD and RATTIGAN. Moreover, although he has, so far, invariably written about English suburban life, his plays have been successful in many countries.

He left school at 17 and has worked in the theatre ever since, apart from a brief spell as a BBC radio drama producer. His first work was as actor and assistant stage manager in DONALD WOLFIT's company. Later, he joined STEPHEN JOSEPH's company in Scarborough; after other work and on Joseph's death, he became director of productions at the Library Theatre, Scarborough and later artistic director of the Stephen Joseph Theatre in the same town, to which post he has remained committed. Most of his plays have been premièred in Scarborough.

Ayckbourn claims that he is a 'lazy' writer who procrastinates a lot, and that each of his plays is written to a deadline, over a short intensive period of four or five days. The rest of the year he concentrates on directing (a role in which his sense of humour and patience, combined with discipline, wins approval from actors). His plays are regularly built upon a dazzling *coup de théâtre*. Thus *The Norman Conquests* (1973), actually a trilogy, allows us to observe the same events from three locations (garden, sitting room and dining room). *Way Upstream* (1981) brings a cabin cruiser (and section of a river) on stage. Several plays allow us to see what is happening in two locations. The set for *How the Other Half Loves* (1969) contrives to represent living rooms in two different houses at the same time. *Bedroom Farce* (1975) brings three bedrooms on stage. Perhaps the most intricately structured of his plays is *Intimate Exchanges* (1982) which has 16 possible variations resulting from a series of encounters, each of which can go one of two ways. All the characters are played by just two actors.

Although his plays are typically concerned with parochial, domestic or marital disasters, in the 1970s they were always light in tone; but in the late 1980s a darker mood began to dominate. In *Woman in Mind* (1985), domestic farce turns to tragedy as the wife suffers a breakdown. *A Small Family Business* (1987), while a very funny comedy, also explores the corruption and dissembling on which the eponymous business has been built. Indeed, Ayckbourn has regularly demonstrated his ability to present domestic or personal agony in a way that induces laughter in his audiences – yet his is not a THEATRE OF CRUELTY – more what one critic (MICHAEL BILLINGTON) has called a 'theatre of recognition' in which the British theatregoing classes (i.e. the middle classes) can recognize themselves and their problems. All this is achieved within the structure and conventions of farce – for whatever theatrical tricks Ayckbourn chooses to play, he relies heavily on 'old-fashioned' dramatic values such as clarity of plot, narrative thrust and shape. He may not be overtly political, but he is both a satirist and a moralist.

Ayckbourn has also written plays for children, and has collaborated on a number of revues and musicals, including *Jeeves* (1975) with ANDREW LLOYD WEBBER. Other plays include *Relatively Speaking* (originally *Meet My Father*, 1965), *Time and Time Again* (1971), *Absurd Person Singular* (1972), *Joking Apart* (1978), *Sisterly Feelings* (1979), *Henceforward . . .* (1987), *Man of the Moment* (1988), *The Revengers' Comedies* (a two-part play, 1989), *Wildest Dreams* (1991), *Communicating Doors* (1994), the linked plays *House* and *Garden* (both 1999), and *Whenever* (2000). Ayckbourn was knighted in 1996.

DAVID SELF

Paul Allen, *Alan Ayckbourn: Grinning at the Edge* (2001).
Michael Billington, *Alan Ayckbourn* (1983)

Ian Watson, *Conversations with Ayckbourn*, 2nd edn (1988)

Ayers, Lemuel (b. New York, 22 Jan. 1915; d. New York, 14 Aug. 1955) Set and costume designer. After studying at Princeton and Iowa he began designing professionally in 1939. Recognition came when he created the costumes for the 1941 revival of *Macbeth* with MAURICE EVANS and JUDITH ANDERSON. However, although he continued to design clothes, his forte proved to be settings which required a feeling of immense spaciousness within the constricting confines of a proscenium. Among his memorable settings were those for *Angel Street* (1941), *Oklahoma!* (1943), *Kiss Me, Kate* (1948), *Kismet* (1953) and *The Pajama Game* (1954). He also sometimes served as co-producer.

GERALD BORDMAN

Aylmer[-Jones], Felix [Edward] (b. Corsham, Wilts, 21 Feb. 1889; d. Sussex, 2 Sept. 1979) Actor. His long and distinguished career on the West End stage (starting with SEYMOUR HICKS in 1911) and in British films never merited stardom but consistently earned critical praise. A commanding character actor, he was typically cast by OLIVIER as Polonius in his film of *Hamlet* (1948). Aylmer earned distinction off the stage as longtime president of British Actors' Equity Association and vice-president of the Royal Academy of Dramatic Art. He was knighted in 1965. IAN BEVAN

Aymé, Marcel (b. Joigny, France, 28 March 1902; d. Paris, 14 Oct. 1967) Playwright, novelist and short-story writer. Aymé's plays are mainly satires, attacking the corruption and hypocrisy of the contemporary political and judicial systems. Plays include *Lucienne et le boucher* ('Lucienne and the butcher', 1948), *Clérambard* (1950, which gave him an international reputation) and *La Tête des autres* ('Others' heads', 1952).

ANNA MCMULLAN

Dorothy Brodin, *Marcel Aymé* (1968)

Azerbaijan *see* SOVIET UNION

B

Babe, Thomas (b. Buffalo, NY, 13 March 1941) Playwright. His plays show scenes of tortured intimacy against violent moments of historical conflict. In *A Prayer for My Daughter* (1977), a policeman ignores calls from his suicidal daughter to interrogate a suspect for whom he develops a painful erotic attraction. Other plays include *Buried Inside Extra* (1983), *Planet Fires* (1984), *Demon Wine* (1989) and *Born Every Minute* (1997). He also directs. DAN REBELLATO

Babel, Isaak [Emmanuilovich] (b. Odessa, Russia, 13 July 1894; d. Moscow, 27 July 1940) Writer and playwright. Many of his best stories, particularly his *Odessa Tales* (1921–4), and his film script *Benya Krik* (1926), deal with his birthplace, the Jewish quarter, and the Odessa underworld. His first play, *Zakat* ('Sunset', 1928) also deals with the Krik family and his second, *Marya*, went into rehearsal in 1935, but two simultaneous productions were stopped by the Stalinist authorities. CHRISTOPHER HAMPTON adapted the play for the ROYAL COURT (1967). Babel was arrested in 1939, and some of his unpublished manuscripts, seized by the secret police, have still to be found. He was posthumously 'rehabilitated' in 1957 with a one-volume edition of his works, introduced by the journalist, critic and poet Ilya Ehrenburg. VERA GOTTLIEB

Bacon, Frank (b. Marysville, Calif., 16 Jan. 1864; d. Chicago, 19 Nov. 1922) Actor and playwright. Bacon worked as a journalist and photographer before making his belated stage debut in San Jose, California, in 1890. He remained in stock there for 17 years. Moving to New York, he spent time in lesser roles on Broadway or in more important assignments in touring companies before his striking success as the bibulous,

prevaricating Lightnin' Bill Jones in *Lightnin'* (1918), which he co-wrote with Winchell Smith. The play became the longest-running American show up to its day. He played the role more than 2,000 times and was touring with it when he died. GERALD BORDMAN

Baddeley, Angela *see* BADDELLEY, HERMIONE

Baddeley [Clinton-Baddeley], Hermione (b. Broseley, Shropshire, 13 Nov. 1906; d. Los Angeles, 19 Aug. 1986) Actress. Made her first stage appearance in 1918 and achieved success in *The Likes of Her* (1923). Although a notable dramatic actress, she also found fame in REVUES, including *The Punch Bowl* (1924), *On with the Dance* (1925) and *The Little Revue* (1939), and played with HERMIONE GINGOLD in *Rise Above It* (1941), *Sky High* (1942) and *Fallen Angels* (1949). She had an extensive film and television career, and published an autobiography, *The Unsinkable Hermione Baddeley* (1984). Her sister Angela (1904–76) married the director GLEN BYAM SHAW and was also an actress. REXTON S. BUNNETT

Badel, Alan [Firman] (b. Rusholme, nr Manchester, 11 Sept. 1923; d. London, 19 March 1982) Actor, noted for his compelling stage presence, who first appeared in Oxford (1940) and made his London debut in 1941 before joining the Parachute Regiment and appearing with the army play unit. From 1947 he played in the major companies (BIRMINGHAM REPERTORY, STRATFORD-UPON-AVON, OLD VIC) in acclaimed roles, including the Fool in *King Lear* (1949), Romeo (1952) and Hamlet (1956). In 1957 he directed and performed in HOCHHUTH's *The Public Prosecutor*. Other notable performances were in *Ulysses in Night-Town* (which he helped produce, 1959), *Man and Superman*

(1965), *Othello* (Oxford, 1970), *Kean* (Oxford, 1970; London, 1971) and *Richard III* (1949, 1976). A grand actor who went out of fashion, he made many television and film appearances. D. KEITH PEACOCK

Bagnold, Enid [Lady Roderick Jones] (b. Rochester, Kent, 27 Oct. 1889; d. London, 31 March 1981) Writer, artist and playwright. She studied painting with Walter Sickert and spent many years working in France and America. Her novel *Serena Blandish* was dramatized in the United States by S. N. BEHRMAN in 1929 and in 1938 VIVIEN LEIGH took the lead in the London production. Other plays include *Lottie Dundass* (1943), *National Velvet* (1946), adapted from her novel and made into a best-selling film starring Elizabeth Taylor, and *The Chalk Garden* (1955), her most successful play. Her *Autobiography* appeared in 1986. MAGGIE GALE

Bahamas *see* CARIBBEAN

Baker, Bobby *see* FOOD AND DRINK

Baker, George Pierce (b. Providence, RI, 4 April 1866; d. New York, 6 Jan. 1935) Educator. After graduation from Harvard University he joined the English department in 1888 as an instructor. In 1905 he inaugurated English 47, a course in playwriting which in 1912 led to his founding of the famous Workshop 47, a forum for staging the plays written under his tutelage. Baker's work at Harvard attracted many talented young people who in time became world-famous (e.g. EUGENE O'NEILL, PHILIP BARRY, SIDNEY HOWARD). By 1925, Baker was considered too unorthodox for his old school and he moved to Yale, where he headed that university's first department of drama until his retirement eight years later. Scholar and practical man of the theatre, Baker had an enormous influence abroad as well as in his own country. His book on the craft of playwriting, *Dramatic Technique* (1919), became a classic. JOSEPH M. DIAZ

W. Kinne, *George Pierce Baker and the American Theater* (1954)

Baker, [Freda] Josephine [McDonald] (b. St Louis, Mo., 3 June 1906; d. Paris, 12 April 1975) Singer and dancer who left a poor, unhappy home in her teens, joined a touring show and became a member of the black American company which opened in Paris as *La Revue Nègre* (1925). Her explosive dance, which she performed clad only in a few pink feathers, was the unexpected hit of the show. Word went out that Baker was *chic*, and she was lionized by the social, artistic and political elite. Soon she was dancing at the FOLIES-BERGÈRE in a string of bananas, and by the end of 1926

she had her own nightclub. Throughout the 1930s she was a major star in Parisian revues, tried her hand – not altogether unsuccessfully – at operetta in a version of Offenbach's *La Créole* and made several films. Her life during the Second World War was something of a mystery, but was rewarded by the French government with the Légion d'honneur and Rosette of the Resistance. She retired from the stage in 1956 to work with orphans, the cost of which forced her back to performing in 1975, in a revue based on her own life. IAN BEVAN

See also CHOREOGRAPHY; DANCE; MOVEMENT, DANCE AND DRAMA.

Bryan Hammond and Patrick O'Connor, *Josephine Baker* (1988)

Lynn Haney, *Naked at the Feast: The Biography of Josephine Baker* (1981)

Ean Wood, *The Josephine Baker Story* (2000)

Bakst [Rozenberg], Leon [Lev Samoilovich] (b. Grodno, Russia, 27 Jan. 1866; d. Paris, 27 Dec. 1924) Painter, graphic artist and costume and set designer. He was a leading member of the World of Art group with BENOIS and emigrated to France in 1909. Inspired by ancient Greek ceramics and Persian miniatures, Bakst acquired fame as one of the outstanding and most influential designers with DIAGHILEV's Ballets Russes, designing sets and costumes for productions which included Stravinsky's *The Firebird* (1910) and Debussy's *L'Après-midi d'un faune* (1912). He was noted for his use of deep colours, clear line and shape, and sense of movement. NICK WORRALL

See also COSTUME DESIGN; FASHION.

Charles Spencer, *Leon Bakst* (1973)

Balanchine, George [Georgi Melitonovich Balanchivadze] (b. St Petersburg, Russia, 22 Jan. 1904; d. New York, 30 April 1983) Choreographer. He studied at the Imperial Theatre School, St Petersburg, and performed with DIAGHILEV's Ballets Russes before accepting an invitation to the United States in 1933 to establish his own company, first American Ballet and then the New York City Ballet, where he created a distinctive choreography, moving ballet away from traditional story-telling to plotless or abstract dance that presents the essence of music in movement. His collaborations with IGOR STRAVINSKY included *Apollo* (1928) and *Agon* (1957). On Broadway he was less revolutionary, although he did create the first ballet to be a dramatic part of a musical with 'Slaughter on Tenth Avenue' in *On Your Toes* (1936); among the other 15 musicals he choreographed are *I Married an Angel* (1938), *The Boys from Syracuse* (1938), *Cabin in the Sky* (1940), *Song of Norway* (1944) and *Where's Charley?* (1948). He also staged an elephant ballet for a circus

and dances for the AMERICAN SHAKESPEARE FESTIVAL.
DAVID STAINES

See also CHOREOGRAPHY; DANCE.

Bernard Taper, *Balanchine: A Biography* (1974)

Baldwin, James [Arthur] (b. Harlem, New York, 2 Aug. 1924; d. St Paul de Vence, France, 1 Dec. 1987) Activist, novelist, essayist and playwright. A major spokesman in the 1960s civil rights struggle, he left Harlem to find independence denied him at home because of white bigotry, anti-homosexual sentiment and his tyrannical minister stepfather. He became the leading black writer of his time, though he is least celebrated as a dramatist. He wrote four plays; neither *Blues for Mr Charlie* (1964; college production 1955) nor *The Amen Corner* (1965) was a BROADWAY success, yet both continued to be widely read, and a production of the latter at the Tricycle Theatre, London (1987, the first English non-musical all-black production in the WEST END) shifted received opinion. LOWELL SWORTZELL

Bali *see* EASTERN THEATRE, ITS INFLUENCE ON THE WEST; SOUTH-EAST ASIA

Ball, William (b. Chicago, 29 April 1931; d. Hollywood, 30 July 1991) Actor and director. After a successful career as an actor, designer and director in regional theatres across the United States he settled in New York, but became frustrated with his working conditions after directing at the LINCOLN CENTER. He decided to found a company that was not beholden to commercial success, a combination of training centre and performing ensemble with a permanent acting company. In 1965 he started the AMERICAN CONSERVATORY THEATER in Pittsburgh, Pennsylvania, in conjunction with his alma mater, Carnegie Mellon University, and the Pittsburgh Playhouse. Squabbles among the three entities led to the company's departure and it ended up in SAN FRANCISCO. Under Ball, ACT became one of the country's most successful regional theatres, winning a 1979 Tony award for its contribution to repertory performance and actor training. Always a teacher, in *A Sense of Direction* (1984) Ball offers his insight into the craft of directing. The somewhat dictatorial but flamboyant Ball left ACT in 1986 over complaints that he had mismanaged funds. He worked in Los Angeles and committed suicide in 1991.
DAVID A. WILLIAMS

Ballard [Goldsborough], Lucinda [Davis] (b. New Orleans, 3 April 1906; d. New York, 19 Aug. 1993) Costume designer. Having studied in both New York and France, she began her professional career on Broadway in 1937. Although she occasionally worked on both settings and costumes, it was as a clothing designer that she earned wide renown. Her creations were seen in such major Broadway successes as *I Remember Mama* (1944), *The Glass Menagerie* (1945), *Annie Get Your Gun* (1946), *The Dark at the Top of the Stairs* (1957) and *The Sound of Music* (1959). She also created the once-famous murals at New York's Stage Door Canteen during the Second World War.
GERALD BORDMAN

ballet *see* DANCE

Banbury, Frith [Frederick Harold] (b. Plymouth, 4 May 1912) Actor and director. Banbury spent 14 years as an actor, under directors like NORMAN MARSHALL and TYRONE GUTHRIE, before taking over a production at the Royal Academy of Dramatic Art, which set him on a hugely successful directing career lasting over 40 years, working with the finest actors of his generation, including EDITH EVANS, PAUL SCOFIELD, SYBIL THORNDIKE and VANESSA REDGRAVE, whom he directed in her professional debut. He discovered WYNYARD BROWNE and directed *Dark Summer* (1947), commissioning and directing his subsequent plays. Associated with the pre-OSBORNE generation, Banbury's crisp and clipped directing style suited the plays he championed, which included *Waters of the Moon* (1950), *The Pink Room* and *The Deep Blue Sea* (1951), *Marching Song* (1953), *Moon on a Rainbow Shawl* (1957) and *Flowering Cherry* (1958). DAN REBELLATO

Charles Duff, *The Lost Summer: The Heyday of the West End* (1995)

Bancroft, Squire (b. Surrey, 14 May 1841; d. London, 19 April 1926) and **Marie (Effie) Wilton** (b. Glocs, 12 Jan. 1839; d. Folkestone, 22 May 1921) Husband and wife team of actor–managers; they virtually retired in 1885, but their influence on early twentieth-century theatre was considerable. In their long managerial and acting careers at London's Prince of Wales Theatre (1865–80) and Haymarket (1880–5) they introduced many changes in styles of acting, content and presentation which carried forward into the Edwardian era. In complete contrast with the full-blooded melodramas of the day, they featured domestic comedies (notably the plays of T. W. Robertson, 1829–71, which made their reputations and carried their influence to New York). The Bancrofts favoured restrained acting, played in realistic and well-furnished domestic settings, and carefully rehearsed their casts to achieve an ensemble style that set a new standard in the British theatre. Together they wrote *The Bancrofts: Recollections of Sixty Years* (1909), and Squire on his own wrote *Empty Chairs* (1925). Bancroft was knighted in 1897 for his work in the theatre, an honour which his wife justly said 'we have both earned'. IAN BEVAN

Bandele[-Thomas], 'Biyi (b. Kafanchan, Nigeria, 13 Oct. 1967) Playwright. Living and working in Britain, he established himself with his first plays, *Marching for Fausa* (1993), *Resurrections in the Season of the Longest Drought* (1994) and *Two Horsemen* (1994), in each of which his African background and concerns are evident in poetic and satirically humorous dramas of ethical and moral questioning. He has adapted Chinua Achebe's *Things Fall Apart* (1997), *Rasselas* by Samuel Johnson (1997) and Aphra Behn's *Oroonoko* (1999).
CHARLES LONDON

Bangladesh Drama in Bangladesh, in both its folk and modern forms, shares a common tradition with adjoining Bengali-speaking areas of INDIA. Chief among the former is *jatra*, which generally treats historical and legendary subjects in a rhetorical manner and includes erotic interludes. Since the 1960s *jatra* and cinema have influenced each other. Modern theatre was a provincial offshoot of the Calcutta stage till 1947, when the region became East Pakistan. Despite Pakistan's repressive climate – one play was passed by the censors on condition 'that no girls participate' – amateur theatres were active, as were playwrights like the politically conscious Shawkat Osman and Munir Choudhury, and the more experimental Syed Waliullah. Bangladesh's independence in 1971 revitalized drama. Theatre groups proliferated and began regular productions, mainly in Dhaka. Translations and adaptations proved as popular as original plays, for which the war of independence with PAKISTAN, the hopes it engendered and the disillusionment that followed provided ample subject-matter. The influence of EPIC THEATRE and the THEATRE OF THE ABSURD were absorbed and experiments made in blending techniques from Western and Eastern traditions. The impact of radical politics led some groups to experiment with STREET THEATRE. Among prominent post-independence theatre groups are Nagorik, Dhaka Theatre, Theatre Aranyak and Padatik; among playwrights, Sayeed Ahmed, Syed Shamsul Huq, Mumtazuddin Ahmed and Saleem Al Deen. KAISER HAQ

Majumdar Ramendu, ed., *Bangladesher Natyacharcha* ('Drama in Bangladesh') (1986)

Bankhead, Tallulah [Brockman] (b. Huntsville, Ala., 31 Jan. 1902; d. New York, 12 Dec. 1968) Actress who used her family's influence (her uncle was a US Senator, her father a member of the House of Representatives) to get her first part on Broadway in 1918 but did not achieve any great theatrical success until she went to England in 1922. She stayed here for eight years, developed a fanatic following among the so-called 'gallery girls' (several of whom she remembered in her will), and became both a box-office star and a social figure seldom absent from the gossip columns. This transformation from actress into personality earned her considerable attention but scant critical respect when she returned to the American stage in 1933. However, she had both artistic and commercial success when she created the role of Regina Giddens in LILLIAN HELLMAN's *The Little Foxes* (1939) and as Sabina in THORNTON WILDER's *The Skin of Our Teeth* (1942). So many anecdotes, most of them concentrating on her free-wheeling sex life, have been told about her that they have obscured her true worth as an actress, but a fine testimony to her talent remains in the Alfred Hitchcock film *Lifeboat* (1944). An autobiography, *Tallulah*, appeared in 1952. IAN BEVAN

David Bret, *Tallulah Bankhead* (1996)

Banks, Leslie [James] (b. Liverpool, 9 June 1890; d. London, 21 April 1952) Actor, producer and director. Banks appeared in only a few productions before the First World War, during which he suffered permanent facial scarring. After the war he worked in Birmingham and then in Hampstead before securing a West End engagement in 1921. A long series of successful productions followed, notably opposite EDITH EVANS in *The Taming of the Shrew* (1937); as the schoolmaster hero in James Hilton's *Goodbye Mr Chips* (1938); and as the Duke in Patrick Hamilton's *Duke of Darkness* (1942). Banks also had some success as a producer, particularly of plays in which he acted, and he starred in a string of British films during the 1930s and 1940s.
ANDREW SOLWAY

Baraka, Imamu Amiri [Everett LeRoi Jones] (b. Newark, NJ, 7 Oct. 1934) Playwright, novelist and poet, who changed his name as he embraced a revolutionary viewpoint and the Muslim faith. His use of searing language, myth and ritual in his depiction of black–white relationships is seen in *The Toilet* (1964), *The Slave* (1964) and *Dutchman* (1964); the last of these powerfully dramatizes a ritual encounter between a white woman and a black man in a subway car. Baraka founded the Black Arts Repertory Theatre and School in Harlem and the black separatist Spirit House in Newark during the mid-1960s. His growing radical attitude is reflected in *Death of Malcolm X* (1965), *Home on the Range* (1967) and *Slave Ship* (1969). Other works include the AGITPROP piece *The Motion of History* (1977) and *Bumpy: A Bopera* (1993). He has written *The Autobiography of LeRoi Jones/Amiri Baraka* (1997). JANE HOUSE

Kimberly W. Benston, *Baraka: The Renegade and the Mask (1976)*

Lloyd W. Brown, *Amiri Baraka* (1980)

Theodore Hudson, *From LeRoi Jones to Amiri Baraka: The Literary Works (1973)*

Weiner Souors, *Armiri Baraka/LeRoi Jones: The Quest for a Populist Modernism* (1978)

Barba, Eugenio (b. Brindisi, Italy, 29 Oct. 1936) Director and theorist. After university he attended the directors' school in Warsaw and then spent three years at GROTOWSKI's theatre in Opole, Poland. Inspired by this experience, he founded his own international company, the ODIN TEATRET, in Oslo in 1964. The company moved to Holstbro, Denmark, in 1966. Out of the intense work of this tightly disciplined community, which performed only when it was ready and often by preference to small audiences, he developed the notion of THIRD THEATRE to describe the activity of groups like his, in the main itinerant and comprising practitioners dedicated to creating theatre outside both the commercial theatre and the subsidized art theatre centred on the word and the director. In 1979 Barba founded at Holstbro the International Institute of THEATRE ANTHROPOLOGY to bring together those in the East and the West who were working along similar lines. As well as contributing to and assembling Grotowski's book *Towards a Poor Theatre*, Barba has written extensively on his ideas. Publications include *The Floating Islands* (1984), *Beyond the Floating Islands* (1986), *A Dictionary of Theatre Anthropology* (with Nicola Savarese, 1991) and *The Paper Canoe* (1994).

COLIN CHAMBERS

Barbados *see* CARIBBEAN

Barbican Theatre *see* ARCHITECTURE; DESIGN; ROYAL SHAKESPEARE COMPANY

Barker, Harley Granville *see* GRANVILLE BARKER, HARLEY

Barker, Howard (b. London, 28 June 1946) Playwright whose prolific output includes cartoon attacks on England's power-structure (*Claw*, 1974) and mordant twentieth-century chronicles (*No End of Blame*, 1981). Under the Thatcher governments, Barker took historical upheavals from Troy to the Bastille as metaphors for current conflicts over ideology, militarism, gender and art (*The Castle*, 1985). Barker's 'theatre of catastrophe' is grotesque and violent, the language dense and obscene, the characters obsessive. Power is inseparable from sexual hunger; men mutilate the body and the state; but the debased survive. Barker rejects simple polemics. He shows the failure of Marxism and liberal democracy to build justice on Europe's battlefields. Other plays include *Stripwell* (1975), *Fair Slaughter* (1977), *The Hang of the Gaol* (1978), *Victory* (1983) and *Scenes from an Execution* (radio 1984, stage 1990). In 1987 the Wrestling School was founded to perform his plays, which, subsequently, focused even more on an individual truth (e.g. *The Last Supper*, 1988; *Seven Years*, 1989). A volume of essays, *Arguments for a Theatre*, appeared in 1989. TONY HOWARD

Charles Lamb, *Howard Barker's Theatre of Seduction* (1998)

Ian David Rabey, *Howard Barker: Politics and Desire* (1989)

Barlach, Ernst [Henrich] (b. Wedel, nr Hamburg, Germany, 2 January 1870, d. Güstrow, Germany, 25 Oct. 1938) Sculptor, novelist and playwright. His plays were staged in Berlin during the Weimar Republic by EXPRESSIONIST directors, notably Jürgen Fehling – *Der arme Vetter* ('The poor cousin', 1919); *Der blaue Boll* (*The Blue Boll*, 1929) – and LEOPOLD JESSNER – *Die echten Sedemunds* (*The Genuine Sedemunds*, 1920). Banned by the Nazis, his plays were revived in 1956. JUDY MEEWEZEN

Bernard R. Anderson, *Ernst Barlach* (1967)

Kent W. Hooper, *Ernst Barlach's Literary and Visual Art: The Issue of Multiple Talent* (1987)

Alfred Werner, *Barlach: His Life and Work* (1966)

Barnes, Clive [Alexander] (b. London, 13 May 1927) Theatre and dance critic. Barnes began his career writing dance criticism for *Dance and Dancers* in 1950, and went on to write for a number of publications on theatre, music, film and dance. In 1965 he moved to the United States, where he held the coveted post of *New York Times* drama critic from 1967 to 1977 and then became the dance and drama critic for the tabloid *New York Post*. Even if he is not always consistent, Barnes is known for his readable style and for striving to champion what seems to be new. THOMAS F. CONNOLLY

Barnes, Kenneth *see* DRAMA SCHOOLS; VAN BRUGH, VIOLET

Barnes, Peter (b. London, 10 Jan. 1931) Playwright. After his first play, the short, anticolonial *Sclerosis* (1965), Barnes' second, *The Ruling Class* (1968), which used a variety of devices (including slapstick, song and dance) to attack Toryism and class privilege, was lauded by the critics as 'a pivotal play' (Ronald Bryden) and equated by others with the best of BECKETT, OSBORNE and PINTER. Later work – *The Bewitched*

(1974), *Laughter!* (1978) – has had rather more mixed notices, although his Black Death play *Red Noses* (1985) was more widely admired. Besides his own plays, he has edited and adapted many classics, notably works by WEDEKIND, Jonson and FEYDEAU. For radio, he has written three much-praised series of exquisite miniature dramas, *Barnes' People* (1981, 1984, 1986), each remarkable for its subtle characterization and originality. DAVID SELF

B. F. Dukore, *Barnestorm: The Plays of Peter Barnes* (1995)

Barnes Theatre A small cinema in south-west London, converted into a theatre by Philip Ridgeway in 1925. Its brief but surprisingly influential history was remarkable for productions of Russian plays by KOMISSARZHEVSKY, particularly *Uncle Vanya* (with Jean Forbes-Robertson), *Three Sisters* (with JOHN GIELGUD), *The Government Inspector* (with CHARLES LAUGHTON) and *The Cherry Orchard* all in 1926, after which it reverted to being a cinema. G. ROWELL

Barr [Baer], Richard [Alphonse] (b. Washington DC, 6 Sept. 1917; d. New York, 9 Jan. 1989) Producer. A former actor (with the MERCURY THEATER) and director, he began making a name as a producer in the 1950s (with e.g. RUTH DRAPER's SOLO SHOWS of 1954 and 1956), and came to prominence with Clinton Wilder (1920–86) as producer of the early plays of EDWARD ALBEE, *The Zoo Story* (1960), *The Death of Bessie Smith* (1961) and *The American Dream* (1961). Barr's 1962 production of Albee's *Who's Afraid of Virginia Woolf?* established the practice of preview performances in New York. Barr was a great supporter of new playwriting, and produced early works by AMIRI BARAKA, LANFORD WILSON, TERRENCE MCNALLY, JOHN GUARE and A. R. GURNEY. Barr was also a great advocate of experimental theatre, renting the Cherry Lane Theatre in the early 1960s and presenting a repertory season of surrealist plays. President of the League of American Theatres for 21 years, he was responsible for the American premières of works by EUGENE IONESCO and SAMUEL BECKETT. LAURIE WOLF

Barratt, Watson (b. Salt Lake City, Utah, 27 June 1884; d. New York, 6 July 1962) Set designer. After serving a brief apprenticeship, he took employment with the SHUBERTS and quickly became their major set designer, turning out scenery for dozens of productions in the busy years of the 1920s and for many later mountings. His work, including that for *Blossom Time* (1921) and *The Student Prince* (1924), was generally deemed adequate but undistinguished. GERALD BORDMAN

Barrault, Jean-Louis (b. Le Vésinet, France, 8 Sept. 1910; d. Paris, 22 Jan. 1994) Actor, director and manager. CHARLES DULLIN introduced him to the Ecole de l'Atelier, where his aquiline profile well fitted Barrault for romantic juvenile leads. During this time he studied mime with ETIENNE DECROUX, collaborated with writers and painters like Prévert and BRETON, and assisted ANTONIN ARTAUD, who became a friend and major influence on his work and his embracing of TOTAL THEATRE. Barrault directed three adaptations in this vein: one based on Faulkner's *As I Lay Dying* (1935); *Numance* (1937), from Cervantes; and *La Faim* ('Hunger') from the novel by Knut Hamsun. He also played Molière, varying his classical roles with romantic parts and mime. During the war he acted and directed at the COMÉDIE-FRANÇAISE under JACQUES COPEAU (e.g. playing the lead in *Hamlet* and *Le Cid*, 1940). In 1946 his partnership with MADELEINE RENAUD produced the privately run Compagnie Renaud–Barrault which played at the Marigny in Paris (1946–56), opening with GIDE's translation of *Hamlet*, and toured the provinces and abroad. The repertoire was wide, containing both *The Oresteia* (1955) and Kafka's *The Trial* (1947), which he adapted with Gide. The range extended from FEYDEAU's *Occupe-toi d'Amélie* (1948) and Offenbach's *La Vie parisienne* (1959) to works by the playwright with whom he was chiefly associated, CLAUDEL (*Le Soulier de satin*, 1958, already produced in 1943; *Partage de midi*, 1948; and *Christophe Colombe*, 1953).

In 1959 Barrault became the director of the state-subsidized ODÉON-Théâtre de France, the second national theatre. Notable early productions included Claudel's *Tête d'or* (1959) and IONESCO's *Rhinocéros* (1960). In 1968 he was dismissed by the Minister of Culture, André Malraux, for allowing his theatre to be used as a centre for student political activity. His natural buoyancy and unquenchable energy soon found fresh outlets. He created *Rabelais* (1968) and played it later in London with a stage erected over the orchestra stalls. In 1974 he created the Théâtre d'Orsay using a tent inside a disused station, moving in 1981 to the Théâtre du Rond-Point, which he transformed from on old skating rink. He was also to realize his dream of founding a Maison Internationale du Théâtre.

An uncompromising and enterprising administrator, he experimented in all dramatic fields and become the dominant figure in postwar French theatre, as well as one of the major figures of twentieth-century theatre. In films, his most famous role was the mime in Marcel Carné's *Les Enfants du paradis* (1944). He has published his *Reflections on the Theatre* (1949), *New Reflections on the Theatre* (1959), and two autobiographical books:

Journal de bord (1961) and *Souvenirs pour demain* (1972).
TERRY HODGSON

J. Chancerel, *Jean-Louis Barrault* (1953)

Barrie, J[ames] M[atthew] (b. Kirriemuir, Scotland, 9 May 1860; d. London, 19 June 1937) Playwright and novelist. Barrie came to prominence with *The Little Minister* (1897), based on his novel, *Walker, London* (1892), and a costume romance *Quality Street* (1902). A prolific and diverse dramatist, he is remembered primarily for his children's play *Peter Pan* (1904), which became a regular Christmas entertainment throughout the century. Although uncharacteristic in subject, its fantasy and somewhat cloying sentimentality, albeit tempered by an underlying menace, inform much of his work. This is most marked in the supernatural elements of *Dear Brutus* (1917) and *Mary Rose* (1920), less obviously so in the whimsical satire of social comedies such as *The Admirable Crichton* (1902) and *What Every Woman Knows* (1908). He was also noted for his one-act plays. Barrie was knighted in 1913.
IAN CLARKE

Andrew Birkin, *Barrie and the Lost Boys* (1979)
R. D. S. Jack, *The Road to the Never Land: A Reassessment of Barrie's Dramatic Art* (1990)
H. M. Walbrook, *J. M. Barrie and the Theatre* (1922)

Barry, Philip [Jerome Quinn] (b. Rochester, NY, 18 June 1896; d. New York, 3 Dec. 1949) Playwright. The first of some 21 Broadway productions, *You and I* (1923), introduced his recurring theme of marriage. *Paris Bound* (1927) established his name as a comic writer. *Holiday* (1928), dealing with youth's revolt against parents, and the psychodrama *Hotel Universe* (1930) proved less acceptable to audiences than the domestic comedies *Tomorrow and Tomorrow* (1931), *The Animal Kingdom* (1932) and *The Philadelphia Story* (1939), his best work and the only one to remain popular. JOSEPH M. DIAZ

Gerald Hamm, *The Drama of Philip Barry* (1948)
Joseph Patrick Roppolo, *Philip Barry* (1965)

Barry, Sebastian (b. Dublin, 5 July 1955) Playwright. He was an established writer of prose fiction before *Boss Grady's Boys* was produced by the National Theatre Society (1989). This was followed by *Prayers of Sherkin* (Peacock, Dublin, 1990; OLD VIC 1997); *White Woman Street* (Bush, 1992, transferred to Dublin same year); *The Only True History of Lizzie Finn* (Abbey, 1995); *The Steward of Christendom* (ROYAL COURT, 1995, transferred to GATE, Dublin, 1996, and New York, 1997); and *Our Lady of Sligo* (1998). His plays continue the Irish tradition of strongly verbal drama; they tend to

deal obliquely with changes in society and reappraisals of historical contexts, often in a vividly hallucinatory fashion. He has been the recipient of a number of international awards. CHRISTOPHER FITZ-SIMON

Barrymore, Ethel *see* BARRYMORE FAMILY

Barrymore family Lionel, Ethel and John are the outstanding siblings in the American 'royal family' of actors, children of Maurice Barrymore (1847–1905), popular leading man, and Georgianna Drew (1856–1893), the actress daughter of Mrs John Drew (1820–97), famous manager of Philadelphia's Arch Street Theatre. The three sometimes acted together on stage and once on film, in *Rasputin and the Empress* (1932). Their family theatrical tree can be traced back to the mid-eighteenth century and, by folklore, to itinerant players in Shakespeare's day. GEORGE S. KAUFMAN and EDNA FERBER sent up the Barrymores in *The Royal Family* (1927).

Lionel (b. Philadelphia, 28 April 1878; d. Van Nuys, Calif., 15 Nov. 1954) was best known as a gruff yet kindly character actor in his later film career. He began acting with his grandmother and other managers during the 1890s, but in 1906 gave up to paint in France. He returned three years later and achieved his greatest Broadway success in *Peter Ibbetson* (1917), *The Copperhead* (1918) and *The Jest* (1919). He appeared in early movies and after a series of stage flops, including *Macbeth* (1921), he left the theatre in the mid-1920s to play an outstanding series of film roles, even when crippled by rheumatism. His Scrooge in *A Christmas Carol* was an annual radio event for many years, and his autobiography, *We Barrymores*, was published in 1951.

Ethel (b. Philadelphia, 15 Aug. 1879; d. Beverly Hills, Calif., 18 June 1959) had a distinctive personality, beauty and a throaty voice that kept her a front-ranked star for many years. After acting in the 1890s with her grandmother and uncle John Drew and with HENRY IRVING in London, Ethel achieved Broadway stardom in *Captain Jinks of the Horse Marines* (1901). Under producer CHARLES FROHMAN's guidance until his death in 1915, Ethel became the original 'glamour girl' on both sides of the Atlantic. She appeared notably in *Lady Frederick* (1908), *Mid-Channel* (1910), *Déclassée* (1918), and *The Constant Wife* (1928). The role of Miss Moffat in the American production of *The Corn is Green* (1939), which she played for three years, crowned her career. She appeared in VAUDEVILLE in *The 12 Pound Look* (1911). She later played in films. The SHUBERTS named a theatre in New York after her in 1928, and her autobiography *Memories* was published in 1955. Two sons failed to make a career from acting but her daughter Ethel (1912–77) was a successful drama teacher and opera singer.

John (b. Philadelphia, 15 Feb. 1882; d. Los Angeles, 29 May 1942), a late starter in acting, became a much-imitated matinée idol, often known as 'The Great Profile', and a classical actor renowned as the American Hamlet of his time. After a career begun in 1903 in light romantic roles, he surprised audiences by a turn to stronger works, notably *Justice* (1916), *Peter Ibbetson* (1917), *Redemption* (1918), *The Jest* (1919), and an outstanding *Richard III* (1920) and *Hamlet* (1922). He then left the stage for a noteworthy series of roles in silent and talking films, although alcohol and scandal marred his later career. His final stage appearance came in a parody of his own position, *My Dear Children* (1939). His daughter Diana (1921–60) and son John (b. 1932) both had promising acting careers cut short by excesses reminiscent of their father. His granddaughter Drew Barrymore (b. 1975) carries on the family name in films. MICHAEL SOMMERS

See also THEATRE FAMILIES.

H. Alpert, *The Barrymores* (1964)
Gene Fowler, *Good Night, Sweet Prince* (1944)
J. Kobler, *Damned in Paradise: The Life of John Barrymore* (1977)
Michael A. Morrison, *John Barrymore, Shakespearean Actor* (1999)
M. Peters, *The House of Barrymore* (1990)

Barrymore, John *see* BARRYMORE FAMILY

Barrymore, Lionel *see* BARRYMORE FAMILY

Barsacq, André [Anatole Sophocle] (b. Theodosia, Crimea, 24 Jan. 1909; d. Paris, 3 Feb. 1973) Designer and director. After moving to France and working for DULLIN as a designer, he collaborated with SAINT-DENIS and COPEAU and co-founded the Compagnie des Quatre Saisons with Dasté and others in 1937. He succeeded Dullin in 1940 as director of the Atelier, one of the CARTEL theatres, and remained there with the Compagnie until his death, presenting elegant revivals of classics and new plays by popular writers such as ANOUILH and AYMÉ. CHARLES LONDON

Bart [Begleiter], Lionel (b. London, 1 Aug. 1930; d. London, 3 April 1999) Composer and lyricist. He made his name in the mid-1950s as the writer of some of the earliest British rock-and-roll songs (e.g. 'Living Doll'). His first theatre work was in REVUE at the left-wing UNITY THEATRE, where the musical *Wally Pone* (1958), for which he contributed book, lyrics and music, was briefly staged. The following year he found substantial success with his lyrics for the BERNARD MILES/Laurie Johnson *Lock Up Your Daughters* and the

songs for THEATRE WORKSHOP's East End musical *Fings Ain't Wot They Used T'Be* before making an international success with his 1960 musical adaptation of Dickens' *Oliver Twist*, *Oliver!*, which established a long-run record for a home-grown musical in the West End (2,618 performances). The spectacular *Blitz!* (1962) and the splendidly gritty *Maggie May* (1964) were further successes, but a feeble burlesque of the Robin Hood legend, *Twang!!* (1965) was a violent failure. In the period of financial and personal problems which followed, Bart's career foundered as *La Strada* (1969) failed on Broadway and other projects, including a musical based on Hugo's *Notre Dame de Paris*, were announced but not produced. KURT GÄNZL

D. Roper, *Bart!* (1994)

Barter Theater Opened in Abingdon, Virginia in 1933, it was the brainchild of Robert Porterfield, who was distressed that hard times deprived many would-be playgoers of the wherewithal to purchase tickets. He allowed patrons to pay for tickets with produce or anything else they could offer. The policy flourished, and at times the company has operated more than one theatre. In 1946 the group was declared the state theatre of Virginia. Most playgoers pay for tickets with cash, but bartering is still accepted. After Porterfield's death in 1972, he was succeeded by Rex Partington and Pearl Price Hayter. GERALD BORDMAN

M. Dawidziak, *The Barter Theatre Story: Love Made Visible* (1982)

Bartlett, Neil *see* EXPERIMENTAL THEATRE; LYRIC THEATRE

Barton, John [Bernard Adie] (b. London, 26 Nov. 1928) Director. While teaching at CAMBRIDGE, he brought acclaim to Marlowe Society productions through his knowledge of seventeenth-century verse, which led him in 1960 to STRATFORD-UPON-AVON and the new ROYAL SHAKESPEARE COMPANY, where he co-directed, directed and adapted many Shakespeare plays. He became one of the company's guiding spirits across four decades. His productions were noted for the verve and accessibility of the verse speaking. Among his most ambitious work is *The Wars of the Roses* (1963, a condensation of the *Henry VI* plays and *Richard III*), his adaptation of ancient tragedy into a cycle of 10 plays, *The Greeks* (1980), and his 10-(originally 12-)play account of the myths that predate ancient tragedy, *Tantalus* (2000). He has also directed modern drama for the RSC (e.g. IBSEN, GRANVILLE BARKER, WHITING). His book, *Playing Shakespeare*, adapted from a television series, appeared in 1984. TERRY HODGSON

M. L. Greenwald, *Directions by Indirections: John Barton* (1985)

Bataille, Henri [Félix] (b. Nîmes, France, 14 April 1872; d. Malmaison, France, 2 March 1922) Playwright. Bataille's early work consists of romantic dramas in verse, while his later plays are psychological dramas, frequently on risqué subjects. Plays include *L'Enchantement* (1900), *La Marche nuptiale* ('The wedding march', 1905), *La Femme nue* ('The naked woman', 1908) and *La Vierge folle* ('The foolish virgin', 1910).

ANNA MCMULLAN

Bates, Alan [Arthur] (b. Allestree, Derbys, 17 Feb. 1934) Actor, at his best playing outwardly cool but inwardly tormented characters. After training at the Royal Academy of Dramatic Art, he made his debut in Coventry (1956) and then joined the ENGLISH STAGE SOCIETY at the ROYAL COURT where he played many leading roles, including that of Cliff in *Look Back in Anger* (London and New York, 1956). Most of his major successes have been in contemporary work, by writers like PINTER (Mick in *The Caretaker*, 1960; *One for the Road*, 1984), STOREY (*In Celebration*, 1967; *Life Class*, 1974; *Stages*, 1992) and GRAY (title role in *Butley*, 1971; *Otherwise Engaged*, 1975; *Life Support*, 1997). He has also had a considerable film career.

D. KEITH PEACOCK

Bates, Blanche (b. Portland, Oreg., 5 Aug. 1873; d. San Francisco, 25 Dec. 1941) Actress. Born of a theatrical family, she first appeared on stage in San Francisco in 1894, but it was not until she appeared in New York in a tour opposite James O'Neill that she attracted attention. The playwright DAVID BELASCO subsequently gave her leading roles in several productions of his work: *Madame Butterfly* (1900), *Darling of the Gods* (1902) and *The Girl of the Golden West* (1905). She also had a big hit in Belasco's production of *Under Two Flags* (1901). With the waning of Belasco's career by 1910, Bates performed for other managements but with less success, and often resorted to work in VAUDEVILLE.

HELEN RAPPAPORT

Baty, Gaston (b. Pelussin, France, 26 May 1885; d. Pelussin, 13 Oct. 1952) Director. A member of the CARTEL, Baty was much influenced by EXPRESSIONISM, the Russian ballet and PUPPET THEATRE. Not an actor himself (unlike the other Cartel directors), he disputed the primacy of actor and text and sought to integrate song, dance and set design with prose and verse dialogue. In 1951 he made a late and successful venture into the regions. Among his celebrated productions are

Maya (1924), *Phèdre* (1940) and his adaptation of *Crime and Punishment* (1933). TERRY HODGSON

Bauer, Wolfgang (b. Graz, Austria, 18 March 1941) Playwright. His dialect plays caused controversy in the press and regular scandals in the theatre because of their sexual content and obscene language. In his dramatic writings he has applied the aesthetics of pop art and beat culture to the theatre, and used crude effects and extreme situations without offering any apparent explanation or analysis of the events depicted. His first success was *Party for Six* (1967); this was followed by *Magic Afternoon* (1968), *Change* (1969), *Silvester, oder Das Massaker im Hotel Sacher* ('New Year's Eve, or the massacre in the Hotel Sacher', 1971) and *Film und Frau* (1971, performed in English as *Shakespeare the Sadist*). Of his later plays, only two were critical successes: *Gespenster* ('Ghosts', 1974) and *Magnetküsse* ('Magnetic kisses', 1976). In the 1980s his work veered between absurdist, surreal and postmodern styles.

GÜNTER BERGHAUS

Bauhaus A movement established in 1919 by WALTER GROPIUS at his school in Bauhaus, Weimar, Germany, in an attempt to break down the traditional barriers between arts and crafts and thereby end the elitist status of art. In 1923 the painter and dancer OSKAR SCHLEMMER set up the Bauhaus Stage Workshop, which was particularly influential on dance in the 1950s, and the important designer MOHOLY-NAGY taught at the school. Bauhaus moved to Dessau in 1925 and more fully embraced a new unity of art and technology. In 1927 Gropius designed a 'TOTAL THEATRE' for the German director PISCATOR, which although never realized came to be highly influential on later theatre ARCHITECTURE. MARIE PETCHELL

W. Gropius, ed., *The Theatre of the Bauhaus* (1961)
John Willett, *The New Sobriety: Art and Politics in the Weimar Period 1917–33* (1978)

Bausch, Pina (b. Solingen, Germany, 27 July 1940) Dancer, choreographer and ballet director. Probably the most influential modern dance choreographer in Europe, Bausch first studied with KURT JOOSS; later she danced in the United States, where she worked under Anthony Tudor. Since 1973, when she became director of Wuppertal Dance Theatre, she has made pieces only for that company. Her work is epic in scale and combines dialogue, theatre and dance; it is by turns funny, chilling, violent and despairing. Design is always an important component: *Rite of Spring* (1973), for example, was performed ankle-deep in mud. Her signature pieces include *Café Müller* (1978) and *1980* (1980). Her influence has spread where categories such as dance theatre dissolve into others like EXPERIMENTAL drama or PERFORMANCE ART. ANDREW SOLWAY

See also CHOREOGRAPHY; DANCE; MOVEMENT, DANCE AND DRAMA.

Bax, Clifford (b. London, 13 July 1886; d. London, 18 Nov. 1962) Playwright, critic and poet. He began his playwriting career with *The Poetasters of Ispahan* (1912) and continued writing throughout the 1920s, 1930s and 1940s, achieving success with his play about Henry VIII, *The Rose Without a Thorn* (1932). During the Second World War he wrote RADIO DRAMA. He adapted many plays, including, from Czechoslovakia, ČAPEK's *The Insect Play* (1923), with NIGEL PLAYFAIR, and from Russia, *Rasputin* (1929). His translations of European texts include *Mine Hostess* (1944) from Goldoni's *La Locandiera*. He also wrote novels and was a well-known figure in repertory circles. MAGGIE GALE

Baxter, James K[eir] (b. Dunedin, 29 June 1926; d. Auckland, 22 Oct. 1972) Playwright, New Zealand's best-known poet and a controversial literary figure. The first performance of *The Wide Open Cage* (1959), directed for Wellington's Unity Theatre by RICHARD CAMPION, was described by BRUCE MASON as 'a spectacular entry into the theatre'. In 1963 it was produced OFF-BROADWAY and in London. In his 24 plays Baxter exposes aspects of New Zealand society that many would prefer to ignore. Uneven as they are, plays such as *The Devil and Mr Mulcahy* (1967), *The Band Rotunda* (1967), *The Temptations of Oedipus* (1970) and *Jack Winter's Dream* (written for radio in 1956; performed 1958) all express his involvement with and criticism of his country's life. The character of his plays is in general non-naturalistic and poetic, incorporating accumulated images and elements of ritual, myth and folk ballad.

Baxter worked particularly closely with two directors: Campion and Patric Carey. His fresh and vital work was significant in the development of indigenous drama in New Zealand. GILLIAN GREER

Bay, Howard (b. Centralia, Wash., 3 May 1912; d. New York, 21 Nov. 1986) Designer. He began his career when the FEDERAL THEATER PROJECT was established and designed three shows for the company before the gritty realism of his tenement-house set in *One-Third of a Nation* (1938) secured his position as one of the most innovative designers of the time. He stayed with the Project until its demise in 1939. He went on to design many prominent plays and musicals of the next decades, including *The Little Foxes* (1939), *The Corn is Green* (1940), *Finian's Rainbow* (1947), *Show Boat* (1946, 1954 and 1960) and *Man of La Mancha* (1965).

During the 1940s he taught design at the University of Michigan, emphasizing the practical element of scenography and promoting his personal philosophy of design, 'to make each setting an intensification of the play's own theme'. He taught at Brandeis University (1965–82) and wrote *Stage Design* (1974).
LAURIE WOLF

Baylis, Lilian [Mary] (b. London, 9 May 1874; d. London, 25 Nov. 1937) Theatre manager and theatrical pioneer. She brought classical and contemporary opera, ballet and drama to a popular audience. Interrupting a successful musical career in South Africa (where she performed with her parents), she returned to England in 1895 to assist her aunt, social reformer EMMA CONS, with the management of the Royal Victoria Hall and Coffee Tavern (popularly, the OLD VIC) as a temperance amusement hall. In 1912 Baylis assumed full management of the theatre and established it as London's only permanent venue for Shakespearean productions. In 1923 the theatre celebrated the tricentenary of the publication of the First Folio by completing with *Troilus and Cressida* the cycle of all Shakespeare's plays which had started in 1914 with *The Taming of the Shrew* – the first time this had ever been achieved. Devoted also to popularly priced opera and ballet, Baylis engaged NINETTE DE VALOIS as ballet mistress to a troupe that would become the Royal Ballet Company. In 1925 she directed the restoration and reopening (1931) of the SADLER'S WELLS theatre, which had fallen into near-ruin – a feat accomplished primarily through public appeals for funds and benefit performances by SYBIL THORNDIKE and GRACIE FIELDS, among others. The Wells was conceived as a companion theatre in north London to south London's Old Vic. Managing both theatres for several years in an exhaustive repertory, Baylis eventually dedicated the Wells to opera and ballet and the Old Vic to drama, thereby laying the foundations of the English National Opera, the Royal Ballet and the National Theatre – a unique and outstanding achievement in the British theatre. Both theatre managements, however, maintained the mandate of The Sadler's Wells Foundation's Declaration of Trust (1932) that performances be 'suited for the recreation and instruction of the poorer classes' at prices that 'will make them available for artisans and labourers', reserving higher-priced engagements for benefit purposes only. Deeply religious and strong-willed, with a reputation for good housekeeping that veered towards parsimony, Baylis was known simply as 'The Lady' to her associates; she was appointed a Companion of Honour in 1929 and, in

1923, became only the second woman outside the university to be awarded an honorary MA at Oxford.
MICHAEL KARP

Richard Findlater, *Lilian Baylis* (1975)
Sybil and Russell Thorndike, *Lilian Baylis* (1938)

Bayreuth   Town in Germany boasting an eighteenth-century rococo Opera House and, at the other architectural extreme, the Festival Theatre (founded 1876), designed by Richard Wagner with the help of architects Semper and Brückwald. It was one of the first to have one body of audience without tiers of balconies, a 'democratic' design that was highly influential in the twentieth century. It seats 1,800 and is famous for prestigious productions of Wagner's work at its annual festivals, which, unfortunately, for a period became the spiritual home of the Nazis. In the 1950s, the composer's grandson WIELAND WAGNER revolutionized the staging of the operas.   ADRIANA HUNTER
See also APPIA, ADOLFE; ARCHITECTURE.

Beale, Simon Russell   *see* RUSSELL BEALE, SIMON

Beaton, Cecil   (b. London, 14 Jan. 1904; d. Broadchalke, Wilts, 18 Jan. 1980)   Stage and film designer. Best known as a fashion and society photographer, Beaton first designed ballet decor and costume for the COCHRAN REVUE *Follow the Sun* (1936). Witty, sumptuous and nostalgic designs were his trademark for ballet, opera and most notably for lavish WEST END and BROADWAY stage productions such as *Lady Windermere's Fan* (1945), *Quadrille* (1952), *Look After Lulu* (1959) and *Coco* (1969). He also designed the costumes for *My Fair Lady* (1956) and the film *Gigi* (1959). He was knighted in 1972.   MICHAEL SOMMERS

Beaton, Norman   (b. Georgetown, Guyana, 31 Oct. 1934; d. Georgetown, 13 Dec. 1994)   Actor who trained in London as a teacher before taking up a stage career, and was active in establishing groups at the beginning of the movement for BLACK THEATRE in the UK, such as the Black Theatre of Brixton (1974). He made his debut at the NATIONAL THEATRE in 1971 and quickly established a reputation as Britain's leading black actor, in particular in plays by MUSTAPHA MATURA such as *Play Mas* (1974) and *Rum and Coca Cola* (1976) for the ROYAL COURT THEATRE, and *The Coup* (1991) for the National. He appeared in a great range of plays, by BECKETT, PINTER, BRECHT, Molière and Shakespeare, for example, and was especially noted for his comic flair. A composer, singer and musician, he also enjoyed a successful radio and television career, appearing in several long-running TV shows. He wrote an autobiography, *Beaton but Unbowed* (1986).
HELEN RAPPAPORT

Beaumont, Hugh 'Binkie' [Hughes Griffiths Morgan]   (b. London, 27 March 1908; d. London, 22 March 1973)   Impresario. After a hesitant start, H. M. TENNENT LTD, the company co-founded by Beaumont in the 1930s, soon rose to a position of pre-eminence in the WEST END, helped by a lucrative and prestigious association with the wartime entertainment organization CEMA (COUNCIL FOR THE ENCOURAGEMENT OF MUSIC AND THE ARTS). Beaumont, who took over as managing director when Tennent died in 1941, was a charming, witty man with a shrewd commercial mind, and many of his productions were critically as well as financially successful. He encouraged the careers of RATTIGAN, BROOK and SCOFIELD, and later ROBERT BOLT and PETER SHAFFER, and was instrumental in bringing much new American work to Britain, including the early work of TENNESSEE WILLIAMS. He served on the boards of the SHAKESPEARE MEMORIAL THEATRE (1950–60) and NATIONAL THEATRE (1962–8), but after 1956 became a target of the new wave. Beaumont's homosexuality was attacked as symbolic of a supposed 'gay theatrical clique' and he was soon seen as a figure from a bygone era.   DAN REBELLATO

K. Black, *Upper Circle* (1984)
C. Duff, *The Lost Summer: The Heyday of the West End Theatre* (1995)
R. Huggett, *Binkie Beaumont, Eminence Grise of the West End Theatre 1933–73* (1984)

Becher, Johannes   *see* ACTIVISM

Beck, Julian   *see* LIVING THEATER

Beckett, Samuel [Barclay]   (b. Foxrock, nr Dublin, 13 April 1906; d. Paris, 22 Dec. 1989)   Playwright, novelist and poet. Beckett has had as great an impact on the theatre internationally as IBSEN, and like him has brought a new kind of actor into existence to interpret his plays, because of the precision they require in performance. Like his novels and prose texts, Beckett's drama is based on his perception of the human condition: born and mostly living in pain, a short brutish existence at the mercy of chance and nature and the random kindness or cruelty of others, people may yet sometimes, through intelligence, be able to create an aesthetic embodiment of that predicament to ease the pain. His philosophy might be called a disciplined stoicism, based on the reduction of personal needs and desires, rather than on their augmentation in line with the commercial ethics of late twentieth-century society to which his work in its implications is totally opposed.
  A brilliant scholar of French and Italian literature (and a useful cricketer) at Trinity College, Dublin, Beckett found a model for his view of the world in Dante's *Divine Comedy*, in which the dead, whether

damned or blessed, remember their lives and think endlessly about them. But to Beckett no one is blessed, and he has created a world, particularly in his plays, in which the air around us is filled with the voices of the dead, each talking to itself, recreating its past, usually unaware of all the other dead voices. This literary conceit first occurs in *En attendant Godot* (*Waiting for Godot*, 1953), his first play to be performed and still his greatest popular success. In his later plays – for instance *Play* (1963) – he sometimes moves beyond the threshold of death, and ghosts frequently occur in his other work. In 1928 he left Trinity for Paris, where he became a member of the JAMES JOYCE circle and taught for two years at the Ecole Normale Supérieure. In 1930 he published his first poems, and a year later a long essay on Proust, which is remarkable above all for the insight it gives into his own thinking about the nature of literature and art. *More Pricks than Kicks*, a collection of semi-autobiographical stories about a student in Dublin, appeared in 1934, followed in 1938 by *Murphy*, his first novel, the hero of which is a work-shy Irishman in London, preoccupied with astrology and the body–mind relationship and supported by a prostitute. During this time he was living mainly in Paris, with frequent trips to England, Germany and back to Dublin, where he found himself at the outbreak of hostilities in 1939; hurrying back to Paris, he spent the war there, was active in the Resistance, barely escaped capture and hid in Roussillon in the Vaucluse (where *Godot* is set) from late 1942 until the liberation. He was awarded the Croix de Guerre for his Resistance activities.

By the end of the war Beckett had written a second novel, *Watt*, his last in English for some years, which was published by Olympia Press in Paris only in 1953. He then started to work in French, both to develop his fluency in that language and to avoid the richness and loquacity that nearly all Irish writers find it almost impossible to escape. The important works of his maturity followed: first, four novellas, three of them published as *Nouvelles* in 1954, then in English, together with the *Textes pourien* in 1967; *Premier amour* (*First Love*), his first French novella, suppressed in both languages by the author until 1970; then the trilogy of full-length novels, *Molloy*, *Malone Dies* and *The Unnamable*, and *En attendant Godot*. All these works were written in French between 1947 and 1949 when, convinced that he had a malignant growth in his cheek, which later proved after removal to be harmless, he believed he had little time to live and felt impelled to put on paper the fruits of his wartime ruminations. Had he written nothing else, these works would have been sufficient to secure his reputation as one of the most original and seminal of contemporary writers.

During a visit to his dying mother in Ireland shortly after the war, Beckett walked on to the jetty at Dun Laoghaire one stormy night and experienced a sudden realization that his way ahead as a writer lay, not in trying to avoid the blackness of his vision – 'the dark I have always struggled to keep under' – but in accepting it and making it the driving force of his work. The incident is quoted in *Krapp's Last Tape* (1958), his first performed English play. Whereas the prewar work was often hilarious in its black humour and general eccentricity, and very Irish, Beckett was now writing in a disciplined French, novels in the first person that tell the lives of tramps and old men, preparing to die or dragging themselves over an unfriendly planet in a state of increasing decrepitude, their memories as painful as their present dilemmas; and also writing *Waiting for Godot*, which pictures two tramps whiling away the time on an empty road, waiting for the protagonist of the title, who never appears, to offer them a job and the prospect for once of sleeping in his warm hayloft and escaping from the inhospitality of the world. Their boredom is mitigated by the arrival of Pozzo, a slave-master, and Lucky, his slave, who pass through once in each act, their dependency on each other having been reversed during the interval. Metaphorically they catch the essence of our natural callousness and cruelty to our own kind, so different from the solidarity of animals with their own species. What comes out of the play, the poetic masterpiece of postwar drama, is not so much a picture of despair as a lesson in how to cope with it. Beckett beautifully dramatizes one of the most universal traumas of our time, the fear of anonymity. We are born, live and die; and our passing through the world, especially in the light of twentieth-century history, is quickly forgotten, our sufferings counting for nothing, soon to be erased from all memory. Religion no longer holds out any compensation, except to a few. This vital and poignant message in *Godot*, which surfaces again in Beckett's later work, became apparent only from his own production with the Berlin Schiller-theater, when the theatre world for the first time gave him the same recognition as a director that he had long enjoyed as a writer.

After the international success of *Waiting for Godot*, the most discussed play of the 1950s, Beckett was commissioned to write a radio play for the BBC; *All That Fall* (1957), with its combination of sound effects, country dialogue and rural tragedy, transformed the possibilities of RADIO DRAMA. Then came *Fin de partie* (*Endgame*, 1957), on which critical opinion was sharply divided. The controversy revolved round the play's claustrophobic atmosphere and the apparent eccentricity of its stage situations, two of its characters being

· Performing Beckett ·

Music is the key to Beckett's work. I approach his plays more like a musician than an actor, with a concern for sound, rhythm and tone. In *Play* at the NATIONAL THEATRE in 1964 – the first time I had appeared in a piece by Beckett and before I had met the author – the director GEORGE DEVINE allowed us to take the piece slowly. When Beckett arrived, he wanted it to go much faster and the increased tempo made the vital difference. It seemed right because the meaning came alive through the rhythm and music and not by an audience following every word. The make-up was incredible: oatmeal, jelly and surgical glue, which gave the desired effect of our faces crumbling before the eyes of the audience as bits flaked off while we spoke. We were enclosed in large jars and I asked if I could have some kind of bar inside to hold on to, to stop me trembling and to give me somewhere to direct the tension – a device I used again in *Not I*.

I feel in tune with Beckett's direction. We have often talked on the telephone, with him reading parts of a play so that I can hear the music he has in his head. We conduct each other, counting the pauses as one would in music. He has a remarkable gift of being able to give me the key to a character in two or three words. We don't really go into the deeper meaning of a piece – with luck that will take care of itself. In rehearsal, I have occasionally asked him to allow me time to absorb what we have done together before going on to the next section. In *Happy Days* he left me alone for two days to cope with him changing 'ahs' to 'ohs' and vice versa. I had spent three months learning the play before we started rehearsals, which lasted seven weeks, and we performed for only three days. Yet it was only at the end of the run that I felt I had really made the part my own.

BILLIE WHITELAW

immured in dustbins during the whole of the action. *Endgame* is about the acceptance of death, a poignant and poetic melodrama that requires acting of the highest possible standard; the grandeur of its language and the power of its compassion can traumatize an audience. Unusual stage imagery is also characteristic of *Happy Days* (1961), *Play* (1964) and *Come and Go* (1966), all written for the stage. In *Happy Days*, Winnie is a middle-aged woman embedded up to the waist in a mound of earth, trying to ignore her situation while carrying on a desultory conversation with her husband; in the second act she has been sucked down until only her head remains free. *Play* shows the audience three dimly lit heads emerging from urns, each responding to a light that flashes from one face to the other; each recounts his part in a domestic drama where a man is trapped between his wife and his mistress, loving both. In the very short dramaticule (Beckett's apt neologism) *Come and Go*, each of three women hears of the terminal plight of the others, but not of herself.

In *Krapp's Last Tape*, written for the actor Patrick Magee, whom Beckett had not yet met but whose special vocal quality he had appreciated in BBC radio broadcasts of his trilogy, the playwright achieved something close to autobiography. On his 69th birthday, which he believes will be his last, Krapp, a writer, plays back old tapes made on previous birthdays, hearing his younger voice recalling significant moments in his life, especially the death of friends, moments of love and loss, but com-

pensated by the growing knowledge of his power as a writer; and then he makes his last tape.

During the 1970s and 1980s, Beckett wrote a series of highly concentrated one-act plays, usually incorporating unusual visual effects and depicting the protagonists in some kind of claustrophobic hell. *Not I* (1973) was remarkably played by BILLIE WHITELAW, whose long association with Beckett's work had started with *Play* at the National Theatre. *Not I* depicts a spotlit mouth, suspended in space, frantically relating a woman's story, denying it is her own, to an inquisitor (who was later dropped in some productions and in the television version). *That Time* (1976) shows an Irish immigrant on his deathbed, seen from above. *Footfalls* (1976) is about a ghost, probably existing only in the imagination of her dying mother, whose imaginary daughter will remember her and create more ghosts to keep her memory alive into the future. *Rockaby* (1981) pictures a woman rocking herself grimly to death. *Ohio Impromptu* (1981) shows the audience two identical old men, one a ghostly nocturnal visitor: one reads to the other from an old book the tale of a loved lost one. In *Catastrophe* (1982), written at the invitation of the Avignon Festival which requested a play in support of the dissident Czech playwright VACLAV HAVEL, an actor is reduced by a tyrannical director to an impotent but defiant statue in Beckett's most direct political statement about artistic and political freedom. *What Where* (1983) examines the impossibility of believing information derived by force in an extraordinary drama of self-torture.

Besides stage plays, Beckett has written two mimes, *Act Without Words I* and *II* (1956), and many radio and television plays: the latter medium had increasing fascinated him since *Eh Joe* (1966), written for the BBC and the actor JACK MACGOWRAN, who like Magee had become closely associated with Beckett's theatre. Beckett worked with actors in many countries who became accustomed to his uncompromising approach, requiring exactitude in every movement and gesture and perfect voice control, musically timed. Beckett's productions were choreographed more than directed. There is one film, entitled *Film* (1964), in which Buster Keaton made his last appearance. Beckett often adapted his work from one medium to another and never ceased to write in other forms, producing novels and some poetry, always reflecting the same themes and preoccupations, often with similar characters.

From the 1960s onwards Beckett would frequently work on his French and English texts simultaneously, so that it was a matter of chance which version emerged first. With few exceptions he translated all his work between the two languages and directly helped his translator with the German versions. Beckett not only had a profound knowledge of languages, but was fluent in at least four, and an enormous erudition, helped by a good memory, lies behind his writing.

All Beckett's work comprises a unity in which certain attitudes are expressed in different ways with much force and rare imagination: life is cruel and painful; failure is no worse than success because neither matters; what is important is to avoid giving pain to others and to share misfortune. There is much early Christian thinking and ethical philosophy here, and Beckett emerges as a moralist as well as a writer. He is often compared to the great Greeks and to Shakespeare; he has learned from the German Romantics, especially Goethe, as well as from composers, Beethoven and Schubert in particular. His own love of music is apparent in his work, which is often musically constructed. Beckett's integrity to his own principles is such that, in spite of his obvious attraction to women and their attraction to him, and his one marriage, he never had a child.

JOHN CALDER

Ruby Cohn, *Just Play: Beckett's Theatre* (1980)

Anthony Cronin, *Samuel Beckett: The Last Modernist* (1996)

John Fletcher, *Samuel Beckett's Art* (1967)

Hugh Kenner, *Samuel Beckett: A Critical Study* (1968)

James Knowlson, *Damned to Fame: The Life of Samuel Beckett* (1996)

John Pilling, *Samuel Beckett* (1976)

Christopher Ricks, *Beckett's Dying Words* (1993)

Bedford, Brian [Anthony] (b. Morley, Yorks, 16 Feb. 1935)   Actor. Since his first American stage performance in 1959, in PETER SHAFFER's *Five Finger Exercise*, Bedford has appeared almost every single year across the continent, from Ontario to Washington to San Diego, in a tremendous range of plays, several of which, such as *Equus*, have toured extensively. His considerable repertoire includes *The Knack* (1963), *The Cocktail Party* (1968), *School for Wives* (1971, Tony award for Best Actor), *Equus* (1976), *The Seagull* (1980), *Educating Rita* (1988), *Two Shakespearean Actors* (1991–2), *Timon of Athens* (1993–4) and *The Molière Comedies* (1994). He has played a whole range of Shakespearean roles since appearing in *Hamlet* in 1968, many of them, such as Malvolio and Richard II, for the STRATFORD FESTIVAL at Ontario. Bedford's career has been a rich and varied one, including film roles and as a director of stage productions (e.g. *Waiting for Godot*, 1996).

HELEN RAPPAPORT

Beerbohm, [Henry] Max[imilian] (b. London, 24 Aug. 1872; d. Rapallo, Italy, 20 May 1956)   Drama critic and playwright; a wit known for his cartoons and essays. From 1898 to 1912 he was theatre critic of the *Saturday Review* and his reviews are collected in three volumes. Curiously, he was antipathetic to many aspects of theatre and is best read for his waspish evocations of style and delivery.

JOHN STOKES

David Cecil, *Max* (1964)

Lawrence Dawson, *Max Beerbohm and the Act of Writing* (1989)

Behan, Brendan [Francis] (b. Dublin, 9 Feb. 1923; d. Dublin, 20 March 1964)   Journalist, raconteur and playwright. A member of a strongly republican family, he joined Fíanna Eireann, the youth wing of the IRA, serving prison sentences in Ireland and Britain. He gradually renounced terrorism; his best play, *The Quare Fellow* (Pike Theatre, Dublin, 1954), is a subtle call for the abolition of capital punishment. This was followed by *An Gíall* (Halla an Damer, Dublin, 1958), subsequently translated into English by the author and adapted by JOAN LITTLEWOOD in music-hall vein as *The Hostage* (THEATRE ROYAL, STRATFORD EAST, 1958). Both plays achieved widespread popularity through Littlewood's productions, both remain important to the Irish repertoire, and both emphasize the mindlessness of physical violence, somewhat in the tragicomic manner of O'CASEY. A stage adaptation of Behan's autobiography *Borstal Boy* (ABBEY THEATRE, Dublin, 1972) has been produced in other countries. The fragmentary *Richard's Cork Leg* (Olympia, Dublin, 1972) was less successful. He also wrote short comedies for radio, three of which were adapted for the stage by Carolyn Swift (Pike Theatre, Dublin, 1958). A genial and easygoing personality, Behan was temperamentally unable to regulate his reaction to international adulation, descending into alcoholism and early death. CHRISTOPHER FITZ-SIMON

Ulick O'Connor, *Brendan Behan* (1970)
Michael O'Sullivan, *Brendan Behan: A Life* (1997)
Carolyn Swift, *Stage by Stage* (1985)

Behrman, S[amuel] N[athaniel] (b. Worcester, Mass., 9 June 1893; d. New York, 9 Sept. 1973) Playwright and screenwriter. He developed an interest in theatre at an early age and entered Harvard in order to take GEORGE PIERCE BAKER's '47' drama workshop. Moving to New York, he eventually discovered his particular style of playwriting, one that mingled high comedy with a critical yet humane attitude towards society. He had little concern for conventional plot, but considerable interest in creating intelligent, sophisticated characters who are complex beneath the surface. His plays include *The Second Man* (1927), *Meteor* (1929), *Biography* (1932) and *No Time for Comedy* (1939). ALEXIS GREENE

K. Reed, *S. N. Behrman* (1975)

Béjart, Maurice (b. Marseille, France, 1 Jan. 1927) Choreographer. As one of the most innovative choreographers of the twentieth century, he began to experiment with TOTAL THEATRE in the 1960s, synthesizing ballet, theatre, opera and film techniques to create more complete theatrical productions, such as *Divertimento* (1961), *Les Sept péchés capitaux de la petite-bourgeoisie* (1961) and *Neuvième symphonie de Beethoven* (1964). This exploration of dance as rite and visual music rather than moving sculpture had great influence on the theatrical use of movement. ADRIANA HUNTER

Bekederemo-Clark, J. P. [John Pepper Clark] (b. Kiagbodo, Bendel State, Nigeria, 11 April 1935) Playwright, poet and scholar. Clark blends aspects of the form and structure of classical tragedies with folklore motifs and the structure of his Ijaw culture to make contemporary statements. His plays include the trilogy *Song of a Goat* (1961), *The Masquerade* (1962) and *The Raft* (1964). His major play is *Ozidi* (1965), a massive communal spectacle recreating an Ijo revenge saga. He founded the PEC Repertory Theatre in Lagos (1981). He

has also written the *Bikoroa Plays* (1983), another trilogy based on generations of the life of an Ijo family, and *The Wives Revolt* (1985). OLU OBAFEMI

Robert M. Wien, *J. P. Clark* (1984)

Bel Geddes, Norman [Melancton] b. Adrian, Mich., 27 April 1893; d. New York, 8 May 1958) Designer for industry and the stage. After studying in Cleveland and Chicago and desigining a show in Los Angeles, Bel Geddes came to New York and in 1918 began designing for the Metropolitan Opera before moving to BROADWAY (e.g. *Lady Be Good*, 1924: *Ziegfeld Follies of 1925*). A modernist and master at streamlining, ironically Bel Geddes' settings were sometimes monumental in scale. None the less, they always emanated from the text and consisted of the brilliant three-dimensional manipulation of space, form and light.

Bel Geddes' most famous setting was, perhaps, for the MAX REINHARDT production of *The Miracle* (1923), for which, in a startling experiment with the audience-stage dialectic, he literally turned the theatre into a cathedral. He is known also for *Hamlet* (1931), with its advanced use of steps and rostra, and for the naturalistic composite set of *Dead End* (1935). A pioneer in the use of lenses in stage lighting, he was an influential visionary whose unrealized plans included an enormous circular set for Dante's *Divine Comedy* and an innovative project for a THEATRE IN THE ROUND. His daughter Barbara (b. 1922) became a successful stage and TV actress. ANNE FLETCHER

Belasco, David (b. San Francisco, 25 July 1853; d. New York, 14 May 1931) Producer and playwright. Although Belasco started his theatrical career as an actor, he soon was staging and writing plays in his native city. His first New York hit was *The Wife* (1887), which he wrote in collaboration with Henry C. DeMille. Among his subsequent writing successes, usually collaborations, were *The Heart of Maryland* (1895), *Madame Butterfly* (1902), *The Girl of the Golden West* (1905), *The Return of Peter Grimm* (1911) and *Kiki* (1921). Other writers' plays which he staged included *The Music Master* (1904), *The Easiest Way* (1909) and *Lulu Belle* (1926). Regardless of the nature of the play, he mounted his productions with the utmost care and realism, using the latest stage machinery and experimenting with lighting effects. At the turn of the century he broke with the THEATRICAL SYNDICATE and ran two theatres, one built by himself and both bearing his name at different times. He was also famous for creating his own stars, such as BLANCHE BATES, MRS LESLIE CARTER, FRANCES STARR and DAVID WARFIELD. GERALD BORDMAN

L. Marker, *David Belasco: Naturalism in the American Theatre* (1975)

Craig Timberlake, *The Bishop of Broadway* (1954)

W. Winter, *The Life of David Belasco* (1925)

Belfast Born of a flamboyant regional nationalism, the Ulster Literary Theatre (ULT) was founded in 1904. The first theatre company to put on stage characters that were ordinary Ulster people, it did so against a spate of theatre-building occasioned by a VARIETY and MUSIC HALL boom. The Empire Theatre opened in 1894, the MATCHAM-designed Grand Opera House in 1895 and the Royal Hippodrome in 1907. Meanwhile, the latest incarnation of the century-old Theatre Royal had become a home to MELODRAMA. Within a few years, however, most would be losing the battle with the cinema, the Royal becoming a picture-house in 1913 and the Hippodrome in 1931. It was the ULT, then, rather than the popular theatre, that set a pattern which would endure longest throughout the century: that of a theatre struggling to articulate an artistic and political line presenting its society's 'own way of things'. From the very beginning, this was problematic. The founders had initially designated the group the Ulster branch of YEATS's Irish Literary Theatre and it was only when snubbed by him that they renamed the company in 1904 the Ulster Literary Theatre – and the debate began: was its work, by playwrights such as RUTHERFORD MAYNE and Gerald McNamara (1865–1938), presenting an Ulster or an Irish way? Were its players part of a national or a regional theatre? Never resolved, the original nationalist propagandist aims rapidly fell away and the company's emphasis increasingly fell on the social realities around it. It attracted a galaxy of talent and successfully premiered comedies, tragedies, farce, melodrama and satire to popular acclaim. After a decline it was renamed again, in 1915 as the more modest Ulster Theatre. Further decline led to disintegration in the 1930s. Some former ULT members joined the Belfast Repertory Theatre Company, a resident company of the Empire Theatre founded in 1929 which briefly assumed the mantle of new writing. In the sense that it presented a set of working-class dramas about urban Belfast to a working-class Empire audience, its plays were unique events. This was particularly the case with the popular work of Thomas Carnduff, a Belfast shipyard worker who reportedly utilized everyday Ulster speech for the first time in the city's drama. Despite such popularity, with regular tours to DUBLIN's ABBEY THEATRE and ambitions to become a form of national theatre, the Belfast Rep closed in

1937; the Empire itself struggled on as a variety theatre until 1961, when it was demolished. None the less, again a line continued. Among the former Rep members were some of the finest actors in the Ulster theatre; together with other, amateur players they became part of the influential Ulster Group Theatre. Created in 1940, this company premièred a significant amount of new work by Ulster writers such as JOSEPH TOMELTY, GEORGE SHIELS and ST JOHN ERVINE. It acquired a strong reputation for ensemble playing, and members went on to achieve stage and screen recognition both at home and abroad. In 1946 the Belfast Arts Theatre was founded by Hubert and Dorothy Wilmot to be an international repertory theatre, and presented an impressive roll-call of writers such as SARTRE, SALACROU, COCTEAU and BORCHERT until its move to larger premises in 1961. Thereafter it became a home for popular entertainment, and remained so until the latest spate of the Troubles began.

The final company in the mid-century Belfast theatre triumvirate was the Lyric Players Theatre. Founded by Mary O'Malley in her own house in 1951, this was dedicated to poetic drama, particularly that of Yeats. It staged challenging programmes of Irish and international work in the capacity of a private theatre until 1968, when it acquired a new purpose-built home. Unfortunately, this was also the year in which the Troubles reignited. During the early, particularly brutal disturbances in Belfast, every theatre in the city except the Lyric went dark. The Group company, in any case, had collapsed in 1960, when a furore arose over SAM THOMPSON's *Over the Bridge*, which overtly had sectarianism as its theme. The board refused to stage it, in a decision perceived as thinly disguised state censorship. Few other new plays with strong political ideology had been staged in the previous decades, and so the Ulster theatre approached the 1970s with little practical experience of direct original representation of the political life of their community. This was to change sharply in the next 30 years. In the difficult 1970s and early 1980s, plays were staged at the Lyric by writers such as John Boyd, Patrick Galvin, Christina Reid, Graham Reid, STEWART PARKER and Martin Lynch which directly addressed the socio-political realities around them. In the 1980s other companies did likewise, particularly Charabanc (founded 1983), whose early new work was collectively written out of the life of working-class communities in the city. Their productions, such as *Somewhere Over the Balcony* (1987) set in Belfast's Divis Flats, reacquainted a whole new Belfast audience with theatre. It regularly toured internationally and launched the career of playwright Marie Jones, who enjoyed much success with *Stones in His Pockets*, first seen in 1996 and rewritten in 1999 for a production that went on to London and New York. The late 1980s and early 1990s saw the arrival of a clutch of new independent companies, including Tinderbox and Prime Cut; the former has become Northern Ireland's main originator of new writing, while the latter presents international work. Replay THEATRE IN EDUCATION company has commissioned an impressive amount of new writing, while Kabosh focuses on a more physical style of theatre. Throughout, the Belfast Festival at Queen's University has brought international theatre, opera and dance companies to the city each year; events are regularly staged at the Grand Opera House, which was magnificently restored in 1980 with government funds to become the principal theatre in Northern Ireland for such large-scale performances. The Group Theatre, meanwhile, was re-opened in 1976 to become the home of amateur drama, amateurs having done much to keep theatre alive during the Troubles.

At the end of one century and the start of a new one – a time of 'not peace, not war' in Belfast – audience figures were increasing. New civic spaces, such as the Belfast Waterfront Hall (1997), were opened as part of official attempts to re-house the Belfast arts in a planned, comprehensive way. Tellingly, older venues such as the Belfast Civic Arts Theatre, kept alive by funders during the Troubles, were closed (1999) as part of this process. New playwriting voices, such as Owen McCafferty and Damian Gorman, have emerged; and, from a Protestant working-class Unionist background, Gary Mitchell, with *In a Little World of Our Own* (1997) and *Force of Change* (2000), is making an impact after a century in which theatre in Ulster predominantly saw itself in an Irish context. Meanwhile, companies such as DUBBELJOINT are causing regular controversy by presenting single-identity work which is not seeking to offer a 'balanced' picture, as were many of the so-called 'Troubles plays', but looks to make particular experiences, such as that of the predominantly nationalist West Belfast, understood. In so doing, the company has worked regularly with COMMUNITY THEATRE, a sector that has become one of the strongest in Belfast theatre. It regularly features work from both Protestant and Catholic working-class communities, both of which previously lacked much theatrical articulation. OPHELIA BYRNE

S. H. Bell, *The Theatre in Ulster* (1972)

O. Byrne, *The Stage in Ulster from the Eighteenth Century* (1997)

D. Grant, *Playing the Wild Card: Community Drama and Smaller-scale Professional Theatre* (1993)

Belgium Until the end of the First World War Belgian theatre was a continuation of the nineteenth century. The French-speaking theatre kept on catering for a bourgeois audience – its most famous writer, MAETERLINCK, was achieving his successes in Paris – whereas the Dutch-speaking theatre in the Flemish part of the country offered popular successes without any cultural aspiration. That landscape changed unrecognizably after 1920 when in Antwerp a young director, Jan Oscar de Gruyter, launched his company on a cultural programme that stressed professionalism, skill and interpretation; with Joris Diels, his successor in the 1930s, there appeared for the first time a theatre that could rival the best in the Netherlands. From 1925 until 1929 the Flemish People's Theatre, with its director Johan de Meester and Anton van de Velde, developed an artistic repertoire (notably by CLAUDEL and the Flemish writer DE GHELDERODE) presented by means of a highly idiosyncratic variant of Soviet directing methods (principally those of TAIROV), trying to reconcile the AVANT-GARDE and the popular within an international spirit. In 1946 a theatrical policy was elaborated at government level, and subsidized repertory companies were founded in Antwerp and Brussels, as well as a touring company, a youth company and a theatre academy in Antwerp. Their repertoire consisted of classical works and more entertaining plays, and there were efforts to stimulate Dutch playwriting. The leading playwright to emerge was HUGO CLAUS.

Flemish theatre became increasingly vigorous in the 1950s. The range was broadened by several small chamber companies (in Ghent, Antwerp, Brussels) and new initiatives soon took shape in provincial centres (Bruges, Kortrijk, Mechelen). Most of these companies favoured the European drama of the EXISTENTIALIST or ABSURD breed. BECKETT, IONESCO and SARTRE were being programmed here long before they were welcomed on the larger stages. These chamber companies kept close to the acting style of the larger houses and there was no real break with their no-nonsense realism. A few of these small companies survived, playing for larger audiences, but no longer in the spirit of protest in which they were born.

In the 1970s the Flemish theatre blossomed out of dissatisfaction with the hierarchical and fossilized working methods adopted by the larger 'official' companies. Several Marxist-oriented companies were founded and, following examples from abroad, introduced a COLLECTIVE writing method, more often than not emphasizing their didactic aims at the expense of any concern for artistic form. They contributed considerably to establishing avant-garde trends; formal and textual concepts hitherto unknown were introduced, and when the home-made play ceased to offer any interest they moved to international texts and found themselves equipped in concept and in skill to perform at the highest aesthetic level to an audience able to appreciate that. Although in the 1980s there were many such companies (like De Blauwe Maandag, De Tijd, Needcompany, and some 20 or so more), each had its own identity in range, style, topics and audience. They do not present a homogeneous movement – rather, they foreshadow international activity within a united Europe. As the concept of repertory theatre increasingly came under attack, a group of young directors (among others, Franz Marijnen, Jean-Pierre De Decker, Dirk Tanghe, Herman Gilis, Luk Perceval, Guy Joosten, Ivo van Hove, Lucas Vandevost, Jan Lauwers, Jan Fabre), in close partnership with outstanding scenographers (e.g. Jan Versweyfeld, Marc Knops, Niek Kortekaas), often also working in the Netherlands, with which they shared a common language, seemed capable of responding to the demands of a new generation.

In French-speaking Belgium, as well as the adventurous Théâtre du Marais (Brussels, 1920–6; director Jules Delacre), there was the Comédiens Routiers which in the 1930s started to take theatre to the people; in 1942 it settled in Brussels under the director Claude Etienne, and revealed a newborn French written drama as well as becoming a springboard for numerous Belgian artists. It took on the spirit of JEAN VILAR and toured the country with great classics and modern Belgian playwrights (de Ghelderode, Willems, Kalisky). For a long time both traditional and new companies were concentrated in Brussels. Only towards the end of the century did new centres appear in Wallonia, mainly Liège and Charleroi. Decentralization then became the norm.

In the 1970s in Brussels the Théâtre de l'Esprit Frappeur, the Théâtre de l'Alliance, the Théâtre du Parvis and especially the Théâtre Laboratoire Vicinal developed the most daring experiments of GROTOWSKI and BARBA. By 1975 these alternative initiatives were officially recognized and this changed the theatrical landscape, with important centres of new work arising, such as L'Atélier Saint-Anne, Théâtre Varia, La Balsamine, Le Plan K (all in Brussels) and Le Groupov (in Liège), and their young directors (e.g. Philippe Van Kessel, Philippe Sireuil, Michel Desoteux, Martine Wyckaert, Isabelle Pousseur, Bernard De Coster).

Armand Delcampe, the motive force behind the Centre d'Etudes Théâtrales (University of Louvain), launched a theatre association influenced by Vilar, L'Atélier Théâtral, and invited international directors (including BESSON and KREČJA), hosted international theatre (BROOK and MNOUCHKINE) and helped open up an international perspective for Belgian audiences; the same was done at De Singel in Antwerp (with, for example, Wajda, KANTOR and BERGMAN). Together with the Belgian dance companies, a new theatre was produced in this way within an international context, laying the foundation of what may become a European theatre culture. CARLOS TINDEMANS

S. Lilar, *The Belgian Theatre since 1890* (1950)

Belgrade Theatre, Coventry *see* ARCHITECTURE; REPERTORY MOVEMENT

Bell, John (b. Newcastle, NSW, Australia, 1 Nov. 1940) Actor and director. After acting with the ROYAL SHAKESPEARE COMPANY (1964–9), Bell returned to Sydney in time for a local theatre boom and directed its first national success, *The Legend of King O'Malley*. In 1970, he co-founded the NIMROD THEATRE COMPANY, of which he was artistic director for 15 years, directing many Australian premières. The performances for which he will be remembered – Cyrano, Arturo Ui, Shylock, C. S. Lewis – have rarely been 'Australian'. In 1991 he founded the Bell Shakespeare Company, which continues to tour nationally and internationally, employing innovative directors such as STEVEN BERKOFF, MICHAEL BOGDANOV and Barrie Kosky. JEREMY ECCLES

Bell, John Joy (b. Glasgow, 7 May 1871; d. Aberdeen, 14 Nov. 1934) Playwright. His career as a dramatist began at the Glasgow Repertory Theatre (1909–14), where Alfred Wareing produced both *Oh! Christina* (1910) and *Wee Macgreegor* (1911). The latter is a slight, if appealing and to a degree sentimental, comedy, based on Bell's own popular newspaper serial, recounting the adventures of the eponymous hero, a small boy living in a vibrant working-class community in Glasgow. If Scottish drama of the period is often condemned as nostalgic, backward-looking and rural, Bell's play is none of these things. Here is a character and an environment determinedly contemporary, urban, familiar to its audience and speaking in a vivid Glaswegian vernacular. ADRIENNE SCULLION

Belorussia/Belorus *see* SOVIET UNION

Bely, Andrey [Boris Nikolaevich Bugaev] (b. Moscow, 26 Oct. 1880; d. Moscow, 8 Jan. 1934) Poet, novelist, critic and theorist. He was one of the founders of Russian SYMBOLISM and collaborator (1903–8) with Valery Bryusov on *Vesy*, the chief journal of the movement. His plays, *He Who Was Come* (1903) and *The Jaws of Night* (1907), come from a period when he stressed the mysterious rather than the real and were less important than his theoretical writings, which influenced theatre artists such as BLOK and MEYERHOLD. MARVIN CARLSON

International Symposium on Andrey Bely, *Andrey Bely: A Critical Review* (1978)

Ben-Ami, Jacob [Jacob Schtchrin] (b. Minsk, Belarus, 1890; d. New York, 2 July 1977) Actor and director. His theatrical grounding was with a troupe of YIDDISH players in Odessa, which later became well known as the Vilna Troupe when they successfully toured Europe in highly stylized productions with Ben-Ami as their leading actor. In 1918 he joined MAURICE SCHWARTZ's company in New York. His success in *The Lonely Inn*, combined with artistic disagreements with Schwartz, led him to take the Madison Square Theater on his own, where he ran a season of plays by SHOLOM ALEICHEM, HAUPTMANN, Tolstoy and Osip Dymov which were a huge success with New York's large population of Yiddish-speaking immigrants. His own highly acclaimed performances soon ensured a successful career for him on Broadway, and he subsequently divided his time between Yiddish- and English-speaking productions, appearing in his first major English-speaking role in *Samson and Delilah* (1920) and earning accolades for his stage work into the 1970s.
HELEN RAPPAPORT

Benatzky, Ralph [Rudolph Josef František] (b. Mährisch-Budwitz, Moravia, 5 June 1884; d. Zurich, 16 Oct. 1957) Composer. He began his composing career as a songwriter before turning to the theatre with a series of scores for short and full-scale Viennese cabaret musicals and operettas. In the 1920s he moved to Berlin, where his Johann Strauss pasticcio *Casanova* (1928) with its famous 'Nuns' Chorus' was produced, before, in 1930, he found outstanding success with his score for the spectacular operetta *Im weissen Rössl*. As *White Horse Inn* this work, with its appealing combination of light comedy, attractive music and hugely extravagant staging, became an international success. He continued a prolific output of operetta, REVUE, musical comedy and film scores as he moved his centre of operations successively to Vienna, Paris, America and, ultimately, Switzerland, in a career of some 40 years and more than 50 stage shows. KURT GÄNZL

Benavente [y Martinez], Jacinto (b. Madrid, 12 August 1866; d. Galapagar, Spain, 12 July 1954) Playwright, awarded the Nobel Prize for Literature in 1922 in recognition of his attempted revitalization of the Spanish theatre, which he dominated for over half a century. Although progressively attacked by the liberal intelligentsia for the conservative nature of his drama, Benavente's satirical social comedies were sharp in their criticism of the moral degradation and hypocrisy of upper-middle-class life. His 172 plays include *El nido ajeno* ('Another's nest', 1894), *Los intereses creados* ('Bonds of interest', 1907) and *La última carta* ('The final letter', 1941). MARIA DELGADO

John E. Diall, *Jacinto Benavente and his Theatre* (1972)
M. C. Peñnelas, *Jacinto Benavente* (1969)

benefit The twentieth century saw a shift away from the traditional benefit performance that dates back to the late seventeenth century and provided additional income for individuals (actors, managers, occasionally playwrights), to benefits for organizations and causes. These events can either be one-off performances with casts specifically gathered, or a specially designated – and often extra – performance during the run of a show. MUSIC HALL and VARIETY artists have a particularly strong record of support for colleagues in need and for charities. (In Britain, they have an organization for this purpose called the Grand Order of Water Rats, which was founded in 1890 following a party the year before that celebrated the achievements of Water Rat, a racehorse.) The profession in general has spread its solidarity wide; benefits have been given to support trades union struggles, civil rights, liberation movements, famine relief and, in the last decades of the twentieth century, those involved in AIDS campaigns. The role of benefits to help individuals was taken over by charities, which were usually less open to abuse, avoided possible embarrassment of the individual and provided a more reliable return. There are many, the oldest of which, like the Royal Theatrical Fund, date back to the early nineteenth century.
CHARLES LONDON

Benin *see* FRENCH AFRICAN THEATRE

Benmussa, Simone (b. nr Tunis, French Tunisia, 5 June 1932; d. Paris, 4 June 2001) Playwright, adaptor, director and editor. Working in a variety of capacities for the RENAUD–BARRAULT Company in Paris for about 40 years, she started by editing the 10-year correspondence between Barrault and PAUL CLAUDEL, then became editor of *Cahiers Renaud–Barrault*, a bi-monthly literary magazine, helping to resurrect the reputation of ANTONIN ARTAUD. She was also responsible for the first production of a play by MARGUERITE DURAS. Although she later wrote original plays, Benmussa's greatest successes were dramatizations of other people's work, in particular *La Vie singuliere d'Albert Nobbs* (*The Singular Life of Alfred Nobbs*, 1978), based on the true story by George Moore about a young Irish girl who masquerades as a man in order to earn a living as a hotel waiter. Other works – often with a feminist perspective – include adaptations from Freud, Edith Wharton, Virginia Woolf and NATHALIE SARRAUTE. After Barrault's death in 1994, she formed her own theatre company and created mixed-media works with composers and dancers.   NEIL DOWDEN

Bennett, Alan   (b. Leeds, 9 May 1934) Playwright and actor. After his early success in the revue *Beyond the Fringe* (1960), Bennett's first play was a satirical celebration of the English establishment (*Forty Years On*, 1965). Subsequent stage successes include a rumbustious seaside farce, *Habeas Corpus* (1973), and the more cerebral *The Old Country* (1973). *Enjoy* (1980) and *Kafka's Dick* (1986) were followed by *Single Spies* (1988) and *The Madness of George III* (1991, later filmed), both staged by the NATIONAL THEATRE. His successful career as a television writer reached a peak with *Talking Heads* (1988 and 1998), two series of monologues in which unprepossessing characters chatter about their humdrum lives – and win our amused sympathies. Individual monologues from the series have subsequently been staged. Screenplays include *A Private Function* (1984), and *Prick Up Your Ears* (1986) about JOE ORTON. Because he regularly writes about the humdrum (with a mixture of pathos and humour), he is sometimes unfairly under-rated as a dramatist. His autobiographical *Writing Home* was published in 1994. This includes a compilation of diary entries, *The Lady in the Van*, which he subsequently dramatized for the stage (1999).   DAVID SELF

Daphne Turner, *Alan Bennett: A Critical Survey* (1997)
Peter Wolfe, *Understanding Alan Bennett* (1999)

Bennett [Enoch] Arnold   (b. Hanley, Staffs, 27 May 1867; d. London, 27 March 1931) Novelist and playwright. Bennett's first play, *Cupid and Commonsense* (1908), an adaptation of his novel *Anna of the Five Towns* produced by the STAGE SOCIETY, suggested he would be a minority dramatist working with regional subject matter. However, *The Great Adventure* (1913), produced by GRANVILLE BARKER, and a collaboration with EDWARD KNOBLOCK, *Milestones* (1912), both ran for over 600 performances. The success of the former allowed Granville Barker to concentrate on Shakespearean production; the latter was an influential forerunner of COWARD's *Cavalcade*. Other plays, *The Honeymoon* (1911), *Sacred and Profane Love* (1919), and *The*

Title (1918), also had long initial runs, but his work has rarely been revived. Bennett has the honour of having an egg dish named after him.   IAN CLARKE

Margaret Drabble, *Arnold Bennett: A Biography* (1985).

Bennett [di Figlia], Michael   (b. Buffalo, NY, 8 April 1943; d. Tucson, Ariz., 2 July 1987) Choreographer and director. He went to dancing school aged three, and at 17 played Baby John in a European tour of *West Side Story*. After being a chorus dancer in three failed Broadway shows and choreographer on three more failures, in 1968 he choreographed his first hit, *Promises, Promises*, and from then on was one of Broadway's busiest choreographers. He worked with SONDHEIM and PRINCE on the creation of the 'party' musicals *Company* (1970) and *Follies* (1971, which Bennett co-directed). In 1971 he directed a straight play, *Twigs*, and about this time conceived the idea of a show about dancers. The result was *A Chorus Line*, which evolved from workshops with dancers and a long rehearsal period. With Bennett as director and choreographer, it opened a season at JOSEPH PAPP's NEW YORK PUBLIC THEATER on 21 May 1975, then moved to the Shubert Theatre in July to become the longest-running musical in Broadway history (6,104 performances). Bennett followed this with one other successful Broadway musical, *Dreamgirls* (1981), and one failure, *Ballroom* (1978). He started work on the British musical *Chess* (1986) but had to retire because of AIDS; he died a year later.   IAN BEVAN

See also CHOREOGRAPHY; DANCE.

K. Kelly, *One Singular Sensation: The Michael Bennett Story* (1990)
K. Mandelbaum, *A Chorus Line and the Musicals of Michael Bennett* (1989)

Bennett, Richard   (b. Deacon's Mills, Ind., 21 May 1873; d. Los Angeles, 22 Oct. 1944) Actor. After a time in stock and touring, he made his first success in *The Lion and the Mouse* (1905), then scored again as John Shand in *What Every Woman Knows* (1908). He often was rewarded by taking leads in plays with seemingly little commercial potential, such as *Damaged Goods* (1913), *Beyond the Horizon* (1920), *The Hero* (1921), and *He Who Gets Slapped* (1922). Later hits included *They Knew What They Wanted* (1924) and *Jarnegan* (1928). A small but virile and handsome man, with a fine voice, he was sometimes criticized for over-deliberate readings.   GERALD BORDMAN

J. Bennett and L. Kiffee, *The Bennett Playbill* (1970)

Bennett, Robert Russell (b. Kansas City, Mo., 15 June 1894; d. New York, 18 Aug. 1981) Orchestrator. Both his mother and father were musicians. He studied with Carl Busch and Nadia Boulanger, and performed as a composer–pianist before turning to orchestrating. His first orchestrations were heard in *Hitchy Koo* (1919). From the 1920s to the mid-1960s he was one of the busiest and most respected of Broadway orchestrators, his rich, singularly balanced work coming to epitomize the Broadway 'sound' of the 1940s onward. His assignments included classic successes such as *Rose-Marie* (1927), *Show Boat* (1927), *Oklahoma!* (1943), *Kiss Me, Kate* (1948), *My Fair Lady* (1956) and *The Sound of Music* (1959). *'The Broadway Sound': The Autobiography and Selected Essays of Robert Russell Bennett* appeared in 1999. GERALD BORDMAN

Benny, Jack [Benjamin Kubelsky] (b. Waukegan, Ill., 14 Feb. 1894; d. Beverly Hills, Calif., 26 Dec. 1974) Comedian. A gifted violinist, Benny started his professional life in VAUDEVILLE and scored many successes, culminating in the Broadway show *The Earl Carroll Vanities* (1930). He made his film debut in 1928 and went on to appear in many more films. His droll, deadpan style of humour, coupled with the trademark of his fiddle-playing, earned him a huge popular following, first on radio (from 1932) and then with the highly successful television series *The Jack Benny Show*, which ran from 1950 to 1965. He also performed SOLO SHOWS. His memoir, *Jack Benny*, appeared in 1974. HELEN RAPPAPORT

See also STAND-UP COMEDY.

J. and J. Benny, *Sunday Nights at Seven* (1991)
I. Fein, *Jack Benny: An Intimate Biography* (1976)

Benois, Alexandre [Alexander Nikolayevich Benua] (b. St Petersburg, Russia, 21 April 1870; d. Paris, 9 Feb. 1960) Painter, theatre designer, art historian, critic and director. A leading member of the World of Art group in St Petersburg, he designed initially for the local Hermitage and Marinsky Theatres. He was briefly artistic director of the Ballets Russes, whose 'look' he created with BAKST, and thereby had an enormous impact on European and international theatre. He designed *Petrushka* for DIAGHILEV/NIJINSKY (1911) and worked for a while at the MOSCOW ART THEATRE as both designer and director. Benois emigrated in 1926 and thereafter designed opera and ballet mainly in France and Italy. His *Reminiscences of the Russian Ballet* appeared in 1941. NICK WORRALL

Benson, Frank [Robert] (b. Tunbridge Wells, Kent, 4 Nov. 1858; d. London, 31 Dec. 1939) Actor–manager. A keen sportsman, Benson is most remembered for his company, formed in 1883, which toured Shakespeare and performed (between 1886 and 1916) during the summer SHAKESPEARE FESTIVALS in STRATFORD-UPON-AVON, giving in 1899 an historic uncut *Hamlet*. He eventually produced all of Shakespeare's plays bar *Titus Andronicus* and *Troilus and Cressida*. Though traditionally Victorian in his productions, Benson was noted for his employment and encouragement of young, inexperienced actors, and his company became a training ground for many who would later establish significant careers in the theatre, such as HENRY AINLEY, OSCAR ASCHE, CEDRIC HARDWICKE, MATHESON LANG and HARCOURT WILLIAMS. Benson wrote *My Memoirs* (1930) and *I Want To Go on the Stage* (1931). He was knighted in 1916 during the Shakespeare Tercentenary celebrations at the THEATRE ROYAL, DRURY LANE – the only actor to be honoured in a theatre. IAN CLARKE

J. C. Trewin, *Benson and the Bensonians* (1960)

Benthall, Michael [Pickersgill] (b. London, 8 Feb. 1919; d. London, 6 Sept. 1974) Director. Having appeared in small parts at the OLD VIC in 1939, he co-directed *Hamlet* for the company, with GUTHRIE. His frequent collaborator ROBERT HELPMANN played Hamlet (1944). After successes at STRATFORD-UPON-AVON and in the WEST END, including Webster's *The White Devil* (1947) and SHAW's *The Millionairess* (1952), Benthall became the Old Vic's artistic director (1953–62). He presented all Shakespeare's First Folio plays in five years. Budgets were low and many actors were inexperienced, but Benthall attracted young audiences with imaginative, populist casting: e.g. RICHARD BURTON and JOHN NEVILLE, alternating as Othello and Iago; FRANKIE HOWERD as Bottom; KATHARINE HEPBURN as Portia and Kate on an Australian tour. He emphasized movement and narrative, often cutting heavily, and gradually discarded spectacle for simple light and shade. TONY HOWARD

Bentley, Eric [Russell] (b. Bolton, Lancs, 14 Sept. 1916) Teacher, editor, critic, translator and playwright. British by birth, he became a US citizen by naturalization in 1948. He was instrumental in bringing BRECHT to the American public through his translations, essays and recordings. From his position at the *New Republic* (1952–6) he established himself as a demanding and stimulating critic. His many books include: *The Playwright as Thinker* (1946), *In Search of Theater* (1953), *The Life of the Drama* (1964), *The Brecht Commentaries 1943–1980* (1981) and *Thinking About the Playwright* (1987). He has also adapted plays by SCHNITZLER and PIRANDELLO and championed European drama. Several of Bentley's original plays have been collected in *Are You Now or Have You Ever Been and Other Plays* (1977) and *The Kleist Variations* (1982). A distinguished academic, he has also directed in the United States and elsewhere.   THOMAS F. CONNOLLY

Bérard, Christian-Jacques (b. Paris, 12 Aug. 1902; d. Paris, 12 Feb. 1949) Theatre, film and fashion designer. As well as designing for some of the greatest choreographers – FOKINE, BALANCHINE, Petit, Massine – Bérard excelled in designs for new plays, such as COCTEAU's *La Voix Humaine* (1930) and GIRAUDOUX's *La Folle de Chaillot* (1945) and *Amphitryon 38* (1947). His work on revivals of Molière plays (e.g. *L'Ecole des femmes*, 1936 and *Les Fourberies de Scapin/Scapin* 1949) won him acclaim too, and his fashion sketches were said to have prompted the Dior New Look of the 1940s.
ADRIANA HUNTER

See also FASHION.

Berg, Alban   *see* OPERA

Berghof, Herbert (b. Vienna, 13 Sept. 1909; d. New York, 5 Nov. 1990) Actor, director and teacher. He studied with such practitioners as MAX REINHARDT and LEE STRASBERG, as well as at the ACTORS' STUDIO, where he was a charter member. He made his professional debut in *Don Carlos* (Vienna, 1927), and was introduced to Broadway in 1940, when he co-directed and acted in *Reunion in New York*. He directed the first US production of BECKETT's *Waiting for Godot* (1956). He is best known as a distinguished teacher of acting. After teaching at several important establishments he founded the Herbert Berghof Studio in 1945 (which he co-directed with his wife, UTA HAGEN), and the HB Playwrights Foundation in 1946.   LAURIE WOLF

Bergman, Hjalmar [Frederik Elgerus] (b. Örrebro, Närke, Sweden, 19 Dec. 1883; d. Berlin, 1 Jan. 1931) Playwright and novelist who led a restless existence, never staying for long in his home country. His early plays, published collectively as *Marionettspel* ('Marionette plays', 1917), were written under the influence of MAETERLINCK and share the same elements of the grotesque and gloomy. But it is his comedy *Swedenhielms* (1925) that is best remembered alongside his more successful work as a novelist, and this play has remained in the Swedish repertoire.
HELEN RAPPAPORT

E. H. Linder, *Hjalmar Bergman* (1975).

Bergman, Ingmar (b. Uppsala, Sweden, 14 July 1918) Film and stage director, scriptwriter and playwright. A man of great energy, honesty, perception and charisma, he created conditions of creative trust in which artists and actors such as Bibi Andersson, Liv Ullman, Ingrid Thulin, Harriet Andersson, Max von Sydow, Gunnar Bjornstrand and Erland Josefson produced brilliant film and stage work. Famous films such as *Summer with Monica* (1952), *Persona* (1966), *Cries and Whispers* (1973) and his last, *Fanny and Alexander* (1982), focus on human behaviour under extreme pressure: the threat of death, pressure of sexual need, isolation and loss. His fame as a film director runs in parallel with his brilliant – and longer – Swedish (and German) stage directing career. He began in Helsingborg in 1940, moved to Gothenburg (1946–50) and Malmö (1952–8), and then to the prestigious Dramaten (1963–6) in Stockholm, where he reformed the programme and improved acting conditions. After his resignation in 1966 he returned for guest productions but in 1976 exiled himself to Germany for nine years as a result of false charges of tax evasion. He rejoined Dramaten in 1985, after the end of his directing career in film (though he continued scriptwriting and TV directing) to stage STRINDBERG's *Miss Julie* and *A Dream Play*. Plays by Strindberg, IBSEN, Molière, CHEKHOV and Shakespeare figure strongly among his productions, but his range is wide. His autobiography, *The Magic Lantern* (translated by J. Tate), appeared in 1988. Bergman has lived and worked intensely and generously. His legacy is evident in the cinema. In the theatre it continues to be mediated by actors, technicians, directors, audiences and critics. We have reason to be grateful.   TERRY HODGSON

Stig Bjørkman, ed., *Bergman on Bergman* (1973)
Peter Cowie, *Ingmar Bergman: A Critical Biography* (1982)
Marc Gervais, *Ingmar Bergman: Magician and Prophet* (1999)
F. J. and L-L. Marker, *Ingmar Berman: A Life in the Theatre* (1992)

Bergner [Ettel], Elisabeth (b. Drohobyz, Poland, 22 Aug. 1900; d. London, 12 May 1986) Actress. After making her stage debut in Zurich in 1919, she established herself as a Shakespearean actress in roles such as Ophelia, Rosalind, Kate, Viola, Juliet, and found international fame in Berlin in MAX REINHARDT's 1924 production of SHAW's *St Joan*. The rise to power of the Nazis forced Bergner to move to England in 1933, where she attracted attention with her first English-language performance (in Margaret Kennedy's *Escape Me Never*) and the lead in *The Boy David* (1936) – BARRIE's last play, which he wrote for her. She was successful on both sides of the Atlantic and after the Second World War toured Germany and Austria in RATTIGAN's *The Deep Blue Sea* (1954) and O'NEILL's *Long Day's Jour-*

ney into Night (1957). She became a British citizen in 1938. HELEN RAPPAPORT

Berkoff, Steven (b. London, 3 Aug. 1937) Actor, director and playwright. He founded the London Theatre Group (1973), which has produced many of his plays. Berkoff's athletic performance style is neo-EXPRESSIONIST and 'Artaudian'. His productions are intense and bare, restricted to mimed props, choric movement and startling vocal effects. He adapted Aeschylus, Poe and, especially, Kafka; but Berkoff's original scripts show modern Londoners – brutalized East Enders, the frustrated young and the grotesquely rich – who speak a remorselessly dazzling fusion of slang, inventive obscenity and Homeric/Shakespearean pastiche. The structure is often Oedipal. Women are presented as sexual objects, but Berkoff gives his actresses witty and angry set-piece monologues. His work became hugely influential for the development of British physical theatre in the 1980s and early 1990s. Plays include *East* (1975), *Decadence* (1981), *Sink the Belgrano!* (1986) and *Kvetch* (1986). An autobiography, *Free Association*, was published in 1996. TONY HOWARD

Berlin Although there were numerous high-ranking regional stages in Germany, the capital, Berlin, held the centre of theatre life. The Deutsches Theater, led by MAX REINHARDT from 1905, predominated until 1918 with classical authors and contemporaries like IBSEN, STRINDBERG, SHAW, GERHART HAUPTMANN and FRANK WEDEKIND. Reinhardt's Shakespeare cycles began with the famous *A Midsummer Night's Dream*, later to be filmed in Hollywood. The social ferment of the Weimar Republic (1919–33) produced anti-illusionist and socio-critical innovations, stimulated by EXPRESSIONIST writers like ERNST TOLLER, GEORG KAISER and BERTOLT BRECHT. New staging techniques were evolved by LEOPOLD JESSNER at the Schauspielhaus and ERWIN PISCATOR at the Volksbühne. Under Nazi rule (1933–45) the theatre declined, but after the Second World War it revived in both parts of the now divided city. In the East, Brecht's BERLINER ENSEMBLE claimed worldwide attention with *Mother Courage* featuring HELENE WEIGEL. Also prominent were the Deutsches Theater (Wolfgang Langhoff, Alexander Lang, Adolf Dresen) and the Volksbühne under BENNO BESSON in the 1970s. New playwrights like PETER HACKS and HEINER MÜLLER came to the fore. In West Berlin, the representative Schiller Theater was eclipsed by the Schaubühne led by PETER STEIN from 1970, staging plays by Ibsen, Kleist, GORKY, CHEKHOV and contemporaries like PETER HANDKE and BOTHO STRAUSS. Piscator continued his political stagings at the Freie Volksbühne. Reunification was marked by Heiner Müller's seven-hour production of *Hamlet/Machine* at the Deutsches Theater in 1990. An unfortunate sequel to reunification was the closing of the Schiller Theater for reasons of economy in 1993. The year 1999 brought radical changes at three of the foremost houses: CLAUS PEYMANN, as new head of the Berliner Ensemble, finally ended the post-Brechtian era; 30-year-old Thomas Ostermeier took over the Schaubühne and resolved to break fresh ground; and the announcment of a newcomer to replace Thomas Langhoff (son of Wolfgang) at the Deutsches Theater in 2001 heralds a sweeping away of long-standing traditions there too.
M. HAMBURGER

Ruth Freydank, *Theater in Berlin* (1988)
Ronald Hayman, ed., *The German Theatre* (1975)
Dieter Kranz, *Berliner Theater* (1990)
Michael Patterson, *The Revolution in German Theatre 1900–1933* (1981)
John Willett, *The Theatre of the Weimar Republic* (1988)

Berlin, Irving [Israel Baline] (b. Temun, Russia, 11 May 1888; d. New York, 22 Sept. 1989) Composer and lyricist. After an early career as a songwriter, Berlin provided his first full BROADWAY score for the 'syncopated musical show' *Watch Your Step* (1914), which featured the ragtime rhythms he had been instrumental in popularizing. He subsequently provided the songs (including a number which have become popular standards) for several large-scale REVUES, including editions of the ZIEGFELD FOLLIES, his own *Music Box Revues* (1921–4), *As Thousands Cheer* (1933) and the forces spectacular *This Is the Army* (1942). His first attempt at a book musical, the Marx Brothers vehicle *The Cocoanuts* (1925), and two subsequent pieces following the fashion for political musicals (*Face the Music*, 1932, and *Louisiana Purchase*, 1940), emphasized Berlin's talent as a writer of individual songs rather than show scores. It was not until his 58th year that he achieved an international hit with a book musical, with the production of Herbert and Dorothy Fields' *Annie Get Your Gun* (1946). Another vehicle for *Annie* star ETHEL MERMAN, *Call Me Madam* (1950), also found success, but two later efforts, again in the political vein (*Miss Liberty*, 1949, and *Mr President*, 1960), were failures.
KURT GÄNZL

L. Bergreen, *As Thousands Cheer* (1990)
D. Ewen, *The Story of Irving Berlin* (1950)
C. Hamm, *Irving Berlin: Songs from the Melting Pot* (1997)
A. Woolcott, *The Story of Irving Berlin* (1974)

Berliner Ensemble German theatre company founded in 1949 in East BERLIN by BERTOLT BRECHT and HELENE WEIGEL. Their production of *Mother Courage* at the Deutsches Theater (January 1949) served as a basis for the creation of a theatre ensemble where Brecht's advanced form of EPIC THEATRE could be given shape. In April 1949 the project received official recognition and plans were made for a repertoire which was to include model productions of Brecht's plays, topical political plays by contemporary authors and classical plays of world dramatic literature. Taking Picasso's peace dove as its symbol, the company was officially inaugurated on 12 November 1949 with a première of Brecht's *Puntila* at the Deutsches Theater. This was the Ensemble's home until 19 March 1954, when the company moved to the Theater am Schiffbauerdamm, scene of an earlier Brecht triumph with *The Threepenny Opera*.

Of the 21 plays produced between 1949 and 1956, when Brecht died, only five were original plays by Brecht, and only seven productions were directed by Brecht himself. The company experimented with various styles and methods in order to enable the members of the ensemble to become all-round actors, and not just Brecht specialists. They included some of Germany's leading actors, such as Ernst Busch, Therese Giehse and EKKEHARD SCHALL.

Weigel continued to be the company's director until 1970. Most key productions were directed by Brecht's old collaborator, Erich Engel, and his former assistant director, Manfred Wekwerth. In 1971 a new artistic team under the directorship of Ruth Berghaus aimed at a new direction. They tried to overcome the recent development of the Ensemble into a Brecht museum by producing some of Brecht's less well-known plays, introducing new dramatists, re-evaluating some of the classics of world literature, and introducing new actors and directors. Several of their productions caused controversy because of their innovative character. In 1977 Berghaus handed in her resignation, and Wekwerth was appointed new artistic director. He trod a middle ground between preserving an established Brecht tradition and modern reinterpretation of his works, complemented by modern East German and Soviet authors and European classics. After German reunification he was forced to step down. A collective leadership that included Matthias Langhoff, Fritz Marquardt, HEINER MULLER, Peter Palitzsch and PETER ZADEK was unable to give the theatre a new direction. In 1999 the Berlin Senate decided to sever the theatre's connections with Bertolt Brecht and appointed the controversial CLAUS PEYMANN as the new artistic director.

GÜNTER BERGHAUS

Karl-Heinz Drescher, *Plakate für das Berliner Ensemble* (1988)

Berman, Ed *see* INTER-ACTION

Bernard, Jean-Jacques (b. Enghien, France, 30 July 1888; d. Meulan, France, 14 Sept. 1972) Playwright. Bernard's THEATRE OF SILENCE presents sensitive studies of shy or reticent characters whose silences betray more than their speech. Plays include *Martine* (1922, revived at the NATIONAL THEATRE, London, 1985), *L'Invitation au voyage* ('Invitation to a voyage', 1924), *Les Soeurs Guedonec* ('The sisters Guedonec', 1931) and *Notre-Dame d'En-Haut* ('Notre-Dame from on high', 1961). ANNA MCMULLAN

Kester Adrian Branford, *A Study of Jean-Jacques Bernard's 'Théâtre de l'Inexprimé' (1977)*

Bernhard, Thomas (b. Heerlen, Netherlands, 10 Feb. 1931; d. Ohlsdorf, Austria, 12 Feb. 1989) Playwright and novelist, whose often florid theatrical style may contribute to an obstinate neglect by English-speaking directors. Many of his plays, which are structured like music, concern the obsession of artists with the potential – or lack of it – of their craft. In *Die Macht der Gewohnheit* (*The Force of Habit*, 1974; London, NATIONAL THEATRE, 1976 – a notable flop), a circus director is compelled to perform Schubert's Trout Quintet. *Minetti* (written in 1976 for the leading German actor Bernhard Minetti) shows an elderly thespian failing to achieve his ambition to play Lear. *Der Theatermacher* (*Histrionics*, or *The Theatremaker*, 1986) is a brilliant and illuminating study of art and autocracy characteristically requiring a virtuoso performance for the central part, an ageing theatre director. Other plays include *Der Ignorant und der Wahnsinnige* (*The Ignoramus and the Madman*, 1972), *Elisabeth II* (1989) and *Heldenplatz* (1988). JUDY MEEWEZEN

Denis Calandra, *New German Dramatists* (1983)

Bernhardt [Bernard], Sarah [Henriette Rosine] (b. Paris, 22 Oct. 1844; d. Paris, 26 March 1923) Actress and manager who became, deservedly, a legend. She began as an erotically charged *ingénue*, graduated to the mature heroines of neoclassical drama, and survived as an icon into old age. Having been dubbed 'divine' she became known for her boldness, as much off stage as on. Her strengths remained the thrilling musicality of her voice and her great ability to exploit the visual resources of theatre: talents that first became apparent in revivals of plays by Hugo and Racine in the 1870s. The international potential of her style became clear when she visited London with the COMÉDIE-FRANÇAISE in 1879. Soon after that she went into independent management in Paris and embarked on the first of a series of highly remunerative American tours. In the 1880s and 1890s she developed, with the playwright VICTORIEN SARDOU, a brand of spectacular romantic MELODRAMA (*Fédora*, 1882; *Théodora, 1884; La Tosca, 1887*), best considered as opera without music. Together with *La Dame aux Camélias* (1884) by Dumas *fils*, these increasingly defined her range, though there were brave experiments, most intriguingly in male roles: *Hamlet* (1899) and ROSTAND's *L'Aiglon* (1900). In 1905 she suffered an injury to her leg that eventually led to amputation, but she continued acting and made forays into the new art of moving pictures and cameo appearances in London MUSIC HALLS. She also painted, sculpted and wrote plays, poetry and her *Memoirs*, which were published in 1907. (*My Double Life: The Memoirs of Sarah Bernhardt*, translated by Victoria Teitze Larson, appeared in 1999.) If her appeal became difficult to grasp decades later it is because her kind of acting, together with her repertoire, had passed out of fashion. Feminist historians, however, have begun to re-evaluate her heroic and salutary career. JOHN STOKES

Elaine Aston, *Sarah Bernhardt: A French Actress on the English Stage* (1989)
Ruth Brandon, *Being Divine: A Biography of Sarah Bernhardt* (1991)
Arthur Gold and Robert Fizdale, *The Divine Sarah: A Life of Sarah Bernhardt* (1992)
John Stokes, Michael R. Booth and Susan Bassnett, *Bernhardt, Terry, Duse: The Actress in Her Time* (1988)
Gerda Taranow, *The Bernhardt Hamlet: Culture and Context* (1996)

Bernstein, Aline [Frankau] (b. New York, 22 Dec. 1880; d. New York, 7 Sept. 1955) Set and costume designer. Bernstein began her theatrical career at the NEIGHBORHOOD PLAYHOUSE, where her work included the sets and costumes for *The Little Clay Cart* (1924) and the EXPRESSIONISTIC designs for *The Dybbuk* (1926). She served as resident designer for EVA LE GALLIENNE's CIVIC REPERTORY THEATER, then worked for the THEATER GUILD. She began a fruitful association with Herman Shumlin on *Grand Hotel* in 1930, and through him became known as the designer for LILLIAN HELLMAN's plays. Bernstein won a Tony award for her costumes for *Regina* (1949). She was also instrumental in founding the Costume Institute at the Metropolitan Museum of New York. ANNE FLETCHER

C. Klein, *Aline* (1979).

Bernstein, Leonard (b. Lawrence, Mass., 25 Aug. 1918; d. New York, 14 Oct. 1990) Composer. He won recognition as a symphonic conductor at an early age. He entered the theatre as a composer with *On the Town* (1944), a light comedy song and dance piece which had success on BROADWAY and as a film. Incidental music for *Peter Pan* (1950) and another successful musical in the standard Broadway style, *Wonderful Town* (1953), were followed by a much more ambitious score for a musical version of Voltaire's *Candide* (1956). The music for *West Side Story* (1957) took yet another path, combining the substance of the *Candide* score and the dance-orientation of *On the Town* in a driving and exciting contemporary version of the Romeo and Juliet story. Although the worldwide stage and screen success of *West Side Story* established it as an all-time Broadway great, Bernstein concentrated thereafter on other areas of his internationally successful musical life as conductor and composer and wrote only one further stage musical, *1600 Pennsylvania Avenue* (1976). In 1974 a rewritten and more humorous version of *Candide* found Broadway success and the piece has subsequently been played in opera houses. KURT GÄNZL

J. Briggs, *Leonard Bernstein* (1961)
H. Burton, *Leonard Bernstein* (1994)
D. Ewen, *Leonard Bernstein* (1960)
J. Peyser, *Bernstein: A Biography* (1987)
M. Secrest, *Leonard Bernstein: A Life* (1994)

Berry, Cicely [Frances] ('Cis') (b. Berkhampstead, Herts, 17 May 1926) Voice teacher. She trained at the Central School of Speech and Drama and was later a teacher there. She joined the ROYAL SHAKESPEARE COMPANY part-time in 1969 and became its voice director in 1970, establishing what was the first permanent voice department to be integrated into a theatre company. She is notable both for this engagement with the theatre voice and because of her political approach to language. Her concern is not with the formation of well-produced sound in itself, but rather that clarity should result from the actor's involvement in and active physical ownership of the text. As well as influencing many actors, directors, playwrights, educationalists and academics, she has worked in schools and prisons and has run workshops worldwide with a range of practitioners, from community groups to leading figures like AUGUSTO BOAL and EDWARD BOND. A director in her own right, she is also the author of several books which have become seminal texts in DRAMA SCHOOLS and universities: *Voice and the Actor* (1973), *Your Voice and How* *to Use It* (1975), and *The Actor and the Text* (1987). *Text in Action* appeared in 2001. LYN DARNLEY

See also VOICE; VOICE TRAINING.

Besson, Benno (b. Zurich, Switzerland, 1922) Director. He made his acting debut in 1942 under the direction of JEAN-MARIE SERREAU in Lyon, and along with Jean-Marie and Genevieve Serreau, presented the first productions of BERTOLT BRECHT's work in Paris. Besson initially met Brecht in Switzerland, following the playwright's return from exile in America. Brecht invited Besson to join the BERLINER ENSEMBLE as an actor and assistant for *mise-en-scène* in 1949, and Besson ultimately collaborated with Brecht on many productions, both as actor and director, until 1958. An important figure in Europe with a striking style, Besson continued to work in East Germany as director of the Deutsches Theater (1960–9) and of the VOLKSBÜHNE (1969–77) when he returned to the French theatre, directing versions of *As You Like It*, *Hamlet* and *The Caucasian Chalk Circle* at the AVIGNON FESTIVAL. He was director of the Comédie de Genève (1982–9) and then resumed a freelance career in opera and theatre. LAURIE WOLF

Betti, Ugo (b. Camerino, Italy, 4 Feb. 1892; d. Rome, 9 June 1953) Poet, playwright and critic. Son of a physician, Betti graduated in law (Parma, 1914) with a thesis on revolution and in 1930 became a judge. His war experiences had made his views more liberal and humane, if still austere. The first of his 26 plays, which range from light comedy to stark symbolism, is *La padrona* (*The Mistress*, 1927), the last *La fuggitiva* (*The Fugitive*, 1953). Betti explores ambitious themes like responsibility, morality and justice in fascinating detail. At its best, as in *Corruzione al palazzo di giustizia* (*Corruption at the Palace of Justice*, 1944), with which he achieved international success, and *L'aiuola bruciata* (*The Burnt Flower-Bed*, 1952), his drama reaches formidable heights of tragical lyric intensity. Other plays include *Frana allo scalo Nord* (*Land Slide at North Station*, 1935), *Delitto all'isola della capre* (*Crime on Goat Island*, 1950) and *La regina e gli insorti* (*The Queen and the Rebels*, 1951). G. H. MCWILLIAM

Emanuele Licastro, *Ugo Betti: An Introduction* (1985)

Beuys, Joseph *see* PERFORMANCE ART

Bijou Theatre A small auditorium in Bayswater, west London, used for amateur productions. It was known as the Bijou from 1886 until 1925, when it was renamed the Century under LENA ASHWELL. The Bijou presented the 'copyright performance' of a number of SHAW's plays (used by him to establish his performing

rights) and the first production of WILDE's *Salome* (1905). ADRIANA HUNTER

Bill-Belotserkovsky, Vladimir [Naumovich] (b. Aleksandriya, Ukraine, 9 Jan. 1884; d. Moscow, 1 March 1970) Playwright. A member of the Communist Party from 1917, between 1911 and 1917 he had worked as a navvy and stevedore in the United States (hence his nickname Bill). The themes of his 12 or more plays became prominent in Soviet drama; for example, *Shtorm* ('Storm', 1925), a Civil War documentary drama, demonstrates the suspicion of the intelligentsia as hidden or potential counter-revolutionaries, and *Zhizn zovyot* (*Life is calling*, 1953) shows the subjection of the personal and individual to the needs and supremacy of the collective. VERA GOTTLIEB

Peter Yershov, *Comedy in the Soviet Theater* (1956)

Billetdoux, François (b. Paris, 7 Sept. 1927; d. Paris, 3 Nov. 1991) Playwright, novelist and radio producer. In his whimsical mixture of BOULEVARD theatre and ABSURDISM, pairs of characters usually confront problems of exploitation and non-communication. *Tchin-tchin* (1959) brought him to prominence and was seen in the UK (adapted by WILLIS HALL) and the United States (adapted by Sidney Michaels). Titles suggesting his characteristic tone include *Il faut passer par les nuages* ('You must go via the clouds', 1964) and *Comment va le monde, Môssieu? Il tourne, Môssieu!* ('How goes the world, sir? It turns, sir!', also 1964). TERRY HODGSON

Jacques Guicharnaud, *Modern French Theatre* (1967)

Billington, Michael [Keith] (b. Leamington Spa, Warks, 16 Nov. 1939) Critic, broadcaster and author. He began writing theatre reviews for the Oxford University undergraduate magazine *Cherwell*. Early journalistic experience in Liverpool was followed by repertory management experience in Lincoln, before coming to London in 1964. After writing reviews for *Plays and Players* and *The Times* (1965–71), he joined the *Guardian* as theatre critic in October 1971. He has also been the London correspondent for the *New York Times* since 1978. Billington has built a reputation for being one of a few first-rate critics to stand alongside AGATE, HOBSON and TYNAN. His writing is balanced, constructively critical and informed by a breadth of knowledge of theatre. He has published on *The Modern Actor* (1973), *Alan Ayckbourn* (1983), *Tom Stoppard* (1987), *Peggy Ashcroft* (1988) and *Harold Pinter* (1996). *One Night Stands: A Critic's View of Modern British Theatre*, an anthology of his reviews from 1971 to 1991, was published in 1993. BRIAN ROBERTS

biomechanics Practice for training actors developed by MEYERHOLD in 1922. Deriving from MIME and the COMMEDIA DELL'ARTE, it sought to generate emotion and 'reflex excitability' from physical exercises. TERRY HODGSON

Birmingham By 1901 this major English manufacturing city boasted ten theatres, including the newly built Tivoli and the Lyceum (subsequently renamed the Hippodrome and the Alexandra), which offered a broad range of MELODRAMA, PANTOMIME, CIRCUS and VARIETY acts. Leading actor–managers toured productions of modern and classical drama to the Theatre Royal and the Prince of Wales, which had dispensed with their resident stock companies. The opening in 1913 of the first purpose-built British repertory theatre, the BIRMINGHAM REPERTORY, introduced innovative play production by a permanent acting ensemble. In the 1920s and 1930s the theatres which survived the threat posed by the cinema competed for the popular market. At the Alexandra Theatre from 1927 until 1937 the owner Leon Salberg maintained a repertory company which performed a weekly change of play twice nightly. From 1935 until it was bombed in 1941, the Prince of Wales offered visiting star companies and nationally famous pantomimes under the management of Emile LITTLER. The Theatre Royal lost status and finally closed down in 1956. A wartime 'Plays in the Parks' scheme led in 1948 to the Arena Theatre, one of the first OPEN-STAGE experiments, which was initially constructed in a circus tent. In 1962 the Midland Arts Centre for Young People (later known as the MAC), which included a studio theatre and a permanent OPEN-AIR Arena Theatre, opened in Cannon Hill Park. The Crescent Theatre, built in 1964, offered radical opportunities for flexible staging to the city's leading amateur company. In 1968 the establishment of the Birmingham Arts Laboratory inaugurated more than a decade of an energetic Birmingham FRINGE which included Banner and Second City as home-grown companies and attracted many of the nationally touring ALTERNATIVE companies which also appeared in the studio theatre of the 'new' (1971) Birmingham Rep. In the 1990s, after the economically turbulent 1980s had seen much alternative theatre collapse, Birmingham City Council pursued an active arts policy which nurtured ventures like Big Brum THEATRE IN EDUCATION company and Stans Cafe as well as several youth theatre groups. In 1992 the Birmingham Stage Company moved into the 'Old' Rep; other venues include the Library Theatre, The Drum (for black performance) and the Custard Factory arts complex. The Alexandra receives mainstream touring productions while the MAC promotes radical PERFORMANCE ART. The Hippodrome has become the home of Birmingham Royal Ballet. CLAIRE COCHRANE

Fred Norris, *Birmingham Hippodrome 1899–1999* (1999) Derek Salberg, *Ring Down the Curtain: A Fascinating Record of Birmingham Theatres and Contemporary Life through Three Centuries* (1980).

Birmingham Repertory Theatre A leading regional theatre and resident company since 1913, when it was founded as Britain's first purpose-built REPERTORY theatre by BARRY JACKSON, who was both owner and artistic director. Among its early successes were *Abraham Lincoln* (1918) by its general manager JOHN DRINKWATER, modern-dress productions of Shakespeare, and the British première of SHAW's *Back to Methuselah* (1923). Jackson had established the theatre's national reputation by 1935, when financial problems led to a board of trustees taking it over. Both LAURENCE OLIVIER and RALPH RICHARDSON were members of the company early in their careers, and CEDRIC HARDWICKE established himself here as a leading actor. Later PAUL SCOFIELD and ALBERT FINNEY achieved recognition. Its directors have included H. K. Ayliff, PETER BROOK and Douglas Seal, and for many years Paul Shelving was resident designer. A new theatre complex, including a Studio Theatre, was opened on a different site in 1971, but without a resident company. Former ROYAL SHAKESPEARE COMPANY director Bill Alexander took over in 1992, revived its fortunes and oversaw a major refurbishment in 1999. He was succeeded in 2001 by Jonathan Church. G. ROWELL

Claire Cochrane, *Shakespeare and the Birmingham Repertory Theatre 1913–1929* (1993)

J. C. Trewin, *The Birmingham Repertory Theatre 1913–1963* (1963)

Birtwistle, Harrison (b. Accrington, Lancs, 15 July 1934) Composer. Distinctive and controversial, he has always been interested in the relationship between words and music. His reputation for theatrical composition was established with *Punch and Judy* (1967) and *Down by the Greenwood Side* (1969), based on the medieval English Mummers' Play. Other dramatic work includes *The Mask of Orpheus* (1986), *Yan Tan Tethera* (1984–6) and *Gawain* (1991). In 1975 he became an associate director of the NATIONAL THEATRE and briefly its music director. Among his most notable work there were *Bow Down* (1977) and the *Oresteia* (1982), both with words by TONY HARRISON. He was knighted in 1988 and made a Companion of Honour in 2000. CATHY JOYCE

M. Hall, *Harrison Birtwistle* (1999)

Bjørnson, Bjørnst Jerne [Martinus] (b. Kvikne, Norway [then linked to Sweden], 8 Dec. 1832; d. Paris, 26 April 1910) Playwright, director, novelist and political campaigner, awarded the Nobel Prize for Literature in 1903. He helped modernize Norwegian theatre as he moved from romantic to realist 'problem' plays akin to those of his contemporary IBSEN, culminating in his greatest work, the two plays *Over Aevne I* (1883) and *II* (1895), the first of which was staged in London as *Beyond Human Power* in 1901. Bjørnson's actor–manager son Björn (1859–1942) campaigned for a Norwegian national theatre and became its first director in 1899. HELEN RAPPAPORT

Bjørnson, Maria (b. Paris, 16 Feb. 1949) Set and costume designer. She began a prolific career in designing for the theatre and OPERA in 1969. Most prominent in her career are the sets and costumes for ANDREW LLOYD WEBBER's *Phantom of the Opera* (1986), which has been seen around the world. She has collaborated with such directors as HAL PRINCE and TREVOR NUNN, and is known for her expressive, stylish approach. DENISE L. TILLES

Black, George (b. Birmingham, 20 April 1890; d. London, 4 March 1945) Impresario. He made MUSIC HALL respectable at the beginning of the twentieth century by bringing to it the lavish production values of REVUE. He began the Royal Command Variety Performances (1912). As head of General Theatre Corporation and Moss Empire running 40 theatres, he established a reputation for fast-paced entertainment, especially at the LONDON PALLADIUM, where he formed the CRAZY GANG in 1932, and at the London Hippodrome, where he staged a series of extravagant revues, such as *Black Velvet* (1939). COLIN CHAMBERS

black comedy Term coined in the twentieth century to describe a type of COMEDY that finds humour in material normally associated with tragedy. The term is probably derived from ANOUILH, who classified his early plays as *prèces roses* or *pièces noires*. The outstanding example is ORTON's *Loot* (1965). Also called ironic or dark comedy. MARVIN CARLSON

See also DRAMATIC THEORY.

black theatre

In Britain
Although a few black actors and playwrights had been at work in Britain since early in the twentieth century (Kobina Sekeye's *The Blinkards* was published in 1907) and black people had fought for Britain in both world wars, it was not until the 1950s that economic need led to mass migration from the non-white colonies and provided the beginnings of a community out of which 'black theatre' was to emerge as a term in general usage two decades later.

Documentation of the earlier period is imperfect; historian and journalist C. L. R. JAMES adapted his work on the Haitian revolution into a theatrical pageant, *The Black Jacobins* (known at its 1936 première as *Toussaint L'Ouverture*), starring PAUL ROBESON, who appeared in several plays in Britain in the 1920s and 1930s. A small group of black actors, including Robeson, performed at the left-wing UNITY THEATRE, out of which came the London Negro Repertory Theatre (1943), probably the first but short-lived attempt to found a British black theatre company. Black productions visited – from the United States, *Anna Lucasta* (1947, 1952 and 1954), *The Jazz Train* (1955), *A Raisin in the Sun* (1959), *The Amen Corner* (1965) and, from South Africa, *King Kong* (1961) – but of more immediate use to the fledgling local movement were the experimental Sunday night programmes at the ARTS THEATRE, ROYAL COURT and Tower Theatre organized by Pearl Connor, the first black theatrical agent and producer in England.

During the 1950s and 1960s, emerging black playwrights from abroad who were then working in London were supported by the Royal Court, which presented Barry Reckord's *Flesh to a Tiger* (1958), *You in Your Small Corner* (1960, staged by the Cheltenham Theatre Company) and *Skyvers* (1963), ERROL JOHN's *Moon on a Rainbow Shawl* (1958), and *The Invention* (1959) and *The Lion and the Jewel* (1966) by WOLE SOYINKA, a member of the theatre's Writers' Group whose play *The Road* was seen at the THEATRE ROYAL, STRATFORD EAST in 1965. With few exceptions, however, major theatres did not employ black actors or programme plays by black writers, and it was left up to the movers and shakers in the black community to agitate for what they wanted; NORMAN BEATON, Mona Hammond, Isabelle Lucas, Carmen Munroe and Rudolph Walker are among those who continued to be active into the 1990s.

By the early 1970s black theatre was beginning to be an indentifiable force as the ALTERNATIVE THEATRE movement grew; occasional and temporary black initiatives gave way to more permanent black groups; more playwrights emerged, some of whom had been born in Britain; and, while directors were hard to come by, technicians rare and producers rarer still, there was a greater number of skilled black actors from whom to choose. Jamaican actor Frank Cousins founded the Dark and Light Theatre in 1970 in Brixton, south London, to provide acting opportunities in a white culture and to serve the new black community, throwing open the venue to a host of projects, including in 1972 the first all-London tour of a black play, *Smile Orange* by TREVOR RHONE. INTER-ACTION's lunchtime theatre, which had presented plays by the black American writer ED BULLINS in its opening year, 1968, followed this with a Black Power season in 1970, and its success helped Dark and Light transform itself into the Black Theatre of Brixton under Jamal Ali, Norman Beaton and Rufus Collins.

A variety of groups emerged around the country, from Leeds to Birmingham and Nottingham to Bristol, but London remained the central force; companies such as TEMBA, founded in 1972 by South African actor Alton Kumalo, survied until 1993, promoting new and established black writers as well as interpretations of the classics, while most, like Calabash or the Fasimbas, disappeared quite quickly. The Keskidee Centre in Islington, north London, founded in 1976, became an important focus for training and production. Under the artistic directorship of Collins and the management of Oscar Abrams, this converted church presented work by Caribbean, African and American (though few British) playwrights such as Lincoln Brown, Steve Carter, YULISA AMADU MADDY and DEREK WALCOTT.

It was also in the 1970s that new plays were beginning to reflect the day-to-day preoccupations of the black community in Britain, and a distinctive group of black writers became visible; MUSTAPHA MATURA has reached the widest audience through his association with a range of theatres, from the BLACK THEATRE CO-OPERATIVE , which he co-founded in 1978 with Charlie Hanson, and FOCO NOVO to the Royal Court and NATIONAL THEATRE. The BTC touring production of his *Welcome Home Jacko* (1979) marked a sea change in the fortunes of black theatre, capturing the imagination of a large young audience of overwhelmingly first-time theatregoers.

Alongside Matura were Ali, whose multimedia performances prefigured rap; Michael Abbensetts; Alfred Fagon; Tunde Ikoli, whose *Scrape Off the Black* (1977) has been produced up and down the country; Jimi Rand; EDGAR WHITE; and T Bone Wilson. In the 1980s women playwrights came to the fore, such as Trish Cook, Maria Oshodi, WINSOME PINNOCK – a quiet, effective and surprisingly vigorous voice – and Jacqueline Rudet. Carib Theatre, founded in 1980 by Anton Phillips and Yvonne Brewster, filled the gap left for children, touring innovative plays, most of them written by black playwrights.

The issue of buildings and the level of subsidy continued to be thorny subjects. The different groups, all with their different policies, have lobbied for control of their own premises and hence of their production

processes. Unfortunately, although a huge sum of money had been earmarked for turning the ROUND HOUSE into a black arts centre, the project did not materialize. However, a breakthrough was achieved in 1992 when Talawa Theatre Company, established in 1986 by Yvonne Brewster as a middle-scale company undertaking residencies in regional theatres, for three years from 1992 to 1995 occupied its own fully equipped theatre, the Cochrane in central London, which had been refurbished for the purpose.

Outside London, too, the situation remained poor; the Cave, established in Birmingham in 1983, closed in 1991. It had provided various cultural facilities in conjunction with the probation service. In Manchester the Nia Centre for black arts was opened in 1991, but closed in 1997, though the Drum Arts Centre opened in 1998 funded by the National Lottery.

For black performers the situation had improved, both in DRAMA SCHOOLS and in the profession (the actors' UNION Equity had set up an Afro-Asian Committee to replace the defunct Coloured Actors' Committee), although there was still much to be done to achieve proper equality of opportunity and 'integrated casting' – casting that ignores the colour of the performers' skin – was by no means generally accepted.

Some practitioners argue that sufficient progress has been made to drop the term 'black theatre', but however integrated the work of actors has become, it has not extended to black playwrights, directors and designers. Thus the term 'black theatre' was still firmly in place at the end of the twentieth century.

Use of labels such as 'black' – or, similarly, 'gay' or 'women's' – theatre is always problematic, contested and changing. It is governed by particular circumstances which themselves are changing, and can vary in meaning and effect depending on who is making use of the labels and to whom. It might be to defend gains, assert rights and ambitions, or regain control of self-identity, and in the process the labels will themselves be altered to keep up with and/or advance the altered perceptions and realities, especially where imperialism and immigration/emigration have been or are involved.

Although theatres such as the TRICYCLE in north London, the THEATRE ROYAL, STRATFORD EAST and the HACKNEY EMPIRE have collaborated with black practitioners to give a new platform to black theatre, the practitioners have always valued the importance of organizing themselves. In 1985 Black Theatre Forum was founded to stimulate the development of black theatre in Britain, running black theatre seasons, a magazine and a network of contacts, and embracing individuals and groups from a wide range of backgrounds, primarily Afro-Caribbean and Asian British, while questioning the basis of ethnic definitions; however, ten years on it began to run out of steam. The Rastafarian company Double Edge and the Black Theatre of Women could be found alongside the British Asian Theatre or TARA ARTS. Asian theatre in Britain, while often brought under the black theatre umbrella, has a distinct and variegated life of its own, but is usually not highly visible in the mainstream media. Its traditions do not recognize the separation of categories such as dance or theatre that is common in Britain, and many of its activities are not in English. As new generations grow up, a new aesthetic emerges, sometimes bi- or multi-lingual, sometimes offering a new take on conventional English theatre, sometimes appropriating Western classics in mainstream situations. Individual writers like Hanif Kureishi, Karim Alrawi, Ayub Khan-Din and Harwant Bains have appeared – and the success of Khan-Din's *East is East* (1996, West End 1997, filmed 1999) briefly raised the profile of Asian theatre – but it is the existence of companies like Tara Arts and the Tamasha Theatre Company (founded 1989) that have kept the notion of an Asian theatre alive as the British social context evolves.

YVONNE BREWSTER & COLIN CHAMBERS

In the United States

African American theatre began with victims of the slave trade from western Africa, who retained many of their performance traditions, such as ENSEMBLE IMPROVISATION, in the New World. Early performances were carried out on plantations and in homes, and ultimately had a wide influence on American culture, first demonstrated in the creation of minstrel shows in the 1820s and 1830s. Black characters in early white plays were always played by whites in black make-up. The first black theatrical company in America was the African Grove, a group of black actors organized in the 1820–1 season by a Mr Brown in New York's Greenwich Village. Until forced to close by the city authorities, the African Grove presented performances of Shakespeare and other plays, including Brown's *King Shotaway*, now lost but the earliest recorded play by a black American. The African Grove also gave a start to Ira Aldridge, the first black actor to achieve an international reputation. Dramatic performing opportunities for blacks remained limited to MINSTRELSY and unstaged readings of classics until the turn of the century, when a series of black musicals appeared on Broadway. *Clorindy, or The Origin of the Cakewalk* (1898), by the poet Paul Laurence Dunbar and the composer Will Marion Cook, and starring the comic Ernest Hogan, was the first black show to play to a white Broadway audience, albeit as a midnight entertainment on a roof garden. *In Dahomey* (1902), a full-length musical by Cook, Dunbar and Jesse Shipp, and starring the comedy team of BERT WILLIAMS and GEORGE WALKER, became the first black show to play a Broadway main stage. And Scott Joplin, a composer now best known for piano rags, also produced a complete ragtime opera, *Tremonisha* (1914), which was under-appreciated in its day but has recently enjoyed a resurgence of popularity.

After the First World War, Northern cities – New York, Philadelphia, Washington, Chicago and Detroit – became crowded with Southern blacks in search of work and better lives. In the booming 1920s, New York's Harlem became the North's largest African American community, and attracted so many artists that its creative ferment has come to be known as the 'Harlem Renaissance'. EUBIE BLAKE and NOBLE LEE SISSLE's ragtime musical *Shuffle Along* (1921) sparked a revival of interest in black musicals. In addition, small theatre groups specializing in black-written plays briefly thrived, for the 1920s were the first major period of black playwriting. Angelina Grimke's *Rachel* (1916) asked whether black couples should bring children into America's racist society. Willis Richardson's one-act folk play *The Chip Woman's Fortune* (1923) and Garland Anderson's full-length courtroom drama *Appearances* (1925) were the first non-musical black-written plays to reach Broadway stages. Short, pithy, generally realistic works such as John Matheus' *'Cruiter* (1926), Willis Richardson's *Flight of the Natives* (1927) and Randolph Edmonds' *Bad Man* (1934) show the influence of the Irish folk-play movement. Others, such as Marita Bonner's *The Purple Flower* (1928), are non-realistic, symbolic works that owe much to the French SURREALISTS. Harlem also managed – sometimes barely – to support its own all-black theatre troupe, the LAFAYETTE PLAYERS. Founded by Anita Bush in 1915, the Lafayette was the most important black ensemble since the African Grove. It produced mostly mainstream white plays, but trained a generation of fine black actors, including CHARLES GILPIN, Rose McClendon, Frank Wilson and Edna Thomas.

At the same time that black theatre thrived, white dramatists began trying – often feebly – to examine the place of blacks in American society. The black characters in EUGENE O'NEILL's *The Emperor Jones* (1920) and *All God's Chillun Got Wings* (1924) and in MARC CONNELLY's *The Green Pastures* (1930) are little better than stereotypes, though PAUL GREEN's *In Abraham's Bosom* (1926) and DUBOSE HEYWARD's *Porgy* (1927) are somewhat more perceptive. Black characters also became common in white-written musicals, notably HAM-

MERSTEIN and KERN's *Show Boat* (1927) and Heyward and the GERSHWINS' *Porgy and Bess* (1937). In the Great Depression of the 1930s, most black theatre companies folded, and many black theatre artists, like poor Americans of all backgrounds, became politically radicalized. LANGSTON HUGHES, a young poet and playwright, founded the Harlem Suitcase Theater to produce his short plays, such as *Don't You Want to be Free?* (1937), which combined the political activism of white AGIT-PROP drama with black music and Hughes' own poetry. The United States' only foray into theatrical production, the Works Progress Administration's FEDERAL THEATER PROJECT (1935–9), organized a Negro Theater as one of its major production units. Under the supervision of Rose McClendon, and, after her death, of JOHN HOUSEMAN, a white producer, the Negro Theater created dozens of productions in major cities around the country. Many of their shows were black adaptations of well-known works, such as the 'voodoo' *Macbeth* (1936) directed by ORSON WELLES, and *Swing Mikado* (1938), which was copied by a Broadway producer as *Hot Mikado* (1939). The Negro Theater employed a number of promising young black writers, and produced several of their plays, including Theodore Brown's *The Natural Man* (1936), a musical about the mythic figure John Henry; J. A. Smith and Peter Morell's *Turpentine* (1936), an exposé of southern work-gangs; Hughes Allison's *The Trial of Doctor Beck* (1937), a courtroom drama dealing with black self-hatred; and Theodore Ward's *Big White Fog* (1938), a domestic drama advocating an alliance between blacks and left-wing unions. The Federal Theater Project was dissolved in 1939 by Congressional red-baiters, and the Second World War further fragmented the black theatre world. It began to rebuild in the early 1950s, finding a new voice in the growing civil rights movement. In the tradition of Grimke's *Rachel* (1916), plays such as Louis Peterson's *Take a Giant Step* (1953) and LORRAINE HANSBERRY's now-classic *A Raisin in the Sun* (1957) portrayed solid, working-class black families struggling to achieve the same ethnic self-respect and living standards as their white counterparts. Others, like ALICE CHILDRESS's metatheatrical *Trouble in Mind* (1954) and OSSIE DAVIS's comedy *Purlie Victorious* (1961), dramatized the clash of traditionalist whites with thoughtful blacks. JOSEPH PAPP's NEW YORK SHAKESPEARE FESTIVAL helped break down barriers to black actors by encouraging multiracial casting, both in classics and in contemporary works.

In the 1960s, activism became the dominant theme of much black theatre. An all-black cast set an OFF-BROADWAY record with its long run of *The Blacks* (1961), a parable of colonialism by the white French-man JEAN GENET. The interracial Free Southern Theater brought an eclectic array of plays to the rural South as part of the civil rights movement. LeRoi Jones (who later adopted the name AMIRI BARAKA) wrote *Dutchman*, an inflammatory one-act play in which a white woman murders a black youth on a New York subway, and JAMES BALDWIN wrote *Blues for Mister Charlie* (1965), an embittered view of the civil rights movement. In the middle to late 1960s, after the passage of the Civil Rights Act (1965), and concurrent with the escalation of the Vietnam War and the Black Power movement, there was a huge explosion of black theatre nationwide. Over 600 new companies were founded: most existed only briefly, but others, including the National Black Theater and the New Federal, lasted for years and made major contributions. The New Lafayette Theater (1966–72) produced group-created 'rituals' on racial and political themes, as well as many plays by ED BULLINS, including *In the Wine Time* (1968) and *Goin' a Buffalo* (1968). In 1967 DOUGLAS TURNER WARD, author of the satiric civil rights play *Day of Absence* (1965), co-founded New York's NEGRO ENSEMBLE COMPANY. This prolific group produced many important works, including LONNE ELDER's *Ceremonies in Dark Old Men* (1969), Joseph A. Walker's *The River Niger* (1972) and CHARLES FULLER's *A Soldier's Play* (1981), and trained hundreds of black actors, designers and stagehands. By the early 1990s, though, the NEC was struggling to survive.

In the 1970s, several shows created and performed by blacks were mainstream successes. NTOZAKE SHANGE's *for colored girls who have considered suicide / when the rainbow is enuf* (1976), a series of poetic dance monologues in support of black women, set the standard for much feminist theatre. *The Wiz* (1975), *Ain't Misbehavin'* (1978), *Eubie!* (1978) and *Dreamgirls* (1981) rekindled interest in all-black musicals. By the 1980s and early 1990s, black theatre, while still struggling, was becoming an accepted part of the American mainstream, with well-trained playwrights, directors, designers and actors turning out quality work on Broadway and elsewhere. LLOYD RICHARDS, whose work on *A Raisin in the Sun* had made him Broadway's first black director, became head of the Yale School of Drama, and brought to Broadway AUGUST WILSON's dramas of black life, including *Ma Rainey's Black Bottom* (1983), *Fences* (1985) and *Joe Turner's Come and Gone* (1987). In 1993 GEORGE C. WOLFE, the author of *The Colored Museum* (1986) and the director of ANNA DEAVERE SMITH's *Fires in the Mirror* (1991) and *Jelly's Last Jam* (1992), and TONY KUSHNER's *Angels in America* (1993), was named JOSEPH PAPP's and JOANNE

AKALAITIS' successor as the head of New York's PUBLIC THEATER. PAUL NADLER

See also ETHNIC THEATRE.

Doris E. Abramason, *Negro Playwrights in the American Theater 1925–1959* (1969)

Rena Fraden, *Blueprints for a Black Federal Theater 1935–1939* (1994)

N. Khan, *The Arts Britain Ignores: The Arts of Ethnic Minorities in Britain* (1976)

James V. Hatch, *Black Theater, USA* (1974)

Errol Hill, *Shakespeare in Sable* (1984)

Edith R. Isaacs, *The Negro in the American Theater* (1947)

Loften Mitchell, *Black Drama* (1967)

K. Owusu, *The Struggle for Black Arts in Britain: What Can We Consider Better than Freedom?* (1986)

—— *Black British Culture and Society: A Text Reader* (1999)

Maxine Schwartz Seller, *Ethnic Theater in the United States* (1983)

A. Woll, *Black Musical Theater from Coontown to Dreamgirls* (1989)

Black Theatre Co-operative Founded in 1979 by MUSTAPHA MATURA and Charlie Hanson, BTC is a one of the most important BLACK THEATRE companies in Britain. It has offered opportunities to black people, denied elsewhere, in a range of the theatrical skills and, in its early days, developed a powerful, muscular style full of sharp humour with actors like Victor Romero, Gordon Case, Judith Jacobs, Malcolm Fredericks, Bert Caesar and Trevor Laird. Successes include Matura's *Welcome Home Jacko* (1979), Farrukh Dhondy's *Mama Dragon* (1980), EDGAR WHITE's *Redemption Song* (1984) and a fine revival of LORRAINE HANSBERRY's *A Raisin in the Sun* (1985) with Carmen Munroe. BTC created a TV show and has had a major influence on the representation of black people on British television. Its increasing interest in MUSIC THEATRE led in 1998 to the founding of an annual FESTIVAL and a year later to a change in the company's name to Nitro. COLIN CHAMBERS

Blair, Ron (b. Sydney, 14 Oct. 1942) Playwright, editor and radio producer. From his first play, the 'entertainment' *Biggles* (1970, written with Michael Boddy and Marcus Cooney), which opened the NIMROD THEATRE, Blair's work has been marked by its wide-ranging choice of forms and themes, from large-scale revues and updated ballad operas to monodramas and historical plays. *The Christian Brothers* (1975), which in spite of its title is a one-man play, stands as one of the most penetrating treatments of themes familiar from the works of other Australian writers such as BARRY OAKLEY and PETER KENNA – religion,

bigotry, frustrated love, and a life constructed around an ordered and destructive social routine. Other plays include *Hamlet on Ice* (1971), *President Wilson in Paris* (1973) and *Mad, Bad and Dangerous to Know* (1976). MICHAEL MORLEY

Blake, James Hubert 'Eubie' see SISSLE, NOBLE LEE

Blakeley, Colin [George Edward] (b. Bangor, Northern Ireland, 1930; d. London, 7 May 1987) Actor. After a late start at 28 with the Ulster Group Theatre he quickly achieved prominence; his quirky, abrasive quality was appreciated in films and on television as much as in the theatre, where he worked on the FRINGE as well as the ROYAL COURT and with the two British national companies: in 1961 he joined the ROYAL SHAKESPEARE COMPANY, where his parts included Touchstone; at the NATIONAL THEATRE from 1963 they included Philoctetes, John Proctor in *The Crucible*, Kite in *The Recruiting Officer*, Hobson in *Hobson's Choice*, Captain Boyle in *Juno and the Paycock* and the creation of the craggy conquistador Pizarro in *The Royal Hunt of the Sun*. Returning to the RSC, he played Titus Andronicus, and Torvald in *A Doll's House*. He also created James in Thomas Murphy's *The Morning After Optimism* (Abbey Theatre, Dublin, 1971). CHRISTOPHER FITZ-SIMON

Blakemore, Michael see NATIONAL THEATRE

Blau, Herbert (b. New Rochelle, NY, 3 May 1926) Director, playwright, scholar, critic and teacher. His several books, including *The Impossible Theatre: A Manifesto* (1964), *Take Up the Bodies* (1982), *Blooded Thought* (1982), *The Eye of Prey* (1987), *The Audience* (1990), *To All Appearances* (1992) and *Nothing in Itself: Complexions on Fashion* (1999), constitute an important dialogue on the development of performance studies as a subject of serious debate. His theories of performance, beginning with a concern for theatre as socially relevant and progressing to an examination of performance as resistant to the representative nature of theatre, are influenced by Freud, French post-structuralism, and his own theatre practice. For Blau, whose writing style complements his theories in its dense, often self-reflective prose, the act of performance is about what is created that was not present before. With Jules Irving (1924–79), Blau founded San Francisco's ACTOR'S WORKSHOP (1952–65), where they introduced American audiences to major European playwrights like BRECHT, BECKETT and GENET. Blau and Irving then co-directed the Repertory Theater of LINCOLN CENTER (1965–7). Blau was influential in the founding of the

California Institute of the Arts and formed Kraken (1971–81), a radical theatre group with a physical ensemble style that sought to explore questions about the nature of theatre. DAVID A. WILLIAMS

Bleasdale, Alan see LIVERPOOL PLAYHOUSE

Blin, Roger [Paul Jules] (b. Neuilly-sur-Seine, France, 22 March 1907; d. Paris, 20 Jan. 1984) Actor and director. A student of CHARLES DULLIN with an interest in the visual and surreal, his talent was more austere than exuberant. He worked with ARTAUD and BARRAULT before turning to directing with STRIND-BERG's *The Ghost Sonata* (1949). He directed the first ADAMOV play to be staged (*La Grande et la petite Manoeuvre*, 1950) and directed BECKETT's *Endgame* (*Fin de Partie*, 1957), *Krapp's Last Tape* (*La Dernière Bande*, 1960) and *Happy Days* (*Oh les beaux jours*, 1963), having made his reputation with the seminal *Waiting for Godot* (*En attendant Godot*, 1953) for which he designed the famous tree. In *Les Nègres* (*The Blacks*, 1959) and *Les Paravents* (*The Screens*, 1966) he brilliantly illuminated GENET's counterposing of the real and the imaginary. Every stage object was significant for Blin and he took extreme care, working with architect or sculptor, to design his stage spaces. TERRY HODGSON

O. Aslan, trans. R. Cohen, *Roger Blin and Twentieth Century Playwrights* (1988)

B. Knapp, *Off-stage Voices* (1975)

Blitzstein, Marc (b. Philadelphia, 2 March 1905; d. Martinique, 22 Jan. 1964) Composer. He sacrificed a possibly outstanding career as a concert pianist to write for the stage in the style of BRECHT and WEILL. His first important work was *The Cradle Will Rock* (1937). This account of a steel strike was written at the suggestion of Brecht, and gained notoriety because of problems concerning its inaugural production by the MERCURY THEATER, which later became the subject of a film (2000) bearing the folk opera's name. An opera, *Regina*, based on LILLIAN HELLMAN's play *The Little Foxes* (1949), was less didactic but also less interesting. His greatest success (both commercially and artistically) was a textual and musical adaptation of the work of his old friends Brecht and Weill – *The Threepenny Opera*. This opened at the tiny Theatre de Lys, New York, in 1954, and ran for 2,707 performances. It did wonders for the reputations of Brecht, Weill and Blitzstein, and had the unexpected spin-off of making 'Mack the Knife' a hit song. Blitzstein also wrote *Juno* (1959), an unsuccessful musical version of O'CASEY's *Juno and the Paycock*. IAN BEVAN

E. A. Gordon, *Mark the Music: The Life and Work of Marc Blitzstein* (1989)

J. Houseman, *Run-Through* (1972)

Blok,   Alexander   [Alexandrovich] (b.   St Petersburg, 28 Nov. 1880; d. Petrograd, 7 Aug. 1921) Poet and playwright. His first book of poetry was published in 1904, and he became the leading figure in the Russian SYMBOLIST movement. He wrote several plays, but it was his first which made him famous: *Balaganchik* (*The Fairground Booth*, *The Fair Show Booth* or *The Puppet Show*, 1906, directed by MEYERHOLD). A combination of the Russian folk theatre's CLOWN show, or *balagan*, and COMMEDIA DELL'ARTE, the production was crucial in Meyerhold's artistic development in his stylized and grotesque use of the *commedia* characters and his rejection of static staging.

Blok greeted the February 1917 Revolution with enthusiasm and in November was one of only five leading   figures   (along   with   Meyerhold   and MAYAKOVSKY) to accept an invitation from LUNACHAR-SKY (the People's Commissar for Education) to a conference reorganizing the arts. In 1919 Blok wrote *Poslednie dni starogo rezhima* ('The last days of the old regime'), formed the board with GORKY and others which opened the Bolshoi Dramatic Theatre, Leningrad, and was briefly arrested. He was also the author of other, though lesser known, plays: *Korol na ploshchadi* ('The king in the square', 1906), denied production by the censorship; *Pesnya sudbi* ('Song of fate', 1908); *Neznakoma* ('The unknown woman' or 'The female stranger', 1906); *Snezhnaya maska* ('Snow mask', 1907); the more famous *Roza i Krest* ('Rose and cross', 1913); *Kaimen* (1914); and *Ramses* (1919). VERA GOTTLIEB

Avril Pyman, *The Life of Alexander Blok*, 2 vols (1979–80)

Bloolips see DRAG; GAY THEATRE; LESBIAN THEATRE

Bloom, Claire (b. London, 15 Feb. 1931) Actress who established an early reputation in Shakespeare, moving from STRATFORD-UPON-AVON (1948) to the OLD VIC (1952), where her roles included Cordelia, Ophelia, Viola – and, most notably, Juliet, as whom she toured Canada and the United States in the mid-1950s and made her BROADWAY debut in 1956. She starred in major revivals of such classics as *A Doll's House*, *Hedda Gabler* (both New York, 1971), *Rosmersholm* and *A Streetcar Named Desire* (both London, 1977). In the 1980s she devoted her acting more exclusively to film and television, although she continued to appear on stage in her SOLO SHOW, *These Are Women: A Portrait of Shakespeare's Heroines*. She has written two memoirs, *Limelight and After: The Education of an Actress* (1982) and *Leaving a Doll's House,* (1996).

DAVID STAINES

Blue Blouse Theatrical movement that began with an agitational theatre group in Moscow in 1923, taking its name from the workers' clothes which it adopted as a basic costume. Both the name and style were rapidly emulated throughout the Soviet Union, and Blue Blouse became a massive organization of amateur and professional troupes, with its own journal, and trades union backing. Influenced by the ideas of MEYERHOLD and EISENSTEIN, the troupes combined techniques of LIVING NEWSPAPER with variety and folk forms to create topical propaganda presentations aimed at proletarian audiences in workers' clubs. By 1928, Blue Blouse boasted 484 professional and 8,000 amateur troupes. Its influence spread to other worker theatre movements in Europe and the United States. IAN SAVILLE
See also PEOPLE'S THEATRE.

Richard Stourac and Kathleen McCreery, *Theatre as a Weapon* (1986)

Blythe, Ernest *see* ABBEY THEATRE; IRELAND

Boal, Augusto (b. Rio de Janerio, Brazil, 16 March 1931) Director, playwright, theoretician and teacher. He trained in the United States and worked as director of the Arena Theater, São Paulo (1956–71). His early work was drawn predominantly from the traditional repertoires of European and North American drama, but in the wake of the 1964 military coup, he began experimenting with popular forms and rapidly developed a radical theatre relevant to increasingly repressive conditions. He was gaoled and subsequently, in 1971, left Brazil, moving first to Argentina and then into European exile.

Major influences in Boal's work include Marx, STANIS-LAVSKY, BRECHT and the educationalist Paulo Freire, author of *Pedagogy of the Oppressed* (1972). In 1973 Boal worked on a Freire-inspired literacy project in Peru, developing many of the methods which he systematized under the title of the 'theatre of the oppressed'. The book of the same name was written in 1974. The theatre of the oppressed is essentially a system of participatory theatre techniques: at its heart is the aim of changing the passive spectator into a protagonist, first in the theatre and then in the real world. In Boal's own words, it is 'a rehearsal for revolution'. Its different forms include 'image theatre', 'forum theatre' and 'invisible theatre'.

From 1978 to 1986 he was based in Paris, developing his work in the European context and becoming increasingly interested in subjective oppressions and therapy. (He called these techniques the 'rainbow of desire' and published a book of that name in 1994.) He returned to Brazil in 1986, and in 1992 was elected a city councillor, a duty he undertook with his theatre company. It used theatre to address local issues and in some cases campaigns led to new laws – hence the name 'legislative theatre' which Boal gave to the process. He published a book entitled *Legislative Theatre* in 1998 and in 2001 *Hamlet and the Baker's Son: My Life in Theatre and Politics*. A major figure on the international WORKSHOP circuit, he is an important influence on THEATRE IN EDUCATION, popular theatre and theatre at the margins of society, in prisons and with the dispossessed. CHRIS VINE
See also THEATRE FOR DEVELOPMENT.

A. Hozier, ed., *Documents on the Theatre of the Oppressed* (1985)
T. Jackson, ed., *Learning through Theatre* (1993)
Mady Schutzman and Jan Cohen-Cruz, eds, *Playing Boal: Theatre, Theory and Activism* (1994)

Bock, Jerry [Jerrold Lewis] (b. New Haven, Conn., 23 Nov. 1928) Composer. After studying at Wisconsin, he started writing music for television shows and for summer camp revues. In 1955 he interpolated some songs into a Broadway revue and the next year wrote the score for *Mr Wonderful*. For the remainder of his career, until his early, self-imposed retirement, he worked with lyricist SHELDON HARNICK to create such successes as *Fiorello!* (1959), *She Loves Me* (1963), and *Fiddler on the Roof* (1964). Probably the most gifted melodist among his generation of Broadway composers, he also revealed in his music a sense of place and time.

GERALD BORDMAN

body art Within the realms of PERFORMANCE, the expression first enjoyed currency as part of the late MODERNIST explosion of forms and categories that occurred in the United States and (swiftly thereafter) elsewhere during the 1970s. As such, it overlapped and was to some extent confused with the terms conceptual art and PERFORMANCE ART. Principal exponents included (in the United States) Carolee Schneemann, Vito Acconci, Dennis Oppenheim, Chris Burden; (in Britain) Bruce McLean; (in Australia) Stelarc; (in Yugoslavia) Marina Abramović; and (in France) Orlan. The range of these artists' interests was considerable, as were the forms that their work took. As a consequence, changes in the arts during the 1980s saw some develop as film-makers, sculptors or painters. Others – most notably Schneemann, Stelarc, Abramović and Orlan – remained constant to what united the various approaches to body art: a concentration upon the capabilities and limits of the artist's body (often demonstrated by its violation) as the subject matter and the material of their art; a form that tended away from the theatrical and towards the 'action', 'gesture', 'intervention' or demonstration; and very often an extreme diligence in documentation through which the work might subsequently be disseminated. With the postmodern absorption into the arts of concerns around sexuality, gender, race, politics and various interpretations of belief, and, no less important, the proliferation of theoretical interest in the corporeal, these artists' work has proven inspirational to younger generations of artists and those emerging from the popular arts, including sado-masochist and fetish clubs. Stelarc, who gained notoriety for his 'suspensions' – in which he hung from hooks inserted through his flesh – emerged during the 1990s as a forward-thinking proponent of the body's obsolescence in a world dominated by technology. Marina Abramoviú's early durational works with her partner Ulay provided the platform for her emergence as one of the more influential artists at the turn of the millennium. Schneemann is now seen as a heroic pioneer of art that declared and reclaimed the female body (territory contemporarily and subsequently explored variously in the work of Linda Montano, Rachel Rosenthal and Annie Sprinkle, *inter alia*). Orlan has gained a popular notoriety for subjecting herself to a series of videotaped cosmetic-surgical operations permanently to transform her physical appearance. Elsewhere, modern primitive beliefs about the cathartic properties of pain are most powerfully embodied in the ritualistic works of Fakir Musafar. Ron Athey (notable among many artists who have used the body as the vehicle for queer political concerns) has employed theatrical settings of autobiographical themes that are rendered entirely anti-traditional by his employment of blood-letting, body piercing and a range of sexual acts. Significantly, the expression 'body art' is also widely employed popularly to denote any form of more or less radical fashionable body modification, including drastic hair cutting or colouration, body painting, piercing and adornment, tattooing, scarring and subcutaneous inserts. It is similarly used even less precisely to denote any form of body modification or adornment. ROBERT AYERS

Lucy R. Lippard, *Six Years: The Dematerialization of the Art Object from 1966 to 1972* (1997)
Paul Schimmel et al., *Out of Actions. Between Performance and the Object, 1949–1979* (1998)
Sarah Wilson et al., *Orlan* (1996)
David Wood, ed., *Body Probe Torture Garden 2* (1999)

Bogart, Anne *see* ACTORS THEATRE OF LOUISVILLE; AMERICAN REPERTORY THEATER; EXPERIMENTAL THEATRE; TRINITY REPERTORY COMPANY

Bogdanov, Michael *see* ENGLISH SHAKESPEARE COMPANY; WALES

Bogosian, Eric *see* EXPERIMENTAL THEATRE; SOLO SHOW

Boleslavsky, Richard [Ryszard Srzednicki Boleslaw] (b. Warsaw, 4 Feb. 1889; d. Hollywood, 17 Jan. 1937) Actor, director and teacher. He acted with the MOSCOW ART THEATRE until 1920 and in 1922 emigrated to the United States, where he rapidly established himself as a director and introduced the ideas of STANISLAVSKY. Following MAT's first US visit in 1923, he and another ex-MAT performer, **Maria Ouspenskaya** (b. Tula, 29 July 1876; d. Hollywood, 3 Dec. 1949) founded the Theatre Arts Institute, a Stanislavsky-based school later called the American Laboratory Theater, which lasted until 1933. The Lab ran a theatre modelled on MAT from 1925 to 1930. Its pupils set up the influential GROUP THEATER and went on to transform American and world theatre through the ACTORS' STUDIO and the METHOD, although Boleslavsky disagreed with the direction taken by his most famous student LEE STRASBERG. Boleslavsky gave lectures which he turned into a book, *Acting: The First Six Lessons* (1933), as well as writing two autobiographies and directing on Broadway and in Hollywood. ADRIANA HUNTER

J. W. Roberts, *Richard Boleslavsky: His Life and Work in the Theatre* (1981)

Bolger, Dermot *see* ABBEY THEATRE

Bolger, Ray[mond Wallace] (b. Boston, Mass., 10 Jan. 1904; d. Los Angeles, 15 Jan. 1987) Zany dancer and singer who, despite his successful stage career, is best-remembered as the scarecrow in the film version of *The Wizard of Oz* (1939). Bolger developed his unique comic talent in VAUDEVILLE and performing in musical comedies for a stock company during the 1920s, appearing most notably in a tour of the REVUE *The Passing Show of 1926*, which attempted to rival the success of the ZIEGFIELD *FOLLIES*. His trademark 'rubber-legged' style of dancing became increasingly popular after he appeared in *George White's Scandals of 1931*, culminating in his hit show, the musical comedy by RODGERS and HART, *On Your Toes* (1936). In 1948 he had his biggest hit yet, in *Where's Charley?*, a musical version of *Charley's Aunt*, in which he sang the show-stopper and one of the songs forever after associated with his name, 'Once in Love with Amy'. After a TV series and several films, he resumed his stage career in the 1960s, but never repeated his earlier successes.

HELEN RAPPAPORT

Bolivia *see* SOUTH AMERICA

Bolt, Robert [Oxton] (b. Sale, Manchester, 15 Aug. 1924; d. Chithurst, Hants, 21 Feb. 1995) Playwright. His first models in *The Critic and the Heart* (1957) and *Flowering Cherry* (1957) were MAUGHAM and the well-made play. Bolt campaigned against atomic weapons and was briefly gaoled (see his play *The Tiger and the Horse*, 1960). His immensely successful *A Man for All Seasons* (1960, filmed 1967), on Thomas More's martyr-dom, places private conscience above duty to the state and established Bolt, a former history teacher, as a popular portraitist of charismatic historical figures. *Vivat! Vivat Regina!* (1970), about Elizabeth I and Mary Queen of Scots, made less impact, however. He adopted mildly Brechtian techniques but rejected Marxist determinism. In *State of Revolution* (1977), Bolt's Lenin is a great man serving a dangerous ideology. Bolt's LUNA-CHARSKY says, 'The personal is of course peripheral'; all Bolt's plays and screenplays (including the unusually complex *Lawrence of Arabia*) argue otherwise. He won Oscars for *Dr Zhivago* (1965) and the More film. Other plays are *Gentle Jack* (1963), *The Thwarting of Baron Bolligrew* (1965) and *Brother and Sister* (1967).

TONY HOWARD

R. Hayman, *Robert Bolt* (1969)
S. Miles, *Serves Me Right* (1994)
—*Bolt from the Blue* (1996)
A. Turner, *Robert Bolt: Scene from Two Lives* (1998)

Bolton, Gavin *see* THEATRE FOR YOUNG PEOPLE

Bolton, Guy [Reginald] (b. Broxbourne, Herts, 23 Nov. 1884; d. London, 5 Sept. 1979) Playwright and librettist. Bolton was a prolific writer, best known for the accomplished witty librettos he produced in collaboration with P. G. WODEHOUSE and the composer JEROME KERN. His output of librettos for musicals and of straight comedies continued from 1915 until 1965 and included collaborations with many other comedy writers. His work includes *Oh, Boy!* (with Wodehouse, 1917), *Tip Toes* (with Fred Thompson, 1925), *Girl Crazy* (with Jack McGowan, 1930) and *Anything Goes* (with Wodehouse, 1944). He co-authored with Wodehouse an autobiography, *Bring on the Girls* (1953).

ADRIANA HUNTER

Bond, Chris (C. G.) *see* LIVERPOOL PLAYHOUSE; MON-STROUS REGIMENT

Bond, Edward [Thomas] (b. Holloway, London, 18 July 1934) Playwright. After submitting two plays to the ROYAL COURT, Bond was invited to join their Writers' Group. *The Pope's Wedding* (1962), which portrays the experiences of a gang of youths, one of whose members develops an obsession with an old man looked after by his girlfriend, was given a one-off 'production without décor'. It was *Saved* (1965) that made Bond's name, largely for its central scene, in which a group of young lads find an abandoned baby in a park; they begin joking and playing with the baby and end up stoning it to death. That scene, and several other parts of the play, were banned by the LORD CHAMBER-LAIN; when the Royal Court presented the play as a CLUB performance, they were prosecuted under the 1843 Theatres Act and fined £50 for presenting the play without a LICENCE. Bond's response was *Early Morning*, a huge, complex and metaphorical play which pictures British (notionally Victorian) society run by corrupt and cannibalistic leaders; its pugnaciously iconoclastic portraits of Queen Victoria, Florence Nightingale, Disraeli, Gladstone and, indeed, the Lord Chamberlain himself, make unsurprising its terse rejection by the CENSOR ('His Lordship would not allow it'). It was premièred only in 1969, after the abolition of the Lord Chamberlain's power as theatre censor (which Bond and the Court had no doubt somewhat hastened). *Narrow Road to the Deep North* (1968) recast the life of the poet Bashō and attempted missionary incursions into Japan in a parable play which draws equally on the simplicity of the *haiku* and the work of BERTOLT BRECHT. In 1971 Bond's *Lear* transforms Shakespeare's *King Lear* in a sprawlingly generous structure, reminiscent of *Early Morning*. Lear's understanding is reforged by a series of bloody civil wars, only to be fully realized in the play's final, desperate moments. With *The Sea* (1973), Bond came to the end of a series of plays investigating the possibilities of freedom and acting rightly in an iniquitous world, usually focusing on characters struggling to comprehend the world around them, and only dimly glimpsing the broader contours of its dehumanizing force.

The next phase of his work builds on this intellectual achievement. *Bingo* (1973) shows an ageing Shakespeare collaborating with a landowner in the enclosure of common land; *The Fool* (1975) concerns John Clare's exclusion and final incarceration by his culture, at a time of rural unrest. Like *Narrow Road to the Deep North*, with its ironic image of the 'great poet' Bashō refusing to accept responsibility for the cruelty around him, these plays argue powerfully for the ineluctable implication of the writer in society, seen in Shakespeare's dying recognition of his failure of responsibility: 'Was anything done?' *The Bundle* (1978) and *The*

Worlds (1980) display an increasing commitment to revolutionary politics as the only genuine way of achieving social freedom. *The Woman* (1978), a massively powerful rewriting of the end of the siege of Troy, explores the possibilities of strategic resistance. *Restoration* (1980) uses witty Restoration comedy pastiche to examine the complexities of class allegiance. *Summer* (1982) uses the conventional theatrical device of a middle-class family on holiday; Bond shows how the family's bourgeois attitudes mask an historical complicity with fascism and a deliberate, willed refusal to accept that the liberal values of justice and kindness are meaningless in a society built on brutality and inequality.

From the mid-eighties Bond's work came increasingly to focus on the politics of nuclear war. Nowhere is this better shown than in his trilogy *The War Plays*, made up of *Red, Black and Ignorant* (1984), *The Tin Can People* (1985) and *Great Peace* (1985). The first play uses an episodic style to show how a life can be brutalized to the point where nuclear destruction can be contemplated. The second and third plays pick up Bond's habitual themes, dwelling on the few survivors of a nuclear holocaust and showing them working out how to rediscover and preserve their humanity. The plays respond to the imagined nuclear bombardment with a bombardment of metaphors and moments of fractured, appalling linguistic fragility, and represent one of the most sustained and uncompromising products of an imagination confronting Armageddon.

The figures and motifs of *The War Plays* have haunted Bond's work ever since: the defiant mother with her baby bundled in her arms; lounging, brutalized soldiers; the casual rapacity of the arms industry. These images resonate through plays like *Human Cannon* (written 1983), *Jackets* (1989), *In the Company of Men* (1992, AVIGNON FESTIVAL), *At the Inland Sea* (1995), and *Coffee* (written 1995).

Bond's work had been staged by the ROYAL SHAKE-SPEARE COMPANY and the NATIONAL THEATRE, but he was increasingly frustrated by the limitations of such institutions and began to have his plays premièred by amateur, student or youth groups. Bond's stagecraft is unrivalled in its rigorous working through of ethical issues of duty and responsibility in a structurally violent society; in *Narrow Road to the Deep North* a man commiserates with himself for nearly drowning while a priest commits *hari-kiri* behind him; Shakespeare, in *Bingo*, sits unconcernedly on a bench in front of the dead body of a gibbeted young woman. Images like these present moral concerns with a rare clarity and force. Such moments should act as a corrective to those who see Bond as simply the playwright of 'violence';

he certainly uses violent images, but if they are meant to shock, they are meant to shock us into a wider understanding of the social forces from which they issue. Bond has called these moments 'aggro-effects', a direct reference to Brecht's ALIENATION EFFECTS; Bond shares with Brecht the uncompromising intelligence, but believes that violently emotional images can be a tool to greater understanding. Bond also shares with Brecht his relentless theorizing of theatrical politics; no playwright since SHAW has produced such a wealth of prefaces, notes, commentaries and poems to accompany the plays, supporting his call for a 'rational theatre' and adding a richness of speculation and argument to his formidable body of dramatic writing.

Other plays include *Black Mass* (1970), *Passion* (1971), *A-A-America!* (1976), *Stone* (1976, for GAY SWEATSHOP), *Derek* (1982), *After the Assassinations* (1983) and a television play, *Olly's Prison* (1993). He has produced TRANSLATIONS AND ADAPTATIONS of *A Chaste Maid in Cheapside*, *Three Sisters*, *Spring Awakening* and *The White Devil*, as well as providing the texts for three music theatre pieces in collaboration with Hans Werner Henze, *We Come to the River* (1976), *Orpheus* (1979) and *The Cat* (1983). Three volumes of his letters were published in the mid-1990s, two volumes of selections from his notebooks in 2000/2001, and in 2000 a collection of essays *The Hidden Plot: Notes on Theatre and the State*.   DAN REBELLATO

Malcolm Hay and Philip Roberts, *Edward Bond: A Companion to the Plays* (1978)
—— *Bond: A Study of his Plays* (1980)
David L. Hirst, *Edward Bond* (1985)
Jenny S. Spencer, *Dramatic Strategies in the Plays of Edward Bond* (1992)

Bondy, Luc (b. Zurich, Switzerland, 1948) Director. Well known in Europe, notably in Vienna, Berlin and Paris, for intelligence, harmony and control. His productions range from Marivaux's *Triomphe de l'amour* (1985) to Shakespeare's *The Winter's Tale* (1988) and in particular those of BOTHO STRAUSS (*Kalldewey Farce*, 1982; *Time and the Room*, 1989; *Final Chorus*, 1992; *Balance*, 1993).   TERRY HODGSON

Bonfils Theatre A non-profit-making theatre in Denver, Colorado founded in 1929 as the University Civic Theater of Denver. In 1953 the actress, producer and local newspaper publisher Helen Bonfils donated the theatre to the company, offering a 550-seat main auditorium and a smaller 'cabaret' auditorium with a capacity of 90. The company is dedicated to giving amateur performers the opportunity to work in an otherwise professional theatre; it also runs drama classes, and presents children's theatre and free open-air summer shows in city parks. In 1980 the Helen Bonfils Theatre Complex – the Bonfils Theatre's companion site with three different performance spaces – was opened as a base for the Denver Center Theater Company. ADRIANA HUNTER

Booth, Shirley [Thelma Booth Ford] (b. New York, 30 Aug. 1907; d. North Chatham, Mo., 16 Oct. 1992) Actress. Her first appearance was in *The Cat and the Canary* (1919) in New England. After making her New York debut in 1925 in *Hell's Bells*, she scored major successes in *The Philadelphia Story* (1939) and *My Sister Eileen* (1940). She received the first of her two Tony awards for *Goodbye My Fancy* (1948), but it was her outstanding performance in WILLIAM INGE's domestic drama *Come Back Little Sheba* (1950) that caught the public's attention and garnered many acting accolades for her, including another Tony as well as an Academy award for the 1952 film version. Her stage successes continued with *A Tree Grows in Brooklyn* (1951) and a third Tony for her performance in *The Time of the Cuckoo* (1952). HELEN RAPPAPORT

Boothe [Luce], Clare (b. New York, 10 April 1903; d. Washington DC, 9 Oct. 1987) Playwright, author and politician. Born of a poor family but endowed by her mother with a love of books, she took up a journalistic managing career after her first marriage ended, becoming editor of *Vanity Fair*. She is best known for *The Women* (1936), a satirical look at what she called 'a very small, special group of rich, idle, social female parasites' which played for 657 performances. In *Margin for Error* (1939), one of the few successful Broadway plays to depict Nazism, a German consul (a thinly veiled Hitler) is mysteriously killed, but it is a young policeman's ironically comic discourse on the virtues of America versus the ills of Germany that gives the play its political undertones. Her plays are known for their wit as well as for an underlying, if not always successful, social commentary. Many received film treatments, including *Come to the Stable* (1949), which was nominated for an Academy award. Her marriage in 1935 to Henry Luce, president of *Time*, lasted 32 years. She served two terms as a Congresswoman and was the first woman to be appointed a US ambassador, to Italy. DAVID A. WILLIAMS

S. Shadagg, *Clare Boothe Luce: A Biography* (1970)
W. Sheed, *Clare Boothe Luce* (1982)

booths Simple, often portable, theatres providing light entertainment at the seaside, they derived from the booths that first appeared at fairs and in town squares. These little theatres consisted of a small stage and rudimentary seating erected inside a tent. Temporary theatres erected along the seafront and on piers became very popular in the nineteenth and early twentieth centuries, offering cheap entertainment for holiday audiences. The main survivor of the form is *Punch and Judy*. ALEXANDER BLOK used the idea for his play *The Fairground Booth* (1906). ADRIANA HUNTER
See also PIERROT; SEASONAL THEATRE.

Borchert, Wolfgang (b. Hamburg, Germany, 20 May 1921; d. Basle, Switzerland, 20 Nov. 1947) Actor, cabaret performer, poet and author of the semi-autobiographical *Draussen vor der Tür* (*The Man Outside*, 1947), the first great postwar drama in German, which was originally produced as a RADIO play. An anti-Nazi, Borchert was drafted to the Russian front, was later imprisoned for informing and sent to Switzerland fatally ill. He died the day before the play's stage première in his native Hamburg. Concerning a German who returns home an outcast and struggles to discover how to live in a shattered world, it became an icon of contemporary European drama. JUDY MEEWEZEN

K. J. Fickert, *Signs and Portents: Myth in the Work of Wolfgang Borchert* (1980)

Bosnia-Herzegovina *see* YUGOSLAVIA

Boston The puritan ethos of colonial Boston virtually prevented live performances; later, misplaced Anglophobia inhibited 'English' entertainments on local stages, even after the American Revolution. During the nineteenth century, however, several playhouses were built and Bostonians came to accept theatre, even though they promulgated the strictest CENSORSHIP laws in the nation. 'Banned in Boston' became the playwright's dread and the press agent's boon. In spite of this, the BROADWAY try-out system was inaugurated here in 1891 with Charles H. Hoyt's *A Trip to Chinatown*, and for most of the next 80 years Boston's theatre consisted largely of plays being tested for New York or touring from there. VARIETY entertainments proved so consistently popular that the first all-VAUDEVILLE theatre, the Colonial, was opened here in 1894. The out-of-town try-out system was finished by the close of the twentieth century, but by then two resident companies, the Huntington Theatre Company and the AMERICAN REPERTORY THEATER, had secured niches for themselves and a place for Boston as a vital regional theatre centre. THOMAS F. CONNOLLY

Elliot Norton, *Broadway Down East* (1978)

Boublil, Alain (b. Tunis, 5 March 1941) and **Schönberg, Claude-Michel** (b. Vannes, France, 6 July 1944) Composer Schönberg first teamed up with lyricist and musical book writer Boublil on a rock opera, *La Révolution française* (1973), under the influence of *Jesus Christ Superstar*. Continuing the epic theme, they then wrote a musical based on Victor Hugo's novel *Les Misérables* (1980). It was staged in Paris but taken up by the British producer CAMERON MACKINTOSH, revised and mounted in 1985 by the ROYAL SHAKESPEARE COMPANY in London to become one of the most successful musicals of its time, with productions in many countries. The pair worked with Mackintosh again on *Miss Saigon* (1989), a reworking of the opera *Madame Butterfly* in the setting of the Vietnam war, and on *Martin Guerre* (1996).

CHARLES LONDON

Boucicault, Dion G. [Darley George] ('Dot') (b. New York, 23 May 1859; d. Hurley, Bucks, 25 June 1929) Actor who used a middle initial to distinguish himself from his father Dion Boucicault (1822–90), one of the most popular actors and dramatists of the nineteenth century. Dion G. started his career in New York in 1879, went to Australia with his father in 1885 and stayed there, producing plays, for 11 years, then returned to London in 1897, married IRENE VANBRUGH and had a successful career as an actor–manager. He directed and wrote plays and was famous for teaching his women stars. MARIE TEMPEST said she owed her comedy technique to him. IAN BEVAN

Bouffes du Nord *see* BROOK, PETER; INTERNATIONAL CENTRE FOR THEATRE RESEARCH

boulevard Taking its name originally from the Boulevard du Temple in Paris, which boasted several theatres, the term *théâtre de boulevard* was applied loosely to the undemanding and highly entertaining plays preferred by rich bourgeois audiences during the *belle époque* around the turn of the twentieth century. Boulevard playwrights of that period include Augier and FEYDEAU; their plays and the works of contemporary boulevard writers continued to be produced in the commercial theatres in Paris throughout the century. The term is also more generally applied to any light plays with commercial appeal. ADRIANA HUNTER

Bourchier, Arthur (b. Speen, Berks, 22 June 1863; d. South Africa, 14 Sept. 1927) Actor and manager; one of the founders of the OXFORD University Dramatic Society. He had a busy and varied acting and managerial career from 1889 until he died on tour abroad. His biggest commercial success was in *The Better 'Ole* (1917), which ran for 811 performances. He followed this with *Tilly of Bloomsbury* (1919) and was the original Long John Silver in the stage version of *Treasure Island* (1922). He was notoriously intolerant of criticism. He was married first to VIOLET VANBRUGH and then to another actress, Kyrle Bellew. IAN BEVAN

Bourdet, Edouard *see* LESBIAN THEATRE

Bourne, Bette *see* DRAG

Bovell, Andrew [John] (b. Kalgoorlie, Western Australia, 23 Nov. 1962) Playwright. An impressive and varied body of work marks him off as one of the most versatile of the younger generation of playwrights. He has written plays in a variety of styles and forms, and for an equally wide range of venues. *After Dinner* (1988), a colourful, lively FARCE, demonstrates his command of the essential theatrical elements such as strong characterization, sharp dialogue and a sure grasp of dramatic structure, while other works, such as *State of Defence* (1987) and *The Ballad of Lois Ryan* (1988), both written for the Melbourne Workers' Theatre, show his political and social concerns. His plays examine the intersection of public and private lives, and offer an adventurous exploration of dramatic forms: *Ship of Fools* (1988), for example, juxtaposes two plot lines 500 years apart, and *Speaking in Tongues* (1996), his most successful play to date, is an assured exploration of emotional landscapes which uses a provocative approach to narrative and dramatic exchanges. He has also written for film (*Strictly Ballroom*, co-author) and television. Other works include *Distant Lights From Dark Places* (1994) and *Who's Afraid of the Working Class* (1998, co-author).

MICHAEL MORLEY

Boyce, Raymond (b. London, 20 May 1928) Designer. After training at the Slade and the OLD VIC Theatre School, Boyce began his career as resident designer at the Dundee Repertory. In 1953 he was invited to New Zealand by the NEW ZEALAND PLAYERS. A major influence on young designers and others in New Zealand theatre, he has designed or directed over 250 productions in all fields of the performing arts, including opera and ballet. He was chairman of DOWNSTAGE from 1968 to 1976. He designed the embroidered hangings for New Zealand's gift to the GLOBE THEATRE (London).

GILLIAN GREER & LAURIE ATKINSON

Brady, Alice (b. New York, 2 Nov. 1892; d. New York, 28 Oct. 1939) Actress and singer. Daughter of the theatrical impresario William A. Brady, she trained as a singer and, after making her stage debut in 1909, appeared in a succession of GILBERT and SULLIVAN productions. There followed several parts in long-running productions such as *Forever After* (1918), *Zander the Great* (1923), *Bride of the Lamb* (1926) and *A Most*

Immoral Lady (1928). Brady had also established a career in silent films and she continued to work in both media until her film career took precedence in the 1930s. Her most acclaimed performance came in the gruelling part of Lavinia in the five-hour THEATER GUILD production of *Mourning Becomes Electra* (1931). HELEN RAPPAPORT

Brahm, Otto (b. Hamburg, 5 Feb. 1856; d. Berlin, 28 Nov. 1912) Director and theatre manager. Brahm began his career as a critic. In 1889 he emulated ANTOINE's Théâtre Libre when he founded his FREIE BÜHNE to produce the plays of the new naturalistic writers, especially HAUPTMANN. Brahm consistently promoted naturalism and ENSEMBLE playing, rejecting the dramatic conventions that still encumbered German theatre. His modern approach made him an important influence but put a strain on his collaboration with directors such as REINHARDT. ADRIANA HUNTER

Branagh, Kenneth [Charles] (b. Belfast, 10 Dec. 1960) Actor, director, producer, and writer. A graduate of the Royal Academy of Dramatic Art, he made his mark in *Another Country* (1981) by Julian Mitchell (1935). He appeared with the ROYAL SHAKESPEARE COMPANY for two seasons, most notably as Henry V, then in 1987 founded the touring Renaissance Theatre Company, with which he acted and directed productions including *Twelfth Night*, *A Midsummer Night's Dream* and *King Lear*. He has also played Coriolanus (CHICHESTER FESTIVAL, 1992) and Hamlet (RSC, 1992). His screen performance in the title role of *Henry V* (1989) signalled an increasing interest in film and led to more actor–director outings in the cinema (e.g. *Dead Again*, 1991; *Peter's Friends*, 1992; *Much Ado About Nothing*, 1993; and *Hamlet*, 1997). He became a showbiz phenomenon at a young age as he emulated the actor-managers of a bygone era, published a very early autobiography (*Beginning*, 1989) and enjoyed a media marriage to the actress Emma Thompson before it ended in 1996. DAVID STAINES

Brandane, John (pseud. for Dr John MacIntyre) (b. Rothesay, Isle of Bute, Scotland, 1869; d. Lochgoil, Argyllshire, 17 Oct. 1947) Playwright. He is best known as the author of *The Glen is Mine* (1923), a play written for the most influential of Scotland's early twentieth-century amateur companies, the SCOTTISH NATIONAL PLAYERS. Its Highland backdrop, and its theme of traditional values threatened by modernisation, is typical of the locus of drama associated with the Players and with Brandane. Despite his commitment to writing in Scots, a tendency to see the Highlands as peopled by cosy, comic characters, as in *Glen-*

forsa (1921) and *Rory Aforesaid* (1928), marks Brandane's drama as at best sentimental, and at worst cliched and parochial. He was an early influence on JAMES BRIDIE and ROBERT McLELLAN. ADRIENNE SCULLION

Brando, Marlon (b. Omaha, Nebr., 3 April 1924) Actor and director. One of the most influential actors of his generation, he gained singular eminence in his only starring role on Broadway as Stanley Kowalski in TENNESSEE WILLIAMS' *A Streetcar Named Desire* (1947). His intensely realistic acting became synonymous with so-called METHOD acting, which he had learned from his teacher Stella ADLER and at the ACTORS' STUDIO. He forsook the stage for film, where he starred in such movies as *On the Waterfront* (1954) and *The Godfather* (1972). DAVID STAINES

P. Manso, *Brando: The Biography* (1994)
R. Schickel, *Brando: A Life in Our Times* (1991)

Braun, Volker (b. Dresden, 7 May 1939) Playwright and poet. He began his theatrical career in 1965, when he was accepted as assistant director at the BERLINER ENSEMBLE. He became one of the German Democratic Republic's leading dramatists with his plays *Die Kipper* ('Tippers', 1972), *Hinze und Kunze* (1968), *Tinka* (1976), *Guevara, oder Der Sonnenstaat* ('Guevara, or the sun state', 1977), *Grosser Frieden* ('Great peace', 1979), *Dmitri* (1982) and *Die Übergangsgesellschaft* ('Transitional society', 1987). His plays deal with the contradictions within the emerging socialist society in the then GDR and the role of the individual in the progress of history. GÜNTER BERGHAUS

L. Arnold, *Volker Braun* (1977)
J. Rosselini, *Volker Braun* (1983)

Brazil *see* SOUTH AMERICA

Bread and Puppet Theater American experimental group, founded (1962) and still led by German-born Peter Schumann. Initially based in New York, it responded to America's growing involvement in Vietnam by touring overt POLITICAL THEATRE pieces (e.g. *Gas for Vietnam*, Washington DC, 1965), usually outdoors at rallies and parades, and, whenever possible, for free; theatre is seen as a staple of life, like bread, which the group would distribute to the audience. The group's work was ceremonial and stark, with large, monochromatic puppets expressing pain, suffering, incomprehension. As the Vietnam War wound down, Schumann, in a strategy for reinvigoration, moved the group to his family farm in Glover, Vermont, where since 1975 the group has presented annually a Domestic Resurrection Circus inspired by the cycles, fairs and pageants of medieval theatre, as well as essaying scripted plays (e.g. *Woyzeck*, 1981). In the 1980s it focused on Latin America (e.g. *Nicaraguan Passion Play*, 1987). Still based on Schumann's farm in Glover, the continually reforming ensemble makes occasional forays into New York and other places, carrying its spiritual message into the new millennium.

GERALD RABKIN

Stefan Brecht, *The Bread and Puppet Theater* (1988)

Brecht, Bertolt [Eugen Berthold Friedrich] (b. Augsburg, Germany, 10 Feb. 1898; d. Berlin, 14 Aug. 1956) Playwright, poet, director and thinker. 'Bert' Brecht, as he styled himself, was not a closet playwright: all his plays were intended for the stage, even at times when he was denied access to it. As a theorist no less than as a practitioner, he challenged orthodoxy throughout his career. His personality, convictions and work constantly involved him in controversy.

Born into a middle-class Bavarian family, Brecht showed precocious literary talent. A one-act satire written in 1919, *Die Hochzeit* (*The Wedding*), was surprisingly accomplished for so young an author. The First World War, Germany's defeat and the troubles following the botched revolution of 1918 sharpened his eye for the fault-lines in his society. But the fact that he was later to turn against his own class and become a spokesman for revolutionary change was only dimly foreshadowed in the first play of his to be staged, *Trommeln in der Nacht* (*Drums in the Night*, 1922), the tale of a soldier returning from the war to find his fiancée pregnant, and in *Baal*, that often revised, larger-than-life portrait of an amoral poet. *Baal* caused a riot when premièred in Leipzig in 1923. So did *Im Dickicht der Städte* (*In the Jungle*), the story of two men's mysterious fight to the death, at its Munich première in the same year. *Mann ist Mann* (*Man Equals Man*), the parable of a docker whose personality is restructured in order to turn him into a 'human fighting machine', was similarly ambivalent in its message. While the text of the Darmstadt production (1926) took a positive view of this reshaping of a man, the Berlin version (1931) presented it as sinister. In Berlin, Brecht moved in important theatrical and intellectual circles, mixing with people like MAX REINHARDT, LEOPOLD JESSNER, ERWIN PISCATOR and GEORGE GROSZ, and it was there that his commercial breakthrough happened, with *Die Dreigroschenoper* (*The Threepenny Opera*, 1928), a commissioned adaptation of *The Beggar's Opera*. The unhappy rehearsals of this musical piece left everyone unprepared for its sensational success, much of which was due to KURT WEILL's catchy and sophisticated score ('Mack the Knife' has been an international hit tune ever since), as well as the play's ambiguity: its attack

on capitalist ethics could be misread as cycnical endorsement. The Brecht–Weill team – also responsible for *Happy End* (1929), with text by Elisabeth Hauptmann, who edited Brecht's works – met with a very different reception in 1930, when the opera *Aufstieg und Fall der Stadt Mahagonny* (*Rise and Fall of the Town of Mahagonny*) was premièred in Leipzig: bourgeois audiences reacted violently against this lampoon on the destructiveness of consumer society.

In notes to the published texts of *The Threepenny Opera* and *Mahagonny*, in a letter to the press concerning *Man Equals Man* and in other polemics, Brecht defined the concept of a new theatre towards which he was working, calling it EPIC THEATRE. By (partially) denying the audience the pleasures of empathy, he sought to arouse its critical sense – critical, that is, of the social realities represented on the stage. Whatever the theory, his plays up to that point had carried an ambiguous message. However, from 1926 onwards he turned to the study of Marxism in order to put his social critique on a sounder basis, and he tried to integrate his new insights into the structure of his plays and their style of performance. He never actually joined the German Communist Party, but he was ideologically close to it. Around this time he wrote a number of teaching plays or *Lehrstücke*, such as *Das Badener Lehrstück vom Einverständnis* (*The Didactic Play of Baden on Consent*, with music by Paul Hindemith, 1929); two school operas based on a Japanese *noh* play, *Der Jasager/Der Neinsager* (*He Who Says Yes and He Who Says No*, with music by Kurt Weill, 1930); and *Die Massnahme* (*The Measures Taken*, with music by HANNS EISLER, 1930). When the latter was premièred in Berlin it had a workers' choir with over 400 singers. *Die Ausnahme und die Regel* (*The Exception and the Rule*), completed in the 1930s after Brecht's emigration from Germany, was first produced in Palestine in Hebrew (1938). The dramatization of Gorky's *Die Mutter* (*The Mother*) is not a *Lehrstück* but it, too, has didactic features. Premièred in 1931, it had Brecht's second wife, HELENE WEIGEL, playing the lead. This play, which describes a Russian working-class mother's growth into revolutionary consciousness, resists a naturalistic approach, as Brecht angrily pointed out when the New York Theatre Union produced it that way in 1935, against his explicit intentions. *Die heilige Johanna der Schlachthöfe* (*St Joan of the Stockyards*), the fruit of his study of capitalist market forces, was published in 1932 (the year of his film, *Kuhle Wampe*) – too late to be staged before Hitler's seizure of power in 1933. It was premièred (in Hamburg) only in 1959, nearly three years after Brecht's death.

Forced to flee by the coming of Nazism, Brecht left

Germany with his family and entourage, going first to Scandinavia (Denmark 1933–9, Sweden 1939–40, Finland 1940–1) and then, via the Soviet Union, to the United States (1941–7). During this period Brecht was cut off altogether from the theatre, apart from contacts with some small left-wing groups. He failed to make any impact on Hollywood, selling only one script, *Hangmen Also Die* (written 1942). Yet it was a time in which he systematized his theories and wrote a number of plays, many of which have since been incorporated into the world repertoire. The first was a ballet–cantata, *Die sieben Todsündender Kleinbürger* (*The Seven Deadly Sins*, written 1933), which brought together the *Threepenny Opera* team of designer CASPAR NEHER, actor LOTTE LENYA and Weill. *Die Rundköpfe und die Spitzköpfe* (*The Roundheads and the Pointed Heads*), inspired by *Measure for Measure* and written between 1932 and 1934, has only rarely been performed. But the 27 disconnected sketches gathered in *Furcht und Elend des Drittten Reiches* (*Fear and Misery of the Third Reich*, 1935–8; also known in English as *The Private Life of the Master Race*), and the one-act play about the Spanish Civil War, *Die Gewehre der Frau Carrar* (*Señora Carrar's Rifles*, 1937), have been very popular in many countries, although (or because?) written in a more traditional manner than the rest of his work. One of Brecht's relatively few history plays, *Leben des Galilei* (*Galileo*, written in 1938–9 but extensively revised in the English-language version he prepared in Hollywood with CHARLES LAUGHTON, 1945–6), dealt with the problem of the 'great man's' social responsibility. *Mutter Courage und ihre Kinder* (*Mother Courage and Her Children*, 1939), intended as a warning against the war which Brecht saw was imminent, proved to be one of his most accomplished and best-loved works, its loose structure covering 12 years of the Thirty Years' War. *Mother Courage* looks at war from the viewpoint not of the leadership but of the ordinary, though by no means guiltless, folk at the bottom of the pile. The parable of *Der gute Mensch von Setzuan* (*The Good Person of Setzuan*), which was written between 1938 and 1941, though based on much earlier ideas, shows the insoluble contradiction between personal goodness and the dog-eat-dog ethics of free enterprise; the heroine Shen Teh's alter ego, the tough unfeeling Shui Ta, is represented by a mask. *Herr Puntilla und sein Knecht Matti* (*Mr Puntila and His Man Matti*), written in Finland in 1940 and based on local stories, comments in comic terms on class conflict in the countryside. *Der aufhaltsame Aufstieg des Arturo Ui* (*The Resistible Rise of Arturo Ui*), quickly composed in 1941 after a good deal of earlier work, traces Hitler's rise to power in a gangster story à la Al Capone. It aims to lay bare the analogies between big business, crime and fascism and is done in the grand manner of an Elizabethan history play. *Schweik im zweiten Weltkrieg* (*Schweyk in the Second World War*, 1942–3) harks back to a figure Brecht had dramatized before as a member of the writing team working for the director Erwin Piscator (*see* GERMAN-LANGUAGE DRAMA): Schweyk, the 'little guy' whose dumb subservience masked sly subversiveness. This play, too, was produced only posthumously, as was *Der Gesighte des Simone Machard* (*The Visions of Simone Machard*, 1942–3), the story of a young woman inspired by dreams of Joan of Arc to resist collaborators as well as Germans in occupied wartime France. Brecht had used the Joan of Arc image before (in *St Joan of the Stockyards*); he was to dramatize her again, but directly, in *Der Prozess der Jeanne d'Arc zu Rouen 1431* (*The Trial of Joan of Arc at Rouen in 1431*, 1952). Another play written in American exile, *Der kaukasische Kreidekreis* (*The Caucasian Chalk Circle*, 1944) was actually premièred in English, at the Nourse Little Theatre in Northfield, Minnesota. It remains one of the most frequently performed in English of Brecht's plays. When put on by Brecht's own company in the German Democratic Republic in 1954 in a very elaborate production with music by PAUL DESSAU, it did not win immediate approval; but its success in Paris at the Théâtre des Nations in 1955 fed back into a warm domestic reception in both East and West Germany. In the latter it was made more palatable by playing down the politics and stressing its picturesqueness and poetry.

In 1947, during the Cold War witch-hunt, Brecht was summoned to appear before the House Committee on Un-American Activities. Warned by this, he quickly left the United States and returned to Europe, spending some time in Switzerland and then going to East Berlin in 1948. *Die Tage des Kommune* (*The Days of the Commune*) dates back to that period; this examination of the failure of the Paris Commune of 1871, from which lessons were to be drawn for present-day struggles, was premièred in Karl-Marx-Stadt (now Chemnitz) shortly after the author's death in 1956. For his comeback Brecht directed *Mother Courage* at the Deutsches Theater in Berlin in 1949, with Helene Weigel in the title role. The production was widely regarded as exemplary. In the same year he founded his own company, the BERLINER ENSEMBLE, which under his wife's management was to give him an opportunity of putting his theatrical ideas into practice. But though most of his work enjoyed official support, his opera *Das Verhör des Lukullus* (*The Trial of Lucullus*), with music by Paul Dessau (originally written as a radio play in 1939), ran into government opposi-

· Performing Brecht ·

Initially, my interest is in the philosophical problem of a play. This concerns me personally as an actor in the play and at the same time exists in the world outside my head. I try to solve it in its social context through getting into the character I'm to portray. Before rehearsals, I broaden my knowledge – when I was preparing for Coriolanus in the Brecht–Shakespeare play, I occupied myself more intensively and in greater detail with Roman and Greek history than would seem necessary. At the start of rehearsals, I had to make the knowledge that I had accumulated become effective in order to be creative. To do this you need to have learnt your lines. When I learn a text, I also learn the entire environment of the given situation so as to be able to move logically in the plot.

You must, however, keep yourself open for the rehearsal process, in which you have to find the external expression for what you think and what you want. You have to move away from intellectual acquisition to make your acting reflexive and convincing, and this only comes through training. Everything you do on stage must be a reaction, not independent or original, otherwise it does not belong there. Any work of art is a self-contained world and outside explanation is irrelevant. This was one of the difficulties of dogmatized socialist realism, which presumed a fixed moral position. I have to defend my characters on stage through their reactions, which become actions when they affect other people. I have to deliver them to history, which means to the story of the play and the judgement of history.

Take *Galileo*. I'm not interested in Galileo the great physicist. Brecht's Galileo is a man who has pleasure in using reason. At first, he believes in 'the gentle power of reason over mankind', yet at the end, reason for him 'is nothing but man's selfishness'. I must show that change not as the wisdom of age but as the prod-surrenders the struggle. Playing this relates to what is known as the gestus – the presentation of an attitude which exists over and above the words in the text. For example, you can perform 'no' in many different ways and mean many different things, including its opposite, 'yes'.

EKKEHARD SCHALL

tion when staged at the Staatsoper in 1951 and had to be revised and retitled.

Brecht's work with the Berliner Ensemble left him little time to write more plays, though he did do a number of adaptations for its repertoire. His last piece was *Turandot, oder Der Kongress der Weisswäscher* (*Turandot, or The Congress of the Whitewashers*, 1953–4, but based on much earlier work), an attack on the venality of intellectuals in the guise of an oriental parable. This was premièred in Zurich only in 1969, and not staged by the Berliner Ensemble until 1973.

This brief and far from complete listing of Brecht's plays omits – among other things – his numerous and important adaptations. In reworking plays by Sophocles, Shakespeare, Marlowe, Molière, Lenz or Farquhar he managed to give each text a characteristic twist. What is so impressive about his *œuvre* is not only its quantity and its quality but also its diversity. No matter whether in parable, 'folk-play', comedy, *Lehrstück* or history, we always hear his unmistakable tone of voice: terse, challenging, ironical, tough, at times tender but always unsentimental.

It is vital to be familiar with Brecht's theoretical writings – such as *The Messingkauf Dialogues* (1939–42) or *The Short Organum for the Theatre* (1947) – if one wishes to stage his plays. It is only a shade less important for the reader to have them at the back of his or her mind. Many elements of epic theatre were not new in themselves; what *was* new was the total mix and its philosophical basis. The preference for a discontinuous, scene-by-scene structure rather than that of the 'well-made' play had sound precedents not only in WEDEKIND and Büchner but also in Lenz and the young Goethe, and indeed ultimately in Shakespeare and the Elizabethans; the rejection of naturalism was a common theme among theatrical innovators from the turn of the century onwards; some of the points of 'epic' acting techniques were gleaned from popular and oriental (Chinese and Japanese) theatre (*see* EASTERN THEATRE, ITS INFLUENCE ON THE WEST). But the central and distinctive thrust of Brecht's argument was that the theatre should not aim to present a slice of life (something it cannot do anyway) but to put forward a *model* of reality, frequently in the form of a parable, which remains recognizable as a model. Not pretending to imitate everyday life, the play would invite spectators to speculate about and take a critical view of the reality behind it. Since the dominant images in any society are controlled by the ruling group, Brecht sought to bring about what from about 1936 onwards he called *Verfremdung* (somewhat unhappily translated as ALIENATION; 'distanciation' is not ideal but fits better). The point of this 'distanciation', or making strange that which is normally unremarked-on, is to make the spectator question all that seems ordinary, natural, mere common sense: in other words, all that he has unknowingly internalized of ruling-class ideology. Brecht intended his plays to show the world as full of contradictions but accessible to reason, greatly in need of change but (with much effort) changeable.

His staging devices, evolved with his lifelong friend Caspar Neher, are well known. Scenic design should avoid naturalism: individual items may be lifelike and detailed, but the overall picture flaunts its theatricality. Incomplete in itself, it allows for the moves and groupings of the actors as an essential part of the design. Costumes and props must be characteristic and suggest use; they should be seen to be the products of labour. Lighting is to be non-atmospheric, i.e. white and saturated; light sources are to remain visible. Title cards are often used to indicate place. The half-height curtain, which can be used for projection, allows the scene-shifting to remain partly visible, thus reminding the audience that mounting a play is a working process.

Brecht often used music in his plays. He collaborated with such distinguished composers as Paul Hindemith, Kurt Weill, Hanns Eisler and Paul Dessau. Like other elements of epic production, the music does not simply blend imperceptibly into the flow of events: songs do not arise, as it were 'naturally', out of the action but are clearly separate from it; the score does not simply illustrate the text but makes its own, frequently contrapuntal, statement; the instrumentalists may play in full view of the audience.

The most widely discussed aspect of Brechtian stagecraft is the so-called 'A-effect' in acting – an alienation whereby the actor does not *fully* identify himself with the character he or she is portraying. It is an attitude of showing rather than total embodiment. This is intended to leave some room for a detached attitude on the part of actors and audience alike. (In fact this has always been an important aspect of comic acting.) Clearly this is in contrast to STANISLAVSKY's concept of the actor drawing on his or her inner resources to create a fully three-dimensional being on stage. Brecht was interested not so much in characterization developed from inside the autonomous individual as in the readable gestures of human interaction (what Brecht called the 'gestus' of the play); his perspective was social rather than psychological.

Towards the end of his life he seems to have preferred to call his concept of theatre 'dialectical' rather than 'epic'. He continued to believe in the activist function of theatre, but felt that the word 'epic' had given rise to too many misunderstandings. In his later theoriz-

ing, such seeming opposites as reason and emotion, instruction and pleasure, interpenetrated rather than excluded one another.

Brecht has made a worldwide impact both as a theorist and as a practitioner – even (appropriately enough) in the Far East. A production in 1979 of *Galileo* by the Chinese Youth Art Theatre in Beijing was considered an important cultural event after the fall of the Gang of Four; it used some indigenous stage conventions such as cloth doors and brightly coloured emblematic costumes. When a West Bengal left-wing theatre group produced *Puntila* it adapted it to the local folk idiom: there was a chorus and a dancer. The set – trees, houses, a motor car, the moon – consisted of unpainted paper sculpture.

Brecht's name is frequently invoked in Britain and the United States, often in a merely ritual way. How deep is the influence really? Some of his plays certainly appear in the repertoire. His example, and that of Neher, have encouraged simplicity in stage design. Acting techniques like direct address to the audience and stepping out of one's role have become commonplace. But many of these formal devices are merely surface decoration. The use of the Common Man as commentator in ROBERT BOLT's *A Man for All Seasons* or the episodic structure of JOHN OSBORNE's *Luther* hardly qualify as Brechtian in any meaningful sense. JOHN ARDEN has shown some Brecht influence in plays like *Armstrong's Last Goodnight*. DAVID HARE's *Fanshen* has many elements derived from Brecht in its description of the coming of communism to a remote Chinese village – episodic structure, direct address, no sets or lighting cues, authentic props and costumes; more fundamentally, it portrays social change as a constant series of contradictions. But English theatre, with its empirical bias, has on the whole resisted Brecht's philosophical approach, while the dominant tendency of American theatre to involve the audience emotionally is diametrically opposed to a Brechtian style.

It would be contrary to the spirit of Brecht himself to treat his work as sacrosanct or unalterable. Thus, the model books of the Berliner Ensemble productions (richly illustrated with scenic details and production stills) should not hamstring *future* directors of Brecht plays for all time. Life moves on, and with it the reception of Brecht and his teachings. GEORGE BRANDT

Graham Bartram and Anthony Waine, eds, *Brecht in Perspective* (1982)

Walter Benjamin, *Understanding Brecht*, trans. Anna Bostock (1973)

Peter Demetz, ed., *Brecht: A Collection of Critical Essays* (1962)

Martin Esslin, *Brecht: A Choice of Evils*, rev. edn (1984)

Frederick Ewen, *Bertolt Brecht* (1967)

John Fuegi, *Bertolt Brecht: Chaos, According to Plan* (1987)

P. Kleber and C. Visser, eds, *Re-interpreting Brecht: His Influence on Contemporary Drama and Film* (1990)

Siegfried Mews, ed., *A Bertolt Brecht Reference Companion* (1997)

Peter Thomson and Glendyr Sacks, eds, *The Cambridge Companion to Brecht* (1994)

Klaus Völker, *Brecht: A Biography*, trans. John Nowell (1978)

John Willett, *The Theatre of Bertolt Brecht*, rev. edn (1977)

——, *Brecht in Context* (1984)

Brenton, Howard (b. Portsmouth, 13 Dec. 1942) Playwright. A committed socialist, Brenton writes with an angry humour as he challenges established myths (*The Churchill Play*, 1974) and warns of the erosion of civil liberties. He wrote deliberately shocking plays for the ALTERNATIVE theatre before achieving wider fame with *Epsom Downs* (JOINT STOCK, 1977), which re-creates Derby Day by bringing dozens of characters on stage in a variety of interwoven plots. More controversial was *The Romans in Britain* (NATIONAL THEATRE, 1980) – as much about British imperialism and the troubles in Northern Ireland as about the (literal) rape of ancient Celts by Roman colonialists which gave rise to a private prosecution, later abandoned. Brenton is no stranger to political rows, from his anti-Tory *A Short Sharp Shock* (1980, with Tony Howard) to *Iranian Nights*, a play about the Salman Rushdie affair which tackled the issue of Islamic fundamentalism (1989, with Tariq Ali). He has often collaborated with other dramatists, notably DAVID HARE (*Brassneck*, 1973; *Pravda*, 1985). A prolific writer, he has written for the major subsidized theatres, the National (e.g. *Weapons of Happiness* 1976; versions of BRECHT's *Galileo*, 1980, and Büchner's *Danton's Death*, 1982), the ROYAL SHAKE-SPEARE COMPANY (e.g. *Sore Throats*, 1979; *Thirteenth Night*, 1981; *H. I. D.*, 1989) and the ROYAL COURT (e.g. *Magnificence*, 1973; *The Genius*, 1983; a 1988 season that included a revival of *Bloody Poetry*, 1984; and *Berlin Bertie*, 1992). His book of essays and diaries, *Hot Irons*, appeared in 1995. DAVID SELF

See also CENSORSHIP.

Richard Boon, *Howard Brenton* (1992)

Colin Chambers and Mike Prior, *Playwrights' Progress* (1987)

Breton, André (b. Tinchebray, France, 18 Feb. 1896; d. Paris, 28 Sept. 1966) Writer and founder of the SUR-REALIST movement, which made a considerable impact on twentieth-century drama. Breton, strongly influenced by Freud, was profoundly experimental. Under a form of hypnosis he wrote several 'automatic' plays with Philippe Soupault (e.g. *Les Champs magnétiques* and *S'il vous plaît*, both 1920) and, with the poet Louis Aragon, a prophetic war play, *Le Trésor des Jésuites* (1929). Bréton helped establish the playwright ALFRED JARRY as a crucial modern influence. ADRIANA HUNTER

Breuer, Lee (b. Philadelphia, 6 Feb. 1937) Director and writer. He worked in Berlin and Poland in the mid-1960s, and was a founding member of the avant-garde collective MABOU MINES. Since 1970 he has written and directed much of the group's most important work, including a notable series of BECKETT productions and his own plays *The Red Horse Animation* (1970), *The B. Beaver Animation* (1974), *The Shaggy Dog Animation* (1978) and *Prelude to Death in Venice* (1978). With composer Bob Telson he created *The Gospel at Colonus* (1983), whose black-church setting gives Sophocles' tragedy a joyous contemporary life.

M. ELIZABETH OSBORN

See also AVANT-GARDE; COLLECTIVE.

Brewster, Yvonne see BLACK THEATRE

Brice, Fanny [Fannie Borach] (b. New York, 29 Oct. 1891; d. Hollywood, 29 May 1951) Comedienne and singer. She began by performing in her parents' saloon, then played in BURLESQUE before she landed a spot in ZIEGFELD's show, billed simply as FOLLIES of 1910. From then on, until she went to Hollywood in the late 1930s, she appeared in numerous Broadway revues and several book musicals. Although her first success came from clowning and comic songs (e.g. 'I'm an Indian'), she also proved to be a superb torch singer, introducing 'classics' such as 'Rose of Washington Square' and 'My Man'. On radio she was celebrated as the voice of the brattish Baby Snooks. The musical *Funny girl* (1964) was based on her life.

GERALD BORDMAN

B. Grossman, *Funny Woman: The Life and Times of Fanny Brice* (1991)

Bridges-Adams, William (b. Wealdstone, Harrow, 1 March 1889; d. Bantry, Co. Cork, Ireland, 17 Aug. 1965) Director. Bridges-Adams's early career included working with the STAGE SOCIETY, LENA ASHWELL, GEORGE ALEXANDER, WILLIAM POEL and HERBERT BEER-BOHM TREE. After experience in regional repertory theatre, most notably as co-director of the LIVERPOOL PLAYHOUSE for the 1916–17 season, his major achievements began in 1919 when he took control of the annual SHAKESPEARE FESTIVAL at STRATFORD-UPON-AVON and became director of the SHAKESPEARE MEMORIAL THEATRE. He held this post until 1934, during which time he directed 29 of Shakespeare's plays and oversaw the design and building of the new Memorial Theatre after the destruction of the original by fire. He spent the latter part of his career as drama adviser to the British Council. His book *The Irresistible Theatre* was published in 1957. IAN CLARKE

S. Beauman, *The Royal Shakespeare Company: A History of Ten Decades* (1982)
R. Speaight, ed., *A Memoir: A Bridges-Adams Letter Box* (1971)

Bridie, James (pseud. for Dr Osborne Henry Mavor) (b. Glasgow, 3 Jan. 1888; d. Edinburgh, 29 Jan. 1951) Playwright: principal founder of the Glasgow CITIZENS' THEATRE (1943), co-founder of Glasgow's School of Drama (1950) and first chairman of the Scottish Committee of the COUNCIL FOR THE ENCOURAGEMENT OF MUSIC AND THE ARTS (forerunner of the ARTS COUNCIL). A medical graduate, for a time Professor of Medicine at the University of Glasgow, Bridie wrote about 40 plays between 1928 (*The Sunlight Sonata*) and 1950 (*The Queen's Comedy*), including a biblical drama, *Tobias and the Angel* (1930); *The Anatomist* (1931), his best-known play, about a doctor who works with resurrectionists; *A Sleeping Clergyman* (1933); *Mr Bolfry* (1943); and *Daphne Laureola* (1949).
JAN MCDONALD

Winifred Bannister, *James Bridie and his Theatre* (1955)
J. T. Low, *Devils, Saints, and Sinners: A Critical Study of the Major Plays of James Bridie* (1980)
Helen Luyben, *James Bridie: Clown and Philosopher* (1966)
Ronald Mavor, *Dr Mavor and Mr Bridie* (1988)
Terence Tobin, *James Bridie* (1970)

Briers, Richard (b. Croydon, Surrey, 14 Jan. 1934) Actor. Briers' name is generally associated with light comedy, due to successful television sitcoms and a clutch of AYCKBOURN roles: Greg in *Relatively Speaking* (1967), Sidney in *Absurd Person Singular* (1973) and Colin in *Absent Friends* (1975). In these productions he cultivated his likeably vague persona, underpinned by immaculate timing and an ability to reveal a flinty cruelty beneath the comedy. In the late 1980s, his Malvolio for Renaissance Theatre Company revealed a character deep in tired, humiliated despair. With them he also had success in *Uncle Vanya* (1992) and *Lear* (1990). In 1997 he appeared with GERALDINE McEWAN in a successful revival of *The Chairs*. DAN REBELLATO

Brieux, Eugène (b. Paris, 19 Nov. 1858; d. Nice, 6 Dec. 1932) Playwright. Brieux's plays are naturalistic dramas which expose social and moral problems and advocate reform. His early work was presented by ANDRÉ ANTOINE at the Théâtre Libre in Paris and championed by SHAW. Plays include *Blanchette* (1892), about a country girl whose education does her more harm than good, *Les Trois filles de M. Dupont* (*The Three Daughters of M. Dupont*, 1897), satirizing the financial transactions of bourgeois marriage, *La Robe rouge* (*The Red Dress*, 1900), criticizing ambition in the legal profession, and two plays that fell foul of the censor – one about venereal disease, *Les Avariés* (*Damaged Goods*, 1902), and one about abortion, *Maternité* (*Maternity*, 1903). ANNA MCMULLAN

Thomas P. Vaughan, *The Plays of Eugène Brieux* (1913)

Brighouse, Harold (b. Eccles, Lancs, 26 July 1882; d. London, 25 July 1958) Playwright and novelist. Associated with the MANCHESTER SCHOOL, he wrote some 70 plays, including over 50 one-act dramas, in a variety of styles; but he was at his most assured in comedy. His most enduring play, often revived, is *Hobson's Choice* (1916), in which a domineering cobbler is tamed by his daughter. It was made into a successful film staring CHARLES LAUGHTON. Brighouse edited the *Works* (1914) of his collaborator STANLEY HOUGHTON.
IAN CLARKE

Rex Pogson, *Miss Horniman and the Gaiety Theatre, Manchester* (1952)

Bristol Before 1939 Bristol's theatrical centre was the Prince's Theatre, opened in 1867, which had eclipsed the Georgian Theatre Royal and housed leading touring companies. The Hippodrome (built 1912) survived the People's Palace (1892) and Empire (1893), offering VARIETY and musical entertainment. It was reopened in 1949 after a fire and became a major touring venue, with one of Britain's largest stages. The Little Theatre, in the Colston Hall, was opened by Rupert Harvey in 1923 as a repertory theatre and continued after the first company broke up in 1934 in this capacity under the Rapier Players until 1963. The bombing of the Prince's in 1940 left a vacuum filled by the restoration of the Theatre Royal, which reopened in 1943 and became the home of the influential BRISTOL OLD VIC Company in 1946. The Bristol Old Vic Theatre School was founded in 1946, moving to more spacious premises in nearby Clifton in 1956, and the first UNIVERSITY DRAMA DEPARTMENT in Britain was inaugurated at Bristol in 1947. This department produced PINTER's first play, *The Room*, in 1957 before it was taken up by the theatre school, in a production that brought him to the attention of a London producer. Bristol also has a history of non-traditional theatre, ranging from the Bristol Unity Players of the 1930s and 1940s to Avon Touring in the 1970s. This spirit has contined since then with the emergence of a number of small-scale companies, notably Show of Strength, founded in 1989 to present mainly new writing, and a company based at the converted Tobacco Factory, founded in 2000, to present Shakespeare. Other venues, such as the theatre attached to Queen Elizabeth's Hospital School and the Wickham Theatre in the university drama department, present work by touring professional companies. Also, The Basement at the Bristol Old Vic has developed an active programme in new writing.   G. ROWELL

See also DRAMA SCHOOLS.

Kathleen Barker, *The Theatre Royal, Bristol 1766–1966* (1974)

Don Carlton, *The Prince's of Park Row* (1983)

Terry Hallett, *Bristol's Forgotten Empire: The History of the Empire Theatre, Bristol* (2000)

Christopher Robinson, *A History of the Bristol Hippodrome (1912–1982)* (1982)

Bristol Old Vic   A leading repertory company, established by the ARTS COUNCIL in conjunction with London's OLD VIC in 1946 at the Theatre Royal, BRISTOL (built 1766). Since then it has presented a continuous programme of classical and new plays and fostered the careers of many players. The first director was HUGH HUNT; among his successors have been Denis Carey (1950–4) and Val May (1961–74). Early members of the company who achieved pre-eminence include ROBERT EDDISON, PAUL ROGERS, DOROTHY TUTIN and ERIC PORTER. Later PETER O'TOOLE and JANE LAPOTAIRE started their careers by playing a wide variety of parts for the company, which also launched the collaboration of Dorothy Reynolds and JULIAN SLADE, culminating in the production there of *Salad Days*. Among new plays staged have been the European première of *The Crucible*, the first production of *The Killing of Sister George*, and the British premières of plays by J. B. PRIESTLEY, Angus Wilson and others, and of translations from GIRAUDOUX and IONESCO. The company has undertaken a number of foreign tours, notably to North America in 1966–7. From 1963 to 1974 it also operated in the Little Theatre, Colston Hall, and, after reconstruction of the Theatre Royal, in the New Vic studio theatre (1973). Following the winding up of the Old Vic in London the Bristol company became the only Old Vic Company. The BOV Theatre Trust also runs the BOV Theatre School.   G. ROWELL

Kathleen Barker, *The Theatre Royal, Bristol, 1766–1966* (1974)

S. Brown, *Bristol Old Vic Theatre School—The First Fifty Years, 1946–96* (1997)

Audrey Williamson and Charles Landstone, *The Bristol Old Vic: The First Ten Years* (1957)

Brith Gof   Founded in 1981, it means 'speckled memory' in Welsh and it is for many people the one Welsh theatre company they know, thanks partly to legendary large-scale productions like *Gododdin* (1988), *Pax* (1990) and *Haearn* ('Iron', 1992) but also to the extensive theorizing to come from company members in their own publications, academic magazines, conference papers and university lectures – in fact, since 1997 Brith Gof has been part of the University of Wales drama department at Aberystwyth.

Founders Lis Hughes Jones (a Welsh speaker) and Mike Pearson (an English archaeology graduate who had worked with RAT [Reflex Action Theatre] in the 1970s) were original members of the innovatory CARDIFF LABORATORY THEATRE, but left to form Brith Gof; the arrival of an architect, Cliff McLucas, as co-director in 1988, saw a change from the GROTOWSKI-influenced work in rural communities to more scenographic productions, and McLucas's fascination with space and time, and new technology, has dominated later work. Composer John Hardy joined in 1987 and had a major input until he left, as did Lis Hughes Jones, in 1982. Pearson has concentrated on solo projects since 1997 and left in 1999.

Undoubtedly one of the major groups in Wales and the UK, Brith Gof has also forged strong links with companies and audiences in Scandinavia, Spain, Germany, Poland, Argentina, Italy, Ireland and Scotland.   DAVID ADAMS

British Actors' Equity Association   *see* UNIONS

British Drama League   *see* BRITISH THEATRE ASSOCIATION

British Theatre Association   Until 1972, it was called the British Drama League (BDL), which was conceived by GEOFFREY WHITWORTH one winter evening in 1918 when, after lecturing on drama to munitions workers in Kent, he was invited to remain for a reading of a one-act play by members of the club, one of a series of such play readings organized by the Workers' Educational Association. This example of what he described as 'community drama' so stirred his imagination that he set about creating a Drama League to foster drama in the community and to promote his long-cherished desire to see a NATIONAL THEATRE, which he thought of as 'COMMUNITY THEATRE, writ large'. Inaugurated with considerable enthusiasm in 1919, the BDL's first priority was to campaign for a national theatre. Among other activities to that end, it sponsored a competition for a design for a national theatre, the winning plans and model of which were exhibited at the British Empire Exhibition in 1924, the first of a long series of aborted designs. The BDL rapidly became the most vocal and active advocate of a national theatre, more so than the somewhat lethargic Shakespeare Memorial National Theatre Committee.

The second major object for which the BDL campaigned was a place for drama in education, for which it lobbied the Board of Education in 1920. This was eventually crowned by the publication in 1926 of the Board's official report, *The Drama in Adult Education*. Later, in 1942, it was the BDL that launched a detailed scheme for civic theatres (including a national theatre). There is little doubt that this campaign influenced the inclusion in the Local Government Act of 1948 of Section 132, which gave municipalities the power to set up theatres and to levy a rate for the purpose. In the same year the National Theatre Act became law.

Amateur dramatic societies had been invited into membership of the BDL on the principle that drama was 'the art of the people' and the theatre was 'everybody's business'. It was regarded as essential, therefore, that the League should include representatives of every interest involved. The number of affiliated groups multiplied rapidly and the BDL became an important influence in the development of the AMATEUR THEATRE movement. One factor in the growth of membership was the inauguration in 1925 of the library, grant-aided by the Carnegie UK Trust, which provided dramatic societies with virtually unique facilities. The major factor, however, was the inauguration in 1927 and the rapid expansion of the National Festival of Community Drama. This proved immensely popular with dramatic societies and in many quarters the FESTIVAL came to be seen as the BDL's main function.

The festival continued to dominate the BDL's affairs for many years. Area representatives on the Council were often primarily concerned with the amateur festival and less interested in the League's wider campaigning; increasingly it was seen as an organization for amateur theatre, which was only one part of its initial purpose. When Whitworth retired in 1948, E. MARTIN BROWNE was appointed director, largely in the hope that with a working professional at the head, the BDL might re-establish its contact with the professional theatre. While this aim was substantially achieved, by the mid-1950s rising costs necessitated a period of contraction and reductions in staff. The work with amateurs continued, particularly in the expanding training department, but it became increasingly hampered by financial considerations and could no longer be sustained by the subscriptions of the members.

The BDL's functions in respect of amateur theatre were performed in Scotland by the Scottish Community Drama Association (SCDA) and in Wales by the Drama Association of Wales (DAW), both of which were represented on the BDL board. The former was formed in 1924 at a BDL meeting organized by David Glen MacKemmie. In 1933 it broke away from the national festival and successfully ran its own festival for Scottish groups, later including a festival of full-length plays as well as of one-acters. It developed a vigorous policy of training and help for Scottish amateurs. The DAW was formed many years later by the amalgamation of the Drama Council of Wales, which had developed from the Drama Department of the Council of Social Service for Wales, and the Welsh Area of the BDL Festival.

It was to emphasize its wider concern with the theatre that in 1972 the BDL changed its name to British Theatre Association. Shortly afterwards the BTA shed responsibility for the national festival, which continued as an independently administered activity. Despite the BTA's unique role as the only central theatre resource in Britain, it was forced to close in 1990 through lack of funding. Its archive was given to the THEATRE MUSEUM. ALFRED EMMET

broadcasting *see* RADIO DRAMA; TELEVISION DRAMA

Broadway A street running from the southern tip of Manhattan to its northern end, its name has become synonymous with New York theatre in particular and American commercial theatre in general. A 1735 map shows a 'Playhouse on Broadway', and in the ensuing years numerous important playhouses continued to be erected on the street. From the 1920s on many of these theatres were converted to more profitable film houses, but a few, such as the Winter Garden and the Broadway, remain devoted to mainstream theatre, while most playhouses sit on side streets just off Broadway, particularly between Times Square and 53rd Street. With the introduction of electric LIGHTING the area also became known as 'The Great White Way'.
GERALD BORDMAN
See also OFF-BROADWAY; OFF-OFF-BROADWAY.

K. Bloom, *Broadway* (1991)

L. Botto, *At This Theatre: An Informed History of New York's Legitimate Theaters* (1984)

M. Henversson, *Places Please: Broadway's Historic Theaters* (1984)

William Morrison, *Broadway Theatres: History and Architecture* (1999)

N. Van Hoogstraten, *Lost Broadway Theaters* (1991)

Bronnen, Arnolt [Arnold Hans Bronner] (b. Vienna, 19 Aug. 1895; d. Berlin, 12 Oct. 1959) Playwright who wrote a number of EXPRESSIONIST plays with a strong left-wing tendency: *Geburt der Jugend* ('Birth of youth', 1925), *Vatermord* ('The patricide', 1922), *Anarchie in Silian* ('Anarchy in Silian', (1924), *Die Katalaunische Schlacht* ('The Catalonian battle', 1924), *Exzesse* ('Excesses', (1925), *Rheinische Rebellen* ('The Rhineland rebels', (1925) and *Ostpolzug* ('Journey to the East Pole', 1926). In the early 1930s he relinquished his allegiance to his hitherto close friend BERTOLT BRECHT and became a fascist supporter, but by 1943 he had joined the Austrian resistance. After the war he became dramaturg at the Scala Theater in Vienna, and in 1955 he moved to the German Democratic Republic, where he worked as theatre critic and novelist.

GÜNTER BERGHAUS

Brook, Peter [Stephen Paul] (b. London, 21 March 1925) Director, of Russian descent; one of the twentieth century's most innovative and productive practitioners. In an industrious career beginning in wartime in London's CLUB THEATRES and then the BIRMINGHAM REPERTORY THEATRE, he has worked on a variety of different kinds of performance and text, including Shakespeare, Seneca, major European and American voices (SARTRE, ANOUILH, GENET, DÜRRENMATT, FRY, MILLER) and seminal modernists (ELIOT) as well as overtly commercial forms, such as musical comedy (*Irma La Douce*, 1958). In addition, he has directed opera and films. Collaborators have included many of the finest contemporary performers, including ALEC GUINNESS, ORSON WELLES, LAURENCE OLIVIER, JOHN GIELGUD, the LUNTS, PAUL SCOFIELD and GLENDA JACKSON. As co-director of the ROYAL SHAKESPEARE COMPANY in the 1960s, and director of his own Paris-based international company since the early 1970s, he has consistently fused uncompromising experimentation with showmanship and commercial acclaim.

Brook's early work can be characterized as an attempt to explore widely divergent forms, styles, themes, working conditions and processes, in the elaboration of a 'theatre of images': stage reality as romantic fantasy, decorative lyricism and escape. His bitter-sweet *Love's Labour's Lost* (1946), for instance, was indebted visually to Watteau. The mid-1950s to early 1960s saw the genesis of a new iconoclastic aesthetic founded on provocation and disturbance, both intellectual and sensory (e.g. *Titus Andronicus*, 1955, with Olivier, sets and *musique concrète* – music constructed by mixing recorded sounds – by Brook; and the RSC THEATRE OF CRUELTY season, 1964). Productions such as *King Lear* (1962) and WEISS's *Marat/Sade* (1964) attempted to synthesize the political nihilism of BECKETT and the THEATRE OF THE ABSURD, BRECHT's techniques of distancing and the ecstatic theatricality of ARTAUD. His book *The Empty Space* (1968) became essential reading for anyone interested in the future of theatre.

Brook's RSC swansong was an airborne *A Midsummer Night's Dream* (1970), with its roots in Chinese CIRCUS: a startling re-reading of a classic text, celebrating the physicality and theatricality of actors as acrobats. Since that time – apart from a return to STRATFORD-UPON-AVON in 1978 to direct ANTONY AND CLEOPATRA – Brook has collaborated with a multicultural, multi-skilled group (*see* INTERNATIONAL CENTRE FOR THEATRE RESEARCH) in a radically utopian search for an intercultural theatre language. Cushioned from the crippling demands and impositions of commercial theatre by government and private subsidy, the company has been able to combine ongoing private research into the specificity of theatre with public performances around the world in an extraordinary range of performance spaces. His pursuit of a 'necessary' theatre has come to focus increasingly on myth and storytelling, culminating in his nine-hour adaptation of the sprawling Sanskrit epic *The Mahabharata* (1985). In the 1990s Brook focused increasingly on intimate chamber pieces concerned with the internal landscapes of neurological disorders (*The Man Who*, 1993), the nature of acting (*Qui est là?*, 1995) and memory (*Je suis un phéomène*, 1998). His thoughts on acting and theatre, *There Are No Secrets*, appeared in 1987, his observations on 40 years of exploration, *The Shifting Point*, also in 1987 and his memoir, *Threads of Time*, in 1998.

DAVID WILLIAMS

See also DIRECTING.

John Heilpern, *Conference of the Birds: The Story of Peter Brook in Africa* (1979)

Albert Hunt and Geoffrey Reeves, *Peter Brook* (1995)

Garry O'Connor, *The Mahabharata: Peter Brook's Epic in the Making* (1989)

David Selbourne, *The Making of A Midsummer Night's Dream* (1982)

A. C. H. Smith, *Orghast at Persepolis* (1972)

J. C. Trewin, *Peter Brook: A Biography* (1971)

David Williams, ed., *Peter Brook: A Theatrical Casebook* (1988)

—, ed., *Peter Brook and the Mahabharata: Critical Perspectives* (1991)

Brooklyn Academy of Music New York nonprofit presenting organization. It originated in the 1860s, but burned down in 1903. The new building (1908) had four auditoriums and was the first multi-space theatre in the United States. Its modern history begins in 1967, when Harvey Lichtenstein took charge of a moribund institution. The sponsor of such AVANT-GARDE art as ROBERT WILSON's early pieces, Lichtenstein is best known for his Next Wave Festival, the country's most prominent showcase for innovative theatre, dance and music from around the world. It has also been home to the Chelsea Theatre (1968–78), the BAM Theatre Company (1977–9 under FRANK DUNLOP, 1979–81 under DAVID JONES) and the Dodger Theatre (1978–80). BAM's annual autumn festival began in 1982. Resident companies include the Brooklyn Philharmonic and 651 Arts, a multicultural, community-based organization that presents the annual DanceAfrica festival and other work. The Next Wave Festival is supplemented at other times by more productions of world-class opera and theatre by such companies as the ALMEIDA, ROYAL SHAKESPEARE COMPANY and Les Arts Florissants. Artists presented at BAM include PINA BAUSCH, INGMAR BERGMAN, PETER BROOK, ARIANE MNOUCHKINE and PETER SELLARS.

M. ELIZABETH OSBORN

Broome, John see CHOREOGRAPHY; JOOSS, KURT; LABAN, RUDOLPH; PHYSICAL PREPARATION

Brown, Ivor (b. Penang, 25 April 1891; d. London, 22 April 1974) Theatre critic. Having worked on *New Age* during the First World War, Brown became theatre critic for the *Manchester Guardian* in 1919 and then for the *Observer*, which he later edited, greatly supporting the new European dramatic forms reaching Britain. Much admired for his wit, intelligence and erudition, he was professor of drama to the Royal Society of Literature (1939), chairman of the BRITISH DRAMA LEAGUE (1954–65), drama director for CEMA (COUNCIL FOR THE ENCOURAGEMENT OF MUSIC AND THE ARTS; 1940–2), and a governor of the OLD VIC and ROYAL SHAKESPEARE COMPANY. He wrote novels, a popular series of books on word usage, and others on Shakespeare.

DAN REBELLATO

Brown, John Mason (b. Louisville, Ky., 3 July 1900; d. New York, 16 March 1969) Drama critic. Unabashedly stagestruck from childhood, Brown studied under GEORGE PIERCE BAKER, and from 1925 to 1931 lectured at the American Laboratory Theater. He was drama critic and associate editor of *Theatre Arts Monthly* (1924–8) and drama critic for the New York *Evening Post* (1929–41), New York *World-Telegram* (1941–2) and *Saturday Review* (1945–55). A founding member of the New York Drama Critics' Circle, he was

its president in 1941–2 and 1945–9. Brown's combination of enthusiasm and sophisticated judgement permeates his more than 20 books. *Dramatis Personae* (1963) offers a retrospective sampling of his reviews from six decades. FELICIA HARDISON LONDRÉ

Brown, Lennox (b. Trinidad, 1934) Playwright who wrote his more than 40 plays while living in Canada, the United States and England. Many of these works were originally written for radio or television, and some have won multiple awards. He is the only playwright to have won Canada's National One-Act Playwriting Competition for four years in succession, with *Snow Dark Sunday* (1965), *The Meeting* (1966), *Night Sun* (1967) and *Jour Ouvert* (1968). He has won numerous other national playwriting awards in Canada and in the United States. His stage plays have been performed in North America, Europe and the Caribbean. Several plays appear in collections. His own collection, *The Twilight Dinner and Other Plays*, which contains *The Blood Promise of a Shopping Plaza* and *Fog Drifts in the Spring* along with the title play, was published in 1981.

Some of Brown's plays, such as the *Behind the Bridge* cycle, draw powerfully on Afro-Caribbean mythology and ritual, incorporating symbolism of the slavery experience. The first play in this cycle, *A Ballet Behind the Bridge*, had its première in New York by the NEGRO ENSEMBLE COMPANY. Others of Brown's plays explore a wide range of cultural themes, both historical and contemporary. His work tends to question traditional values, and resonates with concern for the human condition. JUDY S. J. STONE

Brown, Lew see DESYLVA, BROWN AND HENDERSON

Brown, Pamela (b. London, 8 July 1917; d. London, 18 Sept. 1975) Actress of great ability and emotional intensity who was inclined to give audiences the impression that she was too good for them. After more than a decade of classical roles, including Juliet (1936), Cressida (1936), Hedda Gabler (1940), Ophelia (1944) and Goneril (1946), she made an outstanding success as Jennet in CHRISTOPHER FRY's verse play *The Lady's Not For Burning* (1949), which she played in London, New York and Washington DC. Her career faded after this, and lack of a comedy sense worked against her.

IAN BEVAN

Brown, Trisha (b. Aberdeen, Wash., 25 Nov. 1936) Dancer and choreographer. She studied with Anna Halprin and Robert Dunn and was a founder of the JUDSON Dance Theater, New York (1962–6). Her choreography has used a huge variety of improvisational, compositional and theatrical means. They range from her 'equipment pieces' of the 1970s, such as *Walking* *on the Wall* at the Whitney Museum of Modern Art (1971), to her 'musical' works of the 1990s, such as *M.O.* (1994), set to Bach. She has extended her method in collaboration with many artists and musicians, especially Robert Rauschenberg. She has pushed the bounds of the 'performative' and the theatrical in dance, especially in *Set and Reset* (1983). She continues to work in New York, from where her company (founded in 1970) tours the world.   MICHAEL HUXLEY

See also CHOREOGRAPHY; DANCE.

S. Banes, *Terpsichore in Sneakers: Post-Modern Dance*, 2nd edn (1987)

C. Brunel, T. Brown and G. Delahaye, *Trisha Brown* (1987)

Browne, E[lliot] Martin   (b. Zeal, Wilts, 29 Jan. 1900; d. London, 27 April 1980)   Actor and director. He founded the PILGRIM PLAYERS in 1939, and between 1945 and 1947 ran the MERCURY THEATRE, London, introducing several verse dramatists, notably CHRISTOPHER FRY (*A Phoenix too Frequent*, 1946). He founded the Religious Drama Society and persuaded T. S. ELIOT to write for the theatre, directing all his full-length plays: *Murder in the Cathedral* (1935), in which he later played Becket many times; *The Family Reunion* (1939); *The Cocktail Party* (1950); *The Confidential Clerk* (1953); and *The Elder Statesman* (1958). He also staged the first productions of the revived York Mystery Cycle (1951) and Coventry Mysteries (1962). He served as director of the BRITISH DRAMA LEAGUE (1945–57) and in 1952 became the first president of the International Amateur Theatre Association.   G. ROWELL

See also RELIGIOUS DRAMA; VERSE DRAMA.

Browne, Maurice   (b. Reading, Berks, 12 Feb. 1881; d. Torquay, Devon, 21 Jan. 1955)   Actor–manager and playwright. In 1919 Browne founded the Chicago Little Theater; he directed productions there for several years and was a leading figure in the LITTLE THEATRE movement. He moved to BROADWAY in 1920 and then returned to England. In 1929 he became manager of the SAVOY THEATRE, where he put on acclaimed productions of SHERRIFF's *Journey's End* (1929) and *Othello* (1930), in which he played Iago to PAUL ROBESON's Othello and PEGGY ASHCROFT's Desdemona. In the 1930s he took over the management of the Globe and Queen's Theatres, and put on a series of well-received contemporary plays, including *Wings Over Europe* (1932) which he co-wrote with Robert Nichols.
ADRIANA HUNTER

Browne, Wynyard [B.]   (b. London, 6 Oct. 1911; d. Norwich, Norfolk, 19 Feb. 1964)   Playwright. Browne achieved great acclaim for *The Holly and the Ivy* (1948),

revealing tensions at a family Christmas, but his well-made-play writing was eclipsed by the theatrical revolutions of 1956 associated in the UK with the ROYAL COURT and THEATRE WORKSHOP, which brushed the gentleness of his irony aside. Other plays include *Dark Summer* (1947), *A Question of Fact* (1953) and *The Ring of Truth* (1959).   DAN REBELLATO

Charles Duff *The Lost Summer: The Heyday of the West End Theatre* (1995)

Bruant, Aristide   *see* CABARET

Bruce, Lenny [Leonard Alfred Schneider]   (b. New York, 13 Oct. 1935; d. Los Angeles, 3 Aug. 1966) Comedian and philosopher whose running battle with the contradictions and double-thinking in American society – not to mention with the police, who arrested him often on drugs and blasphemy charges – drove him to a form of comedy based not on jokes but on autobiography of the most painful and shocking kind. He was banned from performing in Britain in 1964, but, after he died of a drugs overdose, he became an anti-establishment symbol of his times, beyond the cult following he already enjoyed. His autobiography, *How to Talk Dirty and Influence People*, appeared in 1965 and a collection of his sketches, *The Essential Lenny Bruce*, in 1973.He inspired later generations of comics and a play, *Lenny* (filmed 1974).   CLIVE BARKER

See also STAND-UP COMEDY.

Bruckner, Ferdinand [Theodore Tagger]   (b. Vienna, 26 Aug. 1891; d. West Berlin, 5 Dec. 1958) Playwright. Between 1923 and 1928 he established the Renaissance Theatre in Berlin, and was its manager until 1929. He rose to fame with two plays: *Krankheit der Jugend* (*Malady of Youth*, 1926) and *Die Verbrecher* (*The Criminals*, 1928). Bruckner's plays of this period depicted the dark side of human existence. His style was influenced by the EXPRESSIONISTS, but he aimed at a detached, more objective view of his society. Before emigrating to the United States on Hitler's seizure of power, he wrote *Die Rassen* (*The Races*, (1933), which became one of the most successful plays of German exile theatre, alerting audiences the world over to the crimes committed against Jews in the Third Reich.

In the United States, Bruckner wrote two historical dramas and two resistance plays. In 1951 he returned to the Federal Republic of Germany. His last plays were existentialist tragedies in the classical tradition.
GÜNTER BERGHAUS

H. F. Garten, *Modern German Drama* (1964)

Bruford, Rose   *see* DRAMA SCHOOLS; VOICE TRAINING

Brustein, Robert [Sanford] (b. Brooklyn, New York, 21 April 1927) Critic, manager, educator and director. As provocative theatre and culture critic in the *New Republic* and the *New York Review of Books* in the 1960s, Brustein initially championed a 'Third Theatre' as an alternative to commercial mediocrity. If his enthusiasm waned in the face of radical dogmatism, it was revived by the emergence of a new postmodern experimentation. In the late 1960s Brustein's critical voice receded as he turned from theory to practice as founder and artistic director of the Yale Repertory Theater (1966–79) and Dean of the Yale Drama School. Moving to Harvard in 1979 as head of the Loeb Drama Center, he founded the AMERICAN REPERTORY THEATRE (1980). In recent years he has reactivated his critical voice in the *New Republic* (from 1978). Major books include: *The Theatre of Revolt* (1964), *Seasons of Discontent* (1966), *The Third Theatre* (1968), *The Culture Watch* (1975), *Making Scenes* (1981), *Reimagining American Theater* (1991), *Dumbocracy in America: Studies in the Theater of Guild, 1987–1994* (1994) and *Cultural Calisthenics: Writings on Race, Politics, and Theater* (1998). GERALD RABKIN

Bryant, Michael [Dennis] (b. London, 5 April 1928) Actor. Early work with the ENGLISH STAGE COMPANY led him to the ROYAL SHAKESPEARE COMPANY, where he appeared in, among other things, the first production of PINTER's *The Homecoming* in 1965. Since 1977 his theatre work has been exclusively at the NATIONAL THEATRE, where he is an associate director and has played in many of the theatre's most important productions, including award-winning performances in Shakespeare (Prospero, Polonius, the Fool in *King Lear*), SHAW and DAVID HARE (*Racing Demon, Murmuring Judges, The Absence of War*). He is an actor of profound humanity and quiet integrity, with a wry, self-deprecating humour, engagingly displayed in his performance as Badger in ALAN BENNETT's adaptation of *The Wind in the Willows* (1990). GENISTA MCINTOSH

Bryceland [Heilbuth], Yvonne (b. Cape Town, 18 Nov. 1925; d. London, 13 Jan. 1992) Actress. She took her stage name from her first husband and was a respected actress with the Cape Performing Arts Board before she and her second husband, Brian Astbury, founded an inter-racial theatre, The Space, in 1972. Here, as later abroad, she became known for her roles in the plays of ATHOL FUGARD (e.g. *Hello and Goodbye, Boesman and Lena, Statements After the Arrest under the Immorality Act, Dimetos* and *The Road to Mecca*). She came to Britain with Astbury and spent eight years with the NATIONAL THEATRE from 1978 to 1986, playing many roles and giving one of the most powerful

performances ever seen in the Olivier Theatre as Hecuba in EDWARD BOND's *The Woman* (1978). CHARLES LONDON

Bryden, Bill [William Campbell Rough] (b. Greenock, Scotland, 12 April 1942) Director and playwright. After being an assistant at the Belgrade, Coventry, to WILLIAM GASKILL, and at the ROYAL COURT (1966–8), Bryden became associate director of the LYCEUM THEATRE, Edinburgh (1971), producing new writing, including his own *Willie Rough* (1972) and *Benny Lynch* (1974), and giving Scottish drama a high profile. He joined the NATIONAL THEATRE (1973), becoming associate director (1975) responsible for the Cottesloe, where his outstanding productions included pioneering work in PROMENADE theatre with *The Mysteries*, developed by TONY HARRISON and the company from the York cycle (1977–85, revived 1999). Bryden became Head of Television Drama at BBC Scotland (1985) and continued to direct theatre, including *The Ship* in Glasgow (1991) and *The Son of Man* (1995, The Pit). CATHY JOYCE

Buchanan, Jack (b. Helensburgh, Scotland, 2 April 1890; d. London, 21 Oct. 1957) Actor, manager and producer. He began as a dancer in 1911 and starred in REVUE, musical comedy and plays. Known for his debonair, throwaway style, he appeared in *A to Z* (1921), *Toni* (1924), *That's a Good Girl* (1928) and *Mr Whittington* (1934), and enjoyed an extensive film career which included many adaptations of his stage successes. REXTON S. BUNNETT

Michael Marshall, *Top Hat and Tails* (1978)

Buenaventura, Enrique *see* MEXICO AND CENTRAL AMERICA; SOUTH AMERICA

Buero Vallejo, Antonio (b. Guadalajara, 29 Sept. 1916; d. Madrid, 29 April 2000) Playwright, little known outside his native Spain but a major figure. Although he had originally studied art, his ambitions to be a painter were cut short by the Civil War, in which he served as a Republican medical orderly, and by his subsequent imprisonment until 1945. Drawing on a variety of techniques that include the symbolic realism of his early plays and the Brechtian distancing of his historical dramas, he sought for 25 years to escape the watchful eye of the Franco censor while exploring concepts of freedom and oppression. Plays include *Historia de una escalera* ('Story of a staircase', 1949), *Las Meninas* ('The maids of honour', 1960), *El concierto de San Ovidio* (*The Concert at Saint Ovide*, 1960) and *El sueño de la razón* (*The Sleep of Reason*, 1970). MARIA DELGADO

Carmen Caro Dugo, *The Importance of the Don Quixote Myth in the Works of Antonio Buero Vallejo* (1995)

Martha T. Halsey, *Buero Vallejo* (1973)

Robert L. Nicholas, *The Tragic Stages of Buero Vallejo* (1972)

Jocelyn Ruple, *Buero Vallejo: The First Fifteen Years* (1972)

Bulgakov, Mikhail [Afanasievich] (b. Kiev, Ukraine, 15 May 1891; d. Moscow, 10 March 1940) Playwright and novelist. Son of a professor of theology, Bulgakov studied medicine at the University of Kiev and practised with the Red Cross before turning to writing in 1920. The following year he moved to Moscow and became a journalist, working for a number of revolutionary papers. In 1924 his story *The Diaboliad* was published, follwed a year later by the first two parts of *Belaya Gvardia* (*The White Guard*; stage version presented in London in 1938 and 1979). An invitation from the MOSCOW ART THEATRE to turn this into a play was the prelude to all manner of difficulties with the Central Repertory Committee because of the sympathetic light in which officers of the White army were portrayed. Revisions, including a change of title to *Dni Turbinykh* (*Days of the Turbins*) did little to disarm criticism, and permission was granted for performance only by the Art Theatre. The production opened in 1926 but was removed from the repertoire in 1929 at the same time as rehearsals were discontinued for *Beg* (*Flight*); *Zoykina Kvartira* (*Madame Zoyka* or *Zoya's Apartment*) and *Bagrovy Ostrov* (*Crimson Island*) were taken off at respectively the Vakhtangov and Kamerny theatres. When *Molière* (originally *Kabala Svyatosh*, seen at the ROYAL SHAKESPEARE COMPANY in 1982) was also banned, Bulgakov wrote a letter of protest to the Soviet government. This provoked the personal intervention on his behalf of Stalin, who approved *The White Guard* on the grounds that it showed Bolshevism triumphing over a powerful and intelligent opposition. The production returned to the Art Theatre stage and remained in the repertoire until the sets were accidentally destroyed in 1941. Though much of his work was still banned, Bulgakov was able to work at the Art Theatre as an assistant director. He adapted Gogol's *Myortvye Dushi* (*Dead Souls*) for the stage in 1932 and turned it into a film script in 1934. At the same time he began work on a fantastical and influential novel, *Master I Margarita* (*The Master and Margarita*), which was banned, later filmed, and staged in 1977 by LYUBIMOV, and a biography of Molière. His play on the French actor/playwright had been released for performance but rehearsals continued from 1932 until 1936, when the production ran for only three weeks at the Art Theatre. Bulgakov left to work at the Bolshoi and began another novel, *Black Snow* (originally known as *Tetralnyi Roman*). This 'theatrical novel' catalogues the experiences of a young playwright suffering from the vagaries of a world-renowned director who has a 'method', a thin disguise for STANIS-LAVSKY. (A dramatization by Keith Dewhurst was presented at the NATIONAL THEATRE, London, in 1991.) Bulgakov's last years saw further disillusion, with abandoned productions of *Posledniye Dni* (*The Last Days*) and *Ivan Vasil'evich* in 1936, and *Batum*, about the young Stalin, in 1939. He did complete a number of opera libretti but fell ill with a kidney disease in 1939 and died the following year. He was said to have written over 20 plays but several have been lost. Others include *Adam i Eva* (*Adam and Eve*, written 1931) and *Blazhenstvo* (*Bliss*, written 1934). J. MICHAEL WALTON

J. A. E. Curtis, *Bulgakov's Last Decade: The Writer as Hero* (1987)

Lesley Milne, *Mikhail Bulgakov: A Critical Biography* (1990)

Ellendea Proffer, *Bulgakov: Life and Works* (1984)

Harold B. Segel, *Twentieth Century Russian Drama from Gorky to the Present* (1979)

Anatoly Smelyansky, *Is Comrade Bulgakov Dead?* (1993)

Bulgaria Bulgarian theatre began to develop only in the 1840s and 1850s, as part of the movement for spiritual and political liberation at the end of a long period of Turkish rule (1396–1878). By 1900 there were several professional companies. In 1904 the Laughter and Tears company was transformed into the National Theatre, which officially opened in a new building in Sofia in 1907. By that time Bulgarian drama had become more open to European influences, trying to overcome the cultural isolation of the past. Moralistic or historical dramas were replaced by plays with modern form and ideas. Petko Todorov's (1879–1916) SYMBOLIST dramas were a fusion of IBSEN's techniques and mystic themes from Bulgarian folklore. Anton Strashimirov (1872–1937) wrote realistic social plays but also symbolist dramas on legendary themes. The modern tragedies of passion of Peio Yavorov (1877–1914), who was for several years artistic director of the National Theatre, contributed to the modernization of the Bulgarian stage. The first two decades of the twentieth century saw intensive developments, and many forms and styles, together with a strong sense of national identity, were established.

The dominant figure after the First World War was the remarkable actor K. Sarafov (1876–1952), who spent more than 60 years acting, directing and producing for the National. By this period the Bulgarian stage had become strongly influenced by Soviet theatre. In 1926 Nikolaj Masalitinov, a Russian actor from the MOSCOW ART THEATRE, became a leader of the National Theatre, and a new drama school, which had a major role in the development of drama education, was opened. In the 1920s and 1930s the satirical comedies on bourgeois life of Stefan L. Kostov (1897–1939) and the peasant tragedies of Yordan Yovkov (1880–1937) were first produced. They are considered Bulgarian classics and continue to be part of the repertoire.

After 1945 and the establishment of communist power, the state gave strong financial support to theatre companies as centres for political propaganda, but the following decade was marked by strict censorship and stagnation. Only in the 1960s did new theatrical processes begin. Playwrights like Yordan Radichkov and Stanislav Stratiev – the Bulgarian dramatists of the ABSURD – Valery Petrov, Stefan Zanev and Konstantin Iliev transformed the image of Bulgarian drama and received international recognition. In the 1980s the first experimental works were made. The feeling of total freedom after the democratic changes of 1989 was very stimulating. Several private companies were formed, trying to expand the theatre's vocabulary and aesthetic. Bulgarian achievements in animation, puppets and circus have influenced the work of young directors, and in the 1990s Bulgarian theatre became better known for its export of shows to European festivals than for its original writing. ANNA KARABINSKA

Bulgarian International Theatre Institute, *The Bulgarian Dramatic Art* (1979)
Iosif Shoulov, *The Bulgarian Theatre*, trans. Elena Mladenova (1964)

Bullins, Ed [pseud. Kingsley B. Bass, Jr.]   (b. Philadelphia, Pa., 2 July 1935)   Playwright. He turned from novel-writing to theatre and was inspired by BARAKA's plays. An integral force in the emergence in the 1960s of BLACK THEATRE IN THE UNITED STATES, in 1967 he became resident playwright at Harlem's New Lafayette Theater and edited its magazine *Black Theatre*. His plays are rooted in naturalism, yet he experiments in form, using JAZZ, blues and RITUAL. A prolific writer, his best-known titles include *Clara's Ole Man* (1965), *Goin'a Buffalo* (1966), *Electronic Nigger* (1968), *The Taking of Miss Janie* (1975) and *Boy X Man* (1995). *In the Wine Time* (1967) and *In New England Winter* (1968) form part of a cycle about black American ghetto life.
JANE HOUSE

Nicholas Canady, 'Towards Creation of a Collective Form: The Plays of Ed Bullins' in *Studies in American Drama* (1986)

Samuel A. Hay, *Ed Bullins: A Literary Biography* (1977)

Bunyan, Carole   *see* MONSTROUS REGIMENT

Burian, Emil [František]   (b. Plzeň, Bohemia [now Czech Republic] 11 June 1904; d. Prague, 9 Aug. 1959)   Director. With directors Jiří Frejka and Jindřich Honzl, Burian was one of the outstanding representatives of the Czech AVANT-GARDE in the interwar period, which was influenced by the Soviet theatre (MEYERHOLD, TAIROV, VAKHTANGOV) in seeking new forms and procedures and in committing contemporary theatre to revolutionary content. At his D Theatre in Prague (1933–41; the D was followed each year by the number of the current season), he combined social comment and attacks against petty-bourgeois values until the Nazis closed him down. Burian was a playwright, scholar, composer, actor and producer, and the first consistently to practise in a Czech environment the concept of director's theatre. He always adapted the plays he staged, whether they were by Shakespeare, Goethe or WEDEKIND. He used film and slide projection innovatively both for design purposes, achieving a dynamic and seemingly weightless environment, and for evoking the emotional states of his characters, making the drama both more metaphorical and more concrete. He created a visual and acoustic synthesis, using vocal rhythms, music dance gestures and movements, as well as projections (known as the theatregraph system) to achieve an internationally acclaimed poetic and lyrical style that influenced later experiments of SVOBODA and the LATERNA MAGIKA. After being deported as a communist to a concentration camp, he returned following liberation and adopted socialist realism. In the mid-1950s, with new stagings of his older productions, he began to break out of the dogmatic shell in which Czech theatre found itself.   EVA ŠORMOVÁ

A. Scherl, 'E. F. Burian', in M. Obst and A. Scherl, *K dějinámčeské divadelní avantgard* ('On the history of the Czech theatrical avant-garde') (1962)
B. Srba, *Poetické divadlo E. F. Buriana* ('The poetic theatre of E. F. Burian') (1971)
—— *Inscenační tvorba E. F. Buriana 1939–1941* ('The staging methods of E. F. Burian, 1939–1941') (1980)

Burkina Faso   *see* FRENCH AFRICAN THEATRE

burlesque   In American parlance, a bawdy variety show featuring striptease dancers and low comics. In most English-speaking countries, this is the primary definition of the term, and such burlesque shows were popular in the United States from 1930 until 1950, when politically motivated officials banned them as immoral. By subsequent standards in entertainment, those shows now seem innocent and even childlike. In earlier times, the term 'burlesque' referred to a literary mockery less derisive than lampoon, not so acerbic as SATIRE nor as clever as parody. In this literary sense, burlesque can be found in the works of Geoffrey Chaucer and in the plays by W. S. GILBERT before he graduated to satire with ARTHUR SULLIVAN, but this application of the term 'burlesque' is as archaic as, alas, the burlesque show itself.

By the beginning of the twentieth century, there were two burlesque 'wheels', or theatre circuits, in America — the Columbia in the east and the Empire in the west. In such theatres as the Comique in Washington DC, Boston's Old Howard, Philadelphia's Olympic and New York's Miner's Bowery, the CLOWNS who were now too broad for pretentious VAUDEVILLE continued to swat each other with noisy slats of wood ('slap sticks'), flapping about in fright wigs and baggy pants, and yammering in the dialects of America's immigrants. So burlesque shows wallowed in Irish clowns, German, Jewish, Italian or black ones, and nothing was sacred except the laughs. FANNY BRICE, later to be celebrated by BARBRA STREISAND in the musical *Funny Girl*, began her career in such circumstances. Male audiences yearned for lustier fare, and that was already forthcoming. 'Cootch dancing' had become a national rage after being introduced in 1893 by one Fahreda Manzar Spryopolos, a belly dancer who billed herself as 'Little Egypt'. A host of imitators soon gyrated across America, variously billed as 'cootch dancers', 'hootch dancers' and 'hootchy-kootchy dancers'. They were last on the programme so that, should the forces of law and order unexpectedly descend, they could be judiciously cancelled. The other founding mother of latter-day burlesque was a beautiful chorus girl named Hinda Wassu, whose version of the cootch dance was the 'shimmy'. One now-legendary night in 1928, Wassu made her entrance on a Chicago stage only to discover that a crucial element of her act was amiss – her on-stage change of costume. Half out of one costume, half into the other, and in mid-shimmy, she tugged frantically until she discovered herself partially exposed. The audience did not protest. At more or less the same time in Cleveland, a rather buxom interpretive dancer by the name of Carrie Finnell discovered the entertainment appeal of suspenseful delayed disrobement. She announced her intention to take this to the limit, almost, and then stretched the suspense for a nearly a year. The invention of the striptease dance is credited to these pioneers, the ladies Spryopolos, Wassu and Finnell, especially after the last accelerated her routine. Finnell proceeded to develop the basic striptease

vocabulary, from 'bumps' (pelvic thrusts) and 'grinds' (hip gyrations) to the ultimate costume of a 'G string' (a triangle of cloth covering the pubes) and 'pasties' (sequinned buttons to conceal the nipples). She even created the fine art of tassel twirling. With such artistic trailblazing, the ritual of striptease began. Various and quasi-fabulous stars created their own variations – SALLY RAND with her fans, Lili St Cyr with her bathtub. Stars like GYPSY ROSE LEE, Georgia Southern, Ann Corio or the reckless Margie Hart would appear just before the intermission and at show's end. The other acts on the bill included lesser strippers ('ecdysiasts') who doubled as foils for such comedians as Jackie Gleason, Phil Silvers, W. C. FIELDS and the team of Bud Abbott and Lou Costello. But when New York's mayor Fiorello LaGuardia closed down the biggest burlesque theatre chain (Minsky's) in 1937, the end was at hand. A slow death followed, a dozen years in which these sex goddesses fanned the embers of lust in dusty, ever seedier theatres. Then they were gone, ultimately to be replaced by today's pornographic generation of sexual entertainers, decidedly less imaginative and hardly as breathtaking. MARTIN GOTTFRIED

See also EROTICISIM IN THE THEATRE.

R. C. Allen, *Horrible Prettiness: Burlesque and American Culture* (1991)
Ralph Allen, *The Best Burlesque Sketches* (1955)
Ann Corio, *This Was Burlesque* (1968)
S. Lonner, *Steve Mills and the Twentieth Century Burlesque Show* (1979)
Michael Minsky, *Minsky's Burlesque* (1986)
B. Sobel, *Burlycue* (1931)
I. Zeidman, *The American Burlesque Show* (1967)

Burma   *see* SOUTH-EAST ASIA

Burns, George [Nathan Birnbaum]   (b. New York, 20 Jan. 1896; d. Beverly Hills, Calif., 9 March 1996) Comic who began in VAUDEVILLE as a boy but achieved stardom only when he partnered **Gracie [Grace Ethel Cecile Rosalie] Allen** (b. San Francisco, 25 July 1906; d. Los Angeles, 27 Aug. 1964). She began as a singer and dancer in vaudeville with her sisters at 14, and teamed up with Burns in 1923. They married in 1926 and Burns supervised the pair's material and career. The duo quickly became vaudeville headliners in 'Lamb Chops' and other comic routines which displayed Allen's wacky but warm personality and Burns' dry asides. Burns and Allen starred on radio from 1932 to 1949 and television from 1950 to 1958 in their own shows, and made 13 feature films and numerous shorts. Allen retired in 1958, but Burns kept performing, achieving grand old man of comedy status by the mid-1980s, complete with his trademark cigar. He wrote or co-wrote several books, including *Gracie, a Love Story* (1988). MICHAEL SOMMERS

C. Blythe and S. Sackett, *Say Good Night, Grace!* (1986)

Burrows, Abe [Abram Solman Borowitz] (b. New York, 18 Dec. 1910; d. New York, 17 May 1985) Playwright and director. Burrows wrote for radio and early television before turning to the stage as co-librettist with Jo Swerling for *Guys and Dolls* (1950). His later hits, often written in collaboration with others, were *Can-Can* (1953), *Silk Stockings* (1955), *How to Succeed in Business Without Really Trying* (1961, Pulitzer Prize) and his translation of a French comedy, *Cactus Flower* (1965). He served as director for many of the plays which he wrote and for those of others, as well as being a play-doctor behind the scenes. GERALD BORDMAN

Burstyn, Ellen [Edna Rae Gillooly] (b. Detroit, 7 Dec. 1932) Actress. Hers is the classic tale of a fine talent ultimately making good after years of dogged persistence, which began in the 1950s playing in Broadway comedies, as a showgirl on television and taking bit parts in films. She won a Tony award for her 1975 Broadway performance in *Same Time, Next Year*. She has also appeared in *Three Sisters* (1977), *84 Charing Cross Road* (1982), *Driving Miss Daisy* (1988) and *Shirley Valentine* (1989). In 1971 her film career took off, and she won an Oscar for *Alice Doesn't Live Here Anymore* (1974). She has campaigned for better roles for actresses, and has served both as artistic director of the ACTORS' STUDIO (1982–8) where she studied, and as president of American Actors' Equity (1982–5) (*see* UNIONS). HELEN RAPPAPORT

Burton [Jenkins], Richard [Walter] (b. Pont-rhydyfen, Wales, 10 Nov. 1925; d. Geneva, 5 Aug. 1984) Actor who first appeared in EMLYN WILLIAMS' *The Druid's Rest* (1943). In 1949 he appeared in *The Lady's Not For Burning* (London; New York, 1950), followed by two other FRY plays, *The Boy with a Cart* and *A Phoenix Too Frequent* (both 1950). He was acclaimed a classical actor in *Henry IV* (Stratford, 1951), a view confirmed by his Shakespearean work at the OLD VIC (1953–6), especially as Hamlet. Although the publicity surrounding his tempestuous marriages to Elizabeth Taylor and his high-living career in films detracted from the appreciation of Burton's genius as an actor, he had successes with *Camelot* (New York, 1960 and 1980), *Hamlet* (New York, 1964), *Dr Faustus* (Oxford, 1966) and *Equus* (New York, 1976). D. KEITH PEACOCK

M. Bragg, *Rich: A Biography of Richard Burton* (1988)

Bury, John (b. Aberystwyth, Wales, 27 Jan. 1925; d. Burleigh, Glos., 12 Nov. 2000) Designer. In 1946, after University College London and the Royal Navy, he began working with JOAN LITTLEWOOD's THEATRE WORKSHOP (where he was known as 'Camel'), both as an actor and doing the lighting. Soon he was designing for the company, including *Mother Courage and Her Children* (1955), *The Quare Fellow* (1956), *A Taste of Honey* (1958), *Fings Ain't Wot They Used T'Be* (1959) and *Oh! What a Lovely War* (1963). He began designing for ROYAL SHAKESPEARE COMPANY in 1962 and was named head of design in 1964. This marked the beginning of his long-term association with PETER HALL, which continued when Hall became artistic director of the NATIONAL THEATRE in 1973 and Bury became head of design there (1973–85). Bury's many notable RSC credits range from *The War of the Roses* (1963), *The Physicists* (1964) and *Henry V* (1964) to *The Homecoming* (1965), *Hamlet* (1965) and *A Delicate Balance* (1969). At the National, his credits include *Happy Days* (1975), *No Man's Land* (1975) and *Amadeus* (1979), for which he won a Tony on Broadway (1981). After 1980 he worked mostly in opera, usually with Hall. His design aesthetic is firmly rooted in realism: his sculptural use of wood and metal was a reaction to the previous generation of British designers, who had favoured a pretty painted-scenery look. Through his association with Hall, he designed the premières of most of HAROLD PINTER's major works. An influential presence in British design, with an international reputation, Bury was chair of the Society of British Theatre Designers (1975–85) and a champion of cultural exchange. DAVID BARBOUR

Tim Goodwin, *Britain's Royal National Theatre: The First 25 Years* (1988)
Peter Hall, *Peter Hall's Diaries: The Story of a Dramatic Battle* (1983)
Ellen Lampert, 'Designer on Design: John Bury', *Theatre Crafts International*, January 1992.

Busch, Charles *see* EXPERIMENTAL THEATRE

Busch, Ernst *see* BERLINER ENSEMBLE; GERMAN-LANGUAGE THEATRE

Bush Theatre Founded in 1972 by Brian McDermott in a cramped room over a pub on one corner of Shepherd's Bush Green in west London, it quickly became an important FRINGE venue with a mix of new plays, EXPERIMENTAL THEATRE and touring shows: LINDSAY KEMP and Phantom Captain were in the programme alongside DAVID EDGAR, HULL TRUCK and 7:84. It soon concentrated on new writing, giving wider recognition in 1975 to STEPHEN POLIAKOFF with *Hitting Town* and *City Sugar* (which later played in the West End and on television – an impulse for popularization that has

continued). As well as presenting the work of playwrights such as ROBERT HOLMAN, Dusty Hughes, Doug Lucie, Sharman MacDonald and SNOO WILSON, it has sustained an interest in Irish writing, being situated in a neighbourhood with a large Irish community; BILLY ROCHE's three Wexford plays (*A Handful of Stars*, 1988; *Poor Beast in the Rain*, 1989; and *Belfry*, 1991) visited his home town and source of their inspiration in 1993 after a successful run as a trilogy at the Bush (1991). A refurbished theatre reopened in 1997.   COLIN CHAMBERS
See also PUB THEATRE.

M. Bradwell, ed., *Bush Theatre* (1997)

Butterworth, Jez [Jeremy Penfold]   (b. London, 4 March 1969)   Playwright and film-maker. *Mojo* (1995) was the first unsolicited play in years to be given a main stage production at the ROYAL COURT. Set in Soho when rock'n'roll arrived in Britain, it almost effortlessly creates a convincing period slang, with witty, theatrical wisecracking dialogue, and an almost classical deployment of violence and tragedy. The play's affinity with the films of Quentin Tarantino, although written before these appeared, helped the Royal Court reinvent itself again with a younger, rather 'laddish' image. A film version was released in 1998.
DAN REBELLATO

Buzo, Alexander [John]   (b. Sydney, 23 July 1944) Writer of 16 plays, two novels and sundry collections. With an Albanian father, Buzo has maintained an outsider's view of the tribal rituals of ordinary life and a Stoppardian love of language. From the controversial *Norm & Ahmed* (1967) to *Martello Towers* (1976), he has mixed the absurdism of IONESCO and BECKETT with the psychological cruelty of PINTER. Romanticism has crept into plays such as *Makassar Reef* (1978) and *The Marginal Farm* (1983), which set suburbanites in exotic locales. Buzo's most revived play around the English-speaking world is the stylishly articulate *Coralie Lansdowne Says No* (1974). His *A Young Person's Guide to the Theatre and Almost Everything Else* appeared in 1988. He is also a writer on and aggressive player of cricket.   JEREMY ECCLES

John McCallum, *Buzo* (1987)

Buzzati, Dino   (b. Belluno, Italy, 16 Oct. 1906; d. Milan, 28 Jan. 1972)   Journalist and writer of plays, novels and short stories. His surreal plots are infused with a sense of mystery and menace. Recurring themes are the fear inspired by the machinery of bureaucracy and the tricks played on the mind by hope, time and mortality. His work for the theatre includes *Un caso clinico* ('A clinical case', 1953) and *Un verme al Ministero* ('A worm at the ministry', 1960). A painter, he also designed stage sets, notably for La Scala, Milan and for the Maggio Musicale Fiorentino.   FELICITY FIRTH

Byrne, John   (b. Paisley, Scotland, 6 Jan. 1940)   Playwright and designer. After *Writer's Cramp* (1977), the comic biography of an invented and talentless local artist, Byrne drew on his experiences in a carpet factory for *The Slab Boys* trilogy (1978–82), which he later filmed. Byrne creates intricate plots, vivid regional dialogue and gangs of oversized characters; farce, nostalgia, aggression and romance overlap, and American music culture saturates parochial worlds. He continued in this vein in his television work (e.g. *Tutti Frutti*, 1987).   TONY HOWARD

Byrne, John Keyes   *see* LEONARD, HUGH

C

cabaret The term – from the French word for a drinking place or tavern – came to be applied to any type of popular or topical entertainment for which the audience is seated at tables rather than on fixed seats. For many years, from before the First World War to the 1970s, it had a specific connotation as an after-dinner entertainment, often in restaurants and clubs in which the entertainment was a central feature. In some, the performers worked from a small stage, in others upon the dance floor itself, on which were presented small-scale productions called floorshows. In its original form, however, it was an artistic offshoot of the French café-concert, which had itself developed, in the manner of the British MUSIC HALL, from tavern entertainment. Its founders are generally accepted as being the Hydropathes, a society of Paris writers who hired a room for weekly meetings at which they read their own works. Gradually, the emphasis changed from the literary to the topical and satirical, and in 1881 the painter Rodolphe Salis found a permanent home for the group in Montmartre, which he named Le Chat Noir. Here the entertainment became more structured and included such features as Théâtre d'Ombres, a shadow show with special effects that pre-dated the cinema, and Montmartre rapidly became the leading cabaret district of Paris. One of the most famous rooms was Le Mirliton, which had taken over the Chat Noir premises. Its leading artist was the singer Aristide Bruant, whose personal style, topical songs and insulting of the customers were influential in determining the path of cabaret. In the 1920s Berlin became the cabaret capital of Europe, though cabaret had taken root earlier in Munich, planted by Albert Langen, founder of the satirical weekly *Simplicissimus*, and developed by the playwrights WEDEKIND and BRECHT,

who made their names as cabaret performers and writers. Other European cities had followed suit, notably Moscow, St Petersburg, Zurich, Barcelona and Cracow, usually linked to the literary and artistic AVANT-GARDE: in Zurich, for example, DADA had emerged from the Cabaret Voltaire. But in Berlin there also came into being dozens of *Amusierkabaretten*, which had few intellectual ideals and catered for every taste. The Nazis banned cabaret in 1935; glimpses of the period can be seen in the musical *Cabaret* and the play *Mephisto* based on the novel by Klaus MANN. The dissenting tradition of European cabaret probably derived from a repressive and conservative press, and did not thrive in Britain and the United States. In the 1960s, however, the Second City company from Chicago and the Establishment in London (following the success of the REVUE *Beyond the Fringe*) revived satirical cabaret with considerable success, and their lead has to a certain extent been followed by the hundreds of comedy clubs which have been opened in both countries, though these have increasingly relied upon solo artists or STAND-UPS. Since the 1980s cabaret, though in a slightly different form, has been revived in New York and, to a lesser extent, in London. The performances are usually by solo singers, with piano accompaniment, and have proved particularly popular with the gay community. PETER HEPPLE

See also NEW VARIETY.

Lisa Appignanesi, *Cabaret* (1975)
J. Jelarich, *Berlin Cabaret* (1993)
Laurence Senelick, *Cabaret Performance: Europe 1890–1940*, 2 vols (1989, 1992)

café theatre A loose term deriving from the French

café concerts of the nineteenth century in which drinkers and diners were offered an accompanying programme of entertainment. It had similarities with VARIETY, VAUDEVILLE, MUSIC HALL and CABARET. Its informality was resurrected and recalled by CAFFE CINO and café LA MAMA at the heart of OFF-OFF-BROADWAY in the United States and in Britain by LUNCHTIME THEATRE and PUB THEATRE. CHARLES LONDON

Caffè Cino American café theatre where the OFF-OFF BROADWAY movement may be said to have begun when, in December 1958, Joe Cino started his coffeehouse at 31 Cornelia Street in Greenwich Village and began presenting plays. Starting out with revivals of classics by SHAW, WILDE and CHEKHOV, the Caffè became a primary home for the presentation of new experimental drama with the arrival of LANFORD WILSON in 1962. Soon it was offering new plays by Wilson, Tom Eyen, JOHN GUARE, H. M. Koutoukas, Robert Patrick and others. Without affiliation, grants or church support, Caffè Cino was the only Off-Off Broadway organization that was self-supporting. On 2 April 1967 Joe Cino died of wounds self-inflicted a few days earlier. Without its guiding spirit, Caffè Cino closed for good the following year. GERALD RABKIN

Cage, John (b. Los Angeles, 15 Sept. 1912; d. New York, 12 Aug. 1992) Musician and composer. Cage studied music in Europe and America, working for a time in 1935 with Schoenberg. From 1937 onwards he developed a strong interest in music for dance, and in 1938 began a collaboration with the dancer MERCE CUNNINGHAM that lasted over 50 years. An influential figure in the experimental arts (e.g. on ROBERT WILSON), Cage was also interested in performance and theatre. He was responsible for developing the 'prepared' piano (a piano on which the sound is changed by inserting objects between the strings) and in the 1950s he created some of the first HAPPENINGS. He has experimented with many compositional techniques, including aleatory music (the use of chance in composition), electronic music and the use of environmental sounds. A former gardener, he was also an expert on mushrooms. ANDREW SOLWAY
See also DANCE; EXPERIMENTAL THEATRE; HAPPENING.

David Revill, *The Roaring Silence: John Cage* (1992)
Sam Richards, *John Cage as . . .* (1996)

Cairns, Tom *see* DESIGN

Caldwell, Zoe [Ada] (b. Hawthorn, Victoria, Australia, 14 Sept. 1933) Actress and director. A leading actress who is equally at home in comic and tragic roles in both classical and modern plays, Caldwell made her

professional debut in 1953 as one of the original members of the Union Repertory Theatre Company (Melbourne). She appeared notably at STRATFORD-UPON-AVON's SHAKESPEARE MEMORIAL THEATRE (1958–9), Canada's STRATFORD FESTIVAL (1961, 1967), and the GUTHRIE THEATER, Minneapolis (1963, 1965). She was acclaimed on Broadway for starring roles in *Slapstick Tragedies* (1966), *The Prime of Miss Jean Brodie* (1968) and *Medea* (1982), and as Maria Callas in *Master Class* (1995). Her directorial work includes *An Almost Perfect Person* (Broadway, 1977) and *Richard II* (Stratford, Ontario, 1979). She is married to producer ROBERT WHITEHEAD. DAVID STAINES

Callow, Simon (b. London, 15 June 1949) Actor, director and author, whose book *Being an Actor* (1984) vividly conveys his working life at the time. After appearing in new plays with GAY SWEATSHOP, at the BUSH and with JOINT STOCK, major classical parts followed: Titus Andronicus (1978), Arturo Ui (1978) and Orlando in JOHN DEXTER's cerebral *As You Like It* (1979) at the NATIONAL THEATRE, where he starred as Mozart in PETER SHAFFER's *Amadeus* (1979) and gave a reading of all Shakespeare's Sonnets (1980). A flamboyant and energetic personality, he has also written biographies of CHARLES LAUGHTON (1987) and ORSON WELLES (1996) and a memoir of his relationship with the play agent PEGGY RAMSAY (1999). Known popularly for his film acting (e.g. *Four Weddings and a Funeral*), he has increasingly turned to directing (e.g. *Shirley Valentine*, 1988; *Carmen*, 1991; and *The Pajama Game*, 1999). TERRY HODGSON

calypso *see* CARNIVAL

Cambodia *see* SOUTH-EAST ASIA

Cambridge A market town in the east of England and home to the country's second oldest university, Cambridge has a long tradition of theatre dating back to the Middle Ages – a tradition upheld by many of its graduates. Although touring companies visited the town, the practice of college performance that had been interrupted by the seventeenth-century civil wars did not really pick up again until the latter half of the nineteenth century, most notably with the founding in 1855 of the Amateur Dramatic Club (ADC) and in 1883 of the FOOTLIGHTS CLUB. There was also from 1882 on a production every third year of an ancient Greek play in the original language. These activities were joined in 1908 by those of the Marlowe Society, following a successful production the year before of Marlowe's *Dr Faustus*. This remained an all-male environment until in 1928 the Cambridge Mummers were founded and women admitted. Other groups followed suit in the next decade.

The productions of these groups and others based in individual colleges, many of which built their own theatres after the Second World War, have provided an extraordinarily fertile seedbed for the professional theatre, producing actors ranging from MICHAEL RED-GRAVE and ROBERT EDDISON to IAN MCKELLEN and DEREK JACOBI as well as playwrights like DAVID HARE, MICHAEL FRAYN and STEPHEN POLIAKOFF. The influence of former Cambridge students was particularly felt in the field of comedy, courtesy of the FOOTLIGHTS annual revue, and in the era of publicly subsidized theatre when directors such as PETER HALL, JOHN BARTON, TREVOR NUNN and RICHARD EYRE dominated the national companies. The university, ironically, does not have a drama department.

Professional theatre in the town at the start of the century was centred on the New Theatre, which became a cinema in the 1930s, until TERENCE GRAY opened his FESTIVAL THEATRE in 1926 offering an adventurous international repertoire presented with advanced staging techniques. It did not survive long after John Maynard Keynes opened his Arts Theatre in 1935, borrowing from Gray the idea of having a good restaurant attached. It was also, unusually in a university town, run by a trust and not by the dons; but it did host student productions and flourished under the chairmanship of a formidable academic, GEORGE RYLANDS, a key figure in Cambridge theatrical life after the Second World War. The Arts Theatre saw the first performances of several important contemporary plays, including PINTER's The Birthday Party (1958), and also housed productions by leading touring companies such as PROSPECT and the local Cambridge Theatre Company, founded in 1969 and renamed Method and Madness in 1995. The Arts closed for refurbishment in 1993 and reopened in 1996 thanks to a National Lottery grant. COLIN CHAMBERS

See also STUDENT THEATRE; UNIVERSITY DRAMA DEPARTMENTS.

Cambridge Festival Theatre A disused Georgian playhouse transformed in 1926 by Egyptologist TERENCE GRAY and Harold Ridge, a metallurgist and author of the standard book Stage Lighting for Little Theatres, into an open-stage theatre, without proscenium arch and employing a solid cyclorama and innovatory lighting. The opening production – Aeschylus' Oresteian Trilogy, directed by Gray with chorus work by NINETTE DE VALOIS – used masks and a set of screens in the manner of CONSTRUCTIVISM. Poetic and dance drama figured prominently; productions of familiar plays were highly

unconventional and controversial. Obsessively daring, it waned in importance after Gray's withdrawal in 1933, and it closed in 1939. G. ROWELL

R. Cave, Terence Gray and the Cambridge Festival Theatre (1980)

Cameri Theatre The municipal theatre of Tel Aviv, Israel; founded 1944 by Yosef Millo (b. 1916) as a youthful, Western-orientated company reacting against the stagnation of HABIMAH in its classical and east European traditions. Most of the original members, some of whom were trained at the Habimah studio, failed to enter the elitist 'closed shop' of the Habimah collective. Cameri's first box-office success, which established it alongside Habimah and OHEL, was Millo's production of Goldoni's The Servant of Two Masters (1945). Unsuccessfully attempting LORCA and ANOUILH, the Cameri soon reverted to English and American box-office hits, whose fresh translations often used everyday language. Moshé Shamir's He Walked through the Fields (1948), a topical patriotic melodrama presented in the middle of the war of independence, enhanced the attraction of the Cameri for the younger generation. With the years the repertoire discrepancies between the Cameri and Habimah diminished, and both competed for the same Tel Aviv audience. Millo left in 1958, and since 1970 the Cameri has been established as a public theatre, its original structure as a COLLECTIVE of artists abolished, and proclaimed the principal theatre of Tel Aviv. It was fiercely attacked in 1970 for producing HANOCH LEVIN's political cabaret The Queen of the Bath, and six years later over Josef Mundi's The Governor of Jericho (prompting the resignation of managing director Jeshaiah Weinberg). Generally considered a successful theatre, its work often being shown abroad in international tours and festivals, the Cameri has, however, often (and increasingly) been reproached for seeking easy box-office hits and not opening up to new talents of unproven success. AVRAHAM OZ

Cameron, Norman (b. Guyana, 1903; d. 1983) Educator. The prejudices he met at Cambridge University, where he was an exceptional student, helped to shape his black nationalist views. He made a particular study of African history, art and traditions. He came to believe that if his people were to claim independent status, as well as better education, they needed a sense of pride in African achievements. He returned to Guyana, then British Guiana, in 1926, and shortly afterwards founded a private high school in Georgetown.

Having completed his two-volume The Evolution of

the Negro (1929, 1934), Cameron embarked on a series of didactic epic plays that honoured black heroes of Africa's history. *Balthazar* (1931) features the third wise man at Christ's birth; *Adoniya* (1943) is about the Ethiopian wife of Moses, and discusses colour prejudice; *Sabaco* (1947) is on the Nubian conquest of Egypt; *Ebedmelech* (1953) again treats colour prejudice, in the rescue of Jeremiah by the Ethiopian; *Kayssa* (1959) deals with conspiracy at the court of the King of Melli in the Sudan; and the most ambitious, *The Price of Victory* (1965), is based on a Yoruba legend about Morimi, wife of Ogun. These plays, designed as teaching tools, were overwritten and do not make good theatre. They have been more often read than staged. However, in their introduction of heroic black characters they were a significant development in the indigenous dramatic writing of the time. Theatrically, Cameron's most successful work was *Jamaica Joe* (1946), which explores black relationships during the Second World War.

JUDY S. J. STONE

Cameroon *see* FRENCH AFRICAN THEATRE

Campbell, Douglas (b. Glasgow, Scotland, 11 June 1922) Actor and director. After beginning his professional career in Britain (working with, among others, SYBIL THORNDIKE and TYRONE GUTHRIE) in the 1940s and early 1950s, he joined Ontario's STRATFORD FESTIVAL company for its inaugural 1953 season, and has remained a stalwart of the company ever since, playing a wide range of roles, most successfully in the comic vein. An actor of great panache but less introspection, he is Canada's RALPH RICHARDSON to WILLIAM HUTT's JOHN GIELGUD. In addition to some celebrated Falstaffs, Campbell's Toby Belch (1957) counts among his finest Stratford achievements, as does (in a different bent) his exuberant Doolittle (opposite JOHN NEVILLE's Higgins) in *My Fair Lady* (1988). Campbell has directed frequently at Stratford, and at the GUTHRIE THEATER, Minneapolis, where he was associate director for the 1963 opening season and artistic director for the 1965 season. L. W. CONOLLY

Campbell, Ken[neth V.] (b. Ilford, Essex, 10 Dec. 1941) Playwright, director and actor. Working in regional theatres in the 1960s and 1970s, he created the Ken Campbell Roadshows: pub entertainments with stunts, songs and storytelling (bizarre 'urban myths'). He founded the Science Fiction Theatre of Liverpool to stage paranormal subjects and devise new popular forms. Campbell worked on a shoestring but appropriated high technology whenever possible; one audience floated on a hovercraft. Epic shows include *Illuminatus!* (a nine-hour-long conspiracy theory fant-

asy with songs and puppets, co-adapted with Chris Langham; it began in Liverpool in 1976 but opened the Cottesloe auditorium of the NATIONAL THEATRE in 1977) and Neil Oram's *The Warp* (the history of alternative culture: 21 hours). Campbell's plays include *The Great Caper* (1974) and such one-man-shows as *Confessions of a Nudist* (1991): strange 'true' tales of modern quests. His Pidgin-English *Macbeth* (1998) reached the West End.

TONY HOWARD

Campbell, Mrs Patrick [Beatrice Rose Stella Tanner] (b. London, 9 Feb. 1865; d. Pau, France, 9 April 1940) Actress who made her professional debut in 1888 and created a sensation in the title role of PINERO's *The Second Mrs Tanqueray* (1893). For the next 20 years she was the most discussed actress on the London and New York stages. She appeared both in new plays written for her (e.g. *The Masquerades*, 1894, by HENRY ARTHUR JONES) and classics (e.g. Juliet and Lady Teazle, 1896; Ophelia, 1897; Lady Macbeth, 1897). She played in the British première of MAETERLINCK's *Pelléas and Mélisande* (1897). Her career climaxed, aged almost 50, when she created the role of Eliza Doolittle in SHAW's *Pygmalion* (1914), but then declined with age and the loss of her remarkable Italianate looks. Her last significant appearance was in 1929 in G. B. STERN's *The Matriarch*. Opinions on her acting ability differed widely, but the critic JAMES AGATE listed her as one of the six greatest actresses he had seen, and JOHN GIELGUD (who acted with her in Ibsen's *Ghosts*) was a firm admirer of her talent although not of her unpredictable temperament. Twice married, she was also the sometime lover of two of her leading men – JOHNSTON FORBES-ROBERTSON and GERALD DU MAURIER – but more interest attaches to her relationship with Shaw. Loudly proclaimed in a series of impassioned letters (published in 1952), their 'affair' seems to have been one of words rather than deeds. IAN BEVAN

Margot Peters, *Mrs Pat: The Life of Mrs Patrick Campbell* (1984)

Campion, Edith *see* CAMPION, RICHARD

Campion, Richard (b. Wellington, New Zealand, 13 Dec. 1923) Director. He trained in London at the OLD VIC, then toured Europe with the YOUNG VIC after the Second World War. On returning to Wellington, he and his wife, Edith, set up the important touring company NEW ZEALAND PLAYERS. During the 1960s Campion was guest producer at the Adelaide Festival. His major commitment to a new kind of uniquely New Zealand theatre resulted in his directing a number of unusual epic projects, such as Expo 70 at Osaka and *Waitangi* (1986), reworked for the celebration of the sesquicentenary at Waitangi in 1990. He has directed first productions of plays by dramatists such as BRUCE MASON and JAMES K. BAXTER, and developed productions for the MAORI Theatre Trust. He was a founder of New Zealand Ballet (1960) and has directed opera in Wellington and Hawkes Bay. His most recent productions reaffirm his commitment to young people in theatre.   GILLIAN GREER & LAURIE ATKINSON

Campton, David   (b. Leicester, 5 June 1924) Playwright. Prolific writer for children, amateurs, regional theatres, television and radio. Campton's humane, sometimes Gothic, sketches of everyday foibles and their startling consequences include *Little Brother, Little Sister* (1961) and *The Life and Death of Almost Everybody* (1970): a 'God's eye view of the history of the world'.
TONY HOWARD

Camus, Albert   (b. Mondovi, Algeria, 7 Nov. 1913; d. Villeblevin, France, 4 Jan. 1960) French journalist, novelist, playwright, actor, director; winner of the Nobel Prize (1957). Born into a working-class *pied noir* community of non-Arab, European ethnic stock (an allegiance which was to cause him intense difficulties during the Algerian War), Camus made his mark in Algiers in the 1930s as the driving force behind a socialist theatre company using some of the AGITPROP techniques of PISCATOR. When the Second World War broke out, the tuberculosis which threatened his life more than once caused Camus to be rejected from call-up into the French army; he was active instead as a Resistance journalist, mainly in the south of France. During the 1940s his four plays were a major contribution to the French theatre at a time of exploration and renewal.

Camus' best play is his first, *Caligula* (1944), which is ostensibly about the short and violent life of the mad Roman emperor but also mirrors the apocalypse of Nazi Germany. Like all of Camus' work at this time, the play examines the limited options open to the individual who discovers the 'absurdity' of the world. In *Le Malentendu* (*Cross-purposes*, 1944) a son returning home from a long exile in the warm, sensuous South is murdered by his mother and sister, who are unaware of his identity. His intention was to bring them the material ease and release from the chill sterility (as the 'Mediterranean' Camus would see it) of northern Europe craved by the spinster sister. *L'Etat de Siege* (*State of Siege*, 1948) is a naïvely didactic political melodrama, conceived on a grandiose theatrical scale (created in collaboration with BARRAULT and calling on some of the fashionable ideas of ARTAUD). Despite the relationship to Camus' successful novel *The Plague*, it deserved to fail. *Les Justes* (*The Just Assassins*, 1949) had

a successful run, and addresses itself to a moral problem still current: does a worthwhile cause justify political assassination? Are there no limits? Camus argued passionately that there are. During the 1950s Camus devoted himself to directing plays, notably his own translations and adaptations (of Calderon, Lope de Vega, Dostoevsky, Faulkner). He died in a car crash.
TED FREEMAN

J. Cruickshank, *Albert Camus and the Literature of Revolt* (1960)
E. Freeman, *The Theatre of Albert Camus* (1971)
Olivier Todd, *Albert Camus: A Life*, trans. Benjamin Ivry (1997)

Canada: theatre in English   Until the twentieth century the history of theatre in Canada, a nation formed only in 1867 and not fully independent until 1931, is a record of domination by foreign touring companies offering standard fare from the classic English repertoire with generous doses of MELODRAMA. The example of such art theatres as GREIN's INDEPENDENT THEATRE SOCIETY in London and Dublin's ABBEY THEATRE inspired the development of a Canadian LITTLE THEATRE movement dedicated to innovation and experimentation. The Arts and Letters Players of Toronto (founded 1908), led by Roy Mitchell, presented plays by MAETERLINCK, YEATS, SYNGE and other contemporary writers. In 1919 the University of Toronto's semi-professional HART HOUSE THEATER opened under Mitchell's direction, regularly performing new Canadian plays in addition to contemporary drama and the classics. The most significant playwright associated with Hart House was Merrill Denison, who produced a number of plays superior to any yet written in English Canada. His *The Unheroic North: Four Canadian Plays* (1923) contains three short plays and the full-length *Marsh Hay*, a powerful portrayal of life in northern Ontario which bears comparison with the work of Synge.

The example provided by the Hart House Theater was emulated in Canada's other major cities; the most innovative contribution was HERMAN VOADEN's work with the Sarnia Little Theater, founded in 1927 in Sarnia, Ontario. Voaden, much influenced by German EXPRESSIONIST drama, drew heavily on music, painting and dance to develop what he called 'Symphonic Expressionism' in plays like *Rocks*, *Earth Song* and *Murder Pattern*, produced between 1932 and 1936.

The Dominion Drama Festival, founded in 1932, helped focus and develop amateur theatre of a high quality – including the presentation of new Canadian plays – in annual competitions held throughout Canada between 1933 and 1970. Among the playwrights associated with the festival were JOHN COULTER and ROBERTSON DAVIES. Coulter is important for demonstrating in his trilogy about the Métis (mixed race) rebel Louis Riel that Canadian history and attendant mythology could provide the substance of an indigenous drama. *Riel*, the first play of the trilogy, was produced by Toronto's New Play Society in 1950. Davies, who had worked under TYRONE GUTHRIE at London's OLD VIC before returning to Canada in 1940, brought to his craft a rare professionalism. In plays written between 1950 and 1975, he explored wittily what he termed the 'theme of the portion of life that is unlived'.

Radio drama played an important role between the 1930s and 1960s, a period during which the Canadian Broadcasting Corporation broadcast more than 3,500 original Canadian plays.

GWEN PHARIS RINGWOOD, the most important of western Canada's playwrights, is best known for her folk plays, *Still Stands the House* (1938) and *Dark Harvest* (1945), sombre tragedies that derive their power from a deep sense of place and the poverty of the Depression era. Ringwood's trilogy – *Maya, The Stranger* and *The Furies*, first produced in 1982 – is a biting indictment of white society's treatment of British Columbia's native peoples.

Following the Second World War the number of professional theatres in Canada increased, with the establishment of, for example, Vancouver's Everyman Theater (1946–53), Toronto's New Play Society (1946–71) and the Crest Theatre (1954–66), and these institutions encouraged the production of new Canadian plays. The STRATFORD FESTIVAL opened in 1953, the Shaw Festival at Niagara-on-the-Lake in 1962 and the CHARLOTTETOWN FESTIVAL in 1965 (its perennial favourite a musical based on L. M. Montgomery's novel *Anne of Green Gables*). Perhaps the most important influence on professional theatre in Canada was the creation in 1957 of the Canada Council, a federal agency which provided substantial funding to create new theatres and sustain new professional companies.

In 1967 three important new plays symbolized the growth of Canadian drama: John Herbert's prison drama *Fortune and Men's Eyes*, which went on to international success; JAMES REANEY's *Colours in the Dark*; and GEORGE RYGA's *The Ecstasy of Rita Joe*, about a Native girl destroyed by white society. Both Reaney and Ryga have written a large body of dramatic work since then; especially notable is Reaney's Donnelly trilogy, produced between 1973 and 1975. Following the example of Coulter, Reaney draws on Canadian history (the murder in 1880 of an Ontario Catholic family, the Donnellys) to forge new symbols and myths within a theatrical context.

Despite large government subsidies and the hope generated by these new plays, in the 1960s the country's major professional theatres, such as Edmonton's Citadel Theater and Toronto's St Lawrence Center, still relied heavily on imported plays. But in the 1970s, prompted by a strong sense of nationalism and a groundswell of interest in Canada's past, a new theatre movement – the 'alternate theatre' – emerged, and alternate theatre companies multiplied across the country. They included Vancouver's Tamahnous Theater (1971), Edmonton's Theater 3 (1970), Newfoundland's Mummers Troupe (1972), and Toronto's THEATRE PASSE MURAILLE (1968) and TARRAGON THEATER (1971). The most influential of these has been Théâtre Passe Muraille, under director Paul Thompson, who pioneered the development of the COLLECTIVE creation, where actors (perhaps with a writer) addressed Canadian social, political and cultural issues by means of a collectively devised script, as in *The Farm Show* (1972). The form became very popular in the 1970s: Newfoundland's Mummers Troupe's 1978 *They Club Seals, Don't They?* was a defence of the sealing industry; Saskatoon's TWENTY-FIFTH STREET THEATRE scored a hit in 1977 with *Paper Wheat*, a collective about the prairie farming cooperative movement.

Founded by BILL GLASSCO, Tarragon Theater emphasized professionalism in production values, and although its mandate did not exclude the production of non-Canadian plays, about three-quarters of the approximately one hundred works it has produced have been Canadian, and over half of these have been premières. Significant playwrights associated with Tarragon include David Freeman, DAVID FRENCH and Quebec's MICHEL TREMBLAY (whose plays have been performed in English). Freeman's best play is the 1971 *Creeps*, a long one-act drama set in the men's washroom of a workshop for victims of cerebral palsy. French is probably English Canada's most accomplished playwright. His tetralogy about the Mercer family – *Leaving Home, Of the Fields, Lately, Salt-Water Moon* and *1949*, produced between 1972 and 1988 – draws on memories of his own Newfoundland background to describe an archetypal father–son conflict as well as a clash between supposed old heroic values (represented by rural Newfoundland) and the mores of a deracinated urban society (Toronto).

Another alternate theatre, Toronto's FACTORY THEATER Lab, has premièred many of the plays of GEORGE WALKER. Walker's early works are derivative, part surreal, part melodrama, with strong affinities with the B-movie. His trilogy *The Power Plays*, published in

1984, examines the value of liberalism in a world dominated by political and military power through the persona of a private eye, Tyrone M. Power.

While Toronto was undoubtedly the centre of English Canadian theatre in the 1970s, a number of playwrights emerged dedicated to articulating the social, cultural and physical character of Canada's regions. MICHAEL COOK's *The Head, Guts and Sound Bone Dance* (1973) is the best of a number of his plays that dramatize life in the outports of Newfoundland. DAVID FENNARIO's *Balconville* (1979, at Montreal's CENTAUR THEATER), is rooted firmly in its Montreal milieu of the poor working class. Written in French and English, the play is a brilliant piece of naturalistic writing with a strong Marxist viewpoint. Ken Mitchell, the regional dramatist *par excellence*, draws extensively on his Saskatchewan environment. His *Cruel Tears* (1975), for example, is a musical based on *Othello* that transforms Shakespeare's tragedy into a tale of love and rivalry among Saskatchewan truck drivers. SHARON POLLOCK has also written a number of plays with a regional interest: *Walsh*, for example (about the Canadian government's treatment of Sioux chief Sitting Bull and his people after their escape to Canada in 1881). Her best play, *Blood Relations* (1980, at Edmonton's Theater 3), is about the American Lizzie Borden, accused of murdering her parents. JOHN MURRELL has written many plays with a west Canadian background and subject matter, but his greatest success has been with *Memoir* (1977), about the last months in the life of SARAH BERNHARDT. It has been performed in many countries and has been translated into some 15 languages.

New theatre companies and promising new dramatists appeared in the 1980s: Thomson Highway, Judith Thompson, Brad Fraser, Allan Stratton, Ann-Marie MacDonald, Sally Clark, Wendy Lill, Joan MacLeod and Jason Sherman. There has also been a significant growth in companies addressing specialized issues – feminism, children's theatre (there are now some 60 professional theatres for young people), homosexuality – and there has been a dramatic increase in low-budget theatre favouring the one-actor show. Significant examples here include JOHN GRAY's *Billy Bishop Goes to War*, which played London and New York after great success in Canada, and ANTONINE MAILLET's *La Sagouine* as performed by Viola Léger (in French and English). The attendant and necessary infrastructure of professional organizations, theatre publishers, professional critics and awards established in the 1970s was strengthened in the 1980s and 1990s so that it can be said with confidence that Canadian theatre has finally been liberated from its colonial past and is now playing an important role in the nation's culture.
EUGENE BENSON

Eugene Benson and L. W. Conolly, *English-Canadian Theatre* (1987)
——, eds, *The Oxford Companion to Canadian Theatre* (1989)
Eugene Benson and William Toye, eds, *The Oxford Companion to Canadian Literature*, 2nd edn (1997)

Canada: theatre in French Despite its relatively long history (the first recorded performance was in 1606, in present-day Nova Scotia), French-language theatre in Canada entered the twentieth century in precarious condition. Since its origins, theatre in French Canada has had to struggle to survive, its existence threatened by demographic and economic factors (a relatively small population spread over a vast area with, until the second half of the nineteenth century, a poorly developed transportation system) and, most importantly, by frequent, stubborn opposition from the Roman Catholic Church, to which the overwhelming majority of Canadian francophones adhered until late into the twentieth century. Primarily because of these factors, the stage arts remained resolutely amateur, cyclical and marginal until the last decade of the nineteenth century. A hundred years later, it is obvious that theatre, despite the many obstacles it has faced, has managed not only to survive, but to flourish brilliantly.

The last quarter of the nineteenth century had been marked by more and more frequent visits of professional troupes from FRANCE, notably those accompanying SARAH BERNHARDT on the nine tours she made to Quebec and Montreal in the period 1880–1918. The church had reacted strongly to the sexually permissive BOULEVARD plays these troupes offered, and to the 'immoral' actors who offered them. But, naturally, local amateur groups had begun to emulate this repertoire, often adapting it for local sensitivities. At the same time, American entrepreneurs tightened their control of commercial theatre, replacing the traditional stock companies with the 'star system', a development which favoured the establishment of local semi-professionals who could, at little cost, supply the supporting cast and supernumeraries necessary for New York-style productions. As a result, the first professional companies grouping local French-language actors began to appear in Montreal in the 1890s, initiating a period often referred to as the 'Golden Age' of theatre in that city.

This Golden Age died with the beginning of the First World War, but even before then its glitter had begun

to fade with the advent of film and of American VARI-
ETY theatre. After the war, movies and touring companies from abroad vied with *burlesque* (the French
term includes VAUDEVILLE, variety and English
BURLESQUE), the last influence becoming more and
more insidious as it adapted to local diction and
themes. With the introduction of radio and soundtrack
films, the place for traditional theatre was scant; and
much of that was occupied by shallow MELODRAMAS
such as *Aurore l'enfant martyre*, based on a sensational
local crime (the play would be performed at least 5,000
times between 1923 and 1950). But a surprising quantity of drama – much of it devoted to patriotic, religious
or historical themes – continued to be written and published in French Canada, although little of it was performed.

By the early 1930s radio had become the most
important vehicle of cultural solidarity French Canada
had known, since now for the first time the fundamental problem of demographic dispersal could be
overcome. Many of those who worked on radio had
come from the theatre, and the successful new
medium, initially pernicious to the stage arts, soon
helped them indirectly, as for the first time something
approaching financial security was possible through
radio performance. Actor–scriptwriters such as Henry
Deyglun and Henri Letondal moved easily back and
forth between stage and airwaves, writing prolifically
for both media, with their most successful works
(Deyglun's *Coeur de maman*, for example) occasionally
made into films as well. Meanwhile, throughout the
worst years of the Depression, *burlesque* continued to
prosper, and to make its influence felt on stage and
radio.

The 1930s also brought two major developments that
led directly to the full flowering of theatre in the 1960s
and beyond. The first of these was the emergence of
a group of well-trained amateurs, the Compagnons de
Saint-Laurent – ironically, under the supervision of a
Catholic priest, Emile Legault, and based initially at a
Montreal college, itself under church control. From
these amateurs came the professional actors, directors,
designers and technicians who continued to shape
Quebec's theatre to the present. The other factor is
even more closely tied to one individual, GRATIEN GÉL-
INAS, who was learning his trade as actor and writer for
radio and stage revues. By the end of the Second World
War Legault's dedicated graduates had infused new life
into the theatrical process; and the première of Gélinas' first full-length stage play, *'Tit-Coq* (1948), permanently changed indigenous playwriting. The full
effect of these two factors would be felt over the next
decade, but it was only after the end (in 1959) of the

repressive premiership of Maurice Duplessis – the
period since characterized, with some exaggeration, as
'La Grande Noirceur' (The Great Darkness) by some
historians – that Quebec's society, and therefore its culture, truly came of age.

It was in this period also that the major theatrical
institutions were established: Le Rideau Vert (1948), a
company founded by Yvette Brind'Amour; Le Théâtre
du Nouveau Monde (1951), the most respected and
influential of existing theatrical companies in French
Canada, founded by former members of Legault's
Compagnons; and the National Theatre School/Ecole
nationale du théâtre (1960), with Jean Gascon and
MICHEL SAINT-DENIS as its first directors. The 1950s witnessed as well the introduction of summer theatre and
the sudden profusion of small *théâtres de poche*, often
operating in direct opposition to the policies and repertory of established, traditional companies like the
Théâtre du Nouveau Monde.

Television came to Canada in 1952, immediately
drawing writers, artists and spectators from stage and
radio and, for the first time, threatening even the survival of *burlesque*. Its influence was immediate and pervasive, in every aspect of theatrical arts. The major
author of the decade, MARCEL DUBÉ, began writing for
national television in 1952, and all his major works
(some three dozen, to date) are visibly influenced by
that medium, notably *Florence* (1957) and *Un Simple
Soldat* (1957). His example was soon followed by
others, and the transition of a production from stage
to television, or vice versa, became commonplace.
Finally, the 1950s saw the establishment at the federal
level of the Canada Council, followed by provincial
and municipal funding agencies whose subsidies and
the policies they reflect have had a profound and lasting effect upon theatre in all of Canada.

Consequently, the 1960s was a decade of great effervescence in theatre, marked by enthusiastic iconoclasm, much of it directed, ironically, against existing
institutions, especially the governmental ones from
which the stage's economic lifeblood flows. The prolific Dubé dominated the first two-thirds of the decade,
passing the baton after 1968 to Quebec's best-known
dramatist to date, MICHEL TREMBLAY, whose epoch-
making *Les Belles-soeurs* was staged in that year. The
revolution inspired by Tremblay was first centred on
the choice of language (in his case, the form of Quebec
French known as *joual* – the impoverished, heavily
anglicized dialect of the urban proletariat, hitherto
considered unfit for public use except in burlesque).
Critics, at first too scandalized by that language to
appreciate the splendid originality, poetry and strength
of Tremblay's drama, were, in the main, hostile. But

within a few years the battle had been won in that arena as well, as amply demonstrated by the sudden surge of plays composed in *joual,* many of them less than memorable. By 1970 half of the annual stage productions in Quebec were of indigenous works, a crucial development indeed in the evolution of theatre in the province.

The provocative, adversarial and separatist tone of most of the drama written in the early 1970s – much of it composed and performed by collectivist troupes, many of them anarchistic or Marxist in sympathy – changed perceptibly after 1976, the year when the first *indépendantiste* government came to power in Quebec. Thereafter, mainstream drama and theatre were less narrowly introspective and much more universal in focus, representing a healthy antidote to some of the excesses of the preceding 15 years. The early 1980s brought serious problems, most of them economic in origin. With national and international economic recession, public subsidies declined markedly, even as the number of companies continued to increase and the theatregoing proportion of the population remained static. Quebec boasted some 125 professional and at least 425 amateur companies in 1986, more than the total of the other nine provinces combined. Judicious pruning would be necessary to ensure the viability of those companies which deserved to survive. At the same time, the overall quality of stage and costume design, directing and acting continued to rise impressively, as did the level of dramatic composition. Tremblay continued to write major plays (his *Albertine en cinq temps,* 1984, is considered by many to be his finest play to date), joined now by a dozen dramatists of the first order, most notably Michel-Marc Bouchard, Normand Chaurette, René-Daniel Dubois, ROBERT LEPAGE and Jean-Pierre Ronfard. An imposing generation of female writers, most of them actively feminist in their views, also appeared, led by Marie Laberge, Jovette Marchessault, Elisabeth Bourget and Maryse Pelletier. Many of the latters' plays have been produced by women's troupes such as Montreal's Théâtre Expérimental des Femmes and Quebec City's Commune à Marie. As Quebec enters the new millennium its theatre remains, despite persistent economic problems, varied, vibrant and self-confident.

It was in Acadia (roughly consistent with today's Maritime Provinces and part of the state of Maine) that theatre began in 1606, with the performance of Marc Lescarbot's *Théâtre de Neptune en la Nouvelle-France,* but thereafter it disappeared for some 260 years. Its rebirth in Acadia was timid, mainly confined to the college stage, and this was the venue for nearly all theatrical activity until the 1950s, consisting mainly of historical and patriotic texts performed by amateurs for local audiences. Acadia's first major playwright, and still the dominant literary and dramatic voice for her homeland, was ANTONINE MAILLET. Now internationally known (she received France's prestigious Prix Goncourt in 1979), she sought to exorcise, in works such as the enormously successful one-woman play, *La Sagouine* (1971) and *Evangéline Deusse* (1976), Acadia's troubled, mythological past as crystallized in the great Deportation of 1755. Other Acadian playwrights of importance in the 1980s and 1990s are Laval Goupil, Jules Boudreau, Germaine Comeau and Herménégilde Chiasson, all of them concerned with the recuperation of a lost cultural identity and the affirmation of that identity in a linguistically split and economically troubled present.

In Ontario there are three major francophone cultural centres: the Ottawa–Hull area, where theatre in French began in the 1860s and has since been heightened by the growing prominence of the federal capital in the arts as in other spheres; Sudbury; and Toronto. Sudbury is the home of the major Franco-Ontarian dramatist to date, André Paiement (dead, tragically, by suicide in 1978, at the age of 28), and of a rising star, Jean-Marc Dalpé, whose *Le Chien,* dealing evocatively with the problems of a Franco-Ontarian in an Anglo-Saxon sea, won the Governor-General's Award for Drama in 1989. There are at present some two dozen French-language troupes active in the province, one of the most enduring and most dynamic being Toronto's Théâtre du P'tit Bonheur, recently renamed Le Théâtre Français de Toronto. In Manitoba and the West, French-language theatre has been surprisingly widespread, considering the small and declining proportion of French-speakers there. As elsewhere in French Canada, theatre in Manitoba began in educational institutions, in this case in the 1870s. By the 1920s local amateur groups flourished, most notably the Cercle Molière in Saint-Boniface, established in 1925 and still vigorous today. As in Acadia and Ontario, the principal preoccupation of local dramaturgy has been the plight of embattled francophones, as exemplified in the plays of Roger Auger, Claude Dorge and Rose-Marie Bissonnette.

LEONARD E. DOUCETTE

Archives des lettres canadiennes, vol V: *Le Théâtre canadien-français* (1976)

E. Benson and L. W. Connolly, eds, *The Oxford Companion to Canadian Theatre* (1989)

Dictionnaire des œuvres littéraires du Québec, 6 vols (1978–94)

L. E. Doucette, *Theatre in French Canada: Laying the Foundations, 1606–1867* (1984)

Anton Wagner, ed., *Contemporary Canadian Theatre: New World Visions* (1985)

Jonathan M. Weiss, *French-Canadian Theater* (1986)

Canetti, Elias   *see* AUSTRIA

Cannan [Pullein-Thompson], Dennis   (b. Oxford, 14 May 1919)   Playwright. His witty anti-war comedy, *Captain Carvallo* (1950), was the first of several eloquent and increasingly bitter attacks on contemporary moral pieties. He collaborated on four PETER BROOK productions, including the Vietnam War play *US* (1966) and the almost misanthropic *Les Iks* (1975).
TONY HOWARD

Cantor, Eddie [Isidore Itzkowitz]   (b. New York, 31 Jan. 1892; d. Beverly Hills, Calif., 10 Oct. 1964) Singer and comedian. A small, slim, pop-eyed man who bounced all over the stage as he performed, he began his career as a vaudevillian and singing waiter. His Broadway debut in the ZIEGFELD FOLLIES of 1917 brought him stardom in many other revues, and in *Kid Boots* (1923) and *Whoopee* (1929). Except for a later appearance in *Banjo Eyes* (1941, a musical version of *Three Men on a Horse*), the remainder of his career was in radio and films. Many of his early performances were in the MINSTREL blackface. He co-wrote two memoirs, *My Life is in Your Hands* (1928) and *Take My Life* (1957)   GERALD BORDMAN

Cape Verde *see*   PORTUGUESE-SPEAKING AFRICAN THEATRE

Čapek, Josef   *see* ČAPEK, KAREL

Čapek, Karel   (b. Malé Svatoňovice, Bohemia, 9 Jan. 1890; d. Prague, 25 Dec. 1938)   Playwright and novelist; a leading representative of the literati who supported the democratic and humanitarian ideals of the new state established in 1918. With the exception of his first two lyrical plays – *Lásky hra osudná* (*Love's Fateful Play*, written 1910, with brother Josef [1887–1945]) and *Loupežník* (*The Robber*, 1921) – Čapek concentrates on the profound problems of humankind. Apprehensive about its future, he used utopian allegories and fantasic parables to point to the danger of totalitarianism, the dehumanization of people and the negative consequences of technical development. He was sceptical, however, about changing the existing order. *RUR* (*Rossum's Universal Robots*, 1920) is an imaginative vision of a machine civilization of artificial people-robots, who rise up against their human creators and destroy their world. It brought Čapek world fame and introduced the word 'robot' into English. The satirical

morality play *Ze života hmyzü* (1922; several titles in English, including *The Insect Play*, *The Life of the Insects*, *The World We Live In (The Insect Comedy)*, *From the Life of Insects*, *And So Ad Infinitum*), and *Adam Stvořitel* (*Adam the Creator*, 1927), which demonstrates the futility of attempts to create a new and better world, were written together with his brother Josef, an outstanding painter and man of letters who died in Bergen-Belsen concentration camp in 1945; in 1923 he had written his own play, *Zemé mnoha jmen* (*A Country of Many Names*).

Karel Čapek's plays have attractive and captivating plots which develop original ideas (e.g. *Věc Makropoulos* (*The Macropulos Secret/Affair*, 1922), about human immortality); confrontation of points of view replaces conflict to discover the truth. This relativism is more a dramatic and poetic method than a philosophical concept, and in his last plays his imaginary visions expressed a warning in relation to current events and strove to mobilize people for the defence of freedom and democracy. *Bílá nemoc* (*The White Disease*, 1937, also known as *Power and Glory*) and *Matka* (*The Mother*, 1938) opposed German expansion, fascism and militarism, and were performed throughout the world.
EVA ŠORMOVÁ

Brońuslava R. Bradbrook, *Karel Čapek: In Pursuit of Truth, Tolerance and Trust* (1998).

F. Černý, *Premiéry bratří Čapku* ('First nights of Brother Čapek') (2000)

W. E. Harkins, *Karel Čapek* (1962)

J. Klíma, *Karel Čapek* (1962)

A. Matuška, *Člověk proti skaze* ('Man against destruction') (1963)

capsule criticism American critic ALEXANDER WOOLLCOTT coined the phrase to refer to the concise put-down. Examples are 'I watched this play at a disadvantage. The curtain was up,' which was penned by GEORGE S. KAUFMAN, or WALTER KERR's verdict on *I Am a Camera*, 'Me no Leica.'   CHARLES LONDON

Cardiff   Having superseded Aberystwyth as the capital of Wales as late as 1958, the city has become a European cultural centre, with one of the leading arts centres in the world, CHAPTER; a major concert space, St David's Hall; a multi-purpose two-auditorium theatre, the Sherman; a classic Edwardian theatre, the New; and the imminent erection of an ambitious lyric theatre style multi-space Millennium Centre for the Performing Arts in Cardiff Bay.

Indigenous professional theatre provision arrived in Wales only in the 1960s, and at first Swansea was more of a theatre centre than Cardiff; visiting professional productions came to the capital relatively late. The Crockherbtown Theatre opened in Cardiff 1826, but there was no high-profile touring work until impresario Robert Redford first took over the Theatre Royal and then opened the New Theatre in December 1906 with BEERBOHM TREE as Malvolio in *Twelfth Night*. The programme became more commercial in the 1920s as the New Theatre became a try-out house for potential London productions. In 1928 the Cardiff Empire had Fred and Adele ASTAIRE's *Funny Face* as well as Beecham's National Opera Company. By the mid-1930s the lack of a serious theatre venue in Cardiff had become an issue, and the Playhouse and Prince of Wales both publicly stated the case for subsidized repertory theatre.

The first attempt at creating a Welsh national theatre company was launched at the New Theatre in 1914. Another attempt was made in the 1930s, but both companies suffered from not having their own premises. Another Cardiff-based Welsh national theatre company was formed in the 1960s and found a home at the small 80-seater Casson Theatre, outside the city centre, until it was wound up in 1978.

The Welsh Arts Council initiated a planned provision of professional theatre that included, in Cardiff, the creation in 1973 of the Sherman Theatre (originally as part of the University of Wales) and support for innovative groups like CARDIFF LABORATORY THEATRE and MOVING BEING. The New was bought by the city council in 1969 and became the base for the Welsh National Opera as well as a receiving house for major tours. The Sherman Theatre formed a resident company in 1985, one which took on a distinctive flavour as it acquired a brief to appeal specifically to younger audiences under director Phil Clark.

Today Cardiff has a vibrant theatre culture, thanks to the Chapter Arts Centre's programme of international performers and support for radical Welsh work, and provides a home for many companies and performers. The Welsh College of Music and Drama, with two theatre spaces, has offered professional training since 1952 – ANTHONY HOPKINS and PETER GILL were both students in the early days – and many of the new companies springing up are formed by its graduates.

DAVID ADAMS

Cardiff Laboratory Theatre Founded by English émigrés Richard Gough and Mike Pearson in 1974, Cardiff Lab was one of the most influential companies in the early days of Welsh theatre. Based on JERZY GROTOWSKI's POOR THEATRE and influenced by EUGENIO BARBA's ODIN TEATRET (which toured Wales in 1980) and American experimental companies like the LIVING THEATER, OPEN THEATER and PERFORMANCE GROUP, Cardiff Lab attracted exciting performers to Cardiff and was the breeding ground for BRITH GOF, the MAGDALENA PROJECT, Man Act, Arad Goch and other shorter-lived radical companies.

Based, like most Welsh experimental practice, at CHAPTER ARTS CENTRE, Cardiff Lab enjoyed success abroad, where its style of image-based physical theatre was perhaps more appreciated; it also meant director Richard Gough could organize visits to Britain by the cream of European experimentalists like Odin, Akademia Ruchu, Wroclaw Laboratorium and Piccolo Teatro di Pontedera. This role as impresario continued after Cardiff Lab's demise in 1984 and the subsequent re-invention of itself as the Centre for Performance Research (CPR) with, for a few years, a separate performing arm, The Practice. The CPR maintains a commitment to THIRD THEATRE practices and since 1996 has been based in Aberystwyth, concentrating on producing an impressive journal, *Performance Research*, and organizing major international conferences.

DAVID ADAMS

Caribbean The Caribbean region consists primarily of a chain of islands, 2,000 miles long, that frames the northern and eastern boundaries of the Caribbean Sea. The chain curves from Cuba, the largest and most westerly of the Greater Antilles, down to Trinidad and Tobago, the most southerly of the Lesser Antilles. Culturally, the region also includes the Bahamas and Bermuda to the north of Cuba, and certain coastal countries of Central and South America, in particular Belize, Guyana, French Guiana and Surinam.

These mainland countries are allied with the Caribbean islands through their shared history of colonization. Over the five centuries since Spain first colonized Jamaica and the other islands claimed by the Portugese explorer Christopher Columbus, the various Caribbean territories have changed hands from nation to nation repeatedly, some of them with remarkable frequency, through settlement, conquest, barter or outright purchase. The last major exchange in the region before Britain began to grant independence to its West Indian colonies in the 1960s was in 1917, during the First World War, when the United States of America purchased a cluster of 40 Virgin Islands from Denmark.

One result of this multinational colonial history is that there are four major languages in use in the Caribbean today: English, Spanish, French and Dutch. Patois in various forms is also common in several islands, such as St Lucia, and Papiamento in some Dutch territories. Hindi is still in use, particularly for religious and cultural functions, and, to a lesser extent, some

Chinese is spoken. Throughout the region the European languages have been modified over the centuries by successive superimpositions of one over another, as in Trinidad's English over French over Spanish, for instance. The languages have been further modified by the language patterns, vocabulary and accents of immigrants from other parts of the world, most noticeably Africa. Following the early Caribbean colonists' decimation of the original Amerindian inhabitants, Africa was for some 300 years the source of the region's slave labour, and a majority of the Caribbean population today is black or of mixed race. The second largest ethnic group comprises the descendants of the indentured labourers from India, who were brought to the West Indies after the emancipation of the African slaves in the 1830s.

A prevailing concern of the twentieth-century writers responsible for developing today's body of West Indian literature has been the search to establish a distinctive, acceptably authentic regional voice. This search is most noticeable in the broadness of the range of West Indian theatre. In addition to the conventional drama of social realism and the yard theatre, the range includes popular farce and roots theatre, musical folk theatre, PANTOMIME, COMMUNITY THEATRE, Jamaica's Gun Court theatre, POLITICAL THEATRE, church theatre, children's theatre, storytelling, the STREET THEATRE of CARNIVAL and carnival theatre, calypso theatre, theatre of RITUAL, and the poetic theatre of St Lucia's DEREK WALCOTT. There is also a considerable body of dramatic work written for film, television and radio. Cuba, in particular, has a comparatively vibrant film industry.

In the latter half of the twentieth century progressively more Caribbean theatre companies turned from staging imported scripts to staging, and even at times collectively creating, indigenous works. At the same time, other companies continued the colonial tradition of staging productions of scripts from Europe, and in more recent times ventured into scripts from America, and also from Africa, India, China, South America, the Middle East and other parts of the world. Productions are often staged in makeshift performance spaces, as there are few buildings in the region specifically designed for theatre, the Reichhold Center for the Arts in St Thomas being a notable exception. For a variety of reasons, which include the geographical fragmentation of the Caribbean and the region's cultural history, audiences for imported theatre and for all but the most popular forms of indigenous theatre are small. Performance runs are more often counted in days than in weeks, even when a production is taken on tour of one or more islands. Jamaica is the only English-speaking island able to sustain any commercial theatre. There is comparatively little support for theatre from the private sector, though a few companies help to underwrite the costs of arts festivals, schools' drama festivals, and playwriting competitions. Caribbean governments tend to subsidize amateur folk theatre in preference to more challenging and less popular theatres. Even Carifesta, the sporadically staged Caribbean Festival of Creative Arts, which was originated in 1972 by the government of Guyana as an extraordinary showcase and meeting-ground for the region's leading artists in all disciplines, has over time been reduced by political influence and financial constraints to little more than an unambitious folk festival.

Under these conditions, theatre producers usually struggle to raise essential funds to stage each production. Not surprisingly, most theatre practitioners earn their living in some other profession, with theatre as their second career. Even so, the abundance of talent in the Caribbean quite frequently generates theatre of the highest calibre. And there is today a small but growing body of full-time practitioners, including producers, directors, actors, designers and technicians, most of whom trained overseas in Britain or America. There is also a pioneering School of Drama in Jamaica which, under the direction of playwright Dennis Scott, has conducted important experiments in the creation of West Indian theatre, in particular the theatre of ritual.

The first coherent developments in West Indian theatre took place in the 1930s, in response to the black nationalist movement active throughout the colonies. Over the preceding 200 years, various original dramatic works had been published or performed within the Caribbean, but these were, virtually without exception, derivative of European theatre. Such theatre had been popular in the English-speaking islands since the seventeenth century, when Jamaica boasted one of the first theatres to be built in the region. Theatre companies from England would tour the West Indies on their way to America. Local amateurs would fill in as extras in these professional productions, and would stage their own productions using the latest scripts from London, or favourite classics. Few of the occasional original works set in the West Indies employed any vernacular dialogue, other than as the object of ridicule.

Until emancipation, this conventional European theatre was almost exclusively the province of the colonial masters. The descendants of the former slaves and other immigrants continued to dismiss theatre as an elitist pastime until well into the twentieth century. This widespread lack of appreciation for the potential of theatre for the masses persisted partly because of inadequate schooling. Throughout the islands, it was to take a century or more after emancipation for comprehensive systems of national education to be organized. Until the emergence in the early twentieth century of writers of popular farces, such as Jamaica's Ranny Williams, British Guiana's Sam Chase and Trinidad's Arthur Roberts, and of stand-up comedy teams such as Jamaica's Bim and Bam, and Abe and Cupes, all of whom wrote their own material, the only formally staged theatre to have a wide popular appeal was storytelling. This latter is still popular today, the most widely known exponents being Jamaica's Louise Bennett-Coverly and Trinidad's Paul Keens Douglas. In the late nineteenth century the most popular storytellers were the Jamaican Henry Garland Murray and his sons.

Over the same post-emancipation period, however, a different kind of popular theatre flourished throughout the Caribbean. This alternative form was the folk theatre that had been brought to the region by the immigrants from Africa, India and other countries and which, like the 'nation language' of each island, had gradually adapted to the mélange of West Indian life. Trinidad's newly emancipated slaves had taken the carnival that had been a private diversion of the French Creoles and turned it into a public celebration of freedom infused with echoes of Africa's Egungun masquerades, as well as the BURLESQUES of their former colonial masters. Jamaica had its Jonkunnu and its Pocomania. St Lucia had its flower festivals of Lawoz and Lamagrit. Barbados, British Guiana, Dominica and other territories had their Cropover, Cumfa, Hosay, pappyshows, Phagwa, Ram Leela, Shango. Because they were not then performed on stage in a building, but in the streets and in fields and at hillside shrines and wherever large masses of people might gather together, these folk festivals and rituals were not considered to be theatre, until the twentieth-century playwrights began to draw on the old immigrant traditions as a resource for the creation of a new West Indian theatre. The traditions of the original Amerindian inhabitants of the region have been largely lost as a resource, but several late twentieth-century playwrights, such as Guyana's Michael Gilkes and Trinidad's Raoul Pantin, have explored the Amerindian experience.

Although the Caribbean region is highly fragmented, there are parallel trends in the development of theatre throughout the islands, just as there are parallels in the islands' shared history of colonization, slavery, emancipation, war, emigration, independence and industrialization. Some of these trends are visible even in territories such as the three French overseas departments, Martinique, Guadeloupe and French Guiana, which in 1946 opted not to seek independence, but to remain administratively dependent on the metropole. Only Haiti, with its isolated political history of eighteenth-century revolution and self-rule, dictatorship and extreme poverty, has a theatre that has evolved along rather different lines, resulting in today's powerfully allegorical form in the work of writers such as Franck Etienne. The Haitian experience has, however, like the Amerindian experience, inspired several important works by playwrights around the Caribbean, such as Derek Walcott, Martinique's AIMÉ CÉSAIRE and Trinidad's C. L. R. JAMES.

James was one of the pioneering West Indian playwrights of the 1930s, at the time of the black nationalist movement. Others included British Guiana's NORMAN CAMERON, Jamaica's MARCUS GARVEY, Frank Hill and UNA MARSON, and Trinidad's DeWilton Rogers. The nationalists' principal objective was to gain the region's independence from its various colonial powers. They found that before they could create a sense of national pride that would draw the people of each territory together, they first had to develop a sense of individual self-esteem, particularly among the black peasantry with its legacy of slavery. Literature, the arts and theatre were the tools with which the nationalists planned to educate and inspire the population. Even after independence had been achieved, a number of the region's playwrights continued to write works imbued with messages of community uplift.

Playwrights such as Cameron, Garvey, James and Marson shared the disconcerting experience of discovering, as young black adults sojourning in England, that the 'mother country' exalted by their colonial education was prejudiced against their race. Cameron reacted by writing didactic plays that extolled the lives of African heroes of the past. Garvey wrote epic works about the panoramic struggles of black people generally. James explored the characters of the Haitian revolutionaries, why they succeeded and where they failed. Marson became one of the earliest Caribbean playwrights of social realism. She wrote about ordinary middle-class Caribbean life, and was the first to bring on stage the then socially unacceptable cult of pocomania.

Other playwrights, such as Jamaica's Archie Lindo, and later the poet and novelist Roger Mais, followed the movement to feature West Indian life in their works. Several Caribbean novels, by writers such as Herbert G. De Lisser, were adapted for the stage. Louise Bennett was already gaining wider acceptance for the vernacular through her poems and storytelling. Dominica's Mabel Caudeiron also worked tirelessly to promote folk traditions. But with the outbreak of the

Second World War in 1939, the momentum of the nationalist movement was temporarily slowed. The establishment of new American bases in the region during the latter years of the war, and the resultant influx of American servicemen, left an indelible mark on the life of the islands, still apparent today in West Indian theatre, carnival and calypso.

One West Indian theatre form which first appeared during the war is the Jamaican pantomime. Traditional English Christmas pantomimes, with songs and dances, the principal boy played by an actress, the DAME played by a comedian, and a large animal played by two actors linked together, had been staged in the island on occasion since the previous century. In 1941 Jamaica's LITTLE THEATRE MOVEMENT, inaugurated that same year by Greta Bourke Fowler, staged the first of its annual pantomimes, using a British script that had been adapted to incorporate satirical commentary on local current events. Such satirical commentary became a hallmark of the Jamaican pantomime. Satirical commentary in a musical form of theatre had been earlier established in Trinidad with the initial experiments in calypso theatre, begun in 1933 with *The Divorce Case* by Raymond Quevedo, who performed as calypsonian Attila the Hun. In 1943 the LTM staged the first original Jamaican pantomime, Vera Bell's *Soliday and the Wicked Bird*. In 1949 Louise Bennett and Noel Vaz collaborated on the second original script, and since 1954 a variety of collaborations by leading Jamaican playwrights has produced an original script for each year's pantomime, with few revivals. Fifty years after its inception, the Jamaican pantomime has developed into a West Indian institution that bears little resemblance to its British source. Each production costs 2 million Jamaican dollars to mount, employs some 100 performers, and plays to a total audience of 70,000 over a three-month run.

In the decade immediately after the war, four phenomena affected the development of West Indian theatre. One was the resurgence of the nationalist movement, which influenced the course of several newly founded West Indian theatre companies, and led to the creation of the genre of yard plays. Another was the pan-Caribbean work of ERROL HILL and Noel Vaz, for Jamaica's Extra-Mural Department of what was then the University College of the West Indies (UCWI). A third was the emergence of the Walcott twins in St Lucia's theatre. The fourth was the 1950s exodus of West Indians, playwrights and other artists among them, who emigrated to look for greater career opportunities in England and North America.

In spite of the work of the nationalists and individual artists, during the 1950s much of middle-class West Indian society, and most vocally schoolteachers, continued to resist any attempt to use the vernacular on stage. The script for the first of the yard plays, Douglas Archibald's *Junction Village*, won an award for Trinidad's best play of 1952, yet it was to be another two years before the playwright could persuade a theatre company to risk production of this vernacular comedy. It became the most successful play of its time, and Archibald went on to write another 14, yard plays and others. A West Indian yard play is in essence a naturalistic drama with the single set of a barrack-yard, where several households struggle for their day-to-day existence. The prototypical yard play is *Moon on a Rainbow Shawl* by another Trinidadian, ERROL JOHN. This play, which won Britain's 1957 Observer playwriting competition, continues to be produced around the world, in English and numerous other languages and adaptations. Other popular yard plays, and variations on the yard form, have been written by Barbados's Anthony Hinkson, Grenada's Francis Urias Peters, Guyana's Slade Hopkinson, Jamaica's Samuel Hillary and Barry Reckord, and Trinidad's Errol Hill, Freddie Kissoon and Eric Roach. In 1986 Trinidad's Earl Lovelace staged the adaptation of his novel *The Dragon Can't Dance* in a musical version of the yard form.

While the yard playwrights were developing the earliest regional form of West Indian theatre, Jamaica's Extra-Mural Department of the UCWI was developing the region's theatre from a more technical aspect. As the Department's Drama Officer, despite the total absence of budget, Hill travelled the islands, lecturing, researching, conducting workshops and producing plays. He assisted in the establishment of several community and other theatres. He encouraged the collective creation of West Indian plays. He collected original scripts and raised funds to have the best of them published, so that they could be circulated more widely. Hill also wrote a number of plays, articles and books which illustrate the progress of his thinking on West Indian theatre. He developed a theory of a regional theatre inspired by the national folk festivals, and wrote his musical *Man Better Man* in support of this theory. In 1972 he published his thesis, *Trinidad Carnival, Mandate for a National Theatre*. Hill's thesis won immediate recognition around the Caribbean. Playwrights who have worked in the genre of carnival theatre, in its widest application, include Dominica's Alwin Bully, Jamaica's Samuel Hillary, Sylvia Winter and the all-woman company Sistren, Montserrat's Edgar White, Trinidad's Ronald Amoroso, Felix Cross, Felix Edinborough, Rawle Gibbons, Anthony Hall, Ronald John, Earl Lovelace, Ralph Maraj and MUSTAPHA MATURA, and the Walcott twins.

Derek and Roderick Walcott, who died in 2000, grew up without exposure to formal theatre, but Derek was already the author of several plays when, at the age of 20, he co-founded the St Lucia Arts Guild. Roderick ran the Guild for nearly twenty years, long after Derek had moved to Trinidad and founded what is still the Caribbean's leading theatre company, the TRINIDAD THEATRE WORKSHOP. Both Derek and Roderick are multi-talented in the arts. Both are painters, designers, directors; and both are influential playwrights in the Caribbean, but their writing styles are quite dissimilar. Roderick is best known for his folk musicals such as *The Banjo Man*, and for his popular comedy *The Harrowing of Benjy*. Derek, who gained international recognition when he won the 1992 Nobel Prize for his poetry, wrote his early plays, such as *Henri Christophe*, in blank verse. It was his ambition to create a heroic West Indian theatre that would be unique in its poetic rendering of the vernacular. His *Dream on Monkey Mountain* is generally considered to be his finest achievement in this respect. In later years Derek came to write in a more naturalistic style, as in his popular two-actor play *Pantomime*, but his plays and other scripts, some 40 in number, are never without a heightened sense of language.

Both the Walcotts eventually settled outside the Caribbean, Roderick in Canada, Derek in America, emulating the West Indian emigrants of the 1950s. It was that earlier emigration that was largely responsible for today's flourishing black British theatre. Among the West Indian playwrights who have settled or sojourned in England, and who have developed careers there in stage, film or television, are Barbados's Jimi Rand, Guyana's Michael Abbensetts and Jan Carew, Jamaica's Alfred Fagon, Evan Jones and Barry Reckord, Montserrat's EDGAR WHITE, St Kitts' Caryl Phillips, and Trinidad's Felix Cross, Errol John, Mustapha Matura and Samuel Selvon. The pioneering work of these immigrant writers, and of other theatre practitioners, helped to open up opportunities for British productions of the work of other West Indian playwrights, such as Derek Walcott, Earl Lovelace and Jamaica's TREVOR D. RHONE.

Trevor Rhone co-founded Jamaica's Barn Theatre in 1965, in the garage of a private home. He has become one of the Caribbean's most successful writers, whose plays are repeatedly performed around the region to record runs. His comedies are written with a rare depth of character and insight into human frailty, and his most popular include exposés of the tourism industry (*Smile Orange*), the education system (*School's Out*), racism (*Old Story Time*) and male chauvinism (*Two Can Play*). Rhone's work is rooted in Jamaica, but his themes are for the most part universal, and he has proved that it is possible to write in a Caribbean vernacular which is true to the ear and at the same time readily comprehensible outside the region.

In addition to Rhone and those playwrights already cited above, many others contributed over the last decades of the twentieth century to the continuing development of different forms of West Indian theatre, the most influential including Antigua's Dorbrene O'Marde, the Bahamas' Winston Saunders, Barbados's Glenville Lovell, the Caymans' Frank McField, Dominica's Daniel Caudiron, Grenada's Wilfred Redhead, Guyana's Francis Quamina Farrier, Frank Pilgrim and Sheik Sadeek, Jamaica's Ginger Knight, Easton Lee and Louis Marriot, Montserrat's David Edgecombe, St Lucia's Stanley French and Kendel Hippolyte, Tobago's Bernadette Allum, Trinidad's Dwight Arthur, LENNOX BROWN, Zeno Constance, Neville Labastide, Ian MacDonald, Ralph Maraj, Victor Questel, Lennox Raphael and Efebo Wilkinson, and the Virgin Islands' Rudolph Wallace. Perhaps largely for cultural reasons, the region has produced comparatively few women playwrights, and those mainly in Jamaica, such as Enid Chevannes, Pat Cumper, Barbara Gloudon, Carmen Tipling, Cicely Waite-Smith, Jeanne Wilson and Sylvia Winter. Others include Antigua's Tulip Fleming, Guyana's Paloma Mohamed, Trinidad's Valerie Belgrave, Sonya Moze, Seeta Persad and Eintou Springer. Most of these playwrights are unknown outside the Caribbean. However, even those, such as Rhone, who enjoy international productions, for the most part find that, to be seen at their most effective, their plays require a genuine West Indian cast. The West Indian style of acting has an uncommon robustness and vigour. It is a style that, at its least skilled, can result in stereotyped performances, particularly in the more popular theatre forms. At its best, whatever the form and whatever the language, West Indian theatre is exuberant, intense, provocative and exceptionally powerful.

JUDY S. J. STONE

Martin Banham, Errol Hill and George Woodyard, *The Cambridge Guide to African and Caribbean Theatre* (1994)
Ken Crosbie, *Theatre in the Caribbean* (1984)
Errol Hill, *The Trinidad Carnival, Mandate for a National Theatre* (1972)
Kole Omotoso, *The Theatrical into Theatre: A Study of the Drama and Theatre of the English-Speaking Caribbean* (1982)
Judy Stone, *Studies in West Indian Literature: Theatre* (1994)

Cariou, Len (b. Winnipeg, Canada, 30 Sept. 1939) Actor and director. He appeared in numerous productions at Stratford, Ontario, between 1961 and 1965, and went on to perform a string of classical roles for TYRONE GUTHRIE's theatre in Minneapolis (including Lear), the GOODMAN MEMORIAL THEATER, Chicago (including Othello) and the AMERICAN SHAKESPEARE FESTIVAL (including parts in *Much Ado About Nothing* and *Three Sisters*). He made his name on Broadway in the musical comedy *Applause* (1970), following this with *A Little Night Music* (1973; film version 1977) and his most acclaimed role, as the demon barber *Sweeney Todd* (1979), for which he won a Tony award. Despite numerous roles on television and in the cinema, he continued to return to the stage in productions such as *Touch of the Poet* (1992) and *Papa: The Legendary Lives of Ernest Hemingway* (1994). He has also directed several plays, including *Death of a Salesman* (1984).

HELEN RAPPAPORT

Carnegie Mellon   *see* DRAMA SCHOOLS

carnival   Popular street festival. The pre-eminent carnivals that developed and became established in the latter twentieth century are Caribbean-derived. The carnivals of Trinidad and Tobago and other Caribbean islands have generated similar large-scale festivals wherever in North America and the British Isles cities received significant Caribbean immigration since the Second World War. These contemporary 'Caribbean' carnivals share a common heritage with those of South America, most notably of Brazil. The significant common element in their histories lies specifically in the collision of the cultures of Catholic European colonizers and of enslaved West Africans. Not only do the art forms of Caribbean carnival derive from the festival performance traditions of both, but much of carnival's nature, both as popular celebration and as resistance art, derives from the historic situation of colonization and slavery and the social and political relations inherent in it.

From its earliest incarnations carnival has challenged order and authority. The pagan revels of pre-Christian Europe, that celebrated rites of fertility and spring, gave licence to feasting and temporary disorder, from which society could regenerate. The Catholic Church absorbed pagan spring revels into its pre-Lenten festival, now widely known as 'Mardi Gras'. The term 'carnival' is generally agreed to derive from Latin *carnem levare*, 'to put away flesh'. Throughout medieval and Renaissance Europe, the days preceding Ash Wednesday, on which, in the Catholic calendar, the Lenten fast begins, were given over to masking, street performance and feasting. For the duration of carnival, traditional boundaries of class and gender were transgressed and the order of everyday life was reversed. Such publicly enjoyed freedom and licence among working

people was frequently seen as threatening by those in authority, and by the early 1600s laws controlling street celebration among ordinary people were so rigorously and oppressively enforced that carnival died out in all but a few places. Popular masking traditions survived in a few rural communities in Europe, while among the upper classes, as in France, the tradition flourished in masquerade balls.

It is with the elite masquerade balls of the French that the story of carnival in Trinidad takes shape. In 1783 the Spanish, who then ruled Trinidad, invited Catholic allies to take up offers of land to accelerate development of sugar and cocoa production. The French who responded to the Spanish Cedula of Population brought to Trinidad their Mardi Gras tradition of elaborate masked balls. Subsequently the British, who seized Trinidad in 1797, introduced to the island Christmas activities of carol singing and mumming. In 1834, when freed Africans took to the streets to celebrate emancipation from slavery, Caribbean carnival was born. From this freedom celebration, initially enacted in August and subsequently moved to coincide with Mardi Gras, today's carnivals in Britain and North America still take inspiration.

Despite, and indeed in reaction to, the colonizers' repeated attempts to control and limit carnival, with bans in the nineteenth century on the wearing of MASKS, the carrying of burning torches and the playing of skin drum, and with strict licensing of calypso lyrics in the Depression years of the 1930s, carnival has grown into a world-class festival of complexity and magnificence, rooted in African, European, Indian and Amerindian cultures and manifesting a remarkable range of art forms. It is one of the performance wonders of the world.

In the 1940s and 1950s Britain invited immigration from the Caribbean to help in postwar redevelopment. In London, many of the Trinidadian arrivants settled in Notting Hill. The carnival dances organized by Trinidadian writer and activist Claudia Jones in 1958 and 1959 mark carnival's beginnings in Britain. Notting Hill Carnival took shape on the streets in 1965 in a community event organized by Rhaune Laslett, a London-born woman of Amerindian and Russian parentage. Trinidadian Russell Henderson and his steel band took to the road that year with other residents, initiating a street festival that has taken place on the last weekend of August ever since. Then as now, it was characterized by the cultural diversity of its arts and the rich racial mix of its participants. Similar developments took place wherever Trinidadians and other West Indians settled, in New York and Toronto as well as in cities across Britain, while the older carnivals, similarly derived from the meeting of West African and European Catholic cultures, continued, and continue, to be celebrated, in Rio and Salvador, in the coastal regions of Colombia and Venezuela, in Haiti and Cuba, Martinique, St Lucia and Trinidad, together with parallel festivals such as Crop-over in Barbados and Jonkonnu in Jamaica. Today, London's Notting Hill Carnival provides the largest and most spectacular street performance in Europe.

Caribbean carnival is TOTAL THEATRE. Its holistic form integrates dance, music, commentary and visual arts. Distinctions between performer and audience dissolve: in carnival everyone is participant. The venue is the street, the players are the people. All regular traffic ceases. The air fills with the aromas of roti, peas and rice and spicy corn fritters, and vibrates with the newest Caribbean, Latin, African and urban sounds. Traditional to carnival are steel band and calypso. In Trinidad the calypsonian has been at the heart of carnival, calling attention to topical issues, commenting on social behaviour, informing and entertaining, invariably witty and provocative, while the fluid, syncopated rhythm and melodic qualities of calypso compel the body to dance. In Britain every popular music form is present in carnival, and music trucks and 'walls' of static sound systems vie to meet every taste from rap to jungle, reggae and hip-hop to salsa and township jive. Carnival bands of 2,000 and more mas players, in Trinidad, or 50 to 500 at Notting Hill, are costumed to different themes each year. The *Port of Spain Gazette* of 14 February 1834 reported on a group of freed Africans coming on to the streets costumed in accurate imitation of the British artillery. Such targeted mimicry, particularly by one race or class of another, has always been at the heart of carnival and is evident in Notting Hill today. Pride themes explore African history, Indian legend, black inventors and heroes; fantasy themes turn mas players into a dazzling shoal of fish or a rainbow. To 'play mas' you join a band whose costume designs you like or to whom you have a special loyalty, paying for your costume to be prepared for you. In Britain, mas players often help to make the costumes, as was once regularly the case in Trinidad.

For the two days of carnival, ingeniously and often elaborately costumed characters 'chip' and 'wine' through streets packed with revellers. Floats play little part in this festival. Here 50 'fancy sailors' with ship head-dresses and classy braid and buttons on their sailor whites are followed by a shimmering band of butterflies, with wide gauzy yellow wings edged in glittering sequins, faces painted black and gold. Right behind comes a traditional ol' mas band, led by a cross-dressed Dame Lorraine, with outrageous bust and buttocks.

Competition has always been present in carnival in one way or another. In nineteenth-century Trinidad, stickfighters provided tests of skill and spectacular entertainment in street or yard; such traditional characters as PIERROT or Midnight Robber were characterized by their extravagant speeches and their competitions in verbal dexterity. Today, in Trinidad and in Britain, annual competitions are hotly contested to find the Calypso Monarch, the leading steel band, the finest, wittiest or most ingeniously costumed King or Queen. To 'play mas' is to step out of yourself and become other than you usually are: the counter clerk becomes king or queen; the bank manager dances anonymously on the street, stripped naked and daubed in clay; a child doubles her height as a stilted Jumbie; a man cross-dresses as a whoring Jamette or importuning Baby Doll. To play Devil is to explore your own darker self. Cross-dressing gives space to play. Such reversals allow briefly for release from all that constrains in ordinary life. It is both exploration and celebration of self. The use of the street is a statement of presence. Much of carnival performance is resistance art. Music, costuming and themes of bands, the very claiming of space, make statements about black identity and presence. Carnival is a way of saying 'I am here'. In the 1980s London carnival met with the kind of establishment antagonism, in the form of police action, that Trinidad carnival experienced in the 1880s. Authority fears the free and frank affirmation of self by ordinary people, and the use of the street as stage.

Carnival is universal and specific, sacred and profane. It is of the moment, ephemeral. When carnival is over it is forgotten – until next time. RUTH TOMPSETT

Abner Cohen, *Masquerade Politics* (1993)

John Cowley, *Carnival Canboulay and Calypso: Traditions in the Making* (1996)

Errol Hill, *The Trinidad Carnival: A Mandate for a National Theatre* (1972)

Earl Lovelace, *The Dragon Can't Dance* (1979)

John W. Nunley and Judith Bettelheim, *Caribbean Festival Arts* (1988)

Kwesi Owusu and Jacob Ross, *Behind the Masquerade: The Story of Notting Hill Carnival* (1988)

Milla C. Riggio (guest ed.), 'Trinidad and Tobago Carnival', *The Drama Review*, special issue, vol. 2, no. 3 (Fall 1998)

Elizabeth Saft, (ed.), *Insight Guide: Trinidad and Tobago* (1998)

Carnovsky, Morris (b. St Louis, Mo., 5 Sept. 1897; d. Easton, Conn., 1 Sept. 1992) Actor, director and teacher. Carnovsky acted at the THEATER GUILD (1924–30) and was a member of the GROUP THEATER where he gave one of his most memorable performances as the grandfather in CLIFFORD ODETS' *Awake and Sing* (1935). From 1940 to 1950 he worked with the Actors' Laboratory Theater as both director and actor. After refusing to name names to the House Un-American Activities Committee, he was barred from Hollywood and subsequently performed predominantly in Shakespearean drama, in roles such as Claudius, Lear and, pre-eminently, Shylock, with the AMERICAN SHAKESPEARE FESTIVAL in Stratford, Connecticut and the NEW YORK SHAKESPEARE FESTIVAL. Carnovsky developed an approach to acting that utilizes the emotional 'reality' of the METHOD to work with elevated texts. His autobiography, *The Actor's Eye*, appeared in 1984. ANNE FLETCHER

Carr, Marina (b. Dublin, 17 Nov. 1964) Playwright. Came to prominence with the National Theatre Society's production of *Ullaloo*, a comedy of Beckettian resonances (1991). Since then the Society has presented *The Mai* (Peacock, Dublin, 1995, national tour, and ROYAL COURT, London) and *Portia Coughlan* (Peacock and Royal Court, 1996); these two plays have also been produced in the United States and several European countries. In 2000 DRUID presented *Rafferty's Hill*. Her work is characterized by the expression, in richly scabrous language, of unhappy personal relationships in a comparatively wealthy new society only one generation removed from peasant culture. CHRISTOPHER FITZ-SIMON

Carroll, Paul Vincent (b. Dundalk, Co. Louth, 10 July 1900; d. Bromley, Kent, 20 Oct. 1968) Playwright and co-founder of Glasgow CITIZENS' THEATRE. His plays divide roughly into two genres: sympathetically critical comedies of Irish life, and especially of narrow religiosity (e.g. *Shadow and Substance*, Dublin, 1934; New York, 1939; *The White Steed*, New York, 1939) and realistic dramas set in Glasgow (e.g. *Green Cars Go East*, Glasgow, 1940; *The Strings, My Lord, Are False*, Dublin and New York, 1942). CHRISTOPHER FITZ-SIMON

Paul A. Doyle, *Paul Vincent Carroll* (1971)

Carte, Richard D'Oyly (b. London, 3 May 1844; d. London, 3 April 1901) Theatre manager, chiefly remembered for his close artistic and business involvement with GILBERT and SULLIVAN. He was an innovative manager (the first to initiate a regular system of licensing amateur productions; the leader of the fight to secure copyright protection for British plays in the United States; and the organizer of world-wide tours). He left a rich inheritance, which was ably managed by his heirs: first his widow, who had been his secretary

(Helen Lenoir [Black], d. 5 May 1913), then his son Rupert (b. 3 Nov. 1876, d. 12 Sept. 1948) and lastly his grand-daughter Bridget (b. 25 March 1908, created a dame 1975, d. 2 May 1985). Copyright in the SAVOY Operas expired in 1961 and the D'Oyly Carte Opera Company ran into difficulties but it continued to function, largely financed by Dame Bridget's bequest which stemmed from her shareholding in the multi-million-pound Savoy Hotel group. IAN BEVAN

Cartel An informal alliance formed in 1927 between four eminent French theatre directors, GASTON BATY (1885–1952) of the Chimère and Théâtre de Montparnasse, CHARLES DULLIN (1885–1949) of the Théâtre de l'Atelier, LOUIS JOUVET (1887–1951) of the Athénée and Comédie des Champs-Elysées and GEORGES PITOEFF (1885–1939) with his actress wife Ludmilla. It aimed to promote high standards of acting and production of foreign and contemporary French plays by such writers as PIRANDELLO, GIRAUDOUX and especially CHEKHOV. All four directors owed a great deal to JACQUES COPEAU (1879–1949), and although the cartel ended with the Second World War its influence continued in the work of the postwar CENTRES DRAMATIQUES. TERRY HODGSON

F. Anders, *Jacques Copeau et le Cartel des quatre* (1959)
Donald Roy, *Copeau and the Cartel des Quatre* (1993)

Carter, Huntly (b. 1861/2; d. London, 29 March 1942) Writer and lecturer. His prominence is largely confined to the period immediately after the First World War, when he travelled widely. Through his books he attempted to bring the 'new movements' in European theatre into the British theatre, and these books constitute a valuable eye-witness account of this theatre at work. As a major contributor to the arts pages of the *Sunday Worker*, from its inception in 1925, Carter laid the basis for the theory and aesthetics of the Workers Theatre Movement, which came into being in 1926. He was an important progenitor of POLITICAL THEATRE and working-class aesthetics in Britain. His books include *The Theatre of Max Reinhardt* (1914), *The New Spirit in the European Theatre* (1925) and *The New Spirit in the Russian Theatre* (1929). CLIVE BARKER

Carter, Mrs Leslie [Caroline Louise Dudley] (b. Lexington, Ky., 10 June 1862; d. Santa Monica, Calif., 13 Nov. 1937) Actress. She entered the profession in 1890 on the heels of a messy divorce case; DAVID BELASCO shrewdly realized that her notoriety could be a crowd puller and gave her roles in lurid MELO-DRAMAS. Their first big success was *The Heart of Maryland* (1895), which Belasco wrote as a vehicle for Carter and which toured for three seasons, followed by *Zaza* (1899); both productions were also seen in

London. The series continued with *Du Barry* (1901, in a part she reprised in the silent film version in 1915) and one of her best roles, *Adrea* (1905). Leaving Belasco's management in 1906 on her remarriage, she toured widely for her own and other touring companies, appearing to considerable acclaim in SOMERSET MAUGHAM's *The Circle* (1921). She retired from the New York stage after a production of *She Stoops to Conquer* in 1928, but continued touring on the West Coast into her seventies. Hollywood made a biopic of her life in 1940. HELEN RAPPAPORT

Cartwright, Jim (b. Farnsworth, Lancs, 27 June 1958) Playwright. Came to prominence in a rugged PROMENADE production at the ROYAL COURT's Theatre Upstairs of his first play, *Road* (1986), a humorous, compassionate, picaresque look at the inhabitants of a run-down street in his home county which came to stand as an emblematic comment on the Thatcherite era. *Bed* (1989), a surreal trip through the memories of seven old people in the same bed, *The Rise and Fall of Little Voice* (1992, later filmed), a more conventional, sequential story of a young woman with a private gift for singing like female superstars, and *Hard Fruit* (2000), which explores male sexuality, confirm both his strong sense of the theatrical and the demotic and his loose sense of form and narrative.
COLIN CHAMBERS

Casarès [Quiroga], Maria (b. Coruña, Spain, 21 Nov. 1922) Actress, who first appeared in a Paris production of SYNGE's *Deirdre of the Sorrows* (1943). Her enigmatic, almost haughty charm earned her leading roles in the existentialist works of CAMUS and SARTRE. In 1952 she joined the COMÉDIE-FRANÇAISE, then the THÉÂTRE NATIONAL POPULAIRE, and in the 1960s the Théâtre de France under BARRAULT. One of the greatest French actresses of the twentieth century, her successes in contemporary works were matched by memorable performances in classical roles such as Lady Macbeth, Margaret of Anjou and Racine's Phèdre.
ADRIANA HUNTER

Casona, Alejandro [pseud. of Alejandro Rodriguez Alvarez] (b. Besullo, Asturias, Spain, 23 March 1903; d. Madrid, 17 Sept. 1965) Theatre director and playwright. The greater part of his work was written in exile. His plays explore the relations between the real and the imaginative, drawing largely on the hauntingly lyrical traditions of Asturian folklore. His major works includes *Prohibido suicidarse en primavera* ('Suicide prohibited in spring', 1937) and *La dama del alba* ('Lady of the dawn', 1944). MARIA DELGADO

Harold Kay Moon, *Alejandro Casona* (1985)

Cassidy, Claudia (b. Shawneetown, Ill., 1905; d. Chicago, 21 July 1996) Drama critic. She held Chicago's theatre community to the highest standards for 40 years, and though she incurred a reputation for brutality, she insisted that her opinions were based on a desire to encourage the best. The most powerful critic in the Midwest, she was also a tireless advocate for the arts, helping to build the Chicago Lyric Opera and aiding the Chicago Symphony Orchestra. She published *Europe: On the Aisle* in 1954, chronicling her yearly trips abroad to take in European arts. After her formal retirement, she continued to exert an influence through her weekly radio commentary (1968–83).
DAVID A. WILLIAMS

Casson, Lewis [Thomas] (b. Birkenhead, Ches., 26 Oct. 1875; d. London, 16 May 1969) Actor and director. A Fabian socialist, Casson joined ANNIE HORNIMAN's company in 1908, inaugurating his lifelong association with SYBIL THORNDIKE, whom he married. He worked with POEL, GRANVILLE BARKER and SHAW, and played Troilus under Charles Fry in the first recorded modern performance of the play 'as written' (1907). During a distinguished career lasting more than 60 years, he was remembered for his pioneering directorial work with actors like GIELGUD and OLIVIER and with classical texts, as well as for his wide range of acting. Casson worked for many years at the OLD VIC, and frequently toured London productions in the regions. He was a founder organizer of British Equity (*see* UNIONS), and during the Second World War worked in close conjunction with the COUNCIL FOR THE ENCOURAGEMENT OF MUSIC AND THE ARTS, directing and playing in *Macbeth* on a tour of South Wales mining villages. He was knighted in 1945. MAGGIE GALE

John Casson, *Lewis and Sybil* (1962)
D. Devlin, *A Speaking Part: Lewis Casson in the Theatre of his Time* (1982)

CAST Pioneering British POLITICAL THEATRE group; the acronym stands for Cartoon Archetypical Slogan Theatre. It was set up by Roland and Claire Muldoon in 1965 while at UNITY THEATRE, from which they were later expelled, to produce socialist cartoon AGITPROP comedies they styled 'agitpop' for new, working-class audiences. Their furious, hilarious style, the seedbed of NEW VARIETY, was seen in shows like *John D. Muggins is Dead* (1966), *Harold Muggins is a Martyr* (1968) and *Confessions of a Socialist* (1978). DAN REBELLATO
See also HACKNEY EMPIRE.

Cathy Itzin, *Stages in the Revolution* (1980)
B. Kershaw, *The Politics of Performance* (1992)

casting In the twentieth century, the act of matching a role to a performer, as well as organizing the necessary AUDITION, became a specialism, no longer simply the gift of the theatre owner or leader of the troupe. The popular myth of the casting-couch tyrant who makes and breaks careers is not an unknown figure in the theatre, but is more a creature of Hollywood. Theatrical casting agents or casting directors – overwhelmingly women – emerged in order to meet a need; as theatre diversified, so the need grew. Major American regional theatres employ casting specialists, sometimes hiring them for part of their time, sometimes putting them on the staff. Depending on location and requirement, however, theatres might use New York-based agents. In Britain, a producing management such as H. M. TENNENT, the dominant force in the West End after the Second World War, running a commercial as well as a not-for-profit company, employed a casting director, as did the ENGLISH STAGE COMPANY at the ROYAL COURT. Changes in theatrical style, the increase in new plays and the expansion of the acting profession in London and the regions required this service, a trend consolidated by the establishment of the ROYAL SHAKESPEARE COMPANY and the NATIONAL THEATRE, which needed actors who could play a variety of different characters in both contemporary and classical plays throughout a season. Unlike in America, the British casting director might negotiate the actor's salary and would certainly be working within a budget.
CHARLES LONDON

· The casting director's view ·

It is the talent of the actors and their personas that make a play work. These are the elements that make each production a unique experience for the participants and the public. It is for this reason that 'type-casting', a term considered derogatory now, is exactly what casting is about.

The casting director is the pale, harassed creature who by day sits hunched up over the telephone and by nights turns up at various theatres around the country or at a venue in town. S/he is a fork with three prongs – firstly as someone who translates the concept of the director into living actors; secondly as the person who finds a relationship with the actor in order to prepare him or her to meet and read for the director; and finally as the commercial negotiator and holder of the purse. The budget is usually given and the company has to be found who will suit the needs of the play and conform to the demands of the budget. One expensive actor can throw the financial balance of a cast and put in jeopardy the overall success of a company.

Casting is about taste, and the developing of a language to describe that taste. It is subject to fashion, attraction and whim, and it is always serious. It involves the understanding of the director's sensibilities and those of the actor and an assessment of a play often before the play has spoken.

The accolades for the success of an actor's performance go elsewhere, the penalty for his/her failure sits right on the casting director's lap. The most successful casting director is invisible. **GILLIAN DIAMOND**

---

celebratory theatre A form of festive and popular theatrical entertainment which may celebrate and dramatize some important event or events. It may combine elements of PAGEANT, TABLEAU, SON ET LUMIÈRE, the CIRCUS and the tattoo. It may also include song, music, dance, MIME, acrobatics and ritual. There is an emphasis on spectacular and ceremonial presentation. A notable example was the celebration of the French Revolution in LE THEATRE DU SOLIEL'S 1789, created by ARIANE MNOUCHKINE in 1970. PETER BROOK has been a pioneer of celebratory theatre in Britain and abroad. CLIVE BARKER
See also CARNIVAL.

CEMA *see* COUNCIL FOR THE ENCOURAGEMENT OF MUSIC AND THE ARTS

censorship Political, religious and moral censorship is as old as theatre and operates in a variety of ways, from overt suppression by the state to self-censorship by producers, managers and artists themselves. In Britain, modern censorship dates back to 1737 when the then Prime Minister, Sir Robert Walpole, goaded beyond endurance by caricatures of himself in the plays of Henry Fielding, introduced legislation empowering the LORD CHAMBERLAIN to close down theatres and imprison actors as 'rogues and vagabonds' for uttering any unlicensed speech or gesture. A new Theatres Act was passed in 1843 to consolidate the Lord Chancellor's powers. Repressive licensing was in some measure responsible for the sterility of British drama at the beginning of the twentieth century. IBSEN's plays were prohibited and many serious writers eschewed the drama. Those few who persisted suffered intolerable restrictions. SHAW's *Mrs Warren's Profession* was banned from 1894 to 1925, as were a number of other ventures into social realism by him and GRANVILLE BARKER. Not even GILBERT and SULLIVAN were sacred: in 1907 licences for all performances of *The Mikado* were withdrawn for one year to avoid offence to a visiting Japanese prince. In 1909, in response to complaints from Shaw, Granville Barker, BARRIE, GALSWORTHY, Gilbert and other literary figures, a Joint Parliamentary Committee was set up to investigate censorship. Reform was strongly opposed by theatre managements, who cared less for the future of drama than for their own immunity from prosecution afforded by the Lord Chamberlain's LICENCE. The committee laid down guidelines for stage censorship which persisted until the 1968 Theatres Act. Plays were to be licensed unless reasonably held to be indecent; to contain offensive personalities; to represent on the stage in an invidious manner a living person or a person recently dead; to do violence to the sentiment of religious reverence; to be calculated to conduce to crime or vice; to be calculated to impair relations with a foreign power; or to be calculated to cause a breach of the peace. The Lord Chamberlain operated a broad definition of 'indecency', and excised all vernacular references to intercourse, genitalia, birth control and venereal disease. In 1930 he settled rules for stage dress (or undress): actresses in movement must not wear less than briefs and an opaque controlling brassiere; actresses may pose completely nude provided the pose is motionless and expressionless, or is artistic and something rather more than a mere display of nakedness. The lighting must be subdued. For many years the Lord Chamberlain maintained an absolute ban on all references to homosexuality; casualties of this stricture included LILLIAN HELLMAN's *The Children's Hour*, SARTRE's *Vicious Circle*, ARTHUR MILLER's *A View from the Bridge* and ROBERT ANDERSON's *Tea and Sympathy*. In 1946, and again in 1951, he secretly consulted 'a wide circle of persons prominent in clerical, legal, scholastic, ethical, governmental, judicial and artistic circles' on the merits of lifting the prohibition, but they decided it should stay. In 1958 he indicated that serious plays on homosexual themes would at last be considered for licensing, but only if homosexual characters were essential to the plot, and the play was not written to propagandize for changes in the law. 'Embraces or practical demonstrations of love between homosexuals will not be allowed.' Notwithstanding this cautious advance, he refused to license JOHN OSBORNE's *A Patriot for Me*, which won the 1965 Evening Standard Drama

Award when presented as a CLUB performance at the ROYAL COURT. The following year he ordered the deletion of e. e. cummings' poem 'I Sing of Olaf' from a presentation by the ROYAL SHAKESPEARE COMPANY, although it had been broadcast on radio and television without complaint. The offending lines were published in permanent form in the theatre programme. Irreverent references to fascist dictators were suppressed throughout the 1930s and plays sympathetic to communism were banned. This obsessive deference to heads of state extended in the 1960s to satires on the Kennedy family, and to aspersions on long-deceased relatives of royalty – in 1960 SADLER'S WELLS Opera were forced to rewrite the libretto of EDWARD GERMAN's *Merrie England* to remove scenes where Elizabeth I conspired to poison a rival. The Lord Chamberlain refused permission for the RSC to perform ROLF HOCHHUTH's *The Representative* (attacking the Pope's complicity in the Holocaust) unless a Vatican apologia was printed in the programme, and declined to license HEINAR KIPPHARDT's *The Trial of J. Robert Oppenheimer*, a documentary critique of McCarthyism. Commercial managements accepted political discipline without demur, but state-subsidized companies had no profits at stake, and the RSC launched an all-out attack as part of a wider campaign against the Lord Chamberlain after he had objected to *US* on the grounds that it was 'beastly, anti-American, and left-wing'. Political censorship was tolerable only so long as unlicensed plays and satires could be performed at theatre CLUBS to AVANT-GARDE audiences. This device was exposed in 1951, when the left-wing amateur UNITY THEATRE was prosecuted in connection with an unlicensed presentation of a satirical revue, and it was declared unlawful in 1966, when the Royal Court was convicted of an offence under the 1843 Act for a club performance of EDWARD BOND's *Saved*. It followed from this decision that no word could be uttered on any stage without the Lord Chamberlain's prior approval, and even ad-libbing by an actor who had forgotten his lines was technically an offence.

In 1966 the Joint Committee on Theatre Censorship commenced its deliberations. Dramatists, state-supported theatre companies and drama critics overwhelmingly demanded abolition of the Lord Chamberlain's powers, but West End theatre managers lobbied to retain their 'father confessor' who dispensed the indulgence of 'total security in relation to substantial investments'. Lord Cobbold, the incumbent Lord Chamberlain, was content to be divested of the censor's mantle because his position as senior courtier to the Queen had associated the monarch too closely with criticism of his decisions. But he argued that *some-*

body had to protect the royal family, heads of foreign states, and the sensitivities of theatregoing families. The Joint Committee rejected his paternalism, and was satisfied that pre-censorship provided a service neither to playgoers nor to dramatic art. Its report recommended repeal of the 1843 Act, and new legislation subjecting the theatre to control by the law of obscenity. Legislation should, however, echo the Race Relations and Public Order Acts by prohibiting any performance designed to stir up racial hatred or calculated to provoke breaches of the peace. The Joint Committee's recommendations were embodied, almost without exception, in the 1968 Theatres Act. Decisions on the interpretation of the Obscene Publications Act applied thereafter with equal force to stage plays, so that no play contravenes the law unless, 'taken as a whole', it would tend to deprave and corrupt a significant proportion of its audience. Obscenity is defined by reference to the circumstances of the staging and to its impact upon an audience more readily ascertainable than the readership for books on general sale. A more stringent test would apply to West End theatres, trading for tourists and coach parties, than to FRINGE theatres or clubs with self-selecting patronage. A 'public good' defence admits expert evidence to justify stage performances which are 'in the interests of drama, opera, ballet or any other art, or of literature or learning'. The 'merit' to which experts must testify attaches not to the play itself, but to 'the giving of the performance in question', so that pedestrian writing may be redeemed by the excellence of acting, direction or choreography. Experts who have not witnessed the performance may none the less testify to its dramatic, literary or educative value by reference to the script, which 'shall be admissible as evidence of what was performed and of the manner in which the performance ... was given'. The penalty provided by the Act is a maximum of three years' imprisonment and/or an unlimited fine. The only prosecution brought since the Act came into force in 1970 related to a 'live sex show' masquerading as a stage play. The organizers were sentenced to 15 months' imprisonment.

The Theatres Act makes no reference to the liability of dramatists, who are consequently liable only if their script incites blatant obscenity, or if they assist in some other way to mount a performance calculated to deprave or corrupt.

In 1981 a private prosecution was brought against Michael Bogdanov, a NATIONAL THEATRE director, charging that he had procured an act of gross indecency between two actors on the stage of the Olivier Theatre as part of a scene in the play *The Romans in Britain* by HOWARD BRENTON, contrary to section 13 of the Sexual Offences Act 1956. This was a bold attempt to side-step provisions of the Theatres Act which require the Attorney-General's consent to any prosecution of a stage play (to prevent frivolous actions), and to avoid the defences which would otherwise be available under that legislation, notably the strict test of obscenity and the public good defence. The prosecution, in the event, collapsed in mid-trial for technical reasons (a not uncommon risk in private prosecutions). It did, however, occasion some concern in theatrical circles. The Theatres Act does not protect persons connected with a play from prosecution for actual criminal offences, simply because they happen to be committed on stage. What it is intended to protect them against is subjection to any form of legal censorship other than is provided for by the Theatres Act itself.

After the collapse of the *Romans in Britain* trial, there were no further prosecutions of plays. The Royal Court Theatre occasionally took legal advice about obscene language and simulated sexuality, and director Bill Alexander challenged the sedition laws with a play at the BIRMINGHAM REPERTORY THEATRE calling for the overthrow of the monarchy, but (probably to the company's disappointment) the authorities took no action. The INSTITUTE OF CONTEMPORARY ARTS held shows that were visited occasionally by the police after stirs by tabloid newspapers, but failed to provoke legal action. The ICA did stop one American performance artist from showing his audience with (his own) HIV-infected blood, but this was because of health regulations rather than the obscenity law. By the turn into the twenty-first century that law had become a dead letter as far as the theatre was concerned – a result that can be attributed variously to the liberality of the 1968 Act, the common sense of prosecuting authorities, or the innate caution and conservatism of British dramatists and theatre managements. GEOFFREY ROBERTSON

Europe, America and elsewhere

In other European countries, censorship was more brutal and openly political, except for France, which ended pre-production censorship in 1905; western and central Europe up until 1945 was dominated by oppressive regimes and then fascism, which banned the entire works of individual artists as well as using theatre for propaganda purposes. In the SOVIET UNION, the picture was much the same after an initial release of tremendous theatrical energy, with artists suffering the ultimate in censorship, murder by the state. Cultural orthodoxy imposed by a centralized censor strangled the drama of the countries that came under Soviet domination but gave rise to a vigorous though personally dangerous theatre of dissent. When Soviet rule was ended a new economic censorship of capitalist anarchy filled the vacuum while official state censorship was relaxed or abolished.

In the United States, free speech is guaranteed by the constitution. There is no national censorship or legislation dealing explicitly with drama. Each state has its own local laws and moral code, so commercial instinct usually operates as the effective censor. The police are always on hand, however, if public decency is thought to be outraged. They frequently raided BURLESQUE shows because of the stripteases, and they arrested actors in New York in a 1905 production of *Mrs Warren's Profession* and MAE WEST in 1924 when she appeared on stage as a prostitute. ALTERNATIVE THEATRE groups such as the LIVING THEATER also met trouble with the police and the authorities, especially when STREET THEATRE became highly political in the Vietnam era. Withdrawal of FUNDING or denial of work is another form of censorship practised in the United States (and in Britain), most notoriously during the McCarthyite period when the livelihoods of playwrights, actors and others were affected by 'blacklisting' or smear tactics. Political attacks in the late 1980s and 1990s on the NATIONAL ENDOWMENT FOR THE ARTS represented another aspect of this kind of oppressive crusading.

Censorship in other parts of the world also follows the vagaries of the various political systems and their relationship to particular religions. Solidarity in the face of extreme forms of such censorship has been rife in the theatre, notably against WOLE SOYINKA's imprisonment and exile, apartheid in South Africa and the devastation of the former Yugoslavia.

CHARLES LONDON

Anthony Aldgate, *Censorship and the Permissive Society: British Cinema and Theatre 1955–1965* (1995)

Nicholas de Jongh, *Politics, Prudery and Perversions: The Censoring of the English Stage, 1901–1968* (2000)

Richard Findlater, *Banned* (1968)

John Johnston, *The Lord Chamberlain's Blue Pencil* (1990)

Alan Travis, *Bound and Gagged—A Secret History of Censorship in Britain* (2000)

Centaur Theater Montreal's leading English-language theatre, founded in 1969, with MAURICE POD-BREY as artistic director. In 1974 the company bought a building in Old Montreal and converted it to two theatres – Centaur 1 and Centaur 2 – seating 255 and 440 respectively. The Centaur company presents seven plays between October and June each year, drawn mainly from the contemporary international' repertoire, with special emphasis on the plays of ATHOL

FUGARD. Podbrey has also promoted the work of such Canadian playwrights as DAVID FENNARIO, Rod Langley, Rick Salutin and MICHEL TREMBLAY (in translation).

EUGENE BENSON

Central African Republic *see* FRENCH AFRICAN THEATRES

Central America *see* MEXICO AND CENTRAL AMERICA

Central School of Speech and Drama *see* DRAMA SCHOOLS

central staging *see* THEATRE IN THE ROUND

Centre for Performance Research *see* CARDIFF LABORATORY THEATRE

Centre 42 *see* ALLIO, RENE; COMMUNITY THEATRE; ROUND HOUSE; WESKER, ARNOLD

Centrepoint Theatre New Zealand's smallest regional professional theatre, in Palmerston North, was opened in 1974. It has survived despite losing its government funding for a period. Since 1986 under director Alison Quigan it has provided a programme to suit a mixed community that is both a farming service centre and a university city. Although it presents contemporary plays from overseas, its most popular productions have been New Zealand plays, e.g. Greg McGee's *Foreskin's Lament*, ROGER HALL's *The Share Club Footrot Flats*, and comedies written by Alison Quigan and Ross Gumbley, the theatre's associate director.

GILLIAN GREER & LAURIE ATKINSON

centres dramatiques Theatres throughout France that receive state and municipal funding so that the regions need not rely on touring companies bringing hits from Paris. The decentralization idea was encouraged by GÉMIER, COPEAU and DULLIN; it was not taken up until 1946 when the first five theatres were built. The centres and their resident repertory theatre companies number more than 20; they present a diverse repertoire of plays, ranging from the classics to contemporary works. The most famous centre is the THÉÂTRE NATIONAL POPULAIRE. ADRIANA HUNTER

Césaire, Aimé (b. Martinique, 26 June 1913) Playwright, poet and revolutionary. The leading creative writer, intellectual and politician of the French-speaking Caribbean, he shares with a similar figure in Senegal, Léopold Senghor, the status of being the leader of the *négritude* movement. Césaire's three original plays all in different ways condemn colonialism and racial prejudice against blacks, as does his adaptation of *The Tempest* (*Une tempête*, 1969) with a white 'colonial' Prospero, mulatto Ariel and black Caliban. Césaire's first work for the theatre, *Et les Chiens se taisaient* ('And the dogs keep their silence', 1956), a dramatization of a long incantatory poem, contains surrealistic imagery reminiscent of his famous *Cahier d'un retour au pays natal* (*Return to My Native Land*). A far more genuinely dramatic work is *La Tragédie du Roi Christophe* (*The Tragedy of King Christopher*, 1964), which explores the traumas that beset the independent black state of Haiti (ex-Saint Domingue) at the beginning of the nineteenth century. In *Une Saison au Congo* (*A Season in the Congo*, 1965), the hero is Patrice Lumumba, who had not long been murdered as a result of the disastrous Congo–Katanga conflict, cynically exploited by Belgian and other international mining interests and one of the first major setbacks to the anti-colonial movement of the early 1960s. Césaire's eldest daughter Ina (b. 1942) became a playwright and his niece Michèle (b. 1951) a writer and director.   TED FREEMAN

Chad   *see* FRENCH AFRICAN THEATRE

Chagall, Marc   *see* DESIGN

Chaikin, Joseph   (b. Brooklyn, New York, 16 Sept. 1935)   Actor, director and teacher. Chaikin joined the experimental LIVING THEATER in 1959, taking over several leading roles and joining the group's influential 1961–2 European tour. He started a workshop within the group to develop a more concrete experimental technique. After the group was forced into exile in 1963, Chaikin expanded his non-naturalistic workshop into a group which named itself the OPEN THEATER. Until its dissolution in 1974, it became one of the preeminent collaborative ENSEMBLES of its era, with such productions as *Viet Rock* (1965), *America Hurrah!* (1966), *The Serpent* (1968), *Terminal* (1969) and *The Mutation Show* (1971). Since 1974 Chaikin has continued to work as a director and actor; even though felled by a stroke in 1984, he persevered and used the experience in plays such as *The War in Heaven* (1985), co-authored with SAM SHEPARD. He wrote *The Presence of an Actor* in 1972 and, with Shepard, published an account of their collaboration, *Letters and Texts 1972–84* (1989).   GERALD RABKIN

Eileen Blumenthal, *Joseph Chaikin* (1984)
Robert Pasolli, *A Book on the Open Theater* (1970)
Arthur Sainer, *The Radical Theatre Notebook* (1975)

Chambers, Jane   *see* LESBIAN THEATRE

Champion, Gower   (b. Geneva, Ill., 22 June 1920; d. New York, 25 Aug. 1980)   Dancer, actor, choreographer and director. While still in his teens, Champion began his career as a nightclub dancer. He also appeared in a few Broadway shows before creating dances for *Small Wonder* (1948). His choreographic wit, style and sense of period charm were then displayed in the REVUE *Lend an Ear* (1948), and in the following, which he also directed: *Bye Bye Birdie* (1960), *Carnival* (1961), *Hello, Dolly!* (1964), *I Do! I Do!* (1966), *The Happy Time* (1973), *Sugar* (1972), a 1973 revival of *Irene*, and *42nd Street* (1980), which opened just as he died.   GERALD BORDMAN

Champion, Harry   (b. Shoreditch, London, 1866; d. London, 14 Jan. 1942)   MUSIC HALL and VARIETY artist. Only 15 when he made his debut on the London halls as Will Conray, a blackface singer of 'coon songs', he soon changed his name and persona for that of the 'Quick-fire Comedian', which brought him immediate popularity and was to sustain the remainder of his long career. Its essential ingredients were simple but inimitable: Cockney patter and songs delivered with gusto and at a breathless pace. These included such ethnic gems as 'Any Old Iron', 'I'm 'Enery the Eighth, I Am', 'Boiled Beef and Carrots' and others about working-class culinary delicacies.   DONALD ROY

Channing, Carol [Elaine]   (b. Seattle, 31 Jan. 1921)   Actress and singer. Following her Broadway debut in the chorus of *No for an Answer* (1941) she appeared in nightclubs and became a star through the revue *Lend an Ear* (1948) and the comedy *Gentlemen Prefer Blondes* (1949) in which she played the gold-digging Lorelei Lee and introduced, among other songs, 'Diamonds Are a Girl's Best Friend'. She took over the lead in the musical comedy *Wonderful Town* (1954), was the eponymous heroine of *The Vamp* (1955) and appeared in a revue, *Show Girl* (1961), which was tailored to her talents, before creating the role for which she will be remembered: the meddling matchmaker Dolly Levi in the popular musical *Hello, Dolly!* (1964). A new version of *Gentlemen Prefer Blondes* called *Lorelei* (1974) lasted only a short time, but Channing returned in style for an anniversary tour of *Hello, Dolly!* in 1994. A comedienne with a large vocal range and a warm, outsized stage personality, who could be coy as well as brazen, she was awarded a Tony in 1995 for lifetime achievement.   CHARLES LONDON

Channing, Stockard [Susan Williams Antonio Stockard]   (b. Seattle, 13 Feb. 1944)   Actress. She worked in experimental theatre in Boston and OFF-BROADWAY, making her debut in 1969. She first appeared on Broadway in 1971 in JOHN GUARE's musical adaptation of *Two Gentlemen of Verona*. Moving to California in the mid-1970s, she appeared in *Vanities* (1976), *Absurd Person Singular* (1977) and *As You Like It* (1979), as well as in numerous television shows and films. Her wit and comic flair finally received recognition when she won a Tony award in PETER NICHOLS' *A Day in the Death of Joe Egg* (1985), a part she had first toured with in New England in 1981–2. Notable performance followed in ALAN AYCKBOURN's *Woman in Mind* (1988) and in two plays by JOHN GUARE, *The House of Blue Leaves* (1986) and *Six Degrees of Separation* (1990) – a part she reprised in London and in a film (1993). She has also appeared in *Four Baboons Adoring the Sun* (1992) and *Hapgood* (1994).

HELEN RAPPAPORT

Chaplin, Charlie *see* ACTING (AN ACTOR REFLECTS); CINEMA

Chapman, John *see* COONEY, RAY; RIX, BRIAN; WHITEHALL FARCE

Chappell, William [Evelyn] (b. Wolverhampton, 27 Sept. 1907; d. Hastings, E. Sussex, 1 Jan. 1994) Actor, designer, dancer, choreographer and director. Chappell always showed a precocious and bewildering ability to express himself at a high level in all his chosen activities throughout a long career. He danced in the 1920s for RAMBERT with Ashton and HELPMANN, and began appearing and designing at SADLER'S WELLS in 1934. Elegant and well read, he was involved in many successes in revue, musicals, ballet, straight plays and opera. He assisted WELLES as director on *Moby Dick* (1955) and choreographed the film *Moulin Rouge* (1953) for John Huston. CLIVE BARKER

See also CHOREOGRAPHY; DANCE.

Chapter Arts Centre One of the major arts centres (with Glasgow's Tramway and London's ICA) in the UK, both as a base for a wide range of performers and artists and as a venue for radical non-mainstream cultural events. Without Chapter, CARDIFF would not be an important player on the international stage and WALES would probably have no experimental theatre.

Chapter, converted in 1971 from an old school in the Canton neighbourhood, was the base for pioneering Welsh companies like CARDIFF LABORATORY THEATRE, PAUPERS CARNIVAL and MOVING BEING. Many of the dominant names in Welsh theatre have been associated with Chapter: Caricature Puppet Theatre, BRITH GOF, Man Act, the MAGDALENA PROJECT, Fiction Factory (formerly Y Cwmni), Earthfall, Alma, ELAN, Made in Wales, Wales Independent Dance, are or have been based there. Chapter has commissioned groups like PIP SIMMONS, IOU, Lumiere & Son, THE PEOPLE SHOW and Music Theatre Wales and playwrights like Alan Osborne, as well as bringing over to the UK for the first

time the WOOSTER GROUP (in 1986) and hosting the 30 village performers of the Naya Theatre of India. Previous directors Mik Flood (1971–81) and Neil Wallace (1983–7) subsequently ran the ICA and the Tramway respectively; theatre programmer Janek Alexander, for 20 years responsible for both encouraging Welsh experimental drama and importing small-scale work from around the world, became centre director in 1995, after which Gordana Vnuk, Croatian director of Zagreb's Eurokaz Festival, took over the theatre direction. In her first year she staged a Japanese season, Body Radicals (including Ron Athey and Annie Sprinkle), a Wales Without Borders festival and a pan-European Iconoclastic Theatre season. Ms Vnuk left in 1999, during implementation of the Arts Council of Wales's controversial new drama strategy.

DAVID ADAMS

See also BODY ART; EXPERIMENTAL THEATRE; PERFORMANCE ART.

Charabanc Theatre Company *see* BELFAST

Charley, Dele (b. Freetown, Sierra Leone, 27 March 1948; d. Freetown, 8 May 1998) Playwright and director. Co-founder of the Tabule Theatre, he was an advocate of and worked in Krio, the language of the Creole people of Freetown, rather than in English or an indigenous Sierra Leonian language. His plays include *The Blood of a Stranger*, *Petikot Kohna* and *Fatmata*. KOLE OMOTOSO

Charlot, André (b. Paris, 26 July 1882; d. Hollywood, 21 May 1956) Theatre manager and producer. After running theatres and music halls, including the FOLIES-BERGÈRE, he became the joint manager of London's Alhambra (1912) where he produced successful REVUES (e.g. *Kill That Fly*, 1912; *5064 Gerrard*, 1915). His *Charlot's Revue* (1924, 1925) brought stardom to such artists as JACK BUCHANAN, GERTRUDE LAWRENCE, JESSIE MATTHEWS and BEATRICE LILLIE in both England and America. He moved to California in the 1930s to work in the movies. REXTON S. BUNNETT

Charlottetown Festival Founded in 1965, the festival has always emphasized MUSICAL THEATRE, which is staged in a 1,108-seat theatre in Charlottetown, Prince Edward Island, Canada. The musicals are often adaptations of Canadian novels or stories; they offer accessible theatre directed to the family and summer tourists, and usually feature lavish sets and dance routines. Central to the repertoire is the musical *Anne of Green Gables*, based on the novel by L. M. Montgomery. In the 1980s the Festival turned to Broadway-type musicals such as *Swing*, a 1985 salute to the big-band era, and the 1987 *Are You Lonesome Tonight?*, a musical biography of Elvis Presley. The musicals *Johnny Belinda* (1997) and *Emily* (1999) provided financial stability following a period in the early 1990s when the Festival's future seemed threatened by falling box-office returns. Artistic directors include Mavor Moore (1965–7), Alan Lund, one of Canada's finest choreographers (1968–86), Walter Learning (1987–91) and Jacques Lemay (1991–7). EUGENE BENSON

Chayefsky, [Sidney] Paddy (b. New York, 29 Jan. 1923; d. New York, 1 Aug. 1981) Playwright. After making a name for himself with realistic television dramas in the early 1950s (e.g. *The Mother*, 1954) and the Oscar-winning film *Marty* (1955), which began as a television drama, he wrote three interesting dramas for Broadway. *Middle of the Night* (1956), a study of an ageing manufacturer, was followed by the more metaphysical *The Tenth Man* (1959), recounting a synagogue's attempt to exorcise a girl's demons, and the biblical *Gideon* (1961). When two later plays failed – even though the latter, *The Latent Heterosexual* (1968), was produced also in Britain – he began to concentrate on screenplays. His tally of three Oscars for best screenplay (*Marty*; *The Hospital*, 1971; *Network*, 1976) has yet to be surpassed. GERALD BORDMAN

J. Chem, *Paddy Chayefsky* (1976)
S. Considine, *Mad as Hell: The Life and Work of Paddy Chayefsky* (1994)

Cheek by Jowl British small-scale touring theatre group. They were formed by director Declan Donnellan (b. Michael Declan Martin Donnellan, Manchester, 4 Aug. 1953) and designer Nick Ormerod in 1981, concentrating on developing ensemble and physical performance skills, through mainly classical revivals, both well known (e.g. *Othello*, 1982) and lesser known (e.g. Sophocles' *Philoctetes*, 1988). With productions like *Vanity Fair* (1983), *Twelfth Night* (1986), *Macbeth* (1987) and *As You Like It* (1992), their colourful, imaginatively theatrical work brought them world acclaim. Donnellan and Ormerod have also worked for the NATIONAL THEATRE (e.g. Lope de Vega's *Fuente Ovejuna*, 1989, TONY KUSHNER's *Angels in America*, 1992, and *Sweeney Todd*, 1988), the Maly Theatre, St Petersburg (*The Winter's Tale*, 1999), and on the musical *Martin Guerre* (1996). The company took a sabbatical in 1998.
DAN REBELLATO

Simon Reade, *Cheek by Jowl: 10 Years of Celebration* (1991)

Cheeseman, Peter (b. Portsmouth, 27 Jan. 1932) Director. Influential founder director with STEPHEN JOSEPH of the VICTORIA THEATRE, Stoke-on-Trent (1962), he was committed to THEATRE IN THE ROUND

and to COMMUNITY drama in industrial north Staffordshire. Cheeseman adapted local fiction (especially Arnold Bennett) and encouraged new Stoke writers, directing 17 plays by PETER TERSON between 1965 and 1976. A long series of collectively created local documentaries explored historical subjects, including the English Civil War and the impact of the railways. *Fight for Shelton Bar* (1974) publicized the successful campaign to save a local steelworks. It included songs, reconstructions of key meetings, and nightly updates from labour leaders in the audience. TONY HOWARD
See also COLLECTIVE; DOCUMENTARY.

Chekhov, Anton [Pavlovich] (b. Taganrog, Russia, 17 Jan. 1860; d. Badenweiler, Germany, 2 July 1904) Playwright and short story writer. He is regarded by Russian theatre historians, practitioners and the theatregoing public as the greatest Russian dramatist since Ostrovsky. His plays have been performed in Russia throughout the years of upheaval from 1887 on, although less frequently after the Revolution and during the Stalin years. In the English-speaking theatre Chekhov is the most frequently performed foreign dramatist: since the first British production (*The Seagull*, Glasgow Repertory Theatre, 1908) and the first American productions (Civic Repertory Theater, New York, 1926–33), the plays have become a 'classical' challenge for directors and actors alike.

Chekhov's contemporary Russia provides the material and the setting for both his stories and plays, and the backcloth is accelerated economic change. Money, or the lack of it, is a constant leitmotif and source of conflict and frustration among the characters inhabiting or visiting the decaying country estates of the increasingly impoverished landed gentry (*The Seagull*, 1896; *Uncle Vanya*, 1898; *The Cherry Orchard*, 1904), while in *Three Sisters* (1901) the house inhabited by the Prozorovs is sub-let and then mortgaged. Ecology, industrialization, and the simultaneous need for and the cost of change are explored in *Uncle Vanya* and *The Cherry Orchard*, while in all of the plays the nature of Russian provincialism (the actual distance from Moscow of the small provincial town setting of *Three Sisters*, for example) is organic to both structure and setting. The Act 2 country setting of *The Cherry Orchard* captures the sense of historical change and movement with its combination of tombstones, neglected shrine, telegraph poles and distant outline of a big town.

Chekhov's short stories and the production of some of his one-act farce–vaudevilles (such as *The Bear* and *The Proposal*, 1888–9) were greeted with popular acclaim, but the first productions of his first full-length plays – the untitled work usually known as *Platonov*

(1878), *Ivanov* (1887), *The Wood Demon* (1889) and the original production of *The Seagull* – all proved disastrous failures which demonstrated the shortcomings of contemporary theatre practice and the innovatory nature of Chekhov's dramatic work. The critical tide turned in Chekhov's favour only when *The Seagull* opened at the MOSCOW ART THEATRE in STANISLAVSKY's production. It was only three years later that Chekhov finally saw this production (when he was well enough to travel from the Crimea), and conflicts between Chekhov and Stanislavsky, which were to become legendary, began to emerge and deepen. The disagreements ranged over casting and the interpretation of individual characters, over Stanislavsky's insistence on detailed naturalism (as in his excessive use of sound effects) and his view of the plays as tragedies. As Chekhov wrote after the first production of *Three Sisters*, 'You tell me that people cry at my plays . . . It is Stanislavsky who made my characters into cry-babies. All I wanted was to say honestly to people: "Have a look at yourself and see how bad and dreary your lives are!"'

Chekhov's own view of his method and intention as a writer closely parallels his professional training and practice as a doctor: 'First of all, I'd get my patients into a laughing mood, and only then would I begin to treat them.' The objectivity of the scientist is no more absent from his 'amateur dabbling', as Chekhov called his writing, than it was from his professional work as a doctor among the urban poor in Moscow, and the rural poor in the countryside: a sense of proportion, treatment for the curable, and the rejection of the explicitly moral and didactic.

Mainstream Russian realism may have taken the form of satire, parody or the grotesque, but never before had irony and understatement been used as Chekhov used them in both his short stories and the plays, and this allows for the detached, the subtle and the implicit. As Chekhov wrote in 1892: 'The more objective you are, the greater the impression you will make.' In many of his letters Chekhov makes it clear that irony does not imply indifference, and that what is needed is the combination of objectivity and yet commitment and compassion in the depiction of what he called 'the sad-comicality of everyday life'. This phrase sums up not only the subject matter of the plays, but also the dramatic method in which one is juxtaposed with the other to avoid sentiment, provoke thought and ensure an objective understanding from the spectator. Chekhov's philosophical and political awareness of the coexistence of the 'tragic and the ridiculous' in life made him reject the existing classifications of drama and create a new form which cuts across their artificial barriers.

His plays defy any neat critical labels. The settings and action are apparently mundane, and because of this emphasis on everyday life, on the avoidance of the explicitly dramatic and melodramatic and of the conventionally theatrical climax (which prefigures much twentieth-century modern drama), he has been called a 'naturalist'. But Chekhov's work goes further than the naturalist's acceptance and depiction of that which *is*, and suggests life as it should be. This suggestiveness is rarely overt and is closely related to Chekhov's use of symbols (the most obvious being the seagull, the storm in *Uncle Vanya*, the illusion of Moscow in *Three Sisters*, or the cherry orchard as 'all of Russia'). This has resulted in Chekhov being labelled a SYMBOLIST. Yet, like SHAW, he uses elements of nineteenth-century popular theatre, and makes something quite new out of the conventions and stock situations: melodrama exposes the melodramatic in character and situation; farce deflates yet heightens the tragic; vaudeville tricks reveal unhappiness (Charlotte Ivanovna in *The Cherry Orchard*); love triangles provide much of both the comedy and the unhappiness in *The Seagull*, and the conventional pistol shot ends both *Ivanov* and *The Seagull*.

Both contemporaries and subsequent critics and directors (particularly Western) have confused Chekhov's poor physical health with his mental rigour, viewing him as 'soulful' rather than humorous, and as somehow living separately from the harsh conditions of his contemporary Russia. The different facets of his life have been compartmentalized, but as the grandson of a former serf, as a struggling medical student writing short stories for comic newspapers to make a living, as a theatregoer in Taganrog and Moscow, and as a practising doctor, Chekhov's life and work reflect the very engagement with contemporary reality which so many of the characters of his plays are unable to face. In 1890 Chekhov made the gruelling journey across Russia to the prison island of Sakhalin, and subsequently published a book which resulted in some crucial reforms of the Penal Code; in 1892 he bought an estate in the country, and involved himself directly in medical, educational and charitable work; and from 1897 onwards he followed his conscience when it was unfashionable and risky, first by his public support of the French writer ZOLA in the Dreyfus Affair against a wave of anti-semitism, and then when he resigned in protest in 1902 from the Academy of Sciences when GORKY was refused membership at the Tsar's insistence.

Chekhov's implicit and understated style was also a result of tsarist CENSORSHIP, which prompted his description of 'writing with a bone stuck in the throat'. There was censorship by the church too. The one-act play *On the High Road* (1885) was banned and neither published nor performed in Chekhov's lifetime, and extensive rewrites were required for the full-length plays, particularly *Uncle Vanya* and *The Cherry Orchard*.

After Chekhov's death, it seemed as though political and cultural change would date his plays. Stanislavsky's style and emphasis on human impotence was out of step with the direct poster-art culture of the Bolsheviks. The new attitude to Chekhov's plays, illustrated by MAYAKOVSKY in the Prologue to his play *Mystery Bouffe* (1921), was more of a reaction to Stanislavsky than to the work itself: in 1921 VAKHTANGOV mounted a production of *The Wedding* (1889) in the highly stylized, anti-naturalistic form of 'fantastic realism'; in 1935 MEYERHOLD staged *33 Swoons* (*The Bear*, *The Proposal* and *The Anniversary*, 1891) in a deliberately non-naturalistic style; and in 1944–5 TAIROV staged a symbolist *Seagull*. For the most part, however, under Stalin it was the Stanislavsky model which held sway, and it was only after 1956 and the relative 'thaw' in Soviet culture that directors such as TOVSTONOGOV and EFREMOV, working within the Stanislavsky tradition, found ways of bringing the theories up to date, retaining the positive elements and discarding aspects which retarded new staging methods. Other directors and designers – Knebel, LYUBIMOV, EFROS and Lider, for example – combined the best of the Russian theatrical tradition, added their own originality and took the production of Chekhov's plays in new and exciting directions.

Stanislavsky's emphasis on character exploration, on detailed naturalism, and on a dominant sadness, coincided with the mood of dejection and disillusionment which characterized western Europen and America between the two world wars. It was assumed that the voices or forces of change are potential agents of destruction, and that the other characters are charming and blameless victims of tragic circumstances beyond their control. This attitude was reinforced by the translation (largely by Constance Garnett) in those years of Chekhov's short stories, of Dostoevsky and Gogol, in which English views of the 'Slav soul', of the 'typically Russian' and 'Russian philosophizing' seemed to be confirmed by, and were overlaid on, Chekhov's dramatic characters. The interpretation was on tragic character to the virtual exclusion of social comedy.

America continued to be influenced by its introduction to Chekhov when the Moscow Art Theatre toured Stanislavsky's productions in 1923–4 – productions which the Soviet theatrical AVANT-GARDE already found old-fashioned. The first American attempts, directed by EVA LE GALLIENNE, were poor imitations with mediocre acting and a slow pace, but perhaps the main

barrier between Chekhov and an American audience has been the evolution of the METHOD school of acting, inaccurately based on Stanislavsky's teachings though extending to areas and extremes which he never envisaged.

From the original Stanislavsky productions by the Moscow Art Theatre, the Russian and Soviet emphasis has been on ensemble playing, and later productions have combined this with an emphasis on the ideas, issues and conflicts raised by the plays. In western Europe and America, however, the emphasis has been primarily on individual characters and on the star system, ensuring good box office returns.

The differences between Russian- and English-language productions are also to be found in the assumptions behind the interpretation of the ideas. Chekhov is neither a revolutionary nor a reactionary, but he is certainly not apolitical in his treatment and depiction of his contemporary Russia. British productions until the 1970s tended to assume that Chekhov was essentially reactionary – 'the voice of twilight Russia', the 'poet and apologist of ineffectualness' – and that his plays deal with the tragedy of dispossession. The dominant tone and mood in the Western theatre have been those of pessimistic tragedy. Soviet Russian productions, on the other hand, have been equally political in stressing the positive and optimistic values. Issues and debates about the nature and cost of change, about the control individuals have in shaping their own destiny, or about human ability to face reality, have all been emphasized, and the plays are generally seen as optimistic.

British Chekhov for many years assumed both tragedy and naturalism, and, in a 'naturalization' process, developed an alien, nostalgic approach. Perhaps the most 'culpable' of directors was the émigré THEODORE KOMISSARZHEVSKY, whose famous productions in London between 1925 and 1936 harnessed the talents of JOHN GIELGUD, CHARLES LAUGHTON, PEGGY ASHCROFT and EDITH EVANS, and yet sentimentalized and romanticized the plays on the grounds that 'the English public always demand a love interest'. The most alive productions have been those in which the plays were 'naturalized' into an American context: *Platonov* in 1940 became *Fireworks on the James* (Princetown Playhouse), and *The Cherry Orchard* was transferred to a Southern plantation setting in *The Wisteria Tree* (1950, Martin Beck Theater).

It was only from the 1970s, in productions by ANTHONY PAGE, JONATHAN MILLER, LINDSAY ANDERSON, MIKE ALFREDS, PETER GILL and RICHARD EYRE, that British readings of Chekhov began to break free of the patrician straitjacket and treat the plays as acute social comedies in which the ridiculous and the unhappy exist side by side. This move towards a greater realization of Chekhov's intentions coincided with the use of new versions or adaptations, often by playwrights already established in their own right, such as CHRISTOPHER HAMPTON, PAM GEMS, TREVOR GRIFFITHS or MICHAEL FRAYN. The plays were also given different settings, from Ireland to the Caribbean, to clarify the class context, while the movement away from naturalism crystallized in PETER BROOK's production of *The Cherry Orchard* (1981), staged on a carpet with a few cushions, making it a timeless play about life and death and transition and change.

New versions of Chekhov's works have come from the cinema. He is one of the few writers of his period to have work filmed as early as 1911. Between 1964 and 1966 there were major Russian, American, Hungarian and British films of *The Seagull, Uncle Vanya* and *Three Sisters*. In 1990 Trevor Griffiths developed a virtually new play, *Piano*, from the film script of Mikita Mikhalkov's brilliant 1976 *Unfinished Piece for Mechanical Piano*, based on Chekhov's unfinished and untitled play, usually entitled *Platonov*. In 1994 Louis Malle filmed *Vanya on 42nd Street* from ANDRÉ GREGORY's stage production of *Uncle Vanya*, with a screenplay by DAVID MAMET, blending rehearsal, debate and the script of the play into a seamless whole. In 1996 ANTHONY HOPKINS also used *Uncle Vanya*, setting the play in Wales, under the title *August*.   VERA GOTTLIEB

David Allen, *Performing Chekhov* (1999)

Jean-Pierre Barricelli, ed., *Chekhov's Great Plays: A Critical Anthology* (1981)

Walter H. Bruford, *Chekhov and his Russia: A Sociological Study* (1948, repr. 1971)

Toby W. Clyman, ed., *A Chekhov Companion* (1985)

Victor Emeljanov, ed., *Chekhov: The Critical Heritage* (1981)

Vera Gottlieb and P. Allain, eds and trans, *The Cambridge Companion to Chekhov* (2000)

Ronald Hingley, *A New Life of Anton Chekhov* (1976)

David Magarshack, *Chekhov: A Life* (repr. 1970)

Patrick Miles, ed., *Chekhov on the British Stage* (1993)

Laurence Senelick, *The Chekhov Theatre: A Century of the Plays in Performance* (1997)

· Performing Chekhov ·

Chekhov is a playwright for actors of all ages. Young actors, starting out as Irina in *Three Sisters* or Konstantin in *The Seagull*, can look forward to ageing through these plays until they end up as Anfisa and Sorin. Chekhov wrote no conventionally leading roles; and so, the very best of actors line up to join the team. Self-effacement, however, is inappropriate. Each character is self-absorbed, convinced that he/she is the centre of the action.

The mature plays inhabit pre-revolutionary Russia: time and places are precise. The text contains all the specifics of the characters' origins and of their current life. The actors need invent nothing extra but be wrapped up in that passionate temperament, where tears overlap laughter. For non-Russians, the all-revealing text is obscured in translation: speakable it may be, but how reliably does it reflect the original idiosyncrasies?

Naturalism abounds but is fused with other styles. Some characters soliloquize their thoughts out loud, even speaking directly to the audience (e.g. Andrei in Act IV of *Three Sisters*). Chekhov's actors need to accomplish the vaudeville silhouette of farce and yet be light comedians, flirting with darker tragedy. The atmosphere of season, of climate, and of offstage events and sounds provides symbolic settings, just as potent as realistic scenery. The poetry of *The Cherry Orchard*'s distant 'twang' defies analysis.

In the great quartet – the plays mentioned above and *Uncle Vanya* – there is so much to achieve that any unifying style would be distorting. Spontaneity is of the essence. The audience, not the actors, are the interpreters. They must be left to respond as fully as they are able; to measure their own lives against the challenge of Chekhov's humanity.

IAN MCKELLEN

Chekhov, Michael [Mikhail Aleksandrovich] (b. St Petersburg, Russia, 29 Aug. 1891; d. Beverly Hills, Calif., 30 Sept. 1955) Actor, director and teacher. Nephew of playwright ANTON CHEKHOV, he joined the MOSCOW ART THEATRE (MAT) in 1912. Under his mentor VAKHTANGOV, Chekhov's acting style evolved away from STANISLAVSKY's psychological realism towards an intuitive approach based in mysticism. His 1924 Hamlet was characterized by a gloomy spirituality. To avoid arrest following open dissent at the MAT, he emigrated to England in 1927; he acted under MAX REINHARDT in Vienna (1928–30) and directed the HABIMAH in Berlin in 1930. He moved to the United States, where he acted in films and founded the Chekhov

Theater Studio (1936–42). His books include *The Path of the Actor* (1928), *To the Actor: On the Technique of Acting* (1953) and *To the Director and Playwright* (1963). The Michael Chekhov Studio was established in New York in 1980 to continue his teaching and an alternative school, the Michael Chekhov Study Center, was founded in Los Angeles. FELICIA HARDISON LONDRÉ

L. Black, *Mikhail Chekhov as Actor, Director and Teacher* (1987)

Chelsea Theater Center   One of the leading OFF-OFF-BROADWAY companies, set up in 1965 under the direction of Robert Kalfin and for the next 25 years was to stage American productions of some of the most important new foreign plays, by writers like GENET, HANDKE and BOND. The company began its operation in Chelsea, Manhattan, and after moving to the BROOKLYN ACADEMY OF MUSIC in 1968 staged productions in both Brooklyn and Manhattan for several years. One of its more notable commercial successes was HAL PRINCE's 1973 chamber production of BERNSTEIN's *Candide*, which later transferred to Broadway.
HELEN RAPPAPORT

Chéreau, Patrice   (b. Lézigné, France, 2 Nov. 1944) Theatre and film director. He joined PLANCHON in 1970 as co-director of the new Villeurbanne THEATRE NATIONAL POPULAIRE, where he first collaborated with the designer RICHARD PEDUZZI. His best-known production of this period was *La Dispute*, a little-known one-act play by Marivaux which he approached as if it had been by de Sade. He also directed operas, and his *Ring* cycle at BAYREUTH in 1976 (conducted by Boulez and designed by Peduzzi), which recast the Norse legends in images of the industrial revolution, brought him international recognition. In 1982 he moved to Paris, taking over direction of the newly rebuilt Théâtre des Amandiers in the suburb of Nanterre. His productions are characterized by great scenic brilliance together with an ability to create modern archetypes, as seen in his productions of the four major plays of BERNARD-MARIE KOLTES. In 1983 he directed the only professional revival to date of GENET's *The Screens*.
DAVID BRADBY

Chevalier, Albert [Onésime Britannicus Gwathveoyd Louis]   (b. London, 21 March 1861; d. London, 10 July 1923)   Actor and MUSIC HALL artist of French/Welsh parentage. First engaged by the BANCROFTS (1877), he worked inconspicuously for years in 'legitimate' theatre until, in 1891, an unexpectedly successful appearance as a coster comedian (associated with Cockney barrow traders) transformed his career and he became the 'Costers' Laureate' of the

halls. Lacking the raw demotic appeal of some fellow performers such as Gus Elen (1862–1940), who was considered a true Cockney, Chevalier was admired by royalty, and gave private recitals to society audiences. He brought an actor's sense of timing and polished modulation of tone between humour and pathos, plus detailed costuming and make-up, to such unexceptionable ditties as 'My Old Dutch' and 'The Future Mrs 'Awkins'. He toured the United States alone and with YVETTE GUILBERT, and made several films. He wrote an autobiography, *Before I Forget* (1901). DONALD ROY

Chevalier, Maurice [Auguste]   (b. Paris, 12 Sept. 1888; d. Paris, 1 Jan. 1972)   Actor and MUSIC HALL singer. He joined the FOLIES-BERGÈRE in 1909 and two years later partnered MISTINGUETT at 1,800 francs a month; she added polish to a professional persona which always retained the knowingness of his café concert origins. He had extraordinary success in REVUES before moving to Hollywood in 1928 to become a star among stars. He returned to Paris in 1936. His screen personality betrayed something of its artificial origins but on stage his blue eyes, straw hat and expansive charm had immense popular appeal.
TERRY HODGSON

Chiarelli, Luigi   (b. Trani, Italy, 7 July 1880; d. Rome, 20 Dec. 1947)   Playwright. With his play *La maschera e il volto* (*The Mask and the Face*, 1916) he inaugurated the genre known as 'grotesque', in reaction against the traditional bourgeois theatre, questioning accepted notions of reality and preparing the way for the anti-realism of PIRANDELLO and others. FELICITY FIRTH

Chicago   Theatre dates back to the earliest days of the city when, in 1837, Harry Isherwood and Alexander McVicker transformed a tavern into a playhouse. By the 1860s new theatre buildings and performance halls were opening every year. In the 1890s, as thousands of immigrants and farmers arrived in Chicago each month, Jane Addams founded the Hull-House Theater. In marked contrast to the entertaining MELODRAMA and VAUDEVILLE which characterized the theatres of the downtown area, the Hull-House Theater earnestly attempted to educate and politicize by representing the deprived living conditions of the tenement dwellers of the West Side community.

While few Chicago theatres have stood the test of time, the GOODMAN MEMORIAL THEATER has emerged as one of the city's most enduring theatrical institutions. From its beginnings in 1925 the Goodman established itself as a professional theatre company. In 1969 it revitalized its ties with the Chicago community and in the 1980s, through a close collaboration between artistic director GREGORY MOSHER and rising Chicago playwright DAVID MAMET, the Goodman became, according to the *New York Times*, possibly 'the most exciting theater in the country'. Around this same time, the Goodman's main competitor, the STEPPENWOLF, also rose to national prominence.

Another specifically Chicagoan contribution to national and international theatre lies in 'improv' comedy. Developed by University of Chicago students and finding its inspiration in Viola Spolin, this spontaneous, freely structured comedy has successfully played since 1955.

Chicago's particular style of theatre, ranging as it does from nineteenth-century melodrama to contemporary comedy, reflecting the rich history and cultural heritage of the almost three million residents who make up the city, may well elude definition.
SUSAN PASTIKA

Sheldon Patinkin, *The Second City: Backstage at the World's Greatest Comedy Theater* (2000)

Chicano theatre   *see* HISPANIC THEATRE IN THE UNITED STATES

Chichester Festival Theatre   The brainchild of local tradesman Leslie Evershed-Martin (1903–94) and funded by public subscription, the 1,400-seat theatre situated in a West Sussex park in the south of England opened in 1962, under LAURENCE OLIVIER. Its innovative open thrust stage, based on the GUTHRIE–MOISEW-ITSCH design of Canada's STRATFORD FESTIVAL Theatre, was the first on this scale to be built in England. Since the early 1960s, when it housed outstanding NATIONAL THEATRE productions, such as *Uncle Vanya* (1962), *The Royal Hunt of the Sun* (1964) and *Armstrong's Last Goodnight* (1965), its programming under JOHN CLEMENTS and his successors has been less ambitious. In 1989 it opened a studio theatre, the Minerva, to try out more challenging work.   DAN REBELLATO
See also ARCHITECTURE.

L. Evershed-Martin, *The Miracle Theatre: The Chichester Festival Theatre's Coming of Age* (1987)
R. Hayman, *The First Thrust: The Chichester Festival Theatre* (1975)

children's theatre   A term employed to denote the performance of plays by professional actors for a children's audience. These plays are usually constructed along conventional lines using writers, directors, designers and occasionally puppetry, music and dance. The plays may include some form of seated vocal participation. The term usually distinguishes work for children under 12 years of age as opposed to the term

'young people's theatre', which includes work aimed at teenagers.

In the first half of the twentieth century, children's theatre in Britain (for the United States, *see* THEATRE FOR YOUNG AUDIENCES) amounted to occasional productions with spectacular visual effects mounted for short seasons, often at Christmas time in large commercial theatres, exemplified by *Peter Pan* (1904) by J. M. BARRIE or *Where the Rainbow Ends* (1911) by Clifford Mills and John Ramsey. The content of such plays was often myth or fantasy, and frequently drew on well-known literature for its source. As regional repertory theatres developed they regularly produced the few classics from the repertoire, such as MAETERLINCK's *The Bluebird* or adaptations of popular books such as Dickens's *A Christmas Carol*, in addition to the traditional Christmas PANTOMIME.

In the late 1940s a number of specialist companies began to tour work for audiences of children in both schools and theatres with a more serious intent. These companies, of which the most enduring have been Caryl Jenner's UNICORN THEATRE (founded 1947) and Theatre Centre (founded in 1949), drew on the model of the work developing in the Soviet Union since the 1920s, and after the Second World War in eastern Europe, where cultural enrichment was seen to be a vital adjunct to education and where major building-based companies with considerable financial subsidy had been established, working with the same resources and expertise as theatre for adult audiences.

Jenner's company, after touring into schools and theatres all over Britain as Caryl Jenner's Mobile Theatre and The English Children's Theatre, found a home as Unicorn Theatre in 1967 at the ARTS THEATRE in London's West End and continued to grow after Jenner's death in 1973, laying claim to being the only theatre for children in Britain along the east European model. In 1999 the Unicorn company left the Arts Theatre with a view to setting up its own purpose-built theatre in the centre of London. Brian Way's Theatre Centre continued its policy of touring into schools but, abandoning its tradition of seated participation, became by its working methods and content more closely allied with the emergent THEATRE IN EDUCA-TION (TIE) movement, particularly after Way's retirement in 1977. Since the 1980s Theatre Centre has focused on and cultivated new writing for children and young people.

By the late 1960s many more peripatetic companies had replaced the traditional companies which toured into schools. These latter had largely been superseded by the TIE companies, whose educational criteria and close links with schools had been welcomed by radical newcomers to the teaching profession. The new children's theatre companies offered a challenging alternative to TIE, relying much more on physical and musical skills and playing as happily in parks, playgrounds or street fairs as in the school hall. Many were the same fringe groups that were finding new audiences among the adult population by playing where theatre groups had not traditionally played before.

In the 1970s DAVID WOOD, whose plays on original themes had become a standard part of the repertoire of regional repertory theatres in the 1960s, replacing traditional stories, formed Whirlygig Theatre to mount major tours in large touring theatres which would preserve the high standard of production values that increased subsidy had brought to the reps and the specialist children's theatre companies. At the same time a touring group, Polka Theatre, presenting largely puppet plays in theatres, founded in 1967 by Richard Gill and Elizabeth Waghorn, created in south-west London the only purpose-built children's theatre in Britain and expanded its work to include more plays performed by actors alone as well as, or with, puppets.

The growth of TIE from the mid-1960s led to a vigorous debate among those working for younger audiences as to the primacy of form or content. The increasingly political motivation of TIE practitioners led them away from myth and fantasy, with its adherence to hierarchical and heroic protagonists, magical solutions to problems and the passive role of women. Contemporary subjects, many of them sensitive ones in the eyes of parents and teachers, became the standard repertoire. In the early 1970s one of the most influential children's theatre companies to draw on the experience of children's own lives in urban situations was the Grips Theatre of West Berlin, whose plays were first performed in Britain by Unicorn Theatre in Roy Kift's translations. They now form part of the standard repertoire of companies all over the Western world. In Canada companies such as Green Thumb from Vancouver brought the adventurous social dialectic of British TIE to the production values of traditional theatre for children. It was the work of such mobile and contemporary companies which now influenced the emergent children's theatre companies in the English-speaking world more than the large-scale, building-based companies of eastern Europe. French-speaking theatre for children in both Europe and Canada meanwhile pursued a more abstract and intellectual strain.

The arts in schools, which had been gaining momentum since the 1960s, were set back as successive governments established a national curriculum based on traditional core subjects and values. Reduced local authority expenditure and standstill state funding for the arts led to the demise of the TIE movement in the 1980s and 1990s.

Novel writing for children in Britain took great strides forward in the 1960s with the work of such writers as Joan Aiken, Helen Cresswell and Alan Garner; many writers being nurtured by the benevolent editing of Kaye Webb at Puffin Books. The 1970s and 1980s in the theatre saw an upsurge in the commissioning of work for children from both established writers such as poet and playwright ADRIAN MITCHELL and adult playwrights such as ANN JELLICOE or KEN CAMPBELL. Many playwrights (e.g. DAVID HOLMAN or Canada's Dennis Foon) learned their trade and established international reputations writing for children's theatre. Their plays reflect a simple, unpatronizing style that addressed itself to the issues affecting children and the concerns of children growing up in the 1980s.

From their inception, however, children's theatre companies in Britain and elsewhere have had to fight a continuing battle to have their work recognized by funding bodies such as the ARTS COUNCIL OF GREAT BRITAIN or local authorities, and by critics and other members of the theatre profession who do not accord the same value or level of seriousness to the needs of children's theatre. The struggle for levels of remuneration and critical recognition which would attract artists of similar stature to those working in adult theatre has been a preoccupation of all practitioners. There has been considerable discussion within the children's theatre movement about the means necessary to create work of the highest standard. This, as well as lobbying for and promoting children's theatre, has been the central preoccupation of the APT (Association of Professional Theatre for Children and Young People). The APT has also produced a journal, *Theatre First*, and helped to organize an annual festival of work for children in the north of England. Much has been done by ASSITEJ (the International Association of Theatre for Children and Young People), founded in 1965 by Britain and the Soviet Union, to sustain an international debate about the need for and means of creating high-quality work, and to share worldwide experience. But product which is available all the year round, from numerous companies, some of high standard but too many underfunded, still goes largely unrecognized by critics and professionals alike.

Since the 1990s the children's theatre movement has witnessed something of a renaissance. The growth of the international sector has been a powerful spur to both aesthetic and organizational development in Britain. Children's theatre festivals are now a regular annual event in many cities in North America, Europe and other international centres. The New Victory Theater, located in the heart of New York's 42nd Street, specializes in programming theatre for children and young people. Artistically, the 1990s witnessed a remarkable new aesthetic in design, writing and direction emerging from Belgium, the Netherlands, Sweden, Denmark and Canada. The Scottish International Children's Festival, which takes place every spring, is a major focus for this new movement. Founded in 1990, it was renamed Inaugurate in 2000 and has moved from purpose-built tents in Edinburgh's Inverleith Park to the theatres of the city centre.

NICK BARTER & TONY GRAHAM

See also THEATRE FOR YOUNG PEOPLE; YOUTH THEATRE.

Nicholas Barter, *Playing with Plays* (1979)
L. Swortzell, ed., *International Guide to Children's Theatre and Educational Theatre* (1990)

Childress, Alice (b. Charleston, SC, 12 Oct. 1920; d. Queens, New York, 14 Aug. 1994) Playwright, actress and novelist. An actress with the AMERICAN NEGRO THEATER, she was the first black woman to have a play produced OFF-BROADWAY with *Gold Through the Trees* (1952). Her plays are concerned with sexism, racial prejudice and insensitivity, and her characters are often 'losers'. Plays include the award-winning *Trouble in Mind* (1955), *Wedding Band* (1966), *Wine in the Wilderness* (1969), *Sea Island Song* (1979) and *Moms* (1987).

JANE HOUSE

Childs, Lucinda (b. New York, 26 June 1940) Dancer and choreographer. Childs planned initially to become an actor, but then became involved in dance. She was a member of the JUDSON CHURCH COLLECTIVE that spawned postmodern dance (1962–4) and influenced many disciplines, including what became known as PERFORMANCE ART. In 1976 she choreographed her own solo material in ROBERT WILSON and PHILIP GLASS's spectacle *Einstein on the Beach* (1976), and has appeared in subsequent work with Wilson (e.g. *Patio*, 1977; *La Madie de la Mort*, 1997) as well as making dances for many companies internationally.

ANDREW SOLWAY

See also CHOREOGRAPHY; DANCE; MOVEMENT, DANCE AND DRAMA.

Chile *see* SOUTH AMERICA

China The two main theatrical forms in China in the twentieth century are Chinese opera (*xiqu*), which originated in Chinese traditional culture, and the spoken drama (*huaju*), imported from the West. The earliest fully fledged Chinese opera arose at the latest in the twelfth century, although its origins can be traced back to the Zhou dynasty (1028–256 BC). Beijing opera (*jingju*) emerged in the nineteenth century as the representative Chinese opera, which consists of some 300 types of local operas. The spoken drama appeared at the beginning of the twentieth century, although the term 'spoken drama' was given later. In 1907 a group of Chinese students in Tokyo founded the Spring Willow Drama Society (*chunliu she*) and staged a scene adapted from *La Dame aux Camélias* by Alexandre Dumas *fils*. Their first full-length play was *Hei nu yu tian lu* ('The black slave's cry to heaven'), adapted from a Chinese translation of the influential American novel *Uncle Tom's Cabin* by Harriet Beecher Stowe.

The main differences between Chinese opera and the spoken drama are that the former is a special song-and-dance drama based on a role-type system which synthesizes singing, acting, reciting and acrobatic fighting and which mainly describes legend, myth and history, while the latter essentially uses actions and words to express modern life or a few historical stories seen from contemporary ideological viewpoints.

At the beginning of the twentieth century, radical ideas in culture and politics were closely linked. The New Cultural Movement that began in 1915 was a prelude to the May Fourth Movement of 1919, whose assertion of national sovereignty was a great turning point in modern Chinese history. In the New Cultural Movement, Confucianism and traditional culture were intensely criticized; scientific thought and democracy were actively propagandized. Some intellectuals, influenced by Western culture, violently criticized Chinese opera for both its form and content, seeing it as hidebound and superfluous. They strongly advocated the spoken drama. However, their criticisms were divorced from the practice of Chinese opera and did not influence its practitioners. In addition, the spoken drama, a mixture of adaptations and translations of Western plays, for example those of IBSEN, and some Chinese stories, was still only performed on a small scale among urban intellectuals.

In the 1920s the spoken drama made progress slowly and gradually came to reflect life in China. In its artistic form, foreign styles were becoming weaker and national colour was increasing. A number of dramatists attacked the traditional system of family and marriage. The most famous was Tian Han (1898–1968), who organized and led the drama company, the South China Society (*nanguo she*), which studied performance and toured its productions. In the 1930s the most prominent playwright was Cao Yu (1910–96). His *Leiyu* ('Thunderstorm', 1934), *Richu* ('Sunrise', 1936) and *Yuanye* ('Wilderness', 1937) successfully examined social issues and won praise from both audiences and critics. Also successful were Xia Yan (1900–95) and Hong Shen (1894–1955), who had studied in the United States and was also an important director, bringing to bear techniques from the West and challenging the prevailing custom of men playing women's parts. It is Hong Shen who first employed the term 'spoken drama' to designate the imported theatrical genre from the West.

In Chinese opera a few outstanding artists, such as MEI LANFANG, began to reform the genre. At first, they created some 'modern costume plays' (*shizhuangxi*), in which plots, themes, characters and costumes were all contemporary, but they were not successful. Then they changed their method. They did their best to improve the singing, dancing and acrobatics in their repertoire and created some historical plays which alluded to realistic life. From 1919 to 1935 Mei Lanfang visited Japan, the United States and the Soviet Union, and introduced Chinese opera through his brilliant performances.

Following Japanese attacks in the early 1930s, the government suppressed left-wing theatre but the Communist Party, which had declared a republic in Jiangxi, organized its own propaganda groups. However, the Japanese invasion in 1937 united Chinese from all walks of life. Patriotic drama groups travelled throughout the country, and Chinese theatre, particularly the spoken drama, attracted larger audiences than ever before. In the early 1940s, despite being censored, the spoken drama was very lively in Chongqing, temporary capital of the Nationalist government, while in Yan'an, the base of the central committee of the Communist Party, drama, and Chinese opera in particular, flourished. Some 'newly written historical plays' (*xinbian lishiju*) were created, which praised peasant uprisings in ancient China. The *yangge*, a rice-planting song and dance, was widely used to carry patriotic and revolutionary themes. A *yangge* drama, *Baimao nü* ('The white-haired girl'), which contained elements of the spoken drama, became very popular and was especially influential in the civil war period (1946–49).

After the People's Republic of China was established in 1949, all theatre soon came under state and party control. The Ministry of Culture led the reform of traditional Chinese opera and the many leading artists who chose to stay were ideologically retrained. Hundreds of traditional plays were revised while thousands of plays which were in danger of disappearing – some oral, some incomplete, some poorly written down – were collected and properly recorded. A few plays, which were deemed immoral or superstitious, or used terror, were prohibited. In the late 1950s 'contemporary plays' (*xiandi xi*) of Beijing opera, borrowing from

the spoken drama and using modern plots, themes and characters, were introduced as an experiment. At the same time, the spoken drama developed quickly, especially in its performing and directing. Artists seriously studied the STANISLAVSKY system as well as Chinese opera, and then the artistic form of the spoken drama became more mature. As a result of propagating the Communist Party's policies, however, most scripts of the period lack vitality, with some exceptions, such as Tian Han's *Guan Hanqing*, about the life of a great playwright of the thirteenth century, or *Chaguan* ('Tea house'), a realistic drama about changes in the lives of Chinese people, by Lao She (1899–1966).

In 1964, as a prologue to the Cultural Revolution (1966–76), all the traditional repertoire of Chinese opera was banned. During the early years of this period, there were virtually no performances except those of the 'model revolutionary plays' (*geming yangbanxi*), the contemporary versions of Beijing opera and ballet such as *Hongdeng ji* ('The red lantern') or *Zhiqu weihushan* ('Taking Tiger Mountain by strategy'). After the fall of Lin Biao in 1971, some contemporary works of local opera and spoken drama appeared, but they had to follow the so-called 'creation principles' of the 'model revolutionary plays'.

After the Cultural Revolution, the traditonal repertoire of Chinese opera was restored, and was extremely popular; research into its history and theory was widespread and fruitful. However, the young urban audiences were bored because they found it difficult to understand and appreciate, and the programmes were limited and old-fashioned. In comparison, the spoken drama carried on its tradition of exposing social problems. Plays criticizing the privilege of officials were enthusiastically received, but the trend was interrupted by the government. In opposition to Stanislavsky, the work of BRECHT was studied and an anti-realistic style of performance emerged in the spoken drama. The THEATRE OF THE ABSURD was introduced to theatrical circles. A number of experimental productions appeared, some of which incorporated a blend of techniques from Chinese opera as well. In the first Shakespeare Festival (1986), Shakespeare's plays were mounted not only as spoken drama but also in the forms of the Beijing opera and other local operas. There were visits from Western companies: the OLD VIC played *Hamlet* in 1979, and ARTHUR MILLER directed his own *Death of a Salesman* in Beijing in 1983. However, the influence of both the spoken drama and Chinese opera was weakening in the 1980s. Chinese theatre, the main entertainment in China in the past, was being challenged by the rising popularity of television, popular music and modern dance, and was engaged in a struggle for its survival. SUN MEI

See also EASTERN THEATRE, ITS INFLUENCE ON THE WEST.

William Dobly, *A History of Chinese Drama* (1976)

Yan Haiping, ed., *Theater and Society: An Anthology of Contemporary Chinese Drama* (2000)

Elizabeth Halsom, *Peking Opera: A Short Guide* (1966)

Roger Howard, *Contemporary Chinese Theatre* (1978)

Colin Mackerras, ed., *Chinese Theatre from its Origins to the Present Day* (1983)

Sun Mei, '*Xiqu*'s Problems in Contemporary China', *Journal of Contemporary China*, vol. 6 (1994)

Arthur Miller, *Salesman in Beijing* (1984)

Chong, Ping *see* ASIAN AMERICAN THEATRE; EXPERIMENTAL THEATRE; LA MAMA EXPERIMENTAL THEATER COMPANY

choreography Choreography is always regenerating itself, alive to trends and influence, both current and past, foreign and indigenous. For theatre and opera it is primarily a collaborative process in which the choreographer is not sole arbiter, but combines with the talents of author, director, designer and composer to create a seamless whole. Together, but drawing on the particular expertise of the choreographer, they combine to discover a movement of vocabulary appropriate to the special dynamic of the setting. Sometimes drawing from mundane behavioural activity, sometimes from the more stylized and lavish language of dance styles, this input serves to develop plot and character, interpret score and generally enhance the playing of a scene.

In the early 1900s most choreographic influences in PANTOMIME, MUSIC HALL and REVUE were mainly balletic, reflecting the paucity of DANCE activity at the time, although it may be possible to identify the contribution of the disciples of Delsarte and EMILE JAQUES-DALCROZE at work. Later, in the 1920s and 1930s, choreographers with links with the Ballets Russes, notably Frederick Ashton and WILLIAM CHAPPELL, became involved in the lavish staging of the COCHRANE revues, and contributed to the development of the musical theatre of IVOR NOVELLO and NOËL COWARD.

In the United States, the careers of choreographers such as AGNES DE MILLE, HANYA HOLM and JEROME ROBBINS spanned ballet, contemporary dance and JAZZ, embracing a great cross-fertilization of dance styles and techniques. They and others had a considerable influence on the American musical theatre and film industry, culminating with *West Side Story*, for which Robbins was both choreographer and director.

In Britain, ballet-based choreographers also incorporated other dance styles and had an important influence on the indigenous British musical, notably in the work of WENDY TOYE and GILLIAN LYNNE (e.g. in ANDREW LLOYD WEBBER's *Cats*).

It is also possible to identify influences deriving from sources other than ballet, in particular in language-based theatre. Directors such as JOAN LITTLEWOOD worked for a while with RUDOLPH LABAN, father of the central European modern dance movement, incorporating his principles of movement training into her own work with actors. Similarly, drama schools witnessed the importance of movement training for the actor, particularly in the work of John Broome, LITZ PISK, Yat Malmgren and Fedora Toshka, having strong links with the central European approach to bodily training for actors and singers.

The explosion of native American modern dance – MARTHA GRAHAM, MERCE CUNNINGHAM, Jose Limon, Paul Taylor, ALWYN NIKOLAIS and ALVIN AILEY – has made the most impact in the second half of the twentieth century, both at home and abroad. STUART HOPPS

See also MOVEMENT, DANCE AND DRAMA.

Martha Bremser, ed., *Fifty Contemporary Choreographers* (1994)

Svetlana Grody and Dorothy Lister, *Conversations with Choreographers* (1997)

Christie, Agatha (b. Torquay, 13 Sept. 1890; d. Wallingford, Oxon, 12 Jan. 1974) Crime writer and playwright. Christie was dissatisfied by others' dramatization of her mystery fiction. She wrote 15 stage plays, from *Black Coffee* (1930), featuring Hercule Poirot, to *Fiddlers Three* (1971). In 1952 in London THE MOUSETRAP began the longest run in theatre history. Christie wrote one historical drama, *Akhanaton* (1937). TONY HOWARD

Christie, John *see* OPERA

Christiné, Henri [Marius] (b. Geneva, Switzerland, 27 Dec. 1867; d. Nice, 12 Nov. 1941) Composer. Christiné was a schoolteacher when he married a café-concert vocalist and began writing songs for her to perform. The couple subsequently moved to France, where his songs found their way into the repertoires of leading popular vocalists and one, 'La Petite Tonkinoise', won worldwide popularity as performed by Anna Held ('How Delightful To Be Married'). He provided the songs for several small-scale musicals mounted in Paris before the First World War, and then, after a decade's absence from the stage, returned to the theatre with a little musical comedy, *Phi-Phi* (1918). It proved a landmark show which introduced the 'songwriter's musical' to the French stage. His sparkling, light-footed melodies, allied to a particularly funny classic burlesque libretto and lyrics by ALBERT WILLEMETZ and Fabien Sollar, set the musical model for the following two decades of French musicals, in which his own *Dédé* (1921), *Madame* (1923), *P.L.M.* (1925) and *Arthur* (1929) found considerble and significant success.

KURT GÄNZL

church drama *see* RELIGIOUS DRAMA

Churchill, Caryl (b. London, 3 Sept. 1938) Playwright. Churchill had some early acclaim with radio plays like *The Ants* (1962), *not not not not not enough oxygen* (1971) and *Schreber's Nervous Illness* (1972). However, it was through contact with feminism that she developed the language and structures to carry the complexity of her ideas. *Owners* (1972), about a woman using her property business to exert power over an ex-lover, *Objections to Sex and Violence* (1975), with its middle-class woman becoming involved in revolutionary anarchism, and the HANDKE-influenced *Traps* (1977) were all staged at the ROYAL COURT. Her *Light Shining in Buckinghamshire* (1976), for JOINT STOCK, set at the end of the English Civil War and marking the start of her long-lasting collaboration with director MAX STAFFORD-CLARK, and *Vinegar Tom* (1976) for MONSTROUS REGIMENT, which refracted modern women's struggles through the seventeenth-century witch-hunts, displayed a burgeoning political and dramatic complexity. This culminated in her second Joint Stock play *Cloud Nine* (1979), which juxtaposed a hilarious sexual farce in Victorian colonialist Africa with the fragmented identities of late 1970s sexual politics.

Top Girls (1982), perhaps Churchill's best play, keenly predicted the rise of bourgeois 'post-feminism' in the Thatcherite 1980s, raising stimulating questions, notably in its *tour de force* opening where the stories of six women from history overlap, clash and connect over a restaurant meal. *Fen* (1983) dissected economic and sexual oppressions in the Fenlands; the Foucault-inspired *Softcops* (1984) considered the meanings of criminality and punishment; and *Serious Money* (1987) was a witty verse thriller about the City, substantially attended by its objects of attack. After *Ice Cream* (1989) Churchill wrote *Mad Forest* (1990), a breathlessly expansive meditation on the 1989 Romanian revolution. *The Skriker* (1994) constructed a fantastic menagerie of creatures to theatricalize the wilder shores of the mind, building on her experiences on *Midday Sun* (1984), *A Mouthful of Birds* (1986, with DAVID LAN), *Fugue* (1988) and *Lives of the Great Poisoners* (1991, with

Orlando Gough and Ian Spink), to develop a language of physical movement as complex and shifting as the dense, punning text. She continued experimenting in *Blue Heart* (1997) and *Far Away* (2000). Churchill's witty, powerfully intelligent dialogue and her uniquely imaginative sense of structure saw her at the forefront of British playwriting in the 1980s and 1990s.

DAN REBELLATO

Colin Chambers and Mike Prior, *Playwright's Progress* (1987)
Geraldine Cousin, *Churchill the Playwright* (1989)
Amelia House Kritzer, *The Plays of Caryl Churchill* (1991)

cinema The cinema has pioneered more innovations in dramatic narrative than either of its fellow media, RADIO and TELEVISION. Like them, it is the child of twentieth-century technology; but it appeared on the scene before them. A whole series of inventions and discoveries had to come together to make the cinema possible. Some of these were not new. Thus the projection of backlit images through a lens, in other words the magic lantern, went back as far as the seventeenth century. The discovery of the phenomenon of persistence of vision, i.e. a rapid succession of static images producing the illusion of movement on the retina, resulted in a number of optical toys in the nineteenth century, such as the phenakistoscope, the zoetrope and the praxinoscope. The development of photography, from the work of Daguerre and Fox Talbot in the 1830s onwards, was the crucial preparatory step. With the last missing link, celluloid-based rolls of film, provided in 1889, the way was clear for Auguste and Louis Lumière to create the cinematograph – camera, printer and projector all in one. We can date the birth of the new art precisely. The first public screening of a Lumière film on 28 December 1895 in Paris may have consisted largely of reportage items (workers leaving a factory, the arrival of a train, etc.), but the sight gag of a gardener tricked into having a jet of water from his hose squirted into his face was the first, albeit primitive, story film.

It was soon discovered that the new medium opened up fresh narrative possibilities. Early studio work owed much to theatrical practice, but the dramatic effectiveness of location shooting was established as early as 1903 by Porter's *The Great Train Robbery*. Of course, it took time before film-makers realized that the new medium enabled them not only to tell old stories in a new way but to tell different stories, beyond the reach of the theatre. Trial and error revealed that the camera could select angles other than a fixed frontal viewpoint, that it could pick out significant details and that it could move. It was seen that non-human elements – natural scenery, animals and that durable emblem of locomotion, the train – could carry much of the dramatic action. Slow and speeded-up motion as well as other camera tricks became favourite devices. The two features that particularly excited early film-makers and spectators were the close-up and editing. The close-up was a means of focusing an audience's attention. It gave exceptional value to an actor's or actress's features, and thus formed the technical basis for the cult of the star. Editing, elaborated by the American D. W. Griffith, the Frenchman Abel Gance and the Russian SERGEI M. EISENSTEIN, was seen to be far more than the joining of one shot to another. It could foreshorten time, create cinematic space, suggest ideas, construct acting performances out of fragments of action and, by the control of shot rhythms, guide an audience's emotional response.

The silent cinema's emphasis on the image brought about the rapid evolution of a new dramatic language. Film proved to have perhaps more in common with the novel than with the stage play (though scenarios were in fact drawn from both sources). This visual bias, which contrasted with the theatre's reliance on speech to convey meaning, did not exclude supplementary means of signification. There were titles: these narrated and commented on the plot, or served as brief passages of dialogue. There was music (by a single pianist, an organ or a whole orchestra): this would underline the action somewhat in the manner of early MELODRAMA. With the coming of the sound film (from *The Jazz Singer*, 1927, onwards) the supremacy of the visual element gave way to a sound–image symbiosis. This may initially have caused the cinema to fall back on the plays, acting techniques and personnel of the theatre, but that was a passing phase. Film sound is far from being a mere transcription of unmediated reality, and the cinema's inherent characteristics were soon to reassert themselves. Though the most crucial single invention, sound has not been the only technical innovation to affect the cinema's expressive arsenal. Colour – notably Technicolor, Agfacolor and Eastman Color – was to have a fundamental influence on art direction. Widescreen systems such as Todd-AO, CinemaScope, Panavision and VistaVision offered a panoramic image beyond the range of television, well suited to battles and any kind of action on the horizontal plane. Other technical advances, such as faster and faster film stocks; improved lenses, including the development of the zoom lens; sophisticated stabilizing gear for helicopter and other moving shots; more lightweight camera, sound-recording and lighting equipment, which have made greater slices of 'reality' available to the film-maker – all these have been reflected in the cinema's enlarged means of expression.

The wide range of specialist crafts that go into the making of a film calls for coordination. Hence the strong position of the director, the person ideally able to hold all the threads in his (or, more rarely, her) hands. This role has not been identical at all times and in all places. European directors have tended to work by the principle, 'One man one film'. But the average American director in the heyday of the Hollywood studio system had as little say over the script he was given to shoot as he had over the final cut. Only men of the stature of John Ford, Howard Hawks and Frank Capra had full control over their films. The film director is inherently more in command of the end product than his theatrical *confrère*. A play makes its impact through the direct interaction of performers and audience. In a film, actors perform in the first instance for the director rather than an audience, and what they do is mediated by the camera, the editing process, the dubbing studio and the laboratory before reaching the public. In 1948 Alexandre Astruc claimed, in an article entitled 'Le caméra-stylo', that the film-maker with his camera was equivalent to the writer wielding his pen. It has often been claimed that the director ought to write his own scripts. Desirable as this may seem, in practice only a minority of directors have done so wholly unaided – men like COCTEAU, INGMAR BERGMAN, FASSBINDER and Woody Allen. Even major directors, *auteurs* by critical consensus such as VISCONTI, Hitchcock or Truffaut, employed writers at the pre-production stage – some in long-standing partnerships like that of Buñuel with Luis Alcoriza and Jean-Claude Carrière.

The writer's status, like the director's, has had its ups and downs. The screenwriter tends to be more affluent but less powerful than the playwright. (He may well be one and the same person, but wearing different hats.) In the Hollywood studio system contract writers had little choice in their assignments, and group rather than solo writing was common practice. Even in the more favourable conditions of independent production there are many factors – budgetary, logistical, personal, etc. – which prevent a script being realized exactly as the writer had in mind. The producer's role has historically been no less varied. His influence has depended not only on prevailing conditions in general, but on the force of his personality. Producers like Darryl Zanuck and David Puttnam have put their own stamp on the films they caused to be made. Indeed, there may be a house style transcending the bias of the individual director or producer – such as the blood and fangs of Hammer or the gloss and production values of

Metro-Goldwyn-Mayer which used to boast that it 'had more stars than there are in heaven'.

It used to be, and to some extent still is, the case that actors rather than other members of the production team attract most public attention. The star system, associated primarily with the American industry, can be said to have begun in 1910 with the build-up of Florence Lawrence, 'The Biograph Girl'. The image of the Hollywood star as a role model, dream lover and exemplar of success was puffed up by an enormous publicity machine with regular press releases, fan magazines, eye-grabbing stunts and a manufactured lifestyle. Stardom has not always been synonymous with, though it need not exclude, acting talent. Sex appeal tends to be a normal ingredient in star quality. Clearly Rudolph Valentino, Mary Pickford, Greta Garbo, Clark Gable, Gary Cooper, Bette Davis and Joan Crawford represented very different levels of acting skill. The decline of the studio system has dimmed but not extinguished the lustre of the star. Paul Newman, MARLON BRANDO, DUSTIN HOFFMAN, Robert de Niro and BARBRA STREISAND were box-office attractions in the latter part of the century. International stardom has not been an exclusively American phenomenon, as witness Max Linder and Asta Nielson in the silent days, or Jean-Paul Belmondo, Brigitte Bardot and Toshiro Mifune in more recent times.

The First World War ended the screen hegemony briefly enjoyed by France and Italy. The United States, not directly hit by hostilities, could use its industrial and financial muscle to conquer the world's screens. With a domestic market large enough to cover production costs, it reaped vast profits from overseas outlets. The glamour, fast pace and narrative expertise of Hollywood films fascinated foreign audiences and laid them open to the ideological messages encoded in them in the guise of entertainment. Taste, fashion and ways of thinking in many countries were affected. America created a number of film genres with recognizable styles and narrative conventions. Silent comedies with a good deal of slapstick became universally popular, raising performers like Charlie Chaplin, Buster Keaton and Harold Lloyd to worldwide fame. Many genres, like the Western and the gangster film, rose directly out of American experience. Others, like the sophisticated (i.e. dialogued) comedy and the horror film, owed not a little to European inspiration. A wholly American genre of the sound era was the musical, universally acclaimed for its melodic invention and choreographic attack. Other countries – first England, France and Italy, then Germany and Russia in Europe, India and Japan in Asia – had been supplying their own home markets from the early years of the

century onwards. Genre films were not unknown there either. Thus costume films were frequent in the British, 'white telephone' films in the Italian cinema. The 1917 Revolution set the Russian industry on a very different course. Lenin regarded the cinema as the most important art for the young Soviet state. The industry was nationalized and turned out a great many films with a communist propaganda message.

Overt propaganda was not confined to the Soviet Union. A good many, though not all, German films carried an open Nazi message after Hitler's rise to power. During the Second World War, all the countries involved used the cinema as a stiffener of morale and a lever on neutral opinion. In the occupied countries, control of the cinema was a major aspect of policy. After the shooting war, the Cold War had unpleasant echoes in films made on either side of the East–West divide. The war left Hollywood still in possession of a dominant position: in 1946 it turned out more than 500 features. But the accelerating rise of television – in the 1940s and 1950s in the developed world, in the 1960s in the Third World – helped to displace the cinema as the chief provider of mass entertainment. Large numbers of cinemas closed down everywhere. In the developed countries, film was in danger of becoming a minority culture, though the odd blockbuster (*Star Wars*, *Jaws*) would still pack in vast audiences. The gap between glittering success and financial disaster widened. Co-productions between different countries, and collaboration of the film with the television industry have become common practice. At the same time, countries which had not previously been in the forefront of the international film scene, such as Argentina, Poland or Hungary, commanded attention. Indeed, countries only recently freed from colonial status – Sri Lanka, the Philippines and Senegal are cases in point – have begun to find their cinematic voice.

The cinema has generated a great deal of literature. Screenplays are published, though often in a format more readable than that of the shooting-script. Many aspects of film history have been written up – the cinema of various countries, the work of individual film artists. There is a sizeable body of criticism and theory, with magazines like *Cahiers du cinéma* in France, *Screen* in the UK and *Film Culture* in the United States at the sharp end of the debate. Early theorists aimed to establish film as being on a level with the older, more respectable arts. Practitioners like Eisenstein and Pudovkin systematized the principles of composition and especially editing as the key features of the new medium. After the Second World War, André Bazin argued that it was the essential task of film faithfully to reflect reality. Later on, critical ingenuity was expended in laying down a canon of *auteurs* (i.e. genuine creators) as against mere *metteurs-en-scène* among directors. Those interested in genre studies read film texts in the light of adherence to, or deviation from, generally understood conventions. Feminism, Marxist sociology, Freudian and Lacanian psychoanalysis, semiology and structuralism have all meshed in with later film theory. Theory tends to follow practice, but it may in turn help practitioners to break the mould of routine. Virtually from the beginnings of the cinema there has been a tributary current, variously called experimental, AVANT-GARDE and underground film, running alongside and feeding into mainstream work. Often in danger of self-indulgence, experimental cinema has contributed new techniques and narrative conventions to the commercial cinema. Methods once regarded as inaccessible have featured in the work of film makers like Godard, Buñuel or Tarkovsky and won a wide measure of audience approval. If the style and methods of drama had to adapt in order to meet the needs of the screen, there has in turn been a feedback from this into the theatre. Much of the fluidity of modern stage practice is indebted to the cinema, and acting styles in the theatre have become more naturalistic at least partly in response to the norms of screen acting. GEORGE BRANDT

Ellen Baskin and Mandy Hicken, *Enser's Filmed Books and Plays* (1993)

André Bazin, *What is Cinema?*, 2 vols (1967, 1971)

Sergei M. Eisenstein, *The Film Sense* (1943)

—— *Film Form* (1951)

Robert Giddings, Keith Selby and Chris Wensley, *Screening the Novel: The Theory and Practice of Literary Dramatisation* (1990)

Denis Gifford, *Books and Plays in Films 1896–1915* (1991)

Torben Grodal, *Moving Pictures: A New Theory of Film Genres, Feelings and Cognition* (1997)

Siegfried Kracauer, *Theory of Film: The Redemption of Physical Reality* (1965)

Gerald Mast and Marshall Cohen, *Film Theory and Criticism*, 3rd edn (1995)

Edward Murray, *The Cinematic Imagination: Writers and the Motion Pictures* (197)

David Robinson, *World Cinema: A Short History*, 2nd edn (1983)

David Shipman, *Cinema: The First Hundred Years* (1993)

Sue Thornham, *Passionate Detachments: An Introduction to Feminist Film Theory* (1997)

Christopher Williams, ed., *Realism and the Cinema* (1980)

Peter Wollen, *Signs and Meaning in the Cinema*, 2nd rev. edn (1973)

Cino, Joe *see* CAFFÉ CINO; OFF-OFF-BROADWAY

Circa Theatre An actors' co-operative theatre in Wellington, New Zealand, founded in 1976 by a group of leading actors disaffected with DOWNSTAGE THEATRE. With its 'actors' theatre' policy and a carefully mixed programme of modern plays, classics and New Zealand works, Circa soon established itself as a leading theatre, particularly after its runaway successes with ROGER HALL's *Glide Time* (1976) and *Middle Age Spread* (1977). In 1994 it moved into a new, harbourside building with a main auditorium seating 263 and a small studio theatre. GILLIAN GREER & LAURIE ATKINSON

John Reid and Ruth Jeffrey, eds, *Circa Theatre 1976–1996* (1996)

Circle in the Square OFF-BROADWAY theatre, founded in 1951 by José QUINTERO and others as a nonprofit offshoot of the Loft Players. It played in the round in a small theatre on Sheridan Square – hence the name. It was active in the early days of the Off-Broadway movement, nurturing a new generation of American playwrights, directors and actors, including GERALDINE PAGE (in a famous 1952 revival of WILLIAMS's *Summer and Smoke*), GEORGE C. SCOTT, Cicely Tyson, JASON ROBARDS (in an acclaimed 1956 production of O'NEILL's *The Iceman Cometh*) and DUSTIN HOFFMAN. In 1961 the Circle opened a theatre school and in 1972 a new theatre on West 50th Street. In 1994 the company moved to the Circle-In-The-Square Downtown theatre, and subsequently went out of business. ELLEN LAMPERT-GRÉAUX

Circle Repertory Company OFF-BROADWAY theatre. Founded in 1969 by Tanya Berezin, Marshall W. Mason, Robert Thirkield and LANFORD WILSON, who had worked together at LA MAMA and CAFFÉ CINO and at the American Theater Project in 1968. It champions the production of new plays by American playwrights, many of which have moved on to BROADWAY and secured places in the regional theatre repertory. Among its successes are: Wilson's *Hot l Baltimore* (1973), *The Fifth of July* (1978), *Talley's Folly* (1979) and *Burn This* (1987); SAM SHEPARD's *Buried Child* (1979) and *Fool for Love* (1983); ALBERT INNAURATO's *Gemini* (1976); JULES FEIFFER's *Knock Knock* (1976); and William M. Hoffman's *As Is* (1985), one of the first plays to deal with AIDS. The Company's dedication to excellence and its vision of truth and humanity have been recognized by the Pulitzer Prize, Tony and a host of other awards. In 1994 it moved to CIRCLE IN THE SQUARE

Downtown, where it performed until going out of business in 1996. ELLEN LAMPERT-GRÉAUX

M. Ryzuk, *The Circle Repertory Company: The First Fifteen Years* (1989)

circus In 1919 the Georgian artist Nikolai Foregger lectured the Union of International Artists of the Circus on his conviction in a renaissance of the circus. He evoked theatre as the Siamese twin of circus, drawing on Elizabethan England and seventeenth-century Spain as models of perfect circus–theatre marriages. Circus has both renewed itself in the twentieth century, primarily from the 1980s on when the standard of new circus was raised, and influenced theatre through directors such as MEYERHOLD, BRECHT and BROOK.

Despite the Latin origins of the word 'circus' meaning 'ring', the gladiatorial amphitheatres of ancient Rome have nothing to do with the modern idea of circus. Its genesis lies elsewhere, going back to prehistoric societies and the figure of the shaman, the medicine man or woman of nomadic tribes, in the magical control of wild animals, the ecstatic flights of the trapeze artist and the metaphor of balance inherent to the tightrope artist who crosses the threshold and narrow bridge between the two worlds. The tradition comes through the ancient classical world of rope dancers, ladder balancers, acrobats and jugglers, a medieval Europe populated by itinerant jongleurs and minstrels, to the *COMMEDIA DELL'ARTE* figure of Arlecchino, who would stilt-walk, tumble and run across tightropes as a normal means of locomotion, and the boulevards of the nineteenth century popularized by Marcel Carné in his film *Les Enfants du Paradis*. Modern circus was born in England in the eighteenth century among the exhibitions of the riding schools; Philip Astley, popularly known as 'the master of the circus', presented equestrian displays in a circle, and this shape, being the most practical for good horsemanship, became a permanent part of the circus. A Mr and Mrs Woolton beat him by three months in mixing other acts with horses, and Charles Dibdin christened the circus when he housed his horsemanship entertainment in a theatre called the Royal Circus in 1782. Circus continued to expand the use of other acts such as strong men, contortionists, acrobats and fakirs, but it was Astley who originated the CLOWN entrée that parodies an act of skill with his 'drunken' tailor pretending bad riding. He also had a flair for publicity and showmanship that connects him to the circus proprietors that colour the history of circus: Abraham Saunders, whose squire outfit probably inspired the traditional costume of the Ringmaster; Barnum and Bailey in the United states; Fossett in Ireland; Billy Smart, Jimmy and Dick Chipperfield, Bertram Mills and Jerry Cottle in England. Parallel elements to the events in England, travelling showmen and John Bill Ricketts' riding school in Philadelphia, inspired the creation of the circus in the United States. And the circus spread across Europe, too, with rich developments in Russia, leading to famous circuses such as Circus Knie in Switzerland and Cirque Medrano in Paris.

Circus at the end of the twentieth century has retained many of its traditions but presents an interesting tapestry. Concern for animal welfare has changed some practices, while new circus has drawn on past traditions yet revitalized and reinvented circus for a new audience, impelled by a generation of young performers eager to redefine circus and to find new theatrical mediums for it. Whereas the circuses of the past transferred their skills through their family line, there has been a blossoming of training opportunities in circus skills since the 1980s, encouraging the emergence of new energies into the mainstream. Reg Bolton's 'suitcase circus' movement was a peripatetic community-oriented circus access scheme in the 1980s. The Centre National des Arts du Cirque from France brought their students to perform at London's New Circus Festival, as did the grassroots community circus, Circus Belfast. Fool Time and Circamedia have been major centres for studying the circus arts in the southwest of England. Circus Space in London continues to flourish and expand, offering opportunities for students to undergo comprehensive training as well as producing shows since 1989. In partnership with the Central School of Speech and Drama, Circus Space now runs the first BA degree in circus arts

There have been many leading lights among the new circus companies. Ra Ra Zoo, originally from London, produced shows that combined aerial acts with juggling, clowning, acrobatics, live music and movement in an innovative way; shows were inspired by complex juggling moves, Beijing Opera and BAUHAUS design, and were characterized by a zany, surreal style – as shown in their tea party balanced on the performers' heads. Cirque Du Soleil from Montreal have toured the world with sophisticated shows that juxtapose lights, music, acrobats and clowns with arresting visual images of transformation and magic. By contrast Archaos, a French company that evolved from a young troupe from the 1970s, Circus Bidon, have offered a contemporary show of motorbikes, chainsaws and macabre clowns, with punk rock overtures; the Big Apple Circus from New York is a sawdust spectacle of status and power turning on the subversion of the beauty and the grandeur of the acts by the clowns; the Pickle Family Circus from the United States saw themselves as an extended family reaching out and embracing the audience; Circus Oz from Australia have produced striking images such as a drummer walking upside down on the roof to play drums upside down; Circus Senso offered a training and performing outlet for young performers under the tutelage of Brian Andro, who has performed and directed with Soleil; Hot and Neon from the United States combined juggling, music, martial arts, dance, magic and acrobatics in spontaneous and captivating theatre.

Concurrent with the explosion of new circus as indoor spectacle was the growth of STREET THEATRE and outdoor performance utilizing circus elements. Companies and individuals from Canada, the United States, Britain and the Netherlands brought stilts, fire juggling, wire and rope walking and unicycling on to the streets. Names included Les Voilà, Original Mixture, the Flying Dutchmen, John Lee, Samande Jugglers, Chris and Alex, the Uncles, and Bernie Bennet. The all-women company Skinning The Cat toured an outdoor trapeze show of extraordinary visual power throughout Europe. Jugglers such as Tim Bat, Venus, Steve Rawlings and Paul Morocco were regular performers on the alternative cabaret circuit that began in the 1980s. Becky Truman was a regular performer at the Leeds Variety theatre with her aerial act in the 1990s, thus perpetuating the tradition of VARIETY bills that included jugglers such as the early W. C. FIELDS and the Swiss acrobat GROCK, who was later to find fame as a clown in the 1920s.

Some companies associated with new circus explored the expression of theatre text through circus. Circus Burlesque adopted *Alice In Wonderland* and No Fit State Circus *Dr Faustus* as circus theatre extravaganzas. Mummerandada integrated circus skills into theatrical stories and the Medieval Players used fire-juggling demons in their medieval epics. The Flying Karamazov's juggling troupe were central figures in a highly physicalized version of *The Comedy of Errors* produced by GREG MOSHER at the Goodman Theater in Chicago. The fear of death and jealous rage were explored through circus metaphor, embodied in aerial trapeze and sword spinning.

Theatre practitioners have often turned to circus for its imagery, staging and popularity in times of exploration and experimentation. In Russia in the 1920s, EISENSTEIN staged Ostrovsky's *Diary of a Scoundrel* using clown and circus acts, MAYAKOVSKY and Meyherhold collaborated on circus-influenced shows such as *Mystery Bouffe* which had the circus clown Lazerenko sliding down a wire and performing acrobatic tricks. Some companies and directors have been interested in the relationship between audience and performer evident

in circus. Meyerhold wrote that he wanted to free his actors from the proscenium stage frame and stage productions so that, 'like a circus arena, ringed on all sides by spectators, the stage apron comes close to the audience'. Peter Brook staged JARRY's *Ubu Roi* in a circus tent. JEROME SAVARY's Le Grand Magic Circus used circus intimacy in presenting the epic theatre show *From Moses to Mao*. FOOTSBARN TRAVELLING THEATRE perform their Shakespearean plays in circus TENTS. GENET called circus 'an instance of the ultimate truth'.

The imagery of circus has also exercised a fascination for the theatre. DARIO FO united politics and circus in his 1967–8 production of *Throw the Lady Out*, with its circus allegory of militarism and government. Peter Brook evoked the dislocation of the lost lovers in *A Midsummer Night's Dream* with a stilt-walking Puck and the otherness of the fairy world through trapezes and plate spinning. ROBERT LEPAGE, in his production of the same play, had Puck performing on a circus web rope as he 'puts a girdle round the earth'. Michael Bogdanov, in his tenure at the Phoenix Theatre in LEICESTER, the YOUNG VIC and the NATIONAL THEATRE, experimented with circus forms in productions of *Gawain and the Green Knight* and *Bartholomew Fair*. The Turkish potentate in TERRY HANDS' production of *Tamburlaine the Great* at the ROYAL SHAKESPEARE COMPANY with ANTHONY SHER appears on stilts as symbol of power. Peter Schumann's BREAD AND PUPPET THEATER also uses stilts and rope walkers as part of its theatre vocabulary. JACQUES COPEAU visited the Cirque Medrano, where he was fascinated by the subtle performance nuances of an English juggler and by the Fratellini Brothers circus clown troupe. This intensified his sense of investigation into popular forms of theatre. And while theatre has investigated circus for revitalization, new circus has sought to theatricalize its imagery.

MITCH MITCHELSON

See also MEDIEVAL THEATRE IN THE TWENTIETH CENTURY.

RoseLee Goldberg, *Performance Art* (1988)
Ron Jenkins, *Acrobats of the Soul* (1988)
George Speaight, *A History of the Circus* (1980)
Rogan Taylor, *The Death and Resurrection Show* (1985)

Citizens' Theatre Founded in 1943 by a group of prominent GLASGOW citizens, most notably JAMES BRIDIE, whose play *Holy Isle* launched the company at the Athenaeum Theatre. Two years later the company moved to the Gorbals and gave its name, taken from a 1909 Glasgow Rep manifesto, to the theatre that was to remain its home. Scottish drama, including some of Bridie's finest work, Sir David Lindsay's *The Three Estates* and a series of celebrated pantomimes – for example, *The Tintock Cup* – dominated the early years, and many distinguished Scottish actors regularly appeared there. Since 1969 artistic director Giles Havergal, who was joined in 1970 by co-directors PHILIP PROWSE and ROBERT DAVID MACDONALD, has presented a repertoire bolder and broader than any in Britain, ranging from COWARD, WILDE, GENET and Goldoni to Jacobean revivals, new plays, German classics and adaptations of novels. A cheap ticket policy and a commitment to accessibility have helped secure strong local support. Not only has the 'Citz' nurtured many fine performers, its unusual, flamboyant and distinctive style has established it as one of the most vital theatres in Europe. Two studio theatres were opened in 1992 to extend the experimental work beyond the main house. JAN MCDONALD

Michael Coveney, *The Citz* (1990)
Jan McDonald and Claude Schumacher, *The Citizens' Theatre Season: Glasgow 1990* (1991)
Cordelia Oliver, *Magic in the Gorbals* (1999)

Ciulei, Liviu (b. Bucharest, 7 July 1923) Director, designer and teacher. His formal training in theatre and architecture influences his productions, which are often visually and metaphorically stimulating. He was artistic director of ROMANIA's leading theatre, the Bulandra (1963–72), but was dismissed in 1972 after allowing a production of Gogol's *The Inspector General* that authorities deemed politically disrespectful. He then worked freelance in Canada, Germany and Australia before coming to America at the invitation of Zelda Fichlander to direct at the ARENA THEATER. He also worked at Julliard, CIRCLE IN THE SQUARE, the NEW YORK SHAKESPEARE FESTIVAL and the GUTHRIE THEATER, where he was artistic director (1980–6), and his bold visual style and importation of guest directors like PETER SELLARS and RICHARD FOREMAN generated tremendous controversy and excitement. His film *The Forest of the Hanged* earned the 'best direction' award at the Cannes Festival in 1965. He has directed and designed operas in various parts of the world while serving on the graduate acting faculty of New York University. DAVID A. WILLIAMS

Civic Repertory Theater Founded in New York in 1926 by EVA LE GALLIENNE with an all-women staff, it aimed to provide a modern repertory at low prices in the mould of publicly subsidized European theatres. New American plays were presented alongside CHEKHOV, IBSEN, Goldoni, Shakespeare and GIRAUDOUX. Always in economic trouble, the company moved out of its theatre in 1933 with a transfer of Le Gallienne's adaptation of *Alice in Wonderland* and folded in 1935, but not without leaving an important legacy to companies such as the MERCURY THEATER and the GROUP THEATER. CHARLES LONDON

civic theatre Term used to describe theatres usually built and mainly supported by a local community or funded by local government, often along with other funding sources, for the betterment of the community's cultural health and standing. Also known as municipal theatre. Britain's first locally funded civic theatre, the Belgrade in Coventry, was named in honour of a gift, from the Yugoslav capital, of wood that was used in the building. It was also the first new theatre to be opened – in 1958 – after the Second World War. Scotland's first civic theatre was Edinburgh's nineteenth-century LYCEUM, which the Corporation bought in 1964. In the United States, where the term is less widely applied, it tended to be used before the Second World War in relation to amateur companies that received public grants. After the war, local subscriptions did found professional theatres, such as the GUTHRIE in Minneapolis. The tradition of civic theatre, however, is most strongly established in continental Europe. CHARLES LONDON
See also ARCHITECTURE.

Cixous, Hélène *see* THÉÂTRE DU SOLEIL

Claire, Ina [Inez Fagan] (b. Washington DC, 15 Oct. 1895; d. New York, Feb. 1985) Comedienne who made her New York debut aged 14, when she was already a noteworthy mimic and VAUDEVILLE singer. In 1911 she performed in her first musical comedy, *Jumping Jupiter*. Claire was a beautiful woman with an unusual gift for high comedy; she was hailed as the finest comedienne of her generation and was called the 'Comic Spirit incarnate' by the critic JOHN MASON BROWN. She enjoyed many great successes in the 1920s and continued acting until 1954, when she made her final performance in *The Confidential Clerk*.
ADRIANA HUNTER

Clark, Bobby [Robert Edwin] (b. Springfield, Ohio, 16 June 1888; d. New York, 12 Feb. 1960) and **McCullough, Paul** (b. Springfield, Ohio, 1883; d. Boston, Mass., 25 March 1936) Comics. They established an act, drawn from the antics of clowning that they learnt in the CIRCUS, that lasted from 1905 until McCullough's death, and during which they made 36 two-reel comedies as well as popular appearances on stage in musical REVUES. Their first big success was in London in *Chuckles of 1922*, which they followed with appearances in IRVING BERLIN's *Music Box Revue of*

1922, and stole the show with their routine in GEORGE and IRA GERSHWIN's *Strike Up the Band* (1930). Despite the blow of the stooge McCullough's suicide in 1936, Clark managed to sustain his irrepressible style of humour in shows like ZIEGFELD, *Star and Garter* (1942) and *Mexican Hayride* (1944), playing a mix of musical comedy and operetta, culminating in *Damn Yankees*, with which he toured in 1956.   HELEN RAPPAPORT

R. L. Taylor, *The Running Pianist* (1950)

Clark, Brian [Robert] (b. Bournemouth, 2 June 1932)   Playwright and publisher. Clark taught drama and contributed to Portable Theatre's controversial group projects, including *Lay By* (1971). He then wrote popular, well-crafted studies, with strong leading roles, of menopausal crises and disrupted bourgeois lives (e.g. *Whose Life Is It Anyway?*, televised 1972, staged 1978, filmed 1981; from the proceeds he founded a theatre publishing firm, Amber Lane Press).   TONY HOWARD

Clark, J. P.   *see* BEKEDEREMO-CLARK, J. P.

Clark, Michael   *see* DESIGN; GAY THEATRE

Clarke, Austin [Augustine Joseph] (b. Dublin, 9 May 1896; d. Dublin, 19 March 1974)   Poet, critic and playwright. He founded the Dublin Verse-Speaking Society in 1940 and, during his lifetime, was considered the natural successor to YEATS. His plays include *The Son of Learning* (1927), *The Flame* (1932), *Black Fast* (1942), *The Kiss* (1944), *The Plot is Ready* (1943), *The Second Kiss* (1946), *The Plot Succeeds* (1950) and *The Moment Next to Nothing* (1958). His plays, many set in medieval times, often have a satiric tinge.
CHRISTOPHER FITZ-SIMON

Clarke, Doreen (b. Middleton, Lancs, 6 May 1928) Playwright. She left school at the age of 14 to work in cotton mills and factories, and emigrated to Australia in 1958. Largely self-taught as a writer, she turned to plays in the mid-1970s after short stories and television sketches, and has worked extensively in COMMUNITY THEATRE, for which she has written over 20 plays. Her strengths are her women characters, who stand at the centre of her work; whether they are former prostitutes, battered wives or simply working-class women asserting themselves in a difficult environment, they are notable for their vitality, humour and sense of themselves. Plays include *Roses in Due Season* (1978), *Bleedin' Butterflies* (1980), *Farewell Brisbane Ladies* (1981) and *Cornerstone* (1990).   MICHAEL MORLEY

Clarke, Martha (b. Baltimore, Md., 3 June 1944) Trained as a dancer, this AVANT-GARDE director boldly experiments with the relationships between dance,

movement and theatre. *A Metamorphosis in Miniature* (1982), based on the work of Kafka, established the form with which she would experiment throughout her career: a blending of movement, images and fragmentary texts to create a dream-like but visceral collage. She followed this with *The Garden of Earthly Delights* (1948), an interpretation of the hallucinatory Hieronymus Bosch painting. For *Vienna: Lusthaus* (1986), she collaborated with playwright Charles Mee, Jr and set designer ROBERT ISRAEL to create a world of decay and decadence in *fin-de-siècle* Vienna. Clarke distilled texts by Kafka and Italo Calvino into haunting visual and textual tapestries to create, respectively, *The Hunger Artist* (1987) and *Miracolo d'Amore* (1988). The recipient of several awards, Clarke became disillusioned with the theatre, and shifted her focus to OPERA in the 1990s, staging works for such companies as the Glimmerglass Opera and the New York City Opera.
SARAH STEVENSON

classical drama   *see* ANCIENT GREEK DRAMA IN THE TWENTIETH CENTURY; ROMAN DRAMA IN THE TWENTIETH CENTURY

Claudel, Paul [Louis Charles Marie] (b. Villeneuve-sur-Fère, France, 6 August 1868; d. Paris, 23 Feb. 1955)   Playwright, poet and diplomat. Despite his reputation as a reactionary (based mainly on his political and religious views), in the theatre he was a radical experimenter. At every stage he subtly adapted contemporary techniques to serve his own ends. His idiosyncratic form of Catholicism created a highly dramatic form of poetic theatre, both by portraying conflict, and by imagery and atmosphere. The rhythmic energy, vocal beauty and emotional intensity of Claudel's highly original form of free verse dominates.

His first plays (1889–94) were on the model of the contemporary SYMBOLIST theatre. In place of that theatre's comparative looseness, incoherence and passivity, Claudel brought a new vitality and a new coherence based on recognizable families of symbols, Nietzschean in *Tête d'Or* ('Golden head', written 1889), anarchistic in *La Ville* (*The City*, written 1893), Catholic throughout. During the 1890s this model was modified to yield far greater simplicity of action and a situation whereby a very real, contemporary world and a super-real world of mystery exist alongside each other, the one illustrating the other. *Partage de Midi* (*Break of Noon*, written 1905) is both the climax of these trends and the basis for a new departure. In this depiction of an adulterous love affair, the roles of the two planes of reality are reversed. Where human relationships had served merely to reflect symbolic meanings on a higher plane, now the highly charged emotions of the protagonists are the central theme, to be explained by that higher reality. The reality of unhappy love dominates Claudel's subsequent plays; the lovers' salvation through suffering is transformed into the universal theme of the salvation of the world through vicarious suffering. These plays are now set in the past: in the Middle Ages – *L'Annonce faite à Marie* (*The Tidings Brought to Mary*, 1912); *Jeanne d'Arc au bûcheric* (*Joan at the Stake*, 1938); 1789–1870 – *L'Otage* (*The Hostage*, written 1912); *Le Pain dur* (*The Crusts, or Hard Bread*, written 1914); *Le Pere humilié* (*The Humiliated Father*, written 1916); and the Counter-Reformation – *Le Soulier de Satin* (*The Satin Slipper*, written 1924); *Le Livre de Christophe Colomb* (*The Book of Christopher Columbus*, 1930).

With *Le Soulier de Satin* we enter on Claudel's most exciting phase, in which he uses all the techniques of the modern theatre, but adds his own twist. Everything is geared to show that this is not reality, but the author's play; using the same techniques, Claudel shows that the world, similarly, is merely God's play.

Claudel's interest in the integration of drama and music, shown by his collaborations with the composers Milhaud and Honegger, is merely one aspect of his interest in practical theatre in this period. His remarkable collaboration with JEAN-LOUIS BARRAULT, from 1941 to 1954, caused him completely to recast certain plays. Their productions, starting with *Le Soulier de Satin*, revealed a completely new Claudel, and he continues to be performed in France, being seen as a major force. Outside France he has had less success. RICHARD GRIFFITHS

Joseph Chiari, *The Poetic Drama of Paul Claudel* (1954)
Richard Griffiths, ed., *Claudel: A Reappraisal* (1968)

Claus, Hugo [Maurice Julien] (b. Bruges, 5 April 1929) Playwright, novelist and poet. Erudite, eclectic and prolific, he writes in Dutch and Flemish, often depicting themes from rural life, as in *Bruid in de Morgen* (*A Bride in the Morning*, 1953), *Suiker* (*Sugar*, 1958) and the play for which he is best known internationally, *Vrijdag* (*Friday*, 1969; Royal Court 1971). Claus has also written epics (e.g. *Serenade*, 1984) and many translations and adaptations of classical plays (e.g. by Seneca, Shakespeare, Ben Jonson and De Rojas). He is a leading postwar Belgian writer of experimental novels and poetry. HELEN RAPPAPORT

Clements, John [Selby] (b. London, 25 April 1910; d. Brighton, 6 April 1988) Actor–manager. Clements founded the Intimate Theatre in Palmers Green, north London, in 1935, planning and performing in its weekly repertory of contemporary and classical plays.

He was an accomplished actor, enjoying many triumphs – some alongside his wife, Kay Hammond – in his own and other productions, but it was in his capacity as a manager that he excelled; he managed the St James's, the Phoenix, the Saville and the CHICHESTER FESTIVAL THEATRE, and was renowned for his spirited though conventional revivals of classic comedies (e.g. PINERO, SHAW, WILDE). He was knighted in 1968. ADRIANA HUNTER

Cleveland Play House America's oldest producing regional theatre, founded in Ohio in 1915 as an amateur group to present native plays. Its opening season came in 1916 under its first president Charles S. Brooks and its first director Raymond O'Neil. The company became professional under Frederic McConnell in 1921. In 1927 a two-theatre complex was opened (the 500-seat Drury and the 160-seat Brooks) and in 1983 a third theatre was added (the 625-seat Bolton). The Cleveland Play House concentrates on producing new and classic plays and ranks among the country's premier regional theatres. ELLEN LAMPERT-GRÉAUX

J. M. Flory, *The Cleveland Play House: How It Began* (1965)

Close, Glenn (b. Greenwich, Conn., 19 March 1947) Actress. She studied drama and anthropology before joining the New Phoenix Repertory Company, making her Broadway debut in Congreve's *Love for Love* (1974), followed by *The Rules of the Game* and *The Member of the Wedding* in 1974–5. A varied stage career followed in regional productions such as *King Lear*, *Uncle Vanya* and *A Streetcar Named Desire*, as well as an OFF-BROADWAY appearance in WENDY WASSERSTEIN's *Uncommon Women and Others* (1977) and a return to Broadway in *The Crucifer of Blood* (1978). A supporting role in the Broadway musical *Barnum* (1980) – which she played for over 300 performances – brought her to the attention of Hollywood and a major film career. On stage, Simone Benmussa's *The Singular Life of Albert Nobbs* (1982) was followed by Tony awards for *The Real Thing* (1984), Ariel Dorfman's *Death and the Maiden* (1992) and *Sunset Boulevard* (1993). HELEN RAPPAPORT

closet drama A play – often in verse – written to be read rather than performed, such as *The Dynasts* (1904–8) by THOMAS HARDY (which later was adapted for performance by GRANVILLE BARKER). The form found most favour among the nineteenth-century English Romantic poets, but survived into the twentieth century as a branch of literature. CHARLES LONDON

clown The word made its first appearance in the English language in the sixteenth century, derived from the term 'clod' or country bumpkin. A lineage can be traced from the COMMEDIA DELL'ARTE through the English PANTOMIME tradition and clowns like Grimaldi to the MUSIC HALL tradition of Laurel and Hardy, Keaton and Chaplin.

Whether in the form of Vidusaka (literally 'one given to abuse') and Vita – the clever rogue – of Hindu epic drama, the clever and verbal *wen ch'ou* or the dim and physical *wu ch'ou* of classical Setzuan Chinese theatre, the medieval *jongleur,* the *commedia*'s Zanni, European court jesters, Coco of British circus fame or even television slapstick comedians (e.g. Benny Hill), the figure of the clown is an archetype of irreverence and burlesque that continually reappears regardless of geography and culture. In ritual drama or Western CIRCUS, the clown is known both by exaggerated costumes (motley) and grotesque, colourful makeup (in the West, whiteface signifies the 'straight' clown; 'august', the bumbling comic fool). The clown acts out the human impulse to anarchy inherent in the most solemn occasions. Despite his lofty ritual function, the aim of the professional clown is above all to provide comic entertainment. As 'Prince' Paul Alpert, the celebrated dwarf clown of America's Ringling Circus often advised beginners, 'When in doubt, drop your pants.'

Twentieth-century drama has been deeply influenced by the clown, most notably in the work of BRECHT. With the outstanding exception of BECKETT in *Waiting for Godot*, the influence has mostly been to enhance social comment or satire – a thread that links the works of WEDEKIND, MEYERHOLD and MAYAKOVSKY with that of LITTLEWOOD, MNOUCHKINE, FO and the ALTERNATIVE THEATRE of El TEATRO CAMPESINO, BREAD AND PUPPET THEATER and the SAN FRANCISCO MIME TROUPE. TREVOR GRIFFITHS subverted the routine of GROCK in *Comedians*, and PETER BARNES's visionary clown monk Flote in *Red Noses* is a medium for mirth.
MICHAEL KARP & MITCH MITCHELSON

Joel Schechter, *Durov's Pig* (1985)
Tony Staveacre, *Slapstick* (1987)

club theatre Theatre that is open only to club members, usually in order to circumvent legal restrictions and/or to be innovative. Club theatres are often short-lived. After both world wars, for example, they flourished briefly in Britain, offering a challenge to the plays of the commercial theatre. While CENSORSHIP was operated by the LORD CHAMBERLAIN, many theatres turned themselves into clubs to stage plays that had been refused a licence; for example, the New Watergate Club at the Comedy Theatre, London (1956–7) presented plays by ARTHUR MILLER, TENNESSEE WILLIAMS and ROBERT ANDERSON on homosexual themes, and

the ROYAL COURT became a club to stage EDWARD BOND's *Saved* in 1965. CHARLES LONDON

clubs Mostly a hangover from earlier eras, theatrical clubs survived into the twentieth century but rarely caught up with it. Membership of London's Garrick Club, founded in 1831 in honour of the actor David Garrick and situated in Covent Garden, remains limited in number and gender (i.e. men). It boasts a notable library, a collection of memorabilia and outstanding portraits. New York's equivalent – the Players Club, founded in 1888 – also houses a fine collection of ephemera and an extensive library, but on Shakespeare's birthday in 1989 it admitted women. HELEN HAYES became its first female member and in 1994 Lynn Redgrave became its first female president.

There are many audience clubs, such as Britain's Gallery First Nighters (1896–1996), usually offering cut-price tickets. Theatres have their own subscription and supporters clubs and actors have their own clubs too, such as the Theatrical Ladies Guild. Most of these follow the lead given by HENRY IRVING when he founded the Green Room Club in London in 1877 as a place to relax and, most importantly, get a drink after hours. CHARLES LONDON

G. Boas, *The Garrick Club, 1831–1947* (1948)

Clunes, Alec [Alexander Sheriff de Moro] (b. London, 17 May 1912; d. London, 13 March 1970) Actor, director and manager. Clunes began his career in 1934 with BEN GREET's company, the OLD VIC and later the Malvern Festival. His acting was eclipsed when he took over the small ARTS THEATRE Club in 1942, running it for eight years as a producing venue. Clunes championed SHAW and new work, with premières from FRY (who wrote *The Lady's Not For Burning*, 1948, on a salary from Clunes, who played the lead), USTINOV and WHITING (whose *Saint's Day*, 1951, was defiantly produced to critical hostility). He also brought new European drama and forgotten British work to public attention, and the Arts earned the nickname of the 'mini' NATIONAL THEATRE before the real thing existed. His acting included an admired Claudius to SCOFIELD's *Hamlet* (1955), and the Bishop of Chichester in *Soldiers* (1968). DAN REBELLATO

J. C. Trewin, *Alec Clunes* (1958).

Clurman, Harold [Edgar] (b. New York, 18 Sept. 1901; d. New York, 9 Sept. 1980) Director, critic, manager, author and lecturer. As co-founder and co-artistic director of the GROUP THEATER, as successful Broadway director, as working theatre critic for three decades, as educator in and out of the academy, Clurman was one of the most influential figures in modern American theatre. After an apprenticeship in the 1920s with EUGENE O'NEILL and ROBERT EDMOND JONES at the Greenwich Village Theater, study with JACQUES COPEAU in France and RICHARD BOLESLAVSKY in America, and play-reading for the THEATER GUILD, Clurman, together with LEE STRASBERG and CHERYL CRAWFORD, founded the Group Theater in 1930. As the young Group searched for its voice, Clurman essentially served as manager, dramaturg, and master teacher. After the sensational debut of *Waiting for Lefty* by Group member CLIFFORD ODETS outside Group auspices, Clurman decided to direct (for the first time) an earlier Odets script, *Awake and Sing!* This successful effort in 1935 initiated the symbiotic relationship between Odets and his theatre, with Clurman directing all of Odets' subsequent plays during the life of the Group.

After the demise of the Group in 1941, Clurman turned briefly to films, serving as producer/director for several Hollywood studios from 1941 to 1946. His heart, however, remained in the New York theatre, where he soon returned to resume his career as director. During the 1950s he directed some of the most important plays of the decade, including McCULLERS' *The Member of the Wedding* (1950), HELLMAN's *Autumn Garden* (1951), INGE's *Bus Stop* (1955), WILLIAMS' *Orpheus Descending* (1957), and O'NEILL's *A Touch of the Poet* (1958).

Always highly verbal (often circulating long analyses to the Group membership), Clurman formally began to write theatre criticism in the late 1940s, first for the *New Republic* (1949–52) and then for the *Nation* (1953 to the end of his life). During 1959 and 1963 he was guest critic for the London *Observer*. As a critic he was knowledgeable without being pedantic, forceful without being strident or personal. In the 1960s he initiated yet another career in academe, serving as professor of theater at the City University of New York from 1964 until his death. He wrote *The Fervent Years* (1945, a history of the Group Theater), *Lies Like Truth* (1958, collection of theatre essays and reviews), *On Directing* (1973, reflections on the craft of directing) and *All People Are Famous* (1978, a loosely structured autobiography). His *Collected Works: Six Decades of Commentary on Theater, Dance, Music, and Film* appeared in 1996.

GERALD RABKIN

Cobb, Lee J. [Leo Jacoby] (b. New York, 9 Dec. 1911; d. Woodland Hills, Calif., 11 Feb. 1976)   Actor. He made his debut in 1929 and from 1935 to 1942 appeared on Broadway in numerous plays, many with

the GROUP THEATER, and then went to Hollywood. His most famous role was Willy Loman in MILLER's *Death of a Salesman* (1949).   GERALD BORDMAN

Cochran, Charles [Blake] (b. Brighton, 25 Sept. 1872; d. London, 31 Jan. 1951)   Producer. After acting in New York he soon transferred to the other side of the footlights as a publicist, agent, personal manager, promoter (of boxing, wrestling, rodeo, roller-skating, CIRCUS) and eventually a fully fledged theatrical producer whose taste ranged from IBSEN (*John Gabriel Borkman*, 1897) to REINHARDT (*The Miracle*, 1911). He claimed to have personally supervised 128 productions in London between 1914 and 1950. His great success was with REVUE and his trademark was 'Mr Cochran's Young Ladies' who rivalled the ZIEGFELD Girls in America. He had a close professional association with NOEL COWARD and first presented his *On with the Dance* (1925), *This Year of Grace* (1928), *Bitter Sweet* (1929), *Private Lives* (1930), *Words and Music* (1932), *Cavalcade* (1931) and *Conversation Piece* (1934). After the Second World War his favourite writer was A. P. Herbert, who gave him two comparative failures and a major success in *Bless the Bride* (1947). His main talent was as a showman, as he acknowledged in the titles of two of his four autobiographical volumes (*Secrets of a Showman*, 1925; *Showman Looks On*, 1945) and his skill at recognizing talent to which he then gave ample opportunities and creative freedom. He was knighted in 1948, and in 1973 he was celebrated in a show using his nickname, *Cockie*.   IAN BEVAN

Cocteau, Jean [Maurice Eugène Clément]   (b. Maisons-Lafitte, nr Paris, 5 July 1889; d. Milly-la-Forêt, nr Paris, 11 Oct. 1963)   Poet, novelist, set designer, choreographer, actor, stage director and celebrated film-maker; as a playwright he was the great innovator. Overwhelmed by the Russian ballet in 1909, when DIAGHILEV invited the young man to astonish him, he did just that. He dabbled in MIME and SURREALISM (*Parade*, 1916; *Les Mariés de la Tour Eiffel/The Eiffel Tower Wedding Party*, 1921), he launched the fashion for modernizing Greek myth (*Antigone*, 1922; *Orphée*, 1926; *La Machine infernale* – his seminial *The Infernal Machine*, 1934; *Oedipe-roi*, 1937), and he flirted with mystical legend (*Les Chevaliers de la Table Ronde/The Knights of the Round Table*, 1937), French classical tragedy (*Renaud et Armide*, 1943), romatic melodrama (*L'Aigle à deux têtes/The Eagle Has Two Heads*, 1946), boulevard drama (*La Voix humaine/The Human Voice*, 1930; *Les Parents terribles/Intimate Relations*, 1938) and even philosophy à la SARTRE (*Bacchus*, 1951). He often successfully combined in the same play elements considered until then impossible to fuse.

Following the nineteenth-century poet Mallarmé's call for a pure theatre in which all the arts participate and 'anything can happen', he collaborated with PICASSO, Chanel and the new composers: SATIE, Honegger, Milhaud and STRAVINSKY. Yet he remained bewitched by the great stars of the boulevard, from *les monstres sacrés* such as SARAH BERNHARDT to Arletty, EDITH PIAF and Edwige Feuillère, with whom he worked. He 'created' the actor Jean Marais.

Often reviled as an effete dilettante or mere publicity-seeker, this 'frivolous prince', as GENET called him, always maintained he was sugaring the pill, inviting the audience to look beyond the *parade* for a deeper significance conveyed not by 'poetry *in* the theatre' but by the 'poetry *of* the theatre'. Like the actor's art, a play should both attract and repel belief. It is a lie that tells the truth. Our life is an enigma. All the poet can do to unravel 'the difficulty of being' is to unveil the complex relationship of life and form, illusion and reality.

Cocteau popularized theatrical metaphor and metaphysical drama, anticipated the ABSURD, recalling JARRY's use of objects by his use of mirrors, chess pieces, talking flowers and horses – and, with his plays and films, became an international icon.
DONALD WATSON

Francis Fergusson, *The Idea of a Theatre* (1949)
Neal Oxenhandler, *Scandal and Parade: The Theatre of Jean Cocteau* (1957)

Codron, Michael [Victor] (b. London, 8 June 1930)   Producer. He gained his early theatrical experience as an assistant to JACK HYLTON, who recommended him to produce the record-breaking *Salad Days* (1954). He became an independent producer with the safely commercial *Ring for Catty* (1956), but soon distinguished himself by recognizing the worth of such writers as HAROLD PINTER (first productions of *The Birthday Party*, 1958, and *The Caretaker*, 1960) and JOE ORTON (first production of *Entertaining Mr Sloane*, 1964) as well as finding solid commercial returns in such plays as *There's a Girl in My Soup* (2,547 performances), *The Philanthropist* (1,114) and *Noises Off* (1,912). He also helped begin the careers of, among others, SIMON GRAY, HENRY LIVINGS, FRANK MARCUS, JAMES SAUNDERS and CHARLES WOOD. After the death of HUGH BEAUMONT in 1973 he was without rival as London's leading commercial producer of straight plays, with the unusual reputation of placing first emphasis on writers and directors rather than on stars. As a result he is the favoured producer of such writers as MICHAEL FRAYN and ALAN AYCKBOURN. He entered a business association with the American producer JAMES NEDERLANDER to operate the Aldwych and Adelphi Theatres in London, as well as running on his own account the Vaudeville Theatre until 1996.   IAN BEVAN

Coghlan, Rose (b. Peterborough, England, 18 March 1851; d. Harrison, NY, 2 April 1932)   Child star and actress. Her first performances were in London and on provincial tours before she settled in the United States in 1877. Here she became a star player with Lester Wallack's ensemble until it folded in 1888, appearing in a string of classic roles which included *School for Scandal* and *As You Like It*. Returning to London in the 1890s, she appeared most notably in *A Woman of No Importance* (1893) – which she also produced in the United States – and *Mrs Warren's Profession*, with which she toured the United States in 1907. Her long stage career continued to bring her success in America after it had waned in Britain, where her acting style had begun to seem stilted and out of date. She saw in her acting jubilee in 1916, making her last appearances in *Our Betters* (1917) and *Deburau* (1920).   HELEN RAPPAPORT

Cohan [Keohane], George M[ichael] (b. Providence, RI, 3 July 1878; d. New York, 5 Nov. 1942)   Performer, producer and playwright. Born into a family of VAUDEVILLE artists, Cohan played with the family act from a young age before, in his early twenties, developing their performance into a show on the lines of nineteenth-century musical farce comedies (*The Governor's Son*, 1901). His brash, colloquial, back-chat dialogue, his breezy, catchy songs, his vigorous performance of his own numbers and his accomplished dancing first found significant success in what remained his best musical, *Little Johnny Jones* (1904). Thereafter he became, both as an author and a performer, the epitome of home-grown American musical comedy theatre – much of it in his own theatre and produced by SAM HARRIS. His subsequent career embraced all aspects of the musical theatre – writing, composing, performing, directing and producing – but he is largely remembered for the best of his show songs: 'The Yankee Doodle Boy', 'Give My Regards to Broadway' (*Little Johnny Jones*), 'Mary's a Grand Old Name' (*Forty Five Minutes from Broadway*, 1905), 'Harrigan' (*Fifty Miles from Boston*, 1908), 'Nellie Kelly, I Love You' (*Little Nellie Kelly*, 1922). He was also seen as a performer in his later years in O'NEILL's *Ah, Wilderness!* (1933) and the musical *I'd Rather Be Right* (1937). His autobiography, *Twenty Years of Broadway and the Years It Took to Get There*, appeared in 1925. His life was the basis for a film (1942) and the musical *George M* (1968).
KURT GÄNZL

John McCabe, *George M. Cohan, The Man Who Owned Broadway* (1973)

W. Morehouse, *George M. Cohan: Prince of the American Theater* (1943).

Cohan, Robert   *see* DANCE

Cole, Jack   (b. New Brunswick, NJ, 27 April 1914; d. Los Angeles, 17 Feb. 1974) Dancer and choreographer. He first danced on Broadway in a 1934 failure, *Caviar*. In 1943 he was given his initial chance to choreograph a Broadway show, *Something for the Boys*. Later that year he both choreographed and danced in the ZIEGFELD FOLLIES of 1943. Subsequent successes included *Kismet* (1953), *A Funny Thing Happened on the Way to the Forum* (1962) and *Man of La Mancha* (1965). His style reflected his interests in JAZZ and orientalia.
GERALD BORDMAN
   See also CHOREOGRAPHY; DANCE.

G. Loney, *Unsung Genius: The Passion of Dancer–Choreographer Jack Cole* (1984)

Coleman, Cy [Seymour Kaufman]   (b. New York, 14 July 1929)   Composer. Coleman gave concerts as a child prodigy and also studied in New York. His fondness for JAZZ prompted him to become a nightclub pianist. Although he had interpolated songs earlier, his first full score was not heard until *Wildcat* (1960). This was followed by the success of *Little Me* (1962), *Sweet Charity* (1966), *I Love My Wife* (1977), *On the Twentieth Century* (1978), *Barnum* (1980), *City of Angels* (1989) and *The Will Rogers Follies* (1991). Coleman is the most prolific and consistently successful of his generation of Broadway composers. His melodies are often catchy, if slightly honky-tonk.   GERALD BORDMAN

Coliseum   Designed by FRANK MATCHAM as a VARIETY theatre for Oswald STOLL, the 'Collie' opened in 1904 with several innovations: the first revolve in Britain, three revolves that moved separately, a mobile lounge, lifts to upper levels, postal facilities in the foyer and an Italianate terracotta exterior topped by a cupola and globe that have made the theatre a landmark, just off Trafalgar Square. Seating 2,358, it is London's largest working theatre, and has hosted the likes of SARAH BERNHARDT, LILLIE LANGTRY and GROCK as well as spectacle (a jockey was killed during a Derby Day recreation), fantasy (HELPMANN's *Peter Pan*), ballet (courtesy of DIAGHILEV), musicals (*Annie Get Your Gun* ran for more than 1,000 performances), cinema and opera (it became the home of the English National Opera, which brought the freehold in 1992).
CHARLES LONDON

F. Barker, *The House that Stoll Built* (1957)

collective   Theatre group in which financial, aesthetic and executive responsibilities are shared by all the members. This model found most favour in the 1960s and 1970s with ALTERNATIVE and THEATRE IN EDUCATION groups like the SAN FRANCISCO MIME TROUPE, La Commune, FOCO NOVO and MONSTROUS REGIMENT. In practice, many groups found collective methods difficult when negotiating with hierarchical venues and funding authorities, and groups like JOINT STOCK, MABOU MINES and the WOOSTER GROUP retained elements of hierarchical organization while using methods of collective creation. Inspired by pioneering collectives such as the LIVING THEATER, this method encouraged the equal collaboration of all and often used IMPROVISATION to this end. Many POLITICAL THEATRE groups embraced this form of creativity which is popular also with alternative companies (e.g. WELFARE STATE), feminist groups (e.g. AT THE FOOT OF THE MOUNTAIN) and in THIRD THEATRE.
DAN REBELLATO

Colombia   *see* SOUTH AMERICA

Colum, Padraic   (b. Longford, Ireland, 8 Dec. 1881; d. Connecticut, 11 Jan. 1972)   Poet and playwright. He may be said, with SYNGE, to be the creator of the Irish rural drama. *Broken Soil* (1903) was produced by the National Theatre Society a year before it took out the lease on the ABBEY THEATRE; later retitled *The Fiddler's House*, it concerns a young man's choice in leaving home for the life of the vagrant musician, implying that the truly creative opt for the difficult road. *The Land* (1905) was highly successful but has proved too particular to its period to warrant major revival. *Thomas Muskerry* (1910), a realistic play of workhouse life, is probably the most likely to survive. *Mogu of the Desert* (1931) is a romantic fantasy. *Moytura* (1961) is a short drama in the *noh* convention. Colum spent the latter half of his life lecturing in the United States.
CHRISTOPHER FITZ-SIMON

Zack R. Bowen, *Padraic Colum: A Biographical-Critical Introduction (1970)*

Colway Theatre Trust   *see* COMMUNITY PLAY

Comden, Betty [Basya Cohen]   (b. New York, 3 May 1915)   Having begun as a performer in a nightclub act, Comden established a lyric writing partnership with fellow performer **Adolph Green** (b. New York, 2 Dec. 1915) which grew from devising cabaret material for themselves and others to a first full BROADWAY musical in *On the Town* (1944). That show's success set in orbit the most durable lyric and occasionally book-writing pairing in musical theatre history, in which *Wonderful Town* (1953), *Bells Are Ringing* (1956), written

169

to feature Judy Holliday who had been a member of their act, *Applause* (1970) and *On the Twentieth Century* (1982) have been notable successes. A sizeable period of the pair's early career was spent in Hollywood where they provided scripts and songs for many musical films, including *Singin' in the Rain*, which they subsequently adapted for an unfortunate Broadway version. KURT GÄNZL

Comédie-Française France's national company, formed in 1680, but not at the cutting edge of theatre in the twentieth century. Four great directors, BATY, COPEAU, DULLIN and JOUVET, tried to revive its reputation in the 1930s and another, BARRAULT, briefly brought it new recognition during the Second World War. Various reforms have been attempted since, under Jean-Pierre Vincent (1983–6) and notably ANTOINE VITEZ (1988–90) who died in post, but it remains a heritage theatre. CHARLES LONDON

J. Lorcey, *La Comédie-Française* (1980)

comedy One of the basic categories of Western drama, taking its name from the Greek word meaning 'to revel' and considered since ARISTOTLE as opposed to TRAGEDY, although far more varied in its manifestations. The rise of realism at the end of the nineteenth century and the subsequent tradition of MODERNISM continued an indifference to the classic genres that had been found among the romantic dramatists and theorists who were following Shakespeare's example. In the twentieth century, playwrights freely mixed serious and comic elements and sought to maintain a delicate balance between these moods (as does CHEKHOV in *The Cherry Orchard*); individual productions may vary widely in how seriously or comically they regard the work.

The main Western comic tradition derives from the ROMAN authors Plautus and Terence, combined with various popular, non-literary comic forms of the Renaissance such as COMMEDIA DELL'ARTE. Both strands drew heavily on stock characters and situations – e.g. young lovers, elderly characters who thwart them, clever servants – which have been utilized ever since through to the present. Traditional comedy deals with ordinary people, is written in prose, seeks to provide amusement and laughter, and ends happily, often with a marriage. Conventionally, the so-called higher forms emphasize thought, language and character, as in the comedy of manners, a tradition of wit and intrigue exemplified by WILDE and COWARD. In its 'lower' forms, such as FARCE, comedy emphasizes physical humour, crude jokes, and thinner, more stereotyped characterizations. Such distinctions have

been challenged throughout the modern era (e.g. by writers such as FEYDEAU or ORTON) while maintaining the moral function of comedy as a social release or corrective, a theme explored by GRIFFITHS in *Comedians* (1975).

Distinctions within comedy have multiplied: SHAW developed an influential comedy of ideas; the strategies of SATIRE took on different comic forms (e.g. in plays by BENNETT, HARE, MAMET, STOPPARD); but the major shift came in the wake of the Second World War. Many dramatists felt that the Kafkaesque modern world of mass destruction, anonymous bureaucracies and apparently meaningless suffering could best be represented by grotesque comedy or by comedy utilizing the materials of tragedy, variously called tragicomedy, dark comedy or BLACK COMEDY. Closely related to such work was the THEATRE OF THE ABSURD, as its title, derived from CAMUS' and Kierkegaard's explorations of meaninglessness, suggests. In a subversion of domestic and drawing-room comedy, the related comedy of menace arose, as seen in the work of PINTER.

An important subdivision of comedy in the modern theatre is the MUSICAL comedy, differing from OPERA in being a spoken drama with interspersed songs. The background of musical comedy is extremely complex, and includes the continental *opera buffa* and operetta, the English ballad opera and works of GILBERT and SULLIVAN (all indebted in turn to the classic comedy tradition), and such American forms as the BURLESQUE, extravaganza and VAUDEVILLE. MARVIN CARLSON

See also DRAMATIC THEORY.

James Feibleman, *In Praise of Comedy* (1939)
Paul Lauter, ed., *Theories of Comedy* (1964)
Elder Olsen, *The Theory of Comedy* (1968)
Wylie Sypher, ed., *Comedy* (1956)

command performance A stage show given by order of, and in the presence of, a reigning ruler. In Britain the tradition dates back to Richard III, who maintained a company of players at court. During the twentieth century, the Royal Command Performance became an annual VARIETY showcase featuring popular comedians, singers and light entertainers who gave their services free of charge. The show is presented to an invited audience and is televised worldwide. Proceeds from the performance are donated to charity. MARIE PETCHELL

commedia dell'arte Literally 'comedy of professional actors', it probably has its roots in ROMAN times but became a recognizable genre of POPULAR THEATRE in the sixteenth and seventeenth centuries, when troupes of Italian performers toured Europe with plays they improvised from agreed scenarios based on typical characters who were known by their masks, e.g. Arlecchino, who became Harlequin. Shakespeare, Molière, Marivaux and Goldoni adapted *commedia*, and the twentieth century has seen renewed interest in its use, most notably by DARIO FO, who has become an expert on its history and adapts its techniques in his political plays and productions. It has influenced other innovators from MEYERHOLD to BARRAULT and, via COPEAU

and SAINT-DENIS, GEORGE DEVINE, as well as attracting new followers in the post-1970s touring FRINGE groups.
TERRY HODGSON

A. Allardyce Nicholl, *The World of Harlequin* (1963)
G. Oreglia, *The Commedia dell'Arte* (1968)
K. and L. Richards, *The Commedia dell'Arte: A Documentary History* (1990)
J. Rudkin, *Commedia dell'Arte* (1994)

· The community play ·

As produced by the Colway Theatre Trust, a relatively new form which bridges the gap between, AMATEUR and professional theatre and introduces a new concept of theatre practice. These community plays aim to involve as many people as possible within a given community, using every available resource: schools, drama societies, local skills and talents grouped around a small professional core. Casts may consist of 180 or more amateur actors of every age and social background. Hundreds more may be involved in every aspect of the work from making costumes to helping with publicity, fundraising, etc. The aim is to produce an original work of art of the highest standard which shall reflect and celebrate the community creating it.

The first such community play was set up in 1978 in Lyme Regis, when Ann Jellicoe wrote and directed a PROMENADE performance of *The Reckoning*, a play about the Monmouth Rebellion which started in Lyme.

As a result of the immense success of this pioneering production, she formed in 1979 the Colway Theatre Trust, based in the south-west of England, to develop the work.

The essential features of a community play, as developed by the Colway Theatre Trust, include the following four elements: (1) a very slow build-up to production (two years is usual) when the community thoroughly and deeply takes on the play as their own, and enthusiasm is generated among as wide a spectrum of the community as possible; (2) a small professional core, including a writer of national standing or the best possible local writer; (3) most of the organizational work being done by the town itself, usually through a system of committees; (4) active follow-up work by the town itself. Community plays always generate new energy and throw up fresh blood. Many participants remark upon a greatly increased social awareness and friendliness. **ANN JELLICOE**

community theatre Lying outside, and usually in opposition to, mainstream theatre, it responds to the concerns and serves the needs of the community in which it is performed.

In the United States, the term refers to a strand of AMATEUR THEATRE, the core of which at the beginning of the twentieth century was the LITTLE THEATRE movement, briefly known also as CIVIC THEATRE. This was seen as having a beneficial effect on the communities in which it flourished. These companies performed in found spaces such as churches, halls or stables, rather than in purpose-built theatres, and were mostly supported by local subscription. They often carried out educational work as well. There were more than 500 by the end of the 1930s, the number rising tenfold in the subsequent three decades. However, some by this Washington, Houston and Cleveland, for example,

had been turned into professional theatres, while others had remained only partly amateur and offered full-scale programmes. The National Theater Conference, which emerged in the 1920s and was formally college theatres, but dissatisfaction with its academic representation led to the founding in 1936 of the American Theater Association. In 1958 this became the umbrella organization for the National Association of Community Theaters, which in 1986 gave way to the American Association of Community Theaters. There was also a movement, triggered in the 1920s by work in North Carolina, called outdoor drama, which specializes in celebrating a noteworthy event in a community's history. The dramas are often repeated annually. CHARLES LONDON

In Britain, community theatre may be defined either geographically or in terms of a 'constituency of interest' (e.g. the working class, an ethnic group, women, the elderly, etc.). Historically, it may be seen as a more radical development from the drive in the 1960s to develop indigenous theatre away from the centre of the metropolis, a development marked by the building of new subsidized regional theatres, and artistically most successful in THEATRE WORKSHOP, east London, and the VICTORIA THEATRE, Stoke-on-Trent.

Although its roots can be traced back to the work of political groups that originated before the Second World War, such as UNITY THEATRE, and later initiatives like Centre 42, community theatre itself originated in the mid-1970s with theatre companies like the HALF MOON, Common Stock and the Combination at the Albany Empire in London; Pentabus and Theatre Foundry in the West Midlands; Perspectives in the East Midlands, Pit Prop in Lancashire, DAC in Yorkshire; Solent People's Theatre in Southampton, Avon Touring in the South-West; Bruvvers in the North-East; and others. Most of these companies' work was performed in local halls, arts centres, clubs, pubs and studio theatres. The very existence and aims of such companies encouraged arts funding bodies like the ARTS COUNCIL, regional arts associations and, much later, some local authorities to establish an administrative structure through which the work of these companies could be brought to their target audiences. The role of local arts officers became much enhanced in this process, and they, along with the general administrative restructuring which took place, comprise some of the more enduring legacies of this period.

Seeking more to relate the content of their work and a democratic method of organization to perceived community concerns than to aim for a specific aesthetic model, different companies brought widely varying artistic approaches to their productions. Radicalism was both aesthetic and organizational. Most companies called themselves COLLECTIVES or 'co-operatives' and, following the 'arts lab' movement of the late 1960s, the wave of HAPPENINGS and visits by American companies like LA MAMA and the LIVING THEATER, companies talked of 'shows' rather than 'plays'. Much of the emphasis was on vivid, physical, non-naturalistic works, often with music and song and various forms of audience participation. BRECHT, GROTOWSKI, MEYERHOLD and COMMEDIA DELL'ARTE were all cited as influences at different times, and to these were added (towards the end of the 1970s) the more indigenous traditions of MUSIC HALL and STAND-UP COMEDY. The latter was aided by the arrival of the Comedy Store in London, giving actors the opportunity to work and sharpen their skills between engagements with the touring companies. Significantly, at this time, actors began to call themselves 'performers'.

An important distinction organizationally was that companies were often performer-led. Instead of seeing themselves as responsible for only their own performances, actors took on responsibility for the content of their work. This led inevitably to their running companies collectively, often devising shows themselves or commissioning writers and hiring directors to fulfil a company 'brief'. Although this brought a greater commitment in performance, it also led increasingly to shows based on generalized issues. The inherent problem of separating collective organization and policy from the need for a unified artistic vision was rarely overcome and generally led to less satisfying work artistically for both actors and playwrights.

Most British community groups were touring companies, though venues which have housed community-orientated theatre (beyond those mentioned above) include CHAPTER ARTS in CARDIFF, Phoenix Arts in LEICESTER, the TRON in GLASGOW, Croydon Warehouse and the Leadmill in SHEFFIELD. Examples of plays include *Taking Our Time* (1978) by RED LADDER, *My Mother Says I Never Should* (1975) by the WOMEN'S THEATRE GROUP, the plays of Les Miller for Inner City (including *Finger in the Pie*, 1985, and *Hot Stuff*, 1987); the plays of JOHN MCGRATH for 7:84 and the LIVERPOOL EVERYMAN, and the plays of STEVE GOOCH at the Half Moon.

In both its organizational and artistic concerns, British community theatre shared much common ground with radical TOURING theatre (7:84, FOCO NOVO, Belt & Braces), and feminist theatre (the WOMEN'S THEATRE GROUP and MONSTROUS REGIMENT), as well as with THEATRE IN EDUCATION and YOUNG PEOPLE'S THEATRE; many companies provided both 'community' and 'young people's' productions, and many actors moved freely between the companies. Always a form of professional theatre, it has less in common with the COMMUNITY PLAY, a term for the production model established by ANN JELLICOE's Colway Theatre Trust, employing professional directors and playwrights (HOWARD BARKER, NICK DARKE, DAVID EDGAR, ARNOLD WESKER) to work with large numbers of amateur performers drawn from the local (usually rural) community, to which the play (usually on a local historical subject) is also performed.

Community theatre offers a vision of a radically different experience for the audience. It seeks to expand that audience in terms of class, age and other social distinctions. It also seeks to expand the aesthetic range of British theatre away from its traditionally realist, verbal, middle-class 'well-made plays'. Requiring as it did huge organizational effort to establish both alternative performing spaces and proper conditions of employment, as well as a new way of seeing theatre, its vision was one of the first casualties of the diminishing real-terms arts subsidy effective in Britain from the late 1970s on. But many of its structural initiatives survived. STEVE GOOCH

See also DOCUMENTARY; OPEN-AIR THEATRE; PLAYWRITING.

'Community Play Archive and Database', held at the Theatre Museum, London
Steve Gooch, *All Together Now* (1984)
Ann Jellicoe, *Community Plays: How to Put Them On* (1987)
Baz Kershaw, *The Politics of Performance: Radical Theatre as Cultural Intervention* (1992)
Albert McCleery and Carl Glick, *Curtains Going Up* (1939)
Percy Mackaye, *The Civic Theatre* (1912)
Eugène Van Erven, *Community Theatre: Global Perspectives* (2001)

Compagnie des Quinze Highly reputed and influential French stage company (1929–34). The artistic descendant of JACQUES COPEAU'S company, its main emphasis was on acting and not scenic spectacle. Its first director was MICHEL SAINT-DENIS. In a characteristic production such as *The Battle of the Marne* (1931), resident writer ANDRÉ OBEY worked closely with the company, improvising domestic and war scenes until casting, staging, costuming, dramatic framework and dialogue became an organic whole. Scenes were played simultaneously, and a kind of EPIC THEATRE evolved at a time before BRECHT was well known in France. The company's visits to London (1931–3) affected a generation of artists who came to shape English Theatre, such as ASHCROFT, DEVINE, GIELGUD and OLIVIER. TERRY HODGSON

Michel Saint-Denis, *Training for the Theatre* (1982)

composing *see* MUSIC

Compton, Edward *see* COMPTON FAMILY

Compton family Family of actors and actor–managers. Henry Compton (1805–77) was a successful actor and theatre manager whose seven children and many remoter descendants made contributions to the English stage. His son Edward (1854–1918) was a celebrated actor–manager who in 1881 founded the Compton Comedy Company, a repertory touring company devoted to the works of great English dramatists such as Shakespeare and Goldsmith. Edward's daughter Fay (1894–1978) was a celebrated actress whose career spanned several decades. She shone in many leading

roles, such as Constance in MAUGHAM's *The Constant Wife* (1927), Ruth in COWARD's *Blithe Spirit* (1941), Marya in CHEKHOV's *Uncle Vanya* (1962), Ophelia in *Hamlet* (1925, 1939) and Lady Bracknell in WILDE's *The Importance of Being Earnest* (1959). ADRIANA HUNTER
See also THEATRE FAMILIES.

L. Warwick, *The Mackenzies Called Compton* (1977)

Compton, Fay *see* COMPTON FAMILY

Congo Republic *see* FRENCH AFRICAN THEATRE

Connelly, Marc [Marcus Cook] (b. McKeesport, Pa., 13 Dec. 1890; d. New York, 21 Dec. 1980) Playwright, producer, director and actor. Born into a family of actors, Connelly developed a love for theatre early in life. He eventually moved to New York, where from 1921 to 1924 he collaborated with GEORGE S. KAUFMAN on several hit comedies, such as *Beggar on Horseback* (1924), bringing a gentle sentimentality to their writing partnership. Connelly's main achievement, however, was *The Green Pastures* (1930), his Pulitzer Prize winning adaptation of Roark Bradford's *Ol' Man Adam and His Chillun* (1928). In this all-black fable, Connelly demonstrated his penchant for the grand theme and an innovative ability to juxtapose fantasy and reality. His autobiography *Voices Offstage* appeared in 1968. ALEXIS GREENE

Paul T. Nolan, *Marc Connelly* (1969)

Conrad, Joseph [Josef Teodor Konrad Nalecz Korzeniowski] (b. Berdczow, Polish Ukraine, 3 Dec. 1857; d. Canterbury, 3 Aug. 1924) Novelist and playwright who translated Shakespeare, Hugo and Bruno Winawer's Polish play (*The Book of Job*, 1931). Conrad developed two plays from short stories (*One Day More*, 1905; *Laughing Anne*, 1920) and wrote two stage versions of *The Secret Agent*, his novel of anarchist London; the second was produced commercially (1923: 11 performances). His situations and psychological mastery remained powerful, but Conrad never found a theatrical substitute for his extraordinary narrative voice. Adaptations by others include Basil Macdonald Hastings' *Victory* (1919) and Howard Brenton's *The Saliva Milkshake* (1975), inspired by *Under Western Eyes*. TONY HOWARD

Cons [Konss], Emma (b. London, 4 March 1838; d. London, 24 July 1912) Philanthropist. She was involved for most of her life in social work in south London, and was one of the first female members of the London County Council. In 1880 she took over the Royal Victoria Hall to create the first temperance music hall in London. Its programme of scientific and cultural lectures developed into Morley College for adult education; its programme of music, ballad concerts, opera and drama established the OLD VIC as a centre of culture, a tradition continued after Cons' death by her niece, LILIAN BAYLIS.   MARVIN CARLSON

constructivism   Soviet artistic movement of the 1920s, inspired by the cubism of PICASSO and by engineering and technology. Its theatrical application of utility over aesthetics is exemplified in MEYERHOLD's version of CROMMELYNCK's *Magnanimous Cuckold* (1922), designed by Liubov Popova (1889–1924). Her 'machine for acting', a set complete with stairs, chutes and a revolving disc, and work-clothes costumes, provided a perfect analogy to Meyerhold's experimental BIOMECHANICS. Through artists such as El Lissitzky, EISENSTEIN and MOHOLY-NAGY constructivism became internationally important, especially via the BAUHAUS. Collectivist in spirit, it influenced contemporary Germany, and its technical elements were later adopted by designers like KOLTAI.   CAROLYN TALARR

Stephen Bann, ed., *The Tradition of Constructivism* (1974)

John Willett, *The New Sobriety 1917–33* (1978)

Cook, Michael   (b. London, 14 Feb. 1933; d. Stratford, Ont., 1994)   Playwright. He migrated to Canada in 1965. His first three stage plays – *Colour the Flesh the Colour of Dust* (1972), *The Head, Guts and Sound Bone Dance* (1973) and *Jacob's Wake* (1975) – constitute what has been called his Newfoundland trilogy, plays linked not by common characters or events but by the spirit and way of life of Newfoundland. Other plays include *Quiller* (1975), *Therese's Creed* (1977), *The Gayden Chronicles* (1980) and *On the Rim of the Curve* (1977).   EUGENE BENSON

Cooney, Ray[mond George Alfred]   (b. London, 30 May 1932)   Playwright, manager, director and actor. As an understudy employed by farceur BRIAN RIX at the WHITEHALL THEATRE, Cooney used his spare time sitting in a dressing room to collaborate with another under-employed member of the company, Tony Hilton, on writing a FARCE of their own. This was *One For The Pot*, which Rix produced at the Whitehall in 1961 for a run of 1,221 performances. Cooney went on to become (often in collaboration with John Chapman, 1927–2001) the most successful writer of stage farces since BEN TRAVERS. Although his plays have not conquered America, they have been played in translation in many countries; and for many years London's West End was seldom without one, and sometimes two, of them. Cooney also directs and produces, and sometimes acts in his own plays. As a manager he was

instrumental in founding the cooperative Theatre of Comedy, which acquired London's Shaftesbury Theatre in 1983 and launched a policy of producing comedies and farces. Unfortunately they ran into financial problems when they produced plays other than those written by Cooney himself – an embarrassing situation which had to be solved by letting the theatre to outside managements. Among Cooney's many successes have been *Chase Me, Comrade* (1964), *Not Now Darling* (1967), *Move Over, Mrs Markham* (1969), *There Goes The Bride* (1974), *Two Into One* (1988) and *Run For Your Wife* (1989). He has also written a book on his favoured genre, *Life in the Farce Lane* (1996).   IAN BEVAN

Cooper, Giles [Stannus]   (b. Carrickmines, Co. Dublin, Ireland, 9 Aug. 1918; d. London, 2 Dec. 1966)   Playwright. Although he wrote successfully for stage and television, Cooper is best remembered for his BBC radio plays. He was preoccupied with the 'inner world' of the mind – as in the bathroom fantasies of the central character in *Under the Loofah Tree* (1958) – and the ease with which we abandon 'respectability'. In *Unman, Wittering and Zigo* (1958), civilized schoolboys become homicidal. In his stage play *Everything in the Garden* (1962), bored suburban housewives turn to prostitution. But despite the 'blackness' of his stylish, economic writing, his work is richly comic. He is commemorated in the annual Giles Cooper awards for radio drama.   DAVID SELF

Cooper, Gladys [Constance]   (b. Lewisham, London, 18 Dec. 1888; d. Henley, Oxon, 17 Dec. 1971)   Actress and manager. She was a much photographed postcard beauty when she was in the chorus and later played small parts in GEORGE EDWARDES' productions of musical comedies. With the help of SEYMOUR HICKS she became an accomplished light comedy actress, and under her own management for some years played leading roles at the Playhouse (London), including the first production of SOMERSET MAUGHAM's *The Sacred Flame* (1929). Her career lasted for more than 60 years and successfully embraced films and television. She wrote two volumes of autobiography, *Gladys Cooper* (1931) and *Without Veils* (1953). Thrice married, she was the mother of actors John Buckmaster and John Merivale, and the mother-in-law of actor ROBERT MORLEY. She was created a dame in 1967.   IAN BEVAN

S. Morley, *Gladys Cooper* (1979)

Cooper, Tommy [Thomas Frederick]   (b. Caerphilly, 19 March 1921; d. London, 15 April 1984)   Conjurer and comedian, an influential giant zany whose main characteristic was incompetence. He was never at ease on a stage, always unsure in what place he ought to stand. He was known by his fez and the catchphrase 'just like that!' His magic tricks either did not work or worked in the most unexpected ways. His jokes were invariably bad. The concealed skill which underlay his acts and his exploitation of the art of anti-climax explored new ways of relating to an audience, of holding their attention and making them laugh. He was the comedian other comedians watched and enjoyed a huge following.

CLIVE BARKER

See also STAND-UP COMEDY.

Copeau, Jacques (b. Paris, 4 Feb. 1879; d. Beaune, 20 Oct. 1949) Actor, director and teacher. As a critic, Copeau was indignant at the 'unbridled commercialization' of the star-based BOULEVARD theatre in Paris, so he set up the tiny Latin Quarter Théâtre du Vieux Colombier (1913) to establish a bridgehead for the total regeneration of the theatre through a return to basic principles: all that was needed was a bare stage. In order to entice writers of quality back to the theatre, Copeau wanted reform in three main areas which pre-occupied him in varying degrees throughout his career: the text, the acting area and training. Celebrated for his public dramatic readings, he was one of the first to emphasize that great texts have rhythms and implicit stage instructions to be deciphered when the director and actors interpret them as if they were musical scores. As with the ENSEMBLE playing of his troupe, the key words for the acting area were simplicity and flexibility. A postwar permanent set, modifiable by the addition of lighting changes and stage elements, provided a foil for the actors speaking the all-important text. It had evolved largely from the stage world dictated by Copeau's hit production of *Twelfth Night* (1914, in part inspired by GRANVILLE BARKER's, seen the year before in London). War closed the theatre but, on the evidence of one season, the company was selected for a propaganda mission to New York where (in the Garrick Theater) a first version of the permanent set, owing much to the efforts of JOUVET, evolved (1917–19).

The ideal of the troupe as a community working together to educate their bodies as expressive instruments appealed to Copeau from the beginning when, like STANISLAVSKY, he took his new company for a stay in the country. His school, the focus of his strongest hopes, opened in 1921, after much experimentation and with the help of his Viola, Suzanne Bing. The classes in MIME stimulated the development of that art in following generations from DECROUX through BARRAULT to MARCEAU. The use of IMPROVISATION and MASKS, especially as developed by the Copiaus (those students who followed Copeau to work for five years in Burgundy after he closed his theatre in 1924) and particularly by his nephew, MICHEL SAINT-DENIS (who carried the torch to both Anglophone and Francophone theatres), contributed to the widespread use of WORKSHOPS and inspired the COLLECTIVE creation of 'communauté' companies such as the LIVING THEATER or ARIANE MNOUCHKINE's THÉÂTRE DU SOLEIL. In addition, JACQUES LECOQ learned the use of masks from Jean Dasté, married to Copeau's mask-making actress daughter, Marie-Hélène.

From 1930 on Copeau became an occasional director, notably at outdoor FESTIVALS, administrator – briefly running the COMÉDIE-FRANÇAISE (1940–1) – and playwright.

Copeau's staging style has had lasting influence (though he has been reproached with taking only what he found useful from the work of theorists like APPIA and CRAIG, thereby blunting their impact in France). His Copiaus were one of the early attempts at taking theatre to the provinces and at developing popular theatre, two tasks that concerned him at the end of his life and were later to be undertaken by the state. He left a body of persuasive writings (listed in the Paul bibliography below), and his training methods have been fruitfully developed. However, these specific debts are less important than the moral inspiration, which has leavened French theatre ever since, reinforced by his family and by the CARTEL, two of whom, Jouvet and DULLIN, had been companions of the pioneering days. For theatre practitioners of several generations and many countries, for HAROLD CLURMAN as for GIORGIO STREHLER, Copeau has been acknowledged as 'le patron'. An anthology of his writings appeared in English in 1990 as *Copeau: Texts on Theatre*, edited and translated by John Rudlin and Norman H. Paul.

ROBIN SLAUGHTER

Maurice Kurtz, *Jacques Copeau: Biography of a Theatre* (1999)

Paul-Louis Mignon, *Jacques Copeau ou le mythe du Vieux Colombier* (1993)

Norman H. Paul, *Bibliographie Jacques Copeau* (1979)

John Rudlin, *Jacques Copeau* (1986)

copyright In Britain, the twentieth century saw the various constituents of the dramatic event gradually brought under copyright protection. The 1911 Copyright Act repealed all previous acts and instituted the modern understanding of 'copyright' as the ownership rights of the author to control legally the reproduction and distribution of his/her work. However, developments in film and television soon made this redundant and a further act was passed in 1956, with an amendment in 1971. The individual problems of designers, actors and technicians in controlling their work were covered by various acts including the Registered Designs Act 1949, the Dramatic and Musical Performers Protection Act 1958, and the Performers' Protection Act 1972. All of this legislation was repealed and replaced by the Copyright Designs and Patents Act 1988. This has its broad equivalent in the United States' Copyright Act 1976, which was enacted from 1978 and replaced the previous Act of 1909 and the system of common-law copyright that applied at state level to works that had not been published or publicly disseminated. The 1988 Act, the most recent piece of major copyright legislation in the UK, guarantees the 'moral rights' of the author over their work, that a play may not be adapted, translated or converted into a different form without his/her permission. (The United States is less receptive to this right, but changes have taken place.) Titles of plays and characters have no protection in law, though if a character is sufficiently complex, duplicating it in another work would inevitably infringe the general copyright laws. This act further guarantees a 'performance right' in the original production. This means that the consent of every performer is required for the further exploitation of their performance. UNION rules forbid the simultaneous video or audio recording of a live performance, and this must be treated, for copyright purposes, as a separate performance. However, the same act legalized tape recording for private purposes, and thus the regulations forbidding tape recorders on theatre walls are not statutory, but have not as yet been tested. This legislation also brings under the provisions of one act protection for specially composed music, sound, set and costume designs. Thanks to European law, all of these protections expire 70 years after the last copyright holder's death, or the first performance, whichever is the later. The term is different in the United States, depending on whether the work was protected before 1978. There are generally two terms, beginning on the date of first performance; copyright has to be renewed after the first 28-year term, if the work is not to fall into the public domain; the second term lasts 48 years, making a total of 76 years. Clause 301 of the British act makes special provision for the copyright in respect of productions of *Peter Pan* by J. M. BARRIE, the royalties from which go to Great Ormond Street Children's Hospital in London in perpetuity.

The main international copyright treaty is the Berne Convention, which is the largest and oldest (founded 1886) such agreement. DAN REBELLATO

See also LICENCE.

John Feather, *Publishing, Piracy and Politics: An Historical Study of Copyright in Britain* (1995)
G. MacFarlane, *A Practical Introduction to Copyright* (1989)
Lyman Ray Patterson, *Copyright in Historical Perspective* (1968)

Corio, Ann *see* BURLESQUE

Cornell, Katharine (b. Berlin, 16 Feb. 1893; d. Vineyard Haven, Mass., 12 June 1974) Actress and producer. Of an unconventional beauty with a rich, vibrant voice, Cornell toured extensively and created an extraordinarily devoted audience. She made her stage debut with the WASHINGTON SQUARE PLAYERS in 1916, achieved stardom with *A Bill of Divorcement* (1921), gained serious critical recognition as SHAW's Candida (1924) and became a Broadway sensation with *The Green Hat* (1925) and *The Letter* (1927). Later roles included Elizabeth Barrett in *The Barretts of Wimpole Street* (1931) and Shakespeare's Cleopatra (1947). With HELEN HAYES and LYNN FONTANNE she was one of the leading actresses of her time, and was dubbed 'First Lady of the Theatre' by the critic ALEXANDER WOOLLCOTT. She retired when her husband GUTHRIE MCCLINTIC, who had directed her in many of her roles, died in 1961. Her memoir, *I Wanted to be an Actress*, appeared in 1938. THOMAS F. CONNOLLY

Guthrie McClintic, *Me and Kit* (1955)
Tad Mosel with Gertrude Macey, *Leading Lady* (1978)

Corrie, Joe (b. Slamannan, Scotland, 1894; d. Alloway, Scotland, 14 Nov. 1968) Playwright. He formed a company of miner–actors in Bowhill in Fife, for which he wrote plays. His most celebrated work, *In Time of Strife* (1929), deals with the effects on a coal-mining family of the General Strike of 1926. This toured all over Scotland and was later revived in a modified version by Glasgow UNITY THEATRE in 1951 and as part of 7:84 (Scotland)'s Clydebuilt season in 1982. Later in life he turned to writing one-act plays of a rather sentimental nature for amateur companies. JAN MCDONALD

Costa Rica *see* MEXICO AND CENTRAL AMERICA

costume design Costume design is something we all do every day, whether dressing for work or for a special occasion. The choice you make is design in itself. A costume designer also has to make a choice. A costume designer goes through a similar process as a scenic designer, and in fact may be the same person. This is more usual in Europe than in the United States or Canada, where the two are usually separate occupations. Most designers are freelance, as are directors.

In his book *The Empty Space*, PETER BROOK relates his own experience of costume in the theatre: 'The actor who is asked his views about his costume design before rehearsals start is in a similar position to the director who is asked for a decision before he is ready. He has not yet had a physical experience of his role, so his views are theoretical. If the designer draws with panache and if the costume is of an actual historical moment the actor will often accept it with enthusiasm only to discover weeks later that it is quite out of tune with all that he is trying to express.' This can be one of the hardest problems for designers as demands are made from the company, costume supervisors and costumiers to have finished designs before the rehearsal starts.

The designer gets to work: having read the play script many times and talked with the director, who may give a lead to the period and style of the production, he or she may take inspiration from an artist, a photograph or a film which captures the essence of the production. The designer will spend much time looking at paintings and photographs within the boundaries of the director's brief. Whether the character is a fishmonger or lord of the manor, there will be much in common with the modern eye within the reference chosen. The drawing process will add or eliminate details and lead to a style of clothes that encompasses the designer's personality and taste, as with any other work of art. A costume design will be diverse in style and medium. Mstislav Dubujinsky's design for Kutuzov in *War and Peace* at the Metropolitan Opera is in pencil and watercolour, and is a character study rather than just a general's uniform. MARGARET HARRIS's sketch (for Kutuzov at the English National Opera) used the same reference but approached the design in a more stylistic form and made the clothes in painted canvas and painted medals as opposed to cloth with gold metal medals. Both designs illustrate the character who in both productions remains historical in a recognizable way. The convention of drawing a costume design was established early and did not really change until the twentieth century, with the aid of the photocopier and computer. Even now, many designers maintain the traditional style.

Although there was a time when actors were responsible for supplying their own clothes, this now only happens where their clothes may evolve during rehearsal. This is not always possible due to budgeting restrictions and the time factor. One costume can take over a week to make, so with a three-week rehearsal period one would need many costumiers; it can also become difficult to control the 'look' of the play. It is not just a case of making drawings that the designer and the director are happy with. The clothes are an extension of the character that the actor has created. The designer is working with vital, constantly changing human beings who will have definite ideas and prejudices about their appearance. The designer has to be aware of these human feelings, and, in order to get the design on stage intact, has to exude a great deal of confidence in the design and the actor's physical appearance as cast for the character. Once colour, shape and style are established, the designer then becomes more detailed. If it is an eighteenth-century play, for example, the designer would choose the exact bodice shape and coat cut; there are many variations – a man's coat may have a three-quarter circle of pleats in the back or hardly any at all. The designer would choose either a 'soft' look or a 'hard' one with much canvas and net inside. The modern eye is able to appreciate different versions more and more, and diverse productions are available from all over the world.

Whatever the concept, the designer is bound by the restrictions of the human figure. Costume making has become as sophisticated as scenery has become high-tech. Costumiers apply modern methods and fabrics to create a period look, as will a milliner or dyer, but they will sometimes yearn for the old materials that are no longer produced.

Costume makers may be presented with a simple line drawing, a splash on a page, a photocopy from a book or a detailed painting. They have to be versatile, as does the costume supervisor, who plays an important role in interpreting the design, budgeting and finding the fabrics. Weight, texture and colour of fabric are all important to the design. The supervisor will work closely with the designer and in some cases will also be the costumier. The job of transferring the design from the page to the stage is as difficult as designing the clothes. The supervisor's position is quite recent; it used to be taken care of by the wardrobe mistress, who would also maintain the clothes during the run of the play. As design has become more sophisticated and demanding, so an artistic supervisor has come into being.

The first showing of the designs to the actors usually takes place on the first day of rehearsals. The STAGE MANAGEMENT will be the link with the rehearsal room and will be in touch with the supervisor on a daily basis. Someone may need gloves, a handbag, a watch. There may be quick changes not clear from the text; many ideas will come from the rehearsal room. The actor may find the coat designed is unsuitable for the action as the rehearsals develop, so the communication with the stage management is essential.

Having purchased the fabrics and discussed the design with the costumiers, the next stage will be to meet the actor and have a fitting. An actor whose work seems real in rehearsal clothes can lose integrity when dressed in period clothes or stylist costume. In Britain, costumes are often made in a local set-up with many individuals who have small workshops or work at home. The fitting will probably take place at the rehearsal room. If working for a company that has its own production wardrobe, like the ROYAL SHAKESPEARE COMPANY at STRATFORD-UPON-AVON, the actor will be fitted in the wardrobe fitting room. There are some commercial companies in Britain where everything is dealt with under one roof; this is more usual in the United States, especially on BROADWAY.

Costume design encompasses millinery, dying, painting, shoes, MAKE-UP and hair as well as the actual clothes. All the decisions are the costume designer's: the size of ring or the length of watch chain, the weight of fabric from which the stockings will be made. On a large costume production it can be beneficial to have everything made in one place; it will reduce the stress factor of travelling to many homes and workshops.

The fitting is the only chance to establish shape and proportion in relation to the actor. There would usually be two fittings. The first would be fairly basic, as the costumier will not want to go too far until everyone has seen the start. What construction is used underneath is as important as the final product. Corsets, padding, petticoats and crinoline shapes, even the right bra or underpants, are important. The second fitting will be more complete but still at a stage where final adjustments to the shape and trimmings can be made; the proportions of the hat with the shoes and outfit, the lengths and size of cuffs and collars. The next time the costume will be on-stage and seen in relation to the other characters, the scenery and lighting.

Costume design reflects its period. Randolph Schwabe's design for *Romeo and Juliet* in 1919 reflects the *art nouveau* period he lived in. Nadine Baylis's design for *Romeo and Juliet* in 1979 related the clothes to the fashion of the time, but also kept some essence of the Renaissance period. EDWARD GORDON CRAIG's *Hamlet*, designed in 1911 (opened 1912), resembled the woodcuts of the period, very stark and black and white. RALPH KOLTAI's costumes for *Hamlet* took the same monochromatic approach 60 years later, although the clothes had more sympathy with the modern day.

Costume designers are often drawn from other professions, as with PICASSO, CHIRICO, Hepworth and HOCKNEY, who are primarily artists and FASHION designers such as Chanel or more recently the Emanuels and Jasper Conran, continuing a crossover from and to fashion that includes ERTÉ and BEATON. Some designers are artists also, such as Yolanda Sonnaband and John McFarlaine, and some are directors, like PHILLIP PROWSE, David Fielding and Tom Cairns. Design is often heavily influenced by the style of fashion and art of the period, and then developed to create the atmosphere surrounding the play. If a production is long-running, much care is given to the updating of design styles during the run, especially with modern productions like *The Mousetrap*, for example, which brings in new designers periodically. The musical *Cats* at its 10th anniversary looked as innovative as it did years earlier. MARIA BJØRNSON's designs for *Phantom of the Opera* are seen through the eyes of an imaginary Victorian opera designer and are thought of as Victorian in flavour regardless of the period the scenes may be set in (e.g. the shape and fabric choice of the fancy dress clothes in the masked ball). The innovative use of modern fabrics and trim, whether it be cheap nylon lace, Indian trimmings, old curtains, antique trim or painted stretch velvet, all give the costumes a Victorian look.   SUE WILLMINGTON

See also DESIGN; DESIGNING; WIGS.

Janet Arnold, *Patterns of Fashion* (1977)

François Boucher, *A History of Costume in the West* (1987)

The Hermitage, Leningrad, *The Art of Costume in Russia: 18th to early 20th Century* (n.d.)

Georgina Howell, *In Vogue,* (1978)

Barbara Johnston, *Album of Fashions and Fabrics* (1987)

Frances Kennett, *The Collector's Book of Twentieth Century Fashion* (1983)

Richard Martin, *Fashion and Surrealism* (1987)

Richard Martin and Harold Koda, *The Historical Mode* (1989)

Men's Fashion Illustrations from the Turn of the Century (1990)

Musée des Arts, *Moments de Mode* (1986)

Julian Robinson, *The Fine Art of Fashion* (1989)

Alexander Schouvaloff, *Theatre on Paper* (1990)

Norah Waugh, *The Cut of Women's Clothes 1600–1930* (1968)

Côte d'Ivoire   *see* FRENCH AFRICAN THEATRE

Cottesloe Theatre *see* ARCHITECTURE; NATIONAL THEATRE

Cottrell, Richard   (b. London, 15 Aug. 1936)   Director, manager and translator. Having trained as an actor in Paris, Cottrell became manager of PROSPECT THEATRE (1962–9), with which he began his directing career, and of HAMPSTEAD THEATRE CLUB (1964–6). He was director of the Cambridge Theatre Company (1970–5) and of the BRISTOL OLD VIC (1975–80). In Canada he was associate director of the STRATFORD FESTIVAL (1983) before moving to Australia, where he ran the NIMROD THEATRE COMPANY (1986–7) and directed commercial and subsidized theatre and opera. He has translated much drama, including work by CHEKHOV, Racine and FEYDEAU.   JEREMY ECCLES

Coulter, John   (b. Belfast, 12 Feb. 1888; d. Toronto, 1 Dec. 1980)   Playwright. Influenced by the playwrights of the Irish literary renaissance, Coulter began writing plays for the BBC in 1920. In 1936 he married the Canadian Olive Clare Primrose and migrated to Toronto. Plays with Irish themes include *The House in the Quiet Glen* (1937) and *The Drums Are Out* (1948), premièred at Dublin's ABBEY THEATRE. Coulter is best known for his *Riel* (1950), *The Crime of Louis Riel* (1967) and *The Trial of Louis Riel* (1967), a trilogy that dramatizes with sympathy and considerable dramatic skill the life of Louis Riel, a Métis (mixed race) leader hanged by the government of Canada in 1885.

EUGENE BENSON

Council for the Encouragement of Music and the Arts   Concern for Britain's national morale during the Second World War led to the founding of CEMA in 1940 to take the arts to factories, isolated rural areas and evacuation districts and to promote local arts initiatives. Started with private funding, by 1942 CEMA was supported solely by the state and, under the arts patron Lord Keynes, increased its grant nearly fivefold before the end of the war. With the slogan 'The Best for the Most', CEMA made a variety of the arts accessible to an enormous number of people. SYBIL THORNDIKE toured classics to Welsh mining villages and the north of England; the bombed-out OLD VIC was taken north; the leading commercial management H. M. TENNENT was helped to establish a non-profit wing; JAMES BRIDIE was helped to establish the CITIZENS' THEATRE, GLASGOW; the Theatre Royal, Bristol, was saved from destruction and became the first theatre to be financed by the state when, after the war, a group from the Old Vic was installed there. Wartime experiences of CEMA, its armed forces partner the ENTERTAINMENTS NATIONAL SERVICE ASSOCIATION (ENSA), the BBC and other initiatives convinced parliament of the need to continue state cultural support and in 1946 CEMA was incorporated into the ARTS COUNCIL OF GREAT BRITAIN.

COLIN CHAMBERS

CEMA, *The Arts in War Time* (1944)

Charles Landstone, *Offstage: A Personal Record of the First Twelve Years of State Sponsored Drama in Great Britain* (1953)

J. Minihan, *The Nationalization of Culture* (1977)

Court Theatre   Since the earliest settlers, Christchurch, New Zealand, has enjoyed a tradition of theatrical entertainment. This was particularly strong in the 1940s when celebrated crime writer Ngaio Marsh first directed students of Canterbury University College in a series of remarkable productions. Some Canterbury students, like James Laurenson, Jonathan Hardy and Sam Neill, made their careers overseas; others like MERVYN THOMPSON were involved in the founding of the Court in 1971 with its first artistic director Yvette Bromley. ELRIC HOOPER, who acted with Marsh and was appointed artistic director in 1979, commissioned a number of New Zealand plays including BRUCE MASON's controversial *Blood of the Lamb* and the musical comedy *Footrot Flats* (ROGER HALL, Philip Norman, A. K. Grant), which has been popular in New Zealand and Australia. On its site in the former university the theatre has two auditoriums presenting a variety of theatre.   GILLIAN GREER

Courteline, Georges [Georges Victor-Marcel Moinaux]   (b. Tours, 25 June 1858; d. Paris, 25 June 1929)   Comic writer. His 28 plays, reflecting satirical aspects of daily life, include *Boubouroche* (1893, his most popular farce), *Les Gaités de l'Escadron* ('The delights of the cavalry', 1895), *Hortense, couche-toi!* (*Hold on, Hortense!*, 1897), which helped launch the GRAND GUIGNOL theatre, and *La Paix chez soi* (*Peace at Home* or *A Private Account*, 1903). A sequel to Molière, *La Conversation d'Alceste* ('Alceste's conversation', 1905) was a success at the Comédie-Francaise.

WENDY SCOTT

Courtenay, Tom [Thomas Daniel]   (b. Hull, Yorks, 25 Feb. 1937)   Actor who made his stage debut with the OLD VIC in 1960 and won critical acclaim the next year as Billy Liar, a role he repeated in the 1963 film version. He was part of a generation of actors who kept their own regional accents and helped redefine their profession in the 1960s. A remarkable comic actor who brings pathos and vulnerability to his tragic roles, he has starred in such plays as *Time and Time Again* (1972), *The Norman Conquests* (1974), *The Fool* (1975) and *The Dresser* (1980), first seen in MANCHESTER at the ROYAL EXCHANGE, a theatre with which he has had a long association, also playing there, among other roles, Hamlet, King Lear and Peer Gynt. His many films include *The Loneliness of the Long Distance Runner* (1962) and *Doctor Zhivago* (1965). He was knighted in

2000. His memoir *Dear Tom: Letters from Home* appeared in 2000. DAVID STAINES

Courtneidge, [Esmeralda] Cicely (b. Sydney, 1 April 1893; d. London, 26 April 1980) Actress. Her early career was spent in musical comedy and REVUE. She appeared in many shows with her husband JACK HULBERT (e.g. *Clowns in Clover*, 1927; *Under Your Hat* 1938), which he produced. She entered films in the 1930s and developed into a dramatic actress later. Her autobiography, *Cicely*, appeared in 1953; she was created a dame in 1972. REXTON S. BUNNETT

Cousin, Gabriel (b. La Perche, France, 1918) Playwright. A writer for the popular, decentralized French theatre, he usually celebrates, in poetry, song and powerful physical movement, love relations which persist in appalling conditions. *Le Drame du Fukuryu-Maru* ('The drama of Fukuryu-Maru', 1963) is set on a radioactive fishing-vessel, *Le Cycle du crabe* ('The crab cycle', 1969) in a shanty town in a marsh.
TERRY HODGSON

J. Chambers, *Théâtre Populaire*, 45 (1962)

Cousse, Raymond (b. Saint Germain-en-Laye, France, 1942) Playwright, performer and novelist. Cousse's monologues, or 'one-man-shows', are frequently adapted from his novels. They are notable for their imaginative and verbal energy, and for their black humour. Main work includes *Stratégie pour deux jambons* ('Strategy for two hams', 1979) and *Enfantillages* ('These childish things', 1984). ANNA MCMULLAN

Coward, Noël [Pierce] (b. London, 16 Dec. 1899; d. nr Port Maria, Jamaica, 26 March 1973) Actor, dramatist, composer and director. He turned his hand to almost every job in the theatre, including designing the posters, but his enduring fame will be as the author of light comedies, at least three of which – *Hay Fever* (1925), *Private Lives* (1930) and *Blithe Spirit* (1941) – rank as masterpieces of their genre; several others – *Design for Living* (1932), *Tonight at Eight-Thirty* (1935), *Present Laughter* (1942) – run them close. He was also a master of the REVUE form, with many successes in the 1920s culminating in the dramatized patriotic pageant, *Cavalcade*, in 1931. An early triumph in the musical theatre with *Bitter-Sweet* (1929), which he both wrote and composed, led him to further endeavours in this form, but without real success, and his disastrous *Pacific 1860* (1946), which re-opened DRURY LANE after the war, so discouraged English managements about the native ability to create musicals that it may be said to have opened the gates for the invasion of Broadway musicals which immediately followed. Coward was a

brilliant light-comedy actor with immaculate timing and a clipped vocal style which was a gift to impressionists and earned him yet another successful career as a cabaret entertainer. He was, above all else, a man of the commercial theatre, and was genuinely surprised when the NATIONAL THEATRE chose *Hay Fever* for a major revival in 1964 – a revival which restored his critical fortunes after a pronounced slump. Known as 'The Master', he wrote two volumes of autobiography. The final accolade came in 1970 with a knighthood which, not immodestly, he felt he had earned by almost 60 years' service to the theatre (he began as a child actor in 1911). Not even his greatest detractors could say his had been anything other than a lifetime's devotion. IAN BEVAN

John Lahr, *Coward the Playwright* (1982)
Cole Lesley, *The Life of Noël Coward* (1976)
Sheridan Morley, *A Talent to Amuse* (1969)
— and Barry Day, eds, *The Theatrical Companion to Coward* (1999)
Graham Payn with Barry Day, *My Life with Noël Coward* (1994)

Cowl, Jane (b. Boston, Mass, 14 Dec. 1884; d. Santa Monica, Cal., 22 June 1950) Actress. Known for her dark-eyed beauty, she began acting under the charismatic actor–manager DAVID BELASCO in *Sweet Kitty Bellairs* (1903), and worked with him until 1910. She achieved star status in *Within the Law* (1912), and from then multiplied her successes in new plays – some of them co-written by herself (e.g. the melodramatic *Smilin' Through*, 1920); in the work of contemporaries such as NOËL COWARD (e.g. *Easy Virtue*, 1925); and in great classical roles such as her celebrated Juliet (*Romeo and Juliet*, 1923). ADRIANA HUNTER

Cox, Brian [Dennis] (b. Dundee, 1 June 1946) Actor. His first professional appearance, with Dundee Repertory Theatre (1961), was followed by seasons at the Royal LYCEUM, Edinburgh and BIRMINGHAM REPERTORY THEATRE. Since 1968 he has appeared with all the major theatre companies in Britain and on tours abroad in a vast range of roles. He received an Olivier best actor award for *Rat in the Skull* (ROYAL COURT, 1984) and again for *Titus Andronicus* (ROYAL SHAKESPEARE COMPANY, 1988), and played the title role in *King Lear* (ROYAL NATIONAL THEATRE, 1990 and world tour). In America, he has been seen in Los Angeles in *Skylight* (1997), and in New York in *St Nicholas* (1998) and *Art* (1999). Cox is one of those reliably good actors who has never achieved 'star' status, but who has worked continuously and consistently well. He has made many television and film appearances, and has also directed.

Cox received an INTERNATIONAL THEATRE INSTITUTE award for services to international theatre in 1990 for his work in promoting student theatre exchanges. He has published *Salem to Moscow: An Actor's Odyssey* (1991) and *The Lear Diaries* (1992). BRIAN ROBERTS

Craig, Edith [Geraldine Ailsa] ('Edy') (b. Wheathampstead, Herts, 9 Dec. 1869; d. Tenterden, Kent, 27 March 1947) Actress and director, the illegitimate daughter of ELLEN TERRY and the architect E. W. Godwin. Her early stage career began as a child and included playing at the Lyceum with her mother and HENRY IRVING. She studied music, worked with her brother EDWARD GORDON CRAIG on his costume designs and stage-managed her mother's tour of the United States in 1907. However, her most notable achievements were with the ACTRESSES' FRANCHISE LEAGUE, for which she directed *How the Vote Was Won* (1909) and *The Pageant of Great Women* (1909), and a women's company that grew out of it, the PIONEER PLAYERS, which she founded in 1911 and for which she directed and designed most of its 150 or so productions. Described by SYBIL THORNDIKE as a 'genius', the innovative Craig, who lived in a *ménage à trois* next door to her mother, found it virtually impossible to find freelance directing work. In 1929 she inaugurated a series of Shakespeare productions commemorating the anniversary of her mother's death and performed in a Tudor barn converted by Edy at her mother's home, Small Hythe Place, Kent, where Edy lived. The productions gave rise to a subscription society (1931) based at the Barn Theatre. She turned the farmhouse and barn into a Terry museum and ended her directing days staging PAGEANTS. IAN CLARKE

See also WOMEN IN THE THEATRE.

Katherine Cockin, *Edith Craig (1869–1947): Dramatic Lives* (1998)

,Julie Holledge, *Innocent Flowers: Women in Edwardian Theatre* (1981)

Joy Melville, *Ellen and Edy: A Biography of Ellen Terry and Her Daughter, Edith Craig 1847–1947* (1987)

Craig, Edward [Henry] Gordon (b. Stevenage, Herts, 16 Jan. 1872; d. Venice, 29 July 1966) Director, designer and theorist, the illegitimate son of ELLEN TERRY and the architect and designer E. W. Godwin. Given his huge influence on twentieth-century theories of theatre and stage design, Craig's own practical ventures in the theatre were remarkably few. After an acting career of minor distinction with HENRY IRVING (about whom he wrote a book in 1930) he turned

under the influence of SYMBOLISM to directing and stage design, with an amateur production in 1900 of the opera *Dido and Aeneas*. Between a revival the following year and 1903 there followed productions of the operas *The Masque of Love* and *Acis and Galatea*, Laurence Housman's nativity play *Bethlehem*, Calvert's *For Sword or Song* and, with his mother, IBSEN's *The Vikings at Helgeland* and Shakespeare's *Much Ado About Nothing*. His extraordinary liaison with ISADORA DUNCAN had a great effect on the arts they both practised. Craig was then invited by OTTO BRAHM to design Otway's *Venice Preserved* in Berlin, in 1905. He also designed Ibsen's *Rosmersholm* for ELEANOR DUSE in Florence (1906), YEATS' *The Hour Glass* at the ABBEY (1911), and *Hamlet* (1912), which he directed for STANISLAVSKY at the MOSCOW ART THEATRE. His last real practical engagement with the theatre was a production of Ibsen's *The Pretenders* in Copenhagen in 1926, although in 1928 he drew a set of designs for a New York *Macbeth*.

Craig's importance and influence derive not so much from his practice, much of which was beset by problems and rows, as from his theoretical writings, most notably *The Art of the Theatre* (1905) and the more complete *On the Art of the Theatre* (1911). Other works include *Towards a New Theatre* (1913), *The Marionette* (1918), *The Theatre Advancing* (1921), and his autobiography *Index to the Story of My Days* (1957). Craig advocated a move away from the concretely pseudo-realized representational settings of the late nineteenth and early twentieth centuries and proposed a theatre based on non-realistic lighting and setting in order to create atmosphere through colour and abstract shapes (e.g. his use of screens, first seen in *The Hour Glass*). For Craig the overall effect was all-important, and he accordingly diminished the priority of the written text and, indeed, of the actor in relation to the control of the unifying director. Better known than his like-minded contemporary APPIA, for whom he had great admiration, Craig has had an immense influence on production methods and values in America and Europe among directors, from REINHARDT and COPEAU to BARRAULT and KANTOR, as well as among designers like SVOBODA and ROBERT EDMOND JONES.

Uncherished in England, Craig lived abroad from 1908, mainly in Italy and later in Spain too. In Florence, he published and largely wrote the journal *The Mask* (1908–29), in which he ranged from specific arguments (e.g. proposing a national theatre in England) to evolving his general theories for theatre as an art form with a deep spiritual significance. He also founded in Florence the short-lived theatre school Arena Goldoni (1913–14). His once radical ideas have become an established part of the general grammar and vocabulary of twentieth-century theatre.   IAN CLARKE

Denis Bablet, *The Theatre of Edward Gordon Craig* (1981)
Edward Craig, *Gordon Craig: The Story of his Life* (1968)
Christopher Innes, *Edward Gordon Craig* (1983)
J. Michael Walton, ed., *Craig on Theatre* (1983)

Cranko, John   *see* DANCE

Craven, Frank   (b. Boston, Mass., 1875; d. Beverly Hills, Calif., 1 Sept. 1945)   Actor, director and playwright. Once a child actor, he scored his most notable success playing the original Stage Manager in THORNTON WILDER's *Our Town* (1938). His plays were generally light comedies about simple people and their domestic troubles, such as *Too Many Cooks* (1914), *New Brooms* (1924) and *That's Gratitude!* (1930).
ALEXIS GREENE

Crawford, Cheryl   (b. Akron, Ohio, 24 Sept. 1902; d. New York, 8 Oct. 1986)   Producer and director. She made her BROADWAY acting debut with the THEATER GUILD (1926) but found her niche there in management, enjoying a reputation for diplomacy and common sense. One of the first women to parlay her way to the top in producing, Crawford, as a co-founder of the GROUP THEATER (1931), the AMERICAN REPERTORY THEATER (1946) and the ACTORS' STUDIO (1947), was involved in some of the most important projects in modern US drama. As a successful independent producer, Crawford mounted, among others, a *Porgy and Bess* revival (1942), *One Touch of Venus* (1943) and *Brigadoon* (1947), as well as four TENNESSEE WILLIAMS premières: *The Rose Tattoo* (1951), *Camino Real* (1953), *Sweet Bird of Youth* (1959) and *Period of Adjustment* (1960). She wrote an autobiography, *One Naked Individual: My Fifty Years in the Theatre* (1977).
ANNE FLETCHER

Crawford [Dumble-Smith], Michael   (b. Salisbury, Wilts, 19 Jan. 1942)   Actor. He appeared on stage as a boy soprano (e.g. in the original productions of Britten's *Noyes Fludde* and *Let's Make an Opera*) and in juvenile roles on television and film before making his adult West End debut in 1965 in *Travelling Light* by Leonard Kingston. He was in the original cast of the long-running farce *No Sex Please, We're British* (1971) by Anthony Marriott and Alistair Foot, and played the eponymous hero in *Billy* (1974) in the Dick Clement/Ian La Frenais musical of *Billy Liar*. National popularity came with his television appearances, notably as the simpering star of *Some Mothers Do 'Ave 'Em*, but he found international fame with his athletic performances in musical theatre, particularly in *Barnum* (1981)

and *The Phantom of the Opera* (1986). *The Music of Andrew Lloyd Webber* (1991) and *EFX* (1995) followed, and his autobiography, *Parcel Arrived Safely: Tied With String*, appeared in 1999.   CHARLES LONDON

Crazy Gang   A group of MUSIC HALL comedians, brought together by impresario GEORGE BLACK, who appeared together in VARIETY bills and REVUES at the LONDON PALLADIUM in an almost unbroken sequence from 1932 until 1940 and then in a series of variety revues at the Victoria Palace from 1947 to 1962. Membership of the 'gang' sometimes changed from show to show, but the group is mainly remembered as consisting of three double acts – FLANAGAN and ALLEN, Naughton and Gold, Nervo and Knox. Another frequent member was the solo comedy juggler, 'Monsewer' Eddie Gray. Allen retired from the stage in 1946, leaving Flanagan to continue with the gang as a solo artist. The style of their work was broad, knockabout, slapstick, often bawdy comedy laced with the sentimental ballads in which Flanagan specialized.
IAN BEVAN

Maureen Owen, *The Crazy Gang: A Personal Reminiscence* (1986)

Cregan, David [Appleton Quartus]   (b. Buxton, Derbys, 30 Sept. 1931)   Playwright. Cregan writes highly theatrical political comedies that use fantasy to emphasize questions of identity, power and outsider status. Associated with the ROYAL COURT in the 1960s, Cregan has also written successful radio and children's plays. Plays include *Miniatures* (1965), *Three Men For Colverton* (1966), *The Houses by the Green* (1968), *The Land of Palms* (1972) and *Poor Tom* (1976).
DAN REBELLATO

Crest Theater   Founded in 1954 by brothers Donald and Murray Davis to offer professional repertory theatre to Toronto audiences. The company's home was a renovated movie theatre, seating 842. In its 13 seasons the Crest presented 140 plays, including works by T. S. ELIOT, JEAN ANOUILH, SAMUEL BECKETT and IBSEN. It also promoted Canadian plays by such dramatists as ROBERTSON DAVIES, MARCEL DUBE and Bernard Slade. Leading actors were the Davis brothers and their sister Barbara Chilcott. In its final years the theatre accumulated an unmanageable deficit, and it closed in 1966.   EUGENE BENSON
See also DAVIS, DONALD.

Crimp, Martin [Andrew]   (b. Dartford, London, 14 Feb. 1956)   Playwright and translator. Crimp's early work was championed by the ORANGE TREE THEATRE, London, where he evolved a pared-down and steely verbal style. From *Dealing with Clair* (1988) and *Play with Repeats* (1989) to *No One Sees the Video* (1990), *Getting Attention* (1991) and *The Treatment* (1993) his work offers a totally convincing vision of social and moral collapse, and a wit, intelligence and theatrical control that has marked him out as one of the finest, most exciting playwrights of his generation. *Attempts on Her Life* (1997) took his sense of social fracture a stage further; the play features a series of scenes, each of which concerns 'Anna' – but who is she? Is each 'Anna' the same person? The text does not even assign lines to specific characters, let alone meanings to itself. His unique ear for theatrical nuance and his attention to language has also been shown in a series of acclaimed translations, including Molière's *The Misanthrope* (1996), IONESCO's *The Chairs* (1997) and KOLTÈS' *Robert Zucco* (1997). *The Country* (2000), a satirical portrait of rural life, was part of the ROYAL COURT's first season at its reopened, refurbished premises in Sloane Square, London. DAN REBELLATO

Cristofer, Michael *see* GAY THEATRE; LONG WHARF THEATER

criticism Theatre criticism in the twentieth century saw an increasing – and regrettable – dichotomy between academic criticism and journalistic evaluation, with the contribution that the latter has made to the evolution of drama greatly under-estimated. British newspapers at the beginning of the century gave their critics enough space to launch personal crusades: Clement Scott (1841–1904) persistently attacked IBSEN and other naturalistic writers, deeming their subject matter inappropriate and their language indecorous; WILLIAM ARCHER was equally impassioned in his dislike of plays notable only for their violence and superficial realism, becoming best known as the translator of Ibsen; and GEORGE BERNARD SHAW was forthright in his defence of plays that introduced a new realism to the British stage, and merciless in his upbraiding of myopic critics after he had become a successful playwright. In 1908 he claimed that *Getting Married* was his revenge upon the critics for their 'gross ingratitude . . . their arrant Philistinism, their shameless intellectual laziness, their low tastes, their hatred of good work, their puerile romanticism, their disloyalty to dramatic literature, their stupendous ignorance, their susceptibility to cheap sentiment, their insensibility to honour, virtue, intellectual honesty, and anything that constitutes strength and dignity in human character'. Shaw's successor at the *Saturday Review*, MAX BEERBOHM, was the last theatre critic to enjoy the luxury of extended column space, and the best subsequent newspaper critics are those who exploit, rather than capitulate to,

the restriction of ever-decreasing column inches and avoid Shaw's list of pitfalls. Since the Second World War, critics writing for weekly publications have had the advantage over daily practitioners of a greater period of consideration, with many of the finest reviews being written in response to other notices – such as 'The Screw Turns Again', a passionate defence in 1958 by HAROLD HOBSON, in the face of universal critical opprobrium, of HAROLD PINTER's *The Brithday Party* that prevented the destruction of the playwright's infant career. Daily critics must also contend with the pressure of a deadline shortly after the curtain has fallen, quickening the temptation to arrive at a performance with the skeleton of a review already formulated. This said, there are no set rules for effective journalistic criticism and many of the daily practitioners champion the value of the expert's first impressions. Some critics, such as JAMES AGATE, employed the precept of 'touchstone' criticism, comparing performances and productions to acknowledged models of theatrical excellence; others, such as IVOR BROWN, relied upon an intimate voice, developed over a period of time, that created resonances in the minds of a familiar, trusting readership. The reorientation of British drama after the Second World War demanded less grandiloquent and more analytical writing, and the type of article, symbolized by W. A. Darlington, which related the plot, listed the actors and conveyed a personal impression, began to be seen as too inflexible to cope with new theatrical approaches from France (existentialist drama), America (the new realism of ARTHUR MILLER) and Germany (the EPIC THEATRE of BERTOLT BRECHT). Hobson's work at the *Sunday Times* (1947–76) was conceived as an historical record of the plays he had witnessed and represents the best example of elegant, incisive writing by a critic aware of the literary tradition in which he was writing. He also possessed no practical experience of the theatre, and was thus not hamstrung by an insider's approach to evaluation – first-hand knowledge not always being an advantage. Notable critics beneficially influenced by their practical experience of the stage include the *Observer*'s KENNETH TYNAN, an actor and director, whose passionate denunciation of the insipid nature of postwar drama in modern, fashionably radical language suited the temper of the 1950s, aided the arrival of the new dramatists and won him a devoted following. Both IRVING WARDLE and MICHAEL BILLINGTON developed approaches to criticism from the 1960s onwards that pay more attention to the social and theoretical context of drama, taking into account European theatrical trends; but even by the end of the century British journalistic criticism was still generally descriptive, averse to literary theory and frequently dependent on the distinctive personalities of the critic to invest the writing with an appealing vibrancy.

At the turn of the century in the United States, James G. Huneker (1857–1921) vigorously championed the European theatre of ideas, especially Ibsen and Shaw. Following in his footsteps came GEORGE J. NATHAN, who added American writers to his crusade, most notably O'NEILL and SAROYAN, a support of native talent also strongly expressed by ROBERT BURNS MANTLE. More directly, the American educator GEORGE PIERCE BAKER offered a playwriting course at Harvard University in 1905 which expanded in 1912 into Workshop 47, a laboratory theatre for the plays written. Baker's inspirational teaching methods drew promising dramatists such as O'Neill, EDWARD SHELDON and SIDNEY HOWARD to Harvard in one of the few twentieth-century examples of academia nurturing contemporary theatre, although WALTER KERR, the foremost critic of his time, was a journalist who invested his criticism with an intellectual dimension missing in his colleagues. ALEXANDER WOOLLCOTT became a celebrity critic at the *New York Times*, although it was BROOKS ATKINSON, with objective, accurate reviews, who established the post as the pivotal one on Broadway, a tradition consolidated by Kerr and continued by CLIVE BARNES and FRANK RICH, who was the most influential critic at the beginning of the 1990s. JOHN MASON BROWN and STANLEY KAUFFMANN at the *Saturday Review* have been influential, as have magazine critics, with perceptive writing by HAROLD CLURMAN (*Nation*), ERIC BENTLEY, STARK YOUNG and JOHN GASSNER (*New Republic*) and John Lahr and Michael Feingold (*Village Voice*).

Theatre critics are often regarded as a necessary evil by actors, playwrights and managers alike, generating welcome publicity with a favourable review (without which few plays would prosper), yet capable – if they write for the most influential publications – of having a catastrophic effect on a production with a few ill-chosen words. The higher the public perception of the worth of the critic, the less likely he or she is to abuse the position in the search for destructive, short-term popularity. DOMINIC SHELLARD

James Agate, *The English Dramatic Critics: An Anthology 1660–1932* (1932)
M. E. Comtois and L. F. Miller, *Contemporary American Critics* (1977)
B. Hewitt, *Theatre USA: 1665 to 1959* (1959)
Harold Hobson, *Verdict at Midnight* (1952)
Irving Wardle, *Theatre Criticism* (1992)

Croatia   *see* YUGOSLAVIA

Croft, Michael   *see* NATIONAL YOUTH THEATRE; YOUTH THEATRE

Crommelynck, Fernand   (b. Paris, 19 Nov. 1886; d. Saint-Germain-en-Laye, 17 March 1970)   Playwright. Though Belgian he lived mostly in France, and his tragicomic FARCES, indebted to Molière's studies of jealousy and avarice and the lyricism of French Romantic and SYMBOLIST poets, evoke the coarse realism and grotesque cruelty of the Flemish painters (Brueghel, Bosch or Ensor); in time and spirit he ranks among the Belgians between MAETERLINCK and GHELDERODE. *Le Cocu magnifique* (*The Magnificent Cuckold*, Paris, 1920; famously produced by MEYERHOLD in Moscow, 1922) launched him internationally. His plays appeared throughout Europe, especially in Paris and Brussels, often with himself as director. His surreal imagination appealed greatly from the 1950s to 1970s, but he wrote little after 1934, except a *Falstaff* in 1954, drawn from Shakespeare, an idea pursued by Orson Welles in his film *Chimes at Midnight*. Sometimes obscure, he is always exciting and arguably severely underrated. DONALD WATSON

Bettina L. Knapp, *Fernand Crommelynck (1978)*
Alain Piette and Bert Cardullo, *The Crommelynck Mystery: The Life and Work of a Belgian Playwright* (1997)

Cronyn, Hume   (b. London, Ont., 18 July 1911) Actor and director. Hume Cronyn began his acting career in Canada and Washington DC, and trained at various schools before joining the BARTER THEATER in Abingdon, Virginia. During the 1930s he acted and directed in many Broadway productions. In 1950 he began performing alongside his wife JESSICA TANDY; as a twosome they enjoyed considerable success, especially in serious, intimate dramas, such as ALBEE's *A Delicate Balance* (1966). He directed Tandy in TENNESSEE WILLIAMS' *Portrait of a Madonna* (1946), which led to her creating the role of Blanche Dubois in *A Streetcar Named Desire* (1947). Cronyn was also noted for his performances of great classic roles, and he won a 1964 Tony award for his portrayal of Polonius to BURTON's Hamlet. He performed opposite his wife for the last time in *Foxfire* (1982), of which he was co-author. His autobiography, *A Terrible Lear*, appeared in 1991. ADRIANA HUNTER

cross-dressing   *see* DRAG; IMPERSONATION

Crothers, Rachel   (b. Bloomington, Ill., 12 Dec. 1878; d. Danbury, Conn., 5 July 1958)   Playwright, director and actress. An early feminist, she operated in the commercial theatre and wrote 38 plays. Through strong women protagonists she explored such themes as the problems faced by the educated, financially independent, professional woman; the effects of divorce; woman's honour; her position in marriage; and man's place in a woman's life. Her tone was often ironic and satirical. The optimism of her earlier heroines changes to confusion and disillusionment in the later plays. Plays include *The Three of Us* (1906), *Myself Bettina* (1908), *A Man's World* (1910), *He and She* or *The Henfords* (1911), *Nice People* (1921), *When Ladies Meet* (1932) and *Susan and God* (1937), starring GERTRUDE LAWRENCE with set design by JO MIELZINER.

JANE HOUSE

Lois C. Gottlieb, *Rachel Crothers* (1979)

Crouch, Julian *see* IMPROBABLE THEATRE

Crouse, Russel [McKinley] (b. Findlay, Ohio, 20 Feb. 1893; d. New York, 3 April 1966) and **Lindsay [Neike], Howard [Herman]** (b. Waterford, NY, 29 March 1889; d. New York, 11 Feb 1968) Playwrights, librettists and producers. Although individually each had a modicum of success before their partnership, it was not until they joined forces to write the libretto for *Anything Goes* (1934) that the duo achieved full recognition. Crouse was a playwright, producer and librettist who started his writing career as a journalist in Cincinnati and New York. In the late 1920s he tried his hand at acting, and then became press agent for the THEATER GUILD. He wrote the books for *The Gang's All Here* (1931) and *Hold Your Horses* (1933) before teaming up with Lindsay, who had already established himself on Broadway as an actor and director before his work with Crouse. He appeared in VAUDEVILLE and BURLESQUE, and was a member of MARGARET ANGLIN's company (1913–18). After the First World War, he returned to the stage as an actor and director. The first straight play written by Crouse and Lindsay was *Life with Father* (1939), a hugely successful play that held Broadway's contemporary long-run record until the 1970s. Other collaborations included *Red, Hot and Blue!* (1936); *State of the Union* (1945), which won the Pulitzer Prize; and two major musical hits, *Call Me Madam* (1950) and the internationally renowned *The Sound of Music* (1959). As producers, Crouse and Lindsay presented *Arsenic and Old Lace* (1941), *The Hasty Heart* (1945) and *The Detective Story* (1949), as well as several of their own plays. LAURIE WOLF

C. Otis Skinner, *Life with Lindsay and Crouse* (1976)

Crowley, Bob [Robert James] (b. Cork, Ireland, 10 June 1952) Designer. In the 1980s, Crowley developed a postmodern design language for the ROYAL SHAKESPEARE COMPANY's large theatres. He used the entire stage space and freely intercut Brechtian curtains, heraldic imagery, historical anachronisms and EXPRESSIONIST effects to underline the texts' diverse range and rhythms. RSC productions with ADRIAN NOBLE include *King Lear* (1982), *Macbeth* (1987), *The Plantagenets* (1988), *Henry IV* (1991) and *Hamlet* (1992), as well as *Les Liaisons Dangereuses* (1986) with HOWARD DAVIES. At the NATIONAL THEATRE, his many designs include the DAVID HARE Trilogy (1990–3) and *Carousel* (1992). He has also designed for the ABBEY THEATRE, FIELD DAY, several OPERA companies and, on BROADWAY, the Paul Simon musical, *The Capeman* (1998).

TONY HOWARD

Crowley, Mart *see* GAY THEATRE

cruelty, theatre of *see* THEATRE OF CRUELTY

Crutchley, Kate *see* LESBIAN THEATRE

Cruttwell, Hugh *see* DRAMA SCHOOLS

Cuba *see* HISPANIC THEATRE IN THE UNITED STATES; MEXICO AND CENTRAL AMERICA; THEATRE FOR DEVELOPMENT

Cummings [Halveerstadt], Constance (b. Seattle, Wash., 15 May 1910) Actress. At home in both classical and contemporary plays, Cummings made her professional debut with the Savoy Stock Company (San Diego, 1926). After her marriage to English playwright Benn Levy (1900–73), she worked mainly in England. Her London stage triumphs include Juliet and SHAW's St Joan (both OLD VIC, 1939), Martha in *Who's Afraid of Virginia Woolf?* (1964) and Mary Tyrone in *Long Day's Journey into Night* (NATIONAL THEATRE, 1971). In 1979 her performance in New York as an aviatrix recovering from a stroke in ARTHUR KOPIT's *Wings* won a Tony award, and later that year she played the role in London. DAVID STAINES

Michael Roy Gartside, *For All Seasons: The Story of Stage and Screen Star Constance Cummings* (1999)

Cunningham, Merce (b. Centralia, Wash., 16 April 1919) Dancer and choreographer. He danced with MARTHA GRAHAM (1939–45) before presenting his first programme of solo works in 1944. He worked extensively with JOHN CAGE, especially in ventures at Black Mountain College, and formed the Merce Cunningham Dance Company in 1952, for whom he has choreographed ever since, making dance, theatrically, for its own sake. He began using chance operations as a method in 1951. In 1964 he presented the first of his *Events*, where dances and parts of dances from his repertoire were recombined into a choreographic collage. His stage work includes *Walkaround Time* (1968), which pays homage to Marcel Duchamp. He has collaborated with many musicians and artists, including Robert Rauschenberg, Frank Stella, Andy Warhol, Jasper Johns and Charles Atlas. MICHAEL HUXLEY

See also CHOREOGRAPHY; DANCE; MOVEMENT, DANCE AND DRAMA.

Melissa Harris, ed., *Merce Cunningham: Fifty Years* (1997)

Richard Kostelanetz, ed., *Merce Cunningham: Dancing Through Time and Space* (1998)

Curel, Françoise de *see* ANTOINE, ANDRÉ

Currency Press *see* AUSTRALIA

Cusack, Cyril (b. Durban, South Africa, 26 Nov. 1910; d. London, 7 Oct. 1993) Actor and producer. As a child he played Little Willie in the hardy Victorian stand-by *East Lynne* on tour in Ireland, subsequently (1932) joining the ABBEY THEATRE, where he appeared in over 70 productions, returning famously many times in later years (as Gaev in *The Cherry Orchard*, Uncle Vanya, Shylock, the title role in Boucicault's *The Shaughran*, Drumm in HUGH LEONARD's *A Life*). He directed the Gaelic Players (1935–6), and later in 1947 in his own play *Tar Éis an Aifrinn* ('After the Mass'). He played in all the other Dublin theatres, and, unhappy with the Abbey, he took over the GAIETY in 1945 and then formed Cyril Cusack Productions to present SYNGE (he was a noted Christy in *The Playboy of the Western World*), BECKETT, Shakespeare, SHAW, O'CASEY (including the première of *The Bishop's Bonfire*, 1955) in Ireland and on tour abroad. Cusack was memorable in *Krapp's Last Tape* (1960) and in a wide range of leading roles with the ROYAL SHAKESPEARE COMPANY, the NATIONAL THEATRE, and other British and US managements. His wistful vein of comedy and his delicate underplaying in dramatic roles have been much admired in the international cinema.

His four daughters, Sorcha, Sinéad, Niamh and Catherine, all lead distinguished careers in the theatre and cinema; the former three appeared at the Dublin GATE THEATRE in 1990 as CHEKHOV's *Three Sisters*, with their father as Chebutykin. Cyril Cusack was noted for cutting remarks uttered in a deceptively whimsical tone of voice, such as (of directors): 'I'm antipathetic to the director regime in theatre. It didn't exist in my early days, and I wonder to myself, what is their contribution?' CHRISTOPHER FITZ-SIMON

Czech Republic In Bohemia, which in 1620 became part of the Austrian Empire, Czech theatre developed alongside German, seeking its own image and attempting to catch up with European developments. The National Theatre, built in Prague in 1881 by national subscription, came to embody the idea of national independence. Besides Prague, only Plzeň and Brno had permanent theatres, while in rural areas travelling troupes played. There were many active amateur societies. In general, theatre played an 'extra-artistic' role of a national, educational and political nature.

At the beginning of the twentieth century new stylistic trends – SYMBOLISM, impressionism, psychological drama – made their appearance. Jaroslav Kvapil, at the National Theatre from 1900 to 1918, represented these trends and became the founder of modern Czech stage direction. A follower of REINHARDT and STANISLAVSKY, his eclectic repertoire was dominated by Shakespeare, IBSEN and the Czech playwright Alois Jirásek. Kvapil also produced plays by other Czech authors (Viktor Dyk and Fráňa Šrámek), as well as foreign ones (e.g. BJÖRNSON, CHEKHOV, CLAUDEL, HAUPTMANN, MAETERLINCK). With outstanding actors such as Eduard Vojan, Marie Hübnerová and Hana Kvapilová, Kvapil created a stylistic unity that was not, however, to survive the First World War, when the symbolist EXPRESSIONISM of Karel Hugo Hilar (at the other major Prague theatre, the Municipal, from 1911 to 1920) became dominant. Hilar and Vlastislav Hofman, a pioneer of modern Czech stage design, became known for their dynamic productions with moments of extreme grotesqueness and poignant heroism, representing great ideas, social movements and strong instincts.

The birth of an independent Czechoslovak Republic in 1918 created favourable conditions for the development of theatre, which no longer had to take on the role of defender of national interests. In Prague and other cities (Olomouc, Ostrava, České Budějovice), repertory theatres were founded. Besides official municipal theatres there were a number of 'opposition theatres' with a socialist orientation and/or proletarian theatres (the Revolutionary Stage, the Socialist Stage, Dědrasbor and others). The National Theatre continued to predominate under Hilar (1921–35), who had abandoned his extreme style in renowned productions such as *Hamlet*, *Oedipus Rex* and *Mourning Becomes Electra*. Other prominent directors at municipal theatres were Karel Dostal, Jan Bor and Kvapil. During the 1920s Czech plays gained world renown, thanks to the ČAPEK brothers. Alongside some outstanding actors there was also a flourishing of stage design, with such practitioners as Josef Čapek, Bedřich Feuerstein and Antonín Heythum. The mid-1920s brought the AVANT-GARDE too, under the influence of Soviet theatre (MEYERHOLD, TAIROV, VAKHTANGOV) and French drama, which was frequently staged (JARRY, APOLLINAIRE, COCTEAU,

BRETON). Small experimental theatres (the Liberated Theatre, Dada, the Modern Studio), grouped around young directors (EMIL FRANTIŠEK BURIAN, Jiří Frejka, Jindřich Honzl) were seeking inspiration in poetry, dance, PANTOMIME, the CIRCUS. They staged plays (e.g. by V. Vančura and V. Nezval) in which artistic opposition was combined with social opposition. By the 1930s they had attained significant positions in the Czech theatre. Frejka at the National Theatre (1930–45), with a group of young actors and designer František Tröster, made the classical repertoire very timely (*Julius Caesar*, *Fuente Ovejuna*, *The Government Inspector*). Burian in his theatre (called D-1933 to D-1944, depending on which year it was) developed his own social yet lyrical testimony to the times using music and highly original lighting and design effects (a system of combined projections). From 1929 to 1938 the Liberated Theatre changed into a satirical and anti-militaristic company which produced variety-type shows, written and played by JIŘÍ VOSKOVEC and JAN WERICH; their intellectual clowning, accompanied by the jazz music of Jaroslav Ježek, became an extremely popular hallmark of the times.

Outside Prague there was the director Jan Škoda with designer Jan Sládek (in Ostrava), the director Oldřich Stibor and designer Josef Gabriel (in Olomouc), the director Viktor Šulc (Czech language ensemble, Bratislava) and others of international acclaim. The great majority of those who worked in both official and unofficial theatres united to defend democracy and freedom against fascist expansion. The significance of ideas increased and the themes of power and dictatorship reverberated (in e.g. Čapek's *The White Disease*, 1937, and *The Mother*, 1938).

Theatre continued even after Czechoslovakia ceased to exist (1938) and the Czech lands were occupied by Nazi Germany (1939–45), though many outstanding artists emigrated, or were forbidden to appear, arrested or executed. With the aid of allegories and the inventive staging of the classics, theatres attempted to deal with contemporary problems and strengthen national awareness. A number of semi-amateur groups of young people were founded, strongly influenced by the prewar avant-garde, while productions of classical plays by Dostal and Frejka at the National Theatre continued to represent the pinnacle of artistic achievement.

After liberation, the theatre was proclaimed to be a national cultural institution, which was to cater to the popular masses. All private licences to operate theatres were abolished and all theatres became a part of the public realm. Travelling troupes were closed and regional repertory theatres were established on the basis of decentralization, creating an oversized network that was later slimmed down. An Academy of Performing Arts was founded as an institution of higher learning. After the communist victory in 1948, the theatre was expected to serve as a propaganda medium to promote socialism. Following the Soviet Union, so-called socialist realism became the predominant style from 1948 to 1953, and the simplified (and not properly understood) Stanislavsky method of acting was considered mandatory. Contemporary Czech plays were devoted to officially sanctioned subject matter, and modern plays from the West, considered the product of an alien and bourgeois ideology, were taboo. Theatres survived by playing the 'unproblematic' classics (Goldoni, Shakespeare's comedies). As direction and design were straitjacketed, the significance of the actor's interpretation increased. After criticism of Stalinism in the Soviet Union in 1956, cultural policy in Czechoslovakia became freer. Directors (OTOMAR KREJČA, Alfréd Radok, Jaromír Pleskot), designers (JOSEF SVOBODA) and playwrights (František Hrubín, Josef Topol, Pavel Kohout, František Pavlíček and Vradislav Blažek) strove for a more truthful and critical image of society's problems. Also, contacts with theatres abroad and with foreign playwrights became more regular. Gradually, the profile of different theatres became more individual. A number of small theatres at the end of the 1950s and beginning of the 1960s (in Prague: Semafor, the Theatre on the Balustrade, the Drama Club; in Liberec: the Y Studio) combined poetry, song, pantomime and puppetry to offer an authentic voice.

The 1960s represented a culmination of postwar development in the theatre, with great variety (Brechtian aesthetics, Chekhovian psychology, the strong influence of the THEATRE OF THE ABSURD), evident not only in staging methods (Krejča at the National Theatre and at his Theatre Behind the Gate) and the quality of direction (Radok, JAN GROSSMAN, Jan Kačer), but in new plays (by Milan Kundera, Ladislav Smoček, VÁCLAV HAVEL).

Svoboda, creator of the famous LATERNA MAGIKA, used modern technology as an art medium and thus created one of the major branches of not only Czech, but world stage designs. LADISLAV FIALKA revived classical pantomime (under the influence of MARCEAU). The struggle of the individual against dehumanization gave Czech theatre civic and ethical values at a time when it was internationally influential.

The Soviet occupation in 1968 and the process of so-called 'normalization' which followed had a highly negative impact. Creative teams were broken up, outstanding artistic personalities lost their jobs and a number were denied the opportunity to work in the profession (some found work abroad). During the 1970s the focus of the Czech theatre moved to theatres outside large cities, where a number of 'un-normalized' theatrical people (Grossman, Kačer, Hynšt, Hajda) were able to continue their work, and where young people (Kříž, Engelova', Rajmont) had more of an opportunity. Attempts to force the theatre back into a propaganda mould proved unsuccessful, but the artistic quality and social commitment of the theatre suffered. A general period of decline was interrupted only by individual productions (by directors Schorm, Macháček, Pistorius) in various short-term projects and ad hoc circumstances. Pantomime came to the forefront; a so-called second, 'grotesque' wave appeared. Also, the puppet theatre (the Dragon, the Naïve Theatre) flourished, as did stage design. The authorities again carefully controlled the selection of plays. Interesting performances were produced by the second line of small, studio-type theatres, some of which started as amateur groups (Theatre on a String in Brno, the Ha Theatre in Prostějov, the Drama Studio in Ústí n. Labem). From the end of the 1960s and beginning of the 1970s they created experimental theatre, which, because of its nonconformist content, increasingly contrasted with the hesitant ideas and rigidity typical of the permanent repertory or so-called 'stone' theatres in their grand buildings. It was from this milieu that K. Steigerwald, the most interesting playwright of the period, appeared.

Theatre workers played an important role in the 'velvet revolution' of 1989. They were the first to join the students' strike, opening the theatres for public gatherings and taking part in meetings in factories and villages throughout the country. However, after the fall of the communist regime the theatre's standing changed completely. The era of a ruling state ideology had come to an end; but so had the time when the entire expenses of the theatres could be paid out of the state budget. Dozens of new theatre groups emerged in the new liberal conditions, but a number of existing theatres ceased to exist. The financial pressure of the free market and a drop in attendances at the beginning of the 1990s fostered a trend towards commercialization. At the same time, new groups of an alternative orientation established themselves. Representatives of a new generation of directors, notably Petr Lébl, Vladimír Morávek and J. A. Pitínský, brought into the Czech theatre a response to postmodernism and a highly aesthetic conceptual approach.   EVA ŠORMOVÁ

Jarka M. Burian, *Modern Czech Theatre: Reflector and Conscience of a Nation* (2000)

F. Černý and L. Klosová, eds, *Dějiny českého divadla III* ('The history of the Czech theatre, III') (1977)

F. Černý and A. Scherl, eds, *Dějiny českého divadla IV* ('The history of the Czech theatre, IV') (1983)

M. Goetz-Stankiewicz, *The Silenced Theater* (1979)

V. Just, ed., *Česká divadelní 1945–1989 v datech a souvislostech* ('Czech theatre 1945–1989 in dates and contexts') (1995)

P. Trensky, *Czech Drama since World War II* (1978)

D

dada 'Anti'-art movement. In a Zurich nightclub in 1916, German poet Hugo Ball led a group of artist refugees in founding the Cabaret Voltaire to denounce all oppressive hierarchies, including rationality, in favour of absolute freedom. With an emphasis on personal performance and adapting techniques from FUTURISM, dada staged manifestos, cacophonous noise pieces, and phonetic, chance and simultaneous poetry, often in cubist-inspired costumes; all this activity exclaimed 'Hurrah for life!' even in a nihilistic way. After the First World War dada spread through Europe, notably to Paris, where, led by Tristan Tzara, it demolished literary structure from syntactical connection to plot coherence before yielding in the early 1920s to the more methodical SURREALISM. In Berlin, dada was more political and, through the involvement of PISCATOR and others, helped develop EPIC THEATRE, albeit tangentially. Despite the brevity of dada's flowering, it engendered much later EXPERIMENTAL performance.
CAROLYN TALARR

See also CABARET; EXPRESSIONISM; HAPPENINGS; PERFORMANCE ART.

Lisa Appignanesi, *Cabaret* (1975)
J. H. Methews, *Theatre in Dada and Surrealism* (1974)
Laurence Senelick, ed., *Cabaret Performance*, vol. I: *Europe 1890–1920* (1989) and vol. II: *Europe 1920–40* (1992)

Dadié, Bernard [Binlin] (b. Assinie, Ivory Coast, 1916) Playwright. He began to write plays when he was at school, and continued later when he founded a cultural group and needed to provide them with material to perform. His mode is satire and his theme the use of power. In *Monsieur Thôgô-gnini* (Algiers, 1969) a freed slave comes back to enrich himself by getting the indigenous people to trade with European slave dealers. *Béatrice du Congo* (AVIGNON FESTIVAL, 1971) deals with the European conquest of the Kingdom of Zaïre. *Les Voix dans le Vent* ('Voices in the wind', 1970), Ubu-like, shows a nonentity assuming the powers of a king, and *Ile de Tempête* ('Island in the storm', 1973) deals with the Haitian revolutionary Toussaint L'Ouverture. Many of his plays have been published in French and performed both in Africa and in France.
KOLE OMOTOSO

Daldry, Stephen (b. Bridport, Dorset, 2 May 1961) Director. After graduating from Sheffield University, he trained with Il Circo di Nando Orfio in Italy before beginning his career as a director. He was artistic director of the GATE THEATRE, west London, from 1989 to 1992, leading it from relative obscurity to a position of great influence, by creating epic productions in a tiny space and by introducing audiences to unfamiliar work from the European repertoire (e.g. HORVÁTH, FLEISSER). In 1992 he was appointed artistic director of the ROYAL COURT THEATRE, and in the same year he and his collaborator, designer Ian MacNeil, produced a groundbreaking re-interpretation of J. B. PRIESTLEY's *An Inspector Calls* which simultaneously reclaimed the play as a socialist masterpiece and catapulted Daldry to international success. While he was at the Royal Court he directed relatively little, though he transformed the auditorium for a revival of ARNOLD WESKER's *The Kitchen* (1994). The bulk of his time was taken up with planning and carrying through a complete rebuilding of the theatre, for which all his energy, charisma and political skill were necessary. He resigned as artistic director in 1996, retaining responsibility for completing

the building scheme while the theatre was in residence in the West End, and turned his attention to film.
GENISTA MCINTOSH

Wendy Lesser, *A Director Calls: Stephen Daldry and the Theatre* (1997)

Dale, Charlie *see* SMITH, JOE

Dallas Theater Center American regional theatre. Founded in 1959 under the leadership of local professor Paul Baker, the centre's main stage is in the 516-seat Kalita Humphreys Theater, named after a Texas actress and the only theatre designed and built by American architect Frank Lloyd Wright. The company also performs in the 56-seat Arts District Theater, a flexible space which allows for creative environmental productions. DTC presents contemporary plays, classics and revivals. Its renowned annual production of *A Christmas Carol* is performed for over 30,000 adults and children.
ELLEN LAMPERT-GRÉAUX

dame A comic female role in PANTOMIME traditionally played by a man, e.g. Aladdin's mother Widow Twankey, Cinderella's Ugly Sisters or Mother Goose. Outrageously or extravagantly dressed in several different costumes, the dame is often the cornerstone of the plot. Although a DRAG role, it is not usually taken by a cross-dresser, as the custom is to remind the audience that it is a man on stage. Some actors hone their craft as dames over a lifetime of service, while other dames are celebrity comedians playing the occasional Christmas show. The roll-call includes DAN LENO, GEORGE ROBEY, G. S. Melvin, George Lacey, Clarkson Rose, Arthur Lacan, Douglas Byng (unusual because he was posh – the housekeeper, not the cook – and a noted female IMPERSONATOR), Shaun Glenville, Nat Jackley, Norman Evans, Harry Gordon, ARTHUR ASKEY, Jack Tripp, Wyn Calvin, Stanley Baxter, JIMMY LOGAN, Les Dawson and DANNY LA RUE (like Byng, a celebrated female impersonator). The dame figure can also be found in CARNIVAL. There were a few notable female dames, such as the MUSIC HALL comedienne NELLIE WALLACE. CHARLES LONDON

P. Ackroyd, *Dressing Up* (1979)
D. Byng, *As You Were* (1970)

dance Having emerged as a vital, diverse and challenging theatrical force, today dance encompasses a range of forms, including the classical, modern and postmodern. As a body of work it includes the narrative, formal, abstract and experimental. It is an established academic discipline and includes a vibrant variety of participatory activity. In the late nineteenth century estab-

lished theatrical dance forms had seen a decline, yet the seeds of a revival that would lead to twentieth-century forms had been planted. Dance had reached an all-time low in its visibility and status. European ballet seemed to be in decline; in Russia, where Marius Petipa had led a nineteenth-century transformation of ballet into a polished virtuoso art, there was dissatisfaction and a sense of stagnation; in the UK, ballet had become part of the MUSIC HALL and PANTOMIME but there was no established ballet company, let alone a national one. Elsewhere, indifferent ballets provided vehicles for star performers to show off their technique. In America, ballet was an import; in New York the stars were European, and beyond, ballet was often a pale imitation of European originals.

At the same time, a number of growth points were emerging; some of them from the very music hall and VAUDEVILLE into which ballet had gone. A number of individual dancers, especially women, emerged from this milieu in the last years of the nineteenth century, experimenting with new ideas and moving away from traditional forms. A singular, albeit indirect, influence on many of them was the French actor and theorist François Delsarte (1811–71). His successors spread the Delsarte system of expression throughout the world and expression, especially individual expression, became a watchword for modern dancers at the turn of the century, including ISADORA DUNCAN and RUTH ST DENIS, and for the musician EMILE JAQUES-DALCROZE, whose eurythmics in turn influenced many European innovators, including MARY WIGMAN, HANYA HOLM and MARIE RAMBERT, who was hired by SERGE DIAGHILEV to use the method with his company, the Ballets Russes (1909–29).

It was Diaghilev who reinstated the artistic respectability of ballet and brought it into the twentieth century. He devised collaborations among innovative composers, designers and choreographers. His dancers displayed new levels of virtuosity and artistry, and his productions were spectacularly theatrical. Along with Rolf de Maré's Ballets Suédois (1920–5), the Ballets Russes redrew the boundaries of ballet in a modern European way, their choreographers and dancers giving the form new meanings. Following Diaghilev's death in 1929, members of the company led the establishment of resident ballet companies with modern works in their repertoires – in Britain, through MARIE RAMBERT and NINETTE DE VALOIS, and in America through GEORGE BALANCHINE. Much of the ballet repertoire is narrative based, using a combination of MIME, dance and character dance. The choreographers that Diaghilev chose extended the traditional boundaries and drew on contemporary behaviour and manners in their works: FOKINE created the first abstract ballet, *Les Sylphides* (1907), and, for *L'Après-midi d'un faune* (1912), NIJINSKY developed a new movement vocabulary. Balanchine created in America a new kind of ballet that was cool, formal and athletic, first for American Ballet (1935–41) and then for New York City Ballet (1948–). This style can be seen in ballets such as *The Four Temperaments* (1946). The other major US company to emerge at this time, American Ballet Theater (1940), drew on Fokine. British ballet – especially through Ballet Rambert and the company that became the Royal Ballet – built on the narrative tradition. De Valois created dramatic works, such as *The Rake's Progress* (1935). Frederick Ashton (1904–88) added wit, as in his *La Fille mal gardée* (1960), and lyricism, as in abstract works like *Monotones* (1965). Kenneth MacMillan (1929–92) took ballet to new heights of expression and fluidity, notably in classic dramatic productions such as *Romeo and Juliet* (1965). As the breadth of work expanded, so the popularity of ballet increased, especially after the Second World War.

While Western theatre dance has had a narrative tradition, its twentieth-century development explored much more than that. Pushing the limits of what dance is, and what it can be, was a subject of enquiry throughout the period. Dance communicates through the dancer in action, so its meanings and significance are mediated by prevailing attitudes to physical behaviour and attitudes towards the body, gender, race and nation. Traditionally, ballet reflected the behaviours from which it originated in the sixteenth and seventeenth centuries, with an emphasis on male gallantry. The social and political changes under way at the opening of the twentieth century allowed for and encouraged different types of dance. Some of these were evident in the work of the Ballets Russes and Ballets Suédois. However, the changes initiated in the last years of the nineteenth century, especially those by women dancers, found their fullest realization in a new type of theatrical dance, modern dance.

Modern dance, as a new form, developed almost simultaneously in Europe and the United States. Its main growth period was the first three decades of the twentieth century. The pioneering work of Isadora Duncan, Ruth St Denis, LOÏE FULLER, TED SHAWN and RUDOLF LABAN typified the new and diverse experiments of the early years of the century as dancers sought to create a fresh mode of expression. Many of the earliest pioneers of modern dance found inspiration in other cultures, traditions, arts and forms. They found many ways of responding to the challenges of the modern world and especially the modern industrial city. In doing so they created a form that encompassed a diversity of points of view and approaches, a reaction against the conformity of tradition. This range is evident in the idealism of Isadora Duncan's work in Europe; the African American roots of the dancing of JOSEPHINE BAKER in Paris; the eclectic cultural mix of DENISHAWN, Ted Shawn and Ruth St Denis's company and school in California; Delsarte-inspired dancers throughout the United States; and the EXPRESSIONISM found in European modern dance. Influences from this latter movement can be seen in many early modern dance works of the 1920s and 1930s. Rudolf Laban's work, his companies, movement choirs and ideas, dominated European modern dance until the 1930s. In Germany he achieved his greatest recognition in the late 1920s and early 1930s, as ballet director of the Berlin State Opera and leader of the state's dance organizations. KURT JOOSS's work drew on the analysis and methods of his teacher Laban on expressionist theatre, especially that of KAISER, and the politics of the time. His signature work *The Green Table* (1932) is the definitive statement of dance of the time – a powerfully crafted anti-war dance-drama that received international acclaim and exemplified the theatrical heights that the new modern dance had reached in Europe. Mary Wigman gave voice to the individual European woman, her dances reflecting the changes in how women saw themselves and were seen through three decades from 1914 to 1944, in dances such as *Witch Dance* (1914). The debacle of modern dance in Germany under Nazism, where some equivocated, some collaborated and many left, led to its demise. Jooss's departure in 1933 and his arrival in England invigorated the emerging British scene, with his Ballets Jooss, and then South America in the 1940s. Hanya Holm's departure for the United States in 1931 helped plant the seeds of a new approach to group CHOREOGRAPHY, the pioneering of American modern dance as a form and the reinvigoration of the stage MUSICAL. Laban's arrival in the UK in 1938 helped establish a strong tradition of MOVEMENT and dance education in British schools, and the internationally recognized Laban Centre London still bears his name. During the 1940s he, and his early British books, had a marked influence on approaches to movement on the stage (on e.g. JOAN LITTLEWOOD).

America developed its own distinctive modern dance tradition, and this continued despite radical changes to dance in the latter half of the century. Its foundations in the late 1920s and 1930s owe debts to individual men and women, to Denishawn, to European modern dance, to workers' dance organizations and to Roosevelt's New Deal. Doris Humphrey (1895–1958), Charles Weidman (1901–75), MARTHA GRAHAM and

Hanya Holm are often credited as the four pioneers of the American modern dance. The changes they helped make in the 1930s, exemplified by dances such as Humphrey's *New Dance* (1935), Graham's *American Document* (1938) and Holm's *Trend* (1936), formed the basis for an American art form. Modern dance in America has stressed the theatricality of the group, as opposed to the individual. Many American modern dance companies typically show work by the founder choreographer only. The dances have a diversity of approaches, both narrative and abstract, but are marked by being clearly 'choreographed' with an evident technique. This twentieth-century 'tradition', a marked change from its roots, continues with the work of Paul Taylor (b. 1930) in the United States and the many 'contemporary dance' companies around the world. It was this form that had a marked influence on British theatrical dance in the 1960s, leading to the establishment of London Contemporary Dance Theatre under Robert Cohan (b. 1925) in 1967 and the revival of Ballet Rambert as a modern company in 1966.

Although the history of ballet and that of modern or contemporary dance are generally treated separately, the development of the two forms shows many similarities. The reclamation of ballet by the Ballets Russes coincided with the work of Duncan, St Denis, Laban and Wigman. Just as Diaghilev's heirs, like Balanchine, typified the creation of modern ballet, so Graham, Holm, Humphrey and their contemporaries in the 1930s motivated generations of modern dancers. America was also home to the development of other distinctive dance forms that have had an international impact. African American dance forms had been developed in the 1930s as modern dance by Americans such as KATHERINE DUNHAM, theatricalizing Caribbean dance in particular. Other dances were adapted by black Americans into JAZZ dance forms in the 1920s. Many were taken and introduced into film and theatre, especially in the musical. Such choreographers as JEROME ROBBINS, AGNES DE MILLE and Hanya Holm introduced elements of jazz dance into their ballets, and there has subsequently been much cross-fertilization between jazz dance, ballet and modern dance. Asian dance forms have found theatrical expression in the United States and Europe. Early exemplars of the forms, such as UDAY SHANKAR and RAM GOPAL, have been followed by many others, especially since the 1970s. They appear in their own right and as expressed through Western forms.

Arguably the single most influential dancer of the twentieth century is MERCE CUNNINGHAM. His work spans the distance from the early modern dance of the 1930s to the digital dancing of the twenty-first century. If any one dancer typifies the monumental changes in the theatricality of dance in the latter half of the twentieth century, it is he. He danced with Graham in her modern dance works; he developed a new formal approach to dance with the musician JOHN CAGE, insisting that dance and music should coexist as equal independent arts on stage; he experimented with the nature of dance as art itself, echoing Marcel Duchamp's fundamental changes to the idea of art; he experimented with the theatricality of dance and its place on stage and screen. He brought all such considerations together in works such as *Biped* (1999). The experimentation with the nature of dance and the redefining of its theatricality in postmodern terms happened in the 1960s and 1970s, primarily in the United States. Dancers like YVONNE RAINER, TRISHA BROWN, Steve Paxton (b. 1939), MEREDITH MONK and LUCINDA CHILDS helped redefine the theatrical limits of dance. The works of Judson Dance Theater (1962–6) at JUDSON CHURCH had a considerable influence. The debate about what defines dance and how it might be postmodern is typified by Rainer's *Trio A* (1966). In this work and others Rainer redefined the conceptual framework within which dance is made and 'spectated'. Here and in the other Judson works the clearly drawn technical and theatrical lines of early modern dance are deconstructed. The postmodern dance of this generation and those, like BILL T. JONES and Mark Morris (b. 1956), who came later, allow for an open, fluid, frequently ironic, approach to matters of gender, race and politics. Theatrical limits were breached by drawing on artistic, filmic and other frames of reference. The blurring of boundaries led to collaborative approaches to making work that go way beyond the ideas of collaboration initiated by Diaghilev and questioned by Cunningham.

It was not until the 1970s that German dance fully recovered from Nazism and the war to which it led. Ballet in Germany underwent a much-needed revival in the 1960s, especially through the work of John Cranko (1927–73) and the highly acclaimed Stuttgart Ballet, which put the country back on the international map. The *Tanztheater* that emerged in Germany in the last three decades of the century has many exponents, most of whom studied with the early moderns such as Jooss and Wigman. However, it gained international recognition for the innovations of PINA BAUSCH in such works as *Café Müller* (1978). Bausch presents 'people as they really are', and her approach has been likened to that of BRECHT. *Tanztheater* is characteristically large scale (either theatrically or in length), presenting real people, real events and real emotions. The situations that explore the intimacies of life also reflect how it is socially constructed, especially through the analysis and portrayal of gender. These are facilitated by formal means that stress discontinuity, deconstruction and collage. Bausch is unquestionably the main figure in late twentieth-century European dance, her stature being comparable to that of HEINER MÜLLER in theatre. *Tanztheater* has been an almost exclusively European form and led to a renaissance of European dance in the years leading up to the millennium. In Japan, the distinctive form of postwar dance has been *butoh*, a dance of darkness that has had an at times unsettling influence on accepted notions of form and narrative in the West. One of its best known proponents was TATSUMI HIJIKATA.

Ballet since the nineteenth century has relied on and continues to rely on conventions and traditional theatrical buildings – the Royal Opera House, the Bolshoi, the LINCOLN CENTER. While the twentieth century's new form, modern dance, did not rely on the theatre as a building, many of its later developments did. It is not surprising, therefore, to find formal and narrative characteristics that have much in common with the play. Dance can consume large quantities of space in its enactment, and the space around the action affects the way in which it is seen and appreciated. Few theatres have been built with the requirements of dance in mind, so performances are often marred by sightlines which do not permit a clear view of the whole stage, especially the floor. The experimental theatres of the twentieth century, such as THEATRE IN THE ROUND and thrust or OPEN STAGES, can be particularly problematic for dance. However, the late twentieth century saw a breaking down of such links and, at the turn of the new century, dance's reference points had become wider than they had ever been. The experimental work has much in common with visual theatre forms, and many of its developments take place outside the theatre altogether. Since the HAPPENINGS of the 1950s, Judson in the 1960s and *butoh* in the 1970s, the theatricality of dance has been less and less defined by the theatre space itself. Where postmodern and *Tanztheater* dancers have used the traditional theatre, they have deconstructed its meaning and redefined the purpose of the space. This can be seen in Brown's work, where the properties of the stage space are subverted, and in Bausch's works, where the stage is redefined and the dancers then use it to different effect. In both instances, audiences are asked to look at dance, theatre and themselves in a different way.

The story of Western dance in the twentieth century is of a quest for a new respectability, new forms and new meanings. From uncertain beginnings, dance has gained artistic, theatrical and intellectual credibility and popular acclaim. It has much to say in its own right and contributes continually to the way art and theatre are seen and redefined.

MICHAEL HUXLEY, JEANETTE SIDDALL & ANDREW SOLWAY

See also ARCHITECTURE; DESIGN; MOVEMENT, DANCE AND DRAMA; PHYSICAL PREPARATION.

Dane, Clemence [Winifred Ashton] (b. London, 21 Feb. 1888; d. London, 28 March 1965) Novelist, journalist and playwright. She began her career as an artist and actress under the name Diana Cortis. As a playwright she is best known for her first play, *A Bill of Divorcement* (1921). Other of her 30 or so plays include *Will Shakespeare* (1921), *Granite* (1926), *Wild Decembers*, about the Brontë family (1932), *Cousin Muriel* (1940), and *Eighty in the Shade*, specially written for SYBIL THORNDIKE (1959). Two of her several novels reflect a theatrical theme: *Broome Stages* (1931) and *The Flower Girls* (1954). She also wrote for radio, television and film. ELAINE ASTON

Daniels, Ron *see* AMERICAN REPERTORY THEATER

Daniels, Sarah (b. London, 1957) Playwright. A fruitful relationship with the ROYAL COURT THEATRE produced work of feminist energy drawing on both pagan and Christian myth (e.g. *Ripen Our Darkness*, 1981; *Neaptide*, 1986; *Beside Herself*, 1990). Controversy surrounded *Masterpieces* (1983), a powerful study of a young woman's angry response to a snuff movie, and *Byrthrite* (1987), about genetic engineering. She continued to explore and validate female experience in her later plays, *The Madness of Esme and Shaz* (1994), *Blow Your House Down* (1995), and a radio play, *Purple Side Coasters* (1998). FRANCES GRAY

Michelene Wandor, *Post-war British Drama: Looking Back in Gender* (2001)

D'Annunzio, Gabriele (b. Pescara, Italy, 12 March 1863; d. Gardone, Italy, 1 March 1938) Poet, novelist and playwright; aesthete, man of action and bon viveur. He was a man of excess in life, art and politics; his extreme patriotism opened the way for his support of fascism. His plays include *La città morta* (*The Dead City*, 1898), a vehicle for BERNHARDT; *La Gioconda* (1899), *Francesca da Rimini* (1901) and *La figlia di Iorio* (*Iorio's Daughter*, 1904). With ELEONORA DUSE he hoped to create a national theatre on a Wagnerian scale, and with his plays aspired to replace bourgeois realism with high tragedy. FELICITY FIRTH

John Woodhouse, *Gabrielle D'Annunzio: Defiant Angel* (1998).

Darby, Eileen   *see* THEATRE PHOTOGRAPHY

D'Arcy, Margaretta   *see* ARDEN, JOHN

Darke, Nick [Nicholas Temperley Watson]   (b. Wadebridge, Cornwall, 29 Aug. 1948)   Playwright. Darke gave up acting to write, working with many forms, notably children's theatre and COMMUNITY history plays like *A Tickle on the River's Back*, *Landmarks* (both 1979); and *The Earth Turned Inside Out* (1984), which later played at the NATIONAL THEATRE, retitled *Ting Tang Mine*. For the ROYAL SHAKESPEARE COMPANY he wrote *The Body* (1983); *The Dead Monkey* (1986), perhaps his best play, depicting the macabre recriminations of a Californian couple haunted by the animal of the title; and the under-rated *Kissing the Pope* (1989), on the Nicaraguan conflict. He is noted for sensitivity, dark wit and vigour. Many of his plays were produced by Cornwall's Kneehigh Theatre, including *The King of Prussia* (1996) and *The Riot* (1999).   DAN REBELLATO

Dasté, Jean   *see* COPEAU, JACQUES; FRANCE; LECOQ, JACQUES

Daubeny, Peter [Lauderdale]   (b. Wiesbaden, Germany, 16 April 1921; d. London, 6 Aug. 1975)   Producer. Daubeny trained as an actor under MICHEL SAINT-DENIS, but after losing his left arm at Salerno in 1943 he moved into management and mounted several successes, including WERFEL's *Jacobowsky and the Colonel* (1945). In 1951 he started bringing international dance companies to London and arranged first visits by MARTHA GRAHAM and the BERLINER ENSEMBLE as he graduated from the non-verbal to the verbal. He presented the LIVING THEATER in London in 1961, and in 1964 he inaugurated his landmark annual WORLD THEATRE SEASONS at the ALDWYCH THEATRE, presented with the ROYAL SHAKESPEARE COMPANY but without government grants. His commitment to international theatre had important consequences in widening the tastes of audiences and practitioners, informing the work of directors like GASKILL and BROOK. He wrote two autobiographical books, *Stage by Stage* (1952) and *My World of Theatre* (1971). He was knighted in 1973. DAN REBELLATO

Davidson, Gordon   *see* MARK TAPER FORUM

Davies, Howard   (b. Reading, 26 April 1945)   Director. Davies's career started at the BRISTOL OLD VIC Studio, which he ran, specializing in new and modern drama, and in COMMUNITY THEATRE, commissioning plays for the Studio, and directing for Avon Touring and the Welsh Drama Company. Buzz Goodbody persuaded him to overcome his suspicion of Shakespeare and the 'Cambridge clique' and join the ROYAL SHAKE-SPEARE COMPANY, where he directed a fine *Man is Man* (1975). He became an associate director, responsible for their new writing theatre, the Warehouse, for five years. His clear, uncluttered, intelligent direction was seen in all the RSC theatres, in several BOND productions including *The Bundle* (1978), in *Good* (1981), *Henry VIII* (1983) and *Les Liaisons Dangereuses* (1985). Davies then joined the NATIONAL THEATRE as an associate director, directing (among others) *Cat on a Hot Tin Roof*, *The Shaughraun* and *The Secret Rapture* (1988), *Pygmalion* (1992), *Chips with Everything* (1997) and *All My Sons* (2000).   DAN REBELLATO

Davies, Robertson   (b. Thamesville, Ont., 28 Aug. 1913; d. Toronto, 2 Dec. 1995)   Playwright and novelist. Internationally known for his novels, he also made an important contribution to Canadian theatre. Central to his dramatic oeuvre is a challenge to the forces that stifle imagination, and an exploration of human affairs conducted within the areas of myth, magic and religion. In the best of his one-act plays, *Overlaid* (1947), the puritanism of Canadian rural life is contrasted with the freedom of art. In such full-length plays as *Fortune, My Foe* (1949) and *At My Heart's Core* (1950) Davies contrasts European values with those of Canada and finds the latter wanting. Other full-length plays include *A Jig for the Gypsy* (1954) and *Hunting Stuart* (1955). His themes of the revenge of the unlived life and the need to establish one's true identity are dramatized in *Question Time* (1975), which suggests that the roots of the national psyche must be found in Canada and not in the colonial past. Davies wrote further works for the theatre, including the libretto for the opera *The Golden Ass* (1998), but his later years were dominated by his work as a novelist.
EUGENE BENSON

Daviot, Gordon [Elizabeth McKenzie]   (b. Inverness, Scotland, 1896; d. London, 13 Feb. 1952)   Novelist and playwright. Daviot's first full-length play, *Richard of Bordeaux* (1931), starring JOHN GIELGUD, ran for over a year and enabled her to give up her career as a PE teacher. *Queen of Scots* and *The Laughing Woman* (both 1934) were less successful in production and Daviot turned successfully to writing detective novels under the name of Josephine Tey.   MAGGIE GALE

Davis, Donald   (b. Newmarket, Ont., 26 Feb. 1928)   Actor and director. A stalwart of Ontario and Toronto theatre in the 1940s and 1950s (with his brother, Murray, he founded the Straw Hat Players in 1948 and the CREST THEATER in 1953), Davis remains active in the contemporary and classical repertoires in theatres across Canada. In the early 1950s he appeared at the

Glasgow CITIZENS' THEATRE and the OLD VIC, and in the 1960s performed with major companies in the United States. In 1960 he starred in the North American première of BECKETT's *Krapp's Last Tape*, directed by ALAN SCHNEIDER, with whom he subsequently mounted other North American premières of Beckett's plays. L. W. CONOLLY

Davis, Henrietta Vinton (b. Baltimore, ?1860/3; d. Washington DC, 23 Nov. 1941) Actress. As a black actress at the turn of the century, she was for the most part restricted to giving public readings and excerpts of leading Shakespearean roles such as Juliet, Portia, Desdemona, Ophelia, Rosalind, Cleopatra and Lady Macbeth, all of which proved very popular. She appeared in and produced plays by black authors: *Our Old Kentucky Home* (1898), written for her by John E. Bruce, and *Dessalines* (1893) and *Christophe* (1912), by William Edgar Easton. Thwarted in her acting career by racial prejudice, she dedicated much of her time to working for civil rights for black people, both in the United States and in Africa. HELEN RAPPAPORT

See also BLACK THEATRE.

Davis, Jack [Leonard] (b. Perth, Australia, 11 March 1917; d. Freemantle, Western Australia, 17 March 2000) Indigenous playwright, poet, activist; best known for his trilogy *The Dreamers* (1981), *No Sugar* (1986) and *Barungin* (1988), which rivals the achievement of any sequence by an Australian playwright. The plays deal with black Australians in a drama which is overwhelmingly white, recording the struggles of his people, the Nyoongah – the first Australians of the south-west of the continent – from 1929 to the present. Each play recalls Davis's initial work, *Kullark* (1979), a history of Aboriginal resistance from the death of Yagan in 1933 to the present: 'Kullark' means home. His other plays and performed poetry include *Wahngin Country*, *The First Born*, *Honey Spot* (1987) and *In Our Town* (1992). His book *A Boy's Life* was published in 1991. Davis was a community leader and was honoured for his services to indigenous culture and education. His work charted shifts in consciousness and indigenous identity in their counter-discourse to whiteness. They are admired at home and abroad. Much of his theatrical success came through collaboration with the Marli Biyol ensemble and a non-indigenous director, Andrew Ross. Their working relationship testifies to David's belief that 'This is ours together/This nation'. GUS WORBY

K. Chesson, *Jack Davis: A Life Story* (1998)
H. Gilbert, *Sightlines: Race, Gender and Nation in Contemporary Australian Theatre* (1998)

G. Turcotte, *Jack Davis: An Introduction* (1994)

Davis, Joe (b. London, 18 Dec. 1912) LIGHTING designer. After working for STRAND Electric, he joined producers H. M. TENNENT at its founding in 1936 as head of lighting and as such worked with major directors and actors on the firm's stylish shows which came to epitomize the best of commercial theatre in their era (e.g. *Ring Round the Moon*, 1950; *Waters of the Moon*, 1951; *The Millionairess*, 1952). For over two decades he was the personal lighting designer to the glamorous MARLENE DIETRICH. He was founder, chair and life president of the Association of Lighting Designers and the inaugural chair of the Association of British Theatre Technicians. CHARLES LONDON

Davis, Ossie (b. Cogdell, Ga., 18 Dec. 1917) Actor, director, playwright, social activist. After acting with a Harlem-based group he made his Broadway debut in the title role of *Jeb* (1946). Other New York roles include *The Leading Lady* (1948), *Stevedore* (1949), *The Smile of the World* (1949), *The Wisteria Trees* (1950), *The Green Pastures* (1951), *Jamaica* (1957), *A Raisin in the Sun* (1959, succeeding Sidney Poitier), *The Zulu and the Zayda* (1965) and *I'm Not Rappaport* (1986). He wrote and starred in *Purlie Victorious* (1961), a spoof of racial prejudice, and co-authored the successful musical version, *Purlie* (1970). He has acted in film and television and directed films (e.g. *Cotton Comes to Harlem*, *Countdown at Kusini*). He often appears with his wife, the actor and writer RUBY DEE, with whom he suffered in the blacklisting of the 1950s. They wrote a joint autobiography, *With Ossie and Ruby: In this Life Together* (1998). DAVID BARBOUR

Davis, R. G. *see* SAN FRANCISCO MIME GROUP

De Angelis, [Thomas] Jefferson (b. San Francisco, 30 Nov. 1859; d. Orange, NJ, 20 March 1933) Comedian, dancer and singer. The son of an original member of the San Francisco Minstrel Company, his colourful career began in comedy sketches at the age of 12 in Baltimore. After an international career as a comedian, he turned to light opera. Setting up his own production company, he gained considerable popularity in *The Jolly Musketeers* (1898), *The Emerald Isle* (1902) and *Fantana* (1905), moving on to appear in several GILBERT and SULLIVAN operas. In the public mind he was associated with the song 'Tammany', which he had made his own in *Fantana*. His autobiography, *A Vagabond Trouper*, appeared in 1931. HELEN RAPPAPORT

De Chirico, Giorgio (b. Volos, Greece, 10 July 1888; d. Rome, 19 Nov. 1978) Painter and designer. He created his first stage work for the Ballets Suedois' *La Jarre* (1924). DIAGHILEV commisioned him to design sets and costumes for *Le Bal* (1929), which harkened back to the SURREALIST motif which had characterized his work before his return to classicism. His dream-like, spacious designs were influential in international scenography and among directors like VITRAC.

DENISE L. TILLES

See also DANCE; DESIGN.

Rupert Martin, ed., *Late De Chirico, 1940–76* (1985)

De Filippo, Eduardo (b. Naples, 24 May 1900; d. Rome, 31 Oct. 1984) Playwright, actor and director. He was well known as a champion of popular dialect theatre and as a highly versatile and expressive actor in the COMMEDIA DELL'ARTE tradition, collaborating in his early life with his actor brother Peppino De Filippo, and for a longer period with his sister Titina. He ran his own company and starred in his own productions. His plays were preponderantly realist and imbued with the spirit of his native Naples. A unique mixture of social concern, tragedy, irony and farce, their underlying theme could be said to be the triumph of human optimism and traditional values in the face of extreme poverty, deprivation and corruption. A cult figure in his own lifetime, it was his magnetic presence on stage that revealed his genius.

Although his early plays show traces of the influence of PIRANDELLO, whom he knew, from 1954 onwards, when he established his company at the Teatro San Ferdinando in Naples, he devoted his energy to the creation of a truly popular Neapolitan dialect theatre. His best-known plays, in many of which Naples itself functions as a protagonist, and even as a symbol of a universal condition, include: *Napoli milionaria* ('Millionaire Naples', 1945); *Questi fantasmi* (*These Phantoms*) and *Filumena Marturano* (both 1946); *Grande magia* (*Grand Magic*) and *Le voci di dentro* (*Inner Voices*, both 1948); *Sabato, domenica e lunedì* (*Saturday, Sunday, Monday*, 1959); and *Il sindaco del rione Sanità* (*The Local Authority*, 1961).

His three last plays, *Il contratto* ('The contract', 1967), *Il monumento* ('The monument', 1970) and *Gli esami non finiscono mai* ('Exams go on forever', 1973) showed a tendency to deal in allegorical vein with questions of moral priorities. These were less successful than the masterpieces of his Neapolitan heyday with their wealth of physical, emotional and domestic detail.

FELICITY FIRTH

Mario B. Mignone, *Eduardo De Filippo* (1984)

de Graft, Joe (b. Ghana, 1924; d. 1978) Playwright, director and actor. One of the earliest graduates in English from what was the University College of the Gold Coast, de Graft became a teacher of drama and set up the theatre programme of the University of Ghana School of Music and Drama in 1963. Plays include *Sons and Daughters* (1964), which looks at the generation gap in modern Africa, *Through a Film Darkly* (1970) and *Muntu*, written after de Graft went to Nairobi in 1969 as an explanation to the World Council of Churches of what African churches were about. KOLE OMOTOSO

De Groen [Mathers], Alma (b. Foxton, New Zealand, 5 Sept. 1941) Playwright and DRAMATURG. She began writing for theatre in Canada with the award-winning *The Joss Adams Show* (1970), and has since produced eight other plays. Among her best work is *The Rivers of China* (1987), which explores a long-standing preoccupation with role-play, with spiritual and sexual freedom, and with the social, political and gender structures which keep people in their place – especially women and artists, and women who are artists. *Available Light* (1993) also touches on these matters. In a world of norms, there is always one who sees beyond and whose actions conform to vision rather than convention, as in *The Girl Who Saw Everything* (1993) and *The Woman at the Window* (1999). This dysfunction sometimes brings here-and-now horror – neglect and isolation in *Going Home* (1976), or persecution for alleged deviance in *Chidley* (1976); sometimes a tenuous creative freedom is achieved from dislocation, disruption and exile, in *Vocations* (1982), for example. One thing is certain; her characters will not rest with the histories they have been given, nor the limitations of the here and now. De Groen explores 'bleak' futures in a theatre of transformation and virtual experience through myth, mysticism, politics and science.

GUS WORBY

E. Perkins, *The Plays of Alma De Groen* (1994)

L. Radic, *The State of Play: The Revolution in the Australian Theatre since the 1960s* (1991)

de Keersmaeker, Anne Teresa (b. Mechelen, Belgium, 11 June 1960) Leading European postmodern choreographer of the generation following PINA BAUSCH. She trained at Mudra, MAURICE BÉJART's school in Brussels, and at New York University before receiving international acclaim at the age of 22 for *Fase, Four Movements to the Music of Steve Reich* (1982). Her work is characterized by a rigorous, often minimalist formalism usually set to music by serious twentieth-century composers, but she has also used text in her choreography – for example, excerpts from TENNESSEE

WILLIAMS and PETER WEISS – and in 1987 staged HEINER MÜLLER's *Verkommenes Ufer* (*Despoiled Shore*). Her company Rosas has received increasingly generous state subsidy and since 1992 has been resident at the Monnaie Théâtre in Brussels. In 1996 she founded the important dance school P.A.R.T.S. RAMSAY BURT

See also CHOREOGRAPHY; DANCE.

Rita Feliciano, 'A Love–Hate Affair with Dance', *Dance Magazine*, March 1998

De Koven, [Henry Louis] Reginald (b. Middleton, Conn., 3 April 1861; d. Chicago, 15 Jan. 1920) Composer. Educated in England and continental Europe, he married wealth on his return to America and devoted his remaining time to music. With lyricist HARRY SMITH he became briefly the doyen of comic opera there, remembered for *Robin Hood* (1891) and *Rob Roy* (1894). Although overtaken by the likes of composer VICTOR HERBERT, he continued to be popular in the early years of the new century and was an important figure at the outset of American musical theatre. CHARLES LONDON

A. De Koven, *A Musician and His Wife* (1926)

de Mille, Agnes [George] (b. New York, 18 Sept. 1905; d. New York, 5/6 Oct. 1993) Dancer and choreographer. Daughter of playwright William C. and niece of the film director Cecil B., Agnes de Mille trained under such dance luminaries as MARIE RAMBERT and Antony Tudor and made her BROADWAY debut as a dancer in 1927. In 1929 she choreographed a popular revival of a melodrama, *The Black Crook*, and then worked in London for a few years before returning to New York. A friend of MARTHA GRAHAM, she was at home in both ballet and musicals. In her choreography for *Rodeo* (1942), *One Touch of Venus* (1943), *Oklahoma!* (1943), *Tally-Ho* (1944), *Carousel* (1945), *Brigadoon* (1947), *Fall River Legend* (1948), *Gentlemen Prefer Blondes* (1949), *Paint Your Wagon* (1951) and others, de Mille created a new American dance style incorporating humour and character psychology. The enormous success of her contribution to *Oklahoma!*, in particular the dream ballet sequence, changed the nature of musical theatre dance for years to come, though it later dated quickly. She founded the Heritage Dance Theater in 1973 to preserve American folk dance forms. A stroke in 1975 left her partially paralysed but intrepid in her arts activism. She is the author of 12 books, including the autobiographical volumes *Dance to the Piper* (1951), *And Promenade Home* (1956), *Speak to Me, Dance with Me* (1973) and *Reprieve: A Memoir* (1981).
FELICIA HARDISON LONDRÉ

See also CHOREOGRAPHY; DANCE.

Carol Easton, *No intermissions: The Life of Agnes de Mille* (2000)

de Montherlant, Henri *see* MONTHERLANT, HENRI DE

de Niro, Robert *see* ACTORS' STUDIO

de Valois, Ninette [Edris Stannus] (b. Baltiboys, Blessington, Co. Wicklow, Ireland, 6 June 1898; d. London, 8 March 2001) Dancer, choreographer, teacher and ballet director. A soloist with DIAGHILEV's Ballet Russe (1923–6), she was the choreographic director at the OLD VIC, CAMBRIDGE FESTIVAL THEATRE and ABBEY THEATRE (1926–30). She became the most important figure in British ballet as founder and director of the Royal Ballet (1931–63) and its school. She was created a dame in 1951 and a Companion of Honour in 1982. Among her books are *Come Dance with Me* (1957) and *Step by Step* (1977).
CHARLES LONDON

See also CHOREOGRAPHY; DANCE.

Kathrine Sorley Walker, *Ninette de Valois: Idealist Without Illusion* (1987)

Deaf West Theater Company Founded in Los Angeles in 1991 by artistic director Ed Waterstreet, it has become a cultural institution serving as a model for deaf theatre worldwide, changing people's perceptions regarding the capabilities of and opportunities for deaf artists. Deaf West is located in the NoHo Arts District of North Hollywood with a 65-seat theatre, complete with a state-of-the-art sound system so that sound can be 'felt' as well as heard. All productions are presented in American Sign Language with voice interpretation (voice actors are integrated as cast members) and supertitles for hearing and non-signing audiences. It is the first professional resident sign language theatre in the western United States, dedicated to directly improving and enriching the cultural lives of the 1.2 million deaf and hard-of-hearing individuals in the Los Angeles area. Deaf West productions, actors and directors have won more than 40 theatre awards for artistic merit; in 1991 the company received a record-breaking five Los Angeles Ovation awards, including best play (*A Streetcar Named Desire*) and best musical (*Oliver!*), the first production of its kind to incorporate American Sign Language fully in a classic musical theatre piece. In 2000 Deaf West established the first professional training conservatory of its kind for talented deaf and hard-of-hearing students, with the goal of helping them to achieve theatrical careers as actors, directors, writers, designers and technicians.
LUISA CARIAGA

See also DISABILITY.

Dean, Basil [Herbert] (b. Croydon, 27 Sept. 1888; d. London, 22 April 1978)   Defined himself as 'actor, producing manager, stage director and dramatic author'. He was a complete man of the theatre – arrogant, opinionated, rude, intolerant, but creative, perceptive, supportive to new writers and, reflecting his original training as an analytical scientist, keen-eyed for detail and relentless in his pursuit of perfection. A graduate from Miss HORNIMAN's Repertory Company, he enlisted in 1914, and in 1917 was transferred to the War Office as head of the Entertainment branch of the Navy and Army Canteen Board. After the war he formed a management partnership with a wealthy businessman, Alec Rea, which lasted until 1926; then he went solo, recognized as the most important individual producer and director in the West End. Among his many successes were JAMES ELROY FLECKER's *Hassan* (1923), which he 'arranged' for stage representation, *The Constant Nymph* (1926), *Young Woodley* (1928), *Autumn Crocus* (1931), the early NOEL COWARD plays and J. B. PRIESTLEY's *When We Are Married* (1938). In the Second World War he was again appointed head of entertainment for the armed services (at the ENTERTAINMENTS NATIONAL SERVICE ASSOCIATION) and made friends of the troops but enduring enemies of many members of the theatrical profession. These enmities contributed to his declining postwar career, which was relieved by several festival revivals of *Hassan*. His autobiographies are *Seven Ages* (1970) and *The Mind's Eye* (1973).   IAN BEVAN

Dean, James   *see* ACTOR'S STUDIO; METHOD

Dear, Nick [Nicholas J.] (b. Portsmouth, Hants, 11 June 1955)   Playwright. Playing with language and form, Dear writes with an abrasive intensity that reveals the world as dark and comic. In *Pure Science* (1983) and *Temptation* (1984) the assumptions of human progress are questioned with humorous élan, and his portrait of George III in *In the Ruins* (1984) is both shocking and spry. His most powerful play, *The Art of Success* (ROYAL SHAKESPEARE COMPANY, 1986), evokes the stinking world of the engraver and painter William Hogarth, whose savaging of social ills Dear links to Hogarth's own immoral behaviour. Dear's ADAPTATIONS, from *A Family Affair* (Ostrovsky, 1988) and *The Last Days of Don Juan* (Tirso de Molina, 1990) to his award-winning screenplay of Jane Austen's *Persuasion* (1995), have won him many plaudits.   CHARLES LONDON

deconstruction   *see* DRAMATIC THEORY

Decroux, Etienne[-Marcel] (b. Paris, 19 July 1898; d. Paris, 12 Mar. 1991)   Actor, MIME and teacher. A pupil of COPEAU, he worked with DULLIN from 1926 to 1934 and taught the young JEAN-LOUIS BARRAULT, appearing with him in the film *Les Enfants du paradis* (1944). He renewed the art of mime by placing emphasis on movements of the body, rather than on the hands and face as had been the practice of earlier masters, Séverin and Wague. He rejected all externals, such as costume, scenery, music and words, concentrating on scenes from modern life – in the factory, on the sports field, in the office. He taught *mime corporel* (to, among others, MARCEL MARCEAU) and describes his work in *Paroles sur le mime* (1963).   TERRY HODGSON
See also PHYSICAL PREPARATION.

Dee, Ruby [Ann Wallace] (b. Cleveland, Ohio, 27 Oct. 1924)   Actress and writer, who, with her husband OSSIE DAVIS, was 'blacklisted' in the 1950s for social activism. She took the title role in the tour of *Anna Lucasta* (1946) and was noted in LORRAINE HANSBERRY's *A Raisin in the Sun* (1959) and for her award-winning performances in ATHOL FUGARD's *Boesman and Lena* (1970) and ALICE CHILDRESS's *Wedding Band* (1972). She was the first black actress at the AMERICAN SHAKESPEARE FESTIVAL, Stratford, playing Katharina in *The Taming of the Shrew* and Cordelia in *King Lear* (both 1965). For the NEW YORK SHAKESPEARE FESTIVAL she played Gertrude in *Hamlet* (1975). Also active in radio, films and television, she was elected to Broadway's Hall of Fame in 1988. She is also the author of several plays, and with her husband wrote an autobiography, *With Ossie and Ruby: In This Life Together* (1998).   JANE HOUSE

Deevey, Theresa (b. Waterford, Ireland, 21 Jan. 1903; d. Waterford, 19 Jan. 1963)   Playwright. Though congenitally deaf, she wrote radio plays from 1936 that are masterpieces of that medium. Her stage plays, *Temporal Powers* (1932), *The King of Spain's Daughter* (1935), *Katie Roche* (1936) and *The Wild Goose* (1936) were first produced at the ABBEY THEATRE, Dublin. *Katie Roche* is often revived.   CHRISTOPHER FITZ-SIMON

Delaney, Shelagh (b. Salford, Lancs, 25 Nov. 1939)   Playwright. Chiefly famous for her first play, *A Taste of Honey* (1958), completed when she was only 18, Delaney has nevertheless other stage plays (e.g. *The Lion in Love*, 1960; *The House that Jack Built*, 1978) and television credits to her name, as well as a number of successful screenplays – notably *Charley Bubbles* (1968) and *Dance with a Stranger* (1985). *A Taste of Honey* was produced by JOAN LITTLEWOOD's THEATRE WORKSHOP, seen in the West End and New York, and filmed in 1962. This earthily realistic, moving story of a reluctant teenage mother-to-be was a definitive play of its period and has been constantly revived; perhaps because it raises issues which were later to become prime concerns of feminist writers, but also because of its undating, vital dialogue. DAVID SELF

H. Keyssar, *Feminist Theatre* (1984)
M. Wandor, *Look Back in Gender* (1987)

Delfont, Bernard *see* GRADE FAMILY

Demarcy, Richard (b. France, 1942) Playwright, performer and academic. Demarcy's plays are exuberantly anti-naturalistic, and draw on folklore, popular songs, satire, fantasy and the grotesque. Plays include *L'Etranger dans la maison* ('Stranger in the house', 1982), *Voyages d'Hiver* ('Winter trips', 1986) and *Les Rêves de Lolita et Laverdure* ('Lolita's dreams and Laverdure', 1987). ANNA MCMULLAN

Democratic Republic of Congo *see* FRENCH AFRICAN THEATRE

Dench, Judi [Judith Olivia] (b. York, 9 Dec. 1934) Actress, admired for her warmth and intelligence. Her acclaimed debut was as Ophelia to JOHN NEVILLE's Hamlet (OLD VIC, 1957). Since 1961, as a member of the first ROYAL SHAKESPEARE COMPANY, she has performed a wide range of leading roles, including Titania (*A Midsummer Night's Dream*, 1962), Hermione and Perdita (*The Winter's Tale*, 1969), Beatrice (*Much Ado About Nothing*, 1976), Lady Macbeth (*Macbeth*, 1976), Juno (*Juno and the Paycock*, 1980) and Mother Courage (*Mother Courage*, 1984). Other parts include Sally Bowles in the musical *Cabaret* (1968) and Cleopatra in *Antony and Cleopatra* (1987) at the NATIONAL THEATRE. She directed *Much Ado About Nothing* (1988) and *Look Back in Anger* (1989) for the Renaissance Theatre Company. In 1999 she received an Academy Award for Best Supporting Actress for her portrayal as Elizabeth I in the film *Shakespeare in Love* (1998) and a Tony for her first stage role on Broadway, in *Amy's View*. Her husband was the popular actor Michael Williams (1935–2001). She was created a dame in 1988.

D. KEITH PEACOCK

G. Jacobs, *Judi Dench: A Great Deal of Laughter* (1986)
John Miller, *Judi Dench: With a Crack in Her Voice* (1999)

Denishawn Dance School Founded in 1915 and run until 1932 by **Ruth St Denis** (originally Ruth Dennis; b. New Jersey, 20 Jan. 1877; d. Hollywood, 21 July 1968) and **Ted Shawn** (b. Kansas City, 21 Oct. 1891; d. Orlando, Fla., 9 Jan 1972). St Denis had her first success with the exotic ballet *Radha* (1906), which she toured extensively in America and Europe. In 1914 she married Shawn, who had first appeared on stage in

1911 and was then touring with a small company. Their school was crucial to the development of American modern dance, providing training for such pioneers as MARTHA GRAHAM and Doris Humphrey, who both influenced contemporary drama. Shawn also headed a Men's Group (1933–40) that did much to destroy the prejudice against male dancers in the United States. ANDREW SOLWAY

See also CHOREOGRAPHY; DANCE; MOVEMENT, DANCE AND DRAMA.

Denison, Merrill *see* CANADA: THEATRE IN ENGLISH

Denison, [John] Michael [Terence Wellesley] (b. Doncaster, Yorks, 1 Nov. 1915; d. Amersham, Bucks, 21 July 1998) and **Gray, Dulcie** [Winifred Catherine] (b. Kuala Lumpur, Federated Malay States, 20 Nov. 1919) One of the the best-known husband and wife acting teams in the British theatre, although no rivals to the Oliviers. They met at drama school and pursued a busy joint stage career from then on. Accomplished without being inspired, they often seemed to have been cast when other more glittering names were not available, but in true British fashion they never let the side down. Gray was also a modestly successful writer of detective stories. Denison's memoir *Overture and Beginners* appeared in 1973. IAN BEVAN

Denmark The twentieth century was heralded with the advent of naturalism and the world premières of plays by IBSEN and STRINDBERG. The Casino, Dagmar and Betty Nansen theatres in Copenhagen were the main exponents of new drama, and works by Henri Nathansen and Gustav Wied are among those from that period still performed. Bodil Ipsen and Poul Reumert were actors encouraging new styles of theatre and, along with film actress Asta Nielsen, they ensured that the Nordisk Filmkompagni was foremost in the world until the 1914–18 war. Although no experimental ground was broken in the theatre until KJELD ABELL's *Melodien, der blev væk* (*The Melody that Lost*, 1935), the patriotic dramas of KAJ MUNK during the 1940s German occupation enshrined his name in Danish theatre. After 1945 came a wave of foreign influence led by the French, followed by the Americans and, finally, by leading British and German dramatists, whose successors continued to dominate the Danish repertoire in the 1990s.

In the 1950s the provincial repertory theatres in Odense, Århus and Ålborg became recipients of state funding, enabling them to champion the absurdists and newer writers and providing powerful alternatives to the Royal Theatre in Copenhagen, which still maintains a key position. Leif Panduro and Klaus Rifbjerg were the modern dramatists of the 1960s, taking a closer look at individual and social values within the Danish welfare system; also, at this time of political and experimental activity, smaller companies established themselves around the country, the most notable of these being the ODIN TEATRET in Holstebro, whose performances, training methods and research into the origins of acting have won international acclaim. Children's theatre developed and solidified its position in the 1970s, as did the importance of the smaller companies throughout the 1980s; notable among these was Dr Dante in Copenhagen. Among the dramatists of the 1990s, Morti Vizki, Sven Holm, Peter Asmussen, Nikoline Werdelin, Line Knutzon, Gerz Feigenberg and Erling Jepsen should be mentioned.

A theatrical institution as popular in Denmark as the pantomime in Britain, is the summer CABARET, and a renowned apprentice of this art was the comedian Victor Borge. It has survived the century. KIM DAMBÆK

P. Brask, ed., *Drama Contemporary: Scandinavia* (1989)
F. J. and Lise-Lone Marker, *The Scandanavian Theatre* (1996)
P. M. Mitchell, *A History of Danish Literature* (1957)

Dennis, Nigel [Forbes] (b. Bletchingley, Surrey, 16 Jan. 1912; d. Warks, 19 July 1989) Playwright and novelist. Dennis's stage plays, *Cards of Identity* (1956), *The Making of Moo* (1957) and *August for the People* (1961), are satires on psychology, religion and democracy, combining a powerful intelligence with hilarious theatricality. They were performed by the ENGLISH STAGE COMPANY in its early years. DAN REBELLATO

Denver Center Theater *see* BONFILS THEATRE

Derain, André (b. Chatou, France, 10 June 1880; d. Chambourcy, France, 8 Sept. 1954) Painter and designer. A member of the Fauve movement, a group of figurative painters known for their bold simplicity and energy, he created wildly colourful decors for DIAGHILEV's *La Boutique Fantastique* (1919). APOLLINAIRE supported his work, which, through Diaghilev, was influential beyond his own circle. DENISE L. TILLES

Derwent, Clarence (b. London, 23 March 1884; d. New York, 6 Aug. 1959) Actor and producer. Derwent spent the early part of his career as an actor in England, working under FRANK BENSON, ANNIE HORNIMAN and finally BEERBOHM TREE. In 1915 he moved to New York and began a very successful Broadway career as both an actor and a producer. Derwent respected the craft as well as the needs of performers. In 1945 he created the Clarence Derwent award, to be presented annually in both New York and London to the performer who

has excelled in a supporting role. The following year he became president of the American Actors' Equity (*see* UNIONS) and later he was president of the AMERICAN NATIONAL THEATER AND ACADEMY. He wrote an autobiography, *The Derwent Story* (1953). ADRIANA HUNTER

design Of all the participants in the act of making theatre, the designer has seen his or her function change most dramatically during the twentieth century, a change reflected not merely in the designer's self-perception, but also in the perceptions of the public. Many people still do not know what designers do – either presuming that design is no more than surface decoration of the stage, or imagining that the physical aspect of a production hardly needs to be designed at all – but this state of ignorance or innocence is in decline. For economic as well as artistic reasons, the designer has been forcibly ejected from the back rooms of the theatre and projected into the creative forefront.

The state of the art is energized by a new awareness of the dynamics of the theatre space, its geometry and its spatial relationship to the spectator. Design is increasingly a three-dimensional activity, affirming GORDON CRAIG's dictum to his students: 'A designer must design with his feet, not merely with his eyes.' What is frequently taken for radical contemporary directing is often in fact imaginative design.

The move out of conventional theatre spaces into alternative or SITE-SPECIFIC localities has provided some theatre artists with an opportunity to redefine the form of theatre and its visual content. The intimate surroundings of TADEUSZ KANTOR's tiny theatre Cricot 2 in Kraków, Poland, and GROTOWSKI's experiments in Opole and Wroclaw, are two small-scale examples. By contrast, ARIANE MNOUCHKINE's Théâtre du Soleil has occupied a vast abandoned cartridge factory in a suburb of Paris. Within the framework of its walls, the performance space is reinvented for each production; the design often begins as a collective attempt to solve the problem of how to perform a given play or subject.

The Italian director LUCA RONCONI, collaborating with the designer Uberto Bertacca, has worked in a series of found spaces – warehouses, industrial buildings, tents – producing astonishing theatre pieces such as *Orlando Furioso* (1968), in which startling visual images were created in response to the challenge of the space. At the Schaubühne in Berlin, PETER STEIN, in collaboration with the designer KARL-ERNST HERMANN, has created multiple environments within the walls of his cavernous theatre, using the audience as a design component in the created world of the play, sometimes moving it inventively from place to place. In Britain, the ROYAL SHAKESPEARE COMPANY's small-scale touring policy has given designers the freedom to explore the form of theatre most suitable for the play, by creating for each production a design encompassing a travelling stage and auditorium, which is then toured to a succession of towns and cities that do not have theatres of their own. Such reinventions of theatre space have made possible new versions of the classics as well as original theatre pieces conceived collectively by theatre groups to exploit all the possibilities of the performing space. In the process, the roles of director and designer inevitably become integrated.

A related development has been the exploitation by theatre artists of the cubic stage space of existing theatre buildings, accepting the given architecture of a traditional theatre space, but so manipulating that space that the spectator's eye is stretched to the very maximum in every dimension. PETER BROOK employed a disused variety theatre in Paris, Les Bouffes du Nord, stripped to its bare brick walls, to show a crowd clambering up the back wall of the theatre in *Timon of Athens* (1987), or, in *Les Ik* (1975), conveying the desperation of poverty and the fragility of a shelter by placing a solitary figure kneeling on the stage surrounded by six small bricks. RICHARD PEDUZZI, a painter working with the director PATRICE CHÉREAU at the THEATRE NATIONAL POPULAIRE, created for Marivaux's *La Dispute* (1976) scenes of astonishing and breathtaking beauty that taught audiences a new visual language of the theatre. A series of giant buildings more than 12 metres high, using the entire vertical dimension of the space, were placed along one side of the stage, taking the audience's eye up to the very top of the proscenium arch. At the same time, a tiny row of real bushes and a small lake of real water, placed at the very back of the stage along a horizontal plane, pulled the audience's attention to the opposite extreme. Directors ROGER PLANCHON and GIORGIO STREHLER, working with many artist–designers but notably EZIO FRIGERIO, have also emotionally and provocatively evoked for audiences the vision of the stage as a cube of space to be sculpted by the imagination of the artist. PHILIP PROWSE, director–designer at the Glasgow CITIZENS' THEATRE, has consistently animated the different stages of this small popular theatre with distinctively vivid and personal visual style, rediscovering new spatial dimensions in familiar plays as well as rarely seen classics. All of these diverse theatrical innovators share in common the ability to choose and implement their own repertoire.

Traditionally the designer has been considered to be the purveyor of background scenery, against which the actors would perform. It was not considered to be part of the designer's function to be involved in the textual exploration of the rehearsal process. In this sense, the emergence of the theatre designer as a distinct professional, and a major creative force in stage production, is a twentieth-century phenomenon; and old ways die out slowly. Traditionally, even up to the 1950s, stage managers could order stock scenery from scenic artists, and these elements would be assembled for the dress rehearsal, where actors who had learned their lines and moves elsewhere would encounter for the first time the physical environment in which they were to perform. Today the role the designer is expected to play, taking charge of the entire visual dimension of a production, and being responsible for managing the production budget, ideally requires the designer's work to be integrated completely into the production from its inception, if an optimum artistic and economic product is to be achieved. The theatre's move away from a flat performance within a picture frame, towards a three-dimensional theatrical event, creates a very different kind of involvement, both in space and time, for the designer of the physical production.

On a traditional painted set there was an invented language of stage naturalism that represented reality pictorially as painted doors, painted fireplaces, etc. – but which audiences had learned to accept as reality. ADOLPHE APPIA and Gordon Craig had visionary concepts of breaking with these conventions; they began the process of moving theatre away from artificial representations of reality by inventing systems of visual metaphors to embody a locality for the play. This was the beginning of the theatre's systematic departure from stage naturalism, and towards the development of an iconography of scenic design. It became increasingly clear to designers that a play did not always necessitate the representation of a geographical reality. Through the use of symbols on the stage, as a depiction of the metaphysical world of the play, powerful resonances can be set up in the audience's mind that make the actuality of the play more vivid than any mere represented place could possibly be. Sometimes this can be achieved by taking real objects out of their natural context and using them poetically and symbolically in the stage space. For example, the use of real trees against an artificial sky, in Peter Stein's production of GORKY's *Summerfolk* (1975), made a strong interpretive statement about the Russian landscape – a crucial component in the meaning of the play. David Borovsky's designs for YURI LYUBIMOV's production of *Crime and Punishment* (1983) used a series of real mobile doors without any visible means of support as a metaphor for the houses that they symbolically represented. Though the audiences saw only the doors, they could utterly believe in the reality of the houses to which the doors belonged, which they did not see. Carefully selected objects put together on the stage can tell a visual story which reinforces the text without illustrating it, informing the audience of a dimension of meaning beyond what they can hear in the dialogue of the play.

Theatre design is closely related to the fine arts, and the word 'designer', which popularly implies surface decoration, does not adequately describe visual artists who choose to express their visions through the medium of theatre. Such authentic artists as Lucio Fanti, Richard Peduzzi, Ezio Frigerio and ROBERT ISRAEL are exploring form, dimension and surface, using theatre in all its dimensions as their medium. This is not the same thing as the work of painters who are invited into the theatre from time to time, and who essentially do no more than transfer their paintings on to a larger scale as backdrops for stage action, thus creating a neo-decorative school of theatre design, and perpetuating an artificial hierarchical distinction between the painter and the stage designer. The design work of such prominent painters as DAVID HOCKNEY, Sidney Nolan and Howard Hodgkin is primarily decorative and pictorial rather than theatrical, and has proved more apt as atmospheric background for ballet and opera than as organic stage design. These guest painters, visual artists *in* the theatre but not *of* the theatre, bring an independent vision to a production which superimposes and projects a personal style, rather than integrating itself into a unified theatre event.

Such ephemeral ventures of painters should not be confused with the productive and influential creative ferment of the interwar years in Europe, where painters entered the theatre out of a need to use it as a powerful medium to express their revolutionary artistic and political beliefs. In this period artists, whether involved in DADA, FUTURISM, CONSTRUCTIVISM, EXPRESSIONISM or SURREALISM, sought to use the resources of the theatre to communicate their ideas to the public. What was important to these artists was to convey directly and immediately their message through the public medium of theatre, rather than to explore the possibilities of dramatic form.

One branch of this movement stems from DIAGHILEV's visions in the early decades of the century, and the creation of the Ballets Russes. Diaghalev's talent was to bring artists together and to give them the opportunity to create new works, not necessarily with a narrative content, but which, through a synthesis of line, form and colour with music, would appeal powerfully to the emotions of the spectator. Modern painters such as Marc Chagall, PABLO PICASSO, JEAN COCTEAU and Natalia Goncharova were ideally suited to exploit these possibilities, since they were talented, young and living in a creative climate where anything and everything was possible. None the less, these painters' aesthetic orientation, their concentration on the sensual impact of their painting, ensured that their designs for the theatre were ultimately no more than paintings – however dynamic – translated into backdrops, scenery within the existing conventions of theatre; their revolution was contained in their surface decoration. Goncharova's designs for *The Firebird* (1910) of STRAVINSKY and Picasso's designs for De Falla's *The Three Cornered Hat* (1919), as well as FEDERICO GARCÍA LORCA's own designs for his plays, share this limitation.

The descendants of this variety of aesthetic experiment manifest themselves in PERFORMANCE ART, in which the visual artist *is* the theatre. ROBERT WILSON and PINA BAUSCH present living paintings which, like the postmodern art of their time, have a certain shock value and use space, form and colour in unconventional arrangements on the stage. The objective is not to illuminate or embody the narrative text, but to create a theatrical image which is complete and self-contained as a work of art.

To find the true roots of contemporary scenography, however, one must look to the Russian constructivist movement. There, in the aftermath of the 1917 Revolution, and in the collective need to create a new society in which the arts no less than other facets of life would play a leading role, the fusion of political and artistic innovations produced a new theatrical reality. The theatre of MEYERHOLD and MAYAKOVSKY used the stage space dynamically and geometrically, alluding constantly to the graphic arts of the period – which were themselves the most direct form of communication to the public. Crucially, the content of theatre as well as its form became an essential component. Meyerhold's famous production of Gogol's *The Government Inspector* (1926) was, in an immediate visual sense, totally non-naturalistic. It used an abstract scaffolding structure to provide different stage levels, thrusting the performers vividly into the perceptions of the audience, while providing multiple points of focus on the stage, creating an appropriately complex arena for the play's satirical patterns of action. Mayakovsky's own visions of the scenography of his plays *The Bedbug* (1929) and *The Bath House* (1930) borrow familiar industrial machinery from the audience's contemporary experience, but project it into a poetic and sometimes highly stylized context. In these productions the power of visual communication is acknowledged and

· Designing ·

The starting point for designing a particular production is usually the play. In the ROYAL COURT tradition, the ethic was that you should follow the playwright. With a new play and a playwright who is willing to rewrite and share in the discovery of the play there is a specially exciting process, both before you get into the rehearsal room and when you are in there, bouncing ideas off each other until, if things have really gone well, you don't know who has thought of what. Even if the designer is working only with the director, it should not be a case of just one ego blazing forth; the designer is trying to attain an intimate understanding of the text and gathers as much information as possible in order then to be able to demonstrate the direction to proceed in.

As a designer I was taught that you had to have 360-degree vision so that you could take in everything, whether it is a civil war in the Balkans or a beetle walking across the road, because you never knew what might feed you, what might be of use in your work. Inevitably, much of the evidence you gather is photographic and, given what is available from around the globe, it isn't always immediately or obviously linked to the play.

At the Royal Court, before one designed a play, one went to find out about the social situation that lay behind it. These were the days that were labelled the period of social realism. For example, when I designed the D. H. LAWRENCE trilogy for PETER GILL, we went to the East Midlands mining community to see the poverty, the spaces they had to live in, the food they had to eat. Sketches will be made but, as theatre is a three-dimensional medium, making the model is the important next step. Design has to be understood in space, not just on paper, however beautiful the drawings may be. Stage one of the process ends with the model creation, getting it approved by the director and judging that the design can be delivered within budget. This can be difficult to assess given the range of variables involved, from workshop time to costs and availability of materials, and in principle budgetary considerations should not interfere with a designer's original conception. However, if a design is going to cost a great deal more than is affordable then the designer is going to face artistic compromise in order to come within budget. It is worth noting here that the contribution of the LIGHTING designer is essential, and that his or her earliest possible involvement can only benefit the end result of the design.

The second stage lies in the workshops. Here the designer has to be flexible to be able to impart his or her ideas to various third parties in order to get them, through their talent and personal contribution, to express what the designer wishes to achieve. The third and final part of the process – the most terrifying – is getting the design on stage through the technical preparation period up to the first performances. This is when the director, actors and playwright see the design on stage for the first time and offer their criticisms, accepting and rejecting on the way.

Following weeks of isolation in the rehearsal room which have ideally produced a collective understanding of the play, the actors go through a difficult time when they first come on to the stage and into their costumes and have to put the production together slowly in its technical parts, with moves being readjusted, lighting cues set. They lose the play for a while until gradually it comes back into shape, and for a designer it is very exciting to see them finally take possession of the stage and to feel that you have helped the actors portray their roles and bring the play to life.

If a design does not go through this process, in which a certain vulnerability allows for creative discovery, then it can easily become an attraction that wins a round of applause and says all that it has to say in 30 seconds, leaving the actors to prove or disprove it for the rest of the performance. This happened in the 1980s when advances in technology allowed a tendency for theme-park designing, in which the mechanics take over the piece. There was a reaction against this lavish phase, particularly from actors, in which design knocked everything else off the stage and damaged the audience by focusing too completely on image.

Every production is a learning process and every piece of design – a statement sublimated through the direction, the actors and the script – demands something from the designer and, more importantly, something of the designer. **JOHN GUNTER** harnessed to the purposes of the play; the scenography achieves equal weight with the stage action.

At the same time in Germany, ERWIN PISCATOR and the artist John Heartfield brought new technology into the theatre, with the intention of relating drama to contemporary events. Through the use of film, photomontage and projection, they provided an external comment on the play simultaneously with its performance, so that the audience was at once subjectively and objectively involved. This produced a fusion of strong black-and-white newsreel images with industrial artefacts and invented stage machinery, related to groupings of actors on the stage to create a contemporary reality at once familiar and strange.

BERTOLT BRECHT and his designer CASPAR NEHER were the inheritors of these revolutionary discoveries, and together they refined them into a new system of theatre characterized by simplicity and clarity, motivated by the need to tell a story and to reaffirm and redefine the art of the performer as storyteller. Neher, a talented painter, worked with Brecht from the time both were schoolboys; his fine sense of artistic quality and vision had a major impact on the creation of Brecht's plays during their formative periods of gestation and composition. Neher knew above all how to paint pictures with people, and create telling stage pictures with the most economical of means. His drawings were often impressionistic, and frequently show no more than alternative groupings of actors, related to one or two very carefully chosen objects. Emphasizing the history and poetry of such stage objects for an actor to work with is of the greatest importance, for it permits the background against which the actor performs to be conveyed impressionistically.

Neher and Brecht used a mainly monochromatic palette, and Neher was a master of the judicious use of tiny accents of colour, as for instance in his design for *Coriolanus* (1925), to underline and give significance to the characters in the play. KARL VON APPEN, Neher's successor as a visual collaborator with Brecht, moved the work into a more photo-naturalistic phase. By cleverly exploiting the placing of scenic elements in the stage space, he created the dramatic excitement of seeing real objects, but knowing that one is seeing them within the context of the theatre. Von Appen's designs for *The Days of the Commune* (1962) provide stage elements that evoke the authentic Paris of 1848, while never letting the audience forget that they are involved in the game of theatre.

The influence of Brecht has so permeated the theatrical language of our time that it is hardly possible to imagine a time before theatre was capable of presenting us with an empty stage, with one actor and a chair appearing through a white half-curtain, and then being revealed in the setting of a plain white box. However, the importance of the theatre of Brecht and Neher transcends its own accomplishments, and compels those who truly understand it to resist any impulse to preserve the style in its pure form, as a series of visually striking museum pieces. The challenge for a generation of post-Brechtian directors and designers has been to reinterpret Brecht's discoveries for their own times and needs – as Strehler and Planchon notably have done. Strehler's production of Shakespeare's *The Tempest* (1978) unfolded with startling clarity and economy in a practically bare space of astounding beauty which opened the audience's sympathies and understanding to the text. Similarly, Planchon's production of Molière's *The Miser* (1986), designed by Frigerio, opened onto a huge basement wall pierced by a row of tiny windows placed at the absolute extreme of the height of the stage. Linked to the stage floor by a mobile vertical ladder, the setting provided an illumination of the social and economic circumstances that define the world and characters of the play.

What Brecht's legacy also suggests is that when two sources of direct creativity in the theatre, the designer and the writer, are conceptually linked together (with or without the intervening presence of a director), a whole new form of expression can occur. At the ROYAL COURT in London, under the direction of GEORGE DEVINE, the designer JOCELYN HERBERT was actively involved in the work of such new writers as ARNOLD WESKER, JOHN OSBORNE and DAVID STOREY during the period before the completion of their plays. Working on minimal budgets in a cramped space, she produced simple yet dramatically thrilling visions that gave life and definition to these evolving scripts. Herbert often found it necessary to use the existing architecture of the theatre, and exploit its every possible advantage. Following Brecht, she realized that the stage floor (often artificially raked) could serve as a major scenic element, so that what the actors stood upon became more crucial than what they stood against.

In the postwar era, a profusion of new theatres were built in many countries. In a few isolated cases theatre designers were invited to serve as consultants in the design of their buildings, as for instance JOHN BURY in the design of the auditoriums of the NATIONAL THEATRE of Great Britain and the RSC's Barbican Theatre in London. In most cases, however, buildings were designed without reference to the kind of plays that might be performed in them, or their scenic requirements. Too often the prime function of such schemes was to create edifices to embody regional cultural aspirations – ironically, these structures have often proved economically as well as artistically impractical. Some of these buildings also came equipped with studio-type theatres with flexible staging and seating provisions. Though seemingly providing much less opportunity for design creativity, these studio spaces have often produced more interesting work than has been achieved on the main stages. The proximity of the audience to performer in studio spaces and thrust theatres has lent new importance to the art of costume design, and made it all the more necessary that a single vision be exerted over every visual aspect of a production.

Concurrent with the development of studio spaces has been the flourishing of FRINGE theatre, inevitably staffed and energized by young performers and designers. Out of necessity such venues emphasize simplicity, directness and a close audience–actor relationship. A new generation of theatre makers has emerged, design conscious in their daily lives and attuned to fashionable postmodern images that speak loudly and clearly to a new audience of young people – as witnessed by the phenomenal success of the Michael Clark Ballet Company, using the FASHION designer Body Map to create extraordinary and daring visual images. Even opera, hitherto the most conventional of forms, has found a new life and audience in smaller, more intimate productions.

As a result of all these developments, designers are now in a position of unparalleled power in the theatre at every level. If they are to create truly dynamic theatre, today's directors must depend upon and entrust creative responsibility to enterprising designers. This necessitates an erosion of the 'old' hierarchical structure of theatre (itself only as old as STANISLAVSKY) based on the idea of theatre as a director's medium. This process leads inevitably to an interdependence between director and designer or even to a combining of the functions. In the highly successful touring company CHEEK BY JOWL, the functions of directing and design are jointly and seamlessly carried out by Declan Donnellan and Nick Ormerod. Meanwhile designers such as Tom Cairns and Ultz have begun to direct their own design concepts into reality. The influences of the British THEATRE DE COMPLICITE, a physical theatre company using the language of JACQUES LECOQ, have permeated all the major national companies. From this collective, the design talents of Tim Hatley and Rae Smith have risen to national prominence.

New technology has given the theatre designer yet another kind of unprecedented freedom and power. Electrical engineering, laser technology and computer lighting – wedded to a willingness to demand that spaces be utterly transformed to allow the creation of spectacle sparing no expense – have led to the invention of such design-based and overwhelmingly popular attractions as the 'Great British Musical' (e.g. *Cats*, 1981; *Starlight Express*, 1984; *Les Miserables*, 1985, designed by JOHN NAPIER). These 'masques for the masses' have led to an outcry of complaint from other theatre practitioners and critics that a new tyranny of designer's theatre has been created; but it is insufficiently recognized that these developments are directly related to, and follow logically from, the revolutionary theatre work of Brook, Strehler, Planchon, Chéreau, Stein and the other major innovators of serious theatre in our own times. Richard Hudson's set designs, with JULIE TAYMOR's costumes and direction, for the musical of Disney's *The Lion King,* summarize the symbiosis of Art and Popularity.

Nevertheless, it is clear that designers do need to demonstrate that they have a clear sense of responsibilities and priorities for their profession. In their new visibility, charged with the expenditure of large sums of public or private money, designers will properly be held accountable for artistic standards and any wastage in production budgets. Most crucially, designers must be dedicated to the criteria of a unified work of theatrical art, based on a respect for and a responsibility to the text of the play – which must remain the focus and the impetus for the production, and in whose service it has its only justification. PAMELA HOWARD

See also COSTUME DESIGN; LIGHTING; SOUND.

Dessau, Paul (b. Hamburg, 19 Dec. 1894; d. Königs Wusterhausen, Germany, 28 June 1979) Composer and conductor. A music director and film composer, he left Germany for exile in Paris in 1933, and the United States in 1939. He composed songs for the 1938 Paris première of Brecht's *Fear and Misery in the Third Reich* before meeting the playwright in Santa Monica in 1942. A newly conscious political style employing Marxist dialectics then becomes evident, resulting in the atmospheric scores of *Mother Courage and Her Children* (1946), *The Good Person of Setzuan* (1947–8), *Mr Puntila and his Man Mati* (1948), which he also made into an opera, and the opera *Lucullus* (1951). He also composed for the BERLINER ENSEMBLE.
DOMINIC SHELLARD

DeSylva, Brown and Henderson Songwriters. Lyricists [George Gard] 'Buddy' DeSylva (b. New York, 27 January 1895; d. Hollywood, 11 July 1950) and Lew Brown [Louis Brownstein] (b. Odessa, Russia, 10 Dec. 1893; d. New York, 5 Feb. 1958) teamed up briefly with composer Ray Henderson [Raymond Brost] (b. Buffalo, NY, 1 Dec. 1896; d. Greenwich, Conn., 31 Dec. 1970) to write what many deem the quintessential musical comedy and revue scores of the late 1920s. Their first show was *George White's Scandals* of 1925; their last, *Flying High* (1930). Their biggest hit was *Good News* (1927). The team's songs have been described as 'low-down in rhythm, piquant in love'. GERALD BORDMAN

development *see* THEATRE FOR DEVELOPMENT

Devine, George [Alexander Cassidy] (b. London, 20 Nov. 1910; d. London, 20 Jan. 1966) Actor and director. Devine's career began at OXFORD when, under his presidency of the Oxford University Dramatic Society, GIELGUD directed his first show, *Romeo and Juliet* (1932), with PEGGY ASHCROFT and EDITH EVANS. In 1935, after acting with KOMISSARZHEVSKY and the OLD VIC, Devine met MICHEL SAINT-DENIS, who was directing Gielgud in *Noah*. Inspired by the story of COPEAU and the Vieux-Colombier school, Devine joined Saint-Denis, his vision complementing Devine's practicality, to open the London Theatre Studio in 1936, aiming at integrating the diverse theatrical crafts and promoting IMPROVISATION, ENSEMBLE and MASK work. Devine, an impressive secondary role actor specializing in physical comedy, continued to work outside the school, notably playing Andrey in (and lighting) Saint-Denis's acclaimed *Three Sisters* (1938); but both the school and Devine's career were halted by the onset of war.

In 1944, at the Old Vic, the suggested home of the NATIONAL THEATRE, plans were drawn up to continue the work of the London Theatre Studio with a school, a children's theatre and an experimental laboratory stage run respectively by GLEN BYAM SHAW, Devine and Saint-Denis, referred to as the Three Boys. The bomb-damaged Old Vic, the bureaucratic hostility of the governors to the school's aims and an imposed administrator from the Arts Council made working increasingly difficult and in May 1951 the Three Boys resigned, creating a public storm. For five years, Devine worked as an actor and director, at Covent Garden, STRATFORD-UPON-AVON and SADLER'S WELLS, giving a memorable performance as Tesman in *Hedda Gabler* (1954). In 1955 a group of entrepreneurs appointed Devine artistic director of their new ENGLISH STAGE COMPANY at the ROYAL COURT. Devine, influenced by the BERLINER ENSEMBLE, which he had seen in 1955 while touring Europe, was committed to reviving British drama through ensemble work on new plays. The company's first such success was with *Look Back in Anger* (1956) by JOHN OSBORNE, whom Devine consistently championed in the teeth of critical disdain, as he did ARDEN, JELLICOE and WESKER. He also acted, memorably in *Cards of Identity* (1956), *The Chairs* (1957),

Endgame (1958) and *A Patriot for Me* (1965), and directed *The Crucible* and *The Good Woman of Setzuan* (1956).

Devine wrote, 'You should choose your theatre like you choose a religion', and his pipe-smoking, paternal commitment inspired the atmosphere that fostered the right to fail, the Writers' Group and the 'Sunday nights without décor' to present new, untried work, and nurtured new playwrights, actors, designers and directors. In 1966, the George Devine Award was internationally sponsored to encourage young theatre workers.
DAN REBELLATO

Irving Wardle, *The Theatres of George Devine* (1978)

Devlin, Anne *see* IRELAND

Dewhurst, Colleen (b. Montreal, 3 June 1926; d. South Salem, NY, 22 Aug. 1991) Actress and great interpreter of O'NEILL; she gave one the American theatre's greatest performances as Josie in *A Moon for the Misbegotten* (1973). She was given her second Tony Award for this role; her first was for her portrayal of Mary Follett in *All the Way Home* (1960) by Tad Mosel. A powerful actress with a commanding presence and a deep, resonant voice, at the start of her career she was associated with the CIRCLE IN THE SQUARE company; later she frequently worked with JOSEPH PAPP's NEW YORK SHAKESPEARE FESTIVAL and his PUBLIC THEATER, and made numerous appearances in films. *Colleen Dewhurst*, her autobiography, was completed after her death (by Tom Viola) and appeared in 1997.
THOMAS F. CONNOLLY

Barbara Lee Horn, *Colleen Dewhurst: A Bio-Bibliography* (1993)

Dexter, John (b. Derby, 2 Aug. 1925; d. London, 23 March 1990) Director. He joined the ENGLISH STAGE COMPANY as an actor but didn't appear, and soon made his mark as a director through ARNOLD WESKER's early work (the Trilogy, 1958–60; *The Kitchen*, 1959; *Chips with Everything*, 1962). He joined the new NATIONAL THEATRE (1963–6), where successes included OLIVIER's *Othello* (1964) and PETER SHAFFER's *The Royal Hunt of the Sun* (1964). Subsequent NT productions included TONY HARRISON's versions of *The Misanthrope* (1973) and *Phaedre Britannica* (1975, from Racine), TREVOR GRIFFITHS' *The Party* (1973, which saw Olivier in his last stage role), Shaffer's *Equus* (1973) and BRECHT's *Galileo* (1980). As well as many freelance achievements, he was also director of productions at the Metropolitan Opera House, New York (1974–81). Dexter's disciplined theatricality encompassed both photographic realism and spectacular stylization. Notoriously outspoken and candid, Dexter demanded tight ensemble work while encouraging star performances; he became famous for brilliantly choreographed set-pieces (e.g. *The Kitchen*'s mounting hysteria; the ritualized masked horses of *Equus*). Writers acknowledging Dexter's influence on their work include Wesker, Shaffer, Harrison and Brenton. An autobiography, *The Honourable Beast*, was published poshumously in 1993. TONY HOWARD

Jim Hiley, *Theatre at Work* (on Dexter's NT *Galileo*, 1981)

Diaghilev, Serge [Sergei Pavlovich] (b. Selitschev Barracks, Novgorod, Russia, 31 March 1872; d. Venice, 19 Aug. 1929) Impresario, founder of the Ballets Russes. Diaghilev went to St Petersburg to study law in 1890, and founded, with a circle of young artists, the magazine *The World of Art,* which he edited until 1904. In 1907 he presented his first Paris season of Russian music, in 1908 a performance of Russian dance as part of an opera programme, and then in 1909 the Ballets Russes. The company stunned Paris audiences. They broke with classical ballet tradition to present short, one-act dances in which choreography, design, music and lighting combined to form an integral dramatic whole. Between 1909 and Diaghilev's death in 1929, many of the greatest dancers, artists and musicians of the period worked with the Ballets Russes, changing internationally notions of stage DESIGN, CHOREOGRAPHY and composing as well as DANCE.
ANDREW SOLWAY

See also COSTUME DESIGN; MOVEMENT, DANCE AND DRAMA.

R. Buckle, *Diaghilev* (1979)
S. Lifar, *Serge Diaghilev: His Life, His Work, His Legend* (1977)
W. MacDonald, *Diaghilev Observed* (1976)

Dickins, Barry (b. Melbourne, Australia, 6 Nov. 1949) Playwright, essayist and humourist. Imagine the MARX BROTHERS, BARRY HUMPHRIES and MAX WALL in one ancient overcoat and you almost have Dickins – unruly, surreal, corny, hilarious, essentially a fantasist. In his more than 20 plays, alligators live in refrigerators, ageing theatricals eat rubber sandals or bicycle pumps, Yiddisher grandmothers play tunes on lobsters, the poor and forgotten find refuge in performance, and life is celebrated and cherished. Most of Dickins's short plays have haunted alternative theatre venues, like La MaMa and the Pram Factory. Encouragement from JACK HIBBERD led him to write a string of plays ranging from monodramas, such as the suicide-comedy *The Death of Minnie* (1980), to full-length, quirky and passionate quasi-naturalistic renderings of suburban

working-class life in *Royboys* (1987) and *Remember Ronald Ryan* (1994). He is known, some say feared, for impromptu performances of his work. Other plays include *Mae's Cafe* (1973), *The Rotten Teeth Show* (1977), *The Banana Bender* (1981), *Lennie Lower* (1982), *Beautland* (1985) and *A Dickins Christmas* (1992). There are seven unpublished performance pieces and three film scripts. His book *I Love to Live: The Fabulous Life of Barry Dickins* was published in 1991. GUS WORBY

Dietrich, Marlene [Maria Magdalene von Losch] (b. Schoenberg, Germany, 27 Dec. 1900; d. Paris, 6 May 1992) Actress who studied for the stage with REINHARDT before her appearance in 1929 in the film *The Blue Angel* won international acclaim and Hollywood contracts for her and the film's director, Josef von Sternberg. For almost 20 years thereafter she was one of the screen's most glamorous stars. An anti-Nazi, she became a US citizen on the eve of the Second World War and then entertained the Allied troops as a symbol of Europe. She never returned to the stage as an actress, though she was often imitated, having become a legend. In 1950 she devised a solo singing act which, in the light of her limited ability as a vocalist, was acting of a high order; it packed theatres all over the world during the next 25 years. PAM GEMS wrote a show about her, *Marlene* (1997). IAN BEVAN

S. Morley, *Marlene Dietrich* (1976)
D. Spoto, *Marlene Dietrich* (1992)

Dietz, Howard *see* SCHWARTZ, ARTHUR

Digges, Dudley (b. Dublin, 9 June 1879; d. New York, 24 Oct. 1947) Actor and director who came to America with the ABBEY company in 1904, after joining them in 1901, and stayed. He served as stage manager for GEORGE ARLISS, then, in 1919, helped found the THEATER GUILD. In the next 11 years he performed nearly 3,000 times with the company in such plays as *Liliom* (1921), *The Adding Machine* (1923), *Marco Millions* (1928) and *Major Barbara* (1928), also directing many of the Guild's productions of SHAW. After leaving the group he continued to assume important roles, especially in *On Borrowed Time* (1938) and *The Iceman Cometh* (1946), appeared in many films and was active in the UNION Actors' Equity. GERALD BORDMAN

digital performance The invention of and exponential rise in theatre-related applications of the computer at the end of the twentieth century (in word-processing, DESIGN, scenography, INTERNET events, theatre administration and data, box-office and MANAGEMENT) gave rise to the term 'digital performance'. The nature of its products being screen based, its attributes were perhaps closer to film, television, moving image and media activities, but it commanded its own group of theatre and performance aficionados, experimenters, inventors and archivists. Because of its interdisciplinary and mixed media attributes, the defining characteristic of 'digital performance' is generally held to be that the outcome has to involve a human live presence undertaking a performative action with regard to or as a response to a digital input. The abstract qualities of dance were foremost in experimenting with digitized movement capture and simulation (used for dance productions and also developing on-screen lifelike animations for cartoons and games applications). The instantaneous qualities of email, chatlines, website access and interactive software rapidly led to the development of 'interactive dramas' where participants could involve themselves either as audience or in some instances as dramatic characters in cyberspace dramas (symbolized on screen by 'avatars', an electronic representation capable of movement and 'speech' by textual display). VR (virtual reality) performance, although more advanced and demanding, had a lower public profile due to its much greater dependence on specialist, expensive equipment: VR tended to require either headsets or large-scale screens which could produce for the audience/ participant a completely immersive environment – for example, negotiating a virtual maze, entering themed environments and/or conflicting with various forces (usually 'evil' in the form of monsters or aliens). As such it came closer to 'games technology' than theatre. New interdisciplinary interests between the arts and sciences – particularly involving digital AI (artificial intelligence), a hybrid largely occasioned by the development of IT (information technology) and the internet – were leading to a new interest in cybernetic performance and robotics: actors were not necessarily going to be (or at least always be) 'human' and the theatre venue was not necessarily going to be located in one physical place but could be in cyberspace, a 'virtual reality field'. For many theatre professionals and theatregoers this sudden eruption of new forms of theatre practice was both threatening and mysterious, lost in the intricacies of a new technology prone to glitches and failures but all the time gathering speed and greater competence, and undertaking more experimental applications. In many ways the onset of 'digital performance' paralleled the early, faltering steps of radio, film and television technologies. BARRY SMITH

Johannes Birringer, *Media and Performance: Along the Border* (1998)

Dillingham, Charles [Bancroft] (b. Hartford, Conn., 30 May 1868; d. New York, 30 Aug. 1934) Producer. A clergyman's son, he was a journalist before turning to the theatre. He began an extended career as producer only after serving as a press AGENT and production assistant for CHARLES FROHMAN and as JULIA MARLOWE's manager. Between 1898 and 1930 he produced more than 200 plays. A few were distinguished comedies and dramas but most were musicals. Only ZIEGFELD was considered to have more of a flair for these than Dillingham. In a trade notorious for its sharp practices, Dillingham's gentlemanly behaviour was a noted exception. GERALD BORDMAN

directing in the twentieth century There have always been directors in the theatre, but only since the end of the nineteenth century has their function been seen as artistic rather than managerial. Before that the arrangement of the actors' movements, their COSTUMES, PROPERTIES, etc., were their own responsibility and were decided by convention, by a given actor's seniority or by personal taste. From the Restoration to the nineteenth century, the monopoly enjoyed by one or two companies, together with the restricted social range of their audiences, gave rise to a consensus between actors and audiences as to the function of theatre. But in the course of the nineteenth century monopolies were abolished and the role of theatre in relation to its society began to be questioned. As the theatre entered an age of commercial expansion, demand grew for spectacular scenic effects. The old oil lamps and candles were replaced in the 1820s by gas light and then, in the last two decades of the century, by electricity. As the stage technology grew more complex, so did the need for the stage manager to ensure that all the effects worked well together. By the end of the century it was common for one person, often the leading actor and manager of the company, to assume artistic responsibility for all aspects of a performance; the word used to designate this function was 'producer', though EDWARD GORDON CRAIG employed the term 'stage director', and can thus be seen as the first person to use the term in its modern sense. By using it, he intended to emphasize the director's role as master of all the signifying practices peculiar to the stage: 'action, which is the very spirit of acting; words, which are the body of the play; line and colour, which are the very heart of the scene; rhythm, which is the very essence of the dance.' Craig's words have proved to be prophetic: many contemporary directors with international reputations, e.g. KANTOR, ROBERT WILSON, GROTOWSKI, BARBA, have succeeded in establishing themselves as the sole source of creative author-

· Directing ·

The word 'director' conjures up two completely different meanings: one, a person who gives direction to an activity involving a large number of people so that it does not go in all directions at once; the other, a person who directs an activity by instilling what is right and therefore what is wrong and who eventually has the last word. Theatre directors combine both elements, and they must constantly ask themselves – and be challenged by other people to answer – how much of their time, how much of their capacities and how much of their ego is to be spent on giving direction and how much on saying the last word.

The latter notion of the theatre director as the enlightened boss has its roots in the nineteenth century; and even in the middle of the twentieth century, when democracy was held to be a good thing for society, autocracy was still seen as highly desirable in art. Only subsequently has this tradition come under sustained fire. STANISLAVSKY or REINHARDT, for example, would conceive a production in the same way that a writer of their times would conceive a play – working alone, crystallizing the total form by an enormous act of creative imagination, and then reproducing it in production down to the last detail. This method is justified only if it is total, in the way that, for instance, a film by Fellini is created out of nowhere except the resources of his own quirky imagination as an act of total authorship. It is a tradition that has become distorted and disastrous, with directors, like absentee conductors, pinning down everything in a foolproof, failsafe way, grinding people into puppets to serve their conception.

At the other extreme, there is a team which, in order to discover a play, goes without preconceptions on a journey of exploration. The director acts as a sort of guide, animating and liberating, knowing that there are a thousand barriers between the potential of a work and its realization. The process cannot and does not happen by itself; it has to be helped, and one main function of the director is to be the person through whose actions barriers are removed and energy flows, and who, when the energy is not there, infuses it. The director's role is to remove psychological barriers, personality barriers, and barriers in schematic thought, in obstructions of understanding and in obstructions of feeling. This has to be done through a million devices that range from discussion and conversation to physical and emotional exercises, from experiements with the text to experiments outside the rehearsal space.

However, with no preconceptions of the direction in which one is going, while one may achieve an honourable production, it is unlikely to bear that stamp which makes theatre work carry conviction. For that to happen – and this, for better or worse, is where the director becomes an artist – there has to be an instant birth at some moment deep inside the director of what can be called a pre-shape that the director recognizes weeks or months later as being the shape towards which he or she was always working. I think this goes for writers, painters and actors too.

In *A Midsummer Night's Dream* (1970), everything was done in rehearsal to free the actors. They made their individual contributions in such a degree that the production really belonged to everyone and everyone felt that without them the production would not be possible, which was true. Yet if we had started with just those actors and the space, without any idea of a pre-shape, we would never have discovered the particular form that heightened our reading of the play, which was the image of acrobats. The image was not there at the very beginning, but by the time we came to rehearse I knew enough to start with exercises and acrobatics because clearly three weeks later we were not going to dress the actors in ballet tutus and bring on fairies with little wands. Within the blend of attributes that one needs to be a director there has to be this ability to have in one's imagination an overall 'smell' of an event and then to allow all the elements the greatest possible liberty while not abdicating from ultimate responsibility.

Ironically, the most important moment in the process comes at the point at which the director must disappear completely, when the work and the audience come together. Yet the director must aim the work so that this important moment can take place in the fullest way possible. This is the exact opposite of the orchestra conductor, who, while aiming at the same degree of realization as the theatre director, is most fully present and not absent at this moment.

The relationship between performance and audience is fundamental, although generally it is not respected in our age. In the commercial theatre it is respected in terms of 'success' and not in human terms; 'they' have to be pleased or 'they' will not come again; and that is not the basis of a genuinely human relation. Attempts to move away from the norms of commercial theatre have carried with them all sorts of emphases – on the body of the actor or the play of words, for example – but at the expense of that moment of truth when the performer encounters the audience. This relationship must be at the centre of all theatre work. When an architect builds a theatre, it is important to discover whether the human relation is the centre of the thinking about the building, or if the centre of thinking includes this relation only as an obvious but secondary necessity.

The same problem faces the director in the choice of space and method of work. The drift of theatre today is guided by cost. Time becomes expensive, and the one thing that should not be under pressure is time. When I started in the theatre, I always lit my shows myself. Nowadays, the director of a big Broadway production cannot do the lighting as well. Time is limited, and it requires a specialist to cope with the technology while the director has to get on with the director's job. In my work in Paris I have tried to go against this tide, reducing theatre to a smaller scale, to something handmade which starts from the human relation between actor and audience and the essential image of that, the image of the storyteller. Here is one simple example. In *Carmen* (1983) we did not set out to prove anything or to destroy any conventions. We placed the storyteller's relation to the audience at the centre of our work. Each experiment was tested and each question answered in the light of this preoccupation. For instance, we had to find out where to place the orchestra. We tried it on two sides of the audience and found that this created barriers. We tried it under the roof of the gallery. We tried it everywhere and resolved the problem only by continually referring back to the central issue through which everything – scenery, lighting, costume, movement, character – found its relative and different place, and through which it gained its meaning. Every decision that in the end made up what we call 'the production' came from this one central axis: the flow between actor and audience.

PETER BROOK

---

ity in what has been dubbed 'directors' theatre'; in other words, they have claimed the function of author, often dispensing entirely with written play texts. These are the directors referred to by BROOK as 'absentee conductors', but not all of them are guilty of 'grinding people into puppets to serve their conception'. In fact, this tendency towards autocracy was present from the very origins of the emergence of the artistic director, in the shape of Ludwig Chronegk, stage director for the company founded by Duke Georg of Saxe-MEININGEN in 1866. This company's productions struck everyone who saw them by the power of the stage groupings, achieved by well-drilled actors, whether they were in leading roles or in walk-on parts. They made a strong impression on ANDRÉ ANTOINE, who established his Théâtre Libre in 1887 in order to promote the new naturalist drama. Antoine regarded himself as the inventor of the art of *mise-en-scène* (the term still used for directing in France). His aim was to ensure detailed realism in *both* acting and stage setting, since he believed that 'it is the environment that determines the movements of the characters, not the movements of the characters that determine the environment'.

A similar emphasis on the harmony between actor and environment was fundamental to STANISLAVSKY's work, but although he placed great emphasis on the creation of a realistic stage picture, Stanislavsky's main efforts were devoted to developing the creative potential of the actor. In this respect he can be seen as the originator of a trend that includes directors as different as COPEAU, LITTLEWOOD, STRASBERG, Grotowski, MNOUCHKINE, Brook, Barba and many others who have placed as much emphasis on the training of actors as they have on the completion of finished productions. Such directors often used their work to challenge society's view of the role of the performing arts, and they were frequently hampered by lack of funding.

The other major trend in twentieth-century directing has followed Craig in seeing the actor as just one element in the vast expressive palette at the disposal of the creative director. MEYERHOLD was the first great exponent of a style of directing in which the actor would not necessarily be in harmony with the stage environment, but might find himself playing *against* it. BRECHT developed the implications of this dialectical approach and was followed, among many others, by STREHLER in Italy, PLANCHON and CHEREAU in France, STEIN in Germany, LYUBIMOV in Russia. The work of these directors at its best has succeeded in combining political commitment with self-reflexive mastery of the stage and has resulted in productions of dazzling brilliance. It has flourished in countries where generous state subsidy is available to support theatres with rich technical resources.

The man who is arguably the most influential of all twentieth-century directors fits into neither of these two trends: ANTONIN ARTAUD was a visionary who wanted theatre to act like the plague, culminating in one of two things, either death or violent catharsis. His essays on the theatre (collected as *The Theatre and its Double*, 1938), pleaded for a return to the roots of drama in religious RITUAL, where a whole society's relation to the world, both physical and metaphysical, could find expression. He has had a profound influence on a vast number of ALTERNATIVE theatre practitioners, from the LIVING THEATER to the present day, and has sometimes been used as an alibi by directors seeking to establish their precedence in the theatrical hierarchy. In fact his theories go far beyond such matters, and question the whole relationship between culture and society in the twentieth century. His promotion of Eastern theatre models has been prophetic; much of the most innovative work in contemporary directing (e.g. NINAGAWA) is concerned with intercultural practices and with how the Western and Eastern theatre traditions may meet or learn from one another.

DAVID BRADBY

See also ACTING; EASTERN THEATRE, ITS INFLUENCE ON THE WEST.

A. Barstow, ed., *The Director's Voice: Twenty-One Interviews* (1988)

D. Bradby and D. Williams, *Directors' Theatre* (1988)

E. Braun, *The Director and the Stage* (1982)

Toby Cole and Helen Crich Chinoy, eds, *Directors on Directing* (1963)

Edward Gordon Craig, *On the Art of the Theatre* (1911)

P. Heritage and M. Delgado, *In Contact with the Gods? Directors Talk Theatre* (1996)

disability The issue to be addressed is not just a matter of providing ramps and parking spaces, but of integrating disabled people into the theatrical world as artists, as production staffs, as administrators and as audience. Exciting new developments in this area are affecting all aspects of theatre, from well-known companies in huge theatre buildings to small groups of disabled people working to set up their own drama organizations. With the growth in political consciousness of disabled people, their involvement in the arts is generally no longer seen in terms of therapy and charitable provision, but rather in terms of professional involvement and rights of access.

At its most obvious, accessibility means the provision of physical facilities which enable people with disabilities to use theatre buildings. Although ramps and lifts can be expensive, many improvements can be made without enormous expenditure: low-level telephones, flexible seating, even water bowls for guide dogs are easily provided. Hand rails, clear signs, firm floors and plain decor, in spaces free from obstruction, are usually incorporated into building improvement programmes. (In the United States this approach has been taken further and is called 'universal design', in which physical and non-physical accessibility are so incorporated that the distinction is not noticeable.)

Performance interpretation – the provision of services which enable people with sensory impairments to particpate fully as audience – is also being implemented. Sign-interpreted performances, audio description, taped synopses or hire of scripts are some of the ways in which performances can be made accessible. The provision of such services is no longer seen as a philanthropic gesture, but rather as part of a marketing strategy to increase audiences. The high percentage of the population who are disabled are an important target in the development plans of many theatres. Performances can make use of signed interpretation in a variety of ways. Conventionally, a signer stands in a well-lit position at the side of the stage and interprets the dialogue for the benefit of deaf people or those with limited hearing. However, signers can also 'shadow' individual actors; or signing can be incorporated into the action, to be carried out by the actors as they perform. Each method has advantages and disadvantages, but all require adequate rehearsal time with the signer(s). Often artistic decisions will be affected. In recent years the possiblities of incorporating sign languages (and mime) as part of the performance have been explored by theatres which use deaf and hearing actors.

Audio description in theatre is a service for blind and partially sighted/low vision people. It requires a describer who sits in a soundproofed area with a clear view of the stage. S/he describes any part of the action which is not obvious from the dialogue: for instance, a fight, or stage directions. Usually this is preceded by a description of the set and costumes. The description is relayed to those who want to select it on a loop system connected to headphones. It is not audible to the general audience. When well done, audio desciption makes an enormous difference to most blind people's enjoyment of theatre. Describing is a skilled task which needs training and careful preparation: the dialogue must not be interrupted, and the describer must decide which aspects of the action are sufficiently significant to describe. This means that s/he must study the script and see the play sufficiently often before describing to an audience.

Less obvious facilities, but equally important, are the provision of taped and large-print scripts or synopses, or a hearing enhancement system, which amplifies sound from the stage for hearing-aid users only. Many theatres have a hearing induction loop or infra-red enhancement system. When any of these facilities are offered, it is essential that publicity about them reaches disabled people. Most disabled people incur extra expense on a theatre visit through the need for a premium seat, often near the stage, or an additional seat

· The performer and disability ·

I was with a CIRCUS once for four days. Being in a wheelchair caused quite a stir. Since there is a tradition of 'freaks' being associated with circus, probably the earliest avenue for the disabled in entertainment, I was perhaps much more readily accepted than an able-bodied stranger. Circus folk are not normally welcoming to outsiders. I was hoping to get work during the summer vacations. Since I am very small, they assumed I wanted to be a clown, but no, I wanted to be a lion-trainer! I asked the incumbent trainer, 'Are there any special qualities needed for the job?' He replied, 'Look at me: I'm scared of heights, spiders, the dark. Until last year I was a clown, then our previous trainer got killed and my Dad said I had to take his place. There are no special qualities, except for one. You have got to be able to con the lions into thinking you are bigger and stronger than they are.' 'How do you do that?' I asked. 'You have to believe it yourself. If you believe it, the lions will.' And that is the most important trick to acting. If you believe you are what you say you are, then the audience will. So being a disabled actor in a wheelchair will not necessarily prevent or disrupt the illusion of being, say, Hamlet, Jesus or Hailie Selassie. The audience will believe and accept it, if you are totally committed to the character and situation. My experience in all the above three roles has taught me that.

In addition to possessing a means to convey a belief, to be an actor you have to have certain other contributory prerequisite qualities: imagination, passion and a capacity to learn. What you don't have to have are two arms, two legs, two eyes and a so-called 'pretty face'. You don't have to be physically dextrous or mobile as defined by the dominant able-bodied culture. For too long, disabled performers have been denied access to the great mirrors of life. This very denial renders the reflected visions distorted and cracked. The medium of theatre, with a few exceptions, has rarely grown beyond an impotent infancy with its facile and fallacious belief that physical beauty equals the good. The romantic leads, the heroes and heroines, are inevitably played by the so-called handsome and beautiful, and yet, in life, neither love nor greatness is the preserve of the physically perfect. Because the performing arts have been responsible for this lopsided portrayal of history and society, people with disabilities have felt inferior and excluded. And when, on occasion, they are included, it is rarely on their own terms. With the active and self-governing involvement of people with physical and mental differences in the performing arts, there is a chance that the more truly representative visions of the world will more effectively lead the world to a greater maturity, tolerance and safe-keeping. Disabled performers, like other minority artists, are creating their impact, either as independent operators within the mainstream or by provoking consciousness-raising through organized disability theatre.

A distinction has to be made between theatre *for* the disabled – suggesting that disabled people have been targeted to be passive recipients of able-bodied thespian activity – and theatre *of* the disabled – suggesting that disabled people have much greater control over their own activity. Clearly it is the latter that has provoked questions and found answers concerning the performer and disability.

Until the mid-1970s, in the history of theatre, the disabled person's active participation in the performing arts was neither promoted nor allowed for. With the growth of radical ALTERNATIVE theatre, whether it be feminist, left-wing, black or gay, came a growing self-awareness and confidence among disabled people that they too had a right to exercise an artistic control of society's cultural existence. In Britain, the public expression of disabled people's theatrical aspirations can be dated back to the mid-1970s as local deaf drama groups coalesced into the Theatre of the Deaf and Interim Theatre, with the emphasis on sign language as a new art form; and drama workshops in a few colleges for the disabled began to devise their own REVUE-type shows centring on disability issues. It was at one such college that the seeds of the GRAEAE THEATRE, Britain's only theatre company that gives regular employment to disabled performers, were first sown. Yet, despite the existence of Graeae, the opportunities for the disabled person to perform professionally remain scandalously scant. One of the principal reasons for this is the appalling lack of training opportunities. Too frequently the problems a prospective disabled student is perceived to be bringing to a drama school (whether it concerns independent access to buildings, toilets, braille facilities, sign language interpreters, etc.) are grossly exaggerated and conveniently provide excuses for continued debarment. The provision of appropriately facilitated venues is also an important issue. The ROYAL COURT's Theatre Upstairs, one of the most inaccessible theatres in London for wheelchair-users, is, ironically, responsible for giving me my biggest breaks in the late 1980s; but it is not a comfortable experience working in an inappropriately designed theatre. As a disabled person, I could regard myself as being lucky for being small, light and portable, and therefore easily carried up and down the stairs between toilets, dressing rooms and stage; but that is no consolation to other disabled people who do not have these advantages. If all the varieties of disabled people are to have equal participation in the thespian arts, then all theatres must receive funding to render all areas, including backstage, 'disability-friendly'. When a production has decided to employ the services of a disabled performer, then the design of the set should take this into account and there should be constant consultation with the performer over this.

Another problem that besets the aspiring disabled performer is the plays – stereotyping, want of disabled characters, lack of plays to perform in. Casting directors, when challenged by disabled lobbyists, try to pass the buck by blaming writers and producers for not creating roles for disabled performers. To a degree this may be true; but whenever plays (and films) about disability are produced the lead roles are given to able-bodied stars, e.g. *Whose Life Is It Anyway?*, *Duet For One*, *Crystal Clear*. But that is only one aspect of the problem. If the disabled performer is unable even to get a look in where disability is the central feature, then what hope is there for obtaining work where it is not the issue? People with disabilities are active in all 'wheels' of life. Disability is not our only preoccupation. In fact, 'our' disability is more usually the unhealthy preoccupation of the non-disabled person – which invariably reinforces our inferior status in the world. Therefore it is not unrealistic to cast a disabled performer as a lawyer, a lover, a mother, a shoplifter, a freedom fighter. For theatre to remain vibrant and blossom beyond incestous sterility, adventurous casting is vital. **NABIL SHABAN**

for an escort/helper. Ticket concessions are sometimes available to accommodate these extra needs, but many theatres do not advertise them. It is always worthwhile to ask, as many theatres are happy to supply almost any type of provision if they know what is needed.

Of course, some disabled people will never be able to attend events in conventional theatre settings. For them it is necessary to bring performance into residential institutions, day centres and other non-arts venues. Several arts organisations are devoted entirely to this type of provision. The 'Shape' network in England of 12 autonomous regional organizations, with affiliated services in Wales and Scotland, works to create participatory arts opportunities for disabled and disadvantaged people. Originally Shape was set up to provide arts workshops and professional performances in hospitals, day centres and prisons, but most regions have expanded from this to develop their own schemes. Some provide training for care staff; others advise local authorities on arts provision in their own establishments. Many small drama companies exist solely to work with disabled people in institutional settings. Using WORKSHOP techniques, they devise, encourage and produce shows with their clients, often liaising closely with social services and involving care staff in their activities. Other (larger) theatre companies run extensive schemes of such 'outreach' work alongside their main schedule, sometimes involving several weeks' residency at an institution which culminates in a large public performance. Some companies with a building base have established programmes of workshops on their premises for disabled people.

Very Special Arts, affiliated to the KENNEDY CENTER in Washington DC, provides arts programmes for disabled young Americans and has related schemes in 47 countries.

Perhaps the most innovatory and interesting aspect of disability and theatre is the gradual movement of more disabled people into the acting profession. This is taking place in mainstream theatre; in the development of companies of disabled actors; and in integrated groups of disabled and able-bodied people. Acting UNIONS have a register of disabled members, and some, though not enough, progress has been made in seeing them on stage in standard roles, not written specifically for a disabled person. However, there are still instances of able-bodied actors playing disabled parts. The problem is partially one of training, and partially one of prejudice. Poor educational opportunities and bad physical access at drama schools compound the difficulties of prejudice which most aspiring disabled actors still face. (A small number of charitable trusts, and also pressure groups, are attempting to redress the balance. Some theatre companies provide theatre skills training schemes for young disabled people, and there are bursaries and placements with theatres for disabled trainee administrators.)

The movement of disabled people into professional theatre is exciting because it has important artistic implications. To see an accomplished professional actor, such as Nabil Shaban, for example, play Hamlet in a wheelchair is to see a new interpretation of Hamlet. To explore these possibilities, many groups of performers have established themselves as disabled or integrated companies. In 1994 Battersea Arts Centre, south London, hosted Britain's first Disability Theatre Festival. Foremost among the British groups is GRAEAE, the only professional full-time theatre company consisting entirely of disabled people. In addition to national tours, Graeae undertakes THEATRE IN EDUCATION work and runs an annual training course in theatre skills for disabled people . At least 30 other professional organizations promote work created, produced and performed by their own disabled members. Sometimes this has educational intent through a focus on the experience of being disabled. Most of this work, however, explores other themes using the particular abilities of the company. For instance, a combination of sign, mime, gesture and dialogue can be used to produce a show which is equally accessible to deaf and hearing people.

Theatre incorporating disability in the United States breaks down into roughly four categories. The first consists of professional, disability-specific theatres such as DEAF WEST THEATER COMPANY in Los Angeles, Theater by the Blind in New York City, and Cleveland Signstage Theater. Second, there are larger not-for-profit professional theatres that either house a continuing disability-specific programme, for example the MARK TAPER FORUM in Los Angeles, under which The Other Voices Project operates, or incorporate artists with disabilities of stories of disability into their seasons, whether as a disability-specific production or a production using both disabled and non-disabled artists. The Mark Taper Forum also falls into this category, as do the NEW YORK SHAKESPEARE FESTIVAL, Center Stage (Baltimore), The Shakespeare Theater (Washington DC), Seattle Children's Theater and MILWAUKEE REPERTORY THEATER, to name a few. In third place, there are disability-specific theatres or companies that operate primarily as community theatres; and in fourth place, there are access organizations, such as Hospital Audiences, Inc., that bring the arts to people with disabilities in institutions or bring the people from institutions to the theatre. In addition, many professional theatres provide outreach, access and/or educational programmes, and there are several organizations that provide a variety of resources, services and/or programmes to people with disabilities; some focus on artists, some target audiences, and some serve both.

LINDA MOSS & SHARON JENSEN

Dockstader, Lew [George Alfred Clapp] (b. Hartford, Conn., 1856; d. New York, 26 Oct. 1924) Minstrel who began as an amateur blackface performer. In 1876 he met Charles Dockstader, and changed his name to form the Dockstader Brothers' Minstrels. In 1898, when blackface MINSTRELSY had virtually disappeared, Dockstader joined forces with the traditional minstrel George Primrose to present a VAUDEVILLE and minstrelsy show which enjoyed success, especially thanks to the up-to-the-minute jokes and satire, as, dressed in outsize clothes and shoes, he lampooned politicians instead of plantation black people.

ADRIANA HUNTER

documentary Terms using 'documentary' and 'drama' in combination (most of which relate more to the world of television than to the stage) can be confusing. 'Documentary drama', describing plays with a close relationship to their factual base, is a twentieth-century extension of historical drama or the *pièce à thèse* where the factual basis gives the action its credibility. In 'documentary theatre', documents themselves are projected into text and performance. Documentary theatre has a declared purpose and an *evident* factual base. It follows the model pioneered in the 1920s by ERWIN PISCATOR. Non-naturalistic EPIC THEATRE techniques are used in documentary theatre to present oppositional critiques of dominant ideologies. Its four major functions are to reassess national/local histories; to celebrate communities/marginalized groups and their histories; to investigate important events and issues past and present; and to be openly didactic in its use of information. In documentary theatre, photographs and/or film project actualities; placards and/or slides project quotations from source documents; actors and/or loudspeakers address the audience directly with facts and information; voices of participants in historical events are used on tape/film. In addition, authentic music and song can add a critique of events, and acting techniques like BRECHT's *Verfremdungseffekt* (*see* ALIENATION EFFECT) can enable representation (rather than impersonation) of historical figures to take place. Information becomes the protagonist through a rhetoric of fact (printed documents, statistics, graphs, maps, actuality tape, film and photograph, song), as it did in the FEDERAL THEATER's LIVING NEWSPAPER. Such theatricalization is the opposite of naturalistic drama, which seeks to mask performance techniques in favour of surface realisms, especially of character. Documentary theatre was sometimes called THEATRE OF FACT in the 1960s, following Piscator's Berlin productions of ROLF HOCHHUTH's *The Representative* (1963), HEINAR KIPPHARDT's *The Case of J. Robert Oppenheimer* (1964) and PETER WEISS's *The Investigation* (1965). THEATRE WORKSHOP's *Oh, What a Lovely War!* (1963) and PETER BROOK's *US* (1966) were landmark productions in Britain, where the methodology derived from these plays became briefly a staple in REPERTORY theatre, having been pioneered by PETER CHEESEMAN at the VICTORIA THEATRE, Stoke-on-Trent. The 'verbatim play' was a 1980s variant of the local documentary. Britain's 7:84 and America's SAN FRANCISCO MIME TROUPE were notable ALTERNATIVE THEATRE exponents of documentary theatre, and the British THEATRE IN EDUCATION movement used it extensively as does radical theatre in the Third World. DEREK PAGET

See also THEATRE FOR DEVELOPMENT.

Gary Fisher Dawson, *Documentary Theatre in the United States: An Historical Survey and Analysis of its Content, Form and Stagecraft* (1999)
Herbert Lindenberger, *Historical Drama: The Relation of Literature and Reality* (1975)
Derek Paget, *True Stories? Documentary Drama on Stage, Screen and Radio* (1990)
John Willett, *The Theatre of Erwin Piscator: Half a Century of Politics in the Theatre* (1978)

Dodd, Ken[neth Arthur]   (b. Knotty Ash, Liverpool, 8 Nov. 1931)   Comedian and compulsive performer, whose ambition it is to play every venue in the British Isles. 'Doddy' confronts audiences with rambling conversations which sometimes go into wild areas of surrealism. Noted for his shock of straggling hair, protruding teeth and 'tickling stick', he charts the responses to all his performances and has elaborated a theory of regional variations in humour. His ability to switch from anarchic humour to sentimental song has provided him with several hit records. He played Malvolio in Liverpool (1971). CLIVE BARKER

See also STAND-UP COMEDY.

E. Midwinter, *Make 'Em Laugh* (1979)

Dodin, Lev   (b. Siberia, 16 May 1944)   Director. He was closely associated with the Maly Drama Theatre (MDT) of St Petersburg before becoming its artistic director in 1983. His first production in this capacity was *Brothers and Sisters* (1985), from the trilogy by Fedor Abramov devoted to peasant life in the Archangel region immediately after the Second World War. Its critical perspective on the Soviet regime made it a precursor of Mikhail Gorbachev's *glasnost* (1986–8). This six-hour work toured internationally to great acclaim after 1988 and belongs to Dodin's 'theatre of prose', as do *The House* (1980, also Abramov), *Lord of the Flies* (1986), *The Possessed* (from Dostoevsky, 1991) and *Chevengur* (1999, from the 1928 novel by Andrey Platonov, not published until 1989). These productions are not adaptations but are devised by the whole company and bear Dodin's hallmarks of long gestation (three years, for example, for *The Possessed*), large scale

(some 40 people perform *Brothers*) and maturation (productions continue to grow over the years of performance). Dodin trained the three generations of actors comprising the MDT at the Leningrad Theatre Insitute, thus developing the studio-company tradition established by STANISLAVSKY. With his last student ensemble incorporated in the MDT, he devised *Gaudeamus* (1991) and *Claustrophobia* (1994). He has staged contemporary Soviet plays (VOLODIN, GALIN) and foreign plays (e.g. Kleist's *The Broken Jug* and O'NEILL's *Desire Under the Elms*, both 1992) as well as CHEKHOV's *The Cherry Orchard* (1994) and *A Play Without a Title* (often known as *Platonov*, 1997). Since 1996 he has directed four operas, of which the most recent is *Mazepa* by Tchaikovsky, which he staged at La Scala (1999), conducted by Mstislav Rostropovich. MARIA SHEVTSOVA

Maria Shevsova, 'Resistance and Resilience: An Overview of the Maly Theatre of St Petersburg', *New Theatre Quarterly*, vol. 13, no. 52 (1997)
—— 'Drowning in Dixie: The Maly Drama Theatre Plays Chekhov Untitled', *Theatre Forum*, vol. 13 (1998)
—— 'War and Ash at La Scala: Lev Dodin Rehearses *Mazepa*', *Theatre Forum*, vol. 16 (2000)

Dominica   *see* CARIBBEAN

Donleavy, J[ames] P[atrick]   (b. Brooklyn, New York, 23 April 1926)   Playwright and novelist, who dramatized four of his novels: *The Ginger Man* (1959), *A Singular Man* (1964), *The Saddest Summer of Samuels* (1981) and *The Beastly Beatitudes of Balthazar B* (1981). The raw humour and picaresque heroes that characterize his novels were also seen in *Fairy Tales of New York* (1960), which won the *Evening Standard* award for most promising playwright in 1961. ADRIANA HUNTER

Donmar Theatre   This former banana warehouse in Covent Garden, London, was bought in 1960 by theatre manager Donald ALBERY and dancer Margot Fonteyn (hence Don-Mar), converted into a theatre and used for ballet. The ROYAL SHAKESPEARE COMPANY soon took it over for rehearsals and it housed part of the company's THEATRE OF CRUELTY season in 1964. Continuing this 'other space' strategy of diversifying its venues, the RSC adopted it as a studio theatre in 1977. Known as The Warehouse, it was committed to new writing and opened with HOWARD BARKER's *That Good Between Us*. After the RSC left in 1982, the theatre was used by touring and other groups until it was completely refurbished within a new shopping mall and reopened in 1992 under SAM MENDES, who turned it into one of London's liveliest small houses, noted particularly for its contemporary plays and musicals (e.g. revivals of SONDHEIM's *Assassins, Company* and *Merrily*

We Roll Along, and of KANDER, EBB and Masteroff's *Cabaret*). ADRIANA HUNTER

Donnellan, Declan *see* CHEEK BY JOWL

Donnelly, Dorothy [Agnes] (b. New York, 28 Jan. 1880; d. New York, 3 Jan. 1928) Lyricist, actress. Daughter of the manager of New York's Grand Opera House, she enjoyed a career as an actress in, among other productions, the US premières of YEATS' *Kathleen-ni-Houlihan* and SHAW's *Candida* (both 1903) and her best known role of *Madame X* (1910), a woman who faces her abandoned husband as the judge trying her for blackmail. Whilst acting, she wrote librettri and lyrics and then gave up performing on the success of her collaboration with SIGMUND ROMBERG on Franz Schubert's life and melodies, *Blossom Time* (1921). She worked on five more shows, including *Poppy* (1923) with Stephen Jones and her biggest hit, *The Student Prince* (1924), with Romberg. CHARLES LONDON

Lorraine Arnal McLean, *Dorothy Donnelly: A Life in the Theatre* (1999)

Doone, Rupert [Ernest Reginald Woodfield] (b. Alcester, Warks., 14 Aug. 1903; d. Northampton, 3 March 1966) Actor and choreographer. In 1931 Doone gave up a promising dance career with DIAGHILEV's Ballets Russes to work as an actor at the CAMBRIDGE FESTIVAL THEATRE. Out of a play-reading group he formed the GROUP THEATRE, in which he took a choreographer–director's role, adapting his own training to the needs of this COLLECTIVE TOTAL THEATRE group. Influenced by COCTEAU, with whom he had had an affair, he aimed for an EXPRESSIONIST political theatre, 'not portraiture but a cartoon'. From 1939 he was director of Morley College's theatre school. He spent his last years in a psychiatric hospital. DAN REBELLATO

Rupert Doone Remembered by His Friends (1966)
M. Sidnell, *Dances of Death: The Group Theatre of London in the Thirties* (1984)

Dorfman, [Vladimiro] Ariel (b. Buenos Aires, 6 May 1942) Playwright, novelist and human rights campaigner. As a child, Dorfman was forced with his liberal parents to flee Argentina in 1945, then McCarthyite America in 1955. Exiled once again from his adopted country, Chile, in 1973 – after General Pinochet's military coup had deposed President Allende's democratic government – he became an internationally renowned advocate of human rights. His play *Death and the Maiden* (1992), in which a woman has the chance to gain revenge on the man she thinks tortured her during the military dictatorship, caused a sensation around the world. It was turned into a suc-

cessful film by Roman Polanski in 1994. The protagonist of *Reader* (1955) is a state censor, whilst *Widows* (revised version 1997) gives a voice to the mothers, wives and daughters of 'the disappeared'. Other plays include *Mascara* and *Who's Who* (both written with his son Rodrigo, 1998) and *Purgatory* (2000), also dealing with the themes of fear, betrayal, justice and reconciliation. All are written in both Spanish and English. In addition, he has written novels, short stories, poetry, essays, memoirs and screenplays. NEIL DOWDEN

Dorst, Tankred (b. Oberland bei Sonneberg, Germany, 19 Dec. 1925) Playwright. He began his career in the late 1950s in the marionette theatre. His plays for stage and television employ a wide variety of styles and include: *Die Kurve* (*The Bend*, 1960), *Grosse Schmährede an der Stadtmauer* ('Great diatribe at the city wall', 1961), *Toller: Szenen aus einer deutschen Revolution* ('Toller: scenes from a German revolution', 1968) and *Eiszeit* ('Ice age', 1973). His collaboration with ZADEK led to a film script of *Eiszeit*, a television play, *Rotmord*, and a revue, *Kleiner Mann – Was Nun?* From 1974 he created a body of work (radio dramas and plays for television and stage) centred on the Merz family, which offer a panoramic view of developments in the Federal Republic of Germany since 1945. His eight-hour play *Merlin oder Das wüste Land* ('Merlin or the waste land', 1981) employed Arthurian legends to reflect on German history, whereas *Eisenhans* (1983) used the Grimm fairytale to show the individual's deformation due to historical and environmental forces. GÜNTER BERGHAUS

Rainer Taëni, *Tankred Dorst* (1977)
Günther Erken, ed, *Tankred Dorst* (1989)

Dotrice, Roy (b. Guernsey, 26 May 1925) Actor and director. He worked with various repertory theatres before founding the Guernsey Repertory Theatre in 1955. In 1958 he joined the SHAKESPEARE MEMORIAL THEATRE Company (later the ROYAL SHAKESPEARE COMPANY), enjoying success in many leading roles. In 1967 he played the seventeenth-century writer John Aubrey in the one-man piece *Brief Lives* (HAMPSTEAD THEATRE CLUB) and re-created the role with great success on Broadway, in the West End (creating a SOLO show record of 213 performances at the Criterion Theatre) and around the world. ADRIANA HUNTER

Douglas, James (b. Co. Wicklow, Ireland, 4 July 1929) Playwright. His serious comedies are often presented in a surrealistic mode; all were first produced in Dublin – *North City Traffic Straight Ahead* (Gaiety, 1961), *The Ice Goddess* (Gate, 1964), *Pices, the Cod* (Abbey, 1964), *A Tale After School* (Eblana, 1969), *And*

Marlene Never Knew (Abbey, 1972) and *Catalogue* (Project, 1972). He has writtten a very large number of radio plays. CHRISTOPHER FITZ-SIMON

Douglas-Home, William (b. Edinburgh, 3 June 1912; d. Winchester, Hants, 28 Sept. 1992) Playwright, prolific light-comic portraitist of the eccentric upper classes. The career of his brother Alec, the Conservative prime minister, inspired *The Chiltern Hundreds* (1947) and *The Reluctant Peer* (1964). More sober works include *Now Barabbas* (1947), reflecting his own wartime court martial and imprisonment for condemning the shelling of French civilians, and *Portraits* (1987), inspired by the career of Augustus John.
TONY HOWARD

Dowling, Eddie [Joseph Nelson Goucher] (b. Woonsocket, RI, 9 Dec. 1894; d. Smithfield, RI, 18 Feb. 1976) Actor, song-and-dance man, director and playwright. Much of Dowling's apprenticeship was spent in musicals and he appeared in three ZIEGFELD *FOLLIES*. In the 1920s he co-authored and starred in three musicals: *Sally, Irene and Mary* (1922), *Honeymoon Lane* (1926) and *Sidewalks of New York* (1927). He also toured in VAUDEVILLE with his wife, Ray Dooley. Later he was acclaimed for directing and acting in more serious works, notably the premières of *The Time of Your Life* (1939) and *The Glass Menagerie* (1945), which gave WILLIAMS a new lease of life. He also directed the première of *The Iceman Cometh* (1946). GERALD BORDMAN

Dowling, Joe (b. Dublin, 27 Sept. 1948) Director. He joined the ABBEY company in 1967 while still a student at University College, Dublin, and founded Ireland's first THEATRE IN EDUCATION company, the Young Abbey, in 1970. From 1973 to 1976 he directed at the Peacock Theatre, was artistic director of the Irish Theatre Company (1976–8) and then at the Abbey (1978–85), and was managing director of the Gaiety Theatre, Dublin (1985–9), where he founded the Gaiety School of Acting. His productions include the première of HUGH LEONARD's *A Life* (1979) and a number of BRIAN FRIEL's plays, *Living Quarters* (1977), *Aristocrats* (1979) and *The Communication Cord* (1982). His Abbey production of Friel's *The Faith Healer* (1979) transferred to the ROYAL COURT in London, and his Gate production of *Juno and the Paycock* (1993) transferred to London's West End. Dowling has also directed in Washington DC, New York, Montreal and Stratford, Ontario. In 1995 he was appointed artistic director of the GUTHRIE THEATER. BRIAN ROBERTS

Downes, Cathy (b. Wellington, New Zealand, 6 Nov. 1950) Actress and director. Trained at the New Zealand Drama School, she worked in Britain and helped establish the English Speaking Theatre of Amsterdam and the Heartache and Sorrow Company (London). She has toured internationally with her SOLO play *The Case of Katherine Mansfield* (1995). She continues to act on radio and on stage (e.g. as Antony in *Julius Caesar*, 1999), but has become one of New Zealand's leading directors with plays such as *Closer*, *Lady Windermere's Fan* and *Amy's View*, and New Zealand plays such as *Woman Far Walking*, *Purapurawhetu* and many others.
GILLIAN GREER & LAURIE ATKINSON

Downstage Theatre Beginning in a coffee bar in Wellington, New Zealand, in 1964, with a membership of 110 and a limited fund to provide small, local, professional theatre, it grew with public and private support to become the Hannah Playhouse (opened 1973). Its artistic directors – Sunny Amey (1970–3), MERVYN THOMPSON (1974–6), Anthony Taylor (1976–82), John Banas (1982–4) and COLIN MCCOLL (1984–1992) – have been committed to local drama. A number of Downstage initiatives have included education schemes and youth classes and performances, collaborations with Playmarket, which it helped set up, and the national Young Playwrights Festival (1987–9). Its writers in residence have included VINCENT O'SULLIVAN, Peter Hawes (*Goldie*, *Aunt Daisy*) and Sarah Delahunty (*Stretchmarks*, *Loose Connections*). Many of New Zealand's best-known directors, designers and actors have been closely associated with Downstage. Particular mention should be made of RAYMOND BOYCE, associate director/designer 1976–88, and BRUCE MASON, who, fully involved from the beginning until his death in 1982, averted many a crisis through his willingness to write or perform a play that would be guaranteed to attract the desperately needed audiences. A second space was opened in the early 1980s which became Taki Rua, with a commitment to MAORI THEATRE.
GILLIAN GREER AND LAURIE ATKINSON

Rebecca Simpson and Susan Ord, *Downstage: A Celebration* (1989)

drag 'Drag' is the wearing of the costume of a sexual role not your own for the purposes of a performance. It is not a sexual or psychological phenomenon, though it may be associated with transvestitism or transsexuality, which are. The word itself dates, along with 'gay' and 'camp', from the late nineteenth century. It usually refers to women's clothes worn by men; in gay slang, 'drag' can refer to any kind of artificial finery; 'butch drag' refers to ritualized masculine clothes worn by a man who does not live as he dresses (or to a woman in men's clothes) and a 'drag queen' is someone who does it for a living. No assumptions should be made about the equivalence or even similarity of different kinds of drag in different cutltures. A Native American *berdache* (an androgynous communicator with the supernatural), a British panto DAME, an American female IMPERSONATOR and an *onnagata* from the Japanese *noh* theatre are not the same thing. It is customary to observe that someone who wears drag is not necessarily a homosexual. This is true; it is equally true that in the twentieth century it is the drag queens who have maintained and elaborated the traditions which straight artists have occasionally adopted and illuminated.

Theatrical drag has always been acceptable on certain well-defined occasions; in the professional theatre, in amateur theatricals in schools, universities and the armed forces, and during CARNIVAL. Street drag has always been unacceptable because of its associations with homosexuality; homosexuals have been allowed to bring their distinctive culture into the theatre on condition that they make only concealed or apologetic reference to that culture; this has been true for PANTOMIME dames, female impersonators and pop singers. Female drag is not often condemned either on or off stage. This is so for two reasons: first, female theatrical drag is usually perceived as being designed for the titillation of men (a principal boy's exposed legs or DIETRICH'S sexual 'mystique'); second, it is acceptable for a woman to dress as a member of the 'stronger' sex but not for a man to dress as the 'weaker'. This last offensive truism should remind any student or admirer of drag that any drag act neccessarily (and dangerously) plays with and confronts sexual images, making theatre out of the distinctions between man and woman and between homosexual and heterosexual. Drag always, whatever the artist's declared or implied intentions, suggests that the adoption of a sexual image is never natural and never straightforward; it may be a fashionable, professional, playful, political, radical, conservative, self-conscious or just perverse act. An evidently gay dame may entertain with a string of sexist or homophobic jokes directed against his (female) principal boy; a heterosexual actress showing her legs to a male audience may become an icon of both lesbian and gay male desire; a VARIETY bill in a drag PUB may feature sincere acts of homage to female strength, wit and beauty alongside inane parodies.

The prehistory of drag includes the ritually cross-dressed grotesques of European folk drama (for instance, the Bessie of the English Mummers' play) and the professional boy- and character-actors who created the female roles in English Renaissance drama. The drag of these first 'actresses' was a necessary convention in a theatre which – like the church – excluded women as either performers or authors. Once the real thing – female actors – came along, drag might have been expected to lose its potency as a theatrical language. Far from it; it has retained its place at the troubled and troubling centre of what 'performance' is and can be.

Drag has always been a popular entertainment. Since the nineteenth century men have worked as actresses both in major cities and on tour, in the MINSTREL shows in America and in MELODRAMA, operetta and the MUSIC HALL in Britain. Well-documented careers include those of Ernest Boulton ('Stella, Star of the Strand'), who toured with his drag colleague Frederick Park ('Fanny Graham'), often playing the ingénue opposite his own real-life lover, Lord Arthur Clinton MP; and of Raymond de Montmorency Lecky Brown-Lecky, an Irish actress famous for his rendition of *Lady Audley's Secret*. Drag was a common feature of musical acts in the early music halls; E. W. Marshall did songs in drag at the very first London hall, the Canterbury, in 1852, though we do not know whether he appeared as a female impersonator, a drag queen or a straight comedian. At the turn of the century Malcolm Scott played the London Pavilion in character as Salomé, Catherine Parr and Boadicea; in 1912 Fred Emney and Wilkie Bard played the first Royal Command variety performance as a drag double act. The nineteenth century saw the first of the pantomime dames – grotesqely costumed mother-figures who lead the annual Christmas entertainment, always recognizable as men. Great dames have included DAN LENO, GEORGE ROBEY, Arthur Lucan ('Old Mother Riley') and Douglas Byng. Byng also appeared in revue; NOEL COWARD wrote a drag sketch for him and ERNEST THESIGER in the COCHRANE revue for 1925, *Oranges and Lemons*. Byng was the exception among dames, bringing a regal elegance and understated gay wit to the role; the rest were great popular comedians who sometimes played character parts as women. The influence of the great dames can be seen in the 'cod' repertoire of gay drag, in which being dressed as a women is treated as a grotesque joke.

In America, a very different tradition developed, that of 'glam' drag: female impersonation dependent on wit, charm and (especially) lavish and expensive costumes. The first and most successful big-time impersonator was JULIAN ELTINGE, who had his own Broadway shows built around him; he was followed by Charles Renault (who rose from a First World War concert party to giving solo galas at the Met), Karyl Norman, Charles Pierce, BERT SAVOY (star of the ZIEGFELD *Follies* for 1917) and Lynne Carter, whose Jewel Box Revue toured across America and internationally, taking in upmarket nightclubs, popular theatres and Broadway.

In Europe, theatrical drag has been more closely allied to transvestitism; its home is the transvestite CABARET or REVUE. Its greatest artists have assumed the beauty of female performers so perfectly that the transformation creates a sexual magic of its own. COCTEAU's idol, the feathered trapeze artist Barbette (born in Texas in 1899), began work billed as a woman. He was followed in the 1950s by Coccinelle; in the 1970s by the dancers of the Parisian troupe La Grande Eugène; and by LINDSAY KEMP, whose company unashamedly relies on the beauty and sexual appeal of its performers.

As music hall and variety began to fail, drag as a performing art was transformed by the Second World War. Homosexual soldiers in drag provided the staple of forces' entertainment; when the war was over, the gay drag revues dazzled a drab culture with hugely successful touring shows – *Soldiers in Skirts*, *Forces Showboat*, *Misleading Ladies*. The artists did not appear in public as gay, but as glamorous variety entertainers. Individual members of the troupes went on to work the variety circuit as singers and comedians, playing to straight audiences; in the 1960s they were the originators of the boom in pub drag, first in mixed pubs, singing the same songs as female singers and telling the same jokes as male comedians, then increasingly in the post-1968 network of gay pubs and clubs. Pub drag is a predictable mixture of glam and cod acts, offering the usual pleasures of variety – frocks, jokes and music, often taped. Occasionally the scene is graced by a comedian as talented as Rex Jamieson (the legendary 'Mrs Shufflewick') or Lily Savage; but at all times this brand of drag is a vital form of popular theatre, as vulgar as it is stylized, glamorous and often strangely moving. Drag has a capacity for intimacy between artist and public rare in other contemporary Western theatre; it is also able to present images of gay culture at its most radical and its most conservative. Amid the Americanization of gay men's culture in the 1970s, British drag has remained a working-class style, maintaining the virtues of pre-liberation culture (vicious humour, strength and unapologetic outrageousness) against the contemporary fashion for exaggerated masculinity and social acceptance. Pub drag has a very complex attitude to the female artists it copies; it may be sexist, misogynist or radically feminist. The most successful entertainer to come out of the forces revues was DANNY LA RUE. In 1964 he opened his own club in London, and was patronized by royalty, who came to see him parody Dame Margot Fonteyn; in 1970 he was the highest-paid performer in London's West End. La Rue's act is extraordinary. He

continually reassures the audience that he is a virile working-class man (his catch phrase is 'Wotcher Mates!'); he chats to the women about the lavish frocks his dame wears; entertains the men with blue jokes and comic humiliations of the attractive younger actress playing principal boy; and occasionally acknowledges the other queens in the audience with old-fashioned cryptic innuendoes that are completely missed by the majority of the audience.

Contemporary drag is developing in several different directions. Gay pub drag, American and European female impersonation continue. In America, radical drag (street drag traumatized by contact with radical gay and feminist politics) began with New York's Hot Peaches and their 'Divas of Sheridan Square'. The older styles of Broadway and VAUDEVILLE were added to the mix, together with the formal radicalism of EXPERIMENTAL THEATRE and PERFORMANCE ART, resulting in the work of Charles Ludlum and the THEATRE OF THE RIDICULOUS, Ethyl Eichelberger and Ekatherina Sobechanskaya and her Trockadero Gloxinia Ballet. In Britain similar work was being done by Bloolips, whose leading lady is Bette Bourne; he embodies all the talents and traditions of British music hall, but in fact began working with Hot Peaches in New York during the political fervour of gay liberation and went on to play Lady Bracknell in *The Importance of Being Ernest* as Billy James, Quentin Crisp and Patrick Fyffe (Dame Hilda Bracket) had before him. In 1974 Kemp created his greatest drag role, Divine, in his homage to GENET, *Flowers*, and also briefly tutored David Bowie; in 1972 Tim Curry, who had dragged up in the musical *Hair*, played the transvestite lead in *The Rocky Horror Show*; thus began the appearance of drag in the performance vocabulary of pop music and video. Drag here does not function as a sign of gay culture but ritualizes the power of popular entertainment, making singers like Bowie, Boy George, Divine and Annie Lennox into sexualized icons or asexual clowns.

The tradition of straight drag comics has reached new heights of popularity in the live and TV performances of Dick Emery and BARRY HUMPHRIES ('Dame Edna Everage, Housewife and Superstar'). The tradition of gay drag performers who make no reference to their gayness in public continues in the work of Danny La Rue and Hinge and Bracket, who started in the Black Cap, London (with the Vauxhall, the most important London drag venue) but went on to tour the country in a popular and respectable musical comedy show.

Women and drag is a separate story. Female music hall artists also appeared in drag – the most famous were Hetty King and VESTA TILLEY, who first appeared in male evening dress in 1869. This costume was also used by Judy Garland and Dietrich, and is occasionally borrowed by lesbian comics Robyn Archer (Australia) and Robin Tyler (United States). Feminist and lesbian critiques of gender roles have also led to satirizing through drag by groups like SPLIT BREECHES. Actresses from BERNHARDT and Esmé Beringer to Frances de la Tour have responded to the fact that men can't or won't write sufficient great parts for women by playing male roles; all of them were famous Hamlets. Although women playing parts written by Shakespeare for boys (Cleopatra, Juliet, Lady Macbeth, etc.) does not cause comment, women playing parts he wrote for men does; SYBIL THORNDIKE played Prince Hal and the Fool in *King Lear*, FIONA SHAW Richard II. In the classical ballet, Evil Fairies and Ugly Sisters are played by male dancers; in opera, women are allowed to play men without comment – Cherubino in *Figaro*, Oscar in *Un Ballo in Maschera* and Octavian in *Der Rosenkavalier* are all played by women; and a woman is expected to play the principal boy in British pantomime, a tradition which began when Madame Vestris (the first woman to manage a London theatre, the Olympic) displayed her legs to great commercial advantage in a Planché pantomime in 1831. A principal boy wears clothes which a real man would never wear – skin-tight high-cut shorts, thigh-high boots or stiletto shoes. Similarly, drag queens appear in costumes which pay homage to their originals but which no real woman entertainer has ever worn, even at her most gorgeous or bizarre. Men dress up as women, and women dress up as men; and men and women both drag up, a style of dress which has its own laws and meanings and history.

NEIL BARTLETT

Roger Baker, *Drag: A History of Female Impersonation in the Performing Arts* (1994)

K. Bornstein, *Gender Outlaw* (1994)

L. Ferris, ed., *Queering the Stage* (1992)

Marjorie Garber, *Vested Interests: Cross Dressing and Cultural Anxiety* (1992)

Kris Kirk and Ed Heath, *Men in Frocks* (1984)

Kenneth Marlowe, *Mr Madam* (1967)

Laurence Senelick, ed., *Gender in Performance* (1992)

—, *The Changing Room: Sex, Drag and Theatre* (2000)

Drake, Alfred [Alfredo Capurro] (b. New York, 7 Oct. 1914; d. New York, 25 July 1992) The finest American musical actor of his day, who created the roles of Curley in *Oklahoma!* (1943), Fred Graham in *Kiss Me, Kate* (1948) and Hajj in *Kismet* (1953). He began his musical career in GILBERT and SULLIVAN and then in the chorus of *White Horse Inn* (1936), from where he went on to larger roles in such hits as *Babes in Arms* (1937) and *Two for the Show* (1940). His rich baritone and strutting stage presence later brought him success in several non-singing roles. In the late 1950s Drake's classical skills were shown as Othello and Benedick at the AMERICAN SHAKESPEARE FESTIVAL, and he was widely praised when he played Claudius to RICHARD BURTON's Hamlet (1964). He also directed and helped adapt several Italian plays.   THOMAS F. CONNOLLY

drama schools

In Britain

'Actors are born, not made' is an oft-quoted maxim; but there is no doubt that any actor or actress, whatever natural gifts he or she may possess, can benefit from teaching and training – not only from a drama school but from studying at a university, where drama societies flourish. In the early years of the nineteenth century, however, becoming an actor meant joining an established company – generally touring the provinces and learning the craft as an apprentice, through practical experience, particularly by observing the work of the leading artists in the company. Drama training as we came to know it in the late twentieth century was virtually unknown. The longest-established training establishment in Europe was the Paris Conservatoire, which started life as the L'Ecole de Déclamation in 1786. Many of this establishment's successful students became teachers later in their careers. This happened in Britain in the early years of the nineteenth century, generally when the actor or actress concerned had retired from the stage. Several attempts to establish training schools were initiated then but none survived more than a few years. The oldest school that did survive was founded by Dr Henry Wilde in 1861 as the London Academy of Music and later became LAMDA – the London Academy of Music and Dramatic Art. The first wholly successful drama school in the UK was run by Sarah Thorne (1837–99), a very accomplished actress and manageress, who owned the Theatre Royal in Margate and was a friend of the TERRY family. Many books had been published about preparing for the theatre, notably Gustave Garcia's *The Actor's Art* in 1882, and this new interest in training encouraged Thorne to open a school attached to the Theatre Royal in the early 1880s, where the curriculum included voice production and dialects, mime and gesture, as well as stage movement and combat, subjects her company had been working on for some years. Among her actors/students were HARLEY GRANVILLE BARKER (who was soon to revolutionize British theatre), the VANBRUGH sisters, Irene and Violet (whose brother Kenneth Barnes was later to become principal of the Royal Academy of Dramatic Art), Louis Calvert and Sir BEN

GREET, who were to become two of the leading Shake-spearean actor–managers of their day, and her favourite pupil, Ellen O'Malley, for whom SHAW wrote Nora in *John Bull's Other Island* and Ellie Dunn in *Heartbreak House*. Apart from the Conservatoire in Paris, the other major training school in Europe was founded in Moscow in 1878 as the School of Music and Drama, but became recognized as a conservatoire and known as the Moscow Philharmonic Society in 1886. VLADIMIR NEMIROVICH-DANCHENKO became leader of the drama course in 1891 and introduced a less rigid style of acting.

In Britain, FRANK BENSON and Greet followed Thorne's system of attaching a training school to their companies. Most teaching, however, was given privately in London by eminent actors and actresses – notably Hermann Vezin, who concentrated on the text and beauty of the spoken word. Many prestigious artists trained with him, and one of his most successful pupils was Rosina Filippi, who taught Vezin's methods but used music to emphasize the rhythm of the voice. Her teaching was rivalled only by ELSIE FOGERTY, whose training at the Paris Conservatoire gave an even stronger emphasis to pure and natural speech. Her students presented the Greek classics in her classrooms at the Albert Hall. Most schools – apart from the academies run by Benson and Greet – were music orientated, notably the London Academy of Music and the Guildhall School of Music (founded 1880), although classes in stage training were part of their curriculum. Then Cairns James, who was a professor at the Guildhall School, left to establish his own School of Musical and Dramatic Art, which – although it included music in the curriculum – specialized in stage training, with particular emphasis on the musical theatre, having close links with the legendary GEORGE EDWARDES. However, training for the legitimate theatre was in short supply until HERBERT BEERBOHM TREE founded the Academy of Dramatic Art in the dome of His Majesty's Theatre in 1904. ADA, as the Academy was known, was reconstituted in 1906, after taking new premises in Gower Street, in order to house the expanding number of applicants; here it has remained. Control was vested in a council consisting of Sir SQUIRE BANCROFT as president, actors and managers GEORGE ALEXANDER, ARTHUR BOURCHIER, JOHNSTON FORBES-ROBERTSON, John Hare, CYRIL MAUDE, Tree himself and the playwrights BARRIE and PINERO. Once again Thorne's influence was mainly responsible, for O'Malley confirmed that Tree's decision was prompted after discussions with Arthur Bourchier, who had married Violet Vanbrugh, a graduate from Margate. Bourchier encouraged Tree to utilize the unused space

at His Majesty's for the new venture and employ distinguished teachers like Filippi and persuade distinguished actors and actresses to teach. Shaw joined the Council of ADA in 1912 and insisted upon the appointment of a woman – Irene Vanbrugh – to the council, and when in 1920 a Royal Charter was granted, ADA became RADA. The original refurbishment of the Gower Street premises took place in 1931 and when Shaw died in 1950 he bequeathed a generous proportion of his royalties to RADA. Thanks to a grant from the National Lottery, the Gower Street premises were refurbished at the end of the century and the main theatre there, the Vanbrugh, re-opened (along with the other amenities) in the autumn of 2000.

Fogerty had worked with Benson at Stratford in 1903 and he was very impressed with the progress of his students studying with her. In 1906 she opened the Central School of Speech Training and Dramatic Art (later Speech and Drama) at her rooms at the Albert Hall, bringing students from the Benson School with her. Her training principles were clear, but she was flexible and aware of the necessity for new methods. Within a few years she was recognized as the foremost authority on speech training and she initiated training for teachers and speech therapists alongside her drama course. At the same time as Filippi and Fogerty were making their names, another young actress from a very famous musical family, Italia Conti, was specializing in preparing children for the theatre. After assisting CHARLES HAWTREY by directing the children appearing in *Where the Rainbow Ends* in 1911, she set up her own school, which also offered a general education for its pupils. This was so successful that similar establishments soon proliferated and survived. During the period before the Second World War other drama schools were founded all over Britain, but only two from that period survive. The Webber–Douglas School of Singing opened in 1926; the principals, Amherst Webber and Walter Johnstone-Douglas, decided their singers lacked acting prowess and decided to employ a teacher to help students appear more natural. Susan Richmond arrived to teach stage training and enlisted the help of O'Malley in the early 1930s. Within a few years the success of the acting training meant the organization was renamed the Webber–Douglas School of Singing and Dramatic Art. Meanwhile, in the midlands, Pamela Chapman, a respected teacher of speech training, founded the Birmingham School of Speech and Drama in 1936. Another important development happened when MICHEL SAINT-DENIS founded the London Theatre Studio in 1935, where his very successful productions, particularly the *Electra* of Sophocles and the *Alcestis* of Euripides in 1938 and 1939, respectively, were the talk of London. When the Second World War came, however, Saint-Denis closed the school and became head of the French Section of the BBC, and many London-based schools closed or moved out of London while the bombs fell. RADA continued its work in London and its principal, Sir Kenneth Barnes, was also general secretary of the ENTERTAINMENTS NATIONAL SERVICE ASSOCIATION (ENSA) from 1939 to 1946.

While most of the pupils at the various drama schools before the Second World War were from families who could afford the fees, most establishments provided scholarships, which provided free tuition for talented but poor students. RADA, in particular, offered the majority of such opportunities. When the war was over, interest in drama training increased and a number of schools opened, including the Mountview Theatre School (1945), the Welsh College of Music and Drama (1946) and the Royal Scottish Academy of Music and Drama (1950), mainly through the influence of Scots dramatist JAMES BRIDIE. Meanwhile, in 1946 Saint-Denis became general director (with GLEN BYAM SHAW) of the OLD VIC Theatre School, and training took place in the war-damaged building from 1946 to 1952. In 1946, soon after the foundation of the BRISTOL OLD VIC Theatre, a sister company – the Bristol Old Vic Theatre School – commenced training. Fogerty had retired as principal of the Central School in 1942 and had been succeeded by Gwynneth Thurburn; one of the school's most valued teachers, Rose Bruford, left to found the Rose Bruford College of Speech and Drama in 1950. After the war, local authorities were empowered to award discretionary grants to pay fees and cover maintenance for promising students who could not otherwise afford to study. As the demand for places increased, new schools opened: Margaret Bury founded the East 15 Acting School (1961), Christopher Fettes and Yat Malmgren left the Central School to open Drama Centre (1963) and Bice Bellairs founded the Guildford School (1964). Many polytechnics and training colleges for teachers introduced drama training into their courses, and, similarly, some of the established drama schools incorporated a musical theatre course into their training. Conversely, the Arts Educational Schools, which had been founded in 1939, mainly concentrating on dance training, opened a course for actors as well as a musical theatre course. Several schools ran technical and stage management courses alongside the acting programme and a few drama schools trained theatre directors. Most of the schools of art now run a specialized department for theatre designers.

The major factor in acknowledging acting as a valid course of study was the formation of the CDS – the Conference of Drama Schools. In 1966 George Rossiter, principal of the Webber–Douglas, appointed a young theatre director, Raphael Jago (who had been recommended by JOHN GIELGUD) to succeed him. Jago was quick to realize that a link had to be established among the drama schools and approached Hugh Cruttwell, then principal of RADA, who backed him to the hilt, realizing the possibilities of such a body, composed of members committed to the raising of standards and communicating with each other so that all students had full information on every subject, particularly when dealing with local authorities on funding. Within a matter of months the CDS was in session and, with the backing of the actors' UNION Equity and the Council of Regional Theatres (CORT), persuaded the Gulbenkian Foundation to conduct a thorough investigation into drama training. Their official report advocated the formation of the National Council for Drama Training, the purpose of which was to accredit training courses for actors. Because fees for full-time courses are relatively high, several drama schools have been founded offering training over a period of two years, operating every evening and over weekends. This enables students to obtain daytime work to fund their tuition and cover their maintenance. Although facilities are limited, which means NCDT accreditation is not a possibility, the standard is generally high and the teachers work for minimum salaries. The most notable of such establishments is the Poor School, founded by Paul Caister in 1986, which was the first in this field. Courses run in drama schools at the end of the twentieth century were infinitely more comprehensive than those running in the earlier part. While most remain grounded in the classical tradition and follow STANISLAVSKY's teaching, which MICHAEL CHEKHOV developed in Europe and the United States, the METHOD technique, pioneered by LEE STRASBERG in the United States after the Second World War, also plays its part in some training. Generally initial teaching covers speech and movement (where the ALEXANDER technique and the teachings of the LABAN School play their part) and the work undertaken combines to develop and strengthen both voice and body. When these technical skills are understood, the process of learning to inhabit the personality of any character an artist is called upon to play predominates in the training, alongside detailed knowledge of work in film, television and radio techniques. In some schools a thorough understanding of MASK and CLOWN studies is developed. Since the 1950s, singing has become a vital element in theatre skills and this has motivated an alteration to the curriculum, so that at most schools each graduate can cope with the demands of the musical theatre – and Brechtian-type productions – by a thorough grounding in the subject. During the last year of training, drama schools present full-scale productions of plays and public auditions, when agents, theatrical managements, directors, producers and casting directors are invited to attend. Besides giving the opportunity for each student to appear in a leading role in a play, every student can perform audition pieces – generally of his or her own choice – in a showcase presentation, so that those attending can make a sound assessment of their potential

Since the formation of the NCDT, funding has become increasingly limited for actors. There are not enough scholarships with maintenance grants, and financial assistance for talented students from local authorities responsible for awarding such grants has become extremely limited. The NCDT has worked consistently towards ameliorating the position. Some schools have established links with universities, so that degree courses in acting and kindred subjects (which are eligible for state support) are available to their students. However, some major establishments do not wish to formalize training in this way, and the NCDT was mainly responsible for initiating the Marchant Report (2000) into the state of funding for drama training. Negotiations at the highest level seem likely to prove successful, providing future students with an adequate level of support. PIETER ROGERS

In the United States

Mention of American actor training tends to conjure up the spirit of the Russian director KONSTANTIN STANISLAVSKY. Years after the MOSCOW ART THEATRE's artistically triumphant American tour, several strains of Stanislavskian thought continue to dominate, though before Stanislavsky and company arrived in the early 1920s, the theatre was served by training models dating back to the nineteenth century. Stock companies were the fertile training grounds in the mid- to late 1800s. They offered aspiring actors opportunities to perform small roles while learning their craft by watching veteran performers. In this quasi-apprenticeship system, there was little formal training. Actors might occasionally take a class in a variety of related areas such as boxing, fencing, elocution and acrobatics, but there was no unified approach to training. Unusual for his time, stock producer Augustin Daly (1838–99) is regarded as an early trainer who taught novices and veterans alike through careful rehearsal and attention to the details of ensemble performance. Daly also helped support Dion Boucicault's School of Acting in

the late 1800s, although its curriculum seems to have relied on what is now called 'scene study'.

Many of the noted actors of the time were opposed to training on the grounds that proficiency must be self-acquired. To these professionals the stage was the only training ground. That any discussions were happening at all is due in large part to the work of Steele MacKaye (1842–94), who began arguing for a conservatory training model in 1871. Based on the teachings of François Delsarte (1811–71), MacKaye's work manifested itself in several training projects. The first three were all short lived. There is some disagreement over who created MacKaye's final project, the Lyceum Theater School. It is unquestioned, though, that both MacKaye and his successor, Franklin Sargent (1856–1923), had a hand in the Lyceum's founding in 1884. In 1885, the Lyceum became the American Academy of Dramatic Arts, which continues to operate successfully more than 100 years later.

The early decades of the twentieth century saw the sprouting of professional theatre training schools in cities such as Detroit, Kansas City, Denver and Seattle, as well as in larger metropolitan areas. Although these schools were dotted across a wide range of urban areas, they were training graduates for an American theatre increasingly centralized in the large cities of the northeast and upper mid-west. Institutions of higher education also began offering professional training in the theatrical arts. In addition to the American Academy, other early-century drama schools in New York included the National Dramatic Conservatory, established by character actor F. F. Mackay (1832–1923), the Stanhope–Wheatcroft Dramatic School, the American School of Playwriting and the Theodora Irvine Studio. Each built around the talent and personality of one person, these schools quite naturally foundered over time. That the American Academy is an exception is partly due to its recognition as an institution of higher education by the State of New York in 1899. It was the Russian invasion of 1922–3 that changed the way American actors were trained. Following the successful tour of the Moscow Art Theatre, RICHARD BOLESLAVSKY – a former member of Stanislavsky's group – founded the American Laboratory Theater (1923–33) in New York. ALT combined a rigorous training programme with a producing theatre company, but it is less important for the splash it made than for the ripples that came later. Among the perfervid followers of Boleslavsky at ALT were HAROLD CLURMAN, LEE STRASBERG and STELLA ADLER. In 1931 Clurman and Strasberg teamed up with CHERYL CRAWFORD to form the GROUP THEATER, which Adler joined as an actor. Even before the Group was under way, Strasberg had begun his approach to actor training that evolved into the vaunted METHOD. His interpretation of Stanislavsky, which was later honed during his more than 30 years (1949–82) at the famed ACTORS' STUDIO – founded by Group members Crawford, ELIA KAZAN and ROBERT LEWIS – relies on the actor plumbing the depths of personal psychology to produce a genuine, affective performance.

After a stint in Paris during 1934, where she studied at length with Stanislavsky, Adler returned to the United States to tell her compatriots that they (including herself) had misinterpreted the Russian director's emphasis on affective memory. She and Strasberg became embroiled in a feud over technique that was never reconciled. In 1949 Adler formed the Stella Adler Theater Studio (now the Stella Adler Conservatory of Acting) and began teaching actors to focus on using text and the playwright's intent to find emotional triggers. Her work also treated emotion as one of many elements of performance; the others included voice and speech, movement, and classical style.

A third member of the Group, Sanford Meisner, began to teach acting at the NEIGHBORHOOD PLAYHOUSE in 1935. While Meisner was undoubtedly influenced by all of the Stanislavskian activity around him, his technique relied strongly on spontaneity and being 'in the moment'. As with Strasberg's Method, Meisner's technique has evolved in recent years, with various acolytes and institutions (Meisner Extension, Atlantic Theater Company) teaching versions of it.

Each generation makes new discoveries in theatrical training, although the 'new' is often tied to something or someone not so new. When they created the Drama Division at the Juilliard School, veteran theatre producer JOHN HOUSEMAN and French actor–teacher MICHEL SAINT-DENIS focused on training that seemed to synthesize much of what was being taught at individual studios bearing Group pedigrees. Saint-Denis' approach, inspired by his uncle, the respected theorist and director JACQUES COPEAU, emphasized a total approach to training. Some have referred to it as a 'European' model in which students receive intensive work in improvisation, movement, mask work, voice, speech and text analysis. It is also an approach that eschews naturalism – a common (and perhaps misguided) complaint about Stanislavsky-based training – in favour of spontaneous and theatrical performance. In 1972 Houseman formed the Acting Company from the first graduating class of the school as a permanent repertory group. Over the next three decades the Acting Company toured widely. Nowadays, though, company members are chosen by audition, not merely by graduation from Juilliard.

The trend for the past several decades has been for conservatories to offer degrees that are acceptable for teaching in higher education. Although some institutions continue to offer certificates upon completion of training, most have begun to offer Masters of Fine Arts degrees as well. The Institute for Advanced Theatre Training, which is attached to the AMERICAN REPERTORY THEATER and is loosely affiliated with Harvard University, recently added MFA degrees to its Certificates of Achievement under a two-tier arrangement with the Moscow Art Theatre School. Elsewhere in the United States, conservatory programmes connected to theatres – such as the National Theater Conservatory in Denver and the AMERICAN CONSERVATORY THEATER in San Francisco – operate comprehensive actor-training programmes that recall, to some extent, the apprenticeship system of the nineteenth century. Although neither is attached to a college or university, both also offer MFA degrees. Indeed, the term 'drama school' is somewhat misleading. The early 'drama departments' at Yale University and Carnegie Institute of Technology (now Carnegie Mellon University) have become schools of drama. In the early part of the century, 'drama departments' were viewed with consternation as too vocationally oriented; at the century's end, though, all of the studios and training programmes mentioned above offered some sort of degree. Most grant the Bachelor of Fine Arts degree; an exception is the American Academy, which offers a two-year Associate degree. While some top-quality acting schools do not offer higher education-based degrees, the more prominent programmes understand that professional credentials are of growing importance as we enter a competitive new age in drama education and training.

JEFFREY ERIC JENKINS

See also PHYSICAL PREPARATION; UNIVERSITY DRAMA DEPARTMENTS; VOICE TRAINING.

Kenneth Macgowan, *Footlights Across America: Towards a National Theater* (1929)

Karl R. Wallace, ed., *History of Speech Education* (1954)

dramatherapy The application of drama and theatre as a programme of treatment in settings such as psychiatric hospitals, day centres, prisons, special schools, rehabilitation and after-care centres and child and family clinics, as well as in private practice. Dramatherapists apply movement, sound, masks, improvisation, text work and all forms of dramatization in order to bring about 'personal growth' and 'social skills'. Peter Slade first used the term in a talk entitled 'Dramatherapy as an Aid to Becoming a Person' in 1954, although many accounts exist over several hundred years, scattered in diverse sources such as biographies and medical history, of drama and theatre having a recreational and a healing function. RITUAL drama may also be seen as healing, and the shaman is sometimes compared to the dramatherapist. However, the contemporary practice of dramatherapy has moved away from 'folk medicine' and allied itself with medical and, in some cases, psychotherapeutic models of practice. In Britain dramatherapists have to be state registered, having completed one of the seven postgraduate dramatherapy diplomas, and 'dramatherapist' is a protected title, regulated by the Health Professions Council and the British Association of Dramatherapists. People wishing to maintain their artistic and folk roots find other ways to describe their practice. SUE JENNINGS

See also THEATRE IN PRISONS; THEATRE FOR OLD PEOPLE.

R. Grainger, *Drama and Healing: The Roots of Dramatherapy* (1990)

S. Jennings, *Introduction to Dramatherapy* (1999)

dramatic theory The main lines of Western dramatic theory were laid out in ARISTOTLE's *Poetics*, which dates from the fourth century BC. The other great classical source for subsequent theorists was the Roman author Horace (65–8 BC), who, like Aristotle, gives central attention to the drama, but with a number of more prescriptive rules and with a typically ROMAN emphasis on a high moral tone, decorum, balance and moderation. Even more than Aristotle, Horace emphasizes the writing of drama over its performance, establishing a strong theoretical bias in favour of the written text which has persisted in the West until modern times. A very different view of theatre is found in oriental theory, where the great classic texts either give equal attention to script and performance, as we find in the monumental Sanskrit *Natyasastra* (*A Treatise on Theatre*), dated between 200 BC and AD 800, or give almost exclusive attention to performance, as in the Chinese *Analytics of Acting* (*c.*1776) or the theoretical treatises of Zeami (1363–1443), the founder of the *noh* theatre of Japan.

Doubtless the rise of a middle-class public, with its preoccupation with the world of material objects, encouraged the trend towards realism in both dramatic theory and practice from the late eighteenth century onwards. For some theorists, such as Lillo (1691–1739), the turn to prose drama and to bourgeois realism was justified on moral grounds – the theatre could best serve as a moral force if its lessons were set in familiar surroundings. Others, such as Hebbel (1813–63), saw realism as the best vehicle for bringing modern bourgeois audiences to the kind of deep insights into the human condition formerly offered by high TRAGEDY.

For still others, such as ZOLA, morality or mystic insights were less important than an accurate recording of the dynamics of social existence. Zola felt that a rigour comparable to that of experiments in the physical sciences could be applied to such recording, to which he applied the term naturalism. Later, Zola's scientific concern faded and naturalism came to mean extreme realism, especially of the grimmer aspects of life.

The enormous impact of IBSEN and the other great realists in the late nineteenth century established this form as the standard for the modern drama, as classicism had been two centuries before, and much theory of the twentieth century, especially that which defined itself as AVANT-GARDE or in opposition to mainstream theatre, has in one way or another involved a rejection of realism. Scarcely had realism become the dominant dramatic mode of the late nineteenth century when it was challenged by the first of the modern anti-realist 'isms', SYMBOLISM. In the new century first FUTURISM, then DADA, SURREALISM (especially in the influential work of APPIA and CRAIG), EXPRESSIONISM and other less well-known movements differed in their specific programmes but were united in their rejection of the realist mainstream exemplified by the core work of a company like the MOSCOW ART THEATRE and its leading figure, STANISLAVSKY. With several notable exceptions, socially engaged drama tended, as may be seen in SHAW and later in the French existentialists such as SARTRE and CAMUS, to become closely associated with realism. Nowhere was this association more important than in the Soviet Union, where socialist realism, politically engaged realist drama, became the official state-sanctioned dramatic form. The defenders of this form frequently attacked non-realistic drama as formalist, arguing that it evaded essential political concerns for the sake of hollow artistic display.

ERWIN PISCATOR and BERTOLT BRECHT, one of the most influential dramatists and theorists of the modern theatre, opposed this position, arguing that a truly political theatre must open up new perspectives, and could do this only by disrupting traditional expectations, especially those of realism. Although Brecht's position naturally brought him into conflict with more traditional Marxists, setting off a complex and continuing debate, his influence, especially in the West, was instrumental in encouraging a strong measure of non-realistic experimentation in POLITICAL THEATRE, often reminiscent of the theatrical experiments in the early years of the Russian Revolution.

Before the twentieth century, classicism's tendency to favour distinct, 'pure' genres meant that much theoretical speculation was devoted to genre analysis, with particular attention to tragedy, considered, since Aristotle, the highest dramatic form. The triumph of realism, with its indifference to traditional generic distinctions, shifted theoretical speculation in other directions. Nevertheless, generic concerns continued to play an important role in subsequent theory and practice. Several important American dramatists, including MAXWELL ANDERSON, EUGENE O'NEILL and ARTHUR MILLER, argued that traditional tragic insight was still possible in the modern theatre. (Lionel Abel coined the term METATHEATRE for this development.) On the contrary, argued such theorists as Joseph Wood Krutch and George Steiner, the modern world, with its loss of faith in both God and man, no longer possessed a 'tragic vision'. Perhaps the most important development of this debate was carried out by writers like FRIEDRICH DÜRRENMATT, who, while denying the possibility of modern high tragedy, felt that tragic insight could still be gained through development of the ironic and grotesque elements in tragedy and farce. This approach was developed in detail during the 1960s by such theorists as J. L. Styan, Cyrus Hoy, Jan Kott and Karl Guthke, and their theoretical work was both inspired and reinforced by the appearance at this same time of the century's most successful group of non-realistic dramatists in France, headed by SAMUEL BECKETT, EUGÈNE IONESCO and JEAN GENET. Though never really a coherent 'movement', these dramatists were connected, at least in English-speaking areas, as playwrights of the THEATRE OF THE ABSURD, a somewhat misleading title applied to them in an influential book by MARTIN ESSLIN.

Despite the almost infinite variety of modern dramatic theory, two major opposing currents seem to persist, both with a history going back to the very beginnings of theoretical speculation on this art. On the one side are theorists like Brecht, who see the drama primarily as reflective of and involved with the social world of which it is a part. On the other side are theorists like the symbolists, who feel that the true goal of drama should be the reflection or expression of a hidden, deeper reality which has little to do with specific political or social concerns. A major modern voice for this metaphysical position was ANTONIN ARTAUD, who rejected not only the realistic theatre, but the entire literary tradition and even language itself, in a search for a visionary theatre of incantation. During the 1960s the cerebral, political theatre of Brecht and the visceral, metaphysical theatre of Artaud seemed for many to define a necessary choice in the meaning and function of drama, a choice perhaps most strikingly embodied in the drama itself in PETER WEISS's *Marat/Sade*, ingenious and complex both in its structure and

in the dramatic debates of its title characters. It should be noted that this choice involved not only the aim and content of drama – metaphysical versus socio-political concerns – but also its form, since the followers of Artaud looked back through symbolist theory to Wagner and his idea of the *Gesamtkunstwerk*, the 'total work of art', in which all elements of production were unified in a single harmonious effect, while the followers of Brecht specifically rejected this idea of TOTAL THEATRE, feeling that audiences should be encouraged to think rather than to feel, and could be stimulated to do so by disjunctures and disharmonies in the production apparatus.

Socialist and Marxist theory, in many variations, remained the central sources for socio-political theories of the drama for much of the century, while theories emphasizing inner reality, recently reinforced by psychoanalytic approaches, remained an important alternative to such socio-historical theories. Formalism, the traditional enemy of Marxist aesthetics, has been most associated with yet another important group of theatrical approaches headed by structuralism and semiotics, derived from linguistic theory by way of literary analysis. Modern semiotic analysis of the drama began in the 1970s in France and entered English studies with Kier Elam's 1980 book on the subject. Such analysis has been most commonly applied to the dramatic script, but Marco de Marinis, Patrice Pavis and others have given close attention to the relationship between the so-called 'dramatic text' and its embodiment in the theatre, the 'performance text'. Semiotic analysis has also been applied to many aspects of the performance event, such as costume (Roland Barthes), historic and contemporary acting styles (Erika Fischer-Lichte, Jiri Veltrusky) and even the theatre building and its urban context (Marvin Carlson). During the 1980s theatre semiotics, like literary semiotics, began to move from almost exclusive attention to sign-production to a concern also with how those signs are received and interpreted. Post-structuralism challenged the tendency of semiotics and structuralism to emphasize stable, self-authenticating meanings or systems of meanings behind or beneath the drama. Deconstruction became the best-known post-structuralist theory, exposing logical and linguistic contradictions in traditional drama and seeking open and multiple meanings rather than closed and singular ones. Jacques Derrida, the best known of the deconstructionist theorists, has, for example, challenged Artaud's theory of a hidden primary reality by arguing that any attempt to capture pure presence is illusory, PERFORMANCE itself being already haunted through consciousness by recurrence and reproductions. This line of argument has been more recently and more fully applied to the theatre by HERBERT BLAU. In quite different ways, phenomenological theorists of theatre and drama, such as Bert States or RICHARD FOREMAN, have also challenged the assumptions of semiotics and structuralism. They have been concerned with what is absent rather than what is present. For such critics, stage objects may well be signs of absent realities, values or concepts, but what is more interesting is that they are also real objects inhabiting the same space as the audience.

In addition to these theories derived from linguistics, political science and philosophy, the modern social sciences have provided a variety of other stimulating models for dramatic analysis, including the post-structuralist writings of the French neo-Freudian psychoanalyst Jacques Lacan. Sociologist Erving Goffman has utilized theatre models in his analysis of human interaction, and certain theatre theorists have turned his insights back upon the study of that art. Similarly, anthropologist Victor Turner, using a structure based on drama to describe general cultural phenomena, inspired Richard Schechner and others to apply anthropological models to the study of drama, and Turner himself in his final writings contributed importantly to this endeavour. This chimed with the work of GROTOWSKI and his disciple EUGENIO BARBA, who developed the ideas of THEATRE ANTHROPOLOGY alongside the theatre of the oppressed of AUGUSTO BOAL, which evolved into a theatre of empowerment through psychodrama.

An important theoretical orientation, new historicism or cultural materialism, appeared in dramatic theory in the late 1980s. This approach, particularly associated with the neo-Marxist theories of Raymond Williams in England and with the explorations of the English Renaissance stage by Stephen Greenblatt and Steven Mullaney in the United States, seeks to combine insights from history, literary theory and the social sciences to generate a new poetics of cultural production. Like semiotics, it seeks to understand how people in a given culture make sense of themselves and their world; but, more in the manner of post-structuralism, new historicism sees the cultural scene as a site of continual power struggles between the dominant institutions and their belief structures on the one hand and, on the other, and a constantly shifting set of challenges to these stabilizing forces by marginal or residual alternative possibilities. Such analysis tends to reveal a play of forces rather than the stable system of traditional structuralist theory.

Feminist and gender studies of the drama have provided one of the richest and most varied sources of theoretical writing since the 1980s. Although as a whole they have a natural affinity with the socially oriented theories, and an important part of feminist and gender theory draws heavily upon socialist and Marxist strategies, the psychoanalytic models of Lacan, the tools provided by semiotics, deconstruction and reader-response theory, and even certain theoretical techniques developed in conscious opposition to these products of a male- and heterosexual-dominated analytical tradition, have all proved useful in various ways within this rapidly developing and highly diverse area of theoretical exploration. They have been apparent in the field of postmodernism, a term applied widely since the 1970s to drama experiments, usually highly self-reflexive or self-conscious, and often parodic and mixing elements of 'high' and 'popular' culture.

MARVIN CARLSON

See also MODERNISM.

Eric Bentley, ed., *The Theory of the Modern Stage* (1980)

Marvin Carlson, *Theories of the Theatre* (1984).

Sue-Ellen Case, *Feminism and Theatre* (1988)

Barrett H. Clark, ed., *European Theories of the Drama* (1947)

Bernard F. Dukore, *Dramatic Theory and Criticism* (1974)

Keir Elam, *Semiotics of Theatre and Drama* (1980)

Steven Mullaney, *The Place of the Stage* (1988)

Michael J. Sidnell, ed., *Sources of Dramatic Theory* (vol. 1, 1991; vol 2, 1994)

dramaturg   A term that can be traced back to eighteenth-century German theatre and the playwright Lessing (1729–81). It denotes a play adviser to a theatre company rather than a one-off play doctor, and is generally a role to be found in the publicly subsidized or not-for-profit sector, rather than the commercial world. The word 'dramaturg' is related to 'dramaturgy', which comes from the Greek, meaning the art or principles of dramatic writing. In some languages it still means someone who writes plays (e.g. *dramaturge* in French), and the work is often undertaken by playwrights. It is only in the twentieth century that the role has arisen in the English-speaking theatre, taking its cue, though not the status, from continental Europe. The advice tendered is primarily literary; hence the use in many companies of the alternative term 'literary manager'. The job is often not very precisely defined; depending on the theatre, it can involve choosing, or advising on, the repertoire; reading scripts that are sent in, or managing that process; adapting or translating plays or commissioning others to do so; commissioning and working on new plays; writing programme notes; undertaking research for directors;

and giving or planning talks on aspects of the repertoire. In the latter half of the century more of a distinction was made between the advisory literary function and the practical production function, with production dramaturgs forming part of the team that created a particular show.

In America, dramaturgs and literary managers are organized and their skills are taught at university. In Britain, the role is less structured and only a few theatres outside of the two national companies can afford to employ such a person on a full-time basis. CHARLES LONDON

Draper, Ruth (b. New York, 2 Dec. 1884; d. New York, 30 Dec. 1956) Monologist. Although she made her debut in a small role in a Broadway play, her snobbish upbringing reputedly made her disdainful of working with ordinary theatre folk, so she elected to appear in SOLO programmes. She wrote her own material, treating the widest range of figures, most notably women, from the lowly to the high and mighty, and finding sometimes humour, sometimes tragedy, in their situations. With her gift for mimicry and improvisation, she used a minimum of props on a bare stage and earned international renown. She first offered her monologues in London in 1920 and in New York in 1921, and was still performing just hours before her death. Her letters were published in 1979. GERALD BORDMAN

Dorothy Warren, *The World of Ruth Draper: A Portrait of an Actress* (1999)
M. Zabel, *The Art of Ruth Draper* (1960)

Dreiser, Theodore [Herman Albert] (b. Sullivan, Ind., 27 Aug. 1871; d. Hollywood, 28 Dec. 1945) Novelist and playwright. His short plays, collected in *Plays of the Natural and the Supernatural* (1916), and his full-length *The Hand of the Potter* (1918) share his naturalistic fiction's preoccupation with and indictment of the industrialization and materialism of modern society. His novel *The American Tragedy* (1925) was dramatized in 1926 and 1936 (in the latter year as *The Case of Clyde Griffiths* by ERWIN PISCATOR for the GROUP THEATER) and filmed in 1931 and 1951. DAVID STAINES

Drew-Barrymore Family *see* BARRYMORE FAMILY

Drexler, Rosalyn [pseud: Julia Sorel] (b. Bronx, NY, 25 Nov. 1926) Playwright, novelist and painter. Influenced by the MARX BROTHERS, IONESCO, the Beatles and her wrestling experience, her plays are highly original. She received awards for *Home Movies* (1964), called the 'first musical of the absurd', *The Writer's Opera* (1979) and the trilogy of *Room 17C*,

Lobby and *Utopia Parkway* (1985), which were published as *Transients Welcome*. Other plays include *Hot Buttered Roll* (1966), *The Line of Least Existence* (1968) and *Dear* (1997). JANE HOUSE

drink *see* FOOD AND DRINK

Drinkwater [Darnley], John (b. Leytonstone, Essex, 1 June 1882; d. London, 25 March 1937) Actor and playwright. In 1907 he founded the PILGRIM PLAYERS, the basis for the BIRMINGHAM REPERTORY THEATRE. A producer, actor (under the name John Darnley) and general manager at the Rep for many years, he was associated with attempts to revive VERSE DRAMA, but was better known for his play *Abraham Lincoln* (1918) which ran for over a year at the LYRIC Hammersmith and started a 'craze' for the 'chronicle' play during the early 1920s. He was the author of many biographies and translated *Napoleon: The Hundred Days* (1932) by Giovacchino Forzano and Benito Mussolini, for which he was decorated by the dictator. MAGGIE GALE

Druid Theatre Company Founded in Galway, Ireland, by Garry Hynes, Marie Mullen and Mick Lally in 1975, its aim was to provide a permanent professional theatre in Galway and to tour productions of high quality in the provinces. Since then, the company has also appeared with enormous success abroad. A new gloss has been given to several plays from the established Irish repertoire. Foreign works have also been produced. Among the Irish plays premièred have been *Bailegangaire* (1985) by TOM MURPHY, at that time the company's playwright-in-association, *Wild Harvest* by Ken Bourke and *The Beauty Queen of Leenane* by MARTIN McDONAGH, for which Garry Hynes won the Tony Award for Best Director on BROADWAY in 1998. The company has also presented McDonagh's *Leenane Trilogy*. Druid's success contributed to the building of a new municipally funded theatre in Galway, which opened to celebrate the company's 21st birthday in 1996 with *The Beauty Queen of Leenane*. Hynes (b. 1953) has established a reputation abroad, working at the ROYAL COURT, with the ROYAL SHAKESPEARE COMPANY and on Broadway. CHRISTOPHER FITZ-SIMON

Drury Lane *see* THEATRE ROYAL, DRURY LANE

du Maurier, Gerald [Hubert Edward] (b. Hampstead, London, 26 March 1873; d. London, 11 April 1934) Actor–manager. Son of the novelist George, who wrote *Trilby*, and father of the novelist Daphne, who wrote *Rebecca*, he was himself the reigning matinée idol of the London stage for almost three decades. After working with FORBES-ROBERTSON and TREE, his early involvement (1900–1), on and off stage, with MRS PATRICK CAMPBELL is credited with launching his career. He scored great successes as Raffles, the gentleman crook (1906), as Brewster in *Brewster's Millions* (1907) and as Bull-Dog Drummond, the schoolboy's favourite detective (1921). For J. M. BARRIE he created the parts of Woolley in *The Admirable Crichton* (1902), Mr Darling and Captain Hook in *Peter Pan* (1904), and Mr Dearth in *Dear Brutus* (1917). For 15 years (1910–25) he was associated with Frank Curzon in managing Wyndhams Theatre, and for five years with Gilbert Miller in running the St James's. Du Maurier was knighted in 1922.   IAN BEVAN

D. du Maurier, *Gerald: A Portrait* (1934)

DubbelJoint   Theatre company. Formed in 1991 and based in west BELFAST, it is committed to creating quality, accessible theatre with and for its local communities, involving a collaboration between professionals and local people. The company enjoys a unique artistic identity through its skills development, empowering individuals and groups to explore and develop creativity, and with its record of touring and a growing presence on the international stage. It has been closely involved with Feile an Phobail, the West Belfast Festival, and from 1995 has developed a very successful relationship with the women's group, JustUs Community Theatre. Pam Brighton has been the artistic director since its formation.

New work includes *A Night in November* (1984), *Women on the Verge of HRT* (1995), *Stones in his Pockets* (1996), and *A Mother's Heart* (1998). In 1997 Dubbel-Joint combined with JustUs to produce *Binlids*, which later transferred to New York. DubbelJoint has also brought work by O'NEILL (*A Moon for the Misbegotten*), Gogol (*The Government Inspector*) and Peter Sheridan (*The Mother of All the Behans*) to west Belfast.
BRIAN ROBERTS

Dubé, Marcel   (b. Montreal, 3 Jan. 1930) French-Canadian playwright. Considered the major dramatist of the 1950s and 1960s in Quebec because of the quality and number of his works produced (some 40 by the end of the century) on stage, radio and television. His earliest works feature young, economically disadvantaged urban characters in conflict with their society's basic values. This iconoclastic spirit also infuses the middle-class characters who populate his later works, which focus more closely on universal social problems. His major plays include *Zone* (1953), *Un Simple Soldat* ('Private soldier', 1957), *Florence* (1958) and *Au Retour des oies blanches* ('The white geese', 1966).
LEONARD E. DOUCETTE

Edwin C. Hamblett, *Marcel Dubé and French-Canadian Drama* (1970)
Maximilian Laroche, *Marcel Dubé* (1970)

Dublin   Following the Act of Union of 1802, Dublin became little more than a colonial outpost of London, and indigenous theatre lost its creative force. Throughout the nineteenth century Dublin theatres were largely receiving houses for English touring productions of Shakespeare, popular MELODRAMA, opera and MUSIC HALL. The foundation of the Irish Literary Theatre in 1898 and the National Theatre Society Ltd (ABBEY and Peacock Theatres) in 1903 altered this situation radically. While several leading Irish playwrights (e.g. WILDE, SHAW) continued to work in London, the National Theatre Society provided a vital outlet for new Irish plays, producing over 800 between 1904 and 1988. As the century progressed, other Dublin managements began to present the work of Irish as well as foreign authors. By 1940 the influence of the London impresarios had almost completely disappeared.

The chief commercial theatres at the turn of the century were the fine neo-classical Theatre Royal, successor to a much earlier local production house; the Capitol (formerly La Scala); the Queen's (formerly Adelphi), noted for its remarkable neo-Celtic plasterwork; the Tivoli, mainly a variety house; and the Victorian rococo Gaiety and Olympia. Several halls (e.g. Rotunda, Antient Concert Rooms, Molesworth) were occasionally used as theatres. All the major theatres presented a very varied fare; of these, only the Gaiety and the Olympia remain. The Gaiety became the home of the Dublin Grand Opera Society (now Opera Ireland) for two annual seasons; ballet, musicals and pantomime are given in both, and both are increasingly used for large-scale productions of plays.

The period following the foundation of the new Irish state in 1922, though noted for the first plays of O'CASEY at the Abbey, was not remarkable for theatre of a more widespread nature. In 1928 MÍCHEÁL MAC-LÍAMMÓIR and HILTON EDWARDS, members of ANEW McMASTER's Shakespearian Players, formed Dublin Gate Theatre Productions principally to introduce the work of modern European and American dramatists. They also introduced new techniques of staging. Their patron – only the Abbey Theatre received a state subsidy at this time – the seventh Earl of Longford, formed his own company in 1936 mainly to produce British and European classics. The two companies alternated at the GATE until 1961, after which a state subsidy ensured continuity.

During the Second World War the Dublin theatre was thrown back upon its own resources. A number of ad hoc managements were formed, and there was a great deal of theatrical activity. The variety theatre flourished as never before with work from comedians such as JIMMY O'DEA, Cecil, Sheridan, Danny Cummins, Noel Purcell, Jack Cruise and others topping the bill in their own shows. Some AVANT-GARDE theatres were formed in the 1940s and 1950s, notably Toto Cogley's Studio, and Alan Simpson and Carolyn Swift's Pike. The postwar Illsley–McCabe management reintroduced West End productions to Dublin at the Olympia, but the venture succumbed to rising touring costs.

The Dublin Theatre Festival, inaugurated in 1957, created an annual focus for international companies, and also broke the virtual monopoly of the National Theatre Society in producing new plays by Irish authors. Plays by BRIAN FRIEL, THOMAS KILROY, HUGH LEONARD and TOM MURPHY were given first productions at early festivals. The arrival of television in 1961 greatly increased employment opportunities for actors and resulted in a continual movement of actors and playwrights between Dublin and London, reminiscent of the eighteenth century but on a much larger scale.

The late 1950s and 1960s saw the Abbey and the Gate challenged for the first time as the centre of Dublin's (and Ireland's) theatrical life. The Abbey had mixed success in adapting itself to the rapid cultural changes and stagnated under the conservative leadership of its managing director Ernest Blythe. Meanwhile the Gate foundered in the post-Edwards/MacLíammóir era. Innovation happened elsewhere in the capital – at Simpson and Swift's Pike Theatre, at the Globe (founded 1954) in Dun Laoghaire, at Phyllis Ryan and Norman Rodway's Gemini company (founded in the late 1950s) and, since the late 1960s, at the PROJECT ARTS CENTRE.

The 1980s saw a burst of theatrical energy in Dublin that continued through to the next century, particularly in the independent sector. Some companies, such as Passion Machine (1984) and Calypso (1993), brought theatre to, and expressed the concerns of, a rapidly changing urban Dublin. Others (ROUGH MAGIC, 1984; Co-Motion, 1985; Bedrock, 1993) opened up Irish theatre to new plays and theatrical ideas from Britain, America and Europe, and also nurtured new Irish writing, as did Pigsback (which was founded in 1988 and changed its name to Fishamble in 1997). Still others – Barabbas (1993), CoisCeim (1995) and Corn Exchange (1995) – opened up Irish theatre to physical and visual forms of expression. A scarcity of mid-sized venues in the city in some ways limited the possibilities of growth for these non-building-based groups, which rented space in venues including Andrew's Lane, Project, the Crypt, the Tivoli

and the SFX Centre. The founding in 1984 of the first dedicated centre for third-level theatre education in Ireland, the Samuel Beckett Centre at Trinity College, meant that young people no longer had to leave the country to train as theatre artists; it was followed by other dedicated centres for education and training, including the Gaiety School of Acting.

CHRISTOPHER FITZ-SIMON & KAREN FRICKER

Brenna Katz Clarke and Harold Ferrar, *The Dublin Drama League* (1979)

Seamus de Burca, *The Queen's Royal Theatre Dublin* (1983)

Christopher Fitz-Simon, *The Arts in Ireland* (1982)

Mícheál MacLíammóir, *All for Hecuba* (1946)

P. B. Ryan, *The Lost Theatres of Dublin* (1998)

Carolyn Swift, *Stage by Stage* (1985)

Dudley, William [Stuart] (b. London, 4 March 1947) Designer. Dudley's early, elegantly minimalist designs included sets for PETER GILL's ROYAL COURT productions of *The Duchess of Malfi* (1971) and BOND's *The Fool* (1975). The former consisted of rows of old hospital doors. Dudley recycled domestic and industrial objects for BILL BRYDEN's NATIONAL THEATRE *Mysteries* (1985) to match the crafts background of the medieval texts: God, wearing a miner's helmet, rose heavenwards on a fork-lift truck. In the 1980s Dudley devised increasingly lavish scenic stage metaphors – a futurist vortex (Dusty Hughes' *Futurists*, 1986), a mobile book of hours (*Richard II*, 1986) – and experimented with complex engineering. For Bryden's *The Ship* (1990), Dudley's team built and launched a replica liner in a disused Glasgow shipyard. He has also worked in opera (e.g. *The Ring*, Bayreuth, 1983).

TONY HOWARD

Tony Davis, *Stage Design* (2001)

Duhamel, Georges *see* ANTOINE, ANDRÉ

Dukes, Ashley (b. Bridgwater, Som., 29 May 1885; d. London, 4 May 1959) Playwright, critic and theatre manager. With the profits of his play *The Man with a Load of Mischief* (1924) Dukes founded the MERCURY THEATRE in 1933 as a permanent home for his wife MARIE RAMBERT's ballet company. In books like *The Youngest Drama* (1923) and the pages of *Theatre Arts Monthly*, which he edited from 1926 until his death, he encouraged new playwrights, and after 1935 he staged much VERSE DRAMA, including works by AUDEN, DUNCAN, FRY, ELIOT and RIDLER. Having travelled widely, he worked to bring the theatre of high European modernism to Britain, notably EXPRESSIONISM, translating many of its plays and also championing neglected writers like Kleist, WEDEKIND and Machiavelli. His memoir, *The Scene is Changed*, appeared in 1942. DAN REBELLATO

Dullin, Charles (b. Yonne, France, 12 May 1885; d. Paris, 11 Dec. 1949) Actor and director. With LOUIS JOUVET, Dullin was the most important disciple of COPEAU. He appeared at ANTOINE's theatre and then, interested in popular theatre, he worked with GÉMIER. Dullin directed the Atelier Theatre (1922–40) and in 1927 became a founder of the directors' CARTEL. Seeking always to serve the text, his directing style ranged from austere to opulent. His school of acting, which drew on CIRCUS skills, Eastern theatre and COMMEDIA, formed a whole generation of actors, including ARTAUD, BARRAULT, BLIN, MARCEAU and VILAR. Famous productions include Calderón's *Life is but a Dream* (1922) and Jonson's *Volpone* (1928). Continuing his aim of reaching wider audiences, he argued for the decentralization of French theatre and moved into a larger theatre where, during the Occupation, he directed SARTRE's first play, *Les Mouches* (*The Flies*, 1943), and a sombre version of Molière's *L'Avare* (*The Miser*). His *Souvenirs et notes de travail d'un acteur* appeared in 1946. TERRY HODGSON

L. Arnaud, *Charles Dullin* (1959)

Dunbar, Andrea *see* ENGLISH STAGE COMPANY; STAFFORD-CLARK, MAX

Duncan, [Angela] Isadora (b. San Francisco, 26 May 1877; d. Nice, France, 14 Sept. 1927) Dancer. The foremost liberator of dance from the bondage of classical ballet, she was a self-styled 'expressioniste of beauty' who performed barefoot in simple flowing garments, her movements inspired by great music, the elements and a powerful sense of classical Greece. Rebellious in morals and in politics, she was revered by and had an impact on leading artists of the day, including in the theatre the directors STANISLAVSKY and her lover GORDON CRAIG. Her influence on performance was profound, most famously in the work of MARTHA GRAHAM and her pupils. With Graham, she transformed dance from an entertainment into a serious art form. Duncan's autobiography, *My Life* (1927), reveals her unique character and high ideals. JOHN BROOME

See also CHOREOGRAPHY; DANCE; MOVEMENT, DANCE AND DRAMA.

Frederika Blair, *Isadora: Portrait of the Artist as a Woman* (1986)
Ann Daly, *Done into Dance* (1995)
Gordon McVay, *Isadora and Esenin* (1980)
V. Seroff, *The Real Isadora* (1971)

Duncan, Ronald [Frederick Henry] (b. Salisbury, Rhodesia, 6 Aug. 1914; d. Barnstaple, Devon, 3 June 1982) Playwright and author, prominent in the postwar poetic drama revival with *This Way to the Tomb* (1945). He adapted COCTEAU's *The Eagle has Two Heads* (1946), was librettist for Benjamin Britten's *The Rape of Lucretia* (1946) and had a success with *Abelard and Heloise* (1970). He was co-founder of the ENGLISH STAGE COMPANY, in whose first season his double bill *Don Juan* and *The Death of Satan* (1956) appeared, but became critical of its policy, as he describes in his autobiography *How to Make Enemies* (1968). TONY HOWARD
See also VERSE DRAMA.

Dunham, Katherine (b. Chicago, 22 June 1909) Leading dancer and choreographer whose company toured nationally and internationally from the late 1930s until the mid-1960s. She initially studied anthropology at the University of Chicago while training as a dancer. She used field research into social and ritual dance in the Caribbean (for an unfinished doctorate) as a resource for creating ballets with which to educate audiences about black culture. Outspoken and politically active, she fought against segregated audiences in the United States during the 1940s, which she had suffered, and angered the US State Department when she refused to withdraw her 1952 ballet *Southlands* about a recent lynching incident from her company's programme in Paris at the height of the Cold War. Her controversial 1964 *Aida* for the Metropolitan Opera House showed the Egyptians as black Africans. She has written several books, including *Dances of Haiti* (1947) and *Island Possessed* (1994). RAMSAY BURT
See also CHOREOGRAPHY; DANCE.

V. Clark and B. Wilkerson, eds, *Kaiso! Katherine Dunham: An Anthology of Writings* (1978)

Dunlop, Frank (b. Leeds, 15 Feb. 1927) Director and administrator. Dunlop has concentrated on bringing accessible classical work to wide – especially young – audiences. He was director of the NOTTINGHAM Playhouse from 1961 to 1964 and in 1966 founded Pop Theatre, casting comedians, jazz and pop singers alongside classical actors in Shakespeare and Euripides. In 1967 he joined the NATIONAL THEATRE, where he directed BRECHT, Webster and MAUGHAM, and in 1969 founded the YOUNG VIC, originally as the NT's youth wing. Dunlop's energetic, funny and physical productions here included *Scapino!* (1970) and *A Comedy of Errors* (1971), lampooning Anglo-Scots relations. As director of the EDINBURGH FESTIVAL (1983–91) Dunlop shifted its emphasis to drama, introducing

World Theatre seasons, inviting companies in from the FRINGE, and (typically) directing Gluck, Schiller and *Treasure Island* (1990). He resigned over the Festival's low funding. TONY HOWARD

Dunn, Nell *see* THEATRE ROYAL, STRATFORD EAST

Dunnock, Mildred [Dorothy] (b. Baltimore, Md., 25 Jan. 1900; d. Oak Bluffs, Martha's Vineyard, Mass., 5 July 1991) Actress. The mousy-looking, sad-but-strong-voiced Dunnock made her debut in 1932 and subsequently played supporting roles in such plays as *The Corn is Green* (1940), *Foolish Notion* (1945) and *Another Part of the Forest* (1946). She is best recalled for three major roles: the dutiful wife in *Death of a Salesman* (1949), the toping Mrs Constable in *In the Summer House* (1953) and the intimidated wife in *Cat on a Hot Tin Roof* (1955). She also directed and appeared many times on film and television. GERALD BORDMAN

Durang, Christopher [Ferdinand] (b. Montclair, NJ, 2 Jan. 1949) Playwright and performer. Durang's work is fuelled by the satirist's rage at the absurdity and injustice of mortal life, and by the comic's delight in the folly he sees everywhere. His *Sister Mary Ignatius Explains It All for You* (1979) exposes the destructiveness of narrow-minded religion to such telling effect that performances have often evoked protests. *Beyond Therapy* (1981) skewers the self-importance of meddling psychoanalysts. In *The Marriage of Bette and Boo* (1985) and *Laughing Wild* (1987), the comedy is deepened by an awareness of pain and by compassion; Durang has acted a leading role in both plays, making their autobiographical roots manifest. Other plays include *Media Amok* (1992), a group of short works; *Durang/Durang* (1994); and *Sex and Longing* (1996), which satirized both sexual mores in America and their effect on politics, and was not well received in its initial Broadway production. *Betty's Summer Vacation* (1999), however, won an Obie Award and once more showed Durang with teeth bared, this time satirizing television talk shows and reality-based programming. He has also performed his comedic nightclub satire, *Chris Durang and Dawne*. M. ELIZABETH OSBORN

Durante, Jimmy [James Francis] (b. New York, 10 Feb. 1893; d. Santa Monica, Cal., 28 Jan. 1980) Comedian, known for his prominent 'schnozzola' nose and brash energy. Having begun his 60-year career at 17 as a ragtime piano player, Durante teamed up with Eddie Jackson and Lou Clayton in 1920s nightclub appearances that led to Broadway in *Show Girl* (1929) and *The New Yorkers* (1930). As a solo performer, Durante starred in *Strike Me Pink* (1933), *Jumbo* (1935) and *Red, Hot and Blue!* (1936), and made many film appear-

ances. Several of his trademark lines – 'Goodnight, Mrs Calabash, wherever you are,' for example, or 'Stop the music' – became catchphrases. MICHAEL SOMMERS

L. Adler, *I Remember Jimmy* (1980)
G. Fowler, *Schnozzola* (1951)
J. Robbins, *Inka Dinka Doo* (1991)

Duras [Donnadieu], Marguerite (b. Gia Dinh, French Indochina [now Vietnam], 4 April 1914; d. Paris, March 1996) Writer. Duras wrote novels and films as well as drama, frequently reworking material across genres. She first turned to the theatre when asked to adapt her novel *Le Square* for the stage in 1956. Many of her plays focus on female figures, and the gaps and spaces in identity and language occasioned by the dynamic of memory and desire. Her plays challenge traditional notions of character, action and dialogue. Plays include *Des Journées Entières dans les Arbres* (*Days in the Trees*, 1965, performed by the ROYAL SHAKESPEARE COMPANY in 1968 with PEGGY ASHCROFT), *La Musica* (1965), *Suzanna Andler* (1968), *Eden Cinéma* (1977) and *Savannah Bay* (1983), written for and performed by MADELEINE RENAUD.
ANNA MCMULLAN

Alfred Cismaru, *Marguerite Duras* (1971)
Liliane Papin, *L'Autre Scène: Le Théâtre de Marguerite Duras* (1988)

Dürrenmatt, Friedrich (b. Konolfingen bei Bern, Switzerland, 5 Jan. 1921; d. Neuchâtel, Switzerland, 14 Dec. 1990) Playwright, novelist and essayist whose work is permeated by an overriding sense of the absurd in human existence. Although he studied literature and philosophy at Berne and Zurich Universities, his original interest was in painting, and in particular the art of caricature, an interest which is reflected in the satirical style of his first play, *Es steht geschrieben* (*It is Written*, 1947). His manipulation of historical facts, translating them into grotesque, black comedy in this play about the sixteenth-century Münster Anabaptists, evoked an uncomfortable response in his audiences. Two further plays again exploited historical fact to chilling, but comic effect: *Der Blinde* (*The Blind Man*, 1948) and *Romulus der Grosse* (*Romulus the Great*, 1949) – the latter bringing Dürrenmatt his first critical success. With *Die Ehe des Herrn Mississipi* (*The Marriage of Mr Mississipi*, 1952) and *Der Besuch der alten Dame* (*The Visit*, 1956), Dürrenmatt finally reached a wider audience. The latter was given a memorable production in London and on Broadway by the LUNTS, while the former was taken to the United States as *Fools are Passing*

Through in 1958. In 1962 Dürrenmatt's international reputation was consolidated with his widely acclaimed play *Die Physiker* (*The Physicists*, 1962). This work, in which Dürrenmatt casts a pessimistic eye over the development of atomic science and highlights the moral bankruptcy of the postwar world, was given a highly successful production by the ROYAL SHAKESPEARE COMPANY in 1963. In 1989 *The Visit* enjoyed a stylized and idiomatic revival by the THEATRE DE COMPLICITE at London's ALMEIDA THEATRE, which transferred to the ROYAL NATIONAL THEATRE.

In his later years, Dürrenmatt's interest in challenging established theatrical techniques led him to adapt STRINDBERG's *The Dance of Death* in 1969 as *Play Strindberg*, a work that has proved to be one of the most popular in his repertoire. In 1970 he announced his decision to abandon writing plays himself, in preference to adapting the works of others, such as *Woyzeck* (1972). He published several critical essays discussing his theatrical theories, notably *Theaterprobleme* (1955), in which he reinforces his belief that humanity's fate is inherently tragic and can be dealt with only through comedy. Dürrenmatt's grotesque, EXPRESSIONIST style, while at times difficult and convoluted, has led to his general appreciation as this century's most important German-language playwright alongside BRECHT.

HELEN RAPPAPORT

Tuino Tiusanen, *Dürrenmatt: A Study in Plays, Prose and Theory* (1977)
Jenny Urs, *Dürrenmatt: A Study of His Plays* (1978)
S. Kenneth Whitton, *Dürrenmatt: Reinterpretation in Retrospect* (1990)

Duse, Eleonora   (b. Venice, 3 Oct. 1859; d. Pittsburgh, 27 Oct. 1924)   Actress. Born into a theatrical family, she acted as a child and first won recognition in Emile Augier's *Les Fourchambault* (1878), followed by success in ZOLA's *Thérèse Raquin* (1879) and VERGA's *Cavalleria Rusticana* (1884). She worked with the major actor–managers Emanuel and Rossi, and then, with the prominent actor Flavio Ando, formed in 1887 the Citta di Roma company, taking lead roles and touring abroad with great success. Duse played both classical and contemporary parts with beguiling emotional intensity and physical grace.

Her most celebrated performances were in roles created by IBSEN – Nora in *A Doll's House*, Hedda Gabler, Rebecca in *Rosmersholm* (with revolutionary design by GORDON CRAIG), Ellida in *The Lady from the Sea* – and she was hailed internationally as one of the finest tragediennes of her generation. She earned the admiration of CHEKHOV, ISADORA DUNCAN and SHAW, who preferred her modernist style to that of BERNHARDT, with whom she was inevitably compared. Duse sought out and encouraged young dramatists, especially D'ANNUNZIO, whose career she helped immeasurably by creating the lead in several of his poetic dramas. After her relationship with him had ended, she toured, mainly for financial reasons, and died abroad. An important cultural figure, her body was returned to Italy.

ADRIANA HUNTER

Giovanni Pontiero, ed., *Duse on Tour* (1982)
—— *Eleonora Duse, in Life and Art* (1986)
J. Stones, M. R. Booth and S. Bassnett, *Bernhardt, Terry, Duse: The Actress in Her Time* (1988)
William Weaver, *Duse* (1984)

E

Easmon, Raymond [Sarif] (b. Freetown, Sierra Leone, 15 Jan. 1913; d. Freetown, 3 March 1997) Playwright who trained as a doctor in Britain. *Dear Parent and Ogre* (1961) won first prize in a playwriting competition and was performed in Lagos, Nigeria, by the 1960 Masks directed by WOLE SOYINKA. Other plays include *The New Patriots* (1966), dealing with corruption in the civil service, and *Mate and Checkmate* and *Dilys Dear Dilys*, both of which were shown on Nigerian television. Easmon has also published two novels.

KOLE OMOTOSO

Eastern theatre, its influence on the West Unlike Western theatre, many of the theatrical forms of the East can claim continuous acting traditions stretching back over several centuries, during which the precise details of the acting have been codified and passed on from master to pupil with very little change. Because these traditions have been so well preserved – usually through direct links with religious or court life – performances have an authority and technical precision that often defy criticism.

Almost without exception, these forms survive, not as spoken drama, but as a blend of music, dance, mime, acrobatics, recitation and singing. The text represents only one element. This has made Asian theatre an irresistible source of inspiration for playwrights and directors who have felt dissatisfied with the literary or naturalistic bias of Western drama and tried to create a more TOTAL THEATRE. JAPAN, CHINA and Bali have exerted the strongest influence, making an immediate impact when companies from these countries first visited Europe in the early part of the twentieth century.

If anything, the influence has grown with the increased Western understanding of these forms. More recently there have been direct exchanges of knowledge, through actors and directors studying in the East, through Asian performers teaching in the West and through productions from both spheres visiting each other. But the first uses of Eastern theatre were often based on serious misunderstandings. W. B. YEATS's *Four Plays for Dancers* (1917–20) were intended to be in the manner of the Japanese *noh* theatre, yet he missed the spirit entirely. Yeats, who had never seen a *noh* performance, was working mainly from translations by the American Ernest Fenollosa in collaboration with Ezra Pound. As with so many Eastern theatre forms, the words alone give very little idea of the total theatrical experience.

Noh was also an inspiration for the French director JACQUES COPEAU. He set up his famous school, the Vieux Colombier, in the 1920s to try to develop a theatre that would be refined, stylized and religious in essence. From his reading Copeau saw many similarities between the *noh* theatre and the Catholic mass. Although no one at the school had seen an authentic *noh* performance, they did attempt to rehearse a *noh* play in 1924. The attraction for Copeau was its refinement of the emotional expression within a highly disciplined form.

This work was carried further by the actor and director JEAN-LOUIS BARRAULT. Barrault was enchanted with the idea of *noh*, though when he first saw a performance, in Paris in 1957, he was greatly disappointed. It was not until he visited Japan three years later that he was able to see this theatre in its proper context and to begin to understand it. 'It seemed to me that I had lived physically inside a soul', he wrote about the performance.

The strict form of *noh*, with its avoidance of dramatic

234

conflict, has made it difficult for Western writers to use as a literary influence. There are, however, two notable exceptions: BERTOLT BRECHT based *The Yes Sayer, The No Sayer* (1930) on Arthur Waley's translation of *Taniko*; and the composer Benjamin Britten based his church parable, *Curlew River* (1964), on *Sumidagawa*, which he saw performed in Japan. Inevitably, there are bound to be coincidental similarities between Eastern and Western forms. It has often been rightly pointed out that SAMUEL BECKETT, through his extreme reduction of language and image, came closest to the spirit of *noh*. But he disclaimed any knowledge of Japanese theatre.

Stylization on a more lavish scale can be seen in *kabuki*, which appealed strongly to the playwright PAUL CLAUDEL while he was French Ambassador in Tokyo during the 1920s. His MIME play *The Woman and her Shadow* was performed in Tokyo (1923) by professional *kabuki* actors and musicians. It was at this time that Claudel wrote his best-known play, *Le soulier de satin* (*The Satin Slipper*), which has many of the qualities of *kabuki* without consciously employing *kabuki* techniques.

The colour and boldness of *kabuki* also appealed to Russian directors in the 1920s. MEYERHOLD explored some of the techniques in his experimental productions, and the film-maker EISENSTEIN was strongly influenced by the *kabuki* company that visited Moscow in 1928. 'Sound and movement, space and voice here do not accompany each other, but function as elements of equal significance', he wrote.

A more explicit use of *kabuki* has been made by the American composer STEPHEN SONDHEIM, who used it as the idiom for his musical *Pacific Overtures* (1976).

One of the most influential figures of twentieth-century European theatre was ANTONIN ARTAUD, and his ideas on the THEATRE OF CRUELTY were shaped partly by a single performance of Balinese dance-drama that he saw in Paris at the Colonial Exposition of 1931. Artaud insisted that theatre should communicate directly through the senses, using symbolic gestures that would physicalize spiritual states. He saw in the Balinese theatre an embodiment of almost everything he believed theatre should be, especially in the way it was linked to the religious and ceremonial life of the community. For Artaud, the Balinese theatre represented 'a new physical language based upon signs and no longer upon words'. Accordingly, the actors became 'animated hieroglyphs'. Artaud's observations on the dance-drama were acutely perceptive, though his lack of knowledge of Balinese culture led him to read certain features into the performance that were simply not there. For example, he interpreted the dancers' mime

language as 'mysterious signs which correspond to some unknown, fabulous and obscure reality which we in the Occident have completely repressed'.

The Beijing Opera, with its dazzling acrobatics, its colourful make-up patterns and conventionalized characters, has had an enduring influence on European theatre from the time it was first seen in the West. Touring the Soviet Union in 1935, the actor MEI LAN FANG and his troupe made a strong impression on STANISLAVSKY, NEMIROVICH-DANCHENKO, Meyerhold and Eisenstein. Also in the audience was Bertolt Brecht, then in exile from Hitler's Germany. It was in his subsequent essay, 'Alienation Effects in Chinese Acting' (1936), that Brecht first used the term *Verfremdungs-effekt* to describe the way Chinese actors kept a distance between themselves and their character. 'By comparison with Asiatic acting,' wrote Brecht, 'our own art still seems hopelessly parsonical.' Brecht's plays share many similarities with the Chinese theatre: his use of episodic scenes, his emphasis on a didactic story before psychological character, his rejection of lighting effects for mood and atmosphere, and of naturalism in favour of meaningful stage pictures. *The Caucasian Chalk Circle* (1954), adapted from a translation of a Chinese opera, comes closest in spirit, particularly in its extensive use of stylized mime.

In France, JEAN GENET's knowledge of oriental theatre led him to rethink radically what Western theatre could be like. He saw the Beijing Opera when a company visited Paris in 1955 and his subsequent plays, *The Balcony* (1957), *The Blacks* (1959) and *The Screens* (1961), used many of the techniques of Chinese theatre: masks, exaggerated costumes and make-up, music, RITUAL and ceremony. *The Screens* also used a 'day-for-night' effect that was featured in the Chinese play *The Inn at the Crossroads*. PETER SHAFFER used the same device in *The Private Ear and The Public Eye* (1962) after seeing this play when a Beijing Opera company visited Britain.

The Polish director JERZY GROTOWSKI visited China and India in the 1960s, then incorporated exercises from the Beijing Opera and *kathakali* (the dance-drama of Kerala) in the training of his own actors. Significantly, Grotowski came to be recognized as the principal disciple of Artaud's 'theatre of cruelty' in the late 1960s.

Another director who investigated Artaud's ideas and also had a great interest in Eastern theatre at this time was PETER BROOK. Before launching his legendary production of *The Mahabharata* (1986), Brook embarked on a long and detailed study of traditional Indian theatre styles. Although his Paris-based international company had a regular *kathakali* teacher, Brook aimed

235

to find an idiom that was somewhere between East and West. It is in this synthesis that some of the richest possibilities of theatre exist, which is why the classically trained Japanese actor Yoshi Oida has played such a vital role in the development of Brook's company, both as a performer and as a teacher.

The French director ARIANE MNOUCHKINE has been influenced by Eastern theatre styles in several of her productions for the THÉÂTRE DU SOLEIL. *Richard II*, *Twelfth Night* and *Henry IV* (1982–3) were notable for the way they drew on elements of Beijing Opera, *noh* and *kabuki*. Comparisons are often made between Greek tragedy, which made extensive use of dance, and classical Asian dance-drama. In 1992 Mnouchkine completed her cycle *Les Atrides*, a spectacular version of *The Oresteia* and *Iphigenia at Aulis*, for which her international cast studied several styles of Asian dance, including *kathakali*, Bharata Natyam and Balinese dance. The resulting synthesis produced a highly successful solution to the problem of re-creating the spirit of Greek tragedy as total theatre.

On a more commercial scale, JULIE TAYMOR borrowed many techniques from Asian theatre in her spectacular staging of the Disney musical *The Lion King* (1998). Despite a lavish budget, the Asian influence served to emphasize the resources of the actor rather than swamp the stage with technology. The show became almost a celebration of the actor's art.

The whole question of influences is now made more complex by the cultural crossovers that frequently take place, especially between Japan and the West. Experimental companies like Stomu Yamashta's Red Buddha Theatre, Terayama's Tenjosajiki, Sankai Juku or the NINAGAWA Company have each absorbed Western influences. But by blending these with their native traditions of *noh* and *kabuki*, they have produced strikingly original styles of theatre that have in turn created a strong impact in the West on both audiences and directors. KENNETH REA

Christopher Innes, *Avant Garde Theatre 1892–1922* (1993)
Leonard C. Pronko, *Theatre East and West* (1967)
Kenneth Rea, 'Theatre in India: The Old and the New', *Theatre Quarterly*, vol. 9, no. 34, 1979

Ebb, Fred *see* KANDER, JOHN

Echegaray [Y Eizaguirre], José (b. Madrid, 19 April 1832; d. Madrid, 15 Sept. 1916) Engineer, mathematician, politician and playwright. A man of many parts – MP and minister, founder of the Bank of Spain, academician – Echegaray wrote possibly up to 100 plays, about half in verse, and was a major yet much derided figure in Spanish drama at the beginning of the twentieth century. A popular success, though rarely revived, he won the Nobel Prize in 1904, to the chagrin of many contemporaries. CHARLES LONDON

Julio Mathias, *Echegaray* (1970)
Y. R. Young, *José Echegaray: A Study of his Dramatic Technique* (1936)

Ecuador *see* SOUTH AMERICA

Eddison, Robert (b. Yokohama, 10 Dec. 1908; d. London, 14 Dec. 1991) Actor. His career was long – beginning in 1930 – successful and varied, but he is best remembered as a classical actor with a voice of great beauty and musicality. An essential modesty enabled him to play both major and minor roles with equal commitment and success. This made him an obvious and valued member of the democratically organized Actors' Company when it formed in 1972. For them he was an impressive Lear (1974). He also produced a chilling performance as the assassin Lightborn in the PROSPECT production of Marlowe's *Edward II* (1969). It was fitting that as the prologue in *Tamburlaine* he spoke the first words on the NATIONAL THEATRE stage in 1976. CLIVE BARKER

Edgar, David (b. Birmingham, 26 Feb. 1948) Playwright. Edgar's writing began with AGITPROP plays like *Tedderella* (1971), *Rent* (1972) and *Dick Deterred* (1974). With his anti-nuclear *O Fair Jerusalem* (1975) and *Teendreams* (1979), co-written with Susan Todd for MONSTROUS REGIMENT and narrating the rise of contemporary feminism, he began working with epic forms, well displayed in *Destiny* (1976), his breakthrough play seen at the ROYAL SHAKESPEARE COMPANY, which contemplated the rise of the National Front and the political prevarication's around racism. *The Jail Diary of Albie Sachs* and *Mary Barnes* (both 1978) showed a firm handling of largely pre-existing material, experiences put to hugely successful use in his adaptation for the RSC of *Nicholas Nickleby* (1980). *Maydays* (1983), following a postwar socialist to New Right authoritarianism, the Dorset COMMUNITY PLAY *Entertaining Strangers* (1985), and a domestic play about the 1984 miners' strike, *That Summer* (1987), dominated his output in the 1980s. *The Shape of the Table* (1990) looked at tensions and struggles in the Eastern European revolutions, a theme he developed in *Pentecost* (1994). *Albert Speer* (2000) was a powerful adaptation of Gitta Sereny's best-selling biography of Hitler's architect. In the late 1980s he began coordinating Britain's first MA in playwriting at Birmingham University, where he became Professor of Playwriting Studies. A book of his essays on contemporary theatre, called *The Second Time as Farce*, appeared in 1998. DAN REBELLATO

Susan Painter, *Edgar: The Playwright* (1996)
Elizabeth Swain, *David Edgar: Playwright and Politician* (1986)
Simon Trussler, ed, *File on Edgar* (1991)

Edinburgh Despite the international significance of the EDINBURGH INTERNATIONAL FESTIVAL and EDINBURGH FRINGE, these annual August jamborees represent only a fraction of theatre activity in SCOTLAND's capital. The LYCEUM began the century managed by Howard and Wyndham and was purchased in 1964 by the Edinburgh Corporation, which launched the Royal Lyceum Theatre Company in 1965. This initiative superseded the GATEWAY, an earlier attempt to rival the CITIZENS' as Scotland's major repertory company, which achieved success with a programme founded on new Scottish work.

Although the Lyceum continues as Edinburgh's main repertory house and 1994 saw the opening of the fully renovated MATCHAM-designed Festival Theatre (the city's premier receiving house), its most radical theatre remains the TRAVERSE, whose commitment to new writing and innovative production dates from its debut season of 1963. ADRIENNE SCULLION

Edinburgh Fringe The 'unofficial' Fringe runs concurrently with the annual EDINBURGH INTERNATIONAL FESTIVAL and is, in its own right, the largest arts festival in the world; it gave rise to the general use of the term FRINGE. It started in the same year as the official festival (1947) when eight groups arrived in Edinburgh, uninvited, to 'showcase' their productions in whatever venues they could find and hire in protest at the absence of Scottish representation at the festival. Thus the Fringe's defining characteristics were established at the outset: it is non-selective, and groups perform in whatever spaces are available, many of which must be converted into 'theatres' by their stage crews. By 1955 a central box office and club for performers had been established, and 1958 saw the establishment of a Fringe Society which now coordinates the booking of halls – but which does not in any way act as a selection agency. The Fringe has grown steadily, even rapidly. In 1969, 57 groups presented 100 shows. In 1975, 123 groups took part. By 1982, almost 500 groups were visiting Edinburgh, giving 800 different productions and selling 460,000 tickets. By 1999, 600 companies were offering 1,600 shows. Nevertheless, the problem of finding an audience remains one of the hardest tasks for those who choose to visit the Fringe and performers have outnumbered audience at many a Fringe show.

The Fringe has always embraced AMATEUR, STUDENT and professional drama. From the late 1980s, both amateurs and students (but perhaps not the audiences) have complained of the 'professionalization' of the Fringe as more and more small-scale professional groups (and solo performers) use the Fringe to catch a critic's eye. These years also saw the growth of three or four 'super venues', where a number of lucky groups are professionally promoted in different performance spaces within one building (e.g. the Assembly Rooms) as well as the ascendancy of comedy and, in particular, of the solo STAND-UP performer.

The Fringe has seen many historic premières (e.g. TOM STOPPARD's *Rosencrantz and Guildenstern are Dead*, 1966) and a strong tradition of late-night REVUES (especially from student groups such as the Cambridge University FOOTLIGHTS) has been maintained. Notable contributions to the Fringe have been made by Edinburgh's own innovative theatre, the TRAVERSE; by Scotland's socialist company 7:84; and by leading foreign groups. The Fringe has also been a home for much experimental work, some of it denounced as 'outrageous' by the staider citizens of Edinburgh and some of it panned (for different reasons) by seasoned critics – for one of the cherished aspects of the Fringe is the performer's right to fail. DAVID SELF

See also FESTIVALS.

Alistair Moffat, *The Edinburgh Fringe* (1978)

Edinburgh International Festival [of Music and Drama] The foundation of this arts FESTIVAL in 1947, in the midst of postwar austerity, was seen by some as an inspired act of cultural defiance and optimism – an attempt to bring harmony and healing to war-torn Europe; by others (including some local politicians) as foolhardiness in those straitened times. Since then, it has been held annually for three weeks each August/September and has become Britain's premier and, with its unofficial FRINGE, biggest festival.

Its originator (and first director) was Rudolf Bing, general manager of Glyndebourne Opera, who wanted to establish a British rival to the Salzburg and BAYREUTH festivals. Under his direction and that of his immediate successors, drama was very much a poor cousin compared to music. But there were productions of Shakespeare (with starry casts), and from the first year leading foreign companies were invited to appear. A constant problem was the shortage of suitable theatres. In 1948 the Church of Scotland's Assembly Hall was first used as a dramatic venue, for TYRONE GUTHRIE's production of the morality play *An Satyre of the Thrie Estaites* – an event which marked the reintroduction of the large-scale open stage in Britain after a lapse of several centuries and, in choice of play, a nod towards regenerating Scottish theatre. In the following year, T. S. ELIOT was commissioned to write *The Cocktail Party* for the Festival. Subsequent commissions were awarded to, among others, O'CASEY and IONESCO, and again to Eliot (*The Confidential Clerk*, 1953; *The Elder Statesman*, 1958).

In 1960, the breakthrough revue *Beyond the Fringe* was premièred at the Festival, and during the 1970s the PROSPECT THEATRE COMPANY was a regular visitor, bringing energetic and innovative productions of Shakespeare (e.g. IAN MCKELLEN as Richard II in tandem with his Edward II). It was followed by several of the leading provincial repertory companies. Under later directors (notably John Drummond, FRANK DUNLOP and Brian McMaster), drama has had a fairer share of the budget – and a higher profile. Dunlop (once director of Prospect) did much to answer charges that the Festival is elitist, while he and others ensured it remained one of the few opportunities in Britain to see first-class world theatre (e.g. the work of LEPAGE, STEIN and ROBERT WILSON), as well as promoting Scottish culture. There are also annual book, jazz, folk, television and film festivals at the same time.

Although the Festival is supported by national (i.e. Scottish), regional and local bodies, funding remains a problem. Edinburgh's first ever socialist council (elected in 1984) seemed more generously disposed to the arts (and aware of the value of the Festival to the city), but there is, as yet, no definite sign that the city is to build a modern, large-scale theatre space.
DAVID SELF

Bruce George, *Festival in the North: The Story of the Edinburgh Festival* (1975)

education *see* DRAMA SCHOOLS; THEATRE IN EDUCATION; UNIVERSITY DRAMA DEPARTMENTS

Edwardes [Edwards], George (b. Clee, Lincs., 14 Oct. 1852; d. London, 4 Oct. 1915) Theatre manager, known as 'the Guv'nor'. He created the glamorous Gaiety Girls chorus line after establishing musical comedy at London's Gaiety Theatre, which he managed. In 1893, he built and opened Daly's Theatre for the American impresario Augustin Daly (1839–99). At the start of the twentieth century, running both theatres and the Adelphi too, he was the single most important producer of light MUSICAL THEATRE, with productions across the English-speaking world and as far beyond as Russia and Brazil. His hits included *The Geisha* (1896) and *The Merry Widow* (1907). Among the many stars he launched were SEYMOUR HICKS and MARIE TEMPEST. CHARLES LONDON

U. Bloom, *Curtain Call for the Guv'nor* (1954)

Edwards, Hilton (b. London, 2 Feb. 1903; d. Dublin, 18 Nov. 1982) Director and actor who spent most of his professional life at the Dublin GATE THEATRE, which he founded with MÍCHEÁL MACLÍAMMÓIR in 1928. His early acting experience was with Charles Doran's Shakespearean Company (1920–2) and the OLD VIC (1922–4). He joined ANEW MCMASTER's company for an Irish tour in 1927, and it was here that he met Mac-Líammóir. He directed over 300 plays in Dublin, including many first Irish productions of works by modern British, European and American authors. His emphasis on visual effects, especially movement and lighting, had an exemplary influence on the over-literary Irish theatre of the time. He directed all the Gate's productions which visited Britain, Europe, Africa and North and South America between 1936 and 1978, his own stage appearances becoming all too rare; among his best parts were Broadbent in *John Bull's Other Island*, Willie Loman in *Death of a Salesman*, Sir John Brute in *The Provok'd Wife* and Claudius in *Hamlet*. CHRISTOPHER FITZ-SIMON

C. Fitz-Simon, *The Boys* (1995)

Efremov, Oleg [Nikolaevich] (b. Moscow, 1 Oct. 1927; d. Moscow, 24 May 2000) Actor and director. He graduated from the NEMIROVICH-DANCHENKO School Studio in 1949 and worked at the Moscow Central Children's Theatre before becoming artistic director of the Sovremennik (Contemporary) Theatre, Moscow, which spearheaded the 'thaw' in post-Stalinist Soviet theatre. It presented indigenous plays by writers such as ROZOV, VOLODIN and SHVARTS as well as work from abroad, e.g. by OSBORNE and ALBEE, and developed an ENSEMBLE style in contrast to the conservative MOSCOW ART THEATRE, which Efremov joined in 1970 as artistic director in order to revitalize it. NICK WORRALL

Anatoly Smeliansky, *Oleg Yefremov* (1988)
——, *The Russian Theatre after Stalin* (1999)

Efros, Anatoli [Vasilevich] (b. Moscow, 3 June 1925; d. Moscow, 13 Jan. 1988) Director. After being artistic director of two Moscow theatres he made his mark in the city's Malaya Bronnaya Theatre during the 1970s with a number of highly energized ENSEMBLE productions, including Gogol's *Zhenit'ba* (*Getting Married*) and Turgenev's *A Month in the Country*, both seen abroad. He was known for lively interpretations of classics (Shakespeare, Molière, CHEKHOV) and his staging of contemporary plays (by ROZOV and RADZINSKY). He was put in charge of the TAGANKA

THEATRE following YURI LYUBIMOV's decision to live abroad (1985). NICK WORRALL

Anatoly Smeliansky, *The Russian Theatre after Stalin* (1999)

Egypt *see* MIDDLE EAST AND NORTH AFRICA

Eichelberger, Ethyl *see* EXPERIMENTAL THEATRE

Eisenstein, Sergei [Mikhailovich] (b. Riga, 10 Jan. 1898; d. Moscow, 11 Feb. 1948) Film director, theatre director/designer, theoretician, teacher. He worked with mobile AGITPROP theatre troupes at the front during the Civil War before becoming director/designer at the First Proletkult Workers' Theatre in Moscow (1920), where he staged experimental productions exploiting popular forms derived from the CLOWN show and the CIRCUS in a style which was to become characteristic of his later film technique, and based on theories of montage which he elaborated in a famous essay, 'Montage of Attractions' (1923). His most original work from this period was a production of Alexander Ostrovsky's nineteenth-century realistic play *Na vsyakogo mudretsa dovol'no prostoty* (*The Scoundrel* or *Even the Wise Can Err*), which he adapted as an 'eccentric' performance for circus arena involving high-wire acts and slapstick comedy while breaking the original play down into a series of turns with a political slant, integrating personalities from the contemporary political scene. Before, in his own words, 'dropping out of the theatre into the cinema', Eisenstein worked as assistant to MEYERHOLD on productions of *Nora* (IBSEN's *A Doll's House*, 1922) and *Smert' Tarel'kina* (*Tarelkin's Death*, 1922). He also studied COMMEDIA DELL'ARTE techniques at Nikolai Foregger's workshop, where he worked as production designer between 1921 and 1922. NICK WORRALL

Robert Leach, *Revolutionary Theatre* (1994)

Eisler, Hanns (b. Leipzig, 6 July 1898; d. Berlin, 6 Sept. 1962) Composer. By 1926 Eisler had become dissatisfied with the direction of modern music and had broken with his former teacher Schoenberg. He joined the Communist Party and began to seek a new social role for music. Instead of writing for the concert hall he composed marching songs and other vocal pieces for AGITPROP groups and workers' choruses, and began to write for the theatre, working with two people who were to become long-term collaborators: the actor and singer Ernst Busch and BERTOLT BRECHT, whose partnership with KURT WEILL was coming to an end. In Eisler Brecht found someone with an acute political intelligence who combined artistic sophistication with a feeling for popular musical idiom. Together they wrote a film, *Kuhle Wampe* (1931), two major stage works, *Die Massnahme* (*The Measures Taken*, 1930) and an adaptation of Gorky's novel *Die Mutter* (*The Mother*, 1932), and *Die Rundköpfe und Die Spitzköpfe* (*Round Heads and Pointed Heads*, begun 1931).

Eisler went into exile in 1933, first in Europe and later in the United States. During this period he worked intensively. With Brecht he composed some of his finest political songs, set poems, and wrote the music for *Schweyk im Zweiten Weltkrieg* (*Schweyk in the Second World War*, from 1943) and *Galileo* (1947). He also wrote film scores, chamber pieces, cantatas and his German Symphony.

In 1948, like many left-wing artists, he was called before the House Committee on Un-American Activities. When international protests helped secure his release he returned to Europe and subsequently settled, as did Brecht, in the German Democratic Republic, where he avoided concert performance in favour of 'applied music', continuing to compose for theatre, film, cabaret, festivals and public events. ANTHONY HOZIER

Manfred Grabs, ed., *Hanns Eisler: A Rebel in Music* (1978)

Eisteddfod *see* NATIONAL EISTEDDFOD

Ekster [Grigorovich], Alexandra [Alexandrovna] (b. Belestok, Russia, 6 Jan. 1884; d. Paris, 17 March 1949) Designer. She studied in Paris, where her acquaintances included PICASSO, Braque, APOLLINAIRE and MARINETTI. She designed for TAIROV (e.g. WILDE's *Salome*, 1917; *Romeo and Juliet*, 1921) and helped him develop his idea of theatre fused as a total entity. Influenced by cubism and futurism, she was a reformer of stage costume and set design. She treated material as a fluid, plastic entity and reduced sets to mobile, three-dimensional geometric forms and levels. NICK WORRALL

Nancy Van Norman Baer, *Theatre in Revolution: Russian Avant-Garde Stage Design 1913–1935* (1991)

El Salvador *see* MEXICO AND CENTRAL AMERICA

El Teatro Campesino *see* TEATRO CAMPESINO, EL

Elder, Lonne, III (b. Americus, Ga., 26 Dec. 1931; d. Los Angeles, 11 June 1996) Playwright, actor and screenwriter. Along with LORRAINE HANSBERRY, IMAMU AMIRI BARAKA, ED BULLINS and DOUGLAS TURNER WARD, Lonne Elder III formed part of the late 1950s BLACK THEATRE movement. He acted in Hansberry's *A Raisin in the Sun* (1959) and in Ward's *Day of Absence* (1967). From 1968 to 1978 he directed the playwriting programme for the NEGRO ENSEMBLE COMPANY which was committed to developing black American playwrights. His *Ceremonies in Dark Old Men* (1969) is a compassionate view of the lives of men in Harlem and the ceremonies they use to escape from the harshness of their environment. Screenplays include *Sounder, Sounder II* and *Bustin' Loose*. JANE HOUSE

Eldridge [McKechnie], Florence (b. Brooklyn, New York, 5 Sept. 1901; d. Santa Barbara, Calif., 1 Aug. 1988) Actress. After her first appearance on Broadway in the chorus of the musical *Rock-a-Bye Baby* (1918), she starred in *The Cat and the Canary* (1922). In 1927 she married FREDRIC MARCH and they embarked on a year-long tour, appearing in *Arms and the Man*, *The Silver Cord*, *The Guardsman* and *The Royal Family*. After the cinema beckoned in the 1930s, she and March became one of the great American theatrical couples, appearing together in several films between 1929 and 1960. They frequently returned to the stage, in, for example, *The American Way* (1939) and long runs of *The Skin of Our Teeth* (1942) and *Long Day's Journey into Night* (1956). HELEN RAPPAPORT

Elen, Gus [Ernest Augustus] (b. London, 22 July 1862; d. London, 17 Feb. 1940) MUSIC HALL performer. A busker in the early 1880s, he joined a blackface minstrel troupe in 1883 and made his music hall debut, as part of a minstrel duo, in Hackney, east London the following year. In the 1890s he established himself as the 'true' voice of the London costermongers (Cockney barrow traders). Unlike the more idealized coster songs of his rival ALBERT CHEVALIER, Elen's songs were full of finely observed, life-like characters. 'It's a Great Big Shame', 'Don't Stop My 'Arf Pint o' Beer', 'Wait Till the Work Comes Round', 'If It Wasn't For the 'Ouses in Between', ' 'E Dunno Where 'E Are', and 'Down the Road' became standards. He toured the US in 1907, retired during the First World War and made a comeback in 1931. He returned to the LONDON PALLADIUM for the 1935 COMMAND PERFORMANCE and made a BBC broadcast in 1937. Recordings from the 1930s reveal a cracked voice full of pathos and irony. CHARLES LONDON

Eliot, T[homas] S[tearns] (b. St Louis, Mo., 26 Sept. 1888; d. London, 4 Jan. 1965) American-born, naturalized (1927) British poet, essayist and playwright. Eliot, who settled in London in 1915, was an established MODERNIST poet when he turned to writing plays – a natural development, as the relationship between drama and poetry had been a central concern of his literary criticism and theory, and his poetry displayed many theatrical qualities. The short, incom-

plete *Sweeney Agonistes* (1933), which mirrored the spiritual alienation of his poem *The Waste Land* and prefigured aspects of the THEATRE OF THE ABSURD, showed Eliot attempting to bridge the gap between poetry and drama and regain the appeal that theatre had enjoyed in Shakespeare's time by drawing on popular forms such as the MUSIC HALL and vernacular speech. His writing on seventeenth-century dramatists helped revive several of their fortunes.

In 1934 Eliot joined the important GROUP THEATRE and was linked with its leading playwright W. H. AUDEN at the core of a new poetic dramatic revival. The chorus work of Eliot's Christian pageant *The Rock* (1934), co-directed by a Group founder RUPERT DOONE and E. MARTIN BROWNE, fed directly into what became probably the most successful verse play of the century, *Murder in the Cathedral* (1935), which Browne directed in the Chapter House of Canterbury Cathedral – the cathedral where the subject of the play, Thomas à Becket's martyrdom, occurred.

Eliot continued to pursue this mix of the popular and the professorial in his four remaining plays, but increasingly secreted his spiritual concerns within the web of conventional comedies of manners which diluted their dramatic power. All are inspired by classical Greek drama – *The Family Reunion* (1939) by Aeschylus, *The Cocktail Party* (1949) and *The Confidential Clerk* (1953) by Euripides, and *The Elder Statesman* (1958) by Sophocles; the latter three were first seen at the EDINBURGH FESTIVAL, bolstered by the author's status as a Nobel Prize winner for his poetry (1948).

With FRY, he represented a rarefied if often suburban world that social realism came to sweep away in the mid-1950s. A decade after his death, however, a reassessment began that included innovative revivals (e.g. MICHAEL ELLIOTT's production of *A Family Reunion*, 1979), a MICHAEL HASTINGS play about his private life (*Tom and Viv*, 1984, filmed 1994) and the longest-running musical of its time, *Cats* (1981), based on his poems *Old Possum's Book of Practical Cats* (1939). COLIN CHAMBERS

E. Martin Browne, *The Making of T. S. Eliot's Plays* (1969)

D. E. Jones, *The Plays of T. S. Eliot* (1961)

Carol H. Smith, *Eliot's Dramatic Theory and Practice* (1962)

Elisha, Ron (b. Jerusalem, 19 Dec. 1951) Playwright and doctor who emigrated from Israel to Melbourne in 1953. His earlier dramas are not set in Australia, nor does he treat distinctively Australian themes, preferring questions which reflect his Jewish concerns, combining these with questions of ethics and moral and political responsibility. He ranges from the two-hander (*Two*, 1982) to the epic (*Einstein*, 1981), and from the almost cinematic treatment of the complexities of a human biography (*Pax Americana*, 1984) to shrewd domestic comedy (*The Levine Comedy*, 1986). Other plays include *Safe House* (1989) and *Esterhaz* (1990). MICHAEL MORLEY

Elizabethan and Jacobean theatre in the twentieth century The twentieth century represented something of a renaissance in the attention paid to the drama of Shakespeare's contemporaries and immediate successors. Their works, with few exceptions (and then in bowdlerized adaptations), disappeared from the eighteenth- and nineteenth-century English stage: their robust language, visceral action, unsentimental and often brutally cynical characters, and their treatment of the darker recesses of human behaviour all contributed to ensuring that they were kept away from audiences. The movement from the beginning of the twentieth century, in academia and the theatre, towards rediscovering Renaissance theatrical conventions and returning to the original texts of Shakespeare created a climate of renewed curiosity about Shakespeare's contemporaries too – an interest furthered in print in the influential reassessments by T. S. ELIOT (*Elizabethan Essays*, 1934), Una Ellis Fermor (*The Jacobean Drama*, 1936) and others.

In terms of the modern performance circumstances of these dramatists, there is one striking difference from Shakespeare: whereas the latter's dominance ensures production at all levels, from village schools to the star-studded stages of London's West End theatres, productions of the plays of Shakespeare's contemporaries, never sure of gaining large audiences (and almost always requiring large casts), have taken place, intermittently, at either amateur or non-profit FRINGE level, or under the auspices of publicly subsidized companies. Nevertheless, there have been enough productions for a repertoire of the most-revived plays to have emerged: Marlowe's *Doctor Faustus*, *Edward II* and, in three major productions, *Tamburlaine the Great*; Ben Jonson's *Volpone*, *The Alchemist* and *Bartholemew Fair*; Francis Beaumont's *The Knight of the Burning Pestle*; Thomas Middleton's *The Changeling* (with Rowley) and *Women Beware Women*; the anonymous *Revenger's Tragedy* (generally ascribed now to Middleton); Philip Massinger's *A New Way to Pay Old Debts*; John Webster's *The Duchess of Malfi* and *The White Devil*; and John Ford's *'Tis Pity She's a Whore*. This list has been supplemented by occasional productions of other works by these and other authors, although productions of the plays of Shakespeare's Elizabethan forebears and rivals

(George Peele, John Lyly, Thomas Kyd, Robert Greene) are extreme rarities, and the stock of Beaumont and Fletcher diminished considerably.

The major impetus in the resuscitation of professional performance of these plays was the formation in the early 1960s of the two subsidized national companies, the ROYAL SHAKESPEARE COMPANY and the NATIONAL THEATRE, with briefs to reinvestigate Britain's dramatic heritage. The opening in the 1980s of the RSC's third Stratford venue, the Swan, with its interior reminiscent of an Elizabethan thrust stage, was heralded as an opportunity to further the company's expansion into the plays of Shakespeare's contemporaries. Inevitably, economic pressures diluted the purity of such a plan, but significant work has been produced there, including the disinterment of some of Jonson's less well known works and a revealing comedy of the transitional Caroline writer James Shirley, *Hyde Park*.

Approaches to production have varied from exploitation of the historically reconstructive period style to the appropriation of other eras as a means of translating the plays into terms meaningful for a modern audience (RICHARD EYRE's NT productions of *Bartholemew Fair* and *The Changeling*, both recast into nineteenth-century contexts, were good examples of the latter). However, since many of these writers reflected more concretely than Shakespeare the particularities of their contemporary world (particularly those writers of the 'city comedies', set in London), they have provided fewer opportunities to directors and designers for the more abstract experiments in style.

Potential readers of these plays have been served, since the 1960s, by two important series of single editions, the New Mermaids (in Britain) and the Regents Renaissance Dramatists series (in the United States), and these have been complemented in recent years by newly edited collections from Cambridge University Press.

These writers are, as yet, unable to escape their historical contemporaneity with, and consequent dependence upon, Shakespeare: while this fact has enabled their emergence and recognition in critical study (especially Marlowe and Jonson) and, to a lesser extent, on the stage, it also ensures they remain in Shakespeare's shadow. While few books focus on modern productions of the plays, useful information and comment can be found in books by or about relevant directors, actors and designers. MARK HAWKINS-DADY

Michael Scott, *Renaissance Drama and a Modern Audience* (1987)

Elliot, Denholm (b. London, 31 May 1922; d. Ibiza, 6 Oct. 1992) Actor. Elliot moved from success in supporting roles (e.g. Edgar in *Venus Observed*, 1950) to establish himself as a romantic lead and excellent speaker of verse (e.g. *The Confidential Clerk*, 1953). He came to concentrate on films, where, with enviable assurance and apparent lack of effort, he specialized in the shabby, the failed and the vulnerable. His selective returns to the stage were often considerable successes, as with Trigorin in *The Seagull* (1963), Judge Brack in *Hedda Gabler* (1972) and Dick in *Chez Nous* (1974). In 1989 he was persuaded to leave his life in the cinema for MAMET's *A Life in the Theatre* (1989), where he played the old actor, Robert, with autumnal dignity and poignancy. DAN REBELLATO

Susan Elliott, with Barry Turner, *Denholm Elliott: Quest for Life* (1994)

Elliott, Gertrude *see* ELLIOTT, MAXINE

Elliott, Maxine [Jessie Dermot] (b. Rockland, Maine, 5 Feb. 1868; d. Juan Les Pins, France, 5 March 1940) Actress. A sea captain's daughter who took to acting as a means of livelihood, she recognized that her black-haired, dark-eyed beauty helped win her international stardom far more than her limited dramatic abilities. She made her New York debut in 1890, then caught the public's eye playing with the producer Augustin Daly's ensemble. Her career peaked between *An American Citizen* (1897) and *Her Great Match* (1905), during which time she often appeared with her husband, Nat Goodwin, and had plays written for her by CLYDE FITCH. Curiously, the decline of her acting career coincided with the opening of her own theatre in 1908. Her sister Gertrude (1874–1950) was also an actress. GERALD BORDMAN

D. Forbes-Robertson, *My Aunt Maxine* (1964)

Elliott, Michael [Paul] (b. London, 26 June 1931; d. Manchester, 30 May 1984) Director. After a remarkable *Brand* (1959) at the LYRIC Hammersmith, with the 59 Company, Elliott directed *As You Like It* (1961) with VANESSA REDGRAVE at the ROYAL SHAKESPEARE COMPANY. He ran the OLD VIC in its last season (1962) before it became the NATIONAL THEATRE, directing *The Merchant of Venice* and *Peer Gynt* here. At the NT in 1966 he directed ALBERT FINNEY and MAGGIE SMITH in *Miss Julie*. In 1969 Elliott re-formed the 59 Company as the 69 Company, notably directing *When We Dead Awaken* (1969). They found a permanent home in 1976 at the ROYAL EXCHANGE THEATRE, Manchester, where Elliott directed *Uncle Vanya* (1977), *The Lady from the Sea* (1978) and *Moby Dick* (1984). Elliott helped to re-establish the integrity of regional theatre, and, although he did direct new plays, like *The Dresser* (1980), he was acclaimed for his pioneering productions of classics, notably of late and early IBSEN.
DAN REBELLATO

Elliott, Sumner Locke (b. Sydney, 17 Oct. 1917; d. New York, 23 June 1991) Playwright and novelist. Before the Second World War, Elliott served his time among the dedicated amateurs at Doris Fitton's Independent Theatre, where eight of his plays were produced between 1939 and 1953. Fitton's links with GREGAN MCMAHON (and, through him, with SHAW) and her belief in the STANISLAVSKY 'system' of acting, ensured that the serious business of entertainment, to which Elliott was committed, was dealt with professionally. It was this professionalism, before the days of a 'legitimate' profession, which saw *Rusty Bugles* (1948) being performed against all odds and becoming the most popular Australian play between Steele Rudd's *On our Selection* (1912) and RAY LAWLER's *The Summer of the Seventeenth Doll* (1954).

When the storm broke over this frank 'documentary' rendering of his time in an ordinance camp in the Northern Territory during the war, Elliott had already embarked on what was to become a highly successful career in the United States, as novelist, short-story writer and television scriptwriter. He remained lost to Australia until two of his novels of revelation and retrospection, *Water Under the Bridge* (1977) and *Careful He Might Hear You* (1963), were adapted for television and film, providing much-needed roles for talented female performers. Other plays include *Interval* (1939), *Goodbye to the Music* (1942) and *Buy the Blue Ribbon* (1953). His novel *Eden's Lost* (1974) was adapted for television by MICHAEL GOW and directed by Neil Armfield. GUS WORBY

R. Arnold, *Sumner Locke Elliott's Rusty Bugle: A Critical Introduction* (1983)
S. Clarke, *Sumner Locke Elliott 'Writing Life': A Biography* (1996)

Ellis, Vivian [John Herman] (b. London, 29 Oct. 1903; d. London, 19 June 1996) Composer. Trained as a pianist, Ellis first composed for the REVUE theatre, before supplying the scores for several touring light musical plays. The best of these, *Mr Cinders* (1929), was highly successful when restaged in London and, over the next eight years, Ellis supplied regular scores and songs for WEST END shows, one of the few British composers to find favour as a theatre composer at a time when the rage was for anything American. His most successful works from this period were the revues

Streamline and *Jill Darling* (both 1934), and the CICELY COURTNEIDGE vehicles *Hide and Seek* (1937) and *Under Your Hat* (1938). After the war, Ellis resumed the partnership begun in *Streamline* with author A. P. Herbert and producer C. B. COCHRAN in four musicals of a more substantial kind. Most suffered from pretentious libretti, but *Bless the Bride* (1947), a conscious attempt at a period operetta of subtle charm, was an outstanding success. His autobiography, *I'm On a See-Saw*, came out in 1953. KURT GÄNZL

Eltinge, Julian [William Julian Dalton] (b. Newtonville, Mass., 14 May 1883; d. New York, 7 March 1941) Female IMPERSONATOR who made his debut in Boston at the age of ten, playing a little girl. After his Broadway debut in 1904 he was soon a VAUDEVILLE 'headliner' and also starred in such specially written vehicles as *The Fascinating Widow* (1911), *The Crinoline Girl* (1914), and *Cousin Lucy* (1915). When vaudeville died away in the 1920s, his career faded too. A big man, he had a large female following and a theatre named after him. He was generally acknowledged as the best of American female impersonators, appearing in beautiful clothes and deriving his humour from situations, rarely from 'camp'. GERALD BORDMAN

See also DRAG.

Laurence Senelick, *The Changing Room: Sex, Drag and Theatre* (2000)

Elyot [Lee], Kevin [Ronald] (b. Birmingham, 18 July 1951) Playwright. His first play, *Coming Clean* (1982), was an award-winning examination of sexual passion and infidelity in a gay relationship, which broke new ground in the explicitness of some of its handling of homosexual themes. After a series of well-regarded adaptations, he scored his next major success with *My Night with Reg* (1994), which transferred from the ROYAL COURT Theatre Upstairs to the WEST END, and was later filmed. The play features a reunion of a group of friends all linked by their relationships with the off-stage Reg. The play's crafted dialogue and artful time structure gave it an emotionally dislocating power. Other plays include *Consent* (1989), *The Day I Stood Still* (1998) and *Mouth to Mouth* (2001).
DAN REBELLATO

Embassy Theatre Built in 1927 in north London, it took over from the neighbouring EVERYMAN as a suburban venue for WEST END try-outs but made its special contribution in the early 1930s as a CLUB THEATRE under actor–manager Ronald Adam (1896–1979) and André Van Gyseghem (1906–79) when they mounted important productions of foreign plays such as the anti-war *Miracle at Verdun* by the Austrian Hans

Chlumberg, O'NEILL's *All God's Chillun Got Wings* and *Stevedore* by Americans George Sklar and Paul Peters. The latter two included PAUL ROBESON in their casts. Adam transferred 28 plays to the West End. Run by actor–manager Anthony Hawtrey (1909–54) from 1945 until his death – a period during which the theatre launched O'CASEY's *Red Roses for Me* in England in 1946 – it was taken over by the Central School of Speech and Drama (1957). Not to be confused with the smart Embassy Club, frequented by the rich and the famous, from royalty to the theatre cat. CHARLES LONDON

Emmet, Alfred (b. Ealing, West London, 29 March 1908; d. Ealing, 16 Jan. 1991) Director. He took over the local QUESTORS company in west London in 1933, and, although a purely amateur enterprise (Emmet worked full-time for a tea manufacturer), it was soon noticed for its innovative repertoire and staging. Emmet, a leading international figure in the AMATEUR THEATRE world, ran International Theatre seasons and a student group (from which directors Alan Clarke and DECLAN DONNELLAN graduated). He also encouraged new dramatists, including RODNEY ACKLAND and JAMES SAUNDERS. Proud of his amateur status, always refusing offers of professional work, Emmet helped found the LITTLE THEATRE GUILD OF GREAT BRITAIN in 1946 and the INTERNATIONAL AMATEUR THEATRE ASSOCIATION in 1956. DAN REBELLATO

Emney, Fred (b. London, 12 Feb. 1900; d. Bognor Regis, W. Sussex, 25 Dec. 1980) Actor, son of a successful BURLESQUE comedian and VARIETY artist with the same name. Emney first found fame in the United States in VAUDEVILLE during the 1920s and worked there for 11 years. On his return he moved to musical comedy and REVUE, including *All Clear* (1939), *Big Top* (1942), *Big Boy* (1945), for which he was part author, and *Blue for a Boy* (1950), and also appeared in straight plays. He was known for his great bulk, his eyeglass and his cigar. REXTON S. BUNNETT

Gerald Fairlie, *The Fred Emney Story* (1960)

Empire Theater Considered BROADWAY's most venerable playhouse in the years before its demolition in 1953, it was built by Al Hayman and CHARLES FROHMAN and stood on Broadway just below 40th Street. It was designed by J. B. McElfatrick, and opened in 1893 with *The Girl I Left Behind Me*. A long lobby, in later years hung with portraits of famous players, led to a red-and-gold rococo auditorium. In Frohman's day it was regularly home to such stars as John Drew, MAUDE ADAMS and ETHEL BARRYMORE Among its subsequent successes was the long-running *Life with Father* (1939). GERALD BORDMAN

En Garde *see* EXPERIMENTAL THEATRE

Engel, Erich *see* BERLINER ENSEMBLE; GERMAN LAN-GUAGE THEATRE

England British imperial power thrived on stratification, and the nineteenth-century theatre that entertained those at the heart of the empire was no exception. In one corner there was the so-called legitimate theatre, which was starting to enjoy a new-found respectability as the old century came to a close; in the other there was MUSIC HALL and other forms of popular performance whose commercial establishment wanted also to be socially accepted. Much of the innovation of the new century came about as a result of attempts, however unsuccessful, to close this gap, as well as to create a national drama of serious purpose.

The music-hall managers sought the ultimate accolade of royal sanction by persuading the new King George V to attend a COMMAND PERFORMANCE in 1912. They underlined their drive for acceptance by omitting from the line-up MARIE LLOYD, the highest-paid music-hall star of the time. She openly flouted moral convention and had recently helped organize a strike of fellow artistes for better wages and conditions. On the other side of the fence, the profession of rogues and vagabonds had already won in 1895 its first knight, the actor–manager HENRY IRVING. He had turned the Lyceum Theatre into the equivalent of a National Theatre, a still elusive monument that would take another six decades to come into being, yet he promoted a conservative repertoire and, though supporting his leading lady ELLEN TERRY, denied her the range of roles her talent deserved.

Thanks to Irving and his usually despotic fellow actor–managers – for example OSCAR ASCHE, Charles Wyndham, JOHN MARTIN-HARVEY, HERBERT BEERBOHM TREE and SQUIRE BANCROFT – the standard of acting had generally risen and the long run had become established as the desired aim of any production. The glorious days of the actor–manager, however, were numbered; one of the last of the old school was FRANK BENSON, who began the SHAKESPEARE FESTIVAL in STRATFORD-UPON-AVON and toured the country playing the Bard. The actor–manager tradition, however, did survive, albeit fitfully and in different guises, in the likes of DONALD WOLFIT, LAURENCE OLIVIER, ANTHONY QUAYLE, BRIAN RIX, STEVEN BERKOFF and KENNETH BRANAGH.

Major change had come about through technological advance, especially in the way theatres were lit, through the partial emergence of a new theatrical function in the figure of the director, and through the ownership and expansion of theatre buildings. The two largest London theatres, DRURY LANE and Covent Garden, which had held a monopoly protected by royal patent until 1834, could not fill their capacity with new plays and opted for a florid style of spectacle which became a benchmark for other productions and against which there was a fierce reaction among those trying to improve the quality of the drama on offer to the theatregoing public.

While there were attempts by writers like JOHN MASE-FIELD and JAMES ELROY FLECKER to initiate a poetic upsurge, and J. M. BARRIE launched his fantasy *Peter Pan* ten years before the First World War, the dominant writing style followed on from the naturalistic conventions of T. W. Robertson (1829–71) in the hands of ARTHUR WING PINERO, HENRY ARTHUR JONES, OSCAR WILDE (whose playwriting was curtailed by gaol and calumny), JOHN GALSWORTHY and WILLIAM SOMERSET MAUGHAM, who had four plays running in the WEST END in 1908. GEORGE BERNARD SHAW, the first major writer for a century to devote his energies to the theatre, was leading the fight to create a modern drama of ideas; he derided Irving for not joining the struggle and championed foreign playwrights like IBSEN. Ranged alongside the Irishman Shaw in challenging English insularity were the Scottish critic and translator WILLIAM ARCHER and the Dutchman J. T. GREIN and his London-based INDEPENDENT THEATRE SOCIETY. This interest in a new international drama coincided with a re-evaluation of the staging of classics, especially of Shakespeare's plays, and an accompanying concern for the integrity of the text. A key character in this trend was WILLIAM POEL, whose experiments bore early fruit in the work of another critical figure, HARLEY GRANVILLE BARKER. With J. E. VEDRENNE, Granville Barker mounted seasons at the ROYAL COURT and SAVOY THEATRES that were protoypes of National Theatre seasons to come, using ensemble acting and simple staging and design, and promoting a repertoire that included international plays (e.g. by SCHNITZLER, MAETERLINCK, HAUPTMANN), new British drama (e.g. Shaw, Galsworthy and ST JOHN HANKIN) and Shakespeare. Such experiment inspired the development of the regional REPERTORY MOVEMENT, with, initially, its short runs of new and classical drama: ANNIE HORNI-MAN, who in 1904 had put her legacy from the tea trade into the ABBEY THEATRE in DUBLIN, switched her fortune to Manchester to found the first British 'rep' in 1908. Reps opened in GLASGOW (1909, under Alfred Wareing), LIVERPOOL (1911, under a trust), BIRMINGHAM (1913, under BARRY JACKSON, another wealthy heir) and BRISTOL (1914, short lived at the time, though not later). Despite the home-grown likes of STANLEY HOUGHTON, HAROLD BRIGHOUSE and JOHN DRINKWATER, the movement could not match the standard of the contemporary Irish writers, and when SEAN O'CASEY was rejected by the Abbey and came to live and work in England, he was rejected here too.

Ethical and political drama was strong among AMATEUR groups in the cooperative and labour movement, in the YIDDISH THEATRE and among the suffragettes. In fact WOMEN played an important role in shaping the theatre, whether as innovative artists such as director–designer EDITH CRAIG (active in the PIONEER PLAYERS and the ACTRESSES' FRANCHISE LEAGUE) or as managers, such as Horniman, LENA ASHWELL, EMMA CONS and her niece LILIAN BAYLIS – who ran the OLD VIC as a people's theatre, setting out to perform the entire cycle of Shakespeare's plays at affordable prices, a feat she achieved between 1914 and 1923.

Entertainment during the First World War, however, was mostly in a lighter vein: based on the Ali Baba story, the spectacular *Chu Chin Chow* opened in 1916 and ran for 2,242 performances, a record that stood for four decades. Commercial theatre held sway but was facing stiff competition from cinema, which ousted live performance from many theatre buildings. Sharply rising rents and costs meant a rise in sub-letting, theatre becoming more of a business without even the individual artistic input of an actor–manager. In such circumstances, the long run anchored in the star system became even more necessary for commercial success. Improvements in transport made more touring possible, but this increased the reliance on commercial productions from London and their values. Individual attempts to counter these forces, like NIGEL PLAYFAIR's reign at the LYRIC, Hammersmith, inevitably succumbed to economic reality, though Baylis survived at the Old Vic and in 1931 took over SADLER'S WELLS as a venue for ballet and opera. The reps, too, tried to resist these trends, but economics undermined their original impetus. Nevertheless, Bristol Little Theatre, SHEFFIELD and OXFORD all opened in 1923 and, along with CAMBRIDGE (1926), Northampton (1927), Birmingham and Liverpool, managed to keep the flame alight. Cambridge was a special case; inspired by the pioneer theorists EDWARD GORDON CRAIG and ADOLPHE APPIA, TERENCE GRAY had redesigned the FESTIVAL THEATRE by dismantling the proscenium and thrusting the stage into the audience, and staged there influential modernist productions of classics. Most experiment took place in LITTLE THEATRES (in line with the European tradition of the independent theatres, the MOSCOW ART THEATRE and its studios, and MAX REINHARDT's

chamber theatre in Berlin). These little theatres were often run as CLUBS (e.g. the EVERYMAN, GATE, BARNES, MERCURY) where managements could escape the CENSORSHIP of the LORD CHAMBERLAIN. NUGENT MONCK's amateur MADDERMARKET THEATRE, Norwich, continued the experiments of Poel and used an open stage for his repertoire of sustained courageous choices. The social role of theatre became a vital force; sometimes it was wedded to aesthetic experiment, as in the GROUP THEATRE, which staged plays by T. S. ELIOT, W. H. AUDEN and CHRISTOPHER ISHERWOOD, and sometimes it was overtly agitational, as in the amateur UNITY THEATRE and similar left-wing groups which flourished around Britain in the 1930s.

In writing, NOËL COWARD and TERENCE RATTIGAN have come to stand out in this period from the immensely popular IVOR NOVELLO, or from Sutton Vane, CLEMENCE DANE, BEN TRAVERS, EMLYN WILLIAMS, R. C. SHERRIFF, JOHN VAN DRUTEN, FREDERICK LONSDALE and J. B. PRIESTLEY, despite successful revivals of plays by some of the aforementioned playwrights. In 1925 Coward equalled Maugham's record of having four plays in the West End at the same time. By now, the actors who were to dominate the middle of the century had come to the fore: SYBIL THORNDIKE, EDITH EVANS, JOHN GIELGUD, PEGGY ASHCROFT, RALPH RICHARDSON, LAURENCE OLIVIER, MICHAEL REDGRAVE. Designers such as MOTLEY and TANYA MOISEWITCH took their craft in new directions alongside increasingly powerful directors like TYRONE GUTHRIE. European ideas remained potent through directors like THEODORE KOMMISSARZHEVSKY and MICHEL SAINT-DENIS, whose work at the London Theatre School was to be highly influential if little publicized. In 1929 the UNION Actors' Equity was founded, just over a decade after the Actors' Association had become a trade union. It joined the ranks of the stage hands and musicians who were already unionized at the start of the century.

The Second World War closed many theatres and destroyed one-fifth of those in the capital, yet at the same time it saw the growth of a popular interest in the performing arts through a number of initiatives. There was the shelter, factory and armed forces entertainment which often took place away from conventional theatre buildings; there were official organizing bodies like the COUNCIL FOR THE ENCOURAGEMENT OF MUSIC AND THE ARTS (CEMA) and the ENTERTAINMENTS NATIONAL SERVICE ASSOCIATION (ENSA); and there was the theatrical work of armed forces groups like the Army Bureau of Current Affairs play unit (in which TED WILLIS and other Unity Theatre associates developed the LIVING NEWSPAPER tradition) or of those affiliated to the active amateur BRITISH DRAMA LEAGUE (founded

1919). The Old Vic – the nearest company to a national theatre at the time – had moved north out of London and eventually set up a residency in Liverpool as well as touring. It returned to the capital, to the New Theatre, in 1944, remaining there for five years while the Old Vic building was repaired following blitz damage. But the inheritance of Baylis, who had died just before war broke out, was broken up and the company was separated from Sadler's Wells, from ballet and opera.

Out of the war came a political consensus in favour of public SUBSIDY for the arts; CEMA became the ARTS COUNCIL OF GREAT BRITAIN, which moved away, however, from the former's democratic impetus and focused on metropolitan patrician interests instead of regional, community and amateur initiatives. It did, nevertheless, help establish the BRISTOL OLD VIC in 1946 at the Theatre Royal, which CEMA had saved from destruction, thereby making it the first British theatre to be financed by the state. Although the arts were low on the list of postwar priorities, in 1948 the Labour administration passed the Local Government Act, which allowed local authorities to spend a percentage of the rates on leisure but did not make it a statutory requirement. The National Theatre Act was passed in 1949, but more than a decade was to pass before a national company was founded.

Despite the hopes of some, who were represented at an important Theatre Conference in 1948 chaired by J. B. Priestley but boycotted by the West End managers, public subsidy did not offer a serious challenge to the commercial sector. This became dominated by fewer but more powerful managements in the wake of a doubling of rents for those buildings that had survived the bombing. A network of companies, known as The Group and headed by Prince LITTLER, controlled almost half the West End theatres and more than half the major touring theatres. The leading producer was H. M. TENNENT under HUGH 'BINKIE' BEAUMONT, who operated a nonprofit arm for supposedly riskier enterprises. The standard commercial fare comprised elegant plays with elegant decor, farces, 'whodunnits' (led by *The Mousetrap*, which opened in 1952 and was to become the world's longest-running play) and American musicals. JEAN ANOUILH and JEAN GIRAUDOUX outshone native talent, which, with a few exceptions from earlier times like Rattigan, seemed to have deserted the theatre. VERSE plays by Eliot and CHRISTOPHER FRY briefly posed an intelligent but apparently too rarefied alternative.

In a spirit of using the arts to heal the wounds of war, the EDINBURGH INTERNATIONAL FESTIVAL of Music and Drama opened its arms in 1947 to world culture, though rather narrowly interpreted. This led the left to spearhead the EDINBURGH FRINGE and, in the shape of Glasgow and London Unity, to enter briefly the realm of professional theatre before being assimilated and reverting to the traditional amateur work. Club theatres continued to offer experiment, and ALEC CLUNES at the ARTS THEATRE in London assumed the mantle of the pocket-size national theatre, while the project to build the real thing was given renewed stimulus in 1951 with the laying of the foundation stone – but in what turned out to be the wrong place. The search for the right place rumbled on through countless committees. The Old Vic school was revived with a new wing, the YOUNG VIC, which, in that incarnation, lasted until 1951. ALEC GUINNESS came out of the war period in top form while a new generation of actors – led by PAUL SCOFIELD and RICHARD BURTON – made its mark. PETER BROOK was the young director to watch.

Postwar disillusion with the post-Holocaust and post-Hiroshima world cast its shadow over the playwrights; JOHN WHITING appeared ahead of his time as did, from Ireland via France, SAMUEL BECKETT, whose *Waiting for Godot* opened at the Arts in 1955. Alongside came other members of the so-called THEATRE OF THE ABSURD, like EUGENE IONESCO. Running counter to this ethos was the socially oriented work of JOAN LITTLEWOOD and THEATRE WORKSHOP, in the East End of London as well as in the West End, and the growing influence of BERTOLT BRECHT and the BERLINER ENSEMBLE, which visited England in 1956. That year also saw the founding under GEORGE DEVINE of the ENGLISH STAGE COMPANY at the Royal Court, which, following the success of JOHN OSBORNE's *Look Back in Anger* – triggered by the showing of an excerpt on television – stimulated a resurgence of British playwriting and a new style of urgent poetic realism.

The following 20 years saw the creation of a serious theatre of debate at the centre of national cultural consciousness. There was a new confidence in the air which saw a wave of theatre building and conversion unmatched since the end of the nineteenth century. The publicly financed Belgrade Theatre, Coventry, was opened in 1958 as the first purpose-built repertory theatre in England for two decades; and within a dozen years after that, 20 new theatres had been built, about three-quarters dedicated to repertory theatre outside of London. THEATRE IN THE ROUND became a major influence, especially in the north of England, at Stoke, then Scarborough, and in Manchester at the ROYAL EXCHANGE. Actors such as ALBERT FINNEY and TOM COURTENAY no longer had to assume the voice of standard English but could use their own accents.

Designers – JOCELYN HERBERT, SEAN KENNY, JOHN BURY, FARRAH, RALPH KOLTAI – revolutionized the look of theatre, and writers like JOHN ARDEN, ARNOLD WESKER, ANNE JELLICOE, HAROLD PINTER and many others in the years to come, such as DAVID RUDKIN, EDWARD BOND and JOE ORTON, created a body of work unparalleled since Shakespeare's time. With all its limitations, here was a major cultural achievement of international significance which put English theatre centre stage once more.

For a while the commercial world, in the shape of risk-takers like producer MICHAEL CODRON, played its part, but it was eclipsed when publicly subsidized theatre took off in the 1960s in the shape of the two national companies, the ROYAL SHAKESPEARE COMPANY (RSC) and, finally, after decades of wrangling, the NATIONAL THEATRE (NT). PETER HALL managed to achieve what his predecessors at Stratford-upon-Avon had not, an ensemble dedicated to exploring the plays of Shakespeare. In a direct line from William Poel, the RSC went back to the texts and used vigorous but simple and fluent staging; they transformed verse speaking and treated Shakespeare as their contemporary. Hall opened a base for the RSC in London at the ALDWYCH THEATRE, where he staged classical work as well as modern and new plays. With Peter Brook and others, through their powerful main-stage productions as well as experimental work in smaller spaces, such as the ARTAUD-influenced THEATRE OF CRUELTY season, Hall made the RSC an international force. Brook later departed for Paris and the company under TREVOR NUNN necessarily became the new establishment, expanding in order to survive and eventually running five theatres.

Laurence Olivier, the inaugural artistic director of the National Theatre, formed a company first at the newly opened CHICHESTER FESTIVAL THEATRE and then took them as the NT to the Old Vic in 1963. Aided in his planning by his literary manager, the flamboyant critic KENNETH TYNAN, he built an extraordinary group of performers, including many young actors who hailed from the Royal Court. In 1973 Olivier ceded power to Hall, who oversaw the company's move to its new home on the South Bank of the River Thames in 1976–7 where, despite inevitable controversies, it enjoyed a sound reputation under him and his successors, RICHARD EYRE and TREVOR NUNN, although, as the new century got under way, questions about its future and role were increasingly being asked.

Jennie Lee, appointed by the Labour government in 1964 as the first arts minister, oversaw a rise in grant to, and influence wielded by, the Arts Council as well as an overall improvement in the general health of the theatre. An historical anomaly – the censorship powers of the Lord Chamberlain, which had been tested and mocked in the West End in the late 1950s over the issue of homosexuality – was subjected to a concerted campaign for its abolition. Spurred by the prosecution of the Royal Court in 1966 for performing the banned *Saved* by Edward Bond, the campaign was victorious in 1968.

An alternative network of arts centres and arts laboratories, theatres in pubs, basements and old halls, spread quickly in the late 1960s and 1970s, inspired by international developments and visits from the United States of groups like OPEN THEATER, LIVING THEATER and BREAD AND PUPPET THEATER. Women's, gay and black theatres were emerging, given a boost by seasons at the Almost Free Theatre, a FRINGE venue run by the dynamic INTER-ACTION group. Innovation and collective creation mixed with a new politics in a flourishing fringe scene, ranging from the PIP SIMMONS THEATRE GROUP and the PEOPLE SHOW to 7:84 and MONSTROUS REGIMENT. A new generation of actors, directors, designers, and writers from the fringe reinvigorated the conventional theatre. The work of HOWARD BARKER, HOWARD BRENTON, CARYL CHURCHILL, DAVID EDGAR, TREVOR GRIFFITHS and DAVID HARE could be seen alongside that of MICHAEL FRAYN, PETER NICHOLS, PETER SHAFFER and TOM STOPPARD. Stage playwrights became militant and in 1976 formed the Theatre Writers' Union – to the left of the existing Society of Authors and Writers Guild of Great Britain – to better both their financial rewards and their influence over production. After a strong campaign, which included a boycott of the NT, a minimum contract was agreed for subsidized theatre managements.

Much of the new energy of the time was channelled into COMMUNITY THEATRE and THEATRE IN EDUCATION as well as into small new-play theatres like the BUSH, SOHO POLY and TRAVERSE. As the regional impetus continued – the SHEFFIELD Crucible was founded in 1971, the NOTTINGHAM Playhouse was a focus of important new writing, PROSPECT toured major productions – many theatres opened studios to allow new work to proliferate. As it turned out, this also had the effect of siphoning off the new work. When television, which developed its own distinctive drama output, helped kill off the reps and public funding was reduced for regional theatres, the studios closed, leaving quite a few theatres able to offer only conventional productions reliant on the output of London and on a new star system based on media personalities.

The British musical came into its own, thanks largely to ANDREW LLOYD WEBBER and his collaborators. There had been earlier landmarks – SANDY WILSON'S *The Boy*

Friend and *Salad Days* by DOROTHY REYNOLDS and JULIAN SLADE in the 1950s had been followed by LIONEL BART's cockney exuberance, notably in the 1960 hit *Oliver!* Lloyd Webber's *Cats* opened in 1981 and became the world's longest-running musical. During that decade Lloyd Webber and producer CAMERON MACKINTOSH were able to emulate the touring shows at the start of the century and export popular musicals abroad, even coming to conquer Broadway, the home of the modern musical. A measure of the shift this represented is the fact that the BOUBLIL & SCHONBERG musical *Les Misérables* was launched outside the commercial sector in England at the RSC, and the NT offered successful productions of musicals such as *Guys and Dolls, Carousel, Oklahoma!* and *My Fair Lady* – something that would have been unthinkable to its early pioneers.

The major reason for this embrace of the commercial world by the publicly subsidized sector was the policy of the Conservative governments from 1979 to 1997, which saw theatre funding suffer severe cuts. The Labour government elected in 1997 continued in similar, though less draconian, vein. By 2000 the Arts Council of England had pronounced theatre an art form in crisis, and reported declining audiences, fewer performances and tours, less challenging plays and increasing deficits thanks to prolonged underfunding. However, an announcement in 2001 of the biggest ever rise in grants suggested this parlous situation might eventually be tackled. During her time, Margaret ('There's no such thing as society') Thatcher had given English philistinism new rein, debasing culture generally and marginalizing theatre in particular. While devolution in public funding was encouraged, she forced the Arts Council to abandon in practice (though not in rhetoric) its 'arm's length' principle and become a tool of government. Following the American model, but without access to either the wealth or the tradition, she pushed the arts into the arms of private sponsorship, claiming it would not replace core public funding, which, inevitably, it did. This was no fault of the business partners but entirely of government, which in 1995 introduced the National Lottery and further destabilized arts funding by making more money available to the arts through this channel than through the public funding agencies. A new wave of theatre building and restoration took place thanks to the Lottery, but money was not provided to support individuals or companies who could fill these buildings with quality performances, let alone run them. An insistence on the award of Lottery grants being dependent on securing matching funding from the private sector also meant increasing numbers of arts bodies competing for the same small pot of private capital. There was a massive cost in Lottery administration and in the amounts spent on feasibility studies for projects that were subsequently denied funding. Theatre, which had become increasingly professionalized since the Second World War, saw the rise of an arts bureaucracy, particularly in middle MANAGEMENT and in the numbers of accountants and consultants that had to be hired to satisfy funders that their money was being used efficiently and effectively.

The subsidized theatre had become the driving force of English drama, and the commercial theatre had come more and more to rely on the public sector for its productions. (AWARDS ceremonies were dominated by the subsidized sector, which also was the original source of the five plays by ALAN AYCKBOURN that played simultaneously in the West End in 1975, thereby breaking the record set by Maugham and Coward.) Yet public funding was insufficient to allow the public sector to remain vigorous on its own terms – it could not even sustain a true ensemble – and public and private began to merge within the world of the marketplace. Against the backdrop of a hostile government, the still craft-based theatre had to compete with the effects of the rise of new technologies, in particular the growth of home entertainment through video, cable and digital television, computer games and the INTERNET. There were also challenges from other art forms, particularly DANCE, and it was common for directors and designers to work in both OPERA and theatre. Experiment and the influence of EASTERN thinking changed notions of drama and playmaking, and broke down barriers between forms, as seen in the growth of PERFORMANCE ART and SITE-SPECIFIC work and productions by companies such as DV8 and Frantic Assembly.

As is often the way, the fringe – in the guise of groups such as CHEEK BY JOWL and THEATRE DE COMPLICITE, and the work of innovators like Julian Crouch and Phelim McDermott (who, with Lee Simpson, founded IMPROBABLE THEATRE) – revitalized the mainstream and showed that creativity could still surface in the new cultural landscape, however difficult it might be. The diversity of English theatre was remarkable; and there were other positive signs, such as the welcome increase in the participation of women, with more women playwrights, directors, designers and administrators making their mark. But the commanding heights were still occupied by men; the glass ceiling had yet to be removed, and was indeed reinforced by a male backlash of acceptable 'laddism' in the 1990s. The theatre also remained very white, unable to speak for, through or to its multicultural citizenry; despite the survival of groups like Talawa and TARA ARTS, the number of such companies dropped badly, and television rather than theatre became the magnet for performers.

With the increased cost of attending DRAMA SCHOOLS, training was in a parlous state, a bad situation made worse by the decline in regional theatre which had previously been the lifeblood of the theatre system. Companies like the Yorkshire-based NORTHERN BROADSIDES under actor Barrie Rutter fought back, and the WEST YORKSHIRE PLAYHOUSE, which opened in 1990, bucked this trend and showed under Jude Kelly what a resourceful regional theatre could achieve when imaginatively serving its own community.

In new writing the Royal Court offered a platform to another 'new wave' of playwrights, yet was caught in the 'event' culture and rarely sustained a developing relationship with a playwright. There was a vitality and emphasis on storytelling and language in plays from IRELAND, like those of SEBASTIAN BARRY and CONOR McPHERSON, while some writers from England, like SARAH KANE in *Blasted* (1995) and MARK RAVENHILL in *Shopping and Fucking* (1996), were sending out high-voltage shocks that reverberated through the mass media. A crop of knighthoods and damehoods for actors – TOM COURTENAY, JUDI DENCH, MICHAEL GAMBON, NIGEL HAWTHORNE, IAN HOLM, DEREK JACOBI, IAN MCKELLEN, DIANA RIGG, ANTONY SHER – and for writers – Alan Ayckbourn, David Hare, JOHN MORTIMER, Tom Stoppard – suggested that English theatre at the end of the century was acknowledged to be a cultural leader and was seen to be playing its part in the world of entertainment, even if the theatre itself was less certain of its own direction and social function. COLIN CHAMBERS

English, Rose   *see* EXPERIMENTAL THEATRE

English Shakespeare Company (ESC) A professional touring theatre company devoted to the production of Shakespeare's plays in a contemporary style. It was founded in 1986 by director Michael Bogdanov [Bogdin] (b. 15 Dec. 1938) and actor Michael Pennington (b. Cambridge, 7 June 1943). Bogdanov had made his reputation running the YOUNG VIC and at the ROYAL SHAKESPEARE COMPANY and the NATIONAL THEATRE. He was later in charge of the Deutsches Schauspielhaus in Hamburg. Pennington had established himself as a fine classical actor, mainly with the RSC (1964–6, 1974–81). Between 1985 and 1989 the ESC presented a cycle of seven of Shakespeare's historical plays under the title *The Wars of the Roses*, with Bogdanov directing Pennington in the key roles. They told its story in a book called *The English Shakespeare Company* (1990). The cycle, which was performed for

television as well as toured abroad, earned nearly 20 awards and nominations. In 1990 the ESC opened a very productive education department. The company was forced to close in 1994 through lack of funding but was relaunched in 1997 by Bogdanov, who added a stage version of the Anglo-Saxon poem *Beowulf* to the repertoire as the prelude to founding a children's touring theatre. Later that year he relocated the ESC to Newcastle.   ADRIANA HUNTER

English Stage Company The most influential post-Second World War English theatre company. It grew out of two parallel initiatives in the early 1950s. GEORGE DEVINE and a younger fellow Oxford graduate TONY RICHARDSON were unsuccessfully negotiating a tenancy at the ROYAL COURT in order to put the bite back into a moribund English theatre, which, however glamorous it might be, had become cut off from contemporary life; at the same time, playwright RONALD DUNCAN and a group of friends were forming what became the English Stage Company to present non-commercial plays, after discovering that their West Country festival, founded in 1953, was not the springboard they had sought. The Court's general manager, OSCAR LEWENSTEIN, brought the ESC together with Devine, who became artistic director in March 1955 with a brief to establish a real REPERTORY theatre with writers at its centre. Richardson was his associate and businessman Neville Blond the chairman. The ESC was to move into the KINGSWAY THEATRE, but renovation costs trebled. Alfred Esdaile, a former music hall performer who ran the theatre, offered ESC his other venue, the Royal Court in south-west London, the stage of which was redesigned for Devine by Margaret Harris of MOTLEY.

The company opened on 2 April 1956 with a revival of Angus Wilson's *The Mulberry Bush* and ARTHUR MILLER'S *The Crucible*. The first new play came next: *Look Back in Anger*, by an actor in the ESC, JOHN OSBORNE. It was the only one deemed worthy of production from more than 700 Devine had received in answer to an advertisement he had placed seeking new plays. The first season also included two plays by Duncan, a novel adaptation by Nigel Dennis, the British première of *The Good Woman of Setzuan* (BRECHT's was an important spirit at the Court) and Devine's revival of Wycherley's classic *The Country Wife*, which, ironically given the ESC's ambition, saved the company's immediate future by its transfer to the WEST END.

It was, however, the Osborne play that changed the ESC's longer-term fortunes; yet it was not a success straight away. It had to wait nearly six months for that, when the BBC televised an excerpt with only three weeks of its run left. It then transferred to the LYRIC Hammersmith (it had to wait another 12 years before being seen in the West End) and earned the ESC salvation money through performance and film rights. The ESC was to stage 11 more Osborne plays, seven of which transferred to the West End, including *The Entertainer* (1957), *Luther* (1961) and *Inadmissible Evidence* (1964), and he was to be a central figure in the company's film offshoot, Woodfall Productions, for which he wrote *Tom Jones* and won an Oscar.

The start of the second year was marked by the world première of *Fin de Partie* and *Acte Sans Paroles* by BECKETT, another influential figure at the ESC – 13 of his plays were to be presented at the Court, including three more world premières: *Krapp's Last Tape* (1958), *That Time* and *Footfalls* (both 1976). In these days, the ESC was quite French-oriented because of Devine's interest; GIRAUDOUX, IONESCO and SARTRE followed quickly before the company's identification with new English writing beyond Osborne began to be more fully cemented through Sunday night experiments without decor and productions in 1958, such as *The Sport of My Mad Mother* by ANN JELLICOE, *A Resounding Tinkle* by N. F. SIMPSON, *Chicken Soup with Barley* by ARNOLD WESKER (in a link-up with the Belgrade, Coventry) and *Live Like Pigs* by JOHN ARDEN. Those four highly regarded shows, however, did, respectively, 23 per cent, 41 per cent, 26 per cent and 25 per cent at the box office at a time when the ESC's ARTS COUNCIL grant (reduced by 28 per cent between 1956 and 1957) was only about 7–8 per cent of total box office takings.

Several important groups were established behind the scenes; one for supporters, one for schools (begun in 1960 and later transformed into the excellent Young People's Theatre Scheme, which supported the innovative Young Writers' Festival), one for actors (under ANTHONY PAGE and LINDSAY ANDERSON) and one for writers, which, under BILL GASKILL and KEITH JOHNSTONE, included Jellicoe, Wesker, EDWARD BOND, DAVID CREGAN and WOLE SOYINKA (an indication of early support for black writing that saw productions at the Court of *Flesh to a Tiger* by Barry Reckord and *Moon on a Rainbow Shawl* by ERROL JOHN in 1958).

The colliding talents within the ESC had established a challenging and at times rebellious identity with which to enter the 1960s: Devine's production of IBSEN'S *Rosmersholm*, WILLIS HALL's *The Long and the Short and the Tall*, Arden's *Serjeant Musgrave's Dance* and NOEL COWARD's adaptation of FEYDEAU, *Look After Lulu* – all 1959 – LAURENCE OLIVIER in *The Entertainer* and Ionesco's *Rhinoceros*, and JOHN DEXTER's productions of the Wesker Trilogy, designed by JOCELYN HER-

BERT and with JOAN PLOWRIGHT outstanding as Beatie in *Roots* – all 1960. These revealed the breadth and style of the ESC's new approach, which became known by the name of the theatre rather than the name of the company. The Court style embraced acting and design as well as writing; the look and sound of a production were crucial, and the ESC helped revolutionize the use of space and colour and the character of performance, with actors like ALAN BATES and KENNETH HAIGH, using their own regional accents, representing a break from prevailing metropolitan convention with a move towards greater naturalness.

ESC founder Ronald Duncan was increasingly at odds with the company, criticizing it as too left-wing, yet it was not the proletarian redoubt of contemporary legend. There was a lucidity, an economy and a poetry, rooted in realism, as well as a catholicity and an unfussy vigour, that defied such labels as 'kitchen sink' or 'ANGRY YOUNG MAN' (first coined by the Court's press officer George Fearon) which were used to try to pigeon-hole the ESC and were supported by only a limited amount of the repertoire and well-reported external activities such as the participation of Court personnel in the annual Campaign for Nuclear Disarmament Easter march.

Renovations were carried out in the early 1960s, a period dominated again by Osborne: *Luther* with ALBERT FINNEY, *Inadmissible Evidence* with NICOL WILLIAMSON, and *A Patriot for Me* (1965). This ran into serious trouble with the censor, was staged as a CLUB performance and began the battle that led to the abolition of stage CENSORSHIP. It also marked Devine's last performance. When he retired, not long before he died (January 1966), he had failed to create the permanent ensemble he desired but had established in its stead not a popular theatre but a theatre that would be part of the intellectual life of the country. It was a testament to Devine that the founding of the NATIONAL THEATRE in 1963 owed so much to the ESC, and that a core of Court actors, like COLIN BLAKELY, FRANK FINLAY, Plowright and ROBERT STEPHENS, and the directors Gaskill and Dexter, played such an important part in its early life.

Gaskill took over as artistic director (1965–9) and directed Bond's *Saved* in his first season (also as a club production, though that did not stop a police visit and summonses) and the following year the critically savaged but hugely successful (98.1 per cent box office) *Macbeth* with ALEC GUINNESS and Simone Signoret. Under Gaskill's stewardship and his time as co-artistic director (1969–72) with Anderson and Page, Bond became an international figure, DAVID STOREY, CHRISTOPHER HAMPTON and JOE ORTON were introduced to the Court, PETER GILL directed the influential D. H. LAWRENCE season (1968) and the Theatre Upstairs was opened (1969), which, among many achievements, launched HEATHCOTE WILLIAMS' *AC/DC* (1970) and the commercial hit *The Rocky Horror Show* (1973). It became a venue for ALTERNATIVE and FRINGE groups, like Portable Theatre, Freehold and the PIP SIMMONS THEATRE, and staged plays by a new wave of writers who were later to command the auditorium downstairs, such as HOWARD BARKER, HOWARD BRENTON, CARYL CHURCHILL, DAVID HARE, MUSTAPHA MATURA and TED WHITEHEAD. The ESC continued to attract leading performers from different traditions to appear in its new work (e.g. MAX WALL in a new version of *Ubu Roi*, 1966; Diana Dors in Donald Howarth's *Three Months Gone*, 1970; or JOHN GIELGUD in CHARLES WOOD's *Veterans*, 1972), and it maintained its international outlook too; the BREAD AND PUPPET THEATER and OPEN THEATER visited and important work from abroad was seen (e.g. by ATHOL FUGARD and SAM SHEPARD).

Oscar Lewenstein (1972–5), Robert Kidd and NICHOLAS WRIGHT (1975–7), Stuart Burge (1977–9) and Max STAFFORD–CLARK (1979–92) continued the ESC tradition, bringing in new writers (e.g. Andrea Dunbar, JIM CARTWRIGHT, SARAH DANIELS, ROBERT HOLMAN, BARRIE KEEFFE, DAVID LAN, TIMBERLAKE WERTENBAKER and NIGEL WILLIAMS) and re-presenting some, like MICHAEL HASTINGS, from earlier days. Most new playwrights, however, had their first plays staged at a fringe venue, and as the economic situation changed for the worse from the mid-1970s on, the approach begun under Devine of the right to fail was increasingly circumscribed. Despite the success of bold productions like *Bent* (1979) by MARTIN SHERMAN, Churchill's *Top Girls* (1982) and JONATHAN PRYCE's Hamlet (1980), directed by RICHARD EYRE, times remained hard and more co-productions were mounted (e.g. with the group JOINT STOCK, which was closely linked to the ESC), and a remunerative exchange with New York producer JOSEPH PAPP was entered into.

Critics felt the ESC was losing direction in the late 1980s, a view not helped by an act that stood in stark contrast to the company's anti-censorship legacy, the cancellation just before opening of Jim Allen's *Perdition* (1987), a play alleging Zionist complicity in the Holocaust. In a much-publicized campaign, Stafford-Clark stood for re-appointment as artistic director at the end of his second term, but the governing council chose STEPHEN DALDRY from the tiny GATE THEATRE to succeed him in 1993. Daldry brought with him a more entrepreneurial approach and put the company back in the public spotlight; the media took note of a new generation of writers – JEZ BUTTERWORTH, SARAH KANE,

MARTIN MCDONAGH, CONOR MCPHERSON, MARK RAVENHILL – and many awards were won. He also oversaw the temporary move to the West End at the Duke of York's and Ambassadors while the Sloane Square theatre was being renovated. His successor, Ian Rickson, was appointed in 1998 and led the company back to the Royal Court in 2000. COLIN CHAMBERS

Terry Browne, *Playwrights' Theatre: The English Stage Company at the Royal Court* (1975)

G. A. Doty and B. J. Harbin, eds, *Inside the Royal Court Theatre 1956–81: Artists Talk* (1990)

Richard Findlater, *At the Royal Court: 25 Years of the English Stage Company* (1981)

William Gaskill, *A Sense of Direction: Life at the Royal Court* (1988)

J. Osborne, *Almost a Gentleman* (1991)

Philip Roberts, *The Royal Court Theatre and the Modern Stage* (1999)

M. Tschudin, *A Writer's Theatre: George Devine and the ESC at the Royal Court 1956–65* (1972)

I. Wardle, *The Theatres of George Devine* (1978)

A. Wesker, *As Much as I Dare* (1994)

Enright, Nick [Nicholas Paul] (b. Newcastle, NSW, Australia, 22 Dec. 1950) Playwright, actor and director. As one of Australia's most versatile theatre practitioners, Enright has written over 20 plays, scripts for film (*Lorenzo's Oil*, 1993), radio and television, translations and adaptations, and collaborated with director and composer Terena Clarke on music-theatre works with witty, incisive lyrics and catchy, yet never banal, melodies. These works range from more traditional musicals (*The Venetian Twins*, 1979; *Summer Rain*, 1983) through cabaret-shows to the political pageant-revue *On the Wallaby* (1980), a portrait of an Adelaide family at the time of the Depression. Other plays include *Daylight Saving* (1990), *St James Infirmary* (1992), *Good Works* (1994) and *Cloudstreet* (1999), adapted with Justin Monjo from Tim Winton's novel. MICHAEL MORLEY

ENSA *see* ENTERTAINMENTS NATIONAL SERVICE ASSOCIATION

ensemble A term that came to the fore in the twentieth century as an ideal for many of its pioneers, though its use varies; it is applied both loosely, to denote a group with shared aims formed around an outstanding figure, and more specifically, to describe a democratically organized company that creates and administers itself collectively and collaboratively. The common thread is that, instead of coming together at random for a single production, people work together over a period of time, developing an identifiable approach that is shaped by generally agreed objectives. The MEININGEN COMPANY at the end of the nineteenth century spread the idea, which was most famously taken up by the MOSCOW ART THEATRE and later by the BERLINER ENSEMBLE. The inspiration is often a mix of the political and the aesthetic, and covers a very wide range of theatrical practice from the likes of the GROUP THEATRE, THEATRE WORKSHOP and 7:84 to THEATRE DU SOLEIL or TEATRO CAMPESINO. Ensembles have proved hard to sustain and seem to require constant regeneration and the right ideological, economic and artistic circumstances.   CHARLES LONDON

See also ALTERNATIVE THEATRE; COLLECTIVE; COMMUNITY THEATRE; POLITICAL THEATRE; TOTAL THEATRE.

Ensler, Eve   see SOLO SHOWS

Enters, Angna   (b. New York, 28 April 1907; d. New York, 28 Feb. 1989)   Dancer, MIME artist and writer. Enters made her debut as a professional dancer in New York in 1924 and evolved a unique style of one-woman performance based on dance–mime sketches of her own devising, with costumes and sets also designed by her. Enters devised more than 300 of these mime vignettes, with which she successfully toured the United States between 1928 and 1960. Her repertoire of haunting sketches include The Queen of Heaven, Pavana and Pierrot, but she is probably best known for Moyen Age, a mime sequence she devised in 1926 based upon a live incarnation of a medieval stone carving of the Virgin. Enters was also an accomplished artist; she exhibited in her own right first in 1933 and subsequently in several museums and galleries, including the Metropolitan Museum of Art in New York. Her skills as a screenwriter were exploited by Hollywood in the 1940s and she later wrote three volumes of autobiography, as well as a novel, a play and a study of her own work, On Mime (1966).   HELEN RAPPAPORT

See also SOLO SHOW.

Entertainments National Service Association
ENSA was founded in 1938 and funded by the Treasury to entertain British and allied armed forces and war workers at home and abroad. Under BASIL DEAN, based at the THEATRE ROYAL, DRURY LANE, ENSA worked with the NAAFI (Navy, Army and Air Force Institute) to provide a wide range of entertainment, from Shakespeare to symphony orchestras, from mobile cinemas to popular singers. It employed thousands of performers on National Service pay (many of whom were or became prominent theatre personalities) and by the end of the war had staged over two and a half million performances. Its characteristic broad English humour and style of show was parodied by ex-ENSA member PETER

NICHOLS in Privates on Parade (1977). ENSA, along with its civilian counterpart CEMA, the BBC and initiatives such as the Army Bureau of Current Affairs Play Unit, focused a public appetite for theatre and the arts that led to the establishment of state cultural funding through the ARTS COUNCIL, though with a narrower approach than ENSA.   COLIN CHAMBERS

Basil Dean, The Theatre at War (1955)
R. Fawkes, Fighting for a Laugh: Entertaining the British and American Armed Forces, 1939–45 (1978)

Enthoven [Romaine], [Augusta] Gabrielle [Eden]   (b. London, 12 Jan. 1868; d. London, 18 Aug. 1950)   Theatre historian. Enthoven was a passionate chronicler and historian as well as a talented amateur actress, a playwright and a translator (The Honeysuckle, New York, 1921, was her adaptation of D'ANNUNZIO's Le Chèvrefeuille, 1913). She collected material about the theatre in eighteenth- and nineteenth-century England: texts, reviews, engravings, letters, prints, models and books. In 1924 she presented the formidable collection to the Victoria and Albert Museum; until her death she administered the collection, which bears her name and continues to expand in the THEATRE MUSEUM. In 1948 she became the first president of the Society for Theatre Research, under whose initiative the Theatre Museum came into being in 1974.
ADRIANA HUNTER

environmental theatre   Although the type of performance represented by the term can be found throughout theatre history, the specific term gained wide currency during the late 1960s and 1970s, primarily due to the practice and theoretical writings of the American theorist/director Richard Schechner. He began his 'environmental' work with a production of IONESCO's Victims of Duty in New Orleans in 1967. The following year he published in The Drama Review 'Six Axioms for Environmental Theatre' and acquired for his PERFORMANCE GROUP the Performing Garage in New York. This became a centre for environmental theatre, the best-known example being Dionysius in 69 (1969). Its designer, Jerry Rojo, also became closely associated during the next decade with environmental theatre.

Most of Rojo's and Schechner's projects were closely related to the 'open space' or 'black box' EXPERIMENTAL THEATRES popular in the 1960s, but with a somewhat different emphasis. 'Open space' theatres, converted from non-theatre spaces, or specifically built for this purpose, are small, calculatedly neutral and flexible performance spaces which can vary seating arrangements for each production. The emphasis in such theatres is on adaptability, while environmental theatres, similarly small and flexible, stress the interpenetration of acting and audience space and the uniqueness of each spectator's view of the work. As Rojo has said, the production is experienced 'from within'.

Although the mixing of actor and audience space has a long tradition in folk performance, it became significant in modern experimental theatre from the early years of the twentieth century, especially as a revolt against proscenium staging. APPIA, FUCHS and MEYERHOLD pursued such activity, followed by COPEAU and SAINT-DENIS in France, REINHARDT and PISCATOR in Germany, and OHKLOPKOV in Russia. Although this European experimental tradition had essentially died out by the 1940s, it was powerfully revived during the 1960s in the enormously influential environmental stagings of GROTOWSKI.

In America and Western Europe, modern environmental theatre was also powerfully influenced by the experiments during the 1950s of artists like CAGE and Allan Kaprow, who sought to integrate audiences and indeterminacy into art works in HAPPENINGS and environmental art; indeed, Schechner took the term 'environmental theatre' from Kaprow. Certain happenings or environments were created within art galleries, just as 'open space' stagings were created within a neutral theatrical space, but others were created in 'found spaces', which could add their own significance to the experience. From such work has developed another approach to environmental theatre, an approach more recently called SITE-SPECIFIC THEATRE. Brooks McNamara, a historian of popular culture and a founding member (in 1971) of the American organization Environmental Theater Associates, has noted that non-theatrical spaces have been so used throughout history, particularly for folk and popular performances, which traditionally favour such popular gathering places as the street, the market or the public square. The twentieth century has, however, been more consciously experimental in pursuing theatrical activity in non-theatrical spaces. In the 1880s the British Pastoral Players presented Renaissance dramas in actual woodlands, and in 1912 Interlaken in Switzerland began regularly offering a William Tell spectacle in natural surroundings, early examples of a widespread interest in OPEN-AIR THEATRE during the twentieth century. EVREINOV re-created the 1917 storming of the Winter Palace upon the actual site of that event. Reinhardt offered influential productions of *Everyman* on the steps of the Salzburg Cathedral and *The Merchant of Venice* in an actual Venetian square. More recently, during the 1960s, when American experimental companies had a great international impact, many of these were involved with some form of environmental work, among them the LIVING THEATER, the BREAD AND PUPPET THEATER, the OPEN THEATER and the Manhattan Project. Such interest was reinforced by politically active theatre groups in the late 1960s, which sought new publics by performing in streets and factories, and by the experiments of such contemporary choreographers as Ann Halprin, TRISHA BROWN and MEREDITH MONK, who were interested both in moving closer to theatre and in performing in new spaces. A series of works in the late 1960s and early 1970s marked a kind of peak of environmental theatre activity: RONCONI's *Orlando Furioso* (1969), the THÉÂTRE DE SOLEIL's *1789* (1970), BROOK's *Orghast* (1971) and ROBERT WILSON's *Ka Mountain* (1972).

The 1980s saw fewer experimental companies and major directors emphasizing environmental theatre, but the approach continued to provide an important element of international production. Ronconi, ARMAND GATTI and Grotowski's disciple EUGENIO BARBA mounted major environmental productions, and in New York Ann Hamburger, a performing artist and environmental sculptor, founded in 1985 En Garde Arts, an organization devoted to developing site-specific theatre. One of the most discussed AVANT-GARDE productions of the early 1990s in New York, Reza Abdoh's *The Law of Remains*, used an environmental approach. The 1980s also saw environmental theatre enter the theatrical mainstream, most notably with John Krizanc's *Tamara*, a production in several cities presumably set in the home of GABRIELE D'ANNUNZIO, in which audience members could follow individual actors from room to room. This was followed in New York by a series of other popular environmental offerings: *Song of Singapore*, in which the audience attends a Southeast Asian nightclub on the eve of the Second World War, and *Tony 'n' Tina's Wedding* and *Bennie's Bar Mitzvah*, in which they become participating guests in these theatricalized celebrations. Audiences can watch real murders re-created or pay to be placed under surveillance, kidnapped and videoed, with the results transmitted to a website. Companies perform on boats, on the underground or even in public lavatories, and can be hired to perform in your own home. MARVIN CARLSON

See also INTERNET; PERFORMANCE ART.

Arnold Aronson, *The History and Theory of Environmental Scenography* (1981)
Brooks McNamara, Jerry Rojo and Richard Schechner, *Theatres, Spaces, Environments* (1975)
Richard Schechner, *Environmental Theater* (1973)

Enzensberger, Hans Magnus (b. Kaufbeuren, 11 Nov. 1929) Poet, playwright, translator, editor and social critic, a leader in seeking a political role for the contemporary author, especially through his periodical *Kursbuch* (1965–75). As an attack on theatricality, his DOCUMENTARY plays are drawn directly from their sources, such as newspapers or legal transcripts, e.g. *Das Verhör von Habana* (*The Havana Inquiry*, 1970), a dramatization based on the Bay of Pigs hearings.

MARVIN CARLSON

epic theatre In the *Poetics* ARISTOTLE drew a distinction between TRAGEDY and epic, though conceding that they had much in common. The separateness of the two genres has been acknowledged down the centuries. Linking them is therefore something of a paradox. This originated after the First World War with German radical theatre practitioners who felt that the linear plot and focus on the individual characteristic of Aristotelian dramaturgy were inadequate tools for representing the clash of vast social forces. They also rejected naturalism as providing too limited an angle of vision for revolutionary times.

The term 'epic theatre' was coined by the left-wing director ERWIN PISCATOR in the early 1920s. For him, the chief connotation of epic was that of scale, of social dimension. In his work in Berlin – at the Proletarisches Theater, the VOLKSBÜHNE and particularly in his own house, the Theater am Nollendorfplatz (1927–9) – he sought, often with less than ideal texts, to make the stage respond to the political battles of the moment. He included a good deal of DOCUMENTARY and indeed didactic material in his shows. In order to demonstrate the connection between widely separated events or to provide a historical context for the stage action, he made a bold use of theatrical machinery: lifts, treadmills, multiple stages, even a huge globe that opened up to reveal acting areas inside. In particular, Piscator pioneered the projection of slides and films as an integral part of a stage performance. What mattered, however, was not so much the technical ingenuity of these devices as the social vision they brought to his productions. His commitment to factual drama resurfaced in the final period of his life, when he ran the Freie Volksbühne in West Berlin (1962–6); here he premièred documentary plays by HOCHHUTH, KIPPHARDT and WEISS.

BRECHT – unlike Piscator not only a director but also, indeed primarily, a playwright and a theorist – appropriated the term 'epic theatre' in the mid-1920s. For him, the chief connotation of epic was that of a narrative mode. (In his definitions he drew on and modified from a Marxist perspective the work of Goethe and Schiller, who had collaborated in the 1790s on reformulating Aristotle's concepts of drama and epic for the modern world.) Brecht's plays were fictional rather than documentary; they were intended to be models (in the laboratory sense) of human interaction. Their form was non-Aristotelian, i.e. open and structurally closer to Elizabethan drama than to the well-made plays of nineteenth-century bourgeois theatre. Since he wanted his audience to react rationally rather than emotionally, he built his plays on a non-linear storyline, with each scene standing on its own, which often avoided a climax; thus the spectators were denied a catharsis. Brecht introduced the so-called ALIENATION effect and would employ a number of distancing devices, some borrowed from oriental theatre, such as direct address to the audience; stylized speech, including rhyming, free and blank verse; the insertion of songs in sharp contrast to the surrounding dialogue; a narrator or a chorus; miming and masks. He would expose stage lighting and illuminate the action with bright, untinted light, openly show the source of (live or recorded) music, identify scenes by means of dropped-in or projected captions and use half-tabs (curtains) that only partially concealed scene changes, thus reminding the audience that they were in a theatre.

Towards the end of his life Brecht had come to doubt whether epic theatre was a really useful description; it could be applied too easily to other kinds of non-Aristotelian plays, such as those by CLAUDEL and THORNTON WILDER, which had no bearing on social conflict and the class struggle. He was tempted to substitute the term 'dialectical theatre' but never found time to evolve a suitable theory.

Epic theatre represents at the same time thematic and technical innovations and a reversion to some pre-naturalist styles of theatre. If it did not bring about the total revolution in the theatre (and elsewhere) that its advocates polemically claimed it would, it did at any rate make a major impact on twentieth-century drama and staging practice. GEORGE BRANDT

See also DRAMATIC THEORY; MODERNISM.

Bertolt Brecht, *The Messingkauf Dialogues*, trans. John Willett (1965)
C. D. Innes, *Erwin Piscator's Political Theatre: The Development of Modern German Drama* (1972)
Janelle Reinelt, *After Brecht: British Epic Theatre* (1994)
John Willett, *Brecht on Theatre* (1964)
——, *The Theatre of Erwin Piscator: Half a Century of Politics in the Theatre* (1978)

Epidauros Surviving open-air Hellenistic theatre in Greece, built *c.*340 BC. It has excellent natural accoustics and a circular acting area fronting a narrow raised stage with tiered seating for 15,000. The Greek National Theatre stages an annual summer festival there, and in 1982 the NATIONAL THEATRE of Great Britain performed its acclaimed masked version of Aeschylus' *The Oresteia*.   MARIE PETCHELL

See also ANCIENT GREEK DRAMA IN THE TWENTIETH CENTURY.

Equity   *see* UNIONS

Equity Players   *see* ACTORS' THEATER

Erdman, Nikolai [Robertovich]   (b. Moscow, 16 Nov. 1902; d. Moscow, 10 Aug. 1970) Playwright. Beginning as a REVUE sketch writer, his first full-length play, *Mandat* (*The Mandate*, 1925), directed by MEYERHOLD, was an enormous success, but his next, *Samoubytsa* (*The Suicide*, 1928), was banned. His career was virtually over. These two plays combine a kaleidoscope of virtuoso dramatic effects with quickfire punning dialogue to create disturbing political farce. Erdman transforms the depressing selfishness of everyone (the 'little man' as much as the powerful) by the energy of the action into a life-enhancing celebration of humanity. *The Suicide*, which first appeared outside the Soviet Union in 1969, became popular in Erdman's homeland after its first performance in Moscow in 1982.
ROBERT LEACH

eroticism in the theatre   Some intrinsic link between theatre and sexuality has often been proposed. One might look at the *déclassée* actresses of SCHNITZLER's Vienna with their dizzying whirl of class and sexual transgression, the late-nineteenth-century London theatres notorious for the prostitutes that worked their foyers and bars, and even the legendary, though partly apocryphal, domination of theatre by gay men. Another formulation is that the theatre is founded on erotic contracts between writer, performer, director and spectator. Certainly, one could cite STRINDBERG shaking with jealous rage as he watched his wife, Siri von Essen, play Miss Julie, or WEDEKIND playing Jack the Ripper to his wife Tilly Newes's Lulu, or TENNESSEE WILLIAMS declaring that he always desired one of his characters. But these approaches presuppose fixed categories both of theatre and of the erotic. In fact, in the modern period both have undergone fundamental change. The voyeurism that characterizes the cinema is more unstable when the images can look back and where the auditorium perches uneasily on a boundary between private and public. This shifting terrain has proved a site for many contesting readings of desire, sexuality and the body.

The nineteenth century, according to the philosopher Michel Foucault, was a time not of repression but rather of an incitement to speak of sex. It became established as the ultimate key to ourselves, the explanatory factor *par excellence*. It is perhaps for this reason that naturalism, with its gung-ho scientism, took such meticulous pains to reveal the truth of sex to us: venereal disease (IBSEN's *Ghosts*, 1882; BRIEUX's *Damaged Goods*, 1902), prostitution (PINERO's *The Second Mrs Tanqueray*, 1893; SHAW'S *Mrs Warren's Profession*, 1902), adultery (ZOLA's *Thérèse Raquin*, 1873), and so on. In the general project of lifting the lid on bourgeois morality, sex ranked high in the list of truths requiring urgent disclosure. However, these plays are not themselves erotic; the coolness of Ibsen's rhetoric doused any ardour that might have been inflamed by the mention of free love, and it fell to the writers and performers of high MODERNISM to make sex more explicit. From MAETERLINCK's teasing *Monna Vanna* (1902), through the provocative explicitness of Wedekind's *Spring Awakening* (1906) and Lulu plays (1898, 1905), to the outrages of DADA and SURREALISM, sexuality had become something that needed to be staged, examined, accounted for. Sex, for the European AVANT-GARDE, was a serious business. Schnitzler's fastidious inventories of sexual permutation in *Anatol* (1910) and *La Ronde* (1912) are like parodies of sexology's taxonomies of erotic variation, just as modernism's declared aims echoed nothing so much as the anatomy lectures of the nineteenth century, lectures largely attended for only quasi-medical reasons.

The less high-minded search for sexual arousal was sustained in different forms for popular audiences. The MUSIC HALL traded on the roguish sexual presence of stars like MARIE LLOYD, and exotic dance routines, Salome's being ever popular. The kind of eroticism that developed after the First World War in secret Berlin sex theatres, or that Paul Derval developed in the FOLIES-BERGÈRE, was impossible in Britain, where the LORD CHAMBERLAIN forbade women to move, even when semi-naked. British erotic REVUES took the form of motionless nude women (male nudes came later) in a number of exotic, historical or mythical settings ('Diana the Huntress', 'Desert Scene', and the like), titled, rather archly, Living Statuary or *poses plastiques*. The Windmill Theatre, for example, which ran continuously from 1931 to 1964, staged 341 'Revudevilles', which combined clothed dance routines (often teasing affairs with parasols and fans), with nude TABLEAUX. The critic Philip Hope-Wallace fondly recalls 'the wartime days when the stately Phyllis Dixey would expose her rigidly motionless hindquarters for ten seconds at a time in the light of a Bengal flare'. Precise negotiations, fractional adjustments in posture, fastidious notes on fabric, shape and use of costume, and meticulous directions on movement and expression served to constitute a docile female body, delivered neatly up to the male gaze. The critic John Elsom has argued that when these living statues were finally permitted movement a great liberation for the women performers was entailed. But in the America of the 1910s, the popular BURLESQUES and 'leg-shows' of the nineteenth century were turning into striptease, a French creation reputedly introduced to the United States by accident when a strap on Beatrice Vivian's dress broke. Other versions trace its origins to a trapeze artist, Charmian, losing her tights mid-performance; but, as a dance, it developed from the 'cootch' via Hinda Wassu and her 'shimmy' through to SALLY RAND with her flashing fans. This type of act, while mobile, had equally stringent rules, passing through the initial 'parade', then the 'grinds' and 'bumps', before the fleeting 'flash' (a routine which GYPSY ROSE LEE made famous). There seems little suggestion that these performers had any more control than the British *poseuses*. In any case, the gradual incorporation of these techniques into mainstream theatre and increasing legal controls led to a falling off in popularity and an outright ban in 1942.

While northern Europe in the 1950s and 1960s saw striptease become the presentation of live sex with audience participation, British censorship was making even the nude *tableaux* difficult to maintain. The touring shows of the 1920s now found that each county council had different rules about what was permissible on stage. In 1953 the London County Council banned strip shows from the music hall altogether. These restrictions saw a series of private strip clubs open in London: first the Irving in 1956, followed by the Raymond Revuebar and Casino de Paris in 1958. Entrepreneur Paul Raymond insisted that the performances in these hand-me-down Folies-Bergère were erotic rather than pornographic, a notoriously hazy distinction but one which seemed to involve the assertion of some measure of 'taste' and 'artistry'.

In the 1950s and 1960s a number of gay playwrights used eroticism in their plays to break up the holy trinity of body, gender and desire. Notable examples are GENET's blend of homoeroticism and rivalry in *Deathwatch* (1949), and his brothel-bound political satire *The Balcony* (1957), while ORTON, in plays like *Entertaining Mr Sloane* (1964), found audiences highly responsive to his polymorphous subversion of the traditionally sexless British farce: 'much more fucking,' he remarked, 'and they'll be screaming hysterics in next to no time.'

In taking the silenced sexuality to the private club, striptease was following in the footsteps of the THEATRE CLUBS established to perform works refused a licence by the Lord Chamberlain. Both movements built up a head of steam that led to the lifting of theatre-specific CENSORSHIP in Britain in 1968. It was now that erotic theatre began in earnest. *Hair* opened in London's West End the day after censorship was abolished. Although this American musical dealt with a number of contemporary concerns, it attracted particular attention for the scene where, in semi-darkness, the cast disrobe. This tentative work was trounced by a FRINGE production of John Herbert's *Fortune and Men's Eyes*, which had opened earlier in the year but later transferred, complete with its full male nudity. The indefatigable Paul Raymond submitted *Pyjama Tops* (1972), featuring a real swimming pool on stage, cunningly designed to motivate the nudity of the three women actors. But it was the liberatory pretension of *Hair* that inspired the subsequent series of ever more revealing productions: there was TYNAN's *Oh! Calcutta!* (1968), billed as an 'evening of civilized erotic stimulation' with its legendary nude *pas de deux* opening the second half; in the same year an actress in TERRENCE MCNALLY's *Sweet Eros* appeared nude throughout. Tom Eyen's OFF-BROADWAY *The Dirtiest Show in Town* (1970), billed as 'a documentary of the destructive effects of air, water and mind pollution in New York City', seemed more clearly designed to display, in the words of playwright HUGH LEONARD, 'as much pubic hair as would upholster a small settee'. The ostensible aim of these shows was a kind of primal release, a profound transgression of puritanical mores. But liberation was still utterly regimented, Eyen observing, 'the conception is very military, very disciplined in form and direction, very physical'; and while 1974's *Let My People Come* featured an explicit representation of lesbian sex, in the two gay scenes the men kept their clothes on, and the bacchanal only extended to a hand on the shoulder.

There was a more serious-minded wave of American work in the 1960s and 1970s. During shows like the PERFORMANCE GROUP's *Dionysus in 69* (1968) or LIVING THEATER's *Paradise Now* (1968), the cast would undress at a crucial moment, inviting the audience to join them, moments informally known as 'group gropes'. The Living Theater played on the ambiguous location of performance, eventually leading the audience into the street in an attempt to subvert the distinction between private and public. The gay Andy Warhol worked against this tradition, and his *Pork* featured auto-eroticism of such an uncommitted sort that the performance became ultimately anti-erotic.

While a series of shows like *The Bed Before Yesterday* (1975), *Funny Peculiar* (1973) and *A Bedful of Foreigners* followed the seaside postcard tradition of *Pyjama Tops* in the early 1970s, the British avant-garde was placing sex at the centre of their plays; Portable Theatre's multi-authored *Lay-By* (1971) and Chris Wilkinson's *I Was Hitler's Maid* (1971) and *Plays for Rubber Go-Go Girls* (1972) explicitly presented pornography and sexual violence, and GRIFFITHS's *Apricots* (1971) features a position that he would doubtless call strategic penetration. But their view of sex was far more pessimistic. The PIP SIMMONS GROUP used nudity to evoke the humiliation and violence of the concentration camps in *An Die Musik* (1975), and BRENTON's characters in the 1970s regularly seem to be as disgusted as they are excited by their desires. In the mainstream theatre, nudity moved beyond being a sign of truthful representation (e.g. DAVID STOREY's *The Changing Room*, 1971) and ceased to be remarkable (e.g. in JOHN GUARE's *Six Degrees of Separation*, 1990, or DAVID HARE's *The Judas Kiss*, 1998). Right-wing activists did not accept this, however, as the attempt at a private prosecution of Brenton's *The Romans in Britain* (1980) and a revival of censorship in the United States in the 1990s showed.

What links the three main forms of sexual theatre is a veneration of the body as the site of sexuality, and an urge to display this body as a means of displaying the truth of sex. A number of changes have seen a shift away from this notion. The first is that, once the body was revealed, scrutinized, made to perform, it soon became clear that enlightenment was not instant. The body does not wear its secrets on its skin. The body was manifestly not an answer, just another question. Second, the women's and gay liberation movements discovered that the body was by no means neutral; it was not a 'privileged pre-social' space, but entirely implicated in politics. It was subjected, controlled, disciplined. Third, there was a general drift away from the Freudian–Marxist synthesis which had tried to claim that sexual liberation was a route to pure freedom. The complexities of a woman's position, e.g. in her right to refuse sex, were increasingly being compromised, and in certain performances of *Dionysus in 69* and *The Dirtiest Show* the barriers between consent and rape became dangerously blurred.

Noticeable in the late 1970s was a move away from this affirmative view of the body to new forms of theatre that examined the limits of the body. The use of the body in dance or LIVE ART, e.g. by Michael Clark's group, or DV8, or the work of KAREN FINLEY, would more often be to confront audiences with the banality and materiality of the body than to affirm it as possessing some spiritual quality. The self-mutilations that characterized some of those performances may be seen as an extension of this project. From a different angle, the eroticism of gay performances like 1991's *Copper's Bottom* or Neil Bartlett's *A Vision of Love* used nakedness and fantasy, while refusing to ascribe metaphysical or moral meaning to these displays. Whereas the political performances of the late 1960s, like Michael McClure's *The Beard* (1967), in which Billy the Kid performs cunnilingus on Jean Harlow, or Lennox Raphael's *Ché* (1969), in which a naked Uncle Sam indulges in buggery and fellatio, had seen sex as a secret which could explain social phenomena (and explained societies in terms of repression), the 1980s increasingly saw sex as effect rather than cause. The explicit sexual scenes in WINSOME PINNOCK's *Talking in Tongues* (1991) or MARTIN CRIMP's *The Treatment* (1993) carried no liberationist pretensions, siting sex within complex grids of power and interpretation.

In the late 1980s, the AIDS health crisis promoted an exploration of alternative forms of sexual pleasure and voyeurism began to swing back into fashion. For the first time, troupes of male strippers, like the Chippendales, Adonis, Dream Boys and Megahunks, offered a teasing spectacle of male muscle for strictly all-female audiences. Although the object of frequent derision, criticized for being facile, excessive and witless – as if female striptease had been an infinitely sophisticated spectacle – the significance of these events was a newfound confidence in the heterosexual world with eroticizing the male body.   DAN REBELLATO

John Elsom, *Erotic Theatre* (1973)
Lucinda Jarrett, *Stripping in Time: A History of Erotic Dancing* (1997)
J. W. McCullogh, *Living Pictures on the New York Stage* (1983)

Erté (pseud. for Romain de Tirtoff) (b. St Petersburg, 23 Nov. 1892; d. Paris, 21 April 1990) Illustrator and designer, whose pseudonym was taken from the French pronunciation of the initial letters of his forename and surname. In 1913 he created his first costumes for a production of *Le Minaret* featuring Mata Hari, and his distinctive Art Deco style, subsequently much copied, was soon to establish him as the doyen of French REVUE design. Over the next 35 years Erté produced elaborate costumes and sets for ballet, opera and musical revues. Particularly notable is his work for the FOLIES-BERGÈRE (1919–30) and the costumes he designed for BROADWAY shows like George White's *Scandals* (1922) and the legendary ZIEGFELD's *Follies* (1923).   HELEN RAPPAPORT

See also FASHION.

C. Spencer, *Erté* (1986)

Ervine, St John [John Greer Ervine] (b. Belfast, 28 Dec. 1883; d. Iping, Sussex, 24 Jan. 1971) Playwright, novelist and critic. On the strength of his plays he was made manager of the ABBEY THEATRE, Dublin, in 1915 before turning exclusively to writing. His acutely observed social comedies of Ulster life – *Mixed Marriage* (1911), *The Magnanimous Lover* (1912), *John Ferguson* (1915, described by LENNOX ROBINSON as 'his masterpiece'), *Boyd's Shop* (1935, his most frequently revived play) and *Friends and Relations* (1941) – were first produced at the Abbey. Success in the UK was aided by his choice of leading ladies: *Jane Clegg* (1913, with SYBIL THORNDIKE), *The First Mrs Frazer* (1929, with MARIE TEMPEST), and *Robert's Wife* (1937, with EDITH EVANS). His later plays are *Private Enterprise* (1947), *My Brother Tom* (1952) and *Esperanza* (1957).
CHRISTOPHER FITZ-SIMON

escapology A branch of MAGIC in which the performer escapes from apparently secure restraints. These might consist of handcuffs, straitjackets, boxes, safes, milkchurns or buried coffins. The escape may take place in a theatre as part of a conventional magic show, or outdoors, or at some significant place, such as a police cell. While some escapes are achieved by physical dexterity, and are impressive as a display of athleticism, others are presented primarily as mysterious magic tricks. In this category must be included the 'substitution trunk', in which the magician and his or her assistant seem to change places instantaneously, after one of them has been locked in a large box. The man whose name is inextricably linked with escapology is HARRY HOUDINI, who performed a series of daring escapes which captured the public imagination in Europe and America at the beginning of the twentieth century. Although he virtually invented escapology as a separate performance category, Houdini did not describe himself as an escapologist, and never used the word on his publicity material. The performer who popularized the term 'escapology' in the 1930s was the Australian Leo Murray Carrington Walters, who styled himself 'Murray the Escapologist'. Murray's most spectacular and dangerous feat was an escape from a straitjacket while locked in a cage full of apparently ferocious lions. Others who have specialized in this branch of magic have included David Deval in Britain, and the Canadian James Randi in the United States. Houdini's original inspiration of escaping from a regulation straitjacket was taken further by Alan Alan and Shahid Malik. These two, and others, have made a feature of performing the escape while hanging upside down on a rope suspended from a crane, the rope having previously been set alight. IAN SAVILLE

Milbourne Christopher, *Houdini: The Untold Story* (1969)
——, *Magic: A Picture History* (1990)
Edwin A. Dawes and Arthur Setterington, *Making Magic* (1986)

Esmond, [Jack] Henry V[ernon] (b. Hampton Court, Surrey, 30 Nov. 1869; d. Paris, 17 April 1922) Actor–manager and playwright who was an important contributor to the huge success of PINERO's *The Second Mrs Tanqueray* (1893) in his role as Cayley Drummle, and similarly in his role as Little Billee in the first production of du Maurier's *Trilby* (1895). His own plays, in which he often toured with his wife Eva Moore (1870–1955, a vice-president of the ACTRESSES' FRANCHISE LEAGUE) and which number roughly 30, did not last, but his sentimental comdedies (e.g. *Elija Comes to Stay*, 1913) had considerable contemporary success.
IAN CLARKE

Espert [I Romero], Núria (b. Barcelona, Spain, 11 June 1935) Actress, director and unofficial global Spanish cultural ambassador. She formed her own company in 1959 in order to stage classical Spanish theatre as well as contemporary international drama and has enjoyed collaboration with directors such as Jorge Lavelli and VICTOR GARCIA, with whom she worked on memorable productions of such plays as *The Maids* (1969), *Yerma* (1971) and *Divinis Palabras* (1975). She has been acclaimed for her interpretations of roles ranging from Medea and Anna Christie to Gigi and Salome. From 1979 to 1981 she served as director of the Spanish National Drama Centre in Madrid. In 1986 she made her directorial debut in London, at the LYRIC Theatre, with LORCA's *The House of Bernarda Alba*, which paved the way for Espert to develop an international career as a stage director and allowed her to enjoy a career split between acting and directing, between theatre and opera (e.g. *Carmen*, 1991, seen in London, Barcelona and Seville), and between Spain and England. Espert continued her stage appearances with the one-woman monologue, *Make-up*, by Hisashi Inoue, which she has presented in major cities around the world. ELLEN LAMPERT-GRÉAUX

Esslin, Martin [Julius Pereszlenyi] (b. Budapest, Hungary, 8 June 1918) Theatre critic and educator. His career began with BBC Radio in 1940, and he served as head of the RADIO DRAMA department from 1963 to 1976, championing new and continental plays. Recognized internationally as a professor of theatre (at Florida State University and Stanford University, California), Esslin has been a member as well as chairman of the ARTS COUNCIL OF GREAT BRITAIN's drama panel. An accomplished author, he has written numerous scholarly books on contemporary theatre, including *Brecht: A Choice of Evils* (1959), *The Theatre of the Absurd* (1962, helping to coin the phrase), and *Artaud* (1976).   ELLEN LAMPERT-GRÉAUX

Esson, [Thomas] Louis [Buvelot] (b. Leith, Scotland, 10 Aug. 1878; d. Sydney, 27 Nov. 1943) Playwright. In Australia, where he had moved with his family in 1881, he struggled to define and set popular standards. With the support of his wife, Dr Hilda Bull, and a group of literary friends and mostly amateur actors, he founded the PIONEER PLAYERS (1922) in Melbourne. He wrote 13 plays between 1908 and 1928, and published astringent articles on theatre, literature, national culture and social institutions for magazines at home and abroad.

Esson's conversion to the cause of an Australian national theatre came from a meeting with W. B. YEATS in 1905. His short play *The Drover* (1920) has been compared favourably with SYNGE's *Riders to the Sea*. *The Woman Tamer* (1910) is an equivalent, but comic, achievement; but the longer plays, *The Time is Not Yet Ripe* (1912), *Mother and Son* (1923), *The Bride of Gospel Place* (1926) and *The Southern Cross* (1946), struggle to find form and sustain character. They address Australia's political conservatism and the subordination of revolutionary spirit, the survival struggles of petty criminals, the tension between loyalty to the land and family, and the yearning for freedom of artistic expression and physical passion. Esson's influence far exceeds his dramatic output and stands in posthumous juxtaposition to the disillusionment of his later years when he abandoned theatre.

Other plays include *Dead Timber* (1911), *The Sacred Place* (1912) and *The Battler* (1922).   GUS WORBY

H. Anderson et al., *Ballades of Old Bohemia: An Anthology of Louis Esson* (1980)

P. Fitzpatrick, *Pioneer Players: The Lives of Louis and Hilda Esson* (1995)

N. Krauth, *Muse of Fire* (1985)

Vance Palmer, *Louis Esson and the Australian Theatre* (1948)

Estonia   *see* SOVIET UNION

Etchells, Tim   *see* FORCED ENTERTAINMENT

Ethiopia   The country consists of up to 70 different nationalities, such as Tigreans, Gurageans, Eritreans (who have won independence, though still with some dispute), Oromos, Somali, and Sudanic peoples. They were brought together through conquest in the nineteenth century to add to the original Amhara highlanders, whose emperors claim descent from a liaison between the Queen of Sheba and King Solomon. Some of the traditional performing arts of these many nationalities incorporate elements of storytelling, music, dance and RITUAL enactments, while within the dominant Amhara culture there exist certain exclusive performances such as priestly dances (*shibsheba*), religious music (*aquaquam*) and oral poetry (*qene*). There is also a tradition of noble praise singers, called *azmaris*. Modern Ethiopian drama started through the action of Tekle Hawariat, a nobleman who had lived in Europe. He wrote a satire, *Fabula: Yawreoch Komediya* ('Fable: the comedy of the animals', c. 1916), based on the fables of La Fontaine but directed at the conservative and corrupt officials of the court. Because the play was anti-establishment, theatre in general was banned at court by the Empress Zauditu – a ban later lifted by Emperor Haile Selassie, who commissioned plays which glorified his reign, the church, and Ethiopian history and culture. In 1935 the Ager Fikir (the Patriotic Theatre Association) was formed with a group of *azmaris*. It was banned during the Italian occupation but reformed in 1942.

In the late 1940s and early 1950s, serious and often moralistic but poorly structured plays were written, mainly for the consumption of the nobility. The best examples are *David and Orion*, *The Voice of Blood* and *King David III*, all by Makonnen Endalkachew. Others were *Hannibal* by Kebede Michael and *The Light of Science* by Romana Kasahun. This period helped set the style and tone of later drama, which is usually characterized by long speeches, often in verse, minimal and often slow-moving dramatic action, and very sketchy character development, as exemplified in Ethiopia's best-known English play, *Oda Oak Oracle* (1965), by its foremost dramatist, Tsegaye Gabre-Medhin.

Ethiopian theatre is the only one in Africa not to be directly influenced by European theatre. It is mostly written in the local language, Amharinya, with few translations and plays written in European languages. It explores national themes, and its production aesthetics and infrastructure are a clear reflection of Ethiopian society and the dominance of Amharic culture and the Ethiopian Orthodox Church. The country has one of the best-organized infrastructures for theatre on the African continent, with some five state-funded theatre companies in the capital, Addis Ababa, alone, which also boasts an active theatre department at its university. There are also state-funded performance art groups called *kinets* in all the regions and considerable amateur theatre activity in the towns. Most of the early theatre was sponsored and controlled by the ruling class, which it in turn supported. By the 1960s new voices of protest and criticism of the ruling elite began to emerge among a young generation of dramatists, notably Gabre-Medhin, Mengistu Lemma, Abe Gubegna, Debebe Eshetu, Tsefaye Gessesse and Wogayehu Nigatu. These writers introduced an element of social criticism in plays such as *The Crown of Thorns* (1958), *Mumps* (1959) and *A Man of the Future* (1965) by Gabre-Medhin; *Marriage of Unequals* (1963), *Balekabara Baledaba* ('The mighty and the lowly', 1974) and *Kassa* (1980) by Lemma; *The Fall of Rome* by Gubegna; and *Yeshi* and *Tehaddiso* ('Renaissance', 1979) by Gessesse. These plays examine issues such as poverty, the oppression of the poor, absence of cultural values in the urban centres – especially among youth, who, the plays argue, seem to lack any sense of direction – urban prostitution, the ignorance and arrogance of the aristocracy, and state coercion. This style of theatre, very popular with city audiences, continued until the revolution in 1974 which swept the aristocracy away. Theatre under the revolutionary government became a weapon for politicizing the population, and this gave rise to a number of cultural groups who created Soviet-style AGITPROP plays such as *The Red Sickle* and *Struggle for Victory*. With this style and with new theatres opening up in the capital, new dramatists emerged who specialized in popular propaganda plays. The main exponents of this style are Ayalneh Mulat, Tekle Desta and Getachew Abdi, with plays like *Isat Sined* (*When the Fire is Burning*, 1975), *The Peasant Woman's Beacon* (1977) and *Pumpkin and Gourd* (1979).

A third generation of dramatists emerged who reacted against the CENSORSHIP and crackdown of the revolutionary dictatorship, which had virtually driven serious drama out of the Ethiopian theatre. Among these were Fisseha Belay, who wrote plays such as *Simen Sintayehu* (1984) and *Hoda Yifejew* (1985), and Astelkachew Yihun. Belay is significant because his plays are based on an understanding and utilization of Ethiopian traditional customs, values and rural life. His other plays include *Alkash Na Zefegn* ('The mourner and the minstrel', 1988). However, the plays of Gabre-Medhin remain the most enduring. They reflect the many stages and changes in the political and artistic landscape and temper of the country. For the first time in Ethiopian drama, he brought the affairs of ordinary people centre stage – a model which other dramatists adopted and which makes Ethiopian theatre a truly people's theatre. OSITA OKAGBUE

ethnic theatre A term used mostly since the 1970s to refer to theatre practised by, and usually for, ethnic minorities in a particular country. While it may have had some limited use in highlighting an area of drama often ignored or undervalued, like many such labels it

raises problems. There is little in common between, for example, a Jamaican farce, a dramatization of a Hindu myth or a Polish tragedy, though all may be performed in the same town and categorized under the same heading. Often what is described as ethnic theatre depends for its vitality on the position within the country concerned of the community that has given rise to the drama, and how close the language used is to that of the 'host' language. It may offer a means of sustaining a distinct culture and language, but that may wane with time and assimilation; it may also offer a way of forging new identities as the community changes, and of challenging the very notion that ethnic theatre encourages of being seen as separate and exotic. CHARLES LONDON

See also BLACK THEATRE; COMMUNITY THEATRE; THEATRE IN EXILE; THIRD THEATRE.

eurythmics *see* JAQUES-DALCROZE, EMILE

Evans, Edith [Mary] (b. London, 8 Feb. 1888; d. Kent, 14 Oct. 1976)   Actress. A milliner and amateur actress (under WILLIAM POEL), she became a professional actress almost by accident at the age of 25 and rose to be, in JOHN GIELGUD's words, 'the finest actress of our time'. After touring with ELLEN TERRY, she played mainly in contemporary roles and originated the parts of the Serpent and She-Ancient in *Back to Methuselah* by SHAW (1923) and Orinthia in Shaw's *The Apple Cart* (1929). She is best remembered, however, for her many fine performances in the classics – notably in Shakespeare, in the 1925–6 Old Vic season, the Nurse in *Romeo and Juliet*, Rosalind in *As You Like It*, Cleopatra in *Antony and Cleopatra* (all of which she repeated later); in Restoration plays, as Millamant (1924) and Lady Wishforth (1948) in Congreve's *The Way of the World* and Mrs Malaprop (1945) in Sheridan's *The Rivals*; in CHEKHOV as Arkadina (1936) in *The Seagull* and Madame Ranevskaya (1948) in *The Cherry Orchard*, and, above all, as Lady Bracknell (1939) in WILDE's *The Importance of Being Earnest*. Yet she also had great success in many modern plays, including her first box-office hit, *Evensong* (a satirical study of Dame Nellie Melba by Beverley Nichols, 1932), *The Late Christopher Bean* (1933), *Robert's Wife* (1937), *Daphne Laureola* (1949), *Waters of the Moon* (1951) and *The Chalk Garden* (1956). In 1964 she made a striking success at the NATIONAL THEATRE as Judith Bliss in the notable revival of NOEL COWARD's *Hay Fever*. The film of *The Importance of Being Earnest* (1951) made her Lady Bracknell internationally famous, and her emphatic delivery of the words 'A *handbag?*' was a gift to impressionists. IAN BEVAN

Bryan Forbes, *Ned's Girl: The Authorised Biography of Dame Edith Evans* (1977)
— and Jean Batters; *Edith Evans: A Personal Memoir* (1977)
J. C. Trewin, *Edith Evans* (1954)

Evans, Maurice [Herbert] (b. Dorchester, Devon, 3 June 1901; d. Rottingdean, Sussex, 12 March 1989) Actor, producer and director. He began his career in London, and appeared with the OLD VIC. Playing Raleigh in *Journey's End* (1929) established him as a star, and in 1934 he performed an uncut version of *Hamlet*. The following year took him to the United States, where he played Romeo to the Juliet of KATHARINE CORNELL and, in 1936, the Dauphin to her St Joan. He then became the most popular Shakespearean actor of his period, often under the direction of MARGARET WEBSTER, playing Richard II, Hamlet, Falstaff, Malvolio and Macbeth. He became a naturalized American in 1941 and during the Second World War performed a *G. I. Hamlet* at military bases, which cut the play to its plot essentials. Evans had further success in SHAW, toured extensively, presented Shakespeare on television and was a major force in the American theatre. Strangely, his stage career petered out in the late 1950s and he took on roles in popular films and television serials. He completed his autobiography, *All This – and Evans Too!* just before his death; it was published in 1989. THOMAS F. CONNOLLY

Evans, Will (b. London, 29 May 1873; d. London, 11 April 1931) MUSIC HALL and PANTOMIME performer who made his debut, aged six, with his father's theatre troupe and toured with them for many years. He and his wife Ada played a double act. Once widowed, he played solo in halls and pantomimes, and was an innovator of the halls' eccentric, knockabout humour, drawing much of his inspiration from chaotic domestic situations such as 'Papering a House'. He created most of his own material and co-authored the celebrated FARCE *Tons of Money* (1922). ADRIANA HUNTER

Eveling, [Harry] Stanley (b. Newcastle upon Tyne, 4 Aug. 1925) Playwright and moral philosopher. Eveling's thoughtful and witty plays seem preoccupied with people's longings, with the disparity between dreams and gross physical reality: e.g. the would-be sailor in *Mister* (1970), and the yachtsman's fantasies in *Our Sunday Times* (1971). He writes skilfully about many sombre themes from approaching death to the aftermath of Nazism (*The Dead of Night*, 1975, shows Hitler's bunker). For Eveling, tragedy always leaves traces of laughter behind. Other plays include *Dear Janet Rosenberg, Dear Mr. Kooning* (1969) and *Caravaggio, Buddy* (1972). TONY HOWARD

Everyman Theatre (Liverpool) A small theatre, formerly a chapel, opened for the presentation of serious contemporary works in 1964 by three ex-Birmingham University students, TERRY HANDS, Peter James and Martin Jenkins, as an alternative to the LIVERPOOL PLAYHOUSE. Its early productions included work by BOND, BECKETT and PINTER. In the 1970s, under Alan Dossor (1970–5), the Everyman saw a shift towards work by local authors such as Alan Bleasdale, JOHN MCGRATH, Bill Morrison and WILLY RUSSELL, whose Beatles musical, *John, Paul, George, Ringo . . . and Bert* (1974) transferred to the West End and launched his career. Actors at the Everyman in this period included Julie Walters, ANTONY SHER and JONATHAN PRYCE. The theatre, which is owned by an independent trust, was restructured in 1976–7 and a 430-seat auditorium was built. KEN CAMPBELL took over as artistic director in 1980; his jubilantly experimental productions, including the ten-play cycle *The Warp* (written with Neil Oram), attracted younger audiences, a counterpoint to the formation from the Everyman of the Merseyside Young People's Theatre by Paul Harman. The theatre hit financial problems and an uncertain future in the 1990s. ADRIANA HUNTER

Everyman Theatre (London) Founded by Liverpool businessman Norman Macdermott (1889–1977) in 1920 in a small converted drill hall in Hampstead, north London. His non-commercial repertoire promoted new plays (e.g. NOËL COWARD's *The Vortex*, 1924) and translations of foreign plays, including early O'NEILL, CHIARELLI's *The Mask and the Face* (1924) and PIRANDELLO's *Henry IV* (1925). Macdermott was succeeded in 1926 by Malcolm Morley, who continued the foreign exploration, particularly of IBSEN, and who directed the first English production of Ostrovsky's *The Storm* (1929). In the 1930s the theatre was used by other groups and in 1947 was turned into a cinema, which followed the theatre's art-house policy in its own programming.
CHARLES LONDON

N. MacDermott, *Everymania: The History of the Everyman Theatre, Hampstead, 1920–26* (1975)

Evreinov, Nikolai [Nikolaevich] (b. Moscow, 26 Feb. 1879; d. Paris, 7 Feb. 1953) Playwright, director, theatre historian and inventor of the theory of 'monodrama', which conceives of stage reality in terms of a single controlling consciousness. Like many other MODERNISTS, he reacted against realist tendencies in post-Renaissance theatre and his creation of the Starinny (Antique) Theatre in St Petersburg led to attempts, between 1907 and 1912, to recapture the stylization of medieval performance. Likewise, his co-founding of the Krivoye Zerkalo (Crooked Mirror) Theatre in 1908 (he was a director there from 1910 to 1917) gave rise to satirical attacks on conventional dramatic and theatrical forms. His many plays, which include *Vesyolaya smert'* ('A merry death', 1910), *V kulisakh dushi* ('The theatre of the soul', 1911) and *Samoye glavnoe* ('The main thing', 1921), anticipated the work of PIRANDELLO and the THEATRE OF THE ABSURD. Evreinov's belief in the theatricalization of life led, after the Revolution, to his master-minding a mass spectacle, *Vzyatiye zimnego dvortsa* ('The storming of the Winter Palace', 1920), involving thousands of participants. A genuinely original spirit, Evreinov set out his ideas in a number of works which include the three-volume *Teatr dlya sebya* ('Theatre for oneself', 1915–17). He also wrote *The Theatre in Life* (1923). He emigrated to Paris in 1925.

NICK WORRALL

Sharon M. Carnicke, *The Theatrical Instinct: Nikolai Evreinov and the Russian Theatre of the Early Twentieth Century* (1989)

Spencer Golub, *Evreinov: The Theatre of Paradox and Transformation* (1984)

experimental theatre A loose term, often meaning AVANT-GARDE, that has been widely used since the middle of the twentieth century and has gone by many other names: 'event' or HAPPENING in the 1950s; 'multi-media' in the 1960s; 'visual theatre' in the 1970s; PERFORMANCE ART in the 1980s; LIVE ART in the 1990s. Rarely have these names been chosen by the practitioners; they have for the most part been coined for the sake of critical convenience, often (particularly in Britain) because when critics are confronted by theatre which is not a play – by work not based in text – they see it as so foreign to their tradition that it must be defined as separate, an 'experiment'. They have been unable to develop a vocabulary which can cope with the physicality and volatility of experimental performance or its multiplicity of meaning. (The work of ROBERT WILSON, for example, was reviewed in one paper early in his career by its dance critic.)

A glance at the history of world theatre, however, reveals the dramatic play as a comparatively recent and primarily European preoccupation. There is another, ancient tradition at work in the great folk theatres of the world; in *COMMEDIA DELL'ARTE*, MUSIC HALL and popular MUSICAL THEATRE; in the consummate combined artistry of *kabuki*; even in Greek theatre, the other elements of which have been largely forgotten in the single legacy of the text. It is in this other tradition

that theatre now defined as 'experimental' has its roots, a tradition which seeks to yoke together as a single live event all the necessary but disparate skills of spectacle – DESIGN, music, CHOREOGRAPHY, performance and text. Such theatre has always been – and still is – a compromised art of process, a mucky, mutable, dirty, competitive, collaborative business. From within this ancient and variegated work, the development of printing permitted the recording of just one element: the text. Theatre no longer had to be discovered or taught in the body. It had achieved a means of distribution through the immutable word from which other productions could be reconstructed. Soon, the word *preceded* production, the solitary task of the writer was born, and the intellectual domination of the play took hold.

The making of a play can be the most authoritarian theatre process: in the beginning of rehearsals is The Word; the director is the Papal power that interprets The Word, and guides all others in service of It. There is a less authoritarian approach which leaves more to the individual conscience – to the actor, for instance, at an extreme in the devised theatre work of MIKE LEIGH. But even in comparison with this approach, experimental theatre is truly heretical. For here, at the beginning of rehearsals, there is no word – there is nothing but the artists and the potential work which they will uniquely create together.

By the end, the music may drown out the text, the performers may be reduced to ciphers by the design, the demands of the choreography may condition all other aspects of the work. It is by virtue of the unpredictability of the creative process that such theatre is most appropriately dubbed 'experimental'. And the most successful experiment is likely to allow equal significance to design, music, performance, choreography *and* text.

Just as the process of experimental theatre differs from playmaking, so does the product. A play's performance aims at singularity of meaning. It seeks to control all the theatrical elements in an accurately repeatable form, proposing an interpretation of the writer's meaning with the greatest precision and clarity. Ask ten different members of an audience about this meaning, though, and paradoxically they will probably come up with ten different interpretations – and ten more if they go to see it again. That is one of the joys of the richness of theatre, and one which experimental work turns to advantage. For here there is a *conscious* multiplicity of meaning. The work is poetic, allusive, ambiguous, possibly contradictory, certainly asking its audiences to trust their own perceptions as to its truth for them. It is also fluid and rarely 'finished'.

Discoveries are made through performance, and the final showings are likely to be very different from the first. Thus each performance is a development of the work as product. By comparison, a play is fixed. In an age dominated by the recorded media of film and television – dead drama – experimental work keeps live theatre at its liveliest.

The confusion between experimental theatre and dance is innocuous; the confusion with performance art, however, is not. Performance art is a term of the fine arts, with a fully documented tradition of its own, and, at the end of the twentieth century, displaying a vigour which experimental theatre lacks. Here, artists use themselves as material. They do not necessarily adopt the mask of character, nor make fictitious use of time and space. These are qualities of theatre. To misunderstand such distinctions is not simply professionally inept – it points to a history of journalistic criticism which has constantly ducked issues of theoretical analysis.

Experimental theatre is born of long creation periods, and the single-minded commitment of genuine ENSEMBLE companies has become a rarity – such circumstances have long since become a financial impossibility. Many of those who might once have advanced experimental theatre now work in the equally innovative and collaborative fields of opera, video, television or film. Those few who continue to experiment do so increasingly intermittently, or as solos or duos.

JOHN ASHFORD

In Britain

In Britain, as elsewhere, the collapsing of definitions from the 1950s onwards resulted in an eclectic history. Groups from the PEOPLE SHOW, PIP SIMMONS, WELFARE STATE INTERNATIONAL, IOU and Impact Theatre to Crystal Theatre of the Saints, Forkbeard Fantasy, IMPROBABLE THEATRE, Rational Theatre and FORCED ENTERTAINMENT can be accommodated under one rather misshapen umbrella. Much of the work was allied to fine art; for example Hesitate and Demonstrate, founded by Geraldine Pulgin and Janet Gold Art in 1975, came out of LEEDS Polytechnic Fine Art Department; yet dance-theatre companies such as DV8 or Second Stride or the David Glass Ensemble can also find shelter under the experimental theatre umbrella, as could the company Gloria and its director Neil Bartlett or THEATRE DE COMPLICITE, who have taken on the challenge of the mainstream with great success. A leader in the field was Lumière and Son, founded in 1973 by Hilary Westlake and David Gale, who performed in a range of spaces – from a TENT for *Circus Lumière* (1980) to Kew Gardens for *Deadwood*

(1986) – and opened the way for SITE-SPECIFIC theatrical events and INSTALLATION projects, which were much encouraged by the LONDON INTERNATIONAL FESTIVAL OF THEATRE (LIFT) and producing organizations like Artangel or Artsadmin.

Influenced by the United States, an arts lab network arose outside London from the 1960s on which nurtured experimental work in places like EDINBURGH, BIRMINGHAM, NOTTINGHAM and CARDIFF, where the CHAPTER ARTS CENTRE and MOVING BEING, founded by Geoff Moore, were important catalysts. Another foreign influence was crucial: the MICKERY THEATRE in Amsterdam commissioned a lot of work that came to Britain, much of it seen at the ICA in London, a tradition consolidated by John Ashford in the 1970s and continued since.

Feminism and sexual politics have played a vital role in this innovatory work, whether in a collective, like the women's touring ensemble Blood Group founded by Anna Furze, or in solo performance, e.g. Rose English or Annie Griffin.

Britain was not very receptive to such challenges, and many artists were forced to perform as much abroad as at home. Without more support from funding bodies, it was not surprising that the major theatre players – for instance, ROBERT LEPAGE, PINA BAUSCH, Robert Wilson, the WOOSTER GROUP – continued to come from abroad. CHARLES LONDON

In the United States

In the United States, 'experimental theatre' encompasses a large, amorphous but vibrant body of work. The artists – directors, performers and designers – cross boundaries of genre and form and discipline, whether working in ALTERNATIVE THEATRE, ENVIRONMENTAL THEATRE, DANCE THEATRE, STREET THEATRE, performance art, AGITPROP or IMPROVISATIONAL theatre, to 'experiment' with a perceived 'norm' that remains elusive. As one mainstream, STAND-UP comedian was reported to mutter after an unsettling silence greeted several jokes, 'Another spell like that and I'll be a performance artist.' Ironically, the only certainty is that one decade's experiment soon becomes the next's tradition.

Nevertheless, if WILLIAM ARCHER could assert – dubiously – that American drama began in 1916 in Provincetown, Mass., with the first production of a play by EUGENE O'NEILL, then, for argument's sake, experimental theatre in the United States could be said to have hatched in 1959, after being incubated at Black Mountain College in North Carolina. That year saw several important theatre events whose many manifestations would, by the end of the century, combine to encompass the whole of American experimental theatre. Allan Kaprow's multi-art-form adventure *18 Happenings in 6 Parts* was offered at New York's Reuben Gallery, spurring the performance art movement; Julian Beck and Judith Malina's LIVING THEATER, in existence since 1947, helped spark actor–ensemble experimentation OFF-OFF BROADWAY with their production of JACK GELBER's *The Connection*; and across the continent, R. G. Davis founded the SAN FRANCISCO MIME TROUPE, an ensemble dedicated to agitprop performance in a *COMMEDIA DELL'ARTE* style, the first of many radical political theatre groups that rose to prominence in the 1960s.

Kaprow's 1959 piece helped generate an interdisciplinary phase of performance art that has done away with the very word 'theatre'. His happening featured many characteristics evident in today's performance experimentation: the use of simultaneous but seemingly unrelated action and movement; the audience as participant/performer; and a fragmented, non-narrative structure using an inter-disciplinarian collage of dance, live and recorded sound, and multimedia technology. Soon after, other artists – Nam June Paik, Jim Dine, Carolee Schneeman, to name a few – experimented with art environments, often using their bodies as both canvas and armature, engaging gallery and 'found' (street) audiences in what has now become an institutionalized subgenre of experimental theatre: performance art. In the early 1990s, for example, Blue Man Group brought the exploration of the question 'What *is* art?' to a zany zenith by, among other tricks, projectile vomiting brightly dyed marshmallows at high velocity at blank, framed canvases from ten feet in their long-running OFF-BROADWAY show.

Indeed, by the 1990s most performance art had begun to emphasize the first of those two words, perhaps because actors, dancers, and musicians – rather than painters and sculptors – were initiating the experiments. Not surprisingly, the concerns of these mostly solo performers often revolve around the self and its identity in relation to society, a subject of special interest to those communities traditionally on the margins of power, whether women, gays or ethnic groups. Performers like KAREN FINLEY, Holly Hughes, Rachel Rosenthal, John Leguiziamo, Tim Miller and the trio PoMo Afro Homos, Laurie Carlos and Margaret Cho have given voice to such concerns. But the form also suits those performers, like ANNA DEAVERE SMITH, Eric Bogosian, Danny Hoch, Jeff Weiss and Leguiziamo, who singly embody a chorus of characters – historical and fictional. Other performers have deconstructed sprawling epic adaptations of classics to the ultimate extreme. Fred Curchack's mid-1980s one-man

The Tempest re-explored the theme of magic and primitivism through a deceptively simple production using dolls and disposable lighters, while Ethyl Eichelberger (1945–90) did for classics what Charles Busch and the RIDICULOUS THEATRICAL COMPANY under Charles Ludlam and later Everett Quinton did for dramatic genre – show audiences a classic's underbelly by coaxing our gender preconceptions and sexual stereotypes out from the closet of ignorance.

In fact, performance venues for such work now exist across America: New York's P.S. 122, Painted Bride in Philadelphia and the Walker Arts Center in Minneapolis are a few of the most notable. In addition, more tradition-bound institutions began sponsoring experimental performance: the BROOKLYN ACADEMY OF MUSIC's annual Next Wave Festival became one of the few to embrace large, adventurous work by artists like Robert Wilson, Pina Bausch, RICHARD FOREMAN, ARIANE MNOUCHKINE and LEE BREUER; the LINCOLN CENTER now regularly presents such work in its annual summer festival of international work; and finally, resident theatres started presenting work on their 'second' stages that ranged from NEW VAUDEVILLIANS like BILL IRWIN or the postmodern juggling troupe the Flying Karamazovs to the monologuist/Wooster Group member Spalding Gray, and the ethereal expressionistic fantasies of Ping Chong. However, no American has embraced the Black Mountain interdisciplinary approach more, or expanded the theatrical imagination further, than director/designer Robert Wilson, whether creating an epic multinational, multi-part unfinished work (*the CIVIL WarS*) or an intimate black-box student production (HEINER MÜLLER's *Hamletmachine*), or re-visioning classics (Euripides' *Alcestis*; Büchner's *Danton's Death*).

Like Wilson, his contemporary Richard Foreman began directing his own plays in the late 1960s. Foreman's Ontological-Hysteric Theatre (since 1992 in the same East Village theatre that harboured SAM SHEPARD's early work) offers enigmatic chamber pieces featuring broken, hallucinatory narrative, backed by amplified and recorded sound, glaring light punctuated with sudden blackouts and video monitors, within sets resembling Joseph Cornell boxes—all in an effort to renew his audiences' perception of familiar phenomena and, like Wilson, give them a chance to perceive stimuli without the burden of interpreting it. MABOU MINES, one of the foremost experimental ensembles of the 1970s, often used classical sources as inspiration. Director JOANNE AKALAITIS deconstructed Colette's writings in *Dressed Like an Egg* (1977) and Breuer snatched bits of Thomas Mann for *Prelude to a Death in Venice* (1979).

Mabou Mines, the Living Theater and the San Francisco Mime Troupe have struggled on, albeit without some important founders and with correspondingly reduced influence. But back in 1950s San Francisco, when HERBERT BLAU and Jules Irving's ACTOR'S WORKSHOP experimented successfully with European avant-garde classics, Davis, a member of the company, founded the Mime Troupe under their auspices. In turn, LUIS VALDEZ got his agitprop training from Davis's group and then formed El TEATRO CAMPESINO, a company devoted to agitprop for the largely Chicano migrant worker population. Soon, small GUERRILLA THEATRES began performing all over the country, using experimental techniques and avowedly non-commercial means to try to enlighten 1960s America to alternative political and social realities.

Meanwhile in New York, Theater Genesis, CAFFE CINO, LA MAMA ETC and the OPEN THEATER, among other groups and venues, sprang into existence, providing shelter for such playwrights as Sam Shepard, MARIA IRENE FORNES, LANFORD WILSON and TOM O'HORGAN, for example. One-time Living Theater actor JOSEPH CHAIKIN's ensemble improvisations helped bring forth influential works like MEGAN TERRY'S *Viet Rock* and JEAN-CLAUDE VAN ITALLIE's *The Serpent*. No New York producer, however, did more to boost and popularize the burgeoning alternative theatre movement than JOSEPH PAPP. As producer of the NEW YORK SHAKESPEARE FESTIVAL for 40 years, he managed to present free 'classics' in the park (from the beginning with multicultural casting, which was seen as radical at the time) while simultaneously nurturing and popularizing experimentalists. He gave BROADWAY the rock musical *Hair*, as well as *A Chorus Line* and NTOZAKE SHANGE's *for colored girls who considered suicide/when the rainbow was enuf* in the early 1970s.

Much alternative theatre since the 1960s has also been energized by the experiments of dancers and choreographers who began moving away from the abstract expressionism of MERCE CUNNINGHAM. Some of the more notable American dance-theatre artists include MARTHA CLARKE, Ping Chong, MEREDITH MONK, John Kelly and David Gordon. Dance Theatre Workshop, based in New York, is one of the country's foremost producers and presenters of experiments in this genre, and it annually hosts the Bessie Awards honouring the year's best achievements in dance theatre.

Ironically, directorial experiments – ORSON WELLES' famous 1930s 'voodoo' *Macbeth* set in Haiti and staged with a black cast at Harlem's LAFAYETTE Theater, for example, once considered daring and innovative for its 'concept' and use of 'non-traditional casting' – are now the tradition at most major regional theatres. Further mainstreaming has occurred as the generation of directors once acclaimed for their youth and innovation in the late 1970s and early 1980s – Des McAnuff, Mark Lamos, Robert Falls – staged classics while running the country's major institutional theatres, before moving on to film, opera and other commercial ventures. Since 1990 the most vigorous experimental directors— Robert Wilson, Robert Woodruff and Anne Bogart, for example – have begun more regularly to test regional theatre audiences' taste for non-naturalistic production.

The most stridently experimental ensemble working in the United States during the last two decades of the century was the Wooster Group. Formed by actors that splintered off from Richard Schechner's Performance Group, they were led by director Elizabeth Lecompte. Productions deconstructed classic works by ARTHUR MILLER, THORNTON WILDER and especially O'Neill – once considered experimental playwrights themselves – by splicing these texts with all manner of found material, including a technological overlay of video images and amplified voice, and a performance style laden with a jokey, affected irony. Their work is similar to the theatrical experiments of the Squat Theater, which came from Hungary to New York and performed against a window looking out on to a street, so that passers-by became part of the action, as did the audience for the passers-by. Wooster also may have influenced a whole generation of US theatre artists, including the idiosyncratic John Jesurun, whose technological soap operas appear digitized through multi-layers of text, sound and large amounts of video.

Arguably, the now defunct En Garde Arts company, based in New York City, consistently produced some of the best experimental theatre in the United States in the 1990s. En Garde's productions are notable not only because of the remarkable ready-made 'sets' the company appropriates (a Central Park lakeside, a decaying Hudson River pier, the yard of an abandoned asylum, the streets of Manhattan's meat-packing district), but because the texts presented are written by vigorously experimental writers like Fornes, Mac Wellman, and Charles L. Mee, and staged by some of the country's foremost directors, including Bogart, Tina Landau, and Reza Abdoh (1963–95). JOHN ISTEL

See also DANCE; DESIGN; MULTIMEDIA THEATRE.

Robert Brustein, *Revolution as Theatre: Notes on the New Radical Style* (1971)
Roselee Goldberg, *Performance Art: From Futurism to the Present* (1988)
Michael Kirby, *Happenings* (1965)
—*The Art of Time: Essays on the Avant-Garde* (1969)

Bonnie Marranca, *Theater of Images* (1977)

James Roose-Evans, *Experimental Theatre* 1981)

Theodore Shank, *American Alternative Theatre* (1988)

expressionism   The term originally referred to painting. Used very occasionally during the nineteenth century, it was popularized in 1901 by the French painter J.-A. Hervé. The German art dealer and publicist Herwarth Walden took it up from 1910 onwards and applied it to the German revolt against academicism and naturalism in all the arts. But, unlike the parallel movements of FUTURISM and SURREALISM, expressionism was never a single school guided by an intellectual leader. Hence the work of very different artists, including playwrights, has been called expressionist – united by common characteristics rather than a strict programme.

In a narrow sense, expressionism was a specifically German phenomenon. Prefigured by WEDEKIND, its theatrical history was brief: from the (non-professional) performance in Vienna in 1909 of OSCAR KOKOSCHKA's *Murderer, Hope of Women* to some time in the early 1920s. Its reign was never unchallenged. Landmarks were productions in Prague and Dresden of WALTER HASENCLEVER's *The Son* (1916) and REINHARDT's memorable staging of REINHARD SORGE's *The Beggar* (1917) in Berlin. These and similar plays dramatized the conflict of the generations, violently rejecting the father figure and expressing a faith in youth in messianic terms.

Military defeat and the collapse of the old order in 1918 gave expressionist drama a more overtly political thrust, as in FRITZ VON UNRUH's *A Family* and ERNST TOLLER's *Transfiguration*, both first staged in 1919. Termed a *Denkspieler* or playwright of ideas, GEORG KAISER, who had satirized bourgeois life in *From Morn to Midnight* (written 1916, performed 1917), now forecast industrial society's race to extinction in the *Gas* trilogy (written in 1912, published in 1916 and premièred in 1917).

Expressionist drama felt no commitment to the depiction of everyday reality; it was subjective and arbitrary. In the wake of STRINDBERG's *A Dream Play* (1907), it often featured dream imagery. Action as well as language throbbed with nervous energy. The unities were discarded, the narrative line frequently being a series of 'stations' rather than a well-knit plot – an approach which, through the work of PISCATOR and BRECHT, gave rise to EPIC THEATRE. Diction, too, became fragmented: grammar was violated and sentences collapsed; there were sudden lyrical outbursts; speech became a cry. These new demands called for a new acting style. The playwright Paul Kornfeld

advised: 'Let not the actor . . . behave as though the thoughts and words he has to express have only arisen in him at the very moment in which he recites them . . . Let him dare to stretch his arms out wide and with a sense of soaring speak as he has never spoken in life; let him not be an imitator or seek his model in a world alien to the actor.'

Such plays could not be staged by conventional methods. A new approach to stage design revealed the close links between expressionism in drama and the visual arts. Sets became simplified, angled, distorted, fantasticated. The stage was conceived as a space rather than a picture. Spotlights – as in Jürgen Fehling's notable production in 1921 of Toller's *Masses and Man* – created the acting areas and shifted the focus from one spot to another; some expressionist lighting techniques had an impact on the CINEMA of the period.

By the mid-1920s inflation was over and stability returned. The expressionist wave passed. The playwrights mentioned above, as well as WERFEL, WOLF, Johst and others, adapted their style to a less ecstatic idiom. The nebulous unity of the expressionist camp fragmented into different ideologies. But expressionism in the wider sense – a technique rather than a specifically German sense of life – can be traced in other countries too. In the 1920s, American theatre was open to experimentation. ELMER RICE's *The Adding Machine* (1922) mocked the depersonalized drudges of capitalism. JOHN HOWARD LAWSON used expressionism for radical purposes in *Roger Bloomer* (1922) and *Processional* (1925). A late example of agitational expressionism was IRWIN SHAW's anti-militarist *Bury the Dead* (1937).

The most notable American exponent of expressionism – in some of his work – was EUGENE O'NEILL. In *The Emperor Jones* (1920) he put subjective visions on the stage; in *The Hairy Ape* (1922) he turned both oppressors and oppressed in a class society into puppets; in *All God's Chillun Got Wings* (1924) he portrayed racial conflict in boldly two-dimensional imagery.

English playwrights failed to respond to continental example, but some Irish writers took to it more readily. DENIS JOHNSTON's *The Old Lady Says 'No!'* (1929) was – among other things – expressionistic. SEAN O'CASEY made the third act of *The Silver Tassie* (1929) one of the peak achievements of expressionist writing. *Within the Gates* (1933) was still inspired by expressionism. Even some of his later plays – the third act of *Red Roses for Me* (1942), or *Cock-a-Doodle Dandy* (1949) – were touched by it.

POLITICAL THEATRE from the 1960s on rediscovered elements of expressionism and in the 1980s theatre DESIGN borrowed heavily from it. But its increasingly loose definition, while a tribute to its influence, made it a less and less useful term for critical debate.

GEORGE BRANDT

See also MODERNISM.

David F. Kuhns, *German Expressionist Theatre: The Actor and the Stage* (1997)

R. M. Ritchie, *German Expressionist Drama* (1976)

Walter Sokel, *The Writer in Extremis: Expressionism in Twentieth Century Germany* (1959)

John Willett, *Expressionism* (1970)

Eyen, Tom *see* CAFFÉ CINO; LA MAMA EXPERIMENTAL COMPANY

Eyre, Richard [Charles Hastings] (b. Barnstaple, Devon, 28 March 1943) Director. Eyre worked at the Phoenix, Leicester, and then the Royal Lyceum, EDINBURGH, becoming director of productions in 1970 and staging fine versions of BRECHT and CHEKHOV. At the same time, he developed his taste for large-scale non-domestic plays, directing for 7:84, the Liverpool EVERYMAN and new work by DAVID HARE, CHARLES WOOD and STEPHEN LOWE. In 1973 he took over the NOTTINGHAM Playhouse at a time of crisis, and built a national reputation for imaginative political plays like *Brassneck* (1973), *The Churchill Play* (1974) and *Comedians* (1975). In the 1980s Eyre's versatility was visible in a series of successful productions including his stark *Hamlet* (1980) with JONATHAN PRYCE at the ROYAL COURT and his slick, intelligent *Guys and Dolls* (1982) for the NATIONAL THEATRE, where he became an associate director in 1981 and later artistic director (1988–97). His time at the National was marked by successful exploitation of commercial possibilities and an increasing openness to experimental groups like THEATRE DE COMPLICITE and directors like ROBERT LEPAGE. Eyre's productions, notably *The Voysey Inheritance* (1989), *Napoli Millionaria* (1991), the DAVID HARE trilogy (1990–3) and *John Gabriel Borkman* (1996), were praised for their clarity, fluidity and wit. He is also a successful television and film director. His autobiographical *Utopia and Other Places* was published in 1993. He was knighted in 1997. DAN REBELLATO

F

Fabbri, Diego (b. Forlí, Italy, 2 July 1911; d. Riccione, 14 Aug. 1980) Playwright and literary critic. A deeply committed Catholic, he commanded respect, even from Marxist critics, for his intense intellectual honesty. Plays such as *Inquisizione* (*Inquisition*, 1950), *Processo di famiglia* (*Family on Trial*, 1953) and *Processo a Gesù* (*Jesus on Trial*, 1955) brought his work to the attention of an international audience. G. H. MCWILLIAM

fact, theatre of *see* THEATRE OF FACT

Factory Theater Founded in 1970 in Toronto as Factory Theatre Lab by Ken Gass and Frank Trotz to present only Canadian plays. Artistic directors have included Gass (1970–7), Bob White (1977–87) and Jackie Maxwell (from 1987). The most important playwright associated with the theatre is GEORGE F. WALKER, who has had 12 plays produced there since 1972. The theatre has also promoted such Canadian playwrights as David Freeman, Herschel Hardin, Bryon Wade, Hrant Alianek and Gass. In 1984 the company, renamed Factory Theater, moved into a new, permanent 230-seat theatre. It went through a period of financial difficulties in the mid-1990s, after which Ken Gass returned as artistic director in 1999. EUGENE BENSON

Fagan, J[ames] B[ernard] (b. Graigneaverne, Queen's County, Ireland, 10 May 1873; d. Los Angeles, 17 Feb. 1933) Actor, director and playwright. He was a member of BENSON's and TREE's companies as a young man but turned to writing, notably *False Gods* (1909, from Brieux) for Tree and *Bella Donna* (1911, from Robert Hichens's novel) for the manager GEORGE ALEXANDER. Between 1918 and 1921 he ran the ROYAL COURT THEATRE, London, where his work included several innovatory productions of Shakespeare and the British première of *Heartbreak House* (1921). In 1923 he founded the OXFORD PLAYHOUSE, where he staged many important artistic productions, notably an early and influential *The Cherry Orchard* (1925). This weekly REPERTORY company helped the early careers of GIELGUD, GUTHRIE, MASSEY and ROBSON among others, yet, at the close of the 1929 season, with Oxford unable to support Fagan's theatre, it closed to become a mini-golf course. He presented many productions by the Irish Players and was the author of a successful comedy, *And So To Bed* (1926), based on Pepys' *Diary*, as well as an adaptation of *Treasure Island* (1922) that ran annually until 1931. G. ROWELL

Fagon, Alfred *see* BLACK THEATRE

Falkland, Samuel *see* HEIJERMANS, HERMAN

Fall, Leo[pold] (b. Olmütz, Moravia, 2 Feb. 1873; d. Vienna, 16 Sept. 1925) Composer. Originally a violinist and conductor, Fall tried his hand at both opera and cabaret songs before the production of his first operetta, *Der Rebell* (1905). His next three works, *Der fidele Bauer* (*The Merry Peasant*, 1907), *Die Dollarprinzessin* (*The Dollar Princess*, 1907) and *Die geschiedene Frau* (*The Girl in the Taxi*, 1908), won him international recognition and a place alongside LEHÁR, OSCAR STRAUS and KÁLMÁN at the forefront of the European operetta tradition. Among his later works, a rewrite of *Der Rebell* as *Der liebe Augustin* (1912), *Die Rose von Stambul* (1916) and *Madame Pompadour* (1922) were varied and outstanding examples of contemporary operetta, combining soaring lyrical music and crisply rhythmic and tuneful comic songs in scores of exceptional beauty and cheerful charm. KURT GÄNZL

Falls, Robert *see* EXPERIMENTAL THEATRE; GOODMAN THEATRE

Fanti, Lucio *see* DESIGN

farce Derived from the Latin for 'to stuff', farce as genre or comic technique has seldom been absent from the popular or bourgeois stage. Rooted in ancient drama yet scorned by critics as vulgar, its physicality and ability to please or shock have placed it consistently at the core of popular entertainment. In the hands of skilled dramatists and performers it offers more than a purely mechanical formula for provoking instant laughter. Much modern farce derives from the 'well-made play' whose complex plotting, intricacy of planted detail, structural precision and liberal deployment of coincidence and oscillating action were pushed to comic extremes in the nineteenth-century farces of Labiche and those of FEYDEAU which span the two centuries. English farces, such as those of PINERO, are less risqué in tone and generally less frantically constructed. Although more reliant on eccentricity or playfulness of character and language, they share an enactment of accelerating social or sexual transgressions, creating opportunities for physical comedy, and generating an embarrassing or dangerous madness released in audience laughter. Rapid entrances, exits, concealments and chases contained within precise settings furnish immediate physical demonstration of social transgressions, complemented by transgressions of dress or costume and verbally by transgressive puns, *double entendres* and nonsense. Such orchestration demands exceptional skill and stamina of dramatist and performers, and the English theatre has enjoyed a strong tradition of farce ensemble acting companies such as were assembled for Pinero's ROYAL COURT farces (1880s), BEN TRAVERS' ALDWYCH FARCES (1920s), the WHITEHALL FARCES (1950s) staged by BRIAN RIX, and RAY COONEY's Theatre of Comedy at the Shaftesbury (1980s). In the contemporary theatre, social and sexual restrictions have been relaxed, encouraging writers such as JOE ORTON to expand the boundaries of comic material beyond the merely titillating for more trenchant purposes. Playwrights as diverse as NEIL SIMON, ALAN BENNETT, CARYL CHURCHILL, TOM STOPPARD, SAMUEL BECKETT, EDWARD BOND and ALAN AYCKBOURN have been attracted to farce as a way of renegotiating society's organized structures and categories, or of expressing a contemporary sense of disorder and confusion. MICHAEL FRAYN has inherited the elegant cleverness of Feydeau, while Alan Bleasdale and Bill Morrison have raised desperate laughter from acute social and political problems. The genre remains remarkably healthy and disturbingly perceptive. RONALD W. STRANG

Eric Bentley, *The Life of the Drama* (1964)
Henri Bergson, 'Laughter', in Wylie Sypher, ed. *Comedy* (1956)
Albert Bermel, *Farce: A History from Aristophanes to Woody Allen* (1982)
Jessica M. Davis, *Farce* (1978)
Brian Rix, *Life in the Farce Lane* (1995)
Leslie Smith, *Modern British Farce* (1989)

Farr, Florence [Beatrice] (b. Bromley, Kent, 7 July 1860; d. Ceylon, 29 April 1917) Actress and director. Named after Florence Nightingale and a noted occultist, Farr was a pioneer in London productions of IBSEN, YEATS and SHAW, playing Rebecca West in the London première of *Rosmersholm* (1891), which she directed, and Blanche in *Widowers' Houses* (1892). She also arranged music, choreographed and performed in GRANVILLE BARKER's productions of Euripides' *The Trojan Women* (1905) and *Hippolytus* (1906). MARVIN CARLSON

Julie Holledge, *Innocent Flowers: Women in Edwardian Theatre* (1981)
Josephine Johnson, *Florence Farr: Bernard Shaw's 'New Woman'* (1975)

Farrah [Abd' Elkader] (b. Boghari, Algeria, 28 March 1926) Designer and painter. After extensive work in continental Europe he designed *The Cherry Orchard* for MICHEL SAINT-DENIS (ROYAL SHAKESPEARE COMPANY, London, 1961) and remained with the company, developing his baroque but stark style in *The Tempest* (1963) and *Dr Faustus* (1968). Bold and expressive, his creation of dynamic stage space became an RSC hallmark, especially in his many designs for TERRY HANDS, beginning with a *Richard III* in 1970 that showed his interest in masks to great effect, and including eight Shakespearean histories in the following decade (up to 1981) as well as GENET's *The Balcony* (1971). TONY HOWARD

Farrell, Bernard (b. Dublin, 21 July 1940) Playwright. He came to prominence at the ABBEY THEATRE, Dublin, where all his early work was hugely successful. Most of his comedies are disturbing and sharply observed satires on middle-class pretensions in a changing society; there is often a grotesquely corrosive element, where the past is uncomfortably revealed.

269

Among his best-known plays are *I Do Not Like Thee, Dr Fell* (1979), *Canaries* (1980), *All In Favour Said No!* (1981), *All The Way Back* (1985) and *The Last Apache Reunion* (1993 – all at the Abbey); *Happy Birthday, Dear Alice* (Red Kettle Theatre Company, Waterford, 1994); *Stella by Starlight* (Gate Theatre, Dublin, 1997); and *Kevin's Bed* (Abbey, 1998). He has also written extensively for television and radio. CHRISTOPHER FITZ-SIMON

Christopher Murray, *Twentieth-century Irish Drama* (1997)

fashion Theatre is inextricably bound up with fashion, in terms both of theatregoing – audience dress codes, a theatre's architecture or interior design – and of theatre-making – set, COSTUME, WIGS, MAKE-UP; even the LIGHTING. The first productions of OSCAR WILDE's plays reflected the fashions of the day among a certain section of society represented in the audience as much as musicals in the 1980s, like the roller-skating pop spectacle *Starlight Express* (1984), reflected fashion trends among a different, younger social group who formed much of its audience. Innovatory designers such as Mariano Fortuny (1871–1949), CHRISTIAN-JACQUES BÉRARD, LEON BAKST and ERTÉ made an impact on the worlds of both fashion and theatre; and by the end of the century the 'catwalk' had become completely theatricalized. CHARLES LONDON

Joel H. Kaplan and Sheila Stowell, *Theatre and Fashion* (1995)

Fassbinder, Rainer Werner (b. Bad Wörishofen, Bavaria, 31 May 1945; d. Munich, 10 June 1982) Film and theatre director, actor and playwright. He trained as an actor in Munich and founded there in 1967 the *Antiteater* ('anti-theatre'), where he worked for several years with a group of actors who also formed the core cast in his early films. He wrote a large number of adaptations and original plays for the company, some of which he later turned into films. As a stage director he worked in some of the leading West German theatres and was responsible for productions of FLEISSER, Büchner, WEISS, HANDKE and JARRY. After 1975 he concentrated on his work as a film director, for which he is mainly remembered. A controversial as well as influential figure, his plays include *Katzelmacher* ('Cock-artist', (1968), *The Bitter Tears of Petra von Kant* (1971), *Bremen Coffee* (1971) and *The Garbage, the City and Death* (1976). GÜNTER BERGHAUS

Faversham, William (b. London, 12 Feb. 1868; d. Long Island, NY, 7 April 1940) Actor–manager. Engaged by CHARLES FROHMAN in 1893, for eight years

he played a number of classical and contemporary roles. In 1909 he directed and took the title role in STEPHEN PHILLIPS's *Herod*. Three years later his talents as an actor and director were fully realized when he played Mark Antony in his own production of *Julius Caesar*, which enjoyed a successful run in New York and on tour. Faversham won acclaim for his subsequent productions of Shakespeare's work and of contemporary plays. ADRIANA HUNTER

Fay, Frank *see* FAY, WILLIAM

Fay, William George (b. Dublin, 12 Nov. 1872; d. London, 24 Oct. 1949) Actor and producer. With his actor brother Frank (1871–1931) he formed a small theatre company in Dublin which flourished until both joined the Irish Literary Theatre in 1902; here Willie was largely responsible for creating the economic style of production for which the ABBEY THEATRE became famous. He created many roles, including Christy in SYNGE's *The Playboy of the Western World* (1907) and Bartley in *Riders to the Sea* (1904). Following a rift with the management, the Fays worked in the theatre in Britain and the United States. CHRISTOPHER FITZ-SIMON

Feder, Abe (b. Milwaukee, Wisc., 27 June 1909; d. New York, 24 April 1997) Lighting designer. After studying at the Carnegie Institute of Technology, he launched his career by creating the LIGHTING for *Trick for Trick* (1929). He then did much designing for the FEDERAL THEATER PROJECT, and in later years often devoted himself to working with interesting productions that promised little commercial success. At the same time he also worked on dozens of major Broadway shows, such as *I'd Rather Be Right* (1937), *The Skin of our Teeth* (1942), and *My Fair Lady* (1956). He also designed the basic lighting for many new theatres, including those in Washington's KENNEDY CENTER, and taught in WORKSHOPS. GERALD BORDMAN

Federal Theater Project American theatre organization. Born during the Great Depression in response to widespread unemployment in the arts, the project was a unique phenomenon in a culture that has always resisted government patronage. The scale of America's only attempt at a national theatre was huge: over 1,200 individual productions in 35 states with, at its peak, an employment roster of over 13,000 theatre personnel. Nor were activities exclusively tied to production: the project encouraged community drama (e.g. in predominantly black, Jewish or Catholic districts) and theatrical training; it established a National Service Bureau to conduct theatre research; it published its own periodical; it created a Federal Theater of the Air.

The project was founded in 1935 by the Works Progress Administration, which had been been empowered to remove the stigma of the dole by offering the unemployed work within their own skills and trades. To meet the needs of unemployed artists, the WPA established four major arts projects: in Art, Music, Writing and Theatre. But the Theater Project's director, HALLIE FLANAGAN (chosen from the non-commercial theatre) conceived of her mandate as more than the administration of relief. She and her collaborators strove to create out of the fact of unemployment a theatre that would express the needs and attitudes of its era.

The dual aims of the Federal Theater were to some extent contradictory, for how could a major theatre be created if its most talented personnel had to be dismissed when they became employable? Moreover, its government support made it vulnerable to congressional attacks on the grounds of wastefulness and radicalism. The heaviest barrage of criticism was directed at those plays produced by the LIVING NEWSPAPER unit (an innovative experiment in stage DOCUMENTARY created with the collaboration of unemployed journalists). The living newspaper dramatized social problems in such works as *Injunction Granted* (labour) and *One-Third of a Nation* (housing), usually from a liberal, reformist point of view. Conservative opposition, however, saw a dangerous political agenda, and, as the economic crisis abated, the Project's days were numbered. Despite widespread support from established theatre artists endorsing the project's 'value to the life of the community', on 30 June 1939 Congress denied funds to the arts projects and the experiment was over.

A host of noted professionals began or consolidated their careers in the Project, among them MARC BLITZSTEIN, PAUL GREEN, JOHN HOUSEMAN, CANADA LEE, ARTHUR MILLER, ELMER RICE and ORSON WELLES. Major productions included Sinclair Lewis's *It Can't Happen Here* (1936), which played simultaneously in over 20 towns, Welles's black *Macbeth* (1936), ARTHUR ARENT's *Triple-A Ploughed Under* (1936), TOLLER's *No More Peace* (1937), William DuBois' *Haiti* (1938) and the American première of ELIOT's *Murder in the Cathedral* (1937). GERALD RABKIN

Hallie Flanagan, *Arena* (1940)
Rena Fraden, *Blueprints for a Black Federal Theater, 1935–1939* (1994)
Malcolm Goldstein, *The Political Stage* (1974)
George Kazacoff, *Dangerous Theatre: The Federal Theater Project as a Forum for New Plays* (1990)
Gerald Rabkin, *Drama and Commitment* (1964)
John O'Connor and Lorraine Brown, eds, *Free, Adult, Uncensored* (1978; publ. London, 1980 as *The Federal Theater Project*)
Wilson Whitman, *Bread and Circuses* (1972)

Feiffer, Jules (b. New York, 26 Jan. 1929) Cartoonist, novelist and playwright; a sharply satirical writer whose work probes the neuroses of modern urban men and women. Plays include the award-winning *Little Murders* (1967), *God Bless* (1968), *The White House Murder Case* (1970), *Knock, Knock* (1976), *Grown Ups* (1981), and *Elliot Loves* (1990). He also wrote the screenplays for *Carnal Knowledge* (1970) and *Popeye* (1980). DAVID BARBOUR

Feldenkrais, Moshe (b. Slavuta, Russia, 6 May 1904; d. Tel Aviv, Israel, 1 July 1984) Scientist and physical analyst. In his meticulous examination of human movement, Feldenkrais emphasized the inseparable relationship of brain and body, and the necessity for a detailed analysis (and therefore an increased awareness) of habitual actions. The process revealed that both body and mind, when undirected, can fall into repetitive and often harmful patterns. The changing of patterns by teacher-manipulation and personal practice can lead to a greater efficiency and sense of well-being ('functional integration'). Thus, by breaking old habits, expanding movement possibilities and developing critical awareness, remarkable improvements in the performance of actors, athletes, musicians and indeed the physically impaired become possible. JOHN BROOME

See also ALEXANDER, F[REDERICK] MATTHIAS; DANCE, MOVEMENT AND DRAMA; PHYSICAL PREPARATION.

female impersonation see DAME; DRAG; IMPERSONATION; PANTOMIME

feminism see LESBIAN THEATRE; WOMEN IN THEATRE

Fennario [Wiper], David (b. Point St Charles, Montreal, 26 April 1947) Playwright. The poverty of his childhood led him to embrace Marxism, an ideology which informs all his work. The one-act *On the Job* (1975) is about a wildcat strike, and the two-act *Nothing to Lose* (1976) is about a group of truckers preparing to strike. *Joe Beef* (1984), *Doctor Neill Cream* (1988) and *The Murder of Susan Parr* (1989) constitute a trilogy which further emphasizes Fennario's Marxist ideology. *Gargoyles* (1997) is a one-act play about the history of Montreal. EUGENE BENSON

Ferber, Edna (b. Kalamazoo, Mich., 15 Aug. 1885; d. New York, 16 April 1968) Novelist, short-story writer and playwright. Her six collaborations with GEORGE S. KAUFMAN are noted for good plots, character development and bright dialogue: *Minick* (1924), *The Royal*

Family (1927), *Dinner at Eight* (1932), *Stage Door* (1936), *The Land is Bright* (1941), and *Bravo* (1948). Her novel *Show Boat* (1927) was made into a successful musical and film. JANE HOUSE

Julie Goldsmith Gilbert, *Ferber* (1978)

Ferrer, José [Vicente Ferrer de Otero y Cintron]
(b. Santurce, Puerto Rico, 8 Jan. 1912; d. New York, 26 Jan. 1992) Actor, producer and director. Ferrer made his debut in 1934, taking his first substantial role as Dan Crawford in *Brother Rat* (1936). Noted for his energy and powerful voice, he enjoyed further success in revivals of *Charley's Aunt* (1940) and *Othello* (1943, playing Iago to ROBESON's Othello), and in the title role in *Cyrano de Bergerac* (1946; filmed 1950, for which he won an Oscar). Ferrer's appointment as general director of the New York City Theater Company in 1948 coincided with his debut in films. He subsequently worked in both media as a director and actor, and was the first actor to receive the National Medal of Arts (1985). HELEN RAPPAPORT

Festival Theatre, Cambridge *see* CAMBRIDGE FESTIVAL THEATRE

festivals Traditionally times of communal celebration, by the end of the nineteenth century local festivals still enjoyed the presence of a variety of amateur and professional theatrical performances, whereas those with a national and international dimension took the form of the earliest modern theatre festival, a seasonal honouring of a single world artist, for example of Wagner at BAYREUTH or of Shakespeare at his birthplace STRATFORD-UPON-AVON. In the twentieth century the idea of a festival as a series of linked events mounted at a particular time of year (usually the summer) came to prominence in 1917 when the director MAX REINHARDT, the composer Richard Strauss and the playwright HUGO VON HOFMANNSTAHL founded the Salzburg Festival. In 1920 Reinhardt initiated what became an annual performance there of Hofmannsthal's adaptation of *Everyman* and subsequently opened up the festival to revivals of European classic plays and operas (at first, following the Bayreuth and Stratford model, mostly by Mozart). In Britain, the Malvern Festival founded in 1929 by the director Sir BARRY JACKSON aimed to explore British drama and came to be associated with GEORGE BERNARD SHAW, though plays from as far back as the sixteenth century were staged. After the divisions of the Second World War, the establishment of both the EDINBURGH INTERNATIONAL FESTIVAL of Music and Drama and the AVIGNON FESTIVAL in 1947, and in 1954 of the THÉÂTRE DES NATIONS in Paris, presented festivals as ways of build-

ing the peace and of fostering new understanding across Europe through displaying the work of an international community of artists. Edinburgh embraced 'high art' (and gave rise to an oppositional FRINGE in response), while Avignon under the direction of JEAN VILAR stressed the importance of youth. This 'healing' trend held through the 1960s, as seen in the annual WORLD THEATRE SEASONS held in London, organized in association with the ROYAL SHAKESPEARE COMPANY. A new direction was heralded in Nancy, France, where an international student festival launched by Jack Lang in 1963 grew into a world theatre festival that not only offered outlets to, but actively promoted through commissioning, radical theatre from around the globe. Such challenges to conventional theatre and theatre-making (and, in Central and Eastern Europe, to state-controlled theatre as well) led to new questions being asked about the role of festivals, particularly in reaction to the government-sanctioned showcase art of the established ones. While festivals such as BITEF in Yugoslavia or the Festival of Fools in Amsterdam provided a platform for cross-cultural, cross-form developments in performance that often took place away from conventional theatre buildings, a new awareness was dawning of community and place. Questions about the nature and role of theatre as well as about the societies in which it was produced featured strongly in the festivals that were created in the late 1970s and early 1980s, such as Theater der Welt in Germany, the LONDON INTERNATIONAL FESTIVAL OF THEATRE (LIFT), the Festival des Ameriques in Montreal and the Zurich Festival. A greater sensitivity in Europe and the United States to the performance traditions of other cultures also influenced the type of artists invited to these festivals, which expanded their remit in the wake of Avignon and Nancy to include workshops, seminars and debates. Some important practitioners – The WOOSTER GROUP, TADEUSZ KANTOR, PETER SELLARS, PETER BROOK, for example – were seen internationally through the emerging festival network. Inevitably, this network influenced the older festivals and, as a result, a new hierarchy of international artists emerged; the once AVANT-GARDE, like ROBERT WILSON or ROBERT LEPAGE, became the new establishment. Dissatisfaction with what had become another international cherry-picking exercise led directors of festivals to re-examine their relationships to the places where the exotic events took place. Festivals established a different relationship to their locales, and became again a place where theatre was made, a creative force, linked to those locales and their history as well as to the people who lived there now. A crucial shift came when Peter Sellars took over the Los Angeles festival, a white Beverly Hills affair on the international supermarket model, and invited participation from artists who were associated with the original cultures of the neglected citizens of the city, such as the Hispanics, the Koreans, the Japanese, the Jewish, the Native Americans. Local artists were involved in the decision-making and also took part in the 1990 festival, which boasted an unprecedented cultural mix, from Hawaiian dancers and Australian aborigines to Cambodian folklore troupes. This democratization and expansion of festival culture quickly influenced other festivals, such as LIFT. For example, in 1993 LIFT brought Hanoi Water Puppets to the banks of the river Thames in a borough with a significant but ignored Vietnamese population at the same time as they presented the culmination of a six-month project working with local children of Vietnamese background telling their own story. Similarly, the Brussels festival established in the early 1990s celebrates the richness of a culturally diverse city – expressive of the French, Walloon and Arab populations, for instance – in long-term work which tries to overcome the conventional problem of festival artists parachuting into communities. Groups like WELFARE STATE tried to overcome this dilemma by taking up residence in the community where the festivals would be produced. Alongside continual re-evaluation came the consolidation of festivals as tourism and as civic pride – every town worth its salt must have one. Yet even within the consumerist model of festivals radical activities are possible (as can be seen at Brighton or Salisbury), and festivals can also play a positive role in their host towns, as part of the regeneration of decayed urban areas, for example. Art and life are brought closer together as festivals return to the notion of being an enjoyable yet exploratory collective experience rooted in a particular place. Handing over more of the choices involved to artists and artistic producers drawn from all the cultures and generations to be found in the places where the festivals are held is opening up the prospect of a healthy future for the festival phenomenon. COLIN CHAMBERS

festivals (amateur)   Amateur drama festivals were originally conceived purely as competitions and were so called. In 1923 the British Drama League (*see* BRITISH THEATRE ASSOCIATION) set up an annual play competition among London drama clubs, attracting some 40 entries; in New York a Little Theatre Tournament for the DAVID BELASCO Cup was inaugurated about the same time. When the New York organizers invited the BDL to nominate a British group to take part with a one-act play in the tournament in 1926, the selection was made by competition among the seven groups that

put themselves forward. This was the germ of the idea that led to the holding of a National Community Theatre Competition the following year, partly to select a group to participate in the 1927 New York tournament. The word 'festival' was substituted for the word 'competition' somewhat arbitrarily in the course of planning, but this was no more than a euphemism. The competitive element, together with the public adjudication, proved attractive and within a few years an elaborate organization had developed for the National Festival, with preliminary rounds, divisional finals, area finals and national final. The establishment of many independent festivals followed, some of which were more truly festival in character, bringing people together to share a week of theatre, with other events in addition to the performances. In many cases, however, competition remained a strong element.

The idea of drama festivals soon spread to other countries, where national festivals at various levels often became a central feature of AMATEUR THEATRE work, regarded as the chief expression of amateur theatre and representing, in a festival's final stages, the peak of achievement. In England leading amateur societies and LITTLE THEATRES seldom take part in the national festival as they rate their work in their own community as of greater importance. Thus the UK Festival does not necessarily represent the best in amateur theatre.

International amateur festivals were a later development and are usually more festival than competition. International youth theatre festivals have been of particular value in encouraging the sharing of theatre internationally among young people. International festivals which attract groups, usually by invitation, from a wide range of different cultures have been held in a number of European countries, in the United States and in Japan. The largest purely amateur festival is the World Festival of Amateur Theatre held every four years in Monaco.   ALFRED EMMET

See also INTERNATIONAL AMATEUR THEATRE ASSOCIATION.

Patrick Carleton, ed., *The Amateur Stage: A Symposium* (1939)

Fettes, Christopher   *see* DRAMA SCHOOLS

Feuchtwanger, Lion   (b. Munich, Germany, 7 July 1884; d. Los Angeles, Cal., 21 Dec. 1958)   Playwright and novelist. His work focuses on the political and Jewish issues which touched his own life. He wrote historical novels; plays loosely adapted from Greek classics; three plays in collaboration with BRECHT (*Edward II, The Visions of Simone Machard, Calcutta 4 May*); and five original plays, including *Jud Süss* (*Jew Süss*, 1917; London, 1929; adapted as a novel 1925).

ADRIANA HUNTER

Feydeau, Georges[-Léon Jules-Marie] (b. Paris, 8 Dec. 1862; d. Rueil Malmaison, 5 June 1921) Playwright. Being a comic writer, it is not surprising that few of Feydeau's contemporaries regarded him as worthy of serious comment. Comprehensive nineteenth- and early twentieth-century literary studies rarely mentioned him. Even his admirers saw little beyond the jokes and fiendishly ingenious plots. Much later, despite his persistent popularity, perceptions finally changed, even in academia. For those no longer content with received opinions, Feydeau is placed alongside Molière. He is, of course, funnier and less obsequious.

In France the literary awakening was complete when the critic Paul Morand hailed the master of FARCE as the heir to Greek tragedy because 'he poses the intolerable problem of fatality'. It has always been more difficult for a comic writer to achieve classic status than a writer of tragedy, for tragedy feeds humankind's sense of self-importance; comedy never does. Yet Feydeau has become a classic: for, once experienced, he refuses to be eradicated from the mind, lingering long in the memory, always fresh and unexpected, never finishing saying what he has to say to us, the creator of a world and of the adjective 'Feydeauesque'. With his wild plots and characters such as Lapige in *La Main Passe* (1904; performed in English as *Chemin de Fer*) who is afflicted with the uncontrollable congenital habit of barking whenever he becomes excited, Feydeau anticipates SURREALISM by some 15 years and the abortive THEATRE OF THE ABSURD by half a century.

Feydeau's 39 plays are extraordinarily diverse, ranging from the maniacal farce *Un Fil à la Patte* (1894; produced in English under several titles, including *Cat among the Pigeons*) to the dream comedy *L'âge d'Or* (1905, 'The Golden Age'). They are also very different from the conventional view of the boulevard farce, for by no means all of them deal with illicit sex in hotel bedrooms, like *L'Hôtel du Libre-Echange* (1894; *Hotel Paradiso*) or *Occupe-toi d' Amélie* (1908; *Keep an Eye on Amelia*). Being a Frenchman, Feydeau is equally interested in money, class, the state of his bowels, religion and madness – the madness both inside and outside: the madness of Bigot in *Le Marriage de Barillon* (1890; *On the Marry-Go-Wrong*), who turns up an hour early for every appointment and if the person he is to meet does not arrive within 30 minutes leaves, furious at this example of bad manners; or the madness which makes it seem perfectly normal that when the simple provin-

cials of *Les Fiancés de Loches* (1888, 'The Fiancés of Loches') mistake an employment agency for a marriage bureau they should all end up in a lunatic asylum – as Feydeau did, dying of syphilis.

Feydeau shows us the world we still live in, for violence against order and respectability runs like a dark thread through his work. Major assaults pose no real danger, but anything that destroys dignity and self-esteem always succeeds. In *La Puce à l'Oreille* (1907; *A Flea in Her Ear*) Chandebise easily escapes a bullet through the head but cannot dodge repeated kicks up the backside. Yet Feydeau's treatment of violence changed over the years. In his last, short, Strindbergian plays, the violence is verbal and psychological; no limbs are broken, only hearts and souls.

Like all good comic writers, Feydeau is basically serious. He plays for real, which means he must be played for real. His own productions were praised for their commonplace realism, intensity and speed. Feydeau's comic realism is very apparent in *Le Dindon* (1896; *Sauce for the Goose*), where a wife is pursued by two would-be lovers, and *Le Bourgeon* (1907, 'The Bud'), an Ibsen-like comic study of an aristocratic family trying desperately to maintain their piety in a fallen world. His characters are ourselves writ large, blind to emotional pain and guilt; lost in a universe ignorant of our existence. We recognize them and laugh; but our laughter is tinged with relief that it is someone else who, for once, is suffering endless comic humiliations at the hands of that ridiculous, banal demon called 'chance'. PETER BARNES

Stuart E. Baker, *Georges Feydeau and the Aesthetics of Farce* (1981)

Leonard C. Pronko, *Georges Feydeau* (1975)

Ffrangcon-Davies, Gwen [Lucy] (b. London, 25 Jan. 1891; d. Braintree, Essex, 27 Jan. 1992) Actress. English of Welsh extraction, she was a concert soprano whose voice earned her a place in touring musicals such as *Tonight's the Night* and *The Arcadians*. In 1921 a singing engagement with Barry Jackson's BIRMINGHAM REPERTORY THEATRE led to her becoming the company's leading lady. When Jackson took his production of *The Barretts of Wimpole Street* to London in 1930 she went with it as Elizabeth Barrett Browning, to achieve considerable success. She consolidated this with her performance as Anne of Bohemia opposite JOHN GIELGUD in *Richard of Bordeaux* (1932), and from then on played a wide range of leading parts in both classic and modern plays, climaxed by an award-winning performance as Mary Tyrone in the 1958 EDINBURGH FESTIVAL production of EUGENE O'NEILL's *Long Day's Journey into Night*. She was created a dame in 1991. IAN BEVAN

Fialka, Ladislav (b. Prague, 22 Sept. 1931; d. Prague, 22 Feb. 1991) MIME artist who trained as a ballet dancer. In 1958 he was a founder member of the Theatre on the Balustrade in Prague, where he set up his own ensemble of mimes, recreating traditional PANTOMIMES using the classical PIERROT white face. Inspired by the nineteenth-century French mime Deburau, Fialka became internationally influential through his productions, such as *Les Amants de la Lune* ('Lovers of the moon', 1959) and *The Fools* (1965), which depicted the evolution of mime through history and was seen in London in 1967 as part of the WORLD THEATRE SEASON. Fialka toured America as well as Europe. HELEN RAPPAPORT

Fichandler, Zelda *see* ARENA STAGE

Field, Sid (b. Birmingham, 1 April 1904; d. London, 3 Feb. 1950) Comedian who toured Great Britain and Australia in VARIETY for 27 years. Arguably the funniest English comedian since Chaplin, he was unknown in London prior to 1943, when he starred in *Strike a New Note*. Other shows include *Strike It Again* (1944), *Piccadilly Hayride* (1946) and *Harvey* (1949). The critic KENNETH TYNAN described him as the bumpkin droll, a burly man of blunt ways who was, nevertheless, 'a soul in bliss', blending mundane observation with a celestial stance. REXTON S. BUNNETT

John Fisher, *What a Performance!* (1975)

Field Day Theatre Company Founded in Derry, Northern Ireland, in 1980 by the playwright BRIAN FRIEL and the actor Stephen Rea with the object of touring new plays throughout Northern Ireland and the Irish Republic. Field Day recieved annual subsidy from the two Arts Councils in Ireland and established itself as one of the island's major companies. There has usually been one major production in Derry each year followed by an extensive tour, although since 1985 the company has not been in continuous production. Plays by Friel, including the première of *Translations* (1980), ATHOL FUGARD, Tom Paulin, Derek Mahon, THOMAS KILROY, STEWART PARKER and Seamus Heaney have been presented. Pamphlets on current cultural and political issues have been published, as well as an anthology of Irish writing from 850 to 1990. CHRISTOPHER FITZ-SIMON

Roland Rees, ed, *Fringe First: Pioneers of the Fringe on Record* (1992)

Fields, Dorothy *see* FIELDS FAMILY

Fields, Gracie [Grace Stansfield] (b. Rochdale, Yorks, 9 Jan. 1898; d. Capri, 27 Sept. 1979) Actress and singer. She was popular in regional REVUES produced and written by her first husband, Archie Pitt, before she made her name in London in such revues as *It's a Bargain* and *Mr Tower of London*, in which she toured for eight years. She commenced a successful film career in 1931 with *Sally in our Alley*, a reference to her theme song. 'Our Gracie' was greatly loved by audiences for her down-to-earth warmth. During the Second World War she was torn between being with her deported Italian-American husband and the country she loved, and so undertook extensive fund-raising activities in America and entertained the troops in Europe. Her career continued until her death. Her autobiography, *Sing As We Go*, appeared in 1960. She was created a dame in 1979. REXTON S. BUNNETT

Fields, Herbert *see* FIELDS FAMILY

Fields, Joseph *see* FIELDS FAMILY

Fields, Lew *see* FIELDS FAMILY; WEBER AND FIELDS

Fields, W. C. [William Claude Dukenfield] (b. Philadelphia, 10 Feb. 1879; d. Pasadena, 25 Dec. 1946) Comedian. Left home at 11, taught himself juggling, to which he added comic patter, entered VAUDEVILLE at 14 and, after touring Europe, became a star performer in the ZIEGFELD *Follies* (1915 and later 1920, 1921, 1925). In 1923 he played an unscrupulous confidence man in the Broadway musical comedy *Poppy*, a part he repeated in both screen versions (1925, 1936), and from which he developed the acerbic, misanthropic character with the disdainful drawl, piggy eyes and onion-shaped nose through which he immortalized himself in a succession of major films, some of which he scripted. He wrote film scrips and stories under various pseudonyms: Charles Bogle, Mahatman Kane Jeeves, Otis Criblecoblis. BRIAN BIRCH

W. K. Everson, *The Art of W. C. Fields* (1967)
W. D. Gehring, *W. C. Fields: A Bio-Bibliography* (1984)

Fields family Theatrical family, prominent in the American muscial theatre. Comedian and producer **Lew [Lewis Maurice Schanfield]** (b. New York, 1 Jan. 1867; d. Beverly Hills, 20 July 1941), came to fame in the 1880s as a dialect comedian in a double act with Joe Weber, who was later his partner in the management of the hugely successful Broadway BURLESQUE house WEBER & FIELDS' Music Hall. Fields went on to produce musicals, having an early success with VICTOR HERBERT's *It Happened in Nordland* (1904), and resurfacing in the mid-1920s with four early RODGERS and HART musicals for which his son **Herbert** (b. New

York, 26 July 1897; d. New York, 24 March 1958) had written the libretti. Herbert was a frequent librettist for the Broadway stage of the 1920s and 1930s, notably for Rodgers and Hart (*The Girl Friend*, *A Connecticut Yankee*), COLE PORTER (*DuBarry was a Lady*, *Panama Hattie*), VINCENT YOUMANS (*Hit the Deck*) and GEORGE GERSHWIN (*Pardon My English*). From the early 1940s he wrote in tandem with his sister, **Dorothy** (b. New Jersey, 15 July 1905; d. New York, 28 March 1974), who had worked as a lyricist since the late 1920s, mainly with Jimmy McHugh (e.g. 'I Can't Give You Anything But Love'). Dorothy and Herbert produced books for Porter's *Let's Face It!*, *Something for the Boys* and *Mexican Hayride* and ROMBERG'S *Up on Central Park* before supplying the libretto for their most important success, *Annie Get Your Gun* (1946). They subsequently worked with ARTHUR SCHWARTZ and CY COLEMAN; following Herbert's death, Dorothy supplied the lyrics for Coleman's *Sweet Charity* (1966), including hits such as 'Big Spender', and *See-Saw* (1973). Their brother **Joseph [Albert]** (b. New York, 21 Feb. 1895; d. Beverly Hills, 3 March 1966), the co-author of the hit plays *My Sister Eileen* and *Junior Miss*, also worked as a librettist in the musical theatre, collaborating on *Gentlemen Prefer Blondes* (1949), *Flower Drum Song* (1958) and the adaptation of *My Sister Eileen* as *Wonderful Town* (1953). KURT GÄNZL

A. and L. Fields, *From the Bowery to Broadway: Lew Fields and the Roots of Popular American Popular Theatre* (1993)
F. Isman, *Weber and Fields* (1924)

Fiennes, Ralph [N.T.W.] (b. Ipswich, Suffolk, 22 Dec. 1962) Actor. After a short spell in regional theatre he joined the NATIONAL THEATRE in 1986, before moving to the ROYAL SHAKESPEARE COMPANY in 1988. Here over the following three years he played many parts, including Henry VI, Troilus and Berowne. He then began what has become an extremely successful film career, appearing in highly praised films such as *Schindler's List* and *The English Patient*. In 1995 he returned to the stage to play Hamlet for the ALMEIDA THEATRE at the HACKNEY EMPIRE and on Broadway, for which he won a Tony award. In 1997 he played CHEKHOV's Ivanov and in 2000 Richard II and Coriolanus, again for the Almeida. The somewhat introspective, 'English' style for which he is best known conceals a capacity for passion and anger which was startlingly apparent in this performance. His ability to move effortlessly between the different demands of film and theatre places him among the most successful actors of his generation. GENISTA MCINTOSH

Y. Membery, *Ralph Fiennes: The Unauthorised Biography* (1997)

Fierstein, Harvey [Forbes] (b. Brooklyn, New York, 6 June 1954) Playwright and performer. Developed OFF-OFF BROADWAY, his *Torch Song Trilogy* (1978–81) was, in its celebration of gay life, a breakthrough Broadway production in 1982. Both the play and Fierstein's performance as the DRAG queen determined to create a home and family won Tony awards. He also wrote the libretto for the huge hit *La Cage Aux Folles* (1983). Since then, he has been visible primarily as an actor in mainstream film and television. Other plays include *Manny and Jake* (1987), *Safe Sex* (1987) and *Forget Him* (1988). M. ELIZABETH OSBORN
  See also GAY THEATRE.

fights During the twentieth century the staging of fights moved away from the artificial swordplay of veteran actors passing on the pretence to juniors, or the occasional visit of an acknowledged swordsman (*sic*) offering brief instruction to the province of a specialist. Whenever a script calls for violence, it is the fight director's responsibility to provide the action, in a convincing but safe manner for both the participants and the audience. The fight director, like the dance CHOREOGRAPHER, provides movements that are prearranged and can be reproduced daily; these movements are for the body as well as the weapons that are to be used. There are two basic forms of staged combat, armed and unarmed. The number and variation of weapons that can be incorporated in a fight, which can involve two combatants or a battle sequence, are endless. If a script calls for certain weapons or the piece is set in a specific historical period, the fight director will use the required weaponry and method of usage. There are legal considerations in the provision and use of stage weapons which have to be adhered to, whether the play is contemporary or not. Unarmed combat does not necessarily mean that no weapons are in use; knives, baseball bats, chains or dustbin lids are just some of the various spontaneous weapons that can be called upon in an unarmed sequence. Societies of fight arrangers exist in Britain, the United States, Canada and elsewhere, and proper training and certification are now standard. STEVE WILSHER

R. Lane *Swashbuckling: The Art of Stage Combat and Theatre Swordplay* (1998)

films *see* CINEMA

Finland The twentieth century began against a background of Finnish–Swedish tension. Finland was united with Sweden from the middle ages until 1809, when it became a grand duchy of Russia. Swedish, the language traditionally used by the upper classes, continued alongside Finnish as one of the country's two tongues. Russian was not used culturally. The first professional theatre was founded in 1872 as the Finnish Theatre, rather than as a bilingual one, and became the National Theatre in 1902. Theatrical activity began to broaden within the circles of both domestic language groups, including a strong tradition of amateur theatre (e.g. drama groups of workers' organizations). Many amateur groups turned professional. Following independence from Russia in 1917 and the ensuing civil war, moves were made towards uniting the professional and amateur wings, and in the depression of the 1930s it was common for towns to have a single professional theatre.

Up until the Second World War four well-known Finnish dramatists had emerged: the national author Aleksis Kivi (1834–72); Minna Canth (1844–97), who was strongly influenced by IBSEN; and the early feminists Maria Jotuni (1880–1943) and Hella Wuolijoki (1886–1954). Wuolijoki is also known for her cooperation with BERTOLT BRECHT over *Herr Puntila and His Man Matti*. Finnish theatre has always been open to international influences, and the German influence was especially strong before the Second World War. EXPRESSIONISM was still much in evidence as late as the 1920s, but there were signs of a new movement in, for example, *The Threepenny Opera*, which was performed both in Finnish and in Swedish as early as 1929–30. However, a deeper Brechtian influence can only be seen after the war, along with that of others from abroad, like STANISLAVSKY.

The first important changes after the war took place in the 1950s, at the same time as literary MODERNISM flourished. Some small theatres were founded at that time, and old institutional theatres began to build small stages. The THEATRE OF THE ABSURD arrived in several waves from 1950 on, and the Swedish Little Theatre staged the world première of *The New Tenant* by IONESCO in 1955. This postwar period ended in the 1960s when a new burst of dramatic activity made vigorous inroads. Social questions attracted interest, and there was a desire to use art to make a stand on contemporary issues. The idea of 'group theatre' also developed around the 1970s. Especially in their early years, new kinds of drama and theatrical expression developed in these circles and they influenced the traditional theatre. At the same time THEATRE IN THE ROUND productions began to appear.

Among postwar directors Eino Kalima (1882–1972) is especially known for his interpretations of CHEKHOV. Ralf Långbacka (b. 1932) has been strongly influenced

by the Brechtian movement, and Kalle Holmberg (b. 1939) and the unique personality Jouko Turkka (b. 1942) represent particularly Finnish views of performance. Many Finnish plays were written after the war, but only a few dramatists achieved a particular reputation or attracted interest outside Finland. Among these are Eeva-Liisa Manner (b. 1921) and Paavo Haavikko (b. 1931).

At the beginning of the 1990s there were about 50 professional companies. Many have their own new theatre complexes, with two or three stages, the result of a period of active building between 1955 and 1987. In the 1990s Finnish theatre was in a state of flux, as the traditional structure of the professional theatre was questioned. The number of small groups had grown and the old unity disintegrated. While in the main the work staged by the professional theatre has been traditional in character, the incorporation of other art forms and rejection of the dominance of the text has had a revitalizing effect, and the need for reform has been realized by the old theatrical institutions.

PIRKKO KOSKI

Pirkko Koski, 'The Dramatic Arts', in Päivi Molarius, ed., *From Folklore to Applied Arts: Aspects of Finnish Culture* (1993)

Pirkko Koski and Pirjo Vaittinen, 'The Theatre System of Finland', in H. van Maanen and S. E. Wilmer, eds, *Theatre Worlds in Motion* (1998)

F. J. and L-L. Marker, *A History of Scandinavian Theatre* (1996)

Irmeli Niemi, 'Finnish Popular Theatre', in David Mayer and Kenneth Richard, eds, *Western Popular Theatre* (1970)

M. Savutie, *Finnish Theatre* (1980)

S. E. Wilmer, ed., *Portraits of Courage: Plays by Finnish Women* (1997)

Finlay, Frank (b. Farnworth, Lancs, 6 Aug. 1926) Actor. Finlay made his name at the Belgrade Theatre, Coventry, and the ROYAL COURT, in ARDEN's *Serjeant Musgrave's Dance* (1959) and as Harry Kahn in *Chicken Soup with Barley* (1962) and the rest of the WESKER trilogy. OLIVIER spotted him as Corporal Hill in *Chips with Everything* (1962) and invited him to the NATIONAL THEATRE, where he played a memorably insidious and softly spoken Iago to Olivier's Othello (1964). Finlay is much admired for his versatility, equally able to take on major roles in television (these have included Jesus, Hitler and Casanova), in new plays (like Bernard Link in MERCER's *After Haggerty*, 1970, and Sloman in GRIFFITHS' *The Party*, 1973), and in European classics (he played Peppino in *Saturday, Sunday, Monday*, 1973, and

Domenico in *Filumena,* 1978, both by DE FILIPPO). DAN REBELLATO

Finley, Karen (b. Chicago, 1956) Performance artist. Trained as a visual artist, she turned to performance shortly after her father commited suicide when she was 21. Her performances typically express a rage towards the social conventions and beliefs in American culture, often offering a critique of male attitudes towards the female body. She appears SOLO on relatively bare stages, and her work is self-consciously rough and unfinished. She uses minimal props, her most evocative one being her nude body which she covers with feather boas, glitter, or more famously, chocolate. Finley's desecration of her body has incited national debate, as some politicians have tried to censor her work. She creates in other mediums such as painting, photography and video, but many critics judge that her best work lies in her confrontational PERFORMANCE ART. SUSAN PASTIKA

See also BODY ART.

L. Champagne, ed, *Out from Under: Texts by Women Performance Artists* (1990)

Finnell, Carrie see BURLESQUE

Finney, Albert (b. Salford, Lancs, 9 May 1936) Actor who made his debut with the BIRMINGHAM REPERTORY THEATRE (1956–8). CHARLES LAUGHTON cast him in Jane Arden's *The Party* (1958) and introduced him to STRATFORD-UPON-AVON in 1959. Finney, a stocky northerner with an independent spirit, became the symbol of a new acting style, less disembodied, more physical, both intelligent and popular. He gained widespread acclaim as the comic anti-hero *Billy Liar* (1960) but avoided typecasting by appearing in widely differing plays, creating, most notably, the leads in OSBORNE's *Luther* (Paris and London, 1961; New York, 1963) and ARDEN's *Armstrong's Last Goodnight* (1965) in a NATIONAL THEATRE season that also saw him play an antique collector in SHAFFER's *Black Comedy* and Jean in STRINDBERG's *Miss Julie.* He co-presented PETER NICHOLS' *A Day in the Death of Joe Egg* (1967), and appeared as Bri in New York (1968). He was an associate director of the ROYAL COURT (1972–5), during which time he played Elliot in E. A. WHITEHEAD's *Alpha Beta* (1972) and directed. He rejoined the National, playing Hamlet in its inaugural production on the South Bank (1976) and opening its Olivier Theatre with Marlowe's Tamburlaine (1976). Later, he made two rare stage appearances in HARWOOD's *Reflected Glory* (1992) and REZA's *Art* (1996). Finney was also a leading figure in the British film renaissance (*Saturday Night and Sunday Morn-*

ing, 1960; *Tom Jones,* 1963; *Charlie Bubbles,* 1967, as actor and director). D. KEITH PEACOCK

Q. Falk, *Albert Finney in Character: A Biography* (1992)

fireworks A traditional feature of outdoor theatrical performance, especially in RELIGIOUS DRAMA and PAGEANT. With the advance of the microchip, a spectacular computer-controlled 'theatre of fire' has been developed, especially by Groupe F and its leader Christopher Berthonneau, whose work ranges from the finale of the 1992 Olympic Games in Barcelona to using musicians, actors and sculptors in a cross between COMMUNITY THEATRE and STREET THEATRE. CHARLES LONDON

Fiske, Minnie Maddern [Mary/Marie Augusta Davey] (b. New Orleans, 19 Dec. 1865; d. Hollis, NY, 15 Feb. 1932) and **Harrison Grey Fiske** (b. Harrison, NY, 30 July 1861; d. New York, 3 Sept. 1942) Born into a performing family, Minnie Maddern made her acting debut at the age of five and went on to become an actress, producer, director and playwright. Even as a youngster she was singled out for exceptional abilities. Some of her most distinguished moments came in *A Doll's House* (1894), *Tess of the D'Urbervilles* (1897), *Becky Sharp* (1899), *Leah Kleschna* (1903), *The New York Idea* (1906), *Salvation Nell* (1908) and *Mrs Bumpstead-Leigh* (1911). The small, red-headed actress, with her nervous movements and delivery, was often called the best of her generation. Her husband was a producer, playwright, director and crusading tradesheet publisher who helped establish the benevolent Actors' Fund of America (1882) and opposed with Minnie the monopoly of the THEATRICAL SYNDICATE, which barred her from its theatres. Ironically, his biggest hit, *Kismet* (1911), was produced in association with his former adversaries. GERALD BORDMAN

A. Binns, *Mrs Fiske and the American Theatre* (1955)

Fitch, [William] Clyde (b. Elmira, New York, 2 May 1865; d. Châlons-sur-Marne, 4 Sept. 1909) Playwright. The most popular playwright of his era, his examinations of (generally) high society were looked on as theatrically effective but superficial, although some critics regard their documentary qualities highly. Among his best plays were *Barbara Fritchie* (1899), *The Climbers* (1901), *The Girl with the Green Eyes* (1902), *The Truth* (1907) and *The City* (1909). GERALD BORDMAN

A. Bell, *The Clyde Fitch I Knew* (1909)
M. Moses, and V. Gerson, eds, *Clyde Fitch and his Letters* (1924)

Fitzgerald [Shields], Barry [William Joseph] (b. Dublin, 10 March 1888; d. Dublin, 4 Jan. 1961) Actor. At first a civil servant, he took on his stage name in 1916 when he started appearing in roles at the ABBEY THEATRE on a part-time basis. He had a roguish, laconic manner on stage and excelled in character parts; he premièred the O'CASEY roles of Captain Boyle in *Juno and the Paycock* and Fluther Good in *The Plough and the Stars* (both 1924). He left the civil service in 1929 to become a full-time actor and toured America with the Abbey in 1934, his Fluther earning the New York critics' best character actor award. He toured the United States again in 1936 and settled in Hollywood the following year, remaining there for over 20 years. He appeared in many films, winning an Oscar for *Going My Way* (1944). He returned to Dublin in the late 1950s. KAREN FRICKER

Fitzgerald, Geraldine (b. Dublin, 24 Nov. 1914) Actress whose earliest engagement was at the Dublin GATE THEATRE in *Blood and Sand* (1933). Leading roles in O'NEILL, WILDER and WILLIAMS demonstrated her brilliant acclimatization to the American theatre scene, though she was equally at home in Shakespeare and European classics. *Wuthering Heights* (1939) and *Easy Money* (1983) are among her many films. CHRISTOPHER FITZ-SIMON

Fitzmaurice, George (b. Co. Kerry, 28 Jan. 1878; d. Dublin, 12 May 1962) Playwright. His 16 plays may be divided into three categories, realistic, fantasy and folk, though all contain a folk element and all are expressed through a very particular English-language dialect of North Kerry. *The County Dressmaker* (1907) is the archetypal realistic Irish rural drama; with *'Twixt the Giltinans and the Carmodys* (1923) it was often revived up to mid-century. Many of his plays were neglected, largely, it has been said, due to differences of opinion with YEATS and AUGUSTA GREGORY. The best of his fantasy plays, *The Magic Glasses* (1910) and *The Dandy Dolls* (1945) are almost SURREALIST in style. CHRISTOPHER FITZ-SIMON

Flanagan, Bud [Chaim Reuben Weintrop] (b. London, 14 Oct. 1896; d. Kingston-upon-Thames, Surrey, 28 Oct. 1968) Comedian and song writer. Known as a boy as 'Robert Winthrop'. During his long partnership with CHESNEY ALLEN, Flanagan appeared in VARIETY entertainments, most notably as part of the CRAZY GANG, REVUES and films, toured abroad, and, during the 1930s and 1940s, created many popular songs, among them 'Underneath the Arches', 'The Umbrella Man', 'Dreaming', 'Music, Maestro, Please', 'Run, Rabbit, Run' and 'On the Outside Looking In'.

After Allen's retirement due to illness, Flanagan appeared alone in such popular reviews as *Together Again* (1947) and *Knights of Madness* (1950). In the celebration show, *Underneath the Arches* (1981), he was played by music hall expert, the comedian Ross Hudd. Flanagan's autobiography *My Crazy Life* appeared in 1961. MARVIN CARLSON

Flanagan [Davis, born Ferguson], Hallie (b. Redfield, S. Dak., 27 Aug. 1890; d. Old Tappan, NJ, 23 July 1969) Producer, professor and playwright. She was an assistant to GEORGE PIERCE BAKER's 47 workshop for playwrights at Harvard University (1922), and established an experimental theatre at Vassar College (1925–42). On leave from Vassar, she was the visionary director of the FEDERAL THEATER PROJECT (1935–9) which created a national, non-discriminatory, socially relevant theatre. She worked at Smith College (1942–55) before retiring, and wrote *Shifting Scenes of the Modern European Theater* (1928), *Arena: The History of the Federal Theater* (1940) and *Dynamo: The Story of a College Theater* (1943), and the plays *Curtain* (1920), *Incense* (1924) and *Can You Hear Their Voices?* (1931), with Margaret Even Clifford. JANE HOUSE

J. Bentley, *Hallie Flanagan: A Life in American Theater* (1988)

Flannery, Peter (b. Jarrow, 12 Oct. 1951) Playwright. Flannery's two best-known plays display his talent for large-scale political panoramas: *Our Friends in the North* (1982), a state-of-the-nation piece looking at recent British history, and *Singer* (1989), which uses similar material but, in focusing on the life, death and rebirth of a Rachman-like figure, considers the meaning and effects of history and particularly the Holocaust. Both were written for the ROYAL SHAKESPEARE COMPANY, which also staged in 1978 *Savage Amusement* and *Awful Knawful*. His television series dramatizing the work of radical lawyers, *Blind Justice*, was a controversial success in 1989, and was followed in 1996 by an award-winning television serial adaptation of *Our Friends in the North*. DAN REBELLATO

Flecker, [Herman] James Elroy (b. London, 1884; d. Davos, Switzerland, 3 Jan. 1915) Poet and playwright. Author of two verse plays, *Hassan* and *Don Juan*, neither of which was performed in his lifetime. *Hassan* (first produced 1923) enjoyed an unusually long West End run for a verse play and is remembered for the sumptuous decadence of its settings and for the music, by Delius. Both plays were revived during the vogue for VERSE DRAMA in the 1950s, but neither has established itself in the repertoire. CLIVE BARKER

Fleisser, Marieluise [Luise Marie Haindl] (b. Ingolstadt, Germany, 23 Nov. 1901; d. Ingolstadt, 1 Feb. 1974) Playwright and novelist. She is known mainly for her plays *Fegefeuer in Ingolstadt* (*Purgatory in Ingolstadt*, 1926) and *Pioniere in Ingolstadt* (*Pioneers in Ingolstadt*, 1928). Fleisser was a close friend of FEUCHT-WANGER and BRECHT and went with them to Berlin, where productions of her two plays caused a considerable stir. Her dramas contributed to the revival of the *Volksstück* tradition in Germany (*see* HORVATH) and were rediscovered by a new generation of playwrights after the Second World War (e.g. KROETZ, FASSBINDER). GÜNTER BERGHAUS

Donna L. Hoffmeister, *The Theatre of Confinement: Language and Survival in the Milieu Plays of Marielouise Fleisser and Franz Xaver Kroetz* (1983)

Fleming, Kate *see* VOICE

Fo, Dario (b. San Giano, Lombardy, Italy, 24 March 1926) Playwright, performer, director and artist. One of the most influential forces in Italian theatre since the 1950s, gaining widespread international recognition from the late 1970s. The secret and success of Fo's style lie in its peculiar blend of popular theatre, learned sources and contemporary themes. After studying painting and architecture and working as a set designer, he spent 15 years (1952–67) of rebellious though light-hearted activity as a popular entertainer, beginning with a series of comic radio monologues and the collaborative writing, production and performance of the satirical review *Il dito nell'occhio* ('The finger in the eye', 1953). In 1954 he married the actress FRANCA RAME and they set up the Fo–Rame Company (1959), successfully performing on the commercial circuits for a middle-class audience. Even by Fo's standards the plays of this period are notable for their bizarre titles, including *Aveva due pistole con gli occhi bianchi e neri* ('He had two pistols with black and white eyes', 1960), *Chi ruba un piede è fortunato in amore* ('He who steals a foot is lucky in love', 1961) and *Isabella, tre caravella e un cacciaballe* ('Isabella, three sailing ships and a conman', 1963). With the political events of 1968 came Fo's decision to abandon his role of 'fool of the bourgeoisie' and adopt a more directly political stance. Nuova Scena (New Stage) emerged out of the original nucleus of the Fo–Rame Company, and under the auspices of the Communist Party it began touring alternative venues – factories, prisons, stadia – performing to audiences of thousands. The author's criticism of the Communists provoked a split, and Fo and Rame formed a new company, La Comune, allied to the 'new left'. Turning an abandoned market into a 600-seat theatre, Fo made it his home for eight years, until forced to leave in 1982. To this central period belong Fo's most famous works: the solo *Mistero Buffo* (1969), in which he demonstrated his brilliant histrionic and improvisatory skills, *Morte accidentale di un anarchico* (*Accidental Death of an Anarchist*, 1970), *Non si paga, non si paga* (*Can't Pay, Won't Pay*, 1974), *Clacson, trombette e pernacchi* (*Trumpets and Raspberries*, 1980) and *Coppia Aperta* (*Open Couple*, 1983), written with Rame. After 1982 Fo returned to perform in mainstream theatres with *Quasi per caso una donna: Elisabetta* (*Almost by Chance a Woman: Elizabeth*, 1984), *Zitti! Stiamo precipitando!* ('Shut up! We are plunging!', 1988), dealing with AIDS, and *Il papa e la strega* (*The Pope and the Witch*, 1989–90). A collection of his writings on theatre, *The Tricks of the Trade*, appeared in 1991. He won the Nobel Prize in 1997. FIRENZA GUIDI

See also MEDIEVAL THEATRE IN THE TWENTIETH CENTURY

Tom Behan, *Dario Fo: Revolutionary Theatre* (2000)
Joseph Farrell and Antonio Scuderi, eds, *Dario Fo: Stage, Text, and Tradition* (2000)
David L. Hirst, *Dario Fo and Franca Rame* (1989)
Tony Mitchell, *Dario Fo: People's Court Jester* (1984)

Foco Novo British touring company, principally for new writing. Foco Novo took its name, a Portuguese idiom meaning 'new starting point', from its first production, a play by BERNARD POMERANCE, who in 1972 set up the company with Roland Rees and David Aukin and wrote their successful *The Elephant Man* (1977). They premièred plays by BRENTON, MATURA and Tunde Ikoli before their funding was cut in 1988. DAN REBELLATO

Roland Rees, *Fringe First: Pioneers of Fringe Theatre on Record* (1992)

Fogerty, Elsie (b. London, 1865; d. Warwick, 4 July 1945) Actress and educator. She was a pioneer of VOICE TRAINING and speech therapy who gave lessons in 'poetic speech' at Crystal Palace, south London, and at the Albert Hall, where in 1906 she founded the Central School of Speech Training and Dramatic Art (later the Central School of Speech and Drama). She tutored numerous great British actors, including LAURENCE OLIVIER and PEGGY ASHCROFT, and had a profound influence on the theatre. She was an indefatigable campaigner for the establishment of a National Theatre. ADRIANA HUNTER

Marion Cole, *The Life of Elsie Fogerty CBE* (1967)

Fokine, Mikhail [Mikhailovich] (b. St Petersburg, Russia, 8 May 1880; d. New York, 22 Aug. 1942)

Dancer and choreographer. An outstanding reformer of ballet, he made the dancer use the whole body as an interpretative and expressive artist within a production that was an integrated whole. From 1909, with DIAGHILEV's company, he put his ideas into practice, in such landmark ballets as *Les Sylphides* (1909), *Carnaval* (1910), *Scheherazade* (1910), *Firebird* (1910) and *Petrushka* (1911). After the war he worked in theatre in London and New York (with BASIL DEAN and MAX REINHARDT). His melding of music, dance and stage design in a wholly original way influenced CHOREOGRAPHY and movement beyond the world of ballet.
ROBERT LEACH

See also DANCE.

Folger, Henry [Clay] (b. New York, 18 June 1857; d. Brooklyn, New York, 11 June 1930) Businessman and collector who, inspired by the philosopher Emerson, began acquiring Shakespeare's works with a 13-volume set of his plays. In 1930 he founded and gave his name to the huge Shakespeare Library in Washington, and bequeathed his collection – which includes 79 First Folios and rivals those in the British Museum and the Bodleian Library – to the nation. The Folger Shakespeare Memorial Library was opened in 1932. In 1970 the Library's director, O. B. Hardison Jr, with Raymond Coinkley, founded the Folger Theater Group, which stages Shakespeare and modern plays in the Elizabethan-style theatre inside the library.
ADRIANA HUNTER

Folies-Bergère The first major Parisian MUSIC HALL, which opened in May 1869, offering a programme of light opera and PANTOMIME. Inspired by London's Alhambra, it became under Paul Derval (1919–66) the most famous music hall in the world, home to international stars such as Chaplin, GUILBERT, CHEVALIER, MISTINGUETT, JOSEPHINE BAKER, Fernandes, PAVLOVA and Matattari. Its trademark was the lavish REVUE spectacle featuring exotic settings and parades of scantily clad women. ANNA MCMULLAN

Charles Castle, *The Folies-Bergère* (1982)

Follies Series of REVUES started by FLORENZ ZIEGFELD in New York in 1907 and taken over after his death in 1932 by the SHUBERT brothers. These opulent 'leg-shows' launched many stars, such as FANNY BRICE, EDDIE CANTOR and W. C. FIELDS, and songs such as 'Shine on Harvest Moon', 'Second Hand Rose' and 'My Man'. From 1915 to 1932 they were designed by JOSEPH URBAN, who gave them their distinctive extravagance. STEPHEN SONDHEIM drew on this tradition for his musical *Follies* (1971). The name was also given to a PIERROT troupe founded by Harry Gabriel Pélissier

(1874–1913) – the only such troupe to find fame in the West End, where they made their debut in 1907. Their programme followed a set pattern of songs, both comic and sentimental, potted plays and burlesques. They never regained their unique position after Pélissier's death though they did become the forerunners of The Co-Optimists, who played successful seasons in London from 1921 through to the 1930s.
REXTON S. BUNNETT

M. Farnsworth, *The Ziegfeld Follies* (1956)

Fonda, Henry [Jaynes] (b. Grand Island, Nebr., 16 May 1905; d. Los Angeles, 12 Aug. 1982) Handsome actor who often portrayed justice-seeking dreamers or archetypical Americans. He worked in community and university companies prior to early Broadway roles in *New Faces of 1934* (1934) and *The Farmer Takes a Wife* (1935), which led to more than 80 films during his career, including *The Grapes of Wrath* (1940) and *On Golden Pond* (1981) for which he won an Academy Award. Fonda returned to Broadway as the officer hero of *Mr Roberts* (1949), for which he won a Tony, notably appearing in *The Caine Mutiny Court Martial* (1954), *Two for the Seesaw* (1958), *A Gift of Time* (1962), *Clarence Darrow* (1974) and *First Monday in October* (1978). His children Peter and Jane Fonda became successful actors. *Fonda: My Story* was published in 1981.
MICHAEL SOMMERS

A. Roberts and M. Goldsterin, *Henry Fonda: A Biography* (1984)

Fontanne, Lynn *see* LUNT, ALFRED

food and drink The rise of naturalism towards the end of the nineteenth century, and the development of the technology to deliver it on stage, transformed eating in plays into an interest in the preparation of food as part of the dramatic action. More than a century later, audiences were still fascinated by an actor making a meal in front of their very eyes, as productions of plays like *Skylight* (1995) by DAVID HARE, in which a teacher cooks for a restaurant owner, confirm. ARNOLD WESKER, once a pastry cook himself, recognizes in his work the social importance of the way people prepare and consume food and drink, and builds the whole of *The Kitchen* (1959) around the usually unseen rituals that lie behind the production and delivery of public eating. Throughout the twentieth century, comedies of manners have been structured around meals: from F. Anstey, who contents himself with a dinner party in *The Man from Blankley's* (1901), and William Collier, who runs the gamut from afternoon tea through dinner to breakfast the next day in

Never Say Die (1912), to playwrights decades later such as ALAN AYCKBOURN or RICHARD NELSON, in whose plays meals frequently occur as central, defining events. FREDERICK LONSDALE has cocktails served in *Spring Cleaning* (1925) to mirror the new fashion in sophisticated drinking habits. However, the food and drink used on stage are often not what they seem. Those in charge of PROP-MAKING have to bear in mind several factors, of which the most important are cost and actor-friendliness. Early in the century in Italy, FUTURISM investigated the theatricality of eating as part of a renewal of both theatre and cuisine. In 1915, the futurists toured a play called *Sempronio's Lunch* by Emilio Settimelli and Bruno Corra, in which the five stages of a man's life are shown in the form of a five-course meal served in five different locations. Led by MARINETTI, the movement opened clubs and restaurants where food was served and consumed in futurist style, including banquets that were themselves theatrical productions. Following in their wake, the relationship of the performer to food also changed, particularly towards the end of the century in PERFORMANCE ART, where artists explored the performance qualities and social meanings in the making and consuming of food. In the 1990s the American Blue Man Group, for instance, challenged the notion of art by regurgitating garishly coloured marshmallows on to a blank screen; South African Jeanne Goosen and Briton Bobby Baker turned the domestic kitchen itself into the performing space in order to challenge constraining notions of gender roles. Cuisine can also play its part off-stage, when companies such as THÉÂTRE DU SOLEIL or TARA ARTS link the food on offer to the AUDIENCE to the shows they are performing. In 1930 ANDRÉ CHARLOT's production of *Wonder Bar* at the SAVOY merged the front stalls with the set and those seated there were served with drinks – a relationship that to varying degrees can be seen in theatres where food and drink can be consumed during performance and in CAFÉ as well as some PUB theatre and in some CABARET. In popular forms such as CARNIVAL, food and drink are integral to the whole experience, and this is reflected in the celebratory work of groups like WELFARE STATE INTERNATIONAL. CHARLES LONDON

E. Aston, ' "Transforming" Women's Lives: Bobby Baker's Performances of "Daily Life" ', *New Theatre Quarterly* 61, vol. 16, part 1, Feb. 2000
G. Berghaus, 'The Theatricality of Food at Futurist Banquets', *New Theatre Quarterly* 65, vol. 17, part 1, Feb. 2001
M. Blumberg, 'Domestic Place as Contestatory Space: The Kitchen as Catalyst and Crucible', *New Theatre Quarterly* 55, vol. 14, part 3, Aug. 1998
Performance Research, vol. 4, no. 1, 1999, 'On Cooking'.

Footlights Club Britain's most famous amateur dramatic society, based at Cambridge University, devoted to comedy and founded in 1883 by Morten Henry Cotton. An elitist club, it admitted only men until the early 1960s (women had appeared sporadically since 1932, but not as members). Before then only a handful of its graduates had entered the professional theatre (e.g. JACK HULBERT, Jimmy Edwards, Richard Murdoch), but after the success of the revue *Beyond the Fringe* (Edinburgh, 1960; London, 1961) drawn from both Cambridge and Oxford, many were to do so who had considerable influence on British and even international humour: Peter Cook, Bill Oddie, Tim Brooke-Taylor; three of the Monty Python team, Eric Idle, Graham Chapman and John Cleese; and Griff Rhys Jones. ADRIANA HUNTER
See also CAMBRIDGE.

Robert Hewison, *Footlights! A Hundred Years of Cambridge Comedy* (1983)
Roger Wilmut, *From Fringe to Flying Circus* (1980)

Footsbarn Travelling Theatre Founded in Cornwall in 1971 by Oliver Foot and John Paul Cook as a publicly funded itinerant COLLECTIVE, which achieved international recognition with *COMMEDIA DELL'ARTE* style Shakespeare (*Hamlet, Lear, Macbeth*). The company moved to France in 1980. ALLEN SADDLER
See also TENT THEATRE.

Forbes-Robertson Jean *see* FORBES-ROBERTSON, JOHNSTON

Forbes-Robertson, Johnston (b. London, 16 Jan. 1853; d. St Margaret's Bay, Dover, Kent, 6 Nov. 1937) Actor–manager. Forbes-Robertson first made a name for himself in Gilbert's *Dan'l Druce, Blacksmith* (1876). His fine features, graceful bearing and much-praised flawless diction qualified him best for classical and Shakespearean roles, and he became a favourite with West End audiences. In 1895 he became actor–manager at the Lyceum; it was here in 1897 that he reached the pinnacle of his career as Hamlet, a part that he continued to play until his retirement in 1913. He was also actor–manager at the St James's Theatre, where his greatest success was as the stranger in Jerome's *The Passing of the Third-Floor Back* (1908). His daughter Jean (1905–62), as well as his three brothers, were also on the stage. He wrote an autobiography, *A Player under Three Reigns* (1925), and was knighted in 1913. ADRIANA HUNTER

Forced Entertainment Theatre Company

Founded in 1984 and based in Sheffield, England, the group defines itself through the mythologies of popular culture by highlighting the contradictions that exist in the codes of social discourse. There is a strong narrative element in its ensemble pieces, although the treatment of the material is completely non-realistic. Instead, they deconstruct the *mise-en-scène* and deliberately destroy any sense of conventional theatre practice: *Red Room* (1993) was a performance INSTALLATION, *Speak Bitterness* (1994) a 'durational' installation and *Paradise* (1997) a project on the INTERNET. Led by artistic director Tim Etchells, the group addresses many disparate issues in any single piece and juxtaposes them, seemingly at random. A piece may begin with a list of words or phrases, as in the case of *Emanuelle Enchanted* (1992) where the opening segment consists of performers running on and off stage carrying a series of signs, indicating attitudes and emotions. The ultimate meaning may never be clearly stated; however, part of the unusual quality of the work is the sense that the narrative is potentially out of control at any given moment. This ever-present threat of anarchy places the COLLECTIVE in the AVANT-GARDE tradition of the twentieth century and makes it one of the most innovative companies in Europe. LAURIE WOLF

T. Etchells, *Certain Fragments* (1999)

Forde, Florrie [Florence Flanagan] (b. Melbourne, 14 August 1876; d. Aberdeen, 18 April 1940) MUSIC HALL and VARIETY artist. Already established as a singing comedienne at home, she moved to London in 1897 and soon became a firm favourite throughout Britain. Her tall, buxom but well-proportioned figure gave her an imposing presence which, coupled with a resonant voice and great clarity of diction, made her the ideal singer of chorus songs like 'The Old Bull and Bush', 'Has Anyone Here Seen Kelly?' and 'Pack Up Your Troubles'. She also appeared often as principal boy in PANTOMIME. In the 1920s and 1930s her touring REVUES and seaside summer seasons introduced many newcomers, notably FLANAGAN and ALLEN.
DONALD ROY

Foreman, Richard (b. New York, 10 June 1937) Playwright, director and designer. Founder of the Ontological-Hysteric Theater in 1968, Foreman has written, directed and designed over 30 original works which have been performed throughout the United States and Europe. His plays break theatre down into its component parts and represent the act of creation as he sees it. He often works like a puppet-master, conducting untrained actors in a philosophical exercise which is defined by the process itself. With composer Stanley Silverman, he has collaborated on a series of MUSICAL THEATRE works. He has also staged the works of classic and contemporary playwrights, from BRECHT and Molière to Kathy Acker and VACLAV HAVEL, and has directed OPERA. ELLEN LAMPERT-GRÉAUX

Kate Davy, *Richard Foreman and the Ontological-Hysteric Theater* (1981)
Gerald Rabkin, ed, *Richard Foreman* (1999)

Formby, George (b. Wigan, Lancs., 26 May 1904; d. Preston, Lancs., 6 March 1961) Comedian, whose stage career began as George Hoy. He took on his famous father's stage name and act after he died, but developed his own stage style of Lancastrian knowing childishness to find success, complete with his trademark ukelele. He entered films in 1934 with *Boot, Boots* and became the top male English box-office performer, famous for comedy songs such as 'Leaning on a Lamp-post' and 'Mr Wu'. During the Second World War he entertained the troops. Later he appeared in musical comedy and REVUE. REXTON S. BUNNETT

John Fisher, *George Formby* (1975)

Fornés, María Irene (b. Havana, Cuba, 14 May 1930) Playwright, director and teacher. The quintessential OFF-OFF-BROADWAY playwright, she is also the Hispanic American theatre's seminal artist. Hatred of brutality and compassion for the dispossessed inform the texts she stages with austere beauty. Her many plays include *Promenade* (1965), *Fefu and Her Friends* (1977), *The Conduct of Life* (1985), *The Mothers* (1986), *And What of the Night?* (1989) and *Oscar and Bertha* (1991). M. ELIZABETH OSBORN
See also HISPANIC THEATRE IN THE UNITED STATES.

Maria M. Delgado and Caridad Svich, eds, *Conducting a Life: Reflections on the Theatre of María Irene Fornés* (2000)
Marc Robinson, *The Theatre of María Irene Fornés* (1999)

Forrest, George *see* WRIGHT, ROBERT

Forsyth, James (b. Glasgow, 5 March 1913) Playwright and designer. After distinguished war service, he became resident playwright at the OLD VIC (1946–8). His plays include *Heloïse* (1951), *The Other Heart* (1952, based on the life of the poet Villon); *Trog* (1959, based on the case of the Elephant Man); and the miracle plays *Emanuel* (1960) and *If My Wings Heal* (1966). Forsyth's highly verbal treatment of historical themes relates him to the revival of VERSE DRAMA in the 1940s and 1950s associated with FRY and others.
PHILIP HOBSBAUM

Forsythe, William (b. New York, 30 Dec. 1949) Choreographer. After training and performing with the Joffrey Ballet and choreographing for the Stuttgart Ballet, Forsythe became the artistic director of Ballet Frankfurt in 1984. While also choreographing ballet pieces for other companies, including the British Royal Ballet, in work with his own company and in collaboration with other artists he has influentially abandoned traditional concepts of PERFORMANCE. In the 1997 *Tight Roaring Circle* he installed a large white bouncy castle in the ROUND HOUSE in London, and from 1989 onwards he collaborated with architect Daniel Liebeskind in the projected redesign of Groningen. In 1999 he became general director of TAT (Theater am Turm), which resulted in a co-production between Ballet Frankfurt and Jan Lauwers Needcompany of a dance/theatre piece *DjamesDjoyceDead* (2000). Taking a deconstructive approach to choreography, Forsythe has developed a CD-ROM that explores improvisational technique through notions of fragmentation and dissolution. MARTIN HARGREAVES

See also CHOREOGRAPHY; DANCE.

Forte, Dieter (b. Düsseldorf, 14 June 1935) Playwright noted for his DOCUMENTARY-style presentation of historical themes. After working as a photographer and painter, Forte began writing plays for radio, with his first play broadcast in 1965. He attracted attention in 1970 with his first stage work *Martin Luther and Thomas Münzer; oder, Die Einführung der Buchhaltung* (*Luther, Münzer, and the Bookkeepers of the Reformation*), a controversial reinterpretation of the period. Forte has continued his re-examination of events and figures in other plays, such as *Jean-Henri Dunant; oder die Einführung der civilisation* (*Jean-Henri Dunant or the Introduction of Civilisation*, 1978) and *Das Labyrinth der Träume; oder, Wie man der Kopf rom Korper trennt* (*The Labyrinth of Dreams or the Separation of the Head from the Body,* 1983), which explores the evils of fascism.
HELEN RAPPAPORT

Fortunato, Depero see FUTURISM

Fortune Theatre Founded in 1974, in Dunedin, New Zealand, it is probably the southernmost English-speaking professional theatre in the world. A century after the gold rush in Otago led to the establishment of early Dunedin theatre, Patric and Rosalie Carey's Globe Theatre made a unique contribution to New Zealand theatre, especially through the plays of JAMES K. BAXTER, yet the Fortune's professional predecessor, the Southern Theatre Trust, foundered in 1970. From its establishment, the Fortune's intention was to produce New Zealand plays, contemporary drama and classics.

Dunedin's audiences have, therefore, been the first in New Zealand to see many plays, including FO's *Accidental Death of an Anarchist* and CHURCHILL's *Cloud Nine*. It has developed close links with Otago University and with local writers ROGER HALL and Leah Poulter. GILLIAN GREER & LAURIE ATKINSON

Fortuny, Mariano *see* FASHION; LIGHTING

forum theatre *see* BOAL, AUGUSTO

Fosse, Bob [Robert Louis] (b. Chicago, 23 June 1927; d. Washington, 23 Sept. 1987) Choreographer and director. Fosse began dancing professionally at the age of 14 and was a chorus boy before providing dances for *The Pajama Game* (1954). Subsequently he choreographed *Damn Yankees* (1955), *New Girl in Town* (1957), *Redhead* (1959), *How to Succeed in Business Without Really Trying* (1961), *Little Me* (1962), *Sweet Charity* (1966), *Pippin* (1972), *Chicago* (1977) and *Dancin'* (1978), among others. He directed many of these shows and co-authored *Chicago*, in which his one-time wife GWEN VERDON had a starring role. His influential style drew on JAZZ and ghetto street dancing and was often marked by tight groupings, angular positions and open, splayed hands. He directed the film *All That Jazz* (1979) about a figure very much like himself. A compilation of his dances called *Fosse* won a Tony Award in 1999 and came to London in the following year.
GERALD BORDMAN

See also CHOREOGRAPHY.

M. Beddow, *Bob Fosse's Broadway* (1997)
M. Gottfried, *All This Jazz: The Life and Death of Bob Fosse* (1990)
K. Grubb, *Razzle Dazzle: The Life and Work of Bob Fosse* (1989)

Foster, Gloria (b. Chicago, 15 Nov. 1936) Actress. Since her OFF-BROADWAY debut in *In White America* (1963), Foster has broken many casting barriers, appearing in roles originally written for white actors, in plays such as *Yerma* (1966), *Coriolanus* (1979), *Mother Courage* (1980) and *Blood Wedding* (1992), and in an all-black production of *Long Day's Journey into Night* (1981). Her appearance in the title role of *Medea* (1965) garnered her a Theater World Award and was one of a string of roles in Greek tragedy, which have included Jocasta, Hecuba, Andromache and Clytemnestra. In 1995 she appeared on Broadway in Emily Mann's *Having Our Say*. HELEN RAPPAPORT

Foy, Eddie [Edwin Fitzgerald] (b. New York, 9 March 1856; d. Kansas City, Mo., 16 Feb. 1928) Comedian and actor who began his career in VAUDEVILLE and touring mining towns with a MINSTREL troupe. After serving as the featured CLOWN in several Chicago musicals he rose to stardom in New York. Among his hits were *Mr Bluebeard* (1903), *Piff! Paff!! Pouf!!!* (1904), *The Earl and the Girl* (1905), *The Orchid* (1907) and *Mr Hamlet of Broadway* (1908). In 1910 he formed a vaudeville act, Eddie Foy and the Seven Little Foys, employing his children. He soon abandoned Broadway and spent the rest of his career with this popular turn. Several of his children went on to success in the entertainment field. *Clowning through Life*, his autobiography, appeared in 1928.

GERALD BORDMAN

Armond Fields, *Eddie Foy: A Biography of the Early Popular Stage Comedian* (1999)

France

1900–1960

The originality and variety of the French theatre in the twentieth century are beyond dispute. As far back as 1882 Henri Becque's naturalist *Les Corbeaux* (*The Ravens*) had left its mark, as did EDMOND ROSTAND's Romantic *Cyrano de Bergerac* in 1898; and in 1924 Simon de Gantillon's *Maya* was translated and played worldwide, daringly modern in its mixture of poetic symbolism and down-to-earth realism as well as its presentation of the multiplicity of identity as seen in the relationship of a prostitute to her various clients. There were 'imported' writers like MAETERLINCK, CROMMELYNCK and DE GHELDERODE from BELGIUM, of considerable merit and some influence, though not as seminal as PIRANDELLO, whose international reputation owed as much to France as to his native Italy. Others who were popular in their day, like EUGÈNE BRIEUX, HENRI BATAILLE, Henry Bernstein and Edouard Bourdet from the earlier years of the century, appeared to fade from the scene, but may yet return. JEAN-JACQUES BERNARD's understated plays of the 1920s and 1930s, in which the silence of intuition expresses what words fail to convey, later awoke interest, as evidenced by the NATIONAL THEATRE's revival in London of *Martine* in 1985. Many – JULES ROMAINS, MARCEL ACHARD, ANDRÉ OBEY, Georges Neveux, ARMAND SALACROU, MARCEL AYMÉ, Félicien Marceau, RENÉ DE OBALDIA, ARTHUR ADAMOV, FRANÇOIS BILLETDOUX, MARGUERITE DURAS, BORIS VIAN, NATHALIE SARRAUTE – have had their work presented abroad. Others, such as JACQUES AUDIBERTI, GEORGES SCHÉHADÉ, JEAN TARDIEU and ARMAND GATTI, are less well known outside France. Yet these, like most of the others, seem assured of some survival, even if only in the number of academic theses they have spawned. And this is not to mention the more light-hearted, such as MARCEL PAGNOL, SACHA GUITRY or ANDRÉ ROUSSIN, whose names have been familiar to many.

As Europe emerged into the twentieth century, the theatre was waking up. France had been more distinguished for its novelists and poets than for its playwrights; theatre was thought of as either an inferior branch of literature or a frivolous pastime. The year 1896 produced three events prophetic of changes to come. The 'Shakespearean' tragedy *Lorenzaccio* by the long-dead Alfred de Musset was staged for the first time. This was symptomatic. The French view of Shakespeare was beginning to change. Perhaps tragedy did not have to be Racinian after all. Yet even the Romantic and melodramatic tragedies of Victor Hugo had maintained certain elements of classical form, which Musset had dispensed with. SARAH BERNHARDT still felt the play had to be tidied up and adapted a bit, but she put it on, assuming the role of the male protagonist herself, a *tour de force* with great appeal to an audience and one she was to repeat three years later when she played Hamlet. Also in 1896, HENRY DE MONTHERLANT was born, one of France's greatest dramatists of the coming century, yet one who still maintained his links with the French classical tradition. Finally, one of the new theatre companies performed ALFRED JARRY's *Ubu Roi*, a staggering novelty that in retrospect seems to have started a highly AVANT-GARDE trend which continued through APOLLINAIRE's *Mamelles de Tirésias* (*The Breasts of Tiresias*, 1917) and in the 1920s and 1930s in early COCTEAU, the SURREALISTS, ROGER VITRAC's *Victor* (seen in London in 1964) and ANTONIN ARTAUD, leading eventually to the THEATRE OF THE ABSURD.

France had started a new revolution, not one that devoured its children but one that invested in their future. The first stage of the revolution came with the establishment of little theatre companies, sometimes as clubs, and the general emergence of a long line of director–managers with three main aims: first, to re-theatricalize the theatre; second, to open French eyes to the international repertoire of drama, classical and contemporary; third, to attract the best contemporary writers back to the theatre and so find a new audience which would no longer be content with 'after-dinner' well-made plays about adultery and money or those lively farces, good as they were, which had built up the reputation of a Labiche or a FEYDEAU.

The two principal literary movements had been NATURALISM and SYMBOLISM. The first directors attempted to make them stageworthy. ANDRÉ ANTOINE and his Théâtre Libre, founded in 1887, was soon followed by LUGNÉ-POE and his Théâtre de l'Oeuvre, where Jarry's *Ubu Roi* was first performed. These threads were drawn together by JACQUES COPEAU, founder of the Théâtre du Vieux Colombier in 1913, who wanted to concentrate on a sound text spoken by good actors on the barest of stages. He later established a school in Burgundy and so was one of the first to take good theatre to the provinces. *Le Théâtre Populaire*, which he published in 1941, also did much to foster decentralization. He familiarized the French with Molière's neglected farces and Shakespeare's mostly unknown comedies; though, like them, a complete 'man of the theatre', he failed to find his ideal playwright. In spite of the support of writers like PAUL CLAUDEL and ANDRÉ GIDE, the directors he trained proved his most important legacy. CHARLES DULLIN and LOUIS JOUVET, both members of Copeau's troupe, went on to form their own separate companies in the 1920s. Dullin worked a great deal with Armand Salacrou and helped to introduce Jean Cocteau and JEAN-PAUL SARTRE. He also founded an influential school of his own, where JEAN-LOUIS BARRAULT rubbed shoulders with Antonin Artaud and a younger generation of future directors such as JEAN VILAR, ROGER BLIN and ANDRÉ BARSACQ. Jouvet's company was richer and more prestigious, and he had the good luck to find an outstanding playwright: JEAN GIRAUDOUX, who soon gained an international reputation for his verbally highly wrought, yet classically inspired and penetrating fantasies. Jouvet went on to direct plays by Sartre and GENET.

Out of Copeau's school came his nephew, MICHEL SAINT-DENIS, who founded the COMPAGNIE DES QUINZE (with his own writer, André Obey). His later career took him to London, where he helped to found the OLD VIC Theatre School and so brought to England a tradition that induced GEORGE DEVINE to form the ENGLISH STAGE COMPANY at the ROYAL COURT THEATRE.

Copeau's example also inspired the Catholic-oriented Léon Chancerel to tour round France with his Comédiens Routiers, several of whose members – such as Hubert Gignoux – went on to head some of the new Centres Dramatiques in the provinces after the war. Chancerel did much to foster a community-based theatre with social implications. Jean Dasté (1904–94), Copeau's son-in-law, went on to become director of the Comédie de Saint-Etienne in 1947 – the second Centre Dramatique to be founded, after Strasbourg – bringing the theatre to an audience of miners and industrial workers. In association with Dullin and Jouvet, GEORGES PITOËFF and GASTON BATY, who also had their own companies, formed the Cartel des Quatre in 1927. Respecting the differences in emphasis between them, the Cartel's policy of mutual help and encouragement furthered the acceptance of Copeau's

ideals, most of which they shared, and in 1936 they captured the citadel of French tradition by taking over the COMÉDIE-FRANÇAISE. Baty, who continued the rediscovery of Musset's drama, was noted for his brilliant lighting techniques, and, like Pitoëff, raised the reputation of HENRI-RENÉ LENORMAND's steamy 'Freudian' dramas in the 1920s.

If Dullin had first introduced Pirandello to the French, it was above all Pitoëff who made him famous with his production of *Six Characters in Search of an Author* in 1923. He then became the chief purveyor of a wide international repertoire of plays by SCHNITZLER, CHEKOV, Tolstoy and SHAW, among others. With Louis Jouvet, all three directed plays by Jean Cocteau, the odd-job man of all the arts and a representative figure of the 1920s and 1930s, comparable perhaps to, though far more versatile than, NOËL COWARD in Britain. Pitoëff was also the first to promote JEAN ANOUILH, later to be linked above all with André Barsacq, whose productions helped him to become possibly the most widely performed French dramatist outside France.

During the Second World War and, more importantly, in the 1950s, Barrault and Vilar came into prominence. Barrault had learned much from the MIME artist DECROUX. He believed strongly in the importance of movement and gesture, lessons he put brilliantly into practice in the film *Les Enfants du Paradis* (1944), and he laid great stress on breathing patterns in the actor's use of voice. Though working most often on texts that belong firmly to literary drama, he delighted in farce and at the end of the 1960s in spectacular 'celebrations', as of *Rabelais* and *Jarry*, displaying all the theatrical arts in vast spaces not unlike the more egalitarian creations of ARIANE MNOUCHKINE in the 1970s. His close acquaintance with Artaud and his theories led him into productions which conveyed SYMBOLIST and EXPRESSIONIST ideas in physical and highly theatrical terms, enhanced by full use of modern technical facilities, not excluding cinema, to create an experience of TOTAL THEATRE.

The author with whom he collaborated most intimately was the Catholic writer Paul Claudel, most of whose plays were conceived in the early part of the century, in many ways the new poetic dramatist Copeau had tried to promote. More than anyone Barrault was responsible for enhancing Claudel's reputation as a dramatist. After a spell with the Comédie-Française, Barrault and his wife, MADELEINE RENAUD, for many years ran a successful company of their own. He was never afraid of the avant-garde and encouraged many new writers, helping to make Eugène Ionesco respectable with his *Rhinoceros* in 1960.

Vilar, like FIRMIN GÉMIER, who in 1920 had first founded a theatre for 'the people' in Paris, wanted to make the theatre accessible to all classes of society. In 1947 he founded the AVIGNON FESTIVAL and in 1950 the THÉÂTRE NATIONAL POPULAIRE at the Palais de Chaillot, where he had vast stages and huge audiences at his disposal. Décor and costume were to remain simple, with great stress laid on the power of communication of disciplined actors. His collaboration with the idolized actor GÉRARD PHILIPPE won him great triumphs in Corneille's *Le Cid* (1949), Kleist's *Prince of Homburg* (1951) and Musset's *Lorenzaccio* (1952). Although he tackled plays by Shakespeare, Hugo, Jarry and Claudel, he also encouraged new writers such as ADAMOV. His taste for EPIC and political drama soon led him through Büchner to BRECHT; and the first major production of *Mother Courage* in 1951, notwithstanding the severe criticisms levelled at his interpretation, launched a tradition new to the French and laid the foundations on which directors like ROGER PLANCHON later built.

All these 'men of the theatre', in spite of differences in emphasis and experimental flair, were fundamentally inspired by Jacques Copeau, who had been so responsive to the international stirrings of his day, to the work of APPIA, CRAIG and STANISLAVSKY, and had thus led the French theatre out of the closet of a narrowly French and Parisian tradition. The generation of directors that followed were to stray variously from his path, but the importance of theatre as a serious art form was by this time firmly established.

The various attempts that had been made to build up a regional and working-class public for the theatre received governmental support with the arrival in 1936 of the Front Populaire, which fostered a number of young companies. During the Second World War, in a divided France, their activities started to drift away from Paris, which under German occupation suffered a stifling censorship. In 1943 Barrault was able to stage a memorable production of Claudel's *Soulier de Satin* (*The Satin Slipper*), but if Dullin got away with Sartre's *Les Mouches* (*The Flies*), and in 1941 Barsacq with Anouilh's *Antigone*, it was doubtless because these naked appeals for resistance were still draped in the mythology of ancient Greece, so fashionable in earlier years in the updated interpretations of Cocteau and Giraudoux.

From 1946, however, after the liberation, the founding of countrywide regional centres, which could radiate into local areas, decentralized theatre as a matter of official policy. Paris was no longer the lure. Confronted by so many subsidized companies presenting the classical repertoire and the work of many talented new writers of serious intent, the frivolous commercial theatre of the boulevards was gradually eclipsed. Fashion was turning to drama that was more intellectual and philosophical – and, after the visit of Brecht's BERLINER ENSEMBLE in 1954, increasingly concerned with politics and society in a Marxist context. The new trend was most apparent in the work of ALBERT CAMUS and Sartre. Their reputation outside the theatre as moral philosophers was rapidly growing when Sartre's *Huis Clos* (*No Exit*) and Camus' *Caligula* were staged in 1944 and 1945. Extending into the 1950s, their drama did much to accustom the world to the concept of the absurd – absence of meaning in a godless universe. Man must invent meaning for himself. Their plays, then, which are conventional in form, are the exposure of a problem, its exploration and the search for a solution. The human condition had long been the true subject of the best French playwrights. Unsurprisingly, Sartre's and Camus' assessment was shaped by the war and by death, overlaid by considerations of revolt and dictatorship, freedom and moral responsibility. Both writers leaned towards melodrama. Sartre was more Marxist, Camus more of a humanist, but both developed their ideas and shifted their ground. Sartre was much concerned with identity, picking up France's debt to Pirandello and preparing himself and his audience for Genet.

With the appearance in the 1950s of SAMUEL BECKETT and Ionesco, a new movement emerged, giving rise, in MARTIN ESSLIN's coinage, to the theatre of the absurd. Antecedents were found in the work of Jarry, Apollinaire, Cocteau and several surrealists. Absurd in both form and content, these later plays may well have expressed postwar fatigue and disillusionment in their pessimism and hopelessness, but they bristled with shock, surprise and humour. Untrammelled by convention or tradition, their authors broke fresh ground in play-making, and a stream of writers emerged, loosely associated but all sharply differentiated: the early Adamov, Tardieu, Romain Weingarten, Obaldia, Vian, Roland Dubillard, Fernando ARRABAL and others, all specializing in the unlikely, the imaginative, the grotesque, often veined with laughter, puns and wordplay. They are anti-realists in every sense, evoking dreams and nightmares, personal and idiosyncratic, accepting all that is opposed to reason, logic and common sense, rejecting ideas and concepts, mostly indifferent to social or political argument. Yet they demonstrated that you could make a play without plot or character development, devoid of a significant message or logical progression, that could yet liberate the imagination, draw attention to spiritual or metaphysical values, reveal an unexpected depth in your complacent everyday self and at the same time allow you to stand back and laugh.

Irish Beckett, writing in English or French and able to translate himself, not surprisingly made the biggest impact in the English-speaking world with his *Waiting for Godot*, *Endgame* and *Happy Days*. Ionesco too established himself strongly, especially with his early plays *The Lesson*, *The Chairs*, *The Bald Prima Donna* and *Exit the King*, in which a whole generation of distinguished British actors were to appear, including LAURENCE OLIVIER and ALEC GUINNESS.

While Anouilh continued in the 1950s and 1960s to fill the BOULEVARD theatres with pseudo-realistic plays that shocked and titillated his bourgeois audiences, the anti-realist French tradition was confirmed not only by the absurdists, whose work was performed largely in the tiny theatres that then proliferated in Paris, but also by new writers such as Adamov and Genet. They were promoted by Jouvet, Vilar, Barrault and Blin in the spirit of the visionary Artaud, whose essays in *The Theatre and its Double*, first published in 1938, became known internationally at this time. An admirer of Jarry, briefly a surrealist, Artaud knew all the major theatrical figures of the interwar years and, absorbing many of the existing trends, built up his own highly personal theories. His own experiments as a director appeared too off-beat and his THEATRE OF CRUELTY – 'cruel above all for myself' – was imperfectly understood, but his rejection of a bourgeois theatre of words, his belief that a stage was pre-eminently 'a space to be filled' and that the theatre should convey a metaphysical experience through the creation of a new theatre language, stimulated many, including PETER BROOK, to test out his ideas.

Adamov was a writer who believed, like Artaud, that the essence of the theatre lay in performance and that the concrete world of objects on stage could achieve a metaphysical dimension. But his dream-like early plays – he much admired STRINDBERG – gradually took on a more social orientation. First adopted by Vilar, and later by Planchon, he had a natural affinity with Blin, who directed *La Parodie* in 1950 and then the first production of Beckett's *Godot* in 1953. Blin went on to become the perfect interpreter of Genet, directing *Les Nègres* (*The Blacks*) in 1959 and *Les Paravents* (*The Screens*) in 1966.

In Genet's plays anti-realism reaches a peak. Though himself an outcast, with scant connection to the theatre, he comes closest perhaps, thanks to Blin's familiarity with Artaud, to the sort of theatre Artaud dreamed of; yet, unlike Artaud, he still conceived his creations in highly coloured poetic language. Violent, shocking, ambiguous in every sense, by inverting and subverting the rituals of power and belief he presented the conflicts of class, politics and racialism in complex, mythical and symbolic celebrations.

DONALD WATSON

1960–2000

When de Gaulle set about consolidating the Fifth Republic in the early 1960s, he was determined that French language and culture should once again assume the dominant role that they had played in the time of Louis XIV. He appointed André Malraux Minister for Culture, authorizing him to make big increases in spending on all aspects of the arts, especially a programme of new buildings to house the performing arts. Malraux had a vision of Maisons de la Culture covering France with a freemasonry of artists and performers as the great Gothic cathedrals had done in the Middle Ages.

The pioneers of decentralized theatre, men such as Jean Dasté, Hubert Gignoux and ROGER PLANCHON, who until now had felt rather isolated, found sudden encouragement from the Ministry; an expansion of theatre provision outside Paris began, which was to continue until the century's end, faltering only in the 1970s. The result is that today no French town of any size is without its municipal theatre or Maison de la Culture. In 1996, as well as the five National Theatres, there were 35 CENTRES DRAMATIQUES Nationaux and 63 Scènes Nationales (some formerly Maisons de la Culture) as well as around 60 independent Paris theatres and over 500 small-scale companies in receipt of government money. The level of subsidy needed to keep this great theatre network operating is more than double the amount allocated by the British government (for a population of about the same size).

At first this expansion met with approval from all sections of the theatre community. The example of JEAN VILAR had shown that new life could be breathed into the classical repertoire, and it was Vilar's example that most of the new young companies sought to emulate. Their work was further fuelled by the discovery of a modern playwright whose plays could speak to all classes of society (not just the habitual theatregoers) and whose reputation had only just been established in France: BERTOLT BRECHT. In the course of the 1960s, the decentralized theatres performed the works of Brecht more frequently than those of any other author except Molière and Shakespeare.

The heady atmosphere of expansion and the conquest of new audiences created a demand for new work of social relevance. The plays of the Martiniquan AIMÉ CÉSAIRE and of the Algerian KATEB YACINE were performed in France, and prompted French authors to create dramas out of the struggles of once colonized peoples. ARMAND GATTI and GABRIEL COUSIN both wrote a number of plays dealing with oppression in different parts of the world.

With the upheavals of 1968 many of the new young theatre workers began to question the state's cultural expansionism. Perhaps it served only to reinforce the power of the bourgeois state, they argued, and while it appeared to give a voice to opposition and dissent, perhaps it was really no more than 'repressive tolerance'. The sacking of theatre directors (including JEAN-LOUIS BARRAULT) who had allowed their theatres to be used for political meetings, confirmed feelings that the state was more repressive than tolerant, and a sharp change of mood swept through much of French theatre: Vilar's broadly humanist goal of a theatre open to all was rejected in favour of a more frankly partisan POLITICAL THEATRE.

Coinciding with this new mood, there came the discovery of COLLECTIVE devising methods known as *la création collective*. The leader in this was ARIANE MNOUCHKINE and her company Le THÉÂTRE DU SOLEIL, who staged two remarkable productions tracing the history of the French Revolution, *1789* (1970) and *1793* (1972). Her initiative was followed by many other companies up and down the country and the success of these devised performances led to a sharp decline in the number of new plays reaching the stage. At the same time there was a crisis in theatre publishing, so that even fewer plays were getting into print. The combination of these things led some to declare that the playwright was dead.

This perception was reinforced by the growing power of the theatre directors in the course of the 1970s. Directors such as Roger Planchon, PATRICE CHÉREAU, Ariane Mnouchkine, ANTOINE VITEZ, Jean-Pierre Vincent, JÉROME SAVARY, Jorge Lavelli and PETER BROOK became the acknowledged stars of the French theatre. Most of these charismatic directors preferred to stage the classics or adaptations of prose writing, and so the writing of new plays suffered. By the beginning of the 1980s much of the playwright's traditional authority in the French theatre had been eroded by directors with a talent for putting on large-scale visual displays of great brilliance, a tendency that was reinforced by examples from the German theatre such as PETER STEIN's Schaubühne.

In the 1980s, however, the playwrights staged a come-back. The plays of GENET were revived (he entered the COMÉDIE-FRANÇAISE repertoire for the first time) and there was a renewed interest in the work of women playwrights, both those of the older generation, such as MARGUERITE DURAS and NATHALIE SAR-RAUTE, but also those of younger authors, many of whom had learned their craft as performers, such as YASMINA REZA, Catherine Anne, Philip Minyana and Olivier Py. The most notable new playwright to emerge in this period was BERNARD-MARIE KOLTÈS whose play *Struggle of the Dogs and the Black* was chosen by Chéreau to open his new Théâtre des Amandiers at Nanterre in 1983. Chéreau went on to stage all of Koltès' major plays until the premature death of the playwright in 1989.

The other major playwright of the period was MICHEL VINAVER, though his early plays date from the mid-1950s. Most of his works are set in offices or commercial businesses and deal with everyday situations that are the opposite of those found in Koltès, being remarkable only for their ordinariness. But he employs a highly original dramatic technique which proceeds by fragmentation and dislocation, so that his characters may find themselves placed in several different situations simultaneously. As a result, different layers of dialogue and theme overlap, building up a dense, poetic texture.

'Theatre of the everyday' was a term employed by critics to designate the work of playwrights who shared Vinaver's exploitation of details drawn from ordinary life. The plays of Jean-Paul Wenzel, Michel Deutsch, Daniel Lemahieu and Daniel Besnehard, use contradictions and discontinuities to dramatize situations that are often banal and characters who are frequently inarticulate. Some of these authors have shown a tendency to return again and again to events set in wartime France under the Nazi occupation, as if the alienation and brutality experienced by certain sections of contemporary French society could all be traced back to those years. Others, such as Jean-Christophe Bailly and Valère Novarina, aim to recreate a theatre of mythical dimensions. At the same time, there is a proliferation of work in MIME, PERFORMANCE ART and other experimental areas.

After the events of 1968 the theatre became more inward-looking, more self-critical, but also more self-absorbed. Amid all the diversity of contemporary work, the pioneering spirit of the years following the liberation was lost, and with it went the confidence in the notion that a vigorous cultural life could help to reinforce democratic freedoms. DAVID BRADBY

David Bradby, *Modern French Drama* (1991)

David Bradby and Annie Sparks, *Mise en scène: French Theatre Now* (1997)

H. Hobson, *French Theatre since 1830* (1978)

D. Knowles, *French Drama of the Inter-War Years, 1918–39* (1967)

Franceschild, Donna *see* WOMEN'S THEATRE GROUP

Frank, Bruno (b. Stuttgart, Germany, 13 June 1887, d. Beverly Hills, Calif., 20 June 1945) Writer who emigrated from his native Germany to America in 1933. In contrast to his early EXPRESSIONISM, he is best known for BOULEVARD/'folk' dramas, notably *Die Schwestern und der Fremde* (*The Sisters and the Stranger*, 1918), *Zwölftausend* (*Twelve Thousand*, 1927) and *Sturm im Wasserglas* (produced in Britain as *Storm in a Teacup* and in the United States as *Storm over Patsy*, 1930). JUDY MEEWEZEN

Fraser, Claude Lovat (b. London, 15 May 1890; d. London, 18 June 1921) Set and costume designer. He was often credited with launching a new era with his designs for *The Beggar's Opera* (LYRIC, Hammersmith, 1920). These challenged the tradition of detailed romantic realism with a single unit setting and simple bright and stylish costumes. His designs were compared to those of CRAIG and BAKST, but Fraser's charming style was unique. During his brief career he produced designs for a variety of ballets, operas, and classical and contemporary plays. MARVIN CARLSON

Fraser, Toa (b. Kingston, Surrey, 4 Jan. 1975) Playwright. Born of Fijian and English parents, he was educated in Auckland, New Zealand, where his first play, *Bare*, was premièred in 1998. It has since been staged to great acclaim at the EDINBURGH FESTIVAL and on tour in Australia. A *tour de force* for its two performers (one male, one female) who play 15 roles in the course of its 110 minutes, it reflects the author's own experiences growing up in an environment where Maori, *pakeha* (those of European descent) and Islanders across the generations find themselves alternately at odds with and in search of their own histories. His second play, a series of monologues baldly titled *No. 2*, also received enthusiastic reviews in Edinburgh, and was staged at the inaugural Tasmanian Arts Festival in 2001. Fraser has also worked in film and television. MICHAEL MORLEY

Frayn, Michael (b. Ewell, Surrey, 8 Sept. 1933) Playwright, novelist, journalist and translator. Frayn is a highly regarded translator and adapter of CHEKHOV, and several of his own plays are of similarly tragic-comic style. Others are fuelled by more frenetic comedy. *Noises Off* (1982) is perhaps his most successful: a brilliantly crafted FARCE about a company of actors touring a production of 'Nothing On'; a farce-within-a-farce. *Noises Off* is also a witty parody of a dated style of comedy, acting and production. Other of his plays reflect similarly shambolic institutions: the library of a provincial paper (*Alphabetical Order*, 1975)

and a university college (*Donkey's Years*, 1976). Other plays include *Clouds* (1976, about a journalists' trip to Cuba), *Benefactors* (1984, about a fifteen-year battle between a journalist and an architect), *Now You Know* (1995, based on his novel of the same title), *Alarms and Excursions* (1998, a collection of revue sketches) and *Copenhagen* (1998, about a possible meeting beetween two nuclear scientists in 1941). He has also written screenplays, notably *Clockwise* (1986), which starred John Cleese as a time-obsessed headmaster. DAVID SELF

free theatre Term designating the revolutionary NATURALISM developed by ANDRÉ ANTOINE in a small theatre (the Théâtre Libre) in Montparnasse, Paris, from 1887. Free from the pressures of the dominant commercial BOULEVARD theatre, Antoine created a new realism of speech, characterization and set design which stimulated other experimental 'free' theatres. OTTO BRAHM founded his FREIE BÜHNE in Berlin in 1889 and J. T. GREIN followed with his INDEPENDENT THEATRE SOCIETY in London in 1891. These theatres, brilliantly staging IBSEN, STRINDBERG and HAUPTMANN, as well as more traditional plays, helped change the expectations of theatregoers. They established the 'fourth wall' convention, encouraged new writing and created a more natural acting style. TERRY HODGSON
See also INDEPENDENT THEATRE.

John Stokes, *Resistible Theatres* (1972)

Freedley, George [Reynolds] (b. Richmond, Va, 5 Sept. 1904; d. Bay Shore, NY, 11 Sept. 1967) Theatrical historian. After studying with GEORGE PIERCE BAKER he took work with the THEATRE GUILD as an actor and technical director. In 1931 he joined the New York Public Library where he established a theatre collection, becoming its curator in 1938. He was a founder of both the Theatre Library Association and the Equity Library Theatre, and served as secretary to the New York Drama Critics' Circle. For a brief time he was drama critic for the *Morning Telegraph*. He was a co-author of or contributor to numerous books on theatre. GERALD BORDMAN

Freehold *see* ARTS CLUB

Freeman, David *see* CANADA: THEATRE IN ENGLISH

Freie Bühne (Free Stage) Theatrical production and membership organization founded by critic OTTO BRAHM in Berlin in 1889. Inspired by ANTOINE's Théâtre Libre, though more consistently devoted to naturalistic drama, it operated as a private theatre CLUB to avoid CENSORSHIP. It championed IBSEN, introduced HAUPTMANN, launched a journal that became a leading German periodical and became the experimental wing of the Deutsches Theater when Brahm was made director. IAN SAVILLE

See also FREE THEATRE; VOLKESBÜHNE.

John Osborne, *The Naturalist Drama in Germany* (1971)

French, David (b. Coley's Point, Newfoundland, 18 Jan. 1939) Playwright. French moved to Toronto with his family when he was seven, and the contrast between the values of rural Newfoundland and urban Toronto has been the theme of a number of his plays. Both *Leaving Home* (1972) and *Of the Fields, Lately* (1973) dramatize the conflict between a father, Jacob Mercer, born in Newfoundland, and his son, Ben, born in Toronto. The third Mercer play, *Salt-Water Moon* (1984), takes place in 1926 and dramatizes Jacob's courtship of his wife, Mary. The final play of the tetralogy, *1949* (1988), deals with the Mercer family and their friends on the eve of Newfoundland's joining Canada in 1949. The most commercially successful of French's plays is *Jitters* (1979), a sparkling comedy about a small Toronto theatre producing a new Canadian play. His *That Summer* (2000) was directed by BILL GLASSCO at the Blyth Festival, Ontario. EUGENE BENSON

French African theatre (sub-Saharan) Unlike the British, who used a policy in Africa of indirect rule, the French aimed to create French citizens out of the natives of their colonies. This had serious implications for the theatre of the francophone countries, both during and after colonialism. Although individually unique as nations, the former French and Belgian colonies, because of this centralizing policy of assimilation, shared a similar colonial experience out of which has developed what appears to be a similar cultural identity based on a synthesis of African and French and Belgian cultural values and traditions. It is, therefore, possible to speak of a francophone African culture south of the Sahara in a way one cannot speak of an Anglophone African culture. The countries referred to comprise a group of states formerly colonized by either France or Belgium, and in some cases Germany, in which French has become the official language of government, business and education. Countries included are Benin, Burkina Faso, Cameroon, Central African Republic, Chad, Congo Republic, Côte d'Ivoire, Gabon, Guinea, Madagascar, Mali, Niger, Senegal, Togo, and Zaire (later the Democratic Republic of Congo). (For French-speaking theatre in north Africa, *see* MIDDLE EAST AND NORTH AFRICA).

As with other African countries, the French-speaking nations have very vibrant traditional theatre performances. These range from the ubiquitous dances and ritual drama to the oral narratives that have produced enduring classics such as the Sundiata and the Mwindo epics of Mali and Zaire, and the widespread masquerade tradition, such as the *Gelede* of Benin and the funeral masques of the Dogon of Mali. In Mali, there is also a highly developed, effective and popular satirical theatre, the *koteba* of the Bambara.

Literary theatre has only a recent history, emerging between the two world wars as the French expanded their influence, yet it boasts nearly 300 published plays of very high quality. Some of the Francophone playwrights are among the best to emerge from sub-Saharan Africa, such as BERNARD DADIE and Zadi Zourou of Côte d'Ivoire; Jacques Rabemanjara of Madagascar; Sony Labou Tansi, Felix Tchikaya U'Tamsi and Sylvia Bemba from Congo; GUILLAUME OYONO-MBIA and Werewere Liking from Cameroon; Cheik N'dao, Abdou Ka, Seyni Mbengue and Amadou Cisse Dia from Senegal; Seydou Badian from Mali; and Senovou Zinsou from Togo. Christian missionaries made extensive use of the theatre to teach the Bible. This practice eventually led to a gradual emergence of European-style dramatic sketches and playlets, which were widespread, especially in Gabon and Dahomey (now Benin), and were the first examples of Francophone African theatre. European-style theatre in French West Africa started at the Ecole Primaire Supérieure in Bingeville, Côte d' Ivoire, but really flowered at the Ecole Normale William Ponty, founded in Goree, Senegal, in 1913. This was a preparatory school for future African civil servants, teachers and doctors for the whole of French West Africa. The school authorities encouraged the students to write plays for various occasions, based on their respective national histories and cultures. Although modelled on European theatre, diverse African themes began to be presented. This was to remain the pattern for many years as most of the early dramatists, such as Dadié and Fodeba Keita, were Pontians and have been instrumental in shaping the political as well as artistic development of their countries both before and after independence. Two major plays to emerge from the Ponty era were *Banyol et Behanzin* (1933) by a group of Dahomean students, and Dadie's *Les Villes* ('The cities', 1931). The Ponty style of historical drama and return to roots dominated French-African theatre well into the 1980s.

To help promote cultural activity as part of its cultural policy, in 1953 the colonial government initiated a programme of cultural centres or circles in each of the major cities of the federation, and to this was added a drama competition in 1955. It was compulsory for all centre groups to participate and it lasted until 1958 when the wave of independence movements began among the French West African states. Independence brought the establishment of schools of theatre in countries such as Senegal, Mali and Côte d'Ivoire, and there emerged a drive to research, preserve and use as much as possible African traditional performance aesthetics while remaining acutely aware of styles and traditions from around the world. This was more evident in the works of dramatists who went to study in France and returned after independence.

Thematically, Francophone African theatre can be divided into three broad categories: historical, social and political. A preoccupation with historical themes dominated in the early period and for some time after independence. In these plays it was usual for heroes and events from the African past to be exalted, both in stature and in the language of representation. Good examples of this are Rabemanjara's *Les Dieux mala-gaches* ('The Malagassy Gods', 1964), *L' Exil d'Albouri* ('The exile of Albouri', 1967) by N'dao, *La Mort de Chaka* ('The death of Chaka') by Badian, Dia's *Les Derniers de Lat Dior* ('The last days of Lat Dior', 1966), Dadié's *Beatrice du Congo* ('Beatrice of the Congo', 1970) and Senyi Mbengue's *Le Process de Lat Dior* ('The trial of Lat Dior', 1971). By stressing the glories and nobility of the African past and the valiant resistance to European occupation by nineteenth-century African leaders, the plays hoped to discredit colonialism. The writers also hoped to rehabilitate African history, which had been denigrated or denied by colonial history. This theatre was, therefore, right from its beginnings political and functional, stressing through its portrayals the validity and importance of the African past. Other plays in this category are *Lat Dior ou le Chemin de l'honneur* ('Lat Dior or the path of honour') by Thierno Ba, *Chaka, roi visionaire* ('Chaka, visionary king') by M. Fall, *Continent-Afrique suivi de Amazoulous* ('Continent-Africa followed by Amazulu', 1970) by Guinean Condetto Nenekhaly-Camara, and D. T. Niane's *Sikasso ou la dernier citadelle suivi de Chaka* ('Sikasso or the last citadel followed by Chaka', 1976).

Plays in the social category concern themselves with exploring the tensions in, as well as the dislocations to, traditional values and belief systems brought about by encounters with modern culture, especially the foreign West European culture which arrived via the cultural imperialism of the colonial assimilation policy. Even though most of these social plays emphasize the evils of colonialism, their exploration of traditional African values and customs avoids extolling them or glossing over their inadequacies, anachronisms and tyrannous impositions. Indeed, they criticize traditional values, especially some of those customs which have become discredited or been found inadequate in dealing with new realities. The social plays are more

contemporary in the themes and situations which they present, such as the hilariously comic plots and situations one finds in Oyono-Mbia's Molièresque *Trois pretendants ... un mari* ('Three suitors ... one husband', 1964) and Menga's *La Marmite de Koka Mbala* ('Koko Mbala's pot', 1969). Other plays in the social category are Rabemanjara's *Agapes des dieux, Tritriva* (*The Reunion of the Gods* or *The Lovers of Tritriva*, 1962), a tragic love story which attacks traditional oppressive marriage customs; Dadié's *Monsieur Thogo-Gnini* (1970), a play about the destructive individualism of a self-seeker; U'Tamsi's *Le Destin glorieux du Marechal Nnikon Nniku* ('The glorious destiny of Marshal Nnikon Nniku', 1979); Maxime N'debeka's *Equatorium* (1989); and Labou Tansi's *La Paranthèse de sang* ('Parenthesis of blood', 1981) and *Je soussigné cardiaque* ('I, the undersigned cardiac case', 1981). The latter plays are more critical of the political tyrannies and dictatorships, the corruption and inefficiencies of these kingdoms and their rulers, which they use as metaphors for the politics of post-independence African states. There are numerous other plays in French-African theatre which fall within this category and they are quite popular with audiences, for whom the realities presented are quite close to home.

The political plays, which overlap with the social (as in Tansi's later plays), began to emerge in the late 1980s and early 1990s. However, there were during the colonial period a few plays which were overtly political and attacked the racism and unequal nature of the colonial relationship. For example, Antoine Letembet-Ambily's *L'Europe inculpée* ('Europe convicted', 1970), an allegorical verse play, was set as a trial of Europe for her colonial crimes against Africa, with other continents as characters prosecuting or defending. French-African dramatists of the later period are more militant, seeming to have outgrown the outmoded appeals to Europe which the Negritude style and philosophy of their predecessors had favoured. They seem also to be more experimental, both in their subject matter and in their theatre styles and forms. This new generation, who very often are actors in or directors of their own theatre companies, includes Werewere Liking, who explores the ritual form in her plays while her company, Kiyi-Mbok, uses masks, puppets, dance, music and mime. She lives and works in Côte d'Ivoire and her plays, which are feminist, include *La Queue du diable* ('The devil's tail', 1976), *La Puissance de Um* ('The power of Um', 1979), *Une nouvelle terre* ('A new earth', 1980), *Les Mains veulent dire* ('Hands have meaning', 1987) and *La Rougeole arc-en-ciel* ('Rainbow measles', 1987). Others are Sony Labou Tansi (e.g. *La Rue des Mouches*, 'The Street of Flies', 1985); Senouvo Zinsou, best known for *La Tortue qui chante* ('The singing tortoise', 1986), *La Femme du blanchisseur* ('The laundryman's wife', 1987) and *On joue la comedie* ('We are acting', 1977), in which he exploits ancient Togolese performance traditions and modern concert party and cantata styles; Zarourou, founder of the Digida Theatre Company and author of *L'Oeil* ('The eye', 1974) and *La Termitière* ('The anthill', 1981), an initiation ritual play; and Jean Pierre Guigane from Burkina Faso, best known for *Le Fou* ('The Fool', 1986).

The majority of later dramatists borrow and adapt folk forms of their respective cultures in bold imaginative ways in a blend with the European models which they have inherited as part of their colonial legacy. To this extent there is a convergence in form and subject matter between francophone and anglophone African practice. As in anglophone Africa, some countries in the francophone zone are more productive than others, with Côte d'Ivoire, Cameroon, Congo, Senegal and Guinea being in the forefront. There is quite a lot of theatre activity in Burkina Faso, which has a vibrant and internationally recognized THEATRE FOR DEVELOPMENT, but unfortunately very few published dramatists. Benin, which was prominent during the Ponty years, has not matched that early promise with much activity or many publications. Its only published playwright is Jean Pliya, who is best known for his popular historical drama *Kondo le requin* ('Kondo the shark', 1981) and *La secretaire particuliere* ('The private secretary', 1973, a social satire). Gabon's only known dramatists are Paul Nyonda, with two published plays, *La mort de Guykafi* ('Guykafi's death', 1981) and *Le soulard* ('The drunkard', 1981), and Josephine Kama Bongo, one of the few female dramatists in French African theatre and author of *Obali* (1974), a play which explores the problems of forced marriages. There are as yet no published plays from the Central African Republic, even though there are sporadic theatrical activities around the country. OSITA OKAGBUE

John Conteh-Morgan, *Theatre and Drama in Francophone Africa* (1994)

Friel, Brian [Bernard Patrick] (b. Killyclogher, Co. Tyrone, Ireland, 9 Jan. 1929) Playwright The landscape of Friel's drama is generally confined to Ballybeg, from the Gaelic *baile beag*, meaning, literally, small town. He focuses usually on the affairs within one clan, or family, exploring their political and psychological hierarchies. His first major play, *The Enemy Within* (1962), concentrated on the monastic settlement of Iona, and the sixth-century Irish saint and scholar, Columba. This play expressed Friel's detached examination of Catholicism's hold over a section of the Irish

population, and to a lesser extent the troubled relations between Ireland and England, a subject he looks at in *The Freedom of the City* (1973) and returns to in *Translations* (1980) and *Making History* (1988). Family life and its divisive obsessions are at the centre of the action of the highly successful *Philadelphia, Here I Come!* (1964), *Crystal and Fox* (1968), *Aristocrats* (1979) and *Dancing at Lughnasa* (1990), which was internationally acclaimed. Experiments in theatrical narrative begun in *Lovers* (1966) and *The Gentle Island* (1971) climax in *Faith Healer* (1979), the same tale told three ways, none and all of them true. Other plays include *The Lover of Cass Mcguire* (1966) and *The Communication Cord* (1982). He has written short lyrics, adapted CHEKHOV and Turgenev, and co-founded the FIELD DAY THEATRE COMPANY in 1980. FRANK MCGUINNESS

Elmer Andrews, *The Art of Brian Friel* (1995)

F. C. McGrath, *Brian Friel's (Post) Colonial Drama: Language, Illusion and Politics* (1999)

Christopher Murray, *Brian Friel* (1999)

George O'Brien, *Brian Friel* (1990)

Richard Pine, *Brian Friel and Ireland's Drama* (1990)

Frigerio, Ezio (b. Erba, Italy, 1930) Designer. He started his career as a painter, and his designs are typified by an indebtedness to sixteenth-century Venetian art. In 1955 he joined STREHLER's company in Milan as a costume designer (e.g. for BRECHT's *The Threepenny Opera*, 1956, and PIRANDELLO's *The Mountain Giants*, 1958), and in 1958 he became a stage designer (e.g. for Goldoni's *The Servant of Two Masters*, 1958). He was an essential collaborator for Strehler and as such influential in Europe; he also worked with others, notably ROGER PLANCHON (e.g. *The Miser*, 1986). His designs were always both practical and painterly.
ADRIANA HUNTER

See also COSTUME DESIGN; DESIGN.

Friml, [Charles] Rudolf (b. Prague, 8 Dec. 1879; d. Hollywood, 12 Nov. 1972) Composer. Friml settled in America in 1906, where he initially made a career as a pianist and composer of light instrumental and vocal music. His first stage musical, *The Firefly* (1912), a vehicle for *Naughty Marietta* star Emma Trentini, established his reputation, *High Jinks* (1913) and *Katinka* (1915) confirmed it, and his two most significant works, the internationally successful romantic musicals *Rose Marie* (1924) and *The Vagabond King* (1925), made him one of the most important BROADWAY composers of the era. Of his subsequent works, ranging from ZIEGFELD REVUE to period operetta, only one, *The Three Musketeers* (1928), was successful, but Friml was by then based in Hollywood. With lyric musicals no longer the vogue, his last Broadway show, *Music Hath Charms* (1934), written for another operatic star, Maria Jeritza, was a failure and he abandoned the theatre to do his remaining work, including film versions of *Rose Marie* (three between 1928 and 1954), *The Vagabond King* (1930 and 1956) and *The Firefly* (1937), for the screen. KURT GÄNZL

fringe The word derives from the EDINBURGH FESTIVAL, where groups led by Glasgow UNITY appeared outside the auspices of the first official programme to press the case for greater Scottish representation. A critic noted that one of these shows had happened on the 'fringe' of the Festival. The following year playwright ROBERT KEMP used the word again, and it was then taken up by all concerned. The term was popularized by the Cambridge FOOTLIGHTS' *Beyond the Fringe* REVUE (1960). The fringe compares with the US OFF-OFF-BROADWAY movement, whose work was showcased at Edinburgh's TRAVERSE THEATRE and London's Quipu, OPEN SPACE and ROYAL COURT. This encouraged the growth of the fringe, which flourished in the counter-cultural 'underground' of the late 1960s and 1970s. The ARTS LAB, INTER-ACTION, the Brighton Combination, the SOHO POLY and others hosted HAPPENINGS, PERFORMANCE ART, LUNCHTIME THEATRE, and the emergent fringe theatre groups.

The original aesthetic of both groups and venues was to be inexpensive, COLLECTIVE, hostile to mainstream theatre, presenting an anarchic, subversive combination of artistic events, enabled in part, at least, by the 1968 abolition of theatre CENSORSHIP. Eventually, some groups and venues began to achieve more attention and funding than others, and the EDINBURGH FRINGE and venues like the BUSH, ORANGE TREE and KING'S HEAD became more established, and distanced from their origins, for which ALTERNATIVE is often the preferred term. DAN REBELLATO

See also LONDON.

Peter Ansorge, *Disrupting the Spectacle: Five Years of Experimental and Fringe Theatre in Britain* (1975)
Sandy Craig, ed., *Dreams and Deconstructions* (1980)
Catherine Itzin, *Stages in the Revolution: Political Theatre in Britain since 1968* (1980)
Roland Rees, *Fringe First: Pioneers of Fringe Theatre on Record* (1992)

Frisch, Max [Rudolf] (b. Zurich, Switzerland, 15 May 1911; d. Zurich, 4 April 1991) Playwright and novelist who, together with his compatriot DÜRRENMATT, is considered one of the most important postwar playwrights writing in German. Frisch originally studied philology and art at university, before aban-

doning his studies to become a journalist. After serving in the Swiss army during the Second World War, he took up architecture and pursued this profession until the 1950s, when he became a full-time writer. Frisch had written his first play at the age of 16, but having rejected his early work, it was not until 1944 that he returned to writing plays, with *Santa Cruz*. His second play, *Now They Are Singing Again* (1945), took its inspiration from BRECHT, dealing as it does with the moral responsibility for war. This Brechtian theme was continued in his next two plays, *The Chinese Wall* (1946) and *When the War Was Over* (1949). With the romantic comedy *Don Juan, or the Love of Geometry* (1953) Frisch offers a new interpretation of the mythical character of the Great Lover.

As a result of his increasing disenchantment with what he considered Swiss complacency in the face of mounting totalitarianism and fascism, Frisch wrote two of his most important plays. *Biedermann und die Brandstifter* (*The Fire-raisers*, written in 1958 as a radio play), satirizes the moral lethargy of the self-satisfied middle classes. This powerful play was seen in London at the ROYAL COURT THEATRE in 1961, and in New York (as *The Firebugs*) in 1963. It was closely followed by *Andorra* (1961), his most disturbing and controversial play, in which Frisch exposed and explored anti-semitism.

Frisch's blending of fantasy with brutal reality owes much to the work of Brecht and THORNTON WILDER, both of whom influenced the playwright in his early years. His later plays, like *Biography* (1968) and *Triptych* (1979), continue to use the device of the modern morality play as a means of exploring the place of humanity in a difficult world. HELEN RAPPAPORT

Michael Butler, *The Plays of Max Frisch* (1985)
Malcolm Pender, *Max Frisch: His Work and its Swiss Background* (1979)
Gertrud B. Pickar, *The Dramatic Works of Max Frisch* (1978)

Frohman, Charles (b. 17 June 1860; d. at sea, 7 May 1915; **Daniel** (b. 22 Aug. 1853; d. New York, 26 Dec. 1940); and **Gustavus** (b. 1854/5?; d. New York, 16 Aug. 1930) Three brothers born at Sandusky, Ohio, who became theatrical managers in New York. The most successful was Charles, whose combination of English plays and American stars dominated the stage first in New York and then in London. He was a partner in the infamous THEATRICAL SYNDICATE which aimed at a booking monopoly, and by 1910 he claimed, with some truth, to have 'the largest theatrical business in the world'. He played a significant role in the playwriting careers of SOMERSET MAUGHAM and J. M. BARRIE, and presented the original productions of *Peter Pan* in London (1904) and New York (1905). After his death in the sinking of the *Lusitania*, his business was headed with diminishing returns by his elder brother Daniel, who had been successful with his New York Stock Company. He wrote *Memories of a Manager* (1911), *Daniel Frohman Presents* (1935) and a volume of essays, *Encore* (1937). Gustavus brought his two brothers into theatre business, but never achieved their success.

IAN BEVAN

I. F. Marcosson and D. Frohman, *Charles Frohman, Manager and Man* (1916)

Fry [Harris], Christopher (b. Bristol, 18 Dec. 1907) Playwright. Fry's rich and exuberant drama was hailed during the austerity of the late 1940s when he was the most commercially successful of the poetic dramatists (e.g. *The Lady's Not For Burning*, 1948). Later plays, like *The Dark is Light Enough* (1954), were not light enough for audiences who preferred the earlier sparkling wit. The style and Christianity of this ex-schoolteacher, who had been an actor and director of repertory theatres, soon fell out of fashion. His verse, unlike ELIOT's, is self-conscious, delighting in the artifice of his chosen form, and is often dazzling enough to obscure frequent weaknesses of plot and character. Plays include *The Boy with a Cart* (1938), *A Phoenix too Frequent* (1946), *Thor, with Angels* (1948), *Venus Observed* (1950), *A Sleep of Prisoners* (1951) and *Curtmantle* (1961). Fry was also a notable adapter of ANOUILH, ROSTAND, GIRAUDOUX and IBSEN.

DAN REBELLATO

See also VERSE DRAMA.

Glenda Leeming, *Christopher Fry* (1990)
Emil Roy, *Christopher Fry* (1968)
S. Krishna Sarma, *Imagery in the Plays of Christopher Fry* (1972)
Derek Stanford, *Christopher Fry* (1962)

Fuchs, Georg (b. Beerfelden, 15 July 1868; d. Munich, 16 June 1949) Author, stage designer and theorist. Inspired by the non-illusionistic Shakespearian productions of the Munich Court Theatre, in 1908 Fuchs and designer Fritz Erler founded the Munich Artists' Theatre. With a wide but shallow relief stage, on which individual actors appeared as if on a bas-relief, it frankly embraced stylization in acting and decor, placing the actor near the audience against simple scenic elements that emphasized painted scenery and coloured light. In his influential books *The Theatre of the Future* (1905) and *Revolution in the Theatre* (1907) Fuchs rejected pictorial realism and called for a 're-theatricalization of the theatre'. MARVIN CARLSON

Fugard, [Harold] Athol [Lannigan] (b. Middelburg, Cape Province, South Africa, 11 June 1932) South Africa's foremost playwright, and the only one to have gained an international reputation. The product of an Afrikaner mother and an Anglo-Irish father, Fugard has always been especially conscious of his mixed linguistic heritage; his plays, written in a demotic form of South African English, naturally incorporate many regional dialects and slang derived from various vernacular registers. Following university, his real education began when – like EUGENE O'NEILL – he knocked about the world as a seaman for several years. As clerk to a Native Commissioner's Court in Johannesburg in 1958, he saw at first hand the daily regimen of apartheid. Becoming a stage manager with the National Theatre Organization (Kamertoneel) in 1959, Fugard worked, part-time, as actor and director, while writing his earliest plays about life in Sophiatown, then Johannesburg's black ghetto. *No-Good Friday* (1958) and *Nongogo* (1959) are immature but realistic studies of slum deprivation and violence. It was not until Fugard returned to Port Elizabeth, where he had been brought up, that his playwriting began to take on a life of its own. The breakthrough was *The Blood Knot,* set in Port Elizabeth but first staged in Johannesburg (1961). Though unwieldy and overwritten, it was the play South African theatre needed in the early 1960s. The love–hate relationship of two coloured brothers (one who could pass for a white man, the other very dark) mirrors much of the country's anguished racial history. Establishing Fugard as a playwright, it set a pattern for his future dramas, using small casts and one simple set with minimal action but one or two powerful stage images and opportunities for acting out intense racial confrontations. *Hello and Goodbye* (1965) and *Boesman and Lena* (1969; filmed 1973) were written for the Serpent Players, an ensemble of black actors founded by Fugard in 1962. Like *The Blood Knot*, both embody tragic family situations.

In 1967, influenced by the AVANT-GARDE director JERZY GROTOWSKI, Fugard and the Serpent Players began to experiment with improvisational theatre. Fugard provided basic images and situations and directed the process by which John Kani and Winston Ntshoni improvised the dialogue; the texture and force of *Sizwe Bansi is Dead* (1972) and *The Island* (1973) emerged from the inner experiences of the actors, who are credited as co-authors in the published texts. The absurdities and cruelties of South Africa's pass laws and of political imprisonment on Robben Island are, respectively, the plays' subject matter. *Statements after an Arrest under the Immorality Act* (1972) completes this workshop phase of Fugard's development.

Fugard has spoken of his next three plays as a trilogy, though not consciously planned as such. *A Lesson from Aloes* (1978), *'Master Harold' ... and the Boys* (1982), his most autobiographical play, and *The Road to Mecca* (1984) are more private and inward-looking, less obviously political and far more concerned with the white man's social responsibilities and conscience than any of the earlier works. After the unconvincing *A Place with the Pigs* (Yale Repertory Theatre, 1987; London's NATIONAL THEATRE, 1988), *My Children! My Africa!* (1989), directly confronted hatred and violence within the black community and answered criticism that this phase of his stage work had turned its back on immediate social and racial problems.

In the 1990s Fugard produced three dissimilar dramas that recall earlier stages in his career while, at the same time, they show an awareness of his country's post-apartheid dispensation. First produced in 1993 at the MARKET THEATRE in Johannesburg, *Playland* is in some ways a companion piece to *The Blood Knot*. Both are two-handers, where one character is black and the other is white (or appears to be white); but whereas *The Blood Knot* propheticlaly enacted apartheid's evils, *Playland* depicts the difficulties of reconciliation in the regime's aftermath. *My Life*, premièred to critical acclaim at the Grahamstown Arts Festival in 1994, has, unusually for Fugard, an all-female ensemble, with him arranging material but (unlike his practice in the earlier improvisational collaboration with two male actors) severely restricting his own authorial contribution. *Valley Song* (Johannesburg and Princeton, NJ, 1995) tenderly dramatizes the increasingly troubled relationship between a simple, inadvertently selfish old widower and his naïve, fun-loving granddaughter, who wants to leave their desolate Karoo farm for the big city.

Throughout a long career, Fugard's most significant contribution to South African theatre has been his involvement at all levels with black theatre practitioners. The strength of his work lies in its enactment – often in racial role-playing – of apartheid situations seen from the victims' point of view. First and foremost a man of the theatre, Fugard has also assayed other literary forms; he has published a novel, *Tsotsi* (1980), a volume of selections from his remarkable diary, published as *Notebooks: 1960–1977* (1983), and *Cousins: A Memoir* (1997). RONALD AYLING

Mary Benson, *Athol Fugard and Barney Simon: Bare Stage, a Few Props, Great Theatre* (1997)
Stephen Gray, *File on Fugard* (1991)
Margarate Seidenspinner, *Exploring the Labyrinth: Athol Fugard's Approach to South African Drama* (1986)
Russell Vandenbroucke, *Truths the Hand Can Touch: The Theatre of Athol Fugard* (1985)
Dennis Walder, *Athol Fugard* (1984)
Albert Wertheim, *The Dramatic Art of Athol Fugard: From South Africa to the World* (2000)

Fuller, Charles [H., Jr.] (b. Pittsburgh, Pa., 3 March 1939) Black playwright. His plays, all staged at New York's NEGRO ENSEMBLE COMPANY, include *In the Deepest Part of Sleep* (1974), *The Brownsville Raid* (1976), *Zooman and the Sign* (1980) and *A Soldier's Play* (1981), which won the Pulitzer Prize (and was filmed as *A Soldier's Story*). Beginning in 1989, he has written instalments of a play cycle, set after the Civil War, under the title *We*. DAVID BARBOUR

Fuller, Loïe (b. Fullersburg, Ill., 22 Jan. 1862; d. Paris, 21 Jan. 1928) Dancer. At first a singer and actress, she made her DANCE debut in the FOLIES-BERGÈRE in 1893, but soon established her own distinctive solo style, in which she manipulated enormous lengths of drapery in fluid patterns, enhanced by the skilful use of moving electrical theatre lights. She influenced the development of stage costume and LIGHTING, and her performance at the Paris Exposition of 1899 impressed the young ISADORA DUNCAN, whom Fuller encouraged. Her *Fifteen years of a Dancer's Life* appeared in 1913. ANDREW SOLWAY

See also CHOREOGRAPHY; MOVEMENT, DANCE AND DRAMA.

Fuller, Rosalinde (b. Portsmouth, 16 Feb. 1892; d. London, 15 Sept. 1982) Actress and singer who went to America on the advice of folk song specialist Cecil Sharp. After giving folk concerts and appearing in REVUE, she starred opposite JOHN BARRYMORE in *Hamlet* (1922). She made her London debut in 1927. A series of roles in SHAW and a notable Irina in CHEKHOV's *Three Sisters* followed before Fuller joined DONALD WOLFIT's Shakespeare Company in 1940. Here she played many of the great Shakespearean roles such as Viola, Katharina, Portia and Desdemona. In the 1950s and 1960s Fuller toured extensively in the Middle and Far East, Africa, Australia and the United States with her own one-woman shows *Masks and Faces* and *Subject to Love*. HELEN RAPPAPORT

funding Ever since it turned professional, theatre has always required funding beyond the income derived directly from its audience; patrons have ranged from the church, the monarch and the court to wealthy individuals and companies or the state, via both central and local government. Every country has its own history and traditions of funding and subsidy, enlightened or otherwise, related to its own stages of social and political development, and crucial to understanding how theatre is made and for whom. By the end of the twentieth century, the mixed economy was dominant; several sources of funding was the norm, involving various permutations of multinational corporations, media conglomerates, banks and leisure industry giants or national, regional and local arts councils and charitable foundations or trusts as well as the box office and the merchandizing of production-related commodities. The balance and the relationship between the sources are matters of shifting negotiation and politics, and much energy is expended by artists and funding specialists alike on undertaking and refining the techniques of fund-raising, subsidy-seeking and income-generation. The biggest source of subsidy, however, remains the creators of theatre, who, with notable exceptions, have low status and low pay for the long and unsociable hours they work.

CHARLES LONDON

See also ARTS COUNCIL; MANAGEMENT; NATIONAL ENDOWMENT FOR THE ARTS; PRODUCING.

W. J. Baumol and W. G. Bowen, *Performing Arts: The Economic Dilemma* (1966)
Justin Lewis, *Art, Culture and Enterprise: The Politics of Art and the Cultural Industries* (1990)
J. Pick, ed., *The State and the Arts* (1980)

futurism Early twentieth-century AVANT-GARDE movement which began in Italy. FILIPPO MARINETTI's 1909 manifesto published in Paris called for the destruction of museums and libraries and the glorification of masculinity, youth, speed, machines and war. Visual artists such as Enrico Prampolini and Fortunato Depero applied futurist ideas to theatre design, and, in the spirit of GORDON CRAIG, who was living in Italy, developed the idea of theatre as an ensemble of kinetic forms. Futurist theatre shocked audiences with brief, alogical mixed-media pieces called *sintesi* ('synthetic'), noise 'music' (known as 'bruitism'), and recitations of *parole-in-libertà* (words free of context). In Russia, a more populist strain produced MAYAKOVSKY's manifesto 'A Slap in the Face of Public Taste' (1912) and Malevich and Kruchenykh's opera *Victory over the Sun* (1913). The horrors of the First World War discredited Marinetti's ideology, which turned to fascism, but CONSTRUCTIVISM, DADA and SURREALISM absorbed many futurist methods and its influence on experimenters in many arts is widespread. CAROLYN TALARR

See also FOOD AND DRINK; HAPPENINGS; PERFORMANCE ART; THEATRE OF THE ABSURD.

M. Kirby, *Futurist Performance* (1971)
M. W. Martin, *Futurist Art and Theory, 1909–15* (1968)

Fyffe, Will (b. Dundee, 16 Feb. 1885; d. St Andrews, 14 Dec. 1947) Actor and comedian who began in his parents' touring company, gravitated to REVUE and thence into PANTOMIME and VARIETY. Real success came when he began singing patter songs of his own composition like 'I'm 94 Today' and 'I Belong to Glasgow'. These, together with his shrewdly observed character studies (the railway guard, the local doctor, the village idiot, the ship's engineer) soon endeared him to an international public. He visited the United States twice, appeared in four Royal Variety Performances, became a regular broadcaster and made numerous films. DONALD ROY

G

Gabon *see* FRENCH AFRICAN THEATRE

Gaelic theatre in Ireland Gaelic culture has a strong tradition of storytelling, poetry and music, but had none of drama, until the Irish Literary Theatre (1899–1901) produced the first Gaelic one-act play, *Casadh an tSugáin* ('The twisting of the rope'), by DOUGLAS HYDE at the Gaiety Theatre, Dublin, in October 1901. The Government of the Irish Free State, having subsidized the ABBEY THEATRE in 1925, also subsidized two Gaelic theatres in the 1920s, An Comhar Dramaíochta (The drama assembly, Dublin, 1926) and An Taibhdhearc (The image-stage, Galway, 1928), both relying on amateur players but with professional directors. From the Galway theatre came the first notable full-length Gaelic play, *Diarmuid agus Gráinne* by the actor MICHEÁL MACLIAMMÓIR. In 1941, the former finance minister in the Irish government who had granted the subsidy to the Abbey became managing director of that theatre, and proceeded to have productions in Gaelic on a regular basis, a policy which has continued at the smaller Peacock Theatre, with tours to the Gaeltacht areas from time to time. In order to have a proper Gaelic theatre in Dublin, the Gaelic organization Gael-linn founded a small theatre, An Damer, in 1955; relying for the most part on amateur players, it continued with marked success until 1975, presenting many new plays and translations and becoming fully professional in 1978, with a state subsidy, which unfortunately ceased in 1981. In 1974 SIAMSA TIRÉ was founded in Tralee, County Kerry, as a semi-permanent Irish-language company of dancers and singers. Despite many efforts, it is true to say that the Gaelic theatre has not as yet achieved a place in Ireland comparable to that of the English theatre

movement there. However, a small professional company of Gaelic players has been formed, Amharclann de hIde (The Hyde theatre), which performs newly written plays from time to time but has not yet managed to mount a regular season. TOMÁS MACANNA

Gaelic theatre in Scotland The Gaidhealtachd, the Gaelic-speaking heartlands of the Highlands and islands of Scotland, do not, on a superficial level, appear to have a tradition of theatre, but the briefest acquaintance with the cultural tradition of the region shows that this view is misleading. In a society which depended little on the written word, the prominence and value attributed to differing kinds of performing skills, specifically in song, dance, musicianship, and above all, the art of storytelling, display a highly developed regard for 'theatre' in its purest form, and the lack of 'theatres', in the sense of bricks and mortar, is quite irrelevant. Theatre occurred wherever people were gathered together, and performed. Nowadays the word 'ceilidh' has transmigrated into English usage to mean 'concert', but in Gaelic it meant (and still means) simply the act of visiting friends in their own homes, which then became the space where 'theatre' happened.

In recent years the main focus of Gaelic drama has been Commun na Drama Ghaidhlig, organizing competitive drama festivals in different regions in Scotland, with regional winners going forward to compete at the National Mod (the Scottish equivalent of the Welsh Eisteddfod), and following rules similar to those of a body with a parallel function in English, the Scottish Community Drama Association.

From 1978 to 1981, a Gaelic repertory company, Fir

Chlis (Aurora Borealis), briefly existed, which toured throughout Scotland, providing the first opportunities for Gaelic actors to view the theatre professionally, but this initiative, at a still embryonic stage, became an easy victim of economic 'cut-backs'. Then, at the end of the 1980s and the beginning of the 1990s, official attitudes to Gaelic began to turn round (with, e.g., government funding of Gaelic TV to the tune of £9.5m annually); a Gaelic THEATRE IN EDUCATION company, Ordag is Sgealbag, a child of the National Gaelic Arts Project, toured Scottish schools, and Combairle Nan Eilean, the Western Isles Council, employed a full-time drama instructor for the first time, reflecting the acceptance of drama as a powerful tool in education, particularly in a linguistic context. The Arts Project continued to give drama a high priority, and in 1989 established Drama na h-Oigridh, the National Gaelic Youth Theatre, an initiative which helped to expand the range of theatrical experience available in Gaelic, moving away from, as well as complementing, the amateur competitive arena. In 1996 a new full-time professional Gaelic theatre company, Tosg, was founded. DOMHNALL RUADH

Gaiety Theatre Built in 1884, it was a run-down music hall in MANCHESTER when ANNIE HORNIMAN bought it in 1907. She had it refurbished and redesigned, halving its seating capacity to 1,250, and in 1908 established Britain's first and pioneering repertory company there, with the managerial support of BEN IDEN PAYNE from 1907 until 1911, when LEWIS CASSON took over. The Gaiety's repertory spanned Euripedes, Shakespeare and SHAW, and was fashioned on the inspirational GRANVILLE BARKER–VEDRENNE management of the ROYAL COURT. This entailed a firm commitment to the 'new drama' and the support of plays by local dramatists who became known as the MANCHESTER SCHOOL. Local playwright STANLEY HOUGHTON provided the Gaiety with its most celebrated drama, *Hindle Wakes* (1912). Gaiety productions were given London seasons and were toured extensively in Canada and the United States until the disbanding of the permanent company in 1917. In 1921 the Gaiety ceased to be a theatre when Horniman sold it to a cinema chain, and in 1952 it was demolished.
ELAINE ASTON

Alan Hyman, *The Gaiety Years* (1975)
Rex Pogson, *Miss Horniman and the Gaiety Theatre, Manchester* (1952)

Galin, Aleksandr [Mikhailovich] (b. Alekseyevka, Matveye-Kurgansk district, Rostov region, Russia, 10 Sept. 1947) Playwright. His first play to be performed,

by fellow students at Leningrad University's Student Theatre, was *Here Fly the Birds*. His next play, *Retro* (1980), about an elderly widowed pensioner and his well-meaning daughter, was an instant hit both at home and abroad. This was followed by *The Eastern Rostrum* (1982), about an elderly orchestral violinist who resumes an acquaintance with five women who were his childhood friends. Galin's third play, *The Delusion* (1983), was followed by the work which brought him further international acclaim, *Stars in the Morning Sky*, premièred in Moscow in (1987) and dealing with a group of prostitutes who are 'tidied away' from public view during the Moscow Olympics. LEV DODIN's Leningrad Maly Theatre production was well received when performed at the GLASGOW Mayfest and at the London Riverside Studios in 1988.
NICK WORRALL

Gallagher, Ed[ward] (b. San Francisco, 1876; d. New York, 28 May 1929) and **Shean, Al[bert Schoenberg]** (b. Dornum, Germany, 12 May 1868; d. New York, 12 Aug. 1949) VAUDEVILLE duo. They formed their double act in 1910 and appeared on Broadway in the musical *The Rose Maid* (1912) and in the REVUE *The Big Banner Show*, only to go their separate ways in vaudeville for six years; they re-formed in 1920 to star in *Cinderella on Broadway*, and established their respective trademarks of pith helmet and fez and their popular catchphrase: 'Absolutely, Mr Gallagher?' — 'Positively, Mr Shean!' Their appearance in a 67-week run of the ZIEGFIELD FOLLIES of 1922 and again in *Greenwich Village Follies of 1924* made them hugely popular, but unfortunately a series of problems in Gallagaher's personal life led to the duo's second break-up in 1925 and the effective end of Gallagher's career. Shean, however, continued with a varied career, playing character roles in more than 25 films, and appearing in vaudeville and on Broadway in *Betsy* (1926), *The Prince of Pilsen* (1930) and *Father Malachy's Miracle* (1937). The legacy of Gallagher and Shean's act can be seen in the work of Shean's nephews – the MARX BROTHERS.
HELEN RAPPAPORT

Galsworthy, John (b. Kingston Hill, Surrey, 14 Aug. 1867; d. Hampstead, London, 31 Jan. 1933) Playwright and novelist, noted for serious and sombre social drama aimed at demonstrating the unfairness of English society. His first play, *The Silver Box* (1906), written for the VEDRENNE–GRANVILLE–BARKER management at the ROYAL COURT, presents parallel legal cases, one involving a wealthy man and the other an unemployed labourer, revealing the inequality of their treatment in the courts. Galsworthy attempts to efface himself as author and attain an impartiality which will let the facts speak for themselves. In *Strife* (1909), which deals with a strike, he presents without prejudice both sides of the argument. In *Justice* (1910) the judicial and penal systems are examined. Here, as in his other plays, it is not the individuals administering the systems who are castigated but the systems themselves; one of the play's scenes, showing the effects of solitary confinement, was instrumental in bringing about penal reform. Noting the contrast with the commercial theatre's preoccupation with high society, contemporaries praised Galsworthy's highlighting of working-class characters. Other plays – *Joy* (1907), *The Eldest Son* (1912), *The Fugitive* (1913) – were more familiar in theme and setting, but nevertheless showed a jaundiced attitude that denied them much commercial success.

Galsworthy continued his earnest, well-crafted writing into the 1920s, most notably in *The Skin Game* (1920) and *Loyalties* (1922). In 1929 he was awarded the Order of Merit and in 1932 the Nobel Prize. He became best remembered for his series of novels *The Forsyte Saga*, which won great popularity in adaptations on television and radio. IAN CLARKE

Dudley Barker, *A Man of Principle: A View of John Galsworthy* (1963)
Catherine Dupré, *John Galsworthy: A Biography* (1976)
H. V. Marrot, *The Life and Letters of John Galsworthy* (1935)

Galvin, Patrick *see* BELFAST

Gambon, Michael [John] (b. Dublin, 19 Oct. 1940) Actor. He joined the NATIONAL THEATRE in 1963 at the OLD VIC and has been continuously associated with it ever since, while also working in the West End, notably in the work of ALAN AYCKBOURN, and at the ROYAL SHAKESPEARE COMPANY, where he was an acclaimed (and unusually young) King Lear in 1982. His performances at the National have included BRECHT's Galileo (1980), an unforgettable Eddie Carbone in ARTHUR MILLER's *A View From The Bridge* (1987), directed by Ayckbourn, and the original production of HAROLD PINTER's *Betrayal* (1978). In 1995 he played Volpone and created the role of Tom in David Hare's *Skylight* (1995), which he also played in New York. His extensive television work includes DENNIS POTTER's *The Singing Detective* (1986), in which he played, with scabrous humour and no self-pity, a man suffering from the same disfiguring illness which afflicted Potter himself. Gambon is a large man with delicate hands and a passion for the intricate mechanisms of antique weapons. His acting displays a similar capacity to be both epic and intimate, putting him among the finest, and most consistently surprising, actors of his generation. He was knighted in 1998. GENISTA MCINTOSH

García, Victor (b. Argentina, 1934) Director. Since leaving his homeland, he has been based in France and gained an international reputation with his controversial interpretation of the work of ARRABAL (e.g. *The Architect and the Emperor of Abyssinia*, which came to the NATIONAL THEATRE, London, 1971) and GENET (e.g. *The Maids* for NURIA ESPERT in Spain, 1969). He also collaborated with Espert on LORCA's *Yerma*, which was set on a huge trampoline and seen at the WORLD THEATRE SEASON, London (1972) and on VALLE-INCLAN's *Divine Words* (also seen at the National Theatre, 1977). HELEN RAPPAPORT

García Lorca, Federico (b. Fuentevaqueros, nr Granada, Spain, 5 June 1898; d. Viznar, Spain, 19(?) August 1936) Playwright and poet. He spent his childhood close to the natural world, village life and popular tradition. Teenage years in Granada developed his musical and poetic talents, broadened his knowledge of Spanish culture, but also revealed homosexual tendencies and deep public antipathy. Ten years at the Residence for Students in Madrid (1919–29) stimulated interest in the European AVANT GARDE, especially through friendship with Salvador Dali and Luis Buñuel, and saw the composition of five plays, mostly puppet-plays and farces. In 1929 depression took Lorca away from Spain, first to New York, then to Cuba. The advent of the Second Republic (1931–6) allowed his talents to flourish in two directions: as director of the government-sponsored touring theatre group La Barraca, and as author of his acclaimed trilogy, *Bodas de sangre* (*Blood Wedding*, 1933), *Yerma* (1934), and *La casa de Bernarda Alba* (*The House of Bernarda Alba*, not produced until 1945). His brutal murder at the hands of Franco partisans in August 1936, the outcome of right-wing hatred of his growing fame, left-wing sympathies and homosexual reputation, has often attracted more attention than his work. It inspired LINDSAY KEMP to create the ballet *Cruel Garden* in 1977.

The themes of Lorca's theatre are rooted in his life: passion, frustration, passing time and death. In particular, deep instinctive needs, countered by social attitudes, are the mainspring of the plays with Spanish subjects, comic and tragic alike: the farces, *La zapatera prodigiosa* (*The Shoemaker's Prodigious Wife*, 1926–30) and *El amor de Don Perlimplín* (*The Love of Don Perlimplín*, 1928); the rural tragedies, where the clash of instinct and social convention is particularly powerful; and *Doña Rosita la soltera* (*Doña Rosita the Spinster*, 1935). On the other hand, they are issues which colour the less obviously Spanish plays: the SURREALIST *El público* (*The Public*, 1930) and *Así que pasen cinco años* (*When Five Years Pass*, written in the United States, 1931). But the true power of Lorca's theatre lies in its universality, in its exposure of the true nature of men and women beneath the masks of appearance, and in its suggestion of the often tragic nature of human experience.

Lorca's stated aim of freeing the Spanish theatre from its stifling conservatism linked seriousness of theme to bold formal experiment, combining traditional and modern elements: puppet-play and Greek tragedy, SYMBOLISM and SURREALISM. The influences of Sophocles, Shakespeare, Buñuel and Dali often mix magically, while the integration of dialogue, song, setting, costume and lighting puts Lorca at the forefront of theatrical innovation in the 1920s and 1930s.

The neglect of Lorca's theatre in the English-speaking theatre is due in part to the absence of actable translations, although he is probably the best-known Spanish playwright of the twentieth century. Good translations require a sound knowledge of Spanish, familiarity with Andalusian tradition, the source of Lorca's imagery, and an instinctive feeling for the emotional power of his language. They are criteria not easily satisfied.
GWYNNE EDWARDS

Reed Anderson, *Federico García Lorca* (1984)
Gwynne Edwards, *Lorca: The Theatre Beneath the Sand* (1980)
Ian Gibson, *Federico García Lorca: A Life* (1989)
R. Martínez Nadal, *Lorca's 'The Public'* (1974)

Gardner, Herb[ert] (b. Brooklyn, New York, 28 December 1943) Playwright. A self-confessed entertainer – and creator of a popular syndicated cartoon, *The Nebbishes* – Gardner looks at life wryly as a comedy. *A Thousand Clowns* (1962), in which a TV writer abandons his career in order to educate his 12-year-old nephew, ran for over a year in New York and was made into a successful film (1965). The appeal of two defiant 80-year-olds in Central Park – a Jewish radical and a black janitor – made *I'm Not Rappoport* (1985) a hit on Broadway and in the UK following its première at the SEATTLE REPERTORY THEATER. Gardner's next play, *Conversations with My Father* (1991), took a similar journey and also starred JUDD HIRSCH. Other plays include *The Goodbye People* (1968) and *Thieves* (1974).
CHARLES LONDON

Garrick Club *see* CLUBS

Garvey, Marcus (b. St Ann's Bay, Jamaica, 17 Aug. 1887; d. London, 10 June 1940) Political activist. A controversial figure on the world stage, he founded the Universal Negro Improvement Association (UNIA), which in the 1920s became the largest pan-African mass movement in history. He travelled widely through North and South America and Europe, promoting his 'Back to Africa' scheme. The scheme eventually failed, along with his other ventures in shipping and politics, but he is venerated as one of Jamaica's national heroes for his selfless dedication to bettering the lives of black peoples worldwide.

While the UNIA headquarters were in New York, Garvey was a major influence in the Harlem Renaissance. Leading black performers found a platform at the UNIA's Liberty Hall, and black writers in Garvey's weekly newspaper, *The Negro World*. He himself wrote 'three great dramas' in support of his efforts to raise black self-esteem. In Jamaica in 1930, after Garvey had been deported from America, the UNIA staged all three plays on consecutive nights: *The Coronation of an African King*, *Roaming Jamaicans* and *Slavery – From Hut to Mansion*. The dramas were epic in form, but in them Garvey was able to break the black stereotypes of his day, and for the first time black audiences could see on stage real people recognizably like themselves. A fourth play by Garvey, *Wine, Women and War*, was staged in 1932 JUDY S. J. STONE

Gascon, Jean (b. Montreal, 21 Dec. 1921; d. Stratford, Ont., 19 April 1988) Actor and director. He studied acting at L'Ecole du Vieux-Colombier, Paris, in 1946 and acted for some years in France before returning to Canada in 1951. He helped found Montreal's Théâtre du Nouveau Monde in 1951; he was its artistic director between 1951 and 1966 and one of the company's most distinguished actors. Between 1968 and 1974 he was artistic director of Canada's STRATFORD FESTIVAL and between 1972 and 1984 artistic director of Ottawa's National Arts Center. Gascon's versatility was evident in his acting in both French and English, and as a much sought-after opera director. EUGENE BENSON

Gaskill, William (b. Shipley, Yorks, 24 June 1930) Director. Having been a nurse, baker, actor and stage manager, he joined the ENGLISH STAGE COMPANY in 1957 and became artistic director at the ROYAL COURT THEATRE (1965–75). Early productions included N. F. SIMPSON's *A Resounding Tinkle* (1957), JOHN OSBORNE's *Epitaph for George Dillon* (1958) and JOHN ARDEN's *The Happy Haven* (1960). Gaskill became known as British theatre's leading Brechtian, directing the professional London premières of *The Caucasian Chalk Circle* (1962), *Mother Courage* (1965), *Baal* (1963) and *Man is Man* (1971), and applying BRECHT's techniques elsewhere (e.g. in a controversial *Macbeth*, 1966, with ALEC GUINNESS, set in a sandpaper-coloured box and lit fully throughout). He joined the new NATIONAL THEATRE, where *The Recruiting Officer* (1963) was the first of Gaskill's many outstandingly clear and realistic productions of seventeenth-century comedy which redefined the genre. At the Royal Court, he directed EDWARD BOND's early plays – *Saved* (1965), *Early Morning* (1968), *Lear* (1971), *The Sea* (1973) – and supported them against censorship. He created the Royal Court Theatre Upstairs (1969) for experimental work and co-founded the innovative JOINT STOCK COMPANY (1974), involving actors and writers in a COLLECTIVE process of workshops and research. As well as directing abroad, he has returned frequently to the NT. He wrote the autobiographical *A Sense of Direction* (1988).

TONY HOWARD

Gassman, Vittorio (b. Genoa, Italy, 1 Sept. 1922; d. Rome, 29 June 2000) Actor–manager and director. Gassman achieved instant stardom in his native Italy with his first stage appearance in Niccodemi's *Nemica* (1943). He went on to play key roles – such as Stanley Kowalski in TENNESSEE WILLIAMS' *A Streetcar Named Desire* (1948) – for a number of eminent directors. In the 1950s he began producing plays himself, and starred in many of these productions. He was an internationally respected actor who excelled in a number of great title roles, such as SARTRE's *Kean*, Othello, Richard III, Lear and Prospero. He also championed the popularization of theatre in ITALY: in 1960 he founded the Teatro Popolare Italiano, inspired by the French THÉÂTRE NATIONAL POPULAIRE. He established a theatre school and wrote several books of memoirs and thoughts on theatre. ADRIANA HUNTER

Gassner, John [Waldhorn] (b. Máramaros-Sziget, Hungary, 30 Jan. 1903; d. New Haven, Conn., 2 April 1967) Critic, producer, educator, author and editor. The broadly talented, indefatigable Gassner taught, usually briefly, at universities around the world and served on numerous committees, boards and literary juries. He also wrote plays and produced, albeit unsuccessfully, in New York. His claim to enduring fame lies with the many anthologies he compiled and with such books as *The Theatre in Our Times* (1954), *Form and Idea in Modern Theatre* (1956), and *Theatre at the Crossroads* (1960). GERALD BORDMAN

Gate Theatre (Dublin) Founded by the Irish actor and designer MÍCHEÁL MACLÍAMMÓIR and the English actor and director HILTON EDWARDS in 1928 in order to bring modern European and American plays to the Dublin stage. Their initial seasons took place in the Peacock Theatre; then, in 1930, they leased the eighteenth-century Rotunda Concert Rooms which the architect Michael Scott transformed into a 370-seat theatre with near-perfect actor–audience rapport. Plays by IBSEN, O'NEILL, EVREINOV, RICE and CAPEK were performed. The company found the playwright it needed in DENIS JOHNSTON, whose *The Old Lady Says 'No!'* (1929) did much to establish the company's style, in which so-called EXPRESSIONIST techniques were favoured. Later, Shakespeare and other European classics were produced, always with emphasis on the visual interpretation. The principal financial benefactor, there being no state support, was Edward, 7th Earl of Longford; following a policy disagreement he formed Longford Productions, which shared the theatre from 1935 until 1960. The Gate company undertook a number of successful tours to the United States, Canada, Eastern Europe and Egypt. During the Second World War, when visiting companies were a rarity in Dublin, seasons were given in the much larger Gaiety Theatre. New Irish dramatists, such as Maura Laverty, Donagh MacDonagh, Desmond Forristal and MacLíammóir himself, were introduced. In 1960 MacLíammóir wrote and appeared in a series of one-person shows: *The Importance of Being Oscar* was performed worldwide. The Gate Theatre continued after the death of its founders, concentrating on very stylish productions of established plays, and enjoying an annual state subsidy. CHRISTOPHER FITZ-SIMON

C. Fitz-Simon, *The Boys* (1994)

Gate Theatre (London) Founded in 1925 by Molly Veness and her husband Peter Godfrey (1899–1970), a conjuror and clown who had acted with BEN GREET, the 90-seat Gate was situated in a garret in Covent Garden, central London, and then moved in 1927 to a skittle alley that had been the site of the Charing Cross Music Hall under the arches just off the Embankment. (In 1946 it housed the PLAYERS' THEATRE). For nearly a decade the Gate was at the cutting edge of challenging drama, a pioneer of CLUB THEATRE and forerunner of the FRINGE. Inspired primarily by EXPRESSIONISM, Godfrey staged some 350 plays by an extraordinary range of playwrights, mostly from abroad, beginning with GLASPELL and moving on through BERNARD, CAPEK, KAISER (*From Morn to Midnight*, reviewed by AGATE, put the Gate on the map), MAETERLINCK and O'NEILL to RICE, STRINDBERG, TOLLER and WEDEKIND. Godfrey attracted or helped launch many leading actors, e.g. GWEN FFRANGCON-DAVIES, Eric Portman, FLORA ROBSON and ROBERT SPEAIGHT.

Godfrey also mounted successful Christmas entertainments, two of which included HERMIONE GINGOLD who went on to star in a series of intimate Gate revues after the theatre had been taken over and refurbished (in 1934) by NORMAN MARSHALL. He remade the Gate's reputation with new and modern plays from around the world – by AFINOGENOV, COCTEAU, HELLMAN and STEINBECK, for example – and by sustaining the quality of performance with actors as different as BEATRIX LEHMANN, ROBERT MORLEY, Vincent Price and DONALD WOLFIT. The Gate closed in 1941 when the roof was blown off by bombing. The name and the spirit was taken up in 1979 by a small PUB THEATRE in west London (and yet another in south London) specializing in foreign work. Kaiser and Cocteau both resurfaced, along with BERNHARD, BULGAKOV, FASSBINDER, FLEISSER, Kleist, Marivaux and MROZEK; special seasons of plays were mounted, e.g. by women, and from the Golden Age of Spain. Much fêted, the 56-seat Gate expanded in 1993 to double its capacity and introduced flexible staging. It again proved to be a valuable seedbed for actors, directors and designers, and includes STEPHEN DALDRY among its alumni.

COLIN CHAMBERS

Norman Marshall, *The Other Theatres* (1947)

Gateway Company Founded in EDINBURGH in 1953 in a theatre owned by the Church of Scotland, by the playwright ROBERT KEMP and actors Tom Fleming and Lennox Milne. It presented a high proportion of Scottish plays in its repertoire. These included dramas by JOHN BRANDANE, JAMES BRIDIE, ROBERT MCLELLAN, Moray McLaren and Kemp. Some of Scotland's finest actors played here regularly, for example Duncan Macrae, Russell Hunter, Iain Cuthbertson, Archie Duncan, Walter Carr, Jean Taylor Smith, Irene Sunters and Edith MacArthur. The Gateway closed in 1965 with the opening of the Edinburgh Civic Theatre at the Royal LYCEUM, designed in part to continue the Gateway policy under Tom Fleming. JAN MCDONALD

The Twelve Seasons of the Edinburgh Gateway Company (1953–1965) (1965)

Gatti, Armand [Dante Sauveur] (b. Monaco, 26 Jan. 1924) Journalist, playwright and film-maker who combines a sense of poetic adventure with a social commitment in a unique way. Born of immigrant Italian parents, he was deported to a labour camp under the German occupation. After the war, he worked as a journalist and special reporter, travelling worldwide, from Guatemala to China, from Korea to Siberia. These experiences resurface continually in his work. He was encouraged to write for the theatre by ERWIN PISCATOR and JEAN VILAR, who directed his first play, *Le Crapaud buffle* ('The buffalo toad'), for the prestigious THÉÂTRE NATIONAL POPULAIRE in 1959. His first notable success, *La vie imaginaire de l'éboueur Auguste G* ('The imaginary

life of the street-swepper Augustus G', 1962) uses the experience of his father, fatally wounded in a clash with riot police. Since then he has written some 30 plays, confronting problems of human dignity, identity and survival, such as *Un Homme seul* ('One man alone', 1966), *La Naissance* ('The birth', 1968) and *La Cigogne* ('The stork', 1968). Following a period of self-imposed exile in West Germany, after his play *La passion du Général Franco* ('The Passion of General Franco', 1969) had been banned from performance in France, Gatti returned to France in 1975 and worked on a series of large-scale community-based projects, in which video provided a major new medium. At the same time, he was continuing his writing for the theatre. The dissident movement in Soviet Russia and the tradition of European anarchism had become a predominant theme, notably in *Le cheval qui se suicide par le feu* ('The horse that burns itself to death', 1977). In 1981 he completed a five-month project with a group of unemployed youth in Derry, Northern Ireland, making a full-length film, *Nous étions tous des noms d'arbres* ('Our names were the names of trees', distributed in Britain under the title *The Writing on the Wall*). Other work includes *Le Labyrinthe* ('The maze', AVIGNON FESTIVAL, 1982), *Opéra avec titre long* ('Opera with long title', Montreal, 1986), *Ces empéreurs aux ombrelles trouées* ('Those emperors with their ragged parasols', Avignon, 1991) and drama workshops with young delinquents and detainees. A humanist and utopian outsider, Gatti offers a potential for the renewal of dramatic language unique in postwar French theatre. JOSEPH LONG

Dorothy Knowles, *Armand Gatti in the Theatre: Wild Duck against the Wind* (1992)

Gay [Armitage], Noel [Reginald Moxon] (b. Wakefield, Yorks., 15 July 1898; d. London, 4 March 1954) Songwriter. Trained for a career in church music, Gay changed course aged 25 and, after success as a songwriter in REVUE (*Clowns in Cover*, 1927; *Folly to Be Wise*, 1931), teamed up with STANLEY LUPINO and lyricist Desmond Carter on the Gaiety musical comedy *Hold My Hand* (1931). Several similar shows over the next four years produced little more than a few successful single songs, until Arthur Rose's vehicle for another member of the Lupino family, the acrobatic little singing comedian LUPINO LANE, hit the bullseye. Following a fine initial run at the Victoria Palace on the brink of the Second World War, *Me and My Girl* (1937) became a perennial Lupino family production, both in the provinces and in regular London return seasons, and its favourite songs, 'The Lambeth Walk' and 'Me and My Girl', became the best known of Gay's many popular songs. Several further vehicles for Lane and the cheeky Cockney character he favoured followed, along with songs for a number of other musical comedies and revues of the lightest kind, mostly written with lyricist Frank Eyton. Gay founded his own music publishing company, which, in 1984 under the management of his son Richard, staged a revised version of *Me and My Girl* which found international success. KURT GÄNZL

Gay Sweatshop British touring theatre company. In 1974, *Gay News* reported INTER-ACTION's plans to run a gay season at the Almost Free Theatre, from which emerged Gay Sweatshop, the pioneer British gay group. Its first independent productions were *Mister X* by Roger Baker and Drew Griffiths, and *Any Woman Can* by Jill Posener (both 1975). The success of the tour established the need for an 'out' gay theatre for both performers and audience. After EDWARD BOND's *Stone* (1976), the company split into lesbian and gay men's companies, coming together for their successful panto-mime *Jingleball* (1976). They maintained a commit-ment to new writing, with premières including Noël Greig's *The Dear Love of Comrades* (1979) and *Poppies* (1983), Michelene Wandor's *Care and Control* (1977) and Jackie Jay's *Twice Over* (1988). They also helped launch the careers of MARTIN SHERMAN, ANTONY SHER and SIMON CALLOW. In 1990, public outcry reversed an Arts Council decision to end their grant and they returned with *The Last Enemy* (1991) by Carl Miller and an innovative explosion of plays, adaptations, cabaret, workshops and seminars, under the dual directorship of James Neale-Kennerley and Lois Weaver. However, in 1997 funding was finally withdrawn.
DAN REBELLATO

See also ALTERNATIVE THEATRE; GAY THEATRE; LESBIAN THEATRE.

Philip Osment, ed., *Gay Sweatshop: Four Plays and a Company* (1989)

gay theatre If 'gay theatre' is taken to mean plays written by and for homosexuals, then it is true that there was almost no 'gay theatre' before that produced in the aftermath of the gay liberation movement of the early 1970s. Such a definition, however, dismisses the formal variety of twentieth-century gay culture, and fails to take account of the specific contradictions and complications produced by the double movement of that culture since the beginning of the century. One direction of movement has been towards the elabora-tion of an autonomous subculture with its own sites and styles; the second, occurring simultaneously, has been towards the integration (often superficial and always troubled) of gay images, languages and indi-viduals into the culture as a whole. Between these two

ideals of autonomy and integration lies a spectrum of cultural operations devised by those who have sup-ported, challenged, appropriated and exploited the existing order. It is within this spectrum that we must try to place a diversity of theatres – a glam DRAG act in a working-class pub, a radical drag version of Mar-lowe's *Dido, Queen of Carthage* in a FRINGE arts venue, a lesbian comedy thriller in the same venue, a play about AIDS with a gay cast, a play about AIDS with a straight cast, LINDSAY KEMP's staging of *A Midsummer Night's Dream*, a wildly camp version of COCTEAU'S *Oedipus* staged by a leading gay actor in a respectable repertory theatre, a lesbian cabaret act, and an utterly straight staging of Otway's *Venice Preserv'd* in which both dir-ector and star (playing one-half of an eighteenth-century 'heroic friendship') are gay men. The twentieth century has been a period of extraordinarily rapid social and cultural change for gay people, but within all this diversity and change one factor has remained until recently constant. The writing and production of theatre have remained largely male operations, and it is not until the early 1970s that the phrase 'gay theatre' can be honestly used to describe work by, for or about lesbian women as well as gay men.

The complications of what might be meant by the phrase 'gay theatre' pre-date the coining of the terms (and indentities) 'homosexual' and 'gay' in the late nineteenth century. The often homoerotic and always transvestite theatre of Marlowe, Shakespeare and Fletcher was attacked by contemporary critics such as Prynne as the home of catamites and Ganymedes; John Wilmot, Earl of Rochester, rewrote Fletcher's *Valentin-ian* in the late 1670s as a maelstrom of confused desires whirling around an outspoken boy-loving emperor; Shadwell, Southerne, Dilke, Farquhar and Vanbrugh all exploited cross-dressing on stage at the same time as the development of an off-stage subculture by men who described themselves as mollies, meeting in pri-vate brothels and semi-public taverns in women's clothes as part of their sexual and social life. By the turn of the nineteenth century, at the end of a 40-year period in which both the subculture and its collisions with the world of culture had produced increasingly confident gay styles, the distinctive features of the gay theatre of our own century had been set.

This formative period was not, however, character-ized by a collective sense of gay culture. Few of the fol-lowing artists active at that time would have been aware of each other's work, or would have perceived themselves as differing practitioners within a single culture: WILDE, the most famously homosexual of all theatre artists, who never created a gay character – if we discount the page-boy in *Salomé* – but whose obsessive demolition of polite sexual and social relations in works as diverse as *The Importance of Being Earnest* (1895) and *La Sainte Courtisaine* (unfinished) was surely profoundly informed by his observations from the perspective of a social and sexual outlaw; DIAGHILEV, who was about to commence the lifelong series of works created with and for his lovers Lifar, Massine, Dolin and NIJINSKY; Malcolm Scott, billed as 'The Woman who Knows' in a series of drag routines at the London Pavilion in 1903; JULIAN ELTINGE, the first, greatest and most successful of the BROADWAY drag queens, who crossed the Atlantic to play to royalty in 1906; John Gray and André Raffalovich, a homosexual couple, both published poets, whose play *The Blackmailers* portrays the strengthening of a male homosexual relationship under the pressure of a family melodrama and was produced by J. T. GREIN at the Prince of Wales, London on 7 June 1894; John Todhunter, whose 1893 play *The Black Cat* decorates a standard marital crisis with a caricature of a homosexual dandy; or John B. Fuller, whose play *At St Judas* (New York, 1896) climaxes in the forced suicide of a best man in love with the groom at a society wedding.

All the categories of contemporary 'gay theatre' are there in that catalogue, with the exception of theatre created for rather than by or about gay people – although Gray and Raffalovich may be seen as having written the first play clearly intended to hearten the gay people in its audience as well as educate its liberals and shock its conservatives.

The most continuous and the richest theatrical tradition built upon these early works has been that of the drag artists – though their work has been the least honoured and the least documented, because it is a popular (i.e. working-class) tradition, and is rarely dependent on scripts or playwrights. The least continuous – since each artist apparently attempts to reinvent theatrical language in isolation – has been the series of acknowledged 'great artists' who are recognized by the critical establishment as gay but whose work is rarely if ever 'about' gay characters or incidents. WILLIAMS, Cocteau, GENET, LORCA and ORTON were not the product of some generalized 'gay sensibility', but each is similar to the others in that his work was decisively influenced by the language, role-playing, bitterness and need to either decisively conform to or disrupt conventions of the very different gay cultures in which he lived.

The 'problem play' is the most extensive section of any bibliography of gay theatre; it will include both plays in which homosexuality is a minor, decorative problem (*The Black Cat*) and plays in which 'the problem of homosexuality' is the main dramatic interest (*The Blackmailers* or Mart Crowley's infamous *The Boys in the Band*, 1968). The popularity of the genre arises from the fact that incidental gay stereotypes or stereotyped gay incidents provide ample opportunity for the bestselling theatrical ingredients of sex, misery and disguise. Also, homosexuality as a construct is the site of many of the culture's most-discussed social crises – sexual licence and sexual identity, the conflicting demands of liberalism and conservatism, parenthood and marriage. It would be a mistake to see such plays as *The Captive* (Eduard Bourdet, 1926), *Rope* (PATRICK HAMILTON, 1929), *The Children's Hour* (LILLIAN HELLMAN, 1934), *A Taste of Honey* (SHELAGH DELANEY, 1958), *A Patriot For Me* (JOHN OSBORNE, 1965) and *Staircase* (Charles Dyer, 1966) as 'merely' commercial or exploitative. They rather form a genuine acknowledgement that the formation of homosexuality in the twentieth century has been inextricably mixed up with the formation of other controversial identities – the 'nonconformist', the 'pervert', the 'independent woman', the 'virile', 'promiscuous' or 'effeminate' man. Some 'problem plays' are sympathetic to or actually militant on behalf of homosexuals – MAE WEST's 1927 *The Drag* or Sewell and Leslie Stokes's *Oscar Wilde* (1936). Some are the work of homosexuals themselves: J. R. Ackerley's *Prisoners of War* (1925), James Fugate (Barr)'s *Game of Fools* (1954), Roger Gellert's *Quaint Honour* (1958). Others are cryptic or transposed homosexual works by authors unable or unwilling to write explicitly – the works of COWARD, RATTIGAN and MAUGHAM, for instance. The cryptic or implicit use of gay themes should not, however, be simplistically read as evidence of the author being 'in the closet'. Somewhere in the category of 'problem play', for instance, one would have to locate the series of works by BRECHT in which the 'problem' of an intense relationship between two men in love is used to expose and tear apart the workings of the society in which they live – *Baal*, *In the Jungle of Cities*, *Edward II* and *Galileo* – the portrayal of the hero and his beloved pupil in the latter surely influenced by Brecht's collaboration with the great gay actor CHARLES LAUGHTON.

The watershed of twentieth-century gay culture is 1969, the year in which the Stonewall riots in New York dramatized the beginning of the gay liberation movement. Before neatly dividing gay culture into 'before' and 'after' Stonewall, it is salutary to consider the scale and diversity of the earlier work and to remember that all of the cultural forms pre-dating gay liberation have survived and developed. On the London stage (London is used throughout as an example of the complex development which might be traced in any English-speaking or European metropolitan gay culture; not because it was the centre of or leader) in 1968, for instance, you would have been able to watch the following shows, all of them by or featuring homosexual women or men: SIMON GRAY's *Wise Child*; Colin Spencer's *Spitting Image*; Orton's *Loot*; SHAFFER's *Black Comedy*; Peter Luke's *Hadrian the Seventh*; John Bowen's *Trevor*, with its depiction of a lesbian couple; Brecht's *Edward II*; Wilde's *The Importance of Being Earnest*; the NATIONAL THEATRE's all-male production of *As You Like It*; CHARLES MAROWITZ's production of *Fortune and Men's Eyes*; CHRISTOPHER HAMPTON's *Total Eclipse*; PADDY CHAYEFSKY's *The Latent Heterosexual*; LANFORD WILSON's *The Madness of Lady Bright*; EDWARD BOND's *Early Morning*, with its lesbian affair between Queen Victoria and Florence Nightingale; Benjamin Britten's *Peter Grimes*; the musical *Hair*; drag queens Rogers and Starr in the *Gaiety Box Revue*; and DANNY LA RUE fronting his own drag club in Hanover Square as well as playing DAME in *Sleeping Beauty* at the Golders Green Hippodrome.

Gay liberation did, however, decisively disrupt this spectrum of theatrical forms, and indeed the meaning of the phrase 'gay theatre'. First, and most importantly, it created a theatre which had not only gay writers, performers and producers but also a gay audience; a theatre not only by and about but also entirely for homosexuals. Although there had been explorations of the idea of playing to a gay audience in the club and cabaret culture of, for instance, the Harlem Renaissance and pre-Hitler Germany, this theatre had in fact never existed before. Second, it proposed that gay women and gay men should work togther to create a radical gay culture. Third, its main political tactic, 'coming out' – ceasing to pretend, behaving in public as an evident homosexual – made the enormous number of plays in which straight writers and performers had made such a drama of speaking as or for gay people seem immediately dated and rather distasteful.

In six years (1971–7) the impact of gay liberation on London theatre produced a development of new forms from STREET THEATRE (the drag disruption of the Miss World contest in 1971) to the complex operations of an established gay company, GAY SWEATSHOP. Their work included influencing the establishment of venues friendly or dedicated to new gay work (INTER-ACTION, ICA, Oval House); extensive regional touring of radical community work; major new plays like *Dear Love of Comrades* by Noël Greig; commissioning work from established writers (Bond's *Stone*); and moving into youth theatre work (ROYAL COURT, 1977). All successive work in this area – the establishment of community companies; the continuing existence of fringe venues promoting radical gay work; the influence of gay

writers and gay sexual politics on EXPERIMENTAL THEATRE as a whole – has been built on their pioneering efforts. The United States and to a lesser extent Europe have also seen the parallel establishment of numerous venues, authors and companies dedicated to the gay audience both as a cultural and political ideal.

Later gay theatre was a continuation of the variety of older forms, complicated further by the intervention of gay liberation. The more-or-less exploitative 'problem play' remained, in several forms. Homophobic details and narratives continued to be common in mainstream film and television. An upmarket version of the old style is provided by the work of Peter Shaffer, whose highly successful plays *The Royal Hunt of the Sun* (1964), *Equus* (1973) and *Amadeus* (1979) all sensationally portray the obsessive admiration of an older man for a younger. Most interestingly, gay writers themselves are producing what are in effect problem plays – commercially successful character-dramas focused on popular and painful issues – which are also explicitly the polemic writings of gay authors: Michael Wilcox, LARRY KRAMER, TONY KUSHNER, William Hoffman, MARTIN SHERMAN. Noel Greig and Michelene Wandor produce work which brings to 'issue' drama the full richness of perspective of their involvement in gay and women's liberation – the result of their early polemic work is, paradoxically, a theatre whose politics are expansive and wide-ranging, embracing multiculturalism and formal experiment as necessary results of the cracks first opened in the theatrical establishment by the demands of the new gay theatre. Drag continues to be a popular tradition, with its inimitable and vital mixture of artistic and political awfulness with rare artistry. It is still the most challenging and the most gay of our theatres; most importantly, it is the only art form which has actual premises – buildings and stages – dedicated to an exclusively gay public. The Broadway musical and the ballet both survive as art forms whose history has often been determined by gay performers and producers, which have a large gay male audience and whose iconography has been much loved and used by metropolitan gay male culture, but neither of which is thought of as 'gay theatre'. Perhaps the most exciting work is that of those artists in whom the new confidence made possible by the expansion of the subculture, and by the radical politics of liberation, has collided head on with the older traditions of drag, VAUDEVILLE, CABARET and the sex industry. In the performances of Lindsay Kemp, CHARLES LUDLUM (New York) and Bloolips (London), in the ballets of Michael Clark and the films of Derek Jarman there is a theatre which seems distinctively and uniquely gay. These spectacles have an uncompromising strength which is the result of our liberation, an eccentricity which acknowledges that we are still outside of the culture and a gorgeousness which is motivated largely by a desire to avenge all the repression and gloom which others have sought to stamp on our culture. They propose a theatre which goes beyond the simple categories of a theatre by, for or about gay people, since they are not always about the 'gay world'. They imagine, attack and talk about the world in gay language.

NEIL BARTLETT

In the United States

Playwright Robert Patrick once quipped that a 'gay play' is one that 'sleeps with other plays of the same sex'. His humour sidesteps an entrenched critical debate. Anthologies sporting such unambiguous titles as *Gay Plays: The First Collection* (1979, ed. William M. Hoffman), *Out Front: Contemporary Gay and Lesbian Plays* (1988, ed. Don Shewey) and *The Actor's Book of Gay and Lesbian Plays* (1995, ed. Eric Lane and Nina Shengold) examine the term 'gay play' carefully: Must it denote the work of an openly gay author? Must it be written for primarily gay audiences? Must it have gay characters, or just gay SUBTEXT? Many gender theorists argue that the very term 'gay' is specious; sexuality manifests too fluidly for language to contain it.

There has, however, been little ambiguity in the American public's animated consumption of '[male] gay plays'. Ever since Jazz Age heterosexuals thronged Greenwich Village cafeterias for 'fairy-watching', US audiences have devoured male homosexuality. New York State law, which from 1927 to 1967 forbade theatrical treatment of 'sex degeneracy, or sex perversion', may have prevented MAE WEST's *The Drag* (1927) from reaching Broadway; but soon thereafter West crashed New York with *The Pleasure Man* (1928), and its soaring ticket prices and heaving reviews revealed a public taste for forbidden gay spectacle. With its presentation of sinister effeminacy, the British import *The Green Bay Tree* (1933) by Mordaunt Shairp also thwarted New York law and allowed thousands of spectators ample opportunity for sordid sexual interpretation. Ironically, ROBERT ANDERSON, TENNESSEE WILLIAMS and ARTHUR MILLER soon profited by Senator McCarthy's terrifying implication that American audiences, blind to homosexual subversives, were not such savvy readers of maleness. Anderson's *Tea and Sympathy* (1953) depicts the brutality foisted on effeminate, heterosexual Tom Lee by Bill Reynolds, his hypermasculine, closeted headmaster. In Williams's *Cat on a Hot Tin Roof* (1955), Brick's former athletic glory and seductive masculinity cannot stem sexual suspicions surrounding his friendship with Skipper. In Miller's *A View From the Bridge* (1955), Brooklyn longshoreman Eddie Carbone unleashes frustrated sexual desire for his niece by slamming a frenzied kiss on her effeminate fiancé's mouth as 'proof' of the boy's deviance. As with Bill and Brick, Eddie's audience must ponder whether his homophobia reveals the attacker's sexuality more than that of his target. Although this equation no longer shocks, *View's* popular 1998 Broadway revival demonstrates America's continuing need to plumb male performance for potential secrets.

In the 1960s OFF-BROADWAY theatres such as the CAFFE CINO in Greenwich Village began to showcase work by openly gay authors for equally open audiences. The Cino, which offered such writers unprecedented freedom, influenced the DRAG- and allusion-heavy dramaturgies of much subsequent gay theatre. For example, through his Ridiculous Theatrical Company, Charles Ludlam convulsed audiences until his death in 1987 with such works as his drag *Camille* (1974) and Gothic spoof *The Mystery of Irma Vep* (1984) – a 1998 revival of which sold out Off-Broadway under the direction of Everett Quinton, Ludlam's longtime lover and successor. Encouraged by audience interest in these ventures, gay theatre troupes outside New York, such as San Francisco's Rhinoceros and Gay Men's Theatre Collective, began to flourish as well. While the Cino and Ludlam began to galvanize gay audiences, far more diverse masses flocked uptown to over 1,000 performances of Mart Crowley's *The Boys in the Band* (1968), an instantly notorious play which spectators alternatively declared either the first 'true' portrait of homosexual misery or a gallery of dated stereotypes. This debate, which overlooks the play's fairly progressive notions of gay relationships and effeminate-male courage, has followed *Boys* through a controversial film adaptation (1970) and a hot Off-Broadway revival (1996). As with *A View from the Bridge*, audiences continue to scrutinize staged maleness; witness the continuing amazement that Cliff Gorman, *Boys'* original Emory, could convincingly play Crowley's queen despite his heterosexuality.

Following *Boys* and the Stonewall Riots (1969), gay characters began to appear in mainstream drama that did not posit tortured (or torturing) homosexuals as its wrenching *raison d'être*. However, such works as James Kirkwood and Nicholas Dante's *A Chorus Line* (1975) and Michael Cristofer's *The Shadow Box* (1977) feature quipping queens who do encourage audiences' associations of homosexuality with constant carnival. In TERRENCE MCNALLY's *The Ritz* (1974), DAVID RABE's *Streamers* (1976), Ira Levin's *Deathtrap* (1978) and MARTIN SHERMAN's *Bent* (1979), gay protagonists figure within the lurid *mises-en-scène* of a bathhouse, a deadly army barracks, a murderous playwright's cottage and a Nazi work camp, respectively.

Fittingly, the arresting visuals of drag and disease helped audiences to process emerging themes of homophobia and AIDS. HARVEY FIERSTEIN's *Torch Song Trilogy* (1982) and book for *La Cage aux Folles* (1984) posit a politics of gay pride against a backdrop of glittering gowns. Larry Kramer's *The Normal Heart* (1985) and William M. Hoffman's *As Is* (1985) plunged American audiences into AIDS's visceral horrors by staging the shouting, shattered bodies suppressed in spotty journalism. In *Jerker* (1986), Robert Chesley updated *Bent*'s infamous sex talk by having his characters masturbate on stage, even while demonstrating their vulnerability to AIDS.

By the early 1990s, the commercial demand to see gay bodies and to hear gay wit prompted such acclaimed Broadway musicals as William Finn's *Falsettos* (1992) and JOHN KANDER, FRED EBB and McNally's *Kiss of the Spider Woman* (1993). Tony Kushner and Terrence McNally shared the Best Play Tony Award four years running with Kushner's two-part epic *Angels in America: A Gay Fantasia on National Themes* (1992, 1993) and McNally's *Love! Valour! Compassion!* (1994) and *Master Class* (1995), his Valentine to gay icon Maria Callas. Off-Broadway, the drag performance troupes SPLIT BREECHES and Bloolips presented *Belle Reprieve* (1991), their queer take on *A Streetcar Named Desire*, to strong reception; Pomo Afro Homos enjoyed considerable vogue for their *Dark Fruit* (1992). With *The Night Larry Kramer Kissed Me* (1992) and *My Queer Body* (1992), David Drake and Tim Miller drew substantial audiences to autobiographical queer monodramas.

Watchers of gay drama have made themselves into spectacle through heated politicking over McNally's *Corpus Christi* (1998). Protesters (and counterprotesters) ironically mounted their own fiery drama by excoriating *Christi*'s suggestion of sexual involvement between Christ and his disciples. The play's tepid reviews provided a startling anticlimax to months of anticipatory demonstrations. Clearly, American investment in the staging of male homosexuality did not languish as the century drew to its close. No other framed body allows spectators so ripe an opportunity to exercise their critical muscles. MICHAEL R. SCHIAVI

See also EROTICISM IN THE THEATRE; IMPERSONATION; LESBIAN THEATRE; QUEER THEATRE; THEATRE OF THE RIDICULOUS.

John M. Clum, *Acting Gay: Male Homosexuality in Modern Drama* (1992)

Kaier Curtin, *'We Can Always Call Them Bulgarians':*
The Emergence of Lesbians and Gay Men on the American Stage (1987)

Nicholas de Jongh, *Not in Front of the Audience: Homosexuality on Stage* (1992)

Terry Helbeing, ed, *Gay Theatre Alliance Directory of Gay Plays* (1980)

William M. Hoffman, 'Introduction', in *Gay Plays: The First Collection* (1979)

Carl Miller, *Stages of Desire: Gay Theatre's Hidden History* (1996)

David Savran, *Communists, Cowboys, and Queers: The Politics of Masculinity in the Work of Arthur Miller and Tennessee Williams* (1992)

Alan Sinfield, *Out on Stage: Lesbian and Gay Theatre in the Twentieth Century* (2000)

Robert Vorlicky, *Act Like a Man: Challenging Masculinities in American Drama* (1995)

Michelene Wandor, *Carry On Understudies* (1986)

Geary, David (b. Fielding, New Zealand, 19 Sept. 1963) Playwright. He studied law at Victoria University but turned to writing and drama, attending the New Zealand Drama School in 1987, then worked as an actor in Wellington and Palmerston North, and wrote several television scripts. In 1991 he wrote a play about a women's rugby team, *Pack of Girls* (1991), following it with the successful *Lovelock's Dream Run* (1993). His rural background is often reflected in his plays, for example *The Learner's Stand* (1994) and *The Farm* (1997). GILLIAN GREER & LAURIE ATKINSON

Gelbart, Larry [Simon] (b. Chicago, 25 Feb. 1923) Writer for radio, stage, screen and television; humorist. After some success with radio shows, he moved into television and became one of the top comedy writers. In *M*A*S*H*, Gelbart first introduced multiple plot lines to half-hour television programmes. His stage works include *Shy Fox* (1976), *Mastergate* (1989), *Power Failure* (1990), *Feats of Clay* (1991) and musical libretti for two hit shows, *A Funny Thing Happened on the Way to the Forum* (1962) and *City of Angels* (1990). In 1998, his autobiography *Laughing Matters* was published. ANNA WHEELER GENTRY

Gelber, Jack (b. Chicago, 12 April 1932) Playwright and director. He has had some 15 plays produced in New York, but he is chiefly remembered for just one, *The Connection* (1959), produced by the LIVING THEATER, an innovative play about drug addiction. ADRIANA HUNTER

Gélinas, Gratien (b. Saint-Tite, Canada, 8 Dec. 1909; d. Oka, nr Montreal, 16 March 1999) French-Canadian playwright, director and actor. Gélinas was a major pioneer in the establishment of modern Quebec theatre, the birth of which is usually dated from the performance of his best-known play, *Tit-Coq* ('Little rooster'), on 22 May 1948, with the author in the title role. He already had long experience in radio and satirical revues, and this experience was central to his success. Founder of the Comédie Canadienne in 1958, he continued to direct, to perform in French and English (he played in Shakespeare at Canada's STRATFORD FESTIVAL), and to write to an advanced age, his last work being *La Passion de Narcisse Mondoux* ('Narcisse Mondoux's passion', 1986), the stage versions of which starred himself and his wife. LEONARD E. DOUCETTE

Mavor Moore, *Four Canadian Playwrights* (1973)
Anne-Marie Sicotte, *Gratien Gélinas: La Ferveur et le doute*, 2 vols (1995)
Renate Usmiani, *Gratien Gélinas* (1977)

Gelman, Alexander [Isaakovich] (b. Dondyushany, Moldavia, 25 Oct. 1933) Playwright. Previously a construction worker and a fitter and later a journalist, he was 40 when he started writing plays. In 1989, in the climate of *glasnost* and *perestroika*, he was elected to the increasingly democratized Supreme Soviet of the USSR. Gelman inverted and then subverted the Soviet theatre's genre of 'production drama', usually set in a factory, boardroom or building site, where a 'keen young (or wise old) Party member' exposes a corrupt and/or inefficient manager and the dénouement involves the unmasking and sacking of the 'villain'. His first play, variously translated as *The Bonus*, *A Party Committee Meeting* and *The Proceedings of a Meeting*, was filmed in 1974 and won the state prize for best film script in 1975, the year it was staged. Several of Gelman's plays have been adapted for film or television: *Feedback* (1977), *We, the Undersigned* (1978), *A Man with Connections* (1981), *The Bend* (1984) and *Zinulya* (1985). *Misha's Party* was co-written with RICHARD NELSON for the ROYAL SHAKESPEARE COMPANY (1993) and the MOSCOW ART THEATRE (1994), and *Czech Photo* was seen in 1998. VERA GOTTLIEB

Gémier, [Tonnerre] Firmin (b. Aubervilliers, France, 21 Feb. 1869; d. Paris, 26 Nov. 1933) Actor, director and teacher who made his début with ANTOINE (Théâtre Libre, then Théâtre de l'Œuvre, where he played JARRY's *Ubu Roi*). He made several attempts to found a People's Theatre, establishing the first THÉÂTRE NATIONAL POPULAIRE but without a company to produce anything. His national touring theatre failed, but he established a Shakespeare Society, ran popular festivals at the ODÉON (1922–30), taught the value of systematic work and improvisation (his best-known pro-

tégé was DULLIN) and created a predecessor of the INTERNATIONAL THEATRE INSTITUTE.
TERRY HODGSON

P. Blanchart, *Firmin Gémier* (1954)

Gems [Price], [Iris] Pam[ela] (b. Bransgore, Dorset, 1 Aug. 1925) Playwright. Initially associated with INTER-ACTION's women's theatre season, out of which came the WOMEN'S THEATRE GROUP, for which she wrote *Go West Young Woman* (1974), Gems first came to wider notice with *Dusa, Fish, Stas and Vi* (1976), comparing four women's views on sex and sisterhood. *Loving Women* (1984) wittily and perceptively retells the eternal triangle story with a lesbian conclusion. But Gems's subtle and cool playwriting can be best seen in *Queen Christina* (1977), her earthily vulgar *Piaf* (1978) and *Camille* (1984), all staged by the ROYAL SHAKESPEARE COMPANY and each dramatizing the struggle of a woman from history to free herself from cultural roles of gender and class. She has also had success with adaptations, including *Uncle Vanya* (1979) and *The Blue Angel* (1990). *Stanley* (1996), her story of the painter Stanley Spencer starring ANTONY SHER, was a success in London and New York. DAN REBELLATO

K. H. Burkman, 'The Plays of Pam Gems' in *British and Irish Drama Since 1960*, ed. J. Acheson (1993)

Genet, Jean (b. Paris, 19 Dec. 1910; d. Paris, 13 April 1986) Playwright. Thief, deserter and homosexual, Genet spent many years in prison, and in his novels and plays fully assumed the role in which society had cast him. Befriended and, as he thought, overinterpreted by SARTRE, who campaigned for his release, he won an international reputation over 20 years with five plays: *Les Bonnes* (*The Maids*, 1946), *Haute Surveillance* (*Death-watch*, 1949), *Le Balcon* (*The Balcony*, 1956), *Les Nègres* (*The Blacks*, 1959) and *Les Paravents* (*The Screens*, 1961). It is a mystery how he did it.

Only chronologically an ABSURDIST, a mirror image of CLAUDEL, to whose Christian symbolism he lends a satanic gloss, Genet is PIRANDELLIAN in his theatricals, his shifting personalities, his reflections on and of reflections, evoking ARTAUD's metaphysical leanings and COCTEAU's view of the theatre as a no-man's-land between the poetry of words and of space. Unsurprisingly, he is concerned with power and dominance: mistress and maids, prison hierarchy, political revolution, blacks versus whites, colonized against colonizers. But nothing in Genet is as it seems. Illusion and reality are interchangeable. Conflicts are worked out in game-playing and play-making. He stands morality on its head, or reflects it in so many mirrors that it becomes fluid. He is scandalous because he challenges the dominant values of society. His whores must look like saints. Genet hated the first production of *The Balcony* (in English at the ARTS THEATRE in 1957) because of its naturalism. In his three last plays, condemned as subversive, the revolutionaries, Blacks and Algerians are seen in a dimension beyond the political. The everlasting minuet continues the other side of the screens.

DONALD WATSON

Robert Brustein, *The Theatre of Revolt* (1965), ch. on Genet
Richard Coe, *The Vision of Jean Genet* (1968)
——, *The Theatre of Jean Genet: A Casebook* (1970)
Bettina L. Knapp, *Genet* (1968)
Joseph H. MacMahon, *The Imagination of Jean Genet* (1963)
Jean-Paul Sartre, *Saint-Genet* (1963)
Philip Thody, *Jean Genet: A Critical Appraisal* (1968)

Georgia *see* SOVIET UNION

German [Jones], Edward (b. Whitchurch, 17 Feb. 1862; d. London, 11 Nov. 1936) Composer. German's earliest substantial compositions were orchestral pieces, both for the concert hall and the theatrical stage, where his dance music for IRVING's production of *Henry VIII* (1892) and for *English Nell* (1900) won particular success. On the death of Sir ARTHUR SULLIVAN, he was commissioned to complete the score of Sullivan's unfinished light opera *The Emerald Isle* and thereafter was teamed with librettist BASIL HOOD on the durable *Merrie England* (1902) and *A Princess of Kensington* (1903). German composed the music for a highly successful stage musical version of *Tom Jones*, produced for the Fielding bicentenary in 1907, and an unfortunate collaboration with W. S. GILBERT on a musical adaptation of his 1873 play *The Wicked World as Fallen Fairies* (1909). He was knighted in 1928.

KURT GÄNZL

B. Rees, *A Musical Pacemaker* (1988)
W. Scott, *Edward German* (1932)

German-language theatre The theatre in the German-speaking world, as an important public institution, looks back on a long tradition of serving as a purveyor of culture rather than of 'mere' entertainment. The latter is in any case amply catered for by the private sector. The generously subsidized playhouses owned by state or municipality – a prominent fact of life since the nineteenth century – tend, instead of the continuous runs customary in the WEST END or on BROADWAY, to present a constantly changing programme of domestic and foreign classics as well as important new plays from anywhere: in other words, a richly varied, exemplary and demanding repertoire. Translations have always formed a considerable part of this 'official' theatrical fare; the German plays discussed below are therefore only a part, and not necessarily the greater part, of what is seen on the stage in German-speaking countries at any given time.

In contrast to the role played by LONDON or PARIS, there is no single theatrical metropolis in the German-speaking world. This is not simply due to the fact that there are three very different German-speaking countries – Germany, AUSTRIA and SWITZERLAND. Regionalism even within Germany has deep historical roots, and at various times Hamburg, Munich, Dresden, Leipzig, Düsseldorf, Bremen, Stuttgart, Bochum and many other cities have been key centres of theatrical energy. The eminence of BERLIN during the Weimar period was never absolute, although it was and still is exceptionally well endowed with theatres of different types. Its high postwar profile while Germany was politically divided owed much to the fact that both East and West put their cultural wares in competing shop windows; even so, the premières of new plays would often take place elsewhere. Outside Germany, VIENNA in particular and Zürich to a somewhat lesser extent are theatrical centres in their own right.

Massive funding as well as the advanced technology characteristic of the German-speaking world account for the prevalence of sophisticated theatrical architecture and machinery. Here wagon stages, hydraulic lifts and revolves have been common features longer than elsewhere. This technical complexity, as well as a bias towards authority figures, has given the director in the German-speaking theatre a particularly dominant position. From MAX REINHARDT, LEOPOLD JESSNER, Jürgen Fehling and Erich Engel in the pre-Hitler period to the actor–director GUSTAF GRÜNDGENS who pre-dated Nazism, worked through it and outlived it, and on to the later generation of Hans Lietzau, BENNO BESSON, PETER ZADEK and PETER STEIN (to mention just a few names out of a galaxy of talent), there has been a succession of powerful directors, often associated with particular writers (as in the case of CLAUS PEYMANN and THOMAS BERNHARD) who have put their stamp on the stage of their day.

At the beginning of the twentieth century two playwrights who had already done part of their work loomed large on the theatrical scene: FRANK WEDEKIND and GERHART HAUPTMANN. The former's provocative drama of adolescent sexuality, *Spring's Awakening*, though published in 1891, could not be performed on the stage until 1906. Wedekind's plays, which oscillated between realism and fantasy, drew obliquely on his own colourful life, as for instance *The Marquess of*

Keith (1900), a satirical comedy of fraud; *King Nicolo, or Such is Life* (1901), the story of a deposed king who becomes a court jester; or *Hidalla* (1904), the tragicomedy of an ugly eugenist. Sexual melodramas like the two Lulu plays, *Earth Spirit* (1895) and *Pandora's Box* (1902), *Castle Wetterstein* (1910) or *Francisca, a Modern Mystery* (1912) were to leave their imprint on the work of later playwrights. The young BRECHT was a great admirer of Wedekind.

In the work of Hauptmann, for a long time the representative German man of letters (he won the Nobel Prize for Literature in 1912), there was a pendulum swing of styles: naturalism, which he had pioneered in German drama, on the one hand, and a vein of fantasy on the other. His tragedy of seduction, *Rose Bernd* (1903), was a realistic and compassionate rural picture; plays like *Michael Kramer* (1900) and *Gabriel Schilling's Flight* (1906) depicted crises in the lives of artists. Fantasy had full play in *Schluck and Jau* (1900), a comedy on the Christopher Sly pattern, as well as in the fairy tale-like quest for the ideal, *And Pippa Dances* (1906), *Poor Henry* (1902), *Charlemagne's Hostage* (1908) and *Griselda* (1909) were set in the middle ages. *The White Saviour* (1920), the story of Montezuma conquered by the Spaniards, and *Indipohdi* (1921), a tragic restatement of *The Tempest*, reflected Hauptmann's despair during and after the First World War. The Second World War was to drive him back to classical themes – *Iphigenia in Aulis, Agamemnon's Death, Electra* and *Iphignia in Delphi*, all written between 1940 and 1944.

Like Hauptmann, the Austrian novelist and playwright ARTHUR SCHNITZLER had an established reputation by the turn of the century. Like Wedekind, he was ahead of his time in the matter of sexual outspokenness. His piece of erotic musical chairs, *Reigen* (best known in the English-speaking world by its French film title, *La Ronde*), was written in 1900 but considered so shocking that it could not be performed until 1920. While the relationship of the sexes in the setting of the final days of the Habsburg Empire was a recurrent theme, in *Professor Bernhardi* (1912) he attacked the problem of anti-semitism in Vienna's medical circles. The plays he wrote after the First World War were still rooted in a prewar universe.

His fellow Viennese Hermann Bahr (1863–1924), in turn the champion of naturalism, SYMBOLISM and baroque art, was a prolific playwright whose farcical comedy, *The Concert* (1909), was performed throughout Europe. Poet, essayist and dramatist HUGO VON HOFMANNSTHAL was also a profoundly Austrian writer. A traditionalist, he adapted Greek, Golden Age Spanish and English Restoration plays for the modern stage. Together with Max Reinhardt he founded the Salzburg

Festival in 1920; his version of *Everyman*, performed at the first Festival, has remained a fixture there ever since. For the 1922 Festival he reworked a Calderón *auto sacramental* into *The Great Salzburg Theatre of the World*. A more original aspect of his talent was shown in the subtle comedy of character, *The Difficult Man* (1918). He supplied distinguished libretti for Richard Strauss operas such as *Der Rosenkavalier* (1911), *Ariadne on Naxos* (1912) and *The Woman Without a Shadow* (1919).

Very different from these essentially metropolitan Austrian writers was the Tyrolean Karl Schönherr (1867–1943). One of his peasant dramas, *The She Devil* (1914), was a Strindbergian battle of the sexes ending in the husband's violent death. The banker's son CARL STERNHEIM spoke with the voice of the new century. It was his ambition to be the German Molière. Indeed, his comedy *The Strong Box* (1912) had echoes of *The Miser*. He named a cycle of satirical comedies *Scenes from the Heroic Life of the Middle Classes*. Part of this cycle is the trilogy *The Bloomers* (1911), *The Snob* (1913) and *1913* (1914), which chronicles the humble Maske family's rise to a position of social and industrial power by cunning role-playing and intrigue.

The First World War, once its devastating effect had begun to sink in, found its theatrical reflection in EXPRESSIONIST drama. A high-pitched, somewhat hysterical style of presentation developed. Though some expressionist plays had been written before the war, they were produced only when the air was heavy with crisis. Thus Reinhard Sorge's *The Beggar*, written in 1912, was staged in 1917, the year which also saw the performance of KAISER's *From Morn to Midnight* and *The Burghers of Calais* (dating back to 1912 and 1913 respectively). Of all the expressionist dramatists Georg Kaiser was the most prolific, with some 70 plays to his credit. His trilogy of industrial life in the age of high technology – *The Coral* (1917), *Gas I* (1918) and *Gas II* (1920) – touched prophetically on future problems of employment, ecology and wars of mass destruction. Kaiser continued to write long after the vogue of his plays had passed. Again and again his plays proclaimed humankind's need for spiritual change. A dramatist who straddled the expressionist period without ever quite belonging to the movement is ERNST BARLACH. A distinguished sculptor and graphic artist as well as author, he went from the symbolism of *The Dead Day* (published in 1912, staged in 1919) to the earthy description of small-town life, *The Genuine Sedemunds* (1920), and the biblical drama *The Flood* (1924).

Protest was a basic expressionist stance. The Prussian officer FRITZ VON UNRUH pleaded for peace in *A Generation* (1917). ERNST TOLLER, gaoled for his pacifist views, described his own conversion from militarism in the ecstatic *Transfiguration* (1919). Imprisoned once more for taking part in the 1919 communist uprising in Munich, he pleaded for non-violence even in the midst of revolution in *Masses and Man* (1921). In *Hinkemann* (1923) he portrayed a soldier-victim reminiscent of Büchner's Woyzeck, within the framework of the post-war genre of *Heimkehrer* drama. The name of this category of plays about soldiers returning to civilian life was derived from *Heimkehr* ('Homecoming', 1918) by Hans José Rehfisch (1891–1960).

An outstanding play of this kind was *Drums in the Night* (first produced in 1921) by the young Bertolt Brecht, whose tough, cynical tone of voice cut through the humanitarian pathos of expressionism. Equally unsentimental was his *In the Jungle* (later called *In the Jungle of the Cities*; staged 1923), the story of a mysterious struggle between two men. The *Threepenny Opera* (1928), Brecht's updated version of Gay's *Beggar's Opera*, owed much of its spectacular success to KURT WEILL's hard-boiled musical score. Brecht and Weill collaborated again on the opera *The Rise and Fall of the Town of Mahagonny* (1930). Having become a Marxist, Brecht contributed to the sharpening struggle between left and right with didactic plays (LEHRSTÜCKE) such as *The Measure* (1930), which was performed by a workers' choir.

In fact the theatre, professional as well as non-professional, had been an embattled political forum since the fall of the Hohenzollern monarchy in November 1918. A militant workers' theatre sprang up. The postwar period spawned such forms as the political revue, the LIVING NEWSPAPER and choral speaking. From the mid-1920s onwards regular AGITPROP groups – the Red Blouses, the Red Rockets, the Red Megaphone and many others – performed in meeting halls, at workplaces and out of doors. By 1930 the movement had gone on to mount complete plays with the active support of sympathizers like the communist playwright FRIEDRICH WOLF.

The outstanding professional advocate and practitioner of political theatre was the director ERWIN PISCATOR. Though his punchy, indeed spectacular, productions were intended to mobilize the masses, his audiences came largely from the radical middle class (*see* EPIC THEATRE). Brecht was a member of his writing team which dramatized *The Good Soldier Schweyk* (1928) from the Czech writer Hašek's famous novel. Piscator's production of this – using animated film by GEORGE GROSZ and treadmills for transporting actors and scenery across the stage – was a landmark in Weimar theatre history.

Even when not committed, theatre aroused intense passions. CARL ZUCKMAYER drew enthusiastic crowds with his comedy *The Merry Vineyard* (1925), in which he made effective use of his native Hessian dialect; but it provoked storms of protest from right-wing elements who saw themselves lampooned in the play. *The Captain of Köpenick* (1931) was a more overtly satirical piece with its true-to-life prewar story of the poor cobbler who helped himself to some cash from officials bamboozled by his military uniform. Many authors wrote what were called *Zeitstücke* (topical plays) with a strongly critical inflection. Peter Martin Lampel (1884–1965) based *Revolt in the Reformatory* (1929) on his experiences as a social worker. The Austrian FERDINAND BRUCKNER examined cynical attitudes among the young in *The Malady of Youth* (1926), and challenged notions of the law in the courtroom drama *The Criminals* (1928). Friedrich Wolf (1888–1953) dealt with abortion in *Cyanide* (1929), with a revolt in the Austro-Hungarian navy in *The Sailors of Cattaro* (1930) and with revolutionary stirrings in China in *Tai Yang Awakens* (1931). MARIELUISE FLEISSER showed up the exploitative relations of soldiers with local girls in her Bavarian play, *Pioneers in Ingolstadt* (1929). In the 1970s her work was to inspire a new generation of playwrights like FASSBINDER, SPERR and KROETZ. ÖDÖN VON HORVÁTH, a writer of Hungarian origin who worked in Berlin and Vienna, was a close observer particularly of lower middle-class lifestyles and speech patterns. His plays, conventional in structure and in some instances labelled 'folk-plays', uncovered the tensions and hypocrisies of everyday life. He too was rediscovered in the 1960s, an eye-opener to audiences as well as to young playwrights.

Not all interwar playwrights saw life from a progressive angle. Hanns Johst (1890–1978), who had turned from expressionism to Nazism, dedicated his anti-French play *Schlageter* (1932) to Hitler 'in affectionate veneration and unchanging loyalty'. It featured the notorious line, 'When I hear the word culture, I slip back the safety catch of my revolver.'

Hitler's coming to power in Germany on 30 January 1933 made a deep, immediate and lasting incision in the theatre as in every other walk of life. All plays at variance with Nazi ideology were banned; 'unsuitable' personnel – Jews, Communists, in fact anybody whose face didn't fit – were thrown out of work. Many left the country, often precipitately – authors like Brecht, Zuckmayer, Bruckner, Hasenclever, Toller, Werfel, Kaiser, Lampel and Horváth; directors like Reinhardt, Piscator and Viertel; actors like KORTNER, Deutsch, Pallenberg, Bassermann, Busch, ELISABETH BERGNER and HELENE WEIGEL. Barlach, who stayed on, was forbidden to write. When Austria was overrun by Germany on 12

March 1938, Nazi cultural policy was imposed on that country as well. The exiles struggled to keep some sort of German theatre alive abroad – in Austria (before the *Anschluss*), Czechoslovakia, France and elsewhere. Plays continued to be written even if they could not be staged for the time being. Such outstanding items of the postwar theatre as Brecht's *The Caucasian Chalk Circle* and Zuckmayer's *The Devil's General* were written in the United States during the Second World War.

Switzerland, the one German-speaking country never under Hitler's domination, played a key role in theatrical culture during the Nazi period. The Zürich Schauspielhaus in particular, where a number of exiled theatre workers were active, staged plays banned in Germany such as Brecht's *Mother Courage and Her Children* (1941), *The Good Person of Setzuan* and *Galileo* (both 1943). FRITZ HOCHWÄLDER, who had fled from Austria to Switzerland, became well known with *The Holy Experiment* (1943), which dramatized the abolition of the progressive Jesuit state in eighteenth-century Paraguay. (The play ran in London after the war under the title *The Strong are Lonely*.) Later work by this skilful though traditional writer, who stayed on in Switzerland, included *The Fugitive* (1945) and *The Public Prosecutor* (1949).

Meanwhile in Germany, where Hanns Johst became President of the Reich Chamber of Literature in 1935, attempts were made to create new forms of ideological theatre. An example of the *Thingspiel* – a type of open-air mass spectacle which emphasized ritual – was *The Frankenburg Game of Dice* (1936) by Eberhard Wolfgang Möller (1906–72): this gave a symbolic and politically acceptable picture of the sixteenth-century Peasants' War. *Thingspiele* and other kinds of Nazi drama vanished without a trace after the defeat of fascism.

During the early phase of the Second World War theatres continued to operate normally in Germany. But from 1942 onwards, as air raids intensified, there were increasing disruptions; many theatres were bombed; and around the middle of 1944 all playhouses were closed. When the country collapsed on 7 May 1945 the theatrical situation was desperate. Over 100 theatres had been damaged or destroyed; the spiritual damage was unquantifiable. Nevertheless immediate efforts were made to revive theatrical activity, whatever the conditions, in all four Allied occupation zones, the Soviet zone of Berlin leading the way. When currency reform in 1948 started to bring economic recovery to the West, the rebuilding of theatres started in earnest. From the 1950s to the 1970s there was a wave of intensive theatre construction – both the restoration of old houses and the building of new ones, some of

them technically so complex as to impose a far from intimate style on productions.

In the early postwar period foreign drama flooded the stage in order to make up for 12 years of cultural isolation. Authors like ELIOT, PRIESTLEY, GIRAUDOUX, ANOUILH and SARTRE were popular; THORNTON WILDER's *The Skin of our Teeth* struck a particular chord. A breakthough for German-language drama occurred in 1946 when Zuckmayer's *The Devil's General* was premièred in Zürich and performed subsequently at a great many West German theatres. The story of the Luftwaffe general who, though contemptuous of Nazism, serves the war effort until he is finally driven to suicide, gave a reassuring view of the 'decent German'. Technically conventional, the play showed Zuckmayer's uncanny (for an exile) insight into the wartime atmosphere of Berlin. Later plays of his, such as *The Cold Light* (1956), *The Life of Horace A. W. Tabor* (1964) or *The Pied Piper* (1975), failed to make anything like the same impact. The voice of the wartime generation itself was first heard in 1947 with *Draussen vor der Tür* (literally, 'Outside the door', but known in English as *The Man Outside*) by WOLFGANG BORCHERT (1921–47). Originally a radio play, this was premièred in Hamburg the day after the author's death. It was a highly emotional piece of the *Heimkehrer* type which reverted to the idiom of expressionism.

The founding in the eastern part of the country of the German Democratic Republic on 7 October 1949 set the seal on Germany's division into two states with radically different ideologies; this included cultural policies. Brecht returned to East Berlin in that year, first to produce *Mother Courage* at the Deutsches Theater and then to install his own company, the BERLINER ENSEMBLE, in the Theater am Schiffbauerdamm. Within a few years the Berliner Ensemble came to be recognized as one of the world's leading theatres, with Brecht's own plays and his adaptations of classics like Lenz's *The Tutor*, Farquhar's *The Recruiting Officer* (retitled *Drums and Trumpets*) and Molière's *Don Juan* serving as the foundation of its repertoire.

The vacuum left by the relative absence of German or Austrian playwrights was filled by two Swiss authors – MAX FRISCH and FRIEDRICH DÜRRENMATT. The fact that Switzerland had been spared the experience of occupation and war gave them a grip on the current scene that other German speakers closer to recent events could achieve only with difficulty. Though influenced by Brecht, neither of the Swiss playwrights wished to propagate any clear-cut, let alone Marxist, message. Frisch pointedly gave the satirical subtitle 'A didactic play without a lesson' to his satire on bourgeois spinelessness in the face of determined aggression, *Biedermann und die Brandstifter* (*The Fire Raisers* in Britain, *The Fire Bugs* in America, 1958). His first play, *Now They Sing Again* (1945), was a requiem for the war dead. *The Great Wall of China* (1946, repeatedly revised since) examined the role of ideas in a romp through history. With *Andorra* (1961), Frisch touched on a sensitive issue: racism. This murderous parable, for which the minuscule Pyrennean country is only a tongue-in-cheek pretext, deals not merely with anti-semitism but with scapegoating as such. Premièred like other Frisch plays in Zürich, it then played in no fewer than 23 German theatres. With *Biography* (1968) Frisch departed from the parable form.

Dürrenmatt, an advocate of black comedy as the only meaningful dramatic genre for the present, projected a grotesque view of the world. *The Marriage of Mr Mississippi* (1952) reduced all ideological stances to equal absurdity. In *The Visit* (really *The Old Lady's Visit*, 1956) he demonstrated the corruption of a whole town, bribed into lynching a fellow citizen; this 'tragical comedy' was an enormous success both in London and New York. So was *The Physicists* (1962), an intrigue among nuclear scientists appropriately set in a madhouse. Dürrenmatt's rewrite of Strindberg's *Dance of Death* with the English title *Play Strindberg* (1969) proved to be one of the most popular plays in the German theatre of the 1970s.

Absurdist influences from France touched some of the younger German writers like Wolfgang Hildesheimer (1916–91); his collection of short pieces was characteristically called *Plays in Which Darkness Falls* (1958). GÜNTER GRASS wrote several plays in this vein, e.g. *Ten Minutes to Buffalo* (1959) and *The Wicked Cooks* (1961), but achieved greater fame as a novelist than as a playwright. TANKRED DORST, the author of absurdist pieces like *The Bend* (1960) and *Grand Tirade at the Town Wall* (1961), has had a more long-term commitment to drama (both for stage and for screen). Even though it has coloured a good deal of subsequent German-language drama, simon-pure absurdism did not last long. Thus, Grass's *The Plebeians Rehearse the Uprising* (1966) was not absurdist but ironical: it viewed the 1953 uprising in East Berlin from the perspective of a Brecht at work on a revolutionary stage production while failing to respond to what was happening right outside his own theatre. Dorst, in his play *Toller* (1968), blended fragments from *Masses and Man* with scenes from that author's biography; his *Ice Age* (1973) is a study of the aged Norwegian author and Nazi collaborator Knut Hamsun.

By the 1960s confronting the painful past had at last become possible. The appropriate dramatic vehicle for this seemed to be the DOCUMENTARY mode. In fact, the play which initiated the trend, *The Representative* (1963) by ROLF HOCHHUTH, was more of a Schillerian tragedy than a strictly documentary effort. First produced by the veteran director Piscator, *The Representative* questioned the ineffectual role of Pope Pius XII during the Holocaust; this aroused bitter controversy in many countries. Hochhuth's next play, *Soldiers: An Obituary of Geneva* (1967), which also blended documentary aspects with theatricalism, proved no less contentious. The National Theatre in London was stopped by its board of governors from putting it on because it was seen as an attack on Churchill. With *Guerrillas* (1970), a fictional drama in an American setting, as well as with his later plays, Hochhuth has demonstrated that he was not really wedded to the documentary idea. HEINAR KIPPHARDT, however, was a genuinely documentary playwright. *In the Matter of J. Robert Oppenheimer* (1964) actually drew on transcripts of the investigation of the witch-hunted atomic scientist. In *Joel Brand, the History of a Business Deal* (1965) he cut even closer to the bone with a reminder of the SS trade in Jewish lives during the war. HANS MAGNUS ENZENSBERGER dramatized the aftermath of the failed Bay of Pigs invasion by Cuban counter-revolutionaries in *The Havana Inquiry* (1970).

A play which aroused enormous interest in a great many countries was *The Persecution and Assassination of Marat as Performed by the Inmates of the Asylum of Charenton under the Direction of the Marquis de Sade* (1964) – usually shortened to *Marat/Sade* – by PETER WEISS, an author living in Swedish exile. This debate between the history-shaping forces of collectivism and individualism combined Brechtian alienating devices with those of Artaud's THEATRE OF CRUELTY – and thus became something truly original. Its triple perspective – 1804 (the framing action), 1793 (the play within the play) and 1964 (the date of performance) – invited the audience constantly to ponder and evaluate the events shown on the stage. Its subdivision into 33 scenes recalled the number of cantos in the latter two parts of *The Divine Comedy*. Because Weiss gave equal weight to the opposing arguments, different productions have interpreted the play very differently.

In the Auschwitz play *The Investigation* (1965), which was based on the record of the Frankfurt trial of concentration camp guards (December 1963–August 1965), Weiss made unbearable events theatrically tolerable by his cool documentary approach. The oppressive material was distanced in that it was formally subdivided into 11 cantos, each canto falling into three parts: this again resulted in the Dantesque number of 33. The 'perfect' number of three informs the cast:

three judges, nine witnesses, eighteen accused. *The Investigation* bridged the country's political divide: it was staged in both East and West Germany. Weiss came to adopt an overtly socialist posture in later plays. *The Song of the Lusitanian Bogeyman* (1967) and *Vietnam Discourse* (1968) were close to agitprop. In *Hölderlin* (1971), he interpreted that poet's life from a political perspective.

MARTIN WALSER preferred a more fantasticated approach to national self-examination. *Oak and Angora* (1962; *The Rabbit Race* in the English version) and *The Black Swan* (1964) looked at the ongoing consequences of Nazism with enough grotesquery to abort any stock responses. He maintained his special tone of voice in *Child's Play* (1970) and *In Goethe's Hand* (1982).

Having peaked in 1968, much of the radicalism of the 1960s dwindled into disillusionment and retreat into the private sphere in German-speaking countries as elsewhere. The Austrian novelist and playwright PETER HANDKE drastically questioned the theatre's claim to social relevance. He wrote a number of self-referential *Sprechstücke* ('speaking plays'). In the first, *Offending the Audience* (1966), four actors perform no action other than provoking the spectators. Similarly, *Self Accusation* (1966) and *Cries for Help* (1967) confine themselves to the verbal plane. *Kaspar* (1968) demonstrates in schematic form the conditioning nature of language by a process described as 'speech torture'. The *Slow Homecoming* tetralogy (1982) uses a symbolic perspective on modern consciousness.

The plays of Handke's compatriot THOMAS BERNHARD (also a novelist) viewed life from the perspective of death. Both in *A Feast for Boris* (1970), a drama peopled by cripples which has been compared to Beckett's *Endgame*, and in *The Ignoramus and the Madman* (1972), Bernhard dissolved action into bleak absurdity. *Minetti* (1976) employed the actual stage veteran of that name to question theatre – and thereby life itself. Bernhard posthumously made his attitude towards his native land abundantly clear in a will which banned all further productions of his plays in Austria until the expiry of copyright. The Austrian novelist and playwright Elfriede Jelinek has also managed to provoke her more conservative compatriots with plays such as *Burgtheater* (1985): this exposé embarrassingly highlights the conduct during the Nazi period of some members of the prestigious Viennese National Theatre.

When the German playwright BOTHO STRAUSS shows contemporary life on the stage it is seen at an oblique angle. *Well Known Faces, Mixed Feelings* (1974) portrays a commune in an isolated hotel, signifying non-communication. *Great and Small* (1978) traces the loneliness of its heroine in disjointed scenes. *The Park*

(1983) is an alienated vision of *A Midsummer Night's Dream* in modern urban terms.

An approach that some, notably Bavarian, authors have adopted since the 1960s for the depiction of reality is that of the 'folk play'. If that term ever suggested a cosy view of the 'people' – heart-warming comedy expressed in racy dialect – Horváth had long since given it a darker inflection. RAINER WERNER FASS-BINDER, better known internationally as a film-maker, wrote about xenophobia among Bavarian proletarians in *Katzelmacher* (a local term of abuse for foreign workers; 1967) and about the life of a woman poisoner in *Bremen Coffee* (1971). His fellow Bavarian MARTIN SPERR recalled not only Horváth but EDWARD BOND's *Saved* (which he had adapted for the German stage) in his unmasking of the baseness of everyday life, *Hunting Scenes from Lower Bavaria* (1966). He pilloried the ruthless competition between two building firms in *Tales from Landshut* (1967). FRANZ XAVER KROETZ, another Bavarian author of folk plays, depicted life among farm workers with unblinking harshness in the double-bill *Dairy Farm/Ghost Train* (1971). In his *Wunschkonzert* (variously translated as *Family Favourites* or *Request Programme*, 1972) a woman prepares for suicide in a wordless one-hour-long play. *Neither Fish nor Flesh* (1981) is more stylized than some of his earlier plays.

In the German Democratic Republic (DDR) the stage was an institution equally important as its counterpart in the capitalist West; perhaps even more so. The country's more than 100 theatres were state-controlled and enjoyed ample financial support – some as much as 80–90 per cent, even in the expiring days of the regime. Programming tended to reflect the current official government line. This was particularly the case from 1951 onwards, when a campaign was launched against formalism in the arts. In that year even Brecht, opposed to doctrinaire socialist realism, found himself in difficulties with his *The Trial of Lucullus*. Over the years there was an exodus of writers to the West, including Kipphardt and Hartmut Lange (b. 1937), whose collective-farm play *Marski* (first performed in 1968) was banned. After the 8th Congress of the ruling Socialist Unity Party in 1971 the situation eased to some extent, and the barrier between the two Germanies became somewhat more permeable.

East German playwrights tried with varying success to portray their contemporary reality. 'Positive' plays reflecting the growth of a new society, such as *Katzgraben* (premièred 1953) by the working-class author Erwin Strittmatter (b. 1912) or *Mrs Flinz* (1961) by Helmut Baierl (b. 1926), were acceptable enough. On the other hand, the poet VOLKER BRAUN had many difficulties with the authorities, from his repeatedly revised industrial play *Tipper Paul Bauch* (1972) to *Lenin's Death*, written in 1970 but not staged until years later. (However, his factory-based tragedy *Tinka*, 1972–3, was performed in both the East and the West.) When PETER HACKS, who had been invited to Berlin by Brecht, dealt with such ticklish matters as contemporary industrial conflict in *Anxieties and Power* (1960), or rural politics in the immediate postwar period in the verse drama *Moritz Tassow* (1965), these plays were allowed only a fleeting stage life. Not surprisingly, he turned to less contentious themes drawn from Greek mythology, such as *Amphitryon* (1967), which also became very popular in West Germany, and *Omphale* (1972). His *Prexaspes* (1976) was a tale of the court of King Cambyses of Persia.

A similar shift from an initially Brechtian style to a very different vision can be traced in the work of director–playwright HEINER MÜLLER. Though often regarded as the outstanding German playwright of the 1970s and 1980s, he too experienced a good many difficulties with the East German authorities. Plays like *Tractor* (1961) and *Cement* (1972) were not produced until 1975; the same year saw the performance of *The Battle*, a blood-boltered sequence of scenes from the fall of Berlin, which had been written as early as 1951. The Brechtian piece *The Correction* itself had to be corrected before it was produced in 1958; *The Building Site* (written 1965) was staged only in 1976, after thorough revision. No wonder he often fell back on his lifelong interest in Greek themes. *Philoctetes*, premièred in Munich in 1968, changed Sophocles' storyline and stressed the brutalizing effect of war. *Depraved Shore* (1982) was based on Euripides' *Medea*. Müller has also reworked Shakespearean themes, e.g. *Macbeth* (1972) and *Hamletmachine* (1977) – texts for performance rather than autonomous literary works: formalism rules. The performance element is uppermost, too, in *Quartet* (1982), variations played on themes from Choderlos de Laclos' *Les Liaisons Dangereuses*.

From 1987 onwards, the political pressure on East German theatre eased up. Some thinly coded critical works were staged: *The Round Table* (1989) by Christoph Hein (b. 1944) clothed the decay of ideology in the guise of an ageing King Arthur and his superannuated knights. When the Berlin Wall was breached on 9 November 1989, as the first step towards the reunification of the two Germanies which was to be consummated less than a year later, the theatrical situation in the East also began to undergo a rapid change – for better or worse. In a united country the free exchange of theatrical personnel and ideas has at last become possible, whatever underlying differences remain and whatever dismantling of existing institutions the process may have entailed.

In responding to the immense range of social and political experiences of the age – many of them catastrophic – the drama of the German-speaking countries has attained a deep significance not only domestically but also for the world at large. True, some national experiences are not transferable: not all of these plays have proved suitable for export. Nevertheless, in the second half of the twentieth century more plays translated from the German enriched the world repertoire than ever before.   GEORGE BRANDT

Denis Calandra, *New German Dramatists* (1983)

H. F. Garten, *Modern German Drama*, 2nd edn (1964)

Glen W. Gladberry, *Theatre in the Third Reich: The Prewar Years* (1995)

Ronald Hayman, *The German Theatre: A Symposium* (1975)

Christopher Innes, *Modern German Drama: A Study in Form* (1979)

Michael Patterson, *German Theatre Today* (1976)

——, *The Revolution in the German Theatre, 1900–1933* (1981)

Leroy R. Shaw, *The Playwright and Historical Change: Dramatic Strategies in Brecht* (1970)

Gershwin [Gershvin], George [Jacob] (b. New York, 26 Sept. 1898; d. Hollywood, 11 July 1937) Composer. Gershwin found his first success as the composer of the song 'Swannee' (1919) but, in spite of individual song hits in REVUE, it was not until 1924, the same year that his 'Rhapsody in Blue' brought him international celebrity, that he achieved success with stage scores in both London (*Primrose*) and New York (*Lady Be Good* with Fred and Adele ASTAIRE). Both used lyrics by his brother, **Ira [Israel]** (b. New York, 6 Dec. 1896; d. Beverly Hills, 17 Aug. 1983). In the following decade, up to his premature death, George combined the composition and performance of piano and symphonic music, mostly based on dance and jazz rhythms, with regular writing for the BROADWAY stage. The requirements of the popular light dance-and-song shows of the era fitted his style impeccably and, if the musicals were ephemeral and often not very successful, many of the Gershwins' individual songs survived them vigorously as popular standards. After the lively, rhythmic frivolities of *Tip-Toes* (1925), *Oh, Kay!* (1926), *Funny Face* (1927) and *Girl Crazy* (1930), the Gershwins provided the songs for three politico-satirical musicals, *Strike up the Band* (1927, revised 1930), *Of Thee I Sing* (1931) and *Let 'Em Eat Cake* (1933); but it was with the 'American folk opera' *Porgy and Bess* (1935), a stunning amalgam of contemporary popular and serious musical and textual styles, that George as composer and Ira as co-lyricist achieved their most substantial and durable stage work. George's final work, for Hollywood films, was again in his early popular songwriting style, the style to which he most naturally gravitated and the character of which gave to his more ambitious writing melodic, rhythmic and structural qualities which encouraged their popular acceptance. After George's death, Ira collaborated on several other Broadway musicals, of which *Lady in the Dark* (1941), composed by KURT WEILL, was the most successful. Broadway's Uris Theater was renamed the Gershwin Theater in 1983. KURT GÄNZL

I. Goldberg and E. Garson, *George Gershwin: A Study in American Music* (1931)

E. Jablonski, *George Gershwin* (1962)

A. Kendall, *George Gershwin* (1987)

R. Kimball and A. Simon, *The Gershwins* (1973)

J. Peyser, *The Memory of All That* (1993)

D. Rosenberg, *Fascinating Rhythm* (1991)

'gestus' *see* ACTING; BRECHT, BERTOLT

Ghana The country has a population of about 19.3 million made up of peoples from around 44 different ethnic groups with individual languages. Of these, the most important are Akan, Ewe, Ga, Dagabani, Hausa Moshi, Nzima and Fanti. Because of its colonial history, English is Ghana's official language, although a significant proportion of the population can speak and understand Akan.

Ghana was the first black African nation to emerge from colonial domination when it achieved independence from the UK in 1957, with Dr Kwame Nkrumah as its first prime minister. In 1960 it became a republic. Through a *coup d'état* in 1966 it came under military rule and, except for brief spells under civilian presidents, it remained under military rule until 1992 when Flight-Lieutenant Jerry Rawlings transformed himself into a civilian president. Throughout this period, Ghanaian politics had a close association with and impact on the development of the country's theatre, beginning with Dr J. B. Danquah, politician and playwright and one of the key figures in the nationalist movement which brought about independence. He used his plays to attack colonial rule, and his outspoken criticisms of the government led to his imprisonment; he died in gaol during Nkrumah's regime. EFUA SUTHERLAND was close to the Nkrumah government, which encouraged and used the theatre to promote its agenda of 'African socialism' and its stance of non-alignment in the Cold War manoeuvres between East and West. Other dramatists, such as AMA ATA AIDOO, Asiedu Yirenkyi and Mohammed Ben-Abdallah, served as ministers at different times under Rawlings.

The development of theatre follows the familiar pattern found in most of the colonial and postcolonial African countries. It particularly shares similarities in source and orientation with NIGERIA in that most of the successful and well-known playwrights come from the universities – notably Sutherland, JOE DE GRAFT, Aidoo, Martin Owusu, Ben-Abdallah, Yirenkyi, Kwesi Kay, Jacob Hevi, Darlene Clems, Patience Addo, Kofi Awoonor and Yaw Asare. Before these playwrights, Ghanaian theatre had developed along two distinct lines of the concert party and the literary theatre, with each borrowing elements of and sometimes structures from numerous traditional performances. The concert party, like the Yoruba Opera in Nigeria, is a syncretic popular theatre based on indigenous performance aesthetics, but which has been transformed by colonial contact to respond to social developments. The main sources for this form were precolonial Akan and Fanti traditions of oral narratives – the same that were later to inspire literary playwrights such as Sutherland, de Graft, Owusu, Ben-Abdallah and Yirenkyi, who all show an interest in the *anansesem,* tales of the trickster spider Ananse.

One of the most influential pioneers of the concert party form in Ghana, Ishmael Johnson (Bob Johnson), was deeply influenced by the *anansesem* performances which he had witnessed as a child. But the real pioneer of the concert party style is Master Yalley, who began his one-man VAUDEVILLE performances in Sekondi in 1918. Although native oral narratives provided the base source and structure for the concert party, its emergence and development were also influenced by elements of colonial culture such as Empire Day concerts, church plays, hymns and cantatas, African-American vaudeville performance styles, and Hollywood movies of the 1920s and 1930s. This syncretism was also reflected in the costume, which ranged from traditional African costumes to Western European dress and stage make-up. The concert party used satirical lyrics and slapstick humour to deal with or comment upon contemporary social issues, and it borrowed from indigenous African forms such as the masquerades and the *anansesem* the use of stereotypes and caricatures. It also borrowed from the masquerade the practice of male actors playing female roles. The popularity of the concert parties has diminished somewhat, with only a few companies surviving. Unlike the Yoruba operatic tradition in Nigeria, the concert troupes in Ghana have not adopted and adapted to the new technology of video and film.

Ghanaian literary drama began in the same period as the Victorian cantatas and comic plays of 1910s and 1920s. The first literary drama, published in 1974 but reputedly written in 1915, was Kobina Sekyi's *The Blinkards*. It is a pioneering and progressive play, both in theme and in aesthetic framework. Its populist stance against cultural domination and apish imitation of Western culture by the elite is innovative, as is the way it uses language levels and registers and mixes Fanti and English to reflect the social gradations and classes whose attitudes to Western culture were the main subject of the play. Unfortunately, Sekyi's adventuorous dramaturgy was not copied by his immediate successors such as J. B. Danquah and F. K. Faiwoo, who wrote in the 1940s. Yet it was these two who led the flowering of a genuine Ghanaian literary dramatic tradition. Their two best-known works, *The Third Woman* (1943) and *The Fifth Landing Stage* (1943) respectively, in spite of being deeply influenced by Western dramatic models with which they had come into contact through education, were attempts to evolve a true native dramatic literature. For instance, Faiwoo's play was originally written in Ewe as *Toko Atolia* and shows the playwright's awareness of, but deliberate departure from, 'Aristotelian demands' by constantly using an African cyclic dislocation of time and space. He successfully captures the 'cadences of spoken Ewe' and this is what makes his characters alive and convincing. In him, therefore, we see the first serious attempts to marry knowledge of Western theatre tradition with an essentially African subject and viewpoint. Another significant theatre achievement of the pre-independence period was the adaptation of *Antigone* as *Odale's Choice* by Caribbean poet Edward Kamau Brathwaite, as part of the active theatrical work carried out in Cape Coast in the 1950s. However, the further development of this hybrid form finds its fullest flowering in the post-independence dramas of such writers as Sutherland, de Graft and Aidoo.

The impetus for a genuine modern Ghanaian theatre came from Sutherland, who in 1957 initiated the process which was to culminate in the creation of the Ghana Drama Studio. The studio played a major role in the formation of the careers of a good many successful Ghanaian dramatists such as de Graft, Kwesi Kray, Aidoo and Owusu. Their post-independence plays were markedly different from those of the 1940s. For one thing, unlike the earlier playwrights, they wrote with the stage in mind, and a lot of the plays benefited from being produced before being published.

Another quality which distinguished them was a conscious and vigorous creative experimentation with performance forms and a marrying of the numerous traditional Ghanaian forms such as storytelling, ritual, dance and music with Western theatrical models. This syncretic process is reflected in plays such as Aidoo's *Anowa* and *The Dilemma of a Ghost* (1965), and de Graft's *Through a Film Darkly* (1970), *Sons and Daughters* (1964) and *Muntu* (1975). Sutherland's experiments were the most adventurous, resulting in her adaptation and development of the *anansesem* storytelling tradition into a contemporary style which she calls the *anansegro* – a hybrid form of traditional storytelling with elements of Western theatre sensibilities added on. The best example of this style is her highly successful and still very popular *The Marriage of Anansewa* (1975). Other playwrights who followed and showed an interest in the *anansesem* include de Graft in *Ananse and the Gum Man*, Yirenkyi in *Anna Pranaa* and Owusu in *The Story Ananse Told* and *Anane*. Latter-day playwrights of note are Mohamed Ben-Abdallah, whose plays include *Ananse and the Magic Drum*, *Ananse and the Rain God*, *The Land of a Million Magicians* (his own reworking of BERTOLT BRECHT's *The Good Woman of Setzuan*), *The Trial of Mallam Ilya*, *The Verdict* and *The Cobra*. Ben-Abdallah is remarkable for his versatility and range of both subject and theatrical styles, from storytelling to puppet theatre, as well as being an articulate scholar and theoretician of the theatre. Asare's *Ananse in the Land of Idiots* (1994) and *Who Raped the Ramatu Sisters* (1994, with choreography by Cecilia Yelpoe) show a successful deployment of the African theatrical arts of dance, music, mime, songs and dialogue to achieve TOTAL THEATRE performance pieces. OSITA OKAGBUE

Kofi Awoonor, *The Breast of the Earth* (1975)

Ghelderode, Michel [Adémar-Adolphe-Louis Martens] de (b. Ixelles, Belgium, 3 April 1898; d. Schaerbeek, Belgium, 1 April 1962) Prolific AVANT-GARDE playwright and story writer. Although Ghelderode was the driving force in Belgian theatre during the interwar years, many of his 60 plays have languished in obscurity and he is yet to find an audience in the English-speaking world. Written originally in French, some of his plays, like the better-known biblical drama *Barabbas* (1928), were first performed in Flemish, and some, like *Le Sommeil de la raison* (1934) in Dutch (*Der Zeren Hoofzonden*). Several of Ghelderode's plays were seen in Paris in the late 1940s (*Escurial*, 1929; *Hop Signor!*, 1942; and *Mademoiselle Jaïre*, 1949). While his grotesque, Gothic style using puppet-like characters in mad, macabre settings (such as in *The Death of Dr Faustus*, 1928, and *Pantagleize*, 1930), never found an international audience, he was influential in the

French development of TOTAL THEATRE and ARTAUD's THEATRE OF CRUELTY.   HELEN RAPPAPORT

Anne M. Beckers, *Michel de Ghelderode* (1985)

Ghéon, Henri [Henri Léon Vangeon]   (b. Bray sur Seine, France, 15 March 1875; d. Paris, 13 July 1944) Poet and playwright. Abandoning medicine for poetry, he sought to establish a poetic theatre for which, in 1911, he published a manifesto. In 1913 he was caught up in COPEAU's adventure at the Théâtre du Vieux Colombier. After his conversion to Catholicism during the First World War his attention turned to the writing of mystical and Christian plays for the company he created, Les Compagnons de Notre Dame. These include *Le Pauvre sous l'escalier* (*The Poor under the Stairs*, 1921), *Le Noël sur la place* (*Christmas in the Market Place*, 1935) and *Mystère de la Messe* (*The Mystery of the Finding of the Cross*, 1936).   TERRY HODGSON

ghosts   *see* SUPERSTITION

Gibson, William   (b. New York, 13 Nov. 1914)   Playwright, novelist and poet. He has had numerous productions of his work in regional theatres throughout the United States. His first Broadway production was *Two for the Seesaw* (1958). He is best known for biography drama: about Helen Keller, who could not see or speak, and her persevering teacher Annie Sullivan, in *The Miracle Worker* (1959, filmed 1962) and its sequel *Monday After the Miracle* (1982); Shakespeare in *A Cry of Players* (1968); and Golda Meir in *Golda* (1977). ADRIANA HUNTER

Gide, André   (b. Paris, 22 Nov. 1869; d. Paris, 19 Feb. 1951)   Novelist, essayist and playwright, awarded the Nobel Prize in 1947. His prose drama *Oedipe* (*Oedipus, 1932)*, modern but closer to Sophocles and simpler than COCTEAU's *La Machine infernale* (*The Infernal Machine*), explores the struggle between individualism and submission to religious authority. Gide was responsible for many adaptations, including Kafka's *The Trial* (*Le Procès*, 1946, with JEAN-LOUIS BARRAULT), as well as translations (e.g. Shakespeare, TAGORE and his own plays). WENDY SCOTT

Giehse, Theresa   *see* BERLINER ENSEMBLE

Gielgud, [Arthur] John   (b. London, 14 April 1904; d. Wooton Underwood, Bucks, 21 May 2000)   Actor and director. He was born into a family heavy with theatrical tradition – his great-aunt was ELLEN TERRY and a dozen or more of his close relatives were active in the British theatre when he started his career as an unpaid student extra at the OLD VIC in 1921. Although the sense of tradition was a strong influence with him, he pursued an independent and often adventurous course, gaining experience in modern plays as well as the classics; his first important job involved understudying and then taking over from NOEL COWARD in Coward's own play *The Vortex* (1925). He took over from Coward again in *The Constant Nymph* (1926) but, despite some well-regarded young man's performances as Romeo and Hamlet – a part he was to perform over 500 times – his reputation with the public at large was not truly established until he directed and played in the modern costume play *Richard of Bordeaux* (1932) by GORDON DAVIOT. This was not only an artistic success but a box-office hit, and at the same time he was seen playing the romantic lead in the immensely successful film of J. B. PRIESTLEY's *The Good Companions*. All at once, he was a star with solid commercial appeal, and managements were willing to back him in almost anything he wanted to do. For five years he worked with BRONSON ALBERY, the manager who had presented *Richard of Bordeaux*; then Gielgud became his own manager for a season of classic plays at the Queen's Theatre. This was his sense of tradition asserting itself: there is no doubt that he saw himself in the role of the old-style actor–manager like IRVING, TREE and his uncle Fred Terry. But times had changed, theatre organization had become much more complex, and Gielgud lacked the necessary one-track, autocratic mind. After this one season (1937–8), he was content to leave managerial problems to others, and for many years he worked mainly with HUGH BEAUMONT of H. M. TENNENT LTD. It was an effective alliance which led to some of Gielgud's outstanding achievements – in *The Importance of Being Earnest* (1939); CHRISTOPHER FRY's modern VERSE DRAMA *The Lady's Not For Burning* (1949); a revival of Congreve's *The Way of the World*, played in repertoire with Otway's *Venice Preserv'd* (1953). Beaumont also entrusted him with the direction of many plays, mainly modern, including works by TENNESSEE WILLIAMS, TERENCE RATTIGAN, ENID BAGNOLD, GRAHAM GREENE and PETER SHAFFER. Throughout his career Gielgud performed in and directed important productions of CHEKHOV and essayed all the major Shakespearean roles. Yet for someone who is most often thought of as a man of the classics, with his Roman profile and golden voice, he was very much in tune with contemporary theatre, and two of his finest performances came late in life, partnering RALPH RICHARDSON in DAVID STOREY's *Home* (1970) and HAROLD PINTER's *No Man's Land* (1975). In 1958 he made a 13-week tour of America with a solo recital programme of Shakespearean excerpts, *Ages of Man*, which he later played in London and toured in many countries. He enjoyed filming and was amused by much of the publicity nonsense that went with it, especially when he won an Academy Award for his comedy performance as the valet in *Arthur* (1981). He has published four books on theatre, including an autobiography, *Early Stages* (1938). The Globe Theatre in Shaftesbury Avenue was renamed after him to mark his 90th birthday. Although he never achieved the heroic heights of LAURENCE OLIVIER, or the inspired eccentricity of RALPH RICHARDSON, he was in many respects the outstanding British actor of the twentieth century, and a fixed compass point from which a bearing could be taken on all the others. Gielgud was knighted in 1953 and awarded the Order of Merit in 1996.   IAN BEVAN

Giles Brandreth, *John Gielgud: An Actor's Life* (2000)
Jonathan Croall, *Gielgud: A Theatrical Life* (2000)
Sheridan Morley, *John G: The Authorised Biography of John Gielgud* (2001)

Gilbert, W[illiam] S[chwenck]   (b. London, 18 Nov. 1836; d. Harrow Weald, Middlesex, 29 May 1911)   Playwright and librettist. Gilbert's early plays were in the comic and fantastic vein of late Victorian dramatic writing and are generally taken to be of largely historical interest, although some are noted for their satirical edge. Although a prolific dramatist, his presence on the twentieth-century stage was assured by his hugely successful collaboration as librettist with ARTHUR SULLIVAN on a series of comic operettas which began with *Trial by Jury* (1875). The most frequently revived are *HMS Pinafore* (1878), *The Pirates of Penzance* (1880), *The Mikado* (1885), *Ruddigore* (1887), *The Yeomen of the Guard* (1888) and *The Gondoliers* (1889). Gilbert was knighted in 1907.   IAN CLARKE

Leshi Ayre, *The Gilbert and Sullivan Companion* (1972)
Caryl Brahms, *Gilbert and Sullivan: Lost Chords and Dischords* (1975)
David Eden, *Gilbert and Sullivan: The Creative Conflict* (1986)
Max K. Sutton, *W. S. Gilbert* (1975)

Gilder, [Janet] Rosamond [De Kay]   (b. Marion, Mass., 17 July 1891; d. New York, 5 Sept. 1986)   Writer and arts activist. She was assistant editor and drama critic for *Theatre Arts Magazine* from 1936, and editor 1946–8. The first woman elected to membership of the New York Drama Critics' Circle, Gilder served as its secretary 1946–50. Best remembered as a tireless promoter of international understanding through theatre exchanges, she was a founder of the INTERNATIONAL THEATRE INSTITUTE in 1947, serving as its vice-president and president, and as director of its US

centre. She wrote or edited numerous books and publications, including *Enter the Actress* (1931).
FELICIA HARDISON LONDRÉ

Gilford, Jack [Jacob Gellman]   (b. New York, 25 July 1907; d. New York, 4 June 1990)   Comic actor. His brand of New York Jewish humour was best displayed in the stage and film versions of *A Funny Thing Happened on the Way to the Forum* (1962 and 1966). Gilford's long stage career, built on a grounding in REVUE and VAUDEVILLE, featured appearances in *The World of Sholom Aleichem* (1953), *The Diary of Anne Frank* (1955) and *Cabaret* (1966). He also had an extensive career in films.   HELEN RAPPAPORT

K. Mostel and M. Gilford, *170 Years of Showbusiness* (1978)

Gill, Peter   (b. Cardiff, 7 Sept. 1939)   Playwright and director. Gill left acting and achieved recognition as a director at the ROYAL COURT (from 1965), notably with his production of three D. H. LAWRENCE plays. In 1976 he was the founding director of the RIVERSIDE STUDIOS, where he directed a huge body of work including influential, spare productions of *The Cherry Orchard* (1978, in his own translation) and *The Changeling* (1978), and which he turned into an innovative arts centre with an international reputation. He joined the NATIONAL THEATRE as an associate director (1980) and was instrumental in setting up the NT Studio (1984), a separate company directing and developing new work. Their first festival of new plays (1985), held in the Cottesloe Theatre, included Gill's *As I Lay Dying* (adapted from FAULKNER) and *In the Blue*, which was followed there by *Mean Tears* (1987). He has continued to write and direct. Other plays include *The Sleeper's Den* (1965), *Small Change* (1976), *Kick for Touch* (1983), *Cardiff East* (1997) and *Certain Young Men* (1999), many of which draw on his Cardiff roots and were directed by himself.   CATHY JOYCE

Gillette, William [Hookes]   (b. Hartford, Conn., 24 July 1855; d. Hartford, 29 April 1937)   Playwright and actor. The handsome son of an American senator, he made his acting debut in 1875. He rose to prominence in his own comedy, *The Professor* (1881), then scored huge successes in two melodramas of his own, *Held by the Enemy* (1886) and *Secret Service* (1896), and in his comedy, *Too Much Johnson* (1894). By far his biggest hit was *Sherlock Holmes* (1899), which he adapted from Conan Doyle's stories. His later career was spent largely acting in others' plays or in revivals of his own plays – especially *Sherlock Holmes*, which was revived by the ROYAL SHAKESPEARE COMPANY in 1974. As a performer he was sparing in his gestures and delivered lines in a curious staccato fashion. He was considered a master of timing. GERALD BORDMAN

D. Cook, *Sherlock Holmes and Much More* (1970)

Gilpin, Charles [Sidney] (b. Richmond, Va., 20 Nov. 1878; d. Eldridge Park, NJ, 6 May 1930) Actor. Gilpin was apprenticed as a printer before beginning to tour in black shows in 1903. He became director of the stock company at Harlem's LAFAYETTE Theater in 1916. On Broadway he scored a success as a black clergyman in *Abraham Lincoln* (1919), which led EUGENE O'NEILL to cast him in the title role of *The Emperor Jones* (1920), for which he garnered high praise. Increasing drunkenness and argumentativeness alienated potential employers and thereafter, though his exceptional abilities were acknowledged, he worked very little. GERALD BORDMAN

Gingold, Hermione [Ferdinanda] (b. London, 9 Dec. 1897; d. New York, 24 May 1987) Actress who had a modest career until just before the Second World War, when an appearance at London's tiny GATE THEATRE led to a decade during which she was the capital's leading comedienne in a series of intimate REVUES, mainly at the Ambassadors Theatre, which were immensely popular (e.g. *Sweet and Low*, 1943; *Sweeter and Lower*, 1944; *Sweetest and Lowest*, 1946). In 1949 she and HERMIONE BADDELEY made mayhem in an hilarious revival of NOEL COWARD'S *Fallen Angels*, to the author's annoyance but financial benefit, after which Gingold left for America. There she had great success as an acid-tongued guest on television chat shows, a triumph as Madame Armfeldt in Stephen Sondheim's *A Little Night Music* (1975), and an enduring cameo opposite Maurice Chevalier in the film *Gigi*, in which they sang 'I Remember It Well'. IAN BEVAN

Giraudoux, Jean [Hippolyte] (b. Bellac, France, 29 Oct. 1882; d. Paris, 31 Jan. 1944) Playwright. As with so many other French dramatists, an unrealistic gloss of charm, surprise or irreverence conceals a harsh appraisal of reality. His much-stigmatized 'preciosity' is a matter of style, not content. Supremely literary, a diplomat and distinguished man of letters, he owes his theatricality to COPEAU's disciple, LOUIS JOUVET, who moulded his work for the stage in a collaboration of unique empathy. Characterized as a drama of debate – reminiscent of SHAW – his work presents the conflict, sometimes tragic, within and between men and women, dealing with identity, private and social justice, politics and nationhood, war and peace, the real and the ideal; a conflict of worlds in which magic and the supernatural play their part, pitting the narrow egoism of human reason against the mad illogicality of destiny. The more pessimistic plays (*La guerre de Troie*

n'aura pas lieu, 1935, and *Pour Lucrèce*, 1953 – *Tiger at the Gates* and *Duel of Angels* in CHRISTOPHER FRY's translations; *Electre*, 1937, and *Sodome et Gomorrhe*, 1943) contrast with the more light-hearted *Amphitryon 38* (1929) and *Intermezzo* (*The Enchanted*, 1933), and the more fantastic *Ondine* (1939) and *La Folle de Chaillot* (*The Madwoman of Chaillot*, 1945). The distinctions of genre and mood, however, are hardly significant when, for example, in his fashionable Greek plays Andromache's eyelash can prompt Ulysses to decide not to pursue the Trojan War, and Clytemnestra's hatred of Agamemnon is sparked off by his beard and his little finger. This playwright's intellectual arguments are often as emotional as they are moral. The language sets the tone. In spite of their at times excessive wordiness, prestigious productions of most of his plays have been seen in Britain and the United States. He can be seen as the epitome of French dramatists in the twentieth century. DONALD WATSON

Robert Cohen, *Giraudoux: Three Faces of Destiny* (1968)
Donald Inskip, *Jean Giraudoux: The Making of a Dramatist* (1958)
Laurent LeSage, *Jean Giraudoux, His Life and Works* (1959)

Gish, Lillian (b. Springfield, Ohio, 14 Oct. 1893; d. New York, 27 Feb. 1993) and **Dorothy** (b. Dayton, Ohio, 11 March 1898; d. Rapallo, Italy, 4 June 1968) These sisters' acting careers spanned most of the twentieth-century American theatrical scene, from traveling VAUDEVILLE shows, silent films and legitimate theatre to television and talking film. As young girls, they were recruited to the stage by a tenant in their mother's boarding house, and in 1912 they made their film debuts together in the D. W. Griffith film *An Unseen Enemy*. Between then and 1928 Dorothy appeared in over 60 of his films, and then spent the remainder of her career switching between film and Broadway, including a spell in the long-running *Life with Father*. Lillian also worked extensively with Griffith and starred in his controversial *The Birth of a Nation* (1915). One of the first film celebrities, she took the opportunity to return to the stage when silent films disappeared. She starred in *Camille* (1932) and was Ophelia to JOHN GIELGUD's *Hamlet* (1936). As late as 1969 she toured a SOLO SHOW. DAVID A. WILLIAMS

J. E. Frasher, *Dorothy and Lillian Gish* (1973)
Stuart Oderman, *Lillian Gish: A Life on Stage and Screen* (2000)

Glasgow The largest city in SCOTLAND has been the base for the majority of pioneering initiatives in Scottish theatre in the twentieth century. The Glasgow Repertory Theatre (1909–14) staged the first production of a play by CHEKHOV (*The Seagull*, 1909); the SCOTTISH NATIONAL PLAYERS (1921–47) aimed to develop Scotland's national drama and to found a Scottish National Theatre: Glasgow UNITY THEATRE (1941–51), formed by an amalgam of various amateur clubs, was committed to socialist writers, such as ODETS, O'CASEY and GORKY; the CITIZENS' THEATRE, founded in 1943 on principles similar to those of the first Repertory Theatre, came to enjoy an international reputation. THE TRON, named after the kirk (church) where it is housed, opened in 1982, having begun life a year before as a café-bar theatre; it presents new Scottish plays and hosts touring companies. Glasgow is also the home of 7:84 (Scotland), Wildcat, Clyde Unity and the Scottish Youth Theatre, as well as Scottish Opera, Scottish Ballet, the Royal Scottish National Orchestra and the Centre for Contemporary Arts, a major venue for PERFORMANCE ART. Scotland's principal training school for professional actors is sited in the Royal Scottish Academy of Music and Drama, and the University of Glasgow has the only Department of Theatre Studies in Scotland, as well as housing within its library the Scottish Theatre Archive, a valuable resource and referral centre for scholars, theatre practitioners and the public. In 1990 Glasgow was nominated Cultural Capital of Europe, an accolade that not only brought leading international theatre companies and theatre practitioners to the city (e.g. the Maly Theatre, the WOOSTER GROUP from America, INGMAR BERGMAN, PETER BROOK) but encouraged many local initiatives. A new concert hall was built, a major art gallery was refurbished, and two new theatre venues emerged: the Arches in the undercroft of the Central Station, and the Tramway, the former Transport Museum which was converted into several flexible playing and exhibition areas. A city that moved from eighteenth-century elegance through nineteenth-century commercial prosperity to a twentieth-century reputation for gang warfare and social deprivation entered the next millennium as an international centre of the creative and performing arts. JAN MCDONALD

Glaspell, Susan (b. Davenport, Iowa, 1 July 1876; d. Provincetown, Mass., 17 July 1948) Playwright, actress, director, novelist and short-story writer. In 1915 she co-founded with her husband George Gram Cook the PROVINCETOWN PLAYERS where, by 1922, she would have 11 plays produced and EUGENE O'NEILL 15. She was concerned with women's issues as well as with exploring dramatic form. *Suppressed Desires* (1914), which she co-wrote with Cook, is a spoof on psychoanalysis and one of her many one-act plays, of which

Trifles (1916) is the most revived. In *The Verge* (1921), an EXPRESSIONIST play, the state of mind of a woman undergoing a nervous breakdown is depicted through the use of lights, sound effects and scenery. *The Inheritors* (1921) is a play about idealism; *Alison's House* (1930), based on the life of poet Emily Dickinson, won the Pulitzer Prize. As director of the FEDERAL THEATER PROJECT in Chicago (1936–8) she produced the famous, all-black *Swing Mikado*. JANE HOUSE

Arthur E. Waterman, *Susan Glaspell* (1966)

Glass, David *see* EXPERIMENTAL THEATRE; MIME

Glass, Philip (b. Baltimore, Md., 31 Jan. 1937) Composer. Known for his unique approach to music, with a style that utilizes repetitive and cyclical rhythmic structures, Glass has written for theatre, OPERA, film and dance chorus. He composed music for the theatre company MABOU MINES in the mid-1970s and is author of five operas, two of which were collaborations with theatre artist ROBERT WILSON: the landmark epic *Einstein on the Beach* (1976) and *The Photographer* (1982). Glass has also directed. DENISE L. TILLES

Glassco, Bill [William] (b. Quebec City, 30 Aug. 1935) Director. With his wife Jane Gordon he founded TARRAGON THEATER in Toronto in 1971, primarily to produce new Canadian plays with a high degree of professionalism, and to introduce, in English translation, the work of key Quebec playwrights. Under his artistic directorship (1971–82) Tarragon became one of the most important theatres in Canada. Glassco became artistic director of Toronto's CentreStage in 1985, and in 1988 co-artistic director of the Canadian Stage Company. He freelanced widely in the 1990s. EUGENE BENSON

Globe Theater (Regina, Saskatchewan) Founded in 1966 by Ken Kramer and Sue Kramer, this company employed THEATRE IN THE ROUND staging to produce Brian Way's participation plays for children. In its first 20 years the company visited more than 2,700 prairie communities. In 1970 the Globe company obtained space in the Saskatchewan Centre for the Performing Arts; in 1981 it acquired its own Regina theatre seating 400. Since 1972 Rex Deverell has contributed a large number of plays to the company's repertoire; other playwrights who have written for the company include Carol Bolt and Rod Langley. EUGENE BENSON

Globe Theatre (London) Shakespeare and the sixteenth-century Globe Theatre where he worked have inspired several later Globe Theatres, the most notable being in Oregon and SAN DIEGO, until in 1996 one was built in London, home of the original, when the dream of SAM WANAMAKER to raise an Elizabethan replica theatre finally came true, albeit three years after his death. The way had been cleared for unrivalled use of the name because the West End theatre called the Globe had been renamed the Gielgud in 1994. Situated on the south bank of the Thames next to the towering Tate Modern art gallery at the easternmost end of a mile-long riverside stretch of national cultural buildings, the new Globe seats 1,500, is polygonal and was built according to traditional methods. It is limewashed, timbered, open to the sky and thatched – the first thatched building to be permitted in London since the Great Fire of 1666. It has an education centre and presents plays by Shakespeare's contemporaries as well as the staple diet of the Bard. Its first full summer season was held in 1997, opening with the artistic director Mark Rylance in *Henry V*.   COLIN CHAMBERS

See also SHAKESPEARE FESTIVALS; SHAKESPEARE IN THE TWENTIETH CENTURY.

Barry Day, *This Wooden 'O': Shakespeare's Globe Reborn* (1996)

J. R. Mulryne, and Margaret Shewring, *Shakespeare's Globe Rebuilt* (1997)

Glover, Sue   (b. Edinburgh, 1 March 1943) Playwright. Her work often focuses on a female perspective and she is interested in the untold stories of people and communities, as in her modern classic *Bondagers* (1991), which explores the lives of 'bondaged' women farm labourers in the Borders of Scotland during the nineteenth century. Known for a strong atavistic streak in both her subject matter and her language, which has a poetic, lyrical quality, she has written most of her theatre work in a Scots dialect, though this has not prevented her plays being toured and produced internationally. Other plays include *The Bubble Boy* (1980), *The Seal Wife* (1980), *The Straw Chair* (1988), *Sacred Hearts* (1994) and *Shetland Saga* (2000).   JOHN TIFFANY

Godber, John   *see* HULL TRUCK THEATRE COMPANY

Godfrey, Paul [C.]   (b. Exeter, 16 Sept. 1960) Director and playwright. His work is marked by an intense lyricism through which the texture of his characters' lives is given dramatic power, as the stillness and beauty of the lines lend a degree of awe and wonder to their profound questioning. Godfrey turned from directing to playwriting with *Inventing a New Colour* (1988). After numerous rejections, the work was accepted by the BRISTOL OLD VIC and the ROYAL COURT. It has a mournful and moving sense of loss and bewilderment that lift the story into the realms of the mythic. *Once in a While the Odd Thing Happens* (1990) draws on the life of Benjamin Britten, exploring the

mysteries of love, music and creativity. *A Bucket of Eels* (1994) is a modern midsummer night's dream, and *The Blue Ball* (1995) is concerned with questions raised by space flight in an attempt to comprehend the mysteries of the experience. Other plays include his *Trilogy of Plays from Different Sources*, comprising *The Modern Husband* (1995) from Henry Fielding, *The Invisible Woman* (1996) from Plautus and *The Candidate* (1997) from Balzac.   DAN REBELLATO

Goering, Reinhard   (b. Fulda, Hesse, Germany, 23 June 1887, d. Jena, Germany, 7 Nov. 1936) Playwright. His greatest play, *Seeschlacht* (*Naval Encounter*, about the Battle of Jutland, staged privately by MAX REINHARDT in 1917), was seminal in the development of German EXPRESSIONISM. His last play, *Die Südpolexpedition des Kapitäns Scott* (*Captain Scott's Expedition to the South Pole*, 1930) was adapted as an opera, *Das Opfer* ('The sacrifice', 1937) by Winfried Zillig.
JUDY MEEWEZEN

Robert C. Davis, *Final Mutiny: Reinhard Goering, His Life and Art* (1987)

Goll, Yvan   (b. Saint-Dié, France, 29 March 1891; d. Neuilly, 14 March 1950) Poet, playwright, editor and translator. A pacifist with no homeland – born Jewish in the disputed Alsace-Lorraine territory, he left for Switzerland in the war – he brought out *Requiem pour les morts d'Europe* in 1916. DADA and APOLLINAIRE influenced his satirical drama *Methusalem*, published with two other plays in *Le nouvel Orphée* (1924) and produced with masks by GEORG GROSZ. Poetry in French and German included *Poèmes d'Amour* (1925), illustrated by Marc Chagall.   TERRY HODGSON

Gombrowicz, Witold   (b. Maloszyce, Poland, 4 Aug. 1904; d. Vence, France, 24 July 1969) Playwright and author of novels, diaries and short stories. He wrote three outstanding plays: *Iwona, Ksiezniczka Burgunda* (*Yvonne, Princess of Burgundy*, 1938); *Slub* (*The Wedding*, 1946); and *Operetka* (*Operetta*, 1967). The Second World War found him in Argentina, which he left in 1963 to settle in France. He was a nobleman, an enfant terrible of Polish prewar intellectual society, and a forerunner of existentialism and the formal innovations of the THEATRE OF THE ABSURD. His plays are not rooted in any homogeneous literary tradition: *Yvonne* (seen at the World Theatre Season, London, 1971) relates to FARCE – a fairy-tale of the futile rebel against official and personal conventions; the Shakespearean character of *The Wedding* is prompted by the dream tradition, introducing the inner drama of existence; and *Operetta* is a musical comedy on revolution, decay and the fall of the old civilization. All his writings share an obsession with the suppression of nature by convention, both in social relations and personal attitudes. Quests for independence, however futile, challenge the products of humanity's dependence on its environment.

JOANNA KRAKOWSKA-NAROŻNIAK

Ewa M. Thompson, *Witold Gombrowicz* (1979)

Goncharova, Natalia see DESIGN

Gooch, Steve (b. Surrey, 22 July 1945) Playwright. Gooch's early work, mostly premièred in ALTERNATIVE venues, especially the HALF MOON, divides between plays playfully dramatizing aspects of working-class experience and history like *Will Wat, If Not, Wat Will?* (1972) and *The Motor Show* (1974), and fluent translations, notably of BRECHT's *Man is Man* (1971) and *The Mother* (1973). His *Female Transport* (1973) and *The Women Pirates* (1978) widened his political range to consider gender. His 1984 book *All Together Now* is a salutary look at the ambitions and realities of COMMUNITY and FRINGE theatre. Other plays include *Landmark* (1980), *Taking Liberties* (1984) and *Star Turns* (1987). DAN REBELLATO

Goodbody, Buzz see ROYAL SHAKESPEARE COMPANY

Goodman Memorial Theater America's second and CHICAGO's oldest (and largest) resident theatre was founded in 1925 as a gift to the Art Institute of Chicago from the family of playwright Kenneth Sawyer Goodman, who was killed in the First World War. From 1925 to 1930 it was a repertory theatre, then operated as a drama school until 1969, when professional productions were again presented. In 1977 the theatre separated from the Art Institute and Goodman School of Drama to become the Goodman Theater. Under the artistic directorship of GREGORY MOSHER and later Robert Falls, it presented a mixture of innovatively staged classics and new works, including the world première of DAVID RABE's *Hurlyburly* (1984), Scott McPherson's *Marvin's Room* and the American première of DAVID MAMET's *Glengarry Glen Ross* (1984). Important revivals include *Death of a Salesman* (1998) and *A Moon for the Misbegotten* (2000), both of which were later seen in New York. The Goodman Theater was honoured with a special Tony Award in 1992. DAVID BARBOUR

Gopal, Ram (b. Bangalore, India, 20 Nov. 1912) Dancer and choreographer. Trained in *bharatanatyam* dance by a traditional guru, Meenakshisundaram Pillai of Pandanallur village, and in *kathakali* dance-drama by guru Kunju Kurup at the Kerala Kalamandalam, he imbibed the classical movements and the dramatic narratives of India's performance repertoires. He was discovered by American ethnic dancer La Meri, whom

he joined in a 1936 tour in India and east Asia, where they presented classical and creative dance-dramas with Indian themes in Burma, Malaya, Indonesia, the Philippines, China and Japan. Later he toured in Europe and America, and was hailed as the 'Indian NIJINSKY'. Gopal founded a school and company where he trained contemporary dancers and choreographers, including Shevanti, Kumudini Lakhia, Shanta Rao and Mrinilini Sarabhai. His theatricality, brilliant stage presence and daring costumes enhanced his elegant figure and classical training, educating audiences about India's great epics and divinities, as well as pleasing them with his performances. A film, *Lord Shiva Dances* (1948), revealed his dramatic and dynamic impact in both classical and creative solo dances. He wrote *Indian Dancing* (1951, with Serozh Dadachanji) and *Rhythm in the Heavens* (1957). He lives in retirement in England, still planning future projects.

JOAN L. ERDMAN

Susheela Mishra, *Some Dancers of India* (1992)

Gordon [Jones], Ruth (b. Wollaston, Mass., 30 Oct. 1896; d. Edgartown, Mass., 28 Aug. 1985) Actress and writer. She first appeared on stage in 1915 in *Peter Pan*, but it wasn't until the 1930s that she attracted attention, for her roles in *Ethan Frome* (1936), *The Country Wife* (1936) – which she also played at the OLD VIC, London – and *A Doll's House* (1937). In the 1940s she took time off to write her own plays: *Over 21* (1944) and *Years Ago* (1946). Her idiosyncratic comedic style eventually lent itself perfectly to the role she made her own, the meddlesome matchmaker Dolly Levi, a part written for her by THORNTON WILDER in *The Matchmaker* (1955). In the 1960s Gordon appeared in several oddball character roles in cult films, most notably *Rosemary's Baby* (1968), for which she won an Academy Award, and *Harold and Maude* (1971). Gordon also wrote three autobiographies and, with her second husband GARSON KANIN, several screenplays.

HELEN RAPPAPORT

Gordone, Charles [Edward] (b. Cleveland, 12 Oct. 1925) Actor, director and playwright. Gordone was the first black playwright to win the Pulitzer Prize, for his *No Place to be Somebody* (1969, produced by JOSEPH PAPP). This dark piece about the anguish of its black characters was also the first OFF-BROADWAY production to win the Pulitzer Prize. ADRIANA HUNTER

Gorelik, Mordecai ('Max') (b. Shchedrin, Russia, 25 Aug. 1899; d. Sarasota, Fla., 7 March 1990) Scene designer, theorist and playwright. A protégé of ROBERT EDMOND JONES, Gorelik started at the PROVINCETOWN PLAYERS and was in the vanguard of theatrical activity of the 1920s and 1930s, most prominently serving as the GROUP THEATER's primary designer (e.g. *Golden Boy*, 1937). As the only true theorist, Gorelik was unique to his generation of designers, winning a Guggenheim Fellowship that culminated in his seminal work *New Theatres for Old* (1940). A believer in theatre's ability to incite society's change, Gorelik was known as a POLITICAL THEATRE practitioner and promoter of the theories of BERTOLT BRECHT. He turned to playwriting as a forum for his ideas. ANNE FLETCHER

Gorky, Maxim [Alexei Maximovich Peshkov]   (b. Nizhny Novgorod, Russsia, 28 March 1868; d. Moscow, 18 June 1936)

Playwright and novelist. Gorky grew up in great poverty and was sent out early to earn his living. Here he met many of the down and outs, the students and political thinkers, about whom he was later to write in his plays and novels. In 1892 he took for himself the name Gorky, meaning 'bitter'.

Gorky's first play, *Meshtchane* (*Philistines*), was staged by the MOSCOW ART THEATRE in St Petersburg in 1902. It portrays the strong, vigorous 'new man' from the working class and contrasts him with the narrow-minded meanness of the lower middle class. Also in 1902, Gorky's second play, *Na dne* (*Lower Depths*), was premièred in Moscow, with STANISLAVSKY himself in the main role. This play is set in the slums of Moscow and portrays the have-nots of society with whom Gorky grew up. In 1903 MAX REINHARDT acted in this play in Berlin, in a production that included over 500 performers, and it was produced by the STAGE SOCIETY in London in the same year. In 1905 *Lower Depths* was performed in Paris with ELEONORA DUSE; it was filmed by both Renoir (1936) and Kurosawa (1957), and became part of the repertoire of many international theatres.

After *Dachniki* (*Summerfolk*, 1904), which exposed the ignorance, selfishness and urban disregard for the countryside characteristic of the middle-class 'summer visitors', Gorky was arrested and imprisoned for his part in the workers' demonstrations against tsarism. He finished his next play, *Deti solnsa* (*Children of the Sun*, 1905), while in prison. In 1906 *Varvary* (*Barbarians*) was premièred in Riga; it deals with his contemporaries' moral purpose and motivation. It was not produced in Moscow until the 1930s.

In 1906 Gorky had to leave Russia to escape political persecution; he went to America, where he wrote *Vragi* (*Enemies*), which has industrial conflict as its main theme and was based on actual Russian protests. It was first performed in Berlin, being banned in Russia, where it was not staged until 1933. In 1908 Gorky finished *Poslednie* (*The Last Ones*), which was also banned,

for its negative portrayal of the tsarist police; it was, however, produced in Tashkent and later (1918) in Petrograd. The same year Lenin visited Gorky on Capri, a first meeting which initiated the uneasy relationship between them.

Gorky finished two plays on Capri, both in 1910: *Chudaki* (*Queer People*) and *Vassa Zheleznova*, which received a prestigious prize but was produced only once. Gorky revised it in 1935. In 1911 *Zykovy* (*The Zykovs*) was completed, but because the Moscow Art Theatre required less emphasis on the political aspects, Gorky refused permission for production and it was staged only later (1918) in Petrograd.

Gorky returned to Russia in 1913; after the February Revolution in 1917, he opposed Lenin's plan for a further Bolshevik uprising, and found himself attacked by both the left and the right. From 1918 to 1921 he consistently argued with the Party on behalf of intellectuals, and was finally persuaded by Lenin in 1921 to leave Russia for medical treatment. He lived abroad, mainly in Italy, until 1932.

Between 1930 and 1932 he finished three plays: *Somov i drugie* (*Somov and Others*), *Yegor Bulychov i drugi* (*Yegor Bulychov and Others*) and *Dostigaev i drugie* (*Dostigayev and Others*) – a trilogy concerned with the times between 1917 and 1930. On his return to Russia he was declared a 'proletarian writer', and Nizhny Novgorod was renamed Gorky. Stalin's use and exploitation of Gorky ironically ensured honours hitherto denied, and his role in the launch of socialist realism raises many questions about the ambivalence of his position. Stalin twice refused Gorky's subsequent application to leave Russia, and the exact circumstances of his death remain clouded (and are unlikely to be clarified); yet Stalin and other Soviet leaders were pall-bearers at Gorky's funeral and subsequent burial in the walls of the Kremlin.

Gorky's reputation abroad rests less on his plays than on his literary works: *The Mother* (dramatized and adapted by BRECHT) and the autobiographical trilogy *Childhood, My Apprenticeship* and *My Universities* (filmed by Mark Donskoi, 1938–40). His visit to the United States in 1906 to raise money for the Bolsheviks and meet with, for example, Mark Twain, attracted the attention of the Hearst press, which attacked the immorality of his common-law marriage with the actress Maria Andreyeva. It was only in the 1970s that his reputation as a dramatist was officially recognized in Britain with what became a string of seven ROYAL SHAKESPEARE COMPANY productions, the first four directed by DAVID JONES. IRENE SLATTER

F. M. Borras, *Maxim Gorky the Writer* (1967)

Gerhard E. Habermann, *Maxim Gorky*, trans. E. Shlans and Frederick Ungar (1971)

Nina Gourfinkel, *Gorky*, trans. A. Flashbach (1975)

Dan Levin, *Stormy Petrel: The Life and Work of Maxim Gorky* (1965)

Alexander Ovcharenko, *Maxim Gorky and the Literary Quests of the Twentieth Century* (1985)

Gotanda, Philip Kan   *see* ASIAN AMERICAN THEATRE

Gow, Michael   (b. Sydney, 14 Feb. 1955) Playwright and director. Founding member of the Thalia Theatre Company in Sydney, committed to staging experimental productions of the classics and reviving important and neglected works of European theatre. His first play, *The Kid*, was workshopped at the 1982 Australian National Playwrights' Conference and performed throughout the country. However, it was *Away* (1986), a portrayal of three Australian families on holiday in the summer of 1967–8, framed by scenes from school productions of *A Midsummer Night's Dream* and *King Lear*, that established him as one of the most important new voices in Australian theatre. With a blend of lyricism and prosaic detail, he breaks with naturalistic approaches to character and situation. Other plays include *On Top of the World* (1986), *Europe* (1987), *1841* (1988), *Furious* (1991) and *Sweet Phoebe* (1994).
MICHAEL MORLEY

See also QUEENSLAND THEATRE COMPANY.

Grace-Smith, Briar   (b. Whakatane, New Zealand, 23 March 1966; tribal affiliations Nga Puhi, Ngati Wai) Playwright. Trained as a journalist, Grace-Smith made her debut as a writer with the award-winning *Nga Pou Wahine* (1995). She also won a best play award for *Purapurawhetu* (1997) which revealed a powerful mix of myth, poetry, and realism in a MAORI setting, also evident in *Haruru Mai* (2000).
GILLIAN GREER & LAURIE ATKINSON

Grade [Winogradsky] family: Lew [Louis]   (b. Tokmak, Russia, 25 Dec. 1906; d. London, 13 Dec. 1998); **Leslie [Lazarus]** (b. London, 3 June 1916; d. Fréjus, France, 15 Oct. 1979); and **Delfont, Bernard [Boris Winogradsky]** (b. Tokmak, Russia, 5 Sept. 1909; d. Angmering, Sussex, 28 July 1994) Three brothers of a Russian Jewish family who migrated to England in 1912. All three were important in British light entertainment after the Second World War. The eldest, Lew, began a theatrical career in 1926 as a dancer specializing in the then fashionable Charleston, and became a VARIETY booking agent in the 1930s. The youngest, Leslie, started as an agent and combined with Lew in 1943 to form Lew and Leslie Grade Ltd, which quickly became the biggest light entertainment

booking agency in Britain, with a worldwide business. Bernard was also a dancer and then an agent, but his real interest was in producing. One of his earliest successes was the musical *Old Chelsea* (1943), which was followed by many variety, REVUE and musical productions, including a remarkable number of new British musicals, among them *Stop The World – I Want To Get Off* (1961), *Pickwick* (1963), *Maggie May* (1964), *Our Man Crichton* (1964), *The Four Musketeers* (1967), *The Matchgirls* (1966), *Joey Joey* (1966), *Queenie* (1967), *The Good Old Bad Old Days* (1972) and *The Good Companions* (1974). In 1955, Lew went into commercial television, where he became a key figure for quarter of a century. Bernard sold his agency to the Grade Organization, which was run by Leslie until 1966, when his place was taken by his son **Michael** (b. London, 8 March 1943). In 1967 the Grade Organization was sold, but the agency side was re-formed under Michael's control as London Management. He left in 1973 to become a television executive. Bernard, alone of his family, remained involved in live entertainment, but as an executive rather than as an active producer. Lew was knighted in 1969 and Bernard in 1974. They were both created life peers in 1976.   IAN BEVAN

Grade, Leslie   *see* GRADE FAMILY

Grade, Lew   *see* GRADE FAMILY

Graeae Theatre   Small-scale British theatre company of disabled people, formed in 1980 by Nabil Shaban and Richard Tomlinson. The company has toured to great acclaim both nationally and internationally. Graeae also offers workshops, provides theatre training courses for disabled people, and advises other organizations on the employment of disabled artists.
ANDREW SOLWAY

See also DISABILITY.

Graham, Martha   (b. Pittsburgh, 11 May 1894; d. New York, 1 April 1991) Dancer and choreographer. Influenced by oriental dance and the non-traditional work of ISADORA DUNCAN, Graham developed her own dance technique, where new angular and tension-dominated movements embodied internal emotions. She formed her own school and company in New York City, which gave its first performance in 1926. During her career she choreographed more than 180 works, including *Appalachian Spring* (1944) and *Clytemnestra* (1956), the first full-length work in modern dance. She created a new form of performance which not only changed dance but deeply affected the theatre, from visionaries like ANTONIN ARTAUD to modern choreographers and those who crossed boundaries in the less verbal theatre forms.   DAVID STAINES

See also CHOREOGRAPHY; DANCE.

Martha Graham, *The Notebooks of Martha Graham* (1973)

grand guignol A type of theatre devoted to short plays of violence, horror, the macabre and ghostly appearances. The genre originated in Paris salons in the late nineteenth century. In 1899 a Théâtre de Grand Guignol, devoted exclusively to this type of theatre, was opened in Montmartre's Rue Chaptal. It closed in 1962. Such plays also appeared in modified form in America and in Britain, including a celebrated season (1920–2) starring SYBIL THORNDIKE. These were antiseptic in comparison to the French fare. Some continental writers, like DE GHELDERODE and ARRABAL, however, have come closer to the original spirit. The name *guignol* derives from an eighteenth-century French puppet character. ANDREW SOLWAY

See also MELODRAMA; PUPPET THEATRE; THEATRE OF CRUELTY.

Mel Gordon, *The Grand Guignol: Theatre of Fear and Terror* (1988)

Grand Magic Circus Popular theatre group based in Paris, founded by JÉROME SAVARY (from the Grand Théâtre Panique, 1965), which sought in the 1970s to develop the techniques of CIRCUS and MUSIC HALL in a variety of often unusual venues. With shock tactics, nudity and deliberate vulgarity the group trampled on established conventions. (In *De Moïse a Mao*, 1973, Molière was compelled to wipe Louis XIV's backside.) This emphasis gradually gave way to highly expert technical effects, circus acts, and song and dance. TERRY HODGSON

J. Savary, *Album du Grand Magic Circus* (1974)

Granville Barker, Harley (b. London, 25 Nov. 1877; d. Paris, 31 Aug. 1946) Playwright, actor, director and scholar. Although Granville Barker's initial theatrical experience lay in acting in the conventional stock pieces of the mid- and late Victorian commercial stage, he was to become a major figure of the early twentieth-century progressive theatre. He acted in productions for the Elizbethan Stage Society, taking the leads in *Richard II* (1899) and *Edward II* (1903), and for the Stage Society he created important roles in SHAW's plays, most notably Marchbanks in *Candida*. Similarly, his own dozen plays, including *The Marrying of Ann Leete* (1902), *The Voysey Inheritance* (1905), *The Madras House* (1906) and *Waste* (written 1907), were written for and promoted by Edwardian non-commercial theatre ventures and, although at first overshadowed by Shaw's work, later came justifiably to be held in

high critical esteem. *Waste*, which deals with cabinet-level political scandal, became prominent in a campaign when it was banned by the CENSOR, ostensibly for its treatment of an abortion. Refused a licence until 1920, it was first publicly performed in a revised version in 1936.

Committed to the ideal of short-run repertory as opposed to the long runs of the commercial theatre, Granville Barker made his most significant and influential achievements in the roles of manager and director. He did much to establish in England the concept of the independent theatre director at a time when the major controls over play production were exerted by the actor–manager and dramatist. His hallmarks as director, in both realist and non-realist pieces, were balanced ensemble playing, uncluttered staging and meticulous attention to detail. Between 1904 and 1907 Granville Barker's partnership with JOHN VEDRENNE, who acted as business manager, resulted in a series of repertory seasons at the ROYAL COURT THEATRE. The repertoire included works by YEATS, MAETERLINCK, HAUPTMANN, IBSEN, GALSWORTHY and MASEFIELD, as well as Gilbert Murray's translations of three plays by Euripides. Most significant was the repertory's contribution to the establishing of Shaw's reputation and success; over the three seasons 11 of his plays were presented for a total of 701 performances. The Court seasons made a small profit, but the financial failure of later repertory ventures in which Granville Barker was involved, at the Savoy (1907–8) and the Duke of York's (1910), further entrenched his belief in the need for a subsidized national theatre, which he advocated in his *A National Theatre* (1930) and his earlier collaboration with WILLIAM ARCHER, *A National Theatre: Scheme and Estimates* (1907).

In 1911 Granville Barker's adaptation of SCHNITZLER's *Anatol* inaugurated a period of joint management ventures with his first wife, the actress LILLAH MCCARTHY, which continued to 1915. The most noteworthy productions were of *The Winter's Tale*, *Twelfth Night* and *A Midsummer Night's Dream*, which, although indebted to WILLIAM POEL and GORDON CRAIG, are often considered milestones in Shakespearean production. Granville Barker's marriage in 1918 to his second wife, Helen Huntington, has often been offered by biographers to account for his virtual retirement from active involvement in the theatre and for a pretentious gentrification exemplified in his hyphenation of his last two names. Though he became chairman of the newly founded BRITISH DRAMA LEAGUE in 1919, his interest in the theatre in the 1920s and 1930s seems to have been primarily scholarly, as in the collaboration with his wife in translations from the Spanish of plays by Martinez Sierra and the ALVAREZ QUINTERO brothers, and the publication of *The Exemplary Theatre* (1922), *On Dramatic Method* (1931) and several more volumes of lectures initially delivered at prestigious universities. His most considerable and lasting achievements during this period were his five volumes of *Prefaces to Shakespeare*. They combine serious Shakespeare scholarship with the insights of a practical man of the theatre and exerted some influence on Shakespearean production in the middle years of the twentieth century; directors such as HARCOURT WILLIAMS, BRIDGES-ADAMS, JOHN GIELGUD and TYRONE GUTHRIE acknowledged their various debts to the *Prefaces* in the planning of their own productions of Shakespeare's plays. IAN CLARKE

Dennis Kennedy, *Granville Barker and the Dream of Theatre* (1985)

Margery M. Morgan, *A Drama of Political Man: A Study in the Plays of Harley Granville Barker* (1961)

C. B. Purdom, *Harley Granville Barker: Man of the Theatre, Dramatist and Scholar* (1955; repr. 1971)

Eric Salmon, *Granville Barker: A Secret Life* (1983)

Grass, Günter [Wilhelm] (b. Danzig, Germany [now Poland], 16 Oct. 1927) Novelist, journalist, political activist and playwright. Best known for his novels, he has made a valuable, if idiosyncratic, contribution to postwar theatre. The early plays are rare German examples of ABSURD theatre – e.g. *Noch zehn Minuten bis Buffalo* ('Ten minutes till Buffalo', 1954); *Hochwasser* ('High water', 1957); *Onkel, Onkel* ('Uncle, Uncle', 1958); and *Die bösen Köche* ('The angry cooks', 1961). Controversy arose in 1966 with the production of *Die Plebejer proben den Aufstand* (*The Plebeians Rehearse the Uprising*; ROYAL SHAKESPEARE COMPANY, 1970) in which Grass combines a critique of a perceived historical inability by the Germans to conduct a revolution with a strong dose of scepticism about BRECHT. He was awarded the Nobel Prize for literature in 1999. JUDY MEEWEZEN

Ronald Hayman, *Günter Grass* (1985)

Alan Frank Keele, *Understanding Günter Grass* (1988)

Patrick O'Neill, *Günter Grass Revisited* (1999)

Gray, Dulcie *see* DENISON, MICHAEL

Gray, John (b. Ottawa, 26 Sept. 1946) Playwright and composer. After theatre experience in Vancouver, Gray moved to Toronto in 1975 where his first musical, *18 Wheels*, was premièred in 1977. His greatest success, *Billy Bishop Goes to War* (1978), written with Eric Peterson, is a musical based on the life of the First World War Canadian flying ace. *Rock and Roll* (1981),

a musical about 1960s rock bands, was complemented by *Don Messer's Jubilee* (1985), a musical about a famous Canadian traditional fiddler. *Amelia* (1994), about the famous pilot Amelia Earhart, premièred at Ottawa's National Arts Center, directed by Gray. EUGENE BENSON

Gray, Simon [James Holliday] (b. Hayling Island, Hants, 21 Oct. 1936) Playwright, novelist and lecturer. In many ways, Gray is a traditionalist. His 'well-made' plays typically feature a small, closely knit group of people in a single setting, often one of the milieux with which he is particularly familiar: the academic and publishing worlds. His protagonists are often egocentric, possibly in need of psychiatric help and wittily bitchy – like the eponymous 'hero' of *Butley* (1971), a lazy, belligerent university teacher obsessed with a sense of failure. The homosexual theme of this play is evident in many of Gray's works, notably *Wise Child* (1967) and *Spoiled* (1971). Other plays include *Otherwise Engaged* (1975), *The Rear Column* (1978), *Quartermaine's Terms* (1981), *The Common Pursuit* (1984) and *The Late Middle Classes* (1999), directed like many of his other plays by HAROLD PINTER. He has also written extensively for television, including *Unnatural Pursuits* (1992), based on his published diary, *An Unnatural Pursuit* (1985), which records problems encountered during the production of *The Common Pursuit*. DAVID SELF

Gray, Spalding *see* PERFORMANCE GROUP

Gray, Terence (b. Felixstowe, Suffolk, 14 Sept. 1895; d. 1986) Director and theatrical innovator. In 1926 he founded the FESTIVAL THEATRE, CAMBRIDGE, making it among the first British theatres to explore continental staging and lighting methods. An anti-realist influenced by CRAIG, his preference was for VERSE DRAMA and dance-drama, EXPRESSIONIST plays (American and particularly German), and highly unconventional productions of Shakespeare (with e.g. Toby Belch on roller skates or Rosalind dressed as a Boy Scout). He rejected 'trade theatre' (his term) and 'picture-frame' staging in favour of 'isometric scenic design' – neutral shapes (ramps, steps, rostra) allowing movement and grouping of actors to be vividly and variously lit – appealing to university audiences and minority taste. Among the young company he enlisted were performers like Robert Donat and FLORA ROBSON, and directors like TYRONE GUTHRIE and NORMAN MARSHALL. He left CAMBRIDGE in 1933 after directing the first English production of *The Supplicants* by Aeschylus, and abandoned the theatre altogether to become a wine grower in France. G. ROWELL

R. Cave, *Terence Gray and the Cambridge Festival Theatre* (1980)

Norman Marshall, *The Other Theatres* (1947)

Greece Modern Greek theatre has its roots in *karagiozis* (traditional shadow-puppet theatre) and *epitheorisi* (satirical revue) on the one hand, and in foreign influences on the other. *Karagiozis* relied on stock characters, but could be used to present anything from ancient Greek tragedy to events and personalities from recent Greek history; its popularity continued to be widespread until the late 1940s. European naturalist and SYMBOLIST drama were introduced to Greece by Constantinos Christomanos (1867–1911), who established the influential 'new stage' movement (1901–5). The 'well-made play' was represented by the problem plays of Gregorios Xenopoulos (1867–1951), which expounded psychological and social issues to middle-class urban audiences. Except for the consciously literary theatre of the poet Anghelos Sikelianos (1884–1951) and the poet and novelist Nikos Kazantzakis (1883–1957), there were no other significant developments before the advent of the influential (and controversial) director KAROLOS KOUN, who founded the Theatro Technis (Art Theatre) in 1942 and developed its attendant drama school. Koun created a more sophisticated public through productions of foreign plays ranging from SHAW to ALBEE and reinterpretations of Greek classics. He also fostered a new generation of Greek playwrights whose work was subsequently taken on by other experimental groups and by the National Theatre. The major writers of the postwar period include Loula Anagnostaki, Iakovos Kambanellis (b. 1922), Margarita Lyberaki (b. 1919), Pavlos Matesis (b. 1934), Yiorgios Skourtis (b. 1940) and Vassilis Ziogas (b. 1935). Although they have rejected traditional notions of plot and characterization in favour of ABSURDIST or BRECHTIAN forms, they all, in various ways, combine the expression of existentialist and post-existentialist philosophical values with exploration of the ethical and political problems of contemporary Greece.

Before Koun's initiative, the major serious theatre was the National Theatre, founded as the Royal Theatre (1900–8), then refounded and reorganized under state control in 1930, with the poet Ioannis Gryparis (1870–1942) as its director. While broadening its repertoire over the years, the National Theatre has continued to specialize in ancient Greek drama. It presents an annual summer season in the amphitheatres in Athens and EPIDAUROS. In 1961 a further state-controlled company, the State Theatre of Northern Greece, was opened in Thessaloniki.

Greece has seen two periods of severe disruption. During the first – the Nazi occupation of 1941–4 and the ensuing civil war of 1944–9 – AGITPROP was used by the resistance while artists like the actress KATINA PAXINOU and her husband, the director Alex Minotis (1904–90), revived classical Greek drama at the National Theatre. Drama was also politicized during the second period – that of the colonels' junta (1967–74) – and many artists left the country before democracy was restored.   CHRISTOPHER ROBINSON

See also ANCIENT GREEK DRAMA IN THE TWENTIETH CENTURY.

Alekos Chrysostomidis, *Popular Theatre* (1989)

Karolos Koun, *We Make Theatre for Our Soul* (1987)

G. Michaelides, *Modern Greek Playwrights* (1975)

Yannis Sideris, *History of Modern Greek Theatre* (1990)

Green, Adolph   *see* COMDEN, BETTY

Green, Paul (b. Lillington, NC, 17 March 1894; d. Chapel Hill, NC, 4 May 1981)   Playwright. Green first came to prominence with a one-acter, *The No 'Count Boy* (1925). The following year he won a Pulitzer Prize for his play about poor blacks, *In Abraham's Bosom*. Among his later Broadway plays were *The House of Connelly* (1931), the first play to be produced by the GROUP THEATER, the anti-war *Johnny Johnson* (1936) and a dramatization of Richard Wright's novel *Native Son* (1941). These earlier plays generally dealt with the downtrodden, and either explicitly or by implication were left-wing in tone. In subsequent years Green specialized in elaborate outdoor historical pageants, starting with *The Lost Colony* (1937), which was followed by *The Common Glory* (1947) and *Faith of Our Fathers* (1950).   GERALD BORDMAN

L. G. Aveny, ed., *A Southern Life: Letters of Paul Green, 1916–1981* (1994)

V. S. Kenny, *Paul Green* (1971)

Greene, [Henry] Graham (b. Berkhamsted, Herts, 2 Oct. 1904; d. Vevey, Switzerland, 3 April 1991)   One of England's leading novelists and a minor, conventional playwright. A rebel Catholic, Greene was in vogue in the 1950s theatre, dealing with faith and morality in such plays as *The Living Room* (1953), *The Potting Shed* (1957) and *The Complaisant Lover* (1959). He also wrote *Carving a Stone* (1964) and *The Return of A. J. Raffles* (1975). Novels dramatized include The *Heart of the Matter* (1950), *The Power and the Glory* (1956) and *Travels with My Aunt* (1991). He was made a Companion of Honour in 1966.   COLIN CHAMBERS

Greet, Ben [Philip Barling] (b. London, 24 Sept. 1857; d. London, 17 May 1936)   Actor–manager.

329

Already an established actor, Greet became famous in 1886 for his OPEN-AIR productions of Shakespeare plays, following the Elizabethan staging ideas of WILLIAM POEL, and for his successful touring company which also visited America. He produced numerous English classics at the OLD VIC, including 24 Shakespeare plays during the First World War. He nurtured and trained many young actors, and introduced hundreds of youngsters to Shakespeare and the theatre by taking his productions to schools and town halls during the 1920s and 1930s. He re-opened the OXFORD Repertory Company in 1930. He was knighted in 1929. ADRIANA HUNTER

W. Isaac, *Sir Philip Ben Greet and the Old Vic* (1964)

Gregory, André (b. Paris, 11 May 1934) Director. Co-founder of the SEATTLE REPERTORY THEATER and associate director (1963–5), he became artistic director of the Theater of the Living Arts in PHILADELPHIA, where his tenure was short-lived (1965–6) and controversial as his AVANT-GARDE inclinations placed him at odds with a conservative board of directors and audience. He founded the Manhattan Project in New York City in 1968. Its first production, after two years of intensive rehearsal with students from New York University, was an adaptation of *Alice in Wonderland* which displayed the influence of GROTOWSKI in its collaborative method of development and physicalized acting style. After an extensive leave of absence from the theatrical world, Gregory collaborated on the 1981 cult film *My Dinner with André* with WALLACE SHAWN. Directed by Louis Malle, it took the form of a simple dinner conversation between the director and the playwright, exploring their philosophies about theatre and life. This creative team joined forces again in 1994 to create *Vanya on 42nd Street*, a film documenting a rehearsal of the CHEKHOV play. SARAH STEVENSON

Joseph Wesley Ziegler, *Regional Theater: The Revolutionary Stage* (1977)

Gregory [Persse], [Isabella] Augusta, Lady (b. Co. Galway, Ireland, 5 March 1859; d. Dublin, 22 May 1932) Playwright and co-founder in 1899 with W. B. YEATS, EDWARD MARTYN and GEORGE MOORE of the Irish Literary Theatre, which became the Irish National Theatre Society. She was the principal administrative driving force behind the ABBEY THEATRE from 1904, when the society moved there, until her death. She wrote over 20 plays, the most frequently revived being *Spreading the News* (1904), *The Rising of the Moon* (1907) and *The Workhouse Ward* (1908). It is now accepted that she contributed much of the text of Yeats's *Cathleen ni Houlihan* (1902) and *The Pot of Broth* (1904).

Her memoir *Our Irish Theatre: A Chapter of Autobiography* appeared in 1913. CHRISTOPHER FITZ-SIMON

Elizabeth Coxhead, *Lady Gregory* (1961)
Mary Lou Kohfeldt, *Lady Gregory: The Woman Behind the Irish Renaissance* (1984)

Greig, David (b. Edinburgh, 17 Feb. 1969) Playwright. Unlike the majority of playwrights, he explored unfamiliar territory in his early work, such as *Stalinland* (1994) and *Europe* (1995), and became much more personal later, as in the Edinburgh-based middle-class world of *The Architect* (1996). He is interested in themes of belonging, communication and the lack thereof, focusing on in-between places such as borders, stations, airports and hotel rooms. In 1990 he co-founded the internationally successful theatre group Suspect Culture with Graham Eatough and became DRAMATURG for the company. Other plays include *Caledonia Dreaming* (1997), *Danny 306 + me 4 ever* (1999), *The Speculator* (1999), *The Cosmonaut's Last Message to the Woman He Once Loved in the Former Soviet Union* (1999) and *Victoria* (2000). His work with Suspect Culture includes *One Way Street* (1995), *Airport* (1996), *Timeless* (1997), *Mainstream* (1999) and *Candide* (2000). JOHN TIFFANY

Greig, Noël *see* GAY SWEATSHOP; GAY THEATRE; SHERMAN, MARTIN

Grein, J[acob] T[homas] ('Jack') (b. Amsterdam, 11 Oct. 1862; d. London, 22 June 1935) Critic and manager. A key figure in the campaign for advanced drama at the end of the nineteenth century, Grein made his greatest contribution in 1891 when he founded the INDEPENDENT THEATRE SOCIETY and gave as its inaugural production IBSEN's *Ghosts*, for which Grein was much abused, to be followed by the first production of a play by SHAW, *Widowers' Houses*. By its demise in 1898, Grein's society had proved to be crucial in establishing a model and stimulus for non-commercial theatre and the sorts of drama, particularly from abroad, that it might offer. He wrote on the Continent and in England for the paper that became the *Sunday Times*. Born Dutch, he took English nationality in 1895. He published seven books of dramatic criticism, and his wife wrote his biography, *J. T. Grein: The Story of a Pioneer* (1936). IAN CLARKE

Grenada *see* CARIBBEAN

Grenfell, Joyce [Irene Phipps] (b. London, 10 Feb. 1910; d. London, 30 Nov. 1979) Described herself as an actress and author, a combination of talents which enabled her to create a series of sharply observed and mildly satirical dramatic monologues which developed from a private entertainment for friends in the 1930s, through a run of West End REVUES, starting with *The Little Revue* (1939), into a series of one-woman shows which she launched in the mid-1950s and toured through the English-speaking world until she retired from the stage in 1973. Her gallery of characters included the society woman of infinitely refined gaucherie, the kindergarten teacher who could not quite control her charges, and above all the games mistress of St Trinian's who enlivened a series of minor British films. She wrote three books, including her autobiography, *Joyce Grenfell Requests the Pleasure* (1976), and was president of the Society of Women Writers. A popular figure on stage and television, Grenfell and her characters were the subject of a revue, *Re: Joyce!*, devised and played by Maureen Lipman (1989). IAN BEVAN

Griffin, Annie *see* EXPERIMENTAL THEATRE

Griffiths, Drew *see* GAY SWEATSHOP; SHERMAN, MARTIN

Griffiths, Trevor (b. Manchester, 4 April 1935) Playwright. Characterized by its dialectical confrontation of ideas, Griffiths's revolutionary Marxist playwriting includes *Occupations* (1970), which pits Italian communist Antonio Gramsci against Soviet machiavel Kabak; in *The Party* (1973), staged at the NATIONAL THEATRE with OLIVIER, representatives of the left argue during the events of May 1968; *Real Dreams* (1984) links a group of fumbling US revolutionaries in the 1960s with the history of political resistance. Perhaps his best play is *Comedians* (1975), where a stand-up comedy class is the scene for a sustained and provoking debate on the relations between humour and politics; it features each would-be comedian's act and culminates in an extraordinary display of revolutionary class hatred by Gethin Price (played originally by JONATHAN PRYCE). Griffiths, frustrated by the small audience for theatre, turned successfully to television drama (*Through the Night*, 1975; *Country: A Tory Story*, 1981; and the acclaimed series *Bill Brand*, 1976). After disillusionment, partly due to a clash with Hollywood over *Reds* (1981), he returned to the theatre with *Piano* (1990), a Chekhovian pastiche; *The Gulf Between Us* (1992), a meditation on the Gulf War; and *Thatcher's Children* (1993). Other plays include *Sam, Sam* (1972) and *Oi for England* (1982). DAN REBELLATO

John Bull, *New British Political Dramatists* (1984)
Mike Poole and John Wyver, *Powerplays: Trevor Griffiths in Television* (1984)

Gripps Theatre *see* THEATRE FOR YOUNG PEOPLE

Grock [Charles Adrien Wettach] (b. Reconvilier, Bern, Switzerland, 10 Jan. 1880; d. Imperia, Italy, 14 July 1959) Circus CLOWN and MUSIC HALL star. He partnered his father, a clockmaker, as an acrobat for 14 years before touring Europe and South America and taking the name Grock in 1903. He stayed in Britain and joined a clown named Brick until 1911, when he went solo as a white-faced, bald clown who wore an enormous coat and grinned a lot. His performance, in which he did not speak but did utter cries, involved planned disasters relating to the unsuccessful playing of many instruments, which he could do brilliantly but which on stage turned into a nightmare. He returned to continental Europe in 1924, performed for the Nazis during their time in power, and founded his own CIRCUS in 1951. He was the inspiration behind the central routine in TREVOR GRIFFITHS' *Comedians* (1975). His autobiography, *Grock, King of the Clowns*, appeared in English in 1957. CHARLES LONDON

J. Schechter, *Durov's Pig* (1985)

Gropius, Walter (b. Berlin, 18 May 1883; d. Boston, 5 July 1969) Architect, director of the BAUHAUS (1919–28), the highly influential arts and crafts school. With PISCATOR, Gropius designed in the 1920s a new style of flexible theatre building, incorporating machinery and projection, to advance the concept of TOTAL THEATRE. Although never built, the project had a considerable impact on later theatre ARCHITECTURE. Among his books are *The New Architecture and the Bauhaus* (1931, trans. 1936) and *The Theatre of the Bauhaus* (ed., 1961). CLIVE BARKER

M. Franciscono, *Walter Gropius and the Creation of the Bauhaus in Weimar* (1971)
O. Schlemmer, L. Moholy-Nagy and F. Molnár, *The Theatre of the Bauhaus* (1961)

Grossman, Jan (b. Prague, 22 May 1925; d. Prague, 10 Feb. 1993) Director. Together with the MIME artist LADISLAV FIALKA, he was a founder member of the Theatre on the Balustrade in Prague. Under his directorship the theatre staged several of the works of the dissident playwright VACLAV HAVEL. Two of Grossman's acclaimed productions – of JARRY's *Ubu* plays (1964) and Kafka's *The Trial* (1966) – were brought to the WORLD THEATRE SEASON in London in the late 1960s, but on his return to Czechoslovakia in 1968 he faced mounting official criticism of his artistic policies and left the country. After working abroad for several years, Grossman returned to Czechoslovakia and later became director of the Balustrade, where he directed Havel's *Largo Desolato* (1990) and *Temptation* (1992). HELEN RAPPAPORT

Grossmith, [Walter] Weedon (b. London, ?1852/3; d. London, 14 June 1919); **George** (b. London, 9 Dec. 1847; d. Folkstone, 1 March 1912); **George 'G. G.'** (b. London, 11 May 1874; d. London, 6 June 1935); and **Lawrence** (b. London, 29 March 1877; d. Hollywood, 21 Feb. 1944) Family of comic actors and writers who left extensive memoirs of life on the English stage. Weedon began touring the United States and at the turn of the century enjoyed a reputation as a playwright. His brother George billed himself as a comic entertainer for high society, having played with GILBERT and SULLIVAN and toured America. The brothers wrote *The Diary of a Nobody* (1892), which was dramatized in 1954. George's sons 'G. G.' and Lawrence had long stage careers. 'G. G.' also played with Gilbert and Sullivan at the SAVOY THEATRE, had a long-standing connection with the Gaiety Theatre and introduced the 'dude' figure to musical comedy.
CLAUDIA DURST JOHNSON
See also THEATRE FAMILIES.

Grosz, George (b. Berlin, 26 July 1893; d. Berlin, 6 July 1959) Painter, satirist and designer whose images have come to sum up the Weimar Republic. He worked briefly but notably in the theatre, with luminaries such as REINHARDT, BRECHT and PISCATOR, for whom he most famously designed *Adventures of the Good Soldier Schweik* (1928). Grosz was often chastized for his satire and was fined for blasphemy for lithographs of projections he had created for *Schweik*. This production also included technical ideas that Grosz experimented with which were to become integral to contemporary theatre, such as conveyor belts to move scenery and performers and the projections. DENISE L. TILLES

Andrew DeShong, *The Theatrical Designs of George Grosz* (1982)

grotesque, theatre of *see* THEATRE OF GROTESQUE

Grotowski, Jerzy (b. Rzeszów, Poland, 11 Aug. 1933; d. Pontedera, Italy, 14 Jan. 1999) Director. Early productions reveal his study of STANISLAVSKY, MEYERHOLD and VAKHTANGOV. He engaged in political activity after the death of Stalin, then grew interested in oriental philosophy. In 1959 he became the director of a small, subsidized experimental company, the LABORATORY THEATRE, where he stripped away everything not essential for the theatrical event and aimed for total control over the actor's body and voice and over all the means of expression. His work there, which he toured, and his espousal of POOR THEATRE, became widely known and he powerfully influenced American and European directors, including PETER BROOK, in the 1960s. His book, *Towards a Poor Theatre*, was published in 1968. In 1982 he became a drama professor in the United States, and in 1986 he opened a research centre in Pontedera, Italy.
TERRY HODGSON & JOANNA KRAKOWSKA-NAROŹNIAK
See also EASTERN THEATRE, ITS INFLUENCE ON THE WEST; ENVIRONMENTAL THEATRE; IMPROVISATION.

Jennifer Kumiega, *The Theatre of Grotowski* (1985)
Richard Schechner and Lisa Wolford, eds, *The Grotowski Sourcebook* (1996)

Group Theater (US) Less for the legacy of the plays it produced than for the artists it nurtured, the Group Theater is the most influential theatre ensemble in American history. Founded in the tradition of the MOSCOW ART THEATRE in 1930 by HAROLD CLURMAN, LEE STRASBERG and CHERYL CRAWFORD, it was politicized by the imperatives of the decade with which its life coincided. While rejecting commercial values, it chose to work within the Broadway framework rather than on the experimental FRINGE. Although committed to plays about contemporary social realities, it did not have a specific political agenda, as its diverse roster of playwrights reveals: MAXWELL ANDERSON, JOHN HOWARD LAWSON, SIDNEY KINGSLEY, PAUL GREEN, WILLIAM SAROYAN and CLIFFORD ODETS. Its greatest influence lay in Americanizing the acting system of STANISLAVSKY as the METHOD, particularly *after* the Group's demise when members such as Stella ADLER, MAURICE CARNOVSKY, Sanford Meisner, ROBERT LEWIS and, pre-eminently, Strasberg, Clurman and ELIA KAZAN became master teachers and directors, albeit with different emphases.

The impact of the Group Theater was felt in other English-speaking countries among pioneering left-wing groups such as UNITY THEATRE. Major productions include Lawson's *Success Story* (1932); Kingsley's *Men in White* (1933), *Awake and Sing!* (1935), *Waiting For Lefty* (1935), *Golden Boy* (1937) and *Rocket to the Moon* (1938) by Odets; *The Case of Clyde Griffiths* (1936) by ERWIN PISCATOR, based on Theodore Dreiser's *An American Tragedy*; Irwin Shaw's *The Gentle People* (1939); Green's *Johnny Johnson* (1936); and *My Heart's in the Highlands* (1939) by Saroyan. The company disbanded in 1940.
GERALD RABKIN

Harold Clurman, *The Fervent Years* (1945)
Wendy Smith, *Real Life Drama: The Group Theater and America* (1990)

Group Theatre (UK) Founded in February 1932 by RUPERT DOONE, John Ormerod Greenwood and others around a nucleus of idealists who had worked at the WESTMINSTER THEATRE and the FESTIVAL THEATRE, CAMBRIDGE. They formed a COLLECTIVE of committed artists and performers, including variously YEATS, ELIOT, MACNEICE, SPENDER, Britten, GUTHRIE, ISHERWOOD, AUDEN and many others who were to be important in the future of theatre. Their highly physical training was influenced by KURT JOOSS, LABAN and Doone's dance disciplines, aiming, like COPEAU, for a permanent ensemble company, but dedicated to a socialist, TOTAL THEATRE unifying the different arts. Their main successes were with verse plays like *The Dance of Death* and *Sweeney Agonistes* (1934), *The Dog Beneath the Skin* (1936), *The Ascent of F6* (1937) and *The Trial of a Judge* (1938). Briefly revived in 1950, they declined by 1954 and wound up finally in 1956, despite an acclaimed production of Sartre's *The Flies* (1951), the first English production of one of his plays. DAN REBELLATO

Robert Medley, *Drawn from the Life* (1983)
Michael Sidnell, *Dances of Death: The Group Theatre of London in the Thirties* (1983)

Grumberg, Jean-Claude (b. Paris, 1939) Playwright, director and actor. Grumberg's plays combine formal experiment with social comment, exposing past and present racism and intolerance. Plays include *Dreyfus* (1973), *En R'venant d'l'Expo* (*Returning from the Exhibition*, 1975), *L'Atélier* (*The Workshop*, 1979) and *Zone Libre* (*Free Zone*, 1989), both of which use material from his Jewish family's past. These latter two and *Dreyfus*, which explores anti-semitism, have been seen in London. ANNA MCMULLAN

Gründgens, Gustaf (b. Düsseldorf, 22 Dec. 1899; d. Manila, 7 Oct. 1963) Actor, director and manager. He began his career in 1921 and worked in several provincial theatres before being engaged by REINHARDT in 1928. Between 1934 and 1944 he was manager of the Staatstheater Berlin, which gained the reputation of being the best theatre in Nazi Germany. After the war he was interned because of his collaboration with the Hitler regime; but his formidable qualities as a manager soon saw him offered the post of director at the Düsseldorf Schauspielhaus (1947–55), making it one of the outstanding theatre centres of the Federal Republic. From 1955 to 1962 he was manager of the Schauspielhaus Hamburg. Gründgens often played the lead in his own productions, which were usually taken from the classical repertoire. His main achievement was Goethe's *Faust I and II* (Berlin 1932–3, Düsseldorf 1949, Hamburg 1957–8), in which he played Mephisto, the name used by Klaus MANN for a novel attacking Gründgen during the fascist years (it was also turned into a play, by ARIANE MNOUCHKINE, 1979, and a film by István Szabó, 1981). GÜNTER BERGHAUS

H. Goertz, *Gustaf Gruendgens* (1982)

Guare, John [Edward] (b. New York, 5 Feb. 1938) Playwright. Depicting a culture that fuses glamour with crime, Guare populates his plays with victims of their own or another's fantasies. Nurtured within 1960s OFF-OFF-BROADWAY, he launched his career with one-act plays, including *Loveliest Afternoon of the Year/A Day For Surprises/Something I'll Tell You Tuesday* (1966), *Muzeeka* (1968) and *Cop Out/Home Fires* (1969). His outrageous playfulness expanded with the full-length *The House of Blue Leaves* (1971). Other plays include the musical *Two Gentlemen of Verona* (1971, book and lyrics), *Rich and Famous* (1976), *Landscape of the Body* (1977), *Bosoms and Neglect* (1979), *Lydie Breeze* (1982) and, his most successful play yet, *Six Degrees of Separation* (1990). He wrote the screenplay for Louis Malle's film *Atlantic City* (1981). LEONARD BERKMAN

Guatemala *see* MEXICO AND CENTRAL AMERICA

guerrilla theatre A form of 'hit-and-run' POLITICAL THEATRE usually performed outdoors and carrying a strong message, like the early AGITPROP plays of the California farmworkers' group, El TEATRO CAMPESINO, the anti-capitalist pieces of the SAN FRANCISCO MIME TROUPE or the oppositional plays of WOLE SOYINKA's Nigerian guerrilla unit which was based at the University of Ife. COLIN CHAMBERS
See also STREET THEATRE.

H. Lesnick, ed., *Guerrilla Street Theatre* (1973)
J. Weisman, *Guerrilla Theatre* (1973)

Guilbert, Yvette [Emma Laure Esther] (b. Paris, 20 Jan. 1867; d. Aix en Provence, 4 Feb. 1944) Singer whose flexible face, clear diction and risqué songs made her a great innovator and favourite. International fame was achieved with such traditional songs as 'Le Fiacre' and 'Madame Arthur'. She wrote *How to Sing a Song* (1918), possibly the first book of its kind, and founded a school in America (1920). She played Mrs Peachum in *The Threepenny Opera* (1937) in Paris. Cabaret composer Aristide Bruand wrote for her, and Toulouse-Lautrec's portraits and posters depict a rough and witty popular entertainer with sharp features, enquiring eyebrows, red hair, white face and long black gloves. TERRY HODGSON

G. Harris, 'Yvette Guilbert—La Femme Moderne on the British Stage' in *The New Woman and Her Sisters*, eds V. Gardner and S. Rutherford (1991)

Guildhall School of Music and Drama *see* DRAMA SCHOOLS

Guinea *see* FRENCH AFRICAN THEATRE

Guinea-Bissau *see* PORTUGUESE-SPEAKING AFRICAN THEATRE

Guinness, Alec (b. London, 2 April 1914; d. Midhurst, W. Sussex, 5 Aug. 2000) Actor, renowned for his meticulous technique. His debut was in Ward Dorane's *Libel* (1934), but he first gained recognition at the OLD VIC as Sir Andrew Aguecheek in *Twelfth Night* (1937) and in GIELGUD's Queen's Theatre season the same year. Back at the Old Vic he played Hamlet (1938), uncut and in modern dress. During the Second World War he served in the Royal Navy but made a brief New York debut in 1942 in *Flare Path*. In 1946 he appeared in his own adaptation of *The Brothers Karamazov* and, rejoining the Old Vic, played, among other roles, the Fool in *King Lear* and Khalestakov in *The Government Inspector* by Gogol (both 1946). He also played Richard III (1953) in the inaugural production of the STRATFORD FESTIVAL in Ontario. He has displayed his versatility in *The Cocktail Party* (1949), *Ross* (1960), *Incident at Vichy* (1966), a startling Macbeth at the ROYAL COURT (1966), and *The Old Country* (1977). He has enjoyed a popular career in television (especially as the Le Carré spycatcher George Smiley) and film (e.g. the Ealing Studio comedies such as *Kind Hearts and Coronets*; 1949; international epics like *The Bridge on the River Kwai* 1957; and *Star Wars*, 1977, which he disliked but which made him a fortune). Among his memoirs are *Blessings in Disguise* (1985), *My Name Escapes Me* (1996) and *A Positively Final Appearance* (1999). He was knighted in 1959 and made Companion of Honour in 1994. D. KEITH PEACOCK

John Russell Taylor, *Alec Guinness: A Celebration* (2000)
K. Tynan, *Alec Guinness* (1961)

Guitry, Lucien-Germain *see* GUITRY, SACHA

Guitry, Sacha [Alexandre-Pierre-Georges] (b. St Petersburg, Russia, 21 Feb. 1885; d. Paris, 24 July 1957) Actor, film-maker, playwright; son of **Lucien-Germain Guitry** (b. Paris, 13 Dec. 1860; d. Paris, 1 June 1925), actor, playwright and manager. An actor of sober power, Lucien returned to Paris in 1891 after nine years in St Petersburg and later appeared in several of his more famous son's productions. Sacha wrote some 130 BOULEVARD plays and REVUES, mostly frothy comedies (e.g. *La Jalousie*, 1915), fantasies (e.g. *L'illusioniste*, 1917) or quasi-biographies (e.g. *Mozart*, 1925). Married five times to actresses, he is remembered as a colourful, highly energetic and ironic maker of popular, large-cast historical films (e.g. *Si Versailles m'était conté*, 1954). TERRY HODGSON

Gunter, John [Forsyth] (b. Billericay, Essex, 31 Oct. 1938). Designer. After working in rep, Gunter became resident designer at the ROYAL COURT (1965–6) and subsequently designed some 30 productions there, notably *Saved* (1965). Its monochrome austerity characterized much of his early work, including his detailed designs for the D. H. LAWRENCE trilogy (1968). After extensive work in German theatres, Gunter's style began to explore the theatricality of the stage space. For *Guys and Dolls* (1982) at the NATIONAL THEATRE an urban forest of neon signs created a dynamic Times Square for the play to work in; for *The Rivals* (1983), Gunter used the Olivier's sweeping curves to re-create Bath's Royal Crescent which elegantly divided to form gardens and interiors. He has garnered many awards during his work for the NT and ROYAL SHAKESPEARE COMPANY, in the West End and Broadway, and in opera. DAN REBELLATO
See also DESIGNING.

Gurik, Robert (b. Paris, 16 Nov. 1932) Playwright and novelist. Gurik, an engineer by training, moved to Canada in 1950, and began writing for the stage a decade later. The success of *Le Pendu* ('The hanged man') brought him to national attention in 1967; his savagely political satire, *Hamlet, Prince du Québec* (1968), marked a turning point in a career which had hitherto concentrated on universal concerns. Apart from these, the best known of his plays are *A Coeur ouvert* ('With open heart', 1969) and *Le Procès de Jean-Baptiste M.* ('The trial of Jean-Baptiste M.', 1972). LEONARD E. DOUCETTE

Gurney, A[lbert] R[amsdell] (Pete), Jr (b. Buffalo, NY, 1 Nov. 1930) Playwright and novelist. Frequently produced both on and off Broadway, as well as in numerous regional theatres across the United States, Gurney's award-winning work often looks with humour on the upper-middle-class WASP lifestyle in America. His plays include *The Middle Ages* (1977), *The Golden Age* (1981), *The Dining Room* (1982), *The Perfect Party* (1986), *Another Antigone* (1986), *The Cocktail Hour* (1988), *Love Letters* (1988, produced internationally), *The Snow Ball* (1991 based on his novel), *A Cheever Evening* (1994), *Overtime* (1995) and *Sylvia* (1995). Gurney serves on the artistic board of PLAYWRIGHTS HORIZONS in New York, where several of his plays have been premièred. ELLEN LAMPERT-GRÉAUX

Guthrie, [William] Tyrone (b. Tunbridge Wells, Kent, 2 July 1900; d. Monaghan, Ireland, 15 May 1971) One of the foremost stage directors of his time, mounting more than 170 productions throughout the world. He was a student at Oxford and acted with

FAGAN's company there before directing for the SCOTT-ISH NATIONAL PLAYERS (1926–8) and at the FESTIVAL THEATRE, CAMBRIDGE (1929–30). Much of his finest work occurred with REPERTORY companies: the OLD VIC, where he directed frequently and served as admin-istrator (1939–45); Canada's STRATFORD FESTIVAL, where he served as the first artistic director (1953–7); and the Minneapolis Theater, later the GUTHRIE THEATER, where he was artistic director (1963–6) and built on two of his Stratford innovations: the creation of ENSEMBLE playing and, with the designer TANYA MOISEWITCH, a thrust stage style that was influential in postwar English theatres. He returned often to both Stratford and Minneapolis as a visiting director. Never afraid to experiment in his productions, with a stress on agile speech and choreography of actors, he often used modern dress (most notably in *Hamlet*, 1938, with ALEC GUINNESS) in his Shakespearean stagings, for which he was best known. A long list of outstanding productions includes *Hamlet* and *Henry V*, both with LAURENCE OLIVIER (1937), *Peer Gynt* (1944) with RALPH RICHARDSON, *The Three Estates* (1948, at the EDIN-BURGH FESTIVAL) and *Tamburlaine the Great* (1951), with DONALD WOLFIT. A RADIO DRAMA producer early in his career, he also wrote two important radio plays (1929–20) and was the author of *A Life in the Theatre* (1959) and *In Various Directions: A View of the Theatre* (1966). He was knighted in 1961.   DAVID STAINES

James Forsyth, *Tyrone Guthrie: A Biography* (1976)
A. Rossi, *Astonish Us in the Morning: Tyrone Guthrie Remembered* (1977)

Guthrie Theater   This theatre, which opened in Min-neapolis in 1963, was the fulfilment of a desire by TYRONE GUTHRIE and his collaborators Oliver Rea and Peter Zeisler to set up a regional repertory theatre in the United States which would be free from commer-cial constraints in the choice of its repertoire. With a substantial grant and a site provided by the Walker Art Center, a theatre seating 1,437 was designed by the architect Ralph Rapson to Guthrie's specifications, and, together with the designer TANYA MOISEWITCH, Guthrie devised a seven-sided thrust stage to accom-modate his staging of such classics as *Hamlet*, *Three Sis-ters* and *Death of a Salesman* in its opening season. After Guthrie's death in 1971, the theatre was renamed in honour of him and a smaller auditorium was added. MICHAEL LANGHAM was artistic director from 1971 to 1975 and, after a period of decline, the theatre was revived in 1981 under the innovative directorship of the Romanian LIVIU CIULEI, who staged new American and European plays as well as classics. He was suc-ceeded by Garland Wright (1986–95) and JOE DOWLING (from 1995).   HELEN RAPPAPORT

Guyana   *see* CARIBBEAN

H

Habimah Theatre Named after the Hebrew word for 'stage', Habimah had its roots in a group formed in Bialystok, Byelorussia, in 1909 by Nahum Zemach, Hannah Rovina and Aaron Meskin. Its four one-act plays by Jewish writers were seen in Moscow in 1918 by STANISLAVSKY, who subsequently agreed to start a studio for the group, with VAKHTANGOV in charge, as part of the MOSCOW ART THEATRE. The most famous production was of ANSKY's *The Dybbuk* (1922), taken on tour over the next six years to Leningrad, Riga, America and Palestine, and kept in the repertoire for almost half a century. Habimah, the first professional Hebrew company, left the Soviet Union in 1926 and, following a tour of Europe and a split in North America, went to Palestine. After a short period in Berlin, it settled in Tel Aviv in 1931 and inaugurated its permanent building in 1945. The scope of its repertory was gradually widened to include classical and modern drama, and apart from fostering several home directors it attracted foreign directors such as MICHAEL CHEKHOV, LEOPOLD JESSNER, TYRONE GUTHRIE, HAROLD CLURMAN and LEE STRASBERG. In 1958 Habimah was proclaimed Israel's National Theatre, but only in 1968 did it abandon the ineffective collective system (whereby all decisions, including the distribution of parts, were made by vote) and acquire the official status of a state theatre. In the 1990s it was often reproached for being commercialized, betraying its vocation as the National Theatre. VERA GOTTLIEB & AVRAHAM OZ

Hackney Empire Designed by FRANK MATCHAM, this 2,000-seat MUSIC HALL in east London opened in December 1901 and numbered Charlie Chaplin, LILLIE LANGTRY, LITTLE TICH, MARIE LLOYD and VESTA TILLEY among its attractions. After its demise in the mid-1950s (having pioneered the transition from music hall to VARIETY) the Empire was used as a television studio and bingo hall, but was saved in 1986 by CAST New Variety, showcasing 'alternative comedy' and restoring the broad popular programming of the past that could range from comedian Lenny Henry or the talent show *291 Club* to *Black Heroes in the Hall of Fame*, OPERA, PANTOMIME, clowning (e.g. Slava Palunin) and visits from the NATIONAL THEATRE and ALMEIDA THEATRE, which premièred RALPH FIENNES in *Hamlet* there.
DAN REBELLATO
See also CLOWN; NEW VARIETY.

Hacks, Peter (b. Breslau, 21 March 1928) Playwright. After his studies and early work in theatre and television in Munich, he moved to the German Democratic Republic in 1955. His large number of plays earned him several national prizes and prestigious awards in both East and West Germany. During his first years in the GDR he wrote six plays which were major successes, the most important of these being *Moritz Tassow* (1965). He also wrote a number of successful adaptations of classical plays for East and West German theatres, as well as several opera libretti. His dramatic output since the early 1960s is characterized by the use of classical themes treated in a manner which combines elements of Brechtian and neoclassical theatre, e.g. in *Beautiful Helena* (1964), *Amphitryon* (1967) and *Adam and Eve* (1973). Hacks is also a prolific writer of polemical essays on all aspects of the dramatic art. He had his biggest success, in both East and West Germany, with the monologue *Conversation in the House of Charlotte von Stein about the Absent Mr Goethe* (1976). GÜNTER BERGHAUS

Michael Mitchell, *Peter Hacks: Theatre for a Socialist Society* (1990)

Hagen, Uta (b. Göttingen, Germany, 12 June 1919) Actress and teacher who made her debut as Nina in the LUNT–Fontanne *The Seagull* (1938). She played Desdemona to PAUL ROBESON's Othello (1943) in the first recorded US integrated production, and notably replaced JESSICA TANDY as Blanche DuBois in *A Streetcar Named Desire* (1948). In a distinguished career, she also played Georgie in *The Country Girl* by ODETS (1950), Shen Te in *The Good Woman of Setzuan* (1956), created Martha in *Who's Afraid of Virginia Woolf?* (1962), the title character in *Mrs Klein* (1995) and Ruth Steiner in *Collected Stories* (1998). She teaches at the Herbert Berghof Studio, which she founded with her husband HERBERT BERGHOF, and she has written *Respect for Acting* (1973), *Sources* (1983) and *A Challenge for the Actor* (1991). JANE HOUSE

Haifa Municipal Theatre The first regional public theatre in Israel, founded in 1962 by Yossef Millo after his forced departure from the CAMERI THEATRE which he had founded in 1944. After a few seasons of varied repertory, it emerged in the early 1970s under Oded Kotler as a haven for young Israeli playwrights, such as HANOCH LEVIN, JOSHUA SOBOL and others. Some offered critical perspectives on predominant ideologies by way of documentary, satirical or political plays, such as *Co-Existence* (Wattad, 1969), *Status Quo Vadis* (Sobol, 1971), *Shitz* (Levin, 1974) and *The Poisoned Mushroom* (Mittelpunkt, Nizan, and Oz, 1984). This caused friction between the theatre and its rather conservative, provincial subscribers. Given Haifa's ethnically mixed population, the theatre was also criticized for competing with Tel Aviv while neglecting its role as a community and regional theatre. In spite of some daring seasons, the Haifa Theatre never managed to recruit an attractive company of permanent actors willing to leave the professional comforts of Tel Aviv and cater for higher artistic standards. AVRAHAM OZ

Haigh, Kenneth (b. Barnsley, Yorks., 23 March 1931) Actor. He made his first professional appearance in 1952 and created the role of Jimmy Porter in OSBORNE's *Look Back in Anger* in the first ENGLISH STAGE COMPANY season at the ROYAL COURT in 1956, re-creating the part on Broadway and on tour to great acclaim. He has worked in classical and contemporary theatre, and on film and television in Britain and America. SARAH A. SMITH

Haim, Victor (b. Paris, 22 July 1935) Journalist and playwright; a writer of 'burlesque tragedy'. *Abraham et Samuel* (1976) achieved great success. *Mourir en chant-*ant ('Die singing', 1989) and *La Peau d'un fruit sur un arbre pourri* ('Rind on a rotten tree', 1971) suggest his characteristic tone. TERRY HODGSON

Haiti *see* CARIBBEAN

Half Moon Theatre Founded in 1972 in a disused synagogue in east London, it aimed to be a PEOPLE'S THEATRE combining left-wing politics and an appeal to the local working-class community. It became noted for its BRECHT productions – *In the Jungle of Cities*, *The Mother*, *St Joan of the Stockyards*, *The Resistable Rise of Arturo Ui* – and for campaigning DOCUMENTARY-based plays on current issues, which, in the case of *George Davis is Innocent, OK?* (1975), about the wrongful imprisonment of a local figure, had an identifiable impact on life beyond the theatre. It also mounted its own productions drawing on the buried history of struggle (e.g. *Will Wat? If Not, What Will?*, 1972, about the peasants' revolt of 1381, and *Female Transport*, 1973, about women convicts sent to Australia, both by STEVE GOOCH). It became an important date for touring socialist groups such as 7:84 and Belt and Braces (who transferred FO's *Accidental Death of an Anarchist* from the Half Moon to the WEST END in 1980). It moved locally in 1979 to an old Methodist chapel (refurbished in 1985 as a modern theatre) and saw *Pal Joey* (1980) and *Trafford Tanzi* (1980) make commercial transfers before the theatre closed through lack of funding in 1989. The Half Moon Young People's Theatre, its THEATRE IN EDUCATION and youth wing, became an independent organization and in 1994 moved into a new home in nearby Limehouse. COLIN CHAMBERS

Hall, Peter [Reginald Frederick] (b. Bury St. Edmunds, Suffolk, 22 Nov. 1930) Director. Hall acted and directed at CAMBRIDGE University, where he was influenced by the critic F. R. Leavis and GEORGE RYLANDS, and many of Hall's later close colleagues are Cambridge graduates, e.g. JOHN BARTON, PETER WOOD, Guy Wolfenden and TREVOR NUNN. His first professional engagement was to direct MAUGHAM's *The Letter* (Theatre Royal, Windsor, 1953). In 1954 he became assistant director and in 1955, director of the ARTS THEATRE, London, where he established his position as a first-rate director with the British premières of BECKETT's *Waiting for Godot* (1955) and other international plays. Hall formed his own company in 1957, for which he directed the British première of WILLIAMS' *Camino Real* (1957). After several productions at the SHAKESPEARE MEMORIAL THEATRE he was appointed its director (1960) and founded the ROYAL SHAKESPEARE COMPANY (1961), fulfilling his dream of an ensemble theatre company based on a continental model. As well as transforming a summer festival theatre into a permanent national one, he added the ALDWYCH in London to the operation, making possible a mix of the classical and the contemporary, and turned the RSC into one of the world's leading companies. Among his many productions with the RSC was the defining *The Wars of the Roses* (1963), *Hamlet* (1965) and the premières of *The Homecoming* (1965), *Landscape* and *Silence* (1969) and *Old Times* (1971) by HAROLD PINTER. Hall left the RSC in 1968 and, after a brief spell as Covent Garden's director of productions, took over from LAURENCE OLIVIER as director of the NATIONAL THEATRE (1973–88), negotiating the opening of its new site on the South Bank. Major productions there include ALAN AYCKBOURN'S *Bedroom Farce* (1977), Pinter's *Betrayal* (1978), *Amadeus* (1979) by PETER SHAFFER and *The Orestia* (1981), which visited EPIDAURUS in Greece. Since then he has formed his own company again and presented several highly successful productions in the West End, such as the revival of *Piaf* by PAM GEMS in 1994, and with a new ensemble at the OLD VIC, where his revival of *Waiting for Godot* (1997) was highly acclaimed. He went to work in the United States in 1999 and a year later opened JOHN BARTON's epic cycle *Tantalus* in Denver prior to a European tour. Hall has also directed opera internationally, including Covent Garden, BAYREUTH and Glyndebourne, where he became the Festival artistic director in 1984. Hall's productions are theatrical and meticulous. He enjoys power and theatre management, and likes working long hours and under pressure. He was knighted in 1977 and has published his *Diaries* (1983) of his time at the National, an autobiography, *Making an Exhibition of Myself* (1993) and a manifesto, *The Necessary Theatre* (1999). DANIEL MEYER-DINKGRÄFE

Stephen Fay, *Power Play: The Life and Times of Peter Hall* (1995)

Hall, Roger [Leighton] (b. London, 17 Jan. 1939) Playwright. A prolific author, he has written over 15 stage plays, as well as PANTOMIMES, musicals (with Philip Norman and A. K. Grant), television series, revue sketches and an autobiography, *Bums on Seats* (1998). His most successful plays have been *Glide Time* (Circa, 1976), described by director RICHARD CAMPION as 'one of the few New Zealand theatrical events that changed society', as New Zealanders showed a willingness to laugh at themselves, and *Middle Age Spread* (1977), probably his best-known play, which won the Society of West End Theatres Comedy of the Year Award in 1979 and was made into a successful film. *Prisoners of Mother England* (1979), *The Share Club* (1987), *After the*

Crash (1988), *Market Forces* (1995), and *C'Mon Black!*, a solo play about a fanatical rugby supporter, illustrate his mix of comedy, satire and social comment. His more serious *State of the Play* (1978) provides a thoughtful commentary on the world of drama. GILLIAN GREER AND LAURIE ATKINSON

Hall, Willis (b. Leeds, 6 April 1929) Playwright. He began writing for radio and then achieved success with *The Long and the Short and the Tall* (1959), a tight, anti-heroic story of young British servicemen fighting in Malaya which was a revelation in its day. Hall's children's plays and his collaborations with KEITH WATERHOUSE often dramatize dreams of fulfilment in a comfortable, dull world (e.g. *Billy Liar*, 1960). He writes a great deal for television. TONY HOWARD

Halliwell, David [William] (b. Brighouse, Yorks, 31 July 1936) Playwright. Halliwell's first major success was *Little Malcolm and his Struggle Against the Eunuchs* (1965), which follows a boy's ambitious attempt at vengeance for his expulsion from art school. Would-be Hitlers appear throughout his work, notably in *K. D. Dufford* (1969), an experiment in 'multiperspectivism', refracting action through its many perceptions. His *Who's Who of Flapland* (1967) brought two of his paranoiacs together, characteristically using language drawn from his native county as the site of their confrontations. In 1966 Halliwell set up an experimental LUNCHTIME THEATRE group, Quipu, but in the 1970s his nuanced psychologizing plays fell out of fashion. DAN REBELLATO

Hamilton [Hammill], Cicely [Cecily Mary] (b. London, 15 June 1892; d. London, 6 Dec. 1952) Actress, playwright and activist. Her first job was as a pupil-teacher; disliking it, she joined a touring company as an actress. She then turned to playwriting and her first play, *The Traveller Returns*, was performed in 1906. Her next, *Diana of Dobsons* (1908), was very successful. In 1908 she joined the Women's Freedom League and wrote two propaganda plays, *How the Vote Was Won* (1909) and *A Pageant of Great Women* (1909). She was a founder member of the ACTRESSES' FRANCHISE LEAGUE and of the Women Writers' Suffrage League. During the First World War she nursed soldiers at the Battle of the Somme and in 1917 was asked to form a repertory company to perform plays for the Allied troops on the Western Front. After the war she became a freelance journalist. She wrote a number of books, including her autobiography, *Life Errant*, which was published in 1935. FRANCESCA GREATOREX

Julie Holledge, *Innocent Flowers: Women in Edwardian Theatre* (1981)

Hamilton, Patrick [Anthony Walter] (b. Hassocks, Sussex, 17 March 1904; d. Worcester, 23 Sept. 1962) Novelist and playwright. He achieved success with the novel *Twopence Coloured* (1928), which had a theatrical setting, and with the play *Rope* (1929), a taut GRAND GUIGNOL thriller that exposes the decadence of the spoilt young rich. It was based on the real case of murderers Leopold and Loeb and was filmed by Hitchcock. Hamilton was also well known for another thriller, *Angel Street* (1938), first staged, and subsequently filmed, as *Gaslight*. Other plays include *The Duke in Darkness* (1942) and *The Governess* (1945). His sister Diane was an actress and playwright, and married the dramatist Sutton Vane. COLIN CHAMBERS

N. Jones, *Through a Glass Darkly: The Life of Patrick Hamilton* (1991)

Hamlisch, Marvin [Frederick] (b. New York, 2 June 1944) Composer. Trained in classical piano, he served as assistant vocal manager on *Funny Girl* (1964) and dance arranger for *Henry, Sweet Henry* (1967), which was choreographed by MICHAEL BENNETT. After working on Las Vegas club acts, he began scoring films, and in 1974 he won three Academy Awards for *The Way We Were* and *The Sting*. He then turned to BROADWAY, with Bennett again, and wrote the music for the outstanding hit of its time, *A Chorus Line* (1975), with lyrics by Edward Kleban. He also wrote the music for the highly successful *They're Playing Our Song* (1979) with lyrics by Carole Bayer Sager, as well as two failures, *Jean Seberg* (1983) and *Smile* (1986). His music, like his own background, combines traditional musical comedy idioms and contemporary popular music. Although his songs are bright and energetic, he can reveal a depth and poignancy far removed from the popular world. His musicals have almost continuous underscoring, reflecting his own film scoring. DAVID STAINES

Hammerstein, Oscar, II (b. New York, 12 July 1895; d. Doylestown, Pa., 23 Aug. 1960) American lyricist and librettist. Grandson of the impresario Oscar Hammerstein (1846–1919), Oscar II made his first essays as a musical writer in collaboration with composer Herbert Stothart and with librettist Otto Harbach, in tandem with whom he was subsequently responsible for the words of several extremely successful Broadway musicals in both the light comic and romantic styles of the 1920s: *Wildflower* (1923), *Rose Marie* (1924), *Sunny* (1925) and *The Desert Song* (1926). He provided texts for all the most important composers of the time – FRIML, ROMBERG, YOUMANS, GERSHWIN, KERN – often in collaboration, but worked alone on book and lyrics

for his most enduring work from this period, *Show Boat* (1927), in which he also made his Broadway debut as a director. After *The New Moon* (1928), his output proved less successful, until he began a partnership with composer RICHARD RODGERS, with whom, in the 17 years from *Oklahoma!* (1943) to his death, he wrote and produced four further staple musical shows of the American repertoire, *Carousel* (1945), *South Pacific* (1949), *The King and I* (1951) and *The Sound of Music* (1959).

His early texts are often utilitarian and his lyrical work mostly in the slickly banal style then favoured in both musical comedy and comic opera, best when, as in *Show Boat* and *The New Moon*, there was character and substance in the piece. He was best suited by the Rodgers shows, where his simple, often inspired song ideas, his frequently sentimental but unhackneyed lyrics and his tightly constructed libretti were popular models in Broadway's most successful years. KURT GÄNZL

Hugh Fordin, *Getting to Know Him* (1977)
S. Green, *The Rodgers & Hammerstein Story* (1963)
E. Mordden, *Rodgers and Hammerstein* (1992)
F. Nolan, *The Sound of Their Music* (1978)
D. Taylor, *Some Enchanted Evening: The Story of Rodgers and Hammerstein* (1953)

Hampden [Dougherty], Walter (b. Brooklyn, New York, 30 June 1879; d. Hollywood, 11 June 1955). Actor. After apprenticeship with FRANK BENSON in England, he returned to make his American debut in 1907, appearing with ALLA NAZIMOVA in several plays, including *The Master Builder* and *A Doll's House*. The tall, lean, handsome actor soon was playing leads in such important new works as Charles Rann Kennedy's *The Servant in the House* (1908) and CLYDE FITCH's *The City* (1909), as well as in such fluff as *Good Gracious Annabelle* (1916). A proponent of an older, romantic school, his heyday came in the 1920s when he starred in several Shakespearean revivals, in *Cyrano de Bergerac* and in Bulwer-Lytton's *Richelieu*. His last part was as the cruel judge Danforth in *The Crucible* (1953). GERALD BORDMAN

Hampstead Theatre Club One of England's leading new play theatres, it was founded by director James Roose-Evans (b. 1927) in a hall in north London in 1959. It moved to its own premises in a prefabricated hut in the same area in 1962, and in 1970 to a similar neighbouring site, seating about 150 with an end stage. An avid band of local theatregoers has always supported its new play policy, which has bridged the role of CLUB THEATRE, FRINGE venue and WEST END try-out house – a policy sustained by successive directors Vivian Matalon (1970–3), Michael Rudman (1973–8), David Aukin (1978–84), Michael Attenborough (1984–8) and Jenny Topper (from 1988), who broadened the repertoire to include revivals.

In the 1960s, several plays transferred commercially, such as Donald Howarth's *A Lily in Little India* (1965), John Bowen's *After the Rain* (1966) and *Little Boxes* (1968), and *Brief Lives* (1967) starring ROY DOTRICE. This trend continued into the next decade and beyond, with plays such as *Alphabetical Order* (1975) by MICHAEL FRAYN, *Dusa, Fish, Stas and Vi* (1976) by PAM GEMS, *Abigail's Party* (1977) by MIKE LEIGH, *Bodies* (1978) by JAMES SAUNDERS and *Gloo Joo* (1979) by MICHAEL HASTINGS. A policy of hosting, or co-producing with, visiting companies led to such successes as *The Elephant Man* (1977) by BERNARD POMERANCE and *Translations* (1981) by BRIAN FRIEL. Hampstead has also premièred plays from abroad – e.g. by DÜRRENMATT, HANDKE, SHEPARD, TENNESSEE WILLIAMS and DAVID WILLIAMSON.   COLIN CHAMBERS

Hampton, Christopher [James]   (b. Fayal, Azores, 26 Jan. 1946)   Playwright. His first play, *When Did You Last See My Mother?* (1964), made him the youngest playwright of the century to be produced in London's West End. His 'bourgeois comedy' *The Philanthropist* (1970) was successful both in London and on Broadway, and demonstrated his ability to write witty, subtle and revealing dialogue. A gifted linguist, he is also a translator – of CHEKHOV (*Uncle Vanya*, 1970); of IBSEN (*Hedda Gabler*, 1970; *A Doll's House*, 1971; *Ghosts*, 1978; *The Wild Duck*, 1979; *An Enemy of the People*, 1997); of Molière, FEYDEAU and Laclos, achieving considerable commercial success with his reworking (1985) of Laclos' *Les Liaisons Dangereuses*, which he adapted as an Oscar-winning screenplay (1989); and of the Austro-Hungarian dramatist ODÖN VON HORVÁTH. Besides his versions of von Horváth's *Tales from the Vienna Woods* (1977), *Don Juan comes Back from the War* (1978) and *Faith, Hope and Charity* (1989), Hampton also featured the dramatist (anachronistically) alongside BRECHT in his own play *Tales from Hollywood* (1982). Other plays include *Total Eclipse* (1968), *Savages* (1973), *Treats* (1976) and the quasi-autobiographical *White Chameleon* (1991). His translation of YASMINA REZA's *Art* (1997) had considerable commercial success, and he also wrote the book for ANDREW LLOYD WEBBER's *Sunset Boulevard* (1993).   DAVID SELF

Ben Francis, *Christopher Hampton: Dramatic Ironist* (1996)

R. Gross, ed., *Christopher Hampton: A Casebook* (1990)

Hamsun, Knut   *see* BARRAULT, JEAN-LOUIS; NORWAY

Hancock, Sheila   (b. Blackgang, Isle of Wight, 21 Feb. 1933)   Actress and director. Her early work was mainly in comedy, musical theatre and REVUE, to which her quirky looks and raffish style were especially suited, and she also had considerable success in television. Her formidable intelligence led her towards more serious work, including roles for the ROYAL SHAKESPEARE COMPANY in 1969 and 1981. She began directing for the Cambridge Theatre Company in the late 1970s and subsequently directed *A Midsummer Night's Dream* for the RSC and *The Critic* for the NATIONAL THEATRE. In 1980 she created the role of Mrs Lovitt in the original London production of STEPHEN SONDHEIM's *Sweeney Todd* Her political, personal and professional courage have kept her at the cutting edge, often working with new writers and younger directors. Her autobiography, *Ramblings of an Actress*, appeared in 1987.
GENISTA MCINTOSH

Handke, Peter   (b. Griffen, Carinthia, Austria, 6 Dec. 1942)   Writer of novels, stories, poems, essays, films and plays. Though better known for novels and associated screenplays (e.g. *The Goalkeeper's Fear of the Penalty*, 1971), he has written a number of innovative plays and influential essays on theatre. Handke argues fiercely that politics have no place in the arts, and remains a controversial figure. In 1966 he interrupted an American university gathering of German writers with an outburst which ensured instant celebrity, declaring that all contemporary literature was descriptive nonsense. His subsequent works offered a new subjectivity in a variety of literary and dramatic forms. *Publikumsbeschimpfung* (*Offending the Audience*, 1966), was conceived as a pamphlet about the impossibility of theatre, but directed as a kind of philosophical beat show. An instant success in Frankfurt, the play soon attained cult status, with audiences more than willing to respond to the ironic stream of abuse. A number of similarly styled pieces followed, e.g. *Selbstbezichtigung* (*Self-Accusation*, 1966), and in 1968 *Kaspar* seemed to herald a new direction for the German theatre. With acknowledged influences as disparate as Wittgenstein, John Lennon and BECKETT, it challenges the way language organizes the world and restricts human freedom. Later plays, e.g. *Quodlibet* (translated with the same title, 1970) and *Der Ritt Über den Bodensee* (*The Ride Across Lake Constance*, 1971), develop similar themes, albeit with startlingly fresh theatrical methods. *Die Unvernünftigen Sterben Aus* (*They Are Dying Out*, 1973), set in the world of business, equates money with language and questions a perceived human obsession with behaving rationally and reasonably at the cost of instinct and nature. This theme is developed in *Über die Dörfer* (*The Long Way Round* or *Beyond the Villages*, 1982), a study of man's inhumanity to man and nature. The plays are almost prohibitively complex and have suffered from weak interpretations in Germany and abroad, but at their best are brilliant and entertaining signals of our time. JUDY MEEWEZEN

Nick Hern, *Peter Handke: Theatre and Anti-Theatre* (1971)
Michael Linstead, *Outer World and Inner World* (1981)

Hands, Terry [Terence David] (b. Aldershot, Hants, 9 Jan. 1941) Director. One of the founders in 1964 and the first artistic director of LIVERPOOL's EVERYMAN THEATRE. He joined the ROYAL SHAKESPEARE COMPANY as artistic director of Theatregoround, its travelling group, in 1966, becoming an associate director of the main company (1967), joint artistic director with TREVOR NUNN (1978), and sole artistic director and chief executive (1987–91). With the RSC, his major Shakespearean work has been marked by visual flair and includes *The Merry Wives of Windsor* (1968 and 1975), *The Merchant of Venice* (1971), *Coriolanus* (1977) and the history cycle starring ALAN HOWARD: *Henry IV Parts I and II* (1976), *Henry V* (1976), *Henry VI Parts I, II and III* (1977), and *Richard II* and *Richard III* (1980); his non-Shakespearean work includes ARBUZOV's *Old World* (1976) and ROSTAND's *Cyrano de Bergerac* (1983). From 1975 to 1977 he was consultant director of the COMÉDIE-FRANÇAISE. He took over THEATR CLWYD in 1997, and in 2000 directed TV's *Frasier* star Kelsey Grammer as Macbeth in New York. DAVID STAINES

Hankin, [Edward Charles] St John (b. Southampton, 25 Sept. 1869; d. London, 15 June 1909) Critic and playwright. Between 1901 and 1909 Hankin, influenced by SHAW and BRIEUX, created a series of dark satires of middle- and upper-class English life. The most popular of these, *Return of the Prodigal* (1905), was revived by GIELGUD in 1948. MARVIN CARLSON

Jan McDonald, *The New Drama, 1900–1914* (1986)

Hanna, Gillian *see* MONSTROUS REGIMENT

Hannan, Chris[topher John] (b. Glasgow, Scotland, 21 Jan. 1958) Playwright. He found early success and critical acclaim with *Elizabeth Gordon Quinn* (1985) drawing on Scotland's tradition of plays set in tenement slums but transforming it into something poetic and universal, as its central character memorably cries 'I refuse to learn how to be poor!' His work oscillates between the populist and the intellectual, often fusing the two to create a surreal world of mythological reference for his working-class characters, as in *Shining Souls* (1996); this interest in the classical world finds clear expression in *The Baby* (1990), with its imperial Roman setting. His characters seem to be attracted to mess and chaos, often trying to save themselves in deformed or exotic ways, like Ann in *Shining Souls* and Sammy and Tracky in *The Evil Doers* (1990). Other plays include *The Orphans' Comedy* (1986) and *The Pretenders* (1991), a version of the IBSEN play. JOHN TIFFANY

Hansberry, Lorraine (b. Chicago, 19 May 1930; d. New York City, 12 Jan. 1965) Playwright. Hansberry's feminism and her commitment to the civil rights movement can be found in her plays. *A Raisin in the Sun* (1959), a turning point for black professionals in the American theatre, touched the pulse of black Americans looking for a voice. This realistic play explores the struggles of a black family living in Chicago. Mama, a strong matriarchal figure, affirms life in the face of racial prejudice, poverty and despair. Hansberry became the first black American woman and the youngest person to win the New York Drama Critics' Circle Award. Her next play, *The Sign in Sidney Brustein's Window* (1964), was not a success. After she died from cancer, Robert Nemiroff, to whom she had been married, made two compilation shows from her writing, *To Be Young, Gifted and Black* (1969) and *Les Blancs* (1970). JANE HOUSE

S. Carter, *Hansberry's Drama: Commitment Amid Complexity* (1991)
Anne Cheney, *Lorraine Hansberry* (1984)
Richard M. Leeson, *Lorraine Hansberry: A Research and Production Sourcebook* (1997)

happening A type of multi-media theatrical event that emerged in America in the 1950s from Black Mountain College, North Carolina, where, among others, the painter Robert Rauschenberg, the composer JOHN CAGE, the dancer MERCE CUNNINGHAM and the poet Charles Olson experimented with non-naturalistic forms. The Vienna Group in Austria devised happenings, but the genre was most prominently explored in America, particularly by the painter Allan Kaprow (b. 1927), who had studied under Cage and whose *18 Happenings in 6 Parts* (1959) gave the form its name.

Happenings often involved a series of pre-planned actions, carried out in non-theatre spaces by performers from different disciplines and/or spectators, partially improvised and without the normal dramatic parameters of character and fictional world. Influences were diverse – FUTURISM, DADA, the ABSURD, Zen – as were the directions taken, from fun chaos (a nude woman wheeled on stage during the 1963 Edinburgh Festival) to environmental art (covering a cliff face with plastic), pop art (Andy Warhol's work) and rock music (Pink Floyd concerts). MARVIN CARLSON

See also ENVIRONMENTAL THEATRE; EXPERIMENTAL THEATRE; INSTALLATION; PERFORMANCE ART.

Allan Kaprow, *Assemblage, Environments and Happenings* (1966)
Michael Kirby, *Happenings* (1965)
M. Sandford, *Happenings and Other Acts* (1994)

Harburg, E[dgar] Y[ipsel] ('Yip') (b. New York, 8 April 1896; d. Brentwood, Cal., 5 March 1981) Lyricist and librettist. Born Erwin Y. Hochberg, the son of Russian Jewish immigrants, he graduated from City College and changed his name after he married in 1923 and began publishing poems. The stock market crash left his electrical appliance business in debt, which is when he became a song lyricist. Harburg found his first collaborator, composer Jay Gorney, through his life-long friend IRA GERSHWIN. Harburg and Gorney wrote 35 songs, including 'Brother Can You Spare a Dime' (*Americana*, 1932), theme to millions during the Great Depression. In 1932 Harburg had more songs on BROADWAY than any other lyricist. In 1939 he and composer HAROLD ARLEN won an Academy Award for 'Over the Rainbow' (*The Wizard of Oz*). Harburg was blacklisted by the House Un-American Activities Committee in the 1950s for writing 'Happiness is a Thing Called Joe' (1942, *Cabin in the Sky*, Arlen). Harburg's innovative musicalization of comic speech infused a new type of recitative into the American musical comedy style. He used metaphor, illusion and belief, and comic neologisms in many of his more than 537 songs, including 'It's Only a Paper Moon' (1932, *The Great Magoo*, Arlen), 'April in Paris' (1932, *Walk a Little Faster*, Vernon Duke), 'The Eagle and Me' (1944, *Bloomer Girl*, Arlen) and 'Old Devil Moon' (1947, *Finian's Rainbow*, Burton Lane). ANNA WHEELER GENTRY

Harold Meyerson and Ernie Harburg, *Who Put the Rainbow in The Wizard of Oz? Yip Harburg, Lyricist* (1993)

Harcourt, Peter [Millais] (b. Wellington, New Zealand, 26 June 1923; d. Wellington, 1995) Theatre historian, radio journalist, scriptwriter, REVUE writer and performer. After eight years in London gaining experience of management, production and journalism, he returned to Wellington where he wrote and co-directed a number of successful revues with David Tinkham. Author of a history of radio in New Zealand and of *A Dramatic Appearance: New Zealand Theatre 1920–1970* (1978), he was a driving force behind saving the St

James Theatre in Wellington from demolition. His wife **Kate [Catherine Winifred]** (b. North Canterbury, New Zealand, 16 June 1927) is an actress well known on radio for her appearances with her husband in a children's programme and more recently in the women's comedy collective Hen's Teeth. She has also appeared in numerous plays at DOWNSTAGE and CIRCA. She was created a dame in 1996 for services to the theatre. Peter and Kate's daughter **Miranda [Catherine Millais]** (b. Wellington, New Zealand, 4 Nov. 1962) established herself as a playwright and as an actor on stage and radio, and became nationally known in the television series *Gloss*. She appeared with her mother in the autobiographical *Flowers from My Mother's Garden* (1998, co-written with Stuart McKenzie), and turned to directing plays with an award-winning production of *Much Ado About Nothing* (1999) and McKenzie's *Double Dare* (2000).
GILLIAN GREER & LAURIE ATKINSON

Harding, Michael (b. Cavan, Ireland, 6 August 1953) Novelist and playwright. His first five plays were produced by the ABBEY THEATRE, Dublin: *Strawboys* (1987), *Una Pooka* (1988), *The Misogynist* (1990), *Hubert Murray's Widow* (1993) and *Sour Grapes* (1997). Highly 'theatrical', his work to date satirically exposes the festering wounds of modern Irish society.
CHRISTOPHER FITZ-SIMON

Hardwicke, Cedric [Webster] (b. Lye, Worcs, 19 Feb. 1893; d. New York, 6 Aug. 1964) Actor. Hardwicke made his stage debut when he was 19 and joined the OLD VIC company in 1914. After the First World War he joined the BIRMINGHAM REPERTORY THEATRE company, where his career as a versatile male lead took off. He was especially applauded for his Shavian roles, and he created the role of King Magnus in SHAW's *The Apple Cart* (Malvern Festival, 1929), which transferred to London to great critical acclaim. He worked with equal success in film and theatre, dividing much of his career between London and New York. His memoirs were published as *Let's Pretend* (1932) and *A Victorian in Orbit* (1961). He was knighted in 1934. ADRIANA HUNTER

Hardy, Thomas (b. Higher Bockhampton, Dorset, 2 June 1840; d. Dorchester, 11 Jan. 1928) Poet, novelist and playwright. As a dramatist Hardy is most famous for *The Dynasts* (1904), a theatrically intractable CLOSET DRAMA of the Napoleonic Wars in 19 acts, staged in considerably truncated form by GRANVILLE BARKER in 1914. Stage and screen versions of Hardy's novels have attracted much larger audiences than his plays. IAN CLARKE

Hare, David (b. Bexhill, Sussex, 5 June 1947) Playwright and director. Co-founder of ALTERNATIVE companies Portable Theatre and JOINT STOCK, for which he wrote *Fanshen* (1975), Hare came to prominence with *Knuckle* (1974) and *Teeth 'n' Smiles* (1975). Although sometimes pigeon-holed as a left-wing writer, Hare has proved to be an independent, even ironic, commentator on the political and social scene, frequently concerned with the effect of the past on the present and not without his own strong convictions. Prominent among these is his mistrust of institutions. Some of his best work probes such institutions – for example, a newspaper empire in *Pravda* (with HOWARD BRENTON, 1985); the Church of England in *Racing Demon* (1990); the judiciary in *Murmuring Judges* (1991); the Labour Party in *The Absence of War* (1993) – all seen at the NATIONAL THEATRE, as were other notable plays, including *Plenty* (1978), which explores the history of postwar Britain; *Map of the World* (1983); *The Secret Rapture* (1988), a commentary on the Thatcher years; and *Skylight* (1995), a play which considers not a corrupt institution but truthfulness in personal relationships. *Amy's View* (1997) and *Via Dolorosa* (1998), his monologue play about Palestine in which he appeared as himself, both transferred from London to New York, and his account of his voyage on to the stage appeared as *Acting Up* (1999). In *My Zinc Bed* (2000) he continues his exploration of faith. He has also directed in the theatre, and both written and directed for television (notably *Licking Hitler*, 1978) and for the cinema (e.g. *Wetherby*, 1985). His essays, *Writing Left-Handed*, appeared in 1991. He was knighted in 1998. DAVID SELF

Colin Chambers and Mike Prior, *Playwrights' Progress* (1987)
Joan F. Dean, *David Hare* (1990)
Carol Homden, *The Plays of David Hare* (1995)
Judy I. Oliva, *David Hare: Theatricalizing Politics* (1990)

Harlem Renaissance *see* BLACK THEATRE; HUGHES, LANGSTON

Harnick Sheldon [Mayer] (b. Chicago, 27 Dec. 1924) Lyricist and librettist. Harnick began his career as a composer and lyricist writing college musicals while attending Northwestern University. He moved to New York as a professional violinist but had greater success writing songs for musical REVUES: *New Faces of 1952* (1952), *Two's Company* (1952), *John Murray Anderson's Almanac* (1953), *Shoestring Revue* (1955), *The Littlest Revue* (1956), *Shoestring '57* (1957), *Kaleidoscope* (1957), *Take Five* (1959) and *Vintage '60* (1960). He began writing lyrics for BROADWAY musicals with *The Amazing Adele* (1955) and *Shangri La* (1956). His most successful creative partnership was with composer

JERRY BOCK, yielding *The Body Beautiful* (1958), *Fiorello!* (1959, Pulitzer Prize), *Tenderloin* (1960), *She Loves Me* (1963), *Fiddler on the Roof* (1964), *The Apple Tree* (1966), and *The Rothschilds* (1970). He has also collaborated with RICHARD RODGERS, CY COLEMAN, Michel Legrand, and, on a stage version of Frank Capra's film *It's a Wonderful Life* (1991), with Joe Raposo. Harnick has written several opera libretti, including an adaptation of Lehár's *The Merry Widow* (1978) for New York City Opera, and two new works, *Captain Jinks of the Horse Marines* (1975, Jack Beeson) and *Coyote Tales* (1998, Henry Mollicone), both premièred by Lyric Opera of Kansas City. ANNA WHEELER GENTRY

Harris, Aurand *see* THEATRE FOR YOUNG PEOPLE

Harris, Jed [Jacob Horowitz] (b. Vienna, 25 Feb. 1900; d. New York, 15 Nov. 1979) Producer and director. Harris spent time in journalism before turning to the stage. His initial efforts as a producer met with little or no success, but he soon had four smash hits in quick succession: *Broadway* (1926), *Coquette* (1927), *The Royal Family* (1927) and *The Front Page* (1928). For a time he was viewed as a wonderboy, but his viciousness and rudeness, which became legendary, alienating many of the theatre's best artists, quickly branded him an *enfant terrible*. He began directing his own productions in the 1930s (e.g. *Uncle Vanya*, 1930; *The Green Bay Tree*, 1933, with OLIVIER as a homosexual; *Our Town*, 1938). In later years his knack failed him, yet he had a few more hits, among them *The Heiress* (1947) and *The Crucible* (1953). He wrote memoirs, *Watchman, What of the Night?* (1963, about *The Heiress*) and *A Dance on the High Wire* (1979). GERALD BORDMAN

M. Gottfried, *Jed Harris: The Curse of Genius* (1984)

Harris, Julie [Julia Ann] (b. Grosse Pointe Park, Mich., 2 Dec. 1925) Actress who has received an unprecedented five Tony and two Emmy Awards. Her first great success, five years after her Broadway debut, was as the motherless 12-year-old tomboy Frankie Addams in CARSON MCCULLERS' *Member of the Wedding* (1950), followed by the bohemian Sally Bowles in VAN DRUTEN's *I Am a Camera* (1951). She has played classical as well as modern roles, including Joan of Arc in ANOUILH's *The Lark* (1955), Mary Todd Lincoln in *Last of Mrs Lincoln* (1973), Emily Dickinson in a one-person show, *Belle of Amherst* (1976), Charlotte Brontë in *Currier Bell Esquire* (1987) and Isak Dinesen in *Lucifer's Child* (1991). In 1994 she appeared in a 50th anniversary production at the Roundabout Theater of *The Glass Menagerie*. Known for her sound technique, she combines robustness and vulnerability. She wrote the semi-autobiographical *Julie Harris Talks to Young Actors* (1971, with Barry Tarshis). JANE HOUSE

Harris, Margaret *see* MOTLEY

Harris, Robert [Louis A.] (b. Axbridge, Somerset, 28 March 1900; d. London, 18 May 1995) Actor. Harris began his career in 1923, in J. M. BARRIE's *The Will*, and made his New York debut in NOEL COWARD's *Easy Virtue* (1925). During the 1930s and 1940s he played many major roles for the OLD VIC and the SHAKESPEARE MEMORIAL THEATRE in Stratford, including Hamlet, Mark Antony, Prospero, Richard II, Marlowe's Dr Faustus, and Marchbanks in SHAW's *Candida*. During 1963–4 Harris toured in the United States as Thomas More in *A Man for All Seasons*, and in 1966 he played Oppenheimer in KIPPHARDT's *In the Matter of J. Robert Oppenheimer*. ANDREW SOLWAY

Harris, Rosemary [Ann] (b. Ashby, Suffolk, 19 Sept. 1930) Actress, better known in the United States than in her native Britain. She made her American debut in 1952 in *The Climate of Eden*. She has been a member of many important companies, both in the UK (BRISTOL OLD VIC, OLD VIC, NATIONAL THEATRE, CHICHESTER FESTIVAL THEATRE) and in the United States (Association of Producing Artists, LINCOLN CENTER, American Shakespeare Theater, WILLIAMSTOWN THEATER FESTIVAL). Her most successful roles have exploited her special blend of sweetness and regal elegance, and have ranged widely across Shakespeare, SHAW, CHEKHOV, COWARD, PINTER and WILLIAMS. One of her most memorable performances was as Eleanor of Aquitaine in *The Lion in Winter* (1966). She has continued to divide her versatile career between Britain and the United States, appearing in theatre, film and television productions. ADRIANA HUNTER

Harris, Sam[uel] H[enry] (b. New York, 3 Feb. 1872; d. New York, 3 July 1941) Producer. A former stage hand, he moved into producing as manager of the prizefighter Terry McGovern, who appeared in BURLESQUE and melodramas. After producing with Paddy Sullivan and A. H. Woods, he formed a partnership with GEORGE M. COHAN in 1904 that was to last for 16 years and was responsible for over 50 plays, including Cohan's *Little Johnny Jones* (1904) and *Forty-five Minutes from Broadway* (1905). When the partnership dissolved, Harris went into independent management and produced a string of successes, including *The Jazz Singer* (1925), *Animal Crackers* (1928), *The Man Who Came to Dinner* (1939) and *Lady in the Dark* (1941). Three shows, *Icebound* (1923), *Of Thee I Sing* (1932) and *You Can't Take It With You* (1937), were awarded Pulitzer Prizes, and a fourth, John Steinbeck's *Of Mice and Men* won

the New York Critics' Circle Award in 1938. He was part owner and manager of the Music Box Theater, which he built with IRVING BERLIN, and managed Sam H. Harris theatres in Chicago and New York. He was one of the most prolific Broadway producers of his time, and had a record for producing successful shows unparalleled by any of his contemporaries. LAURIE WOLF

Harris, Sophie *see* MOTLEY

Harrison, Rex [Reginald Carey] (b. Huyton, Lancs, 5 March 1908; d. New York, 2 June 1990) Actor; an urbane master of high comedy. After his debut with the LIVERPOOL PLAYHOUSE (1924–7), he entered films (1929) for a long and distinguished career. Harrison's first London stage success was in *French Without Tears* (1936). Following wartime service with the RAF, he won a Tony on Broadway in *Anne of a Thousand Days* (1948) and appeared in *The Cocktail Party* (1950). His best-known role was as the speech professor Henry Higgins in *My Fair Lady* (New York, 1956; London, 1958; on film, 1964). Other successes of his apparently effortless technique include *Platonov* (1960), PIRANDELLO's *Henry IV* (New York, 1973; London, 1974), *Heartbreak House* (London and New York, 1983) and *The Circle* (New York, 1990). His autobiography, *Rex*, appeared in 1974 and *A Damned Serious Business: My Life in Comedy* posthumously in 1991. He was knighted in 1989. D. KEITH PEACOCK

Patrick Garland, *The Incomparable Rex: The Last of the High Comedians* (2000)

A. Walker, *Fatal Charm: The Life of Rex Harrison* (1993)

Harrison, Tony [William] (b. Leeds, 30 April 1937) Poet and playwright. Blending keen intelligence with an unexpectedly colloquial humour and clarity, Harrison's dramatic verse work includes a Nigerian *Lysistrata* (1965) as well as libretti for opera and collaborations with contemporary composers. He is best known for his plays and translations that have been premièred at the NATIONAL THEATRE: *The Misanthrope* (1973); *Phaedra Britannica* (1975); *The Oresteia* (1981), also performed at EPIDAUROS; *The Mysteries* (1985); his speculation on a newly-discovered fragment by Sophocles, *The Trackers of Oxyrhynchus* (1988); and *Square Rounds* (1992), on the use and abuse of science. In 1995 he staged his *The Kaisers of Carnuntum*, about Marcus Aurelius, in a Roman stadium near Vienna, and his *The Labourers of Herakles* in Delphi, in an attempt to recapture the public aspect of theatre. He has also made an impact with poems filmed for television, and he wrote and directed the feature film *Prometheus* (1999). DAN REBELLATO

Neil Astley, ed, *Essays on Tony Harrison* (1990)
Joe Kelleher, *Tony Harrison* (1996)
Marianne McDonald, *Ancient Sun, Modern Light* (1992)

Harrower, David (b. Edinburgh, 26 Sept. 1966) Playwright. His first play, *Knives in Hens* (1995), set in a late medieval village, stages the seduction of a young woman by the miller, a figure feared and despised for his ability to write. The play's tautly lyrical dialogue and its immensely confident plotting immediately marked Harrower as a major talent. His second original play, *Kill the Old Torture their Young* (1998), consists of a series of interwoven stories. Unusually, it is a play whose central character is a city, which, at the end of the century, is no longer able to contain or bring together its inhabitants, none of whom seems able to identify who they are. DAN REBELLATO

Hart, Lorenz [Milton] (b. New York, 2 May 1895; d. New York, 22 Nov. 1943) Lyricist and librettist. From his college days Hart formed a partnership with composer RICHARD RODGERS and, after a slow beginning, the pair became established in the mid-1920s as regular contributors to Broadway, providing the scores for a sequence of mostly ephemeral contemporary musical comedies including *The Girl Friend* (1926) and *A Connecticut Yankee* (1927), most of which produced at least one detachable hit song. After a spell in Hollywood, the partners returned to Broadway and, in the eight years before the dissolution of their partnership and Hart's death, turned out a flow of musical theatre scores covering most styles of established musical comedy and, occasionally, as in *On Your Toes* (1936) and their most remarkable piece, the wryly misanthropic *Pal Joey* (1940), taking less common tones. In the popular Broadway style of the time, Hart and Rodgers worked as songwriters, their scores consisting of groups of songs easily detachable from their texts and, in their case, providing regular and outstanding contributions to the standard American song repertoire. At their best, Hart's songs were unusually attractive in their ideas, with lyrics that were unostentatiously clever and complex, easy and pleasantly ingenious in their rhyming, and sufficiently general to allow them a life away from the shows in which they were introduced. KURT GÄNZL

Dorothy Hart, *Thou Swell, Thou Witty; The Life and Lyrics of Lorenz Hart* (1976)
Samuel Marx and Jan Clayton, *Rodgers and Hart: Bewitched, Bothered and Bewildered* (1976)
F. Nolan, *Lorenz Hart: A Poet on Broadway* (1994)

Hart, Moss (b. New York, 24 Oct. 1904; d. Palm Springs, 20 Dec. 1961) Playwright. Success came with his collaboration in 1930 with the arch-collaborator of the New York theatre, GEORGE S. KAUFMAN, in a spoof of Hollywood (where at that time neither of them had been) entitled *Once in a Lifetime*. He wrote eight more plays with Kaufman, including the Pulitzer Prize winner *You Can't Take it with You* (1936) and *The Man who Came to Dinner* (1939), and dramatized his own experience of psychoanalysis in the musical *Lady in the Dark* (1941), with a score by KURT WEILL. He also developed a career as a director which culminated in the production of *My Fair Lady* (1956), whose author and composer, LERNER and LOEWE, paid eloquent tribute to the contribution Hart had made to its phenomenal success. One of his most notable, and certainly one of his most enduring, contributions to the theatre is his autobiography *Act One* (1959), which ranks as one of the best and most truthful books ever written about a life in the theatre. IAN BEVAN

Hart, Roy[den] (b. Johannesburg, South Africa, 30 Oct. 1926; d. nr Frejus, France, 18 May 1975) Voice expert. He studied English and psychology in South Africa before coming to England to study at the Royal Academy of Dramatic Art. He studied with ALFRED WOLFSOHN from 1947 to 1962 and developed a vocal range of between six and eight octaves. When Wolfsohn died, Hart set up experiments in the use of an extended vocal range as a basis for a style of theatre and, with his wife Dorothy, formed the Roy Hart Theatre Company. JERZY GROTOWSKI and PETER BROOK were inspired by this work, which aimed to liberate a greater range of sound and emotion by releasing tensions in the performer. Roy and Dorothy died in a car crash, but the company continues to operate from a base in southern France. PAUL NEWHAM

See also THIRD THEATRE; VOICE.

Hart House Theater A 500-seat theatre incorporated in Hart House, University of Toronto, and built in 1919 to provide facilities for the university's undergraduates. The first director was Roy Mitchell (1919–21). A season generally offered eight or nine plays, each running for a week, including at least one Canadian play. The repertoire was ambitious, including, in the theatre's first ten years, plays by O'CASEY, SYNGE, MAETERLINCK, SHAW and YEATS. In 1966 the theatre came under the control of the university's Centre for Study of Drama, which used it to stage productions under guest directors. Since 1986 the theatre is offered on a rental basis to theatrical groups from both the university and the community. EUGENE BENSON

Hartford Stage Non-profit professional theatre in Connecticut, founded by Jacques Cartier in 1964. From

345

1980 to 1998 it flourished under Mark Lamos (b. 1946). Although the theatre did its share of contemporary plays, its most imaginative work was with the classics (e.g. SCHNITZLER, Molière, IBSEN). Lamos was trained as a classical musician and is also an actor: his romantic and lyric sensibility led to exceptional productions of Shakespeare, filled with visual splendour, music, high intelligence and present-day feeling (e.g. *Twelfth Night*, 1985; *Pericles*, 1987). His *Peer Gynt* (1989) was both lucid and breathtakingly beautiful, and his production of TIMBERLAKE WERTENBAKER's *Our Country's Good* (1990) transferred to Broadway. Michael Wilson succeeded Lamos and has re-emphasized American contemporary classics such as those by TENNESSEE WILLIAMS or AMIRI BARAKA. Hartford Stage won the 1989 Tony award for outstanding regional theatre.

M. ELIZABETH OSBORN

Harvard *see* STUDENT THEATRE; UNIVERSITY DRAMA DEPARTMENTS

Harvey, Jonathan [Paul] (b. Liverpool, 13 June 1968) Playwright. A 'gay playwright' with a mainstream following, his first big hit was *Beautiful Thing* (1993), a romantic comedy about two teenage boys falling in love on a south London working-class housing estate, turned into a film in 1996. *Babies* (1994) is a comic, semi-autobiographical story of a young gay teacher who is afraid of being 'outed' at a pupil's birthday party, whilst *Boom Bang-a-Bang* (1995) is a celebration of the kitsch Eurovision Song Contest. But his later plays are more serious: *Rupert Street Lonely Hearts Club* (1995) takes a darker view of gay relationships within a group of young Liverpudlians; *Guiding Star* (1998) deals with the Hillsborough football disaster; and *Hushabye Mountain* (1999) is concerned with drugs, AIDS and family bereavement. Harvey has been criticized for being sentimental and insufficiently political, but his talent to engage and amuse audiences is undeniable. He has also written for film and TV, including the sitcom *Gimme, Gimme, Gimme*. NEIL DOWDEN

Harwood [Horvitz], Ronald (b. Cape Town, 9 Nov. 1934) Playwright and novelist, an emigré writer in Britain (*Tramway Road*, 1984) who acted with DONALD WOLFIT (which inspired *The Dresser*, 1980) and is concerned with international human rights (*The Deliberate Death of a Polish Priest*, 1985) and loss of faith (*J. J. Farr*, 1987). He wrote the screenplay for Solzhenitsyn's *Ivan Denisovitch* (1970). Other plays include *Another Time* (1989), *Reflected Glory* (1991) and *Taking Sides* (1995). TONY HOWARD

Hasenclever, Walter [Georg Alexander] (b. Aachen, Germany, 8 July 1890; d. Aix-en-Provence, France, 22 June 1940) Playwright. He is known mainly as the author of the EXPRESSIONIST plays *Der Sohn* ('The son', 1916) and *Der Retter* ('The saviour', 1919), and also of *Antigone* (1917) and *Die Entscheidung* ('The decision', 1919). *Der Sohn* was a sensational success in many German theatres and helped to launch expressionism as a new theatrical movement. Hasenclever's plays after his expressionist phase are abstract mystical dramas in the late Strindbergian tradition. During the Nazi period he emigrated to France, where he wrote some tragi-comic social satires and two topical plays dealing with the Nazi regime in an only slightly veiled form. When the German army invaded the south of France he took a drugs overdose in internment and died in hospital in Aix the next day.

GÜNTER BERGHAUS

Hastings, Michael [Gerald] (b. London, 2 Sept. 1938) Playwright. Hastings was a truly young ANGRY YOUNG MAN when his first two plays, *Don't Destroy Me* (1956) and *Yes – And After* (1957) had their premières, the latter only the second Sunday night production without décor at the ROYAL COURT. The failure of a large-scale history play, *The World's Baby* (1964), to achieve full production drove Hastings to semi-silence for several years, from which he returned with a series of plays focusing on black politics and culture: *For the West* (1977), *Gloo Joo* (1978) and *The Emperor* (1986). His biggest successes were once again at the Royal Court, with *Tom and Viv* (1984), filmed in 1994, depicting the relationship between T. S. ELIOT and his first wife Vivienne Haigh-Wood, and his work on the adaptation of Ariel Dorfman's *Death and the Maiden* (1991). DAN REBELLATO

Hatley, Tim *see* DESIGN

Hauptmann, Elizabeth *see* BRECHT, BERTOLT

Hauptmann, Gerhart [Johann Robert] (b. Ober-Salzbrunn, Silesia, 15 Nov. 1862; d. Agnetendorf, Silesia, 8 June 1946) Playwright; the most important representative of German naturalism in the theatre. Between 1885 and 1889 he lived in Erkner, near Berlin, and was a member of the naturalist circle Durch (Through). His breakthrough in the theatre came in 1889 after he was discovered by OTTO BRAHM, the director of the Freie Bühne, a naturalist stage modelled on ANTOINE's Théâtre Libre. *Vor Sonnenaufgang* (*Before Sunrise*, 1889) was quickly followed by a string of other equally successful plays, among them *Das Friedenfest* (*The Reconciliation*, 1890), *Einsame Menschen* (*Lonely Lives*, 1981), *Die Weber* (*The Weavers*, 1893), *Der Biberpelz* (*The Beaver's Coat*, 1893), *Fuhrmann Henschel* (*Drayman Henschel*, 1898), *Der rote Hahn* (*The Con-*

flagration, 1901), *Rose Bernd* (1903) and *Die Ratten* (*The Rats*, 1911).

Hauptmann's international fame rests on the plays of his first phase. His later dramas venture into the realm of the symbolic, mysterious and fantastic, signs of which can already be detected in his earlier plays, e.g. *Hanneles Himmelfahrt* (*Hannele's Assumption*, 1893). Despite their poetic quality and their greater range of argument and depth of vision, the later works do not reach the standard of the earlier. His last plays, written in the 1930s and 1940s, were historical or neoclassical dramas. They developed out of his earlier interest in classical tragedy, but have not gained any popularity on the German stage.

Hauptmann established naturalism in the German theatre and contributed largely towards overcoming the narrow and highly untheatrical aims of ZOLA's followers in Germany. His sense of the dramatic, his interest in the deeper problems of the human existence, and his skilful handling of character and language enabled his plays to transcend the limitations of the first naturalist generation. Hauptmann used the stage to reveal the invisible and permanent values behind the surface of everyday reality and sought to unveil eternal truths beyond the world of actuality. His philosophical roots lay within the mystic Protestantism of his native Silesia. His Christian humanism already pervaded his early plays, where the lower strata of society – the starving workers and struggling peasants – were depicted as humbly bearing their fate and emerging as true conquerors of the spiritual realm, redeemed by the purifying force of their suffering.

Hauptmann saw drama in all human existence; tragedy springs not from the heroes' actions, but from life itself. Attempts to rebel against this tragic world law lead only to more suffering and bloodshed, and are doomed to futility. GÜNTER BERGHAUS

H. F. Garten, *Hauptmann* (1954)
K. G. Knight and F. Norman, eds, *The Hauptmann Centenary Lectures* (1964)
Alan Marshall, *The German Naturalists and Gerhart Hauptmann* (1982)
W. R. Maurer, *Gerhart Hauptmann* (1982)
Margaret Sinden, *Gerhard Hauptmann: The Prose Plays* (1975)

Havel, Václav   (b. Prague, 5 Oct. 1936)   Playwright who became president of his country in 1989. His plays are a highly original synthesis of the ABSURD, the conventional and the satirical, reflecting Czech reality under the communists – bureaucracy, cliches, the deformations of the individual, and the nonsensical functioning of the social and political system – while addressing important general problems of the contemporary world. In *Zahradni slavnost* (*The Garden Party* 1963), *Vyrozuměni* (*The Memorandum*, 1965) and *Ztížená možnost soustředění* (*Increased Difficulty of Concentration*, 1968) an inconsequential individual identifies with this system and strives to maintain or improve his position and status. It is no mere coincidence that he is an official or an administrator fulfilling commands. He lacks an inner dimension, as well as his own identity or past and the ability to reflect on himself or the world. The plays' formal structures create a clear image of emptiness and futile activity; the dialogue is composed of banalities and distorted in a surprising manner to complete nonsense, giving the plays their special sense of humour and absurdity.

Havel's role in the Prague Spring of 1968 and later as a founder of the human rights movement Charter 77 made him a leading spokesmen of opposition ideas and led not only to his persecution and repeated imprisonment, but also to a performance and publication ban on all his plays. With the exception of a single performance of his adaptation of Gay's *The Beggar's Opera*, staged by an amateur group in 1975, all his other plays after 1969 were performed outside Czechoslovakia.

His one-act plays, *Audience* and *Vernisáž* (*Unveiling* or *The Private View*), both first seen in Vienna in 1976, contain new aspects: human beings are no longer the mere products of a social mechanism but become its involuntary victims and begin to become aware of their situation. This shift was even more marked in the full-length play *Largo Desolato* (Vienna, 1985), whose hero is already seeking and clarifying his own identity. *Pokoušení* (*Temptation*, Vienna, 1986) also develops in a new direction, with its Faustian theme. An ambitious scholar who longs to penetrate forbidden knowledge concludes a contract with a modern Mephistopheles, a dubious character who is a police informer. *Asanace* (*Redevelopment* or *Slum Clearance*, Zurich, 1989) is a brilliant satire about the power of the system to transform itself like a chameleon and implies that the author wanted to show that humans represent a great unknown.

Havel's dramas extend beyond their domestic context and rank among the outstanding achievements of world theatre. EVA ŠORMOVÁ

John Keane, *Václav Havel* (2000)
Eda Kriseova, *Václav Havel: The Authorized Biography* (1991)
Antonin J. Liehm, *The Politics of Culture* (1970)

Havergal, Giles   *see* CITIZENS' THEATRE

Hawes, Peter (b. West Coast, New Zealand, 30 Sept. 1947) Playwright who uses a range of comic techniques to explore serious social and philosophical issues. Plays include *Alf's General Theory of Relativity* (1983), *Ptolemy's Dip* (1984), *Goldie* (1986), *Aunt Daisy: The Musical* (1989), and *1946: The Boat Train* (1991). He also translated LORCA's *The House of Bernarda Alba* (1988). SIMON GARRETT

Hawthorne, Nigel [Barnard] (b. Coventry, 5 April 1929) Actor. Educated in South Africa, where he began his professional life in 1950 before returning to Britain in 1951, he has built a reputation for stylish comedy chiefly based on his award-winning television role of Sir Humphrey in the successful series *Yes, Minister* and *Yes, Prime Minister*. Although there have been such comedy roles in the theatre – e.g. in *Privates on Parade* (1978), *Tartuffe* (1983) and *The Magistrate* (1986) – later work has confirmed him as an actor of greater versatility. *Shadowlands* (London, 1989; Broadway, 1990) won him a Tony Award, and *The Madness of George III* (ROYAL NATIONAL THEATRE, 1992; American tour, 1993; European tour, 1994) won him an Olivier Award for best actor. He successfully repeated the title role in the film (1994). In 1999 he appeared as King Lear in Japan and at the ROYAL SHAKESPEARE COMPANY in a production directed by YUKIO NINAGAWA. He was knighted in 1998. BRIAN ROBERTS

Hawthorne, Raymond (b. Hastings, New Zealand, 3 May 1936) Actor and director. A member of the New Zealand Players (1955–7), he travelled to London on a government bursary in 1957 and, after training at the Royal Academy of Dramatic Art, joined the staff as a tutor. In 1971 he joined Auckland's MERCURY THEATRE under Tony Richardson as an actor and director, before becoming director of Theatre Corporate in 1973, where he directed the première production of the highly successful *Foreskin's Lament* by Greg McGee (1980). As Mercury's artistic director, he extended his acting reputation in roles such as Oedipus Rex, and directed a number of outstanding opera productions and a variety of plays. GILLIAN GREER & LAURIE ATKINSON

Hawtrey, Charles [Henry] (b. Eton, Berks, 21 Sept. 1858; d. London, 30 July 1923) One of the last of the Edwardian actor–managers, he specialized in urbanely comic or romantic roles, and was known as the best 'stage liar' of his day. Hawtrey originated the role of Lord Goring in OSCAR WILDE's *An Ideal Husband* (1894). Notable appearances include *Lord and Lady Algy* (1898), *The Man From Blankley's* (1901) and *Jack Straw* (1908). Hawtrey passed his casual stage manner on to NOEL COWARD, who appeared with him as a boy actor in *The Great Name* (1911). Hawtrey provided information against Wilde for the 1895 Bow Street trials. He produced the Christmas children's show *Where the Rainbow Ends* (1911) for many years, and was knighted in 1922. His memoir *The Truth at Last* appeared in 1924. MICHAEL SOMMERS

Háy, Julius [Gyula] (b. Abony, Hungary, 5 May 1900; d. Ascona, Switzerland, 7 May 1975) Playwright; a major European figure. After the defeat of the Hungarian Commune in 1919 he lived in Germany where he wrote *Isten, császár, paraszt* (God, Emperor and Peasant, 1933), a historical play in the manner of SHAW's *Saint Joan* about compromise and martyrdom. Although a success, performances were stopped when Hitler came to power. Later, in Austria, Háy was imprisoned as a communist. Invited to the Soviet Union in 1935, Háy remained there until the end of the Second World War and finished his second masterpiece, *Tiszazug* (Have, 1934–6), a Hungarian peasant tragedy about the murderous consequences of greed. The BBC broadcast the play in 1969 as *To Have and to Hold*, JOAN LITTLEWOOD staged it as *The Midwife* (1954), and the ROYAL SHAKESPEARE COMPANY presented it in 1990 as *Have*. Háy returned to Hungary in 1945, became the leading social realist dramatist and wrote some of his worst plays; but he joined those Hungarian communist writers who became the first openly to defy Stalinist rule. When the 1956 revolt was crushed Háy was gaoled again, now as an anti-communist. Released in 1960, Háy left for Switzerland, where he spent the rest of his life. Most of his plays have been translated into more than ten languages and performed in more than 18 countries, but have not been staged in Hungary for some years. Among them are *A pulykapásztor* (The Turkey-Boy, 1938); *Mohács* (written in prison between 1958 and 1960); *A ló* (The Horse, 1961); *Attila éjszakája* (Attila's Night, 1962); and *A nagy inkvizitor* (The Grand Inquisitor, 1967). His memoirs, *Born 1900*, appeared in English in 1974. GÁBOR MIHÁLYI

Hayes [Brown], Helen (b. Washington DC, 10 Oct. 1900; d. Pittsburgh, 17 March 1993) Actress, who, along with KATHARINE CORNELL and LYNN FONTANNE, was often called the First Lady of the American Theatre. The modest, even coy, daughter of an actress and a travelling salesman, she first performed when she was five. Since 1909, when LEW FIELDS gave her her Broadway debut as Little Mimi in *Old Dutch*, she was continuously active in New York theatre, maturing from child star, to light romantic ingénue, to serious actress, to character comedienne; she ranged from BOOTH TARKINGTON's *Clarence* (1919) and SHAW's *Caesar and Cleopatra* (1925) to J. M. BARRIE's *What Every*

Woman Knows (1926) and GEORGE ABBOTT's *Coquette* (1927), but two of her most famous roles were as queens, in MAXWELL ANDERSON's *Mary of Scotland* (1933) and *Victoria Regina* (1935) by Laurence Housman. Her West End debut came in 1948 as Amanda in TENNESSEE WILLIAMS's *The Glass Menagerie*. After her appearance in O'NEILL's *A Touch of the Poet* in 1958, she mostly performed in revivals (e.g. GEORGE KELLY's *The Show Off*, 1967), playing abroad as well as in the United States. She toured Shakespeare recitations with MAURICE EVANS (1962–3) and formed her own company (1964) to promote similar work.

Hayes was small but had a straightforward style and a strong, low voice that commanded huge appeal. She retired from the stage in 1971, hosted a radio programme for older people and continued to act on television and in film. She was married, in 1928, to the playwright CHARLES MACARTHUR.

Two theatres in New York were named after her and in Washington, where she was born, the major theatrical awards carry her name. She wrote several autobiographies including *On Reflection* (1968) and *My Life in Three Acts* (1990, with Katherine Hatch). JANE HOUSE

D. B. Murphy and S. Moore, *Helen Hayes: A Bio-Bibliography* (1993)

Haynes, Jim   *see* ARTS LAB; TRAVERSE THEATRE

Haynes, John   *see* THEATRE PHOTOGRAPHY

Hayward, Leland   (b. Nebraska City, 2 Sept. 1902; d. Yorktown Heights, NY, 18 March 1971)   Producer. At various stages a reporter, press agent, silent movie, television and film producer, he first gained recognition as a formidable Hollywood talent agent before becoming one of the most successful producers in Broadway history. His hits include *State of the Union* (1945, winner of Pulitzer Prize), *Mister Roberts* (1948), *South Pacific* (1949, winner of Pulitzer Prize), *Call Me Madam* (1950), *Gypsy* (1959), *The Sound of Music* (1959) and *The Trial of the Catonsville Nine* (1971). While he never pandered to popular taste, nor did he break barriers with experimentation or controversy. Rather, Hayward, considered one of the most civilized men in the theatre business, proceeded according to his own artistic instincts. He was one of the last of the breed to act as sole producer for a Broadway production, and in that capacity he took a strong leadership role in artistic matters. He was married to the actress Margaret Sullavan from 1936 to 1948. DAVID A. WILLIAMS

S. Berman, *The Crossing – Adamo to Catonsville: Leland Hayward's Producing Career* (1995)
B. Hayward, *Haywire* (1977)

Heathcote, Dorothy   *see* THEATRE FOR YOUNG PEOPLE

Hebrew theatre   *see* ISRAEL

Hecht, Ben   (b. New York, 28 Feb. 1894; d. New York, 18 April 1964)   Playwright, screenwriter, author and film producer. With his frequent collaborator CHARLES MACARTHUR, the failed acrobat and former journalist Hecht wrote *The Front Page* (1928, first filmed 1931), a frenzied send-up of the newspaper world, and *The Twentieth Century* (1932), a farcical satire on BROADWAY. Hecht spent most of his career in Hollywood, but intermittently wrote for the theatre until 1953, either on his own (e.g. the Zionist *A Flag is Born*, 1946, with music by KURT WEILL) or with others (e.g. *The Great Magoo*, 1932, with Gene Fowler). He wrote a raucous autobiography, *Child of the Century*, published in 1953. THOMAS F. CONNOLLY

W. MacAdams, *Ben Hecht: The Man Behind the Legend* (1990)

Hedgerow Theater   Founded in Moylan, Pennsylvania, near Philadelphia, in 1923 by Jasper Deeter (1893–1972), the group used a converted mill to present a variety of plays in true repertory style. Before this policy was abandoned in 1956, some 200 works were offered, ranging from modern masterpieces by CHEKHOV, SHAW and O'NEILL to premières of new works such as *The Cherokee Night* (1932) by Lynn Riggs and *In the Summer House* (1951) by Jane Bowles. After the mill was damaged by fire, plays were presented for short runs in a newly built auditorium. The company has long operated a school teaching all aspects of theatre.   GERALD BORDMAN

Hedley, Philip   *see* THEATRE ROYAL, STRATFORD EAST

Heggie, Iain   (b. Glasgow, Scotland, 23 April 1953) Playwright. Having had various occupations, including PT instructor and drama teacher, he began writing in 1984 and within three years had won the coveted Mobil Playwriting Award for *A Wholly Healthy Glasgow* (1987). This dark and scabrous play, set in a seedy health club and characterized by Heggie's precise and stylized Glaswegian dialogue, was the only new British play to be presented at the official 1987 EDINBURGH FESTIVAL. His characters are often ill-matched and all too recognizable seekers after sex, romance and affection. When writing *An Experienced Woman Gives Advice* (1995) he is quoted as saying that his real and only constant theme is love. He teaches acting at the Royal Scottish Academy of Music and Drama, where he created a unique improvisation method used to develop his ideas. Other plays include *Politics in the Park* (1985),

American Bagpipes (1988), *Clyde Nouveau* (1989) and *Sex Comedies* (1992). JOHN TIFFANY

Heijermans, Herman (pseud. Samuel Falkland)
(b. Rotterdam, 3 Dec. 1864; d. Zandvoort, Netherlands, 22 Nov. 1924) Novelist, journalist, playwright and director. A social realist in the manner of IBSEN and HAUPTMANN, Heijermans wrote several hundred short stories and novels in addition to his nearly 50 plays. Several of these plays, most notably *Op Hoop van Zegen* (*The Good Hope*, 1900), dealing with the exploitation of Dutch fishermen, gained a major international reputation. His early one-act play, *Ahasverus* (1893), was presented by the Théâtre Libre in Paris, and *Ghetto* (1898), set in Amsterdam's Jewish community, was produced in London and New York. MARVIN CARLSON

Seymour Flaxman, *Herman Heijermans and his Dramas* (1954)

Held, Anna *see* ZIEGFELD, FLORENZ

Hellman, Lillian [Florence] (b. New Orleans, 20 June 1906; d. Martha's Vineyard, Mass., 30 June 1984) Writer. Her 12 plays are notable for their expert dramatic craft, controversial themes, and strong sense of social justice and social responsibility. All but a handful were successful. In *Children's Hour* (1934), a community casts out two women whom a malicious child has accused of lesbianism. In *Little Foxes* (1939), *Another Part of the Forest* (1946) and *The Autumn Garden* (1951), the greed of Southern capitalists in the post-Civil War period is seen to be the cause of destruction of the old South. Other work includes *Watch on the Rhine* (1941), an anti-fascist war play, the libretto for *Candide* (1956), *Toys in the Attic* (1960) and several film scripts. 'Blacklisted' during the McCarthy period, she is also known for her memoirs. JANE HOUSE

Peter Feibleman, *Lilly: Reminiscences of Lillian Hellman* (1988)
Richard Moody, *Lillian Hellman: Playwright* (1972)
William Wright, *Lillian Hellman: The Image, the Woman* (1986)

Helpmann, Robert [Murray] (b. Mount Gambier, Australia, 9 April 1909; d. Sydney, 28 Sept. 1986) Ballet dancer, choreographer, actor and director. After beginning his career in Australia, in ballet and musicals, Helpmann made his London debut in 1933 and was a leading dancer with SADLER'S WELLS until 1950. His first major acting role was Oberon in *A Midsummer Night's Dream* at the OLD VIC (1937) and he subsequently appeared as Hamlet (1944) and in many other roles by Shakespeare and SHAW at the Old Vic, STRATFORD-UPON-AVON and elsewhere. He choreo-graphed works for the Royal Ballet and the Royal Opera and directed many major productions of classic and contemporary drama, musical comedy and opera. Knighted in 1968, he was director of the Adelaide Festival of Arts in 1970. MARVIN CARLSON

See also CHOREOGRAPHY; DANCE; MOVEMENT, DANCE AND DRAMA.

Elizabeth Salter, *Helpmann: The Authorised Biography* (1978)

Henare, George [Winiata] (b. Te Araroa, New Zealand, 11 Sept. 1945) Actor. After formal singing tuition at the College of Education, he toured New Zealand and Australia in *Porgy and Bess* (1965), remaining with the New Zealand Opera Company until 1981 as a soloist and member of the chorus. He worked in radio and television, and at DOWNSTAGE in numerous roles until he moved to the MERCURY THEATRE (Auckland) as lead actor in 1971. He toured internationally with the Maori Theatre Trust, and in commercial productions such as *The Pirates of Penzance*, as well as in the MAORI plays *Purapurawhetu* (1999) and *Hururu Mai* (2000) in his search for a unique form of New Zealand theatre.
GILLIAN GREER & LAURIE ATKINSON

Henderson, Ray *see* DESYLVA, BROWN AND HENDER-SON

Heneker, David [William] (b. Southsea, Portsmouth, 31 March 1906; d. Llechryd, nr Cardigan, Wales, 20 Jan. 2001) Songwriter. After some success as songwriter while a brigadier in the regular army, Heneker resigned his commission and became a club pianist to concentrate on writing. He provided material for several REVUES before combining with librettist WOLF MANKOWITZ, Monty Norman and Julian More on the music and lyrics for *Expresso Bongo* (1958), the best of the British wave of 'realistic' musicals of the 1950s. The songwriting team won a wider success with their English version of the Paris hit *Irma la Douce* (1958), and a third successive hit with *Make Me an Offer* (1959), before Heneker went solo on a commission to turn H. G. Wells' *Kipps* into a stage musical for rock star Tommy Steele. As *Half a Sixpence* (1963), the show gave Heneker his greatest success and put the phrase 'Flash, Bang, Wallop' into the world's dictionaries. His 1965 show *Charlie Girl* was a long-running West End hit, but the five musicals staged over the next 20 years failed to find the success of his early work in a theatrical world where his combination of unambitious musical elegance and precise lyrical charm were no longer favoured. KURT GÄNZL

Henley, Beth [Elizabeth Becker] (b. Jackson, Miss., 8 May 1952) Playwright and screenwriter. The vividness and tragicomic tone of her writing have led to comparisons with another Southern writer, Flannery O'Connor. Her eccentric characters are seen in bizarre situations, usually in Mississippi. *Crimes of the Heart* (1980) won a Pulitzer Prize. Other plays include *The Wake of Jamey Foster* (1982), *Am I Blue?* (1982), *The Miss Firecracker Contest* (1984), *The Debutante Ball* (1985), *The Lucky Spot* (1986), *Abundance* (1990), *Control Freaks* (1992) and *Signature* (1995). JANE HOUSE

Henry, Martha (b. Detroit, Mich., 17 Feb. 1938) Actress and director. After appearing in SUMMER STOCK in Ontario and at Toronto's CREST THEATER (1959–60), she attended the National Theatre School in Montreal and subsequently established herself as one of Canada's most versatile actresses. A long association with the STRATFORD FESTIVAL (where some of her best work was done with ROBIN PHILLIPS in the late 1970s) has been supplemented by appearances at most major Canadian theatres. In addition to Shakespearean and other classical roles, Henry has excelled in contemporary plays, most notably those of JOHN MURRELL. She has appeared on British and Canadian television and in films, and in 1988 became artistic director of Theater London in London, Ontario. L. W. CONOLLY

Henshaw, James [Ene] (b. Calabar, Nigeria, 29 Aug. 1924) Playwright who pre-dates WOLE SOYINKA and BEKEDEMERO-CLARK in the writing of plays for secondary school and amateur theatre groups. He began to write in the 1950s and has published over 20 plays, including *The Jewels of the Shrine* (1957) and *Magic in the Blood* (1964), where the dictates of today's humanism and liberalism contend with ancient African beliefs and rites. KOLE OMOTOSO

Henson, Leslie [Lincoln] (b. London, 3 Aug. 1891; d. Harrow Weald, 2 Dec. 1957) Actor and manager who made his West End debut in *Nicely, Thanks* (1912). Other shows include *Yes, Uncle* (1917), *Funny Face* (1928) and *And So To Bed* (1950). He began theatrical production (in association with TOM WALLS) with Evans and Valentine's *Tons of Money* (1922). During the Second World War he helped found the ENTERTAINMENTS NATIONAL SERVICE ASSOCIATION (ENSA) with BASIL DEAN and toured, entertaining the troops (1943–5). He was noted for his charity work. He published two autobiographies, *My Laugh Story* (1926) and *Yours Faithfully* (1948). His son Nicky (b. 12 May 1945) became a well-known actor. REXTON S. BUNNETT

Henwood, Ray (b. Swansea, Wales, 15 Jan. 1937) Actor. Originally a scientist, he has worked in New Zealand mainly in Wellington at DOWNSTAGE and CIRCA, which he co-founded in 1974. His successful appearance there in the première production of ROGER HALL's comedy *Glide Time* (1976) and the subsequent long-running television series established him as one of New Zealand's most popular actors, with a wide range of roles from Iago to Dylan Thomas – the latter in his own *Nogood Boyo* (1980), a solo performance which he has toured successfully. GILLIAN GREER & LAURIE ATKINSON

Henze, Hans Werner see BOND, EDWARD; OPERA

Hepburn, Katharine [Houghton] (b. Hartford, Conn., 12 May 1907) Actress. She made her BROADWAY debut in 1928 and went on to play many starring roles, e.g. in *The Philadelphia Story*, written for her by PHILIP BARRY (1939), *The Millionairess* (1952) and *The West Side Waltz* (1981). She first appeared in Shakespeare as Rosalind (1950), and later toured with the OLD VIC Company (1955) as Portia, Katherine and Isabella, adding Beatrice (1958), Viola and Cleopatra (1960) at Stratford, Connecticut. Her illustrious film career included several Academy Awards (e.g. for *Morning Glory*, 1933; *Guess Who's Coming to Dinner*, 1967; *On Golden Pond*, 1982). On stage and on screen she portrayed women of independence, precursors of the 'liberated' woman, whose professional success reflected and resulted from their personal strength and intelligence. She wrote *Me: Stories of My Life* (1991).
DAVID STAINES

A. Edwards, *A Remarkable Woman* (1985)
B. Learning, *Katharine Hepburn* (1995)

Herbert, Jocelyn (b. London, 22 Feb. 1917) Designer. Herbert joined GEORGE DEVINE's ENGLISH SHAKESPEARE COMPANY at the ROYAL COURT in 1957 to design Devine's production of IONESCO's *The Chairs*, beginning her long-working relationships with TONY RICHARDSON, JOHN DEXTER, WILLIAM GASKILL and LINDSAY ANDERSON. Believing design to be at the service of the text, she cleansed the stage of unnecessary detail: in WESKER's *The Kitchen* (1959) the back wall and lighting rig were revealed as part of her set, while *Richard III* (Stratford-upon-Avon, 1961) pioneered the use of metal. Her fragmented elements and projections provided poetic indications rather than naturalistic settings for the first productions of works by Wesker, ARDEN and OSBORNE in the 1950s and 1960s, and in the 1970s her evocative designs were the perfect counterbalance for DAVID STOREY's plays. Herbert's precision and restraint made her the natural collaborator for SAMUEL BECKETT, with whom she worked from 1958. *The Oresteia* (NATIONAL THEATRE, 1981) and BIRTWISTLE's *The Mask of Orpheus* (English National

Opera, 1986) enabled her to extend her work with masks. The daughter of playwright A. P. Herbert, she was the defining visual influence of the ESC and one of the leading designers of her day. CATHY COURTNEY

C. Courtney, ed., *Jocelyn Herbert: A Theatre Workbook* (1993)

Herbert, John *see* EROTICISM IN THE THEATRE; OPEN SPACE

Herbert, Victor [August] (b. Dublin, 1 Feb. 1859; d. New York, 24 May 1924) Composer. He arrived in America in 1886 and worked as a cellist and conductor before his first stage work was produced in 1894. In 1895 his BURLESQUE operetta *The Wizard of the Nile* won him a first success. In the following 30 years he produced a steady stream of BROADWAY scores – often two or three a year – for pieces as widely disparate as: the comic opera style of *The Serenade* (1897), *The Fortune Teller* (1898), *Mlle Modiste* (1905), *Naughty Marietta* (1910) and *Sweethearts* (1913), featuring opera and operetta singers; vehicles for low comedy stars (*The Red Mill*, 1906); and even juvenile music theatre (*Babes in Toyland*, 1903) and a grand opera (*Natoma*, 1911). Herbert became the acknowledged leader among American show composers in an era where the English, Viennese and French traditions in turn led the way. He was also a founder of the American Society of Composers, Authors and Publishers. His work gained little recognition outside America until the 1935 film version of *Naughty Marietta* won international success. KURT GÄNZL

E. N. Waters, *Victor Herbert: A Life in Music* (1955)
J. Kaye, *Victor Herbert* (1931)

Herlie, Eileen (b. Glasgow, 8 March 1920) Actress. She worked and toured in repertory during the 1940s, playing in both classical and modern roles, such as Regina in *The Little Foxes* (1944), the Queen in *The Eagle has Two Heads* (1946) and Andromache in *The Trojan Women* (1945). She made her Broadway debut as Mrs Molloy in *The Matchmaker* (1955), and, after marrying an American, spent a great deal of her career working in the United States and Canada, in television and film as well as theatre. MAGGIE GALE

Herman, Jerry [Gerald] (b. New York, 10 July 1932) Composer and lyricist. Although his mother taught piano and music, he had no formal musical training. At college he majored in drama. At the same time he wrote his first REVUE, which was later presented OFF-BROADWAY. Additional Off-Broadway revues preceded his initial Broadway success, *Milk and Honey* (1961). Subsequent successes have been *Hello,*

Dolly! (1964), *Mame* (1966) and *La Cage aux Folles* (1983). He composes good, traditional, if slightly old-fashioned show music. His skill as a lyricist may be underestimated. GERALD BORDMAN

Herrmann, Karl-Ernst (b. Neukirch, Germany, 12 Aug. 1936) Designer. Trained as a hand-weaver, he studied set design in Berlin and then worked in several German theatres during the 1960s. He met PETER STEIN in Bremen and went with him as a core member to the SCHAUBÜHNE in Berlin, where he designed the defining productions of this outstanding company, ranging from Shakespeare, IBSEN, GORKY and CHEKHOV to GENET, KROETZ and STRAUSS. He was noted for transforming the theatre environment and for meticulously realized conceptions. He has also worked with other eminent German directors: CLAUS PEYMANN, Klaus Michael Grüber, Frank-Patrick Steckel, Niels-Peter Rudolph, LUC BONDY and Christoph Nel. Since 1982 he has also directed and designed operas in Brussels and elsewhere, sometimes together with his wife, Ursel. DANIEL MEYER-DINKGRÄFE

Hersey, David (b. Rochester, NY, 30 Nov. 1939) LIGHTING designer. He began as an actor, and then a stage manager and lighting designer in the United States, before coming to Britain in 1968 to join Theatre Projects. He became head of lighting at the NATIONAL THEATRE in 1974 and has designed for most of the leading companies in dance, ballet and opera as well as theatre, and has won many awards. Among his notable credits are *Evita* (1979), *Nicholas Nickleby* (1981), *Guys and Dolls* (1982), *Cats* (1983), *Les Misérables* (1985) and *Starlight Express* (1985). He is known for creating huge banks of computer-controlled light and spectacular effects. CHARLES LONDON

Hewett, Dorothy [Coade] (b. Perth, Australia, 21 May 1923) Playwright, poet and novelist. In almost all her writings Hewett pays homage to the Romantics, Shakespeare and bawdy Jonson, BRECHT, the SYMBOLISTS and EXPRESSIONISTS, and popular theatre. Closer to home, she values and emulates PATRICK WHITE's eclecticism in her creation of unruly psychic landscapes. It is the work of a sort of comrade-seer, a 'wildcard' who, after the Second World War, survived an attempted suicide, early academic failure, marriage, childbirth, divorce, a university teaching career and the Communist Party. Since her first play, the social realist *This Old Man Comes Rolling Home* (1966), she has moved steadfastly through 'ritual poetry', to deal publicly with her private subject matter: disappointment, double-edged sexuality, mortality and the forthright quest for love without surrender. Her characters provide a store of roles which represent a unique gift to a theatre not long liberated from the '6M, 1F' and 'something with a cow in it' format.

Her most successful musical play, *The Man from Mukinupin* (1979), shows Hewett, Prospero-like, attempting a reconciliation of conflicting histories and mythologies in a fantasy which brings a European past and presence into personal and planetary alignment with indigeneity. In her 12 plays she has also written works for young people stressing the need for tolerance and conservation.

Other plays include *The Chapel Perilous* (1971), *Bon-Bons and Roses for Dolly* (1972), *The Tatty Hollow Story* (1976), *The Golden Oldies* (1977), *Pandora's Cross* (1978) and *Song of Seals* (1983). Her autobiography, *Wildcard*, was published in 1990. GUS WORBY

B. Bennett, *Dorothy Hewett: Selected Critical Essays* (1998)
H. Gilbert, *Sightlines: Race, Gender and Nation in Contemporary Australian Theatre* (1998)
M. Williams, *Dorothy Hewett: The Feminine as Subversive* (1992)

Heyward, Dorothy   *see* HEYWARD, DUBOSE

Heyward, DuBose [Edwin]   (b. Charleston, SC, 31 Aug. 1885; d. Tryon, NC, 16 June 1940) and **Dorothy [Hartzell Kuhns]** (b. Worcester, Ohio, 6 June 1890; d. New York, 19 Nov. 1961)   Playwrights. The Heywards hold a special place for opening up possibilities for black people in theatre through their dramatization of two of DuBose's novels about the experiences and aspirations of American blacks: *Porgy* (1927), a Pulitzer Prize winner and the inspiration for the musical *Porgy and Bess* (1935) for which DuBose wrote the book and lyrics; and *Mamba's Daughters* (1939). DuBose, a poet as well as a novelist and playwright, wrote one other (unsuccessful) play, and Dorothy saw five of hers staged. ADRIANA HUNTER

Frank Durham, *DuBose Heyward, The Man who Wrote 'Porgy'* (1954)
W. Shavick, *DuBose Heyward* (1981)

Hibberd, Jack [John Charles]   (b. Warracknabal, Victoria, Australia, 12 April 1940)   Playwright. His affinities with popular forms have conditioned all of his writing for the theatre. His best-known play, the monodrama *A Stretch of the Imagination* (1972), quickly achieved classic status, and stands as an Antipodean version of BECKETT's *Krapp's Last Tape*, with its central figure re-enacting memories, fantasies, encounters and conversations from his past and going on with the banal and necessary rituals of his present. He is at once one of the most theatrical and literary of Australian playwrights, with his fondness for the physical reality of theatre and for the colour and evocative power of language. In a sad comment on Australian drama, in the 1980s Hibberd announced he was leaving the theatre to return to medical practice; nevertheless, he continued to write plays (though most are unperformed) and remains a regular and provocative commentator on the Australian theatre. Plays include *White with Wire Wheels* (1967), *Dimboola* (1969), *The Les Darcy Show* (1974), *A Toast to Melba* (1976), *Sin* (1978), *A Man of Many Parts* (1980), *Odyssey of a Prostitute* (1984) and *Slam Dunk* (1995). MICHAEL MORLEY

Hicks, [Edward] Seymour   (b. Jersey, 30 Jan. 1871; d. Fleet, Hants, 6 April 1949)   Actor, playwright and manager. His stage career began in 1887 and he was popular on both sides of the Atlantic. He wrote and appeared in *Under the Clock* (1895), one of London's first REVUES, and was at home in MUSIC HALL, musical comedy and straight drama. Married to Ellaline Terriss, with whom he shared an extensive theatre and film career, Hicks wrote many plays, such as *A Runaway Girl* (1898); a Christmas classic, *Bluebell in Fairyland* (1901); *The Gay Gordons* (1907); and *Sleeping Partners* (1917). He managed several London theatres, including the ALDWYCH (1905) and the Globe (1907), which he built and opened with plays of his own. His reminiscences include his autobiography *Twenty-Four Years of an Actor's Life* (1910) and *Me and My Missus* (1939). Knighted in 1935, he received the Order of Chevalier of the Legion of Honour from the French government in 1931 in recognition of his services to French drama, both on the English stage and in entertaining troops in France in the First World War. REXTON S. BUNNETT

Hijikata, Tatsumi   (b. Akita, Japan, 1928; d. Tokyo, 21 Jan. 1986)   Dancer and choreographer. He trained in Japan with Kazuko Matsumura. He opened his career in 1959 and in 1960 termed his work *Ankoku Buyo* ('Dance of Darkness'), later *Ankoku Butoh*. It is for the foundation of *Butoh* that he is famous, along with his collaborator Kazuo Ono. His work dealt with death, darkness and sex. It portrays the body, theatrically, as fundamentally chaotic and broken. He is noted for *Butoh Genet* (1967); with Ono, *Admiring La Argentina* (1977); with Yoko Ashikawa, *G Senjo No Okugata* (1976). His work became more widely seen in the West in the early 1980s, shortly before his death.
MICHAEL HUXLEY
See also CHOREOGRAPHY; DANCE.

N. Masson-Sekine, ed., *Butoh: Shades of Darkness* (1988)

Hikmet [Ran], Nazim (b. Salonika, Ottoman Empire [now Thessaloniki, Greece], 1902; d. Moscow, 2 June 1963) Playwright. After 13 years' imprisonment for membership of Turkey's banned Communist Party, Hikmet escaped to the Soviet Union and became one of the most successful playwrights in the socialist countries. His most noted play is *Byl li Ivan Ivanovich?* (*Did Ivan Ivanovich Exist?*, Moscow, 1956).
ADRIANA HUNTER

S. Goksu and E. Timms, *Romantic Communist: The Life and Work of Nazim Hikmet* (1999)

Hill, Benny *see* CLOWN

Hill, Errol [Gaston] (b. Port of Spain, Trinidad, 5 Aug. 1921) Playwright, producer, actor, author, director, lecturer, archivist, theorist and commentator; perhaps the most important of all the West Indian theatre pioneers. Certainly his contribution has been the most wide-ranging. In 1946 Hill co-founded with actor–playwright ERROL JOHN the Whitehall Players, a theatre company which was to have a profound influence on the development of West Indian theatre. In 1947 the company staged the first original works by its founders, Hill's *Brittle and the City Fathers* and John's *How Then Tomorrow*. Like most playwrights of his time, Hill initially wrote in standard English. His first play to be written in the vernacular, *The Ping Pong* (1953), on the steel band, became so popular that it is still frequently staged. He wrote several more short plays, such as *Strictly Matrimony* (1960). His major work, the calypso verse-musical *Man Better Man*, was first staged in 1960 at the Yale School of Drama, where Hill was studying, and represented Trinidad and Tobago at the Commonwealth Arts Festival in Britain in 1965. It was produced by the NEGRO ENSEMBLE COMPANY in New York in 1969.

As drama tutor at the Extra-Mural Department of the University (College) of the West Indies (UWI) in Jamaica from 1953 to 1958, Hill travelled the region, actively encouraging the development of theatre through workshops, the establishment of theatre companies, productions, COLLECTIVE creation, and the collection and publication of plays. In 1962 Hill moved back to Trinidad. Working with the CARNIVAL Dimanche Gras shows, he developed his theory of a theatre based on the folk festivals of the region, which he published in *The Trinidad Carnival: Mandate for a National Theatre* (1972). His *Dance Bongo* and *Man Better Man* illustrate the potential of his thesis, which is opposed by the St Lucian writer DEREK WALCOTT.

After secondment to Nigeria's University of Ibadan in 1965, Hill emigrated to America, where he taught at Richmond College, Staten Island, and then at Dartmouth College. He retired from Dartmouth in 1989 as Willard Professor of Drama and Oratory, Emeritus. He has edited several collections of plays, and his many articles and books on African American and Caribbean theatre include *Shakespeare in Sable* (1985) and *The Jamaican Stage, 1655–1900* (1992). JUDY S. J. STONE

Hill, Ken *see* THEATRE ROYAL, STRATFORD EAST

Hiller, Wendy (b. Bramhall, Cheshire, 15 Aug. 1912) Actress. A student at the MANCHESTER Repertory Theatre, where she made her acting debut in 1930, she first appeared in the West End as Sally Hardcastle in *Love on the Dole* (1935), making her Broadway debut in the same role the following year. At various times appearing with the BRISTOL OLD VIC, the BIRMINGHAM REPERTORY company and the NATIONAL THEATRE, she is equally at home in comedy and tragedy, Shakespeare and SHAW, O'CASEY and O'NEILL. Her principal stage roles include Catherine Sloper in *The Heiress* (1949), Evelyn Daly in *Waters of the Moon* (1951) and the title role in *Driving Miss Daisy* (1988). She was created a dame in 1975. DAVID STAINES

Hindemith, Paul *see* BRECHT, BERTOLT

Hirsch, John (b. Siofok, Hungary, 1 May 1930; d. Toronto, 1 Aug. 1989) Director. The only member of his family to survive the Holocaust, he immigrated to Canada in 1947. With Tom Hendry he founded Manitoba's Theater 77, which merged with Winnipeg's Little Theater in 1958 to form the Manitoba Theater Center, one of Canada's most influential regional theatres, with Hirsch as its artistic director (1958–66). In 1967 he was appointed associate director of Canada's STRATFORD FESTIVAL and in the same year he made his debut as director at New York's LINCOLN CENTER FOR THE PERFORMING ARTS. His production of *The Seagull* (1970) opened HABIMAH's new theatre in Israel, though he directed mainly in the United States between 1970 and 1974 before becoming head of Canadian Broadcasting Corporation Drama for English-language television (1974–7). In 1981 he returned to Stratford as artistic director (1981–5); while he delighted in melodramatic effects he could also convey the subtleties of a text, as his memorable 1976 *Three Sisters* revealed. EUGENE BENSON

Hirsch, Judd (b. New York, 15 March 1935) Actor. His first appearance on Broadway, in 1966, was in the hit NEIL SIMON comedy *Barefoot in the Park*. He followed this with a season in experimental theatre in Philadelphia, returning to New York to appear in several OFF-BROADWAY shows, including *Mystery Play* (1973). For the CIRCLE REPERTORY COMPANY he appeared to critical acclaim in a long run of LANFORD WILSON's *The Hot l Baltimore* (1973), JULES FEIFFER's *Knock, Knock* and Simon's *Chapter Two* (1977), which ran both in California and on Broadway. He appeared in the highly popular TV series *Taxi*, and returned to the Circle in a role written specially for him by Wilson in *Talley's Folly* (1979). He fulfiled a personal ambition by playing Trigorin in *The Seagull* (1983, also at the Circle) and won Tony Awards for HERB GARDNER's *I'm Not Rappaport* (1985) and *Conversations with My Father* (1991).

HELEN RAPPAPORT

Hirschfield, Al[bert] (b. St Louis, Mo., 21 June 1903) Universally recognized as the leading American theatrical caricaturist of his day, he began his artistic career by studying fine arts, hoping to become a sculptor. By the age of 18 he had moved into the film world and become art director for Selznick Pictures. He developed his distinctive drawing style, marked by long, fluid penstrokes, with the aid of a friend, Miguel Covarrubias. In 1927 Hirschfield became Moscow theatre correspondent for the *New York Herald Tribune*; from 1929 he worked almost exclusively for the *New York Times*, specializing in drawings of current BROADWAY shows, personalities and events. Following the birth of his daughter Nina in 1945, he began concealing her name in almost all of his drawings. His works are included in collections in the Metropolitan Museum of Art, the Museum of Modern Art and the Whitney Museum. He has written several books, including *Hirschfield: Art and Recollections from Eight Decades* (1991). A documentary about his life, *The Line King: Al Hirschfield*, was released in 1996.   LAURIE WOLF

Hispanic theatre in the United States Hispanic theatre in the United States, which dates back to the sixteenth century, is as diverse as the people it portrays. The word 'Hispanic' itself has diverse meanings which reflect a hetereogeneity that the word obscures. In New Mexico, 'Hispanic' refers only to the descendants of the Spaniards who settled there in the sixteenth century. In the East, 'Hispanic' is the generic term for people with Spanish surnames, although some consider it to be an elitist term, so that many with Spanish surnames prefer 'Latino' as a generic term of identification. The terms 'Chicano' and 'Mexican American' also evoke different connotations. 'Chicano' has been in common usage in California and the Southwest for generations; some believe it derives from the word *mexicano*. It frequently connotes political activism among Mexican Americans.

Most Hispanics living in the United States cannot trace their ancestors directly to Spain, but are rather descendants of different cultures, be they mestizo (Spanish and Indian), mulatto (African and Spanish), or a combination of Spanish, Indian and African. Other Hispanics have Chinese, Lebanese, English and European heritages; but their cultural identity remains Latino/Hispanic.

Though Hispanic theatre in the United States represents all of these diverse cultures, the majority of its artists are of Mexican, Puerto Rican, Cuban and, more recently, Central American backgrounds. The principal centres of Hispanic theatre activity are California, the Southwest, New York and Miami.

The Mexican presence in the United States is the longest and most complex of all the Hispanic groups, dating back to pre-Columbian times. 'We did not, in fact, come to the United States at all,' says Luis Valdez, founder of El TEATRO CAMPESINO in California: 'The United States came to us.' Puerto Rican and Cuban migration to the United States began in the latter part of the nineteenth century, when increasing Spanish political oppression forced people to flee northward to open businesses and organize independence movements. Puerto Rican merchants and political exiles went to Philadelphia and New York. Cubans migrated to Florida, settling in Key West and Tampa. The Cuban population of the United States swelled after the Castro revolution of 1959 and concentrated in Miami. Puerto Rican migration to the United States expanded after the Second World War, when large groups of working-class people poured into New York City. Immigrants from Central and South America, more scattered throughout the United States than other Hispanic groups and covering a broader economic range, migrated primarily for economic reasons until the 1980s, when political turmoil sparked new and considerable waves of migration. At least 1.6 million immigrants from El Salvador alone are said to be living in the United States, and most of them have arrived since 1980.

According to 1999 census data, Hispanics constitute 11.6 per cent of the total US population and are the United States' fastest-growing minority group. Now, with Hispanic residents in every state, the country has the fifth largest Hispanic population in the world, after Mexico, Spain, Argentina and Colombia. Over the last decade of the century, the US Hispanic population increased by almost 10 million, from 22,372,000 in 1990 to 31,767,000 at 1 November 1999. They include 31.8 million Mexican Americans, Cubans, Puerto Ricans, Dominicans, Central and South Americans in the 50 states and 3.9 million Puerto Ricans living in Puerto Rico. Mexican Americans make up 61 per cent of the US mainland Hispanic population; Puerto Ricans

11 per cent; and Cubans 5 per cent. The remaining 25 per cent are from other Latin American and Caribbean countries. According to the US Census Bureau, Hispanics are expected to overtake blacks as the country's largest minority group by 2005, and to account for 25 per cent of the population by 2050.

Hispanic theatre has a long and varied tradition in the United States. The first play in Spanish staged in what is now the United States, *Los moros y los cristianos*, was produced in 1598 by Spanish colonizers in Nuevo Mexico. By the 1860s professional Mexican theatre troupes that had toured the northern Mexican provinces before they were ceded to the United States had become resident companies in Los Angeles and San Francisco. They presented Spanish melodramas and *zarzuelas* (operettas) and an occasional Mexican or Cuban play. Theatre was also used for political ends, written to raise funds for people who, from the perspective of the community, were wrongly accused of crimes. By the beginning of the twentieth century touring circuits for Mexican companies and artists had been established all along the Mexican border in Texas, New Mexico and Arizona, and along the California coast from San Diego to San Francisco. The influx of Mexicans after the Mexican Revolution of 1910 brought even more artists to the United States and created a greater demand for Spanish-language theatre, which reached its high point in the 1920s.

In Los Angeles and San Antonio, the largest centres of Hispanic theatre in the West, more than 20 theatres presented Spanish melodramas, *zarzuelas*, local plays and *tandas de revista*. Even Chicago, with recent migrants from the Southwest and Mexico, contained at least five community theatre groups. Another genre of Mexican theatrical tradition that toured small border towns and rural areas in the Southwest from the turn of the century to the 1920s was the *carpa* (tent) theatre. *Carpa* troups were composed largely of families or extended families. Rooted in circus and clowning techniques, *carpa teatros* were known for their biting humour, social and political satire, and music. The central figure in this shows was the *pelado*, which means 'naked' in Spanish, a Mexican everyman who is both irreverent and sympathetic – the prototype for the Cantinflas character and similar to Charlie Chaplin's Little Tramp. In the 1920s *tandas de variedad* (variety shows), a form of popular theatre that openly used Anglo vaudevillian techniques and styles, incorporated aspects of both cultures and, as such, appealed to a younger generation. Together the *carpas* and *tandas de variedad* created an alternative vaudeville circuit in the United States that lasted until the 1950s, three decades longer than Anglo-American VAUDE-VILLE. The style and content of these genres formed the basis for the contemporary Chicano theatre that emerged in the mid-1960s.

New York and Tampa were the eastern centres of the Hispanic theatre boom of the 1920s. Spanish-language theatre had been introduced in both cities by touring companies from Spain and Cuba at the turn of the century. Mexican and Argentine troupes also visited New York. The first professional resident theatre company in New York, La Compañía de Teatro Español (founded in 1921) catered to middle-class Spaniards and Cubans who made up over 50 per cent of New York's Hispanic population at that time. The Depression years, the Spanish Civil War and the Second World War took their toll on Hispanic theatre throughout the country. Legitimate theatre reappeared among the Hispanic communities in New York and Chicago in the mid-1950s. In 1954 a young Puerto Rican director Roberto Rodríguez produced a new Puerto Rican play, *La carreta* ('The oxcart') by the then-unknown René Marques. The play was a success and, as a result, Rodríguez and Miriam Colón, one of the actresses and an important figure in US Hispanic theatre, founded the first Hispanic theatre group in New York with its own theatre, El Círculo Dramático.

The Hispanic community of the Chicago area lost its small community theatres, along with half of its population, with the mass deportation of Mexicans and Mexican Americans during the Depression. Theatre activity was revived in the 1950s when Puerto Ricans who had migrated to the Midwest in the 1940s began to express themselves theatrically, usually through church groups and mutual aid societies, as Mexicans had done before them. The Depression years and the deportation of Mexicans did not wipe out the *tandas de variedad*, which had strong popular support on the West Coast and in the Southwest. On the contrary, the *tandas* became more explicitly political, many depicting the fate of the 500,000 Mexican American servicemen who went overseas to fight in the Second World War. The growing popularity of movies and the advent of television, however, were disastrous for *tandas* and *carpas*, which died out in the 1950s.

The political upheaval of the 1960s, sparked by the civil rights movement and an escalating Vietnam War, had a strong impact on the growth of contemporary Hispanic theatre. Nowhere was this relationship as clear as with the emergence of El Teatro Campesino in 1965, which grew directly out of the ferment of the United Farmworkers' struggle in California.

The growth of the Latino theatre movement from Chicago westward for two decades was intimately tied to the work of El Teatro Campesino. Its founder, Luis

Valdez, was a theatre student at San Jose State College when Cesar Chavez's farmworkers' movement began to gain momentum. In the early 1970s, almost 100 Chicano theatre groups, largely encouraged, inspired and trained by El Teatro Campesino, flourished throughout the Southwest and the West. Most of the founders of these groups had no formal theatre training. An exception was Jorge Huerta, who founded El Teatro de la Esperanza in 1969 and 20 years later, in 1989, created a Masters of Fine Arts programme in Hispanic Theatre at the University of California in San Diego.

During the first decade, most *teatros* were organized as collectives, a conscious political choice underscoring the position that farmworkers and minorities should take a more active role in the political process and allowing *teatro* members to practise the underlying ideologies of the plays. By the beginning of the 1990s the era of the collective was all but over. Of the almost 100 campesino-inspired *teatros* that sprang up throughout the West Coast, the Southwest and the Midwest between 1965 and 1975, only five survived. Theatres founded in the 1980s were more diverse in style, mission and structure than the early *teatros*.

In 1976 two of the stronger groups created pieces that have become milestones in the history of Chicano theatre: El Teatro de la Esperanza introduced its most notable collective piece, *La Victima*, and El Teatro Campesino opened Valdez's *Zoot Suit* at the MARK TAPER FORUM in Los Angeles. *La Victima*, based on documented fact about the immigration and deportation of Mexicans, is still performed by Latino groups throughout the country. *Zoot Suit* caused a stir when it opened that is still not forgotten. It is based on the famous zoot suit riots of 1943 in Los Angeles and the sensational Sleepy Lagoon trial of 16 young Mexicans and Mexican Americans. After its run at the Taper, *Zoot Suit* went on to enjoy a long commercial success in Los Angeles, a first for a Chicano play. It opened on Broadway, another first, but did not fare as well in New York. In 1986, Valdez wrote and directed his first major film, *La Bamba*, a popular national and international success when it was released the following year. A new play, *The Mummified Deer*, opened in autumn 2000 at the San Diego Repertory Theater in California.

Although there was greater diversity, ethnically and economically, among the Hispanic population on the East Coast, and they lacked a unifying cause like the farmworkers' struggle, Hispanic artists in the East were also caught up in the unrest and social change of the 1960s. Some of the first public and private monies that became available to minority arts in 1967 were offered in direct response to racial tensions and riots. The New York State Council on the Arts, which receives its funds from the state legislature to assist artists and arts organizations throughout New York State, and the Ford Foundation, on a national basis, were in the vanguard of supporting the development of minority arts.

Among the first organizations to receive funding for minority arts in New York were Colon's Puerto Rican Traveling Theatre and the Real Great Society, a community-based organization with an arts component located on New York's Lower East Side. Cuban refugees also began to produce plays in New York in the late 1960s. Some had theatre backgrounds, but others did not. Gilberto Zaldivar and Rene Buch, who founded Repertorio Español in 1968, were theatrically trained. INTAR, on the other hand, founded in 1966, was run by a group of young Cuban and Puerto Rican professionals with little or no theatre experience. Now, more than 30 years after they were founded, Repertorio Español, which specializes in Spanish classics and Spanish-language contemporary plays; Puerto Rican Traveling Theatre, which produces its plays in both Spanish and English; and INTAR, whose productions are only in English, have become the most stable Hispanic theatre organizations in New York. The Real Great Society, by now known as CHARAS, Inc., is still active, under the leadership of Carlos Garcia. The Bilingual Foundation of the Arts in Los Angeles and GALA Hispanic Theater in Washington DC have also weathered the test of time. Both have grown into stable producing organizations since they were founded in the 1970s.

In Miami, audience predilections coupled with Cuban distrust for government arts funding presented serious handicaps to the development of Hispanic theatre. Moreover, an ongoing rift between the Miami Cuban-American and non-Latino communities has made it difficult for Latino theatres to attract non-Hispanic audiences. Even the established mainstream Coconut Grove Playhouse loses audiences when it produces Hispanic adaptations of classic plays. Mario Ernesto Sanchez, who founded his Teatro Avante in Miami in the early 1970s, has worked hard, with limited success, to bring non-Hispanics into his theatre and into his International Hispanic Theater Festival, which celebrated its 15th year in June 2000.

A 1987 survey of US Hispanic theatre conducted for the Ford Foundation included 101 theatre groups, 28 presenting organizations and 16 service organizations. Of the 101 theatre groups surveyed, 29 were run by Chicanos; 24 by Cubans; 11 by US-resident Puerto Ricans; 17 by San Juan-based Puerto Ricans; and 20 by Hispanics of other national backgrounds, non-Hispanics or people of mixed cultural heritage.

There were 34 theatre organizations in New York City and 31 in California, 11 of them Los Angeles; and 32 in the Southwest, 16 of them in Texas. Florida had 18 organizations, with 17 in Miami and one in Tampa. The Midwest had the fewest theatres, with four organizations in Chicago and one in Minneapolis. The survey included 21 theatre organizations in San Juan, Puerto Rico.

Data collected from 87 of the 101 theatre groups showed that 30 of those 87 groups were founded since 1980 and that seven were 20 years old or more. Most were small and produced an average of three plays a year in 100- to 199-seat houses. Only 13 were affiliated with Actors' Equity Association. Although almost 50 per cent of the theatres did not have paid staff, 85 per cent paid their actors. Fifty-one groups received state and local funding and money from private philanthropists; 34 received funding from the NATIONAL ENDOWMENT FOR THE ARTS; all groups earned some revenues which made up from 5 per cent to 35 per cent of their annual budgets.

Hispanic theatres in the United States are highly diversified in artistic expression, cultural heritage, use of language, managerial expertise and degree of professionalism, with a wide range of artistic focus, priorities and taste. None the less, they face challenges similar to those of almost every theatre organization at the beginning of the twenty-first century: exploring artistic identities and funding strategies for survival.

Developing playwriting talent has been an ongoing priority among Hispanics working in theatre as key to their survival. Veteran playwright MARIA IRENE FORNÉS has made a substantial contribution to that end through her playwrights' labs in New York, California and universities throughout the country, encouraging Latino playwrights who write in English to develop their craft. The better-known playwrights, such as Eduardo Machado, Milcha Sanchez Scott, Migdalia Cruz and Nilo Cruz, have benefited from Fornés' formidable and effective techniques in playwriting. Other incentives include the Hispanic Playwrights' Festival at South Coast Repertory Company in southern California, initiated in 1985. Juliette Carrillo, a second-generation Mexican American and a 1993 graduate of the Yale University School of Drama, has headed this annual two-week programme of plays by emerging Latino dramatists since 1996. Carrillo describes the programme's progress as 'slow, but the quality of the work is way up'. The Latino Theater Initiative at the MARK TAPER FORUM in Los Angeles and the five-year-old National Hispanic Playwriting Award sponsored by the Arizona Theater Company, in association with the Centro Cultural Mexicano in Phoenix, are other not-able programmes that encourage the Latino playwright. A substantial number of women playwrights have emerged, including Lynn Alvarez, Migdalia Cruz, Fornes and Dolores Prida in New York; Josefina Lopez, Milcha Sanchez Scott, Caridad Svich and Edit Villareal in Los Angeles; Denise Chavez in Las Cruces, New Mexico; Estela Portillo Tramblay in El Paso, Texas; and Silviana Wood in Tucson, Arizona.

Although the last decade of the century saw a widespread influence of Hispanic culture on mainstream America, in music, food, dance, visual arts and language, with Jennifer Lopez, Rosie Perez, Gloria Estefan and Ricky Martin becoming celebrity household names, the flurry of Latino cultural icons has not trickled down to theatre. Playwrights like Eduardo Machado, Jose Revera and Edwin Sanchez, who have had their plays produced in mainstream theatres nationally, are exceptions. Most plays written by people with Hispanic surnames do not reach the main stages of US regional theatres. According to Christine Dolen, Miami's leading theatre critic, in an article published in *The Miami Herald* on 28 April 2000, 'Last season, at 79 major regional theaters, only 1.8 per cent of the 549 plays produced were by playwrights with Hispanic surnames.' It is difficult to break a long tradition of theatre in the United States with its formidable historical reference to Great Britain and its many producers whose roots go back to Jewish immigrants from eastern Europe.

Diane Rodriguez, who co-directs the Latino Initiative at the Mark Taper Forum, feels that Latino plays have simply been shut out of the mainstream: 'Los Angeles is 60 per cent; Hispanic, and yet there is a colonial attitude toward us.' Machado, who has headed Columbia University's playwriting programme since 1997, contends that '[even] Latino theatres have done little to help Latino writers. You have to get yourself done, reinvent yourself.' Eddie Sanchez has noticed that critics often use another language when describing a Latino play: 'They like to use the word *sabroso* [tasty] and seem to have a hard time using "intelligent, clever, complex".' Another talented Hispanic American playwright, Rogelio Martinez, one of three Hispanics among the eight playwrights accepted in 2000 at New Dramatists in New York, views the situation with a realistic eye: 'You have to come from a place of optimism if you work in theatre. So little theatre is being done. But I can't look at it from that point of view; I have to keep getting my plays done. Being cynical is no good for a writer.'

The significant changes taking place in US demographics are enabling Latino theatre artists to maintain, consciously and unconsciously, their ethnic identity. These artists are also demonstrating that what they have to say is universal. Despite the difficulties of arts funding shortages in the United States or an inherent cultural bias, Latino/Hispanic theatre expression is making itself heard and becoming more and more viable and recognized as an important US voice.

JOANNE POTTLITZER

Jorge A. Huerta, *Chicano Theater: Themes and Forms* (1982)
Joanne Pottlitzer, *Hispanic Theater in the United States and Puerto Rico* (1988)
Alberto Sandoval-Sanchez, *Jose, Can You See?: Latinos on and off Broadway* (1999)
Joseph Sommers and Tomas Ybarra-Frausto, eds, *Modern Chicano Writers* (1979)
Caridad Svich and Maria Teresa Marrero, eds, *Out of the Fringe: Contemporary Latina/Latino Theatre and Performance* (2000)

Hoar, Stuart (b. New Plymouth, New Zealand,17 June 1957) Playwright; winner of the 1988 BRUCE MASON Playwrights' Award. He was the author of a large number of radio plays before he turned to writing for the theatre. His *Squatter* (1987) achieved success at MERCURY and CIRCA. Other plays include *The Boat* (1992) and *A Long Walk Off a Tall Rock* (1991). He has written the libretto for the opera *Bitter Calm*, composed by Christopher Blake, the award-winning screenplay for the short film *Lovelock*, a novel and plays for children.   GILLIAN GREER, LAURIE ATKINSON & SIMON GARRETT

Hobson, Harold (b. Thorpe Hesley, nr Rotherham, Yorks, 4 Aug. 1904; d. Westhampnett, Sussex, 12 March 1992) Theatre critic. He became the London drama critic of the *Christian Science Monitor* in 1931, having converted to the religion following a childhood attack of polio which kept him out of school until he was 16. In 1939 he inadvertently discovered the government's plans for the evacuation of schools and sold the story to the *Sunday Times*, thereafter being taken on to the paper's staff. Appointed assistant literary editor in 1944, he succeeded the drama critic JAMES AGATE in 1947 and held the post until 1976. His championing of the AVANT-GARDE (e.g. BECKETT's *Waiting for Godot*), his love of French drama (he was awarded the Légion d'Honneur in 1959 but returned it in 1968 when BARRAULT was sacked from the ODÉON), his encouragement of innovative British work (his review of PINTER's *The Birthday Party* in 1958 saved the play from annihilation) and his ability to encapsulate the sense of occasion in great acting performances like those of his favourite Edwige Feuillère marked him out as one of the twentieth century's most accomplished

critics. Hobson had had no practical experience of the theatre, but his desire to create a historical record of the plays that he witnessed (stemming from his Oxford University training as a historian) ensured that he maintained an intelligent, objective approach. His elegant style exploited rather than capitulated to the necessary compression of a journalistic review and for a period, in the late 1950s and early 1960s, he famously did battle every Sunday with the brash *Observer* critic KENNETH TYNAN. His books include *Verdict at Midnight* (1952), his autobiography *Indirect Journey* (1976) and *Theatre in Britain* (1984) He was knighted in 1977.

DOMINIC SHELLARD

Hochhuth, Rolf (b. Eschwege, Switzerland, 1 April 1931) Playwright and leading representative of DOCUMENTARY theatre. His play *Der Stellvertreter* (*The Deputy*, 1963; performed in Britain as *The Representative*) was one of the most widely discussed plays of the 1960s. In its depiction of Pope Pius XII's failure openly to challenge the Holocaust, it shuns most traditional dramatic requirements and places more emphasis on historical truth than on literary quality. However, its irregular blank verse lifts it out of the realm of journalism. Less successful were *Guerrillas* (1970) and *Die Soldaten* (*Soldiers*, 1967), which was refused a production at Britain's NATIONAL THEATRE because of its critical portrayal of wartime prime minister Winston Churchill. Hochhuth's later plays mix elements of documentary theatre with the more traditional requirements of the stage: *Die Hebamme* ('The midwife', 1972, premièred simultaneously at six theatres), *Lysistrate und die NATO* ('Lysistrata and NATO', 1974), *Juristen* ('Lawyers', 1980), *Ärtztinnen* ('Women doctors', 1980) and *Judith* (1984).

GÜNTER BERGHAUS

E. R. Bentley, ed., *The Storm over* The Deputy (1964)
M. E. Ward, *Rolf Hochhuth* (1977)
Rainer Taëni, *Rolf Fochhuth* (1977)

Hochwälder, Fritz (b. Vienna, 28 May 1911; d. Zurich, 20 Oct. 1986) Playwright. An Austrian, who worked mostly in Switzerland, he is best known for three conventional historical dramas of ideas. *Der heilige Experiment* (*The Holy Experiment*, 1943), about the Spanish Church's attitude to Jesuit life in eighteenth-century Paraguay, was seen in London with WOLFIT as *The Strong are Lovely*, translated by LE GALLIENNE, and was the inspiration for the BOLT film *The Mission* (1986). *Der Öffentliche Ankläger* (*The Public Prosecutor*, 1948) is a tragedy set in the French Revolution; and *Donadieu* (1953) is based on a ballad about the Huguenot aristocrat of that name. *Esther* (1940) was one of

359

the first plays to tackle the Nazi extermination of the Jews. JUDY MEEWEZEN

George E. Wellwarth, *The Theatre of Protest and Paradox* (1964)

Hockney, David (b. Bradford, Yorks, 9 July 1937) Painter, designer and multimedia artist. Best known for his colourful paintings as well as his work with photocopy and facsimile machines, Hockney began designing for the theatre and OPERA in 1966, when he designed *Ubu Roi* (ROYAL COURT). Since then he has worked mostly in opera (e.g. *The Rake's Progress*, 1975) in England and America. He was made a Companion of Honour in 1997. DENISE L. TILLES

Marco Livingstone, *David Hockney* (1982)

Hoffman, Dustin (b. Los Angeles, 8 Aug. 1937) Stage and screen actor. His first artistic aspirations were as a musician, but he switched to acting and eventually gained admittance to the ACTORS' STUDIO, where he studied under LEE STRASBERG. His debut on Broadway in 1961 was followed by a lean patch before he gained critical attention in *Harry, Noon and Night* (1965) and *The Journey of the Fifth Horse* (1966). It was while appearing OFF-BROADWAY in a production of *Eh?* by HENRY LIVINGS that he was spotted by director MIKE NICHOLS for the part in *The Graduate* (1967), a film that made him a star overnight. Hoffman's diffident style and unconventional looks broke the mould of the classic movie star and set a new trend in cinema of the 1960s; since then he has won two Academy Awards. In 1984 Hoffman returned to Broadway as Willy Loman in *Death of a Salesman* and in 1989 he made a belated stab at Shakespeare with his role as Shylock in *The Merchant of Venice* in London and on Broadway, to mixed reviews. HELEN RAPPAPORT

R. Bergan, *Dustin Hoffman* (1991)

Hoffman, William M. *see* GAY THEATRE

Hofmannsthal, Hugo [Laurenz August Hofmann, Edler] von (b. Vienna, 1 Feb. 1874; d. Rodaun (now Wien-Rodaun), 15 July 1929) Poet, playwright and librettist. In his youth, he wrote some of the most beautiful poetry and poetic drama of the time (e.g. *Der Tor und der Tod/Death and the Fool*, publ. 1894). An acute mental crisis in 1902 led to his abandonment of Vienna's SYMBOLIST and aesthetic circles in 1905. Language seemed to lose all meaning for him, and his later work reveals a deep understanding of the subtextual qualities of drama: *Der Schwierige* (*The Deep Man*, 1921) and *Der Turm* (*The Tower*, 1925), an adaptation of Calderon's *Life is a Dream*. *Jedermann* (*Everyman*, 1911) is

performed annually as part of the SALZBURG FESTIVAL, which the play inaugurated in 1920, directed by MAX REINHARDT who founded the festival with Richard Strauss and Hofmannsthal. Outside Germany and Austria he is best known for collaborations with Strauss, such as *Elektra* (1909), *Der Rosenkavalier* (1911), *Ariadne auf Naxos* (1912) and *Die Frau ohne Schatten* (*The Woman Without a Shadow*, 1919). JUDY MEEWEZEN

Benjamin Bennett, *Hofmannsthal: The Theatres of Consciousness* (1988)

Thomas A. Korach, *Hofmannsthal and Symbolism: Art and Life in the Work of a Modern Poet* (1985)

Holbrook, Hal [Harold Rowe, Jr] (b. Cleveland, 17 Feb. 1925) Actor and writer. From 1942, Holbrook played SUMMER STOCK and toured a two-hander with his wife, including a sketch based on Mark Twain which he reprised as a one-man show on television, *Mark Twain Tonight*. He alternated between national tours and appearances in various TV shows and series, reviving his immensely popular *Mark Twain* performance at various venues between 1959 and 1964. He has also appeared in *Marco's Millions* (1964), *Tartuffe* (1965), *Man of La Mancha* (1968), *Lake of the Woods* (1972), *King Lear* (1990), *Merchant of Venice* (1991) and *Death of a Salesman* (1994). HELEN RAPPAPORT

Hole in the Wall Theatre Set up in Perth in 1965 by two local theatre practitioners, John Gill and Frank Baden Powell, as an alternative to what they saw as 'the dominating English repertory tradition'. The company aimed at a more experimental approach, initially also expressing a commitment to Australian, and particularly West Australian, drama. It has changed locale three times, but on each occasion has sought to provide an intimate open stage environment, seating between 150 and 300. Since its move into the Subiaco Theatre Centre in 1984, and the uncertainties following from the Australia Council's withdrawal of subsidy in 1981 (subsequently reinstated), the programming has shifted from the innovative to one that reflects the demands of the box office, coinciding with the amalgamation with the Western Australian Theatre Company to form the State Theatre Company of Western Australia. MICHAEL MORLEY

Holland *see* NETHERLANDS

Holloway, Stanley (b. London, 1 Oct. 1890; d. London, 30 Jan. 1982) Actor, famous for his monologues. For three decades from his 1919 debut he performed in concert parties, musicals and PANTOMIMES. He played the First Gravedigger in *Hamlet* (1951) and Bottom in *A Midsummer Night's Dream* (OLD VIC, 1954).

His best-known role was that of Alfred P. Doolittle in *My Fair Lady* (New York, 1956; London, 1958; film, 1964). A character actor in many films from 1921, he continued to appear internationally in plays, including *Candida* (1970) and *The Pleasure of His Company* (1977). D. KEITH PEACOCK

Holm, Celeste (b. New York, 29 April 1919) Actress who made her Broadway debut as Mary in WILLIAM SAROYAN's *The Time of Your Life* (1939). She next won acclaim by creating Ado Annie in *Oklahoma!* (1943). She played the title role in *Anna Christie* (1952), replaced Gertrude Lawrence on Broadway in *The King and I* (1952) and led a tour of *Mame* (1967). She has had an active film career, winning an Academy award (*Gentlemen's Agreement*, 1947) and being nominated twice again (*Come to the Stable*, 1949; *All About Eve*, 1950). She was knighted by the King of Norway in 1979. JANE HOUSE

Holm [Eckert], Hanya [Johanna] (b. Worms, Germany, 3 March 1893; d. New York, 3 Nov. 1992) Dancer, teacher and choreographer. Holm studied eurythmics with EMILE JAQUES-DALCROZE before becoming a pupil of MARY WIGMAN in 1921. In 1931 she emigrated to New York, where she established a Wigman School (later renamed the Hanya Holm School) of modern dance. She was one of the pioneers of modern dance, especially with *Trend* (1937). In America Holm became a renowned teacher, and choreographed such musicals as *Kiss Me Kate* (1948), *My Fair Lady* (1956) and *Camelot* (1960). ANDREW SOLWAY

See also CHOREOGRAPHY; DANCE; MOVEMENT, DANCE AND DRAMA.

W. Sorell, *Hanya Holm: The Biography of an Artist* (1969)

Holm, [Cuthbert] Ian (b. Ilford, Essex, 12 Sept. 1931) Actor. For nearly ten years at STRATFORD-UPON-AVON and with the ROYAL SHAKESPEARE COMPANY, in 1954–5 and again from 1958 to 1967, he gave performances of exemplary lucidity, wit, truthfulness and steely charm (Puck, Gremio, Troilus, Hal, Henry V, Richard III; and Lennie in *The Homecoming*, 1965 and Broadway, 1966). Holm is an actor of paradoxes: flamboyant yet self-effacing, extravagant but austere, demonic but reserved, humane but detached. From the mid-1970s on, he increasingly withdrew from the theatre in favour of television and film, with only the odd live appearance (e.g. in *Uncle Vanya*, 1979) tantalizing audiences and fellow actors with a rare glimpse of great talent. With his King Lear (1998) at the NATIONAL THEATRE, directed by RICHARD EYRE, he gave a performance that more than compensated for the years of voluntary exile from the theatre. He was knighted in the same year. RICHARD EYRE

Holman, David (b. London, 4 March 1942) Leading playwright for youth. His works, performed worldwide, include *Drink the Mercury* (1975), *No Passeran* (1977), and *Peacemaker* (1981). The NATIONAL THEATRE, London, produced *Whale* (1990) and *Elephant* (1992). Theatre of South Australia and Magpie Theatre commissioned *No Worries* (1984), *The Small Poppies* (1986) and *Beauty and the Beast* (1988). NANCY SWORTZELL

See also THEATRE FOR YOUNG PEOPLE.

Holman, Robert (b. Guisborough, Cleveland, 25 Aug. 1952) Playwright. Holman depicts with immense sensitivity and precision people caught on battlegrounds of race, age, gender and class, notably in *Making Noise Quietly* (1986). He has shown compelling handling of historical material in *Other Worlds* (1983) and *Today* (1984), written after months spent with the ROYAL SHAKESPEARE COMPANY, which eventually performed it. He has turned towards environmental themes and metaphors in *The Overgrown Path* (1985), *Across Oka* (1988) and *Rafts and Dreams* (1990), where his forte for atmosphere controls often fantastic events which are brought to heartrendingly tragic ends. *Bad Weather* (1998) explored the impact of a violent crime on a family in northern England. DAN REBELLATO

Holocaust Nazi attempts to exterminate European Jewry gave rise to theatrical performances of an extraordinary kind under extraordinary conditions. It also led to many plays being written that seek to express the enormity of those conditions and question the capacity of drama to deal with such human extremities. In the Introduction to *The Theatre of the Holocaust* (1982), an anthology of plays on the Holocaust, the editor Robert Skloot lists five aims of playwrights who tackle this subject: honouring the victims, educating audiences, evoking responses, airing ethical dilemmas and posing possible solutions to contemporary issues. The plays themselves range across the stylistic spectrum, from the DOCUMENTARY approach of PETER WEISS' *The Investigation* and the detailed realism of JEAN-CLAUDE GRUMBERG's *The Workshop* to the SURREALISM of GEORGE TABORI's *The Cannibals*, the EPIC sweep of JOSHUA SOBOL's *Ghetto* and the grim humour of PETER BARNES' *Laughter!* First-hand experiences have been important: *The Diary of Anne Frank* has proved popular, dramatized as a play and a musical while concentration camp survivors have written plays themselves, such as Charlotte Delbo's *Who Will Carry the Word?* Such experiences have provided others with subject matter for wider considerations, whether PETER

FLANNERY in *Singer*. his indictment of postwar Britain, or MARTIN SHERMAN's *Bent*, which shows that Nazi victims were not only Jewish.   CHARLES LONDON

See also ISRAEL; YIDDISH THEATRE.

V. M. Patraka, *Spectacular Suffering: Theatre, Fascism and the Holocaust* (1999)
R. Rovit and A. Goldfarb, eds, *Theatrical Performance During the Holocaust: Texts, Documents, Memoirs* (1999)

Holt, Bland [Joseph]   (b. Norwich, 24 March 1851; d. Melbourne, 28 June 1942)   Actor–manager and play adapter. He began his stage career as a pantomime clown and comic actor. His first Australian productions in the 1880s were careful reconstructions of earlier successes at the THEATRE ROYAL, DRURY LANE. In the 1890s he discovered the appeal of local settings and specialized in re-setting spectacular MELODRAMAS from their English origins. An important figure at the start of the twentieth century, he retired a wealthy man in 1909.
JEREMY ECCLES

Katharine Brisbane, *Entertaining Australia* (1991)
Margaret Williams, *Australia on the Popular Stage* (1983)

Holt, Thelma   *see* OPEN SPACE

Home, William Douglas   *see*   DOUGLAS-HOME, WILLIAM

Honduras   *see* MEXICO AND CENTRAL AMERICA

Hong Kong   While Hong Kong's population is almost entirely Chinese, its drama has been shaped by its situation for most of the century as a British colony on China's south coast, and displays a mix of traditions from Europe, America and Asia. The two prime influences from CHINA are the Cantonese opera, which has been heavily modified over the years, and *huaju*. This modern Chinese theatre grew out of attempts by students returning from Japan to spread Western ideas into China after the revolution of 1911 which overthrew the Manchu dynasty. The Sino-Japanese war of 1937–1945 popularized *huaju* and it reached as far south as Hong Kong, where drama faced serious problems of apathy and anxiety over local language and identity. *Huaju* scripts had to be rendered into Cantonese, the major dialect used in Hong Kong. After the war, plays from the mainland and from Europe were staged, and, following the communist revolution of 1949, an influx of refugees added to the cultural scene. Local writers began to emerge in the 1950s.

Hong Kong is a bilingual centre, and local English groups, of which the main two were the Hong Kong Stage Club and the Garrison Players, performed contemporary Western plays in the 1960s, inspiring local Chinese students to do the same. In the 1960s and 1970s a booming economy prompted the government to sponsor the arts. The Urban Council founded the HK Repertory Theatre Company in 1978, and the government subsidized the Chung Ying Theatre Company almost entirely, as well as funding other groups on a project basis. By the late 1980s, subsidy had peaked; television and film were offering better opportunities, the drama remained derivative of the West, publishers were unwilling to publish scripts written in a dialect used only in Hong Kong and the neighbouring Guangdong province, and audiences were more concerned with the impending political changes. By the end of the century only ad hoc local groups were producing work in English. The future of Hong Kong theatre depends on the actions of the Chinese government which took back control of the colony in 1997.
VICKI OOI

Hood, Basil   (b. Croydon, 5 April 1864; d. London, 7 Aug. 1917)   Librettist. An army career officer, Hood resigned his commission when the production of his first full-length show, *Gentleman Joe* (1895), coincided with his regiment being ordered abroad, and devoted himself to writing for the theatre. *Gentleman Joe* was a major success, and Hood collaborated thereafter on a series of shows with its composer, Walter Slaughter, including the international hit *The French Maid* (1896). When the GILBERT and SULLIVAN partnership split up, Hood was given the opportunity to collaborate with Sullivan on *The Rose of Persia* (1899), and subsequently worked with EDWARD GERMAN, most notably on *Merrie England* (1902), and LESLIE STUART before GEORGE EDWARDES employed him to anglicize SARDOU's libretto for *Les Merveilleuses*. When Edwardes began to import operettas from Vienna, the literate and versatile Hood was hired to write the English versions and thus became the author of the standard English texts of *The Merry Widow*, *A Waltz Dream*, *The Dollar Princess*, *The Count of Luxembourg* and *Gipsy Love*. His last work was on *Bric à Brac*, one of the first successful British REVUES (1915).   KURT GÄNZL

Hooper, Elric   (b. Christchurch, New Zealand, 1936)   Actor and director. After a scholarship to the London Academy of Music and Dramatic Art (1958–60) and work with the OLD VIC (ZEFFIRELLI's *Romeo and Juliet*), THEATRE WORKSHOP and OXFORD PLAYHOUSE, he returned to act and direct in all the leading New Zealand theatres before becoming artistic director of Christchurch's COURT (1979–2000), where he commissioned, among a repertoire of overseas classics and contemporary plays, the work of local writers such as

BRUCE MASON, ROGER HALL, and Michelanne Forster.
GILLIAN GREER & LAURIE ATKINSON

Hopgood, Alan (b. Launceston, Tasmania, 22 Sept. 1934) Playwright and actor. His first play, *And the Big Men Fly* (1963), is a humorous yet affectionate look at the world of Australian Rules Football, while his second, *Private Yuk Objects* (1966), is a satirical treatment of things relating to the Vietnam War, conscriptions and 'All the way with LBJ'. During the 1970s and 1980s he wrote extensively for film and television (including *Neighbours*), while not entirely neglecting the stage, both as writer and as performer. Other plays include the 'musical biographies' *Callas* (1992) and *The Mario Lanza Story* (1994), and *The Carer* (1999).
MICHAEL MORLEY

Hopkins, Anthony (b. Port Talbot, Wales, 31 Dec. 1937) Actor. He joined the NATIONAL THEATRE in 1966 and made his mark with strong physical performances in roles including Coriolanus (1971) and Macbeth (1972). New York appearances have included PETER SHAFFER's *Equus* (1974) and HAROLD PINTER's *Old Times* (1984). Hopkins returned to the National to star in *Pravda* (1985), *King Lear* (1986) and *Antony and Cleopatra* (1987). A prolific film and television actor with a rich, distinctive voice, he won an Academy Award for *The Silence of the Lambs* (1992). Hopkins was knighted in 1993 and became an American citizen in 2000.
DAVID BARBOUR

Quentin Falk, *Anthony Hopkins: The Authorized Biography* (2000)

Hopper, DeWolf [William D'Wolf] (b. New York, 30 March 1858; d. Kansas City, Mo., 23 Sept. 1935) Comedian and singer. His parents intended him for a career in law, but a taste of amateur acting led him into the theatre. Displaying a good singing voice, he was taken on by John McCaull's opera company and during the next five years developed his fine bass voice. Success followed success in the next few productions. His first appearance in a GILBERT and SULLIVAN opera came in 1911, in *HMS Pinafore*, which he followed with his favourite role, as Jack Point in *Yeoman of the Guard*, and *Iolanthe*. A brief career in silent films failed and Hopper returned to the stage in 1918. By now, public tastes had changed, and Hopper toured with REVUES, Gilbert and Sullivan operas and revivals of earlier performances, such as *El Capitan* (with his wife EDNA HOPPER), as well as productions of the operetta *The Student Prince* and the MELODRAMA *The Monster* (1932). His recitation of the poem 'Casey at the Bat' became a trademark. In 1927 the six-times married Hopper wrote a lively account of his colourful career, *Once a Clown, Always a Clown*. HELEN RAPPAPORT

Hopper, Edna Wallace (b. San Francisco, 17 Jan. 1864?; d. New York, 14 Dec. 1959) Diminutive comedienne and singer. With CHARLES FROHMAN's stock company she played her first lead in a comedy created for her by DAVID BELASCO, *The Girl I Left Behind Me* (1893). Married to the actor DEWOLF HOPPER, her overnight success in this production led to a string of appearances in hit musical shows during the 1890s, such as *El Capitan*, *The Silver Slipper*, *Girl O' Mine* and *Yankee Doodle Dandy*; Hopper's tiny stature made her ability to impersonate boys a particular success with audiences. One of her biggest hits was in the landmark musical *Floradora* (1900), which introduced the novelty of the chorus line. Hopper's musical career continued with productions like *Fifty Miles from Boston* (1908) and *Jumping Jupiter* (1911) until 1920, after which, with her popularity waning, she went on a series of tours promoting her own cosmetic products. She made a nostalgic farewell performance in *The Girl I Left Behind Me* at the age of 89 in 1953.
HELEN RAPPOPORT

Hordern, Michael [Murray] (b. Berkhamsted, Herts, 3 Oct. 1911; d. Oxford, 2 May 1995) Actor. Hordern was praised for his Caliban, Jaques and Sir Politick Would-be at STRATFORD-UPON-AVON, and for lead roles in *Ivanov* (1950) and *Saint's Day* (1951) at the ARTS THEATRE, but his gift for comedy was considered to have overwhelmed his 1958 Pastor Manders and Macbeth. He regained recognition with an eccentric *Lear* (Nottingham, 1969), performances in STOPPARD premières, notably George Moore in *Jumpers* (1972), and diverse roles from Pinfold in an adaptation of *The Ordeal of Gilbert Pinfold* (1977) to Prospero in *The Tempest* (1978). Hordern's Sir Anthony Absolute in *The Rivals* (1983) at the NATIONAL THEATRE was acclaimed for the expert comic timing, instantly recognizable vocal style and physical mastery of high comedy that also distinguished his performances in radio, film and television. His autobiography, *A World Elsewhere*, appeared in 1993. He was knighted in 1983.
DAN REBELLATO

Horniman, Annie [Elizabeth Fredericka] (b. Forest Hill, London, 3 Oct. 1860; d. Shere, Surrey, 6 Aug. 1937) Theatre manager and patron, a pioneer of the REPERTORY MOVEMENT. Daughter of a wealthy tea merchant, she began her patronage of intellectual theatre by financing a season of plays, which included SHAW's *Arms and the Man*, at the Avenue (later the Playhouse) Theatre, London, in 1894. Admiration for the work of W. B. YEATS led to her financing the ABBEY THEATRE, Dublin in 1904. From 1906 she also subsidized the company so that it could become wholly professional, and was notable for the introduction of SYNGE's plays. She was subsequently eased out of the Abbey directorate, and, determined to found a REPERTORY company in Britain, her choice fell on MANCHESTER, where she staged a trial season early in 1907 at the Midland Hotel Theatre and then in 1908 bought and converted the neighbouring GAIETY THEATRE. She interfered very little with its running, but placed complete trust in her artistic directors, particularly the first, BEN IDEN PAYNE. The theatre became most closely identified with plays of the 'MANCHESTER SCHOOL', notably those of STANLEY HOUGHTON, whose *Hindle Wakes* (1913) was the first Lancashire play to achieve worldwide success, and of HAROLD BRIGHOUSE, several of whose early plays (*The Price of Coal*, *Lonesome Like*) were staged at Manchester, though he did not reach international status until 1916 with the production of *Hobson's Choice* in America and London. Nevertheless, Horniman's work was by no means limited to local plays and playwrights; she often presented Shaw, and staged Shakespeare and other classics, including little-known works by IBSEN and Greek drama. She greatly furthered the careers of LEWIS CASSON, both as actor and director of the theatre after Payne, and SYBIL THORNDIKE, and encouraged many local actors, notably Herbert Lomas. The outbreak of war in 1914 seriously reduced the audience for intellectual drama, and in 1917 she had to allow the Gaiety to revert to a touring theatre. Finally in 1921 she was compelled to sell it, and then severed all links with the theatre, though her example had been followed at such repertory centres as LIVERPOOL, GLASGOW and BIRMINGHAM. She received the honorary degree of Master of Arts from Manchester in 1910, and was created Companion of Honour in 1932. She left her extensive library to the BRITISH DRAMA LEAGUE. G. ROWELL

Sheila Goodie, *Annie Horniman* (1990)

Rex Pogson, *Miss Horniman and the Gaiety Theatre, Manchester* (1952)

Horovitz, Israel [Arthur] (b. Wakefield, Mass., 31 March 1939) Playwright, screenwriter and novelist. A prolific and fertile playwright, Horovitz focuses on betrayal, passion and violence. His best work evokes a stern proletarian work ethic. His most successful dramas are the short plays *The Indian Wants the Bronx* (1966), *Line* (1967) and *The Primary English Class* (1975). Among his longer works, *Henry Lumper* (1985) and *North Shore Fish* (1986) are his most dramatically accomplished. They are part of a cycle centring on the

fishing community of Gloucester, Massachusetts, and complement his Wakefield cycle of seven plays (1974–9) which are also set in New England. As well as contributing regularly to the *Village Voice* newspaper, Horovitz has been artistic directory of the New York Playwrights Laboratory and the Gloucester Stage Company. THOMAS F. CONNOLLY

Leslie Kane, ed., *Israel Horovitz: A Collection of Critical Essays*

Horváth, Ödön [Josef] von (b. Fiume, Italy [now Croatia], 9 Dec. 1901; d. Paris, 7 June 1938) Playwright. Though Hungarian, he wrote in German and is associated with the Austrian theatre tradition. Interest in Horváth's dramas and innovative dramatic theory was revived in the 1960s, when many German and Austrian playwrights and directors were becoming disillusioned with BRECHT and sought new heroes. Though CHRISTOPHER HAMPTON has achieved some success with versions of these modern, ironic 'folk' plays – *Tales from the Vienna Woods* (*Geschichten aus dem Wiener Wald*, 1931, trans. 1977), *Don Juan Comes Back from the War* (*Don Juan Kommt aus dem Krieg*, written 1937, produced 1952, trans. 1978) and *Faith, Hope, and Charity* (*Glaube, Liebe, Hoffnung*, 1932, trans. 1989) – Horváth's plays are extremely difficult to translate. An understanding of the writer's distinctive approach and use of language, as described in his *Gebrauchsanweisung* (*Manual for My Works*) is a useful key to a scarcely tried dramatic treasure trove, notably *Figaro lässt sich scheiden* (*Figaro Gets a Divorce*, 1937), *Italienische Nacht* ('Italian night', 1930) and *Kasimir und Karoline* (1932). He fled the Nazis twice, in 1933 to Austria and in 1938 to France, where he was killed in a freak accident during a storm. JUDY MEEWEZEN

Christopher B. Balme, *The Reformation of Comedy: Genre Critique in the Comedies of Ödön von Horváth* (1985)

Krishna Winston, *Horváth Studies: Close Readings of Six Plays* (1977)

Hot Peaches *see* DRAG; LESBIAN THEATRE

Houdini, Harry [Ehrich Weiss] (b. Budapest, 24 March 1874; d. Detroit, 31 Oct. 1926) Magician and escapologist, whose mother and father – a Hungarian rabbi – emigrated with him to the United States when Houdini was a young child. In his teens he became fascinated with magic tricks and, taking his stage name from the nineteenth-century French conjurer Jean Eugene Robert-Houdin, began his performing career as a conventional magician. Success eluded him until he concentrated on the part of his act in which he escaped from handcuffs, and issued challenges to the police to contain him. Using this formula, Houdini achieved enormous success and publicity in England in 1900, and subsequently throughout Europe and beyond. Houdini's challenges seemed more impossible as his career progressed, and he escaped from prison cells, straitjackets, bank safes, packing cases, steel chests and underwater boxes. He died of a ruptured appendix, after a student aimed a blow at Houdini's stomach without giving him time to brace his abdomen. Also a silent film star, his career gave rise to the circus-opera *Houdini* (1977) by ADRIAN MITCHELL and Peter Schat. IAN SAVILLE

Christopher Milbourne, *Houdini: The Untold Story* (1969)

Adam Phillips, *Houdini's Box* (2001)

Houghton, [Charles] Norris (b. Indiana, 26 Dec. 1909) Educator, producer, designer and writer. Between 1932 and 1957 he designed eight Broadway productions and directed four, and founded the OFF-BROADWAY Phoenix Theatre, where between 1953 and 1964 he was involved in some 75 productions. Best known as an educator, he taught at various institutions and wrote six books, including the influential *Moscow Rehearsals* (1936) and *Advance from Broadway* (1941). His autobiography, *Entrances and Exits*, appeared in 1991. LAURIE WOLF

Houghton, [William] Stanley (b. Ashton-upon-Mersey, Cheshire, 22 Feb. 1881; d. Manchester, 11 Dec. 1913) Playwright and critic. Most of Houghton's dramatic work seems a mediocre apprenticeship for his best play, *Hindle Wakes* (1912), in which a young woman exposes the double standards of society. In its non-metropolitan setting and reversal of theatrical expectations, *Hindle Wakes* is the most successful fulfilment of ANNIE HORNIMAN's aims for the GAIETY THEATRE and MANCHESTER drama. IAN CLARKE
See also BRIGHOUSE, HAROLD; MANCHESTER SCHOOL.

Rex Pogson, *Miss Horniman and the Gaiety Theatre, Manchester* (1952)

Houseman, John [Jacques Haussmann] (b. Bucharest, 22 Sept. 1902; d. Malibu, Calif., 30 Oct. 1988) Producer and director. Houseman gained fame in 1934 with his stagings of *Four Saints in Three Acts*, *The Lady from the Sea* and *Valley Forge*, and in 1935 with *Panic*. In 1937 he helped found the MERCURY THEATER with ORSON WELLES, and together they later produced *Native Son* (1941). He directed several distinguished Shakesperean revivals before becoming artistic director for the AMERICAN SHAKESPEARE FESTIVAL. From 1972 until his death he also headed the Acting Company, an off-

shoot of the Juillard School. He was an erudite man with excellent taste who brought a fresh but never outlandish approach to the classics. He wrote useful accounts of his theatrical career: *Run-Through* (1972), *Front and Centre* (1981) and *Final Dress* (1983) brought together as *Unfinished Business* (1986). GERALD BORDMAN

Howard, Alan [Mackenzie] (b. London, 5 Aug. 1937) Actor; nephew of LESLIE HOWARD. After National Service, Howard worked backstage and took his first acting job with the Belgrade Theatre, Coventry, before coming to London in their production of WESKER's *Roots* (1959) and remaining to perform in the Wesker trilogy (1960). Howard's commanding acting style and his skilful handling of verse made him ideally suited to the ROYAL SHAKESPEARE COMPANY, where he quickly established himself with his first major role in Tourneur's *The Revenger's Tragedy* (1966), following this with a striking Achilles in *Troilus and Cressida* (1968). As a leading RSC actor he has appeared in many notable productions, including PETER BROOK's innovative staging of *A Midsummer Night's Dream* (1970). He has played many of the great Shakespearean roles, such as Benedick (1968), Hamlet (1970), Coriolanus (1977), Antony (1978), Richard II and Richard III (both 1980) and, to particular acclaim, Prince Hal/Henry V and Henry VI in productions by TERRY HANDS (1975–7) that defined the RSC at that time. He demonstrated his versatility by appearing successfully for the RSC in O'Keeffe's *Wild Oats* (1976), GORKY's *Enemies* (1971) and *The Children of the Sun* (1979), Ostrovsky's *The Forest* (1981) and C. P. TAYLOR's *Good* (1981). He made his debut at the NATIONAL THEATRE in 1992 in a well received *Pygmalion*, had a less happy experience there as Macbeth (1993), but came back to form as Oedipus (1996). For the PETER HALL Company, he partnered BEN KINGSLEY in an acclaimed *Waiting for Godot* (1997). With *King Lear* (1997), he surpassed other outstanding English actors, such as Garrick, IRVING, OLIVIER and GIELGUD, in the number of Shakespearean kings he had played. HELEN RAPPAPORT

Howard, Joe [Joseph E.] (b. New York, 12 Feb. 1867; d. Chicago, 19 May 1961) Composer and performer. Howard supposedly ran away from home as a young boy and sang in the streets before reaching VAUDEVILLE. His early rags won widespread fame, but his main work in the theatre came between 1905 and 1910, when he wrote a series of shows for Chicago. The most successful was *The Time, the Place and the Girl* (1906). His songs generally had an infectious lilt or beguiling warmth, but how many of them he actually wrote is moot. A lawsuit revealed he had purchased the melody for 'I Wonder Who's Kissing Her Now' from another composer. However, he remained a performer until the very end of his life. GERALD BORDMAN

Howard, Leslie (b. London, 3 April 1893; d. at sea, 1 June 1943) Actor. Noted for his quiet English reserve in his performances, he enjoyed immense success on the London and New York stages and equal acclaim when he made the first of his many films in 1930. His more notable stage triumphs included *Her Cardboard Lover* (1927), *Berkeley Square* (1929), *The Petrified Forest* (1935) and *Hamlet* (1936), which he also directed. During the Second World War he was killed when the plane bringing him from Lisbon to London was shot down. His nephew is the actor ALAN HOWARD.
DAVID STAINES

L. R. Howard, *A Quite Remarkable Father* (1960)

Howard, Sidney [Coe] (b. Oakland, Calif., 26 June 1891; d. Tyringham, Mass., 23 Aug. 1939) Playwright. A key figure in the movement towards more realistic problem plays in the 1920s, Howard wrote, co-wrote or adapted more than two dozen plays before a fatal accident cut short his career. He was an able craftsman who provided effective vehicles for actors; the Pulitzer Prize-winning *They Knew What They Wanted* (1924) features a kindly Italian grape grower in California, while at the centre of his best-known play, *The Silver Cord* (1926), is a ferociously possessive mother. Howard also wrote a number of screenplays, including *Gone with the Wind* (1939). Other plays include *Ned McCobb's Daughter* (1927) and *Lucky Sam McCarrer* (1925). M. ELIZABETH OSBORN

Sidney H. White, *Sidney Howard* (1977)

Howard, Willie [Wilhelm Levkowitz] (b. Neustadt, Germany, 13 April 1886; d. New York, 12 Jan. 1949) and **Eugene [Isidore Levkowitz]** (b. Neustadt, 7 July 1881; d. New York, 1 Aug. 1965) VAUDEVILLE comedians and singers. Willie first appeared as a boy soprano in vaudeville, turning to slapstick comedy after his voice broke. He teamed up with his elder brother Eugene in 1903 as a singing duo and together they popularized songs such as 'Sweet Adeline'. But it was in comedy that they soon excelled; Willie's gift for madcap mimicry and improvisation soon began to steal the show from his brother as straight man, and their act became hugely popular on the touring circuit. A long career on Broadway followed, with six appearances in *Passing Show of 1912* as well as other REVUES. They also appeared six times in George White's *Scandals*, while during the 1930s Willie appeared in the ZIEGFELD FOLLIES and a few films. In 1940 Eugene retired from the stage, but continued to manage the

irrepressible Willie, who appeared in *Crazy with the Heat* (1941), *My Dear Public* (1943) and *Star and Garter* (1944) HELEN RAPPAPORT.

S. Green, *The Great Clowns of Broadway* (1984)

Howe, Tina (b. New York, 21 Nov. 1937) Playwright. The elegant worlds of Howe's literate comedies move towards chaos, revealing her affinity for IONESCO and the MARX BROTHERS. Her central characters are frequently children, artists or both. Howe's plays include *Museum* (1976), *The Art of Dining* (1979), *Painting Churches* (1983), *Coastal Disturbances* (1986), *Approaching Zanzibar* (1989) and *One Shoe Off* (1993).
M. ELIZABETH OSBORN

Howerd, Frankie [Francis Alex Howard] (b. York, 6 March 1921; d. London, 19 April 1992) Stand-up comedian. His act, ludicrous gossip admixed with 'accidental' innuendoes feeding off audience rapport, began with VARIETY and PANTOMIME, extended to radio and television shows, and was adapted to 'legitimate' theatre and cinema. In a fluctuating career, theatre highspots include his own shows in the late 1940s; the long-running revue *Pardon My French* (1953); a brilliant revival of *Charley's Aunt* (1955); the critically acclaimed Bottom in the OLD VIC's *A Midsummer Night's Dream* (1957); and *A Funny Thing Happened on the Way to the Forum* (1963). Prior to his death he enjoyed a return to favour with the young, for whom he was a legend revived. His autobiography, *On the Way I Lost It*, appeared in 1976. BRIAN BIRCH

William Hall, *Titter Ye Not!: The Life of Frankie Howerd* (1992)

Hughes, Barnard (b. Bedford Hills, NY, 16 July 1915) Actor. He made his New York debut in *The Taming of the Shrew* (1934) and established a niche for himself in a string of supporting roles and 'character' parts in plays including *The Teahouse of the August Moon* (1956), *Advise and Consent* (1960), *A Doll's House* (1963), GIELGUD's *Hamlet* (1964), *Hogan's Goat* (1965), *Much Ado About Nothing* (1970, as Dogberry), *Uncle Vanya* (1973), *The Merry Wives of Windsor* (1974, as Falstaff), *Angels Fall* (1983) and *End of the World* (1984). His most notable performance was in the title role of HUGH LEONARD's *Da* (1978). HELEN RAPPAPORT

Hughes, Dusty [Richard H.] (b. Boston, Lincs., 16 Sept. 1947) Playwright. After a spell as theatre editor of the London listings magazine *Time Out* (1973–6) he became artistic director (1976–9) of the BUSH THEATRE, an influential FRINGE venue. It was here that *Commitments* was seen in 1980, which won him attention for its portrayal of contemporary disillusioned leftists. For the ROYAL SHAKESPEARE COMPANY he adapted BULGAKOV's *Molière* (1982), which deals with the problems of a writer caught up in the machinations of the state, and GORKY's *Philistines* (1985), an indictment of the petit-bourgeoisie. These political themes were explored further in *Futurists* (1986, NATIONAL THEATRE), in which celebrated poets, including MAYAKOVSKY, inevitably succumb, as did Bulgakov, to the political system and their protector, Gorky, can no longer save them. Other plays, such as *Heaven and Hell* (1981), *Bad Language* (1983), *Jenkin's Ear* (1987) and *A Slip of the Tongue* (1992), were similarly questioning but less successful. CHARLES LONDON

Hughes, Holly *see* EXPERIMENTAL THEATRE; LESBIAN THEATRE

Hughes, [James Mercer] Langston (b. Joplin, Mo., 1 Feb. 1902; d. New York, 22 May 1967) Story writer, editor, playwright and poet. A key figure in the development of black letters and black autonomy within culture, he was brought up by his grandmother, from whom he learned about radical politics and art. His first public writing was the 1921 play *The Gold Piece*, and he continued to create theatrical pieces – lyrics, libretti, revue contributions, ballet choreography and plays for the stage as well as for radio, television and film – throughout his life, alongside his prolific output in fiction and verse. His next staged play, *Mulatto* (1935), based on a short story of his about interracial mixing in the South, was turned from a tragedy into a melodrama by its producer and became a Broadway hit. The original was produced four years later at KARAMU HOUSE, Cleveland, which he had attended as a boy. Karamu premièred five of his plays, including *Troubled Island* (1935) and *Joy To My Soul* (1937), and several other of his plays were given first performances at other community theatres, some of which he founded, such as the Harlem Suitcase Theater (1938), the New Negro Theater, Los Angeles (1939) and the Skyloft Players, Chicago (1942). His plays were grounded in the culture that most of white America ignored or denigrated, and even when not formally innovative, as in *Little Ham* (1935), *Soul Gone Home* (1937), or *Simply Heavenly* (1957), they contested stage convention by depicting and celebrating black experience from the inside. Influenced by POLITICAL THEATRE he saw in the Soviet Union and in the United States, he experimented with AGITPROP in the poetic *Scottsboro Limited* (1932) and developed this form as political revue in *Don't You Want To Be Free?* (1938), which fed into his later civil rights success *Jericho-Jim Crow* (1963). Music was often important: his adaptation of his novel *Tambourines to Glory* with music by Jobe Huntley

(1963) was very popular, as were his three gospel shows, *Black Nativity* (1961), *Gospel Glow* (1962) and *The Prodigal Son* (1965). His body of work was a powerful inspiration to future generations who built on his achievements, and in 1991 the LINCOLN CENTER staged his previously unseen play *Mule Bone*, written with Zora Neale Hurston in 1930. His autobiographical books *The Big Sea* and *I Wonder As I Wander* appeared in 1940 and 1956 respectively. CHARLES LONDON

James A. Emmanuel, *Langston Hughes* (1967)
Milton Melzer, *Langston Hughes: A Biography* (1968)
Edward J. Mullen, *Critical Essays on Langston Hughes* (1986)
Therman B. O'Daniel, ed., *Langston Hughes: Black Genius* (1971)
Arnold Rampersad, *The Life of Langston Hughes*, vol I: *1902–41 – I, Too, Sing America* (1986); vol. II: *1941–67 – I Dream a World* (1988)

Hughes, Ted [Edward James] (b. Mytholmroyd, Yorks, 17 Aug. 1930; d. North Tawton, Devon, 28 Oct. 1998) Poet and playwright. His plays, which mix the mythic and the real, include a number for radio and for children: *The Coming of Kings* (1970), *Orpheus* (1971) and *The Tiger's Bones* (1974). *The Iron Man* (1968) was adapted for the stage (1993). His version of Seneca's *Oedipus* (1968) was directed by PETER BROOK, with whom he collaborated on *Orghast* (1971), written in a language invented by Hughes. He also adapted LORCA's *Blood Wedding* (1996, YOUNG VIC), WEDEKIND's *Spring Awakening* (1996, for the ROYAL SHAKESPEARE COMPANY, which presented a stage version of his *Tales from Ovid*, 1999), Aeschylus' *The Oresteia* (1999, ROYAL NATIONAL THEATRE) and Euripides' *Alcestis*, presented posthumously in 2000 by NORTHERN BROADSIDES. Hughes was appointed British Poet Laureate in 1984. LOWELL SWORTZELL

Hulbert, Claude (b. London, 25 Dec. 1900; d. Sydney, 22 Jan. 1964) and **Jack** (b. Ely, 24 April 1892; d. London, 25 March 1978) Actors; Jack also produced and wrote for the theatre. Jack married CICELY COURTNEIDGE, with whom he often appeared in shows that he produced. He and Claude also performed together (in e.g. *The Hulbert Follies*, 1941) and both had successful stage and film careers. Jack's autobiography, *The Little Woman's Always Right*, appeared in 1975. REXTON S. BUNNETT

Hull Truck Theatre Company British regional company. Founded in 1971 by Mike Bradwell (b. 1948) and based in the Yorkshire city of Hull, the company first specialized in plays developed through improvisation and quickly won national recognition by its appearances in London and on the EDINBURGH FRINGE. Since 1978 it has concentrated on scripted plays, and in 1983 acquired a permanent base in its intimate Spring Street Theatre (refurbished in 1994). In 1984, the playwright John Godber (b. 1956) became its artistic director and the company toured many of his very popular (but telling) comedies in his own productions: notably *Bouncers* (1984); a play about the northern sport of rugby league, *Up 'n' Under* (1985); and *Teechers* (1987) – all of which entered the repertoire of other regional companies. The company continues to stage and tour a variety of productions, attracting non-traditional theatregoers. DAVID SELF

Humphrey, Doris *see* DANCE

Humphries, [John] Barry (b. Melbourne, 7 Feb. 1934)   Actor and author. By 1956 a sharp tongue and a wild imagination had created two imperishable personae, housewife Edna Everage and suburbanite Sandy Stone. Humphries took them with him to London (1959) and opened his first of several SOLO shows, *A Nice Night's Entertainment*, in 1962. Other characters, Sir Les Patterson and Barry McKenzie, were created at this safe distance from Australia – the latter, a comic strip anti-hero, appearing in two films. The gladioli-brandishing Edna was elevated to megastar dame and consolidated a career which disturbingly confused life and art on stage and, increasingly, television. In 2000, a special category of Tony Award was created to reward Humphries. JEREMY ECCLES

Peter Coleman, *The Real Barry Humphries* (1990)
John Lahr, *Dame Edna Everage and the Rise of Western Civilisation* (1991)

Hungary   At the beginning of the twentieth century the Hungarian National Theatre, founded in 1837 with the goal of promoting national self-consciousness, was still the country's most important and respected theatre. Its most serious rival, the Comedy Theatre, opened its doors in 1896. Under Mór Ditrói (1851–1945) it offered mostly light comedies from Hungarian and foreign authors (Labiche, Scribe, FEYDEAU) and became the home of FERENC MOLNÁR. Yet this company was the first to stage the realistic and naturalistic plays of IBSEN, CHEKHOV, HAUPTMANN, GORKY and O'NEILL, and Ditrói encouraged Hungarian naturalistic drama, presenting the plays of Sándor Bródy (1863–1924) – *A dada* ('The nanny', 1902), *A tanitónó* ('The schoolmistress', 1908) and *A medikus* ('The med', 1911). Unfortunately, the attempts of the Thalia Society (1904–8), one of whose founders was the young Georg Lukács, failed in its efforts to follow the pioneering path of ANTOINE's Paris Théâtre Libre and Ber-

lin's FREIE BÜHNE, and the AVANT-GARDE theatre of EXPRESSIONISM, SURREALISM and DADA had even less chance to gain ground.

In between the two world wars most of the best Hungarian writers and artists opposed the ultra-conservative and chauvinistic Horthy regime which ousted the short-lived communist government. Even the state-controlled National Theatre had to be offered in 1922 to a man of the left, Sándor Hevesi (1873–1939), who directed most of the plays at the Thalia Theatre. Hevesi modernized not only the National's repertoire but also its acting style, and, with his writings and productions, promoted a new Shakespeare cult in Hungary.

In 1935 Antal Németh (1903–68), a specialist in German drama, was appointed head of the National Theatre. He did his best to comply with the political requirements of those in power, but at the same time maintained decent although very conservative artistic standards. He presented the standard classical works of world literature, Hungarian classical drama of the nineteenth century and contemporary Hungarian authors favoured by the regime, such as Ferenc Herczeg (1863–1954). The liberal-minded middle-class public continued to back the Comedy, which had been run since 1921 by Dániel Jób (1880–1955) who continued successfully the policy of his predecessor. The same audience also supported the City Theatre, run by a very professional theatre man, the 'Hungarian REINHARDT', Artur Bárdos (1882–1974). Andor Pünkösti (1892–1944) led the Madách Theatre (named after a famous Hungarian playwright) from 1941 and tried to use his theatre as an artistic forum against fascism. When in 1944 the Germans occupied Hungary, Pünkösti committed suicide.

In 1945 the communist Tamás Major (1910–86) became the director of the National Theatre and hoped to convince the actors of the benefits of the STANISLAVSKY system. With the very talented director, Endre Gellért (1914–60) he succeeded in staging excellent productions of classics, but unfortunately dogmatic thinking gained the upper hand in the 1950s and a lot of bad socialist realist plays were included in the repertoire.

In 1949 the private theatres were nationalized. State subsidies were considerably increased, but the price to be paid was strict obedience to the Stalinist cultural policy of József Révai (1898–1959), the Hungarian equivalent of the Soviet Zhdanov. After 1956 a more enlightened cultural policy, originated by György Aczél (1917–91), the right-hand man of Premier Kádár, eased the constraints considerably. Once more modern authors like O'Neill, TENNESSEE WILLIAMS and SAMUEL

BECKETT could be staged. A new generation of Hungarian playwrights – Imre Sarkadi (1921–61), ISTVÁN ÖRKÉNY and István Csurka (b. 1934) – started to analyse in their plays in a frank although indirect way the causes and consequences of the suppressed 1956 revolution. A trio of directors, Ottó Ádám (b. 1928), Géza Pártos (b. 1917) and László Vámos (1928–96), leading the Madách Theatre, rediscovered the so-called 'bourgeois dramatists' of the 1910s and 1920s, Milán Füst (1888–1967), Ernö Szép (1884–1953) and Dezsö Szomory (1896–1944). In 1962 Vamos produced the most successful *Hamlet* of the Hungarian theatre, which remained in the repertoire for five years. The actor Miklós Gábor (1919–98) confronted the public with a disillusioned intellectual Hamlet who does not want to accept any compromise with the existing order.

The avant-garde was alive among young directors like Péter Halász (b. 1943), who, after being forced to leave Hungary, became the founder of the Squat Theater in New York (*see* EXPERIMENTAL THEATRE), and István Paál (1942–98). With their non-professional companies they were the first to adapt the teachings of BRECHT, ARTAUD and GROTOWSKI.

A new generation of young directors followed in their footsteps at the end of the 1960s and worked in regional theatres: Gábor Zsámbéki (b. 1943) attracted talented directors such as László Babarczy (b. 1941) and Tamás Ascher (b. 1948) to the theatre of Kaposvár. Gábor Székely (b. 1944) worked in Szolnok with Paál. József Ruszt (b. 1937) allied himself with Gábor in the theatre of Kecskemét. The productions they presented – mostly classics – avoided the direct methods of political theatre, but nevertheless were highly critical of the regime. These new directors were the first to break the star system and create a director's theatre based on the collective work of actors. In 1978 Zsámbéki and Székely were invited to lead the National Theatre, but as their programme was considered too anti-establishment and they were accused of anti-national sentiments they had to leave after two seasons. The most talented young actors of the National followed them and they set up a new company at the small Katona József Theatre. They established a reputation quite quickly and won international acclaim with productions of works including *Three Sisters*, *Platonov*, *The Inspector General* and *Ubu Roi*.

With the transformation of Hungary from a socialist into a market-orientated society since 1989, the theatres gained far more freedom but far less money. Ten years later, Katona is still the best Hungarian theatre, although Gábor Székeley broke with Zsámbéki and left the company. After the death in 1997 of

STREHLER Zsámbéki was invited to be president of the Union of European Theatres. Interest has come to centre on a new generation of very talented young directors, adherents of postmodernism. One of the most talented, János Szász (b. 1958), working in Nyíregyháza, was praised for his productions of *Woyzeck*, *Uncle Vanya* and *A Streetcar Named Desire*.   GÁBOR MIHÁLYI

Loránt Czigány, *The Oxford History of Hungarian Literature* (1986)
Mályusz-Császár, *A Brief Outline of Hungarian Theatre History* (1985)
Albert Tezla, *Hungarian Authors: A Biographical Handbook* (1970)
György Székely, ed., 'A Theatre Guide to Hungary', *Theatre Research* (Budapest), vol. 9, no. 1 (1967)
Hungarian Theatres, photo album (1973)

Hunt, Hugh [Sidney]   (b. Camberley, Surrey, 25 Sept. 1911; d. Criccieth, Gwynedd, Wales, 22 April 1993) Director, theatre historian and playwright. In the 1930s Hunt wrote two plays and, more importantly, staged classics in English REPERTORY theatres and new Irish plays at the ABBEY THEATRE, Dublin. After the Second World War he became the inaugural director of the BRISTOL OLD VIC (1945–8) and then director of the OLD VIC, London (1949–53). He was one of the first directors to work from a concept of a play, but not at the expense of the play or to advertise his own talents. Major London productions included *Love's Labour's Lost* (1949) and MICHAEL REDGRAVE's *Hamlet* (1950). Subsequently he was influential in Australian theatre as director of the AUSTRALIAN ELIZABETHAN THEATRE TRUST, Sydney. He was director of the Abbey Theatre (1969–71), where his production of *The Shaughraun* regenerated interest in Dion Boucicault. He was the first professor of drama at Manchester University (1961–73), where he was instrumental in the founding of the Contact Theatre (1973) for young people. Among his books are *Shakespeare and the Producer* and *Old Vic Prefaces* (both 1954).   TONY HOWARD

Hunter, Kathryn [Ekaterini Hadjipateras]   (b. New York, 9 April 1957)   Actress and director. Despite a suicide attempt while at the Royal Academy of Dramatic Art which smashed her body and left her with a limp, she continued with her acting, worked in fringe theatre and, through THEATRE DE COMPLICITE, became one of her generation's leading performers. She has bought a fierce, physical energy and challenging humour to classical roles – Juliet, the Countess in *All's Well That Ends Well*, Paulina in *The Winter's Tale* and, most daringly, Lear – as well as to contemporary ones, most notably in CHURCHILL's *The Skriker*, WHITING's

The Devils and DÜRRENMATT's *The Visit*, for which she received an Olivier Award, and as BRECHT's Mother Courage. She has directed at THEATR CLWYD and the ROYAL SHAKESPEARE COMPANY (*Everyman*, with Marcello Magni), and, for the ALMEIDA and the Right Size Company, Brecht's *Mr Puntila and His Man Matti*.
CHARLES LONDON

Hunter, N[orman] C[harles] (b. Derbyshire, 18 Sept. 1908; d. Merioneth South, Wales, 19 April 1971) Playwright. In the early 1950s, Hunter's sad bourgeois comedies provided strong roles for EDITH EVANS, SYBIL THORNDIKE, WENDY HILLER (*Waters of the Moon*, 1951), JOHN GIELGUD and RALPH RICHARDSON (*A Day By the Sea*, 1953) and many others. Hunter was seen as an English CHEKHOV. In *Waters*, a Rolls-Royce accident brings an outsider into a snowbound Dartmoor hotel, once a country house, and she disrupts the residents' pipe-dreams. Other plays deal with mediocrity, lost love and bitter domestic frustrations. Within commercial limits, Hunter suggested the passing of a comfortable era, and its emotional constriction. Other plays include *A Touch of the Sun* (1958) and *The Tulip Tree* (1962). TONY HOWARD

Hurok, Sol (b. Pogar, Russia, 9 April 1888; d. New York, 5 March 1974) Impresario. He arrived in the United States in 1906 and, starting with a benefit concert in 1911 at which he persuaded the violinist Efrem Zimbalist to play, rapidly transformed himself from a penniless immigrant into a leading impresario. He staged a succession of ever bigger and better tours – many of them featuring performers from Russia such as the MOSCOW ART THEATRE, the Bolshoi Ballet and the Kirov Ballet, as well as leading theatrical companies like the OLD VIC, HABIMAH Theatre, Compagnie BARRAULT-RENAUD and the COMÉDIE-FRANÇAISE. Thanks to Hurok's efforts American audiences were also introduced to some of the greatest performers of their time: PAVLOVA, Chaliapin, Rubinstein and Callas, to name but a few. His memoir, *Impresario*, appeared in 1946.
HELEN RAPPAPORT

Hurry, Leslie [George] (b. London, 10 Feb. 1909; d. London, 20 Nov. 1978) Designer. Hurry, a neo-Romantic painter, first transplanted his highly personal vision to the theatre in the nightmare backcloth for ROBERT HELPMANN's wartime *Hamlet* ballet (1942). His brooding mannerist designs used a narrow range of dark, morbid or opulent colours; complex private symbolism; and elongated El Greco-like costumes. After *Swan Lake* (1943), Hurry designed many ballets, OPERAS (e.g. a barbaric *Turandot*, 1947) and Shakespeare productions. Surprisingly, his *Troilus and Cres-*

sida set in a sandpit (ROYAL SHAKESPEARE COMPANY, 1960) heralded STRATFORD-UPON-AVON's new style of sculptural/metaphorical simplicity. Many of Hurry's last designs were for the Stratford, Ontario, open stage. His *Paintings and Drawings* was published in (1950).
TONY HOWARD

Hurt, William (b. Washington DC, 20 March 1950) Actor. After several roles for the NEW YORK SHAKESPEARE FESTIVAL, including Henry V (1977), he won further acclaim the same year in the CIRCLE REPERTORY THEATER production of Corinne Jacker's *My Life*. Major parts in other Circle productions followed: *Ulysses in Traction*, *Lulu* and *The Fifth of July* (1978), by which time he was being hailed as one of the most promising young actors on Broadway. A film career intervened, but he soon returned to the Circle Rep, in *Hamlet* and *Mary Stuart* (1979); the stage again became his refuge from intermittently successful screen roles during the 1980s, in particular his sensual performance in *Childe Byron*. *Hurlyburly* (1984) kept him on Broadway for a year; but since then films have taken precedence.
HELEN RAPPAPORT

T. Goldstein, *William Hurt: The Man, the Actor* (1987)

Huston [Houghston], Walter (b. Toronto, 6 April 1884; d. Beverly Hills, Calif., 7 April 1950) Gruff-voiced actor. Huston began his career in VAUDEVILLE and in cheap-priced touring shows. His most successful Broadway roles included parts in *Desire Under the Elms* (1924), *The Barker* (1927), *Dodsworth* (1934) and *Knickerbocker Holiday* (1938), introducing WEILL's 'September Song'. He was popular in films, including *The Treasure of the Sierra Madre* (1948), directed by his son John.
GERALD BORDMAN

Hutchinson, Ron (b. nr Lisburn, Co. Antrim, Northern Ireland, 8 Nov. 1946) Playwright. Brought up in England, in Coventry, Hutchinson worked at a variety of jobs, from carpet seller to social security investigator, before his first play to be produced, *Says I, Says He* (1977, Sheffield Crucible) revealed his potential as a humorous chronicler of internecine Irish squabbles in urban Britain. *Eejits* (1978) and *The Irish Play* (1980) continued the story of clashing clans and were topped by the award-winning *Rat in the Skull* (1984, ROYAL COURT), in which Hutchinson explores his own response to the events in Ireland through a vicious confrontation between two Irishmen in a London police station as a suspected Catholic bomber is interrogated by a Protestant detective inspector. Following *The Dillen* (1983) and *Mary, After the Queen* (1985), adaptations for the ROYAL SHAKESPEARE COMPANY of the story of a Stratford family, he had an adaptation of a Sinclair Lewis novel, *Babbit: A Marriage* (1987), produced in Los Angeles and decided to move there, where his flair for fast talking dialogue and narrative verve served him well in television. CHARLES LONDON

Hutt, William (b. Toronto, Ont., 2 May 1920) Actor and director. After beginning his professional career in summer stock in Ontario in the 1940s, Hutt joined the STRATFORD FESTIVAL company in its 1953 inaugural season; it was here that his reputation was built, and much of his subsequent career has been spent playing a wide range of Shakespearean roles as well as leads in Molière, Jonson, SHAW, CHEKHOV and WILDE. He has toured abroad with Stratford and has directed for the company. He also directed extensively while artistic director of Theater London in London, Ontario (1976–1979). The JOHN GIELGUD of Canadian theatre – dignified, eloquent, master ironist – Hutt is as comfortable in the contemporary as in the classical repertoire. He has created roles in many new plays, including ALBEE's *Tiny Alice* (1964) and JOHN MURRELL's *New World* (1984), directed by ROBIN PHILLIPS, with whom he has developed a special affinity; Hutt's 1988 Lear with Stratford's Young Company, directed by Phillips, was one of their (and Stratford's) finest achievements. L. W. CONOLLY

Keith Garebian, *William Hutt: A Theatre Portrait* (1988)

Hwang, David [Henry] (b. Los Angeles, 11 Aug. 1957) Playwright. Having grown up in a Chinese American community, Hwang uses a non-realistic theatricality from his cultural roots to explore issues of identity, and became the first playwright of the ASIAN AMERICAN THEATRE to gain a national standing. From his first play *F.O.B.* ('fresh off the boat', Stanford 1978), which uses role playing and myth to explore self-esteem, through *The Dance and the Railroad* (1981), *Family Devotions* (1981) and the sci-fi *1000 Airplanes on the Roof* (1998, with music by PHILP GLASS and projections by Jerome Sirlin) to his biggest success, *M. Butterfly* (1988, UK 1989), a deconstruction of sexual and ethnic stereotyping, he questions the nature of the American dream through a fusion of illusion and reality. Other plays include *Rich Relations* (1986), *The Voyage* (1992, with Glass again), *Face Value* (1993) and *Golden Child* (1996). He was Artist-in-Residency at TRINITY REPERTORY COMPANY (1995–7). CHARLES LONDON

Hyde, Douglas (b. Co. Sligo, Ireland, 17 Jan. 1860; d. Dublin, 13 July 1949) Scholar, playwright and first President of Ireland (1938–45). He wrote under the pseudonym Craoibhin Aoibhinn (the Beautiful Branch). His collection of translations *The Love-Songs of Connacht* (1893) had an immense influence on younger writers such as SYNGE. His first drama, *Casadh an tSugáin* ('The twisting of the rope', 1901), was the first GAELIC play to be seen in a Dublin theatre; it opened the third season of the Irish Literary Theatre with the author acting in it. It was followed by two more charming folk comedies, *An Tincéar agus an tSidheóg* ('The tinker and the fairy', 1902), and *An Pósadh* ('The marriage', 1902). CHRISTOPHER FITZ-SIMON

D. Coffrey, *Douglas Hyde* (1938)

Hyland, Frances (b. Shaunavon, Sask., 25 April 1927) Actress. She entered London's Royal Academy of Dramatic Art in 1948 and became a contract player for the TENNENT organization. In 1954 she returned to Canada to the STRATFORD FESTIVAL to play Isabella opposite James Mason in *Measure for Measure*. She played eight seasons at Stratford (1955–67) in such leading roles as Portia, Ophelia, Desdemona, Goneril and Mistress Ford. In 1955 she was a widely praised St Joan in a Canadian Players' production of SHAW's play. She was also a leading member of Toronto's CREST THEATRE (1954–65). She made her BROADWAY debut in Thomas Wolfe's *Look Homeward, Angel* (1957). In the 1960s she starred increasingly in Canada's regional theatres (e.g. in the title role in the première of GEORGE RYGA's *The Ecstasy of Rita Joe*, 1967), and in the 1970s and 1980s she turned to directing (e.g. HAROLD PINTER's *The Birthday Party*, 1970; *Othello*, 1979; and STRINDBERG's *Playing with Fire*, 1987). An actress of unusual range, Hyland is noted for her classicism and a presence often termed 'aristocratic'. EUGENE BENSON

Hylton [Hilton], Jack (b. Bolton, Lancs, 2 July 1892; d. London, 29 Jan. 1965) English band leader and impresario. After appearing with a PIERROT troupe, he became a conductor for touring revues, a cinema organist and, in 1924, the leader of a dance band. Radio broadcasts and gramophone recordings made his band a star attraction in Britain and on the European continent. In 1940 he rescued the London Philharmonic Orchestra from a wartime slump by organizing a provincial tour, and this launched him on a managerial career which included the London presentation of many American musicals (*Can-Can*, *High Button Shoes*, *Kiss Me Kate*, *Pal Joey*, *Kismet* and others). He co-presented the long-running British musical *Salad Days* but his greatest postwar success was achieved by reuniting the CRAZY GANG comedians and starring them in a sequence of seven VARIETY REVUES which ran at London's Victoria Palace for 15 years from 1947 to 1962. IAN BEVAN

Hynes, Gary *see* ABBEY THEATRE; DRUID THEATRE COMPANY

Hytner, Nicholas (b. Manchester, 7 May 1956) Theatre, opera and film director. He began directing professionally at the Northcott Theatre, Exeter and LEEDS Playhouse, subsequently becoming associate director at the ROYAL EXCHANGE THEATRE, MANCHESTER. In 1987 he directed *Measure for Measure* for the ROYAL SHAKESPEARE COMPANY, followed by *The Tempest* (1988) and *King Lear* (1990), both with JOHN WOOD. In 1989 his production of *Ghetto* by JOSHUA SOBOL began a distinguished association with the Royal NATIONAL THEATRE, leading to *Wind in the Willows* (1990), *The Madness of George III* (1991), *Carousel* (1993) and *The Cripple of Inishman* (1997). In 1989 he directed the musical *Miss Saigon*, which became an international success. His work in opera includes *Xerxes* (1985), *The Magic Flute* (1988) and *La Clemenza di Tito* (1991). His first film, of ALAN BENNETT's *The Madness of King George* (1995), was quickly followed by others, keeping him away from the theatre for several years. In 1999 he returned, directing *Twelfth Night* at the LINCOLN CENTER, New York, and *The Lady in the Van* (renewing his relationship with Bennett) in London. In 2001 the National announced that he would succeed TREVOR NUNN as artistic director in 2003. His work is characterized by a cool, clean aesthetic allied to great skill in the animation of large spaces and an ability to inspire confidence in actors.   GENISTA MCINTOSH

I

Ibsen, Henrik [Johan] (b. Skien, Norway, 20 March 1828; d. Christiana (now Oslo), 23 May 1906) Playwright. In 1862, when Ibsen was 34, no one could have imagined that he would one day be regarded as the father of twentieth-century European drama. The theatre at which he had been working as a director for the past five years had just gone bankrupt, he was without a permanent job, and he had not yet written any of the plays by which he is now known. Ibsen experienced early humiliation, for in 1835 the whole family was forced to move out of town to a smaller house on account of his father's financial difficulties. From the age of 15 to to 22 Ibsen worked as an apothecary's assistant in the nearby coastal town of Grimstad, and here he wrote his first play, *Catalina* (*Catilinè*), in 1850), the material for which he found in the Latin syllabus he was studying in order to sit his university matriculation examinations. Although it was Ibsen's first play, it contains typically Ibsenian motifs: a man caught between two women, one gentle, one fiery. These two, Aurelia and Furia, are the forerunners of many women in Ibsen's play, from Agnes and Gerd in *Brand* (1866 – all dates are dates of writing), through Thea and Hedda in *Hedda Gabler* (1890) to Asta and Rita in *Lille Eyolf* (*Little Eyolf*, 1894). Another typically Ibsenian motif is the fact that the protagonist is overtaken by a forgotten guilt from the past.

The Christiania to which Ibsen came in 1850 hoping to enter university was a small town with 30,000 inhabitants and only one professional theatre. Norway had gained independence from Denmark in 1814 and was now part of a union with Sweden. In this state of recently won independence, painters, poets and musicians were seeking out what they considered to be the true spirit of Norway in the history, folklore and landscape of the nation. This movement, known as National Romanticism, had a profound influence on the cultural life of the capital throughout the 1840s and 1850s.

It was in order to help foster this movement in the theatre that Ole Bull, the Norwegian virtuoso violinst, in 1851 invited Ibsen to come to Bergen as 'dramatic author' at the recently founded Bergen Norwegian Theatre. The aim of this theatre was to put on plays with Norwegian themes, written by Norwegian dramatists and performed by Norwegian actors. The six years in Bergen were crucial in Ibsen's development as a dramatist, for it was here that he learnt the practicalities of his craft. It was also here that he wrote his early National Romantic plays, *Fru Inger til Østrât* (*Lady Inger of Østrât*, 1855), *Gildet pa Solhaug* (*The Feast at Solhaug*, 1856) and *Hærmændene på Helgeland* (*The Vikings at Helgeland*, 1858), and met his future wife, Suzannah Thoresen.

In 1857 the Christiania Norwegian Theatre invited Ibsen to return to Christiania to help revive its flagging fortunes. The theatre had been set up in 1852, one year after the Bergen Norwegian Theatre, and for the same purpose. From the beginning its survival had been precarious, and shortly before Ibsen's arrival it had seriously considered closing down. Because of the impossibility of pleasing both the public and the critics, Ibsen's years in Christiania between 1857 and 1864 were the most difficult of his life. During this time he wrote only one play, *Kjælighedens komedie* (*Love's Comedy*), which was published in 1862 and which, though a comedy, gives some hint of the scathing critic of bourgeois marriage conventions which Ibsen was to become.

When the Christiania Norwegian Theatre finally

went bankrupt in 1862 Ibsen was left without a job, and from now on had to survive on casual earnings and grants. In 1863 he attended a Student Choral Festival in Bergen and was received with such warmth and appreciation that he found the idea for his last, and most successful, National Romantic play, *Kongs-Emnerne* (*The Pretenders*, 1864). This play about vocation and doubt revolves round the political battle between King Haakon and Earl Skule in thirteenth-century Norway. It was the last play Ibsen ever directed, for the following year he left Norway for Rome, and did not to return to visit his native country till 1874, nor to settle till 1891.

Norway's refusal to help Denmark in its war against Prussia over Schleswig-Holstein in 1864 had profoundly troubled Ibsen, and the anger he felt at his country's faint-heartedness was part of the inspiration for his first masterpiece, *Brand*. Another influence was in all probability the writings of the Danish philosopher and theologian Søren Kierkegaard, though Ibsen himself denied this. There is no half-heartedness in Brand, a clergyman, who believes that man was created in the image of God, but that this image has become botched. For the divine stamp to shine with its original brightness, Brand believes that man has to make his eternal destiny a matter of absolute concern, 'all or nothing', and it is this that he asks of himself and others. In the course of so doing he sacrifices his mother, his son, his wife and finally his own life. *Brand* is a monolithic play in which Ibsen gives full expression to some of his most abiding concerns: the struggle of the individual to be fully him- or herself, whatever the odds; and the conflict between vocation and human relationships.

According to Ibsen, 'after *Brand*, *Peer Gynt* [1867] followed as it were of its own accord,' and it is in many ways the other side of the coin to *Brand*. Where *Brand* is taut and austere, *Peer Gynt* is rich and relaxed, covering a lifetime and half the globe, and moving back and forth between the worlds of fantasy, folklore and reality. Where Brand is himself, Peer is 'himself – enough' or, in the words of a recent translation of the Old Man of Dovre's words from the play, 'self-ish'. He is a role-player who, as he peels the onion in Act V, wonders whether he has a core, a self. Both plays have the subtitle 'dramatic poem', and in Scandinavia *Peer Gynt* was not performed until 1876, nor *Brand* until 1885. In Britain, where Ibsen first became known through his social plays, *Peer Gynt* was not performed until 1911 nor *Brand* until 1912.

Ever since his arrival in Rome in 1864 Ibsen had been grappling with the material of his next play, *Kejser og Galilær* (*Emperor and Galilean*, a vast, two-part, ten-act work about Julian the Apostate (*c.* 331–60), which was not published until 1873. Conceived at a time when the prevailing religious and metaphysical world views were being challenged by the findings of science and particularly Darwinism, the play had, according to Ibsen, 'a closer connection with the currents of our own age than one might at first think'. This is because the struggle between Christianity and paganism which is at the heart of *Emperor and Galilean* can be seen as a parallel to the conflict between religion and science which was raging in the nineteenth century. The fact that Ibsen subtitled the play 'a world-historical drama' suggests that he regarded the conflict of values and beliefs in both periods as being of world-historical significance. The play marked a watershed in Ibsen's career, for it was his last historical play and the last play he conceived on the grand scale. After that he chose to present his themes through the medium of the social reality of contemporary Norway, where the struggle between Christianity and the joy of life becomes the struggle between Pastor Manders and Osvald in *Gengangere* (*Ghosts*, 1881) or between Rosmer and Rebekka in *Rosmersholm* (1886), which in some ways may be regarded as a chamber version of *Emperor and Galilean*.

More drafts exist of *Samfundets støtter* (*The Pillars of Society*, 1877, sometimes called *The Pillars of the Community*) than of any other Ibsen play. The reason is perhaps that with this play Ibsen was branching out into what was for him new territory: the realistic bourgeois drama, acted out within the four walls of the bourgeois home. That it is something of an apprenticeship piece may be seen by comparing it with his next play, *Et dukkehjem* (*A Doll's House*, 1879). Whereas *Pillars* has 19 named characters, *A Doll's House* has six. The secret guiltily kept hidden in *Pillars* is one of cowardice and deceit for business gain, whereas in *A Doll's House* the motives are more complex. The greatest development between the two plays is, however, that of concentration, and Ibsen achieves this by using all the resources of the theatre. Now it is not just the spoken word, but setting, dress, gestures and actions, like lighting a lamp, that become eloquent means of expression. As one scholar long ago observed, even a deaf person could get a lot out of a performance of *A Doll's House*, for Nora expresses herself as much through what she does as through what she says. If this play caused a furore with its idea that a wife could walk out on her husband, it was nothing compared to the storm provoked by Ibsen's next play, *Ghosts*, with its discussion of inherited venereal disease, euthanasia and incestuous liaisons. However, these elements belong to the sensational surface of the play, and beneath this there is enacted the tragic darma of Mrs Alving's quest for a more honest way of life than that permitted by the morality of the day.

With *A Doll's House* and *Ghosts*, Ibsen leapt into the position of the leading European dramatist. How? One reason is that he was the first playwright to make the theatre the forum for the serious consideration of contemporary issues and to show that high drama, even tragedy, could take place within the confines of the domestic sitting room. Furthermore, his characters were not types, but ordinary yet complex individuals questioning the rules under which society made them live.

En folkefiende (*An Enemy of the People*, 1882) was in many ways a response to the reception of *Ghosts*. As Dr Stockmann tries to warn the inhabitants of his home town that the waters of the spa are infected, so Ibsen had tried to warn his countrymen of the corruption at the heart of their society. Neither community had wanted to listen, and as Stockmann is ostracized and rejected for his pains, so Ibsen was vilified when *Ghosts* was published.

In a letter to his publisher, Ibsen wrote that *Vildanden* (*The Wild Duck*, 1884, produced 1885) 'occupies a place of its own among my dramas; the method is in various respects a departure from my earlier ones'. This difference is also evident in the three plays which follow: *Rosmersholm, Fruen fra havet* (*The Lady from the Sea*, 1888) and *Hedda Gabler*. In these plays human unhappiness seems no longer attributable to social ills, but to lie deeper, either in the individual psyche or in the very fabric of human existence. In *The Wild Duck* the characters unable to face reality have sought refuge in a comfortable world of illusion and life-lies. This is shattered by the entry of Gregers Werle who, equally unable to face naked reality, has taken refuge in a sick idealism which he inflicts on the Ekdal household with tragic results. Ellida Wangel in *The Lady from the Sea* believes that humankind might have been happier if it had learnt to live on, perhaps even *in*, the sea. But there is no turning back; civilization may cause discontent, but that which is not tamed, such as the sea, is associated not only with freedom but with death and destruction. Likewise, Rebekka in *Rosmersholm* may originally have come to Rosmersholm as a free, uninhibited individual, but when passion for Rosmer overwhelmed her, she had no learned cultural inhibitions with which to resist the urge to drive his wife to suicide. It is no coincidence that Freud wrote a study of Rebekka West, for in his late plays Ibsen was making the same discoveries as the founder of psychoanalysis, namely that men and women are driven by forces which they do not understand, and that language is a means of concealing as much as revealing. *The Lady from the Sea* was once described as the dramatization of a psychoanalytical cure, and though this description ignores the suggestive poetry of the play as a whole, it is true that when Ellida Wangel, the lady from the sea, is allowed to express more and more of what preoccupies her, the knot of the past is unravelled and she can take responsibility for her life. No such possibility exists in *Hedda Gabler*, where the conflict between Hedda's psychological predisposition and social conditioning, her poetic vision and the reality in which she is caught, runs so deep that she can find no freedom save in death.

Ibsen's last four plays, *Bygmester Solness* (*The Master Builder*, 1892), *Little Eyolf, John Gabriel Borkman* (1896) and *Når vi døde vågner* (*When We Dead Awaken*, 1898) form a more homogeneous group than the previous four, for all focus on an ageing artist figure (in the loosest sense of the word) who, when he casts a retrospective glance over his life, feels that somewhere it took a wrong turn. The first, third and fourth plays of this group also contain a strong autobiographical and metadramatic element, being about the nature and cost of artistic talent, and in the first and fourth the stages of the respective 'artistic' projects have some correspondence to phases in Ibsen's career. In all four cases the protagonist is married to a woman he does not love, and in every play except *Little Eyolf* this situation is radically changed when a woman whom the protagonist has known in the past suddenly appears on the scene. Unlike the self-sacrificing women of the early plays, such as Agnes in *Brand* and Solveig in *Peer Gynt*, the woman from the past in *John Gabriel Borkman* and *When We Dead Awaken* challenges the male protagonist for having used her and then sacrificed her to his vocation. In these two plays and in *The Master Builder* there is an attempt to retrieve what was lost, and regain sexual and creative potency; but the attempt, though heroic, is doomed.

Despite the time that has passed since Ibsen's death, he is still very much alive and with us. Critics and scholars give very different reasons for why this is, but the fact that they do demonstrates the fruitfulness of Ibsen, the fact that however much our interpretations of the world change, he still seems relevant. Some see him as a realist and as a critic engaged in unmasking our illusions and showing up our ideals and most elevated projects as fig-leaves that we use to cover up our fear of life and relationships. Others see beneath the realist a poet exploring the eternal questions which give humans their tragic dignity. But the fact that Ibsen explores profound issues does not in itself make him a major European dramatist. What makes him one

· Performing Ibsen ·

Ibsen talks about 'mining' his plays. Beneath the banal everyday phrases lie words of ambiguity and inference. Every stone on the way must be picked over to expose the damp worm coiled beneath. Take *Hedda Gabler*. I have played Hedda twice; first on television and a few years later on the stage. Hedda Mark I was lighter, quicker, more pensive than Mark II. She tired of herself more obviously, dismissed people more charmingly and was, I suppose, altogether more heartless. In my second attempt I played her less light-headed, more impulsively, more driven by demon winds. If Hedda were merely callous, merely unreasonably calculating, she was much less interesting to me. What satanic script was she writing for herself?

There seems to be some doubt among commentators about whether Hedda is pregnant. Of course she is. There is no play otherwise. Hedda's secret is central to understanding her predicament. I could not forget that she kills not one, but two people at the end. It is a precipitate thing: she wakes in the morning spoiling for trouble, and by the following midnight she is dead.

The play is rife with missed opportunities, hair's-breadth moments when a word could soothe, a rela-trail, but when finally she sees her own salvation gleaming darkly, she hugs to herself the greatest power she has ever experienced, that of escape and liberty, and cocks a mighty snook at all the provincial paraphernalia of which she was fancied the very mark and glass.

In the century which saw the emancipation, in principle, of half the world's population, Hedda's struggle, like that of other Ibsen characters, to make sense of a life beset with dated structures continued to enthral and puzzle. Her modernity lies in her unwillingness to explain herself, in her spiritual laziness. Poorly educated, religiously undirected, physically healthy, aware of a world elsewhere (*sans* television soaps or women's glossies), suffering the pangs of social greed, she is the distillation of Western dissatisfactions – small-town dissatisfactions. That said, like all great dramatic inventions, she resists definition. The free spirit roams in Hades, mysterious, amused. In *Hamlet*, that other black diamond of a play, death also appears strangely desirable. But where Shakespeare ponders and illumines, Ibsen implies.

JANET SUZMAN

of the most performed dramatists after Shakespeare is surely the fact that he makes these issues concrete and specific in the human dramas which he unfolds before our eyes. His questions may be unanswerable and his characters inexhaustible, but as actors and directors take up the challenge and engage in the exploration and questioning we too become involved as readers and theatre-goers. MARIE WELLS

Robert Ferguson, *Henrik Ibsen: A New Biography* (1996)
J. W. McFarlane, *Henrik Ibsen* (1970)
——, *Ibsen and Meaning: Studies, Essays and Prefaces, 1953–87* (1989)
——, ed., *The Cambridge Companion to Ibsen* (1994)
Frederick Marker and Lise-Lone Marker, *Ibsen's Lively Art: A Performance Study of the Major Plays* (1989)
David Thomas, *Ibsen* (1983)

Iceland Ruled by Norway and Denmark from the tenth century to the twentieth, the country became fully independent only in 1944. Although there are references to actors and jugglers in thirteenth-century Icelandic sources, and in spite of the very dramatic nature of the ancient Eddic poems (e.g. dialogue, impersonation) and the fact that some dance-games in Iceland are very old, it is not until the mid-eighteenth century that theatre activities are clearly documented, when a religious festival at Skálholt gave rise to the comedies of Sigurður Pétursson (1759–1827), considered the father of Icelandic playwriting. Theatre activity in the nineteenth century was concentrated in the growing towns, especially in the capital, Reykjavík, where the painter Sigurður Guðmundsson (1833–74) promoted national consciousness and inspired some young authors (e.g. Matthías Jochumsson, 1835–1920, and Indriði Einarsson, 1851–1939) to write plays that became classics. In 1897 the semi-professional Reykjavík Theatre Company was founded, democratically run by the actors but officially subsidized. (Professionally trained actors joined during the 1920s and 1930s.) Soon there emerged some major dramatists: Jóhann Sigurjónsson (1880–1919) with *Eyvind of the Mountains* (1911) and *The Wish* (1913), and Guðmundur Kamban (1888–1945) with *We Murderers* (1919). Another popular play is Davíð Stefánsson's *The Golden Gate* (1941). In 1989 the RTC moved into the new Municipal Theatre.

The National Theatre opened its gates in 1950, increasing the number of plays produced each season by two-thirds. Today these two major companies together employ together more than 100 permanently engaged actors. The National Theatre also fostered a ballet company, now an independent, state-subsidized enterprise, and started opera in Iceland in 1951. There are also 15–18 small professional groups (including marionette groups and an opera house), as well as a professional resident theatre in Akureyri and some 80 amateur groups. Radio theatre started in 1931 and television drama in 1967.

A contemporary season in Reykjavík can offer up to 50 different productions of which 40 per cent are new Icelandic plays by authors such as Halldór Laxness (1902–98), Jökull Jakobsson (1933–78), Guðmundur Steinsson (1926–96), Jónas Árnason (1922–98) and Birgir Sigurðsson (b. 1936), all of whom have been produced abroad, and a number of younger playwrights, e.g. Kjarian Ragnarsson (b. 1945) and Alni Ibsen (b. 1948). The number of spectators in a season can often outnumber the island's population of 250,000. Recent research has brought to light new facts about the popularity of the theatre, and each week during the winter up to 30 different productions in 13 different venues are offered to the Reykjavík audience. SVEINN EINARSSON

Ikoli, Tunde *see* BLACK THEATRE; FOCO NOVO

Ilf [Ilya Aranldovich Fainzilberg] (b. Odessa, Russia, 15 Oct. 1897; d. Moscow, 13 April 1937) and **Petrov [Evgeny Petrovich Kataev]** (b. Odessa, 13 Dec. 1903, d. on flight between Sebastopol and Moscow, 2 July 1942) Playwrights. *The Twelve Chairs* (1928, translated as *Diamonds to Sit On*) and its sequel *The Little Golden Calf* (1931) satirically describe the less savoury aspects of Soviet life: corruption, greed, bootleggers and gangsters. During the Depression, the pair travelled around America humorously detailing their experiences and observations in *Tonya* (1935), *One Storied America* (1936) and *Columbus Puts To* (1937). Petrov wrote of their collaboration in *Notebooks* (1939). *The Twelve Chairs* was filmed by Mel Brooks in 1967.
IRENE SLATTER

illusion *see* ESCAPOLOGY; MAGIC

impersonation In the twentieth century, usually taken to mean more than simply playing a character because it is associated with portraying a real as opposed to a fictional person. Some performers earn a living as 'look-alikes' (whether it be as Madonna or Margaret Thatcher) and some as impressionists where the real figure is conjured up through look, sound and gesture, often reaching beyond imitation and mimicry to lampoon or satire. When actors are cast as real people in plays it may be important to impersonate

accurately, or perhaps to create an authentic impression, or even not to bother at all with verisimilitude, depending on the nature of the performance. In a PAGEANT or some forms of STREET THEATRE, impersonation tends to be no more than symbolic; in WAXWORKS, however, realism is at a premium, while with PUPPETS it will depend on their use and the medium in which they are appearing. CHARLES LONDON
See also DRAG; POP MUSIC AND THEATRE.

Roger Baker, *Drag: A History of Female Impersonation in the Performing Arts* (1994)

Improbable Theatre Founded in 1996 by Lee Simpson, Julian Crouch and Phelim McDermott, it took theatre-making in new directions with a mix of puppetry, improvisation, comedy and storytelling, transforming the unlikeliest of material into striking, idiosyncratic entertainment. From the first show, *Animo* (1996) through the award-winning *70 Hill Lane* (1997), to its adaptation of novelist Angela Carter's *Cinderella* (1998) and *Coma* (1999), Improbable won national and international recognition for crossing boundaries and redefining theatrical culture. Crouch and McDermott also teamed up for equally distinctive productions elsewhere, such as *A Midsummer Night's Dream* (1996) for the ENGLISH SHAKESPEARE COMPANY and *Shockheaded Peter* (1997), which began at the WEST YORKSHIRE PLAYHOUSE before being revived to great acclaim several times in London. CHARLES LONDON

improvisation An important book, *Improvisation in Drama* (1990) by Anthony Frost and Raiph Yarrow, offers this definition: 'The skill of using bodies, space, all human resources, to generate a coherent physical expression of an idea, a situation, a character (even, perhaps, a text); to do this spontaneously, in response to the immediate stimuli of one's environment, and to do it *à l'improviste*: as though taken by surprise, without preconceptions.' Improvisation has three major areas of application: first, it can serve as a tool to assist traditional theatre training; in this area, STANISLAVSKY and MEYERHOLD were precursors. Stanislavsky placed much emphasis on improvisation in his theories; however, there is little evidence that he actually used improvisation in his practical work. Meyerhold developed BIOMECHANICS in his experimental physical work with actors; however, his aim was to enable the actors to comply more efficiently with his demands as a director – he was little concerned with the actors' creativity. The modern tradition really begins with JACQUES COPEAU. The second area is pure improvisation giving rise to an 'alternative' kind of theatrical experience; representatives of this area are Theatre Machine, associated with the ROYAL COURT THEATRE, French clown JACQUES LECOQ, DARIO FO and FRANCA RAME. Finally, there is the extension *beyond* theatre itself, with GROTOWSKI as main exponent.

There is a wide variety of improvisation techniques, given different emphases by different theatre artists. Most improvisation, as indeed most theatre work in general, will start with preparatory exercises, e.g. relaxing the body, ridding it of *unwanted* tension, and theatre games, which help to 'socialize the training' and prepare the actor to be concentrated, *present*, physically and mentally, in space and time. Another set of exercises is about working together: it includes establishing trust and respect among the cast; the actors support each other, in showing events rather than merely telling them, in not leaving each other stranded, or in not blocking new ideas whose further development in improvisation might not be clear at first. More difficult exercises, still geared to enhancing the actors' performing abilities, are aimed at their sensory alertness and awareness of status. Often, work with masks proves helpful. The last group of techniques involves '*applied* improvisation work'. Viola Spolin's 'who/where/what' exercises provide a guideline for the actor's imagination, helping him/her to overcome discomfort resulting from his/her feeling that in improvisation s/he does not know where s/he is going. Whereas pure improvisation does not focus specifically on a dramatic character, in applied improvisation, used in rehearsal, character is the main concern. Such applied improvisation is not about the character's inner life, but about the actor's, and helps the actor to succeed in realizing the Stanislavskian 'As If'.

Improvisation activities serve to free, unblock and alert the performer's mind and body. The performer's self, creativity and imagination are affected, as well as his or her interaction and communication with others, producing 'an extension of being, knowing and interacting'. Such techniques have been applied outside theatre, in therapy and management training, for example. DANIEL MEYER-DINKGRÄFE

Clive Barker, *Theatre Games: A New Approach to Drama Training* (1977)
Keith Johnstone, *Impro: Improvisation and the Theatre* (1981)
Viola Spolin, *Improvisation for the Theater* (1973)
R. Yarrow, *Improvisation in Drama* (1990)

independent theatre A term current at the end of the nineteenth century and beginning of the twentieth to denote theatres operating against the established patterns of state patronage and commercial management. The aim was to create a new theatre which, in its various forms, would be a response to the materialist values of the bourgeoisie from whose ranks its practitioners came. There are no obvious ties which bring together the many independent theatres which sprang up throughout Europe after 1887 to form the first AVANT-GARDE, but theatres were aware of one another's existence and drew support and example from each other. The specific conditions and pattern of activity in each country varied widely. First came ANTOINE's Théâtre Libre, which gave rise to the term 'FREE THEATRE', which overlapped with 'independent theatre'. As well as the first SYMBOLIST theatre, Théâtre d'Art, there were STRINDBERG's Intimate Theatre, OTTO BRAHM's FREIE BUHNE and the MOSCOW ART THEATRE. Some theatres aspired to a broader repertoire (COPEAU and the Vieux Colombier), while another strand tried to widen the composition of the audience to include the lower social classes (ROMAIN ROLLAND, the VOLKSBUHNE), or to participate in the class struggle (PISCATOR and the Proletarian Theatre). The means by which these theatres were financed were many and various: the private purse of rich individuals, subscription seasons, joint stock companies and, often, commercial success. Many existed as private societies not open to the public. The term 'independent theatres' was dropped, or dropped out of use, when the general movement became so successful that it was established as the most vital form of theatre available. The term does occur specifically in connection with J. T. GREIN's INDEPENDENT THEATRE SOCIETY in London, which introduced IBSEN and SHAW to the British stage and which began the move towards the REPERTORY MOVEMENT in Britain and the founding of the NATIONAL THEATRE. CLIVE BARKER

A. Miller, *The Independent Theatre in Europe* (1966)
J. Stokes, *Resistible Theatres* (1972)

Independent Theatre Society This London-based subscription society, inspired by ANTOINE and founded in 1891 largely through the efforts of J. T. GREIN, aimed to give performances of plays of literary and artistic rather than commercial value. Its inaugural 'invitation' production of IBSEN's then banned *Ghosts* (allowed as a private society) provoked a notorious storm of hysterical outrage in the English press. The Society went on to present an eclectic range of plays, including *Widowers' Houses*, SHAW's first play to be performed. Although shortlived (it folded in 1898) its example was crucial to the development of early twentieth-century progressive theatre through the STAGE SOCIETY, the GRANVILLE BARKER–VEDRENNE reign at the ROYAL COURT, and the REPERTORY MOVEMENT. IAN CLARKE

India Geographically termed a subcontinent, India's area is one-third of Europe's but their populations are roughly equal. India's culture lives up to the implications of such comparisons, for four major religions (Hinduism, Sikhism, Buddhism and Jainism) originated and exist within its territorial limits, while sizeable communities of three other religions (Islam, Christianity and Zoroastrianism) have made India their home. Eighteen constitutionally recognized languages are spoken, all with fully developed literatures, many of which date back to the twelfth century or earlier. India is the single largest nation with such a multitude of major languages, and they use nine separate scripts so that – unlike in most of Europe – an Indian may not be able even to decipher the characters printed in a newspaper of a neighbouring state. To discuss Indian drama is therefore like discussing the drama of, say, western Europe (which has about the same number of major literatures): a daunting task fraught with the risk of oversimplifications.

Having made this qualification, one can say that India has three broad theatrical traditions. The oldest, the classical Sanskrit courtly drama, flourished in the first ten centuries of the Christian era; its gradual decline corresponded with that of the ancient language itself, the rise of the various vernacular tongues and the political upheavals accompanying consecutive waves of Muslim invasions. For the folk theatre it is impossible to ascertain a timeframe because it belongs to the oral tradition, with no written documentation. Performed in the dialects of the common people of rural India, which change from district to district, and with myriad varieties, each one quite different from the next, it may have run parallel to the Sanskrit theatre just as it offset the sophisticated urban theatre of the twentieth century. This latter, modern drama, a product of the nineteenth century in the rapidly evolving regional literatures influenced by the artistic ideals and achievements of the imperial West, became more consciously indigenous in the twentieth century and attained the status of *the* serious Indian drama.

Classical theatre

Remnants of Sanskrit theatrical practice linger in the twentieth century. The art of *kutiyattam* (literally, 'group-drama') performed in Hindu temples in the southern state of Kerala maintains an unbroken continuity of at least 1,000 years, making it one of the world's oldest extant theatrical forms. *kutiyattam* groups enact scenes from classical Sanskrit plays in a mix of Sanskrit, Prakrit (the lower-class language of those times) and old Malayalam (the language of Kerala), adhering strictly to manuals of performance handed down from generation to generation. Stylized acting with the aid of *mudras* (codified signs and gestures), ornate and colourful costumes and make-up, heightened vocal delivery and substantial use of music characterize *kutiyattam*, which typically warms up with several nights of introductory episodes before exhaustively interpreting one full act on the last night or couple of nights from about 9 p.m. to dawn.

Closer investigation of the texts preserved by *kutiyattam* troupes led to the sensational discovery in 1909 of plays by Bhasa, a Sanskrit dramatist of nearly 2,000 years ago regarded highly by Kalidasa, himself the finest Sanskrit author. Till then, none of Bhasa's plays appeared to have survived the centuries. By 1914, however, as many as 13 were recovered after a thorough search in Kerala. This find in turn stimulated an interest in reviving his works, and many of them have since been staged in Sanskrit – technically a dead language. Writer–director K. N. Panikkar (b. 1928) was responsible for some of these productions, employing the method of *kutiyattam* and the *kalari* martial arts of Kerala in modernized fashion.

Folk theatre

The convenient labels 'classical' and 'folk' facilitate categorization, but they are also deceptive, just like the division between traditional drama and dance in India. The prominence of devotional ritual, symbol, music and conventionalized expression and movement in both pairs effectively blurs distinctions. Where, for example, does one pigeonhole the Chhau masked performances of eastern India, containing both terpsichorean and thespian elements? Not surprisingly, Indian dance and drama separately claim several performing arts, yet differ upon their classification. For instance, the dance establishment considers south Indian dance-dramas like *kathakali* (literally 'story-performance', from Kerala) and *kuchipudi* (named after the village of its origin in Andhra Pradesh) as 'classical' due to their intricacy and high degree of stylization, apparently derived from the precepts laid down by the Sanskrit theorist Bharata in antiquity, whereas theatre historians place these two among 'folk' idioms on the basis of dialogue, distinguishing the classical drama in Sanskrit from these relatively recent forms that emerged as late as the seventeenth century in modern languages like Malayalam (of *kathakali*) and Telugu (of *kuchipudi*). Consequently some scholars prefer to use the blanket term 'traditional' for all such genres.

Despite the competitive inroads made by electronic media like cinema, radio and television, causing theatre audiences to dwindle and performances to become fewer, the time-honoured live presentations by itinerant troupes in India's villages continue. These are extremely diverse in content and structure: there are about 50 main folk forms across the country, plus another score or so of various PUPPET styles embracing all four kinds of puppetry – string, rod, glove and shadow puppets. Folk plays deal with secular or sacred subjects, though not necessarily Hindu ones. For example, the *chavittu natakam* ('kicking theatre', because it emphasizes footwork) initiated in Tamil in the sixteenth century relates tales from Christian history meant for the Roman Catholic population of Kerala. Folk theatre is generally enacted overnight, in the open or in makeshift pavilions (sometimes near temples on religious occasions) and is full of song, dance and colloquial vocabulary. The mood ranges from farcical horseplay to spiritual intensity, both often coexisting in the same play.

In addition to those mentioned above, some important traditional forms are (with the language area of the best-known variety in parentheses): the devotional *ankiya nat* ('one-act theatre'; Assamese), the satirical *bhand pather* ('clown show'; Kashmiri), the rumbunctious *bhavai* (probably from *bhav*, 'emotion'; Gujarati), the narrative *burrakatha* ('*burra*-story', since accompanied by the *burra* stringed instrument; Telugu), the iconographical *dashavatar* ('ten avatars', alluding to Vishnu; Konkani), the declamatory *jatra* ('processional', because of its religious source; Bengali), the ritualistic *krishnattam* ('Krishna-drama'; Sanskrit done in Kerala), the robust *nautanki* (perhaps from the name of a princess in one of its popular plays; Hindusthani or Urdu), the legendary *prahlad nataka* ('Prahlad theatre', after the protagonist's name; Oriya), the festive *ramlila* and *raslila* ('Rama-play' and 'Ras-play', *ras* being Krishna's typical dance style; Hindi), the comic *suang* ('imitation'; Punjabi), the lyrical *sumang lila* ('courtyard play'; Manipuri), the scurrilous *tamasha* ('fun'; Marathi), the proletarian *terukkuttu* ('street-enactment'; Tamil) and the mythological *yakshagana* ('Yaksha-songs', Yaksha possibly synonymous with the Telugu caste known as Jakkula who specialize in performance; Kannada). Most seem to have developed in medieval times. Their earthy vigour encouraged many late twentieth-century urban directors to borrow their techniques as well as their TOTAL THEATRE approach combining poetry, art, music and dance, in attempts to root modern drama in 'Indianness' – as, for example, in the striking resurrection of folk material by B. V. Karanth (b. 1928). Some critics find this trend merely superficial and opportunistic, but theatre workers tend to disregard this controversy, arguing that theatre has always been eclectic and syncretic.

Modern theatre

Inspired by the British colonial theatre, Indian-owned professional companies and proscenium auditoriums (the concept of permanent playhouses in the Western sense was alien to India) sprang up in the main cities in the nineteenth century. Their date of establishment varied from state to state, with the result that movements in dramatic literature of the major languages similarly varied in chronology, by years and sometimes by decades, although in general one can discern a common evolutionary pattern. This new urban theatre aimed to entertain the lower and middle classes with lavish and garish spectacles based on either Hindu mythological or quasi-historical Indian themes. Liberally garnished with song and dance, often in verse, sentimental or melodramatic, these plays proved immensely popular well into the twentieth century, their reach spreading beyond the cities by virtue of touring companies.

Some proprietors realized the provocative power of theatre fairly early and started using thinly disguised stories from Indian history to arouse patriotic passions in spectators. Recognizing the dangers of such potentially subversive art, specifically after certain plays staged in Calcutta (then India's capital), the British clamped down with the Dramatic Performances Control Act in 1876, under which every script had to pass police approval; the law stood for many years, even after Indian independence in 1947. In the two or three decades prior to independence, the number of historical plays (safe from censorship because not overtly political) performed all over the nation registered a sharp increase, in parallel with the growth of the freedom movement.

Simultaneously, the theatre began to confront hard times caused by the desertion of audiences to the fascinating new world of the talkies. Not just theatregoers, but actors, directors and backstage hands too gravitated to cinema studios, lured by the prospects of quick and easy money. Many public companies and commercial playhouses had to pull down their shutters as once-loyal spectators shifted allegiance; meanwhile, the Indian film industry, centred in Bombay, readily took over the fantasy, glitter and razzmatazz that appealed to these viewers and continued to exploit these devices profitably into the last decades of the century.

The theatre clientele changed radically. A more dedicated, educated and sophisticated customer who looked superciliously at the newfangled fancy called film began frequenting the playhouses. Apart from the undercurrent of protest, an emphasis on realistic and socialistic plays followed, as opposed to the cinema's escapism. In the vanguard of this school was the Indian People's Theatre Association (IPTA), a nationwide body of leftist intellectuals founded in 1943, the year after Mahatma Gandhi launched his 'Quit India' campaign against the British. As the professionals waned, amateurs, beginning with the IPTA in Calcutta, took charge for the next half-century. Calcutta, the heart of Bengali theatre, continued to sustain professional theatres in its old sector, but also boasts the largest number of amateur groups (over 2,000) of any Indian city: Bohurupee, People's Little Theatre and Nandikar are the most prominent, though many splinters from them do good work. Bombay (now renamed Mumbai) had around 500 groups performing in four languages, among them the Indian National Theatre, Avishkar and Rangayan. In south India, Bangalore is home to the energetic Kannada theatre, along with younger groups like Spandana. India's capital, New Delhi, hosts some reputed companies such as the Naya Theatre. These organizations remain amateur because full-time serious theatre is not financially viable. Most members have other regular careers; a few manage to make ends meet through contractual work for feature films, television serials, advertising agencies and even the commercial stage (where it exists). The central and state governments do not subsidize theatre systematically, though autonomous academies under them present annual awards to distinguished dramatists and theatre workers. Amateur groups typically rehearse in the evenings after office hours and, not having their own halls, must book performance spaces in advance. They try their best also to arrange 'call shows' in towns outside their base to raise extra funds; occasionally they successfully negotiate corporate sponsorship. Payments to cast and crew, if any, are arbitrarily decided for each show or production. The limited budgets inevitably cause them to skimp on sets, lights and costumes. Each group usually revolves around its director, whose name is the single most important factor in drawing crowds.

Acknowledged as the pathfinder of modern Indian theatre, the Bengali professional stage at the turn of the century featured the nationalistic historical tragedies of actor–manager Girish Chandra Ghosh (1844–1912) and D. L. Roy (1863–1913). Later, TAGORE's uniquely lyrical drama and stagecraft captivated sensitive audiences across India with their indigenous artistry, their best interpreter after his death being director Sombhu Mitra (1915–97). Bengali amateur groups of the 1960s and 1970s were profoundly influenced by BRECHT; their most original dramatist–director was the witty revolutionary, Utpal Dutt (1929–93). The most substantial experimentation in India

arguably comes from Badal Sircar (b. 1925), who deliberately left the proscenium in the 1970s first for more flexible studio spaces, then for the open air; finally, in the 1980s, he took his group to villages 'where no theatre has gone'. His concept of socially committed THIRD THEATRE, without sets, lights or costumes, grew into a STREET THEATRE movement exemplified by Saturday afternoon performances in a park in Calcutta's central business district. Sircar does not charge admission fees: he passes a cloth around for donations after each show.

The other languages of eastern India followed Bengal's lead at first. In Assamese, Jyotiprasad Agarwala (1903–51) is remembered for his romantic tragedies and comedies, while Arun Sarma (b. 1931) is the most acclaimed contemporary dramatist. In Oriya, the versatile Aswinikumar Ghosh (1892–1962) tried every genre from the devotional to the social and ran the first professional theatre in Orissa. Actor, director, writer and composer Kalicharan Patnaik (1899–1978) established the Orissa Theatre in 1938, the first in that state to present actresses, and produced realistic plays with common people as characters. Oriya's professional companies closed in the 1960s; dramatists of the amateur stage include Manoranjan Das (b. 1921), known for his themes of alienation and man's self-destructive capacities, insightful characterization and unconventional form, and Bijay Misra (b. 1936), who depicts human hypocrisy. The theatre in Manipur, a small north-eastern state, attracted national attention in the 1980s for its aesthetic synthesis of folk traditions, tribal rituals and contemporary staging under directors like H. Kanhailal (b. 1941) and Lokendra Arambam (b. 1939).

In western India, Bombay nurtured the Marathi and Gujarati theatres. For the first three decades of the twentieth century, lengthy Marathi musicals proved immensely popular, their classical music becoming so conspicuous as to relegate the dramatic element to second place; the female impersonations of actor and singer Bal Gandharva (1885–1967) were legendary. In the second half of the century, Marathi professional and amateur theatre coexisted, with naturalistic actor–directors like Shreeram Lagoo (b. 1927) and Vijaya Mehta (b. 1934) respected widely for their perfectionism. Among dramatists, Vijay Tendulkar (b. 1928) is renowned for his psychological portrayals, Mahesh Elkunchwar (b. 1939) for his charged atmosphere and Satish Alekar (b. 1949) for his metatheatricality. Gujaratis initially adopted the theatre style of the Parsi (the Zoroastrian community in India), showy and entertaining, delivered in a Gujarati mixed with Urdu and English. The career of actor and director Jaishankar

Sundari (1889–1975) straddles the old and new stages. But the professionals disappeared by 1950. Credited with the birth of modern Gujarati theatre, C. C. Mehta (1901–91) composed realistic drama and comedy, while the prolific Pragji Dossa (1907–97) churned out prizewinners in the 1950s. Subsequently, the Gujarati amateur stage has mainly cultivated translations and adaptations – a lack of originality that also besets theatre in Sindhi, which started with translations and farces, but had its best period before independence under the Rabindranath Literary and Dramatic Club in Hyderabad (Sind, now in Pakistan), jointly founded by M. U. Malkani (1896–1980), writing 'unpleasant plays' on marital problems, and Khanchand Daryani (1898–1965), revealing social evils. Dramatist and director Gobind Malhi (b. 1921) revived theatre in India after Hindu Sindhis emigrated there, but the displacement of Sindhi from their homeland adversely affected their drama.

The south Indian states also share a background of musical extravaganzas on mythological subjects, originally in Tamil, which dominated the region in the early twentieth century. For over 50 years companies like TKS Brothers drew huge attendances for a wide range of theatrical offerings. Madras (now renamed Chennai) retains this professional milieu, tempered by the reformist P. Sambandha Mudaliar (1873–1964) and the political plays of C. N. Annadurai (1909–69). Malayalam culture felt the Tamil influence most, the farces and histories of E. V. Krishna Pillai (1894–1938) reflecting that relationship. N. Krishna Pillai (1916–88) ushered in modernist Malayalam drama with his Ibsenite techniques. In the 1970s and 1980s Malayalam theatre made rapid anti-illusionistic strides through the EXPRESSIONISTIC mythical plays of C. N. Srikanthan Nair (1928–77) and the SYMBOLIST work of G. Sankara Pillai (1930–89).

Kannada theatre is perhaps the most vibrant in the south. As in Marathi and Tamil, fantastic and spectacular mythological productions held a captive audience until the 1930s, with their performances by famed musicians and touring troupes such as that of Gubbi Veeranna (1890–1972) marshalling horses and chariots on stage. This commercial stage persists, but amateurs now provide the serious activity. The first Kannada dramatist of middle-class social problems was T. P. Kailasam (1884–1946), also a language stylist who fluently melded English with Kannada. He was followed by Adya Rangacharya (1904–85), a Gandhian visionary whose plays grew more and more intellectually complex. A new generation of very theatrical playwrights is represented by folklorist Chandrasekhar Kambar (b. 1937), who applies folk devices effectively in his dram-

aturgy, and actor Girish Karnad (b. 1938), preoccupied by the individual's desire to transcend. Telugu drama had its first major author in P. Lakshminarasimha Rao (1865–1940), who wrote moralistically in all conceivable genres. Plays like those of Gudipati Venkatachalam (1894–1979) on women's emancipation gained acceptance much later. Telugu theatre tends to remain, like Tamil, a fairly conservative area, typified by the many patriotic and poetic tragedies of Viswanatha Satyanarayana (1895–1976). The chief architect of protest drama was Acharya Atreya (1921–89), an actor, director and playwright

The interrelated Hindi and Urdu theatres of north India spent their formative years in the school of Parsi theatre, whose travelling companies scored heady box-office hits but earned opprobrium from orthodox Islamic commentators in Urdu for disrupting family life and children's education by protracted nightly performances. Jaishankar Prasad (1890–1937), regarded as the greatest Hindi dramatist, reacted against Parsi theatre by offering historical and covertly nationalistic plays, whereas Lakshminarayan Mishra (1903–87) undertook comparatively realistic problem plays on social and gender issues. However, only the rise of Hindi cinema finally put paid to Parsi theatre. For all the castigation levelled at the new film stars, some pioneers, like Prithviraj Kapoor (1906–72) of Prithvi Theatres, idealistically maintained a parallel career on the stage. The thoughtful drama that came afterwards included Urdu plays on religious schisms and the Hindi plays of Mohan Rakesh (1925–72) on malfunctioning human communications. In the 1970s and 1980s, writer, director and composer Habib Tanvir (b. 1923), who works in both Hindi and Urdu, won fame for Brechtian folkish productions employing artists speaking the Chhattisgarhi dialect. Some excellent groups in Calcutta and Mumbai enable Hindi theatre to thrive outside its heartland.

Urban theatre arrived in the Punjabi and Kashmiri languages relatively late. Punjab's first leading dramatist, I. C. Nanda (1892–1961), wrote credibly about injustices in marriage and generational differences. The most renowned later playwrights were both Marxist thinkers: Sant Singh Sekhon (1908–97) polemicized on the dialectics of class struggle, while Balwant Gargi (b. 1916) dealt with human passions and folk technique. Composer–director Sheila Bhatia (b. 1916) of the Delhi Art Theatre received acclaim for her montage-like song-dramas in the 1970s. In Kashmiri, Dinanath Nadim (1916–88) started a trend of musical plays that has remained strong, while Motilal Kemmu (b. 1933) revived Kashmiri folk theatre in his dramas.

A minor English-language theatre movement exists

in the six metropolises, the groups in Mumbai attaining considerable technical prowess and slickness of presentation during the 1980s. However, little original drama has appeared from this sector, excepting the topical plays of Asif Currimbhoy (1928–94) and the explorations of family relationships by Mahesh Dattami (b. 1958).

One drawback in post-independence Indian theatre is the paucity of opportunities for formal theatre education. Of over 150 universities, only seven have departments exclusively devoted to dramatics, and the National School of Drama in New Delhi has faced severe censure after its halcyon days under Ebrahim Alkazi (b. 1925) for virtually requiring fluency in Hindi from students and for practically functioning as a prep school for careers in film. Another controversy of the 1980s focused on the intercultural productions of famous Western directors like GROTOWSKI and BROOK, many of whom visited India and in some form or another borrowed Indian ideas for their work. Some outspoken critics term this 'cultural tourism' – a cursory but premeditated appropriation on unequal terms that misrepresents and trivializes Indian culture abroad by highlighting exotica and making no attempt at a deeper understanding of the Indian context or tradition. In the 1990s the debate shifted to introspection, as the rapid expansion in television channels threatened many rural and urban forms of drama with extinction, and theatre found it increasingly difficult to attract younger audiences. ANANDA LAL

See also EASTERN THEATRE, ITS INFLUENCE ON THE WEST.

Rustom Bharucha, *Theatre and the World* (1990)
C. Choondal, *Contemporary Indian Theatre: Interviews with Playwrights and Directors* (1989)
Sisir Kumar Das, *A History of Indian Literature, 1911–1956* (1995)
Shanta Gokhale, *Playwright at the Centre: Marathi Drama from 1853 to the Present* (2000)
Ananda Lal and Chidananda Dasgupta, *Rasa: The Indian Performing Arts in the Last Twenty-five Years* (1995)
Kironmoy Raha, *Bengali Theatre* (1993)
Adya Rangacharya, *The Indian Theatre* (1971)

Inge, William [Motter] (b. Independence, Kan., 3 May 1913; d. Los Angeles, Calif., 10 June 1973) Playwright. His first major success, *Come Back Little Sheba* (1950), was followed by *Picnic* (1953), *Bus Stop* (1955) and *The Dark at the Top of the Stairs* (1957). All four plays were adapted for the screen, and *Picnic* won the Pulitzer Prize and the New York Drama Critics Circle Award. Inge's works, generally drawn from his back-ground, portray the narrow world of the weak, flawed, lower-middle-class Midwesterner whose speech he captured perfectly. Inge's fame was shortlived, for he soon suffered a succession of failures: *A Loss of Roses* (1959), *Natural Affection* (1962) and *Where's Daddy?* (1966). Despite winning the Academy Award for his screenplay *Splendor in the Grass* (1963), Inge's career declined drastically. No longer acclaimed, struggling with alcoholism and depression, he took his own life. JOSEPH M. DIAZ

Arthur F. McClure, *Memories of Splendor: The Midwestern World of William Inge* (1989)
R. Baird Shuman, *William Inge* (1966)
Ralph F. Voss, *The Life of William Inge: The Strains of Triumph* (1989)

Innaurato, Albert (b. Philadelphia, 2 June 1948) Playwright. He writes about difficult and intimate issues, such as neurosis and compulsive behaviour, with a refreshing humour and lightness that make them surprisingly digestible. His most lauded play, *Gemini* (1977), explores ambivalent sexuality; other plays include *The Transfiguration of Benno Blimpie* (1973) and *Ulysses in Traction* (1977). ADRIANA HUNTER

installation A meeting point of expanding, enveloping sculpture; theatrical space that has spilt beyond the confines of a stage; and the potential of locations borrowed from other art forms or from outside the arts altogether. The installation has been an increasingly important and widely practised art form since the end of the 1950s (though earlier examples might be cited, particularly in the work of Kurt Schwitters and Marcel Duchamp). Not by any means always the location for PERFORMANCE, the installation has nevertheless proven an attractive and fecund international art form, particularly for artists seeking to acknowledge the character of the architectural setting of their work, to render it an active component of its meaning, or to increase the intensity of experience that an audience might enjoy by physically entering the work. Its relevance to late MODERNIST performance was probably most significantly articulated by Allan Kaprow. Although he termed it an 'environment', the settings for his HAPPENINGS, and those of his contemporaries, particularly Robert Whitman and Claes Oldenburg, are characteristic of at least one sort of installation. Under postmodernism, a near-ubiquitous interest in the nature of artistic context has elevated the installation to the status of an art discipline, and virtually all intelligent sculpture (in the work of Joseph Beuys, Janis Kounnelis, Joseph Turrell, Jonathan Borofsky and Rebecca Horne, for example) and much performance (by Jan Fabre, ROBERT WILSON and Station House Opera, *inter alia*) has employed one or another sort of installation. In addition, for artists frustrated by the lack of a physical environment that is apparently the formal consequence of currently predominant virtual technologies, the installation continues to intrigue.

ROBERT AYERS

See also ENVIRONMENTAL THEATRE.

Nicolas de Oliviera, Nicola Oxley and Michael Petry, *Installation Art* (1994)

Allan Kaprow, *Assemblage, Environments and Happenings* (1966)

Institute of Contemporary Arts Arising from the modern art world with an exhibition in a basement in London's Oxford Street in 1948, the ICA moved to Piccadilly in 1950 and became a meeting place for artists from many disciplines as well as a platform for their work, including play readings. Its move to The Mall in 1968 allowed it to broaden the range of its public events. It used its new theatre to promote innovative dance and drama, particularly in the field that became known as PERFORMANCE ART.

CHARLES LONDON

integrated casting *see* BLACK THEATRE

Inter-Action Set up in 1968 as a cooperative by American Ed Berman, producing THEATRE IN EDUCATION and pioneering LUNCHTIME THEATRE, they eventually ran many COMMUNITY THEATRE projects, running the Fun Art Bus (children's activity bus), The Other Company (performance art group first run by Berman's assistant Naftali Yavin), Dogg's Troupe (Children's Street Theatre), the Ambiance Theatre Club and the Almost Free Theatre. Their projects spawned GAY SWEATSHOP, Black Theatre of Brixton and the WOMEN'S THEATRE GROUP. In 1977 they gained a new centre in Kentish Town embracing a staggering range of activities from establishing the British American Repertory Company to silk-screen printing, skateboarding, running a 'city farm' and organizing a trades union for Father Christmases. DAN REBELLATO

See also FRINGE.

International Amateur Theatre Association The idea of some kind of international cooperation in amateur theatre first took shape in 1926, when an International Committee for Popular Theatre was formed, with headquarters in Prague. This held a number of international congresses, but ceased to function with the outbreak of the Second World War. Nevertheless a seed had been sown, though it did not bear fruit until after the war. At an exploratory conference in Rotterdam in 1947 it was decided to form an entirely new

organization rather than attempt to revive the old one, and at an inaugural congress in Brussels in 1952 IATA was founded with 22 members (national federations of AMATEUR THEATRE) from 11 countries. The constitution was to some extent based upon that of the INTERNATIONAL THEATRE INSTITUTE (ITI), but there was the important distinction that unlike the ITI, created by UNESCO, IATA was an entirely spontaneous association.

With no funds, no subsidies and an entirely amateur administration, there were few signs of life until in 1957 the Principality of Monaco founded its World Festival of Amateur Theatre. This provided both a focus and a shop window, and for some years this festival appeared to be the main function of IATA. The only other activity was a biennial congress, which every fourth year was held in conjunction with the Monaco festival.

In 1967 financial support from the Prince Bernhard Foundation and the European Foundation for Culture made possible the appointment of a full-time secretary-general; in consequence there was a great increase in activity and also in membership. There followed an alteration in the constitution by which each member country was invited to form its own national centre, bringing together its national federations to do so. This was easier to achieve in some countries than in others where different federations, separated perhaps by a difference in language or in culture, were unaccustomed to cooperate.

In 1973 a corollary to the name of the Association was adopted: 'Organization for understanding and education through theatre', following which IATA was accepted as a member of UNESCO in the category of a non-governmental Status C Organization.

ALFRED EMMET

International Centre for Theatre Research
Theatre company, founded in 1970 by PETER BROOK and administrator Micheline Rozan. The centre is a multicultural theatre research and production group based since 1974 at the Bouffes du Nord, a nineteenth-century theatre in Paris that had been gutted by fire and refurbished to a state of studied disrepair. The organization has also become known as the International Centre for Theatre Creation: the titles are interchangeable, reflecting the interconnected twin aspects of activity (private research/public performance). Funded by the French government and various international foundations (Ford, Gulbenkian, Anderson, etc.), the company has performed major productions of classic texts in both French and English, including

Shakespeare, JARRY, CHEKHOV and epic fables (notably *The Mahabharata*, 1985). DAVID WILLIAMS

Brook, Peter, *Threads of Time: A Memoir* (1998)
Margaret Croyden, *The Centre: A Narrative* (1980)
David Williams, ed., *Peter Brook: A Theatrical Casebook* (1988)

International Federation for Theatre Research
Founded in 1955 at the instigation of the Society for Theatre Research, London. The federation collects theatrical material from all over the world and publishes *Theatre Research International* three times a year. Its International Institute of Theatre Research in Venice catalogues theatrical archive material. The federation has 27 member countries and meets every four years. ADRIANA HUNTER

International Theatre Institute In the aftermath of the Second World War, as nations were drawing up new boundaries, a group of theatre leaders met in Paris under the auspices of UNESCO to find a way for artists to cross those boundaries. Rosamond Gilder, J. B. PRIESTLEY, JEAN-LOUIS BARRAULT, LILLIAN HELLMAN and Julian Huxley, the first director general of UNESCO, were among those concerned. From that meeting in 1947, an organization emerged that would link theatre people of all nations and, in June 1948, the charter of the International Theatre Institute was signed in Prague by eight countries. The ITI grew to a network of theatre centres in more than 75 countries on five continents, and it founded the major international festival THÉÂTRE DES NATIONS. MARTHA W. COIGNEY

internet In the final years of the twentieth century the internet rapidly penetrated all aspects of theatre (as indeed most walks of life). It was both a new medium about theatre – a massive and burgeoning encyclopaedic reference tool, with implications for access to facts and knowledge, and educational and commercial opportunities – and a new medium for theatre itself, known in this context as DIGITAL PERFORMANCE. Because of the relative ease and cheapness of obtaining web space, websites and ezines (electronic journals) proliferated on all manner of theatre-related activities: information – libraries, theatres, archives, venues, companies, listings, theatre reviews; discussion (on genres, academic studies, personal opinions of things seen); commercial sites advertising forthcoming productions, ticket availability, theatre equipment, special effects; 'official' and amateur websites devoted to particular actors, playwrights, trends, publications, grant opportunities. A simple internet search at the end of the century on the words 'theatre'/'theater' produced approximately 4 million different web pages. Inevit-

ably bound by technical developments and in particular 'bandwidth' (the speed and complexity of any transmission), the major internet development at this time was in 'webcasting', broadcasting both live and archived moving image and sound via a website. BARRY SMITH

Rob Shields, ed., *Cultures of Internet* (1996)

Intimate Theatre *see* INDEPENDENT THEATRE; STRINDBERG, AUGUST

invisible theatre A type of free performance developed from the work of AUGUSTO BOAL in which theatregoing rituals are abandoned as actors appear in 'real' public situations as 'real' people and instigate an unscripted event. For example, an actor orders a meal in a restaurant for which s/he cannot pay, which leads to an argument involving other actors as well as non-actors present about the cost of living, low wages, the right to eat. CHARLES LONDON

Ionesco, Eugène (b. Slatina, Romania, 13 Nov. 1909; d. Paris, 28 March 1994) Playwright. He confessed that in the 1950s, when he was a startling 'young dramatist' of the ABSURD, a critic suggested he lower his age, so he gave the year of his birth as 1912 and departed from the Russian Orthodox calendar to make the day 26 November. His French mother took him to France for his early education, but he returned to Romania to study French at the University of Bucharest, where he soon became known as a literary critic and won a scholarship back to Paris in 1938. In 1950 a failure to learn English led to the first of his one-act plays, *La Cantatrice Chauve* (*The Bald Prima Donna* or *The Bald Soprano*), described by the author as a 'tragedy of language' and inspired by his encounter with an English primer; together with *La Leçon* of 1951, it has filled the tiny theatre of La Huchette ever since. These two plays, together with *Les Chaises* (1952), which was boosted by ANOUILH, were at once taken up internationally, the last two at the ROYAL COURT by GEORGE DEVINE, who went on to promote the full-length *Rhinocéros* (1960) with LAURENCE OLIVIER and *Le Roi se meurt* (*Exit the King*, 1962) with ALEC GUINNESS.

Wonder, amazement and horror are the keys to his work. Too monstrous for him, the real world appears as a death-haunted nightmare, a wild distortion of everyday banality pushed to paroxysm, a tragic farce. Chairs, coffee cups and briefcases proliferate, corpses grow, mushrooms sprout; a professor kills with words, a crippled assassin terrorizes a city, an English Sunday morning walk is beset by apocalyptic visions; in his version of *Macbeth* (*Macbett*, 1972) the witches run wild and Malcolm turns tyrant.

Harassed from right and left, he saw himself as a fighter for freedom against all ideologies. He could never forget Romania, but for Ionesco our real problems are not social or political; drama should open out on another world to ease humankind's sense of isolation and spiritual vacuum. His theories on the theatre spring from his own practice (*Notes and Counternotes*, 1962). His originality lies in his theatrical style and creative inventiveness, often inspired by his dreams and his own short stories, owing something to French SURREALISM. Rejecting psychological character development, his longer plays are episodic, one-act situations often linked by the quest of one thinking hero, usually a Bérenger, expiating guilt, nostalgic for love or a lost paradise, coping with revolutions or a plague and, though trapped on a treadmill of -isms in an incomprehensible universe, still left standing on his feet, against all reason.

A humanist asking unanswerable questions, a paradoxical specialist in non-communication: Ionesco's contradictions and illogicalities express estrangement in nonsense, appealing greatly to the young. English-speakers are reminded of the *Goon Show* and Monty Python, not to speak of Lewis Carroll and Edward Lear. Few French plays this century have been so widely performed outside France, and for many these modern classics define the very notion of absurd theatre.

DONALD WATSON

Richard N. Coe, *Ionesco* (1961)

Iran   *see* MIDDLE EAST AND NORTH AFRICA

Iraq   *see* MIDDLE EAST AND NORTH AFRICA

Ireland   Up to the arrival of W. B. YEATS in the 1890s, the Irish theatre was colonial. Yeats, with a little help from his friends EDWARD MARTYN and AUGUSTA GREGORY, made it anti-colonial. After the founding of the Irish Free State in 1922 it became postcolonial. Theatre and drama were thus not native art forms; the idea of a theatre in the conventional sense lay outside Irish culture. Its importation was part of England's cultural imperialism in the late sixteenth century, and as theatre developed after the foundation of the first royal patent was granted in Dublin in 1662 it became a 'semi-governmental institution' and an expression of Anglo-Irish supremacy. Needless to say, its appeal was always to a minority audience, the vast majority of the population being excluded. What was truly vitalizing about Yeats's modest proposal in 1897 to establish the Irish Literary Theatre in Dublin was its determination to redress 300 years of colonialist theatre in one revolutionary moment. The call was for 'a Celtic and Irish school of dramatic literature' endowed with 'that freedom of experiment which is not to be found in theatres of England'. There were two main aims: to counteract the 'stage Irishman' or stereotypical view of the Irish, and to raise Irish consciousness of identity and of history by staging 'the deeper thoughts and emotions of Ireland'. The project was both ambitious and idealistic, appealing to the nationalist impulses of those who had been followers of Charles Stewart Parnell and were committed to Home Rule. It had about it a certain naïveté not lost upon the sophisticated GEORGE MOORE: 'The Celt wants a renaissance, and badly; he has been going down in the world for the last two thousand years.'

Yet when the time arrived, in May 1899, for the launching of the Irish Literary Theatre George Moore had cast off his cynical reservations and thrown in his lot with the founding idealists. With his experience as playwright for J. T. GREIN's INDEPENDENT THEATRE in London, Moore rightly feared for the amateurism of Yeats's plans. So he took a hand in rehearsals and tried to ensure that the programme was professional in style and production. After a visit to the SHAKESPEARE MEMORIAL THEATRE in Stratford, Yeats persuaded FRANK BENSON and his company to stage two new plays, Yeats's *The Countess Cathleen* and Martyn's *The Heather Field*. If there was a certain amount of irony in these plays appearing alongside *King Lear* (now there's a Celtic play!) during the week of the Irish Literary Theatre's debut in Dublin, it was lost amid the uproar surrounding the charge of blasphemy directed against *The Countess Cathleen*. The Catholic Archbishop of Dublin condemned the play unread (although it had been published); on opening night crowds of students from Cardinal Newman's University College attacked the play and the police had to be summoned. This inauguration was to set the mould for the reception of controversial Irish plays hereafter. 'Not what you want but what we want' became the attitude of Yeats and his theatre towards the audience – and, he added with pride, 'we were the first modern theatre that said it.' The new Irish theatre had to be fought for. The audience may have been divided, yet the theatre's commitment to the freedom of artistic expression carried the day from the outset. The first week's productions (and one week was all that was planned) proved a triumph, and allowed two similar experiments to be conducted in 1900 and 1901, during which plays by Moore and Martyn in the Ibsenist mode were added to Yeats's poetic drama (in which Moore collaborated) *Diarmuid and Grania*. The Irish Literary Theatre then dissolved.

Because of the incongruous involvement of the Benson Company, this venture was at best but an interesting episode. Yet while Moore and Martyn were happy to abandon the project Yeats was determined to press on in the search for a more authentic Irish theatre. A one-act play in Irish which completed the bill with *Diarmuid and Grania* in 1901 gave him his way forward. This was *Casadh an tSugain* ('The twisting of the rope') by DOUGLAS HYDE, a simple peasant play in a realistic setting acted by amateurs trained by WILLIAM GEORGE FAY. Yeats admired the simple acting style and made contact with Fay and his brother Frank, two enthusiasts who knew more about modern theatre than Yeats did, for they ran their own little company and were well aware of the new ideas on naturalism coming from Paris. They admired the Irish Literary Theatre but thought Yeats too immersed in vague symbolism. 'In Ireland', wrote Frank Fay as critic for the patriotic *United Irishman*, 'we are at present only too anxious to shun reality. Our drama ought to teach us to face it. Let Mr Yeats give us a play in prose or verse that will rouse this sleeping land.' Yeats obliged with the propagandist *Cathleen ni Houlihan* (1902), with Maud Gonne playing the lead, staged by the National Dramatic Society formed between the Fay brothers, Yeats and the poet George Russell, who offered a verse play, *Deirdre,* to make a double bill.

The way was now open for the development of a form of realism which was close to the people, simple yet deeply moving, and staged with all the authenticity of setting, costume and acting style that naturalism commanded. Yet it would have to be said that the Fays' ideas on acting, while including ensemble playing, were not altogether naturalistic (in the STANISLAVSKY sense) but combined an element of poetic SYMBOLISM. The style thus evolved to suit the repertory, which was predominantly realistic but never entirely so: there was always an other-worldly aspect hovering over or under the dramatic action. JAMES JOYCE, then only 22, disagreed violently with this new development of the Irish theatre and in *The Day of the Rabblement* (1902) accused Yeats of betraying the mission IBSEN had laid down for modern drama by turning to peasant life for theme and representation. Joyce went his own way, not acknowledging that the aim he proposed for himself in fiction, to attend to 'the reality of experience and to forge in the smithy of my soul the uncreated conscience of my race', was being pre-empted by Yeats, the Fays and the new playwrights flocking to the theatre. In his only play, *Exiles*, Joyce remained true to Ibsen but showed how far removed his preoccupations were from this theatre. Yeats, with the backing of ANNIE HORNIMAN, an English admirer, went on to found the Irish National Theatre Society with premises in Abbey Street in 1904. This little theatre (capacity just over 500) and its small stage (only 21 feet at proscenium opening and

just over 16 feet to back wall) was to establish a remarkable repertory of new plays of Irish life. The Fays became the main creators of the Abbey's acting style, while the theatre itself was managed by three writers: Yeats, Lady Gregory and J. M. SYNGE. It was to be, first and foremost, a writers' theatre.

Synge was the first genius to stamp the new dramatic movement with greatness. For him truthfulness and poetry were the primary ingredients for dramatic representation. Or, as he put it, 'On the stage one must have reality, and one must have joy, and that is why the intellectual modern drama has failed.' In his short career he compressed with Keats-like intensity a vision of life as harsh, fleeting and filled with sensuous experience. *Riders to the Sea* (1903), while only a one-acter, selects the lives of the Aran fisherfolk as representative of traditional and yet timeless endurance. In contrast, *The Shadow of the Glen* (1903) shows the mocking side of Synge's sensibility, which enraged certain nationalists because it seemed to signal a return to the sneering comedy of former times. *The Well of the Saints* (1905) was more subversive: in elevating personal choice over religious authority, Synge insisted in symbolic fashion on the individual's right to be blind rather than cured. But it was in his masterpiece, *The Playboy of the Western World* (1907), that Synge showed himself at his most comically inventive and most iconoclastic. There is something mythic about this play, with its Oedipal implications, and at the same time something robustly anarchic and archetypal. It enacts the Irish imagination's disdain of law and order. It caused serious riots at the Abbey, ostensibly over his use of the word 'shifts' (women's slips) but actually over Synge's exposure of the darker side of what Lady Gregory called 'the Irish genius for mythmaking'. In spite of Yeats's brave defence of the play, and his insistence that it continue despite opposition, *Playboy* divided Abbey audiences and many of the nationalists – actors, writers and supporters – seceded.

Not far behind Synge in importance as Abbey playwright was Lady Gregory, who began by supplying dialogue for some of Yeats's plays (notably *Cathleen ni Houlihan*) and quickly developed a knack for farces with a local setting and dialect. These included *Spreading the News* (1904) and *The Workhouse Ward* (1908). A most versatile writer, Lady Gregory also wrote history plays, comedies, tragedies and what she called wonder plays, such as *The Dragon* (1919) and *The Golden Apple* (1920). Although her plays are now little acted, she made an enormous contribution to the Abbey repertory and influenced many in characterization and the use of dramatic speech.

The Abbey suffered a blow in 1910 when Miss Horniman withdrew her annual subsidy. The following years, up to 1923 and the arrival of SEAN O'CASEY, were difficult ones for the Abbey, which was often threatened with closure. Tours to the United States between 1911 and 1914 both helped it financially and also influenced the rise in America of the LITTLE THEATRE (as well as inspiring EUGENE O'NEILL). But as the political situation worsened at home, culminating in the 1916 Rising and the Anglo-Irish war, the theatre was often under curfew and constantly struggling for survival. By the time the Irish Free State was established in 1922 Yeats and Lady Gregory, the two remaining directors after Synge's premature death in 1909, were ready to hand over the Abbey to the new government. Somewhat taken aback, the government declined the offer and instead awarded the Abbey an annual subsidy, the first such in the English-speaking world. In its jubilee celebrations in 1925 the Abbey looked back on the production of no fewer than 216 new plays (though many of them were one-acters).

The writers who had emerged since 1910 were mostly in the grimmer realistic vein, such as LENNOX ROBINSON and T. C. MURRAY; the only writer in any way to emulate Synge's exuberance was GEORGE FITZMAURICE, with such strange folk plays as *The Dandy Dolls* (1908) and *The Magic Glasses* (1913). Then Robinson suddenly provided what was to be his most successful play, *The Whiteheaded Boy* (1916), a well-made comedy of rural family conflict. Its strong characterization and good-humoured style created the mould for 'Abbey comedy' for a whole generation. Robinson, who was manager at the Abbey, and director from 1923, contributed over 20 plays during his long career, many of which were subsequently produced in London and New York. In Ireland, where his reputation sadly declined after his death in 1958, the highly successful revival of *The Whiteheaded Boy* in 1998 by the inventive, mime-based Barabbas the Company showed young audiences just how clever a playwright Robinson was.

The colonial period came to a violent end with the birth of the Free State and the ensuing civil war. At this point SEAN O'CASEY, arguably the greatest playwright Ireland has produced, had his first play, *The Shadow of a Gunman*, accepted by the Abbey. O'Casey moved resolutely from the peasant play to the modern urban play set in the tenement homes of the working class. Once Lady Gregory pointed out to him that his strong point was characterization, O'Casey was able to subordinate didacticism to creation of colourful characters. In *Juno and the Paycock* (1924) and *The Plough and the Stars* (1926) he gave to the world roles of Shakespearean vigour in Joxer Daly and Captain Boyle, Juno, Fluther Good and the Covey. These plays have held

the stage since, not only at the Abbey, where the number of performances of each is far above that of their nearest rival, Synge's *Playboy*, but internationally. In the 1920s O'Casey's plays were enormously popular in Dublin, attracted huge new audiences and saved the Abbey from bankruptcy. A major factor in the success of these three Dublin plays was the strength of the Abbey company at the time, for whom O'Casey particularly created the roles they played. These included BARRY FITZGERALD, F. J. MCCORMICK [Peter Judge], SARA ALLGOOD and Maureen Delany. However, because of its demythologizing of the 1916 Rising, *The Plough and the Stars* was received with riots to equal those which had greeted the *Playboy* 20 years earlier, and although Yeats once more defended artistic freedom at the Abbey it became clear to O'Casey that his future as playwright lay elsewhere. Moving to London, he wrote his anti-war play *The Silver Tassie* in 1928, intending it for the Abbey. Its rejection caused a great controversy and ensured O'Casey's permanent exile in England where his later, more experimental plays were written.

As Ireland's first great postcolonial playwright, O'Casey showed that historical revisionism and ironic deconstruction were the keys to the new realism. His contemporaries tended to be less iconoclastic. T. C. Murray and GEORGE SHIELS showed that rural tragedies and comedies were by no means defunct, in *Autumn Fire* (1924) and *Professor Tim* (1925) respectively. This conservative streak in Irish drama was to persist for another generation, during which the Abbey repertory dwindled to predictable and conventional representations of mainly rural life. A minority of writers, such as DENIS JOHNSTON and PAUL VINCENT CARROLL, emulated O'Casey in attempting more critical and theatrically daring ways of criticizing Irish society, each, like O'Casey, finding intolerable the growing conservatism at the Abbey and taking his work elsewhere. Johnston became associated with the Dublin GATE THEATRE, founded in 1928 by HILTON EDWARDS and MÍCHEÁL MACLÍAMMÓIR to complement the Abbey by staging modern European and American plays in an experimental style. With brilliant use of EXPRESSIONISM, Johnston dramatized the nightmare of postcolonialism in *The Old Lady Says 'No!'* (1929), and thereafter oscillated between the Abbey and the Gate as playwright, unsure of his direction. In that regard he stands as key to the culture itself in the 1930s and after. Paul Vincent Carroll provides evidence that the intellectual Catholic playwright (the majority up to and including Johnston being Protestant) could also be iconclastic. His fiery interrogations of the growing Catholic hegemony, in *Things that are Caesar's* (1932) and *Shadow and Substance* (1937), led eventually to the rejection of *The*

White Steed, 'on the grounds that it would prove offensive to the priesthood'. The infuriated Carroll had the play staged in New York (1938). The director, HUGH HUNT, then resigned from the Abbey.

With the death of Yeats in 1939, following that of Lady Gregory in 1932, the Abbey fell into the hands of ultra-conservatives. Ireland's neutrality during the Second World War led to a general flight from intellectual discussion. The Abbey narrowed its ambitions. Under the management of Ernest Blythe, a former minister of finance and a fanatic for the restoration of the Irish language, there was a purging from the company of actors who were not bilingual in Irish and English, and at the same time an avoidance of anything experimental in form or content in the repertory. It became more respectable for authors to be rejected by the Abbey than to be staged. When the Abbey burned down in July 1951 there were those who said it had to be from spontaneous combustion, so conspicuous was the decline in artistic standards. From 1951 to 1966 the Abbey company played at the Queen's, an old nineteenth-century home of melodrama and vaudeville, ill-suited to the intimate style of the Abbey, and standards declined further. Long runs of established Abbey favourites became the order of the day. New writers, such as M. J. MOLLOY and Walter Macken, continued in old moulds, inviting laughter rather than thoughtful discussion (much less controversy). Irish drama was in the doldrums. Even the Dublin Gate had little to contribute beyond derivative plays by Mac Líammóir on the Celtic twilight and hard times in the west of Ireland. Only in the basement theatres which sprang up in the 1950s was there hope of renewed vitality.

The Pike Theatre in Herbert Lane was one of these. Founded by Alan Simpson and Carolyn Swift in 1953, this venue brought new plays of adventurous bent to its tiny stage, including BRENDAN BEHAN's *The Quare Fellow* (1954) and SAMUEL BECKETT's *Waiting for Godot* (1955). Beckett asked Simpson to hold back his production until PETER HALL's went up at the ARTS THEATRE in London; otherwise, the Pike would have had another English-language world première to add to the Behan. But in 1957, following a production of TENNESSEE WILLIAMS's *The Rose Tattoo*, the Pike was charged under Ireland's obscenity laws for staging an 'indecent and profane' play. Simpson was convicted, and the legal costs which were incurred before the conviction was quashed by the Supreme Court led to the collapse of the Pike. The case highlights the repressive atmosphere of Irish society at the time. Even though there was no equivalent of England's LORD CHAMBERLAIN, and no official CENSORSHIP of theatre as there was of film and printed matter, Ireland's endemic conservatism worked towards the suppression of whatever might be construed as hostile to Catholic doctrine and morality. The fate of O'Casey's *The Drums of Father Ned*, submitted to the second Dublin Theatre Festival in 1957, underlines this point. It was sufficient that the Catholic Archbishop of Dublin took exception to the inclusion of this play, as well as to an adaptation of Joyce's *Ulysses*, for a controversy to rage in the press and for O'Casey to withdraw in fury, supported by Beckett, three of whose mime plays were also scheduled in the programme. The result was the cancellation of the 1958 Dublin Theatre Festival.

Beckett, it has to be said, had little to do with the Irish theatre. He did not write either for it or about Irish matters. His work lies outside the Irish drama as such, although undoubtedly it was influenced by Synge, Yeats and O'Casey. In contrast, Behan, heavily influenced by O'Casey's plays, wanted very much to be part of the national theatre. When Ernest Blythe rejected *The Quare Fellow* it was clear to Behan that his place was with ALTERNATIVE theatre, such as the Pike in Dublin and THEATRE WORKSHOP in London's Stratford East. He was the complete outsider in an age that began to worship the outsider. Ironically, Behan was assimilated into the new revolution in the British theatre in the mid-1950s. *The Hostage* (1958) kicked Irish drama out of its wartime isolation at last. Its postcolonial stance was altogether mocking. A new phase of that drama, now influenced by new ideas from abroad, was about to begin.

This new phase was led by BRIAN FRIEL, TOM MURPHY and HUGH LEONARD. 'We all came out from under O'Casey's overcoat,' Friel has said, paraphrasing CHEKHOV's acknowledgement of his indebtedness to Gogol. In that sense, they were all iconoclasts, at a time when Ireland was about to undergo a massive series of social changes. Tom Murphy, the most outspoken of the three, was early rejected by the Abbey. In retrospect, it is hardly surprising that Blythe was too shocked to consider *A Whistle in the Dark*, Murphy's hard-hitting play that introduced the THEATRE OF CRUELTY before its time. In September 1961 Murphy then took his play to London, where it was a major success. Hugh Leonard, who actually learned his craft at the Abbey with a couple of early plays, saw success in London with his *Stephen D*, the hit of the 1962 Dublin Theatre Festival. Just five years after the Archbishop had seen red when *Ulysses* was on the programme, this theatrically inventive version of Joyce's *Stephen Hero* was acclaimed. A breakthrough was at hand. Friel's *Philadelphia, Here I Come!* (1964) followed. At first sight a fairly conventional Irish family play, this is actually a series of attacks on Irish certitudes. In particular the priest is held accountable for failing to provide the spiritual nourishment necessary to an emotionally famished family. Further, the main character is divided in two, played on stage by two actors (Private and Public), which serves to define the psychic turmoil of a society torn between worship of authority and the need to be fully independent.

These three writers developed in quite different ways from this decisive moment in the history of Irish drama. Murphy went on to write powerful dramatizations of the modern Irish spirit in search of wholeness, which involved a good deal of bitter denunciation of Irish religious authority, in plays from *Famine* (1968) through *The Sanctuary Lamp* (1975) to his masterpiece *The Gigli Concert* (1983). Leonard, for his part, was content to laugh at Ireland's *nouveaux riches*, ludicrously aping their betters and paying self-serving homage to Irish political heroes, as in *The Patrick Pearse Motel* (1971) and the less successful but topical *Kill* (1982). Friel was somewhere in between, angry like Murphy but at the same time controlled and somewhat amused at the Ireland he saw around him, like Leonard. But Friel's distinctive drama is metadrama, plays in which he questions whether what we apprehend as real is so, or is perhaps dream or illusion. *Faith Healer* (1979) is undoubtedly his masterpiece in this line, although *Living Quarters* (1977) and *Aristocrats* (1979) are not far behind.

Many of these plays saw life on the stage of the new Abbey, opened in July 1966 on the site of the old. With a similar seating capacity (628) to the old Abbey, it was geared up for the technological age. Within five years an experimental annex, the Peacock, was added (capacity 157), with totally flexible stage arrangements, and the position of artistic director was created (the first being Hugh Hunt). The gap between the Dublin Gate and the Abbey then began to narrow, as the Abbey staged Chekhov, WILDE, SHAW and Shakespeare in the best modern designs, alongside exciting new productions of Irish plays, often by new writers such as THOMAS KILROY and EUGENE MCCABE. Room was found for the plays of JOHN B. KEANE, whose *Sive* had been rejected by Blythe in 1959. A Brechtian production of Behan's *Borstal Boy* reached Broadway in the late 1960s (Behan had died in 1964), and the old, hidebound days of the Abbey Theatre came to an end. A policy of grooming young new playwrights at the Peacock led to the emergence over the years of TOM MAC-INTYRE, Graham Reid, FRANK MCGUINNESS, SEBASTIAN BARRY, BERNARD FARRELL and MARINA CARR as major writers. Of these, McGuinness has since proved the most successful, his *Observe the Sons of Ulster Marching*

Towards the Somme (1985) establishing an international reputation.

Gradually the new Abbey became a modern repertory theatre, where the emphasis was on new Irish writing but where a production of *Hedda Gabler* or *Medea* or even KUSHNER's *Angels in America* was also a possibility. There was always to be a tension between tradition and modernity, but it has been carefully turned into a positive, energizing division by succeeding artistic directors from Hunt through TOMAS MAC ANNA and JOE DOWLING to PATRICK MASON and Ben Barnes. One of the casualties along the way has been the dissolution of the Abbey's permanent company, and with it the treasured Abbey acting style.

In 1968, when violence exploded in Northern Ireland, it seemed to many that a new Irish drama must emerge there to chart the events. There had, of course, been a strong Northern theatre prior to 1968, and writers such as ST JOHN ERVINE, RUTHERFORD MAYNE and SAM THOMPSON had shown the gritty, intransigent side of Northern life. The Lyric Players Theatre in BELFAST made a valiant effort after 1965 to establish a genuinely artistic centre but was probably compromised by its undisguised nationalism in a community with a two-thirds unionist majority. The plays of Martin Lynch, for instance, could be seen as partisan, while a Protestant writer like Graham Reid felt more comfortable writing for the Abbey. Women playwrights such as Christina Reid and Anne Devlin offered much promise but failed to reconcile themes of tribal politics and feminist issues. The Charabanc Company, mainly a women's group, flourished in the early 1980s with vigorous community-style theatre.

Then came the FIELD DAY THEATRE COMPANY, founded in 1980 by Brian Friel and the actor STEPHEN REA, ostensibly to tour Friel's *Translations* but in effect to establish a new cultural force in Ireland aiming to transform political discourse through art. With support from Arts Councils on both sides of the Irish border, Field Day toured once a year North and South for ten years. It was an exciting episode in Irish theatrical history. Combative plays were produced by Friel (as well as *Translations*, *The Communication Cord*, 1982, and *Making History*, 1988), THOMAS KILROY (*Double Cross*, 1986 and *The Madame McAdam Travelling Theatre*, 1991) and STEWART PARKER (*Pentecost*, 1987), and there were interesting adaptations from the classics by Tom Paulin, Derek Mahon and Seamus Heaney (who was one of the directors of Field Day). But in the end the attempt to intervene politically in the Northern problem proved too great for Field Day, always hampered by the lack of a home base with a permanent theatre.

The end was inevitable once Friel offered *Dancing at Lughnasa* to the Abbey in 1990.

Since the ceasefire was established in the North in 1997 theatre has expanded, especially in BELFAST. It is only in the wake of the violence there that a sense of identity seems to be finding satisfactory articulation on stage, as in the plays of Gary Mitchell, Marie Jones and Owen McCafferty. It is interesting to note that it is only at this point that a passionate restatement of unionist identity is taking place.

The high ambitions of the original Irish Literary Theatre would seem to have been fulfilled. Moreover, regional theatre has flourished, at Galway's DRUID and Waterford's Garter Lane for instance, expanding the Abbey's original idea. Irish drama is now enjoying extraordinary success internationally. The Celtic Renaissance has entered a whole new phase.

CHRISTOPHER MURRAY

See also GAELIC THEATRE IN IRELAND.

Sam Hanna Bell, *The Theatre in Ulster* (1972)

Eberhard Bort, ed., *The State of Play: Irish Theatre in the Nineties* (1996)

Nicholas Grene, *The Politics of Irish Drama: Plays in Context from Boucicault to Friel* (1999)

Robert Hogan, *After the Irish Renaissance: A Critical History of the Irish Drama since 'The Plough and the Stars'* (1967)

D. E. S. Maxwell, *A Critical History of Modern Irish Drama 1891–1980* (1984)

Christopher Murray, *Twentieth-Century Irish Drama: Mirror up to Nation* (1997)

Anthony Roche, *Contemporary Irish Drama: From Beckett to McGuinness* (1994)

Katharine Worth, *The Irish Drama of Europe from Yeats to Beckett* (1978)

Ireland, Kenny   *see* LYCEUM (EDINBURGH)

Irish Literary Theatre   *see* GAELIC THEATRE IN IRELAND; IRELAND; VERSE DRAMA

Irving [Brodribb], [John] Henry   (b. Keinton Mandeville, Somerset, 1838; d. Bradford, 6 Feb. 1905) Actor–manager. His Mathias in *The Bells* (1871) thrilled audiences as a psychological study of guilt; subsequent hits in Shakespeare, beginning with *Hamlet* (1874), rapidly placed him at the head of his profession. In 1878 he assumed the management of the Lyceum and engaged ELLEN TERRY as leading lady, inaugurating a regime which made the Lyceum first among English theatres until it closed in 1902. Eight North American tours confirmed his status as leading star of the English-speaking theatre as the new century dawned. Irving's Lyceum presented old historical MELODRAMAS, like Boucicault's *Louis XI* (1878), similar pieces by contemporary writers (e.g. W. G. Wills' adaptation of *Faust* 1885), and 12 Shakespeare productions. Interpretations were based on Irving's particular view of Shakespearean themes and characters. Proscenium arch naturalism was tempered by his picturesque idealism, and late productions like *Cymbeline* (1896) flirted with SYMBOLISM. While SHAW saw him as devoted to naturalism, his dance-like movement and unique speech were far from naturalistic. Fierce concentration won spectators to share his belief in his roles, and technically, his face, body and voice were so perfectly controlled that the designer and theorist GORDON CRAIG saw him as the prototype actor of the future. In 1895 Irving became the first actor knight. His two sons entered the theatre: H. B. Irving (1870–1919) was an actor and Lawrence (1871–1914) a playwright and actor. H. B.'s son, Laurence (1897–1983), was a stage and film designer, and author of a biography (1951) of his grandfather.   ALAN HUGHES

Edward Gordon Craig, *Henry Irving* (1930)

Alan Hughes, *Hentry Irving, Shakespearean* (1981)

Laurence Irving, *Henry Irving: The Actor and His World* (1951)

Irwin, Bill [William]   (b. Santa Monica, Cal., 11 April 1950) Unconventional actor, particularly notable for his surreal comedic and clowning skills. Irwin picked up his feel for comic rhythms and timing watching television shows like *The Phil Silvers Show* as a child. He studied under HERBERT BLAU at the experimental California Institute of the Arts and later at Oberlin College, Ohio, in particular assimilating the techniques of Blau's experimental method of 'impulse work'; in the mid-1970s he moved on to attend Clown College, where he learnt acrobatics and juggling. He appeared with Larry Pisoni's Pickle Family Circus, but, hungry for more experimentation in his work, began exploring postmodern choreography, appearing with the Dance Collective in 1977. Irwin now began developing his own skits in AVANT-GARDE theatres on the West Coast, finally blending his skills into a one-man show, *The Regard of Flight*, in the late 1970s; he later toured with it in Europe, and scored a huge success at the American Place Theater in 1982. Irwin has regularly revived the show since, complementing it with other shows of his own devising such as *The Clown Bagatelles*, the Kafkaesque *The Courtroom* (1985), *On and Off* (1987) and *Largely New York* (1989). He has also appeared in straight acting roles in *Waiting for Godot* (1988), *Accidental Death of an Anarchist* and *Texts for Nothing* (1992). HELEN RAPPAPORT

See also CIRCUS; CLOWNS; NEW VAUDEVILLE.

R. Jenkins, *Acrobats of the Soul* (1988)

Isaacs, Edith J[uliet] R[ich] (b. Milwaukee, 27 March 1878; d. White Plains, NY, 10 Jan. 1956) Editor and author. After a stint in 1913 as drama critic for *Ainslee's Magazine*, in 1919 she became editor, and for a time principal stockholder, of *Theatre Arts*. She remained in charge until 1945. Under her leadership the magazine was the leading intellectual theatrical periodical of its day, balancing high aesthetic aims with a practical commercial understanding. She also edited or wrote *Theatre: Essays on the Arts of the Theatre* (1927), *Plays of American Life and Fantasy* (1929), and *The Negro in the American Theatre* (1947).

GERALD BORDMAN

Isherwood, Christopher [William Bradshaw] (b. Wyberslegh, Cheshire, 26 Aug. 1904; d. Santa Monica, Calif., 3/4 Jan. 1986) Novelist and playwright. After deliberately leaving CAMBRIDGE University without a degree, Isherwood took a variety of jobs and then went to Weimar Berlin to teach English, staying for five years until Hitler came to power. His stories about this time were dramatized by VAN DRUTEN as *I am a Camera* (1951), which was filmed (1955) and turned into the musical *Cabaret* (1966), which in turn was filmed (1972). Isherwood also wrote with his friend from schooldays W. H. AUDEN the anti-capitalist poetic plays *The Dog Beneath the Skin* (1936), a satire on English fascism mixing GILBERT and SULLIVAN and BRECHT, *The Ascent of F6* (1937), a modernist political allegory, and *On the Frontier* (1938), an anti-war melodrama. In 1939, he and Auden went to their new home, America. Isherwood embraced Indian philosophy, openly espoused his homosexuality, wrote film scripts, novels and other books which were mostly autobiographical, and dramatized Plato's *Dialogues* (1960, with CHARLES LAUGHTON), a SHAW satire and his own novel *A Meeting by the River* (1970, with his lover Don Bachardy). His autobiography, *Christopher and His Kind* (1977), covers his time with the GROUP THEATER. COLIN CHAMBERS

Brian Finney, *Christopher Isherwood: A Critical Biography* (1979)

Israel Hebrew drama is mainly a product of the twentieth century. Revived as a spoken language by the late nineteenth century, modern Hebrew was still making hesitant steps by the turn of the century, when the Jewish national movement of settlement in Palestine was started. In the absence of a theatrical tradition or an established current practice, Hebrew drama first emerged as an occasional offshoot of literature, written almost exclusively by novelists or poets who hardly had theatrical production in mind. Sporadic attempts at mounting stage productions or forming amateur groups in Palestine and the diaspora culminated with the triumph of HABIMAH (since 1958 the National Theatre of Israel), which was founded as a studio beside the MOSCOW ART THEATRE in 1918 and made its name especially with VAKHTANGOV's highly expressionistic production of ANSKY's *The Dybbuk*. The success of Habimah gave rise to several permanent companies in Palestine: first the TEI, the OHEL and the satirical theatre Mat'até ('Broom') in the 1920s and then, after the final settlement of the Habimah in Palestine (1931), the companies constituting the contemporary theatrical scene: first, in 1944, the CAMERI THEATRE (then a youthful, West-orientated company reacting against the stagnation of Habimah in its classical and east European traditions; later, the established Municipal Theatre of Tel Aviv), the Haifa Municipal Theatre in 1961, the Be'er Sheva Theatre and the Jerusalem Khan Theatre in the 1970s.

The establishment of the state of Israel in 1948, following the terrors of the HOLOCAUST and a tense struggle against Arab–Palestinian hostility and British restrictions on Jewish immigration, was marked by lively theatrical activity, attentive both to world theatre and to the immediate problems of the newborn state. However, most leading Israeli playwrights of the period were still prose writers who turned to drama. A new era began in 1949 with *In the Wastes of the Negev* by Vig'al Mossinsohn (b. 1917) and *He Walked in the Fields* by Moshé Shamir (b. 1921), two topical melodramas about patriotism and the generation gap, set against the background of the War of Independence and performed at the Habimah and the Cameri respectively, while the war was still going on. Like Shamir's play, the successful *They Will Arrive Tomorrow* (1950), a war thriller with political touches by Nathan Shaham (b. 1925) – including the controversial scene in which an Israeli officer lets an old Arab prisoner loose in what is, unbeknown to the prisoner, a minefield, in order to 'eliminate' an unlocated mine – was a dramatic adaptation of an earlier work of fiction by the author. The themes involved in the plays of Shamir, Mossinsohn, Shaham and Aharon Meged (b. 1920) were mostly topical: the frustrating encounter of the veteran soldier with the compromising reality of postwar society; kibbutz and socialist ideals versus the cynicism of emerging bourgeois society and capitalist state; newborn bureaucracy and the corruption of the system (*His Name Goes before Him*, 1951, by EPHRAIM KISHON); and above all, Israel as a problematic melting pot of the conflicting traditions and cultures comprising the Jewish diaspora, highlighted especially in the confrontation of Holocaust survivors with Israeli reality (e.g. in Leah Goldberg's *The Lady of the Palace*, 1956, and Ben-Zion Tomer's *Children of the Shadow*, 1963). Significantly, hardly any of these plays touched upon the Palestinian problem, which was rapidly emerging as an important factor in the political, moral and social development of the Jewish state. This attitude was well in keeping with the predominant ideology: as late as the early 1970s Prime Minister Golda Meir still denied the existence of a Palestinian nation.

While most plays of the 1950s were well-made problem plays, NISSIM ALONI's *Most Cruel the King* (1953) read topical conflicts into the biblical narrative of the split of the kingdom, and several plays were to follow this pattern. During the 1960s Aloni emerged as the most distinguished writer to turn to the theatre as a full-time career. Most of his plays were based on borrowed narratives (an Andersen fairytale, a Mark Twain story, the Oedipus myth), commenting indirectly on Israeli themes. He uses allegorical and symbolic patterns to create metaphysical thrillers, invested with colourful Ghelderodean theatricality, melodrama or the picaresque (*The King's Clothes*, 1961; *The American Princess*, 1963; *Aunt Lisa*, 1969). The 1960s also saw the major poet and translator Nathan Alterman (1910–69) emerge as a writer of verse drama (notably *The Inn of Ghosts*, 1962, a complex dramatic study of the interrelation between life, love, freedom and art).

The June 1967 war, followed by a long era of military occupation of neighbouring territories by Israel (longer, eventually, than that of the existence of the state prior to the occupation), saw a rapid change of attitude towards the Israeli–Palestinian conflict. The sharp satirical cabarets by HANOCH LEVIN, especially *The Queen of the Bath* (Cameri, 1970), shocked the public and rendered Kishon's popular bourgeois satires rather obsolete. The Haifa Municipal Theatre emerged as a lively workshop for new Israeli drama, critical of predominant ideologies by way of documentary, satirical or political plays. *Co-Existence* (Wattad, 1969) pioneered the theatrical theme of being an Arab in Israel; *Status Quo Vadis* (JOSHUA SOBOL, 1971) satirized the orthodox religious laws imposed on the secular majority in Israel, where there is no separation between state and religion; *Kriza* (Sobol, 1976) exposed ethnic relations; and *The Poisoned Mushroom* (Mittelpunkt, Nizan and Oz, 1984), a documentary about the rise of fascism in Germany in the 1930s, drew the menacing analogy between past experience and topical, local dangers.

From the late 1970s, the Israeli–Palestinian conflict and the reality of occupation figured as a major theme in the theatre. The most significant playwright to have emerged of the 'Haifa School' was Sobol, who developed from a writer of documentaries into a major dramatist questioning national myths (notably *Weininger's Last Night*, 1982, and *Ghetto*, 1984). Yet the most popular and controversial Israeli playwright of the 1970s and 1980s remained Hanoch Levin, who abandoned satirical cabaret for a witty and sour theatre of cruelty (notably *Heffetz*, 1971; *Ya'acobi and Leidental*, 1972; *Shitz*, 1974; *Rubber Merchants*, 1978; *The Execution*, 1980; *The Sorrows of Job*, 1981). Some marginal attempts to delve into Jewish mysticism to redeem an allegedly dormant tradition of 'Jewish theatre' resulted in an awkward ritual theatre, failing to convince audience or critics that any such tradition ever existed.

Since the beginning of the 1980s the annual Akko Fringe Festival has served as a hothouse for new playwrights, directors, actors and designers. Most established companies started travelling frequently to various international festivals. Several plays, especially by Sobol and Levin, were translated and produced in Europe and the United States.

Current Israeli theatre is often described as nonconformist and critical of the political establishment. The case of Itzhak La'or's *Ephraim Returns to the Army* (1986), banned by official CENSORSHIP for 'defamation of the military forces in the [occupied] territories' and then released by ruling of the Supreme Court of Justice, epitomizes the heated discussion concerning theatre and politics in Israel. The National Children and Youth Theatre's production of Daniella Carmi's *The Blast in Ahalan Street* (1986), whose child heroine lives with her Jewish mother and Arab father in a Jewish quarter in Jerusalem, was reproached by the Minister of Education and Culture for 'encouraging inter-marriages between Jews and Arabs' (the couple in the play live unmarried, since there is no civil marriage in Israel). And the opening night of Sobol's *Jerusalem Syndrome* (1988), an historical parable attempting to allude to the current political situation, was physically interrupted by members of right-wing groups. A closer look at mainstream Israeli drama reveals, however, a self-imposed reticence as far as a deep-down analysis of Zionist ideology is concernerd. Even plays dealing openly with acute political issues related to the effects of the occupation on Israeli society (such as Motti Lerner's *Throes of Messiah* or Benni Barabash's *One of Us*, both 1987) are reluctant to transcend the portrayal of the conflict as an internal Jewish problem. In the politically charged climate within which Israeli culture is still seeking self-identity and definition, such a reluctance leaves much to be desired. The Gesher ('Bridge') company, founded by Russian immigrants headed by director Yevgeny Aryeh, in spite of some fine theatrical achievements, has so far failed to plug itself into the Israeli cultural identity, whereas the attempt to create a state-supported Palestinian repertory theatre, based in Haifa, proved a short-lived venture. The mainstream Israeli theatre of the 1990s became stale and commercialized, barely open to ideological or aesthetic daring, a closed shop run by a narrow cultural clan of managers, directors and playwrights, hardly allowing for the emergence of new voices. Mediocre box-office hits dominated the repertory houses, marginalizing the more creative theatre events: some promising fringe work, a few feminist plays (by Miriam Kayni, Shulamit Lapid or Hagit Ya'ari), Rina Yerushalmi's often intriguing aesthetic experiments with her Itim Ensemble, and the work of some regional theatrical groups. One of the latter, Dudi Ma'ayan's in Akko, staged a five-hour performance of *Arbeit Macht Frei . . .*, a breathtaking theatrical experience exploring the tension between the memory of the Holocaust and Israeli treatment of the Palestinians, which proved one of the most exciting and singular achievements of Israeli political theatre. AVRAHAM OZ

See also MIDDLE EAST AND NORTH AFRICA; YIDDISH THEATRE.

Glenda Abramson, *Drama and Ideology in Modern Israel* (1998)

Linda Ben-Zvi, ed., *Theater in Israel* (1996)

Mendel Kohansky, *The Hebrew Theatre: Its First Fifty Years* (1969)

Emanuel Levy, *The Habima – Israel's National Theater 1917–1977: A Study of Cultural Nationalism* (1979)

Israel, Robert (b. 17 Sept. 1939) Designer. His work spans the worlds of theatre and OPERA. He designs both sets and costumes, believing the two to be inextricable visual elements that must work together to create the overall stage picture. His designs centre on the relationship between illusion and reality, and project what he characterizes as an 'aggressiveness about space', a tension between what is comfortable and uncomfortable. Israel has designed for the majority of the major opera houses worldwide, and is particularly well known for his collaborations with composer PHILIP GLASS, including the premières of *Satyagraha* (1980), for which he co-wrote the libretto, *Akhnaten* (1984), and *Orphée* (1992). As a theatre designer he has worked extensively with AVANT-GARDE director MARTHA CLARKE, on projects including *Vienna: Lusthaus* (1986), *The Hunger Artist* (1987) and *Alice's Adventures Underground* (1994). His designs have been exhibited at the Whitney Museum and the Museum of Modern Art in New York. SARAH STEVENSON

Ronn Smith, *American Set Design 2* (1991)

Italy

1900–1970

Even after political unification in 1861, Italy remained a country of the city state, of the region. No unity was to be found in arts and literature. In drama there were major differences in language, form and audience make-up, particularly between the north (the locus of economic and political supremacy, concentrated in cities like Turin, Milan and Venice) and the south (Naples and Sicily). Marked differences were also to be found among the main northern cities.

While theatre in general was dominated by the opera, 'straight' drama at the end of the nineteenth century was characterized by the naturalist movement VERISMO, with its faithful and photographic depiction of reality. Its major representative was the Sicilian Giovanni Verga (1840–1922), whose narrative and theatrical works were studies of society in its historical context. His regional perspective underlay denunciations of the conditions of the poor and the working classes in Sicily.

The first two decades of the twentieth century marked the end of the romantic–verismo tradition and saw the emergence of anti-naturalistic movements like FUTURISM and the THEATRE OF THE GROTESQUE, and of important writers such as GABRIELE D'ANNUNZIO and the highly influential LUIGI PIRANDELLO. Interest in the theatre of Carlo Goldoni (1707–93) was still very much alive, especially in the Veneto region from which he came and about which he so famously wrote, while a new enthusiasm grew for the COMMEDIA DELL'ARTE and its masks from the sixteenth and seventeenth centuries; having in the intervening period been suppressed by the literary tradition, it began once more to exercise a fascination for anti-naturalistic authors and directors. In this context the VARIETY theatre and CABARET played important roles, becoming, together with the CIRCUS, a great school for theatre and film actors such as Ettore Petrolini and Totò (Antonio de Curtis), as well as the theoretical model for the later AVANT-GARDE movement. And lyric theatre, which had dominated the nineteenth century, slowly gave ground to drama, although its importance never died.

A novelist and war hero as well as a dramatist, D'Annunzio reacted against verismo, escaping from reality to take refuge in a world of beauty and of opulent and barbaric sensuality. He held both the peasants and the petty bourgeosie in contempt, and yet he created the myths through which the petty bourgeoisie realized their forbidden dreams of exceptional loves and later of nationalist and imperialist longings. He was also the poet and dramatist who personified the last fantasy of Italian tragedy, based on a classical past and an ill-fated grandiose scheme for TOTAL THEATRE in the OPEN AIR. Also well known at home and abroad was the work of Roberto Bracco (1862–1943), who went beyond the world of verismo to present spiritual and religious problems and the conflicts of the subconscious.

The years of political stability and economic prosperity up to 1920 were also marked by a growing industrialization and the formation of a mass society. Nationalist tendencies became more virulent, as seen in colonial expansion in Libya, and this led later to the birth of a single Fascist party and incipient civil war. The spirit of futurism – a literary and artistic movement – represented the modern industrialized world of capitalism. The futurists were eager to destroy the past and the old ways of life in order to build a new world. In the theatre, FILIPPO TOMMASO MARINETTI, the father of futurism, wanted to destroy the concepts of proportion, perspective, time and space. He wrote his first experimental works in Paris, and it was there that he launched in 1909 the Manifesto of Italian Futurism, which provided a platform for new forms of literature and drama in Italy and abroad and had longer-term reverberations, especially in the 1960s and after.

In contrast to futurism, the theatre of the grotesque playwrights reacted against the old bourgeois, sentimental drama by adopting its basic formulae and applying them to their own contemptuous, cynical and disillusioned work. Their mistrust of human beings led them to view people as puppets in a world driven by the machine. The theatre of the grotesque became known to London and New York audiences through the works of LUIGI CHIARELLI, in particular through *La maschera e il volto* (*The Mask and the Face*, 1916), which many considered to be the 'manifesto' of the movement. Also current, and as a reaction to D'Annunzio, was the theatre of the 'Crepuscolari' (twilight) and the 'Intimisti' (intimate) – the former an ironic portrayal of a prosaic provincial view of daily life in languid tones, the latter a serious, demure expression of private feelings and states of mind. Fausto Maria Martini (1886–1931) was the leading 'twilight' dramatist.

During the Fascist period under Mussolini (1922–43), with the exception of a few works that praised the regime and a few escapist plays, the theatre remained substantially unchanged. It continued to be a theatre of famous actors (Ruggero Ruggeri, Ermete Zacconi,

ELEONORA DUSE, Emma Gramatica) and repertory companies. Fascism tolerated some small experimental and avant-garde groups that flourished in Rome and Milan. Most had a very short life, with the exception of the Teatro degli Indipendenti, an experimental studio theatre founded in Rome in 1923 by Anton Giulio Bragaglia (1890–1960), who introduced new ideas of scenography. He saw theatre as a 'technique of visualization' and successfully presented a repertoire of Italian and international avant-garde drama (WEDEKIND, JARRY, Pirandello, the futurists) throughout the 1920s. In 1925, Pirandello created the Teatro d'Arte in Rome – a short-lived experiment, lasting only until 1928 – and a travelling company which toured London and other European cities.

Fascism saw the introduction of state support to the theatre (a subsidy was given to Pirandello's company and to the Teatro degli Indipendenti; financial support was also offered to Duse, which she declined). Among the prestigious institutions founded during the Fascist era were the Accademia d'Arte Drammatica (Academy of Dramatic Arts: a drama school), the Ente Teatrale Italiano (with the aim of promoting and developing theatrical events nationally and abroad) and the Istituto Nazionale Dramma Antico (which promotes classical drama), all of which have survived to the present day.

After the Second World War, with the reorganization of the state and its new republican constitution, there was a strong mood of rebirth. Local councils – many run by the left – promoted cultural events, created networks of activities and venues (including the recovery of disused spaces), and helped establish new companies. Diffusion of culture to the masses and especially to young people was a priority. In the theatre, the main developments were the predominance of the director over the actor – *teatro della regia* – and the formation of permanent theatre companies – *teatri stabili*. The names of some of the leading directors (GIORGIO STREHLER, Luigi Squarzina, Gianfranco de Bosio) were associated with the major *teatri stabili*. In the immediate aftermath of the war, the *stabili* wanted to express the civic ideals of the resistance and of anti-Fascist culture. They were originally formed in order to create a permanent 'home' for the nomadic actors, to research and to promote drama throughout the country while at the same time consolidating regional or even civic identity. For example, the first such theatre (and the most famous), the PICCOLO TEATRO of Milan, explored two genres: the 'national–popular', with plays in Milanese dialect or works by Goldoni, and an international repertoire. It was co-founded by Strehler and Paolo Grassi in 1947. Squarzina directed the Teatro d'Arte of Genoa (founded 1951) and de Bosio the Teatro Stabile of Turin (1955). Famous theatre companies were the Giovani (with de Lullo, Folk, Guarnieri, Valli, Allbani); Nuova Scena, set up by DARIO FO; and the Proclemer–Albertazzi, named after its cofounders.

At the same time, the theatre of UGO BETTI and DIEGO FABBRI was still very popular, an existentialist type of drama with religious overtones based on introspection and moral questioning. The dialect theatre of EDUARDO DE FILIPPO was also very successful. The true inheritor of the old Neapolitan tradition, he moved away from typical dialect theatre to a wider form of drama so that his work became a testament to the problems of his time: centrally, the inevitable conflict between the individual and a corrupt, disintegrating society. The search for moral values and the creation of an ethical code even in the midst of total chaos remain constant and central elements of his plays. In 1931 he formed the group Teatro Umoristico i de Filippo with his sister and brother. In 1945 he founded his own company, Il Teatro di Eduardo, with which he worked as writer, director and actor until his death. His work is played abroad with great success.

Between 1950 and 1960, due to the boom of the film industry and the introduction of television, theatre audiences halved, ticket prices doubled and performances came to be concentrated mainly in Milan and Rome. A counter-attack against this trend was mounted through the formation of permanent theatre companies in other Italian cities, through campaigns in favour of season tickets and through an effort to popularize the theatre, with the support of both private initiative and local and central government. The postwar theatre was still a strongly aristocratic, bourgeois and repertory drama. It lacked rapport with the public and failed to portray the social and political situation of the time – and, therefore, to appeal to wider audiences. Cinema, on the other hand, with its neorealism (VISCONTI, ZEFFIRELLI, Rossellini), was a much more immediate, experimental medium; it successfully managed to attract both theatre people (thanks also to its being more lucrative) and theatregoers, and to become an internationally famous and influential 'school'. It continued to affect the theatre throughout the second half of the century; but by the 1980s most cinema actors (for example Benigni, Moretti) were coming from cabaret and the contemporary theatrical ferment.

The late 1950s saw the first stirrings of the avant-garde experimental movement, linked to a group of writers, actors and directors (e.g. Carmelo Bene, whose best-known works are *Spettacolo Majakowskij*, *Pinocchio*

and *Caligola*, Franco Cuomo, Mario Ricci, Carlo Quartucci and Giuliano Scabia, whose *Zip* marked the first, unsuccessful, collaboration between a *teatro stabile* and an experimental group). The avant-garde groups advocated a new concept of theatre based on the connection between theatrical language and theatrical space, with audience participation and the use of visual techniques, unusual phonic systems, dynamic projections and provocative movements. The performance was seen as work-in-progress.

Another moment of change occurred in the late 1960s and early 1970s, the time of student demonstrations, major workers' disputes, and the beginning of the so called 'strategy of tension' with the formation of extremist left-wing groups. Some protagonists of the 'New Theatre' abandoned the avant-garde and tried experiments outside theatre structures; others felt the need to search for a new theatrical identity, to go beyond institutional theatre (which included the achievements of the previous generation such as the *teatri stabili*), to find urban and peasant communities so that they might create a 'theatre of participation'. Strehler resigned from the Piccolo Teatro in 1968 – only to return to its leadership three years later. A significant event at this time was LUCA RONCONI's production of *Orlando Furioso* (1968), with its experimental use of space and relationship with the audience, showing the influence of the visual and the physical which was strong in Italy. During the 1970s, a *decentramento* trend, which had its roots in left-wing ideology, attempted to redistribute funds and subsidies from government, independent bodies and also private sponsors (generally given to institutional theatre) to alternative companies and venues all over the nation. Decentralization saw the birth of thousands of small companies, community theatres and student groups which tried to find alternative styles, rejecting the conventional concept of theatre and challenging its hierarchies. Only a few (e.g. Teatro d'Elfo, Il Collettivo di Parma, Gruppo della Rocca, Teatro del Sole) survived when in the late 1970s the funds were withdrawn and re-invested in the established theatre.

Standing in a category of his own is Nobel Prize winner Dario Fo. As writer, actor and director he is one of the most vital, courageous and controversial theatre personalities of the century, and his popularity has extended worldwide. Fo's theatre is militant, a 'throwaway' theatre that aims at stimulating the audience's opinions and reactions, the embodiment of a serious political and social commitment that goes far beyond entertainment. EVITA BIER

1970–2000

From 1970 to the end of the century, the group Il Carrozzone (later I Magazzini) – Federico Tiezzi, Sandro Lombardi, Marion d'Amburgo – set the pace for the new avant-garde, from its shocking refusal of theatre convention and *teatro di poesia* in the 1980s to a deepening of its work in the 1990s thanks to the contribution of poets/playwrights such as Edoardo Sanguineti, Mario Luzi and Giovanni Testori. In the 1980s Giorgio Barverio Corsetti emerged, dedicated to urban panoramas of concept-music, video and BODY ART, and involved in explorations of video-theatre and stage adaptations of twentieth-century literature and poetics. In 1999 he became the artistic director of the Théâtre Viennale in Venice, thus bringing the avant-garde experience into established institutions. In the same year, theatre and film director Mario Martone, founder of Teatri Uniti in 1988, became the artistic director of the Teatro di Roma. His reforms, however – theatre in alternative spaces, more projects and stagings at lower costs and for a larger audience – did not fit with the administration's politics of a *teatro stabile*, and he resigned in 2000.

Many interesting groups appeared at the end of the century. Heirs of Pirandello's metaphysics, of the avant-garde 'isms' and of Carmelo Bene's genius, they come from small cities and towns and represent a bright alternative to commercial theatre. Iconography and iconoclasm mark the work of the group Motus, creators of performances lacking any defined structure and characterized by typical postmodern 'hypercitation'. Fanny & Alexander regains the pleasure of words and voices, staging radio-drama versions of Shakespeare; choosing to work with traditional texts, they free themselves from the constraint of giving primacy to storytelling, enabling themselves to deepen their analysis and explore the relationships between the text and other texts and the contemporary scene. Lenz-Rifrazioni affirms the romantic 'impossibility to represent', working with actors with mental illness, by this means reaffirming the body-rite of the actor as original 'locus' of theatre. Societas Raffaello Sanzio takes this aesthetic to extremes, into a real anatomical theatre: a rhetorical work on bodies and figures meant to incite a more radical form of communication.

Working on extra-ordinary, defeated bodies as 'perfect' bodies, this group brings on to the stage a truly postmodern transfiguration of myth and fairytale.

MASSAMILIANO COSSATI

M. Apollonio, *Storia del teatro italiano*, 2 vols (1938, 1950)

Marvin Carlson, *The Italian Stage: From Goldoni to D'Annunzio* (1981)

Enciclopedia dello spettacolo, 9 vols + 1 vol. index (1954–68)

Franco Quadri, *L'avanguardia teatrale in Italia (Materiali 1960–76)*, 2 vols (1977)

——, *Il Patalogo* (from 1979, annually)

ITI   *see* INTERNATIONAL THEATRE INSTITUTE

Ivanov, Vsevolod [Vyacheslavovich] (b. Lebyazh'e, Siberia, 12 Feb. 1895; d. Moscow, 15 Aug. 1963) Writer and playwright. He ran away from school to become a circus clown and sword swallower. He is best known for his novella with a Siberian civil war setting, *Bronepoezd 14–69 (Armoured Train 14–69)*, which he adapted for the stage in 1927. This was followed by *Blokada* ('The blockade', 1929). He also wrote historical plays set in seventeenth- and eighteenth-century Russia.   NICK WORRALL

Harold B. Segel, *Twentieth-Century Russian Drama* (1979)

Ivory Coast   *see* FRENCH AFRICAN THEATRE

Izenour, George [Charles]   (b. New Brighton, Penn., 24 July 1912) Mechanical and electrical consultant famous for his pioneering work in theatre LIGHTING. As director of the electromechanical laboratory of the School of Drama at Yale (1946–77), Izenour developed a dimmer, using the thyatron, a type of electron tube, which brought continuous and instantaneous control to remote lighting systems for the first time. Izenour also perfected a synchronous winch system and the steel acoustical shell; since the 1950s, as a design and engineering consultant to theatres worldwide, he has been a leading influence in theatre design, favouring multi-use/multi-form auditoriums. He has written important books: *Theatre Design* (1971), *Theatre Technology* (1988) and *Roofed Theatres of Classical Antiquity* (1992).   HELEN RAPPAPORT

J

Jackson, Anne *see* WALLACH, ELI

Jackson, Barry [Vincent] (b. Birmingham, 6 Sept. 1879; d. Birmingham, 3 April 1961) Theatre manager, director, designer and playwright. Born into a wealthy shop-owning family, he founded the amateur PILGRIM PLAYERS in 1907, out of which came the BIRMINGHAM REPERTORY Company, whose theatre – the first purpose-built repertory theatre – he financed in 1913. He remained the guiding force behind this company for nearly 50 years. In the 1920s and 1930s he staged many important productions in London at the ROYAL COURT, KINGSWAY and other theatres, including the first British performances of SHAW (*Back to Methuselah*, 1924; *The Apple Cart*, 1929; *Too True To Be Good*, 1932; and other plays), MAUGHAM (*For Services Rendered*, 1932), and the first public production in Britain of PIRANDELLO's *Six Characters in Search of an Author* (1922). An admirer of POEL, he pioneered modern-dress Shakespeare (e.g. *Cymbeline*, 1923; *Hamlet* in plus-fours, 1925). He was responsible for introducing Rutland Boughton's music drama *The Immortal Hour* (1920), and achieved great success with plays by JOHN DRINKWATER (a member of the original Pilgrim Players and Birmingham Repertory), notably *Abraham Lincoln* (1918), and of EDEN PHILLPOTTS (*The Farmer's Wife*, 1916; *Yellow Sands*, 1926). He founded the Malvern Festival and directed it from 1929 to 1937, specializing in productions of Shaw, including several premières, and in revivals of English drama from all periods. Between 1945 and 1948 he was director of the SHAKESPEARE MEMORIAL THEATRE, STRATFORD-UPON-AVON, where he introduced much-needed reform and greatly improved standards by reducing the number of productions, and gave early opportunities to directors such as PETER BROOK and MICHAEL BENTHALL. He wrote several popular children's plays, and a number of adaptations from French and Russian. He was knighted in 1925. G. ROWELL

George W. Bishop, *Barry Jackson and the London Theatre* (1933)
J. C. Trewin, *The Birmingham Repertory Theatre 1913–1963* (1963)

Jackson, Glenda [May] (b. Birkenhead, Merseyside, 9 May 1936) Actress, noted for her authority, intelligence, directness and impression of world-weariness. She made her debut in *Separate Tables* (1957) while still at the Royal Academy of Dramatic Art, and in 1964 joined the ROYAL SHAKESPEARE COMPANY for PETER BROOK's THEATRE OF CRUELTY season at the London Academy of Music and Dramatic Art, which led to *US* (1966) and her celebrated performance as Charlotte Corday in WEISS' *Marat/Sade* (London and New York, 1965). She returned to the RSC to play *Hedda Gabler* (1975) and, less successfully, Cleopatra (1978). Other stage successes – all strong women – include a striking Masha in *Three Sisters* (1967), Solange in *The Maids* (1974), Vittoria in Webster's *The White Devil* (1976), the title roles in *Stevie* (1977) and Andrew Davies' *Rose* (1980), Niva in *Strange Interlude* (1984), Bernada in *The House of Bernarda Alba* (1986) and *Mother Courage* (1990). She was elected a Labour MP in 1992 and 1997. D. KEITH PEACOCK

C. Bryant, *Glenda Jackson: The Biography* (1999)
D. Nathan, *Glenda Jackson* (1984)
I. Woodward, *Glenda Jackson: A Study in Fire and Ice* (1985)

Jacobi, Derek [George] (b. London, 22 Oct. 1938) Actor. After Cambridge University, his early professional work was at the BIRMINGHAM REPERTORY THEATRE. In 1963 he joined the newly formed NATIONAL THEATRE company, where he played many roles including Laertes in *Hamlet*, Cassio in *Othello* and Brindsley Miller in *Black Comedy*, in which he revealed a comic talent later recognized when he won a Tony Award (1984) for his performance as Benedick in a ROYAL SHAKESPEARE COMPANY *Much Ado About Nothing*. In 1972 he began a six-year association with PROSPECT THEATRE COMPANY, for which he played, among many other roles, Hamlet. His combination of lyricism and vocal power place him in the tradition of GIELGUD and OLIVIER, and some of his finest performances were given during a fruitful period at the RSC, culminating in a remarkable *Cyrano de Bergerac* (1983), subsequently seen in the United States and on television. He has appeared many times in the commercial West End theatre, notably as Alan Turing in *Breaking the Code* (1987). He directed KENNETH BRANAGH as Hamlet and subsequently appeared in several of Branagh's films. He became a popular figure on television when he played Claudius in *I, Claudius*, and latterly became even more familiar as 'Brother Cadfael'. He was knighted in 1993. GENISTA MCINTOSH

Jacobi [Jakabfi], Viktor (b. Budapest, 22 Oct. 1883; d. New York, 10 Dec. 1921) Composer. The most gifted and musically effective of the writers of twentieth-century Hungarian musical theatre, his first piece was produced in his native Budapest while he was still a student. He followed it with a series of shows leading up to his two outstanding works, *Leányvásár* (1911) and *Szibill* (1914). Both were given highly successful London productions as *The Marriage Market* and *Sybill* and, although they were less successful in New York, it was there that Jacobi went at the outbreak of war. His work here included a successful collaboration with the violinist Fritz Kreisler on the score for *Apple Blossoms* (1919), but attempts to pair him with that show's author, William Le Baron, in two further pieces, *The Half Moon* (1920) and *The Love Letter* (1921), produced failures. KURT GÄNZL

Jacobs [Rich], Sally (b. London, 5 Nov. 1932) Designer. After assisting JOCELYN HERBERT, she designed two productions in the ROYAL SHAKESPEARE COMPANY's ARTS THEATRE Season (1962) and then became closely associated with PETER BROOK's RSC work, designing his experimental THEATRE OF CRUELTY season (1964), *Marat/Sade* (1964), *US* (1966), and the legendary *A Midsummer Night's Dream* (1970), with its memorable three-sided white box set, strong, brightly coloured costumes, coils, confetti, ladders, stilts and the iconic trapeze. She has also lived and worked in the United States, designing in Los Angeles (regularly for the MARK TAPER FORUM), Houston, New York and San Francisco. She has designed opera, and her work as a designer/director includes *The War in Heaven* by JOSEPH CHAIKIN and SAM SHEPARD. CHARLES LONDON

Jahnn, Hans Henny (b. Altona, Germany, 17 Dec. 1894; d. Hamburg, 29 Nov. 1959) Playwright, novelist and pacifist. He is best known for his first play, the EXPRESSIONIST *Pastor Ephraim Magnus*, staged in 1919 by BRECHT and BRONNEN, in which the pastor's children beg to be tortured, in order to be freed from the agony of self. GRÜNDGENS staged *Thomas Chatterton* (1956) and PISCATOR *Der staube Regenbogen* (*The Dusty Rainbow*, 1961). JUDY MEEWEZEN

Jamaica *see* CARIBBEAN

James, Albie *see* TEMBA

James, C[yril] L[ionel] R[obert] (b. Tunapuna, Trinidad, 4 Jan. 1901; d. London, 31 May 1989) Philosopher, writer and historian. James was something of an intellectual prodigy who developed his own code of living, based on the game of cricket, which led to his most popular book on the subject, *Beyond a Boundary* (1963). He became a widely respected Marxist, and taught at several colleges in Trinidad, the United States and England, where he eventually settled. As well as major historical and political work, and a ground-breaking novel, *Minty Alley* (1936), he wrote *Black Jacobins* (1938) on the classic black revolt against oppression, the Haitian Revolution. James's single play is also titled *The Black Jacobins*, though its world première in London in 1936, when the famous American singer PAUL ROBESON created the leading role, was staged as *Toussaint L'Ouverture*. The play had its most powerful impact when it was staged in 1976 in Nigeria, then also ravaged by civil war. It was not performed in James's homeland until 1979; nevertheless, for its depth of character, its philosophical exploration of the nature of rebellion and its tribute to regional history, *The Black Jacobins* is considered a milestone in early West Indian theatre. JUDY S. J. STONE

James, Henry [Jr] (b. New York, 15 April 1843; d. London, 28 Feb. 1916) Expatriate American novelist, playwright and essayist. His plays never received the acclaim accorded his fiction and others' dramatizations of his work, though he would have wished otherwise. Plays premièred in London include *Guy Domville* (1895), the disastrous reception of which nearly capsized his stage career, *The High Bid* (1907) and *The Saloon* (1908). He wrote 12 plays in all and many essays on the theatre (collected as *The Scenic Art*, 1948) and was an avid theatre-goer. His fiction gave rise to several popular plays, among them *Berkeley Square* (1929), *The Heiress* (1947), and *The Innocents* (1950).

LEONARD BERKMAN

Jameson, Rex *see* DRAG

Janis, Elsie [Jane Bierbower] (b. Columbus, Ohio, 16 March 1889; d. Beverly Hills, Cal., 26 Feb. 1956) Musical comedy actress. The epitome of the turn-of-the-century VAUDEVILLE star, Janis made her debut aged eight; thereafter, performing for stock companies in her home town, she was propelled by her archetypal stage mother into child stardom, touring in the musicals *The Belle of New York* and *The Fortune Teller*. Her first New York success was in *When We Were Forty-One* (1905), which led to the lead in *The Vanderbilt Cup* (1906). Janis's talent for singing, mimicry and dancing won her further roles in *The Fair Co-Ed* (1909), *The Slim Princess* (1911) and *Star for a Night* (1911), but it was her performance in *The Passing Show of 1914*, which was also seen in London, which made her a household name. The sobriquet of 'Sweetheart of the AEF [American Expeditionary Force]' became hers during the First World War, as a result of her tireless performing for the troops on the Western Front. After the war she helped devise and write her own show, *Elsie Janis and Her Gang* (1919), and her own revues kept her busy touring the United States throughout the 1920s. Her autobiography, *So Far, So Good!*, appeared in 1932.

HELEN RAPPAPORT

Japan Since foreigners had been steadfastly excluded from Japanese soil from 1640 to 1854, a sense of intellectual and cultural isolation characterized Japanese society when foreign exchange resumed once again. This quickly changed following the restoration of the emperor system in 1868 and the ratification of the new constitution in 1889, when it became a national goal of Japan to establish its ascendancy as a progressive civilization and avoid colonization by Western powers. By the turn of the century the modernization of Japan had gained sufficient momentum to be greedily consuming all the current Western art and political movements. Naturally, increased contact with the West brought with it a burgeoning appetite for foreign plays.

By the end of the nineteenth century *kabuki* had been purged of its plebeian origins and become an acceptable art form for the new Meiji era. Meanwhile, around 1890 a new form of drama emerged, developing out of the political turmoil of the 1880s and 1890s. This *shimpa* or 'new school' attracted audiences with its realistic treatment of everyday life and its highlighting of social problems, and even served as a vehicle of propaganda for the new regime. While retaining many of the techniques of *kabuki*, *shimpa* theatre sanctioned the appearance of women on stage and embraced the use of Western dress and music.

Yet *shimpa* represented only a tentative break from tradition; the second and more enduring development came with *shingeki* or 'new theatre' in the early part of the twentieth century. The Bungei Kyokai (Literary Society), founded in 1906 by the Shakespearean scholar Shoyo Tsubouchi (1859–1935) and Hogetsu Shimamura (1871–1918), staged a performance of *Hamlet* in May 1911 at the New Imperial Theatre, the first Western-style theatre built in Japan. The first production of the Jiyu Gekijo or FREE THEATRE (named after the Théâtre Libre of Paris) was a performance of IBSEN's *John Gabriel Borkman* in Tokyo in 1909.

The Great Kanto Earthquake of 1923, which destroyed most of Tokyo, gave rise to a new wave of experimentation. In 1924, among the ruins of the quake, Yoshi Hijikata (1898–1959) founded the Tsukiji Little Theatre and built a small Gothic Romanesque theatre of 500 seats – the first theatre to be built specifically for realistic drama. Strongly devoted to Western themes and aspirations, Hijikata invited Kaoru Osanai (1881–1928), who bore a great enthusiasm for STANISLAVSKY, to join him. Prominent playwrights such as Sakae Kubo (1900–58) and Kunio Kishida (1890–1954) also joined Tsukiji, but were less keen on the partiality accorded to Western plays. Tsukiji presented 44 consecutive programmes of Shakespeare, CHEKHOV, STRINDBERG, PIRANDELLO and other foreign dramatists before adding occasional new Japanese plays to their repertoire beginning in March 1926. On the death of Osanai, the company split into two: the Shinkyo Gekidan (New Co-operative Theatre Company) established in 1934 by director and playwright Tomoyoshi Murayama (1901–77) and the Shin-Tsukiji Gekijo (New Tsukiji Theatre) under the leadership of Hijikata. Although the two companies differed in political and literary aspirations, both remained persistently left-wing.

Following the occupation of the province of Manchuria in 1931, government pressure on the left increased. From the start of the Russo-Japanese War in 1904 the government had censored communist publications; from 1910 there had been active repression of the socialist movement; and from 1939 mandatory screening of all scripts was enforced. In 1937 several members of Tsukiji broke off to form the Bungakuza (Literary Theatre). Working from a workshop stage, they survived to the postwar period. However, between 1931 and 1945 (the 'Fifteen Years War'), more than 100 theatre practitioners were arrested, including the leading practitioners of *shingeki*.

During the postwar period a new generation of artists, who had grave misgivings about *shingeki*'s uncompromisingly realistic approach, turned to drama as a means of questioning the new government's unchallenged programmes of 'reconstruction' and 'democratization'. Destruction and recovery were obviously part of a continuing historical narrative; but the atomic bomb, as well as Japan's defeat and surrender to a foreign power, had caused a irreversible rupture with tradition that *shingeki* failed to address. Following the revolution in China and the purging of Japanese communists at the outbreak of the Korean War in 1950 came a revolt against *shingeki*'s authority in the form of the AVANT-GARDE *shogekijo* (small theatre) movement. New plays appeared, including *Yuzuru* (*Twilight Crane*) by Juniji Kinoshita (b. 1914) in 1949, first produced by the Budo no kai (Grape Society). Following the end of the American occupation in 1952, a new generation of writers emerged: Kobe Abe's *Dorei gari* (*Slave Hunt*) was performed in 1955; *Rokumeikan* by YUKIO MISHIMA was produced by Bungakuza in 1956; and Yoshiyuki Fukuda's *Nagai bohyo no retsu* (*Long Line to the Grave*) was staged in 1958. Both morally and politically ambiguous, these new works aimed to hold up an introspective mirror to Japan's legacy of imperialism and ultra-nationalism. During the 1960s the most subversive writers formed their own companies; particularly influential were Shuji Terayama (1936–83), Juro Kara (b. 1940) and the more overtly political Makoto Satoh (b. 1943), who wrote for the Free Theatre, the Theatre Centre and the Kurotento 68/71 troupe (Black Tent Theatre 68/71). Influenced largely by European THEATRE OF THE ABSURD, the new plays were nihilistic and perversely discursive. At the same time, in spite of the many postwar upheavals, *shingeki* still continued to stage prewar literary works; in 1946, for example, Hijiki directed Ibsen's *A Doll's House*. By contrast, the main impetus for the *shogekijo* movement came from the student protests and the failure of the campaign against the Japan–US Security Treaty.

The Seigei (Youth Theatre Arts Troupe, founded 1959) was the first company effectively to challenge *shingeki*'s links with the Japan Communist Party, with a production of *Document No. 1* by Fukuda. Inspired by BRECHT, it was an investigation of protest as experienced by the actors themselves – a dramatization of the demonstrations of the 1960s. Both Satoh and Kara contributed to the activities of Seigei. Also in this period, Satoh wrote *Atashi no biitoruzu* (*My Beatles*,

1966) and *Nezumi Kozo Jirokichi* (*The Rat*, 1969). Satoh was concerned that the Japanese were doomed only to substitute one form of slavery for another, and that the so-called reconstruction of Japan simply created more self-delusion and complacency than before. The student movement had led a whole generation into an era of radicalism in which they resisted all forms of cultural domination, either from Western powers or from the Soviet Union; and yet, the survival of the emperor system and the consequent continuity of Japanese history suggested only that order was to be sustained by both those inside and those outside the social structure.

Kara, who as a student had also been active in Jikken Gekojo (Experimental Theatre), moved on from Seigei in 1963 to form his own group, the Jokyo Gekijo (The Situation Theatre). Satoh and Kara both used TENT THEATRES which they set up in empty plots of land, the precincts of a shrine or park, or at the edge of a pond. Wherever he erected his celebrated Red Tent to perform his 'downtown' *kabuki* full of restless absurd dreaming, Kara infuriated the authorities. Jokyo survived the 1960s and Kara remained active long after. (A six-volume collection of his plays was published in 1979–80). His major productions include *Ren mujutsu* (*Dream Making*, 1965); *Jon Shirub* (*John Silver*, 1965); *Nito monogatari* (*A Tale of Two Cities*, 1971); and *Kyuketsu hime* (*Bloodsucking Maiden*, 1971).

Another prominent figure at this time was Terayama, whose first major work, *Chi wa tattamama nemutteiru* (*He Sleeps with Blood Still Standing*), was produced in 1960 by Bungakuza. He subsequently formed his own highly successful troupe, Tenjo Sajiki (The Peanut Gallery) in 1967. Following many stage and street productions, including *Sho wo steyo machi ni deyo* (*Let's Dump the Books and Go out into the Town*, 1968) and *Nokku* (*Knock*, 1975), his overseas tour of *Nuhi-kun* (*Directions to Servants*, 1978) won him international acclaim. Tenjo Sajiki continued until Terayama's early death in 1983, when the group was disbanded. By that time Terayama had become an idol of the European avant-garde. Although a far more prolific writer, Kara is far less well known in the West, as he toured his Jokyo Gekijo only to less-developed regions such as Bangladesh and Palestinian camps in Syria and Lebanon. Other key playwrights of this 'first generation' of postwar artists include Shogo Ota (b. 1939), whose company Tenkei Gekijo (The Transformation Theatre) was founded in 1968; Kunio Shimizu (b. 1936); and the distinguished novelist Abe, who wrote plays from the 1950s onwards and formed the Kobo Abe Stajio (Studio) which operated from 1973 to 1979. Mishima faced the same postwar dilemmas, but was diametrically opposed to most of the writers working in experimental theatre. Until 1963 he was associated with Bungakuza; then his *Sado koshaku fujin* (*Madame de Sade*) was produced by the Neo Littérature Théâtre, which had broken with Bungakuza, in 1965 and *Waga tomo Hitola* (*My Friend Hitler*) by the Roman Gekijo (Roman Theatre) in 1969. His film *Yukoku* (*Patriotism*) anticipated his own suicide in 1970. This extreme act undermined the radical left, as unresolved feelings connected with defeat in war resurfaced and people felt a sense of the hopelessness of action, despite the fact that Mishima's suicide came from a rather more personal motivation: a simple craving for immortality.

Several other prominent innovators of Japanese theatre emerged during this time of political unrest. Among them was the director TADASHI SUZUKI, who collaborated with playwright Minoru Betsuyaku (b. 1937) to stage *Zo* (*Elephant*) in 1962. In 1966 Suzuki went on to form Waseda Shogekijo (The Waseda Little Theatre) which produced a string of Betsuyaku's works including *Matchi-uri no Shojo* (*The Little March Girl*) that first year. Subsequent years saw an early version of Satoh's *My Beatles*, also in 1966, and Kara's *Shojo kamen* (*The Virgin's Mask*) in 1969. Betsuyaku broke with Suzuki to join with Masakazu Yamazaki (author of *Zeami*, 1963) and form Te no Kai (The Hands Company) in 1973. Suzuki continued his own activities, focusing now on montage works, including *Gekiteki naru mono wo megutte II* (*On the Dramatic Passions II*) in 1970, a work that combined fragments of plays from Japan and the West. This period also saw the emergence within his group of star actress Kayoko Shiraishi and the development of his world-renowned 'Suzuki Method' – a rigorous physical training method based on stomping and rooted in principles of *noh* drama and the martial arts. While continuing with experimental montage works, Suzuki now began to apply his physical method to adaptations of Greek tragedies such as *The Trojan Women* (1974), *The Bacchae* (1978) and an original amalgamation of tragedies entitled *Clytemnestra* (1983). In 1976 the group relocated to Toga, a remote mountain village, converted a thatched farmhouse into a theatre and renamed themselves the Suzuki Company of Toga (SCOT). Over the years the site has expanded into a complex of acting spaces, large and small, including a spectacular lakeside amphitheatre. For nearly 20 years, under Suzuki's direction, the site has hosted the Toga International Arts Festival. Suzuki has toured his works extensively around the world, and, as a result of offering years of workshops in his method, both in Toga and overseas, has produced a number of multilingual, multiracial productions, in particular *Clytemnestra*, *The Tale of Lear*

(1988) and *Dionysus* (1990). Suzuki's group has also established itself in Shizuoka, where they perform in an exquisite complex of indoor and outdoor theatres designed by world-renowned architect Arata Isozaki. Suzuki's group is one of a handful of theatre companies in Japan that can honestly call themselves resident companies. The wide range of works it has performed includes adaptations of *Macbeth* (1991–2), a revival of Kara's *John Silver* (1996), an operatic version of *King Lear* (1999) with the score by Hosokawa Toshio, a comical rendition of *Cyrano de Bergerac* (1999), an adaptation of the *noh* drama *Uto* (2000), staged with translucent mirrors, and an austerely condensed version of *Oedipus* (2000). Suzuki's works overall are marked by a deconstructionist approach to texts. They are austere and powerful, with a typically postmodern mix of violent energy and frivolity. The philosophy behind Suzuki's work and training method (referred to as 'the grammar of the feet'), as well as his aspirations for pursuing a regional theatre, for reviving the Japanese countryside and for revitalizing Japanese culture are well documented in his book, *The Way of Acting* (1986).

The 1960s also saw the emergence of another artist of prominent stature, director YUKIO NINAGAWA, who in 1969 gave up stage and film acting to form the Gendaijin Gekijo (The Modern People's Theatre). By 1974, however, Ninagawa had moved into commercial theatre ventures. Although he has continued to produce works by Japanese playwrights such as Kara, Kunio and Akimoto Matsuyo, he has become most widely known for his manner of rendering Western classics using traditional Japanese theatrical conventions (primarily from *kabuki*) and Japanese cultural references. Although he insists his sole intent is to lend greater familiarity to Western classics for Japanese people, non-Japanese audiences have come to admire his alluring 'intercultural' productions both for their spectacle and for the insights they offer. Ninagawa first earned international recognition for his production of *Medea* (1978) featuring the *kabuki oyama* (female impersonator) Hira Mikijiro and a chorus of kimono-clad 'women' strumming Japanese *shamisen*. It performed in Rome and Athens in 1983, and subsequently on several overseas tours. His 'samurai *Macbeth*' (*Ninagawa Macbeth*, 1980), where Macbeth was an aspiring Japanese warlord and Great Birnam Wood was transformed into a grove of cherry trees in full bloom (a favourite setting in many a *kabuki* play), proved to be an equally compelling *coup de théâtre* at the 1985 EDINBURGH FESTIVAL and thereafter. Since then, Ninagawa has returned to the West with *The Tempest* (1988) performed on a dilapidated *noh* stage, a rather unsuccessful *Peer Gynt* (1994), *A Midsummer Night's Dream*

(1995) staged in a Zen stone garden, and *Hamlet* (1998). Although he understands very little English, in 1999 Ninagawa became the first Japanese director to direct for the ROYAL SHAKESPEARE COMPANY with a production of *King Lear*. Also of note was a production of *Waiting for Godot* in Tokyo (1994) that purportedly incurred the wrath of SAMUEL BECKETT's estate for presenting every other performance with a female cast. Ninagawa and Suzuki represent the only two major directors who have continued to be active over three and four decades, surviving the various trends in theatre.

By the mid-1970s a new generation of theatre practitioners had emerged, including Tetsu Yamazaki's acting company Ten'i 21 (Transposition 21); Kohei Tsuka's Tsuka Studio (1974); Kodai Okabe's Kukan Engi (Space Performance), founded in 1970; Ju'ichiro Takeuchi and his group Hiho Zero Bankan (The Mystical Zero Troupe), begun in 1970; and Hana Kino's all-female company, Aoitori (The Blue Bird Troupe), founded in 1974. The playwright–directors of this period departed from the revolutionary visions of the 'first generation' of the little theatre movement, focusing instead on more immediate concerns of everyday life. At the same time, their work pushed the interchangeability of fiction and reality to extremes, a trend prompted in particular by Tsuka's *Atami satsujin jiken* (*The Atami Murder Case*, 1973).

Yet another generation of artists appeared in the late 1970s, with a style of theatre distinguished by lack of concern with social issues, a postmodern frivolity, and a preoccupation with images of science fiction. The most notable practitioners among this group include Hideka Noda and his Yume no Yuminsha (The Dream Wanderers), founded in 1976; So Kitamura and Suisei '86 (Comet '86) begun in 1978; the New Waseda Theatre of Hiroshi Ohashi, also in 1978; and Koharu Kisaragi and her company NOISE, founded in 1983. These groups are marked by their desire to restructure plays, to re-emphasize the power of the body in performance and to alter the acting space itself using small, often mobile theatres, the street or even tents.

All the changes afforded by these 'second' and 'third' generations of artists constituted a new critique of traditional practices and conventional preconceptions of theatre. Plays of these artists acquired greater complexity, often exhibiting multilayered time-frames as well as sudden shifts of characterization or 'reality'. As theatre critic Kaitaro Tsuno has noted of the works of this period, 'The dynamic of these dramas lies within their fragmented structure and surface.' Subject matter broke away from the ordinary, the realistic and the everyday to penetrate a labyrinthine world of fantasy. Their concern with potency and animation, as well as

their desire to escape from Japan's immediate historical past, also drew many of this period into an obsession with death.

Drama of the little theatre movement has striven to transform experience, metamorphose character and enable spectators to identify with any number of figures, sometimes delving into shamanistic roots in order to redefine a history now laden with horrifying new symbols. Such a theatre, where the character need not be fixed and might be alternately masked and unmasked, and where identity is always in question, reflects the unique Japanese experience. In spite of increasing 'internationalization', Japan's insularity has remained fundamentally unchallenged. As theatre critic Ryuko Saeki once wrote, 'For us, the problem is rather now to dismantle "the will to universality", to dramatize the particular quality of Japanese experience.' The legacy of the atomic bomb and Japan's surrender to Western forces fostered a sense of helplessness and an acute desire to escape from a historical cycle of destruction. But even if the prevailing feeling of the times has been exhaustion, the most recent developments in Japanese theatre demonstrate that a dream can be whipped up. Even though the culture drove itself to the brink of annihilation, it has succeeded in hauling itself back.

LIZZIE SLATER & JON M. BROKERING

Peter Arnott, *The Theatres of Japan* (1969)

David Goodman, *Japanese Drama and Culture in the 1960s: The Return of the Gods* (1988)

Donald Keene, *Dawn to the West: Japanese Literature of the Modern Era, vol. II: Poetry, Drama and Criticism* (1984)

Susan Blakeley Klein, *The Premodern and Postmodern Influences on the Dance of Utter Darkness* (1988)

Benito Ortolani, *The Japanese Theatre: From Shamanistic Ritual to Contemporary Pluralism* (1994)

Thomas J. Rimer, *Towards a Modern Japanese Theatre* (1974)

Akihiko Senda, *The Voyage of Contemporary Japanese Theatre* (1997)

Jaques-Dalcroze [Dalkes], Emile [Jakob] (b. Vienna, 6 July 1865; d. Geneva, 1 July 1950) Music teacher and theoretician. Jaques-Dalcroze developed a system for training musical sensibility through the translation of rhythm into bodily movement. He called the system *gymnastique rhythmique*, or eurhythmics. In 1911 he established a school for Applied Rhythm at Hellerau, near Dresden. He worked here with ADOLPHE APPIA, who designed for him a theatre, much admired by CRAIG, and he was influential through innovators such as COPEAU. His system has attracted thousands of adherents, including dancers like RUTH ST DENIS, Dorothy Humphrey and TED SHAWN, with dance and drama schools, as well as theatre movement directors and choreographers, teaching his principles throughout the world. ANDREW SOLWAY

See also CHOREOGRAPHY; DANCE; MOVEMENT, DANCE AND DRAMA.

Jarman, Derek *see* GAY THEATRE

Jarry, Alfred[-Henri-Marie] (b. Laval, Pays de Loire, France, 8 Sept. 1873; d. Paris, 1 Nov. 1907) Playwright, poet and novelist. At the Lycée in Rennes he joined a group of pupils who composed and performed vitriolic puppet plays directed against a much hated and barracked physics teacher, M. Hébert, severally known as P. H., père Heb, Eb, Ebé, Ebon, Ébance, Ebouille and soon to be immortalized as Ubu.

After failing university entrance exams, Jarry was introduced into the AVANT-GARDE Parisian literary circles and published his first poems (1892). A modest inheritance was spent on an expensive but unsuccessful literary journal, and his writings (poems, novels, plays, articles, philosophy) were not lucrative. He resorted to alcohol to combat his hunger, and died of tuberculosis at the age of 34.

Among Jarry's important output, one text puts all else in the shade: *Ubu Roi* (*King Ubu* or *Ubu Rex*), completed in 1895, published in the summer of 1896 and first performed in a *mise-en-scène* by LUGNÉ-POE in December 1896. In 1900 Jarry published *Ubu enchaîné* (*Ubu Bound*, first performed 1937) and the trilogy is completed with the publication in 1944 of *Ubu Cocu* (*Ubu Cuckold*, written 1888–9). The latter plays do not possess the theatrical effervescence of *Ubu Roi* and are very seldom performed.

Ubu Roi is a grotesque parody of *Macbeth* and of Shakespearean tragedy. The first word uttered by the gross, vulgar, murderous figure of Ubu is 'Merdre' (shit). The insult is unprovoked and hurled at the audience in order to shock. The play uses scatological language and numerous nonsense words and expressions. Contrary to the tragic events in *Macbeth*, what happens in *Ubu* is senseless, unexplained and patently absurd.

Ubu Roi is an attempt at subverting 25 centuries of Western theatrical tradition and undermining the belief in the rationality of language and human behaviour, and breaks with the prevailing bourgeois theatre and naturalism. Jarry announces the twentieth century and is a forerunner of DADA, SURREALISM and the so-called THEATRE OF THE ABSURD. The unbridled savagery of Ubu foreshadows the actions of men like Hitler, Stalin, Franco and Pinochet.

In 'De l'inutilité du théâtre au théâtre' ('On the use-lessness of theatre in the theatre, 1896'), Jarry puts forward his own radical conceptions of the art of the theatre, echoing APPIA and pre-dating CRAIG. For Jarry theatre is, and must be seen as, pure artefact. The actor must become a mere sign, a hieroglyph, not the 'incarnation' of the character. Each role demands a specific voice and an idiosyncratic physical appearance. With the help of a mask and a stylized costume, the actor becomes a 'walking abstraction', an anonymous human-sized puppet vocalizing the playwright's words and performing the implicit choreography just as a musician plays a musical score. Similarly, a set must materialize the essence of the work without attempting to ape nature. (For *Ubu*, Jarry enlisted the help of painters – Bonnard, Vuillard, Sérusier, Toulouse-Lautrec.)

The première of *Ubu* on 9 December 1896 created a theatrical and literary scandal. Spectators were offended by the language and dramaturgy. The play has since become a classic and is regularly revived in France with great success. The first English production took place at Bristol University (1962), and the TRAVERSE in Edinburgh gave a few performances in April 1963, but the 'real' première was staged at the ROYAL COURT in 1966 with MAX WALL as Ubu and design by DAVID HOCKNEY. The LORD CHAMBERLAIN objected to some aspects of the director Ian Cuthbertson's translation and 'Merdre' was spoken in French. Among numerous television versions, the cartoon by Geoff Dunbar, shown on BBC2 in 1978, remains outstanding. In both East and West, the play remains a powerful weapon of subversion, and a list of productions would fill volumes.

Since the 1920s Jarry has been recognized as one of the most important influences on contemporary French theatre. APOLLINAIRE acknowledged his debt, then VITRAC; ARTAUD named his first theatre after him. VIAN and IONESCO were among those who created the College of 'Pataphysics in 1948, 'PATAPHYSICS being the science of 'imaginary solutions' whose principles were formulated by Jarry. In Britain Jarry and 'pataphysics have influenced the Goon Show and Monty Python, and liberated generations of playwrights and directors from the shackles of rationalism.

CLAUDE SCHUMACHER

Keith Beaumont, *Alfred Jarry: A Critical and Biographical Study* (1984)

Maurice Marc LaBelle, *Jarry: Nihilism and the Theatre of the Absurd* (1980)

Nigel Lennon, *Alfred Jarry: The Man with the Axe* (1984)

Claude Schumacher, *Alfred Jarry and Guillaume Apollinaire* (1985)

Java *see* SOUTH-EAST ASIA

jazz Definitions of jazz are as slippery and contradictory as those of any art form, but it is quick and convenient to think of it as a way of playing and singing, rather than a rigid repertoire of tunes and songs. Louis Armstrong or Billie Holiday transformed the crassest of raw material into jazz. AL JOLSON, despite his billing, never sang a note of jazz in his life. The heart of the music is Afro-American: its roots include work-song, blues, spirituals and ragtime; its bloodstream is the experience of slavery and oppression. Yet, paradoxically, it knows no boundaries. The melody of 'Tiger Rag' can be traced to a French quadrille which found its way into the tradition via New Orleans. The music, its players and its audience tend to be outsiders, by definition, by choice and sometimes by decree. Hitler and Stalin sent jazz musicians to labour camps; totalitarianism and the unpredictable are mutually exclusive. Even in relatively enlightened societies, jazz is a marginal music. Thus, Fats Waller, the licensed court jester, begat Miles Davis, the designated subversive. In the halls of mainstream theatre, the place of jazz has always been precarious. Its greatest artists starred in VAUDEVILLE and VARIETY, but were rarely granted a central creative role. Scott Joplin wrote two ragtime operas that were never adequately performed in his lifetime, while Duke Ellington, by common consent the music's outstanding creator, made only spasmodic contributions to conventional theatre. In 1941 he wrote the music for *Jump For Joy*, a REVUE presented in Los Angeles. The show ran for four months, with nightly revisions by Ellington and its team of 15 writers, who included LANGSTON HUGHES and Mickey Rooney. One of the songs had the line: 'Uncle Tom's Cabin is a drive-in now.' In the 1950s Ellington wrote music for the STRATFORD FESTIVAL, Ontario: a Shakespearean Suite including 'Sonnet To Hank Cinq' and 'Lady Mac', of whom he said: 'Though a lady of noble birth, we suspect there was a little ragtime in her soul.' Not untypically, Ellington's music achieved full-blooded Broadway success only after his death, with *Sophisticated Ladies* (1981), an honour also bestowed posthumously on Fats Waller with *Ain't Misbehavin'* (1978), joyously acclaimed in both New York and London. *Five Guys Named Moe* (1990), written by Clarke Peters, celebrated the boisterous talent of the singer and alto sax player Louis Jordan, who helped to create rock-and-roll, without sharing in the resulting largesse. Second cousins to these productions, which honoured individuals, are those drawing on the broader inheritance of jazz, blues and black vaudeville songs, and in the process reviving lovely material too long neglected. *One Mo' Time*, *Bubbling Brown Sugar*, *Blues in the Night* and *Rent Party* each strung a series of precious gems on a narrative thread so fine it sometimes disappeared completely – but no harm done. The celebration was the thing.

Plays that seriously examine jazz as a manifestation of the black experience in America tend to be less comforting. AUGUST WILSON's *Ma Rainey's Black Bottom* (1984) and Caryl Phillips's *All or Nothing at All* (1989) looked at the life and work of two singers: Gertrude 'Ma' Rainey and Billie Holiday. They told their stories with skill, passion, anger and insight. To be sure, the celebration survives, but at a price. The outsider status that hangs around jazz seems to fit snugly around many British dramatists since the late 1950s. JOAN LITTLEWOOD's original production of SHELAGH DELANEY's *A Taste of Honey* had a jazz group on-stage, and it is no coincidence that Jimmy Porter in OSBORNE's *Look Back in Anger* plays jazz trumpet. The blues offers rage and redemption simultaneously, and it is a fair bet that in any group of playwrights over the age of 60 at the millennium, half would be able to sing along with Louis Armstrong's most famous solos. Jazz has remained a continuing obsession with writers: in ADRIAN MITCHELL's *Hoagy, Bix and Wolfgang Beethoven Bunkhaus* (1979), in Kevin Hood's *Sugar Hill Blues* (1990) and in ALAN PLATER's *Going Home* (1990), which had music composed and arranged by the trumpet player Ian Carr.

This illustrates one of the continuing frustrations: it was the first time Carr had been invited to work in theatre, despite a distinguished 30-year career as musician, writer and composer. It is a repeating pattern. The pianist Stan Tracey, whose *Under Milk Wood* suite is a brilliantly inventive blend of words and music, has been ignored by the theatre. Mike Westbrook, whose work is tinged with rather than dominated by jazz, has been similarly neglected. His memorable contribution to Adrian Mitchell's *Tyger* was, it seems, not as memorable as all that. The list is potentially endless: Michael Garrick, Mike Gibbs, Kenny Wheeler . . . and a whole generation following on behind.

As the century closed jazz was in fashion again. Young musicians, black and white, were re-examining the roots of jazz, addressing the ancient question: who am I, how did I get here and what am I going to play tomorrow? They may decide not to storm the theatre's Winter Palace, but it would be good to think that somewhere they will find a small back room, reserved for those of ragtime soul who have heard the blues at midnight. ALAN PLATER

Jeans, Isabel [Isobel] (b. London, 16 Sept. 1891; d.

London, 4 Sept. 1985) Actress who became a key performer with the PHOENIX SOCIETY in 1921, giving successful performances in contemporary plays and classics. A spirited comic actress, her first triumph, as Mrs Erlynne in WILDE's *Lady Windermere's Fan* (1945), heralded a succession of hits in strong feminine lead roles varying from the light comedy of ANOUILH (*Ardèle*, 1951) to the more ironic humour of CHEKHOV (*The Seagull*, 1949). ADRIANA HUNTER

Jefford, Barbara [Mary] (b. Plymstock, Devon, 26 July 1930) Actress. Her roles for the SHAKESPEARE MEMORIAL THEATRE in STRATFORD-UPON-AVON (1950–4) included Desdemona, Isabella and Rosalind. She confirmed her stature as a major classical actress with the OLD VIC (1956–62) where she played, among many roles, Portia, Viola and, most notably, SHAW's St Joan. She has made a few forays into the contemporary theatre (e.g. DAVID MERCER's *Ride a Cock Horse*, 1965, and JULES FEIFFER's *Little Murders*, 1967). Her West End engagements alternate with her continuing work for the major companies. DAVID STAINES

Jeffreys, Stephen (b London, 22 April 1950) Playwright. He had his first play, *Where the Tide Has Rolled You*, produced in 1973 in Southampton, where he was a postgraduate student. In 1975 he moved to Cumbria as a lecturer and had a string of plays performed in Kendal, including an admired adaptation of Dickens' *Hard Times* (1982). After a stint as writer-in-residence for PAINES PLOUGH (1987–9), he came to national notice in 1989 with the HAMPSTEAD THEATRE production of *Valued Friends*, a portrait of four of Thatcher's children exploiting the property boom. His craft skills, cool humour and versatility are shown by his adaptation of Richard Brome's 1641 play *A Jovial Crew* (1992) for the ROYAL SHAKESPEARE COMPANY and his two other seventeenth-century pieces, *The Clink* (1990), set in the dying days of Elizabeth I's reign, and *The Libertine* (1994), based on the scabrous life of the notorious Restoration rake the Earl of Rochester. Since 1991 he has been associated with the ROYAL COURT as literary adviser; in 2000 it staged his *I Just Stopped By To See The Man* about an old blues singer from the American South. CHARLES LONDON

Jellicoe, [Patricia] Ann (b. Middlesbrough, Yorks, 15 July 1927) Playwright, director and teacher. Her first play, *The Sport of My Mad Mother* (1958), looks unpromising on the page, for this story of a group of teenage teddy boys (led by an 'earth mother') relies heavily on its cast's ability to develop vocal rhythms and an exuberant, physical style of acting – showing its author to be an early enthusiast of TOTAL THEATRE.

Her later comedy, *The Knack* (1961, ROYAL COURT; filmed 1965), is a more conventional and very funny picture of the shifting (sexual) power balance between three men and a woman. From 1979 to 1985 Jellicoe was much involved in pioneering community theatre in Dorset (*see* COMMUNITY PLAY). Other plays include *Shelley* (1965) and *The Rising Generation* (1967). DAVID SELF

Jenkin, Len (b. New York, 2 April 1941) Playwright. He has been compared with THORNTON WILDER, another writer known for his observations of American life. However, Jenkin adopts a more forthright approach than Wilder's nostalgic take on small-town America. His characters actively pursue often obscure goals outside the frameworks of their lives, frequently addressing the audience through monologues, thereby illustrating their own isolation. His musical play, *Tallahassee* (1995), co-written with Mac Wellman, is a re-telling of Ovid's *Metamorphoses* set among the poor rural whites of Florida's 'cracker country', and examines themes ranging from the government's disdain for the arts to cosmic regeneration. His *Poor Folk's Pleasure* (1996) is a stylish exploration of America's demimonde, set in a bar and commented on by prostitutes and stalkers. The *New York Times* described his *Dark Ride* (1996) as 'a Borgesian take on American cultural rubble'. His adaptations of children's stories are frequently in the repertoire of children's theatre companies. LAURIE WOLF

Jenner, Caryl *see* CHILDREN'S THEATRE; THEATRE FOR YOUNG PEOPLE; UNICORN THEATRE

Jerome, Jerome K[lapka] (b. Walsall, W. Midlands, 2 May 1859; d. Northampton, 14 June 1927) Playwright, actor and humorist, famous for his novel *Three Men in a Boat* (1889). Jerome's most successful play was *The Passing of the Third Floor Back* (1904), an enigmatic tale of a Christ-like tenement lodger who transforms the lives of his fellow tenants. His humorous reminiscences of late Victorian theatre are contained in *Stageland* (1889) and *On the Stage and Off* (1885). IAN CLARKE

Jessel, George [Albert] (b. New York, 3 April 1898; d. Los Angeles, 23 May 1981) Vaudevillian and comedian whose talents as an after dinner speaker won him the informal title of 'Toastmaster General of the United States'. Jessel played *The Jazz Singer* (1925) on BROADWAY but spurned making the landmark talkie in a contract dispute. Other Broadway shows include *The Passing Show of 1923* and *High Kickers* (1941), which he co-produced. He also produced films and made

frequent television and night club appearances.
MICHAEL SOMMERS

Jessner, Leopold (b. Königsberg, Germany, 3 March 1878; d. Hollywood, 30 Oct. 1945) Director and theatre manager. Alongside REINHARDT, he can be regarded as one of the most important creators of a modern concept of DIRECTING. He began his career as an actor in Hamburg, and became one of the leading German producers between 1919 and 1930 in Berlin. In collaboration with the designers Pirchan and Klein and the actor KORTNER, he created some of the most memorable productions of the Weimar Republic: Schiller's *Wilhelm Tell* (1919), WEDEKIND's *Der Marquis von Keith* (1920), *Richard III* (1920), Grabbe's *Napoleon* (1922), Schiller's *Wallenstein* (1924), *Hamlet* (1926), BRONNEN's *Ostpolzug* (1926) and Sophocles' *Oedipus* (1929). He combined strong theatrical effects with utmost simplicity of form. Yet, despite the clarity and precision of his stagings, there was an underlying irrational and emotive strain. The stage was treated as a 'rhythmic space' and was often bare except for the famous 'Jessner steps', which became the trademark of his abstractionist style. These steps enabled Jessner to create stage pictures which employed vertical as well as horizontal relationships among the actors. The performances gained new dimensions from the use of striking movements on stage, novel lighting effects, which replaced traditional stage designs, and off-stage sound effects, which gave every scene a strong musical quality. GÜNTER BERGHAUS

Michael Patterson, *The Revolution in German Theatre 1900–1933* (1981)
John Willett, *The Theatre of the Weimar Republic* (1988)

Jewish theatre see ISRAEL; YIDDISH THEATRE

John, Errol (b. Trinidad, 20 Dec. 1924; d. London, 10 July 1988) Playwright and actor. He was an actor, director and designer with the Whitehall Players in Trinidad. Arriving in England in 1951, he appeared on the British stage but became increasingly frustrated by the lack of good roles for black actors – with the exception of Othello, which he played at the OLD VIC in 1962. John returned to playwriting, which he began with *The Tout* in 1949, and won a competition with what is considered the definitive 'yard' play, *Moon on a Rainbow Shawl*, in which a bus driver escapes the poor Caribbean backyard life of prostitution and crime. Its successful staging at the ROYAL COURT in 1958 was followed by many productions and revivals worldwide and was a breakthrough in Britain for black writing. Other plays by John also explore the theme of escape.
HELEN RAPPAPORT

See also BLACK THEATRE; CARIBBEAN.

John F. Kennedy Center for the Performing Arts *see* KENNEDY CENTER

Johnson, Albert [Richard] (b. La Crosse, Wisc., 1 Feb. 1910; d. New York, 21 Dec. 1967) Set designer. He began painting scenery as a youngster and subsequently studied under NORMAN BEL GEDDES. He was only 19 when he won the highest praise for his designs for *The Criminal Code* (1929). But he quickly moved away from the realism that this play required, and was best remembered for his work with musicals. It was for these shows that he is credited with perfecting the use of revolving stages. Among his major assignments were *The Band Wagon* (1931), *Jumbo* (1935), *The Skin of our Teeth* (1942), and the 1956 revival of *Show Boat*.
GERALD BORDMAN

Johnson [Fleming], Celia (b. Richmond, Surrey, 18 Dec. 1908; d. Nettlebed, Oxon, 25 April 1982) Actress. She brought distinction to many undistinguished commercial plays during a long career starting in 1928 and highlighted by such West End successes as *Ten Minute Alibi* (1933), *The Wind and The Rain* (1933), *Rebecca* (1940), *The Reluctant Debutante* (1955), *Flowering Cherry* (1957) and *The Grass Is Greener* (1958). She made a memorable film appearance in *Brief Encounter* (1946), adapted from NOEL COWARD's one-act play *Still Life*. She was created a dame in 1981. IAN BEVAN

K. Fleming, *Celia Johnson* (1991)

Johnson, Terry (b. Middlesex, 20 December 1955) Playwright. His plays have some affinities with that of TOM STOPPARD in their representation of real historical characters, such as Monroe and Einstein in *Insignificance* (1982); Freud and Dali in *Hysteria* (1993); members of the 'Carry On' team in *Cleo, Camping, Emanuelle and Dick* (1998). Often they share with Stoppard a delight in adopting and adapting generic theatrical convention; *Unsuitable for Adults* (1984) works with the conventions of stand-up COMEDY; *Hysteria* uses FARCE; *Imagine Drowning* (1990) uses elements of murder mystery and political thriller. His work suggests a serious engagement with the meaning and function of laughter: in *Dead Funny* (1994) members of a dead comics appreciation society find their adored and much-repeated routines fail to conceal the misery of their lives. Yet, unlike Stoppard, devices rarely amount to merely self-conscious artifice and the plays often break through their textual playfulnesss to offer broader perspectives and experiences. *Insignificance*, for example, contains a lengthy exposition of the theory of relativity (delivered by Monroe) yet considers the responsibility of scientists to society, while *Hysteria* is a thrilling meditation on the interplay of ageing, guilt and responsibility. He also directs. DAN REBELLATO

Johnston, [William] Denis (b. Dublin, 18 June 1901; d. Dublin, 8 Aug. 1984) Playwright. Educated in Dublin, Edinburgh and Cambridge. Though called to the Bar in 1925, almost his entire professional life was spent in the theatre, broadcasting, and in later years as a university lecturer. He was associated with the Dublin GATE THEATRE in its formative years, and was a director of the company from 1931 to 1936. His earliest play, *The Old Lady Says 'No!'* (1929), heavily influenced by German EXPRESSIONISM, brought the Gate Theatre to prominence. In this, his most complex and characteristic work, an actor portraying the patriot Robert Emmet in an old-fashioned melodrama is injured on stage; his semi-conscious (and often hilarious) ramblings through post-revolutionary Dublin, and also through a skein of hallucinatory incidents in Irish mythology and history, introduce a new genre in Irish playwriting perhaps best described as 'poetic satire'. Though performed internationally, it is, like JOYCE's *Ulysses*, fully appreciated only by Dublin audiences. *The Moon in the Yellow River* (1931) is Johnston's most frequently performed play. Written in a kind of heightened naturalistic style, it is an allegory on contemporary political events. The plot concerns the building of a power station under the Free State government and the attempt by subversives to destroy it. *A Bride for the Unicorn* (1933), *Storm Song* (1934), *The Golden Cuckoo* (1939) and *The Dreaming Dust* (1940) were all produced at the Gate. *Strange Occurence on Ireland's Eye* (Abbey, 1956) examines legal morality and is presented as courtroom drama. *The Scythe and the Sunset* (Abbey, 1958) is Johnston's coolly cynical response to the emotionalism of O'CASEY's *The Plough and the Stars*. As in all his plays, a sense of detachment, sometimes described as 'Anglo-Irish', prevails. Johnston was a BBC war correspondent 1942–5, a period which resulted in a luminous autobiographical work or 'speculative narrative', *Nine Rivers from Jordan* (1953). CHRISTOPHER FITZ-SIMON

Joseph Ronsley, ed., *Denis Johnston* (1981)

Joint Stock Theatre Group British touring company structured to give each member a full part to play in the theatre-making process. Soon after its foundation in 1973 by MAX STAFFORD-CLARK, DAVID HARE and David Aukin, its then unique brand of collaborative production methods (involving actors, writers and directors equally in the creative process) rapidly won this innovative group attention. This process often necessitated lengthy workshop, discussion and rehearsal periods, but resulted in many notable productions after the first in 1974: Hare's *Fanshen* (1975); CARYL CHURCHILL's *Light Shining in Buckinghamshire* (1976), *Cloud Nine* (1979) and *Fen* (1983); BARRIE KEEFFE's *A Mad World My Masters* (1977) and STEPHEN LOWE's *The Ragged Trousered Philanthropists* (1978), both directed by WILLIAM GASKILL; and *Victory* (1983) by HOWARD BARKER. Joint Stock involved many of the major practitioners of its day and became a leading light in the world of FRINGE theatre but commercial pressures curtailed its later work and it was wound up in 1989.
DAVID SELF

Rob Ritchie, ed., *The Joint Stock Book: The Making of a Theatre Collective* (1987)

Jolson, Al [Asa Yoelson] (b. Srednike or Seredzius, Lithuania, 26 May 1886; d. San Francisco, 23 Oct. 1950) Singer and comedian. After coming to America as a youngster he worked in CIRCUS, VAUDEVILLE, BURLESQUE and MINSTREL shows before making his Broadway debut in *La Belle Paree* (1911). Performing in blackface, with a warmth and gusto that soon made him the leading box-office attraction, he then starred in such shows as *The Honeymoon Express* (1913), *Sinbad* (1918) and *Bombo* (1921). He introduced several songs that were to become 'classics' (e.g. 'California, Here I Come', 'My Mammy') and became famous for his pose down on one knee, arms outstretched. When his vogue faded he became for a time a major radio and film star, appearing in the first 'talkie', *The Jazz Singer* (1927). He returned to Broadway only twice thereafter – in *The Wonder Bar* (1931) and *Hold on to Your Hats* (1940). GERALD BORDMAN

M. Freedland, *Jolson* (1972)
H. Goldman, *Jolson: The Legend Comes to Life* (1988)
P. Sieben, *The Immortal Jolson* (1962)

Jones, Bill [William] T[ass] (b. Bunnell, Fla., 15 Feb. 1952) Among the most famous and articulate dancer/choreographers of the postmodern movement, he first distinguished himself through autobiographical storytelling. In 1982 he formed Bill T. Jones/Arnie Zane & Company with his long-time partner Arnie Zane, and their outspoken commitment to each other onstage and off galvanized the New York art world in works such as *Secret Pastures* (1984). Jones and Zane were both diagnosed HIV positive in 1986, and Zane succumbed to AIDS in 1988. After Zane's death, Jones continued to make large-scale works that addressed themes of racial identity, sexuality and cultural memory, such as the epic *Last Supper at Uncle Tom's Cabin/The Promised Land* (1990), a four-part, three-hour

fantasia loosely based on the Harriet Beecher Stowe novel, including an intergenerational cast, rap poetry, and scores of nude dancers in its final utopian vision; and *Still/Here* (1994), a full-length work that dealt soberly with impressions of premature death. With Peggy Gillespie, he wrote *Last Night on Earth* (1995).
THOMAS DEFRANTZ

See also CHOREOGRAPHY; DANCE; MOVEMENT, DANCE AND DRAMA.

Jones, Daniel see VOICE; VOICE TRAINING

Jones, David [Hugh] (b. Poole, Dorset, 19 Feb. 1934) Director. He directed new plays and twentieth-century classics for the ROYAL SHAKESPEARE COMPANY, including BRECHT, VIAN, NELSON, GRASS, O'CASEY, four by MERCER, and a cycle of detailed ensemble productions which re-established GORKY in English-speaking theatres, from *Enemies* (1971) to *Barbarians* (1990). He was artistic director of the Brooklyn Academy of Music (1979–81). He had worked on the influential TV arts programme *Monitor* and, as producer/director, he later popularized classic and contemporary drama on television. Films include PINTER's *Betrayal* (1982) and *84 Charing Cross Road* (1987). He was co-author with Nelson of *Making Plays* (1995), about the writer–director relationship. TONY HOWARD

Jones, Everett LeRoi see BARAKA, IMAMU AMIRI

Jones, Henry Arthur (b. Grandesborough, Bucks, 20 Sept. 1851; d. Hampstead, London, 7 Jan. 1929) Playwright. Jones, who left school at 12 to become a draper's apprentice, established his reputation with a popular melodrama, *The Silver King* (1882), in the writing of which Henry Herman had a hand. The melodramatic intonation remained strong in *Saints and Sinners* (1884) and *The Middleman* (1889), and continued to underpin the seemingly more sophisticated society plays for which he is most famous: *The Case of Rebellious Susan* (1894), *The Liars* (1897) and *Mrs Dane's Defence* (1900), all of which caused a stir. Although he was a tireless campaigner for an intellectual modern drama – see his *The Renascence of the English Drama* (1895) and *The Foundations of a National Drama* (1913) – few of his more than 80 plays overcome their essential conservatism. An important figure at the turn of the century, he has been overshadowed by his contemporaries PINERO and WILDE and his friend SHAW, who regarded him highly. IAN CLARKE

Richard A. Cordell, *Henry Arthur Jones and the Modern Drama* (1932)
Doris Arthur Jones, *The Life and Letters of Henry Arthur Jones* (1930)
F. M. Northend, *Henry Arthur Jones and the Dramatic Renascence in England* (1940)

Jones, James Earl (b. Arkabutla, Miss., 17 Jan. 1931) Actor. With a large presence and booming voice, he has earned his considerable reputation in important dramas of black life, including *The Blacks* (1961), *The Blood Knot* (1964), *The Great White Hope* (1968), *Boesman and Lena* (1970), *Les Blancs* (1970), *Paul Robeson* (1978), *A Lesson From Aloes* (1982) and *Fences* (1987). He has had a close association with the NEW YORK SHAKESPEARE FESTIVAL, playing, among other roles, Oberon, Caliban, Macbeth, Lear, Claudius and Othello – the last of these a part he has repeated to acclaim several times. Other major New York appearances include *Baal* (1965), *The Cherry Orchard* (1973), *The Iceman Cometh* (1973), and *Of Mice and Men* (1974). He also works extensively in film and television. An autobiography, *Voices and Silences* (written with Penelope Niven), appeared in 1993.
DAVID BARBOUR

Jones, Margo [Margaret Virginia] (b. Livingston, Tex., 12 Dec. 1913; d. Dallas, 24 July 1955) Producer and director. After an apprenticeship that included seven seasons with the Houston Community Players (which she founded in 1936), directing at the PASADENA PLAYHOUSE, and assistant directing the original production of TENNESSEE WILLIAMS' *The Glass Menagerie* (1945), Jones embarked upon her pioneering crusade to decentralize the American theatre. She founded the arena-style Theatre '47 (the name changed each year until her death) in Dallas. There the hard-drinking 'Texas Tornado' launched the modern American regional theatre movement and tirelessly promoted new American playwriting. She wrote *Theatre-in-the-Round* (1951). The Margo Jones Award was established in 1961 to reward a producer of new work.
FELICIA HARDISON LONDRÉ

See also RESIDENT THEATRE; THEATRE IN THE ROUND.

Helen Sheehy, *Margo: The Life and Theatre of Margo Jones* (1989)

Jones, Marie see BELFAST

Jones, Robert Edmond (b. Milton, NH, 12 Dec. 1887; d. Milton, NH, 26 Nov. 1954) Stage designer, writer and director. After graduating from Harvard University he travelled throughout Europe, where he discovered REINHARDT's Deutsches Theater in Berlin and observed numerous instances of the new stagecraft associated with pioneers like CRAIG. This movement emphasized the union of all the elements of design, direction and acting into a dramatic whole and was in direct contrast to the concept of romantic realism which then prevailed in America.

After his return to New York, Jones designed the setting for HARLEY GRANVILLE BARKER's production of *The Man Who Married a Dumb Wife* (1915). This revolutionary design marked the entrance of the new stagecraft into America and the emergence of the artist who was the first and most important link with the established theatre attitude in Europe. In 1918 Jones began an association with the director Arthur Hopkins, which enabled him to design productions of Shakespeare, IBSEN, GORKY, O'NEILL and others. He introduced unit sets, almost unknown at that time, and used light and shadow in a manner that showed the influence of ADOLPHE APPIA. Beginning in the early 1920s, Jones worked at the PROVINCETOWN Playhouse and the Greenwich Village Theater, designing such O'Neill works as *Anna Christie* (1921), *Desire Under the Elms* (1924), *Mourning Becomes Electra* (1931) and *The Great God Brown* (1926), which he also directed. Later, he joined forces with KENNETH MACGOWAN at the Experimental Theatre and designed countless productions for the THEATER GUILD in the 1940s. He was also the designer of NIJINSKY's ballet *Til Eulenspiegel* and STRAVINSKY's opera-oratorio *Oedipus Rex* at the Metropolitan Opera House.

Jones was the undisputed father of American stage design. A unique blend of down-to-earth puritan craftsman, romantic mystic and visionary, he was 'the most practical of dreamers', who initiated a theatrical revolution. His writings include *The Dramatic Imagination* (1941) which states his credo: 'The sole aim of the art of scene-designing, costuming, lighting is . . . to enhance the natural powers of the actor.' He spent 1940–1 on a lecture tour of American colleges and universities. With MacGowan he wrote *Continental Stagecraft* (1922), and Jones' vision of theatre is captured in a recording, *Towards A New Theatre, I & II*, a series of lectures he gave at Harvard in 1952. JOSEPH M. DIAZ

Ralph Pendleton, ed., *The Theatre of Robert Edmond Jones* (1958)

Jooss, Kurt (b. Wasseralfingen, Germany, 12 Jan. 1901; d. Heilbronn, Germany, 22 May 1979) Dancer, teacher and CHOREOGRAPHER. An innovative and unique force in European early modern dance, Jooss worked with LABAN and devised principles of movement for an expressive theatre dance. He created dances of strong dramatic and narrative content. He is particularly noted for *The Green Table* (1932), a powerful comment on the insanity of war, deservedly the most famous work of its time. He established Ballets Jooss and transformed modern dance theatre. With

Sigurd Leeder (b. Hamburg, 14 Aug. 1902; d. Herisau, 20 June 1981), co-founder of his company, he created a school which helped formalize his theatrical approach to dance training and had a great influence on movement in theatre. JOHN BROOME

See also CHOREOGRAPHY; DANCE; MOVEMENT, DANCE AND DRAMA.

A. V. Coton, *The New Ballet* (1946)
Susan Walther, *The Dance of Death: Kurt Jooss and the Weimar Years* (1994)

Jordan *see* MIDDLE EAST AND NORTH AFRICA

Jory, Jon *see* ACTORS THEATRE OF LOUISVILLE; LONG WHARF THEATER

Joseph, Stephen (b. London, 13 June 1921; d. Scarborough, 4 Oct. 1967) Actor and director. Son of HERMIONE GINGOLD, Joseph studied drama at the University of Iowa and returned to England in 1955 when he founded his own company – initially at the public library in Scarborough – specializing in THEATRE IN THE ROUND. From 1956 to 1962 it toured Britain with a portable in-the-round stage, pioneering the use of this form of staging. In 1962, with PETER CHEESEMAN, he founded the VICTORIA THEATRE, Stoke-on-Trent, the country's first permanent theatre with this configuration, and became a lecturer and researcher at Manchester University's Drama Department. As a tribute to him, the Stephen Joseph Theatre in the Round was opened in 1976 in Scarborough under the direction of ALAN AYCKBOURN. His books include *Theatre in the Round* (1967) and *New Theatre Forms* (1968). ADRIANA HUNTER

journals *see* MAGAZINES AND JOURNALS

Jouvet, Louis (b. Crozon, 24 Dec. 1887; d. Paris, 24 July 1951) Actor and director. He was an early member of COPEAU's Théâtre du Vieux Colombier as lighting and technical director, and acted a famous Andrew Aguecheek (1913) and a celebrated Géronte in Molière's *Les Fourberies de Scapin* (1920). He redesigned the theatre but left in 1922 to direct the Comédie des Champs Elysées, where his success in *Dr Knock* (1923) by JULES ROMAINS alleviated financial problems. He co-founded the CARTEL (1927), taught at the Conservatoire (from 1934) and became a well-known screen actor in the 1930s. He worked closely from 1928 until the author's death with JEAN GIRAUDOUX, whom he introduced to the public with *Siegfried*, and, from 1930, with the designer CHRISTIAN-JACQUES BÉRARD, often at the Théâtre de l'Athénée, to which Jouvet's name was added. He was first an adviser to (1936) and then a director of (1940) the COMÉDIE-FRANÇAISE, but spent

the Second World War abroad with his company, in Switzerland and South America, returning in 1945 to play, among many Molière roles, a famous Tartuffe. He died, like Molière, on stage. He wrote several books on the theatre, including *Réflexions du comédien* (1939) and *Témoignages sur le théâtre* (published 1952).
TERRY HODGSON

Joyce, James [Augustine] (b. Dublin, 2 Feb. 1882; d. Zurich, 13 Jan. 1941) Poet, novelist and playwright. *Exiles*, an Ibsenite drama set in suburban Dublin, was published in 1918 and has been performed internationally. Many stage adaptations of his prose works have been produced, including *Ulysses in Nighttown* by Marjorie Barkentin (1958), *The Voice of Shem* by Marv Manning (1961), *Bloomsday* by Alan McClelland (1966), *Stephen D* by HUGH LEONARD (1962) and *Joycity* by Ulick O'Connor (1989). He appears as a character in several plays (e.g. *Travesties* by TOM STOPPARD).
CHRISTOPHER FITZ-SIMON

Judson Church From 1961 to 1973 the Judson Memorial Church, in Manhattan's Greenwich Village, produced some of the strongest experimental work of the burgeoning OFF-OFF-BROADWAY movement. This collaboration between the spiritual and secular worlds of church and theatre came about when Assistant Minister Al Carmine opened the church's rooms for members to give poetry readings. Out of this project developed the Judson Poet's Theater, the Judson Dance Theater and the Judson Art Gallery. Relationships between the three companies yielded experimentation with new forms, combining art, dance, HAPPENINGS and drama. The plays of the Judson Poet's Theater had no direct relationship to religion or the church. The free productions, performed in the church's choir loft, included works by GERTRUDE STEIN, MARIA IRENE FORNÉS, ROSALYN DREXLER, George Dennison, Ruth Krauss and H. M. Koutoukas. SARAH STEVENSON

See also CHOREOGRAPHY; DANCE.

Gerald M. Berkowitz, *New Broadways: Theatre across America. Approaching a New Millennium* (1997)
Al Carmine, 'The Judson Poets Theatre', and Michael Smith, 'Introduction', in Nick Orzel, ed., *Eight Plays from Off-Off Broadway* (1966)

juggling *see* CIRCUS

Juilliard School *see* DRAMA SCHOOLS

Julia [Y Arcelay], Raul [Rafael Carlos] (b. Puerto Rico, 9 March 1940; d. Long Island, NY, 24 Oct. 1994) Actor. He made his New York debut in a Spanish production of Calderón's *La Vida es Sueño* (*Life's a Dream*, 1964). His 16-year association with JOSEPH PAPP at the NEW YORK SHAKESPEARE FESTIVAL began in 1966 with *Macbeth*, followed by *Titus Andronicus* (1967), a musical version of *Two Gentlemen of Verona* (1971), *As You Like it* and *King Lear* (1973), *The Taming of the Shrew* (1978) and *Othello* (1979). Julia made his Broadway debut in *The Cuban Thing* (1968). Other roles followed in *Indians* (1969) and *The Persians* (1969), but real critical acclaim did not come until *The Castro Complex* (1970), *Where's Charley?* (1974) and *The Threepenny Opera* (1976). A return to musicals in *Nine* (1982) consolidated Julia's stage career by the early 1980s, when he became increasingly taken up with a burgeoning film career, although he toured *Man of La Mancha* in 1991 and took it to Broadway in 1992. HELEN RAPPAPORT

Jullien, Jean[-Thomas-Édouard] (b. Lyons, 4 Dec. 1854; d. Ville d'Avray, 3 Sept. 1919) Playwright; an advocate of 'slice-of-life theatre' whose plays were directed by ANDRÉ ANTOINE. *La Sérénade* ('The serenade', 1887) was an early success. He wrote a naturalist manifesto and preferred the style of DUSE to the romantic acting of SARAH BERNHARDT. His work includes *La Poigne* ('A firm hand', 1901). TERRY HODGSON

K

Kahn, Florence (b. Memphis, Tenn., 3 March 1878; d. Rapallo, Italy, 13 Jan. 1951) Actress. Kahn's reputation was established as a leading lady to RICHARD MANSFIELD, after which she became a major early interpreter of IBSEN, appearing in *Rosmersholm* (1904), *When We Dead Awaken* (1905) and *Hedda Gabler* (1907). In 1908, appearing in *Rosmersholm* in London, she met MAX BEERBOHM and married him shortly after. She subsequently acted only rarely as a guest performer, most notably as Aase in the OLD VIC *Peer Gynt* (1935).

MARVIN CARLSON

Kahn, Otto H[ermann] (b. Mannheim, Germany, 21 Feb. 1867; d. New York, 29 March 1934) Philanthropist. His financial patronage of various New York City groups helped ensure the prosperity of American theatre at the beginning of the twentieth century. Kahn's love of the arts began as a child in Germany, and after immigrating to the US in 1893 and amassing his fortune as a banker, he recognized that the US government did not subsidize the arts as European governments did. He facilitated the American tours of the Ballets Russes, the MOSCOW ART THEATRE, the ABBEY THEATRE and COPEAU's Vieux Colombier. As one of the founders and major backers of the New Theatre (1909–11), Kahn was instrumental in introducing European methods of staging to the United States, though he was more concerned with nurturing native American talent. He provided financial support to the WASHINGTON SQUARE PLAYERS, the PROVINCETOWN PLAYERS, the Metropolitan Opera, the New Playwrights' Theater and many others, as well as to many individual artists.

DAVID A. WILLIAMS

M. J. Matz, *The Many Lives of Otto Kahn* (1963)

Kaiser, Georg (b. Magdeburg, Germany, 25 Nov. 1878; d. Ascona, Switzerland, 4 June 1945) Playwright, librettist, novelist and poet. Following an adventurous youth in South America he returned to Germany in 1901 and began an extremely prolific literary career. His 74 plays encompass a great variety of styles and made him the most widely performed German dramatist of the Weimar Republic. He was a leading exponent of EXPRESSIONISM. The most important plays were *David and Goliath* (1915); *Die Bürger von Calais* (*The Burghers of Calais*, 1917); *Von Morgens bis Mitternachts* (*From Morn to Midnight*, 1917); *Die Koralle* (*The Coral*, 1917); *Hölle, Weg, Erde* ('Hell, way, earth', 1919); *Gas I* and *Gas II* (1918, 1920); *Der gerettete Alkibiades* (*Alcibiades Saved*, 1920); *Nebeneinander* ('Next to one another', 1923); *Der Zar lässt sich photographieren* ('The tsar has his photograph taken', 1928), an opera with music by KURT WEILL; *Zwei Krawatten* ('Two ties', 1929), a REVUE; and another opera with music by Weill, *Der Silbersee* (*The Silver Lake*, 1933).

Following Hitler's seizure of power in 1933, Kaiser's works were banned in Germany. He had two of his new plays produced in Vienna, but after the occupation of Austria in 1938 he was forced to flee to Switzerland, where three newly completed anti-fascist dramas were premièred. But neither these, nor some work published in the exile press, could earn him a living, and he died in utter poverty a few weeks after the end of the Second World War. GÜNTER BERGHAUS

Renate Benson, *German Expressionist Drama: Frust Toller and Georg Kaiser* (1984)

B. J. Kenworth, *Georg Kaiser* (1957)

Peter K. Tyson, *The Reception of Georg Kaiser 1915–1945: Texts and Analysis*, 2 vols (1984)

Kálmán, Emmerich [Imre] (b. Siófok, Hungary, 24 Oct. 1882; d. Paris, 30 Oct. 1953) Composer. Kálmán's success in popular songwriting propelled him away from legal studies towards the light musical theatre. His musical comedy *Tatárjárás* (1908, *The Gay Hussars*) gave him an early success which was repeated in Vienna (*Ein Herbstmanöver*). The musical play *Az obsitos* (1910, *The Soldier on Leave*) went round the world, and his 1912 piece *Der Zigeunerprimas* gave him a Broadway hit as *Sari*. Consequently, many of the subsequent musical-theatre successes which Kálmán produced, at a more studied and measured rate than some of his contemporaries, were given widespread productions. The most enduring of his works, the warmly Hungarian-flavoured *Die Csárdásfürstin* (1915), initially disappointed in New York (*The Riviera Girl*) and London (*The Gipsy Princess*), but was successful in France, as was *Die Bajadere* (1921, *The Yankee Princess*). *Das Hollandweibchen* (1920, *The Little Dutch Girl*) had a good London run and America gave a warmer welcome to versions of *Zsuzsi kisasszony* (1915, *Miss Springtime*), *Gräfin Mariza* (1924, *Countess Maritza*) and *Die Zirkusprinzessin* (1926, *The Circus Princess*), leading to the composer providing an original score for the Broadway musical *The Golden Dawn* (1927). Chased from Europe by war, Kálmán spent time in France and America without adding significantly to his opus. However, his principal works remain among the most produced standards of the European musical theatre repertoire. KURT GÄNZL

V. Kálmán, *Grüss' mir die süssen, die reizenden Frauen* (1966)

R. Österreicher, *E. Kálmán, der Wegeines Komponisten* (1954)

Kalmar, Bert *see* RUBY, HARRY

Kander, John [Harold] (b. Kansas City, Mo., 18 March 1927) Composer. After college he served as a theatrical apprentice and an orchestrator. Following the failure of his first show in 1962 he teamed up with lyricist **Fred Ebb** (b. New York, 8 April 1932). Their biggest successes have been *Cabaret* (1966) and *Chicago* (1975). Kander's music is respected by fellow musicians, but few of his songs have become standards. GERALD BORDMAN

Kandinsky, Wassily [Vasili Vasilyevich] (b. Moscow, 4 Dec. 1866; d. Neuilly-sur-Seine, France, 13 Dec. 1944) Painter. A pioneer who advocated a drama which elicited 'inner spiritual vibrations' in the spectator. Examples were his libretto *Der gelbe Klang* ('The Yellow Sound', 1912) and a production he staged in Dessau of Mussorgsky's *Pictures at an Exhibition* (1928) in which the music evoked shapes and configurations of a purely abstract nature with scenes composing and dissolving in harmony with the music. He inspired the BAUHAUS. NICK WORRALL

Kane, Sarah [Marie] (b. Brentwood, Essex, 3 Feb. 1971; d. London, 20 Feb. 1999) Playwright. Her debut, *Blasted* (1995), met with tabloid outrage and almost unanimous critical incomprehension. Inspired by the author's urgent disgust with the ethnic cleansing and rape camps that marked the Bosnian war, the play makes connections between these events and 'ordinary' British domestic cruelty. The critics, who seemed stunned that such a play could be written by a young woman, failed to notice Kane's terse, sinewy dialogue, her skilled sense of theatrical space, her subtle interplay of fantasy and realism and her wry, dark sense of humour: features which continued to characterize her work. *Phaedra's Love* (1996), inspired by Seneca, explores sexual taboos; *Cleansed* and *Crave* (both 1998) show a pitiless yearning to find the possibility of love amid the brutality and power structures of modern society. *Crave* recalls the later BECKETT, with four unnamed characters whose speeches are marked by poetic, rhythmic patterns, giving the characters an almost mythical status, adding resonance and power to their interactions. Kane's suicide in 1999 was mourned across Europe, where her broken, uncompromising work had already been acclaimed as a turning point in theatrical writing. Her last play, *4:48 Psychosis* (2000) was premièred posthumously at the ROYAL COURT's Theatre Upstairs. DAN REBELLATO

Aleks Sierz, *In-Yer-Face Theatre: British Drama Today* (2001)

Michelene Wandor, *Post-war British Drama: Looking Back in Gender* (2001)

Kani, John *see* FUGARD, ATHOL

Kanin, Garson (b. Rochester, NY, 24 Nov. 1912; d. New York, 15 March 1999) Playwright and director. He had performed in JAZZ and VAUDEVILLE, but dates his theatrical career from the early 1930s when he first acted and was assistant director to GEORGE ABBOTT. The best-known of Kanin's plays and screenplays is *Born Yesterday* (1946), which he also directed. He often collaborated with his wife, the actress and playwright RUTH GORDON (1896–1985). His brother Michael (1910–93) collaborated on several plays with his wife Fay (b. 1916), whose best-known play was *Goodbye My Fancy* (1948). FELICIA HARDISON LONDRÉ

Kantor, Tadeusz (b. Wielopole, Poland, 6 April 1915; d. Cracow, 8 Dec. 1990) Painter, stage designer and director. During the Second World War Kantor founded an underground experimental theatre of painters in Cracow; after the war he worked as a stage designer in the traditional theatre and welcomed with relief the liberalization in official policy in 1956 which allowed him to open the important experimental Cricot theatre – a theatre that had its origins in the Polish prewar AVANT-GARDE tradition and was inspired by WITKIEWICZ, whose plays backed up Kantor's successive theoretical manifestos and formal experiments. Kantor passed through a fascination with HAPPENINGS (1965–9) on his way towards performances in which he participated as the conductor of the actors and the existence of the audience was irrelevant, such as *Dead Class* (1975) and *Wielopole, Wielopole* (1980). These productions – collages of expressive images informed by movement and sound – were part of Kantor's 'theatre of death' in which memory is exceptionally sensitive to the past and the boundary between life and death is not necessarily where the audience might think it lies. Cricot remained an experimental theatre with no definite ideology, always searching for new aesthetics. Although it had a base and archives in Cracow, Kantor's theatre remained a company on the road and was heralded abroad. A collection of his essays and manifestos was published in 1993 as *A Journey Through Other Spaces: 1944–90*.

JOANNA KRAKOWSKA-NAROŻNIAK

Kaprow, Allan *see* CAGE, JOHN; ENVIRONMENTAL THEATRE; EXPERIMENTAL THEATRE; HAPPENINGS; INSTALLATION

Karamu House The oldest active African American theatre in the United States, taking its name from the Swahili for 'a place of enjoyment for all'. A private arts centre founded in 1915 in Cleveland, Ohio, from 1921 it housed the Gilpin Players, a mainly black company named after the actor CHARLES GILPIN. Karamu premièred six plays by Langston Hughes. CHARLES LONDON

Katayev, Valentin [Petrovich] (b. Odessa, Russia, 16 Jan. 1897; d. Moscow, 12 April 1986) Novelist and playwright, best known for his 1928 play, *Kvadratura kruga* (*Squaring the Circle*), which Western critics have thought reminiscent of NOËL COWARD's *Private Lives*. Another popular play was the stage version of his satirical novel, *Rastratchiki* (*The Embezzlers*, 1928), dealing with two drunken officials who abscond with public money. He also wrote stage versions of his five-year-plan novel, *Vremya vpered!* (*Time, Forward!*, 1932) and *Belyeet parus odinokiy* (*A White Sail Gleams*), a play for children set in 1905. His novels dealing with the First

and Second World Wars were also adapted for the stage. NICK WORRALL

Harold B. Segel, *Twentieth-Century Russian Drama* (1979)

Kauffmann, Stanley (b. New York City, 24 April 1916) Critic, novelist, essayist and playwright. Kauffmann graduated from New York University in 1935, while working as an actor and stage manager for the WASHINGTON SQUARE PLAYERS (1931–41). His career evolved as he wrote 27 plays (1933–44), seven novels (1941–60), several non-fiction books (1966–86) and then theatre and film criticism. He was theatre critic of the *New Republic* (1969–79), *New York Times* (1966) and *Saturday Review* (1967–73). He has published six collections of film criticism (1966–94). During his career he has received many awards and held distinguished academic positions. In 1964 he received an Emmy for 'The Art of Film' and was a member of the Theater Advisory Panel of the NATIONAL ENDOWMENT FOR THE ARTS (1972–6). His autobiographical *Albums of Early Life* appeared in 1980.
ANNA WHEELER GENTRY

Bert Cardullo, *Before His Eyes* (1986)

Kaufman, George S[imon] (b. Pittsburgh, Pa., 16 Nov. 1889; d. New York, 2 June 1961) Playwright, director, 'playdoctor' and journalist who enjoyed a long and successful career on Broadway as a writer of comic plays. He worked with a number of collaborators, including MARC CONNELLY (*Dulcy*, 1921 and *Beggar on Horseback*, 1924), EDNA FERBER (*The Royal Family*, 1927; *Dinner at Eight*, 1932; *Stage Door*, 1936) and Morrie Ryskind (*Strike up the Band*, 1930; *Of Thee I Sing*, 1931). His partnership with MOSS HART resulted in several hits, such as *Once in a Lifetime* (1930), *You Can't Take it With You* (1936), which captured a Pulitzer Prize, and *The Man Who Came to Dinner* (1939). He wrote for the MARX BROTHERS, and among his directional credits is *The Front Page* (1928). He was one of of the writers who comprised the Round Table group at the Algonquin Hotel. Master of the wisecrack, Kaufman is distinguished for his amusing dialogue, a banter of wit and sarcasm. What his plays may lack in depth, they more than make up for in irony. JOSEPH M. DIAZ

Malcolm Goldstein, *George S. Kaufman: His Life, His Theater* (1979)
Jeffrey D. Maron, *Wisecracks: The Farces of George S. Kaufman* (1988)
Scott Meredith, *George S. Kaufman and His Friends* (1974)
Rhoda G. Pollack, *George S. Kaufman* (1988)

Kaye, Danny [David Daniel Kominsky] (b. Brooklyn, New York, 18 Jan. 1913; d. Los Angeles, 3 March 1987) Actor, comedian and singer. Kaye began as a comedian in VAUDEVILLE, summer camps and the New York nightclub circuit before making his Broadway debut in *The Straw Hat Revue* (1939). In 1941 he moved to Hollywood and began a series of films which enormously increased his popularity, especially in Britain, where in 1948 and 1949 he made record-breaking appearances at the LONDON PALLADIUM.
ANDREW SOLWAY

Kazakhstan *see* SOVIET UNION

Kazan [Kazanjoglon], Elia (nickname 'Gadg', short for gadget) (b. Istanbul, 7 Sept. 1909) Actor, stage and film director and writer. He moved from Turkey to America at the age of four to live a lonely ghetto childhood in New York, speaking Greek and Turkish as well as learning English. He later joined the Communist Party and became closely associated with the GROUP THEATER from 1932, acting in ODETS' *Waiting for Lefty* (1935) before deciding, on being told his gift was not for acting, to become a director. His imaginative response to the offer to direct WILDER's *The Skin of Our Teeth* (1942) changed his life. His productions of WILLIAMS's *A Streetcar Named Desire* (1947), *Cat on a Hot Tin Roof* (1955) and *Sweet Bird of Youth* (1959), and of MILLER's *All My Sons* (1947) and *Death of a Salesman* (1949), made him the leading director of his time. After making his first film in 1944 he worked on both coasts, making films in Hollywood and directing plays in New York. In 1947 he helped found the ACTORS' STUDIO, where he and LEE STRASBERG fostered the METHOD style of acting. Kazan brought this form of intense naturalism to the screen in seminal films – *A Streetcar Named Desire* (1951) and *On the Waterfront* (1954), both starring MARLON BRANDO, and *East of Eden* (1955), starring James Dean. These were made after Kazan named known Communists before the Un-American Activities Committee and left the party. From 1962 to 1965 he was director of the LINCOLN CENTER, for which he directed Miller's *After the Fall* (1964). He also wrote novels, unpublished plays and an autobiography, *A Life* (1988). He received an honorary Oscar in 1999. TERRY HODGSON

Michael Ciment, *Kazan on Kazan* (1973)
B. Murphy, *Tennessee Williams and Elia Kazan* (1992)
T. H. Pauly, *An American Odyssey: Elia Kazan and American Culture* (1983)

Keach [Jr], [Walter] Stacy (b. Savannah, Ga., 2 June 1941) Stage, film and television actor. He claimed attention OFF-BROADWAY for *Macbird* (1967), *Long Day's Journey Into Night* (1971) and *Hamlet* (1964), which he played twice more, and was dubbed the best classical actor of his generation. Other successful appearances include roles in *Hughie* (London, 1981), *Idiot's Delight* (1986) and *Richard III* (Washington DC, 1990) and a critical triumph in *The Kentucky Cycle* (New York, 1993). He also directs. NANCY SWORTZELL

Kean, Marie (b. Dublin, 27 June 1918; d. Dublin, 31 Dec. 1993) Actress. An early member of the Radio Eireann Players, she moved to the ABBEY THEATRE in 1949, where she came to prominence as Bernarda Alba in LORCA's play. She created many new parts, and gradually took over the classic roles. She returned to the Abbey Theatre many times during her career, playing Ma in HUGH LEONARD's *Da*, Madge in BRIAN FRIEL's *Philadelphia, Here I Come!* and Maura in JOHN B. KEANE's *Sive*. She was in BRECHT's *Baal* (West End, 1963) and spent two years with the ROYAL SHAKESPEARE COMPANY from 1976. Her Winnie in BECKETT's *Happy Days* won several awards; she also played in his *Rockaby*. She appeared in films directed by Polanski, Lean and Kubrick. CHRISTOPHER FITZ-SIMON

Keane, John B[rendan] (b. Listowel, Co. Kerry, Ireland, 21 July 1928) Playwright. Probably the most popular of his generation, he continues the tradition of rural 'problem' plays initiated by COLUM and T. C. MURRAY, but exposes darker yearnings. *Sive* (1959), *Sharon's Grave* (1960), *The Year of the Hiker* (1963) and *The Field* (1965) are among the best.
CHRISTOPHER FITZ-SIMON

Keatley, Charlotte *see* MANCHESTER

Keeffe, Barrie [Colin] (b. London, 31 Oct. 1945) Playwright. Inspired by a THEATRE WORKSHOP production, Keeffe began writing plays in the 1970s. They combine humour, violence and a fierce urban sensibility. *A Mad World My Masters* (1977), written for JOINT STOCK and based on Middleton's early seventeenth-century play, is a ferocious and widely aimed satire on a class-ridden society; the same feeling informs the trilogy *Gimme Shelter* (1977: *Gem*, 1975; *Gotcha*, 1976; *Getaway*, 1977), articulating class frustration and hatred. *Sus* (1979) is a chilling indictment of police brutality and racism. In the mid-1980s Keeffe began a long association with the THEATRE ROYAL, STRATFORD EAST, notable for *My Girl* (1989), whose characters yearn to keep love alive in difficult times. Other plays include *Barbarians* (1977), *Bastard Angel* (1980), *Black Lear* (1981) and *Better Times* (1985); Keeffe also wrote a celebrated screenplay for *The Long Good Friday* (1980).
DAN REBELLATO

Keene, Daniel (b. Melbourne, 21 Dec. 1955) Playwright, actor and director. In *Cho Cho San* (1984), a free reworking of some of the themes of *Madame Butterfly*, live actors and puppets interact. *All Souls* (1993) is characterized by a poetic lyricism which echoes that of his earlier play *Low* (1992), in which lost individuals connect with each other and the audience through a naïve eloquence in strong contrast to their often brutal and destructive actions. *Beneath Heaven* (1995) received the Wal Cherry Play of the Year award, while the 1998 Adelaide Festival saw the première of *The Architect's Walk*, a play based loosely on the life of Albert Speer. His plays have been staged throughout Australia, with several also receiving productions in New York, Britain and Europe. In 1999 three of his plays received productions in France – in its use of language and the world from which his characters spring, his work has affinities with that of KOLTÈS – and *Silent Partner* (1988) and *Terminus* (1996) were also broadcast on that country's 'Radio Culture' that year. Keene has also written libretti, and for screen and television. Other works include *The Hour Before My Brother Dies* (1985) and *Because You Are Mine* (1995). MICHAEL MORLEY

Keitel, Harvey *see* ACTORS' STUDIO

Kelly, Emmett [Leo] (b. Sedan, Kan., 9 Dec. 1898; d. Sarasota, Fla., 28 March 1979) Tramp CLOWN who based his 'Weary Willie' character on a cartoon he drew. Famous for cracking a peanut with a sledgehammer and sweeping a moving spotlight on the floor, his sad expression made him America's most beloved hobo figure in the CIRCUS and media. LOWELL SWORTZELL

Kelly, George [Edward] (b. Philadelphia, 16 Jan. 1887; d. Bryn Mawr, Pa., 18 June 1974) Playwright. A member of a noted theatrical family, he was an actor and vaudevillean before turning to writing. His first success was a satirical play, *The Torch-Bearers* (1922). After another popular comedy, *The Show-Off* (1924), he turned to more serious themes in the Pulitzer Prize winner *Craig's Wife* (1925), *Daisy Mayme* (1926) and *Behold the Bridegroom* (1927). Thereafter success eluded him. In his early plays Kelly was a fine technician, a perspicacious observer and sometimes an excellent satirist. But his later writings were marred by a falling away in skill and a growing misanthropy.
GERALD BORDMAN

Mark A. Graves, *George Kelly: A Research and Production Sourcebook* (1999)
F. Hirsch, *George Kelly* (1975)

Kelly, Jude *see* WEST YORKSHIRE PLAYHOUSE; WOMEN IN THEATRE

Kemp, Lindsay (b. Isle of Lewis, Scotland, 3 May 1938) Dancer, actor and MIME. Kemp studied at Bradford College of Art, at the RAMBERT Ballet School, and with MARCEL MARCEAU. He worked in cabaret, chorus lines, theatre, film and television, organizing a range of theatrical events from strip shows to HAPPENINGS and Ziggy Stardust concerts for singer David Bowie. His dance company's theatrical work includes *Flowers* (1974), based on JEAN GENET's *Our Lady of the Flowers*, and WILDE's *Salomé* (1977), which reflect Kemp's eclecticism in their astonishing variety of cultural influences and performance styles. For Ballet Rambert, he created *Cruel Garden* (1977), about the playwright LORCA. ANDREW SOLWAY
See also DANCE; MOVEMENT, DANCE AND DRAMA.

Kemp, Robert (b. Hoy, Orkney, Scotland, 25 Feb. 1908; d. Edinburgh, 22 Nov. 1967) Journalist, novelist, dramatist and radio producer. His most famous original drama was *The Other Dear Charmer* (1951), the story of the romance of Robert Burns with Nancy M'Lehose, but his most celebrated contribution to Scottish theatre was his adaptation of Sir David Lindsay's *Satyre of the Thrie Estaitis*, directed by TYRONE GUTHRIE at the 1948 EDINBURGH INTERNATIONAL FESTIVAL. Through his work in radio and his involvement in the GATEWAY Theatre, Edinburgh, he contributed greatly to the flourishing of Scottish theatre in the mid-twentieth century. He also wrote five novels and was a regular contributor to the *Glasgow Herald*. JAN MCDONALD

Kempinski, Tom [Thomas J. M.] (b. London, 24 March 1938) Playwright. A prolific writer who consistently tackles big themes, he is known primarily through the success of *Duet for One* (1980), in which a classical violinist confined to a wheelchair by multiple sclerosis confronts her life in painful sessions with her psychiatrist. Drawn from his own experiences of therapy, the play boldly explores the nature of hope and survival with a power that is sometimes glimpsed but rarely sustained in his other work. He has adapted three plays by JEAN-CLAUDE GRUMBERG (*The Workshop*, 1979, *Dreyfus*, 1982, and *The Free Country*, 1991) and written a number of pieces that see history from his left-wing position. CHARLES LONDON

Kempson, Rachel *see* REDGRAVE, MICHAEL

Kenna, Peter [Joseph] (b. Sydney, 18 March 1930; d. Sydney, 29 Nov. 1987) Playwright. He wrote one of Australia's best-loved and most-performed plays, *A Hard God* (1973), which deals with partings, the widening gap between time past and time present, and the changing face of Irish Catholic Australia. It is the centrepiece of a life's work in theatre, radio and television and is, to Kenna, profoundly experimental – despite some naturalistic trappings. These merely disguise elements of SYMBOLISM and EXPRESSIONISM.

From the fruits of one play Kenna has coaxed two others: *A Furtive Love* and *An Eager Hope*. The trilogy, called *The Cassidy Album*, was first performed in 1978. There is a strong autobiographical strand in this and other writing, but it has been transformed and distanced to allow for a rendering which avoids both confession and exposé. Kenna was born into a large family and at ten began work as an entertainer. The 1950s saw him established as a radio actor who in 1954 joined the AUSTRALIAN ELIZABETHAN THEATRE TRUST. After 11 years working in London, Kenna returned home permanently in 1971. *Mates* (1973) formed one half of the famous NIMROD THEATRE 'mates and brothers' double bill with RON BLAIR's *The Christian Brothers*. His ten plays include *The Slaughter of St Theresa's Day* (1959), *Talk to the Moon* (1963) and *Listen Closely* (1972). He is celebrated in NICK ENRIGHT's play *Mongrels* (1994).
GUS WORBY

V. Brady, *Playing Catholic: Essays on Four Catholic Plays* (1992)

Kennedy [Hawkins], Adrienne [Lita] (b. Pittsburgh, 13 Sept. 1931) Playwright. In such plays as *Funnyhouse of a Negro* (1964) and *The Owl Answers* (1970), private nightmares become mesmerizing public rituals. This black artist's focus on the mystery of identity is also seen in her equally original and surprisingly sunny autobiography, *People Who Led to My Plays* (1987). Other plays include *A Rat's Mass* (1966), *The Lennon Play: In His Own Write* (with John Lennon and Victor Spinetti, 1967), *A Lancashire Lad* (1980) and *Ohio State Murders* (1992). M. ELIZABETH OSBORN

P. K. Bryant-Jackson and L. M. Overbeck, *Intersecting Boundaries: The Theatre of Adrienne Kennedy* (1992)

Kennedy, [John] Arthur (b. Worcester, Mass., 17 Feb. 1914; d. Branford, Conn., 5 Jan. 1990) Actor. Kennedy made his debut with the GROUP THEATER in 1937, and his talent was fully recognized when he played Chris Keller in MILLER's *All My Sons* (1947). He was acclaimed for his performances of central roles in a succession of new serious dramas, including Miller's *Death of a Salesman* (1949, as Biff) and *The Crucible* (1953, as Proctor). He appeared in many films.
ADRIANA HUNTER

Kennedy Center for the Performing Arts President Eisenhower signed a decree in 1958 providing for the establishment of a national cultural centre, and following the assassination of President Kennedy the project was renamed after him as the John F. Kennedy Center for the Performing Arts. The centre opened in 1971 in Washington DC, housing three auditoriums in one building, designed by Edward Durell Stone. The Concert Hall seats 2,750, the Opera House 2,300 and the Eisenhower Theatre 1,140. There are also three small auditoriums. Its guiding spirit was the producer ROGER STEVENS, the centre's president from 1961 to 1988. CHARLES LONDON

Kenny, Sean [Noel] (b. Portroe, Ireland, 23 Dec. 1932; d. London, 11 June 1973) Designer. Kenny, originally a student of architecture, specialised in large, sculptural shapes and using electronics to manipulate his elaborate hydraulic sets, making the transformation of the scenes part of the spectacle. He first won acclaim for his multiple setting of *Lock Up Your Daughters* (1959, MERMAID); then, again with composer LIONEL BART, his mobile platforms and stairs for the musical *Oliver!* (1960) brought him international fame and influence. He worked with Bart on *Blitz!* (1962) and *Maggie May* (1964) and even branched out to the Las Vegas REVUE *Casino de Paris*. He designed for several prestigious productions of Shakespeare and was an adviser on the design of the CHICHESTER FESTIVAL THEATRE. He designed his 'theatre of the future' when the Winter Garden Theatre was rebuilt from the ground up as the New London Theatre (1971–2) with movable seats, stage, lights and walls, but his vision was not exploited until CAMERON MACKINTOSH, who had revived Kenny's sets when he produced *Oliver!*, took it on for *Cats*, in which the designer JOHN NAPIER was able to use and develop Kenny's machinery and ideas. ADRIANA HUNTER

Kent, Jonathan *see* ALMEIDA THEATRE

Kenya As in most other African countries, formal theatre and drama as understood in the West have not existed in Kenya, but dance, music, RITUAL and other performing arts have always provided a solid means or medium for cultural expression among the many ethnic groups that make up modern Kenya.

Modern literary drama arrived in the country, as it did in other African nations, via the colonial corridor. In the case of Kenya, the colonial administration and the white settler communities initiated amateur theatre groups in the later part of the nineteenth century and the early part of the twentieth. Later, educated Kenyans set up their own separate amateur theatre groups. The study of theatre, both as dramatic literature and in terms of stage production, later became part of the school curriculum, with drama festivals and competitions becoming an essential feature of the educational system. These festivals remain very strong and they played a major role in encouraging and nurturing native playwrights. However, the models for an overwhelming majority of their plays are Western and foreign, often banal and outdated in both dramaturgy and acting styles. It is only established writers such as NGUGI WA THIONG'O who have begun to experiment with and adapt the rich traditional forms of theatre in plays such as *The Trial of Dedan Kimathi* (1976), *Ngaahika Ndeenda (I'll marry when I want*, 1977) and *Maitu Njuriga* ('Mother, sing for me', 1986).

Many reasons have been put forward for the different ways in which the development of modern East African theatre differs from that in West Africa. Chief among these is the peculiar pattern of settler colonialism, in which the British embraced all aspects of life while suppressing indigenous forms of cultural expression. Little wonder that as late as the 1970s, what is regarded as Kenya's national theatre was headed by an expatriate, even though the country had become independent in 1963. It was claimed the Africans found it very difficult to carry through the necessary programme of training and nationalization. Government intervention in and suppression of 'native' criticism coming from theatre remained after independence, and is evident in the detention of Ngugi, the escape into exile of major Kenyan theatre artists such as Micere Mugo, Ngugi wa Mirii and Kimani Gecau, and the demolition of the Kamiriithu Cultural Centre and theatre by the government of Daniel Arap Moi in 1982. Such repression, also seen under the dictatorships of Milton Obote and Idi Amin in UGANDA, has never been witnessed in West Africa.

Nevertheless, Kenya has produced a lot of good and successful playwrights whose works have consistently attempted to negotiate the tensions between the past and the present while using this to examine contemporary postcolonial reality. It is this ability to make a connection and offer a radical perspective on history which has made the theatre a very uncomfortable phenomenon for both the Kenyatta and Moi governments.

The beginnings of a Kenyan literary dramatic tradition can be traced back to Ngugi's first play, *The Black Hermit*, produced with an international cast for Uganda's independence celebrations in 1962. For the first time, a Kenyan experience and story is brought to the stage. Although written in English, the language is used to indigenize his characters and setting, experiments reflected in his choice to write in the vernacular in later plays like *Ngaahika Ndeenda* and *Maitu Njugira*, and his collaborative community theatre projects with writers wa Mirii and Gecau and the Kamiriithu community. Prior to that, he had collaborated with Mugo

to write the hugely popular *The Trial of Dedan Kimathi*, a play in which they try to reinterpret Kenyan history in order to restore the dignity and heroism of the Kenyan men and women who stood up to the British colonial administration during the Mau Mau uprising.

Ngugi is joined by other pioneers such as Jonathan Kariara, who wrote *The Green Bean Patch*, and Rebecca Njau, author of what is widely regarded as the first Kenyan (East African) feminist play, *The Scar*. Kariara also wrote *Tonight We Shall Pray to My Gods* (1969), while Francis Imbuga wrote *The Fourth Trial* (1972), *Kisses of Faho* (1972), *The Married Bachelor* (1973), *Betrayal in the City* (1976), *Games of Silence* (1977) and *The Successor* (1979).

The Asian presence and experience are reflected in the works of Kenyan-born Asian, Kudlip Sondhi, an engineer by profession. Sondhi wrote mainly short, often one-act plays, the best known of which are *Encounter*, *With Strings* and a radio play, *Sunil's Dilemma*. *Encounter* is about the Mau Mau war, but unlike *The Trial of Dedan Kimathi* and Kenneth Watene's *Dedan Kimathi*, Sondhi looks at the war from the point of view of two European officers, one of them foreign but Kenyan-born like the writer himself. His other two plays explore the Asian experience, especially the conflicts of interracial marriage in the context of mutual distrust between the various races that make up modern Kenyan society.

Overall, Kenyan theatre is socially relevant. Alongside the literary theatre of the mainly university-educated and based dramatists, there are two other major strands: the later move into professional theatre by groups such as Sarahasi (founded 1990) and the Miujiza Players (founded 1992), and the non-literary theatre of the THEATRE FOR DEVELOPMENT groups and movement, which began after the Second World War and continued into a highly organized and complex network. OSITA OKAGBUE

Kern, Jerome [David] (b. New York, 27 Jan. 1885; d. New York, 11 Nov. 1945) Composer. After more than a decade providing songs for interpolation into a variety of BROADWAY and London shows, Kern found his first significant theatre success with the scores for a group of small-scale musical comedies written between 1915 and 1918 (e.g. *Very Good, Eddie*, *Oh, Boy!*, *Leave it to Jane*). He progressed to larger stages with the successful song-and-dance musicals *Sally* (1920) and *Sunny* (1925), before shifting into a different style to combine with OSCAR HAMMERSTEIN on the score for the most enduring Broadway operetta of the era, *Show Boat* (1927). He maintained a more classic operetta style in the scores for *The Cat and the Fiddle* (1931) and *Music* *in the Air* (1932) but, as in the case of *Roberta* (1933), his songs outweighed and outlasted unimpressive libretti. One of the most successful and durable of Broadway songwriters, through a long career he helped establish the popularity of the songwriter's musical comedy as a mainstream metropolitan genre, before moving on to display the more substantial side of his expansive musical talent in his later works.   KURT GÄNZL

G. Bordman, *Jerome Kern* (1980)
A. Lamb, *Jerome Kern in Edwardian England* (1985)

Kerr, Alfred   (b. Breslau, Germany, 25 Dec. 1867; d. Hamburg, 12 Oct. 1948)   Theatre critic. Kerr was an enthusiastic admirer of naturalism, and therefore championed the plays of such writers as IBSEN and HAUPTMANN; but he was almost as energetic in his opposition to the advent of EXPRESSIONISM, and of the EPIC THEATRE favoured by BRECHT. His criticisms were unashamedly subjective and sarcastic, if a little self-conscious, but he was an extremely influential figure from 1895 to 1920. His work was collated and published as *Die Welt in Drama* ('The World in Drama', 5 vols, 1917), *Was wird aus Deutschlands Theater?* ('What Will Become of German Theatre?', 1932) and *Die Diktatur des Hausknechts* ('The Dictatorship of the House-servants', 1934).   ADRIANA HUNTER

Kerr, [Bridget] Jean [Collins]   (b. Scranton, Pa., 10 July 1923)   Humorist and playwright, whose witty essays made her a household name. She and her drama critic husband, WALTER KERR, collaborated on several Broadway comedies, e.g. *Touch and Go* (1949). Her major Broadway hit comedy was *Mary, Mary* (1961). Other Broadway plays include *King of Hearts* (1954) and *Lunch Hour* (1980).   JANE HOUSE

Kerr, Walter [Francis]   (b. Evanston, Ill., 8 July 1913)   Drama critic, playwright and teacher. After teaching drama at Catholic University (1938–49) and serving as drama critic for *Commonweal* (1950–1) and the *New York Herald Tribune* (1951–66), he became the *New York Times*'s Sunday critic (1966–83), wielding considerable influence with his thoughtful and lucid commentaries until his retirement. He won the GEORGE JEAN NATHAN Award (1963) and a Pulitzer Prize for drama criticism (1978). Four of his own plays reached Broadway: *Count Me In* (1942, with Leo Brady and Nancy Hamilton), *Sing Out Sweet Land* (1944), and, with his playwright wife JEAN KERR, *Touch and Go* (1949) and *Goldilocks* (1958). Among his many books on theatre are *How Not to Write a Play* (1955), *Criticism and Censorship* (1957), *The Decline of Pleasure* (1962), *Theater in Spite of Itself* (1963), *Tragedy and Comedy* (1967) and *Journey to the Centre of the Theater* (1979).

The Ritz Theater in New York was renamed after him in 1990.   FELICIA HARDISON LONDRÉ

Kester, Paul   (b. Delaware, Ohio, 2 Nov. 1870; d. Lake Mohegan, NY, 20 June 1933)   Playwright. He began his career by collaborating with Mrs Fiske on *Countess Rondine* (1892). Thereafter he wrote primarily vehicles for stars, including *Sweet Nell of Drury Lane* (1901), *When Knighthood was in Flower* (1901) and *The Woman of Bronze* (1920).   GERALD BORDMAN

Kidd, Michael [Milton Greenwald]   (b. New York, 12 Aug. 1919)   Choreographer. A dropout from chemical engineering, he performed with the Ballet Theater and other groups before creating the dances for *Finian's Rainbow* (1947). His singularly raffish, exuberant choreography was seen in such shows as *Guys and Dolls* (1950), *Can-Can* (1953), *Li'l Abner* (1956) and *Destry Rides Again* (1959), for each of which he received a Tony Award. He sometimes also served as director and co-producer. He worked successfully in film, including *The Band Wagon* (1953), *Seven Brides for Seven Brothers* (1954) and *Guys and Dolls* (1955).   GERALD BORDMAN
    See also CHOREOGRAPHY; DANCE.

Kiesler, Frederick   (b. Cernuti, Romania, 22 Sept. 1890; d. New York, 27 Dec. 1965)   Architect and designer. He had a strong influence on the development of mid-twentieth-century theatre ARCHITECTURE, as well as on the evolution of ENVIRONMENTAL THEATRE. His work received recognition in Europe, particularly his idea of an 'Endless Theatre', which utilized a series of spirals and ramps within an ellipsoidal space. These designs, along with his vision of 'space stages' – non-scenic architectural spaces – were introduced to an American audience at the International Theatre Exhibit in 1926. Kiesler settled in the United States following this exhibition; however, with the exception of the Eighth Street Cinema in New York in 1930, his projects never achieved the acclaim they had received in Europe.   LAURIE WOLF

Kift, Roy   *see* CHILDREN'S THEATRE

Kilroy, Thomas   (b. Callan, Co. Kilkenny, Ireland, 23 Sept. 1934)   Playwright. Ecomomy of style, substance and output defines Kilroy's work. *The Death and Resurrection of Mr Roche* (1963) gave voice to sexual politics in Irish theatre, challenging radically the stereotypes of Irish masculinity, threatened by the homosexual Mr Roche. *Talbot's Box* (1977) scrutinized the life of the Catholic working-class ascetic Matt Talbot, finding sympathy in his spiritual excesses. A successful transplanting of CHEKHOV's *The Seagull* (1981) to the west of Ireland preceded *Double Cross* (1984), a precise study of the Irishness confusing two key figures of the Second World War, Brendan Bracken and Lord Haw-Haw (William Joyce). He has also adapted IBSEN's *Ghosts* (1988) and written *The Madame MacAdam Travelling Theatre* (1991) and *The Secret Life of Constance Wilde* (1997). FRANK MCGUINNESS

Kimball King, *Ten Modern Irish Playwrights* (1979)
Christopher Murray, *Twentieth Century Irish Drama* (1997)

Kimberley, Charlotte [A.] (b. Meriden(?), W. Midlands, 1877; d. St. Asaph, Flint, Wales, 27 Dec. 1939) Actor–manageress and playwright. Based at the Grand Theatre, Wolverhampton, Kimberley and her husband toured the country and directed a circuit of six theatres in England and Wales. She was a champion of the MELODRAMA, writing more than 40 popular pieces, including *Tatters* (1919). ADRIANA HUNTER

King [Pratt], Dennis (b. Coventry, 2 Nov. 1897; d. New York, 21 May 1971) Actor and singer. After repertory work in England, he came to America in 1921 and was applauded for his Mercutio to JANE COWL's *Juliet* (1923). A baritone, he was best known as the dashing hero of such musicals as *Rose-Marie* (1924), *The Vagabond King* (1925), *The Three Musketeers* (1928), a 1932 revival of *Show Boat*, and *I Married an Angel* (1938). He also distinguished himself in non-musical productions, ranging from modern comedies (*Petticoat Fever*, 1934; *Lunatics and Lovers*, 1954) to classics (*Three Sisters*, 1942; *The Devil's Disciple*, 1950).
GERALD BORDMAN

King's Head A PUB THEATRE in Islington, north London – possibly the capital's first – opened in 1970 by Canadians Dan and Joan Crawford in a back room that had been used for billiards and boxing. It started as a LUNCHTIME THEATRE and differed from other pub venues in that the Crawfords served at the bar and produced the shows as well. It soon made a name for itself as a leading FRINGE outlet, mixing its own shows with those from visiting companies and becoming a meeting place for soulmates. Takings from drink and food sales subsidized the theatre, which attracted an ARTS COUNCIL grant, allowing the impresario publicans to flourish. A commercial breakthrough came with *Kennedy's Children* (1974) by Robert Patrick, which transferred to the ARTS THEATRE and broke fringe records. It was followed by, among others, *Spokesong* (1976) by STEWART PARKER, *Da* (1977) by HUGH LEONARD, and a revival of *Mr Cinders* (1986) by VIVIAN ELLIS. Funding problems in the 1990s forced the theatre to seek even more commercial success to survive. COLIN CHAMBERS

Kingsley, Ben [Krishna Bhanji] (b. Snaiton, Yorks, 31 Dec. 1943) Actor. Son of a Kenyan Asian physician and an English fashion model, in 1967 Kingsley joined the ROYAL SHAKESPEARE COMPANY, where his roles included Demetrius in PETER BROOK's landmark *A Midsummer Night's Dream* (1970), a breathtaking Hamlet (1975) in Buzz Goodbody's production, Brutus in *Julius Caesar* (1979), Squeers in *Nicholas Nickleby* (1980) and Othello (1986). His outstanding film portrayal of Gandhi (1982) won him an Academy Award and brought international fame and many further leading roles in major films, from PINTER's *Betrayal* (1983) to Spielberg's *Schindler's List* (1994). In 1997 he partnered ALAN HOWARD in PETER HALL's acclaimed revival of *Waiting for Godot* at the OLD VIC.
DANIEL MEYER-DINKGRÄFE
See also REHEARSAL.

Kingsley [Kirschner], Sidney (b. Philadelphia, 22 Oct. 1906; d. Oakland, NJ, 20 March 1995) Playwright, director and producer. Kingsley won a Pulitzer Prize with his first produced play, *Men in White* (1933), a study of a doctor torn between wealth and dedication to his profession. Among his other successes were a study of youth gangs, *Dead End* (1935); *The Patriots* (1943), which looked at early American political struggles; and *Detective Story* (1949), centring on an over-zealous policeman. He also adapted Arthur Koestler's novel *Darkness at Noon* (1951) and wrote a moderately successful comedy, *Lunatics and Lovers* (1954). At his best he incorporated trenchant observations of social problems into gripping dramas.
GERALD BORDMAN

Kingsway Theatre Opened in 1882, it had a chequered history from the start, but included the first performance in England of IBSEN's *A Doll's House* (1889). Reopened in 1900 (as the Great Queen Street Theatre), it hosted the first London appearance of SYNGE's *The Playboy of the Western World* (1907). From 1908 to 1915 it was run by an actress, LENA ASHWELL, who named it the Kingsway and, after divorcing HARLEY GRANVILLE BARKER, in 1918, another actress, LILLAH McCARTHY, took it over. In 1932 it became the home of the INDEPENDENT THEATRE SOCIETY and showed plays banned by the LORD CHAMBERLAIN. DONALD WOLFIT first brought his touring Shakespeare to London here in 1940, the year the theatre closed due to bombing. It was demolished in 1956.
COLIN CHAMBERS

Kinoshita, Junji *see* JAPAN

Kipphardt, Heinar [Heinrich Mauritius] (b. Heidersdorf, Upper Silesia, 8 March 1922; d. Munich, 18 Nov. 1982) Playwright whose first plays were performed in the German Democratic Republic. The comedy *Shakespeare dringend gesucht* ('Shakespeare urgently required', 1952) was his most important play of this period. In 1960 he moved to Munich. Kipphardt's plays deal with contemporary issues and, through the use of historical documents, aim at providing political enlightenment for their audiences. His dramatic style is similar to that of HOCHHUTH's DOCUMENTARY theatre. His international fame rests mainly on *In der Sache J. Robert Oppenheimer* (*In the Matter of J. Robert Oppenheimer*, 1964). Since 1975 he has been concerned with creating a body of works (television drama, novels, short stories, poems) centred on the schizophrenic poet März. His last play, *Bruder Eichmann* ('Brother Eichmann', 1983), reverts to the older style of documentary drama. GÜNTER BERGHAUS

Kirkland, Jack (b. St Louis, 25 July, 1902; d. New York, 22 Feb. 1969) Playwright and producer. After serving as a journalist, Kirkland turned to playwriting in 1928 with *Frankie and Johnnie*. His *Tobacco Road*, which opened in 1933 and ran until 1939, had the longest continuing run on record in New York. He produced or co-produced his own plays *Torilla Flat* (1938) and *I Must Love Someone* (with Leyla Georgie, 1939) and several plays by other authors. After 1930 he was also engaged in writing or co-writing film scenarios.
MARVIN CARLSON

Kishida, Kunio *see* JAPAN

Kishon, Ephraim [Ferenc Koffman] (b. Budapest, 23 Aug. 1924) Playwright, journalist and theatre and film director. He survived the Holocaust and came to Israel in 1949, rapidly mastering Hebrew to become a leading Israeli satirist. His first full-length play, *His Name Goes before Him* (1951), dealt with bureaucracy and the corruption of the system in the newborn country. His subsequent satires went along with common bourgeois prejudices, which helped some of these plays to enormous success: *The Marriage Contract* (1961); *Pull Out the Plug, The Water is Boiling* (1965), a fierce attack on modern art; *Oh! Oh! Juliet!* (1974), a domestic sequel to Shakespeare's play; and *Salah Shabbati*, a satiric stereotype of an oriental Jew, which furnished in turn dramatic sketches, a film and a musical. Kishon has directed several of his plays in Israel and abroad, gaining much success, especially in central Europe.
AVRAHAM OZ

Klein, Debby *see* LESBIAN THEATRE

Klein, Yves *see* PERFORMANCE ART

Kline, Kevin (b. St Louis, 24 Oct. 1947) Actor. Trained at the Juilliard School of Drama, he became a founder member of New York's The Acting Co., appearing regularly with them between 1972 and 1976. He won Tony Awards for *On the Twentieth Century* (1978) and the hugely successful revival of *The Pirates of Penzance* (1980). As well as other Broadway performances, in *Loose Ends* (1979) and *Arms and the Man* (1985), he has also appeared OFF-BROADWAY in a succession of Shakespearean roles: Richard II (1983), Henry V (1984) and Hamlet (1990), the last of which he directed. In 1993 he took time off from his successful film career to appear in *Measure for Measure* for the NEW YORK SHAKESPEARE FESTIVAL, of which he had become artistic associate. HELEN RAPPAPORT

Knipper[-Chekhova], Olga [Leonardovna] (b. Glazov, Russia, 21 Sept. 1868; d. Moscow, 22 March 1959) Actress. A founder member of the MOSCOW ART THEATRE (MAT), her beautiful performance as the Tsarina in the company's opening production of A. K. Tolstoy's *Tsar Fyodor Ioannovich* won CHEKHOV's heart, and they married in 1901. In his plays she created or played the MAT roles of Arkadina (*The Seagull*, 1898); Elena (*Uncle Vanya*, 1899); Masha (*Three Sisters*, 1901); Ranevskaya (*The Cherry Orchard*, 1904); and Anna/Sara (*Ivanov*, 1904), playing opposite STANISLAVSKY, as she did also in Turgenev's *A Month in the Country* (1908). Her correspondence with Chekhov provides invaluable information on the first productions of Chekhov's plays. NICK WORRALL

Jean Benedetti, ed. and trans., *Dear Writer . . . Dear Actress . . . : The Love Letters of Olga Knipper and Anton Chekhov* (1996)
Harvey Pitcher, *Chekhov's Leading Lady: A Portrait of the Actress Olga Knipper* (1979)

Knoblock [Knoblauch], Edward (b. New York, 7 April 1874; d. London, 19 July 1943) Playwright. Knoblock spent his entire career in England, briefly as an actor, then as a writer. His most famous work is *Kismet* (1911). Among his other plays are *The Faun* (1911), *Milestones* (1912, with ARNOLD BENNETT) and *Marie-Odile* (1915). His autobiography, *Round the Room*, appeared in 1939. GERALD BORDMAN

Koch, Frederick [Henry] (b. Covington, Ky., 12 Sept. 1877; d. Miami, Fla., 16 Aug. 1944) Educator. As a university professor in North Carolina, Koch instigated the teaching of playwriting and production. He was a contemporary of GEORGE PIERCE BAKER. Koch's students, the Carolina Playmakers, used Southern folklore as inspiration for their work; they wrote many one-act plays and produced them on tours. Koch's influence has been widespread, triggering a rash of plays about the Southern states in the early 1920s, and encouraging schools and colleges to teach dramatic art. Among his famous former pupils was the playwright PAUL GREEN. ADRIANA HUNTER

Kokoschka, Oscar (b. Pöchlarn, nr Vienna, Austria, 1 March 1886; d. Montreux, France, 22 Feb. 1980) Painter and playwright. He outraged Vienna with his one-act play *Mörder, Hoffnung der Frauen* (*Murderer, The Hope of Women*, 1909), decorating actors' limbs with nerve lines, as in his vivid and violent paintings. It was made into an opera by Paul Hindemith in 1921. His *Sphnix und Strohmann* (*Sphinx and the Strawman*, 1907) launched a DADA theatre in Zurich a decade later, and *Der brennende Dornbusch* (*The Burning Bush*, 1919) caused a scandal at REINHARDT's theatre. His plays, including a dramatization of *Orpheus und Eurydike* (1919), were early examples of EXPRESSIONISM. Later, a renowned painter, he did several stage designs in Salzburg and Vienna. TERRY HODGSON

Koltai, Ralph (b. Berlin, 31 July 1924) Stage designer. Koltai trained at London's Central School of Art and Design before the Second World War. During the war he worked for British Intelligence, and was involved until 1947 with the Nuremberg War Crimes Trials. His first design was for London Opera Club's *Angelique* (1950), and he continued for a time to work almost exclusively in OPERA. In 1962 he designed the ROYAL SHAKESPEARE COMPANY's production of *The Caucasian Chalk Circle*, the beginning of an association that has lasted over 30 years. His designs for the RSC include *The Representative* (1963), *The Jew of Malta* (1964), *Major Barbara* (1970), *Wild Oats* (1976), *Baal* (1979) and *Cyrano de Bergerac* (1983), and the Shakespeare productions *The Tempest* (1978), *Hamlet* (1980), *Much Ado About Nothing* (1982), *Troilus and Cressida* (1985) and *Othello* (1986). He has also worked extensively for the NATIONAL THEATRE, for example on *As You Like It* (1967), *Back to Methuselah* (1969), *Richard III* (1979), *Brand* (1978) and *The Wild Duck* (1979). Other notable work includes dance pieces for Ballet Rambert and the Royal Ballet. He has designed opera internationally.

Koltai's influential work is characterized by the use of bold imagery and a conscious sense of style in its exploration of space. His designs often centre on highly expressive constructions, sculptural or architectural in quality. He works extensively with non-traditional materials such as plexiglass, styrofoam and steel. ANDREW SOLWAY

Sally Backemayer, ed., *Ralph Koltai: Designer for the Stage* (1997)

Koltès, Bernard-Marie (b. Metz, France, 9 April 1948; d. Paris, 18 April 1989) Playwright. In plays both lyrical and harsh, mingling GENET's influence and that of other cultures with an austere classicism, solitary characters combat eternity. PATRICE CHÉREAU directed his later plays, including *Dans la solitude des champs de coton* (*In the Solitude of the Cotton Fields*, 1987), *Combats de nègres et de chiens* (*Struggle of the Black and the Dogs*, 1983) and *Quai Ouest* (*Western Dock*, 1986) achieving great success with *Retour au désert* (*Return to the Desert*, 1988). He also translated FUGARD and Shakespeare. A key figure in European drama of the 1980s, he died of an AIDS-related disease just after completing *Roberto Zucco*, which PETER STEIN premièred in Berlin in 1990. TERRY HODGSON

Komissarzhevskaya, Vera [Fyodorovna] (b. St Petersburg, Russia, 27 Oct. 1864; d. Tashkent, 10 Feb. 1910) Actress; half-sister of THEODORE KOMISSARZHEVSKY. She acted in a STANISLAVSKY production in 1891 before joining the Alexandrinsky Theatre in St Petersburg in 1896. Here CHEKHOV admired her acting in the first, inauspicious, production of *The Seagull*. A very serious actress and a great favourite with the public, she opened her own theatre in St Petersburg in 1904. Following a break with MEYERHOLD, her theatre's artistic director, in 1908, Komissarzhevskaya spent the little that remained of her life on tour. The crowds who flocked to her funeral were testimony both to her greatness and to the sense of loss felt at her untimely death. NICK WORRALL

A. Y. Al'tshuller, ed., *Vera Fyodorovna Komissarzhevskaya* (1964)

V. Borovsky, *Komissarzhevskys: A Triptych of the Russian Theatre* (2001)

Y. Rybakova, *Komissarzhevskaya* (1971)

Komissarzhevsky, Theodore F. [Fyodr Fyodrovich] (b. Venice, Italy, 23 May 1882; d. Darien, Conn., 16 April 1954) Director and stage designer; half-brother to VERA KOMISSARZHEVSKAYA and son of F. P. Komissarzhevsky, an opera singer who gave STANISLAVSKY singing lessons. He trained as an architect before joining his sister's theatre in St Petersburg where, between 1906 and 1908, he worked alongside MEYERHOLD and EVREINOV. He moved to Moscow in 1910, staging productions at the Nezlobin Theatre before setting up his own studio in 1914 at the Komissarzhevskaya Theatre, where he worked until 1918 while also freelancing as an opera director at the Bolshoi and elsewhere. Rather like TAIROV, whom his sister had employed as an actor, Komissarzhevsky dreamt of creating a 'universal actor' and a 'synthetic theatre' and, to this end, set up a further experimental studio known as the New Theatre, which numbered among its trainees the young Igor Il'insky who went on to become a key figure in Meyerhold's theatre. Komissarzhevsky left Russia for good in 1919, and during the 1920s and 1930s worked in England; here he was briefly married to PEGGY ASHCROFT, who, with JOHN GIELGUD, acted in many of his productions of CHEKHOV. For a time he ran the tiny BARNES THEATRE, a converted cinema in south London, where he introduced British audiences to CHEKHOV staged in a style influenced by Stanislavsky but romantically adapted to suit English taste in a manner which became very influential. 'Komis', as he was popularly known, also staged notable productions of Shakespeare at STRATFORD-UPON-AVON, where he was described as the company's 'chartered revolutionary', producing a 'fantasticalized' *Merchant of Venice* (1932) which he designed himself in semi-contructivist style; *Macbeth* (1933) with an aluminium set which, in the banquet scene, mirrored Macbeth's own reflection as the ghost of Banquo; a 'barbarically atmospheric' *King Lear* (1936) with DONALD WOLFIT; and *The Comedy of Errors* (1938) in which the frantic action of a single day was dominated by a town-hall clock. Komissarzhevsky moved to the United States in 1939, where he taught acting at his own school. His autobiography *Myself and the Theatre* appeared in 1929. NICK WORRALL

V. Borovsky, *Komissarzhevskys: A Triptych of the Russian Theatre* (2001)

Koonen, Alisa [Georgyevna] (b. Moscow, 17 Oct. 1889; d. Moscow, 20 Aug. 1974) Actress, who, with her husband ALEXANDER TAIROV, founded the Kamerny (Chamber) Theatre (1914), where she remained the company's leading actress. During the 1920s Koonen gave brilliant performances as Racine's Phèdre, SHAW's St Joan and O'NEILL's Abbie Putnam (in *Desire Under the Elms*), in addition to appearances in operetta and contemporary Soviet satires. During the 1930s she was a remarkable Cleopatra, a fine Madame Bovary and an outstanding Commissar in VSEVOLOD VISHNEVSKY's epic drama *Optimistecheskaya tragediya* (*Optimistic Tragedy*). NICK WORRALL

Kopit, Arthur [Lee] (b. New York, 10 May 1937) Playwright. He quickly drew attention with the absurdist farce *Oh Dad, Poor Dad, Mamma's Hung You in the Closet and I'm Feelin' So Sad* (1960). He continued to explore dramaturgical frontiers, notably with *The Day the Whores Came Out to Play Tennis* (1964); *Indians* (1968), which uses a Buffalo Bill Cody show to portray the destruction of Native Americans by the whites; *Wings* (1978), about a stroke sufferer, written originally

for radio; and a nuclear age comedy *The End of the World* (1984). He tried his hand at musical comedy with the book for *Nine* (1982), a version of *Phantom of the Opera* (1991) and a thriller, *Y2K* (1999), but has never gained as much popularity as reputation.
ALEXIS GREENE

Kops, Bernard (b. London, 28 Nov. 1926) Playwright, best known for a series of poetic, bittersweet portraits of Jewish East End life, including *The Hamlet of Stepney Green* (1958). *The Lemmings* (radio, 1963) is a haunting allegory of conformity and mass destruction, while the very powerful *Ezra* (1981) confronts the anti-semitism of Ezra Pound. TONY HOWARD

Korea *see* SOUTH-EAST ASIA

Korneichuk, Alexander [Yevdokimovich] (b. Khristinovka, Ukraine, 12 May 1905; d. Kiev, 14 May 1972) Playwright. Author of more than 20 plays; the best known are his civil war play with a naval setting, *Gibel' eskadry* ('The sinking of the fleet', 1933); *Platon Krechet* (1934), an idealized portrait of a young Soviet doctor; and the war play *Front* (*The Front*, 1942).
NICK WORRALL

Harold B. Segel, *Twentieth-Century Russian Drama* (1979)

Kortner, Fritz [Nathan Kohn] (b. Vienna, 12 May 1892; d. Munich, 22 July 1970) Actor and director, considered to be one of the greatest actors of his time. He was the leading representative of EXPRESSIONISM, to which he gave, after 1923, a more realist colouring. His vitality and extreme physicality stood in clear contrast to the REINHARDT or GRUNDGENS school of acting. In 1933 he emigrated to England and in 1938 to America, working mainly as a film actor. After his return to Germany in 1948 he became one of the most important theatre directors in the Federal Republic.
GÜNTER BERGHAUS

Kott, Jan (b. Warsaw, Poland, 27 Oct. 1914) Drama historian and critic. Kott, who was appointed professor of drama at Warsaw University in 1946 and survived Nazism and Stalinism, wrote the influential book *Shakespeare, Our Contemporary* (appeared in English in 1964), in which he sees parallels between the twentieth century and the Elizabethan era – both typified by instability and change which gives new licence to fools. The title became a catch phrase and his stimulating and innovative views influenced many productions, particularly those of PETER BROOK, whose *Titus Andronicus* (1955) had fuelled Kott's theories in the first place. Kott has lived in America since 1966.
ADRIANA HUNTER

Kouka, Hone (b. Balcutha, New Zealand, 1966, affiliated with Ngati Porou, Ngati Raukawa, Ngati Kahungunu tribes) Playwright, poet, actor and director. He is best known for his powerful MAORI recasting of IBSEN's *The Vikings at Helgeland* as *Ngati Tangata Toa* ('The warrior people', 1994). He has also written plays, such as *Mauri Tu* (1991), which look at contemporary problems of race and cultural alienation. Other plays exploring family and social conflict are *Waiora* (1996), commissioned for the New Zealand International Festival of the Arts, and *Ahika – Homefires* (1998). He edited *Ta Matou Mangai* ('Our own voice', 1999), a collection of Maori plays.
GILLIAN GREER & LAURIE ATKINSON

Koun, Karolos (b. Bursa, Turkey, 1908; d. Athens, 14 Feb. 1987) Director. Founder in 1942 of the Theatro Technis (Art Theatre) of Athens, the most distinguished theatre company of modern GREECE. Beginning as a theatre devoted to such international dramatists as IBSEN, STRINDBERG and WILLIAMS, the Theatro Technis also encouraged young Greek playwrights, most notably the outstanding 'generation of the sixties', such as Kambanellis, Ziogas, Kechaidis and Anagnostaki. The international reputation of the theatre was established in the 1960s with tours of Koun's innovative revivals of Aristophanes' *The Birds* and Aeschylus' *The Persians*. His book, *We Make Theatre for Our Souls*, appeared in 1987. MARVIN CARLSON

Kramer, Larry (b. Bridgeport, Conn., 25 June 1935) Playwright, novelist and AIDS activist. Worked as a story editor for Columbia Pictures in London in the 1960s, writing the screenplay of *Women in Love* (1969). A gay rights campaigner in the 1970s, he became an outspoken advocate for AIDS victims in the 1980s (he is HIV-positive himself), co-founding Gay Men's Health Crisis and the AIDS coalition ACT UP. His semi-autobiographical *The Normal Heart* (1985) – a huge international hit – was the first play to bring the tragedy of AIDS to the stage, with the sequel, *The Destiny of Me* (1993), following Kramer's alter ego Ned Weeks through an experimental treatment programme. Unashamedly polemical, and written with great anger, he condemns both government inacitivity and the indifference of the gay community, controversially comparing homophobia in the 1980s with anti-semitism in the 1930s: AIDS is 'the gay holocaust'. Other plays include *Sissies' Scrapbook* (1972), *Four Friends* (1973) and *Just Say No: A Play About a Farce* (1988). He has also written essays, poetry and novels, in particular *Faggots* (1978). NEIL DOWDEN

Lawrence D. Mass (ed.), *We Must Love One Another or Die: The Life and Legacies of Larry Kramer* (1997)

Kraus, Karl (b. Gitschin, Bohemia, 28 April 1874; d. Vienna, 12 June 1936) Journalist, poet and playwright. A prolific and influential author in his time, mainly through his satirical magazine *The Torch*, Kraus made innovative experiments in form and language. He adapted Aristophanes, translated Shakespeare and wrote plays, most of which have been forgotten. However, *Die letzten Tage der Menschheit* (*The Last Days of Mankind*, publ. 1922, first produced in a severely shortened form 1964), an epic satirical portrayal and indictment in 200 scenes of Austria during the First World War, made its mark on JOAN LITTLEWOOD's *Oh, What a Lovely War!* and was given a remarkable performance by the GLASGOW CITIZENS' THEATRE in 1975.
JUDY MEEWEZEN

George E. Wellwarth, *German Drama Between the Wars* (1971)

Krejča, Otomar (b. Skrýšov, Czechoslovakia, 23 Nov. 1921) Actor and director. Krejča started in the theatre as an actor with BURIAN and Frejka. From 1951 to 1965, at the National Theatre in Prague, he played leading roles in world drama (e.g. Othello, Don Juan, Malvolio). As a director he was responsible for drama at the National Theatre from 1956 to 1961, with a focus on contemporary Czech plays and non-traditional interpretations of world classics (e.g. *The Seagull*, 1960; *Romeo and Juliet*, 1963). In 1965 he founded the Theatre Beyond the Gate (Divadlo za branou) in Prague and achieved an international reputation in collaboration with the designer JOSEF SVOBODA for an integrity of expression based on meticulous exploration of text (e.g. *Three Sisters*, which came to London's WORLD THEATRE SEASON in 1969). The theatre was closed down by the authorities in 1972, and from 1976 Krejča, a supporter of reform, was allowed to work only as a guest director abroad. In 1990, after the fall of communism, he was appointed head of the revived Theatre Beyond the Gate (where he directed e.g. *The Cherry Orchard*, 1990; *The Mountain Giants*, 1994). Since the closure of this theatre, he has directed only *Faust* at the National Theatre (1997).
EVA ŠORMOVÁ

Kroetz, Franz Xaver (b. Munich, 25 Feb. 1946) Playwright, director and actor. He found his first engagements at various fringe theatres in Munich, including FASSBINDER's *Antiteater* (anti-theatre). He wrote over 12 plays before being discovered as a playwright. The first of his plays to be produced were *Heimarbeit* (*Homework*) and *Hartnäcking* ('Stubbornness'), both 1971, *Michis Blut* (*Michi's Blood*, also 1971), *Männersache* (*Men's Business*, 1972), *Stallerhof* (*Farmyard*, 1972), *Dolomitenstadt Lienz* ('Linz, city in the Dolomites', 1972), *Oberösterreich* ('Upper Austria', 1972), *Wunschkonzert* (*Request Concert*, 1973), *Münchener Kindl* ('Child from Munich', 1973) and *Weitere Aussichten* ('Further prospects', 1973). His later plays include *Das Nest* (*The Nest*, 1975), *Lieber Fritz* ('Dear Fritz', 1975), *Geisterbahn* ('Ghost train', 1975), *Sterntaler* (1977), *Mensch Meier* (*Good Gracious*, 1978), *Wer durchs Laub geht* ('Walking through leaves', 1981), *Nicht Fisch nicht Fleisch* (*Neither Fish nor Fowl*, 1981), *Furcht und Elend der BRD* ('Fear and misery of the FRG', 1984) and *Bauern sterben* ('Peasants' death', 1984).

Nearly all of the plays are written in the Bavarian dialect and belong to the tradition of the *Volksstück* (*see* HORVATH; FLEISSER). They are set in the lower-class and poor farming milieux and are peopled by dumb, animal-like creatures leading lives of boredom, violence, adultery and domestic ritual. Kroetz's cold, sober style bears little resemblance to the dramas of classic naturalism. He is not interested in immediate physical data and protects himself against the naturalists' quest for authenticity by using an extremely terse style, the informative value of which rests upon lack of expressiveness rather than descriptive quality.

GÜNTER BERGHAUS

Richard W. Blevins, *Franz Xavier Kroetz: The Emergence of a Political Playwright* (1983)

Michelle Mattson, *Franz Xaver Kroetz: The Construction of a Political Aesthetic* (1996)

Ingeborg C. Walther, *The Theater of Franz Xavier Kroetz* (1990)

Kumalo, Alton *see* TEMBA

Kureishi, Hanif *see* BLACK THEATRE

Kushner, Tony (b. New York, 16 July 1956) Playwright. One work overshadows the rest of his output and made him the most discussed American playwright of the 1990s. His award-winning, two-part *Angels in America* (*Millennium Approach*, 1991, *Perestroika*, 1992), sub-titled 'A Gay Fantasia on National Themes', is an epic, poetic exploration of power and sexuality seen through the interlocking stories of two distressed couples dominated by the central figure of a monstrous right-wing lawyer dying of AIDS but denying to the end his sexual orientation, and the cause of his death. After being commissioned by San Francisco's Eureka Theatre, where it first appeared, Part One became the theatrical talking-point of both London, directed by DECLAN DONNELLAN at the NATIONAL THEATRE in 1992, and New York, directed by GEORGE C. WOLFE on Broadway in 1993. The two parts together are a hymn to the importance of having dreams and the cost of holding on to them. Material not included in *Perestroika* resurfaced in *Slavs* (1993). Kushner had shown his theatrical ambition in the earlier *A Bright Room Called Day* (1987), which intercuts between Hitler's rise in the 1930s and contemporary America. Kushner has also adapted BRECHT, Goethe, ANSKI and Corneille. CHARLES LONDON

Robert Vorlicky, ed., *Tony Kushner in Conversation* (1998)

Kyrghyzia *see* SOVIET UNION

L

La Jolla Playhouse A not-for-profit resident theatre located on the campus of the University of California, San Diego. The La Jolla Playhouse was founded in 1947 by the Actors' Company, a group of Hollywood players including Gregory Peck, Dorothy McGuire and Mel Ferrer. They acknowledged the inescapable fact that the lucrative motion-picture industry was luring talent away from the theatre, and that although film stars periodically voiced a desire to return to the legitimate stage, sheer economics, as well the distance from Los Angeles to New York City, made this impractical. Therefore they established the La Jolla Playhouse, where they could satisfy their need for the creativity of stage work, while simultaneously fulfilling their motion-picture contracts.

The Actors' Company ceased production in the late 1960s, but the theatre was revived under artistic director Des McAnuff in 1983. No longer an adjunct to the movie industry, the La Jolla Playhouse is now devoted to innovative theatrical work, producing classics and new plays side by side under such prominent experimental directors as Frank Galati, Robert Woodruff, Tina Landau, Lisa Peterson and Michael Grief (who succeeded McAnuff as artistic director in 1994).

The Playhouse has premiered works by Diana Son, TONY KUSHNER, JAMES LAPINE, Keith Reddin, Eric Overmyer and Randy Newman, in addition to sending two hit musicals on to successful Broadway runs, The Who's *Tommy* (1992), and *How to Succeed in Business Without Really Trying* (1994). The numerous awards received by the La Jolla Playhouse include the 1993 Tony Award for outstanding regional theatre.

SARAH STEVENSON

La MaMa Experimental Theatre Club Leading proponent of American EXPERIMENTAL THEATRE. A home for emerging theatre artists and multidisciplinary performers, La MaMa supports artistic research and development, the spirit of theatrical collaboration and creativity. Founded in 1961 by ELLEN STEWART, the first Café La MaMa opened as a coffeehouse/theatre in a basement space seating only 30 on New York City's Lower East Side. In 1964 the company moved to a new location on 2nd Avenue, and in 1968 to its present site on East 4th Street, remaining on the Lower East Side and becoming a vital part of the neighbourhood. In 1974 La MaMa added an annex with additional performance space, also on East 4th Street. Under Stewart's guidance, La MaMa was one of the first ALTERNATIVE spaces to house resident companies, providing a supportive and nurturing environment. Led by leading figures in the American theatre, the companies have included The La MaMa Troupe directed by TOM O'HORGAN, MABOU MINES, The ETC Company directed by Wilford Leach, The Great Jones Repertory directed by ANDREI SERBAN and Elizabeth Swados, the OPEN THEATER directed by JOSEPH CHAIKIN, the Theatre of the Eye directed by Tom Eyen, Ping Chong and Company, and others. Throughout its existence, La MaMa has established a tradition of supporting new playwrights. Among those whose work was first presented at La MaMa are SAM SHEPARD, LANFORD WILSON, ISRAEL HOROVITZ, JEAN-CLAUDE VAN ITALLIE, HARVEY FIERSTEIN, William Hoffman, ROCHELLE OWENS, MEGAN TERRY and ADRIENNE KENNEDY. Among the leading directors who have worked at La MaMa are PETER SELLARS, Michael Kahn, Marshall Mason and LEE BREUER and, from abroad, JERZY GROTOWSKI, Serban, PETER BROOK, TADEUSZ KANTOR and EUGENIO BARBA. In addition, La MaMa has played an important part on the international theatre scene, both in sending American companies abroad for festivals and tours, and in presenting companies from around the world at La MaMa. The La MaMa complex includes four buildings housing two theatres, a cabaret, seven floors of rehearsal space, an art gallery, a performance workshop space, a graphics studio, and an archive documenting OFF-OFF BROADWAY theatre. In 1980, the Third World Institute of Theater Arts and Studies was founded at La MaMa. Since its inception, La MaMa has been honoured with numerous awards. ELLEN LAMPERT-GRÉAUX

La Mama Theatre (Melbourne) After a visit to New York, Betty Burstall set up a tiny café theatre in 1967 based on LA MAMA. Writers like HIBBERD, OAKLEY, ROMERIL and DAVID WILLIAMSON became involved, an actors' workshop was set up and out of both evolved the Australian Performing Group. In 1970 it moved round the corner into a huge warehouse that had been used to manufacture prams (hence the name Pram Factory) and a lively, rough performance style and approach to writing emerged.

Meanwhile, the APG actors were increasingly concerned with theatrical approaches represented by US and European experimental groups, and the constant questioning of aims, direction and identities, coupled with increasing financial uncertainty, finally caused the group to dissolve, though the venue continues in use. By the time of its 25th anniversary, it had hosted 576 productions, almost three-quarters of which were Australian in origin. MICHAEL MORLEY

La Rue, Danny [Daniel Patrick Caroll] (b. Cork, Ireland, 26 July 1927) VARIETY artist, actor and probably the century's most famous English-speaking female IMPERSONATOR. After appearing in PANTOMIME and CABARET, his first straight role, in Bran Blackburn's *Come Spy With Me* (1966), ran at the WHITEHALL THEATRE for over a year. Celebrated for his dresses and hairstyles, he continued to make DRAG popular in Christmas shows such as *Sleeping Beauty* (1967) and *Queen Passionelia and The Sleeping Beauty* (1968), and in variety shows like *Danny La Rue at the Palace* (1970). His autobiography, *From Drags to Riches*, appeared in 1987. FRANK LONG

Peter Underwood, *Life's a Drag! Danny La Rue and the Drag Scene* (1974)

Laban, Rudolf [Jean Baptiste Atiua von] (b. Bratislava, Austria-Hungary, 15 Dec. 1879; d. Weybridge, Surrey, July 1 1958) Dancer, choreographer, theorist and teacher. Laban's detailed analysis of human motion in spatial ('choreutic') and dynamic/emotional ('eukinetic') terms created a foundation for European early modern dance, especially in Germany, where he lived for many years. He taught and influenced many dance and theatre artists, including MARY WIGMAN and KURT JOOSS. In 1928 he published *Kinetographie Laban*, a comprehensive system for recording human movement, from daily actions to complex dances, now known as 'Labanotation'. In 1938 he emigrated to England, where he applied his principles to industry, education and acting, as well as dance. He worked with THEATRE WORKSHOP and was influential among practitioners who sought alternatives to conventional dramaturgy. With Lisa Ullmann he founded the Art of Movement Studio, Addlestone, Surrey. The school is now based in London. His published works include *Modern Educational Dance* (1948), *Mastery of Movement on the Stage* (1950), *Principles of Dance and Movement Notation* (1956), *Choreutics* (1966) and *A Life for Dance* (1975). JOHN BROOME

See also CHOREOGRAPHY; DANCE; MOVEMENT, DANCE AND DRAMA.

John Hodgson, *Mastering Movement: The Life and Work of Rudolf Laban* (1998)

labor unions *see* UNIONS

Laboratory Theatre Centre for practical theatre research. Originally the Theatre of Thirteen Rows, it was founded by JERZY GROTOWSKI (director) and Ludwig Flaszen (literary manager) in Opole, Poland, in 1959, and transferred to Wroclaw in 1965. The actors worked on the body and voice under monastic conditions, using gymnastics, yoga and *kathakali* to explore the connections between physical action and the creative imagination. The theatre seated fewer than 100 people and relations between spectator and actor were always important. Early productions (1959–62) 'deconstructed' modernist drama (COCTEAU, MAYAKOVSKY) and the Polish Romantic tradition. Marlowe's *Dr Faustus* (1963), Calderon's *The Constant Prince* (1965) and *Apocalypsis Cum Figuris* (1969) explored the nature of the sacred, confronting the sublime with the grotesque, the mythic with the modern, rapture with derision and pain. Grotowski's theories and his actors' extraordinary commitment and skill revolutionized AVANT-GARDE theatre worldwide. In the 1970s the Laboratory abandoned every production except *Apocalypsis* and invited participants (actors and audience) to collaborate in open 'para-theatrical' events, e.g. Special Project (1973), the University of Research (1975), the Theatre of Sources (1978–80) and the Tree of People (1979). Paratheatre explored the psychological, communal and spiritual significance of performance and ritual, mixing the structured with the spontaneous.

One final production – *Thanatos Polski* (1981, directed by Ryszard Cieślak) – was a response to the Solidarity movement. After several deaths among the group, the Laboratory disbanded in 1984, but aspects of its work have been continued by other Polish groups.

TONY HOWARD

Jennifer Kumiega, *The Theatre of Grotowski* (1985)
Richard Schechner and Lisa Wolford, *The Grotowski Sourcebook* (1997)

Lacey, Catherine (b. London, 6 May 1904; d. London, 23 Sept. 1979)   Actress who toured with MRS PATRICK CAMPBELL in Bayard Veiller's *The Thirteenth Chair* (1925). She took both classic and modern leads in many West End productions as well as touring frequently. An emotionally powerful actress, she gave acclaimed performances in, among others, *Waste* (1936), *Electra* (1951), *The Seagull* (1953), *The Second Mrs Tanqueray* (1954), *The Oresteia* (1961), and *To See Ourselves* (1952) by E. M. Delafield.   MAGGIE GALE

Lackaye, Wilton (b. Loudon County, Va., 30 Sept. 1862; d. New York, 22 Aug. 1932)   Actor who supported such major nineteenth-century stars as Lawrence Barrett and Fanny Davenport, and appeared in popular plays like *Paul Kauvar* (1887) and *Shenandoah* (1889), before achieving widespread fame as the villainous Svengali in *Trilby* (1895, adapted by Paul M. Potter from George DU MAURIER's novel). In 1904 he produced and led a much-praised version of IBSEN's *Pillars of Society*. He regularly starred or was featured in new plays and classics, but also continued to head revivals of *Trilby* until shortly before his death. He founded the Catholic Actors' Guild and was active in Actors' Equity (*see* UNIONS).   GERALD BORDMAN

Lafayette Players   American theatre company directed by actress Anita Bush, named shortly after moving to Harlem's Lafayette Theatre in 1915. The company presented a wide variety of productions, from comedy and melodrama to Shakespeare, sometimes in abridged versions, to replace the previous fare of MINSTREL shows and VAUDEVILLE that demeaned black people. Being in the heart of New York's main black neighbourhood, the company placed considerable emphasis on the works of contemporary black writers and on promoting promising black actors such as CHARLES GILPIN. The Lafayette Players toured and successfully moved to Los Angeles in 1928 before disbanding in 1932. The Harlem theatre became the Harlem centre for the FEDERAL THEATER PROJECT and it was here that ORSON WELLES staged his 'voodoo' *Macbeth* (1936). The theatre was closed in 1968 due to fire.

Legend has it that a tree in front of the theatre brought good luck to black performers who touched it.

ADRIANA HUNTER

Laffan, Kevin [Barry] (b. Reading, 24 May 1922)   Playwright. Laffan's comedies often sketch tensions within small communities: from drop-out culture in *Zoo, Zoo, Widdershins, Zoo* (1969) to a family's response to the Catholic ban on contraception in *It's a Two Foot Six Inches Above the Ground World* (1970). He created the television soap opera *Emmerdale Farm*, set in rural Yorkshire.   TONY HOWARD

Lagerkvist, Pär [Fabian] (b. Vaxjö, Sweden, 23 May 1891; d. Stockholm, 11 July 1974)   Playwright, novelist and poet. Having embraced socialism as a young man, Lagerkvist adopted a radical, modernist approach in his plays (e.g. the one-act trilogy *Den svåra stunden / The Difficult Hour*, 1918) and attacked the naturalism of IBSEN while supporting the experiment of STRINDBERG. His humanism and concern with social issues was later reflected in the play *Bödeln* (*The Hangman*, 1934), which he adapted from his own novel as a response to the rise of fascism. This also inspired the play *Mannenutan själ* (*The Man Without a Soul*, 1936) and one of his last, and most complex, plays, *Låt människan leva* (*Let Man Live*, 1949), which deals with man's inhumanity to man through the ages. He is best known for his novel *Barabbas* (1950), which he dramatized, and in 1951 was awarded the Nobel Prize for Literature.   HELEN RAPPAPORT

Ray Lewis White, *Pär Lagerkvist in America* (1979)
L. Sjöberg, *Pär Lagerkvist* (1976)

Lahr, Bert [Irving Lahreim] (b. New York, 13 Aug. 1895; d. New York, 4 Dec. 1967)   Comedian and actor. From 1910 he worked in BURLESQUE and VAUDEVILLE, making his Broadway debut in the revue *Harry Delmar's Revels* (1927). His clowning in *Hold Everything* (1928) won him fame, but nothing in comparison to his popularity as the Cowardly Lion in the film *The Wizard of Oz* (1939). His portrayal of Estragon in *Waiting for Godot* (1956) established BECKETT in America, and he gave notable performances in *A Midsummer Night's Dream* (1960), *The Winter's Tale* (1960) and the musical *Foxy* (1964).   D. KEITH PEACOCK

J. Lahr, *Notes on a Cowardly Lion* (1969)

Lamarche, Gustave (b. Montreal, 17 July 1895; d. Montreal, 27 Aug. 1987)   French-Canadian playwright, director and poet. The pageant-plays which he wrote and directed in the 1930s and 1940s, generally staged outdoors and consciously medieval in format and inspiration, attracted scores of thousands for each performance. A Catholic priest, he preferred biblical themes. His 34 published plays include *Jonathas* (1933), *La Défaite de l'enfer* ('Hell defeated', 1938), *Notre-Dame-de-la-Couronne* ('Our Lady of the snows', 1942) and *Notre-Dame-de-la-Couronne* ('Our Lady of the crown', 1947).   LEONARD E. DOUCETTE

See also PAGEANT.

LAMDA   *see* DRAMA SCHOOLS

Lamos, Mark   *see* EXPERIMENTAL THEATRE; HARTFORD STAGE

Lan, David   (b. Cape Town, 1 June 1952)   Playwright. Lan left South Africa to study anthropology, a discipline which has informed his work from *The Winter Dancers* (1977) to *Desire* (1990). His work mixes analysis with compassion, notably in his chronicle play *Flight* (1986). He successfully collaborated with CARYL CHURCHILL on *A Mouthful of Birds* (1986), creating a series of visual and rhythmic events of sexual restraint and freedom. His skill with detailed and profound atmosphere successfully served his translation of SOBOL's *Ghetto* (1989). Other plays include *Bird Child* (1974), *Red Earth* (1978), *Sergeant Ola and His Followers* (1979), and *The Ends of the Earth* (1996). He has produced acclaimed TRANSLATIONS and ADAPTATIONS, including *Ion* (1994), *Uncle Vanya* (1998) and *The Cherry Orchard* (2000). In 2000, Lan became artistic director of the YOUNG VIC, London.   DAN REBELLATO

Lanchester, Elsa   *see* LAUGHTON, CHARLES

Lane, Lupino [Henry George Lupino]   (b. London, 16 June 1892; d. London, 10 Nov. 1959)   A member of the LUPINO family of acrobats and dancers, he was working in one of the family's variety acts from the age of 11, and at 27 appeared in *Afgar*, which also took him to New York. In America he appeared in *Ziegfeld Follies of 1924* and as an acrobatic Ko-Ko in *The Mikado*, then returned to England for other musicals and pantomimes, while continuing to make visits to the United States. In 1935 he found the vehicle he was looking for – a farce with songs called *Twenty to One* in which he played Bill Snibson, a variation of the Cockney 'cheekie chappie'. On tour and in London it ran for 1,025 performances. Lane took Snibson into another farce with songs, *Me and My Girl* (1937), but in this he also had a dance called 'The Lambeth Walk' which became a huge hit and helped the show run for an initial 1,646 performances. Lane made a fortune, but lost most of it trying to restore the Gaiety Theatre to its former glory, and he did not live to see the revival of *Me and My Girl* as a full-scale musical in 1985.
IAN BEVAN

J. Dillon White, *Born to Star* (1957)

Lang, Matheson [Alexander]   (b. Montreal, 15 May 1877; d. Bridgetown, Barbados, 11 April 1948)   Actor and manager. After appearing with FRANK BENSON and then GRANVILLE BARKER during the ROYAL COURT seasons (1904–7), he had his first popular success in a revival of Hall Caine's religious melodrama *The Christian* (1907). Much of his career was spent touring abroad. A tall, well-built and hard-working actor, he specialized in melodrama (especially *Mr Wu*, 1913), modern romantic drama and Shakespeare. His Shakespearean productions at the OLD VIC in 1914 with his wife Hutin [Nellie] Britton (1876–1965) inaugurated the theatre under LILIAN BAYLIS as a home for Shakespeare. Later productions included *The Wandering Jew* (1920) and *Jew Süss* (1929). His autobiography, *Mr Wu Looks Back*, appeared in 1940.   IAN CLARKE

Langer, František   (b. Prague, 3 March 1888; d. Prague, 2 Aug. 1965)   Playwright, author of comedies on the model of SHAW and EXPRESSIONIST dramas. His *Periphery* (1925) was presented in London as *The Outsider* (1931) and in New York as *The Ragged Edge* (1935). *The Camel Through the Needle's Eye* (1923) was offered successfully in 1929 by the THEATER GUILD. Among his other plays were *Cavalry Patrol* (1930) and *The Angel in Our Midst* (1931).   MARVIN CARLSON

Langham, Michael   (b. Bridgwater, Som., 22 August 1919)   Director. His early career was established in the 1940s and 1950s in Britain at the BIRMINGHAM REPERTORY THEATRE, STRATFORD-UPON-AVON, the OLD VIC and the CITIZENS' THEATRE, Glasgow. He moved to North America in 1955 to take up the post of artistic director of the STRATFORD FESTIVAL (Ontario), succeeding TYRONE GUTHRIE, and firmly establishing himself as a classical director by running the Festival in a way similar to English repertory companies. During his tenure he developed the programme to include film and television projects, touring and school activities. He himself appeared in a film in which Guthrie discusses various techniques and theories used in theatre productions. Langham was appointed artistic director at the GUTHRIE THEATER in Minneapolis in 1971. He left to become director of drama at the Juilliard School in 1979, and remained in that position until 1992, when he returned to freelance directing.   LAURIE WOLF

Langner, Lawrence   (b. Swansea, Wales, 30 May 1890; d. New York, 26 Dec. 1962)   Producer and playwright. A patent attorney who balanced a dual career in business and the theatre, Langner arrived in the United States from England in 1910. Assessing the BROADWAY theatre as 'cheap', he sought, as he stated retrospectively in his autobiography, *The Magic Curtain* (1951), 'a better theatre'. He was instrumental in forming, organizing and writing for the WASHINGTON SQUARE PLAYERS (1915–17), and was the instigator and inspiration behind its successor, the THEATER GUILD. Also the founder of the AMERICAN SHAKESPEARE FESTIVAL at Stratford, Connecticut in the early 1950s, as a producer Langner consistently combined financial savvy with artistic integrity. ANNE FLETCHER

Langtry, Lillie (sometimes Lily) [Emily Charlotte le Breton] (b. Jersey, 13 Oct. 1853; d. Monaco, 12 Feb. 1929) Actress of legendary beauty. 'The Jersey Lily' was at various times painter's model, mistress of royalty, friend of both the famous and the talented, and racehorse owner. Her theatrical importance at the beginning of the twentieth century is hard to separate from her raffish life. Her first important part was Kate Hardcastle in *She Stoops to Conquer* (1881), and other classical roles include Rosalind in *As You Like It* (1890); but titles such as *The Degenerates* (1899) by Sydney Grundy and the increasingly outmoded plays of Dumas *fils* and Tom Taylor perhaps more accurately define her range. She was also popular in America. She retired in 1918 and wrote an autobiography, *The Days I Knew* (1921). JOHN STOKES

Laura Beatty, *Lillie Langry: Manners, Masks and Morals* (1999)
James Brough, *The Prince and the Lily* (1975)
Ernest Dudley, *The Gilded Lily* (1958)

Languirand, Jacques (b. Montreal, 1 May 1931) French-Canadian playwright, director, actor, novelist and essayist. Languirand spent several years in Paris in the early 1950s and returned to Canada indelibly influenced by the THEATRE OF THE ABSURD – the only French-Canadian dramatist to compose in this vein. He established his own theatre in Montreal in 1956 and wrote several influential plays for it, notably *Les Insolites* ('The unusual ones', 1956), *Le Roi ivre* ('The drunken king', 1956), *Les Grands Départs* ('Great departures', 1958) and the musical *Klondyke* (1970). LEONARD E. DOUCETTE

Lansbury, Angela [Brigid] (b. London, 16 Oct. 1925) Actress and singer of remarkable talents who was evacuated to America in the Second World War. After over a decade in Hollywood she came to Broadway to play in FEYDEAU's *Hotel Paradiso* (1957). Following success in *A Taste of Honey* (1960), she acted with the ROYAL SHAKESPEARE COMPANY and the NATIONAL THEATRE. She made her musical debut in SONDHEIM's *Anyone Can Whistle* (1964). In 1966, the title role in *Mame* brought her the greatest renown, and the first of four Tony Awards; the others she received for *Dear World* (1969), a revival of *Gypsy* (1974) and for creating the role of the murderous, love-starved Mrs Lovett in Sondheim's *Sweeney Todd* (1979). From 1984 to 1996 she was star and producer of the television series *Murder, She Wrote*. THOMAS F. CONNOLLY

M. Bonanno, *Angela Lansbury: A Biography* (1987)
M. Gottfried, *Balancing Act: The Authorized Biography of Angela Lansbury* (1999)

Lapine, James [Elliott] (b. Mansfield, Ohio, 10 Jan. 1949) Director and playwright. Lapine started his career as a photographer and artist. His first involvement in theatre was as a graphic designer at Yale School of Drama, where he staged his first piece, *Photograph* (1978), using famous images based on a poem-play by GERTRUDE STEIN. He directed for the NEW YORK SHAKESPEARE FESTIVAL. Among the plays he directed for BROADWAY are *The Diary of Anne Frank* (1997) and DAVID HENRY HWANG's *Golden Child* (1998). Musical collaborations with STEPHEN SONDHEIM include directing and writing prize-winning libretti for *Sunday in the Park with George* (1985), *Into the Woods* (1988) and *Passion* (1994). Lapine directed and wrote the book for the musical *Falsettos* (1992) with composer/lyricist William Finn. ANNA WHEELER GENTRY

Lapotaire, Jane (b. Ipswich, Suffolk, 26 Dec. 1944) Actress. Having trained at the BRISTOL OLD VIC School and appeared at the Bristol Old Vic for two years, she joined the NATIONAL THEATRE (1967–71) and then worked at the YOUNG VIC and the ROYAL SHAKESPEARE COMPANY, playing Viola in *Twelfth Night* (1974). She played Rosalind in *As You Like It* (NOTTINGHAM Playhouse, 1975; RIVERSIDE, 1976) and the title role in *The Duchess of Malfi* (Bristol Old Vic, 1976) before returning to the RSC in 1978 as Rosaline in *Love's Labour's Lost* and in her award-winning creation of the eponymous role in *Piaf*, which was seen in New York as well as Stratford and London. Further returns to the RSC, as Gertrude to KENNETH BRANAGH's Hamlet (1992), Mrs Alving in *Ghosts* (1993) and Katharine of Aragon in *Henry VIII* (1996), were also acclaimed. Noted for wit, intelligence and strength of characterization, she has played other major classical roles for companies such as PROSPECT, the NT (e.g. Antigone, 1984) and Compass (as SHAW's St Joan, 1985), scored a popular hit in *Shadowlands* (1989), and has toured her own successful one-woman show, *Shakespeare As I Knew Her*. Her auto-

biography, *Grace and Favour*, appeared in 1989, and *Out of Order*, a memoir of a year in her life, in 1999.
CHARLES LONDON

Lardner, Ring[gold Wilmer] (b. Niles, Mich., 6 March 1885; d. Chicago, 25 Sept. 1933) Sketch writer, librettist, humorist, journalist and short-story writer. A dour alcoholic, he none the less created bright, absurdly antic, comic moments. His works include a baseball play, *Elmer the Great* (1928), written with GEORGE M. COHAN; *June Moon* (1929), written with GEORGE S. KAUFMAN, a send-up of Tin Pan Alley; and several sketches for sundry revues and various editions of the ZIEGFELD *FOLLIES*. THOMAS F. CONNOLLY

laterna magika A mixed media system of counter-pointing live performers and their filmed images projected on to screens. Created by the director Alfred Radok and designer JOSEF SVOBODA, it was first seen at the Czechoslovak pavilion at the 1958 Brussels Exposition and was used in their collaboration, *The Last Ones* (1966). Svoboda has sometimes integrated it into his theatrical designs (e.g. in *The Odyssey*, 1987), and is director of the Laterna Magika Theatre in Prague.
CHARLES LONDON

Latin America *see* HISPANIC THEATRE IN THE UNITED STATES; MEXICO AND CENTRAL AMERICA; SOUTH AMERICA

Latino theatre *see* HISPANIC THEATRE IN THE UNITED STATES

Latvia *see* SOVIET UNION

Lauder, Harry [Hugh MacLennan] (b. Portobello, Scotland, 4 Aug. 1870; d. Strathaven, Scotland, 26 Feb. 1950) 'The Laird of the Halls' was the first Scottish comedian to become a star outside of his own country. On stage he wore a kilt and carried a huge curly walking-stick; he had a strong baritone singing voice and his songs became some of the most popular of the genre, e.g. 'Keep Right On to the End of the Road', 'I Love a Lassie', and 'Roamin' in the Gloaming', the title of his autobiography (1944). He toured abroad and made many recordings. His extensive collection of memorabilia is held by Glasgow University. He was knighted in 1919 for his fundraising during the First World War. REXTON S. BUNNETT

Laughton, Charles (b. Scarborough, Yorks., 1 July 1899; d. Hollywood, 15 Dec. 1962) Actor, director and teacher. Intended by his parents to take over the hotel they ran, he started acting at the relatively late age of 26, when he enrolled at the Royal Academy of Dramatic Art. Graduating with the Gold Medal, he rapidly established himself, despite an unconventional appearance, as the most exciting and original young actor of his time. Initially under the patronage of the Russian director KOMISSARZHEVSKY, he gave a series of characterizations that startled with their emotional and sensual realism. His triumphant performances as the sadistic *Man with Red Hair* (1928), the Al Capone-type gangster in *On the Spot* (1930), and the murderous clerk in *Payment Deferred* (1931) seemed to his contemporaries to be a new kind of acting. *Payment Deferred* took him across the Atlantic, where American critics and actors equally embraced him; the public was slightly more resistant, but Hollywood tried to snap him up. He held out for a contract on his own terms, and when this was forthcoming, made in rapid succession six films which established him as a substantial name. It was on a return visit to England, however, that he made the film that in one stroke transformed his career and the English film industry: Alexander Korda's *The Private Life of Henry VIII* (1933). His belching, scratching, chicken-leg-toting Tudor went round the world, the subject of a million impersonations. Returning to the stage only for an unhappy season at the OLD VIC (1933–4) and an unexpectedly tame Captain Hook (1936), he went back to Hollywood, creating in swift succession some of the most famous of all film performances: Barrett in *The Barretts of Wimpole Street* (1934), Captain Bligh in *Mutiny on the Bounty* (1935), Ruggles (of *Red Gap*, 1935): all portrayals of intense theatrical vividness which nevertheless brilliantly use the medium of film. In England there followed *Rembrandt* (1936), in a more intimate simpler style, and the aborted project of *I Claudius* (1936), in which he promised to give perhaps his greatest performance. To extricate himself from debts arising from a film venture of his own he signed a five-picture contract with RKO, of which the first was *The Hunchback of Notre Dame* (1940). Once again, his performance – as Quasimodo – passed instantly into the public consciousness, a creation on an enormous scale. It cost Laughton a great deal, and afterwards his creative energy seemed to go into channels other than acting: teaching, public readings and directing. He returned to the stage to give the world première of the version of *Galileo* (1947) on which he and BRECHT had worked in the closest collaboration for two years; he directed first his students, then actors like Charles Boyer and TYRONE POWER, in a number of productions that achieved enormous success. In 1955 he directed (and wrote) his only film, *The Night of the Hunter*, one of the greatest of American films, though a failure at the time, which broke his heart. In the few good films he made after 1940 – *This Land is Mine* (1943), *The Big*

Clock (1948), *Hobson's Choice* (1954) and *Spartacus* (1960) – he gave complex and imaginative performances; but by this time, movie acting was purely for profit. His real passion went into the readings which took him all over America and by means of which he could convey some of his love and understanding of great literature and art. He became a well-loved figure in the country of which, since 1950, he and his wife, the actress Elsa Lanchester (1902–86), had been citizens.

In 1958 he returned to England to direct and appear in a new play, *The Party* by Jane Arden, which was only a moderate success. The following year, he was invited to Stratford-upon-Avon to play in *A Midsummer Night's Dream* and *King Lear*, his first Shakespeare since 1933, when he had created an unforgettable Angelo and a disastrous Macbeth. His Bottom was acclaimed, an earthy, vigorous creature; the Lear was more controversially received. It had been his life's ambition to play the role, but when the moment came, he was physically incapable of sustaining its huge demands. A last magnificent film performance in *Advise and Consent* (1962) was of a kind with all his best work, an illumination of the oppressor by the oppressed: a closeted homosexual all his life, Laughton portrayed a queer-hating senator from the South with infinite delicacy, showing the danger behind reactionary charm.

In his work from the 1930s, Laughton transcends psychology or observation in the way a great painter or sculptor might. He creates an image (not purely visual but vocal and emotional) of a scale and an expressive intensity imbued with human feeling that gives it universal resonance. The only actor on film with whom he can be compared is Nikolai Cherkassov, EISENSTEIN's Ivan the Terrible and Alexander Nevsky, but Laughton's touch is more human, which earns him supreme greatness. SIMON CALLOW

S. Callow, *Charles Laughton: A Difficult Actor* (1987)
C. Higham, *Charles Laughton* (1976)
E. Lanchester, *Charles Laughton and I* (1938)

Laurents, Arthur (b. Brooklyn, New York, 14 July 1918) Playwright, screenwriter, librettist and director. His plays, including *Home of the Brave* (1945), about wartime Jewish experience, and *The Time of the Cuckoo* (1952), deal with the lonely and the socially outcast attempting to understand the nature of social conformity. Among his libretti are *West Side Story* (1957), *Gypsy* (1959) and *Do I Hear A Waltz?* (1965), an adaptation of *The Time of the Cuckoo*. On Broadway he has directed *Anyone Can Whistle* (1964), *La Cage aux Folles* (1984) and revivals of *Gypsy* (1974, 1989). His screenplays include *Anna Lucasta* (1949), *Anastasia* (1957),

The Way We Were (1973) and *The Turning Point* (1977) His book *Original Story: A Memoir of Broadway and Hollywood* appeared in 2000. DAVID STAINES

Lavery, Bryony *see* LESBIAN THEATRE; MONSTROUS REGIMENT; WOMEN'S THEATRE GROUP

Lawler, Ray[mond Evenor] (b. Melbourne, 1921) Playwright. He plays down the significance of *The Summer of the Seventeenth Doll* (1956) in direct proportion to his nation's desire to celebrate it. To him it was neither seminal nor pivotal, merely his 13th play, 'a night's entertainment'. The Depression years saw Lawler leaving school at 13, subsequently discovering the amateur theatre at 20, performing in variety, and finally joining Gertrude Johnson's National Theatre Company to write, act and direct. By 1955 Lawler was an old hand as well as an overnight sensation, capable of running the professional Union Theatre Repertory Company in John Sumner's absence, writing its most famous play (about two cane cutters spending the annual 'lay-off' period in the city of Melbourne) and acting in it – as Barney, the debatable mate.

The Doll, the first internationally famous modern Australian play, took its author away in 1957 to West End success, Broadway failure and a brief Hollywood film career. In 1970 he came home again. *The Man Who Shot the Albatross* (1970), a psychological study of Captain Bligh's time as Governor of New South Wales, cast fellow expatriate Leo McKern as Bligh. It was the fourth Lawler play after *The Doll* to be performed in Australia. *The Piccadilly Bushman* (1959) treats the dilemma of artistic exile and homecoming with genuine humour. Lawler offered *Kid Stakes* (1975) and *Other Times* (1976) as 'prequels' to the original *Doll* in an attempt to recapture time already lost at the end of the seventeenth summer. Performances of the trilogy in 1977 and 1978 were greeted with almost ritual reverence and relief; 1996 saw an opera version. In *Godsend* (1982) he reflects on his English–Irish background and religious roots.

Other plays include *Cradle of Thunder* (1949), *The Unshaven Cheek* (1963), and *A Breach in the Wall* (1967). GUS WORBY

D. Carroll, *Australian Contemporary Drama* (1995)
P. Fitzpatrick, *After the Doll: Australian Drama since 1955* (1979)

Lawrence, D[avid] H[erbert] (b. Eastwood, Notts, 11 Sept. 1885; d. Venice, 2 March 1930) Novelist, essayist, poet and playwright. His plays, virtually unperformed until the 1960s because of his scandalous reputation as a novelist on sexual matters, came into prominence then with highly regarded PETER GILL productions at the ROYAL COURT of *The Collier's Friday Night* (written 1906), *The Daughter-in-Law* (written *c.* 1912) and *The Widowing of Mrs Holroyd* (written 1910–13). Critics were impressed by Lawrence's seemingly authentic re-creation of working-class life in the mining community and his realistic dialogue, and productions of *The Merry Go-Round* (written 1912) and *Touch and Go* (written 1920) followed. His other plays include two comedies, a drama based on his own relationship with a married woman, and a biblical play, *David* which, like *The Widowing of Mrs Holroyd*, was given a Sunday night production by the STAGE SOCIETY in the 1920s. IAN CLARKE

Keith Sagar, *D. H. Lawrence: Life Into Art* (1985)
Sylvia Sklar, *The Plays of D. H. Lawrence* (1975)
John Worthen, *D. H. Lawrence: The Early Years, 1885–1912* (1991)

Lawrence [Klasen], Gertrude (b. London, 4 July 1898; d. New York, 7 Sept. 1952) Actress and dancer who first appeared on stage aged 12 and later starred in the revue *A to Z* (1921). She was associated with NOEL COWARD throughout her career and acted with him in *Private Lives* (1930) and *To-Night At 8.30* (1936). She starred in the musicals *Oh, Kay!* (1926) *Lady in the Dark* (1943) and *The King and I* (1951). Her autobiography, *A Star Danced*, appeared in 1945. REXTON S. BUNNETT

Sheridan Morley, *Gertrude Lawrence* (1981)

Lawrence, Jerome (b. Cleveland, Ohio, 14 July 1915) and **Lee, Robert E[dwin]** (b. Elyria, Ohio, 15 Oct. 1918; d. Los Angeles, 8 July 1994) Playwrights. During their 50-year career they collaborated on radio plays, films, plays, and books for musicals. Their most famous play, *Inherit the Wind* (1955), is a dramatization of the Scopes 'monkey' trial, in which a Tennessee schoolteacher was prosecuted for teaching evolution, and was one of the longest-running serious plays on Broadway. The play has been translated into 28 different languages. *The Night Thoreau Spent in Jail* (1970), their homage to the birth of civil disobedience, was performed in Hong Kong in honour of the students who died at Tiananmen Square in Beijing. Their plays are well-crafted, contain very actable characters with strong speeches (a result of their early days writing for the radio), and display a deep concern for the dignity of the human mind. They are often produced by school and COMMUNITY THEATRE groups. Lawrence and Lee have been closely involved with the development of new American dramatists, both in their teaching and in their creation of the American Playwrights' Theater, based in their native Ohio. DAVID A. WILLIAMS

Lawson, John Howard (b. New York, 25 Sept. 1894; d. San Francisco, 11 Aug. 1977) Playwright and screenwriter. An innovative playwright in the 1920s (*Roger Bloomer*, 1923, was the first American EXPRESSIONIST play; *Processional*, 1925, experimented with the theatrical use of JAZZ), Lawson was radicalized by events, becoming the dean of American revolutionary theatre in the 1930s and author of one of the most militant plays of the decade, *Marching Song* (1937). An early defector to Hollywood, he authored many successful screenplays, was founding president of the Screen Writers' Guild and headed the Hollywood branch of the Communist Party. One of the 'Hollywood Ten' who refused to cooperate with the House Committee on Un-American Activities, he was jailed for contempt of Congress from 1950 to 1953. He wrote what has become a standard work, *Theory and Technique of Playwrighting* (1936). GERALD RABKIN

Gerald Rabkin, *Drama and Commitment* (1964)

Lawson [Worsnop], Wilfrid (b. Bradford, 14 Jan. 1900; d. London, 10 Oct. 1966) Actor. Lawson made his name in the 1920s in SHAW revivals. Performances in *The Barretts of Wimpole Street* (1935) and *I Have Been Here Before* (1937) confirmed his skill with gravel-voiced character parts; he was perhaps most famous for his performance as Doolittle in the film of *Pygmalion* (1938). His talent carried him over the 1956 watershed, in spite of his alcoholism, with success in *Live Like Pigs* (1958), *Cock a Doodle Dandy* (1959) and *The Lower Depths* (1962), and as the Button Moulder in *Peer Gynt* (1962). DAN REBELLATO

Lay[e], [Elsie] Evelyn ('Boo') (b. London, 10 July 1900; d. London, 17 Feb. 1996) Actress and singer. The child of theatrical parents, she made her first stage appearance at 15. Within a few years she was playing leading roles in musicals such as *Going Up* (1918), *The Shop Girl* (1920), *Mary* (1921), *The Merry Widow* (1923), *Madame Pompadour* (1923), *Betty in Mayfair* (1926) and *The New Moon* (1929). She made her New York debut in NOEL COWARD's *Bitter Sweet* (1929). After the Second World War she rather faded from view until she made a comeback in the British musical *Wedding in Paris* (1954), which ran for a year. Her later successes were in light comedy plays. Her autobiography, *Boo to My Friends*, appeared in 1958. IAN BEVAN

Le Gallienne, Eva (b. London, 11 Jan. 1899; d. Weston, Mass., 3 June 1991) Actress and producer. Daughter of poet and novelist Richard Le Gallienne, she trained and acted in London before making her American debut in 1915. She won fame in commercial enterprises – *Liliom* (1921), *The Swan* (1923) and *Uncle*

433

Harry (1942) – but her first love was classic theatre, and she played a vital role in introducing many foreign authors to Americans. In the 1925–6 season she produced and played in revivals of IBSEN's *The Master Builder* and *John Gabriel Borkman*. She founded the CIVIC REPERTORY THEATER (1926) and led it for six years, directing and appearing in many of its low-priced classical productions. In 1946 she helped found the ill-fated AMERICAN REPERTORY THEATER. The tiny, tight-faced actress was deemed too self-consciously mannered by many playgoers. Her translations of CHEKHOV and Ibsen have been published, and she has written a biography of ELEONORA DUSE as well as two volumes of autobiography, *At 33* (1934) and *With a Quiet Heart* (1953). GERALD BORDMAN

R. A. Schanke, *Eva Le Gallienne: A Bio-Bibliography* (1989)

——, *Shattered Applause: The Lives of Eva Le Gallienne* (1992)

Lebanon *see* MIDDLE EAST AND NORTH AFRICA

Lecompte, Elizabeth *see* WOOSTER GROUP

Lecoq, Jacques (b. Paris, 15 Dec. 1921; d. Paris, 19 Jan. 1999) Actor, who became recognized as the twentieth century's most influential teacher of the physical aspects of the actor's art. Through his preoccupation with MIME he was also responsible for widening the territory of that genre, away from white-faced solos in the tradition of MARCEL MARCEAU towards a more total view of popular theatre.

Lecoq studied mime under Jean Dasté in 1945 when he became an actor with the Compagnie des Comédiens in Grenoble. It was at this time that he began working with masks, which were later to become a vital component of his teaching. Moving on to Italy, in 1948 he taught and directed at the Padua University Theatre; then, in 1951, he taught at the school of the Teatro Piccolo in Milan. Returning to Paris, he joined the THÉÂTRE NATIONAL POPULAIRE under JEAN VILAR, then opened his own school in 1956, the Ecôle Internationale de Mime et de Théâtre, which he directed until his death. Through his research on movement analysis, body language and gesture, Lecoq has popularized such genres as the CLOWN, bouffons, *COMMEDIA DELL'ARTE*, TRAGEDY and MELODRAMA. Former students of his included members of the British companies Moving Picture Mime Show and THEATRE DE COMPLICITE. Periodically, Lecoq conducted workshops for actors and teachers in Britain. Today there is hardly a single drama school in Britain that has not been touched by his teachings. He also continued to tour his lecture demonstration on the physical art of the actor, *Tout Bouge*. In 1982 he was awarded the Légion d'Honneur. His book, *The Moving Body*, translated by David Bradby, was published in English posthumously in 2000. KENNETH REA

See also PHYSICAL PREPARATION.

Lee, Auriol (b. London, 13 Sept. 1880; d. nr Hutchinson, Kan., 2 July 1941) Actress and director. Having trained in Brussels, she appeared in early ACTRESSES' FRANCHISE LEAGUE productions. She played an enormous number of roles and directed many West End hits during the 1920s and 1930s, being well known for productions of JOHN VAN DRUTEN's plays. Engaged as a director by Hitchcock at Elstree Studios (1932), she spent her later years in America. MAGGIE GALE

Lee, Canada [Leonard Lionel Cornelius Canegata] (b. New York, 3 March 1907; d. New York, 8 May 1952) Actor. After a successful boxing career was cut short by injury, he made his stage debut in 1928 and won attention in a 1934 CIVIC REPERTORY THEATER revival of *Stevedore*. He played Banquo in the FEDERAL THEATER's 'voodoo' *Macbeth* (1936) and really grabbed the spotlight with his portrayal of the hunted-down murder suspect in *Native Son* (1941), adapted by PAUL GREEN and Richard Wright from Wright's novel. Lee earned praise as Caliban in *The Tempest* (1945) and, opposite ELIZABETH BERGNER, as a white-faced de Bosola in *The Duchess of Malfi* (1946). GERALD BORDMAN

Lee, Eugene (b. Beloit, Wisc., 9 March 1939) Scenic designer. From *Slaveship* OFF-BROADWAY in 1970 and the 1993 revival of *Show Boat* to the 1998 musical *Ragtime*, Lee's prolific career includes the Tony award-winning productions of *Candide* (1974) and *Sweeney Todd* (1979). In 1967, Lee designed *The Threepenny Opera* for Trinity Square in Providence, Rhode Island, beginning his tenure as resident designer there. Other US regional theatre credits include ARENA STAGE, Washington DC, Center Stage, Baltimore, and Studio Arena, Buffalo, as well as 25 seasons of NBC's *Saturday Night Live* for television. His hallmarks include the use of real materials and objects in the creation of distinctive stage environments. ELLEN LAMPERT-GRÉAUX

Lee, Gypsy Rose [Rose Louise Hovick] (b. Seattle, 9 Jan. 1914; d. Los Angeles, 26 April 1970) BURLESQUE star and striptease performer. She toured with her sister June under various names in VAUDEVILLE in the 1920s, driven, as always, by their ruthless mother Rose. Around 1929 Rose Louise finally made her solo debut in burlesque in Ohio, eventually perfecting her striptease act as Gypsy Rose Lee into 'seven minutes of sheer art', as producer Billy Minsky put it when she appeared for the first time in New York at his Republic

Theater. By the mid-1930s Lee was commanding high fees for her performances, and appeared in the ZIEGFELD FOLLIES of 1936. At the height of her fame she commanded $4,000 a week for shows like *The Streets of Paris*, staged at the New York World's Fair in 1940. Meanwhile, she pursued a more cerebral life off-stage, befriending many intellectuals and writing newspaper columns as well as plays and murder mysteries. In 1942 she scored a major success in the Broadway musical *Star and Garter*. In 1957 she published her autobiography, *Gypsy: A Memoir*, which was turned into a successful musical (1959) and film (1962). Between 1958 and 1961 she also toured with her own one-woman show, *A Curious Evening with Gypsy Rose Lee*.
HELEN RAPPAPORT

J. Havoc, *Early Havoc* (1959)
E. Preminger, *Gypsy and Me* (1984)

Lee, Ming Cho (b. Shanghai, China, 3 Oct. 1930) Designer. A distinguished and influential elder statesman of American stage design, Lee has enjoyed an expansive career and has developed enduring associations with numerous theatre, opera and dance companies and universities. His early work was spare and modern but later he developed a more detailed realistic style. Lee studied painting before emigrating in 1949 to the United States, where he turned to set DESIGN, serving for five years as apprentice and assistant to JO MIELZINER. His work was first seen in New York in the OFF-BROADWAY production of *The Infernal Machine* (1958). In 1962 he began working at JOSEPH PAPP's NEW YORK SHAKESPEARE FESTIVAL, where he designed the Anspacher and Newman theatre spaces, as well as a long list of productions during his years as the resident designer. He has designed for many regional theatres, including the ARENA STAGE, Washington DC, and the MARK TAPER FORUM, Los Angeles, as well as for leading American opera companies. He has also served as a principal designer for the Juilliard School of Music and has contributed to the design repertoire of American choreographers such as Jose Limon, MARTHA GRAHAM and ALVIN AILEY. Lee's off-stage work has been dedicated to the training of future generations of designers, particularly at the Yale School of Drama. Lee received a Tony Award in 1983 for *K-2*, in which he designed a mountain on stage. Lee has mounted several one-man shows of his watercolours. ELLEN LAMPERT-GRÉAUX

Tony Davis, *Stage Design* (2001)

Lee, Robert E. *see* LAWRENCE, JEROME

Leeder, Sigurd *see* JOOSS, KURT; PHYSICAL PREPARATION

Leeds By the beginning of the twentieth century theatre in Leeds had largely moved from its roots south of the river (where in 1771 Tate Wilkinson had established the first permanent theatre in Hunslet Lane) to the more fashionable, and residentially expanding, north. The Theatre Royal (founded 1876) existed variously as a home for MELODRAMA, 'No. 1 tours' and weekly REPERTORY, until being metamorphosed into a shopping precinct in 1957. Perhaps its highlight was a three-week season of serious repertory presented by Milton Rosmer in late 1913, featuring SHAW, MASEFIELD, ARNOLD BENNETT and GALSWORTHY. This attempt to launch a repertory theatre to parallel Manchester's achievement was not to succeed. Audiences were poor for Shaw and divided by Galsworthy's politics (they liked Masefield). The Grand (founded 1878 by Wilson Barrett) remains a major touring venue and more recently the home of Opera North. VARIETY theatres flourished for long periods. The Moss Empire lasted until 1961 (still residually evident in one of Leeds' commercial arcades) and the City Varieties, sustained at a crucial time by television's *The Good Old Days*, still exists. The Hippodrome offered popular melodrama and variety until 1933, while south of the river from 1898 The Queen's offered cheerful sentiment and variety, becoming a cinema in 1924. The Leeds Playhouse opened in 1970 and grew into the WEST YORKSHIRE PLAYHOUSE (1990), finally establishing serious resident theatre in the city. AMATEUR THEATRE has always thrived, centred on the Civic Theatre, and in the 1930s and 1940s there was a lively UNITY Theatre movement. Since 1970 Leeds has also spawned enterprising independent theatre companies – amongst them RED LADDER, Interplay, Blah,Blah,Blah – and the innovative Leeds THEATRE IN EDUCATION company. MARTIN BANHAM

Léger, Fernand (b. Argentan, Normandy, France, 4 Feb. 1881; d. Gifsuryvette, Oise, France, 17 Aug. 1955) Painter and designer. He explored the spatial conflict between actors and scenery by shunning the use of perspective. Influenced by CIRCUS and VARIETY, he wanted to synthesize all theatrical elements. Léger designed two milestone works for the Ballets Suedois: *Skating Rink*, (1922) and the 'African ballet' *La Création du monde* (1923), inspired by tribal animal costumes.
DENISE L. TILLES

Christopher Green, *Leger and the Avant-Garde* (1976)

legislative theatre *see* BOAL, AUGUSTO

Lehár, Franz [Ferencz] (b. Komárom, Hungary, 30 April 1870; d. Bad Ischl, Austria, 24 Oct. 1948) Composer. Lehár worked as a military bandmaster and tried his composing hand at opera and waltzes before the production of his first stage musicals, *Wiener Frauen* (1902) and *Der Rastelbinder* (1902). The huge worldwide triumph of *Die lustige Witwe* (*The Merry Widow*, 1905) made him the international standard-bearer of the Viennese musical theatre through its most intense period of popularity prior to the First World War, in spite of the fact that only *Der Graf von Luxemburg* (1910) and *Zigeunerliebe* (1910) of a dozen subsequent prewar works achieved significant worldwide success. After the war, *Die blaue Mazur* (1920), *La Danza della Libellule* (1922), *Frasquita* (1922) and *Clo-Clo* (1924) were played internationally, but from 1925 he put aside the lighthearted strains of his *Lustige Witwe* days and began a second period of pre-eminence with a series of romantic operettas written to star the popular tenor Richard Tauber: *Paganini* (1925) *Der Zarewitsch* (1927), *Friederike* (1928) and, most successfully, *Das Land des Lächelns* (1929).   KURT GÄNZL

S. Frey, *Was sagt ihr zu diesem Erfolg* (1999)
B. Grün, *Gold and Silver: The Life and Times of Franz Lehár* (1970)
I. and H. Haffner, *Immer nur lächen* (1998)

Lehmann, Beatrix   (b. Wycombe, Bucks, 1 July 1903; d. London, 31 July 1979)   Actress who built her reputation after her debut in 1924 with many memorable performances, including Susie in *The Silver Tassie* (1929), Emily Brontë in *Wild Decembers* (1933), and Lavinia in *Mourning Becomes Electra* (1937). Politically active (she was an active trades unionist who became president of Equity in 1945; *see* UNIONS), Lehmann signed the Communist Party's People's Convention against the Second World War in 1941, which led to her being banned from the BBC. In the STRATFORD-UPON-AVON 1947–8 season she scored major successes playing Portia, Isabella, Viola and the Nurse. Her versatility cast her in a wide range of plays including *Huis Clos* (1946) and *The Birthday Party* (1958). Lehmann brought a powerful brooding presence to the stage, her voice described as being like a 'taut violin string'.
DAN REBELLATO

lehrstück   Didactic play, whose origins in Germany were musical. The term is associated with plays by BRECHT which, influenced by Japanese theatre, asked questions about political choices. Were evil means permissible to combat fascism? Might individuals be sacrificed in the interests of the group? The plays include: *He Who Says Yes* (1930), *The Measures Taken* (1930) and *The Exception and the Rule* (written 1930, first performed – in Hebrew – in Palestine, 1938).
TERRY HODGSON

Leicester   In the centre of the UK and only an hour from London, Leicester has taken some time to develop a clear theatre culture. Whereas until the 1950s the Palace, Theatre Royal, and Opera House existed, these buildings eventually succumbed to the planners' new developments for the city, leaving the council to build the 340-seater Phoenix Theatre as a temporary building, with only the amateur Little Theatre as any alternative for audiences. Throughout the 1960s and 1970s the Phoenix ran a repertory of new and classic plays, as well as receiving major touring companies such as the PIP SIMMONS GROUP. The new Haymarket Theatre, seating 800, was opened in 1973, with a repertory company directed by Robin Midgely, leaving the Phoenix Theatre to run an alternative repertoire under MICHAEL BOGDANOV as director. These developments coincided with an enlightened county education drama policy, which encouraged a plethora of theatre activity in all schools in the region, thus nurturing a new theatre audience without parallel in the UK. The national developments of performing arts departments at higher education level complemented this, and Leicester's then polytechnic (now De Montfort University) pioneered professional links between higher education and the Leicester theatres. While Leicester has been well served for theatre and dance on a middle scale, the larger-scale operatic and ballet repertoire has rarely been seen. In the 1990s the Haymarket became well known for its musicals, particularly those of STEPHEN SONDHEIM, at one end of the scale, while at the other the recently converted 'Y' Theatre, attached to the YMCA building, established itself as an ALTERNATIVE venue, having pioneered the New Works Festival in 1994, which promoted the work of new young artists.
NOEL WITTS

Leigh, Mike [Michael D.]   (b. Brocket Hall, Hatfield, Herts., 20 Feb. 1943)   Director and playwright. Leigh began to develop his distinctive creative method at the Midlands Arts Centre, Birmingham. His performers work through IMPROVISATION and WORKSHOPS, amassing the material from which Leigh constructs the final script. The proximity of acting and writing has produced some remarkable performances in plays like *Bleak Moments* (1970), *Babies Grow Old* (1974), *Ecstasy* (1979), *Goose Pimples* (1981) and *Greek Tragedy* (1989), in television plays like *Nuts in May* (1976), *Grown Ups* (1980) and *Meantime* (1983), and films like *High Hopes* (1988), *Life is Sweet* (1991), *Naked* (1993) and *Secrets and Lies* (1996). In Leigh's most famous play, *Abigail's Party* (1977), Alison Steadman, to whom Leigh was married, was by turns horrifying and hilarious as Beverley, the suburban tyrant who invites her neighbours for a disastrous drinks party. DAN REBELLATO

P. Clements, *The Improvised Play: The Work of Mike Leigh* (1983)
M. Coveney, *The World According to Mike Leigh* (1996)

Leigh, Vivien [Vivian Mary Hartley] (b. Darjeeling, India, 5 Nov. 1913; d. London, 8 July 1967) Actress, first noticed in *The Mask of Virtue* (1935), an adaptation of a STERNHEIM play. At Elsinore (1937) she played Ophelia opposite LAURENCE OLIVIER, whom she married in 1940 and partnered as Juliet (New York, 1940), Cleopatra to his Shakespeare's Antony and SHAW's Caesar (both 1951, the latter having been filmed with her in 1946 at Shaw's suggestion) and Lavinia to his Titus Andronicus (1955). Other notable performances were in *Duel of Angels* (London, 1958; New York, 1960) and *Ivanov* (New York, 1966). A famous beauty, she is best remembered on film in her Oscar-winning parts of Scarlett O'Hara in *Gone With the Wind* (1939) and Blanche opposite Marlon Brando in *A Streetcar Named Desire* (1951, a role which she had played to great acclaim on stage in 1949).
D. KEITH PEACOCK

A. Edwards, *Vivien Leigh* (1977)
H. Vickers, *Vivien Leigh* (1988)

Leighton, Margaret (b. Barnt Green, Worcs, 26 Feb. 1922; d. Chichester, Sussex, 13 January 1976) Actress. Noted for her elegance and sophistication, and her versatility in comedy and tragedy, she made her debut with the BIRMINGHAM REPERTORY THEATRE in 1938, and later appeared with the OLD VIC. She appeared regularly on the London and New York stages, with brief forays into the world of film. In London she starred in *The Cocktail Party* (1950) and *Separate Tables* (1956); she appeared in the latter play in New York two years later, and then starred in *The Night of the Iguana* (1961). DAVID STAINES

Leivick, Halper [Leivick Halper] (b. Cerva, Russia, 1 Dec. 1888; d. New York, 23 Dec. 1962) YIDDISH poet and playwright. Leivick left Russia as a political exile for New York in 1913 and between 1920 and 1949, the outstanding Yiddish poet of his time, he wrote some 20 plays there, including the world-renowned *The Golem* (written 1920, produced 1925); this story of the legendary monster made of clay has also been filmed and set to music. MARVIN CARLSON

Leno, Dan [George Galvin Wild] (b. London, 20 Dec. 1860; d. London, 31 Oct. 1904) The greatest of the MUSIC HALL comedians and PANTOMIME DAMES. He came from a family of music hall performers and went on the stage at three years old. He began as a clog dancer, winning a championship in Leeds in 1880, and later becoming world champion. A command performance before Edward VII brought him the title 'the King's Jester'. He was famous for his versatility and one-sided dialogues. His first pantomime was *Jack and the Beanstalk* (1886), and from 1888 he played the dame in the Drury Lane pantomimes for 15 years. Mental illness handicapped his last years. An autobiography written in 1901, *Dan Leno Hys Booke*, appeared in 1968, ghosted by T. G. Elder. REXTON S. BUNNETT

J. Hickory Wood, *Dan Leno* (1905)
G. Brandreth, *The Funniest Man on Earth* (1977)

Lenormand, Henri-René (b. Paris, 3 May 1882; d. Paris, 17 Feb. 1951) Playwright. Wrote gloomy but fascinating psychological dramas, notably *Les Ratés* (*The Failures*, 1920) about the deterioration, moral and physical, of an author and his actress-mistress, in which he turns to drink and kills her, then himself. Other plays include *Le Temps est un songe* (*Time is a Dream*, 1919), *Le Simoun* ('The simoon', 1920), *Le Mangeur de rêves* (*The Dream Doctor*, 1922), *A l'ombre du mal* ('In the shadow of evil', 1934) and *La folle du ciel* ('The madwoman of the heavens', 1936). Many plays contain tableaux: short scenes occupying one part of the stage, while the rest is blacked out, thereby emphasizing his dark and depressing view of life. His autobiographical *Confessions d'un auteur dramatique* appeared in 1949, and in English, as *Confessions of a Playwright* in 1952. WENDY SCOTT

Lenya, Lotte [Karoline Blamauer] (b. Vienna, 18 Oct. 1898; d. New York, 27 Nov. 1981) Singer and actress. After being a child tightrope walker, she studied ballet in Switzerland. She achieved her first great success after moving to Berlin, where she created the role of Pirate Jenny in *The Threepenny Opera* (1928) by BERTOLT BRECHT and KURT WEILL; she married Weill and accompanied him to the United States. Her first New York appearance was in WERFEL's *The Eternal Road* (1937). She reprised Pirate Jenny in the historic OFF-BROADWAY revival of *The Threepenny Opera* (1954), revisited her Weimar roots in the revue *Brecht on Brecht* (1961), which helped renew interest in Brecht and Weill, and was acclaimed for her world-weary Frau Schneider in *Cabaret* (1966). Wags decried her voice as an 'octave below laryngitis', but she was a powerful singer and a moving actress. Her recordings of Brecht and Weill, especially *The Rise and Fall of the City of Mahagonny*, *The Seven Deadly Sins* and *The Threepenny Opera*, remain benchmarks for later interpreters.
THOMAS F. CONNOLLY

Donald Spoto, *Lenya: A Life* (1989)

Leonard, Hugh (pseud. for John Keyes Byrne)
(b. Dublin, 9 Nov. 1926) Playwright. The wit, satire and mastery of construction obvious in Leonard's theatre disguise a depth of feeling and sense of disturbance running through his plays from *The Poker Session* (1963) to *Kill* (1982). His comedies, particularly *The Patrick Pearse Motel* (1971) and *Time Was* (1976), scalp the Irish middle class with ruthless insight, subverting their manners and morals. *Da* (1973) and *A Life* (1979) dissect old age and dying with great tenderness, giving to ordinary lives, as Leonard does at his best, extraordinary articulacy. Throughout his work Leonard plays complex games with time, making it, perhaps, the constant character in his theatre. He is a prolific stage and television writer; among his other plays are *Summer* (1974), *The Au Pair Man* (1968), *Moving* (1992) and *Love in the Title* (1998). He has written three volumes of memoirs, *Home Before Night* (1980), *Out After Dark* (1989) and *Rover and Other Cats* (1992).
FRANK MCGUINNESS

Kimball King, *Ten Modern Irish Playwrights* (1979)

Leonov, Leonid [Maksimovich] (b. Polukhino, nr. Moscow, 19 May 1899; d. Moscow, 8 Aug. 1994) Novelist and playwright. His first play, *Untilovsk* (1928), is a psychological study of social conflict, set in Siberia, while *Nashestviye* (*Invasion*, 1942) is one of the best plays to emerge from the war period. *Zolotaya kareta* ('The golden carriage', written 1946, staged 1957) continued the theme of ideological struggle between old and new, positive and negative elements in Soviet society characteristic of his prewar novels and taken up in his play *Polovchanskiye sady* (*The Orchards of Polovchansk*, 1938), staged by OKHLOPKOV in 1957.
NICK WORRALL

Harold B. Segel, *Twentieth-Century Russian Drama* (1979)

Lepage, Robert (b. Quebec City, 12 Dec. 1957) Actor, director. Lepage grew up in a house which revolved around the interaction of the English and French languages. As a result, language and cultural identity have become signature subjects for this French Canadian innovator, whose creation of striking visual imagery in theatre, opera and film has been acclaimed world-wide. Lepage graduated from the Conservatoire d'Art Dramatique in Quebec City in 1978 and then studied in Paris. When he returned to CANADA he became involved with Théâtre Repère, whose techniques were influenced by the San Francisco Dancers' Workshop. He developed his own collaborative working method and in 1984 directed his first show for Repère, *Circulations*, which toured throughout Canada.

Between 1985 and 1986 Lepage became the Artistic Director of Théâtre Repère, opened his first one-man show, Vinci, and directed the first production of *The Dragons' Trilogy*. Like other projects, this production changed its shape as it evolved through different casts and venues, transmuting from a 90-minute show to a six-hour extravaganza. It appeared as part of the LONDON INTERNATIONAL FESTIVAL OF THEATRE in 1987, bringing Lepage international attention and launching his international career. The work which followed includes: devising and directing *Polygraphe* (1987) and *Tectonic Plates* (1988), both of which toured nationally and internationally; a starring role in the film *Jesus of Montreal* (1988); appointment as the Head of the French Theatre section of the National Arts Centre in Ottawa; and the creation of a second one-man show, *Opium and Needles* (1991), at the NAC. In 1992 Lepage directed *A Midsummer Night's Dream* at the National Theatre in London and directed two operas for the Canadian Opera Company, *Duke Bluebeard's Castle* and *Ewartung*, which toured to New York and Edinburgh. At the 1994 EDINBURGH FESTIVAL Lepage opened the first stages of *The Seven Streams of the River Ota* and directed Peter Gabriel's *Secret World* tour. In 1995 he made his first film, *Le Confessionel*, and his one-man adaptation of *Hamlet*, entitled *Elsinore*, opened in Montreal. *Geometry of Miracles*, his play about the architect Frank Lloyd Wright, first toured internationally in 1998. He produced another solo show, *The Far Side of the Moon*, in 2000.

While not all his productions have received unanimously positive responses (*A Midsummer Night's Dream* was the subject of considerable controversy), his work has stirred interest and excitement wherever it has been on view. CHRISTIE CARSON

Remy Charest, *Robert Lepage: Connecting Flights*, trans. Wanda Romer Taylor (1997; first publ. as *Quelques zones de liberté*, 1995)
Joseph I. Donohoe, ed., *Robert Lepage: Theatre sans frontières* (2000)
Alison McAlpine, 'Robert Lepage', in *In Contact with the Gods*, ed. Maria M. Delgado and Paul Heritage (1996)

Lerner, Alan Jay (b. New York, 31 Aug. 1918; d. New York, 14 June 1986) Librettist and lyricist. Educated at Harvard, Lerner did most of his best work with composer FREDERICK LOEWE: *The Day Before Spring* (1945), *Brigadoon* (1947), *Paint Your Wagon* (1951), *My Fair Lady* (1956, based on SHAW's *Pygmalion*) and *Camelot* (1960). His work with other composers was generally less popular. He wrote fine dialogue, but frequently had problems constructing books, unless, as with *My*

Fair Lady, he was a adapting a well-made play. However, his literate and witty lyrics found few equals among the writings of his own generation. His autobiography, *The Street Where I Live*, appeared in 1978.
GERALD BORDMAN

G. Lees, *Inventing Champagne: The Worlds of Lerner and Loewe* (1990)

lesbian theatre

In Britain

The first clearly identifiable lesbian characters appeared on the public stage in Britain in FRANK MARCUS' play *The Killing of Sister George* in 1965. The subject of sexual attraction between women and the threat it might pose to the heterosexual couple, the family and society at large had been treated in a cautious way in *The Prisoner* by the French writer Edouard Bourdet (1887–1945) in 1926, and a translation of this play had been shown at the ARTS THEATRE. However, this was a private performance for CLUB members since the LORD CHAMBERLAIN refused a LICENCE for a public staging. Even in 1965 censorship meant that the word 'lesbian' could not be used, so the audience was led to make assumptions about the relationship of the two main women characters in *The Killing* through its portrayal as a sort of sado-masochistic mutual dependence.

Although lesbian characters were therefore represented before 1975, it is this date that could be said to mark the beginning of what may be properly called lesbian theatre, that is, theatre about lesbian issues controlled by lesbians. Jill Posener's play *Any Woman Can*, first performed by GAY SWEATSHOP in Leicester in November 1975, was written and directed by lesbians and had a mainly lesbian cast and stage crew. It was concerned with the experience of being a lesbian in a predominantly heterosexual society and was a 'coming out' play in which the main character begins and ends by telling the audience that they are looking at a screaming lesbian who is looking right back at them. Building on the success of this first production, the women members of Gay Sweatshop went on to perform pieces commissioned by writers such as Michelene Wandor, Sue Frumin, Maro Green, Jackie Kay and Bryony Lavery. The style was usually experimental and the themes were wide-ranging: some were serious, some were comic, but all were political in the broadest sense, challenging the accepted norms of patriarchal society and giving a central place to lesbian relationships. The characters were generally women.

In addition to Gay Sweatshop, other women's theatre groups began to write plays with lesbian themes. Siren Theatre Company was a group of radical

feminist musicians who met in Brighton in the late 1970s and performed their first show, *Mama's Gone A-Hunting*, in 1980. Loosely constructed from songs, sketches and readings, it demonstrated the violence women had suffered through history. In spite of their strongly feminist messages, the group played to appreciative audiences of both sexes, lasting as a company for nine years before disbanding, ironically just after receiving their first substantial amount of funding from the ARTS COUNCIL. They used both male and female characters in their plays, most of which were written by Tash Fairbanks, the men always being played by women in a caricatured fashion.

The 1970s and 1980s were decades during which lesbian theatre began to flourish, albeit always in minor venues and without proper financial backing. Two London theatres, the Drill Hall and the Oval House, were associated with the various groups which came into being. Julie Parker, in charge of the Drill Hall, and Kate Crutchley, theatre programmer at the Oval House, had both been associated with the first production of *Any Woman Can* and were committed to nurturing such lesbian companies as Hormone Imbalance, Hard Corps, Nitty Gritty, Shameful Practice, Red Rag, Character Ladies and Spin/Stir. Often performers moved from group to group, also appearing in CABARET, thus acquiring a faithful following. For example, Karen Parker and Debby Klein, originally members of Hard Corps, having formed their own company, Parker and Klein, performed both plays and cabaret. The emphasis being on entertainment, many shows had en extremely 'camp' flavour. Klein's *Coming Soon* (1985), described by her as a soap opera, was performed on a bright pink set presided over by a photograph of Joan Collins in her underwear, lit by a glowing pink triangle. This was a reference to one of the leading actresses in a highly popular and melodramatic television soap. Such references to popular culture and topical issues are typical of Parker and Klein's work and of that of Red Rag. Most of this work was aimed at a lesbian audience rather than a broader one, using the kind of humour which relied on 'insider' knowledge. The Oval Howe Theatre and the Drill Hall both provided a safe space in which lesbians could view theatre which for the first time related directly to their own experience.

The success of this work depended on the generous commitment of all involved. It was virtually impossible to find financial support, which meant that actors and technicians alike had to rely on unemployment benefit or have other part-time jobs. Even when audiences were appreciative, the strain of always managing on very restricted means prevented groups from staying together for very long. It is perhaps for this reason that individual performances and cabaret began increasingly to take over from 'straight' plays during the 1990s. Also, there was a growing interest in 'physical' theatre, a communication through the body and sound as well as, or even instead of, traditional dialogue. Spin/Stir (the name given to a collective formed by ex-University of Kent students in 1990) dealt with important social issues such as child abuse and incest through metaphor, using a blend of poetry and physical theatre to break away from a linear narrative to make stories which the audience understand at some deep level. This is what Joelle Taylor, Spin/Stir's writer/performer, described as 'social surrealism'. This kind of theatre, because it depends so much on performance skill, like cabaret, is ephemeral. Even if it exists in scripted form, it is unlikely to find a publisher.

Only one play which deals with lesbian concerns and offers a lesbian point of view has been created in a major theatre outside the FRINGE: that is SARAH DANIEL's *Neaptide* (1986). I would call this a lesbian play because of the obvious sympathies of the author, rather than lesbian theatre, since the director was a man and the whole production was not conceived from a particularly lesbian point of view.

In the United States

The first lesbian character appeared on the American stage in *The God of Vengeance* by Shalom Asch (1880–1957), written in YIDDISH in 1907 and performed in English in New York in 1922. In spite of an explicit love scene between a young girl and a prostitute (considerably cut in the Broadway version), some members of the audience, as well as certain critics, did not fully appreciate the implications of the relationship between the two women. There was a similar response to Edouard Bourdet's play *The Captive*, when a translation of it from the French opened in Broadway in 1926. This play, which had already caused a stir in Paris, was closed by a police raid after a year in New York, since by then no one was in any doubt about the real nature of the attraction between the married heroine, Irene, and her beloved Mme D'Aiguines, although the subject had been very delicately handled by Bourdet, one of the lovers never even appearing. The word 'lesbian' was not spoken in either of the above mentioned plays, nor in the next Broadway production to broach love between women. LILLIAN HELLMAN's *The Children's Hour* (1934) examines the disastrous effect on two young schoolteachers of the scandalous rumours spread by one of their pupils. 'Unnatural love' is finally confessed by one of the teachers before she goes off to die, leaving her partner to marry and have a 'normal' life.

None of the plays described so far could be categorized as 'lesbian theatre', since that phrase is usually reserved for work created by lesbians for lesbians. It was only in the wake of the Women's Liberation Movement in the 1960s that a number of feminist groups identifying as lesbian came into being. The 1970s saw the formation of the Lavender Cellar Theater and the Minneapolis Lesbian Resource Center in Minneapolis, whose productions included two plays by Pat Suncircle – *Prisons*, set in women's detention centres, and *Cory*, the study of a 16-year-old-girl trying to come to terms with her sexuality. Some groups, such as the Red Dyke Theater, founded in Atlanta in 1974, sought to provide entertainment for lesbians themselves; others, for example the Lesbian-Feminist Theater Collective of Pittsburgh (1937), wanted to show 'straights' what lesbianism was really about. During the 1970s and 1980s companies sprang up all over the United States offering a variety of theatrical performances – sometimes scripted plays, often revues or shows of a more improvised nature. Many scripts have been collected and stored in the Lesbian Herstory Archive. When Kate McDermott was looking for a new lesbian play to direct, she found very few were available, a situation which eventually led her to seek out scripts from a number of sources and through different contacts. This enabled her to edit *Places, Please*, the first anthology of lesbian plays, published in 1985.

Two of the plays in this anthology have received several subsequent productions. *Dos Lesbos*, by Terry Baum and Carolyn Myers, having opened in Ollie's bar in Oakland, California, in 1981, went on to run for two years in the San Francisco Bay Area and in Santa Cruz. Publication gave it a new lease of life. Its popularity was due to its light-hearted approach and the mixture of theatrical genres employed, including VAUDEVILLE. It also only requires two actresses. *8 × 10 Glossy* by Sarah Dreher, the second most widely performed play in the anthology, is more straightforwardly realistic, as is most of Dreher's work. Realism is the predominant mode of another well-known lesbian identified writer, Janc Chambers. This resemblance to more conventional theatre is possibly the reason why her work is popular. Two of her plays, *A Late Snow*, published in 1979, and *Last Summer at Bluefish Cove* (1982), have been performed all over the English-speaking world, so that it could be said that Chambers is the best-known and most successful lesbian playwright in the United States.

The rise of critical theory brought a move away from realism, however. In 1989 the feminist theorist Jill Dolan published an article in which she maintained that classical realism was inappropriate to deal with lesbian issues as it necessarily led to the marginalization of the lesbian subject. Other influential literary theorists, such as Sue-Ellen Case, Elin Diamond and Janelle Reinelt, also held the view that the representation of the lesbian subject on stage should be multifaceted, and should involve exploration of lesbianism in all its aspects rather than the realistic portrayal of one or two individuals. The company which has concentrated most extensively on the deconstructed lesbian subject is SPLIT BRITCHES, named after the first play devised by the company members, Peggy Shaw, Lois Weaver and Deborah Margolin. Shaw and Weaver met while touring in Europe; Shaw with Hot Peaches and Weaver with SPIDERWOMAN. Shaw was persuaded to join Spiderwoman and it was within this company that the show *Split Britches* was performed. The separate company Split Britches, formed in 1981, went on to write, devise and perform shows throughout the 1980s and 1990s, including *Upwardly Mobile Home* (1984), *Little Women* (1988), *Anniversary Waltz* (1989), *Belle Reprieve* (with Bloolips, 1991) and *Lesbians who Kill* (1992). They also worked with other authors, for example Joyce Halliday on an adaptation of Isabel Miller's *Patience and Sarah* (1984), and Holly Hughes on *Dress Suits to Hire* (1989).

Hughes, Weaver and Shaw worked together at the WOW Café in New York, which Weaver and Shaw had founded and Hughes administered for a year. Although Hughes had come to New York as a painter, she took easily to performing and writing. Among her other shows are *Lady Dick*, *Well of Hormones* and *World Without End*. The WOW Café was the offspring of the WOW (Women's One World) Festivals in New York in 1980 and 1981, which attracted theatre groups from all over Europe and the United States. Inspired by their success, Shaw, Weaver and others organized benefits to raise money to establish a permanent venue, the WOW Café at 330 E 11th St, New York. It has been described by Weaver as community theatre in its best sense, using volunteers and professionals to put on shows and organize events. It has provided a base for experimental lesbian work in which all aspects of sexuality and sexual representation may be explored in a totally non-realistic way. SANDRA FREEMAN

Sue-Ellen Case, *Feminism and Theatre* (1988)
——, *Performing Feminisms* (1990)
Kaier Curtin, *We Can Always Call Them Bulgarians* (1987)
Sandara Freeman, *Putting Your Daughters on the Stage* (1997)
Lynda Hart and Peggy Phelan, eds, *Acting Out: Feminist Performances* (1993)
Carol Martin, ed., *A Sourcebook of Feminist Theatre and Performance* (1996)
Alan Sinfield, *Out on Stage: Lesbian and Gay Theatre in the Twentieth Century* (2000)

Lessac, Arthur *see* VOICE; VOICE TRAINING

Levin, Hanoch (b. Tel Aviv, 18 Dec. 1943; d. Tel Aviv, 18 Aug. 1999) Playwright, poet, writer and director. He began his playwriting career shortly after the 1967 war, when his bitter political reviews attacked Israeli politics and national euphoria following the occupation of the territories: *You and Me and the Next War* (1968); *Ketchup* (1969); *The Queen of the Bath* (1970). The last of these shocked the public so much that the CAMERI THEATRE stopped its run following fierce attacks in the press and physical assaults on the actors. Except for one later political review (*The Patriot*, 1982), following the Israeli invasion of Lebanon, Levin reverted to full-length plays, exposing grotesquely the vain ambitions underlying human behaviour. His heroes are normally small people who mercilessly compete with others on the portions of success bourgeois life allows them: marriage, own apartment and (especially) sexual conquests (notably *Heffetz*, 1972; *Ya'acobi and Leidental*, 1972; *Shitz*, 1974; *Krum*, 1975; *Popper*, 1976; *Rubber Merchants*, 1978; *Suitcase Packers*, 1983; *The Labour of Life*, 1989; *The Hesitator*, 1990). A third phase of his work carries his THEATRE OF CRUELTY to the cosmic dimensions of mythological parables, in which man is squeezed into his bodily and spiritual elements by the painful presence of imminent destruction and death (notably *The Execution*, 1980; *The Sorrows of Job*, 1981; *The Great Whore of Babylon*, 1982; *Beaten and Defeated*, 1989; *Dreaming Child*, 1991; *Mouth Open*, 1995; *Beheading*, 1996; *The People That Walked in Darkness*, 1998). In *Murder* (1997) his perspective on 30 years of bloodshed in the Middle East, since his dramatic writing began, becomes a shuddering political parable. *Requiem* (1999), written and produced while a terminal disease was conquering his body, is, like his last book of poetry published the same year, a sad, passionate and powerful account of, and resignation to, imminent death. AVRAHAM OZ

Lessac, Arthur *see* VOICE; VOICE TRAINING

Levy, Benn *see* CUMMINGS, CONSTANCE

Levy, Deborah *see* WOMEN'S THEATRE GROUP

Lewenstein, Oscar [Silvion] (b. London, 8 Jan. 1917; d. Hove, Sussex, 23 Feb. 1997) Theatrical manager, producer. Lewenstein cut his theatrical teeth as general manager of Glasgow UNITY (1947–9). In 1952 he became the general manager of the ROYAL COURT, convening in 1954 the first council of the ENGLISH

STAGE COMPANY. Combining socialist principles with effective business sense, Lewenstein presented the work of OSBORNE, FRIEL and GENET, and was responsible for the British premières of BRECHT's *The Threepenny Opera* (1956) and IONESCO'S *Rhinoceros* (1960), and transfers of THEATRE WORKSHOP productions to the WEST END. He was also a successful film producer (e.g. *The Knack, Tom Jones*). In 1972, he was appointed Artistic Director of the Royal Court, and by 1975 he had produced many successes, notably seasons of plays by FUGARD and ORTON. His autobiography, *Kicking Against the Pricks*, was published in 1994. DAN REBELLATO

Lewis, Robert [Bobby] (b. Brooklyn, New York, 16 March 1909; d. New York, 11 April 1997) Actor, director and teacher. A founding member of the pioneering GROUP THEATER in 1931 and in 1947 of its vital descendant, the ACTORS' STUDIO. ELIA KAZAN cast MARLON BRANDO in *A Streetcar Named Desire* after seeing him in one of Lewis' classes there; other pupils who went on to make their mark in theatre or film include ELI WALLACH, Anne Bancroft, Karl Malden, Meryl Streep, Faye Dunawaye and Frank Langella. Lewis argued with Kazan and left the Actors' Studio but continued to teach, act and direct, most notably *Brigadoon* (1947), *Teahouse of the August Moon* (1953) and *Jamaica* (1957). He wrote *Method – or Madness?* (1958) and an autobiography, *Slings and Arrows* (1984). CHARLES LONDON

Lewis, [John] Saunders (b. Wallasey, Merseyside, 10 Oct. 1893; d. Cardiff, 1 Sept. 1985) Playwright. One of the most controversial and prolific writers and scholars in Wales, he was an uncompromising activist on behalf of Welsh nationalism, a fiercely religious convert to Roman Catholicism, a right-wing elitist who was an inspiration to later left-wing playwrights and poets. Despite all this, his plays were seldom produced after his death, Sion Eirian's eloquent translation of the verse drama *Blodeuwedd* ('Woman of Flowers', 1948) for the Actors' Touring Company being a notable exception; during his lifetime, by contrast, he was seen as Wales's major contribution to theatre and compared with Corneille, Molière and ELIOT.

Born of Welsh parents who had moved to Wallasey, Lewis was brought up a Welsh-speaking Liverpudlian and in 1922 went to Wales as a lecturer in Welsh Studies at University College Swansea. In 1936, while president of the newly formed Welsh Nationalist Party, subsequently known as Plaid Cymru (which he headed from 1926 to 1939), he was imprisoned for setting fire to an RAF Bombing School in Caernarvonshire. Lewis went into semi-retirement during the 1940s and 1950s but re-emerged in 1962 urging revolutionary action to save the Welsh language and leading the militant Cymdeithas yr Iaith Gymraeg (Welsh Language Society), later even denouncing Plaid Cymru.

He wrote around 20 plays, only the first (*The Eve of St John*, 1921) in English. His work is often based on Welsh legend, though he berated his fellow countrymen for ignorance of their own mythology; he argued for a Welsh national theatre, but complained that there were no practitioners capable of performing his own plays.

BBC Television produced his last play, *Branwen*, in 1971, and Theatr yr Ymylon produced *Blodeuwedd*, *Siwan* ('A King's Daughter', 1956) and *Gymerwch chi Sigaret?* ('Have a Cigarette?', 1956) in the 1970s, but his work was rarely produced thereafter. DAVID ADAMS

I. M. Williams, *A Straitened Stage: A Study of the Theatre of J. Saunders Lewis* (1991)

librettists The role of the librettist, the playwright who creates the book and often the lyrics of a musical play, has changed tremendously over the course of the twentieth century. However, it can remain a thankless job: the librettist is blamed if a musical fails and is overlooked if it is successful.

In the first decades, in the shadow of W. S. GILBERT, musical libretti ('little books') were either light-minded comedies involving tangled romances or romantic operettas with a strongly middle-European flavour. The former were typified by the works of P. G. WODEHOUSE and GUY BOLTON, authors of several musicals with composer JEROME KERN (*Oh, Boy!, Leave it to Jane*), and such humorists as GEORGE S. KAUFMAN, MOSS HART and Herbert Fields, who frequently wrote vehicles for popular comedians like the MARX BROTHERS (*Animal Crackers*), and William Gaxton and Victor Moore (*Of Thee I Sing, Anything Goes*). Such shows were frequently a series of comic sketches strung together as a loose plot line; continuity and fidelity to reality were not important considerations.

The operetta genre, as seen in the work of Dorothy Donnelly, Rida Johnson Young and Otto Harbach, among others, tended to recycle the same sentimental plot ideas – the romance of an aristocrat and a commoner, for example – against a series of changing backgrounds, although Germany or Vienna were the favourite settings for such works as *The Student Prince* and *Blossom Time*.

The pivotal figure in the history of librettists is OSCAR HAMMERSTEIN II, a former operetta practitioner, who, with *Show Boat* (1927) and *Oklahoma!* (1943), pioneered the integration of musical numbers into a relatively coherent and serious narrative. The success of the latter show ushered in a new generation of sophisticated librettists, many of whom had careers as non-musical playwrights or screenwriters. These included ALAN JAY LERNER (*Brigadoon, My Fair Lady*), ARTHUR LAURENTS (*West Side Story, Gypsy*), Joseph Stein (*Fiorello!, Fiddler on the Roof*), Michael Stewart (*Bye Bye Birdie, Hello Dolly!*), and Peter Stone (*1776*). Such librettists greatly expanded the range of subject matter in MUSICAL THEATRE, treating race relations, politics and important historical events, in addition to the usual romantic comedy topics. During this period the libretto frequently consisted of lengthy scenes of spoken dialogue which shared equal time with the musical numbers.

The advent of the sung-through show in the 1970s, especially with the musicals of ANDREW LLOYD WEBBER, has redefined the librettist's role to that of a 'scenarist-lyricist', a role not unlike that of the opera librettist. These writers include TIM RICE (*Jesus Christ Superstar, Evita, Chess*), Charles Hart (*The Phantom of the Opera*), and ALAIN BOUBLIL (*Les Misérables, Miss Saigon*). In some cases, notably in the work of STEPHEN SONDHEIM, the lyricist on *West Side Story* who usually writes his own music and lyrics, the librettist functions solely as scenarist, e.g. Hugh Wheeler on *Sweeney Todd* or JAMES LAPINE on *Sunday in the Park with George* and *Into the Woods*.

In America, the gradual fading of the sung-through musical has seen a resurgence of librettists, many of whom are established playwrights, such as Lapine, MARSHA NORMAN (*The Secret Garden*) and TERRENCE MCNALLY (*Cragtime*). Playwrights have also worked consistently as librettists in opera, from HOFMANNSTAHL (e.g. *Der Rosenkavalier*) and AUDEN (*Seven Deadly Sins, The Rake's Progress, Paul Bunyan*) to BOND (*The Cat, We Come to the River*). DAVID BARBOUR

licence Rules and regulations covering theatrical performance have changed enormously over the course of the twentieth century. International conventions address some areas (e.g. COPYRIGHT), while others (such as health and safety) depend on local conditions. A licence has to be obtained from the relevant authority both in order to be able to perform a play (i.e. permission from the playwright, usually via an AGENT or the estate of a dead playwright if the work is still in copyright) and in order to have the venue – and the production – passed as fit and safe for public attendance. CHARLES LONDON

See also CENSORSHIP; LORD CHAMBERLAIN; THEATRICAL ESTATES.

G. McFarlane, *A Practical Introduction to Copyright* (1989)

LIFT *see* LONDON INTERNATIONAL FESTIVAL OF THEATRE

Ligeti, György *see* MUSIC THEATRE

lighting, history of Since 1900 the evolution of theatrical lighting technology has progressed with amazing speed. Light in the theatre benefited enormously from the explosion of technological innovation in the electric and computer industries that began just before and continued into the twentieth century. This new technology, growing ever more quickly, combined with the imaginative impulse of directors, producers and designers, produced and sustained major advances in light quality and control, and thereby expanded the variety of uses and facility with which light was used on stage.

The twentieth century's revolutionary change from gas to electricity produced increasing innovation in the brightness and quality of electric light. In the early 1900s electric lamps, which were dim and yellow, were relegated to cramped lives inside bunch lights or in footlight troughs and were used primarily to wash the stage with soft and uneven light. The spotlights used to isolate or pick out special places on the stage still employed the arc or limelight systems developed early in the nineteenth century, despite the high heat, potentially harmful vapours and fire hazards they produced. Not until the introduction of the metallized carbon filament, with its increased durability and output of 3 lumens per watt of electricity (an increase of half a lumen per watt) did spotlights begin to utilize the electric lamp. Less hot than arc light and without the vapours of limelight, this new lamp began to compete actively with the established spotlight sources. In 1905 the major electrical companies began improving the durability and intensity of the lamps available for use on stage. The Schwabe Company of Germany led in pioneering the innovation until the 1930s, when America's General Electric Company and Britain's Strand Electric began active competition.

Arguably the most important development in electric lamps in the first half of the century came in 1907 with the advent of the tungsten filament. The ductile qualities and high gasification or melting point of tungsten enabled electrical engineers to create a filament of high durability and concentrated design. This ability to concentrate the metal filament to as small a point as possible increased the efficiency of these lamps. Between 1911 and 1915 electric lamps became brighter and longer-lived with the development of the drawn tungsten filament lamp. Technicians discovered that introduction of an inert gas, usually nitrogen or argon, into the glass envelope of the lamp or bulb decreased the rapidity with which the filament decayed. These new

· Lighting ·

Light allows us to see – but only when that light is reflected by an object. What is it about the stage that makes one think that light itself can have shape, the source itself seem so compelling – that beam present there in the air? Light is difficult to talk about. It is a thing that human beings tend to ignore, to take for granted, simply not to question. Perhaps the fact that we perceive light only when it strikes an object and is reflected back into our eye makes it difficult to separate light from the object lit. Certainly a discussion of colour in light almost invariably becomes a discussion of the colour of the objects that are revealed by the light, and not the colour of the light itself. The fact that light is controlled and manipulated by design in a theatrical production adds yet another layer. What is it that allows us to understand without being able to articulate? What is it that is satisfying about a visual image in the same way that a metaphor or turn of phrase is satisfying? What is the nature of the fabrication (putting light on the stage is as much a fabrication as putting paint on a canvas) that gives form or shape to a production? Is it the control and manipulation of time? Is it the concealment or revelation and perhaps creation of a space? Is it the changing from one moment to the next of one carefully composed or focused and designed picture to another? The mind tries to make sense of everything it perceives. The human eye has evolved to organize the many little details that it sees at any one time into one unit. The eye only needs a clue or two to allow an entire image to register. Anything that is put on-stage – an actor speaking words, wearing clothes, moving; furniture, architecture, spatial forms, light – is designed to be part of an image, *not* to represent reality. Each detail is a conscious choice of the actor, director or designer made to present an image that will stimulate each of us to create a picture far beyond any single unit that our eye perceives.

Light does not necessarily reveal. It is the pattern of light and dark, brightness and shadow – contrast – that allows our eyes to perceive what is on the stage at any given moment. If it is equally bright everywhere, we may not be able to sense depth or to focus on the important action. Light can reveal a shape, or change it, or destroy it. One sees an object in space only as it is revealed by light. If a circle is hit by one slash of light you see it as a slash, not as a circle. If a yellow costume is hit by a purple light, its true colour is obscured. The wonder of light is that through manipulation of these very things – beams of different coloured light – a lighting designer can control what is revealed to the audience. Light can push and pull, literally throw objects around, causing us to see them differently – in a 'new light' – from moment to moment.

A lighting designer takes certain light sources, places them quite exactly, colours them, and decides whether they should be on or off at any given moment. When a choice is made about a light on-stage – whether it should be soft edged or sharp, whether the source should be visible or not, whether it should be dim or bright, whether it should be bluish lavender or pinkish lavender, whether it should hit a large part of the stage or only a small concentrated area – it implies to the audience that this choice means something. This meaning may be subliminal, perhaps cannot be articulated, but the audience will sense it. The meaning may be the function; the fact that the light helps the focus of the scene by placing emphasis (making it bright) in a certain place, or by creating lines of light or shadow to lead the eye to a given place, or by cooling areas around the point of focus so that the background tends to recede from the eye. Or the use of the light may signal that something in the play that is occurring now relates directly to something that happened at an earlier time. It may imply a deeper meaning, may in some mysterious way make us discover something about our inner selves, what we have been and what we may become. It is perhaps in non-verbal ways running parallel to the words of the play that we discover ourselves in the world of that play.

A lighting designer can learn much about colour and angle in light from studying nature. The rewards not only of looking but of analysing are immense, but one does not put 'natural light' on the stage. It is by studying how painters have taken these natural occurrences and manipulated them for their own effect that a lighting designer can learn why to use such an effect on-stage and how to manipulate it in order to create a certain quality, ambience or sensation. The control and the use of artifice to present the impression of what is found in nature, in the real world, is equal in painting and on the stage. By carefully studying the effect in painting, whether it be dramatic or simple, the lighting designer discovers how humans perceive and react to light. The play of light and shadow is the material of which visual communication in theatre is made. It is through such contrast that our eye discovers the place and the dimension of actors and objects on-stage. By focusing and composing the picture, something that both painter and lighting designer must do, the audience eye is allowed to enter the scene and then follow the action freely through the landscape without jumping nervously from place to place. The opposite is also true. When there is no focus there is gibberish. For the lighting designer the tools are always the same – angle, colour and intensity. It is, however, the kind of production that will determine how these tools are used to make a composition in space and in time. It may be that this particular production needs for the light to seem to come from actual sources on-stage – or it may well be that the light in this production should actually come from those sources. There are two very different theatrical conventions. It may be that the play needs theatrical light defining the actor separate from the surroundings and creating the space (not necessarily the atmosphere) of each scene; or the production may need simple presentational light to reveal the actor. The style or determination of the rules to be followed in any production is set in advance either tacitly or by common agreement among all involved in order to convey some unity of purpose. Light on-stage bears no resemblance to 'real' light. There are certain conventions so accepted by most of us, audience and designer alike, that they are *considered* 'real'. These conventions are methods that have been in practice for so long that their use is unquestioned. For example, light that comes from the front, positioned in the auditorium, is so often used to light faces on-stage that the audience takes it for granted; they seem not to notice it. The light does not seem to come from anywhere; it just is. Conventions came to be accepted over the time that indoor theatre has developed and owe much to the course that lighting technology has followed in this time. Technological advancement has revolutionized the way we make light in theatre, and the conventions that we had established previously are in flux. As we gain more control over the light it becomes important to us to use the light to make its presence felt. By using light in a conventional way a designer allows it to go unnoticed, taken for granted. By breaking with convention a designer can make an audience wake up, sit up and take notice; it is a signal that there are things going on that are not quite what meets the eye at first glance.

The lighting designer has few choices to make – what kind of light should be used, where the light should come from, what colour it is, when it should be on, how bright or dim, and how quickly it should change. Any playing space and players within that space are best revealed by a balance of light from all angles – the front, the side and the back. Often the possibility of having light from these three angles is limited by the scenery. A box set with walls and a ceiling eliminates all backlight and sidelight as well except from the downstage. This makes it difficult (but obviously not impossible) to make the actors visible – particularly if the background is the same colour as the costumes or skin or hair of the actors. A lighting designer fights for at least two of these angles and may feel that the scenery should be redesigned to allow it. But there may be definite stylistic reasons for designing a set that by its nature limits the sources of light. It is the space that must ultimately bring its own light. The lighting designer does not run roughshod over the ideas of the set designer. Instead of being limited by the space provided by the set, the lighting designer accepts it as a statement of the idea on which the production is based. The set designer must accept the responsibility for making sure that the space is indeed as it was intended, that the light the space allows is the light the space calls for. Obviously a situation comedy with no possibility of lighting the set upstage centre is not intended by the set designer. The time spent at the drafting board trying to integrate lighting ideas with possibilities provided by the space is the best dialogue imaginable between lighting designer and set designer, particularly if it happens at a time when the lighting designer may still have some influence over the design of the space.

Economics makes it necessary for a lighting designer to work incredibly quickly. Set and costume designers have weeks or months to execute and refine their ideas. The lighting designer must plan in advance, of course, but the final ideas are put on the stage and polished within relatively few hours. The choices of what kinds of lights to use and where they should be, even what colour they should be, are difficult to change once the lights have been hung in the theatre; but choices of on or off and when and how intensity changes, i.e. the composition of the picture at any given moment, must be determined once the production is on-stage. Getting in touch with one's feelings, with one's deeper intuition, about a production as expressed through light is very difficult, particularly in a quick minute. The lighting designer is 'super' audience and must develop an ability to sense when the dynamic is right, allowing the audience easy entrance to the piece, at the same time being totally involved with the mechanics and problems to overcome in the actual process of lighting the play. It is important that the lighting designer allow the layers of the play to be perceived, perhaps only subliminally; allow the audience to feel the richness, the complexity that is within the play. The designer must help make clear the differences between this scene and that, must allow the audience to be in touch with what is unique to this production.

Lighting is much like performance. Totally ephemeral. **JENNIFER TIPTON** lamps, now available in 750–1000 watt sizes, had an increased output of 20 lumens per watt. The cleanliness, relative lack of heat, low maintenance and greater brightness of these new lamps meant that they were employed widely and remained the advanced technology in lamp design until 1929.

During this period major theatres around the world began the wholesale conversion to electricity. The Paris Opera, London's SAVOY THEATRE, New York's People's Theater and the Baldwin Theater of San Francisco were four of the first to convert totally to electric lighting systems. Innovation in electrical distribution and control grew early in the century, though at a slower pace. Electrical wiring in theatres became easier and safer to install and operate. This facility in installation, combined with the absence of bulky gas pipe and rubber tubing, created a larger variety of possibilities for lighting positions. Lighting fixtures in and over the auditorium, better known as front-of-house lighting, became widespread in the 1930s.

Improvements in reflector and lens design of the spotlight, the workhorse lighting fixture, called for another leap in lamp technology. Following the development in the 1930s of gaseous discharge lamps (fluorescent, neon, etc.), the tungsten halogen lamp was developed. This lamp combined the effective tungsten filament with filament-renewing halogens, such as iodine or bromide gases, creating a stronger, whiter light and a more durable lamp. Experimentation with the size and shape of these new lamps led to increased versatility in their stage application.

As the intensity and qualities of stage lighting instruments improved, the demand for more durable and yet subtle methods for colouring light increased. Turn-of-the-century theatrical practitioners shone light through coloured silks, giving hue to light emanating softly from the wings. The Fortuny system (named after the Italian FASHION designer) of bouncing light into silks and on to the stage quickly became outmoded with the introduction of colour media or filters. Colour filters eliminated from the light all but the desired colour of the spectrum. Initially these filters, made of coloured gelatine, were a great improvement, using light more economically. The plastic industry's development of high heat resistant materials further improved both the efficiency of the light transmitted and the quality and consistency of the hue. By 1960 designers had up to 70 various filtered colours from which to choose, and the variety has continued to increase.

Dimming equipment, a novel electrical technology, evolved from the bulky and primitive water-barrel resistance dimmers, which regulated current and therefore intensity, to coiled-wire resistance dimmers, which were a bit less bulky but generated tremendous heat as current was stored in their repetitive coils. Not until the 1950s when autotransformers and then electronic dimmers reduced the size of the mechanism of dimming, did this technology progress.

The introduction of computerized lighting control in the late 1960s was the significant technological advance of the latter part of the century. Computer control affected theatrical lighting in many and profound ways. Initially, simple memory boards were designed to change light on stage automatically by shifting from one file of information to another in emulation of the manually controlled electronic preset boards. States of light on stage, known as cues, could be quickly and simply recorded into a computer's memory as a file, including cue name or number and instruction of fade time out of the current file into a subsequent one.

Improvements in computer control include streamlined methods of saving accumulated information, an increase in the ability to handle complex timing and an array of special effects programs. This revolution in stage lighting control coincided with and undoubtedly contributed to the emergence of the theatrical lighting specialist: the designer of light. Combining the improvements in light quality developed in the beginning of the twentieth century with computerized control of cueing and focus, the theatrical lighting designer has become a master of dramatic time and space limited only by his or her imagination.

CHRISTOPHER AKERLIND

See also COSTUME DESIGN; DESIGN; SOUND.

Willard P. Bellman, *Lighting for the Stage: Art and Practice* (1967)

Gosta M. Bergman, *Lighting in the Theatre* (1977)

F. Cerny, *Innovations in Stage and Theatre Design* (1972)

Louis Hartmann, *Theatre Lighting* (1930)

W. O'Dea, *The Social History of Lighting* (1958)

Richard Pilbrow, *Stage Lighting* (1970)

Francis Reid, *Discovering Stage Lighting* (1993)

Lillie, Beatrice [Gladys] (Lady Robert Peel) (b. Toronto, 29 May 1898; d. Henley-on-Thames, Oxon., England, 20 Jan. 1989) Comedienne. A child performer in Canada, she first appeared on stage in England in 1914 in MUSIC HALL. She made her reputation ('The Funniest Woman in the World') in a series of REVUES and her American debut in *André Charlot's Revue of 1924*. During the Second World War she travelled extensively entertaining the Allied armed forces. Her one-woman show, *An Evening with Beatrice Lillie*, ran (with minor changes) from 1952 to 1960. Her last appearance was in *High Spirits* (1964), a musical adaptation of NOEL COWARD's *Blithe Spirit*. Elegant and slender, she had a subversive sense of humour, making an audience laugh with the raising of an eyebrow or suddenly swinging a long string of pearls down around her body. Her autobiography, *Every 'Other' Inch a Lady*, appeared in 1972. EUGENE BENSON

Limon, Jose *see* CHOREOGRAPHY

Lincoln Center for the Performing Arts This venue, inaugurated in 1960 and covering an extensive site on the Upper West Side of New York, comprises five buildings which house the Metropolitan Opera, the New York City Opera, the New York Philharmonic and the New York City Ballet, the Vivian Beaumont Theatre and a library for the performing arts. The theatre, conceived along the lines of a national theatre, was opened in 1965 with Büchner's *Danton's Death* and a season combining new American plays with European classics staged by its own resident repertory company. A smaller auditiorium (now called the Mitzi E. Newhouse Theater) was opened in 1966, and both were taken over by JOSEPH PAPP and his NEW YORK SHAKESPEARE FESTIVAL after a somewhat shaky start under the directorship of ELIA KAZAN had failed to ignite critical acclaim for the venue. Financial difficulties forced Papp to abandon his directorship in 1977 and the guiding hand passed to various luminaries such as EDWARD ALBEE and Woody Allen without much success until the arrival of GREGORY MOSHER (1985–92), who was followed by Andre Bishop. HELEN RAPPAPORT

Lindsay, Howard *see* CROUSE, RUSSELL

Linklater, Kristin (b. Edinburgh, 22 April 1936) Voice teacher. Daughter of the writer Eric Linklater, she graduated in 1956 from the London Academy of Music and Drama, where she had been a pupil of Iris Warren. After a spell in Scottish repertory, she returned to LAMDA as a trainee teacher under Warren. When Warren died in 1963, Linklater went to the United States and, as well as working in many repertory theatres, opened her own New York studio where she trains actors and teachers in her psychological and emotional approach. Her widely used book *Freeing the Natural Voice* (1976) was followed by *Freeing Shakespeare's Voice* (1992), which reflects her work with Shakespeare and Company (co-founded with Tina Packer in 1972). In Boston in 1990 Linklater founded The Company of Women, an all-women Shakespeare company which, in addition to touring, also provides outreach and education projects for women and girls. Her influence has spread beyond the United States to Europe and Australia. LYN DARNLEY

See also VOICE TRAINING.

literary manager *see* DRAMATURG

Lithuania *see* SOVIET UNION

little theatre A name applied to small theatres, mostly run on a shoestring, not motivated by profit, usually offering a different play selection from that presented by the predominant stages, and sharing some sense of common identity. In America the focus was on AMATEUR groups with a regional base, and the name superseded the label CIVIC THEATRE at the beginning of the twentieth century. In terms of impact, the most significant 'little theatre' was the PROVINCETOWN PLAYERS through their association with EUGENE O'NEILL. Prominent figures elsewhere in the US included teacher and writer Percy Mackaye; MAURICE BROWNE, who founded the Chicago Little Theater in 1919 with Ellen van Volkenburg, his wife; and the director KENNETH MACGOWAN. As in Britain, the movement was at its strongest between the world wars.

Amateur theatre also played an important part in Britain, through organizations such as the BRITISH DRAMA LEAGUE and the LITTLE THEATRE GUILD OF GREAT BRITAIN, and through individual groups, from the aesthetic, classical work of the MADDERMARKET THEATRE to the political challenge of UNITY. The term occasionally overlapped confusingly with the much less coherent development in the REPERTORY MOVEMENT after the First World War as it reacted to the stultification of the WEST END and prewar theatres, with repertory houses such as those in BIRMINGHAM and LIVERPOOL being joined by new enterprises like the OXFORD PLAYHOUSE, the FESTIVAL THEATRE, CAMBRIDGE, and the GATE, London, in providing a more ambitious repertoire. There were big variations among the theatres (e.g. between Northampton, BRISTOL's Little Theatre and SHEFFIELD), and innovation often gave way to serving a community, as in Hull, MANCHESTER and LEEDS.

Similar little theatre movements grew up elsewhere, e.g. in AUSTRALIA and the CARIBBEAN (*see* LITTLE THEATRE MOVEMENT OF JAMAICA), and shared similar patterns of activity and decline. By the nature of the theatres and their aims, the audiences were likely to be relatively small and not economically sustaining. The movements were also affected by the role of subsidy, both private and public, and by cultural changes, from the rise of cinema and television to the success of the little theatres in influencing the mainstream and thereby giving themselves less of a part to play. CHARLES LONDON

See also RESIDENT THEATRE.

A. McCleery and C. Glick, *Curtains Going Up* (1938)

Kenneth Macgowan, *Footlights Across America* (1929)
Norman Marshall, *The Other Theatre* (1947)

Little Theatre Guild of Great Britain In the mid-1930s the Crescent Theatre, Birmingham (founded 1923), attempted to form an Association of LITTLE THEATRES (that is, non-commercial groups controlling their own buildings). The scheme was aborted by the difficulty of administration. The next attempt was to create a special section within the membership of the British Drama League (*see* BRITISH THEATRE ASSOCIATION), an idea not altogether welcomed although adopted at a BDL conference in 1938. The BDL was not well equipped to deal with the specialist problems of the little theatres, and its Little Theatres Committee, unlike the little theatres themselves, was an early casualty after the outbreak of war in 1939. At the end of the war, four little theatres – Bradford Civic Playhouse (established 1929), Highbury Little Theatre, Sutton Coldfield, (1925), the People's Theatre, Newcastle-upon-Tyne (1911) and the QUESTORS THEATRE, west London (1929) – which had already been consulting together over such matters as entertainments duty, clothing coupons and charitable status, felt the need to end the isolation imposed by the wartime slogan 'Is your journey really necessary?' and to share ideas and experiences with other little theatres. At a meeting in 1946 the LTG was formally inaugurated with nine founder members.

More and more little theatres were subsequently established, as serious-minded amateur groups increasingly realized the artistic and social value of owning their own facilities. By 1987 LTG members had increased in number from the original nine to 61, two-thirds of which had established their theatres after 1946. In seating capacity the theatres ranged from a maximum of 500 down to no more than about 70; half were in the range of 100–200. Annual programmes consisted of as many as over 20 productions or as few as four; the average was about eight. Almost all the groups were registered charities; most had junior or youth groups and a significant proportion their own training schemes. Several also established studio-type theatres for more experimental work.

The Stockport Garrick Society (1901) was the first to be founded. Most were established in adapted buildings, such as chapels, halls, warehouses or barns – and in one case (South London Theatre Centre), a disused fire station. Some, notably the Crescent Theatre, Birmingham, the Newport (Gwent) Playgoers Society and the Questors, replaced their original adapted buildings with new, postwar theatres built to their own adventurous design. At Dumfries and Lancaster the little theatre groups occupy what were originally eighteenth-century theatres and the MADDERMARKET, Norwich, is based on an Elizabethan theatre design.

The LTG has taken a number of initiatives, notably in connection with new plays (commissioning, a new play competition, an association with the Charles Henry Foyle New Play Award, a New Plays Festival in 1987 to mark its fortieth anniversary). It was actively represented at the British Theatre Conference of 1948 and was a founder member of the INTERNATIONAL AMATEUR THEATRE ASSOCIATION in 1952. Its international activities have been substantial and inspired little theatre movements around the world. ALFRED EMMET

Little Theatre Movement of Jamaica Founded by Greta Bourke and Henry Fowler, who later became husband and wife and whose original purpose was to raise funds, by means of theatrical production, for the building of a LITTLE THEATRE. The company's first production was the 1941 PANTOMIME *Jack and the Beanstalk*. The pantomime became an annual tradition, and a major source of funding for the LTM. Over the years, beginning with Vera Bell's *Soliday and the Wicked Bird* in 1943, the company co-opted most of Jamaica's leading playwrights, actors and directors into developing an original, satirical style of Jamaican pantomime. Typical titles include *Bluebeard and Brer Anancy* (1949), *Anancy and the Magic Mirror* (1954), *Queenie's Daughter* (1963), *Johnny Reggae* (1978), *River Mumma and the Golden Table* (1986) and *Man Dey Yah* (1991). The pantomime has been taken on tour within the region, and the 1981 *The Pirate Princess* was produced in London in 1986. Since 1969 the pantomimes and lyrics have been written or co-written by Barbara Gloudon, who eventually took over the chairmanship of the LTM, and also that of the Jamaica School of Drama. The latter had been established by the LTM in 1969, but was handed over to the government in 1975, to become one of the four schools in the Cultural Training Centre.

In 1961, after some 20 pantomimes and 25 other productions, the LTM opened its new 615-seat theatre in Kingston. The pantomime, however, with its massive audiences, continues to be staged at the larger Ward Theatre. JUDY S. J. STONE
See also CARIBBEAN.

Little Tich [Harry Relph] (b. Cudham, Kent, 21 July 1867; d. Hendon, Herts, 10 Feb. 1928) MUSIC HALL comedian whose height was less than the length of the boots he wore. He started his career as a 'coloured' comedian and dancer, and it was part of the stock-in-trade of the 'negro' IMPERSONATOR to don large shoes; even when he stopped using the burnt cork he kept the shoes for his acrobatic dance act, and they gradually extended to the enormous size associated with him. He was well known as an impersonator and was an influence on Chaplin. Little Tich was also popular in the United States and Europe, especially in France where, in 1910, he was made an Officer of the French Academy. REXTON S. BUNNETT

Littler The assumed family name of two brothers and a sister born Raines in Ramsgate, Kent, the children of the lessee of the Royal Artillery Theatre, Woolwich, where all three had their introduction to theatre business. The eldest, **Blanche** (b. 26 Dec 1899; d. Brighton, 7 June 1981) partnered her brother **Prince** [né Frank] (b. 25 July 1901; d. Henfield, W. Sussex, 17 Sept. 1973) in various provincial tours and promotions but is best known as the second wife of the comedy actor GEORGE ROBEY. Prince was an active producer of pantomimes and provincial tours until a shrewdly advised purchase of controlling shares made him the head of Stoll Theatres Corporation (*see* STOLL MOSS THEATRES LTD) in 1942. He then became head of Associated Theatre Properties (London) Ltd (1943), of THEATRE ROYAL, DRURY LANE Ltd (1944), a director of Moss Empires Ltd (1945) and then its chairman (1947), and a director of Howard & Wyndham Ltd (1945). His interlocking directorates made him the most powerful business figure in the British theatre, a power which he exercised with ruthlessness and considerable business acumen. He was often not on speaking terms with his brother, **Emile** (b. 9 Sept. 1903; d. Ditchling, W. Sussex, 23 Jan. 1985), who rivalled him as a producer of provincial pantomimes and outpaced him as a West End producer but – with a mere two London theatres, the Palace and Cambridge, to his name – was very much his inferior as a theatre owner. Neither brother had any great artistic pretensions but, with their financial muscle and popular tastes, they had considerable influence on the British commercial theatre in the 1940s and 1950s. The family rivalries were underlined when Blanche became Lady Robey (1954) and Emile was knighted (1974), while, apart from a CBE, Prince had to remain content with the title he had bestowed on himself. IAN BEVAN

See also THEATRE FAMILIES.

Littlewood, Joan [Maudie] (b. Clapham, London, 6 Oct. 1914) Director. After leaving the Royal Academy of Dramatic Art, she worked in the 1930s with POLITICAL THEATRE groups in MANCHESTER, in partnership with EWAN MACCOLL, and she embarked on a course of self-taught study which embraced theatre history and methods of training and encompassed experiments in theatre forms and styles which were being used in Europe and the United States. Her concept of a theatre company envisaged an ENSEMBLE in which this range of study would be carried out cooperatively. After 1945 she formed THEATRE WORKSHOP with MacColl, some members of the prewar companies and new actors. The company embarked on provincial and European tours until 1953, when Littlewood took a lease on the THEATRE ROYAL, STRATFORD EAST, London E15. Central to her work in the immediate postwar period was the idea that the great theatres of the past had all attracted and held popular audiences and that there was a way of performing the classics which would still hold a popular audience. The company proved this in a string of exciting productions, from the anonymous late sixteenth-century *Arden of Faversham* (1954) to *Richard II* and *Volpone* (both 1955). Her style of work was based on rigorous research and improvisation in rehearsal, and is best expressed through her own statement: 'I do not believe in the supremacy of the director, designer, actor or even the writer. It is through collaboration that this knockabout art of theatre survives and kicks ... No one mind or imagination can foresee what a play will become until all the physical and intellectual stimuli which are crystallised in the poetry of the author, have been understood by a company, and then tried out in terms of mime, discussion and the precise music of grammar; words and movement allied and integrated.' The Stratford period brought honours and success, in the form of transfers to the WEST END of many of her productions (e.g. *The Hostage*, 1958; *A Taste of Honey*, 1959; *Fings Ain't Wot They Used T'Be*, 1959). Although this arguably increased the pool of actors available to her, it also struck at the concept of the ensemble, and from 1960 Littlewood began to withdraw from staging shows. In the early 1960s she worked on a project, *The Fun Palace*, which would use a computerized environment to research and create new artistic forms. The project failed to find sufficient official support to create it and Littlewood moved to working in minimalist ways with children in the streets and parks. She returned to Stratford to stage a few shows (e.g. *Oh, What a Lovely War!*, 1963; *Mrs Wilson's Diary*, 1967), but on the death of her partner, Gerry Raffles, in 1975 she withdrew to live in France. An inspiration to countless theatre people and companies, she published *Joan's Story* in 1994.
CLIVE BARKER

Howard Goorney, *The Theatre Workshop Story* (1981)
Samuel L. Leiter, *From Belasco to Brook* (1991)

live art Expression coined in the early 1980s, originally (and still predominantly) confined to British usage. It was adopted in the first instance by artists dissatisfied with the application to their work of the expression PERFORMANCE ART, feeling that it implied a too obvious relationship with the performing arts and that it was restrictive or suggested that their work was of a less than serious character. Its early, more public applications were in the change of name of the highly influential Nottingham-based annual festival 'Four Days of Performance Art' to the National Review of Live Art, and the adoption of the straplines *The Review of Live Art* and *Live Art Now* by the equally influential *Performance Magazine*. Its breadth of use was encouraged by its incorporation in the title of the *Artists Newsletter* volume *Live Art*, which was widely used in undergraduate teaching, and the ARTS COUNCIL OF GREAT BRITAIN's own *Live Art Now*, which seemed to confer an all-important seal of approval by the then single most important national funding body for independent artists' activity. Its subsequent predominance, and its gradual comprehension outside of Britain, have been encouraged by the establishment of the Live Art Archives at <http://art.ntu.ac.uk/liveart> (where, incidentally, a range of artists' definitions of the term may be found), and the academic mailbase, the Live Art List; the establishment of the journal *Live Art Magazine*; its employment in a range of internationally read theoretical publications; and, no less important, its own breadth, flexibility and, some might say, lack of precision of meaning.

The term embraces a wide range of innovative, interdisciplinary activity deriving from theatre, fine art, music, cinema and video, the new technologies, and the popular arts ranging from CIRCUS to CABARET and clubbing, characteristically combined or refined in ways that question or deconstruct the assumptions of any one of these individual disciplines. This may involve at least the questioning of theatrical pretence and the formality of audience–performer relationships, and may well extend to the apparent abandonment of any recognizable PERFORMANCE situation at all. Ironically, usage of the term 'live art' seems to extend to work in which the live element is not necessarily of prime importance or even present. Video, INSTALLATION, broadcast, publication in all media and web-based projects all seem at various times to be absorbed in this most accommodating of terms. What seems more important is that works of live art exist in, or strongly suggest, real time and place.

For example, works of EXPERIMENTAL THEATRE (by e.g. FORCED ENTERTAINMENT or Desperate Optimists), of BODY ART (by Stelarc or Orlan), of MUSIC THEATRE (by Laurie Anderson), of performance art of all sorts (by Bobby Baker or Andre Stitt or Alastair MacLennan), of experiments in virtual reality (by Blast Theory), of

DANCE (by Jerome Bel), and of social intervention (by Shelley Sacks) were all unproblematically dubbed live art in the late 1990s. ROBERT AYERS

See also DIGITAL PERFORMANCE; INTERNET.

Robert Ayers and David Butler, *Live Art* (1991)
RoseLee Goldberg, *Performance: Live Art since the Sixties* (1998)
Paul Schimmel et al., *Out of Actions: Between Performance and the Object, 1949–1979* (1998)
Tracey Warr et al., *Live Art Now* (1987)

Liverpool The most familiar of Britain's northern cities, as celebrated for its distinctive art and popular culture as it is notorious for its social problems. In 1900 the city was a great seaport, with eight major theatres testifying to its wealth and power. Of these, the Royal Court and Empire have survived. The Theatre Royal had already closed down, providing an early indication of the city's independence from metropolitan influence. In 1911 the Liverpool Repertory Theatre (later the LIVERPOOL PLAYHOUSE) opened to stage the new drama. The long-standing Merseyside UNITY THEATRE (1937–86), founded on socialist principles, provided an important amateur platform for left-wing theatre. The refurbished Unity Theatre building continues to be a major centre for experimental and COMMUNITY productions. In 1964, at the height of the Merseybeat, the EVERYMAN theatre was formed. Funded originally to cater for the young audience, the company subsequently developed a reputation for alternative approaches to both plays and performance. Stimulated by the Everyman, and also by the Playhouse studio, which opened in 1969, an influential school of Liverpool playwrights emerged headed by Alan Bleasdale and WILLY RUSSELL, whose work was popularized on television and film. In the 1990s funding problems made the fate of Liverpool's subsidized theatres increasingly precarious, but drama continued to contribute strongly to the city's regeneration, especially in the spheres of education and training. Since 1978 Merseyside Young People's Theatre has taken specially commissioned plays to local schools. The Hope Street project, founded in 1988, uses theatre as a means of developing vocational skills and placing people in work. BOB MILLINGTON

Liverpool Playhouse The oldest remaining repertory theatre in Britain. The restructured Star Theatre opened in 1911 as the Liverpool Repertory Theatre in the wake of the success of the GAIETY THEATRE, Manchester, and became the Playhouse in 1916 under BASIL DEAN. It has always been intended to suit a wide spectrum of theatregoers and therefore has a varied repertoire comprising popular and conventional pieces as well as more AVANT-GARDE, contemporary works and new plays for children. The main auditorium seats 758; there is also a 120-seat theatre called the Playhouse Studio. The resident Playhouse Repertory Company is subsidized by national and local public funding. Between the world wars it was, with the more attractive BIRMINGHAM REPERTORY THEATRE, the other twin pillar of the REPERTORY MOVEMENT under the firm guidance of William Armstrong as artistic director (1922–44) and Maud Carpenter as business manager (1923–62). It housed the OLD VIC during the Second World War and continued its established policy thereafter, consolidating its reputation for having helped actors such as MICHAEL REDGRAVE and REX HARRISON start their careers. Following the success of the local EVERYMAN, it responded with a change of policy in 1981 and appointed four playwright directors all associated with the neighbouring theatre: Alan Bleasdale (Liverpool-born, 1946, best known for his TV series *Boys from the Blackstuff*, 1982), C. G. (Chris) Bond (b. 1945), Bill Morrison (Irish-born, 1940, author of *Flying Blind*, 1977); and WILLY RUSSELL. Thereafter financial problems rendered its future uncertain, and it went into liquidation in 1998; however, it reopened, refurbished, at the end of 2000. ADRIANA HUNTER

G. W. Goldie, *The Liverpool Repertory Theatre 1911–34* (1935)
Pelham McMahon and Pam Brooks, *Actor's Place: The Liverpool Repertory Company at Liverpool Playhouse, 1911–1998* (2000)

living newspaper Originating with Russian and German AGITPROP troupes (1920–33), the living newspaper was a theatrical DOCUMENTARY which became associated in the English-speaking world with the US FEDERAL THEATER PROJECT, part of Roosevelt's 'New Deal'. Under its director HALLIE FLANAGAN, the Project used its living newspaper units to explore important, and often controversial, social and political questions. The personnel for the units, formed in several major US cities, were unemployed newspaper and theatre workers. The former researched topics, the latter translated research material into theatre. Source material was used in highly theatrical ways, often using the amplified 'Voice of the Living Newspaper' to underline points. Plays like *Triple-A Plowed Under* (1936), *Power* (1937) and *One-Third of a Nation* (1938), all scripted by ARTHUR ARENT, were great successes seen by huge numbers of people. Living newspaper arrived in Britain from America. UNITY THEATRE groups before and after the Second World War produced shows like *Busmen* (London Unity, 1936) and *Man with a Plan* (Merseyside

Unity, 1946). During the Second World War the British Army Bureau of Current Affairs even had a play unit which used living newspapers to inform soldiers about matters such as the welfare state (*Where Do We Go From Here?*, 1945). DEREK PAGET

Colin Chambers, *The Story of Unity Theatre* (1989)
Malcolm Goldstein, *The Political Stage: American Drama and Theater of the Great Depression* (1974)
John O'Connor and Lorraine Brown, *The Federal Theater Project: 'Free, Adult, Uncensored'* (1980)

living statuary *see* EROTICISM IN THE THEATRE

Living Theater An AVANT-GARDE drama company founded in New York in 1947 by **Judith Malina** (b. Kiel, Germany, 4 June 1926) and her husband **Julian Beck** (b. New York, 31 May 1925; d. New York, 14 Sept. 1985), a director, actor and designer who trained under PISCATOR. After staging modernist writing (PIRANDELLO, LORCA, GERTRUDE STEIN, Paul Goodman, BRECHT), their productions became increasingly confrontational, political and intense (e.g. JACK GELBER's *The Connection*, 1959; Kenneth Brown's *The Brig*, 1963). They moved to Europe after tax disputes with the government, closing the theatre they had opened in 1959. The company became an influential multinational travelling commune with a repertoire of aggressive 'anarchist–pacifist' performances, including the ARTAUD-derived *Mysteries*, their audience-participation 'rite' *Paradise Now* (1968) and *Prometheus* (1978). They became counter-cultural symbols at the height of the Vietnam War, and in 1971 began a cycle of 100 short agitational plays, *The Legacy of Cain*. In Brazil, where they worked for 13 months, they were arrested. They returned to New York in 1984 after more spells in Europe and working with steel and coal communities in the United States. In 1993 the company was once more forced out of its house and became itinerant again. Late productions included work derived from KOKOSCHKA and TOLLER, and collaborations with the dispossessed. Beck wrote *The Life of the Theater* (1972) and *Theandric* (1992), and Malina *Diaries 1947–1957* (1984). TONY HOWARD
See also THIRD THEATRE.

P. Biner, *The Living Theater* (1972)
J. Tytell, *The Living Theater: Art, Exile and Outrage* (1995)

Livings, Henry [George] (b. Prestwich, Lancs, 20 Sept. 1929; d. Oldham, Lancs, 20 Feb. 1998) Playwright. Livings acted with, among others, THEATRE WORKSHOP before turning to writing plays which bore the marks of his theatrical apprenticeship and northern upbringing. Although always marked by a subversive intellectual ambiguity, he moved from the early naturalism of *Big Soft Nellie* (1961) and *Nil Carborundum* (1962), which farcically depicts a large-scale military exercise at an RAF base, to the fantasies of *Kelly's Eye* (1963) and *Eh?* (1964), whose protagonists are anarchic but inarticulate outsiders pitted against a brutal society. In such plays as *The Little Mrs Foster Show* (1966) and *The Pongo Plays* (1967–70) Livings revived cartoon, myth and music-hall forms to carry his exuberant, colloquial social commentary. He wrote prolifically for stage, television and radio; his other plays include *Stop It, Whoever You Are* (1961), about a lavatory attendant in a factory; *Jug* (1975), an adaptation of Kleist's comedy; and *This Is My Dream: The Life and Times of Josephine Baker* (1987).

DAN REBELLATO

Lloyd, Marie [Matilda Alice Victoria Wood] (b. London, 12 Feb. 1870; d. Golders Green, London, 7 Oct. 1922) The queen of the MUSIC HALL, a singer and character actress from London's East End who was famed for her broad *double entendre* songs which were popular with her public but, along with a divorce and her politics, kept her out of the first Royal COMMAND PERFORMANCE in 1912. Instead she played in a theatre next door in her own show. In 1907 she joined the great music hall strike for better working conditions. Her funeral attracted 100,000 people. Renowned for her generosity, she spent all she earned. She married three times and found international stardom with her famous wink and saucy songs such as 'The Boy I Love is Up in the Gallery', 'A Little Bit of What You Fancy', 'One of the Ruins that Cromwell Knocked About a Bit', 'Don't Dilly Dally' and 'Oh Mister Porter'.

REXTON S. BUNNETT

Richard Anthony Baker, *Marie Lloyd: Queen of the Music Halls* (1990)

Daniel Farson, *Marie Lloyd and Music Hall* (1972)

Midge Gillies, *Marie Lloyd: The One and Only* (1999)

Lloyd Webber, Andrew (b. London, 22 March 1948) Composer and producer. In collaboration with lyricist TIM RICE, Lloyd Webber developed in the early 1970s a new style of sung-through musical show in which the composer's blend of classical and modern popular musical styles set a new norm for the musical theatre. The pair worked together on three shows. The short cantata *Joseph and the Amazing Technicolor Dreamcoat* (1968–72), later developed into a light-hearted stage show full of musical parody, was followed by *Jesus Christ Superstar* (1972), subtitled 'a rock opera', and *Evita* (1978) – the two most internationally successful musicals of the decade which developed the

style initiated in *Joseph* for use in a substantial dramatic context. Lloyd Webber subsequently took a turn into a lighter vein with his setting of the Old Possum poems of T. S. ELIOT as the song-and-dance spectacular *Cats* (1981), a theatrical sensation which outran even its record-breaking predecessors, and essayed further into the spectacular with the consciously pop-orientated extravaganza *Starlight Express* (1984). There was further success with the staged pairing of his solo song-cycle 'Tell Me on a Sunday' and a choreographed version of his 'cello variations on a Paganini theme as *Song and Dance* (1982), with the romantic musical melodrama *The Phantom of the Opera* (1987), in which opera pastiche and lush love songs were paired with some highly developed ensembles, and the comparatively intimate and sophisticated *Aspects of Love* (1989). At one point in the early 1990s he had a record five shows running in London and three on Broadway. Subsequent projects have included the remake of the classic film *Sunset Boulevard* as a musical (1993), the small-scale *By Jeeves* (1996), in which the composer swapped his usual musical tones for period pastiche, and a version of another well-known screenplay, *Whistle Down the Wind* (1996). His last new musical show of the century was a collaboration with comedian and novelist Ben Elton, *The Beautiful Game* (2000). Lloyd Webber's Really Useful Company has produced all his later works, as well as some by other writers, and is also one of the largest theatre owners in Britain. The works of this most important and innovative theatre composer of his era have shown a considerable musical range within his preferred idiom while not only remaining accessible, but providing several chart hits, and winning worldwide success in a manner achieved by no other theatre composer of his era. He was knighted in 1992 and created a life peer in 1997. KURT GÄNZL

M. Coveney, *Cats on a Chandelier* (1999)

J. Mantle, *Fanfare: The Unauthorised Biography of Andrew Lloyd Webber* (1989)

M. Walsh, *Andrew Lloyd Webber* (1989)

Lochhead, Liz (b. Motherwell, Lanarks, Scotland, 26 Dec. 1947) Playwright, poet. She studied painting and worked as an art teacher until 1979, when she began writing full-time and became an important figure in the renaissance of Scottish theatre. Known for her wit and rich language, she is a prolific writer and has published several acclaimed collections of poetry, as well as critical and review writing. Many of her plays examine the lives of women in history and literature, including Queen Mary and Elizabeth I in *Mary Queen of Scots Got Her Head Chopped Off* (1987) and Mary Shelley in *Blood and Ice* (1982). Other plays include *Dracula*

(1985), a Scots version of *Tartuffe* (1985), *Jock Tamson's Bairns* (1990), *Quelques Fleurs* (1991) and a version of *Medea* (2000). *A Perfect Day* (1998) was well received at the EDINBURGH FESTIVAL and transferred to London's West End. LAURIE WOLF

Loesser, Frank [Henry]   (b. New York, 29 June 1910; d. New York, 26 July 1969)   Songwriter. Loesser did hs earliest work as a lyricist, notably during a seven-year period in Hollywood during which time he supplied the words to a number of standard songs, but he subsequently expanded as a solo songwriter and in 1948 provided the lyrics and music for the successful musical farce *Where's Charley?*. His versatility and unusual ability became more wholly evident with his second show, *Guys and Dolls* (1950), which combined a panorama of musical and lyrical styles and skills in one of the most colourful and characteristic of all musical comedy scores, and which was a major success on English-language stages. *The Most Happy Fella* (1956), for which he provided both text and score, took a different turn, seamlessly mixing operatic vocalizing with broad Broadway show songs in a musical of considerable scope and substance, but in *Greenwillow* (1960) he attempted to step too far away from his genre and met failure for the first time. His final Broadway musical, the brisk, modern *How To Succeed in Business Without Really Trying* (1961), exposed another, more satirical facet of his style, and gave him a fourth major success, although the total was increased posthumously when his 1952 film score *Hans Christian Andersen* was used as the basis for a London stage musical in 1974. KURT GÄNZL

S. Loesser, *A Most Remarkable Fella: Frank Loesser and the Guys and Dolls in his Life* (1993)

Loewe, Frederick ('Fritz')   (b. Berlin, 10 June 1901; d. Palm Springs, Calif., 14 Feb. 1988)   Composer. After a decade attempting to break into the musical theatre in America, Loewe saw his early efforts, first in collaboration with Earle Crooker and then with ALAN JAY LERNER, prove quick failures. The pairing with Lerner paid off, however, when their third attempt, *Brigadoon* (1947), a romantic fantasy following the vogue for BROADWAY operetta recently re-established by *Oklahoma!*, was a solid hit. *Paint Your Wagon* (1951) gave them a second success, but the partnership's memorable triumph came with their musical adaptation of SHAW's *Pygmalion* as *My Fair Lady* (1956). This show had a record-breaking Broadway run and was produced worldwide, penetrating countries where the American musical was otherwise little known, and became the most popular and played show of its era. Further suc-

cess came with a fourth consecutive show, *Camelot* (1960), a humorous musical retelling of the Arthurian legend, before Loewe retired from the theatrical scene, emerging only briefly in 1973 to supply additional material for an unfortunate first stage version of the partnership's 1958 film hit, *Gigi*. KURT GÄNZL

G. Lees, *Inventing Champagne: The Words of Lerner and Loewe* (1990)

Logan [Short], Jimmy [James Allan]   (b. Glasgow, 4 April 1928; d. Clydebank, 13 April 2001)   Actor, entertainer. He appeared as one of the VAUDEVILLE troupe the Logan Family along with his parents and four siblings before becoming the principal stand-up comedian, aged 19, at Glasgow's Metropole, a theatre he later bought but ran without success. He created a series of popular revues, *Five Past Eight*, in which character observation replaced gags, and was by the mid-1950s a radio and TV star. He had his own *Jimmy Logan Show* on BBCTV (1957–61). He regularly appeared in PANTOMIME, mostly as the DAME, and in 'straight' plays such as *The Entertainer, Death of a Salesman* and *Comedians*. He was a legend in Scotland and became the repository of its popular theatre history, notably that of his idol Sir HARRY LAUDER whom he celebrated in a solo show *Lauder: The Golden Years*. A subsequent show, *The Fabulous Fifties*, recreated the dying days of Scots VARIETY. Logan's memoir, *It's a Funny Life*, appeared in 1998. CHARLES LONDON

Logan, [Lockwood] Joshua   (b. Texarkana, Tex., 3 Oct. 1908; d. New York, 13 July 1988)   Director, producer and playwright. Known primarily as a director, he studied briefly with STANISLAVSKY in Moscow and later helped found the University Players. Celebrity came with his staging of *On Borrowed Time* (1938). Among his other hits were *I Married an Angel* (1938), *Knickerbocker Holiday* (1938), *Morning's at Seven* (1939), *By Jupiter* (1942), *Annie Get Your Gun* (1946), *Mister Roberts* (1948) and *The World of Susie Wong* (1958). In later years his direction was perceived as increasingly heavy-handed, possibly because of mental problems he suffered. He sometimes co-produced and co-authored the shows he staged, including the Pulitzer Prize winner *South Pacific* (1949), the film of which he also directed, and *Fanny* (1954). He wrote two autobiographies, *Josh* (1976) and *Movie Stars, Real People and Me* (1978). GERALD BORDMAN

Logue, Christopher   (b. Portsmouth, Hants, 23 Nov. 1926)   Poet and playwright. Logue was briefly diverted from poetry by an interesting attempt to blend Brechtian dialectic with popular forms, as in *The Lily-White Boys* (1960). His best play, a reworking of *Antigone*

453

(1960), was muffled by its pairing with a ham-fisted sexual satire, *Cob and Leach* (1959) at the ROYAL COURT under the title *Trials by Logue* (1960). His translations of *The Iliad* have generated powerful performances as *War Music* with the actor ALAN HOWARD. His memoir *Prince Charming* appeared in 1999. DAN REBELLATO

London The modern history of London theatre begins after the Theatres Act 1834 abolished the monopoly of the seventeenth-century royal patent that allowed only two companies to perform legitimately. Massive expansion followed in the WEST END; most of today's London theatres, like the ALDWYCH (1905), Duke of York's (1892), Garrick (1889) and Wyndham's (1899), were opened around the turn of the century, while the older theatres were rebuilt and refurbished to accommodate larger audiences: the Adelphi in 1901, the Haymarket in 1905 and Her Majesty's in 1897. So-called 'illegitimate' theatre flourished in the MUSIC HALLS.

The domination of London by the West End was challenged first by an 'outer circle' of theatres – notably the OLD VIC, under LILIAN BAYLIS from 1912, and the LYRIC Hammersmith, under NIGEL PLAYFAIR from 1918 – committed to a serious theatre of professional quality; and secondly by CLUB THEATRE, following the example of J. T. GREIN's INDEPENDENT THEATRE SOCIETY. These clubs, which included the EVERYMAN (1920), Q (1924), GATE (1925), ARTS and EMBASSY (1927), MERCURY (1933) and Intimate Theatre (1935), and whose membership-only status exempted them from the LORD CHAMBERLAIN's purview and so from CENSORSHIP, introduced to London many of the works of European modernism which found no home in the West End. Even SHAW and the new drama were not safe bets for commercial theatre.

In the 1930s, the increasing popularity of the cinema saw theatres like the LONDON PALLADIUM converted into lucrative film houses. Several theatres, like the Gaiety and Royalty, proved unprofitable to run and were left empty before being demolished. In 1941, some were damaged in the blitz. While a number were restored after the war, including the THEATRE ROYAL, DRURY LANE, OLD VIC, Palace and ROYAL COURT, others stood empty to be demolished later, like the Holborn Empire and the KINGSWAY.

When war was declared in 1939, theatres were instructed to close, and then later allowed to re-open, with a strict curfew. Many productions used the lighter restrictions elsewhere to tour, leaving London's theatre life sparse and precarious for some years. Apart from the amateur UNITY THEATRE, only the Windmill, with its diet of nude tableaux and revue, was able to claim, as it did for many years after, that 'we never closed'.

After the war the dominance of the American musical and costume drama was undermined by a seismic shift that accompanied the arrival of BRECHT, BECKETT, tough realism from the United States, vibrant popular drama from THEATRE WORKSHOP and a new writing explosion centred on the Royal Court. The Royal Court and THEATRE ROYAL, STRATFORD EAST, however, did not affect London's bricks and mortar, and the first significant postwar realignment 'architecturally' came in the explosion of tiny arts labs and pub theatres that emerged as part of the FRINGE, notably the ARTS LAB, Quipu, SOHO POLY and OPEN SPACE (1968), Oval House and Theatre Upstairs (1969), KING'S HEAD (1970) and INTER-ACTION's Almost Free, BUSH and HALF MOON (1972). This expansion was matched in the 1980s by the proliferation of venues for 'alternative comedy'. By this time, new modern theatres like the MERMAID (1959), NATIONAL THEATRE (1976) and Barbican (1981) had been built but older buildings were crumbling. In 1977 the Theatres Trust was set up to protect them. Nevertheless, the diversity of theatrical activity was impressive, especially when activities in the streets, in the open air, in the communities, in the drama school and college theatres, on tour, late night or at lunchtime were taken into account. At the end of the 1990s London could offer some 5,000 productions per year, and 34 per cent of all visitors said theatre was the sole reason for their visit to the capital. DAN REBELLATO

London Academy of Music and Drama *see* DRAMA SCHOOLS

London International Festival of Theatre Known by its acronym LIFT: originally a biennial, three-week summer theatre FESTIVAL held in venues all over London, founded by Lucy Neal and Rose de Wend Fenton in 1981 as an alternative to mainstream 'showcase' festivals. It was designed to bring to Britain the cream of contemporary performance from around the world; to facilitate cultural exchanges; to stage a maximum of outdoor performances; and to provide a platform for theatrical innovation and for British artists. In its first ten years, LIFT welcomed over 1,500 artists from 31 countries, earning a good reputation in the world theatre network. The festival receives considerable private and public funding. It also staged special seasons in between festivals, called 'out of LIFT'. Following LIFT '99, a growing emphasis on commissioning and education, and an exploration of all the cultures of the host city, London, saw the seasonal festival give way to continuous promotion of events and projects. ADRIANA HUNTER

London Palladium ('The Palladium') The best-

known theatre in London for popular entertainment, it was opened in 1910 on a site famous for its CIRCUS and water spectacles. Designed by FRANK MATCHAM and seating just over 2,300, it soon earned a reputation for VARIETY and, under the direction of GEORGE BLACK, became the home of REVUE and the CRAZY GANG as well. This plush two-tiered auditorium (named 'London' in 1934) was also host to the annual Christmas *Peter Pan* show (1930–8) and after the Second World War it became the venue chosen by major US stars for their London appearances. Scene of many Royal COMMAND Variety Performances, its fame spread through a television variety series, *Sunday Night at the London Palladium,* which always ended with the guests turning on the revolve – a moment that passed into the mythology of popular humour.
COLIN CHAMBERS

Ian Bevan, *Top of the Bill* (1952)

London Theatre School   *see* DEVINE, GEORGE; DRAMA SCHOOL; SAINT-DENIS, MICHEL

Long, John Luther   (b. Philadelphia, 1 Jan. 1861; d. Clifton Springs, NY, 31 Oct. 1927) Playwright, lawyer and short-story writer. A successful adaptation by DAVID BELASCO of his *Madame Butterfly* (1900) prompted him to collaborate with Belasco on *The Darling of the Gods* (1902) and *Adrea* (1904). These hits were followed by less popular efforts, all equally archly romantic.   GERALD BORDMAN

Long Wharf Theatre   Located in NEW HAVEN, Connecticut, in a converted warehouse, this 484-seat venue has become one of the United States' most prestigious regional theatres since it was established by Harlan Kleinman and Jon Jory in 1965 with Arvin Brown as artistic director from 1967 to 1997. Over the years it has staged world and American premieres of several important new plays, some of which have later transferred to Broadway, for example DAVID STOREY's *The Changing Room* (1973) and ATHOL FUGARD's *Sizwe Bansi is Dead* (1975), as well as important new work from American playwrights like DAVID MAMET's *American Buffalo* (1980), DAVID RABE's *Streamers* (1976) and Michael Cristofer's Pulitzer Prize winning *The Shadow Box* (1977). A smaller 'Stage II', seating 199, was opened in the building in 1977. The theatre has won several awards, including a special Tony in 1978 for outstanding regional theatre. In 1999 Doug Hughes took over as artistic director.   HELEN RAPPAPORT

Longford, Edward, 7th Earl of   (b. London, 29 Dec. 1902; d. Dublin, 4 Feb. 1961). Impresario and playwright. He subsidized the Dublin GATE THEATRE from 1930 until his death, and formed Longford Productions which he ran for 25 years with his wife, the playwright and novelist Christine (*née* Patti). His outstanding play is *Yahoo* (1933).   CHRISTOPHER FITZ-SIMON

Lonsdale, Frederick [Leonard]   (b. Jersey, Channel Islands, 5 Feb. 1881; d. London, 4 April 1954) Playwright. He wrote for the most part neat comedies and had three plays running in London in 1908, including *The Early Worm.* He was a librettist, most notably for the musical comedy *The Maid of the Mountains* (1916). The opening night of his thriller *The Last of Mrs Cheyney* (1925) was said to be the theatrical event of the year. His farce *On Approval* (1927) has been revived several times. Lonsdale co-wrote and adapted plays throughout the 1920s and 1930s, his last play being *The Way Things Go* (1950), although *Let Them Eat Cake* was produced posthumously (1959).   MAGGIE GALE

Lopez, Francis [Francisco]   (b. Montbéliard, France, 15 June, 1916; d. Paris, 5 Jan. 1995) Composer. Trained as a dentist, Lopez had success as a songwriter before turning to the theatre with *La Belle de Cadix* (1945), a musical comedy which provided the French musical theatre with the same kind of new acceleration as *Oklahoma!* had recently done for America. Lopez and his librettist/lyricist Raymond Vincy followed up with a series of similar pieces for larger Parisian stages over the next decade, while the composer also worked on more intimate comedy musicals with equal success, dominating postwar French musical stages large and small. After Vincy's death in 1970 the hearty freshness of Lopez's earlier work began to give way to too familiar strains set to predictable libretti and his later shows, most of which were self-produced, were embarrassing imitations of his own early work.   KURT GÄNZL

Loquasto, Santo   (b. Wilkes-Barre, Penn., 26 July 1944) Set and costume designer. A graduate of Yale Drama School who first worked on OFF-BROADWAY in the 1970s, Loquasto's great versatility in design for theatre, film and dance has been seen in a variety of projects ranging from numerous BROADWAY musicals (e.g. *Grand Hotel*, 1989) and more than a dozen films by Woody Allen (e.g. *Radio Days*, 1986) to pieces by choreographers TWYLA THARP and Mark Morris. Loquasto is noted for his outstanding sense of detail and use of colour.   ELLEN LAMPERT-GRÉAUX

Lorca, Federico García   *see* GARCÍA LORCA, FEDERICO

Lord, Robert N.   (b. Rotorua, New Zealand, 18 July 1945; d. Dunedin, New Zealand, 7 Jan. 1992) Playwright. He began writing for the theatre in 1971 with *It Isn't Cricket*, which was followed by *Balance of Payments*

(1972), the popular *Well Hung* (1974), *Heroes and Butterflies* (1974) and *High as a Kite* (1979). From 1974 onwards he divided his time between New Zealand and New York, with his works published and performed in New Zealand, Australia and the United States. He nevertheless retained close links with Wellington's CIRCA THEATRE, which followed the Christchurch Court in staging *Bert and Maisy* (1984; later adapted for television) as well as *Country Cops* (*Well Hung* rewritten, 1985), *China Wars* (1987), *Glorious Ruins* (1992) and the particularly successful *Joyful and Triumphant* (1992), a humorous examination of New Zealand's changing culture. He also wrote the screenplay for the feature film *Pictures* (1979).

GLLIAN GREER & LAURIE ATKINSON

Lord Chamberlain Pre-production CENSORSHIP of plays in Britain was in the hands of the Lord Chamberlain, a functionary of the royal household, from 1737 to 1968. Plays could be banned or refused a LICENCE on a number of grounds – blasphemy, politics, profanity, sacrilege, sedition, indecency, or as likely to cause offence or a breach of the peace – and there was no appeal. CLUB THEATRES emerged to evade such strictures. In the twentieth century, famous victims of the Lord Chamberlain included SHAW, STRINDBERG, PIRANDELLO, O'NEILL, COWARD, OSBORNE, PINTER and ORTON. Mostly, textual changes were required before performance was allowed. The last play to be banned outright was BOND's *Early Morning* in 1968, but by then the campaign to end the Lord Chamberlain's censorship powers had gathered enough steam to be successful later that year.   COLIN CHAMBERS

Anthony Aldgate, *Censorship and the Permissive Society: British Cinema and Theatre 1955–65* (1995)
Nicholas de Jongh, *Politics, Prudency and Perversions: The Censoring of the English State, 1901–1968* (2000)
Richard Findlater, *Banned!* (1968)
John Johnston, *The Lord Chamberlain's Blue Pencil* (1990)

Lortel, Lucille   (b. New York, 16 Dec. 1900; d. New York, 6 April 1999)   Producer, popularly known as the 'Queen of OFF-BROADWAY'. She studied acting at the American Academy of Dramatic Arts and in Germany before making her stage debut in 1924, After her marriage in 1931 she retired from the stage until persuaded by friends in 1947 to convert a stable on her estate in Westport, Connecticut, into a theatre. This became the White Barn Theater – a popular showcase for new plays and actors, which housed many visiting theatrical troupes, including the highly successful 1951 season by the Dublin Players' Company. In 1955 Lortel

acquired the Theatre de Lys in Greenwich Village, opening with a spectacularly successful production of BRECHT's *The Threepenny Opera*, which ran until 1961 and inaugurated the Off-Broadway Matinée Series. Lortel's choice of subsequent productions has always been adventurous, including *Hamlet* (1957) with SIOBHAN MCKENNA in the title role and the 1961–2 production *Brecht on Brecht*. In 1981 the theatre was renamed after her. She promoted European playwrights as disparate as O'CASEY and IONESCO, and put on notable productions of GENET's *The Balcony* (CIRCLE IN THE SQUARE, 1960) and FUGARD's *The Blood Knot* (Cricket Theater, 1964). She also co-founded the AMERICAN SHAKESPEARE FESTIVAL. The Lucille Lortel Awards for outstanding achievement Off-Broadway were inaugurated in 1986.   HELEN RAPPAPORT

Los Angeles   Theatre in southern California since 1911 has had to compete against the major entertainment medium of the twentieth century: film. Hollywood, the entertainment capital of the world, lies completely within the city limits of LA. Los Angeles is the second largest city in the United States, and its population is perhaps the most diverse in America: two-thirds of its people are non-white. During the 1920s theatre and theatre building flourished, and Los Angeles had enough local talent to overcome its early dependence on Eastern road shows; but this vitality was short lived. The FEDERAL THEATER PROJECT helped sustain theatre workers during the late 1930s. However, as film rose in popularity in the 1930s and 1940s, acting in theatre was looked down on as many of the most talented actors discovered the lucrative lifestyle and visibility that the movies offered.

From the 1960s Hollywood began to parcel out its projects to other parts of the country (and even overseas), and this trend, coinciding as it did with an economic and artistic revitalization, led to a resurgence in theatrical activity. One important group to emerge from the racial disparity of this period was the Performing Arts Society of Los Angeles, a black theatre organized out of the 1965 race riots in the Watts section of the city. PASLA's brief but energetic three-year campaign to provide a cohesiveness and sense of history to the city's embattled black population serves as a shining example of the positive effects of COMMUNITY THEATRE.

At the end of the century Los Angeles was home to more than 100 theatre stages, from the large SHUBERT Theatre (1972) to small neighbourhood venues, showcasing the talent of about 33,000 actors, many of whom hope to be 'discovered' by the large film producers. The MARK TAPER FORUM (1967) is perhaps the major theatre in the city: many plays originating here have gone on to BROADWAY, earning Tony Awards and a few Pulitzer Prizes. The real vitality, however, lies in the numerous mid-sized and Equity-waiver (under 99 seats) theatres dispersed throughout the city, often performing challenging work or serving the main ethnic communities and nurturing local playwrights.

DAVID A. WILLIAMS

Losey, Joseph (b. La Crosse, Wisc., 14 Jan. 1990; d. London, 22 June 1984) Stage and film director. Losey's New York directing debut came with Albert Bein's *Little Ol' Boy* (1933), beginning for him activity in left-wing theatre which included several influential FEDERAL THEATER productions using LIVING NEWSPAPER and other experimental techniques he found in the Soviet Union. He directed BRECHT's *Galileo* (1947), the first major Brecht production in the United States. He left the US to avoid the McCarthyite blacklist and settled in England in 1952 where he concentrated on film. ANNE FLETCHER

David Caute, *Joseph Losey* (1994)

Lovelace, Earl (b. Toco, Trinidad, 1935) Trinidadian playwright and novelist. He took up writing poetry and short stories while working as a forest ranger. His first play, *The New Boss*, was staged in 1962 but he was not noticed as a playwright until he dramatized his novel *The Dragon Can't Dance* as a musical in 1986. Using traditional West Indian music, this play became the first 'yard' musical – depicting life in the CARIBBEAN backyard – and was followed by *The New Hardware Store* (1980) and *The Wine of Astonishment* (1988), both of which incorporate the musical elements of CARNIVAL.

HELEN RAPPAPORT

Lowe, Stephen (b. Nottingham, 1 Dec. 1947) Playwright. A former actor, Lowe has written an extremely varied corpus of work, from his excellent adaptation of Tressell's *The Ragged Trousered Philanthropists* (1978) to his remarkable depiction of a group of working-class women at the end of the Second World War before the bombing of Hiroshima and Nagasaki, *Touched* (1977). Although he can be erratic, as in *Divine Gossip* (1988), looking at literary expats in 1930s Paris, or the multimedia *Demon Lovers* (1987), his best work displays a clear-eyed compassion informed by socialism and feminism, as in *Shooting, Fishing and Riding* (1977) and *Tibetan Inroads* (1981). DAN REBELLATO

Lowell, Robert [Traill Spence, Jr] (b. Boston, 1 March 1917; d. New York, 2 Sept. 1977) Eminent Pulitzer Prize winning poet. In the 1960s Lowell worked on a trilogy of historical plays reflecting America's cul-

tural history which were collectively entitled *The Old Glory* (*Benito Cereno*; *My Kinsman, Major Molineux*; and *Endecott of the Red Cross*). Adapted from the work of Nathaniel Hawthorne and Herman Melville, the plays were first performed at the American Place Theater in 1964. Lowell also translated Racine's *Phèdre* (1960) and Aeschylus' *Prometheus Bound* (1966). HELEN RAPPAPORT

Lucas, Craig (b. Atlanta, Ga., 30 April 1951). Playwright. Though often defying categoriszation, his work tends toward highly politicized, intense psychological drama that blurs the boundaries between real and surreal. A former actor, Lucas has written *Missing Persons* (1981), *Reckless* (1983), *Blue Window* (1984), *Prelude to a Kiss* (1988), *God's Heart* (1997) and *The Dying Gaul* (1998), as well as a number of short plays and playlets. He is also responsible for conceiving and developing *Marry Me a Little* with Norman René (songs by STEPHEN SONDHEIM), co-authoring the musical play *Three Postcards* with Craig Carnelia, and co-writing opera libretto for *Cousin Lillie* and *Orpheus in Love* with Gerald Busby. He has also written several screenplays and won a number of awards. SHARON PRESSBURG

Luce, Clare Boothe *see* BOOTHE, CLARE

Luckham, Claire *see* MONSTROUS REGIMENT

Ludlam, Charles *see* QUEER THEATRE; THEATRE OF THE RIDICULOUS

Lugné-Poë, Aurélien[-François-Marie Lugné] (b. Paris, 27 Dec. 1869; d. Villeneuve les Avignon, 19 July 1940) Actor, director, dramaturg and manager. He entered the Théâtre Libre in 1888 but reacted against ANTOINE's naturalism. Influenced by painters such as Vuillard and Bonnard, he advocated a poetic, SYMBOLIST theatre. Dispensing with stage furniture and box-set, he encouraged a slow, singing dramatic delivery in atmospheric settings, curtained and carefully lit. At the Théâtre de Œuvre, after his first success with MAETERLINCK's *Pelléas and Mélisande* (1893), he became a great discoverer of foreign plays. IBSEN, STRINDBERG, GORKY and SHAW were in his repertoire, as well as D'ANNUNZIO, CLAUDEL and JARRY, whom he introduced to the public with the first *Ubu Roi* in 1896. He managed ELEONORA DUSE and wrote several books on theatre.

TERRY HODGSON

Lunacharsky, Anatoli [Vasilevich] (b. Poltava, Russia, 11 Nov. 1875; d. Menton, France, 26 Dec. 1933) Russian theatre critic, dramatist and first head of the Soviet Commissariat of Education and Enlightenment. Appointed to this post in 1919, he took issue with ultra-radical theatrical experimentalism and advocated a return to the realist traditions of the nineteenth century. Generally, however, he fostered a climate of critical tolerance in the arts, despite his own partisan preferences, and encouraged the building of new theatres. A writer of historical plays, as well as an expert on European history and culture, his death in 1933 robbed the AVANT-GARDE of the kind of powerful protector on whom some had relied and whom they so desperately needed.   NICK WORRALL

Sheila Fitzpatrick, *The Commissariat of Enlightenment: Soviet Organisation of Education and the Arts under Lunacharsky* (1970)

lunchtime theatre   As the name suggests, theatre that takes place at lunchtime, sometimes in pubs or cafés, sometimes in venues where FOOD AND DRINK can be consumed. There were sporadic antecedents (e.g. in CLUB THEATRE or during the Second World War), but it was only in the late 1960s and 1970s that the term acquired a distinct meaning as a notable part of the British FRINGE, and to a lesser degree OFF-OFF-BROADWAY. DAVID HALLIWELL and David Calderisi started the trend in Britain in 1966 with their group Quipu at the ARTS THEATRE, London, already noted as a gathering place because of its restaurant. Nothing unifies lunchtime theatre other than the time at which it takes place, and among many enterprises three stand out: INTER-ACTION's Ambiance Basement (1968), which later moved to the Almost Free and helped launch important ventures in women's, gay and black theatre; the Soho lunchtime theatre (1968), which became the SOHO POLY; and the KING'S HEAD (1970).   COLIN CHAMBERS
   See also PUB THEATRE.

Lunt, Alfred [David]   (b. Milwaukee, 12 Aug. 1892; d. Chicago, 3 Aug. 1977) and **Lynn [Lillie Louise Fontanne]** (b. Woodford, Essex, 6 Dec. 1887; d. Genesee Depot, Wisc., 30 July 1983)   Actors. After working in stock and in tours, Alfred won recognition in the title role of *Clarence* (1919) two years after his Broadway debut. Lynn, a dark-haired, willowy, feline actress with a deep, rich voice, came to America in 1910 but did not score a major success until *Dulcy* (1921). The pair married in 1922; most of their subsequent appearances were together and they came to be looked on as the finest American acting couple of the century. (The Globe Theater, New York, which had become a cinema, was reopened in 1958 bearing their name.) Their numerous credits include *The Guardsman* (1924), *Elizabeth the Queen* (1930), *Reunion in Vienna* (1931), *Idiot's Delight* (1936) and *Amphitryon 38* (1937). Except for their last play, *The Visit* (1958), most of their post-Second World War appearances were in superficial vehicles. Detractors lamented something finicky in Alf-

red's style compared with his wife's tigerish assurance.
GERALD BORDMAN

J. Brown, *The Fabulous Lunts* (1986)
P. Runkel, *Alfred Lunt and Lynn Fontanne: A Bibliography* (1978)
Maurice Zolotow, *Stagestruck: The Romance of Alfred Lunt and Lynn Fontanne* (1965)

Lupino, Stanley   (b. London, 15 May 1894; d. London, 10 June 1942). Actor and playwright, a member of the the Lupino/Lane family – known as the 'Royal Family of greasepaint' – who have been associated with the world of entertainment for over 300 years, tracing their roots back to a line of Italian puppet masters. (The Lupinos and the Lanes intermarried in the nineteenth century.) Stanley was trained by his father George and made his first appearance at the Britannia, Hoxton, in London's East End in 1900 – as a monkey. His first West End appearance was at DRURY LANE in *Dick Whittington* in 1910 – as the cat. A trained acrobat, he went on to find fame in REVUE, musical comedy and plays, some of which he wrote himself. Other members of the family include the actor Barry Lupino (1882–1962, elder brother and a leading PANTOMIME DAME), film actress Ida Lupino (b. 1914, daughter) and the cousins, actors LUPINO LANE and Wallace Lupino (1897–1961). Stanley's autobiography, *From the Stocks to the Stars*, appeared in 1934.
REXTON S. BUNNETT

LuPone, Patti   (b. Northport, NY, 21 April 1949) Actress and singer. She studied at the Juilliard School of Drama and for three years undertook a gruelling tour as a founder member of the school's Acting Company before making her OFF-BROADWAY debut with the company in 1972 in *The School for Scandal*. Her performance in *The Robber Bridegroom* (1975) earned her praise and in 1979 she won the lead in the US production of *Evita* from 200 other aspirants, for which she received Tony and Drama Desk Awards. After playing the part for 19 months she changed tack to appear in *As You Like It*. As well as touring with her own CABARET act, she returned to musicals with *The Cradle Will Rock* (1983), *Oliver!* (1984) and *Les Misérables* in London (1985), for which performance she was the first American to receive a Laurence Olivier Award. She followed this with success in revivals of *Anything Goes* (1987) and *Pal Joey* (1995), as well as starring in the London and New York productions of *Sunset Boulevard* (1993). In 1997 she played Maria Callas in *Master Class* on Broadway and in London.   HELEN RAPPAPORT

Lyceum Theater (New York)   The oldest surviving New York playhouse still in regular use, it was built on

45th Street, east of BROADWAY, by DANIEL FROHMAN and named after another theatre he had managed. The firm of Herts and Tallant was the designer. It opened in 1903 with *The Proud Prince*. Among its hits have been *The Lion and The Mouse* (1905), *Berkeley Square* (1929), *Junior Miss* (1941), *Born Yesterday* (1946) and *Look Back in Anger* (1957). In the 1970s and 1980s it was often dark, but Frohman's apartments above the theatre serve as the SHUBERT Archive and this means that the landmark theatre probably has some additional protection. GERALD BORDMAN

Lyceum Theatre (Edinburgh) The Scottish capital's repertory theatre opened in 1883 with HENRY IRVING and ELLEN TERRY as guest artists. Leading companies and performers from London dominated until the introduction of repertory seasons by Brandon-Thomas (1933–7) and the Wilson Barrett Company in the 1940s and 1950s. In 1964 Edinburgh Corporation bought the theatre and established the Edinburgh Civic Theatre Trust, and in 1965 the Lyceum developed its own in-house product, briefly under Tom Fleming (*see* GATEWAY), and later under the overall directorship of Clive Perry (1966–76), assisted by BILL BRYDEN and RICHARD EYRE. The Lyceum was Scotland's leading theatre throughout the 1970s in the encouragement of new indigenous writers, presenting the works of Stewart Conn (*The Burning*, 1971), Roddy Macmillan (*The Bevellers*, 1973) and Bryden (*Willie Rough*, 1972). The accolade of 'Scottish National Theatre' was mooted. The break-up of the Perry/Bryden/Eyre collaboration (the last two departing for England's NATIONAL THEATRE) led to a fallow period, but later a new company became well established under Kenny Ireland (from 1993). JAN MCDONALD

Donald Campbell, *A Brighter Sunshine: A Hundred Years of the Edinburgh Royal Lyceum Theatre* (1983)

Lynch, Martin *see* BELFAST; IRELAND

Lynne [Pyrke], Gillian [Barbara] (b. Bromley, Kent, 20 Feb. 1927) Dancer, choreographer and director. Having joined the Royal Ballet at 16, Lynne soon became a principal dancer appearing in numerous roles between 1944 and 1951. After dancing in VARIETY and musical REVUES in many London venues, Lynne eventually formed her own jazz-dance company, Collages (1963). She started as a choreographer in 1962 and moved from ballet and revue to film and musicals. Her collaboration with TREVOR NUNN at the ROYAL SHAKESPEARE COMPANY on *The Comedy of Errors* (1976) and *Once in a Lifetime* (1980) led to her choreographing ANDREW LLOYD WEBBER's *Cats* (1981), which has been reproduced internationally and won her many awards.

Further successful collaboration with Lloyd Webber followed on *Phantom of the Opera* (1986) and *Aspects of Love* (1989), again with Nunn. Her success as a choreographer and director has led to a string of over 50 London and Broadway shows and operas as well as work in film, ballet and television. HELEN RAPPAPORT
See also CHOREOGRAPHY; DANCE.

Lyric Theatre (West London) After success as a PANTOMIME and MELODRAMA venue and three reconstructions since opening in 1888, the derelict theatre in Hammersmith was taken over by NIGEL PLAYFAIR in 1918 and renamed the Lyric. Under his direction (until 1933) the theatre became a fashionable venue challenging the WEST END with a series of distinguished productions, often from the eighteenth century. They were noted for their elegance and included *The Beggar's Opera* (with vibrant designs by CLAUD LOVAT FRASER), which ran from 1920 to 1924, *The Way of the World* with EDITH EVANS in 1924 and *The Cherry Orchard* with JOHN GIELGUD in 1925. A tradition of REVUES was begun with A. P. Herbert's *Riverside Nights* (1926).

The theatre was a useful showcase outside, but possibly on the way to, the WEST END and housed an early production by PETER BROOK (*The Brothers Karamazov*, 1946), star-led H. M. TENNENT shows (playing COCTEAU, MILLER, SARTRE), a famous Gielgud season (1952–3), PINTER's first full-length play (*The Birthday Party*, 1958) and, in 1959 with the 59 Company that later formed the nucleus of the ROYAL EXCHANGE, Manchester, Büchner's *Danton's Death* and *Brand* by IBSEN. The Lyric closed in 1966, was demolished in 1972 and was reproduced in a new complex a short distance away in 1979 with a studio space attached, continuing under Peter James and his successor Neil Bartlett to stage high-quality and bold revivals, new plays and work from abroad (e.g. LYUBIMOV's production of *Crime and Punishment*, 1983). COLIN CHAMBERS

N. Playfair, *The Story of the Lyric* (1925)

lyricists *see* LIBRETTISTS

Lyttelton Theatre *see* ARCHITECTURE; NATIONAL THEATRE

Lyubimov, Yuri [Petrovich] (b. Yaroslavl, Russia, 17 Sept. 1917) Actor and director. He graduated from the Shchukin Drama School of the Vakhtangov Theatre, 1939, and after the war joined the VAKHTANGOV Theatre company (1946). He held classes at the Shchukin School from 1953 and, as a result of his production of BRECHT's *The Good Person of Setzuan* there, was offered the directorship of the then moribund TAGANKA THEATRE in 1964. The main body of the student group formed the nucleus of a company which, during the course of the next 20 years, was to revitalize Soviet theatre in a manner reminiscent of the early 1920s, providing a focus for the expression of intellectual and artistic dissent in the increasingly stagnant climate of the Brezhnev years. Very much a director's theatre, the Taganka nevertheless depended for its success both on a highly developed and sophisticated sense of a stylized theatre of convention inspired by MEYERHOLD, and also on the outstanding talents of a group of young actors, designers and musicians, including Vladimir Vysotsky, Alla Demidova and David Borovsky. Important productions by Lyubimov there include *Ten Days That Shook the World*, (1965), *The Exchange* (1976), *Hamlet* (1974) and *The Master and Margarita* (1977). In 1985 he left the Soviet Union to work in the West and staged notable productions of, for example, Dostoevsky's *Crime and Punishment* and *The Possessed* before returning to MOSCOW during the Gorbachev era. His autobiography, *The Sacred Flame*, appeared in 1989.   NICK WORRALL

Birgit Beumers, *Yuri Lyubimov at the Taganka Theatre 1964–1994* (1997)

Aleksandr Gershkovich, *The Theatre of Yuri Lyubimov* (1989)

M

Mabou Mines American experimental theatre COL-LECTIVE. With a name derived from a mining village in Nova Scotia near where the group worked in the summer of 1970, when it was formally founded after years of collaborative work in San Francisco and Paris, Mabou Mines has suffused the ensemble spirit of the 1960s with the innovations of new art and music – composer PHILIP GLASS was among the founders – creating new theatre pieces from original texts or by innovative stagings of existing texts. With no single artistic director, it encourages each of its eight members to pursue his/her artistic vision by assuming directorial authority in collaboration with the rest of the company. Significant productions are *Mabou Mines Presents Samuel Beckett* (director: LEE BREUER, 1975); *Cascando* (director: JOANNE AKALAITIS, 1977); *Wrong Guys* (director: Ruth Maleczech, 1981); *Lear* (director: Breuer, 1990). The group, once resident at LA MAMA (1970–3) and the PUBLIC THEATER (1975–85), is now based in Public Space 122, a converted school, and continues working into the new millennium (e.g. *Las Horas de Belén /A Book of Hours*, 1999). GERALD RABKIN

MacAnna, Tomás (b. Dundalk, Ireland, 1926) Designer and director. He moved to DUBLIN in 1944 to take a post with the Irish government's Customs and Excise department. A theatre enthusiast and fluent GAELIC speaker, he volunteered at the ABBEY THEATRE as a scene-painter. In 1947, the Abbey's managing director Ernest Blythe created the position of 'director of plays in Irish' for MacAnna, who in that role directed nearly 20 plays and pantomimes. MacAnna also directed many plays in English for the Abbey, opening up the repertoire to European playwrights. Among the highlights of his tenure was the première of BRENDAN

BEHAN's *Borstal Boy* (1967), which when remounted on BROADWAY in 1970 earned a Tony Award for best production. From 1949 to 1978 MacAnna served as the Abbey's scenic designer, generating over 130 sets. In 1966 he was appointed artistic director, a position he held until 1968, then again from 1973 to 1978, and again for a short time in 1985. He also served as the director of plays in the Peacock, the Abbey's second stage, from 1970 to 1972. KAREN FRICKER

McAnuff, Des *see* EXPERIMENTAL THEATRE; LA JOLLA PLAYHOUSE

MacArthur, Charles (b. Scranton, 5 Nov. 1895; d. New York, 21 April 1956) Playwright, screenwriter and journalist. His writing collaboration with another newspaperman, BEN HECHT, produced a number of Broadway hits and popular Hollywood films. The most luminous theatrical results of their partnership were *The Front Page* (1928), a much-revived insiders' look at the newspaper world which has been filmed three times, and *Twentieth Century* (1932), a showbiz comedy. His solo work includes the political satire *Johnny on a Spot* (1942). ALEXIS GREENE

Ben Hecht, *The Improbable Life and Times of Charles MacArthur* (1957)

McBean, Angus *see* THEATRE PHOTOGRAPHY

McBurney, Simon *see* THEATRE DE COMPLICITE

McCabe, Eugene (b. Glasgow, 7 July 1930) Playwright. *King of the Castle* (1964; frequently revived) introduced a major dramatist dealing in themes of emotional sterility and sexual longing in a milieu set between the traditional rural and emerging entre-

461

preneurial. He has written several novels, television and radio plays, and for the theatre *Breakdown* (1966), *Pull Down a Horseman* (1966), *Swift* (1969), *Gale Day* (1979) and *Heritage* (1980). CHRISTOPHER FITZ-SIMON

McCann, Donal (b. Dublin, 7 May 1943; d. Dublin, 17 July 1999) Actor. Despite bouts of depression and heavy drinking, he established himself in the eyes of many commentators as the leading Irish actor of his generation, noted for a burning, mesmeric intensity on television, film and stage. He studied architecture before joining the ABBEY THEATRE as an actor and first became known in 1969 when he played Estragon opposite PETER O'TOOLE in *Waiting for Godot*. He was particularly successful in O'CASEY, notably as Captain Boyle in *Juno and the Paycock*; also as Frank in a 1980 revival of BRIAN FRIEL's *The Faith Healer* and as the dying police chief in SEBASTIAN BARRY's *The Steward of Christendom* (1995), which was hailed in New York and London as well as in Dublin. CHARLES LONDON

McCarten, Anthony (b. New Plymouth, New Zealand, 28 April 1961) Playwright. After *Invitation to a Second Class Carriage* (1984) and *Yellow Canary Mazurka* (1987), he and Stephen Sinclair wrote *Ladies' Night* (1987), a play about male strippers which became New Zealand's most commercially successful play. Subsequent plays have included *Weed* (1990), *Via Satellite* (1991), for which he also wrote the screenplay, as well as directing the successful screen version in 1998, and *Hang on a Minute, Mate* (1992), an adaptation of a series of novels by Barry Crump.

GILLIAN GREER, LAURIE ATKINSON & SIMON GARRETT

MacCarthy, [Charles Otto] Desmond (b. Plymouth, 1877; d. Cambridge, 7 June 1952) Drama critic and man of letters. One of the most respected reviewers of his time, he became a journalist after completing his education at Eton and Cambridge; by 1904 he was the drama critic for *The Speaker*. In 1920 he became drama critic for the *New Statesman*, and began writing his most characteristic criticism. A familiar voice on the radio, he also reviewed books for the *Sunday Times*. A champion of SHAW's plays, he was admired for the alacrity and acuity of his judgements. He left an autobiography, *Memories* (1953), and his best work is collected in *Drama* (1940) and *Theatre* (1955). He was knighted in 1951. THOMAS F. CONNOLLY

McCarthy, Joseph *see* TIERNEY, HARRY

McCarthy, Lillah (b. Cheltenham, 22 Sept. 1875; d. London, 15 April 1960) English actress and manager. Her career was much associated with that of her first husband, HARLEY GRANVILLE BARKER, with whom she

appeared in several productions. She created many of SHAW's leading roles, including Ann Whitefield in *Man and Superman* (1905), Jennifer Dubedat in *The Doctor's Dilemma* (1906), Margaret Knox in *Fanny's First Play* (1911) and Lavinia in *Androcles and the Lion* (1913). She also played the title role in JOHN MASEFIELD's *The Tragedy of Nun* (1908) and several Greek leads (in *The Bacchae*, *Oedipus Rex* and *Iphigenia at Tauris*). McCarthy went into management with Barker at the SAVOY and on her own account at the Little Theatre (1911), presenting IBSEN, Shaw and SCHNITZLER. She also ran the KINGSWAY THEATRE after divorcing Barker in 1918 and was active in the ACTRESSES' FRANCHISE LEAGUE. Her autobiography, *Myself and My Friends*, appeared in 1933. IAN CLARKE

McClintic, Guthrie (b. Seattle, 6 Oct. 1893; d. New York, 29 Oct. 1961) Actor, director and producer. He studied at the American Academy of Dramatic Arts and made his New York debut in 1914. After acting in stock companies, he became the assistant to producer WINTHROP AMES. In 1921 he started directing and producing plays and married KATHARINE CORNELL. Thereafter he was associated with all of her important productions. He was widely respected for his casting choices, but feared as an exacting taskmaster during rehearsals. He won numerous awards and his nearly 100 stagings include: *The Dover Road* (1921), *The Green Hat* (1925), *The Shanghai Gesture* (1926), *The Barretts of Wimpole Street* (1931), *The Old Maid* (1935), *Winterset* (1935), *Ethan Frome* (1936) and *Hamlet*, with JOHN GIELGUD (1936). His autobiography, *Me and Kit*, came out in 1955; he was lampooned as Carleton Fitzgerald by MOSS HART in *Light Up the Sky* (1948).

THOMAS F. CONNOLLY

McColl, Colin (b. Lower Hutt, New Zealand, 25 Dec. 1948) Director. After experience in the United States, UK and Australia, he returned to New Zealand to become director of the DOWNSTAGE THEATRE. He established a reputation for updated modern classics (IBSEN, BRECHT, DÜRRENMATT), often with New Zealand settings. His *Hedda Gabler* was the first New Zealand production invited to the EDINBURGH FESTIVAL (1990). He has directed Ibsen in Oslo and the Netherlands. He has also had a major influence on New Zealand theatre by encouraging MAORI theatre and promoting and directing New Zealand playwrights such as PETER HAWES, VINCENT O'SULLIVAN, John Broughton and HONE KOUKA. His productions range from *Sweeney Todd* to *She Stoops to Conquer* and *Cat on a Hot Tin Roof*.

GILLIAN GREER & LAURIE ATKINSON

MacColl, Ewan [Jimmy Miller] (b. Salford, near Manchester, 25 Jan. 1915; d. Beckenham, Kent, 22 Oct. 1989) Songwriter, singer and playwright; an inspirational revolutionary figure in oppositional culture. He left school at 14 and two years later had founded the AGITPROP STREET THEATRE group Red Megaphones, a forerunner of the pioneering THEATRE WORKSHOP which he established with his first wife, JOAN LITTLEWOOD, and others in 1945. He was the touring company's main playwright until the early 1950s, when he opposed its move to a permanent theatre in London. He had studied modern theories of drama and was particularly interested in the movement ideas of LABAN, whose assistant Jean Newlove – Theatre Workshop's movement teacher – was his second wife. Mac-Coll was an encyclopedically knowledgeable leader of the folk revival, and his work on radio ballads changed broadcasting and influenced stage DOCUMENTARY. As an enthusiast for language he was a skilful adaptor (of Aristophanes, Jonson, Molière, LORCA and Hašek). His own plays include *Johnny Noble* (1945); *Uranium 235* (1946), one of the first anti-nuclear war plays, if not the first; *The Other Animals* (1948). His third wife was the folk singer Peggy Seeger. His autobiography, *Journeyman*, appeared in 1990. COLIN CHAMBERS

C. Chambers and M. Prior, *Playwrights' Progress* (1987)
H. Goorney, *The Theatre Workshop Story* (1981)
J. Littlewood, *Joan's Book* (1994)

McCormick, F. J. [Peter Judge] (b. Dublin, 1 June 1890; d. Dublin, 24 April 1947) Actor. He joined the ABBEY THEATRE at the age of 19 and played in some 500 productions there, including O'CASEY's Dublin trilogy in which he created Seumas Shields, Joxer Daly and Jack Clitheroe. CHRISTOPHER FITZ-SIMON

McCowen, Alec [Alexander Duncan] (b. Tunbridge Wells, Kent, 26 May 1925) Actor. He began his professional career in repertory theatre in 1943 before making his first London appearance, in *Escapade*, in 1953. He joined the OLD VIC company in 1959 and subsequently the ROYAL SHAKESPEARE COMPANY, where, among many other roles, he was an unforgettable Fool to PAUL SCOFIELD's King Lear in PETER BROOK's seminal 1962 production. He had huge successes in both London and New York, first in Peter Luke's *Hadrian VII* (1967) and then in CHRISTOPHER HAMPTON's *The Philanthropist* (1970), establishing himself as the leading exponent of a fastidious, elegant, particularly English style of acting, which he exploited further at the NATIONAL THEATRE, notably as Alceste in TONY HARRISON's adaptation of *The Misanthrope* and as Dysart in PETER SHAFFER's *Equus*. He has associated himself frequently with new work, as well as giving memorable performances in Shakespeare (as Prospero in *The Tempest*) and CHEKHOV (as Gayev in *The Cherry Orchard*) for RSC productions in the 1990s. His SOLO performance of his own adaptation of *The Gospel According to St Mark*, which he first gave in 1978, was a tour de force. He has written two volumes of autobiography, *Young Gemini* (1979) and *Double Bill* (1980). GENISTA MCINTOSH

McCracken, Esther [Helen] (b. Newcastle upon Tyne, 25 June 1902; d. 9 August 1971) Playwright and actress. McCracken spent eight years with the Newcastle Repertory Company during the late 1920s. She wrote many smash hits, including *The Willing Spirit* (1936) and *Quiet Wedding* (1938), and is seen as having taken over as 'queen of the domestic comedy' where DODIE SMITH left off. *A Quiet Weekend* (1941) played for over 1,000 performances. She played a succession of roles in productions of her own plays, and her work made her into a household name. MAGGIE GALE

McCullers, Carson [Lula] (b. Columbus, Ga., 19 Feb. 1917; d. Nyack, NY, 3 Oct. 1967) Writer. While not primarily a playwright, her 1950 dramatization of her novel, *Member of the Wedding*, starring JULIE HARRIS as the 12-year-old motherless child and ETHEL WATERS as the black cook, ran for 501 performances. It was later filmed, as were her novels *The Ballad of the Sad Café*, which EDWARD ALBEE dramatized in 1963, and *The Heart is a Lonely Hunter*. Her only other play was *The Square Root of Wonderful* (1957). JANE HOUSE

McCullough, Paul *see* CLARK, BOBBY

McDermott, Phelim *see* IMPROBABLE THEATRE

McDiarmid, Ian (b. Carnoustie, Tayside, Scotland, 11 Aug. 1944) Actor and director. He first came to prominence in the early 1970s as a member of the GLASGOW CITIZENS' company, where his ferocious intelligence and bravura style were admirably suited to the theatre's repertoire. In 1974, he began a long association with the ROYAL SHAKESPEARE COMPANY during which he played, among many roles, Shylock in *The Merchant of Venice*. He became a particularly fine exponent of new writing, especially the work of EDWARD BOND and HOWARD BARKER, whose plays he continued to perform in and direct after he moved on from the RSC to become an associate director at the MANCHESTER ROYAL EXCHANGE THEATRE. In 1989 he was appointed, with his long-time colleague Jonathan Kent, joint artistic director of the ALMEIDA THEATRE in north London, which they transformed in the following few years into one of the most important producing theatres in the

UK. Here he gave some of his finest performances, notably as Volpone and as Orgon in *Tartuffe*, and successfully continued to direct both plays and opera. He has also worked extensively in film and television and is probably best known for his performances in the *Star Wars* series of films. GENISTA MCINTOSH

McDonagh, Martin (b. London, 26 March 1970) Playwright. His first major play was *The Beauty Queen of Leenane* (1996), co-produced by DRUID THEATRE COMPANY and the ROYAL COURT. This established McDonagh's style; set in a remote village in the west of Ireland, it follows a mother's determination to crush any possibility of independence for her daughter. The play is structured around a series of thrilling reversals, written with the theatrical confidence of Dion Boucicault; the dialogue, making full use of a certain kind of stage Irish vernacular, is witty, warm and touching. It was the first play in what became the *Leenane Trilogy* (1997), the two others being a grim comedy about two feuding brothers, *The Lonesome West*, and a graveyard story of a man with a past, *A Skull in Connemara*. McDonagh's *The Cripple of Inishmaan* (1997) depicts the effect on a small Irish community when a Hollywood company film in the area.

Garlanded with prizes and honours, his work can seem self-conscious and artificial set against the more sinuous stage language of his contemporaries like BILLY ROCHE and CONOR MCPHERSON. It remains to be seen if his style will develop sufficiently to make it capable of embodying truly powerful emotional and intellectual experiences. DAN REBELLATO

Aleks Sierz, *In-Yer-Face Theatre: British Drama Today* (2001)

MacDonald, Robert David (b. Elgin, Scotland, 27 Aug. 1929) Playwright, dramaturg and director. A self-taught polygot, MacDonald has translated and/or adapted for the stage works by European authors such as Goldoni, Lermontov, Goethe, Tolstoy, LORCA and Proust. His original works include *Dracula* (1972), *Chinchilla* (1977) and *Summit Conference* (1978). *Chinchilla*, set in the world of DIAGHILEV, he described as 'a metaphor' for the company at the CITIZENS' THEATRE, where he is one of an artistic triumvirate with GILES HAVERGAL and PHILIP PROWSE, promoting the policy of theatrical Europeanism. JAN MCDONALD
See also ADAPTATION/TRANSLATION.

MacDougall, Roger (b. Glasgow, 2 Aug. 1910; d. London, 31 May 1993) Screenwriter and playwright. A regular contributor to Ealing Studios, his writing partnership with John Dighton and Alexander Mackendrick produced the celebrated film *The Man in the White Suit*, for which ALEC GUINNESS won an Oscar nomination. His plays include *The Gentle Gunman* and *To Dorothy a Son* (both 1950), *Escapade* (1952) and *The Trouble with Father* (1964). JAN MCDONALD

McEwan [McKeown], Geraldine (b. Old Windsor, Berks, 9 May 1932) Actress, renowned for her idiosyncratic voice, who first appeared in her local rep as an attendant in *A Midsummer Night's Dream* (1946). Her West End debut in John Dighton's comedy *Who Goes There?* (1951) brought her stardom and typecasting. She was a celebrated Beatrice in *Much Ado About Nothing* (STRATFORD-UPON-AVON, 1961) and showed her versatility by playing the prostitute-wife in *Everything in the Garden* the following year. A series of leading roles followed, including many with the NATIONAL THEATRE from 1965 (*Armstrong's Last Goodnight*, 1965; *The Dance of Death*, 1966; *The Way of the World*, 1969; *The Browning Version/Harlequinade*, 1980). In 1995 she won the *Evening Standard* Best Actress Award for the role of Lady Wishfort in another production of *The Way of the World* at the National and in 1997 captivated London in a revival of *The Chairs*. In 1988 she directed *As You Like It* for the Renaissance Theatre Company, and in 1991 *Four Door Saloon* at the Hampstead Theatre. D. KEITH PEACOCK

MacGowan, Kenneth (b. Winthrop, Mass., 30 Nov. 1888; d. Los Angeles, 27 April 1963) Director, author, drama critic and producer. From 1919 to 1925, Macgowan was one of the primary reporters on the international theatre scene. As an editor for and contributor to *Theater Arts Magazine* he was responsible for much of the transmission of theatrical activities abroad to the United States. With ROBERT EDMOND JONES he collaborated on the seminal work on European theatrical innovations, *Continental Stagecraft* (1922). From 1923 to 1926 he served with Jones and EUGENE O'NEILL as part of the triumvirate of directors who gained control of the PROVINCETOWN PLAYERS, and was influential on O'Neill's development as a playwright. ANNE FLETCHER

MacGowran, Jack (b. Dublin, 13 Oct. 1918; d. New York, 13 Jan. 1973) Actor, closely associated with the work of SAMUEL BECKETT. He played at the GATE and ABBEY Theatres in Dublin (1944–50), and was a founder of the Dublin Globe Theatre (1954). A student of mime, he played the lead in IONESCO's *Amédée* (1957) and was a notable Harry in O'NEILL's *The Iceman Cometh* (1958). He acted often in the West End, and in films (directed by Polanski, Rotha, Ford and others), and also directed. He excelled in comically grotesque roles. He was Clov in the British première of *Endgame* (1958), and played in the first productions of two

Beckett radio plays, *All That Fall* (1957) and *Embers* (1958). He performed three solo Beckett presentations – *Beginning to End* (1965) toured internationally – and he lectured on Beckett and O'CASEY, with whose plays he was also associated. CHRISTOPHER FITZ-SIMON

McGrath, John [Peter] (b. Birkenhead, Merseyside, 1 June 1935) Playwright and director. He achieved success with the anti-militaristic *Events While Guarding the Bofors Gun* (1966, filmed in 1968 as *The Bofors Gun*) and wrote episodes for the realistic television series *Z Cars* as well as popular films before aiming at working-class audiences in Liverpool (e.g. *Fish in the Sea*, 1972, for the EVERYMAN) and founding the socialist theatre companies 7:84 (1971) and 7:84 (Scotland) (1973). Most notable among his many plays is the innovative Ceilidh piece, *The Cheviot, the Stag and the Black, Black Oil* (1973). One of the major contributors to POLITICAL THEATRE in the last three decades of the century, McGrath, in his book *A Good Night Out* (1981), produced a seminal work on the theory and practice of popular entertainment. He followed this with a second volume, *The Bone Won't Break* (1990). JAN MCDONALD

Colin Chambers and Mike Prior, *Playwrights' Progress* (1987)
Maria DiCenzo, *The Politics of Alternative Theatre in Britain, 1968–1990: The Case of 7:84 (Scotland)* (1996)
Catherine Itzin, *Stages in the Revolution* (1980)
Baz Kershaw, *The Politics of Performance* (1992)

McGuinness, Frank (b. Buncrana, Co. Donegal, Ireland, 29 July 1953) Playwright, undoubtedly the most brilliant of his generation. His work reflects profound sensitivity to human emotions, expressed in richly allusive language and often mixed with an irreverent vein of satiric comedy. The ABBEY THEATRE, Dublin, first produced *The Factory Girls* (1982), the award-winning *Observe the Sons of Ulster Marching Towards the Somme* and *Baglady* (both 1985), a version of LORCA's *Yerma* (1987) and *Carthaginians* (1989). The GATE THEATRE, Dublin, produced *Innocence: The Life and Death of Michaelangelo Merisi Caravaggio* (1986) and versions of IBSEN's *Peer Gynt* (1988), CHEKHOV's *Three Sisters* (1990) and the BRECHT–WEILL *The Threepenny Opera* (1991). A version of Ibsen's *Rosmersholm* (1987) was given at the NATIONAL THEATRE, London (1987), as was his adaptation of *The Caucasian Chalk Circle* (1997) and his own play, *Mutabilitie* (1997); *Mary and Lizzie* was seen at the ROYAL SHAKESPEARE COMPANY (1989). An Abbey production of *Barbaric Comedies*, his version of a trilogy by VALLE-INCLÁN, was seen at the EDINBURGH FESTIVAL in 2000. Most of his plays have been produced abroad, and he has been the recipient of numerous international awards. He charts the ambition and pain of Irish survival, wracked by civil war and increasingly uncertain of faith and ideology, yet building a new future. In *Someone Who'll Watch Over Me* (1992) three hostages typically transcend differences in an effort to find a common bond; and in *Dolly West's Kitchen* (1999) conflicting personal and national loyalties are set in the frame of the Second World War. CHRISTOPHER FITZ-SIMON

E. Jordan, *The Feast of Famine: The Plays of Frank McGuinness* (1997)

McIntyre, Clare *see* WOMEN'S THEATRE GROUP

MacIntyre, Tom (b. Cavan, Ireland, 10 Dec. 1931) Playwright. Struggling with a tradition that is often extravagently verbal, MacIntyre is one of the few Irish playwrights to have followed YEATS's TOTAL THEATRE and BECKETT's linguistic minimalism. A considerable prose writer, in his theatre writing MacIntyre slowly moved away from dependence on the word towards a physical 'imagistic' style. Early plays – *Eye Winker, Tom Tinker* (1972), based on the life of the Fenian revolutionary James Stephens, and *Find the Lady* (1977), based on the story of Salomé – move from the relatively conventional to somewhere halfway between the literary and the AVANT-GARDE. Influenced by American theatre dance – he produced *Doobally/Black Way* (1979) with the Calque-Hook company – and with director PATRICK MASON and actor Tom Hickey, he moved towards a dream-like, primarily visual theatre with little dialogue. His first and most successful such collaboration, *The Great Hunger* (1983), based on Patrick Kavanagh's poem, was successfully toured abroad. Subsequent works with the same team – *The Bearded Lady* (1984, based on Swift); *Rise Up Lovely Sweeney* (1985); *Dance for Your Daddy* (1986); and *Snow White* (1988) – have been more involuted psychic explorations. FINTAN O'TOOLE

Mackay, Steele *see* DRAMA SCHOOLS

McKellen, [Murray] Ian (b. Burnley, Lancs, 25 May 1939) English actor. After success as an undergraduate actor, when he showed a prodigious appetite and gift for the classical repertoire, he played at the Belgrade, Coventry, and NOTTINGHAM Playhouse before making his London debut in JAMES SAUNDERS's *A Scent of Flowers* (1964). A season at the NATIONAL THEATRE was followed by lead roles in Donald Howarth's *A Lily in Little India* (1966) and ALEXEI ARBUZOV's *The Promise* (1966; Broadway 1967). His Richard II and Edward II (1969) for the PROSPECT THEATRE COMPANY established him as a classical actor. He co-founded the Actors'

Company (1972) with Edward Petherbridge (b. 1936) and in 1974 joined the ROYAL SHAKESPEARE COMPANY, with which he played many notable roles, including Faustus, Romeo, and Bernick in IBSEN's *Pillars of the Community*; and in three celebrated TREVOR NUNN productions, as Face in *The Alchemist*, Macbeth and Iago. McKellen led the RSC's first, annual small-scale tour in 1978. He played one of the incarcerated homosexuals in MARTIN SHERMAN's *Bent* (1980) and, after appearing as Salieri in the New York production of PETER SHAFFER's *Amadeus* (1980), went to the NATIONAL THEATRE under PETER HALL, where he played in MICHAEL FRAYN's CHEKHOV adaptation *Wild Honey* (1984) and Coriolanus (1984) in Hall's production. A year later he led a company of actors at the NT which performed *The Duchess of Malfi*, *The Real Inspector Hound* and *The Critic*, and *The Cherry Orchard*. Under RICHARD EYRE's directorship he gave a gravely comic performance in DE FILIPPO's *Napoli Milionaria*; he also played Uncle Vanya, and Richard III in Eyre's modern-dress production which toured Europe and the United States.

Unquestionably the leading theatre actor of his generation, he has undeviatingly dedicated himself to theatre in all its aspects, directing, frequently becoming involved in running companies (at the RSC and the NT), seeking democracy on and off the stage (the Actors' Company), and tirelessly lobbying and proselytizing for the subsidized theatre as a whole. From the end of the 1980s he also campaigned for gay rights and AIDS charities.

Initially somewhat mannered, McKellen has worked with great determination and increasing self-knowledge to achieve performances that are a model of fastidious detail and truthfulness, underpinned by a ferocious energy and intelligence. He was knighted in 1991. RICHARD EYRE

See also CHEKHOV; SHAKESPEARE IN THE TWENTIETH CENTURY.

Joy Leslie Gibson, *Ian McKellen* (1986)

McKenna, Siobhán (b. Belfast, 24 May 1923; d. Dublin, 16 Nov. 1986) Actress. Perhaps the last of the great heroic actresses, McKenna suffered from working in a theatrical period not particularly sympathetic to heroic acting. Born into a nationalist, Irish-speaking family, which moved from Belfast to Galway where her father was professor of mathematical physics, she came to symbolize Ireland in much the same way that LAURENCE OLIVIER came to symbolize England, and the burden made it difficult for her to establish a long-term relationship with any repertory company. Though she worked for periods with the ABBEY, where her professional career began in 1943 (playing in both English

and Gaelic) and with the ROYAL SHAKESPEARE COMPANY (in 1952), most of her career was spent without the support of a company that would ensure she performed the major classic roles. She did play a range of notable parts (in BRECHT, O'CASEY, FRIEL, CHEKHOV, O'NEILL) and her triumphs tended to be individual ones: as SHAW's St Joan (London, 1954; New York, 1956) as SYNGE's Pegeen Mike in *The Playboy of the Western World* (first in 1951, then on tour, 1960), even as a female Hamlet (New York, 1959). Much of her latter career was spent in one-woman showpieces, such as *Here Are Ladies* (first seen 1970), compilations of her favourite parts. She found, however, a late home in the emerging DRUID THEATRE COMPANY in Galway, giving a magnificent performance in TOM MURPHY's *Baileqangaire* (1985), her last role before her death, which confirmed her extraordinary vocal range and emotional power. FINTAN O'TOOLE

McKenzie, Elizabeth *see* DAVIOT, GORDON

Mackintosh, Cameron [Anthony] (b. Enfield, Midd'x, 17 Oct. 1946) Producer. He credits a childhood visit to the SLADE-REYNOLDS musical comedy *Salad Days* with motivating him to enter the theatre, which he did first as an acting student. He quickly abandoned this to work as a stagehand on his way to becoming a producer, an ambition realized at the age of 21 with a touring version of *Little Women*. At 23 he produced his first West End musical (a disastrous revival of *Anything Goes*) and at 30 he had his first real success with *Side By Side By Sondheim* (1976). For some years his bread and butter came from provincial tours with other people's London successes (notably *Godspell*) but in 1981 he launched *Cats* – a show for which he and ANDREW LLOYD WEBBER (who was both composer and co-producer) had the utmost difficulty in raising the necessary capital. Its worldwide success gave Mackintosh the opportunity to extend his managerial activities to other countries and he set up subsidiary companies in the United States and Australia with the declared intention of becoming a global impresario. Fortune smiled on his next major production, a revised English version of the French musical *Les Misérables* which began with the ROYAL SHAKESPEARE COMPANY in 1985, and smiled again with *The Phantom of the Opera* (1986), giving him three major international hits which for a long time were all playing simultaneously in London, New York and Vienna – a total conquest of the three world capitals of the light musical theatre. The victory was confirmed in 1989 when he launched *Miss Saigon*, an updated treatment of the *Madame Butterfly* story. In the same year his charitable foundation endowed Oxford University with a a chair of contemporary drama, first occupied by STEPHEN SONDHEIM, whose musical *Follies* Mackintosh had produced in 1987. Although fortune has not smiled on him quite so generously since his three outstanding hits, he has continued to mount both new musicals and revivals of classic shows, both solo and in tandem with Britain's NATIONAL THEATRE, and is acknowledged as the world's leading producer of MUSICAL THEATRE. Mackintosh was knighted in 1995.

IAN BEVAN

S. Morley and Ruth Leon, *Hey Mr Producer* (1998)

McLean, Bruce   *see* BODY ART

MacLeish, Archibald   (b. Glencoe, Ill., 7 May 1892; d. Boston, 20 April 1982)   Poet and playwright. After writing in Paris in the 1920s, MacLeish published several poetry collections and won the Pulitzer Prize for *Conquistador* (1932) and *Collected Poems 1917–1952*. Although he wrote several verse dramas for both stage and radio, including *Panic* (1935) and *The Fall of the City* (1937), his only significant stage success was *J.B.* (1958) – a modern-day version of the Book of Job, which again earned him the Pulitzer Prize, as well as a Tony Award for best play.   HELEN RAPPAPORT

McLellan, Robert   (b.Kirkfieldbank, Lanarks, Scotland, 28 Jan. 1907; d. Isle of Arran, 27 Jan. 1985)   The most successful Scottish playwright of the mid-century, McLellan's career is closely associated with Glasgow's Curtain Theatre (1933–8). His most accomplished early play is *Jamie the Saxt* (1936), wherein an intricate, not to say confusing, plot sees the canny King James VI caught in a tangled morass of politicking and intrigue. Greatly influenced by JOHN BRANDANE and the linguistic principles of the Scottish Renaissance, McLellan was committed to writing in Scots. *The Flouers o' Edinburgh* (1947), a satire on the fashion of the eighteenth-century Edinburgh gentry to employ tutors to instruct them in the manners of polite (English) society, has a worthy companion piece in his most significant later play, *The Hypocrite* (1967). Although his plays are historical, their style and wit give them much contemporary resonance.

ADRIENNE SCULLION

MacLíammóir, Mícheál [Alfred Willmore]   (b. London, 25 Oct. 1899; d. Dublin, 6 March 1978)   Actor, designer and playwright; co-founder with HILTON EDWARDS of the Dublin GATE THEATRE in 1928. A leading child actor in London from 1911 to 1914, he then learnt Gaelic and developed a romantic attachment to Ireland while attending the Slade art school, and subsequently became a well-known illustrator and stage designer, much influenced by Beardsley and BAKST. He returned to acting with ANEW MCMASTER's Shakespearean company in 1927, where he met Edwards, and thereafter played and designed at the Gate in over 300 productions. He directed and acted in Gaelic plays for An Comhar Dramuíochta, Dublin, and An Taibhdhearc, Galway, which he also founded with Edwards (1928). His own plays include *Where Stars Walk* (1940), *Ill Met by Moonlight* (1946), *The Mountains Look Different* (1948) and *Prelude in Kazbek Street* (1973). His one-person shows *The Importance of Being Oscar* (1960) and *I Must Be Talking to my Friends* (1963) enjoyed worldwide tours. His memoirs include *All For Hecuba* (1946), *Put Money In Thy Purse* (on the making of the *Othello* film with Orson Welles, 1950) and *Each Actor on His Ass* (1961).   CHRISTOPHER FITZ-SIMON

See also GAELIC THEATRE IN IRELAND.

Christopher Fitz-Simon, *The Boys* (1995)

McMahon, Gregan   (b. Sydney, 2 March 1874; d. Melbourne, 30 Aug. 1941)   Actor and director. Moving from acting to directing in 1911, McMahon was enormously influential in introducing the plays of SHAW, IBSEN, CHEKHOV, GALSWORTHY and GRANVILLE BARKER to Australian audiences by founding both the Melbourne and Sydney Repertory Theatres with amateur casts whom he trained. He also encouraged local playwriting, premièring ESSON's *The Time Is Not Yet Ripe* (1912). In the 1920s, with commercial backing, he founded the first professional repertories in the country. In 1936, Shaw allowed him to direct the English-language première of *The Millionairess*. Shaw once said, 'My impressions of Australia are sheep and Gregan McMahon.'   JEREMY ECCLES

Katharine Brisbane, *Entertaining Australia* (1991)
Dennis Douglas, and Margery Morgan, 'Gregan McMahon and the Australian Theatre', *Komos*, vol. 2, no. 2, 1969

McMaster, Anew   (b. Birkenhead, Merseyside, 24 Dec. 1891; d. Dublin, 25 Aug. 1962)   Actor–manager, brother-in-law of MÍCHEÁL MACLÍAMMÓIR. He is chiefly remembered as the leading Irish Shakespearean actor of his day – an outstanding Shylock – and for his exceptionally popular touring company which he ran in Victorian style between other engagements from 1925 until 1957, the subject of HAROLD PINTER's entertaining monograph *Mac* (1968). He started with Fred Terry's company in 1911 and rapidly became a juvenile lead, culminating in a long run in *Paddy the Next Best Thing* (1920). He played in this and other productions in Australia (1921–4). At STRATFORD-UPON-AVON, he played Bolingbroke, Coriolanus, Hamlet, Macduff and Petrucchio in the early 1930s. He went with the Dublin GATE THEATRE to Cairo in 1937, playing his famous Othello, and Charles Surface in *The School for Scandal*. In 1956 he starred memorably in JOSE QUINTERO's production of *Long Day's Journey into Night* on tour in the United States. CHRISTOPHER FITZ-SIMON

Macmillan, Kenneth *see* DANCE

McNally, Terrence (b. St Petersburg, Fla., 3 Nov. 1939) Playwright. McNally wrote his first play while still in high school, and after studying journalism at university worked as a stage manager at the ACTORS' STUDIO. During the burgeoning of OFF-OFF-BROADWAY he wrote many one-act plays, notably the pair *Witness and Sweet Eros* (1968) and *Next* (1969), which ran for over 700 performances. After failing to find success with his full-length plays, McNally returned to the one-act form with *Bad Habits* (a double bill of *Ravenswood* and *Dunelawn*, 1971), which eventually transferred to Broadway. A bigger box-office hit was the musical *The Ritz* (1975, filmed 1976) but other critical disappointments dogged him until the major success of *Frankie and Johnnie in the Clair de Lune* (1987), which McNally turned into a successful screenplay (1991). He returned to the stage musical with the Tony Award winning *Kiss of the Spider Woman* (1990). His love of opera is shown in *Master Class* (1995), about Maria Callas. *Corpus Christi* (1998), which portrays Jesus as homosexual, outraged fundamentalists of the Christian and Muslim faiths. Police were on guard at the première, and threats and protests have dogged the play in the United States and the UK, including the issuing of a fatwa against McNally by the Shari'ah court in Britain. HELEN RAPPAPORT

MacNamara, Brinsley [John Weldon] (b. Delvin, Co. Westmeath, Ireland, 6 Sept. 1890; d. Dublin, 4 Feb. 1963) Novelist and playwright. All his plays, mainly rural comedies on social themes, received their first productions at the ABBEY THEATRE, of which he became a director. *The Glorious Uncertainty* (1923), *Look at the Heffernans!* (1926) and *Margaret Gillan* (1933) have often been revived. CHRISTOPHER FITZ-SIMON

R. J. Porter, *Brinsley McNamara and George Shiels* (1973)

MacNeice, [Frederick] Louis (b. Belfast, 12 Sept. 1907; d. London, 3 Sept. 1964) Poet, playwright, translator and RADIO dramatist. In the 1930s he was grouped with W. H. AUDEN, not so much for his politics as for his approach to language. A classics lecturer, he joined the BBC in 1941 and became a feature-writer and producer. He wrote plays for radio, such as *Chris-*

topher Columbus (1944) and *The Dark Tower* (1946), and for the stage, e.g. *Out of the Picture* (1937), as well as translations of Aeschylus' *Agamemnon* (1936) and Goethe's *Faust* (1951). His unfinished autobiography *The Strings are False* was published posthumously in 1965. THOMAS F. CONNOLLY

See also VERSE DRAMA.

McNeil, Jim (b. Melbourne, 23 Jan. 1935; d. Sydney, 16 May 1982) Playwright who, while serving a 17-year gaol sentence for armed robbery and wounding a policeman, began writing plays about prison life. Although all of his plays deal with the dispossessed, oppressed, brutalized and often brutal members of society, they are notable for a distinctive combination of comedy and violence, hopelessness and vitality. They include *The Chocolate Frog* (1971), *The Old Familiar Juice* (1972) and *How Does Your Garden Grow?* (1974). MICHAEL MORLEY

McPherson, Conor (b. Dublin, 6 Aug. 1971) Playwright. McPherson's writing career began with an acclaimed series of plays – *Rum and Vodka* (1992), *The Good Thief* (1994) and *This Lime Tree Bower* (1995) – all performed by his own company, the Dublin-based Fly By Night. *St Nicholas* (1997) was an extraordinary monologue, performed by BRIAN COX at the BUSH THEATRE, about a jaded theatre critic, who unwisely pursues a romantic dream and becomes involved with a group of vampires. His most successful play to date, *The Weir* (1997), premièred at the ROYAL COURT, tracks one night in a pub in rural Ireland, when the storytelling efforts of the male regulars are equalled and undercut by the more profoundly upsetting story of a young woman new to the area. *Dublin Carol* (2000), a moving exploration of guilt and reconciliation, re-opened the revamped Royal Court Theatre. McPherson's strikingly confident and witty handling of narrative, and his no less impressive emotional complexity, mark him out as one of the most promising new writers in Irish theatre. DAN REBELLATO

Macedonia *see* YUGOSLAVIA

Madagascar *see* FRENCH AFRICAN THEATRE

Maddermarket Theatre The Guild of the Norwich Players was founded in 1911 by W. NUGENT MONCK, who had worked with and been much influenced by WILLIAM POEL. After a break during the First World War, the group was re-formed and in 1921 Monck bought what had originally been an eighteenth-century Catholic chapel, then being used by the Salvation Army, to convert it into a theatre, which he named the Maddermarket. This was based as far as practicable on an Elizabethan theatre plan. Here he was able to follow Poel's idea of continuous, non-scenic production of Shakespeare's plays, which he did with great success, producing the entire canon. A front curtain hung between the two advanced pillars on the stage facilitated the production of more modern plays.

Monck ruled the theatre as an autocrat. The amateur actors were subject to very strict rules and discipline: no curtain calls, no names in programmes, no taking part in other dramatic performances without permission, two years working as an associate before qualifying for full membership as a player. It was only Monck's own total commitment that enabled him to forge such a tight-knit community, which at its best was capable of a very high standard of work. The Maddermarket achieved a fame and an influence far beyond its limited field of operation.

After Monck's retirement in 1952, the theatre became more professionally staffed, with a paid director, designer, stage manager, wardrobe mistress and house manager: in effect a professional theatre with amateur actors. ALFRED EMMET

See also AMATEUR THEATRE; LITTLE THEATRE GUILD OF GREAT BRITAIN.

C. Rigby, *Maddermarket Mondays* (1933)
The Maddermarket Theatre, Norwich (1975)

Maddy, Yulisa [Amadu] (b. Freetown, Sierra Leone, 27 Dec. 1936) Playwright and director. He has worked in different parts of Africa, including Nigeria and Zimbabwe besides his own country, as well as in Britain, the United States and Scandinavia. A collection of his plays, *Obasai and Other Plays*, was published in 1971. *Pulse* (1979), which Maddy wrote with the Ethiopian writer Alem Mezgebe, deals with dictatorship in African countries and gave Maddy an opportunity to act out his imprisonment in Sierra Leone in 1976. With DELE CHARLEY, he has promoted the use of the Creole language, Krio, especially in *Big Berrin* ('Big burial'), which led to Maddy's imprisonment. KOLE OMOTOSO

Maeterlinck, Maurice [Mauritius Polydorus Maila Bernardus] (b. Ghent, Belgium, 29 Aug. 1862; d. Nice, France, 6 May 1949) Playwright and poet, awarded the Nobel Prize for Literature in 1911. Much of his dramatic output – symbolic and gloomy in tone, written in French – was quickly forgotten, although it was important at the time in the development of a modern European drama. His SYMBOLISM and belief that stillness would reveal the elusive forces of life (e.g. in *Les Aveugles/The Blind*, 1891) had led some commentators to see him as a forerunner of the THEATRE OF THE ABSURD and his suppressed eroticism

to prefigure PINTER. He is best remembered for *Pelléas et Mélisande*, first staged by LUGNÉ-POË in Paris in 1893, which had a memorable production in London in 1904 in which MRS PATRICK CAMPBELL (Mélisande) played opposite SARAH BERNHARDT (Pelléas). It was also used as the libretto for Débussy's opera. Although he wrote many other plays, Maeterlinck's only other enduring, popular success was *The Blue Bird*, first staged by STANISLAVSKY at the MOSCOW ART THEATRE in 1908. Its elements of fairy-tale and fantasy have inspired numerous film versions. HELEN RAPPAPORT

Bettina L. Knapp, *Maurice Maeterlinck* (1975)
Patrick Mahony, *Maurice Maeterlinck, Mystic and Dramatist* (1984)
Patrick McGuinness, *Maurice Maeterlinck and the Making of Modern Theatre* (2000)
Katherine Worth, *Maeterlinck's Plays in Performance* (1985)

magazines and journals Alongside the coverage of theatre in the mainstream news media, there was a proliferation of magazines and journals relating specifically to theatre throughout the twentieth century, coming and going in response to a variety of needs: for more detailed news and comment (often locally or nationally based); for a record and documentation of productions and performances; for expert information and relevant technical discussion; and for critical appraisal of the state of theatre at different times under different conditions, both in the 'home' country and abroad. Some are linked to an individual (e.g. GORDON CRAIG and *Mask*) and some to movements (e.g. promoters of the 'news stagecraft' in the US and *Theater Arts Magazine*. At one end of the range are the general trade papers – VARIETY in the United States and in the UK THE STAGE, which took over the role of the important weekly *The Era* (1838–1939); at the other end, specialist journals for the likes of production managers, electricians and lighting or sound designers. In the UK, the more assiduous can also look to *Theatre Record* as an invaluable monthly compendium of reviews. The keen theatregoer has also been served by a host of magazines that rise and fall with the fashion: *New Theatre, Theatre Today, Drama, Plays and Players* and *Plays International*, to name a few. The most notable was probably *Encore* (1956–65) because of its association with the British 'new wave'. However, the biggest single influence on the evolution – and expansion – of theatre journals was the rapid development in the latter half of the century of the academic study of theatre, which promoted a new readership as well as contributors who have seen in theatre a fruitful source of theoretical writing and discussion of practice. The

United States led the way in 1956 with the *Tulane Drama Review* (subsequently entitled simply *The Drama Review*), a brand leader, which, under the energetic editorship of Richard Schechner (1962–9), navigated the choppy seas of PERFORMANCE studies. The UK brand leader was *Theatre Quarterly* (1971–81) and its successor *New Theatre Quarterly* (from 1985), bridging the worlds of academe and theatrical practice under editors Clive Barker and Simon Trussler. In the United States, *Performing Arts Journal* has developed an international outlook, as have UK-based journals *Contemporary Theatre Review*, *Dance Theatre Journal* and *Total Theatre*. The development of live art from PERFORMANCE ART allowed *Performance* (then *Hybrid*) to develop into *Live Art Listings* and encouraged the growth of *Performance Research* since its founding in 1996. The academic communities are more closely served by *Studies in Theatre and Performance* as well as flourishing specialist journals such as the *Shakespeare Quarterly* and the *Journal of Samuel Beckett Studies*.   NOEL WITTS & COLIN CHAMBERS

See also CRITICISM;   RECORDING AND RESEARCHING THEATRE.

Magdalena Project   An international, Wales-based network of women performers, based at the CHAPTER ARTS CENTRE, Cardiff. It was founded as a result of the First International Festival of Women in Contemporary Theatre in 1986 and co-ordinated by former CARDIFF LABORATORY THEATRE member Jill Greenhalgh, who had left the company in 1986, at the same time that Simon Thorne and Phil McKenzie departed to explore men's role in society through their Man Act company. The Magdalena Project has been non-ideological, exploring a series of questions about women's voices, collaboration and practice, through individual performances and workshops, conferences and joint productions. Major performers from around the world – around 500 independent theatre artists – have worked with Magdalena in 40 projects. Ironically, at the moment when the Arts Council of Wales decided to withdraw its funding as part of its 1999 drama strategy, a whole new generation of Magdalena Projects were born all over the world, and are now thriving; in Wales, it exists only as a website.   DAVID ADAMS

See also WOMEN IN THEATRE.

Magee, Patrick   *see* BECKETT, SAMUEL

magic   It can be defined as the theatrical presentation of phenomena which seemingly defy the known laws of nature, and is among the most ancient of dramatic arts. Documentation dates back at least to ancient Egypt, where it was associated with religious RITUAL, but still had a function as entertainment for the mighty. Its itinerant performers were popular throughout the ancient world. The move to a more settled and respected theatrical performer came via the eighteenth-century magician Isaac Fawkes, whose substantial BOOTHS at Bartholomew and Southwark Fairs were widely publicized, and in the nineteenth century with the Scottish John Henry Anderson (1814–74), 'The Great Wizard of the North', whose spectacular demonstrations of tricks and illusions toured theatres and music halls in Britain, the United States and Australia, and Jean Eugene Robert-Houdin (*c.* 1805–75), the French magician who is generally credited with being the 'father of modern conjuring'. His oft-quoted dictum that the magician is 'an actor playing the part of a magician' represents a conscious break with the former image which magicians cultivated, of an individual inhabiting a world between the real and the supernatural. The enormous popularity of magical performance at the beginning of the twentieth century can be seen in the success of John Nevil Maskelyne (1839–1917), who, with G. A. Cooke (1825–1905) and later with David Devant (1868–1941), presented a full show of magic and illusions at the Egyptian Hall in London's Piccadilly – a show which was continually updated, but ran for more than 30 years from 1873, and then transferred to St George's Hall, where it continued for almost another 30 years, Maskelyne's share of the show being taken over by members of his family after his death.

There have been a few attempts since the days of Maskelyne and Devant to devote a theatre exclusively to the performance of magic – notably The Magic Castle in Hollywood, which opened in 1963 – but these have been exceptional. In the twentieth century, magic has been essentially an adjunct of the MUSIC HALL, VAUDEVILLE or VARIETY stage, with occasional appearances in CIRCUS. Of the magicians who achieved great success in the early part of the twentieth century, undoubtedly the most famous is HARRY HOUDINI, whose name has become almost a synonym for impossible escape. Others include Chung Ling Soo (1861–1918), who died attempting to repeat the feat of catching a bullet in the teeth, the British magician Selbit (1881–1938), who invented the trick of sawing a woman in half, and the American Horace Goldin (1873–1939), who became famous with another version of the same trick. Less well known, but nevertheless an equally consummate performer, was Richard Pitchford, known as Cardini (1895?–1973), whose vaudeville act was performed without words, and presented a drunken man-about-town, complete with top hat and cane, who was continually astounded by the fans of cards, lighted cigarettes and billiard balls which inexplicably appeared at his fingertips.

Magic retained its popularity in the age of television, and a series of magicians have exploited the medium to great effect. Robert Harbin ('Ned' Williams, 1909–78), a suave and polished performer, added a new and intriguing twist to the idea of sawing a lady in half, with his now standard 'zig-zag' illusion, in which the standing assistant is cut into three sections, and the middle one slid to one side. The closeness which television can achieve for the performer was exploited in the 'mentalist' or mind-reading magic of Chan Canasta (b. 1921) in America and Al Koran (1914–72) in Britain. In Britain, the first magician to gain his own weekly television programme, and to achieve the status of a television 'personality' was the rather low-key performer David Nixon (1919–78). In the 1970s and 1980s the tendency, especially in American television magic, has been towards illusions on a grand scale, with the television 'specials' of Doug Henning (1947–2000), and what is probably the definitive 'big illusion', David Copperfield's vanish of an aeroplane. (Henning appeared in the Broadway musical *The Magic Show*, 1974, performing a Houdini trick as well as vanishing a tiger.) In modern times, many of the best-known magicians have exploited the potential for comedy in magic, whether by relentlessly sending up their own pretensions as a magician, as pioneered by the American Frank Van Hoven (1886–1929) and developed hilariously by the British TOMMY COOPER, or by combining their tricks and illusions with a series of one-liners and funny situations, a style which has ensured the success of British magician Paul Daniels.

The role of women in magical performance has, until the later part of the twentieth century, been generally confined to that of assistant to the saw-wielding male. An exception to this rule in the early years of the century was Adelaide Herrmann (1853–1932), widow of the popular Alexander Herrmann, who took on her husband's act after his death, including the dangerous bullet-catching trick. Despite sexist attitudes among some male magicians, women such as Frances Marshall in America and Fay Presto in Britain have shown that it is quite possible for women to perform magic entertainingly and effectively. Like NEW VARIETY, an alternative or new magic circuit was developed in the 1980s.

The use of magic tricks in the 'legitimate' theatre is limited, perhaps the only example which will be widely known being the sequence in CHEKHOV's *The Cherry Orchard*, in which Charlotta performs tricks for guests in the Ranyevskaia drawing-room. However, the theatrical techniques which underlie magical performance are such as can be usefully exploited by per-formers in many branches of theatre, and magicians are frequently used as consultants by theatre companies to help stage effects that are not in themselves magic. Without giving away any secrets ('exposure' to the general public of how a trick is done being the cardinal sin among magicians), it would be worth noting some of these techniques. The central principle which underlies all magical performance is that which magicians call 'misdirection'. This consists not simply of attempts to distract the audience from the magician's true actions, but of subtly leading the audience's attention towards the focus which the magician desires, by the use of natural actions and an understanding of the psychology of observation. The popular belief that it is 'the quickness of the hand which deceives the eye' is very rarely the case, since quick and unnatural actions are more likely to appear suspicious than fluent, natural ones. Thus the magician who wishes to perfect any significant move or 'sleight' will have to observe natural movements as closely, and probably a great deal more closely, than any actor steeped in the principles of naturalism. Magic continues to be popular with the public, both as spectacle and pastime, with enormous numbers of amateur magicians meeting in clubs and societies throughout the world, and even greater numbers of children being given their first introduction to the practice of the performing arts in the form of a set of magic tricks. IAN SAVILLE

See also ESCAPOLOGY.

Milbourne Christopher, *The Illustrated History of Magic* (1973)
Edwin Dawes, *The Great Illusionists* (1979)
Geoffrey Lamb, *Magic Illustrated Dictionary* (1979)
John Mulholland, *The Story of Magic* (1936)

Maillet, Antonine (b. Buctouche, Canada, 10 May 1929) French-Canadian playwright and novelist. The most important writer of francophone Acadia, she was awarded France's prestigious Prix Goncourt for her novel *Pélagie-la-Charette* in 1979. Her first dramatic success came with the one-woman play *La Sagouine* (*The Slattern*, 1971), composed in the archaic Acadian dialect and widely performed in Canada, in French and in English. Other notable plays performed are *Evangéline Deusse* (*Evangeline the Second*, 1976), *La Veuve enragée* (*The Mad Widow*, 1977) and *Margot la Folle* (*Mad Maggie*, 1987). LEONARD E. DOUCETTE

Paul Gilbert Lewis, ed., *Traditionalism, Nationalism and Feminism: Women Writers of Quebec* (1985)
Donald Smith et al., *Voices of Deliverance: Interviews with Quebec and Acadian Writers* (1986)

make-up A misapprehension exists that make-up is

about painting faces. The truth is that, in theatre, the make-up artist is a composite of skilled hairdresser and wigmaker, and a prosthetic and cosmetic artist; as likely to produce a deformed monster as to deal with the problems of ageing from 18 to 80. The twentieth century saw make-up pass from the hands of actors into those of technicians. Less make-up has been worn generally, year by year, and that which is worn has become subtler, defying detection by bright lights and critical audiences. The techniques now in use require several years of training and they advance daily. It is a challenging and exciting area to work in, offering the actor more assistance than has been available ever before. Each actor looks for the appropriate appearance for the characters he is portraying. Much can be done by changing the hair to indicate age, health, social class and historical period. The actor can easily add colour or whitener to his hair, grease it down or brush it through, but fundamental differences in style and length can only be remedied with a WIG. At the beginning of the twentieth century, wigs were made by knotting hair on to a cotton base, and where this met the face, the area known as the join, there was a clear line. The join had to be disguised, and this was achieved with the aid of heavy old-fashioned grease make-up. This make-up not only hid the join, it also wiped out the natural colour of the face, something for which the LIGHTING was often, erroneously, blamed. If even one person was wearing a wig and consequently a heavy make-up, then every one else needed to wear an equally heavy make-up. In practice, this meant that make-up was worn in all productions. What lighting did do, by coming from the side of the stage, level with the actor's face and in front, and from below it, was to flatten out the natural contours. Starting, as it were, from a clean canvas, the actor could completely control his or her appearance by the skilful use of make-up. Notably, at this time several ageing actors were enabled to play parts much younger than their own ages with great success. The Leichner make-up, available since 1876, was a cheap, safe and reliable tool. Its use was part of the training of every actor, whether at a drama school or, more usually, in repertory companies. Grease make-up requires powdering to set or it may run under the heat of the lights; this tends to wipe out any subtlety of colour or shading. But LAURENCE OLIVIER, as Romeo, showed in 1936 what an enormous difference an actor could make to his appearance with a clearly thought-through make-up, well applied. His romantic vision of Italian youth is only one of many make-ups to have been captured by a portrait painter, surely a testament to his skill.

As electric lighting replaced gas, far stronger light was available than previously. It revealed, unkindly, what had been hidden – that for some actors the skill of make-up remained elusive and their efforts, far from giving a natural appearance, made them look stylized and mask-like. A strange situation developed where young actors, learning by observing their elders, began to learn and, in their turn, pass on, the mistakes of a previous generation. It was forgotten that make-up had arrived on the stage in the early nineteenth century to compensate for a lack of light, or out of the need to show the character or to hide the wig join. Make-up continued to be worn on stage, automatically, until the 1960s. Fortunately, most leading actors were good at make-up and adapted to brighter light by applying the Leichner stick in a more subtle way. They mixed the colours in their hands to find a natural base and applied it lightly. Max Factor, while chief perruquier at the MOSCOW ART THEATRE, had devised a method of blending the colours and heating them with oil to form a greasepaint. He was soon producing it commercially, for use in films as well as on the stage. The popularity of this product lay in its wide variety of shades and colours, which saved mixing, and the ease with which it spread in comparison to the stick form of make-up. During the 1930s, films were a great influence on all who saw them. Young actors aspired to become matinée idols and used make-up as a corrective and to emphasize their good features. Although women have always used street cosmetics to supplement their stage kit, this option was not easily open to men until the late 1960s. In the meantime the Max Factor range expanded to cover lip and eye make-up which could be bought by men from theatre make-up stockists without fear or ridicule. The development of pancake make-up was a great step forward. Introduced in 1938, it swiftly became a best-seller on and off stage, and remained so for 30 years. Pancake was a completely water-soluble product, easy to apply with a damp sponge; it came in a wide range of colours which Max Factor was happy to extend for special cases, and, because it incorporated talc, it needed no powdering. It could give a rather flat effect, however, and was superseded in 1950 by the panstick, for the face. The 1960s brought into the theatre an audience familiar with television. To them the romantic style of make-up looked artificial and could be a distraction. Some make-up would always be needed, but now the actor in make-up would be the exception, not the rule. Lighting was now capable of reproducing daylight, showing the bone structure of the face, but strong enough to light through any delicately painted alterations. To make realistic changes under these circumstances is far more difficult. If heavily painted faces stand out like masks and lightly painted ones are too subtle to show, the actor who has only been trained at drama school in painted techniques is at a loss and a specialist make-up artist must be called in.

A make-up artist had been available from the wig-maker, if needed, as one could not be worn without the other, and the make-up suppliers had always been happy to send diagrams and charts to cover most circumstances. In London, Richard Blore at Leichner and Douglas Young at Max Factor would personally teach the use of their products; but three-dimensional effects will usually need specialist application and daily maintenance. Freelance experts brought techniques of film and television to the theatres, training the staff to carry on the care and replacement of prosthetics. Kenneth Lintott and Alan Boyle pioneered the use of PVC in the early 1960s. They used it for noses, in place of the wax used previously, and most notably for balding effects and high foreheads, such as those in TREVOR NUNN's production of *The Revenger's Tragedy* (Stratford, 1966). Chrisopher Tucker has shown what may be achieved with foam rubber and several theatres have successfully reproduced his excellent make-up for *The Elephant Man*.

The bleeding wounds of Shakespeare's history plays call for another of the make-up artist's skills. In Shakespeare's own day real blood was used, but for health reasons a substitute is now mixed up from glucose syrup and food colouring. Until it became too expensive, a vegetable powder called 'dragon's blood' was used. The blood capsules, sponges and bags are made, applied and disguised by the make-up department. Make-up techniques now in use require several years of training, and they advance continually. It is a challenging and exciting area to work in. BRENDA LEEDHAM

Malaysia *see* SOUTH-EAST ASIA

male impersonation *see* DRAG; IMPERSONATION; PANTOMIME

Mali *see* FRENCH AFRICAN THEATRE

Malina, Judith *see* LIVING THEATER

Malkovich, John (b. Christopher, Ill., 9 Dec. 1953) Actor, director and sound designer. Malkovich first appeared OFF-BROADWAY in 1982, after which his career as a stage and film actor, a stage director and sound designer blossomed rapidly. He is a co-founder of the STEPPENWOLF THEATER COMPANY in Chicago, whose style he came to epitomize, and has won acclaim and awards for his physically energized, persuasive performances, such as in SAM SHEPARD's *True West* (1982) and, in London, LANFORD WILSON's *Burn*

This (1991). As a director he was praised for a revival of WILSON's *Balm in Gilead* (1981) and his own adaptation of Don De Lillo's *Libra* (1994). ADRIANA HUNTER

Malleson, [William] Miles (b. Croydon, Surrey, 25 May 1889; d. London, 15 March 1969) Actor, director and playwright whose many character portrayals – Aguecheck, Gobbo, Polonius, Foresight (in Congreve's *Love for Love*), Filch (in Gay's *The Beggar's Opera*), Scrub (in Farquhar's *The Beaux Stratagem*) – and unusual 'chinless moonstruck' face made him a familiar figure both on stage and in film. His play, *The Fanatics* (1927), 'blazed the trail for British sex comedies'. Malleson worked as a director and was famed (though criticized by purists) for his free adaptations of Molière, in which he also appeared. His many plays include *Black 'Ell*, *Conflict* and *Six Men of Dorset*, which he co-authored with H. Brooks. Malleson was also active in the Independent Labour Party in the 1920s. MAGGIE GALE

Malmgren, Yat *see* CHOREOGRAPHY; DRAMA SCHOOLS

Malvern Festival *see* FESTIVALS; JACKSON, BARRY

Maly Theatre, St Petersburg *see* DODIN, LEV

Mamet, David [Alan] (Flossmoor, Ill., 30 Nov. 1947) Playwright. He studied acting with Sanford Meisner and, after working as an actor for a while, took up a post teaching acting; later he would claim to have started writing simply to provide material for his young actors to perform. This impetus produced early versions of *Lakeboat* (1970), *Duck Variations* (1972) and *Sexual Perversity in Chicago* (1972), a flinty portrayal of a relationship blossoming and breaking down, which won a prize when revived in 1974. After a minor success with *Squirrels* (1974), his next major play was *American Buffalo* (1975), his first to be directed by long-time collaborator GREG MOSHER. Set in a junk shop, it ruthlessly unmasks the fragility of masculinity as it follows the almost Chekhovian failure of three incompetent burglars; it aroused controversy with its rhythmic, idiomatic language. Mamet consolidated his growing reputation with *A Life in the Theatre* (1977), pitting an older against a younger actor, delineating the mixture of respect and rivalry between them. That year, this success was complemented by a revival of *American Buffalo* on Broadway, and premières of *The Water Engine* and *The Woods*.

After an acclaimed revival of a rewritten *Lakeboat* in the 1980s, his next major plays were *Edmond* (1982) and *Glengarry Glen Ross* (1983), set in the ruthless world of business among a group of salesmen working in a real estate office in Chicago. Notionally a whodunnit, the play captures the fragility and desperation of these lives, pitched against each other in a cruel sales contest. The play was premièred, after the intercession of HAROLD PINTER, at Britain's NATIONAL THEATRE, later won the Pulitzer Prize, and was successfully filmed in 1992.

A double bill of *The Shawl* and *Prairie du Chien* (1985), both confronting ordinary people with intimations of the supernatural, re-opened the LINCOLN CENTER THEATER, New York. A satire on Hollywood, *Speed the Plow* (1988), achieved considerable success, helped in part by the singer Madonna taking a leading role. In the meantime, Mamet had been writing a series of notable screenplays, among them *The Postman Always Rings Twice* (1978), *The Verdict* (1982), *The Untouchables* (1987) and *Hoffa* (1992). His debut as film director, *House of Games* (1987), was acclaimed, and was followed by *Things Change* (1988), *Homicide* (1991), *The Spanish Prisoner* (1998) and a new adaptation of RATTIGAN's *The Winslow Boy* (1999).

Controversies over Mamet's work reached a new peak in 1992 with the première of *Oleanna*. This play brilliantly depicts the transformations of language and authority in a dramatically shifting power relationship between a student and a university teacher, but was widely interpreted as an attack on the excesses of 'political correctness'. It is on this ground, where power, rhetoric and identity meet, that Mamet has built his work. Few people capture like Mamet the way that language is something we use *in* the world, rather than something we use to *describe* the world; his writing is sparse, but the rhythms and detailed observation of language use, influenced by BECKETT and PINTER, make his plays intensely rich theatrical experiences. Some commentators have criticized his work for lacking subtext; perhaps what they are responding to is that Mamet rarely makes his moral presence felt in his work: moral concerns are open for negotiation, nothing is assumed. This was beautifully shown in *The Cryptogram* (1994), which, as the title suggests, depicts a puzzle, a story about growing up within a maze of clues, betrayal and loss.

Other plays include *Dark Pony* (1977), *Reunion* (1979), *Lone Canoe* (1979), *The Disappearance of the Jews* (1983), *Bobby Gould in Hell* (1989) and *The Old Neighbourhood* (1995). He has written numerous short plays, sketches and monologues, several CHEKHOV adaptations and a handful of radio and television plays. He has produced a volume of verse, *The Hero Pony* (1990), a handful of novels, and several books of essays: *Writing in Restaurants* (1986), *Some Freaks* (1989), *On Directing* (1991), *The Cabin* (1992), *Make-Believe Street* (1996), *True and False* (1997) and *Jafsie and John Henry* (2000).

DAN REBELLATO

C. W. E. Bigsby, *David Mamet* (1985)

Dennis Carroll, *David Mamet* (1987)

Anne Dean, *David Mamet: Language as Dramatic Action* (1990)

John Heilpern, *How Good is David Mamet, Anyway?* (1999)

Mamoulian, Rouben (b. Tiflis [Tblisi], Georgia, 8 Oct. 1897; d. Los Angeles, 4 Dec. 1987)   Director. After studying in Paris and Moscow, where he attended VAKHTANGOV's studio, and a period of relatively minor activity in London from 1918 to 1923, Mamoulian became involved with the THEATER GUILD, first as a teacher, then to direct the premières of *Porgy* (1927) and *Marco Millions* (1928), and of the MUSICALS *Porgy and Bess* (1935), *Oklahoma!* (1943) and *Carousel* (1945), all notable for his sweeping stage compositions and atmospheric charm. Mamoulian's film work includes such pioneering sound musicals as *Applause* (1929), *Love Me Tonight* (1932), and the first Technicolor film, *Becky Sharp* (1935).   MICHAEL SOMMERS

T. Miln, *Rouben Mamoulian* (1969)

M. Spergel, *Reinventing Reality: The Art and Life of Rouben Mamoulian* (1993)

management   In common with many other aspects of theatrical life, management broadened in scope during the twentieth century and gave rise to the emergence of the specialist. The business imperatives of the commercial theatre, where the PRODUCER is usually the manager, were increasingly encouraged in the not-for-profit or publicly subsidized theatre. This still tends to be run by men and women whose primary task is to direct plays and who, therefore, have had to acquire administrative skill and accept financial responsibility while also practising a demanding (and in some ways incompatible) craft. They needed increasing levels of administrative support, which was supplied by a new breed of arts administrators, often the product of expanding theatre studies and arts management courses. In both sectors, financial systems are sophisticated, marketing and production departments are often in control of large budgets, and producers or governing boards require their staff to display a high level of commercial acumen alongside the more traditional artistic skills. Managers may now find themselves with strategic financial duties as well as day-to-day responsibilities ranging from casting plays, running restaurants and organizing the 'front of house', where the public come and go, to negotiating with local authorities on fire, health and safety issues and having the lavatories cleaned. Such duties vary according to the size and nature of the theatre but, wherever it takes place, the business of theatre management involves much more than just putting on plays.

It is not uncommon to find a theatre staff comprising an artistic director, an administrator (general manager or executive director), a finance officer, a MARKETING officer (in charge of media and public relations), a sponsorship officer, a production manager (in charge of technical needs), a box office manager and an education officer (much FUNDING depending on educational or 'outreach' work). Ultimate responsibility will usually rest with a board, often representing local and funding interests. Income will be generated through the box office, through general fundraising, and through various forms of ancillary trading. AUDIENCE research will be carried out in a constant effort to increase both the numbers and the range of people attending performances. Managers will also attempt to forge links with the community of which the theatre is a part, through support and subscription schemes, education work and, if possible, talks, exhibitions, special days and the hiring of parts of the theatre to local groups. The economics of theatre has encouraged co-production between theatres and, in its wake, experiments with the sharing of management functions. Theatre is a highly labour-intensive activity, even in its most pared-down forms. It is also essentially collaborative. Many different kinds of work must be brought together smoothly each time a live performance is given before an audience. Virtually alone among providers of a service to the public, theatres regularly deliver the product specified at the appointed time and place, which is the ultimate task of management. GENISTA MCINTOSH

Manchester The industrial conurbation of Greater Manchester boasts the largest concentration of theatres of any regional city in the UK outside LONDON. The ARTS COUNCIL awarded Manchester the accolade of 'City of Drama' in 1994, recognizing both the liveliness and diversity of Manchester's theatre and its pivotal position in recent British theatre history.

Most significant has been the city's leading role in the REPERTORY MOVEMENT. In 1907 ANNIE HORNIMAN founded the country's first repertory company here and set a pattern soon followed by dozens of theatres elsewhere. In 1952 the Library Theatre Company became the first full-scale civic repertory, wholly funded by the city. It established its reputation for contemporary work under David Scase (1954–63, 1971–83), and was followed in 1971 by the addition in the suburbs of a second theatre, the Forum, which specialized in musicals and other more commercial productions. During the expansive 1960s and 1970s, the Octagon Theatre was built in neighbouring Bolton;

Oldham's Coliseum was radically transformed into a lively, popular community theatre; MICHAEL ELLIOTT founded the prestigious ROYAL EXCHANGE Company, based in the magnificent new THEATRE IN THE ROUND in the Cotton Exchange, quickly building a national reputation for high-quality productions of the classics; and HUGH HUNT (head of the university's Drama Department) created a repertory theatre for young people, Contact, based at the University Theatre and making its name with its inventive reinterpretations of the classics and new plays by young writers (e.g. Charlotte Keatley's *My Mother Said I Never Should*, 1987, which went on to be translated into 20 languages).

ALTERNATIVE THEATRE, too, has played a vital part in the city's theatrical life. JOAN LITTLEWOOD and EWAN MACCOLL together founded the radical Theatre of Action in Manchester in the 1930s, which became THEATRE WORKSHOP after the Second World War before transferring to London. In the 1960s and 1970s, major THEATRE IN EDUCATION/COMMUNITY THEATRE companies were established in Bolton and Wigan. Later, the Green Room, the city's main FRINGE venue, became the focus of a lively alternative theatre scene; the unique Nia Centre for African and CARIBBEAN arts was established; and in 1994 a new fringe venue opened, the Dancehouse Theatre, serving also as a performance base for the Northern Ballet.

Large-scale touring of opera, ballet, plays and musicals is catered for by the two main commercial houses, the Opera House (built 1912) and the superbly refurbished Palace Theatre (built 1891), which was taken over by a trust in 1978 and enlarged to accommodate a bigger stage and an audience of 2,000.

During the 1990s the publicly subsidized theatres found survival a precarious business. Some of the smaller 'fringe' venues disappeared while new ones emerged; the larger 'reps' continued, though with a marked reduction in output and greater reliance on touring productions. Recent positive developments have included the rebuilding of Contact Theatre as a centre for an expanded range of theatre work, both for and with young people, and the wholesale refurbishment of the Royal Exchange Theatre, including the opening of a new studio theatre. The presence in the city of major television and radio studios, several acting academies and university drama departments and a thriving amateur and student theatre scene, have all helped to secure the city's future as a vital centre for the performing arts.

ANTHONY JACKSON

Manchester School A term loosely applied to a group of playwrights associated with the Manchester

GAIETY THEATRE in the early 1900s. The three key members of this group were HAROLD BRIGHOUSE, STANLEY HOUGHTON and ALLAN MONKHOUSE. While GLASGOW and LIVERPOOL repertory theatres supported such writers too, it was only in Manchester that a distinctive body of work emerged inspired by local life, as can be seen in the 'school's' two most famous plays, Brighouse's *Hobson's Choice* (1915) and Houghton's *Hindle Wakes* (1912). ADRIANA HUNTER

Manhattan Theater Club This OFF-BROADWAY venue was founded in 1970, in the converted Bohemian National Hall, by a group of East Side residents who sought to provide a showcase for new work not only in drama, but also in opera, poetry and music. Apart from its three stages, there are also facilities for rehearsals and readings, and within seven years of its opening the club's consistently high standard of productions was recognized by one of the Obie awards set up by the *Village Voice* newspaper in 1955. The club's productions have included award-winners like ATHOL FUGARD's *The Blood Knot* (1976, Obie), the musical *Ain't Misbehavin'* (1978), BETH HENLEY's *Crimes of the Heart* (1981) and TERRENCE MCNALLY's *Frankie and Johnny in the Clair de Lune* (1987). Lynne Meadow (b. 1946) has been artistic director since 1972, with Barry Grove as executive producer. She has directed, among other plays, *Ashes* (1976), *The Jail Diary of Albie Sachs* (1979) and *A Small Family Business* (1992). The theatre stages an average of eight plays a year and has received many awards, including two Pulitzers, 40 Obies and six Tonys. HELEN RAPPAPORT

Mankowitz, [Cyril] Wolf (b. London, 7 Nov. 1924; d. Co. Cork, Ireland, 20 May 1998) Playwright and producer. His prolific output concentrates on the rhythms and concerns of Jewish life. *The Bespoke Overcoat* (1953), a short play about a tailor making a coat for a dying man, exemplifies his sensitive, poignant humour. Other plays include *Make Me an Offer* (1952); *The Last of the Cheesecake* (1956); and the book from his story for the musical *Expresso Bongo* (1958). An early supporter of the ENGLISH STAGE COMPANY, he wrote for film and television, and is the author of novels, short stories and poetry. DAN REBELLATO

Mann, Emily (b. Boston, Mass., 12 April 1952) Playwright and director. Drawing on contemporary history, Mann describes her work as 'theatre of testimony'. Her first play, *Annulla, An Autobiography* (1977), is based on interviews with a survivor of the Nazis; *Still Life* (1980) on interviews with contemporaries in the Vietnam era; *Execution of Justice* (1984) concerns the

1978 homophobic murder of San Francisco's mayor and city supervisor. She collaborated with NTOZAKE SHANGE and musician Baikida Carroll in 1989 on a musical, *Betsey Brown*. Other plays include *Having Our Say* (1994) and adaptations of *Nights and Days* (1984) by Pierre Laville and LORCA's *The House of Bernada Alba* (1997). She has directed across the US and in 1989 was appointed artistic director of Princeton's McCarter Theater. As well as her own work, among her directing credits is the première of ANNA DEVEARE SMITH's *Fires in the Mirror* (1992). CHARLES LONDON

Mann, Erika *see* MANN FAMILY

Mann family German literary and theatrical family. Heinrich (1871–1950), best known for his short stories, wrote a number of plays in different styles. His novel *Professor Unrat* (1905) was filmed famously as *The Blue Angel* (1930), launching MARLENE DIETRICH to stardom, and has been subsequently dramatized (e.g. by PAM GEMS, 1991). His brother Thomas (1875–1955), who won the Nobel Prize for his novels, wrote only one play but many essays on the theatre. His novella *Death in Venice* (1912) has inspired film, opera and drama. Thomas's daughter Erika (1905–69) and son Klaus (1906–49) wrote for and acted in anti-Nazi cabaret in Munich, Zurich and New York. Erika was known for appearances in Klaus's plays, particularly an important work about adolescence, *Anja und Esther* (1925). Klaus wrote comedies, and his novel *Mephisto* (1936), based on Erika's husband GRÜNDGENS, was dramatized by MNOUCHKINE (1979) and also filmed. CHARLES LONDON

Mann, Heinrich *see* MANN FAMILY

Mann, Klaus *see* MANN FAMILY

Mann, Thomas *see* MANN FAMILY

Manners, J[ohn] Hartley (b. London, 10 Aug. 1870; d. New York, 19 Dec. 1928) Playwright. He began his career as an actor and came to America in 1902 in one of his own plays. He found his métier writing vehicles, usually rosy-hued, for his wife, Laurette Taylor, most notably *Peg o' My Heart* (1912). GERALD BORDMAN

Mansfield, Richard (b. Berlin, 24 May 1854; d. New London, Conn., 30 Aug. 1907) Actor and producer who settled in America in 1882 and grabbed overnight fame as a brutal roué in Feuillet's *A Parisian Romance* (1883). Subsequent successes included *Prince Karl* (1886), *Dr Jekyll and Mr Hyde* (1887), *Richard III* (1889), *Beau Brummel* (1890), *Arms and the Man* (1894), *The Devil's Disciple* (1897), *Cyrano de Bergerac* (1898) and *Old Heidelberg* (1903). A producer with a keen eye for detail and lavish sets, he helped introduce SHAW to America, and also IBSEN, including *Peer Gynt*, which he played in 1907 in the first production of the play in

English. An exceptionally tiny man with a pale, squarish face and receding brown hair, his style served as a bridge between the more flamboyant old ways and the more restrained new ones. While he was respected, his mean-spiritedness and vanity offended many.

GERALD BORDMAN

P. Wibtach, *Richard Mansfield: The Man and the Actor* (1908)
W. Winter, *Life and Art of Richard Mansfield*, 2 vols (1910)

Mantell, Robert B[ruce] (b. Irvine, Scotland, 7 Feb. 1854; d. Atlantic Highlands, NJ, 27 June 1928) Actor. He first appeared on stage in Belfast in 1873, making his New York debut in 1878 as a member of the Polish actress Madame Modejska's company. He went back to England to try to make a career for himself, but the attempt failed and it was not until his return to New York and his performance in *Fedora* (1883) that he scored any real success. Hungry to star in his own vehicles, he set up a company, for which he performed in a string of popular MELODRAMAS: *Tangled Lives* (1886), *The Marble Heart* (1887), *The Corsican Brothers* (1890). Keen to prove himself as a classical actor, he embarked on a series of Shakespearean roles, appearing first as Romeo (1887), then as Othello (1888), Hamlet (1890), Richard III (1901) and most of the other great roles. His Shakespearean appearances were, however, far more successful on tour outside New York, where Mantell's by then outmoded and grandiloquent style was still acceptable. HELEN RAPPAPORT

Clarence Joseph Bulliet, *Robert Mantell's Romance* (1918)

Mantle, [Robert] Burns (b. Watertown, NY, 23 Dec. 1873; d. Long Island, NY, 9 Feb. 1948) Critic and editor. A printer turned journalist, Mantle became the *New York Daily News* theatre critic in 1922, a job which gave him considerable influence until he retired in 1943. In 1920 he created and edited *The Burns Mantle Theater Yearbook*, known as the *Best Plays* series – a multi-volume work, which he continued to edit until his death, charting the development of American theatre from 1894 onwards, by indexing and giving extracts from significant plays produced each year.

ADRIANA HUNTER

Manzoni, Piero *see* PERFORMANCE ART

Maori theatre The formal contemporary beginnings of Maori theatre can be traced to the founding of the Maori Theatre Trust in 1966, the culmination of activity by actors and administrators in both professional and amateur capacities – particularly in concert parties

and in educational institutions, and including the Maori Musical Society's 1941 production of *Hinemoa* in Rotorua. Maori theatre itself, however, can be seen as rooted in the structure of the culture.

The 1970s were a period of consolidation for Maori theatre, and the 1980s of building on those foundations. In 1972 Harry Dansey became the first Maori playwright with *Te Raukura: The Feathers of the Albatross*, presented at MERCURY in Auckland by Central Theatre with GEORGE HENARE playing the Maori prophet Te Whiti. In 1976 Jim Moriarty founded Te Ika a Maui Players for a production of Rore (Rowley) Habib's *Death of the Land*. Rawiri Paratene began writing plays in Dunedin in 1978. Maranga Mai, homegrown AGITPROP theatre, was founded in 1979. In 1982 RENEE began her playwriting career, and Rangimoana Taylor directed Selwyn Muru's *Get the Hell Home Boy* for the Maori Writers and Artists Association. Taylor founded Te Ohu Whakaari, which produced plays by Apirana Taylor (*Kohanga*, *Te Whanau a Tuanui Jones*), Riwia Brown (*Roimata*, *Te Hokinga*, *Nga Wahine*), and Haina Stewart (*Iwitaia*). For Wellington's International Festival of the Arts in the country's sesquicenntenial year, 1990, Te Ika a Maui combined with Te Ohu Whakaari and, as Te Rakau Hua O Te Wao Tapu, produced a programme at the Depot which included Bruce Stewart's *Broken Arse* and John Broughton's *Nga Puke* (*The Hills*). In the early 1990s Broughton became a significant playwright with plays like *Te Hokinga Mai*, *Michael James Manaia* and *Marae*. In 1990 Roma Potiki, formerly with Maranga Mai, formed He Ara Hou, which collaborated on the production of their play *Whatungarongaro*. Rena Owen, whose first play, *Te Awa i Tahuti*, had opened in London in 1987, wrote *Daddy's Girl* in 1991 for Taki Rua-Depot, established by DOWNSTAGE in Wellington as a second space in the early 1980s and since 1983 dedicated to New Zealand work. It changed its name in 1991 to Taki Rua-Depot to reflect its growing focus on Maori theatre. In Auckland, Don Selwyn directed the first production of Hone Tuwhare's *In the Wilderness Without a Hat* (1985), and has continued to produce plays at Waiatarua, including Pei Te Hurinui Jones's Maori translation of *The Merchant of Venice* (1990).

The 1990s saw the growth of Maori theatre, with Taki Rua (formerly Taki Rua-Depot) Theatre initiating most of the development. Its own company season, Te Roopu Whakaari, was established in 1994, introducing HONE KOUKA (and plays *Nga Tangata Toa*, *Waiora*) and Briar Grace Smith (with her work *Purapurawhetu*, *Haruru Mai*) as two major Maori playwrights. This decade also saw the growth of plays in te reo Maori (the Maori language), beginning with Taki Rua's 1995

Te Reo Maori Season. The late 1990s introduced a new wave of Maori playwrights with an urban perspective: Mitch Tawhi Thomas, with *Doughboy*, illustrates this well.

The 1990s also saw the development of *marae* theatre. This involves treating the theatre space as a *marae*, the open area in front of a meeting house with which it forms the physical and spiritual centre of the community. Subsequently the protocol of greeting, speaking and farewelling is followed. The audience is called into the theatre space, greeted with *waiata* (songs), encouraged to support the actors during the performance, and expected to reply at its conclusion and in all ways to treat the theatre as a *marae* for the duration of the performance.

SIMON GARRETT & GILLIAN GREER

See also NEW ZEALAND.

Marber, Patrick (b. London, 19 Sept. 1964) Playwright, performer and director. He made his name by writing for and performing on radio and television. His career as a playwright was nurtured by the NATIONAL THEATRE Studio and began with the award-winning *Dealer's Choice* (1995), drawing on his own gambling and card-playing experiences to examine the dynamics of all-male environments, through a witty and mature choreography of a poker game. He followed this up with *Closer* (1997). This marked a more anguished and raw look at sexual incomprehension. A celebrated scene featured two men (one of whom is pretending to be a woman) having sex over the internet, their hunched, screen-befixed figures contrasting ironically with the bravado of the virtual erotic promises they offer each other. Marber has also written a new version of *Miss Julie* and *Howard Katz* (2001), and has begun a successful directing career. DAN REBELLATO

Aleks Sierz, *In-Yer-Face Theatre: British Drama Today* (2001)

Marbury, Elizabeth *see* AGENTS

Marceau [Manager], Marcel (b. Strasbourg, France, 22 March 1923) MIME artist who was responsible for widening the popularity of this hitherto minority art form. Since the late 1940s he has toured the world many times with his acclaimed SOLO shows, playing in more than 80 countries and usually setting himself an average of 300 performances a year. No other mime performer in the twentieth century could match his appeal.

One of the earliest influences on Marceau's work was the silent cinema. As a young boy in Strasbourg, he would dress up in his father's trousers and paint on a black moustache to do Charlie Chaplin impersona-

tions for his playmates. In later life, Chaplin, along with Buster Keaton, remained his idol. But his initial aim was to be an actor. Following a period in the French Resistance, during which he adopted the name Marceau after one of Napoleon's generals, he went to Paris to study at the school of the eminent director CHARLES DULLIN. There, he met ETIENNE DECROUX, who taught him a vocabulary of mime technique that Marceau was quick to extend in his own special way. He also spent a short time with JEAN-LOUIS BARRAULT's company in 1946, when he was praised as Arlequin in the mime play *Baptiste*, adapted from the film *Les Enfants du Paradis*. Marceau went on to create numerous 'mimodramas', as he called them, with companies of his own. *The Overcoat*, adapted from a story by Gogol, was the most accomplished, and was revived over several decades. However, the form often looked stilted and artificial, suffering from the lack of words. It was for his solo performances that Marcel Marceau became internationally famous.

In the style exercises (*pantomimes de style*) he elaborated on the possibilities of the fixed point in space to achieve illusions like leaning against walls, walking on the spot, going up stairs or struggling against the wind — all on a bare stage. It was through the character of Bip, however, that Marceau's mime technique came most vividly alive, blending humour and pathos. Here he departed from the classicism of Decroux to revive the more romantic spirit of Jean-Gaspard Deburau (1796–1846) and the nineteenth-century PIERROTS. Since Bip's first appearance, in the tiny Théâtre de Poche in 1947, the white face beneath the battered top hat with its red flower sticking out has become a trademark for Marceau's work. One of Marceau's most popular compositions is *Bip as David and Goliath*, a dazzling piece of virtuosity in which he plays both characters, separating them by a small screen and changing from one to the other with such rapidity that it soon looks as if there are two actors on stage. By the 1990s Marceau's style appeared increasingly out of tune with the times, especially as mime and PHYSICAL THEATRE had moved on in such an innovative way.

Marceau has made several films of his work. He reopened his international mime school in Paris in 1978 and was awarded the Légion d'Honneur. KENNETH REA

Ben Martin, *Marcel Marceau* (1978)

Marcel, Gabriel (b. Paris, 7 Dec. 1889; d. Paris, 8 Oct. 1973) Philosopher and playwright. His early Christian existentialist plays, written in the 1920s and 1930s, were staged much later, e.g. *Un Homme de Dieu* (*A Man of God*, 1949) and *Le Chemin de crête* (*Ariadne*,

1953). *Rome n'est plus dans Rome* ('Rome is longer in Rome', 1951) is about the Cold War. WENDY SCOTT

March, Fredric [Frederick McIntyre Bickel] (b. Racine, Wisc., 31 Aug. 1897; d. Los Angeles, 14 April 1975) Actor. The sternly handsome performer made his acting debut in 1920 and had an undistinguished career before becoming a film star. His later, more significant stage roles came in *The Skin of Our Teeth* (1942), *A Bell for Adano* (1944), *Years Ago* (1946), *The Autumn Garden* (1951) and *Gideon* (1961). His major achievement was his James Tyrone, the embittered, old matinee idol, in EUGENE O'NEILL's *Long Day's Journey into Night* (1956), where his ageing good looks and the hint of old-fashioned emotive player he had long manifested gave his performance a special conviction. He often played opposite his wife FLORENCE ELDRIDGE. GERALD BORDMAN

M. Burrows, *Charles Laughton and Fredric March* (1969)

Marcus, Frank [Ulrich] (b. Breslau, Germany, 30 June 1928; d. London, 5 Aug. 1996) Playwright and critic. Though Marcus' studies of shifting sexual relationships – e.g. *The Formation Dancers* (1964), *Cleo* (1965), *The Killing of Sister George* (1965), where the lovers are lesbian, and *Notes on a Love Affair* (1972) – are amusing, they emphasize loneliness and obsession with youth. Contemporary England becomes a dowdy parallel to secessionist Vienna (e.g. *Mrs Mouse, Are You Within?*, 1968). Marcus twice translated SCHNITZLER's *Reigen* (1952, and 1982 for television) as well as his *Anatol* (1976) and MOLNAR's *The Guardsman* (1969). Formerly an actor, director and antique dealer, he was a leading Sunday newspaper drama critic from 1968 to 1980. TONY HOWARD

Mardi Gras *see* CARNIVAL

Marinetti, F[ilippo] T[ommaso] (b. Alexandria, Egypt, 22 Dec. 1876; d. Bellagio, Italy, 2 December 1944) Poet and playwright, founder and chief propagandist of the FUTURIST movement. Marinetti's plays, based on principles enunciated in his *Manifesto of the Futurist Synthetic Theatre* (1915), are bombastic and extravagant displays of his contempt for the conventions of the well-made play. He created something of a stir with pieces like *Elettricità sessuale* (*Sexual Electricity*, 1920), *Il tamburo di fuoco* (*Drum of Fire*, 1922), *Prigioneri* (*Prisoners*, 1927) and *Vulcani* (*Volcanoes*, 1927). He turned the manifesto into an art form by issuing so many, and stimulated other areas of creativity (notably painting and cooking) more than the theatre. He embraced Mussolini's Fascism to the end. G. H. MCWILLIAM

See also FOOD AND DRINK.

marionette *see* PUPPET THEATRE

Mark Taper Forum The semicircular auditorium, with a pentagonal thrust stage and a seating capacity of 760, which forms part of the Music Center of Los Angeles County in downtown Los Angeles, California. Named after the benefactor who provided the funds for its establishment, the Forum has since 1967 been the home of the Center Theatre Group, a non-profit organization created in 1959 by the University of California (Los Angeles) Extension and a number of committed individuals, and dedicated to a repertory of classical and modern plays as well as world premières, which have included Michael Cristofer's *The Shadow Box* (1975), MARK MEDOFF's *Children of a Lesser God* (1980) and *Tales from Hollywood* (1982) by CHRISTOPHER HAMPTON. The director has been, since 1965, Gordon Davidson. The Forum has no permanent or resident company. DAVID STAINES

Market Theatre Johannesburg company founded in 1976 by Barney Simon and Mannie Mann to make indigenous theatre that spoke powerfully about life in apartheid SOUTH AFRICA, which it did brilliantly both inside and outside the country. The company converted a fruit market into an arts complex with three theatres, an art gallery, photo gallery, drama school and photographic workshop. It was funded by private donation. By 1980 it was recognized abroad through the success of *Woza Albert!*, created in workshop by Simon and the actors Percy Mtwa and Mbongeni Ngema, and a string of plays by ATHOL FUGARD, including *Master Harold . . . and the Boys*. The main auditorium re-opened in 1997, seating 450, two years after the theatre received its first state subsidy from the new democratically elected government. CHARLES LONDON

M. Benson, *Athol Fugard and Barney Simon: Bare Stage, a Few Props, Great Theatre* (1997)
A. Fuchs, *Playing the Market: The Market Theatre, Johannesburg, 1976–1986* (1990)

marketing From barely scraping an existence in the 1960s and 1970s, marketing by the end of the century had become a fully paid-up member of the entertainment scene and commanded both status and respect. The practice of marketing, and the jargon required to describe it, have become mantras fighting for top spot with the other artistic buzz words and phrases – arts provision, access for all, outreach, customer care. One might ask: what happened to the art?

But what do we really mean by marketing? Word of mouth (or 'recommended by a friend') can still be a major motivating factor; but a few centuries ago there was little else. A town crier, some hastily printed handbills, a sandwich-board person on the high street, a poster or two: these and variations all played their part in informing (not persuading) those who could afford it to buy a ticket for the latest event in town – a CIRCUS, MUSIC HALL, new melodrama. In the second half of the nineteenth century and the first half of the twentieth, POSTERS were the most widely used selling tool, supported by discreet listing-style adverts in the quality press. Toulouse-Lautrec in late nineteenth-century Paris raised the standard of the poster to an art form. Many poster artists followed suit and this tradition continues – the icon/image logo of a successful Lloyd Webber musical can be seen in most major cities around the world.

As the world has become more sophisticated with electronic and digital communications, literally creating a 'global village', new marketing techniques have had to be developed to keep pace. The consumer is king, the marketplace his/her court. The courtiers are highly competitive and are continually devising new and ingenious ways to persuade the consumer to part with their plastic. The same is true in the arts and entertainment field; no longer are we being sold just a ticket, we are being offered the total experience – a night out, the weekend break, or even the complete destination (as in STRATFORD-UPON-AVON, EDINBURGH, Verona, STRATFORD, ONTARIO, ADELAIDE or Vienna). Of course, TV names are still being shoehorned into tired pot-boilers by London producers looking for a juicy hit on the road, but they now perform in new or refurbished buildings with spacious bars and restaurants, on-site parking and, usually, a courteous welcome (unlike many theatres in the capital). This is true the world over. Customers demand better service and value, and the theatre industry is listening. The customer care training is finally paying off.

What, then, are the basic principles of marketing? First you need a mission statement, more commonly called a central proposition; this acts as an aspirational and inspirational yardstick against which all activities in your arts organization can be assessed. Second, you need a business plan, of which the marketing strategy is an essential ingredient. To create the strategy you must first undertake an audit of your organization, traditionally called a S.W.O.T. analysis. What are the Strengths and Weaknesses of, Opportunities for and external Threats to your company or venue within the marketplace? Your strategy should then concentrate on the four key areas which form the building blocks of any strategic plan: *Product* – what do you have to offer and what are its unique qualities? *Price* – what will

it cost the consumer and how will you target specific sectors of the community such as the young, the disadvantaged, the old, the group market, the tourist, the family? Access for all? *Place* – your venue, its ambience, catering/bars, parking, public transport, access and customer care. *Promotion* – the twin objectives must always be to maximize revenue while offering access to the widest possible market, and to position the organization as vibrant, innovative and stimulating; an essential part of the community it serves. Target audiences and techniques for reaching them need to be clearly defined, including the usual mix of advertising, database marketing, print distribution/door to door and special promotions.

Two major leaps forward in the last 20 years of the century were undoubtedly credit card booking over the telephone – easy, direct and guaranteed, it also provides the venue with the customer's name and address – and sophisticated marketing-led ticketing systems. Combined, they have provided a completely new weapon of database marketing, which had often been undertaken previously using out-of-date mailing lists. But the digital age is upon us and we are even now beginning to leave database (or tactical) marketing behind, preferring a more strategic approach – loyalty/reward schemes for both individuals and corporations and the return of subscription; the ladder of commitment versus the impulse buy. It's important for a consumer – in the junk food/fast boil society we live in, where there's too much to do and too little time to do it in – to 'buy into' an arts organization, to share its ethos and values and to feel comfortable with its brand.

When so much bewildering choice is available, a brand provides assurance for the consumer. Calvin Klein, Nike, Porsche, Sony and in the UK Sainsbury, Virgin, the ROYAL SHAKESPEARE COMPANY, the WEST YORKSHIRE PLAYHOUSE, CAMERON MACKINTOSH are all stronger brands than their individual products; such strength is essential if they are to retain the loyalty of their market through the lean times as well as the boom.

Where will all this lead? The digital age of home shopping and banking, 200 TV channels, the web and every household with a PC or a Playstation – how will arts marketing adapt to this 'e' invasion? The INTERNET, offering personal 24-hour direct access, is becoming and will be an essential tool, as will highly targeted and positioned e-mail. Ambient advertising using the environment around us to project messages (particularly to reach the young) is increasingly popular, and TV and radio will remain strong spheres of influence as long as they continue to produce their own icons.

But they may never replace your best friend telling you it's a 'must see' . . . PETER HARLOCK

Keith Diggle, *Arts Marketing* (1994)
Philip Kotler and Gary Armstrong, *Marketing: An Introduction* (1990)

Marlowe, Julia [Sarah Frances Frost] (b. Caldbeck, Cumberland, 17 Aug. 1866; d. New York, 12 Nov. 1950) Actress. Brought to America at the age of four, she began her career, under the name Fanny Brough, in an all-children *HMS Pinafore* (1879). Although she had major successes in such plays as *Barbara Frietchie* (1899) and *When Knighthood Was in Flower* (1900), the dark-eyed, dark-haired, slender actress was best known for her Shakespearean heroines, performed opposite her second husband, E. H. SOTHERN. Surviving records reveal a richly musical voice, but her readings would probably be considered much too florid for later audiences. GERALD BORDMAN

E. H. Sothern, *Julia Marlowe's Story* (1954)

Marowitz, Charles (b. New York, 26 Jan. 1934) Director and critic. Initially METHOD-based, Marowitz's work soon embraced ARTAUD and he co-directed the ROYAL SHAKESPEARE COMPANY's THEATRE OF CRUELTY season with PETER BROOK (1964), out of which came his deconstruction of *Hamlet* (1965) and subsequent 'collage' updatings of Shakespeare (*Macbeth*, 1969; *Othello*, 1972; *The Shrew*, 1973; *Measure for Measure*, 1975). He founded the OPEN SPACE Theater (1968) as a home for international new writing (e.g. SAM SHEPARD, ARRABAL, HOWARD BARKER) and for experiments in acting and design. Back in the US, he founded the Open Theatre of Los Angeles (1982) and two years later became an Associate Director of the Los Angeles Theatre Center. He has written much criticism and many books on theatre, including *Confessions of a Counterfeit Critic* (1973) and the memoir *Directing Action* (1991). His own original plays include *Artaud at Rodez* (1975). TONY HOWARD

Marshall, Norman (b. Rawalpindi, India, 16 Nov. 1901; d. London, 7 Nov. 1980) Director and manager. In 1926 Marshall joined the Cambridge FESTIVAL THEATRE, eventually becoming resident director, taking over for a season in 1932. When, in 1934, he was offered the lease on the ailing GATE THEATRE in London, he took it, and over the following six years transformed its fortunes with plays by ČAPEK, O'NEILL, HELLMAN, GLASPELL and TOLLER, often financing them with hugely successful intimate REVUES. He later set up a production company concentrating mainly on the WEST END. His business skills were often called upon by the NATIONAL THEATRE, OLD VIC and BRITISH THEATRE ASSOCIATION. In 1947 he published a famous account of the early EXPERIMENTAL THEATRE movement, *The Other Theatre*. DAN REBELLATO

Marson, Una (b. St Elizabeth Parish, Jamaica, 6 Feb. 1905; d. Kingston, Jamaica, 6 May 1965) Playwright. One of the few pioneering women playwrights in the West Indies, Marson was a feminist, a black nationalist and an exceptional achiever. She founded *The Cosmopolitan* journal in 1928, when she was only 23. She was a consistent proponent of a Jamaican national theatre, which she saw as a theatre of social realism, based on the lives of the Jamaican people.

In 1932 Marson went to England, where she spent three years as secretary to the League of Coloured Peoples. It was for the League that in 1933 she co-wrote (with Horace Vaz), directed and played the leading role in her first play, the one-act Jamaican comedy *At What a Price*. The play was so well received that it transferred from the London YMCA for a short run at the Scala Theatre. In 1936 Marson returned to Jamaica and founded the Kingston Drama Club, for which she staged her second play, the full length *London Calling* (1937), on student life in the capital. Her most important play was the 1938 *Pocomania*, in which she explored the influence of the African religious cult of the title on an ordinary middle-class family. *Pocomania* was one of the earliest Jamaican plays of social realism, and one of the first to incorporate folk songs and dances. It was also the first to dare to bring the cult of pocomania on to the Jamaican stage.

Marson returned to England in 1938. She worked on the BBC programme *Calling the West Indies*, which featured the work of West Indian writers. She wrote no more plays. JUDY S. J. STONE

See also CARIBBEAN.

Honor Ford-Smith, *Una Marson: Black Nationalist and Feminist Writer* (1986)
Delia Jarrett Macauley, *Life of Una Marson* (1998)

Martin, Mary [Virginia] (b. Weatherford, Tex., 1 Dec. 1913; d. Surrey, Rancho Mirage, Calif., 3 Nov. 1990) Singer and actress who worked as a dance instructor and nightclub performer before winning overnight fame singing 'My Heart Belongs to Daddy' in *Leave It to Me* (1938). Following a brief film career, she returned to Broadway in *One Touch of Venus* (1943) and *Lute Song* (1946), then made her London debut in *Pacific 1860* (1946). With an uncertain theatrical future, she wisely accepted the lead in the American national tour of *Annie Get Your Gun* (1946), produced by RICHARD RODGERS and OSCAR HAMMERSTEIN II, who then offered her the lead in *South Pacific* (1949). Her singing of 'I'm Gonna Wash That Man Right Outa My Hair' and 'A Wonderful Guy,' as Ensign Nellie Forbush, consolidated her position as a major star of the American MUSICAL. She was able to demonstrate again her curious mixture of boyish zest and feminine charm in a musical version of *Peter Pan* (1954); thanks to subsequent television airings, this part became associated with her more than any other. She offered another instance of her versatility as Sabina in a short international tour of *The Skin of Our Teeth* (1955). Her last association with Rodgers and Hammerstein came in *The Sound of Music* (1959), where her pure, rangy soprano was heard in 'Do-Re-Mi,' 'My Favorite Things' and the title song. The musical *Jennie* (1963) was a quick failure, so she accepted the starring part in the international tour of *Hello, Dolly!* (1965). With Robert Preston she turned a mediocre musical, *I Do! I Do!* (1966) into a long-running success. This proved to be her final musical, and she was never again to find a worthwhile vehicle of any sort. In 1976 she published her autobiography, *My Heart Belongs*. GERALD BORDMAN

Martin-Harvey, John (b. Wyvenhoe, Essex, 22 June 1863; d. Surrey, 14 May 1944) Actor–manager, the last great one patterned on HENRY IRVING. His modern repertoire (MAETERLINCK) and bold experiments (REINHARDT's *Oedipus*, 1912) failed to establish him in London. His most famour role was Sidney Carton in *The Only Way*, a romantic adaptation of *A Tale of Two Cities*. Between its first performance in 1899 and his retirement in 1939, he played it 5,004 times, almost entirely in the British provinces and Canada. He was also the author of *The Autobiography of Sir John Martin-Harvey* (1933). He was knighted in 1921. ALAN HUGHES

Nicholas Butler, *John Martin-Harvey: the Biography of an Actor-Manager* (1998)

Martyn, Edward [Joseph] (b. Co. Galway, Ireland, 30 Jan. 1859; d. Co. Galway, 5 Dec. 1923) Philanthropist, art patron and co-founder with AUGUSTA GREGORY, W. B. YEATS and GEORGE MOORE of the Irish Literary Theatre, for which he wrote *The Heather Field* (1899) and *Maeve* (1900), both heavily influenced by IBSEN. His later plays were produced by his own group, the Irish Theatre, which he founded in 1914 to stage plays in GAELIC. He was president of the Republican movement, Sinn Fein (1904–8). CHRISTOPHER FITZ-SIMON

Marie-Thérèse Courtney, *Edward Martyn and the Irish Theatre* (1956)

Marx Brothers: Chico [Leonard] (b. New York, 26 March 1886; d. Hollywood, 11 Oct. 1961); **Harpo [Adolph]** (b. New York, 2 Oct. 1888; d. West Hollywood, 28 Sept. 1964); **Groucho [Julius]** (b. New York, 2 Oct. 1890; d. West Hollywood, 19 Aug. 1977); **Gummo [Milton]** (b. New York, 1893; d. Palm Springs, 21 April 1977); **Zeppo [Herbert]** (b. New York, 25 Feb. 1901; d. Palm Springs, 30 Nov. 1979) Comedy team, a successful VAUDEVILLE musical act (in various family permutations) drilled by their mother, that made Broadway in the musical comedies *I'll Say She Is* (1924), *The Cocoanuts* (1925), and *Animal Crackers* (1928). The latter two were co-authored by GEORGE KAUFMAN, who helped them develop an influential cinema career of anarchic surrealist comedy, beginning with *The Cocoanuts* (1929), in which their stage characters were exploited to the full: Groucho, grotesquely moustached, lasciviously leering, indefatigable wisecracker; Chico, bizarrely Italian, broken-Englished, appalling punster, interpreter of 'crazy' Harpo's mime and instrumental effects; plus romantic lead Zeppo (replacing Gummo). They effectively dispersed after 1950, Groucho continuing as a television quizmaster. BRIAN BIRCH

J. Adamson, *Groucho, Harpo, Chico – and Sometimes Zeppo* (1973)
S. Louvish, *Monkey Business: The Lives and Legends of the Marx Brothers* (1999)

Masefield, John (b. Ledbury, Herefordshire, 1 June 1878; d. Abingdon, Oxon, 12 May 1967) Poet and playwright. He wrote more than a dozen plays in verse and prose, seeking, unsuccessfully, suitable theatrical forms for his vision and drawing on many lost cultures (Greek, Roman, Icelandic, Norwegian, Japanese, etc.). He often portrayed brutal rural poverty (*The Tragedy of Nan*, 1908); in contrast, *The Tragedy of Pompey the Great* (1910) and *The Faithful* (1915) – from the *kabuki* samurai play *Kushingura* – are heroic dramas. A biblical cycle includes *The Coming of Christ* (Canterbury Cathedral, 1928). Masefield was Poet Laureate from 1930 and was awarded to the Order of Merit in 1935.
TONY HOWARD
See also VERSE DRAMA.

masks A covering for all or part of a performer's face, the mask has been employed in the theatre from the earliest times, firstly in religious RITUAL and then in the Greek and Roman theatre to express COMEDY and TRAGEDY in a highly stylized way, conveying general, basic emotions. When more subtle and complex emotions came to be expressed in the more intimate Elizabethan theatre, masks were no longer adequate and fell into disuse, being used only in court dances and masques and carnivals. In Italy in the sixteenth and seventeenth centuries the COMMEDIA DELL'ARTE used half- or demi-masks for their characters, and in the Japanese theatre masks have continued to play an important role in the *noh* plays. In the twentieth century masks have been mainly used in Shakespearean productions, although playwrights such as BRECHT, YEATS, O'NEILL and ARDEN called for them and directors such as COPEAU, SAINT-DENIS and DEVINE have used them more widely. In PETER HALL's 1981 production of the *Oresteia* all the characters wore full masks. ALTERNATIVE and STREET THEATRE also rediscovered the value of the mask in OPEN-AIR situations.

The same basic method of making masks – the casting of the face, or modelling in clay and casting in plaster, followed by the moulding of layers of papier mâché or muslin with glue – has been used for generations. Masks were also made in sheet metal and leather. Lately more modern materials and methods are used, such as latex and vacuum-forming in styrene. The latter method was used to make the mask for MICHAEL CRAWFORD in the musical *The Phantom of the Opera*. This was cast over an elaborate make-up and held on by thin piano wire over the head for easy removal in performance. Animal masks also play a role. Bottom's ass's head in *A Midsummer Night's Dream* is usually made realistically, covered in fur fabric. But the construction of bare frameworks in wire and cane can also be used, as in PETER SHAFFER's play *Equus*.
STUART STALLARD

See also PROPS; PUPPETS; WAXWORKS.

Jennifer Foreman, *Maskwork: The Background, Making and Use of Masks* (1999)
John Mack, ed., *Masks: The Art of Expression* (1994)
John W. Nunley and Cara McCarty, *Masks: Faces of Culture* (1999)

Mason, Bruce   (b. Wellington, New Zealand, 28 Sept. 1921; d. Wellington, New Zealand, 31 Dec. 1982) Playwright, director, performer, musician, critic – by the time of his death the most prominent figure in New Zealand's theatre. Having returned to the country after serving overseas in the Second World War, Mason moved to London to train as a concert pianist. In 1951 he and his wife settled in New Zealand. J. B. PRIESTLEY's advice not to write 'imitation English plays' but to draw on his own environment encouraged him to write indigenous drama. He was closely associated with Wellington's Unity Theatre, which performed his first produced play, *The Bonds of Love* (1953). Exposing the reality behind the utopian ideal of New Zealand, the play won an award but earned the playwright an angry

reaction from the audience. His last stage play, *Blood of the Lamb* (1980), ensured that his career ended as bravely and controversially as it had begun. With *The Pohutukawa Tree* (1957) Mason became the first New Zealand playwright to tackle emerging contemporary race and land issues. This play, a milestone in the country's theatre, was written for the NEW ZEALAND PLAYERS. *Awatea* (1965), with the great MAORI bass Inia te Wiata, and other later plays further explored these themes.

Closely involved in the founding of the DOWNSTAGE THEATRE, Mason was regarded as its saviour on more than one occasion, having rescued it at times of financial crisis by either writing a new play or performing one of his popular SOLO pieces. These solo performances of his own work, in particular *The End of the Golden Weather* (1959), would alone have guaranteed him a lasting reputation. He also wrote New Zealand's first television drama, the controversial *The Evening Paper* (1965). A prolific writer for stage and television, his contribution cannot be overestimated. He captured the magic and pain of New Zealand childhood, the dilemmas of racial relations, the awkwardness of an unsophisticated, puritanical society.   GILLIAN GREER

David Dowling, ed, *Every Kind of Weather: Bruce Mason* (1986)

Mason, Marshall W.   *see* CIRCLE REPERTORY COMPANY

Mason, Patrick [D.]   (b. Romford, Essex, 16 April 1951)   Director. He has worked chiefly in Ireland, where from 1977 he directed over 30 productions for the ABBEY THEATRE; among these have been substantial new works from Irish playwrights, including five plays by TOM MACINTYRE. He has also directed regularly at the GATE THEATRE and for independent managements in Dublin. His Abbey production of BRIAN FRIEL's *Dancing at Lughnasa* (1990) transferred to London's NATIONAL THEATRE, the WEST END and BROADWAY. Mason was artistic director of the Abbey from 1993 to 1999, during which period he restored the company to international prominence.   CHRISTOPHER FITZ-SIMON

mass declamation   A non-naturalistic, group performance used by working-class theatre troupes in Europe and America between the world wars, often at consciousness-raising left-wing political meetings. Distinguished by its use of chanting and choral speech, singing and choreographed movement, the mass declamation belongs to AGITPROP theatre. Its power in performance depended on well-drilled rhythmic awareness; Tom Thomas, of the Workers' Theatre Movement, noted in 1932 that British groups should use mass declamation texts 'like an orator would, with well-marked changes of rhythm, emphasis and intensity'. *On Guard for Spain*, written by Jack Lindsay and performed by UNITY THEATRE at the time of the Spanish Civil War, is a fine example. DEREK PAGET

Raphael Samuel, Ewan MacColl and Stuart Cosgrove, *Theatres of the Left 1880–1935: Workers' Theatre Movements in Britain and America* (1985)
Colin Chambers, *The Story of Unity Theatre* (1989)

Massey, Anna *see* MASSEY, RAYMOND

Massey, Dan *see* MASSEY, RAYMOND; SHAW (PERFORMING)

Massey, Raymond [Hart] (b. Toronto, 30 Aug. 1896; d. Los Angeles, 29 July 1983) Actor and director who moved confidently from leading roles to character parts in a range of work from the classics (Shakespeare, STRINDBERG) to numerous films and the popular television series *Dr Kildare*. Among his successes were the title role in *Ethan Frome* (1936), 1940s revivals of *The Doctor's Dilemma, Candida* and *Pygmalion*, a reading of *John Brown's Body* (1952) and the Godlike Mr Zuss in *J. B.* (1958). The tall, gaunt performer is best recalled for his moving portrayal of *Abe Lincoln in Illinois* (1938). He wrote two autobiographies, *When I Was Young* (1976) and *A Hundred Different Lives* (1979). His second wife, Adrianne Allen, their son, Daniel [Raymond] (b. London, 10 Oct. 1933; d. London, 25 March 1998) and their daughter, Anna (b. Thakeham, Sussex, 11 Aug. 1937), also acted successfully. GERALD BORDMAN

Matcham, Frank (b. Newton Abbot, Devon, 22 Nov. 1854; d. Southend, Essex, 17 May 1920) Theatre architect. Between 1879 and 1912 he designed some 150 theatres, more than twice the number of his great rival Charles John Phipps, whose work turned out to be of less lasting importance. Audience safety and comfort were among his chief concerns, and his theatres were noted for good acoustics and sightlines as well as for being soundly built. Considered the greatest British exponent of his craft, he designed his auditoria like exotic palaces, lavishly decorated with cherubs and extravagant features. More than 20 of his theatres were still in operation a century after their construction, including BELFAST's Grand Opera House, the HACKNEY EMPIRE, the London COLISEUM and the LONDON PALLADIUM, which he redesigned in 1910 complete with palm court. COLIN CHAMBERS

See also ARCHITECTURE.

B. Walker, ed., *Frank Matcham: Theatre Architect*

Matthews, [James] Brander (b. New Orleans, La., 21 Feb. 1852; d. New York, 31 March 1929) Critic,

playwright, and the first person to hold the title of professor of dramatic literature in an American university. Matthews was one of the first scholars to deal seriously with native literature, almost single-handedly creating the field of American literary criticism. From a wealthy family and educated as a lawyer, he was an unsuccessful playwright in his early years. His many reviews and articles on theatre appeared in the most widely read journals of his day, and as the main theatre reviewer for the *Nation* for 20 years (1875–95), he wielded great influence over the country's taste for drama at the outset of the century. He was a staunch proponent of realism in drama and literature, believing that realistic portrayals reveal the life and character of America. Among his two dozen books are *The Development of Drama* (1903), *Principles of Playmaking* (1919) and two memoirs, *These Many Years* (1917) and *Rip Van Winkle Goes to the Play* (1926). DAVID A. WILLIAMS

Matthews, Jessie (b. London, 11 March 1907; d. Pinner, Middx, 19 Aug. 1981) Actress who rose to stardom via the REVUES *London Calling!* (London, 1923), *André Charlot's Revue* (New York, 1924) and *Charlot's Revue* (London, 1925). She also starred in *This Year of Grace* (1928) and *Ever Green* (1930). She began a successful film career in 1923. Latterly she became best known as Mrs Dale in the radio serial *Mrs Dale's Diary* (1963–9) while continuing an active stage career. Her autobiography, *Over My Shoulder*, appeared in 1974. REXTON S. BUNNETT

Matura, Mustapha (b. Trinidad, 17 Dec. 1939) Playwright. He settled in London in 1961, where he worked in various jobs from hospital porter to stockroom assistant. Matura's first full-length play, *As Time Goes By*, was staged on the FRINGE both at EDINBURGH and in London, winning him awards for the most promising playwright of 1971. He depicted life in the CARIBBEAN and for black people trying to survive in England, and wrote challenging roles for black actors. A major success came in the 1974 production of *Play Mas* at the ROYAL COURT, which transferred to the West End, a first for a Caribbean playwright. *Rum and Coca Cola* (1976), *Independence* (1979), *Meetings* (1979) – all set in Trinidad – and *Welcome Home Jacko* (1979) confirmed his position as the leading black playwright in England. He was a founder of the BLACK THEATRE CO-OPERATIVE and made his mark in television too. He has adapted the classics with great wit and humour (e.g. *The Playboy of the West Indies*, 1984, from SYNGE; *Trinidad Sisters*, 1988, from CHEKHOV). His surrealistic farce *The Coup* was staged at the NATIONAL THEATRE in 1991. HELEN RAPPAPORT

Maude, Cyril [Francis] (b. London, 24 April 1862; d. Torquay, Devon, 20 Feb. 1951) Actor–manager and president of the Royal Academy of Dramatic Art. Maude gave his first notable performance in PINERO's *The Second Mrs Tanqueray* (1893) and then entered into partnership with another member of the cast, GEORGE ALEXANDER: in 1896 they took over the management of the Haymarket, then the Royal Avenue Theatre (later the Playhouse) and produced a series of hits in which Maude and his wife Isabel often took leading roles (e.g. *The School for Scandal*, 1900). He also organized and performed in several successful tours. His autobiography, *Behind the Scenes*, appeared in 1927. ADRIANA HUNTER

Maugham, [William] Somerset (b. Paris, 25 Jan. 1874; d. Nice, 15 Dec. 1965) Novelist and playwright. Maugham gave up medicine to be a writer and achieved celebrity in 1908 with the simultaneous London runs of *Lady Frederick*, *Jack Straw*, *Mrs Dot* and *The Explorer*. Although he attempted serious plays, his finest and most characteristic work came after the First World War (during which he served as a British secret agent) in a successful series of elegant and slightly cynical comedies, which include *Home and Beauty* (1919), *The Circle* (1919, regarded as a classic), *The Constant Wife* (1926) and *The Breadwinner* (1930), all dealing with sexual relationships. He treated unconventional topics – miscegenation in *East of Suez* (1922), euthanasia in *The Sacred Flame* (1928) – and wrote bitterly of the glorification of war in *For Services Rendered* (1932). After the relative failure of *Sheppey* (1933), the story of a barber who tries against the odds to live life according to true Christian principles and which O'CASEY thought a masterpiece, Maugham decided he was no longer in touch with the tastes of his audiences and resolved to retire from playwriting.

To Maugham's 29 original plays must be added many stage and screen dramatizations of his novels and short stories, such as *Rain* and *The Moon and Sixpence*, which contributed to his popularity as an author. IAN CLARKE

Ronald E. Barnes, *The Dramatic Comedy of William Somerset Maugham* (1968)
Anthony Curtis, *Somerset Maugham* (1977)
Archie K. Loss, *W. Somerset Maugham* (1987)
Ted Morgan, *Somerset Maugham* (1980)

Mauriac, François (b. Bordeaux, 11 Oct. 1885; d. Paris, 1 Sept. 1970) Novelist, playwright and critic, awarded the Nobel Prize in 1952. His plays, *Asmodée* (1938), *Les Mal Aimés* ('The adored evils', 1945) and *Passage du Malin* ('Unfolding of the ruse', 1947), depict emotional frustration in the conflict between sensual-

ity and the religion which he, as a fervent Catholic, believed purifies the heart. WENDY SCOTT

Mauritius The inhabitants of this small volcanic island in the Indian Ocean largely trace their roots back to African slaves imported by French rulers (1722–1814) and Indian indentured labourers imported under British rule (occupied 1810, sole power from 1814–1968) after slavery was abolished (1834). About 45 per cent of the islanders are Hindu, 30 per cent Christian and 15 per cent Muslim. English is the official language, French is spoken more generally – though French Creole wider still – and there are Asian tongues too. Colonialism brought folk drama from Africa (*sega*) and India, and more formal theatre from Europe, yet it was not until 1932 and the founding of the Mauritius Dramatic Club that English-language theatre began to emerge. A type of Hindustani dance-drama (*natak*) developed in World War II when Hindi films were in short supply, and after the war there were some playwrights writing in Hindi and French. Youth theatre was given a boost in 1951 with the inaugural Youth Drama Festival, which until independence accepted plays only in English, and in 1966 a directors' society was established. Independence in 1968 saw an increase in theatrical interest across the island and the rise of Creole as its principal language (e.g. in the work of Asize Asgarally and Henri Favory). CHARLES LONDON

Mavor, Osborne Henry *see* BRIDIE, JAMES

Mayakovsky, Vladimir [Vladimirovich] (b. Bagdady [later renamed Mayakovsky], Russia, 19 July 1893; d. Moscow, 14 April 1930) Artist, poet and playwright. A Bolshevik from the age of 15, when he was first arrested and spent nearly a year in solitary confinement, he subscribed with no less enthusiasm to new artistic movements. He was a collaborator in 1912 on the FUTURIST manifesto *A Slap in the Face of Public Taste*, and published his first poetry collection in 1913 under the title of *Me*. This precocity and self-absorption extended to his first play, a monodrama called *Vladimir Mayakovsky*, subtitled *A Tragedy* (1913), which he also directed and starred in. *Misteria-Buff* (*Mystery-Bouffe*, 1918) was the first Soviet play to be performed, directed by MEYERHOLD. It is an epic, pseudo-biblical piece set after a new flood with seven pairs of 'Clean' (contemporary world leaders) and seven pairs of 'Unclean' (representative workers) in search of Utopia. A revised version appeared in 1921. By this time Mayakovsky was director of the Bolshevik advertising and propaganda agency, for which he produced cartoons, poems and slogans. He is also given credit for the introduction of the poster boats and trains which carried the new government message to the further corners of the country. Several short agitational plays date from 1920 with titles such as *Chempionat Vsemirnoy Klassovoy Borby* (*The Championship of the Universal Class Struggle*) and *A Chto Y Esli . . . Pervomayskiye Grezy V Burzhuaznom Dresle* (*And What If . . . May the First Daydreams in a Bourgeois Armchair*). During the early 1920s Mayakovsky concentrated on lecturing, poetry recitals and editing the journal *LEF*, which was opposed to aestheticism. Two major plays, *Klop* (*The Bedbug*) and *Banya* (*The Bathhouse*), were produced in 1929 and 1930. These, apart from a further CIRCUS play, *Moskva Gorit* (*Moscow's Burning*, 1930), completed his work as a dramatist. *The Bedbug* and *The Bathhouse* both have a science fiction quality. *The Bedbug* somewhat ambiguously follows the fortunes of Prisypkin, a would-be bourgeois, who is frozen in a block of ice and resurrected 50 years in the future. *The Bathhouse* has a character called the Phosphorescent Woman arriving by time-machine from 100 years in the future to transport the deserving to her own era. Both were directed by MEYERHOLD but met with official hostility for their apparent attack on current values and tendencies. Four weeks after the first night of *The Bathhouse*, overwhelmed by the virulence of his critics, Mayakovsky shot himself. As 'the poet of the Revolution' he was rehabilitated by Stalin in 1935, but it was not until after Stalin's death that Mayakovsky's plays returned to the stage. J. MICHAEL WALTON

See also AGITPROP.

Nikolai A. Gorchakov, *The Theatre in Soviet Russia* (1957)

Alex Miller, trans., *Vladimir Mayakovsky, Innovator* (1976)

Konstantin Rudnitsky, *Russian and Soviet Theatre Tradition and the Avant-Garde* (1988)

Harold B. Segel, *Twentieth Century Russian Drama from Gorky to the Present* (1979).

Marc Slonim, *Russian Theatre from the Empire to the Soviets* (1961)

Mayne, Rutherford [Samuel Waddell] (b. Tokyo, Japan, 1878; d. Dublin, 25 Feb. 1967) Playwright. Active member of Ulster Literary Theatre from its foundation in 1904, for whom he wrote *The Turn of the Road* (1916) and *The Drone* (1903). *Peter* (1930) and *Bridgehead* (1934) first appeared at the ABBEY THEATRE, Dublin. His mordant comedies have been undeservedly neglected since the 1940s. CHRISTOPHER FITZ-SIMON

Meadow, Lynne *see* MANHATTAN THEATER CLUB

Meckler, Nancy *see* SHARED EXPERIENCE

medicine show A North American hangover from the nineteenth-century, offspring of touring European quack doctors selling patent medicines from gaudy caravans by offering skits, MAGIC and music too. A few practitioners survived advances in health, drugs and communications, including the onset of cinema, and continued the tradition late into the twentieth century. CHARLES LONDON

M. Calhoun, *Medicine Show* (1976)

Brooks McNamara, *Step Right Up: An Illustrated History of the American Medicine Show* (1995)

medieval theatre in the twentieth century
Before 1900 there appear to have been no public performances of English medieval plays since the Reformation had suppressed this lively tradition of popular theatre which flourished in the 150 years separating Chaucer and Shakespeare. It was an unsophisticated theatre, by turns pious and vulgar, embracing the rite of the eucharist and the ribaldry of the buffoon – a genre which hardly squares with ARISTOTLE's prescriptions for tragic theatre. Being mostly a representation of a Catholic world-view, it was considered both blasphemous and idolatrous and was outlawed. (This legacy of CENSORSHIP remained until the LORD CHAMBERLAIN's power was removed in 1968, and it has profoundly coloured modern notions of what theatre is, its history and who it is for.) With the majority of texts and records lost or destroyed by reforming zealots, it has been difficult for twentieth-century historians to piece together a picture of medieval theatre.

The first great step forward was taken by Sir Edmund Chambers with the publication in 1903 of *The Medieval Stage*. This will gradually be superseded by the work of *The Records of Early English Drama*, which is cataloguing and publishing all extant references to and information about medieval theatre. The nearest thing to a comprehensive collection of plays, David Bevington's *Medieval Drama* (1975) went out of print quickly, and many plays remain unpublished or available only in expensive volumes destined for academic libraries.

Modern performances of medieval theatre begin with WILLIAM POEL's production of *Everyman* (c. 1500) at the Charterhouse, London, in July 1901. The following February it transferred to the Imperial Theatre in the West End, where the *Guardian* claimed that 'the severe stillness and simplicity of method' were 'beyond praise . . . We have never seen actors grimace less or stand more still.' It was a startling success and the hit of the season. American critics were less receptive when it played on Broadway and toured the West Coast. Having an actor play God was considered idolatrous, and He was reduced to being represented by a blue neon light offstage. Poel soon disowned *Everyman*: 'I did not myself produce *Everyman* as a religious play. As a religious play it is bad . . . But the whole story is beautiful as a piece of art.'

The same religious hackles rose at NUGENT MONCK's production of the Passion sequence from the *Ludus Coventriae* in London in 1909: it was closed by the police as Christ's appearance violated the Blasphemy Act. Though it was reproduced in 1938 for an invited audience at the MADDERMARKET in Norwich, it wasn't until 1952 that the Lord Chamberlain permitted a public performance.

Though Poel's only other 'medieval' production was *Abraham and Isaac* (mid-fifteenth century), he used the earlier theatre as a blueprint for how to produce theatre for a modern audience. His life and personal fortune were dedicated to rewriting the history of theatre, placing Shakespeare at the end of a great tradition of popular theatre stretching back to the mystery plays, and not as the forerunner of contemporary naturalism. Poel (like DARIO FO, years later) was challenging a theatrical establishment which he saw as rotten with commercialism and totally devoid of vitality.

The Festival of Britain in 1951 gave medieval theatre a much wider audience with Christopher Ede's *Chester Cycle* and ELLIOT MARTIN BROWNE's production of the York Mystery Plays in an edition by Canon J. S. Purvis. There followed a burgeoning of interest in the Mystery Plays to the point where they are now a regular feature of the summer calendar in towns like Canterbury, Chester, Coventry, Durham, Lincoln, Pirran's Round in Cornwall, Wakefield and York, and are a fixed point on the tourist itinerary. The plays are marketed as part of Heritage – as English as village greens, real ale and morris men – and are produced in a way which will appeal to the widest possible audience. Heritage, however, turns its back on the present: the past is used to reassure, either through nostalgic escapism or through a jingoistic return to traditional values. The opposite was taken by the ROYAL SHAKESPEARE COMPANY when it staged *The Mysteries* in 1997–8, re-examining them in the light of contemporary debate. As Umberto Eco notes, every age re-creates its own middle ages according to the needs, tastes and contradictions of its culture.

The late 1960s saw a flourishing of university productions of medieval plays; the most prolific university was BRISTOL, with productions by Neville Denny and Glynne Wickham. Realizing they could learn only so much about medieval theatre through studying the texts and records, they started to produce some of the plays in public. This tradition of academic performance has flourished with work at the universities of Lancas-

ter (directed by Meg Twycross), York (with their company The Lords of Misrule) and Leeds (directed by Peter Meredith), where reconstructions of medieval plays are regularly staged. PLS from Queen's University, Toronto, under the direction of David Parry (also a gifted actor) has toured the UK and regularly mounts massive productions in Toronto and throughout Canada. These productions are often meticulously authentic and invaluable to the contemporary director and actor, because information drawn from (or inferred from) orginal documents is translated into exact dimensions, colours, effects, materials and iconography.

The drive behind this renaissance was, in Wickham's words, 'towards a recovery of poetic, imaginative freedom through a return to the use of theatrical conventions appropriate to open stages'. This could just as well apply to, and places the revival of medieval drama in the context of, the radical experiments of FRINGE or ALTERNATIVE THEATRE in the same period, which, recalling Poel, also rejected the limits and limitations of the proscenium arch theatres and the artistic horizons of their patrons.

A huge public awareness of medieval theatre was created around Easter 1977 with two very different accounts of the Mystery Plays, both of which emphasized their essentially 'popular' nature, written, as they were, for common folk, in their language, in all its colour, imagery and vulgarity. The first was *The Passion*, later to become Part II of TONY HARRISON's three-part version of the York Mystery Plays produced by the NATIONAL THEATRE under BILL BRYDEN's direction. The second was the transmission on Italian television of Dario Fo's one-man show *Mistero Buffo* (literally, comic mystery), which was revived by Robbie Coltrane in London (1990).

The National's *Mysteries* took eight years to complete and were a triumphant success both in Britain and abroad. Harrison had seen the plays, still performed from the Canon Purvis text, and was disgusted at how the rich northern dialect had been jettisoned in favour of a bland Home Counties English. He swore to restore the humour and guts of the northern orginal. The other essential and radical element to be restored was the PROMENADE element: the actors walking among the standing audience. This sense of communion was both the production's success and its shortcoming. Harrison and Bryden have admitted that the biggest problem was the frankly religious nature of the plays: as a result, theological problems were given theatrical solutions. For example, designer WILLIAM DUDLEY rejected any religious iconography when tackling hell's mouth in favour of 'a corporation dust cart's jaws, and

Hell itself, a combination of sewage and garbage' because 'these images would be more real for a largely agnostic audience'. The religious content of most medieval drama still generates embarrassment among most contemporary producers and critics, partly as a hangover from our puritan past which still harbours a suspicion of any attempts to represent physically things which are spiritually ineffable, and partly because of the spiritual anguish of our secular society.

Fo's *Mistero Buffo* began in 1969 as a lecture/performance and grew with each presentation into a series of monologues as he re-created for the twentieth century the role of the *giullari* or jester, by turns profound and vulgar. The development was a process of continual negotiation between himself as performer and his audience: the monologues are narrated in Grammalot, an invented dialect, framed by *interventi* on contemporary issues delivered in modern Italian. Fo's socialist beliefs informed his sympathy with the downtrodden, and these 'medieval' monologues were his way of re-creating the voice, the history and the culture of these people. *Mistero Buffo* was screened at the same time as ZEFFIRELLI's *Jesus of Nazareth*, and it was Fo's version of the Passion that was condemned by the Pope. Fo replied that Zeffirelli's Christ was 'a huge, saintly Indian-style guru seized by cathartic trembling every time he's about to perform a miracle' while his was one 'who rolls up his sleeves and produces wine for everyone'.

The most consistent exploration of medieval drama in a contemporary context was by The Medieval Players (1981–93), which toured nationally and internationally. Their approach blends the careful research of the academic pioneers with the pragmatic stagecraft of the professional actor who has to communicate with a paying audience. Performing on a simple trestle stage, the company took its inspiration and repertoire from the itinerant troupes who toured Britain in the gap between Chaucer and Shakespeare. Singing, playing musical instruments, juggling, tumbling, as well as animating puppets and masks, their style owes as much to the ideas of BERTOLT BRECHT as to ancient traditions of storytelling. DICK MCCAW
See also UNIVERSITY DRAMA.

Medoff, Mark [Howard] (b. Mt Carmel, Ill., 18 March 1940) Playwright, director and actor. He had a number of OFF-BROADWAY successes – such as *When You Comin' Back, Red Ryder?* (1973) and *The Wager* (1974) – about people who are victims of society. He is best known for his Tony Award winning *Children of a Lesser God* (1979), about the difficulties a deaf student has coming to terms with her disability in a relation-ship with her hearing instructor. The central character is usually played by a deaf actress. ADRIANA HUNTER

Mei Lanfang (b. T'ai-chou, Kiangsu Province, China, 1894; d. Beijing, 8 Aug. 1961) Actor, great and popular master of Beijing opera. Born into a family of Beijing opera actors, Mei Lanfang began to learn from them the *dan* (female) role at eight years old and first performed in public two years later. When he was 19 he became influenced by Western styles in Shanghai, and began to develop aspects of his work, including make-up, costume and music, in new ways. From 1915 to 1937 he mounted a number of new plays in the Chinese opera style and improved some traditional ones. He drew on the *kunqu* opera, a traditional theatrical form which dominated the Chinese stage between the seventeenth and nineteenth centuries, and he was consistently perfecting his performance. He formed his own theatre school and challenged the exclusion of women from the traditional stage.

Between 1919 and 1935 he visited Japan, the United States and the Soviet Union, becoming the first performer of Chinese opera to influence theatre outside his country. Among others he met Chaplin, BRECHT, EISENSTEIN, STANISLAVSKY, NEMIROVICH-DANCHENKO and MEYERHOLD. In protest against the Japanese invasion of China, he did not perform until the war was over. After the People's Republic of China was established in 1949, he was elected to several important positions, including president of the Beijing Opera Theatre of China. His home has been turned into a museum. SUN MEI
See also CHINA; EASTERN THEATRE, ITS INFLUENCE ON THE WEST.

Wu Zuguang, Huang Zuolin and Mei Shaowu, *Peking Opera and Mei Lanfang* (1981)

Meiningen Company Under the direction of Ludwig Chronegk (1837–91), the court company founded by the Duke of Saxe-Meiningen in 1866 became a major influence on the development of theatre across Europe through its attention to detail and its ENSEMBLE playing. Its impact was felt on naturalism and specifically in Britain on IRVING and the Flower family of STRATFORD-UPON-AVON, the chief local theatre patrons who established the SHAKESPEARE MEMORIAL THEATRE (later the ROYAL SHAKESPEARE COMPANY); in France on ANTOINE; and in Russia on STANISLAVSKY. CHARLES LONDON
See also DIRECTING IN THE TWENTIETH CENTURY.

Ann Marie Koller, *The Theatre Duke* (1984)
John Osborne, *The Meiningen Court Theatre* (1988)

Meisner, Sanford *see* DRAMA SCHOOLS; NEIGHBOR-HOOD PLAYHOUSE

Melbourne Established as a commercial centre in 1835, it grew rapidly in the course of the nineteenth century, and as a consequence of the gold rushes became the second largest city in the southern hemisphere. This expansion also led to the building of large theatres on substantial inner-city sites, three of which are still occupied by theatres. It was also at this time, as the theatre historian Harold Love has noted, that 'the press set standards for the rest of the continent and made theatre the focus of furious disputes between ideologically committed critics.' In spite of the still discernible presence of an 'establishment' in the city, and a residual puritanism in some areas, Melbourne remains notable for its continuing tradition of experimental, AVANT-GARDE theatre. For a time, companies such as Australian Nouveau Theatre and The Church Theatre flourished; subsequently, organizations such as PLAYBOX THEATRE COMPANY and Chamber Made Opera have sought both to promote and to push back the boundaries of local theatre and music theatre. As one critic has pointed out, the tradition of experimental work can be attributed not only to the city's culture of experimentation in political and social terms, but also to the number and type of church halls which have been converted into theatre venues. It is this contrast between the conformism, the 'establishment and church', on the one hand, and an interest in avant-garde ideas, the celebration of art and 'the square', on the other, which has prompted critical or positive comment from many observers, including, latterly, the novelist Thomas Keneally, who noted that 'Melbourne seems to be a secret to which you can obtain the code only if you are born into it or undergo a long initiation.' MICHAEL MORLEY

Melbourne Theatre Company Australia's first professional drama company. It was set up in 1953 as the Union Theatre Repertory Company of the University of Melbourne, taking its present name in 1968. It has occupied a number of spaces, moving into the Playhouse at the new Victorian Arts Centre in 1984, while still retaining access to alternative venues for smaller-scale productions. Under its long-time director John Sumner it established a secure reputation; yet some critics felt that, despite the original aims (a professed commitment to revivals of twentieth-century work and to 'contemporary plays from home and abroad'), there has been a preference for the popular over the more demanding and led to an under-representation of indigenous talent. Under the guidance of Roger Hodgman, who took over in 1987, and, subsequently, Simon Phil-

lips, the company has mounted a wider range of plays, including works by contemporary British and American playwrights. MICHAEL MORLEY

Melfi, Leonard [Anthony] (b. New York, 21 Feb. 1935) Playwright. Melfi's best work is in his early short plays, performed at the Café LA MAMA, like *Birdbath* (1965) or *Times Square* (1966), in which he places his denuded characters in a harshly impersonal New York, where they strive for an undefinable transcendence. His many plays, despite occasional sentimentality, have a stark, violent power. DAN REBELLATO

melodrama A popular theatre genre that came to be equated with sensationalism and excess. Melodramas emerged in the nineteenth century from eighteenth-century French and German productions that combined music (melody) with drama. The use of music and the Gothic influence of virtue overcoming horror diminished, and melodramas turned to more domestic themes and later gave way to realism before succumbing to cinema and subsequently television. Few original melodramas were written; many were simply translations or adaptations from novels. By the beginning of the twentieth century productions were becoming increasingly spectacular. The genre lost its impetus early in the century but survived in various forms. DAVID BELASCO in the United States generated his own version; ALFRED JARRY in *Ubu Roi* wrote a highly influential comic melodrama; and SARTRE wrote an intellectual melodrama in *Crime Passionel*. STOPPARD parodied the form in *The Real Inspector Hound* while ORTON offered a burlesque of it in *Loot*. According to some theorists, a distinction can be made between TRAGEDY, which deals with internal flaws, and melodrama, which deals with external forces.
ADRIANA HUNTER

Melville, Walter (b. London, 1875; d. Hove, E. Sussex, 28 Feb. 1937) and **Frederick [E.]** (b. Swansea, 1876; d. 5 April, Worthing, W. Sussex 1938). Playwrights and PANTOMIME producers. They were respected writers of garish but moral MELODRAMAS with such colourfully evocative titles as *The Worst Woman in London* (1899), *The Ugliest Woman on Earth* (1904) and *The Bad Girl of the Family* (1909). They were joint proprietors of London's Lyceum Theatre and built the Prince's Theatre (later the Shaftesbury). It was at the Lyceum that they became famous, producing gaudy pantomimes for some 20 years consecutively. These grandiose productions, often written by Frederick, guaranteed them full houses for months.
ADRIANA HUNTER

memorabilia *see* RECORDING AND RESEARCHING THEATRE

Mendes, Sam (b. Redding, Scotland, 1 Aug. 1965) Theatre and film director. After gaining a first-class degree and a cricket blue at Cambridge University, he joined the CHICHESTER FESTIVAL THEATRE in 1987, becoming artistic director of the Minerva (studio) Theatre in 1988. Following the sudden departure of another director, he took over the direction of a main stage production, which led to his directing *The Cherry Orchard* with JUDI DENCH in London in 1989. This in turn led him to the ROYAL SHAKESPEARE COMPANY, where his productions include *Troilus and Cressida* (1990), *The Alchemist* (1991), *Richard III* (1992) and *The Tempest* (1993), and the Royal NATIONAL THEATRE (*The Sea*, 1991; *The Rise and Fall of Little Voice*, 1992; *The Birthday Party*, 1994). In 1990 he became the first artistic director of the new DONMAR Warehouse Theatre, which opened in 1992 with his production of SONDHEIM's *Assassins*. Much of his best work has been done in his own theatre, which has become a national and international success under his leadership, particularly with his production of *Cabaret*, which won awards in London and New York, as well as playing in Los Angeles. In 1999 his first film, *American Beauty*, made for Steven Spielberg's Dreamworks studio, established him as an equally accomplished film-maker, winning many awards including an Oscar. Mendes's deceptively affable manner conceals a formidable intellect matched by great emotional intelligence. He is pre-eminent among directors of his generation for the range and consistency of his achievements.
GENISTA MCINTOSH

Menotti, Gian-Carlo (b. Cadgliano, Italy, 7 July 1911) Composer, librettist, director and producer. After studying both in his native Italy and in Philadelphia, he saw his first opera, *Amelia Goes to the Ball*, produced in 1938. Most unusually, he created several operas which were presented at legitimate playhouses rather than at opera houses. The most successful of these were *The Medium* and *The Telephone* (a double bill, 1947), *The Consul* (1950), and *The Saint of Bleeker Street* (1954). GERALD BORDMAN

Mercer, David (b. Wakefield, Yorks, 27 June 1928; d. Haifa, Israel, 8 Aug. 1980) Playwright. Mercer was, first and foremost, a pioneering screenwriter whose work reflects his Marxist beliefs, his northern roots and his own history of mental illness. A recurring theme is the tension resulting from conflicting social (or political) and family pressures, seen in his first West End play, *Ride a Cock Horse* (1965), in which a York-shire writer moves among three women. His television trilogy, *The Generations* (*Where the Difference Begins*, 1961; *A Climate of Fear*, 1962; *The Birth of a Private Man*, 1963) features a dogmatic socialist miner and his son, a left-wing intellectual. His best-known television play, a study of a schizophrenic, is *A Suitable Case for Treatment* (1962), later reworked for the cinema as *Morgan: A Suitable Case for Treatment* (1965). *After Haggerty* (1970) was his first major critical stage success; it was presented by the ROYAL SHAKESPEARE COMPANY, which also produced *Belcher's Luck* (1966), *Cousin Vladimir* (1978) and *No Limits to Love* (1980). Other plays include *The Buried Man* (1962) and *Flint* (1970). He wrote the screenplay for *Providence* (1978). DAVID SELF

Don Taylor, *Days of Vision: Working with David Mercer* (1990)

Mercury Theater (New York) Theatre group established by ORSON WELLES and JOHN HOUSEMAN in 1937. It was an outgrowth of their work on the FEDERAL THEATER PROJECT which had seen, among other productions, a 'voodoo' *Macbeth* (1936). Though it lasted scarcely two years, this group electrified BROADWAY and had a lasting impact on the American theatre. The novelty of its productions and the storm of controversy it aroused made it one of the most dynamic experimental theatres in American history. Among its notable presentations were the modern-dress, 'fascist' *Julius Caesar* (1937) and the legendary musical *The Cradle Will Rock* (1937), which was originally put on in spite of a police ban and started the Mercury project off. It also staged *The Shoemaker's Holiday* and *Heartbreak House* (both 1938) and, two years after it had closed, one last show, *Native Son* (1941). Welles had starred with his company in the notorious 'War of the Worlds' radio broadcast that panicked the nation, and later took it to Hollywood for the film *Citizen Kane* (1940). Among the troupe's members were Agnes Moorehead, Joseph Cotten, Everett Sloane, Paul Stewart, Ray Collins and George Couloris. Houseman's 1972 memoir, *Run-Through*, recalls those heady days.
THOMAS F. CONNOLLY

R. France, *The Theatre of Orson Welles* (1977)
Morgan J. Himmelstein, *Drama Was A Weapon* (1963)

Mercury Theatre (London) Built in 1931 by ASHLEY DUKES to house the Ballet Club of MARIE RAMBERT, his wife, the intimate 150-seat Mercury was licensed as a theatre in 1933. As the London home of Ballet Rambert (until 1966), dance paid the rent while Dukes staged whatever plays he wished to: e.g. *La Parisienne* by Henri Becque (1837–99), Machiavelli's *Mandragola*, *The Ascent of F6* by AUDEN and ISHERWOOD. ELIOT's *Murder* *in the Cathedral* was an early success in 1935, directed by E. MARTIN BROWNE, and the interest in poetry continued after the war with his PILGRIM PLAYERS seasons (1945–7) of work by RONALD DUNCAN, CHRISTOPHER FRY (the popular *A Phoenix Too Frequent*), Donagh Mac-Donagh, Norman Nicholson and ANNE RIDLER. In spite of London premières in 1947 of SAROYAN's *The Beautiful People* and O'NEILL's *SS Glencairn*, and of GENET's *The Maids* in 1952, drama ceased from 1952. Visiting companies, such as LA MAMA, used the theatre from time to time until it closed in 1975.   COLIN CHAMBERS

Mercury Theatre (New Zealand)   The Mercury was established in Auckland's former Playhouse cinema and theatre in 1968 after the Queen Elizabeth II Arts Council decision to support regional professional theatre. Its first director, Anthony Richardson from the Belgrade Theatre, Coventry, England, made an influential contribution to New Zealand theatre, directing some 39 of the 100 plays performed in his nine years at the Mercury. Under director RAYMOND HAWTHORNE, widely recognized both in that capacity and as an actor, Mercury had a resident company including associate artists Lee Grant, GEORGE HENARE, Bridget Armstrong and Elizabeth Hawthorne. Its varied programme included opera and experimental musicals, classics and new plays from home and abroad. It closed in 1992 and its place has been largely filled by the Auckland Theatre Company, directed by Simon Prast.
GILLIAN GREER & LAURIE ATKINSON

Meredith, [Oliver] Burgess   (b. Cleveland, 16 Nov. 1908; d. Malibu, Calif., 9 Sept. 1997)   Actor and director who received his training and made many of his earliest appearances in EVA LE GALLIENNE's CIVIC REPERTORY THEATER. His career peaked shortly afterwards when he played leading roles in three MAXWELL ANDERSON successes: *Winterset* (1935), *High Tor* (1937) and *The Star Wagon* (1937). Subsequently he found work in superficial comedies, as a replacement for other stars, or in films, radio and television. He was a small man with a pixieish manner and voice. He wrote an autobiography, *So Far, So Good* (1994).   GERALD BORDMAN

Mermaid Theatre   Started life in 1951 as a private theatre in north London, designed along Elizabethan lines by Josephine and BERNARD MILES and playing a seventeenth-century repertoire. Two years later the Mileses were asked to help celebrate the coronation of Elizabeth II and the Mermaid arose in the City of London with a 13-week season of more seventeenth-century fare. The Corporation of London then offered a seven-year lease on a blitzed warehouse at Puddle Dock by the River Thames, and in 1959 a new open-stage theatre, funded by public subscription and seating nearly 500 in one raked tier, was opened with *Lock Up Your Daughters*, a musical adaptation from Henry Fielding by Bernard Miles and LIONEL BART which transferred to the WEST END.

One of the liveliest and friendliest theatres in London, the Mermaid presented a bold repertoire that included more than a dozen plays by SHAW, an O'CASEY season, Euripides, HAUPTMANN, BRECHT, IBSEN, Molière and MAYAKOVSKY. It produced many transfers to the West End – *The Bed Sitting Room* (1963) by JOHN ANTROBUS and SPIKE MILLIGAN, three plays by BILL NAUGHTON, Peter Luke's *Hadrian VII* (1968), *Breezeblock Park* (1977) by WILLY RUSSELL and Brian Clark's *Whose Life Is It Anyway?* (1978). It became famous for its Christmas and children's shows – e.g. *Treasure Island* with Miles as Long John Silver – and for a series of musical tributes, to NOËL COWARD, COLE PORTER and STEPHEN SONDHEIM. The Mermaid closed in 1978 for rebuilding and reopened in 1981. In spite of a transfer of *Children of a Lesser God* that year, the theatre was beset with financial problems. Miles left in 1980 and it never recovered.   COLIN CHAMBERS

Merman [Zimmermann], Ethel [Agnes]   (b. Astoria, NY, 16 Jan. 1909; d. New York, 15 Feb. 1984) Singer and actress who appeared in nightclubs and VAUDEVILLE before making a sensational Broadway debut in GEORGE GERSHWIN's *Girl Crazy* (1930), where her singing of 'I Got Rhythm' stopped the show. After *George White's Scandals* (1931) and *Take a Chance* (1932), she consolidated her reputation with *Anything Goes* (1934), in which she introduced such COLE PORTER hits as 'I Get a Kick Out of You', 'You're the Top' and the title song, and became Broadway's musical comedy queen – a position she retained for 25 years. Hitherto this pinnacle had belonged to beautiful, sweet, blondish sopranos, like LILLIAN RUSSELL, JULIA SANDERSON and MARILYN MILLER; Merman, by contrast, was dark-haired, not especially pretty, and brassy. Impeccable enunciation and projection accounted for much of her uniqueness, though she never lost her New York accent. *Red, Hot and Blue* (1936), *Stars in Your Eyes* (1939), *DuBarry Was a Lady* (1939), *Panama Hattie* (1940) and *Something for the Boys* (1943) followed before she had another exceptional hit with *Annie Get Your Gun* (1946), in which she introduced 'There's No Business Like Show Business' and other IRVING BERLIN gems. She sang a second Berlin score in *Call Me Madam* (1950). The failed *Happy Hunting* (1956) was compensated for by her last major success, *Gypsy* (1959), which not only gave her the opportunity to sing excellent JULE STYNE songs but demonstrated she could be a riveting actress. Thereafter her age and changing styles in musical theatre brought an end to her string of successes. She replaced CAROL CHANNING briefly in *Hello, Dolly!* (1970), starred in revivals of her old favourites and gave some vaudeville concert performances, including a visit to the LONDON PALLADIUM in 1974. She published an autobiography with George Eells, *Merman*, in 1978.

GERALD BORDMAN

Merrick [Margulois], David (b. St. Louis, Mo., 27 Nov. 1911; d. London, 25 April 2000) Producer. Merrick grew up in poverty but won a scholarship to Washington University and then went on to practise law in St Louis. After moving to New York City, he changed his name to Merrick, a combination of Margulois and Garrick (the eighteenth-century actor), in an attempt to disown his past. He learnt about theatre from producer–director HERMAN SHUMLIN; even in his first major production, *Fanny* (1954), he exhibited a penchant for flamboyant advertising and aggressive promotion. His most famous productions were musicals, including such major hits as *Gypsy* (1959), *Carnival* (1961), *Hello, Dolly!* (1964), *Promises, Promises* (1968) and *42nd Street* (1980). He introduced American audiences to such British productions as *Look Back in Anger* (1957), *Becket* (1960), *Oliver!* (1963), *Luther* (1963) and *Philadelphia, Here I Come!* (1966). The most celebrated and successful BROADWAY producer of his time – and his producing career spanned four decades – Merrick won 12 Tony Awards. He once paid someone to go on stage and slap an actor in order to get publicity and his promotion schemes earned him such nicknames as 'the Barnum of Broadway' and 'the Abominable Showman'. Renowned for his dourness, he was an unsentimental and lonely man. DAVID STAINES

H. Kissel, *David Merrick: The Abominable Showman* (1993)

Messager, André [Charles Prosper] (b. Montluçon, France, 30 Dec. 1853; d. Paris, 24 Feb. 1929) Composer and administrator. Messager began his wide-ranging musical career as a symphonic composer and a performer and conductor of serious music while also providing ballet music for and conducting at the FOLIES-BERGÈRE. He composed the scores for a dozen light operas and several ballets with some success, but it was not until 1897, with *Les P'tites Michu* and then with *Véronique* (1898), that he found a significant place on the international musical stage. His output over the next 20 years was limited by his activities successively as musical director of the Opéra-Comique, as director of both the Paris Opéra and London's Royal Opera

House, and as a theatre and concert conductor, but after the First World War he returned to the light musical theatre to collaborate successfully with FREDERICK LONSDALE on the impressive musicalized *Monsieur Beaucaire* (1919), with SACHA GUITRY on the plays *L'Amour Masqué* (1923) and *Deburau* (1918), and finally on two suave, jazz-age musical comedies, *Passionnément* (1926) and *Coup de Roulis* (1928). KURT GÄNZL

M. Augé-Laribé, *André Messager: musicien de théâtre* (1951)

J. Wagstaff, *André Messager: A Bio-Bibliography* (1991)

Messel, Oliver [Hilary Sambourne] (b. London, 13 Jan. 1904; d. Barbados, 13 July 1978) Designer. Messel designed costumes and decor for COCHRAN REVUES (1929, 1930), transformed the Lyceum into a cathedral for REINHARDT's *The Miracle* (1932) and worked on several ballets and musical comedies. His graceful and witty pictorial style – opulent, intricate, yet delicate – became increasingly fashionable in the 1930s. He designed the Hollywood film of *Romeo and Juliet* (1936) and TYRONE GUTHRIE's mock-Victorian *A Midsummer Night's Dream* (OLD VIC, 1937). In the postwar period, Messel contributed to the success of FRY's *The Lady's Not for Burning* (1949), ANOUILH's *Ring Around the Moon* (1950) and *Rashomon* (1959) by the KANINS. As well as film work, his many OPERA commissions included Mozart in Glyndebourne, London and New York.

TONY HOWARD

metatheatre A term used by American playwright Lionel Abel (1910–2001) in 1963 to define what he saw as a new genre of contemporary play, such as *Death of a Salesman* by ARTHUR MILLER or *A Man for All Seasons* by ROBERT BOLT, that could not be classified as TRAGEDY, despite similarities, but still held a metaphoric power. The term enjoyed only a brief currency.

CHARLES LONDON

See also DRAMATIC THEORY.

Method An American school of acting particularly associated with LEE STRASBERG, who applied principles derived from STANISLAVSKY to his work at the GROUP THEATER in the 1930s and later at the ACTORS' STUDIO. Stanislavsky, seeking a means to create a consistently emotionally convincing portrayal night after night, asked his actors to project themselves into the imagined emotional lives of their characters. Stressing one aspect of Stanislavsky's ideas, the Method encouraged actors to develop and colour characterizations from their own emotional memories. This created performances of great intensity, although Method actors were sometimes accused of displaying their own private world instead of that of the playwright. It became globally famous through the cinema work of MARLON BRANDO and James Dean, and came to be synonymous with modern American acting.   MARVIN CARLSON

See also ACTING.

David Krasner, ed, *Method Acting Reconsidered: Theory, Practice, Future* (2001)
Robert Lewis, *Method – or Madness?* (1958)
S. Vineberg, *Method Actors: Three Generations of an American Style* (1991)

Mexico and Central America

Mexico

The dawn of the twentieth century saw the continued popularity of the lighthearted *género chico* (minor genres) transplanted from Spain in 1869. The lyric *sainete*, *zarzuela* and *revista* (REVUE) subgenres soon assumed Mexican characteristics. As part of a Mexican nationalist movement in art, theatre defended and catered to the Indian, rural peasant and urban proletariat. Naturalism inspired by ZOLA also continued to survive in dramas that portrayed violent rural conflict.

In the 1920s and 1930s several brief movements had a limited success in transcending deep-rooted Spanish models through seasons of Mexican plays, portrayal of middle-class concerns, and revolution-based themes: examples were El Grupo de los Siete Autores (the Group of Seven Authors), La Comedia Mexicana (the Mexican Comedy) and El Teatro de Ahora (the Theatre of Now, run by Mauricio Magdaleno and Juan Bustillo Oro). The influence of PISCATOR and BRECHT was first seen in Bustillo Oro's epic, political pieces, such as *Justicia, S.A.* ('Justice, Inc.', 1933).

The experimental drama of Teatro Ulises (Ulysses Theatre, 1928) achieved fuller expression in a successor, Celestino Gorostiza's Teatro de Orientación (Theatre of Orientation, 1932–8). Modern North American, European and classic authors (and some original works) attracted new, intellectual audiences. Francisco Monterde's *Proteo* ('Proteus'), the first Mexican piece to be presented in the new style, was mounted in 1931 by Julio Bracho and Los Escolares del Teatro (the Theatre Scholars). Bracho also introduced workers' theatre and founded the Teatro Universitario (University Theatre) in 1936.

Rodolfo Usigli (1905–79), prolific father of the Mexican national theatre, gradually moved from a realist to an EXPRESSIONIST style, achieving profound psychological depth in his characters. In *El gesticulador* ('The gesticulator', 1947) he examines the hypocrisy of Mexican politics. The *Corona* ('Crown') trilogy (1947–61) focuses upon decisive events in Mexico's historical and spiritual development as a nation.

Japanese director Seki Sano had a profound effect on Mexican theatre, introducing STANISLAVSKY to over 6,500 students from 1939 to 1966. In 1941 Sano co-founded the anti-commercial, revolutionary Teatro de los Artes (Theatre of the Arts), and in 1948 created the Teatro de Reforma (Theatre of Reform), a non-commercial centre for professional experimentation.

Reacting against the melodrama and realism of the commercial theatre, the Poesín en Voz Alta (Poetry Out Loud) movement (1956–63) saw explorations by a group of successful artists including Héctor Mendoza, Octavio Paz, Juan José Arreola, Juan Soriano and others. Dramatic and musical collages of Spanish, French, North American and Mexican literary materials were presented.

Several dramatists emerged under Usigli's influence. Emilio Carballido (b. 1925) became Mexico's best-known and most prolific playwright, with a highly original style abounding in humour, poetry and fantasy. *Rosalba y los Llaveros* ('Rosalba and the Llaveros family', 1950) is a provincial comedy of manners. *Yo también hablo de la rosa* ('I also speak of the rose', 1967), one of scores of his one-act plays, poetically questions the essence of reality through multiple perspectives. Outstanding contemporaries of Carballido include Sergio Magaña (1924–90), Elena Garro (b. 1920), Hugo Argüelles (b. 1932) and Luisa Josefina Hernández (b. 1928). Magaña's *Moctezuma II* (1954), Garro's *Felipe Ángeles* (1978) and Argüelles' *Los gallos salvajes* ('The savage roosters', 1986) are attempts at Mexican tragedy utilizing classical structures. Hernández' plays deal with politics, society and metaphysical considerations of human destiny and values. Carballido, Argüelles and Hernández, along with Héctor Azar and Vicente Leñero, have been important teachers for the contemporary generation of dramatists: José Agustín, Oscar Villegas, Willebaldo López, Víctor Hugo Rascón Banda, Oscar Liera (1946–90), Sabina Berman, Jesús González Dávila, Otto Minera, Pilar Campesino, Dante del Astillo, Tomás Espinoza, Juan Tovar, José Ramón Enriquez, Dr Guillermo Schmidhuber, Enrique Ballesté and Enrique Cisneros. This relatively large, struggling group came of age in the context of the political upheaval and the Tlaltelolco massacre of 1968. Themes of social protest and generational conflicts, initially in a realist mould, evolved into a multiplicity of styles and genres, frequently influenced by BRECHT; the reinterpretation of Mexican historical subjects was a major characteristic. Director Luis de Tauira, also of this generation, has staged many major works including Garro's *Felipe Ángeles* (1999). Most of these representative authors have received important prizes. Felipe Santander (b. 1934) and Vicente Leñero (b. 1933) have also

493

made important contributions to the new movement. Santander's themes of violent rural conflict draw on Bustillo Oro, contemporary Cuban theatre, Brecht and Mexican rural life. His *El extensionista* (*The Government Man*, 1978) has been performed perhaps more than any other Mexican play. Novelist and journalist Leñero's historical, Brechtian, documentary theatre has sparked great controversy. *El martirio de Morelos* (*Morelos' Martyrdom*, 1980) humanizes and demystifies a national independence hero. *Nadie sabe nada* (*No One Knows Anything*, 1988), an exposé of high-level corruption in Mexico, was censored by the government.

Traditional Mexican *género chico* styles were updated and reintroduced in 1976 through the Carpa Geodésica (Geodesic Tent Show) and playwright–director Ignacio Merino Lanzilotti. The trend continued in the 1980s with the acclaimed re-creations by Enrique Alonso (b. 1923) of classic revues from the 1930s and 1940s. In the 1990s, Yucatán state's Héctor 'Cholo' Herrera continued a long family tradition of regional, bilingual and bicultural (Mayan–Spanish) revues.

The turbulent politics of 1968 and the early 1970s gave rise to the New Popular Theatre, akin to South American New Theatre, and the pioneering collective Los Mascarones inspired multitudes of young people to form theatre COLLECTIVES and engage in AGITPROP STREET THEATRE aimed at radical political and social transformation. Collectively created works were directed toward the middle and lower classes; models were Brecht, Enrique Buenaventura (Colombia) and AUGUSTO BOAL (Brazil). In 1973 Universidad Nacional Autónoma de México (UNAM) drama students and others formed the Centro de libre Experimentación Teatral y Artística (Centre for Free Theatrical and Artistic Experimentation, CLETA). Since the early 1980s CLETA has been a worker-based cultural organization under the coordination of Enrique Cisneros, a type of Mexican DARIO FO.

In the 1980s several collectives achieved more mature levels of acting, collective creation and direction. The Grupo Zero mastered the tent show revue genre in *La Carpa Zero* ('The Zero tent show', 1982). The Contigo América company successfully united Uruguayan and Mexican independent theatre. Tabasco state's Laboratorio de Teatro Campesino e Indígena (María Luisa Martínez, director) achieved widespread recognition. Independent Indian theatre continued to thrive in many of Mexico's ethnic areas. Mayan companies Lo'il Maxil (Monkey chatter) and FOMMA (Mayan women's strength) are based in Chiapas state.

Many universities have recognized theatre programmes, among them the Universidad Veracruzana (Xalapa) and the UNAM, where dramatist Carlos Solórzano (b. Guatemala, 1922) is professor emeritus. The Instituto Nacional de Bellas Artes (director: Gerardo Estrada), founded in 1947, offers government support for theatrical training, performance and research through the Escuela de Arte Teatral (Theatrical Arts School; director: Ignacio Escárcega), the Compañía Nacional de Teatro (director: Alberto Lomnitz; production: Dora García) and the Centro de Investigacíon y Documentación Teatral Rodolfo Usigli (director: Imar Valdés).

In the 1990s a new generation of playwrights, performers and directors achieved widespread recognition. Playwrights included Antonio Serrano (b. 1955), *Sexo, pudor y lágrimas* ('Sex, shame and tears', 1991); David Holguín (b. 1963), *Puerta del fondo* ('The rear door', 1990); Luis Mario Moncada (b. 1963), *Las historias que cuentan los Hermanos Siameses* ('The stories told by the Siamese twins', co-written with director Martín Acosta, 1999); and Gerardo Mancebo del Castillo Trejo (b. 1970), *Las tremendas aventuras de la Capitana Gazpacho* ('The awesome adventures of Captain Gazpacho', 1998). Performance artists Jesusa Rodríguez and Astrid Haddad gained popularity and notoriety through a cabaret theatre of social and political satire. Among the young directors who moved to the forefront during the 1990s are Claudio Valdez Curi, Mauricio García Lozano and Martín Acosta. A national grass-roots COMMUNITY THEATRE movement flourished in rural areas under the guidance of the Asociación Nacional Teatro Comunidad (1987–97) and general coordinators Domingo Adame, Francisco Acosta, Francisco Navarro and Susan Jones.

The Mexican theatre scene at the end of the 1990s continued to suffer from an acute lack of indoor performance space and state support; nevertheless, Mexican theatre remains rich in dramatists and performing companies – in the capital, the provinces, and traditional rural areas.

Central America and the Caribbean

Since the nineteenth century, travelling troupes from Spain, Italy, Mexico, Cuba and South America have performed lyric and comic 'minor genres' and romantic drama in the region. Their example, which continued into the 1920s and 1930s, was imitated in Guatemala and Costa Rica. In Cuba, a strong lyric theatre tradition survived into the 1980s, rooted in the *bufo* tradition of the late nineteenth century. During the first decades of the twentieth century 'backyard' comedies of manners, with gentle, humorous criticism of social habits and vices, continued to be performed. This thread soon evolved into critical and social realist pieces, supplying in-depth analyses which marked the beginnings of truly national theatres. Puerto Rico's quick shift from colonial to neo-colonial status sparked an early and sustained development of critical realism in that country, with frequent attacks on the United States' military and economic presence. In most cases, criticism was directed at the repressive political/social practices of the oligarchies, particularly their effects on the lives of rural inhabitants. National independence heroes were exalted in their struggle against colonial tyranny.

Outstanding realist dramatists are: Costa Rica – Ricardo Fernández Guardia (1867–1950) and Alberto Cañas (b. 1920); Cuba – José Antonio Ramos (1885–1946); Dominican Republic – Rafael Damirón (1882–1946); El Salvador – Francisco Gavidia (1863–1955) and José Llerena (1895–1943); Guatemala – Manuel Galich (1913–84); Honduras – Alonso A. Brito (1887–1925) and Medardo Mejía (1907–81); Nicaragua – Hernán Robleto (1896–1968); Panamá – Rogelio Sinán (b. 1902); and Puerto Rico – Luis Lloréns Torres (1878–1944) and Manuel Méndez Ballester (b. 1909).

Works by European and North American experimental authors have had their most significant influence in the arena of POLITICAL THEATRE. Psychological, ABSURDIST, GROTESQUE and Brechtian approaches permitted new, critical interpretations of political and social realities, including economic underdevelopment, dictatorships, the disintegration of the family and (in Puerto Rico) migration to the United States. Some outstanding experimental authors are: Cuba (late 1940s–1960s) – Carlos Felipe (1914–75), Virgilio Piñera (1912–79), Rolando Ferrer (1925–76), JOSÉ TRIANA (b. 1931), Antón Arrufat (b. 1935) and Nicolás Dorr (b. 1946); Dominican Republic (1950s) – Máximo Avilés Blonda (b. 1931) and Franklin Domínguez (b. 1931); Guatemala (1930s) – Rafael Arévalo Martínez (1884–1970), Adolfo Drago Bracco (1894–1965), and (1960s) Hugo Carrillo (b. 1929); Honduras (1960s) – Andrés Morris (Spain, 1928–87); El Salvador (1950s, 1960s) – Walter Béneke (b. 1928), Roberto Arturo Menéndez (b. 1931), and Alvaro Menén Desleal (b. 1931); Nicaragua (1930s) – Pablo Antonio Cuadra (b. 1912), José Coronel Urtecho (b. 1906), Joaquín Pasos (1915–47), and (1950s) Rolando Steiner (b. 1935); and Puerto Rico (1950s) – Francisco Arriví (b. 1915), René Marqués (1919–79), Luis Rafael Sánchez (b. 1936), and Juan Pedro Soto.

Latin American New Theatre's influence in the region in the 1960s and 1970s resulted from contact with South American and Mexican theatre. Buenaventura and Boal had a profound effect on university and independent groups. Radical 'GUERRILLA' STREET THEATRE, COLLECTIVE creations, revisions of national histories, interest in popular traditions and legends, political DOCUMENTARY pieces and democratically organized theatre collectives proliferated. Theatre entered the hinterlands, urban streets and factories, becoming a massive, popular form of expression frequently linked to political or social movements seeking radical change from the status quo.

Cuba's and Nicaragua's socialist revolutions (1959, 1979) provided fertile ground for scores of new, revolutionary authors and collectives: Abelardo Estorino (b. 1925), Roberto Orihuela (b. 1950) and the Cubana de Acero and El Escambray collectives in Cuba; Alan Bolt, and the Nixtayolero, Xilonem, Justo Rufino Garay and Teyocoyani collectives in Nicaragua. Also deserving mention are: Costa Rica – Joaquín Gutiérrez, Compañia Nacional and Teatro Universitario; El Salvador – Roberto Salomón's ActoTeatro, Sol del Río 32 and Maíz collectives (all in exile since the 1980s); Guatemala – Manuel José Arce (1935–85) and the Teatro Vivo and Rabinal Achí collectives (both in exile since the 1980s); Honduras – Teatro Nacional, Teatro Experimental Universitario La Merced, La Fragua collective and Rafael Murillo Selva's (b. 1936) Grupo Rascaniguas; Panamá – Roberto McKay, Ernesto Endara (b. 1932), Agustín del Rosario, José de Ávila, Raúl Leis (b. 1947), Junta Teatral Victoriano and Ileana Solís Palma's Oveja Negra collective; and Puerto Rico – Myrna Casas, Victoria Espinosa, Jaime Carrero (b. 1931), Lydia Milagros González (b. 1942), and El Tajo del Alacrán, Anamú; and Teatro del Sesenta collectives.

Into the early 1990s, collectives and dramatists continued to explore drama from the region, the continent and the world, in an attempt to forge a theatrical language adequate to deal with political and social realities. Besides many of those mentioned above, other significant practitioners of the 1980s are: Costa Rica – Samuel Rovinski (b. 1932) and Víctor Valdelomar; Cuba – Freddy Artiles (b. 1946), Ignacio Gutiérrez, Francisco Garzón Céspedes, Fidel Galbán, Abraham Rodríguez, Francisco Fonseca, and Rafael González; Dominican Republic – Iván García (b. 1938) and Reynaldo Disla; El Salvador – Roberto Armijo (b. 1937) and José Roberto Cea (b. 1939); Guatemala – Víctor Hugo Cruz and Manuel Corleto; and Puerto Rico – Roberto Ramos Perea (b. 1956) and José Luis Ramos Escobar.

Repressive regimes have meant the death and exile of many practitioners from Guatemala and El Salvador since the late 1970s, and the depoliticization of those countries' theatres. By the early 1990s most of the region suffered from extreme economic dependence, and – with the noteworthy exception of Cuba – lack of a clearly defined (and economically supported) national cultural project. Nevertheless, a traditional popular theatre (ritual Indian and/or folkloric *mestizo*) continued to thrive in the Guatemalan countryside, and to a lesser extent, in El Salvador, Honduras and Nicaragua, affirming age-old cultures and identities.

DONALD H. FRISCHMANN

See also CARIBBEAN; HISPANIC THEATRE IN THE UNITED STATES; SOUTH AMERICA.

Gabriel Careaga, *Sociedad y teatro modern en México* (1994)

José Ramón Enríquez, ed. and intr., *Teatro para la escene* (1996)

Escenarios de dos mundos: Inventario teatral de Iberoamérica, vols 1–4 (1988)

Donald H. Frischmann, *El Nuevo Teatro Popular en México* (1990)

——, 'Misiones Culturales, Teatro Conasupo, and Teatro Cominidad: The Evolution of Rural Theater', in W. H. Beezley et al., eds, *Rituals of Rule, Rituals of Resistance* (1994)

——, 'New Mayan Theatre in Chiapas: Anthropology, Literacy, and Social Drama', in Diana Taylor and Juan Villegas, eds, *Negotiating Performance* (1994)

Fernando de Ita, ed. and intr., *Teatro mexicano contemporáneo: Antología* (1991)

Rine Leal, *Breve historia del teatro cubano* (1980)

Leon F. Lyday and George W. Woodyard, eds, *Dramatists in Revolt: The New Latin American Theater* (1976)

Daniel Meyran, Alejandro Ortiz and Francis Sureda, eds, *Teatro, Público, sociedad* (1998)

Armando Partida, *Dramaturgos mexicanos, 1970–1990* (1998)

Marina Pianca, gen. ed, *Diógenes: Anuario Crítico del Teatro Latinoamericano*, vols 1–3 (1986–8)

Margaret Sayers Peden, *Emilio Carballido* (1980)

Beatriz J. Rizk, *El nuevo teatro latinoamericano: una lectura histórica* (1987)

Meyerhold, Vsevolod [Emilevich] [until 1895, Karl Theodor Kasimir] (b. Penza, Russia, 28 Jan. 1874; d. Moscow, 2 Feb. 1940) Actor and director. He studied law and music before training at the Moscow Philharmonic under NEMIROVICH-DANCHENKO. He was invited to be a founder member of the MOSCOW ART THEATRE (1898), where he acted the roles of Konstantin and Tuzenbakh in CHEKHOV's *The Seagull* and *Three Sisters*. Tiring of the theatre's naturalistic approach to play production and disappointed at not having been made a shareholder, Meyerhold left in 1902 to found a group, based in the provinces, calling itself The Fellowship of the New Drama. Here he devoted himself to evolving new forms of theatre derived from SYMBOLISM – a theatre of convention in that it was character-

ized by the use of defining symbols – and based on new methods of staging being pioneered in Western Europe by CRAIG, FUCHS, Wagner, APPIA and others. He was invited by STANISLAVSKY to put some of these ideas to the test at a new studio in Moscow, but the experiment was frustrated by the limitations of the actors and by the revolutionary events of 1905. A further invitation was extended to Meyerhold to work at the theatre in St Petersburg which had recently been taken over by the actress VERA KOMISSARZHEVSKAYA. Meyerhold exploited this opportunity to explore an interest in non-realistic theatre forms deriving from medieval mystery plays as well as from pre-Renaissance popular entertainment based on the MIME, the native Russian tradition of the *balagan* or CLOWN show, Italian COMMEDIA DELL'ARTE and the Russian *skomorokh* or strolling player. The spirit of 'the mystery' informed intriguing and highly original productions of *Hedda Gabler* (1906), MAETERLINCK's *Sister Beatrice* (1906) and ANDREYEV's *Zhizn' cheloveka* (*The Life of a Man*, 1907). Another key production from this period was of Alexander Blok's *Balaganchik* (*The Puppet Show* or *The Fairground Booth*, 1906) in which Meyerhold also acted the part of PIERROT. Following disagreements with Komissarzhevskaya, Meyerhold left to become artistic head of the prestigious Imperial Theatres in St Petersburg, a post which he held from 1908 until the Revolution and where he staged sumptuous productions of plays and operas from the classic repertoire (e.g. Molière's *Don Juan*, 1910; Lermontov's *Masquerade*, 1917), working with some of the greatest actors, singers, designers and musicians of the day. Simultaneously, under the pseudonym Dr Dapertutto, he was staging experimental plays in various studios and private apartments in St Petersburg, holding acting classes and editing a journal named after Carlo Gozzi's play *The Love of Three Oranges*. Through these various media, Meyerhold continued to explore methods of presentation and performance based on the Italian comedy of the MASK, the PANTOMIME and the harlequinade while evolving a stylized form of acting, based on physical movement, which, as BIOMECHANICS, was to make a considerable impact after the Revolution.

Appointed by LUNACHARSKY to head the theatrical section of the Commissariat of Education and Enlightenment, Meyerhold threw himself into the revolutionary fray with all the radical zeal of one whose hostility to 'bourgeois' theatrical forms had been anticipated by his pre-revolutionary reputation as an *enfant terrible*. This brought him into conflict with those who thought that the ultra-leftism of the Russian AVANT-GARDE was a form of infantile disorder and that bourgeois realism, albeit of a critical and socialist kind, needed to be the order of the day. Pioneering director's theatre, a number of his productions staged between 1920 and 1924 (such as CROMMELYNCK's *The Magnificent Cuckold*, 1922) were regarded by many as outrageously schematic and formalistic – an eclectic brew of stage forms drawing on cubism, FUTURISM and CONSTRUCTIVISM allied to the disciplined gymnastics of biomechanical performance technique. Removed from his post as theatre commissar, the mood of Meyerhold's productions began to alter under pressure from an increasingly authoritarian bureaucratic structure. From 1926 onwards, in the wake of his extraordinary production that year of Gogol's *Revizor* (*The Government Inspector* or *The Inspector General*), he was increasingly subjected to official criticism as repertory committees demanded changes or even insisted on productions being withdrawn or banned altogether. In the difficult climate of the 1930s, as Stalinist norms began to assert their authority in all walks of life, Meyerhold felt himself increasingly isolated. The suicide in 1930 of MAYAKOVSKY, with whom he had collaborated on productions of *Misteria-Buff* (*Mystery-Bouffe*, 1918, 1921), *Klop* (*The Bedbug*, 1929) and *Banya* (*The Bathhouse*, 1930), affected Meyerhold profoundly. Subjected to charges of formalism, Meyerhold's theatre was closed in 1938 and building work on his new theatre was suspended. Sheltered briefly by Stanislavsky, who offered him work at his opera studio, Meyerhold finally fell victim to the purges carried out in 1939 and was executed in prison the following year. He was officially rehabilitated in 1955 and is now recognized, both in his own country and abroad, as one of the seminal figures in twentieth-century theatre. NICK WORRALL

See also DIRECTING IN THE TWENTIETH CENTURY.

Edward Braun, *Meyerhold on Theatre* (1969)
——, *Meyerhold: A Revolution in Theatre* (1995)
Marjorie L. Hoover, *Meyerhold: The Art of Conscious Theater* (1974)
Robert Leach, *Vsevolod Meyerhold* (1989)

Michell, Keith (b. Adelaide, 1 Dec. 1928) Actor, trained at the OLD VIC Theatre School and a member of the original YOUNG VIC Company. He has starred in plays and musicals in London, STRATFORD-UPON-AVON, BROADWAY and on international tour, including his home country of Australia. He appeared in the opening production of the CHICHESTER FESTIVAL (1962) and was its artistic director 1974–8, directing and designing several productions there. He is most famous as Henry VIII and won five awards for the television series *The Six Wives of Henry VIII* (1970). He is a successful painter and has exhibited in London and New York.
SARAH A. SMITH

Mickery An extraordinary theatre in Amsterdam, founded in 1965 by Ritsaert ten Cate to explore beyond national boundaries all the nooks and crannies of theatrical art. Originally based in ten Cate's farmhouse near Amsterdam, Mickery moved to the city after receiving public funding in 1968. A former cinema without a formal space for actors or audience became the centre for foreign and homegrown experiments, often in the relationship between theatre and other visual media, especially video; in some shows the audience floated on itinerant cubicles. Strong links were forged with companies such as the PEOPLE SHOW, the PIP SIMMONS THEATRE GROUP, the TRAVERSE, and LA MAMA, and with writers like HOWARD BRENTON. Ten Cate decided to close Mickery in 1991 and went out with a bang – a 12-day international multimedia festival, *Touch Time*, held in various locations in Amsterdam, performed by some 20 new and established groups, including KEN CAMPBELL, the WOOSTER GROUP and BREAD AND PUPPET.
CHARLES LONDON

Middle East and North Africa Dominated by Arabic, and mainly Egyptian, traditions, the twentieth-century theatre of the Middle East and North Africa comprises many currents differing in detail but often broadly similar in history and structure depending on religion, language, the nature of the colonial experience and the vicissitudes of post-independence struggles. Old forms – oral narrative, musical clowning, shadow puppets – have mostly declined as Western-influenced and national theatre has asserted itself, although in the process the latter has inevitably been shaped by the former.

Religion
Religion, mainly Islam, plays a decisive role in the development of culture in the region, in respect of what the prevailing orthodoxy allows and what it prohibits. In Iran, for example, where great efforts were made to establish Western-style theatre, particularly after the Second World War, the high-profile Shiraz Festival attracted leading Western practitioners, such as PETER BROOK, TADEUSZ KANTOR and ROBERT WILSON; but this was stopped by the triumph of the Islamic revolution in 1979. However, the tradition of the Muslim passion play, based on the martyrdom of Hussain, the Prophet Mohammed's grandson, continues in Iran, as it does in other countries with a significant Shia population, such as southern Lebanon and Iraq. In the Sunni Muslim countries, notably Egypt, Sufi saints' days often have their own cycle of plays that range from the pious to the rumbustious.

Arab theatre

In the early part of the twentieth century Arab theatre was largely the theatre of the Lebanese and Egyptians. The preponderance of Egyptian plays, and the influence of the Egyptian style of melodrama and pageant play in modern festivals in Tunis (where the important Carthage Festival is held every two years), Egypt, Jordan and Iraq, bears witness to the continuing pre-eminence of Egyptian theatre in the Middle East and North Africa.

Contemporary Arab theatre can be dated from the middle of the nineteenth century when several plays by Molière were translated into Arabic, mainly by Lebanese writers, of whom Maron el-Naquash (1817–55) was the pioneer. These plays were performed in the traditional style developed by the companies of travelling players called *muhabazeen*, whose roots probably extend far back into Egyptian history. Until then these companies had not used written scripts, depending more on improvisation that involved a great deal of interplay with their audiences.

Theatre was used, especially by the poet Abdullah el-Nadim, as a popular means of putting over the nationalist message during the years of ferment before and after the Orabi rebellion of 1881. With the strengthening of the British hold over Egypt, and with the advent of the First World War, there tended to be a preference for escapist historical plays that dwelt on past glories, such as *Saladin and the Kingdom of Jerusalem* by Farag Anton as well as the several plays of Ibrahim Ramzy.

From the war years up to the mid-1950s virtually the only forms of theatre were the melodrama and the farce. The three most notable figures were el-Kassar, who wrote slapstick farces; Naguib el-Rehani (1892–1949), who wrote satirical farces critical of the social corruption of his day; and Yusif Wahaba, whose plays extolled the virtues of the Turkish aristocracy and mocked the simplicity of ordinary people. These three dominated Egyptian and Arab theatre. El-Rehani's and Wahaba's theatre companies toured many of the Arab countries and left their stamp wherever they went – an influence that has not always been healthy.

During the 1930s two other trends started to develop. The first was the poetic play spawned by the romantic movement, whose most important exponents were Ahmed Shawki (1868–1932) and, to a lesser degree, Aziz Abaza. Shawki's plays, such as *Cleopatra's Death* and *Ali Bey the Great*, deal with periods of defeat in Egyptian history in which the larger-than-life heroes often choose to die noble deaths. The second and more enduring trend was that represented by TAWFIQ AL-HAKIM, whose work represents a qualitative leap forward for Arab theatre, dealing with serious and sometimes pressing ideas in a form that is theatrical and accessible. He drew his plots from sources as far apart as Greek myth, Quranic verses, Middle Eastern history, simple folk tales and newspaper reports. Like GEORGE BERNARD SHAW, to whom he is sometimes compared, he wrote his plays initially for publication. He remains, despite his shortcomings, the single most important influence in Arab theatre.

During the economic recession of the 1930s many actors found themselves unemployed. To ease their plight, in 1935 the government subsidized for the first time a national theatre company whose brief was 'to present the world classics in translations by outstanding men of letters'. The main Egyptian writers who had their plays performed alongside those of Shakespeare and Racine were predictably Shawki and al-Hakim, as well as Abaza and Mahmoud Taimour (1894–1973), whose plays drew on the fashionable psychoanalytical ideas of the day. The successes and failures of this company over almost two decades spawned several rival companies that were to establish themselves and prepare the way for the theatre revolution of the 1950s and early 1960s.

The army coup of 1952 put a group of young nationalist officers in power in Egypt. The clash between them and the British government precipitated the Suez crisis. Ahmed Hamrush, a young leftist officer, had been appointed as the new director of the National Theatre in 1955. With the country on the verge of war, Hamrush decided to take a risk. He cancelled the scheduled season and put on three anti-colonial plays by virtually unknown writers. The plays were produced in the afternoon to avoid problems of curfews and blackouts. Within days the theatre was bringing in audiences such as it had never seen before. Young working-class people were forming queues that blocked the traffic in Cairo's streets.

As the theatres started to search out new writing talents, Numan Ashour, Alfred Farag, Yusef Idriss and others had their plays taken up in the seasons that followed. The early Nasser years saw an attempt at building a national culture that was independent of European interests. The result was a relaxing of censorship and an increased subsidy for the arts. This paid off in theatre attendances. The National Theatre achieved unprecedented sellout seasons. Subjects that previously had been treated satirically, and locations, such as the countryside, that had been mere backdrops for romantic plots, now came to the fore. The once invisible world of the poor and the weak became the subject of new plays. This was especially true in the early works of Idriss, Ashour and Lutfy el-Khoully.

By the early 1960s the playwrights were raising questions that were beginning to disturb the regime. El-Khoully asked, in *The Litigation*, how society must be changed. Farag raised issues of war and peace in *The Fall of Pharoah* at a time when Egypt was still at war with Israel. Idriss tackled in a more abstract way the cyclical relationship between master and servant in his most famous play, *Farafeer*, which was the theatrical event of the 1964 season at the National Theatre.

During the 1960s the discrepancy between the rhetoric of the regime and its failings in actuality led to a parting of ways. Farag, probably the most consistently interesting and accomplished playwright of his generation, was imprisoned for almost four years for his politics, as were several other writers. On his release his *Suliman el-Halabi*, about the patriot who assassinated the Napoleonic governor of Egypt, became one of the major productions of the mid-1960s. By then a new generation of writers was emerging, the most significant of them being Muhamad Diab (e.g. *The Old House*, 1964). The reimposition of the full rigours of censorship hit this generation the hardest. Diab was eventually silenced as a playwright in the early 1970s. Other notable writers such as Salah Abdel Sabour, Shawki Abdel Hakim and Naguib Sorour were also to fall foul of the censor, who during the 1970s tightened his grip on the theatre still further. At the same time the state drastically reduced its subsidy, resulting in a heavy dependence on the adaptation of successful European and American musicals; *Hello Dolly!* being one of the biggest hits. The few writers who rose to prominence at this time were of a more commercial bent than their predecessors. Ali Salim, the most significant, has that rare ability to present ideas in a form that is easily digestible and therefore commercial. However, although Lenin el-Ramli's domination of central Cairo's theatres in the late 1980s was based on a commercial approach, his later efforts showed a greater maturity.

Outside Egypt, Arab theatre is dominated by the actor–manager. The most important of these figures are probably the Moroccan Tayib Siddiq, the Lebanese Nidal el-Ashar and Roger Assaf, who has been trying to develop an Islamic theatre, as well as the Syrian Duraid Laham, whose theatre is pan-Arab and nationalist. Each represents a distinctive approach and offers a content tinged with regional concerns. For a short time the audience-participation plays of the Syrian Saadullah Wannus seemed to offer a way forward, yet once the novelty had worn off, they were revealed as another symptom of a general decline.

Arabic has a relatively strict literary form and a looser colloquial form. The language issue has been resolved by words being spelt as they should be when written, but pronounced according to the regional bias of the character. Strict grammatical construction is then modified to fit local speech patterns. This compromise avoids regionalization and allows plays written in one Arab country to be performed in another without loss of meaning.

Any playwright working in Egypt at the close of the twentieth century was hampered by a ruthless censor, crass commercialism and a cultural bureaucracy that controls all aspects of state-subsidized theatre. These conditions are similar, give or take a degree or two and the effects of war, in the rest of the Arab world; Palestinian theatre, though, is a special case due to the Israeli occupation.

Palestinian theatre

In the 1920s and 1930s plays were performed in church schools. In the 1940s a club in Nazareth was actively presenting classical plays in Arabic. The State of ISRAEL, created in 1948, largely suppressed Palestinian theatre through heavy censorship. On the West Bank, theatre continued under the watchful eyes of the Jordanians, while in Egypt and Syria a THEATRE IN EXILE developed that mixed symbolism with slogans. Israeli occupation of the West Bank in 1967 led to Palestinian attempts to create a serious theatre that drew on their experience of being occupied and of exile. During the 1980s the improvisation-based al-Hakawati was the dominant force in Palestinian theatre. Two important companies, Al Kasaba Theatre and Inad Theatre, which established links abroad, were formed on the West Bank in 1974 and 1987 respectively. Over 40 productions later, Al Kasaba opened a new theatre in 2000 in a converted cinema. To cope with the scarcity of performance spaces, Inad Theatre under its director Raeda Ghazaleh has taken to presenting children's plays off the back of an open truck to complement its work in its studio theatre. The flat back of the truck is used for transporting the set and the actors, and then is decked out as a stage. In this way productions like *Sharshoora* (toured 1998) and *Miladeh wa Ramadan* (2000) were seen all around the Bethlehem area. Interactive plays like *Karagoza* (1997) that engage a young audience have been presented throughout the occupied West Bank territory in schools and community centres. However, the *intifada*, beginning in 1987, led to a parting of the ways: while activists resorted to puppetry and traditional storytelling techniques to get their messages across, those with international ambitions left to perform abroad. During the second, al-

Aqsa, *intifada*, which began in 2000, the Inad's theatre was shelled by Israeli tanks and extensively damaged, but Inad as well as other groups, including Al Kasaba, continued performing.

Turkey

Its geographical position, bridging Europe and Asia, and its imperial past have meant that many theatrical influences have shaped Turkish drama. While its adopted religion of Islam did not encourage drama to flourish, popular traditional forms, like that of the actor–storyteller (*meddah*), shadow-puppets (*karagoz*) or comic troupe (*orta-oyunu*), have given way in the tweitheth century to Western forms, often in the spirit of social and political protest.

The National Theatre was founded in 1908, following the establishment of a Turkish constitutional monarchy that year. The First World War saw the country occupied by foreign troops. They were expelled in 1922 by Mustapha Kemal, known as Atatürk, who a year later founded the Turkish republic, paving the way for the creation of a new Turkish drama. Women were allowed on stage, municipal theatres were set up in Istanbul in 1927 and a children's theatre was established in 1935. A state conservatory for theatre, opera and ballet was opened in 1936 with help from Western European artists. Later, private companies grew as the state-backed theatres prospered.

The main figure in this expansion was Mushin Ertugul (1892–1979), who had returned from Germany in 1920 to run the National Theatre. After spending a period in the mid-1920s in the Soviet Union with MEYERHOLD and STANISLAVSKY, Ertugul returned to Turkey to transform his country's theatre in the light of contemporary European practice. Under his aegis, European classics were produced alongside new Turkish plays by writers such as Müsahipzade Celâl (1870–1959), Vedat Nedim Tör and NAZIM HIKMET (1902–63).

New plays have flourished, by writers such as Turgut Özakman, Refik Erduran, Cahit Atay, Haldun Taner, Orhan Asena, Hidayet Sayin and Güngör Dilmen, and there has been a strong musical theatre, particularly associated with the brothers Ekrem Reşit Rey and Cemal Reşit Rey.   KARIM ALRAWI

Metin And, *Culture, Performance and Communication in Turkey* (1980)

M. M. Badawi, *Modern Arabic Drama in Egypt* (1987)

——, *Early Arabic Drama in Egypt* (1988)

Talat Sait Halman, *Modermm Turkish Drama* (1976)

Richard Long, *Tawfiq al Hakim: Playwright of Egypt* (1979)

N. N. Martinovitch, *The Turkish Theatre* (1968)

Matti Moosa, *The Origins of Modern Arabic Fiction* (1983)

P. G. Starkey, *From the Ivory Tower: a critical study of Tawfiq al-Hakim* (1987)

Mielziner, Jo (b. Paris, 19 March 1901; d. New York, 15 March 1976) Set and LIGHTING designer. After making his professional debut as actor and designer with the Jessie Bonstelle Stock Company in Detroit (1921), he went to Vienna and studied under Oscar Strnad. In 1924, as a design apprentice at the THEATER GUILD, he played walk-on roles, then made his BROADWAY design debut with *The Guardsman* (1924). By the 1930s he was known for his suggestive realism enhanced by evocative lighting. With Edward F. Kook of Century Lighting, Mielziner experimented with lighting instruments and techniques. He was a lighting consultant to CBS-TV during the early days of television. In 1937 he became principal designer for the PLAYWRIGHTS' COMPANY. As a designer of musical comedies, he developed the use of the scrim to cut down the time needed for scene changes and to allow a flow of action. He also worked on breaking out of the proscenium arch to bring the action closer to the audience. He was obsessed with the primacy of the text and worked closely with his directors on interpretation. His best-known settings were for MAXWELL ANDERSON's *Winterset* (1935) and ARTHUR MILLER's *Death of a Salesman* (1945). He also designed the première productions of TENNESSEE WILLIAMS' *The Glass Menagerie* (1945), *A Streetcar Named Desire* (1947) and *Cat on a Hot Tin Roof* (1955). The dominant designer of his time, he designed over 300 Broadway shows, including for three decades most of the major new plays and musicals (e.g. *Pal Joey*, 1940; *Annie Get Your Gun*, 1946; *South Pacific*, 1949; *Guys and Dolls*, 1950; *The King and I*, 1951). He won eight Pulitzer Prizes, five Tonys and numerous other awards. He was collaborating designer for the Vivian Beaumont and Forum Theaters in the LINCOLN CENTER and won an Academy Award for best art direction on the movie *Picnic* (1955). He wrote *Designing for the Theatre: A Memoir and a Portfolio* (1965).
FELICIA HARDISON LONDRÉ

Mary C. Henderson, *Mielziner: Master of Modern Stage Design* (2000)

Orville K. Larson, *Scene Design in the American Theater from 1915 to 1960* (1989)

Mikhoels, Solomon Mikhailovich (pseud. for S. M. Vovski) (b. Dvinsk, Russia, 16 March 1890; d. Minsk, 13 Jan. 1948) Actor. A leading member, and later director, of Moscow's Jewish State Theatre until his death when a lorry hit him 'by accident'. He played some 30 roles, ranging from vaudeville to tragedy, and demonstrating mastery of expressive gesture, sculptural plasticity of form and movement plus a profound philosophical temperament. Among his outstanding roles were those of the Jester in I. L. Peretz's *Night in the Old Market* and King Lear in RADLOV's 1935 production. Stalin closed all Jewish theatres in 1948, the year of Mikhoels' mysterious death. NICK WORRALL

Miles, Bernard [James] (b. Uxbridge, 27 Sept. 1907; d. Knaresborough, N. Yorks, 14 June 1991) Actor and director. During the early years of his career he doubled up as a scene painter, designer, stage manager, carpenter and property master. After 20 years in repertory he founded his first MERMAID THEATRE (1951) with his wife and constant collaborator, Josephine Wilson, in their garden in London. Two years later the theatre was re-established in the City of London and became successful enough to convince Miles to found a permanent Mermaid (1959), to which he dedicated the rest of his life. A pioneer of new plays, Miles re-introduced the public to Greek and early seventeenth-century drama and BRECHT, as well as housing subsequent West End hits such as BILL NAUGHTON's *Alfie* (1963) and Brian Clark's *Whose Life Is It Anyway?* (1978). Among his many acting roles were Galileo (1960), John Gabriel Borkman (1961), Schweyk (1963), Oedipus (1965) and Falstaff (1970). He directed and adapted many plays, including Henry Fielding's *Rape Upon Rape*, which, as *Lock Up Your Daughters*, opened the new theatre. He was known nationally for a distinctive burr in his voice through rural monologues on radio, television advertising for eggs and stout, and for numerous film appearances. His most famous role was Long John Silver in *Treasure Island*, which he played more than a thousand times in his own adaptation. He was also the author of four books, including *The British Theatre* (1948). Miles was created a life peer in 1979. MAGGIE GALE

Miles, Julia *see* WOMEN IN THEATRE; WOMEN'S PROJECT

Miller, Arthur (b. New York, 17 Oct. 1915) Playwright. His plays may be characterized as well-crafted, prosaic, realistic dramas in the tradition of IBSEN, usually on themes of guilt and responsibility. His close-knit Jewish family background and the difficulties his parents experienced during the Depression gave him the social awareness that informs his work. His job as a shipping clerk while he saved for college was to become the basis for his short play *A Memory of Two Mondays* (1955). His first professionally produced play, *The Man Who Had All the Luck* (1944), perceived as heavy-handedly earnest, closed after only four performances, although it won the Theatre Guild National

Prize. *All My Sons* (1947), which was directed by ELIA KAZAN and won the New York Drama Critics' Circle Award, demonstrated through the ordinariness of the play's Keller family that irresponsible actions may have consequences far beyond one's own back yard.

Death of a Salesman (1949) is generally regarded as Miller's masterpiece. Staged by Kazan and starring LEE J. COBB, it won both a Pulitzer Prize and the New York Drama Critics' Circle Award. JO MIELZINER's Tony Award winning set design enhanced the play's skilful blend of expressionistic memory sequences within a realistic framework. The central character, Willy Loman, is a travelling salesman whose misplaced values lead him to suicide after he fails in his work and fails as a father. The play aroused much discussion on the nature of tragedy and the common man: was Willy Loman a modern echo of the tragic stature of King Lear or merely a victim? Noteworthy among its numerous revivals was a 1983 production in Beijing, starring the renowned Chinese actor Ying Ruocheng and directed by Miller himself who wrote about this in his book *Salesman in Beijing* (1984).

Miller's adaptation of Ibsen's *An Enemy of the People* (1950) nudged its content toward a sharper focus on the theme that was also to dominate in *The Crucible* (1953): the responsibility of the individual to stand up to the community in the cause of truth. *The Crucible*, a historical drama about the Salem witchcraft trials in colonial America, is often interpreted as political allegory, reflecting Miller's preoccupation with the McCarthy hearings of the early 1950s. *A View from the Bridge* began as a one-act play (1955) and was expanded to full length for a 1956 London première. It is the drama of an Italian American longshoreman who confuses his own motives when he betrays two illegal immigrants to the authorities. United Artists produced *The Misfits* (1961), a screenplay Miller wrote for Marilyn Monroe, whom he had married in 1956. That marriage, which ended in divorce in 1961, and his subsequent marriage to Austrian photographer Morath, inspired his 1964 play *After the Fall*. *Incident at Vichy* (1966) explored individual guilt in the context of the Holocaust. *The Price* (1968), a drama of confrontation between two brothers, has been Miller's most successful play since the 1960s. His 1970 one-acters *Fame* and *The Reason Why* aroused little interest. *The Creation of the World and Other Business* (1972) was dismissed by critic CLIVE BARNES as 'a comic strip version of Genesis'. None the less, Miller collaborated with composer Stanley Silverman on a musical version titled *Up from Paradise* (1974); it was produced at Miller's *alma mater*, the University of Michigan. Neither *The Archbishop's Ceiling* (1977) nor *The American Clock* (1980) fared well in pro-

---

· Performing Miller ·

Apart from playing a small part in *The Crucible* for the NATIONAL THEATRE at the OLD VIC in 1965, my first real experience of acting in Arthur Miller was playing Eddie Carbone in *A View from the Bridge* (also for the National) in 1987. The experience was extraordinary. It's quite a short play and Alan Ayckbourn's production moved with enormous speed. All the images that come to mind when I think about it are to do with trains – the power and inevitability of the play's climax come at you like a speeding express train, and each performance felt like being on that train, speeding along, the landscape outside a blur. Because Eddie doesn't express himself very lucidly, it's a part you have to inhabit even more thoroughly than most – because most of his emotions are internalized. The shoes and clothes I wore were of enormous importance to me (as they always are) and I had a nightly battle with my dresser not to have the costume freshly laundered, which wouldn't have felt right at all. **MICHAEL GAMBON**

---

duction. The one-acters *Some Kind of Love Story* and *Elegy for a Lady* were produced under the title *Two by A.M.* (1982) and published as *Two-Way Mirror*. Similarly, *Danger: Memory!* (1987) comprises two one-act plays, *Clara* and *I Can't Remember Anything*; critic FRANK RICH noted of them that Miller as 'pontificator wins over the playwright'. A more favourable reception greeted Miller's television drama *Playing for Time* (1980), about an Auschwitz inmate whose life is spared because of her musical ability. It explores not only the survivor's sense of guilt but also the seeming paradox that those who perpetrate horrible cruelties on their fellow human beings also have the capacity to love and appreciate the arts.

The 1990s brought a new surge of interest in Miller's plays in the United Kingdom. *The Ride Down Mt Morgan* (1991) premièred in London, which also saw *The Last Yankee* (1992), depicting two couples who meet at a mental hospital where the wives are being treated for depression, and *Broken Glass* (1994), in which a Jewish wife's hysterical paralysis reifies the recriminations of a dysfunctional marriage and the tribulations of Jewish people in 1938 Germany.

In addition to his plays, Miller has published a number of theoretical essays on the drama (e.g. in 2000, *Echoes Down the Corridor: Collected Essays 1944–1999*) as well as his autobiography, *Timebends* (1987). Whatever posterity's verdict on his writing, Arthur Miller himself has earned wide respect as a figure who galvanizes moral issues. FELICIA HARDISON LONDRÉ

Jantosh K. Bhatia, *Arthur Miller: Social Dramas as Tragedy* (1985)

C. W. E. Bigsby, *A Critical Introduction to Twentieth-Century American Drama*, vol. 2: *Williams, Miller, Albee* (1984)

Christopher Bigsby, ed, *The Cambridge Companion to Arthur Miller* (1997)

Dennis Welland, *Miller the Playwright* (1961)

Miller, [John] Henry (b. London, 1 Feb. 1859; d. New York, 9 April 1926).   Actor, producer and director with an infamous explosive temper. The handsome, somewhat stocky Miller made his debut in Toronto (1877) and came to New York three years later. After rising to leading roles under other producers, he set up as an actor–manager and presented himself in such hits as *The Great Divide* (1906), with MARGARET ANGLIN, *The Rainbow* (1912) and *The Famous Mrs Fair* (1919). He launched the career of ALLA NAZIMOVA and produced and directed *The Servant in the House* (1908, starring WALTER HAMPDEN), *Daddy Long Legs* (1914) and *Come Out of the Kitchen* (1916). In 1918 he opened Henry Miller's Theater, which from 1926 to 1968 was managed by Gilbert Heron Miller (1884–1969), the son of Henry and the actress Bijou Heron. Gilbert ran the St James Theatre, London, from 1918 until its closure in 1958 and did much to encourage artistic exchange between London and New York.   GERALD BORDMAN

Frank P. Morse, *Backstage with Henry Miller* (1938)

Miller, Jonathan [Wolfe] (b. London, 21 July 1934)   Director and author. Miller qualified as a medical doctor at CAMBRIDGE, co-authored and appeared in the REVUE *Beyond the Fringe* (EDINBURGH FESTIVAL, 1960; WEST END, 1961) and made his directorial debut with JOHN OSBORNE's *Under Plain Cover* (1962). For a year (1964–5) he took over the BBC arts programme *Monitor*. A production of *The Merchant of Venice* (1970) with LAURENCE OLIVIER at the NATIONAL THEATRE led to Miller becoming an associate there (1973–5) with a reputation for intelligence and originality. Very much his own man, he worked for the ROYAL SHAKESPEARE COMPANY and several repertory theatres, became a noted opera director (e.g. a modern *Rigoletto*, 1984, set among the New York Mafia) and ran the OLD VIC (1988–90), giving new life to many rare and half-forgotten plays. He always maintained his medical interests and in 1985 was appointed Research Fellow in Neuropsychology at Sussex University. The author of several books, including *Subsequent Performances* (1986), he has written and presented medical programmes on television. FRANK LONG

Michael Romain, *A Profile of Jonathan Miller* (1992)

Miller, Marilyn[n] [Mary Ellen Reynolds] (b. Evansville, Ind., 1 Sept. 1898; d. New York, 7 April 1936) Musical comedy actress. The archetypal little trouper, she was thrust on to the stage at the age of four in a family act and toured in VAUDEVILLE until she was spotted by Lee SHUBERT and brought back to New York to appear in *The Passing Show of 1914*. Her popularity ensured her return in later *Passing Shows*, as well as the ZIEGFELD FOLLIES of 1918 and 1919. But her biggest success was her long run (570 performances) in a Cinderella role in *Sally* (1920), featuring songs such as 'Look for the Silver Lining'. By this time her popularity had guaranteed her huge earnings, and when she appeared in the star vehicle *Sunny* (1925), she was the highest-paid musical comedy star of her day. Her popularity was underscored with *Peter Pan* (1924), *Rosalie* (1928) and *Smiles* (1930), and successful film versions of *Sally* and *Sunny* in the early 1930s; but her career was cut short by an early death at the age of 38, after she had returned to the stage in *As Thousands Cheer* (1933). The leading role in JEROME KERN's *The Cabaret Girl* (1922) was loosely based on her and she was portrayed in the musical *Ziegfeld* (1988) as well as on film in *Till the Clouds Roll By* (1946) and *Look for the Silver Lining* (1949). HELEN RAPPAPORT

W. Harris, *The Other Marilyn* (1985)

Miller, Max [Thomas Sargent] (b. Brighton, 1895; d. Brighton, 7 May 1963) Comedian. Known as 'the cheeky chappie', he topped the bill at all of London's main VARIETY houses from the 1920s to the 1950s. He appeared in the revue *Apple Sauce* (1940) and also on film, radio and television. He was famous for his white trilby, loud, baggy silk suits and his two stage books of jokes, one white, the other blue. It was the latter, which was more saucy than risqué, that the audience inevitably chose. 'You're the kind of people who'll get me a bad name,' he would say, and he would have them eating out of his hand. The character of Archie Rice in *The Entertainer* has been said to have been based on Miller, though the author, JOHN OSBORNE, denied it. REXTON S. BUNNET

Milligan, Spike [Terence Alan] (b. Ahmednagar, India, 16 April 1918) Comedian and writer. Irish, born in India, Milligan has sustained his SURREALIST comedy through many radio and television series from *The Goon Show* on. By devising a form of humour which did not rely on narrative progression to a 'punch-line', Milligan precipitated a new style of comedy, taken up by *Monty Python's Flying Circus* and its many spin-offs. He could be said to be the founding father of contemporary television comedy. His play (with JOHN ANTROBUS) *The Bed-Sitting Room* (1963) and his central performance in *Oblomov* and *Son of Oblomov* (both 1964) helped break the deadlock of the post-1956 social realist theatre and pointed forward to the post-1968 ALTERNATIVE THEATRE, liberating later playwrights to establish their own rules and invent new forms through which to express social concern. He also appeared often as Ben Gunn in *Treasure Island*. He was knighted in 2000. CLIVE BARKER

Mills, Florence (b. Washington DC, Jan. 1895; d. Harlem, New York, 1 Nov. 1927) VAUDEVILLE singer and dancer. She displayed a talent for singing aged five, when she appeared in the all-black musical *Sons of Ham*. She spent the early part of her career touring in vaudeville in a singing act, 'The Mills Sisters', where she was spotted for another all-black revue, *Shuffle Along* (1921), in which she appeared with JOSEPHINE BAKER. Like Baker, she became popular in Europe during the 1920s, appearing in shows like *Dover Street to Dixie* in London and Paris; she returned to New York to star in *From Dixie to Broadway* (1924). In 1926 she appeared at the London Pavilion in *Blackbirds*, in which she sang the hit song 'Bye Bye Blackbird'. There was a mass turnout for her funeral in Harlem. HELEN RAPPAPORT

Mills, John [Lewis Ernest Watts] (b. North Elham, Suffolk, 22 Feb. 1908) Stage and film actor. Mills started as a MUSIC HALL song and dance man, and turned actor in 1929, becoming popular in comedy and musicals. He entered film acting in 1932 and established himself as an archetypal stalwart Englishman in films such as *In Which We Serve* and *Scott of the Antarctic*. Married (1941) to playwright Mary Hayley Bell, he ranged more widely in his stage work, from CHARLES WOOD's *Veterans* (1972) to BRIAN CLARK's *The Petition* (1986). He wrote an autobiography, *Gentlemen Please* (1980), and was knighted in 1976. FRANK LONG

Milne, A[lan] A[lexander] (b. London, 18 Jan. 1882; d. Hartfield, Sussex, 31 Jan. 1956) Children's writer, novelist and playwright. Author of the *Winnie the Pooh* series, he was a journalist and assistant editor on *Punch* (1906–14) as well as being a successful playwright with some 30 titles to his credit. His plays include *Belinda* (1918), *Mr Pym Passes By* (1920), *The*

Truth About Blayds (1921), *The Ivory Door* (1927), *Gentleman Unknown* (1938) and the popular adaptation of Kenneth Grahame's *The Wind in the Willows*, staged as *Toad of Toad Hall* (1930). MAGGIE GALE

Milton, Earnest [Ernest] (b. San Francisco, 10 Jan. 1890; d. London, 27 July 1974) Actor; born in America, he made his career in England. His London debut was in Montague Glass and Charles Klein's *Potash and Perlmutter in Society* (1914), and he joined the OLD VIC Company in 1918. Blessed with a mellifluous voice, which the critic HAROLD HOBSON likened to a Stradivarius violin, his reputation is based on several highly interesting and unorthodox interpretations of Shakespearean characters, among them Macbeth, Richard II, Shylock and Hamlet. He was greatly praised for his performance in PIRANDELLO's *Henry IV* (1925), and as Timon in *Timon of Athens* (1935), but from then on never quite fulfilled the promise of the first half of his career. DOMINIC SHELLARD

Milwaukee Repertory Theater Founded in Milwaukee, Wisconsin, in 1954 by Mary John as the Fred Miller Theater to produce commercial plays, it joined the nonprofit movement in 1961. Tuns Yalman (1966–71) was followed as artistic director by Nagle Jackson (1971–7), John Dillon (1977–93) and Joseph Hanreddy. The theatre is notable for its multiracial acting company, freely cast in every kind of play. Its repertoire includes contemporary plays about the Midwest and from abroad, especially from Japan and Latin America. Playwrights Amlin Gray and Larry Shue (1946–85) were nurtured by MRT, which also welcomes such innovative artists as MARÍA IRENE FORNÉS and Ping Chong.
M. ELIZABETH OSBORN

See also RESIDENT THEATRE.

S. O'Connor and S. Myers, *Working Space: The Milwaukee Repertory Theater Builds a Home* (1992)

mime As an art form, it underwent radical changes throughout the twentieth century, mainly because it periodically attracted the interest of people dedicated to theatrical experiment and innnovation. Most of the important work has stemmed from France, where there had been a strong revival of interest in silent mime (known there as *pantomime*) in the early nineteenth century. This centred on Jean-Gaspard Deburau, who adopted the white-faced image of PIERROT, one of the most popular figures of the COMMEDIA DELL'ARTE.

The development of mime in the twentieth century can be traced to the French actor and director JACQUES COPEAU. As a reaction against the increasing preoccupation with naturalism on the French stage at the beginning of the century, Copeau set up his own acting school in Paris, the Vieux-Colombier, to investigate the importance of the body as a means of expression. Copeau's actors played on an almost bare stage, and as part of their training, they studied masks, gesture and Japanese *noh* theatre. One of Copeau's students was ETIENNE DECROUX, who continued his own research into the architecture of the body, eventually developing a system he called *mime corporel* (corporeal mime). This lifted mime once more to the level of an autonomous art, though in many ways it was the opposite to what Deburau had done. Decroux was interested in research more than entertainment. He would rather perform to a handful of invited friends in a drawing room than in a popular theatre. His style was abstract and severe: he usually worked almost nude, with a gauze over his head to neutralize the face. In 1940 he opened his own school in Paris, which continued until his death. Because of his uncompromising attitude towards the performance of mime, Decroux was little known outside the profession; yet within it he is rightly recognized as 'the father of modern mime'. Decroux's closest collaborator during the 1930s was the great French actor JEAN-LOUIS BARRAULT. Together they gave many private performances, and in 1945 they appeared as father and son in Marcel Carné's film *Les Enfants du Paradis*. Barrault played Deburau and re-created for the film some of Deburau's nineteenth-century pantomimes. Great physical sensitivity remained a hallmark of Barrault's later work, both as an actor and as a director. But it was not until the emergence of MARCEL MARCEAU in 1947 that mime was able to reach large audiences around the world. Marceau had studied with Decroux, though he developed a completely different approach, preferring to go back to the romantic tradition of Deburau. He was also influenced by the great mimes of the silent films, in particular Buster Keaton and Charlie Chaplin. In his solo mimes, Marceau became expert at creating an environment of imaginary objects and characters in space. For many people, his clown character, Bip, with its white face and battered top hat, was for decades the quintessence of mime. Ironically, Marceau's international popularity almost drove mime into an artistic cul-de-sac, because it became increasingly difficult to add anything new. The countless imitations to be seen in public squares throughout Europe merely made cliches of the devices Marceau had so meticulously perfected. And despite fine work from respected artists like the Czech mime LADISLAV FIALKA or the Swiss clown Dimitri (b. 1935), the public began to tire of the Pierrot image.

A bold new direction was taken in the late 1950s by JACQUES LECOQ. Through his Paris school, Lecoq extended the territory of mime to include related disciplines like clowning, masks, *commedia dell'arte* and bouffons. He also set out to reassess some of the physical principles of genres like TRAGEDY and MELODRAMA. Although not primarily a performer, Lecoq became one of the most influential figures in twentieth-century mime in that he showed the way forward from Marceau. Whereas Marceau produced a new generation of white-faced solo performers, Lecoq's students have tended to form diverse companies, like the British groups Moving Picture Mime Show and THÉÂTRE DE COMPLICITÉ. The growth of mime in Britain has been further encouraged by the London International Mime Festival which was founded in 1977 to provide a showcase for new mime. Added stimulus was also given through regular workshops conducted in Britain by leading teachers like Lecoq, Philippe Gaulier and the *commedia dell'arte* exponent Carlo Boso. Meanwhile, the influence of Etienne Decroux has strengthened, especially in the United States where his somewhat geometrical style is represented by performers like Daniel Stein and Thomas Leabhart. The French company Théâtre de Mouvement is the finest exponent of Decroux's legacy.

In Britain one of the most influential and enduring figures has been David Glass, first through his solo performances in the 1980s, then through a series of startling productions for the David Glass Ensemble in the 1990s. By the early 1980s it was clear that mime, no longer a silent art, was moving into a fruitful area of overlap with conventional drama, while certain strands of drama were increasingly drawing on mime. British theatre groups like SHARED EXPERIENCE and CHEEK BY JOWL, or French groups like le THÉÂTRE DU SOLEIL, have often resorted to mime in their efforts to restore the supremacy of the actor on a bare stage. Mime techniques of Asian theatre were used to stunning effect in JULIE TAYMOR's big-budget staging of *The Lion King* (1998).

Inevitably, a confusion has arisen as to what is now meant by mime. In order to dispel the Marceau image, some companies prefer to call their work visual theatre, or physical theatre. Others call it new mime or postmodern mime, hoping that the public will eventually recognize that the term 'mime' now means a lot more than a silent world of white-faced figures walking against the wind. KENNETH REA

Jean-Louis Barrault, *Reflections on the Theatre* (1951)
Etienne Decroux, 'Words on Mime', trans Mark Piper, *Mime Journal*, 1985
Giacomo Oreglia, *The Commedia dell'Arte* (1968)
Bari Rolfe, ed., *Mimes on Miming* (1981)

Minack Theatre A fine 600-seat OPEN-AIR auditorium carved out of the granite hillside in Porthcurno near Penzance, Cornwall, in 1932. At first it was privately owned; in 1959 the Minack Theatre Society was set up to generate publicity for the theatre, which hosts companies from all over the country to present performances through the summer months.
ADRIANA HUNTER

Minneapolis/St Paul Following decades of traditional activity – stock companies, educational and academic productions – this middle-sized city, located in Minnesota along the US–Canadian border, was put on the theatrical map in 1963 when TYRONE GUTHRIE established there the GUTHRIE THEATER, which has remained a major American resident theatre. Since then, Minneapolis has developed a distinctive theatre community of its own, with a number of important companies. Theatre de la Jeune Lune, founded in 1979, is an ensemble of actors, designers and directors who create their own productions, which are influenced by COMMEDIA DELL'ARTE, MIME, CIRCUS, VAUDEVILLE and MUSICAL THEATRE. The Children's Theater Company, founded in 1961, presents elaborate and highly professional productions, including both original works and adaptations of children's classics. The Walker Art Center concentrates on AVANT-GARDE work and PERFORMANCE ART. Other Minneapolis companies have included AT THE FOOT OF THE MOUNTAIN (1974, a pioneering women's theatre), Brass Tacks Theater (1979, new works) and Cricket Theater (1971, contemporary works), as well as Illusion Theater (1974, new works), Mixed Blood Theater Company (1976, multicultural theatre), Penumbra Theater Company (1977, in St Paul: African American theatre), and Playwrights' Center (1971, development of new works).
DAVID BARBOUR

C. Beuville, *Theater Magic: Behind the Scenes at a Children's Theater* (1986)
F. Whiting, *Minnesota Theater: From Old Fort Snelling to the Guthrie* (1988)

Minsky Brothers   *see* APOLLO THEATER; BURLESQUE

minstrelsy American VARIETY entertainment performed in blackface. It is generally said to have begun in 1828, when T. D. Rice, a white performer, began copying African American slaves' songs and dances, including the now infamous 'Jump Jim Crow'. The term 'minstrelsy' was taken from the British tradition of travelling singers and musicians, and in fact many minstrel performers were of Irish ancestry. After the American Civil War, many minstrel shows grew into massive spectacles, and some African American minstrel companies were formed – though audience expectations obliged them to perform in blackface and to perpetuate the same racial stereotypes that had been institutionalized earlier by whites. Later in the nineteenth century, VAUDEVILLE drew away minstrelsy's audience, and in the twentieth century film damaged its business further, though early films continued the minstrel tradition of using white actors in blackface to play African American roles. In the 1920s AL JOLSON triumphed on Broadway in blackface, and Hollywood musicals included minstrel-like blackface routines as late as the 1940s. Not until after the Second World War and the emergence of the civil rights movement was blackface minstrelsy killed off.

In its era, minstrelsy gave an outlet to the racial tensions that have existed in the United States since slave times. It reassured the Caucasian majority that African Americans were funny, talented and content with their inferior social status. But minstrelsy was also a finely wrought form of variety entertainment, the influence of which has continued up to the present. CLIFFORD ODETS patterned his classic agitprop *Waiting for Lefty* (1935) after minstrelsy; anti-minstrel plays like JEAN GENET's *The Blacks* (1959) and DOUGLAS TURNER WARD's *Day of Absence* (1965) call for black actors to 'whiten up' to mimic whites; and even the format of Johnny Carson's *Tonight* show can be seen as a modified minstrel structure. There were minstrel troupes in Britain too, in the latter half of the nineteenth century, until 1904. The tradition was revived in the 1960s with *The Black and White Minstrel Show*, popular both on television and on stage; it ran in the West End for a decade and was for many years the longest-running musical London had ever seen. The show was revived in 1992 to much outcry, even though the blackface had been dropped, but this time it did not take.

CHARLES LONDON

Robert C. Toll, *Blacking Up: The Minstrel Show in Nineteenth-century America* (1974)

P. Sampson, *Blacks in Blackface* (1980)

Carl Wittke, *Tambo and Bones: A History of the American Minstrel Stage* (1930)

Mirren, Helen (b. Southend, 26 July 1946) Actress of English–Russian birth. Since her appearance as an astonishingly mature Cleopatra for the NATIONAL YOUTH THEATRE in 1964, she has been known for the intelligence and sensuality she has brought to roles such as Ophelia, Cressida, Lady Macbeth and Cleopatra again (1983 and 1999), principally for the ROYAL SHAKESPEARE COMPANY, though she has played classic parts for a number of companies, including an acclaimed lead in *The Duchess of Malfi* (1980) for the ROYAL EXCHANGE, Manchester. In 1972–3 she worked in Africa and the United States with PETER BROOK's Centre International de Recherches Théâtrales. She has also appeared in notable productions of modern plays (e.g. *Teeth 'n' Smiles*, 1975), in many films and on television (e.g. *Prime Suspect*). ROBERT CHEESMOND

Mishima, Yukio [Kimitaké Hiraoka] (b. Tokyo, 14 Jan. 1925; d. Ichigaya, 25 Nov. 1970) Novelist and playwright, regarded as one of Japan's finest postwar writers, who mixed a narcissistic and romantic concern for an aristocratic past with explorations of sado-masochism, self-will and Zen ideas. He committed *hara-kiri*. Of Mishima's many plays, only a collection of his short plays in the style of *noh*, *Five Modern Noh Plays* (*Kindai Nogakushu*, 1956) and one long play, *Madame de Sade* (*Sado Koshaku Fujin*, 1965) have been produced in English. The latter had a remarkable production by INGMAR BERGMAN in Sweden in 1989.
DANIEL MEYER-DINKGRÄFE

J. Nathan, *Mishima: A Biography* (1975)

Henry Scott Stokes, *The Life and Death of Yukio Mishima* (1975)

Peter Wolfe, *Yukio Mishima (1989)*

Mistinguett [Jeanne-Marie Bourgeois] (b. Enghien les Bains, France, 5 April 1875; d. Bougival, 5 Jan. 1956) Actress, dancer and REVUE star. She achieved fame in MUSIC HALL as a singer and comedienne with eccentric dances, followed by great success at the MOULIN ROUGE (of which she was part proprietor) and then with MAURICE CHEVALIER at the FOLIES-BERGÈRE, where she was famous for her highly insured legs and extraordinary hats and dresses. After the First World War she created a series of revues, went to the United States and returned to Paris with another resounding success: *Ça c'est Paris* (1926) at the Casino. 'Miss' was queen of the Parisian music hall for 40 years, playing in her last revue in 1948. Her book, *Mistinguett: Queen of the Paris Night*, appeared in 1954.
TERRY HODGSON

David Bret, *The Mistinguett Legend* (1990)

Mitchell, Adrian (b. London, 24 Oct. 1932) Poet, playwright and adapter. Mitchell first came to dramatic notice with his adaptation for PETER BROOK of PETER WEISS' *Marat/Sade* (1964), which ably deployed his skills in terse, epigrammatic poetry that still conveyed the steely horror of the play. He collaborated with Brook again at the ROYAL SHAKESPEARE COMPANY on *US* (1966). He is best known for his adaptations, notably of Calderon's *The Mayor of Zalamea* (1981, for the NATIONAL THEATRE) and *Life's a Dream* (1983, with

JOHN BARTON for the RSC), and of Gogol's *The Government Inspector* (1974) and Lope's *Fuente Ovejuna* (1989), both at the NT; and for his many accomplished children's plays. Always politically engaged, Mitchell has had most individual success with *Man Friday* (1972, in its various incarnations), a witty reversal of the cultural assumptions behind *Robinson Crusoe*. Other plays include *Tyger* (1971), *Mind Your Head* (1973), *White Suit Blues* (1977), and *The Tragedy of King Real* (1983), written for WELFARE STATE INTERNATIONAL.   DAN REBELLATO

Mitchell, Ann   *see* MONSTROUS REGIMENT

Mitchell, Gary   *see* BELFAST

Mitchell, Katie [Katrina Jane]   (b. Reading, Berks, 23 Sept. 1964)   Director. After three years (1986–9) working as assistant director at the KING'S HEAD Theatre, PAINES PLOUGH and the ROYAL SHAKESPEARE COMPANY, she founded her own company, Classics on a Shoestring, for which she directed *Arden of Faversham* (1990) and, in co-production with London's GATE THEATRE, *Vassa* (1990), *Women of Troy* (1991) and *The House of Bernarda Alba* (1992). She has worked extensively for both the RSC (including *The Dybbuk*, 1992; *Ghosts*, 1993; *The Phoenician Women*, 1995; *Uncle Vanya*, 1998) and the Royal NATIONAL THEATRE (including *Rutherford and Son*, 1994; *The Oresteia*, 1999). She has also directed opera and worked in Italy (directing MARTIN CRIMP's *Attempts on Her Life*) and in Poland. Her work, minutely detailed and painstakingly researched, has been created almost exclusively for small spaces. It is informed by her passionate belief in the importance of theatre as a medium for discussing big political and social questions.   GENISTA MCINTOSH

Mitchell, Ken   *see* CANADA: THEATRE IN ENGLISH

Mitchell, Langdon [Elwyn]   (b. Philadelphia, 17 Feb. 1862; d. Philadelphia, 21 Oct. 1935)   Playwright. Son of a famous novelist, his best work was his social satire *The New York Idea* (1906). His other successes were adaptations or translations, such as *Becky Sharp* (1899), *The Kreutzer Sonata* (1906) and *Major Pendennis* (1916).   GERALD BORDMAN

Mnouchkine,   Ariane   (b.   Boulogne-sur-Seine, France, 1939)   Director. After university and student theatre she visited the East before founding in Paris the THÉÂTRE DU SOLEIL (1964) along rigorous cooperative lines. WESKER's *The Kitchen* (1967) and a sensual *A Midsummer Night's Dream* (1968) led, after the student upheavals of 1968, to her acclaimed COLLECTIVE creations on the French Revolution, *1789* (1970) and *1793* (1972). *L'Age d'or* (1975), *Méphisto* (1979), adapted by the Algerian-born Hélène Cixous, and two of her own

plays, *Norodom Sihanouk* (1985) and *The Indiade* (1988), a political history play on Indian independence, have followed, as well as a cycle of Shakespeare plays (*Richard II*, 1981; *Twelfth Night*, 1982; *Henry IV, Part 1*, 1984). Oriental theatre has influenced her highly stylized and relentlessly perfectionist methods of direction, which represent a mix of ARTAUD, BRECHT, COPEAU and VILAR. Months of rehearsals ensure supreme choral work. In her *Agamemnon* (1990–1), part of her Greek cycle *Les Atrides*, a final elaborate dance lasted the length of the sustained applause.
TERRY HODGSON

See also EASTERN THEATRE, ITS INFLUENCE ON THE WEST.

A. Kiernander, *Ariane Mnouchkine and the Théâtre du Soleil* (1993)
Travail Théâtral (quarterly), special issue, 'Différent, le Théâtre du Soleil', Feb. 1976

modernism   Writers on literature began making a distinction between classic and modern works and attitudes as early as the Renaissance, although the modern was not widely defended as an alternative until the end of the seventeenth century. A sense that they were involved in creating new forms, suitable to and reflective of a distinctly modern consciousness, pervades both the theory and the practice of romantic writers, and under their influence, the goal of creating a 'modern' art became a central concern during the nineteenth century. By the end of the twentieth century, modernism was most frequently considered to have begun not with romanticism, however, but with realism, which places its beginning around the middle of the nineteenth century if one is speaking of modern painting or the modern novel, and in the 1870s, with the writings of ZOLA and the first plays of IBSEN's realistic period, if one is speaking of the theatre.

The history of the modern theatre is often seen to begin in 1887 with the founding in Paris by ANDRÉ ANTOINE of the Théâtre Libre, which championed the works first of Zola and the naturalists and then of the first major international modern dramatists, such as Ibsen, STRINDBERG and HAUPTMANN. Antoine's theatre in turn served as a model for other experimental theatres across Europe and eventually in America and elsewhere. Although these theatres varied widely in their repertoires, production methods and specific goals, they shared a common dissatisfaction with the mainstream theatre of their time and sought to provide a significant alternative to it. This phenomenon, the INDEPENDENT THEATRE movement, is essentially associated with the years before the First World War, but an ALTERNATIVE theatre tradition, closely associated with the AVANT-GARDE and with modernist experimentation, has remained an important part of the international theatre ever since.

Modernism, somewhat confusingly, is a term applied to various developments in all of the arts in the late nineteenth and early twentieth century, many of these developments having a distinctly anti-realistic orientation. Certain elements in modernism suggest a revival of the romantic spirit of the early nineteenth century, especially the concerns with internal reality. Modernist art was iconoclastic, often with a specific programme of clearing away the debris of the past to make way for a new art of the future. Indeed, the first major modernist movement of the new century was aptly named FUTURISM, a movement that celebrated speed, change, technology and revolutionary upheaval in art and politics. Introversion, sophistication, technical display, mannerism, internal self-scepticism and a consciousness and display of a sense of crisis and rapid movement in culture, in perceptions of reality, in the sense of community, were all features commonly found in modernism.

Modernism was closely associated with the idea of the avant-garde, a term applied to artists involved in introducing original and experimental ideas, forms and techniques, usually with an implication that these ideas anticipated significant directions in the development of modern art, and would gradually become more widely accepted.

The first major modernist movement in the theatre was SYMBOLISM, which produced its own theatres (most notably LUGNÉ-POË's Théâtre de l'Œuvre, founded in Paris in 1893), its own dramatists (headed by MAETERLINCK and the later Ibsen), and its own approach to staging and scenic design (most strikingly expressed in the work of APPIA and CRAIG). Although the famous MOSCOW ART THEATRE, founded in 1898, has most closely been associated with realism and, thanks to the work of its director and leading actor KONSTANTIN STANISLAVSKY, especially with psychological realism in acting, the growing reputation of the symbolist dramatists at the beginning of the twentieth century stimulated this theatre to establish a series of experimental studios to explore alternative approaches. For a time VSEVELOD MEYERHOLD, the leader of Russia's anti-realist directors, worked in the first studio, but his abstract and director-controlled productions, though they anticipated an important line of development in modern theatre, were unacceptable to Stanislavsky. Meyerhold worked for other theatres and on his own in a brilliant series of productions that increasingly aroused the antagonism of the authorities as realism became the preferred national

approach, and led at last to Meyerhold's arrest and execution in 1940.

Although the futurist movements in Italy and Russia, SURREALISM in France, and several other avant-garde movements in poetry and art in the early years of the twentieth century produced a number of striking experiments and a few memorable plays, the first modernist movement in the theatre after symbolism to have a major international impact was EXPRESSIONISM, centred in Germany in the second and third decades of the century. The non-realistic dramas of STRINDBERG and the plays of FRANK WEDEKIND provided the major inspiration for expressionism in the theatre, a movement which often emphasized subjective perceptions of reality through such devices as elliptical and exaggerated speech, and abstract and distorted movement, costume and scenic elements. Not all expressionists focused upon inner reality. An important part of the movement applied the expressionist style and approach to social and political concerns, both in playwriting and in production. During the 1920s ERWIN PISCATOR sought to create a politically oriented theatre for working-class audiences by combining certain techniques and concerns from the expressionist theatre with experimental techniques from the recent post-revolutionary Soviet theatre. He developed a production form mixing traditional theatre with film, cartoons, projections, treadmills and a variety of non-representational devices. BERTOLT BRECHT drew both upon Piscator and upon expressionism to develop his non-realistic EPIC THEATRE, one of the most influential of modern dramatic forms. This approach inevitably involved Brecht, as it did other non-realistic authors, in a conflict with the evolving doctrine of socialist realism in the Soviet Union.

The European modernist movements entered the American theatre just before the First World War through the LITTLE THEATRES, founded in imitation of the independent theatres of Europe, and through the 'new stagecraft', which brought to America new ideas in scenic design, many of them influenced by the work of the symbolists. ROBERT EDMOND JONES and LEE SIMONSON were leading designers of the new movement, and *Theater Arts Magazine*, America's most influential theatre journal, was founded in 1916 to spread the new ideas. One of the first and most famous of the 'little theatres' was the PROVINCETOWN PLAYERS, whose leading dramatist, EUGENE O'NEILL, not only dominated the American theatre for the next generation, but was instrumental in bringing to the American stage many of the concerns and techniques of the European avant-garde theatre.

By the 1930s the first wave of modernist experimentation in the Western theatre was clearly diminishing in strength and variety, and more traditional and realistic work, although from time to time showing the influence of modernist thought, was in the ascendant. Only a few dramatists, such as LUIGI PIRANDELLO in Italy, THORNTON WILDER in America and JEAN COCTEAU in France, gained important reputations with works that could be called primarily modernist. The major works of Brecht and the extremely influential theoretical writings of ARTAUD both date from the 1930s, but neither had any real impact until the next wave of modernism developed in the Western theatre in the late 1950s. The best chronicle of the modernist theatre during these turbulent years was *The Drama Review*, which occupied a position at this time somewhat analogous to that of *Theater Arts* during the earlier period of modernist experiment in the United States.

As in the 1890s, this new wave was launched by French dramatists, several of them with close ties to the first generation of modern writers. SAMUEL BECKETT had served as secretary for JAMES JOYCE; FERNANDO ARRABAL was a member of ANDRÉ BRETON's surrealist circle; and EUGÈNE IONESCO was fascinated by the work of ALFRED JARRY. Jarry's *King Ubu*, one of the most revolutionary works presented at the symbolist Théâtre de l'Œuvre, was now hailed as a precursor of the new modernist theatre movement represented by writers like Ionesco, Beckett and Arrabal, and generally known in English as the THEATRE OF THE ABSURD. The non-realistic characters and settings of these plays naturally posed, as had the coming of symbolism, a challenge to traditional approaches to acting and scenic design. Stanislavsky, who had come to represent, especially in Russia and America, the main line of realistic actor training, was now challenged by a variety of less psychological approaches, most notably that of the Polish experimental director JERZY GROTOWSKI, who was seen as much closer to the rediscovered visionary Artaud.

During the 1960s Artaud became a central reference point for modernism in theatre. In England PETER BROOK devoted a season to studying the implications of his writings, which led, among other things to one of his most acclaimed productions, WEISS' *Marat/Sade*. Another major experimental organisation feeling the Artaud influence was the American LIVING THEATER, which left in 1964 to tour Europe, becoming the best-known avant-garde company of the period and a major voice for breaking down audience/actor barriers, for creating a new community for

theatrical work and for free, even anarchic expression in the theatre. Much of the modernist work in the 1960s, that very political decade, had a distinctly political flavour, and certain groups and individuals combined a central political interest with extremely modernist experimentation. Among these were the SAN FRANCISCO MIME TROUPE and the BREAD AND PUPPET THEATER in the United States, the creations of ARMAND GATTI in France and the experiments of AUGUSTO BOAL in Latin America. Still another important aspect of 1960s modernism was the concept of TOTAL THEATRE derived from Wagner's concept of the *Gesamtkunstwerk*. A pioneer in modern total theatre was JEAN-LOUIS BARRAULT in France, but the concept might be applied to many of the visionary modernist directors from the 1960s onward who placed a personal stamp on every aspect of production – from the work of Peter Brook in England, YURI LYUBIMOV in Russia, ROGER PLANCHON in France, INGMAR BERGMAN in Sweden, GIORGIO STREHLER in Italy and TADEUSZ KANTOR in Poland, on through the epic spectacles of ROBERT WILSON.

The highly visual, non-realistic and director-dominated work was a much more distinctive feature of modernist theatre in continental Europe during the 1970s and 1980s. Such figures as Brook (in France in exile), Lyubimov (also in exile), Strehler, Barrault, Bergman and Planchon continued to produce major works, but they were joined by an impressive group of original younger directors, among them ANTOINE VITEZ, PATRICE CHEREAU, PETER STEIN, PETER ZADEK, LLUIS PASQUAL and Daniel Mesguich.

Director-dominated work never gained much currency in America, where the avant-garde of the 1970s and 1980s went in rather different directions. A certain part of the modernist theatre tradition has always been interested in testing the delicate balance between theatre and reality, from the interest in early twentieth-century Russian avant-gardists like NIKOLAI EVREINOV in 'theatricalizing' everyday life, through DADAIST manifestations and the plays of Pirandello, to the political STREET THEATRE of the 1960s. A closely related concern is that of the relationship between the 'illusion' of the stage and the 'reality' of both the actors and the audience. Explorations of these relationships have been of particular interest to the recent American avant-garde, from the highly politicized Living Theater to the generally apolitical HAPPENINGS of the 1960s. The avant-garde of the 1970s frequently turned away from social concerns to experiment with a more abstract and visual theatre, and with the essence of theatre itself and of its particular relationship with its audiences. This can

509

be seen also in the work of the PERFORMANCE GROUP and its offshoot, the WOOSTER GROUP, one of the best-known experimental groups in America during the 1980s.

Both the Wooster Group and the equally well-known MABOU MINES also experimented with modern technology, such as video and sound amplification. The continually expanding technical means of the theatre, especially in LIGHTING, provided important tools for much experimental theatre production during the twentieth century. The widespread availability of such machinery as computers and video gave the technical element a much increased role after the 1960s, both in modestly funded productions and in elaborate multimedia spectacles like those of Laurie Anderson and the *Europeras* of JOHN CAGE.

The works of Cage are the best-known examples of another important modernist challenge to the traditional boundaries of the art form: the introduction of chance or indeterminacy into the creative or performance process. Cage's experiments in music provided a key model for such work, and moved closer to theatre when Cage began collaborations with dancer MERCE CUNNINGHAM. The introduction of chance elements, and even more importantly, the introduction of non-dance material from everyday life moved the modern DANCE of Cunningham, MEREDITH MONK and others into a realm almost indistinguishable from certain parts of modernist theatre.

During the 1970s and 1980s even the term 'theatre' began to seem inadequate to describe modernist work involving live artists, and the term PERFORMANCE ART steadily grew in popularity. 'Theatre' seemed too tied to a certain tradition, involving an established script, certain invariable presentation conditions and a certain type of narrative structure. 'PERFORMANCE' seemed more clearly to recognize such non-structured events as happenings and chance theatre, the new interest of the avant-garde in CIRCUS, CLOWNS, juggling and so on (represented by the movement called in America the NEW VAUDEVILLE), the increasing utilization of mixed media, especially film and video, in theatre, as well as the development of new mixtures of dance and theatre in the works of such artists as MARTHA CLARKE in America, PINA BAUSCH in Germany and Maguy Marin in France. Many of these experiments fell within the field that became known as post-modernism, with its self-conscious and often parodic mix of elements of 'high' and 'popular' culture.

The tradition of psychological realism and of the realistic drama and realistic stage picture has remained through the twentieth century the continued common enemy of the many modernist movements in theatre, and this common enemy has given the avant-garde, somewhat paradoxically, a rather consistent tradition of its own. That tradition, however, has steadily increased in the range of its experimentation, in its variety, in its technical means and in the complexity of its inter-relationships with other experimentation, with the traditional theatre, and with the cultural and social world in which it occurs. It has long since become clear that modernism is not centrally involved, as its practitioners once thought, in anticipating the art works of the future, but rather in providing the richest possible variety of artistic expression to the ever-changing present.

MARVIN CARLSON

See also BODY ART; DRAMATIC THEORY; EXPERIMENTAL THEATRE; LIVE ART; MULTIMEDIA THEATRE.

Malcolm Bradbury and James McFarlane, eds, *Modernism 1890–1930* (1976)

Oscar Brockett and James Findlay, *Century of Innovation* (1973)

Roselee Goldberg, *Performance Art from Futurism to the Present* (1988)

Ronald Hayman, *Theatre and Anti-Theatre: New Movements since Beckett* (1979)

John A. Henderson, *The First Avant-Garde* (1971)

E. T. Kirby, *Total Theatre* (1969)

Richard Kostelanetz, *The Theatre of Mixed Means* (1968)

Maurice Valency, *The End of the World: An Introduction to Contemporary Drama* (1980)

Moeller, Philip (b. New York, 26 Aug. 1880; d. New York, 26 April 1958) Playwright, producer and director. Moeller's theatrical career flourished in the 'new' American theatre of New York in the 1920s and 1930s. He was a member of the WASHINGTON SQUARE PLAYERS, who produced three of his one-act plays, and served as a director and board member of its successor, the THEATER GUILD. Equally adept at directing comedy and 'drama', Moeller staged the Guild's inaugural production, *Bonds of Interest* (1919), and later proved himself a fine interpreter of the works of EUGENE O'NEILL (e.g. *Strange Interlude*, 1928; *Dynamo*, 1929; *Mourning Becomes Electra*, 1931; *Ah, Wilderness!*, 1933).

ANNE FLETCHER

Moholy-Nagy, Laszló (b. Bacsbarsod, Hungary, 20 July 1895; d. Chicago, 24 Nov. 1946) Teacher in photography, film and theatre in the BAUHAUS. During this period he designed for PISCATOR (*The Merchant of Berlin*, 1929) and several operas. He co-authored, with MOLNÁR and SCHLEMMER, *The Theatre of the Bauhaus,* which contains his influential speculations on new forms of theatre buildings. CLIVE BARKER

Moiseiwitsch, Tanya (b. London, 3 Dec. 1914) Designer. She worked with HUGH HUNT at the ABBEY THEATRE and designed over 50 productions there (1935–9). After weekly rep at the OXFORD PLAYHOUSE (1941–4) she moved to the OLD VIC's branches in Liverpool, London and Bristol. At Liverpool, she designed a modern-dress *Alchemist* for TYRONE GUTHRIE, and they collaborated until his death (1971). She designed a permanent timber setting with no front curtain for Guthrie's *Henry VIII* (STRATFORD-UPON-AVON, 1949) and developed this concept with her single set for Stratford's 1951 histories cycle. She was responsible for many Shakespeare productions. In 1953 she designed the influential open stage for the first STRATFORD, Ontario, Shakespeare Festival, founded by Guthrie, and she designed over 20 productions there. Subsequently she advised on the design for two major OPEN-STAGE theatres: the Tyrone Guthrie Theater, Minneapolis (1963), and the Crucible Theatre, Sheffield (1970). Her important experiments with masks in Greek tragedy include *Oedipus Rex* (Ontario, 1954, filmed 1957) and *The House of Atreus* (Minneapolis, 1968). Internationally renowned, her strong, simple settings and richly textured costumes created the right space and visual statement for the plays they were serving. TONY HOWARD

See also ARCHITECTURE.

Moldavia/Moldova *see* SOVIET UNION

Molloy, M[ichael] J[oseph] (b. Milltown, Co. Galway, Ireland, 3 March 1917; d. Milltown, 27 May 1994) Playwright. Most of his plays deal with rural depopulation and the erosion of local culture. Among those first performed at the ABBEY THEATRE, Dublin are *Old Road* (1943), *The Visiting House* (1946), *The King of Friday's Men* (1948), *The Wood of the Whispering* (1953) and *Petitcoat Loose* (1979).

CHRISTOPHER FITZ-SIMON

Molnár [Neumann], Ferenc (b. Budapest, 12 Jan. 1878; d. New York, 1 April 1952) Playwright and novelist. He studied law in Budapest and Geneva, and changed his name to Molnár in 1896 as the national independence movement gathered pace. He earned his first international success as a playwright with *Az ördög*, (*The Devil*, 1907), which after its first night in the Vigszinház of Budapest was staged all over Europe and in New York. It is a modern variation of the Faust theme transformed into a very spiritual light comedy. *Liliom* (1909), a mixture of realism and fantasy, a bittersweet love story between a roughneck full of hidden goodness and a charming, naïve young woman, is his best-known play, turned into a musical in 1945: *Carousel* had a long run on Broadway and in England. The continuing popularity of his comedies can be explained by perfect theatrical dexterity: an always amusing plot, full of unexpected turns yet faultlessly constructed in the manner of the 'well-made play', is combined with elegant and witty dialogue in the style of OSCAR WILDE, giving excellent parts for outstanding actors, such as the LUNTS in *A testör* (*The Guardsman*, 1910).

The rise of fascism forced Molnár to leave Hungary in 1938. He settled two years later in New York, where he wrote novels, an autobiography and a play, *A Császár* (*The Emperor*, 1946). Most of his plays have been translated into English. Other works include *A farkas* (*The Tale of the Wolf*, 1912); *A hattyu* (*The Swan*, 1920); *Az Üvegcipö* (*The Glass Slipper*, 1924); *Játék a kastély bon* (*The Play in the Castle*, (1924, adapted by P. G. WODEHOUSE as *The Play's the Thing*, 1926); and *Olimpia* (*Olympia*, 1928). GÁBOR MIHÁLYI

Clara Györgyey, *Ferenc Molnár* (1950)

Monck [Walter] Nugent [Bligh] (b. Welshampton, Shropshire, 4 Feb. 1878; d. Norwich, 21 Oct. 1958) Director and producer. Monck was committed to the resurrection of neglected and persecuted plays. He founded the Norwich Players (1911), an amateur group, and created their theatre, the MADDERMARKET (1921), the first permanent reproduction of an Elizabethan playhouse. A disciple of POEL, he excelled in Shakespeare production and presented the entire canon. He championed medieval drama and his private production of the banned Mystery plays (1938) opened the way for subsequent presentations. His adventurous repertoire included work by Calderón, Goldoni, Webster, CHEKHOV, PIRANDELLO, Euripides, and KAISER. SARAH A. SMITH

See also AMATEUR THEATRE; MEDIEVAL THEATRE IN THE TWENTIETH CENTURY.

Moncrieff, Gladys (b. Bundaberg, Queensland, Australia, 13 April 1892; d. Benowa, Queensland, 8 Feb. 1976) Musical star who began as a solo singer in VAUDEVILLE. In a far-sighted move in 1912, the J. C. Williamson management signed her to a long-term contract that led to her breakthrough as the lead in *The Maid of the Mountains* (1921). 'Our Glad', as she was known, became the recognized queen of the Australian light musical stage and a major box-office draw. Efforts to create an Australian musical for her were only partially successful in *Collit's Inn* (1933) and *The Cedar Tree* (1934), and her repertoire until her retirement in 1959

consisted mainly of revivals of her earlier successes, including *The Merry Widow* and inevitably *The Maid* which she played an estimated 2,289 times.
IAN BEVAN

Monk, Meredith (b. Lima, Peru, 20 Nov. 1942) Dancer, choreographer, singer, composer, and film-maker. Monk was involved from 1963 with the New York JUDSON CHURCH postmodern dance COLLECTIVE, but in contrast to much of its early work her work has been MULTIMEDIA, theatrical and rich in imagery. In 1968 she formed her own company, The House. Several of Monk's pieces have used non-theatrical venues: *Juice* (1969), for example, was staged in the Guggenheim Museum. Her first internationally acclaimed work was *Education of the Girlchild* (1971). She has created chamber theatre prices (a travelogue and an archaeology series) and in 1983, at PETER STEIN's request, a multimedia theatre work, *The Games*. Monk has made award-winning films of several of her innovative and influential works, including *Quarry* (1976) and *Turtle Dreams* (1983). ANDREW SOLWAY

See also CHOREOGRAPHY; DANCE; MOVEMENT, DANCE AND DRAMA.

Monkhouse, Allan [Noble] (b. Barnard Castle, Co Durham, 7 May 1858; d. Disley, Cheshire, 10 Jan. 1936) Playwright and novelist. Associated with the MANCHESTER SCHOOL, his early work, though similar in theme, uncharacteristically does not highlight Lancashire working people. The best of his 20 plays is an ironic anti-war drama, *The Conquering Hero* (1924), which prefigures SHERRIFF's *Journey's End*. IAN CLARKE

monodrama see EVREINOV, NIKOLAI

Monroe, Marilyn see ACTORS' STUDIO; MILLER, ARTHUR; STRASBERG, LEE

Monstrous Regiment Founded in 1975 at the instigation of Gillian Hanna by a group of women exasperated at the lack of roles for actresses, it became the most prominent of Britain's feminist companies. Its first production, *Scum: Death, Destruction and Dirty Washing* (1976), was commissioned from Chris Bond and Claire Luckham, and looked at the Paris Commune from the point of view of its washerwomen. The group was a collaborative, though not exclusively female (until 1981) touring company that also commissioned plays from writers such as CARYL CHURCHILL (e.g. *Vinegar Tom*, 1976), DAVID EDGAR, Bryony Lavery, Ann Mitchell, Susan Todd, Micheline Wandor, Melissa Murray, Rose Tremain and Carole Bunyan. It explored many styles from CABARET and REVUE to collage and EPIC THEATRE to reveal and illuminate aspects of

women's experience. It also provided a platform for and a stimulus to women's writing (e.g. Churchill's *Top Girls* drew on workshops she had done with the company). JOOLS GILSON-ELLIS

Montenegro see YUGOSLAVIA

Montgomery, Elizabeth see MOTLEY

Montherlant, Henry [Millon] de (b. Neuilly-sur-Seine, France, 21 April 1896; d. Paris, 21 Sept. 1972) Novelist, poet and playwright. He was already an established novelist when, in 1942, he turned his hand to the theatre, where his subsequent fame was to lie. Originally commissioned as an adaptation of a Spanish Renaissance play, *La Reine morte* (*Queen After Death*, 1942) emerged as a highly original piece of theatre, in which most characteristics of Montherlant's dramaturgy were already present. Its great success led to a profusion of other plays, some historical, others in modern dress. These two strands, which have often been contrasted, share most of the common elements of Montherlant's individual approach to drama. His originality does not lie in his stage techniques, which are surprisingly traditional, but in the introduction of a novelist's ambiguities, and in a rejection of shape, coherence or synthesis, particularly in the field of psychological motivation. He rejects the 'theatre of ideas', and presents us with human situations of infinite complexity, in which there are no certainties, no solutions and certainly no authorial 'message' (hard as many critics have tried to ascribe one to him). Certain themes fascinate him, and recur: heroism, stoicism, the clash of ideals – and, above all, religion. As an agnostic, Montherlant is nevertheless able to depict, from his detached standpoint, Christian problems of grace in a far more convincing way than most Catholic authors. His powerful theatre has aroused much controversy in France; one thing that is sure is that it cannot be ignored. His major plays include *Fils de personne* (*No Man's Son*, 1943); *Malatesta* (1948); *Le Maître de Santiago* (*The Master of Santiago*, 1948); *Demain il fera jour* (*Tomorrow the Dawn*, 1949); *La Ville dont le prince est un enfant* ('The city whose prince is a child', 1951, not staged until 1967); *Port-Royal* (1954); and *La Guerre civile* (*Civil War*, 1965). RICHARD GRIFFITHS

John Cruickshank, *Montherlant* (1964)

Montserrat see CARIBBEAN

Moody, William Vaughn (b. Spencer, Ind., 8 July 1869; d. Colorado Springs, Colo., 17 Oct. 1910) Poet and playwright. The bulk of his work is original poetry and scholarship, for which he is renowned. His early VERSE DRAMAS, *The Masque of Judgement* (1900)

and *The Fire Bringer* (1904) were not produced in his time and his theatrical fame rests on *The Great Divide* (1906). Considered a milestone in American theatre, it breaks from melodrama in its telling of a true story of an East Coast woman going west, and is both a realistic and experimental treatment of the conflict between the Eastern and Western United States, employing a sophisticated lyricism and symbolism to which American playgoers were unaccustomed. His last play, *The Faith Healer* (1909), failed but later critics have admired it. CLAUDIA D. JOHNSON

Maurice F. Brown, *Estranging Dawn* (1973)

M. Halpern, *William Vaughn Moody* (1964)

Mooney, Ria (b. Dublin, 1904; d. Dublin, Jan. 1973) Actress and director. She created several roles at the ABBEY THEATRE from 1924, including Rosie in *The Plough and the Stars* (1926) and Hannie in *Lovers' Meeting*, and ran its experimental theatre, the Peacock. She worked extensively in Britain and the United States before returning to Dublin as director of the Gaiety Theatre School of Acting in 1944. She was producer at the Abbey from 1948 until her retirement in 1963, the first woman to hold the post. CHRISTOPHER FITZ-SIMON

Moore, George [Augustus] (b. Co. Mayo, Ireland, 1852; d. London, 21 Jan. 1933) Novelist, art connoisseur, poet and playwright. He used his experience in London of J. T. GREIN's INDEPENDENT THEATRE SOCIETY, which staged his first play *The Strike at Arlingford* (1894), to help establish in 1899, with W. B. YEATS and EDWARD MARTYN, the short-lived but ground-breaking Irish Literary Theatre in DUBLIN. Its second production was Martyn's *The Heather Field* (1899), on which Moore collaborated, and its third was his rewriting of Martyn's play *The Tale of the Town* as *The Bending of the Bough* (1900), which suffered by comparison with its inspiration, IBSEN's *An Enemy of the People*. Moore collaborated on other plays with both Martyn (*Maeve*, 1900) and Yeats (*Diarmuid and Grania*, 1901) before the project collapsed through disagreement in 1901. Moore was better known for his poetry and fiction, including the novel *Esther Waters* (1894), which he dramatized in 1911. He writes of his colleagues in his autobiographical trilogy, *Hail and Farewell* (1911–14). CHARLES LONDON

Malcolm J. Brown, *George Moore: A Reconsideration* (1956)

Joseph Hone, *The Life of George Moore* (1936)

Morahan, Christopher *see* NATIONAL THEATRE

Morgan, Charles [Langbridge] (b. Bromley, Kent, 22 Jan. 1894; d. London, 6 Feb. 1958) Novelist, drama critic, essayist and playwright. Morgan spent from 1907 to 1918 in the navy until going to Oxford to study literature. He joined the staff of *The Times* in 1921 and was the paper's drama critic from 1926 to 1939. Morgan's plays, which include *The Flashing Stream* (1938), *The River Line* (1952) and *The Burning Glass* (1954), were produced successfully around Europe; *The Flashing Stream* ran for a year in Paris (1945). MAGGIE GALE

Morley, Robert (b. Semley, Wilts, 26 May 1908; d. Reading, Berks, 3 June 1992) Actor and playwright who first attracted favourable notice in 1936 at London's GATE THEATRE in the title role of *Oscar Wilde* by Sewell and Lesley Stokes. Because of its subject the play was not licensed for the West End, but it took him to New York and earned him his first film role, in MGM's *Marie Antoinette* (1938). In 1941 he starred in the London production of *The Man Who Came To Dinner*, which began an amazing sequence of box-office successes in which five plays lasted him for 15 years. The others were *The First Gentleman* (1945), *Edward My Son* (which he co-wrote with Noel Langley, 1947), *The Little Hut* (1950) and *Hippo Dancing* (which he adapted from André Roussin, 1954). His only other long-running show was AYCKBOURN's *How the Other Half Loves* (1970). Success, allied with good living, allowed him to develop the portly figure which, along with a suitably stentorian voice, typecast him on stage and in film as larger than life. He wrote an autobiography (with Sewell Stokes), *Responsible Gentleman* (1966). IAN BEVAN

M. Morley, *Larger Than Life* (1979)

Morocco *see* MIDDLE EAST AND NORTH AFRICA

Morris, Mark *see* DANCE

Morrison, Bill *see* LIVERPOOL PLAYHOUSE

Mortimer, John [Clifford] (b. Hampstead, London, 21 April 1923) Playwright, novelist and barrister. A good-humoured chronicler of the British middle classes, his best play is his very moving *A Voyage Round My Father* (1970), which depicts the dramatist's father (resolutely denying his blindness) as a 'difficult' yet much-loved man. A successful adapter of FEYDEAU, Mortimer favours comedy, but his humour is always mellowed with compassion. Besides his prolific output for stage and screen, he has written extensively for television – notably his dramatizations of *I, Claudius* (1972) and *Brideshead Revisited* (1981), plus his own series about a seedy but successful barrister, *Rumpole of the Bailey* (1975–87). Other plays include *The Dock Brief* (1957) and *The Wrong Side of the Park* (1960). He was knighted in 1998. DAVID SELF

Morton, Martha *see* UNIONS; WOMEN IN THEATRE

Moscow Art Theatre An all-night conversation in June 1897 between KONSTANTIN STANISLAVSKY and VLADIMIR NEMIROVICH-DANCHENKO led to the founding of the MAT with the goal of transcending old-fashioned theatrics, false pathos and insignificant repertoires. They aimed, according to Stanislavsky, 'to create the first rational, moral public theatre', focusing especially upon the training of the actor and raising the standards of the theatre-going public. Influenced by companies such as the MEININGEN and ANTOINE's Théâtre Libre, MAT opened with Alexei Tolstoy's *Tsar Fyodor Ivanovich* on 14 October 1898. The theatre's success was finally assured, as its ensemble style coalesced, with the opening on 17 December the same year of *The Seagull* by CHEKHOV. That play gave the theatre its seagull emblem for the curtain, posters, and programmes. Chekhov's last three plays were also directed by Stanislavsky – wrongly, in Chekhov's view – for the company, and Chekhov married its leading actress OLGA KNIPPER. Other outstanding figures from the MAT's early days include MEYERHOLD, Kachalov and VAKHTANGOV In 1902 GORKY's first plays were staged by the company, and the MAT moved into a theatre in Kamergevsky Street. Over the years Stanislavsky developed his acting system and opened several studios of the MAT (e.g. HABIMAH) as venues for experimentation in acting and production styles. One of the MAT's most noteworthy pre-revolutionary productions was *Hamlet* (1912), directed and designed by CRAIG with help from Stanislavsky. However, the company remained best known for psychological realism, which helped it to weather the difficult years when all theatres were expected to conform to tenets of socialist realism. (BULGAKOV, whose *Days of the Turbins* was produced in 1926, satirized his time at the MAT in his novel *Black Snow*, 1936.) The company was highly influential at home and abroad. On tour to New York in 1923 and 1924, the MAT made a lasting impact on the development of American schools of acting. A period of stagnation followed the deaths of Stanislavsky in 1938 and Nemirovich-Danchenko in 1943, although the mid-1950s then saw the emergence of a new generation of artists. The theatre was revitalized with the appointment in 1972 of OLEG EFREMOV to the artistic directorship, and in 1973 the MAT moved to a new, modern home. The old theatre was refurbished and reopened as a second stage. By 1987, however, the company had grown too unwieldy to function as a single administrative unit and was split into two separate companies, with Efremov running what was called the Chekhov company in the old building and Tatiana Doronina at the head of the Gorky company in the new premises; the two branches were popularly referred to as the 'male' and 'female' Moscow Art Theatres. Adjustment to the post-Soviet market economy, however, has been difficult.
FELICIA HARDISON LONDRÉ

Actors Theater of Louisville, *Moscow Art Theatre: Past, Present, Future* (1989)
Claudine Amiard-Chevrel, *Le Théâtre artistique de Moscou (1898–1917)* (1979)
Jean Benedetti, *Stanislavski: A Biography* (1988)
——, ed., *The Moscow Art Theatre Letters* (1991)
Anatoly Smeliansky, *Is Comrade Bulgakov Dead? Mikhail Bulgakov at the Moscow Art Theatre* (1993)
N. Worall, *The Moscow Art Theatre* (1996)

Mosher, Gregory [Dean] (b. New York, 15 Jan. 1949) Director and producer. After studying at the Juillard School, Mosher worked as director of the Stage 2 programme at the GOODMAN MEMORIAL THEATER in Chicago, becoming its artistic director in 1978. He produced BECKETT's first work as a director in the United States, with *Krapp's Last Tape* (1979) and *Endgame* (1980). He worked as artistic director for the LINCOLN CENTER Theater (1985–91). He has produced and directed new works by many distinguished playwrights, such as EDWARD ALBEE, JOHN GUARE, DAVID RABE and MICHAEL WELLER, but is known in particular for premières of DAVID MAMET's work: *American Buffalo* (1975), *Glengarry Glen Ross* (1984), *Speed the Plow* (1987) and *The Cryptogram* (1994). Mosher has also received Tony Awards as producer of two successful revivals: *Anything Goes* and *Our Town*. HELEN RAPPAPORT

Moss, Edward *see* STOLL MOSS THEATRES LTD

Mostel, [Samuel Joel] Zero (b. Brooklyn, New York, 28 Feb. 1915; d. Philadelphia, 8 Sept. 1977) Actor of giant physique and lugubrious countenance. After various jobs he became a stand-up comic in Greenwich Village nightclubs (1942). He entered films, but was subsequently blacklisted for left-wing sympathies and survived as a painter, re-establishing himself on stage as Bloom in the Off-Broadway *Ulysses in Nighttown* (1958). He played the lead in IONESCO's *Rhinoceros* (1961), in *A Funny Thing Happened on the Way to the Forum* (1962), and, most notably, in *Fiddler on the Roof* (1964), winning Tony Awards for all three. In 1976 he portrayed the blacklisted actor in the film *The Front*, and he died rehearsing Shylock in WESKER's *The Merchant*. His memoirs were published in 1965.
BRIAN BIRCH

J. Brown, *Zero Mostel: A Biography* (1989)

K. Mostel and M. Gilford, *Seventy Years of Showbusiness* (1978)

Motley Design firm consisting of **Margaret 'Percy' [Frances] Harris** (b. Shortland, Kent, 28 May 1904; d. Northwood, Middx, 10 May 2000), her sister **Sophie [Audrey Sophia]** (b. Hayes, Kent, 2 July 1901; d. London, 27 March 1966) and **Elizabeth Montgomery** (b. Kidlington, Oxon, 15 Feb. 1902; d. London, 15 May 1993). They studied at the Slade School of Art and started their distinguished career in the theatre when JOHN GIELGUD asked them to design the costumes for his OXFORD University Dramatic Society production of *Romeo and Juliet* (1932). Throughout the remainder of the 1930s they dominated set and costume design in the more serious quarters of the WEST END and at the OLD VIC (e.g. *Richard of Bordeaux*, 1933; *Hamlet*, 1934; *The Witch of Edmonton*, 1936; *The School for Scandal*, 1937; *Henry V*, 1937; *Three Sisters*, 1938). The beauty they created through simplicity stood in stark contrast to the prevailing fashion for rich, elaborate design. In 1940, after German bombs had destroyed their studio, 'Percy' and Montgomery extended their work to the United States when they were invited by OLIVIER to design *Romeo and Juliet*. (Sophie stayed in England, married GEORGE DEVINE and had a nervous breakdown after the birth of their daughter Harriet; 'Percy' married a furniture designer and returned to the UK in 1946; Montgomery married an American and stayed a quarter of a century.) Motley designed sets and/or costumes for many notable US productions on BROADWAY, for the Metropolitan Opera and for the AMERICAN SHAKE-SPEARE FESTIVAL (e.g. *The Doctor's Dilemma*, 1941; *Three Sisters*, 1942; *The Cherry Orchard*, 1944; *South Pacific*, 1949; *Paint Your Wagon*, 1951; *Long Day's Journey Into Night*, 1956; and *Il Trovatore*, 1961). Motley continued to expand in the UK, in STRATFORD-UPON-AVON (e.g. *Othello*, 1956; *As You Like It* and *Julius Caesar*, 1957; *Hamlet*, 1958; and *King Lear*, 1960); the ROYAL COURT (e.g. *The Country Wife*, 1956, for which 'Percy' designed the first permanent surround) and the NATIONAL THEATRE (e.g. *Hobson's Choice* and *Hay Fever*, 1964). Until retirement in 1976, Motley designed more than 300 productions – Shakespeare, modern classics, new plays, opera, ballet, musicals and film. They were dedicated to the playwright, director and actors, helping to produce shape and meaning rather than attempting to impose their own dominating concepts. Their London studio was a favourite meeting place of the theatrical profession. Their name lives on in a design school in London, founded in 1968 by 'Percy'. Since 1981, more than 5,000 of their designs have been housed in the University of Illinois Library, serving as a basis for research and for an exhibition, 'Designs by Motley', which toured the United States and Britain from 1988 to 1990. They have published *Designing and Making Stage Costumes* (1974) and *Theatre Props* (1976). DANIEL MEYER-DINKGRAFE

M. Mullin, *Design by Motley* (1996)

Motton, Gregory (b. London, 17 Sept. 1961) Playwright. From his debut plays, *Chicken* and *Ambulance* (both 1987) it was clear that here was a compelling and disturbing talent voicing a desire to explore value and communication in an urbanized world of loss and isolation. His next play, *Downfall* (1988), falls prey to a too wild, demotic EXPRESSIONISM, which was more tightly focused in *Looking at You (Revived) Again* (1989). Adaptations of STRINDBERG (*The Ghost Sonata*, 1989; *The Pelican*, 1989; and *The Father*, 1993), WILDE (*The Picture of Dorian Gray*, 1990) and Büchner (*Woyzeck*, 1992) reveal an unsentimental and public concern for the battered fate of humanity, which in the sweep and intensity of his own work can sometimes become obscured. Increasingly he found his dark collages more accepted in continental Europe than in Britain, where the theatrical power-brokers found plays such as *A Message for the Broken Hearted*, *The Terrible Voice of Satan* (both 1993) and *Cat and Mouse* (1994) wilfully remote and portentous. CHARLES LONDON

Moulin Rouge Paris REVUE theatre. Founded by Charles Zidler and Joseph Oller, it opened at the Place Blanche in 1889 on the site of a dance hall. The name evokes Toulouse-Lautrec's posters, cancan dancers and the huge windmill over its entrance which echoes its name. Parisians strolled in its large garden, used for dancing and entertainment in summer, contemplating the colossal elephant in which LE PÉTOMANE exercised his peculiar gift. At 8 p.m orgies of light and movement filled the bizarre Moorish, rustic Norman hall. Here reigned such celebrities as Max Dearly, Valdina and YVETTE GUILBERT. In the early 1900s it turned more to music hall (MISTINGUETT was part proprietor and star) and later to lavish spectacle. It was a cinema from 1930, returning to live shows in 1953 but increasingly became simply a tourist attraction. TERRY HODGSON

P. Pacini, *Moulin Rouge and Caf' Conc'* (1989)

D. and J. Parker, *The Natural History of the Chorus Girl* (1975)

Mousetrap, The A murder mystery play by AGATHA CHRISTIE which opened at London's Ambassadors Theatre on 25 November 1952 and was still running when this book went to print, although in the interim it had transferred (25 March 1974) to the adjacent, and larger, St Martin's Theatre, and become by a huge margin the longest-running play in the history of the world's theatre. (It had also been seen in more than 40 countries and translated into more than 20 languages.) This success owed as much to the shrewd management of Peter Saunders (b. London, 23 Nov. 1911) as it did to the skill of its author. Following its success, Saunders (a former film cameraman and journalist) became a theatre owner, a power in the Society of West End Theatre, a television executive, a multi-millionaire and a Knight of the British Empire – events not to be foreseen when Mrs Christie took him to lunch to console him for the failure of one of her earlier plays and handed him the script in a brown paper parcel with the words, 'Here's a present for you.' IAN BEVAN

movement, dance and drama Movement and sound start in the blood-beat and air-flow. Rhythm and melody are inherent in the pulse and in the in- and out-going of the breath. The demarcations of DANCE, movement and MIME are blurred. They all employ visual forms, sculptured shapes of the human body and designs in space. Movements of everyday activities could be compared with prose, dramatic movement with poetry in prose, dance with measured or free verse and mime could be said to be tales told without words. Dramatic impulses and primal theatrical elements that were at work in ceremonies, celebrations and social occasions before the nature-rites of Dionysus expanded into organized Greek theatre festivals are still extant; they point towards the distinction between participation and performance. The old Greeks wrote of dancing as intoxication, as art, as entertainment and as education. Poets wrote plays in which actors dance and dancers act and rhythmic movements 'represent men's characters as well as what they do and suffer' (ARISTOTLE). The convergence of impulses, rhythms of speech, music, movement, dance, and a sense of visual form evolve from texts of written plays and their invitation to offer a twentieth-century audience and spectator a common experience in the theatre. The plastic substance of the human body continually changes; it shows traces of foregoing and frequently renewed inner and outer movements and inner and outer pressures. Visual images in the theatre and their recognition by the spectator owe much to resources and stimulants gained from pictures and sculptures. There is no reason to think that bodies look and move as they appear to in the plastic and pictorial arts. Different methods of portraying the body and its move-ments, changing attitudes towards the body held by artists and societies, and a number of contributory causes that lie beneath the changes of form reveal themselves in presentations of the human shape in works of art from various cultural stages: distorted and misplaced members of the body (PICASSO), truthful reality (Rembrandt), perfection of the human appearance (Michelangelo), idealized beauty (Praxiteles). The actor fashions himself into beings linked to their appearance from past, present and imaginary worlds, and forms his body into still and moving sculptures of fleeting moments. The demands on the actor's physique are considerable. He must be aware of his body and his surroundings, of tensions and relaxations (tuning); he must detach and coordinate structural parts, the spine and joints (central keys), expand the ligaments (for elasticity and reach of strings), strengthen the muscles (for freedom and power) and also practise various skills (vocal sounds, speaking, singing, dancing, fighting, acrobatics). To 'give play to sight and the imagination' (O'CASEY), the actor's accomplishment may never be found in his physical existence. He frees his body to be in readiness to express inner contents; he does not move for movement's sake; he transforms to embody and communicate a 'moving' image in motion or in stillness.

Twentieth-century dance-theatres combined classical ballet techniques, contemporary movement-languages and ethnic modes of moving and dancing. The American ISADORA DUNCAN refused all rules of the balletic technique; she danced barefoot on a bare stage; her dance was her self-expression. The Ballets Russes under SERGEI DIAGHILEV's direction performed with academically trained dancers non-classical ballets, such as *The Rite of Spring* and *Les Noces* to STRAVINSKY'S music, evoking social rituals. The German MARY WIGMAN combined emotion with intellect in her dances. RUDOLF LABAN in Germany wrote movement theories and invented a dance-notation to be read like a musical score to reconstruct dances and preserve their compositions for future generations. MARTHA GRAHAM in America enlarged the movement and dance vocabulary and condensed entire stories in her cycles of Greek tragedies represented with dance, movement and staging. British ballet companies, under the direction of NINETTE DE VALOIS, Frederick Ashton and Kenneth MacMillan, integrated academic balletic techniques and contemporary dance-movements in their ballets based on romantic literary sources and on dramatic plays. Real people began to appear on the stages of dance theatres. The tap-dance of the American 'negro' joined theatrical presentations. Modes of dramatic expressions of the human body are further enlarged through introductions and influences of theatrical traditions of Japan and China and of mimic displays from France, Poland and the former Czechoslovakia. Multicultural contemporary dance companies were formed and their contributions to the twentieth-century theatre are significant.

In the picture-frame theatre of the spoken and sung word, the function of a dance performed on a strip of stage-space in front of a closed curtain may be intended to do no more than to divert the audience from the noise caused by shifting the scenery and to entertain the public during the time it takes to change the set. There is no reason to think that such a divertissement, if exquisitely made and performed, does not make a pleasurable contribution to an evening in the theatre. Dances, movements, dumb-shows, fights, battles are decisive elements in the stories to be told in Shakespeare's plays. Twentieth-century drama and opera revitalize these components and synchronize audible and visible elements in the totality of ordered meaning in a work for the theatre. In STRINDBERG's *Miss Julie* the 'ballet' becomes a dramatic bridge between two scenes and changes the set at the same time. The servants who stream into the kitchen of the count's household 'form a ring and dance'. They have known their step-patterns and dance-figures since they were servants' children; now, on midsummer night, liberated through drink and the loss of respect for their masters, they turn their dancing into a movement-sequence of revolutionary actions and leave the kitchen in chaos. The tarantella that Nora dances in IBSEN's *A Doll's House* expresses an intensity of feeling and meaning. Choreographed group-formations and movements are synchronized with the spoken chorus in T. S. ELIOT's VERSE DRAMAS. Actors in BERTOLT BRECHT's presentations of his plays and operas cross the dividing line between the proscenium arch and the auditorium; they introduce themselves and their characters and their ways of living and thinking; they address the public with dance-songs and poetic metres that were once forms of ballads; their symbolic movements aim to strike and awaken the public. Brecht's actors also embody elements of physical behaviour and movements from Japanese and Chinese theatrical traditions. In the musical *West Side Story* the American choreographer and director JEROME ROBBINS reworked the plot of *Romeo and Juliet* and set it firmly in a real world with real characters, in a contemporary situation with actors who are equally accomplished in acting, dancing and singing. Multicultural theatre companies incorporate human impulses that result in modes of bodily expressions. The twentieth century recognized the power of the human body, its symbolic shapes and gestures, its power of movement and silent poetry, its sense of time and place, and its link with dramatic manifestations. LITZ PISK

See also CHOREOGRAPHY; VOICE.

Moving Being   One of the few groups from the late 1960s to survive to the end of the century, Moving Being was in the vanguard of MULTIMEDIA experimentation in the late 1960s and 1970s, reached its peak in the 1980s and was still mounting productions, albeit not so regularly, in the 1990s. Founded by art graduate Geoff Moore in that *annus mirabilis* 1968, the company was originally based at The Place in London but moved to CARDIFF's new CHAPTER ARTS CENTRE as its resident company in 1972, and was responsible for much of what happened in the development of Welsh theatre thereafter – including the struggle to define a new Welsh theatre aesthetic that would ignore barriers of language and dramatic form. In 1983 the company moved to its own building, St Stephens Theatre Space, a converted church in Cardiff's docklands. Partly because of problems linked to the financial responsibilities of running St Stephens, the company lost its Arts Council revenue grant in 1993, but continued to produce SITE-SPECIFIC work.

While Moving Being's early work was an intoxicating mix of music, dance, visuals, film and drama in true 1960s style, there was always a political thrust – memorable works after the move to Cardiff include *Body Politic* (1980), based on Blake's writings, *Brecht in 1984* (1981), *The City Trilogy* (1982), celebrating Cardiff, as well as Alan Osborne's *Tiger! Tiger!* (1985), another look at Cardiff working-class history, and *Rising* (1987), an adaptation of Marxist historian Gwyn Alf Williams's classic work on the Merthyr Rising. Moore gradually became more interested in text and directed thrilling versions of HOWARD BARKER's *No End of Blame* (1988) and *The Castle* (1990), as well as *Miss Julie* (1984), *A Doll's House* (1985), *Romeo and Juliet* (1986) and *The Duchess of Malfi* (1990). He was also exploring in complex productions that often involved the audience the ideas and works of William Morris (*Earthly Paradise*, 1984), KARL KRAUS (*In These Great Times*, 1987) and Joseph Beuys (*In Dusseldorf and Nebraska*, 1988). Moving Being has also mounted ambitious versions of the *Mabinogion,* the collection of Welsh myths, in various venues. DAVID ADAMS

Mozambique   *see*   PORTUGUESE-SPEAKING AFRICAN THEATRE

Mrożek, Sławomir   (b. Borzęcin, Poland, 29 June 1930)   Playwright. He made his debut as a cartoonist and author of satirical short stories. His work began to be banned in the early 1960s and from 1963 he lived abroad, first in Italy, then in France. In the generation of writers which emerged after the liberalization of October 1956, Mrożek represents the tradition of the ABSURD in Polish conditions. He combines the universal philosophical significance of IONESCO or BECKETT and Kafka's tenor of menace with political and social involvement, revealing the absurdities of the system and an acute grasp of the comic in the surrounding reality. His plays are either grotesque accounts of social relations, abuses of the state, fanaticism and psychological violence – *Policja* (*The Police*, 1958); *Męczenstwo Piotra Oheya* (*The Martyrdom of Peter Ohey*, 1959); *Indyk* (*Turkey Cock*, 1960); *Karol* (*Charlie*), *Na pelnym morzu* (*Out at Sea*) and *Striptease*, 1961 – or records of submission: *Emigranci* (*Emigres*, 1974); *Pieszo* (*On Foot*, 1980); *Portret* (*Portrait*, 1987). His most successful play in Poland and abroad is *Tango* (1964, adapted by TOM STOPPARD and directed by TREVOR NUNN, London, 1966) – a tragic farce based on the conflict of generations and attacking totalitarianism. *Vatzlav* (*Vatzlau*, 1970), a philosophical allegory, *Garbus* (*The Humpback*, 1975), an ambiguous comedy, *Ambasador* (*Ambassador*, 1981), a political drama, and *Love in Crimea* (1993) confirm Mrożek as a socio-political and philosophical playwright not bound by any label.

JOANNA KRAKOWSKA-NAROŻNIAK

Jan Klossowicz, *Mrożek* (1980)

Mrs Shufflewick   *see* DRAG

Muldoon, Roland   *see* CAST; HACKNEY EMPIRE

Müller, Heiner   (b. Eppendorf, Saxony, 9 Jan. 1929; d. Berlin, 30 Dec. 1995)   Playwright and poet. His theatrical career began in 1957 in East Berlin with his adaptation of John Reed's *Ten Days that Shook the World*. In 1958 he joined the ensemble of the Maxim Gorki Theatre in East Berlin as dramaturgical collaborator after having published his first original play, *Der Lohndrücker* ('The scab', 1958). His next plays, *Die Korrektur* ('The correction', 1958), *Die Umsiedlerin, oder Das Leben auf dem Lande* ('Resettling, or life in the country', 1961) – premièred at a student theatre, with a revised version launched in 1975 under the title *Die Bauern* ('The peasants') – and *Der Bau* ('The construction site', 1980), dealt with the conflicts and contradictions of the emerging socialist society in the German Democratic Republic. They caused a considerable stir and discussion and brought Müller into conflict with influential political groups in East Germany. In these plays, as well as in a group of three LEHRSTÜCKE ('plays for learning') – *Philoctetes*, *The Horatian* and *Mauser* – writ-

ten between 1958 and 1970, Muller revealed himself as the leading German dramatist continuing and expanding BRECHT's model of EPIC THEATRE. In 1970 he was invited to join the BERLINER ENSEMBLE as DRAMATURG. In the two plays *Germania Tod in Berlin* ('Germania death in Berlin', 1978) and *Die Schlacht* ('The battle', 1975) he continued his treatment of German history, artistically stretching Brecht's epic model of the theatre to its limits. The wild, often violent imagery and the grotesque, often surreal style of these plays were even surpassed in his version of *Macbeth* (1972), which led to extended debates in the GDR's leading literary and theatrical journals.

By the early 1970s Müller's plays had been performed in some of the leading West German theatres, and a marked change in East German cultural politics led to an official recognition of his work in 1975, when he was awarded the GDR's most prestigious literary award, the Lessing Prize. In 1975 he left the Berliner Ensemble and became writer-in-residence at the University of Texas at Austin. When he returned to Germany in 1976 he became dramaturg of the Volksbühne, supervising some of the best productions of his own plays.

A last phase in Müller's career as a playwright can be identified starting in the mid-1970s. The plays *Leben Grundlings* (*Grundling's Life*, 1979), *Die Hamletmaschine* (*Hamletmachine*, 1979), *Der Auftrag* (*The Task*, 1980), *Quartett* (1982), *Verkommenes Ufer* (*Despoiled Shore*, 1983) and *Anatomie Titus* ('The anatomy of Titus', 1985) are historical–mythological montages which explore the role of the intellectual in the revolutionary process. They have moved far beyond the confines of traditional realism and are his dramatically most imaginative and complex plays, attracting innovative collaborators internationally, such as ROBERT WILSON. Following German reunification in 1989, Müller became one of the most widely performed playwrights in the country. He directed many major productions, including several of his own plays. From 1990 to 1993 he was president of the Academy of Arts and from 1991 to 1995 artistic director and co-director of the Berliner Ensemble.   GÜNTER BERGHAUS

David Barnett, *Literature versus Theatre: Textual Problems and Theatrical Realization in the Later Plays of Heiner Müller* (1998)
Jonathan Kalb, *The Theatre of Heiner Müller* (1999)
A. A. Teraoka, *The Silence of Entropy* (1985)

multimedia theatre   Name given loosely to performance in which different forms, such as speech, song, dance, film or video, are mixed together. Arising in the 1960s out of experiments like HAPPENINGS and influenced by POP culture, it aspires to a kind of TOTAL

THEATRE and often overlaps with terms such as MUSIC THEATRE, PERFORMANCE ART and other types of EXPERIMENTAL THEATRE. A good example of the versatility of the designation is the work of Laurie Anderson (b. 1947). She constantly reinvents herself as a performer as she uses technology to explore notions of popular music and artistic iconography in highly threatrical work, from her first piece, *Automotive* (1972), orchestrated for car horns, to *The Nerve Bible* (1995), in which she triggers audio samples through electronic sensors padded in a specially designed suit, to *Moby Dick* (1999), a multimedia mediation on Melville's novel.
CHARLES LONDON

multiracial casting *see* BLACK THEATRE

Muni, Paul [Muni Weisenfreund] (b. Lemberg, Austria [now Lviv, Ukraine], 22 September 1895; d. Montecito, Cal., 25 Aug. 1967) Actor who began his career in 1908 playing old men's parts in YIDDISH THEATRE and appeared on English-speaking stages only after 18 years as a leading Yiddish actor. He became prominent on Broadway (*Counsellor-at-Law*, 1931), and in Hollywood (*Scarface*, 1932). Celebrated for his 1930s biographical film roles, studio conflicts led him back to the stage, scoring successes from *Key Largo* (1939) to his last performance, *Inherit the Wind* (1955). Increasing blindness forced the retirement of this master of make-up, a meticulous if over-conscious performer.
BRIAN BIRCH

J. Lawrence, *Actor: The Life and Times of Paul Muni* (1974)

Munich Court Theatre *see* FUCHS, GEORGE

municipal theatre *see* CIVIC THEATRE

Munk, Kaj [Harald Leininger Peterson] (b. Maribo, Denmark, 13 Jan. 1898; d. Silkeborg, 4 Jan. 1944) Playwright and Lutheran pastor. Inspired by Shakespeare and Schiller, he was driven by a fervour to influence the times he lived in. He wrote over 30 plays, many on historical themes, dealing with faith, patriotism and the human will. Munk was a hero-worshipper and an anti-democrat, originally favourably inclined towards the fascist dictators; but during the German occupation of Denmark (1940–5), his persistent and public opposition to the Nazis led to their assassinating him. A controversial martyr, his plays include *Ordet* (*The Word*, 1925, first staged 1932, filmed by Carl Dreyer 1954), *Han sidder ved smeltediglen* (*He Sits at the Melting Pot*, 1938) and a patriotic attack on the Nazi occupation, *Niels Ebbesen* (1942). KIM DAMBÆK

Melville Harcourt, *Portraits of Destiny* (1966)

Munroe, Carmen *see* BLACK THEATRE

Murphy, Tom [Thomas Bernard] (b. Tuam, Co. Galway, Ireland, 23 Feb. 1935) Playwright. Formally the most subversive of Irish playwrights, Tom Murphy explodes the pieties and passions of rural Irish society in his early plays, *On the Outside* (1956) and *A Whistle in the Dark* (1961), the latter portraying an immigrant Irish family in Coventry, rooting their passions and perversions in the fertile foreign soil of England. HAROLD PINTER has acknowledged its influence on *The Homecoming*. *A Crucial Week in the Life of a Grocer's Assistant* (1969) and *Conversations on a Homecoming* (1985) illuminate an Ireland in spiritual, emotional and intellectual decay, turning into a world of political sterility and personal greed. Murphy's moral codes are tempered by a sense of the magical in *The Sanctuary Lamp* (1975), *The Gigli Concert* (1983) and *Bailegangáire* (1986), where feats of mythic proportion are undertaken and, miraculously, accomplished. Other plays include *Famine* (1966), an epic account of Ireland's terrible famine in the 1840s, *Too Late for Logic* (1989) and *The Patriot Game* (1992). FRANK MCGUINNESS

Kimball King, *Ten Modern Irish Playwrights* (1979)
Fintan O'Toole, *The Politics of Magic: The Work and Times of Tom Murphy* (1987)

Murray, Melissa *see* MONSTROUS REGIMENT

Murray, T[homas] C[ornelius] (b. Macroom, Ireland, 17 Jan. 1873; d. Dublin, 7 March 1959) One of the leading Irish playwrights of his day, a member of the 'Cork realists' group, he provided upwards of a dozen plays for the ABBEY THEATRE, Dublin, of which *Birthright* (1910), *Maurice Harte* (1912), *Autumn Fire* (1924) and *Michaelmas Eve* (1932) are the most powerful. *Autumn Fire* continues to be revived in Ireland.
CHRISTOPHER FITZ-SIMON

Murray-Smith, Joanna (b. Mornington, Victoria, Australia, 17 April 1964) Playwright. Her first professionally produced play, *Angry Young Penguins* (1987), explores the Ern Malley literary hoax, an event from the 1940s which has assumed a legendary status on the Australian literary scene. She has since drawn upon the middle-class mores of domestic existence, focusing on female characters who undertake literal and metaphorical journeys away from this family milieu, as in *Love Child* (1993) and *Nightfall* (1999). *Honour* (1995) won the Victorian Premier's Literary Award for Drama and has been staged in many countries, including a successful season on BROADWAY in 1999. She has also written for television, while radio adaptations of her plays have been produced in Korea and Sweden. Other works include *Atlanta* (1996) and *Redemption* (1997).

MICHAEL MORLEY

Murrell, John (b. Lubbock, Tex. 15 Oct. 1945) Playwright. After graduating from the University of Calgary in 1969, he became a teacher. Murrell first gained national attention with *Memoir* (1977), a two-act play about the last days of SARAH BERNHARDT as she attempts to complete her memoirs with the help of her manservant Pitou. The interweaving of the actual play and the scenes 'played' by Bernhardt and Pitou creates arresting theatrical effects. *Memoir* has been performed in more than 25 countries, including a three-year run in Paris. *Waiting for the Parade* (1977), a bitter-sweet play about five Canadian women during the Second World War remembering their loved ones overseas, contrasts with the brutality and sexual degradation dramatized in *Farther West* (1982), which traces the journey of a prostitute westwards. *New World* (1984) and *October* (1988, about a meeting between ISADORA DUNCAN and ELEANORA DUSE) and *Faraway Nearby* (1995) have reinforced Murrell's stature as an important Canadian dramatist. EUGENE BENSON

museums *see* RECORDING AND RESEARCHING THEATRE; THEATRE MUSEUM

music A powerful theatrical tool, it can illuminate and support text and action, define or shift time and space, create mood, and cover a noisy and complicated scene change while simultaneously commenting on the unfolding drama. Music can also transform lyric poetry into memorable song, excite an audience with the cathartic release of DANCE, darken and ennoble TRAGEDY, or lighten and point up COMEDY or FARCE. Playwrights from Aeschylus and Aristophanes, through Shakespeare and beyond BRECHT have all relied heavily on a great variety of musical solutions in their work, which are constantly reinvented in contemporary productions.

Theatre has become increasingly and heavily director led. A typical scenario for the decision-making that leads to a viable score goes something like this. A director chooses a composer who he thinks will be suitable for a particular production and encourages him to read the play. The style of the production is discussed in great detail. If the chosen text is classical (be it Greek, Russian, French or English) will it need a period, pastiche or contemporary score? Any roles in the piece that require the actor to sing, dance or play an instrument are identified, and the composer or his music director invited to auditions. Budgets for musicians, recordings (if any) and SOUND design are

revealed and haggled over. The designer presents the costume drawings and set model – a vital piece of the jigsaw, as it can define where the music is played from. Many distinguished composers have been through this procedure – for example, Pierre Boulez with the Compagnie RENAUD-BARRAULT in Paris, and HARRISON BIRTWISTLE at the ROYAL NATIONAL THEATRE in London. (Coincidentally, they both wrote scores for Aeschylus' *Oresteia* for their respective companies.) Ultimately such great talents instinctively want more control over their music and gain it outside the intensely collaborative world of 'straight' theatre, a world which can, and does, embrace authenticity, imitation of all manner of styles appropriate to a given text and an entirely fresh, contemporary musical approach to the problems set by the playwright and the director.

In the first half of the twentieth century, theatre music was most commonly played from the orchestra pit, but there was a general trend in the mid-1950s to cover over pits – a nod in the direction of the Elizabethan 'thrust' or 'apron' stage, with its more intimate and confrontational relationship of actor to audience. This realignment, coupled with other experiments such as THEATRE IN THE ROUND, resulted in many ingenious solutions to the problem of where music could be played from thereafter.

There are three main locations. First, there is off-stage music: in the Shakespeare canon, for example, the texts, particularly in the histories and tragedies, frequently demand off-stage military music – trumpet calls, or fanfares, variously identified as 'flourishes', 'tuckets', 'sennets', 'retreats' and 'parleys', and battle music ('alarums and excursions') involving the additional use of drums. Shakespeare also creates moments of great peace and stillness through the use of gentle, therapeutic, healing music played off-stage, such as Lear's awakening or Prince Hal's last confrontation with his dying father, King Henry IV. The appearance and disappearance of ghosts and apparitions, or the romantic accompaniment to lovers' trysts, can likewise be played off-stage, or even under the stage. Then there is on-stage music. Another solution to the problem of where music can be played from in a theatre space without an orchestra pit is to place it on the stage itself, a technique commonly found in oriental theatre and often copied in the West. Many plays and production styles benefit enormously from the total integration of music and musicians with stage action. This can involve considerable extra rehearsal time and additional expense. Music cues may have to be memorized, the musicians costumed, special instruments purchased or even designed and made. The results, however, are frequently worth the trouble. Live music, seen to be played live in the theatre, invariably has, as in everyday life, a built-in fascination. A Salvation Army band playing carols round a Christmas tree in a shopping mall is guaranteed to separate the public from its spare change far more easily than a sad Santa with a hi-fi system. Third, there is music above the stage. Modern developments of the Elizabethan 'minstrels' gallery' have been designed for certain specific productions and further adapted in the shape of gantries or catwalks, either overlooking the stage from each side or even jutting out into the auditorium. Theatre music is also frequently amplified and relayed to the audience via carefully placed loudspeakers. A dedicated area, sometimes known as a 'band room' or 'band box', is commonly reserved for this method of providing music. Such band rooms do not have to be on the same level as the stage, as contact with actors, singers and stage management is achieved with closed circuit television and 'show-relay' (the broadcasting of the play to the music director, along with a necessary link with all the technical staff who will cue and balance the music).

From the moment in 1927 when AL JOLSON sang in *The Jazz Singer* (the first 'talkie'), the writing was on the wall for the thousands of musicians worldwide who earned their living playing in cinema orchestras. On a smaller scale, a similar threat hangs over the lives of musicians who play in straight theatres. With sophisticated modern equipment theatre music can be recorded, stored on disc and married to the production with great precision and studio-quality sound. The use of recorded music in the theatre is by no means a new phenomenon. Directors such as PETER BROOK experimented with it in *Titus Andronicus* (1955), for which he created an ingeniously achieved palette of pre-recorded music and sound-effects, known in those days as *musique concrète*. The awesome versatility of the latest synthesizers, which can be coupled with samplers, sequencers and emulators, give the contemporary theatre composer the possibility of creating sounds previously undreamt of, though restraints, such as low budgets, frequently seem to encourage the overuse of this technology as a substitute for so-called 'acoustic' music. A synthesizer pretending to be a harp merely says to the audience, 'We can't afford to hire a harpist.' Some theatres (the ROYAL SHAKESPEARE COMPANY in England, for example) employ musicians on full-time contracts, and add freelance players for particular productions. Elsewhere, musicians tend to be engaged on an *ad hoc* basis, though some theatres retain music directors, who double as rehearsal pian-

ists. The great companies of the world usually take considerable care at the casting stage to find actors who can sing well, if their role requires them to do so, and even learn how to play musical instruments, rather than mime to an off-stage recording. Many contemporary productions employ actors with adequate instrumental skills, dispensing with professional musicians altogether.

Music is frequently used under dialogue in films and television. Underscoring text in the theatre, however, is a more controversial proposition. Film stock and video tape are 'cold', and music can warm them up. Actors in a theatre are warm already, human and fallible. They usually have better lines to declaim than in the average movie, and these have to be clearly heard and understood. A theatre audience, unlike that in a cinema, is a key element in a crucial partnership, and the interaction between the two groups is of paramount importance. Music can help or, if inappropriately used, hinder this relationship.
GUY WOOLFENDEN

See also DESIGN; JAZZ; POP MUSIC.

music hall Regarded as the only truly British popular entertainment form, it was born in the 1840s in London and flourished until the advent of the First World War, after which it was gradually superseded by VARIETY. Music hall sprang from the singing rooms which had been a feature of public houses and taverns throughout the country in the early part of the nineteenth century. In 1843 the Theatre Act required saloons to choose whether to become licensed legitimate theatres or to confine themselves to staging turns by solo artists, in which case drinking was permitted to continue in the auditorium. Though many houses opted for the former course, with some present-day theatres being built on the site of saloons, Charles Morton, licensee of the Canterbury in South London, is credited with having invented the music hall, building a separate hall attached to his pub in 1852, with the intention of upgrading the entertainment so that respectable men and women could attend. His programmes usually included excerpts from opera and the popular classics as well as the now-established comic songs. Inspired by his success, music halls began to spring up throughout London and provincial towns large and small, and by the 1860s music hall had become a widespread industry, with its own structure of agents, managers and booking circuits distinct from the legitimate theatre. In the latter part of the nineteenth century, acknowledged stars had begun to make their appearance and the major artists went on long tours, not only in Britain but also overseas. Although few British music hall stars conquered the United States, a number of American artists found a niche in Britain and music hall established itself in the larger cities of the British Empire. One of the major problems lay in finding material for music hall acts. It was important for artists to create individual characters for themselves, a process that often took several years of trial and error. Once recognized, however, they were able to buy, usually outright, songs suited to their particular persona, though few songwriters wrote specifically for one artist. George Le Brunn, for example, though associated mainly with MARIE LLOYD, wrote for other performers, and several artists not only wrote their own material but provided songs for others. By the beginning of the twentieth century music hall had won favour among all classes, having long since built its most glittering palaces in the West End. The final seal was that of royal approval, granted when King George V attended the first Royal COMMAND PERFORMANCE at the Palace Theatre in 1912, though Marie Lloyd was requested not to appear, as her performance was considered too vulgar for royal ears. Though music hall disappeared after the First World War with startling rapidity, and most of its stars were dead by the 1920s, its legacy lives on to a remarkable extent. There can be few people in Britain even today who are completely unacquainted with such songs as 'My Old Man Said Follow the Van', 'Down at the Old Bull and Bush', 'Roamin' in the Gloamin'', 'Who Were You With Last Night?', 'A Little of What You Fancy', 'Nellie Dean', 'I'm Henery the Eighth I Am' and 'The Man Who Broke the Bank at Monte Carlo', all of which date from before 1914. Moreover, while the artists did not have the benefit of the publicity afforded by radio and television, and the gramophone record was in its infancy (though a surprising number of them were recorded) their names are still remembered. Among them were GEORGE ROBEY, DAN LENO, LITTLE TICH (who made a considerable success on the continent), Sir HARRY LAUDER (the first music hall star to be knighted), FLORRIE FORDE, HARRY CHAMPION, VESTA TILLEY, ALBERT CHEVALIER, GUS ELEN, Vesta Victoria, Eugene Stratton and, of course, Marie Lloyd. Of the halls themselves, many survive, though often used for other purposes, as cinemas, legitimate theatres or for bingo. In London the HACKNEY EMPIRE has come back into service as a working theatre and the PLAYERS' THEATRE preserves the spirit of the more respectable Victorian music hall. In Leeds the City Varieties is still in use for various kinds of theatrical entertainment and is familiar through the long-running television series 'The Good Old Days'. Certainly for much of its existence music hall was unique in being virtually classless, perhaps its greatest virtue. PETER HEPPLE

Roy Busby, *British Music Hall* (1976)

Peter Honri, *Working the Halls* (1973)

Raymond Mander and Joe Mitchenson, *British Music Hall* (1965)

Clarkson Rose, *Red Plush and Greasepaint* (1964)

Brian Rust, *British Music Hall on Record* (1979)

Laurence F. Senelick, David F. Cheshire and Ulrich Schneider, *British Music Hall 1840–1923* (1981)

George Speaight, *Bawdy Songs of the Early Music Hall* (1975)

music theatre The idea of combining speech, action and music in a theatrical performance is as old as theatre itself, and originates in classical Greek tragedy. The term has been used since the 1960s to describe staged or semi-staged musical works for small or moderate forces, and is applied retrospectively to earlier works such as Schoenberg's *Erwartung* (1909) and STRAVINSKY's *The Soldier's Tale* (1918). The staging often lacks scenery and consists of no more than the movement of costumed performers using minimal props; such works are therefore performed as often in the concert hall as in the theatre. Examples are György Ligeti's *Aventures* and *Nouvelles Aventures* (both 1966), Peter Maxwell Davies's song cycle *Eight Songs for a Mad King* (1969) and small-scale operas such as HARRISON BIRTWISTLE's *Bow Down* (1977). The MUSIC-THEATRE GROUP was formed in 1971 in the United States to present chamber pieces by artists such as RICHARD FOREMAN. Distinctions are drawn between music theatre, MUSICAL THEATRE (a term applied to popular forms such as the operetta, musical comedy and the musical) and PERFORMANCE ART (in which song, dance and speech may be combined with film or video images, lighting and special effects). ROSEMARY ROBERTS

See also MULTIMEDIA THEATRE.

Music-Theatre Group New York nonprofit professional theatre, with a summer home in Lenox, Massachusetts; founded in 1971 by Lyn Austin. She has been a major force behind the creation of innovative MUSIC THEATRE in the United States, putting together in a laboratory setting teams of artists who prove to be first-rate collaborators. Also known as Lenox Arts Center, the theatre has been particularly important to RICHARD FOREMAN and Stanley Silverman, director–creator Anne Bogart, and the dance theatre of MARTHA CLARKE. M. ELIZABETH OSBORN

musical theatre The musical theatre of the Western world entered the twentieth century in thrall to the kind of shows written and composed by the GEORGE EDWARDES stable of authors and musicians. They had displaced the nineteenth century's vastly successful fashions in the frothy and foolish *opéra bouffe* and the light-hearted but more dignified *opéra comique* from France and, to a lesser degree, from Austria; in the British comic opera as purveyed by GILBERT and SULLIVAN; and in the song-and-comedy shows which passed on the London stage for latter-day BURLESQUE. As in the cases of those earlier, all-pervasive varieties of musical theatre, the products of Edwardes' theatres were not played solely in their country of origin, but had spread quickly and vigorously throughout the world. They dominated the musical theatres of the principal English-speaking countries, from the most important such as America, where native writers were struggling to establish themselves and their work, and Australia, where they were not, to the outposts of Empire in southern Africa and on the oriental circuit; and they made a more than usually significant impression on European stages where the French- and German-language operetta theatres were, as the new century opened, far from as attractively productive as they had been a few years previously. The new-style musical comedy, as epitomized by one of the most successful of the era, Owen Hall and Leslie Stuart's *Florodora* (1899), was a traditional blend of light romantic and comic elements, written mostly in modern dialogue, played in present-day dress and colourful settings, and illustrated by a selection of songs – not necessarily all the work of the show's nominal composer, and both movable and changeable at will – with sometimes more or often less relevance to the usually slight plot. These shows ranged from the least sophisticated and blatantly song-orientated, where the show virtually came to a halt in the second act to allow a series of out-front solos from the stars, to, in the first decade of the new century, some finely constructed and composed pieces in which story, character and music were carefully worked out. This more dramatic attitude to the musical play, in line with the comic opera tradition of earlier years, had been evident in the second style of 1890s musical theatre, cultivated at Daly's Theatre, where Sidney Jones's *The Geisha* (1896) was Edwardes' most enduring hit. Here, although comedy was not lacking, the romantic portion of the show was given more prominence, the music was more substantial and more vocally demanding, and the light, bright frivolity of the musical comedy sweethearts gave place to genuine scenes of sentiment in the text. *Florodora* and *The Geisha* were well to the fore among the London musical shows which spread through almost every country where light musical theatre was popular in the

first decade of the century, and they were played from St Petersburg to Singapore to Buenos Aires, along with the works of such equally successful London theatre composers as Ivan Caryll, Lionel Monckton and Howard Talbot. Edwardes, however, after twenty years as the most important producer of light musical theatre in the world, was well aware that fashions in theatre change constantly and that novelty is the byword in public taste. As the early years of the new century slipped by, and the generation of writers who had penned his most successful shows looked like thinning out, he began to look elsewhere for inspiration. He tried to vary the popular style with a new form of variety–burlesque, he tried revue and he tried France, but he hit the jackpot when he imported the Austrian musical *Die lustige Witwe* in 1907. As *The Merry Widow*, it was a triumph and, as the stages of the world avidly followed his success, an international craze for the waltzing, laughing musicals of FRANZ LEHÁR and such of his compatriots as OSCAR STRAUS, LEO FALL and EMMERICH KÁLMÁN swept away the latter days of the British dominance of the musical theatre.

From London, the creative heart of the musical theatre moved to Vienna and, in the years prior to the First World War, pieces such as *Die Dollarprinzessin* (*The Dollar Princess*, 1907), *Der tapfere Soldat* (*The Chocolate Soldier*, 1908), *Der Graf von Luxemburg* (*The Count of Luxembourg*, 1909), *Die Keusche Susanne* (*The Girl in the Taxi*, 1910) and *Der lila Domino* (*The Lilac Domino*, 1912) filled the theatres of London, Paris and New York. The war put a damper on the import of German-language shows into Britain and France and, although some of the not inconsiderable postwar Viennese and German shows found overseas success in the 1920s and even after, as the world found itself a new identity and a new lifestyle it also discovered a different form of musical theatre to go with it. It was a more facile style musically than the thoroughly composed Viennese shows, being based, like the cheerfully lowbrow British and American variety musicals of the nineteenth century and the ever-popular French vaudevilles and German comedies with songs, on a combination of light comedy and even lighter music. Ensemble music was out, the often long and involved concerted finales which brought each operetta act to a climax were gone, and the score consisted simply of songs – bright and tuneful, often lyrically banal, but above all dance-music songs. The Viennese waltz bowed out before the jazzy rhythms of ragtime, the fox-trot, the one-step and the tango as the age of the dance-band swept out from America and across the world. The feather-light, foot-tapping *No, No, Nanette* (1923) was the mascot show of the era as theatrical attention became appreci-

· Directing musicals ·

First, a word about taste: I don't know where it comes from. Is any of it genetic? Is all of it acquired? How does it relate specifically to talent? Surely taste defies definition *because* it is largely subjective. Nevertheless, everything that follows on the subject of direction in the musical theatre assumes you possess taste to go with talent (equally impossible to define) and ambition (easy, that!) and an obsession to *work*. How does the direction of musicals differ from that of straight plays? To my mind, very little. The same verities apply. The director stands at the head of the team empowered to bring out, in collaboration with performers and designers, the truth, the clarity – the theatricality in a piece of dramatic literature. His responsibilities begin with an encompassing vision of the play (I have always referred to musicals as plays). The journey the play takes, the motor energy, the route (landscape/scenery) is perhaps the most important thing to be determined before going into rehearsal. Too few plays don't know from the start where they are headed. The director must coalesce the members of his acting company who come to him, all ages and capabilities, with vast experience or almost none. He must see to it, as best he can, that they *belong* on the same stage. The more experienced, inventive, talented actors need him only as an editor to stimulate them, to serve as the critical eye. The least experienced often require a drama teacher: 'Go here,' 'Go there,' 'Raise this finger on that word,' and 'Louder!' Not the most fun for a director, but part of the job.

Truth and clarity immediately come to my mind, possibly because I think they are often overlooked. When a director encourages the easy laugh, the cheap tear, he'll find a dead end in such manipulation. Even in FARCE, the door is slammed because someone is going somewhere for an emotional reason – not for a laugh. The doors I have seen and heard slammed have closed more shows . . .

So, the director of musicals and the director of straight plays should work from the same criteria and impress collaborators with equal respect. Where the musical and the straight play part company is in the area of craft. A new musical, in addition to script, sets, costumes and performers, has a choreographer, dancers, sound design, orchestrations, conductor, musicians. The technology of musicals has exploded in the last few decades, probably provoked by the competitive media – television and film. Though some of the high-tech marvels have enjoyed great success, I believe a better route is in defining what the stage has to offer that is unique to it. After all, a theatre setting invites the audience's collaboration as no other medium can. If you are lucky enough to be working in a black box or can create one, the audience will fill in the blank spaces. They'll add the wallpaper, the veneer, the patina. The more you demand of them in this collaboration, the further they'll sit forward in their seats and participate.

More about craft: prior to 1949, the musical's structure was rather primitive. There were full-stage scenes, and when they were over, the curtain closed or a drop dropped and the upstage scenery was replaced, while downstage (usually competing with the din) an in-one scene took place; a few actors or a full chorus talked or danced or merely ran from left to right or in the opposite direction. If there was dialogue, it was insignificant: an unidentified chorus person carrying a basket and saying to another unidentified chorus person, 'We're thinking of moving to a new neighbourhood.' *Who's* thinking of moving? And why are they? Audiences in those days didn't care. Sometimes – more often, I suppose – nothing happened in front of the curtain while the scenery was being changed; the orchestra played what we call 'utility music' until there was a signal from backstage that everything was ready and the show resumed. But in 1949 everything changed. JOSHUA LOGAN co-authored and directed *South Pacific*. He demanded that the play move as a movie did. Layers of transparent travellers were designed so that movement and pertinent dialogue could continue throughout the performance. There was no filler and the tension of the story remained taut from beginning to end. It was an epic occasion, and the musical was never the same again. Because of this, over the years, the libretti for the musicals I have directed have come to read more and more like film scripts. There are close-ups and long shots and quick cuts and dissolves. Brief scenes can be interpolated into longer ones, new venues introduced in abstract space. The criteria which have come to identify a well-made play are irrelevant to the structure of a well-made musical. A great deal (too much) has been said about the concept musical. I honestly don't know what 'they' are talking about. If it has a beginning, a middle and an end, if it takes place in a space redolent with atmosphere, if if makes a serious point, that would appear to make it a concept musical. I would have thought those are the demands one makes of all musicals. I do not believe one can learn how to direct a musical in school. Does such a school even exist? I do not know of any other way to learn the craft of musical-making other than on the job. And getting such training has become more difficult with the diminution of musical productions.

I took the stage managing route. I started as a second assistant stage manager, called half-hour, kept sign-in sheets, and checked artists' entrances and exits. I also understudied, though I had no desire, no talent for acting. Covering roles went with the contract. I progressed to being a first assistant stage manager which put me in charge of stage left, the less important side of the stage, assisting the stage hands with the change of sets, the wardrobe changes, and, again, dealing with actors' entrances and exits. After two years, I graduated to actually calling the show, giving the cues from stage right via 'biscuits' to the various technical departments on the stage level, on the fly floor, and in the front of the house where lights and sound are usually based. In addition, I ran understudy rehearsals. This was my first practical directing experience, inhibited by the necessity of following the director's original staging and line readings with computer-like dedication. But thanks to this backstage experience, I got to know the space, its capabilities and its limitations.

The process of filling an empty space must be akin to filling an empty canvas. You must know how to paint a realistic picture before you abstract it. But when to know you're ready? Again, I haven't a clue.

I suspect everyone makes the leap before he's ready. What I do know is illustrated by an anecdote. In the mid-1960s, having produced and directed for over a decade, I went to Russia – not my first visit. My wife and I went to LYUBIMOV's TAGANKA THEATRE, where they were performing his political cabaret based on John Reed's *Ten Days That Shook the World*. The production was stunning, unlike anything I had ever seen, an outgrowth of MEYERHOLD's theatre of the 1930s. It also contained LIVING NEWSPAPER segments popularized by PISCATOR. The text was banal; for example, Woodrow Wilson and Kerensky were its villains, and the passion and fervour with which they were vilified was curiously touching because this was about as far as the government would permit its director, Lyubimov, to go. The techniques, however, which he used to batter his store dummies were electrifying. After the show, I couldn't sleep for the excitement of it, and when I went back to New York, nothing that I had done before was acceptable. Nothing had expressed *me*. From that moment forward, I took the techniques I had learned and challenged the space. I questioned the accepted definition of musical material, the conventional motor energy of musicals, the use of sound and scenery. From that moment, the structure of my musicals bore more resemblance to *Citizen Kane* than to *My Fair Lady*. HAL PRINCE

See also CHOREOGRAPHY; DANCE; DESIGN; DIRECTING; LIGHTING; SOUND.

atively fixed for the first time on the musical products of BROADWAY and found there not only a lively set of dancing comedies put to music by JEROME KERN, GEORGE GERSHWIN, VINCENT YOUMANS, HARRY TIERNEY, Louis Hirsch and their songwriting companions, but a memorable half-bred strain of popular continental operetta as displayed in the works of SIGMUND ROMBERG (*The Desert Song, The Student Prince, The New Moon*) and RUDOLF FRIML (*Rose Marie, The Vagabond King*).

Behind the ubiquitous *No, No, Nanette*, some of these American shows found their way beyond the hungry British and Australian stages and back to Europe, but by and large Europe took the dance music elements of the new-style American show song and fabricated their own up-to-date musicals, in which the rhythms of the New World were blended with more traditional local elements. Neither Britain nor the central European nations succeeded in these years in producing more than a tiny group of pieces which were anything better

than ephemeral, but, while Lehár's increasingly dark romantic operettas remained the backbone of the Austrian and German musical theatre, France took up the new sound of theatre music and, in the hands of songwriters HENRI CHRISTINÉ and MAURICE YVAIN and librettists ALBERT WILLEMETZ and André Barde and their contemporaries, stylishly made them their own in a series of intimate jazz age musicals of scintillating Gallic charm, wit and melody.

The 1930s saw much of the sparkle go out of the eyes and the music of the world's jazz-age writers and, although the decade produced a limited range of individual shows, from the lightest of musical comedies to the most romantic and/or serious of operettas, from such musicians as COLE PORTER, George Gershwin, RICHARD RODGERS and KURT WEILL on Broadway, or NOEL COWARD, VIVIAN ELLIS and IVOR NOVELLO in London, the modern light musical theatre, for the first time in the some 70 years of its history, operated under the influence of no one single internationally popular school and style of writing. This wayward situation was altered early in the 1940s when Rodgers and OSCAR HAMMERSTEIN – both celebrated earlier with other partners – teamed up to lead Broadway back into the limelight with a series of richly coloured musical plays, a series beginning with *Oklahoma!* (1943) and written in the best romantic-comic tradition of Daly's Theatre and the classic operetta. In the years that followed, a pantheon of American writers including FREDERICK LOEWE, ALAN JAY LERNER, FRANK LOESSER, IRVING BERLIN, LEONARD BERNSTEIN, ARTHUR LAURENTS, CY COLEMAN, Michael Stewart, JERRY HERMAN, JERRY BOCK, NEIL SIMON, JOHN KANDER, FRED EBB, STEPHEN SONDHEIM and JULE STYNE provided regular new shows for Broadway, shows which combined textual and musical elements in equal and not too aggressively substantial parts and contributed to a quarter of a century of vivid and varied American musical theatre which was as much the focus of international attention as the France of Offenbach and Lecocq, the Britain of Gilbert and Sullivan and George Edwardes, or the prewar Vienna of Lehár and his contemporaries had been. In spite of this new focus, however, there was a difference between the sphere covered by the Broadway musical of the 1960s and that dominated by the musical theatre styles of earlier periods. Under the influence of a whole host of alternative entertainments and attitudes, the world of the musical theatre was both shrinking and changing its nature. Germany, Austria and Hungary, each of which had contributed so much to the genre in the early years of the century, had virtually ceased to produce viable new works and existed largely on repertoire house revivals of old favourites. France, in common with the rest of the continent, almost totally ignored the Broadway musical, preferring to centre its diminishing attentions on a new series of spectacular romantic operettas of its own, prompted by the vast but unexpected success of Francis Lopez's *La Belle de Cadix* (1945), but in serious decline by the late 1960s. In Australia, long a principal outlet for overseas musical shows, live theatres were disappearing fast and only the largest hits were now imported. Only the New York–London axis was still undiminished, with London regularly producing and occasionally exporting a number of fine shows, mostly on a smaller scale than its showier and slicker New York counterparts which, in return, found a welcome home in the West End. There were few other places for a show to go during these Broadway years, and musicals such as *My Fair Lady* (1956), *Fiddler on the Roof* (1964) and *Hello, Dolly!* (1964) which

appeared in significant foreign productions were the exception rather than the rule.

The ultimate and inevitable decline of the American musical, after a period of central importance even longer than and as productive as the great French *opéra bouffe* and *opéra comique* years, into a series of increasingly isolated successes overlapped, as so often in theatrical history, with the rise of significant talents elsewhere. After more than half a century, under the influence of composer ANDREW LLOYD WEBBER and lyricist TIM RICE, the centre of musical theatre action returned to Britain. Rice's individual, contemporary lyric style and Lloyd Webber's colourful and accessible mélange of classical and popular modern musical styles set new standards for a musical theatre which had become too often paralysed in the song-and-scene show and the musical-theatre manners of the previous generation. The sung-through 'rock opera' *Jesus Christ Superstar* (1971) established the young collaborators as worldwide favourites; the more dramatic *Evita* (1978) developed the same style and confirmed their position; and Lloyd Webber's setting of T. S. ELIOT's poetry as the dance-and-song spectacle *Cats* (1981) joined the two earlier record-breaking shows in the centre of musical theatre actuality, spreading vigorously enough to reopen the traditional overseas outlets for musical theatre and even to open new ones in such countries as Japan. Once again the musical theatre became a world entertainment. London continued to lead the way during the 1980s, providing the launching pad for such successes as Lloyd Webber's *The Phantom of the Opera* (1986) and the adapted French musical *Les Misérables* (1980; reworked 1985) in a climate of immense popularity for the musical theatre, and most particularly for the large-scale and spectacular musical pieces which, with their original staging carefully reproduced in country after country, had become the favourite genre of the contemporary theatre, offering a kind of entertainment which could not be matched by the television screen and appealing to the whole spectrum of theatregoers and beyond.

A notable feature of the development towards the large-scale and technically complicated musical during the 1980s was, however, a substantial decrease in the production of new pieces. The extensive finance required to stage an untried musical in a style comparable to that of the major hits being more difficult to raise than that for the small musical farces or dance-and-comedy shows of earlier eras, those shows which did succeed required and secured longer and longer runs in which to recoup their outlay and to move into profit, thereby decreasing the theatre space available for new works. The biggest hits of the era were, however, more lucrative than ever and, as a result, the financing of major musical projects moved largely out of the hands of the man-of-the-theatre producer and into those of the international financiers. The musical theatre became, in these years, a very different business from that of even a decade earlier, and if, at the end of the twentieth century, its rewards and results had become perhaps greater than ever, the bases from which musical theatre plays and productions grow had shrunk in such a fashion as to indicate that another switch in styles and standards will eventually have to come.   KURT GÄNZL

Anton Bauer, *Opern und Operetten in Wien* (1955)

Gerald Bordman, *American Musical Theatre: A Chronicle* (1978)

Florian Bruyas, *Histoire de l'opérette en France* (1974)

Kurt Gänzl, *The British Musical Theatre* (1986)

——, *The Encyclopedia of the Musical Theatre* (1994)

——, *The Musical: A Concise History* (1997)

Stanley Green, *The World of Musical Comedy* (1968)

——, *Broadway Musicals: Show by Show* (1996)

Ethan Mordden, *Broadway Babies: The People Who Made the American Musical* (1983)

Richard Traubner, *Operetta: A Theatrical History* (1983)

Musser, Tharon (b. Roanoke, Va., 8 Jan. 1925) Lighting designer. One of the top names in BROADWAY-LIGHTINGdesign for several decades, her versatility ranges from the spectacular to the highly detailed. She began her career in the late 1940s with the PROVINCETOWN Playhouse. She has toured with dance companies and designed for numerous American regional theatres, productions in London's WEST END and international venues reaching to Australia. Her career has been crowned with numerous awards and includes the original BROADWAY productions of *Long Day's Journey into Night* (1956), *Mame* (1966), *Follies* (1971) and many NEIL SIMON plays, as well as the ground-breaking production of *A Chorus Line* (1975). She has also designed for OPERA, and has shared her vast knowledge as a university lecturer and consultant.

ELLEN LAMPERT-GRÉAUX

N

Nagy, Phyllis (b. New York, 7 Nov. 1962) Playwright. Nagy claims to have been 'the best-known unproduced playwright in America' before she moved to London in 1992. After the première of *Weldon Rising* that year, however, this all changed, and by the end of the century she was widely recognized as one of the most challenging, exuberant and imaginative writers in Britain or America. *Weldon Rising* is set during an apocalyptically hot day in New York, where a delightfully perverse series of characters tumble from their tenements to bear witness to the unclenching of moral certainties as the city is consumed by the heat. *Butterfly Kiss* (1994) has a fragmented but theatrically dazzling structure of flashbacks and memories which reconstruct the processes leading to a case of matricide. *Disappeared* (1995) similarly uses a thriller structure to account for a mysterious disappearance of a woman from a bar, and her mysterious friendship with an eccentric thrift-shop worker. *The Strip* (1995) is a cross-Atlantic play showing echoes and parallels in the picaresque lives of its characters, rich in allusional metaphor. *Never Land* (1998) shows the disintegration of an obsessively anglophile French family. Other plays include *Trip's Clinch*, *Girl Bar* and *The Scarlet Letter*, all premièred in the United States in 1994. Nagy's plays are always surprising and exciting for the sardonic wit of the writing, the daring playfulness of form and structure, and their gallery of firmly drawn but uniquely eccentric characters. DAN REBELLATO

Aleks Sierz, *In-Yer-Face Theatre: British Drama Today* (2001)

Napier, John (b. London, 1 March 1944) Designer. After training under RALPH KOLTAI, he worked at the Phoenix, LEICESTER. Early designs for the OPEN SPACE theatre (*Fortune and Men's Eyes*, 1968), the ROYAL COURT (*Lear*, 1971) and the NATIONAL THEATRE (*Equus*, 1973, at the OLD VIC) led to an anti-realist trilogy of Shakespeare's English historical plays (1974) at the ROYAL SHAKESPEARE COMPANY. He created a permanent timber set for the 1976 Stratford season, establishing a collaboration with TREVOR NUNN which includes *Nicholas Nickleby* (1980) and *Les Misérables* (1985) and established a vogue for extraordinary environments and spectacular musicals drawing on popular culture: *Cats* (1981), *Starlight Express* (1984) and *Sunset Boulevard* (1993). TONY HOWARD

Nash [Nusbaum], N[athan] Richard (b. Philadelphia, Pa., 7 June 1913) Playwright, screenwriter and novelist. Plays include *The Rainmaker* (1954), in which a conman brings rain to a dry landscape and awakens love in a spinster; he adapted it as a film (1956) and a musical, *110 in the Shade* (1963). DAVID STAINES

Nathan, George Jean (b. Fort Wayne, Ind., 14 Feb. 1882; d. New York, 8 April 1958) Drama critic. Educated at Cornell and Bologna, Nathan joined the reporting staff of the *New York Herald* in 1905 and, while writing dramatic criticism for *The Bohemian* and *Outing*, began his championship of the drama of ideas in opposition to the realism prevailing on the American stage. He introduced the new drama of Europe: IBSEN and STRINDBERG, SHAW and HAUPTMANN. In 1909, while serving as co-editor with H. L. Mencken as well as theatre critic of *The Smart Set*, he made his most important American discovery, EUGENE O'NEILL. Nathan published and arranged for productions of O'Neill's early work. In 1923 Nathan and Mencken founded *The American Mercury* and, after their quarrel the following year and Mencken's departure, Nathan continued to write the paper's dramatic criticism until 1932. In 1934 he introduced SEAN O'CASEY and ensured a New York production of *Within the Gates*, and in 1939 he did the same for WILLIAM SAROYAN's first theatre piece, *My Heart's in the Highlands*.

To a degree rarely encountered in American letters, Nathan was a true cosmopolitan and aesthete. He was also an indefatigable worker, whose efforts were always in pursuit of an American drama that could compete with the best of Europe. That he was successful is attested by the world renown which Broadway enjoyed between the world wars and for a generation thereafter. In later years Nathan wrote criticism for, among others, *Saturday Review*, *Esquire*, *Theatre Arts* and *Newsweek* as well as producing a theatre annual from 1943 until 1951 and a total of more than 30 books, most notably *The Intimate Notebooks of George Jean Nathan* (1932). His will established an award for drama criticism and 'intelligent theatre going'. JOSEPH M. DIAZ

C. Angoff, ed., *The World of George Jean Nathan* (1952)
Thonmas F. Connolly, *George Jean Nathan and the Making of Modern American Criticism* (2000)

National Eisteddfod   This important and unique arts festival is held in a different part of WALES each year, and prior to the arrival of professional theatre in Wales was the main showcase for indigenous Welsh theatre – in the Welsh language, and produced by amateurs. The Eisteddfod (untranslatable, based on the word for 'seat'), as a music and poetry competition, can be traced back to medieval times, but the event as we know it, with its bardic chair, stone circle and druidic costume, was started by fervent nationalists in London in 1792 before being adopted as the 'authentic' eisteddfodic form in Wales in 1820. Like all tradition, it is highly suspect but very, very potent.

Drama has always been a contentious ingredient in the National Eisteddfod. Lloyd George's championing of Welsh drama at the 1902 Eisteddfod at Bangor was intended to create a parallel to the Irish theatre revival but, without either the tradition or the resources, the Welsh national theatre movement never really happened, although it was debated at Eisteddfodau regularly throughout the century. There has always been a drama section in the competitions, and for most of the century a special Eisteddfod company produced plays until the advent of Wales's first professional group, Cwmni Theatr Cymru, in 1965, which took over the job. Since its demise, other professional Welsh-

language companies have been invited to perform an Eisteddfod commission.

With the amateur–professional distinction blurred in Welsh culture, it is not surprising that leading playwrights (including GWYN THOMAS) saw their work first performed at the Eisteddfod. Recently a range of professional Welsh-language companies have been invited to perform on the Eisteddfod *maes* (field) as a part of the official programme, while the event also attracts most other Welsh companies to stage new productions in FRINGE venues.   DAVID ADAMS

National Endowment for the Arts   Starting in the 1950s, new not-for-profit arts organizations and regional theatres in the United States experienced unprecedented growth. Most of these companies were created initially with major financial support from local sponsors and foundations – notably the Ford Foundation. This 'movement' was so successful that by 1965 the US government had also begun to finance the not-for-profit arts in America by establishing the National Endowment for the Arts, a federal agency. (A 'sister' agency, the National Endowment for the Humanities, was founded at the same time.) Grants were made available to the performing and visual arts, folk arts, electronic media, literature and other fields. Unlike the federal Works Progress Administration of the 1930s, which was a national employment programme for artists and performers during the Great Depression, the NEA provided direct FUNDING to both not-for-profit institutions and individual artists. With few exceptions, NEA support was never comparable to European arts subsidies. An NEA grant rarely represented more than a small percentage of an applicant company's budget, and was generally offered in partnership with separate funding from state arts agencies and private sources. However, NEA budgets continued to grow in relation to the US arts economy until 1980, when the Reagan administration proposed draconian cuts. Considerable lobbying efforts kept the cuts from being implemented at first, but by 1989 government support for the arts – and the NEA's very existence – became a widely debated political issue. Grants supporting art assumed to be offensive towards religion, in support of left-wing causes or promoting homosexual culture came under severe attack and the NEA's budget was cut substantially in the early 1990s. In many states, the controversies that surrounded the NEA led to similar budget reductions at state and local arts agencies. Although the NEA still exists, most American not-for-profit arts groups now receive little in the way of direct support from the government, and are more reliant than ever upon box-office income, foundation grants,

corporate promotions, donations from private individuals and alliances with commercial organizations.
ROBERT MARX

National Folk Theatre of Ireland *see* SIAMSA TÍRE

National Lottery *see* ARTS COUNCIL

National Theater of the Deaf This American company of deaf actors was set up, with a federal grant, in 1966 in New York by designer David Hays and others, including Anne Bancroft and Arthur Penn (involved in the original production of *The Miracle Worker* about the deaf mute Helen Keller). Under the umbrella of the O'NEILL THEATER CENTER, it set up training and touring programmes, and won a Tony award for theatrical excellence in 1977. It has inspired the creation of nearly two dozen similar companies in the United States. Although the actors employ a modified style of dramatic sign language, the group's productions, ranging from classics to contemporary plays, usually include actors who are not deaf to voice the more expository elements of the story. The company, based since 1983 in Chester, Connecticut, has worked with PETER BROOK in Paris in its exploration of ways of overcoming the barriers created by language. In its distinguished history it has staged 60 national tours and 28 international ones, and received many awards. In 1998 it became the first theatre company to perform on all seven continents when it opened a theatre workshop in Antarctica. HELEN RAPPAPORT

S. Baldwin, *Pictures in the Air: The History of the National Theater of the Deaf* (1993)

National Theatre (London) Unlike many European countries, which perhaps had a clearer sense of the social value of theatre and of its role in symbolizing national aspiration, Britain failed to establish a national theatre before the twentieth century. Even then it had taken nearly 200 years from the first native rumblings – courtesy of the actor David Garrick – to do so. The earliest specific proposal came in 1848 and was linked to erecting a monument to Shakespeare, a connection that remained with the national theatre idea right until the moment of its realization. A proper movement to create a national theatre gathered steam, however, only in the early 1900s. In 1904 the critic WILLIAM ARCHER and playwright–director HARLEY GRANVILLE BARKER, supported by the leading actors and dramatists of the day, circulated privately a detailed and costed plan, including a repertoire outline. It was published in 1907 as *A National Theatre*. The campaign was joined by those who were promoting a revival of Elizabethan stagecraft and those who

had been arguing for a lasting tribute to Shakespeare, and in 1908 they founded together the Shakespeare Memorial National Theatre Committee. It launched an appeal, which raised £100,000 in five years, and lobbied parliament for public money to be contributed. A bill was passed but did not garner sufficient votes to take effect. A site – the first of five – was purchased in 1913 in London's Bloomsbury; then war intervened.

Enthusiasts, particularly the BRITISH DRAMA LEAGUE through its general secretary Geoffrey Whitworth, kept the campaign alive after the First World War, although some in the profession, notably the OLD VIC, came out against it. Granville Barker revised his scheme in 1930 and another site, in Kensington, was acquired in 1938. The prominent architect Sir Edward Lutyens made designs for the theatre, which would have stood opposite the Victoria and Albert Museum, a long way from theatreland. War intervened a second time, and, paradoxically, good things came from it for the NT campaign: state funding for the arts, the London County Council (LCC) offering to locate the theatre on the South Bank of the Thames in exchange for the Kensington site, and a *rapprochement* between the Old Vic and the NT cause.

In 1949 parliament passed the National Theatre Act and voted £1 million for the project. Two years later a foundation stone was laid – only to be moved discreetly the following year. Paralysis set in again. Negotiations led at the end of the 1950s to plans for the ascending STRATFORD-UPON-AVON to combine with the declining Old Vic, but PETER HALL launched the ROYAL SHAKESPEARE COMPANY and, having taken over the ALDWYCH THEATRE, they pulled out of the scheme as unworkable. LAURENCE OLIVIER, who had been asked unofficially if he would lead the putative NT, became in 1961 the first director of productions at the new CHICHESTER FESTIVAL THEATRE just as the Conservative government declared that the nation could not afford a national theatre. The Labour-led LCC applied pressure by saying it would contribute to the cost of the NT and provide the site rent-free. It passed a resolution to proceed with building the NT immediately. In 1962 a National Theatre Board was formed which announced Olivier as the NT's inaugural director. He was to create his new company at Chichester, the first open-stage theatre to be built in Britain since Shakespeare's time. It was to open as the NT the following year at the Old Vic, with PETER O'TOOLE playing Hamlet in what turned out to be for the occasion a rather low-key performance.

Olivier hired the flamboyant critic KENNETH TYNAN as his literary manager and, with JOHN DEXTER and WILLIAM GASKILL, two directors from the ROYAL COURT, assembled an outstanding acting ENSEMBLE in the early years. There was a new generation that had emerged from the Royal Court: COLIN BLAKELEY, FRANK FINLAY, JOAN PLOWRIGHT, ROBERT STEPHENS; and there were other youngsters also destined to become tomorrow's leaders: MICHAEL GAMBON, ANTHONY HOPKINS, DEREK JACOBI, IAN MCKELLEN, MAGGIE SMITH – and already established elders of the profession, such as EDITH EVANS and MICHAEL REDGRAVE. Olivier led from the front, notably with an extraordinary Othello (1964), alongside other sparkling productions – of new plays such as PETER SHAFFER's *The Royal Hunt of the Sun* (1964) and of classics like *The Recruiting Officer*, *Uncle Vanya* (both 1963) and *Love for Love* (1965) with GERALDINE MCEWEN.

Meanwhile a new theatre was being designed by Denys Lasdun. The site was moved again, down the South Bank to where the theatre now stands. Work began in 1969, and after many delays it was decided to open the building in stages. Olivier had resigned through ill-health and was succeeded in 1973 by Hall, who had to cope with soaring building costs. But finally the proscenium Lyttelton Theatre (seating 890) opened in March 1976 with transfers from the Old Vic, led by PEGGY ASHCROFT in BECKETT's *Happy Days*, and the open-stage Olivier Theatre (seating 1,160) opened that October with ALBERT FINNEY as Marlowe's Tamburlaine. The Cottesloe Theatre (a flexible studio seating up to 400) opened in March 1977 with a visit from the Science Fiction Theatre of Liverpool in *Illuminatus!* by KEN CAMPBELL and Chris Langham.

Hall broke with Olivier's regime, losing Tynan, Dexter and his co-directors JONATHAN MILLER and Michael Blakemore, who had added lustre in their Old Vic productions. During Hall's reign he brought in several directors to run their own companies within the NT: MIKE ALFREDS, the writer ALAN AYCKBOURN, MICHAEL BOGDANOV, BILL BRYDEN, PETER GILL, the writer DAVID HARE, the actors Ian McKellen and Edward Petherbridge, and the directors Christopher Morahan, Michael Rudman and PETER WOOD. The country's major actors, from the generation of JOHN GIELGUD and RALPH RICHARDSON to those of younger years like SIMON RUSSELL BEALE, were to be found at the NT, but usually for no more than a few productions during any one run of work. Individuals such as SIMON CALLOW, BRIAN COX, Michael Gambon, ALEC MCCOWEN, DENNIS QUILLEY, DIANA RIGG, PAUL SCOFIELD, and FIONA SHAW would become associated with the theatre for periods of time before they departed; many would return and repeat the pattern. A few, epitomized by MICHAEL BRYANT, did stay more or less permanently, but they were the exception.

Hall had to tackle several critical problems, from what became high-profile labour disputes and, despite being of the latest technology, the shortcomings of the two larger theatres – especially the acoustic – to the worst problem of them all, the monetarist policies of Thatcherism, which pitted the NT and other nationally subsidized theatres against less well-endowed regional theatres and drove the NT into the arms of the market economy. Undaunted, he championed new plays on the big stages – work by EDWARD BOND, HOWARD BRENTON, David Hare – introduced the popular pre-show Platform Performances, in which the theatre and its role in the world could be publicly dissected and explored in three-quarters of an hour, and, in 1984, under Peter Gill, opened the National Theatre Studio, a valuable laboratory both for the NT and for the theatre profession at large. It later set up writers' residencies in South Africa, Scotland and Lithuania.

Hall also broke down the barriers between so-called highbrow and lowbrow art, programming in 1982, for instance, his production in masks of the TONY HARRISON – HARRISON BIRTWISTLE treatment of Aeschylus' *The Oresteia* alongside the Broadway musical *Guys and Dolls*. The director of that successful production, RICHARD EYRE, succeeded Hall in 1988 – the year the NT became 'royal', courtesy of the chairman of the board, who apparently had consulted no one at the theatre. Eyre expanded the range of new work that was presented, from established writers like ALAN BENNETT, HAROLD PINTER and TOM STOPPARD to younger talents such as PATRICK MARBER and MARTIN MCDONAGH, and particularly in his own productions of David Hare's plays. ARTHUR MILLER was given a new lease of life by director David Thacker, and there were forceful revivals of TENNESSEE WILLIAMS's work. Eyre also took children's theatre seriously and ensured an annual offering of good quality. He extended his interest in the musical through another generation of directors – e.g. Steven Pimlott's production (1990) of *Sunday in the Park with George* and *Carousel* directed by NICHOLAS HYTNER (1992) – but large-stage Shakespeare proved problematic, with some exceptions, e.g. the updated *Richard III* (1990) with Ian McKellen. Along with directors known for their controlled lucidity, such as HOWARD DAVIES, Eyre brought in directors of a more explicitly physical and mythical bent: DECLAN DONNELLAN (e.g. with Tony Kushner's *Angels from America*, 1992), STEPHEN DALDRY (e.g. J. B. PRIESTLEY's *An Inspector Calls*, 1992) and Simon McBurney and THEATRE DE COMPLICITE (e.g. *Street of Crocodiles*, 1992). He also gave a berth to French-Canadian experimenter ROBERT LEPAGE and briefly to Jatinder Verma with his Asian company TARA ARTS.

Eyre's good commercial sense, underlined by a series of transfers to the West End and Broadway, underpinned a successful time running the NT during which it eclipsed its old rival the RSC. Ironically, in 1997 he was succeeded by TREVOR NUNN, who had taken over from Hall at the RSC almost 30 years before. Among his successes was the introduction of an ensemble, which was responsible for a powerful *Merchant of Venice* (1999), with Henry Goodman outstanding as Shylock. With further restrictions on public subsidy and an intensifying debate on the meaning of the nation, Nunn faced a big challenge to give the NT a new identity at the dawn of the new millennium. In 2001 it was announced that the challenge would be handed on to NICHOLAS HYTNER as his successor in Spring 2003. COLIN CHAMBERS

S. Callow, *The National* (1997)

J. Elsom and N. Tomalin, *The History of the National Theatre* (1978)

T. Godwin, *Britain's Royal National Theatre: The First 25 Years* (1988)

J. Goodwin, ed., *Peter Hall's Diaries: The Story of a Dramatic Battle* (1984)

P. Lewis, *The National: A Dream Made Concrete* (1990)

National Youth Theatre Name given in 1961 to a project founded in 1956, before the YOUTH THEATRE movement was fully under way, by teacher and former actor Michael Croft (1922–86), to allow his London pupils to perform Shakespeare in the summer holidays. The initiative soon attracted young people from all over Britain. It established a reputation for energetic and often socially aware productions of Shakespeare (e.g. its modern-dress *Julius Caesar* in 1960) and then successfully added new plays (e.g. *Little Malcolm and his Struggle against the Eunuchs* by DAVID HALLIWELL in 1965), including the premières of several plays by PETER TERSON. His football terrace play *Zigger Zagger* (1967), which the NYT also performed abroad, became a school play standard.

After appearing in several London theatres for its summer programme, particularly at the Jeannetta Cochrane during the 1960s, the NYT moved in 1971 to the local authority owned Shaw Theatre in north London, and established there the professional Dolphin Company which produced in 1978 the first full revival of the WESKER Trilogy. With the withdrawal of its Arts Council grant and the demise of Dolphin in 1981, loss of the Shaw in 1984 and the death of Croft in 1986, the NYT continued its long-lasting survival battle to find premises and funding. The public grants were consistently small – on the grounds that the NYT was an amateur organization – and from the 1980s onwards commercial and private sponsorship was increasingly sought.

As well as sustaining a national and international reputation, the NYT has encouraged young writers (e.g. BARRIE KEEFFE) and given a start to many who became leading performers, among them Timothy Dalton, DEREK JACOBI, BEN KINGSLEY and HELEN MIRREN.
COLIN CHAMBERS

S. Masters, *The National Youth Theatre* (1969)

naturalism *see* ANTOINE, ANDRÉ; DRAMATIC THEORY; ZOLA, EMILE

Naughton, Bill [William John Francis] (b. Ballyhaunis, Co. Mayo, Ireland, 12 June 1910; d. Isle of Man, 9 Jan. 1992) Playwright, born in Ireland but brought up in Bolton, Lancashire. Naughton's detailed, sensitive dramas of Lancashire working-class family life, like *All in Good Time* (1963) and *Spring and Port Wine* (1964), labelled him initially as a descendant of the MANCHESTER SCHOOL. But *Alfie* (1963, filmed 1966) was altogether bleaker, while still displaying Naughton's remarkable talent for creating complex, believable characters. He also wrote novels and short stories.
DAN REBELLATO

Nazimova, Alla (b. Yalta, Crimea, 22 May 1879; d. Los Angeles, 13 July 1945) Actress. Played a season at the MOSCOW ART THEATRE before a tour of Europe and America, where she settled and became a famous performer, particularly in IBSEN (e.g. *Ghosts*, 1935) and influenced American views of Russian acting styles. The Nazimova Theatre (later 39th Street Theatre) opened in 1910 with a production of Ibsen's *Little Eyolf*. She had a film career and also appeared with LE GALLIENNE's company and the THEATER GUILD.
NICK WORRALL

G. Lambert, *Nazimova: A Biography* (1997)

NEA *see* NATIONAL ENDOWMENT FOR THE ARTS

Neagle, Anna [Marjorie Robertson] (b. London, 20 Oct. 1904; d. London, 3 June 1986) Actress. She was a chorus dancer until JACK BUCHANAN gave her a leading role in *Stand Up and Sing* (1931), followed by the lead opposite him in the film *Goodnight, Vienna* (1932). This brought her instant stardom and its producer, Herbert Wilcox (1891–1977), whom she married in 1943, cast her in numerous starring roles on screen. On stage she had a much more limited range, but her film name made her a potent draw and she was much loved by a loyal public. She achieved a major success in the critically condemned but vastly popular musical

Charlie Girl (1965). Her autobiography, *There's Always a Tomorrow*, appeared in 1974. She was created a dame in 1969. IAN BEVAN

Nederlander, James [Morton]   (b. Detroit, 31 March 1922) Theatre owner and producer. The son of a renowned theatre owner, David Nederlander (1886–1965), James added to the family collection across the United States, including Chicago, Los Angeles, San Francisco and – especially – New York, to the point where it was second only to that of the SHUBERT ORGANIZATION. In 1968 he was appointed producer of the New York State Theatre's summer season. His career as a producer gained momentum in the late 1960s, and he produced a series of successful musicals (e.g. *Hello Dolly!*, 1978), comedies and straight plays as well as the shows of solo artists. The Nederlander Organization bought a New York theatre in 1979 which became known by the family name in honour of David. ADRIANA HUNTER

Negro Ensemble Company   The early 1960s saw the emergence of a strong African American theatre in the United States in the wake of the civil rights movement, and this company, established in New York in 1967 under the directorship of the black playwright DOUGLAS TURNER WARD, subsequently matured into a potent force in black American theatre. A considerable grant from the Ford Foundation enabled the group to spell out clearly an artistic policy which was not geared to commercial dictates and would promote the work of black writers, actors and directors. Over the years the company collected numerous awards for plays like *Dream on Monkey Mountain* (1971), *The River Niger* (1973) and *A Soldier's Play* (Pulitzer, 1981) as well as a Tony in 1973 for its own special achievement. It was also known for staging workshops and play readings, and touring extensively abroad. Its operations wound down in the 1980s and by the mid-1990s it had ceased to be an effective organization, though producing the occasional one-off show. HELEN RAPPAPORT

Neher, Caspar [Rudolf Ludwig]   (b. Augsburg, 11 April 1897; d. Vienna, 30 June 1962) Stage designer. A classmate of BERTOLT BRECHT, his lifelong collaboration with the playwright went well beyond that of simply staging his plays. He worked on the whole concept of the play, often suggesting ideas for scenes with his drawings. Neher designed the first productions of *In the Jungle of the Cities* (1923) and *Edward II* (1924) – Brecht's first completely independent work as director – and went on to invent stage devices integral to EPIC THEATRE: the famous half curtain stretched across the front of the stage, the hauntingly symbolic use of

texture and colour (usually black or grey), the technique of projecting choric comments on to a screen on stage, and the utilization of props that have a recognizable tactile quality, hewn by human hands. Neher's innovative design for *The Threepenny Opera* (1928) with its anti-illusory devices was part of the reason for the play's enormous success. In a Neher set for a Brecht play, every item that matters is authentic, while everything peripheral needs merely to be indicated. Brecht's admiration for Neher was undiminished by Neher's decision to opt for 'inner exile' during the Nazi era, resulting in his designing propaganda productions such as the 1937 *Coriolanus*, which paid tribute to the Nazi architecture of Albert Speer. The charge that Neher was thus a man of no convictions, however, is harsh, and Brecht was delighted to renew their working relationship in 1948 in Switzerland with a production of his *Antigone* and to take Neher with him to the BERLINER ENSEMBLE. One of the outstanding designers of the twentieth century, Neher worked with many of the leading directors and was noted for his impressive settings to operas (especially by Mozart). He also wrote opera libretti (e.g. for KURT WEILL's *The Pledge*, 1931). DOMINIC SHELLARD

Denis Bablet, *Revolutions in Stage Design of the Twentieth Century* (1977)
John Willett, *Caspar Neher: Brecht's Designer* (1986)

Neighborhood Playhouse   An amateur theatre from 1915 to 1920 in New York's Lower East Side, built by Alice and Irene Lewisohn; when it turned professional it presented a mix of REVUES, serious modern drama from the likes of SHAW, GALSWORTHY and O'NEILL, and folk plays from Japan, India, France and Celtic and Norse myth. It always had a social and educational dimension, and after it closed in 1927 it spawned the Neighborhood Playhouse School of Theater, opened in 1928, and the Costume Institute of the Metropolitan Museum, opened in 1937. The school of theatre was run from 1936–59 by the actor Sanford Meisner (b. 1905), a member of the original GROUP THEATRE who co-directed *Waiting for Lefty* (1935) with CLIFFORD ODETS. CHARLES LONDON

Alice Lewisohn Crowley, *The Neighborhood Playhouse: Leaves from a Theater Scrapbook* (1959)

Neilson, Anthony   (b. Aberdeen, 16 March 1967) Playwright. No contemporary male playwright has trained such an unflinching gaze on his own masculinity as Neilson. While some have criticized his work for misogyny, his sense of masculinity seems to be informed by feminist arguments which have broken down the distinction between the brutal and the ordinary. *Normal* (1991), showing a series of encounters between the Düsseldorf Ripper and his defence counsel, argues for the incoherence of the title word as a means of distinguishing respectable barrister from rapist. *Penetrator* (1993) became controversial for its violent, pornographic language, yet Neilson uses this language to capture the mind of a disturbed army cadet on the run. *The Censor* (1997) traces a series of meetings between a film-maker and a film censor, as they become involved in a perverse and violent erotic relationship. Again Neilson's target seems to be liberal pieties.

Other plays include *Welfare My Lovely* (1990), *Year of the Family* (1994), *Jeffrey Dahmer is Unwell* (1995, co-written with Alan Francis and Mike Hayley) and *The Night Before Christmas* (1995).   DAN REBELLATO

Aleks Sierz, *In-Yer-Face Theatre: British Drama Today* (2001)

Neilson, Julia   *see* TERRY, ELLEN

Nelson, Richard [John]   (b. Chicago, 17 Oct. 1950) Playwright. Nelson's work (which includes many adaptations of classic texts) focuses in a variety of styles on political, social and moral issues, increasingly with sharp but humorous irony; his early characters are often exiles or lovers, displaced in time as well as space. Later work explores the responsibility of the artist and the nature of an individual's commitment and conviction. Influenced by both BRECHT and CHEKHOV, his plays include *The Vienna Notes* (1978), the epic *Rip Van Winkle or The Works* (1981), and *Principia Scriptoria* (1986), with which he began a long-standing collaboration with the ROYAL SHAKESPEARE COMPANY. He has written eight plays for them, including *Some Americans Abroad* (1989), *Two Shakespearean Actors* (1990), *Columbus and the Discovery of Japan* (1992), *Misha's Party* (with the Russian playwright ALEXANDER GELMAN, 1993), *New England* (1994), *General from America* (1996) and *Goodnight Children Everywhere* (1997), which won an Olivier Award for best new play. In 2000 he won a Tony for the book of *James Joyce's The Dead* (1999), which he directed, and his play *Madame Melville*, also directed by him, opened to acclaim in the West End. He co-authored with DAVID JONES a book on the writer–director relationship, *Making Plays* (1995).
M. ELIZABETH OSBORN

Nemirovich-Danchenko, Vladimir [Ivanovich]
(b. Ozurgety [now Makharadze], Russia, 11 Dec. 1858; d. Moscow, 25 April 1943) Director, playwright, teacher, theatre critic and short-story writer; co-founder, with STANISLAVSKY, of the MOSCOW ART THEATRE (1897; first production 1898). Nemirovich

worked as a theatre critic in the 1870s, and during the 1890s wrote both prose and dramatic works, some of which were performed at the Imperial Theatres in Moscow and St Petersburg. He taught at the Moscow Philharmonic (1891–1901), where his students included MEYERHOLD and KNIPPER, whom he invited to join MAT's first season. Despairing of the old-fashioned methods and routines of nineteenth-century Russian theatre production, Nemirovich discovered a kindred spirit in the person of Stanislavsky and, despite many quarrels and disagreements over the years, they jointly managed MAT from its inception until Stanislavsky's death in 1938. Nemirovich assumed responsibility for the literary management of the theatre from the outset while also either directing a number of plays himself or having a hand in Stanislavsky's productions (e.g. the four major CHEKHOV plays, when he exercised a restraining hand though still coming into conflict with the writer). It was Nemirovich who was responsible for recruiting Chekhov to MAT and for commissioning further plays from him, although his own taste inclined more towards the plays of IBSEN, as evidenced by a string of productions which he staged of work by the Norwegian dramatist, including *Brand* (1906), *Rosmersholm* (1908) and *Peer Gynt* (1912). Before the Revolution he also staged notable productions of *Julius Caesar* (1903) as well as adaptations of Dostoevsky's *The Possessed* (1913) and *The Brothers Karamazov* (1910). After the Revolution, Nemirovich became increasingly interested in the staging of opera and operetta, founding his own Musical Theatre in 1926 out of MAT's Musical Studio. Following Stanislavsky's virtual retirement from the live theatre after 1928, Nemirovich became more involved in the day-to-day running of MAT and staged productions of work by Soviet dramatists, including *Vragi* (*Enemies*, 1935) by GORKY, with whom he had worked on *The Lower Depths* (1902); IVANOV'S *Blokada* (*Blockade*, 1929); and POGODIN'S *Kremlyovskiye kuranty* (*Kremlin Chimes*, 1942) of which officialdom greatly approved, conferring virtually canonical status on MAT productions by the end of the 1930s. One of Nemirovich's finest productions was his revival of Chekhov's *Three Sisters* in 1940, with a cast drawn from a new generation of MAT actors and with new settings by Vladimir Dmitriev. His book, *My Life in the Russian Theatre*, was published in 1936.   NICK WORRALL

Neptune Theater   Founded in 1963 in Halifax, Nova Scotia, Neptune is one of Canada's major regional theatres. Its artistic directors have included Leon Major, John Wood, JOHN NEVILLE, Tom Kerr and Richard Ouzounian. Neptune's mandate has been to present a repertoire of international classics, leavened by established and, more rarely, new and experimental Canadian works. Initially housed in a 520-seat former vaudeville theatre and cinema, in 1997 Neptune moved into a new facility; this houses a main stage, a 180-seat flexible space, and a theatre school. Neptune's artistic and financial integrity has wavered from time to time, but it continues to fulfil important regional and national roles. L. W. CONOLLY

Richard Perkyns, *The Neptune Story* (1989)

Nesbitt, Cathleen [Mary] (b. Cheshire, 24 Nov. 1888; d. London, 2 Aug. 1982) Actress with a wide range who worked closely with AUGUSTA GREGORY, DION G. BOUCICAULT, BASIL DEAN and HARLEY GRAN-VILLE BARKER. She joined the Irish Players in 1911 and went with them to America, where she returned in 1915 for four years. She acted in such stage hits as the revival of *A Bill of Divorcement* (1929) and *Love on the Dole* (1935), and made many notable films. Nesbitt spent much of her career working in America after the New York production of *The Cocktail Party* (1950), returning there at the age of 90 to play Mrs Higgins in *My Fair Lady*, a part she had played on Broadway in 1956. Her autobiography, *A Little Love and Good Company*, was published in 1975. MAGGIE GALE

Netherlands For Dutch theatre the twentieth century commenced in 1870. At that time a group of prominent burghers in Amsterdam founded Het Tooneelverbond (Theatre Union) with the aim of 'uplifting' Dutch theatre. They were worried that the theatre had increasingly become the domain of the lower classes. Furthermore, in their eyes the quality of Dutch actors and their repertoire had sunk to an unacceptably low level. Het Tooneelverbond started out with the publication of a magazine, *Het Nederlandsch Tooneel* ('The Dutch Stage'), designed to revive the interest of well-to-do burghers in the theatre. Some time later a school of acting was established to raise the levels of refinement and learning within the acting profession, hoping thus to attract entrants from the upper classes. Finally the union set up its own theatre company, Het Nederlandsch Tooneel (The Dutch Stage), directed by H. J. Schimmel (1825–1906), banker and burgomaster's son. This company would receive the designation 'Royal' in 1882.

Royal recognition indicated that the union had indeed achieved its aims, albeit step by step. During its first years, for example, it was not able to realize its aim of improving the repertoire. It appeared that the general public did not appreciate new and better plays and continued to prefer the repertoire performed

before 1870: PAGEANT plays, MELODRAMA, VAUDEVILLE and the like. In the productions staged by its own company, the union, which was not yet subsidized by the government and therefore depended on box-office receipts, decided instead to concentrate on improving performance. The practice of subordinating a show to the performance of a famous star was scrapped; the *mise-en-scène* and actors' diction and ability to work as an ensemble were improved; and more and more attention was paid to costumes and décor, striving especially after unity of effect and, when necessary, historical accuracy.

After a number of years the general public grew a little more receptive to the idea of a new and better repertoire. The new French theatre (the comedies of manners by Scribe, Augier and SARDOU) was put on, and in 1879 a play by Shakespeare, *Romeo and Juliet*. This production proved an overwhelming success: '22 October deserves a place of honour in the annals of the history of Dutch theatre,' read the review in *Het Tooneel. The Merchant of Venice*, staged a year later, was at least as big a success. This was due substantially to the performance of Louis Bouwmeester (1842–1925), a phenomenal actor, whose rendition of Shylock, a role which he would eventually play more than 2,600 times, rapidly became legendary. His fame led to performances throughout Europe and a French ministerial award.

Despite all these positive developments, criticism was not silenced and even gained strength after 1885. Melodramas remained an important item on the repertoire, as they continued to ensure high box-office receipts. And Schimmel refused to stage anything more modern than French drawing-room plays. The work of BRIEUX, IBSEN and STRINDBERG, as well as realistic or naturalistic stagings, found no favour in his eyes.

The conservative stance adopted by Schimmel led to the establishment in 1889 of De Tooneelvereeniging (The Drama Association), an initiative comparable to ANTOINE's founding of the Théâtre Libre (1887) in Paris, and to the founding by the Dutchman J. T. GREIN of the INDEPENDENT THEATRE SOCIETY (1891) in London. The common aim of these companies was the staging of modern theatre.

On 29 March 1889 De Tooneelvereeniging introduced itself to the Dutch public with a performance of Ibsen's *Nora (A Doll's House)*, which proved to be an overwhelming success. Not only was the subtle and variegated interaction of the actors (the result of no fewer than 30 rehearsals) highly praised, but the décor and lighting were much appreciated as unprecedentedly lifelike. Despite this success, De Tooneelvereeniging was unable to cope financially, and was soon forced to close down. The torch of realism was kept burning into the twentieth century, however, thanks especially to a company established in 1893: De Nederlandsche Tooneelvereeniging (The Dutch Drama Association). HERMAN HEIJERMANS, undoubtedly the most important Dutch playwright of this period, was attached to this company. He was a member of the Socialist Democratic Workers' Party and in his plays he made no secret of his political convictions. Although Heijermans never reached the level of Ibsen, Strindberg or WEDEKIND, to his contemporaries his plays possessed indisputable quality. They were of topical interest, dealt with familiar situations and, in their portrayal of the Dutch bourgeoisie, were entirely credible. They were, moreover, extremely entertaining, because Heijermans was not averse to borrowing numerous elements from popular theatre such as music, antics and jokes.

Heijermans' biggest success was *Op hoop van zegen* (*The Good Hope*, 1900), a play about the miserable life of poor fisherfolk in a Dutch seaside town. No other Dutch play has been translated into so many languages or performed in so many important theatres as this one. A list of famous names linked to *Op hoop van zegen* includes Antoine, ELLEN TERRY and STANISLAVSKY. Heijermans left for Berlin in 1907, among other reasons because Holland had still not become a signatory to the Berne Convention, which meant he could not claim protection for foreign translations and performances of his works. Also in 1907, the first break with realism occurred in the Netherlands. In the village of Laren, an artist's colony near Amsterdam, two medieval plays were put on, one of which was *Elckerlijc* (the Dutch *Everyman*). The persistence of two young directors, Eduard Verkade (1878–1961) and Willem Royaards (1867–1929), was the driving force behind this production.

The role of Verkade was especially important. The son of a major Dutch industrialist, he was intended to follow in his father's footsteps, and was accordingly sent to study relevant subjects in Britain and Germany; however, he was primarily concerned with what the theatrical scene in those countries had to offer him. Back in the Netherlands, he took speech and acting lessons. The favourable reception of his solo performance of *Macbeth* in 1904 confirmed him in his choice of theatre as his profession. The Dutch theatrical world was too constricted for his ambitions, however, and in 1906 he left for Germany to work with REINHARDT. There he met EDWARD GORDON CRAIG. The three months that Verkade and Craig spent in close contact with each other would prove to have far-reaching consequences for Dutch theatre. Verkade was fascinated by

Craig's rejection of illusionistic theatre, in which everything revolved around the text, in favour of suggestive theatre, in which line, colour, sound and movement were at least as important as the spoken word.

In 1907 Verkade and Royaards were given the chance to put some of these ideas into practice. Their *Elckerlijc* was the first non-realistic production in the Netherlands. The décor consisted only of a plain construction with three arches (a triptych) coloured brick-red and sandy-yellow, and an object which functioned as Elckerlijc's bench and grave. A dark-blue cloth spangled with golden stars was stretched across the whole décor. In his use of colours the set designer declared himself to have been inspired by Giotto's frescoes. Almost without exception, the reviews this *Elckerlijc* received were extremely favourable. The feeling was that Dutch theatre had been raised to a form of art for the first time in its history.

Verkade and Royaards would determine the shape of Dutch theatre into the 1920s, although their paths diverged shortly after the production of *Elckerlijc* when each founded his own company. Time and again, financial insecurity forced Verkade and Royaards to cut their coats according to their cloth. This meant removing plays which did not run well from the repertoire ever more rapidly, cutting down rehearsal time and adapting the repertoire to the tastes of the general public. Obviously, in such a climate a performance could only occasionally blossom into a true work of art. The press rarely reported a production as a 'happening' not to be missed. Even so, there were some such 'happenings': *Romeo and Juliet* (1911) and SHAW's *St Joan* (1924), both directed by Verkade, and Vondel's *Adam in Ballingschap* ('Adam in exile', 1908) and *Twelfth Night* (1917), directed by Royaards. Most of the plays put before the public were rather light and played in a manner which was a cross between realism and the grand style of the nineteenth century. The director and actor Albert Van Dalsum (1889–1971) was the only practitioner able to realize a few EXPRESSIONISTIC performances in this climate. This remained the state of affairs until the Second World War.

Of course, some people in the world of Dutch theatre were very dissatisfied with the sorry state of their profession; and to them, the end of the war seemed a suitable moment for change. During the war a group of directors had already drawn up a plan for a new theatrical order. Elements of that plan were implemented after the war, but the Dutch government's decision to subsidize five newly founded companies proved to be the most important innovation. The secure financial position of these five companies did not, however, lead to the spectacular changes in repertoire and staging style that might have been expected. This was chiefly the result of the government's stipulation that the companies would be subsidized only if they presented their work to the Dutch population in its entirety; that is, not only to theatregoers in the big cities in the west of the country (the three main companies were based in Amsterdam, Rotterdam and The Hague), but also to the population in the north, east and south. This stipulation forced the companies again to include several productions in the repertoire simultaneously, to travel a lot at the expense of scarce rehearsal time and to adapt their repertoire to the tastes of a provincial audience, an audience which was presumably less progressive and intellectual than an urban one. In consequence, their repertoire remained on the light side and the staging style did not really progress beyond realism. The most that can be said is that within these limits the companies concerned achieved a certain level of excellence. Dutch theatre after the Second World War is best described as polite entertainment.

Even though the repertoire was compiled for a general public and the quality of the performances was better than before the war, attendance figures started to decrease dramatically in the 1960s (from 5 million a year just after the war to under 2 million in 1965). Two factors were prominent in this trend. First, the rise of television meant that people did not have to go out for entertainment any more; and second, the concerns of the unruly generation of the 1960s were not taken into consideration by the main theatre companies which continued to propagate an orderly and uncomplicated world view.

This view of postwar Dutch theatre needs to be somewhat modified, however. Occasionally the large companies did stage more serious, contemporary work. In the 1950s and 1960s De Nederlandse Comedie (The Dutch Comedy), based in Amsterdam, performed plays by ALBEE, MILLER and TENNESSEE WILLIAMS. A number of works by the Flemish playwright HUGO CLAUS opened in Rotterdam. In these plays Claus candidly pointed out the discrepancy between human desires and the narrow-minded values of Catholic society in Belgium and Holland. His *Een bruid in de morgen* (*A Bride in the Morning, 1955*) and *Suiker* (*Sugar*, 1958), as well as his later play *Vrijdag* (*Friday*, 1969), were soon regarded as modern classics of Dutch theatre.

Furthermore, the number of companies subsidized by the government increased to 12 during these years. In addition to companies which catered for regional audiences or specific groups such as children, a company specializing in experimental theatre had been established: Toneelgroep Studio (Theatre Company Studio), directed by Kees van Iersel (1912–98). The modernization that was going on in post-war Dutch theatre may be primarily ascribed to Kees van Iersel. Not only did he confront Dutch audiences with playwrights like IONESCO and BECKETT and produce plays which featured current events (e.g. VAN ITALLIE's *America Hurrah!*), he also broke with the traditional picture-frame stage and the realistic staging style associated with it. Studio performed on a bare platform stage which jutted diagonally into the house. The audience was seated on three sides around it. Not surprisingly, Studio's slogan ran: 'no curtain, no distance between you and the actors'. Ritsaert ten Cate (b. 1938), who since 1965 has brought such companies as LA MAMA, PIP SIMMONS, the LIVING THEATER and BREAD AND PUPPET THEATER to the Netherlands, gave another important impetus to Dutch theatre with his MICKERY theatre, which became an experimental centre for the avant-garde. However, neither van Iersel's work nor Mickery and a number of other experimental initiatives put on in small, out-of-the-way halls could prevent the continuing growth of dissatisfaction. On 9 October 1969 two students from the Amsterdam school of acting treated a performance by actors from De Nederlandse Comedie not to applause, but to a pelting with tomatoes. The following months were extremely turbulent. Going under the name Aktie Tomaat (Action Tomato), drama students and aspiring young theatremakers repeatedly disrupted performances, called discussion groups and presented new plans. A scheme to abolish all existing companies and to create a whole new order was not adopted; nevertheless, a change in the rules on subsidy cleared the way for the establishment of a large number of small companies devoted to experimental theatre.

It may well be said that Dutch theatre exploded after Aktie Tomaat. That much is made clear by the figures: between 1969 and 1985 the number of subsidized companies grew from 12 to 44. It is impossible to discuss here the whole range of theatrical forms presented to Dutch audiences after 1970. Only the most important innovations in form and content will be mentioned.

Innovation in content amounted to the selection and development of a repertoire that reflected to a larger extent than before what was going on in society. According to the accepted opinion in those days, theatre was supposed to be 'socially relevant'. In the same vein, actors were expected to be 'personally committed'. The main vehicle for this innovative approach was POLITICAL THEATRE. This type of theatre was produced by companies such as Proloog and Sater, whose main concern was not artistic expression but the promotion of class consciousness. Usually these companies aimed at reaching young people and blue-collar workers, preferably in their own environment. They did not perform in theatres, but in youth centres, at schools and in factories. The performances were often the result of improvisation and they dealt with the social problems and living conditions of their audiences. As a matter of course room for discussion was provided after the performance.

The most important formal innovation after 1970 was the downgrading of the playwright's text as the main element of a performance. It was realized that the other elements of a performance – space, décor, lighting, movement – had been neglected and used mainly as a subservient illustration of the text. Directors now started to explore the dramatic potential of those neglected 'sign systems': theatre became an art in which meaning could be transmitted not only by words, but in many other ways. To that end directors would often seek cooperation from artists trained in other disciplines. In the more extreme cases this led to performances dubbed *mengeltheater* (mixed theatre) by a Dutch critic: performances which were a cross between theatre and the visual arts, e.g. by Onafhankelijk Toneel (Independent Theatre) or between theatre and music (Orkater).

Movement theatre – a mixture of theatre and dance or mime – may be deemed the main exponent of formal innovation, precisely because this was theatre operating without a text. The company with the longest record of service in this field of theatre is Bewth (an abbreviation of BEWegingsTHeater, the Dutch word for movement theatre), which dates back to the mid-1960s. Bewth specializes in SITE-SPECIFIC performances. For each production the company chooses a different building (it could be a church, factory building or riding school), the qualities of which are revealed by means of movement and lighting. Because both the history and the architecture of a building are highlighted, Bewth's performances may best be described as voyages of discovery through time and space.

Political theatre and movement theatre define the two extremes of the Dutch theatre landscape after 1970. The numerous other companies, large and small, of which the most important were Het WERKTEATER, De Appel and Baal, can be situated somewhere in between. In these years, too, the young were taken seriously as potential theatregoers for the first time. In the 1980s and 1990s theatre for the young became a fully fledged component of Dutch theatre, thanks to playwrights and diretors like Ad de Bont (b. 1949), Hans van den Boom (b. 1951), Liesbeth Coltof (b. 1954), Suzanne van Lohuizen (b. 1953), Pauline Mol (b. 1953) and Heleen Verburg (b. 1964). It also won acclaim in the rest of Europe.

This outburst of inspiration, creativity and invention continued until about 1980. Then leftist fervour petered out, which inevitably led to the demise of political theatre. At the same time, dramatists who had initiated formal innovation also ran out of enthusiasm. To make matters worse, attendance figures started to decline rapidly once again. It seemed as if a pause was required, in order to reflect on the new accomplishments. During this period of malaise, Flemish theatre appeared on the scene. Under the terms of an exchange treaty with Belgium, Dutch directors were granted a 50 per cent subsidy for staging guest performances by Flemish companies, and because Dutch companies were temporarily indisposed, more and more Flemish productions were billed during the 1980s. The successes these productions achieved led Dutch companies in turn to contract Flemish directors and actors. Nowadays, directors like Ivo van Hove (b. 1958; Zuidelijk Toneel, Toneelgroep Amsterdam) and Dirk Tanghe (b. 1956; Paardenkathedraal) still make important contributions to Dutch theatre. Although it is certainly a simplification, one could say that the Flemish contribution reanimated Dutch theatre when intellectualism and formalism threatened to suffocate it. This process of resuscitation continued and even became reciprocal.

From the end of the 1980s Dutch theatre finally seemed to be reaping the fruits of Aktie Tomaat and everything that it put in motion. Theatre-makers who had had the opportunity to master the art of theatre in all its forms during the 1970s came to present work bearing their own unique signature. There is some irony in the fact that, much to the displeasure of their younger colleagues, they became established figures. The most important amongst them were Gerardjan Rijnders (b. 1949), artistic director of Toneelgroep Amsterdam, Frans Strijards (b. 1952), founder and artistic director of Art & Pro, and Karst Woudstra (b. 1947). Their work is difficult to compare. Rijnders is still known particularly for his large-scale dramatic collages which most resemble video clips. Strijards is able to turn any piece whatsoever, be it *The Cherry Orchard* or *Hedda Gabler*, into a hilarious comedy peopled by screwed-up idiots. And Woudstra, in an almost classical manner, strives for psychological credibility and emotional intensity. Despite their differences, however, there is something they have in common: besides being directors, the three of them are also playwrights. Indeed, Rijnders, Strijards and Woudstra have enriched Dutch drama with several brilliant plays.

Others, too, have set the tone of Dutch theatre at the end of the century. A company like Hollandia has developed the field of site-specific theatre, in which sound and music play a prominent part. Working in small COLLECTIVES like De Trust, Dood Paard and 't Barre Land, the latest generation of theatre-makers has focused on finding an individual, specific style of acting. At the start of the new century smallness of scale and 'mixed theatre' remain characteristic of the Dutch theatre landscape, increasingly involving the new media of video, virtual reality and sound technology.   ROB VAN DER ZALM & E. RUDOLF VALKHOFF

R. L. Erenstein, ed., *Een theatergeschiedenis der Nederlanden: Tien eeuwen drama en theater in Nederland en Vlaanderen* (1996)
Robert L. Erenstein and Robert van Gaal, *Theatre in the Netherlands* (1992)
B. Hunningher, *Een eeuw Nederlands Toneel* (1949)
Hans van Maanen, *Het Nederlands Toneelbestel van 1945 tot 1995* (1997)
——, 'The Netherlands', in H. van Maanen and S. E. Wilmer, eds, *Theatre Worlds in Motion: Structures, Politics and Developments in the Countries of Western Europe* (1998)

Nethersole, Olga [Isabel]   (b. London, 18 Jan. 1870; d. Bournemouth, Hants, 9 Jan. 1951)   Actress, manager and director who ran the ROYAL COURT, Adelphi, His Majesty's and Shaftesbury theatres. She was well known in both London and New York, and pioneered MAETERLINCK's *Sister Beatrice* (1909) and *Mary Magdalene* (1910). She became noted for parts that challenged the repressive morality of the day (e.g. in *The Second Mrs Tanqueray*, *The Notorious Mrs Ebbsmith* and *Camille*). She caused controversy in England and America with her portrayal of the lead in Clyde Fitch's *Sapho* (1900), which was closed in New York, though she was acquitted of indecency. She virtually gave up acting for social work, founding the People's League of Health in 1917.   MAGGIE GALE

Neville, John   (b. London, 2 May 1925)   Actor and director. After graduating from the Royal Academy of Dramatic Art, he joined the BRISTOL OLD VIC (1950–3), then the London OLD VIC (1953–61), where his leading Shakespearean roles included Romeo, Richard II, Mark Antony and, alternating with RICHARD BURTON, Othello and Iago. He appeared in the opening production of the CHICHESTER FESTIVAL (1962) and from 1963 to 1967 was joint and then sole director of the NOTTINGHAM Playhouse Company in its new theatre. He created national interest there, stimulating a new energy in other centres outside London. After emigrating to Canada in 1972, he took leading acting and directing assignments with the companies where he was artistic director: Citadel Theater (Edmonton, Alberta),

Neptune Theater (Halifax, Nova Scotia), and the STRATFORD FESTIVAL (Ontario).   DAVID STAINES

Robert A. Gaines, *John Neville Takes Command* (1987)
J. C. Trewin, *John Neville* (1961)

New Amsterdam Theater   Built by Klaw and Erlanger to serve as their flagship, it was designed in ornate fashion by Herts and Tallant, and opened in 1903 with *A Midsummer Night's Dream*. The playhouse's success helped establish 42nd Street as New York's main theatrical area. Although the theatre's last legitimate attraction was *Othello* in 1937, it served primarily to house large MUSICALS, including most of the ZIEGFELD FOLLIES, *The Merry Widow* (1907), *Sally* (1920) and *The Band Wagon* (1931). Its roof garden housed a cabaret. From 1937 to the late 1980s it was a film house, then was closed for restoration to full glory as a legitimate theatre in 1997.   GERALD BORDMAN

Mary C. Henderson, *The New Amsterdam: The Biography of a Theatre* (1997)

new circus   *see* CIRCUS

New Dramatists   The oldest non-profit workshop for American playwrights, founded in 1949 by Micaela O'Hara. Three to five writers annually are admitted to membership and receive the support of a professional staff for five years. Over 100 readings each year, professionally cast and directed, allow development of scripts without commercial pressures. Other programmes include a composer–librettist studio, a national script distribution service, a Playwrights' Press for non-profit publication of new plays for sale at performances, loan and travel grant funds, temporary lodging in New York, and a theatre library. Among those who have been helped are WILLIAM INGE, ED BULLINS, LANFORD WILSON, JOHN GUARE, MEGAN TERRY, MARIA IRENE FORNES, AUGUST WILSON and PADDY CHAYEFSKY.
FELICIA HARDISON LONDRÉ

New Haven (Connecticut)   In the 1950 film *All About Eve*, the scheming Eve Harrington – after clawing her way to the top – launches her acting career in a play opening at the Shubert Theater in New Haven. At the time the film opened, New Haven, less than 100 miles from New York, was a major try-out city for plays headed to BROADWAY. The Shubert Theater, created in 1914 by the SHUBERT brothers, housed the premières of such classics as *Oklahoma!* (entitled *Away We Go* when it opened in New Haven in 1943), *A Streetcar Named Desire* (1947), *My Fair Lady* (1955) and *Long Day's Journey into Night* (1956). The title of Joseph Heller's 1968 anti-war novel and play, *We Bombed in New Haven*, puns on the importance New York producers placed on this city as a testing ground. Although no longer a try-out theatre, the restored Shubert still presents road tours of plays and musicals.

Two New Haven theatres which were created during the American regional theatre movement in the 1960s present new work as well as classics. LONG WHARF THEATER was founded in 1965 by Jon Jory and Harlan Kleiman in New Haven's Meat and Produce Terminal. Two years later, Arvin Brown took over as artistic director, and continued to run the theatre for 30 years with the help of executive director M. Edgar Rosenblum. It has a 480-seat thrust main stage and a 199-seat 'black box' Stage II. Transfers to Broadway and OFF-BROADWAY include *Broken Glass*, *The Changing Room*, *Sizwe Banzi Is Dead*, *The Gin Game*, *Quartermaine's Terms*, *The Shadow Box* and revivals of *All My Sons*, *American Buffalo*, *A View from the Bridge* and *Requiem for a Heavyweight*. In 1997 Douglas Hughes, former associate artistic director for the SEATTLE REPERTORY THEATER, became artistic director, with Michael Ross as managing director. Long Wharf has received a Tony Award for Outstanding Regional Theatre, and three plays which premièred there have received a Pulitzer Prize, including *Wit* by Margaret Edson in 1999.

In 1966 ROBERT BRUSTEIN, dean of the Yale School of Drama, formed Yale Repertory Theater, a professional company in residence at the school. (The drama department at Yale University was founded in 1925 by GEORGE PIERCE BAKER; it became a graduate school in 1955.) Brustein served as artistic director until 1979, and moved Yale Rep into a 487-seat converted church, while continuing the use of the 654-seat University Theatre. LLOYD RICHARDS was artistic director from 1979 to 1991 and premièred all of AUGUST WILSON's plays, including *Ma Rainey's Black Bottom* and *Fences*, as well as staging several US premières of ATHOL FUGARD's plays, including *Master Harold and the Boys* and *The Road to Mecca*. Stan Wojewodski Jr, artistic director since 1991, introduced the work of playwrights Suzan-Lori Parks and Eric Overmeyer as well as the MINNEAPOLIS-based company Théâtre de la Jeune Lune. Yale Rep also received a Tony Award for Outstanding Regional Theater.

New Haven's smaller theatres continue to thrive; they include Elm Shakespeare, an outdoor Shakespeare company run by artistic director James Andreassi, and the New England Actors Theatre headed by Jerry Prell. The International Festival of Arts and Ideas, started in New Haven by Anne Calabresi, Jean Handley and Roz Meyer in 1996, has grown in artistic calibre and audience size. SARI BODI

new variety It differs from traditional VARIETY both structurally and economically, although the form remains similar. Incorporating all the associated theatrical skills, not just STAND-UP COMEDY, it addresses modern issues and rejects the jingoism, sexism and racism of its forebear. Acts are expected to be able to perform for at least 15–20 minutes as there are rarely more than six acts on any bill. Its greatest achievement is the re-opening of the HACKNEY EMPIRE by Hackney New Variety in 1986. The political touring group CAST set up a new variety format in the 1960s, utilizing light shows, bands, poetry and theatre, having realized the popular format while working on old time MUSIC HALL at UNITY THEATRE. In 1982 CAST started new variety at an old music hall beside the Old White Horse public house in London. Local government funding sustained the artists, enabling them to become professional. Through the artists' own efforts a national circuit of variety and CABARET venues was established, although this had a tendency to focus too specifically on stand-up comedy (e.g. the Comedy Store in London, founded in 1979, where the likes of Alexei Sayle, Ben Elton and Rik Mayall learnt their craft).

ROLAND MULDOON

See also NEW VAUDEVILLE; POLITICAL THEATRE.

new vaudeville The term first appeared in the late 1980s to describe an eclectic group of performers enamoured of the American popular theatre. While some performers and critics resist this label, 'new vaudeville' does capture something about a particularly American fascination with its own theatrical history, and indeed history itself. Coming out of the Reagan era, new vaudevillians revealed an unfashionable political optimism that critics quickly identified with the 1960s. And to be sure, new vaudevillians use experimental theatre COLLECTIVES from that wide-open decade – the SAN FRANCISCO MIME TROUPE, BREAD AND PUPPET THEATER, PERFORMANCE GROUP and HERBERT BLAU's Kraken – as a palette. They are also inspired, however, by *COMMEDIA DELL'ARTE*, the CIRCUS, VAUDEVILLE, CARNIVAL and MEDICINE SHOWS. Abandoning psychological realism for AGITPROP, new vaudevillians, from the macabre, high-flying comics Penn and Teller to the homespun, guitar-strumming story teller Stephen Wade, clown and fly and leap and hurdle and shout their way towards a kind of staged democracy – yet they are as much influenced by BECKETT as by ODETS. These inventive artists present alienated loners, confessional circuses and woeful American anti-heroes through the prism of physical theatre. Indeed, new vaudevillians deploy physical feats to unmask their loneliness. Using juggling, plate spinning, unicycling, slap dancing, stilt walking, banjo playing, puppetry and ventriloquism, as well as techniques like Chaplin's slapstick pratfalls and Keaton's deadpan walk, they seek to amaze their audience, all the while creating heroic stories about the consoling sadness of American life. The Pickle Family Circus, the Flying Karamozov Brothers and the Big Apple Circus, for example, imagine postmodern circuses in which tragicomedies emerge in the crevice where character and derring-do meet. (The acrobat falls in love with the beautiful dancer, who is in love with the cruel ringmaster.) Similarly, virtuoso SOLO performers like BILL IRWIN and Avner the Eccentric invent apocalyptic moments in which dehumanizing modern life threatens to crush the happy–sad clown. Monologists like Spalding Gray and Paul Zaloom have updated storytelling in a similar fashion; anticipating the confessional theatre of the 1990s, these melancholy garrulous performers talk to bring late twentieth-century life's absurdities into sharp focus and to stave off its horror. While modernist geniuses like BRECHT, MEYERHOLD and COCTEAU as well as Beckett used the popular theatre to animate their plays, new vaudevillians, less interested in talk than movement, stage high-wire acts and 'business' itself as a gestural language. Telling parables of failure and success, of love lost and won, they are squarely in the American tradition, the slapstick ARTHUR MILLERS and soft-shoe DAVID MAMETS of their time. RACHEL SHTEIR

R. Jenkins, *Acrobats of the Soul* (1988)

New York City America's spiritual and sometimes practical centre. From the turn of the century until the 1920s, theatre in New York combined two distinct threads: comedy (simple humorous plays and VAUDEVILLE) and theatre from Europe. The plays from Europe had gained recognition first in their countries of origin and were picked up by American producers who brought them to New York, often with the star who had created the leading role. After a New York run, these plays would then tour the country. In the 1920s the MOSCOW ART THEATRE introduced the work of playwrights CHEKHOV and GORKY. It also brought with it its approach to acting, the METHOD of STANISLAVSKY, whose disciple, Polish-born RICHARD BOLESLAVSKY first taught the technique at his American Laboratory Theater. It became the basis, along with a conviction (promulgated by CLIFFORD ODETS) that theatre could engage politics, of the GROUP THEATER, started in 1932. Joined by ORSON WELLES' MERCURY THEATER, with commercial hits by NOËL COWARD, KAUFMAN and FERBER, and S. N. BEHRMAN, this was theatre in the 1930s. Vaudeville continued its tradition through the 1920s with the annual George White FOL-

LIES and the early years of musical comedy, featuring George and Ira GERSHWIN, the entire FIELDS family, IRVING BERLIN and then in the 1940s RICHARD ROGERS and LORENZ HART, followed by Rodgers and OSCAR HAMMERSTEIN. The 1940s ushered in LEE STRASBERG's ACTORS' STUDIO (his interpretation of the Stanislavsky acting technique) and playwrights TENNESSEE WILLIAMS and ARTHUR MILLER, who dominated the stage through the 1950s. There was also a strong representation of French theatre in this decade (ANOUILH, GIRAUDOUX, IONESCO), and LEONARD BERNSTEIN collaborated with STEPHEN SONDHEIM to write the best musicals of the era (*Candide*, *West Side Story*). The 1960s brought EDWARD ALBEE and, through the influence of the ROYAL COURT, the ANGRY YOUNG MEN of England. Though 'straight' plays were still produced on BROADWAY – NEIL SIMON carrying the torch for the next three decades – OFF-BROADWAY became the more viable venue. With anti-Vietnam unrest, the 1960s gave New York HAPPENINGS, performed in unconventional spaces, and theatre of protest, which brought American politics to the stage and enabled the existence of angry black theatre (the NEGRO ENSEMBLE COMPANY). Economics changed the face of theatre in the 1970s. To economize, not-for-profit (tax-exempt) theatres proliferated, generating such future bastions as JOSEPH PAPP's NEW YORK SHAKESPEARE FESTIVAL, the MANHATTAN THEATER CLUB and PLAYWRIGHTS HORIZONS (described as OFF-OFF BROADWAY), with Broadway the almost exclusive home of musical theatre (dominated by Stephen Sondheim and HAL PRINCE). Papp also contributed the musical *A Chorus Line* to Broadway. Of particular significance, after this historical transfer, was that commercial producers would look almost exclusively to the nonprofit world as their fishing ground, as the best place to develop and prove new work. The 1980s yielded playwright DAVID MAMET, the 1990s playwright TONY KUSHNER; Broadway musicals, when new, were spawned in theatres across the country, or were restagings of old favourites or new contributions by England's ANDREW LLOYD WEBBER.
PEREGRINE WHITTLESEY

M. Henderson, *The City and the Theater* (1973)

New York Public Library The Library established the Theatre Collection for research in the performing arts in 1931. The division embraces stage, cinema, radio and television, as well as other forms of popular entertainment. Emphasis is on production rather than literary content, and includes personalities and organizations. Holdings are heavily weighted towards nonbook materials: typescripts and promptbooks, programmes, scrapbooks, reviews and other press cuttings, personal papers and archives; also costume and scenic renderings, prints and photographs, posters and, since 1970, videotapes of live theatrical performances. In 1979, the division was named the BILLY ROSE Theatre Collection in recognition of a gift from the Billy Rose Foundation.   DOROTHY L. SWERDLOVE

See also RECORDING AND RESEARCHING THEATRE.

New York Public Library, Research Libraries, *Catalog of the Theatre and Drama Collections*, Parts I–III, 51 vols (1967–76). *Part I: Drama Collection* (1967); *Part II: Books on the Theatre* (1967); *Part III: Non-Book Collection* (1976). Parts I and II are continued in *First Supplements* (1973) and thereafter in annual *Bibliographic Guides to Theatre Arts*.

New York Shakespeare Festival   Founded in 1954 by JOSEPH PAPP at Emanuel Presbyterian Church, NYSF has grown to become America's largest single theatrical institution and has been the recipient of more than 150 awards. Since 1957 the festival's free open-air summer productions of Shakespeare have been performed in Central Park, at first on a portable stage and from 1962 at its permanent home, the Delacorte Theater. In 1967, NYSF established the PUBLIC THEATER with five auditoriums to diversify its repertoire. Opening with *Hair*, it went on to present new and classic plays: *No Place to be Somebody* (1970), *Sticks and Bones* (1971), *That Championship Season* (1972), *A Chorus Line* (1975), *For colored girls who have considered suicide / when the rainbow is enuf* (1976), *The Marriage of Bette and Boo* (1985), *Aunt Dan and Lemon* (1986), *The Colored Museum* (1986) and *Fires in the Mirror* (1991). In 1982 it founded the Festival Latino de Nueva York. It ran a Young Playwrights festival as well as a fruitful exchange with the ROYAL COURT, London, which brought DAVID HARE (*Plenty*, 1983) and CARYL CHURCHILL (*Top Girls*, 1983) to New York and to London LARRY KRAMER (*The Normal Heart*, 1986). Other companies also visit. JOANNE AKALAITIS from MABOU MINES became artistic director after Papp's death in 1991, but was sacked in 1993, to be succeeded by former NYSF writer-in-residence GEORGE C. WOLFE.

MARIAN J. PRINGLE

New Zealand   For most of its first 100 years New Zealand was frequently described as the 'Britain of the South'; for those who were of British descent, the majority of the population, Britain was 'Home'. Yet as New Zealand approached its sesquicentenary in 1990 its mixed population of indigenous MAORI people, Europeans descended from the early settlers and recent immigrants began a process of re-assessment. Inevitably the theatre played a role in this evolution from

British colony to independent PACIFIC nation. As New Zealanders have sought to find and define a national identity, theatre has become increasingly diverse, both reflecting and initiating change. No longer can it be said, as it was in the 1950s, that the country's theatrical ideal would be a permanent tour of NOEL COWARD's *Private Lives*! As elsewhere, the development of theatre has been directed as much by the expectations of audiences as by the creative talents of those involved in the various aspects of theatre. The small size of the country's population (three and a half million), and its distribution in widely dispersed, often relatively inaccessible small centres, have also been determining factors.

Theatrical performances began in Auckland, Wellington and Nelson in the 1840s, usually as popular entertainment for hotel patrons. Most plays were eurocentric in content, although Lawrence Booth's *Crime in the Clouds* (1871) included New Zealand material and Maori actors in stereotypical roles and events. From the 1850s overseas companies such as Mr and Mrs W. H. Foley, the Australian J. C. Williamson's and Allan Wilkie's Shakespeare Company, and actors like Julius Knight presented a variety of plays including IBSEN, WILDE, Shakespeare and PINERO, as well as musicals. VAUDEVILLE and VARIETY flourished. There was also some locally written and produced theatre, such as *The Land of the Moa*, an 1895 melodrama by George Leitch, and the enormously popular comedy opera by Syd Ribbands, with music by Archie Don, *Marama: The Mere and the Maori Maid* in 1920. By the late 1920s, however, the motion pictures had made their mark, and English, American and Australian tours were rare. Whereas *Marama* had benefited from a surge of national pride and optimism after the First World War, other local attempts at professional theatre in the 1920s, such as the English Comedy Company, inevitably failed as a result of high costs and a small population. The amateur theatre of the various local societies and Country Women's Institutes developed rapidly to fill the vacuum, receiving considerable impetus from the establishment in 1932 of a branch of the BRITISH DRAMA LEAGUE, later merged with the New Zealand Drama Council to form a New Zealand Theatre Federation. The following year *The Wind and the Rain*, by a New Zealand doctor, Merton Hodge, later dubbed 'The English Chekhov', opened its three-year run in London followed by considerable success in New York, Paris and Berlin.

Back home, however, apart from the popularity of the Drama League's one-act playwriting competitions, the flourishing amateur societies generally showed little interest in performing full-length indigenous drama. There were exceptions, such as Allen Curnow's verse drama of 1948, *The Axe*, which attempted deliberately 'to place New Zealand at the centre'. The same year the visit of the OLD VIC Company with LAURENCE OLIVIER and VIVIEN LEIGH raised theatrical consciousness.

Immigrants from Europe like Maria Dronke brought new expertise combined with a social and political commitment. Slowly, through the efforts of such groups as Wellington's Unity Theatre (1942), which produced what BRUCE MASON called 'socially committed' plays by such writers as O'CASEY, MILLER and BRECHT, New Zealand plays by Bruce Mason, JAMES K. BAXTER, Campbell Caldwell, Claude Evans and others became accepted. Unity continued to challenge the social and dramatic status quo for over 30 years. The Canterbury College Drama Society under Ngaio Marsh had built a solid reputation for performance beyond just Christchurch. Newly emerged from the experiences of the Second World War, New Zealanders learned the reality of their isolation from Britain: the ties to the mother country were no longer so necessary or so binding as formerly. Inevitably there was now talk of a national theatre, particularly with the success of Ngaio Marsh's Commonwealth Players in New Zealand and Australia.

Amateur theatre continued to flourish in the 1950s, but what limited enthusiasm there had been for indigenous drama dwindled still further; theatregoers wanted light comedy, not social criticism. Unity's production of *The Trap* by New Zealander Kathleen Ross won the Drama League festival in 1951, but its subject, a deserted mother and an unmarried pregnant daughter, made it difficult to cast and unpopular with audiences. Even the generally lighter, more romantic plays of Claude Evans enjoyed only limited popularity. A major step towards a professional national theatre came in 1953, when Richard and Edith CAMPION, returning to New Zealand after three years in London with the Old Vic School, founded the New Zealand Players. This professional company toured New Zealand for seven years. Among its members was RAYMOND BOYCE, a young Briton who has become the most influential designer in New Zealand's theatre history. The company gave New Zealand a kind of theatre that it had not seen before. In 1960, after the Campions themselves had withdrawn from the Company, the Players closed. However, its Schools Quartet, founded by Richard Campion to train young actors and stimulate interest in the theatre, continued for 17 years, bequeathing a permanent legacy of skills and enthusiasm through its young audiences. Much had been gained, but the dream of a national theatre was over. New Zealand at this point was very far from Aus-

tralia's 1955 theatrical milestone, the Elizabethan Theatre Trust's production of RAY LAWLER's *Summer of the Seventeenth Doll* – an Australian play by an Australian author with an Australian cast which had been a resounding success in every way. Nevertheless, if the most fundamental requirement for the growth of theatre in a country is the writing and production of indigenous drama which delineates the character of that country, there had been some significant steps. The Players had performed not only Shakespeare, SHAW and ANOUILH but also, in 1959, *The Tree* by Stella Jones (premièred in Bristol, 1957). This was the first time a New Zealand play had reached such a wide audience. But far more significant was *The Pohutukawa Tree*, written for the Players in 1956 by Bruce Mason – critic, essayist, actor, playwright and a prominent figure until his death in 1982. A widely used text in schools for many years, it was a landmark work, exploring the different attitudes and heritage of Maori and European New Zealanders, long before these issues were part of the national consciousness. Also in 1956 one of the country's most colourful figures, the poet James K. Baxter, wrote *Jack Winter's Dream* for radio (later followed by a stage and film version), while in 1959 Richard Campion, who remained a vital figure in New Zealand theatre in the 1980s, directed Baxter's next important play, *The Wide Open Cage*, for Wellington's Unity. Although Baxter's plays were not flawless, they were genuine theatrical experiences. The relationship between Baxter and Patric and Rosalie Carey at their amateur Globe Theatre in Dunedin was particularly productive. Mason, on the other hand, disillusioned, turned to solo performance. His *End of the Golden Weather*, a dramatic evocation of New Zealand childhood set performance records throughout the country and was adapted by Ian Mune into an award-winning feature film (1992).

As the New Zealand Broadcasting Corporation developed its production facilities in the 1960s it became, under the guidance of William Austin, a vitally important factor in the development of New Zealand theatre, providing training, employment, encouragement and income for writers and actors. This continued despite limited production facilities and reductions in staff during the late 1980s and early 1990s, but diminished considerably by the end of the century. The New Zealand Drama School (later Toi Whakari) was founded in 1970 by the Queen Elizabeth II Arts Council; under Nola Millar, one of the founders of Unity who was closely associated with the New Zealand Players, the New Zealand Theatre Federation and the semi-professional New Theatre, it ensured professional theatre training while also indicating a growing recognition of the importance of theatre. Whereas for many years aspiring actors had no choice but to study overseas or seek one of the limited number of New Zealand Drama School places, education and training opportunities increased in the late 1980s and 1990s as universities, polytechnics and private training establishments competed to offer a wide variety of courses in performance, design and theatre studies.

Since 1960 the government has contributed some financial support to theatre, mainly through the regional Arts Councils and the Queen Elizabeth II Arts Council, later Creative New Zealand, and some specific funding for Maori and Pacific theatre. Corporate funding and sponsorship have also become increasingly important, although less available following the stock-market collapse of 1987.

After the demise of the Players, New Zealand's professional theatre developed on a regional basis. Wellington's DOWNSTAGE, the FORTUNE in Dunedin, the COURT in Christchurch and CENTREPOINT at Palmerston North are small, intimate theatres, while Auckland's MERCURY, which closed in 1992, had a far larger seating capacity. These regional theatres were expected to operate at a profit in order to qualify for government assistance, but understandably their relative funding stability has been contested by newer theatrical ventures.

Wellington has always enjoyed a particularly strong amateur theatre, notably through the Unity Theatre (1942–78) and the larger but more conservative Wellington Repertory. The location here of the national drama school, the School of Dance, central television and radio studios helped to make Wellington, with its concentration of small professional theatres, the country's most varied and active theatrical centre. CIRCA THEATRE, founded in 1976 by a group of established Wellington actors, many of whom had started with Unity and associated with Downstage, soon gained national recognition with the record-breaking productions of ROGER HALL's *Glide Time* (1976) and *Middle Age Spread* (1977) and Greg McGee's *Foreskin's Lament* (1980). Some of New Zealand's best-known actors, like GRANT TILLY, RAY HENWOOD, Alice Fraser and CATHY DOWNES, work regularly with Circa. In its early years it encouraged the performance of plays by women, such as *The Revenge of the Amazons* (1983) by Jean Betts and Sarah Delahunty's *Stretchmarks* (1985), and New Zealand plays by writers such as Roger Hall, Joseph Musaphia and ROBERT LORD. In 1999 it was the venue for the International Magdalena Aotearoa festival. Wellington's Depot, founded by Downstage, later the Depot-Taki Rua Theatre, was run as an autonomous collective with a commitment to New Zealand drama,

music and dance, commissioning plays by RENEE, James Beaumont and Rore Hapipi (Rowley Habib). It actively encourages Maori and Polynesian theatre (Te Whakarite Theatre Company, Te Ohu Whaakari, Te Kari Kari o te Rangatahi, Taiao, Nga Toa and Te Ika Maui). The tiny Bats theatre was established in 1988 as a venue for the work of young actors, writers and directors, many of whom were NZ Drama School graduates. Nearly all the productions here have been New Zealand works. The theatre also runs the annual Young and Hungry season of new plays performed by young actors as well as housing many of the annual fringe festival performances. Many plays have found national recognition, such as Ken Duncan's *Blue Sky Boys* (1991) about an imagined tour of the Everly Brothers to Wellington in 1964, when the Beatles were there too, and the farce *The Sex Fiend* (1989) by Stephen Sinclair and Danny Mulheron. The latter, along with *Ladies Night* (Stephen Sinclair and Anthony McCarten), featured among the comedies with which young playwrights won extraordinary popular success in attracting non-traditional audiences at the end of the 1980s.

Auckland, a very different city with a widespread population of over one and a half million, was for over 20 years until 1992 the home of the country's largest professional theatre, the Mercury. Auckland has also suffered from the closing of Theatre Corporate, an influential company with a distinctive style, and a lack of theatrical venues for more recently formed companies like Tantrum and The Watershed. Recent developments in Auckland have included the completion of the multi-million-dollar Aotea centre and the Bruce Mason Centre, and the success of the Auckland Theatre Company, directed by Simon Prast. Relocation of the major television drama studios to Auckland will probably generate more theatrical activity and interest, and further fuel the parochial arguments between Aucklanders and Wellingtonians on their respective cities' cultural lives.

Although in the 1960s and early 1970s a considerable number of New Zealand plays were performed before responsive audiences, the staging of Roger Hall's comedy *Glide Time* at Circa attracted record audiences. Its phenomenal success proved that thousands of New Zealanders could laugh at themselves and would support local drama without any sense of 'cultural cringe'. In the country which invented the welfare state all would recognize, in some way, the bureaucrats who bumble through Hall's play. His next, *Middle Age Spread*, exposed the sterility of New Zealand suburbia equally effectively, although in its successful London production any reference to New Zealand was removed.

McGee's *Foreskin's Lament* (Theatre Corporate) provided another theatrical milestone, attracting large new audiences throughout the country. Written by a former All Black triallist at a time when New Zealand was confronting the controversial issue of a Springbok rugby tour, it not only exposed the myths of rugby but challenged its audiences in a wider sense. New Zealanders have continued to try to answer McGee's challenge 'Whaddarya?', to define themselves and their country, and many more plays have been written and performed as part of this quest. The Victoria University Press, assisted by the Literary Fund, has published many plays. Playmarket's 1988 Directory lists 192 playwrights and 276 full-length plays, although many of these have not yet had a professional production. Established in 1973 with the assistance of Downstage, Playmarket is supported by the Arts Council and Victoria University. The country's principal playwrights' agency, it publishes plays in low-cost format, provides script assessment, and organizes readings and national and local workshops. University writing fellowships, the Writers in Residence scheme, awards and commissions have provided further much-needed encouragement in recent years.

As is natural in a country that is still seeking to define its national identity, many plays have dealt with specific historical events; these include MERVYN THOMPSON's popular songplay *O! Temperance!* (1972) about the days of Prohibition; Maurice Shadbolt's *Once On Chunuk Bair* (1982); *The Case of Katherine Mansfield*, a 1979 Edinburgh Festival award winner about the life and work of Katherine Mansfield, devised and performed by Cathy Downes, which has toured throughout New Zealand and extensively overseas; and Renée's movingly powerful drama about the Depression, *Wednesday to Come* (1984), and its sequel. Similarly, STUART HOAR's *Squatter* (1987) examines political attitudes in an historical setting, while a little-known incident involving the killing of Japanese prisoners during the Second World War, provided VINCENT O'SULLIVAN with the chance to confront his 1980s audiences with questions of cultural and racial difference in an innovative style in *Shuriken* (1983). The Japanese tour of *Shuriken* following its 1995 Hamilton production reactivated controversy surrounding the play, and questions of war, peace and forgiveness. This questioning of social values and attitudes has continued, from a different perspective, in the work of Maori writers and directors.

Although some New Zealand playwrights – such as James K. Baxter, Craig Harrison, Robert Lord, Bruce Mason, Joseph Musaphia, Vincent O'Sullivan, Renée, Mervyn Thompson, BRIAR GRACE-SMITH, HONE KOUKA, LORAE PARRY – have been successful with a number of plays, relatively few have produced an integrated, substantial body of significant work. Hall, criticized by some as populist and intellectually unchallenging, remains New Zealand's best-known and most successful playwright.

More sophisticated overseas visitors have frequently commented on New Zealand as a nation of resourceful 'do-it-yourselfers'. New Zealand theatre has similarly always been characterized by an independent energy and creative initiative. This has resulted in remarkable individual innovation and versatility, a continuing strong tradition of amateur theatre in country districts, towns and cities, and a considerable amount of strong experimental theatre. Many of these ALTERNATIVE COLLECTIVES, often generating their own scripts in rehearsal, have been fairly short-lived. The Amamus theatre group and its successor Theatre of the Eighth Day, with its founder–director Paul Maunder, was particularly influential in respect of social commitment and a deliberately confrontational style. Alan Brunton and Sally Rodwell's Red Mole has provided an anarchic mixture of comedy and social comment. Some of the most entertaining and innovative theatre in Auckland and Wellington has come from groups such as Inside-Out, Theatre at Large, Front Lawn and Trouble. Other theatrical forms – CLOWNS, acrobats, PUPPET and stilt theatre – have received greater recognition in recent years with further impetus from the establishment of the Festival Fringe at Wellington's bi-annual New Zealand International Festival of the Arts.

By 1990 New Zealand was a very different country from even 20 years earlier. Auckland has one of the largest concentrations of Polynesian people in the world, and by the end of the century a third of its population would be Polynesian. The Maori language and culture have undergone a dramatic renaissance; the *hikoi* (Maori Land Marches) of the 1970s and 1980s and the subsequent reappraisal of, and commitment to, the Treaty of Waitangi signed in 1840 between representatives of Queen Victoria and Maori, have profound implications for all New Zealanders. This has been increasingly, if slowly, reflected in the country's theatre, bringing indigenous traditions into a new, imaginative relationship with the traditions, facilities, styles and inventiveness of European theatre and a questioning of social values and attitudes.

After Mason's *The Pohutukawa Tree*, his *Awatea* (1965) was written for radio for the great Maori bass Inia te Wiata, who subsequently acted in its first stage production. Subsequently other *pakeha* writers – New Zealanders of European descent, such as Craig Harrison with *The Whites of their Eyes* (1974) and *Tomorrow Will Be a Lovely Day* (1974), and Vincent O'Sullivan's *Shuriken* – challenged *pakeha* New Zealanders' attitudes to Maori people. Though Mason wrote other plays exploring Maori themes, he kept his early promise that he would stop once Maori playwrights themselves were ready to dramatize the experiences and concerns of their people. This was first achieved by writers like Rore Hapipi, Hone Tuwhare and Renée, since joined by others including Hone Kouka, Briar Grace-Smith, John Broughton, Rawiri Paratene, Riwia Brown, Rena Owen and Bruce Stewart. Further incentive has been provided by the achievement of actors like GEORGE HENARE, Kima te Wiata, Nancy Brunning and Rena Owen, directors (Don Selwyn, Jim Moriarty, Roma Potiki, Rangimoana Taylor, Apirana Taylor) and Radio New Zealand workshops. The success of films such as *Once Were Warriors*, *Ngati* and *Ufa*, Maori and South Pacific Arts Council funding, and several television series by Maori writers commissioned by Television New Zealand, the NZ Film Commission and Manu Aute (a Maori media collective) have contributed to further development. For the 1990 International Festival of the Arts, Wellington's Depot became a *marae* — an open area that forms the physical and spiritual centre of the community – for the performance of Maori theatre such as Hone Tuwhare's *In the Wilderness without a Hat*. Certainly the expectations and possibilities of theatre have been extended considerably in recent years by the concept of *marae* theatre, and by major events such as the opera *Waituhi: The Life of the Village*, by short-story writer and novelist Witi Ihimaera, with music by Ross Harris, and Jenny McLeod's *Earth and Sky* – the presentation of Maori myth in a fusion of drama, dance and music. Another development has been the occasional translation into Maori of existing texts, such as Don Selwyn's 1990 production of *The Merchant of Venice*, translated by Pei Te Hurinui. A major event was the performance by Jim Moriarty of John Broughton's *Michael James Manaia* (Downstage, 1991) at the Edinburgh Festival. Major groups have included Te Ohu Whakaari (the Indigenous Theatre Company of Aotearoa) and Taiao. *Le Matau* by Stephen Sinclair and Samson Samasoni (Depot, 1984), which movingly explored the social adjustment confronting Pacific Island immigrants, indicated another direction for New Zealand theatre. New Zealand's increasing ethnic diversity is reflected in Jacob Rajan's sellout *Krishnan's Dairy*, also performed at the Edinburgh Festival, and *The Candlestick Maker* (2000); the award-winning *Tzigane* (1996) by John Vakidis, a European immigrant; the work of Linda Chanwai Earle (*Ga Shui* and *The Box*); and Pacific

writers like Oscar Kightley and popular groups such as The Naked Samoans.

Another striking dramatic feature on the theatrical landscape is the creative vitality and success of women's theatre, beginning with strongly political aims expressed through feminist productions at the United Women's Conventions in 1973 and 1977. From the early days of Mrs Foley women have claimed a significant place in New Zealand theatre, despite difficulties. Over the second half of the twentieth century Edith Campion, Davina Whitehouse, Dame Pat Evison, Yvette Bromley, Elizabeth Moody, Yvonne Lawley, Alma Woods, Dorothy McKegg and Alice Fraxer have made major contributions; but considerable frustration has been felt by many women actors at their lack of administrative power and the shortage of significant women's roles in the established mainstream theatre. Further developments included a Circa season of women's plays in 1979–80, Lorae Parry's *Strip*, Cathy Downes's *Sweet Corn* and Jean Betts's *The Revenge of the Amazons*, the formation of a number of women's theatre groups, such as Cactus Theatre, Bandana, Hen's Teeth, The Women's Equity Caucus and the WOPPA (Women Professional Playwrights' Association) Festival in 1993 with Vivienne Plumb's *Love Knots*, *Farewell Speech* (Cathy Downes), *Lashings of Whipped Cream* (Fiona Samuels), *Ophelia Thinks Harder* (Jean Betts), *Cracks* (Lorae Parrey). The response to these plays by women, and by others such as Renée, Sarah Delahunty, Carolyn Burns (*Objection Overruled*, Court, 1982), Michelanne Forster, Jo Randerson, Briar Grace-Smith, Hilary Beaton and Riwia Brown has provided further encouragement. Feature films and television series written, produced and directed by women – notably Jane Campion (*Angel at My Table*, *The Piano* and *Holy Smoke*), Gaylene Preston (*Mr Wrong*) and Melanie Reed (*Trial Run*) – have also encouraged the increasingly wide, successful involvement and achievement of women in theatre. Certainly by the time of the International MAGDALENA Aotearoa Festival which brought performers to Circa from all over the world, the place of women in New Zealand theatre is very different from 1907, when the Taylor Carrington Company's production of *Is She Guiltless?* was hailed as the 'Best Ladies' Drama ever staged in Dunedin'.

Although some New Zealanders may feel that their theatre is increasingly rich and diverse, others have criticized professional theatres for a failure to market theatre effectively and to stimulate indigenous drama. Some, like Greg McGee, disenchanted with the theatrical establishment, turned mainly to television; also, just as New Zealand opera singers Kiri Te Kanawa, Donald McIntyre, Heather Begg and Nicola Ferner

Waite are based overseas, so many writers, actors and directors now live and work elsewhere; these include Barbara Ewing, Sam Neill, Catherine Wilkin, Lisa Harrow and Temuera Morrison.

Government-owned television and its private competitors have provided considerable if uneven employment for many involved in the theatre through drama series such as *Close to Home*, *Gliding On* (adapted from *Glide Time*), *Shark in the Park* and American-funded series such as *Xena, Warrior Princess* (starring New Zealander Lucy Lawless), some outstanding children's television drama, and *Gloss* – New Zealand's answer to *Dallas* – and later soaps. Argument has continued over the years about the desirability of a quota system for television and radio and equity of funding for Maori performance. Major films by Jane Campion, Vincent Ward, Robert and Duncan Sarkies and, particularly, Peter Jackson (*Lord of the Rings*) have provided further potential employment for actors, writers and others trained in the theatre.

Rapidly rising travel costs and the country's slow economic recovery have made commercial touring increasingly risky. As a result rural districts and cities other than Auckland, Wellington, Palmerston North, Christchurch and Dunedin now seldom see professional theatre, but are generally well served by amateur theatre of a high standard. Exceptions to this generally occur only when a play or musical can be guaranteed a commercially successful tour because of association with a popular television programme or star. The Wellington bi-annual International Festival of the Arts has also provided New Zealanders with the chance to enjoy international and indigenous theatre of a high standard. Whatever one's reservations, the fact remains that New Zealand theatre has become a vital, significant and influential part of national life. The 1990 National Playwrights' Conference expressed the view that lack of funding resulted in a reluctance to stage indigenous drama. Certainly, the country's swing to a market-driven, economic rationalist economy in the 1990s had considerable impact on government funding and company sponsorship for the arts. It can be argued that this has resulted in a more conservative and commercial approach to theatrical production in a highly competitive environment. The willingness of the Prime Minister also to take the arts portfolio, followed by an announcement of additional funding in 2000, may provide further impetus for New Zealand theatre.
GILLIAN GREER

Act: Theatre in New Zealand, 1967–1986
Laurie Atkinson, Pat Hawthorne and Judy Russell, eds, *Playmarket 1963–1994* (1995)

Peter Downes, *Shadows on the Stage: Theatre in New Zealand – The First 70 Years* (1975)
Peter Harcourt, *A Dramatic Appearance: New Zealand Theatre 1920–1970* (1978)
Hone Kouka, ed., *Ta Matou Mangai* (1999)
Howard McNaughton, *New Zealand Drama* (1981)
The Playmarket Directory of New Zealand Plays and Playwrights (1992)
Roger Robinson and Nelson Wattie, eds, *The Oxford Companion to New Zealand Literature* (1998)
Terry Sturm, ed., *The Oxford History of New Zealand Literature* (1991)
John Thomson, *New Zealand Drama 1930–1980: An Illustrated History* (1984)

New Zealand Players Company founded by Richard and Edith CAMPION on their return from Europe to New Zealand intent on establishing a national theatre. They aimed for professionalism, popular appeal and a commitment to touring from Whangarei in the north, to Invercargill in the far south. Fellow OLD VIC Theatre School graduate RAYMOND BOYCE was enlisted as the theatre's designer, and the Players opened with *The Young Elizabeth* in 1953. Other productions included Douglas Stewart's *Ned Kelly*, Ngaio Marsh's *A Unicorn for Christmas* and Stella Jones's *The Tree* (all New Zealand playwrights), as well as *Salad Days*, *Pygmalion* and Shakespeare. Standards remained high and attendances were good – over a million people in the first five years. Many of these joined the Audience Support Organization to billet the players. As intended, the Campions left the Players in 1956. Financial difficulties and other factors resulted in the company's collapse in 1960, but the Schools Drama Quartet continued for another 17 years and cleared much of the company's debt. The New Zealand Theatre Company, set up as a successor, was short-lived.
SIMON GARRETT & GILLIAN GREER

Newcastle upon Tyne A vibrant coastal city in England's north-east with its own proud 'Geordie' accent and culture, in 1788 it gained a Theatre Royal, which was demolished in the 1830s to make way for Grey Street, the site of a new (1837) and still current theatre bearing the same title. After fire damage the theatre was reconstructed and enlarged, and reopened in 1901. In 1973 it was purchased by the local council and, under the management of a trust, has become a major touring venue. Since 1977 it has hosted an annual residency by the ROYAL SHAKESPEARE COMPANY. In 1911 the amateur Clarion Dramatic Society was formed as an antidote to commercial fare; in 1915 it moved to new premises and in 1921 took the name the People's Theatre. It was devoted to serious, even controversial

547

drama; its first full-length play was SHAW's *Major Barbara*. It moved again in 1928 and later expanded to include an art gallery, cinema and restaurant. The Newcastle Playhouse was first named after FLORA ROBSON who appeared there in 1962 in EMLYN WILLIAMS' *The Corn is Green*. It was knocked down to allow road widening, and in 1968 was replaced by the University Theatre, housing the Tyneside Theatre Company and, from 1978 when the theatre was renamed the Playhouse, the Tyne and Wear Theatre Company. In 1987 the company moved to the Tyne Theatre and Opera House under the name Tyne Theatre Company. Two years later it moved again, to Newcastle Arts Centre, and changed its name again, this time to Northern Stage. In 1992 Alan Lyddiard was appointed its artistic director and, to complete the circle, the company moved back to the Playhouse and its Gulbenkian Studio, and became the largest producing theatre company in the north-east, touring regionally, nationally and internationally. In 1998 the company introduced an ensemble-led way of working and became known as Northern Stage Ensemble. It remained at the Playhouse, which also hosts a range of visitors including, along with the Theatre Royal, the RSC during its annual season. Among the Playhouse's noted productions are ALAN PLATER's *Close the Coalhouse Door* (1968) and C. P. TAYLOR's *And a Nightingale Sang . . .* (1979), which came out of the author's work with the Newcastle-based Live Theatre Company. Following Taylor's premature death in 1981 the company named its own theatre after him. CHARLES LONDON & LAUREN BISHOP

See also AMATEUR THEATRE.

Veitch, Norman, *The People's* (1950)

Newman, Paul *see* ACTORS' STUDIO; STRASBERG, LEE

Newson, Lloyd (b. Albury, NSW, Australia, 2 March 1957) Choreographer. After studying for a degree in psychology, Newson trained at the London Contemporary Dance School. He performed with Extemporary Dance Theatre (1981–5) before co-founding DV8 Physical Dance Theatre with Nigel Charnock with their piece *My Sex, Our Dance* (1986). Newson's works involve a highly theatrical dance language, integrating often violent dialogue and physically demanding performance, based around the exploration of issues of gender, sexuality and identity. Newson has achieved international success with pieces including *Dead Dreams of Monochrome Men* (1988), *Strange Fish* (1992) and *Enter Achilles* (1995), which have also been reworked for film. He devises his pieces through improvisation and movement research rather than working with texts or standard dance vocabulary, and has

worked with artists such as Wendy Houston, Russell Maliphant and Lauren Potter. He directed part of the opening ceremony for the 2000 Olympics in Sydney. MARTIN HARGREAVES

See also CHOREOGRAPHY; DANCE.

Ngema, Mbongeni (b. Umkumbane, Durban, South Africa, 1955) Playwright, composer, choreographer and director. With director Barney Simon and actor Peray Mtwa, he created and performed in *Woza Albert!* (MARKET THEATRE, 1981), one of the most internationally renowned plays to emerge from South Africa in the struggle against apartheid. Believing, however, that much of the POLITICAL THEATRE was bad theatre and allowed audiences, particularly in Europe, to patronize his country, he founded the Committed Artists theatre company in a Johannesburg warehouse in 1983, with the goal of training 'disadvantaged black South Africans in music, theatre and dance'. Following *Woza Albert!*, his work – e.g. *Asinamali* (1985), *Sarafina!* (1987) and *Township Fever!* (1990) – carried black South Africa's message of resistance abroad. In *Mama! The Musical of Freedom* he addresses the issue of what direction theatre should take after liberation. He celebrates the change in the country's politics with music, dance and humour, echoing the mixture of sounds heard in the townships. LAURIE WOLF

Laura Jones, *The Harsh Times and Bold Theatre of South Africa's Mbongeni Ngema* (1994)

Ngugi Wa Thiong'o [James T. Ngugi] (b. Kamiriithu, Kenya, 5 Jan. 1938) Novelist and playwright. Working through the Kamiriithu Community Education and Cultural Centre, Ngugi and his main collaborators – Micere Githae Mugo on *The Trial of Dedan Kimathi* (1984) in English, and Ngugi wa Mirii on *Ngaahika Ndeenda* (*I Will Marry When I Want*, 1977) in Kikuyu – attempted to put on plays that challenge the accepted wisdom of the Mau Mau insurrection and anti-colonial struggle and the traditional oppression of females. The government bulldozed the Centre and put Ngugi in prison in 1977–8. He now lives in exile in the United States. KOLE OMOTOSO

D. Cook and M. Okenimpke, *Ngugi Wa Thiong'o: An Exploration of His Writings* (1983)

Nicaragua *see* MEXICO AND CENTRAL AMERICA

Nichols, Mike [Michael Igor Peschkowsky] (b. Berlin, 6 Nov. 1931) Director and producer. After escaping Nazi Germany he studied at Chicago University and the ACTORS' STUDIO. He co-devised and performed in the successful *An Evening with Mike Nichols and Elaine May* (1959–60), a series of skits for BROAD-

WAY. From 1963 to 1971 he successfully staged NEIL SIMON's plays in New York. Later direction has been more serious: STOPPARD's *The Real Thing* (1983), RABE's *Hurlyburly* (1984), Ariel Dorfman's *Death and the Maiden* (1992). Major film direction includes *Who's Afraid of Virginia Woolf?* (1965), *The Graduate* (1968) and *Catch 22* (1970). Nichols co-produced the musical *Annie* (1977) and D. L. Coburn's *The Gin Game* (1977), which he also directed. NANCY SWORTZELL

Nichols, Peter [Richard] (b. Bristol, 31 July 1927) Playwright. A teacher and actor before writing television plays, Nichols came to prominence when he dramatized his family's relationship with their handicapped daughter in *A Day in the Death of Joe Egg* (1967), in which the characters use songs and music-hall routines to cope with their pain. Nichols developed this style in *The National Health* (1969), interweaving a television medical soap opera with death on an underfunded ward; *Privates on Parade* (1977), about an army concert party in Malaya just after the Second World War; and *Poppy* (1982), a pantomime 'satirizing' the Chinese Opium Wars. In contrasting style, *Passion Play* (1981) transforms the sex-comedy genre: *doppelgangers* speak the adulterers' secret thoughts. The autobiographical *Forget-Me-Not-Lane* (1971) and *A Piece of My Mind* (1987) are equally unsentimental and inventive. The NATIONAL THEATRE and the ROYAL SHAKESPEARE COMPANY between them have performed five of his plays. His television output and other stage work (e.g. *Chez Nous*, 1974; *Born in the Gardens*, 1980) also taps a broader vein. His *Diaries* were published in 2000. TONY HOWARD

Niger *see* FRENCH AFRICAN THEATRE

Nigeria Thanks to British political alchemy, what was once Britain's largest colony in Africa is made up of more than 250 ethnic groups, each with its own unique culture and language, though sharing certain cultural features. The main groups are the Yoruba, the Igbo, the Hausa, the Bini, the Ijo, the Kalabari, the Ibibio and the Efik. The Igbo, Yoruba and the Hausa are the biggest and so their respective languages are more often than not spoken by others. The problematic use of English for the Nigerian literary theatre gives it an international standing but more or less alienates it from the majority of Nigerians who are not proficient in English.

The curious mix of Nigerian society, with old traditional values coexisting with borrowed ones, is equally evident in the contemporaneity of different forms of its theatre: namely, traditional theatre, the popular tradition and the literary theatre of the mainly university-educated dramatists. The roots of Nigerian drama are to be found in the early religious Yoruba ceremonies and festivals, the *egwugwu* and *mmuo* masques of the Ibo and the *owu* and *oru* water masquerades of the Ijaw. Both the popular and the literary theatre are connected to the traditional theatre, which provides a veritable fount on which individual Nigerian theatre-makers draw. These range from Hubert Ogunde (1916–90), the pioneer of the popular travelling theatre, Nobel laureate WOLE SOYINKA, OLA ROTIMI, WALE OGUNYEMI, whose indebtedness to Yoruba traditional theatre aesthetics is clear, and both J. P. Clark (BEKEDEREMO-CLARK) and ZULU SOFOLA, who make use of Ijo and Igbo traditional theatre aesthetics respectively, to later playwrights such as Meki Nzewi, FEMI OSOFISAN, BODE SOWANDE, Olu Obafemi, Sam Ukala and Esiaba Irobi, who are also very much influenced by their respective ethnic performance forms.

Traditional theatrical performances have survived and are widespread among the many ethnic cultures. Before the colonial encounter, and the Christianization of the south and the Islamization of the north, these theatrical performances not only served to entertain their respective communities, but were also a means and context for social commentary and societal reflection. Except for the dramatic performances of the Hausa/Fulani to the north, the main focus and style of most forms of traditional Nigerian theatre is the masquerade, generally predicated upon the idea of spirit materiality, which enables the introduction of otherworldly phenomena and actualizing fiction. Nigeria masking theatre, in spite of its entertainment qualities, is a form of active religion, and this has given rise to a mix of religion and art, and a functional dimension to Nigerian theatre. Among the Hausa there is a range of traditional performances generally referred to as *wasannin garajiya* or *wasan kwaikwayo,* in which there is usually a representation of a fictional character or being by an actor in front of an audience. Unlike in Igbo and Yoruba mask theatre, there is an absence of the religious, except the *wasan bori,* in which gods and spirits feature.

The popular theatre is synonymous with the Yoruba operatic tradition of renowned artists such as Ogunde, Kola Ogunmola, Duro Ladipo, Moses Olaiya (Baba Sala), Oyin Adejobi, Isola Ogunsola, Lere Paimo and a host of other practitioners with their successful travelling theatre companies. The origin of this tradition is credited to Ogunde, who in 1946 formed the African Music Research Party. But according to historian Joel Adedeji, there was already in 1826 a record of an *Alarinjo* performance (a traditional Yoruba travelling theatre) in the journals of explorers Hugh Clapperton and Richard Lander. Nevertheless, Ogunde's theatre was pioneering in many respects. First, his was the first in Yoruba theatre in which women appeared on stage in their own right. Second, his theatre was the first authentic Nigerian theatre of the modern era. *Tiger's Empire* (1946) was Ogunde's first independent play, and it was an attack on colonial rule. This was followed by many others such as *Strike and Hunger* (1946), for which he was arrested and fined by the colonial police, *Bread and Bullet* (1950), about the Enugu miners' strike in 1949 in which 18 miners were shot and killed by the police, and the highly political *Yoruba Ronu* (*Yoruba Think*, 1964). This led to his ban from performing in the whole of the western region, which he writes about in *Ottiro Koro* (*Truth is Bitter*). One thing about Ogunde's theatre, and the popular theatre as a whole, is that plays are not only structurally and aesthetically influenced by the traditional *egungun apidan* theatre, but also continue the tradition of using theatre for social reflection and criticism. The literary dramatists already mentioned, and others such as Kole Omotoso, Sonny Oti, Kalu Uka, Emeka Nwabueze, Chimalum Nwankwo, Tess Onwueme, Tunde Lakoju, Ossie Enekwe, Tunde Fatunde, Stella Oyedepo, Akanji Nasiru, Segun Oyekunle, Samson Amali and Chris Nwamuo, keep this functional dimension clearly in focus in their work.

The literary theatre is a product of colonization, a blending of the diverse indigenous folk forms with Western theatre traditions and styles. Freed slaves and Brazilian settlers imported European forms of the concert and drama, and these to some extent provided the framework for the early Nigerian theatre. After a diet of European classics, musicals, operas and cantatas, there was a call, especially during the nationalist movement, for native plays to be written. Awards of money and prizes were offered to encourage this. In 1866 the idea was born of the Academy, which was to be a social and cultural centre for public enlightenment, dedicated to the promotion of the arts, sciences and culture. Several other groups of this nature sprang up between 1866 and 1910, and all of them organized shows of their own, based on the format of the English MUSIC HALL. There were also church groups which put on dramatic performances, of European plays of course. Gradually there began to emerge a blend of the Nigerian and the European in the entertainments, especially in church programmes. The first truly Nigerian plays came from the innovation emanating from the churches, and in 1902 the first Nigerian play, *King Elejigbo and Princess Abeje of Kotangora*, was written by D. Oloyede and performed by the Egbe Ife at the Bethel African Church School Hall.

Contrary to what many think, Nigerian literary drama did not begin at University College, Ibadan, even though the university was to play a major role in the development of modern Nigerian theatre. The first recognized Nigerian playwright was James Ene Henshaw, a medical doctor who wrote *This is Our Chance* in 1956 (first performed 1957). Alongside him were the numerous Onitsha Market plays, which began to emerge in the late 1940s and early 1950s but which, unlike Henshaw's plays, were not written with performance in mind. Henshaw's themes have changed from the earlier preoccupation with tradition versus modernity of plays such as *This is Our Chance, Jewels of the Shrine* (1957) and *Children of the Goddess* (1964) to drawing-room comedies and farces such as *Dinner for Promotion* (1967). However, despite his stated aim of writing 'a truly Nigerian drama for a Nigerian audience', he merely copied European models without any modifications. A truly Nigerian theatre emerged only with the advent of Soyinka and Clark-Bekederemo in the late 1950s.

Theatre scholarship often divides Nigerian literary theatre into two periods, the first generation and the second generation. There is now talk of a third generation, which covers theatre since the 1980s and whose dramatists are even more radical than their predecessors. Among the first generation are Soyinka, Clark-Bekederemo, Rotimi, Sofola, Ogunyemi, Obi Egbuna and Sonny Oti, whose works are characterized by a preoccupation with an animist metaphysics, an essentially tragic vision and an aesthetic of cultural retrieval. They explore contemporary reality by revisiting and reworking ancient myths and rituals, from Soyinka's early plays, such as *A Dance of the Forests* (1960) and *Death and the King's Horseman* (1976), Clark-Bekederemo's classical trilogy, which includes *Song of a Goat* (1961) and *Ozidi* (1966), Rotimi's *The Gods are Not to Blame* (1968) and his historical tragedy *Ovonramwem Nogbaisi* (1971), Sofola's *Wedlock of the Gods* (1972) and *King Emene* (1974), up to Sonny Oti's *The Old Masters* (1977). These plays seem to be saying that the past is very much a part of the present and that it affects and influences it. For Soyinka, as well as for the others, life is an endless cycle of mistakes repeated through generations and it is futile trying to break out of this cycle. This is where the second generation make their departure. Yet one only has to look at plays such as Soyinka's *The Beatification of Area Boy* (1995) or Rotimi's *Hopes of the Living Dead* (1985) to see the level of radical social critique of the first generation, whose playwrights also displayed an awareness and a willingness in their art to engage with and come to terms with the constantly changing socio-political reality of their Nigerian society.

The second generation, made up of playwrights such as Osofisan, Sowande and Omotoso, also make use of the past, but they differ from the first generation in the radical use which they make of this material. For them, there is not that reverential and mystifying attitude to history, ritual or myth which one finds in, say, *Death and the King's Horseman* or Rotimi's *Kurunmi* (1969). What one finds instead is a radical interrogation, reinterpretation and demystification of ritual, history and myth to reveal them as ideological constructs. This is evident in *The Chattering and the Song* (1976), a play in which Osofisan turns ancient myths on their heads as aspects and moments of Yoruba history are rigorously questioned to reveal patterns of social inequality between the aristocracy and the masses. The same is true of Sowande's *A Farewell to Babylon* (1978) and *Tornadoes Full of Dreams* (1990). Despite these differences, however, all Nigerian dramatists from the popular to the first and second generations write as a direct product of the traditional view of the artist as existing and functioning for his or her community.

Since the 1980s, a newer generation of artists has emerged, radical but not specifically reacting to the perceived 'reactionary' bent of the first generation, whose styles and themes range from the linguistically radical pidgin plays of Fatunde, such as *Oga Na Tief Man* (*The Master is a Thief*), to Irobi, who is as comfortable with the mystic ritualism of *Nwokedi* as he is with the frenetic politics of *Hangmen Also Die*. Also in this group are Obafemi, whose socio-political plays, such as *Naira Has No Gender* (1990) and *Nights of a Mystical Beast* (1986), are similar to Osofisan's or Sowande's; Ukala, who uses folk motifs and forms to explore contemporary reality in plays such as *The Slave Wife* and *The Placenta of Death*; and Onwueme, one of the few female Nigerian dramatists, who has written political or ideologically potent dramas that engage directly with the Nigerian socio-political realities, such as in her award-winning *The Desert Encroaches* (1985), *The Broken Calabash* (1984), *The Reign of Wazobia* (1988) and *Ban Empty Barn* (1989).

There is healthy cross-pollination in Nigerian theatre and each tradition is enriched as it grows, although the popular travelling theatre is gradually succumbing to the inevitable lures and economic viability of modern technology and doing away with the punishing touring schedules in favour of film and video making. The literary theatre is moving away from the confines of the academic environment. There is a recognition that theatre about the people should ultimately be for the people. The problem of writing in English, which has been one of the main reasons why the literary theatre tended to be elitist, is being addressed by playwrights in different ways. Rotimi has experimented with 'yorubaenglish' as a means of making his plays accessible to a wider audience. Clark-Bekederemo and Soyinka have also carried out a more sophisticated domestication of English to enable it to express their Nigerian experience. There are also some native-language writers such as Tony Ubesie, who writes in Igbo, and a host of Yoruba-language writers. These plays are limited by the size of the audiences which they can command. The native-language writers remain parochial or provincial unless they are translated, which is not happening very much. The most radical writer is Fatunde, who has elected to write in pidgin, a language spoken and understood by up to 75 per cent of the Nigerian population. Until Nigerian literary theatre deals with this problem of which language it should use, it will continue to suffer the accusation of being elitist and exotic to the majority of Nigerian audiences. OSITA OKAGBUE

O. Obafemi, *Contemporary Nigerian Theatre* (1996)

Y. Ogunbiyi, ed., *Drama and Theatre in Nigeria* (1981)

Nijinska, Bronislava (b. Minsk, Russia, 8 Jan. 1891; d. Pacific Palisades, Calif., 21 Feb. 1972) The most acclaimed female ballet choreographer of the twentieth century. She trained in St Petersburg and joined the Ballets Russes through the support of her more famous brother NIJINSKY, with whom she worked closely as his choreographic assistant. After spending the First World War in Russia, she returned to Europe and rejoined the Ballets Russes in 1921, creating for them her most famous ballets – *Les Noces* (1923) and *Les Biches* (1924). She continued making ballets for her own and other leading companies until retiring in 1952 to live in Hollywood, where she ran a dance school and wrote her autobiography, *Bronislava Nijinska: Early Memoirs*, posthumously published in 1982. Interest in her work revived in the 1960s when she remounted some works for the British Royal Ballet. RAMSAY BURT

See also CHOREOGRAPHY; DANCE.

N. van N. Baer, *Bronislava Nijinskja: A Dancer's Legacy* (1986)

Nijinsky, [Vaslav Fomich] (b. Kiev, Russia, 12 March 1890; d. London, 8 April 1950) Dancer and choreographer. His mixture of athletic agility and daring sensuousness (e.g. in *L'Après-midi d'un faune*, 1912), transcended classical ballet and through his work with the Ballets Russes changed dance and influenced many in the theatre including REINHARDT, BERNHARDT, GIRAUDOUX and CLAUDEL. ROBERT LEACH

See also CHOREOGRAPHY; DANCE.

Richard Buckle, *Nijinsky* (1971)

Nikolais, Alwin (b. Southington, Conn., 25 Nov. 1910; d. New York, 8 May 1993) Choreographer. While he derived his initial inspiration in dance from MARY WIGMAN and her acolyte HANYA HOLM, the eclectic, MULTIMEDIA style that became his hallmark can be traced to his early academic training in scenic design, acting, puppetry and music composition, and even to his brief teenage career playing organ accompaniment to silent films. A true innovator, Nikolais pioneered the abstract-EXPRESSIONIST DANCE theatre that would transform the post-MARTHA GRAHAM world of modern dance, defining dance itself as 'the art of motion, which, left on its own merits, becomes the message as well as the medium'. With his long-time collaborator and leading dancer Murray Louis (a noted choreographer in his own right), Nikolais created what he called 'theatre pieces' of wit, charm and grace – a body of work which earned him accolades worldwide.
MICHAEL KARP

Nimrod Theatre Company Founded in Sydney in 1970 by John Bell, Richard Wherrett and Ken Horler, this was for over a decade Australia's most innovative company. From the outset its hallmark was its production style – a clearly recognizable mix of the local, colourful, comic and irreverent. It fostered new Australian writing, and by the end of 1984 had presented 205 plays, 138 of which were by Australian authors. In 1974 it moved to a converted salt and tomato sauce factory, which became a two-theatre, open-space venue. (The company's first premises at Nimrod Street became the home of the Griffin Theatre Company.) Nimrod premièred major Australian and European works (among them plays by DAVID WILLIAMSON, HANDKE and HARE) and in 1972 received from England the GEORGE DEVINE Award jointly with Williamson for its production of his *The Removalists*. The company also developed a unique, updated and fresh approach to Shakespeare. In 1985, after much discussion and controversy over future directions and artistic personnel, the company moved again (to the Seymour Centre, a difficult complex of three theatre spaces), with the intention of attracting larger audiences. RICHARD COTTRELL was appointed artistic director but, in spite of some positive critical response, audience figures did not improve and his resignation coincided with the closure of the company in 1987. The building became the home of Company B at Belvoir Street, which, under the directorship of Neil Armfield (since

1994) has established a reputation as the key adventurous company in Australia. MICHAEL MORLEY

Ninagawa, Yukio (b. Kawaguchi, Japan, 15 Oct. 1935) Director. He began as an actor and made his directorial debut in 1969 with a production of Kunio Shimizu's *Shinjo Afureru Keihaku-sa* (variously translated as *Hearty but Flippant* or *Sincere Frivolity*). He confirmed his status as an innovative director in a four-year collaboration with Shimizu and in 1974 directed *Romeo and Juliet*. This production marked his move away from small-scale work and began a period of distinctly Japanese productions of Western classics as well as continued staging of contemporary Japanese work. The work during this period was the result of a successful partnership with the producer Tadao Nakane and, later, his production company Point Tokyo (formed in 1987). The key works from this collaboration were *King Lear* (1975), *Oedipus Rex* (1976), *Chikamatu Shinju-Monogatari* (*Suicide for Love*, 1976), Mishima's adaptation of the *noh* story *Sotoba-Komachi* (*Beautiful Lady of Stupa*, 1976), *Hamlet* (1978), Shimizu's *Tango at the End of Winter* (1978), *Ninagawa Macbeth* (1980), *Medea* (1983) and *The Tempest* (1987). Since 1983, many of his productions have been seen in Europe, Asia and North America, winning him critical acclaim for his bold theatricality and the blending of traditional elements of Japanese theatre with classical Western material. In particular, Ninagawa's company visited the ROYAL SHAKESPEARE COMPANY with *The Tempest* (1993), and a multinational cast production of *Peer Gynt* (1994) and, under the RSC banner, he directed *King Lear* (1999), with NIGEL HAWTHORNE in the title role.
BRIAN ROBERTS
See also EASTERN THEATRE, ITS INFLUENCE ON THE WEST.

nineteenth-century theatre, its influence in the twentieth century Stylistic change in art is often misinterpreted as progress. Every generation thinks its greatest actors more 'natural' than their predecessors. Nineteenth-century acting has been as rejected as 'artificial' with the wide dissemination of STANISLAVSKY's 'system', and his disciples' emphasis upon 'psychological truth' has implied that actors before him were largely concerned with technique. It is true that late nineteenth-century actors sought to improve nature rather than imitate it literally; HENRY IRVING wrote in 1893, 'Finally, in the consideration of the Art of Acting, it must never be forgotten that its ultimate aim is beauty.' Moreover, photographs and recordings show that acting style was broader than anything we see today. But this does not mean that acting was merely technical. No matter what convention shapes movement and gesture, only the actor's belief and emotional truth can persuade an audience. Nineteenth-century actors knew that as well as we do, and passed on that ideal to their successors. Stanislavsky was a product of the nineteenth century, and his system is designed to induce a belief and truth that actors have sought since ancient Greece.

Romantic acting flourished well into the twentieth century. Actors like MARTIN-HARVEY and DONALD WOLFIT retained a strong following until the Second World War, and films such as *Richard III* (1956) show us an OLIVIER who was decidedly flamboyant by contemporary standards. Virtually all acting is conventional, and most theatres have always aimed at a convention which audiences will *accept* as natural. SARTRE made one of the great nineteenth-century actors, Kean, the subject of a play, and the styles of performers like BERNHARDT have been reinvestigated at the end of the twentieth century in the wake of new feminist analysis.

In the 1880s and 1890s, growing urban populations and cheap public transport brought audiences to theatres in unprecedented numbers. Theatres prospered and runs lengthened: *Faust* (1885) played for more than two seasons at the Lyceum, and *Charley's Aunt* (Royalty, 1892) ran for 1,466 performances. Thus managements found it possible to design and build sets, costumes and props specifically for a production, regardless of cost. And since the illusion of visual reality was the ideal, a high degree of spectacular realism was achieved. After 1918, however, film began to cut into theatre audiences and budgets; besides, it is easier and more convincing to film the real Niagara Falls than to reproduce it on the stage. Recognizing it could not compete, the theatre retreated from spectacle combined with illusion. Today's spectacles are usually theatrical rather than realistic in nature (e.g. *Cats*). Nevertheless, the norm in most theatres is still the box set, representing a believable room. This is the direct result of nineteenth-century stage convention and theatre architecture.

The proscenium arch was first employed during the Italian Renaissance, but it was not until the late nineteenth century that all action retreated behind it. The arch was regarded as the frame of a huge, moving picture. When MARIE WILTON and SQUIRE BANCROFT rebuilt London's Haymarket in 1880, the arch was decorated as a four-sided picture frame; a delighted spectator wrote that sets and actors now looked like 'a picture projected on a surface'. Such theatres enforced the convention that actors were unaware of the audience. By the 1880s, new LIGHTING technology allowed the house to be blacked out during a performance, reinforcing the illusion. With an interior set, the arch represented a missing or transparent 'fourth wall'. This convention still flourishes, and with it, many successors to the accompanying naturalistic 'cup and saucer' drama pioneered by T. W. Robertson.

Most new British and American plays are written for proscenium arch theatres, because most commercial theatre buildings in London and New York (where many English-language dramatists hope their plays will ultimately be performed) are of late Victorian or Edwardian construction. Until these buildings crumble or burn, the drama will be obliged to conform to an obsolete convention. Canada is different; the major Toronto theatres which produce original work have open stages. But since regional companies use traditional theatre buildings, foreign plays are featured, while productions of Toronto successes are frequently relegated to 'alternative' theatres.

Scenically, the first major challenge to naturalistic illusion was issued by ADOLPHE APPIA and EDWARD GORDON CRAIG, who began their work in the nineteenth century. Craig was the son of ELLEN TERRY, and learned much from Henry Irving's designers at the Lyceum. Appia and Craig pioneered the non-representational unit set, popular in the 1920s (see the designs of ROBERT EDMOND JONES and NORMAN BEL GEDDES) and the 1960s and in eastern Europe. An important variant is the permanent set, like that built for JACQUES COPEAU's Théâtre du Vieux Colombier in Paris. TANYA MOISEWITSCH's stage at the STRATFORD (Ontario) Festival Theatre (1957) is the most conspicuous example in use today.

Electric flood lighting was gradually introduced in theatres during the 1880s and 1890s, but electric spotlights were not available until the twentieth century; in the meantime, limelight remained the normal focusable instrument. Even after theatres were entirely equipped with electric light, control systems were (and remain) based on systems devised in the nineteenth century for gaslight. The modern dimmer board works on the same principles as the 'gas table', an arrangement of gas 'circuits' controlled by calibrated taps analogous to dimmers. Even the names of basic colour medium shades (steel blue, rose, amber, straw yellow) were originally applied to those used with gas limelights.

The contemporary ideal of a single artist who controls all aspects of production was inherited from the nineteenth century, when the controlling artist was normally an actor–manager: it was an 'actor's theatre'. Since the actor–manager was both the star whom the public came to see and the employer of the company, it was expected that the focus would be directed towards him – or her: some of the most successful, such as Marie Wilton and Sarah Bernhardt, were women. While some actor–managers survived into the early twentieth century, they have been gradually supplanted by directors.

The contemporary director is usually a freelance, like the actors and designers he or she directs. Few directors act in their own productions any more; most are not actors at all, unlike the earlier pioneers such as ANTOINE, Stanislavsky and REINHARDT. Early directors learned from actor–mangers to be 'traffic cops', instructing actors exactly how to interpret their parts, move and speak in order to fit the production concept. But innovators stretching back to the Duke of Saxe-MEININGEN and reaching through Craig to PETER BROOK have developed processes designed to enlist the resources of actors, designers and others involved to make a production a group creation. The director has become a creative, rather than an entirely interpretive, artist: his or her interpretation frequently takes precedence over the dramatist's intention and has produced today's 'director's theatre'.

Since the eighteenth century, Western theatre has blended contemporary drama with a 'classical' repertoire (Shakespeare, Racine, Molière). Little drama of the earlier nineteenth century holds the stage. Some playwrights have been rescued from obscurity: Georg Büchner attracted little attention in his own time, but influenced ERWIN PISCATOR and BERTOLT BRECHT and is performed today. The classical repertoire now includes at least three dramatists whose careers began in the late nineteenth century: IBSEN, CHEKHOV and SHAW, who has his own Festival Theater at Niagara-on-the-Lake, Ontario, rivalling the Shakespearean Festival at neighbouring Stratford. From these playwrights the twentieth century derived a genre which deals with contemporary social and political issues. It was not their invention, however. Early nineteenth-century MELODRAMA often presented the appalling problems facing working-class people during the industrial revolution: Hedda Gabler boring herself to death is hardly a social casualty on the same scale as the starving unemployed in *The Factory Lad* (1832) or the slaves in *Uncle Tom's Cabin* (1852). But about mid-century, French dramatists began writing about middle-class problems; this, and the literary quality of their successors (e.g. Ibsen, Shaw, Chekhov as well as a writer like WILDE), ensured their enduring success with the audience that remained after the working class deserted theatre for cinema in the early twentieth century.

Most nineteenth-century artists believed that art should idealize, rather than represent life 'warts and all'. The idea that art can legitimately represent any

phenomenon, however squalid, because it is real, entered the theatre with dramatists like Alexandre Dumas *fils* and Emile Augier, whose *Dame aux Camélias* (1852) and *Mariage d'Olympe* (1855) forced audiences to face sexual fears which social taboos forbade them to discuss. Subsequently, Ibsen and BRIEUX discussed syphilis in *Ghosts* (1881) and *Les Avariés* (*Damaged Goods*, 1902), audacities which paved the way for nudity, profanity and other challenges to conventional morality on stage.

The 'new drama' of the late nineteenth century was unlikely to see production at commercial playhouses. It helped to create the INDEPENDENT THEATRE movement, including ANTOINE's Théâtre Libre (Paris, 1887), FREIE BÜHNE (Berlin, 1889), INDEPENDENT THEATRE SOCIETY (London, 1891), MOSCOW ART THEATRE (1898) and ABBEY THEATRE (Dublin, 1904), which offered clear alternatives to commercial theatre and opened the way for the contemporary twentieth-century pattern of theatres appealing to minority interests: social, political, aesthetic, racial and sexual.

The nineteenth-century novel has also been an inspiration, from Gogol, Tolstoy, Dostoevsky and Eliot to the figure who seems to have come to stand for his time, Dickens, whether in the proliferation of versions of *A Christmas Carol* or the ROYAL SHAKESPEARE COMPANY's *Nicholas Nickleby*.   ALAN HUGHES

Richard C. Beecham, *Adolphe Appia, Theatre Artist* (1987)

Michael R. Booth, *Theatre in the Victorian Age* (1991)

W. R. Fuerst and S. J. Hume, *Twentieth-Century Stage Decoration* (1967)

Christopher Innes, *Edward Gordon Craig* (1983)

David Magarshack, *Stanislavsky: A Life* (1950)

S. M. Waxman, *Antoine and the Théâtre Libre* (1926)

Nobel Prize   *see* AWARDS AND PRIZES

Noble, Adrian [Keith]   (b. Chichester, Sussex, 19 July 1950) Director. After Bristol University and the London Drama Centre, Noble worked in COMMUNITY and young people's theatre in Birmingham. A director's bursary took him to the BRISTOL OLD VIC (1976–9) as resident (later associate) director. Award-winning productions for the MANCHESTER ROYAL EXCHANGE THEATRE (*The Duchess of Malfi*, 1980) and the ROYAL SHAKESPEARE COMPANY (*The Forest*, 1980; *A Doll's House*, 1981) brought him wider recognition. He held overall responsibility for the 1988 STRATFORD-UPON-AVON season, which included his acclaimed *The Plantagenets* (an adaptation of the *Henry VI* plays with *Richard III*) – one of many partnerships with designer BOB CROWLEY that included *Macbeth* (1987, with JONA-

THAN PRYCE) and *Hamlet* (1992, with KENNETH BRANAGH). Establishing a reputation for epic, ensemble productions, Noble went on to direct the *Henry IV* plays and *The Thebans* (an adaptation of Sophocles' plays) in 1991, the year he became artistic director of the RSC. Other successful productions include *King Lear* (1982, with MICHAEL GAMBON as Lear and ANTONY SHER as the Fool, and 1993 with ROBERT STEPHENS), *Antony and Cleopatra* (1982, with Michael Gambon and HELEN MIRREN), *Three Sisters* (1991, Dublin), and *The Cherry Orchard* (1996). In 1997 he took the RSC out of the Barbican for six months of the year and increased the company's touring. In 2001 he announced controversial plans for a leaner company that would leave the Barbican altogether but would redevelop its Stratford base to provide more flexible spaces, and open the building to different artistic activities and a wider public. GILLIAN M. DAY

Noguchi, Isamu (b. Los Angeles, 17 Nov. 1904; d. New York, 30 Dec. 1988) Sculptor and designer. Brought up in Japan from the age of two, Noguchi moved in 1926 to Paris and worked as an assistant to the sculptor Brancusi. That year he created his first theatre design, masks for actress Ito Michio in YEATS' *At the Hawk's Well*. Noguchi began working with choreographer MARTHA GRAHAM in 1935, designing the sets for *Frontier*. A 53-year collaboration ensued, including memorable sets for *Appalachian Spring* (1944), *Seraphic Dialogue* (1955) and *Night Chant* (1988). Noguchi also designed the famous GIELGUD *King Lear* (1955, STRATFORD-UPON-AVON), as well as for GEORGE BALANCHINE and MERCE CUNNINGHAM. An influential figure in exploring form and function, his striking, simple images inhabited an abstract world that defined the performance space in a tactile but non-realistic way. DENISE L. TILLES

Robert Tracy, *Spaces of Mind: Isamu Noguchi's Dance Designs* (2000)

Nordic Theatre Arts Laboratory *see* ODIN TEATRET

Norén, Lars (b. Stockholm, 9 April 1944) Playwright. Originally a poet, his first performed play was *Fursteslickaren* (*The Prince's Bootlicker*, 1973). As a result of poor reviews, he did not produce another play until 1979. The critical success of this work, *Orestes*, followed by *Underjordens leende* (*Smiles of the Underworld*, 1980) and *En fruktansvård lycka* (*A Terrible Happiness*, 1981), firmly established Norén as Sweden's leading playwright. His best known early works – *Natten år dagens mor* (*Night is Mother to the Day*, 1982), *Kaos år med Gud* (*Chaos is God's Neighbour*, 1983) and *Model att döda* (*Courage to Kill*, 1984), a semi-autobiographical trilogy

dealing with a nuclear family – along with his other plays, investigate the discrepancies in human behaviour, the inability to manifest externally inner issues and turmoil. Difficult to translate and several hours in length, his plays are not often produced outside the subsidized theatre. In 1989, however, the world premières of *Hebriana*, *Endagsvarelser* (*Dragonflies*) and *Autumn and Winter*, in the Netherlands, Germany and Denmark respectively, proved more accessible and placed Norén internationally. In 1991 *Och ge oss skuggorna* (*And Grant Us the Shadows*, a play about EUGENE O'NEILL) was premièred in Norway. LAURIE WOLF

S. Osten, 'Lars Norén: A Working Process for the Director', in E. Törnqvist, ed., *Not Only Strindberg* (1985)

Norman, [John] Frank (b. London, 9 June 1930; d. London 23 Dec. 1980) Playwright. He was brought up in a Barnardo's orphanage, worked on farms and fairs, and was imprisoned for passing fraudulent cheques. His book on prison life, *Bang to Rights* (1958), was successful and an *Encounter* article on London slang grew into a 48-page playscript: *Fings Ain't Wot They Used T'Be*, a vivid lowlife comedy set in a Soho gambling house. THEATRE WORKSHOP developed it into a musical with songs by LIONEL BART (1959) that transferred to the West End. Norman wrote novels, non-fiction, and three more stage plays: *A Kayf Up West* (1964), *Insideout* (Royal Court, 1969, based on *Bang to Rights*) and *Costa Packet* (1972). His autobiography *Why Fings Went West* appeared in 1975. TONY HOWARD

Norman [Williams], Marsha (b. Louisville, Ky., 21 Sept. 1947) Playwright. The title of her acclaimed first play, *Getting Out* (1977), points to Norman's primary passion. Trapped by possessive parents and their own limitations, her central characters struggle for independence. In the Pulitzer Prize winning *'Night, Mother* (1983), Jessie kills herself to break free. Other plays include *The Holdup* (1980), *Traveler in the Dark* (1984), *The Shakers* (1988) and *Loving Daniel Boone* (1993). She wrote the book and lyrics for *The Secret Garden* (1991) and *The Red Shoes* (1993, music by JULE STYNE). M. ELIZABETH OSBORN

Northern Broadsides Touring theatre company, based in an old wool mill in Halifax, Yorkshire. Founded in 1992 by Yorkshireman Barrie Rutter to present plays in his regional accent, it opened with him as Richard III and found favour beyond its own constituency with a string of energetic Shakespeare productions, including *A Midsummer Night's Dream* (1994), *Antony and Cleopatra* (1995) and *King Lear* (1999). The company also performs work by other writers: it has staged Yorkshireman TONY HARRISON's *The Trackers of*

Oxyrhynchus (1998), the play which had given Rutter the inspiration to found Northern Broadsides when he appeared in it at the NATIONAL THEATRE, and *Alcestis* (2000), an adaptation of the Euripides play by the Yorkshire Poet Laureate TED HUGHES, his last theatrical work and given to Rutter by the author himself. Rutter, an actor who developed his love of theatre with the NATIONAL YOUTH THEATRE, follows the NYT's no-nonsense approach to staging, interpretation and verse speaking. For the achievement of his company, he won in 2000 the Creative Britons prize, the largest award for the arts in Britain. CHARLES LONDON

Northern Ireland *see* BELFAST; IRELAND

Norway At the dawn of the twentieth century Norway had two national theatres: Den Nationale Scene in Bergen (founded 1876) and the Nationaltheater in Christiania (later Oslo), which opened in 1899. Construction of the monumental Nationaltheater, on a prime plot between the university and the parliament, was funded by the emerging middle class of bankers, merchants and lawyers. Both of these theatres are still in operation. There were also theatres in such coastal cities as Kristiansand, Arendal, Stavanger and Trondheim; but they were used mainly by amateur groups or sporadically by touring companies.

In 1913 Arne and Hulda Garborg founded Det Norske Teatret in Oslo. It was dedicated to furthering the cause of the minority, rural language, Nynorsk, and to presenting themes and characters thought to be specifically 'Norwegian'. Despite its nationalist and rural roots, it quickly became Norway's most international theatre, often presenting challenging new plays from abroad, occasionally guest-directed by some of Europe's finest directors.

The history of Norwegian theatre since the Second World War has been marked by a high degree of decentralization and increasing subsidies. As part of the 'rebuilding' of the country in the postwar era, the ruling Labour party formulated an aggressive programme to strengthen the arts. Theatre companies in Oslo, Bergen, Trondheim and Stavanger were given regular subsidies, thus ensuring their survival. A national touring company, Riksteatret, was founded in 1948, and a school for actors was opened in 1953. (Since 1980 the school has also had a programme for directors.)

At the end of the century there were seven major theatre companies in Norway's five largest cities, and professional or semi-professional companies in eight smaller towns. Of particular note is the Sami (Lapp) theatre in Kautokeino, Beaivvas. All these companies are heavily subsidized, with 60–90 per cent of revenue coming from local and national funding. There is far less corporate sponsorship than in English-speaking countries, and private donations are very rare. Each year these theatres sell about 1.3 million tickets in a country of 4.2 million people.

All the government-funded theatres have permanent companies (except for three of the smaller regionals). The actors' union has achieved a measure of influence in questions of repertoire and casting. The ensemble system is often accused of fostering stagnation, but perhaps because it works against typecasting, the level of artistic achievement in acting is consistently high. Since the 1970s the notion of a 'dialect-free' stage speech has been eroded and young actors typically strive to retain some of their local dialect.

Norwegian theatre has become highly international. Seeing a new play most often means seeing a recent foreign play in translation, and theatres are quick to pick up on new trends and authors abroad, particularly in the English-speaking world. Foreign directors working in Norway have also provided new impulses; they include SILVIU PUCARETE (Romania), Gábor Zsámbéki (Hungary), Krystyna Skuszanka (Poland), Sam Besekow (Denmark), JOHN BARTON (England), Jan Håkanson (Sweden) and Jacques Lasalle (France). The importance of new Norwegian plays has declined steadily since IBSEN's day, and by the end of the century there seemed to be less good, new writing being produced in Norway than in other countries with comparable theatre activity. Three significant writers earlier in the century were Nordahl Grieg, Oskar Braaten and Helge Krog. Their works are occasionally revived. Of contemporary playwrights, Klaus Hagerup, Terje Nordby, Julian Garner, Cecilie Løveid and others have written consistently interesting plays. With the emergence of Jon Fosse (b. 1959) as a playwright in 1994 (by which time he had many successful novels and volumes of poetry behind him), Norwegian theatre seems to have found a new voice of international size. His plays have been produced far afield. Writing in Nynorsk, Fosse often presents primal scenes of family life. In *Sonen* (*The Son*, 1997), a prodigal son returns from the city to his ancestral farm. The only other characters are his father and mother, and the play concerns the gap that has grown between them. Fosse's plays are written in a tightly controlled, minimalistic and mesmerizing style, filled with ellipses and repetitions of stock phrases signifying a failure to communicate. Many critics have proclaimed his body of plays the finest since Ibsen. MICHAEL EVANS

Lise Lyche, *Norges Teaterhistorie* (1991)

F. J. and Lise-Lone Marker, *The Scandinavian Theatre* (1975)
Modern Nordic Plays, intr. E. Eide (1974)

Nottingham Home to the Theatre Royal (since 1760; newly built 1865) and the Nottingham Playhouse. The former has continued from the nineteenth century as a commercial theatre with a programme of tours (including such stars as HENRY IRVING and ANNA PAVLOVA) and PANTOMIME. It was in a poor state in the 1960s, and in 1978 the council finally renovated it as a modern theatre with Victorian character. A VARIETY theatre, the Empire, built alongside in 1897, lasted until 1958. The Playhouse was founded in 1948 by a trust of local people who wanted a theatre to compare with BIRMINGHAM, LIVERPOOL, BRISTOL and GLASGOW. Originally housed in a converted cinema, it achieved a notable reputation under its first artistic director André van Gyseghem (1906–79), a distinguished actor and director and lifelong communist who had great influence in the left-wing theatre groups of the 1930s. A policy of quality classics continued under John Harrison (1952–7), Val May (1957–61), and FRANK DUNLOP (1961–4), who inaugurated a new building in 1963 with JOHN NEVILLE and PETER USTINOV. On his own, Neville (1963–8) took the theatre to new heights, creating in his words, 'a pocket National Theatre for the region'. Stuart Burge (1968–73) consolidated Neville's work and introduced new plays (e.g. PETER BARNES' *The Ruling Class* (1968), an emphasis strengthened under RICHARD EYRE (1973–8), whose tenure included *Brassneck* (1973), by HOWARD BRENTON and DAVID HARE, *The Comedians* (1974) by TREVOR GRIFFITHS and *Touched* (1974) by Stephen Lowe.

The vitality of the Playhouse's work slackened after Eyre's departure, and was only revived under Ruth McKenzie (1990–7). So far as artistic innovation was concerned, the focus had in any case moved across town to The Midland Group Arts Centre by the mid-1970s. Under the directorship of Anthony Everitt, performance programmer Steve Rogers founded the Four Days of Performance Art in 1979. This annual platform for young artists was renamed The National Review of Live Arts by Rogers' eventual successor as its artistic director, Nikki Milican, in 1984. It continued in Nottingham until the financial collapse of the Midland Group in 1987. (It continues biennially in Glasgow.) On the basis of this work, the success of the Nottingham Trent University's Contemporary Arts Course, and the City Council's Contemporary Archives Festival (1989–91), Nottingham swiftly became an internationally regarded centre for live art activity, particularly through its festivals NOW (1992–) and Expo (1991–). Fusions with dance and new media are also significant. Dance 4, the national dance agency for the East Midlands, moved to Nottingham in 1994 and co-promotes the interdisciplinary NOTTDance Festival (1990–) with the Bonington Gallery.
MARIE PETCHELL & ROBERT AYERS

John Bailey, *A Theatre for All Seasons* (1994)

Novello, Ivor [David Ivor Davies] (b. Cardiff, 15 Jan. 1893; d. London, 6 March 1951) Actor, playwright and composer. Success as a songwriter, notably with the wartime 'Keep the Home Fires Burning', preceded Novello's composing debut in the musical theatre with a part-score for the Gaiety hit *Theodore & Co* (1916). He subsequently provided material for REVUE and musical comedy, while leading a higher-profile career as a movie and then a stage matinée idol, collaborating on the musical comedy hit *Who's Hooper* (1919) and on the comic opera *The Golden Moth* (1921). Commissioned to write a large-scale spectacular musical for the troubled THEATRE ROYAL, DRURY LANE, Novello turned out *Glamorous Night* (1935), a lush, romantic light opera in which he starred in the non-singing hero's role. Its success led to a series of six similarly styled works, of which *Perchance to Dream* (1945), *King's Rhapsody* (1949) and, particularly, *The Dancing Years* (1939) were outstanding long-run hits for him as a librettist, composer and sometime lyricist as well as as an actor. His final work, *Gay's the Word* (1951), a vehicle for CICELY COURTNEIDGE, marked a return to the light music of his early days. KURT GÄNZL

J. Harding, *Ivor Novello* (1987)
W. MacQueen Pope, *Ivor* (1952)
P. Noble, *Ivor Novello: Man of the Theatre* (1951)
S. Wilson, *Ivor* (1975)

Nowra, Louis (b. Melbourne, 12 Dec. 1950) Playwright. Instead of fashionably exploring 'Australian' themes, Nowra sets his plays in eighteenth-century Russia, nineteenth-century Paraguay or China. Yet his most powerful and visionary piece, *Inside the Island* (1980), has an Australian setting, with its brooding evocation of the outback in 1912 where a colonial, military society finally erupts in violence. He is interested in the tensions between dream and reality, will and action, madness and insight; he has much in common with a European tradition that includes Kleist, WEDEKIND (both of whom he has adapted), Büchner, CHEKHOV and STRINDBERG. In works like *Inner Voices* (1977) and *The Golden Age* (1985), he creates images of a powerful and disturbing immediacy. He has also written novels, radio and television plays, films and opera libretti. Plays include *Kiss the One-Eyed Priest* (1973),

Visions (1978), *The Precious Woman* (1980) and *Sunrise* (1983); *Cosi* (1992) and *Radiance* (1994), both filmed; and *The Temple* (1993) and *The Language of the Gods* (1998). MICHAEL MORLEY

Ntshona, Winston   *see* FUGARD, ATHOL

Nugent, Elliott [John]   (b. Dover, Ohio, 20 Sept. 1899; d. New York, 9 Aug. 1980)   Playwright, actor and director. The son of vaudevilleans, he wrote two hits with his father, J. C. Nugent: *Kempy* (1922) and *The Poor Nut* (1925). He starred in comedies by other writers, notably *The Male Animal* (1940) and *The Voice of the Turtle* (1943). His autobiography, *Events Leading Up to the Comedy*, appeared in 1965.   GERALD BORDMAN

Nunn, Trevor [Robert]   (b. Ipswich, Suffolk, 14 Jan. 1940)   Director. After Cambridge, he won a director's scholarship to the Belgrade Theatre, Coventry, in 1962, where he became resident director. In 1964 he joined the ROYAL SHAKESPEARE COMPANY, becoming in 1965 an associate director and in 1968 its artistic director; from 1978 to 1986 he was its chief executive and joint artistic director with TERRY HANDS. Under his leadership the RSC was seen as one of the major companies in the world. His many outstanding RSC shows demonstrate an ability to create a convincing world on stage and allow individual actors to flourish. They include *The Revenger's Tragedy* (1966), his own adaptation of *Hedda Gabler* (1975), *Macbeth* with IAN MCKELLEN and JUDI DENCH (1976), *The Life and Times of Nicholas Nickleby* (1980) and an Edwardian *All's Well That Ends Well* (1981). In 1981 he began his successful association with ANDREW LLOYD WEBBER, directing *Cats* (1981), *Starlight Express* (1984), and *Aspects of Love* (1989). The English had caught up with the Americans in the staging of musicals – a point he underlined as co-director with John Caird of the highly successful *Les Misérables* (1985). He became artistic director of the NATIONAL THEATRE in 1997, and was praised for his work with an ensemble there, in particular *Summerfolk* and *The Merchant of Venice* (both 1999). His successor NICHOLAS HYTNER was due to take over from him in 2003.   DAVID STAINES

O

Oakley, Barry (b. Melbourne, 24 Feb. 1931) Playwright, literary editor, novelist, essayist and football enthusiast. In his drama Oakley ranges beyond the suburban mysteries of his other work. His approach to character and circumstance is picaresque, humorous and scathing, though rarely cruel. He reveals an acute sense of the absurdity of belief in the 'order' of things – gained, no doubt, from time spent in the public service, advertising, journalism and academia. Oakley's first of 15 plays, *From the Desk of Eugene Flockhart* (1966), was presented as part of an Australian Play season which marked the untimely end of Wal Cherry's Emerald Hill Theatre. His political satires for the popular theatre, *The Feet of Daniel Mannix* (1971) and *Beware of Imitations*, and the 'ghetto' comedy of manners *Bedfellows* (1975), contributed markedly to the success of the Australian Performing Group and the 'new wave' of Australian playwriting. It was here that the brilliant comic actor Max Gillies realized a series of Oakley's flawed heroes – politicians, prelates, academics, poets – and brought to them his gift for portraying eccentric paranoia and a sustained state of imminent collapse. *Scanlan* (1978) marks the highpoint of this riotous partnership, which also produced 'Orion' Horne, 'the farthing poet', in *The Ship's Whistle* (1978). *A Lesson in English* (1968) is the best known of the short plays. His autobiographical 'Falling on his Feet' was published in 1996 in a collection edited by Gillian Whitlock, *Autographs: Contemporary Australian Autobiography*. GUS WORBY

L. Radic, *The State of Play: The Revolution in the Australian Theatre since the 1960s* (1991)

Obaldia, René de (b. Hong Kong, 22 Oct. 1918) Playwright, poet and novelist; a mercurial writer whose imaginative plays, literary in style, have charm, humour and fantasy, touching on the ABSURD (cf. IONESCO, VITRAC), usually with reference to contemporary matters such as cosmonauts, nuclear war, housing problems, baby-sitters, 'Lolitas', role-playing, etc.: e.g. *Genousie* (*Jenusia*, 1960); *Seven Impromptus for Leisure* (1961, popular with universities and drama schools). Most of his plays have been staged or broadcast in English, including his 'chamber Western', *Wind in the Branches of the Sassafras* (1965). DONALD WATSON

Oberammergau Village in Upper Bavaria, Germany: site since 1634 of a performance every ten years or so of a medieval passion play, in fulfilment of a pledge made by the villagers in the midst of the plague should they be spared further devastation. Until 1990 married women and women over 35 were banned from participating, but the rules were relaxed to exclude from the 1,900-strong cast and crew only those not born in the town or resident for 20 years. The text used in the twentieth century dates from 1810 and has been revised several times, including changes to remove anti-semitism. The whole production, containing a series of TABLEAUX VIVANTS, lasts around six hours and has become a byword for the creation of a theatrical event. CHARLES LONDON

James Shapiro, *Oberammergau: The Troubling Story of the World's Most Famous Passion Play* (2000)

Obey, André (b. Douai, France, 8 May 1892; d. Montsoreau, France, 12 April 1975) Playwright and actor–manager. Obey was COPEAU's dramatist, and his plays *Noé* (*Noah*, 1931), a witty reinterpretation of the biblical theme seen in London in 1935, directed by

559

MICHEL SAINT-DENIS with JOHN GIELGUD as Noah, *Le Viol de Lucrèce* (1931), a dramatization of Shakespeare's *The Rape of Lucrece* that was adapted by THORNTON WILDER as *Lucrece* (1932) and used as a source for the libretto of Britten's opera *The Rape of Lucrece* (1946), and *La Bataille de la Marne* ('The battle of the Marne', 1932) were produced by Copeau's COMPAGNIE DES QUINZE. He also adapted from Greek drama, as well as reworking the Don Juan legend three times.

WENDY SCOTT

Obraztsov, Sergei [Vladimirovich]   (b. Moscow, 22 June 1901; d. Moscow, 8 May 1991)   PUPPET master. Entered the theatre as an actor–singer at the NEMIROV-ICH-DANCHENKO Musical Theatre (1922–30) before joining the Second MOSCOW ART THEATRE (1930–6), which became the State Central Puppet Theatre in 1937. Obraztsov has since travelled widely abroad, presenting puppet shows for both children and adults; he has also made films and written important books on puppetry, including his memoir, *My Profession* (1981, translated by R. Parker, V. Scott and D. Rottenberg).

NICK WORRALL

O'Casey, Sean [John]   (b. Dublin, 30 March 1880; d. Torquay, 18 September 1964)   Playwright, and one of the very few giants of the English-speaking theatre in the first half of the twentieth century. Though he remained true to his working-class and national origins throughout a long and prolific life, the depth of his compassion for suffering humanity, breadth of characterization and pervasive sense of humour combine to give his work a universality that was initially doubted when he achieved fame in the mid-1920s with his tragi-comic trilogy – *The Shadow of a Gunman* (1923), *Juno and the Paycock* (1924) and *The Plough and the Stars* (1926). Falsely seen for many years as primarily a naturalistic delineator of slum life, O'Casey took pains to diversify dramatic speech and action to make drama worthy of comparison with other genres, such as the novel and poetry, that had for many decades outstripped it in artistic and social relevance. His plays from the first show a delight in the poetry of racy idiomatic speech and in the stylization of language as well as in dramatic action; from the late 1920s onwards, moreover, he sought by even bolder theatrical experimentation – expanding expressionistic elements and emphasizing group as well as individual experience – to enlarge the compass of drama in many exciting ways. Few playwrights have explored more exhaustively the modern theatre's possibilities for showing the social conflicts and contradictions of its age.

In his life, as in his writings, O'Casey brought together disparate realities and sought to reconcile them. Born Protestant in predominantly Catholic Dublin, he became an Irish nationalist who lived the last 38 years of his life in England. Though an avowed communist, from the early 1920s onwards he numbered among his personal friends such diverse men as the apolitical hedonist GEORGE JEAN NATHAN and the Conservative politician and publisher of O'Casey's works, Harold Macmillan. The youngest of eight children, of whom only five lived beyond early childhood, O'Casey experienced poverty and illness from an early age. His father's death (when Sean was only six years old) brought the family great hardship. O'Casey's education was retarded by a disease which seriously afflicted his eyes throughout his life; he had little schooling, and it was not until his early teens that he undertook his education seriously.

The future playwright began work at the age of 14 and had a succession of manual jobs – including ten years as a labourer on the Irish railway – until becoming a full-time writer in 1925. O'Casey joined the Gaelic League and the militant Irish Republican Brotherhood, an underground organization that was to mastermind the 1916 Rising. Experience of police brutality during the 1913 Dublin Lockout, however, changed the emphasis of O'Casey's radicalism. Although he continued to support national independence, the cause of international socialism and the need to improve Irish working conditions became his primary concerns. During the Rising, O'Casey was a critical spectator; the Anglo-Irish War (1916–21) and the Civil War (1922–3) were not fought for the ideals that he most wished to see realized in Ireland, and their chief victims – physically and politically – were the country's working people and the civilian population generally.

During his apprenticeship to drama from 1917 to 1922 O'Casey wrote at least four plays, of which just one has survived, before *The Shadow of a Gunman* was accepted for performance at what was soon to become Ireland's national theatre. O'Casey's association with the ABBEY THEATRE has become so famous that it is perhaps surprising to realize just how relatively brief – no more than five years in all – that working relationship was. Much has been made of his debt to the Abbey and its remarkable triumvirate of playwright–directors (W. B. YEATS, AUGUSTA GREGORY and LENNOX ROBINSON), but, though their encouragement and example afforded him considerable inspiration, his work owes very little to them. The acting of the Abbey players – then, in the mid-1920s, at a new height of naturalistic artistry – was perhaps the theatre's most significant gift to him: each of his plays from *Juno* to *The Silver Tassie* contains major characters written specifically for BARRY FITZGERALD, SARA ALLGOOD and F. J. MCCORMICK.

· Performing O'Casey ·

Of the O'Casey canon I state an actor's preference for what I call the 'Dublin plays' as, through the years 1916 to 1922, they come bursting out of the tangled turgid spirit of that unpredictable city, the O'Casey characters clamorously tearing out of its very pores, rescued in passionate embrace from off the streets of the Rising, the War of Independence and the Civil War to be swept up and on to the stage of the Abbey Theatre, there, with great acting, renewed as living personalities of the drama for as long as theatre exists.

Here let me name them, some: from the play to which they give its title – the 'Paycock' and his 'Juno'; 'Fluther' and the young 'Covey' from *The Plough and the Stars*; Seumas Shields from *The Shadow of a Gunman*, a stream of others surrounding the human foundations of O'Casey theatre, figures floating unendingly to and fro between street and stage. These offer the inexhaustible reality, poetically informed, which may draw from the actor, supplementing from actual experience, artistic consummation.   CYRIL CUSACK

The abiding popularity of O'Casey's first three Abbey successes has made him far and away the most frequently performed of all playwrights in his native city. *The Shadow of a Gunman* was the first of several dramas on the Irish 'Troubles' in which O'Casey concentrated on the comic and pathetic aspects of war rather than on its patriotic glories. *Juno and the Paycock* and *The Plough and the Stars* showed the writer expanding his craft in characterization, theme and setting; indeed, the third play is truly of epic compass. Dramatizing the 1916 Easter Rising, *The Plough* greatly offended nationalist opinion in Ireland and the resulting riots at the Abbey were the most serious there since those against Synge's *The Playboy of the Western World* in 1907. Though fortified by the vigorous defence of Yeats, O'Casey experienced a sense of bitterness that persisted for many years; leaving Ireland in March 1926, he spent his remaining years in self-imposed exile.

There followed an intensely experimental phase, inaugurated by *The Silver Tassie* (1928) and including *Within the Gates* (1933) and *Red Roses for Me* (1942). These works are characterized by a daring mixture of disparate elements: lyrical speech mingles with demotic utterance; choric effects and liturgical ceremony are found side by side with everyday realistic elements; knockabout farce is infused with heightened (even incantatory) language and actions; songs and dancing are given increased prominence.

A high price was exacted for such audacity. The Abbey Theatre rejected *The Tassie* and never premièred another play by O'Casey, who found it increasingly difficult to get his work staged. The scarcity of productions of his post-Abbey plays meant that O'Casey was forced to publish work before seeing it performed, and this necessitated textual revisions after publication for most of his later dramas. It also occasioned considerable financial hardship for a man with growing family responsibilities. He had in 1927 married Eileen Carey

Reynolds, an Irish actress, and their three children were born between 1928 and 1939. On and off, from 1930 to 1954, the dramatist was engaged in writing an autobiography which, starting as a few impressionistic sketches of a slum childhood, eventually assumed epic proportions within six volumes that provided the family's principal source of livelihood for almost three decades.

Two dissimilar plays were issued in 1940: *The Star Turns Red*, a somewhat heavy-handed political allegory of a world divided into two armed camps, and *Purple Dust*, in which for the first time O'Casey turned to an Irish rural setting and to a largely farcical treatment of contemporary cultural and social issues. This work inaugurated a new creative phase. O'Casey's later plays – from *Purple Dust* to *Cock-a-Doodle Dandy* (1949), *The Bishop's Bonfire* (1955), *The Drums of Father Ned* (1959) and *Behind the Green Curtains* (1961) – realize dramatically the stultifying conditions of contemporary life in rural Ireland. Each one contains a good deal of satire directed at the narrow-minded materialism of the middle-class businessmen running an increasingly authoritarian country with the support of the church establishment. Artistically, these plays are a mixed bag, yet *Cock-a-Doodle Dandy* and *The Bishop's Bonfire*, in which the more enlightened young people are forced to leave the country, deserve recognition alongside the early Dublin masterpieces.

Though there was towards the end of the century, in some circles, increased appreciation of O'Casey's original contributions to working-class drama (and of his influence on playwrights such as JOHN ARDEN, ARNOLD WESKER, HENRY LIVINGS, BRENDAN BEHAN and BRIAN FRIEL), he was still to come fully into his own, critically, and evaluation of his more AVANT-GARDE writings waited upon their adequate theatrical realization.
RONALD AYLING

Ronald Ayling and Michael J. Durkan, *Sean O'Casey: A Bibliography* (1978)

Heinz Kosok, *O'Casey, the Dramatist* (1985)

David Krause, *Sean O'Casey: The Man and his Work* (1975)

E. H. Mikhail, *Sean O'Casey and his Critics: An Annotated Bibliography* (1985)

Eileen O'Casey, *Sean* (1971)

Bernice Schrank, *Sean O'Casey: A Research and Production Sourcebook* (1996)

Ockrent, Mike *see* TRAVERSE THEATRE

O'Dea, Jimmy (b. Dublin, 26 April 1899; d. Dublin, 7 Jan. 1965) Comedian. He spent his early years touring in VARIETY throughout the British Isles until he became established as Ireland's leading character comedian in the 1940s. He was chiefly associated with the Royal, the Olympia and the Gaiety Theatres in DUBLIN, appearing in Christmas PANTOMIME and summer REVUE in the latter for 20 years with his scriptwriter partner Harry O'Donovan. During the Second World War he had a weekly comedy programme on BBC radio, and in later years his own show on Irish television. He also appeared in Dublin GATE THEATRE productions, notably as Bottom. His most famous stage character was 'Biddy Mulligan, Pride of the Coombe'. CHRISTOPHER FITZ-SIMON

Odéon First built in 1782 to house the COMÉDIE-FRANÇAISE, it became France's second national theatre when it reopened in 1819 after burning down twice. From 1946 to 1959 the company was merged with the Comédie-Française, which used the Odéon as its second house, often for more modern works. Renamed the Théâtre de France (1959) during MALRAUX's reorganization of theatre, it reverted to the Comédie-Française and the title Théâtre National in 1971. Past directors include ANTOINE, GÉMIER and BARRAULT, under whom the company staged major modern productions (e.g. of CLAUDEL, IONESCO, GENET) until he was dismissed by Malraux, who had appointed him, for being too lenient when students occupied the theatre in May 1968. THÉÂTRE DES NATIONS productions appeared at the Odéon from 1967 to 1970 and the international Théâtre de l'Europe is based there. The Odéon is now once again independent from the Comédie-Française. ANNA MCMULLAN

Odets, Clifford (b. Philadelphia, 18 July 1906; d. Los Angeles, 14 Aug. 1963) Playwright and screenwriter. The major plays of Clifford Odets, the Golden Boy of Depression drama, articulate the faith that an economically debilitated society can create a new world in which 'happiness isn't printed on dollar bills.' As a young actor in the late 1920s, Odets was a charter member of the newly formed GROUP THEATER. Making little impact as an actor, he turned to playwriting, though the Group leadership would not produce him until the sensational success of a play Odets wrote for a radical theatre benefit: *Waiting for Lefty* (1935). About the conversion to militancy of a series of taxi-cab workers, *Lefty*, like JOHN OSBORNE's *Look Back in Anger* two decades later, struck the chord of its era, and within a few months of its debut was performed all over the world. The Group rushed into production an earlier play by its new sensation, *Awake and Sing!* (1935), which revealed the young dramatist as not only a fervent revolutionary but a skilful recorder of lower middle-class Jewish life.

Throughout the remainder of the life of the Group, which exactly coincided with the decade, Odets was its major playwright, with HAROLD CLURMAN directing productions of *Paradise Lost* (1935), *Golden Boy* (1937), *Rocket to the Moon* (1939) and *Night Music* (1940). Yet Odets' relationship with the Group was ambivalent and often conducted at long distance, since he had succumbed to Hollywood's blandishments and gone west to write such screenplays as *The General Died at Dawn* (1936) and *Blockade* (1938). Returning to New York in 1937, he offered the Group *Golden Boy*, a cautionary prize-fighting parable about the lust for success, characterized by a revulsion best expressed in his later play *The Big Knife* (1949), a definitive excoriation of Hollywood mendacity. His tortured love affair with the film capital lasted until his death there in 1963.

Odets enjoyed his greatest post-Group success with *The Country Girl* (1950), an apolitical study of an alcoholic actor and his wife. Despite Odets' loss of radical commitment, he was called before the House Committee on Un-American Activities in 1952, where he performed the demanded act of contrition by naming communists in the Group. The last decade of his life was spent largely in the worlds of film and television, his last substantial achievement ironically being the screenplay for *Sweet Smell of Success* (1957). GERALD RABKIN

Margaret Brenman-Gibson, *Clifford Odets: American Playwright* (1982)

Harold Clurman, *The Fervent Years* (1945)

Gerald Rabkin, *Drama and Commitment* (1964)

R. Baird Shuman, *Clifford Odets* (1962)

Odin Teatret (Nordic Theatre Arts Laboratory)
International theatre company, founded in Oslo in 1964 by Italian director EUGENIO BARBA following his three years spent with GROTOWSKI in Poland. After its first production, *Ortofilene*, had successfully toured Scandinavia, the company was invited to move to Hol-

stebro in Denmark. This has been its centre ever since, from which it tours globally, and the site of much international exchange and research. Based on an enclosed community of performers who follow intense physical and vocal training, the company is a COLLECTIVE who create together and together run the organization. Performances are given only when the company is ready, and at first were often for preference presented to small audiences. As Barba began to develop his ideas of THIRD THEATRE – neither protected nor the self-consciously AVANT-GARDE theatre of the subsidized sector – Odin embraced popular forms such as STREET THEATRE more akin to CIRCUS (e.g. *Anabasis*, 1977) but still subjected to its own fierce discipline. It also introduced a barter system, whereby audiences pay with a performance of their own or participation in a community activity. Odin remains one of the most influential groups to have emerged in the 1960s. Productions include *The Book of the Dance* (1974), *Come! and the Day Will Be Ours* (1976), *The Million* (1978), *Brecht's Ashes* (1980), *The Gospel According to Oxyrhincus* (1985), *Talabot* (1988) and *Kaosmos* (1993). In 1979 Barba founded the International School of THEATRE ANTHROPOLOGY at the theatre in Holstebro, to which Odin has made a major contribution. CHARLES LONDON

Ian Watson, *Towards a Third Theatre: Eugenio Barba and the Odin Teatret* (1993)

O'Donoghue, John (b. Newcastle, NSW, Australia, 5 Aug. 1929) Playwright. Though his first published play, *A Happy and Holy Occasion* (1976), is a remarkably assured and powerful piece of writing, it was *Essington Lewis: I Am Work* (1981) which attracted most attention, being hailed by one critic as a 'national treasure'. It is a sorry comment on the artistic policies of the major subsidized companies that this work, an exuberant, celebratory yet incisive and satirical look at the life of the worker turned manager of Australia's biggest company, had to wait four years to be seen in Sydney, and was not published till 1987. O'Donoghue's plays include *In the Field Where They Buried Peter Pan* (1982) and *Abbie and Lou, Norman and Rose* (1993).
MICHAEL MORLEY

Oenslager, Donald [Mitchell] (b. Harrisburg, Pa., 7 March 1902; d. Bedford, NY, 21 June 1975) Scene designer and teacher. He studied under GEORGE PIERCE BAKER and designed sets for the 47 Workshop. After a year of travel in Europe where he saw the work of APPIA and CRAIG, he made his New York design debut with the ballet *Sooner or Later* (1925) at the NEIGHBORHOOD PLAYHOUSE. At the PROVINCETOWN Playhouse he worked with ROBERT EDMOND JONES, who became his

mentor. Oenslager designed over 250 New York productions including *Anything Goes* (1934), *Johnson* (1936), *You Can't Take it With You* (1936), *Of Mice and Men* (1937) and *The Man Who Came to Dinner* (1939), and became especially noted for his elegant interiors. He was particularly influential as a teacher at Yale University (1925–71) and assembled an important collection of historical theatrical designs. He wrote *Scenery, Then and Now* (1936), *Stage Design: Four Centuries of Scenic Inventions* (1975) and *The Theatre of Donald Oenslager* (1978). FELICIA HARDISON LONDRÉ

Off-Broadway The development of an alternative theatre offering experimental work and new plays that were off the mainstream of conventional BROADWAY theatre started around the beginning of the twentieth century, but was particularly a phenomenon of the years following the Second World War. During the 1950s a variety of ad hoc venues, run on shoestring budgets, sprung up in and around Greenwich Village and on the East Side of New York, and soon quickly challenged the complacency of the commercial theatre. Theatres like CIRCLE IN THE SQUARE, Théâtre de Lys, the NEGRO ENSEMBLE COMPANY, the NEW YORK SHAKESPEARE FESTIVAL and the MANHATTAN THEATER CLUB produced some of the best and most adventurous new plays as well as reviving neglected classics. Some of these productions enjoyed long runs, such as *The Threepenny Opera* at the Théâtre de Lys (1955–61), or later transferred to Broadway. The LUCILLE LORTEL awards and the Obie awards (set up by the *Village Voice* paper in 1955) are given for achievement Off-Broadway. Over the years Off-Broadway served not only as a place where new actors and directors could show their talents, but also one where established artists, jaded by their work in commercial theatre and films, could take up new artistic challenges. Inevitably, Off-Broadway became a victim of its own success: as critical acclaim for its productions promoted it to a parallel version of Broadway, so the experimental element of its work became diluted, and newer and untried talent turned increasingly to the OFF-OFF-BROADWAY circuit. HELEN RAPPAPORT

H. Greenberger, *The Off-Broadway Experience* (1971)
S. Little, *Off-Broadway: The Prophetic Theatre* (1972)
J. Price, *The Off-Broadway Theatre* (1962)

Off-Off-Broadway When Joe Cino put on plays in his tiny coffee house in 1959, CAFFÉ CINO launched Off-Off-Broadway. The era of social protest in the 1960s and 1970s saw an increasing demand for plays which would provide a forum for the serious exploration of issues like black, feminist and gay rights, which the commerical theatre is traditionally reluctant to tackle. This movement inspired a whole new generation of playwrights, actors and directors looking for freedom of expression in a non-commercial environment which even OFF-BROADWAY could no longer provide. In its wake, a rash of experimental, AVANT-GARDE and STREET THEATRE groups, many of them short-lived, sprang up in an astonishing variety of spaces – lofts, basements, churches, cafés – which, along with the more influential groups like the OPEN THEATER, LA MAMA, PERFORMANCE GROUP, LIVING THEATER, JUDSON CHURCH Poet's Theater and BREAD AND PUPPET THEATER, challenged social, literary and theatrical convention. Once the intitial period of anarchic or at times undisciplined experimentation had died down, venues began to offer the works of more accomplished playwrights like SAM SHEPARD, DAVID RABE and TERRENCE MCNALLY, and the influence of Off-Off-Broadway was felt on Broadway itself and beyond. Off-Off-Broadway in its turn seems to have lost its original vitality and impetus, and is frequently used as a try-out for pre-Broadway plays. HELEN RAPPAPORT

A. Poland, A. and B. Mailman, *The Off-Off-Broadway Book* (1972)

Ogunyemi, Wale (b. Igbajo, Oyo State, Nigeria, 12 Aug. 1939) Actor, director and playwright. He embraces the totality of African theatre – music, dance, dialogue – to explore the myth, history and politics of Nigeria. His plays are traditional and mythical, such as *The Vow* (1962), *Obaluaye* (1968), *The Scheme* (1967), *Eshu Elegba* (1971), the historical *Ijaye War* (1968, 1970) and *Kiriji War* (1976), the satirical *Skrigo* (1997) and *Queen Amina of ZauZau* (1997). He adapted Fagunwa's and SOYINKA's *Ogboju Ode* as *Langbodo* (1976), and *Macbeth* as *Aare Akogun* (1969). OLU OBAFEMI

Ohel Theatre Founded as a studio in 1925 in Tel Aviv by Moshé Halevi, a former HABIMAH actor, who recruited a group of young Jewish pioneers to whom he passed the rival methods of STANISLAVSKY and his student MEYERHOLD. The Ohel was later adopted by the Histadrut, the trades union organization, and labelled 'The Theatre of Israeli Workers' (1934–62). Organized (like Habimah) as a COLLECTIVE, it was meant to be a Jewish proletarian theatre, and its name (Hebrew for 'tent') revived both biblical and modern pioneering images. In its early period the Ohel did specialize in ideological repertory: biblical, Zionist and social plays. Later it became just another theatre, and it closed in 1969. AVRAHAM OZ

O'Horgan, Tom [Thomas Foster] (b. Chicago, 3 May 1927) Director and composer. O'Horgan made a name for himself in OFF-OFF-BROADWAY, in particular for his work with LA MAMA (e.g. *Futz*, 1967). He is best known, however, for his staging of the musicals *Hair* (1968) and *Jesus Christ Superstar* (1971), winning a Tony award for the former. He has also composed music for numerous stage productions and films. HELEN RAPPAPORT

Okhlopkov, Nikolai [Pavlovich] (b. Irkutsk, Russia, 2 May 1900; d. Moscow, 8 Jan. 1967) Stage and film director and actor. Okhlopkov made his directorial debut in 1921, when he staged a mass PAGEANT on the main square of his home town. In 1922 he joined MEYERHOLD's State Higher Directors' Workshop, acting in several productions between 1922 and 1926 and meeting, among others, EISENSTEIN, with whom he was to work and develop notions of montage. Devoted to the idea of theatre as spectacle and deriving many of his ideas from ancient and oriental theatre and from medieval and Renaissance public festivals, Okhlopkov found himself in charge of Moscow's tiny Realistic Theatre (1931–7). He completely rethought the idea of theatre space, staging plays in the round and even above the heads of the audience, reconceiving the relationship between setting and spectator in a series of radical and innovatory experimental productions of a politically committed nature (e.g. GORKY's *The Mother*, 1933). During the 1950s and 1960s Okhlopkov was artistic director of Moscow's Mayakovsky Theatre, where he staged a notable *Hamlet* (1954). He returned to the notion of theatre as mass spectacle in 1961 with a production of Euripides' *Medea* staged in the central square in Minsk. NICK WORRALL

See also THEATRE IN THE ROUND.

A. van Gyseghem, *A Theatre in Soviet Russia* (1943)
Nick Worrall, *Modernism to Realism on the Soviet Stage: Tairov–Vakhtangov–Okhlopkov* (1989)

Old Globe Theater A reconstruction in SAN DIEGO's Balboa Park of Shakespeare's Globe, it was opened in 1935 as an attraction of the California Pacific International Exposition. Nineteen different Shakespeare plays were presented in 50-minute versions prepared by BEN IDEN PAYNE and Thomas Wood Stevens. When the fair ended in 1936, citizens protested at the theatre's scheduled demolition and raised funds to renovate it for use as a community theatre. A summer Equity company was inaugurated in 1959. The original theatre was destroyed by fire in 1978, but a new outdoor Festival Stage was opened in 1982 as part of a three-theatre complex, named the Simon Edison Centre for the Performing Arts, which mingles première productions with its continuing commitment to Shakespeare. The Festival Stage was itself destroyed by fire in 1984 and was replaced by the outdoor Lowell Davies Festival Theatre in 1985. The company was awarded a Tony in 1984 for excellence in regional theatre.

FELICIA HARDISON LONDRÉ

See also GLOBE THEATRE; SHAKESPEARE FESTIVALS.

old people *see* THEATRE FOR OLD PEOPLE

Old Tote Theatre From 1963 to 1978, the major professional theatre in Sydney, providing a nursery for a generation of actors and directors. It was founded by Professor Robert Quentin, of the University of New South Wales, in a former racecourse totalizator building on its campus. After two years, he handed artistic direction to Robin Lovejoy, who survived until 1974. Thereafter, the Old Tote declined – though ROBERT HELPMANN was briefly a successor. Criticized from 1964 on for concentrating on classic and overseas plays, the Old Tote established the tiny Jane Street Theatre to develop Australian work, and commissioned plays by DAVID WILLIAMSON, ALEX BUZO, PATRICK WHITE and Tom Keneally. In 1970 TYRONE GUTHRIE directed *King Oedipus*, while *The Legend of King O'Malley*, a seminal local work, played at Jane Street. In 1973, the Old Tote took up residence in the new Sydney Opera House Drama Theatre, but, over-extended elsewhere, it lost funding and closed. JEREMY ECCLES

Leslie Rees, *A History of Australian Drama* (1987)

Old Vic A London theatre which opened in 1818 outside 'theatreland' on a site south of the newly built Waterloo Bridge, originally called the Coburg and rechristened the Royal Victoria in 1833, whence it earned its familiar name. In 1880 the tenancy was taken over by the Coffee Music Hall Association, of which the driving force was the social worker EMMA CONS, with her mission to preach temperance and offer entertainment and education to the working classes of south London. The entertainment settled into a pattern of variety and concerts, including concert versions of operas, while the education, developing from lectures, was taken under the wing of Morley College (housed in the theatre until 1924).

In 1898 Cons was joined in the management by her niece, LILIAN BAYLIS, who became director of the theatre after the former's death in 1912. An experiment in staging plays in 1914 developed until the theatre became the home of popular Shakespeare, plainly presented, for local audiences at prices they could afford, while the operatic performances were fully staged. The challenge of wartime conditions gave Old Vic Shakespeare a purpose to which the leadership

of Baylis and her first resident director of productions, BEN GREET, were crucial; by 1923 they had staged all the plays in the First Folio.

In the 1920s, particularly after Morley College gave up occupation of the building, this purpose was developed by a close-knit company offering chiefly Shakespeare but also other classical plays, and was sustained by a line of directors, notably ROBERT ATKINS (1920–4) and HARCOURT WILLIAMS (1929–33). A succession of Old Vic actors dedicated themselves to the demands of the theatre, in which hard work had largely to be its own reward. Among these were Russell and SYBIL THORNDIKE, ERNEST MILTON, Ion Swinley and John Laurie.

Increasingly, established performers were drawn to the company, notably EDITH EVANS (1925), JOHN GIELGUD (1929) and RALPH RICHARDSON (1930). The opera programme continued and a nucleus of dancers was assembled under NINETTE DE VALOIS. In 1931, after lengthy preparations, SADLER'S WELLS Theatre was rebuilt and opened under the joint management of the Old Vic, but the practice of exchanging productions proved unworkable, and from 1935 their functions were divided, opera and ballet being confined to Sadler's Wells.

A new era was initiated by the appointment in 1933 of TYRONE GUTHRIE as director of productions. He reduced the number of plays, raised the standards of performance and recruited his company much more widely, for example bringing in CHARLES LAUGHTON, already an international film star, for the season 1933–4. The Old Vic became a leading London theatre, its productions achieving national acclaim, particularly through the performances of LAURENCE OLIVIER in 1937–8, the return of Richardson, and an extension of the repertoire to include foreign classics as well as a more representative selection of British plays. After Baylis's death in 1937 Guthrie took full control.

The theatre closed on the outbreak of the Second World War, although a company led by Gielgud appeared there in the spring of 1940. Thereafter the Old Vic played elsewhere, and in 1941 the theatre was damaged by bombing. Towards the end of the war Guthrie initiated a period of dazzling success for the company with a season at the New Theatre, London, in which Olivier and Richardson registered a series of acting triumphs, taking over direction of the company in 1945. Meanwhile the Old Vic itself was designated a Theatre Centre, under MICHEL SAINT-DENIS, with an Old Vic School under GLEN BYAM SHAW and GEORGE DEVINE. Richardson left the company in 1947, Olivier in 1949, and its return to the theatre in 1950 involved a conflict with its existing function, leading to the resignation of the Centre and School directors. Guthrie came back briefly, and the theatre found stability with a five-year plan to stage again all Shakespeare's First Folio plays, devised by MICHAEL BENTHALL between 1953 and 1958. In the latter year the adjacent Old Vic Annexe was built.

The creation of a NATIONAL THEATRE Company under Olivier led to the decision to make the Old Vic its temporary home. The Company appeared there between 1963 and 1976, achieving many outstanding productions. After the opening of the National Theatre on the South Bank the function and funding of the Old Vic became increasingly problematic, although the former PROSPECT COMPANY restored its status as a classical house with limited seasons between 1977 and 1981. The withdrawal of the Company's Arts Council grant put an end to this, and in 1982 the theatre was sold to the Canadian impresario Edwin Mirvish, who undertook extensive restoration. From 1983 to 1997, when he put the Old Vic up for sale, he maintained it as a home of chiefly classical plays with directors JONATHAN MILLER and later PETER HALL trying to renew the spirit of the famous place. The Old Vic Trust bought the theatre and offered the dance company Adventures in Motion Pictures a residency while continuing to host mainstream drama. G. ROWELL

John Booth, *The Old Vic 1816–1916* (1917)
Richard Findlater, *Lilian Baylis: The Lady of the Old Vic* (1975)
Cicely Hamilton and Lilian Baylis, *The Old Vic* (1926)
Peter Roberts, *The Old Vic Story* (1976)
George Rowell, *The Old Vic Theatre: A History* (1993)
Harcourt Williams, *Four Years at the Old Vic* (1935)
——, *Old Vic Saga* (1949)

Olesha, Yuri [Karlevich] (b. Elizavetgrad, Russia, 3 March 1899; d. Moscow, 10 May 1960) Playwright. Though he first made his name as a poet and novelist, it was as a playwright who dramatized the dilemmas of the bourgeois intellectual under communism that he achieved his most controversial successes. His two major dramas, *Zagovor Chuvstv* (*A Conspiracy of Feelings*, 1929) and *Spisok blagodeyanii* (*A List of Assets*, 1931, directed by MEYERHOLD), are carefully constructed, yet, despite psychological insight, are somewhat melodramatic in their action. Perhaps this was due to the overbearing nature of the Soviet regime, which virtually silenced him from the early 1930s to 1956. His promise as a playwright remained unfulfilled. ROBERT LEACH

Olivier, Laurence [Kerr] (b. Dorking, Surrey, 22 May 1907; d. Steyning, W. Sussex, 11 July 1989) Actor, director, manager. The son of an Anglo-Catholic priest, Olivier demonstrated few gifts as a child for anything other than acting, but at this he was from the earliest age exceptional. ELLEN TERRY and SYBIL THORNDIKE recognized his talent as a schoolboy actor; his early career, however, was far from meteoric. Slight of build, gap-toothed, his face burdened with continuous eyebrows and a very low forehead, he presented a somewhat wild appearance. Possessed also of enormous high spirits and a propensity for uncontrollable giggling on stage, he clearly needed taming. This was provided first of all by the Central School, then run by its founder ELSIE FOGERTY, by a season or two at the BIRMINGHAM REPERTORY THEATRE (1926–8) and finally by a longish stint in the unrewarding role of Victor Prynne in the London and New York runs of COWARD's *Private Lives* (1930–1), with the author in the cast to keep a sharp eye on him. At this stage, Olivier's ambitions were entirely directed towards achieving the status of romantic leading man. He made a number of miscalculations, however: instead of continuing with the role of Stanhope in *Journey's End* (1928), which he had created, he chose to star in *Beau Geste*, a conspicuous catastrophe; and a brief visit to Hollywood had left him disenchanted with film. The turning point in his career came when, in 1935, JOHN GIELGUD, who had directed him the year before in *Queen of Scots*, invited him to alternate the roles of Romeo and Mercutio with him. Olivier, having had his teeth and hairline adjusted, and having acquired a degree of professional discipline, came to Shakespeare with a passionate conviction that the plays were essentially realistic. His performances, as a highly sexed Mediterranean Romeo and a dangerous wild Mercutio, created a sensation, most particularly by contrast with the lyrical and aesthetic performances of Gielgud. His verse speaking was disparaged, but it was clear that an actor capable of re-inventing the tradition of classical acting had arrived. This was confirmed when in 1937 he joined the OLD VIC company under the direction of TYRONE GUTHRIE, playing in quick succession Hamlet, Henry V, Macbeth, Coriolanus and Iago. Thus established as a leading classical actor, he returned to Hollywood for *Wuthering Heights* (1939). His Heathcliff gave him international stardom, but with England at war, he returned home as quickly as possible (against the instructions of the British Embassy), first to join the Fleet Air Arm, then to direct a film of *Henry V* (1944) as part of the war effort. This triumphant success was followed the same year by co-directorship with RALPH RICHARDSON and MICHAEL BENTHALL of the Old Vic. The company's productions of *Peer Gynt*, *Henry IV*, *Arms and the Man* and *King Lear* became a focus of national pride to such an extent that the theatre became a national theatre in all but name. Richardson's performances and his own, above all as Richard III and in the audacious double bill of *Oedipus Rex* and *The Critic*, were high-water marks of the modern British theatre. It is all the more astonishing that, in one of the most disgraceful episodes of recent theatre history, when plans were laid to establish the NATIONAL THEATRE at the Old Vic in 1946, it was decided Olivier and Richardson would not head it; actors, it was felt, were unsuitable for the task of running so important and complex an organization.

Olivier went into theatre management on his own; for some years he was more involved in directing or presenting than acting. He re-entered the lists as a tragic Shakespearean actor with *Macbeth* and *Titus Andronicus* (Stratford, 1955), the latter directed by PETER BROOK and with Olivier's second wife, VIVIEN LEIGH, as Lavinia. Both performances were acclaimed, the Titus particularly being an adventurous interpretation in a startling production. It seemed to prepare him for the great leap which he took two years later, when he appeared at the ROYAL COURT THEATRE as Archie Rice in JOHN OSBORNE's *The Entertainer* (with his third wife to be, JOAN PLOWRIGHT). The first actor of his generation or stature to associate himself with the new wave of playwrights, he scored an enormous personal success and boosted the new movement. His straddling of the old and the new, his managerial experience and his personal authority made him, belatedly, the inevitable and only choice for the directorship of the National Theatre when in 1962 it was finally voted into being by parliament. Drawing together the best talents from the various theatrical worlds he had inhabited, he created an organization which for some years set new standards of excellence. Directing, acting (his Shylock, Edgar in STRINDBERG's *Dance of Death*, James Tyrone in O'NEILL's *Long Day's Journey into Night* and Tagg in *The Party* by TREVOR GRIFFITHS were among the outstanding creations of those years) and leading very much from the front, he brought the century-old dream of a National Theatre to life in a way that no one else could have done. Towards the end of his tenure tiredness and ill-health led to a slight decline in the vigour of the work, but he had laid the foundations of a flourishing theatre.

After retiring from the National Theatre in 1973, three years before the opening of its new complex with an auditorium bearing his name, he never appeared on stage again, though he continued to make film appearances. After the Second World War he acted in over 20 films, often with great distinction, but without ever quite seeming to belong in the medium. It is his work on the stage that brought him the immortality he so fervently sought, and from the early 1950s it was a commonplace for English-speaking actors (Americans as well as British) to refer to him as the greatest living actor. Certainly no one in the twentieth century has challenged himself more. Transforming himself vocally and physically for every part, he left an indelible stamp on a number of the greatest roles in the repertory. He always sought a realistic core to his characterizations which sometimes robbed them of their poetry or their grandeur; but in compensation he brought comedy verging on the vulgar, physical audacity bordering on the reckless and an emotional intensity that could be terrifying. Olivier never concealed his virtuosity: he wanted his audiences to be as interested in the mechanics of acting as he was. His ambition was so huge, his achievement so great, that his disappearance from the stage left something of a vacuum. This was to some extent deliberate: asked who would inherit Kean's sword (given to Olivier by John Gielgud), he replied: 'No one; it's mine.'

Olivier was knighted in 1947, and created baron in 1970 and Companion of Honour in 1981.

SIMON CALLOW

Melvyn Bragg, *Laurence Olivier* (1989)
Anthony Holden, *Olivier* (1988)
Thomas Kiernan, *Olivier, The Life of Laurence Olivier* (1981)
Raymond Lefèvre, *Sir Laurence Olivier* (1980)
Donald Spoto, *Laurence Olivier: A Biography* (1991)

Olivier Awards   *see* AWARDS AND PRIZES

Olivier Theatre   *see* ARCHITECTURE; NATIONAL THEATRE

Omaha Magic Theater   Theatre company. Founded in 1968 in Omaha, Nebraska, by Jo Ann Schmidman to push to new limits the boundaries of what is recognized as theatre, often using music and EXPERIMENTAL techniques. Joined in 1971 by OPEN THEATER founder member MEGAN TERRY as literary manager and resident playwright, the company, which tours, has won a national reputation with shows such as *Babes in the Bighouse* (1974), *American King's English for Queens* (1978), *Walking Through Walls* (1987) and *Body Leaks* (1990).   CHARLES LONDON

O'Malley, Mary   *see* BELFAST

Omotoso, Kole   (b. Akure, Nigeria, 21 April 1943). Playwright, novelist, actor and journalist. A member of the AVANT-GARDE generation on the Nigerian dramatic scene, he studied in Ibadan and took his doctoral degree in Edinburgh in 1968. His work includes the part-absurdist, part-political plays *The Curse* (1976) and

Shadows on the Horizon (1975), which expose the vulgarity of bourgeios wealth, and the essence of revolutionary action by the oppressed classes for social liberation and equality. Apart from his numerous novels and polemical essays, he has produced 30 serial episodes entitled *Life off the Curse* (1981–2) for the Nigerian Television Authority. OLU OBAFEMI

one man/one woman show *see* SOLO SHOW

O'Neal, Frederick (b. Brooksville, Miss., 27 Aug. 1905; d. New York, 25 Aug. 1992) Actor. He made his first stage appearance in 1927 in *As You Like It* for the Ira Aldridge Players of St Louis, which he founded. After moving to New York and attending the New Theater School, he joined forces with the writer Abram Hill to found the AMERICAN NEGRO THEATER in 1940, appearing to considerable acclaim as Frank in Philip Yordan's *Anna Lucasta* (1944), which ran for three years on Broadway and was also staged in London (1947). As well as appearing in *Lost in the Stars* (1949) and *Take a Giant Step* (1953), he made several films and appeared in the 1960s hit television show *Car 54 Where Are You?* He did much to encourage black actors in the profession, as president of the Negro Actors' Guild (1961–4), as well as serving as president emeritus of American Equity (*see* UNIONS). He also received numerous awards, including five honorary doctorates. HELEN RAPPAPORT

O'Neill, Eugene [Gladstone] (b. New York, 16 Oct. 1888; d. Boston, 27 Nov. 1953) Playwright. The third son of the popular Irish American actor, James O'Neill, and Mary Ellen (Ella) Quinlan, Eugene was taken on tour as an infant while his father performed in his perennial starring vehicle, *Monte Cristo*, a role he played some 4,000 times. Both the melodrama and his father's portrayal of the romantic hero formed an ironic counterpoint to several of O'Neill's later tragedies, including *A Touch of the Poet* and *Long Day's Journey into Night*. In the latter play, O'Neill spoke with candour, accurately depicting both his parents as struggling against entrapment: James from the melodrama which vulgarized his talent, Ella from an addiction to morphine she was given as an anodyne for pain after Eugene's birth.

Eugene was educated in Catholic preparatory schools and spent a semester at Princeton University before beginning a period of wandering he later called a 'seeking flight'. He took ship as a sailor to South America and Europe, and between voyages lived the life of an alcoholic derelict in bars and flophouses on the New York waterfront. There, after a failed suicide attempt, he contracted tuberculosis, and in 1912 was sent to a sanatorium. While recovering, he read STRINDBERG, SHAW, Conrad, Nietzsche, SYNGE, BRIEUX and HAUPTMANN. Discharged in 1913, he began to write. His first book, *Thirst and Other One Act Plays*, was privately printed the following year and displayed the influence of European naturalistic dramas wherein the central characters are crushed by a form of 'ironic fate' they cannot control.

He enrolled for a year in a playwriting course at Harvard University, and in 1916, at Provincetown, Massachusetts, met a group of literati headed by the essayist George Cram Cook, the playwright SUSAN GLASPELL and John Reed, the radical journalist. Playing at theatre as a summer amusement, the group staged O'Neill's one-act sea play, *Bound East for Cardiff*. In this simple, moving account of the death of a sailor, O'Neill's characteristic voice was first heard. Its success encouraged the group, known as the PROVINCETOWN PLAYERS, to continue in New York's Greenwich Village as The Playwright's Theatre at the Provincetown Playhouse, where many of O'Neill's early experimental one-act plays were first staged.

He began to write full-length plays, among them the naturalistic *Beyond the Horizon* (1920), recounting the tragic lives of two brothers, one who 'belongs' to the sea, the other to the land. The theme of 'belonging' was further explored in *Anna Christie* (1921), the story of a woman who 'belongs' to the sea but who, when forced to live inland, far from her right world, becomes a prostitute. Returning to the sea, she is able to purge herself and find spiritual salvation. Both plays received the Pulitzer Prize for drama. *The Emperor Jones* (1920), the first American drama to star a black actor, became a major success, as did the expressionistic account of a stoker in a futile quest for something to which he can belong, *The Hairy Ape* (1922).

During the 1920s, in both Europe and the United States, O'Neill became known as a daring playwright whose theatrical experiments with sound, lighting and monologues (some of which encompassed the entire play) were enlarging the scope of the American theatre. He was befriended by critics like GEORGE JEAN NATHAN, and his work was published in AVANT-GARDE magazines and in book form. In his personal life, he found both joy and sorrow. He had undergone a forced marriage to Kathleen Jenkins in 1909 and fathered a son, Eugene O'Neill Jr. The two were divorced in 1912, and in 1918 he married a young writer, Agnes Boulton. Two children were born of that marriage, Shane Rudraighe in 1919 and Oona in 1925. Between 1920 and 1923, however, Eugene's father, mother and brother died, each in tragic circumstances.

After the production in 1924 of two controversial plays, *Desire under the Elms*, an Oedipal tragedy of life

· Performing O'Neill ·

The most important thing with O'Neill is to trust the words. There's always a mystery, a secret, something you have to find out, but the key is to follow the blueprint he has set up and not to deny it or drastically change it. When I first played Hickey in *The Iceman Cometh* I erased all his stage directions; but I soon discovered that they were just as important as the dialogue. He lays it all out for you and gives you a lead. It may take a while to discover, but it's there. For example, I don't think he overwrites. There is a method in his repetition, and as an actor you have to find his music. O'Neill was such a good writer that I didn't have any problems with phrasing or rhythm and I never found him obtuse in the plays that I did. He was theatrical – he had a bit of melodrama in him, probably from watching his father perform, and that schooled him in theatre. He knew what he was doing as a playwright. When I read *A Moon for the Misbegotten* I thought it was a Freudian soap opera, but suddenly when I played it I realized it wasn't that at all. It's all there in the writing, and he helps you a lot if you stick with him. **JASON ROBARDS**

on a stony New England farm, heavily influenced by the philosophy of Friedrich Nietzsche, and *All God's Chillun Got Wings*, which centres on the marriage of a young black lawyer and a white woman, the O'Neills moved to Bermuda, where he worked on dramas with large philosophical and psychological concerns. The immediate results were impressive excursions into the non-realistic theatre, including *The Great God Brown* (1926), a drama that uses masks to present the inner and outer personalities of the characters; *Strange Interlude* (1928), a nine-act account of a woman's life wherein the characters reveal their inner lives through 'thought asides' addressed directly to the audience; *Marco Millions* (1928), a satire on the materialistic American businessman imagined as Marco Polo at the court of Kublai Khan; and a lavish choral drama, *Lazarus Laughed* (unproduced in New York City), in which O'Neill attempted to formulate the basis of a modern religion.

During this period he worked with the critic KENNETH MACGOWAN and the designer ROBERT EDMOND JONES as a producer in Greenwich Village, but *Marco Millions* and *Strange Interlude* were presented by the THEATER GUILD, the producing organization with which O'Neill was thereafter associated. *Strange Interlude* was an unprecedented success, both on stage and as a best-seller in book form. It won O'Neill's third Pulitzer Prize.

In 1926 O'Neill fell in love with Carlotta Monterey, an actress he had first met when she played in *The Hairy Ape*. In 1928, the two left for Europe and were married in 1929, when the divorce from Agnes was final. O'Neill's major undertaking in France was the trilogy *Mourning Becomes Electra* (1931), a version of the Greek story of the House of Atreus updated to the period immediately following the American Civil War. In Europe and the United States, the trilogy's success was exceptional. It was instrumental in gaining for O'Neill the Nobel Prize for Literature in 1936.

Upon returning to the United States in 1931, the O'Neills moved to Sea Island, Georgia, where Eugene wrote two plays: one a morality play about a man's quest for faith, *Days Without End*; the other a nostalgic, partly autobiographical comedy of turn-of-the-century American life, *Ah, Wilderness!* (Both were produced in 1933.) Thereafter O'Neill was not represented on the stage during his lifetime, but worked slowly and laboriously on *A Tale of Possessors Self-dispossessed*, an 11-play cycle of life in America from the days preceding the Revolutionary War to the then present. Only one of the plays, *A Touch of the Poet* (1958), was completed, although its remarkable sequel, *More Stately Mansions*, exists in unrevised draft form and was produced in a severely cut version in Stockholm in 1962 and in Los Angeles in 1967.

Moving to California in 1936, the O'Neills built Tao House overlooking the San Ramon Valley east of San Francisco. There O'Neill completed his last and greatest works, characterized by superb dramaturgy and profound sympathy for the human condition: the one-act, two-character *Hughie* (Stockholm, 1958; New York, 1964), and three semi-autobiographical works: *The Iceman Cometh* (1946), a deeply sympathetic study of the inhabitants of a slum bar who live without hope; his introspective view of his family's tragedy, *Long Day's Journey into Night* (1956); and its loving sequent play about his brother and the death of his mother, *A Moon for the Misbegotten* (1957). The accomplishment of the Tao House plays was achieved under tragic personal hardship: the estrangement of his children, a psychological depression occasioned by the outbreak of the war in Europe, and an increasingly debilitating health problem. At times he suffered from a tremor so intense that it was impossible for him to hold a pencil, much less to write. Too ill to complete the cycle, O'Neill destroyed it.

At the end of the Second World War the O'Neills moved to New York for the production of *The Iceman Cometh* and thence to Massachusetts. For a time their relationship was in jeopardy, brought about by illness in both partners. In the end, their marriage was restored, and Carlotta cared for her husband in a Boston hotel until he died. Thereafter, as his literary executor, she cared scrupulously for his plays, both in production and in library archives.

At his death, O'Neill was almost a forgotten playwright, but premières of several of the Tao House plays by the Royal Dramatic Theatre in Stockholm, followed by a New York revival of *The Iceman Cometh* in 1956, restored both his critical and his popular reputation. The New York production of *Long Day's Journey into Night* in the same year won O'Neill's fourth Pulitzer Prize and established him unquestionably as America's leading dramatist. TRAVIS BOGARD

Stephen Black, *Eugene O'Neill: Beyond Mourning and Tragedy* (1999)

Travis Bogard, *Contour in Time: The Plays of Eugene O'Neill* (rev. edn 1988).

Arthur Gelb and Barbara Gelb, *O'Neill* (rev. edn 1974)

Michal Mannheim, ed, *The Cambiridge Companion to O'Neill* (1998)

Yvonne Shafer, *Performing O'Neill: Conversations with Actors and Directors* (2000)

Louis Sheaffer, *O'Neill, Son and Playwright* (1968)

——, *O'Neill, Son and Artist* (1973)

O'Neill, Máire [Allgood, Molly] (b. Dublin, 1887; d. London, 2 Nov. 1952) Actress. In 1906 she joined the ABBEY THEATRE, where she subsequently created the part of Pegeen Mike in J. M. SYNGE's *The Playboy of the Western World* (1907). She was engaged to Synge, who died in 1909 before finishing his revisions of *Deidre of the Sorrows*, which he wrote for her; she married G. H. Mair, the *Manchester Guardian* theatre critic, in 1911, after which she acted in Britain with BEERBOHM TREE, J. B. FAGAN and other leading managers, and later in the United States. Her second husband was the Abbey actor Arthur Sinclair, with whom she and her sister SARA ALLGOOD often appeared. CHRISTOPHER FITZ-SIMON

O'Neill Theater Center (Eugene O'Neill Memorial Theater Center) Founded by George White in 1963 in Waterford, Connecticut, and named after America's only Nobel Prize winning playwright, it is dedicated to providing an environment for theatrical experimentation and the exchange of ideas between writers, directors, and actors, and combines the National Critics' Institute, the National Opera/Music Theater Conference and the National Playwrights' Conference. Its principal programme remains the presentation of new plays each summer, though the O'Neill also provides a permanent home for the NATIONAL THEATER OF THE DEAF, the Little Theater of the Deaf and the Creative Arts in Education Program. The National Playwrights' Conference, first held in 1965, helps young playwrights by presenting their work in staged readings and by allowing them to revise their scripts for further performance a week or so later. LLOYD RICHARDS was appointed artistic director in 1968. JOHN GUARE, AUGUST WILSON and LANFORD WILSON are among the beneficiaries. SUSAN PAULY

Open Space Founded in 1968 in Tottenham Court Road, London, by American director CHARLES MAROWITZ and Thelma Holt, who was to become an important producer/impresario breaking down England's theatrical isolation. The Open Space became an influential FRINGE venue inspired by the laboratory model from the United States (e.g. OPEN THEATER, LA MAMA) and Europe's AVANT-GARDE (e.g. GROTOWSKI). Though critical of groups that performed in similar spaces like the ARTS LAB, Marowitz was also more interested in performance style than in new writing, yet he provided an outlet in the evenings and at lunchtime for the likes of HOWARD BARKER, HOWARD BRENTON, DAVID EDGAR, TREVOR GRIFFITHS, DAVID RUDKIN (*Ashes* was premièred in 1974), SAM SHEPARD (*The Tooth of Crime* was premièred in 1972), MICHAEL WELLER and TED WHITEHEAD (*Mecca* was premièred in 1977); the first show, John Herbert's *Fortune and Men's Eyes*, even transferred to the WEST END. The theatre also became known for Marowitz's experimental Shakespeare (e.g. a voodoo *Macbeth*, 1970; a black power *Othello*, 1972; a Watergate-style *Measure for Measure*, 1975) before its closure in 1979, having been forced by office redevelopment to move round the corner two years earlier. A company toured until disbandment in 1981. COLIN CHAMBERS

open stage It may be defined as a theatre in which actors and audience share the same space, whereas in a proscenium theatre the enclosed stage is separated from the auditorium by the proscenium wall and its 'picture frame'. The open stage has been important in the twentieth century for practitioners striving to regain the three dimensional human quality of the actor, compared with the flat, two-dimensional effect of the proscenium stage. What may be seen as a seminal influence was the collaboration in 1911 of ADOLPHE APPIA and EMILE JAQUES-DALCROZE in the design of the Festival House in Hellerau, a suburb of Dresden, for the use of Dalcroze's students. It was Appia's inspiration to do away with proscenium frame and front curtain. The Hellerau summer festivals attracted the notice of many of the leading theatre artists in Europe and the United States. This initiative was sadly short-lived, however, due to the outbreak of war in 1914. JACQUES COPEAU's Théâtre du Vieux-Colombier, opened in Paris in 1913, was another major influence, though Copeau did not go so far as to dispense with a front curtain.

There are three main types of open stage: (1) the open-end stage, in which there is no separating proscenium wall or front curtain, but in which the audience still has a unified single view of the action, as in the proscenium theatre, though the barrier between actor and audience is removed; (2) the thrust, promontory or peninsular stage, in which, properly speaking, the audience embraces the acting area on three sides, thus with a multi-sided view of the action – a form influenced by the Elizabethan platform stage; and (3) THEATRE IN THE ROUND, also called 'central staging' or 'arena theatre', in which the audience entirely surrounds the action. Other forms of open stage include a traverse theatre, with the audience on two facing sides of the action; theatre in the corner, based on a diagonal axis; even PROMENADE THEATRE, in which actors and audience intermingle. ALFRED EMMET

See also ARCHITECTURE; AUDIENCE.

Stephen Joseph, *Actor and Architect* (1964)
——, *New Theatre Forms* (1968)
Richard Southern, *The Open Stage* (1953)

Open Theater Experimental New York theatre workshop founded by JOSEPH CHAIKIN in 1963 after he left the LIVING THEATER. Known for its emphasis on the presence of the performer, its non-naturalistic acting style and its rejection of conventional theatre methods, the company developed productions from theatre games drawing on 'transformation' theory – the concept that a changing context induces a 'transformation' of roles; 'sound and movement' improvisations; and exercises developed by GROTOWSKI's Polish LABORATORY THEATRE. Playwrights reshaped workshop material into productions of which the best known are MEGAN TERRY's *Viet Rock* (1966), JEAN-CLAUDE VAN ITALLIE's *America Hurrah!* (1966) and *The Serpent* (1968), and Susan Yankowitz's *Terminal* (1969). The group was disbanded in 1974. JANE HOUSE

R. Pasolli, *A Book on the Open Theater* (1970)

open-air theatre A form as ancient as drama itself which survives in the twentieth century wherever itinerant companies perform. Some theatre takes place in the open in locations designed and primarily used for other purposes, for example STREET THEATRE, PAGEANTS, religious and secular, or *SON ET LUMIÈRE*.

There are, however, venues built specifically for an audience to enjoy open-air performance – weather permitting. BEN GREET's Woodland Players started to appear in London's Regent's Park in 1900; the theatre was rebuilt in 1975 and is now occupied by the New Shakespeare Company. The Bard is popular in this type of theatre, whether in Cornwall's MINACK THEATRE or Central Park's Delacorte Theater, the home of the NEW YORK SHAKESPEARE FESTIVAL's summer seasons. Europe's biggest open-air theatre is in Scarborough in the north of England. In the United States there is also a type of historical play called outdoor or symphonic drama, which was developed in North Carolina by FREDERICK KOCH and usually tells the story of a local event using music, dance and drama on a grand scale. The largest open-air theatre in the world is claimed by Brazil. It opened in 1968 to present an annual passion play. CHARLES LONDON

See also COMMUNITY THEATRE.

opera The twentieth century opened with opera as a vital and contemporary art form, in many ways leading innovations in music and drama and tackling a number of important issues of the day. The main strength of opera is its multiple layers, in which so much more can be implied and inferred, than in the purely textual, or indeed purely musical.

During the latter half of the nineteenth century Richard Wagner crusaded at length about the need to balance all the elements of opera – singers, orchestra, libretto, staging and design. To ensure that there was complete equality and unity he believed one person should compose, direct and design, and hence achieve a *Gesamtkunstwerk* – a universal art-work of TOTAL THEATRE. Unfortunately, one person is unlikely to be equally skilled in all these disciplines, and if the work has any artistic merit it should outlive its creator and would therefore require others to realize it. However, Wagner's ideas on the equality of the elements were enthusiastically taken up, and composers such as Giacomo Puccini sought out librettists who could provide dramatic but realistic books which required a more naturalistic staging. Puccini was one of the great exponents of VERISMO – meaning truth, or real-life drama. This was taken a step further to heightened realism by composers such as Alban Berg with his operas *Wozzeck* (1925) and *Lulu* (1937). Both these works were inspired by plays, by Georg Büchner and FRANK WEDEKIND respectively, and have such a powerful dramatic force in the story and music that it would be impossible to stage them without an equally forceful production. BERTOLT BRECHT, also experimenting in the 1920s and 1930s, brought his ideas of heightened realism and dramatic intensity into the realm of opera and music drama in his collaborations with KURT WEILL such as *Die Dreigroschenoper* (*The Threepeny Opera*, 1928), *Aufstieg und Fall der Stadt Mahagonny* (*The Rise and Fall of the City of Mahagonny*, 1930) and *Die Sieben Todsünden* (*The Seven Deadly Sins*, 1933). As a result of such developments in dramatic presentation the productions of older, standard repertoire operas were reassessed and, especially after the Second World War, the concept of directors' opera emerged. With directors such as FRANCO ZEFFIRELLI and LUCHINO VISCONTI producing operas in the major houses around the world, audiences came to judge the production and overall performance as well as the quality of singing.

The crossover of directors between theatre, film and opera has opened up many new techniques and has made many extra demands on the performers. The technique required to sing and act simultaneously is much more exacting than in the past. However, it means that singers expect these demands to be made, and directors are able in turn to expect much more from their performers dramatically. There are still some opera houses on the international circuit where the 'star' singers will fly in the day before a performance and therefore require a set production similar to other ones they have been in. Glyndebourne Festival Opera, which was founded in 1934 by John Christie, was one of the first houses to insist on ENSEMBLE opera. The rehearsal period of about seven or eight weeks gave the director, conductor and performers the chance to get to the heart of a work and to explore all its possibilities. It is therefore no coincidence that many of Benjamin Britten's finest works were written for Glyndebourne and that well-known theatre directors such as PETER HALL and TREVOR NUNN made some of their early ventures into opera there. DAVID HOCKNEY also made his first opera stage DESIGNS there and helped to remind audiences that designs are often also impressive works of art.

In Europe, the same ensemble approach was also being used, especially in Germany, with the work of Ruth Berghaus and PATRICE CHÉREAU. The latter's 'deconstructionist' *Ring* cycle at BAYREUTH in 1976 was first greeted as simply out to shock, but within five years was being hailed as a classic production which in its search for the true meaning of the work led the audience to finding it themselves through having to think much more deeply, and more uncomfortably, about all the elements.

In Britain, English National Opera has become the most progressive of houses. In the 1980s, in the so-called 'powerhouse' years, it actively pursued a policy of producing a mixture of standard and less well-known operas but always with an emphasis on interesting, sometimes controversial, productions.

The greater emphasis on the dramatic side of opera productions has also influenced the work of composers, although in terms of output the twentieth century has produced a relatively small number of new works. The musical language of the century has often proved difficult for audiences, which have tended to be backward-looking in regard to repertoire, even though they have become gradually more accepting of newer production styles. The choice of subject matter has often been influenced by the events of the century, for example Bernd Alios Zimmermann's *Die Soldaten (The Soldiers)*. Using a shocking story by Jakob Lenz written in 1776, the opera was just as relevant in 1960 in its theme of war atrocities and the effect they have on individual lives. The American composer John Adams has used news stories for the plots of his operas *Nixon in China* (1987) and *The Death of Klinghoffer* (1991). Hans Werner Henze has used ancient or allegorical plays with libretti by well-known poets and playwrights to draw complex parallels with his own times and to highlight his own socialist ideals and disillusionment with authority. Probably his best-known works which illustrate this are *The Bassarids* (1966), with a libretto by W. H. AUDEN and Chester Kallman after Euripides' play *The Bacchae*, and *We Come to the River* (1976) and *The English Cat* (1983), both with libretti by EDWARD BOND.

Opera has reached a point where directors feel that they can be more experimental than in straight theatre, and PETER SELLARS, for example, is constantly pushing the audience to see how far they can go. Film and MULTIMEDIA have also been used to add extra layers or comment on the drama unfolding. PHILIP GLASS has crossed many of these boundaries in his 'minimalist' operas – where he uses repetition and a clear musical structure – and this may be the reason why he is one of the most often performed contemporary composers. His collaboration with ROBERT WILSON as director–designer on *Einstein on the Beach* (1976) was very much influenced by the latter's views on PERFORMANCE ART, and the dramatic drive stems from many visual elements.

The development of the ensemble view of performers and the expansion of the importance of all elements of a production has led to an increase in the number of smaller opera companies which often present some of the most experimental work. Necessity being the mother of invention, these companies do not have vast resources for lavish sets and costumes or to hire high-earning singers. A great number of smaller companies also tour to venues away from the major operatic centres, thus helping to expand the potential opera audience. This has also been extended through developments in mass media. Not only do videos take opera productions into peoples' homes, but the use of opera arias as film and advertisement soundtracks as well as the success of the Three Tenors have taken opera into mainstream culture. KATHARINE HERBERT

Orange Tree Theatre Founded in 1971 by Sam Walters in an 80-seat room above the Orange Tree pub in west London, the theatre rapidly acquired a reputation for small-scale excellence, attracting national and international notice. In 1991 the company moved into a converted school nearby, mainly designed for performances in the round, with an increased seating capacity of between 150 and 200 on two levels but without losing the intimacy of the original space – which is used under the name of The Room as a second studio space.

The theatre has premiered work by VÁCLAV HAVEL, TOM STOPPARD, MARTIN CRIMP, JAMES SAUNDERS and Fay Weldon as well as 'discovering' such plays as Tolstoy's *The Power of Darkness*, RODNEY ACKLAND's *Absolute Hell* and GRANVILLE BARKER's *His Majesty*.
BRIAN ROBERTS

See also PUB THEATRE; THEATRE IN THE ROUND.

Orchard Theatre Established in Barnstaple, Devon, in 1969 under Andy Noble as Britain's first theatre for rural touring. It took its name from the last line of *Sergeant Musgrave's Dance*: 'Let's start an orchard.' It commissioned plays on regional issues and also played the principal towns in south-west England, but folded in 2000 after being starved of funds. ALLEN SADDLER

Oregon Shakespeare Festival The festival began in Ashland in 1935 when Angus L. Bowmer, professor of drama at Southern Oregon Normal College, presented *Twelfth Night* and *The Merchant of Venice* on a simple platform stage. Apart from a five-year hiatus during the Second World War, the festival has operated continually and grown to an annual attendance of 350,000 for 11 plays in three theatres. (The outdoor Elizabethan stage, based on London's Fortune Theatre of 1599, is the third on the site. An indoor theatre named after Bowmer opened in 1970, allowing the festival to operate nearly year-round.) It has completed the Shakespeare canon twice (1958 and 1978). Bowmer retired in 1971 and was succeeded by Jerry Turner (1971–91), Henry Woronicz (1991–5) and Libby Appel (from 1996). Since 1988, the festival has also presented an annual five-play season in the Portland Center for the Performing Arts. FELICIA HARDISON LONDRÉ

See also SHAKESPEARE FESTIVALS.

Örkény, István (b. Budapest, 5 April 1912; d. Budapest, 24 June 1979) Playwright. He became well known in the 1960s as a leading east European figure in the THEATRE OF THE ABSURD. *Tóték* (*The Toth Family*, 1967) was staged all over the world. The play shows that even the most peaceful person eventually revolts against oppression. *Macskajáték* (*Cats Play*, 1969) was an even bigger hit. It was seen in England in 1972 at the QUESTORS THEATRE and in 1977 it was staged in the United States in 22 theatres. This amusing 'grotesque' comedy of jealousy among three elderly people, at an age when generally one does not think any more of love, is a hymn to women's vital force and also a discreet declaration of love for one's country. Örkény's other plays, dealing with the conflict between the individual and Hungary's dictatorial state, are also outstanding works of modern Hungarian drama, but difficult to follow for those not acquainted with eastern Europe. Nevertheless *Forgatókönyv* (*Screenplay*, 1982), about the show trials and the Hungarian revolt of 1956, was presented in Washington DC in 1983. Other plays include *Vérrokonok* (*Blood Relations*, 1974); *Kulcskeresök* (*The Key-searchers*, 1977); and *Pisti a vérzivatorborn* (*Pisti in the Holocaust*, 1978). GÁBOR MIHÁLYI

Orlan *see* BODY ART

Ormerod, Nick *see* CHEEK BY JOWL

Orton, Joe [John Kingsley] (b. Leicester, 1 Jan. 1933; d. London, 9 Aug. 1967) Playwright. Much publicized through posthumous publication of his diaries and a film (*Prick Up Your Ears*), Orton, a promiscuous homosexual eventually murdered by his lover, Kenneth Halliwell, was flamboyantly antiauthoritarian in his life and writing. He delighted in shocking audiences by breaking taboos surrounding sexuality and death in conventionally structured 'black' FARCES involving epigrammatic dialogue and frenetic, convoluted plots. Thus, in *Entertaining Mr Sloane* (1964), a young lodger attempts to lure a woman and her brother into providing him with all he needs, only to find he has become each one's sexual plaything; *Loot* (1965) is a parody of a detective story involving much comic business with a coffin and a corpse; and *What the Butler Saw* (1969) stylishly turns farce on its head. Other plays for the stage include *The Ruffian on the Stair* (1966) and *The Erpingham Camp* (1967); and for television, *The Good and Faithful Servant* (1967) and *Funeral Games* (1968). He also wrote novels, including two with Halliwell, and a screenplay for the Beatles, *Up Against It*, which was never filmed.   DAVID SELF

C. W. E. Bigsby, *Joe Orton* (1982)
Maurice Chainey, *Joe Orton* (1984)
John Lahr, *Prick Up Your Ears: The Biography of Joe Orton* (1978)
Simon Shepherd, *Because We're Queers: The Life and Crimes of Kenneth Halliwell and Joe Orton* (1988)

Osborn, Paul (b. Evansville, Ind., 4 Sept. 1901; d. New York, 12 May 1988)   Playwright. His early plays, such as *The Vinegar Tree* (1930), *On Borrowed Time* (1938) and *Morning's at Seven* (1939), were original works, sharply observed and affectionately written. Later hits, such as *A Bell for Adano* (1944) and *The World of Suzie Wong* (1958), were adaptations.
GERALD BORDMAN

Osborne, John [James]   (b. London, 12 Dec. 1929; d. Shrewsbury, Shropshire, 24 Dec. 1994)   Playwright. Rarely has so much cultural weight been laden upon a single play as on Osborne's *Look Back in Anger*, which opened in May 1956 at the ROYAL COURT as the third production of the newly formed ENGLISH STAGE COMPANY. In the setting of an attic flat in the midlands, the anti-hero, Jimmy Porter, rails at the world around him, terrorizing his friends and lovers and inspiring a wave of playwrights like ARDEN, WESKER, BOND and BRENTON to confront British society with a searingly passionate realism. Early critical responses were mixed (though not as damning as legend has suggested), but it was KENNETH TYNAN's review in the *Observer* which acclaimed him as a spokesman for postwar youth: 'I doubt if I could love anyone who did not wish to see *Look Back in Anger*,' he wrote. 'It is the best young play of its decade.' After a lengthy extract was televised, audiences picked up enough for the play to be revived, and soon it was being heralded as a turning point for the British theatre. Osborne's next play, *The Entertainer* (1957), paralleled the decline of imperial Britain with the decline of the MUSIC HALL, embodied in the shabby comedian Archie Rice (dazzlingly portrayed by LAURENCE OLIVIER). After success with *Epitaph for George Dillon* (1957), co-written with Anthony Creighton (a writer and actor, the model for Cliff in *Look Back in Anger*, who alleged in January 1995 that he had once been Osborne's lover), and failure with the musical *The World of Paul Slickey* (1959), a curious gender-bending satire on the press, Osborne had great success with the epic *Luther* (1961), which narrated the life of angry Reformation theologian Martin Luther (played by ALBERT FINNEY). *Plays for England* (1962) comprised the unsatisfactory *The Blood of the Bambergs* and the slight *Under Plain Covers*, but Osborne returned to form with *Inadmissible Evidence* (1964), depicting the collapsing life and fragmenting thoughts of a misanthropic lawyer. It maintained a distance between the central character, Maitland (played by NICOL WILLIAMSON), and the audience that had been absent from previous work, challenging his misogyny and homophobia. *A Patriot For Me* (1965), banned by the LORD CHAMBERLAIN for its explicit discussion of homosexuality, played as a CLUB performance at the Royal Court, which in 1968 also staged *Time Present* and *The Hotel in Amsterdam*. The former was moderately well received, but now the target was the 'permissive society', and Osborne was derided as a theatrical reactionary. Subsequent plays, *West of Suez* (1971), *A Sense of Detachment* (1972), *The End of Me Old Cigar* (1975) and *Watch It Come Down* (1976), seemed less careful in their construction, the form now only a platform for increasingly grouchy opinionizing. Osborne wrote nothing for theatre in the 1980s, returning to television, where, with plays like *A Subject of Scandal and Concern* (1960) and *The Gift of Friendship* (1974), he had already distinguished himself. In the early 1990s Osborne wrote *Déjà Vu* (1991), a sequel to *Look Back in Anger*. In this play his characters, 35 years on, blur the boundaries of fiction and reality, of life and art, as the angry old Jimmy Porter comments freely on his own reputation and the Royal Court, and reprises almost verbatim Osborne's own invective journalism.

Osborne adapted Lope de Vega, IBSEN, WILDE and Shakespeare and, for Woodfall Films, of which he was a director, the novel *Tom Jones* (1963), which won him an Oscar.

Osborne was shuttled swiftly into fame by *Look Back in Anger*, but it became something of a curse. The play, and specifically Tynan's description of it, had him labelled as a left-wing political playwright, but his later work shows him to be nothing of the sort. He is perceived to have drifted rightwards politically, and yet a passionate individualism marks all of his work; he looks back not in anger at the past, but in anger at how current society and culture seem to have betrayed the promise of the past. He was a freewheeling, troublemaking opponent of fads, priggishness and dissembling. And yet he is a playwright who can trip simplistic attempts to belabour his non-aligned misanthropy; often his plays tilt ironically against their apparent heroes as much as they support them.

In 1981 and 1991 he wrote two volumes of autobiography, *A Better Class of Person* and *Almost a Gentleman*. In these books he revived his earlier searing rage, writing with a renewed verbal power, settling old scores and wittily, sometimes horrifyingly, cutting through old myths to create new equally potent ones. A collection of his shorter prose writings was published in 1994 under the title *Damn You, England*. DAN REBELLATO

See also ANGRY YOUNG MAN.

Ronald Hayman, *John Osborne*, 2nd edn (1972)
John Heilpern, *Biography of John Osborne* (2000)
Arnold P. Hinchcliffe, *John Osborne* (1984)
Simon Trussler, *The Plays of John Osborne: An Assessment* (1971)

Osofisan, [Baba] Femi [Adeyemi] (b. Ijebu-Ode, Ogun State, Nigeria, 16 June 1946) Playwright and poet, a pioneer of the drama of conscious ideological commitment. His plays deal with topical political issues from a philosophically materialist perspective. His plays, numbering over 40, include *A Restless Run of Locusts* (1975), *The Chattering and the Song* (1976), *Red is the Freedom Road* (1969), *Morountodun* (1979), *Birthdays are not for Dying* (1990), *Yungba Yungba and the Dance Consert* (1993) and *Twingle Twangle A-Twynning Tale* (1995). He adapted *Who is Afraid of Solarin* (1978) after Gogol's *The Inspector General*, *Midnight Hotel* (1986) after FEYDEAU's farce *Paradise Hotel*, *Another Raft* (1988) after BEKEDEREMO-CLARK's *The Raft* and *Tègònni, an African Antigone* after Sophocles' *Antigone* (1998). His most recent pan-African plays are *Nkrumah – ni! . . . Africa Ni!* and *Reel, Rwanda!* (1999). OLU OBAFEMI

Muyiwa P. Awodiya, *The Drama of Femi Osofisan* (1996)

O'Sullivan, Vincent (b. Auckland, New Zealand, 28 Sept. 1937) Playwright, poet, journalist, editor, novelist and short-story writer. Already established as a writer of radio drama, he was appointed playwright in residence at the DOWNSTAGE THEATRE in 1983. *Shuriken* (1983) is based on the fatal confrontation in 1943 between New Zealand soldiers and their Japanese prisoners; then followed *Ordinary Night in Ward 10* (1984). His entertainment *Jones & Jones* (1988) won considerable critical acclaim. *Billy* (written in Australia; first performed in Wellington, 1989), about an aboriginal mute being trained in the European ways of the European settlers, explores many ideas and conflicts central to the development of contemporary society in Australia and New Zealand. The 1996 COURT THEATRE production of *Casement: Saint or Sinner*, in which a priest seeks to persuade the condemned Casement to renounce his homosexuality, was judged to be 'as good as New Zealand theatre gets', while his 1998 radio play *Yellow Bride* relocates Medea in the modern world of New Zealand business, with an Asian heroine.
GILLIAN GREER & LAURIE ATKINSON

Other Place, The *see* ROYAL SHAKESPEARE THEATRE

O'Toole, Peter [Seamus] (b. Connemara, Ireland, 2 Aug. 1932) Actor. Brought up in Yorkshire, he made his first appearance in Leeds, aged 18. His film roles – the most celebrated being Lawrence of Arabia (1962) – brought him early international recognition, but he has constantly returned to the theatre. A three-year engagement with BRISTOL OLD VIC (1955–8) culminating in *Hamlet* introduced him as a leading actor; he played the same role in the inaugural production of the NATIONAL THEATRE (1963) after notable performances as Petruchio and Shylock at STRATFORD-UPON-AVON (1960). A tall, lean actor with emotional and vocal flair, he earned notoriety in a disastrous production of *Macbeth* (1980), which, nevertheless, was extremely popular on tour. He brings an almost mystic quality of introspection to many of his characterizations, excelling in a repressed sense of vulnerability or hurt. Among his outstanding successes have been John Tanner in *Man and Superman* (1958, 1969, 1982), Bamforth in *The Long and the Short and the Tall* (1959), *Baal* (1963), Captain Boyle in *Juno and the Paycock* (1966), Vladimir in *Waiting for Godot* (1969), and the title roles in *Uncle Vanya* (1973) and *Jeffrey Bernard is Unwell* (1991). His autobiographies, *Loitering with Intent: The Child* and (the second volume) *The Apprentice*, appeared in 1992 and 1996 respectively. CHRISTOPHER FITZ-SIMON

M. Freedland, *Peter O'Toole: A Biography* (1983)
N. Wapshott, *Peter O'Toole* (1983)

Otto, Teo (b. Remscheid, Germany, 4 Feb. 1904; d. Frankfurt, 9 June 1968) Designer. His work was visually and dramatically powerful, even magical and extravagant. After working in Berlin and Zurich, during the Second World War he designed the first productions of several BRECHT plays (e.g. *Mother Courage*, 1941; *The Good Person of Setzuan*, 1943), thus playing an important part in the legacy Brecht left subsequent generations. After the war Otto worked with the BERLINER ENSEMBLE, and designed premières by FRISCH and DÜRRENMATT as well as the famous GRÜNDGENS *Faust* (1957). One of his last great successes was the design for GASSMAN's production of the *Oresteia* (1959).
ADRIANA HUNTER

Ould, Hermon (b. London, 14 Dec. 1885; d. London, 21 Sept. 1951) Poet, journalist and playwright. He was joint editor of the journal *Theatre Craft* and founder of two amateur companies, the Curtain Group and the People's Theatre Society. His playwriting career began with *Between Sunset and Dawn* (1913); other plays include *The Black Virgin* (1923, an early play to deal with homosexuality), *Hoppla* (1929, from TOLLER) and *The Shadow and The Substance* (1934). He was the author of *The Art of the Play* (1938, revised 1948).

MAGGIE GALE

Ouspenskaya, Maria *see* ACTING (AN ACTOR REFLECTS); BOLESLAVSKY, RICHARD

Out of Joint Theatre company founded in 1993 by director MAX STAFFORD-CLARK and producer Sonia Friedman with a tour that paired Sue Townsend's adaptation of her novel *The Queen and I* and a revival of JIM CARTWRIGHT's seminal 1980s play *Road*. The company tried to pick up where new play pioneers JOINT STOCK had left off, and in its next tour (1994) had combined a new with a classical play, STEPHEN JEF-FREY's *The Libertine*, about the Earl of Rochester, and Etheredge's Restoration comedy *The Man of Mode*, which offers a contemporary view of the celebrated rake. The company showed its work at the ROYAL COURT, where Stafford-Clark had been artistic director, and through that association came to occupy a central place in the 1990s new play revival with MARK RAVENHILL's *Shopping and Fucking* (1996), the quintessential youth portrait of decaying Cool Britannia.

COLIN CHAMBERS

outdoor drama *see* OPEN-AIR THEATRE

Owen, Alun [Davies] (b. Liverpool, 24 Nov. 1925) Playwright. Owen came to notice with *Progress to the Park* (1958), a radio play subsequently staged (1959), in which the familiar themes of sex and sectarianism are renewed by his hallmark of witty, lyrical dialogue, confident handling of a large cast, and powerful observation of working-class life in Liverpool. After a confused incursion into sexual politics with *The Male of the Species* (1974), Owen abandoned theatre for television and radio. Perhaps his most famous script was the Beatles' film *A Hard Day's Night* (1964). Other plays include *The Rough and Ready Lot* (radio 1958, stage 1959) and *Maggie May* (1964), with music and lyrics by LIONEL BART. DAN REBELLATO

Owens [Bass], Rochelle (b. Brooklyn, New York, 2 April 1936) Playwright and poet. She has been aligned by critics with ARTAUD's THEATRE OF CRUELTY. Her fantastical plays are often grotesque in content while drawing on allegory and primitive myths. They include *Futz* (1965), about a man's love for a pig, *Beclch* (1967), *Istanbul* (1965) and two historical plays, *The Karl Marx Play* (1973) and *Emma Instigated Me* (1977).

JANE HOUSE

Oxford Frowned on by the university authorities, theatre played only a modest part in Oxford life before the 1920s. The New Theatre (built in 1885) housed touring companies, and the Oxford University Dramatic Society (OUDS), founded in 1884, was restricted to Shakespeare and Greek drama. After suspending its activities during the First World War, OUDS began to claim widespread attention for its productions, often under professional directors and using professional actresses in the women's parts. The opening in 1923 of the OXFORD PLAYHOUSE greatly stimulated theatrical interest within the city and made a brief national impact – no thanks, however, to the university. Student actors were acclaimed in the national press (Gyles Isham as the first OUDS Hamlet in 1924; ROBERT SPEAIGHT as Peer Gynt in 1925). EMLYN WILLIAMS proceeded to a long and distinguished career as actor and dramatist, while TYRONE GUTHRIE moved straight from OUDS to the Playhouse before establishing himself as a director. In the late 1920s and 1930s OUDS was able to engage directors of national and international standing: KOMISSARZHEVSKY undertook *King Lear* in 1927; JOHN GIELGUD's production of *Romeo and Juliet* (1932) included PEGGY ASHCROFT as Juliet and EDITH EVANS as the Nurse; for REINHARDT's *A Midsummer Night's Dream* in 1933 a lake was specially constructed on Headington Hill. The foundation by Nevill Coghill (a professor of English closely identified with Oxford theatre for 40 years) of the Experimental Theatre Club (ETC) in 1936 expanded the range of student drama, while the rebuilding of the New Theatre (later the Apollo) in 1934 and the opening of the new Playhouse in 1938 enhanced professional standards. OUDS was again suspended during the Second World War, but was resuscitated in 1947 under Glynne Wickham, later an influential historian and professor of drama, and in the immediate postwar years student theatre brought forward such practitioners as Frank Hauser, John Schlesinger, LINDSAY ANDERSON, KENNETH TYNAN and TONY RICHARDSON. In 1966 RICHARD BURTON (who had been a student actor at Oxford during his National Service) played Dr Faustus for OUDS, with Elizabeth Taylor as Helen of Troy. ETC continued to embrace modern developments, numbering CARYL CHURCHILL and JOHN MCGRATH among its participants. The rise to popularity of the broadcast media gave the impression that Oxford produced more television comedians (e.g. Rowan Atkinson) than leading actors; but Diana Quick became the first woman president of OUDS in 1968, while student theatre has produced directors such as Ronald Eyre, Peter Dews and Patrick Garland, and drama critics including MICHAEL BILLINGTON. Despite the lack of a university drama department, the influence of Oxford as a seed-bed for the theatre is considerable. In 1989 funds were donated by producer CAMERON MACKINTOSH for a visiting chair in theatre, and STEPHEN SONDHEIM inaugurated this annual appointment. G. ROWELL

See also STUDENT THEATRE; UNIVERSITY DRAMA DEPARTMENTS.

Humphrey Carpenter, *OUDS: A Centenary History of the Oxford University Dramatic Society* (1985)

Oxford Playhouse A converted hall known as the 'Big Game' Museum on the outskirts of OXFORD was opened as a theatre in 1923 by JAMES FAGAN, with the first British performance outside London of *Heartbreak House*. It offered a venue for the university drama society, OUDS, and many ambitious and artistic professional productions, including KOMISSARZHEVSKY's 1925 production of *The Cherry Orchard*. After Fagan's departure in 1928 it became a more conventional repertory enterprise. In 1938 a new Playhouse was built nearer the centre of the city, and this maintained performances throughout the war years of 1939–45. Standards reached new heights during the tenancy (1956–73) of the Meadow Players under Frank Hauser, attracting national players and national acclaim. The lease was acquired by the university in 1961, but attendances declined and the theatre closed in 1989. It was reopened in 1991 after an appeal and then refurbished in 1996. G. ROWELL

Oyônô-Mbia, Guillaume (b. Mvoutessi, nr Sangmélina, Cameroon, 1939) Playwright. His comedies – *Trois prétendants ... un mari* (*Three Suitors, One Husband*, 1964), *Jusqu'à nouvel avis* (*Until Further Notice*, 1970), *Notre fille ne sera mariera pas* (*Our Daughter Isn't Going to Marry*, 1971) and *His Excellency's Special Train* (1979) – deal with the ambivalent attitude of rural people to the world of urban dwellers, the conflict between the adherence of the rural population to ancient African strictures and the alluring materialism which the people of the urban areas can display to annul such strictures. Writing in French, it is not surprising that the greatest influence on his comedy is Molière. Educated in Britain and France, Oyônô-Mbia translates his plays into English himself. KOLE OMOTOSO

P

Pacific countries Melanesia, Micronesia and Polynesia are regions where combinations of music, dance, poetry and improvised skits are traditionally more significant than theatre pieces in which actors take on other personae in long narratives. Modern artists are, however, crafting pieces that are closer to Western theatrical displays, and in recent years a number of Pacific nations have founded national or regional theatre companies where indigenous and European models are combining to create a distinctive performance practice.

Dance mimes, which may involve PUPPETS or MASKS, are traditionally popular throughout the Melanesian area, which includes Papua New Guinea, Irian Jaya, Vanuatu, New Caledonia and the Solomon Islands. Prior to Christianization, many performances would take place in conjunction with male ceremonies. An example is the cycle of rites created by the Orokolo of Papua, which took decades to enact and concluded with performers dancing huge masks from the men's club house to the sea. Each area has a distinctive tradition. Though many traditional ceremonies can no longer be enacted in the traditional framework, given the immense social change the region has undergone, still many ceremonies have not lapsed in the memory of individuals now living. Great interest is evident among educated Melanesians in researching and exploring these forms for material that can be reincorporated in the present. Also, as nations have become independent the elite has often created a modern theatre as a vehicle for exploring national identity. Radio, too, has become a venue for sharing dramatic thought.

In Papua New Guinea, classes at the University of Papua New Guinea taught by the German Ulli Beier in the 1960s created a blossoming of modern drama, and theatre became a tool of an independence movement that culminated in the end of colonial rule in 1975. Significant authors include John Kasaipwalova, whose *Sail the Midnight Sun* (1980) was a mythical exploration of the hero's quest in which the hero was a personification of the emerging nation. John Kaniku (*Scattered by the Wind*) and Leo Hannet (*Ungrateful Daughter*) are other playwrights of the 1970s. The Papua New Guinea National Theatre was established in Port Moresby under director/playwright Arthur Jawadimbori in the late 1970s. In the highlands, Raun Raun Theatre has established a lively company that toured the area doing improvised comedies in the open air. Radio drama has flourished in all areas of Papua New Guinea.

Performances in Micronesia (Yap, Truk, Ponape, Kosrae, the Marianas, Marshall Island, Palau, Kiribati and Nauru) involve significant dance and poetry but minimal drama in the conventional sense of the word. Mime does take place in some dances, which may show activities like fishing, canoeing or lovemaking. Some dances involve mimesis of birds or iguana, since in the past possession trance was a feature of this area and the frigate bird and iguana were appropriate possessing entities.

Similarly, poetry and dance were also more important features of Polynesian performance than was drama. The pattern of comic mimes and spirit possession did, however, exist in the area, leading to some forms of indigenous drama. The *Fale aitu* (house of the spirits) of Samoa, for example, involved clowns doing skits in interludes between group song/dances. Performers called *fa'aluma* might take local comic types like the transvestite as their topic, or mock European foibles. Petolo from Western Samoa is a noted exponent of this form in recent years. In Fiji, clowning and mime activities have been incorporated into dance mimes by Manoa Rasignatale, a former pop star who decided to research his island heritage after the first Pacific Arts Festival in 1972. In Tahiti and the Cook Islands this patten of incorporating dance and pageants of traditional life into modern theatre pieces is also evident. Performances at the important annual arts competitions and the quadrennial Pacific Arts Festivals, in which all Pacific nations participate, are apt to follow this model.

In Hawaii, Kuma Kahua at the University of Hawaii produces indigenous plays which focus on the Hawaiian experience. The Honolulu Theater for Youth sponsors performances that articulate tales of the Hawaiians and ethnic groups that have settled in the island in addition to doing classics of the European and American stage. Throughout the Pacific, universities are centres for theatre, dance and training. The University of Hawaii, with its active Asian theatre training programme under James Brandon, is but one example. Out of these institutions grow modern scripts, operas and performances which draw on the older traditions but rework and rethink them for modern times.
KATHY FOLEY

Ulli Beier, ed., *Voices of Independence: New Black Writing from Papua New Guinea* (1980)
Mary Browning, *Micronesian Heritage: Dance Perspectives* (1970)
Norman Simms, *Writers from the South Pacific: A Bio-bibliographical Critical Encyclopedia*

Pacino, Al[fredo] James (b. New York, 25 April 1940) Actor. After studying at the ACTORS' STUDIO and playing OFF-BROADWAY, Pacino made his BROADWAY debut in *Does a Tiger Wear a Necktie?* (1969). His roles, which include Richard III (1973) and leads in *The Basic Training of Pavlo Hummel* (1977) and *American Buffalo* (1980), were often young working-class non-conformists repressed and even victimized by their social environment. His frequent returns to the stage augment and complement his major film roles (e.g. the three parts of *The Godfather*). From 1982 to 1992 he was artistic director (with ELLEN BURSTYN) of the Actors' Studio. DAVID STAINES

A. Yule, *A Life on the Wire* (1991)

Page, Anthony [Frederick Montague] (b. Bangalore, India, 21 Sept. 1935) Director. Page was educated in England, trained in New York and directed many plays at the ROYAL COURT THEATRE (artistic director, 1964–5). His work there was remarkable for its intelligence and emotional force and for powerful, idiosyncratic acting. Page directed PAUL SCOFIELD,

NICOL WILLIAMSON and Jill Bennett in nineteenth-century classics (CHEKHOV, Gogol, IBSEN) and in plays by JOHN OSBORNE (respectively *The Hotel in Amsterdam*, 1968; *Inadmissible Evidence*, 1964; and *Time Present*, 1968). He also directed Osborne's *A Patriot for Me* (1965) and *West of Suez* (1971) and TED WHITEHEAD's *Alpha Beta* (1972). In the 1990s he returned to stage work after a period in Hollywood. His production of Ibsen's *A Doll's House* (1996) with Janet McTeer was a success in London and New York. TONY HOWARD

Page, Geraldine [Sue] (b. Kirksville, Mo., 22 Nov. 1924; d. New York, 13 June 1987) Actress. An exponent of the METHOD school, she first won fame as the unhappy spinster in *Summer and Smoke* (1952). Starring roles followed in *Midsummer* (1953), *The Immoralist* (1954), *The Rainmaker* (1954), and *Sweet Bird of Youth* (1959), in which she created the role of the Princess. She later modified her METHOD style in a 1963 revival of *Strange Interlude*, the double bill of *White Lies* and *Black Comedy* (1967), *Absurd Person Singular* (1974) and *Agnes of God* (1982). She appeared in numerous films. GERALD BORDMAN

Page, Louise (b. London, 7 March 1955) Playwright. Page tackled issues like breast cancer in *Tissue* (1978), the Falklands War in *Falkland Sound/Voces de Malvinas* (1983), and women's athletics and competition in *Golden Girls* (1984), through individuals' experiences; she is best known for the haunting, personal *Salonika* (1982), in which a First World War widow meets the ghost of her husband on the beach where he was killed. Other plays include *Real Estate* (1982), *Beauty and the Beast* (1985) and *Diplomatic Wives* (1989). More recently, she has turned to radio, and she is a regular writer for the long-running radio soap opera *The Archers*. DAN REBELLATO

pageant A spectacular, episodic drama, usually to celebrate or construct the history of a place or community; nearly always an 'occasional' form, done once or for a single run; very frequently performed by amateurs under professional direction. In the late middle ages synonymous with the wagon on which a religious drama was played, 'pageant' is now roughly equivalent to 'procession' or 'parade'. A pageant is a station drama, and two general types occur. First is the street procession in which episodes or TABLEAUX parade past an audience. Second is the arena, field or stadium event in which a seated audience is treated to a series of chronologically arranged episodes – a history is made to 'pass by'. Processions often form an important part here, too. (The first type can still be seen in the annual Lord Mayor's Show in the streets of London.)

The second type gained significance in 1905, when retired schoolmaster Louis Napoleon Parker made his *Pageant of Sherborne* in emulation of the German *Festspiel*. Nine hundred amateurs in middle England marked the 1200th anniversary of the town and private school in 11 episodes. He made similar pageants at Warwick (1906), Bury St Edmunds (1907), Dover (1908), Colchester and York (both 1909). A Book of the Pageant – a souvenir programme including scenario – was published for each, and remained a regular feature in similar events. Parker 'invented' the role of Pageant Master: script organizer, director, (self-)publicist and administrator. Patriotic pageants were held in London theatres during the First World War, and in 1918 Parker mounted *The Pageant of Drury Lane* in the DRURY LANE theatre. Parker's political horizon was conservative; he saw these events as ways of uniting different classes around a sense of communal history, while not disturbing class hierarchy. Such pageants constructed a transcendent as well as local sense of 'heritage', and were popular in Britain and America in the early years of the century.

The modern pageant has relevance to the rhetorics of civic authority, commerce, state and the labour movement. An active mediation between popular celebrations of place and community and the scale and pomposity of the Parkerian pageant can be seen in events such as the 1930 *Salford Pageant*, in which the city is saved by Robin Hood. It was designed to make the unemployed feel cosy rather than disaffected. The 1932 Lancashire Cotton Pageant involved local amateurs in a colourful celebration of the commodity, stimulating trade both through the spectacle itself and through providing a 'community' event.

The historians Hobsbawm and Ranger (1983) have demonstrated how both state and working-class organizations in Europe began to 'invent traditions' from the last quarter of the nineteenth century. Ceremonies were renovated or frankly created so as to construct an aura of the 'immemorial'. These include annual or other memorial events, occasions for looking back – and perhaps to the future. The Parkerian pageant became a staple of state pomp for mass consumption, as in the *Pageant of Empire*, done for the 1924 British Empire Exhibition, or the *London Pageant of Parliament* in 1934.

The Cooperative Movement in Britain scaled up its annual celebrations of International Cooperative Day from the mid-1920s, with scripted pageants emerging out of a standing practice of 'traditional' fairs. In 1934 the London Trades Council mounted an indoor *Pageant of Labour* at Crystal Palace, an episodic drama designed to recruit women and young people to the union movement. Music was by communist composer Alan Bush, script and direction by Matthew Anderson and Edward P. Genn. The last two had cut their teeth on civic pageantry, having made an *Historical Pageant* for the second of Britain's first Civic Weeks in Liverpool in 1926. They were aware of their need to compete with the scale of spectacle furnished by the modern cinema. A technique of 'cutting' between scenes was also adopted from it.

The principal pageants in Britain in the twentieth century were those associated with the Communist Party of Great Britain (CPGB) during the Popular Front. The move from a strategy of class war to one of class compromise against the extreme threat of fascism, effective from 1936, included changes in cultural policy (*see e.g.* UNITY THEATRE). The pageant form afforded the possibility of manufacturing narratives in which communism appeared as the natural outcome of popular democratic struggle through the ages. A platform meeting in Hyde Park in September 1936 was preceded by a mass procession in which banners deployed by various branches formed an historical narrative culminating with present Party leaders. Emulations of this event were made by the Party in its regions, as in Manchester and Liverpool in 1937. The most impressive of these street demonstrations was probably that done in Glasgow for May Day in 1938. These events can be seen as special forms of demonstration; as appropriations of invented traditions such as the May Day parade; and as 'counter-discourses' to the conservative narratives made by civic pageantry. Bush, writer Montagu Slater and director Andre Van Gyseghem (who had mounted pageants in South Africa) collaborated variously on three major arena events, each involving thousands of amateurs, many of them drawn from labour choirs. *Towards Tomorrow*, mounted by four London Cooperative Societies at Wembley Stadium in July 1938, celebrated the history of the movement, and called for peace. The CPGB mounted the *Pageant of South Wales* simultaneously in three outdoor arenas on 1 May 1939, tracing working-class struggle from the 1839 Newport Rising to its centenary. *Heirs to the Charter*, done at the Empress Hall in July 1939, and linking communism to Chartism on its centenary, was part of a Party recruitment drive.

Some pageants have been stage plays, most famously perhaps CICELY HAMILTON's *Pageant of Great Women*, done by the ACTRESSES' FRANCHISE LEAGUE in 1909.

By the 1950s the pageant form was more or less moribund in Britain, although the Trotskyite left revived the tradition briefly. ALTERNATIVE THEATRE groups, motivated by a similar spirit, operated on a smaller scale, in COMMUNITY THEATRE, with indoor or PROMEN-

ADE plays about local history, or in other STREET THEATRE forms, creating popular spectacles in a locality (e.g. WELFARE STATE; BREAD AND PUPPET THEATER). Spectacles for mass consumption *en masse* have tended since not to be made as communal enterprises (e.g. ice pageants and military tattoos). This clearly reflects general changes in social organization, as well as in the technologies of recreation. MICK WALLIS

John Clark, Margot Heinemann, David Margolies and Carole Snee, eds, *Culture and Crisis in Britain in the Thirties* (1979)

Viv Gardner, ed., *Sketches from the Actresses' Franchise League* (1985)

Eric Hobsbawm and Terence Ranger, eds, *The Invention of Tradition* (1983)

Louis Napoleon Parker, *Several of my Lives* (1928)

Mick Wallis, 'Pageantry and the Popular Front: Ideological Production in the Thirties', *New Theatre Quarterly*, vol. 10, no. 38 (May 1994)

——, 'The Popular Front Pageant: Its Emergence and Decline', *New Theatre Quarterly*, vo.. 11, no. 41 (Feb. 1995)

Robert Withington, *English Pageantry: An Historical Outline*, 2 vols (1918, 1920)

Pagnol, Marcel [Paul] (b. Aubagne, 28 France, Nov. 1895; d. Paris, 18 April 1974) Playwright and major film-maker; founder of the magazines *Les Cahiers du Sud* and *Les Cahiers du Film*. Pagnol's plays are largely popular comedies satirizing social and political corruption, particularly in the town of Marseille. They include *Topaze* (1928), *Marius* (1929), *Fanny* (1931) and *César* (1936), the latter three forming the basis of the American musical *Fanny* (1954). Claude Berri's films *Jean de Florette* and *Manon des Sources* (1986) were based on Pagnol's novel and film about Provence, *Manon des Sources* (1952) ANNA MCMULLAN

David Coward, *Pagnol: La gloire de mon père and Le château de ma mère* (1992)

Paige [Bickerstaffe], Elaine [Mary] (b. Barnet, Herts, 5 March 1948) Actress and singer. She made her first appearance out of London in *The Roar of the Greasepaint . . . The Smell of the Crowd* (1964) and her West End debut in *Hair* (1971), the first of several takeovers, including Sandy in *Grease* (1973), before creating her first notable role, as Rita to MICHAEL CRAWFORD's Billy in the musical of that name (1974). She achieved old-style showbiz fame 'overnight' when she appeared as Eva Perón in *Evita* (1978), which won her many awards. Her international celebrity was reinforced by her performance as the original Grizabella in *Cats* (1981) in which she sang 'Memory', making it a stand-

ard. Her starring appearances in *Chess* (1986), *Anything Goes* (1989), which she co-produced, *Piaf* (1993), *Sunset Boulevard* (1994), *The King and I* (2000) and Royal COMMAND PERFORMANCES, and on international concert tours, as well as her successful recording career, confirmed her status as the leading British female performer from the musical theatre of her time.
CHARLES LONDON

Paines Plough British touring production company. Founded in Coventry in 1974 by the playwright DAVID POWNALL with John Adams and Chris Cooks, it quickly established itself as a lively producer of new plays, including several by Pownall himself. Original music has played an important part in many productions, e.g. in Pownall's imaginative study of the composer Peter Warlock, *Music to Murder By* (1976). It has remained at the cutting edge of new play creation and development, nurturing writers at all stages of their careers. Writers originally commissioned by Paines Plough include PAM GEMS, Stephen Jeffreys and TERRY JOHNSON. DAVID SELF

Pakistan The nineteenth-century operatic theatre and Agha Hashar's narrative theatre were made new in the 1930s by Taj, Rafi Peer and the cinema. Nationalist poetic drama in English by Ahmed Ali and Fyzee Rahamin became well known, while social themes dominated the Sindhi and Urdu scripts by Qalich-Beg, Sharar and Manto. Adaptations of European plays thrived and stage technology improved as entertainment of troops and the Parsi theatre created a regular audience in the 1940s to compete with the radio play as a major new genre. Gaining independence as a mainly Islamic state in 1947, modern Pakistan was divided into east and west separated by 1,100 miles of INDIA, but lost the eastern region in 1972 when it became BANGLADESH. Drama in higher education (e.g. at the Government College Dramatic Club and Kinnaird College) and the Arts Council in the 1950s and 1960s promoted a middle-class urban theatre in Urdu and English. In 1956 the Karachi Theatre was founded. Deft productions of adaptations of Western drama (e.g. Shakespeare, Gogol, NEIL SIMON) gave a boost to Urdu comedy and the theatre of ideas. In English, Nasir Farooki and Taufiq Rafat explored existentialist themes. Between 1965 and 1975 such activities became more didactic and centralized around Pakistan Television and Lahore's semi-official stage, Al-Hamra. Martial Law (1977–85) gave rise to both vulgarized forms of the Parsi theatre and also a parallel theatre practising a serious-minded realism by several groups in Lahore, Karachi and Rawalpindi. Folk theatre is waning; puppet theatre has flourished since the 1970s; children's theatre has a chance to grow. Lately, also, a multilingual national theatre movement has gained some ground. ALAMGIR HASHMI

See also EASTERN THEATRE, ITS INFLUENCE ON THE WEST.

Palace Theater (New York) Built on BROADWAY just south of 47th Street by Martin Beck, who lost control of it before it opened, and designed by the firm of Kirchoff and Rose, it was from the night of its unveiling on 24 March 1913 until the early 1930s America's premier VAUDEVILLE house. After vaudeville died it became a film house. A brief attempt to revive vaudeville's two shows a day in the 1950s was short-lived. In 1966 the theatre joined the legitimate fold with *Sweet Charity*. For a time beginning in the late 1980s it was closed while a new highrise was erected atop the old auditorium. It reopened in 1991 with *The Will Rogers Follies*. GERALD BORDMAN

Palestine *see* MIDDLE EAST AND NORTH AFRICA

Palladium *see* LONDON PALLADIUM

Palmer, Vance (b. Bundaberg, Australia, 28 Aug. 1885; d. Melbourne, 15 July 1958) Playwright, novelist and essayist. His most successful dramatization of the 'Australia of the Spirit' comes in the robust, democratic, frugal, unsentimental, communal and masculine *The Black Horse* (1923). Here the outback combines with psychological tension in one simple action, as an embittered couple struggle for emotional control of their son. In *The Prisoner* (1919), *Telling Mrs Baker* (1922), *Travellers* (1924) and *Prisoner's Country* (1960) Palmer strives for mood and inner life. Apart from the four-act comedy *A Happy Family* (1922), the best of that genre presented by the PIONEERS PLAYERS which he co-founded, and a much later work, *Christine*, his other dramatic output was largely confined to adaptations for radio of his short stories. GUS WORBY

D. Carroll, *Australian Contemporary Drama* (1995)
P. Fitzpatrick, *Pioneer Players: the Lives of Louis and Hilda Esson* (1995)
V. Smith, *Vance and Nettie Palmer* (1975)

Palunin, Slava *see* HACKNEY EMPIRE

Panama *see* MEXICO AND CENTRAL AMERICA

panic, theatre of *see* THEATRE OF PANIC

pantomime Since Victorian times it has been a family Christmas entertainment, almost exclusively English, in which stock characters, jokes, slapstick, romance, topical songs, male and female IMPERSONATION, trick scenery and transformation scenes are loosely brought together within the framework of a traditional fairy tale. In the eighteenth century, the earliest panto-mimes (from the Greek 'all mime or imitate'), were short, wordless dramas performed to music, which consisted of an opening derived from classical mythology, followed by a transformation of the gods and heroes into Harlequin, Pantaloon, Pulcinella and other characters from the *COMMEDIA DELL'ARTE*. Later, the opening mythological scene was replaced by a fairy tale, performances grew in length until they took up a whole evening, and the DAME roles were played by men. During Victorian times the pantomime became exclusively a children's Christmas entertainment. The 'principal boy', played by a woman in tights, became the pantomime's hero, and the fairy tale became the main theme of the familiar story — whether *Cinderella*, *Aladdin*, *Dick Whittington*, *Babes in the Wood* or *Puss in Boots*. Other stock panto characters, such as the Widow Twankey, Baron Hardup and Buttons were also established at this time. From 1879 VAUDEVILLE acts and MUSIC HALL performers such as MARIE LLOYD and DAN LENO were introduced. The fairy-tale plots suffered greatly, but it delighted the adults in the audience.

Pantomime continued to enjoy widespread popularity in the twentieth century and was a box-office banker for many theatres. Audience involvement, in the form of shouting 'Behind you!', exchanges such as 'Oh, no it isn't,' 'Oh, yes it is,' and sing-song choruses with the words unfurled on a huge song sheet, became habitual. Stars from television, film and popular music replaced the music-hall performers throughout Britain and the topical references changed, but otherwise pantomime retained its late Victorian character. PETER NICHOLS exploited it in *Poppy* (1983) to lampoon the imperialism that gave it this character. It also threw up its own 'King', John Morley (1924–94), who wrote more than 200 scripts and became panto's archivist.

In the CARIBBEAN, Jamaican pantomime developed its own form quite distinct from its British source. In some countries, e.g. France, the word is still used in its earlier meaning of a mime without words.
ANDREW SOLWAY

Y. C. Clinton-Baddeley, *All Right on the Night* (1954)
G. Frow, *'Oh, Yes It Is!': A History of Pantomime* (1985)
Raymond Mander and Joe Michenson, *Pantomime: A Story in Pictures* (1973)
David Pickering and John Morley, eds, *The Encyclopaedia of Pantomime* (1993)

Paper Bag Players, The *see* THEATRE FOR YOUNG PEOPLE

Papp [Papirofsky], Joseph (b. Brooklyn, New York,

22 June 1921; d. New York, 31 Oct. 1991) Producer and director. His most notable achievement is the founding of the NEW YORK SHAKESPEARE FESTIVAL in 1954. The year before he had founded its forerunner, the Shakespeare Theatre Workshop, after working as an actor, stage manager, producer and director. Papp raised enough financial support from the public and private sectors to inaugurate, in 1962, a permanent outdoor theatre for the Shakespeare Festival Company, the Delacorte in Central Park which seats over 2,000. His relentless perseverance enabled him to realize his twofold objective of attracting a wider audience for Shakespeare and providing consistent work for actors. Admission is free at the outdoor summer theatre and 'blood-and-guts' actors are used in preference to a star system.

In 1967 Papp founded the PUBLIC THEATER, which houses several auditoriums, galleries and workshops for photography and film as well as drama. This OFF-BROADWAY endeavour provided Broadway with several hits, most notably *Hair* (1967) and the record-breaking *A Chorus Line* (1975). Papp also served as director for the Vivian Beaumont and Mitzi E. Newhouse Theatres at the LINCOLN CENTER (1972–8). He established a fruitful exchange with the ENGLISH STAGE COMPANY at the ROYAL COURT which resulted in, among other things, New York seeing CHURCHILL's *Top Girls* (1983) and London LARRY KRAMER's *The Normal Heart* (1986). Despite chronic financial problems, he was a major force in New York theatre. He took creative chances, bringing theatre to schools and championing Off- and OFF-OFF BROADWAY. He received many awards, including a Tony for Distinguished Service to the Theatre in 1958, the year he refused to provide the House Committee for Un-American Activities with names of associates involved in left politics. JOSEPH M. DIAZ

Toby Cole and Helen Krick, eds, *Directors on Directing* (1963)

H. Epstein, *Joseph Papp* (1994)

Stuart W. Little, *Enter Joseph Papp: In Search of a New American Theater* (1974)

Paris Drama in France has inevitably developed where wealth and talent are concentrated in the capital city, and Paris has inherited traditions which date back to the fourteenth century and particularly to the establishment by Louis XIV in 1680 of the COMÉDIE-FRANÇAISE, which continues to provide a programme of Molière, Racine and other seventeenth- and eighteenth-century classics. The twentieth century benefited from the boom in Paris theatres along Haussmann's *grands boulevards* following the removal of restrictions by Napoleon III in 1864, and a tradition of highly professional commercial drama has continued. Artistically, however, the most important development for the twentieth century was the establishment of the new naturalist style of acting at the Théâtre Libre (1887) by ANDRÉ ANTOINE. The century saw many developments. FEYDEAU continued the tradition of French FARCE established by Scribe, SARDOU and Labiche. JACQUES COPEAU established the Vieux Colombier in 1913 in reaction against commercial farce and melodrama, and was the figure behind the powerful CARTEL of JOUVET, DULLIN, PITOËFF and BATY, formed in 1927, which dominated the interwar years with, in particular, outstanding and influential productions of GIRAUDOUX and PIRANDELLO. POLITICAL THEATRE and the ABSURD dominated the mid-century, with SARTRE's *The Flies* daringly produced in 1943 during the occupation and the postwar productions of JEAN VILAR, notably of BRECHT's later drama at the Palais de Chaillot and other Paris theatres, as director of the THÉÂTRE NATIONAL POPULAIRE from 1951. At the same time the new 'absurdist' drama, related to the interwar SURREALIST movement, revealed itself in famous productions by BECKETT and IONESCO: the latter's *La Cantatrice Chauve* (1950) was performed for decades at the tiny Théâtre de la Huchette on the Left Bank, and Beckett's *Waiting for Godot* (1953), directed by ROGER BLIN, was the most influential play of the 1950s. Other names should be mentioned. BARRAULT and RENAUD at the ODÉON created a broad repertory which included CLAUDEL as well as Beckett and Ionesco. MIME flourished with MARCEL MARCEAU and the influential mime school of JACQUES LECOQ has trained not only French but also British actors, such as STEVEN BERKOFF. A more recent internationally known company is that of the THÉÂTRE DU SOLEIL at Vincennes under ARIANE MNOUCHKINE, whose highly original staging and choral work has since the 1960s underpinned dramatic creations with a strong political and social content, such as *1793* (1972). The development of provincial drama centres by André Malraux as de Gaulle's minister of culture and a subsequent increase in funding of provincial theatre by Jack Lang has enabled brilliant young directors in Strasbourg and elsewhere to gain experience and create productions which have subsequently enriched the Paris scene. Paris now has well over 100 theatres and offers in season nearly 200 productions of AVANT-GARDE, classical and staple BOULEVARD theatre. Auditoriums range from huge to tiny. Large, subsidized, highly professional theatres exist in the suburbs where they counter intense but often conventional activity in the centre. Paris's claim to be the centre of European drama in the twentieth century rests on numbers of brilliant performers, theorists and teachers, from Antoine to Vilar and VITEZ, who have vigorously linked classical theatre with the naturalism, EPIC THEATRE and absurdism which quickly took root there. TERRY HODGSON

Parker, Julia   *see* LESBIAN THEATRE

Parker, Louis N[apoleon]   (b. Calvados, France, 21 Oct. 1852; d. Devon, 21 Sept. 1944) Playwright. He produced many of his own plays and popular PAGEANTS. Prolific at the turn of the century, he wrote successfully for the American as well as the English stage; his best-known play is *Rosemary* (1896), but he is chiefly remembered for creating *The Pageant of Drury Lane* (1918). ADRIANA HUNTER

Parker, [James] Stewart   (b. Belfast, 20 Oct. 1941; d. London, 2 Nov. 1988) Playwright. From a Protestant working-class background, Parker playfully depicts individuals struggling against the civil war in Northern Ireland. He is fond of pastiche, exemplified in *Northern Star* (1984), which affectionately parodies several Irish writers. His best-known work, *Spokesong* (1975), is a hilarious musical history of the bicycle set against changes in Irish history. Other plays include *Catchpenny Twist* (1977), *Nightshade* (1980) and *Pentecost* (1987). He also wrote for radio and television.
DAN REBELLATO

Parry, Lorae   (b. Sydney, 28 April 1955) Playwright, actor and director. In 1979 she worked as actor and writer with other New Zealanders in London in the fringe Heartache and Sorrow Company, and while in London co-wrote the successful *Strip* (1979) with Lynne Brandon and Celia West. Returning to New Zealand, she rewrote *Strip*, playing the lead at the CIRCA THEATRE. *Frontwomen* enjoyed sellout seasons in Wellington (1988) and Auckland (1989), examining a rare theme in New Zealand drama, 'the love that exists between women . . . who lead ordinary and sometimes extraordinary lives'. Always committed to empowering women in the theatre, Parry founded the Women's Play Press, co-founded the Women's Professional Playwrights' Association and festival, was an actor and writer with Hens' Teeth, a women's comedy collective, and co-wrote and performed the satirical *Digger and Nudger Try Harder* (1990). *Cracks* (Taki Rua, 1994), 'a rough-edged contemporary fairy tale', examines the effects of class on character; *Eugenia* (Taki Rua, 1996), performed in New Zealand, Sydney and Manchester, explores the nature of sexuality and gender and is her most successful achievement. In 1998 she completed *Vagabonds*, linking early New Zealand theatrical performers with contemporary issues and an oral history of older New Zealand actresses.
GILLIAN GREER & LAURIE ATKINSON

participatory theatre   A term used since the 1960s for theatre involving audience participation (e.g. the LIVING THEATER), usually concerned with the links between political, social and sexual liberation, but which gradually became less political and more frivolous. Personal confrontation gave way to satire and escapism – audiences could judge beauty contests, be kidnapped and videoed, attend weddings and bar mitzvahs, lose themselves in role-play (become a detective hunting a murderer) or take mystery tours on trains and coaches. CHARLES LONDON
See also ENVIRONMENTAL THEATRE.

Pasadena Playhouse   One of the first significant theatres on the West Coast of America, it was founded as a semi-professional venture by Gilmor Brown in 1918 and presented a mixture of classics and new works, including the première of O'NEILL's *Lazarus Laughed* (1928). Brown opened a new theatre in 1925, an acting school in 1928 and a studio space in 1929. Many graduates, such as Randolph Scott and TYRONE POWER, went on to important film careers. After a period of decline, the theatre closed in 1970. It reopened in 1986 and has attained popularity by offering a mixture of musicals, thrillers and topical dramas. Several hit Pasadena productions – *Mail* (1988), *Accomplice* (1990) and *The Baby Dance* (1991) – have been produced in New York, but with little success. DAVID BARBOUR

Pasqual, Lluis   (b. Tarragona, Spain, 3 June 1951) Director. He acted and directed with La Tartana, an independent theatre company, and, while at university in Barcelona, with the Grup d'Estudis Theatrals d'Horta. During his time teaching in the Escola de Teatre de l'Orfeo de Sants, he directed *La setmana tràgica* ('The tragic week', 1975), a devised work with the designer Fabià Puigserver. In 1976 he co-founded the Teatre Lliure Collective with Pere Planella and Puigserver, with whom he has collaborated on many subsequent productions. Between 1976 and 1978 he worked at the National Theatre of Warsaw and at the PICCOLO TEATRO di Milano, assisting GIORGIO STREHLER, before returning to the Lliure Collective. Over the next few years, the Lliure built an outstanding reputation for presenting Catalan drama as well as stylish productions of other European classics, e.g. *Three Sisters* (1979), *As You Like It* (1983) and Goldoni's *One of the Last Afternoons of the Carnival* (1985). In 1983 he was appointed artistic director of the Centro Dramàtico Nacional. His production of LORCA's *El Público* (1986) brought together the Théâtre de l'Europe and the Piccolo Teatro di Milano, and in 1989 he directed *As You Like It* at the COMÉDIE-FRANÇAISE.

In 1990 he succeeded Strehler as the artistic director of the Théâtre de l'Europe, where his policy has been to encourage distinctly European productions. In 1994 he was the first foreign director to work at the Maly Theatre in St Petersburg. BRIAN ROBERTS

'**pataphysics** A parody of a philosophical system, created by ALFRED JARRY as a 'science of imaginary solutions'. In 1949 EUGENE IONESCO, RAYMOND QUENEAU, BORIS VIAN and others formed a 'Pataphysicians College, which published a posthumous play *Le Betrou* (1956) by poet Julien Torma (1902–33) and other dramas. The peak of its influence was the advent of the THEATRE OF THE ABSURD. COLIN CHAMBERS

Patrick [Goggan], John (b. Louisville, Ky., 17 May 1907; d. Delray Beach, Fla., 7 Nov. 1995) Playwright. After some early Broadway efforts and service in the Second World War, he scored a success with the military drama *The Hasty Heart* (1945). Follow-up works included *The Curious Savage* (1950) and *Lo and Behold!* (1951). His biggest hit was the comedy *The Teahouse of the August Moon* (1953), in which American 'get-up-and-go' comes to postwar Okinawa. His subsequent stage works, often played by regional and amateur companies, include *Good as Gold* (1957), *Juniper and the Pagans* (1959), *Everybody Loves Opal* (1962), *Everybody's Girl* (1967), *Love is a Time of Day* (1969), and *Lovely Ladies, Kind Gentlemen* (a musical version of *Teahouse*, 1970). DAVID BARBOUR

Patrick, Robert *see* ARTS LAB; CAFFÉ CINO; GAY THEATRE

Paupers Carnival Founded in 1975, a seminal and much-loved company based in CARDIFF in the heady experimental early days of the emergent Welsh theatre, Paupers Carnival consisted of Vanya Constant and Dek Leverton and did not survive their personal parting in 1990. Based at CHAPTER ARTS CENTRE, the company produced a series of exquisitely detailed miniature fantasies as well as, later, larger-scale spectacles that involved the audience, as *In The Court of the Sun* for Chapter's tenth birthday.

Perhaps with a nod to the presence at Chapter of Jane Phillips's Caricature PUPPET THEATRE, one of the earliest Welsh companies (founded 1965), Paupers incorporated puppetry into their own whimsical productions. But their style and inspiration were entirely their own, with influences as varied as MUSIC HALL, GRAND GUIGNOL, Max Ernst and cinema as much as European THIRD THEATRE. They toured the UK and Europe but as times got tighter, theatre got more political and the constraints of touring forced them to trim their imaginations, Paupers Carnival increasingly looked lost.

Vanya Constant still performs throughout the world and has her own company, Constant Theatre. DAVID ADAMS

Pavlova, Anna (b. St Petersburg, Russia, 12 February 1881; d. The Hague, 23 Jan. 1931) One of the greatest ballerinas of the twentieth century, Pavlova trained at the Russian Imperial Ballet School but had a considerable influence on the development of ballet in the West. Her European tours began in 1907 and included appearances with DIAGHILEV's Ballets Russes in 1909 and 1911. Unattracted to Diaghilev's modernism, Pavlova formed her own company in 1911. This isolated her from the major choreographic, scenic and musical collaborations of her era. However, her extensive worldwide tours, frequently performed on small stages in provincial towns, took an enduring ideal of classical ballet to a wide audience. Pavlova is best remembered for her interpretation of 'The Dying Swan'. This solo, created for her by MIKHAIL FOKINE in 1907, broke away from ballet as virtuosic spectacle; it represented a rediscovery of the poetic and sublime that were the hallmarks of Pavlova's style. LESLEY-ANNE SAYERS

See also CHOREOGRAPHY; DANCE; MOVEMENT, DANCE AND DRAMA.

Oleg Kerensky, *Anna Pavlova* (1973)
Keith Money, *Anna Pavlova, Her Life and Her Art* (1982)

Paxinou [Konstantopoulou], Katina (b. Piraeus, Athens, 15 Dec. 1900; d. Athens, 22 Feb. 1973) Actress who became famous in the 1920s under the direction of Alexis Minotis. They took their successful partnership to New York in the early 1930s (and were married in 1940). Paxinou joined the Athens National Theatre in 1932, by then considered the finest Greek actress of her generation. She worked in Greece, the United States and Britain, appearing in theatre, films and television plays. Her most memorable performances include the title roles in *Electra* (Athens, 1936), *Hedda Gabler* (New York, 1942) and *The House of Bernarda Alba* (Athens, 1954). ADRIANA HUNTER

Paxton, Steve *see* DANCE

Payne, Ben Iden (b. Newcastle upon Tyne, 5 Sept. 1881; d. Austin, Tx., 6 April 1976) Actor and director. Payne's early acting career with FRANK BENSON and his directing at the ABBEY THEATRE led him to the birth of the English REPERTORY MOVEMENT when, from 1907 to 1911, he worked with ANNIE HORNIMAN in MANCHESTER, as manager, director and performer. He left to tour with his actress wife Mona Limerick, and from 1913 to 1934 he pursued a theatrical and academic career in the United States. He was back in England until 1943 as director of the SHAKESPEARE MEMORIAL THEATRE, STRATFORD-UPON-AVON, and thereafter he resumed his career in the States. In 1950 he established a summer SHAKESPEARE FESTIVAL at Balboa Park, SAN DIEGO. He wrote a memoir, *A Life in a Wooden O* (1977).   ELAINE ASTON

Peacock Theatre   *see* ABBEY THEATRE

Pedrolo, Manuel de   (b. L'Aranyó, Spain, 1 April 1918; d. Barcelona, 26 June 1990)   Novelist and playwright. Several of his plays can be defined within the THEATRE OF THE ABSURD. His best works, such as *Cruma* (1957) and *Homes i No* (*Men and No*, 1958), have a simple visual imagery and are both philosophical and political.   JOHN LONDON

Peduzzi, Richard   (b. Argentan, France, 28 Jan. 1943)   Designer. Since 1969 Peduzzi has collaborated extensively with director PATRICE CHÉREAU on numerous projects for the theatre, opera and cinema, notably at Nanterre-Amandiers (1982–90). His influential design talents have also been in numerous museum INSTALLATIONS and in the interior architecture for such monuments as the French National Library and the Arab World Institute in Paris, where he has served as director of the National Institute for Decorative Arts since 1990. He also designed the exhibitions for the French Pavilion at Expo 92 in Seville, Spain.
ELLEN LAMPERT-GRÉAUX

Penhall, Joe   (b. Thames Ditton, Surrey, 23 Aug. 1967)   Playwright. His early work was championed by the ROYAL COURT and he became resident dramatist at the DONMAR Warehouse. From *Some Voices* (1994) and *In Pale Horse* (1995) to *In Love and Understanding* (1997) and *The Bullet* (1998) there is an exploration of male relationships, usually involving one individual whose eccentricity clashes dangerously with the responsible and timid aspirations of the other; this tension, frequently brought into crisis by sudden upsurges of intrusion, violence and sexual threat, is played out in a world of moral confusion and bewilderment. Other plays include *Blue/Orange* (2000), a success at the NATIONAL THEATRE, which examines racism, health care and perceptions of madness and normality. It transferred to the West End (2001).   DAN REBELLATO

Aleks Sierz, *In-Yer-Face Theatre: British Drama Today* (2001)

Pennington, Michael   *see*   ENGLISH SHAKESPEARE COMPANY

People Show   English touring group, founded in 1965 by art teacher Jeff Nuttall and owing much of its sub-

sequent survival to actor Mark Long. The group's prolific improvised COLLECTIVE creations have been described as EXPERIMENTAL, HAPPENINGS and PERFORMANCE ART, and were once a hallmark of the underground culture in venues like the ARTS LAB. SITE-SPECIFIC shows gave way to more mobile acts and an international reputation grew. Their influence on and beyond the FRINGE can be seen in the work of writers such as HOWARD BRENTON and groups like WELFARE STATE or the INTER-ACTION organization.
COLIN CHAMBERS

J. Nuttall, *Performance Art: Memoirs* (1979)
Roland Rees, ed., *Fringe First: Pioneers of the Fringe on Record* (1992)

People's National Theatre   A London company dedicated to non-commercial theatre, run by its founder, actress and theatre manageress NANCY PRICE, from 1930 until the destruction of its base, the Little Theatre, in 1941. She modelled the venture on the Scottish National Theatre Society and the New York THEATER GUILD and presented more than 50 plays from Euripides, PIRANDELLO and GLASPELL to the Chinese writer Hsiung.   ADRIANA HUNTER

people's theatre/popular theatre   These terms have often been used interchangeably and there has been some confusion over to what manner of theatrical presentation each refers. This varies according to class viewpoint and ideological affiliations. The debate goes back to fifth-century Athens when – one view has it – theatre could only be popular, i.e. of the people, since no other theatre existed; by contrast, the hierarchical society of Rome and the city- and nation-states which succeeded it created quite clear distinctions between elite forms of theatre and popular amusements.

It was not until the run-up to the French Revolution of 1789 that consideration was given to theatrical expression of 'the people' as socially unifying, and thence in the 1850s to a concept of theatre to be taken to the people, transcending class conflicts and working for social stability but, in fact, thereby promoting the interests of the middle class. In the second half of the nineteenth century, with the bourgeoisie firmly seated as the rising, if not dominant, class, people's theatre as a possibility was shelved. The Paris Commune of 1871 issued a set of decrees for the theatre (see *Tulane Drama Review* 44, 1969) but was not in power long enough to put them into practice; yet this rising, and the presence of other political unrest towards the turn of the century, restored the matter of a people's theatre to the agenda. After various attempts to create theatres in the suburbs of Paris, ROMAIN ROLLAND set out to establish the case for a people's theatre and became the spokesman for a considerable movement in the 1890s and the early years of the twentieth century to establish theatres in working-class districts, funded by the French government.

In cases where the interests of the middle class could be identified with a movement for national liberation, as they could in Hungary, Czechoslovakia and Bulgaria, the term 'national theatre' had a specific symbolic function. Elsewhere it became the institutional instrument through which the values of the bourgeoisie were disseminated and its traumas depicted and dissected. Such theatres included the original INDEPENDENT THEATRE, ANTOINE's Théâtre Libre, and BRAHM's Deutsches Theater. On these stages, the plays of the reformers IBSEN and HAUPTMANN, and the traumatists CHEKHOV and STRINDBERG, were performed. These theatres, more than Rolland and his cries for an independent people's theatre, were to be the influential instruments of bourgeois proselytization.

What seemed to be wanted was the Freie VOLKSBÜHNE movement, founded in Berlin in 1890, which was a very sophisticated instrument for taking theatre to the people. Backed by a mass membership, the Freie Volksbühne could afford to rent performances or even commission performances (from the middle-class theatres) at times when workers could attend. Almost as soon as it started, the contradictions in its operation were exposed by some members of the organizing body, who preferred to see plays promoted which directly reflected the values and interests of the working class. The questions raised were: 'Should we have theatre for the people or theatre by the people?' and/or: 'Should the purpose be education *in* theatre or education *through* theatre?' The schism provoked a breakaway movement, the Neue Freie Volksbühne, which followed a more political policy, less successfully than its progenitor.

In France, the movement for a people's theatre petered out. FIRMIN GÉMIER created the significantly named Théâtre National Ambulant, which made two tours in the years before the 1914–18 war with a largely populist repertoire but with the important intention of eventually touring the nucleus of productions and involving local people wherever they went. The project was cumbersome and expensive and went no further. Gémier was given a white elephant of a theatre in Paris as the THÉÂTRE NATIONAL POPULAIRE. The Trocadero was sited in a middle-class district and he was given no budget with which to mount productions.

The two events which provoked the next important developments were the First World War and the Russian Revolution. In Germany, ERWIN PISCATOR was at the centre of many initiatives made possible by the existence of a mass membership Communist Party. Piscator redefined the orientation of people's theatre as proletarian theatre. A popular theatre was to ally itself to the most advanced section of the working class, that is the Communist Party. Piscator's theatre aimed at political education. According to BRECHT, Piscator 'saw the theatre as a parliament, the audience as a legislative body. To this parliament were submitted in plastic form all the great questions that needed an answer . . . It was the stage's ambition to supply images, statistics, slogans which would enable its parliament, the audience, to reach political decisions.' Piscator's vision of theatre involved direct intervention in the lives of the audience. His form was that of EPIC THEATRE. The dramatic form would no longer suffice to articulate the questions of the day. The theatre would return to its didactic purpose, reinforced by all the possible resources of the modern theatre. Actuality, in the form of DOCUMENTARY film, was incorporated into the stage action. Scripts were constructed by a COLLECTIVE as Piscator considered it was no longer possible for one writer to understand the full economic and political complexity of the world. For the Communist Party he mounted two large-scale REVUES – utilizing popular theatre forms and using montage to replace the bourgeois drama. The achievements of Piscator were many. The limitations were that he was drawn into a fascination with expensive stage machinery, which could be supported only by solid backing from the wealthier patrons, and the preference of the Communist Party for a less dialectical form which could transmit party propaganda more directly and simply. Much of Brecht's pre-exile work followed Piscator's lead, but the LEHRSTÜCKE were designed to teach by participation; workers learned by taking part in theatre pieces which demanded political decisions.

After the Russian Revolution, people's/popular theatre was located for the first time within a state dedicated to rule by the proletariat and peasantry. As a minority ruling party, the Bolsheviks needed to mobilize quickly the support of these two groups, many of whom were illiterate and could not be reached by printed matter. In a series of imaginative approaches to these problems, theatre was used to inform and arouse through agitational propaganda (AGITPROP) and through the form of LIVING NEWSPAPER – the news performed in a variety of theatrical styles and forms. These techniques were honed to a very fine degree after 1922 by the BLUE BLOUSES. Beginning as one professional group in Moscow, the Blue Blouses became a nationwide movement, incorporating professional and amateur factory groups and involving thousands of people. The Blue Blouses created their programmes out of a montage of 'attractions' or popular theatre forms – dance, song, sketches, acrobatics. The content mixed exhortation with satire against the excesses, corruption and inefficiency of the Soviet bureaucracy. Their programmes were designed to be played in any circumstances with a minimum of resources.

In the years around 1922 the Russians also revived, in their changed context, the form of the people's festival celebrating and sometimes restaging the events of the Revolution. The most famous of these mass spectacles was *The Storming of the Winter Palace* (1924) which reconstructed the revolutionary events in Leningrad. The early living newspapers were later developed to an extraordinary level of skill and sophistication during the FEDERAL THEATER PROJECT in the United States in the mid-1930s. Through this form the political stage was able to counter the bias of the mass capitalist press. However, the form which became the mainstream workers' theatre, as it now became known, was agitprop in the style practised by the Blue Blouses. Ironically, one year before Stalin disbanded the movement in 1928, the original group was sent to Germany as part of the celebrations of the tenth anniversary of the Russian Revolution. Representatives of the working-class movement from all parts of the world were in Germany and saw the group perform. As a result, political agitprop groups sprang up in every place where labour engaged with capital and where popular resistance movements opposed invaders or aggressors. The general pattern of work was based round sketches, MASS DECLAMATIONS and songs, usually written for specific occasions at very short notice. The streets and rallies provided the audiences. Although standards varied from country to country and group to group, the speed of writing, lack of rehearsal and the subjection of aesthetic or artistic means to political necessity of the 'message' limited the growth of this form to any sort of maturity. After 1935, with Hitler in power and fascist aggression rising, class struggles were subdued in the interest of national or popular front movements to resist the dictators.

In those Western countries where workers' theatre was not suppressed, it tended to go indoors and form working-class theatres with a broad rather than aggressive political policy (such as the UNITY THEATRE in London). The material prosperity of most Western societies between 1945 and 1968 led to a decline in overtly political theatre or workers' theatre, though not in people's theatre. In the years after 1945 the term was not used, and it became more common to refer to popular theatre. This term covered two concepts. First,

there was a drive to make theatre more accessible to a wider, more demotic audience. The French pattern of decentralizing the theatre away from the Paris boulevards is the prime example of this, although the search for a new public went much wider than France. In the second use of the term, the 'popular' refers to style, form or technique. Even before the 1939–45 war there had been a long history of experimentation in the European theatre, particularly in France and Russia, to revive and develop both the acting styles of previous ages, like the COMMEDIA DELL'ARTE, which were seen as appealing to a popular audience, and to incorporate acting styles from the CIRCUS or CLOWNING. Postwar prosperity allowed some people to cross the old class lines, which were becoming more blurred and permeable, through increased opportunities in education, and this led to an intermixing of 'high' and 'low' culture.

The various forms of political unrest and action in 1968 led to a resurgence of political theatre in many forms, largely eclipsing popular theatre or relegating it to its populist, social integratory position. For a brief period theatre emerged again on the streets as GUERRILLA THEATRE, theatricalized HAPPENINGS or actions attempting to intervene in political events or, in a situationist manner, provoke authority to show its repressive nature in retaliation. Agitprop also reappeared as STREET THEATRE. After these early days there was a widespread growth of theatre groups usually termed 'radical theatre' in the United States and POLITICAL THEATRE in Britain. The great majority of these groups were formed by left-wing socialist intellectuals operating independently of political parties. In their work they adopted counter-hegemonic stances and, in a world becoming more complex and confusing, tried to raise working-class consciousness and to demystify the operations of international capitalism, its forms of oppression and exploitation. The British writer JOHN MCGRATH defined the function of this form of theatre as promoting 'the social, political and cultural development of the working class towards maturity and hegemony . . . [it is] a form of theatre, which is searching, through the experience and forms of the working-class, for those elements which point forward in the struggle together to resolve humanity's conflict with nature, and to allow all to grow to the fullest possible experience of life on earth.'

By the end of the twentieth century, to a large extent, this movement belonged to the past, although there was still a considerable residue of the groups in existence. The fall of socialist regimes in Europe after 1989 and the revelations of the corruption and incompetence that they had sheltered confused the principles of socialism with its flawed practice. Since most political theatre of an agitational kind had as its aim participating in the process of hastening the end of the capitalist system and supplanting it with socialism, the work of these groups seemed to be rendered generally *un*popular and had to be rethought on more sophisticated lines. Many of those who were previously involved in radical or political theatre now turnerd to attempting political change inside the institutions of bourgeois society. The existence of a mass working-class audience in television, coupled with the failure of many groups to build a solid working-class audience in the theatre, is one reason for this. There has been a movement away from national initiatives towards regional action and this provoked an aggressive growth of new theatre groups. There has similarly been a movement away from mass political action to forms of theatre which work closely with clearly defined specific audiences. Many developments in women's theatre (*see* WOMEN IN THEATRE), GAY THEATRE and BLACK THEATRE, or THEATRE IN PRISONS or with the homeless, follow this line of popular or political theatre.   CLIVE BARKER

See also TENT THEATRE; THEATRE FOR DEVELOPMENT.

D. Bradley and J. McCormick, *People's Theatre* (1978)

K. McCreey and R. Stourac, *Theatre as a Weapon* (1986)

John McGrath, *A Good Night Out* (1981)

Ros Merkin, *Popular Theatres?* (1996)

Erwin Piscator (ed. H. Morrison), *The Political Theatre* (1980)

Romain Rolland, *The People's Theatre* (1919)

K. M. Taylor, *People's Theatre in America* (1972)

Percy, Esmé [Saville]   (b. London, 8 Aug. 1887; d. Brighton, 16 June 1957)   Actor. After training with SARAH BERNHARDT, Percy worked with a number of repertory companies until the First World War, during which he turned to production, laying on nearly 150 plays for the troops. In the 1920s he returned to London and the Charles Macdona Players, with whom he gained recognition as a definitive actor of SHAW's plays. He was a versatile actor – also enjoying special success in Shakespearean roles – and an imaginative director.   ADRIANA HUNTER

performance   In English, theatre, music and DANCE are traditionally spoken of as the 'performing arts', and a specific theatrical, music, or dance event is called a 'performance'. While this usage is still common, the term 'performance' acquired a new prominence during the twentieth century and a much wider association of meanings particularly in the last quarter. During the 1960s and 1970s many of the leading theorists in the social sciences made performance a central term. They stressed such concerns as the analysis of certain patterns of action that conformed to pre-existing models, as well as the relation of those patterns to the situations in which they occurred and the audience for which they were intended. The close relationship between theatre and such analysis, with its images of role-playing and concern with audience effect, called the attention of theatre theorists, most notably Richard Schechner, to the possibility of seeing theatre itself as a particular kind of social action, a performance not only in the conventional artistic sense, but in the same sense that social actions like RITUALS, ceremonies, sporting events and public celebrations of all sorts are performances. From this insight was developed the idea of performance studies as a new academic discipline. Whereas traditional theatre studies had a strong orientation towards high culture and the enactment of texts that were also honoured for their literary value, performance studies looked beyond the theatre which was aligned with literature to that which was involved with movement (giving new attention, for example, to modern dance, and to such pioneers as LOÏE FULLER and ISADORA DUNCAN). It also looked beyond the theatre of high culture to such relatively neglected expressions of popular culture as fairs, circuses, parades and shows of all sorts. Performance studies became much more interdisciplinary in its orientation. It saw even this broader field of entertainment as only part of an even larger area of concern that would include the social and private patterns of activity that recent work in disciplines such as sociology, anthropology, ethnography and psychology had opened up to study as performance. Performance studies has come to occupy an increasingly important place on the cultural scene, first in America and then elsewhere, inspiring the establishment of new university programmes, new professional journals, and major national and international conferences. During this period, the term 'performance' developed a slightly different meaning and set of associations within the art world itself. Influenced on the one hand by experiments like HAPPENINGS and on the other by the works of artists using their own bodies as a medium in the movement often called BODY ART, there developed in America during the 1970s and 1980s a type of artistic presentation that came to be widely designated as 'performance' or PERFORMANCE ART. By the end of the century this concept had become so common that publications like the *New York Times* included a listing of 'performance' along with such traditional listings as 'music', 'theatre' and 'dance'. In this context, the term performance has been applied to a very wide range of artistic activity, but normally it refers to the work of a SOLO artist, using his or her body as a medium and presenting material that is often autobiographical and is in any case original with that artist. The close association of performance with the performer, and with the social and cultural positioning of that performer, means that performance has been a particularly important way for ethnic and sexual issues to gain visibility. This in turn has made performance a target for conservative critics who have particularly resented its often frank involvement with sexual matters. The removal of previously granted FUNDING to four prominent performance artists in America in 1990 by the NATIONAL ENDOWMENT FOR THE ARTS was a central event in the ongoing debate in that country over public funding for the arts. MARVIN CARLSON

Marvin Carlson, *Performance: A Critical Introduction* (1996)

C. Carr, *On Edge: Performance at the End of the Twentieth Century* (1994)

Sue-Ellen Case and Janelle Reinelt, *The Performance of Power* (1991)

Joseph Roach and Janelle Reinelt, *Critical Theory and Performance* (1992)

Richard Schechner, *Between Theatre and Anthropology* (1985)

performance art A meeting of the visual arts and theatre which grew out of mainstream theatre, in explicit and intentional opposition to it and, more generally, to the values traditionally attached to art. Its history reaches back to the beginning of the twentieth century. FUTURISM, which started in 1909, advised the performing artist to shock the audience. By the mid-1920s, the futurists had established performance as an art medium in its own right. In the process, performance art had spread to Moscow and Petrograd, Zurich, New York and London. In Russia, artists such as Burlyuk, MAYAKOVSKY and Khlebnikov assimilated futurist ideas and developed their own forms of performance art.

In 1916 the iconoclastic DADA movement was founded in Zurich by Hugo Ball; he was joined by Jean Arp, Tristan Tzara, Marcel Janco and Richard Huelsenbeck, all appalled by the violence of the First World War. Many dada artists gathered around ANDRÉ BRETON from around 1924, giving rise to the surrealist movement. Inspired by psychoanalysis, SURREALISM had a major influence on mainstream theatre's preoccupation with language, whereas post-Second World War performance art turned more to the core principles of dada and futurism – chance, simultaneity and surprise. In Germany, performance art was pioneered in the 1920s by OSKAR SCHLEMMER at the BAUHAUS, a teaching institution for the arts founded in 1919. In

the United States, performance art started to develop when many European performance artists emigrated to America in the late 1930s. After the Second World War, the individual work by and the collaboration between dancer MERCE CUNNINGHAM and musician JOHN CAGE, as well as Allan Kaprow, stand out in the United States, as do Yves Klein in France, Piero Manzoni in Italy and Joseph Beuys in Germany.

Performance artists rejected traditional conventions of representation and generally did not want to represent a character; instead, they sought to confront the audience directly with a 'real' presence centred on explorations of the body; the worlds of art and real life were merged. The performance, however, was an abstraction, allowing its formal design to make the performer its object and 'decentring' the spectator by a refusal to guide. Such direct exposure of performers to their audience did not aim at catharsis. Performances were single events, not restaged, not rehearsed and not taped. The emphasis was on the process of performance, not the product. In line with these propositions, performance art was opposed to the commercial value of art.

The specific use of imagery plays an important role in performance art. Many images are taken from life, but, in the context of the performance, take on a surrealistic shape. The performing artist's aim will be to seduce the spectators out of their everyday realities into a parallel world of dreams and the subconscious, and to intensify the spectators' receptive faculties. Collage is related to imagery in two ways: it constitutes the images themselves, and it exists between different images. The collages are constituted by collisions of media (such as performers versus PUPPETS); of cultures (such as Eastern versus Western); of rhythm and texture (such as movement versus stillness); or of eye and ear (such as words distorted through visual effects). By removing the linear connection between word and character through lines, performance art reaffirms two central quests of MODERNISM: to achieve the irreducible, and to force the spectator to look at art as art, and not as life.

Since the 1970s, when performance art became institutionalized through festivals, college courses and publications, it has lost many of its distinctive characteristics because it has lost its quality of experimentation; it has become the way art frequently functions. The body is no longer central to performance art – it has become one element among many, and this focus has shifted to LIVE ART and, more so, BODY ART. Performance art nowadays tends to take place in more traditional places like theatres, galleries and multi-purpose halls, rather than some of the original locations like a zoo, a cage or a swimming pool. Finally, performance art has become commercial, with an emphasis on the finished product rather than process.

Its loss of function gives rise to performance art as a form, a genre, in which its original methods – of rupture, fragmentation and repetition – have become the norm themselves. DANIEL MEYER-DINKGRÄFE

See also ENVIRONMENTAL THEATRE; EXPERIMENTAL THEATRE; MULTIMEDIA THEATRE.

Philip Auslander, From Acting to Performance: Essays in Modernism and Postmodernism (1997)

Gregory Battock and Robert Nickas, The Art of Performance: A Critical Anthology (1984)

Herschel B. Chipp, Theories of Modern Art: A Source Book by Artists and Critics (1968)

Josette Féral, 'What is Left of Performance Art? Autopsy of a Function, Birth of a Genre', Discourse, vol. 14 (1992)

RoseLee Goldberg, Performance Art: From Futurism to the Present (1988)

Xerxes Mehta, 'Performance Art: Problems of Description and Evaluation', Journal of Dramatic Theory and Criticism, vol. 51 (1990)

A. David Napier, Foreign Bodies: Essays in Performance, Art and Symbolic Anthropology (1990)

Performance Group American theatre group. Inspired by GROTOWSKI's visit to New York in 1967, Richard Schechner (b. 1934), the editor of Tulane Drama Review (1962–9), set up the group to work on displacing traditional oppositions between life and art or performer and spectator, and the conventional focus on monolinear verbal texts. This project produced several experimental, ritualistic, physical pieces: Dionysus in 69 (1968), Makbeth (1969), and Commune (1970). Later work, like The Tooth of Crime (1972), Mother Courage and Her Children (1974), The Balcony (1979) or Oedipus (1977), was involved more closely with texts but still displayed a characteristic physical invention and fragmenting of focus. Their early performances were structured around improvisation and the release of psychological conflicts and barriers, practices repudiated by Grotowski and some group members who, from 1975, worked in a more formally conscious way as the WOOSTER GROUP. Schechner disbanded the Performance Group in 1980 and continued his teaching at New York University. He formed a new group, East Coast Artists, in 1993, and resumed the editorship of what had become The Drama Review. DAN REBELLATO

Perkins, Osgood (b. West Newton, Mass., 16 May 1892; d. Washington DC, 21 Sept. 1937) Actor. He pursued a career in silent films made by his own pro-

duction company before making his stage debut in Beggar on Horseback (1924). It was his performance in The Front Page (1928) that established his theatrical reputation. His string of stage performances during the 1930s, in Uncle Vanya (1930), Tomorrow and Tomorrow (1931), Goodbye Again (1932) and The School for Husbands (1933), was also combined with further appearances in films such as Scarface (1932). His son Anthony [Tony] (1932–92) was a successful stage and screen actor, noted for Look, Homeward Angel (1957) and, on film, Psycho (1960). HELEN RAPPAPORT

Perry, Antoinette (b. Denver, 27 June 1888; d. New York, 28 June 1946) Actress, director and producer. Her debut in Chicago in 1905 led to supporting roles in New York, but she gave up the stage to have a family after she married in 1909, returning in 1924. She began co-producing plays with Brock Pemberton, starting with Goin' Home (1928) – a creative relationship that lasted through numerous productions into the mid-1940s, most notably the long-running Mary Chase comedy, Harvey (1944). In the late 1930s Perry took on numerous administrative roles, including president of American Equity (1941; see UNIONS) and chairman of the American Theater Wing War Service (1941–4), which in 1947 set up the Antoinette Perry (Tony) awards for distinguished performances and achievements in the theatre as a memorial to her work for the acting profession. HELEN RAPPAPORT

I. Stevenson, ed, The Tony Award (1997)

Perry, Clive see BIRMINGHAM REPERTORY THEATRE

Peru see SOUTH AMERICA

Petherbridge, Edward see ACTING (AN ACTOR REFLECTS); NATIONAL THEATRE

Pétomane, Le [Joseph Pujol] (b. Marseille, 1857; d. Toulon, 1945) Entertainer. The most disconcerting, hilarious and painful of all the MOULIN ROUGE performers, his special talent lay in the orchestration of sonorous effects achieved by controlling and modulating the gases of his alimentary canal. Placed inside the elephant outside the Moulin Rouge, he attracted large crowds, thanks to what he called his anus aspirateur. When his phenomenal gift was no longer a novelty he dwindled to a penurious life with travelling fairs. Victor by the SURREALIST dramatist VITRAC contained a femme pétomane, played by Juliette Greco in a 1946 revival. TERRY HODGSON

J. Nohain and F. Caradec, Le Pétomane 1857–1945 (1968)

Petrov see ILF AND PETROV

Petrushevskaya, Lyudmila [Stefanova] (b. Moscow, 26 May 1938)   Playwright. Influenced by the 'critical realism' of ALEXSANDR VAMPILOV, her plays offer complex yet clear portrayals of commonplace life, particularly of Russia's personal politics: domineering, hypocritical and lazy males and females who collude in the gender status quo. She deals with sobering and challenging humour with many themes suppressed and denied in the pre-Gorbachev era: crime, sex, alcoholism, corruption, unemployment, pollution, homelessness. Her plays began to be published in the 1970s and were staged from 1981 on, beginning with *Love*. Other short plays include *A Bagful of Rubbish*, *The Staircase*, *Cinzano*, *Smirnova's Birthday*, *Andante*, *Columbine's Flat*, *Men's Prison Camp*, and a collection of four published as *The Dark Room*. Full-length plays include *Music Lessons* (1983), *Three Girls in Blue* (1986) and *A Moscow Choir*. The best-known internationally of the Russian women playwrights of the latter part of the twentieth century, she is also the author of short stories and fairytales for children and adults.   VERA GOTTLIEB

Peymann, Claus (b. Germany, 1937)   Director. He joined the Frankfurt Theater am Turm in 1966 when the company was experimenting with democratic self-management, an ideal situation for Peymann, who had trained during the days of the student protest movement. He immediately established his reputation as a provocative director with productions of contemporary writers such as PETER HANDKE (*Offending the Audience*, 1966; *Kaspar*, 1968). He has challenged conservative attitudes in subsequent jobs, as intendant of the Württemberg State Theatre, Stuttgart (1974–9); at Bochum (1979–86), where he established a municipal repertory company at a time when German productions were designed around individual stars; and at Vienna's Burgtheater (from 1986). Peymann has been irreverent with classics and nurtured new writers as well as premièring works by established authors like THOMAS BERNHARD and HEINER MÜLLER. In 1994, his Burgtheater contract was extended to the end of the century, but he was asked to run the BERLINER ENSEMBLE beginning in the 1999/2000 season, to pursue yet another new direction with a now traditional company.   LAURIE WOLF

Philadelphia   In the first half of the twentieth century, Philadelphia's proximity to New York City made it an ideal location for pre-BROADWAY try-outs, reaching the height of its influence with ten theatres in 1927. (Only three of its principal houses survive.) The SHUBERT-owned Walnut Street Theater, America's oldest theatre, presented such productions as *A Streetcar Named Desire*, with MARLON BRANDO (1947), and *A Raisin in the Sun*, with Sidney Poitier (1959), before their transfers. However, with the rise of the regional theatre movement, Philadelphia's theatrical identity shifted. No longer merely an adjunct to New York, Philadelphia – until the early nineteenth century, America's theatrical capital – developed a strong RESIDENT THEATRE culture of its own.

The Philadelphia Drama Guild, a prestigious amateur company founded in 1956, turned into a professional resident theatre in 1970, followed by the opening of the Philadelphia Theater Company and the People's Light and Theater Company four years later. The latter has since captured vast audiences with its free summer theatre festival. The Bushfire Theater for the Performing Arts was founded in 1977. Growth continued in the 1980s with the addition, in 1981, of two theatres devoted to new work, the Philadelphia Festival Theater for New Plays and the American Music Theater Festival. Following suit, the Walnut Street became a resident company in 1983, joined by the multicultural Venture Theater (1987), and the Arden Theater Company (1988). The Theater Alliance of Greater Philadelphia, the organization that promotes professional theatre in Philadelphia and presents the annual Barrymore Awards, currently boasts over 40 member theatres.

Philadelphia also has a thriving alternative theatre scene, represented by such AVANT-GARDE companies as the Brick Playhouse, devoted to workshopping new plays, and the experimental Bloody Someday Productions, a CABARET-style theatre devoted to the fusion of theatre and poetry.   SARAH STEVENSON

Philipe, Gérard (b. Cannes, France, 4 Dec. 1922; d. Paris, 25 Nov. 1959)   Actor who became famous in the role of CAMUS's *Caligula* (1945). He was soon extravagantly fêted as the foremost *jeune premier* in France. At JEAN VILAR's Festival d'AVIGNON he played *Le Cid* (1951) with extraordinary panache and then took principal roles at Vilar's THÉÂTRE NATIONAL POPULAIRE (e.g. *Lorenzaccio*, 1952; *Richard II*, 1954; *Ruy Blas*, 1954). Films by René Clair and René Clément had made him an international star when the sudden extinction of his grace and radiant youth dumbfounded the public. A progressive who was president of the actors' union, he was buried in Provence in the costume of Le Cid.   TERRY HODGSON

Philippines   *see* SOUTH-EAST ASIA

Phillip Street Theatre   For 17 years, the home of intimate revue in Sydney, and training ground for a generation of actors. It opened in May 1954 with *Top of the Bill*. In 1956, BARRY HUMPHRIES made his Sydney debut here in *Mr & Mrs*, and Edna Everage made her first appearance in the 13-month run of *Around the Loop*. In 1965, *A Cup of Tea, a Bex and a Good Lie Down*, by regular John McKellar, introduced that phrase into the language and Ruth Cracknell and Reg Livermore to the professional stage. Intimate review had run its course by 1971. JEREMY ECCLES

Katharine Brisbane, *Entertaining Australia* (1991)

Phillips, Anton *see* BLACK THEATRE

Phillips, Robin (b. Haslemere, Surrey, 28 Feb. 1942) Director. He became associate director of the BRISTOL OLD VIC in 1960, having acted for them and trained at the school. After work at the ROYAL SHAKE-SPEARE COMPANY and the Northcott Theatre, Exeter, he helped found the Company Theatre, Greenwich, where he became artistic director in 1973. In 1974 Phil-lips was appointed artistic director of Canada's STRAT-FORD FESTIVAL. Since leaving it in 1980 he has worked in both England and Canada, returning in 1986 to Stratford as director of its Young Company at the Third Stage. An actor's director, Phillips at his best is able to re-create with startling theatricality texts as different as *King Lear*, *Uncle Vanya* and *Private Lives* because of his ability to integrate design, film-like blocking and visual clarity. Following a period as director-general of Edmonton's Citadel Theater (1990–4), he freelanced widely in North America and England, adding opera to his directorial interests. EUGENE BENSON

Phillips, Stephen (b. Summertown, Oxon, 25 Jan.1864; d. Deal, Kent, 9 Dec. 1915) Poet and play-wright. Exploiting an essentially nineteenth-century tradition of pseudo-Shakespearean VERSE DRAMA, Phil-lips wrote 13 plays: *Herod* (1900) and *Ulysses* (1902), lavishly mounted by BEERBOHM TREE, and *Paolo and Francesca* (1902), similarly mounted by GEORGE ALEX-ANDER, enjoyed a voguish but ephemeral success. IAN CLARKE

Phillpotts, Eden (b. Mt Aboo, India, 4 Nov. 1862; d. Broad Clyst, Devon, 29 Dec. 1960) Writer and play-wright. He went to London at the age of 18, studied for the stage and then became a clerk in a fire insurance company for ten years, during which time he wrote in the evenings. He wrote upwards of 160 books, often using the pseudonym of Herrington Hext. His plays include *The Secret Woman* (1912), *Bed Rock* (1924) and *Jane's Legacy* (1925). *Yellow Sands* (1926) and *The Good Old Days* (1932), were co-written with his daughter Adelaide. Many are English rural comedies, such as the smash hit *The Farmer's Wife* (1916) and *Devonshire Cream* (1924). MAGGIE GALE

Phoenix Society It was founded in London in 1919 as an offshoot of the STAGE SOCIETY, which was to devote itself to contemporary works while Phoenix concentrated on Elizabethan, Jacobean and Restora-tion dramatists. Philip Carr's Mermaid Society had attempted a similar project in the early 1900s, but to little effect. Allan Wade directed most of the Phoenix productions, which, by the Society's demise in 1926, had not only included the better-known earlier English drama (Marlowe, Jonson) but had done invaluable work in restoring many forgotten pieces (e.g. Fletcher's *The Faithful Shepherdess*). IAN CLARKE

See also RESTORATION DRAMA IN THE TWENTIETH CEN-TURY.

Phoenix Theater A company organized in 1953 by T. Edward Hambleton and NORRIS HOUGHTON, it took over the old Yiddish Art Theater in lower Manhattan, renamed it and for eight years offered a series of bril-liant, off-beat and imaginative productions. These included *Madam, Will You Walk?* (1953), *Coriolanus* (1954), *The Golden Apple* (1954), *Phoenix '55* (1955), *The Duchess of Malfi* (1957) and *The Octoroon* (1961). Finan-cial problems forced it to work in collaboration with other groups and in later years at other venues. In 1964 it was joined by the Association of Producing Artists (1960–70), run by ELLIS RABB as a repertory ensemble. Before folding in 1982, the Phoenix presented *Oh Dad, Poor Dad . . .* (1962), *You Can't Take It with You* (1966) and *The Show-Off* (1967). GERALD BORDMAN

photography *see* THEATRE PHOTOGRAPHY

physical preparation The gradual improvement in the concern for bodily health and well-being has had its effect upon acting, that most physically demanding of professions, and has created a growing appreciation for the body as a means of expression. It now goes without question that it is as essential to free the body as it is to free the VOICE, and that both operate in per-fect and inseparable harmony.

Physical emancipation, pioneered with such extra-ordinary artistic strength by ISADORA DUNCAN, and a movement system of scientific accuracy promulgated by RUDOLF LABAN, continue to influence the per-forming arts. Once the iron grip of classical ballet had been broken, the way was open for a natural flow of movement closer to the instincts of the actor. It was the combined and unique talents of such men as KURT JOOSS, theatre DIRECTOR and CHOREOGRAPHER, and Sigurd Leeder, teacher, that sustained the remarkable school of Central European Dance, flourishing in Ger-many, and later in England, during the early part of the twentieth century. It is from this source that per-formers and students, along with those trained at both the Laban Art of Movement Studio and the MIME schools of England and France, moved into education and the performing arts. Unlike the ballet, whose formula was too inflexible, the so-called modern DANCE, with its expressive action and wide-ranging vocabulary, was ready-made for the actor in training, and the critical elements of this technique formed a fine basis upon which to build an actor's physical expertise.

In North America, the movement-tutor, the modern dance schools and the dance/drama departments of the universities, again largely inspired by Laban, were responsible also for bringing the individual performer to the highest point of energy and relaxed readiness. In the right hands it was possible to turn an inert, sleepy, disgruntled and ordinary person into a vibrant, sparkling, ready-to-act marvel, filled with what Coleridge called 'Wonder-exciting vigour'.

It is true that there is nothing so lovely in the world as a feeling of inertia; but if anything competes with that pleasure it is the joy of being fully alive and ready for action. The body is an amazing powerhouse, with such amplitude, such freedom and such variety, that it seems unworthy to reduce it to a negligent and uncaring vessel. (Even fifteen minutes of comparatively mild activity can lift the latent energy a hundredfold.) In training the body it is good to know that two important polarities are involved: flexibility and control. On the printed page these terms signify little, but in action they mean everything. Flexibility suggests freedom; control, restriction. A full command of these seeming opposites will produce a well-ordered, vulnerable actor, moving with imaginative ease and sustained, expressive beauty.

How is this achieved? The word 'exercise' suggests dull rote and a lack of inspiration, but it is through exercise, especially exercises of originality and challenge, that the goal is achieved. 'Inspiration' is the vital word here, for, like the voice, it is upon breath that the edifice is built. The importance of supportive breathing in voice work is unquestioned, but it also gives a life force to movement. The perfect marriage between breath and action creates energy in the body; once that is experienced – and it is impossible not to feel it – everything begins to grow. Here is a good starting point in the awakening of the body, and a movement-tutor makes use of this natural phenomenon, encouraging freedom in the spine and the limbs, and kindling the enjoyment of containing that freedom within simple forms. But structures in movement, whether apparently wild or diminutive and subtle, must be built upon a healthy skeletal foundation. The work of F. MATTHIAS ALEXANDER is the best in this field, and

his technique is widely used in drama schools, musical academies and theatres.

Free from major physical problems and fully prepared in this way, the actor can develop and maintain a remarkably efficient mechanism. What every responsible actor most desires is the confidence born of accomplished skills in physical (and vocal) techniques, from the speed and strength required in armed and unarmed combat to the relaxed poise and easy carriage of complete assurance. This buoyant ease is the enduring quality of historical dance and movement, and gives authenticity and authority of manner in plays of earlier centuries.

However, it is accepted that overt physicality is but a part of the story of movement training. An actor should be also, in a lovely Indian phrase, an 'athlete of the spirit'. Fanciful though this may seem, the truth is that action and non-action live in the same house. Non-action, stillness, the stillness of conscious relaxation, is the perfect blend of flexibility and control. The limbs are free and at rest, the mind is quiet and at peace, the breath has an easy slow depth. From this point all action begins, and to it all action returns. The joints are fully articulated and remain ready; the mind is alert in its emptiness and remains ready; the breath rises and falls like a placid ocean, waiting for the first necessary sounds of communication. This total preparation opens the way for the spoken word, words which flow effortlessly from a clear head on great reserves of energized breath. JOHN BROOME

See also MOVEMENT, DANCE AND DRAMA; VOICE.

physical theatre Generally, a theatre piece in which the physical aspects of the performance are at least as important as the dialogue, often more so. The term has been used to describe the work of GROTOWSKI, whose LABORATORY THEATRE involved extensive and rigorous physical training, and that of his disciples like Schechner. It is also applied to a broader spectrum of work exemplified by companies such as THÉÂTRE DE COMPLICITÉ, in which the performers' training in such disciplines as CLOWNING, MIME and *COMMEDIA DELL'ARTE* techniques provides a completely different perspective on even the most traditional material. ANDREW SOLWAY

See also BODY ART; PERFORMANCE ART.

Piaf, Edith [Edith Giovanna Gassion] (b. Paris, 19 Dec. 1915; d. Paris, 11 Nov. 1963) Singer. The manager of a chic cabaret recognized the talent of this street singer and dubbed her *la môme Piaf*, 'the sparrow kid'. In 1937 she was an immediate success at the ABC. She toured the United States (1945, 1955), and though she did not perform in Britain, her records sold in millions

there. Later, undermined by illness and the effects of alcoholism and drug addiction, she continued to sing in her rough-edged, vibrant voice of the hopes and deceptions of love, her theme song being 'Je ne regrette rien'. Famous songs she wrote herself include 'La Vie en rose' and 'L'Hymne à l'amour'. She appeared in several films and on stage in COCTEAU's *Le Bel Indifférent* (1941), written specially for her, and Achard's *La P'tite Lili* (1951). She also wrote two autobiographies, *Au bal de la chance* and *Ma Vie* (*My Life*, 2000), and was the subject of the play *Piaf* (1979) by PAM GEMS.
TERRY HODGSON

S. Berteaut, trans. G. Boulanger, *Piaf* (1970)
Margaret Crossland, *Piaf in Context* (2000)

Picasso, Pablo [Ruiz y] (b. Málaga, Spain, 25 Oct. 1881; d. Mougins, France, 8 April 1973) One of the most renowned painters, sculptors and graphic artists of the twentieth century, Picasso also designed sets, costumes and occasionally curtains for theatre and ballet. Ballets designed include COCTEAU's *Parade* (1917), *The Three-Cornered Hat* (1919), *Pulcinella* (1920) and *Mercure* (1924) for the Ballets Russes. His theatre décors include *Antigone* (1922) and *Oedipus Rex* (1951). He wrote two experimental plays, and his dove of peace was used by the BERLINER ENSEMBLE for their curtain. DENISE L. TILLES

piccolo teatro Earliest and most renowned *piccolo teatro* (small theatre) is the one in Milan, founded in 1947 by Paolo Grassi and GIORGIO STREHLER with financial and political support from the city to attract young working people. Following Milan's lead, other *piccoli teatri*, established municipally with similar social purpose but less successful, were founded in Rome (1948), Genoa (1952) and Turin (1955), as well as Bolzano, Trieste, Catania, L'Aquila, Naples, Bologna and Palermo. G. H. MCWILLIAM

Picon, Molly (b. New York, 28 Feb. 1898; d. Pennsylvania, 5 April 1992) Actress and singer who began her career, which spanned some 80 years, busking on trams at the age of five. By the 1920s and 1930s, the golden age of the YIDDISH THEATRE, this diminutive performer had established herself as one of its most popular stars, touring all over the world with REVUES, operettas and musical comedies, many of them adapted or written by her husband, Jacob Kalich. Her unrivalled popularity was not confined to Yiddish speakers: in 1938 she topped the bill at the LONDON PALLADIUM, and her long career is peppered with appearances in the West End, on Broadway and in Hollywood films, perhaps most notably as Yente the matchmaker in *Fiddler on the Roof* (1972). Despite being, for many, the very embodiment of the popular Yiddish theatre, Picon's energy and versatility allowed her to remain in demand even after the Yiddish theatre was effectively destroyed by the Holocaust in Europe and assimilation elsewhere. She wrote an autobiography, *So Laugh a Little* (1962). DAVID SCHNEIDER

Pierce, Charles *see* DRAG

pierrot In Britain, 'pierrot show' was a term used to describe a form of summer entertainment popular in seaside resorts around the beginning of the twentieth century, thought to have been inspired by Pellissier's Follies, a REVUE company which had adopted a modified version of the traditional COMMEDIA DELL'ARTE costume. Within a few years pierrot troupes, with the males in baggy pantaloons and the females in short skirts, had sprung up on the beaches around Britain, often working in the open air and earning their wages by 'bottling', amassing small coins from a collection among their audience. The Co-Optimists, a famous company of the 1920s who played West End seasons, reverted to the pierrot costumes, but by this time most of the seaside resorts had built covered theatres and their function was taken over by concert parties, who usually worked in evening dress. With EDWARD KNOB-LOCK and others, J. B. PRIESTLEY successfully adapted for the stage his novel *The Good Companions* about a pierrot company. JOAN LITTLEWOOD had the actors in *Oh, What a Lovely War!* (1963) perform as a pierrot troupe – a link both to the period in which the show was set and to the place of the pierrot in popular theatre. The pierrot, closely related to Harlequin, re-appeared in British PANTOMIME. In continental Europe, mostly through the MIME Debureau, the pierrot survived as a symbolic figure that was to attract the attention of artists from Picasso and Schoenberg to ELIOT, BARRAULT, BLOK and MEYERHOLD, who played the part in Blok's *The Fairground Booth* (1906). Pierrot's white face came to dominate mime until in the 1960s new directions were sought. PETER HEPPLE

A. Sterne and A. de Bear, *The Comic History of the Co-Optimists* (1926)

Pike Theatre Club Founded by Alan Simpson and Carolyn Swift in 1953 in DUBLIN, it was the first of the city's FRINGE venues to exert significant influence, through its own type of intimate late-night REVUE and an international repertoire that included CLAUDEL, IONESCO, SARTRE and TENNESSEE WILLIAMS. It launched the theatre career of BRENDAN BEHAN by staging the première of *The Quare Fellow* (1954) after the ABBEY had rejected it; in 1958 it also presented three of his radio plays (*The Big House, Moving Out* and *A Garden Party*) adapted by Swift for the stage. SAMUEL BECKETT robbed the Pike of another 'first' when his wish to let London see the English-language première of *Waiting for Godot* was granted. The Pike staged it later the same year, 1955, and it enjoyed a good run there. The theatre's adventurous policy became its downfall when it was prosecuted in 1957 under obscenity laws for showing Williams' *The Rose Tattoo*. It was remounted at Belfast's Grand Opera House but Simpson had been found guilty and the legal costs incurred before the conviction was ultimately quashed led to the closure of the Pike. CHARLES LONDON

Alan Simpson, *Beckett and Behan and a Theatre in Dublin* (1962)
Carolyn Swift, *Stage by Stage* (1985)

Pilgrim Players An AMATEUR group formed in Birmingham in 1907 by BARRY JACKSON to present chiefly VERSE DRAMA. In 1911 their name was changed to the BIRMINGHAM REPERTORY Company, and it formed the basis of the professional group for whom Jackson built a home in 1913. It was also the name of a company under the direction of E. MARTIN BROWNE which toured religious drama to theatreless areas from 1939 to 1945, and was among the first theatrical enterprises to be supported by the COUNCIL FOR THE ENCOURAGEMENT OF MUSIC AND THE ARTS (later the ARTS COUNCIL). G. ROWELL

H. and M. E. Browne, *The Pilgrim Story* (1945)

Pinero, Arthur Wing (b. London, 24 May 1855; d. London, 23 Nov. 1934) Playwright. After a series of popular farces at the Old Royal Court Theatre, initiated by *The Magistrate* (1885) and *The Schoolmistress* (1886), Pinero, a former actor, changed tone with *The Profligate* (1889) and then consolidated his reputation with a serious 'social problem' play, *The Second Mrs Tanqueray* (1893), which some critics once celebrated as the first modern English play. Seen as daring by contemporaries, because of Pinero's treatment of a 'tainted' woman, its success derived partly from its accommodation of the outspokenness of IBSEN to the conventional views of the commercial stage. A series of consciously crafted social dramas, which repeated this strategy, and occasional comedies followed; these include *The Notorious Mrs Ebbsmith* (1895), *The Gay Lord Quex* (1899), *Iris* (1901), *His House in Order* (1906), *The Thunderbolt* (1908), and *Mid-Channel* (1909). Altogether he wrote over 50 plays; the leading English playwright at the turn of the century, his FARCES, such as *Dandy Dick* (1887), and a sentimental comedy *Trelawney of the*

'Wells' (1898) have endured better than his serious work. Pinero was knighted in 1909. IAN CLARKE

Wilbur Dwight Dunkel, *Arthur Wing Pinero: A Critical Biography with Letters* (1941)
Walter Lazenby, *Arthur Wing Pinero* (1972)

Pinget, Robert (b. Geneva, Switzerland, 19 July 1919; d. Tours, France, 25 Aug. 1997) Playwright and novelist. Pinget's parents came from Savoy, and he later resumed French nationality. His first book, *Between Fantoine and Agapa* (short, somewhat surrealistic sketches), was published in 1951. Some 20 novels and almost as many plays followed, the first, *Lettre Morte* (*Dead Letter*) being created at the THÉÂTRE NATIONAL POPULAIRE in 1960. Pinget's plays, like all his writing, express his preoccupation with the nature of reality in all its contradictions, and with the connection between art and life. Little interested in realistic stage settings, he nevertheless produces vivid images through his impeccable choice of words. Through words, which he sees as the approach to 'absolute time', he raises banal characters and events to the level of poetry – a poetry suffused with humour, sometimes of the most down-to-earth nature.

Other plays include *La Manivelle* (*The Old Tune*, 1960; English version by SAMUEL BECKETT); *Ici ou ailleurs* (translated as *Clope*, 1961); *Autour de Mortin* (*About Mortin*, 1965); *Abel et Bela* (1971); and *Un testament bizarre* (*A Bizarre Will*, 1986). The AVIGNON FESTIVAL featured several of his plays. BARBARA WRIGHT

M. Renouard, *Robert Pinget* (1988)

Pinnock, Winsome [May] (b. London, 26 Aug. 1961) Playwright. She came to notice with her second play, *Leave Taking* (LIVERPOOL PLAYHOUSE Studio, 1988; ROYAL COURT Theatre Upstairs, 1990), which, in its story of a West Indian mother and her two English daughters, explores the issue of an individual's cultural identity and its expression in fraught dualities (black/white, 'standard' English/dialect). These issues were rarely examined in British theatre and featured in later plays such as *A Hero's Welcome* (1989) and *Talking in Tongues* (1991). The role of culture features again in *Picture Palace* (1988), which deals with women and the media; in *A Rock in Water* (1989), in which she dramatizes the life of black communist Claudia Jones, who, expelled from the United States for 'un-American' activities, came to England where she founded the Notting Hill Carnival; and in *Mules* (1996), about women used as drug carriers. When *Leave Taking* was revived in a production that played at the Cottesloe in 1995, she became the first black British woman to have a play produced at the NATIONAL THEATRE. COLIN CHAMBERS

Pinter, Harold   (b. Hackney, London, 10 Oct. 1930) Playwright, actor and director. Of all the playwrights who came to prominence following the renaissance of British theatre in the late 1950s, Pinter has had the greatest critical acclaim. The word 'Pinteresque' has entered the language to describe his style of writing: dialogue that is both naturalistic and enigmatic, loaded with significant (and insignificant) pauses. Sometimes his plays are classified as belonging to the THEATRE OF THE ABSURD; a more accurate term would be 'comedy of menace'. Typically set in a single room, they depict one or more characters defending a certain territory (be it geographical, like the house in *The Caretaker*, 1960, or a relationship, as in *Old Times*, 1971), into which an intruder insinuates him- or (less frequently, her-) self.

Pinter was born in London's East End, his father a Jewish tailor. He trained as an actor and acted in rep (1949–57, some of the time as David Baron). During this period he was writing poetry and some prose; in 1957 he wrote his first (short) play *The Room*. His first full-length play, *The Birthday Party*, was a critical and commercial failure the following year, but a successful British television production in 1960 brought his name to the public attention. The play's central character is Stanley, whose (temporary) haven of security is a room in a seedy boarding house. Into this setting come two mysterious characters who begin to threaten and humiliate him. The play has no traditional exposition; unresolved mysteries repeatedly perplex the audience; yet it was hailed as a major step in extending the bounds of theatre, just two years after its original dismissal. Its first American production (1960) was by the ACTOR'S WORKSHOP, San Francisco. It has since had many revivals.

Also in 1960, *The Caretaker* consolidated Pinter's position as a leading British playwright. Academics have made ingenious claims about this play's symbolism, but Pinter has insisted it is simply about three people: two brothers (one apparently sadistic, one mentally damaged) and a tramp who is invited into the house. Again, the play is full of non sequiturs and menace as the characters fight to defend their differing 'territories'. *The Caretaker* was filmed in 1962.

The early 1960s were prolific years for Pinter. Notable among his work was *The Collection* (1961), written for television and subsequently directed for the stage by PETER HALL (who has several times directed Pinter's work, notably for the ROYAL SHAKESPEARE COMPANY and the NATIONAL THEATRE) and by Pinter himself. This play has a more elegant setting than the early ones. Its four characters are involved in the fashion trade; various heterosexual and homosexual relationships may or may not exist between them. Written with economy and wit, the play reaches no resolution except to suggest there is no hard distinction between fact and fiction. Like so much of his work, it is both absorbing and disturbing.

Pinter's exploration of sexual themes (and sexual menace) culminated in *The Homecoming* (1965), which originally had a mixed critical reception but won the New York Drama Critics Circle Award; it was successfully revived in London in 1991 (by the original director and designer, respectively Hall and JOHN BURY), and has been described as one of his most important works. Like many Pinter plays, it convinces on stage even if it disappoints on the page. The action is set within a complex mesh of (all-male) family relationships, into which situation Teddy arrives from the United States to see his father and brothers. Inexplicably, when he departs he leaves his wife behind as a kind of family whore. The play's strength is to diffuse the audience's incredulity and replace it with a kind of terror and recognition of the disruptive power of erotic attraction.

Similarly 'Pinteresque' themes are explored in *Old Times*, in which an intruder (this time, a woman) enters a 'haven', disturbs a seemingly happy married relationship, and brings to the surface tensions and contradictions that had remained unspoken. In *No Man's Land* (1975) the relationship is between Hirst, a prosperous writer (originally played by RALPH RICHARDSON) and Spooner, a garrulous, down-at-heel poet (JOHN GIELGUD). Hirst is 'protected' by two servants, but Spooner becomes a threat to this stable household.

In *Betrayal* (1978), a play that received notices as dismissive as those originally given to *The Birthday Party*, Pinter allows his audience for once to feel they know more about the characters than the characters do themselves. It is a triangular love story, largely told in reverse as (scene by scene) we are 'flashed back' in time in a style that is distinctly cinematic. (Pinter has written extensively for that medium, providing the screenplay for, among other films, *The Servant*, 1963; *Accident*, 1967; *The Go-Between*, 1971; *The French Lieutenant's Woman*, 1981; *Betrayal* itself, 1983; *The Handmaid's Tale*, 1990; and *The Comfort of Strangers*, 1990.) Thereafter, he wrote little for the stage but concentrated on directing, screenwriting and, increasingly, political protest. He began to fall out of critical favour. For example, the dramatist JOHN OSBORNE suggested he had been 'mining a very narrow seam for thirty years, and it may be the ore is giving out'. There was more cogent (feminist) criticism of his treatment of women in his plays. His political enthusiasms surprised many, given the complete absence of sermonizing in his writing, but in his youth he had been a conscientious objector rather than perform his National Service. In the 1980s he became increasingly vocal on behalf of such causes as Amnesty International, the Campaign for Nuclear Disarmament, Nicaragua Solidarity and anti-CENSORSHIP movements. These concerns surfaced in two short plays, *Mountain Language* (1988) and *Party Time* (1991).

Pinter has been compared, with good reason, to BECKETT (whom he admires particularly) and the novelist Kafka. For his work in the 1960s and 1970s alone he deserves the approval he has won from critics, both journalistic and academic, and the international acclaim that has greeted his influential and innovative style.

Other plays include *Landscape* (1968), *Silence* (1968), *Other Places* (a trilogy of short plays, 1982), and *Ashes to Ashes* (1996), a typically intense and disturbing play that explores the links between politics and sexuality. His other work includes a novel, *The Dwarfs* (1990), collections of his own poems, and a volume of essays. DAVID SELF

Michael Billington, *The Life and Work of Harold Pinter* (1996)
Bernard F. Dukore, *Harold Pinter* (1982)
Martin Esslin, *Pinter: A Study of His Plays* (1973)
Steven H. Gale, ed., *Harold Pinter: Critical Approaches* (1986)
Elizabeth Sakellaridou, *Pinter's Female Portraits: A Study of Female Characters in the Plays of Harold Pinter* (1988)
David T. Thompson, *Pinter: The Player's Playwright* (1985)

Pioneer Players (London) Founded in 1911 by EDITH CRAIG 'to deal with all kinds of movements of contemporary interest . . . as a play is worth a hundred speeches where propaganda is concerned'. A London-based subscription theatre company which came out of Craig's involvement in the ACTRESSES' FRANCHISE LEAGUE, the Pioneer Players brought new foreign writers such as SUSAN GLASPELL, PAUL CLAUDEL and LEONID ANDREYEV to the British theatre as well as promoting home-grown plays that tackled a range of important topics from war and the vote to work, poverty and the family, usually from a woman's point of view (e.g. GITHA SOWERBY's *Rutherford and Son*, 1912). Actresses such as ELLEN TERRY, LENA ASHWELL, AURIOL LEE and SYBIL THORNDIKE played in early productions. The company was wound up in 1925. MAGGIE GALE
See also WOMEN IN THEATRE.

Katharine Cockin, *Women and Theatre in the Age of Suffrage: The Pioneer Players* (2000)

Julie Holledge, *Innocent Flowers: Women in the Edwardian Theatre* (1981)

Pioneer Players (Melbourne) In 1922 a group of friends and mostly amateur actors centred on the playwright LOUIS ESSON formed a company called the Pioneer Players to present plays written by and for Australians. Until 1926 they staged 18 new plays, including Esson's *The Bride of Gospel Place* (1926) and *A Happy Family* (1922) by VANCE PALMER, one of the co-founders, before lack of funds and audiences forced them to close. CHARLES LONDON

Peter Fitzpatrick, *Pioneer Players: The Lives of Louis and Hilda Esson* (1995)

Pip Simmons Theatre Group British touring theatre group. Formed at the ARTS LAB in 1969, they were forerunners of what became known as PERFORMANCE ART. Named after their founder and director, they performed brash, cartoon-like, often highly political shows which accused and attacked their audiences. They developed a visual, surreal style that won a large following abroad. Their best known works were *Superman* (1969), *Do It!* (1971), *The George Jackson Black and White Minstrel Show* (1973) and *An Die Musik* (1975), an iconic work of the ALTERNATIVE THEATRE. DAN REBELLATO

P. Ansorge, *Disrupting the Spectacle: Five Years of Experimental and Fringe Theatre in Britain* (1975)

Pirandello, Luigi (b. Agrigento, Sicily, 28 June 1867; d. Rome, 10 Dec. 1936) Playwright, poet and novelist. He studied at the universities of Palermo, Rome and Bonn, and settled in Rome where he established his reputation as a writer of novels and short stories. During the last 20 years of his life he concentrated his energies on writing for the stage. He collaborated with the founder of a Sicilian-dialect theatre and later formed his own National Art Theatre (1925) in which he functioned as manager and director, and achieved international renown as Italy's foremost twentieth-century playwright. In 1934 he was awarded the Nobel Prize for literature. His wife was Antonietta Portulano, whose much-publicized chronic mental illness may have served to confirm him in his pessimism, but chronologically could not have been its cause. Although he insisted on the separation of art and politics, his support, however vacillating, for the fascist regime that financed his theatre did not prevent his later plays being censured.

His anti-realist and anti-rationalist plays are open to interpretation on many levels: metaphysical, sociological and theatrical. His dramatic method reflects his message and is characterized by a quality of open-endedness and ambiguity. His play *Sei personaggi in cerca d'autore* (*Six Characters in Search of an Author*, 1921) was seen by his contemporaries to mark a revolutionary step forward in theatrical history, and to liberate the stage from the constraints of nineteenth-century bourgeois realism. In it he analyses the principle of performance in every sense, embodying on the stage the network of relationships (between author, character, actor, director and audience) which is the basis of every theatrical production. Here and elsewhere in his canon, the theatre emerges as the ultimate metaphor for human life, humans being of necessity performers, seeking meaning, identity, expression, direction and relationship.

Pirandello's major dramatic works are all demonstrations of the limitations imposed on his characters by their humanity. Theatrical imagery is repeatedly used to clarify the message. In *Enrico IV* (*Henry IV*, 1922) the modern protagonist seeks refuge from existential anguish by masquerading in the full fustian of a fixed historical character. In *Il piacere dell'onesta* (*The Pleasure of Honesty*, 1917), *Il giuoco della parti* (*The Rules of the Game*, 1918) and *Come tu mi vuoi* (*As You Desire Me*, 1930) the plots are again based on the assumption of a fixed role or stance, and *Ciascuno a suo modo* (*Each in His Own Way*, 1924), *Questa sera si recita a soggetto* (*Tonight We Improvise*, 1930), *Trovarsi* (*To Find Oneself*, 1932) and *I giganti della montagna* (*The Giants of the Mountain*, his last, unfinished play) all make symbolic use of actors and the theatre to explore the human predicament.

Pirandello's plays are grounded in relativism; their premise is twentieth-century uncertainty and the demise of the absolute. The refusal to make judgements or formulate opinions finds dramatic expression in the stylized flight of fancy entitled *Cosi è (si vi pare)* (*Right You Are, If You Think So*, 1917). The tone of sceptical defeatism which underlies the hilarity of such works may account for the early reluctance of British audiences to accept Pirandello's work, while ensuring him an immediate and enduring popularity in France. Many of his themes found echoes and parallels in the output of French dramatists and filtered through to become the commonplaces of the European theatre of the mid-century: the menace of the void; the deceptiveness of appearances; the fallibility of speech; the disintegration of personality; the common need for structure and illusion. Yet few of his more than 40 plays are regularly performed in English, and many are not available in good translations.

Apart from his theatrical trilogy (*Six Characters in Search of an Author*, *Each in His Own Way* and *Tonight*

We Improvise), Pirandello's plays are not overtly experimental in form. They appear to be constructed somewhat along the lines of the nineteenth-century well-made play, but with an element of self-parody and caricature constantly creeping in to disorientate and disconcert. They tend to provoke a sense that the 'happening' is taking place, not on the stage, but in the awareness of the audience.

Other plays include *Il berretto a sonagli* (*Cap and Bells*, 1917), *La giara* (*The Jar*, 1917), *Tuto per bene* (*All For The Best*, 1920), *Vestire gl'ignudi* (*Naked*, 1922), *L'uomo dal fiore in bocca* (*The Man with the Flower in his Mouth*, 1923; the first play to be broadcast on British, and possibly any television), *La vita che ti diedi* (*The Life I Gave You*, 1923) and *Non si sa come* (*No-one Knows How*, 1935). FELICITY FIRTH

Susan Bassnett-McGuire, *Luigi Pirandello* (1983)

Eric Bentley, *The Pirandello Commentaries* (1986)

G. Cambon, ed., *Pirandello* (1967)

Piscator, Erwin [Friedrich Max] (b. Ulm, Germany, 17 Dec. 1893; d. Starnberg, Germany, 20 March 1966)   Director and theatre manager. Piscator studied theatre at Munich University and worked as an actor before being drafted into the army. The war experience totally shattered his artistic beliefs, and when given leave in 1918 he joined the Berlin DADA circle. After the war he worked as an actor in Königsberg and became director of the small Tribunal Theatre there. In 1920 he founded the Proletarian Theatre in Berlin, a working-class amateur theatre which performed short AGITPROP plays. In 1924 he staged the *Revue Roter Rummel* ('Red Revue') for the German Communist Party's election campaign, followed in 1925 by the pageant *Trotz alledem* ('Despite All') for the Communist Party's Berlin conference. These pioneering pieces of agitprop theatre were produced outside his main activity as director at the VOLKSBÜHNE. Between 1924 and 1927 he staged nine large-scale productions for this theatre, making use of the latest technological inventions. Radical changes in the play texts ensured the topicality of his productions but also led to some major controversies and his eventual dismissal from the organization. In 1927 he opened his own theatre, the Theater am Nollendorfplatz, where he directed four shows, which rank among the best and most influential productions of the Weimar theatre: TOLLER's *Hoppla, wir leben!* (*Such is Life*, 1927), Tolstoy's *Rasputin* (1927), Hašek's *Schweik* (*Schweik*, 1928) and Mehring's *Der Kaufmann von Berlin* (*The Merchant of Berlin*, 1929). These classical examples of the 'Piscator style' proved to be so expensive to stage that the Nollendorftheater had to be abandoned. They did, however, lay the foundations of EPIC THEATRE, which was developed by BRECHT, who worked on *Rasputin* and *Schweik*, and was one of the most influential movements of the century.

Between 1931 and 1936 Piscator worked in the Soviet Union, where he directed the film *The Revolt of the Fishermen* and helped to set up an exile-theatre project for German artists who had had to leave their country after the Nazi takeover. After a three-year interlude in Paris he moved to New York where, in January 1940, he set up the Dramatic Workshop of the New School. Initially the emphasis was very much on playwriting; but the acting course, run by Stella ADLER and later by LEE STRASBERG, attracted more and more students and soon surpassed those in directing, design, opera and dancing. Despite its artistic and pedagogical success, the Dramatic Workshop ran into debts, and in 1951 Piscator decided to return to Germany. Despite some successful freelance productions, he was regularly turned down when applying for the post of manager at West German theatres. From 1962 to 1966 he ran the Theater am Kurfürstendamm, which belonged to the Freie Volksbühne organization. His last major successes were three productions at its new theatre: HOCH-HUTH's *The Deputy* (1963), KIPPHARDT's *The Oppenheimer Case* (1964) and WEISS's *The Investigation* (1965), DOCUMENTARY plays that kept Piscator at the centre of POLITICAL THEATRE developments until his death. GÜNTER BERGHAUS

C. D. Innes, *Erwin Piscator's Political Theatre* (1972)
E. Piscator, *The Political Theatre* (1980)
John Willett, *The Theatre of Erwin Piscator* (1978)

Pisk, Litz [Alice Therese] (b. Vienna, 22 Oct. 1909; d. Penzance, Cornwall, 6 Jan. 1997) Movement teacher. Named after her father's favourite book *Alitzia in Wunderland*, she studied painting, theatre design and movement, and worked with REINHARDT and BRECHT before coming to Britain to escape the Nazis in the 1930s. She taught painting, pottery and movement but was best known in the latter role, notably at the OLD VIC School and at the Central School of Speech and Drama. She choreographed the celebrated MICHAEL ELLIOTT production of *As You Like It* (1961, with VANESSA REDGRAVE), and choreographed for him at the Old Vic (e.g. *Peer Gynt*, 1962), at Theatre 69 and its successor, the ROYAL EXCHANGE. She drew on animal studies and used improvization to free the actor physically, and published the influential *The Actor and his Body* (1975) as well as exhibiting her pottery and drawings. CHARLES LONDON

See also MOVEMENT, DANCE AND DRAMA.

Pit, The *see* ROYAL SHAKESPEARE COMPANY

Pitoëff family: Georges [Gyorgy Pitoyev] (b. Tiflis, Georgia, 4 Sept. 1884; d. Geneva, 17 Sept. 1939), **Ludmilla** (b. Tiflis, 24 Dec. 1896; d. Rueil Malmaison, 15 Sept. 1951) and **Sacha** (b. Geneva, 11 March 1920) Famous THEATRE FAMILY. Georges and Ludmilla spent six years in Geneva after he had worked in Russia with STANISLAVSKY and MEYERHOLD. From 1921, at diverse Parisian theatres, he staged plays by CHEKHOV, Shakespeare, SHAW, IBSEN and over a hundred other authors, including new French writing by the likes of ANOUILH, CLAUDEL, COCTEAU and LENORMAND; he directed PIRANDELLO's renowned *Six Characters in Search of an Author* (1923), which demonstrated his characteristic respect for the text and the inventive staging learned from Russia. A co-founder of the CARTEL (1927), he was a total 'man of the theatre', acting, directing, translating, adapting. Ludmilla took over his company after his death.

Ludmilla and Georges formed an intuitive team. An excellent actress, SHAW's *St. Joan* (1925) was her greatest success. Sacha also ran a company, and became a fine actor, especially in film, and director, often recreating his father's famous productions. TERRY HODGSON

Planchon, Roger (b. St-Chamond, France, 12 Sept. 1931) Director, actor, playwright. Planchon is of working-class origins and largely self-educated in the theatre; his work is marked by the originality and excitement of the young man who discovered the theatre classics for himself, not through the classroom. His first company was founded when he was 21, in a disused printing works in Lyon. In this small (110-seat) auditorium he alternated ebullient musical comedies of his own devising with AVANT-GARDE plays by authors such as IONESCO and ADAMOV. He was one of the first directors to put on BRECHT's work in France, and with Adamov evolved a Marxist theatre style of great social and theatrical complexity. In 1957 the company moved to the large municipal theatre of Villeurbanne on the eastern edge of Lyon, where he has remained ever since. Here his work has been particularly characterized by Marxist reinterpretations of plays by Shakespeare, Molière, Marivaux and Racine, the most successful of which were his two versions of Molière's *Tartuffe* (1962 and 1973). Since 1962 he has written over a dozen plays of his own, several of which he has directed. These often present images of peasant life (largely ignored outside of FARCE in the French tradition) in which clashing ideological concepts are dramatized in realistic scenes of great force (e.g. *Old Man Winter* and *Fragile Forest*, 1991). He has been criticized for not producing the work of many contemporary playwrights, though he was the first director to

attempt a version of MICHEL VINAVER's masterpiece *Overboard* (1973). In 1970 Planchon's theatre received the title THÉÂTRE NATIONAL POPULAIRE, and so the mantle of JEAN VILAR passed to him. His style employs a greater visual range than Vilar's, and he does not share Vilar's vision of culture as a socially unifying force, but by continuing to work in Villeurbanne he has placed a similar emphasis on making theatre available to working-class audiences. He is widely admired for his skills as an actor as well as a director and playwright, and has done much to encourage a new generation of directors, e.g. Jacques Rosner, PATRICE CHÉREAU, Georges Lavaudant. Since 1988, when his first feature film, of Molière's *Dandin*, was presented, he has devoted most of his creative energies to the cinema.
DAVID BRADBY

D. Bradby, *The Theatre of Roger Planchon* (slideset, 1984)
Y. Doust, *Roger Planchon: Director and Playwright* (1981)

Plater, Alan [Frederick]   (b. Jarrow, Tyne and Wear, 15 April 1935)   Playwright; possibly the most prolific television dramatist of his time. He first achieved success with scripts for the classic police series *Z-Cars* and *Softly, Softly* (1963–8), while his 'single' TV plays have often reflected life in the north of England (where much of his stage work is seen) and champion liberal values. Several have been adapted by him for the theatre. His early plays were performed at Stoke-on-Trent; his most notable success is *Close the Coalhouse Door* (1968), with songs by Alex Glasgow, based on the stories of pit life by Sid Chaplin. Other stage plays include *I Thought I Heard a Rustling* (1991), *Peggy For You* (1999) and his dramatizations of Bill Tidy's 'northern' strip cartoons, *The Fosdyke Saga* (1977) and *Fosdyke II* (1978). He has also written for radio.   DAVID SELF
   See also JAZZ.

Playbox Theatre Centre   Founded in Melbourne in 1976 by Graeme Blundell, Garrie Hutchinson and Carrillo Gantner as an alternative to the MELBOURNE THEATRE COMPANY. It was originally named the Hoopla Theatre Foundation; in 1977 it moved into its headquarters at the former Playbox Theatre, where it soon established itself as one of Australia's fastest-growing companies, continuing its programme of promoting Australian talent in every area – writing, directing, acting, designing. After a disastrous fire in 1984, it performed in a variety of venues before the conversion of a former malthouse into a two-theatre complex. It has performed many Australian plays and staged Australian premières of important overseas works, particularly from America. In 1990 it changed its name from 'Company' to 'Centre' to coincide with its move into new premises at The Malthouse Theatre. Since 1993, under the direction of Aubrey Mellor, it has had a continuing commitment to new Australian writing.
MICHAEL MORLEY

Players Club   *see* CLUBS

Players' Theatre   A membership club initially called Playroom Six, founded by a small theatre company in 1927, with which PEGGY ASHCROFT made her London debut, and given its present name two years later when it moved from the first floor to the ground floor of 6 New Compton Street in central London. The company moved again several times, maintaining a successful programme of 'song-and-supper' evenings known as *Ridgeway's Late Joys* after its one-time director Peter Ridgeway. In 1946, under Leonard Sachs, noted as chairman of TV's *The Good Old Days* MUSIC HALL series, the Players took over part of Gatti's Under the Arches VARIETY theatre at Charing Cross. (Another part had been occupied by the GATE THEATRE until 1941.) Their greatest success was the première of SANDY WILSON's musical *The Boy Friend* (1953). They continue to present Victorian productions to their members.
ADRIANA HUNTER

Playfair, Nigel [Ross]   (b. London, 1 July 1874; d. London, 19 Aug. 1934)   English actor, producer and manager. From 1918 he was the owner and manager of the LYRIC THEATRE, Hammersmith, where for 14 years he presented a succession of stylish productions, most famously a series drawn from the English eighteenth-century repertoire. His greatest success, revived several times, was Gay's *The Beggar's Opera* (1920), with designs by CLAUDE LOVAT FRASER. Also notable were *The Way of the World* (1924) and *The Beaux' Stratagem* (1927), both featuring EDITH EVANS, and *The Importance of Being Earnest* (1930), with JOHN GIELGUD. He gave his own account of his management in *The Story of the Lyric Theatre, Hammersmith* (1925) and *Hammersmith Hoy* (1930). He was knighted in 1928.
ROBERT CHEESMOND

Playwrights' Company   Founded in 1938 in New York, primarily by a group of writers unhappy with the producing policy of the THEATER GUILD, its initial members included MAXWELL ANDERSON, S. N. BEHRMAN, SIDNEY HOWARD, ELMER RICE and ROBERT E. SHERWOOD. Others joined later, including ROBERT ANDERSON and KURT WEILL. Among its major early successes were *Abe Lincoln in Illinois* (1938), *No Time for Comedy* (1939) and *There Shall Be No Night* (1940). In later years, when several of its original members had died, retired or deserted the fold, it produced plays by non-members. However, by 1960, with few young

playwrights promising a steady output of worthwhile works or willing to join, the company was dissolved.
GERALD BORDMAN

J. F. Wharton, *Life Among the Playwrights* (1974)

Playwrights Horizons An award-winning OFF-BROADWAY producing organization in New York, founded in 1971 by Robert Moss to support, develop and produce the work of contemporary American playwrights, composers and lyricists. Under the direction of André Bishop and Paul S. Daniels from 1981 to 1991, Playwrights Horizons presented the work of over 300 writers, including nine resident playwrights: CHRISTOPHER DURANG, William Finn, A. R. GURNEY, ALBERT INNAURATO, JAMES LAPINE, Peter Parnell, Jonathan Reynolds, TED TALLY and WENDY WASSERSTEIN. Many of their productions have enjoyed successful runs on BROADWAY, including three Pulitzer Prize winners: *Sunday in the Park with George* (1984, book by Lapine, lyrics and music by SONDHEIM); Alfred Uhry's *Driving Miss Daisy* (1987); and Wasserstein's *The Heidi Chronicles* (1988). Don Scardino became artistic director in 1992 and in 1996. ELLEN LAMPERT-GRÉAUX

Pleasance, Donald (b. Worksop, Notts, 5 Oct. 1919; d. St Paul de Vence, France, 2 Feb. 1995). Actor who built a reputation with character roles in plays like *The Brothers Karamazov* (1946), and with the BIRMINGHAM REPERTORY THEATRE and BRISTOL OLD VIC. His major break and best-remembered role was as Davies in *The Caretaker* (1960), which he recreated on Broadway (1961), on film (1962) and under PINTER's direction (1991). Initially cast in 'common man' roles, television in the 1960s created a glassy-eyed, sinister persona whose menacing chill has been cast over numerous films, but was also used to great effect on stage in Robert Shaw's *The Man in the Glass Booth* (1967).
DAN REBELLATO

Plowright, Joan [Ann] (b. Brigg, Lincs, 28 Oct. 1929) Actress. A student at the OLD VIC Theatre School, she acted with the BRISTOL OLD VIC and NOTTINGHAM Playhouse before joining the original ENGLISH STAGE COMPANY, where she was acclaimed as Margery Pinchwife in *The Country Wife* (1936) and the Old Woman in *Chairs* (1957), and above all for creating the role of Beatie in WESKER's *Roots* (Coventry and London, 1959). She later joined the inaugural CHICHESTER FESTIVAL and NATIONAL THEATRE companies, playing such leading roles as St Joan, Hilda in *The Master Builder*, Sonya in *Uncle Vanya*, Portia in *The Merchant of Venice* and the title part in *Mrs Warren's Profession*. A direct but engaging style made her known for realistic performances, e.g. as Jean Rice in *The Entertainer* (1957), Josephine in *A Taste of Honey* (New York, 1960), and in two plays by DE FILIPPO, *Saturday, Sunday, Monday* (1973) and *Filumena* (1977). At the National Theatre she also co-directed *An Evasion of Women* and *The Travails of Sancho Panza*, and directed *Rites* in 1969. She married LAURENCE OLIVIER in 1961. Her memoirs *And That's Not All* appeared in 2001. DAVID STAINES

Plummer, [Arthur] Christopher [Orme] (b. Toronto, 13 Dec. 1927) Actor. Making his professional debut with the Canadian Repertory Theater in 1950, he played nearly 100 roles with this touring company. Equally accomplished in comic and tragic roles, he was especially acclaimed for his Shakespearean performances with the AMERICAN SHAKESPEARE FESTIVAL Theater (Mark Antony in *Julius Caesar*, 1955), the STRATFORD FESTIVAL, Ontario (between 1956 and 1962, many successes including the title roles in *Henry V*, *Hamlet* and *Macbeth*) and the ROYAL SHAKESPEARE COMPANY (Benedict, Richard III, 1961). In the West End he played Henry II in *Becket* (1961), and his Broadway triumphs include *The Royal Hunt of the Sun* (1965) and the musical *Cyrano* (1973). In 1994 he appeared opposite JASON ROBARDS in Roundabout's production of *No Man's Land*. Among his many films is *The Sound of Music* (1965). DAVID STAINES

Podbrey, Maurice (b. Durban, South Africa, 25 April 1934) Director. After graduating in South Africa and studying theatre in England, he became an actor and director before migrating in 1966 to Canada, where he was appointed assistant director at Montreal's National Theater School. In 1969 he became artistic director of Montreal's CENTAUR THEATER, founded in the same year, while also acting in many of its productions. Podbrey has promoted work drawn from the international repertoire, giving special attention to the plays of ATHOL FUGARD, a fellow countryman, and to plays by Canadian playwrights DAVID FREEMAN, DAVID FENNARIO and MICHEL TREMBLAY, among others.
EUGENE BENSON

· Playwriting ·

The Tangible and the Intangible

While it's not possible to teach someone how to become a good playwright, it *is* possible to describe what is required to make a good play; though I'm not sure it's possible to explain *why*.

A play is an event in two parts. The first appears on the page, the second on the stage. Each part is a structure that can be broken down into its elements. The elements are fixed and respond to the laws of stagecraft. What is *done* with those elements on the page by the playwright, and on the stage by the interpretive artists, answers to no laws, only to their imaginations, intellects, skills and sensibilities.

To be specific, the elements in the structure of a play on the page are twofold:

The Tangible	and	The Intangible
Characters		How those characters are perceived by the playwright
Their dialogue		The strength, vividness and rhythm the playwright gives to that dialogue
Their actions		The significance perceived by the playwrights of those actions
Their relationship		The subtlety of characters' relationships
The setting		The metaphoric strength of the setting
The framework of scenes within which characters exist		The poetic impact made by juxtaposition and rhythm of the scenes

Finally: content, substance, what the play is about, which is both

Tangible	and	Intangible
because it could be about love	but	insensitively handled
or about politics	but	dealt with by a limited intelligence
or a comedy about the human condition	but	handled by a feeble comic talent for cheap effect

There is one last and important element for which the 'tangible' and 'intangible' require more space than a tabulated layout: theme and resonance – 'theme' being tangible, e.g. 'old age'; 'resonance' being intangible, resulting from the playwright's powers to raise his theme above the specifics of his setting. Art is not about current street corners: it may be *set* in current street corners, but setting is not to be confused for theme, nor period for substance. I have made this point elsewhere: Euripides may belong to fifth-century BC Greece, Shakespeare to sixteenth-century England, CHEKHOV to pre-revolutionary Russia, but something other than the specifics of their decade or century marks them: a strange chemistry made up of perceptive intelligence, poetic sensibility, imagination, and God knows what other intangibles which result in a power we call art. These writers both reflect and stamp their times, but with a quality of insight from which future generations seem able continuously to refresh themselves.

The elements in the structure of a play on the stage (as opposed to the page) are also twofold:

The Tangible	and	The Intangible
Performance		The actor's performing ability – good or bad
Staging		The director's ability to comprehend and imaginatively lift from the page, and to stage, all the elements in the play
Setting		The quality of the designer's imagination to construct the setting belonging to and enhancing the play
Lighting		The quality of the lighting designer's skills

These elements involve people. Other elements in the staging of a play involve *decisions* made by those people. *Space* – in the round? proscenium? promenade? *Music* – specially composed? existing? *Sounds* – wind, birds, animals, street noises, other-world sounds? In a new play such decisions, if not already indicated in the text, are made with the playwright.

There is one other element without which genius withers: economics – the amount of money available for a production. Money, not inevitably but usually, purchases the best. This applies to everything from a roll of material to a house, from a tailor to a builder, from a cup to a motor car. It applies as well to talent. A play may make its impact or not depending upon how much can be spent on it. Bad actors, the wrong design, a mediocre director can render Shakespeare a third-rate bore. It wasn't always so in the theatre, nor of course is it *always* so today. Risks are still taken; the best will work for less if they care passionately about what they have been offered. In the early 1960s companies like the ENGLISH STAGE COMPANY and THEATRE WORKSHOP cared more about quality than box-office returns, and though one often led to the other the priorities were in the right order. I personally enjoy discovering new talent, and in such cases the best is not then so expensive; however, the problem with unknown talent is few producers or companies will risk investing in it! Catch 22!

Any of the elements identified above would require a chapter to explain fully. My hope here is modest: to show that playwriting is not simply a question of creating characters made to talk on stage by actors helped by directors. Between the first spark and the first night takes place a more complex process. There is no one way in which that first spark is ignited. There are as many different sparks as there are playwrights, perhaps even as there are plays. Personal examples will help convey my meaning. To begin, let us touch on two of the endless debates that affect the climate within which playwrights work.

Imagination or Experience?

It's possible to divide literature into that which attempts to understand life through a re-creation of experience, and that which attempts to understand life through the imagination. O'NEILL's *Long Day's Journey into Night* is experience recreated as theatre. BECKETT's *Waiting for Godot* is theatre shaped by imagination. D. H. LAWRENCE's *The Rainbow* is a novel based on his early life. *The Picture of Dorian Gray* by OSCAR WILDE is an imagined story about evil masquerading as beauty.

Some declare they are not interested in a writer's life. Literature, they say, has nothing to do with autobiography. Others insist autobiography is the *only* ingredient that draws them to a writer's work. 'Now *that*,' they say, 'feels as though it comes from the front line.' There is a third view that declares *all* writing is autobiography, if not of the physical events in the writer's life then of his or her emotional life.

Where does this place Shakespeare? Is he Hamlet? King Lear? Romeo? Was there a friend he talked out of suicide who had said to him 'you know, Will, to be or not to be is the real question', and did he rush to write it down and transform it into his very own and immortal phrasing? Or did the question come to him in his own dark night of the soul? Or did the words assemble in his mind from nowhere in an idle moment while gardening? We know too little of Shakespeare's life to be able to answer such questions, but we can certainly go on to identify others.

Art or Entertainment?

This is the most confused debate of all. The confusion arises from the clash between theatre as an experience and theatre as a commodity in the marketplace. All art is a commodity needing to be sold. The more expensive it is to create, the greater the need to reach the largest audience to obtain maximum return. A film is more expensive to produce than a book; more people are needed to pay for the vast expense of production. This need invariably affects what the artist produces.

I would like my plays to be seen by everybody everywhere forever, but I do not, cannot, write them in order to realize this ambition. Some playwrights attempt to. They apply their skills to crafting plays aimed at the largest possible audience. There are no formulas to guarantee they will succeed, but such writers are clear about their intentions, and what they intend ably meets the wishes of most theatregoers who declare 'I go to the theatre to be entertained.' It certainly encourages theatrical entrepreneurs to invest their money in such work.

Sadly, such a public and such entrepreneurs, though one very happily concedes their right to invest their money where they wish, and though one makes no judgement of *their* taste, become upset and defensive if other playwrights, exercising *their* right to create a different kind of play, suggest their work is more an 'experience' than an 'entertainment'. 'Entertainment,' they say (and I am one of them), 'is a red herring. What we write aims to give an audience a unique experience by *engaging* its intelligence, emotions, imagination and laughter.' It is important for both the writer and the audience to understand such distinctions in order to be aware of the parameters offered.

So, we write our plays against the background of such debates: should a writer *invent* or use *experience*? Is a writer aiming to *entertain* or *engage* an audience? It is not easy to steer through such a landscape.

The Writing Process

We were considering sparks. How do plays take shape? I offer personal examples. My first full-length play was about my two maiden aunts: one, a trades union organizer, tiny, tough and widely read; the other, dumpy, giggly, a reader too, but untogether. Three reasons excited me to write the play, if I remember correctly: the autobiographical one – with myself central to the drama, and my sister and parents existing in the background; a wish to explore why two women remained unmarried and what it felt like to be without children and male companionship; and a wish to provide a play for the amateur drama group to which I belonged. They never performed it. The director was a maiden lady herself and found the questions too raw. When I came to write the first of my plays to be performed, *Chicken Soup with Barley*, I scavenged the maiden aunt play and changed focus. It became a play about my parents, my sister and me, with the maiden aunts in the background. And the prompt to write came from seeing *Look Back in Anger*, which excited me and convinced me theatre was where my writing belonged.

But that is not the full story of *Chicken Soup*. My mother had been a communist. Though not a party member, I considered myself one too until 1956, the year of the Hungarian uprising. I quarrelled with her over the event, which, to my amazement, had not shaken her faith. I said some hurtful things. She said some remarkable and impressive things. What she said became the last speech in the play. Her pleas to me in 1956 were the sparks that ignited it. The play became an attempt to trace the years that lead up to the pleas. My father had become an invalid. My sister had married and moved away. My aunt had been retired from the union. Where to begin? With the halcyon days, inevitably. (And how did I know to begin there? Because I'd read those huge family sagas such as *Fame is the Spur* by Howard Spring, *The Stars Look Down* by A. J. Cronin, Lawrence's *The White Peacock*, Sinclair Lewis's *Main Street*. Literature had taught me how to understand life. I was now taking from life and putting it back into literature.) I reached back to childhood memories, the famous anti-fascist demonstration in 1936 in the East End of London where I lived. Nineteen thirty-six to nineteen fifty-six. Twenty years to span. Could drama encompass the time span of the novel? We are fortunate to live in the light of Shakespeare, who teaches that everything is possible in theatre. The family, like the ideal, disintegrated over 20 years. The parallel was poetic, and the theme – domestic breakup, political disillusion – was resonant. It could be done.

This brings me to another observation about the nature of theatre. From the start of my writing career I was aware of the difference between material that was merely anecdotal and material that was resonant. *Chicken Soup* is not a play of nostalgic memories. The material touched me because I sensed that it had the possibility to survive and cross time and frontiers. Families and ideals disintegrating were universal themes. Whether my talent was sufficient to enable me to handle such material with perception is not for me to say, but everything written since, whether stories or plays, has been written because I have believed the material to be resonant.

Chips with Everything, to take another personal example, grew out of an empty moment. *The Kitchen* and *The Trilogy* had been staged. I was uncertain what to write next. I had been a conscript in the air force between 1950 and 1952. During the first eight weeks of basic training – how to march, salute, handle a rifle – I wrote a letter every day to family, friends, girlfriend, and later collected and collated them and wrote a novel about the experience, *The Reed that Bent*. Not very good. Never published. I took it out of the bottom drawer, reread it and realized that each chapter was a scene in a play. The spark! But wasn't this material merely anecdotal? No. The training camp was a metaphor for the way the powerful in society could mould its citizens unquestioningly to obey orders.

Caritas, a play written almost 20 years later, had a completely different birth. An American friend, a professor of literature, told me the story of Christine Carpenter, a young woman of Surrey in the fourteenth century, who became an anchoress immured in a cell attached to the church in the village of Shere where she hoped to live a life so pure and ideal that she would receive divine revelation. After three years she realized she didn't possess the vocation to pursue an austere life of isolation and deprivation, and begged the church to relieve her of her vows. The church refused. She was doomed to remain imprisoned against her will.

My friend insisted I write the play. I told him not to be silly. I couldn't write from history, only from experience. But over the years the image of poor Christine, doomed to lifelong incarceration because of a conviction not fully thought through, because of a mirage – falling in love with an *idea* of herself rather than facing the reality of herself – grew in my imagination as a powerful metaphor for prisons we all create for ourselves: profession, marriage, political or religious belief, the impulsive act that affects the rest of our lives. I had to write the play. Christine's story was my story, the story of many around me. Research over nine months took me through histories of the middle ages, works of and about mystics and mysticism, books on Catholicism; and, consciously or unconsciously, I repeated the structure of *Chicken Soup*, telling two stories which, because running parallel, I thought poetically commented one upon the other: the story of Christine unfolded over three years against the background of the failed Peasants' Revolt of 1381; the personal and the political, two stories telling of the quest for the ideal that is betrayed by the way in which the quest is pursued.

And so on. As with all playwrights, so each of my 37 plays had a different birth. And though two have historical settings (in which I did not live), and the cycle of *One Woman Plays* is about women and I am not a woman, and *Their Very Own and Golden City* is about an architect which I never was, yet none of them strays far from autobiography.

The Marketplace

How do playwrights sell their work? Well, it depends upon the kind of play they are selling – a thriller, a light comedy, an intellectual comedy, a play exploring social issues, a drama of personal conflict, a satire with or without music, an experimental work – the list is not endless but I've not exhausted it. Whatever the genre, the route to the stage is varied.

Most playwrights have an AGENT – for the new playwright, that can be a problem. (An actor once observed: changing agents is like changing deckchairs on the *Titanic*!) Agents tend to take on clients who either have a track record or, if the writer is a first-timer, have themselves found a theatre to put on their play. An agent should be an enthusiastic champion of a writer's plays, but most prefer to negotiate a contract rather than argue a producer into presenting the work. To argue the virtues of a play, an agent requires the mixed skills of intellectual and entrepreneur. Playwrights constantly search, as though for the holy grail, such a rare soul-mate who is in tune with their work and can both perceive its meaning and describe its impact so vividly that a management will eventually buy the performing rights.

Most playwrights, through a network of contacts built up over the years, struggle to find their own managements. They send plays to directors or actors they have come to know. If their reputation is high enough, they can command the attentions of star actors and directors they *don't* know. It is not so much a marketplace as a jungle in which power is important. To achieve power you need a power base – as Sir PETER HALL had for ten years at the NATIONAL THEATRE; or fortune must smile upon you and make you a marketable property. Actors are crudely assessed within the profession by whether they will 'put bums on seats'. If a play excites such an actor, or a director with a power base (or with a high enough reputation to have access to a power base), then the play stands a chance of being taken up.

Even if an actor or director takes up a play it still has to meet other criteria. Art subsidy has been cut, the cost of mounting a play has risen; playwrights write plays with large casts or more than one set at their peril. All this may change if a government, like those of Scandinavia, France, Germany and Italy, enters the scene and places arts subsidy high in its list of priorities. For now, because it affects the writing of plays, we must record: the arts strive in parched times.

That bleak statement requires tempering by important qualifications. In Britain, the bulk of new writing since the 1960s has been presented by publicly subsidized theatres, most of it commissioned; and though the majority had of necessity to be limited in scope because not all commissioning agents were financially endowed to tell playwrights 'the sky's the limit, cast and sets – no problem!' yet the main houses like the ROYAL SHAKESPEARE COMPANY and the National *could* and did say this. This situation, however, does not invalidate my argument that the theatre is a jungle in which power is important. A playwright is not the writer of one or two commissioned plays; there is a lifetime of writing to be pursued. No theatre, not even the RSC, will nurture a playwright into international fame as they do a director. (The history of 1950s and 1960s playwrights – OSBORNE, BEHAN, DELANEY, PINTER, myself – who *did* instantly rocket into international fame is an exception, part of that curious cycle for which no one, to my knowledge, has yet accounted. First one, then another art form attracts a fierce focus, burns briefly, illuminates fortunate artists who find themselves within its glow, then shifts focus: the British poets of the 1930s; Italian cinema of the 1950s; the pop painters of the 1960s. Even the exceptional history of the 1950s Britishtheatre revolution, so called, has its calamity stories.) No, the rule remains. After the first few daring trials the writer is let loose into that primordial jungle where all manner of wild beasts wait to devour him, and even her!

Actors and directors are prime operators in this raucous and aggressively competitive marketplace. Being interpretive artists they must perforce be opportunists, that is to say they must follow the best career opportunities. This is understood and accepted. Opportunism in the *creative* playwright, however, is rightly despised. Therein lies a central conflict for serious playwrights – they need the talents, skills and courage of the best actors and directors, whose considerations are often completely other than those of the uncommercial playwright calling for risks. With everything (and everyone) costing so much, it is understandable that there are few around who can afford to take risks. So, agents make phone calls, write letters and post off scripts; playwrights make phone calls, write letters and post off scripts. Playwrights also invite to dinner those who run theatres, attempting to persuade them to mount their plays – at least, I have done so – and it should be a meeting of colleagues. It rarely is. Heads of theatres have a power base, the writer is the beggar at the gate. It is a humiliating relationship. We become schizophrenic, living the lives of artist and hustler in the same skin.

Financial rewards fluctuate. If you are a FRINGE writer such as I am – that is to say, my plays rarely reach the commercial circuit – then you depend for your income upon many countries presenting your work. I'm fortunate, an international reputation has kept me going for over 40 years without having to supplement income with other kinds of work, apart from occasional journalism. Further help came from television productions of stage plays generating unexpected and substantial sums of money; and by the occasional and handsomely paid film script. Even so, it has all been rare and sparsely spread, ensuring continual dependence upon an overdraft. Hair-raising! (Many playwrights, following upon a couple of stage successes, are lured from the stage to write television plays, serials, adaptations, or film scripts – a treadmill upon which they become hooked and which they must struggle to get off if they want to return to theatre. I've managed to resist that danger – though, as noted above, at the price of a permanent overdraft. Theatre became my love and I remainedfaithful to her no matter how often the damn whore betrayed me!) I don't complain. Being performed in foreign parts has enabled me to travel the world on the crest of my craft. (Note: since I wrote this essay, Texas University has purchased my archives. The overdraft is gone!)

A guide to earnings: in 1977, had the famous Broadway star ZERO MOSTEL not died out of town in Phila-delphia after giving one performance of *Shylock*, and had the play gone on to Broadway with him in the lead as planned, my box-office income was calculated as £10,000 a week. The 1988–9 revival of *Roots* at the National Theatre, which toured for seven weeks and ran in repertory at the Cottesloe for four months, earned me, 11 years after the death of Mostel, a total of £6,937, less agent's commission of £1,047: £5,890, or £256 a week. One commercial breakthrough – a play performed worldwide and made into a film, or that elusive smash-hit musical – can transform a modern playwright into a millionaire. Superstar playwrights are very rich indeed; but the norm is poverty. Merely fortunate playwrights have a steady, unspectacular income supplemented by extra-mural work. Others, like myself, who are not commercial talents but have international reputations, are sustained by respect and some security.

Lifting a Play from the Page, and Other Obstacles

Many years ago I wrote a lighthearted essay on the hurdles over which the playwright must leap before his work can reach a public ('The Playwright's Obstacles Course', published in *The Burns Mantle Theatre Year Book 1973/74*). The hurdles remain. First, your agent must be enthusiastic about your play or she can't sell it in the marketplace. Then a producer or the artistic head of a subsidized theatre must be fired sufficiently to raise money in the market, or use the state's money. The play must next excite a director – unless you are allowed to direct your own plays. Actors, the fourth hurdle, must be found – and you rarely end with your first choice: they're not available, or your play doesn't offer them the image they wish to present at that moment in their career, or they don't like the play, or they don't like you ... The set designer is another hurdle to negotiate. A bad set, or the wrong set, can cripple the flow, the rhythm, the atmosphere of a play. Then, perhaps the highest hurdle of them all, the critic, whose thumb up or down can open or close a box-office cash-till. And there was one final hurdle the little essay identified: the aftermath commentator, those writers of books who look back, assess and create their beloved top-ten lists. All these must be leapt over to reach – what? Not a winning post. Who is the 'winner' out of IBSEN, STRINDBERG, Chekhov, SHAW? Perhaps 'hurdle' was the wrong metaphor. The 'stages of propulsion into orbit' would have been better, for it is into orbit we want our work to burst, held back by nothing, ever again.

Those hurdles or stages of propulsion were merely

headlines. The miseries of the marketplace are legion: cowardice, rudeness, opportunism – often linked – are three of them; theatres which, or directors who, hang on to a manuscript for half a year without responding; letters unanswered; honest opinions withheld; judgements offered with insufficient thought; miseries which, because there is no excuse for them, can be railed against. Much more difficult to live with are the problems *inherent* in the task of comprehending a complex work crafted over many months – perhaps longer – with years of skill behind it and a great deal of attention to detail. Every writer of drama – whether for film, television or stage – will have one loud lamentation at the top of his/her list of miseries. This: no one, or few, can read a script!

Read again the list of elements that I specified were to be found in the structure of a play on the page. At any one moment in a play several different things can take place simultaneously: two characters whisper in conversation; they are in a room full of objects that hold memories for them; a storm is building up outside; two other people have just departed, their presence and words still lingering, affecting the atmosphere; something that occurred early in the play fills the audience with foreboding that something cataclysmic is about to happen; the exchange between the two characters is full of humour as well as tension; their different speech rhythms reveal different personalities and backgrounds, what they say reflects how each is responding to the charged moment; and so on.

Most people reading the play, even those experienced in the theatre, are likely only to be aware of the words being spoken. If they identify the humour it might confuse them – surely, they think, the moment is a tense one? If they *can* accept that humour and tension can exist side by side, they might nevertheless find the cataclysmic event that follows to be gratuitous because they had forgotten – or had not noticed – the occurrence that took place earlier on in the play which, though an *audience* will register it (because they've had audiovisual help), the *reader* of the page might fail to do. He's had no help, just words on a page. Nor has the reader, literary manager, producer, director or whoever, registered the sound of a growing storm or the visual impact of a room full of memory-laden objects, or the atmosphere left behind by the two previous characters, or the melodies of the dialogue – elements all very carefully assembled so that this moment and the one to follow make a desired impact. Some directors and actors boast, with jocular dismissal, that they always skip the stage directions anyway!

Of course, there are thrills as well as miseries, courage as well as cowardice, humility as well as tyranny. Suddenly, after the humiliation of rejections, one key person locks into what you have written. Director, actor or producer – any one of them can be fired by the play and sufficiently influential to achieve a production of it. I owe the launching of my career to the director, the late LINDSAY ANDERSON – one of the most individual and unopportunistic directors who worked in theatre and film, who in 1957 generously gave time to reading *Chicken Soup with Barley* and pressed for its production at the ROYAL COURT THEATRE. I owe the idea for and the televising of *Love Letters on Blue Paper* to my ex-agent, Robin Dalton. Elizabeth Spriggs, the actress who played in the television version, persuaded Peter Hall to invite me to stage it at the National Theatre. *Caritas* at the National Theatre is due to Peter Hall's enthusiasm. Agent, actress, director; rarely have I, the author, been able to persuade a producer or head of a theatre to present my play. No matter how long a playwright has been writing, no matter how strong his or her track record, no matter how large the reputation throughout the world, the word of the playwright is rarely trusted. A head of the National Theatre who didn't warm to my play *Shylock*, despite a battery of excellent reviews for both the New York and BIRMINGHAM REPERTORY productions, told me that if one of his directors *did* warm to the play he would give their views serious consideration. My own views were of no weight, no value. In any essay on playwriting, this is a fact of the playwright's life that must be recorded.

The Collaborative Process

Two other approaches to playwriting must be touched upon: the group play and the COMMUNITY PLAY. Both are comparatively late developments.

For the community play, simply, a community decides to stage a play specially written for it, either to commemorate an event in its history or for no other reason than that it wants the dynamic social experience which, its leaders have heard, is a way of bringing the community together. Various groups of professional theatre practitioners have emerged who will undertake to work with the community. The most well-known in England, and the one to have originated the idea under the inspiration and guidance of ANN JELLICOE, is the Colway Theatre Trust.

To use a personal example again, the postwar town of Basildon built itself a new theatre in 1988 for £8 million; 1989 saw its 40th birthday. Backed by Basildon's town council, the theatre approached Colway Theatre Trust to help them commission and mount a play commemorating 40 years of existence. I was invited to accept the commission. The brief was wide. I could write what I wanted, provided it called upon the participation of as many as possible of Basildon's inhabitants. I visited the town on many occasions; spoke with and interviewed many people; read official documents, books, the work of local children and townsfolk; listened to history tapes made by the local history society. From all this I fashioned one of my strangest works, *Beorhtel's Hill*, calling for a cast of 120, a choir, a brass band, choreography and an original musical score. A professional team of designer, director, choreographer and composer was engaged; the citizens of Basildon sang and acted, made the sets and props, raised part of the money, organized the sale of tickets, and were called upon to offer general factotum services. The play ran for 15 performances and presented Basildon with its first mirror image of itself.

Community plays are mushrooming in other countries. To date the Colway Theatre Trust has mounted productions in Denmark, Canada and the United States.

The group play is a different animal. Whereas *Beorhtel's Hill*, though executed by hundreds of people, is written by one person, the group play is written by many – often the actors and director together with a writer. In such a situation the writer's function is to shape what the group, after discussion, has decided upon. It is not a method of working to which I could adapt. Playwrights, like composers, must depend upon others for the final realization of their work, but to create the work by committee is a procedure few artists can tolerate. I have seen interesting productions resulting from this method of working, but art is the last and only human activity where the individual's spirit and imagination must not be called upon to compromise its vision of the human condition. Group theatre, needing to accommodate the perceptions and sensibilities of many, inevitably results in such compromise.

The Staging Process

"Twixt cup and lip ... ' and here comes the biggest debate of them all, one to which I have elsewhere devoted a full-blown lecture ('Interpretation – to impose or explain', *Performing Arts Journal*, vol. 32). What is the function of the interpreters – the director and actors? Is their responsibility to comprehend the author's intention and meaning which, with their sensitive skills, they hand on to an audience? Or is the play a vehicle for their own self-expression? The director JONATHAN MILLER refuses to direct new work by living authors; he prefers to exercise his skill, imagination and intelligence on known plays by dead authors who are not around to tell him he has misunderstood their intentions – a somewhat necrophiliac approach to the pleasure of directing. Miller argues that authors do not understand their intentions anyway, are not fully aware of what they have created, imagine they have created one work with only one possible meaning when in fact they have created a work with many possible meanings which it is a director's right to choose from and explore, regardless that with a new play this might involve a form of censorship.

Even in a 50-minute lecture I could only skim the complexities of this argument, one of the most destructive at work in the theatre today between writer and director. It can't be ignored, however. Power lies in the hands of the director, indisputably. (Sometimes in the hands of the actor; I have received reports of very bizarre things actors have done to my plays.) Britain may be the last place where the wishes of writers are respected. Here the writers' unions have won for playwrights the right to attend rehearsals of their work and be paid for so doing; legally, no script may be changed without the author's consent. Many British directors are on record saying their main concern is to present the author's text. My own experiences have ranged from a director telling me he believed the writer should write his play and then 'fuck off', to the director who was happy to sit back and let me take over a three-day refresher rehearsal. I prefer to direct my own plays (see 'The Playwright as Director', in *Distinctions*, 1985), but it's not always possible to command trust. Authors, the argument goes, cannot be objective about their work, though no one expects objectivity about his work from the director. It is an unhealthy state of affairs which in the rest of Europe, Scandinavia and the United States has driven dramatists away from the theatre. Why bother to write that which becomes the plaything of others?

Yet again, all is not misery. Theatre is a difficult profession in which diverse and diverging talents have to work in harmony, and this miraculous fusion can sometimes occur. I believe the miracle takes place when all energies are directed towards realizing the writer's intentions. Then everyone says to the writer: I understand what you intend, but are you certain this action, this phrase, this scene achieves it? Might this phrase, that action be better? I owe many important changes in my plays to directors, actors, designers, translators, friends and family. I listen a great deal to their responses and criticism. The problem is: because we none of us believe we have ever got it right, therefore what most people have to say seems intelligent and workable, one is seduced. Sometimes we forget why we've written what we've written the way we've written it! We must select carefully what feels right and reject the rest. It is not easy.

But structuring the physical play is an exciting process, which is why I enjoy directing. To work with the designer, watch a drawing become a model become a set; to pace rehearsals, shape a scene, find its temperature; to sit day after day and watch actors grow, invent, change direction and take risks; to introduce sounds, light the show, to bring together all the elements from the first spark to the first night is a very intoxicating and emotional experience. Theatre is an unholy profession, but O its lure is wickedly powerful. **ARNOLD WESKER**

Poel [Pole], William (b. London, 22 July 1852; d. London, 13 Dec. 1934) Actor and director. Poel was an iconoclast and an innovator who at first managed what was to become the OLD VIC and worked for FRANK BENSON. He reacted against Victorian 'picture-frame' distortions of Shakespeare and tried to unite theatre practice with scholarship, presenting Elizabethan drama in a method of continuous staging on a bare platform which approximated to the stages for which it was written. Founder of the Elizabethan Stage Society (1895–1905), he was the first to revive many non-Shakespearean Renaissance plays and he introduced several European classics to Britain. He worked outside the mainstream – often using amateurs, performing in small and unconventional venues, subsidizing most productions, touring widely – and promoted an ENSEMBLE performance style and rich vocal delivery which, while innovative, could also be eccentric. He campaigned for theatre reform and his practical and scholarly work was widely influential, especially in the first half of the century and through GRANVILLE BARKER. Poel staged 17 of Shakespeare's plays and a seminal modern production of the morality play *Everyman* (1901). He turned down a knighthood in protest at the establishment's lack of sympathy with his aims. *Shakespeare in the Theatre* (1913) contains some of his many writings. IAN CLARKE & SARAH A. SMITH

See also ELIZABETHAN AND JACOBEAN THEATRE IN THE TWENTIETH CENTURY.

Rinda F. Lundstrom, *William Poel's Hamlets: The Director as Critic* (1984)

Cary M. Mazer, *Shakespeare Refashioned: Elizabethan Plays on Edwardian Stages* (1981)

Marion O'Connor, *William Poel and the Elizabethan Stage Society* (1987)

Robert Speaight, *William Poel and the Elizabethan Revival* (1954)

poetic drama *see* VERSE DRAMA

Pogodin [Stukalov], Nikolai [Fyodorovich] (b. Rostov-on-the-Don, Russia, 16 Nov. 1900; d. Leningrad, Russia, 19 Sept. 1962) Playwright. Of peasant origin, Pogodin became a correspondent for *Pravda* before turning to playwriting. His plays embrace a variety of Soviet themes and he won both Stalin and Lenin prizes. *Aristokraty* (*Aristocrats*), a comedy about the digging of the White Sea canal, was first presented in a celebrated production by OKHLOPKOV in 1934, but Pogodin is best known for his trilogy featuring Lenin as a character, *Chevolek S Ruzhyom* (*The Man with a Gun*, 1937), *Kremlyovskie Kuranti* (*Kremlin Chimes*, 1940) and *Tretya Pateticheskaya* (*The Third, Pathétique*, 1958).

J. MICHAEL WALTON

Poland Polish theatre entered the twentieth century with the political and artistic burden of a past as a stateless country. The memory of two tragic national uprisings and the extraordinary heritage of Polish Romanticism coexisted with the new social and psychological movements in art encouraged by economic and intellectual developments all over Europe. Theatrical life flourished in Cracow under liberal Austrian rule. Naturalism, besides its significant influence upon the style of acting, gave rise to the drama of manners, in for example the work of Gabriela Zapolska (1857–1921), such as *The Moral of Mrs Dulska* (1906). The revival of the Romantic tradition was connected with the arrival of STANISŁAW WYSPIANSKI, poet, painter and designer. His most original plays (*The Wedding* 1901; *Liberation*, 1903; *November Night*, 1904) were deeply rooted in the national tradition. He became a pioneer fighting for a new type of *mise-en-scène* representing a synthesis of the arts.

In Poland's 20 years of independence after 1918, with the exception of state companies supported by the city councils, like the National and the Opera, theatres were either private or belonged to ephemeral dramatic enterprises. The economic crisis of 1929–32 led to the end of all subsidies, but in 1933 a new powerful syndicate joined together the funds of the state, city councils and private business and took care of the several Warsaw companies. The actors union, ZASP, founded in 1918, aimed to protect and assist artists on the one hand, and on the other to propagate professional ethics and raise actors' social status. ZASP set minimum wages and secured yearly contracts and paid holidays. The moral authority it represented was highly important and exemplary in the Second World War.

The post-Romantic traditional theatre, which followed the ideas of GORDON CRAIG, was promoted in the late 1920s and 1930s by the director LEON SCHILLER. Another mainstream influence, the Reduta, came close to STANISLAVSKY's practice. Its leader, Juliusz Osterwa, wanted it to be a theatre, a dramatic studio, an experimental institute and a community all at the same time. His methods of detailed analysis and collective work on the text led actors to an emotional and intellectual identification with their parts and to truthful, precise psychological representation. Reduta made an exceptional contribution to the modern style of acting (e.g. in GROTOWSKI's work).

As well as commercial variety theatres and the drama associated with Schiller and the Reduta, there was an important AVANT-GARDE movement which, because of general hostility, was active more in the field of theory and playwriting than on the stage. Its key figure, STANISLAW WITKIEWICZ, had already advocated the necessity of a formal revolution in the theatre in the early 1920s. He and others in the avant-garde like WITOLD GOMBROWICZ considered that the use of new technical devices, audience involvement, the transformation of theatrical space and the replacement of word domination with that of scene were the aims and necessary conditions of such a revolution. Recognition and appreciation of these ideas came only many years later, in the late 1950s.

Evidence of the growing prestige of the Polish theatre was the fact that prominent European playwrights offered it the rights for the world premières of their works: for example, in 1929 GEORGE BERNARD SHAW gave *The Apple Cart* to Warsaw's Polski Theatre. With no direct state interference and quite liberal censorship, Polish theatre at this period presented a variety of plays and aesthetic forms: from VAUDEVILLE to a world classical and modern repertoire, and from traditional to experimental stagings; politically, it included small leftist companies.

Six years of Nazi occupation wrought a devastating attack on Polish culture. Theatres were closed down and theatrical life moved underground. ZASP forbade its members to take part in the primitive entertainment licensed by the Germans. Most famous actors took jobs as waiters instead. Secret chamber performances were organized in private apartments, theatrical training took place in the underground, and semi-professional companies existed in POW camps and in the Polish army abroad. There were notable underground achievements – performances of Schiller's mystery plays, and the work of the Rapsodyczny theatre of poetry and music in Krakow and of TADEUSZ KANTOR's avant-garde theatre of painters. These were to be continued after the war.

The theatres of the eastern territories occupied by Soviet forces continued to work – usually in a difficult environment controlled by commissars – but nevertheless they could stage the Polish patriotic repertoire. After the war, despite the ruins, the dispersal of the old companies, casualties and emigration, normal theatrical life was quickly restored. Audiences crowded into the theatres, their suppressed social needs and aesthetic aspirations suddenly liberated. The country faced a radical political, cultural and ideological metamorphosis. The people were torn between contradictory emotions and hopes: hostility towards the imposed Soviet system and alien ideology, and a yearning for peace, social justice and a return to normal life after the calamities of war.

The immediate postwar theatre of the Polish People's Republic was eclectic and its beginnings were directly connected to the traditions of the interwar period. This gradually changed with the approach of full-blown Stalinism. The Ministry of Culture and Art gradually took over control of the companies. The process of nationalization structured theatres like other state enterprises: they were highly subsidized, and had a planned budget and detailed artistic schedule which specified the number of premières and performances. This excess of care was accompanied by intensive ideological and personal control. The repertoire had to submit to the rigours of social realism. 'Psychologism', 'existentialism' and 'cosmopolitanism', together with most classical and all avant-garde works, were to be forced out and theatres were to propagate progress and optimism according to ready-made schemes. Plays about workers and factory problems, like *Grinder Karhan's Brigade* by the Czech writer Vašek Jáňa, became the required drama. Actors had to exaggerate the positive and negative features of their characters to make the ideological intention absolutely clear. Any manifestation of individuality was discouraged. Propaganda theatres were established in almost every large town, and the three theatre schools founded in Warsaw, Krakow and Łodz in 1946–9 could not provide enough professionals for the provincial companies.

In 1955, as a first token of the 'thaw', Polish Romantic drama returned with a production of *Forefathers' Eve* by Adam Mickiewicz (1798–1855). As the nightmare of Stalinist terror ended, cultural policy radically altered. The classics returned, although they were overshadowed by modern drama: BRECHT, SARTRE, IONESCO, BECKETT and hundreds of new works from all over the world. The Polish prewar experimental drama of Witkiewicz and Gombrowicz was rediscovered, and SŁAWOMIR MROZEK and Tadeusz Rozewicz made their first appearances. The Ministry of Culture passed its supervisory role to the local authorities, which increased the autonomy of theatres in artistic and economic matters but did not eliminate the pressures exerted by the local administration on the choice of plays for specific occasions, treatment of particular subjects, or participation in festivals and international tours. Censorship was vague and fluid, being sensitive to the demands of individual officials or local Party committees. It traced attacks on the communist system and Poland's political allies, as well as anything that was considered dangerous at a given moment.

In the late 1950s and 1960s in Warsaw two excellent theatre companies took the lead in the promotion of modern drama: the Dramatyczny Theatre, famous for elaborate productions and scenery, and the Wspołczesny (Contemporary) Theatre, which enjoyed the reputation of having a first-class repertoire and highly professional but unobtrusive directing and acting, thanks to the stable, 30-year management (1949–81) of Erwin Axer. The Ludowy (People's) Theatre in Nowa Huta near Krakow should also be mentioned as a controversial company staging classical plays in the modern style.

The general stability of the 1960s was reflected in a prolific period for traditional theatre, and it made a good background for alternative, experimental works; Grotowski's and Kantor's theatres were to win an international reputation. The legacy of JÓZEF SZAJNA, who staged 'anti-literary' productions, was later taken over by the director/designer Jerzy Grzegorzewski, who ran a unique repertory theatre of aesthetic experiment, the 'Studio' Arts Centre, which is also a gallery, a video documentation centre and a place of arts patronage.

There was also a boom in student theatre, which was a powerful focus for change. It began after 1956 with the popular satirical theatres (STS, Bim-Bom), while in the 1970s new socially and politically oriented theatres appeared, like The Theatre of the Eighth Day, whose political involvement caused conflicts with the authorities.

Kazimierz Dejmek, who became director of the National Theatre in 1962 and who excelled in medieval religious and secular drama, was fired after his pro-duction of *Forefathers' Eve* (1967), accused of stimulating anti-Soviet sentiments. It was taken off the stage, which caused student demonstrations and was used in the power struggle within the Communist Party, becoming a pretext for an anti-semitic and anti-intellectual campaign – one of the most disgusting episodes in the history of communist rule.

Since the late 1950s 'TV-theatre' has become very popular, representing a high standard and casting the best actors in an interesting repertoire. Adam Hanuszkiewicz, who succeeded Dejmek, turned the National into a popular theatre of the commercial 'TV' type, and the mantle of national theatre passed to the Stary Theatre from Krakow, thanks to its excellent company and outstanding directors, designers and composers working away from the vanity fair of Warsaw. Konrad Swinarski was, up to his tragic death in 1975, its moving spirit. His productions of the Romantic drama, Wyspianski and Shakespeare are among the most significant in the Polish postwar theatre, as works of passion, universal concerns and aesthetic versatility. Andrzej Wajda's productions of Dostoevsky (*The Possessed*, *Nastassia Filipovna*, *Crime and Punishment*) were also very successful in the Stary Theatre due to their visual and expressive qualities.

In the late 1970s, in the face of growing political dissatisfaction, theatre made great use of allusions and historical costume to refer to hidden views and emotions. The Polish revolution of 1980 revealed, however, the deep crisis of theatre, helpless in the face of dramatic events, trying hard to keep up with reality and unable to sustain its social role. The imposition of martial law in December 1981 reversed the situation for a while, restoring theatre as a place where people could come together. Drawing on the tradition of the underground, actors performed in private flats presenting forbidden texts, such as the plays of VACLAV HAVEL. Many semi-official, mostly patriotic, performances were at that time sponsored by and presented in the Catholic churches, e.g. ELIOT's *Murder in the Cathedral* by Jerzy Jarocki. The actors who refused to work for the military television, which led the campaign against the democratic opposition, expressed the feelings of the people. The authorities reacted hysterically to the boycott: several theatre directors were thrown out of their posts and the actor's union was outlawed.

The remedy for the crisis was seen in the radical reform of the system of financing and organization – to free all the decisions connected with the cultural policy of the state from political criteria. After 1989 the situation of Polish theatre changed radically. Theatre is no longer a substitute for normal public and political life, and therefore politics no longer has any influence on success. As soon as the fall of communism was proclaimed, a new criterion appeared in Polish theatre – profitability – and the problem of how to win audiences and make them visit the theatre became predominant. This new priority brought changes in organization, financing and repertoire.

Polish theatre of the 1990s was dominated by the established avant-garde, represented by Jerzy Grzegorzewski; the new generation of theatre directors who expressed their chaotic selves and the brutal outer world, like Grzegorz Jarzyna or Kryzysztof Warlikowski; and young experimental companies spread all over the country. JOANNA KRAKOWSKA-NAROŻNIAK

Bohdan Drozdowski Cawer, ed., *20th Century Polish Theatre* (1979)
Edward Csato, *The Polish Theatre* (1965)
Martin Esslin, *The Theatre of the Absurd* (1962)
August Grodzicki, *Directors in the Polish Theatre* (English version, 1979)
August Grodzicki and Roman Szydowski, *Theatre in Modern Poland: Text and Selection of Photographs* (1963)
Jerzy Grotowski, *Towards a Poor Theatre*, with preface by Peter Brook (1968)
Boleslaw Taborski, *Polish Plays in English Translation* (1968)

Poliakoff, Stephen (b. London, 1 Dec. 1952) Playwright. Poliakoff had his first play produced when he was 16. His early work, like *The Carnation Gang* (1973), *City Sugar* and *Hitting Town* (both 1975), all at the BUSH, and *Strawberry Fields* (1977), written while he was writer in residence at the NATIONAL THEATRE, captured with alienated horror the brutal urban emptiness of precinct Britain. After *Shout Across the River* (1978) and *American Days* (1979), which saw Poliakoff experimenting with greater stylization and psychological insight, he began exploring elements of his Russian émigré family history; in *Breaking the Silence* (1984), a scientist is holed up in a train with his family fleeing the Russian Revolution, and *Playing with Trains* (1989) shows an inventor's struggle against bureaucracy. Both were staged by the ROYAL SHAKESPEARE COMPANY. Poliakoff has also produced acclaimed screenplays, including *Caught on a Train* (1980). Other plays include *Sweet Panic* (1996), *Blinded by the Sun* (1996) and *Remember This* (1999). DAN REBELLATO

political theatre A term denoting theatre used for political purposes, usually as part of a campaign or movement, sometimes as part of the work of a political party. At its loosest, it can have a wide application ranging from COMMUNITY THEATRE to consciousness-raising by groups with a specific identity such as women's, black or gay companies. Its usage is often imprecise, overlapping with other terms like ALTERNATIVE, GUERRILLA or radical theatre. Each country has its own tradition of political theatre. In the twentieth century the peaks of activity in the industrialized world coincided with two periods of social and political upheaval, the first and major one triggered by the Russian Revolution of 1917 and its aftermath, and the second coming in the 1960s and 1970s. Common themes emerged – for peace against war, for democracy and justice against exploitation and tyranny – and common forms too, e.g. AGITPROP. Most of this theatre was socialist- or communist-inspired, and often involved professionals working with amateurs in non-traditional venues. By its nature much of the work is ephemeral, but it has also had an important effect on the theatre world through inspirational practitioners like PISCATOR, BRECHT, LITTLEWOOD and BOAL.
COLIN CHAMBERS

See also POPULAR THEATRE; STREET THEATRE; THEATRE FOR DEVELOPMENT.

Augusto Boal, *The Theatre of the Oppressed* (1979)
Colin Chambers, *The Story of Unity Theatre* (1989)
Malcolm Goldstein, *The Political Stage: American Drama and Theatre of the Great Depression* (1974)
Morgan Y. Himmelstein, *Drama was a Weapon: The Left-Wing Theatre in New York 1929–1941* (1963)
Cathy Itzin, *Stages in the Revolution: Political Theatre in Britain since 1968* (1980)
R. Samuel, E. MacColl and S. Cosgrave, *Theatres of the Left 1880–1935* (1985)

Pollock [Chalmers], Sharon (b. Fredericton, New Brunswick, 19 April 1936) Playwright. Her early plays, such as *Walsh* (1973), focus on historical and political issues. *Walsh* dramatizes the events surrounding the expulsion from Canada of the Sioux chief Sitting Bull and his people in 1881. *The Komagatu Maru Incident* (1975) is about a boatload of Sikh immigrants refused entry to Canada in 1914. *Blood Relations* (1980) re-creates the events of the infamous Lizzie Borden murders. By using a play-within-a-play device, Pollock rises above mere 'docudrama' to create a work of rich moral complexity. Other plays include *Whiskey Six Cadenza* (1983), *Doc* (1984) and *Fair Liberty's Call* (1995). EUGENE BENSON

Pomerance, Bernard (b. Brooklyn, New York, 1940) Playwright. He moved to London in the early 1970s and wrote *Foco Novo* (1972), set in an unnamed South American dictatorship, the first play produced by the theatre company of the same name which Pomerance helped to establish with David Aukin and

Roland Rees. Pomerance's greatest success was *The Elephant Man* (1977), produced by FOCO NOVO, which transferred to Broadway and was later restaged at the NATIONAL THEATRE and made into a successful film in 1980. Other plays include *Someone Else is Still Someone* (1974), *Melons* (1984), and adaptations of Brecht's *A Man's a Man* (1975) and *The Elephant Calf* (1977).
BRIAN ROBERTS

Poor School   *see* DRAMA SCHOOLS

poor theatre   Term associated with JERZY GROTOWSKI and the influential LABORATORY THEATRE. He called his theatre poor because it dispensed with theatrical trappings and the technological resources of 'rich' theatre. Grotowski made the actor's voice and body central to the performance. Only stationary light sources were used; the only masks were the actors' faces; costume was nondescript; vocal effects replaced instrumental music and sound 'off'; the auditorium became an intimate space divided in varying ways to allow the utmost contact and exchange between performers and audience.

Grotowski sought for something beyond drama. He worked to develop physical and emotional responses so that 'impulse and reaction are concurrent'. He moved beyond the early influence of STANISLAVSKY towards a ritualized intensity. At moments of shock or terror, he argued, human beings use 'rhythmically articulated signs' and begin to dance and sing. 'A sign, not a common gesture, is the elementary integer of expression for us'. Grotowski sought to explore moments of extreme pressure and moved naturally towards 'archaic situations' expressed in myth and often involving taboo. In a world where myths are myths and not truths, we must attempt to assume myth's 'ill-fitting skin' he proclaimed. When the theatre confronts us with brutal situations where 'the life mask cracks and falls away' it can expose an 'intimate layer' which returns us to common human truths. The aims of poor theatre are reminiscent of the theories of ARTAUD. But Artaud aimed to synthesize the work of the actor with 'rich' technology of noise, light and costume. The writings of Nietzsche, Durkheim and Jung are also frequently invoked as influences on Grotowski, but the practical work of Stanislavsky, MEYERHOLD and the MIME MARCEL MARCEAU seem of more direct importance. The idea of poor theatre was very influential, both in the art theatre (e.g. PETER BROOK) and in ALTERNATIVE THEATRE. From it EUGENIO BARBA developed his own theories that led to the notion of THIRD THEATRE.   TERRY HODGSON

Jerzy Grotowski, *Towards a Poor Theatre* (1969)

Jennifer Kumiega, *The Theatre of Grotowski* (1985)

pop music and theatre   Through MUSICAL THEATRE, MUSIC HALL, VAUDEVILLE and VARIETY, popular music has enjoyed a close relationship with modern popular theatre, the source of many well-known songs. Since the Second World War and the advent of a distinct pop music, with as many forms as there are theatrical variations, the picture has changed and broadened: an innovator like Andy Warhol works with a Brechtian theatre COLLECTIVE and produces his 'total environment' cross-over theatre/rock touring show, The Exploding Plastic Inevitable featuring the Velvet Underground; rock concerts become more theatrical, from the psychedelic HAPPENINGS of Pink Floyd through to the glam showbiz style of Queen; The Who even write a rock opera, *Tommy*, while ANDREW LLOYD WEBBER draws heavily on rock and pop genres in his globally successful musicals. BRECHT and WEILL influenced many rock musicians, some of whom, like Lou Reed or Tom Waits, recorded their songs. David Bowie, an important figure in the theatricalization of pop, has acknowledged the influence of LINDSAY KEMP, with whom he worked. Bono and The Edge from U2 composed the music for the ROYAL SHAKESPEARE COMPANY's production of *A Clockwork Orange*, and singer–composer Paul Simon wrote his own musical, *The Capeman*. By the end of the twentieth century, theatre was awash with tribute bands and 'clone-zone' shows, a form of dramatic biography that has embraced Patsy Cline, Nat King Cole, Buddy Holly, Roy Orbison, The Sex Pistols, Elvis Presley and others, standing alongside their more reflective cousins such as WILLY RUSSELL's Beatles show, *John, Paul, Ringo and . . . Bert* or AUGUST WILSON'S *Ma Rainey's Black Bottom*.   CHARLES LONDON
See also JAZZ; MULTIMEDIA THEATRE; SOUND.

Popova, Lyubov   *see* CONSTRUCTIVISM

popular theatre   *see* PEOPLE'S THEATRE/POPULAR THEATRE

Portable Theatre   *see* ARTS LAB; HARE, DAVID; WILSON, SNOO

Porter, Cole [Albert]   (b. Peru, Ind., 9 June 1891; d. Santa Monica, Calif., 15 Oct. 1964) Songwriter. Wealthy and well-living, Porter purveyed from his early writing days a kind of songwriting which reflected his lifestyle: crisply suave, self-aware lyrics blended with smoothly insinuating melodies or comical blips of tune to produce material of a kind often more suitable to the newly popular CABARET world than to the theatre. His early songs were largely used in REVUE or as interpolated numbers in less sophisticated scores but, although a number of shows written in the 1930s and 1940s had good runs on BROADWAY, only *Anything Goes* (1934), with its happily nonsensical libretto and a bundle of Porter's most irresistible songs, proved to have any theatrical durability until, in 1948, he temporarily abandoned his habitual style to provide a classic score of lyric and comic music for Sam and Bella SPEWACK's backstage musical *Kiss Me, Kate* (1948). The songs of *Can-Can* (1953) and the film score for *High Society* (1956) gave him later successes. His work has been pushed back into the theatre in varying and usually unfortunate forms since his death. KURT GÄNZL

G. Ells, *Cole Porter: The Life That Late He Led* (1967)
D. Ewen, *The Cole Porter Story* (1965)
D. Grafton, *Red, Hot and Rich!* (1987)
W. McBrien, *Cole Porter: A Biography* (1998)

Porter, Eric [Richard] (b. London, 8 April 1928; d. London, 15 May 1995) Actor. He made his debut in 1945 as a spear carrier with the SHAKESPEARE MEMORIAL THEATRE company (later the ROYAL SHAKESPEARE COMPANY) and then toured with LEWIS CASSON and DONALD WOLFIT, played in repertory at BIRMINGHAM and the OLD VIC, and joined GIELGUD's season at the LYRIC, Hammersmith, in 1952 after an eye-catching performance as Solyoni in *Three Sisters* (1951) at the Aldwych. His versatility in tragedy and comedy, in old and new plays, was shown by his seasons with the BRISTOL OLD VIC, when he played the leading roles in *Murder in the Cathedral* (1954), *Uncle Vanya, Volpone* and *King Lear* (1955–6), and afterwards in the West End when he took over the male lead in PETER USTINOV's frothy *Romanoff and Juliet* (1956). His award-winning performance as Rosmer in *Rosmersholm* (1959) at the ROYAL COURT was followed by a return to Shakespeare at Stratford-upon-Avon in the first season under PETER HALL's new regime, playing Malvolio, Ulysses and Leontes. He played many roles for the company of which he was a founder member, now the RSC, including *Becket* (1961), Bolingbroke in *Richard II* (1964) – a role he had played to acclaim before – and a daring combination in the one season of Shylock and the title role in Marlowe's *The Jew of Malta* (1965). A highly successful television career – in *Cyrano de Bergerac* and *Anna Karenina*, for example, and as the callous lawyer Soames in *The Forsyte Saga*, which became the country's obsession – was topped by success on stage as Big Daddy at the NATIONAL THEATRE in *Cat on a Hot Tin Roof* (1988) and another Lear, at the Old Vic (1989). A private man off-stage, he was a compelling actor with a strong presence whose unsentimental sharpness prevented him from becoming as well loved as comparable contemporary talents. CHARLES LONDON

Porter, Hal (b. Melbourne, 16 Feb. 1911; d. Melbourne 29 Sept. 1984) Playwright and eminent short-story writer. Porter is a conservative, self-conscious stylist whose theatre work is overshadowed by his other writings, yet his ability to write dialogue has translated itself into entertainment of great theatrical craft if not great intellectual or social substance. He has also written a book of theatre biography entitled *Stars of the Australian Stage and Screen* (1965).

Porter's full-time writing career began at age 50. Before that, as a sometime actor and theatrical producer, he contributed to the life of Australia's LITTLE THEATRE. His plays helped sustain the tenuous thread of Australian content within that movement, especially at the Brett Randall–Irene Mitchell St Martin's Theatre in Melbourne. In this important contribution he joins other occasional playwrights, such as Ray Matthew, David Ireland and Dymphna Cusack.

His most serious work, *The Professor* (first produced as *Toda San*, 1965), deals with the gulf between Eastern and Western culture and the relationship between love and lust. Other plays include *The Tower* (1963) and *Eden House* (1969), which was also produced at the ROYAL COURT (1972). GUS WORBY

A. Broinowski, *The Yellow Lady: Australian Impressions of Asia* (1992)
D. Carroll, *Australian Contemporary Drama* (1995)
M. Lord, *Hal Porter* (1974)

Portugal Though drama is Portugal's weakest literary genre, there were invigorating, if controversial, developments after the 1974 Revolution with the long-awaited staging of BRECHT and the emergence of a wry Marxist theatre, notably in *A Noite* ('The night') of Nobel Prize winner José Saramago (b. 1922) in 1979. The fire-gutted National Theatre had been rebuilt by 1978 (even if its state-run company laboured under a top-heavy burden of bureaucrats and maintenance staff), and the Portuguese theatre was liberated from censorship.

In the four centuries before 1900 there emerged, at the most, half a dozen dramatists worthy of note; with the shining exception of Gil Vicente (1460–1536), their names are virtually unknown outside Iberia and such lack of distinction has likewise typified much of twentieth-century Portuguese theatre. The most fertile national literary aptitudes are essentially elegiac or satirical and are often wanting in those interactive qualities that generate true theatre. Portugal has no PIRANDELLO, no LORCA, no COCTEAU, no Brecht. This impoverishment was aggravated from 1926 to 1974 under the repression of a right-wing one-party state. Innovatory or politically sensitive drama might occasionally be published, but only exceptionally was it performed. Until 1945 effete naturalism reigned supreme. There occurred, however, a handful of significant achievements. Three playwrights, Raul Brandão (1867–1930), Alfredo Cortez (1890–1946) and Carlos Selvagem (1890–1973), were moving beyond naturalism. In 1927 came the production of Brandão's *O Gebo e a Sombra* ('The ragamuffin and the shadow'), which veered towards discussion of existential problems concerning life, age, poverty and evil. A heftier impact was created by Cortez in 1934 with *Gladiadores* ('Gladiators'), a play not only aesthetically revolutionary in its EXPRESSIONIST techniques but also boldly controversial in its socio-political satire. As for Selvagem, he had scored a major success back in 1917 with the naturalism of *Entre Giestas* ('Among the broom bushes'), a play of wide appeal concerning the intricacies of love and class in rural Portugal; but it was not until 1944 that he achieved similar acclaim for *Dulcineia* ('Dulcinea'). Billed as 'Don Quixote's last adventure', this production, with its striking sets and hint of the experimental, constituted a third major break with naturalism.

Much credit for the effect of both *Gladiadores* and *Dulcineia* was due to the private company, headed by leading actress Amélia Rey-Colaço, which held the National Theatre franchise from 1929 until the conflagration of 1964. Into an imaginative programme, largely composed of national classics and translated foreign drama, the company incorporated a growing number of contemporary Portuguese plays.

After the Second World War there came a steady shift towards experimentation, with the formation of sundry vigorous enterprises, notably the Salitre Studio in Lisbon in 1946 and the Oporto Experimental Theatre in 1953. A significant contribution was made by university drama groups, especially at Coimbra under the inspiring leadership of Paulo Quintela. Most prominent among the many talented directors of the new generation was the unorthodox Carlos Avilez of the Cascais Experimental Theatre. Postwar attitudes promoted the belated staging of four plays by two eminent writers from earlier generations, namely José de Almada-Negreiros (1893–1970) and José Régio (1901–69). Almada, a boisterous eccentric, had designed the stunning costumes and sets for *Dulcineia*. *Antes de Começar* ('Before beginning') and *Deseja-se Mulher* ('Woman wanted'), both dating from the 1920s, were presented in 1949 and 1963 respectively; they illustrated Almada's passion for fantasy and for making the theatre a vehicle for experiments in the visual arts. *Benilde ou a Virgem-Mãe* ('Benilde or the virgin-mother'), by the established poet and novelist

Régio, was staged in 1947, exhibiting despite its colloquial naturalism a strong hint of reactionary idealism; but Régio's principal dramatic achievement had much longer to wait: *Jacob e o Anjo* ('Jacob and the angel') was written in 1937, published in 1941 and performed in Paris in 1952; but came to Lisbon only in 1968–9. This 31-years delay exemplifies the quite extraordinary crisis in Portuguese twentieth-century theatre. With its baroque declamatory style, *Jacob e o Anjo* was pure Régio in its successful exploration of his lifelong *idée fixe*, the dichotomy between matter and spirit, man and God.

The postwar generation of dramatists fell into three main camps. First, there was the continuing naturalist theatre as represented by Romeu Correia (b. 1917), a prolific and popular playwright; gradually, however, he began to add magical elements and Pirandellian touches. A typical example was his rural parable *Sol na Floresta* ('Sun in the forest'), performed in 1957. Second, there was the THEATRE OF THE ABSURD; here the most successful practitioner was Hélder Prista Monteiro, as in *A Rabeca* ('The fiddle'), professionally staged in both 1961 and 1966 with echoes of IONESCO, BECKETT and PINTER. Third, and most importantly, there emerged an apparently historical theatre, intent, however, not on reconstructing the past but on applying it to illumine the present. A prominent contribution came from the novelist José Cardoso Pires (1925–98), whose *O Render dos Heróis* ('The relief of the heroes'), was staged in 1965 and which, with Brechtian traces, took its stance on an 1846 revolt against oppression. Also acclaimed was Luzia Martins (b. 1927), whose *Bocage, Alma sem Mundo* ('Bocage, worldless soul'), directed by the authoress in 1967, refocused the attitudes of a runaway eighteenth-century poet.

The leaders in this third group were the gifted playwrights Bernardo Santareno (1920–80) and Luís de Sttau Monteiro (1926–93). Santareno's steady output of plays drew on religious doubt, sexual repression and social injustice, as in *O Pecado de João Agonia* ('The Sin of John Agony'); produced in 1969, this drama was notable for its hysterically violent dénouement. Arguably Santareno's most powerful play is *O Judeu* ('The Jew'), which presents the burning at the stake of an eighteenth-century Jewish playwright; yet – as with *all* the plays of Sttau – *O Judeu* had to wait until after the Revolution to be performed. Significantly, Sttau's masterpiece, *Felizmente Há Luar!* ('Good job there's moonlight!'), based on the 1817 execution of a general on false charges, had won a prize in 1962 and been staged in Paris in 1969. But at last the shackles fell away.

R. C. WILLIS

Luiz Francisco Rebello, *História do Teatro Português*, 4th edn (1989)

Portuguese-speaking African theatre Angola, Mozambique, Guinea-Bissau, Cape Verde and Sao Tome e Principe make up lusophone Africa. These former colonies, except for Cape Verde, declared independence in 1975 after a military coup overthrew the dictatorship in Portugal the year before. Armed struggle for independence had begun in 1956 in Guinea-Bissau and Cape Verde, in Angola in 1961, and in 1964 in Mozambique. Although these countries shared a common colonial history, they each have a unique historical and social heritage. Angola is made up of the Bakongo, Kimbundu and Ovimbundu ethnic groups, all of Bantu origin, who it is believed moved into the area from central Africa in the late fifteenth century and early sixteenth century. It is a fairly large country, as big as Portugal, France and the United Kingdom put together, with a population of about 10 million. Guinea-Bissau is much smaller in area, with a population of 1.5 million people made up of 26 ethnic groups, of which the Balanta, Peul (Fulani), Mandingo (Malinke) and Mandyako are the major ones. Mozambique has a population of approximately 17.5 million, made up mainly of people of Bantu origins with three main subgroupings, the Changana, the Makway and the Senas. In all these countries, although numerous African languages are spoken, Portuguese is the official language, and in some, like Guinea-Bissau, Crioulo (a Portuguese-derived Creole) is spoken by many.

Angola, Mozambique and Guinea-Bissau have developed theatre traditions and some published plays. Cape Verde has very little theatre activity, while in Sao Tome e Principe theatre seems to be insignificant. This, to a large extent, is down to the fact that the Portuguese neither encouraged nor developed any infrastructure for theatre in their colonies. In those colonies that have managed to develop theatre, Negritude and Pan-Africanism, which provided the philosophical framework for the independence struggle, also provide an aesthetic underpinning. European-style theatre was introduced by missionaries while an extremely repressive colonialism stifled traditional African forms of cultural expression. The early European plays were religious in character, since their aim was to propagate Catholic doctrine to the exclusion of everything else. The result is that much Portuguese-speaking theatre is European-influenced.

In Angola, which had a theatre tradition going back to the seventeenth century, amateur theatre companies specializing in European-style farces and melodramas emerged in the capital, Luanda, and in other parts of the country by the early part of the twentieth century. In spite of Portuguese suppression; some Angolan playwrights did emerge in the mid-1930s and 1940s, such as Henrique Galvao, who wrote *Como se faz um homen* ('How a man is made', 1935), *O velo d'ocio* ('The golden fleece', 1936) and *Colonos* ('The colonists', 1939); Padre Benevato, who wrote *O' Condestavel* ('The supreme commander', 1940); and Alfredo Cortez, who wrote *Moema* (1940). The greatest impetus for the emergence of Angolan theatre was the formation in the early 1940s of the National African League, which produced and encouraged plays reflecting local culture or dealing with local socio-political issues.

Indigenous Angolan theatre began in the 1950s and 1960s with street carnivals and processions, though these efforts were often frustrated by the colonial police. Ngongo Theatre Group's attempts to present the legends and myths of Angola were built upon during the independence struggle in performances on the streets and in factories, schools and hospitals, and these efforts produced didactic and anti-colonial plays such as *Poder Popular* ('People power', 1975) by Tchingange Theatre. Much theatre after independence sought to awaken the socio-political consciousness of the people: other plays in this mode are Manuel Santos Lima's *A pele do Diablo* ('The devil's skin', 1977), and *A corda* ('The rope', 1978) and *A revolta da casa dos idolos* ('A revolt in the house of idols', 1980) by Pepetela ('Artur Pestana dos Santos'). Other notable plays are *O circulo de giz de Bombo* ('Bombo's chalk circle', 1979), an adaptation of BRECHT's *The Caucasian Chalk Circle* by Henrique Guerra, and Jorge Macedo's *Sequira Luis Lopes on o Mulato des prodigos* ('Sequira Luis Lopes or the prodigal mulatto', 1991).

In Mozambique before independence, the most popular form of entertainment was the VAUDEVILLE. As in the other Portuguese colonies, it was difficult to write or produce theatre with a clear political theme because of CENSORSHIP, but in 1959 Afonso Ribeira wrote *Tres setas apontadas para a o Futuro* ('Three arrows pointing to the future'), a play which criticizes the colonial status quo. Its example was followed by other plays which bravely began to challenge colonial ideology, such as Lindo Longhos' *Os noivos au conferencia dramatica sobre o lobolo* ('The engagement, or Dramatic discourse on the purchasing of a bride', 1971), later banned by the colonial authority for its Pan-Africanism and support of local culture. Longhos also wrote *As trinta mulheres de Muzelene* ('The thirty wives of Muzelene') on polygamy and European reactions to it. Similar plays written in the years preceding independence include *Filhos da noite* ('Children of the night') by

Antonio Francisco, and *Feitico e a religiao* ('Sorcery and religion') by Joao Fumene.

After independence, theatre became part of the new government's drive to heal colonial wounds, and was used to put across the ideology of the new socialist state. Soviet-style AGITPROP theatre became the vogue, giving birth to new plays such as *Un minuto de silencio* ('One minute of silence') and *Na machamb de Maria – sabado as tres de tarde* ('On Maria's small farm – Saturday afternoon, three o'clock', 1975) by Orlando Mendes, and *A estrada* ('The road', 1979) by Leite Vasconcelos. Others are *O destino: inimigo do povo* ('Destiny: an enemy of the people') by a workers' collective and *A Commune* ('The commune', 1979) by the railway workers and the students of Eduardo Mondlane University. Theatre projects created by groups such as Maputo Theatre Group and Mutumbela Gogo were common, using adaptations of novels and stories by Mia Cuoto, Luis Honwana and others. Unlike individually written pieces, the collective creations are deeply influenced by African theatre aesthetics of song, dance, music, mime, improvisation and, above all, active audience participation.

In Guinea-Bissau, alongside the traditional forms such as storytelling, music, dance, mime and movement, European-style theatre was carried on by amateur groups in the 1940s for purposes of satiric and social commentary. Some early plays performed included *Don Beltrano de Figueira* and *Don Ramon de Chapishuela* by Julio Dantas. In the 1950s a form of children's theatre emerged in which dramatizations of both African and European folktales featured, e.g. *Festival of Arrows*, *The Cicada and the Ant*, *Cinderella* and *Sleeping Beauty*. In the early 1960s a group made up entirely of natives of Guinea-Bissau emerged in Bolana; because it was part of the nationalist movement, it was regularly censored by the colonial police and was eventually hounded out of existence because of its overtly cultural politics.

After independence, many theatre groups emerged, including Afrocid (Occidental Africa), which is significant both because it was the umbrella under which many Guinean dramatists such as Rosalina Gauffin, Rui Borges (Pantcho) and Umbani N'Kesset gained their experience and because it produced two very important plays: *Africa Liberada* ('Free Africa', 1975), about the meaning of independence for both the Africans and the Portuguese colonials, and *Milo* (1976), about individual and communal crises arising from independence. *Chasso* was collectively created by some former members of Afrocid and tackles the brutality of the colonial police towards prisoners during the struggle for independence as well as the emancipation and role of women. The same collective also produced *Se Cussa Murri, Cassa cu Matal* ('Nothing dies without a cause') under the direction of Carlos Vaz, dealing with colonial repression, especially atrocities in prisons.

Although not much theatre has been written and produced in Cape Verde since independence, much of what has been done has been used to raise the socio-political awareness of the people. The most prominent example is Oswaldo Osorio's *Gervasio*, a play very much influenced by Brechtian techniques and based on a slave uprising. It shows the fighting spirit of the Africans who stood up against their enslavers. Other dramatists of note are Kaoberdiano Dambara, who wrote *Os disanimados para os infernos* ('To hell with the pessimists', 1977) and Donaldo Pereira de Macedo, author of the Crioulo play *Descardo* ('Shameless', 1979), the first Cape Verdean play to be published. The only major theatre troupe is Korda Kaoberdi, formed in 1976 by Kwame Konde. There are bold attempts at cultural retrieval which show the influence of the radical Brazilian educationalist Paulo Freire and theatre philosopher AUGUSTO BOAL. OSITA OKAGBUE

See also THEATRE FOR DEVELOPMENT.

Posenor, Jill *see* GAY SWEATSHOP; LESBIAN THEATRE

posters *see* RECORDING AND RESEARCHING THEATRE

postmodernism *see* DRAMATIC THEORY; MODERNISM

Potter, Dennis [Christopher George] (b. Coleford, Glos, 17 May 1935; d. Ross-on-Wye, Hereford and Worcester, 7 June 1994) Playwright, who for 40 years repeatedly redrew the formal and moral boundaries of TELEVISION DRAMA. His masterpiece, the postmodern mystery serial *The Singing Detective* (1986), typically cuts between comic pastiche, old escapist songs and harrowing emotional realism. Many forces cripple his characters, sometimes literally: guilt, social frustrations, childhood traumas, sex, and most of all memory. God is a silent judge (*Son of Man*, television play staged 1969), evil is active (*Brimstone and Treacle*, banned by the BBC, staged 1978). Yet the plays press therapeutically towards recognition and catharsis – for the spectator and, Potter hints, the author. His frank discussion of his own fatal cancer on Channel Four television was in many ways the true climax of his career. He wrote one original stage play, *Sufficient Carbohydrate* (1983). TONY HOWARD

H. Carpenter, *Dennis Potter: A Biography* (1999)
S. Gilbert, *Fight and Kick and Bite: The Life and Work of Dennis Potter* (1995)

Power family The Powers have been actors since the eighteenth century. [Frederick] Tyrone [Edmond]

(1869–1931) was the grandson of a successful actor and playwright who had made a transatlantic career playing stage Irishmen. Power was a leading man in Daly's Company, later he was a well-regarded Shakespearean actor, most notably playing Claudius to BARRYMORE's *Hamlet* (1922). His son, Tyrone (1914–58), had a brief stage career, making his debut as Benvolio in the GUTHRIE–CORNELL *Romeo and Juliet* (1935), but he left the stage to became a Hollywood star. Strikingly handsome, possessed of a good voice, he became dissatisfied with films and returned to the theatre to appear in *Mister Roberts* (1950) and *The Dark is Light Enough* (1955), among other plays. His son, Tyrone Jr, is also an actor. THOMAS F. CONNOLLY

See also THEATRE FAMILIES.

H. Arce, *The Secret Life of Tyrone Power* (1979)
W. Winter, *Life of Tyrone Power* (1913)

Power, Tyrone *see* POWER FAMILY

Pownall, David (b. Liverpool, 19 May 1938) Playwright. Pownall's style changes with each play, and he has written many, for stage, television and radio. They blur the borders between the concerns of morality and politics, as in *Motocar* (1977) and *Barricade* (1979), combining a challenging intellect and profound enquiry with a keen sense of theatrical fantasy, as in *Richard III, Part Two* (1977). Although he has never won wider recognition, his interest in creativity and history (*Music to Murder By*, 1976; *An Audience Called Edouard*, 1978; *Elgar's Rondo*, 1993) achieved acclaim in 1983 with *Master Class*, which considers politics, art and responsibility through a hilarious meeting in 1948 between Stalin, Zhdanov, Prokofiev and Shostakovich. In 1975, Pownall co-founded PAINES PLOUGH, a company committed to new writing. He has also written novels and poetry. DAN REBELLATO

Prampolni, Enrico *see* FUTURISM

Price, [Lilian] Nancy [Bache] (b. Kinver, Worcs, 3 Feb. 1880; d. Worthing, W. Sussex, 31 March 1970) Actress and manager who played hundreds of roles and directed more than 80 plays. She founded in London the PEOPLE'S NATIONAL THEATRE (1930), producing over 50 plays in seven years. During the late 1930s she founded the English School Theatre Movement, touring Shakespeare to working-class children, often using star actors willing to work for low wages. She wrote several books, including the autobiographical *Shadows on the Hill* (1935). MAGGIE GALE

Prichard, Katherine Susannah (b. Levuka, Fiji, 4 Dec. 1883; d. Greenmount, Western Australia, 2 Oct. 1969) Novelist and playwright. Her first play, *The Burglar* (1909), an otherwise conventional comedy, hinted at a socialism that in years to come would see Prichard writing AGITPROP. During a six-year stint as a journalist in London, she wrote two curtain-raisers for the ACTRESSES' FRANCHISE LEAGUE: *Her Place* (1913) and *For Instance* (1914). With her return to Australia in 1916 came two film versions of her successful novel *The Pioneers*; she wrote a one-act adaptation of this work (1923) and later a three-act version. Success as a playwright came with a prize for *Brumby Innes* (written 1927; production followed 45 years later). Then with the Depression came Prichard's agitprop 'strike' plays. In 1951 she wrote a long biographical piece on the father of the Australian Federation, *Deakin* (1951), into which she incorporated much of the politician's remarkable oratory. *Persephone's Baby* (1959), her last play, deals with the true story of a child – SUMNER LOCKE ELLIOTT – raised by three sisters after the death of his mother. Of her 17 plays, 11 were produced by small amateur or left-wing theatre groups, including the PIONEER PLAYERS (*The Great Man*, 1923). Revivals by the Australian Performing Group and the Canberra Repertory have ensured that the title 'playwright' will stand alongside that of 'eminent novelist' in any description of Prichard. GUS WORBY

P. Fitzpatrick, *Pioneer Players: The Lives of Louis and Hilda Esson* (1995)

Priestley, J[ohn] B[oynton] (b. Bradford, 13 Sept. 1894; d. Alveston, Warks, 14 Aug. 1984) Playwright, novelist, essayist and broadcaster. Priestley was already established as a novelist when his first stage work appeared in 1931: an adaptation, with EDWARD KNOBLOCK, of his novel about a touring PIERROT troupe, *The Good Companions*; like several of his later plays, it was also filmed. Among his most interesting works of the 1930s are those influenced by the philosophers Dunne and Ouspensky, which explore theories of parallel and serial time – *Dangerous Corner* (1932), *Time and the Conways* (1937) and *I Have Been Here Before* (1937) – making difficult concepts popularly accessible. The most popular of his 'time' plays is *An Inspector Calls* (1945), which enjoyed a remarkable revival in 1992 directed by STEPHEN DALDRY. Priestley wrote his own theoretical account of time in *Man and Time* (1963). He also experimented in *Music at Night* (1938), in which characters attending a concert are liberated from consecutive literal time, and *Desert Highway* (1943), which presents parallel actions in the Syrian desert, one during the Second World War and the other in 703 BC. The former was presented by his own company, the London Mask Theatre, at the Westminster Theatre, which Priestley had taken over in 1938. Other plays are

· Preparing a part ·

Rehearsing a part begins, in a way, long before being offered the role. Beyond everything else, and before even confronting the craft of acting, let alone the preparation for a particular part, comes the need to be an actor. This quest to be seen and heard has to be the product of an intellect and imagination that has an insatiable appetite for knowledge, for experience and for sharing that experience in company.

Likewise, no craft preparation can properly enhance the development and life of a character and the validity of its psychological reality unless the actor at some stage either before entering the rehearsal room or during rehearsal feels that he or she really needs to play the role. When I played BRECHT's Baal, I had a hunger to play the part. He was an entertainer, a narcotic, an extremely volatile, unpredictable addict. I had to confront those aspects of my psychology and articulate them as a craftsman by polishing my need and my intuition, not so that I could be introverted, having a private fix on stage, but in order to present me in the role to the audience as a compelling narrative whole. That you can only do by breaking down the role and, with the help of the director, finding where are the rest periods, where the peaks, and what is the recurring theme. If it's too obvious, it's boring for both the actor and the audience; but if the actor has joy in finding it, then so will the audience.

The energy invested in the rehearsal process in discovering the secret resonance of the role should radiate into the theatre when the time comes to perform. I found that profoundly when I played Hamlet, which forced me to re-examine the turning points in my life, my relationship with my parents, with my female and male friends, and with my craft. After ten weeks of rehearsing with the director Buzz Goodbody, the revelations she induced in me and the others in the cast were provoked in the audience and you couldhear the realization exploding throughout the run. The preparation for that demanded great stamina to deal with the intellectual, vocal and physical dexterity required.

The intellectual preparation, the reading, the research, feeds the joy of exploring and digging and hunting. If you are rehearsing a Restoration comedy, for example, it is extraordinary to study the dress and the modes of combat – you are bewigged and yet armed to the teeth at the same time. This practical historical knowledge can provide channels through which to release your intuitive grasp of the character. In playing Othello, I felt my interest in his Moorish background sharpened my understanding and helped me find a context for his code of behaviour, especially in how to treat the loss of face, which is completely different from the way an Englishman, Frenchman or Italian would react. With Hamlet, apart from reflecting on the alarmingly high suicide rate in Scandinavia, I thought about the effect on one's imagination and metabolism of living through endless nights and endless days and saw him as the Prince of Light – as opposed to the Prince of Darkness – whose journey was towards lucidity.

In the end, all the clues are to be found in the text. The actor has to return to the text continually, even when the lines are learnt, to check, to see how it punctuates, to ensure you are not using an 'and' instead of a 'but' because that could trigger off an avalanche of wrong clues for the audience.

Vocally and physically, the actor has to be properly exercised, fit and relaxed. It can be very frustrating if you can hear in your head what the voice should be but cannot produce it, and, in striving to achieve it, actually prevent the realization by holding on to something that you should have let go. Exercises such as those associated with the ALEXANDER Technique help; you trace your spine and your limbs, relax your gut, release the neck, and unknot the muscles that tense when you are about to face an audience. Fitness also helps the memory and the reflexes and allows the actor to develop as full a physical vocabulary as possible. It's great news when your body finds an image that expresses the character without using a word. As Kean I had to practise extremely hard to convince an audience that I could do his sprightly, frog-like Harlequin dances with their acrobatic leaps and hops that kill the thigh muscles.

All this preparation ultimately has to lead to the point at which the actor feels that he or she is truly the custodian of the character as presented by the playwright – and then, paradoxically, the actor is free. This requires sensitive handling of the rehearsal process by the director. For example, it is terrifying and inhibiting to be told by a director that you can do what you like in a scene. A director needs to set limits in order to liberate the actor; yet the director must let the actors discover for themselves because you only learn by making mistakes. An actor, however, will require the right atmosphere to be created in which mistakes can be made. If this atmosphere is endangered – by exhaustion or trivialization – the director has to act to pump new energy into it.

Rehearsal is a delicate process of gestation and what

the audience sees depends on the common discovery during that process and the bonding of those taking part, with each other, with the text and the subtext. There are times when rehearsals are tremendously hard work and times when they are fun. They can also offer great privilege, when you work with an actor who represents a link with the ancient craft of glamour, intelligence, wit and danger – what has been called 'a touch of the old'. Watching RALPH RICHARDSON rehearse the death of the old servant Firs, the entire cast of *The Cherry Orchard* saw a rare piece of bravura theatre that affected everyone's feelings towards one another and the production – a true reminder that in the age of cinema and television the starting point for the rich, scary, beautiful craft of acting is still the live performance. **BEN KINGSLEY**

See also MOVEMENT, DANCE AND DRAMA; PHYSICAL PREPARATION; VOICE; VOICE TRAINING.

more conventional – *Laburnum Grove* (1933), a comedy crime drama; *Eden End* (1934), a gently ironic comedy; and *When We Are Married* (1938), a farce with a conventionally familiar Yorkshire setting. *The Linden Tree* (1947) was a notable realist family drama dealing with political views, about a professor fighting his enforced retirement. More interesting are the undisguised allegories of *Johnson over Jordan* (1939), a modern morality drama, and *They Came to a City* (1943), which presents a utopian vision that caught the contemporary mood of hopes for postwar reconstruction. More explicitly propagandist were Priestley's wartime broadcasts, in which he embodied the commonsense voice of Labour Party politics. His dramatic output declined sharply in the 1950s, although he did collaborate with Jacquetta Hawkes on two plays and with Iris Murdoch on a dramatization of her novel *A Severed Head* (1963), which ran in the West End for two and a half years.

Author of nearly 50 plays, some of which have become standards in the nation's repertoire, he was also UK delegate to UNESCO, chair of three postwar theatre conferences and first president of the INTERNATIONAL THEATRE INSTITUTE. Among his prolific non-dramatic output are the memoirs *Margin Released* (1962) and *Instead of the Trees* (1977). He was awarded the Order of Merit in 1977. IAN CLARKE

John Atkins, *J. B. Priestley: The Last of the Sages* (1981)
Gareth Lloyd Evans, *J. B. Priestley: The Dramatist* (1964)
Holger Klein, *J. B. Priestley's Plays* (1988)

Prince, Hal [Harold Smith]   (b. New York, 30 Jan. 1928) Producer and director. 'The only child of a privileged upper-middle, lower-rich class, Jewish family', to use his own words, Prince graduated from the University of Pennsylvania (1948), then took an assistant's job at the GEORGE ABBOTT office in New York, where he met Robert E. Griffith, Abbott's production stage manager. Prince, also a stage manager, formed with Griffith and Frederick Brisson a producing partnership in 1953, their first productions being the successful *The Pajama Game* (1954) and *Damn Yankees* (1955). With Griffith, he produced an even bigger hit in *West Side Story* (1957); the many major MUSICALS Prince produced alone include *A Funny Thing Happened on the Way to the Forum* (1962) and *Fiddler on the Roof* (1964). His first directorial effort was the musical *A Family Affair* (1962), and he went on to direct and produce such other musicals as *She Loves Me* (1963) and *Cabaret* (1966).

For four decades Prince was the major directorial force in the musical theatre. 'A musical has an arc,' he observed, 'which only the director is in charge of; I learned about that arc from George Abbott and JEROME ROBBINS.' His most distinguished and daring musical achievements are his six collaborations with STEPHEN SONDHEIM, sometimes known as 'concept musicals': *Company* (1970), *Follies* (1971), *A Little Night Music* (1973), *Pacific Overtures* (1976), *Sweeney Todd* (1979) and *Merrily We Roll Along* (1981). He also collaborated with ANDREW LLOYD WEBBER on *Evita* (1978) and *The Phantom of the Opera* (1986). Complementing his immense work in the musical theatre are the plays he has directed, including *The Visit* (1973), and the many operas he has staged for such companies as the New York City Opera, the Chicago Lyric Opera and the Vienna State Opera. He has won more Tony awards than anyone else.

One of the major features of Prince's career is the extent to which he is attracted to unconventional – and perhaps at first glance unpromising – subject matter that challenges audiences. His stagings, developed in close collaboration with his designers, emphasize the theatrical possibilities and power of the production. Without forsaking the traditional appeal of the musical comedy genre, he explores and expands its thematic and theatrical boundaries. His autobiography, *Contradictions: Notes on Twenty-six Years in the Theater*, was published in 1974. DAVID STAINES

See also MUSICAL THEATRE (DIRECTING MUSICALS).

Foster Hirsch, *Harold Prince and the American Musical Theatre* (1989)
Carol Ilson, *Harold Prince: A Director's Journey* (2000)

Printemps, Yvonne [Wignolle] (b. Ermont, Seine-et-Oise, France, 25 July 1895; d. Paris, 19 Jan. 1977) Actress and singer who made her first stage appearance in a REVUE, *Nue, Cocotte!!* (1908). She stayed in revue until 1916 when she joined a company directed by SACHA GUITRY, whom she married in 1918. This match with the brilliant son of one of France's leading actors (Lucien-Germain) brought her into the theatrical establishment, and Guitry, with his skills as writer, director and actor, transformed her from a follies soubrette into a star comedienne. At the height of her success, in 1932, she left him for a young actor, Pierre Fresnay. She played the lead in NOËL COWARD's *Conversation Piece* (London, 1933), a part she had to learn phonetically until Coward, in despair, rewrote much of her dialogue into French. In 1937, with Fresnay, she had one of her greatest successes with the operetta *Trois Valses*. IAN BEVAN

prisons *see* THEATRE IN PRISONS

prizes *see* AWARDS AND PRIZES

producing The producer is the person responsible for coordinating the artistic, technical, financial and managerial aspects of a production. In the first half of the twentieth century, the term was also used to mean DIRECTOR. A producer may originate an idea and commission its execution, but more often buys an idea from somebody else; if creative, a producer may help develop that idea. In the commercial sector, the producer is all-powerful and takes on all the responsibilities of MANAGEMENT. In the not-for-profit or publicly subsidized sector, the artistic director of a theatre may be the producer and many of the producer's functions will be devolved to the theatre's staff. Given the nature and economics of theatre, producing is a complex activity that involves many partnerships and therefore requires a range of considerable skills. Successful exponents include LELAND HAYWARD, HAL PRINCE, HUGH BEAUMONT, MICHAEL CODRON and CAMERON MACKINTOSH. Stories of their mercenary and philistine counterparts are legendary, as are some of their stunts. DAVID MERRICK publicized *Fanny* (1954) by commissioning a statue of its belly dancer, naked, which he put opposite a bust of Shakespeare in Central Park. CHARLES LONDON

James Inverne, *The Impresarios* (2000)

Project Arts Centre Following a three-week festival of experimental arts and music at DUBLIN's GATE THEATRE in 1966, the organizers, Colm O Briain and Jim Fitzgerald, decided to create a permanent alternative centre for the performing and visual arts. It had a number of homes around Dublin before settling, in 1974, in the then-dilapidated central Temple Bar area. The Centre presents and, to a lesser extent, produces theatre. Among the notable theatre and film artists who worked there in its early days are Peter and Jim Sheridan, Vinnie McCabe, Neil Jordan, Gabriel Byrne and Liam Neeson. In the 1980s ROUGH MAGIC THEATRE COMPANY made Project its primary performance venue, as did the experimental MUSIC THEATRE group Operating Theatre. In the mid-1990s the Centre shut for refurbishment and performances were held off-site. The new Project, which reopened in 2000, features three convertible, state-of-the-art performance spaces. KAREN FRICKER

promenade A type of theatre in which the actors walk around or through the audience, if they share one space, or lead them to different acting locations, if there is more than one space. Tracing its origins back to medieval times and before, it can occur outdoors, as a form of COMMUNITY PLAY, STREET THEATRE, CARNIVAL or PAGEANT, pioneered by ALTERNATIVE THEATRE groups like BREAD AND PUPPET THEATER, ODIN TEATRET and WELFARE STATE, as well as indoors. THÉÂTRE DU SOLEIL's 1789 (1970), *The Mysteries* (1979–83) performed by BILL BRYDEN's company at the NATIONAL THEATRE, and JIM CARTWRIGHT's *Road* (1986) are notable examples of the latter. Conventional plays have also been restaged in promenade, especially the works of Shakespeare (e.g. PETER STEIN's 1977 production of *As You Like It*). CHARLES LONDON

prop-making The basic skills of the prop-maker remained the same throughout the twentieth century. However, they have proved more adaptable to the use of new materials than those of the scenic artist, and this has changed the status of prop-making. Since the 1960s it has no longer been seen as an aspect of scenic construction, but as a distinct area of expertise, whose scope encompasses aspects of both costume and scenery. Props (short for stage property) may be loosely defined as anything used, carried or handled by an actor. However, the areas where props and costume and props and set meet can be very vague. For instance, the majority of three-dimensional decoration on a set, e.g. trees, mouldings, sculptures and set dressing, would fall within the province of the prop-maker. As for costume, the prop-maker is often called upon to make armour, helmets, masks, animal bodies and heads, jewellery and other adornments. There are three sections to props: running props, props buying and prop-making. *Running props* is the department responsible for the setting, storing and care of props during the production period and run of the show. The property master and crew would carry out minor repairs to props; major repairs would be done by the prop-maker. In some theatres this department would come under the auspices of STAGE MANAGEMENT; in others it would be a separate division of the technical department. The *props buyer*, as the title suggests, is responsible for the purchase or hire of props, furniture, etc., which either go straight to running props for immediate use or to the prop-maker for painting, alteration or to be copied in more durable materials. Any props not bought are manufactured by the *prop-maker*, who must be able to work from both drawings and scale models, and also from discussion with the designer. A good working knowledge and appreciation of period is also desirable. The skills of a property workshop must cover everything from carpentry and furniture-making, upholstery and soft toys, metalwork and welding, modelling and sculpture, to mould making and casting in fibreglass (GRP), polyurethane and other foams and vacuum- and heat-formed plastics. In addition, the more traditional materials such as latex, scrim, canvas, plaster and *papier mâché* are still much used. Prop-making continues to rely heavily on traditional skills, methods and materials, yet since the 1960s new materials (GRP, vacuum-formed plastics, isocyanates, acrylics, etc.) have been used increasingly. There are several reasons for this: not only are they relatively strong and light, but the majority of these materials as used in the theatre are available in fireproof formats. As a result of increasingly stringent fire regulations, the use of inherently fireproof materials has become more widespread. In the case of soft props such as fabrics and papers, many better and more versatile fireproofing agents have become available. Another reason for the expanding use of such media as GRP is an increasing awareness by both designers and producers of the possibilities of these materials. Thus designers are free to design props which would be difficult or unrealistic to produce in other media. Many of the modern plastics, however, can only be used in the larger property and scenic workshops.

It was, ironically, the very need for well-ventilated areas in which to fabricate GRP and other modern materials that, in the 1970s and 1980s, led to the expansion of props workshops. Prior to their widespread use, even in the large companies, such departments would be housed in small rooms backstage or in an annexe of the theatre. As their use became more widespread, prop-making moved out of the theatre itself, opening the way for a widening of the prop-maker's scope and importance. PHIL DALE

See also COSTUME DESIGN; DESIGN.

Prospect Theatre Company English touring company, originally called Prospect Productions, founded in OXFORD in 1961. Acclaimed for the quality of its performers, the company under TOBY ROBERTSON moved its base to the CAMBRIDGE Arts Theatre for several years and enjoyed a close association with the EDINBURGH FESTIVAL. In 1977 the company moved to the OLD VIC and became the Old Vic Company. Prospect's reputation as a classical touring company was built on such productions as *Richard II* (1968) and *Edward II* (1969), both title roles being played by IAN MCKELLEN, *Saint Joan* (1977) with EILEEN ATKINS, and *Hamlet* (1978) with DEREK JACOBI. This production was also performed in Elsinore and China – the first visit by a British company to the People's Republic. The company folded after its ARTS COUNCIL grant was withdrawn in 1981 because it was curtailing its touring programme, not long after its new artistic director Timothy West (b. 1934) had toured as Shylock and PETER O'TOOLE had barnstormed the country as a popular but critically slaughtered Macbeth. ADRIANA HUNTER

Timothy West, *A Moment Towards the End of the Play* (2001)

Provincetown Players A most important American pioneering and experimental theatre. In the summer of 1915 a group of Greenwich Village bohemians staged several of their own plays in Provincetown, Massachusetts. They were fired by the artistic zeal of George Cram ('Jig') Cook, whose life's mission was to bring the spirit of Athenian drama to the American theatre. In 1916 EUGENE O'NEILL submitted his play *Bound East for Cardiff*, and the group's activities soon focused on producing his work. O'Neill's plays brought the players enough success to move from Provincetown's Wharf Theater to take over a small playhouse at 139 Macdougal Street in Greenwich Village and present seasons in the city. Operations began on 3 November 1916.

Writers such as SUSAN GLASPELL, Edna St Vincent Millay, John Reed, EDNA FERBER, Edmund Wilson, THEODORE DREISER and PAUL GREEN had their plays presented by the group. Provincetown's goal was to provide 'American playwrights a chance to work out their ideas in freedom'. The Provincetown Players presented plays that challenged conventional theatre, morality and politics. Initially a united and cooperative group of artists, the anarchistic philosophy that originally linked Cook and his colleagues frayed their aesthetic bonds, and tensions mounted through the 1921 season. Feeling ill-used, Cook sailed for his spiritual homeland, Greece, with his wife Susan Glaspell, and soon died there. Provincetown resumed productions in 1923 under the 'triumvirate' of KENNETH MACGOWAN, ROBERT EDMOND JONES and O'Neill. They carried on for two more years, but their demand for thoroughly polished productions now conflicted with the other members' vision of continuous experimentation, so control was peacefully passed to James Light. The Players fitfully continued, but outlived the boom of the 1920s by only a month, presenting their last bill in November 1929. Almost all of O'Neill's early plays were first presented by Provincetown, but the entire history of the group is significant. Its influence reaches to the mainstream THEATER GUILD, the radical GROUP THEATER and beyond. Cook, Glaspell, Jones and O'Neill created a theatre whose idealism brought American theatre into the twentieth century by connecting it to the aims of Europe's AVANT-GARDE and providing a stage for a uniquely American drama to be created. THOMAS F. CONNOLLY

See also LITTLE THEATRE; RESIDENT THEATRE.

Helen Deutsch and Stella Hanau, *The Provincetown: A Story of the Theatre* (1931)

Robert K. Sarlos, *Jig Cook and the Provincetown Players* (1982)

Prowse, [John] Philip (b. Worcester, 29 Dec. 1937) Designer and director. He joined the GLASGOW CITIZENS' THEATRE as a designer (all-male *Hamlet*, 1970) and became one of its triumvirate of directors with Giles Havergal and ROBERT DAVID MACDONALD. Prowse made the most visible and distinctive contribution to the Citizens' international success, with his severely elegant, beautiful and allusive sets and costumes. His productions of familiar or forgotten Jacobean tragedies were remarkable, and other important work at Glasgow included his ambitious GENET trilogy and Macdonald's Proust adaptation *A Waste of Time*, de Sade, COWARD, WILDE and BRECHT. Prowse inspired the emergence of British stage designers as major interpretive artists in the 1980s. He has directed and designed for both the NATIONAL THEATRE and the ROYAL SHAKESPEARE COMPANY. TONY HOWARD

Michael Coveney, *The Citz* (1990)
Cordelia Oliver, *Magic in the Gorbals* (1999)

Pryce, Jonathan [John Price] (b. Holywell, Wales, 1 June 1947) Actor who studied at art college prior to the Royal Academy of Dramatic Art. At the LIVERPOOL EVERYMAN THEATRE he was part of a group of gifted actors under Alan Dossor's direction which included ANTONY SHER, Trevor Eve and Bernard Hill. Pryce joined RICHARD EYRE's company at NOTTINGHAM Playhouse and gave many outstanding performances, including Khlestakov in *The Government Inspector* and Gethin Price in TREVOR GRIFFITH's *Comedians* (1975; later OLD VIC and BROADWAY). This was the quintes-

sential Pryce performance: astonishingly energetic, acerbically witty, mercurial and dangerous, underpinned by a small boy's vulnerability and a strong layer of melancholy. His performance of Hamlet (ROYAL COURT, 1980), also with Eyre, exhibited these qualities to their utmost. He played the lead role in the musical *Miss Saigon* (1989 and, after controversy over his playing an Asian part, in New York, 1991). He stayed in musicals with Fagin in LIONEL BART's *Oliver!* (1996). With the exception of Macbeth (ROYAL SHAKESPEARE COMPANY, 1986) and *The Seagull* (West End, 1985), he appears to be a formidable actor in search of a formidable role sufficiently extreme and demanding to liberate his talent. RICHARD EYRE

pub theatre The British answer to CAFÉ THEATRE. Theatre in pubs developed from the 1960s on as part of the FRINGE, and sometimes as LUNCHTIME THEATRE. Each strand has its own culture: DRAG in pubs goes much further back and links up with the song-and-supper tradition of early MUSIC HALL; the annual Festival of Fools (1965–71) led by EWAN MACCOLL offered political entertainment that gave way to NEW VARIETY, which grew up on small stages in large pub rooms, vying for customer attention amid the hurly-burly of social drinking; and plays in pubs – mostly in London except at festival time – take place away from the carousing, in rooms converted into theatres above or at the side of pubs. The KING'S HEAD, the BUSH, the ORANGE TREE, the GATE, the Old Red Lion and others have established excellent reputations for programming new work and are a vital part of the country's theatre life. CHARLES LONDON

Public Theater The downtown Manhattan home of the NEW YORK SHAKESPEARE FESTIVAL, founded by JOSEPH PAPP. A leading force in American theatre producing during the 1970s and 1980s, the Public Theater opened in 1967 with the original version of the musical *Hair*. Other benchmark productions include Charles Gordone's *No Place to be Somebody* (1970), the first play by a black writer to win the Pulitzer Prize, and *A Chorus Line* (1975), which went on to become one of the longest-running musicals on Broadway, winning nine Tony awards and a Pulitzer Prize. A former public library dating back to the 1850s, the theatre building was converted under Papp to house multiple performance spaces, and in 1992 on Shakespeare's birthday it was renamed the Joseph Papp Public Theater. George C. Wolfe was appointed artistic director in 1993. ELLEN LAMPERT-GRÉAUX

publicity *see* MARKETING

publishing   *see* THEATRE PUBLISHING

Pulitzer Prize   The prize was one of several set up by the publisher Joseph Pulitzer (1847–1911). That for drama was to be awarded to 'the original American play performed in New York which shall best represent the educational value and power of the stage in raising the standards of good morals and good manners'. It was given first in 1918 to *Why Marry?* by Jesse Lynch Williams. While many of the winners have been truly distinguished and are revived with some regularity, time has suggested some probably did not merit the award. Although the prize remains prestigious, the televised Tony awards increasingly have become more important at the box office.   GERALD BORDMAN

See also AWARDS AND PRIZES.

Punch and Judy   *see* BOOTHS; PUPPET THEATRE

puppet theatre   The 'puppet' is defined as an inanimate object given life by human agency to project a dramatic idea or concept, and the term includes hand, string or marionette, shadow and rod types. There are also unique types, which are often combinations of the general techniques. Puppetry is concerned with the object as an actor as well as with representations of the human form; also with MASKS.

Over the centuries there has been a continuous borrowing between the puppet and the dramatic theatre, and the visual and plastic arts; it is also clear that the puppet has been a major influence on the theatre and the allied arts. At the beginning of the twentieth century, the dramatic theatre saw the need to revolt against naturalism. This gave rise to experiments in TOTAL THEATRE and a departure in the use of the puppet, which until then had imitated its live counterpart. Many of the outstanding personalities involved in early Soviet theatre show the influence of the puppet in their work, among them several of DIAGHILEV's collaborators, BENOIS, STRAVINSKY and COCTEAU. There were also the artists of the BAUHAUS, Alexandra Exter and followers of FUTURISM; their first performance, *A Marionette Ballet*, was performed in the puppet theatre of Vittorio Podrecca, whose Teatro dei Piccoli was to become a major influence on the marionette theatre in many countries. Then there were the writers ALFRED JARRY, GARCIA LORCA and MICHEL DE GHELDERODE and the director–designer EDWARD GORDON CRAIG, who dreamed of the actor becoming an *über*-marionette. His vast literary output included 12 small magazines devoted to the puppet theatre with the title *The Marionette*, published in 1918. In the 1920s ERWIN PISCATOR used huge manikins in *The Adventures of the Good Soldier Schweyk*. Unfortunately, the puppet theatre itself made little use of the many important experiments and discoveries made by these artists.

The year 1925 saw the formation of the British Model Theatre Guild, later to be renamed the British Puppet and Model Theatre Guild, with the support of such personalities as Craig, Sir BARRY JACKSON and G. K. Chesterton. The early work of the Guild was devoted to the juvenile drama or the TOY THEATRE, as well as hand puppets and the development of more sophisticated string puppets, which were used to perform mimes, ballads, folk dramas, Japanese *noh* plays and the works of MAETERLINCK, CHEKHOV, Shakespeare and others. Gradually much of the more sophisticated material was to be replaced by popular material more suited to the child and family audience. The international organization of puppeteers, UNIMA, was formed in 1929, the year the actor and painter SERGEI OBRAZTSOV was invited to form a State Puppet Theatre in Moscow. His practical and theoretical work influenced the nature and development of puppeteers and puppet theatres all over the world.

New and popular developments had taken place in imaginative productions for children (the puppet Muffin the Mule was the first star created by British television), yet some puppeteers and puppet companies continued to produce important work for the adult audience. Many found it difficult to survive with this work alone, and found increasing audiences in VARIETY and VAUDEVILLE theatres, CABARETS, and on luxury cruise liners. It also became clear that the puppet could be of great value and importance in the fields of education, therapy and diagnostics. From the 1960s, film and television made increasing demands on the skills of puppeteers, from simple hand puppets to the most sophisticated animatronic puppets. The rod puppet, more commonly found in Asia and the Far East as well as in areas of European folklore, was involved with greater frequency in the large-scale productions of Obraztsov and others; it was discovered that they were far better suited to the performance of more complex dramatic material. With the development of large-scale puppet theatres, multi-media production techniques using combinations of all types of puppets and actors, with or without masks, became a familiar feature of international puppet theatre festivals from the end of the 1950s, as did 'black theatre' and the ultra-violet light puppet specialities seen in PANTOMIMES, summer shows and variety theatres. Unrest in many parts of the world in the 1960s led to the increasing theatrical use of the puppet as a means of projecting political argument. In the United States, BREAD AND PUPPET THEATER involved large numbers of people with giant puppets in outdoor presentations of a highly political nature.

which were to be influential globally, particularly in 'hot-spots' such as Nicaragua. The development of large-scale subsidized theatres attracted large numbers of talented writers, designers and directors who were aware of the growing potential of the modern creative puppet theatre. Their ideas required the interpretive skills of imaginative actor/puppeteers, which led to the establishment of professional training faculties. Theatre academies in Czechoslovakia, the Soviet Union, Bulgaria, Hungary, Poland and Sweden created special departments for the training of puppeteers. In 1981 UNIMA, in collaboration with the French Ministry of Culture and the town of Charleville Mezières, opened the Institut de la Marionnette. The outstanding Czechoslovak company Drak produced some of the most important MULTIMEDIA puppet theatre productions of great international influence, with its talented director Josef Krofta in great demand. The much neglected shadow puppet theatre was given new life and meaning with a range of large-scale innovative productions in France, and also in Italy – particularly those by the company Gioco Vita, designed by the outstanding graphic artist and film maker Emanuele Luzzati. In the 1980s there was an increasing interest in the traditional comic puppet characters, led by Mr Punch. His popularity was seen during the celebrations that marked the 320th anniversary of his first appearance in London in 1662. The Japanese bunraku puppet theatre, with a history as old as that of Mr Punch, became a major influence as a result of performances in the WORLD THEATRE SEASONS in London and subsequently elsewhere. A number of of puppeteers and directors in the dramatic theatre used the bunraku technique with varying degrees of success, e.g. in *A Midsummer Night's Dream* (1981) at the ROYAL SHAKESPEARE COMPANY, *The Tempest* (1983) at the Phoenix Theatre, Leicester, and SONDHEIM's *Pacific Overtures* (1988) at the English National Opera. In fact, the dramatic theatre in search of a new dynamic continues to make extensive use of all types of puppets in dramas, musicals, and performances in non-theatrical venues and other situations (e.g. the original production of *Little Shop of Horrors* in 1982 featured an enormous plant which was operated by puppeteers). In the United States, where JULIE TAYMOR has been innovative in her use of puppets, the first International Festival of Puppet Theater was held in 1992 at the PUBLIC THEATER. However, the expansion of puppeteering has been threatened by financial restraints and, in many cases, a discrimination by funding bodies against children's and puppet theatres, which has led to the closure or severely restricted operation of important puppet theatre companies.

JOHN M. BLUNDALL

See also IMPERSONATION; SEASONAL THEATRE; WAXWORKS AND DUMMIES.

Bil Baird, *The Art of the Puppet* (1965)

John Bell, *Puppets, Masks and Performing Objects* (2000)

Cyril Beaumont, *Puppets and Puppetry* (1958)

Olive Blackham, *Shadow Puppets* (1960)

Gunter Bohmer, *Puppets through the Ages*, trans. Gerald Morice (1971)

Donald Keene, *Bunraku: The Art of the Japanese Puppet Theatre* (1965)

Paul McPharlin, *The Puppet Theatre in America* (1969)

George Speaight, *The History of the English Puppet Theatre* (1955)

S. Tillis, *Towards an Aesthetics of the Puppet* (1992)

Purcarete, Silviu (b. Bucharest, 6 April 1950) Director. After directing 14 productions between 1974 and 1988, mostly in Romania, but also in Israel and Germany, he began working at Romania's National Theatre of Craiova, where his productions, notably *Ubu Rex with Scenes from Macbeth* (1990), *Titus Andronicus* (1992) and *Phaedra* (1993), won him and the theatre international recognition. During this period he also directed seven puppet shows for children. He was appointed director of the Bulandra Theatre of Bucharest in 1992, where he produced *Il Teatro Comico* by Goldoni. In 1995 he was invited to direct two productions of *The Tempest*: the first in Oporto, the second at the NOTTINGHAM Playhouse, which subsequently toured internationally. In the same year he produced a large-scale reconstruction of the ancient Greek trilogy *Les Danaïdes*, involving a chorus of 100. The production was premièred at the AVIGNON FESTIVAL before playing in New York and throughout Britain, France and Germany, securing Purcarete's reputation as one of Europe's most innovative directors. Since 1996 he has been the artistic director of Théâtre de l'Union in Limoges, where he has produced his own version of *The Orestia* (1996), CHEKHOV's *Three Sisters* (1997) and Molière's *Don Juan* (1998). BRIAN ROBERTS

Q

Q Theatre

From 1924 to 1956 it was one of the London's leading LITTLE THEATRES, producing a play a week at its premises near Kew Bridge, west London, with WEST END actors, ready for possible transfer. Under the determined leadership of Jack (1902–56) and Beatie (1900–91) de Leon, Q not only played host to a number of distinguished performers, but gave a start to many, such as Dirk Bogarde, Joan Collins, VIVIEN LEIGH, Margaret Lockwood and ANTHONY QUAYLE. PETER BROOK directed his second production there, having been inspired by Shakespeare as a child at Q, and TONY RICHARDSON and WILLIAM GASKILL also directed at Q early in their careers. TERENCE RATTIGAN and WILLIAM DOUGLAS HOME had their first plays presented there. COLIN CHAMBERS

Kenneth Barrow, *On Q* (1992)

Quayle, [John] Anthony

(b. Ainsdale, Lancs, 7 Sept. 1913; d. London, 20 Oct. 1989) Actor and director. Starting out as a straight man in MUSIC HALL, Quayle went on to perform on stage, on television, and in more than 30 films. An accomplished Shakespearean actor in a wide variety of roles, he performed often and toured widely with the OLD VIC company during the 1930s. He served as director of the SHAKESPEARE MEMORIAL THEATRE at STRATFORD-UPON-AVON from 1948 to 1956, performing in or staging more than a score of productions and making the theatre into one of Britain's and Europe's leading stages. He was a notable Falstaff there in 1951 in a pioneering Shakespeare history cycle, which Quayle directed. A solid, unshowy style rarely bought him great acclaim but, alongside some notable performances in London (e.g. in *Chin-Chin*, 1960, or *Old World*, 1978), he continued to offer major classical theatre to the regions as actor (e.g. King Lear, 1978) and director (e.g. *The Rivals*, 1978) with the Prospect Theatre Company and, after its demise, by founding the Orbit (1981) and Compass (1984) companies. He was knighted in 1985, and his autobiography, *A Time to Speak*, appeared in 1990.
MARVIN CARLSON

Queensland Theatre Company

The first Australian theatre company to be established under an Act of Parliament, in 1970. It received the 'Royal' epithet in 1984. Its aims were similar to but wider than those of the MELBOURNE THEATRE COMPANY, although no reference was made to the promotion of Australian works. Unlike the MTC, however, the company decided from the beginning that it would serve not just Brisbane and the metropolitan area, but the whole state of Queensland. It ran a THEATRE IN EDUCATION company until 1986, when funding from the Australia Council ceased. Like the MTC, it had a long-serving artistic director whose background was in British theatre – Alan Edwards, who finally stepped down in 1988. However, partly as a reflection of the deeply conservative political environment in Queensland, the QTC's programming over many years mostly avoided plays with any radical political content. With the 1990s, a change occurred, and the dropping of the 'Royal' epithet coincided with a change in the artistic direction of the company under successive directors Aubrey Mellor, Robyn Nevin and the playwright MICHAEL GOW. An annual production of a play by a Queensland playwright and the establishment of the George Landen Dann Award raised the profile of the state's dramatists and indicated a commitment to new Australian work, while continuing with a repertoire that included contemporary American and British drama, and classics from the European theatre.   MICHAEL MORLEY

queer theatre   Term for transgressive theatre that arose OFF-OFF-BROADWAY in the 1960s. It was related to BURLESQUE and VAUDEVILLE and went beyond, though it arose from, GAY and LESBIAN theatre. In its comic critique of life and ideology as meaningless and mendacious, it focused its energy in the aesthetic, in the language (verbal and visual) of PERFORMANCE. Its poet laureate was Charles Ludlam, an actor with The Play-House of the Ridiculous, founded in 1965 by director John Vaccaro and writer Ronald Tavel. In 1967 Ludlam founded the THEATRE OF THE RIDICULOUS, where he acted and directed in his own plays. Other notable pioneers were Hot Peaches. The camp and kitsch spirit of queer theatre spread wider in the 1980s and 1990s when 'trash' became acceptable and fashionable.   CHARLES LONDON

See also GAY THEATRE; LESBIAN THEATRE.

S. Brecht, *Queer Theatre* (1978)

S. Samuels, ed., *Ridiculous Theatre: Scourge of Human Folly – The Essays and Opinions of Charles Ludlam* (1992)

Queneau, Raymond   (b. Le Havre, France, 21 Feb. 1903; d. Paris, 25 Oct. 1976)   Poet and novelist who used language in an audacious and comical way. His novel *Zazie dans le Métro* (*Zazie in the Underground*, 1959) was adapted for the stage by Olivier Hussenot and for the screen by Louis Malle. *Loin du Rueil* ('Far from Rueil', 1961) was staged by VILAR.
WENDY SCOTT

Questors Theatre   An AMATEUR THEATRE group in Ealing, west London, founded in 1929. In 1933 it established its first theatre in what had been a Catholic chapel of temporary construction. In 1952, after purchase of the site, research and planning started for a new theatre to be built in replacement of the old and inadequate building. At a time when there was much discussion as to what form of theatre building best met contemporary needs, a decision was made to build an adaptable playhouse in order to explore various actor–audience relationships, from proscenium stage, with forestage, through thrust stage to in-the-round. The ancillary buildings were put up first, largely by the members themselves, and the new playhouse was opened in 1964, with a seating capacity of around 350 varying in accordance with the stage form. The design has had some influence on the planning of other new theatres, as was the expressed hope.

The Questors established a considerable reputation, not only for adventurous and experimental work, but particularly for the production of new plays. After the Second World War it became policy to include at least one new play in every season's programme; the silver jubilee in 1954/5 was celebrated by a season entirely of new plays, and 1960 saw the first of a series of annual Festivals of New Plays (three new plays presented in repertoire with nightly discussions with the audience and usually with the author), which continued for 18 years, thus creating a specific market for new playwrights. Writers whose plays have been premièred by the Questors include RODNEY ACKLAND (e.g. *The Dark River*), JAMES SAUNDERS (e.g. *Next Time I'll Sing to You*) and Dannie Abse (b. 1923, e.g. *The House of Cowards*). In 1986 a new play competition restricted to full-time students was organized, both the winning play and the runner up receiving production.

A number of International Amateur Theatre Weeks have been held, in which three selected foreign companies are invited to perform their plays in repertoire and share a week of theatre-making with their hosts. Leading companies from 12 countries have visited, and Questors companies have visited France, Germany, Japan, Sweden and the United States in return.

Since 1947 The Questors have run a two-year training course for amateur actors (the 'Student Group'); groups for children and young people from age five upwards have weekly practical drama work; and Questors companies have performed in local schools. A smaller, studio theatre has been established with a regular programme of more experimental work.   ALFRED EMMET
See also LITTLE THEATRE GUILD OF GREAT BRITAIN.

G. Evans, ed, *A Few Drops of Water: The Story of the Questors Theatre, 1929–1989* (1989)

Quilley, Dennis [Clifford]   (b. London, 26 Dec. 1927)   Actor. He began his career at the BIRMINGHAM REPERTORY THEATRE which he joined, aged 17, as an acting assistant stage manager. He was an early member of the NATIONAL THEATRE Company at the OLD VIC, where he played a remarkable range of parts from Macbeth (1973) and Jamie in *Long Day's Journey Into Night* (1971), to a memorably hilarious Hildy Johnson in *The Front Page* (1972). He has also worked extensively in musicals, creating, among many other things, the role of Sweeney Todd in the original (1980) London production of STEPHEN SONDHEIM's melodrama, a work to which he returned at the National Theatre in 1993. One of his most remarkable performances was in PETER NICHOLS' 1976 *Privates on Parade*, in which his musical comedy skills were dazzlingly displayed alongside a moving evocation of isolation and pain. He repeated this performance on film. In 1995 he played Falstaff in *The Merry Wives of Windsor* at the National Theatre, and was a member of the NT's award-winning 1999 ensemble. His career has demonstrated an exemplary, and increasingly rare, commitment to acquiring and using all the skills to which an actor can aspire; there are few who have covered so much ground with such distinction.   GENISTA MCINTOSH

Quintero, José [Benjamin]   (b. Panama City, 15 Oct. 1924; d. New York, 26 Feb. 1999)   Director, noted for his focus on O'NEILL. He was an actor's director who concentrated on realizing the play as a whole rather than on imposing his particular vision of it. After directing a season at the Woodstock, New York, Summer Theater (1949), he co-founded the CIRCLE IN THE SQUARE in 1951. He attracted critical recognition for his 1952 staging of WILLIAMS' *Summer and Smoke*, and in 1956 began the renewal of interest in O'Neill with his historic revival of *The Iceman Cometh* and the American première of *Long Day's Journey into Night*, both with JASON ROBARDS. Other O'Neill productions include *Desire under the Elms* (1962), *Strange Interlude* (1963), *Hughie* and *Marco Millions* (1964) *More Stately Mansions* (1967), *A Moon for the Misbegotten* (1973), *Anna Christie* and *A Touch of the Poet* (1977) and *Welded* (1981). Among his other successful productions are BEHAN's *The Quare Fellow* (1958) and *The Hostage* (1962). Quintero also directed for film, radio and television. His autobiography is called *If You Don't Dance, They Beat You* (1972).   THOMAS F. CONNOLLY

Edwin J. McDonough, *Quintero Directs O'Neill* (1991)

Quinton, Everett   *see* GAY THEATRE; THEATRE OF THE RIDICULOUS

R

Rabb, Ellis (b. Memphis, Tenn., 20 June 1930; d. Memphis, Tenn., 11 June 1998) Actor and director. Founder in 1960 and artistic director of the Association of Producing Artists, a group which moved from Bermuda to Princeton, Milwaukee, New York, Ann Arbor and back to New York, and for which he appeared in and/or directed dozens of works. In 1964 the APA merged with the PHOENIX THEATER; it disbanded in 1970. Rabb worked to sustain repertory theatre in the United States and won several awards for his directing, including *The Royal Family* (1975). He was married for a time to actress ROSEMARY HARRIS. DAVID BARBOUR

Rabe, David [William] (b. Dubuque, Iowa, 10 March 1940) Playwright. A Vietnam veteran, Rabe is best known for three plays – *The Basic Training of Pavlo Hummel* (1971), *Sticks and Bones* (1971) and *Streamers* (1976) – that examine the lethal shortcomings of American society which that war revealed. In *Hurlyburly* (1984), set in Hollywood, Rabe continued his exploration of male rivalry, corruption and violence. Other plays include *Goose and Tomtom* (1982), *Those the River Keeps* (1991), a prequel to *Hurlyburly*, and *A Question of Mercy* (1998). M. ELIZABETH OSBORN

P. Kolm, *David Rabe: A Stage History* (1988)

RADA *see* DRAMA SCHOOLS

radical theatre *see* POLITICAL THEATRE

Radio City Music Hall This 1932 Art Deco edifice with a seating capacity of 6,200 struck on a successful formula for providing family entertainment, by combining film with a VAUDEVILLE stage show during the heyday of cinema when there was a high and rapid turnover of audiences to fill its vast auditorium. Featuring a tap-dancing ensemble called the Rockettes, the stage shows played up to four times daily, with technical facilities like a motorized turntable and elevated sections making it ideal for large-scale spectaculars. Since being fully restored under the auspices of the Landmark Preservation Commission in 1979, the theatre has continued to be used for concerts and recitals by major international stars. HELEN RAPPAPORT

C. Francisco, *The Radio City Music Hall: An Affectionate History of the World's Greatest Theater* (1979)

radio drama When sound broadcasting was introduced as a public communication channel after the First World War, the purveying of drama was one of its many functions. Indeed, radio drama was to overtake the theatre in quite a few countries, in terms of both output and audience figures. By 1930 the BBC was putting on twice as many plays as the London stage. Half a century later, its annual production of new plays was somewhere in the region of 600.

Radio was the first broadcast medium to bring drama into one's sitting room; so it is not surprising that it took some time to find its voice. It all began with a transmission by the British Broadcasting Company, on 16 February 1923, of three different scenes from Shakespeare plays. Theatre plays have figured in the radio repertoire ever since, in Britain and elsewhere. But it was soon realized that radio also needed a new kind of drama specially written for the medium. Because it lacks any visual element, radio drama has been defined as a 'theatre for the blind'. Richard Hughes's *A Comedy of Danger*, Britain's, and perhaps the world's, first original radio play, broadcast on 15 January 1924, exploited this aspect in a tale of people trapped in a mine shaft in total darkness. Later plays such as MAC-NEICE's *The Dark Tower* (1946), THOMAS's *Under Milk Wood* (1954), PINTER's *A Slight Ache* (1959) and Barry Bermange's *No Quarter* (1962) – to mention but a few – have all used the theme of blindness. It is true that sightlessness imposes certain constraints on radio drama. Any character who fails to speak for a while vanishes from the mind's eye. A prolonged general silence might mean the end of the programme rather than a significant pause. Too large a number of speakers may well confuse the listener. Gestural communication does not read. But the listener's 'blindness' is not just a handicap. It is often said that radio drama paradoxically gives us the best pictures. It appeals to the imagination, conjures up different images in each listener's head and thus enjoys the advantages of multivalence and fluidity. It has the greatest freedom in the handling of time and space. A purely aural medium, it gives enormous value to the actor's vocal expressiveness, which has to convey character, intention and feeling without any facial or gestural signals. Radio drama is particularly well suited to rendering inner processes: it easily accommodates the monologue. However, to conclude from this – as some critics have done – that radio drama naturally inclines towards an ABSURDIST view of life is itself an absurdity.

Besides the human voice, sound effects – recorded or produced on the spot, naturalistic, suggestive or symbolic – create place, action and atmosphere. Music, too, can play a role as mood setter or bridge between scenes. Actually, at certain periods in the history of radio drama, effects and music have been used to excess. With its emphasis on dialogue, radio drama is a writer's medium. Its technology being relatively inexpensive (at least compared to film and television), it is a useful launching pad for new playwrights; JOHN MORTIMER, Harold Pinter and TOM STOPPARD all wrote for radio in the early parts of their careers. For established playwrights, too, radio offers a stimulating challenge though only relatively modest fees. After the success of *Waiting for Godot*, BECKETT showed his grasp of the sound medium with *All that Fall* (1957) and *Embers* (1958).

Technological change was bound to affect the nature of radio drama. The dramatic control panel, introduced in 1928, made a multi-studio technique possible; the voices of actors working from several studios with different acoustics could be modulated and combined. Concepts like 'fades' and 'superimpositions' were borrowed from the cinema. Later, filters served to modify microphone characteristics, providing such effects as telephone conversations. A major innovation pion-

eered in Germany and quickly adopted everywhere after the end of the Second World War was the audio tape recorder. Drama had gone out live before; now it became normal to pre-record it. In such a recording there was no longer any need to run a play through from start to finish in one go; it became possible to take individual scenes and then edit them together, just as in film-making. The highly portable tape recorder can also be taken outside to record a play, or parts of it, on location (though this is by no means universal practice).

The institutional framework of broadcasting cannot fail to have a bearing on the type of drama produced or indeed whether any drama is produced at all. In the United States, radio has been a commercial enterprise from the start. By 1927 two large networks, NBC and CBS, completely dominated the hundreds of local radio stations. As more and more programmes were commercially sponsored, it became imperative to maximize audiences. Not surprisingly, controversy and experimentation were frowned upon. Mystery and detective series were popular. But the staple fare of US radio drama was the family serial – intellectually untaxing, but involving. Because many of these were sponsored by soap manufacturers in the early days, they came to be known as soap operas. By 1938 there were as many as 38 of these on the air, aimed chiefly at women listeners housebound during the daytime. But throughout the 1930s competition between the networks produced what has hyperbolically been called the Golden Age of Radio Drama in America. It was to last barely a decade and a half. 'Columbia Workshop' (CBS) created a stir with MACLEISH's verse play, *The Fall of the City* in 1937 – a forecast of fascist aggression to come. Several series by the writer–producer Norman Corwin were the CBS drama flagship; his rival at NBC was Arch Oboler. Perhaps the most talented person in American radio drama was ORSON WELLES. His company was given a regular spot on CBS as 'Mercury Theater on the Air'. When he directed H. G. Wells's *The War of the Worlds* for Hallowe'en 1938, his reportage style of presenting a Martian invasion was so convincing that it triggered off a mass panic: people rushed off in their cars to escape instant destruction; telephone switchboards were flooded. Welles's knowledge of radio technique rubbed off on his subsequent film work, notably *Citizen Kane*. With the coming of television, high-quality drama virtually disappeared from American radio.

In the United Kingdom, on the other hand, the BBC has represented public service broadcasting and has built up a solid tradition of drama. (The contribution to drama of Independent Local Radio, set up in 1973, has been negligible.) A good many BBC plays have been avowedly popular, from the detective series *Dick Barton – Special Agent*, which by 1947 had some 15 million listeners, to that longest-running of all family serials, *The Archers*. By the end of the century this rural saga was in its fifth decade and enjoyed a devoted following, many listeners believing in the characters with astonishing literal-mindedness. Relieved of the pressure of ratings, the BBC has been able to appeal to a wide spectrum of tastes, with the Third Programme (Radio 3 since 1970) explicitly featuring works with a minority appeal. Not all BBC plays have actually come out of the Drama Department. From 1933 onwards, Features rivalled it in drama output for some 30 years. Thus *Christopher Columbus* (1942), one of the most successful plays by the prolific poet-producer Louis MacNeice, was classed as a feature. So was Dylan Thomas's *Under Milk Wood*. This investigation of a non-existent small Welsh seaside town was a work of the imagination, though in quasi-documentary guise. Feature or drama, it turned out to be probably the most acclaimed radio play of all time – repeated three times within three months of the original broadcast, transmitted overseas six times in the following year and put out again many more times in subsequent years. It quickly appeared on the market as a book and a record. When adapted for the stage, television and the cinema, it obstinately remained what Thomas had called it – a 'play for voices'. Over the years the BBC has kept up a remarkable volume of excellent productions, with writers like Henry Reed, GILES COOPER, JAMES SAUNDERS, Don Howarth, BILL NAUGHTON, Fay Weldon and a host of others supplying scripts of real quality. Television has long since cut into the audience figures of the 1940s and 1950s, but a weekday afternoon play will still draw hundreds of thousands of listeners.

Interest in radio drama has been worldwide. Italy's commitment was demonstrated by the establishment in 1948 of the international Prix Italia for the year's best radio play. Germany's Radio Drama Prize of the War Blinded was set up in 1951 for the best German-language offering of the year. Radio drama has been particularly important in postwar Germany. The broadcast on NWDR of BORCHERT's *Draussen vor der Tür* (*The Man Outside*, 1947) was a significant event in the country's facing up to its recent past. The leading radio playwright of the 1950s and 1960s was the poet Günter Eich, but many other writers – Ilse Aichinger and Wolfgang Hildesheimer among them – have also contributed to radio drama. Indeed, a great many countries from the Czech Republic to Canada, from Switzerland to Japan, have all laboured to built up a vast, though unfortunately to the reader mostly inaccessible, corpus

of plays for broadcasting. It is true that television has decimated the audience for radio drama. But the latter continues to be an interesting, if insufficiently regarded and remunerated, form of playwriting – different in form from, but closely affiliated to, other forms of drama and literature in general.

GEORGE BRANDT

Erik Barnouw, *A History of Broadcasting in the United States*, 3 vols (1966–70)

Asa Briggs, *A History of Broadcasting in the United Kingdom*, 4 vols (1961–79)

John Drakakis, ed., *British Radio Drama* (1981)

Martin Grams, *Radio Drama: A Comprehensive Chronicle of American Network Programs 1932–1962* (2000)

Peter Lewis, ed., *Radio Drama* (1981)

Donald McWhinnie, *The Art of Radio* (196)

Radlov, Sergei [Ernestovich] (b. St Petersburg, Russia, 18 July 1892; d. Riga, 27 October, 1958) Director. Trained with MEYERHOLD (1913–17) before staging a range of EXPRESSIONIST productions in Leningrad (1923–7) and experimenting with multiple and simultaneous staging at his own Theatre of Popular Comedy (1920–2). Staged a notable production of *King Lear*, starring SOLOMON MIKHOELS, in 1935.

NICK WORRALL

Radzinsky, Edvard [Stanislavovich] (b. Moscow, 23 September 1936) Playwright. His plays range stylistically from the lyrical to the grotesque and from history and philosophy to farce; a recurring theme is the loneliness of women and the egotism of men. Especially associated with the director ANATOLI EFROS and the actress Tatyana Doronina, his plays have been widely staged abroad. They include *104 stranitsy pro lyubov'* (*104 Pages about Love*, 1964), *Obolstitel' Kolobashkin* (*The Seducer Kolobashkin*, 1968), *Besedy s Sokratom* (*Conversations with Socrates*, 1980) and *Ona, v otsutstviy lyubvi i smerti* (*She, in the Absence of Love and Death*, 1980). NICK WORRALL

Rainer, Yvonne (b. San Francisco, 24 Nov. 1934) Dancer and film-maker. She trained with MARTHA GRAHAM and then with Anna Halprin. In 1962 she formed the JUDSON Dance Theater with Steve Paxton and Ruth Emerson. A short trio with Steve Paxton and David Gordon, *Trio A*, (1966), heralded the emergence of postmodern dance. The extended version, *The Mind is a Muscle* (1968), consolidated the corporeal democracy, irony and juxtaposition that marked out her approach. Both versions questioned existing ideas of theatricality in dance and established a precedent for a postmodern approach to dance. She was part of the renowned improvisation COLLECTIVE, Grand Union, from 1970 to 1971. In the 1970s she gave up dancing to concentrate on film-making. She returned to dancing in 1999 with a reconstruction of *Trio A* at Judson Memorial Church, three decades after the original. She published *Work 1961–73* in 1974, and in 1999 a book of essays and interviews, *A Woman Who . . .* appeared.

MICHAEL HUXLEY

See also CHOREOGRAPHY; DANCE.

Rambert, Marie [Cyvia Rambam, later Miriam Ramberg] (b. Warsaw, 20 Feb. 1888; d. London, 12 June 1982) Choreographer and teacher. After working with EMILE JAQUES-DALCROZE, the creator of eurhythmics, and The Ballets Russes she moved to Britain, where in 1918 she married the playwright ASHLEY DUKES. She founded a ballet school in London in 1920 and from the mid-1920s presented new and classical ballets through small companies which in 1936 crystallized as the Ballet Rambert. She developed young choreographers and dancers such as FREDERICK ASHTON and Antony Tudor, and encouraged the collaboration in DANCE of painters and musicians as DIAGHILEV had done. She also worked at the OLD VIC and with TERENCE GRAY at the CAMBRIDGE FESTIVAL THEATRE. In the 1960s her company embraced modern dance and renewed itself as a driving force of the contemporary scene. Her influence spread beyond the dance world to theatre, in MOVEMENT teaching and CHOREOGRAPHY. She was created a dame in 1962 and her autobiography, *Quicksilver*, appeared in 1972. CHARLES LONDON

Rame, Franca (b. Milan, 18 July 1929) Actress and playwright. Her most important contribution to contemporary theatre is the creation of strong comic and tragic parts for women which challenge and help to redress the balance in a Western theatre dominated by male roles. Coming from a long-established family of actors, Rame became a vital presence – and collaborator – in the works of her husband DARIO FO. In 1977 she began her own career as playwright with *Tutta casa, letto e chiesa* ('She is all home, bed and church'), a series of monologues since translated and performed in many languages (in English, as *One Woman Plays*, NATIONAL THEATRE, 1981), which was followed by *Parti femminili* (*Female Parts*, 1988) and, with Fo, *Coppia aperta, quasi spalancata* ('The open couple', 1991).

FIRENZA GUIDI

David L. Hirst, *Dario Fo and Franca Rame* (1989)

Ramsay, Peggy [Margaret Francesca Venniker] (b. Molong, Australia, 27 May 1908; d. London, 4 Sept. 1991) The outstanding play agent in Britain after the Second World War. Brought up in South Africa, she came to England in 1929 and toured with an opera company before becoming an actress. She read scripts for various managements and briefly ran the Q THEATRE in west London before becoming an agent in 1954. While representing AVANT-GARDE writers from abroad like IONESCO and ADAMOV, her first home-grown discovery was ROBERT BOLT, who became internationally renowned with *A Man for All Seasons* (1960). She nurtured outsiders like DAVID MERCER and, famously, JOE ORTON as well as writers in their youth, taking on CHRISTOPHER HAMPTON when he was 20 and STEPHEN POLIAKOFF when he was 16. Her remarkably catholic range of clients included the major names of their time, from ALAN AYCKBOURN, EDWARD BOND and CARYL CHURCHILL to DAVID HARE and WILLY RUSSELL. A larger-than-life figure who helped change the status of playwrights in the theatre, she was known for her formidable candour and her outrageous indiscretions, but above all for her commitment to talent. She figured in several plays, either as the basis for a character or as herself, most notably in ALAN PLATER's *Peggy For You*. After her death, the Peggy Ramsay Foundation was established by her estate in order to help playwrights.

COLIN CHAMBERS

Simon Callow, *Love is Where it Falls* (1999)
Colin Chambers, *Peggy: The Life of Margaret Ramsay, Play Agent* (1997)

Rand, Sally [Helen (Hazel) Gould Beck] (b. Elkton, Miss., 3 April 1904; d. Glendora, Cal., 30 Aug. 1979) Dancer. She had worked her way through the grind of the showgirl chorus, VAUDEVILLE and CIRCUS, as well as working as a 'cigarette girl' and artist's model and playing bit parts in movies, before she changed her name and hit on her winning crowd-puller of dancing naked (or so the audience thought – she usually wore a body stocking) with ostrich plumes in Chicago nightclubs in the early 1930s. At the 1933 World's Fair she scandalized the public with her famous fan dance, for which she used two seven-foot pink fans; despite the tasteful accompaniment of music by Debussy and Chopin, she soon found herself in court charged with performing an act that was 'degrading to public morals'. But, as she herself later put it, 'I haven't been out of work since the day I took my pants off,' and indeed, the coy titillation of her act made Rand an overnight star – a position she managed to hold on to for the next 30 years. During this time she opened a nude show of her own in Dallas in 1936 as well as 'Sally Rand's Nude Ranch' at the 1939 Golden Gate Expo. She later developed another act involving the use of a 60-inch see-through plastic bubble, and she was still performing her act into her sixties. HELEN RAPPAPORT

Rattigan, Terence [Mervyn] (b. London, 9 June 1911; d. Hamilton, Bermuda, 30 Nov. 1977) Playwright. *French Without Tears* (1936), an elegant, well-observed comedy about a group of diplomats learning French, won Rattigan fame and fortune, with over 1,000 performances. *After the Dance* (1939) was critically respected, though commercially unsuccessful. After a disastrous attempt at political satire, he re-established himself with the moving semi-autobiographical *Flare Path* (1942) about servicemen and their partners. After two more light comedies (*While the Sun Shines*, 1944, outran his prewar hit), Rattigan began to win acclaim as a serious writer and came to dominate the West End. *The Winslow Boy* (1946) was based on the trial of a young boy wrongly accused of stealing a postal order; in 1948 Rattigan revived the one-act play with *Playbill*, comprising the theatrical farce *Harlequinade* and *The Browning Version*, depicting the retirement of a schoolmaster and his momentary redemption through a schoolboy's gift. Neither *Adventure Story* (1949), about Alexander the Great, nor *Who is Sylvia?* (1950), a lightweight bachelor farce, was a hit, and Rattigan's attacks on the 'play of ideas' lost him favour with critics. But he recovered to write perhaps his best play, *The Deep Blue Sea* (1952). With bleak optimism, revealing an affinity with late IBSEN, it tells of a woman whose suicide attempt leads to her abandonment by husband and lover. After the superficial *Sleeping Prince* (1953), Rattigan wrote *Separate Tables* (1954), another double bill, set in a boarding house. *Table by the Window* portrays the attempted reconciliation of a woman with her ex-husband, a disgraced Labour MP; *Table Number Seven* follows the events after an elderly resident, the 'Major', is fined for groping women in a cinema, and is exposed as a charlatan; the play is a humane and liberal plea for tolerance.

By 1956, Rattigan's success and outspoken belief in craft and character, expressed in the prefaces to his plays, in which he invoked 'Aunt Edna' as the barometer of ordinary taste, made him a target for the new generation of playwrights. Subsequent plays – *Variation on a Theme* (1958), *Ross* (1960), *Man and Boy* (1963), *Bequest to the Nation* (1970) – were marked more by sentiment than passion, and he briefly gave up the theatre for lucrative film work. In the 1970s revivals were admired by new audiences, who saw that he understood the contradictions and limitations of his characters' lifestyles. With the acclaimed *In Praise of Love* (1973) he regained his former emotional complexity. By the time of his death, with *Cause Célèbre* (1977) still running, his writing was once again appreciated for its aching compassion and bleak realism, with much discussion about the 'gay' sensibility of his work. Rattigan was knighted in 1971. DAN REBELLATO

Michael Darlow, *Terence Rattigan: The Man and His Work* (2000)
Geoffrey Wansell, *Terence Rattigan* (1995)
B. A. Young, *The Rattigan Version: Sir Terence Rattigan and the Theatre of Character* (1986)

Ravenhill, Mark (b. Cuckfield, W. Sussex, 7 June 1966) Playwright. He came to prominence with *Shopping and Fucking* (1996), populated by mainly gay, clubbing, E-taking twentysomethings. Its taut, witty, ironized dialogue and its unusual sexual explicitness propelled it from two runs at the ROYAL COURT Theatre Upstairs into a national tour, a WEST END run and finally a transfer to NEW YORK. Despite the play's flamboyant breaking of taboos, it finally refuses to endorse this life, and is rather a play about the collapse of a collective social consciousness, trying to explore what space there may be for friendship and a genuine sense of community in a fragmented, market-driven, postmodern culture. After a reworking of the Faust myth, in *Faust (Faust is Dead)* and a contribution to the group-written *Sleeping Around* (both in 1997), he scored another success with *Handbag* (1998), a witty meditation on *The Importance of Being Earnest*, intertwining the play with contemporary themes around gay sexuality and parenting. *Some Explicit Polaroids* (1999) was a more consciously political play, tracing the effects of globalization on personal relationships and political aspirations. DAN REBELLATO

Aleks Sierz, *In-Yer-Face Theatre: British Drama Today* (2001)
Michelene Wandor, *Post-war British Drama: Looking Back in Gender* (2001)

Rawlings, Margaret (b. Osaka, Japan, 5 June 1906; d. Wendover, Bucks, 19 May 1996) Actress. She began her career in 1927 touring SHAW with the Macdona Players, and returned to them in the 1930s to tour more of his work. She appeared at the innovative GATE THEATRE (e.g. as a highly sensual Salome in WILDE's play, 1931) and established a reputation for intense, passionate acting in a series of roles on both sides of the Atlantic that spanned 60 years, such as Helen in *The Trojan Women* (1937), Vittoria Corombona in *The White Devil* (1947), *Lady Macbeth* (1950), *Phèdre* (1957 and 1963) and Jocasta in *Oedipus the King* (1964). CHARLES LONDON

Rayson, Hannie (b. Melbourne, 13 March 1959) Playwright. Co-founder of, and actor and writer with, Theatre Works. Her experience in group projects there and at the Mill Theatre, Geelong, shows to good effect in her early work (e.g. *Please Return to Sender*, 1980; *Mary*, 1981). This is combined with a sharp eye for male–female relationships; *Room to Move* (1985) is a cleverly constructed, satirical look at the domestic battlefield, while her best-known work, *Hotel Sorrento* (1990; also filmed), depicts the familial rivalries of three sisters. Other plays include *Falling from Grace* (1994). MICHAEL MORLEY

Razumovskaya, Lyudmila [Nikolayena] (b. Riga, Latvia, 2 Feb. 1948) Playwright, trained as an actor and director. Since her first produced play, *Poor Yelena Sergeyevna*, was staged in Tallinn in 1981 she has been prolific and popular across mainland Europe. Her rich and complex yet accessible plays include *Under the Same Roof, Dream of the Old House, The Garden without Soil, My Sister, The Mermaid, To Be Back Home ... !* (1989), *The End of the Eighties* (1994) and *French Passions in a Dacha near Moscow*. VERA GOTTLIEB

Rea, Stephen (b. Belfast, 31 Oct. 1949) Actor. He started his career with the Young Abbey in DUBLIN in the 1960s and then in the 1970s moved to Britain, where he made a name for himself in regional theatres, at the ROYAL COURT and with PETER HALL at the new NATIONAL THEATRE on London's South Bank. Rea became frustrated with the experience of living outside his home culture and approached BRIAN FRIEL, whom he had met while appearing in Friel's play *The Freedom of the City* at the Royal Court in 1973, about the possibility of touring a play around Ireland. The result was the FIELD DAY THEATRE COMPANY and the 1980 world première of Friel's *Translations* in Derry, in which Rea played the role of Owen. He continued as one of the core members of Field Day throughout its active life in the 1980s, appearing in leading parts in many of its productions and directing several others. He achieved international recognition as a film actor in 1992 in *The Crying Game* and enjoys a high-profile career in television and film. KAREN FRICKER

realism *see* DRAMATIC THEORY; MODERNISM

Reaney, James [Crerar] (b. South Easthope, Ont., 1 Sept. 1926) Playwright and poet. After winning two Governor-General Awards for Poetry, in 1949 and 1958, Reaney turned to drama. The best of the plays he wrote in the 1960s is *Colours in the Dark* (1967), in which multiple incidents and rapid mood changes are linked by means of a group of striking poems to dramatize aspects of innocence and experience. Reaney is best known for a trilogy based on the 1880 murder of a notorious south-western Ontario family, the Donnellys. The first part, *Sticks and Stones* (1973), is the strong-est; the others, *The St Nicholas Hotel* (1974) and *Handcuffs* (1975), too often allow the key figures of the plays to be submerged in a welter of incidents and historical trivia. None of Reaney's later plays approaches the strength of his best work. His libretti include *Crazy to Kill* (1988) and *Serinette* (1990). EUGENE BENSON

recording and researching theatre

Theatre on the page
The first English playwright to owe a fair proportion of his wealth to the publication rather than the performance of his plays was the dogged HENRY ARTHUR JONES. The four-volume edition of *Representative Plays* (1925), released simultaneously on both sides of the Atlantic, was the culmination of his careful cultivation of publishers. It was also an irascible man's bid to assert the authority of the literary drama over the tawdry theatre: 'twin arts', as he called them in his introduction to *The Shadow of Henry Irving* (1931), in 'eternal opposition'. Jones had less cause for grievance than many finer playwrights, e.g. than Webster after the failure of *The White Devil* or CHEKHOV after the first performance of *The Seagull*. Great plays fouled by actors have been a regular feature of the theatrical calendar, though not as common as second-rate plays lifted to brief glory by their treatment in the theatre, and it is appropriate to begin an account of the recording and researching of theatre with an acknowledgement of the contribution made by publishers of books. We have moved a long way since Sir Thomas Bodley, at the height of the greatest period of English drama, wrote to the keeper of his library: 'Haply some plays may be worth the keeping: but hardly one in forty.'

Playwrights have been the chief, but by no means the sole, beneficiaries of developments in twentieth-century THEATRE PUBLISHING. The awakening of the Western world to the cultural significance of PERFORMANCE was accelerated by Frazer's *The Golden Bough* (1890–1915) and by the impact of Freud's parading of the subconscious. Developments in theatrical biography are an indicator of the distance travelled. Recent outstanding studies of, among many others, Susannah Cibber, Talma, Harriet Smithson, Shchepkin, Lemaître, Macready, Rachel, TREE and DUSE have replaced mere theatrical anecdote with cultural history. Actors may reflect, represent or even lead the society they gratify. Repressive regimes, whether in the Greece of the colonels, 'nationalist' South Africa or strife-torn Nigeria, have found it necessary to silence actors. Nazis murdered Hans Otto; Stalinists murdered Zinaida Raikh; and in the United States one actor killed a president and another became president. One political historian has already likened the misguided patriotism of Ronald Reagan to that of John Wilkes Booth, but the two men represent, more overtly, the polar contrast of the actor as rebel/outsider and the actor as social success. Sensitive to the polarity, modern biographers have claimed for their subjects a rightful place as representatives of, or challengers to, the taste of the time. The craft (or art?) of acting has come under new scrutiny, too. STANISLAVSKY's work, however obscured by the unfortunate history of its translation into English, remains seminal. The quest is for a vocabulary that will be analytical and accurate rather than emotional and approximate. The interest in semiotics, in particular, has drawn attention to the ways in which the actor's body materializes stage discourse. GROTOWSKI's early work was, in part, a search for a reliable semiotic discipline, lacking the political impetus of BRECHT's *gestus*, but striding ahead of MEYERHOLD's generative experiments. It is hard to resist an argument that the VOICE has lost its vaunted primacy in the complex visual theatre of the twentieth century.

Advances in the recording of theatre history have augmented the call for a sharpening of theatrical vocabulary. Shakespeare has been pushed predictably into the centre by the pioneering work of scholars like G. C. D. Odell and A. C. Sprague. The outcome has been a prompt-book industry, with its own reference work in C. H. Shattuck's *The Shakespeare Prompt-books* (1965). The painstaking reconstruction of historical performances offers reliable rewards to the patient reader, but attempts to stage such reconstructions suffer from the impossibility of reconstructing an audience. SAM WANAMAKER's brave endeavour to rebuild Shakespeare's GLOBE already feels that pinch. This is not to downgrade the value of prompt-books, only to caution against asking of them more than they can provide. The diligence of scholars may have discovered sufficient detail of a 'moving diorama' by Clarkson Stanfield (1793–1867) to allow craftsmen and painters to reconstruct it, for example, but spectators will no longer pay with anticipation and gaze with wonder to see it unfold. It is not, then, surprising that research into the composition of past AUDIENCES is striving to reduce the established lead of research into past performance. Theatre students are seeking – and finding – the collaboration of historians, architects and sociologists. The contribution of universities to the broadening and deepening of theatre research has been grudgingly acknowledged, not only in universities themselves ('Drama is not an academic subject'), but also in the theatre ('What do academics know?'). Even so, Topsy-like, drama departments have 'just growed', almost all with a strong investment in the practice as well as the study of theatre. As guardians of archives and special collections, they are a vital resource, but they are also an implicit challenge to the lingering insularity and philistinism of national theatres. The greater proportion of influential theatre journals, from the *Tulane Drama Review* to the *New Theatre Quarterly*, have been university-based or university-edited. Nor is drama in the universities as self-regarding as many of the older disciplines. It is a subject that compels contemporaneity and the recognition of research as an *activity*. It might, indeed, be argued that an exploration of the *uses* of drama has been the universities' most valuable achievement. It is no longer necessary to defend the teaching of drama in schools, nor the deployment of dramatic techniques in the teaching of other subjects. Simulation and role-play are accepted practices in industry and the police force as well as in therapy. Reminiscence theatre for the elderly, performances for and by the disabled, the invention and testing of theatre games – these and others are areas of active research in higher education. DRAMA THERAPY, like drama-in-education, has its own learned journals, and its own inroads to the curative imagination. Against the twentieth-century decline in theatre audiences must be set an increase in participants.

Much of this activity goes unrecorded. For researchers and would-be recorders of the twentieth-century theatre, newsprint is a disappointment. Reviewers, even the best of them, are quick to formulate opinions and sadly neglectful of their responsibility, not only to observe, but also to record their observations. From Hazlitt and Leigh Hunt, we can go some way towards reviving the voice and gesture of Edmund Kean. The great reviewers have always endeavoured to describe what it was like to be in a particular place at a particular time. The modern reviewer, restricted in column space, delivers a judgement and is gone. Researchers may weigh and balance favourable and unfavourable notices – just as actors and directors do – but the particularity that preserves what is otherwise ephemeral has been abandoned. Against the verbal loss, the twentieth century can set visual gains. Theatrical events have been captured, with unavoidable distortions, on film, on video, in photographs and in slide collections. Thoughtfully mounted exhibitions and television documentaries embody research and encourage more. There have been aural gains, too. The faint scratchings of Irving's voice, with its barely distinguishable eccentricities of pronunciation, are more a torment than a resurrection, but records and cassettes can richly represent the living and the recently dead.

In 1900, actor–managers led the theatre. By mid-century, and increasingly since then, directors had replaced them. More cerebral perhaps, certainly more reflective, many of the finest directors have described their own practices. CRAIG served himself, almost exclusively. BROOK and Meyerhold have been particularly well served by others. It is impossible to know how much the rise of the articulate director has been fronted by articulate critics and students of the theatre. There has certainly been persuasive support from leading publicists of drama, as of film. What Stanislavsky, Meyerhold, VAKHTANGOV, COPEAU and Brecht did not say for themselves is being hunted out by others. The ironic possibility at the close of the twentieth century was that the Western world would see a theatre in decline amid a burgeoning of the research it has provoked. PETER THOMSON

Art and artefacts

A theatrical offering, by its nature, disappears once the curtain falls. Nevertheless, much can be learned about it from a study of contemporary manuscripts, printed and pictorial sources and, more recently, electronic media. Many dramatists keep notebooks of ideas for plays. These, together with various drafts of the script, show the evolution of the play as envisioned by its author. A director's notes and an actor's script clarify the creative process of transferring the play from the page to the stage through rehearsals. Once the action has been 'set' by the director, the stage manager's prompt-book records the blocking (stage movement) of the finished production, as well as lighting and sound cues, notes on costumes and properties for each scene, and other relevant instructions or observations. In the case of a classic which is often revived, a comparison of prompt-books for several productions reveals cuts, revisions and staging ideas followed by directors at different times and under various circumstances. Three-dimensional objects (costumes, properties, etc.) can add information about a production, as can personal memorabilia (diaries, correspondence, autobiographies, contracts), financial accounts, government decrees (e.g. CENSORSHIP rulings) and, occasionally, transcripts of legal proceedings.

There may be several versions of the printed play. A relatively cheap acting edition will include blocking notes, as well as lists of props and costumes and diagrams of the scenic plots. A more elaborate reading version may contain special introductory material by the playwright or other authority. Large 'coffee-table' books (as produced for e.g. *The Phantom of the Opera* or The Who's *Tommy*), generally do not reproduce the script, but are profusely illustrated and usually have essays by the major creative personnel involved in the production. A popular and prolific dramatist's work

may appear in various editions and collections, affording the playwright an opportunity to review and revise the work with each new appearance. Translations and adaptations can also differ markedly from the original. Biographies and histories add another dimension to the study of a play by placing it in an historical context.

Theatrical posters began to appear in the mid-seventeenth century. Early English posters were small handbills nailed to wooden posts in the street and to theatre entrances. They were usually simple heralds advertising a forthcoming production, but sometimes they included a rough woodcut depicting a scene. In the nineteenth century posters became larger and more elaborate, with more information and better illustrations as lithography replaced woodcuts; today serigraphy (silk-screen) or offset printing is commonly used. Modern poster artists normally study the script and the production designs in order to create a poster which captures the spirit of the play being advertised. A strong commercial market exists for posters as works of art, in addition to their theatrical interest. Playbills, like posters, were originally simple public announcements of a performance. Gradually, more information was added for the use of audiences inside the theatre, and the modern programme contains lists of everyone connected with a production in any capacity. Today's programme is the official record of the play. Normally issued weekly or monthly, and dated accordingly, it records cast changes, the running order of scenes and musical numbers, and often includes special articles about the production. In the United States, programmes are issued to patrons free of charge, but one may also purchase a souvenir programme which contains colour production photographs and additional commentary. In Britain, programmes are paid for, though some theatres issue free cast lists.

Reviewers from the various media appraise the merits of the finished production. While most drama critics have had training in the art of reviewing, their opinions often differ widely and occasionally reveal personal bias. Sometimes a researcher or journalist is invited to sit in on the rehearsal process and to attend several performances of a play, enabling the writer to compose a detailed casebook of the entire production, including audience reaction. News accounts, feature articles, interviews and similar items appearing in general and specialized publications, contribute additional information. As far back as the eighteenth century printed reviews were often accompanied by theatrical caricatures, line drawings that are deliberately distorted to emphasize certain significant details of a scene or character. ALBERT HIRSCHFELD, whose drawings have appeared in the *New York Times* since 1925, is perhaps the most famous artist working in this genre today. Some actors are also talented artists (e.g. ANTONY SHER in Britain and ZERO MOSTEL in the United States) and use sketches and caricatures to help them develop their characters.

Since the time of Inigo Jones (1573–1652), costume and scene designs and, more recently, three-dimensional models (maquettes) have provided an artist's concept of the visual aspects of a production. Elevations, floor plans and lighting plots used for the actual construction of the set are the essential technical data needed to re-create accurately the physical production for future study. For documentation on prior periods, the researcher must look to paintings, prints (including 'penny plain and twopence coloured' sheets), woodcuts, etc., although these were often based on a literary concept rather than the play as staged. With the development of the camera in the nineteenth century, photographs offered a more accurate depiction of costume, but the 'scenery' was often a photographer's studio backdrop. Modern cameras, using fast film, record the actual stage action. Audio and video equipment can now be used to record a production from rehearsal through to final presentation. Besides their archival value, audio and video recordings have a strong commercial appeal, and CDs, cassettes, videotapes and similar items are often manufactured specifically for the commercial market; in the case of musicals, a popular singing star may record his or her own version of the songs.

Libraries, museums and certain university departments collect, catalogue and preserve theatrical artefacts, but technological advances have made it easier and faster for researchers to obtain the data. Computers allow institutions to update the record of their holdings continually, and co-operative information networks make this information immediately available at many different sites. The older means of reproduction have been supplemented or replaced by improved tools, including data banks, electronic mail, facsimile reproductions transmitted via telephone, and the INTERNET. Many researchers now use personal computers to gain access to information while working in their private offices or at home. Libraries and museums also contribute by mounting special exhibitions and talks, acting as venues for performances and helping to devise educational programmes and productions. Several theatrical CLUBS have important archives, too, sometimes supplemented by private collections, which can range from postcards to porcelain, when these do not go to a university or museum. Furthermore, theatre artefacts change hands as a very small wing of the art

market, though this concentrates mainly on the eighteenth and nineteenth centuries. DOROTHY L. SWERDLOVE
See also CRITICISM; MAGAZINES AND JOURNALS; THEATRE PHOTOGRAPHY; UNIVERSITY DRAMA DEPARTMENTS.

Mary C. Henderson, *Broadway Ballyhoo: The American Theatre Seen in Posters, Photographs, Magazines, Caricatures, and Programs* (1989)

Red Ladder   At a CAST   meeting in 1968, the AgitProp Street Players were formed, later presenting *The Little Artist* at a Trafalgar Square rally. They operated as a COLLECTIVE and performed to workers wherever possible. In 1972 they changed their name to Red Ladder, after a regularly used prop, and moved away from AGITPROP incorporating sexual politics into their work (e.g. *Strike while the Iron is Hot*, 1974). This led to some members forming Broadside Mobile Workers Theatre. Red Ladder moved to Leeds and focused on youth and community work.   DAN REBELLATO
See also POLITICAL THEATRE; STREET THEATRE.

Redgrave, Corin   *see* REDGRAVE, MICHAEL

Redgrave, Lynn   *see* REDGRAVE, MICHAEL

Redgrave, Michael [Scudamore]   (b. Bristol, 30 March 1908; d. London, 21 March 1985)   Actor and director. After some time as a schoolmaster, Redgrave made his professional acting debut at the LIVERPOOL PLAYHOUSE in 1934; his London debut came in 1936 at the OLD VIC, as Ferdinand in *Love's Labour's Lost*, and in 1937 he joined GIELGUD's company at the Queen's. In his long and distinguished career Redgrave, described by his wife, actress Rachel Kempson (b. 1910), as a perfectionist, played all the major Shakespearean characters, mostly at either the Old Vic or the SHAKESPEARE MEMORIAL THEATRE, Stratford: Macbeth (1947), Berowne (1949), Hamlet (1949, 1958, both toured), Richard II, Hotspur, Prospero (all 1951), Shylock, Antony, King Lear (all 1953), Benedick (1958) and Claudius in the inaugural production of the NATIONAL THEATRE Company at the Old Vic in 1963. His intelligent, sensitive playing came to the fore in modern work too, from ELIOT's *The Family Reunion* and RATTIGAN's *The Browning Version* (1948) to *Uncle Vanya* in the inaugural season of the CHICHESTER FESTIVAL in 1962; he repeated that role at the NT and followed up with *Hobson's Choice* and *The Master Builder* (both 1964) before being forced to leave due to ill-health. His last role was Jasper, the silent academic, in SIMON GRAY's *Close of Play* at the National in 1979. Redgrave also had a long and very successful film career, appearing in films as varied as *Thunder Rock*, *The Brown-*

ing Version, *The Lady Vanishes*, *The Dam Busters* and *The Importance of Being Earnest*. He successfully directed for the theatre and opera, and wrote a novel, several plays and two books on acting – *The Actor's Ways and Means* (1953) and *Mark or Face* (1958) – and finally, in 1983, his autobiography, *In My Mind's Eye*. A theatre in Farnham, Surrey, was named after him in 1965. He came from a THEATRE FAMILY and his three children, VANESSA, Corin (b. 1939) and Lynn (b. 1943), as well as two grandchildren, Natasha (b. 1963) and Joely Richardson (b. 1965), also became actors. Michael Redgrave was knighted in 1959. His archive was placed in the THEATRE MUSEUM in London in 2000.

DANIEL MEYER-DINKGRÄFE

Richard Findlater, *Michael Redgrave: Actor* (1956)
Rachel Kempson, *A Family and its Fortunes* (1986)
Corin Redgrave, *Michael Redgrave, My Father* (1995)

Redgrave, Vanessa (b. London, 30 Jan. 1937) Actress, born to theatrical parents, MICHAEL REDGRAVE and Rachel Kempson. Trained at the Ballet RAMBERT and Central School of Speech and Drama, she made her West End debut in 1958, and since that time has alternated with success between leading roles in classical and contemporary dramas. She established her reputation with the ROYAL SHAKESPEARE COMPANY as Helena in *A Midsummer Night's Dream* (1959), Rosalind in MICHAEL ELLIOTT's acclaimed *As You Like It* (1961), and Katharina in *The Taming of the Shrew* (1962); other major roles in revivals include Nina in *The Seagull* (1964), directed by her then husband TONY RICHARDSON, Ellida in *The Lady from the Sea*, directed again by Elliot (New York, 1976; London, 1979), Hesione Hushabye in *Heartbreak House* (1992), Ella Rentheim in *John Gabriel Borkman* (1996) and Carlotta in *Song at Twilight* (1999). Her breakthrough in contemporary plays came with the title role in Muriel Spark's *The Prime of Miss Jean Brodie* (1966), which demonstrated both her sense of the comic and a luminous passionate quality. Redgrave has always complemented her stage work with major roles in such films as *Camelot* (1967), *Isadora* (1968) and *Julia* (1977), and is an outspoken left-wing political activist. Her *Vanessa Redgrave: An Autobiography* appeared in 1991. Her daughters Natasha and Joely are also actresses. DAVID STAINES

regional theatre *see* REPERTORY MOVEMENT; RESIDENT THEATRE (US)

rehearsal *see* PHYSICAL PREPARATION; PREPARING A PART; VOICE

Reid, Christina *see* BELFAST; IRELAND

Reid, Graham *see* ABBEY THEATRE; BELFAST; IRELAND

Reid, Kate [Daphne] (b. London, 4 Nov. 1930; d. Stratford, Ont., 27 March 1993) Actress. Following study with UTA HAGEN in New York and student appearances at Toronto University's HART HOUSE THEATRE, Reid acted on radio and television before starring in CHEKHOV's *Three Sisters* at the CREST THEATRE, Toronto, in 1956. In 1959 she first played Canada's STRATFORD FESTIVAL, where she became a leading member of the company, playing the nurse (*Romeo and Juliet*), Cassandra (*Troilus and Cressida*), Katherina (*The Taming of the Shrew*), Lady Macbeth, and Madame Ranevskaya (*The Cherry Orchard*). In New York, she played Martha in ALBEE's *Who's Afraid of Virginia Woolf?* (1962), and on television, Queen Victoria in *Disraeli* (1963). In 1964 she scored a triumph opposite ALEC GUINNESS as Caitlin in Sidney Michael's *Dylan*. In the 1970s, now recognized as one of Canada's leading actresses, she played at theatres throughout North America, expanding her repertoire to include Gertrude in *Hamlet*, Big Mama in TENNESSEE WILLIAMS's *Cat on a Hot Tin Roof*, and Juno in O'CASEY's *Juno and the Paycock*. She co-starred with Katharine Hepburn in *A Delicate Balance* (1972), and her Linda Loman opposite Dustin Hoffman in a 1985 New York revival of MILLER's *Death of a Salesman* won critical acclaim. She has also appeared successfully on television and in films.

EUGENE BENSON

Reinhardt, Max [Goldmann] (b. Baden, Austria, 9 Sept. 1873; d. New York, 31 Oct. 1943) Director, actor, theatre manager and educator. He began his theatrical career as an actor, becoming between 1894 and 1902 a principal actor at the Deutsches Theater, Berlin, under OTTO BRAHM, from whom he learned the fundamental principles of modern directing. Between 1895 and 1897 he led a small group of actors from the company, which became a separate unit in the Brahm ensemble when they took over the cabaret Schall und Rauch in 1901. He came under the influence of the SYMBOLIST movement, and the productions of the small Reinhardt troupe moved away from the naturalist mode which had been Brahm's hallmark. In 1903 he severed his connection with Brahm and became manager of a second theatre.

In both houses he presented a number of productions in an impressionist/symbolist style, where the acting had a strong gestural quality, novel lighting designs and use of atmospheric music created a sensuous mood, and the scenic designs effused a beautiful and captivating quality. Reinhardt aimed at stimulating the spectator's feelings and awakening his or her senses through new and daring theatrical devices. He established the idea of the director as the leading artistic

639

force, tightly knitting together all the elements of theatre. Reinhardt's style found instant recognition. Critics as well as audiences responded very favourably to his productions, and in 1905 he was offered the post of managing director of the Deutsches Theater, replacing his old master Brahm. Unlike most managers Reinhardt bought the theatre he was running, thereby laying the foundation of an empire, which in 1932 included no fewer than eight leading houses. Within a few years Reinhardt became Germany's and Europe's leading director, residing periodically at the Deutsches Theater (1905–11, 1929–32), the Künstlertheater in Munich (1909–11), the VOLKSBÜHNE in Berlin (1915–18), the Grosses Schauspielhaus in Berlin (1919–20), and the Theater in der Josephstadt in Vienna (1924–29). In between he produced major works in SALZBURG, LONDON, Stockholm and Venice. His prolific output during these years can be divided into four categories: the intimate theatre, or *Kammerspiel* (e.g. WEDEKIND's *Spring Awakening*, 1906), where formal divisions between stage and the small auditorium were abolished and the spectator was encouraged to engage fully in the theatrical illusion; the impressionist manner (e.g. *A Midsummer Night's Dream*, 1905); the literary comedies, which demanded a highly developed acting style from stars and ENSEMBLE; and the great spectacles, like *Oedipus* at the Circus Schumann (1910), Vollmöller's *The Miracle* at the Olympia Hall, London (1911), or the Salzburg *Jedermann* (*Everyman*, 1920), which was repeated annually for many years and initiated the international music and drama festival there.

After the Nazi takeover of Germany, Reinhardt worked in America, where he started a school of acting in Hollywood and directed a film version of *A Midsummer Night's Dream* (1935). He emigrated there following the occupation of Austria and directed a number of relatively unsuccessful plays. GÜNTER BERGHAUS

See also DIRECTING; ENVIRONMENTAL THEATRE.

M. Jacobs and J. Warren, eds, *Max Reinhardt: The Oxford Symposium* (1986)
O. M. Sayler, *Max Reinhardt and his Theatre* (1924)
J. L. Styan, *Max Reinhardt* (1982)
G. E. Wellwarth and A. G. Brooks, eds, *Max Reinhardt, 1873–1973* (1973)

Réjane [Gabrielle-Charlotte Réju] (b. Paris, 6 Dec. 1856; d. Paris, 14 June 1920) Actress. Beginning in Paris in 1875, she later played in London and New York, and was greatly admired (by SHAW, for example) as a light comedy actress, though she possessed a wider range. Her successes included *Germinie Lacerteux* (1888) by the brothers Goncourt and SARDOU's *Madame Sans-Gêne* (1893), and she was the first French actress to play IBSEN's Nora in *A Doll's House* (1886). From 1906 to 1918 she ran her own Théâtre Réjane (where she staged Ibsen's *John Gabriel Borkman*) and played in early films. When she died, ISADORA DUNCAN danced in tribute the Funeral March of Schubert, requesting no applause.
TERRY HODGSON

religious drama CENSORSHIP prohibited the stage representation of Christ for many years, yet Jesus figures in many modern plays (e.g. in work by MAXWELL ANDERSON, ARRABAL, DE GHELDERODE, KAISER, LLOYD WEBBER, POTTER, STRINDBERG, WILDER, WILLIAMS, WYSPIANSKI) as well as in the medieval mystery plays that are often revived and in passion plays, like the one performed at OBERAMMERGAU or the popular American one, *Eyes upon the Cross*. In Brazil, what was claimed to be the largest OPEN-AIR THEATRE in the world was opened in 1968 to mount annually a passion play; thirty years later it faced competition from another Easter Brazilian production that used FIREWORKS and lasers to tell the story of Christ's final days. Twentieth-century plays habitually deal with religious themes and faith, from ANOUILH's *Becket* (1959) or DAVID HARE's *Racing Demon* (1990) to *Waiting for Godot* (1953), yet, outside the mostly amateur drama of organized religion, few are explicitly religious in intent. Some British VERSE DRAMA has been linked to a Christian movement, in which the Religious Drama Society and the Canterbury Festival were active. It was at Canterbury that another play about Becket, ELIOT's *Murder in the Cathedral* (1935), was first performed. FRY's Christianity speaks through all his work but is specifically manifest in *The Boy with a Cart* (1938), *Thor, with Angels* (1948, written for Canterbury) and *A Sleep of Prisoners* (1951). In France, HENRI GHÉON wrote for religious groups and the work of CLAUDEL is predicated on his Catholicism, achieving an aesthetic suffused with the Liturgy.
CHARLES LONDON

See also PAGEANT; SEASONAL THEATRE.

Relph, Harry see LITTLE TICH

Renaud, Madeleine[-Lucie] (b. Paris, 21 Feb. 1903; d. Paris, 23 Sept. 1994) Actress. In 1921 she won first prize at the Paris Conservatoire and went on to play notably in Marivaux and Molière at the COMÉDIE-FRANÇAISE, where she met her future husband JEAN-LOUIS BARRAULT. From the 1940s her career runs together with his, she the epitome of classical training, he of modern experiment. Her administrative talents became clear when they formed the famous Renaud–Barrault company (1946), which toured the world and changed the face of French theatre. With Barrault she played great roles in modern plays (*Amphytrion*, 1947;

Christophe Colomb, 1953; *The Cherry Orchard*, 1954). In later years, with fine intelligence and unquenchable energy, she embraced the work of BECKETT, notably the extremely demanding role of Winnie in *Happy Days* (1963), which was seen in London (1965).

TERRY HODGSON

Renée (b. Napier, New Zealand, 19 July 1929) Writer and influential woman playwright. Born of MAORI (Ngati Kahungunu), Scots and Irish ancestry, she left school at 12, but later completed a BA degree. After working in amateur theatre, she began writing plays in 1980. She is best known for her remarkable trilogy of historical plays. *Wednesday to Come* (1984), the most widely read and performed, is set in the Depression and explores the experiences of a group of women striving to hold their families together at a time of social dislocation. Her other two most significant plays are *Pass It On* (1986) and *Jeannie Once* (1990). Later plays have explored contemporary New Zealand issues.

GILLIAN GREER & LAURIE ATKINSON

repertory movement The name widely applied to a British theatrical movement, operating chiefly in the provinces, which originated in the early years of the twentieth century, was extended between the two world wars, and became after 1950 the prevailing form of theatrical organization outside London. Although the term 'repertory' strictly indicates a number of plays presented 'in repertoire' (i.e. in rotation), this has always been exceptional in the majority of British repertory theatres, due to the cost and difficulty of such a system (sometimes called 'true repertory'). What has characterized most repertory theatres has been a resident company and director, limited runs, close links between theatre and community, and a commitment to drama of quality, sometimes associated with 'regional' drama. In the second half of the century the repertory theatre became increasingly dependent on public funding, either national or local, and most of the buildings erected or adapted during this period have been publicly financed.

The earliest repertory companies were conceived as a protest against the capital's domination of the provincial theatre (then exercised through the universal system of touring companies and receiving theatres), and the commercial exploitation of 'WEST END successes'. This protest was often fired by regional loyalty (e.g. in DUBLIN, where the ABBEY THEATRE, opened in 1904, grew out of several nationalist dramatic movements) and amateur organizations: the BIRMINGHAM REPERTORY THEATRE, built in 1913, developed from the PILGRIM PLAYERS, a group of local enthusiasts active since 1907. The work of local play-

wrights was notable at Dublin, with YEATS, SYNGE and others, and at MANCHESTER (at the Gaiety Theatre, taken over in 1907), with the Lancashire School represented by STANLEY HOUGHTON and HAROLD BRIGHOUSE. All the financing of these early companies was found privately, either through wealthy patrons (e.g. ANNIE HORNIMAN, partly responsible for the Abbey and wholly responsible for the Gaiety, Manchester; and BARRY JACKSON at Birmingham) or by local support, as at the LIVERPOOL PLAYHOUSE, founded in 1911, and the GLASGOW Repertory at the Royalty Theatre from 1909 to 1914. All the pre-1914 companies acknowledged the inspiration of the seasons at the ROYAL COURT THEATRE, London, under GRANVILLE BARKER, and most drew extensively on their repertoire, notably SHAW and GALSWORTHY.

Only Liverpool and Birmingham survived the 1914–18 war, and Birmingham gave the movement a lead during the interwar years not only in its own home, but in numerous associated achievements at various London theatres and in the Malvern Festival Theatre from 1929. The repertory movement during these years was extended in at least two ways: by the appearance of 'art' theatres with resident companies (notably at the OXFORD PLAYHOUSE from 1923 and the FESTIVAL THEATRE, CAMBRIDGE, from 1926 to 1935), and by the growth, particularly in the 1930s, of 'commercial' repertory companies, organized in circuits by managers chiefly concerned with making a return on their investment (e.g. Alfred Denville, and Harry Hanson with his Court Players). They achieved a defence of the live theatre against the conquering forces of the cinema, particularly after the introduction of the 'talkies' in the late 1920s, but their standards of performance and choice of play were basic, and tended to devalue the term 'repertory'.

The importance of the arts to national morale during the 1939–45 war, acknowledged by government funding for the first time, through the COUNCIL FOR THE ENCOURAGEMENT OF MUSIC AND THE ARTS (later the ARTS COUNCIL), resulted in a steady increase of subsidy for repertory companies after 1945. These included survivors (Birmingham, Liverpool, Sheffield, Northampton) and new companies, particularly the CITIZENS' THEATRE, Glasgow, and the BRISTOL OLD VIC Company, the latter housed in the Georgian Theatre Royal which the Arts Council had actually leased and renovated. There was also a marked growth of local funding for resident companies (increasingly identified as 'regional' theatres), made possible by an Act of 1948 authorizing rates expenditure on the arts. This began as subvention to existing companies, but by the end of the 1950s had progressed to the funding of purpose-built homes, starting with the Belgrade, Coventry, in 1958, and leading to such prestigious projects as the new NOTTINGHAM Playhouse (1963), the Crucible, SHEFFIELD (1971), the new Birmingham Repertory (1971), and the ROYAL EXCHANGE THEATRE, Manchester (1976). Most of the new theatres and many of those rebuilt included studios for experimental work and undertook educational theatre both inside and outside their own buildings. In addition, the regional scene was greatly enlivened by the creation and financing from local funds of smaller companies wholly dedicated to experimental work, e.g. the VICTORIA THEATRE, Stoke-on-Trent (1962), the LIVERPOOL EVERYMAN (1964) and the Contact Theatre, Manchester. These companies may be seen as a new movement of protest against the increasingly 'established' reputation of the bigger repertory companies, and the growing importance in the theatrical world of national companies, publicly funded and devoted to quality drama, notably the ROYAL SHAKESPEARE COMPANY, with a London base from 1960, and the NATIONAL THEATRE, operating at the OLD VIC from 1963 and finally moving to the South Bank in 1976.

The extensive development of the regional theatre in the 1960s and 1970s was followed by contraction in the 1980s, and a sense of frustration and disappointment, fed in part by the high but sometimes conflicting expectations of the preceding years. Cutbacks in funding meant shorter seasons, including the closing of some studio theatres, and the rewards offered by television meant the virtual abandonment of the resident company in favour of casting each production independently (a method always favoured by repertories within travelling distance of London, e.g. Windsor, Guildford, Leatherhead, as being both more practical and preferable). But the contraction has not been universal: in 1989 the LEEDS Playhouse, a converted building, was replaced by the new WEST YORKSHIRE PLAYHOUSE, with thrust stage and large auditorium, which under Jude Kelly proved a great success. If the repertory movement seems to be struggling, its achievements should not be discounted, nor can the importance outside London of the regional theatre be overvalued, as has been shown by excellent work in the 1990s and at the turn of the century at the Nottingham Playhouse (under Ruth McKenzie), Bolton Octagon (under Lawrence Till), NEWCASTLE Playhouse (Alan Lyddiard's Northern Stage) and Mercury Colchester (under Dee Evans and Gregory Floy). G. ROWELL

Cecil Chisholm, *Repertory: An Outline of the Modern Theatre* (1934)

Council of Repertory Theatres, *The Repertory Movement in Great Britain* (1968)
Kate Dunn, *Exit Through the Fireplace: The Great Days of Repertory* (1998)
John Elsom, *Theatre Outside London* (1971)
Phyllis Leggett, 'The Repertory Movement in Great Britain', in *Who's Who in the Theatre*, 15th edn (1972)
Norman Marshall, *The Other Theatre* (1947)
George Rowell and Anthony Jackson, *The Repertory Movement: A History of Regional Theatre in Britain* (1984)

resident theatre   America's professional, nonprofit theatres are interchangeably referred to as 'resident theatres' and as 'regional theatres'. The term 'resident' refers to the presence of a permanent company of actors and directors, as contrasted to theatres that import touring productions. The alternative term, 'regional', successfully captures the geographic diversity of the non-profit theatre network, with theatres in over 40 states, yet it implies a certain provincialism, and a limited importance in comparison to the New York theatre. On the contrary, as BROADWAY becomes increasingly plagued by escalating production costs and commercialism, regional theatres have become the home to much of the serious theatre in America. As a result, the resident theatre movement – at the end of the twentieth century a network of over 300 theatres – has been called a collective national theatre.

The historical roots of the resident theatre movement lie in the amateur LITTLE THEATRES that arose in the early century, both outside New York City, to compensate for the demise of the professional stock companies that had toured throughout the country in the late nineteenth century, and in New York City itself, where they were formed in order to challenge Broadway's commercial structure. The WASHINGTON SQUARE PLAYERS (established 1914), and the PROVINCETOWN PLAYERS (established on Cape Cod in 1915 and relocated to New York City the following year) were devoted to creating an atmosphere of experiment and innovation, and fostering the work of new playwrights. Other antecedents to the resident theatre movement include early repertory theatres such as EVA LE GALLIENNE's Civic Repertory Theater (1926), which followed the example of the subsidized European theatres by instituting a rotating repertory of plays and low admission costs, and theatre collectives such as the GROUP THEATER, formed in 1931, that were based on the model set by the MOSCOW ART THEATRE.

Although scattered resident theatres appeared as early as the 1920s, such as the CLEVELAND PLAYHOUSE (an early little theatre that became professional in 1921), the resident theatre movement truly came into being after the Second World War. Founding the Theater '47 in 1947, MARGO JONES articulated what would become the movement's guiding mission: 'I want to live in an age where there is great theater everywhere.' In elaborating her desire to create, in Dallas, Texas, 'a permanent repertory theater with a staff of the best young artists in America; a theater that will be a true playwright's theater; a theater that will give the young playwrights of America (or any country, for that matter) a chance to be seen; a theater that will provide the classics and the best new scripts with a chance for good production,' Jones and the Theater '47 provided the inspiration and a working model for the rise of future resident theatres. Early followers included Nina Vance, who created the ALLEY THEATER in Houston, Texas that same year, and Zelda Fitchandler, the founder of Washington DC's ARENA STAGE (1950). In 1954 MILWAUKEE REPERTORY THEATER opened its doors. The two decades that followed saw the establishment of a tremendous number of theatres, as the resident theatre movement spread quickly through the country. This meteoric rise was aided by grants from the Ford Foundation, whose extensive support of the resident theatre movement, initiated in 1957, was crucial to the survival of many theatres. In 1961 Ford funded the creation of the THEATER COMMUNICATIONS GROUP, the umbrella organization that represents the resident theatres and publishes *American Theater* magazine. Of TCG's end-of-the century members, 55 were created in the 1960s and a startling 105 came to being in the 1970s. Networks were formed and in 1972 Adrian Hall, artistic director of TRINITY REPERTORY COMPANY (1963), convened a meeting of regional theatre leaders, resulting in a newfound cooperation that signalled, according to Hall, 'a first step in the "coming of age" of regional theaters, which in our view is a flourishing national theater.'

Resident theatres are predominantly subscriber-based institutions and employ actors under professional Equity UNION contracts. They maintain a commitment to the goals outlined by Margo Jones, providing their communities with high-quality productions of both classic and new plays. Within that scope, numerous theatres have distinguished themselves in specific areas, whether their emphasis be on the creation of new work, directing, acting or community outreach. The ACTORS' THEATER OF LOUISVILLE (1964) premières new works through the Humana Festival of New American Plays. Two California theatres, the LA JOLLA PLAYHOUSE (1954) and the MARK TAPER FORUM (1967), have also earned reputations for developing new playwrights. Theatres known for innovative directing and design include the Yale Repertory Theater (1966) and

the AMERICAN REPERTORY THEATER (1979), whose commitment is to staging 'classics as new plays and new plays as classics'. Resident theatres that place their primary focus on acting and actor development include the AMERICAN CONSERVATORY THEATER in San Francisco (1965), 'devoted to the growth of the actor', and the STEPPENWOLF THEATER COMPANY (1976), which pioneered a style of tight ensemble work and naturalistic acting known as the 'Chicago style'. In addition, many resident theatre programmes extend their commitment to actor training through their affiliation with theatre conservatories, such as the American Repertory Theater Institute for Advanced Theater Training at Harvard, the Yale School of Drama and the GOODMAN THEATER School.

Many regional theatres develop solid identities with the community and state in which they perform. Juneau, Alaska's Perseverance Theater (1979) declares its mission to 'hold up a mirror to our region of the world', and devotes one slot per season to premièring the work of a new Alaskan playwright. New Stage Theater (1965) in Jackson, Mississippi is dedicated to educating the state about its rich literary history through the creation of the 'Mississippi Writers Program'. Of note also is the Cornerstone Theater (1986), whose 'urban residencies' are devoted to 'building an inclusive community-based theater'. Educational and outreach programmes, crucial to the success of the regional theatre movement, became even more important in the 1990s, as part of an attempt to fill in the gap left by dwindling arts funding in education. Numerous theatres maintain productions that tour to schools, performing and offering workshops for teachers and students. These programmes serve to develop the audiences of the future, and provide a vital link between the theatre and the community, a link that is at the heart of the resident theatre movement.

SARAH STEVENSON

See also STUDENT THEATRE.

S. Langley, *Theatre Management in America: Principle and Practice: Producing for the Theatre* (1990)

Theatre Profiles 12: The Illustrated Guide to America's Non-Profit Theatres (1996)

J. W. Ziegler, *Regional Theatre: The Revolutionary Stage* (1977)

Restoration drama in the twentieth century

Restoration drama, the body of plays first written for the London stage between 1660 and 1710, had to be entirely rediscovered in the twentieth century. None of the plays had had anything even approximating to a continuous performance tradition through the nineteenth century; Restoration comedy was abandoned under the attack of moral censors who found the plays far too disgusting for public performance and almost too obscene even for the private reading of gentlemen. In 1841 Lord Macaulay had successfully attacked the plays for their apparent acceptance of sexual promiscuity, refuting the earlier claims by Charles Lamb that they could be tolerated because they were 'artificial', disconnected from reality and hence not requiring a moral judgement on the part of the audience.

The first stage performances of any Restoration plays in the twentieth century were under the auspices of the STAGE SOCIETY, beginning with Farquhar's *The Recruiting Officer* in 1915. With the establishment of the PHOENIX SOCIETY in 1919, founded for 'the adequate presentation of the plays of the older dramatists' by Montague Summers, eccentric editor of modern editions of many of the plays, the combination of aristocratic patronage and scholarship made it marginally respectable to stage, between 1919 and 1925, 14 Restoration plays for two performances each in semi-professional productions. After the 1924 production of Wycherley's *The Country Wife* with a cast including ERNEST THESIGER, Baliol Holloway and ATHENE SEYLER, a correspondent to the *New Statesman* wondered: 'Did the Phoenix players really give it unbowdlerized? And did none of the audience suffer from a feeling of sickness, retching – such as I felt when I first read it?' But Macaulay-like horror was rejected both by the audience's enjoyment and by a new factor, a definition of an appropriate style for Restoration comedy as 'comedy of manners'.

In 1924 NIGEL PLAYFAIR directed Congreve's *The Way of the World* at the LYRIC THEATRE, Hammersmith, with EDITH EVANS as Millamant. Through her performance Congreve's dramatic language was suddenly revalued and the critic JAMES AGATE could judge the play 'the greatest prose comedy in the English language'. Agate, calling Lamb's defence of the drama as artificial 'a world of mischief', recognized that the play had a startling reality, 'as real as any canvas of old Hogarth or modern page of Zola'. But the assumption that Restoration comedy had its own distinct style readily modulated into the assumption that style was the only quality the plays had; JOHN GIELGUD praised Edith Evans' performance as 'the finest stylized piece of bravura acting'. Style appeared to be nothing more than acting technique: actors began to be trained in handling fans as the only necessary skill to perform the plays.

Playfair's production depended on lightness and vitality, a firm denial that the play was concerned with anything serious. Similar values marred productions for the next 40 years, even though the plays' theatrical viability had now been established. A production of

The Country Wife ran for five months at the Ambassadors Theatre in 1934, and the play was produced at the OLD VIC in 1936 with MICHAEL REDGRAVE and Ruth Gordon in the cast. When the ENGLISH STAGE COMPANY in its first season at the Royal Court in 1956 wanted a classical revival to shore up the company's finances at Christmas, GEORGE DEVINE directed the play with JOAN PLOWRIGHT as Margery Pinchwife; a reviewer, praising the production's 'fastidious grace' and 'rococo charm', believed that 'without style and pace there would be more rough than smooth in *The Country Wife*', as if roughness was a danger to be kept under control.

The range of Restoration comedy performed in this period was far narrower than that explored by the Phoenix: two plays each by Congreve, Vanbrugh and Farquhar and one by Wycherley constituted the full professional repertory.

Since the Phoenix productions the theatre had ignored Restoration tragedy completely. PETER BROOK directed Otway's *Venice Preserv'd* at the Lyric Theatre in 1953 with Gielgud and PAUL SCOFIELD in the cast, finding a tragic heroism in the play and an unnerving modernity in its analysis of political conspiracy. Brook's is still the only significant production to represent the entire genre, in spite of later productions of Otway's play by the NATIONAL THEATRE and of Dryden's *All for Love* (his version of Shakespeare's *Antony and Cleopatra*) by PROSPECT.

In 1963 WILLIAM GASKILL directed Farquhar's *The Recruiting Officer* for the National Theatre at the Old Vic. Gaskill's choice was influenced by the BERLINER ENSEMBLE's visit to England in 1956 with Brecht's adaptation of Farquhar's play as *Trumpets and Drums*. Gaskill saw the play as a troubling reflection of Farquhar's experiences in recruiting in Shrewsbury in its attack on the Act of Impressment as well as 'Farquhar's genuine desire to find a solution for marital problems, so unlike the complacent acceptance of adultery of other Restoration writers'. While KENNETH TYNAN worried that 'the text is not quite strong enough to stand up to the realistic scrutiny to which Gaskill subjected it', he also recognized that the play was 'stripped of the veneer of camp that custom prescribes for plays of its period'. Gaskill's production was the first to accept the essential seriousness of a Restoration comedy, even though it made Farquhar too much of a precursor of Brecht.

Subsequent productions have followed the three paths taken so far. Comedies by Otway, Etherege, Ravenscroft, Shadwell, Southerne and Aphra Behn have received their first productions for centuries. A few plays have been repeatedly performed within the conventional canons of what has come to be believed to be Restoration style. Even fewer have been allowed serious and imaginative production with the intellectual respect Gaskill gave Farquhar. The best productions have consistently sought to reinvent a style, to find a contemporary form in which a society whose power-games and promiscuity seem disconcertingly modern can be reimagined. At the same time such productions have seen the pain, cynicism and anxiety behind the style, recognizing that the dramatic style mirrors a set of social forms needed to protect vulnerable individuals. Almost all these major productions have been by the ROYAL SHAKESPEARE COMPANY: TREVOR NUNN directed a witty version of Vanbrugh's *The Relapse* in 1967; JOHN BARTON brilliantly revealed the serious tensions behind the plot of Congreve's *The Way of the World* in 1978; John Caird's discovery of Farquhar's *The Twin Rivals* in 1981 found in Ultz's design a visual metaphor for the play's jaggedly conflicting styles; and MAX STAFFORD-CLARK used the Swan Theatre to show a watchful society of unhappy people in Southerne's *The Wives' Excuse* in 1994. In such productions the theatre has begun to make manifest the serious and troubling qualities academics have long argued for the plays.   PETER HOLLAND

William Gaskill, 'Finding a Style for Farquhar', *New Theatre Quarterly*, vol. 1 (1971)

Kenneth Muir, 'Congreve on the Modern Stage', in Brian Morris, ed., *William Congreve* (1972)

M. Stafford-Clark, *Letters to George* (1990)

Retta M. Taney, *Restoration Revivals on the British Stage, 1944–1979* (1985)

Kenneth Tynan, ed., *George Farquhar 'The Recruiting Officer': The National Theatre Production* (1965)

reviewing   *see* CRITICISM

revue   A stage production generally regarded as consisting of songs, dances and comedy sketches, though the term has been applied broadly to everything from Las Vegas spectaculars to shows involving a handful of performers in tiny theatres. The word first occurs in French fairground theatre in the early part of the eighteenth century as applied to a topical entertainment, and from 1828 to 1848 a survey of the year's events was part of the programme at the Théâtre de la Porte-Saint-Martin in Paris, this feature being called a *revue*. There is some evidence of a similar series of topical songs and sketches in the productions in London by J. R. Planché in the early part of the Victorian era, but it did not survive as entertainment in its own right. Towards the end of the nineteenth century, however, the term began to be used in Paris in connection with

the *grands spectacles*, the first of which was produced at the FOLIES-BERGÈRE in 1886. These shows had little or no topical content and consisted of TABLEAUX, imaginative in concept and inevitably featuring a large number of scantily clad and, later, nude females. In between there were song and dance numbers and eventually the inclusion of VARIETY acts. By the late 1920s the Folies-Bergère productions had grown to such an extent that they employed about 500 performers and musicians, and had been copied and occasionally emulated by other Parisian theatres. Many of the great French stars of the period, for example, MISTINGUETT and JOSEPHINE BAKER, rose to fame through their appearances in these large-scale revues. In other European countries, revue took rather a different path. Though there were some spectacles after the Parisian fashion in capital cities, the more topical tradition became firmer established, particularly in Germany, though here it became subsumed into the thriving between-the-wars CABARET scene. But the structure of revue made it attractive to theatre producers, particularly the AVANT-GARDE element. ERWIN PISCATOR mounted a production in 1924 which used hundreds of non-professional actors; it was called *Revue Rote Rummel*. Red Revue groups operated in Germany during the later 1920s, many of BRECHT's works, for example, owing a good deal to the revue style, as did some of the Soviet productions by MEYERHOLD and MAYAKOVSKY. Though there were a few attempts to produce topical revues in the 1890s, the form did not catch on in Britain until Albert de Courville presented Hello Ragtime in 1912, which in essence was a more sophisticated form of MUSIC HALL. However, it appealed to a wide section of the British public, particularly during the First World War, offering modest spectacle, comedy sketches and solo turns from a number of music hall stars. After the war, particularly at the Hippodrome, a number of French revues were imported.

In the 1920s a more distinctive style of English, more specifically London revue made its appearance, the main producers being C. B. COCHRAN and the Frenchman ANDRÉ CHARLOT. Both these men were instrumental in furthering the careers of a large number of British writers, composers and performers, among them NOËL COWARD, GERTRUDE LAWRENCE and BEATRICE LILLIE.

Revue survived as a staple of the British theatrical scene for nearly 40 years. The Little Revue at one of London's smallest theatres, which introduced JOYCE GRENFELL, was at one end of the scale, and this tradition was carried on during the war years with the Sweet and Low series at the Ambassadors, and later with what was called 'intimate revue' as practised by such writers as Alan Melville, Peter Myers and Ronald Cass. At the other end of the scale was a long series of what were in effect revues at the LONDON PALLADIUM, starting with the CRAZY GANG. From the 1920s, touring revue was part of the programming of most British variety theatres, though in the last years these often degenerated into an excuse for nude *tableaux*. Nevertheless, some remnants of the style can still be seen in summer shows.

The United States had its own type of revue (*see below*), though largely based on the French model, in the productions of FLORENZ ZIEGFELD, GEORGE WHITE and Earl Carroll, which were among the biggest theatre attractions from the 1920s to the 1940s. Las Vegas and other American resorts continue the tradition, though the emphasis is now on spectacle rather than content. Many of the essentials of the format continue, especially in television light entertainment and in some FRINGE and ALTERNATIVE THEATRE productions, usually in a deliberate subversion of the form.   PETER HEPPLE

In the United States
Some eighteenth- and early nineteenth-century productions may seem with hindsight to be prototypical examples of musical revue, but their relationship to the genre is tenuous at best. Only one mounting, John Brougham's *Dramatic Review for 1868*, with its blend of songs, satirical sketches and spectacle, makes any serious claim to priority. But it was a failure and spawned no imitators. The real progenitor of the American musical revue is almost always seen to be *The Passing Show*, which was produced at the fashionable Casino Theater in New York 1894. The show tied together its skits, songs and spectacle with a thin storyline, something most American revues continued to do until the First World War. It was also perceived as a 'summer show', again setting a precedent for its most immediate followers. ZIEGFELD's earliest *Follies* (beginning in 1907) consolidated the vogue for the genre. These spectacular productions, with huge scenery, dozens upon dozens of women in elaborate costumes, a cast filled with major stars and songs by the best composers, flourished from about 1915 to the mid-1920s. Besides the *Follies*, other long-lived annuals included the SHUBERTS' *Passing Shows* (unrelated, but for title, to the 1894 production) and GEORGE WHITE's *Scandals*. In the 1920s smaller, faster-paced, wittier revues began to supplant the behemoth spectacles. *The 49ers* (1922) and the London importation, *Charlot's Revue* (1924), served as models. Choice later instances of this type would be *The Band Wagon* (1930) and *As Thousands Cheer* (1933). They remained popular throughout the

1930s. But their popularity began to wane in the 1940s and the coming of television effectively put an end to the traditional genre. However, in the late 1970s a new type of revue emerged, generally very small in scale and devoid of sketches. These shows concentrated on the music of one bygone composer and so could be thought of as retrospectives. *Ain't Misbehavin'* (1978), featuring the music of Fats Waller, is an example.
GERALD BORDMAN
See also EROTICISM IN THE THEATRE.

R. Baral, *Revue: The Great Broadway Period* (1962)
Gerald Bordman, *American Musical Revue: from 'The Passing Show' to 'Sugar Babies'* (1985)

Reynolds, Dorothy   *see* SLADE, JULIAN

Reza, Yasmina   (b. Paris, 1 May 1959) Playwright. During a period as an unemployed actor she began writing plays to help fill the time. Her best-known work is her third play, *L'Art* (*Art*, 1994), an intelligent, adult comedy, produced in a CHRISTOPHER HAMPTON translation in London's West End in 1996, then on Broadway in 1999, after being seen across mainland Europe. Her other plays are *Conversations après un Enterrement* (*Conversations After a Burial*, 1987, ALMEIDA, London, 2000), *La Traversée de l'Hiver* (*Winter Crossing* (1996), *L'Homme du Hasard* (1996, performed as *The Unexpected Man* by the ROYAL SHAKESPEARE COMPANY, 1998, and in New York, 2000) and *Trois Versions de la Vie* (2000, performed by the NATIONAL THEATRE, London, as *Life × Three*, 2000). She has also written a novel and for the cinema.   LAURIE WOLF

Rhone, Trevor [D.]   (b. Kingston, Jamaica, 24 March 1940) Playwright. Rhone has been termed the father of Jamaican theatre. The youngest of his parents' 21 children, he had his first stage experience in the Jamaican secondary schools drama festival. In 1960 he went to England for a three-year course in acting and teaching at Rose Bruford College. Unable subsequently to find any openings in theatre in either Jamaica or England, in 1965 he co-founded his own theatre, Barn Theatre 77, in the garage of a private home in Kingston.

Although his youthful ambition had been to be an actor, the dearth of suitable West Indian scripts now prompted Rhone to turn playwright. In 1969 he won an award with his first full-length play, *The Gadget*, the original version of what was to become one of his most popular comedies, *Old Story Time* (1979). With an eye to the international market, Rhone wrote his early plays in standard English. *Smile Orange* (1971), a Molière-like exposé of the tourism industry, was the first of what were to become Rhone's characteristic vernacular comedies. It was also the first of his plays to enjoy a record première run (245 performances), and the first to be turned into a film. Rhone has written other award-winning screenplays; his most successful stage plays include *School's Out* (1975) and the two-hander *Two Can Play* (1982).

Rhone uses his fast-paced comedies to explore serious themes of universal concern. He writes with a depth of character not usually found in works of mass appeal. His plays draw exceptional audiences wherever they are staged, and his use of the vernacular has been no drawback to the success of productions outside the CARIBBEAN. JUDY S. J. STONE

Ribman, Ronald [Burt] (b. New York, 28 May 1932) Playwright. His literate dramas are sombre and surprising, often tragicomedies depicting fallen worlds. They include grotesque characters and events, and are marked by a powerful sense of loss. Among Ribman's plays are *Harry, Noon and Night* (1965), *The Journey of the Fifth Horse* (1966), *Cold Storage* (1977), *Buck* (1983) and *Dream of the Red Spider* (1993). M. ELIZABETH OSBORN

Rice [Reizenstein], Elmer [Leopold] (b. New York, 28 Sept. 1892; d. Southampton, Hants, 8 Aug. 1967) Playwright and director. For over five decades, Rice's well-crafted plays in divergent styles were prominent on Broadway: *The Adding Machine* (1923, EXPRESSIONISM); *Street Scene* (1929, naturalism); *We, the People* (1933, social drama); *Cue for Passion* (1958, psychological drama). He frequently exploited his background as a lawyer in such courtroom dramas as *On Trial* (1914), *For the Defense* (1919) and *Counsellor-at-Law* (1931). He was a longstanding opponent of censorship. His plays and other activities (head of the New York regional branch of the FEDERAL THEATER PROJECT, co-founder of the PLAYWRIGHTS' COMPANY) reflect the evolution of a liberal sensibility from the 1910s through to the 1950s. His autobiography, *Minority Report*, appeared in 1963. GERALD RABKIN

A. F. Palmieri, *Elmer Rice: A Playwright's Vision of America* (1980)
Michael Vanden Heuvel, *Elmer Rice: A Research and Production Sourcebook* (1996)

Rice, Tim[othy Miles Bindon] (b. Amersham, Bucks., 10 Nov. 1944) Lyricist. In collaboration with composer ANDREW LLOYD WEBBER, Rice pioneered a breakaway in the early 1970s from the long popular book-and-songs musical show and returned to a cantata form, a sung through text with no intervening dialogue, scarcely used in the musical theatre since GILBERT and SULLIVAN. The composer's mixture of modern popular and classical elements was blended for their first work, *Joseph and the Amazing Technicolor Dreamcoat* (1968–72), with Rice's individual and contemporary verse style, part speech-patterned, part lyrical, combining everyday language with occasional more fanciful flights and an enjoyable and youthful comic sense.

This combination of styles was developed further in their 'rock opera' *Jesus Christ Superstar* (1972), and in *Evita* (1978), internationally the two most successful musical stage shows of the 1970s. Generally, other writers failed to encompass the style but Rice, in a sadly rare return to the theatre, secured a further success in the same mode with *Chess* (1986), written in collaboration with Bjorn Ulvaeus and Benny Andersen, former members of the Swedish pop group Abba. The bulk of his subsequent work has been for the animated screen, whence *Beauty and the Beast* (1993) and *The Lion King* (1997), each containing lyrics by Rice, were brought with success to the live spectacular stage. Rice was knighted in 1994, and in 1999 his memoir *Oh, What a Circus* appeared. KURT GÄNZL

Rich, Frank (b. Washington DC, 2 June 1949) Theatre critic. Rich entered journalism after graduating from Harvard. A direct, unambiguous style earned him the posts as film critic of the *New York Post* (1975–7), film and television critic of *Time* (1977–80) and chief drama critic of the *New York Times*, the most powerful critic's post in America (1980–93). He then became a columnist for the paper. He is also the author of *The Theatre Art of Boris Aronson* (1987, with Lisa Aronson). DOMINIC SHELLARD

Richards, Lloyd [George] (b. Toronto, 1923) Director and educator. After beginning as an OFF-BROADWAY actor, he achieved major directorial success with the BROADWAY production of LORRAINE HANSBERRY's *A Raisin in the Sun* (1959). He taught at Hunter College and New York University before his 1968 appointment as artistic director of the National Playwrights' Conference at the O'NEILL THEATER CENTER, Connecticut, where each summer new works are nurtured. As dean of Yale School of Drama and artistic director of Yale Repertory Theater (1979–91), he developed and directed plays by, among others, ATHOL FUGARD and particularly AUGUST WILSON (*Ma Rainey's Black Bottom*, 1984; *Fences*, 1985; *Joe Turner's Come and Gone*, 1986; and *The Piano Lesson*, 1988). NANCY SWORTZELL

Richardson, Ian [William] (b. Edinburgh, 7 April 1934) Actor. His early work at the BIRMINGHAM REPERTORY THEATRE (where he played Hamlet) was followed by a long period at the ROYAL SHAKESPEARE COMPANY, which he joined in 1960. Here he quickly

647

emerged as one of the most gifted of the young ensemble put together by PETER HALL, playing with equal skill in the comedies (Aguecheek, Antipholus, Oberon and most notably Ford in *The Merry Wives of Windsor*) and the tragedies (Edmund, Coriolanus and – alternating with Richard Pasco – Richard II and Bolingbroke). He created the role of Marat in PETER BROOK's production of *Marat/Sade* (1965) and played Vendice in *The Revenger's Tragedy* (1967) in a production which established TREVOR NUNN's reputation. During the late 1970s he spent some time in the United States and Canada, playing Henry Higgins in *Pygmalion* on Broadway and appearing at the Shaw Festival. In the 1990s he was seen more on television and in films than in the theatre. His distinctive voice and impeccable technique, honed in the classical theatre, have adapted with remarkable success to the different demands of modern television acting.
GENISTA MCINTOSH

Richardson, Joely *see* REDGRAVE, MICHAEL; REDGRAVE, VANESSA

Richardson, Natasha *see* REDGRAVE, MICHAEL; REDGRAVE, VANESSA

Richardson, Ralph [David] (b. Cheltenham, Glos, 19 Dec. 1902; d. London, 10 Oct. 1983) Actor. He made his debut in 1921 in East Anglia, and toured before making his name with the BIRMINGHAM REPERTORY THEATRE, which he joined in 1926. His reputation was confirmed at the OLD VIC in 1930, where his Shakespearean parts included Hal, Bolingbroke, Caliban and Enobarbus; on the re-opening of SADLER'S WELLS in 1931 he played Toby Belch. He continued to play Shakespeare (e.g. Prospero, STRATFORD-UPON-AVON, 1952; Timon, Old Vic, 1956), yet defined himself as one of the quartet of great British male actors alongside GIELGUD, REDGRAVE and OLIVIER as much in contemporary work like MAUGHAM's *Sheppey* (1933) and PRIESTLEY's *Eden End* (1935) as in the classical repertoire. His trademark was not heroic rhetoric but making the ordinary extraordinary, with a touch of the naive or the innocent, as in Priestley's *Johnson over Jordan* (1939) and later in BOLT's *Flowering Cherry* (1957), a performance that established the reputation of the playwright.

After serving in Fleet Air Arm in the Second World War, he was appointed joint director with Olivier of the Old Vic, and they presented four historic seasons at the New Theatre; among his own successes there were Peer Gynt and Vanya (both 1944), Falstaff (1945), Inspector Goole in Priestley's *An Inspector Calls* (1946) and Cyrano (1946).

His list of outstanding performances embraced Dr Sloper in *The Heiress* (1949), Vershinin in *Three Sisters* (1951), Volpone (1952) and Sir Anthony Absolute in *The Rivals* (1966); two roles opposite Gielgud, in STOREY's *Home* (1970) and PINTER's *No Man's Land* (1975); the title role in *John Gabriel Borkman* (with the Pinter at the NATIONAL THEATRE); and the main part in *The Kingfisher* (1977), written for him by WILLIAM DOUGLAS HOME.

Richardson appeared in more than 200 stage roles and 50 films, and was much loved for his eccentricities – such as riding his motorbike with pipe in mouth and parrot on shoulder. Although his ease and timing seemingly made him more suited to comedy, his ability to touch an audience in tragedy made his career remarkable for its breadth and diversity. He was knighted in 1947. COLIN CHAMBERS

H. Hobson, *Ralph Richardson* (1958)
John Miller, *Ralph Richardson* (1995)
Gary O'Connor, *Ralph Richardson* (1982)

Richardson, Tony [Cecil Antonio] (b. Shipley, Yorks, 5 June 1930; d. Los Angeles, 14 Nov. 1991) Stage and film director. He was a key figure in the 1950s renaissance of British playwriting and filmmaking. After television work, he became associate artistic director of the new ENGLISH STAGE COMPANY and directed JOHN OSBORNE's first successes, *Look Back in Anger* (1956), *The Entertainer* (1957) and *Luther* (1961). The first two he also filmed for the company's cinema offshoot, Woodfall Films, which he co-founded to encourage British screen realism and to popularize major new authors; he won an Oscar for *Tom Jones* (1963), as did Osborne for the screenplay. His classical credits include PAUL ROBESON's *Othello* (1959), NICOL WILLIAMSON's *Hamlet* (1969), and *Antony and Cleopatra* with VANESSA REDGRAVE (1973), to whom he had been married. His autobiography, *Long Distance Runner*, was published posthumously in 1993. TONY HOWARD

John Osborne, *Almost a Gentleman* (1991)

ridiculous, theatre of *see* THEATRE OF THE RIDICULOUS

Ridler, Anne [Anne Barbara Bradby] (b. Rugby, Warks, 30 July 1912; d. Oxford, 15 Oct. 2001) Poet and playwright. Ridler emerged through the VERSE DRAMA movement, presenting a less flamboyant, more colloquial verse line than FRY or ELIOT, and displayed a social sensibility alongside the usual Christian theology prominent in verse drama of the time. Best known for *The Trial of Thomas Cranmer* (1956) and *Henry Bly* (1947), her reflection on the politics of corporate art,

The Shadow Factory (1945), sounds a disturbingly prophetic note.   DAN REBELLATO

Rigg, Diana   (b. Doncaster, Yorks, 20 July 1938)   Actress. She started in repertory in Chesterfield and York before joining the SHAKESPEARE MEMORIAL THEATRE (later the ROYAL SHAKESPEARE COMPANY) in 1959; she remained here for four years, playing, among other parts, Helena and Cordelia. On her return in 1966 she played Viola. Her striking good looks took her quickly into television, where she became widely known (and is still remembered) for her role as Emma Peel in *The Avengers*. She joined the NATIONAL THEATRE in 1971 to play Dottie in *Jumpers* and remained to play Lady Macbeth and Célimène in *The Misanthrope*. She returned in 1976 to play Phèdre. Her career continued with great success in the West End and in film and television throughout the 1980s, including an appearance in SONDHEIM's *FOLLIES*. In 1991 she played Cleopatra in Dryden's *All For Love*, beginning a fruitful association with the ALMEIDA THEATRE and in particular with the director Jonathan Kent, for whom she later (1993) played Medea, winning awards in London and New York. In 1995 she returned to the National Theatre to play Mother Courage, directed by Kent. In 1996 she was again at the Almeida, playing Martha in *Who's Afraid of Virginia Woolf?*. She was created a dame in 1994.   GENISTA MCINTOSH

Ringwood, Gwen Pharis   (b. Anatone, Wash., 13 Aug. 1910; d. Williams Lake, Canada, 24 May 1984)   Playwright and educator. Ringwood first attracted attention for the series of radio plays she composed in the 1930s. Her most successful stage play is the one-act *Still Stands the House*, first produced in 1938 and now a Canadian classic. Most of her texts are local (western Canadian) in setting, notably *Dark Harvest* (1945), *The Rainmaker* (1946) and *Stampede* (1946); her last work was a trilogy (*Maya*; *The Stranger*; *The Furies*), dealing with the plight of native Canadian Indians, produced in 1982.   LEONARD E. DOUCETTE

Geraldine Anthony, ed., *Stage Voices: 12 Canadian Playwrights Talk About Their Lives and Work* (1978)
——, *Gwen Pharis Ringwood* (1981)

riots   The definition of a riot varies across different cultures and different periods. When the revolutionary Russian audience stormed the stage to acclaim the sentiments of STANISLAVSKY's Dr Stockmann in *An Enemy of the People* (1905), this unleashing of energy was part of the mode of the production; similarly, the calculated stage invasions built into productions by DARIO FO or the LIVING THEATER incorporate the audience's response into the dramatic event. Early MODERNIST performances, notably of JARRY's *Ubu Roi* (1896), MARINETTI's *Roi Bombance* (1909) and COCTEAU's *Parade* (1917), were habitually disrupted by aesthetic opponents, as were the premières of DIAGHILEV's *Rite of Spring* (1913) and *Romeo and Juliet* (1926), immediately guaranteeing their artistic credibility. Politically organized disturbance is also common, from the Irish nationalist outrage at SYNGE's *Playboy of the Western World* (1907) and O'CASEY's *The Plough and the Stars* (1926), through the fascists who stormed the stage in support of the COMÉDIE-FRANÇAISE's anti-democratic *Coriolanus* (1932), to the Nazi sympathizers who objected to GENET's depiction of the army in *The Screens* (1966) and BRENTON's treatment of Northern Ireland in *The Romans in Britain* (1980).   DAN REBELLATO

ritual   A term usually associated with religious practice but often used to describe any formal set of human actions which function primarily at a symbolic level. The preoccupation with theatre's relation to ritual began in the nineteenth century with Wagner's operas and Nietzsche's theories about the Dionysiac origin of Greek drama in the primitive collective musical form of the Chorus (before it was superseded by the Apollonian principles of rationality and individual character). By the early twentieth century comparative studies in anthropology, religion and language, supported by archaeological research (and often under the misleading influence of Frazer's *The Golden Bough*), had encouraged extensive and enduring speculation about not only theatre's descent from primitive religion but also the survival and revival of ritual forms in theatre itself.

In the 1920s SURREALIST and primitivist movements developed in response to new ideas in psychology, and artists attempted to base their work on the unconscious and irrational impulses in individual and collective life. One of the early surrealists, ARTAUD, went on to assimilate oriental, occult and neoplatonist concepts and to develop an aesthetic for theatre based largely on its affinity with religious ritual. Although initially neglected, some of his ideas were realized in the 1950s in the plays of GENET.

The late 1960s saw the convergence of a number of developments. The innovative work of GROTOWSKI and, to a lesser extent, BROOK provided the focus for a revival of Artaud's work and for the growing interest in Asian theatre (which offered contemporary models for theatre in a ritual context). Neither Brook nor Grotowski subscribed to Artaud's metaphysics and used only those aspects of ritual which suited their purposes. However, the liberal climate of the 1960s provided the necessary conditions for fresh attempts to bring theatre and ritual together. At a theoretical level this was encouraged by the increasing use of the concept at a technical level in psychiatry and the social sciences.

The main initiatives were counter-cultural and came from companies committed to communal lifestyles and COLLECTIVE modes of work. To assert and define a radical group identity, the most effective strategy was to ritualize the performance itself. Companies in the United States like the LIVING THEATER and BREAD AND PUPPET set out to engage spectators with aspects of real life through active participation in a symbolic or fictional event. Typical of this period was the PERFORMANCE GROUP's *Dionysus in 69*. The production aimed to combine text, rites, games, celebration and audience interaction in a ritual confrontation with the Dionysus myth. Much of the theory, however, has outlived the practice, and it is in theoretical work that the Performance Group's director, Richard Schechner, has done most to develop the creative dialogue between theatre and the social sciences which continued into the 1990s. This body of theory has demonstrated that the different media dissolve the frontiers between theatre, society and politics in advanced capitalist countries, and that the theatricalization of public life – from HAPPENINGS and the Situationists' engagement with a Society of the Spectacle in the 1960s to the televised trial of O. J. Simpson and the funeral of Diana, Princess of Wales, in the 1990s – can also be seen as a process of ritualization. ANTHONY HOZIER

See also EASTERN THEATRE, ITS INFLUENCE ON THE WEST; RELIGIOUS DRAMA.

Margaret Croyden, *Lunatics, Lovers and Poets: The Contemporary Experimental Theatre* (1974)

Jane Harrison, *Ancient Art and Ritual* (1913; reissued 1978)

C. D. Innes, *Holy Theatre: Ritual and the Avant Garde* (1982)

Richard Schechner, *Public Domain* (1969)

——, *The Future of Ritual: Writings on Culture and Performance* (1993)

Riverside Studios A foundry converted into film studios between the world wars and afterwards the largest television centre in Europe, this two-auditorium arts centre by the River Thames in west London was opened in 1975 with local authority support under PETER GILL (until 1980) and became internationally renowned through visitors from home (like JOINT STOCK) and abroad (such as TADEUSZ KANTOR, La Claca from Catalonia, Tereyama from Japan) and Gill's own productions (e.g. *The Cherry Orchard* in 1978). Beset by funding problems, it nevertheless survived under different managements and continued with a similar mix (e.g. *Hamlet* directed by the Georgian ROBERT STURUA; O'NEILL's *A Moon for the Misbegotten* from resident director David Leveaux, which transferred to Broadway; and regular exciting shows in the LONDON INTERNATIONAL FESTIVAL OF THEATRE). A third studio was added when Riverside re-opened after refurbishment in 1994 along with its cinema, bar and café. COLIN CHAMBERS

Rix, Brian [Norman Roger] (b. Cottingham, Yorks, 27 Jan. 1924) Actor, director and manager. He first appeared on stage in 1942, and started his own repertory company in Yorkshire when he was discharged from the RAF in 1948. Within two years he had brought a wartime comedy, *Reluctant Heroes* by Colin Morris, to the WHITEHALL THEATRE, London, and began a phenomenal reign as the West End's king of FARCE. In 15 years at that theatre he presented five plays – the others were John Chapman's *Dry Rot* (1954) and *Simple Spymen* (1958), *One For The Pot* (1961) by RAY COONEY and Tony Hilton, and Cooney's *Chase Me Comrade* (1964) – which together ran an astonishing total of 6,483 performances, in most of which Rix played as the principal farceur. His work was distinguished by quick changes, acrobatic manoeuvres, frequent double takes and the inevitable lost trousers. The early farces were also successfully broadcast on television. In 1980 he retired from the stage to work full-time for Mencap, a society for the mentally handicapped. He has written an autobiography, *My Farce from My Elbow* (1975). In 1992 he was created Lord Rix of Whitehall in acknowledgement of his charitable work. IAN BEVAN

Robards, Jason, [Jr] (b. Chicago, 26 July 1922; d. Bridgeport, Conn., 26 Dec. 2000) Actor and greatest interpreter of O'NEILL. Robards' voice and bearing are distinctive and commanding. The son of an actor, he studied at the American Academy of Dramatic Arts. After ten years as an actor and stage manager (and work as a sailor), he first won acclaim as Hickey in the historic CIRCLE IN THE SQUARE revival of *The Iceman Cometh* (1956). He created the roles of Jamie in *Long Day's Journey into Night* (1956) – also playing in the film (1962) – and Erie Smith in *Hughie* (1964). Other O'Neill roles include Jim Tyrone in *A Moon for the Misbegotten* (1973), Con Melody in *A Touch of the Poet* (1977), James Tyrone in *Long Day's Journey* (1976 and 1988), and Nat Miller in *Ah, Wilderness!* (1988). Robards also distinguished himself in Shakespeare and in contemporary comedy and drama, from *After the Fall* (1964) and *You Can't Take It With You* (1983) to *No Man's Land* (1994). He frequently appeared in film and on television. THOMAS F. CONNOLLY

Robbins [Rabinowitz], Jerome (b. New York, 11 Oct. 1918; d. New York, 29 July 1998) Choreographer and director. Robbins appeared in several musicals as a dancer and returned to Broadway, after establishing himself as a choreographer with the Ballet Theater, to choreograph the LEONARD BERNSTEIN musical *On the Town* (1944), a piece which had originated in the ballet *Fancy Free*. He devised dances for a number of musicals, including *High Button Shoes* (1947), with its 'Keystone Kops' scena, and *The King and I* (1951), with its 'Small House of Uncle Thomas' pantomime, before sharing the direction, but not the choreography, of *The Pajama Game* (1954).

He was both director and choreographer for the musical version of *Peter Pan* (1954), and subsequently for *Bells Are Ringing* (1956), *West Side Story* (1957), *Gypsy* (1959) and *Fiddler on the Roof* (1964), setting the fashion for choreographer-turned-director which pervaded musical theatre afterwards. Robbins' work for the hugely successful *West Side Story*, on the dramatic form of which he had a considerable influence, epitomized his skill at expressing contemporary action in a strong combination of dance and drama. He subsequently returned to ballet as Ballet Master-in-Chief of New York City Ballet and an international choreographer, but was back on Broadway in 1989 to stage a musical show made up of items taken from his earlier works. KURT GÄNZL

See also CHOREOGRAPHY; DANCE.

Christine Contrad, ed, *Jerome Robbins: That Broadway Man, That Ballet Man* (2000)
C. Schlundt, *Dance in the Musical Theatre: Jerome Robbins and His Peers* (1989)

Robertson, Toby [Sholto David Maurice] (b. London, 29 Nov. 1928) Director. Robertson became an actor after studying at Cambridge, but turned to directing in 1958. After working in several regional theatres between 1959 and 1963, he became artistic director of the touring PROSPECT THEATRE COMPANY in 1964, for which he directed over 40 productions, including critical successes such as *Richard II* (1968), *Edward II* (1969) and *A Month in the Country* (1975), and a production of *Hamlet* which was seen in China in 1980 – the first visit there by a British theatre company. From 1985 to 1992 Robertson was artistic director of THEATR CLWYD. He has also directed abroad as well as staging operas and directing for television. HELEN RAPPAPORT

Robeson, Paul [Leroy Bustil] (b. Princeton, NJ, 8 April 1898; d. Philadelphia, 23 Jan. 1976) Actor and singer, with one of the most famous bass voices of the twentieth century. His father was a former slave who became a poor preacher, but Robeson overcame adversity to graduate at Columbia University. He was called to the Bar, became a national football star and was self-taught in 20 languages. A huge man in physique and spirit, he was striking in O'NEILL's *All God's Chillun Got Wings* (1924), controversial because of its depiction of love between a black man and a white woman, and *The Emperor Jones* (1925), in *Porgy and Bess* (1927) and, in London, as Joe in KERN and HAMMERSTEIN's musical *Show Boat* (1928). The part had been written with him in mind, and he gave lasting currency to the song 'Ol' Man River', the words of which he later changed to make it into an affirmative and challenging protest anthem. He triumphed as Othello in London (1930), in a record-breaking revival on Broadway (1943), and at STRATFORD-UPON-AVON (1959).

He faced racism thoroughly in his life and, although he was an internationally celebrated concert singer and film actor, he was pilloried and denied his passport during the McCarthy period for his politics – his communist sympathies, his struggle for peace and black culture – but his lustre remained undimmed.

JAMES EARL JONES appeared as Robeson in Philip Hayes Dean's solo play about his life, *Paul Robeson* (1977), and Actors' Equity give an annual prize bearing his name to those who follow his struggle for equality and justice. His book, *Here I Stand*, was published in 1958, and *Paul Robeson Speaks*, a collection of speeches, writings and interviews edited by Philip S. Foner, came out in 1978. FRANK LONG

Martin Bauml Duberman, *Paul Robeson* (1989)

Robey, George [Edward Wade] (b. London, 20 Sept. 1869; d. London, 29 Nov. 1954) Comedian and actor. An engineer and amateur comedian, he made his professional debut in 1891 and quickly became a MUSIC HALL star, dubbed 'the Prime Minister of Mirth'. In 1916 he appeared in the revue *The Bing Boys Are Here* when he sang the famous duet, 'If You Were The Only Girl In The World' with Violet Lorraine. From then on his career was mainly in VAUDEVILLE revues at London's major variety theatres, but he achieved some reputation as an actor by being skilfully typecast as Sancho Panza in two films of *Don Quixote* (1923 and 1933), on stage as Sir John Falstaff in *Henry IV, Part One* (1935), and again as Falstaff in OLIVIER's film of *Henry V* (1944). He was knighted in 1954. IAN BEVAN

P. Cotes, *George Robey* (1972)

Robins, Elizabeth (b. Louisville, Ky., 6 Aug. 1862; d. Brighton, Sussex, 22 Feb. 1952) Actress and author. Robins toured in the 1880s with the great actors Edwin

Booth and Lawrence Barrett, but after 1889 performed primarily in London, where she was a pioneer in introducing such modern dramatists as IBSEN, ECHEGARAY and PHILLIPS. She worked on her own and with such experimental groups as J. T. GREIN's INDEPENDENT THEATRE, and wrote on IBSEN and on the theatre. Her memoir, *Both Sides of the Curtain*, appeared in 1940. MARVIN CARLSON

Joanne E. Gates, *Elizabeth Robins, 1862–1952* (1994)
Angela V. John, *Elizabeth Robins: Staging a Life* (1995)

Robinson, Bill [Luther] ('Bojangles') (b. Richmond, Va., 25 May 1878; d. New York, 25 Nov. 1949) Legendary tap dancer and singer. Having received little or no schooling, Robinson began his dancing life busking on street corners. From there he moved into VAUDEVILLE, where he worked for many years before finding fame in several films with Shirley Temple in the 1930s. Robinson made his Broadway debut in *Blackbirds of 1928*, and followed this with several other black musical comedies such as *Brown Buddies* (1930) and *Blackbirds of 1933*. His grace and skill as a tap dancer were much emulated and he was particularly renowned for his famous 'stair dance'. HELEN RAPPAPORT

J. Haskins and N. R. Mitgang, *Mr Bojangles: The Biography of Bill Robinson* (1988)

Robinson, [Esmé Stuart] Lennox (b. Cork, 4 Oct. 1886; d. Dublin, 14 Oct. 1958) Playwright and director. One of the principal figures of the Irish theatre between 1910 and 1950, during which period he enjoyed several important roles at the ABBEY THEATRE, Dublin – play director (he directed over 100 plays there), manager, producer and member of the board. He was also the founder of the Abbey's experimental stage, the Peacock Theatre (1925), and its School of Acting (1926). The most frequently revived of his plays are *The White-Headed Boy* (1916), *The Far-Off Hills* (1928) and *Drama at Inish* (1933), gently satiric and superbly constructed comedies of provincial life. Almost all of his 18 plays were highly popular in their day. *The Big House* (1926) and *Killycreggs in Twilight* (1937) are Chekhovian in tone and milieu. *Church Street* (1934) introduces a Pirandellan note. He edited J. B. Yeats's *Letters* (1920), *The Irish Theatre* (essays, 1939) and AUGUSTA GREGORY's *Journals* (1946). He wrote *Ireland's Abbey Theatre: A History 1899–1951* (1951). CHRISTOPHER FITZ-SIMON

Michael J. O'Neill, *Lennox Robinson* (1964)

Roblès, Emmanuel (b. Oran, France, 4 June 1914) Novelist and playwright. His work portrays many forms of oppression as well as the search for freedom and dignity. He employs a variety of genres from farce to tragedy. Plays include *Montserrat* (1948, adapted by LILLIAN HELLMAN, seen in London with RICHARD BURTON), a historical tragedy, *Porfirio* (1953), *L'Horloge* ('The clock', 1958), and *Plaidoyer pour un rebelle* (*Case for a rebel*, 1966). ANNA MCMULLAN

Robson, Flora (b. South Shields, Durham, 28 March 1902; d. Brighton, Sussex, 7 July 1984) Stage and film actress. Robson made her debut in 1921, when she appeared in CLEMENCE DANE's *Will Shakespeare*. Her successful career was due largely to her ability to excel in a wide variety of roles. In the early 1930s she was seen in dramas by PRIESTLEY, MAUGHAM and O'NEILL. A season at the OLD VIC in 1933 demonstrated that she had a talent for playing comedy as well as the classics. In 1938 she went to the United States and on to Hollywood, though she did not abandon London's West End, where she continued to perform until 1969. Robson was created a dame in 1960. ELAINE ASTON

J. Dunbar, *Flora Robson* (1960)

Roche, Billy (b. Wexford, Ireland, 11 Jan. 1949) Playwright. He has devoted his playwriting career to chronicling the life and language of his home town – a hamlet south of Dublin on the country's east coast. He began writing after his own band, for which he was the lead singer, broke up in 1980. In 1986 he published a novel, *Tumbling Down*, fictionalizing the lives of regulars in his father's pub on Wexford's waterfront, and his first play, *Johnny Nobody*, was produced in Wexford. A year later *The Boker Poker Club* was also seen in his home town. As *A Handful of Stars* it was produced at London's BUSH THEATRE, and, like many Irish dramatists, Roche's first theatrical success came in Britain: the play, set in a pool hall, won the JOHN WHITING, Plays and Players, and Thames Television awards, and heralded a new interest in Irish writing. *Poor Beast in the Rain* (1989), set in a betting shop, won Roche the GEORGE DEVINE award; this play and *Belfry* (1991), set in a sacristy, were also produced at the Bush and were subsequently grouped together with *A Handful of Stars* as the 'Wexford Trilogy'. Roche's interest in community was also the focus of *Amphibians* (first seen in Wexford, 1987; revised for the ROYAL SHAKESPEARE COMPANY, 1992), a family drama set in the declining fishing industry in Wexford. *The Cavalcaders* (1993), which focuses on a barbershop quartet, is a companion to the 'Trilogy' and was his first major work to première in Ireland, at the ABBEY's Peacock Theatre. KAREN FRICKER

Rodgers, Richard [Charles] (b. Hammels Station, NY, 28 June 1902; d. New York, 30 Dec. 1979) Composer. Teamed with lyricist LORENZ HART, Rodgers moved from early songwriting work for college shows, through REVUE and musicals in New York and London and a period of filmwriting in Hollywood, to a varied series of mostly successful light musical shows. These ranged from conventional Broadway song, dance-and-laughter musicals (*Babes in Arms*, 1937) and classic BUR-LESQUE (*The Boys from Syracuse*, 1938; *By Jupiter*, 1942) to shows with libretti which effectively explored much less usual areas as ballet (*On Your Toes*, 1936) and the seedy side of town (*Pal Joey*, 1940). The tunefully effective style of traditional Broadway songwriting which had ensured takeout song hits in almost every Rodgers and Hart show was replaced by a different form of musical writing when Rodgers ended his partnership with Hart and combined with OSCAR HAM-MERSTEIN II on a succession of modern Broadway operettas. *Oklahoma!* (1943), *Carousel* (1945), *South Pacific* (1949), *The King and I* (1956) and *The Sound of Music* (1959) won worldwide popularity both as stage shows and in the cinema, and became established as an essential part of the American classic repertoire. More lyrical, often more musically substantial and vocally demanding than Rodgers' earlier work for the musical theatre, they also produced a large number of song standards.

After Hammerstein's death Rodgers wrote several further musicals without success. His autobiography, *Musical Stages*, was published in 1975. The quality of his major works and the impetus he gave to the Broadway musical stage in the 1940s and 1950s both as a writer and as a producer make him one of the most significant and successful figures of his period in the MUSICAL THEATRE.   KURT GÄNZL

D. Ewen, *With a Song in His Heart* (1957)
S. Green, *The Rodgers and Hammerstein Story* (1963)
S. Marx and J. Clayton, *Rodgers and Hart: Bewitched, Bothered and Bewildered* (1976)
E. Mordden, *Rodgers and Hammerstein* (1992)
F. Nolan, *The Sound of Their Music* (1976)
D. Taylor, *Some Enchanted Evening: The Story of Rodgers and Hammerstein* (1953)

Rogers, Ginger [Virginia Katherine McMath]   (b. Independence, Mo., 16 July 1911; d. Rancho Mirage, Cal., 25 April 1995) Actor, comedian and dancer. Rogers began her career as a dancer and singer on the VAUDEVILLE circuit in south and west America. She is best known for a series of 1930s films with FRED ASTAIRE, widely acknowledged as the best and most influential dance partnership ever seen on film. After a solo film career, she appeared in several stage musicals, including *Hello Dolly!* in New York (1965–7) and *Mame* in London (1969).   ANDREW SOLWAY

Rogers, Houston   *see* THEATRE PHOTOGRAPHY

Rogers, Paul   (b. Plympton, Devon, 22 March 1917) Actor. Trained by MICHAEL CHEKHOV, Rogers joined the BRISTOL OLD VIC, demonstrating a versatility that encompassed SHAW, IBSEN and PANTOMIME. In the 1950s, at the OLD VIC, he played many Shakespearean roles including Shylock (1953), Macbeth (1954), Falstaff (1955) and Hamlet (1957, in Australia). Returning to Britain, he was competing with a new generation and the parts became fewer; however, one of his greatest performances was as the crude patriarch Max in *The Homecoming* (1965), for the ROYAL SHAKESPEARE COMPANY, earning Rogers a Tony Award on Broadway, where he increasingly worked.   DAN REBELLATO

Rogers, Will[iam Penn Adair]   (b. Oglagah, Indian Territory (Oklahoma), 4 Nov. 1879; d. Point Barrow, Alaska, 15 Aug. 1935). Folksy humorist. Rogers began as a rodeo and Wild West show performer. His elaborate rope tricks led to a topical monologist act ('All I know is what I read in the papers . . . '), which led to VAUDEVILLE by 1905 and later the *ZIEGFELD FOLLIES* of 1916 and four more editions of the show. He appeared in silent films but achieved great national recognition in radio, in talking films such as *State Fair* (1933) and for his syndicated newspaper column. He died in a plane crash; an autobiography appeared in 1949, and his life was musicalized as *The Will Rogers Follies* (1991).   MICHAEL SOMMERS

R. Ketchum, *Will Rogers: His Life and Times* (1973)
B. Yagoda, *Will Rogers: A Biography* (1993)

Rojo, Jerry   *see* ENVIRONMENTAL THEATRE

Roland, Betty [Mary Isobel Maclean]   (b. Kaniva, Victoria, Australia, 22 July 1903; d. Sydney, 12 Feb. 1996) Playwright and novelist. Her first play, *The Touch of Silk* (1928), stands as one of the most distinctive and impressive of early Australian plays; though the plotting is somewhat contrived, her portrayal of the central figure and the evocation of the isolated farm community where she lives are memorable and intense. She returned to Australia in 1935 after 15 months in the Soviet Union, and wrote a number of short political plays and sketches. Disillusioned with communism in 1939, she turned to writing for radio and magazines, and continued with this into the 1950s in Australia and Britain. She has written plays for television and radio, children's books, novels and a compelling, if somewhat episodic, autobiography, *The Eye of the Beholder* (1984). A short radio play from 1931 was the basis for one of the first Australian sound feature films, *The Spur of the Moment* (1932).   MICHAEL MORLEY

Rolland, Romain [Edmé Paul Emile] (b. Clamecy, France, 29 Jan. 1866; d. Vézelay, 30 Dec. 1944) Playwright and novelist. Awarded the Nobel Prize for Literature, 1915. He published an influential essay in 1903 advocating a People's Theatre, and wrote two enormous play cycles, including several epic dramas about the French Revolution (e.g. *Danton*, 1900; *Le quatorze juillet* (*The Fourteenth of July*, 1902); and *Robespierre*, 1939). *Les Loups* (*The Wolves*, 1898) was inspired by the Dreyfus affair. ANNA MCMULLAN

Pierre Sipriot, *Romain Rolland* (1968)

Romains, Jules [Louis Farigoule] (b. Saint-Julien-Chapteuil, France, 26 Aug. 1885; d. Paris, 14 Aug. 1972) Poet, playwright and novelist. His several successful farces were produced and performed in the 1920s by JOUVET, notably *Knock, ou le triomphe de la médicine* (*Dr Knock*, 1923), in which the doctor, finding no patients in his new rural practice, creates a neurotic need for his services. He also adapted Jonson's *Volpone* (1928) from STEFAN ZWEIG's version.
WENDY SCOTT

P. J. Norrish, *Drama of the Group* (1958)

Roman drama in the twentieth century Few, if any, major genres of Western drama have been so unjustly neglected on the modern stage as Roman comedy and tragedy. Such neglect is particularly surprising in light of the fact that the works of Plautus, Terence and Seneca have, since the early Renaissance, more decisively influenced theatrical practice, and been more imitated by dramatists, than those of any Greek playwright.

Scholarship is partly to blame. Seneca was routinely (if dubiously) characterized as a 'CLOSET dramatist' whose works were never intended for performance. Plautus' reputation suffered from a somewhat disdainful attitude and an inability to take him entirely seriously, partly out of the (mistaken) belief that he had done little more than rework to their detriment earlier Greek masterpieces, and partly from an ambivalent attitude towards practical theatre in general, and comedy in particular. In the absence of scholarly espousal and encouragement, theatre practitioners have tended to avoid Roman dramatists.

That situation has changed a little. The discovery and analysis in the twentieth century of several original works by the Greek comic playwright Menander, whose plays Plautus was charged with corrupting, have tended to raise his reputation, while somewhat diminishing Menander's. At the same time, the willingness of scholars (in the wake of Shakespearean studies) to evaluate ancient plays not merely as texts, but also as scenarios for performance, has helped to reveal what Renaissance investigators had realized earlier: that Plautus and Terence have a superb theatrical sense, a sure grasp of comic potential, and deft dramaturgical skills. What may seem bland on the page comes exuberantly alive on stage, particularly when such performance eschews scenic realism and verisimilitude, to embrace a frankly presentational and deliberately self-conscious production style. Seneca's tragedies are more problematic, but similarly benefit from an analogous approach, as PETER BROOK's 1969 'THEATRE OF CRUELTY' production of his *Oedipus* vividly displayed.

This developing awareness is reflected in a number of critical books and articles which have explored the performance occasion and staging potential of Roman drama, as well as in new translations endeavouring to capture the innate theatrical sense of the original texts and convey it through stageworthy English. Such activity has, in turn, slowly emboldened actors and directors – whose only awareness of Roman drama may have derived from musical comedies such as *The Boys from Syracuse* (1938) or *A Funny Thing Happened on the Way to the Forum* (1962) – to attempt stagings of the original plays.

In the 1930s a series of influential performances of Plautus and Terence were given in Cassel, Germany, and revivals of Roman comedy are regularly presented in the Roman theatres at Pompeii and at Ostia. In the 1970s a number of new translations of Plautine comedies were staged at Dartmouth University in America, and successive productions making use of a stage believed to replicate the type on which Roman drama was first performed have been presented at the University of Warwick in Britain and the J. Paul Getty Museum in California. However, neither Britain's NATIONAL THEATRE nor its ROYAL SHAKESPEARE COMPANY has yet presented a comedy by Plautus or Terence. RICHARD BEACHAM

Richard Beacham, *The Roman Theatre and its Audience* (1992)
Erich Segal, *Roman Langhter* (1968)
Niall Slater, *Plautus in Performance* (1985)

Romania Historically, Romania is the bridge between Europe and Byzantium, and though it has been a united country only since 1859, it has had the advantage, over the centuries, of a rich traffic of cultures. Its theatre springs from ancient pagan rites, liturgical drama and puppet plays, challenged by the presence of large Hungarian and German communities, and by travelling theatre companies from France, Italy and, later, Russia. The Ceauşescu dictatorship stopped the traffic, but this only served to consolidate Romanian theatre as a national force, and to increase its desire to be seen on the international stage.

Two playwrights from the nineteenth century have had an enduring influence on Romanian theatre. Vasile Alecsandri (1821–90) co-founded the first Romanian National Theatre in Iasi in 1840. His plays, mostly topical or historical comedies, are frequently revived, to mark historic occasions or to throw a slant on contemporary events. His *Ovid* (1885) and *Tyrant Prince* (1879) were both used to open or re-open national theatres, and it was a production of his *Iasi in Carnival* at the National Theatre of Cluj, with its outrageous portrayals of the dictator and his wife, which prefigured the fall of the Ceauşescus in December 1989. Ion Luca Caragiale (1852–1912) is generally considered to be the greatest Romanian playwright. All his plays were premièred at the National Theatre of Bucharest, which later took his name, and where he was briefly artistic director (1888–9). His period of playwriting lasted only ten years, starting with *A Stormy Night* (1878) and reaching a peak with *A Lost Letter* (1884). His subject was generally petty-bourgeois life and provincial intrigue, which so irritated him in real life that he left Romania for good in 1904, and died in Berlin.

It was the advent of the AVANT-GARDE, during and after the First World War, that began to give Romanian theatre a modern identity. For the first years of the twentieth century, the trend had been for Shakespearean drama and historical romances, competing, as elsewhere in Europe, with the rise of realism. But the SYMBOLISTS, particularly MAETERLINCK, struck a chord with Romanian dramatists, among them Zaharia Barsan (1878–1948) and Victor Eftimiu (1889–1972), both directors at the National Theatre of Cluj who sought to combine the avant-garde with elements of traditional Romanian theatre. The EXPRESSIONIST poet Lucian Blaga (1895–1961) added his own touch to the genre, going back to the roots of the national culture with his play *Zamolxis* (1922). Between the wars, French influence was much in vogue, with Bucharest fêted as the 'Paris of the East'. Many writers travelled to France, and some stayed there: Tristan Tzara, founder of the DADA movement, settled in Paris in 1920; Mihail Sebastian (1907–45), author of *The Final Hour* (1954) and considered the finest social comedy writer since Caragiale, spent long periods in France; EUGENE IONESCO studied in Bucharest, but returned to Paris to become a French citizen in 1938.

The end of the Second World War forms the dividing line for twentieth-century Romanian theatre. Up to 1945 there were only 16 theatres throughout the country, very few of which were state-aided. By the 1970s there was a network of 36 national and state theatres,

supporting permanent companies and performing all year round; linguistic minorities were catered for by six Hungarian theatres, two German and one Yiddish. Two Institutes of Drama, at Bucharest and Tirgu Mures (the latter serving both the Hungarian- and Romanian-speaking theatres) ensured a continuous flow of trained talent into the profession. According to official statistics, the number of regular theatregoers expanded from 1,577,000 in 1938 to 12,500,000 in 1973. In the capital the number of theatres rose to 17, the most prestigious and adventurous being the Bulandra, the Mic, the Nottara, the Giulesti and the National Theatre.

Two actors stand out as the founding parents of modern Romanian theatre. Radu Beligan was artistic director first of the Comedy, then of the National Theatre Bucharest. Actor, entrepreneur, essayist and cultural ambassador, he was president of the INTERNATIONAL THEATRE INSTITUTE through the dark years of the 1970s and kept open a vital lifeline between Roman theatre and the rest of the world. Lucia Sturdza Bulandra (1873–1961) was one of the foremost actresses of her day and a woman of immense versatility and flair. In 1914, with her husband Tony Bulandra, she founded the company which now bears their name. After his death in 1943 she became general manager of the theatre, and was still acting at 88, playing the mother in TENNESSEE WILLIAMS's *The Glass Menagerie* until a few days before she died. The running of the theatre then passed to the actor, director and designer LIVIU CIULEI. This period saw the flowering of a prolific generation of Romanian writers, notably Camil Petrescu, Aurel Baranga, Alexandru Mirodan, Horia Lovinescu.

Ciulei, Radu Penciulescu, Lucian Pintilie, David Esrig and the young ANDREI SERBAN were the leading directors in the 1960s and early 1970s, when Romanian theatre reached a peak, liberating itself from STANISLAVSKY and social realism, exploring new uses of space and form, and beginning to challenge the emergent Ceauşescu dictatorship. Matters were brought to a head with Pintilie's 1973 production of Gogol's *The Government Inspector*, with its closing image of a mass of robot-like bureaucrats stumbling about the stage in an ever-thickening fog. By the mid-1970s, all five above-named directors had been obliged to emigrate, but not before they had established a rich seed-bed of imaginative successors (Catalina Buzoianu, Mircea Cornisteanu, Ion Caramitru, SILVIU PURCARETE, Dinu Cernescu, Cristian Hadjiculea and, later, Victor Ioan Frunza, Alex Darie and Dominic Dembinski) who would advance theatre's role as a covert forum for dissent and a resistance movement, and lead it through to revolution.

From the end of the 1970s, CENSORSHIP, power cuts

and cuts in funding were putting theatres under siege – at the same time as two-thirds of the national arts budget was being diverted into the annual 'culture' festival in praise of the country's leaders. By the late 1980s theatre funding had shrunk from 80 per cent to 10 per cent, with theatre workshops having to develop sidelines to reduce the shortfall: in Iasi they made birdcages; in Craiova, it was coffins. But this pressure served only to sharpen the vision of theatres, both in classical productions and in new work by writers such as the Nobel nominee Marin Sorescu. Plays began to take on darker, 'Aesopian' meanings. The Bulandra's *Hamlet*, directed by Alexandru Tocilescu, became the tragedy of a country crumbling away from within through the corruption of its government; Marin Sorescu's *The Third Stake* (1978) told of Vlad Dracula, who founded Romania on the impaled bodies of his countrymen; and in 1989, at the same time as the massacre was happening in Timisoara, *Iasi in Carnival* was presenting a battery of solo burlesque acts, aimed directly at the dictatorship.

Actors and directors were in the front line when events broke in December 1989. Controversial writers such as Paul Everac, Dumitru Solomon and Mihai Ispirescu just happened to have plays in rehearsal or planned. Ion Caramitru, the Bulandra's Hamlet, led the tanks in the assault on the television studios, and was appointed one of the country's five interim vice-presidents. For a time after 1989 the theatre was on the streets, in parliament and on television, and theatres themselves faced empty houses. Previously forbidden foreign attractions were suddenly available, and with artistic independence came the economic onslaught of the marketplace. To stem the dilution of Romanian theatre, UNITER (the Romanian Theatre Union) came into being, in 1990, to promote creativity, set up international exchanges and arrange festivals and tours. Exiled directors returned – Serban as general director of the National Theatre of Bucharest; Liviu Ciulei to the Bulandra. Each brought experience of working in the West, and opened the way for the best of current Romanian theatre to tour abroad, notably the National Theatre of Craiova – *Ubu/Macbeth*, *Titus Andronicus*, *The Danaides*, *Phaedra* – under director Silviu Purcarete, and the Odeon Theatre Bucharest with *Richard III* (1994), directed by Mihai Maniutiu, starring Marcel Ures. The acclaim abroad helped invigorate audiences at home.

Throughout the Ceaușescu years, Romanian authors had been compulsory fare, with the accent on ideological correctness, so it was natural, with the rush of freedom in the early 1990s, that imported culture should predominate. However, as the new century approached, and the crypto-Communists receded from government, Romanian theatre began to re-emerge with a new strength, thanks to UNITER and the presence in government of theatre writers and practitioners (Andrei Plesu, Ion Caramitru, Marin Sorescu, Marian Popescu). The 1990s saw acclaimed premières both from established writers – Dumitru Solomon (*The Recurrent Balcony Piece*, 1995), Dumitru Radu Popesecu (*A Scarf Floating on the Danube*, 1997) – and from a new generation of 'international' Romanians: writers Matei Visniec (*Clown for Hire*, 1991), Vlad Zografi (*Tsar Peter*, 1998) and directors Vlad Mugur, Tompa Gabor and Alexandru Darie.

Romania has shown how a national theatre can endure, entertain, stir the conscience and take a lead during times of oppression and political madness, and can then draw on, and contribute to, the experience of other cultures, without losing its unique and peculiar destiny. RICHARD CRANE & FAYNIA WILLIAMS

Ion Dodu Balan, *Cultural Policy in Romania* (1975)
Ion Caramitry, *Britain and Eastern Europe* (1992)
Charles Carpenter, *Modern Drama, Scholarship and Criticism 1966–80: An International Bibliography* (1986), pp. 427–36
Alice Georgescu, *A Mirror of Times* (2000)

Romberg, Sigmund (b. Nagykanizsa, Hungary, 29 July 1887; d. New York, 9 Nov. 1951) Composer. Arriving in America in 1909, Romberg survived at first on musical piece work, making his entrée on to BROADWAY as the composer of melodies for REVUE and as made-to-order interpolations into American versions of continental operettas. His own ability to write a score in this currently fashionable style was first seen in *Maytime* (1917), but another seven years of hack writing, including the successful American adaptation of *Das Dreimäderlhaus* (*Blossom Time*, 1921) intervened before the production of *The Student Prince* (1924) brought him fame. *The Desert Song* (1926) and *The New Moon* (1928), both on stage and film, confirmed his reputation, placing him with RUDOLF FRIML at the helm of the most substantial period of Broadway operetta to date, albeit one which was deeply rooted in continental traditions. As the fashion for this type of work passed, Romberg had less success, although his music was heard on Broadway up to and even after his death. KURT GÄNZL

See also DONNELLY, DOROTHY.

E. Arnold, *Deep in My Heart* (1949)

Rome, Harold [Jacob] (b. Hartford, Conn., 27 May 1908; d. New York, 20 Oct. 1993) Composer and lyricist. He turned to songwriting only after studying law and architecture. Before creating his first Broadway score for the long-running trades union REVUE, *Pins and Needles* (1937), he wrote shows for summer camps. Although he subsequently enjoyed several major successes, such as *Call Me Mister* (1946), *Wish You Were Here* (1952) and *Fanny* (1954), virtually none of his songs have become standards. Best known are probably the title songs from the last two mentioned musicals. GERALD BORDMAN

Romeril, John (b. Melbourne, 26 Oct. 1945) Playwright. With over 30 plays to his credit, he is one of Australia's most prolific and most produced playwrights. He is also one of the most celebrated (for his masterly *The Floating World*, 1975); one of the most unorthodox (in his long-term commitment to collective creations and causes); and one of the most controversial (for his part in the writing of *A History of Australia – the Musical*, 1988, a fêted adaptation of Manning Clarke's six-volume magnum opus). In 1968 Romeril joined the radical La Mama Company as actor and 'public pen'. After early AGITPROP plays came *Chicago, Chicago* (1970) and *I Don't Know Who to Feel Sorry For* (1969), and later a share of *Marvellous Melbourne* (1970), the first Australian Performing Group production. These plays represent three strands of development: a JAZZ-like fusion of clipped themes, intuitions and speedy responses; a quasi-naturalistic treatment of social problems; and popular-theatre celebrations with song, dance, spectacle and satire. In each his writing is angular, volatile, comic and compassionate.

He has travelled Australia as scribe to schools, community theatre, universities and occasionally the large subsidized theatres – as with his adaptation of Louis Stone's novel *Jonah* (1985) for the Sydney Theatre Company. Socialism and a determined anti-imperialism have led him to champion the cause of the underdog and to examine contradictions in class, gender and racial conflict as well as Australia's geopolitical identity. This is evident in his version of *Love Suicides* (1997) and his involvement in the Landmines Project (from 1999).

Other published plays in include *A Nameless Concern* (1968), *Mrs Thally F.* (1971), *Bastardy* (1972), *The Kelly Dance* (1986) and *Top End* (1989). GUS WORBY

J. Davidson, *Sideways from the Page: The Meanjin Interviews* (1983)
G. Griffiths, ed., *John Romeril* (1993)

Ronconi, Luca (b. Sousse, Tunisia, 8 March 1933) Actor and director. He is particularly associated with ENVIRONMENTAL THEATRE through his imaginative staging of classic and little-known work, most notably the epic poem *Orlando Furioso* (1969). His innovative productions of Shakespeare, Greek tragedy, opera and other works have been mounted in Italy, Germany, Austria and Switzerland. Since 1989 he has been director of the Teatro Stabile in Turin. MARVIN CARLSON

Rose, Billy [William Samuel Rosenberg] (b. New York, 6 Sept. 1899; d. Montego Bay, Jamaica, 10 Feb. 1966) Songwriter, producer and theatre owner. A tiny, self-publicizing opportunist, Rose began his career writing lyrics and occasional melodies. He subsequently produced *Sweet and Low* (1930), *Billy Rose's Crazy Quilt* (1931), *Jumbo* (1935), *Carmen Jones* (1943), and *Seven Lively Arts* (1944). He used this last show to restore the magnificent ZIEGFELD THEATER to the legitimate fold, only to later sell the playhouse to developers for demolition. He also purchased the out-of-the-way National Theatre, which he renamed for himself. His foundation funded the Billy Rose Theatre Collection at the NEW YORK PUBLIC LIBRARY. One of his five wives was FANNY BRICE. His autobiography was called *Wine, Women and Work* (1948). GERALD BORDMAN

E. Conrad, *Billy Rose: Manhattan Primitive* (1968)
S. Nelson, *'Only a Paper Moon': The Theatre of Billy Rose* (1987)

Rose, Reginald (b. New York, 10 December 1920) Playwright and screenwriter. Made his name as an outstanding TV scriptwriter in the 1950s and 1960s, winning three Emmy Awards for realistic dramas with a social conscience. He also wrote screenplays for a number of largely undistinguished films. Best known as the author of *Twelve Angry Men*, originally a TV play, then turned into a celebrated film starring HENRY FONDA, which Rose adapted for the stage in 1964. Set in the jury room of a court, a dissenting juror slowly manages to convince the other 11 – who are forced to confront their own prejudices and preconceptions – that there is insufficient evidence to find a young Hispanic guilty of murdering his father. HAROLD PINTER directed a successful revival in the West End, London in 1996. Other plays include *Black Monday* (1962), *The Porcelain Year* (1965), *Dear Friends* (1968) and *This Agony, This Triumph* (1972), but none achieved the iconic status for liberal humanism of *Twelve Angry Men*. NEIL DOWDEN

Rosenthal, Jean (b. New York, 16 March 1912; d. New York, 1 May 1969) Lighting designer, lifelong associate of MARTHA GRAHAM. She worked with ORSON WELLES' MERCURY THEATER (1937–199) and lit *The Cradle Will Rock* (1937). In 1940 she opened a design firm, Theater Production Service, and continued to work in dance, opera, musicals and theatre, including the AMERICAN SHAKESPEARE FESTIVAL (1953–8). Among her many notable shows are: *Show Boat* (1954), *The King and I* (1956), *Kiss Me, Kate* (1956), *West Side Story* (1957), *The Sound of Music* (1959) and *Fiddler on the Roof* (1964). She wrote an autobiography, *Magic of Light* (1972) with Lael Wertenbaker. JANE HOUSE

Roshchin, Mikhail [Mikhailovich] [M. M. Gibel-man] (b. Kazan, Russia, 10 February 1933) Playwright. Popular at home and abroad, his romantic comedy, *Valentin and Valentina* (1971), and Second World War play, *Eshelon* (*The Evacuation Train*, 1975) have been staged both in the Soviet Union and in the United States. He has also adapted Tolstoy's *Anna Karenina* for the stage (1984). NICK WORRALL

Harold B. Segel, *Twentieth-Century Russian Drama* (1979)

Rossiter, Leonard (b. Liverpool, 21 Oct. 1926; d. London, 5 Oct. 1984) Actor. Having made a name at the BRISTOL OLD VIC (1959–61), in London as Brennan the Moor in O'CASEY's *Red Roses for Me* (1962), and on Broadway as Fred Midway in David Turner's *Semi-Detached* (1963), Rossiter went on to display his matchless sense of timing in a series of comic roles, particularly delighting audiences as pretenders: Corvino in *Volpone* (1967), his hilariously hubristic Arturo Ui (1968), a pseudo-genteel Davies in *The Caretaker* (1972), and *Tartuffe* (1976). These talents came together as Truscott in *Loot* (1984). His ability to project a neurotic ordinariness, coupled with a doomed but boundless ambition, also earned him great acclaim in film and television. DAN REBELLATO

Rostand, Edmond [Eugène Alexis] (b. Marseille, France, 1 April 1868; d. Paris, 2 Dec. 1918) Playwright. Best known for *Cyrano de Bergerac* (1897), a heroic verse comedy featuring a love-sick courtier in seventeenth-century France who is unattractive because of his huge nose. The play combines patriotic sentiment with lyricism and verbal energy. It has been adapted internationally by several leading writers, including Augustin Daly, Anthony Burgess, CHRISTOPHER FRY and LOUIS NOWRA, and filmed. *Cyrano* was followed by *L'Aiglon* (*The Eaglet*, 1900), about Napoleon's son, and *Chantecler* (1910), based on the *Roman de Renart*, an allegorical drama which satirizes contemporary politics and literature, and in which all the characters are animals. Rostand's plays draw on the tradition of Romantic drama. *The Fantasticks* (1960), a musical version of his comedy *Les Romanesques* (1894), became the longest running show in New York.
ANNA MCMULLAN

Alba Amoia, *Edmond Rostand* (1978)

E. J. Freeman, *Edmond Rostand, Cyrano de Bergerac* (1995)

Rotimi, [Emmanuel Gladstone] Ola [Wale] (b. Sapele, Bendel State, Nigeria, 13 April 1936; d. Obafeme, Nigeria, 18 Aug. 2000) Playwright, director and actor. Studied playwriting and directing at Boston and Yale Universities. Founded the Ori Olokun Players (1966), a company which gained immense popularity among students and workers in Ile-Ife, owing to its accessibility and familiar use of indigenous ways of performing. He writes historical plays (e.g. *To Iron God*, 1966; *Kurunmi*, 1969; *Ovonramwen Nogbaisi*, 1966), absurdist dramas (e.g. *Holding Talks*, 1970), political plays (*If . . .*, 1979; *Hopes of the Living Dead*, 1985) and domestic comedy (*Our Husband Has Gone Mad Again*, 1967). He has also adapted Sophocles' *Oedipus Rex* as *The Gods Are Not to Blame* (1967) and Adegoke Durojaiye's *Abe Kude* as *Grip-Am* (unpublished). OLU OBAFEMI

Rough Magic Theatre Company Founded in 1984 in DUBLIN by a group of recent graduates from Trinity College breaking away from what they saw as an outdated focus on 'ruralism' and poverty in Irish theatre. Its early programme was made up of British and American plays which had not been seen on Irish stages, and then expanded to include new interpretations of classic plays by writers including WILDE and John Webster. In the late 1980s and 1990s, the company also began to present new Irish plays and was instrumental in nurturing the early careers of writers such as Declan Hughes, Gina Moxley, Donal O'Kelly and Paula Meehan. Nine of the company's debut plays were published in *Rough Magic: First Plays* in 1999. Like most Dublin-based independent theatre companies, Rough Magic has never owned its own performance space; its principal venue in Dublin is the PROJECT ARTS CENTRE, and it has toured extensively at home and abroad. In the late 1990s, with the departure of founding producer Siobhán Bourke, the company entered a period of re-evaluation and in 2000, under founding artistic director Lynne Parker and new executive producer Deborah Aydon – it is one of the few Irish theatre companies staffed almost exclusively by women – it decided to produce only new work. KAREN FRICKER

Peter Thompson, 'Rough Magic', in *Theatre Ireland*, 9/10 (1985)

round, theatre in   *see* THEATRE IN THE ROUND

Round House With its landmark domed roof supported by iron pillars, this nineteenth-century north London shed for turning locomotives is listed as a building of historic and architectural importance, and was taken over in 1966 to be the headquarters of Centre 42, a movement aiming to return art to the people (named after the number of a resolution at a Trades Union Congress on the importance of culture). Under ARNOLD WESKER, Centre 42 mounted six arts festivals around England, but failed to achieve its plan for the Round House, which nevertheless became an important THEATRE IN THE ROUND, housing innovative work by BROOK (*The Tempest*, 1968), ARDEN and D'Arcy (*The Hero Rises Up*, 1968), MNOUCHKINE (*1789*, 1971), BARRAULT (*Rabelais*, 1971), the OPEN THEATER (1973) and the GRAND MAGIC CIRCUS (1973). It was an important focus for the counter-culture, with the LIVING THEATER, HAPPENINGS, liberation conferences and pop concerts, and, later, for companies wishing to show their work in London (e.g. ROYAL EXCHANGE, MANCHESTER) or as a stepping stone to the WEST END (e.g. *Oh! Calcutta*, 1970, and *Godspell*, 1971). A plan to turn it into a black arts centre in the 1980s floundered, and in the 1990s there were plans to sell it to become an architectural library, but it was still operating intermittently as a theatre space at the end of the century.

COLIN CHAMBERS

Roussin, André (b. Marseille, 22 Jan. 1911; d. Paris, 4 Nov. 1987) Actor and playwright. While performing with the director Louis Ducreux he wrote and directed polished sexual comedy and melodrama. *Am-Stram-Gram* (1941) made his name. Subtle use of Molière's recipes ensured continuing success in works such as *La Petite Hutte* (*The Little Hut*, 1947, an international hit), *L'Amour fou* ('Crazy love', 1955) and *La Locomotive* (1966). TERRY HODGSON

Royal Academy of Dramatic Art *see* DRAMA SCHOOLS

Royal Alexandra Theater Built in 1906–7, this 1,525-seat touring house in downtown Toronto opened on 26 August 1907. In its early years a home to several stock companies, the Royal Alexandra has always been a key venue for touring theatrical troupes and opera and ballet companies. Typically, the theatre offers a popular mix of serious drama, musical hits, and star performers. It was bought by Edwin Mirvish in 1963 and meticulously refurbished; it is the most beautiful and functional of Toronto's theatres.

EUGENE BENSON

Royal Court Theatre Opened in 1888 on the east side of Sloane Square in west central London as a replacement for a nearby theatre of the same name that was pulled down to widen the road, the Royal Court came to prominence after staging PINERO's hit

Trelawny of the Wells (1898), with ground-breaking seasons (1904–7) under the management of J. E. VEDRENNE and HARLEY GRANVILLE BARKER. Revivals of early SHAW plays and premières of important new ones put it firmly on the theatrical map, and challenging work from abroad – IBSEN, MAETERLINCK – was seen alongside Shakespeare, HANKIN, GALSWORTHY and Barker himself. After the First World War there was more of interest – and more Shaw – from J. B. FAGAN and BARRY JACKSON (who brought his BIRMINGHAM REPERTORY company with modern-dress Shakespeare as well as Shaw), and three seasons of the Irishman's plays from the Macdona players. A 642-seater located away from commercial theatre's heartland was not a good business prospect, however, and in 1932 the Court became a cinema. It was damaged in the war and did not return to full-time theatre use until 1952.

In 1956, the arrival of the ENGLISH STAGE COMPANY under GEORGE DEVINE heralded the most important period for the Court, which after the success that year of JOHN OSBORNE's *Look Back in Anger* became known as the leading English theatre for new writing. While BRECHT, BECKETT and IONESCO found a home there, it was the company's promotion of playwrights such as Osborne, WESKER and ARDEN, and then, under WILLIAM GASKILL after Devine's retirement in 1964, of BOND and STOREY, that secured the theatre's place in contemporary cultural history. In fact, it was the name of the theatre (which was renovated in 1964) rather than that of the English Stage Company that became synonymous internationally with the company's distinctive approach, embracing along with new writing a new realist style of acting and design. The Court influenced not just the theatre profession but the wider arts world too, and became a kind of unofficial school for hosts of artists, both those already established and those who were to become leaders of their craft.

The Court played a crucial part in the abolition of stage CENSORSHIP and continued its radical, controversial tradition with subsequent generations of theatregoers and theatre workers, although survival was always a struggle. By the late 1980s there was a need for its identity to be renewed. Audiences beyond the liberal-minded intelligentsia were attracted to enter the famous frontage carrying in lights the name of the current play and playwright and to sample the equally famous interruptions from the noise of passing underground trains.

A studio space, the Theatre Upstairs, was opened in 1969 under NICHOLAS WRIGHT in the wake of counter-cultural HAPPENINGS and the establishment of an 'arts laboratory' network. It provided a platform for a new generation of writers, such as HOWARD BRENTON,

HEATHCOTE WILLIAMS and CARYL CHURCHILL, and later offered a try-out for downstairs, with plays like *Class Enemy* (1978) by NIGEL WILLIAMS transferring. It also became the venue of the excellent annual Young Writers' Festival and of many exciting productions by the Young People's Theatre Scheme, which had its roots in Devine's own work for children and schools' schemes first launched at the Court in 1960. It closed in 1996 for renovation and the Royal Court–English Stage Company took up temporary residence in the West End. The refurbished theatre re-opened in 2000. COLIN CHAMBERS

Richard Findlater, *At the Royal Court: 25 Years of the English Stage Company* (1981)

D. MacCarthy, *The Court Theatre 1904–7* (1907)

Philip Roberts, *The Royal Court Theatre and the Modern Stage* (1999)

Royal Exchange Theatre Opened in 1976, a remarkable steel and glass structure housing a THEATRE IN THE ROUND suspended within Manchester's old Royal Exchange building. It was designed by Richard Negri (1927–99), one of the team of artistic directors who came to Manchester as 69 Theatre Company, with the declared aim of presenting work of the highest standard – mainly classics – outside London. Other key founder members were Caspar Wrede (1929–98), James Maxwell (1925–95), Braham Murray (b. 1943) and MICHAEL ELLIOTT. The nucleus had trained under MICHEL SAINT-DENIS and started out as the 59 Company for a season at west London's LYRIC THEATRE. From 1968 to 1973 they occupied the University Theatre in Manchester and in 1973 built a temporary theatre in the Royal Exchange, which then gave way to the new theatre. There is no permanent acting company; each production is individually (and therefore, theoretically, ideally) cast. The high standards set have made it one of the major theatres in Britain and ensured regular appearances by actors of international standing (e.g. ALBERT FINNEY, VANESSA REDGRAVE, BEN KINGSLEY, HELEN MIRREN, TOM COURTENAY). It has also helped in the early stages of careers of directors such as ADRIAN NOBLE and NICHOLAS HYTNER. With the oil company Mobil, it ran an annual playwriting competition for several years. The theatre was damaged by an IRA bomb in 1996 and had to move to temporary premises pending renovation. It re-opened in 1998 with a new studio theatre alongside. ROBERT CHEESMOND

R. D. H. Scott, *The Biggest Room in the World: A Short History of the Manchester Royal Exchange* (1976)

Royal National Theatre *see* NATIONAL THEATRE

Royal Scottish Academy of Music and Drama *see* DRAMA SCHOOLS

Royal Shakespeare Company (RSC) Founded in 1961 by PETER HALL as Britain's first national theatre company nearly three years before the official body bearing that name began performing, the RSC emerged out of two traditions, one English, the other continental. Its English roots go back to David Garrick's 1769 Shakespeare Jubilee celebrations in STRATFORD-UPON-AVON and the opening there in 1879, after a national fund-raising campaign led by the local brewers, of the SHAKESPEARE MEMORIAL THEATRE. The cricket-loving FRANK BENSON became the first director of the summer festival of plays, which extended to spring and autumn with touring in between under his successor from 1919, WILLIAM BRIDGES-ADAMS. Benson's ideal, influenced by the continental MEININGEN COMPANY, was to train an ENSEMBLE, every member of which would be an essential part of an organic whole dedicated to performing the plays of Shakespeare. Although Bridges-Adams established the practice of having a resident company in Stratford, neither he nor his successors – until Hall – were able to realize Benson's dream; but its flame was never snuffed out in the meantime.

Bad luck followed the granting of the royal charter in 1925: the next year, fire ripped through the theatre. Productions continued in a local cinema while money was raised around the world to build a new theatre, which opened in 1932 (seating 1,500) and, though modified several times, was still standing at the close of the century. There were mixed fortunes in the 1930s under artistic directors BEN IDEN PAYNE, ROBERT ATKINS and THEODORE KOMISSARZHEVSKY, whose production of *King Lear* (1936, with Randal Ayrton in the lead) was one of the outstanding successes of the decade. BARRY JACKSON in the 1940s tried to introduce new ideas and brought from Birmingham the exciting young partnership of director PETER BROOK and actor PAUL SCOFIELD. ANTHONY QUAYLE took over in 1948 and was joined in 1953 by GLEN BYAM SHAW. Together they brought international as well as national recognition through a series of star performances by the likes of PEGGY ASHCROFT, RICHARD BURTON, JOHN GIELGUD, CHARLES LAUGHTON, LAURENCE OLIVIER, MICHAEL REDGRAVE, VANESSA REDGRAVE, RALPH RICHARDSON and PAUL ROBESON. Quayle resigned in 1957 and Byam Shaw stayed on alone until Hall took over as managing director in 1960, aged 29.

Inspired by the example of the great European ensembles – the MOSCOW ART THEATRE, the BERLINER ENSEMBLE, the THÉÂTRE NATIONAL POPULAIRE – Hall proposed the creation of a new company to the then chairman of the board, Fordham Flower, whose brewing family had donated the site by the River Avon on which the Memorial Theatre stands. Under the guidance of first Charles, then Archibald and now Fordham Flower, the Memorial Theatre enjoyed a healthy balance sheet which Hall's radical plan would seriously test. State support for the arts was underdeveloped in Britain, and funding a group of artists on long-term contracts as Hall proposed was unprecedented. It was made all the more risky because the theatre was based in a tourist trap 100 miles from the capital. Nevertheless, Flower agreed and, extraordinarily, Hall delivered very fast. Ashcroft agreed to lead the new company as its first three-year contracted player; the Stratford stage was redesigned; a London theatre, the ALDWYCH (seating 1,000), was leased – against the wishes of the West End's commercial managers and only after some smart footwork by Hall; leading playwrights were commissioned, among them JOHN ARDEN, ROBERT BOLT, PETER SHAFFER and JOHN WHITING; and, in the most public break with the past, the Memorial Theatre was renamed the Royal Shakespeare Theatre and the company became known as the Royal Shakespeare Company.

The London home helped attract actors and allowed Hall to extend the repertoire beyond Shakespeare to other classical plays and, most importantly, to new work as well. Verse speaking within a contemporary context became a priority, matched by urgent, fluid staging. Through outstanding productions – e.g. CLIFFORD WILLIAMS' *The Comedy of Errors* (1962), Brook's *King Lear* (1962) with Scofield, the cycle of history plays called *The Wars of the Roses* (1963) directed by Hall and JOHN BARTON and designed by JOHN BURY – the RSC within a few years became a byword globally for innovation and a new theatrical energy. Brook and MICHEL SAINT-DENIS, who ran an Actors' Studio in Stratford for the company, joined Hall in the artistic direction of the company which featured actors like JUDI DENCH, ALAN HOWARD, IAN HOLM, GLENDA JACKSON, ALEC McCOWEN, IAN RICHARDSON, DIANA RIGG, JANET SUZMAN, DOROTHY TUTIN and DAVID WARNER.

The company's profile was further raised by challenging new plays, such as Whiting's *The Devils* (1961) and HAROLD PINTER's *The Homecoming* (1965), and by experimental seasons at smaller venues, for example at the ARTS THEATRE in 1962 and the THEATRE OF CRUELTY work at the LAMDA school in 1964. This fed into the main stage work both by transfers (e.g. *Afore Night Come* by DAVID RUDKIN moved to the Aldwych in 1964) and by direct influence (e.g. Brook's productions of *Marat/Sade* by PETER WEISS in 1964 and *US* in 1966).

Negotiations to receive state funding were entangled with the establishment of the NATIONAL THEATRE, which, until just after the creation of the RSC, had been entwined with Stratford throughout the century, often with bitterness. In a series of complex events, the RSC withdrew from a plan to be part of the new NT and eventually received public subsidy for the 1963–4 season but less than the amount awarded the NT, a gap that remained thereafter despite the RSC's larger size and greater output. When Hall left in 1968, his policy of expanding to survive – he trebled audience figures – had turned the early surplus into a worrying deficit, despite rises in grant.

After the departure of Brook to Paris following *A Midsummer Night's Dream* (1970), one of the landmark productions of the era, further expansion was the order of the day. TREVOR NUNN was artistic director from 1968 to 1978, joined in the latter year by TERRY HANDS, who took sole charge in 1986. A tin-hut rehearsal room became The Other Place in 1974 under Buzz Goodbody (1946–75). It was a small space (seating up to 180) dedicated to a new, low-budget aesthetic and community service. Goodbody, a feminist and communist, produced startling work, including an electric *Hamlet* (1975) with BEN KINGSLEY, before killing herself in a tragedy that marked the company for years to come. The Other Place housed some of the company's finest work, both new (e.g. DAVID EDGAR's *Destiny*, 1976, CHRISTOPHER HAMPTON's *Les Liaisons Dangereuses*, 1986) and old (e.g. Nunn's production of *Macbeth* in 1976 with IAN McKELLEN and Judi Dench). In London, DAVID JONES' modern work, from new plays by DAVID MERCER to powerful stagings of plays by MAXIM GORKY, was followed up by the opening in 1977 under HOWARD DAVIES of The Warehouse (seating 200), which took shows from The Other Place and originated its own distinctive brand of new plays by playwrights such as HOWARD BARKER, EDWARD BOND, PETER FLANNERY and C. P. TAYLOR.

Two major annual commitments to projecting the company outward were instituted in 1977: a tour of the company's repertoire to Newcastle upon Tyne and a small-scale tour to areas that had little access to theatre. Epic stagings in the tradition of *The Wars of the Roses* – the complete Roman plays (1972), the *Henry VI* trilogy (1977) – became a company hallmark that was recognizable later in *The Greeks* (1980), *Nicholas Nickleby* (1980), *The Plantagenets* (1988), *The Thebans* (1991) and the staging of all the history plays that began in 2000.

In 1982 the RSC moved into the Barbican Arts Centre in the City of London. Despite an increase in audience figures and some splendid productions, the company never recovered artistically from this move, which was first mooted in 1965 when the RSC became involved in planning its new home. Like The Pit, the RSC's new 200-seat theatre there, the company could not establish a new identity isolated in the east of the capital, even with the new resources of the larger theatre (seating 1,150). Nunn exploited these in his more populist work, which culminated for him in *Peter Pan* (1983) and *Les Misérables* (1985), and was followed in the RSC by productions such as *Kiss Me Kate* (1987), *The Wizard of Oz* (1987) and the disastrous musical *Carrie* (1988).

In 1986 Stratford acquired a new theatre, The Swan, thanks to the generosity of an American patron, Frederick R. Koch. Seating 430 and inspired by early seventeenth-century theatres, it is built in timber inside part of the shell of the original Memorial Theatre, with a stage that thrusts into the audience sitting in a horseshoe shape in tiers. The Swan's repertoire is drawn from Shakespeare's time as well as world classics and new plays, and has been noted for revivals of long neglected British plays like James Shirley's 1632 comedy *Hyde Park*. In 1991 the old Other Place was replaced by a new building and continued to house workshops, the annual teachers' summer school, and other projects alongside its own repertoire.

That year saw ADRIAN NOBLE take over from Hands and concentrate on redefining the RSC as a classical company, but without the core of associate directors who had been the RSC's backbone for many years. In the new freelance arrangement it became harder to sustain the ensemble ideal and, notwithstanding the restoration of ROBERT STEPHENS' reputation with a highly praised Falstaff in *Henry IV Parts 1 and 2* (1991) and Lear (1993), the company's fortunes were mixed and began to rely on star performances, such as KENNETH BRANAGH's Hamlet (1992). Under threat was its ability to nurture and be a home for actors across the generations – whether JANE LAPOTAIRE, FIONA SHAW, ANTONY SHER, JULIET STEVENSON, Patrick Stewart, HARRIET WALTER and JOHN WOOD, or SIMON RUSSELL BEALE, RALPH FIENNES and ZOE WANAMAKER.

In the struggle to survive, the RSC, which had been a pioneer in gaining business sponsorship, concluded major private deals as public funding was being constricted. Yet financial problems led the company to close its Barbican Theatre for four months in 1990, and in 1996 it announced that it was pulling out of the Barbican altogether for half of every year. Instead, it would tour more, and added Plymouth, at the opposite end of the country to Newcastle, as its second regional residency, though this only lasted a few years. Its administration swelled and, even with the addition of

a few associate directors, the company's sheer size had become a problem beyond the control of the artistic director. With five theatres, two companies of around 80 actors each, productions in the West End and two or three on tour in Britain and abroad at any one time, it had become as much an entertainment corporation as a theatre company, carrying an unhealthy deficit and in need of artistic renewal. Plans for a major rebuilding programme in Stratford at the beginning of the new millennium were seen as central to the company's future direction, which took a new turn in 2001 when Noble announced that the company would no longer have a London base, and would cut its workforce to become a fleeter, slimmer operation. It looked as if the RSC had come full circle and, in a necessary process of re-invention, would cease to be anything like its founder dreamed of forty years before.

COLIN CHAMBERS

D. Addenbrooke, *The Royal Shakespeare Company: The Peter Hall Years* (1974)
S. Beauman, *The Royal Shakespeare Company: A History of Ten Decades* (1982)
C. Chambers, *Other Spaces: New Theatre and the RSC* (1980)
P. Hall, *Making an Exhibition of Myself* (1993)

Ròżewicz, Tadeusz (b. Radomsko, Poland, 9 Oct. 1921) Poet and playwright. He was a member of the Resistance movement during the Second World War, one of the 'lost generation' cruelly affected by the tragedy of the conflict, which became the predominant subject of his poetry and shaped his perception of the world and existence. Ròżewicz's radical, adventurous concept of 'open drama' goes beyond established theatrical forms, whether traditional or AVANT-GARDE. His first play, *Kartoteka* (*The Card Index*, 1960), a Polish modern classic, is considered a testimony to his generation, its trauma and disillusionment. *Grupa Laokoona* (*The Laocoon Group*, 1961) and *Swiadkowie, albo Nasza mala stabilizacja* (*The Witnesses*, 1962) are both formal experiments, and the spirit of BECKETT is present in *Stara kobieta wysiaduje* (*The Old Woman Broods*, 1968). Other plays include *Smieszny staruszek* (*The Funny Old Man*, 1964), *Akt przerywany* (*The Interrupted Act*, 1964), *Na czworakach* (*On Hands and Knees*, 1971), *Biale malżenstwo* (*The White Marriage* or *Mariage Blanc*, 1974), *Do Piachu* (*Below Ground*, 1979) and Kafka's biography, *Pulapka* (*The Trap*, 1982).

JOANNA KRAKOWSKA-NAROŻNAIK

Halina Filipowicz, *A Laboratory of Impure Forms: The Plays of Tadeusz Ròżewicz* (1991)
Henry K. Volger, *Ròżewicz* (1976)

Rozov, Viktor [Sergeyevich] (b. Yaroslavl, Russia, 8 August 1913) Playwright. He began his career as an actor and director in 1938 before writing plays for children's theatre during the 1950s in an association with the director EFROS. He achieved wide success with a play which became synonymous with the post-Stalin 'thaw': *Vechno zhivye* ('Alive for ever', 1957), staged by EFREMOV before reaching an international audience via Kalatozov's film *The Cranes are Flying*. The many plays which Rozov has written since are concerned with moral and ethical themes. He has described himself as 'a Romantic' who deals with 'the spiritual atmosphere' which can surround life's most commonplace events.
NICK WORRALL

Harold B. Segel, *Twentieth-Century Russian Drama* (1979)

Ruby and Kalmar Songwriters. Lyricist and librettist **Bert Kalmar** (b. New York, 16 Feb. 1884; d. Hollywood, 18 Sept. 1947) and composer **Harry Ruby** [Rubinstein] (b. New York, 27 Jan.1895; d. Woodland Hills, Calif., 23 Feb. 1974) gained fame on Tin Pan Alley before providing the scores to such lighthearted Broadway romps as *The Ramblers* (1926), *The Five O'Clock Girl* (1927) and *Animal Crackers* (1928).
GERALD BORDMAN

Rudkin, [James] David (b. London, 29 June 1936) Playwright of Anglo-Irish descent. Rudkin's dense, many-layered texts have haunted the British theatre since his stunning debut, *Afore Night Come* (Oxford, 1960; London, ROYAL SHAKESPEARE COMPANY, 1962), in which an itinerant vagrant is ritually killed on a midlands farm. *Ashes* (1974) juxtaposed the political and sexual problems of a Belfast couple, in a more naturalistic vein. His three-part, nine-hour allegory *The Sons of Light* (produced in 1976 after 11 years of writing, and revised to a single play in 1978) is strikingly original, rich in pagan mysticism and overwhelming theatrical imagination, showing the overthrow of an oppressive kingdom. *The Saxon Shore* (1986) set Celts against Saxons in the last years of Britain's Roman occupation; as in most of Rudkin's plays, Northern Ireland's 'troubles' are not far away. His astonishing allusive power, his sense of theatrical rhythm, the imagination that interweaves sexuality, identity, politics and environment, make him a complex and rewarding playwright. Other plays include *Cries from Casement as his Bones are Brought to Dublin* (1973), *The Triumph of Death* (1981) and adaptations of Euripides' *Hippolytus* (1978), GENET's *Deathwatch* and *The Maids* (1987), and

IBSEN's *Peer Gynt* (1982) and *When We Dead Awake* (1990). DAN REBELLATO

David Ian Rabey, *David Rudkin: Sacred Disobedience: An Expository Study of his Drama, 1959–96* (1997)

Rudman, Michael *see* NATIONAL THEATRE

Russell, Annie (b. Liverpool, 12 Jan. 1864; d. Winter Park, Fla., 16 Jan. 1936) Actress. Thrust upon the stage as a child by her impecunious parents in Montreal in 1872, she made her debut in New York in *HMS Pinafore* (1879) and then went on to tour South America and the West Indies. On her return to New York in 1881 she became an overnight success as the winsome eponymous heroine of *Esmeralda*, a part she went on to play through 900 performances. Her London debut in *Sue* (1898) had also brought her huge success in the United States. Her enduring popularity saw further successes in the first production, under SHAW's direction, of *Major Barbara* (1905), as well as *A Midsummer Night's Dream* (1906), *Twelfth Night* (1909), *Much Ado About Nothing* (1912) and *The School for Scandal* (1914). In 1932 she became director of the theatre named after her at Rollins College in Florida, where she also taught acting. HELEN RAPPAPORT

Russell, Lillian [Helen Louise Leonard] (b. Chicago, 4 Dec. 1861; d. Pittsburgh, 6 June 1922) Singer. In 1880 she was hired to sing ballads at the Bowery variety theatre, and after touring California, she scored her first New York success in *The Grand Mogul: or, The Snake Charmer* (1881), followed by appearances in GILBERT and SULLIVAN and other comic operas. After an ill-judged elopement and disastrous marriage to the composer Edward Solomon and some appearances in London, she returned to reclaim her undimmed popularity in New York, singing in Offenbach's *The Brigands* (1889) and *The Grand Duchess* (1890) and numerous other musicals such as *Princess Nicotine* (1893), *The Tzigane* (1895) – and *An American Beauty* (1896), the title of which was forever after identified with her. In 1899 she turned her hand to BURLESQUE, joining WEBER AND FIELDS' company for five years to appear in whimsical-sounding shows such as *Fiddle-dee-dee*, *Twirly-Whirly* and *Whoop-dee-doo*. Her last major appearances were in the MELODRAMA *Wildfire*, and another Weber and Fields musical, *Hokey Pokey*. After her fourth marriage in 1912 she effectively retired from the stage, and took up writing a newspaper column. HELEN RAPPAPORT

Parker Morell, *Lillian Russell* (1940)

Russell, Willy [William Martin] (b. Whiston, Liverpool, 23 Aug. 1947) Playwright and songwriter.

After a variety of jobs, the commercial success of his musical about the Beatles (*John, Paul, George, Ringo . . . and Bert*, 1974) allowed Russell to concentrate on writing. Many of his plays, rooted in his native city, are cheerful and unpatronizing pictures of its aspiring working classes. *Educating Rita* (1979), a dialogue between a university lecturer and his unsophisticated (female) student, and *Shirley Valentine* (1986), a witty monologue, have both been filmed to international acclaim. *Blood Brothers* (1981; musical version 1983), about two brothers brought up in very different families, succeeded as a long-running West End hit and also a perceptive social critique. One of the most produced writers of his time, Russell has also written for television and for schools. His other plays include *Breezeblock Park* (1975), *One for the Road* (1976), *Stags and Hens* (1978; filmed as *Dancin' thru the Dark*, 1990) and *Our Day Out* (television 1977; stage musical version 1983). His novel, *The Wrong Boy*, appeared in 2000. DAVID SELF

J. Gill, *Willy Russell and His Plays* (1996)

Russell Beale, Simon (b. Penang, Malaya, 12 Jan. 1961) Actor. After early work in REPERTORY theatre, and at the ROYAL COURT, he joined the ROYAL SHAKESPEARE COMPANY in 1986 and remained there for most of the following decade, playing many roles including the King of France (*Love's Labour's Lost*), Edward II, Konstantin (*The Seagull*), Edgar (*King Lear*), Oswald (*Ghosts*), Thersites (*Troilus and Cressida*), Richard III, and Ariel (*The Tempest*) – these last three directed by SAM MENDES . For the Royal NATIONAL THEATRE he has played Mosca (*Volpone*, 1995), Guildenstern (*Rosencrantz and Guildenstern Are Dead*, 1996) and Iago (*Othello*, 1997, directed again by Mendes, with whom he has formed a particularly creative partnership). In 1999 he returned to the RNT to play in its ensemble (e.g. in *Summerfolk* and as Voltaire in *Candide*, for which he won an Olivier award), and the following year gave another award-winning performance there as Hamlet. He has appeared many times on radio and television, notably in a remarkable TV performance as Widmerpool in an adaptation of Anthony Powell's novel sequence *A Dance to the Music of Time*, a portrayal that earned him another award. He is one of the finest of the younger generation of classical actors, combining dazzling technical skill and great intelligence with charm and painful vulnerability. GENISTA MCINTOSH

J. Croall, *Hamlet Observed* (2001)

Russell Bennett, Robert *see* BENNETT, ROBERT RUSSELL

Russia *see* SOVIET UNION

Rutherford, Margaret (b. London, 11 May 1892; d. Chalfont St Peter, Bucks, 22 May, 1972) Actress. Initially a teacher of elocution and pianoforte, she studied acting at the OLD VIC, and there made her first appearance, in 1923. Her first huge success was as Madame Arcati in NOËL COWARD's *Blithe Spirit*, and she became famous for portrayals of *grande dames*. After WILDE's Lady Bracknell she became an equally devastating Lady Wishfort in Congreve's *The Way of the World*. From 1936 she appeared in many films and television dramas, and a host of classical plays. She was created a dame in 1967. FRANK LONG

G. Robyns, *Margaret Rutherford* (1972)
D. L. Simmons, *Margaret Rutherford: A Blithe Spirit* (1983)

Ryga, George (b. Deep Creek, Alta., 27 July 1932; d. Summerland, BC, 18 Nov. 1987) Playwright. Ryga wrote 15 stage plays characterized by a strong populist bent. He first gained attention with the one-act *Indian* (1962), which depicts a confrontation between an anonymous Indian worker and an official of Canada's Indian Affairs Department. *The Ecstasy of Rita Joe* (1967), Ryga's best play, dramatizes events in the life of a young Indian woman who, at the play's close, is murdered by a gang of brutal whites. Later plays include *Grass and Wild Strawberries* (1969), *Captives of the Faceless Drummer* (1971), *Sunrise on Sarah* (1972), *A Letter to My Son* (1981) and *Paracelsus* (1986). EUGENE BENSON

Rylands, George [Humphrey Wolferstan] ('Dadie') (b. Tockington, nr Bristol, 23 Oct. 1902; d. Cambridge, 16 Jan. 1999) Director, scholar and anthologist; an important educator and university administrator. From 1946 to 1982 he was chair of the Arts Theatre, CAMBRIDGE, and directed many Renaissance and Greek plays. He was a governor of the OLD VIC for many years and served on the board of TENNENT Productions Ltd. He staged *Hamlet* at the Haymarket in 1944 with JOHN GIELGUD and the following year directed a controversial *Duchess of Malfi* with, among other innovative touches, CANADA LEE playing Bosola in whiteface. Acclaimed for *The Ages of Man*, his Shakespeare compendium which Gielgud toured in from 1958 and also filmed, Rylands supervised the recording of the uncut Shakespeare canon for Cambridge University's Marlowe Society. He influenced generations of students, many of whom, including JOHN BARTON, PETER HALL, TREVOR NUNN and PETER WOOD, became prominent theatre practitioners. THOMAS F. CONNOLLY

S

Sackler, Howard (b. New York, 19 Dec. 1929; d. Ibiza, 14 Oct. 1982) Playwright. Sackler was a recording director, a screenwriter, a poet and author of several plays produced at American regional playhouses. However, he was best known to mainstream theatregoers for his drama based on the career of Jack Johnson, an early black prizefighter, *The Great White Hope* (1968). GERALD BORDMAN

Saddler, Frank (b. Pennsylvania; d. Brewster, NY, 28 March 1921) Orchestrator. Saddler was educated in Munich. He played in and eventually conducted pit orchestras in American BURLESQUE houses before turning to orchestrating. At the time he began to orchestrate, in the early years of the twentieth century, only the better operettas had orchestrations of pronounced sophistication. Saddler is said to have been the first to bring this sound to American musical comedy. GEORGE GERSHWIN referred to him as 'the father of modern arranging'. Among the shows he orchestrated were *Watch Your Step* (1914), *Very Good Eddie* (1915), and *Sally* (1920). GERALD BORDMAN

Sadler's Wells ('The Wells') When it closed in 1906 it was London's oldest surviving theatre, dating back to 1765 and before that to a wooden hall built in 1683 on the site of a spring that was said to have miraculous powers. In 1927 LILIAN BAYLIS took over the derelict shell used as a playground and in 1931 – playing *Twelfth Night* on Twelfth Night, 6 January, with GIELGUD as Malvolio – opened a new theatre as the north London partner to her OLD VIC south of the river. From 1934 on, with the occasional visit from a theatre company, it concentrated on opera and DANCE. It was demolished in 1996 to be replaced by a new, multi-art theatre, which opened in 1998. COLIN CHAMBERS

D. Arundell, *The Story of Sadler's Wells* (1965)

E. J. Dent, *A Theatre for Everybody* (1945)

Sadur, Nina (b. Novosibirsk, Russia, 1950) Playwright, novelist and short story writer. Her authorial voice and themes belong to women's, though not feminist, writing, and even in an apparently domestic setting she turns firmly away from social realism, revealing an interest in the spiritual and mystical. Her plays include *A Strange Woman* (1982), *The Swallow Exposed* (1982), two short plays, *Go* and *Dawn Will Come* (both 1983), *The Force of Hair* (1984), *Nose* (1986) and *Frozen* (1987), as well as *Pannochka* (1985), based on Gogol's *Viy*, and *Mystification* (1998), a dramatization of his *Dead Souls*. VERA GOTTLIEB

Saint-Denis, Michel [Jacques] (b. Beauvais, France, 13 Sept. 1897; d. London, 31 July 1971) Actor, director, teacher and consultant, with a career spanning the Channel and the Atlantic. Saint-Denis, the nephew of COPEAU, worked as stage manager at his Théâtre du Vieux Colombier, then, with other pupils, followed him to his school in Burgundy in 1924. There they formed a disciplined team with multiple theatrical skills, working on IMPROVISATION and the use of MASKS. They eventually became the COMPAGNIE DES QUINZE (1929–34) under the leadership of Saint-Denis and inspired ANDRÉ OBEY to write such plays as *Noah*, reliant on their ability to conjure up fictional worlds with simple means. After successful but unprofitable English tours, and a production in English of *Noah* (1935) with GIELGUD, Saint-Denis set up the short-lived but influential London Theatre Studio. He directed a memorable *Three Sisters* (1938), and during the Second World War worked for the BBC as Jacques

Duchesne of the Free French Radio. In 1945, the season of his direction of OLIVIER as Oedipus, he became involved in running with his friends GEORGE DEVINE and GLEN BYAM SHAW the OLD VIC Theatre Centre which embraced the YOUNG VIC and a school. The pre-war LTS was reborn as the Old Vic School until its closure in 1952, when Saint-Denis returned to France as director of one of the new decentralized theatres and founded a school there, both of which moved to Strasbourg in 1953. In North America he became a consultant, particularly to the LINCOLN CENTER's Juilliard School and to Canada's National Theater School. Saint-Denis joined the ROYAL SHAKESPEARE COMPANY as a director and adviser in 1962 and, even there, he set up an experimental studio. He wrote *Theatre: the Rediscovery of Style* (1960) and *Training for the Theatre* (1982).
ROBIN SLAUGHTER

St Denis, Ruth *see* DENISHAWN DANCE SCHOOL

St Kitts *see* CARIBBEAN

St Lucia *see* CARIBBEAN

St Martin's Theatre (Melbourne) In 1980 the Australian State of Victoria's Ministry for the Arts set up a Centre for Youth Arts of which the St Martin's Theatre Company was a central element. The centre is located on a site which, from the beginning of the century, had been occupied by a chapel functioning both as a place of worship and as an educational centre for the teaching of drama and related subjects. Over the years this theatre has undergone a number of transformations: first as the Melbourne Little Theatre, then, in the 1960s and 1970s, as St Martin's Theatre, before Rex Cramphorn's Performance Syndicate became the resident company from 1973 to 1977. During the 1990s St Martin's Centre functioned as home to the Youth Theatre Company as well as a focus for the state's Youth Arts Programme, encompassing literature, theatre, visual arts and music. MICHAEL MORLEY

Sainthill, Loudon (b. Hobart, Tasmania, 9 January 1919; d. London, 9 June 1969) Designer who moved to England after designing for several ballet companies in Australia, and achieved immediate recognition with his poetic designs for MICHAEL BENTHALL's production of *The Tempest* (Stratford-upon-Avon, 1951). He designed GIELGUD's production of *Richard II* (1952), *Orpheus Descending* (1959) and COWARD's *Sail Away* (1962). Two of his most remarkable productions were elaborate PANTOMIMES at the Coliseum: RODGERS and HAMMERSTEIN's *Cinderella* (1958) and COLE PORTER's *Aladdin* (1959), which were said to rival the splendour of nineteenth-century pantomimes at DRURY LANE. Perhaps the most acclaimed of all his work were the

sets and costumes for the Rimsky-Korsakov opera *Le Coq d'Or* at Covent Garden (1954). IAN BEVAN

Saks, Gene (b. New York, 8 Nov. 1921) Actor and director. Saks began his career acting OFF-BROADWAY, and after appearing in several plays on Broadway turned to directing in 1963. He made his reputation with a string of hit comedies: ALAN AYCKBOURN's *How the Other Half Loves* (1971), Bernard Slade's *Same Time Next Year* (1975), and *Brighton Beach Memoirs* (1983) and *Biloxi Blues* (1984) by NEIL SIMON. He has also directed screen adaptations of several Broadway comedies and musicals. HELEN RAPPAPORT

Salacrou, Armand (b. Rouen, France, 9 Aug. 1899; d. Lettavie, 23 Nov. 1989) Playwright. His early plays mingle farce and tragedy, poetry and vaudeville, fantasy and metaphysics, while his later plays draw more upon naturalism and social satire. Plays include *L'Inconnue d'Arras* ('The unknown woman of Arras', 1935), in which a man who has just committed suicide relives his past in the few moments before his death; *L'Archipel Lenoir* ('The Lenoir archipelago', 1948), a satire on bourgeois manners; *Les Nuits de la colère* (*Nights of Wrath*, 1946), set during the Resistance; and *Boulevard Durand* (1961), about a trades union activist wrongfully accused of murder. Many of his plays were directed by CHARLES DULLIN. ANNA MCMULLAN

David Loosely, *A Search for Commitment: The Theatre of Armand Salacrou (1985)*

Salvini, Tommaso (b. Milan, 1 Jan. 1829; d. Florence, 31 Dec. 1915) Actor, one of the best known of the late nineteenth century's international stars and a pioneer of modern realistic acting; for this he was admired by STANISLAVSKY who, in *My Life in Art*, describes his most famous role, Othello. He also appeared as Hamlet, Macbeth, Lear, and Coriolanus, as well as in Italian dramas by such authors as Vittorio Alfieri (1749–1803) and Paolo Giacometti (1816–82). His memoir *Leaves from the Autobiography of Tommaso Salvini* appeared in 1893. MARVIN CARLSON

Salzburg Festival *see* FESTIVALS; GERMAN LANGUAGE THEATRE; HOFMANNSTHAL, HUGO VON; REINHARDT, MAX

San Diego Located in the southernmost part of California, with miles of ocean-front land, an ideal, sunny climate with mild winters, and a leisurely lifestyle, San Diego plays host to thousands of tourists – and theatregoers – every year. The city has a thriving arts community, including over 100 theatre, dance and music companies.

At the beginning of the twentieth century the city

already had several active theatres. The Spreckels Theater (*c.* 1912) opened up the touring circuit and hosted several popular road shows from the East Coast. For the 1935 California Pacific Exposition a replica of Shakespeare's Globe Theatre was erected in Balboa Park, and after the Second World War this theatre began producing all year. The award-winning OLD GLOBE now has a national reputation for outstanding new works as well as classics. The LA JOLLA PLAYHOUSE, founded in the late 1940s by film actors Gregory Peck, Mel Ferrer and Dorothy McGuire, was for many years the preferred stage home for Hollywood actors. La Jolla's new home on the campus of the University of California, San Diego marks a successful association between professional and academic theatres, evidenced by its own collection of Tony awards. Other theatres include the San Diego Repertory Theater; the San Diego Light Opera, which offers outdoor musical performances; and the Lamb's Players. The Gaslamp Quarter Theater (1980) produces mainly twentieth-century popular plays on the site of a 1920s dance hall in what is now an area of downtown refurbished to evoke its Edwardian past. Virtually any kind of performance can be found in the city, including numerous children's and puppet theatres, ethnic performing groups, and a host of community and college theatres.

DAVID A. WILLIAMS

San Francisco   Situated in northern California on a peninsula jutting into the Pacific Ocean, San Francisco has emerged as one of the leading cultural centres of the United States, if not the world. Its steeply sloping streets, colourful houses and ethnically diverse population host a variety of theatrical entertainments. By 1900 San Francisco already had a 50-year theatrical tradition and, thanks to the completion in 1869 of the Transcontinental Railroad, had witnessed performances by the greatest actors and actresses from both sides of the Atlantic.

San Francisco theatre faced an early challenge with the great earthquake in April 1906. All but one of the city's theatres were destroyed, but by December of that same year theatres were rebuilt and theatrical life was thriving once more. The first quarter of the century saw a boom in VAUDEVILLE and the beginnings of a world-class opera company. Spoken drama during this period waned alongside the commercial influence of the THEATRICAL SYNDICATE and the popularity of vaudeville and film. By the 1930s, the Depression and the exodus of actors to film had left San Francisco theatre in a pretty dismal state, but the FEDERAL THEATER PROJECT helped sustain the drama. In 1952 the ACTOR'S WORKSHOP started up, and for the next 15 years dominated

the theatre scene with its daring but often esoteric productions.

During much of the first half of the twentieth century San Francisco theatre relied heavily on imports from BROADWAY. Since the 1960s, however, the city's international reputation has been represented on three home-grown fronts. The famous AMERICAN CONSERVATORY THEATER is one of the pre-eminent theatres in America, offering a classical and contemporary repertoire, and the award-winning SAN FRANCISCO MIME TROUPE is the longest-running POLITICAL THEATRE group in the country. Finally, San Francisco's cultural diversity has produced a rich tapestry of traditional, ethnic, and community-based theatrical forms, including ASIAN AMERICAN, GAY, WOMEN'S and HISPANIC theatre. These examples barely touch the surface of a fertile arts community boasting over 250 theatre companies.   DAVID A. WILLIAMS

San Francisco Mime Troupe   Founded by R. G. Davis in 1959 as a classical mime company, the San Francisco Mime Troupe evolved into one of the foremost political theatres of the 1960s. Guided by Marxist precepts and run communally, the Mime Troupe incorporated an eclectic array of techniques and scripts: from the *COMMEDIA DELL'ARTE* and blackface MINSTREL shows to modern DANCE, traditional MIME, puppetry and mask-making; from POPULAR MUSIC, flip cards, AVANT-GARDE HAPPENINGS, Molière and JARRY to, most importantly, BERTOLT BRECHT's EPIC THEATRE – all used to craft scathing commentaries on capitalist politics and bourgeois values. A GUERRILLA THEATRE, the Mime Troupe continues its collectivist approach to topical theatre, and tours extensively, having appeared in Cuba, at the KENNEDY CENTER in Washington DC and at the First National Theater Festival in Nicaragua. In 1987 the Troupe won a Tony award for excellence in regional theatre.   MICHAEL KARP

R. G. Davis, *The San Francisco Mime Troupe: The First Ten Years* (1975)

Sanderson [Sackett], Julia   (b. Springfield, Mass., 20 Aug. 1887; d. Springfield, Mass., 27 Jan. 1975)   Singer, actress. With her father an actor, she made her stage debut as a child and her Broadway chorus debut aged 15 before starring in the 1904 revival of *Wang*. Appearances in New York and London were topped by her playing of Eileen in *The Arcadians* (1910), which made her the star of the US MUSICAL THEATRE, a role she held through the next decade in shows such as *The Siren* (1911), *The Girl from Utah* (1914, in which she introduced JEROME KERN's 'They Didn't Believe Me'), *The Canary* (1918), and *Tangerene* (1921). Known for her voice more than her personality, she later toured in *No, No, Nanette* (1925) and *Oh, Kay!* (1927) and played in VAUDEVILLE. CHARLES LONDON

Sandow, Eugene [Friedrich Wilhelm Möller] (b. Königsberg, Germany, 2 April 1867; d. London, 14 Oct. 1925) Strongman who came from Germany to the United States in 1893, making a fortune for FLORENZ ZIEGFELD and himself by such feats as lifting pianos and opening safes with his teeth. With TABLEAU VIVANT in vogue, Sandow, in tights, struck familiar classical poses. He was also well known as a promoter of physical culture. He died supposedly from injuries suffered after lifting a car from a ditch.

CLAUDIA DURST JOHNSON

Sands, Diana (b. New York, 22 Aug. 1934; d. New York, 12 Sept. 1973) Actress whose successes included *A Raisin in the Sun* (1959), *Tiger, Tiger Burning Bright* (1962), *Blues for Mr Charlie* (1964), *The Owl and the Pussycat* (New York, 1964; London, 1966), *St Joan* (1968), *Tiger at the Gates* (1968), *We Bombed in New Haven* (1968) and *The Gingham Dog* (1969). She was the first black actress to play St Joan, and her achievement in a wide variety of modern and classical roles was unusual for a black actress of her time. DAVID BARBOUR

Sardou, Victorien (b. Paris, 5 Sept. 1831; d. Marly, France, 8 Nov. 1908) Playwright. After abandoning medical studies and experiencing failure with his first play, *La Taverne des étudiants* ('The students' tavern', 1854), he became, with the encouragement of his actress wife, the natural successor to the nineteenth-century vaudeville master Eugène Scribe and embarked on a triumphant career which lasted into the early years of the twentieth century. His work includes interesting historical plays and the technically well-crafted farces which nourished what GEORGE BERNARD SHAW called 'sardoodledom'. They include *Les Premières armes de Figaro* ('Figaro's first coat of arms', 1859), *Pattes de mouche* (*A Scrap of Paper*, 1860), *La Famille Benoiton* (1865), *Divorçons* (*Let's get a Divorce*, 1880), *La Tosca* (1887, one of several vehicles for SARAH BERNHARDT and used by Puccini for his opera, *Thermidor*, 1891) and the famous *Madame Sans-Gêne* (*Madam Devil-May-Care*, 1893). TERRY HODGSON

Sargent, Franklin *see* DRAMA SCHOOLS

Saroyan, William (b. Fresno, Calif., 31 Aug. 1908; d. Fresno, 18 May 1981) Playwright, screenwriter, novelist and short-story writer who burst upon Broadway in 1939 as an original voice with *My Heart's in the Highlands* and *The Time of Your Life*. The former is a sometimes disturbing allegory about an embittered,

impoverished poet, his son and a fanciful Shakespearean actor who pays them a visit before dying. The latter play is a bittersweet comedy about several regulars of Nick's Pacific Street Saloon. This play was the first play to win both the Drama Critics' Circle Award and Pulitzer Prize and is continually revived. Saroyan refused the Pulitzer and wrote many more plays but none achieved popular appeal. After the failure in 1957 of two ambitious pieces, *The Cave Dwellers* and *The Slaughter of the Innocents*, he turned more to other forms of writing. THOMAS F. CONNOLLY

Lawrence Lee and Barry Gifford, *Saroyan: A Biography* (1984)

Sarraute [Tcherniak], Nathalie (b. Ivanova, Russia, 18 July 1900; d. Paris, 19 Oct. 1999) Playwright and novelist. She was taken at the age of two to Paris, where she had her schooling and took a law degree. Sarraute's first book, *Tropismes* (1938), already concentrates on what she later termed the 'sub-conversation' that underlies all human relationships; she sees this book as containing in germ everything she subsequently developed in her essays, her seven novels and her eight plays. Seen by critics in the 1950s as a member of the school of 'New Novelists', Sarraute published her first play, *Le Silence* in 1967. Other plays include *Le Mensonge* (*The Lie*, 1967); *C'est beau* (*It's Beautiful*, 1975); *Elle est là* (*It is There*, 1978); and *Pour un oui ou pour un non* (*For No Good Reason*, 1986).

BARBARA WRIGHT

S. Bell, *Nathalie Sarraute* (1982)
V. Minogue, *Nathalie Sarraute and the War of the Words* (1981)

Sartre, Jean-Paul (b. Paris, 21 June 1905; d. Paris, 15 April 1980) Philosopher, novelist and playwright; offered, but refused, the Nobel Prize (1964). Like ALBERT CAMUS, with whom he is often associated, Sartre came to prominence in France at the end of the Second World War, and his plays reflect similar concerns. The apocalyptic events of 1935–45 (followed by the Cold War), the metaphysical anguish of how best to resist fascism and kindred tyrannies, the universal moral scandals of the age, genocide, racism, torture, political corruption – these are central to his eight original plays spanning the years 1943–60. Sartre's is a theatre of razor-edge crisis, the once-in-a-lifetime situation when ordinary men and women have a chance to claim their freedom, to authenticate themselves by courageous and lucid action. Sartre came to the theatre relatively late – as a result, he claimed, of discovering its potential for communicating with his fellow men while a prisoner of war of the Germans in 1940–1. His first performed play, *Les Mouches* (*The Flies*, 1943), is in the neo-Greek vein popularized by COCTEAU, GIRAUDOUX and ANOUILH. Like Anouilh's *Antigone*, *Les Mouches* contains (among other things) a disguised message – beneath the nose of the German censors – of courageous resistance to tyranny. Sartre had lectured to the director DULLIN's drama students on Greek tragedy, and maintained an interest until a long time later (adapting Euripides' *Trojan Women* in 1965), yet he soon expressed his dissatisfaction with *Les Mouches* and similar modernizations of Greek myths. What the age required, he wrote, was theatre about the precise dilemma of Resistance fighters who know that innocent fellow-citizens will be executed in reprisal for the *necessary*(?) sabotage they have committed. What are the consequences for the conscience of the average man or woman who thus ends up with bloody hands: paralysing guilt? suicide? a brutalising cynicism? or the weary but courageous attempt of Canoris (*Morts sans Sépulture*; *Dead without Shadows*, 1946) to live on and continue the struggle (similarly, Hoederer in *Les Mains Sales*; *Dirty Hands* or *Crime Passionnel*, 1948)? At all events, not the blithe exit of Orestes at the end of *Les Mouches*, leaving the citizens of Argos to pick up the pieces.

Sartre acknowledged his affinity with the seventeenth-century theatre of conflict and debate, notably Corneille, and he depicts protagonists debating responsibility for their actions in his major works: *Morts sans Sépulture*, *Les Mains Sales*, *Le Diable et le Bon Dieu* (*The Devil and the Good Lord*, 1951) and *Les Séquestrés d'Altona* (*The Condemned of Altona*, 1960).

The three characters in *Huis Clos* (*In Camera* or *No Exit* or *Vicious Circle*, 1945), arguably Sartre's finest play and the one that travels best internationally, are destined to torment each other for eternity in hell; they are dead, and there is nothing they can do to change their (unheroic) lives and the way they will be remembered on earth.

Even Sartre's less often performed works, such as *Kean* (1953; known in the UK via BADEL, HOPKINS and JACOBI) and *Nekrassov* (1955; first play of the ENGLISH STAGE COMPANY to go to the EDINBURGH FESTIVAL), contain much that is of interest beyond France. He also wrote some film scripts and a huge book on GENET.

TED FREEMAN

Ted Freeman, *Theatres of War: French Committed Theatre from the Second World War to the Cold War* (1998)
Robert Lorris, *Sartre Dramaturge* (1975)
Dorothy McCall, *The Theatre of Jean-Paul Sartre* (1969)

Sastre, Alfonso (b. Madrid, 20 Feb. 1926) Playwright and theorist, whose refusal to comply with the strict CENSORSHIP of the Franco regime in Spain meant that his work remained largely unperformed in his native country. Imprisoned repeatedly for political dissent, Sastre has produced a body of subversive work which reflects his uncompromising political stance, protesting against oppression in all its manifestations. During the 1980s he drew increasingly on the Goyaesque tradition of the grotesque and the legends of the Basque region where he had settled. Plays include *Escuadra hacia la muerte* ('The condemned squad', 1953), *La cornada* ('Death thrust', 1960), *El banquete* ('The banquet', 1965), *El escenario diabólico* ('Diabolical scenario', written 1958, published 1973) and *Los últimos días de Emmanuel Kant contados por Ernesto Teodoro Hoffman* ('The last days of Emmanuel Kant, as told by Ernest Theodore Amadeus Hoffman', 1990). MARIA DELGADO

Farris Anderson, *Alfonso Sastre* (1971)
T. Avril Bryan, *Censorship and Social Conflict in the Spanish Theatre: The Case of Alfonso Sastre* (1983)

Satie, Erik [Eric Alfred Leslie] (b. Honfleur, France, 17 May 1866; d. Paris, 1 July 1925) Composer. One of the great influences on modern DANCE, Satie composed music that was part of the evolution of 'modern' music as well. His first ballet score, for the Ballets Russes' *Parade* (1917), produced by DIAGHILEV, PICASSO and COCTEAU, associated him with cubism. He wrote a play with incidental music, *Le Piège de Meduse* (1913), a symphonic drama, *Socrate* (1919), and composed the score for the Ballet Sudeois' last work, *Relâche* (1924), which was considered one of the first SURREALIST theatre works. His influence was wide and can be seen notably in the work of JOHN CAGE and in HAPPENINGS.

DENISE L. TILLES

satire A term that comes from the Latin for 'medley' and may have had origins in cooking, though not in the Greek satyr play, as the first Elizabethans believed. Satire uses various types of comic exaggeration to ridicule human institutions or behaviour, in the hope of their being changed or corrected. Among the common devices of satire are irony, parody and caricature. The first known dramatic satires are the plays of Aristophanes, and the tradition extends back beyond these to pre-dramatic Greek lampoons making fun of local figures. Satire, a favourite ROMAN form, has ever since been associated with the emphases of its two leading practitioners, Horace and Juvenal; Horatian satire is gentler, with some sympathy for its victims, while Juvenal lashes his victims without mercy. Both types of satire have a long and important tradition in the drama: the Horatian from Molière through the good-natured comedies of Goldsmith to the humane comedies of CHEKHOV, a good deal of SHAW and the generally sentimentalized tradition of the modern MUSICAL comedy; the harsher Juvenalian strain from Jonson through much of the 'English' comedy of manners tradition – Wycherly, WILDE, COWARD – to many modern BLACK COMEDY authors (e.g. JOE ORTON) and THEATRE OF THE ABSURD writers such as IONESCO. Juvenalian satire has also long been a favourite device of politically engaged drama, a tradition that can be traced back to Aristophanes and that would include Henry Fielding and BERTOLT BRECHT. Together with plays such as *Pravda* (HARE and BRENTON, 1985) or *Serious Money* (CARYL CHURCHILL, 1987), these examples suggest that Juvenalian satire is often closely related to the political cartoon or caricature, a relation that has been made explicit by modern AGITPROP and STREET THEATRE companies like the American TEATRO CAMPESINO and the BREAD AND PUPPET THEATER. MARVIN CARLSON

Ronald Paulson, ed., *Satire: Modern Essays in Criticism* (1971)
Peter Petro, *Modern Satire: Four Studies* (1982)

Saunders, James [A.] (b. London, 8 Jan. 1925) Playwright. Saunders' lengthy career is marked by its imaginative variety. The Beckettian *Next Time I'll Sing To You* (1962), which influenced STOPPARD, and the EXPRESSIONIST *A Scent of Flowers* (1964) contrast with the satire of *The Borage Pigeon Affair* (1962); the ABSURDISM of *Alas, Poor Fred* (1959) or *A Slight Accident* (1961) gave little hint of what was to come in the intellectual marital drama *Bodies* (1977), Saunders' biggest West End success. This story of two couples meeting to come to terms with their interrelated infidelities still demonstrates his underlying compassion and humanism. Supported by the local ORANGE TREE and QUESTORS theatres, and his higher European profile, Saunders has defied characterization, constantly testing new forms in his prolific output for stage, television and radio with enormous integrity and invention.
DAN REBELLATO

Saunders Lewis, J. *see* LEWIS, J. SAUNDERS

Savage, Lily *see* DRAG

Savary, Jérome (b. Buenos Aires, 27 June 1942) Actor, director and playwright. Famous as the leader of the GRAND MAGIC CIRCUS, much of Savary's work derives from the LIVING THEATER, JEAN VILAR and nineteenth-century popular entertainment. Harsh early work, including ARRABAL's *Le Labyrinthe* (1967) and *Adventures of Zartan, Ill-loved Brother of Tarzan* (1971), achieved desired notoriety, yet a somewhat mellower

Cyrano de Bergerac (1984) also won acclaim. *Cabaret* (1986) was an international triumph, and in 1988 he succeeded VITEZ at the THÉÂTRE NATIONAL POPULAIRE. In his technically brilliant *Frégoli* (1991), a formerly celebrated quick-change artist stepped with precise timing into and out of a pre-recorded film. TERRY HODGSON

Savoy, Bert [Everett Mackenzie] (b. Boston, 1888; d. Long Island, NY, 26 June 1923) Female IMPERSONATOR, effectively the pioneer of the contemporary DRAG act. Savoy, who learnt his trade appearing in CARNIVALS, was the first to depart from the traditional style of MUSIC HALL female impersonation which depicted women as grotesque battle-axes and attempt something more outrageous, both in content and in the use of flamboyant costumes. He used a fictional character, 'Margie', as his vehicle, coining the popular catchphrases of 'You don't know the half of it, dearie' and 'You must come over' – the latter indicative of his probable influence on the later characterizations of MAE WEST, who also adopted his penchant for large, picture hats and *double entendre*. He was joined as his 'feed' in 1913 by Jay Brennan (1883–1961) who continued to perform after Savoy's death, both with other partners and as a solo act. HELEN RAPPAPORT

Savoy Theatre Opened in London in 1881 by Richard D'Oyly Carte as the home of GILBERT and SULLIVAN. Their collaborations – previous as well as subsequent – became known as the Savoy Operas. The theatre also housed the pioneering VEDRENNE–GRANVILLE BARKER management and received many successful WEST END transfers. COLIN CHAMBERS

F. Cellier and C. G. Bridgeman, *Gilbert, Sullivan and the D'Oyly Carte* (1927)

Scase, David *see* MANCHESTER

scenography *see* DESIGN

Schall, Ekkehard (b. Magdeburg, 29 May 1930) Actor, director and formerly a leading member of the BERLINER ENSEMBLE, which he joined in 1952, and ran as artistic director from 1977 to 1992. He is best remembered for his performances in BRECHT plays, e.g. as Puntila, Arturo Ui, Coriolan, Azdak and Galileo. His wife Barbara is the daughter of the founders of the Ensemble, BERTOLT BRECHT and HELENE WEIGEL.
GÜNTER BERGHAUS

Schaubühne am Halleschen Ufer A theatre in West Berlin, founded in 1962 by students with the aim of pursuing theatrical activity outside the conventional pattern of subsidized municipal or state theatres on the one hand, or commercial theatres of the WEST END type on the other. In 1970 the lessees of this FRINGE theatre, situated in the run-down area of Kreuzberg outside the city centre, invited a group of theatre artists working with the director PETER STEIN to produce a programme of inexpensive, experimental and left-wing plays and to continue the theatre's tradition of cooperative and democratic working methods. The new Schaubühne ensemble was run by a directorate consisting of the two lessees, the directors Stein and CLAUS PEYMANN and the dramaturg Dieter Sturm. Final decisions in controversial matters lay with a general meeting of all employees, which met monthly. A subcommittee, elected by the general meeting, met the directorate twice weekly and reported back to the appropriate body. Appointment of new staff and casting of plays were democratically decided on, and a redistribution of wages was initiated to prevent the development of a star system and to abolish status differences between artistic and technical staff.

This organizational model became a blue print for several similar attempts in West Germany. Apart from fulfilling its political aims, the Schaubühne also sought to be a place for continuous theatrical research. The inspiration received from BRECHT's BERLINER ENSEMBLE showed itself in the political as well as aesthetic dimension. The heightened realism of Stein's work was supplemented by the more overtly political stagings of Frank-Patrick Steckel and the experimental performances directed by Klaus Michael Grüber. The company became influential abroad as well as at home for its interpretations of the classics (GORKY, CHEKHOV, IBSEN, Shakespeare, Aeschylus) and new plays (by writers such as HANDKE, KROETZ and STRAUSS, who was also dramaturg there).

Over the years, the model of democratic decision-making was modified, and on receipt of colossal subsidies from public funds, political compromises also had to be made. In 1980 the company moved to its new residence at the Lehniner Platz, which had been adapted to its needs with the help of huge public subsidies. The old theatre at the Hallische Ufer was handed over to a fringe company, the Theatermanufaktur. In 1984 Stein resigned his post and from 1985 to 1991 the theatre had a succession of interim directors, until the appointment in 1992 of Andrea Breth, who continued the tradition established by Stein a decade earlier. When she left in 1998, the theatre undertook a radical change of direction by appointing two young artistic directors from outside the ensemble, the choreographer Sasha Waltz and the head of a small Berlin fringe theater, Thomas Ostermeier.
GÜNTER BERGHAUS

Jack Zipes, 'The Irresistible Rise of the Schaubühne am Halleschen Ufer', *Yale Theater*, vol. 9, no. 1 (1977)

Schechner, Richard *see* ENVIRONMENTAL THEATRE; MAGAZINES AND JOURNALS; PERFORMANCE GROUP

Schehadé, Georges (b. Alexandria, 2 Nov. 1907; d. Paris, 17 Jan. 1989) Poet and playwright; Lebanese, he wrote in French. His plays *Monsieur Bob'le* (1951), *La soirée des proverbes* ('Party of the proverbs', 1954), *Histoire de Vasco* (*Vasco*, 1956), *Voyage* (1961) and *Les Violettes* ('The violets', 1966) contain mysterious adventures, in which characters seek some kind of truth through the innocence of poetry. WENDY SCOTT

Schiller, Leon [Jerzy Wojciech De Schildenfeld] (b. Cracow, 14 March 1887; d. Warsaw, 25 March 1954) Director, essayist, historian of theatre and teacher. Schiller was influenced by GORDON CRAIG's theories which inspired his quest for TOTAL THEATRE – a synthesis of acting, music and scenery. His productions of Polish romantic drama (e.g. Krasinski's *Undivine Comedy*, 1926; Mickiewicz's *Forefathers' Eve*, 1932) in modern, cubist settings became known as his 'monumental' style. Sensitive to the social and political problems of his times, he created a new type of spectacle – *Zeittheater*, a politically involved theatre of current ideas (e.g. BRECHT's *The Threepenny Opera*, 1929; TRETYAKOV's *Roar China*, 1932). He also drew on Polish mystery and folk plays. Schiller was the outstanding figure in Polish theatre between the world wars and is considered the founder of modern Polish direction. JOANNA KRAKOWSKA-NAROŹNIAK

Schisgal, Murray [Joseph] (b. New York, 25 Nov. 1926) Playwright. He gained recognition in America with a double bill, *The Typists* and *The Tiger* (1963), although the former had been performed in London in 1960. His big hit was the comedy *Luv* (London, 1963; New York, 1964). His later plays have not found success. GERALD BORDMAN

Schlemmer, Oskar (b. Gerboren, Germany, 4 Sept. 1888; d. Baden Baden, 13 April 1943) Designer. From 1923 to 1929 he was head of the BAUHAUS stage workshop, where he developed his influential ideas on relating the moving human form to the stage space via his geometric analysis of the body. Through this work he became a pioneer of PERFORMANCE ART and applied his abstract architectural notions to CHOREOGRAPHY as well as to painting. Among the productions he designed are the KOKOSCHKA–Hindemith opera *Mörder, Hoffnung der Frauen* (*Murderer, The Hope of Women*,

1921), *Don Juan und Faust* (1925) and *Hamlet* (1925). His own *Triadic Ballet* was performed in 1922. He was denounced by the Nazis and ended his life as a factory worker. His book, *New Stage Forms*, appeared in 1928 and *Letters and Diaries* in 1990.   CHARLES LONDON

W. Gropius, ed., *The Theatre of Bauhaus* (1916)
A. Huneke, ed., *Idealist der Form: Oskar Schlemmer* (1990)
A. L. Lehmann and B. Richardson, *Oskar Schlemmer* (1986)

Schneeman, Carolee   *see* BODY ART

Schneider, Alan [Abram Leopoldovich]   (b. Kharkov, Ukraine, 12 Dec. 1917; d. London, 4 May 1984) American director. In a full career which began in 1941, Schneider moved easily between Broadway and neighbourhood and regional theatres in the United States. A prolific director, he placed great store by casting the actor who was 'right' for the part, but also the actor no one else would have thought of. (The process came unstuck when he cast Bert Lahr and Tom Ewell in *Waiting for Godot*, 1956, when Lahr insisted as 'top banana' on having the laughs.) In general this approach served Schneider well, motivating actors to energetic performances following a smooth rehearsal period. Although his range of dramatists and styles was wide, Schneider is celebrated as the interpreter of BECKETT and ALBEE; he directed the world premières of *Who's Afraid of Virgina Woolf?* (1962), *Tiny Alice* (1964) and *A Delicate Balance* (1967), and the US premières of Beckett's *Waiting for Godot*, *Endgame* (1958), *Happy Days* (1961) and *Play* (1964). With Buster Keaton performing, he directed. Beckett's film script *Film* (1964). His autobiography, *Entrances: An American Director's Journal*, appeared in 1986, and a collection of his correspondence with Beckett, *No Author Better Served*, in 1999.   CLIVE BARKER

Schnitzler, Arthur   (b. Vienna, 15 May 1862; d. Vienna, 21 Oct. 1931) Playwright and novelist. He came from a well-established doctor's family and was himself a practising doctor until his literary fame allowed him to live off his royalties. His youth in Vienna was characterized by erotic adventures, gambling, visiting balls and suburban dance halls, and intellectual debates in coffee houses and artists' bars. His first play, *Anatol* (1893), describes the lifestyle of such bourgeois youths as himself, who have no sense of direction and drift through a life of endless, superficial pleasures. Attempts to perform *Anatol* led to censorship problems, and when *Das Märchen* (*The Fairytale*) opened at the Deutsches Volkstheater in 1893, it caused a scandal and performances had to be cancelled after two nights. However, through this play he made the aquaintance of Adele Sandrock, the leading star of the Viennese stage, which launched his career at the Burgtheater. Here in 1895 *Liebelei* (*Love Games*) was given its première with Sandrock in the lead. The play was an enormous success and was taken into the repertoire of BRAHM's Deutsches Theater and nine other German theatres. A publishing contract with S. Fischer Verlag made Schnitzler an established writer at the age of 33. However, the plays *Überspannte Person* ('Eccentric person', published 1896), *Freiwild* (*Free Game*, 1896) and especially *Der Reigen* (*La Ronde*, published 1903; subsequently filmed by Max Ophuls) brought him notoriety and the reputation of being the most immoral poet writing in the German tongue. Not surprisingly, his plays were banned by the Nazis.

Between 1903 and 1914 Schnitzler was one of the most widely performed playwrights in the German-speaking countries. His developed form of psychological realism and the impressionist structure of his plays was brought out most clearly in productions by Brahm and REINHARDT, while the Vienna Burgtheater preferred his historical dramas. His later works were mainly of a novelistic nature. He also wrote one-act plays, of which the best known is *Der grüne Kakadu* (*The Green Cockatoo*, 1899).

Schnitzler was an acute observer of the disintegration of the Habsburg Empire, and the impact capitalism and industrialization had on the Viennese population. In *Professor Bernhardi* (1912), he dealt with the very personal issue of anti-semitism. He possessed a highly developed sensitivity for the subtle changes in various social milieux, but concentrated on exemplifying his observations with brilliantly drawn character portraits. He has often been called a *Doppelgänger* of Sigmund Freud. The two men were aware of each other's work. They lived in close proximity, yet consciously avoided meeting each other and pursued independently their analysis of the pathological tendencies and neuroses of a moribund society (for example, in *Das weite Land*, 1911, seen in London in 1979 in a version by TOM STOPPARD entitled *Undiscovered Country*). In Schnitzler's works, some of which predate modernist writers like Joyce, the erotic element is of prime importance. The depth and subtlety of his insight into the human soul were expressed through ordinary and everyday plots and situations. But this apparently unpretentious material is knit together by elegant, charming dialogue and a dramaturgy where, under an apparent formlessness, a precise structure of musical quality is hidden.
GÜNTER BERGHAUS

Brigitte L. Schneider-Halsvorson, *The Late Dramatic Work of Arthur Schnitzler* (1983)

M. Swales, *Arthur Schnitzler* (1971)

R. Urbach, *Arthur Schnitzler* (1973)

Schoenberg, Arnold *see* EISLER, HANNS; MUSIC THEATRE

Schönberg, Claude-Michel *see* BOUBLIL, ALAIN

Schreyer, Lothar (b. Blasewitz, Saxony, 19 Aug. 1886; d. Hamburg, 18 June 1966) Playwright, director, designer and essayist. After two years of military service, in 1916 he joined EXPRESSIONIST circles in Berlin and edited their journal, *Der Sturm*. He organized several theatrical soirées and founded, in 1918, the Sturmbühne, a small private theatre wholly dedicated to the performances of expressionist plays. The first production was STRAMM's *Sancta Susanna* (1918). In 1919 Schreyer returned to Hamburg, where he founded the Kampfbühne and mounted eight productions, financed by a local organization called 'Friends of Expressionism'. In 1921 Schreyer was offered a teaching post at the BAUHAUS in Weimar, where until 1923 he ran their theatre workshop. GÜNTER BERGHAUS

M. S. Jones, *Der Sturm: A Focus of Expressionism* (1984)

Schumann, Peter *see* BREAD AND PUPPET THEATER

Schwartz, Arthur (b. Brooklyn, New York, 25 Nov. 1900; d. Kintnersville, Pennsylvania, 3 Sept. 1984) Composer, producer and librettist. Initially trained as a lawyer, he composed for VAUDEVILLE and contributed to several shows before teaming up with lyricist **Howard Dietz** (b. New York, 8 Sept. 1896; d. New York, 30 July 1983). The partnership was responsible for a series of successful REVUES, including *The Little Show* (1929), *Three's a Crowd* (1930), *The Band Wagon* (1931) and *At Home Abroad* (1935). Schwartz worked with lyricist DOROTHY FIELDS on *Stars in Your Eyes* (1939), *A Tree Grows in Brooklyn* (1951) and *By the Beautiful Sea* (1954). He composed 46 film scores between 1939 and 1946, and re-formed his collaboration with Dietz to write the musicals *The Gay Life* (1961) and *Jenny* (1963). Many of their songs have become standards of popular music, including 'You and the Night and the Music', 'That's Entertainment' and 'Dancing in the Dark'. Schwartz was director of the American Society of Composers, Authors and Publishers from 1958 until 1983. LAURIE WOLF

Schwartz, Maurice (b. Sedikor, Russia, 18 June 1890; d. Petah Tikva, Israel, 10 May 1960) Actor and producer who came to America in 1901 and was still in his teens when he began performing in YIDDISH play-

houses. In 1918 he took over the ageing Irving Place Theater in New York, and converted it into the Yiddish Art Theater. The company moved to other playhouses, but Schwartz always led it, with occasional breaks, until 1950. His dark hair, piercing eyes and rumbling voice allowed him to dominate, although younger playgoers increasingly complained about his old-style flamboyance. He had a wide repertoire in Yiddish of roles in both classics and newer plays, including Shylock and the title part of the rabbi in *Yoshe Kalb* (1932), which he adapted from I. J. Singer's novel. GERALD BORDMAN

Scofield, Paul [David] (b. Hurstpierpoint, Sussex, 21 Jan. 1922) Actor, equally at home in comic and tragic roles, in classical and contemporary drama. After studying at the London Mask Theatre School and making a West End debut in 1940, he first made his mark at the BIRMINGHAM REPERTORY THEATRE under BARRY JACKSON, who took him to STRATFORD-UPON-AVON in 1946. For two decades Scofield played major Shakespearean roles, including Hamlet (1948) and Lear (1962) in PETER BROOK's outstanding production, one of the key performances of the time. He appeared with Canada's STRATFORD FESTIVAL in 1961, and in the 1970s, 1980s and 1990s worked with England's NATIONAL THEATRE (e.g. Othello, 1980; Oberon, 1982; John Gabriel Borkmann, 1996). He has played leading roles in such contemporary plays as *The Power and the Glory* (1956), most famously *A Man For All Seasons* (1960), in which he made his Broadway debut the following year and the film in 1966, and *Amadeus* (1979). He was made a Companion of Honour in 2000. DAVID STAINES

J. C. Trewin, *Paul Scofield* (1956)

Scotland

1900–1970

During the early twentieth century, the Scots were all too aware of the inadequacies of their theatrical past and, in particular, their lack of a coherent, continuously developing dramatic tradition. They attributed this deficiency to a variety of causes. Murray McClymount blamed English cultural dominance, which began with the departure of King James VI's court to London in 1603 and reached its height in the heyday of the British Empire in the late nineteenth century. Robert Mitchell, a working-class activist, argued that the fault lay with religion, with the curbs imposed by Calvinism and Presbyterianism. At the turn of the century, there was plenty of theatre available in Scotland, but very little of this was indigenous. While Scottish dramatists such as J. M. BARRIE found fame and fortune in London, Scottish cities and towns became largely dependent on the visits of English actor–manager troupes such as FRANK BENSON's Shakespeare Company or the MARTIN-HARVEY Players. There were some very successful commercial tours of Scottish plays, such as Isack Pocock's *Rob Roy MacGregor* or Graham Moffat's *Bunty Pulls the Strings*. However, these plays presented images of Scottish life which were divorced from reality, and immensely trite. The former was an historical drama, presenting the Scotsman as a violent, hairy man in a kilt, the latter an example of what was known as a kailyard drama, set typically in a Lowland parish, portraying a minor event in the lives of two-dimensional village folk in a sentimental and comic fashion.

The Scottish MUSIC HALLS, with their VARIETY programmes and long-running PANTOMIMES, likewise presented a more distinctly Scottish fare, and in the era of comedians such as HARRY LAUDER, WILL FYFFE, Harry Gordon, Tommy Lorne, Tommy Morgan and George West, the pantomime, as LEWIS CASSON put it, became the national theatre of Scotland. But the legacy of the music-hall programme, with its comic sketches and songs, is a mixed one. While the comedians themselves tended to indulge and exploit the tartan and kailyard images of Scotland for their comic potential, the playwright JOHN MCGRATH has used some features of the music-hall programme as part of a new dramatic form, and performers from Duncan McCrae and Molly Urquhart to John Bett, Billy Paterson and Elizabeth McLennan readily acknowledge their debt to music-hall skills.

During the early twentieth century a new national awareness spread through the arts in Scotland, and in its wake two independent theatre movements, competing but in many ways complementary, came into being. First there was a new bourgeois movement, founded by Alfred Wareing's Scottish Repertory Theatre (1909–14) and revived after the First World War by the SCOTTISH NATIONAL PLAYERS. Its development in the interwar years was furthered by two early provincial repertory theatres in Dundee and Perth, a series of LITTLE THEATRES including the Curtain Theatre, Glasgow (1930–9), and the MSU Theatre, Rutherglen (1939–44), as well as the many middle-class AMATEUR theatre clubs which took part in the Scottish Community Drama Association's annual FESTIVAL of one-act plays, instigated in 1926. Second was the emergence of working-class drama groups in the industrial centres, notably GLASGOW and the mining villages of Ayrshire, Fife, Lanarkshire and Lothian. Some of these had links with two British movements, the Workers' Theatre Movement and the UNITY THEATRE Society.

Many more were formed independently by Scottish socialist organizations – local branches of the Communist, Labour and Independent Labour parties, the Scottish Labour College, the Clarion and Co-operative Societies – as well as apolitical working-class groups such as the local Burns club or, in the case of Glasgow, the Jewish Institute. The two most important clubs of this kind were JOE CORRIE's Bowhill (or Fife) Miner Players (1926–31) and Glasgow Unity Theatre (1941–51).

These two traditions remained discernible in postwar Scotland. The middle-class companies of the interwar years were the precursors of wartime and postwar repertory theatres, including the CITIZENS' in Glasgow (from 1943), the GATEWAY in EDINBURGH (1943–65), the Royal LYCEUM (also in Edinburgh from 1965), and the Scottish Theatre Company (1981–6), as well as smaller experimental theatre clubs including the TRAVERSE (from 1963), the Close (1965–73) and the TRON (from 1981). Similarly, the working-class theatres of the 1920s, 1930s and 1940s prepared the way for the popular political groups of the 1970s, including 7:84 (Scotland) and Wildcat Stage Productions. Their fortunes have fluctuated due to external developments such as the advent of television and access to state funding. During the interwar years, the vast majority of Scottish theatre groups were amateur and drew on the fact that people were used to making their own entertainment. After the war, a change in the habits of the general public, notably a growing reluctance to adopt pastimes which would take them outside the home, threatened amateur theatre, and there was increasing emphasis on a theatre's capacity to survive as a professional organization. During the immediate postwar period, state funding became available. The Citizens' had received help from the COUNCIL FOR THE ENCOURAGEMENT OF MUSIC AND THE ARTS during the war, and other bourgeois theatres soon found themselves in receipt of grants from the Scottish Committee of the ARTS COUNCIL OF GREAT BRITAIN (1947–67). Working-class groups were less fortunate. Forced back on their amateur status at a time when working-class communities were being broken up by the closure of traditional centres of work, the clearance of slums for high-rise flats and ring roads, the working-class theatre of the interwar years virtually disappeared. In 1967 the Scottish Arts Council replaced the Scottish Committee of the Arts Council of Great Britain and, under its auspices, new theatres were built and new companies formed, the latter including new popular political groups. In the 1980s circumstances changed again, and theatres catering for bourgeois and working-class audiences were faced with the possibility of a major reduction of resources or complete loss of funding.

Scotland, then, has forged two independent drama traditions. They have been dominated by two major concerns. First, there is the concept of the Scottish national theatre, the Scots' urge to create a native drama and, allied to this, their desire to assert their independence of English drama. While this has led some playwrights, directors and individual performers to turn inwards to aspects of their native culture, others have looked to international models for inspiration. During the interwar years, both theatre traditions were influenced by the ABBEY THEATRE, Dublin, early bourgeois companies like the Scottish National Players leaning towards YEATS and SYNGE, working-class theatres such as the Fife Miner Players or Glasgow Unity towards SEAN O'CASEY. Similarly, both traditions recognised the need to stage a range of international works, bourgeois reps turning to IBSEN and CHEKHOV, their working-class counterparts to Americans such as ODETS and European authors such as GORKY and TOLLER. Some Scottish theatres offered Scots adaptations of the classics: the Gateway Theatre presented ROBERT KEMP's Scots adaptations of Molière. Since the Second World War, the Scots have been brought into regular contact with international developments thanks to two annual festivals, the EDINBURGH INTERNATIONAL FESTIVAL of Music and Drama (from 1947, and latterly also the FRINGE), and Glasgow's MAYFEST (from 1983), and thanks to the policies of individual companies, notably the Traverse and the Citizens', under the artistic directorship of Giles Havergal, ROBERT DAVID MACDONALD and PHILIP PROWSE.

The second major concern has been to create a tradition of native writing. At the start of the twentieth century the number of Scottish plays was minute, but since then Scottish writers have acknowledged the need to produce a body of native drama, poets and novelists alike attempting to write a play at some point in their careers. Naturally, the bourgeois and working-class traditions had different views about what a Scottish play should ideally be like, though both recognized the need to abandon or re-examine the myths behind the tartan and kailyard images of Scottish life. At this point, it is important to mention JAMES BRIDIE. He was the founder of the Citizens' and of the Drama College attached to the Royal Scottish Academy of Music, chairman of the Scottish Committee of the Arts Council of Great Britain and of the Scottish Community Drama Association, and Drama Adviser to the Edinburgh Festival, and as such his influence on the development of Scottish drama was very considerable. His plays made less impact, for the vast majority were first performed outside Scotland and their content and style remain unique to Bridie, the next generation of playwrights preferring to follow other trends. None the less, his 'Scottish' plays, which include *The Anatomist* (Masque Theatre, Royal Lyceum, London, 1930), *The Sleeping Clergyman* (Malvern Festival, 1933), *Mr Bolfry* (Westminster Theatre, London, 1943) and *Mr Gillie* (King's Theatre, Glasgow, 1950), became very popular in Scotland and can be seen as a response to the needs of Scottish drama. They present archetypal Scottish characters (the doctor, the minister, the schoolteacher), the familiar figures of kailyard comedy. At one level, they portray these characters as exceptional, exploring their intellectual or moral stature in an effort to restore their credibility as subjects for serious drama. At another, they seek a measure of detachment – through the inclusion of lengthy academic discussion about the nature of man and God and through a somewhat subversive mocking humour – which seems to have been Bridie's answer to the excessive sentimentality of earlier Scottish plays.

Bridie aside, various patterns of playwriting have emerged. Many bourgeois exponents of the Scottish national theatre called for subjects which were 'abstract' or 'general' in the belief that this would elevate and universalize the works. The playwright JOHN BRANDANE, a leading member of the Scottish National Theatre Society and the Scottish National Players' Play Reading Panel, was particularly enthusiastic about plays concerning Scottish antiquity, the 'Celtic Twilight'. He was the prime mover behind the production of Neil Gunn's *The Ancient Fire* (Scottish National Players, Lyric Theatre, Glasgow, 1929) which stimulated a great deal of discussion about the direction which Scottish drama should be taking. His own plays, including *The Glen is Mine* (Athenaeum Theatre, Glasgow, 1923), fell into another of the Scottish National Players' favourite categories, portraying rural, preferably Highland experience as the true Scottish experience, free from the influence of English culture, which had corrupted the cities. A third type of play was the Scottish history drama, which included some fine works such as ROBERT MCLELLAN's *Jamie the Saxt* (Curtain Theatre, Glasgow, 1937), but which at its worst descended into formulaic renditions of the same well-known episodes, notably the 1745 Rebellion. The playwrights debated at length the kind of language they should use; McLellan, like many poets of the day, wrote in Lallans, or old Scots.

By contrast, working-class playwrights such as Joe Corrie, Robert McLeish and ENA LAMONT STEWART argued that a national drama should portray some of the concrete realities of the present day. They wrote plays – *In Time O'Strife* (Bowhill Players, 1927), *The Gorbals Story* (Glasgow Unity, 1946) and *Men Should Weep* (Glasgow Unity, 1947) respectively – about the life of the urban working class, partly because at that time Scotland was a depressed industrial nation, but mainly because this was the life they knew. They wrote not in Lallans but in the regional dialects they used every day. Following in their footsteps, the plays of John McGrath – from *The Cheviot, the Stag and the Black, Black Oil* (7:84 Scotland, 1973) to *Border Warfare* (Freeway Films and Wildcat, 1989) – bring together many of the themes which have dominated Scottish playwriting in the twentieth century, portraying experience which might be historical or contemporary, Highland or urban.

While dramatic developments have dominated the Scottish theatrical scene, the twentieth century has also seen an expansion in other performing arts. Despite the decline of the music hall, traditional pantomime remains as popular as ever. Scottish Opera presents an international repertoire which includes Scottish works, while since 1970 the Scottish Ballet – which traces its origins back to Margaret Morris's Celtic Ballet of 1947–58 and the Scottish National Ballet of 1960 – has also been immensely active.

LINDA MACKENNEY

1970–2000

The distinct concerns of Scottish theatre, as noted above, were still identifiable in the last quarter of the century but found new and vibrant expression. A flourishing cultural independence substituted for the political independence that failed to appear in 1979 when the devolution vote was lost, and Scotland's playwrights became vital to its sense of identity.

The three notable movements of abstract expressionism, historical nostalgia and contemporary social realism remain but are no longer mutually exclusive, often assimilating each other's strengths. SUE GLOVER's *Bondagers* (1991), portraying female farm labourers in the Borders towards the end of the nineteenth century, strikes an emotional chord in Scotland with its story of a forgotten community, but the lyricism of the language and expressionistic images of the women working in the fields give the piece an epic quality, borne out by the international success of the play. Similarly, the majority of CHRIS HANNAN's work is set in working-class tenements but has a distinct absurdist streak running through it, as exemplified by *Elizabeth Gordon Quinn* (1985), whose eponymous heroine cries 'I refuse to learn how to be poor!'

The strong tradition of writing in a Scots language has always been important for the country's sense of

identity, but its use developed and changed remarkably over the last three decades of the century. During the 1970s many dramatists eschewed both the artificial form of older Scots used for historical plays and the accented dialogue used for contemporary plays in favour of a demotic Scots they felt to be real. The resulting plays harnessed a great energy, as in Tom McGrath's *The Hard Man* (1977), about a Glasgow gangster, and Hector MacMillan's *The Sash* (1974), exploring religious sectarianism. Questions of identity, both of gender and of nation, and of how these are expressed through language have become a fascination for many playwrights. A defining moment in this progression is LIZ LOCHHEAD's *Mary Queen of Scots Got Her Head Chopped Off* (1987) in which the Scots of Queen Mary is set against the English of Queen Elizabeth. This relationship is made all the more interesting by giving Mary's Scots a heavy French accent and having her switch roles (and languages) with Elizabeth, each becoming the other's maid. There has always been an element of fantasy in Scots, and over the last 30 years of the century the exotic metaphors which characterize working-class speech in west central Scotland were best expressed in the work of JOHN BYRNE, Chris Hannan and IAIN HEGGIE.

As well as linguistic expression, questions of national identity have also been a rich source of subject matter for Scottish theatre. In Liz Lochhead's devised piece *Jock Tamson's Bairns* (1990) the central character (androgynously) embodies the whole of Scottish identity in 'his' head. Another fine example is Stephen Greenhorn's *Passing Places* (1997), which can be seen as the ultimate Scotland play as its two heroes journey north and discover that their country is bigger and much more disparate than they had bargained for.

This inward focus has been matched by a strong drive to look at Scotland's relationship with Europe and the rest of the world, which has found expression in the work of both playwrights and theatre companies. The Citizens' Theatre has gained a reputation for bringing the best of European drama to Scotland, and the effect on audiences, and in shaping a new generation of playwrights, has been immense. Since the early 1980s Communicado Theatre Company has brought a performance style inspired by JERZY GROTOWSKI and TADEUSZ KANTOR to a whole host of Scottish and international plays. New Scots translations/versions of both classic and contemporary texts have been produced to great acclaim; highlights are Liz Lochhead's *Tartuffe* (1985) and *Medea* (2000), Hector MacMillan's *The Hypochondriak* (1987) and Edwin Morgan's *Cyrano de Bergerac* (1992). Scotland, 'a country within a country', has also found dramatic parallels in other such nations around the world. The Tron Theatre's production of Bill Findlay and Martin Bowman's Scots translation of the Québecois playwright MICHEL TREMBLAY's *The Guid Sisters* (1989) was successful in both Scotland and, surprisingly, Montreal. In fact this, and much of Tremblay's other work, has found such resonance that he has been called the finest playwright Scotland never had. The Traverse Theatre, which has a long history of presenting international work alongside native new writing, produced plays by DAVID GREIG (*The Speculator*, 1999) and Lluisa Cunïllé (*The Meeting*, 1999) at the Edinburgh International Festival under the banner *Caledonia/Catalonia*. David Greig has also found great success on an international platform with his own theatre company Suspect Culture, which has developed a unique visual and gestural performance style inspired by European working methods. This fusion of new writing and a physical, visual style has also characterised the productions of Ktc and their work with DAVID HARROWER.

During the 1990s much original work was produced with a keen eye on Europe and the rest of the world. This saw plays written in a more standard English (though no less Scottish because of it) finding great success at home and abroad. John Clifford's plays have a style, and often subject matter, illuminated by his interest in seventeenth-century Spanish drama. Latin America has also had an impact on his writing, resulting in affinities with the work of the magic realists. David Greig's work has a strong international streak running through it, from the east European setting of *Stalinland* (1994) and *Europe* (1995) to the multinational *The Cosmonaut's Last Message to the Woman he Once Loved in the Former Soviet Union* (1999). Mike Cullen has been strongly influenced by the American playwright DAVID MAMET, as can be clearly seen in his multi-award-winning play *Anna Weiss* (1997).

This is not to say that writing in a dialect has precluded international success for Scotland's playwrights. David Harrower's atavistic *Knives in Hens* (1995) has become something of a European classic, translated into over ten languages and produced in countless countries worldwide, as has Liz Lochhead's romantic comedy *Perfect Days* (1998).

In 1997 Scotland overwhelmingly voted to regain its own parliament. Scottish theatre is as political as ever, although there is now much less overt agitprop in its plays. It currently has a generation of vital playwrights inspired by a strong tradition of indigenous work. The new Scottish parliament is responding to the theatre community's appeal for a national theatre, one of the most powerful arguments being that there is now a repertoire of Scottish plays worth producing.

Might this not be as a result of the confidence that has grown up around the prospect of constitutional change? JOHN TIFFANY

Douglas Allen, 'The Glasgow Workers' Theatre Group and the Methodology of Theatre Studies', *Theatre Quarterly*, vol. 9 (1980)

Winifred Bannister, *James Bridie and His Theatre* (1955)

Frank Bruce, *Scottish Showbusiness: Music Hall, Variety and Pantomime* (2000)

Donald Campbell, *Playing for Scotland* (1996)

V. Devlin, *King's, Queens and People's Palaces: An Oral History of the Scottish Variety Theatre 1920–70* (1991)

John Hill, 'Towards a Scottish People's Theatre: The Rise and Fall of Glasgow Unity', *Theatre Quarterly*, vol. 7 (1977)

David Hutchison, *The Modern Scottish Theatre* (1977)

W. Isaac, *Alfred Wareing* (1951)

J. H. Littlejohn, *The Scottish Music Hall 1880–1990* (1990)

Linda Mackenney, *The Activities of Popular Dramatists and Drama Groups in Scotland, 1900–52* (2000)

Randall Stevenson and Gavin Wallace, *Scottish Theatre since the Seventies* (1996)

Scott, Bertie   *see* VOICE TRAINING

Scott, George C[ampbell]   (b. Wise, Va., 18 Oct. 1927; d. Westlake Village, Cal., 22 Sept. 1999)   Actor and director who made his New York debut as Richard III with the NEW YORK SHAKESPEARE FESTIVAL (1957), for which he later played Shylock and Antony. He complemented his successful stage career, where he had leading roles in such plays as *The Andersonville Trial* (1959), *Plaza Suite* (1968), and *Sly Fox* (1976), which he also directed, with equally successful acting forays into film and television. His long association with New York's CIRCLE IN THE SQUARE involved starring roles in such plays as *Children of Darkness* (1958) and *Uncle Vanya* (1973) and directing revivals of *Death of a Salesman* (1975) and *Present Laughter* (1982), in which he also starred, and *Design for Living* (1984). These last two performances showed off his comic skills in contrast to his reputation for gritty, intense acting. Campbell Scott, his son with COLLEEN DEWHURST, is also an actor. His many films include *Dr Strangelove* (1964) and *Patton* (1970), for which he was awarded the best actor Oscar – but, not believing in the Oscar system, he refused to accept it, the first actor to do so. DAVID STAINES

Scottish National Players   The company first performed in 1921, under the auspices of the St Andrew Society, and aimed to produce plays of Scottish life and character; to encourage in SCOTLAND a public taste for good drama of any type; and to build a national theatre. Based in Glasgow, the SNP toured Scotland, and were an important training ground for Scottish theatre and for the BBC. At its height in the 1920s, the company produced some 60 new plays. TYRONE GUTHRIE was its director in 1926–7, and among those whose work was staged were JOHN BRANDANE, JAMES BRIDIE, JOE CORRIE (who fell out with the Players) and ROBERT KEMP. The movement folded in 1948.

KAREN MARSHALSAY

seasonal theatre Many people go to the theatre during the Christmas or summer holidays, and managements cater specifically for this trade. At Christmas, the shows are generally aimed at children. In Britain, since Victorian times, the tradition at this time of year has been to present a PANTOMIME, with its stock characters and situations that are constantly updated. Edwardian times saw the addition of *Peter Pan* (1904), which continued the pantomime convention of a woman playing the lead male until the ROYAL SHAKE-SPEARE COMPANY (1982) offered a new dramatization in which Peter is played by a man. Edwardian values were still to the fore when the fairy play *Where the Rainbow Ends* (1911) opened; it was a regular December offering through to the mid-1950s. Joining *Peter Pan* were other adaptations from fiction, either thematically appropriate, like *A Christmas Carol* (a favourite in America), or suitably adventuresome, like *Treasure Island*; these became more popular from the 1960s on. Theatres also present shows such as *The Wizard of Oz* or its black version, *The Wiz*, and RADIO CITY MUSIC HALL in New York has its own Christmas and Easter shows. In the summer months there is light entertainment in many British coastal resorts. A successor to PIERROT shows and concert parties, it generally takes the form of a VARIETY or REVUE-type production. In the larger resorts, notably Blackpool, it is built around star artists. BOOTHS can also be found on beaches and piers, typically showing Punch and Judy (*see* PUPPET THEATRE). For more serious theatregoing, FESTIVALS, such as the EDINBURGH INTERNATIONAL FESTIVAL or the NEW YORK SHAKESPEARE FESTIVAL, are often held in the summer. In America, there were also travelling 'tent shows' (until 1950) and still are SUMMER STOCK companies performing in parks and resorts. Outside the ranks of organized Christianity, which still mounts nativity plays at Christmas time and passion plays at Easter, the professional theatre occasionally sees Easter performances of passion plays or of sections of the medieval mystery plays. COLIN CHAMBERS & PETER HEPPLE

See also MEDIEVAL THEATRE IN THE TWENTIETH CENTURY; RELIGIOUS DRAMA; TENT THEATRE.

Seattle Although located in the relative isolation of America's Pacific north-west, this city of 500,000, in the state of Washington, is home to an extraordinarily large and diverse theatre community. VAUDEVILLE peaked here at the beginning of the twentieth century, and from then until the 1960s local drama was dominated by the Seattle Repertory Playhouse, which promoted O'NEILL and ODETS. Following the 1962 World Fair, the founding in 1963 of SEATTLE REPERTORY THEATER marked the birth of Seattle's indigenous professional theatre community. Since then many lively companies have found a home in Seattle (although not all have survived). They include A Contemporary Theater (1965, focusing on the modern repertory); Bathhouse Theater (1970, known for revivals of Shakespeare and other classic works); Empty Space (1970, contemporary works); Fifth Avenue Musical Theater (new and classic musicals); Group Theater Company (1978, multi-ethnic theatre); Intiman Theater Company (1972, new and classic works); Seattle Children's Theater (1975, new works for children – the largest such organization in the United States); New City/Theater Zero (1982, AVANT-GARDE), Alice B Theater (1984, GAY and LESBIAN theatre), Northwest ASIAN AMERICAN THEATER (1972) and On the Boards (1979, PERFORMANCE ART). Nearby in Tacoma can be found Tacoma Actors' Guild, which presents mostly new works. Also located in Seattle is the Cornish School conservatory (founded 1914) and the University of Washington, whose drama department, founded in 1941 by noted theatre educator Glenn Hughes, has dozens of graduate students studying acting, playwriting, directing and design. In addition, Seattle is home to a flourishing FRINGE theatre scene, with more than 40 companies in existence at any one time, promoted by an organization named LOFT (League of Fringe Theaters). An annual Fringe Festival (named after the similar event in EDINBURGH) highlights the work of these theatres. DAVID BARBOUR

David Barbour, 'Seattle', *Theatre Crafts International*, March 1992.
Steven Samuels, ed., *Theater Profiles 10: The Illustrated Guide to America's Nonprofit Professional Theater* (1992)

Seattle Repertory Theatre Founded in 1963 in a building designed for the World Fair the previous year, SRT has developed into one of the most important RESIDENT theatres in the United States. After a difficult start, SRT established itself under W. Duncan Ross. In 1974 a second building was taken, called Stage 2. Under the artistic directorship of Daniel Sullivan (1981), SRT has premièred a series of new American plays, including Herb Gardner's *I'm Not Rappaport*

(1985) and *Conversations With My Father* (1991), WENDY WASSERSTEIN's *The Heidi Chronicles* (1988), Richard Greenberg's *Eastern Standard* (1988) and BILL IRWIN's *Largely New York* (1989). However, classic works from the world repertory are also staged. In 1983, SRT opened the Bagley Wright Theatre at the Seattle Center, which also houses a small Forum for new work. The twenty-first century began with Sharon Ott as artistic director. The company was honoured with a special Tony Award in 1990. DAVID BARBOUR

Seldes, Marian (b. New York, 23 Aug. 1928) Actress, writer and teacher. Born into an artistic family, she studied acting and became a protégée of director GUTHRIE MCCLINTIC and his wife, actress KATHARINE CORNELL. A diligent, often brilliant, performer, Seldes' Broadway appearances span 40 years. Though some critics cite a tendency to 'overact', her extensive stage, television and film career has garnered many awards, including a Tony for *A Delicate Balance* (1967). Other notable performances came in *The Ginger Man* (1964), *Isadora Duncan Sleeps with the Russian Navy* (1976) and *Painting Churches* (1984). In 1969 she began teaching at the Juilliard School. DAVID A. WILLIAMS

Sellars, Peter [Mark] (b. Pittsburgh, Pa., 27 Sept. 1957) Director and producer. During the 1980s Sellars was the *Wunderkind* – some would say the *enfant terrible* – of the American theatre. Energetic and constantly productive, his audacious productions for his short-lived American National Theater at the KENNEDY CENTER in Washington DC and for many other theatres ranged through the world repertoire: Gogol's *The Inspector General* (1980), BRECHT's *The Visions of Simone Machard* (1983), Sophocles' *Ajax* (1986) and Aeschylus' *The Persians* (1993). Many of them were epic and most involved music. Less iconoclast than idealist, Sellars seeks to link contemporary life with the sublime, as should be clear from his innovative work on operas by Handel, Mozart, Wagner and John Adams. The 1990 Los Angeles Festival he produced featured the spiritual arts of Pacific Rim cultures. The production of *The Merchant of Venice* he directed for Chicago's GOODMAN MEMORIAL THEATER (1994) set the play in the high-tech age of riot-torn contemporary California. Sellars was appointed artistic director of the 2002 Adelaide Festival in Australia (*see* FESTIVALS).
M. ELIZABETH OSBORN

A. Green, *The Revisionist Stage: American Directors Reinvent the Classics* (1994)
Adrian Rigelsford, *Peter Sellars* (2000)

Senegal *see* FRENCH AFRICAN THEATRE

Serban, Andrei (b. Bucharest, Romania, 21 June 1943) Director. Serban was introduced to Western audiences in 1970, when he worked at LA MAMA in New York and subsequently at the PUBLIC THEATER and several regional theatres, including the AMERICAN REPERTORY THEATER in Boston, where he has been directing for more than two decades. He worked with PETER BROOK in Europe and developed a reputation as a leading director on the international theatre and opera scene through a series of innovative, physical productions, such as *The Cherry Orchard* (1977), *The Marriage of Figaro* (1982) and *The King Stag* (1984). Serban returned to his native country as artistic director of the Romanian National Theatre in 1991. In 1992 he was appointed director of the Oscar Hammerstein II Center for the Performing Arts at Columbia University in New York City, and he has taught at several other American universities. ELLEN LAMPERT-GRÉAUX

E. Menta, *The Magic World Behind the Curtain: Andrei Serban in the American Theater* (1995)

Serbia *see* YUGOSLAVIA

Serpent Players *see* FUGARD, ATHOL

Serreau, Jean-Marie (b. Poitiers, France, 28 April 1915; d. Paris, 1 June 1973) Director. Formed by DULLIN and strongly marked by BRECHT, he staged ADAMOV, IONESCO and BECKETT, and linked the ABSURD with POLITICAL and EXPERIMENTAL THEATRE. Michel Parent's *Gilda appelle Mae West* ('Gilda calls Mae West', 1962) was mounted (in Dijon) on a multiple set to show the pilots', victims' and general reactions to the dropping of atomic bombs. He fought to find theatres for plays about Third World problems, such as KATEB YACINE's *Le Cadavre encerclé* (*The Besieged Corpse*, 1963). Other productions include CÉSAIRE's *La Tragédie du Roi Christophe* (*The Tragedy of King Christopher*) and CLAUDEL's *Pain Dur* (*Hard Bread*) at the COMÉDIE-FRANÇAISE (1970). TERRY HODGSON

Elizabeth Auclaire, *J-M. Serreau, découvreur de théâtre* (1986)

7:84 A socialist touring theatre company founded by director and playwright JOHN MCGRATH in 1971; 7:84 (Scotland) was launched two years later with a core of talented performers including John Bett, Elizabeth MacLennan, Alex Norton and Bill Paterson. The name derived from the statistic that 7 per cent of the population of Britain owned 84 per cent of its wealth. Despite many successes by the English company, notably *Fish in the Sea* and *Yobbo Nowt* (both 1975), the Scottish company is the more celebrated, with its Highland tours initiated by McGrath's brilliant piece, *The Chev-*

iot, the Stag and the Black, Black Oil (1973), and with the 1982 'Clydebuilt' Season – revivals of four plays that dealt with working-class issues in the years between 1930 and 1950. 7:84 (Scotland) flourished after the parent company's last performance, All The Fun of the Fair, (1985), but had its own political and artistic problems that led to McGrath's resignation in 1988, though not to the collapse of the Scottish company, which is one of the four main touring companies in the country. JAN MCDONALD

Maria DiCenzo, The Politics of Alternative Theatre in Britain, 1968–1990: The Case of 7:84 (1996)
John McGrath, A Good Night Out – Popular Theatre: Audience, Class and Form (1981)
——, The Bone Won't Break: On Theatre and Hope in Hard Times (1990)
E. McLennan, Theatre Belongs to Everyone: Making Theatre with 7:84 (1990)

Sewell, Stephen (b. Sydney, 13 March 1953) Playwright, the most adventurous and politically committed of his generation. Sewell centres his plays on the themes of the family, politics, power, male–female relations and his characters' attempts to understand themselves and the world they inhabit. An 'internationalist' vein in his plays can be seen in their varied milieux and historical/contemporary settings: Australia of the real yet fictionalized present and potential future; Russia prior to and during Stalin's reign of terror; Germany of the 1950s and 1960s. In The Blind Giant is Dancing (1983), he achieves an intensity unmatched by any other contemporary Australian dramatist. He has also written for television and the cinema, including the script for the award-winning The Boys (1998). Plays include The Father We Loved on a Beach by the Sea (1977), Traitors (1979), Welcome the Bright World (1982), Dreams in an Empty City (1986), Sisters (1991) and The Garden of Granddaughters (1993). MICHAEL MORLEY

Seyler, Athene (b. London, 31 May 1889; d. London, 12 Sept. 1990) Actress. Seyler made her name in a number of Restoration roles at the LYRIC Hammersmith, including Melanthea in Marriage à la Mode (1920) and Mrs Frail in Love for Love (1921). At the OLD VIC in 1933 she played, among others, Lady Bracknell, and later had long runs with two American plays, Watch on the Rhine (1942) and Harvey (1949). Seyler was admired for her Ranevskaya in The Cherry Orchard (1941) and starred in RATTIGAN and EMLYN WILLIAMS premières; but she was best known for her expert, intelligent performances in Restoration comedy and FARCE, which established her as the finest clown of her genera-

tion. In 1944, she published The Craft of Comedy (co-written with Stephen Haggard), outlining the principles of her technique. DAN REBELLATO

Seymour, Alan (b. Perth, 6 June 1927) Playwright, film and theatre critic, and educational writer, who has lived mostly outside Australia since 1961. His theatre writing falls into two categories: plays that are rooted in naturalistic detail with sensitive observations of ordinary people, albeit with satirical touches; and plays that break with the naturalistic mode, introducing grotesque, bizarre and extravagantly drawn characters and situations. Though self-confessedly untypical, The One Day of the Year (1960), a well-crafted, three-act, naturalistic play, has marched into the nation's folklore, its title (which refers to Anzac Day, the day of remembrance of war) having been absorbed into colloquial usage, while a television sitcom based on its characters appeared in the early 1970s. He has also written radio and television plays, broadcast both in Australia and Britain. Plays include Swamp Creatures (1958), The Gaiety of Nations (1965), The Saltering (1973) and The Float (1980). MICHAEL MORLEY

Shaffer, Peter [Levin] (b. Liverpool, 15 May 1926) Playwright, former coal miner and librarian. Shaffer's first stage play, a hit in London and New York, was Five Finger Exercise, a well-made play set in a country retreat: in 1958 a genre missing, presumed dead. After two more comedies, both short, The Private Ear and The Public Eye (1962), and a best-forgotten pantomime for JOAN LITTLEWOOD, Shaffer wrote The Royal Hunt of the Sun (1964), an epic history of the Spanish conquest of Inca Peru, using an innovative mixture of MIME, dialogue, RITUAL and music, soon labelled TOTAL THEATRE. Its success —the first for the new NATIONAL THEATRE with a contemporary play—was matched at the NT by Black Comedy (1965), a brilliant farce which takes place during a power cut, but on a lit stage. White Liars (1967) joined it in the West End, but was followed by a failure, The Battle of Shrivings (1970), meditating on the limits of pacifism. Two more NT hits – Equus (1973), about a psychiatrist treating a boy who has blinded six horses, in a return to the theatricality of 1964, and the equally popular Amadeus (1979), narrating the rivalry between Mozart and Salieri – preceded Yonadab (1985, NT), depicting the Old Testament fall of the House of David, which saw Shaffer treading old ground. The comedy Lettice and Lovage (1987) was a major West End success, starring MAGGIE SMITH and Margaret Tyzack as two eccentric middle-aged women who celebrate individuality and display contempt for the 'mere' present by re-enacting historical scenes.

Shaffer's long association with the NT allowed him

to develop his famously extravagant style, but some critics have suggested that the bombastic theatricality hides an intellectual shallowness. The constant search for divinity and the celebratory individualism of his characters have not always been fashionable. However, Shaffer remained popular for his seemingly effortless ability to marshal the resources of theatre to tell his enigmatic stories. His twin brother Anthony [Joshua] (1926–2001) was also a playwright, best known for his new take on the country-house thriller genre, *Sleuth* (1970), and the cult film *The Wicker Man* (1974). Peter was knighted in 2000. DAN REBELLATO

Virginia Cooke and Malcolm Page, *File on Shaffer* (1987)
C. J. Gianakaris, *Peter Shaffer* (1992)
Dennis A. Klein, *Peter Shaffer* (1979)
——, *Peter and Anthony Shaffer: A Reference Guide* (1982)
M. K. MacMurragh-Kavanagh, *Peter Shaffer: Theatre and Drama* (1998)

Shaftesbury Avenue A road forming the core of LONDON's WEST END and a term used as a synonym for commercial theatre. The needs of transport and communication saw slums being destroyed to make way for the opening of Shaftesbury Avenue in June 1886, running between Piccadilly and Holborn. Two years later, the Lyric and Shaftesbury theatres were built on it, followed by the Palace (1891), Apollo (1901), Globe (1906), Queen's (1907) and Princes (1911). The last was renamed The Shaftesbury in 1963, the former Shaftesbury having been destroyed in the air raids of 1941. The most recent addition, the Saville (1931), was converted into a cinema in 1970, but in the late 1930s, when all eight theatres were open, they had a combined capacity of over 11,000. All of the theatres, except the Globe (renamed the Gielgud in 1994), are Grade II listed buildings. DAN REBELLATO

Raymond Mander and Joe Mitchenson, *The Theatres of London* (1975)

Shairp, Mordaunt *see* GAY THEATRE

Shakespeare festivals Festivals to celebrate the work of William Shakespeare became increasingly popular in the twentieth century following in the footsteps of David Garrick's Shakespeare Jubilee of 1769. The tercentenary celebrations of 1864 in London and STRATFORD-UPON-AVON led to the foundation, in 1879, of the SHAKESPEARE MEMORIAL THEATRE for annual festivals of plays in the dramatist's native town. Every April Stratford-upon-Avon holds birthday celebrations, including a floral procession from Shakespeare's birthplace to his grave, with representatives from many countries taking part. This is followed by a performance at the nearby theatre, in which, since its founding in 1961, the ROYAL SHAKESPEARE COMPANY presents a repertoire of Shakespeare plays in seasons that now cover ten months each year.

Significant annual overseas festivals include those in Germany (in Weimar and in Bochum) and in China (the Chinese Shakespeare Society was inaugurated in 1981 with performances in both Shanghai and Beijing). Shakespeare festivals have grown up in over 30 North American centres since OREGON led the way in 1935. The most notable are held at STRATFORD, Ontario; NEW YORK; Colorado; and Stratford, Connecticut. Several are presented in reconstruction Elizabethan theatres, such as that at SAN DIEGO.

At most festivals not only are Shakespeare's plays performed and recitals presented, but often also gatherings of enthusiasts and scholars discuss and share contemporary views on the continuing significance and importance of the plays. MARIAN J. PRINGLE

See also SHAKESPEARE IN THE TWENTIETH CENTURY.

Sally Beauman, *The Royal Shakespeare Company: A History of Ten Decades* (1982)
Roberta Krensky Cooper, *The American Shakespeare Theatre, Stratford 1955–1985* (1986)
T. C. Kemp and John Courtnay Trewin, *The Stratford Festival* (1953)
Louis Marder, *His Exits and His Entrances: The Story of Shakespeare's Reputation* (1964)

Shakespeare in the twentieth century The twentieth century saw a consolidation of Shakespeare's position as the pre-eminent writer in the English language. But this status does not necessarily imply stasis, for it means that Shakespeare has been the first focus of debate and controversy in theatrical practice, critical theory, English literature syllabuses, government arts policy and cultural studies.

Unlike those of his fellow dramatists, Shakespeare's works remained in the repertoire through the eighteenth and nineteenth centuries, although largely in so-called 'improved' versions to suit prevailing tastes for visual decoration and actor–managers' desires for opportunities for histrionic display. While twentieth-century approaches to Shakespeare have hardly been uniform, there has been a basic trend towards restoring the seventeenth-century texts, and extracting their themes, ideas, images and metaphors to determine production style – a movement inextricable from both the rise of the director and designer as arbiters of theatrical style, and the gradual acceptance of theatre (Shakespeare being the standard bearer) as something of educative and social value.

WILLIAM POEL, who stripped away scenery to experiment with Shakespeare on a bare stage, is credited by the commentator J. L. Styan with being 'the father of modern thinking about Shakespeare on the stage', and the playwright–director HARLEY GRANVILLE BARKER elaborated upon Poel's experiments in his SAVOY THEATRE Shakespeare productions of 1912–14, eventually putting into print his accumulated thoughts in the highly influential *Prefaces to Shakespeare*. Poel, Barker, actor–director FRANK BENSON (who staged an uncut *Hamlet* in 1899), designer EDWARD GORDON CRAIG and other innovators shared a desire to strip away the lavish visual accretions that characterized nineteenth-century Shakespeare. LILIAN BAYLIS's OLD VIC produced all of Shakespeare's plays (1914–23), and, between the world wars, was also nurturing the century's foremost Shakespearean actors, OLIVIER, GIELGUD and RICHARDSON, in a distinctly unglamorous atmosphere of straitened circumstances. In Stratford, the modern SHAKESPEARE MEMORIAL THEATRE (1932) was obliged by its Royal Charter to implement 'the advancement of Shakespearean drama and literature', and the appointment of Sir BARRY JACKSON as head of the theatre in 1945, shortly followed by the young director PETER BROOK's first production there, testified to a new seriousness of approach, and one in which the director (often now not an actor–producer), aided by a designer often lured from the world of AVANT-GARDE art or FASHION, was coming to dominate.

The true era of 'director's Shakespeare' was ushered in with PETER HALL's inheritance of the stewardship of the Memorial Theatre in 1960. The granting of the first government subsidies allowed Hall to establish the ROYAL SHAKESPEARE COMPANY, and opened the way for a generation of young, university-educated (mostly CAMBRIDGE) directors like himself, and for a new and younger generation of Shakespearean playgoers. Productions at Stratford and elsewhere looked in Shakespeare's texts for those elements that would have most resonance in the world as experienced by a modern audience, and sought to highlight them through bold characterization, design, and *mise-en-scène*: Peter Brook's playfully surreal and acrobatic *A Midsummer Night's Dream* of 1970 seemed remarkably in tune with its age. The most radical experiments with 'director's Shakespeare' have, however, taken place abroad, notably in Germany (e.g. by PETER STEIN) and in eastern Europe (e.g. LYUBIMOV, STURUA), where Shakespearean histories and tragedies became usefully remouldable metaphors for the vicissitudes of life under political tyranny.

During the 1970s and 1980s there began a reaction against some forms of director's Shakespeare. Hall recanted his 1960s radicalism, and instead adopted 'militant classicism' as his philosophy, refusing to cut texts for performance (perhaps overlooking the dubious authority of those texts anyway) and using sober design concepts harking back to the Elizabethan open stage; the actor-turned-entrepreneur SAM WANAMAKER, in his valiant endeavour to build a working replica of Shakespeare's GLOBE THEATRE (posthumously realized), was following in Poel's historicist impetus; and something of Olivier's vigour as a populist Shakespearean actor/director/producer re-emerged in the stage and film work of KENNETH BRANAGH. By the 1990s Shakespearean production was characterized by eclecticism and variety, although market forces combined with reduced subsidies were beginning to threaten those qualities.

Of course, Shakespearean production has not existed in a vacuum, and the century was notable for the bewildering growth of critical literature on every aspect of the playwright and his work. The texts of the plays themselves remain the subjects of constant philological re-examination: most sensationally, Stanley Wells' and Gary Taylor's *Oxford Shakespeare* (1986) included two King Lear plays, rather than conflating the different original versions as previous editors had tended to do. Academia and the theatre, while maintaining their mutual suspicion, have never been more closely intertwined than with respect to Shakespeare. Hall brought the Shakespearean scholars JOHN BARTON to Stratford (as a director), and John Russell Brown to the NATIONAL THEATRE (as literary manager). In the classroom and lecture hall, the teaching of Shakespeare as poet rather than as dramatist has largely given way to a more stage-centred approach.

In the United States, which was visited at the turn of the century by SALVINI from Italy, BERNHARDT from France, and IRVING and TERRY from England, there were indigenous Shakespearean productions in the languages of the immigrant population, from German to YIDDISH as well as English. Granville Barker's innovative *A Midsummer Night's Dream* came in 1916 and along with other European influences helped challenge the overblown style represented by MANTELL. With few exceptions (e.g. ORSON WELLES), what little Shakespeare there was tended to be conventional. The development of SHAKESPEARE FESTIVALS from the 1950s on – e.g. the AMERICAN SHAKESPEARE FESTIVAL or the NEW YORK SHAKESPEARE FESTIVAL – saw a notable rise in the number of productions, and from the 1980s an increasing number of visiting foreign productions enriched the American scene, contributing to a greater willingness by American directors such as PETER SELLARS to challenge orthodox readings.

· Performing Shakespeare ·

From Burbage onwards, styles of acting Shakespeare have changed in keeping with contemporary pre-occupations. The nineteenth-century obsession with heroes, in an age of moral certainty, led to large displays of emphatic leading performances, with texts cut to exaggerate the star actor. Twentieth-century Shakespeare performances, in tune with the concerns of the time, are more psychologically dense, and a more democratic spirit illuminates every area of the play. The actor–manager's ego has been ousted by a collective company strength, led by an offstage director, who, at best, has developed Shakespeare's own staging. Pageantry is avoided so that the text (often very full) is dominant. Actors explore stylistic variety, from bombast and rhetoric, through naturalism to the complicated ambiguities of the late plays. Small theatres have been designed on a human scale, allowing a direct and intimate relationship with the audience.

Among actors who have regularly returned to Shakespeare, two main styles have prevailed, most notably embodied in the influential achievements of GIELGUD and OLIVIER. The 'head' actor concentrates on the complications of verse and language, tending to a vocally adept essay on the role. The rival 'heart' actor relishes the language as a starting-point for a fully embodied characterization that tends to naturalism. The most affecting Shakespeare acting has combined both.   IAN MCKELLEN

Since the 1980s there has been a reaction by younger, feminist and gay critics against the scale and ideological implications of what they see as a 'Shakespeare industry', arguing that the *a priori* assumption of the author's brilliance reveals an attempt to appropriate the plays for the reinforcement of an Establishment view of historical continuity and national identity. There are also objections to the marketing of this identity as a commodity, particularly through the tourist industry (as is ever more apparent in Stratford-upon-Avon), which is seen as encouraging an unhealthy and unthinking 'bardolatry'. While these arguments contain their own contradictions, they do suggest an element of fragility in Shakespeare's status: one wonders how intact it will remain, and of what it will consist, in an increasingly multicultural world.

MARK HAWKINS-DADY

Regular reviews of Shakespeare in performance appear in *Shakespeare Quarterly* and other journals. Books by and about directors, designers and actors frequently contain important material.

David Addenbrooke, *The Royal Shakespeare Company: The Peter Hall Years* (1974)
Richard David, *Shakespeare in the Theatre* (1978)
Graham Holderness, ed., *The Shakespeare Myth* (1988)
Jan Kott, *Shakespeare Our Contemporary* (1964)
Glen Loney and Patricia Mackay, *The Shakespeare Complex* (1975)
K. Parsons and P. Mason, eds, *Shakespeare in Performance* (1996)
C. H. Shattuck, *Shakespeare on the American Stage*, 2 vols (1976, 1987)
J. L. Styan, *The Shakespeare Revolution: Criticism and Performance in the Twentieth Century* (1977)
J. C. Trewin, *Benson and the Bensonians* (1960)
——, *Shakespeare on the English Stage 1900–1964* (1964)

Shakespeare Memorial Theatre STRATFORD-UPON-AVON's theatre opened in 1879 to stage short annual festivals of Shakespeare's plays. Seasons were extended by FRANK BENSON's Company (1888–1918). The original theatre burned down in 1926 and was replaced, to Elisabeth Scott's design, in 1932. The theatre has seen the work of many of the best directors and actors of the twentieth century, from THEODORE KOMISSARZHEVSKY and PETER BROOK to LAURENCE OLIVIER, JOHN GIELGUD, PEGGY ASHCROFT, PAUL SCOFIELD and JUDI DENCH. A strong international reputation was established under ANTHONY QUAYLE and GLEN BYAM SHAW in the 1950s. In 1961 the theatre became the Royal Shakespeare Theatre, home of the ROYAL SHAKESPEARE COMPANY.   MARIAN J. PRINGLE

Sally Beauman, *The Royal Shakespeare Company: A History of Ten Decades* (1982)
Susan Brock and Marian J. Pringle, *The Shakespeare Memorial Theatre 1919–1945* (1984)
M. C. Day and John Courtnay Trewin, *The Shakespeare Memorial Theatre* (1932)
Marian J. Pringle, *The Theatres of Stratford-upon-Avon: An Architectural History* (1994)

Shange, Ntozake [Paulette Williams] (b. Trenton, NJ, 18 Oct. 1948) Poet and playwright. Best known for her 'choreopoems' which use poetry, song, and dance. *For colored girls who have considered suicide/when the rainbow is enuf* (1976), which won a Tony Award, is a strongly feminist work about the American black woman's experience. Other plays include *Spell No. 7* (1978), *Boogie Woogie Landscapes* (1980), *Batry Brown* (1991) and *The Love Space Demands* (1995), all of which confirm her unique voice. JANE HOUSE

Neal Lester, *Ntozake Shange: A Critical Study of the Plays* (1995)

Shankar, Uday [Uday Shankar Chaudhry] (b. Udaipur, Rajputana, India, 8 Dec. 1900; d. Calcutta, 26 Sept. 1977) Dancer, choreographer and creative teacher. Shankar made his theatrical debut at a Covent Garden production by his father, Shyam Shankar Chaudhry, of *The Great Moghul's Chamber of Dreams* in 1923. Discovered by prima ballerina ANNA PAVLOVA in the same year, he created *Hindu Wedding* and *Radha-Krishna* for her company, dancing the latter with Pavlova. In 1930, with his Swiss patron sculptor Alice Boner, he founded the first Indian dance company, Uday Shankar Company of Hindu Musicians and Dancers. They opened at the Théâtre des Champs Elysées in Paris on 3 March 1931, in a programme of divertissements and a dance-drama, *Tandava Nrittya*. His company performed 889 shows in seven years in 30 countries. Later dance-drama themes included the play of the gods, the freedom of India and the oppressions of industrialization. In India, in 1939, he founded the Uday Shankar India Culture Centre at Almora, which became the inspiration for India's modern dancers and theatrical presentations (including *Discovery of India*) by his disciples in the 1940s, and dance-drama productions by his students and brother, renowned sitarist Pandit Ravi Shankar. His film, *Kalpana* ('Imagination'), released in 1948, was an artistic but not a financial success. JOAN L. ERDMAN

See also CHOREOGRAPHY; DANCE; MOVEMENT, DANCE AND DRAMA.

Joan L. Erdman, 'Performance as Translation: Uday Shankar in the West', *Tulane Drama Review* (1987)
Mohan Khokar, *His Dance His Life: A Portrait of Uday Shankar* (1983)

Sharaff, Irene (b. Boston, Mass., 1910?; d. New York, 16 Aug. 1993) Costume designer. She studied at the New York School of Fine and Applied Arts and at New York's Art Students League, and at the Grand Chaumière in Paris, then was an apprentice under ALINE BERNSTEIN. Although Sharaff was probably better known for her well-publicized Hollywood designs, she enjoyed a fruitful career for nearly half a century on Broadway, beginning in 1929. Her stylish, often highly colourful costumes graced such successes as *Idiot's Delight* (1936), *On Your Toes* (1936), *I'd Rather Be Right* (1937), *Lady in the Dark* (1941), *The King and I* (1952), *West Side Story*

(1957), *Sweet Charity* (1966) and the 1973 revival of *Irene*. Her book *Broadway and Hollywood Costume Designs by Irene Sharaff* appeared in 1976.
GERALD BORDMAN

Shared Experience British touring company. Since it launched itself in 1975 with a trilogy of plays based on the Arabian Nights, followed by a stunning adaptation of Dickens's *Bleak House*, this company has become known especially for its inventive storytelling, minimalist staging and the physicality of its acting style. In particular, it has concentrated on dramatizations of epic novels, including *Anna Karenina*, *War and Peace* and *The Mill on the Floss*. Shared Experience was influential in paving the way for the visually and physically strong theatre of companies such as CHEEK BY JOWL and THÉÂTRE DE COMPLICITÉ. Leading directors include its founder, MIKE ALFREDS, and, from 1987, Nancy Meckler, who was noted for her work with the Freehold Theatre Company, HAMPSTEAD THEATRE CLUB and the ROYAL COURT. DAVID SELF

Shatrov [Marshak], Mikhail [Filippovich] (b. Moscow, 3 April 1932) Playwright. The success of his first play, *Chistye ruki* ('Clean Hands', 1955), led him to give up his job as a mining engineer. There followed plays about Young Communists (e.g. *Mesto v zhizni*, 'A place in life', 1956) and several – nine in all – about Lenin, such as *Imenem revolyutsii* ('In the name of the Revolution', 1957), *Shestoye iyulya* ('6 July', 1964) and *Tridtsatatoye avgusta (Bolsheviki)* (*The Bolsheviks*, 1966). Although he joined the Communist Party in 1964, his historical views were considered at the time to be 'revisionist', particularly in humanizing Lenin and treating his opponents seriously, and the plays were often banned or censored. He became a key figure, however, in the Gorbachev era of *glasnost* or 'openness' but subsequently, in the new 'post-communist' context, his work seems weakly journalistic and overly deliberate. CHARLES LONDON

Shaw, Fiona (b. Cork, Ireland, 10 July 1958) Actress. After a short period in repertory and touring theatre, and an early appearance as Julia in *The Rivals* at the NATIONAL THEATRE (1984), she joined the ROYAL SHAKESPEARE COMPANY in 1985, where she remained for five years, playing a series of parts (Celia, Portia, Beatrice, Kate, Mistress Carol in James Shirley's *Hyde Park*) in which her agile wit and piercing intelligence quickly established her reputation. In 1990 she played Electra in a production for the RSC directed by DEBORAH WARNER, beginning one of the most productive actor–director partnerships of the period. Under Warner's direction she played Shen Te/Shen Ta in *The*

Good Person of Setzuan at the National Theatre, Hedda Gabler and Medea for the ABBEY THEATRE, Dublin, May in BECKETT's *Footfalls* at the Garrick Theatre and the title role in *Richard II*, again at the National Theatre, all strikingly original interpretations of familiar texts. In 1993, working with STEPHEN DALDRY, also at the National Theatre, she brought an unfamiliar play, SOPHIE TREADWELL's *Machinal*, to startling life in one of her finest performances as a young woman driven to murder. Her film career, though not extensive, has included successful Hollywood comedies as well as more serious work (e.g. *My Left Foot*). Her huge talent has sharp edges, making her one of the most uncomfortably brilliant of her generation.   GENISTA MCINTOSH

Shaw, George Bernard (b. Dublin, 26 July 1856; d. Ayot St Lawrence, Herts, 2 Nov. 1950) Playwright, socialist pamphleteer, critic and novelist. Born into a shabby-genteel Protestant household, ill-educated and intellectually restive, he settled in London in 1876. He addressed political, religious and literary groups and reviewed for *The Hornet, Pall Mall Gazette, The World, The Saturday Review* and *The Star* on music, art and drama. His theatre criticism, collected in three volumes (*Our Theatres in the Nineties*, 1931), provides a remarkable and highly opinionated view of British drama at that time. Having seen *A Doll's House* in 1889 he defended IBSEN in the ensuing controversy, publishing *The Quintessence of Ibsenism* (1890). His first play, *Widowers' Houses*, an expansion of an unsuccessful collaboration with WILLIAM ARCHER, was produced by J. T. GREIN at the Independent Theatre, London (1892); he later described it as 'my first and worst play'. He had difficulty finding producers for other early plays, some of which were published (*Plays Pleasant* and *Plays Unpleasant*, 1898) prior to staging. Written under the immediate influence of Ibsen, and fired by his own engaging enthusiasm for social causes and theories, these were, in order of composition, *The Philanderer* (1905) on ethical considerations in love and marriage; *Mrs Warren's Profession* on female prostitution (privately produced by the ENGLISH STAGE COMPANY 1902), and with *Widowers' Houses* and *The Philanderer* comprising *Plays Unpleasant*; *Arms and the Man* (Avenue Theatre, London, 1894) on the false idealization of war; *Candida* (produced on tour in England by JANET ACHURCH, 1897) on male philistinism and chauvinism; and *You Never Can Tell* (Strand Theatre, London, 1900) on the irrationality of love. (With *The Man of Destiny*, 1897, these last three comprised *Plays Pleasant*.)

Shaw wished for 'a pit of philosophers' and aimed to attract the minds of theatregoers rather than simply to amuse them – though in fact he did both. Widely scorned – 'the unspeakable Irishman', said Henry James – as using the stage in place of soap-box or pulpit, these plays made little impact outside a small 'advanced' circle.

Three Plays for Puritans (published 1901) contained *The Devil's Disciple* (Albany, New York, 1897), *Captain Brassbound's Conversion* (Strand Theatre, London, 1900) and *Caesar and Cleopatra*, which had to wait five years for production (by MAX REINHARDT at the Neues Theater, Berlin, 1906). It was not until he met the actor–manager HARLEY GRANVILLE BARKER who, with J. E. VEDRENNE, produced 11 of his plays (701 performances) at the ROYAL COURT Theatre, London, between 1904 and 1907, that Shaw experienced the popularity which attended his work for the rest of his life.

Barker and Vedrenne produced several of those plays which had previously been performed by coterie groups, as well as *John Bull's Other Island* and *How He Lied to Her Husband* (1904), *Man and Superman* and *Major Barbara* (1905), and *The Doctor's Dilemma* (1906). In *Man and Superman* he introduced the notion of the 'life force'.

The Shewing Up of Blanco Posnet, having been refused a licence by the LORD CHAMBERLAIN on account of its alleged blasphemy, was produced by the ABBEY THEATRE, Dublin (1909). The play's Christian theme was continued in *Androcles and the Lion* (1913). By this time Shaw was at the height of his powers. Critics began to realize that his plays succeeded not only on account of the promulgation of specific ideas but also because these ideas were expressed by vibrant, exuberant and witty characters. Shaw was inviting his audience to revel in the absurdities of conventional moral attitudes in a lighthearted manner of which Ibsen was incapable: his verbal paradox is in the same vein as WILDE's, but he also makes use of paradoxical situation.

Pygmalion (Hofburg, Vienna, 1913), probably his most popular play, treats of human relations by means of a sparkling dissertation on the question of class mobility through the study of phonetics. *Heartbreak House* (New York THEATER GUILD, 1920) is a sombre comedy written during the First World War in which Shaw looks with foreboding on the future of the human race; it anticipates the lengthy 'metabiological Pentateuch' *Back to Methuselah* (New York Theater Guild, 1922), in which he casts a visionary eye on the place of man in creation. *St Joan* (New York Theater Guild, 1923) is perhaps Shaw's greatest play. He saw Joan as 'one of the first Protestant martyrs', staking her

---

· Performing Shaw ·

It is easy to strike attitudes in Shaw, resting on the surface rhetoric of all that coruscating wit and wisdom. But when I worked with TREVOR NUNN on *Heartbreak House*, in which I played Hector Hushabye, we found that just beneath that surface there was a texture and a dimension to the relationships every bit as rich and raw as any you might find in CHEKHOV or Shaw's great master, IBSEN. In general terms, though, I think speed is of the essence with Shaw. Not pace and gabble; but the Shavian mind of ideas is a racing mind, and you do need, together with agility and a lightness of touch, an extraordinary amount of mental energy in animating those ideas. When I played Charteris in Shaw's early treasure, *The Philanderer*, at the NATIONAL THEATRE, the director, Chris Morahan, described what I should be striving for in this way: 'You should feel yourself prancing along the beach with sand cascading from your coat pocket. Now, remember to stay one step ahead of the audience trying to catch it.' Shaw's Irishness pervades his work, nowhere more so than in the cadences and rhythms of his dialogue. On occasions, neither meaning nor rhythm is immediately clear. In some of the love scenes, for example, given Shaw's complex and fascinating relationship with women, meaning is often wrapped in an almost Shakespearean ambiguity. When this happens, try working the phrases through with a gentle Irish lilt to what you are saying. Very often the mists will begin to lift, and all will become clear. That's the Irish for you! DANIEL MASSEY

---

conscience innocently against the dogma of a corrupt and collusive established order.

Of the 14 plays written during the last 25 years of his life, only *The Apple Cart* (Warsaw, 1929), *Village Wooing* (Dallas, 1934) and *The Millionairess* (Akademie, Vienna, 1936) are often revived. In 1934 the *Prefaces* to his plays were published in a single volume. A towering figure of the English-speaking theatre in the first half of the twentieth century, Shaw wrote 53 plays, some of them merely sketches, containing almost 500 characters. He refused public honours, except the Nobel Prize for Literature (1923) and the Freedom of the City of Dublin (1946). When he died, the lights of Broadway were extinguished as a mark of respect. Royalties from his plays, including the musical version of *Pygmalion*, LERNER and LOEWE's *My Fair Lady* (1957), continue to support the chief beneficiaries of Shaw's estate: the National Gallery of Ireland, the British Library and the Royal Academy of Dramatic Art, London.
CHRISTOPHER FITZ-SIMON

Eric Bentley, *Shaw* (1957)

Harold Bloom, ed., *George Bernard Shaw: Modern Critical Perspectives* (1987)

Bernard F. Dukore, *Shaw's Theater* (2000)

Michael Holroyd, *Shaw: The Search for Love, The Pursuit of Love, The Lure of Fantasy*, 3 vols (1988–91)

C. Innes, ed, *The Cambridge Companion to George Bernard Shaw* (1998)

Morgan Meisel, *Shaw and the Nineteenth-century Theatre* (1963)

Margery Morgan, *The Shavian Playground: An Exploration of the Art of George Bernard Shaw* (1972)

Shaw, Glen[cairn Alexander] Byam (b. London, 13 Dec. 1904; d. Goring-on-Thames, Oxon, 29 April 1986) Actor and director. A successful acting career (1923–40) was broken by war service, after which he was appointed director of the OLD VIC School and of the Old Vic Theatre Centre (1947). He also directed for the YOUNG VIC. He joined ANTHONY QUAYLE as co-director of the SHAKESPEARE MEMORIAL THEATRE in 1952, and took sole charge in 1956. When he resigned in 1959, the actors he had attracted to STRATFORD-UPON-AVON, his intelligent, sensitive interpretations of Shakespeare's plays, and his encouragement of young talent had laid the foundations for the ROYAL SHAKESPEARE COMPANY. His appointments to SADLER'S WELLS (1962) and the COLISEUM, as Director of the English Opera (1968), led to 19 years of operatic achievement, marked by the grace and integrity that were the hallmarks of all his work. LORNA FLINT

Shaw, Irwin (b. New York, 27 Feb. 1913; d. Davos, Switzerland, 16 May 1984) Playwright. His early plays, *Bury the Dead* (1936) and *The Gentle People* (1939), both pacifist and leftist in tone, were well received. However, all his subsequent plays were failures, and from the 1940s he more or less abandoned the theatre to become a popular novelist.
GERALD BORDMAN

M. Shnayerson, *Irwin Shaw: A Biography* (1989)

Shaw, Peggy *see* LESBIAN THEATRE

Shaw Festival Founded in 1962 by Brian Doherty, this festival in Niagara-on-the-Lake, Ontario, offers some 500 performances in three theatres. The main

Festival Theatre, which opened in 1973, seats 861. Although the plays of SHAW are central to the repertoire, the festival's various artistic directors have interpreted their mandate to include plays by Shaw's contemporaries. Thus productions of IBSEN and STRINDBERG are offered as well as more popular fare like BEN TRAVERS' *Thark* (1977) and NOËL COWARD's *Cavalcade* (1985) and *Easy Virtue* (2000). EUGENE BENSON

The Shaw Festival 1962–1998: The Record of Performances (1999)

Shawn, Ted *see* DENISHAWN DANCE SCHOOL

Shawn, Wallace (b. New York, 12 Nov. 1943) Actor and playwright. Known as a film actor, he also appears live; he performs his own anguished monologue *The Fever* (1990) to limited audiences in unconventional places. His examinations of cruelty – primarily sexual, in *Marie and Bruce* (1979); primarily political, in *Aunt Dan and Lemon* (1985) – are sophisticated, shocking and intelligent. Films include *My Dinner with André* (directed by Louis Malle, an adaptation of Shawn and ANDRÉ GREGORY's play of the same name, 1981). Other plays include *A Thought in Three Parts* (1977), *The Hotel Play* (1981) and *The Designated Mourner* (1996). M. ELIZABETH OSBORN

Shean, Al *see* GALLAGHER, ED

Sheffield Before and just after the Second World War, there existed a Sheffield Playhouse which housed what was for a time the third most important national REPERTORY company in England (after BIRMINGHAM and LIVERPOOL). It began in 1919 as an amateur dramatic society founded by rail clerk Herbert Prince, who was an important figure in the interwar repertory movement. He changed its name to the Sheffield Repertory Theatre in 1920. It played in halls and became professional, gaining its own auditorium in 1928. During the war it played in Southport in the north-west. After the war, local legend Geoffrey Ost held sway, presenting what were in all but name West End productions, the while helping launch actors like Patrick McGoohan, DONALD PLEASANCE and Peter Barkworth.

The Empire and Palace theatres catered for VARIETY or VAUDEVILLE enthusiasts ('Fats' Waller composed 'Hush, Hush, Baby' while appearing at the former in 1938) but they have since gone; HAROLD HOBSON, the great post-war critic, grew to manhood in Sheffield. After redevelopment started by Hitler's bombs and concluded by council fiat, the rotunda of the Crucible Theatre arose in 1971 to replace the Playhouse. Seating 1,000, and with a 250-seat studio, it quickly became known as an innovator and under Peter James (1974–81) established

a reputation for staging new plays and lively revivals (e.g. *Cabaret*, 1977) as well as successful British premières (e.g. *Chicago*, 1978; *The Wiz*, 1980). A stone's throw away lies the much older Lyceum, dark for many years but refurbished in the 1980s and dedicated to commercial productions in a joint enterprise with the Crucible. FRANK LONG

Sheldon, Edward [Brewster] (b. Chicago, 4 Feb. 1886; d. New York, 1 April 1946) Playwright. A pupil of GEORGE PIERCE BAKER at Harvard, Sheldon achieved success with his first play *Salvation Nell* (1908), starring Mrs FISKE. *The Nigger* (1909) and *The Boss* (1911) continued his serious realistic vein, but the public preferred the emotion of *Romance* (1913). FELICIA HARDISON LONDRÉ

Eric W. Bernes, *The Man Who Lived Twice: The Biography of Edward Sheldon* (1956)

Shepard, Sam [Samuel Shepherd Rogers Jr] (b. Fort Sheridan, Ill., 5 Nov. 1943) Playwright, actor and director. Shepard's work was first produced OFF-OFF-BROADWAY in 1964, and his work retains a vitality, imagery and hallucinatory quality redolent of the 1960s. He explores American popular culture and the lives, prejudices and pain of its stereotypical or even mythic characters through his imaginative and imagistic use of colour, music and distinctive language. He charts the demise of the American Dream, the strengths and tensions of family and the quest for roots in an alienated world. Hard to pin down, he has bucked the system by emerging as a leading, critically acclaimed playwright without embracing the delights of BROADWAY. His early short stories – spare and potent, like *Cowboys #2* (1967) – were followed by full-length plays of similar style, like *The Tooth of Crime* (1972, written while staying in London), which showed two rock stars locked in a power struggle. He then drew on a more realistic poetic impulse in plays like *Curse of the Starving Class* (1977) and *Buried Child* (1978), which won a Pulitzer Prize for its shattering demolition of family relationships. His prolific, award-winning work includes *Icarus's Mother* (1965), *La Turista* (1966), *Operation Sidewinder* (1970), *True West* (1980) and *Fool for Love* (1983, both staged at the Magic Theatre, San Francisco, where he was resident playwright), and *A Lie of the Mind* (1985). After a gap of six years, he returned to playwriting with *The States of Shock* (1991) and *Simpatico* (1994). Successful as a film actor, his screenplay *Paris, Texas* (1984) was widely acclaimed. He has also co-written three plays with JOSEPH CHAIKIN. ADRIANA HUNTER

Stephen J. Bottoms, *The Theatre of Sam Shephard: States of Crisis* (1998)

D. DeRose, *Sam Shepard* (1993)

Lynda Hart, *Sam Shepard's Metaphorical Stages* (1987)

Ron Mottram, *Inner Landscapes: The Theatre of Sam Shepard* (1984)

Ellen Oumano, *Sam Shepard: The Life and Work of an American Dreamer* (1986)

Sher, Antony (b. Cape Town, 14 June 1949) Actor and writer; an émigré who started his career in the company of many highly gifted actors at the LIVERPOOL EVERYMAN where he played a variety of roles, including Ringo in WILLY RUSSELL's *John, Paul, George, Ringo . . . and Bert* (transferred to the West End, 1974). Even at an early age he showed the characteristics which reached fruition in his quintessential performance as Richard III (ROYAL SHAKESPEARE COMPANY, 1984): grotesque, quirky, cartoon-like, formidably inventive, energetic, and, above all, funny. Roles in his seasons with the RSC include the Fool in *King Lear*, Shylock, the title role in BULGAKOV's *Molière*, the lead in PETER BARNES' *Red Noses* and PETER FLANNERY's *Singer*, and the eponymous role in Marlowe's *Tamburlaine*. At the NATIONAL THEATRE he was an alluringly unconventional Astrov in *Uncle Vanya*, as well as Stanley in PAM GEMS' play of that name and Titus Andronicus in a production that began in his homeland. He returned to the RSC in 1998 as Cyrano de Bergerac, and played an outstanding Macbeth the following year. Sher is a unique figure in British theatre, a polymath: actor, cartoonist, novelist and playwright. His book *Year of the King: An Actor's Diary and Sketchbook* appeared in 1985 and his autobiography *Beside Myself* in 2001. He was knighted in 2000. RICHARD EYRE

Sherman, Martin (b. Philadelphia, 22 December 1938) Playwright. He wrote his first play, *A Solitary Thing*, in 1963, but his career did not take off until 1975, when *Passing By* (written in 1972) was presented in London as one of GAY SWEATSHOP's first productions in Almost Free Theatre's lunchtime season of gay plays. Sherman moved to London and was inspired by the section of Noël Grieg and Drew Griffiths' Gay Sweatshop play *As Time Goes By* set in 1933 Weimar Germany to write his ground-breaking *Bent*. Productions at the ROYAL COURT with IAN MCKELLEN and Tom Bell in 1979, and on Broadway with Richard Gere, ensured the success of a play which has been produced all over the world. *Bent* focuses on sexual identity, first in the closeted 'fluff' world of Berlin and later in the brutalizing extremities of Dachau's labour camp, where the central relationship triumphs over the regime's attempts to silence homosexual love. Sherman's sub-

sequent plays – *Messiah* (1982), set in seventeenth-century Poland; *When She Danced* (1985), about ISADORA DUNCAN; *A Madhouse in Goa* (1989); *Some Sunny Day* (1996); and *Rose* (1999) – all attracted strong casts and appeared in mainstream venues, but made none of the impact of the earlier *Bent*. BRIAN ROBERTS

Sherriff, R[obert] C[edric] (b. Hampton Wick, Surrey, 6 June 1896; d. Kingston-upon-Thames, Surrey, 13 Nov. 1975) Playwright and novelist. After several years of writing he was asked for an all-male play and achieved sudden fame with his anti-jingoistic *Journey's End* (1928), which drew on his experiences of the First World War. It played abroad in many languages. Later plays are less noteworthy than his screenplays, which include *Goodbye, Mr Chips* (1939), *The Four Feathers* (1939) and *Lady Hamilton* (1941). IAN CLARKE

Sherwood, Robert E[mmet] (b. New Rochelle, NY, 4 April 1896; d. New York, 12 Nov. 1955) American writer; most famous as playwright. With the success of his anti-war comedy, *The Road to Rome* (1927), Sherwood was set on a full-time career as playwright. Although the works which immediately followed were not notable, Sherwood ensured his position as a leading dramatist with *Reunion in Vienna* (1931), a comedy starring the LUNTS; *The Petrified Forest* (1935), a drama on idealism; *Idiot's Delight* (1936), an anti-war play; and his most important work, *Abe Lincoln in Illinois* (1938), a chronicle play drawing political parallels between Lincoln's day and the 1930s (the last three plays won Pulitzer Prizes). He wrote screenplays and became president of the Dramatists' Guild and a founder of the PLAYWRIGHTS' COMPANY. *There Shall Be No Night* (1940) decried America's policy of isolation, and led to Sherwood taking government positions and writing speeches for Roosevelt. JOSEPH M. DIAZ

John Mason Brown, *The World of Robert E. Sherwood* (1965)

——, *The Ordeal of a Playwright* (1970)

Walter J. Meserve, *Robert E. Sherwood: Reluctant Moralist* (1970)

Shields, Arthur (b. Dublin, 1896; d. Santa Barbara, Calif., 27 April 1970) Actor. Brother of BARRY FITZGERALD, he joined the ABBEY THEATRE, Dublin, in 1916 and created parts in plays by COLUM, GREGORY, JOHNSTON, MURRAY, O'CASEY, LENNOX ROBINSON, YEATS and many others until 1937, when John Ford started him on his Hollywood career. CHRISTOPHER FITZ-SIMON

Shiels, George (b. Ballymoney, Co. Antrim, Ireland, 24 June 1881; d. Ballymoney, 19 Sept. 1949) Playwright, one of the most popular of his generation. *The Rugged Path* (1940) broke the ABBEY THEATRE's attendance record. *Paul Twining* (1922), *Professor Tim* (1925), *Cartney and Kevney* (1927), *The New Gossoon* (1930), *Grogan and the Ferret* (1933) and *Quin's Secret* (1937), all produced at the Abbey, are gentle comedies of Ulster life. *The Passing Day* (1936), a *comédie noire* on the baleful influence of a Molièresque family tyrant, is much harsher, as are *The Rugged Path* and *The Summit* (1941). His reputation suffered at the hands of Ulster amateurs, but TYRONE GUTHRIE's production of *The Passing Day* (London, 1951) and subsequent Abbey revivals have been acclaimed. CHRISTOPHER FITZ-SIMON

R. J. Porter, *Brinsley McNamara and George Shiels* (1973)

Shostakovich, Dmitri [Dmitrevich] (b. St Petersburg, Russia, 12 Sept. 1906; d. Moscow, 9 Aug. 1975)   Composer who was attracted to the theatre and wrote several ballets and OPERAS among his internationally renowned output. For a time he supported himself by working as resident pianist at MEYERHOLD's theatre, where he also composed music for a firemen's band to accompany a scene in MAYAKOVSKY's *The Bedbug* (1929). It was here that he was inspired by Meyerhold's production of Gogol's *The Government Inspector* to write his first opera, *The Nose* (1928), based on Gogol's story and echoing the structure of Meyerhold's piece. He also wrote incidental music for Bezymyensky's *The Shot* and for AKIMOV's formalist production of *Hamlet* (1932). NICK WORRALL

Elizabeth Wilson, *Shostakovich: A Life Remembered* (1994)

showboats   Developed in the 1830s, these popular American 'floating palaces' had their heyday after the dislocations of the Civil War. The largest seated over 1,000 people. Several managements in the 1920s, notably the Bryants and the Menkes, still operated boats offering the tried and trusted favourites of VAUDEVILLE, musical comedy and MELODRAMA, but the Great Depression of the early 1930s and with it the increasing popularity of the cinema killed their trade. By 1938 only five boats remained, operating along the Mississippi and Ohio rivers. Although only a few survive as museum pieces, the colourful history of these floating theatres has been immortalized in KERN and HAMMERSTEIN's 1927 musical *Show Boat*. HELEN RAPPAPORT

Shubert Organization   This theatrical management and production company was originally set up by three Lithuanian immigrants, the Shubert [Szemanski] brothers Sam[uel] S. (1876?–1905), Lee [Levi] (1873–1953) and J[acob] J. (1879–1963). They arrived in New York in 1882. Lee and Sam worked in local theatres, and in 1894 Sam bought the area touring rights of Charles Hoyt's play *A Texas Steer*. They challenged the domination of the THEATRICAL SYNDICATE and rapidly built up a network of leasehold theatres in New York and around the United States in the early 1900s. Despite the early death of Sam, the first to be involved in theatre, the other two continued to build on their empire by buying theatres, vaudeville halls and cinemas until they had a virtual monopoly on the American theatrical industry. They built many of BROADWAY's theatres and named one after Sam. Their shrewd business sense led them to plump for the musical as their most regular money-spinning venture, and by 1954 the organization had staged 520 productions on Broadway alone, where it owns and manages some 16 theatres. Anti-trust action in the mid-1950s forced them to sell a number of their properties. Some of their more recent musical productions, such as *Ain't Misbehavin'* (1978), *Dream Girls* (1981) and *Little Shop of Horrors* (1982) have been hugely successful, as have been imported shows like the ROYAL SHAKESPEARE COMPANY's production of *Nicholas Nickleby* (1981) and the New York staging of *Cats* (1982).

J. J.'s son John (1909–62) ran the organization in the 1950s until his death, when he was succeeded by Lawrence Shubert Lawrence Jr (1916–92), a great-nephew of the founding brothers. The enterprise was reorganized in 1973 as the Shubert Organization under Bernie [Bernard] B. Jacobs (1916–96) and Gerald Schoenfeld (b. 1924). HELEN RAPPAPORT

Foster Hirsch, Brooks McNamara and Jerry Stagg, *The Brothers Shubert* (1968)

Shumlin, Herman   *see* HELLMAN, LILLIAN

Shvarts, Yevgenii [Lvovich] (b. Kazan, Russia, 1896; d. Leningrad, 1958 [actual dates of birth and death not recorded])   Playwright best known for fairytale plays. The son of Jewish medical students outlawed for political activities, Shvarts studied law before becoming an actor and writer. Some of his plays were realistic but he was much influenced by Andersen, Hoffman and Perrault in such pieces as *Goly Korol* (*The Naked King*, 1934), *Ten* (*The Shadow*, 1940) and *Drakon* (*The Dragon*, 1943). Despite the apparently innocuous plots, he encountered difficulty with the censors over the satirical style; *The Naked King* remained unperformed until 1960, other plays were banned after an initial production. Shvarts also wrote puppet plays and film scripts, including *Don Kikhot* (*Don Quixote*, 1957). J. MICHAEL WALTON

Siamsa Tíre (National Folk Theatre of Ireland)

Founded by Pat Ahern at the old Theatre Royal, Tralee, in 1974. The permanent Irish-language company creates its material initially in workshops and improvisations inspired by traditional stories and customs, projecting the finished stage material chiefly through dance, mime and song. Siamsa Tíre has performed widely abroad. A new theatre building was opened in Tralee in 1990. CHRISTOPHER FITZ-SIMON

See also GAELIC THEATRE IN IRELAND.

Siedle, Caroline (b. England, ?1867; d. Yonkers, NY, 26 Feb. 1907) Costume designer. Possibly the first woman in the American theatre to become famous for her clothing designs, she came to prominence in the mid-1890s. Until her early death she created costumes primarily for musicals (e.g. *The Wizard of Oz*, 1903) and for prima donnas of the era, such as LILLIAN RUSSELL.
GERALD BORDMAN

Sierra Leone The country achieved political independence from Britain in 1961, and became a republic in 1973. It is made up of 14 ethnic groups, each with its own distinctive language. The country's modern history can be traced back to the later part of the eighteenth century when a group of blacks made up of maroons from the West Indies, liberated slaves from North America, some poor former slaves from England, and some slaves freed from illegal slave ships by anti-slavery patrol vessels, were resettled in Freetown by the British government on land bought from the indigenous peoples. This resettled group are the Creoles, who make up 1 per cent of the total population. The Creoles (commonly called Krios), unlike their indigenous neighbours, were essentially Christian with European acculturation, and their formal education also made them very British in outlook. However, despite their small size, this group has exerted enormous political and cultural influence, and Krio (the language which they developed from a mix of varieties of English, and the various native languages of the slaves from the slave ships) is officially recognized as Sierra Leone's lingua franca, even though English remains the official language.

Precolonial theatre (such as the very strong storytelling traditions of the Mende and the Limba) was not an end in itself but rather a means to an end, and this has largely remained the case, except for writers such as RAYMOND SARIF EASMON, the source of inspiration and material for much contemporary theatre. Starting in the 1930s with Gladys Casely-Hayford, who dramatized Sierra Leonean folk tales, and N. J. G. Ballanta-Taylor, who wrote 'African operas', through John Akar in the 1950s, who wrote and produced plays with distinctive African themes realized through indigenous songs and dances, to Thomas Decker, Juliana John, YULISA AMADU MADDY and DELE CHARLEY, who began the real process of writing and producing indigenous Krio theatre, dramatists have relied on the traditional theatre. Other indigenous forms are the rituals and ceremonies of the various ethnic groups, cults and secret societies, such as the Poro and Bundu; there were also masquerades (which are still very popular), and the mimes, music and dances which are commonly found among all the indigenous groups.

Contemporary theatre began as a quest for cultural and national identity in response to and rejection of the colonial literary and theatrical models which sidelined indigenous forms as 'primitive' or non-existent. European-style spoken drama began during the colonial period with the introduction of Christian and Western education. The model was the nineteenth-century Christian church, which had used dramatic methods to explain stories from the Bible. This activity became transformed into a kind of variety-concert performance with a dramatic sketch around which all other activities associated with the gathering were structured. It remained very popular and was the major form of entertainment in Freetown up until the 1950s. Evangelical and moralistic dramas, such as *Everyman*, *The Bishop's Candlesticks* and other church-inspired classics such as T. S. ELIOT's *Murder in the Cathedral,* are still performed in some areas.

In 1948 Nada Smart, who had attended a British Council drama course in England, returned and helped found the British Council Dramatic Society, which did much to set the pace and tone of theatre development over the next decades, as well as being the model for other dramatic groups formed in its wake. But, because of its leadership and patronage, it was more or less a colonial outpost. The plays it produced, as well as those of the other societies influenced by it, were mainly British, European or American. For example, in its first year the BCDS produced NOËL COWARD's *Blithe Spirit* and J. B. PRIESTLEY's *Laburnum Grove*. Other dramatists who were popular choices for the societies were Shakespeare, Sheridan, Goldsmith, OSCAR WILDE, SOMERSET MAUGHAM, Eliot and EMLYN WILLIAMS.

The staging in 1957 of the first Sierra Leonean Festival of the Arts brought about a significant change, encouraging the writing of indigenous play scripts, many of which were eventually staged. As part of the independence celebrations in 1961 a drama competition was organized, an event which produced the country's first major dramatist, Sarif Easmon. His prize-winning *Dear Parent and Ogre* (1961) became the first African play to be performed by the BCDS. Easmon, who also wrote *The New Patriots* in 1965, explores cultural and generational conflicts, conspicuous materialism, patriotism, and the dilemmas as well as the often misguided idealism of the new political elite. However, he seems to endorse the values of the elite, who are more British than African, and he makes no attempt to use the various indigenous theatre traditions. That came only with a new generation who ushered in the Krio theatre. Independence significantly altered the membership of the country's elite, and out of moves towards cultural independence grew a more open and easily accessible theatre which those not highly educated or literate in English could enjoy and feel at home in.

It was this kind of atmosphere which produced a dramatist such as Thomas Decker, whose translation of Shakespeare's *Julius Caesar* into Krio in 1964, and performed to great acclaim by the National Theatre League, effectively announced the emergence of Krio theatre. Decker also translated *As You Like It* which he entitled *Udat Di Kiap Fit* ('Who the cap fits'). However, it was other dramatists such as John, Maddy and Charley who ensured its development into an alternative and mass-based theatre. John wrote the first full-length Krio plays, notably *Na Mami Born Am* and *E Day E No Du* (both 1966). Her example led to an upsurge in theatre activity all over the country in the late 1960s and early 1970s and the formation of new theatre groups. Among them were companies such as Tabule Experimental Theatre, founded by Charley and Adeyemi Meheux in 1968, Gbakanda Tiata formed by Maddy in 1969, Songhai founded by Clifford Garber and John Kolosa Kargbo in 1973, and Belangi Dramatic Group formed in 1974. These new theatre groups showed their difference in subject matter and theatrical mode as well as in their names.

Maddy's significance lies in the fact that he was the first complete artist of the theatre to emerge in the country. To begin with, he was the exact opposite of Easmon; he was a professional actor completely aware of the possibilities of the stage, whereas Easmon was a medical doctor who wrote plays. And whereas Easmon's characters belonged to the elite, Maddy's were thugs, urban slum-dwellers, prostitutes, school dropouts and criminals. Unlike Easmon, Maddy made extensive use of song, dance, mime and other elements of traditional African performance in structuring his plays – the first Sierra Leonean dramatist to do so.

Other notable writers of this generation are Charley, whose *Wan Paun Flesh* ('A pound of flesh', 1978) was stopped by the police because it had not been passed by the censorship board introduced by the government that year to curb the theatre's criticism of its activities.

Charley was detained and had to go into exile on his release. Maddy also had close brushes with government, and went to prison before going into exile in the 1980s. Kargbo is best known for *Poyo Ton Wahala*, a socio-political satire of life in the country since the 1970s, and a play instrumental in the introduction of CENSORSHIP. Other playwrights are Raymond DeSouza George of Tabule Experimental Theatre; Julius Spencer, founder of Freetong Players and author of *Modelloh*; Bobson Kamara of Ronko Theatre and author of *Sonny Boy*; and Akmid Bakarr, director of Ronko Theatre, who wrote *Sugar Daddy Na Case* ('Sugar daddy is trouble', 1983) and *Are Go Die For Me Mama* ('I will die for my mother', 1983) and an English play, *The Great Betrayal* (1980). Each of these playwrights is attached to a specific theatre group for which they write and which they sometimes lead.

Since the late 1960s more than 150 plays have been written and produced by Sierra Leonean dramatists, but only a handful of these have been published. Nevertheless, the state of the theatre is quite healthy, with newer groups emerging and a certain professionalism becoming noticeable. There are now dramatists and actors who actually survive on earnings from theatre, and the occasions for performance are as diverse as there are human events or ceremonies.

OSITA OKAGBUE

silence, theatre of *see* THEATRE OF SILENCE

Sim, Alastair (b. Edinburgh, 9 Oct. 1900; d. London, 19 Aug. 1976) Actor and director, a professor of elocution who began a stage career at 30 and a film career at 35, and was active in both until his death. Doleful-eyed, skilled at portraying eccentrics, master of ironic wit, he came to attention in JAMES BRIDIE's plays, which he also directed, first with *Mr Bolfry* (1943, revived 1956). A frequent Hook in *Peter Pan*, he was superb in *The Clandestine Marriage* (CHICHESTER, 1966; London, 1975), *The Magistrate* (Chichester, 1969) and *Dandy Dick* (London, 1973), and was widely popular through such films as *The Belles of St Trinian's* and *Scrooge*. BRIAN BIRCH

Simon, John [Jovan Ivan] (b. Subotica, Yugoslavia, 12 May 1925) Drama critic. He taught at universities before turning to criticism and has been drama critic for *The Hudson Review, Theater Arts Magazine, The New Leader*, WNET-TV and, most notably, *New York Magazine*. His awards include the GEORGE JEAN NATHAN (1970) and American Academy of Arts and Letters (1976). Often attacked for his vitriolic personal comments, he confesses only to being an elitist in service to higher standards of theatre. He is the author of several books, including *Singularities: Essays on the Theatre 1964–73* (1976).   FELICIA HARDISON LONDRÉ

Simon, [Marvin] Neil   (b. New York, 4 July 1927) Playwright, television and screenwriter. After writing radio and television scripts and then comedies for the theatre, Simon became so successful that he has had a Broadway theatre named after him. Since *Come Blow Your Horn* (1961), with almost yearly regularity, he produced a string of comic hits, from *Barefoot in the Park* (1963), *The Odd Couple* (1965), *Plaza Suite* (1968) and *Last of the Red Hot Lovers* (1969) to *The Prisoner of Second Avenue* (1971), *The Sunshine Boys* (1972) and *Laughter on the 23rd Floor* (1993). In *Brighton Beach Memoirs* (1983), *Biloxi Blues* (1984), *Broadway Bound* (1986) and *Lost in Yonkers* (1991) he draws on his own background. He wrote the books for the musicals *Sweet Charity* (1966) and *Promises, Promises* (1968), and the screenplays for many films of his own work.
GERALD RABKIN

Robert K. Johnson, *Neil Simon* (1983)
Edythe M. McGovern, *Not-so-Simple Neil Simon: A Critical Study* (1979)

Simonov, Konstantin [Kirill Mikhailovich]   (b. Petrograd, Russia, 15 Nov. 1915; d. Moscow, 28 Aug. 1979)   Novelist and playwright. He wrote plays based on his observations as a war correspondent, including *Russkiye lyudi* (*The Russian People*, 1943) staged by TYRONE GUTHRIE at the OLD VIC that year. His postwar play *Russkiy vopros* (*The Russian Question*, 1947) anticipated the Cold War in both mood and theme.
NICK WORRALL

Harold B. Segel, *Twentieth-Century Russian Drama* (1979)

Simonson, Lee   (b. New York, 26 June 1888; d. Yonkers, NY, 23 Jan. 1967)   Scene designer, art critic and author. A visual artist, influenced by the work of Maxfield Parrish, Simonson studied under GEORGE PIERCE BAKER and in Paris, returning to the United States inspired by Europe's new stagecraft. He began designing for the WASHINGTON SQUARE PLAYERS, then notably for the THEATER GUILD, for which he also served as a board member from 1919 to 1940. An advocate of simplified realism and plasticity, Simonson designed one of America's finest examples of EXPRESSIONISM in ELMER RICE's *The Adding Machine* (1923). His thoughts on stage design through the ages are presented in *The Stage is Set* (1932) and his personal experience in *Part of a Lifetime* (1943).   ANNE FLETCHER

Simov, Viktor [Andreyevich]   (b. Moscow, 2 April 1858; d. Moscow, 21 Aug. 1935)   Designer. He became the MOSCOW ART THEATRE's chief designer, working there until 1912 and returning in 1925. Trained in a realistic tradition, Simov designed settings for plays by CHEKHOV, IBSEN and GORKY in addition to providing the lavishly opulent and archaeologically precise settings for MAT's opening production, *Tsar Fyodor Ioannovich* (1898).   NICK WORRALL

Simpson, Alan   *see* ABBEY THEATRE; BEHAN, BRENDAN; PIKE THEATRE

Simpson, N[orman] F[rederick]   (b. London, 29 Jan. 1919)   Playwright. He brings the English prose tradition of surreal whimsy to the theatre. In *One Way Pendulum* (1959) one man trains weighing machines to sing while another builds a courtroom in his house; in *The Hole* (1958), people form a queue behind a tramp who is watching a man at work; in *A Resounding Tinkle* (1957) there is an elephant in a suburban front garden; and in *Was He Anyone?* (1972) a character learns the piano as he waits 27 months for someone to save him from drowning. Simpson's popularity in the late 1950s, when he was linked to the THEATRE OF THE ABSURD, soon faded.   TONY HOWARD

Sinden, Donald [Alfred]   (b. Plymouth, 9 Oct. 1923)   Actor. He began his career in the late Second World War with Mobile Entertainments, a touring company performing plays for the armed forces in southern England, then worked with the SHAKESPEARE MEMORIAL THEATRE Company for two seasons before joining the BRISTOL OLD VIC in 1948. Equally adept at comedy and tragedy, he often alternates between classical roles and contemporary commercial West End plays. His starring roles with the ROYAL SHAKESPEARE COMPANY include Richard Plantagenet in *The Wars of the Roses* (1963), Lord Foppington in *The Relapse* (1967), *Henry VIII* (1969), Sir Harcourt Courtly in *London Assurance* (1971) and King Lear (1977). Noted for his fruity, resonant voice, he has also appeared in over 30 films, among them *The Cruel Sea* (1953) and *The National Health* (1973), and in many television series. His *A Touch of the Memoirs* appeared in 1982 and *Laughter in the Second Act* in 1985. He was knighted in 1997.   DAVID STAINES

Singapore   *see* SOUTH-EAST ASIA

Sissle, Noble Lee   (b. Indianapolis, Ind., 10 July 1889; d. Tampa, Fla., 18 Dec. 1975) and **Blake, James Hubert 'Eubie'**   (b. Baltimore, Md., 7 Feb. 1883; d. Brooklyn, New York, 12 Feb. 1983)   Composer–lyricist team who inspired a new era of African American BROADWAY musicals. Singer, lyricist and bandleader Sissle began singing in his youth and served in the First

World War as a regimental drum major. Pianist, composer and bandleader Blake began playing ragtime piano professionally at age 15, and wrote his first composition, 'Charleston Rag', at age 16. Sissle and Blake met in summer 1915 and soon launched their VAUDE-VILLE partnership as The Dixie Duo. Their first song, 'It's All Your Fault' (1916), was written for SOPHIE TUCKER. Their collaboration *Shuffle Along* (1921) was the first musical written, produced and performed by African Americans during a regular Broadway season. It included 'I'm Just Wild About Harry', later chosen as Harry Truman's presidential campaign song. Other musicals include *The Chocolate Dandies* (1924), *Shuffle Along of 1933* and *Shuffle Along of 1952*. Their songs can also be heard in the musicals *Bubbling Brown Sugar* (1976) and *Eubie* (1978). They were the first black people to be in talking pictures when filmed (1923) in synchronized sound by inventor Lee De Forest.

ANNA WHEELER GENTRY

R. Kimball and W. Bolcom, *Reminiscing with Sissle and Blake* (1973)
A. Rose, *Eubie Blake* (1979)

site-specific theatre A term that gained currency in the late twentieth century to describe theatre designed for a specific space or location that is not itself designed for theatrical use. Coming at the fine art end of an unconventional spectrum – often also called INSTALLATION – there is usually an emphasis on the visual and/or the technological, and there is overlap with PERFORMANCE ART and ENVIRONMENTAL THEATRE. A performer has spent seven days asleep in a glass case in an art gallery; classical drama has been staged in former Nazi submarine docks; and computer artists from different countries have beamed images on to buildings surrounding a once thriving shipyard while a MULTIMEDIA event among the yard's swivelling cranes is able to be seen by 30 million people on the INTERNET. On one industrial estate in the north of England, a play starred 75 cars, three buses and an excavator. The audience drove in, sat in their cars in a circle, and played their part by hooting their horns and slamming their doors. The play was broadcast on radio. An early fashion for the spectacular began to give way to more ordinary, non-theatrical locations.

CHARLES LONDON
See also EXPERIMENTAL THEATRE.

Skinner, Cornelia Otis (b. Chicago, 30 May 1901; d. New York, 9 July 1979) Actress and writer. She followed in the footsteps of her renowned father OTIS SKINNER as an actor, touring for three decades in one-woman shows, many of which she wrote (e.g. *The*

Wives of Henry VIII, The Loves of Charles II). Her acting career, begun in 1921 with her father, included film and television and embraced such notable stage performances as Mrs Erlynne in *Lady Windemere's Fan* (1946). She also wrote theatrical histories (e.g. *Madame Sarah*, 1967, about BERNHARDT), memoirs (e.g. *Family Circle*, 1948, about her family), plays, and a popular travelogue with Emily Kimbrough, *Our Hearts were Young and Gay* (1942). CLAUDIA DURST JOHNSON

Skinner, Otis (b. Cambridge, Mass., 28 June 1958; d. New York, 4 Jan. 1942) Actor, producer and author. He made his debut in Philadelphia stock in 1877; moving to New York several years later, he performed with Edwin Booth, Lawrence Barrett, Helena Modjeska and Daly's ensemble. The flamboyantly romantic performer's stardom began with *His Grace de Grammont* (1894) and continued with a 1901 revival of *Francesca da Rimini* (1855); The Honour of the Family (1908); *Kismet* (1911), in which he created the part of the beggar Hajj; *Mister Antonia* (1916), written for him by BOOTH TARKINGTON; and *Blood and Sand* (1921). Later he played in Shakespeare and wrote several fascinating books about the theatre, including an autobiography, *Footlights and Spotlight* (1924). He was the father of CORNELIA OTIS SKINNER. GERALD BORDMAN

Slade, Julian [Penkivil] (b. London, 28 May 1930) Composer. He studied for the stage at the BRISTOL OLD VIC Drama School after an education at Eton and Trinity College, Cambridge. He started to write for the theatre while at Bristol in collaboration with Dorothy Reynolds (1913–77). Their musical comedy *Salad Days* (1954) transferred to London and ran for 2,283 performances. Other shows include *Free As Air* (1957), *Follow That Girl* (1960, both with Reynolds), *Vanity Fair* (1962), *The Pursuit Of Love* (Bristol, 1967) and *Trelawny* (1972). REXTON S. BUNNETT

slang Many professions tend to encourage insiders' jargon, if only to magnify their importance and heighten the fascination of the laity. Theatre is no exception, replete as it is with taboos, SUPERSTITION and apprehensions – the transgression of uttering the name *Macbeth* instead of 'The Scottish Play' is well known and often parodied. Much theatrical slang remains in common usage backstage. The 'green room' is the rest area, while to 'strike' a set is to remove it. George Spelvin is an American version of Walter Plinge – a name used in a programme to conceal the identity of the actor. 'To dry' means to forget one's lines at the very worst moment, i.e. just when they have to be uttered before an audience. 'To corpse' does not mean to drop dead on stage but to dissolve into uncontrollable giggles. 'To joey' means the responsibility of carrying a burden, usually another actor, across the stage. Greasepaint is known as 'slap', and some thespians, not all of them women, defying long-standing superstition, even wear it offstage and in public. 'Dying the death' means failing to register with the audience, and more often refers to VARIETY performers. 'Business' is stage activity of one sort or another, merely to beguile or aid plot progression. (In *Dry Rot*, a famous WHITEHALL FARCE of the 1950s, the late John Slater had to hold a cup of tea in one hand, a bowl of sugar cubes in the other, and by gripping the sugar tongs in his teeth negotiate cubes from bowl to cup. This always elicited sustained applause; but then, any 'business' longer than 30 seconds in a British stage production always does.) 'Resting' is a well-known euphemism among actors for being out of work. 'Ham' is a term for an actor who tends to overact, who loves 'centre stage' and 'upstages' his fellows. 'Wott' is just another term for the same weakness, being an acronym for 'Way Over The Top'. 'Cue' has entered the language generally and means it is high time to introduce oneself to the audience. To 'cover' means to understudy. Sometimes an actor will 'cover' three or even four roles in a play. When a theatre is 'dark' it is closed and unused. ' The bird' is what an unappreciated performer receives from his or her customers: a spontaneous burst of total indifference. When LITTLE TICH was informed, much to his horror, that he was to be the opening act in a new show, he observed dolefully: 'It's the early worm that catches the bird!' FRANK LONG

Walter Parker Bowman and Robert Hamilton Ball, *Theatre Language: A Dictionary of Terms in English of the Drama and the Stage from Medieval to Modern Times* (1962)
Martin Harrison, *A Book of Words: Theatre* (1993)
Colin Winslow, *The Oberon Glossary of Theatrical Terms: Theatre Jargon Explained* (1991)

Slovakia The centuries-old forced priority of German and Hungarian and the economic backwardness of a poor agrarian region caused theatre in Slovakia to develop much later than in the Czech lands. Until the 1920s only amateur theatres existed, and the national and educational aspects dominated over the artistic. Slowly a Slovak professional theatre was created with Czech aid after Slovakia became a part of Czechoslovakia in 1918. The Slovak National Theatre was founded in Bratislava in 1920.

At first a Czech-language ensemble, which included several Slovaks, began to perform; then, from 1925 on, plays in the Slovak language were occasionally performed. A shortage of audiences, actors and plays in Slovak delayed the creation of an independent Slovak ensemble, which was finally established in 1932 under the leadership of Ján Borodáč. The founders of the Slovak theatre (Borodáč, Bagár, Borodáčová-Országhová, Meličková) were influenced by STANISLAVSKY and the MOSCOW ART THEATRE; their programme of national revival was founded on domestic classics and contemporary plays. Foremost of the playwrights was Ivan Stodola (1888–1977), who wrote historical plays, tragedy, satirical plays and farce, as well as social drama. After Slovakia seceded from the Czechoslovak Republic in 1938 and an independent, strongly nationalistic Slovak state was created, professional theatres were founded in towns other than Bratislava (in Nitra, Martin, Prešov) and rapidly developed. The generation of the 1940s (which includes the director Ján Jamnický) created a stylized theatre, influenced by MEYERHOLD and BURIAN.

At the end of the Second World War, when a united Czechoslovakia was restored, Slovak theatre developed in the same environment as the Czech, yet differently. It was only after the war that the theatre became fully professional, including a network of permanent repertory theatres. Culture was not burdened by as strong a tradition of non-artistic functions as in the Czech lands, and current artistic impulses (such as socialist realism, BRECHT, the THEATRE OF THE ABSURD) were not accepted as unequivocally. The development of the more uniform Slovak theatre was smoother and its mainstream was concentrated to a greater extent within traditional drama theatres (with fewer small, studio-type theatres). Despite the emphasis on propaganda in the postwar years, a group of individual and expressive directors did appear (Budský, Zachar, Rakovský), as well as the outstanding representative of Slovak stage design, Ladislav Vychodil. The designs of Bezáková, with their ornamental and moulded elements, influenced costume in both parts of Czechoslovakia.

In Bratislava, a studio theatre, the Theatre on the Promenade (1968–71), staged very interesting, anti-conventional performances (e.g. Gogol's *Marriage*; BECKETT's *Waiting for Godot*). This was the only theatre in Slovakia not to survive the post-occupation 'normalization' process which otherwise had much less of an impact on the Slovak theatre. (Theatre was less politically and socially committed than in the Czech lands.) There was no clear-cut interruption of continuity and Slovak theatre remained highly creative. An alternative was offered by the Naïve Theatre from Radošina, founded in 1963, which uses actors without professional training, the local dialect, and methods typical in the theatre of the absurd. Its foremost personality is

Stanislav Štěpka (b. 1944). Among the Slovak playwrights of the postwar period a special place belongs to Štefan Králik (1909–83), who wrote SYMBOLIST, philosophical plays, and to Peter Karvaš, a critical analyst of important moral and social problems, whose work (such as *Midnight Mass*, 1959; *Antigone and the Others*, 1962; *The Scar*, 1963; *The Big Wig*, 1964; *The Damocles Experiment*, 1967; *Absolute Prohibition*, 1969) has been banned since the beginning of the 1970s.

There were also theatres for minorities living in Slovakia – Hungarians, Ruthenians and Ukrainians and, later, for Gypsies.

In the 1970s and 1980s the work of the Slovak National Theatre (directors P. Haspra, L. Vajdička; later V. Strnisko, M. Huba) and other theatres in Bratislava (New Stage, where directors M. Pietor and V. Strnisko worked, and Studio S, with the comedy partnership J. Satinský and M. Lasica) was marked by vigorous directorial interpretations and a mature acting style. Distinctive personalities also established themselves in the regions, for example the director J. Bednárik in Nitra. In November 1989 theatre workers in Slovakia, just as in the Czech Republic, took an active role in the 'velvet revolution'. After the fall of communism there was an upsurge of alternative theatres (e.g. GunaGu, Stoka) which brought completely new, provocative aspects to the Slovak theatre and expanded its spectrum quite considerably. The writer V. Klimáček and director B. Uhlár formulated their work within this circle. A new Bratislava theatre, Astorka-Korzo (director R. Polák), re-adopted the 'grotesque' tradition of the Korzo Theatre at the end of the 1960s and beginning of the 1970s. EVA ŠORMOVÁ

M. Mistrík, ed., *Slovenské divadlo v. 20. storočí* ('Slovak theatre in the twentieth century') (2000)
Z. Rampák, *Dějiny slovenského divadla* ('The history of Slovak theatre') (1948)
V. Štefko, ed., *Otvorené divadlo v uzavretej spoločnosti* ('Open theatre in the closed society') (1997)

Slovenia *see* YUGOSLAVIA

Smallest Theatre in the World Started in 1972 by ex-KEN CAMPBELL Roadshow member Marcel Steiner (1931–99), it measured 6ft long × 6ft high × 2ft 3ins wide and was built complete with box office and stage door on the sidecar of a Russian motorbike. Based in the UK but peripatetic, it seated one and toured a dozen countries with its epic repertoire that ranged from *A Tale of Two Cities* and *The Hunchback of Notre Dame* to *War and Peace* and *The Guns of Navarone*. CHARLES LONDON

Smith, Anna Deveare (b. Baltimore, Maryland, 18 Sept. 1950) Playwright, performer. She gained widespread attention for two SOLO pieces that are part of a series of such work collectively titled *On the Road: A Search for American Character*, derived from interviews with people about particular topics in which she plays the entire cast: *Fires in the Mirror: Crown Heights, Brooklyn, and Other Identities* (1992) is her response to racial differences in the Crown Heights area of Brooklyn between black and Jewish communities following a three-day riot, and *Twilight: Los Angeles, 1992* (1993) tackles similar cultural tensions in Los Angeles. CHARLES LONDON

Smith, Dodie [Dorothy Gladys] (b. Whitefield, Lancs, 3 May 1896; d. Great Dunmow, Essex, 24 Nov. 1990) Playwright, novelist and actress. Having trained at the Royal Academy of Dramatic Art, she gave up acting in 1922 and joined the London furniture store Heals as a buyer. While there she wrote the successful play *Autumn Crocus* (1931, under the pseudonym C. L. Anthony). Her six West End hits during the 1930s (including her best, *Dear Octopus*, 1938) inspired GIELGUD's description of her as the 'Queen Bee of the London stage'. She remains best known for her children's story *101 Dalmatians* (1956), written after her theatre work lost favour with audiences and filmed twice, once as an enormously popular cartoon, and for her novel, *I Capture the Castle* (1949). She wrote four volumes of autobiography. MAGGIE GALE

Valerie Grove, *Dear Dodie* (1996)

Smith, Ellie [Lilian Enis-Smith] (b. Auckland, New Zealand, 1950) Actress, singer and director, known particularly for her outstanding performances in lead roles at DOWNSTAGE, in *Piaf* (1982) by PAM GEMS and in *Shirley Valentine* and *Educating Rita* (1983) by WILLY RUSSELL; also in *Master Class* (1996) and *Sweeney Todd* (1999) at CIRCA. She was director of Downstage 1998–9. GILLIAN GREER & LAURIE ATKINSON

Smith, Harry B[ache] (b. Buffalo, NY, 28 Dec. 1861; d. Atlantic City, NJ, 2 Jan. 1936) Librettist, lyricist and adapter. A Chicago journalist, he teamed up with composer REGINALD DE KOVEN to emulate GILBERT and SULLIVAN in America, and wrote 16 libretti for him, of which the most successful was the comic opera *Robin Hood* (1891). He worked with other composers, notably VICTOR HERBERT, and, although few of his songs became standards, he was immensely popular and influential in his day. His count of some 300 libretti, 6,000 lyrics and 123 Broadway shows put him in a category of his own, and he was the first such lyricist to be honoured with a published collection of his songs, issued in 1900 as *Stage Lyrics*. His autobiography, *First Nights and First Editions*, appeared in 1931. His younger brother Robert was also a librettist.

CHARLES LONDON

Smith [Sultzer], Joe (b. New York, 17 Feb. 1884; d. Englewood, New Jersey, 22 Feb. 1981) and **Dale, Charlie [Charles Marks]** (b. New York, 16 Sept. 1881; d. Teaneck, New Jersey, 16 Apr. 1971) VAUDE-VILLE duo. Their association began after they performed in MINSTREL shows in the late 1890s. They went on to form the Avon Comedy Four, with several different comedians making up the foursome at different times, perfecting sketches such as their most famous one, 'Dr Kronkeit and His Only Living Patient'. In 1909 Smith and Dale led the first all-American VARIETY show on tour to Europe. They were the inspiration for NEIL SIMON's comedy about two old, warring comedians, *The Sunshine Boys*, and for several noted duos, such as Dean Martin and Jerry Lewis, and Cheech and Chong. HELEN RAPPAPORT

Smith, Maggie [Margaret Natalie] (b. Ilford, Essex, 28 Dec. 1934) Actress. Her early roles in REVUE (e.g. *Share My Lettuce*, 1957) established her as a remarkable comedienne; as her career developed via the OLD VIC and the West End, she became at home in the classics as well as in contemporary plays (e.g. *The Rehearsal*, 1961; *The Private Ear* and *The Public Eye*, 1962). In the mid-to-late 1960s she worked in the first NATIONAL THEATRE company, achieving acclaim in such roles as Desdemona to OLIVIER's *Othello* (1964), and the leads in *Miss Julie* (1965) and *Hedda Gabler* (1970). However, with her quick wit and precision delivery, she was still best known for her comedy, which was shown to great effect in two performances opposite her then husband ROBERT STEPHENS, as Beatrice to his Benedick (1965) and Amanda in *Private Lives* (1972). In the 1970s she spent four seasons at Canada's STRATFORD FESTIVAL, where her roles included Beatrice, Cleopatra and Lady Macbeth. Other successes include *Lettice and Lovage* (1987), Lady Bracknell in *The Importance of Being Earnest* (1993) and *The Lady in the Van* (1999). She has also enjoyed stardom on the screen, winning Academy awards for *The Prime of Miss Jean Brodie* (1969) and *California Suite* (1978), to accompany her many stage awards. She married the playwright Beverley Cross (1931–98) in 1975, and was created a dame in 1990.

DAVID STAINES

Michael Coveney, *Maggie Smith* (1992)

Smith, Oliver [Lemuel] (b. Waupaun, Wisc., 13 Feb. 1918; d. Brooklyn, New York, 23 Jan. 1994) Set designer and producer. After studying at Penn State, he began his career working for ballet companies before designing the sets for *Rosalinda* (1942). His settings were later seen in numerous successes, including *On the Town* (1944), *My Fair Lady* (1956), *West Side Story* (1957), *The Sound of Music* (1959) and *Hello, Dolly!* (1964), as well as in non-musicals. The wide range of plays and musicals on which he worked allowed him to employ an equally wide range of styles, but he brought to all of them his taste, imagination and elegance. He also often served as co-producer of the shows he designed and won many awards, including seven Tonys. GERALD BORDMAN

T. Mikiotowicz, *Oliver Smith: A Bio-Bibliography* (1993)

Smith, Rae see DESIGN

Smoktunovsky, Innokenti [Mikhailovich] (b. Tat'yanovka, Soviet Union, 28 March 1925; d. Moscow, 4 Aug. 1994) Actor who came to prominence at the Bolshoi Gorky Dramatic Theatre in Leningrad, where he acted a stunning Prince Myshkin in TOVSTONO-GOV's adaptation of Dostoevsky's *The Idiot* (1957), subsequently seen in London (1966). He became a world star as Hamlet in Grigori Kozintsev's film (1964).

NICK WORRALL

Sobol, Joshua (b. Tel Mond, Israel, 24 Aug. 1939) Playwright. He wrote documentaries on social and political issues for the Haifa Municipal Theatre in the early 1970s, and later wrote several fully-fledged plays, such as *Sylvestre 72* (1972) and *The Night of the Twentieth* (1973), the latter about a group of Jewish pioneers on the eve of their settling in a new spot in Galilee. He widened his questioning of national myths (notably in *Weininger's Last Night*, 1982, on the life of the Viennese Jewish philosopher, and in *Ghetto*, 1984, on the Jewish theatre in the Vilnius ghetto during the Holocaust) and openly criticized the deteriorating Zionist dream in the political reality of Israel (*The Palestinian*, 1985). The opening night of his *Jerusalem Syndrome* (1987), an historical parable alluding to the current political situation, was physically interrupted by members of right-wing groups. The incident lead to Sobol's resignation from his joint artistic directorship of the Haifa Theatre, and his following plays (*Adam*, 1989, a less successful sequel to *Ghetto*; *Solo*, 1991, on the life of Spinoza) were produced elsewhere. In the late 1980s, some of Sobol's plays (especially *Ghetto*) were discovered outside of Israel and produced in Europe and the United States, but he did not sustain this international position in the 1990s. His best-known play of the period, *Village* (1995), a nostalgic depiction of his native village during his childhood, won great success, but its ideological consistency with his earlier writing is at best questionable. AVRAHAM OZ

social realism *see* DRAMATIC THEORY

Sofola, Onuxkwuke Nwazuluoha [Zulu Sofola] (b. Issele-Ukwu, Nigeria, 17 June 1935; d. 7 Sept. 1995) Playwright and director. Writing mainly from a traditional perspective about contemporary women and their situation in a male-dominated world, she employed elements of magic, myth and legend as dramaturgy and for examining age-old conflicts between traditionalism and modernism in which male supremacy persists. She was also Professor of Performing Arts at Ilorin, Nigeria. Her many plays include *The Disturbed Peace of Christmas* (1969), *Wedlock of the Gods* (1971), *King Emene* (1975), *The Sweet Trap* (1975), *Old Wines Are Tasty* (1975), *The Wizard of Law* (1976), and *Songs of a Maiden and Memories of Moonlight* (1977). OLU OBAFEMI

Soho [Poly] Theatre A pioneer of new writing, founded by Verity Bargate and Fred Proud in 1968 as a LUNCHTIME THEATRE in the basement of a condemned Chinese restaurant in Soho, central London. Poly was added to its name in 1972 when the theatre moved to another basement, owned by the Polytechnic of Central London. Here it became a vital part of the FRINGE, helping many writers, in particular HOWARD BRENTON, PAM GEMS, BARRIE KEEFFE and Tony Marchant, and maintaining high standards of production and performance. It attracted many leading actors, such as COLIN BLAKELEY, SIMON CALLOW and DAVID WARNER. An annual new play award was named in 1983 after Bargate, who had been sole artistic director since 1975 and had died in 1981. From 1990, the company continued in different venues under its old name of Soho Theatre. In 1996 it moved into its new premises in Soho, which were being redeveloped to provide a new theatre; it opened in 2000. COLIN CHAMBERS

solo show A show presented by only one person. It has a long history, including *rhapsodes* (classical Greece) and *scops* (Anglo-Saxon England). In the nineteenth century, reading tours became very successful for Charles Dickens, Edgar Allan Poe and Mark Twain. In America, the one-person show was popularized by the Chautauqua Assembly, an educational and religious institution founded in 1875. In the twentieth century, one-person shows came to be regarded as integral to theatre, as opposed to a form of entertainment distinct from it. John S. Gentile, in *Cast of One* (1989), differentiates several subgenres: biographical shows centred on the life of a famous artist or politician; performers presenting their own lives in autobio-

graphical shows; solo Shakespeare recitals (e.g. GIELGUD's *Ages of Man*, 1957; MCKELLEN's *Acting Shakespeare*, 1977); and contemporary monologues (shows that do not fit any of the above), often characterized by social criticism, such as the solo pieces based on interviews performed by ANNA DEVEARE SMITH or Eve Ensler's *The Vagina Monologues* (1997), which has been seen in 20 countries and heard in 20 languages. Among the genre's American representatives are LILY TOMLIN, Whoopi Goldberg and Eric Bogosian; in Britain, STEVEN BERKOFF's *One Man* (1985) or shows by Clive Merrison fit that category. ALEC MCCOWEN's recital of *St Mark's Gospel* (1978) is unique. For the dramatist, writing a one-person show may offer particular opportunities (e.g. ALAN BENNETT, PETER BARNES, SAMUEL BECKETT, DAVID MAMET, LANFORD WILSON) or be a good creative exercise (e.g. DAVID POWNALL), while actors tend to like doing one-person shows to overcome patches of unemployment. Theatres, more and more subjected to tight budgets, find one-person shows financially attractive because they are relatively inexpensive.

Others who have performed successful solo shows include MAX ADRIAN, RUTH DRAPER, JOYCE GRENFELL, BEATRICE LILLIE, MÍCHEÁL MACLÍAMMÓIR, CORNELIA OTIS SKINNER, EMLYN WILLIAMS, JAMES EARL JONES, JULIE HARRIS and ZOE CALDWELL.

DANIEL MEYER-DINKGRÄFE

Sybille Demmer, *Untersuchungen zu Form und Geschichte des Monodramas* (1982)
Alan Sinfield, *Dramatic Monologue* (1977)

Sologub, Fyodor (pseud. for Fyodor Kuzmich Teternikov) (b. St Petersburg, 1 March 1863; d. Leningrad, 5 Dec. 1927) SYMBOLIST poet, novelist and playwright. Author of some 18 plays and associated with pioneering directors like MEYERHOLD and EVREINOV, his most interesting contribution is his essay *Theatre of One Will* (1908), which argues for the 'mystery' of a subjective theatre. His plays add an element of delicious eroticism to this. ROBERT LEACH

***son et lumière* (sound and light)** An outside, evening entertainment using various media. The Son et Lumière, which was introduced in 1952 by the Châteaux of the Loire, combines the use of lighting with a soundtrack of music, narrative and dramatized sequences to entertain and to inform. The first British example dates from 1957 at Greenwich, London, and in the United States, from 1962 at Independence Hall, Philadelphia. The settings for *son et lumière* are usually of historical interest, for example the Egyptian Pyramids or the Tower of London. ADRIANA HUNTER

Sondheim, Stephen [Joshua] (b. New York, 22 March 1930) Lyricist and composer. Sondheim began his BROADWAY career as lyricist to LEONARD BERNSTEIN on *West Side Story* (1957) and to JULE STYNE on *Gypsy* (1959) but, following his first lyrics and music assignment on *A Funny Thing Happened on the Way to the Forum* (1962), he has, with the exception of an impressive collaboration with RICHARD RODGERS on *Do I Hear a Waltz?* (1965) and some additional lyrics for the 1974 revival of Bernstein's *Candide*, written words solely to his own scores. His successful early works showed a considerable versatility, beginning with the wittily uncomplicated burlesque of *A Funny Thing*, followed by the sharply observed and exposed New Yorkery of *Company* (1970), the showbizzy foolishness of *Follies* (1971), and a serenely lovely score for Hugh Wheeler's INGMAR BERGMAN adaptation, *A Little Night Music* (1973). From *Pacific Overtures* (1976) on through the musical melodrama *Sweeney Todd* (1979), *Merrily We Roll Along* (1981), *Sunday in the Park With George* (1984), *Into the Woods* (1988), *Assassins* (1991) and *Passion* (1994), Sondheim made a series of attempts to stretch various limits of the established style and structure of the contemporary musical, both textually and musically. He gained as a result an international reputation and fervent following, but less often the wide success enjoyed by his early work, which displays a mastery of literate lyrical style, both comic and sentimental, unequalled in the modern MUSICAL THEATRE.
KURT GÄNZL

S. Banfield, *Sondheim's Broadway Musicals* (1993)
J. Gordon, *Art isn't Easy* (1990)
M. Gottfried, *Stephen Sondheim* (1993)
Craig Zadan, *Sondheim & Co.* (1974)

Sorge, Reinhard [Johannes] (b. Rixdorf, nr Berlin, 29 Jan. 1892; d. Ablaincourt, the Somme, 20 July 1916) Poet whose play *Der Bettler* (*The Beggar*, 1917) was of central importance for the development of EXPRESSIONIST drama. Originally called the *Ich-Drama* ('Drama of the self'), the play was the first to contain the full range of devices and stylistic characteristics of expressionism. Sorge saw the stage as a 'healing-place' where humanity's deepest spiritual concerns could be revealed. His other plays were mystical, dramatic poems of no significant importance for theatre history. Sorge volunteered for army service and died in the First World War. GÜNTER BERGHAUS

Sothern, E[dward] H[ugh] (b. New Orleans, 6 Dec. 1859; d. New York, 28 Oct. 1933) Actor and producer, son of the famous comedian E. A. Sothern. He planned to be a painter but, changing his mind, made his stage debut in 1879 and rose to fame under DANIEL FROHMAN in comedies such as *Lord Chumley* (1888) and in the swashbuckling *The Prisoner of Zenda* (1895). Having a gift for poetry, the soberly handsome performer offered his Hamlet in 1900. From 1904 to 1924 he and his second wife, JULIA MARLOWE, became America's leading Shakespeareans, although many critics prefered Sothern's comic interpretations, for example of Benedick and Malvolio, to his tragic readings.
GERALD BORDMAN

sound At the beginning of the twentieth century, sound in the theatre was strictly limited to the production of off-stage noises and sound effects, and was the preserve of the properties department. The PROPS man would have thunder sheets, wind and rain machines, glass crashes and door knocks, as well as a variety of machines of his own design for other effects. The properties lists for two popular shows of the 1920s, *The Ghost Train* by Arnold Ridley and *Journey's End* by R. C. SHERRIFF, include such diverse items as a garden roller, a water tank, various orchestral drums and whistles, and a milk churn. The full list for *The Ghost Train*, which includes the operating instructions for the arrivals and departures of an invisible train, makes fascinating reading, and can be found in the Samuel French edition of the play. Today, much use is still made of 'live' glass crashes and door knocks, although the majority of other sound effects are prerecorded. Like sound with film, the creation and manipulation of sound in the theatre by electronic means came to the fore in the United States. Using techniques of both broadcasting and film studios, sound effects replayed from disc and amplification of speech and music became an accepted part of theatre in North America in the 1930s, and the Bell Telephone Company demonstrated three-channel relay of an orchestra playing in one theatre to an audience in a separate theatre as early as 1933. With the development and commercial availability of the magnetic tape recorder after 1945, replay of both sound effects and music became commonplace in the American theatre. British theatre was somewhat slower in embracing this new technology, and eleborate consoles employing disc reproducers and special devices to allow accurate cueing of sound effects and music were to be found in most of the larger theatres. These consoles were known as Panatropes, and it was common for the sound operating position to be known as 'The Pan', long after these consoles had been replaced by more modern equipment. Effects and music were replayed from disc, and the comparatively coarse and heavy replay arms meant that discs had to be replaced regularly. With the adoption of magnetic tape as a storage medium, replay of effects and music became far less problematic, and many exciting and ambitious soundtracks were incorporated into drama productions. The arrival of low-cost digital storage of audio in the 1980s, and the use of computers – in particular, of the MIDI (Musical Instrument Digital Interface) standard as a control protocol – has meant that what is now possible is limited by little more than the imagination of the artist/technician. The range of equipment available to theatre sound is bewilderingly large, and encompasses digital audio samplers which store audio in digital format in random access memory (RAM) for instant playback, digital audio tape (DAT), mini-disc and compact disc (both with their associated recorders), digital cartridge machines, and multi-track hard-disc recorders as a component of digital audio workstations.

The reinforcement of voice and music in theatre remained limited to an overall pick-up of the entire stage or orchestra, with specific microphones being used for effect only. The arrival of a new type of musical under the auspices of such composers as JULE STYNE, STEPHEN SONDHEIM and JERRY HERMANN, heralded a change in sound reinforcement techniques that is still under way. Before the musical *South Pacific* (1949), musical numbers were mostly staged separately from the main plot, and it was not until this show that songs were seen as a means to advance and comment on the plot, rather than to interrupt it. Increasingly complicated libretti and orchestrations, and auditoriums that were acoustically poor, led the directors of such shows to seek ways of increasing the intelligibility of the lyrics. The use of directional microphones, and later miniature microphones coupled to radio transmitters, together with a sound control board, or mixing desk, in the auditorium, enabled the director or the composer to have a measure of control over the balance between singer/actor and orchestra, and also allowed the use of actors who were not primarily singers. The freedom that these techniques allowed was exploited to the full in the 1960s and 1970s, and reached a plateau with the 'rock musicals' of the latter decade, when the theatre stage became little more than a platform for dramatized rock music concerts, with little form or content. The appearance of the team of ANDREW LLOYD WEBBER and TIM RICE in the UK, ALAIN BOUBLIL and CLAUDE-MICHEL SCHÖNBERG in France, and the continued presence of Stephen Sondheim in the United States, did much to revitalize and rehabilitate the musical, and the involvement of respected drama directors such as TREVOR NUNN, as well as the long-established masters of the genre like HAL PRINCE, led to the emergence of a new type of technician, the sound designer, to handle the intricacies of presenting these musical spectaculars to a demanding audience who are far more used to listening to high-quality sound in their homes than their predecessors. Through-composed musicals, where there is little or no spoken dialogue, place great demands on the skills of the sound designer; the casting of actors who can sing reasonably well, rather than singers who can act reasonably well, and demanding, eight-performances-a-week schedules have increased the reliance on technology to make complex lyrics understandable over the top of musical arrangements that are not always sympathetic to the natural range of the human voice. This has led to the use of higher levels of sound reinforcement than might previously have been felt desirable, although an increasing number of musical productions have started to reverse this trend by returning to a less complex style of orchestration and a more natural level of reinforcement.   JOHN A. LEONARD

David Collison, *Stage Sound* (1976)
John Huntington, *Control Systems for Live Entertainment* (2000)
John A. Leonard, *Theatre Sound* (2000)
Burris Meyer et al., *Sound in the Theatre* (1979)
Graham Walne, *Effects for Theatre* (1995)

South Africa   Like most other African countries with a colonial history, South Africa is made up of different ethnic groups and cultures. The country's cultural history in many ways reflects the many tensions and struggles which characterize a complex socio-political history and landscape which saw the introduction of the divisive system of apartheid. The original dwellers of the country were the San (who it is believed have lived in the area for over 8,000 years) and the Khoi (who came from what is now Botswana about 2,000 years ago). These two ethnic groups, now collectively known as the Khoisan, originally settled in the Eastern and Western Cape regions and they eventually met up with the Bantu groups, most of whom had migrated from central Africa. They were later joined by the European settlers, who first arrived in the fifteenth century after the evolution of the distinctive ethnic cultures expressed today in the dances, rituals, songs and narratives which constitute the indigenous/traditional performances of South Africa. Sustained military confrontations between African farmers and the European settlers in the nineteenth century succeeded in pushing the native population further inland and marginalizing them. This remained the position, except for the contest for political control between the Dutch and the English, until the end of apartheid and the coming to power in 1994 of the African National Congress.

European domination also meant an undermining and sidelining of the natives' cultural basis as they were sucked into the whirlpool of capitalist expansion resulting from the diamond discoveries in the late nineteenth century which brought European touring theatre companies and other entertainers to the country.

Traditional performance, such as dance, storytelling – for example, the Xhosa *intsomi* and Zulu *inganekwane* – oral praise poetry (*izibongo*), religious rituals, and military and political ceremonies, existed before the introduction of European written and spoken drama as a distinct and separate theatre style. Thus, two performance traditions and systems developed side by side. First there were the indigenous forms, with their new variants such as the *sifela* to be found in the urban centres and mining compounds. These forms were completely excluded from the colonial theatre system, and ignored by scholars and the mainly white theatre historians. Then there was the European-style theatre which the English, the Dutch and the Germans introduced and which, not surprisingly, provided the basis for the current system in style, form of spaces and organization. This imported theatre began to naturalize itself as local writers began to produce original South African texts. Foremost in this group were Stephen Black, Melt Brink, C. Langenhoven, and the first black playwright and critic Herbert Dhlomo, who in 1935 wrote *Nongquase, the Liberator: The Girl Who Killed to Save*. The first Afrikaans play was *Magrita Prinsolo*, written by S. du Toit in 1897. After the Anglo-Boer war of 1899–1902, Afrikaner nationalism found expression in a wave of patriotic writings such as Langenhoven's *Die Hoop Van Suid-Afrika* ('The hope of South Africa', 1912).

The victory of Afrikaner nationalism in 1948 and the subsequent establishment and experience of apartheid became the major subject matter for theatre thereafter. Even in post-apartheid South Africa, the effects of the years of racial segregation, the official denial of recognition to forms of cultural expression that were not European, and the deprivation and exclusion of non-European artistic forms from the funding structure have had both negative and positive impacts. Having said that, the cultural mix means that there is a diversity in the forms of cultural expression, which became even more obvious from the 1970s on – a healthy cross-fertilization between artists from different cultural and ethnic backgrounds that brings nearer the ever-increasing possibility of a uniquely South African style of theatre evolving.

Such crossover between the European style and traditional and usually oral forms can be seen in the work-shop theatre technique pioneered by Theatre Workshop '71 in productions such as *Women at the Crossroads* and made famous by ATHOL FUGARD, John Kani and Winston Ntshona in internationally popular plays such as *Sizwe Bansi is Dead* (1972) and *The Island* (1973). It was also used by Barney Simon, Percy Mtwa and Mbongeni Ngema in *Woza Albert!* (1981), in *Sophiatown* (1986) by Junction Avenue Theatre, and in the township musicals of dramatists such as Gibson Kente. The 'workshop play' with its economy – spartan and highly mobile – became the format of most of the nationally and internationally successful anti-apartheid plays.

The musical, on the other hand, owed its beginning to the hugely successful collaboration of white capital and black artists under the umbrella of Union Artists, an organization formed in opposition to the exclusive and government-promoted white (English and Afrikaans) theatre and determined to defy government policies of racial segregation that made *King Kong* possible in 1959. It was Gibson Kente who was to popularize this genre later and to evolve a peculiar musical style of presentation and highly melodramatic content in shows like *Hard Road*, *Lobola* and *Mama and the Load*. Kente, who was highly popular with the township audience, has been criticized for the apolitical nature and extreme commercialism of the shows. However, he also wrote more political plays like *How Long?* which landed him in trouble with the authorities.

Abroad, musicals such as *Ipi-Tombi* and *Umbatha* (a Zulu *Macbeth*) were successful but criticized as commercial exploitations of tribal forms. Theatre was in the forefront of the struggle to establish a direction for African art and to create a new social order. Internationally, the country faced a writers' boycott. Internally, the white commercial theatre flourished, but from the 1970s an alternative theatre movement developed in opposition to the government-sponsored provincial performing arts councils and the state supported National Theatre Organization, founded in 1947. Foremost in this movement were directors and groups such as Robert Kavanagh, who founded Theatre Workshop '71 in 1971, Molefe Phetoe, who helped found MDALI in 1972, The People's Experimental Theatre (1973) and Junction Avenue Theatre (1976) under the directorship of Malcolm Purkey. Other alternatives emerged in theatres such as the MARKET THEATRE in Johannesburg and the People's Space Theatre in Cape Town. There is also a corpus of literary drama by native African playwrights such as Lewis Nkosi, Zakes Mda, Maishe Maponya, Matsemela Manaka, Small Ndaba and Fatima Dike, as well as the work of white and Asian writers who write in either English or Afrikaans, foremost of these being Fugard, Simon, Batho Smit, Paul Slabolepsy, Reza de Wet, Anthony Akerman, Kirben Pillay, and P. G. du Plessis. These literary dramas evidence a wide variety of styles, ranging from du Plessis, whose plays comfortably mix tragedy, comedy and melodrama, to the surface realism of de Wet's psychic dramas, and from the political and explosive praise poetry style of direct address to the audience of playwrights such as Maponya and Manaka to Mda's plays, which are firmly rooted in African communal performance traditions. Of all these writers, Fugard stands taller than most, both in the breadth of his styles and in the complexity and spread of his dramatic output.

Since 1994 great steps have been taken to develop theatre, from the creation of a new performers' union to the transformation of management and funding structures to represent better the interests of the majority. OSITA OKAGBUE

D. Coplan, *In Township Tonight: South Africa's Black City Music and Theatre* (1985)

Lizbeth Goodman, *Women, Politics and Performance in South African Theatre Today* (1999)

Robert Kavanagh, *Theatre and Cultural Struggle in South Africa* (1985)

A. von Kotze, *Organise and Act: The Natal Workers' Theatre Movement, 1983–7* (1988)

Loren Kruger, *The Drama of South Africa: Plays, Pageants and Publics since 1910* (1999)

South America During the period 1890–1920, a period of realism and naturalism, an American consciousness began to be manifested in South American theatre, with Argentina as the point of departure. It can be said that twentieth-century theatre started under the influence of the *gaucho* literature of the Argentina pampa horsemen, in the form of the epic poem *Martin Fierro* (1872) by José Hernández (1834–86). From this poem was derived the serial novel *Juan Moreira* by Eduardo Gutiérrez (1851–89), which was adapted for the stage in 1886 by actor–playwright José Podestá and enjoyed unprecedented success in Buenos Aires. Numerous works followed with the same *gaucho* theme, among them *Calandria* (1898) by Martiniano P. Leguizamón (1858–1935) and *Jesús Nazareno* (1909) by Enrique García Velloso (1880–1935), which also received public acceptance but no critical acknowledgement. Towards the end of the nineteenth century, two theatrical currents were defined that prevailed well into the next century. The first consisted of popular forms of entertainment represented by the CIRCUS and the so-called *tabladillos* (a kind of VAUDEVILLE); the second, of the theatre known as *mayor* (major), comprising stagings of classical plays (Shakespeare, Molière, etc.)

As a hybrid of these two currents, the *sainete* (a comedy of manners), probably the most widely disseminated theatrical form in Latin America, began to take shape. The *sainete criollo* was different in themes and language from its European counterpart. As the *sainete* evolved in the realistic period, its content increasingly included strong social commentaries that eventually ran at cross-purposes with its quasi-parodic style of acting. Among the most important *sainete* playwrights were the Argentinian Nemesio Trejo (1862–1916) and Alberto Vacarezza (1886–1959), and the Uruguayan Carlos Mauricio Pacheco (1881–1924).

The rural setting of the early *gaucho* plays gave way to the urban scene, in which the idealized epic *gaucho* was replaced by the common man. Thus emerged the realistic drama of South America, which was also influenced by European naturalism. During the first two decades of the twentieth century, realistic drama practically dominated the River Plate region. This genre's most representative authors included the Uruguayan Florencio Sánchez (1875–1910) and the Argentinians José León Pagano (1875–1964) and Gregorio de Laferrère (1867–1913). Their plays depicted social conflict with resolutions that stressed conformity rather than rebellion. In some cases the characters were predestined to self-destruct, as in *M'hijo el dotor* ('My son the doctor', 1903), and *Barranca abajo* ('Down the ravine', 1905) by Sánchez.

The First World War put an end to the prevailing positivistic thinking, and as a result of the AVANT-GARDE tendencies of the period after the war, realistic drama did not fully develop, and the 15 years from 1920 to 1935 are seen as its period of gradual decadence. In the rest of South America, this movement produced only a few plays worth mentioning, such as *Víboras sociales* ('Social vipers', 1911), by the Colombian Antonio Alvárez Lleras (1892–1956). The most important realistic plays written in Latin America came from later generations, written by authors such as the Ecuadorian Raúl Andrade (1905–83), the Venezuelan César Rengifo (1915–80) and the Uruguayan Mauricio Rosencof (b. 1933).

The Mexican (1910) and Russian (1917) revolutions underscored the problems of the peasantry and the Indians stemming from the unjust distribution of land. In the theatre these concerns were reflected in efforts to interpret national realities with a new focus on culturally marginal groups, and to incorporate Latin America definitively into the context of Western civilization.

In the River Plate area, the *sainete* had already paved

the way for its utmost expression: the *grotesco criollo* (1921–50), which reached its highest level with Armando Discépolo (1887–1971) in plays such as *Mateo* (1923), *Stephano* (1928) and *Relojero* ('Watch maker', 1934). Influenced by the Italian *grottesco*, the *grotesco criollo* made the connection with its own social reality by adopting the popular dialect spoken in Buenos Aires. The *grotesco* was basically a theatre of identification in which emotion played an essential role. The spectators were to share the sufferings of the characters, usually poor immigrants full of illusions about a world that existed only in their minds.

The *grotesco*'s thematic exhaustion contributed to the arrival of the INDEPENDENT THEATRES. Influenced partly by STANISLAVSKY's theories, a re-evaluation of the roles to be played by directors, playwrights and actors within a theatre group became a necessity. The independent theatre made its appearance with the founding in Buenos Aires of the Teatro del Pueblo (People's Theatre) in 1931 by Leonidas Barletta. At the end of the decade there were more than 30 stages in the city dedicated to the independent theatre. Among them, the group Fray Mocho is of special importance because of its contribution to the formative years of prominent figures such as the playwright Osvaldo Dragún (1929–99).

In Montevideo, the independent theatre was founded when its own Teatro del Pueblo was established in 1937. Soon after that, several groups were formed. An offspring of the movement, the group El Galpón (The Shed), set the guidelines to be followed later by the 'new theatre' groups. From 1949 to 1976 they produced more than 80 plays in Uruguay drawn from both Latin American and world theatre. During the group's exile, from 1976 until 1985, they staged more than 25 productions, mostly Latin American plays, all under the direction of some of the most highly renowned directors in the country such as Atahualpa del Cioppo, César Campodónico and Rubén Yáñez, among others.

During this period the universities began to take part in the shaping of national theatres. Chile is a case in point. In 1941 the Teatro Experimental of the Universidad de Chile was founded; and in 1943 the Teatro de Ensayo de la Universidad Católica opened its doors. In addition, new groups started to develop in other educational centres such as the Universidad de Concepción and the Universidad de Autofogasta, among others. The university theatres carried out a programme similar to the independent theatres: the elimination of the star system, the search for new forms and the application of technical innovations. Their repertoire started with traditional classical drama and, little by little, incorporated local plays. Most theatrical

activities in Chile since the 1960s, not only within the experimental and popular milieux but also in the professional arena, are the offspring of the university theatres.

There were efforts to create national theatres even in countries with little theatrical tradition: for example, in Bolivia by Raúl Salmón and his Grupo de Teatro Social. In Paraguay, during the 1930s, Julio Correa collected a good number of plays in Guaraní, mostly from the oral tradition, which he performed all over the country. In Colombia, Luis Enrique Osorio (1896–1966) left a monumental dramatic legacy of more than 50 plays, *costumbrista* (folk literature) in nature, with which he entertained his audiences at his own Teatro de la Comedia.

At the end of the 1950s, a theatrical movement known as the 'new theatre', or 'new popular theatre', spread throughout the continent. It was 'new' in the sense of 'renovation', but also indicated a major break with certain theoretical and practical aspects of the theatrical tradition, especially those associated with naturalism. The political context, mainly the class struggle and economic colonialism, once again made obvious by the Cuban Revolution (1959), renewed the social commitment of the New Theatre practiioners. Aspiring to take an active part in the transforming historical process, they adopted working methods such as the so-called 'COLLECTIVE creation'. In this approach, the hierarchical organization of traditional theatre companies was to be abolished and every member of a group would become involved in every step of the production, assuming responsibility for the totality of the process. The Colombian director and playwright Enrique Buenaventura (b. 1925), leader of the group Teatro Experimental de Cali, has been the foremost theoretician of the widely used collective creation method.

Thus, since the 1950s, a series of plays started to appear that depicted the realities of each country seen, for the first time, through the eyes of the 'other', the marginal, voiceless majority of the people. In many instances the authors rewrote the history of their countries from this new point of view, appealing to their audiences through the spontaneity and vigour of popular theatre. In Colombia, for example, the 'Bananera Massacre' of 1928 was the subject of *Soldados* ('Soldiers', 1968), by Carlos José Reyes (b. 1941) and Enrique Buenaventura. The latter also wrote *La denuncia* ('The accusation', 1974), on the same topic. The turbulent period of 'La Violencia' ('The violence'), from 1948 to 1957, was reviewed in *Guadalupe años sin cuenta* ('Guadalupe, the fifties', 1976), a collective creation by the group La Candelaria, directed by Santiago

García (b. 1928). In Brazil, the Teatro Arena de São Paulo, under AUGUSTO BOAL – one of the best-known innovators of Latin American theatre – and Gianfrancesco Guarnieri, dedicated one of the plays of the series *Arena conta . . .* ('Arena Tells . . .') to the eighteenth-century popular hero Tiradentes, who rebelled against Portuguese rule.

In every country in Latin America we find similar historically conscious plays. In Ecuador, the Group Ollantay created a piece entitled *S + S = 41* about the 1941 Oil War between Peru and Ecuador, whose actual protagonists were the Shell and Standard Oil companies. In Argentina, the 1969 'Cordobazo', a popular uprising against the military dictatorship, was dramatized in *El asesinato de X* ('The assassination of X', 1970), a collective creation by the Libre Teatro Libre (Free Theatre) of Córdoba, directed by María Escudero.

The anxiety of living in constant danger under an absolutely repressive regime and the topic of the 'disappeared' began to be reflected in the cycle of one-act plays performed from 1980 to 1985 under the name of Teatro Abierto (Open Theatre). More than 200 directors, playwrights, actors and theatre artists participated in these events as a reaction to government oppression. Two of the most memorable plays were *Decir Si* ('To say yes', 1972) by Griselda Gambaro (b. 1928) and *Lejana tierra prometida* ('Distant promised land', 1981) by Ricardo Halac (b. 1935). The Indians' plight was depicted in plays such as *Puño de cobre* ('Copper fist', 1972) and *Allpa Rayku* (1978), both by the collective group Yuyachkani of Peru, under the direction of Miguel Rubio, and *Velada* ('Soirée', 1977) by Alcibíades González del Valle (b. 1936) with the group Aty Ñee of Paraguay.

On the other hand, a lack of written plays resulted in groups exploring other literary genres for material. The Latin American novel has been an inexhaustible source. The group Rajatabla from Venezuela, directed by Carlos Giménez (1945–93), developed its imagistic style through versions of novels such as *El Señor Presidente* ('Mr President', 1946) by Miguel Angel Asturias and *El coronel no tiene quien le escriba* ('No one writes to the colonel', 1961) by Gabriel García Márquez. In Ecuador audiences still remember the 1970 Teatro Ensayo's adaptation of *Huasipungo* by Jorge Icaza, and in Brazil the Centro de Pesquisa Teatral (Theatre Research Centre) has dedicated itself to the creation of a national theatre through adaptations of other literary genres. Under the direction of José Alves Antunes Filho the group Macunaima, affiliated to the Centre, started in 1978 with the highly acclaimed theatrical version of the novel *Macunaima* by Mário de Andrade.

As to its style, the new theatre welcomed dramatic forms and conventions developed by historical, political, AGITPROP, EPIC, dialectic, DOCUMENTARY and STREET THEATRE, among others. BRECHT has been singled out as its most important influence, with PETER WEISS in second place. In fact, every device used by Brecht to 'destroy the stage illusion' has been effectively used by the new theatre artists.

Simultaneously with the new theatre movement, realism in its multiple forms – 'magic realism', 'poetic realism', 'reflexive realism', 'social realism' – continued to yield works. The authors are many but there is space here to mention only a few of them, not already included above: in Argentina, Carlos Gorostiza (b. 1920), Roberto Cossa (b. 1934), Eduardo Pavlovsky (b. 1933) and Eduardo Rovner (b. 1942); in Brazil, Nelson Rodrigues (1912–80), Oduvaldo Vianna Filho (1936–74) and Alfredo Dias Gomes; in Chile, Egon Wolff (b. 1926), Sergio Vodanovic (b. 1926), Jorge Díaz (b. 1930), Alejandro Sieveking (b. 1934) and Marco Antonio de la Parra; in Colombia, Jairo Aníbal Niño (b. 1941) and José Manuel Freidel (1951–90); in Peru, Sebastián Salazar Bondy (1924–65) and Julio Ortega (b. 1942); in Uruguay, Carlos Maggi (b. 1922); and in Venezuela, Isaac Chocrón (b. 1932), Román Chalbaud (b. 1931), José Ignacio Cabrujas (1937–95) and Rodolfo Santana (b. 1944).

This period brought another development to the Latin American theatre: the theatre of exile. Fleeing from the rigours inflicted by dictatorships, theatre artists from all parts of the continent scattered throughout the Western world, bringing with them their art and creating new groups, new plays and new audiences wherever they went. Outstanding examples are the Chilean groups the Compañía de los Cuatro (The Foursome Company) exiled in Venezuela, the Teatro del Angel (Angel's Theatre) in Costa Rica and the Grupo Aleph in France.

Just like the rest of the Western world at the *fin de siècle*, Latin America experienced changes towards the end of the century that transformed the way Latin Americans perceive each other and the way they express their reality through the arts. Politically, while the continent was moving towards democratization, after long periods of military dictatorships in more than half its territory, the evidently heterogenous character of its culture and its people called into question the very essence of any presupposed 'national collectivity'. Furthermore, with the loss of utopian thinking and the general decline of the left, caused by the fall of the Eastern bloc, a new kind of artist emerged from Latin America. These individuals directed their attention away from the centre to the periphery, and were motivated to articulate the problems and needs of groups traditionally overlooked by the elites, from the right or the left, whether culturally or otherwise, such as women, gays and lesbians, Indians, African Latin Americans, etc. Some of the women playwrights who are making a considerable impact on the field are Diana Raznivoch, Cristina Escofet and Susana Torres Molina in Argentina; Leilah Assunçâo, Consuelo de Castro and Maria Helena Kühner in Brazil; Isadora Aguirre and Inés Margarita Stranger in Chile; Patricia Ariza and Piedad Bonnett in Colombia; Sara Joffré and Celeste Viale in Peru; and Mariela Romero in Venezuela. Also, the performers/authors Maritza Wilde from Bolivia and Edda de los Rios from Paraguay have greatly contributed to their countries' dramaturgy. The popular banner 'anything goes', symptomatic of the times, characterized the region's dramatic production. There is probably no other place in the world where the convergence of trends brought about by postmodernism could have found a more fertile soil than in Latin America, for it is precisely there that one can find cultures considered 'high' and 'low' coexisting side by side; if there is a consensus to which most scholars adhere, it is that the continent's culture is a superimposition of layers of historical moments that persist simultaneously, having different modes of production – no one of which prevails over the others – and using a variety of artistic forms: archaic, folkloric, modern and postmodern, to express this simultaneity. Theatre artists are experimenting with the old and the new, exemplifying more than ever the diversity of Latin American theatre. All the dramatic forms employed by the new theatre have remained in use along with new forms imported from a diversity of outside influences. One such influence is the Italian/ Danish director EUGENIO BARBA and his ODIN TEATRET, with his theories on the Tercer Teatro (THIRD THEATRE); another is the Japanese director TADASHI SUZUKI; another is the Chinese Beijing Opera. The United States' pop culture, disseminated through its powerful media, is another source ingrained in the theatrical imagery emerging from Latin America. Theatre-dance, or dance-theatre, and the performance arts have become solid additions to the theatre's repertoire in the region. Among the best-known dancers and choreographers are Susana Zimmerman, Ana Itelman, Miguel Angel Robles and Brenda Angiel from Argentina; Marcia Duarte and Henrique Rodovalho from Brazil; Patricio Bunster from Chile; Alvaro Restrepo and Mónica Gontovnic from Colombia; Wilson Pcio from Ecuador; Hebe Rosa, Elsa Vallarino and Florencia Varela from Uruguay; and David Zambrano and Hercilia López from Venezuela. As to the theatre-makers, a number of young directors are leaving a definitive imprint on their national theatres, among others the Brazilians Gerald Thomas, Bia Lessa, Gabriel Villela and Leon Góes; the Argentinians Alberto Félix Alberto and Ricardo Bartis; the Chileans Andrés Pérez, Mauricio Celedón and Alfredo Castro; and the Peruvians Edgar Saba and Oscar Naters.

Finally, the theatre FESTIVALS have contributed enormously to the growth of Latin American theatres. In 1992, for example, there were international festivals in almost every South American country with ample participation from all over the continent. The future of the Latin American theatre looks very promising.

BEATRIZ J. RIZK

See also HISPANIC THEATRE IN THE UNITED STATES; MEXICO AND CENTRAL AMERICA.

David George, *The Modern Brazilian Stage* (1992)

Willis Knapp Jones, *Behind Spanish American Footlights* (1966)

Catherine Larson and Margarita Vargas, eds, *Latin American Women Dramatists* (1998)

Gerardo Luzuriaga, ed., *Popular Theater for Social Change in Latin America* (1978)

Leon F. Lyday and George Woodyard, eds, *Dramatists in Revolt: The New Latin American Theatre* (1976)

Rosalina Perales, *Teatro hispanoamericano contemporáneo 1967–1987* (1989)

Beatriz J. Rizk, *El Nuevo Teatro Latinoamericano, una lectura histórica* (1987)

Diana Taylor, *Theatre of Crisis: Drama and Politics in Latin America* (1991)

Diana Taylor and Juan Villegas, eds, *Negotiating Performance: Gender, Sexuality and Theatricality* (1994)

Adam Versenyi, *Theatre in Latin America Religion, Politics and Culture from Cortes to 1980* (1993)

Judith Weiss et al., *Latin American Popular Theatre: The First Five Hundred Years* (1992)

south-east Asia The two major variants of theatre in south-east Asia, which includes the wide area from Burma to the Philippines, are traditional performances and the modern drama of the educated urban elite. The former continue to maintain links to RITUAL and ceremonial functions, although the competition of modern media has increased focus on humour and entertainment. Meanwhile, modern theatre practitioners trained in the universities and conversant with the latest innovations from Japan and the West create AVANT-GARDE performances that tour large cities. These artists move freely from stage to film and television. Indonesia is perhaps the most theatrically active nation of the area. Its *wayang* is the theatre of the Javanese speakers who live in central and east Java, the Sundanese speakers who live in west Java, and the Balinese speakers who live on the small island of Bali. *Wayang* is the art of a *dalang* (narrator, puppeteer) who, to the accompaniment of an orchestra of bronze metallophones (*gamelan* in Java and Sunda), tells stories of Hindu derivation (*purwa*) or local origin (*babad*) while PUPPETS he manipulates, or dancers he oversees, act out episodes in an all-night performance at rites of passage ceremonies like weddings. Different ethnic groups have their own preferred form of *wayang*. *Wayang kulit purwa*, literally, 'leather (shadow) puppets telling Hindu stories', is the prime form of Java. *Wayang golek purwa*, which uses round wooden puppets, is popular with the Sundanese. Balinese audiences prefer *wayang parwa*, in which leather figures are used. Numerous other forms of *wayang* exist but are more rarely seen. About 95 per cent of the stories tell tales related to the *Mahabharata* epic. While local *dalang* complain that their business has deteriorated due to the competition of modern media, a small number of highly gifted performers use the media to expand their popularity, becoming superstars of their own language area. They often perform on television and their live performances earn them fees astronomical by local standards. Currently among the most admired performers are Asap Sunandar Sunarya in the Sundanese area, I Wayan Wija and I Made Sija of Bali, and Anom Suroto and Ki Manteb of central Java. Characteristic of these performers is their ability to improvise creatively within the traditional format incorporating modern tunes, new puppets and other innovations in their work.

In addition to *wayang*, traditional performances of masked theatre (*topeng*) or dance drama (*sendratari*) thrive. Areas like Bali boast numerous trance, ritual and entertainment forms. New experiments using traditional dance, music and characterization are staged by top artists who often come from the regional performing arts schools such as SMKI (the Conservatory of Music) and STSI (the Indonesian Academy of Performing Arts). Works of these groups can be seen at the Bali Arts Festival in June and July each year.

Another form of traditional performance is popular theatre, in which actors generally improvise their dialogue to act out a chosen scenario. This includes genres that grew up at the end of the nineteenth century in urban areas. *Sandiwara* is the Sundanese-language popular theatre, *ketoprak* is a Javanese-language form of central Java, while *ludruk* of the Surabaya area of east Java is noted for its transvestite performers. *Arja* is a Balinese form which features female singer–performers. These forms can borrow their repertoire from traditional *wayang*, Islamic romances, local legends or new stories. The forms do not have a *dalang* to do nar-

ration and, though *gamelan* may accompany some forms, electronic instruments and popular music are often incorporated. CLOWN characters are central to performances, and clashes between true love and economic incentives to marry become the crux of many episodes. In recent years some genres, including *sandiwara* and *arja*, have lost popularity while other genres retain large audiences. Srimulat, a troupe that has branches in Surabaya and Jakarta, is a good example of the most viable groups. Srimulat performers appear on television as well as in their live performance venues. Comic actors often play the same clown whatever the story, while other troupe members may specialize in a particular role (ingénue, hero, mother, villain, father).

Modern theatre flourishes in Jakarta and other major cities. This is the first instance of scripted drama (as contrasted to drama improvised within set constraints of character, story, music and movement) and has emerged in the twentieth century. Malay language performances with improvised dialogue in the early 1920s, inspired what has been considered the first scripted drama in Indonesian language, *Bebasari* (1926) by Rustam Effendi, a metaphorical call for independence from colonial domination. Since then this modern drama movement has largely stemmed from playwright/directors. Umar Ismail was a noted writer/director of the 1940s but abandoned the stage for film in the 1950s.

With the founding of a national theatre complex, Taman Ismail Marzuki, in Jakarta in 1968, there was a flowering of modern theatre. W. S. Rendra, a central Javanese playwright/director, returned from studying theatre in New York in the 1960s. Many of the actors who initially worked with Rendra's Workshop Theatre (Bengkel Teatre) went on to found their own groups in later years. A powerful actor and charismatic poet, Rendra has created work that spans a number of styles and periods, from minimal language (*mini-kata*) pieces focused on movement to dramas that borrow elements from *wayang* and deliver political/social messages (e.g. *Struggle of the Naga Tribe*, 1974). Arifin C. Noer, who also worked extensively in film and television, studied with Rendra then founded his own Little Theatre (Teatre Kecil) in the late 1960s. *Moths* (1970) remains his most frequently produced work. Balinese artists Putu Wijaya and Ikranagara are also active. Wijaya's group is Teatre Mandiri (Standing Theatre); their performance combines poetry, absurd whimsy and political criticism. Ikranagara, a premier actor, leads Teatre Siapa/Saja (Anyone's Theatre, Pure Theatre). Wisran Hadi from Sumatra, and Nano Riantarno and Teguh Karya from Java, are other important director/playwrights. Riantiarno's *Coackroach Opera* (1985) is a tragicomic look at the underside of national development. Teguh Karya's work in drama and film is a realistic and psychologically based examination of the upwardly mobile urban elite confronted with the realities of a nation where many remain poor and disempowered.

Other south-east Asian nations maintain a similar range, from traditional improvised performances to script-based modern performance. In Malaysia, traditional forms like *wayang siam* puppet theatre, *mayong* dance, and the once thriving urban popular theatre (*sandiwara*) have waned as modern drama has emerged. The first Malay-language drama was created in the *purbawara* style, a nationalistic genre that glorified Malay heroes to promote independence: writer Shahrom Hussain (*The Hunchback of Tanjung Puteri*, 1961) was active in this style from the 1940s to the 1960s. In the 1970s and 1980s Norridin Hassan has been the premier playwright. His *It is Not the Tall Grass that is Blown by the Wind* (1970) referred to the 1969 race riots between Chinese and Malays which tore the nation apart. His work in the 1980s became more Islamic in themes (e.g. *Don't Kill the Butterflies*, 1983). Dinsman, a performer/cult figure among Malay youth since the 1970s, creates characters that showed disenchantment with both tradition and modern values. Krishan Jit has been a major director and scholar of Malay theatre. Singapore, which broke off from Malaysia in 1963, has traditional Malay, Chinese and Tamil performances and a growing modern drama movement. Most notable of modern artists here is perhaps Kuo Pao Kun, an Australia-trained playwright/director, who despite being detained by government in the 1970s for his leftist leanings has emerged to create pieces which speak powerfully of the cultural homogenization of Singapore. Recent years have seen the emergence of the Singapore Arts Festival from low-key beginnings in around 1977 to a large government-supported event from 1986. Companies like Kuo Pao Kun's Substation and Ong Keng Sen's Theatreworks create major pieces for this biannual festival. Michael Chiang's comic examinations of Singapore life have been popular pieces performed by Theatreworks.

The Philippines has a lively theatre tradition that grows from both local indigenous performance and *zarzuela* models of the Spanish colonial period. 'Seditious plays' (anti-American performances) were staged at the beginning of the century by playwrights like Aurelino Tolentino and Juan Matapang Cruz, provoking government suppression. Since the 1950s a lively drama scene has been developed by writers coming from the universities. Nick Joaquin (*A Portrait of the Artist as Filipino*, 1952) was one of the early writers of this movement. In 1967 the Philippine Educational Theatre Association (PETA) inaugurated STREET and GUERRILLA performances in Tagalog in contrast to the earlier preference for English as the language of performance. PETA remains both a training company and a performing organization, and in recent years has mined the Filipino theatre tradition for models for its rich new work. Amelia Lapena Bonifacio's *The Journeying of Sisa* (1976) grafted ideas borrowed from Japanese *noh* on to an indigenous style of singing that tells the story of Christ's passion. Political work with Brechtian approaches is representative of the company, which is currently led by Cecile Guidote.

In Thailand's Malay-language area, traditional puppet theatre has continued to flourish, while *likay*, a modern Thai urban form that mounts romances for middle-class female viewers, has attained popularity in the central region of the country. Classical music, dance and theatre descended from the Thai palace tradition continue under the direction of the Department of Fine Arts at the National Theatre in Bangkok. Modern drama (*lakon phut*) began in 1904 when Prince Vajiravudh wrote the first piece. Most writers and actors engage in live theatre as a vocation and many also work in film and television.

The lively traditions of countries in the northern area of the peninsula have been hampered by the persistent military conflicts that have plagued the region. Cambodian traditional court performance was revived during the reign of Norodum Sihanouk (1941–70) under the influence of the Queen Mother Kossamak, and cultural and diplomatic performances of the palace arts were important in the cultural politics of this period. After the king was deposed and the south-east Asian war grew in intensity, the performing arts collapsed and many artists fled the country or were killed. Today, artists struggle to revive the traditions at the Academy of Fine Arts while other court-influenced troupes have tried to reconstitute themselves in France under Princess Bopha Devi and in the United States.

In Vietnam, the *hat boi* traditional opera and the more modern popular theatre of the country, *cai luong* and *cheo*, have also had difficulties in the economically depressed postwar period. Vietnamese water puppetry (*mua rôi nuoc*) has enjoyed some resurgence in urban performance as students at the National Film and Theatre Academy have trained in this genre. *Kich nôi* (spoken drama) has been popular with young urban audiences and supported by the government. Burma's performance traditions are maintained in government academies, but touring has been hampered for regional performers in recent decades by fighting in outlying areas. Burmese puppetry, *rokthe pwe*, is currently undergoing a revival in Mandalay under the leadership of Ma Ma Naing of Mandalay Marionettes. KATHY FOLEY

See also EASTERN THEATRE, ITS INFLUENCE ON THE WEST.

I Made Bandem and Frits deBoer, *Kaja and Kelod: Balinese Dance in Transition* (1981)

James Brandon, *Theatre in Southeast Asia* (1967)

B. De Zoete and W. Spies, *Dance and Drama in Bali* (1973)

Doreen Fernandez, 'From Ritual to Realism: Brief Historical Survey of Philippine Drama', *Philippine Studies*, vol. 28 (1980)

——, 'Philippine Theatre after Martial Law', *Asian Theatre Journal*, vol. 4, no. 1 (1987)

Claire Holt, *Art in Indonesia* (1967)

Maung Htin Aung, *Burmese Drama* (1957)

Gunawan Mohamad, *Modern Drama of Indonesia* (1991)

Matani Rutnin, *Dance, Drama, and Theatre in Thailand* (1993)

——, ed., *The Siamese Theatre* (1975)

Southern, Richard *see* UNIVERSITY DRAMA DEPARTMENTS

Soviet Union Until August 1991, the Soviet Union consisted of 15 republics: the Russian Republic (which came into being after the Revolution of 1917); Belorussia, the Ukraine, Armenia, Azerbaijan, Georgia, Uzbekistan, Kyrghyzia, Kazakhstan, Turkmenistan, Tajikistan (incorporated between 1918 and 1922, though the last two were not given autonomy until 1936); Lithuania, Estonia, Latvia and Moldavia (1940). Across these republics, which span two continents and which gained independence with the break-up of the Soviet Union, are 21 main nationalities, many other smaller national or ethnic groups, and 72 languages. Among these national and ethnic groups there is an immense range of 'theatrical' activity – drama, comedy, music drama, dance, the folk arts – but Russian-language culture has been the dominant one, and for most of the twentieth century only works performed or written in Russian had wide access to the Soviet and international general public. While the Russian-centred nature of Soviet culture initiated conventional Western drama in republics which prior to federation had had different and separate traditions – such as the Kazakhs, Uzbeks, Tajiks, Turkmens or Kyrghyzes – it dominated the theatrical traditions of other nationalities, such as the Georgians, Latvians and Estonians.

This historical centralization of Russian Soviet culture must be related to other means of production and exchange in the Soviet economy: theatre, the other arts and the media were state-owned until 1986, and until 1987 the ideological content was controlled by the Communist Party. As such, the history of Soviet theatre, as with the other arts, is inseparable from the political history of the Soviet Union – a history alternating between 'freeze' and 'thaw', and falling roughly into seven periods after the end of tsarist Russia: (1) the Revolutionary period, 1917–28; (2) the first Stalin period, 1928–41; (3) the war years, 1941–6; (4) Stalin and the postwar purges, 1946–53; (5) the 'thaw' under Khrushchev, 1953–63; (6) the period of 'stagnation' under Brezhnev, 1964–82; and (7) the contemporary scene, from 1985.

(1) *The Revolutionary period, 1917–28.* In one sense, the artistic revolution began to take place some 20 years before the political revolution: the 'Silver Age' of the 1890s and first decade of the twentieth century saw the formation of the MOSCOW ART THEATRE (1898), the works of DIAGHILEV, BAKST, BENOIS, PAVLOVA, NIJINSKY, and the Ballets Russes; the plays of CHEKHOV, GORKY, BLOK and ANDREYEV, and an emerging conflict about the nature of theatre and art represented by 'the realists' and 'the decadents' (the SYMBOLISTS and Imagists). All artistic activity was controlled by the tsarist censors, and one of the measures introduced by the Provisional Government in February 1917 was their abolition. With the Bolshevik Revolution of October 1917, Lenin put education and the arts in the charge of ANATOLI LUNACHARSKY as People's Commissar of Enlightenment – a crucial post which he held until inevitably sacked by Stalin in 1929. Author of 14 plays, a Marxist, pluralist and democrat, Lunacharsky ensured the preservation of the best of pre-revolutionary Russian culture, and, while committed to the need for art to serve the Revolution, he also protected and encouraged professionalism. For the Bolsheviks, military and economic priorities were joined by culture as 'the third front' to open up and make accessible to the workers 'all the artistic treasures which were created on the basis of the exploitation of their labour and which have, up until now, been available exclusively to the exploiters' (8th Party Congress, 1919). Conflicts arose between (often sympathetic) professionals and revolutionary iconoclasm or dogma, and a number of organizations reflected these clashes: Proletkult (1917–32), created to provide 'proletarian culture', had control of its theatre groups taken over by the trades unions in 1922; Repertkom, the theatrical censorship committee, which then became Glavrepertkom; and RAPP, the Russian Association of Proletarian Writers, which, though disbanded in 1922, gradually won the battle over style, characterization and experimentation: plays should be positive portrayals of Soviet society with 'realistic' characterization and immediately accessible to the broad masses – one definition of the 'socialist

realism' which came to dominate Soviet theatre. Different perceptions of 'art in the service of the Revolution' were practised by other organizations, such as LEF (Left Front in Art), formed by AVANT-GARDE artists such as TRETYAKOV, EISENSTEIN, Rodchenko, MEYERHOLD and MAYAKOVSKY, whose 'utilitarian' but non-realistic forms created revolutionary new techniques and styles aimed at the broad masses of the largely illiterate population, and ranging across FUTURISM, CONSTRUCTIVISM, symbolism, DOCUMENTARY DRAMA, mixed media performance, and montage.

Thus, throughout the period there were three significant trends: (1) the revolutionary and avant-garde rejection of realism; (2) the emerging dogma of socialist realism; and (3) the fear of political interference and imposition of a repertoire, as expressed by STANISLAVSKY in 1920: 'that the writing of plays to order on the great events of the day and the direction of the work of actors to order instead of at their own volition creates not real art but a mere parody of it'. Ironically, Stanislavsky's 'naturalism' was to be taken up by Stalin and used in the cause of socialist realism. In 1919 all theatres were nationalized under Lunacharsky's Commissariat, and Meyerhold briefly ran the Theatre Section.

Plays and productions of the period included an extraordinary range of styles and approaches. There were mass theatre festivals (such as the staged storming of the Winter Palace on 7 November 1920); AGITPROP theatre groups (such as BLUE BLOUSE); CABARETS; MUSIC HALL; CIRCUS; PANTOMIME; smaller 'Agitka' – propagandist 'agitational' works, like LIVING NEWSPAPERS; PUPPET THEATRES; children's theatres (the first opening in Moscow on 7 November 1918), which by 1939 numbered over 200; 'theatre brigades' performing at the Civil War fronts; and the work of directors, designers and actors such as Meyerhold, VAKHTANGOV, TAIROV, Granovsky, Foregger, TRETYAKOV, RADLOV, SIMONOV, Diky, Koonen, KNIPPER, Babanova, Ilinsky, Zinaida Raikh, Vesnin, the Sternbergs, Stanislavsky, Les Kurbas in Kharkov and Akhmeteli in Georgia, often staging the European classics.

New plays ranged from Civil War plays – MIKHAIL BULGAKOV's *The White Guard* (*The Days of the Turbins*, 1926); VSEVOLOD IVANOV's *The Armoured Train 14–69*, (1927); VISHNEVSKY's *First Cavalry* (1929); Tretyakov's *Roar, China* (1926) – to satires of the NEP (New Economic Policy) period: plays such as ERDMAN's *The Mandate* (1924) and *The Suicide* (1926–30); Mayakovsky's *The Bedbug* (1928) and *The Bathhouse* (1930), both staged by Meyerhold; KATAYEV's VAUDEVILLE *Squaring the Circle* (1927); Bulgakov's *Zoya's Apartment* (1926) and *Molière* (1929); Alexei Feyko's *The Man with the Briefcase* (1928); YURI OLESHA's *A List of Assets* (1931); and plays by BABEL, Gorky, AFINOGENOV and Kirshon.

(2) *The first Stalin period, 1928–41.* By 1934, the year of the first All-Union Writers' Congress, and 10 years after Lenin's death, the theatre under Stalin had been nationalized (previous imperial and private theatres, like the MOSCOW ART THEATRE, became 'state academic theatres'), unionized, centralized and subsidized. Administrative control was exercised by and through the Theatre Union (professional work dependent on membership), while political control was exercised through the Party's Censorship Committee and, increasingly, by newspaper hacks. The Writers' Congress (with Gorky used as a figure-head), was addressed by Andrei Zhdanov, Stalin's spokesman for cultural matters, and formulated the official policy of 'socialist realism'. This was the beginning of what Babel called 'the genre of silence', and 'Zhdanovism' was to last for 20 years. In 1930 Mayakovsky killed himself; Gorky (in Italy from 1921 to 1932) died suddenly in 1936 in as yet not properly documented circumstances; Babel was arrested in May 1939 and subsequently killed; Meyerhold, under ferocious critical attack throughout the 1930s, was shot in a Moscow prison in February 1940; his actress wife, Zinaida Raikh, was mutilated and murdered in their flat shortly after his arrest; Bulgakov, after a decade of having his plays banned, went blind in 1939 and died in 1940 of neurosclerosis. The 'cultural avant-garde' were increasingly isolated and silenced, and the original RAPP doctrine was reformulated into socialist realism. Definitions of socialist realism vary from the official – 'truthfulness and historical concreteness of artistic representation should be combined with the ideological remoulding and education of the working people in the spirit of socialism' (Zhdanov) – to the satirical: 'Socialist realism is praising the leaders in language they themselves can understand.' It was the end of experiment in non-realistic forms and avant-garde styles, and throughout the 1930s there were three major terms of critical abuse to describe officially unacceptable theatre work: 'Meyerholditis', 'Bulgakovism' and 'formalism' (or 'technical experimentation'). Ironically, the flagship became Stanislavsky's Moscow Art Theatre naturalism, and the Stanislavsky system became the only school of acting allowed in the Soviet Union. Stanislavsky, neither a member of the revolutionary avant-garde nor a Bolshevik (though a staunch defender of Meyerhold), was used by Stalin – as was Gorky – to produce the 'grey realism' which stamped Soviet theatrical life until 1956. There were, however, organizational advantages which emerged in the period: the Theatre Union (like other unions) provided restaurants, clubs, sanatoria

and secure employment; each theatre was made into a permanent repertory company enabling both long-term planning of repertoires and good ensemble playing (both aims of Stanislavsky's). The repertoire, however, was becoming increasingly restricted in a period which saw the Great Purges of 1936–8 and the elimination of all potential opposition to Stalin (real or imaginary), whether from the old Bolsheviks (Trotsky was killed in exile in 1940, Kirov murdered in 1934, Zinoviev, Kamenev, Bukharin and Radek by 1938) or the Red Army (Marshall Tukhachevsky was executed in 1937) – a reign of terror which included the states of Latvia, Lithuania, Estonia and Moldavia (annexed in 1940), and which was slackened only with the German invasion of 1941.

(3) *The war years, 1941–6.* The war aims for Soviet playwrights were clarified in May 1942 by the Committee for Art Affairs: 'By the power of their art-forms, they [the dramatists] were to actualize the spiritual mobilization of the people ... for the destruction of the enemy, to show the maintenance of the patriotic struggle, to honour the heroic deeds of our country's defenders.' Innumerable plays followed: AFINOGENOV's *On the Eve*, LEONOV's *Invasion*, SIMONOV'S *The Russian People* and *Wait for Me*, KORNEICHUK's *The Front* and *Partisans*, POGODIN's *The Ferryboat Girl* (about Stalingrad), ARBUZOV's *The Cottage at Cherkizov*, the Georgian Moivani's *Partisans*, YEVGENII SHVARTS's *A Far Country* and *One Night*, Alexandra Brushtein's *Day of the Living*, Margarita Aliger's *Tanya*, and plays by Kazakov and Kaverin. Under the direction of the Theatre Union, many theatres were evacuated and theatre brigades were formed to perform at the front (actors were often used as stretcher-bearers and under direct attack). The armed forces also formed their own theatre groups, such as the First Black Sea Front-line Theatre, or the Baltic Fleet Theatre which performed in Leningrad during the siege. In Leningrad, cut off from the rest of Russia for 900 days by the German and Finnish armies, there were performances of musical comedy – and an amateur production of *Three Sisters*, at which nearly a third of the audience remained in their seats after the performance, dead from starvation. In that context, the ideal of 'going to Moscow' took on new significance.

(4) *Stalin and the postwar purges, 1946–53.* With the end of the war, which cost at least 27 million Soviet lives, Stalin and Zhdanov renewed their assault on actual and potential oppenents in a new phase of purges. In 1946 Zhdanov's two edicts made it evident that the partial toleration of the war years was over – attacks followed on the writers Akhmatova and Zoshchenko, and on the music of SHOSTAKOVICH, Prokofiev

and Khachaturian, and in 1949 the State Jewish Theatre in Moscow (under MIKHOELS) was closed – as were all other Jewish theatres. Many plays written in the period, such as Shvarts's allegory on tyranny, *The Dragon* (1944), received only one performance and were then banned. Other plays remained in drawers – or unwritten.

(5) *The 'thaw' under Khrushchev, 1953–63.* The 'thaw' effectively began three years after Stalin's death. In 1956 Nikita Khrushchev, First Secretary of the Communist Party since 1953, delivered a 'Secret Speech' at the 20th Party Congress in which he denounced Stalin's 'cult of personality' and advocated 'collective leadership' by the Party. 'The thaw' (the title of a book by Ilya Ehrenburg, 1954) resulted in the 'rehabilitation' of many of the dead, and the release of the living from labour camps or exile in Siberia. Alexander Fadeyev, secretary of the Writers' Union, feared the denunciations of returning exiles and shot himself. The 'rehabilitation' had its effect on the theatrical repertoire: Shvarts's *The Dragon* was allowed performance in 1962, as were his other plays; Bulgakov's *The White Guard* (*The Days of the Turbins*) was revived, and his *Flight* performed for the first time; NIKOLAI AKIMOV (1901–68) directed Sukhovo-Kobylin's *The Affair* (1955), and then the entire trilogy; the Moscow Sovremennik (Contemporary) Theatre was founded in 1956 by a group including OLEG EFREMOV and Galina Volchek, opening with VIKTOR ROZOV's *They Will Live for Ever*. And, in the late 1950s, the Moscow Theatre of Drama and Comedy, directed until 1983 by YURI LYUBIMOV and known as the TAGANKA THEATRE, became the leading avant-garde theatre, opening with productions of BRECHT, readings of poetry by Voznesensky and Mayakovsky, and an innovatory (because non-realistic) dramatization of John Reed's *Ten Days That Shook the World*. In Leningrad, the Gorky Theatre, under the direction of the Georgian GEORGI TOVSTONOGOV, staged innovatory productions of Griboyedov's *Woe from Wit* (1962) and other classics. This period is characterized by new directors and directions, new plays by – for example – Arbuzov and Zorin, and the mass poetry readings by young poets such as Yevtushenko, Voznesensky and Akhmadulina; by the 'rehabilitation' of Babel, OLESHA and Zoschenko, and the excitement generated by each issue of the liberal literary journal *Novyi Mir*, under the editorship of Tvardovsky. By 1963 Yevtushenko's *Babi Yar*, Solzhenitsyn's *One Day in the Life of Ivan Denisovich* and memoirs by Paustovsky, Ehrenburg and Nadezhda Mandelshtam were published, although not Pasternak's *Dr Zhivago* which, like other *tamizdat* ('over there') works (as distinct from *samizdat*, or 'self-published'), was published abroad, in Italy in

1957. But by 1964 the conservatives had won: Khrushchev was dismissed and Brezhnev replaced him, ushering in an 18-year period of economic and cultural stagnation.

(6) *The period of 'stagnation' under Brezhnev, 1964–82.* One characteristic of this period was the number of major Soviet artists living in exile by the time of Brezhnev's death in 1982. They included the musician Rostropovich, the film-maker Tarkovsky, and Lyubimov, whose passport was withdrawn while he was in London with two of his Taganka Theatre productions: Dostoevsky's *Crime and Punishment* and *The Possessed* (1983). For many, the 'consistent inconsistencies' and restrictions of Soviet cultural policy outweighed the advantages of guaranteed employment, fixed salaries and a comparativly high standard of living, combined with an investment in subsidized theatre which resulted in the enviable (from a Western perspective) situation in which every major Soviet city had a drama theatre, often a comedy theatre, maybe also a 'national' theatre (such as the Georgian Rustavelli Theatre, or the Rainis Latvian Theatre), an opera and ballet theatre, a puppet and/or children's theatre (such as the Mikoyan Armenian Theatre for Young Spectators), and a Russian theatre. National and 'ethnic-language' theatres increased given the pursuit of semi-autonomous policies, particularily in the Baltic republics and in Georgia and Azerbaijan. Cultural restrictions were fewer in Tallinn than in Moscow. Playwrights of the period include Arbuzov, ALEXANDER VOLODIN, Rozov, ALEXSANDR VAMPILOV, CHINGIZ AITMATOV, ALEXANDER GELMAN, EDVARD RADZINSKY, MIKHAIL ROSHCHIN, Zoya Boguslavskaya, LUDMILA RAZUMOVSKAYA and LUDMILA PETRUSHEVSKAYA, some of whose plays, however, are only now being fully staged and published. This era of cautious playwriting resulted in strong 'directors' theatre', exemplified by ANATOLY EFROS at the Malaya Bronnaya Theatre. His productions of *Three Sisters* (1967), Molière's *Don Juan* (1974), Gogol's *The Marriage* (1975) and *The Cherry Orchard* (Taganka, 1975) caused critical uproar but popular excitement. Efros, using a 'synthesis of elements' from Stanislavsky, Meyerhold, Vakhtangov and Brecht, moves away from social and socialist realism to the stylized. Other major directors stretching imposed interpretational restrictions include Oleg Tabakov, ROBERT STURUA (of the Rustavelli Theatre), Efremov, Gennady Chenyakovsky, Galina Volchek and Adolphe Shapiro (in Riga).

(7) *The contemporary scene, from 1985.* With the climate of Gorbachev's perestroika and glasnost, more radical changes took place in the Soviet Union – and hence in Soviet theatre – than at any time since the immediate post-Revolutionary period. The changes for theatre are essentially fourfold. First, in 1986, control of theatres was removed from the Ministry of Culture and given to the theatres themselves. Second, also in 1986, the All-Soviet Theatrical Union was disbanded, and replaced by an independent Union of Theatre Workers. Third, a government (Ministry of Culture) directive came into force on 1 January 1987 requiring democratization of theatre management and administration: 'one person, one vote'; election of artistic directors; free choice of repertoire; decision-making over distribution of profits; box-office accountability; freedom for companies to set their own ticket prices, and to hire and fire actors according to requirements; reallocation of subsidy in direct ratio to box-office takings. Fourth, CENSORSHIP was abolished.

The implications, both economic and artistic, of these radical changes are only fully realized with hindsight, but were part of the Soviet move towards democratization and market forces. Some results, however, were quickly evident. Lyubimov returned to work at the Taganka Theatre in May 1988; the number of theatres in Moscow increased from 30 to 45 between January 1986 and June 1988; considerable numbers of studio or FRINGE theatres opened (the most prominent being Tabakov's Studio Theatre and ANATOLY VASILIEV's School of Dramatic Art); and previously banned Western dramatists (such as BECKETT, PIRANDELLO, IONESCO) have been translated, published and performed. Most significant are the controversial new Russian plays: *Sarcophagus*, by the journalist Vladimir Gubaryev, on Chernobyl (1986); MIKHAIL SHATROV's trilogy *The Bolsheviks* (1985–8), one of which – *The Peace of Brest-Litovsk* – was directed by Robert Sturua in November 1987; Viktor Slavkin's *Cerceau*; ALEXANDER GALIN's *Stars in the Morning Sky* (1988); director–playwright Alexander Chervinsky's 1987 dramatization of Bulgakov's story, *Heart of a Dog*. Also important is the growing number of women playwrights – Petrushevskaya, Ludmila Razumovskaya, NINA SADUR and the self-avowedly feminist Maria Arbatova. Splits and schisms, mirroring the political diversity both within Russia and among the rapidly changing federated republics, resulted in the replacement of artistic directors – Efremov, for example, led the younger part of the now split Moscow Art Theatre back to the old theatre building. The fragmentation of the Soviet Union itself led to other splits: the Lithuanian Theatre Union had already declared independence from the new Union of Theatre Workers before the abortive coup and 'gentle revolution' of August 1991, and the recognition of the Baltic states as independent countries. 'National' and 'ethnic' theatres will now take on a new meaning. Market forces have proved to have no more positive effect on theatre in Moscow, Tbilisi, Riga or Baku than in London or New York. VERA GOTTLIEB

R. W. Davies, *The Soviet Union* (1989)

Julian Graffy and Geoffrey Hosking, eds, *Culture and the Media in the USSR Today* (1989)

Mikhail Guerman, *Art of the October Revolution* (1979)

Geoffrey Hosking, *A History of the Soviet Union* (1990)

Konstantin Rudnitsky, *The Russian and Soviet Theatre Tradition and the Avant-Garde* (1988)

Robert Russell, *Russian Drama of the Revolutionary Period* (1988)

Robert Russell and Andrew Barratt, *Russian Theatre in the Age of Modernism* (1990)

Harold B. Segel, *Twentieth-Century Russian Drama: From Gorky to the Present* (1979)

Harold Shukman, ed., *The Blackwell Encyclopedia of the Russian Revolution* (1988)

Anatoly Smeliansky, *The Russian Theatre after Stalin* (1999)

Nick Worrall, *Modernism to Realism on the Soviet Stage* (1989)

Sowande, Bode (b. Kaduna, Nigeria, 2 May 1948) Actor, director and playwright. He studied at the universities of Ife (now Obafemi Awolowo University), Nigeria, Dakar, Senegal and Sheffield, England. He belongs to the second generation of dramatists who espouse a materialistic and revolutionary aesthetic for the theatre. He was resident playwright for SOYINKA's Orisun Theatre, Lagos from 1968 to 1971, and in 1972 he founded the Odu Themes which later became Odu Themes Meridian, the professional company which he has managed since his retirement in 1990 as a lecturer in Theatre Arts at the University of Ibadan. His plays are informed by a humanist vision that places the individual at the centre of the historical process and sees society as progressing to better and better states. In spite of the tragic ironies that his plays contain, there is very often an optimism underpinning his dramatic structuring. His plays, which he usually directs and acts in, include *The Night Before*, *A Farewell to Babylon*, *A Sanctus for Women*, *Flamingoes*, *Afamako*, *The Master and the Frauds*, *Circus of Freedom Square*, *Tornadoes Full of Dreams* and *Ajantala Pinocchio*. His other plays include the Yoruba *Arede Owo* and *Arelu*, a Yoruba adaptation of Molière's *L'Avare*. He has also written for television. OSITA OKAGBUE

Brian Cox, ed., *African Writers*, vol. 2 (1997)

Chris Dunton, *Make Man Talk True: Nigerian Drama in English since 1970* (1992)

Sowerby, [Katherine] Githa (b. Gateshead, Co. Durham, 6 Oct. 1876; d. London, 30 June 1970) Playwright and children's writer. Best known as the author of *Rutherford and Son* (1912), a powerful drama about the eponymous, domineering owner of a glassworks in north-east England in bitter conflict with his daughter and sons. Written in muscular dialect, with both feminist and Marxist overtones, this 'suffrage play' was originally a success but was almost forgotten until 'rediscovered' in the 1980s and given a landmark production by KATIE MITCHELL at the NATIONAL THEATRE in 1994. Sowerby wrote five other plays — *Before Breakfast* (1912), *Jinny* (1914), *Sheila* (1917), *The Stepmother* (1924) and *The Policeman's Whistle* (1934) — as well as several children's stories illustrated by her sister Millicent, but nothing matched the emotional force of *Rutherford and Son*, now often regarded as one of the best plays of the century. NEIL DOWDEN

Soyinka, Wole [Akinwande Oluwole] (b. Ìsarà, Western Nigeria, 13 July 1934) Playwright, poet, novelist and essayist; the first African to win the Nobel Prize for Literature (1986). Of distinguished Yoruba stock, his paternal grandfather was a local chieftain while his father became a highly respected headmaster and school inspector in the Anglican educational system at Abeokuta. The many apparent contradictions and ironies within this background – vividly realized in his first two superb autobiographical books, *Aké: The Years of Childhood* (1981) and *Ìsarà* (1989) – involve tribal life and modern Western ways, Yoruba mythology and Christian belief, and Nigeria's complex colonial inheritance as well as contemporary neocolonial problems. Soyinka's art pays homage, consciously as well as intuitively, to traditional values; but, at the same time, he can be scathing about an often unthinking regard for past modes of thought, for empty ceremony and ruthless autocratic rule.

Educated at University College, Ibadan (1952–4) and at the University of Leeds (1954–7), Soyinka worked at the ROYAL COURT THEATRE – as, officially, a playreader – during its most dynamic phase under GEORGE DEVINE. While there, he wrote and staged the still unpublished *The Invention* at a Sunday try-out in 1957 and produced an early tragedy, *The Swamp Dwellers*, at a student drama festival in London in 1958. Returning home early in 1960, he was commissioned to write a play to inaugurate Nigeria's independence celebrations: *A Dance of the Forests*, an ambitious and prescient though over-elaborate mythological parable, was produced in both Lagos and London in the same year. Subsequent productions in Nigeria of *The Swamp Dwellers*, as well as a ribald comedy *The Lion and the Jewel* (1960) and

The Strong Breed (1963), established him as a force to be reckoned with on the by then burgeoning Nigerian literary scene.

Soyinka has always kept a close working relationship with the practical theatre, not only the legitimate professional stage (in England and the United States as well as Nigeria) but also various forms of STREET or agitational protest theatre, which he has termed GUERRILLA THEATRE. He founded the amateur Masks theatre company in 1960 and, four years later, the professional Orisun Repertory Theatre, whose plays, though in English, drew creatively upon the traditional festive drama of the Yoruba people, which – like much of his own work – uses music, dance and ritual freely. In 1965 Soyinka published *The Road*, a tragedy centred on the criminal gangs that scavenge upon the Nigerian highways like eighteenth-century English highwaymen; it is remarkable for its creative exploitation of a wide range of linguistic registers. *The Trials of Brother Jero* (1960), a picaresque romp exposing the greed and hypocrisy of a self-appointed religious evangelist-cum-prophet, was produced successfully OFF-BROADWAY in 1967. *Requiem for a Futurologist* (published 1986) carries on, in much the same spirit, Soyinka's Jerovian fun at the expense of what the critic James Gibbs has called 'the credulous and exposed apostates'. *Jero's Metamorphosis* (1972), meanwhile, continued the irrepressible adventures of the religious trickster, though with a darker satirical edge.

In 1965 Lagos was to view an even more sombre work in *Kongi's Harvest*, the first of several full-length portraits of modern African tyrants. Soon afterwards, in taking the dictatorial title role in a film version (1970) that he subsequently disowned, he was to earn for himself among his friends the nickname of Kongi. There is no hiding in the play itself, however, the author's loathing and contempt for the new breed of absolutist rulers – many of them military figures heading army coups – that was increasingly to dominate African politics from the mid-1960s. This strain within Soyinka's work reaches its apotheosis in two savage works. *Opera Wonyosi* (1977) is an African *Beggar's Opera* which, following BRECHT's lead in *Arturo Ui*, is passionately critical of corruption in Nigeria under its military government. *A Play of Giants* (1984), subtitled 'a fantasia', daringly follows up the theme by dramatizing a group of gangster-politicians held hostage at a New York embassy while attending the United Nations.

Though Soyinka has written a great deal about the Nigerian civil war (1967–9), during which he was incarcerated for two years in solitary confinement, only one of his plays embodies his sense of horror and outrage

at this conflict. He has described *Madmen and Specialists* (1971) as an exercise in exorcism. Cannibalism and mutilation provide perverse yet powerful rituals as well as stage metaphors; the final effect, however, is somewhat confused, perhaps because Soyinka was still too close to the experience when writing the work. His next play, *Death and the King's Horseman* (1975), is a masterpiece. A tragic study of ritual suicide and conflicting codes of honour, it is perhaps most notable for its daring admixture of ritual threnody (hauntingly reminiscent of SYNGE, whose plays are much admired by Soyinka), vibrant representation of Yoruba market life, and hilarious satire at the expense of British officials and their African employees. Preoccupied by immediately pressing social issues, Soyinka's drama has since turned away from ritual, tragedy and poetry to a sombre satire reminiscent of Ben Jonson. Spending most of the century's last decade in exile – with a death sentence, passed in absentia, hanging over him while the military remained in power – Soyinka has written much polemical prose on cultural, political and literary topics, a third volume of memoirs covering the years from 1946 to 1965, entitled *Ibadan* (1994), and three dissimilar plays. *From Zia, With Love* (Siena, Italy, 1992), based on an appalling situation in Nigeria under the military regime of Generals Buhari and Idiagbon, is set in a gaol where political prisoners coexist with criminals and are treated like them. Several of the same characters are presented in a radio play, *A Scourge of Hyacinths* (BBC Radio 4, 1991). A more powerful indictment of the avarice and megalomania of the country's rulers, *A Beatification of Area Boy*, was premièred at the West Yorkshire Playhouse, Leeds in 1995 as the centrepiece for the 'Africa 95' festival. Arguably a companion piece to *Opera Wonyosi* as well as to Jonson's *Bartholomew Fair*, it is a roistering satire depicting the bustling street-corner life, colourful conmen and women and area boys in what the subtitle calls 'A Lagosian Kaleidoscope'. The truly outstanding feature of Soyinka's career has been its unflagging imaginative inventiveness, its prodigious variety and its consistent linguistic ingenuity.

Director, actor and film-maker as well as playwright and poet, Soyinka has written several other radio plays – most notably, *Camwood on the Leaves* (1960) – and two screenplays, as well as four books of verse, three highly original novels, and much criticism, including a volume of essays on the ritual and mythic roots of drama. Editor of several influential African journals, including *Black Orpheus* and *Transition*, his courageous resistance to dictatorship has been sustained at considerable danger to his life throughout the last three decades of the twentieth century.

RONALD AYLING

James Gibbs, *Critical Perspectives on Wole Soyinka* (1980)

——, *Wole Soyinka* (1986)

Ketu H. Katrak, *Wole Soyinka and Modern Tragedy: A Study of Dramatic Theory and Practice* (1986)

Adewale Maja-Pearce, ed., *Wole Soyinka: An Appraisal* (1994)

Gerald Moore, *Wole Soyinka* (1971; 2nd rev. edn 1978)

Mpalive-Hangson Msiska, *Wole Soyinka* (1998)

Spain   Restoration of the monarchy in 1875 marked a period of political conservatism, relative economic growth, religious revival and the triumph of traditional values that would last until the First World War. In 1900 Spanish theatre reflected this situation; in the three principal centres of Madrid, Barcelona and Valencia, commercial interests prevailed. Theatres, owned by businessmen and rented to companies run by 'star' actors, survived economically on the basis of two performances a day and a frequent change of programme. The cities also had many theatre-cafés where smaller and shorter pieces could be performed. Statistics for 1908 show an appetite for theatre and the sheer volume of plays presented: in Madrid alone, 414 plays by 290 writers, 70 with some form of music. Audiences, limited to the middle and upper-middle classes and the aristocracy, were essentially conservative, hostile to intellectual ideas and any departure from traditional theatrical formulae. Financial risk and artistic experiment proved impossible. In addition, academies of dramatic art remained ignorant of new developments abroad in acting and staging techniques.

In the 1890s, a challenge was mounted to the clichéd neo-Romantic drama of the day in a reworking of the concerns of seventeenth-century drama – honour, duty, religion and patriotism. Greater realism and seriousness were promised, and the early work of JACINTO BENAVENTE attempted to disturb bourgeois complacency. Soon the theatre public's taste had driven him into a different kind of cliché: the bourgeois 'drawing-room' drama, whose formula of aristocratic or upper-class characters, well-made plots, and elegant and witty dialogue set the fashion for three decades to come.

The early 1900s saw the emergence of two other types of formula drama: first, the almost conveyor-belt production, especially by the brothers SERAFÍN and JOAQUÍN ALVAREZ QUINTERO, of plays which romanticized the characters and customs of southern Spain and ignored the problems of poverty and backwardness in favour of idealized stereotype and cliché-ridden escapism; second, the so-called 'poetic' theatre, a reaction to Benavente's realism, which celebrated Spain's past in historical plays of exotic settings.

The impulse for change is linked largely to a group of intellectuals, philosophers, essayists, novelists, poets and dramatists dubbed the 'Generation of 98'. In response to Spain's loss of Cuba and the Philippines in 1898, they advocated national reassessment and regeneration. This meant rejection of the commercial theatre and the forms and values it encouraged, in particular naturalism and the 'well-made play'. Serious issues were treated in imaginative ways which embraced, for example, SYMBOLISM and, in terms of performance, the integration of settings, costumes, movement and lighting then being championed elsewhere in Europe by APPIA, MAETERLINCK, CRAIG and others.

The early work of RAMÓN DEL VALLE-INCLÁN, the most innovative dramatist of the first quarter of the twentieth century, has an epic scale and heroic flamboyance more suited to the printed page than a stage which could not meet its technical demands. From 1920 onwards he was actively involved with independent groups and developed the *esperpento*, a form which owed much to the puppet tradition now in fashion again and which allowed Valle-Inclán to move from the heroic tone of his previous work to an emphasis on the grotesque which anticipated the THEATRE OF THE ABSURD by 30 years.

The Second Republic (1931–6) ousted a seven-year dictatorship and created a liberal climate in which artistic experiment thrived. An expansionist education programme included peripatetic teachers and also the subsidized touring theatre group La Barraca, directed for four years by FEDERICO GARCÍA LORCA, the greatest modern Spanish dramatist. On the commercial stages of the major cities AVANT-GARDE plays, revealing a broader European influence, vied with popular successes, and between 1933 and 1936 Madrid saw the stylized and poetic masterpieces of Lorca, quickly acclaimed in Spain and abroad. The presence and influence of progressive directors and 'star' actors in particular theatres also made itself felt in programming, production and the formation of drama schools.

The Civil War (1936–9) cut short the promise of these years, though the Europeanizing influence of the period could still be seen in Republican AGITPROP groups, much influenced by German models. Thereafter the triumph of the Nationalists under Franco saw the exile of progressive dramatists and the re-establishment in the theatre of the safe bourgeois drama of Benavente, now taken up by younger men. During the dictatorship (1939–75) theatre which attempted specifically to examine the political, social and moral problems of Spain was driven either to work subversively within the system, or to challenge it directly. The former approach, exemplified by ANTONIO BUERO VALLEJO, frequently employed historical subjects to parallel contemporary situations. The latter, as in the case of ALFONSO SASTRE, was very outspoken and frequently banned. In either case serious themes were explored in forms which ranged from symbolic realism to Brechtian EPIC theatre, challenging the general stagnation and, in the case of Buero Vallejo, often triumphing on the commercial stage. On the other hand, the decision of FERNANDO ARRABAL to live in France and write his plays in French is one of the most serious indictments of the Franco years. There were also, during the 1960s, some signs of a less oppressive policy, which led to commercial productions of the plays of Lorca and others who had supported the Republic. In addition, this was a highly productive time for university and independent groups which throughout the dictatorship did valuable work in relation to the performance of Spanish and foreign plays.

The post-1975 triumph of democracy in Spain has not been matched by the sudden emergence of significant new dramatists, though signs of progress are clear: the removal of censorship; the creation in Madrid, in conjunction with the Ministry of Culture, of the National Centre of Drama – an organization based in two theatres, consisting of a team of professional actors and directors, including NÚRIA ESPERT, and concerned with the rehearsal and performance of serious plays and the training of actors; and new efforts in relation to youth theatre. Also evident are a substantial increase in subsidy from central and local government and financial organizations; the growth of many independent theatre groups such as Els Joglars and Tábano; a more enlightened commercial theatre; the appearance of theatre journals; and the publication and performance of the work of dramatists banned during the dictatorship. In Madrid subsidized theatre at the Teatro Español has done good work, both Spanish and foreign, though a single stage limits the number of annual productions and no new work is undertaken.

As far as the production of Spanish theatre abroad is concerned, Lorca is clearly the best-known dramatist, though COPYRIGHT has in the past impeded effective translations and there have been few commercial productions either in the United Kingdom or the United States. American independent and university groups have proved to be more receptive to Spanish theatre in general, clearly better attuned than their English

counterparts to a more expansive kind of theatre.
GWYNNE EDWARDS

E. Díez-Canedo, *Artículos de crítica teatral: el teatro español de 1914 a 1936*, 4 vols (1968)

L. García Lorenzo, *Documentos sobre el teatro español contemporáneo* (1982)

Gwynne Edwards, *Dramatists in Perspective: Spanish Theatre in the Twentieth Century* (1985)

F. Ruiz Ramón, *Historia del teatro español*, vol. 2: *Siglo XX*, 4th edn (1980)

Martha T. Halsey and Phyllis Zatlin, eds, *The Contemporary Spanish Theatre* (1988)

Speaight, Robert [William] (b. St Margaret-at-Cliffe, nr Dover, Kent, 14 Jan. 1904; d. Tonbridge, Kent, 4 Nov. 1976) Actor. After the Liverpool Repertory Theatre, his first break came at the OLD VIC (1931–2), where his roles included Hamlet, Malvolio and Cassius. In 1935 he created the part of Becket in *Murder in the Cathedral* and played it several times. His rich, resonant voice and his championing of religious poetic drama earned him fame for authoritative, sonorous religious roles, such as Antony in *This Way to the Tomb* (1945), Thomas More in *A Man for all Seasons* (1962) and Jesus in the film *The Man Born to be King* (1965). Later he turned to writing, publishing books on Becket, Mauriac, Belloc, acting and Shakespeare. DAN REBELLATO

Spears, Steve J. (b. Adelaide, Australia, 21 Jan. 1951) Playwright, actor and musician. He has written in a variety of styles, but little to match the success of *The Elocution of Benjamin Franklin* (1976). Other plays include *Africa – A Savage Musical* (1974), *The Resuscitation of the Little Prince Who Couldn't Laugh as Performed by Young Mo at the Height of the Great Depression of 1929* (1977), *King Richard* (1978) and *Those Dear Departed* (1986). MICHAEL MORLEY

special effects *see* STAGE MACHINERY

Spender, Stephen [Harold] (b. London, 28 Feb. 1909; d. London, 16 July 1995) Poet and critic. With AUDEN at OXFORD University, Spender became known as a left-wing poet in the 1930s and wrote in verse the anti-fascist tragedy *Trial of a Judge* (1938) for the GROUP THEATRE. He is best known in the theatre for his translations: of Schiller's *Maria Stuart*, Büchner's *Danton's Death* (with Goronwy Rees), TOLLER's *Pastor Hall* (with HUGH HUNT), five plays by WEDEKIND (with F. Fawcett), and Sophocles' Oedipus trilogy. Spender was knighted in 1983. COLIN CHAMBERS

Sperr, Martin (b. Steinberg, Germany, 14 Sept. 1944) Writer of plays for stage, screen and radio. Best known for *Jagdszenen aus Niederbayern* (*Hunting Scenes from Lower Bavaria*, 1966), which uses a heightened

realism and strong local dialect to portray harsh life in a contemporary rural community in the tradition of HORVÁTH and FLEISSER. He adapted Shakespeare and translated BOND's *Saved* for STEIN. Other plays include *Landshuter Erzählungen* (*Tales from Landshut*, 1967), *Müncher Freiheit* (*Munich Freedom*, 1971) and *Die Spitzeder* (1977), adapted from his own television play.
JUDY MEEWEZEN

Spewack, Sam (b. Bachmut, Russia, 16 Sept. 1899; d. New York, 14 Oct. 1971) and **Bella [Cohen]** (b. Bucharest, 25 March 1899; d. New York, 27 April 1990) Husband-and-wife team of playwrights and screenwriters. Their writing partnership created several Broadway hits, notably *Boy Meets Girl* (1935), a Hollywood satire, and the books for the musicals *Leave It To Me!* (1938, based on their 1932 comedy *Clear All Wires*) and *Kiss Me, Kate* (1948), both of which had music and lyrics by COLE PORTER. ALEXIS GREENE

Spiderwoman Theatre Feminist COLLECTIVE theatre company. Taking its name from the Hopi goddess of creation, it was founded in New York in 1975 by three Native American sisters, Lisa Mayo and Gloria and Muriel Miguel. The high-energy shows mix media, comedy, improvisation and myth to tell their wild, powerful stories. Ex-members formed SPLIT BRITCHES in 1981. CHARLES LONDON
See also LESBIAN THEATRE; WOMEN IN THEATRE.

Split Britches Theatre company, founded in New York in 1981 by three former members of SPIDERWOMAN THEATRE, Lois Weaver, Peggy Shaw and Deborah Margolin, as a feminist lesbian COLLECTIVE. Drawing on BRECHT, they used popular culture to explore gender and sexuality. After first appearing at the East Village's WOW Café, set up by Shaw and Weaver, the group visited Britain with *Dress Suits to Hire* (1987) by Holly Hughes, and later worked with British groups GAY SWEATSHOP and Bloolips.
CHARLES LONDON
See also LESBIAN THEATRE; WOMEN IN THEATRE.

Sue-Ellen Case, ed. *Split Britches: Lesbian Practice/Feminist Performance* (1996)

sport and the theatre Whereas cinema frequently draws on sport for its subject matter, and occasionally for its performers, the relationship between sport and theatre is more tenuous, although both are forms of entertainment that can provide popular spectacle. This connection was seen at the start of the twentieth century in the staging of a horse race (at London's COLISEUM), in which one jockey died, and at the end of the century in a show like *Starlight Express*, which is built around a roller-skate race. The Shakespearean director FRANK BENSON placed great emphasis on sporting prowess among his company and wrote on the beneficial relationship between sport and acting in *I Want to Go on the Stage* (1931). Believing the body to be crucial to performance, JEAN-LOUIS BARRAULT explored the link when he hired a sports stadium in 1941 to stage Aeschylus' *The Suppliant Women* and OBEY's *800 Metres*, in which he and other cast members ran round the track as the story of a runner unfolded. There is an honourable body of cricket-loving playwrights, from SAMUEL BECKETT (apparently the only one to appear in the cricketing Bible, *Wisden*) to HAROLD PINTER, and two former captains of the England cricket team have trodden the boards: Ian Botham, in PANTOMIME, and C. Aubrey Smith, who was cast as the original Professor Higgins in SHAW's *Pygmalion* until sacked by MRS PATRICK CAMPBELL, who complained that 'acting with Aubrey is like being held by a cricket bat'. Her loss was Hollywood's gain. Another leading cricketer, Percy Fender, toured the United States with JACK HULBERT revues in the 1920s, the same period that BRECHT and his colleagues were still caught up in the cult of sport.

KAISER puts a bicycle race in *From Morn to Midnight* (1917) and Brecht casts *In the Jungle of Cities* (1923) as a wrestling match. The sport which seems to have influenced the modern theatre the most, however, both as subject and as metaphor, is boxing. STERNHEIM and APOLLINAIRE were enthusiasts of the link, and when Brecht wanted *Man is Man* (1926) and other works to be presented like a sporting event, the analogy he used was the boxing ring. He befriended the German middleweight champion Paul Samson-Korner, and in 1926 collaborated with him on an unfinished play, *The Human Fighting Machine*. Several other champions have similar connections; they include Gene Tunney, who lectured on Shakespeare and was a friend of Shaw and WILDER, Gentleman Jim Corbett, who briefly became a Broadway leading man, Rocky Graziano, Max Baer and Maxie Rosenbloom, all of whom tried their hand at acting, and, more recently, Barry McGuigan and Frank Bruno, who both appeared in pantomime. *The Great White Hope* (1967) by Howard Sackler was based on the life of Jack Johnson, the first black heavyweight world champion. Boxing also figures in *Golden Boy* (1937) by CLIFFORD ODETS. Other sports that feature in plays include wrestling (Claire Luckham's *Trafford Tanzi*, 1978); association football (PETER TERSON's *Zigger Zagger*, 1967); cricket (R. C. SHERRIFF's *Badgers Green*, 1930; BEN TRAVERS' *A Bit of a Test*, 1933; ALAN AYCKBOURN's *Time and Time Again*, 1971;

Richard Harris's *Outside Edge*, 1979); rugby league football (DAVID STOREY's *The Changing Room*, 1971; John Godber's *Up 'n' Under*, 1984); Australian Rules football (DAVID WILLIAMSON's *The Club*, 1980); athletics (Louise Page's *Golden Girls*, 1984); basketball (Jason Miller's *That Championship Season*, 1972); baseball (the 1955 musical *Damn Yankees*; John Ford Noonan's *The Year Boston Won the Pennant*, 1969; AUGUST WILSON'S *Fences*, 1983); and tennis (Ayckbourn's *Joking Apart*, 1978).

CHARLES LONDON

Spring Thaw A REVUE, first presented in 1948 by Toronto's New Play Society, which became a popular annual event running from 1948 to 1971, and from 1980 to 1986. It featured music, dance and skits on Canadian mores, institutions and politics; the satiric emphasis of the show's early years gradually gave way to song-and-dance routines. The revue was usually mounted in a Toronto theatre but regularly toured Ontario; in 1964 it toured Canada. *Spring Thaw* served as a showcase for a host of Canadian actors, writers, choreographers and composers. EUGENE BENSON

Sprinkle, Annie *see* BODY ART

Spryopolos, Fahreda Manzer *see* BURLESQUE

Spurling, John (Henry Tube, pseud) (b. Kisuma, Kenya, 17 July 1936) Playwright and art critic. His plays are often ambitious kaleidoscopes of world history and culture, of survival and change (e.g. *The British Empire* trilogy, 1980–5). *In the Heart of the British Museum* (1971) interweaves Rome, Mexico and Maoist China. Others 'deconstruct' the reputations of Christopher Marlowe (*On a Clear Day You Can See Marlowe*, 1974) and Che Guevera (*MacRune's Guevara*, 1969). He is also known for his RADIO plays. TONY HOWARD

Squat Theatre *see* EXPERIMENTAL THEATRE

Sri Lanka An island in the Indian Ocean with a majority Buddhist Sinhalese population and a large Hindu Tamil minority which was a British colony (Ceylon) from 1815–1947. Ritual and folk ceremonies connected to worship form the basis of pre-modern indigenous theatre such as the masked *sokari* and *kolam*; the folk drama *nadagama* inspired the *rukada* puppet drama, and towards the end of the nineteenth century, the Christian community enjoyed the *pasku* passion play. The richness of the islanders' Indian ancestors and neighbours is absent, largely because Buddhist monks proscribed drama. However, a 'new drama', *nurti*, arose in the capital Colombo in the 1880s, influenced by a touring Parsi musical company from Bombay. The 'new drama' borrowed from Indian Western-style theatre and introduced women to the stage; it evolved its own style among the urban working-class before declining in the 1930s with the advent of cinema. Briefly, it was replaced by a genre that took its name from its leading actor/writer, Eddie Jayamanna, who lampooned the upper echelons of society. In the 1940s, students at what is now the University of Sri Lanka translated and adapted European plays (e.g. CHEKHOV), and in the 1950s attempts were made (e.g. by Ediriweera Sarachchandra) to create a local dramatic form but theatre remains underdeveloped and often ad hoc even if popular. It is still used to criticize government, particularly in the continuing tense Sinhalese–Tamil conflict.

CHARLES LONDON

Ranjini Obeyesekere, *Sri Lankan Theatre in a Time of Terror: Political Satire in a Permitted Space* (1999)

Stafford-Clark, Max (b. Cambridge, 17 March 1941) Director. Artistic director of the TRAVERSE THEATRE, EDINBURGH (1968–70), in 1974 he co-founded JOINT STOCK THEATRE GROUP, for which he co-adapted and co-directed with WILLIAM GASKILL its inaugural production, *The Speakers*. He was artistic director of the ENGLISH STAGE COMPANY at the ROYAL COURT from 1979 to 1993. He is distinguished in his dedication to the development of new writing and in his focus on theatre as a collaboration between writer, director and actor. Among the young writers he helped was Andrea Dunbar (1961–90), directing *The Arbor* (1980) and *Rita, Sue and Bob Too* (1982). He has collaborated with many of Britain's most renowned writers, including CARYL CHURCHILL, directing notable productions of *Cloud Nine* (1979), *Top Girls* (1982) and *Serious Money* (1987), and TIMBERLAKE WERTENBAKER, directing *Our Country's Good* (1988). He began a brief association with the ROYAL SHAKESPEARE COMPANY in 1992 and formed the OUT OF JOINT company in 1993, for which he directed SEBASTIAN BARRY's *The Steward of Christendom* (1995) and MARK RAVENHILL's *Shopping and Fucking* (1996). He wrote about his experience of directing *The Recruiting Officer* in *Letters to George* (1990).

DEBORA WESTON

Stage, The (The Stage and Television Today) Britain's weekly trade paper for the theatre world. *The Stage* was launched in 1880 by Lionel Carson and Maurice Cummerford to cover news, reviews and features about professional theatre in Britain, and its ownership has remained in the Cummerford family. In 1959 the paper included coverage of television. *The Stage and Television Today* is intended for actors, light entertainment performers, managers, technicians and students of drama. It attracts advertising for the recruitment of performers, technicians and stage managers.

ADRIANA HUNTER

See also MAGAZINES AND JOURNALS; RECORDING AND RESEARCHING THEATRE.

stage machinery So much change in the technical departments of theatre took place in the latter half of the nineteenth century that it would have been practically impossible for this pace to have continued unabated throughout the twentieth. What did happen was a consolidation of much that was begun in the previous century. The early twentieth-century stage in some cases replicated in steel the wooden machinery of the nineteenth. The real innovation of the twentieth century was the revolving stage made possible by engineering and electrical advances. Theatres were proud to say they had one. Some were used to effect fast scene changes, but this use came to be superseded by that of the sliding pallet floors noted elsewhere, after which revolves tended to be something installed for a specific production rather than built-in machinery. Twentieth-century practice is exemplified by the stage lifts at the Royal Opera House in London. Installed in 1903, covering the whole playing area, these five lifts worked for over 90 years. They were disposed of during the major redevelopment of the Opera House in 1997–9. The successor arrangement of lifts and moveable pallets was ready for the re-opening in the very last month of the century and, indeed, the millennium. The Opera House lifts were driven by direct current motors. The incoming alternating current had to be 'rectified' in large mercury vapour devices with all the appearance of Dr Frankenstein's laboratory. Direct current offers easy speed control of motors without loss of power. The theatre found this very useful in the early years, not just for lifts, but also for revolves and other machinery as well. When the NATIONAL THEATRE opened for business at the Old Vic in 1963, an alternating current motor drove a direct current generator which fed a variable speed motor or motors controlling the front curtain via a rotating knob in the prompt corner. The technology had not moved far from 1900. Towards the end of the twentieth century, the beginnings of a new generation of staging usages and equipment emerged that will continue evolving well into the twenty-first.

The Victorian passion for spectacular events on stage continued into the Edwardian years. However, after the First World War and during the inter-war period, this mode became unfashionable, with many new plays taking place in a restricted number of settings, changed during the interval. So marked was this trend that Richard Southern, in his seminal work of the 1950s, *Changeable Scenery*, wrote that there was apparently no need for changeable scenery in the modern theatre. Since the 1980s, however, there has been a resurgence in the use of stage machinery, not only to facilitate increasingly complex production devices but also, in many cases, to increase the efficient working of a building, especially in large-repertoire venues such as opera houses. Stage machinery can also be used to alter the configuration of a venue, for example by changing the angle of the stage floor, or the width of the proscenium opening. These installations are frequently driven by economic factors, the need to maintain or even increase the number of performances justifying expenditure on ever more complex stage machinery.

There is now such a huge range of machinery available that it would be difficult to define any particular set-up as a generic stage for the modern era. Rather, the question has become one of selecting the arrangement of equipment which any particular individual or company feels best suits their intended use of the stage. There is a difference here between stage machinery and mechanical scenery – stage machinery being those things which you would normally expect to find in a theatre as part of the fabric, and mechanical scenery being the pieces of engineering which are built to the DESIGN of any one particular production. We are seeing the emergence of the stage designer, that is, an individual who designs stages, as a distinct and separate creature from the scenery designer (the person who decides what the audience will see on the stage). The pace of advance is so fast that it would be extremely speculative to suggest what practices might be prevalent in even 10 or 15 years' time.

There are many successful theatres, built either as conversions of existing buildings or from scratch, which could be considered 'studio' in type, where there is neither the expectation nor the need for stage machinery. At the beginning of the twentieth century architects felt that they required at least the rudiments of a flying system or stage machinery, but the studio configuration relieves theatres of this need.

Development has taken place in almost every facet of the stage machinery field, not so much in the general principles of use and operation as in the components of its manufacture and control. The theatre has moved from small metal pulleys in wooden blocks to large pulley wheels made of compressed artificial material, capable even of weighing the load passed over them; and from cotton or hemp rope to steel wire rope with terminations pre-marked with the load they are tested to carry.

Technicians at the beginning of the twentieth century would have been happy with a grid twice the height of the proscenium opening. This multiple soon advanced to two and a half times, and, by the end of the century, three times that height was considered a good mark to aim for. Because of advances in building materials and technology, this is well within the realms of possibility and is achieved. The additional height gives greater flexibility to the designer and allows for storage in a suspended position out of sight of the audience.

The most common flying system has been the counterweight, the single purchase variety being normally preferred for ease and precision of manual operation. Some installations have resorted to lead weights in order to increase the lifting capacity. The need for gantries to access the weights has led to stages surrounded by these walkways at successive levels, providing excellent access for staff. In some cases, motorized 'bridges' are installed, carrying lighting instruments and allowing personnel direct access to them without recourse to ladders.

The most common piece of machinery after the flys is probably the orchestra lift. This can be used as a forestage, lowered to auditorium level and used for seating, or lowered again to become an orchestra pit. The mechanized stage will comprise a well in which are installed lifts or revolves, or even a combination of the two, the intention being to offer the set designer the potential for movement and the operators with the means of changing the shape of the space by the use of the lifts.

A stage consisting of separate squares has been tried. As each one can travel upwards or downwards and be ramped, there is the potential for creating all manner of stage platform shapes simply by pre-setting the control system and pressing a button. More than this, the physical effort required from the crew is minimized, because almost anything can be lifted or lowered to be on a level with where it has to be put, practically eliminating physical lifting.

The hydraulic motor has begun to make an impact on stage machinery and mechanical scenery. It enables precise controlled movements to be made at an enormous variety of speeds, shifting loads of widely varying resistance, the power being provided via hydraulic pressure created out of earshot of the stage. As far as flying systems are concerned, the hydraulic or motor-driven system provides some distinct advantages over the counterweight system which was in common use throughout the greater part of the twentieth century. There is no requirement to load and unload weights, and so individual items can be lowered in and left on the stage and the system taken away without any unsafe procedure being involved. The space required

for counterweights is also freed, offering the potential of side stages either side. For a time it appeared that hydraulic systems would be the way forward. However, in the very last years of the century, technology got to grips with the speed control of alternating current motors without significant loss of power. In the UK, this was accelerated development, urged on by the millions of pounds being spent on new theatres and major refurbishments. Significant institutions like SADLER'S WELLS and the Royal Opera House took this route. The space and operational advantages are similar to those of hydraulic systems. Whether they will last as long as the counterweight systems only time will tell. Hydraulic motors are used to drive trucks, revolves and lifts – in fact, in almost any application where movement is required. Control systems are available which can link all manner of movement functions to one console, offering synchronous movement for every performance.

A complex advance in stage machinery has been the increase of side stages, i.e. complete stage areas lying to either side of, below or behind the main performing space. Behind soundproofed shutters, staff can erect and dismantle settings without being heard in the performance space. This enables completed sets to be moved on to the stage, thereby reducing the time spent on changing over or increasing the complexity of what can be changed in a relatively short time. There has been a considerable expansion of this facility, so that some major venues store as many as ten or twelve sets or part sets, completely built, in the nether regions of a building and move them mechanically to the performance space. The advantages are enhanced efficiency of the use of the main space and a more efficient use of working personnel.

For years, the carpenters and 'machinists' in theatres displayed much of their own ingenuity in the productions they presented. This is no longer the case. Settings are now fabricated in workshops removed from the theatre. The complexity of modern engineering has produced specialists in theatrical applications, working closely with designers, to create the mobile scenery needed in modern productions. The increasing range of products available 'over the counter' has made it easier for complex settings to be assembled. There have even been cases where productions have been scheduled so as to dovetail with the engineer's ability to produce the mechanical scenery.

There has been a steady trend, accelerating since the Second World War, towards bulkier and heavier scenery. The traditional canvas and wood are rarely seen now. The wooden frame remains, but steel is increasingly used. Solid sheet materials are now used instead of canvas, providing a wrinkle- and warp-free surface for the painter. Woven materials are still frequently applied on top to offer better paint absorption. The *trompe l'oeil* painted friezes and mouldings of old are replaced by corresponding effects in vacuum form plastic; textures are used to simulate stone or brick. However, massive increases in light levels have resulted in even apparently solid mouldings being flattened by the brightness, so paint is still necessary to emphasize the shadows. The reality is enhanced, yet at the same time, scenic artists are still gilding the lily.

The development in the last 30 years of the century of the square-section metal tube allowed for quick cutting and joining while also providing a flat surface on which decorative panels or other items could be fixed. It had a marked effect, probably greater than any other technical advance. It has become cheaper to work in metal for rostra over a given height; large shapes are more easily assembled, require less bracing and so appear rather neater. This trend is reflected in the building of 'trucks' – those wheeled pieces of scenery representing houses or other solid objects. Once made of standard wooden/canvas flats and fixed to a wheeled wooden rostrum, the current mode is frequently a steel chassis with wheels set to engineering precision, offering smoother movement.

It is difficult to determine what is an 'effect' in terms of the stage, but throughout the century there has often been some form of movement in front of the audience, except perhaps between the two world wars, when 'effects' were unpopular. It is fair to define a scenic effect in this context as something that moves within sight of the audience, pushed by some great unseen hand. This movement will usually be vertical, horizontal or rotatory. It may vary in speed from sudden to ponderous, and may be linked to other movements as well. It will almost certainly be linked to the work of two other departments, LIGHTING and SOUND.

Since the introduction of electric lighting into theatre in the late nineteenth century, there has been a dazzling array of devices available to produce all manner of effects, such as remotely controllable shaped and patterned beams of varying colours, with hard or soft edges.

Technical advances have steadily produced longer-lasting, ever brighter lamps. Theatre responds by asking for ever higher levels of brilliance which bear no relationship to the 10-candle power (literally) bulbs at the turn of the century. The brighter lights also allow lighting instruments to be placed further away and encourage the use of the greater height in the stage space. Performers, too, have had to adjust their

MAKE-UP style to compensate for the higher intensity. Lighting was the first department to get remote control. In the 1930s systems were available to allow one operator rather than several to control a performance. This principle, with the added facility of computerized memory, is now so commonplace that even relatively small installations can afford it. The memory system also eliminates the time formerly taken in working out how the desired states could be reproduced in sequence on a manual control board.

Since the 1950s the role of the lighting designer has emerged. This trend has been fuelled in part by the industrialization of the manufacturing process. Mass-production of lanterns and dimming systems without moving parts after the Second World War meant that larger installations using hundreds of instruments were achievable at relatively low cost compared with previous times. The organization and handling of these larger rigs and installations has become an expert job, calling forth the skills of the aforementioned lighting designer. The real quantum leap, if there was one, came in 1953, when the first die-cast lighting instruments were produced in the UK in large batches. The significance of the change can be appreciated when one considers the earlier system, in which skilled workers made each individual instrument on a bench. The net result is that a greater volume of the stage space is now occupied by lighting equipment than before. The use of that space can become a matter for negotiation between scenic and lighting designers.

Sound, too, has become a distinct specialization. The traditional devices to make the noises of wind, thunder, rain, slamming doors, etc. are still used, but there is also the choice of electronically reproduced sound. Sound has been variously produced from 78rpm discs, 33rpm discs, tape, compact discs, mini discs and microphones. The sound engineer is frequently seen at the rear of the auditorium 'mixing' the sound as the performance progresses. Sound designers specify the nature and locations of loudspeakers to satisfy the needs of each particular production. This development has brought yet another department into the bargaining for use of space.

In common with most other industries, the technical and mechanical sides of theatre have experienced a steady reduction in the numbers of personnel engaged as more and more aspects of the operations involved are computerized, remotely controlled or mechanically handled. Strangely, this has not markedly reduced the amount of time taken in usual circumstances to mount a production, either because expectations are rather higher than they used to be, or because more areas of complexity are being explored than at the beginning of the century. It may also be that there is greater concern for staff welfare, resulting in fewer long shifts being worked, in the interests of safety and economy.

The twentieth century provided the theatre with its first, highly organized competition for the public's pennies in the form of film, recorded sound and television, and this has had an effect on the way the stage is used. Contemporary dramatists are often given to writing multi-scene plays and designers are increasingly using the stage to give impressions which are quickly changeable, rather than the complete picture which was the vogue in the day of the 'well-made play'. This quick-change facility relies upon the ability to raise, lower, revolve or otherwise manipulate the stage in a fluid way to get from one scene to another without a prolonged break in the action.

The stage has come to be seen as an integral, flexible piece of precision engineering providing means of suspension as well as lateral movement, remotely controlled, with computerized facilities, offering low labour-cost operation. By comparison, at the beginning of the twentieth century, although the stage might have had revolving or other stage machinery, each single piece would have been individually controlled. The average stage would not have had facilities for work to be carried on simultaneously with performance or rehearsal work on the stage itself. Scenery would have been much lighter and manually handled far more frequently, and the scene change (where complete sets were struck and others erected during an interval) was a far more common event then than it is now. Crews in large shows could then run up to 70 or so men for each performance. One would be hard put to find a quarter of that number now. JOE AVELINE

See also ARCHITECTURE.

Joe Aveline et al, ed. G. Walne, *Effects for the Theatre* (1995)
——, *Metric Handbook*, 2nd edn (1999)
——, *Production Management* (2000)

stage management In the long history of the theatre, the actual term 'stage management' did not appear until comparatively recently, and at first was used to mean what is now called 'direction'. However, most of the duties that a stage manager does now must always have been needed, whatever the people carrying them out were called. The most central of these duties is probably the responsibility for keeping 'the book', and someone called the 'book holder' was present at performances of miracle plays. By the seventeenth century he was being called the 'prompter', a position which persisted until well into the nineteenth century. He attended rehearsals to record alterations

and stage directions in the prompt copy and, during performances, he 'held the book', or 'was on the book', phrases still in common use. These functions, as well as those of the 'callboy', are now usually taken by the deputy stage manager. Under the stage manager, the stage management team is responsible for the organization and smooth running of the rehearsals and technical periods in the theatre, putting up the 'calls', detailing the props required, as well as being in charge of the physical side of the production for its entire run in the theatre. The increase in the complexity of staging made it preferable for one person to be answerable for all aspects of a production at every performance. HENRY IRVING engaged as stage manager H. J. Loveday. He was not an actor, but had gained his knowledge of the theatre as a musician. He became Irving's right-hand man in everything backstage, from drilling 'supers' (extras) in crowd scenes to responsibility for all the technical departments. Irving himself kept a firm hand on the direction of the acting company, assisted by the prompter.

The beginning of the twentieth century saw the decline of the actor–managers, with many theatres coming to be run by businessmen who employed 'producers' to direct productions. Producers were usually from the acting profession, but not part of the acting company, so they were not present to oversee every performance. This became the prime duty of the stage manager and his assistant. They had taken over the place of the prompter, though not yet of the callboy, who continued to be needed for calling the actors until intercom systems to dressing-rooms were developed. Stage managers still came from the acting profession, often combining small-part playing or understudying with their stage management duties, and the role was still thought of as essentially a man's job. However, during the First World War, with so many men being called up, jobs in many industries previously considered a male preserve were being done by women, and stage management was no exception. An actress called Maud Gill became the stage manager at the BIRMINGHAM REPERTORY THEATRE and continued to hold the position for several years after the end of the war.

The only way of learning stage management was by being taken on as a 'student ASM' (assistant stage manager) with a REPERTORY company, a device also often used for learning to become an actor. In the 1930s in Britain, two acting schools under John Fernald and MICHEL SAINT-DENIS included stage management courses; but then the Second World War intervened, and it was not until 1957 that John Fernald, by now principal of the Royal Academy of Dramatic Art, engaged Dorothy Tenham to establish a separate course to teach stage management students. Several other drama schools soon followed suit with the result that the route to stage management no longer led exclusively through acting. In the Second World War, many stage management jobs were again taken up by women, but this time there was to be no reversion at the end of the war to the idea of it being a male preserve. Another wartime effect was that stage managers often also took on the duties of business managers, an arrangement which has persisted. At first, this double identity led to their being known under other titles, such as stage director or company manager, with the second member of the team being called stage manager and the third, assistant stage manager; but when the UNION Equity started to negotiate with the employers for standard contracts for stage management, the confusion of titles had to be rationalized. It was agreed that the senior member of the team should go back to being called stage manager, with the title of company manager added if business management was also involved. The third member of the team was still to be known as ASM, and the new title of deputy stage manager was introduced for the number two. This title is not used in North America, where the war had not caused a comparable manpower shortage.

DAVID AYLIFF

B. Dilker, *Stage Management: Forms and Formats* (1982)
B. Gruver and F. Hamilton, *The Stage Manager's Handbook* (1972)

Stage Society, Incorporated Founded in 1899 by Frederick Whelen as a successor to the INDEPENDENT THEATRE SOCIETY, the Stage Society was committed to the presentation of contemporary plays of distinction which were usually unacceptable to commercial managements or the CENSOR. Using London West End theatres and professional actors, it relied heavily on Sunday performances when theatres and actors were unengaged (though police raided its inaugural production, SHAW's *You Never Can Tell*, for breaking the ban on Sunday opening). From 1915 to 1919 it revived one Restoration play a year and then founded the PHOENIX SOCIETY to explore the early English repertoire. Before the First World War the Stage Society played a crucial role in the promotion of British progressive drama (beating the censor with plays such as *Mrs Warren's Profession* and GRANVILLE BARKER's *Waste*) and the drama of Russia and continental Europe (e.g. MAETERLINCK, Tolstoy). In the 1920s it introduced many German and American EXPRESSIONIST plays to the English stage, as well as PIRANDELLO's *Six Characters in Search of an Author* and R. C. SHERRIFF's *Journey's End*. In 1926 it

merged with Phyllis Whitworth's Three Hundred Club. By the 1930s its pioneering work was being overtaken by other groups, and it was wound up in 1939 with LORCA's *Blood Wedding*. IAN CLARKE

stand-up comedy Form of entertainment in which one or two performers directly address an audience with the explicit intention of making them laugh. Its immediate origins are in American VAUDEVILLE and British VARIETY theatre, where the spoken patter became more important than the verses of the comic songs between which it was sandwiched. In both vaudeville and variety, the emphasis was on the tried and tested: comics toured the same act for years; and stealing material was widespread, with radio appearances by the likes of JACK BENNY and Bob Hope being a typical target for comic larceny. The dominant joke themes were domestic matters (nagging wives, domineering mothers-in-law) and sexual innuendo, both of which are present in abundance in the work of one of variety's biggest stars, MAX MILLER. In spite of a general tendency to the formulaic, some comics (KEN DODD, TOMMY COOPER) did plough a more experimental, absurdist furrow. After vaudeville spluttered to a halt in the 1930s, it was replaced by a diverse set of venues, principally the 'Borscht Belt': a circuit of as many as 500 hotels in the Catskills catering for a mainly Jewish clientele, which produced comedians like Jerry Lewis and Red Buttons. In Britain, variety lasted longer, stumbling on as late as the 1960s, when it was replaced by the working men's clubs and bigger, privately owned venues like the Batley Variety Club. If anything, club comedy was even more standardized and reactionary than what came before, relying exclusively on packaged jokes, with many comics (e.g. Bernard Manning) turning to racial issues, making immigrants the target of harsh, sometimes violent gags. By this time, the revolution which would redefine stand-up had already started in America. In the 1950s, the so-called 'sick comics' (LENNY BRUCE, Mort Sahl) who emerged from strip clubs and Beat venues rejected established joke formats in favour of more free-flowing, improvisational routines, influenced by JAZZ and laced with hipster slang, which encompassed the Cold War, segregation, sexual repression and illicit drug use. The importance of using original, self-written material was stressed, and in moving the emphasis from simple laughter-making to self-expression these comics paved the way for the likes of Richard Pryor, Robin Williams and Roseanne Barr. In Britain, things started to change when Billy Connolly exploded out of the folk music scene, making the scatological, sacrilegious wit of the Glasgow shipyards into a high art.

However, it was only when the opening of the Comedy Store in 1979 kicked alternative comedy into life that the revolution really began. For the first time, stand-up had an explicit ethical line – Tony Allen pushed the idea that 'altcom' should be non-sexist, non-racist – as well as an overt political agenda, with Alexei Sayle describing himself on stage as a 'Marxist comedian'. Stylistic boundaries were pushed back and audiences were confronted as much as entertained by gratuitous obscenity, barbed attacks on their lifestyle choices, and even, on occasion, physical attack. 'Altcom' has also encouraged a new generation of confrontational women performers (Jo Brand, Jenny Eclair), following the precedent set by gentler acts like Victoria Wood, who forged her career outside the main circuits, and further back, variety comediennes like Suzette Tarri.

OLIVER DOUBLE

See also NEW VARIETY; NEW VAUDEVILLE.

Lenny Bruce, *How to Talk Dirty and Influence People* (1965)

O. Double, *Stand-Up: On Being a Comedian* (1997)

J. Fisher, *Funny Way to Be a Hero* (1973)

John Limon, *Stand-up Comedy in Theory, or Abjection in America* (2000)

R. Wilmut, *Didn't You Kill My Mother-in-Law?* (1989)

Stanislavsky [Alekseyev], Konstantin [Sergeyevich] (b. Moscow, 5 Jan. 1863; d. Moscow, 7 Aug. 1938) Actor, director, teacher and theorist. Born into a wealthy manufacturing family with strong cultural connections, Stanislavsky first trod the boards on a home stage in 1877. His 'Alekseyev Circle' performed vaudevilles and operettas, including GILBERT and SULLIVAN's *The Mikado*. In 1888, together with his singing teacher F. P. Komissarzhevsky and the stage director A. F. Fedotov, Stanislavsky founded the Society of Art and Literature in Moscow, where he gave performances in plays by Pushkin, Pisemsky, Tolstoy, Schiller, Gutzkow and Shakespeare – his performance of Othello inspiring MEYERHOLD to abandon his law studies and enter the theatre. He also took his first steps as a director, staging Tolstoy's *Fruits of Enlightenment* (1891). Stanislavsky drew his inspiration from the past and the present, deriving his notions of an ideal theatre from the theoretical legacy of Gogol, Turgenev and Ostrovsky and his practical inspiration from Mikhail Shchepkin and touring tragedians such as TOMMASO SALVINI and Ernesto Rossi. He was also greatly influenced by the second visit to Russia, in 1890, of the MEININGEN COMPANY under their director Ludwig Chronegk, from whom he learned the importance of ENSEMBLE work.

In 1897, as a result of what was to become a famous eighteen-hour conversation with VLADIMIR NEMIROVICH-DANCHENKO, who had been impressed with Stanislavsky's work, the Moscow Art Popular-Accessible Theatre (as it was first named) was created with a company drawn from students in Nemirovich's classes at the Moscow Philharmonic Society and members of Stanislavsky's Society of Art and Literature. History was made in the company's first season, which opened in October 1898, with Stanislavsky's scrupulously ethnographic, historically naturalist production of A. K. Tolstoy's *Tsar Fyodor Ioannovich*. This was followed in December by the epoch-making production of CHEKHOV's *The Seagull*, for which Stanislavsky prepared detailed prompt-books and on which, as in the case of the Tolstoy play, endless hours of rehearsal had been spent – something quite unique at that time in the history of Russian theatre. A string of great performances followed Stanislavsky's appearance as Trigorin in *The Seagull*, including his Astrov in *Uncle Vanya*, Vershinin in *Three Sisters*, Gayev in *The Cherry Orchard*, Satin in GORKY's *The Lower Depths*, the eponymous hero in *Dr Stockmann* (IBSEN's *An Enemy of the People*), and Rakitin in Turgenev's *A Month in the Country*, for all of which Stanislavsky, as director, prepared detailed production scores. Chekhov, who died in 1904 shortly after the première of *The Cherry Orchard*, was not always happy with the Art Theatre's interpretation of his plays. For example, he disapproved of Stanislavsky's 'romantic' interpretation of Trigorin, whom Chekhov saw as an altogether more 'seedy' character. He also felt that Stanislavsky's productions of *Three Sisters* and *The Cherry Orchard* erred on the side of over-solemnity in ignoring the fact that the author himself considered the plays to be comedies.

Increasingly dissatisfied with naturalist forms of theatre after 1905, as well as critical of his own performances, Stanislavsky began to interest himself in non-realistic modes of theatre production, drawing inspiration from the SYMBOLIST movement. This expressed itself in innovatory productions of MAETERLINCK's *The Blue Bird*, ANDREYEV's *The Life of Man* and the plays of Knut Hamsun. Immersing himself more and more in theories of the actor's creativity and attempting to widen the theatre's experience of theatre production, he extended invitations to MEYERHOLD (in 1905) and to EDWARD GORDON CRAIG (in 1910) to work at the Moscow Art Theatre. The result was abortive attempts at a stylized theatre and a less than totally successful production by Craig of *Hamlet*. Stanislavsky's concern to refine the actor's art and to investigate its creative wellsprings led to the establishment of studios attached to the Art Theatre, the first of which was headed by the exceptionally gifted teacher Leopold Sulerzhitsky, assisted by his equally inspired lieutenant

YEVGENY VAKHTANGOV. The early deaths of both men were a severe blow to Stanislavsky.

His visits with the Art Theatre to the United States, in 1922 and 1924, contributed to the extension of the theatre's and Stanislavsky's worldwide reputation, as did the publication, in English, of his volume of memoirs, *My Life in Art* (1924). Returning to the Soviet Union, Stanislavsky found his theatre trying hard to adjust to a post-revolutionary climate. He made his own contribution as directorial adviser on productions of BULGAKOV's civil war drama *Dni Turbinykh* (*The Days of the Turbins*, 1926) and IVANOV's *Bronepoezd 14–69* (*The Armoured Train 14–69*, 1927). He also staged memorable productions of classic plays – Beaumarchais' *The Marriage of Figaro* (1927) and Ostrovsky's *Goryacheye serdtse* (*The Ardent Heart*, 1926). A heart attack suffered in 1928 forced Stanislavsky into semi-retirement, although he kept in touch with the theatre and conducted rehearsals at home, preoccupied with work on acting theory, the results of which were to appear as *Rabota aktyora nad soboi* (*An Actor's Work on Himself*, 1936).

There are many terms in Stanislavsky's theoretical vocabulary which have become familiar, such as the 'through-line' of action, the 'circle of attention' and the 'magic if', but none more important than 'emotion memory' and 'the given circumstances'. These latter demand that an actor, in rehearsal, plumb the very depths of his or her emotional being in search of those feelings from past experience which will enable the performer to identify with the emotions of the character in the imagined circumstances of the play. The task of rehearsal is to render these emotions instantly retrievable as 'living truth' in the repetitive and routine circumstances of performance with a spontaneous vividness which is devoid of cliché or mere technical virtuosity.

Universally recognized as one of the great figures of twentieth-century theatre, Stanislavsky left a theoretical legacy that has been both controversial and misunderstood. As well as being misappropriated by dogmatic proselytizers of 'socialist realism', in order to idealize and distort the nature of political truth in the name of a 'humanistic' emotional truth, Stanislavsky's actor-centred methodology was also used, especially during the Stalinist 1930s, as a weapon to attack 'formalist' or convention-based methods of theatrical presentation which did not necessarily privilege the status of the living actor. The means were also misapplied in America by so-called METHOD actors in the interests of unfettered emotional self-expression at the expense of theatrical 'ensemble' or a play's wider meanings. The 'system' has also been challenged by those who believe that the theatre has never been concerned with realism as conventionally understood, or with the emotional identification between actor and character implied by the term *perezhivaniye* (the living-through of emotional experience) – a key word in Stanislavsky's theory.

NICK WORRALL

S. D. Balukhaty, trans. David Magarshack, *The Seagull Produced by Stanislavsky: Production Score for the Moscow Art Theatre* (1952)
Jean Benedetti, *Stanislavski: A Biography* (1988)
——, *Stanislavski and the Actor* (1998)
Sharon M. Carnicke, *Stanislavsky in Focus* (1998)
Toby Cole, ed., *Acting: A Handbook of the Stanislavski Method* (1957; rev edn 1971)
Christine Edwards, *The Stanislavsky Heritage* (1965)
Erika Munk, ed., *Stanislavski and America* (1966)

Stanley, Kim [Patricia Kimberly Reid] (b. Tularosa, NM, 11 Feb. 1925) Actress. She studied at the ACTORS' STUDIO in the 1940s and appeared OFF-BROADWAY before taking over the lead in *Monserrat* (1949), following this with a notable appearance in *Picnic* (1953). Although she was praised for her performance in *Bus Stop* (1955), she was supplanted in the film version by Marilyn Monroe. Roles in *A Touch of the Poet* (1958), *Cat on a Hot Tin Roof* (1958, her London debut), *A Far Country* (1961) and *Three Sisters* (1964) testified to her considerable acting skills. She gave up the stage to concentrate on teaching. HELEN RAPPAPORT

Stapleton, [Lois] Maureen (b. Troy, NY, 21 June 1925) Actress. A charter member of the ACTORS' STUDIO (1947), she is a character actress of great power who has played Italian, Jewish and Southern women on stage and screen. She won acclaim as Serafina in *The Rose Tattoo* (1951) by TENNESSEE WILLIAMS, and her comic talent came out as three different people in NEIL SIMON's *Plaza Suite* (1968) and as Evy Meara in his *The Gingerbread Lady* (1970, winning a second Tony Award). Other notable roles include two more by Tennessee Williams: Lady Torrance (*Orpheus Descending*, 1957) and Amanda Wingfield (*The Glass Menagerie*, 1965, 1975), and Birdie in a 1991 revival of *The Little Foxes*. Active in television and film, she was elected to the Theatre Hall of Fame in 1981. She wrote *A Hell of a Life* (with Jane Scovell, 1995). JANE HOUSE

J. M. Woods, *Maureen Stapleton* (1992)

Starr [Grant], Frances (b. Oneonta, NY, 6 June 1881; d. New York, 11 June 1973) Actress. After her first stage performance in 1901, she worked in stock companies until impresario DAVID BELASCO gave her her first break, asking her to take over the lead in the long run of *The Music Master* at his Belasco Theater. She became noted for doe-eyed ingénue roles in a sustained series of leads in other Belasco productions: *The Rose of the Rancho* (1906), *The Easiest Way* (1909), *The Case of Becky* (1911), *Marie-Odile* (1915), *Little Lady in Blue* (1916), *Tiger!, Tiger!* (1918) and *Shore Leave* (1922). After her association with Belasco ended, Starr continued to work until her retirement in the 1950s. During the American actors' strike of 1919, Starr was one of a group of actors who disassociated themselves from American Equity and formed the Actors' Fidelity League (*see* UNIONS). HELEN RAPPAPORT

State Theatre Company of South Australia
Founded in 1965 as the South Australian Theatre Company, it had uncertain beginnings, lacking a permanent venue. In 1972 the company became a statutory body and, with the opening of the Adelaide Festival Centre, resident company at the Playhouse. It has staged productions at other venues – primarily at Theatre 62 and The Space at the Festival Centre – but since 1986 has mounted the majority of its work in the Playhouse. The company has undergone several changes of profile and has had six artistic directors since 1976 who have, with varying degrees of success, sought to establish either a strong subscription list or a definite house style, and concentrated either on importing 'stars' from Sydney or Melbourne for individual plays or on developing an ensemble company which might tackle more adventurous work. Renamed Lighthouse by Jim Sharman during his period as artistic director, it subsequently reverted to its less flamboyant title, and after a period under Keith Gallasch which saw the programming of some unsuccessful new Australian plays – without any attempt at selectivity – and a consequent collapse of subscriber support, it opted for a more conventional repertoire under artistic director John Gaden. Gaden's term saw an improvement in both subscriptions and quality of productions – a trend which continued when Simon Phillips took over in 1990. On his departure in 1993 the position of artistic director was replaced by that of executive producer; the first incumbent was Chris Westwood, whose decision to concentrate on an exclusively Australian repertoire led to a disastrous decline in subscriber support and her subsequent departure. Since 1997, under successive directors, the company has struggled to find an identity. MICHAEL MORLEY

Stavis, Barrie (b. New York, 16 June 1906) Playwright. He writes from history about heroic people in their struggle for social change: *Lamp at Midnight* (1947) about Galileo Galilei, *The Man Who Never Died* (1955) about Joe Hill, *Coat of Many Colors* (1966) about

Joseph in biblical Egypt, *Harper's Ferry* (1967) about John Brown and *The Raw Edge of Victory* (1976) about Washington. Translated into more than two dozen languages, his plays are more honoured abroad than at home. FELICIA HARDISON LONDRÉ

Ezra Goldstein, 'Barrie Stavis', *Dramatics*, April 1986.

Stein, Gertrude (b. Allegheny, Pa., 3 Feb. 1874; d. Neuilly-sur-Seine, France, 27 July 1946) Expatriate American playwright and poet. Her 77 plays are experiments in a non-linear, non-climactic dramaturgy, and many were never performed. *What Happened: A Play* (1913) explores the essence of moments. Her 'landscape plays' express relationships through spatial arrangements. Her story plays are more often performed, e.g. *Yes Is For a Very Young Man* (1949) as well as her opera, *Mother of Us All* (1945) and *Four Saints in Three Acts* (1934), with music by Virgil Thomson. JANE HOUSE

Stein, Peter (b. Berlin, 1 Oct. 1937) Director and theatre manager. After being a dramaturg and assistant director at the Munich Kammerspiele, Stein first directed BOND's *Saved* (1967), followed by Schiller's *Intrigue and love* (1967, Bremen), BRECHT's *In the Jungle of the Cities* and WEISS's *Vietnam Discourse* (both 1968, Munich), and Goethe's *Torquato Tasso* (1969, Bremen). He then directed three productions at the Schauspielhaus Zurich: Bond's *Early Morning*, O'CASEY's *Cock-a-Doodle Dandy*, and Middleton's *The Changeling*. In the course of this work he had met a group of collaborators with whom, in 1970, he founded a company; with them, he moved to the SCHAUBÜHNE AM HALLESCHEN UFER in Berlin. The ensemble's first new production was Brecht's *The Mother*, which Stein co-directed with two other members of the company. His first major success came with a production of IBSEN's *Peer Gynt* (1971), followed a year later by Kleist's *Prince Friedrich of Homburg* and in 1973 by Labiche's *La Cagnotte* (*Pots of Money*). By now Stein had become an international celebrity and visitors arrived from all over the world to see his productions. The theatre proved too small for his enormous following and the poor stage facilities were restricting his imagination. His next production, the *Antikenprojekt* ('Antiquity Project', 1974), was performed in a large exhibition hall, and *Shakespeare's Memory* (1976) and *As You Like It* (1977) at a film studio outside the city centre. The Berlin Senate then agreed to raise the money to convert a former cinema into a large-scale theatre according to Stein's specifications. The new Schaubühne am Lehniner Platz was opened in 1980 with his production of the *Oresteia*, followed by Marivaux's *The Dispute* (1981), GENET's *The Blacks*

(1983), CHEKHOV's *Three Sisters* and STRAUSS's *The Park* (both 1984). In 1985 he resigned as artistic director and became freelance. He produced a number of major plays and operas at various international venues, and from 1992 to 1999 acted as artistic director of the Salzburg Festival. His uncut staging of the two parts of Goethe's *Faust* (2000) lasted 20 hours (over six evenings or one weekend at the Hanover Expo).

Stein has described himself as a pupil of Brecht and KORTNER. He lays great emphasis on fantasy and poetic qualities of performance, and invites the spectator to enjoy the stage illusion, yet at the same time remaining distanced from it. He carries out extensive research with the whole company and uses an extremely detailed rehearsal method which gives his productions an unusual degree of clarity and precision. He creates a theatre of refined beauty, where political relevance is combined with a high degree of aesthetic accomplishment. GÜNTER BERGHAUS

M. Patterson, *Peter Stein* (1981)

Steinbeck, John [Ernst] (b. Salinas, Calif., 27 Feb. 1902; d. New York, 20 Dec. 1968) Novelist and Nobel Prize winner, who made acclaimed dramatizations of two of his books: *Of Mice and Men* (1937) and *The Moon is Down* (1942). His adaptation of *Burning Bright* (1950) was less successful. *Of Mice and Men*, *Sweet Thursday* and *East of Eden* were turned into musicals, and *Tortilla Flat* was dramatized by JACK KIRKLAND (1938). ADRIANA HUNTER

Stelarc *see* BODY ART

Stephen Joseph Theatre In 1976 THEATRE IN THE ROUND pioneer STEPHEN JOSEPH's Library Theatre moved to a new building in Scarborough, Yorkshire — a converted boys' high school — and adopted the name of its founder, who had died in 1967. The theatre has always pursued a policy of launching new writing, most notably that of ALAN AYCKBOURN, who joined the Scarborough company in 1955 as stage manager and aspiring actor, and has been its resident artistic director since 1970. All but three of Ayckbourn's plays received their world premières in the 300-seat main auditorium before the theatre moved again, in 1996, to the Art Deco former Odeon cinema, built in 1937, which houses two auditoriums, the Round, seating 404, and the McCarthy (named after the main benefactor), seating 165. JEANNIE SWALES

Stephens, Robert (b. Bristol, 14 July 1931; d. London, 13 Nov. 1995) Actor. He came to prominence at the start of the ENGLISH STAGE COMPANY at the ROYAL COURT in premières of ARDEN, OSBORNE, WESKER and DENNIS. He joined OLIVIER's new NATIONAL THEATRE, where he played the Dauphin in *St Joan* (1963) and Plume in *The Recruiting Officer* (1963). Tipped as the greatest actor of his generation, he became a cornerstone of the company, using a rich, sonorous voice and committed physicality to create a remarkable Atahuallpah in *The Royal Hunt of the Sun* (1964) and Benedick in ZEFFIRELLI's *Much Ado About Nothing* (1965) opposite his then wife MAGGIE SMITH. He continued to give much-praised performances at the NT (in e.g. *The Cherry Orchard*, 1978; *Brand*, 1978; *The Mysteries*, 1985), without, however, achieving the star status predicted for him. He returned to leading roles with the ROYAL SHAKESPEARE COMPANY as Falstaff (1991) and King Lear (1993). He was knighted in 1994, and his autobiography, *Knight Errant*, appeared in 1995. DAN REBELLATO

Steppenwolf Theater Company Founded in CHICAGO in 1976 by a group of friends from Illinois State University, Steppenwolf has evolved into an ensemble of international reputation. Using the great repertory companies, like the ROYAL SHAKESPEARE COMPANY and the MOSCOW ART THEATRE, as models of their own commitment to a communal approach to theatre, Steppenwolf has developed a raw, gritty style and is noted for the subtlety and 'bare-bones' staging of its classical, contemporary and commissioned repertory. Among its most notable productions are *Burn This* by LANFORD WILSON, *Lydie Breeze* by JOHN GUARE, *True West* by SAM SHEPARD and *Educating Rita* by WILLY RUSSELL. In 1989 the theatre mounted the first adaptation of JOHN STEINBECK's *The Grapes of Wrath* to be sanctioned by the Steinbeck estate. Many of its actors have found recognition beyond the ensemble, most notably JOHN MALKOVICH. In 1991 the company moved into a new, two-auditorium home. Steppenwolf has won many awards, including in 1985 a Tony for excellence in regional theatre. MICHAEL KARP

Stern, Ernest [Ernst J.] (b. Bucharest, 1876; d. London, 28 Aug. 1954) Designer. Stern studied painting and worked in cabaret in Munich. In 1907 he started working as a stage designer in Berlin, collaborating over 16 years with REINHARDT on numerous notable productions, including Shakespeare, IBSEN and contemporary German playwrights. He also designed for OPERA, and spent several years in England designing for COWARD. His autobiography, *My Life, My Stage*, appeared in English in 1951. ADRIANA HUNTER

Stern, G[ladys] B[ertha] (b. London, 17 June 1890; d. Wallingford, Oxon, 19 Sept. 1973) Writer and playwright. She trained as an actress but became a writer and spent many years in Italy. *The Matriarch* (1929), starring MRS PATRICK CAMPBELL, was popularly received. In *The Man Who Pays the Piper* (1931), Stern continued her examination of women's lives in relation to the social and economic climate of the 1930s. She moved into film script writing in the 1940s. MAGGIE GALE

Sternhagen, Frances [Hussey] (b. Washington DC, 13 Jan. 1930) Actress. After studying at Vassar and with SANFORD MEISNER in New York, she made her debut in 1948 with the Bryn Mawr Summer Theatre in *The Glass Menagerie* and *Angel Street*. She first appeared in New York in *Thieves Carnival* (1955) and followed this with a string of distinguished performances, in *The Admirable Bashville*, *The Country Wife*, *The Skin of Our Teeth*, *Great Day in the Morning*, *The Cocktail Party* and *Playboy of the Western World*. She received her first Tony award for *The Good Doctor* (1973), and has since appeared in *Equus*, *On Golden Pond*, *Driving Miss Daisy* and *The Heiress*, the last of which won her another Tony in 1995. She has also appeared in numerous films and television series. HELEN RAPPAPORT

Sternheim, [William Adolf] Carl (b. Leipzig, 1 April 1878; d. Brussels, 3 Nov. 1942) Playwright, novelist and critic. After an inauspicious literary beginning his first major play, the domestic comedy *Die Hose* (*The Bloomers/Underpants*, 1911) was not a great success; however, the extraordinary scandal that accompanied the production stimulated public interest in this satirist of bourgeois society. Over the next five years he wrote six comedies, which proved to be his most lasting achievements: *Die Kassette* (*The Strongbox*, 1911), *Bürger Schippel* (*Paul Schippel, Esq.*, 1913), *Der Snob* (*The Snob*, 1914), *Der Kandidat* ('The Candidate', 1915), *1913* (1919) and *Tabula Rasa* (1919). Thereafter he wrote a number of minor plays before his last masterpiece, *Das Fossil* (*The Fossil*, 1923), a challenge to militarism. Between then and the rise of Nazism he wrote adaptations, more satires, novels, memoirs and criticism.

Sternheim's plays have been compared with Molière's comedies, and his portrayal of society has been called a literary equivalent to GEORGE GROSZ's paintings. The protagonists of his *Aus dem bürgerlichen Heldenleben* (*Scenes from the Heroic Life of the Bourgeoisie*, published collectively in 1922), as he called his cycle of early comedies, are stripped of their fineries, revealing the soul of the German middle class – the very type of person who, a decade later, became the supporter of Hitler's quest for power. GÜNTER BERGHAUS

Burghard Dedner, *Carl Sternheim* (1982)
Rhys W. Williams, *Carl Sternheim: A Critical Study* (1982)

Stevens, Roger L[acey] (b. Detroit, 12 March 1910; d. Washington DC, 2 Feb. 1998) Producer. Stevens turned to the theatre only after making a substantial fortune in real estate. In 1951 he joined the PLAYWRIGHTS' COMPANY, then in 1954 helped found both the Producers' Theatre and the AMERICAN SHAKESPEARE FESTIVAL. In 1971 he was appointed head of Washington's JOHN F. KENNEDY CENTER FOR THE PERFORMING ARTS. Apart from his work with these groups, he also produced numerous successes on Broadway, either alone or with another producer. These included *Bus Stop* (1955), *West Side Story* (1957) and *Mary, Mary* (1961). He was keen on British theatre and fostered in America work by writers such as BOLT, PINTER and STOPPARD. GERALD BORDMAN

Stevenson [Stevens], Juliet [Anne Virginia] (b. Braintree, Essex, 30 Oct. 1956) Actress. She joined the ROYAL SHAKESPEARE COMPANY in 1978, immediately after leaving RADA, and remained for the following eight years, playing many leading roles including Rosalind, Cressida, Isabella, Titania and Madame de Tourvel (*Les Liaisons Dangereuses*). For the Royal NATIONAL THEATRE she played Yerma (1987), Hedda Gabler (1989), Grusha in *The Caucasian Chalk Circle* (1997) and Amanda in *Private Lives* (1999). She has been seen frequently on television, and is probably best known for her performance in Anthony Minghella's film *Truly, Madly, Deeply*, in which her characteristic emotional rawness was eloquently displayed. She has formidable technical resources, possessing a rich, flexible voice and an intelligent ability with complex text, but she is also an instinctive, volatile performer whose mercurial quickness and dangerous unpredictability make her one of the most compelling actresses of her day. GENISTA MCINTOSH

Stewart, Douglas (b. Eltham, New Zealand, 30 Dec. 1913; d. Sydney, 14 Feb. 1985) Poet, playwright and editor. The most famous of Stewart's plays is one of six in verse, *Ned Kelly*, written in 1940, performed first on radio in 1942 and often thereafter in the theatre – despite its reputation as unproducible. It tackles classical themes in modern form: pride, and the struggle between vitality, freedom of spirit, and physical and social entrapment. *The Fire on the Snow* (1941), a radio play about Scott's journey to the Pole, is the best known of Stewart's other dramas, and *Shipwreck* (1951) is reputedly his finest. He scripted the much-loved documentary *The Back of Beyond*. *The Golden Lover*

(1943, 1953) and *Fishers Ghost* (1960) completed his dramatic output. GUS WORBY

K. Inglis, *This is the ABC: The Australian Broadcasting Commission 1932–1983* (1983)
E. Perkins, 'Douglas Stewart', in Phillip Parsons, ed., *Companion to Theatre in Australia* (1995)
C. Semler, *Douglas Stewart: A Critical Study* (1974)

Stewart, Ellen (b. Alexandria, Los Angeles, 7 Oct. 1920) Producer. While working as a fashion designer she opened a boutique theatre in a New York basement in 1961 and launched the influential Café La MaMa, now LA MAMA EXPERIMENTAL THEATER CLUB, the major OFF-OFF-BROADWAY organization. Through world tours she created an international orbit for the theatre, encouraging alternative theatre, international cross-fertilization of ideas and experimentation by theatre artists in an environment free of commercial pressure. An extraordinary creative force, she has fostered, among many others, playwrights Julie Bovasso, Tom Eyen, LEONARD MELFI, ROCHELLE OWENS, SAM SHEPARD, Elizabeth Swados, MEGAN TERRY, JEAN-CLAUDE VAN ITALLIE and LANFORD WILSON; directors TOM O'HORGAN and ANDREI SERBAN; and visiting artists such as PETER BROOK and TADEUSZ KANTOR. In 1985 she won a MacArthur Foundation 'genius' award. JANE HOUSE

B. L. Horn, *Ellen Stewart and La MaMa* (1993)

Stewart, Ena Lamont (b. Glasgow, 10 Feb. 1912) Playwright. Her two most celebrated plays, *Starched Aprons* (1945), a naturalistic portrayal of hospital life, and *Poor Men's Riches* (1947), were written for Glasgow UNITY THEATRE. The latter was rewritten in 1976 and presented under the title *Men Should Weep* in 7:84 (Scotland)'s Clydebuilt season in 1982, directed by Giles Havergal. The feminist revision of the earlier social realist drama produced one of the most vibrant texts of twentieth-century Scottish theatre. JAN MCDONALD

Stoll Moss Theatres Ltd Theatre owners and managers descended from the buccaneering business ventures of two great pioneers of British MUSIC HALL. Oswald Stoll [Gray] (b. Melbourne, 20 Jan. 1866; d. London, 9 Jan. 1942) acquired his first music hall in Cardiff in 1889 and by 1899 owned eight provincial theatres. In that year he joined forces with the Moss and Thornton theatres headed by [Horace] Edward Moss (b. Manchester, 12 April 1852; d. 25 Nov 1912), who had started with the Gaiety Variety Theatre, Edinburgh, in 1877. The combined circuit was known as Moss Empires Ltd. A heavy expansionist programme included building the Hippodrome and COLISEUM theatres in London, but in December 1910 Stoll split from Moss and kept the Coliseum as his flagship theatre, where his variety bills included the DIAGHILEV ballet company. Moss Empires Ltd was merged in 1938 with a circuit which included the LONDON PALLADIUM and stayed in competition with the Stoll circuit until the 1950s, when the rapid growth of television sounded the death knell of variety and many provincial theatres closed, became bingo halls or were sold to local councils. In 1979 the remaining businesses of Stoll and Moss were merged once again. They sold their last provincial theatre, the Bristol Hippodrome, in 1984, and consolidated their business in London, where their 13 major theatres – with the exception of the Coliseum, which they released in 1992 – had no direct descent from Stoll or Moss. The company made an impact briefly on the West End before the theatres were sold in 2000 to ANDREW LLOYD WEBBER. Both men were knighted – Moss in 1905 and Stoll in 1919 – but for their charitable activities, not for their work in the theatre. Their true memorial remains the theatre buildings which they commissioned, many of them designed by the greatest of all English theatre architects, FRANK MATCHAM. IAN BEVAN

F. Barker, *The House that Stoll Built* (1957)

Stoppard [Straussler], Tom (b. Zlin, Czechoslovakia, 3 July 1937) Playwright. While he was an infant, his family moved to Singapore. His father was killed when it fell to the Japanese; his mother and her children had moved to India, where she remarried. Stoppard took his stepfather's name and was educated in England.

A journalist in Bristol, he developed an interest in the theatre through reviewing, and had early plays performed on radio and television. In 1966 his first stage play, *Rosencrantz and Guildenstern Are Dead*, was a success on the EDINBURGH FRINGE and again the following year when it was staged by the NATIONAL THEATRE Company at the OLD VIC, and subsequently on Broadway. It was filmed by him in 1990. The play presents imagined happenings offstage during the action of *Hamlet* and elevates two of that play's minor characters to tragi-comic, heroic status. Several commentators saw their struggle to make sense of the events that engulf them as a metaphor for those times; the play's wit, innovation and theatricality established Stoppard as a major new writer.

His next full-length play, *Jumpers* (1972), also combined the cerebral with the spectacular. Its hero, George, is a lecturer in moral philosophy trying to reconcile theoretical progressions with reality; yet it is a very funny comedy, incorporating a 'whodunnit', a striptease and a troupe of trampolining acrobats.

While *Travesties* (1974) requires its audience to appreciate a large number of literary allusions, his later work has been of wider appeal. *Night and Day* (1978) is about the ethics of journalism; *The Real Thing* (1982) about marriage. Stoppard has also written several adaptations (of MROZEK, LORCA, HAVEL, SCHNITZLER, Nestroy), screenplays and television plays – including the much praised *Professional Foul* (1977), about political dissidence under communism – a theme close to his heart and one which he explored on stage in *Every Good Boy Deserves Favour* (1977, music by André Previn). Other plays include *The Real Inspector Hound* (1968), *Artist Descending a Staircase* (radio, 1973), *Dirty Linen* (1976), *Hapgood* (1988), *In the Native State* (radio, 1991; as stage play *Indian Ink*, 1995), *Arcadia* (1993) and *The Invention of Love* (1997). Among his screenplays are *The Romantic Englishwoman* (1975) and *Empire of the Sun* (1991). He was knighted in 1997. DAVID SELF

R. A. Andretta, *The Plays of Tom Stoppard* (1991)
Paul Delaney, *Tom Stoppard: The Moral Vision of the Major Plays* (1990)
Ronald Hayman, *Tom Stoppard* (1977)
Katherine Kelly, *Tom Stoppard and the Craft of Comedy* (1991)
Thomas R. Whittaker, *Tom Stoppard* (1983)

Storey, David [Malcolm] (b. Wakefield, Yorks., 13 July 1933) Playwright and novelist. His stern poetic naturalism, rejecting overt ideological drama ('life before concepts'), was central to the ROYAL COURT repertoire in the late 1960s and early 1970s. *The Contractor* (1969) and *The Changing Room* (1971) are ensemble studies of Yorkshire working men: erecting and dismantling a wedding marquee (on-stage) or playing professional rugby become resonant images of personal and class relations. Elsewhere Storey, a miner's son, examines family guilt and the harsh, unbreakable bonds between generations (*In Celebration*, 1969; *The March on Russia*, 1989). A third, more surreal group of plays present inner disintegration and madness (*The Restoration of Arnold Middleton*, 1967; *Home*, 1970). He worked closely with the director LINDSAY ANDERSON and scripted the film (1963) of his own novel *This Sporting Life*, which Anderson directed. Other plays include *Cromwell* (1973), *Life Class* (1974) and *Stages* (1992). TONY HOWARD

William Hutchings, *The Plays of David Storey: A Thematic Study* (1988)
John Russell Taylor, *David Storey* (1974)

Stramm, August (b. Münster, Germany, 1874; d. Gorodec, Germany, 1 Sept. 1915) Playwright and poet; one of the most experimental writers of the EXPRESSIONIST era. The AVANT-GARDE nature of his small output of poems and short plays stood in marked contrast to his career as a civil servant in the postal administration. He led a conventional bourgeois life and became an army officer in the First World War, but his political ideals were socialist and his artistic tastes too radical to find acceptance. Most of his works would not have survived had they not been discovered by Herwarth Walden and published in his expressionist magazine *Der Sturm*. Stramm's five most important plays were written between 1912 and 1914: *Sancta Susanna*, *Rudimentär* ('Rudimentary'), *Die Haidebraut* ('The Moor's bride'), *Erwachen* (*Awakening*) and *Kräfte* ('Forces'). Their subject matter is rather conventional, but the language is novel. The plays were first adequately staged by SCHREYER and Blümner. GÜNTER BERGHAUS

Henry Marx, 'August Stramm', *Drama Review*, vol. 67 (Sept. 1975)

Strand Lighting An international lighting manufacturing company, founded in 1914 in London by theatre electricians Arthur Earnshaw and Phillip Sheridan as Strand Electric. In 1968 Strand purchased the American company Century Lighting, which had been founded in 1929 by Ed Kook with Joe, Irving and Saul Levy. Strand Lighting is one of the world's largest manufacturers of lighting fixtures and control systems for theatre, film, television studios, architectural installations, theme parks and cruise ships. Strand manufactures equipment in Scotland, Canada, the United States and Italy, with sales agents and technical support services worldwide. ELLEN LAMPERT-GRÉAUX

Strasberg [Strassberg], Lee [Israel] (b. Budzanow, Galicia, Poland, 17 Nov. 1901; d. New York, 17 Feb. 1982) Actor, director and teacher. The son of an emigrant from the old Austrian empire, he lived in New York's Lower East Side until the early 1920s. He read voraciously and played in amateur productions, then in 1923 saw STANISLAVSKY's MOSCOW ART THEATRE ensemble as well as BARRYMORE's Hamlet and DUSE's last performances. He auditioned for the American Laboratory Theatre (1923–9) run by RICHARD BOLESLAVSKY, a student and disciple of Stanislavsky who had remained behind in America. What he learned underpinned all his subsequent working life.

Strasberg acted with the THEATER GUILD before joining HAROLD CLURMAN in founding the GROUP THEATER. There he co-directed its first play, *The House of Connelly* (1931) by PAUL GREEN, with CHERYL CRAW-FORD; other productions include MAXWELL ANDER-SON's *Night over Taos* (1932) and Green's *Johnny Johnson* (1936). From 1937 to 1949 he directed plays and films in New York and achieved great personal fulfilment as a teacher. In 1949 he joined the ACTORS' STUDIO which ELIA KAZAN, ROBERT LEWIS and Crawford had founded two years before. He became director in 1950 and was identified with the highly naturalistic school of METHOD acting, based on Stanislavsky's 'system', which exerted such a strong influence on post-Second World War American theatre and film through pupils such as MARLON BRANDO, Marilyn Monroe and Paul Newman. 'Everything is our business,' he claimed, including intimate details of actors' private lives which could be used to strengthen performance. He placed strong emphasis on individual work with actors but stressed, at the same time, the importance in 'true' theatre of ENSEMBLE work.

Thorough, energetic, dedicated, his training sessions were recorded and are available in edited form in *Strasberg at the Actors' Studio*. His writing on the Method, *A Dream of Passion*, was published in 1988. He can be seen on film in *The Godfather II* (1974). TERRY HODGSON

C. Adams, *Lee Strasberg: The Imperfect Genius of the Actors' Studio* (1980)

Robert H. Hethmon, *Strasberg at the Actors' Studio* (1966)

Stratford East *see* THEATRE ROYAL, STRATFORD EAST; THEATRE WORKSHOP

Stratford Festival (Ontario) One of the world's major theatre organizations, it began in 1953 in the small Ontario town of Stratford. Founder Tom Patterson and his colleagues raised enough money to mount artistic director TYRONE GUTHRIE's first season of two plays – *Richard III* and *All's Well That Ends Well* – in a tent seating 1,477; in 1990 the festival presented 15 productions in 572 performances. The 1957 permanent Festival Theater seats 2,276 in a 220-degree auditorium; the thrust stage, designed by Guthrie and TANYA MOISEIWITSCH, recreates the Elizabethan open stage. This theatre is complemented by the more conventional proscenium Avon Theatre (1,107 seats) and the experimental Tom Patterson Theatre (493 seats). Artistic directors include Guthrie (1953–5), MICHAEL LANGHAM (1956–67), JEAN GASCON (1968–74), ROBIN PHILLIPS (1975–80), JOHN HIRSCH (1981–5), JOHN NEVILLE (1986–9), David William (1990–3) and Richard Monette (from 1994). While emphasis in early years was placed on presenting the plays of Shakespeare and his contemporaries, the repertoire has in recent years

been expanded to include not only SHAW, IBSEN and BRECHT, for example, but GILBERT and SULLIVAN operettas, and American musicals. Stratford Festival productions have traditionally been characterized by minimal scenery and sets, lavish and meticulously executed costumes, and fluidity and swiftness of movement, especially in group scenes. EUGENE BENSON

John Pettigrew and Jamie Portman, *Stratford: The First Thirty Years* (1985)

J. Alan B. Somerset, *The Stratford Festival Story* (1991)

Stratford-upon-Avon Birthplace of William Shakespeare. This Warwickshire market town has become the international centre for Shakespeare studies as well as the headquarters of the ROYAL SHAKESPEARE COMPANY (RSC). It is also a major tourist attraction. Stratford's famous Royal Shakespeare Theatre, originally named the SHAKESPEARE MEMORIAL THEATRE, produces chiefly the works of Shakespeare; the adjacent Swan Theatre presents a range of classical and contemporary work, and the nearby The Other Place – the third Stratford base for the RSC – has a repertoire of more experimental work. Stratford also boasts a library, a conference centre and the Shakespeare Institute, all dedicated to the celebrated dramatist. During the summer a conference attracts Shakespeare scholars from all over the world to discuss his work, and the RSC holds its annual summer school. Also in his honour are the annual birthday celebrations, held on the weekend nearest to 23 April. ADRIANA HUNTER

See also SHAKESPEARE FESTIVALS.

Straus, Oscar [Nathan] (b. Vienna, 6 March 1870; d. Bad Ischl, Austria, 11 Jan. 1954) Composer. Straus spread his composing and conducting widely, and composed a variety of stage pieces before his breakthrough into mainstream operetta with *Ein Walzertraum* (1907). His *Der tapfere Soldat* (1908), taken from SHAW's *Arms and the Man*, solidified his international fame when, as *The Chocolate Soldier*, it proved hugely popular in America and Britain, introducing the popular waltz song 'My Hero' and becoming the basis of a Hollywood film. In spite of a number of successes on central European stages, no further enduring pieces followed until Straus left Austria and began to follow the international avenues opened up by his first successes. Following the hit of the exciting *Der letzte Walzer* (1920) in Berlin, he provided the music for SACHA GUITRY's *Mariette* (1928) in Paris, scored a number of Hollywood films, and had stage successes with *Eine Frau, die weiss was sie will* (1932) produced in Berlin and in London as *Mother of Pearl*, and in Zurich with *Drei Walzer* (1935), a semi-pasticcio romance which became a part of the standard repertoire in France. His score for the film *La Ronde* gave him a last success at the age of 80.   KURT GÄNZL

B. Grün, *Prince of Vienna* (1955)
F. Mailer, *Weltburger der Musik* (1985)

Strauss, Botho (b. Naumburg, Saale, Germany, 2 Dec. 1944) Playwright, critic and DRAMATURG. First known to the German public through his essays and reviews in the magazine *Theater Heute* (Theatre Today), he worked as dramaturg with PETER STEIN at the influential SCHAUBÜHNE AM HALLESCHEN UFER in Berlin during the 1970s and adapted GORKY, IBSEN and Kleist for him. Strauss's plays are a development of the new subjectivity already evident in HANDKE. Using images of the real world and sometimes mythology, Strauss reconstructs and questions the meaningless attitudes and behaviour of the bourgeoisie. His bleak perception of the world disguises a search for harmony in life and art. His plays include *Die Hypochonder* (*The Hypochondriacs*, 1972), *Trilogie des Wiedersehens* (*The Reunion Trilogy* or *Three Acts of Recognition*, 1976), *Gross und Klein* (*Great and Small*, 1978), *Kalldewey Farce* (1982), *Der Park* (*The Park*, 1984, a fantastic reworking of *A Midsummer Night's Dream*), *Die Fremden Führen* (*The Tourist Guide*, 1985), *Die Zeit und das Zimmer* (*Time and the Room*, 1988), *Schlusschor* (*Final Chorus*, 1991), *Das Gleichgewicht* (*Balance*, 1993) and *Jeffers Akt I und II* (1998).
JUDY MEEWEZEN

Denis Calandra, *New German Dramatists* (1983)

Stravinsky, Igor [Fyodorovich] (b. Oranienbaum [later Lomonosov], Russia, 5 June 1892; d. New York, 6 April 1971) Composer. He achieved fame with a range of major works for DIAGHILEV, including *The Firebird* (1910), *Petrushka* (1911) and the landmark *The Rite of Spring* (1913), a turning point in European music with its liberated rhythms. He worked with all the major figures at the Ballets Russes, which was a major influence on the future of the theatre and other arts. Cut off from Russia by the war, he lived in Switzerland and France, and then emigrated to America where he collaborated with BALANCHINE (e.g. *Orpheus*, 1948, designed by NOGUCHI). Other works for the theatre include *The Nightingale* (1918), staged by MEYERHOLD in Petrograd; an opera oratorio, *Oedipus Rex* (1927); and an opera, *The Rake's Progress* (1951), with libretto by W. H. AUDEN.   NICK WORRALL

Victor Borovsky and Alexandre Schouvaloff, *Stravinsky on Stage* (1982)
Minna Lederman, ed., *Stravinsky in the Theatre* (1949)

Streep, Meryl   *see* ACTORS' STUDIO

street theatre A term used loosely to denote performance outdoors but not in any defined venue. Looking back to the European tradition of COMMEDIA DELL'ARTE and strolling players, modern street theatre is popular in aim and goes to its audience rather than the other way round. Its different manifestations depend on time and place; it can range from PROMENADE theatre through a town or village to AGITPROP outside a factory or on a demonstration, linked up with a social or political campaign. It took on a particular meaning in the 1960s and 1970s with the rise of ALTERNATIVE THEATRE and was often related to COMMUNITY THEATRE or attempts to revive CARNIVAL aspects of playmaking. Examples can be found in the work of groups such as the SAN FRANCISCO MIME TROUPE, BREAD AND PUPPET THEATER, ODIN TEATRET, WELFARE STATE INTERNATIONAL, RED LADDER or BLUE BLOUSE. The anti-globalization and environmental campaigns of the 1990s often used forms of street theatre in their protests.   COLIN CHAMBERS
See also GUERRILLA THEATRE; POLITICAL THEATRE.

Jan Cohen-Cruz, ed, *Radical Street Performance: An International Anthology* (1998)
Henry Lesnick, ed, *Guerilla Street Theatre* (1973)
Bim Mason, *Street Theatre and Other Outdoor Performance* (1992)

Strehler, Giorgio (b. Barcola, Trieste, Italy, 14 August 1921; d. Lugano, Switzerland, 25 Dec. 1997) Director. Co-founder (with Paolo Grassi) of Milan's PICCOLO TEATRO in 1947, Strehler was one of the most influential and innovative directors in postwar Europe. Renowned in Italy, his reputation spread further in the 1980s during his tenure as director of the Théâtre de l'Europe at the ODÉON in Paris, and through international touring. Detailed theatricality and stunning scenography can be seen in his long collaboration with designer EZIO FRIGERIO. Strehler developed a signature style of lyric realism in his productions of playwrights ranging from Goldoni and BRECHT to Shakespeare. Two productions of *The Tempest*, one in 1948, the other in 1978, frame Strehler's long career as benchmarks of twentieth-century theatre.   ELLEN LAMPERT-GRÉAUX

David Hirst, *Giorgio Strehler* (1993)

Streisand, Barbra [Barbara Joan] (b. Brooklyn, New York, 24 April 1942) Actress, singer and director, noted for playing independent women. Streisand made her Broadway debut in *I Can Get It for You Wholesale* (1962), where she stopped the show nightly with her second-act solo, 'Miss Marmelstein'. In *Funny Girl* (1964) she played FANNY BRICE, later recreating the role in the film version (1968) and winning an Academy award. Her two BROADWAY roles led to record albums, television musical specials, and an illustrious film career (e.g. *Hello, Dolly!*, 1969; *The Way We Were*, 1973; *Nuts*, 1987).   DAVID STAINES

Strindberg, [Johan] August   (b. Stockholm, 22 Jan. 1849; d. Stockholm, 14 May 1912) Playwright. He had early ambitions to become an actor and wrote his first plays when he was 20, but his breakthrough came ten years later with a novel, and throughout his life he was to mix drama and prose. He was a prolific writer, and his *œuvre* includes more than 60 plays, well over half of which were written between 1898 and 1909. After spells on the continent, Strindberg had returned to Sweden in 1896. In his native country, however, he was to remain a controversial figure well beyond his death; and theatre directors from abroad have been instrumental in opening up the possibilities of some of his more innovatory plays.

After an abortive attempt to found a Scandinavian experimental theatre in the late 1880s, he established his Intimate Theatre in Stockholm in 1907 and was at last able to influence the total effect of dramatic text and scenic form, elements which to him had increasingly come to constitute an indivisible whole. Early in his *Memoranda* to the members of the Theatre, he sketches his career as a playwright in terms that highlight the extent to which his role as a leading innovator was grounded in a sustained interest in theatre and staging practices. He outlines a dramatic *œuvre* that began as a rebellion against the Swedish theatre conventions of the 1870s and 1880s, and that was subsequently more closely associated with the radical new stages in France and Germany – ANDRÉ ANTOINE's Théâtre Libre in Paris, OTTO BRAHM's Freie Bühne and MAX REINHARDT's Kleines Theater and Kammerspiel-Haus in Berlin – than with theatres in his native Sweden.

Strindberg's first major play, *Mäster Olof* (1872 – all dates are date of writing), exploits the prestigious historical genre only to subvert it. Shunning the habitual blank verse and the solo numbers for star actors, Strindberg used prose and, in his own words, 'composed polyphonically, a symphony, in which all the voices were interwoven (major and minor characters were treated equally), and in which no one accompanied the soloist'. The central character, one of the founding fathers of the Lutheran Reformation in Sweden, is a rebel; and, inspired by Shakespeare's *Julius Caesar*, Strindberg presented this rebel in private as well as in public, replacing the focus on ideas customary in historical drama with a modern, psychological realism.

Strindberg's interest in dramatic form was boosted by the Modern Breakthrough, a period in Scandinavian literature characterized by the prominence of science and positivism in place of the traditional Christian faith, and drawing much of its initial inspiration from the Danish critic Georg Brandes, who emphasized that literature ought to deal with contemporary issues such as class, marriage and sexuality. In Norway, IBSEN had already demonstrated the effectiveness of realist drama in this context; subsequently, Strindberg was also influenced by French naturalism, notably the work of EMILE ZOLA. His first naturalistic drama, *Fadren* (*The Father*, 1887), uses a single setting, a 24-hour timespan, and a plot revolving around a single conflict – a confrontation between husband and wife over their daughter that soon assumes archetypal proportions. The economy of the dramatic form highlights the psychological dimensions of the conflict: having developed an interest in suggestion and hypnotism, Strindberg, who described the warfare between Laura and the Captain in terms of a 'battle of brains', viewed the psychological confrontation as the basis of a modern version of tragedy. The psychological depths, along with a confrontation developed in terms of class as well as gender and sex, are further explored in *Fröken Julie* (*Miss Julie*, 1888). With its exceptional concentration – the plot time nearly coincides with the performance time of about 90 minutes – and its unflinching investigation into the combination of attraction, repulsion and dependence that ties the daughter of a count to her father's servant, the work is probably Strindberg's naturalistic masterpiece. The 'Author's Preface', with its comments on the play's 'characterless characters', confirms the innovatory impact of Strindberg's interest in psychology and points ahead to his post-Inferno drama: 'My souls (or characters) are agglomerations of past and present cultures, scraps from books and newspapers, fragments of humanity, torn shreds of once-fine clothing that has become rags, in just the way that a human soul is patched together.' It is the precision with which these fragmented aspects are presented and the relentlessness with which they are made to engage with each other that make *Miss Julie* at once momentous and convincing. Strindberg further honed his naturalistic style in a number of one-act plays, including *Den Starkare* (*The Stronger*, 1888–9), *Paria* (Pariah, 1889), and *Mode Skärlek* (*Motherly Love*, 1892).

Strindberg's Inferno crisis, in 1894–6, marks a decisive shift in his writing. The crisis, which takes its name from his prose text *Inferno* (1897), was in fact a succession of psychotic states during which Strindberg grappled with the condition of humankind in a metaphysical context. A major source of inspiration was the work of the Swedish scientist and religious thinker, Emanuel Swedenborg (1688–1772), whose notions of correspondences and transformations in particular also appealed to Strindberg the dramatist.

Till Damascus (*To Damascus, I*, 1898) has often been referred to as an early example of EXPRESSIONISM. The Unknown's struggle with the Invisible One, his admission of guilt and his atonement are structured in the form of a pilgrimage, the scenes recalling the stations of certain types of medieval drama and their arrangement, with the second half of the play mirroring the first, illustrating a concept of repetition that is of a piece with the foregrounding of penance in the play. Crucial to the impact of the structure is the innovative handling of the central character; in the words of the leading critic Egil Törnqvist, 'Presumably for the first time in the history of drama we are confronted with a play in which an inner reality is *consistently* dramatized, or better: in which the border between outer and inner reality is blotted out.' The perspective of the Unknown here equals that of the spectator, thus introducing a subjectivity that also includes the other characters, who can be perceived as projections of the Unknown's mind. Having consistently focused on the psychological dimensions, Strindberg here makes identity a central issue, with the Unknown emerging not as an individual character but as a representative of humankind.

Strindberg's dramatic output during the subsequent decade was characterized by an unparalleled breadth. Eight history plays belong to this period. They can be seen as part of a calculated comeback to the Swedish stage, and combine an impressive grasp of the relevant periods with a formal precision and elegance and a continuing preoccupation with psychology. Thus the central character in *Gustav Vasa* (1899) is portrayed as a powerful and decisive ruler who nevertheless wavers at crucial moments; and the king's concluding crisis and new insight echo the experiences of the Unknown in *To Damascus, I*. *Kristina* (*Queen Christina*, 1901) brilliantly exploits the theatricality of the central character and her court, the constant play-acting illuminating the queen's uncertainty in her official role. Strindberg's history plays, which also include works like *Erik XIV* (1899) and *Gustav III* (1902), remain among his best-loved works for the theatre in his native country.

Dödsadansen (*The Dance of Death*, 1900) illustrates a different kind of post-Inferno drama. Of the two parts of the play, the first is the most powerful and original. The focus on a marital conflict has sometimes led to the work being perceived as a new version of *The Father*, albeit with the marriage developed into a Swedenborgian hell where husband and wife continue the mutual torture *ad infinitum*. It is clear, however, that the precision of *The Dance of Death* – the setting in a tower on an island in the sea, the collection of furniture and mementoes in the single room, the superbly economical dialogue with its glimpses of black humour – gradually leads into an unsettling subjectivity. The mounting symbolic significance of the setting combines with the prominence of repetition and the Captain's uncanny oscillation between sickness and health to transport us into a hallucinatory world suggesting the proximity of death. It is the metaphysical hope generated by the Captain's insight into death that imbues the ending of the play with a more positive note.

Kronbruden (*The Virgin Bride*, 1901) is another example of the range of Strindberg's post-Inferno drama. Drawing on Swedish national romanticism, with its interest in folklore in general and in the province of Dalarna in particular, *The Virgin Bride* relies on some highly complex settings, a sometimes abrupt and frequently formulaic dialogue, traditional music, and a cast list that includes supernatural figures such as a water-sprite and a dead child. In a plot that revolves around the plight of a young bride who has hidden the fact that she has had a baby so as to remain entitled to wear the parish wedding crown, the supernatural figures help externalize the central character's mental path from deceit to truth-telling and eventual religious conviction. The role of suffering, which is relatively marginal in history plays like *Gustav Vasa* and *Queen Christina*, is restored to a central ethical function in both *The Dance of Death* and *The Virgin Bride*.

In *Ett drömspel* (*A Dream Play*, 1901), probably Strindberg's most original work for the stage, the text and the scenic form enter into a new relationship. Here the visual elements assume a prominence unparalleled in his previous work as images from the world of dreams are unleashed on to the stage. This exploration of the hidden world of the mind – which is virtually contemporary with Freud's *The Interpretation of Dreams* – has a number of characteristics. Among them are the sharp, detailed settings such as the castle behind a forest of gigantic, brilliantly coloured hollyhocks; Foulstrand, with its exercising machines resembling instruments of torture and its quarantine building with ovens and furnace rooms; and Fingal's Cave, with its majestic geological formations and green waves. The transformations constitute another characteristic: here a tree turns into a coat and hat stand, an office notice-board into a hymnboard in a church, and a flower-bud on the roof of the castle into a huge chrysanthemum. In this play, where the conventional notions of time and space have been suspended, the speed of such changes is essential to the overall effect; as has frequently been pointed out, Strindberg's technique in *A Dream Play* is more akin to that of film than that of drama.

Suffering is central to the plot of this play, in which the Daughter of the god Indra descends to earth to explore the condition of humankind. The structure, which to some extent echoes the mirror arrangement used in *To Damascus, I*, reinforces the curve of the Daughter's journey, with the marital scene between her and the Advocate and Foulstrand-Fairhaven forming the nadir. Although she comes to the conclusion that humankind 'is to be pitied', the overall perspective is less pessimistic than in most of Strindberg's post-Inferno drama as a tone of acceptance and even reconciliation pervades *A Dream Play*.

Founding the Intimate Theatre gave a new impetus to Strindberg's playwriting. 'No predetermined form is to limit the author,' he wrote, 'because the motif determines the form. Consequently: freedom in treatment, which is limited only by the unity of the concept and the feeling for style.' During the theatre's three-year life-span 24 of Strindberg's plays were performed, including his chamber plays, which were written specifically for it. Although *A Dream Play* was never performed at the Intimate Theatre, Strindberg continued to develop his ideas for the staging of the play. These included the use of his radical 'drapery stage', which dispensed with virtually all the props, relied on a few distinctive symbols, and indicated settings and transitions by means of lighting. Strindberg's ideals with regard to production were moving in the direction of dematerialization, and the growing emphasis on simplicity and beauty has been linked to the influence of GORDON CRAIG.

The five chamber plays constitute Strindberg's last major works for the theatre. *Svarta handksen* (*The Black Glove*) was written in 1909, whereas the other four were written in 1907; in plays like *Oväder* (*The Storm*), *Brända tomten* (*After the Fire*), *Spöksonaten* (*The Ghost Sonata*) and *Pelikanen* (*The Pelican*) the sense of disillusion is total, yet these works are imbued with a creative energy and theatrical inventiveness that can render them uniquely powerful on the stage. Strindberg referred to the chamber play as 'the concept of chamber music transferred to drama'; and it is characteristic of these plays that the plot has been made subordinate to themes and motifs which in turn have been formulated in striking theatrical terms. Thus, in *The Ghost Sonata*, given a musical structure based on the sonata form and probably the best known of these plays, the fashionable house becomes the central symbol, the early account of a collapsing house anticipating an irrevocable movement inwards and a process of unmasking that reveal a once beautiful woman turned into a mummy; a grotesque ghost supper culminating in a suicide; and a lady who appears to epitomize youth and perfection but is found to be sick and dying. In this play, inspired not merely by Swedenborg's ideas but also by Buddhism, only death can liberate the human being from a suffering that is all-pervasive.

As the notable critic and translator Inga-Stina Ewbank has pointed out, Strindberg's corpus, like that of Shakespeare, 'suggests the ability to grow and change to have been fundamental to his talent'. And she continues: 'The basic consistency lies in a faithfulness to his own vision, however that vision might change; the consequent inconsistency lies in a refusal ever to cling to a form or a mode of expression for its own sake, however successful it might have proved.' The exceptional artistic insight, sensibility, and curiosity informing this growth have been fundamental to Strindberg's position as a central figure in twentieth-century European drama.   HELENA FORSÅS-SCOTT

Harry G. Carlson, *Out of Inferno: Strindberg's Reawakening as an Artist* (1996)

Michael Robinson, *Strindberg and Autobiography: Writing and Reading a Life* (1986)

Evert Sprinchorn, *Strindberg as Dramatist* (1982)

Birgitta Steene, ed., *Strindberg and History* (1992)

Göran Stockenström, ed., *Strindberg's Dramaturgy* (1988)

Egil Törnqvist, *Strindbergian Drama: Themes and Structure* (1982)

striptease   *see* BURLESQUE; EROTICISM IN THE THEATRE

Stritch, Elaine (b. Detroit, Mich., 2 Feb. 1926) Singer and actress. Stritch made her Broadway debut in *Loco* (1946), was a hit in *Pal Joey* (1952) singing 'Zip', and then went on to starring roles in such musicals as *Goldilocks* (1959), *Sail Away* (1961) and *Company* (1970) and in such plays as *Bus Stop* (1955), *Who's Afraid of Virginia Woolf?* (1962) and *Private Lives* (1968). Her husky, gritty voice was the perfect complement to the acerbic and sardonic characters she frequently portrayed, and she became well known in both America and Britain. Her stage career has been complemented by several television series and films.   DAVID STAINES

Strouse, Charles [Louis] (b. New York, 7 June 1928) Composer. After attending the Eastman School of Music, he continued his studies by working with Nadia Boulanger and Aaron Copland, among others. He served as a rehearsal pianist, and wrote for resort and OFF-BROADWAY shows, before succeeding on Broadway with *Bye Bye Birdie* (1960). His only other subsequent successes have been *Applause* (1970) and *Annie* (1977). He has a gift for melody and a musically imaginative approach to show music, but so many of his shows have been failures that much of his music has been denied the hearing it deserves.

GERALD BORDMAN

Stuart, Aimée [Constance] (b. Glasgow, 1890?; d. Brighton, Sussex, 17 Apr. 1981) Playwright. Her first West End successes, *Clara Gibbing* (1928), *Her Shop* (1929) and *Nine Till Six* (1930), were written in collaboration with her husband Philip. She was criticized for the 'feminine' appeal of her plays, which often focused on the domestic and social life of women of all classes. However, audiences flocked to see her work and many of her plays were either filmed or televised during the 1950s. MAGGIE GALE

Stuart, [Barrett] Leslie [Thomas Augustine] (aka Lester Thomas) (b. Southport, 15 March 1864; d. Richmond, Surrey, 27 March 1928) Songwriter. He began his career as a church organist and as a writer of popular songs (e.g. 'Lily of Laguna'). His earliest theatrical writing was done for the MANCHESTER theatre and, although he interpolated individual numbers into many West End musicals in the 1890s, it was not until 1899 that he completed his first full musical comedy score, *Florodora*, in collaboration with London's most fashionable librettist, Owen Hall. *Florodora*, with its famous double sextet, 'Tell Me Pretty Maiden', was a worldwide success and earned its composer an international theatre reputation. Although none of his later works achieved the same fame, *The Silver Slipper* (1901), *The School Girl* (1903), *The Belle of Mayfair* (1906), *Havana* (1908) and *Peggy* (1911) all had substantial runs in London and some success abroad. In his later years, when his gambling debts outweighed his royalties from the still lively *Florodora*, he appeared in VARIETY performing his most famous songs at the piano. KURT GÄNZL

student theatre

In Britain

If there has never been a defined student theatre 'movement' in Britain, this is largely because the development of theatre originated and performed by students, dating back to the Renaissance, has taken place in a variety of different contexts, and often with widely differing objectives. This merely reflects the often pragmatic development of higher education itself. By the beginning of the twentieth century the major undergraduate dramatic societies such as the ADC (Amateur Dramatic Society, 1855) in CAMBRIDGE, and OUDS

(OXFORD University Dramatic Society, 1885) were already a force which enabled rich, upper-class, public-school educated undergraduates to become professional actors. Performers of the calibre of FRANK BENSON, NIGEL PLAYFAIR and FELIX AYLMER came along this route, and by the time that GEORGE DEVINE, the future founder of the progressive ENGLISH STAGE COMPANY, joined OUDS in 1930, the society had become well established as a feeder to the WEST END. The functions had always been social as well as artistic (the Prince of Wales, later King Edward VII, had been president of the ADC), and corresponded exactly to the rather elitist, middle-class ethos of both acting and drama in Britain at that time. But during the first half of the century a quiet revolution had been in progress; the foundation of new civic universities – Birmingham (1899), Liverpool (1903) and Leeds (1904), to name three – had allowed in some cases the establishment of English departments, the degrees of which incorporated the study of drama and of Shakespeare in particular, albeit in a literary rather than performance context. This all gave an added impetus to the establishment of many AMATEUR drama societies which gave students the opportunity to practise the arts of acting, directing and, in several cases, playwriting. The early societies were also beginning to take risks in the performance of work that the commercial stage would find difficult to sell to the public. For example, in 1925 Birmingham University played a version of Pushkin's *Boris Godunov*, while the first production with which Devine was involved at Oxford was FLECKER's elaborate *Hassan*, with FRITH BANBURY and TERENCE RATTIGAN in the cast, and PEGGY ASHCROFT as a guest performer. By the time the Second World War broke out, student drama societies were well established all over the country, but with few common purposes or common objectives.

The postwar period saw two important developments: the expansion of post-school education, and the foundation of the ARTS COUNCIL OF GREAT BRITAIN, with its spreading of resources to the regions, and the consequent rash of new theatres with studio auditoriums attached, playing work that was often new and highly subsidized, on the continental model. This gave a new force to student theatre; not only was British new dramatic writing reflecting the postwar levelling of society, but the number of state-aided students now at university and college increased tenfold. In the 1960s and early 1970s, some universities built their own theatres (e.g. Northcott Theatre, Exeter), which were used both departmentally and by students, and became part of a network of arts centres that gave life to the burgeoning independent touring groups. The increasingly important student unions subsidized theatre societies, through which many exceptional students were able to gain experience and entry to the profession, and some campuses even supported semi-resident professional groups. Already in the 1950s university groups were appearing on the FRINGE of the EDINBURGH FESTIVAL with premières of important plays, often from abroad, such as UGO BETTI's *Corruption in the Palace of Justice* (Oxford Theatre Group, 1953). When in 1956 the *Sunday Times* first launched what was to become the National Student Drama Festival, the winner of the trophy was Regent Street Polytechnic's production of THORNTON WILDER's *Our Town*, directed by Timothy West. In 1957 Bristol University's production of HAROLD PINTER's *The Room* launched the playwright, and in 1961 Leeds' production of ARDEN's *Serjeant Musgrave's Dance* did much to redress what had been largely disliked by critics at its 1959 première. Under the direction of Kenneth Pearson of the *Sunday Times*, and latterly of Clive Wolfe, this festival, held annually in different campuses, became the only continuing national forum for the best of student drama, in spite of occasional opposition (the *Observer* funded a couple of student theatre festivals in Oxford in the 1970s), and its somewhat chequered history mirrors the changing concerns of students. Having given an initial boost to actors, actresses and directors – such as Elizabeth Shepherd, Henry Woolf, WOLE SOYINKA, TERRY HANDS, Peter James, Michael York, Jane Howell – the festival was virtually taken over by the student power rebellion of the 1960s, which saw it as a necessary focus for some radical theatre experiment.

At this period also, drama societies were making discoveries of major writers unrepresented much elsewhere in the country, and certainly not in the West End – SAMUEL BECKETT (Keele University, Dryden Society, Cambridge), MICHEL DE GHELDERODE (Keele University, Leicester Polytechnic), IONESCO (Oxford), CAMUS (Bradford University) – as well as discovering new British writers such as SNOO WILSON, KEVIN LAFFAN and ANN JELLICOE. Student drama was also producing its own set of concerns, such as the Vietnam War, with performances of MEGAN TERRY's *Viet Rock*, as well as pioneering experiments in ENSEMBLE work and PARTICIPATORY THEATRE on the model of the American LIVING THEATER of Beck and Malina, which had visited Britain. Peter Sykes's Keele University Drama Group produced a series of controversial, physically based theatre pieces that paralleled the discovery of the work of the Polish director JERZY GROTOWSKI – *Paradise Lost* (1971), *Fallacy* (1972) and *Blindfold* (1973). Another strand of theatre pioneered by students – in this case from Rolle Teacher Training College, Exmouth – was improvisationally based performance, little practised

professionally in Britain, and in 1973 Keele University performance group went so far as to present JOHN CAGE's *Theatre Piece*, a rare incursion into the cross-currents of experimental music. (They also performed SATIE's hilarious play, *Le Piège de Meduse*, 'Medusa's trap'). At the same period at Bradford Art College, Albert Hunt was producing a series of performance pieces (emphatically not plays) which for a short while revolutionized the ways in which we looked at our past history. The titles alone give the clues to the approach – *John Ford's Cuban Missile Crisis* (1971), *Looking Forward to 1942* (1970), *James Harold Wilson Sinks the Bismarck* (1972). During the 1970s it was these experiments in theatre practice, unavailable in the professional theatre with the notable exception of PETER BROOK's anti-Vietnam piece, *US*, which gave student theatre its peculiar urgency and immediacy. Here was theatre contributing to a shift in consciousness not being attempted elsewhere on anything like the same scale or with the same resources.

It was at this period that student drama in Britain most closely approached student drama concerns in other European countries – Poland in particular. It had been clear for some time that in eastern Europe, and to some extent in West Germany and Spain, student drama had the function of a young national conscience, in that the political and aesthetic concerns expressed were a reminder of alternatives, of possibilities of change. Above all there was a concern with theatre as a visual and physical event, not simply a literary one, allied with MARTIN ESSLIN's memorable definition of theatre as 'a place where society speaks to itself', which led to some interesting new developments in the late 1970s. Whereas the professional DRAMA SCHOOLS had always seen themselves as training actors to enter an already defined profession, and UNIVERSITY DRAMA DEPARTMENTS had concentrated in the main on theoretical and literary concerns, the new polytechnics and colleges of higher education began to offer innovative degree courses in performing/performance/creative arts, which were designed to examine theatre concerns in a practical sense – producing a new generation of actors, directors, administrators, enablers, who would question and change the position and function of drama in society, and would set up new organizations and new performance structures. Innovative performance material, writers and devisors emerged from such places as Middlesex and Leicester Polytechnics, Crewe and Alsager Colleges, Dartington College of Arts, to be followed by the formation of fringe companies in the regions designed to open up access to drama as a leisure activity not simply to the privileged, but for all the many layers of the by now multicultural society. Student drama now includes a range of material that parallels the cross-over developments evident throughout the country's arts activities.

NOEL WITTS

In the United States

Prior to the twentieth century, theatre had no officially sanctioned place in the university system. Extra-curricular theatricals were tolerated, although officially frowned upon by the administration. Harvard University's Hasty Pudding Club, a literary society, produced its first transvestite musical satire in 1844, a tradition that continues to this day. Other prominent universities had amateur theatrical societies, including Brown University's Thalian Dramatic Association (1866), the University of Pennsylvania's Mask and Wig Club (1892) and Princeton's Triangle Club (1893). The musical BURLESQUE and VAUDEVILLE styles that dominated the collegiate theatre in the nineteenth century remained entirely divorced from the academic study of such legitimate topics as Shakespeare and the classic tragedies, which were the domain of English and Classics departments. At the turn of the century courses devoted to theatre and drama began to filter into the formal curriculum, albeit initially disguised as literature, rhetoric and elocution. In 1902 Columbia University took the pioneering step of appointing BRANDER MATTHEWS as the nation's first professor of dramatic literature, and in the following year GEORGE PIERCE BAKER offered his first playwriting course, 'English 46: The Forms of the Drama', at Radcliffe College, followed by 'English 47' at Harvard. Baker realized the crucial importance of having a student theatre as a complement to academic study, and by 1912 he had established the famous 47 Workshop for this purpose. No longer merely high-spirited antics, student theatre developed the potential to become an integral part of a liberal education, and the chasm that had existed between academic study and practical theatre began to narrow. The complementary curricular and extra-curricular theatre structure that resulted serves as the ideal for theatre study in the university system.

Practical theatre instruction also made its official debut in a university setting in the first decade of the century. In 1906 the University of Wisconsin offered the first college acting classes. After 1911 courses in production and directing began to appear at several other universities. America's first drama department was created soon thereafter when, in 1914, the Carnegie Institute of Technology in Pittsburgh established a four-year programme leading to a baccalaureate degree in theatre, under the chairmanship of Thomas Wood

Stevens. It would be a full decade later, however, before the next major university followed Carnegie Tech's lead. In 1925, Yale successfully wooed George Pierce Baker away from Harvard, which had refused to provide him with a permanent theatre for his workshop. Under Baker's leadership, Yale established its Department of Drama. Yale's endorsement allowed university theatre to achieve curricular legitimacy, and within the next four years large-scale theatres were built on many college campuses for student use, including the Yale University Theater, the GOODMAN MEMORIAL THEATER, the PASADENA PLAYHOUSE and the CLEVELAND PLAYHOUSE. In the 1920s and 1930s, along with the amateur LITTLE THEATRE movement, student theatres such as the Carolina Playmakers, established in 1919 by FREDERICK KOCH, and Vassar College's Experimental Theater, founded in 1925 by HALLIE FLANAGAN, were an important cultural force in America, as virtually no professional theatre existed outside New York City.

The 1930s saw an explosion of student theatre curricula and student dramatic activity. The number of universities offering theatre courses soared, from 100 in 1930 to 800 five years later. Networks began to unify the programmes and numerous organizations arose. In a quest to raise the standards of student theatre, Baker helped to found the National Theater Conference in 1932. Four years later, the American Educational Theater Association was founded. AETA began publication of the *Educational Theater Journal* in 1949 (later retitled *Theater Journal*) and the *Educational Theater News* in 1968. When the AETA went bankrupt in 1986, the new Association for Theater in Higher Education took up its work; it continues to the present. These networks lent further legitimacy to the theatre programmes in the academic world. New play FESTIVALS and tournaments also began to grow rapidly in the 1930s, leading to improved quality in the extra-curricular student theatres. The play festival concept reached a zenith in 1969, with the first annual American College Theater Festival, co-produced by AETA and the AMERICAN NATIONAL THEATER AND ACADEMY. This festival, whose final competition took place in the nation's capital, attracted nearly 200 entries from 44 states.

In the 1940s a major development in the university theatre system occurred. Seeking to enhance the quality of actor training, theatre departments established contacts between students and professional theatre practitioners. The Catholic University in Washington DC invited professional actors to act alongside students in 1941, and Syracuse University established an artists-in-residency programme in 1944. Starting in the 1950s, many theatre programmes became vocationally oriented, and the rise in the number of RESIDENT THEATRES in the 1960s and 1970s led to increased professionalization. Alliances between colleges and resident theatres proliferated tremendously, with representation and promotion from the University/Resident Theatre Association, founded in 1969. As a result, today professional and student theatres often exist side by side, providing students with the opportunity to participate as interns and extras on the resident theatre's main stage while also performing and directing their own work.

The amount of student theatre within colleges is astounding, with the majority of colleges and universities having not one but many student groups. For instance, theatre groups at the University of Pennsylvania include the Penn Players, the African American Arts Alliance, a Jewish theatre, a children's theatre and an experimental theatre (which sponsors a national Alternative Theatre Festival). Likewise, Harvard University's decentralized, extra-curricular Harvard–Radcliffe Dramatic Club produces over 20 plays a semester, ranging from established classics to new plays and experimental works, and staging them in spaces ranging from the main-stage and black box theatre (the most standard theatre for experimental student work, because it offers the ultimate flexibility, accommodating itself to any manner of stage set-up) to temporary theatres set up in common rooms, basements and libraries.

Debates over the ideal relationship between extra-curricular theatre programmes and curricular theatre study continue. As theatre department curricula become increasingly vocational, however, the extra-curricular student theatres are still the province of both the committed theatre student and the liberal arts student. SARAH STEVENSON

B. Beckman, 'The University Accepts the Theatre: 1800–1925', in *The American Theatre: A Sum of its Parts* (1971)
J. H. Butler, 'The University Theatre Begins to Come of Age: 1925–1969', in *The American Theatre: A Sum of its Parts* (1971)
'Choices: Liberal Arts Education or Professional Theatre Training? It's Your Call', *Dramatics*, Dec. 1997

Sturua, Robert (b. Tbilisi, Georgia, 31 July 1938) Director. He was appointed artistic director of the Rustaveli Theatre, Tbilisi, in 1978. His productions of BRECHT's *The Caucasian Chalk Circle* and Shakespeare's *Richard III* were first seen in Britain in 1979. He staged a powerful *King Lear* in the early 1980s and a controversial *Three Sisters* in London in 1990. Sturua's theatrical ideas draw their inspiration from Georgian folk theatre, EPIC THEATRE, notions of Bakhtinian 'carnival',

and cinematic 'montage'. Music also plays an important part in Sturua's productions and he has collaborated fruitfully over the years with the composer Gia Kancheli and the actor Ramaz Chkhikvadze. NICK WORRALL

Styne, Jule [Julius Kerwin Stein] (b. London, 31 Dec. 1905; d. New York, 20 Sept. 1994) Composer. A child prodigy and classically trained, he led a band and made a name for himself writing songs in Hollywood before turning to Broadway rather late. However, from 1947, with *High Button Shoes*, to 1972, when he wrote the score for *Sugar*, he was Broadway's most prolific provider of scores and, along with RICHARD RODGERS, its most successful. Among his long runs were *Gentlemen Prefer Blondes* (1949), famous for 'Diamonds Are a Girl's Best Friend'; his best work, *Gypsy* (1959), with 'Everything's Coming up Roses'; and *Funny Girl* (1964). His catchy melodies have an affinity for the stage, yet have often been immensely popular long after their shows have closed. Albeit largely traditional, his songs frequently take freshly thought-out, unexpected turns. GERALD BORDMAN

T. Taylor, *Jule: The Story of Composer Jule Styne* (1979)

subsidy *see* FUNDING

subtext A term that achieved prominence in the twentieth century, thanks to psychoanalysis, to refer to the implicit, unspoken set of meanings in a play. These meanings can be revealed by performance and/ or constructed by the audience, and there is often much debate as to whether the meanings are intentional and ideological or not. MODERNIST texts since SYMBOLISM have foregrounded the subtext, through imagery, non sequitur, juxtaposition and even absences; in CHEKHOV's satirical comedies, STRINDBERG's chamber pieces and BRECHT's political dialectics, the plays have been understood by attention to the subtext, produced by the clashing of elements in the text. The use of silence, as in work by MAETERLINCK, BERNARD, BECKETT and PINTER, suggests meaning emerging, as the word suggests, from 'underneath the text'; but postmodern authors, like BARKER or MÜLLER, have challenged this kind of reading, producing texts which seem to evade resolution at a subtextual level. DAN REBELLATO

See also THEATRE OF SILENCE.

Sullivan, Arthur [Seymour] (b. London, 13 May 1842; d. London, 22 Dec. 1900) Composer. His association with librettist W. S. GILBERT began in 1871 and their comically satirical operettas became very fashionable. *Trial By Jury* (1875) was so successful that the impresario RICHARD D'OYLY CARTE formed a company exclusively to produce their work; it moved to the new SAVOY THEATRE in 1881. It was for his serious compositions and church music that Sullivan was knighted (1883), although these did not achieve the lasting popularity of his work with Gilbert, which endured throughout the twentieth century in amateur as well as professional productions as a rare survivor of Victorian musical drama. CATHY JOYCE

summer shows *see* SEASONAL THEATRE

summer stock SEASONAL THEATRE that developed in resorts and urban leisure spaces with the decline of the nineteenth-century permanent stock companies and flourished in North America from the 1920 to the 1960s. Theatres varied from groups of amateur collegiate players performing in converted barns to professional operations such as the Westport Country Playhouse, which employed stars. Some theatres would perform popular repertory; alternatively, a star might travel among them with a packaged show, usually a lighter BROADWAY success, such as TALLULAH BANKHEAD in *Private Lives* in the late 1940s. The competition of television and changing theatre economics had dimmed much professional activity by the 1980s. The use of young people as apprentices was a staple of the scene, which was romanticized in films such as *Summer Stock* (1950) and *Babes in Arms* (1939). MICHAEL SOMMERS

superstition The variety of superstition in the theatre is wide, and continued to exert its hold throughout the twentieth century. Objects, events or people can serve as omens of good or bad luck. In many cases, a specific reaction is prescribed in a given event, e.g. immediately destroying the envelope of a first-night telegram. Superstitions can be personal (including the lucky mascot and rituals carried out before first nights or generally before every performance), or general (whistling in the dressing room brings very bad luck). The most well-known general superstition is that of the curse of *Macbeth*. There is also the tradition of theatre ghosts, often said to be the spirits of deceased actors. Sarah Siddons haunts the BRISTOL OLD VIC, John Buckstone continues to rehearse his lines at the Haymarket Theatre, the 'man in grey' (said to be an actor stabbed to death during a stage fight) appears in the upper circle of DRURY LANE, and William Terriss wanders the Adelphi in London, where he was murdered in 1897. Seeing a ghost is considered good luck for the current production. DANIEL MEYER-DINKGRÄFE

See also SLANG.

Richard Huggett, *The Curse of Macbeth and Other Theatrical Superstitions* (1981)

surrealism AVANT-GARDE artistic movement. French poet GUILLAUME APOLLINAIRE coined the term as early as 1917 to characterize such works as his *Breasts of Tiresias* and COCTEAU's *Parade*. In 1924, however, another French poet, ANDRÉ BRETON, split from DADA because of its nihilistic 'merciless iconoclasm' and proclaimed surrealism as the best hope for the human spirit. Based on experiments inspired by Freud in the transcription of subconscious imagery, Breton defined surrealism as the 'transmutation of those two seemingly contradictory states, dream and reality, into a sort of absolute reality', while others dismissed it as 'dada's sawed-off son'. The surrealist programme channelled dada's anarchic method of chance into the syntax of dreams; surrealist drama shifted fluidly among planes of reality, transcending the logical with the 'marvellous'. Such works as Louis Aragon's *The Mirror-Wardrobe One Fine Evening* (1924) or ARTAUD's *Jet of Blood* (1927) suggest the range of surrealism's hallucinatory possibilities. When Breton allied the 'surrealist revolution' with communism and renounced theatre as bourgeois, disagreement over surrealism's role in society dissolved the founding group, alienating Artaud and other dramatists, such as VITRAC. The surrealist movement left more artefacts in visual art and cinema than in drama, but it cleared the way for postwar avant-garde writers as different as IONESCO, GENET and ARRABAL. In addition, dramatists unaffiliated with the movement, e.g. Poland's WITKIEWICZ and Spain's VALLE-INCLÁN, created work classifiable as surreal. Dream-structure also infiltrated conventional theatre (e.g. the dream-ballet in RODGERS and HAMMERSTEIN's *Oklahoma!*). CAROLYN TALARR

Michael Benedikt and George E. Wellwarth, *Modern French Theatre: The Avant-Garde, Dada, and Surrealism* (1964)
J. H. Methews, *Theatre in Dada and Surrealism* (1974)
Maurice Nadeau, *The History of Surrealism*, trans. Richard Howard (1967)

Sutherland [Morgue], Efua [Theodora] (b. Cape Coast, Ghana, 27 June 1924; d. Accra, Ghana, 22 Jan. 1996) Playwright and director. Instrumental in founding in Accra the Experimental Theatre and Ghana Drama Studio, she became the most influential person in the development of drama in Ghana and Africa's most celebrated black woman writer. She received higher education in England, and was conscious of the importance of both English and indigenous languages such as Akan, deliberately encouraging bilingualism in her productions. Her plays, many of them written for children and using traditional material, include *Foriwa* (1962), *Edufa* (1962), *You Swore an Oath* (1963), *Vulture! Vulture!* (1968) and, perhaps the most famous, *The Marriage of Anansewa* (1975).

KOLE OMOTOSO

Suzman, Janet (b. Johannesburg, 9 Feb. 1939) Actress and director. Suzman came to England from a family of anti-apartheid activists and, after training at the London Academy of Music and Dramatic Art, she joined the newly formed ROYAL SHAKESPEARE COMPANY. Over the next two decades she played a wide range of major parts, from Rosaline, Portia, Ophelia (1965), Katharina, Celia (1967), Rosalind (1968) and Cleopatra (1972) to Clytemnestra and Helen in *The Greeks* (1980). She was highly commended for her Masha in *Three Sisters* (1976) and a captivating, intensely powerful Hedda Gabler (1977). Her personal commitment has often seen her in FRINGE productions, notably *Hello and Goodbye* (1973) at the KING'S HEAD. Her subtly nuanced delivery, precise intelligence and striking demeanour have also brought her success in television and film. She directed *Othello* (1987) and *The Good Woman of Sharkville* (adapted from BRECHT, 1996) for the MARKET THEATRE of Johannesburg, and, in association with this company at the BIRMINGHAM REPERTORY THEATRE, her South African version of *The Cherry Orchard* (1997) and a later development of this, *The Free State* (2000). Among her books are *Acting with Shakespeare: The Comedies* and a commentary on *Antony and Cleopatra*. DAN REBELLATO

See also IBSEN (PERFORMING IBSEN).

Suzuki, Tadashi (b. Shimizu City, Japan, 21 June 1939) Director, writer and creator of the Suzuki method of actor training. At university, he studied political science but became involved with the Wasada Free Stage, a leftist company committed to STANISLAVSKY's system. As chairman from 1960 to 1961, Suzuki emphasized artistic concerns over political aims in his stagings of CHEKHOV, MILLER and SARTRE. In 1961 he formed his own company, The Free Stage, with Minoru Betsuyaku as resident playwright. In 1966 the company was renamed the Wasada Little Theatre, opening with Betsuyaku's *The Little Match Girl* (1966). Within his own company Suzuki began to explore and develop his particular style and methods of actor training. His first major production was *On the Dramatic Passion I* (1969), an experimental collage of Western and Japanese references, followed by *On the Dramatic Passion II* (1970), which subsequently played in Paris; it was here that his work began to be noticed in the West.

In 1976 his theatre company moved to the remote mountain village of Toga, although it still has a base in Tokyo. In Toga, the company developed the Suzuki method of actor training and in 1984 officially became the Suzuki Company of Toga (SCOT). The method is a challenging discipline intended to heighten physical and vocal possibilities. Central is a return to 'animal energy' through a grounded approach to movement called the 'grammar of the feet'. The method draws on traditional Japanese theatre forms as well as the material arts and looks for a universality of meaning beyond cultural and national barriers. Suzuki initiated a Toga theatre festival in 1982, introducing the work of international theatre practitioners to Japan, and he has taught his method at the Juilliard School, New York, and the University of Wisconsin. From 1985 SCOT has toured internationally, with productions of Greek plays *(Dionysus*, 1990), Shakespeare *(The Tale of Lear*, 1988; *Macbeth*, 1991) and Chekhov *(The Chekhov*, 1989). Suzuki's book on his method has been translated into English as *The Way of Acting* (1986).

BRIAN ROBERTS

Svoboda, Josef (b. Čáslav, Czechoslovakia, 10 May 1920) Designer. Trained as an architect, Svoboda has designed more than 500 productions in a career that began in the early 1940s. He made a fundamental impact on Czech theatre, working with outstanding directors such as KREJČA, Radok and Kašlík, and for some three decades was the head of design and technical operations at the National Theatre. Among his designs there were *The Government Inspector* (1948), *The Entertainer* (1957), *Hamlet* (1958), *The Seagull* (1960), *Romeo and Juliet* and *Oedipus Rex* (both 1963). Its production of *The Insect Play* was seen in the WORLD THEATRE SEASON, London, in 1966 and this led Svoboda to the OLD VIC (*The Storm*, 1966; *Three Sisters* 1967; *The Idiot*, 1970). Since the 1960s, he has worked extensively abroad in the major international OPERA houses and theatres. His typically monumental designs for Wagner's *Ring* cycle in Covent Garden, BAYREUTH and Geneva have been particularly acclaimed.

Svoboda has a total view of scenography in which he explores space and time through all the media available. He uses kinetics, mechanics and optics to experiment with light, shape and colour, and sees scenography as dramatic rather than visual, an essential element in the meaning of the play which can even become the dominant factor. A pioneer in the theatrical use of technology, he developed a number of important inventions – light walls, colour backdrops, beam splitter mirrors, low voltage footlights – and, in his work on collage and kaleidoscopes, multiple projections. In this field he created the Polyecran system of simultaneous projection and, with Radok, the LATERNA MAGIKA, in which live performers combine with projections and for which Svoboda was awarded a prize at the Brussels Expo 58. Svoboda became director of a theatre called Laterna Magika in 1973; it operates as part of the National Theatre, although primarily as a tourist attraction.

Enormously influential and much honoured, Svoboda has also worked on projects for flexible theatre buildings and is a popular teacher who believes that scenography is a discipline capable of initiating the further development of theatre itself. EVA SORMOVA

D. Bablet, *Revolutions in Stage Design of the 20th Century* (1977)

J. Burian, *The Scenography of Josef Svoboda* (1983)

Swan Theatre *see* ARCHITECTURE; RESTORATION DRAMA IN THE TWENTIETH CENTURY; ROYAL SHAKESPEARE COMPANY

Sweden At the beginning of the twenty-first century, Swedish theatre shows enormous vitality but suffers from alarming uncertainty about its FUNDING base. With a population of over 8.5 million and over 4 million paid attendances a year, Sweden has three national theatres, 31 regional or municipal theatres, and about 100 ALTERNATIVE theatre and dance companies, all receiving or eligible for some degree of public subsidy. Until the last years of the twentieth century commercial productions and business sponsorships were relatively infrequent, and the assumption of Swedish cultural policy has been that permanent, serious theatre cannot survive on box-office takings alone. Approximately 17 per cent of central government funding on culture goes to theatre and dance (compared with just over 3 per cent to film, radio and television, and 23 per cent to adult education). This partly reflects a tradition of centuries of royal patronage that included the founding of the Royal Theatre (1771, now housing the national opera and ballet) and the Royal Dramatic Theatre, or Dramaten (1788), which, thanks to its huge resources, still dominates the production of spoken drama. However, by the time of Sweden's most influential dramatist AUGUST STRINDBERG, the most progressive repertoire and production practices were often to be found in private, commercial theatres, which flourished as public funding declined. Strindberg pioneered the introduction into Sweden of SYMBOLIST aesthetics, through his dream plays and the chamber plays he wrote for the Intimate Theatre. Nevertheless, despite his plays' domination of the Swedish repertoire of the early twentieth century, and significant MODERNIST initiatives by such pioneers as

director Per Lindeberg (1890–1944) and playwright PÄR LAGERKVIST, the pervading early twentieth-century aesthetic was realist, reaching levels of sophistication that resulted in Dramaten giving the world premières of several of EUGENE O'NEILL's late plays, such as *Long Day's Journey Into Night* in 1956, directed by Olof Molander (1892–1966). Social Democratic governments in the 1920s and 1930s made the subsidy of theatre a core element in their creation of the Swedish welfare state. Emphasis on the decentralized distribution of theatre included the creation of the National Touring Theatre (1934), which now gives over 1,300 performances annually; the opening of a number of municipal theatres in major cities; and, later, the establishment of the regional theatres that now serve almost every county in Sweden. Generous public funding in the 1960s and 1970s fostered the development of over 200 so-called 'free groups', many doing theatre for young audiences, many with overtly left-wing or counter-cultural agendas. The late 1980s and 1990s saw public funding compromised by worsening economic conditions and changing politics. The free groups and alternative theatres are now much fewer, though several (such as the Orion Theatre and Teater Galeasen) have become nationally important for the development and premièring of innovative work. While the national theatres continue to be relatively secure, even Dramaten had to reduce staff in the late 1990s. Meanwhile, threats to regional companies that depend on local subsidy are exemplified in Sweden's second city, Göteborg, where, in 1997, municipal politicians threatened to close the Municipal Theatre (founded in 1917, and one of the country's largest). Sweden remains a world leader in creating theatre for young audiences, especially theatre that treats the young as serious, thoughtful spectators. Foremost in a large field have been the Young Klara, Stockholm (led since its founding in 1975 by Suzanne Osten) and Backa Theatre (a section of the Göteborg Municipal Theatre, led by Eva Bergman). Swedish AMATEUR THEATRE has also continued to have particular vitality, and community productions, such as the 1997 *Norberg Strike*, showed an early lead in developing the kind of COMMUNITY PLAYS later popularized in Britain and North America by the Colway Trust. The creativity of Swedish theatre remains vital and progressive, with important and innovative new plays from such writers as Mattias Andersson, Magnus Dahlström, Katarina Frostenson, Jonas Gardell, Margareta Garpe, Staffan Göthe, Stig Larsson, LARS NORÉN, Barbro Smeds, and Thomas Tidholm. Acclaim for the brilliant directorial work of INGMAR BERGMAN seemed to overshadow the work of younger directors well into the 1990s, but his gradual retirement has brought into clearer perspective the work of such talented artists as Peter Oskarson, Karl Dunér, Mats Ek (also a writer and choreographer), Pia Forsgren, Rickard Günther, Staffan Valdemar Holm, Kajsa Isaksson, Lars Rudolfsson and Linus Tunström. HARRY LANE

Gunilla Anderman, ed., *New Swedish Plays* (1992)
Claes Englund and Leif Janzon, *Theatre in Sweden* (1997)
Leif Janzon, *Theatre in Sweden* (1998)
Frederick J. Marker and Lise-Lone Marker, *A History of Scandinavian Theatre* (1996)

Swerling, Jo   *see* BURROWS, ABE

Swift, Carolyn   *see* ABBEY THEATRE; BEHAN, BRENDAN; IRELAND; PIKE THEATRE

Switzerland   With German and French cultures to draw on, Swiss theatre has been variegated if not nationally cohesive. One of the great visionaries of twentieth-century theatre, ADOLPHE APPIA, was born and worked in Geneva, but found little acceptance in his own country, or indeed elsewhere. Switzerland's municipal theatres and lack of censorship attracted the likes of Georges and Ludmilla PITOËFF, who came from Russia to live in Geneva from 1915 to 1921. They presented the new European drama of IBSEN, CHEKHOV and SHAW, and were influenced by Appia's Austrian colleague EMILE JAQUES-DALCROZE who worked in Switzerland. Swiss director Oskar Eberle (1902–56) achieved international fame with modern productions of sixteenth- and seventeenth-century plays.

Refugees from Nazi Germany helped turn Switzerland into an important cultural centre as the only Nazi-free zone of German-speaking Europe. A key part was played by Swiss director Oskar Walterlin, first in Basel and then in Zurich, where the Schauspielhaus became a leading theatre of world renown; BRECHT's three outstanding exile plays, *Mother Courage* (1941), *The Good Person of Setzuan* (1943) and *Galileo* (1943), were given their premières there. The Austrian playwright FRITZ HOCHWÄLDER fled to Switzerland and remained after the war, when two Swiss playwrights, MAX FRISCH and FRIEDRICH DÜRRENMATT, emerged as major figures.

There is a strong amateur and semi-professional tradition in Switzerland, much of it organized around festivals with popular participation and a folklorist bent, whether it is the staging of a classic like Schiller's *William Tell*, a PAGEANT commemorating an historical event, or a celebration of the harvest. Appia was heavily influenced by these OPEN-AIR festival performances. The important network of LITTLE THEATRES that sprang

up after the Second World War offering an AVANT-GARDE repertoire also came from amateur and semi-professional roots.   CHARLES LONDON
See also GERMAN-LANGUAGE DRAMA.

Swope, Martha   *see* THEATRE PHOTOGRAPHY

Sydney   Australia's largest city has always prided itself on a lively mix of the unconventional and the colourful, the bohemian and the sophisticated. First settled in 1788, the young colony saw its first play, *The Recruiting Officer*, in a production staged the following year by convicts to celebrate King George III's birthday, and Australia's first theatre opened in 1796. During the nineteenth century there were regular surges of interest in theatre, marked by the construction and refurbishment of buildings to house visiting companies and local productions. By 1900 at least seven major theatres were operating, and the firm of J. C. Williamson had become the dominating entrepreneurial and production organization in both Australia and New Zealand. In the 1930s, dozens of 'little theatres' sprang up, often with a brief life, followed over the next decades by organizations such as the MERCURY THEATRE, the Ensemble Theatre Company and the AUSTRALIAN ELIZABETHAN THEATRE TRUST. During the 1970s the NIMROD THEATRE COMPANY and Melbourne's Australian Performing Group were between them responsible for the new wave of Australian drama. After its closure in 1987, Nimrod became the home for the Belvoir Street Theatre, subsequently Company B at Belvoir, the major alternative company to the larger SYDNEY THEATRE COMPANY. Both Melbourne and Sydney seek to define their individuality with reference to the other: as one commentator has noted: 'If Melbourne is schooled by Freud, Sydney's guru is Dale Carnegie; Melbourne could be an English city, Sydney a Californian one; Melbourne is loyal to its fine old institutions, Sydney enchanted by the new; Melbourne people give dinner parties which are incomplete without discussions of politics, religion, sex, books and/or football; Sydney has attitude and goes out, splitting the bill in someone else's space.'   MICHAEL MORLEY

Sydney Theatre Company   The largest company in New South Wales, with a brief to serve the four-million-plus population of Sydney. Established in 1978 after the Old Tote was disbanded, it ran an interim season of visiting productions before beginning its own operations in 1980. Since then it has proved to be one of the major success stories in Australian theatre, under artistic director Richard Wherrett, one of the co-founders of the NIMROD THEATRE COMPANY. Initially it was based at the Sydney Opera House, where it staged productions in both the Drama Theatre and the Opera Theatre. However, the Opera House could not support a resident theatre company whose operations were spread over five locations, and in 1984, thanks to the initiative of the New South Wales government, a new home – a disused wharf on Walsh Bay, further round the harbour – was made available and wholly refurbished. Here the company has three spaces: the 320-seat Wharf Theatre, the 140-seat Wharf Studio and the 544-seat Drama Theatre. But whereas in 1983 and 1985 it could afford to mount and tour productions of *Chicago* and *Nicholas Nickleby* respectively, the scale of the company's operations has been increasingly hit by the lack of financial support from the major government funding bodies. MICHAEL MORLEY

symbolism Symbolism is a basic feature in most art, since artists commonly employ language and representations of objects, both real and imagined, as signs of something else, that is, as symbols. They are designed to evoke some concept or emotion in the mind of a receiver while also having a real existence themselves – a rose is a rose but can also stand for love.

As a movement, symbolism is very close to romanticism. A desire to contact a reality beneath or beyond that accessible to reason and everyday observation leads to an art of indirection, suggestion, ambiguity and elusiveness. Drama's traditional emphasis upon action rather than contemplation, and its physical embodiment on the stage, presented formidable obstacles to the spiritual orientation of symbolism. Nevertheless, the symbolists had an enormous influence on theatre. It was symbolism that provided the first clear alternative to the triumphant realist drama, and in its theatres, its dramatists and its search for alternative styles of acting and production, symbolism created the first AVANT-GARDE in the modern theatre and the model for all those that followed. The late plays of IBSEN and STRINDBERG, strongly influenced by symbolism, continue to provide a challenging alternative to the earlier realistic works, and if MAETERLINCK's dramas of internal action are rarely seen on the international stage, the spiritual heirs of this vision, from W. B. YEATS and HUGO VON HOFMANNSTHAL to GARCÍA LORCA and SAMUEL BECKETT, continue to exercise an enormous influence in the modern theatre. In the area of scenic design also, symbolism's impact was very great. Applying its concerns with abstraction and evocation to the visual world of the theatre, ADOLPHE APPIA and EDWARD GORDON CRAIG, among the most influential designers of the twentieth century, provided an alternative vision to the heavy and detailed realistic settings of the early twentieth century, a vision so striking and effective that scarcely any subsequent theatre designer has escaped its influence entirely. MARVIN CARLSON

See also MODERNISM.

Anna Balakian, *The Symbolist Movement* (1967)
Haskell M. Bock, *Mallarmé and the Symbolist Drama* (1963)
Charles Chadwick, *Symbolism* (1971)
May Daniels, *The French Drama of the Unspoken* (1977)
Daniel Gerould, *Doubles, Demons, and Dreams: An International Collection of Symbolist Drama* (1985)
A. G. Lehmann, *The Symbolist Aesthetic in France 1885–1895* (1950)

Synge, [Edmund] J[ohn] M[illington] (b. Rathfarnham, nr Dublin, 16 April 1871; d. Dublin, 24 March 1909) Playwright and poet. Admired as the author of one of the finest stage comedies in the English language, *The Playboy of the Western World* (1907), which has been acknowledged as an influence by dramatists as diverse as LORCA and BECKETT, Synge has yet been the victim of two quite contradictory obfuscations. In his native Ireland he has often been seen, because of his Protestant ascendancy background and ill-disguised antipathy to militant and simplistic Irish nationalism, as an exploiter of a native Gaelic tradition which he did not really understand; in the words of ST JOHN ERVINE, 'a faker of peasant speech'. Outside of Ireland, there has been a tendency to see him as an exotic primitive, a writer concerned with an archaic world. Synge is neither of these things, but an infinitely subtle dramatist, concerned to undercut both the rationalistic theatre of ideas and the heroic romanticism of the Celtic Twilight.

The son of a wealthy barrister, who died when he was just a year old, and a stern and religiously obsessive mother, Synge reacted against the conservative and socially privileged Protestantism of his background with atheism, socialism, a dedicated interest in native Gaelic language and culture, and an element of anarchic exuberance which was to manifest itself in his plays. At the age of 26 he was diagnosed as suffering from the Hodgkin's Disease which was to kill him 12 years later, and to this event may be attributed much of the passion for life, the impatience with mystifications and the intensity which he poured into his six plays.

After a fateful meeting with W. B. YEATS in Paris in 1896, when the latter encouraged Synge to abandon his notions of becoming a critic of French literature and return to Ireland to learn from the language of the peasantry, Synge made five extended annual visits to the remote Aran Islands. Profoundly influenced by his experiences among the islanders, Synge was far from being an antiquarian. His account of the place, *The Aran Islands* (1907), is sharply aware of social contradictions and of imminent change. This same mixture of intimacy and criticism marks all of his peasant plays.

Though, alongside Yeats, Synge became a director of the ABBEY THEATRE in 1906, he was privately sceptical of Yeats' mythologizing tendencies, and the ironic realism of Synge's plays, particularly of *The Playboy*, is a direct deflation of Yeats' romance of violent heroism. As Yeats correctly discerned, Synge used peasant speech – forged into some of the most robustly extravagant stage language since the Jacobeans – not to identify himself with the peasantry but to give himself 'objectivity', allowing him to 'escape self-expression'. That very objectivity brought him into conflict with the nationalist movement's desire to idealize the Irish peasant, a conflict which culminated in the riots which greeted the opening of *The Playboy*.

Synge saw his own task as being to strike a balance between the Gaelic oral and English literary traditions, and his work blends high art (the elements of Sophoclean tragedy in his great one-act tragedy *Riders to the Sea*, 1904) with popular forms (the macabre folk-tale of *In the Shadow of the Glen*, 1903), the broad melodramatic comedy of *The Playboy* and the literary language of the King James Bible with demotic speech. In doing so successfully, he not only created an enduring body of plays but also became one of the first truly postcolonial writers of the century, making a positive achievement out of the tension between a native tradition and a colonial culture.

Synge's other plays are *The Well of the Saints* (1905), *The Tinker's Wedding* (1909) and *Deirdre of the Sorrows* (1910), which he did not live to finish revising.

FINTAN O'TOOLE

David H. Greene and Edward M. Stephens, *J. M. Synge, 1871–1909* (1959)

Nicholas Grene, *Synge: A Critical Study of the Plays* (1975)

Declan Kiberd, *Synge and the Irish Language* (1979)

Mary C. King, *The Drama of J. M. Synge* (1985)

Ann Saddlemeyer, *J. M. Synge and Modern Comedy* (1968)

Robin Skelton, *The Writings of J. M. Synge* (1971)

Syria *see* MIDDLE EAST AND NORTH AFRICA

Szajna, Józef (b. Rzeszow, Poland, 13 March 1922) Painter, designer and director. An Auschwitz prisoner, he co-founded the Ludowy (People's) Theatre, Nova Huta, in 1955. Szajna believed design must communicate meaning, independent of the action. His symbolic sets used collage and mobile sculpture, and helped to establish a new Polish anti-realism. He stressed the contemporary significance of the classics, introducing images of totalitarianism and the camps. Szajna confronted the Auschwitz experience in *Akropolis* (1962), co-directed with GROTOWSKI, and his own *Replika* (1972). He was the director of the Studio Theatre, Warsaw (1972–81), where he created five spectacular performances exploring the vision of artists working during profound historical upheavals, including *Dante* (1974) and *Mayakovsky* (1978). TONY HOWARD

T

tableau vivant (living picture) A formation of silent, still performers, used since medieval times to represent RELIGIOUS or artistic scenes. MELODRAMA used tableaux vivants to enact contemporary paintings, and the passion play of OBERAMMERGAU uses them to show aspects of Christ's story, whereas in REVUE they are used to expose female flesh. In Britain and America, for much of the century, nudity on stage was allowed only if it was immobile; hence the resort to tableaux in the ZIEGFELD *FOLLIES*, GEORGE WHITE's *Scandals* and a succession of shows at London's Windmill Theatre, where the ruling was 'if it moves, it's rude'. Tableau vivant gave rise to its cousin, the *pose plastique*, in which classical statuary is imitated, and MUSIC HALL was the beneficiary of 'living statuary' with naked or semi-naked women powdered all over in white. DAVID POWNALL in *An Audience Called Edouard* (1978) and STEPHEN SONDHEIM in his musical *Sunday in the Park with George* (1983), in which, respectively, a Manet and a Seurat painting come to life, offer rare examples of late twentieth-century use. CHARLES LONDON

See also EROTICISM IN THE THEATRE.

J. W. McCullogh, *Living Pictures on the New York Stage* (1979)

Tabori, George (b. Budapest, Hungary, 24 May 1914) Playwright. A Hungarian-American Jew with a British passport, Tabori is much travelled – Europe, the Middle East, the US – but his main success has been in the GERMAN-LANGUAGE THEATRE, though he writes in English. Noted for sardonic, BLACK COMEDY, his idiosyncratic and dark engagement with fascism and the HOLOCAUST in plays such as *The Cannibals* (1968) and *Mein Kampf* (1989), and other forms of oppression – racism in *The Niggerlovers* (1967), militarism in *Pinkville* (1970) – belies the earlier idealism of *The Emperor's Clothes* (1953). He has adapted BRECHT (*Brecht on Brecht*, 1962, *The Resistible Rise of Arturo Ui*, 1963, *The Guns of Carrar*, 1963, *Mother Courage*, 1970), STRINDBURG (*Miss Julie*, 1956), FRISCH (*Andorra*, 1963) and Shakespeare (*The Merchant of Venice*, 1978), and also directs. CHARLES LONDON

Anat Feinberg, *Embodied Memory: The Theatre of George Tabori* (1999)

Taganka Theatre Theatrical home to the Moscow company founded in 1964 by YURI LYUBIMOV and a group of Vakhtangov Theatre School students. Here they staged a number of radically innovative productions, inspired by the example of MEYERHOLD, VAKHTANGOV and BRECHT, which sought to reanimate the dormant spirit of AVANT-GARDE experimentation typical of Soviet theatre in the 1920s. Their work, frequently seen at European theatre festivals, was characterized by a strong ensemble spirit, imaginative *mises-en-scène* and subtle political commentary, as demonstrated in brilliantly conceived productions of work by Soviet and European writers, including a *Hamlet* (1974) starring the charismatic poet and songwriter/performer Vladimir Vysotsky. Because of the comparative weakness of the Soviet repertoire, many of the theatre's greatest successes, such as BULGAKOV's *The Master and Margarita* (1977), were dramatic adaptations of fictional works. Following Lyubimov's decision to live abroad in 1983, the theatre was headed, briefly, by ANATOLI EFROS and then by Nikolai Gubenko, before Lyubimov resumed control following the collapse of the Soviet Union. NICK WORRALL

Birgit Beumers, *Yuri Lyubimov at the Taganka Theatre 1964–1994* (1997)

Tagore, Rabindranath (b. Calcutta, 7 May 1861; d. Calcutta, 7 Aug. 1941) Writer, director, choreographer, composer, actor; the first non-European to win the Nobel Prize (1913) for his poetry. He is recognized as the most inspirational artistic and creative force in modern INDIA. He wrote 61 plays in Bengali and translated some into English. His unique contribution was the development, after 1908, of symbol-based dramatic forms drawing on Indian folk and classical traditions, culminating in stylized musical dance-dramas. As theorist and practitioner, he opposed the Western naturalistic idiom. He travelled and lectured widely, especially on peace. His major plays are *Raja* (1911, published 1910), *The Immovable Institution* (1914, published 1911), *The Post Office* (world première at the ABBEY THEATRE, Dublin, 1913; published 1912), *Muktadhara* (1925, published 1922), *Red Oleander* (1934, published 1924), *The Dancer's Worship* (1926) and *Tapati* (1929). The dance-dramas include *Chitrangada* (1936), *Chandalika* (1938) and *Syama* (1939).
ANANDA LAL

Sisir Kumar Das, *The English Writings of Rabindranath Tagore*, vol. 2 (1996)
Ananda Lal, *Rabindranath Tagore: Three Plays* (1987)

Tairov [Kornblit], Alexander [Yakovlevich] (b. Rovno, Russia, 24 June 1885; d. Moscow, 25 Sept. 1950) Director. Hostile to both STANISLAVSKY's realism and MEYERHOLD's theatre of convention, Tairov sought a theatre of 'emotionally saturated form' in which all the elements of stage production fused as a total entity. Much enamoured of PANTOMIME in its purest sense, Tairov put his theories to the test at the Kamerny (Chamber) Theatre, which he and his actress wife, ALISA KOONEN, founded in Moscow in 1914 and where they fostered the ideal of a theatre dedicated to art for art's sake — a dangerous undertaking in the increasingly austere political climate of the period. Tairov's credo, expressed in his book *Zapiski rezhissyora* (1921, translated by W. Kuhlke as *Notes of a Director*, 1969), embraced both operetta and high tragedy and required the virtuosity of a 'universal actor' — one capable of combining the grace and plasticity of the dancer with the vocal range of a singer. The finest exponent of this demanding art was Koonen, around whom most of Tairov's productions were built. He also attracted to the theatre a number of outstanding designers such as EKSTER, who assisted his experiments in forms of MODERNIST staging influenced by cubism and CONSTRUCTIVISM.   NICK WORRALL

Konstantin Rudnitsky, *Russian and Soviet Theatre: Tradition and the Avant-Garde* (1988)
Nick Worrall, *Modernism to Realism on the Soviet Stage: Tairov–Vakhtangov–Okhlopkov (1989)*

Tajikistan *see* SOVIET UNION

Talawa *see* BLACK THEATRE

Tally, Ted (b. Winston-Salem, NC, 9 April 1952) Playwright and screenwriter. Tally gained early recognition with his ambitious first play *Terra Nova* (1977), which dramatized Scott's ill-fated 1912 expedition to the South Pole and had an English production at CHICHESTER in 1980 as well as several others abroad. His subsequent work, such as *Coming Attractions* (1982) and *Little Footsteps* (1986), while more populist and satirical, has lacked the dramatic breadth of his first work, and his stage work has since been overtaken by the huge commercial success of his Oscar-winning screenplay for *The Silence of the Lambs* (1990).
HELEN RAPPAPORT

Tamasha *see* BLACK THEATRE

Tamiris [Becker], Helen (b. New York, 24 April 1905; d. New York, 4 Aug. 1966) Choreographer. Considered one of the pioneers of modern dance, she choreographed social protest works during the Depression under the umbrella of the Federal Dance Project, which she brought into existence, and strengthened dance's role as an integral part of BROADWAY musical comedies in the 1940s and 1950s. She worked with experimental theatre groups, like the PROVINCETOWN PLAYERS, and choreographed movement sections for the FEDERAL THEATER PROJECT's controversial *Trojan Incident* (1938), a dance-drama version of Euripides' *The Trojan Women*. She taught movement classes to actors in the GROUP THEATER in return for their giving acting classes to her dancers. Among the musicals she choreographed to a very high standard are *Up in Central Park* (1945), the 1946 *Show Boat* revival, *Annie Get Your Gun* (1946), *Park Avenue* (1946), *Inside USA* (1948), *Touch and Go* (1949), *Fanny* (1954) and *Plain and Fancy* (1955), and the progressive review *Bless You All* (1950).
LINDA SEARS
See also CHOREOGRAPHY; DANCE.

Tandy, Jessica (b. London, 7 June 1909; d. Easton, Connecticut, 11 Sept. 1994) Actress who made her London debut in 1927 and her New York debut three years later. Before moving permanently to America in late 1940, she played, among other important roles, Ophelia to JOHN GIELGUD's Hamlet and several Shakespearean heroines at the OLD VIC. Highlights of her American career began with her creation of Blanche

DuBois in TENNESSEE WILLIAMS' *A Streetcar Named Desire* (1947). Subsequently she won praise in *Hilda Crane* (1950), *The Fourposter* (1951), *Madam, Will You Walk?* (1953), *A Delicate Balance* (1966) and *The Gin Game* (1977). She later starred in several failures, although her performance in *Foxfire* (1982) won her a Tony award. Both her husbands were actors. The first, Jack Hawkins, she married in 1932. From the 1950s on she often co-starred with her second husband, HUME CRONYN, whom she married in 1942. She was also popular on American and British television and won an Oscar in 1990 for *Driving Miss Daisy*. She and Cronyn won a Tony in 1994, just before she died, for their life's work in theatre.   GERALD BORDMAN

S. Bananger, *Jessica Tandy: A Bio-Bibliography* (1991)

Tanguay, Eva (b. Marbleton, Quebec, 1 Aug. 1878; d. Hollywood, 11 Jan. 1947) Singer and actress who appeared in stock, in touring shows and on Broadway before turning to VAUDEVILLE. In one of those touring shows, *The Sambo Girl* (1905), she introduced 'I Don't Care', which not only expressed her hedonism but became her theme song; she was frequently nicknamed the 'I Don't Care Girl'. Her gorgeous figure, frizzled blonde hair, outlandish, often wildly feathered costumes, abandoned movements and raucous, energized delivery soon made her America's most popular and highest-paid vaudevillian. With the demise of twice-daily performances and the onset of health problems she retired in the early 1930s.   GERALD BORDMAN

Tanzania There have been three distinct eras in the development of Tanzanian theatre: the precolonial, the colonial and the socialist or *ujamaa*. In the precolonial era, theatre was essentially traditional but varied as it reflected the many ethnicities that make up what eventually became the Tanzanian nation at independence from Britain in 1961 (then called Tanganyika). The outcome of this ethnic diversity was that theatre displayed an equally wide variety of forms and styles, which include storytelling, dance, ritual drama and ceremonies, and heroic recitations. Like most other African performance traditions, these were functional, usually performed to educate (especially the young), to criticize and regulate social and political behaviour, to mobilize in times of communal need, and generally to gauge and monitor the overall well-being of the communities. Some of the dances, such as the *mkole* or the *digubi* used during initiations and rites of passage, formed part of the traditional educational system. The wide variety functioned in many other capacities, such as *abasimba* for hunting, *bugobogobo* for working the fields, *mbeta* and *selo* at weddings, and *mbayaya*, *livan-gala* and *madogori* for religious worship and healing rituals.

Western theatre was first introduced during the colonial era, and by the early 1920s this tradition, especially the English, was being performed in schools, primarily for the entertainment of the expatriate teachers and colonial administrators and the students. It was also used by the colonial administration as a tool for spreading Western cultural values. To help 'foster and emphasize proper and "correct" English speech', the British Council sponsored an annual Schools Drama Competition, which began in 1957 and became the Youth Drama Festival which continued until 1973. To its credit, this competition was a major catalyst for the emergence of the early Tanzanian dramatists such as Ebrahim Hussein, Faraji Katalambula and George Uhinga.

Expatriate theatre was established and supported in the European and expatriate communities through the formation of drama associations or 'LITTLE THEATRES', the first being the Dar es Salaam Players (or the Dar es Salaam Little Theatre) in 1947, followed by the Arusha Little Theatre in 1953. They ignored any style or tradition other than those of BROADWAY or the WEST END, and as a result played no part in the development of theatre.

Although the missionaries introduced Western-style spoken drama as an evangelical tool, through morality plays and pageants, and through adapting and retelling Tanzanian folk tales during mass, they were equally in the forefront, together with the colonial educators and administrators, in discouraging and suppressing Tanzanian traditional performances. These were described as pagan, barbaric and uncivilized, yet some of these forms stubbornly survived.

Although independence in 1964 (when Tanzania was born by uniting with Zanzibar) brought very little change to the theatre scene, the formation of the Youth Drama Association in 1966, sponsored by expatriates and the Tanzanian elite, did result in the emergence of some original plays written in the adopted national language, Kiswahili. Notable playwrights of this period were M. Mulokozi, who wrote *Mukwava wa Uhehe* ('Mukwava of the Uhehe'), Julius Nyerere (the country's president), who translated Shakespeare into Kiswahili, and Hussein, who was a product of the drama competitions.

The Arusha Declaration of 1967 provided the blueprint for the creation of a socialist state and the philosophical framework for much of contemporary theatre development and practice. Plays by foreigners, especially Westerners, were discouraged and Kiswahili performances were in the ascendancy as dramatists, in response to President Nyerere's call for artists to go forth and propagate the philosophy of *ujamaa*, began to write and compose plays and performance texts which broadly supported the tenets of the Declaration. More than 20 native plays and playwrights emerged at this period, chief among the latter being N'galimecha Ngahyoma, who wrote *Kijiji Chetu* ('Our village'), Penina [Muhando] Mlama, author of *Haitia* ('Guilt'), K. Kahigi, who co-wrote *Mwanzo wa Tufani* ('Beginning of the storm') with A. Ngemera, and Emmanuel Mbogo with his *Giza Limeingia* ('The Dawn of Darkness'). Unlike later work, these early *ujamaa* plays, while pointing out the obstacles on the path of realizing the ideals of socialism, supported it more or less uncritically. With the later plays from 1978, a different note became evident: they became more critical, often presenting the failures of the system arising from the corruption of the public officials responsible for implementing the socialist programme. There were also plays which portrayed the disillusionment and helplessness of the masses who felt exploited and unfulfilled. The major plays of the second period were *Harakati za Ukombozi* ('Liberation struggles', 1982), collectively produced by Amadinha Lihamba and others; *Nguzo Mama* ('Mother, the main pillar', 1982) and *Lina Ubani* ('There is an antidote for rot', 1984) by Mlama; *Kaptula la Marx* ('Marx's capital') by E. Kezilahabi; and Paukwa Theatre Association's *Ayubu* ('Job', 1982).

A strong tradition of didactic theatre was responsible for the development of various syncretic forms, such as the *vichekesho* and the highly politicized and popular *ngonjera*, which was closely associated with an old Swahili poetic tradition. The *ngonjera* is primarily a poetic dialogue couched in a question-and-answer structure. Its popularity, flexibility and adaptability have meant that there exist troupes in virtually all schools, and standard scripts of performances have emerged which are being modified to suit new occasions and contexts.

The newest form to develop has been the THEATRE FOR DEVELOPMENT, also referred to as community or popular theatre. Theatre for development is a form which seeks to identify problems, analyse them and try out solutions within the context of the play. This form emerged in the early 1980s and was initiated by the University of Dar es Salaam's Department of Art, Music and Theatre. It has been influenced by the radical pedagogical theories of Paulo Freire and the 'theatre of the oppressed' techniques of AUGUSTO BOAL, and encourages the active participation of the community at all stages of the theatre process. The first theatre for social development project in Tanzania took place in Malya, a large *ujamaa* village in the Mwanza region; it was sponsored by Oxfam and coordinated by Muhando and Lihamba among others from the university. The project, which lasted for 18 months between 1982 and 1983, has been held up by scholars of the form as the ideal model, first because of its innovative approach, which included the integration and utilization of indigenous Sukuma songs, mimes and dances (particularly the *bugobogobo*, *wigashe* and *burungule*) within the structure of the plays, which were made with members of the community. Second, the catalysts of the process lived in and became accepted by the community, with the result that the usual mistrust and tensions of the outsider–insider encounter were removed. The Malya experience led to many governmental and nongovernmental agencies employing theatre for development to carry through some of their projects: between 1982 and 1996 a total of 11 theatre projects were carried out in different communities across Tanzania.

Theatre in Tanzania has had a successful history, and in many respects has always broken new ground, especially because it is the only African country which in one stroke was able to do away with the language problem that has plagued most of the continent's postcolonial theatres. Kiswahili is spoken and understood by nearly 85 per cent of the population. All theatre styles, from the indigenous to the university-based, Western-influenced tradition, are in Kiswahili, so no Tanzanian dramatist is marginalized or considered elitist or provincial, as is the case with the literary dramatists or even the so-called popular artists who write or perform in non-national languages such as Yoruba, Igbo, Akan or Gikuyu in, say, Ghana, Nigeria, Kenya or Cameroon.
OSITA OKAGBUE

Tara Arts Britain's first professional Asian company, set up in 1976, following the murder of an Asian youth, Gurdeep Singh Chaggar, in west London, in order to explore the experience of being Asian in Britain. Tara has mixed educational, devised and AGIT-PROP work on themes ranging from old age, mental illness and problems at home to alienation among young people and racism in schools, with presentation of classical texts, such as the opening production in 1977, an adaptation of *Sacrifice* by RABINDRANATH TAGORE. After an initial learning phase up to 1982, Tara concentrated on its Asian heritage before, in 1985, drawing on Western and Asian theatre to produce a new drama. Under artistic director Jatinder Verma (b. Dar-es-Salaam, Tanzania, 1954), Tara has become known in Britain and abroad for this fusion, in shows like *Tartuffe* set in the court of a Moghul emperor (1990), *The Little Clay Cart*, a modern reading of an eighth-century Sanskrit play which was seen at the

NATIONAL THEATRE (1991), and *Heer and Romeo* (1991), which combined Varis Shah's *Heer and Ranijha* with *Romeo and Juliet*. In 1998 Tara launched an ambitious trilogy, *Journey to the West* (*Exodus*, 1998; *Genesis*, 1999; *Revelations*, 2000), which is based on interviews among the UK Asian population and tells the stories of three generations of Asians as they travel throughout the twentieth century from India to Africa and from there to Britain. COLIN CHAMBERS

Graham Ley, 'Twenty Years of Tara Arts', *New Theatre Quarterly*, vol. 52, Nov. 1997
J. Verma, 'Sorry, No Saris!', in V. Gottlieb and C. Chambers, eds, *Theatre in a Cool Climate* (1999)

Tardieu, Jean (b. Saint-Germain-de-Joux, France, 1 Nov. 1903; d. Créteil, France, 27 Jan. 1995) Poet and playwright; an influential and prolific writer. Much of his drama is in the form of the short, experimental scenes first performed as *Six pièces en un acte* ('Six plays in one act', 1955), published in his first volume of plays *Théâtre de Chambre* (*Chamber Theatre*, 1955). *Les Amants du métro* (*The Underground Lovers*, 1952), about lovers caught up in an absurd crowd, is published in a second volume, *Poèmes à Jouer* ('Poems to perform', 1960). There are two more volumes, the fourth including *La Cité sans sommeil* (*The Sleepless City*), premièred by LA MAMA in New York in 1987. WENDY SCOTT

Leonard C. Pronko, *The Experimental Theatre in France* (1962)

Tarkington, [Newton] Booth (b. Indianapolis, 29 July, 1869; d. Indianapolis, 19 May 1946) Novelist and author of 21 plays, nine of them (including *The Man from Home*, 1908) written in collaboration with Harry Leon Wilson (1867–1939). Many of Tarkington's most successful dramas were vehicles for particular stars, such as *Monsieur Beaucaire* (1901), written with Evelyn Greenleaf Sutherland (1855–1908) for RICHARD MANSFIELD, and *Clarence* (1919), written for ALFRED LUNT and HELEN HAYES. For OTIS SKINNER, Tarkington created *Your Humble Servant* (1910) and *Mister Antonio* (1916), and for GEORGE ARLISS *Poldekin* (1920).
MARVIN CARLSON

Keith J. Fennimore, *Booth Tarkington* (1974)
J. Woodress, *Booth Tarkington: Gentleman from Indiana* (1955)

Tarragon Theater One of several new theatres that opened across Canada in the early 1970s, The Tarragon, in Toronto, Ontario, has dedicated itself since its foundation in 1971 by BILL GLASSCO to the development and production of new Canadian plays. The works of many leading English Canadian playwrights have premièred there, including DAVID FRENCH, JAMES REANEY, SHARON POLLOCK and Judith Thompson. Most of the English-language premières of the plays of Quebec's MICHEL TREMBLAY have also appeared at Tarragon. Under the artistic direction of Urjo Kareda since 1982, it has sustained its commitment to the playwright and the script. L. W. CONOLLY

tattoo *see* CELEBRATORY THEATRE

Taylor, C[ecil] P[hilip] (b. Glasgow, 6 Nov. 1929; d. Newcastle upon Tyne, Dec. 1981). Prolific and versatile playwright whose early work, inspired by his Glasgow Jewish socialist roots, was staged in 1960s at the TRAVERSE THEATRE in Edinburgh. Plays like *Allergy* (1966), *Lies About Vietnam* (1969), *Passion Play* (1971) and *The Black and White Minstrels* (1972) attest both to his warmth and honesty and to his political ideas. Although plays such as *Bread and Butter* (1966), *Bandits* (1977) and *And a Nightingale Sang . . .* (1979) were seen in London, he remained committed to northern regional theatre, especially in NEWCASTLE where he helped new writers. Aside from writing for television and radio, Taylor produced over 50 plays, including adaptations of other playwrights. His version of CARL STERNHEIM's *Schippel* was seen in the West End in 1975 as *The Plumber's Progess*. Taylor's premature death came only a short time after his most mature and critically acclaimed work, *Good*, had received a fine production, starring ALAN HOWARD, by the ROYAL SHAKESPEARE COMPANY in 1981, which transferred to the West End and New York. The Newcastle Company Live Theatre, for which he wrote, named its theatre after him following his sudden and early death. HELEN RAPPAPORT

Taylor, Laurette [Loretta Cooney] (b. New York, 1 April 1884; d. New York, 7 Dec. 1946) Actress who began in VAUDEVILLE, then performed in cheap-priced touring shows, including those of her first husband, Charles A. Taylor. In 1912 she enjoyed two Broadway successes, *The Bird of Paradise* and the long-running *Peg o' My Heart* written by J. HARTLEY MANNERS, who became her second husband and wrote most of the mediocre vehicles in which she subsequently starred. After his death in 1928 she became a reclusive alcoholic, returning to the theatre only for a 1938 revival of *Outward Bound* and one final triumph in *The Glass Menagerie* (1945). GERALD BORDMAN

M. Courtney, *Laurette* (1955)

Taylor, Paul *see* CHOREOGRAPHY; DANCE

Taymor, Julie (b. Newton, Mass., 15 Dec. 1952) Director and stage designer. Taymor's early theatre experience included Boston Children's Theater workshops, JACQUES LECOQ's mime school in Paris, and acting with The Oberlin Group under HERBERT BLAU. She spent four years in Indonesia learning mask-carving and puppetry, and formed a cross-cultural troupe, Teatr Loh, which collectively created and toured a masked dance-drama, *Tirai* (1977–8). Taymor's American career began with designs for *The Odyssey* (1979) in Baltimore and *The Haggadah* (1980) for the NEW YORK SHAKESPEARE FESTIVAL. Since 1984 she has worked primarily as a director, usually creating works that emphasize visual imagery over literary text. She has also directed and designed three Shakespeare productions, as well as several operas. Her film of *Titus Andronicus*, called *Titus*, was rleased in 2000. Her most acclaimed and visually extravagant productions have been *The King Stag* (1984), *Juan Darién: A Carnival Mask* (1988, revived 1990), and *The Lion King* (1997). The last of these, produced on Broadway by Walt Disney, was hailed for its imaginative evocation of animal figures with masks, puppetry, mime, dance, lighting effects, and cinema-inspired illusions of scale and distance. Taymor works in close collaboration with composer Elliot Goldenthal, whom she describes as like herself in that 'he can work in the popular world and still be true to his artistry.' Her book, *'The Lion King', Pride Rock on Broadway,* appeared in 1998.   FELICIA HARDISON LONDRÉ

See also EASTERN THEATRE, ITS INFLUENCE ON THE WEST.

Eileen Blumenthal, *Julie Taymor, Playing with Fire: Theater, Opera, Film* (1995)

Tearle, Godfrey [Seymour] (b. New York, 12 Oct. 1884; d. London, 8 June 1953)   Actor. Tearle made his debut as a child in his father George's company, and in the 1920s enjoyed success in a series of light comedies. It was later, in weighty Shakespearean roles such as Hamlet (1931), Antony (1946) and Othello (1948), that he achieved recognition as a great actor. He was knighted in 1951.   ADRIANA HUNTER

Teatro Campesino, El (The Farmworkers' Theatre)   Theatre company. Founded to support striking grape-pickers in California in 1965 by Luis Valdez (b. Delano, California, 1940), a former member of the SAN FRANCISCO MIME TROUPE who had been active in student politics and visited Cuba. Valdez created a bilingual theatre to investigate the culture, tradition and struggle of the Mexican-Americans in the US. Early AGITPROP plays rooted in Chicano life also opposed the Vietnam War, and in the 1970s the group set up El Centro Campesino Cultural south of San Francisco to explore their POLITICAL THEATRE in a broader context of drama and myth. The company

mount an annual reworking of a traditional shepherd's play. Among Valdez' most important works are *Las dos Caras del patroncito (The Two Faces of the Boss*, 1965), *Bernabe* (1970), *La gran carpa de los rasquachis (The Great Tent of the Underdogs*, 1973), *Zoot Suit* (1978), which moved to Broadway but was less successful there than it was in Los Angeles, and a musical, *Corridos: Tales of Passion and Revolution* (1986), also adapted by the author for national television. His film credits as director include *La Bamba* (1987).   BEATRIZ J. RIZK

See also HISPANIC THEATRE IN THE UNITED STATES.

Flores, A. C. *El Teatro Campesino de Luis Valdez* (1980)
Huerta, Jorge A. *Chicano Theater* (1982)
Sommers, Joseph and Tomas Ybarra-Frausto, eds, *Modern Chicano Writers* (1979)

television drama   The twentieth century has produced three 'indirect', i.e. recorded and/or transmitted types of drama: radio, film and television. Of these, television is coming to have the greatest impact almost everywhere. Not only are sets increasingly available, reaching near-saturation in countries like Britain and the United States; the intensity of their use leaves the other media behind. If the average viewer in Britain will watch the box for some five hours and the average American viewer for over six hours a day, it is safe to say that he or she will be seeing a great deal of drama in that time.

Television drama is intimately linked with both theatre and cinema; all three, after all, are visual media. The umbilical connection with the stage was more evident in the early days. The first drama ever presented on television was PIRANDELLO's one-act play, *The Man with a Flower in his Mouth*, broadcast experimentally by the BBC as early as 1930. Between the start of regular transmissions in 1936 and their suspension because of the war in 1939, the BBC televised a total of 326 plays; only 14 were written especially for the new medium. In the early postwar period, when television plays went out live, they were necessarily continuous – in other words, very much like theatrical performances. It is true that the action was covered by several cameras from different angles. But there was little of the flexibility and mobility of film production. Only a limited number of sets could be accommodated in the studio, and there were time constraints on costume and make-up changes for the cast. Cables inhibited camera movement beyond certain limits. Film, if used at all, appeared only by way of inserts for outdoor scenes. The introduction of videotape in the late 1950s changed all that. Plays could now be recorded in segments and edited, somewhat in the manner of film.

Moreover, from the 1960s onwards writers and producers increasingly wished to break out of the confines of the studio. Plays would be shot on location, often with a single camera – first on film and later, when electronic cameras become more and more portable, on videotape. The development of sophisticated video effects in the 1970s and 1980s helped to push the television play closer and closer to a cinematic mode. By the end of the century television drama had become very flexible; it could lean towards either theatre or cinema in method and style. The question is, has it achieved a language of its own, distinct from that of its sister arts?

Some doubt whether there is such a thing as television drama at all. They would claim that it is film or theatre transmitted electronically rather than an aesthetic category in its own right. But that is to overstate the case. True, the television play shares a good deal with film, its closest relation – a narrative conveyed by means of images which are passed through a lens, accompanied by sounds which are passed through a microphone. Nevertheless, the two media differ fundamentally in their mode of reception. The key to the nature of television drama lies in its viewing conditions. Cinema-going involves choice and effort; switching on a TV set is little more than a reflex. The cinema shows a limited programme; television drama is embedded in a continuous flow of heterogeneous material. Indeed, the television viewer may not catch the start of a play; he or she may abandon it before the end. The cinema screen is large and placed above; the domestic screen is small and placed at, or below, the viewer's eye level. The dark auditorium focuses attention on the screen action; domestic lighting may bleach the television image, faulty set adjustment may degrade it, while family turmoil, the phone or the dog may interfere with concentration. This suggests that television viewing is less engrossing than a visit to the cinema. Linguistic usage bears this out: film watchers are called spectators, television watchers viewers. But domestic play-watching is not just an inferior sort of dramatic experience; it is an experience different in kind, with its own advantages. The appeal is to the individual or the small group rather than to a mass audience. What television drama loses in intensity it gains – among other things – in extension. Vast audiences share the same experience though physically separated from each other. When the last of the 251 episodes of *M*A*S*H* went out in the United States in 1983, it was seen by the staggering number of 125 million viewers. The social bonding implied by such figures is reinforced by constant repetition. The impact of television drama is not so much that of the individual play as of a routine of viewing, almost a way of life.

Television drama can more easily be a writer's medium than the cinema, where front office, directors and stars exert their own pressures. British television in particular has accorded a high status to playwrights. Authors like DAVID MERCER, ALUN OWEN, HAROLD PINTER, TREVOR GRIFFITHS, ALAN PLATER, PETER NICHOLS, Fay Weldon, Jack Rosenthal, DAVID HARE, DENNIS POTTER and Alan Bleasdale have been featured in pre-transmission publicity and their scripts are frequently published in book form. The writer's status is closely (though not, of course, exclusively) linked with the single, i.e. the non-serialized, play. In the early days of television this tended to be the staple dramatic product, apart from the adaptation of stage plays. During the late 1940s and early 1950s, NBC's Philco *Playhouse* and CBS's *Studio One* provided outlets for single plays, often by previously unknown authors, in the United States. In the late 1950s and early 1960s a similar platform was offered in Britain by ABC's *Armchair Theatre* and the BBC's *Wednesday Play* (renamed *Play for Today* in 1970). This supremacy was to be of short duration. The serial (i.e. the multi-episode drama) and the series (i.e. self-contained episodes involving the same group of characters) were preferred by network executives and producers. These were easier to schedule than single plays, they were more cost-effective and, above all, they consolidated viewer loyalty. In a sense, a serial is only an extension of the single play. It is generally written by one author rather than a committee. At the 'literary' end of the spectrum there is the dramatization of novels, a genre particularly characteristic of British television which has run adaptations of works by Dickens, Thackeray, Trollope, Henry James, Bennett, George Moore, Sartre, Hugo, Flaubert, Dumas *fils* and many other novelists. So original a playwright as Dennis Potter has done adaptations like Hardy's *The Mayor of Casterbridge* (BBC, 1978) and Scott Fitzgerald's *Tender is the Night* (BBC, 1985). Ken Taylor's 14-episode version of Paul Scott's Raj Quartet, entitled *The Jewel in the Crown* (Granada, 1984), handled a tetralogy of some complexity with great skill. But the serial is often an original story rather than an adaptation. Analogous to the nineteenth-century serial novel, it has a more direct ancestor in film serials like the French *Fantômas* and the American *Perils of Pauline* which thrilled audiences in the early days of the cinema. The serial offers certain advantages over the single play. It enables the playwright to develop stories in depth, with ample room for characterization. At the receiving end, the sense of time passing between episodes becomes part of the viewing experience. Latin America is particularly addicted to serials; there they are known as *telenovelas*. The chief provider is Brazil's giant multimedia network Globo, which has been active since 1965. At first *Telenovelas* were a fantasy vehicle for the socially deprived, with their dreams of luxury living and rags-to-riches stories. But they developed into a narrative form with high production values, some literary ambitions and a great appeal to all strata of society. The length of the Brazilian *telenovela* is often prodigious, running perhaps to as many as 200 episodes. Viewing figures of up to 50 million are not exceptional.

A universally popular subgenre of the serial is the sci-fi adventure. The BBC's *Doctor Who* is perhaps the most famous example. First launched in 1963, it has generated a huge following, with fan clubs, a *Doctor Who Monthly* and scholarly publications. A major branch of the serial is the soap opera, so called after a kind of RADIO DRAMA. Soap opera is typically sited within a group – family, workplace or district. The British variety has a strongly regional character – from the *doyen* of its kind, Granada's *Coronation Street* situated in working-class Lancashire, to Central TV's *Crossroads* set in a Midlands hotel, Yorkshire TV's *Emmerdale Farm* (later simply *Emmerdale*), Merseyside Television's *Brookside* (which is actually shot in a Liverpool suburb), and the BBC's London-based *EastEnders*. But soap operas need not always hold up the mirror to working- or lower-middle-class nature. The American soaps *Dallas* (CBS/Lorimar) and *Dynasty* (ABC) filled the world's screens with their tales of super-affluent oil tycoons. France's *Châteauvallon* followed the intrigues of the rich and powerful. Unmistakably an element of wish fulfilment was being pandered to – envy seasoned with curiosity and disapproval. Viewer identification with soaps runs high. The characters are believed by many viewers to be as real as themselves, and unpopular storyline changes raise storms of protest. Soap operas are open-ended. (*Coronation Street*, initially scheduled for a mere 13 weeks, just went on of its own accord.) Having no firm end in view they can be adjusted. Thus, some Brazilian *telenovelas* of the soapier kind have been reshaped in mid-course to accommodate audience research findings. There is an assembly-line element to such authorship. Teams of writers work simultaneously on different narrative strands; relays relieve each other from time to time. On *Coronation Street* an archivist keeps tracks of the characters' biographies for the guidance of writers new to the serial. Typical of soap operas are the weaving together of several plotlines running side by side; a mixture of moods (the banal alternating with the sensational, the comical with the pathetic); and cliff-hanger endings designed to keep the viewer hooked. Plot development

is leisurely since viewers may well miss some episodes.

The series can afford to work a good deal faster. Though it, too, had a forerunner in the cinema (Sherlock Holmes, Fu Manchu, Ellery Queen, etc.) it is an essentially televisual format. It tends to raise few social questions; characters are fixed and rarely learn from experience. Series easily fall into genre patterns. The Hollywood inspiration of many American series is self-evident; indeed, many are made in Hollywood. There are Westerns; medical shows (tales of individual doctors or of hospitals); and polices series (crime being viewed from the angle of law enforcement rather than the criminal's point of view, as in traditional cinema). Comparable genre concepts are at work in other countries too. A popular subgenre of the series is the situation comedy. Its basic pattern is that of a group of characters engaged in permanent conflict, their never-resolved problems giving scope for a maximum number of permutations. Sitcoms tend to be sited in more specialized environments than soap operas; much of the writer's ingenuity lies in finding a new *milieu* to explore. Let us take three British examples. *Porridge* (BBC) was a prison story of wily lags; *Rising Damp* (Yorkshire TV) chronicled the lives of tenants in a run-down apartment building; *Yes Minister* and its sequel *Yes Prime Minister* (BBC) poked fun at goings-on in the corridors of power.

Series and serials have practically driven the single play off American television screens, but for the odd prestige production like Arthur Miller's *Playing for Time* (CBS, 1980). In Britain, any threat to the single play used to stir up heated polemics in its defence. But to see it – rightly – as the cutting edge for innovation in writing and production is not to deny the potential merits of the serial and the series. One must, however, bear in mind the shift in institutional power the dominance of the latter brings about – a transfer of responsibility from individual author to script editor and producer.

Another frequent cause of controversy is the documentary drama. This broad title covers a wide range of plays, all in some ways linked to 'reality'. Stylistic devices typifying the genre – talking heads, jump cuts, unsteady camerawork – are designed to give an unmediated, as it were authentic, impression of actuality. The argument against documentary drama is that it might confuse viewers as to what precisely is demanded of them: are they to enjoy it as fiction or credit it as literal fact? Critics maintain that it may so merge with the flow of factual reportage as to become indistinguishable from it. Actually there are many ways of signalling the real status of the programme. More confusion is caused by soap operas. The attacks on documentary drama are often disingenuous, aimed at socially critical but never at safely conservative programmes.

Television has long since overtaken the cinema, at any rate in the TV-saturated developed world, as a mirror of individual conduct. Jeremiahs claim that it does not merely reflect these patterns but influences them as well – usually for the worse. Such arguments draw more on gut feelings than hard sociological evidence. Nevertheless, one cannot dismiss out of hand the notion that a daily demonstration of how to conduct oneself will leave its mark. Television drama also reflects (and perhaps influences) the broader implicit values of society. Different parts of the world follow different guidelines in their programming policies. While developing countries tend to be frankly interventionist, the pressures and constraints on television drama in the liberal capitalist West are not so apparent. 'Free world' value systems are, however, built into seemingly neutral offerings, including cop shows and soap operas. Problems are always seen in the light of personal malfunction; wider social perspectives are shunned. The very insertion of commercials into plays, regardless of the content of the latter, carries a 'free enterprise' and consumerist message. Only rarely does ideology rear its head openly, as in the case of ABC's Cold War serial *Amerika* (1987).

The influence of television drama is not confined to the home market. A number of countries, like the United States, Britain, France and Brazil, export a great many programmes. The domination of the television screens of quite a few countries by American plays and films is a continuation of Hollywood's traditional supremacy in world cinema. The strong pressure exerted by these products, particularly in Latin America, can be seen as a form of cultural imperialism, whether intended as such or not. Subtle denationalization of culture can take other forms too. The growing demand for glossy TV superproductions may lead to a pooling of resources by two or more countries; such coproductions often result in compromise. Non-American production companies frequently have the American market in mind when devising their drama serials. These are in danger of being mid-Atlantic rather than a true expression of native culture.

The rise of television drama has been meteoric. More drama is currently being 'consumed' than ever before in history. True, there are dangers in the massive substitution of fictional life for real experience, in ideological manipulation dressed up as entertainment. But there are strong positive values on the other side of the ledger. People's mental horizons have been extended beyond the limits of their personal experience. Ima-

ginations have been stretched in a way that only drama can accomplish. GEORGE BRANDT

In the United States

Starting in the 1940s, drama has been the most watched form of American television. Half-hour situation comedies with continuing characters usually head the weekly rating charts, but for quantity and variety, drama comes first and is packaged in six sizes.

(1) Thirty-minute filmed programmes, both anthologies such as *The Twilight Zone* or *Alfred Hitchcock Presents*, and series such as *General Electric Theater* or *Four Star Playhouse*.

(2) Hour-long filmed programmes with continuing characters such as *The Fugitive*, *The Defenders* and *Bonanza* and, subsequently, *Dallas*, *Dynasty*, *Hill Street Blues* and *L.A. Law*. The one-hour dramatic anthology, once the most popular form, has virtually vanished. In the early days *Studio One*, *Kraft Television Theater* and *Armstrong Circle Theater* were among those providing original exciting dramas live or taped. In a longer format (average playing time about 75 minutes), *Playhouse 90* was original American television drama at its best.

(3) The special programme, 90 minutes to three hours, allowed subjects to be treated in greater depth. Sometimes originals, often adaptations of plays and, more recently, 'docudrama', such shows have been the highlights of every season. In the live and tape days the *Hallmark Hall of Fame*, *Dupont Show of the Week* and *Producers' Showcase* provided the greatest performances. The shows were rehearsed like plays, shot with electronic cameras and, with the arrival of tape, electronically edited. Today such shows are no longer produced, but the motion picture made expressly for television has taken their place. These two-hour or longer films are written, directed and produced by our leading artists and often tackle subjects that would be avoided in the risky feature film market.

(4) The long form, a filmed programme that plays over several evenings and allows epic subjects to be treated in depth. *Roots*, *Winds of War*, *Blind Ambition* and *Shogun* are examples. Although requiring an investment by the audience of eight to 30 hours, these shows have proven to be both very popular and very costly.

(5) The daytime 'soap operas', seen five days a week by millions of addicts, present usually lurid domestic crises with surprisingly high standards of performance and technical quality. Once live, these are now all taped.

(6) Most motion pictures made for theatrical distribution end up on television, the new ones on pay

cable, the oldies everywhere, with 15–30 choices every night. A majority of set owners have recorders to tape them for later viewing or storage. As these dramas were not created for the tube, no further comment will be made, except to note the problem of such films being interrupted by commercials, recut for length, slowed or speeded electronically, colourized and, in the case of widescreen pictures, scanned.

The content of all these programmes through the years has ranged from brilliant originality to the most cliché-riddled trash. Presumably the producers, writers, and directors would prefer to do good work, but time restriction, excessive interference from the networks and the pressure from sponsors to reach the largest audience make this difficult, if not inpossible. When dramatic programmes were live, the original impetus came from a producer, usually a single individual such as Martin Manulis or Worthington Miner. Writers were given no limits, other than a code of standards and practices. These were usually personal stories with limited production but great integrity, such as *Marty* or *Twelve Angry Men*. The directors were in control of performances and camera work, and with no time for 'second guessing', a singleness of viewpoint provided the setting for actors and actresses to give first-night once-only performances. These live days are still thought of as the 'golden age' of American television drama.

When live first turned to tape, the same conditions existed because mechanical editing was primitive and even dangerous. But with sophisticated editing the cooks increased from two or three to dozens and the broth lost its unique highly personal flavour. Recently public television has found drama to be too expensive, but at one time *Play of the Week* (live), *Hollywood Television Theater* and *Visions* (taped) provided stunning theatrical productions. Today only one programme, *American Playhouse*, airs a mixture of original films and some seen earlier on cable. Quantities of British televison drama can be seen on public stations and Arts and Entertainment cable, due to the high quality and low cost. Most films made for television are commissioned by a network and sold to many sponsors, whose commercials interrupt the programmes about every 12 minutes. Occasionally a major sponsor such as Hallmark, General Electric or Xerox can afford to pay the entire cost of making a two-hour film. It is amazing how much good filmed drama exists despite the cost and the network interference with casting and content. HBO and other cable companies have also tried with occasional success to produce important drama, and it is to be hoped that they will be the source of more in the future. GEORGE SCHAEFER

Robert C. Allen, ed., *To Be Continued . . . Soap Operas around the World* (1995)
George W. Brandt, ed., *British Television Drama* (1981)
——, *British Television Drama in the 1980s* (1993)
Philip Elliott, *The Making of a Television Series* (1973)
John Ellis, *Visible Fictions: Cinema; Television; Video* (1982)
E. Ann Kaplan, *Regarding Television: Critical Approaches* (1983)
David Self, *Television Drama: An Introduction* 1984)
Irene Shubik, *Play for Today: The Evolution of Television Drama* (1975)
R. W. Steadman, *The Serial* (1977)
Raymond Williams, *Television: Technology and Cultural Form* (1974)

Temba Theatre Company Named after the Zulu word for 'hope' or 'trust', Temba was founded in 1972 in London by Atton Kumalo and became Britain's leading BLACK THEATRE company. It sought to find a spectacular theatrical form which drew on black cultural traditions, and actively promoted new, established, British and international black writing as well as producing interpretations of Western classics informed by black experience and using integrated casting. Productions include *The Dutchman* (1974), MATURA's *Black Slaves, White Chains* (1977), WALCOTT's *Pantomime* (1985) and *Romeo and Juliet* (1988). After a struggle with the founders led by Alby James, artistic director since 1984, Temba closed in 1993 and was wound up in 1996. JOOLS GILSON-ELLIS

Tempest, Marie [Mary Susan Etherington] (b. London, 15 July 1864; d. London, 14 Oct. 1942) Actress. She trained in music in London and Paris, and from 1885 to 1900 pursued a stage career in musical comedies and operetta in England, America and Canada. Her performance in 1900 as Nell Gwyn in *English Nell* marked her departure from musical works. From then on she worked in comedy on a national and international scale, touring America, Australia, New Zealand, South Africa, India and the Far East. Back in England during the 1920s she played in contemporary drama such as COWARD's *Hay Fever* (1925) and ST JOHN ERVINE's *The First Mrs Fraser* (1929). Tempest was created a dame in 1937. ELAINE ASTON

H. Bolitho, *Marie Tempest* (1936)

Temple, Joan (b. London, 1887; d. Battle, Sussex, 5 May 1965) Actress and playwright. She acted with J. B. FAGAN's company as well as with many of the experimental repertory companies of the 1920s and 1930s. By 1947 she had written over 13 plays and had acted in many of the original productions. Her plays include

The Plunge (1922), *The Widow's Cruise* (1926) and *Charles and Mary* (1930). MAGGIE GALE

Templeton, Fay (b. Little Rock, Ark., 1865; d. San Francisco, 3 Oct. 1939)   Musical comedy actress. 'Born in a trunk', she toured with her parents as a child performer in the 1860s and made her New York debut in 1873 at the age of eight, playing Puck in *A Midsummer Night's Dream*. After this she was rarely out of work, appearing in comic operas, musicals – *Hendrik Hudson* (1890), *Excelsior, Jr* (1895) – and finally as a star, for five years, of BURLESQUES at the WEBER & FIELDS Music Hall. She popularized 'Mary is a Grand Old Name', one of the songs particularly associated with her, in the hit show *Forty-Five Minutes from Broadway* (1906). She ostensibly retired from the stage in 1910, but made frequent comebacks in VAUDEVILLE, as well as GILBERT and SULLIVAN operas. Her last great success was in the long-running Broadway show *Roberta* (1933).

HELEN RAPPAPORT

Tennent, H. M., Ltd   A firm of theatrical producers founded in 1936 by Henry ('Harry') Moncrieff Tennent (b. Eltham, 18 Feb. 1879; d. London, 10 June 1941) and HUGH 'BINKIE' BEAUMONT. In 1933 two large provincial circuits, Moss Empires Ltd (*see* STOLL MOSS THEATRES LTD) and Howard & Wyndham Ltd (*see* ALBERY FAMILY), formed a subsidiary to provide their theatres with touring plays. Tennent was made general manager and he co-opted his friend Beaumont from Moss Empires. In 1936 the subsidiary was re-formed as a separate company, H. M. Tennent Ltd, to mount original productions for the West End, but their first efforts were comparative failures. Late that year one of their secretaries saw a Sunday night try-out of *George and Margaret* by Gerald Savory and recommended it for production; it opened on 27 February 1937 and was a smash hit, running for 799 performances. The management rarely faltered for the next 36 years, dominating the West End and often having ten or more shows running simultaneously. Their style featured stars and lush productions, exemplified by the famous 1939 revival of *The Importance of Being Earnest*, directed by and starring JOHN GIELGUD with EDITH EVANS as the archetypal Lady Bracknell, and the luxurious 1945 revival of *Lady Windermere's Fan*, designed by CECIL BEATON. Their many long-running hits included *Blithe Spirit* (1,997 performances), *While the Sun Shines* (1,154), *Traveller's Joy* (954), *Seagulls Over Sorrento* (1,551) and *The Little Hut* (1,261), as well as the London productions of the American musicals *Oklahoma!* (1,543), *My Fair Lady* (2,281), *West Side Story* (1,040), *Hello, Dolly!* (794) and *Godspell* (1,128). The firm continued after Beaumont's death right into the early 1990s, but on a much

reduced scale. His personal taste and energies were the driving force of the firm from its inception.   IAN BEVAN

K. Black, *Upper Circle* (1984)

C. Duff, *The Last Summer: The Heyday of the West End Theatre* (1995)

R. Huggett, *Binkie Beaumont: Eminence Grise of the West End Theatre 1933–73* (1984)

tent theatre   Form of theatre staging offering a multitude of examples, since presumably as long as there were sail-makers, awnings could be erected to protect open-air audiences from the sun, without obscuring the light. Tents came into their own in the eighteenth century in Britain when entrepreneurial showmen began touring BOOTH theatres from fair to fair. Excluding CIRCUSES, which have always used this method, the eighteenth and nineteenth centuries provide many examples of legitimate theatre performances and also equestrian melodramas. FIRMIN GÉMIER, in France, founded the Théâtre National Ambulant in 1911 with a tent seating over 1,500 as part of the campaign to found a PEOPLE'S THEATRE and break the commercial and centralized nature of French theatre. In Britain, Intimate Theatre Group toured in a tent from the late 1940s to the 1960s; in the 1970s Bubble Theatre used this form of staging as the most appropriate to carry out their policy of touring the suburban areas of London, and FOOTSBARN TRAVELLING THEATRE Company extended tours of England into worldwide touring. The term 'tent show' has a quite specific meaning in the United States where from 1850 to 1950 travelling companies toured during the summer months in tents. Some of these companies presented VAUDEVILLE and some straight theatre. The economic troubles of the 1930s contributed to the decline of this form of theatre, as did the rise of the cinema, and by 1950 it had almost ceased to exist, except where, as with the case of Footsbarn, companies choose this form to tour their plays. A tent show collection is held at the Texas Technical University.   CLIVE BARKER

See also HISPANIC THEATRE IN THE UNITED STATES; OHEL THEATRE; SEASONAL THEATRE.

C. Ashby and S. D. May, *Trouping Through Texas: Harley Sadler and the Tent Show* (1982)

J. C. Mickel, *Footlights on the Prairie* (1974)

W. L. Stout, *Theatre in a Tent: The Development of a Provincial Entertainment* (1972)

Terry, Ellen [Alice] (b. Coventry, 27 Feb. 1847; d. Smallhythe, Tenterden, Kent, 21 July 1928)   Actress. Bright particular star of the English-speaking theatre, she flourished in the 1880s and came of a theatrical dynasty which includes her grand-nephew JOHN GIEL-

GUD. As a child she joined Charles Kean's company but her early career was interrupted by marriage to painter G. F. Watts and a liaison with architect E. W. Godwin, father of her children EDITH and EDWARD GORDON CRAIG. When she returned to the theatre, her Portia (1875) and Olivia in W. G. Wills' adaptation of *The Vicar of Wakefield* (1878) persuaded HENRY IRVING that she was essential to his Lyceum venture. Their *Hamlet* (1878) began an acting partnership that endured until 1902, setting the tone for the start of the century. The Lyceum's historical MELODRAMAS offered Terry few satisfying parts; Margaret in *Faust* (1885) was an exception, and Irving mounted SARDOU's *Madame Sans-Gêne* (1897) as a vehicle for her. But her best work was done in Shakespeare.

Terry seemed the Victorian feminine ideal incarnate; charm, vivacity, vulnerability and Pre-Raphaelite beauty made her Portia (1879), Desdemona (1881), Beatrice (1882), Cordelia (1892) and Imogen (1896) triumphant. Conventional interpretations of Lady Macbeth (1888), Queen Katherine (1892) and Volumnia (1901) required more tragic passion and assertiveness than she could command, but by remodelling them to suit her stage personality she produced fresh, original interpretations. Late performances can be seen in silent films or heard on recordings. She is best glimpsed in her correspondence with SHAW, which was published in 1931. Three of her sisters, Kate (1844–1924), Marion (1852–1930) and Florence (1855–96), had successful stage careers, as did her younger brother Fred (1864–1932), who became a notable actor–manager with his wife, the actress Julia Neilson (1868–1957); their combined offspring continued another generation of theatre artists. Her autobiography, *The Story of My Life*, appeared in 1908. ALAN HUGHES

David Cheshire, *Potrait of Ellen Terry* (1989)
Roger Manvell, *Ellen Terry* (1968)
J. Stokes, M. Booth and S. Bassnet, *Bernhardt, Terry, Duse* (1988)

Terry, Fred *see* TERRY, ELLEN

Terry, Megan [Marguerite Duffy] (b. Seattle, Wash., 22 July 1932) Playwright. Founding member of the New York OPEN THEATER and playwright-in-residence, 1963–8. Since 1974 she has been literary manager of the OMAHA MAGIC THEATRE and its playwright-in-residence, writing some 60 plays and librettos there. After an early realistic period she began experimenting with a non-linear, montage-like dramaturgy, and pioneered transformational drama where the established circumstances of a scene can change several times during the course of the action, as in

Calm Down Mother (1965). *Viet Rock: A Folk War Movie* (1966), the best-known of her plays, is a rock musical about the Vietnamese war. *Approaching Simone* (1970) is about philosopher Simone Weil, and *Babes in the Bighouse* (1974) is about women in prison. JANE HOUSE

Lynda Hart, ed, *Making a Spectacle* (1989)
Helen Keyssar, *Feminist Theatre* (1984)
David Savran, *In Their Own Words* (1988)

Terson [Patterson], Peter (b. Newcastle upon Tyne, 24 Feb. 1932) Playwright, associated with the VICTORIA THEATRE IN THE ROUND, Stoke-on-Trent, and the NATIONAL YOUTH THEATRE. His first large-cast NYT play, *Zigger Zagger* (1967), turned the stage into football terraces packed with chanting fans. Terson (an ex-teacher) caricatured society's failure to tap teenagers' potential. In subsequent years he presented the case for other youth subcultures, from apprentices (*The Apprentices*, 1968) to skinheads (*Spring-heeled Jack*, 1970). Terson's style is episodic and direct, and has had an important influence on regional theatre. His Stoke plays include several dark rural comedies (*The Mighty Reservoy*, 1964). A prolific writer for stage, radio and television, Terson often celebrates working people's surprising strategies for enriching their lives, from hobbies like trainspotting and rabbit-breeding to the true story of women forced into striptease during the Thatcherite de-industrialization of Tyneside (*Strippers*, 1984). Other plays include *The Ballad of the Artificial Mash* (1967), and *Mooney and His Caravans* (1968). TONY HOWARD

Thailand *see* SOUTH-EAST ASIA

Tharp, Twyla (b. Portland, Ind., 1 July 1941) Choreographer. Her influential work bridges popular mainstream and more experimental, postmodern concerns. She danced in the early 1960s with the Paul Taylor Dance Company before starting her own company in 1965. At the time she was a leading exponent of experimental choreography, using everyday movement and exploring non-theatrical spaces. Abandoning this around 1970, she began making works in a deceptively loose-limbed, eclectic movement style set to popular music, combining popular social and classical dance styles in a manner likened to postmodern pastiche. With *Deuce Coupe* (1973), for the Joffrey Ballet, she became the first experimentalist to 'cross over' and work with a ballet company. As well as maintaining her own company, she has since made works for many of the world's leading ballet companies. Her autobiography, *Push Comes to Shove*, appeared in 1992. RAMSAY BURT

See also CHOREOGRAPHY; DANCE.

Theater Communications Group A not-for-profit organization created in 1961 by the Ford Foundation to assist America's nascent regional theatre movement by promoting interaction between its far-flung members (more than 300 theatres from more than 40 states in 1992). It does so by awarding travel grants to artists, administering design and director fellowships, sponsoring symposia and conferences, and publishing plays, books, management surveys, an arts employment newsletter and *American Theater* magazine. Ranging from established SHAKESPEARE FESTIVALS to inner-city bilingual troupes, from Alaska's Perseverance Theatre to Appalachia's Roadside Theater, from small ensembles – the WOOSTER GROUP, MABOU MINES – whose theatre experiments have garnered international renown, to large urban institutions – the SEATTLE REPERTORY THEATER, Los Angeles' MARK TAPER FORUM or New York's PUBLIC THEATER – that have produced the new American plays that Broadway producers can no longer afford to develop on their own, the TCG umbrella embraces what some consider to be America's true 'national theatre'. JOHN ISTEL

See also RESIDENT THEATRE.

Theater Guild New York theatre company known in the 1920s for productions of innovative European dramas and new American plays. An outgrowth of the WASHINGTON SQUARE PLAYERS, the Guild was founded in 1919 by LAWRENCE LANGNER, PHILIP MOELLER and actress Helen Westley. This trio was quickly joined by Therese Helburn, who would become the organization's executive director, banker Maurice Wertheim, and LEE SIMONSON. Despite the inherent problems in operating 'by committee', the Guild remained loyal to its concept of rule by a governing board. The Guild's mission was 'to produce plays of artistic merit not ordinarily produced by the commercial managers' and it proved unique in its ability to subsist on a subscription basis, thanks largely to Armina Marshall (1895–1991), who was married to Langner. The Guild's earlier triumphs were in the realm of EXPRESSIONISM (e.g. KAISER's *From Morn to Midnight*, 1922; RICE's *The Adding Machine*, 1923) and in introducing SHAW to America (e.g. *Heartbreak House*, 1920; *Back to Methuselah*, 1922; *Saint Joan*, 1925). Although works by SIDNEY HOWARD, S. N. BEHRMAN, ROBERT SHERWOOD, MAXWELL ANDERSON and, regularly, EUGENE O'NEILL were played there, the organization was sometimes criticized for neglecting American playwrights.

The Guild seemed unable to bend with the artistic and political turmoil of the early 1930s and several members defected to form the GROUP THEATER, while some of its writers began the PLAYWRIGHTS' COMPANY.

The Guild itself turned to comedy and musicals – *Oklahoma!* (1943) and *Carousel* (1945). It no doubt succumbed to producing popular and star vehicles (featuring the LUNTS) in order to survive. None the less, it had earned its place in American theatre history through its managerial principles and practices, the quality of its productions, its extensive national tours, the individual actors and companies it spawned, and its sheer longevity and ability to serve as a model 'art theatre' in a nation that has no national theatre. ANNE FLETCHER

W. P. Eaton, *The Theater Guild: The First Ten Years* (1929)

R. Waldau, *Vintage Years of the Theater Guild 1928–1939* (1972)

Theatr Clwyd Officially renamed in 1998 Clwyd Theatr Cymru (Clwyd Theatre Wales), this is regarded by many, although more by those outside Wales, as the leading Welsh theatre company and from 2000 the base of a new touring Wales National Performing Arts Company. It was founded as the production company of the new Theatr Clwyd arts complex at Mold, just inside the Welsh border from Cheshire, in 1976. (Clwyd was the county, since replaced by several new, smaller local authorities; Mold was the county town and is now in Flintshire.)

A series of high-profile directors (Toby Robertson 1985–92, Helena Kaut-Howson 1992–5, TERRY HANDS from 1997) made the theatre more than a provincial rep and brought much-needed publicity and the possibility of West End transfers. Memorable productions among the familiar staple diet include Robertson's Welsh-based *Enemy of the People* (1991), which some thought turned IBSEN's theme on its head; his brief associate Annie Castledine's startling première of Sheila Yeger's play about Gwen John, *Self Portrait* (1987); Kaut-Howson's often exciting but also too often incoherent application of east European style in *The Devils* (1992) and *Full Moon* (1994); and Hands' assured *Equus* (1997). Hands's arrival saw some political image-changes and the appointment of Tim Baker (erstwhile director of the successful THEATRE IN EDUCATION and COMMUNITY THEATRE company, Theatre West Glamorgan) as Welsh-speaking associate director, so that it could become the National Theatre of Wales by default. DAVID ADAMS

theatre anthropology An area of practical research developed in the 1970s through the influence of EUGENIO BARBA. Since its inception in 1979, the International School of Theatre Anthropology (ISTA), founded by Barba within the Nordisk Teaterlaboratorium (*see*

ODIN TEATRET), has held regular encounters in various countries between theatre practitioners from Western and oriental theatre and scholars working in a wide range of disciplines. The term 'theatre anthropology' is interpreted in the widest possible sense, that is, as the study of human behaviour on both the biological and socio-cultural levels in a performance situation.

Barba's work and the work of similar THIRD THEATRE companies involves rigorous physical training sessions on a daily basis. This emphasis on the physical has resulted in a different kind of theatre work, one that finds its focus elsewhere than in the tradition of psychological realism or building the character that is so much a part of the contemporary Western actor's training. Because of the scarcity of models in the West, Barba turned to oriental theatre and especially to two aspects of the oriental actor's training programme: the existence of a set of codified laws in the transmission of theatrical forms and conventions, and the process of handing down knowledge from one generation to another as actors train from an early age with acknowledged expert teachers. Following BRECHT, Barba asserts that the art of the actor does not exist in the West, where, with the exception of classical ballet, subjectivity and individualism prevail over codified rules and conventions.

In classical ballet and other forms of codified theatre, the human body is used in ways that are notably different from its daily use or from its use in realist theatre. The ISTA research project began with an examination of those extra-daily techniques, studying them on a comparative basis, and discovered that all codified performance forms have as a constant feature the deliberate deformation of the daily technique of body movement, which involves a reconstructing of natural balance. The next phase of the research was to study how those processes of creating imbalance occurred within the body and how they manifest themselves in different forms and in different cultures. The initial work of theatre anthropologists involved close examination of the physical processes in different types of contemporary theatre, and then moved on to consider different moments in time. The historical dimension of theatre anthropology has proved to be particularly fruitful, since it opens up an alternative perspective to that previously offered by Western theatre historians whose starting point was within the conventions established by the predominance of psychological realism.

Work in theatre anthropology in the late 1980s and 1990s focused increasingly on the problem of the actor's pre-expressivity. What is meant by this is the way in which physiological factors modify the muscle tones and result in new body rhythms that bring about a change in the quality of energy used by the actor. A contentious issue emerged in the meeting of ISTA in 1986, when the question of sexuality and pre-expressivity came under scrutiny. There is some division of opinion as to whether the concept of pre-expressivity can be understood as asexual or whether the sex of the actor inevitably conditions the way in which that pre-expressivity takes place.

Work in theatre anthropology draws from a wide range of disciplines, including theatre and performance studies, semiology, traditional anthropology, neurophysiology and psychology. CLIVE BARKER

See also EASTERN THEATRE, ITS INFLUENCE ON THE WEST.

Eugenio Barba, 'Anthropologie théâtrale: première hypothese', in *Theatre International ITI* (1981)
——, *The Dilated Body* (1985)
Franco Ruffini, 'Pour une semiologie concrète de l'acteur', in *Degrés*, no. 30, 1982
Nicola Savarese and Eugenio Barba, *The Dictionary of Theatre Anthropology: The Secret Art of the Performer* (1991)
Richard Schechner, 'Anthropological Analysis', *Drama Review*, vol. 22, no. 3, 1978
——, *Between Theatre and Anthropology* (1985)

Theatre Centre *see* CHILDREN'S THEATRE

theatre clubs *see* CLUB THEATRE

Theatre de Complicite British-based theatre company, formed in 1983, characterized by COLLECTIVE improvisation and a strong physical and comic emphasis. Their work draws on COMMEDIA DELL'ARTE traditions and on the work of Philippe Gaulier and Monika Pagneaux, teachers at the LECOQ school in Paris. The company has toured internationally to build a strong following for its often frenzied but disciplined comedy, and has achieved wider recognition through television appearances and new developments following performances of DÜRRENMATT's *The Visit* at the NATIONAL THEATRE (1991; first performed on tour 1988) where the company also staged *The Street of Crocodiles* (1992) and *Out of a House Walked a Man* (1994). One of the founders, Simon McBurney, who became artistic director of the company, was praised for Complicite's *The Three Lives of Lucie Cabrol* (1994), *The Caucasian Chalk Circle* (1997 at the NT), *Chairs* (1997 at the Royal Court) and *Mnemonic* (1999). Other members, particularly KATHRYN HUNTER and Marcello Magni, have taken Complicite's growing influence to other companies. ANDREW SOLWAY

Théâtre de l'Europe French national theatre given over to the performance of European drama. A. M. Julien conceived of it as a competitor to the THÉÂTRE DES NATIONS, aiming to bring to Paris foreign directors who would direct plays from their own cultures, using French actors. Belgium also wished to establish such a theatre in Liège. Problems of subsidy, administration and temperament set back the anticipated inauguration date (1966). Eventually, under GIORGIO STREHLER, the traditionally adventurous ODÉON national theatre, to which BARRAULT had brought GROTOWSKI in 1966, became Odéon-Théâtre de l'Europe, staging foreign and French plays and hosting many touring productions, such as the ROYAL SHAKESPEARE COMPANY's *Richard III* in 1990. TERRY HODGSON

Théâtre des Nations One of the most visible 'children' of the INTERNATIONAL THEATRE INSTITUTE, it started in Paris in 1957 as a development from the Festival of Paris (1954) which saw the first visit to the West of the BERLINER ENSEMBLE. It was produced annually in Paris until 1972. It then became itinerant, and later biennial, appearing abroad. Its influence stemmed from the calibre of its visitors, who included THEATRE WORKSHOP, LIVING THEATER, BREAD AND PUPPET THEATER, KREJCA, GROTOWSKI and KANTOR. The University of Theatre of Nations was created to involve young artists in every aspect of the festival's season, offering one month of workshops, performances, and discussion with performers, scholars, critics and guest artists. Sessions of the university have also been held in connection with other FESTIVALS, in Barcelona, Damascus and Seoul. MARTHA W. COIGNEY

Théâtre du Soleil Influential theatre cooperative based at the Vincennes Cartoucherie (cartridge warehouse) on the outskirts of Paris. Formed in 1964, it pursues, under the dominant personality of ARIANE MNOUCHKINE, a policy of collective responsibility for writing, casting, technical production and all the chores of theatre work, including collecting tickets and selling drinks. Although a production of Wesker's *The Kitchen* (1967) pointed the way, it was not until after the turmoil of 1968 that group work fully developed. Productions since the remarkable *1789* (1970) have been marked by long rehearsal periods and brilliantly orchestrated choral work. The repertoire, both text-based and company-researched, has included Shakespeare, *1793* (1972), *Mephisto* (1979), *The Indiade* (1998, about Indian independence) and *Les Atrides* (1990–1), consisting of Euripides's *Iphigenia at Aulis* and Aeschylus's *Oresteia*, which displayed the powerful influence of oriental theatre, music and dance. It has worked closely with the feminist writer Hélène Cixous (b.

Oran, Algeria, 1937) since the late 1970s; collaborations include *Mephisto, The Terrible but Unfinished Story of Norodom Sihanouk, King of Cambodia* (1985), *The Indiade*, and *The Perjury City, or the Awakening of the Furies* (1994). TERRY HODGSON

M-L. and D. Bablet, *Le Théâtre du Soleil* (1979)
A. Kiernander, *Ariane Mnouchkine and the Théâtre du Soleil* (1993)
D. Williams, ed, *Collaborative Theatre: The Théâtre du Soleil Sourcebook* (1999)

theatre families It is not unusual that members of a family share the same profession, yet the professional interaction of theatre artists, in rehearsal or on the stage, is at times more intense and more emotionally charged than the interaction of members of other professions. In some cases, several generations of a family will pursue careers in the theatre. Notable modern examples are the ADLER, ALBERY, BARRYMORE, Calvert, COMPTON, CUSACK, POWER, REDGRAVE, TERRY and WEBSTER families. DANIEL MEYER-DINKGRÄFE

Richard Foulkes, *The Calverts: Actors of Some Importance* (1992)
Rachel Kempson, *A Family and its Fortunes* (1986)
Margaret Webster, *The Same Only Different: Five Generations of a Great Theatre Family* (1969)

theatre for development New forms and uses of drama associated primarily with postcolonial rural communities coping with problems of change. Through its widespread use of propaganda, the Second World War inspired a more sophisticated understanding of communication techniques and the theory behind them; following the war, the social needs resulting from postcolonial independence and the availability of the new communication techniques combined to create a variety of new forms and functions for the theatre. Sometimes these endeavour to provoke change or reinforce processes already in operation; sometimes they deal with the necessity, in a time of change, to develop new skills, attitudes or behavioural patterns. In some cases, theatre programmes are promoted by the ruling class to integrate the population into the changing situation and so preserve the status quo; in other cases, oppositional groups use theatre to promote popular movements to resist integration and to destabilize the structures of dominance. In both these strategies it is possible to distinguish two mutually exclusive approaches. The first is the 'top-down' approach in which some external body assesses the needs of the target audience and delivers the solution in the form of a 'message'. The second is the 'grass-roots' approach through which local groups are encouraged to define their own problems and to reach conclusions and solutions cooperatively. In the former case, theatre is useful because it is a direct form of information distribution, more personal, more entertaining, more popular than the impersonal mechanical media. In the latter case, theatre serves in a participatory way as a teaching tool and educational process, and as a force for community social action. In both of these, the popular or traditional appeal of theatre wins out over the mechanical media.

Centrally initiated programmes can take a number of forms. In mobile propaganda programmes, theatre groups are hired to tour plays or concerts made up of a variety of forms or units. In mobilization campaigns, local theatre groups are utilized to work more intensively in specific areas performing plays with a more precise relevance. This approach can also involve an animateur working in a district to form amateur theatre groups, giving a more specific orientation and a clearer identification between performers and audience. This method was widely used in China in the 1950s, where government policy supplied trained animateurs to form a mass movement of over a quarter of a million village theatre groups providing entertainment and an educational tool.

Many groups throughout the world that participate in this work were originally formed to use theatre in literacy and non-formal education programmes. Song, drama and MIME are used as a medium for literacy learning in many parts of the world, and also function as a means for overcoming self-consciousness, feelings of inferiority and psycho-social conditioning, persuading people to learn and express themselves. Literacy programmes form a part of the work of extension workers operating in rural areas in varieties of non-formal education. Plays are rehearsed and scripted, often impromptu, on local issues, usually relating cause to consequence. These plays form a basis for discussion and for cooperation between villagers and experts. Issues such as nutrition, vaccination, alcoholism and family planning are dealt with in this way, through dramatized case-studies. Socio-drama and role-playing exercises are all used in the training of extension workers. A further extension of this form of work can lead to community development and cooperatives. In this work, performance is more process- than content-orientated. It puts across no message but tries to stimulate the identifying of community problems searching for solution through community or group action. Performances are not one-off but are part of an ongoing process of community action. The text continuously evolves through discussion, participation and critical scrutiny.

In all these areas of work there is a dialectic in operation. Although designed for the benefit of the individual and the community, because such theatre operates within government policy and does not seek to challenge the social and political status quo, it can be seen as open to political manipulation, either by government agencies operating through the animateurs or extension workers, or through the influential sections of the community, who are more articulate and better organized, and who speak with traditional vested authority. Ross Kidd, who has worked in development programmes and conducted a comprehensive survey of work throughout the world, cites one example of this: a community problem in Botswana was identified as cattle-rustling and a team of development workers used this as the basis for their theatre programme. Cattle-rustling is, however, only a problem for those who own cattle, not for the poorer members of society who do not.

At the same time, this utilization of theatre often leads to an understanding on the part of those being educated that issues are being subverted or that questions are being begged. Once started, the process of self-education is difficult to stop, and when people gather to identify problems and establish forms of community action it is often difficult to prevent awkward questions arising. There have been cases of literacy groups outgrowing their function and widening their work to share the new awareness with their fellow villagers. The Kamirithu community theatre in Kenya grew out of a literacy programme. In their progress towards literacy the group became very politicized and began to use drama to expose the social ills of corruption, landlessness and unemployment; by this means they went on to organize their fellow villagers into a movement for popular struggle.

In this respect, the non-governmental movement in development theatre begins where the work described above leaves off. The performing arts have a different function to fulfil. They work in the process of educating, politicizing and organizing the lower classes to defend themselves against victimization and to act to transform the existing power structure. In some parts of the world this work is often grouped under the heading 'liberation theatre', giving it a clear relationship to 'liberation theology', which seeks to transform the role of the Roman Catholic Church in the Third World. It is also called 'theatre of the oppressed' after AUGUSTO BOAL's description, derived from the Brazilian educator Paulo Freire's 'pedagogy of the oppressed', the principles of which underlie almost every project in this field.

Various forms of work in this area can be identified.

(1) *Conscientization* or *agitational theatre by outside groups*. Although the general direction of this work (and the nature of some of the performances) is towards a 'top-down' dissemination of political analysis, many groups move beyond simple ideological persuasion and utilize post-performance discussion to encourage people to think through the problems themselves, rather than imposing on them an analysis and ready-made solutions. Boal gives an example of the over-simplification of this field of work. Performing a play which encouraged peasants to rise against landowners and take the land from them by force, he and his actors found themselves conscripted into a peasant uprising with real guns to replace the prop ones in the play. Narrowly escaping from this, Boal learned not to prescribe solutions to other people's problems. A sophisticated example is Teatro Escambray in the mountains of Cuba, which maintains continuous contact with its audiences, scripting its plays on the basis of 'participatory research', exposing the contradictions of post-revolutionary Cuba and encouraging collective efforts among the farmers of the region. The work spills over into animating theatrical productions by the farmers themselves. In some parts of the world the work involves confronting people with issues as a means of moving them to take action. Women's STREET THEATRE groups in India perform plays and instigate discussion on such matters as rape, dowry deaths and other issues of female oppression. Some groups offer participatory workshops as part of their work.

(2) *Conscientization drama workshops* extend this work further. Drawing on Freire's educational principle of 'conscientization' and on Boal's work extending Freire's concepts and ideas through drama, these workshops dispense with the performance and move straight to encouraging peasants and workers to dramatize their situation, to analyse and critically assess the dramatization and to restructure it, moving always to the positing of solutions, which must include all necessary steps along the way from the present to the desired future. In this way, peasants and farmers struggle to objectivize their exploitation and oppression and to move towards controlling it and removing it. Following Freire's principles, it is a complex process of self-enlightenment and education which is necessary if people are truly to liberate themselves and not exchange one master for another.

(3) *Theatre of identity* seeks to revitalize the culture of oppressed groups. Workers in the Ayni Ruway movement among the Indians of Bolivia argue that the Indians know very well that they are exploited and repressed and in what ways. The need is to give them back a sense of identity and self-confidence which will lead to the formation of political organizations to combat and, it is hoped, overcome this oppression.

(4) *Peasants'/workers' theatre* differs from the first category of work in so far as it arises in local communities, which ensures that the theatre is locally produced and there is class identification or identity between the performers and the audiences. Theatre of this type expresses class views and perspectives, seeks to create class consciousness and can mobilize protest against oppression, and often serves to counteract the media propaganda of the dominant class. Because of their local identity, these groups tend to operate independently of any political movement or force, although in the Philippines a network of these groups constitutes a considerable oppositional voice. The Sistren company in Jamaica is a women's COLLECTIVE formed out of women employed to sweep streets. Its work involves research not only into the condition of women in Jamaican society but also into the history of women in that society. Plays are structured out of research carried out among other Jamaican women. The group gives performances as well as workshops, and the collective provides an example of Jamaican women creating their own cooperative structure to work against their own oppression. They are well integrated into Jamaican society because of the links and continuity between research, performance, discussion and workshops.

Some groups who began in this way have become directly politicized by their activities and have become part of a wider organization directly combating oppression and serving as the political arm representing the interests of the people of the locality. In peasants'/workers theatre for conscientization and organizing, the theatre plays an important mobilization role linked to education, politicization, movement-building and political struggle. This work characterized the early years of El TEATRO CAMPESINO in California under LUIS VALDEZ, when he was directly linked to Cesar Chavez' attempts to organize the fruit and grape pickers. The community theatre group in Kamirithu, Kenya, fulfilled this function there.

(5) An organizational variation of the above is *popular movement drama*. The members of a popular political movement utilize drama to present their case, raise morale and rehearse various courses of action. This form of theatre is frequently spontaneous and does not seek to separate out theatre as a distinct form of activity. It is the cultural expression of political activists.

Although it has been possible to make distinctions here between those activities which seek to continue the status quo and those which oppose it, in practice this is not always possible. There has been a considerable takeover of Freire's terminology, and these methods have been used in many of the above areas of theatre work by governments who have utilized them in their own interests under the guise of being liberationists inside the system. In looking at projects it is necessary to distinguish clearly between those projects which serve a view of development in which the object of social transformation is to incorporate the unskilled into a more technologically advanced world in order to increase productivity, and those projects which serve a view of development in which social transformation is achieved, to quote Juan Diaz Bordenave, by 'awakening the intellectual and decision-making potential of rural people so that they themselves can change the very structure of society'. CLIVE BARKER

Kees P. Epskamp, *Theatre in Search of Social Change* (1989)
Kees P. Epskamp and Ad Boeren, *The Empowerment of Culture: Development, Communication and Popular Media* (1992)
Ross Kidd, *The Popular Performing Arts, Non-Formal Education and Social Change in the Third World: A Bibliography and Review Essay* (1982)
R. Kidd and N. Colletta, eds, *Cultivating Indigenous Structures and Traditional Media for Non-Formal Education and Development* (1981)

theatre for old people Form of COMMUNITY THEATRE which is directly addressed to the institutionalized aged. Although there is a clear justification for the offering of entertainment, usually in the accessible form of MUSIC HALL, to the aged (Old Age Theatre Society), other groups have tried ways of utilizing participatory forms of theatre to reverse mental and physical stultification in old people, to awaken interest and to provide mental stimulation for people to go on living (Age Exchange, Reminiscence Theatre). This can provoke people to remember the songs and other performance skills of their youth, or seek to stimulate the memory for historical, documentary or personal recall purposes. CLIVE BARKER

theatre for young people

In Britain
The twentieth century has seen a vast increase in the number of professional theatre companies working largely, and often exclusively, for young people, beyond the traditional fields of PUPPETRY, MAGIC, CLOWNING and Christmas productions of classic 'children's' texts. Many practitioners are loath to categorize their work too closely, perhaps fearing the potential divisiveness and restrictions of such labels when there is much

overlap. However, four main strands of theatre for young people can be identified: CHILDREN'S THEATRE, young people's theatre, THEATRE IN EDUCATION and YOUTH THEATRE. The work of COMMUNITY THEATRE groups who respond to the needs of specific sections of society, including young people, and of subsidized theatres, which include occasional provision for local children in their season, can also fall into one of these categories.

Children's theatre, which has taken many forms, is the precursor of the other, later, developments, but it has retained its original emphasis: the presentation of plays designed specifically for younger audiences, usually aged 12 and under. Young people's theatre has similar roots but its audiences include teenagers and its work is more likely to be based on social issues, rather than the myths and fantasies found in much children's theatre. The work of some young people's theatre companies, influenced by the theatre in education movement, has a defined educative purpose. As early as 1900, when BEN GREET offered performances of Shakespeare at 'very popular prices' for elementary and evening school pupils, theatre for young people was beginning to be linked with education. The struggle for wider acknowledgement of the educational and artistic value of theatre for young people was fought on isolated fronts over the next 40 years. In 1924 the London County Council was providing a grant to enable the OLD VIC to offer free seats for Shakespeare matinées as part of the school curriculum. By 1937 the Scottish Children's Theatre, formed by Bertha Waddell in 1927, was given a grant to provide free performances of her 'combined arts' programme in junior schools. However, the remarkably rapid development of theatre for young people in Britain can be dated from the 1944 Education Act. Although innovative moves could hardly be described as burgeoning in the 20 years following the Act, there are three landmarks worth noting: the establishment in 1947 by Caryl Jenner of the UNICORN THEATRE; the founding by Brian Way and Margaret Faulkes in 1949 of Theatre Centre, which toured to schools; and the publication in 1954 of *Child Drama* by Peter Slade.

Jenner's dream of a National Children's Theatre is yet to be realized. All forms of theatre for young people are still perceived as low-status work by many both inside and outside the theatre profession. The first purpose-built theatre for young people did not open until 1970 with the creation of the YOUNG VIC; now its work is no longer exclusively for young people. Theatre Centre experimented in and researched forms of theatre suitable for children of all ages, while the publication of Slade's *Child Drama* saw a move further away from theatre. His argument that child drama has its roots in play, its purpose being to develop creative self-expression, did give it identity and status; but it also placed it as a separate and different art form. The division of opinion over Slade's views was the genesis of the theatre versus educational drama debate that continued through the 1950s. The publication in 1967 of Way's influential book *Development Through Drama* further encouraged the growth of drama in education as a separate study from theatre arts. The work of Slade and Way influenced the creation of the next major strand. In 1965, at the Belgrade Theatre, Coventry, the first theatre in education (TIE) company was founded through the work of the theatre's director Anthony Richardson and his assistant Gordon Vallins. The fertile environment in which this and other similar initiatives to bring theatre to young people, such as the MERMAID THEATRE's Molecule Club (founded in 1967), took root was the economic boom of the 1960s, the creation of new CIVIC THEATRES and arts centres, and the simultaneous move to liberalize educational theory and practice that was itself rooted in the 1944 Act. The late 1960s and early 1970s saw the creation of a number of TIE companies, and an emphasis on participatory drama, in which company members saw themselves not only as actors but as teachers. Some were independent co-operatives and some, like Coventry, were attached to 'main house' theatres and, as such, developed alongside newly flourishing youth theatre groups, which were themselves a result of moves by the theatres to reach out to their community. In 1975, the Standing Conference of Young People's Theatre (SCYPT) was founded, an organization for professional workers in TIE and young people's theatre. As theatre in education developed, it began to move away from the view of Slade and Way, with a change in emphasis from personal development and self-expression to the recognition of drama and theatre as unique teaching tools for developing understanding about the society in which young people live as well as an understanding about their own potential within that society. The new division was between what might be described as 'art for art's sake' or form-based work (often identified as children's and young people's theatre) and 'content-based' work (TIE). Key to this qualitative shift, and to the reuniting in the 1980s of theatre and drama in education, is the work of Gavin Bolton and Dorothy Heathcote. However, the political and economic climate in Britain from the mid-1980s saw a drastic reduction in the number of companies combining theatre and participatory educational drama. By the end of the twentieth century, children's

theatre and youth theatre were the dominant forms of theatre for young people.

The low status of theatre for young people, together with the need for box-office success, has resulted in a relative dearth of new plays in this area. Most of the innovative and original work is produced in the publicly subsidized sector, but few of these excellent plays are published or performed outside their original specialized field. Few writers have become known solely for their plays for young people. Exceptions to this include Brian Way, DAVID WOOD, DAVID HOLMAN, and Volker Ludwig of Gripps Theatre, Germany. There are a few more, largely unpublished, writers whose plays for theatre in education and young people's theatre companies deserve a wider audience – for example, John Wood, Geoff Gillham, Lisa Evans, Noel Greig, Paul Swift, Charles Way, Bryony Lavery, Tony Coult. Their work can usually be obtained from the producing companies, SCYPT or the national centre of the International Association of Theatre for Children and Young People (ASSITEJ). Young people themselves have increasingly been encouraged to write plays by a host of schemes, usually associated with a particular institution like the ROYAL COURT.

There have been many and varied influences from the wider world of theatre on work for young people; they include JOAN LITTLEWOOD, BERTOLT BRECHT, EDWARD BOND, ERWIN PISCATOR, AUGUSTO BOAL as well as the development of feminist theatre and many elements of BLACK and Asian cultures.   LYNNE CLARK

In the United States
American theatre for young audiences developed in the twentieth century in three separate settings: in the field of education, in regional and community theatres and in professional companies. Despite numerous sporadic efforts by individuals such as Alice Minnie Herts, who opened her Children's Educational Theater in 1903 for New York City's immigrant audiences, no effort was made to organize nationwide operations until 1944, when 80 teachers and directors met to form the Children's Theater Conference. Declaring their goal to improve standards of writing and directing, they held annual conferences and showcases over the next six decades, and, in the 2000s, as the American Alliance for Theater and Education, this organization remains children's theatre's most powerful force. By honouring research, new plays, authors and distinguished companies, AATE in its publications nurtures the development of theatre for young people throughout the country. Almost every US college theatre department includes introductory study in theatre for young audiences, many with specialized courses. Numerous

new plays have had first productions in college productions: e.g. *Step on a Crack* by Susan Zeder (Southern Methodist University, Dallas, Texas, 1974); *The Arkansaw Bear* by Aurand Harris (University of Texas at Austin, 1974); *Cinderella: The World's Favourite Fairy Tale* by Lowell Swortzell (Ferrum College, Virginia, 1991).

Non-professional regional theatre companies came to national notice in the 1930s when Winifred Ward established the Evanston, Illinois, Children's Theater and when Charlotte Chorpenning began directing her own plays at the GOODMAN MEMORIAL THEATER in nearby Chicago. Founded in 1961, the Children's Theater Company of Minneapolis, Minnesota, moved into its modern building in 1975 to establish an impressive record for large-scale productions of original scripts, most appealing to both children and adults. Other important regional theatres exist in Atlanta, St Louis, Louisville and Honolulu. In 1993 the Children's Theater of Seattle opened a new theatre of its own with a commissioned play, *Afternoon of the Elves*, to great local and national acclaim.

In the 1920s Clare Tree Major, a former British actress, established her own professional touring theatre which continued into the early 1950s, offering adaptations of children's classics performed by adult actors. In the mid-1930s the FEDERAL THEATER PROJECT sponsored children's theatre, for the first time supported by the US government. Killed by a hostile Congress in 1939, FTP none the less proved that talent existed for a vital and committed coast-to-coast theatre for young people.

The Paper Bag Players, the best-known modern American professional company, founded in 1958, still plays a New York season and travels widely, at home and abroad. Its performance style combines MIME, music, minimal dialogue and décor made out of discarded cardboard boxes. Theaterworks/USA (1962) also tours, giving more than 850 performances a year of original musicals, often based on the lives of famous young Americans such as Abraham Lincoln, Eleanor Roosevelt and Jim Thorpe. In the late 1970s, BROADWAY became interested in children when the musical *Annie* (1977) ran for 2,377 performances. Subsequently, *Big River* (1985), *The Secret Garden* (1991), *Beauty and the Beast* (1994) and *The Lion King* (1997) demonstrated that productions intended for young audiences at last had entered mainstream commercial theatre.

The need for playwrights is a constant cry from all those working in the field. Before 1945 only one major dramatist, Charlotte Chorpenning, had emerged, with works mostly based on traditional sources (*The Emperor's New Clothes*, 1938). In the 1950s and 1960s Aurand Harris established a national reputation for his still continuing series, now numbering over 50, of adaptations and original plays. His *Androcles and the Lion* (1963) is widely performed around the world, making Harris the most produced American dramatist for young people. Beginning in the 1970s, Susan Zeder contributed a number of popular works, some dealing with contemporary problems such as divorce. By the 1990s, a generation of dramatists had emerged, headed by Joanna Halpert Kraus, Flora Atkin, Max Buxh, Virginia Glasgow Koste, James Still and Laurie Brooks. Dramatists from the adult theatre also write for children: DAVID MAMET, MARK MEDOFF, WILLIAM GIBSON and Wendy Kesselman foremost among them.

The THEATRE IN EDUCATION movement imported from England in the 1970s incorporates theatrical techniques into educational settings. Treating contemporary problems, TIE makes audiences face issues directly and solve problems through post-performance sessions or at various points in the play itself. The Creative Arts Team of New York University has become the leading exponent of American TIE, noted for its work on topics such as child abuse and conflict resolution.

The Young Playwrights' Festival, held in New York each year since 1981, attracts young dramatists (aged under 19) to submit original works which are given professional OFF-BROADWAY productions. More than 1,000 scripts from throughout the country are entered annually, and the Educational Program has conducted writing workshops with more than 4,000 students in the New York area alone.

Clearly, Mark Twain's 1906 prediction that 'children's theatre is one of the very, very great inventions of the twentieth century' has been realized by teachers, professionals and young audiences alike.

LOWELL SWORTZELL

Gavin Bolton, *Towards a Theory of Drama in Education* (1983)

——, *Acting in Classroom Drama* (1998)

T. Jackson, ed., *Learning through Theatre: New Perspectives on Theatre in Education* (1993)

L. Johnson and C. O'Neill, eds, *Dorothy Heathcote: Collected Writings on Education and Drama* (1984)

Nellie McCaslin, *Historical Guide to Children's Theatre in America* (1987)

——, ed., *Theatre for Young Audiences* (1978)

John O'Toole, *The Process of Drama* (1992)

Lowell Swortzell, *International Guide to Children's Theatre and Educational Theatre: A Historical and Geographical Source* (1990)

——, *The Theatre of Aurand Harris* (1997)
Winifred Ward, *Theatre for Children* (1935)
Brian Way, *Audience Participation* (1981)

theatre in education As a generic term coined in England in 1965, it is used to describe theatre forms presented by professionals who are versed in the techniques and methods of both teaching and theatre. It is performed predominantly in or for schools, but also in youth clubs, colleges, theatre buildings and other community venues. The performers are traditionally called 'actor–teachers'. Audiences are usually drawn from a specific age group within the age range of 5 to 19 years. Most companies service one geographical area, maintaining regular contact with their audiences. In its short history TIE has spread and evolved, and taken root in many parts of the world.

The primary distinguishing feature of TIE is its explicit educational purpose. The companies (or 'teams') aim to provide more than entertainment, and to teach something other than theatre appreciation or skills. Teaching objectives vary enormously. A typical selection might include language development; an analysis of racism; exploration of a concept (e.g. power); or the critique of a contemporary issue, such as nuclear energy. The dramatic content chosen to focus the learning is usually drawn from the real world of historical or contemporary events (e.g. a documented experience of eighteenth-century slavery). TIE methodology has also been enlisted for HIV/AIDS education and conflict resolution work.

The form of the TIE event (called a 'programme') is dictated by the educational aims. Companies work in-depth with small audiences, usually 30–40 young people. A programme is longer than an average play, lasting half a day or more. Some programmes are in several parts, presented at intervals, and linked by interim class-work from the teacher. TIE's distinctive formal feature is the use of active audience participation. The degree and kind vary from programme to programme, but possible components include simulation games, role-play, improvised drama, dialogue between the audience and characters from a play ('hot-seating'), audience intervention in the dramatic action (cf. AUGUSTO BOAL), and group discussion. The integration of these methods with more familiar performance techniques is a genuine innovation in theatre form. CHRIS VINE

See also THEATRE FOR YOUNG PEOPLE; YOUTH THEATRE.

Tony Jackson, ed., *Learning through Theatre: New Perspectives on Theatre in Education* (1993)
John O'Toole, *Theatre-in-Education: New Objectives for Theatre – New Techniques in Education* (1976)

Christine Redington, *Can Theatre Teach?* (1983)
Ken Robinson, *Exploring Theatre and Education* (1980)

theatre in exile As the name suggests, theatre performed by people in exile, such as Palestinians in Egypt or Syria, Kurds in Germany or, during the junta's reign, Chileans in London or Paris, to raise consciousness in the host country, encourage solidarity and maintain a sense of identity within the displaced community.
CHARLES LONDON

See also POLITICAL THEATRE.

theatre in prisons An umbrella term for a wide range of activities from formal entertainment to therapy and rehabilitation. There is theatre *for* prisoners, where a visiting company gives performances; theatre *by* prisoners, where inmates create their own productions; and theatre *with* prisoners, where theatre is co-created with drama specialists to serve entertainment and/or therapeutic ends. The term is also applied to work in secure hospitals. There is much debate on whether the theatre is about the prison, i.e. the confined space, or the population, i.e. the prisoners, and about whether people who are being punished should be allowed theatre; some term it a luxury, a soft option, a reward, while people who support or practise theatre in prisons insist either that theatre is a basic human need or that theatre will assist in the rehabilitation process and therefore reduce future offending behaviour.

Groundbreaking work has been carried out by groups such as Geese Theatre Company, Clean Break, and Theatre for Prison and Probation, but the most famous example remains the productions of BECKETT's plays in San Quentin Prison, California, that began in 1961.
SUE JENNINGS

M. Cox, ed., *Shakespeare Comes to Broadmoor* (1992)
S. Jennings, 'The Traveller: Healing Theatre in Magilligan Prison', *Dramatherapy Journal*, vol. 21, no. 2, 1999
J. Thompson, ed., *Prison Theatre* (1998)

theatre in the round A mainly twentieth-century phenomenon, also known as central staging or arena theatre, it is the most extreme form of OPEN STAGE, in which the actors are entirely surrounded by the audience. It is also the most controversial. Some take the view that the impracticability of using conventional scenery is a handicap; thus not infrequently a section of the surrounding seating is removed to accommodate scenic items, when the result is little different from a thrust stage. Others hold that the absence of scenery is itself a gain, the audience's attention and imagination being more fully focused on the actors and the text. Many object to seeing the actors' backs; on the other hand, it is claimed that a trained actor's back can be

· Theatre in the round: practical aspects ·

Modern Western theatre is usually performed in rooms seating up to 1,000, though more comfortably to smaller numbers. Though many productions now incorporate elements of music and dance, the substantial part of a play's content is in the words spoken by the actor, and this prescribes a theatre in this range of capacities. The theatre of which I was Director until 1998, the New Victoria, Newcastle-under-Lyme, seats approximately 600, and the fact that the seating rows completely surround the stage means that large audiences are very close, most of them within 20 feet of the actors. At this distance one encircling row can contain 100 people. No one is further than about 25 feet from the stage. STEPHEN JOSEPH set careful standards for the visibility and audibility of the action. If the essence of performance was the presence of the live actor, then he must be clearly seen and heard. Joseph's touring theatre in the round was a set of small wooden platforms surrounding a rectangular acting area about 19 feet square. ('Round,' he used to say, 'is used in the geographical rather than the geometrical sense.') Each row of the audience was seated at a different level one foot higher than the row in front. The actor was therefore seen clearly. The New Vic is slightly steeper than this and it has a balcony. Given satisfactory acoustics, hearing the actor remains a constant technical discipline for the performers. Other shapes of theatre demand that the actors translate the natural three-dimensional structure of life to project events in one direction, or at least along one central axis. Theatre in the round imitates life more literally. The actors can stand face to face and talk to each other. Stage action needs to be built up in this way from a set of internal focuses – omnidirectional, with the audience looking in. But, of course, it presents the actor with the problem of speaking distinctly when half his listeners are always behind him. If a presentational problem of proscenium theatre is to make unidirectional groupings look natural, then the problem of theatre in the round is to ensure that it is audible. The rewards for the actor are great, for the proximity of the whole audience does enable a wide range of vocal and physical subtleties to be effective. In addition, the encircling audience creates a positive tension which, like a magnetic field, seems to give a greater power to such subtleties. The greater sense of three dimensions also gives stage LIGHTING more impact in defining the space in which the actors are seen. Music and SOUND effects in association with the actors' performances convey a great imaginative charge in the concentrated arena. Properties, furniture, colours and textures also have a stronger presence. Theatre in the round has been used for spectacular musicals. It is a most exciting form for the presentation of dance. But it is also effective with virtually no scenic apparatus at all and is very easy to overdress.

The programmes of the four British professional theatres in the round – at Scarborough, Manchester, Richmond (near London) and Newcastle-under-Lyme – have demonstrated its versatility in plays of all periods and literary traditions. New work specially conceived for it has explored two stylistic extremes. At the old and New Victoria Theatres, adaptation of novels with wide-ranging narratives and the famous musical documentaries have both exploited the capacity of the open stage to shift from scene to scene with minimal scenic devices and great imaginative effect. At the other extreme, theatre in the round can exploit the tangible details of a naturalistic setting in close proximity to an audience. ALAN AYCKBOURN has often demonstrated this in his own first productions of his comic masterpieces at Scarborough, creating simple and complex domestic settings – kitchens, bedrooms, gardens, tennis courts, and even the famous floating river boat of *Way Upstream*. PETER CHEESEMAN

very expressive and that the actors, by playing directly 'in' to each other instead of 'out' to the audience, draw the audience more fully into the action of the play. The last is more true of plays concerned with character relationships or of psychological interest, but less so in the case of artificial comedy.

One undisputed advantage of theatre in the round is financial. It is very much less costly to build a theatre in the round, or adapt an existing building, as well as much less costly to run, because of the savings on making and storing the scenery, and on stagehands to shift it. Also undisputed is its intimacy. It is generally agreed that seven rows of audience is about the maximum in the round, but it would require from three to four times as many rows to seat an equivalent audience in a single-view theatre.

Central staging was being experimented with in America as early as 1914, in the middle of a gymnasium at Columbia University, and the idea spread to other college and community theatres. The first purpose-built theatre in the round, the Penthouse Theater, was constructed in 1940 on the campus of the University of Washington (Seattle). MARGO JONES was the first to establish a permanent professional repertory theatre in the round, in Dallas in 1947. Apart from professional summer theatres, by 1951 there were six other permanent professional theatres in the round in the United States, including the recently formed ARENA STAGE, Washington DC, and the CIRCLE IN THE SQUARE, New York; in her book *Theatre-in-the-Round* (1951), Margo Jones was able to list no fewer than 25 community, college and semi-professional theatres regularly using this medium. The ALLEY THEATER, Houston, went professional in 1954. Theatre in the round did not catch on so quickly in Europe and examples are few and far between. Russian director OKHLOPKOV's famous central stage production of GORKY's *The Mother* at the Realistic Theatre, Moscow, in 1933 does not seem to have led anywhere. In Milan, the Teatro Sant' Erasmo, opened in 1952, though described as in the round, is in fact asymmetrical and nearer in form to traverse theatre; Paris had its circular Théâtre en Rond the following year. These examples were not followed up, however, and further experiment has been confined to some FRINGE groups and amateurs. The proscenium stage tradition, known as 'à l'Italienne', is too firmly embedded.

In England, the pioneer of the form was STEPHEN JOSEPH, who established the first professional theatre in the round (the Studio Theatre Company) in the Central Library in Scarborough in 1955; it became well known as the Library Theatre. Independently, the Pembroke Theatre in the round flourished for a few years in Croydon (1959–62), before making way for the conventional new Fairfield Hall. It was Joseph who, in 1962, established the VICTORIA THEATRE in the round in a converted small cinema in Stoke-on-Trent, with PETER CHEESEMAN as director. This remained the only permanent in the round theatre for some years, until in 1976 the Scarborough company, then led by ALAN AYCKBOURN, was at last able to establish itself. It became known as the STEPHEN JOSEPH THEATRE IN THE ROUND. In the same year the more lavish ROYAL EXCHANGE THEATRE in the round was set up in the Royal Cotton Exchange, MANCHESTER. While the in-the-round form has been frequently used by a number of easily adaptable theatres such as the Barbican Pit, the YOUNG VIC and the amateur QUESTORS THEATRE, there was no permanent custom-built theatre in the round in this country until in 1986 Peter Cheeseman opened the New Victoria Theatre in Newcastle-under-Lyme in replacement of the converted cinema in neighbouring Stoke after 24 years of continuous production there. ALFRED EMMET

Stephen Joseph, *Theatre in the Round* (1967)

Théâtre Libre *see* ANTOINE, ANDRÉ; FREE THEATRE; INDEPENDENT THEATRE

Theatre Museum In London's Covent Garden since 1987, it houses collections of programmes, playbills, manuscripts, photographs, and other material pertaining to the theatre and related arts. It also has a National Video Archive and study facilities. The museum was inaugurated in 1974 by the British Theatre Museum Association (set up in 1957 by the Society for Theatre Research, which donated its collection to the museum). After the demise of the BRITISH THEATRE ASSOCIATION, the museum inherited its outstanding library. Exhibits include the Hinkins Collection of Toy Theatre Sheets, the Houston Rogers Collection of theatrical photographs, the Anthony Hippisley Coxe Collection of CIRCUS materials, and special collections dedicated to UNITY THEATRE and BLACK THEATRE. The museum is the National Museum of the Performing Arts and is administered by the Victoria and Albert Museum. ADRIANA HUNTER
See also RECORDING AND RESEARCHING THEATRE

Théâtre National Populaire A French national theatre for the people, founded in 1920 by FIRMIN GÉMIER who secured government subsidies for productions performed for workers. This enterprise folded in 1937, but in 1951 JEAN VILAR revived it and set up a permanent theatre company. Again it was intended for workers, and presented a repertoire of French and other classics with a few contemporary plays. The TNP became known for the quality of its acting, its experimental staging and its simple, intimate performances. With the decentralization of theatre in France, which it helped pioneer, the TNP lost popularity. In 1972 the title and accompanying subsidies were transferred to PLANCHON's influential theatre. ADRIANA HUNTER
See also CENTRES DRAMATIQUES.

G. Leclerc, *Le TNP de Jean Vilar* (1971)
M-T. Serrière, *Le TNP et Nous* (1959)

theatre of cruelty Term applied after 1932 by ANTONIN ARTAUD to the new theatre he wished to create, opposing literature, discursive structure and repetition with immediate physical presence. The dark physicality of Artaud's images led many to associate cruelty with bloodshed and suffering, but Artaud insisted that cruelty meant rigour, an implacable determination to confront and experience the dark creative principle at the heart of being. His own Théâtre de la Cruauté folded in 1935 after its first production, his adaptation of Shelley's *The Cenci*, but the term was

later applied to plays by writers like CAMUS and GENET, and to experiments in the 1960s and after that were influenced by Artaud (e.g. the ROYAL SHAKESPEARE COMPANY's 1964 season at the London Academy of Music and Dramatic Art under PETER BROOK which led to his productions of WEISS' *Marat/Sade* and *US*.
MARVIN CARLSON

See also GRAND GUIGNOL; THEATRE OF PANIC; THEATRE OF THE ABSURD.

theatre of fact A form of DOCUMENTARY drama exemplified by such plays as *In the Matter of J. Robert Oppenheimer* (1964) by HEINAR KIPPHARDT, in which he draws directly from transcripts of the US Atomic Energy Commission, and *The Investigation* (1965) by PETER WEISS, in which he uses the court transcript of a trial of Auschwitz guards. CHARLES LONDON

theatre of panic Name assumed by a group of writers in France in the 1960s headed by FERNANDO ARRABAL (e.g. *The Architect and the Emperor*, 1967) and Alexandro Jodorowsky (1930–99), who emphasized improvisation, chance and the juxtaposition of unlikely elements within a theatrical ritual. Part revolutionary theory, part carnivalesque SATIRE, theatre of panic recalled the similar earlier experiments of JARRY and DADA. MARVIN CARLSON

See also THEATRE OF CRUELTY; THEATRE OF THE ABSURD.

theatre of silence Also called 'theatre of the unexpressed'. Term applied to a group of French writers of the 1920s, led by GASTON BATY, JEAN-JACQUES BERNARD and Denys Amiel (1884–1977), who rejected traditional 'literary' theatre to emphasize, like MAURICE MAETERLINCK, a 'hidden' dialogue behind the spoken words. CHEKHOV was a precursor of those who exploited silence. Enlisted later were BECKETT and PINTER, whose *The Caretaker* (1960) contains 143 pauses. MARVIN CARLSON

See also SUBTEXT.

M. Daniels, *The French Drama of the Unspoken* (1977)

theatre of the absurd Term drawn by MARTIN ESSLIN from the existentialist ALBERT CAMUS, who used it to describe the situation of humankind seeking meaning in a universe that does not provide it. Esslin applied this term, somewhat misleadingly, to the new, primarily French EXPERIMENTAL THEATRE of the 1950s – especially the works of EUGÈNE IONESCO, SAMUEL BECKETT, JEAN GENET, FERNANDO ARRABAL and ARTHUR ADAMOV. Ionesco suggested the term 'theatre of the unexpected' for his work, and Rosette Lamont proposed 'metaphysical farce', but the existentialist term 'absurd' has remained the most popular, though none of these writers was in fact an existentialist. Although the 'absurdists' were never really a coherent movement, their plays did share a rejection of realistic settings, characters and situations, along with conventional logic, and offered instead portrayals of meaninglessness, isolation and the breakdown of language. The term came to be applied more widely, to playwrights such as EDWARD ALBEE, SLAWOMIR MROZEK and HAROLD PINTER, and its roots were traced back to the THEATRE OF THE GROTESQUE, WITKIEWICZ, VALLE-INCLÁN, JARRY, even Shakespeare and the ROMANS – at which point loose usage rendered it meaningless.
MARVIN CARLSON

See also GRAND GUIGNOL; MODERNISM; THEATRE OF CRUELTY; THEATRE OF PANIC.

Martin Esslin, *The Theatre of the Absurd* (1961)

theatre of the grotesque A movement in Italian drama during and after the First World War involving such authors as CHIARELLI, Roso di San Secondo (1887–1956) and, most prominently, PIRANDELLO. It utilized fantasy to depict contrasts between appearance and reality, faces and masks, pathetic situations and farcical humour. MARVIN CARLSON

See also GRAND GUIGNOL; THEATRE OF THE ABSURD.

theatre of the ridiculous A genre of 'camp', originating OFF-OFF-BROADWAY in 1965 as the Play-House of the Ridiculous with playwright Ronald Tavel, director John Vaccaro and actor Charles Ludlam. The trio soon went their separate ways, but held to the extravagant and anarchic 'ridiculous' style of witty wordplay, satirical poor taste, cross-dressing and ambiguous sexuality. Tavel left to continue as a writer; Vaccaro stayed and directed plays by Ludlam and, when Ludlam left, toured before joining LA MAMA with the Play-House until it closed in 1972. Ludlam (b. Floral Park, New York, 12 April 1943; d. New York, 28 May 1987) founded the Ridiculous Theatrical Company in 1967 and raised the trash style to new heights as actor, director and writer in shows such as *Bluebeard* (1970), *Camille* (1973), *Stage Blood* (1975) and *Galas* (1983). After Ludlam's death, the company was taken over by his partner Everett Quinton. CHARLES LONDON

See also GAY THEATRE; QUEER THEATRE.

S. Brecht, *Queer Theatre* (1978)
B. Marranca and G. Dasgupta, eds, *Theatre of the Ridiculous* (1979)
S. Samuels, ed., *Ridiculous Theatre: Scourge of Human Folly – The Essays and Opinions of Charles Ludlam* (1992)

theatre of the twilight *see* ITALY

Theatre Passe Muraille Unlike the TARRAGON

THEATER (also in Toronto, Ontario), and rather more like TORONTO WORKSHOP PRODUCTIONS, this 'Theatre without Walls' has focused its efforts not so much on the theatrical script as on COLLECTIVE creation, often in a DOCUMENTARY vein. Founded in 1968 by Jim Garrard on the principles of ARTAUD, the theatre's identity was most firmly established by PAUL THOMPSON, artistic director from 1972 to 1982. His production of *The Farm Show* (1972) and *1837: The Farmers' Revolt* (1973) were landmarks in the theatre's history, both shows combining socio-political astuteness with flamboyant yet disciplined performance style, and local colour with universal relevance.   L. W. CONOLLY

theatre photography   When the pressing of the shutter perfectly coincides with the moment of truth on stage, the resulting photograph defines a performance or a production more potently than any other medium. It becomes a window on to the past, reflecting the age in which it was taken and the requirements of the theatre of that time. The story of theatre photography in the twentieth century is one of developing style and techniques responding to the needs of each decade and to the changes in performance and style.

The nineteenth-century actor was confined to the studio, but by the beginning of the twentieth century technical advances in cameras, lenses and film had led to the establishment of companies like White Studios working on Broadway productions in New York, and Daily Mirror Studios and Stage Photo Company in London, who produced full-stage photographs of BEER-BOHM TREE's spectacular productions, DRURY LANE melodramas and pantomimes, or GEORGE EDWARDES' musical comedies. They worked in specially posed photocalls, augmenting the stage lighting with banks of floodlights. This coincided with the rise of the illustrated periodical, which had now developed the technology to reproduce photographs. To later eyes, the two-dimensional overall evenness and static actors lack spontaneity, but the photographs reflect the massive grandeur of the productions and the acting style of the period, and they provide important information about staging and design.

The character and personality of performers of the period are conveyed more vividly in studio studies, mostly taken to feed the pre-1914 mania for postcard collecting. Of the great studio photographers of the period, E. O. Hoppe and Baron de Meyer were celebrated for their sensitive studies of the dancers of the DIAGHILEV Ballet, de Meyer recording NIJINSKY in the ballet *L'Après-midi d'un faune* in soft focus images full of the drowsy eroticism of Nijinsky's interpretation

and the hazy shimmer of Debussy's score. In America, Edward Steichen and later George Platt Lynes produced equally imaginative images of performers both in and out of the studio. By the 1920s, although equipment was still relatively cumbersome, increasingly sensitive film meant that a production could be photographed from the auditorium in available stage light, giving for the first time some idea of what audiences actually saw. Here newspapers were the pioneers, led by Ulric van den Boegarde and John Greenwood of *The Times*, who took what is probably the first stage action colour photograph, of *Die Meistersinger* in 1925. This, however, was almost an isolated example; throughout the century colour was relatively rarely used, partly because of a lack of outlets, but also because it lacked the impact, power and focus of the black and white image. By the 1930s other newspaper photographers were using action photographs taken in performances or dress rehearsals. The greater flexibility provided by the minature camera allowed the photographer to get closer in to the performer and move around the auditorium and wings, varying angles to increase the sense of involvement. As the cameras could capture fast movement in low light, they were particularly suitable for dance photography, and Merlyn Severn explored the new possibilities, creating images that perfectly capture the immediacy of live performance and the emotion, drama and style of ballet in the 1930s.

WEST END and BROADWAY theatre of the 1930s and 1940s demanded a different approach to reflect the glamorous stars and polished productions, and here a posed photocall produced publicity and front of house pictures that conveyed at a glance the style or plot. The director and photographer selected key scenes, and a shooting script was then prepared for the actors. Photographs by a master such as Angus McBean or Houston Rogers in London, or by Vandamm Studios in America, captured the significant dramatic moment, recreating it in photographic terms that conveyed the physical and emotional relationship between the actors in images of great power and insight that enhanced and preserved the theatrical illusion.

Glamour treatment was certainly not required for the realistic 'kitchen sink' drama of the 1950s; a new generation of photographers, including Anthony Armstrong-Jones and John Haynes, developed a more photo-journalistic approach, and the hand-held 35mm camera came into its own. The grainy, harsher images reflected the realism of the plays, and the photographers experimented with unusual viewpoints to draw the viewer into the action. In America, action photographers like Eileen Darby, the Friedman-Abeles Studio and Martha Swope displaced the formal posed

· Theatre photography ·

When I first started to take theatre pictures the photographs outside theatres were the results of long photocalls where actors were posed in fixed positions and lit in the same manner as the sets. Portraits were retouched to flatter. In this way wonderfully sharp pictures could be reproduced without visible grain. This technique, however, had the disadvantage of being unlike the actual production the pictures were trying to record or capture. Although the pictures could be stunning, the photographers had reinvented the play. It was not until I saw the grainy pictures of Antony Armstrong-Jones (Lord Snowdon), which were full of life and animation, that I knew I would work in the theatre.

My parents had retired to the south coast of England and I somehow found myself watching plays at the local repertory company, the Penguin Players. I can still recall my fascination with *Mr Kettle and Mr Moon* by J. B. PRIESTLEY, whose theme – a sudden renunciation of suburban life – struck a resonating chord. It was also at this time, having just returned from national service in Singapore, that I was shown a book by Henri Cartier-Bresson, *The Europeans*. I was stunned: I saw images of people, caught in their own environments, who were unaware of the camera. These photographs were not just documentary or journalistic pictures, they possessed a timeless quality as well as a perfect geometry. I thought they were works of art and still do. My father bought me a Leica camera from his savings, and I moved to London. During the days I took photographs and in the evenings I worked back stage in the theatre to support myself. I was encouraged by Keith Johnstone, who was then an assistant director at the ROYAL COURT THEATRE, to take pictures of the mask classes that he and GEORGE DEVINE led. These experiences allowed me to gain the confidence that I needed to work as a theatre photographer. I also spent two years working for the *Sunday Times* newspaper where I covered news, sport and the arts, always having to meet an urgent deadline. It was an exciting and varied diet, which helped to improve my knowledge of people and photography; when the call came for me to work at the Royal Court as their resident production photographer I was ready.

The Royal Court during the early 1970s was an inspiring place to be: it was an intoxicating fusion of writers, directors and designers. It was also a place that had its own artistic and aesthetic demands, which certainly influenced my style of photography. The Eleventh Commandment decreed that we should all 'Pare everything down to its absolute essentials' and its aesthetic was embodied in the beauty and simplicity of a set designed by JOCELYN HERBERT and lit by the open white Brechtian lighting by Andy Phillips. All this was a gift to a young photographer; it was my training as a photographer of plays.

In that role I often become involved with a production as early as the third week of rehearsal, to take pictures for the programme. The atmosphere is usually relaxed and inquisitive, and the concentration by the director and actors on text and movement I find totally fascinating and a joy to photograph. Later, I will attend a dress rehearsal on stage and photograph the entire play. When the house lights go down I try to respond to the play as I would to an event unfolding on the street. Certain scenes need to reflect the set and others need to be framed as close ups. It is rather like making a film of the play – although the play never stops or waits for you to catch up. Sometimes it is necessary, through a lack of production time, to make a photocall of the play. I consider this to be my most difficult task. The photocall, during which a selection of scenes from the play are performed, never produces the same results or intensity of emotions from the actors as when they perform the whole play. In these circumstances the photographer has to find a way out of the negative conditions and use technique to compensate for the artificial situation which is likely to produce a stilted and posed photograph. By contrast, in the course of a dress rehearsal, two actors alone on stage, engaged in dialogue, can seem inauspicious, but if you are quick enough to catch their peak responses, the outcome may be an exhilarating picture that has a genuine energy. The same scene set up for the benefit of a photocall will guarantee you a dull picture unless you can use technique to change the angles and throw the foreground actor out of focus, thus concentrating your focus on the speech of the sharply focused actor. I prefer to avoid such technical pictures whenever possible and feel that I am most successful when my pictures reflect the actions that the audience will witness later.

I have always worked with 35mm cameras: small, light and quiet, being the operative words. Cartier-Bresson's words 'Of all forms of expression, photography is the only one that seizes the instant in flight' very much apply to my style of photography. I've tried to use larger cameras, whose negative size is supposed to give you better quality pictures, but their disadvantage is that they are slow, heavy and noisy. And there is the risk of missing the picture. I use Ilford HP5 as a general purpose film – it can be rated from its normal 400ASA up to 1600ASA quite easily. If the play is very dark then Ilford's Delta 3200ASA will capture the darkest of *Cherry Orchards*. There is a photographic worry to consider insofar as fast film produces very noticeable grain, and if you enlarge a negative to five foot it will hit you in the face. Personally I find it exciting to achieve a photograph that would have been out of reach if I was using slower film. I use Nikon 5 and F100 cameras – both have silent motors, and Canon EO55 cameras are also quiet. Some of the top of the range so-called professional cameras have shutters which, when pressed, sound like machine guns. I avoid them. I also use a Leica rangefinder camera, quietness always being the main consideration for a theatre photographer. A noisy camera will upset an actor working in a dress rehearsal, who may be on the set for the first time in a sensitive atmosphere where maybe motivation or lines as well as sound, lights, costume and the set itself will need sorting out. I avoided using a tripod for years as it tends to isolate you in one position and can encourage you to become lazy. Now I find it useful with the zoom. I set up a board over the seats behind my tripod, positioned at about row F in the stalls. Then I am better able to line up my lens and films for easier access in the dark. I usually carry three cameras: one with a 20–35mm zoom, one with an 85mm (my most used lens), and the other with a fast 135F2 telephoto lens. With this equipment I can move quickly to change angles when I need to. Sometimes I steady the 300mm lens on top of my 80–200mm tripod mounted zoom.

I think black and white photography is superior to colour in its portrayal of a serious play. (Musicals, opera, and ballet are a different matter.) Today, selling a play has become more important than recording a play and Shaftesbury Avenue is illuminated with colour photography but I don't enjoy its visual impact. I do, of course, use colour when the production company requests it, which is frequent. I use two types of colour film, negative, (and the type of film which we all use to take our holiday snaps with), as well as colour reversal-transparency (slides) film. Transparency film can produce the most accurate colour, and there is one film which is balanced for tungsten (theatre lighting). It has its advantages and its disadvantages, as it has very little exposure latitude, and in the constantly changing theatre lighting, which may even include several daylight balanced lamps, exposures can be difficult. Enlargements for front of house have to be copied onto negative film, which sometimes reduces their impact. My own preference is for colour film that can be enlarged direct from the negative just like black and white. When I took my first pictures of theatre in the late sixties and early seventies I was helped by the technical advances of the small camera. At the start of a new century, the age of the digital camera and computerized images is with us; and DAVID HOCKNEY declares 'From today chemistry photography is dead'. Well, I still feel myself governed by the same ideals that I had when I began. I am still excited when I am asked to work on a play with an inspired director. Still challenged by the thought of taking a picture to equal my 1971 picture of HARRY ANDREWS climbing the hill in EDWARD BOND's play *Lear*. Still trying to capture a play in about twelve images, hopefully with some style and just a little flourish. As the years pass and memory fades, the original perception of a play – the theatre photograph – becomes our only solid reminder of a loved favourite production. Very few plays have been filmed, and even fewer successfully! I want my photographs to be an accurate rendition of the play as it *actually* was.

JOHN HAYNES

sessions. The photocall became an expensive luxury and photographers became invited guests at a run-through, developing the instinctive reflexes that could recognize and capture the significant moment, and new technical skills to compensate for the lower light levels favoured by lighting designers. Nevertheless, demand for the posed photograph did not decline; indeed, it increased to feed the growing publicity and marketing machine of the 1980s and 1990s theatre – actors' directories and programmes, posters, leaflets, illustrations to interviews and articles, all required different approaches. The posed photocall survived for companies like the NATIONAL THEATRE (although now the director alone selected what should be photographed) and front of house publicity shots in the West End, which maintained a glossiness that reflected the productions they celebrated, while in dance, photographers such as Anthony Crickmay and Lois Greenfield brought a new insight into the studio study in images that froze yet still conveyed movement.

Throughout the century photography played an important role in theatre, reflecting changing styles, from the spectacular drama of the actor–managers to the raw realism of the 1990s and responding to the developing outlets, from illustrated magazines to the INTERNET. In an image-conscious world its importance is unlikely to diminish in the next hundred years.
SARAH C. WOODCOCK

See also RECORDING AND RESEARCHING THEATRE.

theatre publishing

In Britain

Up to the end of the nineteenth century, play publishing in Britain had hardly changed since Shakespeare's time. Two precepts governed, with very few exceptions. One was that the play-text was published in the wake of the performed play, giving it the status of a record of that performance, and the other was that the purpose of publication was to provide the means for further performances. Exceptions to the first were, for instance, the plays of Byron and Shelley, published as part of the poet's *œuvre* and performed only long after their deaths. Exceptions to the second were collections of plays, often attractively bound in leather, obviously intended to grace the libraries of the leisured classes rather than for use by working actors. But the end of the nineteenth century saw both precepts undermined, and the reason was the explosive content of the plays of IBSEN and, in his wake, SHAW. Ibsen's plays made their first impact in Britain through their published translations, which were read and discussed – and objected to – on the page: productions came later. Perhaps it was his awareness of the effectiveness of this strategy – first page, then stage – that encouraged Shaw to make a special presentation of his early plays to the reading public after he had failed to get them staged successfully or indeed at all. From this stems Shaw's famous habit of writing the stage directions like narrative in a fiction. They are like that – and the prefaces are as they are – precisely because Shaw was addressing a reader rather than a spectator. The result was that the published play became more than merely a cheaply printed script for use in rehearsal and became a book in its own right – as witness first editions of the plays of Shaw and, after him, GRANVILLE BARKER and J. M. BARRIE, among many others. So it continued, with playwrights of note now appearing in properly bound editions for a reading public. A shift into paperback occurred – suitably – in the late 1950s and early 1960s precisely at the time the ANGRY YOUNG MEN were taking the theatre itself down a social peg or two. But, in the wake of the great explosion of British playwriting, a much more significant shift took place from 1980 onwards with several sustained attempts to publish plays alongside their first productions, most notably at the ROYAL COURT but also at the ROYAL SHAKESPEARE COMPANY's Pit and intermittently at other venues. This changed the status of the published text again: now it was neither a work offered to readers in advance of or instead of a production, nor a *post facto* record of a staged play, carefully revised and prepared for publication by an author anxious to include improvements wrought on the play in the process of rehearsal and production. The simultaneously published script, though often at variance with the play on stage owing to changes made too late in the production process for them to be incorporated, had the effect of enhancing the status of the playwright. His or her contribution to the staged event could plainly be distinguished from other elements by audiences who had the script in their hands at the time they first encountered the play on stage, particularly as these scripts tended to be bound into the theatre's own programme booklet.

What this brief history omits is the development of what is now called the 'acting edition'. These came into being in the 1830s when Samuel French, having acquired the rights to license performances of certain plays, began printing texts of these plays for use in rehearsal. And though rivals – such as Dick's and Evans – have come and gone, French's are still printing acting editions of plays whose performing rights (usually only amateur) they control.

Among the British publishers who have predominated in play publishing in the twentieth century are Ernest Benn, with their series of Contemporary British Dramatists in the 1920s, Paul Elek with nearly 50 annual volumes of Plays of the Year which ended in the 1970s, Penguin Books with their New English Dramatists series (14 volumes from 1959 to 1970), Heinemann in the 1930s, 1940s and 1950s, and Methuen and Faber, which have dominated the scene from the 1960s. NICK HERN

In the United States

The publication of dramatic works in the United States in the twentieth century has always been a sometime thing. In the early decades there was little if any publication of plays, aside from the classics – Shakespeare, Marlowe, Webster, et al. – which were part of the college curriculum in the humanities. During the 1930s and beyond, a fair number of anthologies appeared annually, containing the best BROADWAY plays staged the preceding year. Bennet Cerf, co-founder of Random House, who was as much a performer as a publisher, as happy rubbing elbows with actors and directors as he was lunching with authors, virtually had his pick of the plays with which to feather his theatrical publishing nest. While many of them were light and superficial, the anthologies often contained one or more serious dramas, including the works of SHAW (whose plays were performed in the United States before they were in Britain), NOËL COWARD, EUGENE O'NEILL, STRINDBERG (a major influence on O'Neill), and PIRANDELLO. Cerf had little or no competition in the field: publishing plays was to him more a hobby than a meaningful contribution to his company's bottom line. Thus he was taken aback one day in the early 1950s when he decided to include in that year's anthology the controversial new play starring BERT LAHR entitled *Waiting for Godot* by newcomer SAMUEL BECKETT, only to be told by the producer that the play was already under contract. 'To be *published?*' he is reported to have cried out, as if a poacher had just intruded on his private domain and made off with a piece of prize game. 'Yes,' the producer assured him. 'And by whom, may I ask?' 'By Grove Press.' 'Never heard of it,' Cerf is reported to have said. In fact, that young press, founded in 1951, had contracted a year or two later to publish several works by the virtually unknown Irish writer, who until then had written only prose – novels and short stories – and a slim volume of poetry. Thus Grove's entry into the realm of play publishing was motivated not so much by interest in the genre itself as by an overall commitment to an author's work. During the next two decades Grove became the leading publisher of drama in the United States: not only all of Beckett – and from *Godot* on he focused largely on drama – but that of the Romanian EUGENE IONESCO, the Frenchman JEAN GENET, the Englishmen HAROLD PINTER, JOE ORTON and TOM STOPPARD, the German BERTOLT BRECHT and the Spaniard FERNANDO ARRABAL, to mention only the most illustrious. The essential difference between Grove's almost accidental move into the niche and the Random House anthologies – of fleeting interest at best – was that virtually all the plays it published were single volumes of considerable literary merit, many of them enduring. And because of the plays' intrinsic merits, sales generally followed, often in geometric progression. For example, Grove's first printing of 3,000 copies of *Godot* had still not sold out two years later. But a decade further on, it had topped the 100,000 mark, and in the next decade it reached a million, and by the century's end had reached 2.5 million. While Grove's other drama publishing did not reach such staggering heights, it discovered one truth about drama publishing in America in the latter half of the century: drama, thought of as an integral part of literature, was increasingly being taught at colleges and universities across the land. Younger professors, looking for new voices and new forms, more and more eschewed the SOTs (Same Old Textbooks). Younger students responded to the challenges, wilful ambiguities and innovations of the new playwrights, and because the United States boasts so many colleges and universities, large and small, with a student population in the millions, once these plays were 'adopted' by the rising generation of professors they became a basic – and, more importantly, continuing – part of the curriculum. While bookstore sales alone could not suffice to make drama

publishing profitable, when the 'adoption factor' was added in, the picture changed dramatically (pun intended).

During those same early decades after the Second World War, another smallish publisher, Hill and Wang, also found that what had been a desert could, by choosing carefully, be made into an oasis: small, no doubt, but lush. Founded in 1956, armed with more youthful idealism than hard cash, Messrs Hill and Wang bought from the old A. A. Wyn catalogue the Mermaid Series of English plays, 88 titles in all. Two years before that, a young Doubleday editor, Jason Epstein, who had (correctly) theorized that quality books, in a number of areas, might well find a ready audience if brought out in paperback in attractive formats, on decent paper (as opposed to mass-market newsprint paper, which turned yellow and crumbled after a disturbingly few years), and at roughly half the hardcover price. Taking their cue from Epstein, Hill and Wang issued their Mermaid titles in paperback, and from that springboard began to publish contemporary playwrights: ARTHUR KOPIT, LANFORD WILSON, JULES FEIFFER – all Americans – plus, from abroad, MAX FRISCH, FRIEDRICH DÜRRENMATT, Miguel Piñero and JEAN ANOUILH. To buttress their burgeoning drama list, Hill and Wang also initiated a series of 'Dramabooks', works about theatre, acting and playwriting, by the likes of STANISLAVSKY, STARK YOUNG, HAROLD CLURMAN, George Steiner and John Russell Taylor. Arthur Wang, whose company was bought by Farrar, Straus and Giroux, notes, however, somewhat ruefully, that his problem editorially through those early years was that, 'wherever I went, Grove seems to have been there first.'

By the early 1970s, a serious decline in sales was noted by both these bastions of play publishing, probably due in part to the advent of television plus, in the late 1960s, the student unrest that swept not only the United States but most of the Western world, bringing in its wake a demand for new and radically different curricula. The only new playwright of note added to the Grove list since then has been DAVID MAMET.

More recently, the torch for publishing drama has been taken up by a company aptly called Applause. Unlike Grove or Hill and Wang, both of which were general publishers with strong drama leanings, Applause's focus is wholly on drama: plays, cinema, and in its own words 'entertainment'. Founder and head of the house is Glenn Young, who taught drama and playwriting at Wesleyan University in Connecticut before moving to New York's Columbia University, where he chaired the graduate playwriting seminar. Applause began as a bookstore on New York's Upper West Side specializing in drama. Its evolution into publishing was one of those serendipitous acts of madness out of which so many of our lives are moulded: the attorney for playwright SAM SHEPARD called Young one day, to tell him that Sam's publisher had gone belly up, wanting advice on how to rescue the dramatist's inventory from the clutches of the bankruptcy court. After several deep breaths, Young called back to say *he'd* buy the inventory, which consisted of five major anthologies of Shepard's plays. From that day on, Applause Publishing was up and running. Young, like Bennet Cerf before him, believes strongly in the value of anthologies, though for quite different reasons. In the end-of-the-century overload of hundreds of magazines, each trying to freeze-frame the frenzy of the moment, anthologies, if well chosen, have the virtue of preserving plays of interest and quality that might not survive without the contiguity of more famous theatrical peers. At the century's end, Applause, which publishes about 25 books per year, had more than 300 titles in print. The company is devoted to drama in the largest sense: plays form only about a third of the output, the rest consisting of biographies and autobiographies of theatre luminaries, with another third on the art and craft of theatre and cinema: acting, directing, design – both set and costume. Again, as with Grove, Hill and Wang, and anyone who has ventured into the field of publishing drama, love of the theatre, plus a deep-rooted desire to help encourage, preserve and facilitate the dramatic art, is an essential ingredient for making it work. Most assuredly, in the twentieth century, no one did it for the money. RICHARD SEAVER

Theatre Royal, Drury Lane The most famous theatre in London (seating 2,245) and the oldest still in use (it was founded in 1662). Burned down twice, damaged during riots, bankrupted on several occasions and bombed in the Second World War (during which it was closed, though used as the headquarters of ENSA, it survived to hold its place as the premier venue for musicals – from *Rose Marie*, *The Desert Song* and *Show Boat*, via *Oklahoma!*, *Carousel*, *South Pacific*, *The King and I*, *My Fair Lady* and *Hello Dolly!* to *A Chorus Line*, *42nd Street* and *Miss Saigon*. A custom dating from the eighteenth century, when actor Robert Baddeley left a bequest to provide a Twelfth Night cake, wine and punch annually to the company in residence on 6 January, is still observed. The resident ghost appears in grey at the back of the upper circle at matinées and brings luck. ADRIANA HUNTER

See also SUPERSTITION.

B. Dobbs, *Drury Lane* (1972)
W. Macqueen-Pope, *Theatre Royal, Drury Lane* (1945)

Theatre Royal, Stratford East Opened in 1884, MELODRAMA, MUSIC HALL and VARIETY were the staple diet of this east London theatre until THEATRE WORKSHOP arrived in 1953 and put the theatre on the international map. Its address, Gerry Raffles Square, bears the name of the Workshop's manager. From the late 1970s onwards Philip Hedley continued this popular tradition, bolstered by WEST END transfers, such as Nell Dunn's *Steaming* (1981), Ken Hill's *Phantom of the Opera* (1991) and *Five Guys Named Mo* (1990), and by making a new commitment to new plays and the local, multi-ethnic community. COLIN CHAMBERS

M. Coren, *100 Years of Stratford East* (1984)

Theatre Upstairs *see* ENGLISH STAGE COMPANY; ROYAL COURT

Theatre Workshop Pioneering touring company (1945–52) that settled in the THEATRE ROYAL, STRATFORD EAST from 1953 to 1976 and helped change the face of postwar British drama. Its origins lie in the POLITICAL THEATRE of the 1930s, when JOAN LITTLEWOOD came to Manchester and met EWAN MACCOLL, a founder of Salford Red Megaphones which had grown into Theatre of Action (1934) as they moved from AGITPROP outdoor theatre to an indoor synthesis of different arts. Under the influence of continental ideas (e.g. APPIA), they experimented with writing, staging, movement, sound and light. They broke with other left-wing groups, not in their beliefs or commitment but in how those beliefs should be expressed theatrically. As Theatre Union (1936–42), they intensified their pursuit of study and training and developed the techniques that were to become the hallmark of Theatre Workshop. After the Second World War a small group who had kept in touch started Theatre Workshop in Manchester. Their aim was to reflect the dreams and struggles of the people. Idealism triumphed over hardship, and they toured Britain and abroad (where they achieved greater acclamation) with a repertoire based mainly on new plays by MacColl and classics, including Shakespeare, played in a bold and popular style.

Exhaustion and a need for recognition and stability lay behind the move to the dilapidated music hall in London's working-class East End, which was opposed, however, by MacColl as a betrayal of the company's aims. With Littlewood and Gerry Raffles, the general manager, as the driving force, the company renovated the theatre, encouraged local support, and mounted an extraordinary series of short-run ENSEMBLE productions of new plays and classics including a modern-dress *Volpone*, *Richard II* and *Arden of Faversham* (then a late sixteenth-century rarity).

The Good Soldier Schweik played in the WEST END in 1956, beginning just over a decade of Theatre Workshop transfers that included *The Quare Fellow* (1956) and *The Hostage* (1958) by BRENDAN BEHAN, *A Taste of Honey* (1958) by SHELAGH DELANEY, and the musical *Fings Ain't Wot They Used T'Be* (1959) by FRANK NORMAN and LIONEL BART. Commercial success – required because of inadequate public grants – tied up the company in long runs away from base, and Littlewood left in 1961 while the theatre was leased to other managements. She returned in 1963 to direct the show that was to become synonymous with the name of the company, *Oh What a Lovely War!*, in which a PIERROT troupe enact scenes from the First World War against the backdrop of a screen on to which are projected the horrific facts of the carnage.

An invitation to take *Henry IV* to the EDINBURGH FESTIVAL in 1964 marked some kind of official approval, but it came when Theatre Workshop was all but finished. The theatre was leased again to outside managements up until 1970, with the exception of 1967 when Littlewood returned to direct. Redevelopment of the site, and the consequent battle to preserve the theatre, took its toll; the theatre closed from 1970 to 1972, and in 1974 its completion coincided with Raffles' resignation. Littlewood's last production came in 1973, although the name Theatre Workshop continued to be used until 1978.

Individuals fashioned in the collective spirit of the group took their skills to other theatres and media. Some, like Harry Corbett, became household names through television; others, like the designer JOHN BURY, became leaders of their profession. The great postwar institutions, the ROYAL SHAKESPEARE COMPANY and the NATIONAL THEATRE, as well as many FRINGE companies and those working in communities like PETER CHEESEMAN, have been inspired by Theatre Workshop's exuberant style of muscular, imaginative presentation. It broke a pattern of theatre-making and theatregoing that was strangling the life out of British drama, by offering an alternative, COLLECTIVE expression that drew its inspiration, its language, its art from the people. COLIN CHAMBERS

Howard Goorney, *The Theatre Workshop Story* (1981)
Joan Littlewood, *Joan's Book: Joan Littlewood's Peculiar History As She Tells It* (1994)
Ewan MacColl, *Journeyman: An Autobiography* (1990)

theatrical estates Authors' rights are controlled, for 70 years after their death under current COPYRIGHT convention, by their literary estates, which are often run by their families. In the case of playwrights whose work, although it may exist in script form, comes to three-dimensional life only when it is performed, questions are raised relating to what kind of production may be authorized, and how any proposed production may or may not conform to what is perceived to be the author's original intentions. This can affect same-language productions as well as ADAPTATION AND TRANSLATION, and has led to much tension between guardian estates and subsequent would-be interpreters. If, like BERTOLT BRECHT, the writer leaves, to all intents and purposes, definitive versions of productions by means of documentation and photographs, then is it the task of the estate to preserve these as the only possible contemporary versions, or to allow new productions which may depart from that which the author himself approved. In the case of SAMUEL BECKETT, his plays, or rather theatre pieces, are frequently so meticulous in terms of lighting, sound, and positioning, that they would seem, on the surface, to preclude any contemporary explorations. But the issues thrown up by the refusal of estates to allow deviation from the author's last intentions – for example, the banning of DEBORAH WARNER's production of Beckett's *Footfalls* – relate to the nature of theatre as a live and contemporary performance and a form, therefore, that is never fixed. Is it really conceivable that Brecht, if he were alive today, would insist on the cart, half-curtain and captions in *Mother Courage*? Or would Beckett insist that audiences all sat in theatres to receive his works, when many of them, as KATIE MITCHELL showed at STRATFORD-UPON-AVON in 1995, work well as quasi-INSTALLATIONS? For authors' estates it is therefore important to differentiate between an author's last thoughts and an audience's contemporary perceptions. We may be grateful that there is no Shakespeare estate, an absence which allows for a degree of experiment and variation leading to some innovative and exciting contemporary versions of his work. NOEL WITTS

Theatrical Syndicate [Trust] A virtual monopoly that dominated American theatre at the beginning of the twentieth century, controlling the major venues and insisting its clients did not conduct business with anyone else. In the 1890s there was a free-for-all among booking agents, who had flooded into New York in the wake of a new-found ability to tour America following the massive rail expansion that followed the Civil War. A group of producers, theatre owners and agents representing interests across the states, including Abraham Erlanger, CHARLES FROHMAN, Alfred Hayman, Marc Klaw, Fred Nixon-Nirdlinger and Fred Zimmerman, met in 1895 to bring the situation under control. As the Syndicate, they exercised a stranglehold until beaten at their own game by the SHUBERT brothers, who had

become dominant by the outbreak of the First World War. Near-monopolies were common at the time: BURLESQUE, VAUDEVILLE and low-priced theatres were all subject to monopoly control in this period.
CHARLES LONDON

A. L. Bernheim, *The Business of Theatre* (1932; repr. 1964)

theatricalism An approach to production developed in Germany and Russia at the beginning of the twentieth century that emphasizes theatre as being distinct from 'real' life. The audience's attention is called to the fact that they are in a theatre by a self-conscious use of curtains, backdrops, stage lighting, 'theatrical' gestures, asides and so on, rather than an attempt to present them with realistic representations of the world.
MARVIN CARLSON

Thesiger, Ernest   (b. London, 15 Jan. 1879; d. London, 4 Jan. 1961)   Character actor, particularly known as a performer of high comedy. Thesiger trained initially as an artist, but quickly discovered he preferred acting. He worked initially under GEORGE ALEXANDER and BEERBOHM TREE, then from 1915 appeared in the FARCE *A Little Bit of Fluff*, which ran for over three years. After the First World War, Thesiger became one of SHAW's most valued actors. Shaw created several roles for him, including the Dauphin in *St Joan*. His memoir, *Practically True*, appeared in 1927.   ANDREW SOLWAY

third theatre   Term used to define a new theatrical phenomenon that emerged in the late 1970s. The first Encounter for Third Theatre took place in Belgrade in 1976. A short document written by EUGENIO BARBA served as a manifesto for third theatre and was published after the meeting in most European countries, as well as in Japan, Argentina, Bolivia, Colombia, Peru and Venezuela. Despite a general shift to the right and the decline of the idealism of the 1960s, a new generation of young people in the 1970s began to conceive of theatre not so much as a means to an end, as part of a process of social change, but rather as a way of life. Small FRINGE groups emerged, developing their own pattern of rigorous daily training and devising cooperative performance structures. Many had no previous experience in the theatre or any formal theatrical education, but nevertheless perceived theatre work as central to their existence. Third theatre groups essentially dedicate their lives to the creation of theatre, often working in poverty-stricken conditions, on the streets or in makeshift playing spaces.

Barba uses two metaphors to describe the international phenomenon of the small, highly disciplined third theatre groups. The first metaphor is that of the archipelago or floating islands, without contact among themselves but existing as an alternative to the two 'official' theatres, the institutionalized theatre that is protected and subsidized and the AVANT-GARDE theatre that is consciously in search of innovative techniques. Belonging to neither of these categories, the new theatre follows a third path. The second metaphor is that of the ghetto. Separated from the subsidized theatre and the art theatre, cut off from educational establishments, deliberately and of necessity auto-didactic, third theatre groups exist in a separate, alternative world of individual group training, occasional performances, often based in rural or poor urban communities, and meetings with other, similar groups in the network of encounters and festivals that has sprung up in Europe, Central and South America and the Far East. Barba notes that the ghetto carries connotations of struggle for survival, of poverty and pogrom, of the minority isolated from the majority; but he also points out that the ghetto is the place used for preparing assault on an enemy, the place where the weapons that will be used in the coming struggle can be sharpened.

In the 1980s, the phenomenon underwent certain significant changes. Established as an ALTERNATIVE form of theatre, the groups developed their own didactic processes. In some cases this has led to the establishment of theatre laboratories or training programmes, where the practical work also includes an investigation into related fields such as theatre history and THEATRE ANTHROPOLOGY, and in other cases it has resulted in an exchange of techniques and ideas between practitioners from vastly different theatrical traditions. European third theatre groups have shown evidence of techniques learned from the oriental theatre or from different indigenous theatres, and the process of exchange has led to an exciting combination of styles and traditions in the work of third theatre groups worldwide.

Fundamental to the concept is a notion of universal values and techniques. Practitioners often refer to a 'third theatre family' that transcends national and cultural barriers. One important aspect of this interchange and cultural mixing is the establishment of the multilingual group, without a common language except that of the place in which they are based. This multilingualism has had repercussions in the type of theatre made by the groups: verbal language tends to be less important than the creation of spectacle and the interaction between performers and spectators; many third theatre performances have no texts, or use a collage of textual fragments from different sources, often different languages. This tendency, combined with the importance of improvisation as a technique in the work of third theatre groups and the occasional nature of many of their performances, means that third theatre is a more ephemeral form and less easy to document than the two more orthodox modes of theatre. CLIVE BARKER

See also COLLECTIVE; EASTERN THEATRE, ITS INFLUENCE ON THE WEST.

Eugenio Barba, *Beyond the Floating Islands* (1986)
——, *The Paper Canoe* (1995)
Ian Watson, *Towards a Third Theatre: Eugenio Barba and Odin Teatret* (1993).

Thomas, Augustus (b. St Louis, Mo., 8 Jan. 1857; d. Nyack, NY, 12 Aug. 1934) Playwright, considered by many the best of his period. He made a determined effort to see that American theatre reflected American themes. Among his better plays were *Alabama* (1891), *In Mizzoura* (1893), *Arizona* (1900), *The Earl of Pawtucket* (1903), *Mrs Leffingwell's Boots* (1905), *The Witching Hour* (1907, about the occult and often regarded as his best), *As a Man Thinks* (1911) and *The Copperhead* (1918), in which LIONEL BARRYMORE gave one of his outstanding performances. His autobiography, *The Point of My Remembrance*, appeared in 1922. GERALD BORDMAN

Thomas, Brandon (b. Liverpool, 25 Dec. 1826; d. Leighton Buzzard, Beds, 19 June 1914) Playwright and actor, remembered for his hugely successful farce *Charley's Aunt* (1892). The initial production ran for four years and the play has frequently been revived on both the professional and the amateur stage. IAN CLARKE

Thomas, Dylan [Marlais] (b. Swansea, Wales, 27 Oct. 1914; d. New York, 9 Nov. 1953) Poet and playwright. Thomas wrote short documentary scripts, but his most famous dramatic work is his 'play for voices' *Under Milk Wood* (1953), showing through his rich, allusive poetry moments of sex, love and death over 24 hours in the fictional seaside town of Llareggub. DAN REBELLATO

Thomas, Ed (b. Abercraf, Wales, 17 July 1961) The most interesting playwright to come out of the emergent Welsh theatre scene, a truly modern practitioner not only through his writing for the stage but as a director, producer and writer of television comedies and documentaries for his Cardiff-based company Fiction Factory (formerly Y Cwmni) and a leading light in the Welsh film scene. His first play, *House of America* (1988), was made into a film ten years later, receiving mixed reviews but also winning awards.

His plays tend to be very self-referential, with the same characters and situations cropping up, and all deal with questions of cultural and personal identity and express an exasperation at Wales's lack of self-confidence. He is conscious of Wales's invisibility and its need to create myths and reinvent itself, themes he explored in his 'New Wales' trilogy of *House of America* (1988), *Flowers of*

the Dead Red Sea (1991) and *East From the Gantry* (1992). *Song From a Forgotten City* (1995) and *Gas Station Angel* (1998) have been co-productions with the ROYAL COURT; London critics, however, have not taken to his plays, showing an animosity (and, it must be said, an almost wilful abstruseness) that would only confirm the belief that he has almost single-handedly created a kind of main-stage Welsh theatre that has little in common with the English model. He is, nevertheless, well received in Wales and his work is very popular in the rest of the world, having been produced in Ukraine, Romania, Australia, Belgium, Germany, Spain, Canada and elsewhere. DAVID ADAMS

Thomas, Gwyn (b. Porth, Wales, 6 July 1913; d. Cardiff, 13 April 1981) Playwright. WALES produced a clutch of twentieth-century Renaissance men of the theatre, writers who were also erudite raconteurs and larger-than-life personalities, and Gwyn Thomas, like his namesake Dylan, was as much known for his wit as his work. Born in the working-class mining environment of the Rhondda Valley, where creativity, humour, rhetoric, socialism and disputation seem to have been breathed in the air as freely as coal dust, he was never happy far away from his beloved south Wales valleys, and all his plays are based there.

He first became known as a short-story writer; then, moving into radio drama, he came to the attention of GEORGE DEVINE at the ROYAL COURT in 1956. *The Keep*, a very Welsh play that is notable not only for a rare London success but also for an influence on a later generation of Welsh playwrights, was produced there in 1960 and became an international success. In 1963 *Jackie the Jumper*, set during the 1831 Merthyr Rising, excited Royal Court audiences less. Thomas seems to have become particularly disillusioned when he found his draft for the THEATRE ROYAL, STRATFORD EAST of a First World War play punctuated with songs, which he called *Sap*, superseded by *Oh What A Lovely War! Sap* was later produced at Cardiff's Sherman Theatre in 1974, but Thomas henceforth wrote plays mainly for radio and television. DAVID ADAMS

Thompson, Mervyn [Garfield] (b. Kaitangata, New Zealand, 14 June 1935; d. 13 July 1992) Playwright, actor and director. After leaving school at a young age to work in the west coast coal mines, he later became a student at Canterbury University College, where he acted under Ngaio Marsh. On returning from overseas, he became co-founder and co-director of the COURT THEATRE, Christchurch (1971–4). He was artistic director of Wellington's DOWNSTAGE THEATRE (1975–6); his productions of *Equus* and *Three Sisters* were particularly memorable. He was director of the first New Zealand

Playwrights' Workshops (1980, 1982), run by Playmarket, out of which evolved the highly successful *Foreskin's Lament* by Greg McGee. Thompson's first play, *O! Temperance* (1972), combined history, political commentary and music with a strong Kiwi flavour. His *Songs to Uncle Scrim* (1976) and *Songs to the Judges* (1980) posed questions about politics, race and land. His solo autobiographical plays, *Coaltown Blues* (1984) and *Passing Through* (1991), also involved songs and provocative themes in his desire to develop a popular drama.

GILLIAN GREER & LAURIE ATKINSON

Thompson, Paul (b. Charlottetown, Prince Edward Island, 4 May 1940) Director. Educated in Canada and France, in 1965 he served his apprenticeship with director ROGER PLANCHON. After two seasons as an assistant director at Canada's STRATFORD FESTIVAL, Thompson joined Toronto's THEATRE PASSE MURAILLE in 1969. He was its artistic director 1972–82 and the leading force in COLLECTIVE creation in Canada, emphasizing Canadian and local themes. Notable productions were *The Farm Show* (1972) and *Maggie and Pierre* (created with actress Linda Griffiths, 1979). He was appointed director-general of Canada's National Theater School in 1987, but in the 1990s he returned to freelance directing. He collaborated with Timothy Findley in writing *Elizabeth Rex* (2000), presented by the Stratford Festival.

EUGENE BENSON

Thompson, Sam (b. Belfast, 21 May 1916; d. Belfast, 15 Feb. 1965) Playwright; artistic godfather to a generation of Belfast playwrights. His *Over the Bridge* (1960) succeeded in putting sectarian violence at centre stage for the first time in the city's sparse theatrical history, and against formidable opposition from the whole Unionist establishment. The play's setting is the Belfast shipyard in which Thompson had worked as a painter for over 20 years before trying his hand at radio scripts, and then stage plays. The *Over the Bridge* controversy and triumph turned him into a campaigning public figure, a role he relished, and in 1964 he stood as a parliamentary candidate for the Northern Ireland Labour Party. *The Evangelist* (1963) attacked religious demagoguery, and *Cemented with Love* (1965), a television drama, took on the corrupt practices endemic in Ulster elections. But Thompson died of a heart attack before this last piece – twice postponed by the BBC – was finally transmitted.

STEWART PARKER

Hagal Mengal, *Sam Thompson and Modern Drama in Ulster* (1986)

Thorndike, Sybil [Agnes] (b. Gainsborough, Lincs, 24 Oct. 1882; d. London, 6 June 1976) Actress. Her father was a clergyman, and both her younger brother, Russell (1885–1972), and sister, Eileen (1891–1953), went on the stage; Sybil would have been a musician if not for a broken wrist. In 1904 she joined BEN GREET's Academy, the only recognized drama school at the time, and toured England and America with him. She made her name in contemporary plays, such as *The Madras House* (1910), *Hindle Wakes* (1912) and *Jane Clegg* (1912). Her lifelong association with LEWIS CASSON began while they were both working with ANNIE HORNIMAN at the Gaiety, Manchester. During the First World War Thorndike developed a skill for playing Shakespearean males while working with LILIAN BAYLIS at the OLD VIC. After the war she appeared in CLAUDEL's *The Hostage* (1919) for the PIONEER PLAYERS and in GRAND GUIGNOL (1920–2), but it was her acting in *The Trojan Women* (1919) that inspired SHAW to write *St Joan* for her in 1924. She was also successful as his Candida (1920) and Major Barbara (1929). Both she and Casson revitalized Greek drama and toured London productions widely, performing in Welsh mining villages during the Second World War.

Thorndike worked very closely with artists such as CLEMENCE DANE, who wrote *Eighty in the Shade* (1959) for her and Casson; EMLYN WILLIAMS, with whom she appeared in his play *The Corn is Green* (1938); J. B. PRIESTLEY (she and Casson starred in his play *The Linden Tree*, 1947); RALPH RICHARDSON; and LAURENCE OLIVIER. She supported progressive causes, and was renowned for her intelligent and perceptive portrayals. As for film, she felt the medium truncated plays, although she had several notable film credits, including *Dawn* (1928), based on the life of nurses Edith Cavell and Florence Nightingale.

Still performing at the age of 90, Thorndike was a much loved and admired actress after whom a theatre in Leatherhead, Surrey, was named in 1969. She was created a dame in 1931 and a Companion of Honour in 1970. MAGGIE GALE

John Casson, *Lewis and Sybil* (1962)
Elizabeth Sprigge, *Sybil Thorndike Casson* (1971)
Russell Thorndike, *Sybil Thorndike* (1929)
J. C. Trewin, *Sybil Thorndike* (1955)

thrust stage *see* OPEN STAGE

Thurburn, Gwynneth *see* DRAMA SCHOOLS; VOICE TRAINING

Tierney, Harry [Austin] (b. Perth Amboy, NJ, 21 May 1890; d. New York, 26 March 1965) and **McCarthy, Joseph** (b. Somerville, Mass., 27 Sept. 1885; d. New York, 18 Dec. 1943) Songwriters. Although lyricist

McCarthy and composer Tierney both worked with others, they are remembered as a team because of three successful Broadway shows: *Irene* (1919), *Kid Boots* (1923) and *Rio Rita* (1927). GERALD BORDMAN

Tilley, Vesta [Matilda Alice Victoria Powles] (b. Worcester, 13 May 1864; d. London, 16 Sept. 1952) The most famous male IMPERSONATOR in English MUSIC HALL. She began her career as a child performer known as The Great Little Tilley and played principal boy in PANTOMIME, but is best remembered for her military and 'masher' impersonations, notably 'Burlington Bertie' and 'Algy or the Piccadilly Johnny with the Little Glass Eye'. Her military numbers, such as 'Jolly Good Luck to the Girl who Loves a Soldier', were used as part of the recruitment campaign for the First World War. She led fashion with her neatly tailored suits, yet did not pursue the masquerade vocally off stage. She gave up her stage career after her husband, Conservative MP Walter de Frece, who wrote many of her songs, was knighted. Her autobiography, *Recollections of Vesta Tilley*, appeared in 1934. ELAINE ASTON

See also DRAG.

Sara Maitland, *Vesta Tilley* (1986)

Tilly, Grant (b. Sydney, 12 Dec. 1937) Actor and designer. After an apprenticeship in amateur theatre with Unity in Wellington, he studied in London and returned to New Zealand to become a tutor, actor and designer, particularly at Wellington's DOWNSTAGE THEATRE. In 1974 he was a co-founder and coordinator of Wellington's CIRCA THEATRE, where he has spent most of his career, with success in such roles as Tupper in Greg McGee's *Foreskin's Lament*, the Fool in *King Lear*, Dad in *Joyful and Triumphant* and Dickie Hart in ROGER HALL's *C'Mon Black!*. One of New Zealand's most popular actors, he was senior tutor at the New Zealand Drama School for 14 years, while continuing to work extensively for theatre, radio, television and film.
GILLIAN GREER & LAURIE ATKINSON

Tipton, Jennifer (b. Colombus, Ohio, 11 Sept. 1937) LIGHTING designer. With well over 200 ballets and 80 plays to her credit, Tipton is one of America's best-known and most highly respected lighting designers. After studying astrophysics in college, she embarked on a career as a dancer. This led to lighting when she took a course with Thomas Skelton in 1960 and developed an interest in the use of light as an element in performance. Her award-winning lighting has been applied in DANCE, drama, OPERA and PERFORMANCE ART; she has worked with directors such as ROBERT WILSON, MIKE NICHOLS, ANDREI SERBAN and JOANNE AKALAITIS, as well as with choreographers ranging from

JEROME ROBBINS and TWYLA THARP to Mikhail Baryshnikov and Paul Taylor, with whom she has collaborated since 1965. She teaches lighting at the Yale School of Drama. ELLEN LAMPERT-GRÉAUX

TNP *see* THÉÂTRE NATIONAL POPULAIRE

Todd, Susan *see* EDGAR, DAVID; MONSTROUS REGIMENT

Togo *see* FRENCH AFRICAN THEATRE

Toller, Ernst (b. Samotschin, Germany [now Szamocin, Poland], 1 Dec. 1893; d. New York, 22 May 1939) Playwright and poet. Following his military service he became a pacifist, joined the communist Independent Socialist Party, participated in the 1919 uprising in Bavaria and was sentenced to five years' imprisonment. During his incarceration he became one of Germany's best-known contemporary dramatists, as a result of the successful stagings of *Die Wandlung* (*Transfiguration*, 1919), *Masse Mensch* (*Masses and Man*, 1921), *Die Maschinenstürmer* (*The Machine Wreckers*, 1922) and *Der deutsche Hinkemann* (1923; known as both *Hinkemann* and *Brockenbrow*). He wrote other plays about contemporary events, and several of his historical pageants and speech choirs were staged at trades unions and Communist Party gatherings. After his release, Toller lived in Berlin where, in 1927, PISCATOR opened his Theater am Nollendorfplatz with a production of *Hoppla wir leben* (*Hurray! We're Still Alive*, or *Such is Life!*).

In 1933 Toller was forced to emigrate. For several years he lived in England, where in 1939 he wrote his antifascist drama *Pastor Hall* (premièred in 1947 in Berlin) and was active as a public speaker and pamphleteer, campaigning on behalf of the Spanish Republic and alerting the world to the dangers of Hitler's regime. He committed suicide, feeling impotent as Hitler expanded East.

Toller's early plays, especially their original productions, were exemplary of EXPRESSIONISM in the theatre. They gained international recognition and contributed more to the development of an experimental, political theatre in the 1920s than did the work of his contemporaries such as KAISER. GÜNTER BERGHAUS

See also MASS DECLAMATION.

R. Dove, *Revolutionary Socialism in the Work of Ernst Toller* (1986)
——, *He Was a German: A Biography of Ernst Toller* (1990)
M. Ossar, *Anarchism in the Dramas of Ernst Toller* (1980)
M. Pittock, *Ernst Toller* (1979)

Tomelty, Joseph (b. Portaferry, Co. Down, Ireland, 5 March 1911; d. Belfast, 7 June 1995) Actor and playwright. A founder of the Ulster Group Theatre in 1940, he performed in several productions there while writing

one of the BBC's most popular wartime serials, *The McCooeys*. He played Phibbs in GEORGE SHIEL's *The Passing Day* for TYRONE GUTHRIE's Northern Ireland Festival of Britain Company in London in 1951; this gained him widespread attention and was followed by many stage and film roles. His own plays, *The End House* (1944), *Is the Priest at Home?* (1945) and *All Soul's Night* (1948), retain an important place in the Irish repertoire. His daughter Frances became a successful actress.
CHRISTOPHER FITZ-SIMON

Tomlin, Lily [Mary Jean]   (b. Detroit, 1 Sept. 1939) Comedienne and actress. After dropping out of university, Tomlin developed a cabaret act which she took round the coffee-house circuit in New York in the 1960s. Her talent for IMPERSONATION won her a place in the cast of the long-running television series *Laugh In* from 1969 to 1972. As well as numerous concert appearances, she was acclaimed for two one-woman Broadway shows, *Appearing Nitely* (1977) and *The Search for Signs of Intelligent Life in the Universe* (1986); the latter won her a Tony Award.   HELEN RAPPAPORT

Tony Award   *see* AWARDS AND PRIZES; PERRY, ANTOINETTE

Topol [Haim]   (b. Tel Aviv, 9 Sept. 1935)   Actor, who first graced the stage while serving in the Israeli army. He founded Tel Aviv's popular Theatre of Satire and went on to help found Haifa's Municipal Theatre (1962). He was equally at home in classical roles (such as Petruchio in *The Taming of the Shrew*) as in contemporary works (such as IONESCO's *Rhinoceros* or as Azdak in *The Caucasian Chalk Circle*). He shot to international stardom in the role of Tevye in the musical *Fiddler on the Roof*, in which he starred both on stage and screen.
ADRIANA HUNTER

Toronto   In North America, Toronto is second only to New York in the extent and variety of its theatre scene. The city's first commercial theatre – a converted Wesleyan Church – opened in 1834. Prominent nineteenth-century theatres included the Royal Lyceum (1848–74), the Grand Opera House (1874–1928), the Royal Opera House (1874–83) and the Princess Theater (1889–1930). Twentieth-century theatres include the ROYAL ALEXANDRA THEATER (1907–), Loew's Yonge St Theater (1913–28), the O'Keefe Center (1960), renamed the Hummingbird Centre in 1997, and the Princess of Wales Theater (1993). Of particular note are the Elgin and Winter Garden Theaters (1914–28). This complex, designed by noted theatre architect Thomas W. Lamb, comprised a lower theatre, the Elgin (seating 2,149) and the beautiful Winter Garden Theater above, seating 1,410. Both have been meticulously restored, the Elgin

opening in 1985, the Winter Garden in 1990. The Pantages Theater, opened in 1920 as a VAUDVILLE house, was likewise restored to its former splendour in 1988, and in 1989 opened a ten-year run of the musical *The Phantom of the Opera*.

Until the 1920s Toronto's – and Canada's – theatrical scene had been dominated by American and British companies and plays. The founding of Toronto's HART HOUSE THEATER in 1919 signalled an interest in home-grown drama, but it was not until the 1960s that a truly indigenous Canadian theatre began to establish itself. Such companies as THEATRE PASSE MURAILLE (1968), FACTORY THEATER LAB (1970), and TARRAGON THEATER (1971) emphasized Canadian content, often with a left-wing political and historical ideology. Some – especially Theatre Passe Muraille and TORONTO WORKSHOP PRODUCTIONS (1959–88), Canada's first alternative theatre company – favoured a collective dramaturgy, others the development of Canadian playwrights (GEORGE F. WALKER at Factory Theater Lab, DAVID FRENCH at Tarragon). The 1980s and 1990s saw the emergence of companies with more specific mandates: the promotion of feminist agendas (at Nightwood Theatre, 1979); the articulation of aboriginal concerns (as in plays by Tomson Highway, Drew Hayden Taylor and Daniel David Moses); GAY and LESBIAN concerns (at Buddies in Bad Times, founded by Sky Gilbert in 1979, Toronto's leading QUEER THEATRE). Francophone theatregoers are served by Théâtre Français de Toronto (1987), originally Théâtre du P'tit Bonheur, founded in 1967.
EUGENE BENSON

Toronto Workshop Productions   Before operations were indefinitely and controversially suspended in 1988, TWP was Toronto's oldest theatre company. Founded in 1959 by George Luscombe (who had worked in England with Joan Littlewood's THEATRE WORKSHOP), TWP was consistently committed to COLLECTIVE and ENSEMBLE work, to imaginative but economical theatricality, and to a left-wing political viewpoint. The first of Canada's ALTERNATIVE theatres, it remained distinct from the main alternative trends of the 1960s and 1970s to some extent because of Luscombe's international rather than nationalistic perspectives. None the less, one of TWP's most notable productions was the collective *Ten Lost Years* (1974) about the Canadian Great Depression, which toured Europe in 1976 and was re-created for television. Luscombe remained artistic director until 1986, after which a series of financial crises and legal disputes quickly led to the company's demise. It finally closed in 1989.   L. W. CONOLLY

Toshka, Fedora   *see* CHOREOGRAPHY

total theatre A term derived from Richard Wagner's concept of a *Gesamtkunstwerk*: a total or unified work of art, in which all elements – music, voice, movement and spectacle – work together for a complete and harmonious effect. The concept was central for the SYMBOLISTS and was especially associated with JEAN-LOUIS BARRAULT and his productions of CLAUDEL's *Soulier de Satin* (1943) and *Christophe Colomb* (1953). COCTEAU was another noted exponent of total theatre, which became the precursor of the 'director's theatre' that characterized the post-1960s modernists, from PETER BROOK to ROBERT WILSON, who placed a personal stamp on every aspect of their productions. BRECHT, however, challenged this interpretation of total theatre, seeing it as a form of integration that degraded all the fused elements equally and led to passivity in the audience, left to stew in the melting pot. He explored an alternative interpretation that had begun with ERWIN PISCATOR, who in the 1920s had asked WALTER GROPIUS to design a total theatre that could be used for all types of drama and opera, film, dance, political meetings – even sporting events. Piscator used all the artistic and technical elements available to drama with a clear political intention and lay the foundations of EPIC THEATRE, a tradition carried on by playwrights such as JOHN ARDEN and companies such as THEATRE WORKSHOP. MARVIN CARLSON

See also MODERNISM.

E. T. Kirby, *Total Theatre* (1969)

touring Theatre has a long history of itinerant playing, and in the twentieth century that tradition continued with unprecedented variety. Circuits of theatres were well established by the beginning of the century, either to receive regular touring companies or, as in VAUDEVILLE, under the same ownership in order to guarantee an uninterrupted turnover of acts. Commercial hits in the WEST END or on BROADWAY would be toured, though often with lesser stars, and, in reverse, new productions would be tried 'out of town' before essaying the theatrical capitals. With the decline of the regional REPERTORY system in Britain, companies, such as PROSPECT, were formed especially to tour. Notwithstanding FUNDING problems, the touring scene in the 1980s and 1990s was healthy and of high quality, with groups like Actors Touring Company, English Touring Theatre and SHARED EXPERIENCE regularly producing good work. The rise of the FRINGE and ALTERNATIVE THEATRE saw the emergence of smaller groups dedicated to touring and the development of new circuits; some companies performed their shows in the OPEN AIR, or anywhere other than a traditional theatre, like a TENT or a school hall, and some took their own seating with them. Some travelled to different locations and created COMMUNITY-specific shows.

Economics has regulated touring at all levels of operation, and, as theatre has become technically more complex, touring has become more expensive. Co-productions between different theatres was one way of sharing costs and ensuring a geographically wider viewing. CHARLES LONDON

Tovstonogov, Georgi [Alexandrovich] (b. Tbilisi, Georgia, 15 Sept. 1915; d. Leningrad, 29 May 1989) Director. In the 'thaw' of 1956 Tovstonogov became director of the Bolshoi Gorky Dramatic Theatre in Leningrad, where he acquired an international reputation for boldly conceived, highly disciplined ENSEMBLE work in the realist tradition (e.g. Dostoevsky's *The Idiot*, 1957, with SMOKTUNOVSKY). His productions became known abroad through his theatre's appearances in America and at European festivals. His book, *The Profession of the Stage Director* (1965), was published in English in 1972. NICK WORRALL

Anatoly Smeliansky, *The Russian Theatre after Stalin* (1999)

toy theatre A popular children's toy, the first toy theatres were probably intended primarily as accurate models both for enthusiastic theatre followers and for managers in the provinces hoping to recreate London productions. Toy theatres, which were introduced in the nineteenth century, consisted of some eight to twelve printed sheets on which the stage, performers and costumes of a particular production were accurately reproduced. These elements were cut out and the sets recreated. The figures were mounted on long handles and moved about the stage, while a 'narrator' read from the accompanying potted version of the script. Plays were written for toy theatres until the early twentieth century. Later the theatres represented a valuable record of memorable productions and otherwise forgotten plays. London has a Toy Theatre Museum, which used to be named after one of the main publishers of these plays, Pollock's, and their images have influenced contemporary designers (e.g. Anthony Ward's set for the ROYAL SHAKESPEARE COMPANY's *The Tempest*, 1993). ADRIANA HUNTER

Toye, Wendy (b. London, 1 May 1917) Dancer, director, producer and choreographer. In a varied and distinguished career that began in 1929, Toye has been a major dancer and choreographer with the leading ballet companies of the day and influenced British musicals and light entertainment through her direction and choreography. She arranged the dances for producer GEORGE BLACK's sumptuous REVUES from 1938 to 1945, notably *Black Velvet* (1939), and directed three shows for CHARLES COCHRAN. But she could also be found directing opera, television, film and Shakespeare at the OLD VIC.   CHARLES LONDON

See also CHOREOGRAPHY; DANCE.

trades unions   *see* UNIONS

tragedy   The most highly respected category in the Western drama, accorded first place among literary genres by ARISTOTLE, a position which it retained until the modern era, when its dominance was challenged by the less elevated drama and various mixed gentres. According to the Aristotelian tradition, a tragedy was a serious play dealing with the fall from power of a figure in high position because of a mistaken judgement, the 'tragic flaw'. As this tradition was developed during the Renaissance, other features were also stressed, among them a unity of tone, the famous 'three unities' of time (the action taking place in a single day), place (in a single location) and action (involving no subplots or alternative actions), and the use of poetry (most generally the rhymed couplet the French call the Alexandrine).

The most highly praised works of the most revered dramatists in the West have been tragedies, beginning with the works of the great Greek tragedians, Aeschylus, Sophocles and Euripides, and continuing through the Roman plays of Seneca to the modern works of Shakespeare, Racine, Schiller and IBSEN. Similarly, tragedy has, until quite recently, dominated critical and theoretical speculation about the drama, due in large part to the continuing influence of Aristotle. Thus tragedy remains a central concern for Horace, for the key Renaissance theorists such as Scaliger, Castelvetro and Sidney, for the major theorists of the seventeenth and eighteenth centuries such as Dryden, Boileau, Johnson, Lessing and Voltaire, and for the great German romantics Goethe, Hegel and Nietzsche.

Although the English and French traditions of tragedy, dominated respectively by Shakespeare and Racine, differed in a number of significant ways, most notably in the English willingness to allow comic elements, multiple actions, large numbers of characters, a mixture of prose and poetry, and considerable latitude in the time and space encompassed by the work, the two traditions agreed on the basic subject matter of tragedy, which had to be the suffering and almost inevitably the death of a figure of stature, a king or a prince, whose fall was seen as representative of and involving a whole society. Aside from the differences between the French and English traditions, tragedy has remained a much more stable form than COMEDY, probably due in part to the authority of Aristotle. There has really been only one major variation on tragedy in the Western tradition, and that is the development of modern realistic tragedy, dealing with middle- or lower-class characters and written in prose.

Although a number of important dramatists experimented with prose tragedy involving middle-class characters in the eighteenth and nineteenth centuries, most notably Lillo in England, Lessing and Hebbel in Germany, and Augier and Dumas *fils* in France, it was the Norwegian Ibsen who in the late nineteenth century established this form with a series of works so influential that they have often been said to have begun the modern theatre internationally. They also essentially displaced the traditional concept of tragedy as dealing with the fortunes of kings and princes, so that since Ibsen new works designated as tragedies have essentially followed his model. Among the many playwrights who followed him in creating tragedies of everyday life were STRINDBERG, LORCA, BETTI and SYNGE. This tradition was particularly important in America in the work of such leading serious dramatists as O'NEILL, WILLIAMS and MILLER. Miller in particular looked to Ibsen as a model and wrote a much-quoted defence of the common man as the best hero for modern tragedy.   MARVIN CARLSON

Aristotle, *Poetics*, trans. Ingram Bywater (1954)
W. M. Dixon, *Tragedy* (1924)
Francis Fergusson, *The Idea of a Theatre* (1949)
F. L. Lucas, *Tragedy* (1957)
Friedrich Nietzsche, *The Birth of Tragedy*, trans. Walter Kaufman (1967)
George Steiner, *The Death of Tragedy* (1961)

Tramway   *see* GLASGOW

translation   *see* ADAPTATION/TRANSLATION

Travers, Ben[jamin]   (b. Hendon, 12 Nov. 1886; d. London, 18 Dec. 1980)   Playwright. Travers' first success was *A Cuckoo in the Nest* (1925), which began a series of what later became known as the ALDWYCH FARCES. These ten plays included *Rookery Nook* (1926), *Thark* (1927), *Plunder* (1928), *A Night Like This* (1930) and *Turkey Time* (1931). He also wrote *Banana Ridge* (1939) and *She Follows Me About* (1945) for other West End theatres. In 1976 three Travers plays were playing in London: two revivals and a new farce, *The Bed Before Yesterday* (1975). He wrote film and television versions of his farces and two volumes of autobiography, *Vale of Laughter* (1957) and *A Sitting on a Gate* (1978).
MAGGIE GALE

L. Smith, *Modern British Farce* (1989)

Traverse Theatre   Founded in EDINBURGH   in 1962, the Traverse pioneered both a new vogue for CLUB theatres (to evade CENSORSHIP laws prior to the Theatres

Act of 1968) and a novel actor–audience relationship, with the 60 spectators being seated on two sides of a small room – hence the name. Under the direction of one of the founders, Jim Haynes, then Gordon McDougall (1966–8), who staged productions in larger venues, MAX STAFFORD-CLARK (1968–70), who moved the theatre to new premises, Michael Rudman (1970–3) and Mike Ockrent (1973–5), the Traverse was celebrated as an experimental theatre with an impressive number of premières and an international repertoire. It became a key venue at the time of the annual EDINBURGH FESTIVAL. Stafford-Clark also founded the Traverse Theatre Workshop Company, which laid the basis for his contribution to JOINT STOCK. When Chris Parr took over in 1975, the work of Scottish playwrights took pride of place – JOHN BYRNE's *The Slab Boys* (1978) being the most renowned. The Traverse, a public theatre since 1987, has, under subsequent directors Peter Lichtenfels (1981–5), Jenny Killick (1985–8), Ian Brown (1988–96) and Philip Howard (1996–), continued to nurture new Scottish writers, for example, LIZ LOCHHEAD, Peter Arnott, CHRIS HANNAN, Stephen Greenhorn and Nicola McCartney. The Traverse moved to a new two-auditorium theatre in 1992. JAN MCDONALD

Joyce McMillan, *The Traverse Theatre Story* (1988)

Treadwell, Sophie   (b. Stockton, Calif., 5 Oct. 1885; d. Tucson, Ariz., 20 Feb. 1970) Dramatist. During the First World War, Treadwell was the first accredited woman war correspondent for the American press. Fluent in Spanish, she travelled to the hideout of Mexican revolutionary Pancho Villa for his only interview with an American. She drew on that experience for *Gringo* (1922), her first professionally produced play on Broadway.

Treadwell wrote 54 plays, but only seven were produced in New York. She is particularly remembered for *Machinal* (1928), an expressionistic, proto-feminist drama inspired by the famous Ruth Snyder murder trial. Originally produced by Arthur Hopkins and designed by ROBERT EDMOND JONES, the play had New York revivals in 1960 and 1990, as well as many productions abroad, including one at the NATIONAL THEATRE in London in 1993. Treadwell produced two of her own plays in New York: *O, Nightingale* (1925) and *Lone Valley* (1933). *Hope for a Harvest*, produced by the THEATER GUILD in 1941, expressed Treadwell's belief that Depression America could reinvigorate itself by hard work and ethnic inter-marriage. FELICIA HARDISON LONDRÉ

Jerry Dickey, *Sophie Treadwell: A Research and Production Sourcebook* (1997)
Jennifer Jones, 'In Defense of the Woman: Sophie Treadwell's Machinal', *Modern Drama*, vol. 37, Fall 1994
Yvonne Shafer, *American Women Playwrights, 1900–1950* (1995)

Tree, Herbert [Draper] Beerbohm   (b. London, 17 Dec. 1852; d. London, 2 July 1917)   Actor–manager. Initially noted as an actor for his versatility and mimicry, Tree is mainly remembered for his management of the Haymarket Theatre (1887–96) and then, on the opposite side of the street, Her Majesty's Theatre, which he built, opened in April 1897 and ran until 1915. At the Haymarket he produced several plays by Shakespeare, but more adventurously others by MAETERLINCK, WILDE and IBSEN. At Her Majesty's, his interest in new work was dominated by adaptations that gave him an opportunity to shine (e.g. as Fagin, 1905) and by the poetic dramas of STEPHEN PHILLIPS. In 1914 he created there Henry Higgins to MRS PATRICK CAMPBELL's Eliza Doolittle in SHAW's *Pygmalion*. Tree relished magnificent spectacle, and visited this love on Shakespeare: the *mise-en-scène* for *A Midsummer Night's Dream* (1900) included live rabbits and children dressed up like fairies; *Julius Caesar* (1906) filled its forum scene with a huge cast, intricately arranged and dressed in lavish costumes, a decision which also characterized his famous pageant in *Henry VIII* (1910). His attempts at tragic roles tended to confirm his talent for comedy and character. In 1904, he established what would become the Royal Academy of Dramatic Art. A major figure at the turn of the century, he wrote three books and was knighted in 1907.
DAN REBELLATO

Madeleine Bingham, *The Great Lover* (1978)
Hesketh Pearson, *Herbert Tree* (1956)

Treharne, Bryceson   *see* ADELAIDE; AUSTRALIA

Tremain, Rose   *see* MONSTROUS REGIMENT

Tremblay, Michel   (b. Montreal, 25 June 1942)   Playwright and novelist. Internationally recognized as the most important Quebec dramatist to date, he burst on the scene with his controversial *Les Belles-Soeurs* (*The Sisters-in-Law*), the performance of which in 1968 is considered a turning-point in French Canada's theatre and, indeed, its culture. The first work performed in *joual*, the impoverished, anglicized urban French of Montreal, it soon attracted national and international attention. A series of plays set in similar tawdry conditions ensued, all remarkably successful, notably *A Toi pour toujours, ta Marie-Lou* (*Forever Yours, Marie-Lou*, 1973) and *Sainte-Carmen de la Main* (*Saint Carmen of the Main*, 1976). His later work has moved away from proletarian themes to more universal ones, as exemplified in his powerful *Albertine en cinq temps* (*Albertine, in Five Times*, 1984), considered by many his finest play to date.
LEONARD E. DOUCETTE

Geraldine Anthony, ed., *Stage Voices: 12 Canadian Playwrights Talk About Their Lives and Work* (1978)

Gilbert David and Pierre Lavoie, eds, *Le Monde de Michel Tremblay* (1993)

Renate Usmiani, *Michel Tremblay: A Critical Study* (1982)

Tretyakov, Sergei [Mikhailovich] (b. Kuldiga, Latvia, 20 June 1892; d. Moscow, 20 Sept. 1937) Playwright. A brilliant pianist, artist and futurist poet, he was enthused by the Bolshevik Revolution, and collaborated closely with leading 'left' theatre workers EISENSTEIN and MEYERHOLD. He wrote a number of highly original dramas, mixing grotesque, acrobatic, farcical and monumental elements through a montage technique which was to influence his friend BRECHT's later EPIC drama. His last play was banned, and he turned to screenplays, translation (three of Brecht's plays) and 'factography'. He was arrested and shot in 1937. His plays include *No vsyakogo mudretsas dovolno prostoty* (*A Wise Man*, 1923), *Zemlya dybom* (*Earth Rampant*, 1923), *Rychi Kitai!* (*Roar, China!*, 1926) and *Khochu rebenka* (*I Want a Baby*, 1927). ROBERT LEACH

Triana, José (b. Camagüey, Cuba, 4 Jan. 1931) Playwright. In *El mayor general hablara de teogonia* ('The major general will talk about theogony') and *Medea en el espejo* ('Medea in the mirror'), both 1960, Triana questions supreme authority and tradition, displaying a nihilist attitude towards society. Other plays include *El parque de la fraternidad* ('The fraternity park', 1962), *La muerte del ñeque* ('Ñeque's Death', 1963) and *La visita del angel* ('The Angel's Visit', 1963). His most popular play, *La noche de los asesinos* ('The night of the assassins', 1966), a ritualistic re-enactment of a family murder, has been viewed as a metaphor of pre-revolutionary Cuba. During the 1980s Triana moved to Paris, where he continued writing. *Palabras comunes* was staged as *Worlds Apart* in 1986 by the ROYAL SHAKESPEARE COMPANY, which had presented *La noche de los asesinos* as *The Criminals* in 1967. Other plays include *Cruzando el puente* ('Crossing the bridge', 1991) and *La fiesta* ('The party', 1992). BEATRIZ J. RIZK

Isabel Alvarez-Borland and David George, '*La noche de los asesinos*: Text, Staging and Audience', *Latin American Theatre Review*, vol. 20, no. 1 (Fall 1986)

Frank Dauster, 'The Game of Chance: The Theatre of Jose Triana' in *Dramatists in Revolt: The New Latin American Theatre* ed. Leon F. Lyday and George W. Woodward (1976).

Tricycle Theatre (north London) It was opened in an old music and dance hall in 1980 in the Kilburn area of London by the Wakefield Tricycle Company, a campaigning touring FRINGE group founded in 1972 in a King's Cross pub called the Pindar of Wakefield (hence the company's name). The Tricycle has established a reputation for presenting popular theatre and serving well its local audiences, including distinctive Irish and black communities. As well as giving a platform to new, and especially black writers – for example, TREVOR RHONE – it often presents politically trenchant work when it is unfashionable, such as the DOCUMENTARY plays *Half the Picture* (1994), by Richard Norton-Taylor and JOHN MCGRATH, about UK complicity in arms sales to Iraq, and Norton-Taylor's *The Colour of Justice: The Stephen Lawrence Inquiry* (1999), an edited version of the damning account of police inaction after the racist murder of a black student. Since 1984 the Tricycle has been led by Nicholas Kent. CHARLES LONDON

See also BLACK THEATRE.

Trinder, Tommy (b. London, 24 March 1909; d. Chertsey, Surrey, 10 July 1989) Comedian who appeared in regional VARIETY during the 1920s before starting in a long run of REVUES, including *Band Wagon* (1939), *Best Bib and Tucker* (1942), *Fancy Free* (1951) and *United Notions* (1956). He worked extensively on television, hosted *Sunday Night at the London Palladium*, and served as chairman of the Fulham Football Club for many years. REXTON S. BUNNET

Trinidad and Tobago *see* CARIBBEAN

Trinidad Theatre Workshop DEREK WALCOTT founded the company now known as the Trinidad Theatre Workshop in 1959. It was to become the doyen of theatre companies in the CARIBBEAN region. Under Walcott, the company presented repertory seasons and other productions of the best West Indian playwriting, and also plays from Africa, Europe and the United States. The company was to be most widely recognized, however, as a showcase for the work of Walcott himself, at a particularly fertile period in his development as a dramatist.

The TTW began life as the Little Carib Theatre Workshop, in partnership with the legendary Beryl McBurnie's Little Carib Dance Company. Both were based at the Little Carib Theatre in Port of Spain. The fledgling theatre company gave its first public performance in 1962, with a double bill of BECKETT's *Krapp's Last Tape* and Dennis Scott's *The Caged*. Later the same year, the TTW staged an early version of Walcott's *The Charlatan*. In 1965, Walcott and the TTW left the Little Carib. The company's name changed to, simply, The Theatre Workshop. The TTW camped successively in a hotel basement, a zoo, a school hall and, after years of homelessness, an abandoned fire station. When Walcott began to take productions on tour of the region and to

North America in the late 1960s, the TTW became identified as the Trinidad Theatre Workshop.

Walcott left the Workshop in 1976, when he emigrated to America. Subsequently, the company was run by senior members. With few new works from Walcott to stage, the TTW thrust eventually turned from public production more towards educational theatre and the running of a school for the arts. However, with his 1992 award of the Nobel Prize for Literature, Walcott's involvement with the TTW renewed, and the company's revivals of his works were once again taken on tour to various parts of the world, including Singapore and Boston. JUDY S. J. STONE

Bruce King, *Derek Walcott and West Indian Drama* (1995)

Trinity Repertory Company One of the premier regional theatres in the United States. Founded in 1964 by a group of artistically committed citizens of Providence, Rhode Island, under the leadership of Adrian Hall (1965–89), it was originally called the Trinity Square Repertory Company; the 'Square' was dropped in 1986. The group managed to employ AVANT-GARDE techniques and forge a strong link with its community. Generous government grants gave the company a sound financial base, enabling it to stage dozens of world premières, maintain a flourishing company and create a recognizable 'house' style by its third decade. Presenting a mixed repertoire of up to 12 productions annually on two different stages, Trinity was also able to start a school for actors, playwrights and directors in 1978. The theatre survived Hall's resignation and Anne Bogart's disastrous 1989–90 season, and recovered under the leadership of company stalwart Richard Jenkins. Oskar Eustis became artistic director in 1993.
THOMAS F. CONNOLLY
See also RESIDENT THEATRE.

Jeanne Marlin Woods, *Theatre to Change Men's Souls* (1993)

Tron Theatre Named after the Tron Kirk in Glasgow where it is now housed, it was envisaged as a replacement for the Close, a club theatre destroyed by fire in 1973. It began as a café-bar theatre in 1981, presenting new Scottish works by Marcella Evaristi and LIZ LOCHHEAD among others, as well as a variety of visiting companies. The main playing space opened in 1982, largely as a receiving venue for touring groups. In 1985 Michael Boyd was appointed as the first artistic director, and although leading British and overseas groups still appeared frequently, there was an increasingly high proportion of in-house product. Following his departure in 1996, the policy was maintained but there is a greater emphasis on music and visiting companies from within the UK. JAN MCDONALD

Tucker, Sophie [Sofya Kalish, later Abuza] (b. Russia, 13 Jan. 1887; d. New York, 9 Feb. 1966) Singer and actress. The daughter of immigrant Russian Jews, she sang for the customers in her father's restaurant in Connecticut as a child, coming to New York to seek her theatrical fortune in 1906. She got her first break in the ZIEGFELD FOLLIES of 1909, building up a strong following playing VAUDEVILLE at MUSIC HALLS in New York and Chicago. Her panache with *double entendre* and the gusto with which she belted out a song made her popular with audiences both in the United States and in England, where she toured in 1922 and 1925. By 1926 she had her own CABARET show in New York, and in 1928 she was given the billing for ever after associated with her: 'The Last of the Red Hot Mamas'. By now she was appearing with some of the musical greats of her era – BRICE, CANTOR, FIELDS – in Broadway musicals such as *Leave It to Me!* (1938) and *High Kickers* (1941). After the demise of vaudeville in the 1950s she adapted to working in some of America's top nightclubs. Raucous, larger than life and an indomitable trouper to the end, she was still performing well into her seventies, reprising her classic songs like 'There's Company in the Parlor Girls, Come on Down', 'My Yiddishe Mama', 'Some of These Days' and 'After You've Gone' in her inimitable, gutsy voice. She helped organize vaudeville performers in the American Federation of Actors, of which she was president in 1938. Her autobiography, *Some of these Days*, appeared in 1945. HELEN RAPPAPORT

Tune, Tommy [Thomas James] (b. Witchita Falls, Tex., 28 Feb. 1939) Performer, choreographer and director. After a brief career as a chorus boy he won attention dancing in *Seesaw* (1973). Although the tall, slim entertainer subsequently performed in *My One and Only* (1983) and in a touring 1991 revival of *Bye Bye Birdie*, he is probably better known for his choreography and direction in such shows as *The Best Little Whorehouse in Texas* (1978), *A Day in Hollywood/A Night in the Ukraine* (1980), *Grand Hotel* (1989) and *The Will Rogers Follies* (1991). Since 1992 he has appeared on tour and in New York in a revue, *Tommy Tune Tonite*. He has a gift for making shoddy material theatrically effective. OFF-BROADWAY he directed the long-running plays *The Club* (1976) and *Cloud Nine* (1981). GERALD BORDMAN
See also CHOREOGRAPHY; DANCE.

Tunisia *see* MIDDLE EAST AND NORTH AMERICA

Turkey *see* MIDDLE EAST AND NORTH AFRICA

Turkmenistan *see* SOVIET UNION

Turner, Clifford   *see* VOICE; VOICE TRAINING

Tutin, Dorothy   (b. London, 8 April 1930; d. Midhurst, W. Sussex, 6 Aug. 2001)   Actress. Tutin caused a sensation as Rose Pemberton in *The Living Room* (1953) and Sally Bowles in *I Am a Camera* (1954). After a lull, interrupted by her Jean Rice in *The Entertainer* (1957), she played a series of Shakespearean heroines at STRATFORD-UPON-AVON, including Juliet (1958), Viola (1958), Ophelia (1958), Portia (1960) and Cressida (1960), the last of these proving her capable of more than infectious and bubbly heroines, as was confirmed by her memorable performance as the raving, humpbacked Sister Jeanne in *The Devils* (1961). Lady Macbeth, Lady Plyant in Congreve's *The Double Dealer* and Ranevskaya in *The Cherry Orchard* (all NATIONAL THEATRE, 1978) brought accolades for this coolly powerful, softly spoken actress, whose splinter-sharp timing and subtle inflection distinguished her in a trilogy of PINTER roles; Kate in *Old Times* (1971), Deborah in *A Kind of Alaska* (1985) and Melissa in *Party Time* (1991). She was made a dame in 1999.   DAN REBELLATO

25th Street Theatre   Founded by Andras Tahn and others in 1971, the company (despite its name) has performed in diverse venues in Saskatoon, Saskatchewan, with a repertoire of almost exclusively Canadian works, a mixture of COLLECTIVE creations (influenced by THEATRE PASSE MURAILLE) and more conventional scripts. The company's most notable production remains the collective *Paper Wheat* (1977), a documentary history of Saskatchewan farming. After its opening locally in Sintaluta, it toured nationally and was televised. Ken Mitchell and Linda Griffiths are among the Canadian playwrights whose works have premièred at 25th Street Theatre.   L. W. CONOLLY

Tynan, Kenneth [Peacock]   (b. Birmingham, 2 April 1927; d. Santa Monica, Ca., 26 July 1980)   Theatre critic and DRAMATURG. On leaving OXFORD, where he had cut a dashing figure, Tynan failed to establish himself as an actor/director and turned to theatre criticism. Appointed drama critic of the London *Evening Standard* in 1952, his left-wing views, acerbic style and irritation with the available theatrical fare won him an immediate audience, but he was fired the following year for threatening to sue his employers for libel if they published a proposed page of letters entitled 'Should Actors Be Critics?' As drama critic at the *Observer* (1954–8 and, after a spell at the *New Yorker*, 1960–3), he was notorious for articles which brilliantly ridiculed the middle-class preoccupations of contemporary drama, in a vigorous language that had great resonance for a new generation of theatregoers impatient with the conservatism of their peers. The first British critic to understand how the theoretical background to BRECHT's EPIC THEATRE related to his stage practice, Tynan was a keen supporter of the ROYAL COURT and the 'kitchen-sink dramatists'. In 1963 Tynan was appointed by OLIVIER as literary adviser to the NATIONAL THEATRE, and the innovative feel of the repertoire in the first few years bears his mark. A dispute with the theatre board's chairman over HOCHHUTH's *Soldiers* in 1967 led to his departure in 1969, having co-produced the play in the West End. (He remained a consultant to the NT until 1973.) He devised the first sex revue, *Oh! Calcutta!* (1968), in the aftermath of the abolition of CENSORSHIP, and published several collections, including *He That Plays the King* (1950), *Tynan Right and Left* (1967) and *A View of the English Stage* (1975). Combative, eloquent and capable of intuitive insights, Tynan was a theatre critic whose practical experience of theatre gave an extra dimension to his ironic prose. A smoker to the end, he died from emphysema.   DOMINIC SHELLARD

Elaine Dundy, *Life Itself!* (2001)
Kathleen Tynan, *The Life of Kenneth Tynan* (1988)
——, ed., *Kenneth Tynan Letters* (1994)

Tzara, Tristan   *see* DADA; PERFORMANCE ART

U

Uganda The many kingdoms and ethnic groups which make up Uganda came together as a unit in 1900 with the signing of the agreement which made them a protectorate of the British. The four kingdoms are Bunyoro, Buganda, Toro and Ankole, and they were joined by several other ethnic groups which eventually became independent from British colonial rule in 1962. Each of these kingdoms and ethnic groups had its own forms of performances, some of which happened indoors and privately in the royal courts and palaces, and some of which took place outdoors. Some courts, such as Bunyoro, had teams of professional entertainers made up of dancers, musicians, acrobats and occasionally court jesters. Remnants of this tradition can still be found in bands of itinerant performers who sometimes get invited to perform at occasions such as weddings and other celebrations. These precolonial and colonial traditional forms have many features in common, and it is these shared characteristics which have combined to shape an emergent Ugandan theatre tradition.

Spoken or 'dialogic' theatre was first introduced by the mission schools which used play texts in English to help teaching and learning. However, students began to improvise vernacular farces and satires based on topical issues. A further development occurred when the traditional forms such as the call and response pattern of the storytelling tradition, and music and dance forms, were adapted for didactic purposes by social welfare assistants and the officers of the influential Mothers' Union. Even though the missionaries tried to suppress the traditional forms, the Mukono Theological College in 1946 began teaching its students to use role-play as a means of understanding. The students were also encouraged to create plays based on major stories from the Bible but expressed in the native languages. One of the most notable plays of this phase was *Were You There?* (1949). This activity was further developed when playscripts began to be written based on Ugandan traditional folk tales and stories such as *The Cows of Karo* and *Kitami the Queen*.

From 1946 a more formalized theatrical practice emerged, with all forms of activity being encouraged through national competitions for youth groups, colleges, schools and adult groups. Most if not all of the earliest known dramatists came to public attention through the competitions, and a majority are also products of Makerere University College. Also by the late 1940s and early 1950s, the colonial administration initiated educative drama and theatre performance as a means of improving agricultural production, and so the first signs of what became THEATRE FOR DEVELOPMENT were already in place, to be later reflected in the Makerere Travelling Theatre which took off in 1965.

In 1959 the Ugandan National Theatre in Kampala was built, and in its first years was used largely by expatriate groups. One such group was the Kampala Amateur Theatrical Society (KATS), culturally active expatriates who saw their role as being 'guardians of Western cultural values and the British theatrical tradition'. This role was reflected in the kind of plays and acting styles that the group adopted. Other expatriate groups were the Kampala Kale Kandia Group, which represented the Indian upper-middle class and produced plays not only in English but also in Gujarati and Hindi as well as performing traditional Indian dancing. The Goan community also had its own cultural group. The various groups saw their task as that of asserting, promoting and enhancing their respective group-specific cultural identities and heritages.

The first all-Ugandan theatre group did not emerge until 1954, when Wycliffe Kiyingi-Kagwe founded his African Artists Association, which specialized in producing social satires. Their most prominent play was *Wokulira* ('By The Time You Wake Up'), which was developed into a long-running radio serial. Byron Kawadwa (later murdered by President Idi Amin's secret police in 1977) founded the Kampala City Players and created a new type of music theatre in Luganda, his most successful opera being *Oluyimba Lwa Wankoko* ('Song of Mr Cock'). His first production was *Makula ga Kulabako* ('A gift for Kulabako', 1970). In the former work, Kawadwa successfully combines Bagandan forms of music and mime with elements of Western music hall, revue and cantata in plots that explore serious socio-political issues. His major contribution was to organize the 'mixed-bag' – incidental music, unrelated dramatic sketches, recitals of concert parties and church entertainment – into a coherent form and structure underpinned by an essentially African concept of integrated performance in which dance, music, song and mime, with or without dialogue, are given equal significance. This model of performance has been copied by many of the younger generation of Ugandan dramatists.

The first signs of a politically conscious and committed theatre emerged immediately after independence; in general, post-independence playwrights were preoccupied with exploring the impact of foreign values, especially those of the West. Between independence in 1962 and 1986, Uganda passed through a succession of dictatorships. Kawadwa's fate, and even the mysterious death while in exile in Kenya of another well-known Ugandan dramatist, Robert Serumaga, showed the high risk involved in being an artist in opposition during these years. Most Ugandan dramatists fled, closely followed by other east African writers who had helped make Makerere University the centre of intellectual and theatrical activity in the whole of east Africa. Under Amin, the Asians were expelled and the Europeans left as well, so these sources of theatrical activity dried up. Among those who left were such Asian writers as Laban Erapu and Jagit Singh, who wrote *Beyond the Line* and *Sweet Scum of Freedom* respectively, two plays which explore the Asian dimension and the triangular racial antagonism of east African society.

The banning of *Wokulira* in 1965 marked the introduction of CENSORSHIP and the political reprisals that were to become the hallmark of the relationship between the theatre and subsequent regimes. Serumaga had formed the country's first professional theatre company, Theatre Limited, in 1970. It was later renamed the Abafumi Players in 1972 and became the most important group during the Amin years. The company, which initially was a collection of outstanding actors such as Rose Mbowa, David Rubadiri, Serumaga himself, popular artists Kiyingi-Kagwe and Kawadwa, and backstage personnel who were mainly expatriate, began by producing plays by other writers, but eventually concentrated on producing only Serumaga's plays. He trained his actors in a unique balletic style while his own writing and directing experimented with indigenous forms by drawing upon the visual, on dance and movement, mime and ritual to create plays and performances that dealt with the problems of human relationships from a uniquely African perspective. His best-known plays are *Renga Moi* (1972) and *Amayirikiti* (1974), the latter a play without dialogue dealing with the murders and repression under Amin. *Renga Moi* uses mime and dance to tell the story of a chief's tragic struggle to defend his kingdom from external aggression. His earlier plays, written in English, are *A Play* (1967), *The Elephants* (1970) and *Majangwa* (1971).

Other Ugandan dramatists of note are John Ruganda, author of *The Burdens* (1971), *Convenant With Death* (1973), *Black Mamba* (1973) and *The Floods* (1979). In their very oblique way, Ruganda's plays are attacks on the socio-political ills of his country, even though he now lives and writes in exile in Kenya. *The Burdens*, his response to Amin's repressive regime, used mainly signs and symbols to attack the dictator's penchant for accumulating wives and mistresses. A similar technique of distancing was used by another Ugandan playwright, Nuwa Sentongo, in *The Invisible Bond* (1975), also to attack Amin. Elvania Zirimu, who died in 1979, was an outstanding Ugandan actress, playwright and theatre scholar. She formed the Ngoma Players with the aim of writing and presenting plays which exploit Ugandan modes and styles of theatre and performance. Her first play, *Keeping Up With the Mukasas*, won the English and Original Play award in the 1962 Ugandan Drama Festival. Her themes range from the social satiric and comic mode of *Keeping Up With the Mukasas* to the more serious tone and subject matter of *Family Spear*, a play which explores the conflicts and tensions created by the generation gap and issues of modernity versus tradition. Her other plays are *When the Hunchback Made Rain* (1975) and *Snoring Strangers* (1975).

Mbowa and Clifford Lubwa p'Chong (the latter formerly married to Zirimu) are among the remaining greats of Ugandan theatre, having belonged to the elite group that made up Serumaga's Theatre Limited. Mbowa's plays, which are usually written in response to specific occasions or needs, aspire to an integrated performance aesthetic. The best example is her very popular *Mother Uganda and Her Children*, a political allegory which, borrowing from BRECHT's *Mother Courage*, links dance, music, rituals, folk tales and customs as a means of reflecting the ethnic and cultural diversity of Ugandan society. Chong has written *Generosity Kills* and *The Last Safari* (both 1975), *The Minister's Wife* (1983), *Kinsman and Kinswoman* (1986) and *Song of Prisoner* (1988), which is an adaptation of a well-known novel.

From the mid-1980s, especially with the coming to power of the new Museveni government in 1986, social dramas and moralistic farces seemed to dominate, along with popular farces and development-oriented theatrical activities of the government and non-governmental organizations, also known as theatre for development or campaign theatre. Social plays of note since the 1980s, apart from Chong's *The Minister's Wife*, are Mbowa's *Mine By Right* (1985), *Time Bomb* (1993) by Steven Rwangyezi, Charles Mulekwa's *The Eleventh Commandment* (1994), and *The Riddle* (1991) and *The Hydra* (1992), two AIDs plays jointly authored by Harriet Masembe, Peter Lwanga, Susan Birungi and Kiyimba Musisi. Others are Christopher Mukiibi's *Omuzadde n'Omwana* (1982); John Katunde's *The Dollar* (1988) and *The Inspector* (1990), two detective plays which explore the theme of materialism and corruption in Ugandan society; Charles Senkubuge's *Omunaala* ('The Tower', 1990); Patrick Mangeni's *The Prince* (1995), and Mukulu's popular political musical, *Thirty Years of Banana* (1991). Mukulu had earlier written *Wounds of Africa* (1990), a play heavily influenced by the ABSURDIST production style and political commitment of both Serumaga and Kawadwa. He also pushed further the experimental quest for the common ground between the various traditional Ugandan performance forms; his plays seek to transcend the language barrier by incorporating plenty of dance, music and mime, a style pioneered by his models, Serumaga and Kawadwa.

The freedom and absence of censorship under Museveni, coupled with the government's encouragement of theatre, gave rise to a renewed vigour in theatrical activity, especially in and around Kampala, where many new theatre groups and dramatists emerged. Among them are Fagil Mandy, who wrote *Endless Nights* (1981), a play about the rigged election of 1980, and a host of plays for children, such as *Drunken Mary Anne* (1985), *Bush Trap* (1988) and *Flowers* (1989); Mulekwa has also written *The Woman in Me* (1992), the play by which he is best known.

A pattern emerged whereby writers and actors tended to form their own companies, from Kiyingi-Kagwe,

Kawadwa and Serumaga to Ruganda (who founded the Makonde Players to perform his politically committed plays), Zirimu (who formed Ngoma Players), Mbowa, Jimmy Katumba (the founder of the Ebony Players, later The Ebonitas), Mukiibi, who directs Theatrikos, and the younger dramatists such as Mukulu (founder/director of Impact International) and Andrew Kibuuka, who directs Bakayimbira Dramactors. Experimentation with traditional forms in a blend with Western styles has continued apace, and the search is still on by those working in native-language theatre and those writing in English for a truly native style of dramaturgy and presentation. OSITA OKAGBUE

Ukraine *see* SOVIET UNION

Ulric, Lenore [Leonora Ulrich] (b. New Ulm, Minn., 21 July 1892; d. Orangesburg, NY, 30 Dec. 1970) Actress. She made her New York debut in *The Mark of the Beast* (1915). Spotting her potential, DAVID BELASCO snapped her up and created numerous vehicles for her, such as *The Heart of Wetona* (1916), *Tiger Rose* (1917), *The Son Daughter* (1919) and two of her biggest hits: *Kiki*, which ran for 600 performances, and *Lulu Belle*, in which she appeared in blackface as a Harlem prostitute. Having cornered the market for overblown MELODRAMAS with Belasco, Ulric's career inevitably faded after she left his company in 1929; but she continued her line of loose women and prostitutes with *Pagan Lady* (1930) and *The Fifth Column* (1940), as well as making a few undistinguished films.
HELEN RAPPAPORT

Ulster Group Theatre *see* BELFAST

Ulster Literary Theatre *see* BELFAST

Ultz *see* DESIGN

Unicorn Theatre Founded in 1947 by Caryl Jenner (pseud. for Pamela Penelope Ripman, 1917–73) as a touring company performing both adult and children's work, it became resident at London's ARTS THEATRE in 1967 and, working there until 1999, developed a wide range of adaptations for children, including *Meg and Mog*, *Stig of the Dump* and *The Wizard of Earthsea*, as well as producing new plays for young people. This pioneering company later provided workshops with special programmes for deaf children and a drama club. A liaison team works closely with schools.
CATHY JOYCE

Union Theatre Repertory Company *see* MELBOURNE THEATRE COMPANY

unions The first forms of organization for protection within the modern theatrical profession were charities, which in Britain could be traced back to the eighteenth-century benevolent funds of the two patented theatres at Drury Lane and Covent Garden. In the nineteenth century other theatres followed suit and more general funds were created, such as the Royal General Theatrical Fund and the Actors' Benevolent Fund. The idea of an Actors' Protective Association was mooted by Charles. L. Carson in 1882, but little happened for a decade. With a background in craft guilds and groupings, stage operatives organized first, founding the National Association of Theatre Employees in 1890, affiliated to the Trades Union Congress (TUC). The following year, the Actors' Association (AA) was founded, with HENRY IRVING as president, and in 1893 the Theatrical Choristers' Association was formed.

A rival to the AA was set up in 1905, and in 1906 the Variety Artists' Federation (VAF) came into being affiliated to the TUC, an important factor in its fight the following year in what became known as the 'music hall war'. Stimulated by their variety colleagues, AA members called for their organization to become a trades union, which eventually occurred in 1918. Within a year it had won a London standard contract. Managers, many of them actors themselves, rallied to their cause and, as they saw the rather aloof AA decline, proposed to establish their own all-embracing body for the profession.

The response was the founding in 1929 of Actors' Equity of Great Britain. It came to represent performers in radio, film, television and theatre, and in 1968 absorbed VAF. From the 1970s on, Equity was riven by internal disputes, and in the 1980s and 1990s had to confront not only the rise of new technology but also changes in industrial law that saw the end of the union 'closed shop'. Musicians had long had their own organization, stage managers joined Equity and stage crews continued in their own union, which changed its name as the profession changed, eventually merging with others in the broadcasting business.

Playwrights were able to join the Society of Authors (1884) but set up their own TUC-affiliated organization in 1959, transforming the Screenwriters' Association (1937) into the Writers' Guild of Great Britain. The Theatre Writers' Union (TWU) was founded in 1976, a year after the ALTERNATIVE theatre movement, organizing against cuts in subsidy, had thrown up the Theatre Writers' Group. TWU boycotted the new NATIONAL THEATRE in its campaign to win a standard minimum contract, which was achieved in 1979. In 1997 TWU amalgamated with the Writers' Guild. As the professionalization of theatre gathered pace, bodies were also formed (or loose associations transformed) to organize

and protect directors, theatre technicians, lighting designers, set designers, fight directors, choreographers and critics, many of whom were also members of larger unions.

In the United States, stage hands were the first to achieve collective bargaining; the National Alliance of Theatrical and Stage Employees was founded in 1893 and affiliated with its Canadian counterpart in 1898, as a consequence of which the name changed in 1902 to the International Alliance. As in Britain, actors had organized themselves for social protection, in bodies such as the Actors' Order of Friendship and eventually in one charitable organization, the Actors' Fund of America, before combining for contractual and working protection. The Hebrew Actors' Union was formed in 1899 by those working in YIDDISH THEATRE and won recognition in 1902.

The Actors' Society of America was formed in 1895 but enjoyed little influence and was disbanded in 1912, giving way at the end of that year to Actors' Equity Association. The American Federation of Labor (AFL) had been backing the White Rats vaudeville union until it was destroyed in a lockout in 1916–17. The AFL, through the Association of Actors and Artistes of America, recognized Equity in 1919. It then called its first strike, for better working conditions enshrined in a basic contract, which lasted 30 days, closed 37 theatres in eight cities and prevented the opening of 16 others. It won recognition from the employers, which helped it see off a rival organization, the Actors' Fidelity Association, formed by vaudeville performer GEORGE M. COHAN and the Producing Managers' Association. A union shop agreement was concluded in 1924, protection in dealings with agents in 1929, a minimum wage in 1933 and minimum rehearsal expenses in 1935.

In 1955 Equity merged with Chorus Equity, founded in 1919, and in 1960 another strike was called, which secured pension and health provision. The following year racial discrimination was prohibited – following a tradition of campaigning against racial segregation in theatres; discrimination against women and performers with disabilities has also been tackled.

Equity opened its showcase Library Theatre in 1941, in association with the New York Public Library, and has worked for federal support for the arts, for the creation and continued funding of the NATIONAL ENDOWMENT FOR THE ARTS and for the preservation of historic theatre buildings. Equity represents stage managers as well as performers, and its jurisdiction covers theatres of all sizes and locations, including young people's theatre and OFF-BROADWAY. There are, however, different types of agreement for different types of theatre; a

BROADWAY production would be 100 per cent unionized but this would not be enforced for an OFF-OFF-BROADWAY production. Equity has been involved in the development of not-for-profit theatre, but not always happily, just as its attempts to balance protection of American jobs against support of cultural exchange and its defence of certain working practices has led to controversy within the profession. A branch of Equity was opened in Toronto in 1955, and in 1976 an independent Canadian Actors' Equity Association was formed.

Playwrights organized themselves in 1878 in the short-lived American Dramatic Authors' Society which was succeeded in 1890 by the American Dramatists' Club, subsequently known as the Society of American Dramatists and Composers. Its chief success was in strengthening the COPYRIGHT laws. In 1907 the Society of Dramatic Authors was founded by Martha Morton in the face of resistance to women's membership by the all-male ADC. The Authors' League of America, which included playwrights in its membership, was founded in 1911, and following the Equity strike of 1919 an autonomous committee dedicated to playwrights was set up. This led a year later to the creation of the all-embracing Dramatists' Guild of America Inc.

Costume, set and lighting designers joined the United Scenic Artists of America, which was formed in 1912, probably as a result of the demise of the Protective Alliance of Scenic Painters of America, which had been set up in 1885. In 1959 the Society of Directors and Choreographers was established (recognized by the League of New York Theatres and Producers in 1962). The Association of Theatrical Press Agents and Managers was set up in 1928. Unions or guilds also evolved in other performing arts (e.g. among musical and variety artists) and in relation to radio, film and television. CHARLES LONDON

Alfred Harding, *The Revolt of the Actors* (1929)
Joseph Macleod, *The Actor's Right to Act* (1981)
G. Quinn, *Fifty Years Backstage* (1926)
M. Sanderson, *From Irving to Olivier: A Social History of the Acting Profession 1800–1983* (1984)

United States of America By coincidence, the dawn of the twentieth century saw marked changes in the American theatre. Lester Wallack, whose family led the most prestigious American ensemble for many decades, retired in 1887 and left no successor. Augustin Daly died suddenly in 1899. A. M. Palmer encountered financial problems and withdrew as a major producer. But these men, while supremely important to nineteenth-century theatre, had done little to promote American drama. Wallack's troupe emphasized classic English comedy and contemporary British drama. Daly relied largely on German farces. Palmer was distinguished by his mountings of French melodrama.

Native American playwriting was to a large extent in the hands of a few dedicated pioneers, who usually met with no better than modest success. The most enduring American plays of the nineteenth century were generally associated with major performing stars, who kept them alive season after season. Notable examples would be Joseph Jefferson in *Rip Van Winkle*, Frank Mayo in *Davy Crockett* and Denman Thompson in *The Old Homestead*. But Mayo died in 1896 and Jefferson retired in 1904. Thompson continued a little while longer, but he too died in 1911.

In 1895 a group of Jewish entrepreneurs who had risen to positions of importance as producers and theatre owners met secretly to form an organization that became known as the THEATRICAL SYNDICATE or Theatrical Trust. Publicly they professed that their sole purpose was to bring order out of the chaos that had developed since the growth of railroads had made it convenient for BROADWAY producers to tour their successes or send out road companies. Unfortunately, the group soon proved as unethical and brutal as monopolists in other industries, demanding kickbacks, reducing salaries and denying bookings to anyone who would not acquiesce to their exorbitant terms. Called 'brick and mortar men' by their detractors, their interest in making profits led them to seek safety in tested successes, which at the time generally meant importing shows which had proven their popular appeal in the WEST END. In 1900 the SHUBERT brothers, who had enjoyed some success in upstate New York, came to New York City and announced their intention of defying the Syndicate. Their success was startling and immediate, but as their power grew they became as demanding and as unethical as the group they had replaced.

Inevitably, the hue and cry raised by frustrated American dramatists, by the American press and, in good measure, by American playgoers at a time of growing American self-esteem forced the Shuberts, the Syndicate and smaller producers to heed the call for more native works. Younger American dramatists had the example of Bronson Howard who, between 1870 and 1889, had doggedly persisted in creating plays on American themes, or at least with American settings. There was also the example of the popular actor–dramatist, WILLIAM GILLETTE, especially his Civil War plays, *Held by the Enemy* and *Secret Service*, gripping melodramas mounted in 1886 and 1896. However, Gillette's most popular piece was his adaptation of *Sherlock Holmes* (1899). For the rest of his career Gillette was largely content to revive this tremendous hit or appear in other men's works. CLYDE FITCH rose to fame with his *Beau Brummell* in 1890, but virtually all of his subsequent successes focused on American high society, especially its women. Until his early death in 1909 he was by far the American theatre's most prolific, popular and successful dramatist, though many critics chided him for what they perceived to be his superficiality.

Of course, the critics themselves were changing. The dean of nineteenth-century American play reviewers was unquestionably William Winter, critic for the *Tribune* from 1865 to 1909. Sadly, with the rise of realism in the 1880s and the coming of IBSEN shortly thereafter he became increasingly backward-looking, shrill and vituperative. A truly new and fine school of American critics did not appear on the scene until shortly before the First World War.

But most critics, conservative or progressive, did welcome one play as a harbinger of greater things to come. That play was WILLIAM VAUGHN MOODY's *The Great Divide*, which was produced in 1906 and which powerfully and poetically dramatized the growing differences in the philosophies and ways of life of stodgy Easterners and more openminded Westerners. Like Fitch, Moody died early, leaving unanswered the question how far his promise might have been fulfilled.

One other important playwright of this period was AUGUSTUS THOMAS. His interest in American matters was manifested in the titles of many of his better works, such as *Alabama, In Mizzoura* and *Arizona*. An excellent, devoted constructionist, his plays probed more deeply than Fitch's but lacked Moody's breadth and poetry.

Two technological developments altered the course and nature of the American theatre during these years. The first was the coming of electrification. Auditoriums began to be lit with electric lights in the late 1880s (although for some years most houses kept their gas systems at the ready in case of outages). Very shortly thereafter stage lighting was introduced. For several decades it remained primitive by later standards, and many prominent players detested it for the harsh truths it revealed. To cite one example, the practice of older performers playing much younger characters, a very common occurrence until then, had to be abandoned. The second technological development was the coming of films. When first introduced publicly at VAUDEVILLE houses in the mid-1890s they were, of course, both silent and black-and-white. Some comedies and musicals introduced brief filmed segments to show such broadly moving affairs as bicycle races or automobile chases; but films were still largely dismissed as a passing novelty, and their effect on main-

stream theatres was, indeed, slow to be seen. However, at the turn of the century the United States had a huge circuit of lesser playhouses which charged far lower than first-class prices and offered their seemingly loyal lower-class patrons a steady diet of cliff-hanging melodramas and slapdash musicals. To the surprise of many, the loyalty of these lower-class playgoers was not as unyielding as had been hoped. They embraced the new films and abandoned their playhouses so swiftly and in such numbers that by 1910 the circuit had totally disappeared.

Yet for all the changes occurring in turn-of-the-century American theatre, in retrospect these years are more clearly seen to have been merely a bridge between the patterns which prevailed in much of the nineteenth century and the newer ideas and practices which emerged with remarkable force just as Europe became embroiled in the First World War. Many in an increasingly affluent, better-educated and more thoughtful middle class were becoming restless with a perceived commercialism and shallowness in the theatre. They were not the first to reject the ways of mainstream theatre, but earlier signs of discontent had flared briefly then sputtered out of existence. Not so the new groups, or at least their influence on American stages. In 1914 the Liberal Club, a cluster of intellectuals, rejected the idea of a dramatic branch, so a number of disappointed members banded together to start up their own theatrical group. They named this group the WASHINGTON SQUARE PLAYERS, after the New York City park nearby, where they first worked out their scheme. They began by mounting one-act plays, only later moving on to full-length works, and much of what they presented was of European origin. Although the group was dissolved in 1918, it called attention to the need for fresh thinking in the American theatre, and it gave a significant boost to such figures as KATHARINE CORNELL and LEE SIMONSON. Most importantly, many of its most influential members subsequently founded the THEATER GUILD.

Within months of the founding of the Washington Square Players a coterie of somewhat more determinedly intellectual theatre aficionados began producing plays in a converted wharf in Massachusetts. The PROVINCETOWN PLAYERS, led at first by the husband-and-wife playwrights George Cram Cook and SUSAN GLASPELL, eventually moved to New York City and continued to flourish until the mid-1920s. Called in one history 'more a laboratory than a theatre', Provincetown gave major opportunities to such young hopefuls as ROBERT EDMOND JONES, PAUL GREEN and, most of all, EUGENE O'NEILL.

Besides these professional organizations, adventurous

semi-professional and amateur ensembles began to spring up across the country. Gilmor Brown's Pasadena Community Playhouse, founded in California in 1918, exemplifies the former. MAURICE BROWNE, after several false starts (one of which inspired the Washington Square Players), created the Chicago Little Theater in 1919. During the 1920s and 1930s more than 500 LITTLE THEATRES blossomed all across America. However, these amateur ensembles, although a source of frequently excellent entertainment, soon lost any urge to experiment and, as a rule, were content to mount recent Broadway successes. The Second World War and the coming of television in the late 1940s spelt *finis* for most of them.

These organizations were lucky to have been in the right place at the right time. The First World War was cutting off easy access to European talents and ideas, and was fanning a disenchantment with all things European, all the while encouraging a still greater waxing of American self-esteem (some would say chauvinism). This assured American dramatists, composers, performers, directors, designers, and others an unparalleled opportunity, of which they were quick to take advantage. Furthermore, a war-born prosperity, which was to continue with one minor interruption until late 1929, encouraged theatregoing, which in turn promoted an unparalleled explosion of theatre construction and play production. When Broadway peaked during the 1927–8 season, it boasted more than 80 major theatres and offered playgoers between 260 and 270 productions. Native artists therefore had a fine chance of having their work on stage.

Probably no native artist figured as importantly in this renaissance as Eugene O'Neill. Certainly his contemporaries thought so, and subsequent students have for the most part agreed. The son of a famous actor who had wasted most of his career touring profitably in one popular melodrama, O'Neill was obsessed with a singularly tragic vision of life. His early one-acters were mounted by the Provincetown Players, but it was the Theater Guild's production of his *Beyond the Horizon* in 1920 which established his uniqueness and greatness. In season after season his works not only revealed his unusual perspectives, but demonstrated his willingness to tackle then theatrically dangerous subjects such as miscegenation and tuberculosis as well as to use out-of-the-ordinary forms such as expressionistic drama and plays so long they required a lengthy intermission to allow patrons to have dinner.

However, O'Neill was far from the only new playwright of worth to emerge at this time. The 1910s and 1920s saw the appearance of ELMER RICE, GEORGE S. KAUFMAN, MARC CONNELLY, PHILIP BARRY, MAXWELL ANDERSON, ROBERT E. SHERWOOD and other authors who, among them, offered playgoers a wide variety of high-quality works ranging from tragedy to social drama to farce to high comedy.

The American MUSICAL THEATRE flowered brilliantly at the same time. JEROME KERN's 1914 interpolations in the imported London musical *The Girl from Utah* made him famous and began the years-long popularity of the dance-based love ballad. Later in the same year IRVING BERLIN, already famous for his 'Alexander's Ragtime Band' and other Tin Pan Alley ditties, had a huge success with *Watch Your Step*, a musical whose songs were all composed in the ragtime idiom. In relatively short order a host of brilliant young melodists appeared, including COLE PORTER, GEORGE GERSHWIN, RICHARD RODGERS, VINCENT YOUMANS and ARTHUR SCHWARTZ. These men primarily wrote musical comedies. Their music experimented not only with harmonies and modulations that had hitherto been confined to black music, but also with traditional musical-comedy-song form. They were fortunate in being able to work with some equally brilliant young lyricists and librettists, such as P. G. WODEHOUSE (on his visits from England), OSCAR HAMMERSTEIN II, LORENZ HART, IRA GERSHWIN and DOROTHY FIELDS. (Berlin and Porter served as their own lyricists.) Two middle European immigrants, RUDOLF FRIML and SIGMUND ROMBERG, also called attention to themselves in the 1910s and went on to reinvigorate, at least briefly, the American version of Ruritanian operetta. Many students believe that it was the work of these men and women and their associates that was to be the crowning glory of the American theatre for the next half-century. Certainly the American musical for a time had more success and more influence on foreign stages than non-musical American theatre.

In terms of numbers the Shuberts were Broadway's busiest producers throughout the 1920s, but they leaned heavily on 'girlie' REVUES, old-fashioned operettas, farces and other supposedly surefire entertainments. More venturesome writers turned to other producers. Most notable was the Theater Guild which, from its start, attempted a schedule balanced between exciting importations from Europe and new American plays. Almost immediately it became the producer-of-choice of O'Neill and other leading new playwrights. With its subscription lists, its great contracted players (the LUNTS, Edward G. Robinson, DUDLEY DIGGES, etc.), and its policy of relatively short runs, the Guild for a short time appeared on its way to becoming a national repertory theatre. But there was also a surprising number of artistically minded independent producers who entered the scene in the 1910s and 1920s. Among them were WINTHROP AMES, Arthur Hopkins and Richard Herndon.

When the best producers offered works of the best young writers their productions were assessed by some notably knowing, thoughtful and interesting new critics. The first to appear may have been Walter Prichard Eaton, a knowledgable and reasonable reviewer, now largely forgotten. Better remembered are such observers as GEORGE JEAN NATHAN, STARK YOUNG and BROOKS ATKINSON. Their influence among their contemporaries and their enduring fame owe as much to their ability to stir controversy (as with Nathan) or their long loyalty to a major newspaper (as with Atkinson) as to their general excellence. The best critics of the era all maintained a healthy double standard, judging shows designed purely for light entertainment by one set of criteria and evaluating more serious, demanding works by another. As a corollary of show-by-show criticism, the establishment in 1918 of a PULITZER PRIZE for drama not only reflected the perception that a theatrical revolution had begun but also served to create an ongoing series of exemplars.

The introduction of sound films in 1927, followed two years later by the stock market crash, devastated live theatre in America. Many of the theatre's best talents rushed to Hollywood and never returned to Broadway. By 1937 the number of new productions had dropped to under 100 a season; the number of active playhouses in New York was halved. In outlying cities the case was the same or worse. PHILADELPHIA had ten first-class playhouses at the height of the boom, by the late 1930s only three were open. For the most part, however, Broadway still offered playgoers a wide variety of plays, although 'girlie' revues, operettas and bedroom farces became notably scarce. On the other hand, plays with clearly propagandistic aims came to the forefront. Many were mounted by the FEDERAL THEATER PROJECT, a government-subsidized attempt to keep theatre people employed at a time of long breadlines. At its peak it gave work to 10,000 stage folk. However, the project, having been authorized by Congress in 1935, took on an increasingly militant left-wing stance which alienated many Congressmen, and it was abolished in 1939. Nevertheless, commercial Broadway also reflected the same concerns. In 1931 HAROLD CLURMAN, CHERYL CRAWFORD and LEE STRASBERG, chagrined at the Theater Guild's adamantly apolitical policies, broke away to found the GROUP THEATER. Their most important playwright was CLIFFORD ODETS, and for a few seasons he and others provided the new company with a succession of powerful, unmistakably political plays. But by the late 1930s Odets seemed written out, and deserted the stage for

films. His departure, plus internal wrangling, led to the Group Theater's dissolution in 1940. A more interesting and somewhat longer-lived organization was the PLAYWRIGHTS' COMPANY. Like the Group Theater, it was a breakaway from the Theater Guild, this time by a group of established dramatists who were irked by the Guild's niggardliness and other failings. The initial members included Maxwell Anderson, S. N. BEHRMAN, SIDNEY HOWARD, Elmer Rice and Robert E. Sherwood. Their plays, beginning with Sherwood's *Abe Lincoln in Illinois* (1938), continued to cover the wide variety of styles and approaches that had been their wont. The company continued to produce fine plays until it was disbanded in 1960, by which time other interests or death had removed most of the founders from the scene.

One prominent new writer, whose works were unassociated with any of these groups was LILLIAN HELLMAN. Starting in 1934 with *The Children's Hour*, she provided the theatre with a succession of biting, often controversial dramas. The 1930s also witnessed the growth of union militancy, which led to exorbitant pay scales, featherbedding and other practices which were to have an unfortunate effect on theatrical economics.

The war-bred prosperity of the first half on the 1940s glossed over some growing economic difficulties and led to longer runs for successful shows. Even so, the number of first-class productions continued to drop: for example, the 1949–50 season saw only 57 premières. Although the total rose in some subsequent seasons, worse was yet to come. Nevertheless, two major new playwrights came to the fore in this decade: TENNESSEE WILLIAMS and ARTHUR MILLER. Williams was revealed as a brilliant, poetic apostle of social decadence. Miller's plays were more prosaic studies of familial and social dilemmas. Equally significant was the renaissance in the musical theatre initiated by the success of Richard Rodgers and Oscar Hammerstein's *Oklahoma!* in 1943. In the ballyhoo accompanying the show's popularity claims were made that it had launched a new genre called the musical play, a type of musical that carefully integrated song and story. Actually the show was merely a totally American operetta, combining the use of American musical idioms with a distinctly American setting. Jerome Kern and Hammerstein's 1927 hit, *Show Boat*, had pioneered the style years earlier. What *was* uniquely integrated was the dancing – modern ballets rather than the old tap routines and drills. For better or worse, this school of musicals was more seriously self-conscious in its artistry and, indeed, in its tenor. Even musical comedy became less joyously musical and less carefree in its comedy. New names on the musical scene included LEONARD BERNSTEIN, JULE STYNE and FREDERICK LOEWE among composers; BETTY COMDEN, ADOLPH GREEN and ALAN JAY LERNER among lyricists and librettists.

The diminution of production on Broadway and the consequent falling off of attractions for major touring theatres in outlying cities (to no small extent a reflection of the fast-growing attraction of television) led to the beginnings of two major theatrical developments in the very late 1940s and early 1950s. In 1947 MARGO JONES founded Theater '47 in Dallas. A totally professional company, as opposed to the amateur little theatre groups, it presented programmes of exciting new works and occasional classical revivals. The widespread acclaim accorded the organization heralded the growth of regional theatre, which was to become one of the strengths and glories of the American theatre in the latter half of the century. Miss Jones's theatre closed in 1959, four years after her premature death, but such ongoing groups as Washington's ARENA STAGE and the GUTHRIE THEATER in MINNEAPOLIS exemplified the burgeoning of regional theatre all across America. At the same time, small playhouses, often seating only 100–200 playgoers, began cropping up in Manhattan's Greenwich Village and other areas of New York City away from the main theatre district. Before long, much of the theatrical excitement that Broadway had monopolized was usurped by what became called OFF-BROADWAY.

Broadway in the 1950s witnessed the meteoric career of WILLIAM INGE, whose sentimental social dramas of Midwestern life were tremendously popular. Perhaps more importantly, it saw the posthumous production of several towering Eugene O'Neill dramas, most notably Long Day's Journey into Night. The musical theatre continued to flourish, bringing forth such masterpieces as My Fair Lady, West Side Story and Gypsy.

The 1960s began with the promise of the Kennedys' 'Camelot', soon destroyed by political tragedy, social turmoil and a disheartening inflation. Inevitably, the theatre was affected adversely by these developments, although the number of plays mounted in first-class theatres rose very slightly for much of the decade. The older generation of playwrights continued to die off, while the younger dramatists, especially Williams and Inge, went into slides from which they never recovered. Only Miller brought out interesting new works intermittently. As if the nation wished to laugh away its growing malaise, the lone new writer of major stature proved to be NEIL SIMON, whose very Jewish slant on New York life provided comic relief through the decade and onwards into the 1990s with such plays as Barefoot in the Park, Plaza Suite and the semi-

autobiographical trilogy that started with Brighton Beach Memoirs. Several more serious writers emerged with single notable successes, but only EDWARD ALBEE, who had first won attention with one-acters off Broadway, seemed destined for prolonged development and success. Sadly, only one of his later plays matched the acclaim of his trenchant Who's Afraid of Virginia Woolf? A few of his other dramas received some critical approval, but, too often, his works became increasingly cryptic and ultimately vituperative.

There is some consensus that the American musical theatre's 50-year heyday ended after the première of Fiddler on the Roof in 1964. Its songwriters, JERRY BOCK and SHELDON HARNICK, had come to the fore in the late 1950s, and they were followed by such equally superior composers and lyricists as CY COLEMAN, CHARLES STROUSE, JOHN KANDER and FRED EBB. However, these artists almost never saw their songs achieve the sort of national renown enjoyed by their predecessors', since by the mid-1960s rock and roll had swept more traditional styles off the airwaves and virtually monopolized the lists of best-selling records. Although a handful of fine rock-and-roll musicals did appear (mostly off Broadway), for various reasons, including its largely ageing audience, Broadway itself seemed uncomfortable with rock and roll.

The growth and maturity of Off-Broadway were recognized in the 1970s when works performed here were awarded Pulitzer Prizes for the first time. No fewer than three Off-Broadway plays won the award during the decade. Similarly, one Broadway success which earned the prize and one of the Off-Broadway winners had initially been presented in regional theatres. Indeed, the most important playwrights to emerge in the decade were all at first identified with Off-Broadway, albeit several subsequently enjoyed some success on Broadway. SAM SHEPARD's writing revealed his interest in low types and in the mythology of the American Southwest. DAVID RABE became the spokesman for those unhappily engulfed in the Vietnam War. The most forceful and variegated of the new dramatists was probably DAVID MAMET, who went on to achieve major success on Broadway. In a lighter vein, TERRENCE MCNALLY demonstrated a deft comic touch in dealing with lower-middle-class Easterners. For the musical theatre, one of the most significant events was the coming of age of STEPHEN SONDHEIM, who earlier had shown remarkable skills as a lyricist and then as a songwriter. Beginning with Company in 1970, he presented Broadway with a series of fascinatingly original musicals. His unique, adventuresome musical style, while not as endearing as that of older melodists, was coupled with his exceptional brilliance as an observant, misanthropic lyricist, and he imbued his librettists with his singular outlook. With the perceived paucity of great writing talent, directors and choreographers (and sometimes director–choreographers) became increasingly responsible for the creation of new musicals. HAL PRINCE, GOWER CHAMPION, BOB FOSSE, MICHAEL BENNETT and, later, TOMMY TUNE played primary roles in moulding new musicals. The outstanding example of this trend was *A Chorus Line*, which opened in 1975 and ran for 15 years to establish a long-run record for its time in New York. Concurrently, Broadway began to welcome a relatively large number of English and, eventually, French musicals. In this respect, historians could see the American musical stage come full circle, since, when it first began to flourish in the late 1860s, it was French *opéra bouffe* and then the shows of GILBERT and SULLIVAN and their successors that inspired the earliest American song and dance entertainments.

The history and reception of the two most interesting American playwrights to win wide recognition in the 1980s suggests in some small measure why Broadway suffers from some of its current ailments. Certainly the most trumpeted and garlanded of the new writers has been AUGUST WILSON, who has offered Broadway a number of new plays, each dealing with the lives of American blacks in a different decade. His first success was *Ma Rainey's Black Bottom* in 1984. It depicted the hard, sometimes violent life of a singer in the 1920s. His plays contained magnificently theatrical scenes, but their writing often seemed slapdash, incorporating mysticism, music, violence and whatever else might have momentary effect; overall, his writing seemed sloppy. Nevertheless, in 15 years his plays won two Pulitzer Prizes and five Drama Critics Circle Awards. By contrast, the writings of A. R. GURNEY display superior craftsmanship and are superbly witty. But he deals with American high society and that seems a subject clearly out of vogue. As a result his works have been largely confined to Off-Broadway and regional theatres.

The problem is that in most American cities only one major newspaper survives. In New York, the *Times* is so powerful it can usually make or break a play. Musically, the stage has been dominated by the spectacular productions of Englishmen and Frenchmen, notably the works of ANDREW LLOYD WEBBER.

Financially the picture is distressing. Inflation on Broadway is seemingly out of hand. While annual total grosses have risen steadily, they have risen because of ticket prices, not because of attendance figures, which have usually remained flat and occasionally dropped. Theatregoing has become a special event, not a regular habit, as of old. And most special events have been musicals. Non-musicals have suffered. The trade paper *VARIETY* reported that when KATHARINE HEPBURN's vehicle, *West Side Waltz*, closed during the 1982–3 season, for the first time in memory not a single non-musical play was on tour. *Variety* also bewailed the fact that the total of 31 new Broadway productions (musicals and non-musicals) during the 1984–5 season was the lowest in history. At the end of the century, matters have improved slightly; but it remains to be seen if this good news is a fluke. GERALD BORDMAN

See also EXPERIMENTAL THEATRE; HAPPENING; MULTIMEDIA THEATRE; PERFORMANCE ART.

Unity Theatre Founded in 1936 in a north London hall by activists from the AGITPROP movement who wanted to broaden POLITICAL THEATRE, Unity established itself with a dynamic production of *Waiting for Lefty* by CLIFFORD ODETS and moved to its own premises behind King's Cross in a chapel converted by volunteer labour in 1937. Run mainly by communists, Unity's membership and support was drawn from the left, the trades unions and the cooperatives but included prominent individuals such as BEATRIX LEHMANN, MICHAEL REDGRAVE, ELMER RICE, GEORGE BERNARD SHAW, SYBIL THORNDIKE and H. G. Wells. SEAN O'CASEY served on its board along with PAUL ROBESON, whose appearance there in *Plant in the Sun* by Ben Bengal, followed later in 1938 by international acclaim for its anti-appeasement political pantomime *Babes in the Wood*, marked the high point of Unity's fame. It led a national upsurge in politically committed AMATEUR drama, cut short by the outbreak of war in 1939. Unity, however, was the first theatre in London to reopen after the ban on public entertainment had been lifted and it remained open throughout the war years, also providing shelter and factory entertainment. It briefly ran a professional company (1946–7) when it emerged from the war at the head of a new national movement for socially aware drama, bringing together groups such as those in Aberdeen, Bristol, Cambridge, Leeds, Liverpool, Sheffield and elsewhere that had been active during hostilities. The Glasgow group (see below) also became professional and surpassed the standards set by London, which, from the mid-1950s on, declined as many of the innovations it had pioneered, such as vernacular and DOCUMENTARY drama, LIVING NEWSPAPER and political satire, became accepted by the theatrical mainstream and television. The theatre itself was destroyed by fire in 1975.

Alongside the many new plays and shows created specially for Unity, it had championed the work of GORKY and BRECHT (being the first theatre in England to stage one of his plays, *Señora Carrar's Rifles*, in 1938) and had mounted premières of ADAMOV, Lope de Vega, O'Casey, Odets, SARTRE and SHATROV. Many professionals – e.g. LIONEL BART, Alfie Bass, MICHAEL GAMBON, Bob Hoskins, David Kossoff, Warren Mitchell, Bill Owen, TED WILLIS – learned their craft at this influential theatre, which was working people's most sustained and successful COLLECTIVE contribution to drama and helped lay the groundwork for many postwar theatrical developments.

Glasgow Unity was formed in 1941 by five left-leaning groups. Much of its repertoire was at first similar to that of London Unity, but it contributed significantly to the native drama by staging new Scottish plays by writers like James Barke, George Munro, Benedict Scott and ENA LAMONT STEWART. The company's production of Gorky's *The Lower Depths* in 1945, performed in the actors' own idiom, was an outstanding success and was capped the following year by a natural successor, its professional production of *The Gorbals Story*, set by Robert McLeish in a Glasgow slum. By April 1947 it had been seen by more than 100,000 people and had visited London's West End, the first Scottish play acted by a Scottish repertory company to do so. Glasgow Unity initiated the FRINGE at the EDINBURGH FESTIVAL through its insistence on Scottish representation. The professional group stayed in London, at the EMBASSY THEATRE, and folded in 1951. The amateur wing in Scotland collapsed soon after.

COLIN CHAMBERS

Colin Chambers, *The Story of Unity Theatre* (1989)

university drama departments

In Britain

During the nineteenth century, the long-enduring puritan ban on drama in the universities began to relax, leading to the establishment of informal drama groups at OXFORD and CAMBRIDGE. However, these groups mainly operated despite the university authorities. The birth of English as a university discipline at the beginning of the twentieth century did not entail much more study of drama in the academy. The rise of criticism associated with F. R. Leavis in the 1930s focused primarily on the novel, Leavis often treating some of his favoured writers' habit of also writing plays as little more than an aberration. The contemporary rise of New Criticism, with its emphasis on an asocial and ahistorical close reading of 'words on the page', meant that the crucially social institution of theatre was ruled out of court and that plays (particularly those by Shakespeare) were read as primarily poetic and literary texts. Out of a sense of this absence, a movement

developed in the 1940s to institute the teaching of performed drama in universities as a discipline in its own right. Theatre studies had been taught in universities in the United States for some time, and it was there in the mid-1940s that a working party from Oxford University comprising A. H. Smith, Maurice Platnauer, T. C. Keeley and Nevill Coghill went to explore the possibilities of offering such a course. Their report, published in 1945, while favourably inclined towards the idea of a university degree course, maintained that it was perhaps not quite the thing for Oxford. These Oxford dons were remarkably tentative about the value of such a discipline. Although they ultimately recommended a course, they were wary of two particular aspects of the American experience. First, they noted the vocational leanings of university theatre in America, which had produced a number of the leading lights of American theatre. They also bemoaned a lack of intellectual rigour to the discipline. In this they were spurred on by HARLEY GRANVILLE BARKER, who taught in America during the Second World War and who noted that performances by students, rather than 'increasing their understanding of a particular play, tended to diminish it'.

These factors formed the background to Bristol University's decision in 1947 to institute the first joint honours drama course in a British university. The course faced hostility both within the university, which all too often continued to see theatre studies as a lightweight concern, and also within the theatre profession, which was often prone to characterize it as dustily bookish. Initially taught by theatre historians like Glynne Wickham and Richard Southern, the course soon gained a greater practical emphasis, in a compensatory move designed to break with the literary emphasis of English. The formula was largely successful and in 1961 a chair in drama was funded by Granada Television at Manchester University, and another was instituted at Bristol. In 1962 the Manchester course became a single honours course, thus establishing it as a discipline in its own right. Over the next three years Birmingham, Hull and Glasgow Universities set up drama departments, marking the start of a 20-year explosion in theatre studies departments.

The dominant ethos of theatre studies remained, as it was in the late 1950s, centred on performance as an object in itself, around which all other concerns (theoretical, historical, sociological, psychological) fall into second place. This meant an ever greater distance from the concerns of English studies, which since the war saw an increasing emphasis on literary and cultural theory, a move in which theatre studies with its broadly empirical emphasis was not able to share. The benefits of this practice have been enormous: an exploration of practical methods within an academic environment has meant an enviable proliferation of teaching and learning methods, through workshops and productions as well as through the more traditional university apparatus of lecture, seminar and tutorial. In this it has radically broadened the scope of what is meant by teaching and research.

During the 1990s, however, there was something of a *rapprochement*, triggered partly by the new importance of the notion of 'performativity' within literary and cultural theory. Fifty years of work exploring theatricality, role-playing and the complexities of theatrical and paratheatrical performance meant that British university drama departments were able to contribute significantly to a whole range of disciplines within the humanities. Also, the intense interest in PERFORMANCE ART in British academia celebrated and intensified the kinds of theoretical questioning which had once seemed so alien to the discipline. Lastly, the increasing influence of anthropological and ethnographic approaches to the study of theatre fostered a sophisticated interdisciplinary approach to the subject which greatly broadened the traditional range of objects available for study.

As British theatre and performance studies begin a new century, they appear to be in a healthy state. Student applications for degree courses are rising at an enviable rate. Serious historical, theoretical and textual work is being published in ever greater quantities. Theatre practice is increasingly being recognized as a respectable parallel research activity (practice-based PhDs are beginning to be seen). However, a decade of higher education reforms have insisted on massive increases in student numbers without a concomitant increase in funding. This is a problem across the university sector, yet the prized teaching methods and practical exploration of theatre studies could still be put in jeopardy.   DAN REBELLATO

In the United States

At the beginning of the twentieth century, there were no formal programmes in drama or theatre in colleges and universities in the United States. By the mid-1990s, though, there were some 1,180 institutions throughout the United States and Canada offering theatre education in a two-year, four-year or graduate school setting. Although the influential religious leader Cotton Mather included plays among 'Satan's Library' when addressing pedagogical issues at Harvard College in 1723, performances of dialogues and plays by college literary societies often marked important occasions such as anniversaries and commencements on eighteenth- and nineteenth-century campuses. While antitheatrical attitudes apparently prevented the development of drama and theatre studies programmes until the twentieth century, theatrical performance thrived in early academic settings as well as in the commercial realms of stock and touring companies.

The study of drama and theatre at the college and university level evolved primarily from surveys of dramatic literature within English departments. As dramatic study emerged from the shadows of these departments, early programmes included in their titles words such as 'speech', 'rhetoric' and 'public speaking'. It was only later that the more specific terms of 'drama', 'theatre', 'theatre arts', 'theatre studies' and 'performance studies' were employed. GEORGE PIERCE BAKER is generally credited with introducing the study of theatre to the higher educational curriculum through his playwriting course at Radcliffe College, launched in 1903. However, in 1902 critic and playwright BRANDER MATTHEWS became professor of dramatic literature at Columbia University – the first post of that title in the United States. Even as early as 1899, a course in playwriting and contemporary dramatic study was offered in West Virginia. In addition, courses in 'dramatization' and 'staging' were also springing up in Nebraska and Texas just after the turn of the century. Baker, however, receives the lion's share of note due to the successes of his landmark 47 Workshop (1912–25) at Harvard. Named after the English 47 playwriting course that provided its basis, the workshop counted among its alumni such important BROADWAY figures as PHILIP BARRY, SIDNEY HOWARD, EUGENE O'NEILL, EDWARD SHELDON, GEORGE ABBOTT, Theresa Helburn and others.

Drama and theatre remained on the periphery of college life, despite their advances in the early part of the century. While scores of drama courses and productions were offered in colleges and universities around the country, there was no degree granted until Carnegie Institute of Technology (now Carnegie Mellon University) created a department of drama under the leadership of Thomas Wood Stevens in 1914. Whereas the focus at other educational institutions highlighted theatre as literature – rendering it 'acceptable' for study and praxis – Carnegie Tech (owing to its technical-school roots) emphasized a fusion of the technical elements of acting, directing and design in its training. By 1925 the programme was producing more than a hundred annual performances integrated with the daily rigours of academic life.

Yale University began its long march to primacy among university drama and theatre programmes when Baker moved there, from an inhospitable environment at Harvard, to create a graduate programme of theatre training in 1925. Yale and Carnegie closely rivalled one another for many years, with faculty and students passing from one to the other, until critic ROBERT BRUSTEIN became dean of the Yale School of Drama (1965–79). Brustein's tenure, marked by artistic innovation and controversy, allowed Yale to lay claim to the unofficial title of 'best theatre training school' in the United States – which it retained to the century's end. Among other early twentieth-century programmes that continue to thrive at the end of the century, those run by the University of Iowa and Northwestern University also emphasized production demands akin to those at Carnegie Tech.

As the field grew, a bifurcated focus gradually developed between performance areas (acting, voice and speech, movement, directing and design) and more scholarly areas (history and theory). Institutions such as Stanford University managed to integrate these fields in doctoral programmes that required directing students to demonstrate a command of critical theory while their design counterparts did likewise in history. Mainly, though, doctoral programmes in the late twentieth century continued to spiral outwards and encompass various aspects of critical theory, cultural and performance studies, and history.

As the regional theatre movement began to grow in the early 1960s, it seemed as though there would be a need for well-trained actors, directors and designers to staff nascent theatres. This perceived need created an explosion in the development of fine arts degree programmes. Primarily focused on post-baccalaureat Masters of Fine Arts (MFA) degrees, these proliferating curricula also included Bachelors of Fine Arts degrees. Due to their narrowness of focus, the burgeoning fine arts curricula were of particular concern to educators. The programmes mushroomed from a relatively few high-quality courses to hundreds offering degrees ranging from acting to child drama to puppetry to theatre technology. As the regional theatre movement cooled in the 1980s, practice-based theatre education saw its momentum slow. Although many MFA programmes disappeared as a results of competition and fiscal restructuring in the early 1990s, nearly 200 remained as the decade closed.

Over the course of the twentieth century, the degrees granted in drama, theatre and performance studies multiplied. The ever-increasing specialization of the field, and a move away from the term 'generalist', partially reflected the need to create market niches for teachers and institutions of higher education. The glut of trained practitioners and teachers at both master's and doctoral level led, near the end of the century, to

a new pattern in theatre teaching: in 1999 as many as 60 per cent of drama, theatre and performance studies courses were taught by part-time, adjunct instructors and professors working for low pay and no benefits.

College- and university-based education in the areas of performance and performance study was in a state of near-continuous metamorphosis by the end of the 1990s. Schools such as New York University's Tisch School of the Arts, the University of Texas at Austin, and the University of California at San Diego offer high-calibre training, but performance students are also challenged by critical ideas and historical contexts. The Graduate Center of the City University of New York and the University of Wisconsin at Madison, among others, offer faculties of top scholars who guide their schools' diverse doctoral programmes in theatre. Other well-regarded schools – such as Columbia University, Southern Methodist University, the University of Washington and the University of California at Berkeley – are rebuilding their programmes after administrative reorganizations.

With more than 1,100 institutions looking towards new challenges, the complexities of theatre in higher education – and its occasionally conflicting goals – are being addressed by professional organizations such as the Association for Theater in Higher Education. Early twentieth-century programmes in drama and theatre emphasized the technical aspects of acting, playwriting, design and production. However, the future success of college- and university-based programmes will rely on cooperation between practitioners and scholars as they seek a productive convergence of theory and practice. JEFFREY ERIC JENKINS

See also AMATEUR THEATRE; DRAMA SCHOOLS; DRAMATIC THEORY; STUDENT THEATRE.

D. G. James, *The Universities and the Theatre* (1952)
K. Macgowan, *Footlights Across America: Towards a National Theater* (1929)
Karl R. Wallace, ed., *History of Speech Education* (1954)

Unruh, Fritz von (b. Koblenz, Germany, 10 May 1885; d. Diez an der Lahn, 28 Nov. 1970) Playwright. His experiences at the front during the First World War converted him to pacifism and he emigrated in 1932, eventually reaching the United States in 1940. Plays include the early *Offiziere* (*Officers*, 1911), his two EXPRESSIONIST successes, *Ein Geschlecht* (*One Sex* or *A Generation*, 1917) and *Platz* (*Room*, 1920), and *Duell an der Havel* (*Duel on the River Havel*, 1953). He returned to Germany in 1952. JUDY MEEWEZEN

Urban, Joseph (b. Vienna, 26 May 1872; d. New York, 10 July 1933) Scene designer. He turned from architecture of palaces and exposition pavilions and interior decoration to designing sets for the Vienna Burgtheater, then operas in Paris, London and elsewhere. Invited to become artistic director of the Boston Opera, he came to the United States in 1912 and launched the New Stagecraft movement, which emphasized a painterly, impressionistic beauty, anticipating the work of American designers like ROBERT EDMOND JONES. From 1917 to 1933 he designed at least one new production each year for the Metropolitan Opera. He also designed regularly for the ZIEGFELD FOLLIES (1915–31), Shakespeare revivals and musicals (e.g. *Show Boat*, 1927). He introduced the use of portals (inner proscenium arch) to the American stage and was known for his use of perspective and colour and his beautiful scenic drops. FELICIA HARDISON LONDRÉ & IAN BEVAN

Orville K. Larson, *Scene Design in the American Theater from 1915 to 1960* (1990)

Uruguay *see* SOUTH AMERICA

USSR *see* SOVIET UNION

Ustinov, Peter [Alexander] (b. London, 16 April 1921) Actor, playwright, director and raconteur. Ustinov's manifold talents have been used principally to entertain. Two of his plays, *The Love of Four Colonels* (1951) and *Romanoff and Juliet* (1956), enjoyed long runs. His acting performances have built upon his pro-digious abilities as a mimic and parodist. The combination of his talents enables him to hold audiences charmed by his wit and stories. He wrote an autobiography, *Dear Me* (1977), and was knighted in 1990. CLIVE BARKER

Uys, Pieter-Dirk (b. Cape Town, South Africa, 28 Sept. 1945) Actor, political satirist, writer and playwright. During the 1970s he wrote and directed plays at the Space Theatre, Cape Town and the MARKET THEATRE, Johannesburg. In 1975 his play *God's Forgotten* was produced at LA MAMA in New York. A prolific author, he has written over 35 plays, including *Paradise is Closing Down* (1976), *Beyond All Reason* (1981), *Panorama* (1987) and *Just Like Home* (1989). He is best known for his SOLO SHOWS and satirical performances that excoriated apartheid and challenged the new rainbow nation with equal energy. His first, *Adapt or Dye* (1981), was followed by *Farce about Uys* (1983), *Total Onslaught* (1984), *Beyond the Rubicon* (1986) and *Dekaffirnated* (1984). In the 1980s he created the outlandish character of Evita Bezuidenhout, and in this popular role has since 1994 hosted a weekly television interview with top politicians such as Nelson Mandela. He owns a small theatre and has written a number of books, among them a biography of Evita Bezuidenhout, *A Part Hate, A Part Love*. FRANCESCA GREATOREX

Uzbekistan *see* SOVIET UNION

V

Vaccaro, John *see* THEATRE OF THE RIDICULOUS

Vaganova, Agrippina (b. St Petersburg, Russia, 24 June 1879; d. Leningrad, 5 Nov. 1951) Ballet teacher. A former dancer, Vaganova developed a progressive teaching system which influenced ballet and movement training throughout the world. Her method, emphasizing expressive movement and co-ordination, formed the link between the old Russian school and the new Soviet development. SARAH A. SMITH
See also PHYSICAL PREPARATION.

Vakhtangov, Yevgeny [Bagrationovich] (b. Vladikavkaz, Armenia, 13 Feb. 1883; d. Moscow, 29 May 1922) Director and teacher. Beginning as a sensitive actor at the MOSCOW ART THEATRE, he soon began directing and sought a middle way between the psychologism of STANISLAVSKY's system and the theatricality of MEYERHOLD's, based on the primacy of the actor. His productions were highly choreographed and even schematized, making their strong impressions through frankly theatrical devices, both in design and performance. Most famous were his intense and internationally important *The Dybbuk* (1922, for the HABIMAH) and a fantastic *Princess Turandot* (1922), completed days before his death, which brilliantly mixed conventions of oriental theatre with those of *COMMEDIA DELL' ARTE*.
ROBERT LEACH

L. Vendrovskaya and G. Kaptereva, eds, *Evgeny Vakhtangov* (1982)
Nick Worrall, *Modernism to Realism on the Soviet Stage: Tairov, Vakhtangov, Okhlopkov* (1989)

Valdez, Luis *see* TEATRO CAMPESINO, EL

Valentin, Karl [Valentin Ludwig Fey] (b. Munich,

4 June 1882; d. Munich, 9 Feb. 1948) Comic and actor. Valentin began his career as a club comedian in his late teens. He exaggerated his Bavarian dialect in portraying a workman struggling with his tools and his inability to communicate. In 1911 he met Liesl Karlstadt (Elizabeth Welleno, 1892–1961), with whom he formed a successful and prolific partnership, writing and performing farces and sketches. Valentin's work, much of which was filmed, influenced several contemporary dramatists, especially BRECHT. ADRIANA HUNTER

J. Schechter, *Durov's Pig* (1985)
R. Senelick, *Cabaret Performance*, vol. 2: *Europe 1920–40* (1993)

Valle-Inclán, Ramón [María] del [Ramón José Simón Valley Peña] (b. Villanueva, Galicia, Spain, 28 Oct. 1866; d. Santiago de Compostela, Spain, 5 Jan. 1936) Playwright, poet and novelist. He had a happy, privileged childhood, and, while a law student, he read contemporary French authors and began to write short stories. He settled in Madrid in 1895, leading a bohemian existence, and in a literary activity spanning over 40 years wrote novels, short stories, poetry and 17 plays. Rejecting the commercial theatre, Valle-Inclán's early plays – e.g. *Romance de lobos* (*Ballad of Wolves*, 1907) – reveal the influence of SYMBOLISM and have an epic, mythical character and a bold theatricality. Subsequently, an increasing concern with the ills of Spanish society and the human condition in general inspired a changed vision and a new theatrical style, *esperpentismo*, based on systematic distortion, and led to the highly original grotesque plays, *Luces de Bohemia* (*Bohemian Lights*, 1920), *Divinas palabras* (*Divine Words*, 1920) and *Los cuernos de don Friolera* (*The Horns of Don*

Friolera, 1921). As a dramatist, he greatly influenced LORCA and anticipated the THEATRE OF THE ABSURD. GWYNNE EDWARDS

Robert Lima, *Valle-Inclán: The Theatre of His Life* (1988)
John Lyon, *The Theatre of Valle-Inclán* (1984)
V. Smith, *Ramón del Valle-Inclán* (1973)

Vampilov, Aleksandr [Valentinovich] (b. Kutulik, Siberia, 19 Aug. 1937; d. Lake Baikal, 17 Aug. 1972) Playwright. Vampilov's plays present a devastating and hilarious portrait of life in Brezhnev's Russia. Relatively ordinary people are shown in paradoxical or 'boundary' situations where their behaviour necessarily questions their attitude to such values as truth, innocence, love and conscience. This focus, his innovative stagecraft and the authenticity of his dialogue made Vampilov the hero of the 'new wave' dramatists in Russia after his death. Plays include *Proshchaniye v iyune* (*Farewell in June*, 1966), *Predmeste* (*The Elder Son*, 1969), *Utinaya okhota* (*Duck Hunting*, 1976), *Dvadtsat minut s'angelon* (*Twenty Minutes with an Angel*, 1972), *Istoriya s metranpazhem* (*Incident with a Paginator*, 1972), and *Proshlym letom v Chulimske* (*Last Summer in Chulimsk*, 1973). PATRICK MILES

Van Druten, John [William] (b. London, 1 June 1901; d. Indio, Calif., 19 Dec. 1957) Playwright and director. His sophisticated, often witty, examination of modern life was seen in such plays as *Young Woodley* (1925), *There's Always Juliet* (1931), *The Distaff Side* (1933) and *The Voice of the Turtle* (1943). He also successfully adapted several novels for the stage, most notably *I Am a Camera* (1951), from CHRISTOPHER ISHERWOOD's *Goodbye to Berlin*, which formed the basis of the musical *Cabaret*. His autobiography, *The Widening Circle*, appeared in 1957. GERALD BORDMAN

Van Gyseghem, André *see* EMBASSY THEATRE; NOTTINGHAM; UNITY THEATRE

van Itallie, Jean-Claude (b. Brussels, Belgium, 25 May 1936) American playwright born in Belgium. Heightening social critique through theatrical metaphor, he catapulted into the vanguard of experimentalists with *America Hurrah!* (1966) and *The Serpent* (collaboration with JOSEPH CHAIKIN's OPEN THEATER, 1968). His many other plays include *A Fable* (1976), *Bag Lady* (1979), *Ancient Boys* (1991) and *Struck Dumb* (with Chaikin, 1991). He has adapted CHEKHOV's *The Seagull* (1973), *The Cherry Orchard* (1977) and *Three Sisters* (1979). LEONARD BERKMAN

Vanbrugh, Irene *see* VANBRUGH, VIOLET

Vanbrugh [Barnes], Violet Augusta Mary (b. Exeter, 11 June 1867; d. London, 10 Nov. 1942) and **Irene** (b. Exeter, 2 Dec. 1872; d. London, 30 Nov. 1949) Actresses who had strikingly similar careers. The sisters succeeded in lighter, drawing-room plays, and both were strongly influenced by their actor–manager husbands – Violet by ARTHUR BOURCHIER, Irene by DION G. BOUCICAULT. Violet's daughter, Prudence, achieved success as an actress in Australia. Their brother, Sir Kenneth Barnes (1878–1957), was principal of the Royal Academy of Dramatic Art (1909–55) and named the Academy's Vanbrugh Theatre after his sisters – not, as is often assumed, after the seventeenth-century playwright and architect Sir John Vanbrugh. Violet's memoir was called *Dare to be Wise* (1925) and Irene's *To Tell My Story* (1948). Irene was created a dame in 1941. IAN BEVAN

Vance, Nina *see* ALLEY THEATER

variety The successor to MUSIC HALL in Britain and the equivalent of VAUDEVILLE in the United States, with which it had much in common. Variety essentially stemmed from the efforts of Sir OSWALD STOLL to upgrade music hall at his COLISEUM THEATRE in the West End by including, in addition to the comic singers of the day, a much wider range of entertainment. Though this recipe was not entirely successful at the Coliseum, a rather broader version of it gained appeal after the First World War in the leading provincial theatres and in the West End at the LONDON PALLADIUM. A number of former music hall stars transferred quite happily to the new form of entertainment, though in time they were replaced by other performers with a more informal approach. The character comedians of the music hall were often replaced by a new breed of humorist who specialized in talking directly to the audience or by double crosstalk acts. Singers were expected to present produced acts. There was invariably room on the average variety bill for two or three speciality acts presenting such feats of skill as juggling, magic, acrobatics, balancing and various forms of dance. For 40 years variety was constantly refreshed by new blood from other media, for instance films, radio and gramophone records, and by artists from overseas, notably the United States, which, in the vaudeville circuits that had begun to flourish before the First World War, had created the type of performer particularly suitable for variety.

A medium of infinite flexibility within its preferred two performances a night format, variety theatres presented almost every conceivable type of act. For some years, bands that had gained radio reputations were in demand, taking over the second half of the bill and presenting a variety show in miniature from their own resources. From the early 1930s onwards, radio did much to create a new audience for variety, the public being eager to see their favourites in the flesh. The Moss and Stoll circuits, which controlled the largest theatres in the biggest cities, were the pinnacle of the variety profession, offering long tours to performers from Britain and overseas, but beneath them were numerous No. 2 and 3 theatres in smaller towns, which offered a useful training ground to artists. There were surprisingly few artists who spent their whole career in variety, many appearing part of the year in PANTOMIME and summer shows (*see* SEASONAL THEATRE). Variety was effectively killed by television, many of the theatres being demolished or converted to other uses such as cinemas or bingo halls. Those that have remained have become some of Britain's most successful mixed-programme touring theatres. Through its relatives CABARET and REVUE, variety influenced theatrical innovators throughout the century, and in the 1980s gave rise to NEW VARIETY. PETER HEPPLE

F. Barker, *The House That Stoll Built* (1957)
Roy Hudd with Philip Hindin, *Roy Hudd's Cavalcade of Variety Acts: A Who Was Who of Light Entertainment 1945–1960* (1997)
R. Wilmut, *Kindly Leave the Stage! The Story of Variety 1919–1960* (1985)

Variety The most influential American theatre, film and television magazine, founded in 1905 by the New York critic Sime Silverman, who prided himself on the impartiality of his reviews. These reviews and up-to-date theatre news, written in a distinctive style popularizing shorthand terms such as 'showing' and 'legits', became mainstays of the weekly publication and remain central to its success. It is distributed internationally with offices all over the world. *Variety* has increasingly given more space to film and television than theatre, and it gives takings and attendance figures for theatres and films. *Daily Variety* was first published on the West Coast in the 1930s. Daily editions of *Variety* are also published during major festivals such as the Cannes Film Festival. ADRIANA HUNTER

See also MAGAZINES AND JOURNALS; RECORDING AND RESEARCHING THEATRE.

Vasilyev, Anatoly (b. Voronezh, Russia, 4 May 1942) Director. He made his mark in Moscow when he staged *Vassa Zheleznova* (using GORKY's original, pre-Revolutionary text rather than the 1935 version) and *The Grown-Up Daughter of a Young Man* by Viktor Slatkin in 1979. *Cerceau* (also Slatkin, 1985) travelled to Germany, Britain and France in 1986–7 and, together with *Six Characters in Search of an Author*

(Moscow, 1986; AVIGNON FESTIVAL and Paris, 1987), secured his international reputation. It was after this success abroad that he founded in Moscow in 1987 the School of Dramatic Art, an experimental, laboratory theatre which, during the 1990s, withdrew into monastic seclusion. His research with his students into the art of acting appears to have become an end in itself: public performances are rare and generally confined to extracts and exercises, to what amounts to work in progress rather than completed productions. His style is minimalist, oratorical, hieratic (although actors did dance, sing and play the piano in earlier productions) and suffused in a religious, even spiritualist, atmosphere. MARIA SHEVTSOVA

vaudeville Entertainment is respite from the drudgery and unhappiness of real life, and so it is only right that it be exempt from ordinary rules of order. Scholars have never been able to agree, for instance, on the source of the term 'vaudeville'. While it is plainly a French word, it is all but universally accepted as an American form of entertainment, a bill of acts performed in a VARIETY theatre and popular from the 1890s until about 1930. The likeliest origin of the term would seem the French *voix de ville* (voice of the city), but some scholars have speculated that the term comes from *chanson du vau*, as the ballads of the early troubadours were called, or the *vive vaude* entertainments of thirteenth-century France. French troubadours, like English minstrels and buskers, were the founding fathers of variety entertainment. When these entertainers moved indoors in the middle of the nineteenth century, British MUSIC HALL entertainment began, and it was exported to the United States. There, 'girlie' and 'leg' shows had been playing in beer halls. In 1840 one William Valentine opened the first New York variety theatre. Soon, similar auditoriums began to spring up across the country, called 'honky tonks' or 'free and easies'. Then, at last, in 1871, H. J. Sargent organized Sargent's Great Vaudeville Company in Louisville, Kentucky, and an era of brave solo entertainers began which spread across the country. The bars of such theatres were busy and so were the prostitutes in the curtained boxes. Needless to say, women did not attend these shows, and so vaudeville's turning point came when Tony Pastor decided to seek after this family trade by offering entertainment 'as clean as a hound's tooth'. He tried from the 1860s on and succeeded in his New York theatre on 14th Street which opened on 24 October 1881, marking the birth of classic American vaudeville. Pastor's great star was the beautifully buxom LILLIAN RUSSELL, along with the likes of WEBER and FIELDS, The Four Cohans, Harrigan and Hart, and Buster Keaton. However, he had competition soon enough from two Boston theatre operators who transferred to New York: Franklin Keith and Edward F. Albee (grandfather of the American playwright). They were establishing the first vaudeville 'wheel', or circuit of theatres; and they lured the most attractive acts from Pastor by engaging them not for one theatre but for their entire circuit. Playing this wheel, or circuit, came to be called 'Keith time', and from this expression derived 'big' and 'small' time, meaning major or minor theatres. As the twentieth century began, the Keith wheel was the biggest of all because it paid the most money and offered the most handsome theatres. The vaudeville shows themselves had evolved ritualistically. Each bill would consist of eight acts, beginning with a 'dumb' or silent performer – a bicyclist, acrobat or animal trainer – who did his act while the audience was still arriving. Second on the bill was considered the least desirable spot and would be filled by a newcomer, minor singer or comedian. Then there was a 'tab' (tabloid, or small-sized) version of a Broadway success, or a 'flash' act, meaning one with a large company, elaborate scenery or costumes. The fourth and fifth spots in this typical agenda were usually filled with solid performers, an established comedy team or a rowdy act like the MARX BROTHERS. Sixth on the bill approached the cream of the show and called for a class act, perhaps a ballroom dance team like Vernon and Irene Castle. Then came the headliner, who was always seventh on the bill. The eighth and closing act, like the first one, was a dumb act as the customers began to leave. Vaudeville at its American peak, whether at Hammerstein's Victoria Theater or the legendary PALACE THEATER (both in Times Square), is known for such historic entertainers as GEORGE BURNS and GRACIE ALLEN, JACK BENNY, Fred Allen, W. C. FIELDS and FANNY BRICE. But equally endearing and even mythic were its strange and novel acts such as The Cherry Sisters ('The World's Worst Act'), who were magnificently awful; Francis White ('The World's Smallest Dancer'); 'Willard, The Man Who Grows'; Charlie Chase who ate light bulbs; Swain's Cats and Rats, who raced around a track with the rats atop the cats; or Marguerite Webb and Jack Connelly, who played the piano with fruit. Yet for all this laughter and absurdity, the jewels of vaudeville were its singing women, such as the emotional Nora Bayes, who was banished from the Palace Theater for vociferously complaining that SOPHIE TUCKER (another star singer) was headlined above her; or the fabulous EVA TANGUAY, vaudeville's greatest and sexiest star, liable as not to sock a chorus girl in the jaw for stealing a boyfriend.

Talking pictures began the end of vaudeville, and by 1932 the Palace Theater was fraying at the edges of its reputation. Live entertainment and the bravery of the solo performer were to go the way of all hand-made things. The electronic revolution was beginning, and no longer would the lonely entertainer step through those glittering curtains, risking the spotlight to pluck him from the darkness that might have kept him safe.
MARTIN GOTTFRIED

C. Caffin, *Vaudeville* (1914)
J. E. DiMegho, *Vaudeville USA* (1973)
D. Gilbert, *American Vaudeville* (1940)
J. Laurie, Jr, *Vaudeville: From the Honky-Tonks to the Palace* (1953)
A. Slide, *The Encyclopedia of Vaudeville* (1994)
B. Smith, *The Vaudevillians* (1976)
R. W. Snyder, *The Voice of the City: Vaudeville and Popular Culture in New York* (1989)
S. Staples, *Male–Female Comedy Teams in American Vaudeville 1865–1932* (1984)

Vauthier, Jean (b. Grace-Berleur, nr Liège, Belgium, 20 Sept. 1910) Playwright. His plays, written in French, with two or three characters, e.g. *Capitaine Bada* ('Captain Bada', 1952) and *Les Prodiges* ('The prodigies', 1959), are full of verbal delirium and dissect human relationships. The monologue *Le Personnage combattant* ('The fighting figure', 1956), about a man in search of his past, was brilliantly performed by BARRAULT. WENDY SCOTT

Vedrenne, J[ohn] E. (b. 13 July 1867; d. London, 12 Feb. 1930) Theatre manager. His most notable achievement was his association as business manager with HARLEY GRANVILLE BARKER during the latter's tenure as artistic director of the ROYAL COURT. Between 1904 and 1907 they staged there 32 plays by 17 playwrights and changed the face of English theatre. These seasons were crucial to the promotion of the new drama and in consolidating SHAW's career as playwright. Vedrenne's joint venture with Barker at the SAVOY (1907–8) was less successful and saw the end of their partnership. Usually in association with other actors and managers he continued in management and as a concert agent into the first half of the 1920s.
IAN CLARKE

Venezuela *see* SOUTH AMERICA

Venne, Lottie (b. 28 May 1852; d. 16 July 1928) Comic actress. She made a name for herself in BURLESQUE (Strand Theatre, 1874–8) and then broadened her career to become a popular comedienne in straight comedy, farce and musicals, enriching many productions with her humour and her uncanny ability as a mimic. ADRIANA HUNTER

ventriloquism An ancient form of performance, allied closely with MAGIC, its modern English name deriving from the Latin for 'speaking from the belly'. The misconception that this is how the ventriloquial effect is achieved persists, though ventriloquists, like others, use the vocal cords, not the stomach, to produce and articulate sounds. The definitive aspect of ventriloquism is that its practitioners create the illusion of sound coming from elsewhere than their own bodies. The common belief that this is accomplished by 'throwing the voice' is actually a fallacy. The voice cannot be 'thrown', but the eye and intellect of the observer can be tricked to convince the ear that sound is coming from where the ventriloquist wishes. Early ventriloquists performed without the aid of a doll, puppet or 'dummy', using their vocal skills and facial control to create a scene involving 'distant' voices and the sound of animals. The first use of a doll with a moving mouth as an aid to ventriloquism is attributed to the Austrian Baron Von Mengen in 1750, though this idea of allying ventriloquism and puppetry was not taken up by other performers until the nineteenth century. In the early MUSIC HALL the standard format for the ventriloquist's act involved a number of life-sized figures sitting in a row or semi-circle, being operated by the ventriloquist moving behind them. The innovation of using a single, diminutive doll in a quick and funny crosstalk act was introduced by Fred Russell (1862–1957), whose 'Coster Joe' dummy was the first of the 'cheeky boy' characters which became the familiar companions of ventriloquists in the twentieth century. Ventriloquists using this or a similar format could top the bill in music hall and VAUDEVILLE, though the decline of these arenas in the 1930s threatened to eradicate the art entirely. Surprisingly, the medium in which it was to flourish again was radio. In the 1940s the American ventriloquist Edgar Bergen (1903–78) topped the ratings with his show starring the wisecracking dummy Charlie MacCarthy, trading insults not just with Bergen, but with regular guest W. C. FIELDS. In Britain, similar radio success was later achieved by Peter Brough, whose doll, Archie Andrews, had Tony Hancock as its tutor.

Ventriloquism remains a fascinating and multi-layered performance technique – a form of puppetry in which puppeteer converses with puppet, or can even dispense with the puppet entirely. Some of the best ventriloquists have explored the strange contradictions of the situation. Arthur Worsley, for instance, remained silent and stony-faced while his vociferous dummy goaded him with the challenge of saying 'a bottle of beer' (articulated perfectly by the dummy) without moving his lips. Several films have exploited the notion of the ventriloquist as a psychologically split personality, or the dummy coming to life and taking over its operator, notably *The Great Gabbo* with Eric Von Stroheim (1929), *Dead of Night* with MICHAEL REDGRAVE (1946) and *Magic* with ANTHONY HOPKINS (1978).

Since the 1930s, ventriloquism is rarely seen in the theatre, and in the latter part of the century was best known through the medium of television. IAN SAVILLE
See also PUPPET THEATRE; WAXWORKS AND DUMMIES.

Steven Connor, *Dumbstruck: A Cultural History of Ventriloquism* (2000)
Valentine Vox, *I Can See Your Lips Moving* (1981)

Verdon, Gwen [Gwyneth Evelyn] (b. Culver City, Cal., 13 Jan. 1925; d. Woodstock, Vt., 18 Oct. 2000) Actress, dancer and choreographer. One of the major stars of the American musical theatre, Verdon made her Broadway debut in *Alive and Kicking* (1948) and went on to play starring roles in *Can Can* (1953), *Damn Yankees* (1955), *New Girl in Town* (1957), *Redhead* (1958), *Sweet Charity* (1966) and *Chicago* (1975), the last five choreographed by BOB FOSSE, to whom she was married for a time. Her dancing embodies the sexual and often forlorn women whose lives she depicted with unequalled brilliance. She also appeared in such films as *Damn Yankees* (1958) and *Cotton Club* (1984). DAVID STAINES

Verga, Giovanni *see* ITALY; VERISMO

verismo A term related to the naturalism of ZOLA in France and used in the Italian theatre at the beginning of the twentieth century to describe plays that depicted reality 'truthfully', even if this meant representing poverty and oppression, which was not then fashionable. Not surprisingly, it arose in a depressed region, Sicily, whence came its main theorist Luigi Capuana (1839–1915). The principal playwrights were Giuseppe Giacosa (1847–1906) and Giovanni Verga (1840–1922), whose *La Lupa* (*The She-Wolf*, 1896) was one of the hits of the WORLD THEATRE SEASON in 1969. D. H. LAWRENCE was influenced by Verga and *verismo*, and translated some of his plays. The term has also been applied to melodramatic operas by Puccini and Mascagni. *Verismo* is also related to *verism*, which is similarly dedicated to portraying reality regardless of how unpleasant it may be. It spread across the arts in Europe at the same time, survived the First World War and was particularly strong among politically conscious German artists. CHARLES LONDON

Verma, Jatinder *see* TARA ARTS

verse drama Strictly speaking, drama in which the dialogue is written in verse lines. Some plays not written in verse are often called 'poetic', which normally turns out to mean that the language aims for heightened effect, or, more loosely, that the action departs from the realist mode. The desire to develop verse drama was a recurrent feature in the twentieth century's theatrical and, perhaps especially, literary life. There are a variety of reasons for this. The nature of drama is such that its ancient sources always seem to be within reach. Modern efforts at theatrical renewal refer to origins, especially the Greek theatre, and thus have often been seen to require verse. In English this ambition has of course been buttressed, or beset, by the language's greatest model, Shakespeare. The simple force of tradition has persuaded many that the highest drama will be in verse. These aspirations have frequently resulted in an impatience with the modern theatre's realist manner and commercial interests. The efforts to re-invent verse drama in English have often therefore come from movements outside the theatrical mainstream. But it has always been difficult to decide what shall be the scope and style appropriate to a modern verse drama. In setting, is its particular quality best suited to historical, or transhistorical subjects, or can contemporary characters be represented as speaking verse? Then, what kind of verse should that be? In the seventeenth century Dryden had described Shakespeare's verse as 'pestered with figures', and many writers since have insisted on the need to escape what AUDEN called 'the romantic sham-Tudor'. But was this to mean that the verse should be so self-effacing as to go unnoticed by an audience? If so, the effort to move beyond what Dryden called 'conversation' would scarcely seem worthwhile, even if, as both he and ELIOT argued, the writer is always part way to acknowledging the case for verse in recognizing that 'prose, on the stage, is as artificial as verse' (Eliot). Whatever may have been the omissions of verse dramatists, theoretical self-awareness has not been one of them. However, none of the century's verse dramatists can be said to enjoy a place in the repertory alongside the century's prose dramatists. With a few exceptions – MAXWELL ANDERSON, ROBERT LOWELL – verse drama has been wholly absent from American theatre.

The first significant effort to renew verse drama for this century began in the 1890s with the foundation in 1891 of the Irish Literary Movement. Its major figure was the poet W. B. YEATS (1865–1939). In this period Yeats's Irish nationalism was developing in conjunction with an interest in Irish Gaelic literature and the ancient history of Ireland. His first play, *The Countess Cathleen* (1892), was part of his project to create a 'great distinctive poetic literature' out of Ireland's history and cultural traditions, and contribute to the 'de-Anglicization' of Ireland. In collaboration with two major patrons, the Irishman EDWARD MARTYN and Miss ANNIE HORNIMAN from Manchester, the Irish Literary Theatre was founded and gave its first performances in Dublin in 1899. This was succeeded in 1904 by the foundation of the ABBEY THEATRE; by this time the important creative figures in the movement, especially for the speaking of verse, included the actors FLORENCE FARR and WILLIAM and Frank FAY, and J. M. SYNGE.

Yeats wrote verse plays consistently through this period, among them *The Land of Heart's Desire* (1894), *The Shadowy Waters* (1900), *Cathleen ni Hoolihan* (1902) and *Deidre* (1907). Stylistically they eschew realism and seek to make a poetic stage language out of the common speech of rural Ireland. Yeats continued to write plays throughout his career, and when his work did not prove popular at the Abbey he wrote for private performance. This work included his four *Plays for Dancers* (1921), ritualistic work making great use of music and dance, and influenced by his interest in the Japanese *noh* theatre. His last plays, written in the year of his death (1939), were *The Death of Cuchulain* and *Purgatory*. However, the works from the Irish movement that have continued to be regularly performed have been the more realistic prose dramas of Synge and SEAN O'CASEY.

The Irish movement had contemporary counterparts in England among a number of writers who shared a distaste for realism and the commercial theatre of their day. Among the works staged were STEPHEN PHILLIPS' *Herod* (1900) and *Paolo and Francesca* (1902), and Gordon Bottomley's *The Crier by Night* (1902) and *King Lear's Wife* (1915). Two plays also influenced by the *noh* tradition were JOHN MASEFIELD's *The Tragedy of Nan* (1908) and JAMES ELROY FLECKER's *Hassan*, posthumously produced in 1923. According to Auden, all of these, Yeats included, shared 'only one defect: they won't go'. Auden himself was the next major writer to try to make verse drama go. He shared his predecessors' rejection of realism but also scorned what he saw as their preciosity. In 1926 he wrote that 'the only remaining traces of theatrical art were to be found on the music-hall stage', and that 'later, perhaps, something might be done with puppets'. As this programme suggests, when Auden did turn to write for the stage with the 'charade' *Paid on Both Sides* (1928), he sought to write broad symbolic works with strong burlesque elements. In 1932 Auden began a collaboration with the GROUP THEATRE, founded in London by the painter Robert Medley and the dancer and actor RUPERT DOONE. His first work for the Group was a *danse macabre* in CABARET style, *The Dance of Death*, produced in 1934. In this period Auden's work also included verses for John Grierson's documentary films *Night Mail* and *Coal Face*. Auden's remaining verse plays were all written jointly with CHRISTOPHER ISHERWOOD; they were all produced by the Group Theatre and maintain the same mixed theatrical style. The politics of the 1930s are central to them, and Auden's interest in drama seems tied to his social and political hopes in that period.

The 'alternative' aspect of verse drama was also marked in Eliot's first complete dramatic work, *Murder in the Cathedral* (1935), in that it was written not for the theatre but for festival performance in Canterbury Cathedral. Eliot rapidly decided, however, that the historical and picturesque was 'a dead end'. Poetry, he argued, should be heard from people 'dressed like ourselves . . . using telephones and motor cars and radio sets'. The very titles of his subsequent plays announce the determined contemporaneity of their setting: *The Family Reunion* (1939), *The Cocktail Party* (1950), *The Confidential Clerk* (1954), *The Elder Statesman* (1959). He aimed to 'accustom our audiences to verse to the point at which they will cease to be conscious of it'. But the naturalistic settings of Eliot's plays belie their real interests, which are to reveal larger religiously conceived realities beneath the surface of contemporary, secular sophistication. The paradoxical problem has turned out to be that the very country-house and drawing-room settings whose significance Eliot sought to dissolve as illusion were those he thought necessary to achieve popular dramatic success. By the mid-1950s these settings had become debilitatingly unfashionable.

Although acknowledging Eliot, and frequently working with Eliot's producer E. MARTIN BROWNE, the work of CHRISTOPHER FRY departs from Eliot's precepts. His free verse is eloquent and demonstrative, aiming for a heightened colloquialism. Among his settings are Egypt in the time of Moses (*The Firstborn*, 1948), a sixth-century 'Jutish farmstead' for *Thor, with Angels* (1948), England in 1400 for *The Lady's Not For Burning* (1948), and the twentieth century, which yet could be any time, for *A Sleep of Prisoners* (1951). Again, Fry's work was first seen in non-theatrical spaces, partly because of its 'fringe' status, and partly because the religious dimensions of his work made such settings as Canterbury and Tewkesbury Abbey appropriate. The vigour of his language, his stagecraft and, not least, his

comic vision did, however, bring him considerable mainstream success.

The recurrent feature of modern verse drama has been that of return: the effort to recuperate ancient dramatic and spiritual roots and older social forms. The efforts to do this have, however, been perhaps more literary than theatrical. In view of this it is not surprising that much of the most striking verse drama in recent years has come from outside the metropolitan centres of English. The Nigerian writer WOLE SOYINKA mixes prose and verse, the latter not as song or other interludes, but often extensively, as, for example, in *A Dance of the Forests* (1960) and *Death and the King's Horseman* (1976). DEREK WALCOTT, from St Lucia, has written poetry and drama concurrently throughout his career. His many plays include *Ti-Jean and His Brothers* (1957) of which he writes how the African art of the storyteller and 'tribal memory' works in it at a deeper level than his other influences from GARCÍA LORCA and BRECHT.

In England at the beginning of the 1990s the most successful verse dramatist was TONY HARRISON. Several of his plays have been written in collaboration with composers and feature a strong poetic style using metre and rhyme. They belong to that tendency in verse drama that eschews realism in favour of archaic sources and forms, but does so in ways that aim to re-open relations with aspects of popular culture. These are familiar aims. It will be interesting to see if they can at last be permanently achieved.

JEFFREY WAINWRIGHT

George Steiner, *The Death of Tragedy* (1961)
Kenneth Tynan, 'Notes on a Dead Language' and 'Prose and the Playwright', in *Tynan on Theatre* (1964)

Vezin, Hermann *see* DRAMA SCHOOLS; VOICE TRAINING

Vian, Boris (b. Ville d'Avray, France, 10 March 1920; d. Paris, 23 June 1959) Playwright, poet, novelist and jazz trumpet player. Often linked with the THEATRE OF THE ABSURD, Vian's work satirizes political, military and bourgeois practices. Plays include *L'Equarrissage pour tous* (*Knackery for All* or *The Knacker's ABC*, 1950,); *Les Bâtisseurs d'Empire* (*The Empire Builders*, 1959), his best-known work abroad; and *Le Gouter des généraux* (*Tea for the Generals*, 1962). ANNA MCMULLAN

Victoria Theatre Opened in 1962 in a converted cinema in Stoke-on-Trent, Staffordshire, by STEPHEN JOSEPH's 'Theatre-in-the-Round' touring company as Britain's first permanent THEATRE IN THE ROUND, seating 347 (extended in 1971 to 389). It is run by a trust. PETER CHEESEMAN was artistic director until 1998. The

resident company offered a mixed programme, including classics and new plays (often by PETER TERSON), but is best known for its local musical documentaries including *The Jolly Potters* (1964), *The Knotty* (1966), *The Fight for Shelton Bar* (1974), *Plain Jos* (1980) and *The Dirty Hill* (1990). These documentaries were the realization of Cheeseman's avowed aim of serving and reflecting the local community. In 1986 the company, which has given a start to many successful professionals, moved to a custom-built 600-seat theatre in the round in nearby Newcastle-under-Lyme.
D. KEITH PEACOCK
See also DOCUMENTARY.

Vidal, Gore [Eugene Luther] (b. West Point, NY, 3 Oct. 1925) Writer and politician. After establishing himself as a novelist and writer of teleplays, in 1957 he turned briefly to theatre. There he was most successful with adaptations of two of his teleplays, *Visit to a Small Planet* (1957) and *The Best Man* (1960), a satire on American politics. Other plays include *On the March to the Sea* (1961), *Weekend* (1968) and *An Evening with Richard Nixon and . . .* (1972). ALEXIS GREENE

F. Kaplan, *Gore Vidal: A Biography* (1999)

Vienna Centre of the disintegrating Austro-Hungarian empire, it was both an anti-semitic cauldron of hedonism and cynicism and a theatrical capital at the beginning of the twentieth century, with particular strength in opera and light musical theatre (e.g. LEHAR's *The Merry Widow*, 1905, STRAUS' *The Chocolate Soldier*, 1908). In the years up to World War I it was also a focal point for the AVANT-GARDE in many fields: architecture, psychoanalysis (it was the home of Freud), philosophy (the young Wittgenstein), music (Schoenberg's departure from traditional composition) and art (Klimt and Schiele) as well as theatre. OSCAR KOKOSCHKA's play *Murderer, The Hope of Women* (1909) was a pioneer of EXPRESSIONISM which scandalized Vienna as did his violent paintings of the time; ARTHUR SCHNITZLER, a member of the Young Vienna group who wanted to modernize the city's culture, chronicled those who were scandalized, and his plays, especially *Reigen* (1903) or *La Ronde* as it is better known in English, caused outraged in its turn; fellow group member HUGO VON HOFMANNSTHAL was writing SYMBOLIST poetic drama and libretti for Richard Strauss; and KARL KRAUS, who charted the decadence of the Hapsburgs in the satirical magazine *The Torch* (1899–1936), portrayed the absurdity and cruelty of war in his epic *The Last Days of Mankind* (1922). After the war, while Vienna remained important for stage production with the Burgtheater one of Europe's leading houses, it became subsumed into the German theatre world. Vienna-born FERDINAND BRUCKNER left for Berlin in 1923 and began his playwriting there and fellow Viennese playwright FRITZ HOCHWALDER had two plays produced in his hometown before another world war intervened, and he remained in voluntary Swiss exile afterwards. In the mid-1950s another Vienna Group, including playwrights Conrad Bayer and H. C. Artmann, paved the way for the iconoclastic work of PETER HANDKE in 1966, but he did not have a play produced in Vienna until 1989. Similarly THOMAS BERNHARD, who moved to Austria as a baby, had his plays produced more in German cities than in Vienna, and his will stated that while his work remained in copyright after his death it was not to be produced or published in Austria. However, for playwrights in neighbouring oppressive states, like VACLAV HAVEL in Czechoslovakia, Vienna's theatres could provide a much-needed platform from which to address the rest of the world. CHARLES LONDON
See also GERMAN-LANGUAGE DRAMA.

W. E. Yates, *Theatre in Vienna: A Critical History, 1776–1995* (1996)

Viertel, Bertold (b. Vienna, 28 June 1885; d. Vienna, 24 Sept. 1953) Director. Viertel was associated as playwright and director with EXPRESSIONISM in his early years, promoting the work of HASENCLEVER and KAISER in Vienna, Dresden and Berlin. From 1927 until after the Second World War he was in America, directing films and a New York revival of BRECHT's *The Private Life of the Master Race*. After the war he directed notable revivals of WILLIAMS, SHAW and Brecht in Vienna, Zurich and Berlin, where he worked for the BERLINER ENSEMBLE. MARVIN CARLSON

Vietnam *see* SOUTH-EAST ASIA

Vilar, Jean (b. Sète, Hérault, France, 25 March 1912; d. Sète, 28 May 1971) Actor and director. He studied under DULLIN before discovering popular theatre with a touring company. After spending the war in the tiny Théâtre de Poche, he founded in 1947 the famous annual AVIGNON FESTIVAL. The outdoor techniques he practised – rapid movement and dialogue, strong contrasts of colour, sound and light – served him well when the state granted him the huge Chaillot Theatre in Paris. There between 1951 and 1963 Vilar's THÉÂTRE NATIONAL POPULAIRE, which had been dormant for nearly two decades, sought to become a theatre of debate in the classical (and Brechtian) traditions. Celebrated productions included *Le Cid*, *Dom Juan* and *The Resistible Rise and Fall of Arturo Ui*. He wrote three books on the theatre. TERRY HODGSON

D. Bradby & J. McCormack, *People's Theatre* (1978)

G. Leclerc, *Le TNP de Jean Vilar* (1971)

P. Wehle, *Le Théâtre populaire selon Jean Vilar* (1981)

D. Whitton, *Stage Directors of Modern France* (1987)

Vinaver [Grinberg], Michel (b. Paris, 1927) Novelist and playwright. His two novels and early plays were written in the 1950s, when his first play *Les Coréens* ('The Koreans', 1956) had considerable success. But in between *Iphigénie Hotel* (written 1959) and *Par-dessus bord* (*Overboard*, 1973, written 1969), he wrote no plays, devoting himself to his work as an executive with Gillette International. The world of business provides the material for most of his later plays, such as *La Demande d'emploi* (*Situation vacant*, 1973) and *Les Travaux et les jours* (*Works and days*, 1979). In these, plot is reduced to a minimum, the plays consisting of ambiguous, fragmentary dialogues in which questions and answers do not necessarily correspond, and different streams of consciousness interweave to create a rich dramatic texture. Many have been directed by Jacques Lassalle, including *L'Emission de télévision* ('The television programme', 1990). Vinaver is seen as part of the *quotidien* or 'everyday' school of playwrights because of the realistic nature of his characters and his exclusively contemporary subject matter. But in his more ambitious plays, like *Overboard*, mythical archetypes underlie modern stories and the drama deals with its material in multiple ways, varying from naturalist representation to sequences in which the very possibility of representation is questioned. DAVID BRADBY

D. Bradby, *The Theater of Michel Vinaver* (1993)

Virgin Islands *see* CARIBBEAN

Visconti, Luchino [Conte di Modrone] (b. Milan, 2 Nov. 1906; d. Rome, 17 March 1976) Film and theatre director. Visconti's classic and contemporary stage productions, like his films, for which he is better known, mixed a striking visual imagination with realistic detail and social concern. His productions of Verdi, Shakespeare (*Troilus and Cressida*, 1949), Goldoni (*La Locandiera*, 1952), CHEKHOV (*The Cherry Orchard*, 1965) and PINTER (*Old Times*, 1973) were particularly highly praised. MARVIN CARLSON

Geoffrey Nowell-Smith, *Luchino Visconti* (1968)

Gaia Servadio, *Luchino Visconti* (1982)

Claretta Tonetti, *Luchino Visconti* (1997)

Vishnevsky, Vsevolod [Vitalyevich] (b. St Petersburg, 21 Dec. 1900; d. Moscow, 28 Feb. 1951) Playwright. He engaged in literary polemics from his twenties, and ended his life an ardent Stalinist. His best

plays, episodic, monumental, epic, are *Pervaya konnaya* (*The First Cavalry*, 1929) and *Optimistecheskaya tragediya* (*An Optimistic Tragedy*, 1933). They are flamboyant and energetic, if weakly constructed and ideologically naïve. ROBERT LEACH

Vitez, Antoine (b. Paris, 20 Dec. 1930; d. Paris, 30 April 1990) Actor, director and teacher. A student of Russian and Greek, he became a communist, wrote for *Bref*, the journal of VILAR's THÉÂTRE NATIONAL POPULAIRE, created puppet-play scenarios, adapted Aristophanes, translated Sholokhov and became Louis Aragon's secretary. His first productions were Sophocles' *Electra* and MAYAKOVSKY's *The Bathhouse* (1966). Much influenced by Vilar and BRECHT, he achieved his own style in four famous 1978 Molière productions. Gesture and posture on a bare stage focused critical dramatic moments, creating a desired instability. His productions at Chaillot after 1981 (remodelled to his designs when the Théâtre National Populaire left) from 1981 included *Britannicus* and *Hernani*. Administrator of the COMÉDIE-FRANÇAISE from 1988, he died rehearsing Brecht's *Life of Galileo* (1990). TERRY HODGSON

A-F. Benhamou et al., *Antoine Vitez: toutes les mises-en-scène* (1981)

Vitrac, Roger (b. Pinsac, France, 17 Nov. 1899; d. Paris, 22 Jan. 1952) Playwright and poet; with Tristan Tzara, a founder of DADA. Of all French SURREALIST playwrights the most accomplished, he believed profoundly in the value of theatre and defied the strictest tenets of ANDRÉ BRETON, who expelled him, with ARTAUD, in 1926. Together they co-founded the Théâtre Alfred Jarry in 1927, where his *Mystères de l'Amour* (*The Mysteries of Love*), an experiment with automatic writing, featuring Lloyd George and Mussolini, was followed in 1928 by his tragic farce *Victor ou les enfants au pouvoir* (*Victor or All Power to the Children*), a daringly successful parody of bourgeois drama, whose rebellious hero, though fully grown, is only nine years old, his imminent death prefigured by a beautiful lady unable to control her farting in society. Often revived, in 1962 *Victor* was directed in Paris by JEAN ANOUILH, who considered him a great innovator, and it was seen, as *Victor*, in London two years later. In the 1960s ROGER PLANCHON's company staged his *Le coup de Trafalgar* (1934). Vitrac's work anticipates certain aspects of IONESCO's. DONALD WATSON

Voaden, Herman (b. London, Ont., 19 Jan. 1903; d. Toronto, 27 June 1991) Playwright. Voaden studied theatre at the Yale School of Drama in 1930–1, and widened his knowledge of German EXPRESSIONIST theatre on a number of visits to Germany between

1928 and 1933. He developed a theory, 'symphonic expressionism', which called for the coalescence of diverse art forms – sculpture, music, dance, architecture – to create a new kind of theatre. His theory is exemplified in his own work, in plays like *Wilderness* (1931), first produced at Yale, *Earth Song: A Drama in Rhythmic Prose and Light* (1932), and *Murder Pattern* (1936).

EUGENE BENSON

Vogel, Paula (b. Washington DC, 16 Nov. 1951) Playwright and teacher whose plays are often structured around fantasy and deal from a feminist perspective with human concerns such as domestic violence, molestation, AIDS and the non-traditional family. Her target is almost always a social system that pits the weak against the strong in a life dance that often ends tragically for the powerless. She was awarded the 1998 Pulitzer Prize for *How I Learned to Drive*, in which a young girl's sexual awakening at the hands of her uncle is compared to a driving lesson. Other plays include *The Oldest Profession* (1981), about a group of 70-ish prostitutes, and *The Baltimore Waltz* (1992), in which Vogel tackles AIDS and the hypocrisy of the government's response to a disease that is perceived as mostly affecting those outside the 'norm'. Domestic violence ends up in death for the women in *Desdemona* (1979) and *Hot 'n' Throbbing* (1992).

DAVID A. WILLIAMS

voice training The history of voice training inevitably parallels the history of actor training. The development of voice training has been shaped by changing theatre sizes and has responded to the demands of the texts of each period and the styles of performance. At the beginning of the twentieth century the aspiring actor had little choice about the type of voice training available. The influence of singing training and of the elocutionists was still strongly felt, but now teachers tended to be working actors rather than academics and their training was more directly related to the theatre. In 1885 Sarah Thorne opened a very successful school in Margate on the south coast of England which offered classes during the day and then rehearsal and performance experience alongside professionals in the evenings, thus re-introducing an element of the apprenticeship model of Shakespeare's day. Classes offered by Sarah Thorne's School included voice production, gesture, MIME and the teaching of dialects. Later, in 1896, BEN GREET started a school which offered a similar curriculum to that of Thorne's. He employed his most successful students in his touring company. During this period Herman Vezin, a renowned actor and elocutionist, was the most famous private teacher in London. He had rooms in Lancaster Place and his teaching involved rapid, precise speech with the emphasis on strong consonants. He also taught text analysis and required his pupils to take classes in dance and fencing. Many of his students went on to work with FRANK BENSON's company. Rosina Filippi, a student of Vezin's, became a successful actress and later a respected teacher in her own right. She continued to teach in Vezin's style but also improvised on the piano in order to encourage students to respond to rhythm changes. She ran her own school and taught in groups, with a focus on productions.

There was a perceived need among the theatrical community for a training establishment on a par with the Paris Conservatoire. In 1904 Sir HERBERT BEERBOHM TREE started the Academy of Dramatic Art. He employed teachers such as Filippi in his school. ELSIE FOGERTY, who had studied at the Paris Conservatoire, had been teaching privately at the Royal Albert Hall since 1898. Her mission was to eradicate the old style of recitation. In 1903 she had met Benson while in Stratford-upon-Avon. As well as his company, Benson had a training school and his students followed the apprenticeship system most similar to that of Shakespeare's period. He was keen for his students to acquire greater vocal and physical skills and had heard of the work of Fogerty. In 1906 Fogerty took Benson's students to the Albert Hall and the Central School of Speech Training and Dramatic Art (later Speech and Drama) was founded. It was her belief that a sound speech training was the most important element of training for the actor. During her lifetime she established courses for the training of voice and speech teachers, and started speech therapy in England as well as training actors. Students of hers went on to teach at the major training establishments in London and the English-speaking world. Important individuals who worked with her were Dr W. A. Aiken, who devised the bone prop (a small device for separating the teeth to allow improved vowel production and diction) and the resonator scale. Another was Clifford Turner, who recommended the use of rib reserve breathing. He went on to teach for many years at both the Central School and the Royal Academy of Dramatic Art, and produced the book *Voice and Speech in the Theatre* (1950), which was a standard text for many years.

Fogerty produced many influential teachers; among them was Gwynneth Thurburn, who succeeded her as principal of the Central School from 1942 to 1967 and whose major influence was in the area of verse and language, and Rose Bruford, who went on to establish her own successful training school for actor/teachers in

· Voice ·

The twentieth century has seen radical changes in acting styles; it follows, then, that there have been comparable changes in how the voice is used, and in the manner of speech.

Ideally, every actor wants to know that their voice is carrying what is in their mind and imagination directly across to the audience. They want it to be accurate to their intention and to sound unforced. They want to know that they are carrying the listener with them, for, in the end, it is the voice which sets up the main bond between the actor and the audience: certainly this is true of English mainstream theatre. The actor knows that the audience want to be let into the character, and that this will happen to a large extent through voice and speech. Above all, the voice needs to be interesting. Just how difficult is this, then?

Because everybody talks and uses their voice a great deal in everyday life, many people, when they go to the theatre, imagine that it is relatively easy for actors to speak on stage, that it is just a matter of projection and 'speaking up', and everything will be all right: perhaps you have to work on breathing and even do some singing exercises to strengthen the voice, which is where a voice teacher comes in, but that is all there is to it. As a member of the audience, you know when you like someone's voice, when it gives you pleasure and sounds right, but few people understand the complexity of what this 'rightness' means.

An actor has to find his or her own inner truth – the truth of the character in relation to him- or herself – and then make it big enough to share with the audience. They want to sound natural, as in naturalistic speech, yet one cannot talk naturally, for that would not reach. So a technique has to be found: and that technique is based on four key issues.

The first is *relaxation*. Because there is always a certain pressure on an actor to be interesting, and because simply to go out on stage involves some nervous tension – in other words, the adrenalin is flowing – the actor has to be physically in control of that tension so that it can be used positively. Tension affects the voice adversely: tension in the shoulders and the upper part of the chest means that you cannot use your ribs to the full, and so cannot take deep enough breaths; the breathing then becomes shallow, which then limits the phrasing, and stops the voice being resonated in the chest. Valuable resonance will be lost and the timbre will be thin. Tension in the neck and throat also limits resonance, but more than that, it makes one start to push the voice from the throat, and this cuts out all the natural talking inflections that we normally use. The voice will be unmusical and flat, and will not engage the listener. And, crucially, the louder you need to be, the more tense you will become, to the point where the voice can be damaged. So, exercises must be done for relaxation – and for posture, for often faulty posture produces tension.

Second is *breathing*. The vocal energy lies with the breath, for it is the breath striking the vocal cords and causing them to vibrate that produces vocal sound. If the breath hits the cords too roughly the tone will be harsh and glottal, and damage can be caused to the cords. If the impulse is not firm enough, the resultant tone will be breathy and unfocused and will very likely not carry well. It will also be effortful. So the way the breath is used is vitally important. Also important is that the breath taken is deep, for the deeper the breath the further the sound will carry: as with loosing an arrow, when the further back you draw the bow, the further the shaft will carry. The breath must be used firmly and without restriction.

Because an actor's job has a great deal to do with finding size – both the size of the space that has to be filled, and the size of the character they are playing – they need as much vocal energy at their command as possible. It is the breath, and how it is used, that will give the size that is needed. And, curiously, almost as much energy is needed when working in a small space as in a large one, for energy is not so much to do with volume as with vocal intensity and definition. Exercises for breathing, both for increased capacity and for using it as well as possible, are essential. This is particularly important for classical work, where the phrases are so often long, and where the meaning can be lost if the phrasing is broken up.

Third is *verbal energy*. This involves doing exercises for both consonant firmness and the vibration of the voiced consonants, plus the forward placing of the vowel sounds. Exercises for the muscularity of both the vowels and consonants ensure the clarity and placing of the tone, and this is the most important part of projection: for it is the clarity and verbal energy of consonants that carries the voice to all parts of the theatre, and makes the listener remark the language. Mistakenly, in the past exercises have emphasized the sharpness and explosiveness of consonants with quick patter exercises: this cuts down on the vibrations of the voiced consonants which carry the voice through the space, and it also devalues the language. Always, vowels must be open and free, and care taken that they are not clipped. Vowel sounds vary a great deal in length; this is part of the texture of the language, and we must be aware of this, for they often carry the emotional weight of the text. After all, we probably made open sounds before we made closed ones.

Fourth is *cadence*. Every piece of text has its own music, and we have to train our ears to listen for this. If we are working on classical text, the need for this music is more apparent: but modern text too has its own rhythm, sound and texture. This sense of cadence has to do with variety of intonation within the phrasing, but it also has to do with the music of the whole, and the way the argument builds through a speech and through a whole scene. So we have to do exercises to stretch the voice and increase our range – and also to feel comfortable and right with it.

These are the basic requirements, but there is much more skill needed. The actor's job is to use language as well as possible in order to make the fullest impact on the hearer: to make it 'remarkable', to quote BRECHT. Just as, in everyday life, how someone expresses themselves is part of that person's character, so in a play the character's language is intrinsic to the motive and emotion of that character: we measure the character by the language, for language is always a choice. The actor has to inhabit words other than their own and yet make them their own. The actor has to become very sensitive to what the language is doing, how the phrases and rhythm work, whether it is smooth or broken up – and above all, we have to be alive to the imagery: all these are keys to the nature of the character, and are an intrinsic part of the fabric of the writing.

A steady stream of articles and books on the subject of elocution and the speaking voice has been produced since the early nineteenth century, and research into the physiology of the voice and into acoustics was well under way by 1855. The first great voice teacher who turned his attention to the needs of the actor as opposed to the needs of the singer, Gustave Garcia, joined the staff of the Royal Academy of Music in 1865: he may have been the first teacher to establish a system of work for the actor's voice.

Class has always played a large part in our choice of speech styles, for what has been accepted as 'good' speech has always been what is seen to be 'educated' English, so that rich and musical regional accents have not been accepted in mainstream drama, except when specifically asked for in the text. In the United States a 'mid-Atlantic' speech was developed, again representing what was accepted as 'educated' speech. This has been profoundly detrimental; Shakespeare, for example, was not written in what has come to be accepted as Received Pronunciation, or RP as we now know it, and we have consequently lost much of the muscular richness and music which is in the writing. In training for the stage, much emphasis was put on the 'voice beautiful', based on sound rather than matter, and on rhetorical styles of acting. This idea of the 'voice beautiful', subtly allied to upper-class speech, became irretrievably linked with good stage speech: this concept of speech in the theatre did not alter radically until the 1950s, when new writing changed what we expected from the theatre, and what we wanted to hear.

There were those who were actively opposed to the idea of the 'voice beautiful' and all the connotations of gesture and declamation with which it was associated. WILLIAM POEL, who founded the Elizabethan Stage Society in 1895, aimed to produce the plays of Shakespeare and his contemporaries with the minimum of scenery, to make people listen to the words rather than attend to the effects. He was very conscious that, while honouring the poetry, the voice should sound as natural as possible. This in itself was quite radical. Perhaps his most famous adherent was EDITH EVANS, whose voice was wonderfully musical, yet never rhetorical or over-emotional in performance. However, the technique was still to do with singing rather than speaking.

Perhaps the most important development in voice and voice training in the twentieth century was when ELSIE FOGERTY established a school where the training of the speaking voice was of primary concern in its own right and not necessarily related to singing. Her concern was with the training of the actor's voice, and that this should be backed up as much as possible by scientific research: this, in its way, was revolutionary. The school was the Central School of Speech Training and Dramatic Art, and it became one of the major drama schools in Britain.

Her work at the Central School was carried on by Gwynneth Thurburn, another woman of strength and charisma: she also had great influence on actors of her generation, including LAURENCE OLIVIER, whom she taught, and who was perhaps the first great classical actor to break completely from the singing mode to find a new style of speaking Shakespeare. Her influence was by no means confined to actors, for under her guidance both the speech therapy and the teacher training courses at the Central School flourished: and so her approach was carried through, not only into acting schools throughout Britain, but also into wider areas of education. As a result, many excellent voice teachers emerged in the period just after the war – Iris Warren, Clifford Turner and Kate Fleming, to name a few.

Parallel to all this was the important work of Daniel Jones, who pioneered research into phonetics in the English language, and through that a properly analysed approach to dialects, the knowledge of which was essential both for voice teachers and actors.

All this happened just at the right time, for at the end of the 1940s and in the 1950s there were radical changes in dramatic writing. In the United States, the plays of MILLER, WILLIAMS and others coincided with a new impulse and style of acting. Under great teachers and directors such as BERGHOF, CLURMAN and KAZAN the emphasis was on finding the physical attributes of a character, on inter-character relations and the motivation of a scene: communication through language became in a way secondary. In Britain in the 1950s, playwrights demanded a new kind of realism, different in kind from the American one, in that the emphasis was still very much on text, for always there was a discovery through language, even if that discovery was through an evasion of feeling rather than being verbally explicit. It demanded an ear for the demotic speech, and for naturalistic speech rhythms. This was endorsed by television and film writing, where actors needed to sound as 'of the street' as possible.

Good modern theatre writing, nevertheless, demands more than just a naturalistic 'throw-away' delivery: the very fact that it is being spoken in a theatre requires a certain poise and style in the speaking, for the language is still a choice, and characters are defining themselves through the words. Actors therefore have to be aware of these differences, and must respond to them.

The audience tuned in differently to stage speech; rhetorical styles were no longer acceptable, and, except for high WEST END comedy, a new kind of naturalism became appropriate. Dialects were used seriously, not just for comic relief, though 'Received Pronunciation' was still a requirement for the classics: that tradition has been hard to break. However, the actor who has worked consistently in modern work, and in television and film, now quite often finds it difficult to fulfil the demands of a classical text, where the feelings are explicit in the language, where the shaping and pointing of phrases is important, and where there is a delight in being articulate. PETER BROOK's 1970 production of *A Midsummer Night's Dream* was a landmark, in that he walked the tightrope between the formality of the verse and a naturalistic way of speaking.

As styles of writing and speaking in the theatre are changing all the time, so are the demands and expectations of the audience and consequently teaching methods. Increasingly the voice expert is asked in to work on productions. In the ROYAL SHAKESPEARE COMPANY this work is central to its philosophy, and many regional and experimental companies employ voice teachers as and when their budgets permit. Training of voice teachers has also improved. In the United States, the work of Arthur Lessac and KRISTIN LINKLATER – a protégée of Iris Warren – has had considerable influence on the work of the theatre there.

There remain constant challenges. For example, there has to be a neutral stage accent which everyone can use and which is recognizable as such to give a unity to a production, unless there are specific demands otherwise. This is the case in Britain, and in the United States and elsewhere; it was initiated and refined by the famous voice teacher Edith Skumez, whose analysis of stage speech is accepted and taught in acting schools and conservatoires all over the United States. However, any standardization of accent tends to take away the vitality of the language, and makes it sound careful. The theatre has to be more open to change in this area.

The actor has to find his or her own entry into the truth of the character, while at the same time honouring the form of the writing, i.e. the imagery, the rhythm and the cadence in the language. This is a complex mix in that it involves both a subjective and an objective response to one's own voice. Language therefore has to be practised in order that the actor feels the confidence and freedom to explore the possibilities of the text so that it can make the fullest impact on the hearer – for words are always active and can both inspire and provoke the listener. The actor and voice teacher must never underestimate the primitive delight people have when listening to language which is being fulfilled by the speaker; that pleasure must be preserved, and through that the intention and meaning of the text will be made inescapable.

CICELY BERRY

1950. During the 1930s two important voice teachers were Iris Warren and Bertie Scott. Neither came from the Fogerty tradition. Scott was an Irish singer who later developed an interest in the spoken voice. TYRONE GUTHRIE brought him to London in 1937 to work with the actors at the OLD VIC. He also taught at the London Theatre School started by MICHEL SAINT-DENIS, who, in his book *Training for the Theatre* (1982), displays an integrated attitude to voice and body.

Warren was also teaching at the LTS. Her work was more concerned with the unity of mind and body, and her approach was more psycho-physical than that of her contemporaries. She taught at RADA for a time and later went on to work at the London Academy of Music and Dramatic Art. During her career she worked with the ROYAL SHAKESPEARE COMPANY as well as spending time with the Shakespeare Company in Ontario, Canada. She never published, but her student KRISTIN LINKLATER developed her principles and has been working in the United States since the 1960s. Linklater's book *Freeing the Natural Voice* (1976) gives a clear indication of Warren's methodology, and she has become one of the major influences in both America and Britain.

Voice teaching methods that have moved away from the traditional style and have won a following are the 'sinus tone' method of Ernest White and the vocally liberating work of ROY HART, which grew out of ALFRED WOLFSOHN's pursuit of the eight-octave voice. The singing-based work of Jo Estill has had some influence. The major British influence since the 1970s has been CICELY BERRY, who was trained at the Central School of Speech and Drama during Gwynneth Thurburn's time and was later a teacher there, before becoming voice director of the RSC where she established the first permanent voice department attached to a theatre company.

The training of voice teachers in Britain is eclectic and almost entirely undertaken through the Master's Degree or Postgraduate Diploma in Voice Studies offered by the Central School of Speech and Drama. The course developed from the Advanced Diploma in Voice Studies which was established in 1984 and grew out of the Central School's long tradition of voice teaching. In the United States, training is largely through courses run by specialist institutions offering individual methodologies, such as those of Arthur Lessac and Kristin Linklater. Most training is given regularly over a period of three years, is specifically for the theatre and complements the other skills an actor strives to develop. It should be integrated with acting style and technique and not taught in isolation. Aspects of voice training include physical work on release of restricting tensions, postural alignment, efficiency of effort, rhythm, spontaneity, flexibility and the ability to work away from habitual personal patterns. The teaching should aim to bring together the actor's physical, interpretive and communicative skills. Vocal exercises should relate to actors' intentions and be focused rather than concerned with the development of an attractive but uncommitted sound. Above all, the actor must develop an easy relationship to the delivery of all aspects of language and text.

Specialist training is usually offered in the area of dialect and accent, and instruction is given by specialist teachers. The ability to produce speech in an accent and/or dialect as required by a text is desirable as it offers the actor greater flexibility and opportunity in character terms. Some texts depend on the reproduction of the sounds and rhythms in order to create the sound-scape of the region of period. Status and the political contexts of plays can be effectively defined by the use of accents, but the conventional idea that in Shakespeare and the classics, the characters of the upper echelons should be played in Received Pronunciation, while the clowns and servants should be played in rural accents, has become generally outdated. A phonetician who greatly influenced the teaching of accent and dialect was Daniel Jones (1881–1967), who was professor of phonetics at University College London and wrote *The English Pronouncing Dictionary*, published in 1927. (Its 15th edition was printed in 1997.) At first he described the speech of the privately educated southern English and referred to the model as Public School Pronunciation; by 1926 he had started to use the term 'Received Pronunciation' (RP). In Britain, the introduction of educational grants after the Second World War meant that many more working-class actors trained in the drama schools, and this eventually led to the teaching of Received Pronunciation as an accent to allow the actor greater vocal flexibility and style choices, rather than its imposition as the required sound.

An actor's ability successfully to produce an accent depends on the accuracy of their ear, their ability to distinguish the minutiae of vowel shifts and consonant placement as well as the intonation and musical pattern of the phrase. Teaching dialect and accent often involves the teaching of the international phonetic alphabet, which allows the actor to relate sounds to symbols. It also often examines the physical placement and feel of an accent, the way the tongue is held in the mouth, the tension in the lips and the placement of the resonance. Consideration is given to the drive and energy of the speech and the socio-political and geographical elements that may influence the accent.

LYN DARNLEY

See also ACTING; DRAMA SCHOOLS; PHYSICAL PREPARATION; REHEARSAL.

W. A. Aiken, *The Voice: An Introduction to Practical Phonology* (1937)
Cicely Berry, *Voice and the Actor* (1973)
——, *The Actor and the Text* (1987)
Elsie Fogerty, *The Speaking of English Verse* (1923)
——, trans., *The Art of the Actor Cocquelin* (1932)
Gustava Garcia, *The Actor's Art: A Practical Treatise of Stage Declamation, Public Speaking and Deportment, for the Use of Artists, Students And Amateurs* (1882)
Arthur Lessac, *The Use and Training of the Human Voice* (1967)
Kristin Linklater, *Freeing the Natural Voice* (1976)
Gwynneth Thurburn, *Voice and Speech* (1939)
Ernest G. White, *The Voice Beautiful in Speech and Song* (1922)

Volcano Theatre Founded in 1987 and one of the hottest and most prolific performance groups of the 1990s, this Swansea-based company from the outset differed from most other 'physical' theatre practitioners by having a strong textual element in their ultra-political work. They started out as graduates emulating the style and work of STEVEN BERKOFF but, after a contretemps with their erstwhile hero, rapidly developed their own distinctive style in such controversial shows as *V* (1990), based on TONY HARRISON's poem, and *Medea Sex War* (1991), which utilized the extreme feminism of SCUM (the Society for Cutting Up Men, founded by Valerie Solanas, would-be assassin of Andy Warhol and author of the notorious SCUM manifesto). Their interest in the role of the performer and in deconstruction theory, harnessed to a rather academic socialism, enabled them to capture that end of the cultural zeitgeist, and they attracted a strong young radical following as they toured the arts centres of the UK and soon were taken up by the European festival circuit. With their interest in challenging the established canon, they made exciting productions from such unlikely sources as Marx and Engels (*Manifesto*, 1992), Shakespeare's sonnets (*L.O.V.E.*, 1992), Baudrillard and Nietzsche (*After the Orgy*, 1994), IBSEN (*How To Live*, 1995) and DYLAN THOMAS (*Under Milk Wood/The Town That Went Mad*, 1998). Director Paul Davies (who along with Fern Smith and Andrew Jones make up Volcano) also wrote *Vagina Dentata* (1996) and *Moments of Madness* (2000) for the company.

Their latest move is to take contemporary classics and present them without departing from the script but from a new perspective – ALAN AYCKBOURN's *The Time of My Life* (1998) thus became an even darker comedy and a more incisive critique of modern capitalism and its denial of happiness. DAVID ADAMS

Volksbühne (People's Stage) Originally Freie Volksbühne (Free People's Stage). Theatrical production and membership organization founded in Berlin in 1890, when members of a workers' club sought affiliation to the FREIE BÜHNE and instead formed Freie Volksbühne, devoted to making theatre available to the working classes, under the slogan 'Art for the People'. In 1914 it opened its own theatre, which became one of the most influential venues in Berlin. By 1930 the movement had grown to over 300 local groups wielding considerable cultural power. It had promoted the work of writers such as TOLLER and SHAW and directors like PISCATOR and REINHARDT, and had established an education programme and journals. The Volksbühne was closed by the Nazis in 1939, but reopened in 1947. In East Germany, it ceased to be a movement and as a theatre became best known for the work of the director BENNO BESSON. In West Germany, the movement continued and the Freie Volksbühne was recreated, moving to a new Berlin theatre under Piscator in 1963. IAN SAVILLE

Cecil Davies, *The Volksbühne Movement: A History* (2000)

Vollmer, Lula (b. Keyser, NC, 1898; d. New York, 2 May 1955) Playwright. One of the first Americans devoted entirely to the native folk play, she wrote about the mountain people among whom she grew up. Her best plays were *Sun-Up* and *The Shame Woman* (both 1923). Later, less successful works included *The Dunce Boy* (1927), *Trigger* (1928) and *The Hill Between* (1938). GERALD BORDMAN

Volodin, Alexander [Moiseyevich] [A. M. Lifshits] (b. Minsk, Russia, 10 Feb. 1919) Playwright. He came to prominence in 1957 with *Fabrichnaya devchonka* (*The Factory Girl*), in which the villain is a Young Communist. His *Pyat' vecherov* (*Five Evenings*, 1959), a simple love story, was admired both for its content and its technique, and gained him a wider, international audience. NICK WORRALL

Harold B. Segel, *Twentieth-Century Russian Drama* (1979)

Voskovec, Jiří [Wachsmann] (b. Sázava-Budy, Bohemia [now Czech Republic], 19 June 1905; d. Pear Blossom, Cal., 1 July 1981) and **Werich, Jan** (b. Prague, 6 Feb. 1905; d. Prague, 31 Oct. 1980) Actors and playwrights; creators of the famous Osvobozené divadlo (the Liberated Theatre). Inspired by silent film figures and circus clowns, this duo transformed what was originally an AVANT-GARDE theatre into an extremely popular satirical theatre. At first they were exponents of a non-traditional 'liberated' laughter, based on DADA and poetry (*Vest Pocket Revue*, 1927), but later they gradually became satirists who overtly attacked totalitarianism, fascism and war (beginning with the variety play *Caesar*, 1932). As playwrights they developed a specific form of variety theatre using the forestage to express their opinions on current affairs. It was here that their extraordinary ability to improvise became famous. They co-authored all the plays performed at the Osvobozené divadlo until it was closed down by the Nazis in 1938. Voskovec and Werich emigrated to the United States. After the Second World War, in 1946 they opened their own theatre in Prague again, where they staged such works as *The Finian's Rainbow* (1947). Their work together was abandoned when Voskovec left Czechoslovakia in 1948 to return to the United States after spending some time in Paris. EVA ŠORMOVÁ

Vysotsky, Vladimir *see* LYUBIMOV, YURI; TAGANKA THEATRE

W

Wagner, Robin (b. San Francisco, 31 Aug. 1933) Stage designer. He studied at the California School of Fine Arts and did his first design work for the San Francisco ACTOR'S WORKSHOP. Over the years he has refined and perfected a minimal style of set design, best demonstrated in his striking use of mirrors in the finale of *A Chorus Line* (1975). He has worked on many London and BROADWAY musicals such as *Hair, Crazy for You, City of Angels, Chess, Song and Dance, Dreamgirls, 42nd Street* and *Jelly's Last Jam*. He has also designed sets for the American Ballet Theater and the New York City Ballet, and his versatility is demonstrated by his ability to design both for opera and for the 1975 Rolling Stones tour of the Americas. HELEN RAPPAPORT

Wagner, Wieland (b. Bayreuth, 5 Jan. 1917; d. Munich, 10 Oct. 1966) Director and designer, grandson of Richard Wagner and director of the BAYREUTH Festival after 1951. Beginning with the *Ring* cycle in 1952, Wieland revolutionized the staging of Wagnerian opera, rejecting the traditional realistic approach in favour of abstract settings and symbolic lighting based on the approach of APPIA. He also staged Wagnerian opera in Stuttgart, Vienna, Palermo, Edinburgh, Belgium and the Netherlands, and with his wife Gertrude as choreographer applied the new staging style to operatic works of Gluck, Beethoven, Orff, Bizet and Verdi. MARVIN CARLSON

Wajda, Andrzej *see* POLAND

Walcott, Derek [Alton] (b. Castries, St Lucia, 23 Jan. 1930) Poet and playwright. His first published play, *Henri Christophe* (1950), was performed by the St Lucia Arts Guild, which he founded with his twin brother Roderick (1930–2000), also a playwright and director.

Other early plays were produced by Derek at the University of the West Indies, Jamaica, while he was studying there. While working as a teacher and art critic he devoted his spare time to setting up the TRINIDAD THEATRE WORKSHOP (1959), which he ran for nearly 20 years, directing his prolific output and touring with the company to North America. Unlike ERROL HILL, Walcott believes the typical Caribbean play form to be the musical rather than CARNIVAL theatre. Among his plays are *Ti Jean and His Brothers* (1957), *Dream on Monkey Mountain* (1967, performed in 1971 by the NEGRO ENSEMBLE in New York), *O, Babylon* (1976), *Remembrance* (1977) and *The Odyssey* (1992, performed by the ROYAL SHAKESPEARE COMPANY). Since the 1980s Walcott has concentrated more on poetry and often works in the United States. He is a writer of international stature, the recipient of many awards, including the Nobel Prize in 1992. KOLE OMOTOSO

Edward Baugh, *Derek Walcott: Memory as Vision* (1978)
Robert D. Hammer, *Derek Walcott* (1981)
Bruce King, *Derek Walcott and West Indian Drama* (1995)

Wales It may come as something of a shock to realize that while there may have been professional theatre in Wales for centuries, Welsh professional theatre is a relatively new cultural phenomenon and certainly no older than the twentieth century. The Welsh Theatre Company, with its later and longer-lasting Welsh-language arm Cwmni Theatr Cymru, was initiated by the Welsh Committee for the Arts in 1962: hitherto there had been only amateurs alongside imported touring English and Irish work.

There is possibly a half-hidden tradition of performance whose vestiges are found in folk customs. There are some medieval plays extant in Welsh, and a Welsh version of the Troilus and Cressida drama; there were also itinerant groups of semi-professionals at the end of the eighteenth century, but they flourished for less than 50 years. For much of the twentieth century, drama, like most Welsh culture locked into a robust amateur tradition, was linked to the NATIONAL EIS-TEDDFOD and the LITTLE THEATRE companies. Some of the latter paid their part-time actors, but they were not professional in the sense we would recognize and in any event all but disappeared after the Second World War. There were Welsh dramatists writing in English and Welsh, but they were not producing work for Welsh professional stage performers. Whether we regard the amateur–professional distinction simply as a nicety or as a defining characteristic, there was unquestionably nothing one can describe as a Welsh theatre prior to the 1960s. 'We are the only country in the world,' admitted Wilbert Lloyd Roberts, director of Cwmni Theatr Cymru, 'where television came before theatre.'

Welsh theatre is thus an invention of the late twentieth century. This explains much about the kind of theatre found in Wales – a practice that owes nothing to tradition because there was no tradition. It has evolved into a unique mixture of community-based provision, English-style mainstream productions and non-literary experimental work. There is also the emergence of a distinctively Welsh form of what has been called syncretic theatre – theatre that adapts and subverts the dominant, naturalistic mainstage English model to create something new and distinctive to the culture. However, the future of Welsh theatre hangs in the balance as proposals from the Arts Council of Wales are radically changing existing provision.

For the first half of the twentieth century there was little, if anything, that might be called indigenous Welsh theatre. There were some famous names: Richard Hughes, EMLYN WILLIAMS, DYLAN THOMAS, GWYN THOMAS and the controversial SAUNDERS LEWIS, a Liverpudlian who spoke and wrote in Welsh and was a fiery activist on behalf of Welsh nationalism – and the issues of language and nationalism are interwoven in the fabric of contemporary Welsh theatre.

The national theatre debate bubbled away throughout the century, after Lloyd George championed the idea of an indigenous Welsh drama at the 1902 Eisteddfod, and it has surfaced at moments when nationalism was fashionable rather than when theatre was strong. Lord Howard de Walden, an English émigré, led various incarnations of a national theatre company before and after the First World War. Saunders Lewis

and the newly formed nationalist Plaid Cymru championed the cause in the 1930s. In the 1960s, when Gwynfor Evans became Plaid's first MP, the movement won new followers and almost became a reality with the publicly funded Welsh Theatre Company – but, crucially, without a permanent base. In the 1990s the campaign inevitably found a new lease of life, led by MICHAEL BOGDANOV. Despite his assumed east European name and international reputation, Bogdanov reidentified himself as a born-again Welshman (he was born to a Dr Bogden in Neath) understandably frustrated with the lack of any real professional structure in the land of his birth. But for most practitioners the question of a national theatre is irrelevant, at best a diversion and at worst an elitist conspiracy to channel funding into a large company at the expense of the 30-odd smaller ones which claim they constitute the real national theatre of Wales.

The national theatre campaigners have tended to forget, or be ignorant of, what happens on the ground. They concentrate on only one form of theatre: mainstream literary drama, the sort that has dominated England since Shakespeare but a convention that has not exactly flourished in Wales, despite getting the lion's share of public funding. After the Welsh Theatre Company (1962–78) and Cwmni Theatr Cymru (1965–84), both of which suffered a painfully long-drawn-out demise, there was the bilingual Theatr yr Ymylon (1972–7), praised for its adventurousness but destroyed by its lack of organization, and Theatre Wales (1980–7), dismissively referred to at the time as Theatre 125 because it seemed to depend on London talent dashing to Cardiff and back on the new Intercity 125 train – all aspiring to be the National Theatre of Wales. In literary drama, the leading new-writing company Made in Wales (1981–2000) failed, under both Gilly Adams and more recently Jeff Teare, to make a major impact either in or outside Wales, despite promoting promising work by Alan Osborne, Dic Edwards, Peter Lloyd, Larry Allan and Roger Williams. Hwyl a Fflag (1984–94), the Welsh-language new-writing community-based company, and Dalier Sylw (founded 1988; since 2000, renamed Sgript Cymru and funded as the only new-writing company) are, or were, probably more successful at doing a similar job mainly in the Welsh language, but neither was a conventional main-stage company. There are four production houses – THEATR CLWYD (founded 1976) at Mold in the north-east; Bangor's Theatr Gwynedd (built in 1975 and with its own company since 1985) in the north-west; the Milford Haven Torch (1977) in the south-west; and the Sherman (built 1973, with its own company from 1985) in Cardiff, in the south-east – and all of them have always had both financial and artistic problems. Indeed, the core of the Arts Council of Wales's drama strategy published in 1999 was about mainstream provision, proposing English- and Welsh-language national performing arts companies. Theatr Clwyd, based a few miles from Chester, is generally regarded as attracting its audience from England; Gwynedd, producing only Welsh-language work, recovered in the 1990s but suffers from the dearth of material; the Torch mounts only its own productions, a few times a year, and has no urban or student population to draw on; and the Sherman suffers from a lack of identity, with a brief to concentrate on young people, although it did develop a refreshingly open house-style based on community-theatre techniques when director Phil Clark arrived in 1989, encouraging new writing and offering professional productions of work by the Rhondda-based playwright Frank Vickery, whose work formerly focused on the amateur theatre. Welsh writers often still prefer to follow the footsteps of Gwyn Thomas, Emlyn Williams, Dannie Abse, PETER GILL and Sean Matthias and move to London; others simply absconded to the well-paid pastures of Welsh television.

Despite this lack of tradition, it was perhaps understandable that the embryo Welsh Arts Council (from 1953 to 1967 the Welsh Committee of the ARTS COUNCIL OF GREAT BRITAIN) decided in the 1950s that its first step towards introducing professional theatre to Wales should be the manufacture of a company, even though in 1962 it had no theatre buildings to play in and no known audiences to play to; the second step was to set up the buildings, in many cases in collaboration with universities and local authorities, starting with Theatr y Werin in Aberystwyth in 1972. But the third step was the one really to kick-start Welsh theatre: the creation of a network of small companies in every county (eight of them at that time) that would take small-scale theatre to non-theatre venues and also offer a THEATRE IN EDUCATION (TIE) service. Theatr Powys (1973) was the first and is still the largest. Within a decade Wales had a TIE and COMMUNITY THEATRE provision that was the envy of many other cultures that had enjoyed a centuries-old theatre tradition. The unique Hijinx Theatre (founded 1981), with its commitment to audiences with learning difficulties, came out of this TIE/community movement and still can call on a core of some of the best Welsh-based directors, actors and technicians. The TIE companies also produced many of the admittedly small band of Welsh playwrights: Greg Cullen, Charlie Way, Dic Edwards, Laurence Allan and Lucy Gough are all still associated with TIE/community work. The emphasis given to work with young people has also seen the emergence of Mid Powys

Youth Theatre (founded 1988) on the one hand and a range of companies playing to young people like Green Ginger (1978) and Small World (1992) on the other. At the end of the century, however, TIE/community provision was threatened by the withdrawal of funds triggered by local government reorganization in 1996 and the restructuring of the Arts Council of Wales two years later. TIE/community theatre companies were victims of ACW's 1999 new drama strategy, to be replaced by four franchised Young People's Theatre companies, although they won a temporary reprieve after public protests in 1999–2000.

The third strand of theatre practice was one that could not be planned: the organic growth of small companies that depended on the unpredictable mix of practitioners, economics, politics, audiences and history. It may indeed have been a resistance to the very idea of 'planned provision' that led to the creation in the 1970s of companies like CARDIFF LABORATORY THEATRE (1974), PAUPERS CARNIVAL (1976) and Theatr Bara Caws (1976), and the relocation from London to Cardiff in 1972 of MOVING BEING; all of these did the groundwork for what has developed into a distinctively different Welsh theatre scene. This now includes BRITH GOF, Man Act, Centre for Performance Research and the MAGDALENA PROJECT, all with their roots in Cardiff Lab; Sgript Cymru and the various new dance and performance groups who owe so much to Geoff Moore's Moving Being; and VOLCANO THEATRE and Frantic Assembly, whose unique styles were developed and encouraged in a theatrical climate sympathetic to experiment and radical non-naturalism. ELAN (European Live Arts Network) Wales is a unique Cardiff company under the direction of Italian Firenza Guidi that mounts often stunning community-based 'montages' in Wales and throughout Europe. Other small groups that flourished intermittently in the last decade of the century include the all-women Alma Theatre and Y Gymraes, NoFit State Circus, Thin Language, Theatrig, Theatr Y Byd, Mappa Mundi, U-Man Zoo, Good Cop Bad Cop, Beyond the Border, Wales Actors Company, Castaway, Scala Review, and projects based on the performance talents of such as Eddie Ladd, Marc Rees and Sean Tuan John.

Finally, there is an English-language Welsh theatre that has been labelled syncretic theatre, a term that comes from postcolonial theory and suggests a form of performance that is basically the 'colonized' culture's appropriation of the imposed dominant form (English-style literary theatre) and the indigenous tweaking thereof to create a form that may seem to be English but which is in fact decidedly un-English and indeed distinctively Welsh. Such allegedly syncretic theatre may be seen in the plays of ED THOMAS (with his company Fiction Factory, formerly Y Cwmni) and Ian Rowlands (with his Theatr Y Byd), both of whom subvert recognizable naturalistic theatre by using Welsh language forms and rhythms, Welsh cultural references, Welsh political issues and an aggressively anti-naturalistic style. It has its roots in the attempts by J. O. Francis (e.g. *Change*, 1913), Caradoc Evans (*Taffy*, 1923) and Dylan Thomas (*Under Milk Wood*, 1953) to create an Anglo-Welsh (albeit a much despised term) language, and perhaps also to the work of Welsh-language playwrights like Gwenllyn Parry (*Y Twr*, 1978). Not unexpectedly, English critics have not warmed to Welsh theatre: Ed Thomas's *Gas Station Angel* (1998), commissioned by the ROYAL COURT, though well received in Wales and on the European continent, generally incensed the traditional English press, who found it wordy and whimsical, and unleashed a torrent of racist stereotyping.

The word 'Welsh' is used here mostly to describe practitioners in either of the two main languages of Wales, although there is to a great extent separate development. Such indigenous theatrical tradition as can be claimed is, of course, in Welsh, although only a minority now speak the language. There was for years a ring-fenced funding allocation by the Arts Council of Wales for Welsh-language theatre as part of its commitment to the language, and there are some interesting playwrights who work entirely (Meic Povey and Gareth Miles, notably) or mainly (Sion Eirian) in Welsh; but by common assent the quality and consistency of production are affected by the drawing power of more lucrative Welsh-language television work which attracts writers, directors and actors away from live theatre. Perhaps inevitably, Welsh-language theatre has struggled to achieve a profile as high as the English-language or bilingual companies. Brith Gof perform more in Welsh than in English; but their pedagogic, conceptual, GROTOWSKI-influenced theatre communicates regardless of language: a smattering of postmodernist theory is more useful than Welsh. None of the purely Welsh-language companies looks secure – Cwmni Theatr Cymru folded in financial chaos in 1983, Cwmni Cyfri Tri and Theatr Crwban merged into Arad Goch in 1985, Whare Teg (founded 1984) became Cwmni Mega, which staggers along with little or no funding, Hwyl a Fflag lost its grant in 1994. The success of Sgript Cymru relies on the variable quality of the new plays it produces. Theatr Clwyd under TERRY HANDS worked a neat bit of image manipulation by renaming itself Clwyd Theatr Cymru and producing a Welsh-language programme alongside its glossier English work, but it still has to win the hearts of Welsh audiences. The Welsh-language National Performing Arts Company proposed by the Arts Council of Wales's 1999 drama strategy, initially in the form of a merger of Theatr Gwynedd and Bara Caws, would be expected to develop and deliver work for Welsh-speaking audiences throughout Wales. On the smaller scale, Sera Moore-Williams's Y Gymraes (founded in 1992) may look the best hope for the future.

Welsh theatre in both languages, despite being diverse, different and unpredictable, is virtually invisible in the rest of the UK, although it exports well to Europe. It is unclear how much of this practice and provision will survive. The new Welsh Assembly; a new strategy from a restructured Arts Council of Wales, which drastically reduced its portfolio of 20 revenue-funded companies by half at the start of the twenty-first century; a Millennium Centre for the Performing Arts due to open in Cardiff Bay; a new generation of writers, actors and directors who can be seduced into television rather than the stage – all hold the key to whether Welsh theatre will build on its first 40 years or will turn out to be a remarkable but relatively brief flash in the pan. DAVID ADAMS

Walker, George F[rederick] (b. Toronto, 23 Aug. 1947) Playwright. Early plays like *Bagdad Saloon* (1973), *Beyond Mozambique* (1974) and *Ramona and the White Slaves* (1976) reveal Walker's interest in MELODRAMA, the B-movie and ABSURDIST theatre; his persistent theme is the nature of evil. *Zastrozzi* (1977) is an amalgam of those elements that characterize Walker's style – parody, melodrama, swashbuckling theatricality, and a sending up of other genres such as the revenge tragedy. *Gossip* (1977), a more accessible play than any of the early period, introduces the political reporter Tyrone Power, who returns in *Filthy Rich* (1979) and *The Art of War* (1983). In *Criminals in Love* (1984), Walker exploits his urban Toronto roots in a farcical variation of his criminality–morality theme. Other Toronto or 'East End' plays include *Better Living* (1986), *Beautiful City* (1987) and the highly successful comedy *Love and Anger* (1989). Plays of the 1990s include *Escape from Happiness* (1991) and *Tough!* (1994).
EUGENE BENSON

Walkley, A[rthur] B[ingham] (b. Bristol, 17 Feb. 1855; d. Tendring, Essex, 8 Oct. 1926) Drama critic, noted for his 16-year stint at *The Times* from 1910. His unusually academic and literary approach gave rise to criticism that dealt more with the text of a play than the production or the actors. His characteristic conscientiousness and erudition were satirized by SHAW in the character of Mr Trotter in *Fanny's First Play* (1911).

Several volumes of his collected criticism have been published. ADRIANA HUNTER

Wall, Max [Maxwell George Lorimer] (b. London, 12 March 1908; d. London, 22 May 1990) Actor and comedian. He began in the 1920s as an eccentric dancer in VARIETY, going on to appear in REVUES and musical comedies including *Bow Bells* (1932) and *Panama Hattie* (1943) after being invalided out of the RAF. Later he moved to character roles; Père Ubu in *Ubu Roi* (1966), Archie Rice in *The Entertainer* (1974) and two notable BECKETT performances: Krapp in *Krapp's Last Tape* (1976) and Vladimir in *Waiting for Godot* (1981). Famous for his elastic face and voice, a funny walk in undersized jacket and trousers, and a curious hint of turmoil beneath a deadpan exterior, he created the character of Professor Wallofski and often performed the solo *Aspects of Max Wall* (1974). His autobiography, *The Fool on the Hill*, appeared in 1975. REXTON S. BUNNETT

Wallace, Naomi (b. Louisville, Ky., 17 Aug. 1960) Playwright. She initially gained recognition in London (at the BUSH THEATRE and the ROYAL SHAKESPEARE COMPANY). She describes the theatre as a space for resistance; her plays interweave issues of class, sexuality and power, and force a confrontation between haunting poetry and political social realism. *In the Heart of America* (1994) is set during the Gulf War; *One Flea Spare* (1995) takes place amid the social upheaval wrought by the plague in seventeenth-century England. Its New York première (1997) received the Obie award for best play. *Slaughter City* (1996) uses Brechtian techniques to examine class relations during a strike at a slaughterhouse. *The Trestle at Pope Lick Creek* (1998), set in Depression-era Kentucky, reflects her conviction that the past is always present. SARAH STEVENSON

J. Palmarini, 'Power and Poetry: Playwright Naomi Wallace's Challenge to Mainstream Theatre', *Dramatics*, May 1998

N. Wallace, 'Poetry, Plays, Politics, and Shifting Geographies', in Robert Vorlicky, ed., *Conversations with Tony Kushner* (1998)

Wallace, Nellie [Eleanor Jane] (b. Glasgow, 18 March 1870; d. London, 24 Nov. 1948) MUSIC HALL comedienne who first appeared as a clog dancer. After touring as one of the Three Sisters Wallace and in a theatre troupe, she went solo in music halls and became a star with the billing 'the Essence of Eccentricity'. She appeared in PANTOMIMES (and, unusually for a woman, was successful as a DAME) and REVUES, including *The Whirl of the World* (1924), *Sky High* (1925) and *All Fit* (1928). REXTON S. BUNNETT

Wallach, Eli (b. Brooklyn, New York, 7 Dec. 1915) Actor. An exemplar of the ACTORS' STUDIO or METHOD style of acting, he has taken major stage roles in *The Rose Tattoo* (1951), *Camino Real* (1953), *Major Barbara* (1956), *The Chairs* (1958), *Cafe Crown* (1988) and *The Price* (1992). He has often appeared on stage and film with his wife Anne Jackson (b. 1926), in such shows as *Rhinoceros* (1961), *The Tiger and The Typists* (1963), *Luv* (1964) and *Twice Around the Park* (1982). He enjoyed a late-career success with the Off-Broadway comedy *Visiting Mr Green* (1997). DAVID BARBOUR

Waller, Lewis [William Waller Lewis] (b. Bilbao, Spain, 3 Nov. 1860; d. Nottingham, 1 Nov. 1915) Actor–manager; one of the great matinée idols. He was so popular that women banded into a club known as the K.O.W (keen on Waller) brigade. Waller possessed a dynamic and powerful voice along with handsome looks that were used to best advantage in heroic costume dramas which he played with his wife Florence West (1862–1912). He was much admired for his performances as d'Artagnan in *The Three Musketeers* (1898) and in the title role of *Monsieur Beaucaire* (1902). He produced and acted in WILDE's *An Ideal Husband* (1895), and managed the Imperial and the Lyric. His portrayals of Brutus, Faulconbridge (*King John*), Hotspur and especially Henry V were his most famous Shakespearean roles. BARRY YZEREEF

Walls, Tom [Kirby] (b. Kingsthorpe, Northants, 18 Feb. 1883; d. Surrey, 27 Nov. 1949). Actor, director and producer. Walls specialized in musical comedy and FARCE, achieving great success in *Tons of Money* (1922), which he transferred to the ALDWYCH THEATRE in 1923, thus beginning a ten-year run of ALDWYCH FARCES by BEN TRAVERS. Walls starred in and produced them all; his roguish man-about-town persona perfectly offset his double-act partner Ralph Lynn's 'silly ass' character. He also ran three production companies and a repertory theatre. DAN REBELLATO

Walser, Martin [Johannes] (b. Wasserburg, Germany, 24 March 1927) Playwright and novelist who started out as a writer and director for television. Since 1960 he has produced a substantial dramatic output which oscillates between two poles represented by BRECHT and Kafka. His tragicomical treatment of West German society often verges on the grotesque and is strongly influenced by the THEATRE OF THE ABSURD. The most important plays of his earlier period are *Eiche and Angora* ('Oak tree and angora', 1962, also known as *The Rabbit Race*), *Überlebensgross Herr Krott* ('Death-resistant Mr Krott', 1963) and *Die Zimmerschlacht* ('Indoor battle', translated as *Home Front*, 1967).

Das Sauspiel ('Pig's game', 1975) and *Die Ohrfeige* ('Box on the ear', 1981), indicate a new move towards more realist forms of drama.   GÜNTER BERGHAUS

J. E. Schlunk and A. E. Armand, *Martin Walser: International Perspectives* (1987)
Anthony E. Wayne, *Martin Walser: The Development as Dramatist 1950–1970* (1978)

Walter, Harriet   (b. London, 24 Sept. 1950)   Actress, in some respects of archetypal Englishness: statuesque, with noble good looks, considerable intelligence and immense grace. After early days in alternative theatre with Common Stock, 7:84, PAINES PLOUGH and JOINT STOCK, she began a frutiful relationship with the ROYAL COURT, playing Ophelia in *Hamlet* (1980, CARYL CHURCHILL's *Cloud Nine* (1980), *The Seagull* (1981), *The Lucky Chance* (Aphra Behn's late seventeenth-century satire, which was the inaugural production of the Women's Playhouse Trust) and TIMBERLAKE WERTENBAKER's *Three Birds Alighting on a Field* (1991). For the ROYAL SHAKESPEARE COMPANY she performed in a range of classical and modern plays, including *All's Well that Ends Well* (1981), *Twelfth Night* (1987), HOWARD BARKER's *The Castle* (1985), *Three Sisters* (1988), *The Duchess of Malfi* (1989) and *Macbeth* (1999), as Lady Macbeth. At the NATIONAL THEATRE she appeared in TOM STOPPARD's *Arcadia* (1993) and scored another success in 2000 in YASMINA REZA's *Life × 3*. She has a blend of extreme vulnerability set against a determined severity. Above all, she possesses stillness and the paradoxical virtue of passionate reserve. In 1999 she published a book about acting, *Other People's Shoes*.   RICHARD EYRE
   See also WOMEN IN THEATRE.

Walton, Tony [Anthony John]   (b. Walton-on-Thames, Surrey, 24 Oct. 1934)   Set and costume designer. He has created sets and costumes for productions at the ROYAL NATIONAL THEATRE and in the WEST END, but is better known for his work in New York, on and off BROADWAY. Versatile and inventive, his prolific stage work includes *A Funny Thing Happened on the Way to the Forum* (1962), *Hurlyburly* (1984), *The House of Blue Leaves* (1986) and *She Loves Me* (1993). He has received three Tony awards (including scenic design for *Pippin*, 1972, and *Guys and Dolls*, 1992), a TV Emmy and an Academy award for *All That Jazz* (1979). He has also designed for opera and ballet in the United States, the UK and continental Europe.   ELLEN LAMPERT-GRÉAUX

Wanamaker, Sam   (b. Chicago, 14 June 1919; d. London, 18 Dec. 1993)   Actor, director and producer. Wanamaker came to Britain during the period of McCarthyite anti-communism in the United States,

and directed and starred in a number of successful productions including *The Big Knife* (1954) and *The Rainmaker* (1956). In early 1956 he directed an influential *Threepenny Opera* at the ROYAL COURT before taking over in the following year at the New Shakespeare Theatre in Liverpool, where he directed several new American plays including *Bus Stop*, *The Rose Tattoo* and *View from the Bridge*. He continued acting, performing an admired Iago in *Othello* (1959). In 1970 he became executive director of the Globe Playhouse Trust, campaigning to have built in London a working replica of Shakespeare's GLOBE; it was completed three years after his death. His daughter ZOE WANAMAKER is a noted actress.   DAN REBELLATO

Wanamaker, Zoe   (b. New York, 13 May 1949)   Actress. Her early career was spent in repertory theatre, including periods at the LEEDS Playhouse and the LYCEUM, Edinburgh, working with RICHARD EYRE in both. She subsequently followed him to the NOTTINGHAM Playhouse, where she was a leading member of his company. In 1976 she joined the ROYAL SHAKESPEARE COMPANY, where she remained for seven years, playing a wide range of roles including Toine in PAM GEMS' *Piaf*, which transferred to the West End and to New York. In 1989 she played Emilia in TREVOR NUNN's RSC production of *Othello*, in which she gave one of her richest, most assured performances. In 1997 she played Electra to great acclaim. She has worked extensively at the NATIONAL THEATRE, and in the 1990s became increasingly well known for a variety of fine television work. After the death of her father SAM WANAMAKER, she devoted considerable energy to the realization of his GLOBE THEATRE project. Her unusual looks and idiosyncratic style might have consigned her to a limited range of mainly comic roles, but her intelligence and imagination, combined with great technical skills, place her among the best and most versatile of her generation.   GENISTA MCINTOSH

Wandor, Michelene   *see*   GAY THEATRE;   LESBIAN THEATRE; WOMEN'S THEATRE; WOMEN'S THEATRE GROUP

Ward, Douglas Turner   (b. Burnside, Los Angeles, 5 May 1930)   Actor, director and playwright. He was until 1988 artistic director of the NEGRO ENSEMBLE COMPANY, which he founded in 1967 with Robert Hooks and Gerald Krone on the lower East Side of New York. He has performed in and directed many NEC productions, including *Ceremonies in Dark Old Men* (1969), *The River Niger* (1972) and *The Soldier's Play* (1981). In his comedy *Day of Absence* (1960), Ward shows a South that recognizes its need for its black citizens. His other plays include *Happy Ending* (1960), *The*

Reckoning (1969), *Brotherhood* (1970) and *The Redeemer* (1979). He was inducted into the Theater Hall of Fame in 1996. JANE HOUSE

Warde, Frederick [Barkham] (b. Wardington, Oxon, 23 Feb. 1851; d. Brooklyn, New York, 7 Feb. 1935) Actor. Having unsuccessfully studied law, Warde turned to the stage, touring in English provincial theatre in the late 1860s before travelling to New York to appear in *Belle Lamar* (1874). After further supporting work, mainly in Shakespeare, he went on tour in 1881 playing a string of roles including Shylock, Hamlet, Richard III, King Lear and Henry VIII, so that by the end of the century he had played almost all the great Shakespearean leads. In 1907 he began to combine his acting with lecturing on the theatre, in particular Shakespeare. Reluctant to tackle contemporary drama, he stuck to tried and tested roles in nineteenth-century standards. In 1913 he published some of his lectures as *The Fools of Shakespeare* and in 1920 his autobiography, *Fifty Years of Make-Believe*. He also appeared in silent film versions of, among others, *King Lear* and *Richard III*. Warde took American citizenship in 1922. HELEN RAPPAPORT

Wardle, [John] Irving (b. Bolton, Lancs, 20 July 1929) Theatre critic. Wardle became the deputy theatre critic of the *Observer* under TYNAN in 1960, and then theatre critic of *The Times* (1963–89). His intelligent, considered notices resisted the tendency to sensationalize, and he invested a daily column with a considered feel more associated with weekly publications, providing an accurate chronicle of this period of change in the theatre. He has also written a respected biography, *The Theatres of George Devine* (1974), a play, *The Houseboy* (1974), and a book entitled *Theatre Criticism* (1992). In 1990 he became the first theatre critic of the *Independent on Sunday*, a post he held until 1995. DOMINIC SHELLARD

Warehouse Theatre *see* DONMAR THEATRE

Warfield [Wollfeld/Wohlfelt], David (b. San Francisco, 28 Nov. 1866; d. New York, 27 June 1951) Actor. After an apprenticeship in his native city he moved to New York, where he soon became a favourite comedian in musical comedy, usually playing Jews with thick dialects and long beards. In a second career as a serious actor, he won applause for his characterizations in *The Auctioneer* (1901), *The Music Master* (1904), *A Grand Army Man* (1907) and *The Return of Peter Grimm* (1911). For the next 11 years he performed in one or another of these plays, then retired after offering his Shylock in 1922. GERALD BORDMAN

Warner, David (b. Manchester, 29 July 1941) Actor. Warner was spotted in the film *Tom Jones* (1963) by the ROYAL SHAKESPEARE COMPANY, for which he subsequently played Henry VI and Edward IV in the celebrated *The Wars of the Roses* (1963) and an acclaimed Hamlet (1965) as a young intellectual activist. A starring role in the film *Morgan: A Suitable Case for Treatment* (1966) by DAVID MERCER cemented an image of aggression and revolt that made him an icon for the 1960s. However, he failed to build on this promise and personal problems – causing him, among other things, to jump from a window, which permanently injured both of his feet – made it difficult to work, although he had success in *Tiny Alice* (1970) and in *The Great Exhibition* (1972). DAN REBELLATO

Warner, Deborah (b. Burford, Oxon, 12 May 1959) Director. After training as a stage manager, she founded Kick Theatre Company, directing a number of highly regarded productions between 1980 and 1986, including *The Tempest, Measure for Measure, King Lear* and *Coriolanus*. In 1987 she joined the ROYAL SHAKESPEARE COMPANY to direct *Titus Andronicus* (for which she won both Olivier and Evening Standard awards), and subsequently *King John* (1988) and *Electra* (1989), the latter a production which marked the start of her long association with the actress FIONA SHAW. Warner directed her in *The Good Person of Setzuan* (1989) and *Richard II* (1995) at the Royal NATIONAL THEATRE, where she also directed *King Lear* (1990). Her work in opera includes a controversial *Don Giovanni* (Glyndebourne, 1994), *Wozzeck* (Opera North, 1993) and *The Turn of the Screw* (Royal Opera, 1997). Her first film, *The Last September*, was made in 1999. She directed Shaw in a staging of *The Waste Land* in 1995, which has since been seen all over the world, and she has also created SITE-SPECIFIC works (The St Pancras Project, London, 1995; The Tower Project, London, 1999; Perth Festival, 2000). She is one of the most original talents of her generation, experimenting boldly with form and content, sometimes to the discomfort of her critics. Although her output has recently been small, it is always unusual and challenging. GENISTA MCINTOSH

Warren, Iris *see* LINKLATER, KRISTIN; VOICE; VOICE TRAINING

Washington DC Although Washington DC is the political capital of the United States, it is not its theatrical capital, an honour that belongs to NEW YORK CITY. Often viewed as inhospitable to the arts due to the government's antipathy towards arts funding, it is on the contrary a city with several strong resident theatres, showcasing provocative and engaging work, both new and classical, and musical and dramatic. The first of these, both in chronology and esteem, is the ARENA STAGE, one of the initial vanguard of the RESIDENT THEATRE movement and founded in 1950 under Zelda Fichandler. The historic Ford's Theater, best known as the site where stage death met real death in the assassination of President Lincoln, was restored and reopened in 1968 as a theatre devoted to the growth of MUSICAL THEATRE, the most uniquely American of all art forms. It is joined in this mission by the Signature Theater (est. 1989).

The Shakespeare Theater was established in 1970 in the Folger Shakespeare Library, and since 1986 has been under the artistic leadership of Michael Kahn. Although no longer affiliated with the Folger, it is recognized as the foremost Shakespeare troupe in the country. The Woolly Mammoth Theater, founded in 1980 and led by Howard Shalwitz, is devoted to fostering new plays, with over half its season world premières and the rest American regional premières.
SARAH STEVENSON

Washington Square Players Founded in New York in 1914 by a group of young professionals and amateurs, the organization was modelled on after a similar one in Chicago. Beginning in 1915, they offered evenings of one-act plays and, later, full-length works. Although they hoped to emphasize new American playwriting – they staged EUGENE O'NEILL's *In the Zone* and ELMER RICE's *Home of the Free* – in practice many of their most admired mountings were of then AVANT-GARDE dramas from overseas (MAETERLINCK, CHEKHOV, SHAW). The company disbanded in 1918. Among the founders were LAWRENCE LANGNER, PHILIP MOELLER and the actress Helen Westley, and among the youngsters whose careers they boosted were the actor and designer Rollo Peters, LEE SIMONSON and KATHARINE CORNELL. Many of these people were subsequently instrumental in starting up the THEATER GUILD.
GERALD BORDMAN
See also RESIDENT THEATRE.

O. M. Sayler, *Our American Theatre* (1923)

Wasserstein, Wendy (b. Brooklyn, New York, 18 Oct. 1950) Playwright. In *Uncommon Women and Others* (1977), in which five women reflect on their college days, *Isn't It Romantic* (1980) and *The Heidi Chronicles* (1987, Pulitzer Prize and Tony Award), which explores ideas about the women's movement through the eyes of one woman and her peers, she compassionately examines the hopes and conflicts of the contemporary, educated, well-spoken woman who is seeking

independence without losing romance. She has written several other plays, including *The Sisters Rosensweig* (1992) and *An American Daughter* (1997). JANE HOUSE

C. Barnett, *Wendy Wasserstein: A Casebook* (1999)
G. Ciociola, *Wendy Wasserstein: Dramatizing Women, Their Choices and Their Boundaries* (1998)

Wassu, Hinda *see* BURLESQUE

Waterhouse, Keith [Spencer] (b. Leeds, 6 Feb. 1929) Playwright, novelist and newspaper columnist. With WILLIS HALL, he wrote Northern comedies (e.g. *Celebration*, 1961), bourgeois farces (*Who's Who*, 1971) and adaptations: DE FILIPPO's *Saturday, Sunday, Monday* (1973) and *Filumena* (1977), and novels by ARNOLD BENNETT, J. B. PRIESTLEY, George and WEEDON GROSSMITH, and Waterhouse's own *Billy Liar* (1960). He adapted *Jeffrey Bernard is Unwell* (1990) from Bernard's journalism. TONY HOWARD

Waters, Ethel (b. Chester, Pa., 31 Oct. 1900?; d. Chatsworth, Calif., 1 Sept. 1977) Singer and actress. After appearing in both black and white VAUDEVILLE she made her Broadway debut in *Africana* (1927). Later musicals included *Blackbirds of 1930*, *Rhapsody in Black* (1931), *As Thousands Cheer* (1933), *At Home Abroad* (1935), *Cabin in the Sky* (1940) and *Blue Holiday* (1945). On top of her reputation as a singer and comedienne she also proved to be a fine serious actress, particularly in two dramas, *Mamba's Daughters* (1939) and *The Member of the Wedding* (1950). Her last important appearance was in a one-woman show, *At Home with Ethel Waters* (1953). She published her autobiography, *His Eye is on the Sparrow*, in 1951. GERALD BORDMAN

T. Knaack, *Ethel Waters: I Touched a Sparrow* (1978)

Waterston, Sam[uel Atkinson] (b. Cambridge, Mass., 15 Nov. 1940) Actor. Educated at Yale and in Paris, he made his New York debut in *Oh Dad, Poor Dad, Mama's Hung You in the Closet and I'm Feelin' So Sad* (1962). A succession of OFF-BROADWAY performances followed over the next ten years, in new and experimental work such as *La Turista*, *Posterity for Sale*, *Red Cross*, *Muzeeka* and *The Brass Butterfly*. On Broadway, he played in *Halfway Up the Tree*, *Indians* and *The Trial of the Catonsville Nine*, and for JOSEPH PAPP's NEW YORK SHAKESPEARE FESTIVAL *Prince Hal* (1968), *Benedick* (1972), *Prospero* (1974) and *Hamlet* (1975). By this time, the cinema and television began luring him away from the stage. He returned in *Benefactors* (1986), *A Walk in the Woods* (1988), *Shakespeare and Szekspir* (1994), *Abe Lincoln in Illinois* (1993, as Abraham Lincoln) and *The Master Builder* (1991). HELEN RAPPAPORT

waxworks and dummies Springing from a tradition of anatomical display and royal portraiture, waxworks became a major attraction in the nineteenth century through Madame Tussaud, who had taken death masks from guillotine victims before founding what was to become a world-famous exhibition of dummies in London. Similar galleries opened elsewhere, and during the twentieth century paved the way for the development of the idea and its techniques as part of the tourist and entertainment industry. Stately homes, historic places and theme parks have been enlivened by animatronics, laser effects and other devices that appear to make dummies of real or fictional people come to life. This form of IMPERSONATION is associated with an interest in documentary representation and is linked to theatrical tableaux and PAGEANT. Dummies have their own tradition in the theatre as PUPPETS, as partners to ventriloquists and as items in an extensive armoury of stage effects and props which are related to taxidermy and mummification. CHARLES LONDON

See also TABLEAU VIVANT; VENTRILOQUISM.

Way, Brian *see* CHILDREN'S THEATRE; THEATRE FOR YOUNG PEOPLE

Weaver, Fritz (b. Pittsburgh, 19 Jan. 1926) Actor. After appearing in Virginia and Massachusetts, he made his New York debut OFF-BROADWAY in *Doctor's Dilemma* (1953), and a string of solid performances followed in *Way of the World* (1954), *Family Reunion* and *Power and Glory* (1958), and *Peer Gynt* (1959). He won the Clarence Derwent award for his first Broadway role, in *The White Devil* (1955), following this with *The Chalk Garden* (1956), *Miss Lonelyhearts* (1957), *All American* (1962), *The White House* (1964) and *Child's Play* (1969), for which he won a clutch of awards. Among his noted Shakespearean performances are Henry IV, Hamlet, Macbeth and Lear. Later stage roles include *Cocktail Hour* (1990), *Love Letters* (1989, 1990) and *The Professional* (1995), as well as numerous film and television roles. HELEN RAPPAPORT

Weaver, Lois *see* GAY SWEATSHOP; LESBIAN THEATRE

Webber–Douglas School of Singing and Dramatic Art *see* DRAMA SCHOOLS

Weber and Fields Comedians and producers. The taller, slimmer FIELDS and the shorter, padded **Weber, Joseph Morris** (b. New York, 11 Aug. 1867; d. Los Angeles, 10 May 1942) began their careers together in VAUDEVILLE while they were still children and employed a popular 'Dutch' (i.e. Yiddish) accented act. In 1896 they opened the tiny Weber and Fields Music

Hall, where their mixed bills of short musical comedies, olios, burlesques on contemporary dramas, and a stunning chorus line became for a time Broadway's hottest ticket. After the pair split in 1904, both men continued to produce – mostly musicals – though Fields was considerably more successful than Weber. GERALD BORDMAN

A. and L. Fields, *From the Bowery to Broadway: Lew Fields and the Roots of American Popular Theatre* (1993)
Felix Isman, *Weber and Fields* (1924)

Webster, Margaret (b. New York, 15 March 1905; d. London, 13 Nov 1972) Actress and director, the last in a 150-year-old line of a notable theatrical family. She appeared on stage as a child and made her adult debut in *The Trojan Women* (1924) with SYBIL THORNDIKE, following this the year afterwards with a part in *Hamlet* when JOHN BARRYMORE brought his acclaimed performance to London. Webster worked in BEN GREET's and J. B. FAGAN's companies and at the OLD VIC. In the 1930s she returned to New York, where she had been born during one of her parents' theatrical visits, and established herself as a director as well as an actress. Her Shakespeare productions – such as *Othello* (1943), starring PAUL ROBESON and JOSÉ FERRER and with herself playing Emilia, which broke box-office records for Shakespeare on Broadway – made her reputation, although not without controversy as she often altered the texts. The Margaret Webster Shakespeare Company (1948) toured Shakespeare to schools and colleges. In 1946 she co-founded the AMERICAN REPERTORY THEATER and in 1950 she became the first woman to direct at New York's Metropolitan Opera. She wrote several books, including *Shakespeare Without Tears* (1942), *The Same Only Different* (1969) and *Don't Put Your Daughter on the Stage* (1972). MAGGIE GALE

M. Barranger, *Margaret Webster: A Bio-Bibliography* (1994)

Wedekind, [Benjamin] Frank[lin] (b. Hanover, 24 July 1864; d. Munich, 9 March 1918) Playwright, poet and actor. Wedekind grew up in Switzerland and studied law. He wrote his first plays while working in an advertising and press agency. In 1891 he moved to Paris where he led a bohemian lifestyle, visiting BOULEVARD and VARIETY theatres and CIRCUS shows. His love for unpretentious entertainment and physical forms of theatre influenced his dramatic style and his performances as an actor. In 1895 he returned to Berlin and had his plays rejected by the Freie Bühne, the most AVANT-GARDE theatre in Germany. Back in Munich, publication of *Frühlings Erwachen* (*Spring Awakening*, 1891) and *Der Erdgeist* (*Earth Spirit*, 1895) made his name known among a small circle of modern-art lovers. In 1898, with half a dozen plays to his credit, he joined the Leipzig Literary Society as actor and secretary of their touring company, and soon after became dramaturg, director and actor at the Munich Schauspielhaus. He played Dr Schön in the first production of *The Earth Spirit*. Two poems published in the satirical magazine *Simplicissimus*, of which he was a founder, caused his imprisonment in 1899–1900 for *lèse-majesté*. In the 'comfort' of his prison cell he finished *Der Marquis von Keith* (*The Marquis of Keith*) and enjoyed the publicity his case had brought him. After his release he joined the cabaret team 'The Eleven Executioners'. From now on his plays were widely performed. In 1906 he married Mathilde (Tilly) Newes and performed with her in many of his plays. In his dozen or so later works Wedekind made more use of traditional forms of drama, without, however, losing his satirical undertone. Following in the dramatic footsteps of Büchner, he influenced many writers, particularly BRECHT, and created in the Lulu plays (*Earth Spirit* and *Die Büchse der Pandora*, *Pandora's Box*, 1904), a mythic figure of the twentieth century (cf. Berg's opera *Lulu* and Pabst's film *Pandora's Box*). Wedekind's aesthetic principles were in opposition to the dominant trend of the day, naturalism. He objected not only to the naturalists' artistic tastes, but also to their reformist political attitudes. Wedekind's writings were intended as a protest against bourgeois society. In opposition to Christian, middle-class morality he proclaimed a 'theology of the bordello' and a sensual amorality in which 'the flesh has its own spirit'. In Wedekind's erotic utopia, instinct and sex drive do not conflict with culture but fuse with the world of the intellect and spirituality. In *Spring Awakening* the transition from the natural, vital childhood to repressed adult life is shown to have disastrous results. Lulu is seen as an allegory of untainted natural existence: after her entry into the male world she is tamed and turned into an object of desire. She wreaks vengeance on the men who attempted to possess her, but is herself destroyed in the process.

GÜNTER BERGHAUS

E. Boa, *The Sexual Circus: Wedekind's Theatre of Subversion* (1987)

Weidman, Charles *see* DANCE

Weigel, Helene (b. Vienna, 12 May 1900; d. Berlin, 6 May 1971) Actress. She began her career in Frankfurt in 1919. In 1924 she met BRECHT, whom she married in 1929. She performed in his plays *Man Equals Man* (1927, 1931), *Happy End* (1929), *The Measures Taken* (1930) and *The Mother* (1932). In 1933 she fled Ger-

many, giving a few rare performances elsewhere in Europe, in *The Rifles of Señora Carrar* (Paris, 1937; Copenhagen, 1938) and *Fear and Misery of the Third Reich* (Paris, 1938). After exile, she returned to Europe and in 1948 settled in Berlin, where with Brecht she prepared the foundation of the BERLINER ENSEMBLE. From 1949 until her death she was the director of the company, securing it an international reputation. Her performances as Mother Courage and Pelagea Vlassova in *The Mother* are regarded as perfect examples of Brecht's EPIC acting style. GÜNTER BERGHAUS

Weill, Kurt [Julian] (b. Dessau, Germany, 2 March 1900; d. New York, 3 April 1950) Composer. Weill's early career included both orchestral and theatrical works in which his most notable collaborations were with playwrights GEORG KAISER (*Der Silbersee/Silverlake*, 1933) and BERTOLT BRECHT: *Die Dreigroschenoper* (*The Threepenny Opera*, 1928); *Aufstieg und Fall der Stadt Mahagonny* (*Rise and Fall of the Town of Mahagonny*, 1930); *Happy End* (1929). These scores, whether in the *Singspiel* style of *Dreigroschenoper* or the sub-operatic style of *Silbersee*, have, in keeping with their libretti, a strong and often harsh contemporary tone, muscular and demanding, rarely finding place for sentiment or humour of anything but the bitterest kind. In 1935 Weill moved to America. Having failed with his first Broadway musicals, the anti-war *Johnny Johnson* (1936) and *Knickerbocker Holiday* (1938, from which came the enduring 'September Song'), he made good with the scores for the musically inventive *Lady in the Dark* (1941) and *One Touch of Venus* (1943), a photofit Broadway score in which, if little of the composer's individuality was evident, his gift for melody was. With the 1947 'Broadway Opera' *Street Scene*, Weill produced an excitingly pictorial modern theatre score which richly bestrode the musical and operatic idioms. Subsequent musicals found less success than a 1954 version of *The Threepenny Opera*, which has remained its composer's most widely played work. Weill's influence has grown since the 1970s, and many singers have followed in the footsteps of his wife LOTTE LENYA in performing and recording his songs. KURT GÄNZL

David Drew, *Kurt Weill: A Handbook* (1987)
D. Jarman, *Kurt Weill* (1982)
K. Kowalke, ed., *A New Orpheus: Essays on Kurt Weill* (1986)
R. Sanders, *The Days Grow Short* (1980)

Weiss, Peter [Ulrich] (b. Nowawes, nr Berlin, 8 Nov. 1916; d. Stockholm, 10 May 1982) Playwright, novelist, film-maker and painter, born in Germany of a Swiss mother and a Czech father. After his youth in Berlin and Bremen, Nazism forced his family into exile. He studied at the Art Academy of Prague and after 1939 lived in Sweden. His numerous plays, many of them written in blank verse, combine elements of EPIC and DOCUMENTARY theatre with the traditions of SURREAL-ISM and the THEATRE OF THE ABSURD. He is best known for his asylum play that yokes together BRECHT and ARTAUD *Die Verfolgung und Ermordung Jean Paul Marats, dargestellt durch die Schauspielgruppe des Hospizes zu Charenton unter Anleitung des Herrn de Sade* (*The Persecu-tion and Assassination of Jean-Paul Marat as Performed by the Inmates of the Asylum of Charenton under the Direc-tion of the Marquis de Sade*, known as *Marat/Sade*). First performed in 1964 at the Schiller Theater in West Berlin, the same year saw an important production by BROOK in London. Considerable stir and political repercussions were caused by *Die Ermittlung* (*The Investigation*), premièred simultaneously in 14 theatres on 19 October 1965, which linked Auschwitz and post-war values; *Gesang von Lusitanischen Popanz* (*Song of the Lusitanian Bogeyman*, 1967), dealing with Portuguese colonialism in southern Africa; and *Diskurs über die Vorgeschichte und den Verlauf des . . . Befreiungskrieges in Viet Nam* (*Vietnam Discourse*, 1968). His later plays are *Trotzky im Exil* (*Trotsky in Exile*, 1970), *Hölderlin* (1971) and two adaptations of Kafka's *The Trial*.

GÜNTER BERGHAUS

Robert Cohen, *Undestanding Peter Weiss* (1993)
R. Ellis, *Peter Weiss in Exile* (1987)
I. Hilton, *Peter Weiss: A Search for Affinities* (1970)

Wekwerth, Manfred *see* BERLINER ENSEMBLE

Welfare State International English EXPERI-MENTAL travelling theatre group, the foremost practi-tioners of taking theatre to the audience and making it happen in non-theatre environments. Founded in Leeds in 1968 by John and Sue Fox, the COLLECTIVE of Civic Magicians and Engineers of the Imagination, as members call themselves, crosses and fuses the arts, from firework specialists and sculptors to musicians, puppeteers and actors. This mix is reflected in their elaborate STREET THEATRE and CELEBRATORY ceremon-ies – heralding, maybe, the coming of the seasons – which are often developed around a local issue with the help of the community in order to break down dis-tinctions between art forms, between art and its con-sumers, and between art and life. The company moved to Cumbria in 1979 to explore further its craft-based theatre in a mass technological age staging epic, mythic allegories, such as *The Tower of Babel* (Bracknell, 1982), and local festivals such as *Feast of Furness* (1990). Evolving from HAPPENINGS (e.g. *Earthrise*, 1969) and

spiritual quests (e.g. *The Travels of Lancelot Quail*, 1972) into more popular, social forms, Welfare State have reinvigorated a PROMENADE folk tradition in which theatre can encompass huge processions, barn dances, highly dramatic set pieces, CIRCUS, eating and drinking – 'soup as well as songs'. The work exploits the contrast between the CARNIVAL images the com-pany presents and the reality against which it presents them: the sea, a housing estate, an old rubbish tip redecorated with junk from the dump, or a former cemetery with glass horse-drawn hearse, saxophones and fire sculptures.

They have worked in continental Europe, North America, Japan, Australia and Africa, and have been very influential in the burgeoning of what came to be called PERFORMANCE ART. The well regarded IOU (Independent Outlaw University) was formed in 1976 by ex-members. COLIN CHAMBERS

Tony Coult and Baz Kershaw, eds, *Engineers of the Ima-gination* (1983)
B. Kershaw, *The Politics of Performance: Radical Theatre as Cultural Intervention* (1992)

Weller, Michael (b. New York, 26 Sept. 1942) Play-wright. Depicting his own generation with humour and affection, Weller dramatizes the ways in which such social and political events as the Vietnam War affect individuals. His plays include *Moonchildren* (originally *Cancer*, 1970), *Fishing* (1975), *Loose Ends* (1979), *Spoils of War* (1988), *Lake No Bottom* (1990), *Ghost on Fire* (1995) and *The Heart of Art* (1997); he also wrote the screenplays for *Hair* (1979) and *Ragtime* (1980). M. ELIZABETH OSBORN

Welles, [George] Orson (b. Kenosha, Wisc., 15 Oct. 1915; d. West Hollywood, 10 Oct. 1998) Actor; film and stage director. From the start he was prodigious, adapting, designing, staging and most often starring in productions at his school. At 15 he went to Ireland on a drawing tour; arriving in Dublin, he presented him-self on impulse to HILTON EDWARDS at the GATE THEATRE, claiming that he was 18 and a Broadway star. Undeceived but intrigued, Edwards and his partner MÍCHEÁL MACLÍAMMÓIR took him on: he stayed for a year, making, with his great height (6 feet 4 inches) and sonorous voice, a big impact in parts like the Grand Duke Karl in *Jew Suss* and the Ghost in *Hamlet*. His fame had spread in his own country, and he found himself in KATHARINE CORNELL's prestigious company (1933–4); it was after a performance of *Romeo and Juliet* that he met the man who was the key to channelling his torrent of energy and inspiration: JOHN HOUSEMAN, who extended to him, in his capacity as head of the

Negro Theater Project, an invitation to direct an all-black *Macbeth* (1936). This brought audiences flocking to Harlem, and ensured that Houseman and Welles were given their own project – number 491 – in Roosevelt's FEDERAL THEATER scheme. Despite the innovative brilliance of *Dr Faustus* and *Horse Eats Hat*, Project 491 collapsed with the production of BLITZSTEIN's pro-labour musical *The Cradle Will Rock* (1938), held by their government bosses to be politically subversive. They then formed the MERCURY THEATER, whose first production, a *Julius Caesar* in modern military costumes and pierced with great beams of light *à la* the Nuremburg Rally, created another sensation. Here, it was felt, was a new start for Shakespeare in America, paying full due to the verse, but making it immediate and recognizable. He then turned his attention to radio. Sponsored by Campbell's Soup, Welles created the Mercury Theater On the Air; he took great novels and plays, gutted them, reshaped and transposed them so that they appeared as urgent as the day's news. Most famous was the dramatization of *The War of the Worlds* as a newsflash, interrupting a purported light music programme to describe the arrival of a Martian spaceship in Central Park. The brouhaha provoked by the programme made Welles, still only 23, internationally notorious. Hollywood inevitably called, offering him a film contract of unprecedented scope. He settled on the project that became *Citizen Kane*, which was immediately hailed as one of the most remarkable films ever to have come out of Hollywood, a verdict posterity has had no cause to revise.

A supremely gifted film-maker, Welles encountered nothing but difficulty – some self-created – in his dealings with studios. From time to time there were returns to the stage: *Native Son* (1941), evidence of Welles' passionately held liberal convictions; *Around the World* (1947), a spectacular version of Verne's novel, which aimed to recreate the Victorian theatre, but which was critically and commercially disappointing (though BRECHT thought it the best thing he had seen in the American theatre); a strange double bill of his version of *Dr Faustus* (*Time Runs*), and his own boulevard comedy *The Unthinking Lobster*; a rather conventional *Othello* for his London debut (1951); *Moby Dick* (1955, also London), which Welles claimed was the best thing he had done in any medium; an indifferent *King Lear* (1956, New York, title role and director); and *Chimes at Midnight* (1968, Dublin and Belfast, a trial run for a subsequent Falstaff film). His last stage work was a production of IONESCO's *Rhinoceros* starring LAURENCE OLIVIER (1960, ROYAL COURT and WEST END); the play was a success, but the circumstances were unhappy. It was a rather unexciting end to a stage

career which had started with such elan. After the Mercury, he never found a context in which to do sustained work, but it is hard to know whether he ever really wanted a company. He might have created an American National Theatre; he might have been an American EISENSTEIN; he might have been the greatest American actor of the century. To have achieved any of these things, he would have needed to stay in one place longer than he was ever prepared to. He died with so much of his potential unrealized, a talent mountain, who in the end became bigger than anything he was in. SIMON CALLOW

S. Callow, *Orson Welles* (1996)
R. France, *The Theatre of Orson Welles* (1977)

Werfel, Franz (b. Prague, 10 Sept. 1890, d. Beverly Hills, Calif., 27 Aug. 1945) Novelist, playwright and poet; a friend of Kafka. Austrian by birth, he later worked in Vienna and Germany, emigrating to France in 1938 and to the United States in 1940. An EXPRESSIONIST and pacifist, his anti-war version of Euripides' *Trojan Women* (1915) won great acclaim and, after some ambitious verse plays, his SYMBOLIST *Bockgesang* (*Goat Song*, 1922), on human brutality, caused controversy. It was seen throughout Europe and in America (staged by the THEATRE GUILD, 1926). He won further renown with *Juarez und Maximilian* (1925) and his comedy *Jacobowsky and the Colonel*, adapted by BEHRMAN (1944). WEILL wrote music for his play *Der Weg der Verheissung* (*The Eternal Road*, 1935; directed on Broadway by REINHARDT, 1937). His popular novel *The Song of Bernadette* (1941) was filmed (1943) and made into a play (1946) by Jean and WALTER KERR. JUDY MEEWEZEN

Werich, Jan *see* VOSKOVEC, JIRÍ

Werkteater ('work theatre'.) Innovative NETHERLANDS COLLECTIVE formed in Amsterdam in 1970 and which, until its demise in 1985, was one of the foremost actors' groups in the Western world. A dozen well-trained actors came together to create through IMPROVISATION and without director or script a theatre rooted in their own lives and devoted to subjects of contemporary social reality, such as the handling of patients in a mental institution (*In a Mess*, 1972) or relationships in a home for the elderly (*Twilight*, 1974). DUNBAR H. OGDEN

Dunbar H. Ogden, *Performance Dynamics and the Amsterdam Werkteater* (1987)

Wertenbaker, [Lael Louisiana] Timberlake (b. New York, 1951?) Playwright. Of Canadian heritage, she grew up in the French Basque country, taught

English and French in Greece and then settled in London. Her plays, not unsurprisingly, deal with culture, identity and language. She was resident writer at SHARED EXPERIENCE in 1983, when she wrote for them two highly praised Marivaux translations, *False Admissions* and *Successful Strategies*. She was also resident writer in 1985 at the ROYAL COURT, which produced *Abel's Sister* (1984, Theatre Upstairs), *The Grace of Mary Traverse* (1985), and two award-winning successes, *Our Country's Good* (1988, adapted from a novel by Thomas Keneally) and *Three Birds Alighting on a Field* (1991). For the ROYAL SHAKESPEARE COMPANY she wrote *The Love of a Nightingale* (1988) and translations of MNOUCHKINE and Sophocles. Other plays include *The Break of Day* (1995) and *After Darwin* (1998). ORLA PULTON

C. Dymkowski, 'The Play's the Thing: the Metatheatre of Timberlake Wertenbaker' in *Drama on Drama: Dimensions of Theatricality on the Contemporary British Stage*, ed. N. Boireau (1997)

M. Wandor, *Post-war British Drama: Looking Back in Gender* (2001)

Wesker, Arnold (b. Stepney, London, 24 May 1932) Playwright. Inspired by JOHN OSBORNE's *Look Back in Anger* (1956) and introduced to the ROYAL COURT by LINDSAY ANDERSON, Wesker emerged at the head of the first wave to follow Osborne's shattering debut. GEORGE DEVINE, the theatre's artistic director, was apparently uncertain about his new find and arranged a co-production with the Belgrade Theatre, Coventry, of *Chicken Soup with Barley* (1958), the first part of what became known as the 'Wesker Trilogy' which also comprises *Roots* (1959) and *I'm Talking about Jerusalem* (1960). The whole trilogy is fiercely, tangibly autobiographical and traces the vicissitudes of an east London Jewish family from their socialist high-water mark fighting Mosley's Blackshirts in 1936 through revelations about Stalinist atrocities and the despair of the third Tory election victory in 1959. The three parts were performed at the Royal Court in 1960 to great acclaim, the published edition going on to sell over 350,000 copies.

Wesker followed up this success with an early play, *The Kitchen* (1961), based on his own experience as a pastry cook, and *Chips with Everything* (1962), based on time spent doing National Service. In 1962 he pursued an ambitious project of cultural renewal designed to bring high culture to a popular audience as part of an alternative socialist community. Funded by the trades unions, it was called Centre 42, the number of the TUC resolution that brought it into being. The idealism of this project animated *Their Very Own and Golden City* (1964). Again, Wesker is talking about Jerusalem; the play follows an idealistic socialist architect campaigning for new towns geared to meeting their inhabitants' cultural and community needs. When this play opened in London in 1966, in a penny-pinching production, it was greeted coolly. This came hard on the heels of the disappointing response to his elliptical meditation on love, *The Four Seasons* (1965).

Centre 42 was founded in the spirit of Wesker's (very New Left) belief that cultural standards and judgements were being eroded by mass culture. This enterprise chimed uneasily with the emergence of the 1960s counter-culture, which attacked such visions of culture as elitist and used Centre 42's base, the ROUND HOUSE, London, for disparate activities that seemed to point up how out of step Wesker's vision was with the contemporary scene. His play *The Friends* (1970), which seems obliquely to revisit the characters of the trilogy, is marked by a new disillusionment and despair.

Wesker had a bad time in the 1970s. The decade began with the collapse of Centre 42. He spent two months in the offices of the *Sunday Times* researching *The Journalists*, which was attacked by some of the journalists (perhaps unaware of the irony of their stance) as a breach of confidence. When the play, a fragmented, cinematic presentation of a news room, was presented to the ROYAL SHAKESPEARE COMPANY, the acting company refused to perform it. Wesker sued for breach of contract, tying him up in litigation which would end with an unsatisfactory award of damages in 1980. *The Old Ones* (1972) was dropped by the NATIONAL THEATRE and then performed by the Court. During the 1977 pre-Broadway try-out of his ambitious rewriting of *The Merchant of Venice* as *The Merchant* (since reworked under the title *Shylock*), his Shylock, ZERO MOSTEL, died. The production limped unhappily on to Broadway. Wesker wrote about the experience in *The Birth of Shylock and the Death of Zero Mostel* (1997).

These experiences seem to have embittered Wesker against British theatre. His public comments became increasingly defensive and barbed. He continued producing some fine work which, while continuously successful in Europe, struggled to find venues in Britain. He wrote a series of monologues for women; the best of these, *Annie Wobbler* (1983), offers portraits of an elderly Cockney cleaner, a young graduate and a successful novelist; Wesker questions with great delicacy the place of role-play and identity in their lives. In 1989 there was the première of his COMMUNITY PLAY *Beorhtel's Hill*. While ostensibly a popular history of Basildon in Essex, it is also a sly piece of self-analysis. He returns to the territory of *Their Very Own and Golden City* (which receives a namecheck in the play); but now the narrator is continually out of step with the people he discusses, Wesker casting himself as the 'community drunk'. Its bold message seems to be that a community which defines itself against strangers is not a healthy community.

Wesker's concerns have been fairly constant: the vitality of our common existence, the authenticity of our relationships, the faint possibilities of idealism. His sincerity is at the heart of his writing. His urge for us to appreciate the intensities of our world studs the action of his plays. In more cynical times, his work can seem naïve, even sentimental. Perhaps this is why, while the naturalism of his trilogy seems old-fashioned, his more formal plays, where the emotions are to be found in the interstices of history or institutional life, are proving more durable: *The Kitchen* and *Chips with Everything* saw major London revivals in the mid-1990s. And it may also be that plays like the once-derided *Golden City* may regain their place in the repertoire.

One of his less reported political trajectories has been an increasing exploration of the importance of his Jewish identity; indeed, one of the most politically daring and incisive moments in Wesker's work comes in *The Merchant*, where he places Shakespeare's traditionally celebrated 'Hath not a Jew eyes?' speech in the mouth of the calculating anti-semite, Lorenzo.

Other plays include *The Wedding Feast* (1974), *Love Letters on Blue Paper* (1977), *Caritas* (1981), *One More Ride on the Merry-Go-Round* (1985), *Whatever Happened to Betty Lemon?* (1986), *Three Women Talking* (1992), *Letter to a Daughter* (1992), *Wild Spring* (1994), *Blood Libel* (1996), *When God Wanted a Son* (1997) and *Menace* (for television, 1963). In 1994 he published an autobiography, *As Much as I Dare*, covering the years up to 1957. DAN REBELLATO

See also PLAYWRITING.

Colin Chambers and Mike Prior, *Playwrights' Progress* (1987)
Reade W. Dornan, *Arnold Wesker Revisited* (1994)
Glenda Leeming, *Wesker the Playwright* (1983)
Robert Wilcher, *Understanding Arnold Wesker* (1991)

West, Mae (b. Brooklyn, New York, 17 Aug. 1892; d. Los Angeles, 22 Nov. 1980) Actress and playwright. She had a successful career as a solo comedienne in VAUDEVILLE where she developed a distinctive style of broad, sexual comedy which was part BURLESQUE and part promise of serious action – a combination which provided a problem for censors throughout her career. Along with an over-emphasized, hour-glass Edwardian figure and a technique which allied a drawling voice with suggestively delayed timing, her talent for writing enabled her to create several plays in which she starred on Broadway – notably *Sex* (1926), *Drag* (1927) and *Diamond Lil* (1929). She filmed the last of these in 1933 under the title *She Done Him Wrong*, and followed this immediately with another film, *I'm No Angel*. Both had a huge, worldwide success. Her catchphrases (such as 'Come up and see me sometime') achieved international currency. She made nine more films, but only one (*My Little Chickadee*, with W. C. Fields, in 1940) equalled her early successes and she returned to the theatre to revive *Diamond Lil* and play *Catherine Was Great* (1944). In the Second World War, Allied airmen named their inflatable lifejackets after her. Salvador Dali immortalized her in a sofa designed in the shape of her lips. Her name continued to epitomize bawdy but good-humoured sexuality after her death, when she became an icon for some in the feminist and gay movements. Her autobiography, *Goodness Had Nothing to Do with It*, came out in 1959. IAN BEVAN

G. Eells and S. Musgrove, *Mae West* (1982)
M. Leonard, *Mae West, Express of Sex* (1991)
J. Sochen, *Mae West: She Who Laughs, Lasts* (1992)

West End LONDON's commercial theatre district: an area bounded by Soho, Aldwych, Piccadilly and Westminster to the west (hence its name) of the city. When Sir Squire and Lady BANCROFT bought a small theatre in 1865, renamed it the Prince of Wales, converted the cheap stalls into the expensive seats, encouraged long runs, and attracted the new metropolitan rich created and nurtured by the industrial revolution, they defined the financial parameters of the West End and ushered in 50 years of intensive theatre-building, notably in the two decades either side of the new century; there were 24 West End theatres by 1900. These were clustered into a handful of competing managements who also ran chains of provincial theatres. Ownership has changed, but has continued to rest in the hands of a few huge concerns. Some theatres have closed, some have changed name; around three dozen have survived, ranging from a 300-seater to a 2,300-seater. The last theatre to be built in the West End was the New London in 1973.

The West End has proved remarkably resilient at absorbing challenges to it whether from outside – the cinema and television – or within. After the First World War the CLUB THEATRES which sprung up as an outlet for serious or AVANT-GARDE theatre became used as try-out houses for uncertain work like *Journey's End* (1928). In the 1940s the COUNCIL FOR THE ENCOURAGEMENT OF MUSIC AND THE ARTS, the forerunner of the ARTS COUNCIL, was established to promote and subsidize serious theatre work. The West End, led by TENNENTS, used it to guarantee exemption for some of their work from entertainment tax, which led to the consolidation of their fortunes under 'the Group' which acted as a cartel on London's commercial theatre. From the mid-1950s on, the West End comfortably accommodated occasional products of the rebels at the ROYAL COURT and THEATRE ROYAL, STRATFORD EAST, like *Oh What a Lovely War!* (1963), but by the 1980s, when recession was biting hard, the West End was surviving on a diet of musicals, *The Mousetrap* (since 1952), farces, and a stream of work from the publicly subsidized sector. DAN REBELLATO

See also SHAFTESBURY AVENUE; STOLL MOSS.

Raymond Mander and Joe Mitchenson, *The Theatres of London* (1975)

John Pick, *The West End: Mismanagement and Snobbery* (1983)

West Indian theatre *see* CARIBBEAN

West Yorkshire Playhouse Opened in 1990 in LEEDS, England, it is the largest REPERTORY theatre company in the United Kingdom outside London and STRATFORD-UPON-AVON. Comprising two performance spaces, the Quarry Theatre seating 750 and the Courtyard Theatre seating 350, the Playhouse is funded by Leeds City Council and four other West Yorkshire local authorities, and stages an impressive number of well-attended performances, workshops, readings and community events. Under director Jude Kelly, the Playhouse has become a beacon of regional theatre, attracting actors of the calibre of IAN MCKELLEN, championing new writing and offering a wide repertoire from Shakespeare and CHEKHOV to SOYINKA. It has made a particular contribution in MUSICAL THEATRE – *Carnival Messiah* placed reggae alongside Handel, and it launched the West End hit *Spend, Spend, Spend*. LAURIE WOLF

Westminster Theatre A London chapel that had been converted into a cinema, it was opened as a theatre in 1931 by manager Anmer Hall (1863–1953) to reflect his own tastes following his four seasons at the FESTIVAL THEATRE, CAMBRIDGE. The inaugural production – BRIDIE's *The Anatomist* – marked TYRONE GUTHRIE's London debut and had HENRY AINLEY and the almost unknown FLORA ROBSON as the leads. A bold international repertoire followed, embracing PIRANDELLO, three O'NEILL English premières (*Ah, Wilderness!*, 1936; *Mourning Becomes Electra*, 1937; *Marco Millions*, 1938), the QUINTERO brothers, DENIS JOHNSTON and *Waste* by GRANVILLE BARKER (1936); the GATE THEATRE, Dublin, and the GROUP THEATRE also appeared, and in 1938 J. B. PRIESTLEY and Ronald Jeans established the London Mask Theatre in similar spirit,

with Hall's director Malcolm Macowan staying on. A Christian evangelical movement bought the theatre in 1946. It was reconstructed as part of a new complex in 1966. COLIN CHAMBERS

Whelan, Peter (b. Newcastle-under-Lyme, 3 Oct. 1931) Playwright. He began his career in advertising before starting to write for the stage. Many of his humane, intelligent plays have been premièred by the ROYAL SHAKESPEARE COMPANY, including *Captain Swing* (1978), *The Accrington Pals* (1981), *Clay* (1982), *The Bright and Bold Design* (1991), *The School of Night* (1992) and the award-winning *The Herbal Bed* (1996), based on events when Shakespeare's daughter was publicly accused of adultery, which transferred to the West End and Broadway. His play *Divine Right* (1996), about the future of the monarchy, was produced by BIRMINGHAM REPERTORY THEATRE. BRIAN ROBERTS

Whistler, Rex [Reginald John] (b. Eltham, Kent, 24 June 1905; d. Le Mesnil, Normandy, France, 18 July 1944) Designer and painter. He was discovered by CHARLES COCHRAN and became noted for his uncluttered Georgian and Regency designs which subtly and stylishly recreated the period's atmosphere from a detached viewpoint. Among his successes were *Pride and Prejudice* (1936) and *Old Music* (1938). He also designed operas. MARIE PETCHELL

White, Edgar [Nkosi] (b. Montserrat, 4 April 1947) Playwright. His family emigrated to America when he was eight years old. He was then already a voracious reader, for which he credits Montserrat's excellent education system. He grew up bilingual in Spanish-speaking Harlem. As a teenager he joined a seminary to study for the priesthood, but soon became disillusioned with the church, and turned to the theatre. After some 30 years' success as a playwright, novelist and children's writer, however, he returned to the church, graduating from the New York Theological Seminary to become an ordained minister.

White was only 18 when his first play, *The Mummer's Play* (1965), was produced by JOSEPH PAPP at the New York PUBLIC THEATER (NYPT). Papp also produced White's next four plays, one of which was bilingual, in Spanish and English. In 1981 White moved to England after his *Les Femmes Noir* transferred there from NYPT. Several of his world premières were staged in London, including *Masada* (1980) and *Like Them That Dream* (1983). Others, such as *I, Marcus Garvey* (1987), were staged in the Caribbean. In 1993 New York's Café LA MAMA premièred *Live from Galilee*, a blues opera about the Scottsboro Boys, nine young black men wrongly held in gaol in the South on the accusation of raping two white women. White's published play collections include *Crucificado* (1976), *Lament for Rastafari and Other Plays* (1983), *The Nine Night and Ritual by Water* (1984), *Redemption Song and Other Plays* (1985) and *Underground* (1970).

The over-riding concern in White's *oeuvre* is for the displacement and exile of black peoples generally, and of West Indians in particular. Much of his work is panoramic in vision, and his plays are remarkable for their writer's soaring imagination, his sense of irony and the leanness of his language.   JUDY S. J. STONE

White [Weitz], George   (b. New York, 1890; d. Hollywood, 11 Oct. 1968)   Dancer, producer and director. White began dancing professionally while still a youngster. He afterwards performed in VAUDEVILLE and in BROADWAY musicals. In 1919 he launched the first edition of his revue, *George White's Scandals*, and produced 13 more between then and 1939. These revues were perceived as less cumbersomely ornate, more topical and jazzier than the competing ZIEGFELD revues. Among his other productions were *Runnin' Wild* (1923), *Manhattan Mary* (1927) and *Flying High* (1930).   GERALD BORDMAN

White, Jane   (b. New York, 30 Oct. 1922)   Actress. She made her Broadway debut in *Strange Fruit* (1945), but most of her subsequent work was OFF-BROADWAY or outside New York, in productions such as *Blithe Spirit*, *The Taming of the Shrew* and *Dark of the Moon*. In the mid-1960s she appeared in a run of classical roles for JOSEPH PAPP's NEW YORK SHAKESPEARE FESTIVAL, which was prepared to cast black actors in conventionally 'white' roles, and was awarded an Obie for her performance as Volumnia in *Coriolanus* (1964). Other powerful renditions included Clytemnestra in *Iphigenia in Aulis* (1967) and Goneril in *King Lear* (1975).
HELEN RAPPAPORT

White, Miles [Edgren]   (b. Oakland, Calif., 27 July 1914; d. New York, 19 Feb. 2000)   Costume designer. White studied in California and New York. His first designs were seen in *Right This Way* (1938). His costumes for *Oklahoma!* and the ZIEGFELD *Follies of 1943* won high praise and special attention when the shows opened on successive evenings. From then until the early 1960s he was one of the busiest and most admired of Broadway costumers. Virtually all of his work was done for musicals and includes *Gentlemen Prefer Blondes* (1949), the 1952 revival of *Pal Joey*, and *Bye, Bye, Birdie* (1960).   GERALD BORDMAN

White, Patrick [Victor Martindale]   (b. London, 28 May 1912; d. Sydney, 30 Sept. 1990)   Novelist and playwright. In White's major plays the enduring concerns of love, the us-in-me, renewal and grace are revealed in epiphanies which momentarily unite playwright, character, audience and some greater community in a paradoxical revelation through disguise. A number of comedies and sketches preceded White's first influential play *The Ham Funeral* – an inner portrait of the young artist – written in 1947 and initially rejected for its modernism when premièred in Australia in 1961. *The Season at Sarsaparilla* (1962), *A Cheery Soul* (1963) and *Night on Bald Mountain* (1964) were his prodigal response. In them, 'returning home from England and war to the stimulus of time remembered' was entangled with satire of a loved but limiting and repressed society. In each case the fragmentation of dramatic unities and juxtaposition of EXPRESSIONISM, SYMBOLISM, VAUDEVILLE and SURREALISM, were met with misunderstanding, suspicion and trivialization. White consequently withdrew from the theatre and suppressed his plays until the 1970s, when collaboration with director Jim Sharman saw successful revivals of *The Season at Sarsaparilla* and *A Cheery Soul*. Since then four new plays – *Big Toys* (1977), *Signal Driver* (1982), *Netherwood* (1983) and *Shepherd on the Rocks* (1987) – have appeared, as well as the film of a short story and an opera of *Voss* (1957, libretto by David Malouf).

Critics still baulk at flimsy narratives and schematic characterizations, but respect 40 years of theatrical experiment, service to art and humanity, and a Nobel Prize (1973).   GUS WORBY

May B. Akerholt, *Patrick White* (1988)
D. Carroll, *Australian Contemporary Drama* (1993)
John Colmer, *Patrick White* (1984)
D. Marr, *Patrick White: A Life* (1991)
John A. Weigel, *Patrick White* (1983)

Whitehall farce   A peculiarly British institution, it takes its name from the series of plays produced by and often starring BRIAN RIX at the Whitehall Theatre, London, from 1950 to 1966 which surpassed in popularity the prewar ALDWYCH FARCES. Frequently centred around the bedroom, concerning mistaken or duel identity and laced heavily with innuendo, these included John Chapman's *Dry Rot* (1954) and *Simple Spymen* (1958), and RAY COONEY's *One For The Pot* (1961) and *Chase Me, Comrade* (1964).   MARIE PETCHELL
See also FARCE.

Whitehead, Robert   (b. Montreal, 3 May 1916) American producer and director. Whitehead has served as managing director for the AMERICAN NATIONAL THEATER AND ACADEMY, as a founder of the Producers' Theatre, and as a director of the Repertory Theatre of

LINCOLN CENTER. With these groups, with other collaborators or alone he has compiled a record of memorable productions, including *Medea* (1947), *The Member of the Wedding* (1950), *Bus Stop* (1955), *The Visit* (1958), *A Man for All Seasons* (1961) and *Lunch Hour* (1980). He directed his wife, ZOE CALDWELL, in a 1982 revival of *Medea*. GERALD BORDMAN

Whitehead, Ted [Edward Anthony] (b. Liverpool, 3 April 1933) Playwright. The author of powerful Strindbergian studies of working-class sexual relationships, he highlights domestic brutality and male bafflement. *Alpha Beta* (1972) charts a marriage's vicious decline, but Whitehead arouses compassion for his cannibalistic men and women, who damage themselves as much as their partners and are bound together in ways they cannot understand. In *Mecca* (1977), sexual tourists try to escape their responsibilities and the culture that shaped them: they blunder into rape and racial violence. But *The Man Who Fell in Love with His Wife* (1984) moves towards a tentative, bruised optimism. He adapted STRINDBERG's *The Dance of Death* (1984). TONY HOWARD

Whitelaw, Billie (b. Coventry, 6 June 1932) Actress. The leading English-speaking interpreter of SAMUEL BECKETT's dramas, she performed, at the ROYAL COURT or the NATIONAL THEATRE, in *Play* (1964), *Not I* (1973), *Footfalls* (1976), *Happy Days* (1979), *Rockaby* and *Enough* (1982). From 1964 to 1967 she also appeared with the National Theatre in plays as diverse as *Othello*, *Hobson's Choice* and *Trelawny of the Wells*. She has also appeared with the ROYAL SHAKESPEARE COMPANY (e.g. *After Haggerty*, 1971; *The Greeks*, 1980) and in the WEST END (e.g. *Alphabetical Order*, 1975, transfer from Hampstead Theatre). Her many films include *Charlie Bubbles* (1968). Her autobiography, *Billie Whitelaw – Who He?*, appeared in 1995. DAVID STAINES

Whitemore, Hugh [John] (b. Tunbridge Wells, Kent, 16 June 1936) Playwright. His commercially successful work presents extraordinary events and lives in their domestic contexts: *Stevie* (1977, about the poet Stevie Smith), *Pack of Lies* (1983, about a family drawn into the Kroger spy ring), and *Breaking the Code* (1986, about the career and suicide of Alan Turing, decoder of Hitler's Enigma cypher). Other plays include *The Best of Friends* (1987) and *A Letter of Resignation* (1997). He is also a prolific television writer and wrote the screen play for *84 Charing Cross Road* (1987). TONY HOWARD

Whiting, John [Robert] (b. Salisbury, Wilts, 15 Nov. 1917; d. London, 16 June 1963) Playwright. Championed by many within the theatrical profession in the face of critical and audience resistance, Whiting, an actor who turned to writing during war service, achieved wider popularity with only one play: his last, *The Devils* (1961). It played in the ROYAL SHAKESPEARE COMPANY's first season at the ALDWYCH THEATRE after PETER HALL had lured him back to live drama from earning his living as a film scriptwriter. Cancer cut short his life at 45 just as he had found a new voice, rich and epic, in a play about the possession of nuns that helped change the way English theatre treated historical subjects.

His early plays – *A Penny for a Song* (1951), a fable-like English celebration of eccentricity; *Saint's Day* (1951), an allegory of self-destruction; and *Marching Song* (1954), a morality play about the guilt of war – mix the metaphysical with the whimsical, the spiritual with the cruel, creating theatrically alive but socially narrow, metaphorical worlds. Along with his other work – *The Gates of Summer* (1956), *Conditions of Agreement* (1965), shorter pieces and adaptations of OBEY and ANOUILH – they represent a personal, poetic and painful view of human weakness and regeneration. An influential figure – early PINTER bears the stamp – Whiting stands aloof both from the VERSE DRAMA of FRY and ELIOT, with whom he is often bracketed, and, more obviously, from the radical drama of the ROYAL COURT.

He served on the Drama Panel of the ARTS COUNCIL from 1955 until his death, and in 1965 the Council established the annual John Whiting Award for plays that reflected the state of Britain. His drama criticism is collected in *Whiting on Theatre* (1966). COLIN CHAMBERS

Ronald Hayman, *John Whiting* (1969)
Eric Salmon, *The Dark Journey: John Whiting as Dramatist* (1979)
Simon Trussler, *The Plays of John Whiting: An Assessment* (1972)

Whitworth, Geoffrey (b. London, 7 April 1883; d. London, 9 Sept. 1951) Arts campaigner and critic. Fired by the GRANVILLE BARKER–VEDRENNE seasons at the ROYAL COURT, Whitworth began a campaign for theatrical reform, culminating in the 1919 British Theatre Conference which established the BRITISH DRAMA LEAGUE. Under Whitworth's secretaryship, the League campaigned for the recognition of AMATEUR THEATRE, for a NATIONAL THEATRE and for a raised profile for drama generally. Whitworth's passionate advocacy of a national community of the theatre is documented in his *The Theatre of My Heart* (1930) and *The Making of a National Theatre* (1951). He lived to see local authority theatre funding, the ARTS COUNCIL and the laying of a foundation stone for a National Theatre. DAN REBELLATO

Wigman, Mary (b. Hanover, Germany, 1 Nov. 1886; d. West Berlin, 18 Sept. 1973) Dancer and choreographer whose career as a performer began in 1914 at the outbreak of the First World War. She was an early pupil of, and collaborator with, RUDOLF LABAN, with whom she worked for some years. She established her own school and company in Dresden in 1920, and her pupils included Harald Kreutzberg, Gret Palucca and HANYA HOLM. She ran and choreographed her own company (1920–35), and continued to choreograph for the theatre until 1961. Among her better-known works are her second version of *Witch Dance* (1926), and Albert Talhoff's momentous *Totenmal* (1930). Her book *The Language of Dance* was published in English in 1966. MICHAEL HUXLEY

See also CHOREOGRAPHY; DANCE; MOVEMENT, DANCE AND DRAMA.

wigs The twentieth century saw a revolution in the technique of wig-making, producing a wig for stage use that is lighter weight and more realistic than ever before. Until the 1940s men's stage wigs were made as they had been in the previous two centuries. Pieces of linen or cotton cloth were cut, seamed and tucked to fit over a head-shaped piece of wood called a block. Strong metal springs were sewn on to the front, sides and back of this foundation to help it cling to the actor's head. If an area of wig was to be exposed as skin, it could be constructed with a chamois-leather insert, giving a more realistic skin effect than cotton. Fringe-like strips of hair known as weft could then be added. For a more natural result, hairs were knotted in individually, rather as a rug or carpet is knotted, but on a much smaller scale. For a character wig, perhaps for Shakespeare's Falstaff, the foundation could be padded out with cotton wadding. Beards and moustaches were created by sticking wisps of hair directly on to the face. This was a slow process requiring skills which many actors were proud to have mastered. The cotton front of the wig hid the actor's own hairline. This allowed the production designer freedom to change the actor's appearance to suit the character he was portraying, perhaps giving him a high forehead. Durable and versatile, the cotton-fronted wig continued to be worn in many theatres until the 1960s. During the 1930s an ancient refinement of wig-making was revived for use in films and became established in the theatre during the 1940s. This method involved cutting the cotton front back to just in front of the actor's own hairline, to hide it, and adding a piece of net in front of this for any extra hair to be knotted into. The net was originally made by hand from human hair. This was replaced first by cotton net, then by nylon net, which has become progressively finer. Today 10 denier net is often used and the wig join has become invisible. During the 1960s the entire wig foundation for men began to be made from nylon net and could be washed without fear of shrinking. Ladies' wigs made in this way replaced those caul-net wigs whose stretch bases had allowed hastily arranged hair to give the head a lumpy appearance. These wigs always had to be dry-cleaned in spirits, an expensive and inconvenient practice. The terylene net foundation in common use by the 1970s was strong enough to hold its shape without the addition of springs or reinforcement with galloon. Wig-making had become a simpler process, quicker and cheaper. Beards and moustaches have been made by knotting the hair on to net in the same way as wigs since 1950, and very few actors now have the skill to lay on a beard. The cotton-fronted wigs were stuck down with a strong resin glue, now replaced by medical adhesives or water-soluble gum. In a show like *Cats* these improvements mean a great deal to actors who may be wearing thick wigs which must be firmly stuck to counteract the sweat and rough treatment of a heavily costumed and active performance on many successive nights.

Theatrical wig-making, though often carried out on the same premises, is quite different from fashion wig-making, the end result as often as not being to make the wearer look older or less attractive than his natural appearance, but it is strongly affected by the prevailing fashion in hairstyles. For example, the actress playing Rosalind in the nineteenth century would wear a short wig to disguise herself as a boy. These days the actress is more likely to have her own hair cut short and wear a wig as a girl. The cut of women's hair varied so much through the twentieth century that it is almost always necessary for an actress to wear a wig if playing anything other than a contemporary part. Men's hairstyles alter as quickly; the overall shape of the head was emphasized more in the twentieth century, with hair generally worn shorter at the nape and longer on the top of the head. Any production wishing to reflect men's appearance of even a century ago calls for wigs all round, possibly beards and moustaches too.

In Britain, the commercial sources of these items in the early days were the wigmakers Bert and Gustave, Nathans and, since 1946, Wig Creations. These London-based organizations usually hired out their wigs for each production. During the run of the play they would be cared for by the wardrobe department or the assistant stage manager, or by the actor himself. The larger companies employed a specialist wig person to do this from the 1950s, and by the 1960s most large theatres had established wig departments, employing a team of wigmakers, hairdressers and make-up artists. The subsidized theatres, which had begun to supply their own wigs to save money, discovered that, with a group of skilled people available during the show to assist the company, far more could be done to change appearances by working with the actor's own hair or adding hairpieces or extensions. As many wigs are being worn today as at any time, but audiences are more likely than ever to assume that what they are seeing is the actor's own hair. The new materials and higher standards of care are making realistic transformations possible in even the smallest studio spaces.

BRENDA LEEDHAM

See also MAKE-UP.

Wilcox, Michael   *see* GAY THEATRE

Wild West show   Nineteenth-century exhibitions of frontier culture, exemplified by 'Buffalo Bill' Cody's shows, became a branch of CIRCUS in the twentieth century but were mostly overshadowed by the cinema's portrayals. The musical *Annie Get Your Gun* (1946) was inspired by a Cody celebrity, and ARTHUR KOPIT in *Indians* (1968) uses Cody's show to comment on the subjugation of indigenous Americans as well as on the horror of the Vietnam War.   CHARLES LONDON

Paul Reddin, *Wild West Shows* (1999)

J. G. Rosa and R. May, *Buffalo Bill and his Wild West* (1989)

Wilde, Oscar [Fingal O'Flahertie Wills] (b. Dublin, 16 Oct. 1856; d. Paris, 30 Nov. 1900)   Poet, novelist, belle-lettrist and playwright. He was the son of eccentric parents, (Sir) William, a leading Dublin surgeon and amateur historian, and (Lady) Jane Francesca (née Elgee), author of nationalistic verse and collector of folklore. After attending Portora Royal School and Dublin University he proceeded to Oxford, where he won the Newdigate Poetry Prize for *Ravenna* (1878). He settled in London, contributed to various literary and artistic journals, and promoted the 'new aestheticism'. He married Constance Lloyd of Dublin in 1884, was editor of *Woman's World* (1887–9), published *The Happy Prince and Other Tales* (1888), *A House of Pomegranates*, *Lord Arthur Savile's Crime*, *Intentions* and *The Picture of Dorian Gray* (1891). All his important plays except *Salomé* were written and produced between 1892 and 1895. In 1895 he took a libel action against Lord Queensberry following the latter's allegation of Wilde's homosexual attachment to his son Lord Alfred Douglas; Wilde lost the case and was himself prosecuted. He served two years in gaol and published *The Ballad of Reading Gaol* (1898). His death in 1900 in Paris

was an event ironically anticipated in *The Importance of Being Earnest:* 'In Paris! I fear that hardly points to any very serious state of mind at the last!'

Wilde's plays are: *Vera* or *The Nihilists* (published 1880, performed Union Square Theatre, New York, 1883); *The Duchess of Padua* (published 1883, performed Broadway Theatre, New York, as *Guido Ferrenti*, 1891); *Lady Windermere's Fan* (St James' Theatre, London, 1892); *A Woman of No Importance* (Haymarket Theatre, London, 1893); *An Ideal Husband* (Theatre Royal Haymarket, London, 1895); and *The Importance of Being Earnest* (St James' Theatre, London, 1895). *Salomé* was rehearsed in its original French text in London in 1892, banned by the LORD CHAMBERLAIN, published in Paris 1893, published in London 1894, and produced in Paris 1894; its first professional English-language production was at the Dublin GATE THEATRE in 1928. *A Florentine Tragedy* and *La Sainte Courtisane* are both fragmentary (published 1908). Several of Wilde's non-dramatic works have been adapted for the stage and other media. They include: *The Decay of Lying* (1889), *The Critic as Artist* (1890), *Lord Arthur Savile's Crime* and *The Picture of Dorian Gray*, the last in many versions, of which MÍCHEÁL MACLÍAMMÓIR's (1945) best captures the spirit of *fin-de-siècle* decadence. There have been a large number of stage, television and radio plays based on Wilde's life, taking the Queensberry case as central motif; and many films have been made from his prose fiction, his plays and his life.

Vera was inspired by Russian history and contemporary Russian events. Biographer Richard Ellmann has shown that Wilde's Irish nationalism strengthens the theme of betrayal. The somewhat turgid prose may be taken as a foretaste of the highly allusive and decorative language of *Salomé*. The first production, following Wilde's phenomenally successful American lecture tour, was a failure. His verse tragedy *The Duchess of Padua* also received its first production in New York, and was slightly more enthusiastically received. Somewhat in the style of the Jacobean revenge play, it lacks the full-bloodedness of the genre. The production history of *Salomé* was even more discouraging. Wilde never saw it performed, for LUGNÉ-POË's production at the Théâtre de l'Oeuvre took place while he was in prison. Its progenitors are the Bible, Mallarmé's *Herodiade*, the painting of Gustave Moreau, and SYMBOLIST art and literature in general. A lyrically crepuscular work, it is highly charged with the imagery of eroticism, debauchery and death, and it was praised, significantly, by Mallarmé and MAETERLINCK. Richard Strauss's opera followed as early as 1905.

Lady Windermere's Fan, *A Woman of No Importance* and *An Ideal Husband* are, structurally and thematically, very much in the mode of their time; what distinguishes them from other comedies of society is Wilde's sparkling use of epigram and the inversion of verbal cliché to create a paradoxically witty remark. Though the characters take themselves and their predicaments very seriously, they express themselves most eloquently and with vivid flashes of wit of a kind not at all common among real-life members of the English upper classes.

A quite different tone manifests itself in *The Importance of Being Earnest*, for plot is virtually absent and there is no attempt at any moral stance. (The situation is lifted from Boucicault's *A Lover By Proxy*, 1842). The comedy moves effortlessly on the momentum provided by its own verbal precocity; its structure is conditioned by the permutation of exchanges between the few characters; their seemingly inconsequential repartee carries the action. Late twentieth-century critics tended to view *The Importance of Being Earnest* as anticipating the THEATRE OF THE ABSURD, but Wilde's comedy is far too detached for this categorization. TYRONE GUTHRIE wrote: 'Though it's full of nonsense, it is also full of profound and utterly charming sense. It is the greatest play of all time by an Irish dramatist.' Exactly 100 years after its first performance, Wilde's name was added to Poet's Corner in London's Westminster Abbey. CHRISTOPHER FITZ-SIMON

Alan Bud, *The Plays of Oscar Wilde* (1977)
Richard Ellmann, *Oscar Wilde* (1988)
F. Harris, *Oscar Wilde, His Life and Confessions* (1930)
Montgomery Hyde, *Oscar Wilde, a Biography* (1975)
Walter J. Nelson, *Oscar Wilde and the Dramatic Critics: A Study in Victorian Theatre* (1989)
Kerry Powell, *Oscar Wilde and the Theatre of the 1890s* (1990)
Katherine Worth, *Oscar Wilde* (1983)

Wilder, Clinton   *see* BARR, RICHARD

Wilder, Thornton [Niven]   (b. Madison, Wisc., 17 April 1897; d. New Haven, Conn., 7 Dec. 1975)   Playwright and novelist. His earliest stage successes came with scenery-less, free-flowing, homey works: the one-acters *The Long Christmas Dinner* and *The Happy Journey to Trenton and Camden* (1931), and the Pulitzer Prize winner *Our Town* (1938), an affectionate look at village life that has become one of the most popular plays in America. He won a second Pulitzer with his allegory about man's struggle for survival, *The Skin of Our Teeth* (1942). His last hit, the farcical *The Matchmaker* (1954), later turned into the musical *Hello, Dolly!*, was a rewriting of an earlier failure, *The Merchant of Yonkers* (1938), which in turn was based on an old Austrian play by

Nestroy. He also wrote modern adaptations of *Lucrèce* (1932) and *A Doll's House* (1937).   GERALD BORDMAN

R. Goldstone, and G. Anderson, *Thornton Wilder* (1982)
Gilbert A. Harrison, *The Enthusiast* (1983)

Willemetz, Albert [Lucien]   (b. Paris, 14 Feb. 1887; d. Marnes-la-Coquette, France, 7 Oct. 1964)   Librettist and lyricist. Trained in law, Willemetz worked at first as a civil servant while writing songs and REVUE material on the side. He swept to fame in 1918 as the co-author and lyricist of *Phi-Phi*, the hilarious small-scale musical which started a new fashion in post-war France for light, comic musical plays accompanied by songs in the popular music mode. Willemetz's pithy, satirical jazz-age style quickly became the model for a decade of musicals in which he contributed book and/or lyrics to many of the greatest Parisian successes, notably the works of HENRI CHRISTINÉ, MAURICE YVAIN, Joseph Szulc and Raoul Moretti. He also persuaded the doyen of the French *opérette*, ANDRÉ MESSAGER, into composing two successful musical shows in the new style. As fashions in musical theatre changed, Willemetz smoothly changed with them. He turned out books and lyrics for spectacles and for French versions of American musicals, new libretti for classic works, and original musical plays, while at the same time keeping up a vast flow of songwords for popular vocalists, and maintaining his position as the most important lyricist of the French theatre until the 1950s.   KURT GÄNZL

Williams, Bert [Egbert Austin]   (b. Nassau, New Providence, West Indies, 1876; d. New York, 4 March 1922)   Comedian. Williams came to the United States as a child and performed as a MINSTREL before forming a double act with George Walker in 1895. They acted as a twosome and in Broadway shows. Williams became famous for his portrayal of a gullible, downtrodden, black dope. He became the first black performer in the ZIEGFELD *Follies* (1910–19), in the face of antagonism from some of the white actors. He was the most highly acclaimed black comic and a well-loved VAUDEVILLE performer, but – probably because of the raging racism in the United States at the time – he was never given an opportunity to explore less stereotypical roles and had to 'black' up because of the lightness of his skin. He founded the first all-black friendly society for actors in 1906.   ADRIANA HUNTER

A. Charters, *Nobody: The Story of Bert Williams* (1970)
M. Rowland, *Bert Williams, Son of Laughter* (1923)
E. L. Smith, *Bert Williams: A Biography of the Pioneer Black Comedian* (1992)

Williams, Clifford (b. Cardiff, 30 Dec. 1926) Director. He founded the Mime Company (1950–3), for which he wrote and directed 20 plays, and worked in regional theatre before joining the ROYAL SHAKESPEARE COMPANY (1961) and directing DAVID RUDKIN's *Afore Night Come* (1962). His *Comedy of Errors* (1962) was created to fill a sudden gap in the schedules; it used masks and *COMMEDIA DELL'ARTE* techniques and became the RSC's longest-running Shakespeare production (final revival, 1972). Williams's RSC work explored the entire range of comedy – from farce to black comedy, from Marlowe to SHAW – alongside important contemporary responses to historical and ethical problems (e.g. HOCHHUTH's *The Representative*, 1963). He directed a controversial all-male *As You Like It* (NATIONAL THEATRE, 1967) and Hochhuth's *Soldiers* (1968), which ran into legal problems because of its treatment of Winston Churchill. Many later commercial productions became international successes, particularly *Oh! Calcutta* (1970) and Anthony Shaffer's *Sleuth* (1970). TONY HOWARD

Williams, [George] Emlyn (b. Mostyn, Wales, 26 Nov. 1905; d. London, 25 Sept. 1987) Actor, director and playwright. Born into a poor Welsh family, Williams won a scholarship to OXFORD, where he was active in the university dramatic society, OUDS. His plays include the thrillers *A Murder has been Arranged* (1930) and *Night Must Fall* (1935), and *The Corn Is Green* (1938), a semi-autobiographical piece which ran for almost two years with him in the lead and was later made into a successful film. He wrote adaptations, such as the comic *The Late Christopher Bean* (1933, from the French play by René Fauchois) and IBSEN's *The Master Builder* (1964) for OLIVIER at the NATIONAL THEATRE. He often appeared in and directed his own plays. Williams' acting career spanned many types of role, from Shakespeare to modern parts, in both theatre and cinema, and he was acclaimed internationally for his SOLO shows based on the writings of Dickens and DYLAN THOMAS. He also wrote two volumes of autobiography, *George* (1961) and *Emlyn* (1973). MAGGIE GALE

J. Harding, *Emlyn Williams: A Life* (1993)

Williams, [E[a]rnest George] Harcourt (b. London, 30 March 1880; d. Croydon, Surrey, 13 Dec. 1957) Actor and director. First appearing on stage in 1898 with FRANK BENSON, Williams acted with many of the stars of the Edwardian stage, including IRVING and TERRY. He made his most notable contribution during his directorship of the OLD VIC (1929–34), where his innovations in Shakespeare production, prompted by HARLEY GRANVILLE BARKER's *Prefaces to Shakespeare*, were much emulated throughout the 1930s and 1940s. He paid particular attention to the vigour of the verse-speaking, and brought back to the company actors such as SYBIL THORNDIKE and EDITH EVANS while also attracting new ones like JOHN GIELGUD, RALPH RICHARDSON and PEGGY ASHCROFT. He was also a champion of SHAW. He married the actress Jean Stirling Mackinlay (1882–1958), who was a pioneer in CHILDREN'S THEATRE. Among his books are *Four Years at the Old Vic* (1935), *Vic Wells, the Work of Lilian Baylis* (1938) and *Old Vic Saga* (1949). IAN CLARKE

Williams, Heathcote (b. Helsby, Cheshire, 15 Nov. 1941) Playwright. His theatre derives its power from language. In *AC/DC* (1970), a key play of its time, and *The Speakers* (book 1964; stage adaptation 1974), visionaries, schizophrenics and 'misfits' use frenetic monologues as weapons of survival. Williams soon discarded all semblance of plot to write anarchic counter-cultural manifestos. *The Immortalist* (1977) mocks rationalism. His Whitmanesque ecological poems, including *Whale Nation* (1988), have been performed by Roy Hutchins. Other plays include *The Local Stigmatic* (1966). TONY HOWARD

Williams, Nigel (b. Cheadle, Cheshire, 20 Jan. 1948) Playwright, novelist, screenwriter and journalist. His theatre work was established through the ROYAL COURT. His early plays share a strong left-wing, bitterly comic vision of contemporary politics, from class conflict set in a school classroom in the award-winning *Class Enemy* (1978), which was seen widely abroad, sexual politics in *Sugar and Spice* (1980), and confrontation between army and unions in *Line 'Em* (NATIONAL THEATRE, 1980) to police provocation in *WCPC* (HALF MOON, 1982). *Country Dancing* (Stratford, ROYAL SHAKESPEARE COMPANY, 1986), about the folk-song collector Cecil Sharp, examines conflicting views of the past as romantic myth or grim reality. Williams has more recently turned his attention primarily to television and novels, for which he has established a stronger reputation. BRIAN ROBERTS

Williams, Raymond [Henry] (b. Pandy, Gwent, Wales, 31 Aug. 1921; d. Oxford, 26 Jan. 1989) Cultural theorist. Williams developed the stance of 'cultural materialism', an attempt to relate culture to its material conditions of production which has been very influential in theatre studies. In 1974 he was appointed to the first chair in drama at Cambridge University. His writing on theatre includes *Drama in Performance* (1954), *Modern Tragedy* (1966) and *Drama from Ibsen* *tojyBrecht* (1968). An active lifelong socialist, he wrote two plays for television in the 1960s as well as novels and several outstanding books on culture.

DAN REBELLATO

Williams, Tennessee [Thomas Lanier] (b. Columbus, Miss., 26 March 1911; d. New York, 24 Feb. 1983) Playwright. The son of Edwina Dakin and Cornelius Coffin Williams enjoyed a sheltered early childhood, living at the Episcopal rectory in the small Southern towns where his grandfather Dakin was minister. His life changed abruptly in 1918 when his father moved his wife and children to a small apartment in St Louis. He began writing stories and poems as an escape from his miserable home life. He studied briefly at the University of Missouri, but in 1931 his father insisted that he go to work in a shoe factory warehouse, an experience that was to inspire the autobiographical character of Tom in *The Glass Menagerie* (1945). Several early plays were performed by community theatre groups in St Louis. In 1943 his parents authorized a prefrontal lobotomy on his older sister Rose. He and Rose had always been close; now she became an obsession, her presence permeating much of his work for the rest of his life, from Laura in *The Glass Menagerie* to the sister in *The Two-Character Play* (1975). He adopted the pen-name 'Tennessee' after moving to New Orleans in 1938. He won $100 for a group of one-act plays entitled *American Blues* (1939), followed by a $1,000 Rockefeller Fellowship. The THEATER GUILD opened his *Battle of Angels* (1940) in Boston, but its controversial reception prevented their taking it to New York. Hired as a Hollywood screenwriter, Williams put his best efforts into writing *The Glass Menagerie*. Its openings in 1945 (Chicago) and 1946 (Broadway) signalled the appearance of a major new American playwright and, according to the critic T. E. Kalem, 'galvanized a theatre that had lost its creative momentum'.

Streetcar Named Desire (1947) was the first play to win all three major awards of the time: the Pulitzer Prize, the New York Drama Critics' Circle Award and the Donaldson Award. The play's complex heroine Blanche Dubois remains one of his most compelling creations, an archetypal figure in American drama. *Summer and Smoke* (1948) features a similar clash of the spiritual and the sensual; Williams later revised the play and retitled it *Eccentricities of a Nightingale* (1964). One of Williams' liveliest comedies, *The Rose Tattoo* (1949), was written for Anna Magnani, who finally played the role of Serafina in the 1955 film version. *Camino Real* (1953) mystified audiences at the original production, but the haunting, expressionistic evocation of innocence lost to corruption has steadily gained

admirers over the years. *Cat on a Hot Tin Roof* (1955) illustrates Williams' ability to write a tightly constructed 'continuous action' play, as opposed to the plays of 'cinematic' structure for which he is best known. It features one of Williams' most colourful characters, Big Daddy. The play exists in three versions, but the 1974 revision should now be considered definitive. *Suddenly Last Summer* (1958) is a tightly compressed piece with horrific imagery. *Sweet Bird of Youth* (1959) rounds up several of Williams' perennial themes: violence, loss of purity, the ravages of time, and fear of the decline of creative powers. A slight comedy, *Period of Adjustment* (1960), tends to be overlooked in Williams' canon. *The Night of the Iguana* (1961) brings together several of Williams' most memorable characters: the despairing Reverend Shannon, brassy Maxine Faulk, the inscrutable Hannah Jelkes, and her grandfather Nonno, a poet whose final creation is perhaps Williams' finest poem. *The Two-Character Play* (1967), was produced in several versions, including one entitled *Out Cry* (1971); its beauties have been under-appreciated to date. *Small Craft Warnings* (1972) is an expanded version of *Confessional* (1970), both depicting a collection of drifters in a waterfront bar. In his last years Williams seemed torn between experimentation and a return to his traditional dramas grounded in autobiography. The experimental plays, which never quite caught on with the public, include *The Milk Train Doesn't Stop Here Anymore* (1963), *Slapstick Tragedy* (composed of two one-acters, *The Mutilated* and *Gnädiges Fräulein*, 1966), *In the Bar of a Tokyo Hotel* (1969), *The Red Devil Battery Sign* (1975), and *Clothes for a Summer Hotel* (1980). More accessible, although not as successful as his earlier works, are *Vieux Carré* (1977), set in a New Orleans rooming house in the 1940s, and *A Lovely Sunday for Crève Coeur* (1979), a mix of comedy and pathos set in St Louis. Although tormented by the belief that he had fallen from critical and popular favour, Williams never stopped writing. His *Memoirs* appeared in 1975. Lyle Leverich's two-volume biography, *Tom* (1995) and *Tennessee* (2000), may now be considered the definitive study of his life. FELICIA HARDISON LONDRÉ

Richard F. Leavitt, ed., *The World of Tennessee Williams* (1978)

Felicia Hardison Londré, *Tennessee Williams* (1979)

John S. McCann, *The Critical Reputation of Tennessee Williams: A Reference Guide* (1983)

M. C. Roudane, ed, *The Cambridge Companion to Tennessee Williams* (1997)

D. Spoto, *The Kindness of Strangers* (1985)

M. A. VanAntwerp and S. Johns, eds, *Dictionary of Literary Biography*, vol. 4: *Tennessee Williams* (1984)

· Performing Williams ·

Ever since I decided to act, the part of Blanche DuBois in *A Streetcar Named Desire* was held up as the greatest possible role in American literature for an actress to play. I had the chance to find out over a five-year period, on Broadway, on television and in London's West End, and I discovered that to be true: she is drawn so tenderly, is so rich in colour – there is no other role that offers you so many possibilities.

I couldn't anticipate quite what it was going to be like to play Blanche. For me it turned out to be a very haunting part; it gets under your skin and stays there. After the Broadway production, I felt a longing for her – almost physical. It was hard to shake her off afterwards; I wanted to play her again. The more I played her, the more I loved her, and the last time was the most heartbreaking. But each time I played her there was a different impact, different resonances, and each time it was thrilling.

Williams presents everything in the play so clearly from each of the characters' point of view. They all lose out tremendously. Each one desires so much but they act at cross-purposes. They are lost souls. As you watch Blanche being destroyed by this, you can see how much of your own life is ruled by desire, by wanting. There is sexual desire at the most obvious level, but it goes much deeper than that. What I saw most clearly is the force of youth – specifically, the unforgivingness of youth that makes you act in certain ways; you become more understanding as you get older. The lynchpin for Blanche is the death of her young husband, which she can trace back to her unforgivingness of who he was, and this leads to a lifetime of self-recrimination.

Playing Blanche was a mysterious and fascinating process. I could make a slight adjustment at the very start of the play and it would remain true through to the end. But you can make a radical adjustment, too, and it would still be true. In the PETER HALL production in London, we worked on the more quixotic shifts of character; we found more of them, they happened faster, with a quicker velocity, and the dialogue supported that. That's so rare. Blanche speaks almost nonstop from beginning to end but the words are never a burden. They feed you and energize you. Williams achieves something in the language that is out of the ordinary. On stage I released myself through the words, which took you to where you had to be. To have those words at your fingertips made such a difference. He touches so brilliantly on something universal that I never felt the play was exhausted. It seemed bottomless, and I feel I could play it again and find another million possibilities still. The construction is so solid that the play supports you regardless of the production, like a freight train powering through, more so than in anything else he wrote. It is his most complete and inspired work. JESSICA LANGE

Williamson, David [Keith] Melbourne, 24 Feb. 1942) Playwright. With his second play, *The Removalists* (1971), in which a young policeman finally goes berserk and beats a man to death, Williamson sounded a new note in modern Australian drama. Caustic, savage and comic, it suggested that here was a writer who could both reflect and satirize the society to which he belonged. His later plays (e.g. *Sons of Cain*, 1985; *Emerald City*, 1987; *Money and Friends*, 1992) are more comfortable and comforting, blander and more readily accommodating of his audience, though his dialogue is invariably sharp and clever, and the plays' construction deft and assured. He is Australia's most performed playwright abroad, and has written 25 plays since 1970. These include *The Coming of Stork* (1970), *Don's Party* (1971), *What if you Died Tomorrow* (1973), *The Club* (1977), *Travelling North* (1979), *The Perfectionist* (1982), *Sanctuary* (1994), *Dead White Males* (1995) and *After the Ball* (1998). MICHAEL MORLEY

Williamson, J. C. *see* ADELAIDE; AUSTRALIA

Williamson, Nicol (b. Hamilton, Scotland, 14 Sept. 1938) Actor. Once described as the 'terrible tempered tiger of the English stage', Williamson's temperamental behaviour has overshadowed his earlier achievements. At the ROYAL SHAKESPEARE COMPANY he played Meakin in *Nil Carborundum* (1962), from which followed his towering performance as Bill Maitland in *Inadmissible Evidence* (1964) at the ROYAL COURT. On his return to the RSC he was lauded as Hamlet (1969); *Uncle Vanya* (1973), which he directed at The Other Place, and *Macbeth* (1974) were well received, but his reputation for abusing other actors saw the work dry up in London. Williamson's ability to transform unsympathetic characters into complex, ambiguous creations, and his brooding, savage presence became visible mainly on film and in solo shows.
DAN REBELLATO

Williamstown Theater Festival During the cultural boom after the Second World War, regional theatres in America took root in surprising places. One literally began with a building – the splendid (but idle every summer) Adame Memorial Theater of Williams College in the north-west corner of Massachusetts. Thanks to donations from local residents (including Cole Porter), the doors opened in 1955. The new venture prospered as Nikos Psacharopoulos (artistic director for 33 years) took chances on plays beyond the usual scope of 'summer theatre' – ALBEE, Euripides, GIRAUDOUX, IBSEN, Molière and SHAW; CHEKHOV, hardly a repertory staple at the time, became a fixture. New companies multiplied: an apprentice workshop, a cabaret, literary events, an experimental 'other stage', local outreach to area youngsters, an alfresco 'free theatre'. As its ambitions soared, the theatre formally became the Williamstown Theatre Festival (WTF) and acquired an international reputation.

In essence the theatre's success lies in its double-edged affinity for actors: starting gifted neophytes out on careers and luring established artists to Williamstown. Without its large pool of talent, some of WTF's most daring projects – a two-night celebration of TENNESSEE WILLIAMS, the transfer of *The Seagull* to PBS-TV, the US première of *The Greeks*, a tribute to the GROUP THEATER which became part of an Emmy-winning documentary, an 80th-birthday salute to ARTHUR MILLER on three stages – could never have occurred.

After Psacharopoulos' death in 1989, Peter Hunt guided WTF for six years, with a special emphasis on lost American classics. In 1996 Michael Ritchie became producer, launching a new and concerted effort to link WTF to the cutting edge with the most exciting playwrights and directors in contemporary American theatre. STEVE LAWSON

Willis, Ted [Edward Henry] (b. London, 13 Jan. 1918; d. London, 22 Dec. 1992) Playwright. Formerly a vehicle builder, he learnt his craft at UNITY THEATRE. His pictures of postwar working-class London combined realism, domestic melodrama and humour with faith in traditional community values. Plays include *No Trees in the Street* (1948), *Hot Summer Night* (1959, tackling racial prejudice) and *Woman in a Dressing-gown* (1962). He was a pioneer of the British 'soap opera', scripting the first episodes of the radio serial *Mrs Dale's Diary* (1948) and creating the long-running television serial *Dixon of Dock Green* (1955). He became a Labour peer in 1963, and published two autobiographies, *What Ever Happened to Tom Mix* (1970) and *Evening All* (1991). TONY HOWARD

Wilson, August (b. Pittsburgh, Pa., 27 April 1945) Poet turned playwright who leaped to fame with *Ma Rainey's Black Bottom* (1984), the first in his heavily symbolic cycle of plays depicting the black experience in twentieth-century America. *Fences* (1985, Pulitzer Prize), *Joe Turner's Come and Gone* (1988), *The Piano Lesson* (1987, Pulitzer), *Two Trains Running* (1990), *Seven Guitars* (1995) and *Jitney* (2000) continue this panorama of black life, frequently drawing on his own background and each set in a different decade. Often fierce yet eloquent, his voice, which is particularly associated with LLOYD RICHARDS at the Yale Repertory Theater, has become one of the most prominent in America. Wilson is probably the best known of African American playwrights. LOWELL SWORTZELL

A. Nadel, ed., *May All Your Fences Have Gates: Essays on the Drama of August Wilson* (1994)

Wilson, Francis (b. Philadelphia, 7 Feb. 1854; d. New York, 7 Oct. 1935) Actor and singer. He made his name and fortune in musicals, such as *Erminie* (1886), *The Merry Monarch* (1890), *The Lion Tamer* (1891), *Half a King* (1896) and *The Toreador* (1902). He eventually tried straight acting, in *Cousin Billy* (1904), *The Mountain Climber* (1906) and *When Nights Were Bold* (1907), and writing (e.g. *The Bachelor's Baby*, 1909, a play which ran for three years). Between 1913 and 1921 Wilson was the first president of American Actors' Equity (*see* UNIONS), combining this with writing more plays and books, as well as lecturing. His autobiography, *Francis Wilson's Life of Himself*, appeared in 1924. HELEN RAPPAPORT

Wilson, Lanford [Eugene] (b. Lebanon, Mo., 13 April 1937) Playwright. Wilson emerged in New York's OFF-OFF BROADWAY CAFÉ THEATRES of the 1960s and, with widening success, has gone on to write over 40 short and long plays, many exploring the nature of family relationships. He is best known for *The Rimers of Eldritch* (1966), *Lemon Sky* (1970), *The Hot l Baltimore* (1972), *The Fifth of July* (1978), *Talley's Folly* (1979) and *Burn This* (1987). He was a founder of the CIRCLE REPERTORY COMPANY with his long-time directorial collaborator Marshall Mason. GERALD RABKIN

Anne M. Dean, *Discovery and Invention: The Urban Plays of Lanford Wilson* (1994)
Philip M. Williams, *A Comfortable House: Lanford Wilson, Marshall W. Mason, and the Circle Repertory Theater* (1998)

Wilson, Robert [M.] (b. Waco, Texas, 4 Oct. 1941) Theatre maker. A painter whose canvas is the stage, Wilson uses architectural principles to structure his dream worlds, and lights them with meticulous radiance. The rigorously choreographed actions of his performers reflect the unhurried rhythms of nature and his interest in the orient. His early work, like *A Letter to Queen Victoria* (1974), was influenced by the experiences of autistic children. *The Life and Times of Joseph Stalin* (1973) lasted 12 hours and *Ka Mountain* for a whole week at the 1972 Shiraz Festival, Iran. Wilson has often produced and played in his pieces, many epic in scope; he is always their director and chief designer. The best known is *Einstein on the Beach* (1976), an opera created with composer PHILIP GLASS. He has also collaborated with opera singer Jessye Norman, the singers David Byrne and Tom Waits, the novelist William Burroughs and choreographer LUCINDA CHILDS. From the 1980s, Wilson began to work more in Europe and has staged plays and operas, both classic (e.g. Büchner's *Danton's Death*, 1992) and contemporary, by others (e.g. MÜLLER's *Hamletmachine*, 1986). His *Dr Faustus Lights the Lights* (1993) and *Orlando* (1996, adapted from Virginia Woolf) were both seen at the EDINBURGH FESTIVAL. An important retrospective was mounted at Boston's Museum of Fine Arts in 1991 alongside his production of IBSEN's *When We Dead Awaken*. His visionary art is a major influence on twentieth-century theatre. M. ELIZABETH OSBORN

See also AVANT-GARDE; ENVIRONMENTAL THEATRE; EXPERIMENTAL THEATRE.

Stefan Brecht, *The Theatre of Visions: Robert Wilson* (1984)

A. Holmberg, *The Theatre of Robert Wilson* (1997)

L. Shyer, *Robert Wilson and His Collaborators* (1989)

Wilson, Sandy [Alexander Galbraith] (b. Sale, Manchester, 19 May 1924) Songwriter. Wilson made his initial impact as a writer and composer in the early 1950s, in the heyday of the small CLUB THEATRES into which British REVUE and MUSICAL THEATRE writers had retreated under the postwar barrage of BROADWAY musicals. His 1953 musical comedy *The Boy Friend*, produced at the tiny Players' Theatre, secured his fame. An affectionate pastiche of the *No, No, Nanette* brand of 1920s musical, for which Wilson wrote book, lyrics and music, it was transferred to the West End, where it became one of the longest-running shows of London theatre history, prior to a vast and worldwide succession of productions over the next 40 years. A highly skilful 1958 musical play, *Valmouth*, based on the esoteric works of Ronald Firbank, won as much success with the cognoscenti as *The Boy Friend* had with the public, and an attractive 1930s sequel to *The Boy Friend*, *Divorce Me, Darling* (1964), again progressed from the Players' Theatre to the West End, but Wilson's subsequent works were confined to the small theatres which best suited his intimate style. His autobiography, *Could Be Happy*, came out in 1975. KURT GÄNZL

Wilson, Snoo [Andrew] (b. Reading, Berks, 2 Aug. 1948) Playwright and director. He co-founded one of the key ALTERNATIVE companies, Portable Theatre, in 1968. Early work with them included *Pericles, the Mean Knight* (1970); *Pignight* and *Blowjob* (1971); and two pieces written collaboratively, *Lay-By* (1971) and *England's Ireland* (1972). He also directed for Portable.

He enjoyed a period of controversial success on the FRINGE and at the ROYAL SHAKESPEARE COMPANY and ROYAL COURT, with a number of plays focusing on the individual, cult figures and the subconscious, such as *Vampire* (1973), *The Pleasure Principle* (1973), *The Beast* (1974), *The Soul of the White Ant* (1976), *England-England* (1977) and *The Glad Hand* (1978), for which he received the John Whiting Award. In the 1980s his anarchic dramas fell out of fashion. He worked in the university sector in America and has continued to write, e.g. *Lynchville* (1989), *Callas* (1990), *Darwin's Flood* (1994), *Bedbug* (adapted from MAYAKOVSKY, 1995), and *Sabina* (1998). BRIAN ROBERTS

Wilton, Marie *see* BANCROFT, SQUIRE

Witkiewicz, Stanislaw Ignacy ('Witkacy') (b. Warsaw, 24 Feb. 1885; d. Jeziory, Ukraine, 18 Sept. 1939) Philosopher, painter, novelist and playwright. He was a 'catastrophist' who committed suicide, considering his prophecies fulfilled, the day after the Soviet army, in alliance with the Nazis, entered the Polish eastern territories in 1939. Witkacy was the forerunner of modern trends in literature and theatre and a pioneer of existentialism. Calling in the early 1920s for radical change in the name of audience involvement in 'metaphysical anxiety', Witkacy established an original aesthetic theory based on pure form. This he saw as an absolute freedom of composition, achieved by rejecting any real-life basis of action, behaviour or psychological motivation. Conscious of the decay of the old civilization and its approaching destruction, he broke the dramatic conventions through SURREALISM and grotesque tragedy. Unfortunately, both his aesthetics and his obsessions came too early for European sensibilities, which were illuminated only a few years after his death by similar feelings of despair, fear and moral crisis.

Of his 30 plays, the main ones include *Pragmatysci* (*Pragmatists*, 1919), *Tumor Mozgowicz* (*Tumor Brainowicz*, 1920), *Metafizyka dwuglowego cielecia* (*The Metaphysics of a Two-Headed Calf*, 1921), *W malym dworku* (*In The Small Country-House*, 1921), *Kurka wodna* (*The Water Hen*, 1921), *Matwa* (*The Cuttle Fish*, 1922), *Wariat i zakonnica* (*The Madman and the Nun*, 1923), *Matka* (*The Mother*, 1924) and *Szewcy* (*The Shoemakers*, 1934). JOANNA KRAKOWSKA-NAROŻNIAK

Daniel C. Gerould, *Witkacy: Stanislaw Ignacy Witkiewicz as an Imaginative Writer* (1981)

Wodehouse, P[elham] G[ranville] (b. Guildford, Surrey, 15 Oct. 1881; d. Long Island, NY, 14 Feb. 1975) Author, humorist and lyricist. He began his career as a journalist and was drama critic of *Vanity Fair*. Though now perhaps best known for his *Jeeves* books, he also wrote plays and libretti, many in collaboration with GUY BOLTON, including *Leave it to Jane* (1917), *Oh, Kay* (1926) and *Anything Goes* (1934). He was knighted in 1975. REXTON S. BUNNETT

A. A. Jones, *The Theatre of P. G. Wodehouse* (1979)

Wolf, Friedrich (b. Neuwied, Rhineland, 23 Dec. 1888; d. Lehnitz, Brandenburg, 5 Oct. 1953) Playwright who began his theatrical career with several EXPRESSIONIST plays. After 1923, while pursuing his profession as a physician, he produced a large number of socialist realist dramas, both in Germany and while in exile from the Nazis. They included *Cyankali* ('Cyanide', 1929), about abortion, *Die Matrosen von Cattano* (*The Sailors of Cattano*, 1930) and *Florisdorf* (1935). He participated in the revolutionary workers' theatre movement and became one of the most important and successful political playwrights in Germany. His theories of POLITICAL THEATRE (expounded in, for example, his programmatic speech of 1928, 'Art as a Weapon') influenced many dramatists and theatre practitioners.

Wolf's model of political theatre can be seen as the antithesis of BRECHT's EPIC THEATRE and was usually preferred by socialist theatre artists until the end of the 1950s. Wolf's plays rely on the dramatic mechanisms typical of Aristotelian theatre. His *Professor Mamlock* (1934) was the most successful anti-fascist play of the 1930s and 1940s. After the war he influenced a whole generation of young dramatists in the German Democratic Republic. GÜNTER BERGHAUS

H. F. Garten, *Modern German Drama* (1964)

Wolfe, George C. (b. Frankfort, Ky., 23 Sept. 1954). Playwright, director. He came to prominence with *The Coloured Museum* (1986), a satire on contemporary black life which was also seen in London, and *Spunk* (1989), based on three Zora Neale Hurston stories, which he directed as well. In 1990 he directed BRECHT's *Caucasian Chalk Circle* set in Haiti and in 1992 TONY KUSHNER's *Angels in America*, for which Wolfe won a Tony Award. He also directed his own musical *Jelly's Last Stand* (1992) about Jelly Roll Morton and in 1993 was appointed to run the NEW YORK SHAKESPEARE FESTIVAL. CHARLES LONDON

Wolfit [Woolfitt], Donald (b. Newark-on-Trent, Notts, 20 April 1902; d. London, 17 Feb. 1968) Actor–manager. He toured in his early twenties with Fred Terry's company and seems to have been imbued with the idea of becoming, like Terry, an actor–manager in the old tradition. It was, however, some years before he formed his own Shakespearean company (1937), after earning a reputation as a classical actor at the OLD VIC (1929/30) and at STRATFORD-UPON-AVON (1936). From then on, although economics occasionally obliged him to appear with other companies, he did so with obvious reluctance and he kept his own company on the road as much as possible, playing a largely Shakespearean repertoire. He gave himself all the 'big' parts – Shylock, Macbeth, Volpone – and excelled as King Lear. For other managers, he was a flamboyant Captain Hook in *Peter Pan* (1954), an evil Edward Moulton-Barrett in *The Barretts of Wimpole Street* (1932) and its musical version *Robert and Elizabeth* (1966), and a demonic Svengali in a film version of *Trilby* (1954). But his heart was in Shakespeare and, when it became impossible to run a full company, he toured the world in a Shakespeare recital (1960), just as he had presented scenes from Shakespeare in popular lunchtime performances during the Battle of Britain. He wrote an autobiography, *First Interval* (1955). He was much helped by his third wife, the actress Rosalind Iden, and he was lovingly portrayed by his biographer, Ronald Harwood, in the play *The Dresser* (1980, filmed 1983), which was a bigger success than any Wolfit had had in his lifetime. He was knighted in 1957. IAN BEVAN

R. Harwood, *Sir Donald Wolfit* (1971)

Wolfsohn, Alfred (b. Berlin, 23 Sept. 1896; d. London, 5 Feb. 1962) Medic who suffered aural hallucinations after witnessing horrifying cries of the wounded and dying in the First World War, and who cured himself by training his voice to make these sounds and thereby vanquishing the emotions and memories associated with them. Wolfsohn became influenced by the psychologist Carl Jung, who proposed that the human mind contains a gallery of images, moods, instincts and characters which manifest themselves visually in dreams. Wolfsohn believed that these psychological elements could be expressed audibly through singing and sound-making. In the 1940s he opened a voice studio in London where he trained people to develop vocal ranges of between four and eight octaves. Among his pupils was ROY HART and, though little known, his influence has spread widely among some of the century's greatest innorators, such as BARRAULT, BROOK, CAGE and GROTOWSKI. PAUL NEWHAM

women in theatre Why an article on 'women in theatre'? The most cursory perusal of the panoply of pre-twentieth-century drama will provide the clue to the complex answer to so simple a question. Open a collection of plays by Shakespeare and glance down the list of characters: men first, women second; men in the overwhelming majority. Move on to post-Restoration drama: the imbalance is somewhat redressed, but even in the plays of Aphra Behn (the first professional woman playwright of any substance) the ratio is two to one, in favour of the male characters.

Until the Restoration (1660) women were not officially welcome in the professional theatre (although courtly women wrote plays and masques, and women were an active part of itinerant, popular theatre); through the eighteenth and nineteenth centuries actresses established themselves more and more firmly, along with the popular concomitant assumption that women performers were but a step away from prostitution. It was not until the end of the nineteenth century that a further step forward was taken in establishing women's place as a central part of the theatrical tradition, and this came about as a result of new developments in both the artistic and political spheres.

First, an important new dynamic took charge of developments in playwriting, through the influence of naturalism in the arts. This move, exemplified particularly in the French novel, and to a degree in French theatre, gave rise to the influential work of IBSEN, which was to have a decisive influence in England, indirectly in conjunction with the plays of GEORGE BERNARD SHAW. Plays could be seen to be about present-day life and issues, with ordinary, prose speech, rather than heightened poetry. Also, in the second half of the nineteenth century the waves of feminist activity appropriate to Western industrial society began, culminating significantly in the Women's Social and Political Union (1903) which over the following decades stepped up the campaign for women to gain the vote. That there was a link between these two elements can be seen in the fact that Eleanor Marx (Karl Marx's daughter) organized readings of Ibsen's plays in London in the 1880s and 1890s.

The beginning of the twentieth century saw the birth of the REPERTORY MOVEMENT, thanks to ANNIE HORNIMAN, and the transformation of the OLD VIC under LILIAN BAYLIS into a popular classical theatre of national importance. At the same time, a movement for social change, and a new realistic focus on drama, began a series of individual and organizational waves, each of which shunted the question of the place of women further and further to the surface. The ACTRESSES' FRANCHISE LEAGUE (1908) produced short plays and monologues which were used as illustrative aids to the struggle for the vote, and in the process a number of actresses – such as Gertrude Robins and CICELY HAMILTON – turned playwrights. During the First World War women supplied a large part of the membership of the concert parties which toured with entertainment for the troops. During the 1920s the PIONEER PLAYERS, founded by EDITH CRAIG, daughter of ELLEN TERRY, developed from the earlier AFS; the administration and artistic direction was controlled by women, and they continued producing serious drama into the mid-1920s. Osiris, possibly the first all-women professional touring group, was formed by Nancy Hewins (1902–78) in 1927 and ceased activity only in the 1960s. The campaigning labour movement theatre in the 1930s (UNITY theatre groups, and the network of Left Book Club Theatre Groups) included plays on women's issues, and a rather more secular organization, the Arts League of Service Travelling Theatre (inspired by the League of Nations) functioned during the interwar years (1919–37), managed and produced by Eleanor Elder, putting on plays including those by AUGUSTA GREGORY. The Unity Theatre Movement included, as one of its great successes, *Men Should Weep*, by Glasgow writer ENA LAMONT STEWART. First performed in the 1930s, it was revived during a later resurgence of activism on women's behalf in the 1970s. The AVANT-GARDE arm of the interwar years was represented by the London GROUP THEATRE (1932–39), which included among its members artist Vanessa Bell and actress/writer Antonia White.

After the Second World War, the watershed year of change for British theatre, 1956, when JOHN OSBORNE's *Look Back in Anger* was produced, also included a very successful West End play by a woman writer, ENID BAGNOLD: *The Chalk Garden*. In the next new wave of post-1956 theatre, with the subject matter broadened to focus on ordinary people, and reaching out to more popular forms, the work of JOAN LITTLEWOOD in London's East End was particularly vital. Through her theatre, playwright SHELAGH DELANEY became established; on the other side of London the ROYAL COURT, another home of new writing, put on the work of ANN JELLICOE and Doris Lessing. In 1968 theatre censorship was finally abolished in Britain, and this at long last enabled drama to flex a genuine variety of ideological, aesthetic and political wings, engendering a nationwide movement of drama that ranged from the most avant-garde of performance forms to the most AGITPROP-influenced, and taking in along the way the whole gamut of text-based theatre.

It can be seen, even from this very swift survey of theatre in the first half of the twentieth century, that

· Women in theatre ·

As a child, acting was an escape from myself – from 'you've only got one life.' I wanted at least nine. Boy's lives if possible. They had more fun, and were thought more important. In this I was like most of my friends, until they grew out of playing and left me behind.

Years later, I went to DRAMA SCHOOL, and here there were no such renegades. Make-believe was called Theatre and Play became Work. I was legitimate. For the first two years out of three we were nurtured in the ideals of ENSEMBLE work. 'Stardom' and 'career' were words not in our vocabulary. Then the third year was upon us with a shock. We were being groomed for the status quo. We were to make ourselves sellable; and the prettiest would sell best. I was advised to have my nose changed and my teeth fixed. 'But what has that to do with CHEKHOV?' I wondered. It was as though we had all been running together in the marathon, all aiming in the same direction while going at our own speed, and then suddenly the rules had been changed. Now it seemed we were competing in the Olympics, where only the gold, silver and bronze medals counted, where my success necessarily means your failure (and vice versa) and where everyone else is an also-ran. Luckily, by joining a COMMUNITY theatre and spending most of the next decade on the FRINGE and in political touring companies like JOINT STOCK and 7:84, I could rinse out the nasty taste that the final year at drama school had left in my mouth, and continue where the second had abruptly left off.

When I joined the ROYAL SHAKESPEARE COMPANY, both they and the NATIONAL THEATRE were embracing many of the ideas developed in the fringe, as well as absorbing a lot of the writing and acting talent that had grown up there – my first job, in *Nicholas Nickleby*, was a sort of giant-scale workshop which used all those hat-changing, scene-shifting and quick-fire storytelling techniques that were so familiar to me. Via this bridge of familiarity I embarked on the classics, and unimagined mountain peaks reared up before me. Shakespeare's texts demand all of you. The brain, the heart, the body, the imagination. Of course, all acting should demand that, but it seldom does. With Shakespeare, one must not limit the character one is playing to one's own size. The heightened language forces one to think and feel on a grander scale, and I learnt that acting was a question not of escaping the self, but of transcending the self, and paradoxically one could only do that if truly connected with one's self. A lifetime's work ... but the Shakespearean repertoire for women does not span a lifetime. It barely scrapes you past the wedding day. Just at that point when an actress arguably has the most skill and life experience to contribute, and just when her male counterparts are barely beginning to scale the acting mountains ahead of them, our path runs out, give or take the odd Lady Macbeth. Yet only in the classical theatre is there any semblance of a career ladder; in the freelance world doing a job is the easy bit and having none is hard work. Actresses are weeded out at a punishingly early age, and those few left in the 'contest' have usually a high price to pay in their private lives.

The trick is to keep your feet on the ground while reaching for the clouds, to keep hold of your wildest dreams while looking reality in the eye. And the jugglers! I see them all around me – women managing miraculously to keep several balls in the air: creativity with child rearing, integrity with service, anger with generosity, celibacy with celebrity, ideals with practicalities. Some are mothers whose children have grown up and who want to relaunch their careers, but have missed too many boats; some were too busy with their careers to have a family, and now find it's too late; some have had children late and are overtired and rejuvenated all at once; some are actresses sick of being expected to play parts which reduce rather than expand them, who are re-routing their displaced energy into writing, directing or some other activity.

What an interesting point women have reached in the real world; but how imperfectly this is reflected in drama. Why is such infinite variety usually reduced to a few tired old types? Art is supposed to hold a mirror up to nature, but in this respect it is lagging far behind. Is it a question of how we define what is dramatically interesting? The tradition is that conflict and violence are dramatic, and they are the province of men: moral dilemma is dramatic and is traditionally the burden of men; public life is male, domestic is female and public is more important than domestic. These are outmoded habits of thinking, but on stage (and on screen even more so) they die hard.

True, many more women are writing the scripts now, but that alone won't solve the problem. Great writers of either gender do not grow on trees, and it takes time to hone this exceptional skill. Women playwrights cannot be expected overnight to counterbalance the weight of centuries of male writing. And then there is fashion. The feminism which inspired a generation of female playwrights in the 1970s and 1980s is no longer news, and many of their successors are caught up in a kind of laddism which is something of a double-edged sword for women. Besides all this, women over 40 have seldom counted in the fashion stakes of any generation.

Often we look to the great male playwrights of the early twentieth century (Chekhov, IBSEN, LORCA, BECKETT, COWARD, to name a random few) for the best roles for women. They wrote these roles not to do actresses a favour, but because for various reasons they identified with the female in society and recognized the universal significance of the changes happening to her. This ability to empathize across the genders points the way forward. Empathy is a muscle of the imagination which can be developed through exercise, and women have had to stretch that muscle more than men. As theatregoers starved of female role models we have learnt to identify with King Lear, Othello and Henry V; so why can't men do what we have done for centuries and try identifying with Goneril, Beatrice or Ophelia? Rigid gender defnitions have cramped us all. Whether male or female, writer, performer or spectator, we all need to find new forms of dramatic expression and discussion. Necessity is the mother of Invention; but who says Invention has to be a boy?

HARRIET WALTER

at all points a very small number of women made their influential mark. The occasional energetic and crusading woman remained precisely that. After 1968, a new wave of feminism ensured that for the first time there was a genuinely concerted attempt by women to breach their secondary status in the theatre. The women's liberation movement drew women from all aspects of society into a series of campaigns and debates that for the first time challenged women's secondary social status across the board. In the movement's literature and actions, gender relations in society were analysed with thoroughness, bringing together attitudes to women at work, in the family, in culture, and in the way that men and women internalize ideas about their respective roles in the world. Above all, the movement, and the feminism it produced, challenged misogynist views of 'human nature', based on the assumption that the biological differences between men and women mean that the latter are inferior to the former, and that everything women are and do is inherently less important and less valued than the equivalent activities of men. The alternative view, that women have a 'special' and precious role as wives and mothers, and that therefore all other aspirations are 'unnatural', received equally short shrift.

Although feminism itself contained different political strands, they all, in some form, challenged the assumption that only men were equipped to hold power in all spheres of political and cultural life; and the way women were represented in theatre, as workers, as well as in the work on stage, received new and varied attention. Throughout the 1970s and 1980s a range of groups and individuals drew further active attention to the position of women in the theatre industry: actresses, playwrights, directors, designers, administrators and technicians sought, in a mixture of ways, to redress the gender imbalance in the theatre. Several companies had a self-consciously militant aim in their work: the WOMEN'S THEATRE GROUP, developed out of STREET THEATRE and agitprop theatre, from 1974 onwards commissioned and devised plays which took women's oppression and experience as their subject matter. As an all-women touring company it actively sought out audiences in non-theatre venues (schools, community halls, etc.), often following plays with discussions of the issues among their audiences (very much in the style of the time); GAY SWEATSHOP, also a touring company, took the issue of sexual politics (power based on gender or sexual orientation) on board in its representation of homosexual experience in its drama. Sweatshop consisted of both men and women, although a large part of their work was created by separate single-sex companies; MONSTROUS REGIMENT was a mixed company but with a majority of women deciding policy and programming, which was placed on the divide between 'issue-based' plays and 'art' plays. Some of their work confronted relationships between men and women more directly.

The new debates about the position of women in society, as well as the activities of women themselves, made it possible for new generations of women playwrights to explore new kinds of subject matter. The most successful and well-known of these has been CARYL CHURCHILL, but there are many other women writers who have emerged as dramatists; Churchill's generation includes Olwen Wymark and PAM GEMS, and there are younger generations of writers that have included TIMBERLAKE WERTENBAKER, LOUISE PAGE, SARAH DANIELS, Debbie Horsfield and SARAH KANE. However, despite this genuine increase in the profile of women in theatre, the basic predominance of men remains. A small number of women have latterly become artistic directors of theatres (Clare Venables, Sue Dunderdale, Jenny Topper, Annie Castledine, Yonne Brewster, Deborah Paige, for example) or their theatres' most senior executives (Genista McIntosh, Ruth McKenzie, Sue Storr, Venu Dhupa, to name a few); Jude Kelly combined the two posts. But overwhelmingly the issue of parity in theatre – women as 50 per cent of the work force across the board – is still quite some way off. The basic questions about why women have been relatively absent in influencing theatre work (as opposed to, say, the novel, where they have been, and are, prominent) remain. Terms such as 'women's theatre', 'feminist theatre', 'theatre for women' or 'separatist theatre' are used fairly loosely in both books and journalism to try to define the ways in which women have made their presence felt. All these terms can be used positively, by women seeking to define the nature of their work, or negatively, by hostile critics who accuse women of working in a ghetto by virtue of wanting to represent the 50 per cent of the population they feel has been under-represented. Some arguments put by women journalists have conflated the institutional power held by men with the nature of theatrical form itself – claiming that the structure of plays is in some inherent way gendered and 'male'. This is not a useful argument, because it diverts attention from the more important issues of content and the way argument (or 'message') is conveyed through a work of fiction.

Other aesthetic questions about the relationship between gender and playwriting remain very much open to discussion: can men write well about women? Can women write well about men? How much does it matter? Is each sex confined in its own gendered perspective on the world? Does the genuinely original imagination transcend or harness the differences? The fact is that while all these questions are crucial to an expansion of aesthetic theory of theatre, the basic structure of the industry still operates overwhelmingly in favour of men. In the professional theatre, patterns of employment are pyramid-shaped as regards gender, with women at the base. The higher up the hierarchy one goes, the fewer women there are. Permanent theatre companies have far more men than women, reflecting the fact that although drama schools turn out more or less equal numbers of men and women, plays (ancient and modern) still have predominantly male casts. Thus actresses are more likely to spend longer unemployed than actors. Behind the scenes (literally), although a handful of women technicians have made inroads in the fields of lighting and backstage staffing, they still tend to be relegated to stage management roles, on the grounds, by no means

always justifiable, that the manual work is heavy and unsuitable for women. Other so-called women's jobs tend to reflect professionalized aspects of women's domestic, familial roles. Women are commonly found as CASTING directors, as VOICE coaches and in charge of WIGS, MAKE-UP and wardrobe or COSTUME DESIGN. In keeping with other office-based work, women predominate in the secretarial sphere; and also as publicity officers, reflecting the still prevalent view that a pretty young woman can help sell a commodity (the play) to journalists and critics.

The conundrum which has exercised women is how to go about changing things with the aim of achieving parity across the board, with women as 50 per cent of the work force, and representation from their own varied perspective as part of the subject matter of drama. Counter-arguments include the point of view that artistic directors must always have the freedom to choose what is 'best', and if women simply do not emerge as part of that category, then it must mean that women are not good enough. One answer to that is that aesthetic choice is not based on abstract non-social factors alone, and that the ideological bias of the person making the choice (the stereotype of which is the middle-aged, white, middle-class male) is bound to determine the nature of the chosen object, either to reflect his (sic) concerns, or to create a form of patronage in which work by a different social group (women, or drama of ethnic origin) is given a brief look-in. Additionally, theatre, like many other industries, demands work at unsocial hours; biological differences between men and women are a reality, and in order for women to have genuinely freer opportunities, provision for childcare (social as well as private) remains a consideration. It is no coincidence that some women become playwrights when they have children, since writing is easier than, say, the job of a touring actress to juggle with maternal commitments.

There is another element, more complex and more subtle than the material obstacles outlined above: this is the nature of the (often unrealized) prejudice against the presence of more women as playwrights. It is the case historically that whenever there is an increase in the number of women playwrights there is an increase in the number of parts for women, and a shift to a more woman-centred bias in the plays around. The art of playwriting is a far more public enterprise than, say, the art of novel-writing. The playwright creates a stage world in which dialogue is spoken on a platform to a live audience. It is direct, immediate communication. The fact that theatre censorship was retained until so very recently testifies to the fact that many people still see the theatre as akin to a public political platform,

even though it is the locus for fictional creation rather than factual polemic. Certainly theatre's direct form of communication has made it suitable for the development of the agitprop form (fiction in support of ideological persuasion), but it is not in itself a form of hustings. It is also the case that in public life, in spheres where public speaking is an essential part of a profession, women figure in a tiny minority. The great orators of history are men, and it is simply not a matter of course to be familiar with women as custodians of public speech. Thus for a woman to write the words for men and women to 'speak' in a play, and to increase the number of female voices heard, let alone make public the relatively privatized concerns of women, is – whether she claims to be a feminist or not – a relatively subversive thing for a woman to do. The exception always proves the rule, and the reason for drawing attention to the category of 'women in theatre' is to question the rule that prevents one of our culture's most vital art forms (and in Britain one of its most prolific) from being more fully representative of half the population. Surveys of theatre audiences always show that more women than men go to the theatre; the amateur theatre world is peopled by societies where women are in the majority. This is reflected in drama written for the amateur market, where a higher proportion of women write plays, and where plays for all-female casts outnumber those for all-male casts by nearly three to one. The imbalance is clear.
MICHELENE WANDOR

In the United States
American theatre at the beginning of the twentieth century was influenced by the turmoil of the country's burgeoning economic success – its expanding population, especially in cities; its industrial metamorphosis; widespread education, individual empowerment and increasing sexual freedom. Classical drama was being rejected by the desire of a vast and varied audience to see their own commonplace lives portrayed on stage. A more sophisticated audience exposed to the naturalistic 'new drama' of the socially aware prose plays written by Ibsen and Shaw came to view staged entertainment more as a public forum that could reflect and explore the social changes that were spreading throughout America. Many of the changes involved – indeed, were spearheaded – by women eager to seek equality politically and artistically. The way in which women established themselves in the theatre is the story of their contribution to twentieth-century American theatre. The 'legitimate' stage where women could pursue artistic ambition also became a place where women, eager for political recognition, could speak out

in a socially conscious and acceptable format. By 1910 a proliferation of women playwrights were mirroring, at times implicitly criticizing, their society. Stereotyped off stage and on, the women involved in the theatre countered conventional wisdom with a realistic depiction of the changes and problems in a rapidly evolving America. Women playwrights such as RACHEL CROTHERS, SUSAN GLASPELL, Alice Gerstenberg (1885–1972) and SOPHIE TREADWELL enjoyed major careers, broke new ground, experimented with form, and presented a wide range of subject matter based on their lives.

Ever since the English Restoration, when women were at last allowed to play themselves on stage, actresses have been popular entertainers in many kinds of public performances and have enjoyed respected reputations. MAUDE ADAMS, HELEN HAYES, KATHARINE CORNELL, CORNELIA OTIS SKINNER and ETHEL BARRYMORE are pioneers of the stage. But actresses have often chosen to do double duty as actress–playwrights or actress–directors to ensure their visions would be presented. Despite the entrenched position of men as producers, directors, critics and theatre owners, women have exerted their right to creative expression by becoming playwrights, producers, directors, critics, acting teachers, and theatre owners and founders. Martha Morton (1865–1925), commemorated now as American's first professional woman playwright, wrote popular plays to showcase particular stars, but she directed many of her own plays as well, and, most importantly, in 1907 she founded the Society of Dramatic Authors, 30 of whose original members were women unable to join the exclusively male American Dramatists' Club. In 1921, for her play *Miss Lulu Bett*, Zona Gale was the first woman to win a Pulitzer Prize for Drama. In following decades other women were honoured: Susan Glaspell in 1931 for *Alison's House*; ZOE AKINS in 1935 for *The Old Maid*; Mary Chase in 1945 for *Harvey*; Ketti Frings in 1958 for *Look Homeward, Angel*. Not until the 1980s did plays by women again earn Pulitzer recognition with WENDY WASSERSTEIN, MARSHA NORMAN and BETH HENLEY. The 1950s gave us plays by African American women, including ALICE CHILDRESS and LORRAINE HANSBERRY's *A Raisin in the Sun* on Broadway. Throughout the early and middle decades of the twentieth century women could and did earn a living and in some cases a reputation for writing plays. In addition to professional playwrights women known for other distinctions also wrote plays: MAE WEST, GERTRUDE STEIN, Edna St Vincent Millay, Zora Neal Hurston, CLARE BOOTH LUCE, Dorothy Parker, CARSON MCCULLERS. Perhaps America's best-known woman playwright remains LILLIAN HELLMAN, whose career spanned 30 years from the 1930s to the 1960s.

Her pre-eminence perhaps overshadows the careers of other women playwrights who did not enjoy such mainstream success. Broadway has not been historically hospitable to women, but that has not prevented women from pursuing other avenues. Perhaps taking their cue from playwright Susan Glaspell, who, in 1915, co-founded the PROVINCETOWN PLAYERS in order to produce her own plays as well as those by EUGENE O'NEILL, many actresses and playwrights starting out in the second half of the twentieth century became active career producers: small theatre companies proliferated throughout the country, giving a voice to women and other minority viewpoints. In the 1930s HALLIE FLANAGAN headed the FEDERAL THEATER PROJECT. In 1946–7 EVA LE GALLIENNE, CHERYL CRAWFORD and MARGARET WEBSTER put together the AMERICAN REPERTORY THEATER. Other regional theatres were founded, notably the ARENA STAGE in 1961, headed by Zelda Fichlander, to house a permanent professional company. Theresa Helburn and Cheryl Crawford, a co-founder of the ACTORS' STUDIO, established the THEATER GUILD. Nina Vance, following the example of MARGO JONES who founded the 47–50 Dallas theatre company, founded the ALLEY THEATER, which by 1968 had become a 1,100-seat house producing new work as well as classics.

The women's liberation movement in the volatile 1960s encouraged not just women playwrights but also women producers in their efforts to establish serious theatre communities. The non-profit theatres became a welcoming alternative to playwrights whose work could not be accommodated in mainstream theatre and gave many women a base of power from which to operate. One of the first was ELLEN STEWART's Café LA MAMA (1961), followed by Women's Experimental Theatre, Murial Miguel's SPIDERWOMAN, Women's Interact, Martha Bosing's AT THE FOOT OF THE MOUNTAIN and MABOU MINES, co-founded by Ruth Maleczech, as well as the SPLIT BRITCHES Company producing feminist and lesbian plays at WOW Café. A distinct group of solo artists from RUTH DRAPER to KAREN FINLEY, who write and perform their own stories, are popular; many come from the art world and their texts are powerful. LUCILLE LORTEL has produced plays OFF-BROADWAY for 50 years. Lynn Meadows at the MANHATTAN THEATER CLUB has been actively producing and directing for many years. But while these women have produced male and female playwrights, Julia Miles, founder and artistic director of THE WOMEN'S PROJECT and Productions, is notable as a producer determined to give women a unique theatrical home and support system for their work. Since its debut in 1978, The Women's Project has become the oldest and largest professional theatre dedicated to producing plays exclusively by women. And though some women today produce for the commercial Broadway theatre, women have found a warmer welcome in the smaller non-profit theatres in New York City and across the country where audiences have been able to embrace a wide range of talent, ideology and ethnicity in the works of playwrights such as MARÍA IRENE FORNÉS, NTOZAKE SHANGE, MEGAN TERRY, ADRIENNE KENNEDY, PAULA VOGEL and TINA HOWE.

And so, throughout the century, many women actively and persistently pursued their art, their vision, their passion, defying convention, contradicting stereotypes, exploding myths and sometimes simply entertaining. Playwrights who are women and creative directors such as JULIE TAYMOR, MARTHA CLARKE, Ann Bogart, JOANNE AKALAITIS, Elizabeth LeCompte, ANNA DEVEARE SMITH and EMILY MANN will continue to re-invent the theatrical experience for the new century.

JULIA MILES

Elaine Aston, *An Introduction to Feminist Theatre* (1995)
Lizbeth Goodman, *Contemporary Feminist Theatre* (1993)
Trevor R. Griffiths and Margaret Llewellyn-Jones, *British and Irish Women Dramatists since 1958* (1993)
H. Manfull, *Taking Stage: Women Directors on Directing* (1998)
H. Stephenson and N. Langridge, *Rage and Reason: Women Playwrights on Playwriting* (1997)
Michelene Wandor, *Carry On Understudies* (1986)

Women's Project, The Producing company founded in New York in 1978 by Julia Miles when she was working at the American Place Theatre, which, under Wynn Handman, was dedicated to presenting new American plays. The project set up on its own in 1987 to offer a platform for women writers and directors through publication, rehearsed readings and full production.

CHARLES LONDON

See also WOMEN IN THEATRE.

Women's Theatre Group A British feminist group that grew out of STREET THEATRE activity and INTERACTION'S Women's Theatre Season (1973) and was formed in 1974 in the forefront of gender-based radical theatre. They worked as a COLLECTIVE and often devised plays. Political insight has been matched by experiments with form, from AGITPROP (e.g. *My Mother Says I Never Should*, 1975, about contraception, aimed at teenagers) to a modernist dance of archetypes, *Pax* (1984) by Deborah Levy. In 1991 it changed its name to The Sphinx. Writers who have worked with the group include PAM GEMS, Michelene Wandor, Donna Franceschild, Bryony Lavery, Clare McIntyre, Melissa Murray, TIMBERLAKE WERTENBAKER and WINSOME PINNOCK. COLIN CHAMBERS

See also WOMEN IN THEATRE.

Wood, Aubrey *see* AGENTS

Wood, Charles [Gerald] (b. St Peter Port, Guernsey, 6 August 1932) Playwright. Coming from a theatrical family, Wood turned to playwriting after working backstage, including for a time at THEATRE WORKSHOP. He has tended to draw on his own life and focus on the theatre, as in *Fill the Stage with Happy Hours* (1966); the film industry, as in *Veterans* (1972) and *Has 'Washington' Legs?* (1978); or, most powerfully, on war: *Cockade* (1963), *'H'* (1969) and, perhaps his best play, *Dingo* (1967), a brutal and horrifying satire on patriotic myths of the Second World War and an early influence on HOWARD BARKER. To these themes, Wood brings the skill of one of theatre's great stylists. His inventive, highly charged, dense language mixes slang, poetry, profanity and wit to great effect. His profoundly felt pacifism has also produced some remarkable screenplays, from *How I Won the War* (1967) to the controversial BBC Falklands War drama, *Tumbledown* (1988). Other screenplays include *The Knack* (1965), from the play by ANN JELLICOE. DAN REBELLATO

Wood, David (b. Sutton, Surrey, 21 Feb. 1944) Actor, playwright, director and producer; one of the main forces behind CHILDREN'S THEATRE in Britain. After appearing in the West End in a university anti-capital-punishment revue, *Hang Down Your Head and Die* (1964), to which he contributed as a writer, he made many appearances in repertory while continuing to co-write revues. In 1967 he wrote the book, music and lyrics for a children's show, *The Tinderbox*, which was followed by a long line of work for children, including *The Plotters of Cabbage Patch Corner* (1970) and the much-revived *The Gingerbread Man* (1976). In 1979 with John Gould he co-founded Whirligig, which was to become one of the leading children's theatre companies. His book *Theatre for Children* appeared in 1997. CHARLES LONDON

Wood, John (b. Derbyshire, ?1930/4) Actor. Educated at Oxford Unversity, he made his first West End appearance in TENNESSEE WILLIAMS' *Camino Real* (1957), and worked regularly in London for the next ten years until he was cast as Guildenstern in the New York production of TOM STOPPARD's early success *Rosencrantz and Guildenstern Are Dead*. This was the beginning of a long and successful relationship both with Stoppard and with New York. He first joined the

ROYAL SHAKESPEARE COMPANY in 1970 and remained for four years playing, among many other roles, Brutus and Sherlock Holmes – a part to which he might have been born – at the ALDWYCH THEATRE and subsequently on BROADWAY with enormous success. The following year he created the role of Henry Carr in Stoppard's *Travesties*, for which he won an Evening Standard award in London and a Tony award in New York. He remained in the United States for the greater part of the next decade, returning once to London in 1979–80 to the NATIONAL THEATRE. In 1988 he returned to the RSC to play Prospero for NICHOLAS HYTNER, who directed him two years later as King Lear, a remarkable performance in which lucid textual exposition was combined with painful emotional rawness.

In 1997, at the National Theatre, Stoppard once again provided him with a brilliant vehicle in *The Invention of Love*, in which he gave a dazzling and much-admired performance as the poet A. E. Housman. He is one of the most prodigiously gifted actors of his generation, and yet he remains something of an outsider, a dangerous challenge to comfortable certainties. GENISTA MCINTOSH

Wood, Peter (b. Colyton, Devon, 8 Oct. 1927) Director. Wood worked at the OXFORD PLAYHOUSE and ARTS THEATRE before notably directing *The Devils* (1961) for the ROYAL SHAKESPEARE COMPANY and *The Master Builder* (1964) for the NATIONAL THEATRE. He is best known for directing many of STOPPARD's premières, from *Jumpers* (1972) to *Hapgood* (1988), but he also directed premières of PINTER's *The Birthday Party* (1958) and SHAFFER's *Black Comedy* (1968). He is an accomplished director of Restoration comedy, e.g. *Love for Love* (1965) and *The Rivals* (1983), in which his usual determination to produce a clear, faithful presentation was achieved with classical vocal clarity and physical energy to shape a definitive production. DAN REBELLATO

Woollcott, Alexander (b. Phalanx, NJ, 19 Jan. 1887; d. New York, 23 Jan. 1943) Drama critic. As much a public personality as a voluminous and acerbic writer, Woollcott exercised his verbal talents at the famed Algonquin Round Table of the 1920s, named after the hotel where the leading wits of the day regularly gathered. He was drama critic at the *New York Times* (1914–22), *New York Herald* (1922–5), and *New York World* (1925–8). He then turned to broadcasting as 'The Town Crier' (1929–42) and to writing the *New Yorker*'s 'Shouts and Murmurs' page. Author of a dozen books, Woollcott also collaborated on two plays with GEORGE S. KAUFMAN. Sheridan Whiteside in Kaufman and

HART's *The Man Who Came to Dinner* was modelled on Woollcott and he played the part on tour (1940). His books include *Enchanted Aisles* (1924) and *Going to Pieces* (1928).   FELICIA HARDISON LONDRÉ

M. U. Burns, *The Dramatic Criticism of Alexander Woollcott* (1980)

E. P. Hoyt, *Alexander Woollcott: The Man Who Came to Dinner* (1968)

Wooster Group, The American EXPERIMENTAL THEATRE group. In 1974 Elizabeth LeCompte and Spalding Gray, two members of one of the foremost experimental ensembles of the late 1960s, the PERFORMANCE GROUP, began to develop a distinctive experimental style which combined autobiography, cultural analysis and surreal imagery. Soon, the leadership of the group passed to them, particularly to LeCompte (b. 1944), who became artistic director. The group was rechristened after the street in New York's SoHo, where its theatre, the Performing Garage, was and is located. From pieces based upon Gray's Rhode Island upbringing – *Sakonnet Point* (1975), *Rumstick Road* (1977), and *Nayatt School* (1978) – the group moved to controversial 'deconstructions' of modern American classics: *Our Town* was transformed into *Route 1 & 9* (1981), *The Crucible* became *L.S.D. (. . . Just the High Points . . .)* (1983–4) – disturbing works which present a hallucinatory collage of contemporary American fragmentation. The group's work in the 1990s continued this deconstructive tradition, with *Fish Story* (1994), a reflection on CHEKHOV's *Three Sisters*; experimental productions of O'NEILL's *Emperor Jones* (1993) and *The Hairy Ape* (1995); *House/Lights* (1999), a daring conflation of Gertrude Stein and vintage erotica; and a revised revival (1999) of an earlier work, *North Atlantic*, a scary collage of American military macho on display.   GERALD RABKIN

David Savran, *Breaking the Rules: The Wooster Group* (1986)

Worker's Theatre Movement   see CARTER, HUNTLY

workshop A place in a theatre or elsewhere where scenery and props are made and painted. The term was appropriated gradually in the twentieth century to mean primarily a collaborative exploratory method of creating plays, or a small theatre space where experimental work is staged. Through the influence of COPEAU, BRECHT and others, the term came to prominence in the title of JOAN LITTLEWOOD's THEATRE WORKSHOP company. ALTERNATIVE THEATRE in the 1960s brought renewed interest in workshop creativity. It was popularized in America by director MICHAEL BENNETT with the musical *A Chorus Line* (1975). Instead of taking a full production of a finished script on the road prior to a New York opening, Bennett developed the show, based on the lives of chorus dancers, through a series of workshops, using improvisations, memory exercises, role-playing and other acting games. Professional writers created a script from the workshop, and drafts of the show were presented to small invited audiences. Although similar approaches had been used at the ACTORS' STUDIO Playwrights Lab in the 1950s, JOSEPH CHAIKIN's OPEN THEATER in the 1960s, and in Britain with writers like CARYL CHURCHILL and the JOINT STOCK COMPANY in the 1970s, the critical and popular success of *A Chorus Line* made it the standard method in the musical theatre of the 1980s. Bennett used it again to create the smash hit *Dreamgirls* (1981), as did STEPHEN SONDHEIM with *Sunday in the Park with George* (1984) and *Into the Woods* (1987). The workshop was seen as an attractive alternative to the old-fashioned out-of-town try-out process, which was both expensive and cumbersome. In a workshop, actors worked for a small salary, there was no pressure from a scheduled opening night and, in the absence of a fully designed production, it was relatively simple to make radical script changes if deemed necessary. Many not-for-profit theatres adapted the workshop process to their own uses, testing new plays through a series of readings, staged readings and invitation-only performances to polish new work before committing financially to a full production. However, some playwrights have complained that their plays were frequently marooned in an endless workshop process leading to no productions; and some prominent directors – most notably HAL PRINCE – have never embraced the workshop.   DAVID BARBOUR

See also COLLECTIVE.

Colin Chambers, 'Product into Process', in *Dreams and Deconstructions*, ed. S. Craig (1980)

Stephen Citron, *The Musical from the Inside Out* (1992)

David Garfield, *The Actors' Studio: A Player's Place* (1984)

Ken Mandelbaum, *A Chorus Line and the Musicals of Michael Bennett* (1989)

World Theatre Day Held annually on 27 March. It was established by the INTERNATIONAL THEATRE INSTITUTE in 1962 and is celebrated by most nations. World Theatre Day honours theatre's role in society and its contribution to mutual understanding through international collaboration and exchange. Each year the ITI secretariat invites an esteemed theatre practitioner to issue the World Theatre Day Message.   HELEN SALMON

World Theatre Season The first season in 1964 was planned as a one-off by impresario PETER DAUBENY, who had an outstanding record of bringing foreign companies to Britain, and by the then three-year-old ROYAL SHAKESPEARE COMPANY in order to celebrate Shakespeare's quatercentenary. Seven companies, including the ABBEY, COMÉDIE-FRANÇAISE and MOSCOW ART THEATRE, played at the RSC's London home, the ALDWYCH, and were such a success that the season was repeated in 1965 and subsequently every spring until 1973, with a final season in 1975 just before Daubeny died. More than 40 of the world's leading companies appeared in a unique display of theatrical talent that made a great impact on the often insular British theatre. COLIN CHAMBERS

Worth, Irene [Harriet Elizabeth Abrams] (b. Omaha, Nebr., 23 June 1916) Actress; American, she became a major theatrical star in Britain. An ex-teacher, her debut came with a road company in Margaret Kennedy's *Escape Me Never* (directed by KOMIS-SARZHEVSKY, 1942), followed the next year by her Broadway debut in Martin Vale's *Two Mrs Carrols*, both with ELISABETH BERGNER. She went to London, which she made her home for 30 years, to seek a classical training. Her debut there was in WILLIAM SAROYAN's *The Time of Your Life* (1946). She created Celia Copplestone in T. S. ELIOT's *The Cocktail Party* (1949) at the EDINBURGH FESTIVAL and joined the OLD VIC company (1951–3) as Desdemona and Portia before appearing in the inaugural season of the Shakespeare Festival Theatre in STRATFORD, Ontario (1953), which she helped found and to which she would return. A line of memorable performances followed: Goneril in *King Lear* (directed by PETER BROOK for the ROYAL SHAKESPEARE COMPANY, 1962), Hesione Hushabye in *Heartbreak House* (1967); and Jocasta (directed again by Brook, 1968). Meanwhile she had also appeared in New York, in Schiller's *Mary Stuart* (1957), *Toys in the Attic* (1960) by LILLIAN HELLMAN, and EDWARD ALBEE's *Tiny Alice* (1964). She returned to live in the United States, in New York, in 1975 and played notably in *Sweet Bird of Youth* (1975), *The Cherry Orchard* (1977), *Happy Days* (1979), *The Physicists* (1980), in which she had appeared with the RSC in 1963, *Coriolanus* (1988), in which she had appeared with the NATIONAL THEATRE in London in 1984, and *Lost in Yonkers* (1991). She also toured a solo show based on the writings of Edith Wharton (1993) and performed the one-woman show *The Gypsy and the Yellow Canary* (1997), an adaptation of Mérimée's *Carmen*. An actress of great courage and immense authority with a strong, mellifluous voice,

her awards include three Tonys. She was elected to the Broadway Hall of Fame in 1980. JANE HOUSE

Wright, Frank Lloyd *see* DALLAS THEATER CENTER

Wright, Nicholas (b. Cape Town, 5 July 1940) Playwright and director. A former actor and casting director, Wright was the first director of the ROYAL COURT's Theatre Upstairs in 1969, and co-artistic director of the Court with Robert Kidd for two stormy years (1976–7). After a ten-year absence from playwriting, he wrote *Treetops* (1978), set in Cape Town; *The Gorky Brigade* (1979), a Brechtian examination of the early Soviet Union; *The Custom of the Country* (1983), an ironic and sophisticated look at southern Africa in the 1890s which was a reworking of a Fletcher and Beaumont play; the satirical *The Desert Air* (1984); and his portrait of psychoanalyst Melanie Klein, *Mrs Klein* (1988). *Cressida*, set among Shakespeare's boy-players, opened in the West End in 2000. He has also adapted Balzac, PIRANDELLO, IBSEN and WIEDEKIND. DAN REBELLATO

Wright, Robert [Craig] (b. Daytona Beach, Fla., 25 Sept. 1914) and **Forrest, George [Chichester]** (b. New York, 31 July 1915; d. 10 Oct. 1999) Collaborators since their teens, they worked together on music and lyrics for stage and film projects before finding success with *Song of Norway* (1944), a fictionalized biography of Edvard Grieg illustrated by songs arranged from the composer's own music. A series of other projects utilizing music adapted from the works of celebrated composers followed, the most successful of which were *Kismet* (1953), a musical version of the famous KNOBLOCK play using the music of Alexsandr Borodin, and a new version of the Johann Strauss pasticcio *Walzer aus Wien* under the title *The Great Waltz* (1965). KURT GÄNZL

Wyckham, Glynn *see* MEDIEVAL THEATRE IN THE TWENTIETH CENTURY; UNIVERSITY DRAMA DEPARTMENTS

Wyndham, Charles *see* ALBERY FAMILY

Wyndham, Mary *see* ALBERY FAMILY

Wynn, Ed [Isaiah Edwin Leopold] (b. Philadelphia, 9 Nov. 1886; d. Los Angeles, 19 June 1966) Comedian. He joined forces with Jack Lewis as a VAUDEVILLE team, The Rah! Rah! Boys, for two years and in 1904 struck out on his own, developing an act based on wild antics and flamboyant costumes. After his first Broadway appearance in *The Deacon and the Lady* (1910), he performed in the ZIEGFELD FOLLIES of 1914 and 1915 and by 1920 had written a comedy REVUE, *Ed Wynn's Carnival*. This was so successful that he quickly followed it with other shows of his own devising: *The Perfect Fool* (1921), *The Grab Bag* (1924) and *Laugh Parade* (1931). In the 1930s he combined his stage career with a hit radio series, which eventually had a following of 20 million listeners, and by the late 1940s was appearing in his own television VARIETY shows. His son Keenan was a prominent actor and wrote a book, *Ed Wynn's Son* (1959). HELEN RAPPAPORT

S. Green, *The Great Clowns of Broadway* (1984)

Wynyard, Diana [Dorothy Isobel Cox] (b. London, 16 Jan. 1906; d. London, 13 May 1964) Actress, one of the most popular of her time. A member of the Liverpool Repertory Company (1927–9), her first of many West End successes was as Charlotte Brontë in CLEMENCE DANE's *Wild Decembers* (1933). She appeared in hits like *Petticoat Influence* (1930) and played Gilda in COWARD's *Design for Living* (1939). Her early film work included *Cavalcade*, *Rasputin* and *Gaslight*. She toured with the ENTERTAINMENTS NATIONAL SERVICE ASSOCIATION and worked many seasons at STRATFORD-UPON-AVON (e.g. as Desdemona, Beatrice, Lady Macbeth), but was equally at home in new plays. Well known for her beauty and intelligence, Wynyard's acting brought the work of writers such as LILLIAN HELLMAN, JOHN WHITING and ANDRÉ ROUSSIN to public notice. MAGGIE GALE

Wyspiański, Stanisław (b. Cracow, Poland, 15 Jan. 1869; d. Cracow, 28 Nov. 1907) Poet, playwright, painter and designer. His influence upon modern Polish theatre has been tremendous. As a stage manager, Wyspiański became a pioneer of the 'great reform' fighting for a new type of *mise-en-scène*, a synthesis of the arts. His most original plays (e.g. *Wesele/ The Wedding*, 1901; *Noc listopadowa/November Night*, 1904; *Wyzwolenie/Liberation*, 1903) were deeply rooted in the national tradition and, together with his idea of theatre, are both symbolic and romantic.
JOANNA KRAKOWSKA-NAROŻNIAK

Leon Schiller, 'The New Theatre in Poland: Stanisław Wyspiański', *The Mask*, vol. 2, 1909/1910
Tymon Terlecki, *Stanisław Wyspiański'* (1983)

Y

Yacine, Kateb (b. Constantine, Algeria, 26 August 1929; d. Grenoble, France, 28 Oct. 1989) Novelist, poet and playwright. His highly poetic plays deal with the struggle of the Algerian people against French colonialism. Plays include *Le Cadavre Encerclé* ('The surrounded corpse', 1958), *Les Ancêtres redoublent de férocité* ('Ancestors become more ferocious', 1967) and *L'Homme aux sandales de caoutchouc* ('The man with rubber sandals', 1971), about the Vietnam War.

ANNA MCMULLAN

Yale *see* NEW HAVEN; STUDENT DRAMA; UNIVERSITY DRAMA DEPARTMENTS

yard play *see* CARIBBEAN

Yavin, Naftali *see* INTER-ACTION

Yeats, W[illiam] B[utler] (b. Sandymount, Co. Dublin, 13 June 1865; d. Cap Martin, France, 28 Jan. 1939) Playwright and poet. For a playwright who had nearly 30 plays produced and published, a man who spent half a century virtually obsessed with the theatre, W. B. Yeats has gathered a curiously indifferent dramatic reputation. His years of writing plays, founding theatrical movements, helping to run theatres, instructing actors, hectoring audiences, inventing dramatic theories, even designing stage sets, have been dismissed by no less a critic than ERIC BENTLEY with the comment that Yeats 'did not really like the actual theatre'. Just as, for instance, BERTOLT BRECHT's stature as a poet has been overshadowed by his achievement as a playwright, so Yeats's standing as a man of the theatre has suffered from being seen as a footnote to the career of one of the greatest lyric poets of the century. Yeats, however, stands not just as a founder and

prime mover of the Irish dramatic movement (he was a director of the ABBEY THEATRE from 1906 until his death), nor only as a major Irish playwright in his own right, but as a link between the nineteenth- and twentieth-century theatres, between French SYMBOLISM on the one hand and the 'holy theatre' of ARTAUD, GROTOWSKI and BROOK on the other. One of the great synthesizers of the modern theatre, he brought together sources as diverse as Celtic legend and Japanese *noh* drama (though his knowledge of both was always second-hand and often amateurish) with the modern AVANT-GARDE's desire for a non-naturalistic theatre of action. The son and brother of important painters, who himself spent three years studying painting at the Dublin School of Art (1883–86), Yeats, unlike most poets in the theatre, retained a strong sense of the visual and physical elements of drama, leading him to important collaborations with GORDON CRAIG and NINETTE DE VALOIS, among others. The great irony of Yeats's dramatic career is the increasing contradiction between the actual theatrical institution which he was instrumental in creating, the Abbey, and his own work as a playwright and theorist. With his links to Irish nationalism, his idealization of the Irish peasantry and his confusion of the Abbey company's naïve naturalistic acting with the 'static theatre' of MAETERLINCK and LUGNÉ-POË, Yeats helped to create a theatre company that would be incapable of performing his own highly stylized plays. Most notoriously, in the late 1920s he rejected, on behalf of the Abbey, the beginnings of an Irish EXPRESSIONISM with SEAN O'CASEY's *The Silver Tassie* and DENIS JOHNSTON's *The Old Lady Says No!*, which would have been much more in keeping with his own understanding of theatre. That view of theatre constitutes one of the earliest and most profound critiques of the Ibsenist and Shavian play of ideas (he described the characters of *Ghosts* as 'little whimpering puppets'). Yeats sought primarily to create a tragic theatre drawing not on ideas or characters, but on 'rhythm, balance, pattern, images that remind us of vast patterns, the vagueness of past times, all the chimeras that haunt the edge of trance'. It is this search which unifies the vast range of his work, from the allegorically nationalistic sweep of *The Countess Cathleen* (1899) and *Cathleen ni Houlihan* (1902, with AUGUSTA GREGORY), to the taut Beckettian atmosphere of *Purgatory* (1938); from the Celtic Twilight poeticism of *The Shadowy Waters* (1900) to the total theatricality of *Fighting the Waves* (1929).

Yeats's great achievement is his cycle of plays, written over 35 years, using the legendary hero Cuchulain, particularly *On Baile's Strand* (1903), *At the Hawk's Well* (1916), *The Only Jealousy of Emer* (1919) and *The Death of Cuchulain* (1939), with their increasingly stark grandeur. His great tragedy, given the profound theatricality of his work, is his gradual retreat into a disdainfully aristocratic and avowedly 'unpopular' ideal of what his audience should be. His plays were quarantined into the drawing rooms of the mystical rich, and they have remained, even for his own Abbey Theatre, a rare and rarefied pursuit. Yeats's other major plays include *King Oedipus* (1926) and *Oedipus at Colonus* (1927), translations from Sophocles; *Deirdre* (with Lady Gregory, 1907); *The Player Queen* (1919); *The Dreaming of the Bones* (written 1917); *Calvary* (written 1920); *The Resurrection* (1927); and *The Words Upon the Window Pane* (1930).   FINTAN O'TOOLE

See also VERSE DRAMA.

Seamus Deane, *O'Casey and Yeats, Exemplary Dramatists in Celtic Revivals* (1985)
Denis Donoghue, *Yeats* (1972)
Richard Ellmann, *Yeats, The Man and the Masks* (1979)
James W. Flannery, *W. B. Yeats and the Idea of a Theatre* (1976)
Peter Ure, *Yeats the Playwright* (1963)
Helen Vendler, *Yeats' Vision and the Later Plays* (1963)

Yiddish theatre   Until the last decades of the nineteenth century, it was virtually impossible to speak of a Yiddish theatre. With the exceptions of the *purimshpil* (Purim play, usually telling the apocryphal story of Queen Esther) and performers such as the *badkhn* (wedding bard), drama was not a part of traditional Jewish life. It was only when Moses Mendelssohn's Haskalah (Jewish Enlightenment) movement became influential in the early years of the nineteenth century that things began to change. Committed to bringing Jews into the modern world, several of Mendelssohn's

disciples wrote highly didactic, anti-traditionalist plays in Yiddish. By the 1860s these were widely read by followers of the Haskalah, but were rarely, if ever, performed, and were certainly of no interest to the great mass of Yiddish speakers.

All this changed largely through the efforts of one man, the so-called 'father of Yiddish theatre', Avrom Goldfaden (1840–1908). In 1876, in a wine bar in Jassy, Romania, Goldfaden, a relatively well-known songwriter, staged his first plays. They were semi-improvised, with Goldfaden's two actors, the *Broderzinger* (café entertainer) Israel Grodner and his assistant, Sakher Goldstein, creating their own dialogue around songs and a rough plot. The plays were a great success and soon Goldfaden was touring extensively, writing ever more substantial plays for his rapidly expanding troupe. Even his more ambitious later plays and operettas may have been, as he himself admitted, of limited literary value. But their folk quality and their melodramatic mix of moralizing, music and broad comedy made them extremely popular.

Within a few years, Goldfaden's troupe had spawned many others throughout eastern Europe. By the turn of the century, in the wake of the tsar's brutal edicts and increasing anti-semitism, over a million Jews had fled to the New World. New York quickly established itself as the centre of Yiddish theatre, with playwrights such as Hurvitz and Lateiner 'baking' (i.e. mass-producing) bombastic operettas and domestic melodramas to satisfy the demand for escapism. The public had their favourite stars – JACOB P. ADLER, David Kessler, Boris Thomashevsky and the like – and had little or no interest in the roles they were meant to be playing. It was the era of the so-called *shund* (literally: trash, rubbish) drama.

Shund may have been popular with the theatregoers (and it remained so throughout the history of the Yiddish theatre), but it was a thorn in the side of Jewish intellectuals. One of these was a recent arrival in the United States from the Ukraine, Jacob Gordin (1853–1909). Gordin was committed to improving the standards of the Yiddish theatre. His plays, often adapted from European classics, may not have been outstanding, but he persuaded Yiddish actors and audiences to accept a realism which had hitherto been foreign to them. The Gordin era, the so-called 'Golden Age' of the Yiddish theatre, had begun.

Meanwhile, in Europe, a rich literature in Yiddish was rapidly developing. Inspired by the efforts of the 'classicists' Mendele Moykher Sforim, SHOLOM ALEICHEM and I. L. Perets, and thriving on contacts with their non-Jewish colleagues, a whole generation of Yiddish playwrights was emerging: Ash, Pinski, Kobrin, Leyvik,

Hirshbeyn. The heirs of Haskalah idealism and didacticism, they wrote plays, largely from a left-wing perspective and ranging in style from the naturalist to the SYMBOLIST, that explored contemporary Jewish questions, highlighting the plight of the Jew, the relationship with tradition and the duty of the individual towards society. Initially, however, the more successful of these writers were reliant on non-Yiddish producers such as MAX REINHARDT to stage their works. It was only in 1908, when the playwright Perets Hirshbeyn (1880–1948) founded his touring troupe in Odessa, that a Yiddish company existed capable of doing justice to the new repertoire. Hirshbeyn's troupe split within two years, but their commitment to ensemble playing and the production of quality drama bore fruit and, by the 1920s, the Yiddish art theatre had arrived.

In many ways, this was the true golden age of Yiddish theatre. Yiddish companies earned respect throughout the world and were often at the forefront of the theatrical AVANT-GARDE. Among the most influential were Dovid Herman's Vilna troupe, best known for its 1920 première of ANSKY's *The Dybbuk*, which toured throughout the Yiddish-speaking world between 1916 and 1924; and the Moscow State Yiddish Art Theatre or GOSET, founded in 1919 under the direction of Alexander Granovsky, the most influential of some 20 state-subsidized Yiddish theatres in the nascent Soviet Union. Both these companies, together with the Hebrew-speaking HABIMAH, became associated with a broad, EXPRESSIONIST style which, for many, was synonymous with 'quality' Yiddish drama. Also worthy of note were the Kaminska family's Warsaw Yiddish Art Theatre (VYKT) and Vaykhert's experimental Yung Teater (Young Theatre), which survived despite increasingly rigorous censorship in Poland; and, in America, the radical amateur companies ARTEF and the Folksbine (People's Stage) as well as the very popular Yiddish Art Theatre run by MAURICE SCHWARTZ. Although not always as faithful to its ideals as its European counterparts, Schwartz's theatre fought to maintain high standards in a brutally commercial world and provided a much-needed platform for new writing from 1918 until it closed in 1950.

With the HOLOCAUST, Stalin's purges and assimilation, the Yiddish theatre declined as rapidly as it had grown. In postwar Poland and Romania, state Yiddish theatres performed largely to non-Jewish audiences, while elsewhere small groups of actors staged occasional performances, mostly musical comedies, wherever some Yiddish speakers could be found. Nevertheless, a resurgence of interest in Yiddish culture during the last years of the century (not least in the former Soviet Union) led to the creation of professional Yiddish companies in the United States and Israel, as well as several amateur groups throughout the world. The future of Yiddish theatre may be uncertain, but its fate is by no means sealed. DAVID SCHNEIDER

Evelyn Torton Beck, *Kafka and the Yiddish Theatre* (1971)
The Drama Review, Jewish Theatre edition (1980)
Hutchins Hapgood, *The Spirit of the Ghetto* (1902)
Joseph C. Landis, *The Dybbuk and Other Great Yiddish Plays* (1986)
David Lifson, *The Yiddish Theater in America* (1965)
Nahma Sandrow, *Vagabond Stars: A World History of Yiddish Theater* (1986)
Jeffrey Veidlinger, *The Moscow State Yiddish Theatre: Jewish Culture on the Soviet Stage* (2000)

Youmans, Vincent [Millie] (b. New York, 27 Sept. 1898; d. Denver, Colo., 5 April 1946) Songwriter. At first a song-plugger and rehearsal pianist, Youmans had an early success as a songwriter when he contributed several numbers to the 1923 Harbach/HAMMERSTEIN musical *Wildflower*. Later the same year he wrote the complete score for his most successful show, *No, No, Nanette*, with its memorable tunes 'Tea For Two' and 'I Want To Be Happy'. *No, No, Nanette* has come to be remebered as the archetypal show of the American 1920s musical stage. Youmans subsequently wrote nine more musical comedy scores, but only one (*Hit The Deck!*, 1927) gave him a comparable success. He also wrote the songs for the first FRED ASTAIRE/GINGER ROGERS musical film, *Flying Down to Rio*. KURT GÄNZL

G. Bordman, *Days to Be Happy, Days to Be Sad* (1982)

Young, Stark (b. Como, Miss., 11 Oct. 1881; d. New York, 6 Jan. 1963). Critic, translator, playwright and novelist. One of the most respected reviewers of the American theatre, Young brought knowledge and erudition untinged by pedantry to drama criticism. He was a polished stylist, particularly skilled in describing acting. He translated plays from Spanish, Italian and Russian, his CHEKHOV translations being especially well regarded. He was associated with *The New Republic* from 1922 to 1947 – save for an unhappy one-season stint at the *New York Times* in 1924–5 – and with *Theatre Arts* (as associate editor 1921–40). Young's books include *The Flower in Drama* (1923), *Glamour* (1925), *The Theatre* (1927) and *Immortal Shadows* (1947). His own plays were unsuccessful but he did direct on occasion, including the première of O'NEILL's *Welded* (1924), through his association with the PROVINCETOWN PLAYERS. THOMAS F. CONNOLLY

John Pilkington, *Stark Young, A Life in the Arts: Letters 1900–1962*, 2 vols (1975)

young people *see* CHILDREN'S THEATRE; THEATRE FOR YOUNG PEOPLE; THEATRE IN EDUCATION; YOUTH THEATRE

Young People's Theatre Canada's leading theatre for young audiences, YPT was founded in 1966 in Toronto by Susan Douglas Rubes, who remained artistic director until 1979. She was succeeded by Richard Ouzounian and, in 1980, by Peter Moss, who resigned in 1990. Many of Canada's leading actors, directors, playwrights and designers have worked at YPT, and its productions have toured Canada and abroad. Housed in a large Victorian building, the company operates two theatres as well as a school tours programme that frequently addresses sensitive and controversial issues, particularly in the plays of Dennis Foon, co-founder of Vancouver's Green Thumb Theatre for Young People (1975). L. W. CONOLLY

Young Vic Originally a touring children's and young people's theatre run by GEORGE DEVINE as part of London's OLD VIC and its school from 1946 to 1951, during which time it established a formidable reputation, beginning with its first production, Carlo Gozzi's *King Stag*. Financial and internal problems led to its demise. Nineteen years later, in 1970, its second incarnation appeared under the wing of the Old Vic's successor, the NATIONAL THEATRE, and was run by a former Devine student, FRANK DUNLOP. The Young Vic became independent in 1974. It was the first purpose-built theatre for young people in England, and in 1984 a studio space was added alongside the 450-seat main auditorium. Dunlop developed an energetic physical approach to classical and new work which was carried on in 1978 under MICHAEL BOGDANOV, who also set up the Young Vic Education Service. Under David Thacker (1984–93), the theatre also became associated with ARTHUR MILLER, reviving and premièring several of his plays. Tim Supple (1993–2000) developed an imaginative programme in tune with new directions in theatre, and was succeeded by DAVID LAN. Groups such as the ROYAL SHAKESPEARE COMPANY also use the theatre. COLIN CHAMBERS

See also THEATRE FOR YOUNG PEOPLE.

Youngman, Henny [Henry] (b. London, 16 March 1906; d. New York, 24 Feb. 1998) Violin-playing comedian, dubbed 'king of the one-liners'. The son of Russian Jewish immigrants, Youngman made a name for himself with his own band in the early 1930s before settling for a solo career as a comedian. He toured exhaustively for the next four decades, appearing in casinos and nightclubs throughout the United States, as well as in films and on television comedy shows. He also published an autobiography (1974) and *10,000 One-Liners: An Encyclopedia of One-Liners* (1989). HELEN RAPPAPORT

youth theatre A term used since the Second World War to denote the creative use of young people's spare time through the medium of theatre and drama. The activity has grown out of schools drama, enlightened AMATEUR theatre and COMMUNITY drama initiatives, but is not now tied to any single institutional allegiance and involves theatrical performances created by many different groupings of young people. In 1999 there were more than 700 youth theatre groups in the United Kingdom. Those aged between 11 and 20 are the most active participants but the age range has extended to cover those from 5 to 30 years and older. Nearly all work with groups is undertaken on a full or part-time basis by leaders from a wide range of professional backgrounds, primarily education, theatre and youth work.

In the summer of 1956 Michael Croft undertook a production of Shakespeare's *Henry V* with a group of former pupils from Alleyn's School, south London, where he had been teaching. Youth theatre's first major public manifestation in Britain was thus an emancipation of the school play whose tradition had been long but fairly conservative. Croft's project grew in scope and reputation, despite many struggles for official recognition and funding, and was in 1961 given the title NATIONAL YOUTH THEATRE. Croft's initiative inspired a number of developments in youth theatre during the following two decades, including the annual National Festival of Youth Theatre, which lasted from 1977 to 1986. At the National Festival in 1982 the initiative was taken to set up a National Association of Youth Theatres, and this body has continued to act as a support and development agency for youth theatre work since that date. In the 1970s County Youth Theatres were set up by local education authorities in places like Leicestershire and Devon, and a number of regional repertory theatres established their own groups. The momentum of youth theatre development was picked up in the 1980s by local government departments concerned with recreation and in the 1990s by national funding agencies as a medium for youth arts work. Many groups have set up independently, and youth theatre continues to owe its rather ad hoc growth to a number of committed and hardworking individuals. There has always been an awareness, however, that through youth theatre work young people's performances provide a radical renewal of social perspective both for the participants and for the communities to which they belong.

Youth theatre advances in line with the differing social and cultural emphases of individual countries. Throughout mainland Europe, where there are huge discrepancies in support and development, it enjoys a wide variety of cultural affiliations. In Austria and Finland, for example, it has evolved out of a strong amateur theatre tradition with the help of supportive youth work. Danish youth theatre has also received its greatest encouragement from youth work and the great diversity of the educational system, and plays an important role in social education and theatrical experimentation. In Portugal, a similar tradition has been recovered since the return to civilian government in 1974, which has lent a strong socio-cultural dimension to the work. In France and Malta, by contrast, there are strong links with formal education, particularly drama training, and in the Netherlands much work is centred on professional theatre companies. Whether youth theatre development is sparse, as in Flanders, or strong and well-supported, as in Germany, it is generally felt that the work is given insufficient public support and status.

There are strong developments in the United States and in India and south-east Asia, where subsidized professional theatre is less common, and youth theatre forms part of a strong community drama movement. In Australia an impressive tradition of innovation and social relevance has developed out of the creative coalition of young performers and professional practitioners.

Despite the lack of a worldwide organization, a spirit of internationalism has been greatly advanced by the increasing number of international exchange visits between groups. In 1982 the first European Children's Theatre Encounter was held in Belgium, and in 1987 young people from 19 European countries attended the first European Youth Theatre Encounter in STRATFORD-UPON-AVON in Britain. Both events have continued to be hosted by European countries on a regular basis in the 1990s.

Youth theatre in the UK continues to develop, thanks mainly to the work of the National Association. It established the Big Youth Theatre Festival in 1994 as a major focus of growth for the medium, and in 2000 the Festival attracted 800 participants from seven countries to a greenfield site in the south of England. Increasing numbers of groups experiment with the language of performance and across art forms to produce hybrid work which is 'postmodern' in spirit. History may characterize youth theatre by such radicalism, see it as one creative element in a leisure-based culture or

acknowledge its enduring value as the best of youth work; in any event, thanks to the participation of generations of young people, its effects will be felt for many decades and in many cultures. ROGER HILL

See also CHILDREN'S THEATRE; THEATRE FOR YOUNG PEOPLE.

Ginny Graham, *How to Start a Youth Theatre* (1993)
Roger Hill, *Coming into Majority: Support for Youth Theatre in the 1980s* (1985)
Nicholas Ripley and Patrick Canning, *Strategies for Success* (1996)

Yugoslavia At the beginning of the twentieth century, the people living in what was to become Yugoslavia, or the South Slav state, were ruled by the Austro-Hungarian Empire. At this time, Belgrade (Serbia), Zagreb (Croatia) and Novi Sad (Vojvodina), each with national theatres founded in the 1860s, rediscovered two outstanding national personalities, Marin Držiú (1508–67), a Renaissance comic writer who surpassed his Italian models, and Jovan Sterija Popoviú (1806–56), the first Serbian realist comic writer and 'father of Serbian drama'. During the nineteenth century, playwrights willing both to describe their own nation in a humorous way and to liberate it from its own myths and errors had not been able to count on support from audiences, critics and theatre managements. Yet this type of drama is what Držiú and Popoviú offered and, for most of the century, their works remained cornerstones of the national repertoire.

Alongside their reappearance came the release of theatres in the Slavic south, in the above-named towns and in Ljubljana in Slovenia (New National Theatre, founded 1892), from the dominant influence of German theatre which had spread through the Austro-Hungarian Empire. Vienna's Burgtheater had been the focus, in repertoire as well as styles of acting, directing and design, but it was now replaced by the influence of French theatre by way of people educated in France who were returning home, especially to Belgrade. However, it is characteristic of the period that this influence came not from new French theatre, such as ANTOINE's Théâtre Libre, but from the traditional COMÉDIE-FRANÇAISE and the popular Parisian theatres. New European drama did gradually find its way into Yugoslav theatre, through dramatists such as Ivo Vojnoviú (1857–1929), Milan Begoviú (1876–1948), Milutin Bojiú (1892–1917) and Vojislav Jovanoviú Marambo (1884–1968). Ivan Cankar (1876–1918) introduced a certain liveliness into Slovenian drama, and tried to base it on contemporary social and moral problems, in the way that IBSEN had, by balancing naturalism and SYMBOLISM. His plays were also influenced by MAETER-

LINCK and WEDEKIND. Josip Kosor (1879–1961), an autodidact, fixed brutal, primitive instincts, especially a hunger for land, into his dramas, which were performed on various European stages. (His first play, *The Fire of Passion*, was seen in Germany and England before Yugoslavia.) Said to be influenced by Tolstoy, GORKY and ANDREYEV, Kosor later turned to Freud and Nietszche and ended up in EXPRESSIONISM.

After the First World War and the formation of the Yugoslav kingdom in 1918, many theatres were founded in major towns and country centres. A National Theatre was established in Sarajevo (Bosnia) in 1920, and theatre life was re-established in Skopjie in Macedonia (National Theatre founded 1913, with performances in the Serbian language) and Cetinje in Montenegro (under the name of Zeta Region; National Theatre founded 1910). Since state theatres were only modestly supported, the struggle for audiences and complaints about the lack of funding were the leitmotif of theatre talk. There were also commercial, usually travelling, theatres.

Between the two world wars, tours by the MOSCOW ART THEATRE (1920/1 and 1924) fascinated theatre people and the work became a model to be equalled; Belgrade, Zagreb, Ljubljana and Novi Sad boasted companies of a central European standard. Branko Gavella (1885–1962) became a renowned director, and other directors, such as Mihailo Isailoviú, Ivo Raiú and Tito Strozzi, were also distinguished. Two dramatists of European standing also emerged; Branislav Nušiú (1864–1938), author of *Godpodja ministaka* ('Madam Minister's wife'), *Ožalošúena porodica* ('The bereaved family') and *Pučina* ('High seas'), belongs to the main stream of Serbian comedy that begins with Sterija, and Miroslav Krleža (1893–1981) showed in his cycle of plays *Legends* (the most characteristic of which is *Kralievo*, a religious holiday celebrated as a carnival) a new approach to theatre art that preceded ARTAUD. Krleža's most famous work is *The Glembays*, concerning the fate of a rich bourgeois family; however, some critics claim *Aretheus* to be his best play. Opponents usually call it a 'dramatized encyclopedia'.

During the Second World War, many theatres were closed and others merely vegetated, although occupying Bulgarian and Italian forces had drama in their own language. Numerous actors were prisoners of war or joined the resistance, and great enthusiasm burst out after liberation. In 1945 Yugoslavia became a federation of socialist republics. Theatres were opened for the first time in some 30 towns, although not always on a realistic basis. Altogether about 70 companies were active (including puppet and children's theatres) supported by federal finance. In the mid-1960s cities began to finance theatres, and some 20 closed throughout Yugoslavia before the numbers gradually increased again, back to around 70. Faculties for Dramatic Arts were established in Lubljana, Belgrade and Zagreb, and, in the 1970s, in Sarajevo, Novi Sad and Skopjie, where the first Macedonian National Theatre had been founded in 1945. There were also theatres performing in Hungarian, Albanian, Turkish, Italian and other languages spoken by national minorities in the six federal republics, and there was a Romany theatre in Skopjie.

The early postwar years were marked by Soviet influence and a dogmatically conceived STANISLAVSKY system. By the beginning of the 1950s, after the break with Stalin, Yugoslavia gradually 'opened up' to the rest of the world; the most outstanding companies were, first, the Belgrade Theatre of Drama, with a new repertoire including plays by ARTHUR MILLER and TENNESSEE WILLIAMS and then JOHN OSBORNE, and later Belgrade Atelier 212, the first theatre in Yugoslavia to perform plays by SAMUEL BECKETT and EUGENE IONESCO. Yugoslavia has had many fine actors and directors, but it was not until after 1960 that there was an important development in playwriting. It lasted over 20 years and produced several writers who ranked among the best in Europe, such as Ranko Marinkoviú (b. 1913), Dominik Smole (1929–92), Alexandar Popoviú (1929–96), Ivo Bresšan (b. 1936), Ljubomir Simoviú (b. 1935), Dušan Jovanoviú (b. 1939) and Dušan Kovačevič (b. 1948). Little of this work was known abroad, although some of it was toured and seen at festivals. Small, independent groups sprang up outside the main subsidized repertory system, and the influence of Artaud's ritual and physical theatre was particularly strong. Ljubljana was considered by many experts to be a centre of modern theatrical experiment.

Yugoslavia's rich and varied theatre life was characterized by numerous festivals. The most important were the Dubrovnik Summer Festival, established in 1949, with a repertoire dominated by world and national classics, using many non-theatre sites for performance and attracting a high proportion of tourists in the audiences; Sterija Festival, established in Novi Sad in 1956 as a festival of national drama with mostly contemporary plays – a precious incentive to the faster development of national playwriting and associated with Sterijino Pozorje, a publishing and research institution which also played an important role in international relations; and BITEF, an influential international autumn festival established in Belgrade in 1967, enabling Yugoslav spectators to see achievements in new theatre from around the world.

All these developments were interrupted in 1991 by

the dismemberment of the Yugoslav federation and the creation through often savage war of separate states: Slovenia, Croatia, Serbia-Montenegro, Bosnia-Herzegovina and Macedonia. International solidarity was expressed by many theatre artists during these wars, the most high-profile example being a production of *Waiting for Godot* in 1993 directed by the American writer Susan Sontag during the siege of Sarajevo.

PETAR MARJANOVIĆ

Nikola Batušić, *Povjest hrvatskog kazališta* ('History of Croatian theatre') (1978)

Dragan Klaić, *Theatre in Yugoslavia* (1986)

Josip Lešić, *Istoria jugoslavenske moderne režije* ('History of modern Yugoslav directing') (1986)

Petar Marjanović, *Srpski dramski pisci XX stoleúa* ('Twentieth-century Serbian playwrights') (1997)

Dušan Moravec, *Slovensko gledališce o vojne do vojne* ('Slovenian theatre between the wars from 1918 to 1941') (1980)

Savremena drama i pozorište u makedoniji ('Modern drama and theatre in Macedonia'), selected by Blagoje Ivanov (1982)

Savremena drama i pozorište u bosni i hercegovini ('Modern drama and theatre in Bosnia and Herzegovina'), selected by Josip Lešić (1984)

Savremena drama i pozorište u sloveniji ('Modern drama and theatre in Slovenia'), selected by Vasja Predan (1986)

Savremena drama i pozorište u crnoj gori ('Modern drama and theatre in Montenegro'), selected by Sreten Perović and Radoslav Rotković (1987)

Borivoje Stojković, *Istorija srpskog pozorišta od srednjeg veka do modernog doba (drama i opera)* ('History of Serbian theatre from the middle ages to the modern era – opera and drama') (1979).

Yvain, Maurice [Pierre Paul] (b. Paris, 12 Feb. 1891; d. Suresnes, France, 28 July 1965) Composer. Conservatoire-trained, he worked as pianist and songwriter, making his greatest hit with MISTINGUETT's 'Mon Homme', later sung by FANNY BRICE as 'My Man'. A commission from Gustave Quinson, who had launched the new-style French musical with *Phi-Phi*, produced the hugely successful show *Ta Bouche* (1922), written with *Phi-Phi* lyricist ALBERT WILLEMETZ, and promoted Yvain alongside CHRISTINÉ to the forefront of jazz-age musical theatre composers. His second musical, *Là-Haut* (1923), a frothy vehicle for his friend MAURICE CHEVALIER, was again a success, and, over the next dozen years, while also writing a number of film scores, he kept up a steady stream of light, jazzy and mostly popular musicals, mainly to libretti by André Barde. Of these, *Pas sur la Bouche* (1925) was the outstanding success. Tempted with the change in musical-theatre fashions to larger stages, he later scored with *Au Soleil de Mexique* (1935) and his last Parisian show, *Chanson Gitane* (1945). KURT GÄNZL

Z

Zadek, Peter (b. Berlin, 19 May 1926) Director and theatre manager. He grew up in England, where he received his training as an actor and director. He first worked for the BBC and some small theatre clubs. His productions of GENET's *Les Bonnes* (*The Maids*, 1952) and *Le Balcon* (*The Balcony*, 1957) caused a stir and gave a first indication of his directorial style, which he continued to develop after his move to West Germany in 1959. After productions in Cologne, Hanover, Cassel and Ulm he became artistic director at the Stadttheater Bremen, where, between 1963 and 1967, he earned himself the reputation of the *enfant terrible* of the German stage. From 1972 he pursued his vision of a new popular theatre using brash staging techniques at the Stadttheater Bochum, but was less successful as artistic director at the Schauspielhaus Hamburg (1985–9). From 1992 to 1995 he was a co-director of the BERLINER ENSEMBLE.

Besides his interest in 'deconstructing' the classics (e.g. *Othello*, 1976), he has shown great skill in producing large-scale REVUES. Less well known are his IBSEN productions which reveal him as equally well versed in the art of psychological realism. His first volume of autobiography, *My Way: eine Autobiographie*, appeared in 1998. GÜNTER BERGHAUS

Zaïre *see* FRENCH AFRICAN THEATRE

Zambia The territory came under direct British control in 1924, and for a time both Northern and Southern Rhodesia joined with Nyasaland (now Malawi) to form the Federation of Rhodesia and Nyasaland. In 1964 Zambia became independent, with Kenneth Kaunda as president. Ethnically, Zambia is divided into 73 different groups of Bantu origin who speak lan-guages that are quite similar. Of these, Bemba, Lozi, Nyanja, Tonga, Lunda and Kaonde are used for teaching at primary school level and for broadcasting on radio and television. English, which is part of the colonial heritage, is the language used for national administration and for education at the secondary and university levels.

Like other African countries, Zambia has numerous traditional performance forms, which include dances, dance-dramas, ritual dramas, rites of passages and initiation such as the *makishi* masquerades and the *gule wa mkulu*, and royal ceremonies (*mutomboko*). There are also vibrant storytelling traditions, the most famous of which are the tales about *kazulu*, the wily hare. Colonization ensured that these forms survived in 'pure' form only in rural communities, being modified in the urban centres into new syncretic forms involving music, song, dance and dramatic sketches blended with the newly encountered dramatic styles from Europe. A good example of this syncretism is the *mbeni* (a form of militaristic mime similar to the *beni* found in parts of east Africa) created by African soldiers during the Second World War. *Mbeni* is rooted in Zambian music and dance aesthetics, while some of its music, movement style and costume reflect contact with the European military culture of hierarchy, uniforms, bands and parades. Other similarly syncretic forms are the *kalela*, a dance form satirical of white dress and manners and performed by the Bisa and Ushi ethnic groups of the Luapula Province; the *kayowa*, a dance which mirrors the courtship of the cock and the hen; *fwembu*, an acrobatic dance developed by returning Second World War soldiers; *kachala*, a dance form derived from the *mashawe* spirit-possession dances of the Tonga of southern Zambia and northern

Zimbabwe; and *nachsungu*, the puberty rites which feature satiric mimes of contemporary issues and behaviour. By the 1950s there were regular weekend performances of these new forms, especially in the mining towns of the copper belt, which eventually became organized into local and regional competitions. Their popularity, coupled with their didactic potential, made them effective weapons during the nationalist movement years. They also provided the base for the dance aesthetics and repertoire of the National Dance Troupe formed in 1965, which, under the leadership of Edwin Manda, made use of traditional and syncretic forms to create full-length dance dramas such as the popular *Nsombo Malimba*.

European missionaries, teachers and settlers introduced Western spoken drama into Zambia, and by 1945 dramatic literature was a regular feature of English studies in schools. In 1950 a number of British and South African performing companies undertook a tour of the country with European-style plays and operas. The tour provided the impetus for the formation of a number of theatre clubs, especially within the European settler community. In 1952 six of these formed the all-white Northern Rhodesia Drama Association, which became the Theatre Association of Zambia at independence. In 1953 it organized the first National Drama Festival, with only Western plays in English allowed to enter.

Between 1954 and 1958 a number of theatres were built or existing buildings were converted by some of the theatre clubs for the exclusive use of the expatriates and settler communities. In 1958 a British theatre expert, Adrian Stanley, was engaged to help train theatre artists; also that year, the Waddington Club, the colony's only multiracial theatre club, was formed in Lusaka under the leadership of Reverend John Houghton. The club challenged the colour bar of the other clubs in the NRDA and was denied membership of the association's festivals until 1960. However, Waddington's entries were still Western and American: OBEY's *Noah* in 1960 and HANSBERRY's *A Raisin in the Sun* in 1963. Because of NRDA's exclusion of Africans, an alternative association, the Northern Rhodesian Youth Council, organized its own annual drama and choir festival between 1958 and 1962, stopping only when its members became actively involved in campaigns for independence. Also in 1958, a 15-minute radio programme broadcasting short plays/sketches in Zambian languages was introduced. Prominent writers for this programme were Edward Kateka, Asaf Mvula, Wilfred Banda, Patterson Muhanda and M. Zulu. Two weekly series, one in Tonga called *Malikopo* and the other, *Tambwali*, in Nyanja, were extremely popular in the late 1950s. Zambia's first full-length play (written for radio) was Andreya Masiye's *The Many Lands of Kazembe*.

Prior to 1960 spoken drama was mainly west European plays in English or adaptations of them for the Zambian stage, with the works of Shakespeare, BRECHT and Molière being commonly performed to cater primarily for the tastes and interests of the mainly British settler community. At and immediately after independence there was a lack of plays that reflected the culture of Zambian society, and white Zambians and expatriates still controlled all aspects of theatre through their domination of the Theatre Association of Zambia. For instance, each year TAZ organized a national drama festival which was open to all theatre clubs. Plays entered for the competition were assessed by adjudicators invited from England, whose criteria for assessment were essentially foreign, a practice that led to friction in later years.

The emergence of dramatic activity at the newly established University of Zambia marked a significant shift in the direction of the development of theatre. UNZADRAMS, a student dramatic society formed in 1969, became active on the campus, championing locally written plays such as Kabwe Kasoma's *The Long Arm of the Law* and Michael Etherton's adaptation of Ferdinand Oyono's novel *Houseboy*. The society challenged the continued imposition of European dramatic criteria on post-independence Zambian theatre, especially when in 1972 and 1973 British adjudicators rated its entries in the TAZ festival among the poorest. UNZADRAMS pulled out of the competition and set up ZANTAA, an alternative association for black Zambians. ZANTAA and TAZ were forced by the government to merge in 1986 to become the National Theatre Arts Association of Zambia (NATAAZ).

The development of a truly Zambian theatre, however, must be traced to the construction of an open-air theatre which transformed the student dramatic society into Chikwakwa Theatre. One of its founders, Michael Etherton, describes its vision as 'to develop a style of drama that used the dances, songs and music of the rural areas and the urban townships, the masks and the fabulous costumes, the artifacts, the fires and the lamps of traditional storytelling'. Chikwakwa was part research and part active performance, modelled on the travelling theatre style already tried out by the universities of Ibadan in NIGERIA and Makerere in UGANDA. Its members (staff and students of the university drama section) took theatre, both in English and Zambian languages, to different regions; the plays were either already written, or were developed collectively and with local schoolchildren. They began in 1971 with literary texts such as AUGUSTA GREGORY's *Spreading the News*, *Return of Nsata* by Ezekiel Mphalele and *Homecoming* by Musisimi Fwanyanga; the tour of the Southern Province in 1972 saw some adaptations of literary texts such as OYÔNÔ-MBIA's *Three Suitors, One Husband*, *Cheelo Ca Madaala* from Plautus' *Mostelleria*, and *Unity* from CLIFFORD ODETS' *Waiting for Lefty*. Two of the plays for this tour, *Kalyabantu* by Obi Nazombe and *Mucaala* by Patrick Hamugompa, were adapted directly from local Tonga oral narratives, and these, not surprisingly, proved the most popular. By the 1973 tour of the Northern Province, all the plays were derived from Zambian material. They included *Drown in a Drink* by Whitney Lukulu, *The District Officer Visits a Village* by Stephen Chifunyise and Kasoma's *The Poisoned Cultural Meat*. Subsequent tours continued this move towards locally based performances. Chikwakwa's lead was enthusiastically followed by other artists and theatre groups, inside and outside the university. Bazamai Theatre, founded in 1970 by Masauto Phiri and Steven Moyo outside the university, produced that year an adaptation of Chinua Achebe's novel *Things Fall Apart* and a play, *Nightfall* by Phiri. It also produced a dance-drama, *Kuto*, and Moyo's *The Last Prerogative*. Another offshoot was Tikwiza Theatre, founded in 1975, which dominated Zambian theatre for almost a decade. Its plays were noted for their radical politics, best exemplified by Phiri's *Soweto* and Dickson Mwansa's *The Cell*.

The late 1980s and the early 1990s saw a spectacular growth in community theatre projects, and eventually the emergence of THEATRE FOR DEVELOPMENT using traditional forms and local languages to explore and address local issues. Numerous theatre groups are involved in this movement, including Kanyama Theatre (which became the first full-time professional company in Zambia), Africa 2000, Mwanga Theatre, Fwebena Africa, Modern Images and Tiyende Pamodzi.

The number of Zambian plays is still quite small but progress has been made since Masiye's *The Many Lands of Kazembe*. Notable playwrights of the 1960s include Gideon Lumpa, who wrote *Iyi Eyali Imukalili* ('The way we lived') and *Kalufyanya* for the Zambian Arts Trust (a national organization of indigenous theatre enthusiasts who toured the country with plays in English and local Zambian languages). His plays reflect the tensions of a society caught in the throes of transition and the challenges between the new and old African ways of life. Kabwe Kasoma, with feet in the literary and popular traditions, also wrote for ZAT as well as for Chikwakwa. His other notable work includes *The Fools Marry* and *Black Mamba Lobengula*, about Kaunda and the nationalist struggle for independence. In general,

his plays focus on Zambian history and social life. Fwanyanga Mulikita is best known for *Shaka the Zulu*, about the famous Zulu warrior-king.

In the 1970s newer writers emerged, notable among them the Zimbabwean Stephen Chifunyise, whose major plays are *The Blood* and *I Resign* as well as the popular *The District Officer Visits a Village*. He has also written numerous sketches and scenarios for the Chikwakwa travelling programme and is one of the driving forces of contemporary theatre in Zambia and Zimbabwe. Darus Lungu is known for *The Graduate* and *The Mishanga Sellers and the Man in the Street*, which deal with the betrayal of the hopes raised at independence and the problem of unemployment among the urban youth. Dickson Mwansa has also written *What's in a Title?*, *Father Kalo and the Virus* and *The Family Question*, which explore the social contradictions to be found in a society in transition. The other well-known Zambian playwright is Masauto Phiri, best known for his Soweto trilogy – *Soweto*, *Soweto Remembered* and *Soweto Flowers Will Grow*, which focus on the upheavals in the wake of the 1976 Soweto uprising. Other significant dramatists are Craig Lungu, whose plays have been successfully adapted for both stage and television and include *Farewell to Babylon*, *Imbangala* and *School Leaver's Notebook*; Kwaleyala Ikafa, Moses Kwali, Julius Chongo, Killian Mulaisho and Nora Mumba. Among the expatriate (British Zambian) dramatists are David Kerr, Stewart Crehan and David Wallace, who started out as a harsh critic of Chikwakwa but later became a champion of the use of traditional forms to create plays that are uniquely Zambian. OSITA OKAGBUE

Zamyatin, Yevgeny [Ivanovich] (b. Lebedyan, Russia, 1 Feb. 1884; d. Paris, 10 March 1937) Novelist and playwright; a comic and satirical writer whose best plays questioned all forms of orthodoxy – e.g. *Ogni sv. Dominika* (*The Fires of St Dominic*, 1922) and an extremely successful adaptation of a Nikolai Leskov short story, *Blokha* (*The Flea*, 1925). He emigrated to Paris in 1931, and is best known for his novel *My* (*We*, 1920), which influenced Orwell's *1984*. ROBERT LEACH

Alex. M. Shane, *The Life and Works of Evgenij Zamjatin* (1968)

Zeffirelli, [Gian]Franco [Corsi] (b. Florence, Italy, 12 Feb. 1923) Director and designer. Zeffirelli began his career acting in VISCONTI films, and later became his assistant director and designer for films and theatrical productions such as *A Streetcar Named Desire*. In 1953 Zefirelli directed his first opera, *La Cenerentola*, for La Scala, Milan, and has since gone on to work as a theatre, film, television and opera director and designer of worldwide renown. His romantic cinematic versions of Shakespeare, *Romeo and Juliet* (1967) and *The Taming of the Shrew* (1960), were hugely successful. Theatre productions of note include a disastrous *Othello* (1961, ROYAL SHAKESPEARE COMPANY, with GIELGUD), *Much Ado About Nothing* (1965, OLD VIC), Verga's *La Lupa* (*The She-wolf*, 1965; seen in London's WORLD THEATRE SEASON, 1969), and two productions of DE FILIPPO's work – *Saturday, Sunday, Monday* (1973, London, NATIONAL THEATRE; 1974, New York) and *Filumena* (1977, London) – that helped spread his reputation internationally. DENISE L. TILLES

Ziegfeld, Florenz [Jr] (b. Chicago, 21 March 1867; d. Los Angeles, 22 July 1932) Producer; the archetypal showman who never produced a show outside the United States but whose name, more than half a century after his death, was still known worldwide for the glamorous women who paraded in his famous glittering *Follies*. He established himself as the manager of a VAUDEVILLE strongman EUGENE SANDOW, and then took the idea of a Parisian-style REVUE from his first wife, the singer Anna Held (1873–1918). He produced 21 editions of the *Ziegfeld Follies* in New York between 1907 and 1931, most of them lushly designed by JOSEPH URBAN. Ziegfeld also produced many musical comedies, including *Sally* (which made a star of MARILYN MILLER in 1920), *Rio Rita* (1927), *Whoopee* (1928) with EDDIE CANTOR, the New York production of COWARD's *Bitter Sweet* (1929) and, his greatest theatrical achievement, *Show Boat* (1927). Incurably extravagant on and off stage, he died deeply in debt but all his debts were paid by his widow, the actress Billie Burke, who worked ceaselessly in Hollywood to earn the money. His life was made into a film, and the SONDHEIM musical *Follies* (1971) was probably inspired by the theatre that bore Ziegfeld's name.) IAN BEVAN

R. Carter, *The World of Flo Ziegfeld* (1974)
Eve Golden, *Anna Held and the Birth of Ziegfeld's Broadway* (2000)
Charles Higham, *Ziegfeld* (1972

Ziegfeld Theater New York playhouse, considered by many the finest and most beautiful built in America. Named after the producer FLORENZ ZIEGFELD who had it built, it was paid for by William Randolph Hearst and designed by JOSEPH URBAN and Thomas Lamb. The auditorium was boxless and egg-shaped, and the backstage and public rooms exceptionally spacious. The undecorated proscenium and jutting apron were gilt, while the cornerless walls and ceiling were given over to Urban's huge, imaginative mural, done in burnished tones. The playhouse opened in 1927 with *Rio Rita*, which was followed by such hits as *Show Boat* (1927) and *Bitter Sweet* (1929). After ZIEGFELD's death in 1932 the theatre became a film house until 1944. In later years it housed, among others, *Brigadoon* (1947), *Gentlemen Prefer Blondes* (1949) and *Kismet* (1953). It was demolished in 1967. GERALD BORDMAN

Zimbabwe Formerly called Southern Rhodesia, Zimbabwe has a population of about 10.9 million made up of predominantly Shona and Ndebele peoples of Bantu origin. The Shona make up 70 per cent and include the Kalanga, Zeruru, Manyika, Ndau and Korekore. Shona is also the dominant language, but other languages spoken are Ndebele, Tonga, Venda and English, the colonial language which has become the official language. From the late 1880s white settlers dispossessed the indigenous peoples of their lands and in 1923, on the basis of a whites-only election, voted to become a self-governing colony rather than join the Union of South Africa. In 1964 the minority white community declared the country independent from British rule and renamed it Rhodesia, still completely excluding the black majority from the political process and government. A number of black nationalist political parties adopted armed struggle as the only means of wresting power from minority occupation, and in 1979 a peace agreement formulated a new constitution. The country became independent in 1980.

When the white settlers arrived, the country had its traditional performing arts. These were an integral part of the respective communities, associated with occasions such as after-harvest, funerals, storytelling sessions, praise-poetry performances, ritual ceremonies and chants, and traditional dances and dance-dramas of various kinds. The Christian church tried its utmost to discourage these vital and joyous occasions, labelling them pagan and evil practices, but they survived to provided a foundation for new experiments in theatre forms and styles.

As in SOUTH AFRICA, colonial theatre historians conveniently ignored this wealth of theatre tradition, claiming that theatre began in Zimbabwe in 1890 with a production of *Regiment Sergeant* by William King. Again as in South Africa, a number of British-style theatre clubs were formed, the best known being the Salisbury Repertory Players (1931). The Rhodesian Institute of Allied Arts (formed in 1947) organized competitive drama festivals, and these, with the national theatre festival of the Association of Rhodesian Theatrical Societies (ARTS, formed in 1958), provided the backbone and organizational framework for all colonial theatre activities. There was overwhelming west European influence, as seen by the popularity of

Shakespeare, ARTHUR MILLER, HAROLD PINTER, SAMUEL BECKETT, EDWARD ALBEE, HENRIK IBSEN, GEORGE BERNARD SHAW, Molière, GILBERT and SULLIVAN, OSCAR WILDE, AGATHA CHRISTIE, W. B. YEATS, EUGENE IONESCO and JOHN OSBORNE in the repertory of the visiting companies from South Africa and Britain, as well as in the Rhodesian little theatres. There was also the fact that adjudicators at the festivals were from either South Africa or Britain, which pointed to the dominance of the British tradition. Even though there were some white settler playwrights who wrote about local issues, such as George Yiend's *Someone in the House* (1973), a play performed by the University of Rhodesia Players, there was a marked preference for either WEST END or BROADWAY plays.

Theatre was encouraged in schools through the teaching of English literature and through ARTS, which organized a drama festival for high schools. As in ZAMBIA, the rules and regulations, as well as the choice of plays, were Eurocentric, and no mention of theatre activity within the native African communities was ever made. Indigenous performances were discouraged or ignored. Even black imitations of Western theatre (such as translations of Shakespeare and other European classics into indigenous languages) were ignored by the colonial press. But there was significant activity by groups that had formed to promote music, dance and drama within the native community. One such club was the Ecumenical Arts Workshop, formed in the early 1960s. This group was later to play a significant role in producing playwrights for the black majority theatre movement. Another group was the College Drama Association, which produced notable Zimbabwe dramatists such as Ben Sibenke, Tobby Moyana and T. K. Tsodzo. There was also a host of other clubs which, through festivals and drama competitions, helped to develop theatre within the black communities. Because of the predominance of church organizations and mission schools such as the Ecumenical Arts Workshop, Mabvuku Catholic Youth Club and Senka Christian Youth Club, passion and religious plays were the most popular, and the first to be performed in Shona was *Mutambo Wapanyika*, an adaptation of a morality play. The most frequently performed in the mission schools was *Mazuva Ekupedzisiva* ('The last days') by Dummi Maraire, about the passion of Christ. There were also regular productions of *Everyman* and versions of the Nativity.

A significant shift was the emergence of multiracial theatre groups, beginning with John Haigh's Sundown Theatre Company in 1974 which provided a platform for black actors in plays such as *Othello* (1979), WOLE SOYINKA's *Kongi's Harvest*, and ATHOL FUGARD's *The*

Blood Knot, *Master Harold and the Boys*, *Boesman and Lena* and *The Island*. Other such companies followed, including ZAP (founded by playwright/director Andrew Whaley and the black actors from Sundown), People's Theatre Company (formed by playwright/directors Carl Dorn and Ben Sibenke), and Zambuko/Izibuko Theatre (a socialist-oriented company founded by Robert McLaren at the University of Zimbabwe in 1985). These multiracial groups, coupled with the introduction of THEATRE FOR DEVELOPMENT and COMMUNITY THEATRE when independence came, have been responsible for both encouraging and staging native plays.

Major playwrights to have emerged include Ben Sibenke, author of plays such as *My Uncle Grey Bonzo*, a comedy set in a traditional Shona community, *Dr Madzuma and the Vipers* and the very popular *Chidembo Chauhuwa* ('The polecat stank'), and Stephen Chifunyise, who trained and lived in Zambia where he did a lot of his writing but is equally popular in his native Zimbabwe, and whose plays include *Talenda* ('Thank you', 1983), *Shocks and Surprises* (1988), *Temporary Market* (1992), *Jehesa* (1994), *Tsotso* (1994), *Two Angry Youngmen* (1994), *The Candidate* (1994), *Inmates* (1995) and *Strange Bedfellows* (1995). He deals with problems of the disabled and the environment, and high government corruption. Andrew Whaley's *Platform Five*, about tramps on the streets of Harare, looks at the plight of the indigenous peoples whose lives seem not to have changed in spite of independence. Whaley has also written *Nyoka Tree* (1988) and *The Rise and Shine of Comerade Fiasco* (1990). Carl Dorn wrote *Home Holds the Heart* (1987), a play which, like most of Sibenke's and Chifunyise's, examines the high level of alienation and disorientation among black Zimbabwean youth arising from years of west European education and cultural imperialism. Many plays have also emerged from the theatre for development and community theatre groups which use a collective creation and workshop process to generate their texts. Key groups in this style include Glen Nora Women Theatre Company, which has produced *Who is to Blame?* (1991), *Ngozi* (1992), *Mai Tapiwa* ('Mother of Tapiwa', 1993) and *My Piece of Land* (1994). Glen Nora's plays are designed to raise awareness among women of social problems and the possibilities of how to solve them. Amakhosi has produced action-packed plays such as *Book of Lies* (1982) and *Diamond Warriors* (1982), which deals with the loss of African cultural heritage through European colonization. Its other plays include the Ndebele-language *Ngizozula Lawe* ('I will elope with you', 1984); *Nansi Lenduda* ('Here is the man', 1985), which won five awards at the national festival and also launched the

863

group nationally; *Workshop Negative* (1986) and *Children on Fire* (1987), both of which were highly critical of the government, especially the corruption and hypocrisy of its officials; *Cry Silho, Citizen Mind, Stitsha* and *Jazzman; The Story of My Life* (1990); and *Dabulap* and *Hoyaya* (1994), which looks at the spread of AIDS in the country. Zambuko/Izibuko is a socially oriented theatre group with links to the university under the leadership of Robert McLaren, whose plays attempt to raise public consciousness and mobilize support in the struggle for peace, unity and social justice among the many peoples of Zimbabwe, and between the country and its neighbours. The company's major plays are *Katshaa!* ('The sound of the axe', 1986), *Samora Continua* (1987), *Mandela: The Spirit of No Surrender* (1990) and *Simuka Zimbabwe* ('Arise Zimbabwe', 1994). It has also produced two shorter plays, *Socialism or Death* and *Chris Hani: Revolutionary Fighter* (both 1993). All the company's plays illustrate the socialist and revolutionary perspective which the company adopted.

The national liberation movements used theatre (especially the *ngonjera* and other traditional forms and styles such as praise-poetry, storytelling, mime and dance) to show the history and injustice of the colonial occupation. After independence, dramatists and theatre artists tried to find ways of employing theatre to articulate and explore issues of national unity and cultural identity. Unfortunately, not many of the numerous plays of the very active theatre for development and community theatre groups are published. But the major published dramatists such as Sibenke, Chifunyise, Court Mhlanga (of Amakhosi) and Tsodzo Thompson, who writes in Shona and English and whose usually moralistic plays include *The Talking Calabash* (1976), *The Storm* (1982), *Tsano* ('The brother-in-law', 1982) and *Shanduko* (1983), also work within the theatre for development and community theatre format, which seems to be the prevailing style of much recent Zimbabwean theatre. OSITA OKAGBUE

Martin Rohmer, *Theatre and Performance in Zimbabwe* (2000)

Zimmerman, Bernd Alios *see* OPERA

Zinaida, Raikh *see* SOVIET UNION

Zindel, Paul (b. Staten Island, NY, 15 May 1936) Playwright and novelist. After four undistinguished plays, *The Effects of Gamma Rays on Man-in-the-Moon Marigolds*, originally written for television in 1965, won the former science teacher overnight success in 1970. Its central female role was compared with the best of TENNESSEE WILLIAMS. The ghoulish story of a widowed mother who terrorizes her daughters at home, where the younger one survives by conducting scientific experiments, it was only the second OFF-BROADWAY production to receive the Pulitzer Prize. Four more plays by Zindel were staged in the early 1970s, including *And Miss Reardon Drinks a Little* (1972), but none enjoyed the same success as his first big hit and he has since increasingly turned his attention to writing screenplays and children's novels. HELEN RAPPAPORT

Zipprodt, Patricia (b. Evanston, Ill., 24 Feb. 1925) Costume designer for theatre, ballet, opera and film. She made her BROADWAY debut with the costumes for *The Potting Shed* (1957); her later shows include *Fiddler on the Roof* (1964), *Cabaret* (1966), *Plaza Suite* (1968), *Pippin* (1972) and *Sunday in the Park with George* (1984). Among her opera work are the costumes for *La Bohème* (1962) and *Tannhäuser* (1977) and her film credits include the costumes for *The Graduate* (1967) and *1776* (1972). The winner of many awards, she has been a lecturer at many colleges and universities and is noted for her highly textured designs. DAVID STAINES

Zola, Émile [Edouard Charles Antoine] (b. Paris, 2 April 1840; d. Paris, 29 Sept. 1902) Novelist, playwright and man of letters. Of Italian and French parentage, he grew up in Aix-en-Provence. At 18, poor and unqualified, he went to Paris, became a journalist and began to advocate the literary realism embodied in his famous 20-volume novel cycle, *Les Rougon-Macquart* (1871–93). In *Le Naturalisme au théâtre* (1878) he attacked the melodrama, farce and costume drama which dominated the 'debased boards' of the Paris theatres and sought a new theatrical style. He was an influential figure in the theatre as a pioneer of naturalism, and his short story 'Jacques Damour', adapted by Léon Hennique (1851–1935) opened the Théâtre Libre of his friend and disciple ANDRÉ ANTOINE and embodied the principles of his own 'scientific' social novels. Of his plays, libretti and collaborative dramatizations, only *Thérèse Raquin* (1873), based on his earlier novel, is revived. TERRY HODGSON

Lawson A. Carter, *Zola and Theatre* (1963)

Zuckmayer, Carl (b. Nackenheim am Rhein, Germany, 27 Dec. 1896; d. Visp, Switzerland, 18 Jan. 1977) Playwright and novelist. One of many Berlin-based writers to leave Germany in 1933, he divided his time after the Second World War between the United States and Switzerland, where he settled in 1958. He was a prolific writer, and many of his plays proved controversial, from his EXPRESSIONIST *Kreuzweg* (*Crossroads*, 1920) and his adaptation of Terence's *Eunuchs* (1923), banned as obscene, to his best-known works: the satirical comedy debunking the military and bureaucracy *Der Hauptmann von Köpenick* (*The Captain of Köpenick*, 1931); the anti-nazi *Des Teufels General* (*The Devil's General*, 1946, a triumphant success in Frankfurt, despite the reluctance of the American authorities who feared civic unrest; and *Der Gesang im Feuerofen* (*The Song in the Fiery Furnace*, 1950), on the resistance. He adapted American plays into German and scripted several major films (e.g. *The Blue Angel*, 1930).

JUDY MEEWEZEN

William Grange, *Partnership in the German Theatre: Zuckmayer and Hilpert, 1925–61* (1991)
Siegfried Mews, *Carl Zuckmayer* (1981)

Zurich   *see* GERMAN-LANGUAGE THEATRE; SWITZERLAND

Zweig, Stefan   (b. Vienna, 28 Nov. 1881; d. Petropolis, Brazil, 22 Feb. 1942)   Novelist, poet and playwright. A much travelled writer, he took exile in Switzerland in the First World War, emigrated to England in 1938, then to the United States and Brazil. Best known for novels and short stories, he adapted two Ben Jonson plays: *Volpone* (1926), which was widely performed and made into a film by JULES ROMAINS, and *Die Schweigsame Frau* (*The Silent Woman*, 1935), as a libretto for Richard Strauss. The most popular of his half dozen plays is *Jeremias* (*Jeremiah*, 1917). He also translated the plays of ROLLAND, PIRANDELLO and ROMAINS.

JUDY MEEWEZEN